The College Board

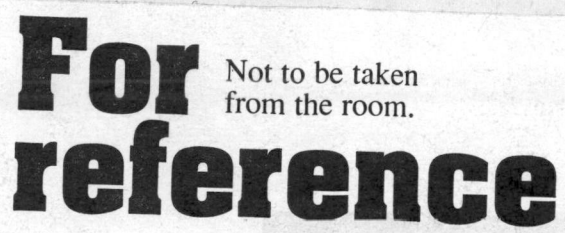
For reference

Not to be taken from the room.

The College Board Index of Majors and Graduate Degrees 2004

The College Board Index of Majors and Graduate Degrees

2004

Twenty-Sixth Edition

The College Board
New York

Editorial inquiries concerning this book should be directed to College Planning Services, The College Board, 45 Columbus Avenue, New York, NY 10023-6992; or telephone 212 713-8000.

Copies of this book are available from your local bookseller or may be ordered from College Board Publications, P.O. Box 869010, Plano, TX 75074-0998. The book may also be ordered online through the College Board Store at www.collegeboard.com. The price is $23.95.

Library of Congress Catalog Card Number: 80-648202
International Standard Book Number: 0-87447-696-8

Printed in the United States of America

Contents

Preface 1

How to use this book 3

Glossary of special programs 5

Majors by discipline 7

Brief descriptions of majors 15

Majors 49

Special academic programs

Accelerated program 589
Combined bachelor's/graduate program in:
    Accounting 593
    Architecture 593
    Business administration 593
    Chemistry 595
    Dentistry 595
    Education 596
    Engineering 596
    Environmental studies 597
    Fine Arts 598
    Forestry 598
    Law 598
    Mathematics 599
    Medicine 599
    Nursing 600
    Occupational therapy 601
    Optometry 601
    Osteopathic medicine 601
    Pharmacy 602
    Physical therapy 602
    Podiatry 603
    Psychology 603
    Social work 603
    Veterinary medicine 604
Combined liberal arts/career program in:
    Accounting 604
    Architecture 606
    Aviation 607
    Business administration 607

    Computer science 610
    Criminal justice 613
    Education 615
    Engineering 617
    Environmental studies 619
    Forestry 621
    Medical technology 621
    Natural resource management 623
    Nursing 623
    Occupational therapy 625
    Pharmacy 626
    Physical therapy 627
    Physician assistant 628
    Radiology technician 628
    Social work 629
Cooperative education 631
Distance learning 635
Double major 641
Dual enrollment 647
ESL program 653
External degree 657
Honors program 658
Independent study 664
Internship 671
Semester at sea 679
Student-designed major 679
Study abroad 683
Teacher certification 688
United Nations semester 693
Urban semester 693
Visiting/exchange student 694
Washington semester 696
Weekend college 698

Colleges in this book 703

Alphabetical index of majors 721

Dear Friend,

The College Board is dedicated to preparing, inspiring, and connecting students to college and opportunity, while emphasizing the principles of excellence and equity. With the College Board's Handbook series, we hope to put an authoritative source of college information at your fingertips and help connect you to a college education.

College is a dream for many, a dream worth working hard to achieve. I've been a businessman, a governor, and now the president of the College Board, but nothing makes me prouder than to say that I graduated from college. With perseverance, anyone who desires a college education can attain one. College Board publications can help you get there.

My best wishes on your journey to success—

Gaston Caperton
President
The College Board

Preface

The College Board Index of Majors and Graduate Degrees is designed to help students, counselors, and educators identify colleges that offer particular fields of study at the associate, bachelor's, master's, doctorate, and first-professional levels.

Over 900 majors, listed alphabetically, are included in this book. The colleges and graduate institutions that offer those majors or provide in-depth specialization approximating a major are listed state by state.

The list of majors is based on the Classification of Instructional Programs (CIP) 2000, developed by the National Center for Education Statistics, and on data collected for the College Board's Annual Survey of Colleges.

Each year the College Board's annual survey provides colleges with the CIP and asks them to report their majors (even though their own names for majors may not match the CIP names exactly). Colleges can add the names of the majors they offer that do not conform to any major in the CIP. These additional fields (at the undergraduate level) can be found in *The College Board College Handbook* but are not represented in the *Index of Majors*.

In a separate section, there are 61 special academic programs. These are organized alphabetically and include state-by-state listings of colleges offering that program.

To help students who are undecided about a major, two other sections of the *Index of Majors* are of particular use. "Majors by discipline" breaks down each broad discipline into a list of the specific majors offered within it. "Brief descriptions of majors" offers succinct descriptions of the scope of study for each major.

About this book

This edition is based on all-new curriculum and academic program information provided by nearly 3,000 institutions in the College Board's Annual Survey of Colleges 2003–2004. For the first time this year, colleges reported the majors they offer in concordance with the new Classification of Instructional Programs (CIP) 2000. This new taxonomy nearly doubles the number of majors described, allowing for a far more accurate reporting of the fields of study available.

The survey was completed by participating colleges, universities, and graduate institutions in the spring of 2003. The information they supplied was verified with the institutions by a staff of editors to ensure that the data are as complete and accurate as possible. However, program changes occur, and students are urged to contact institutions directly to confirm facts related to their own major of choice.

To be eligible for inclusion, an institution must be accredited by a national accrediting association at the institutional or program level. Graduate programs are listed only for those institutions that also have undergraduate programs. A complete list of the colleges, universities, and graduate institutions included in the *Index of Majors* can be found at the back of the book, along with an alphabetical index of the majors.

The enormous task of data collection, management, and verification for *The College Board Index of Majors and Graduate Degrees* was accomplished by a staff of editors under the direction of Shauna Morrison, Vice President of Content; Renée Gernand, Senior Director, College Planning Services; Stan Bernstein, Associate Director; and with the assistance of Cathy Serico, Associate Director, and Susan Bailey, Administrative Associate.

collegeboard.com

If you have Internet access, visit the College Board at www.collegeboard.com to find out more about colleges, scholarships, and majors. While you're there, you can also register for the SAT®, visit the SAT Learning Center™, look for scholarships, do a career search, and browse the College Board Store.

We welcome any comments and suggestions that will help us make our publications and services useful to you. Please contact us by mail or telephone: College Planning Services, The College Board, 45 Columbus Avenue, New York, NY 10023-6992; 212 713-8000.

Tom Vanderberg
Editor, Database Publications
College Planning Services

How to use this book

Two of the most important factors in choosing a college are programs of study and location. *The College Board Index of Majors and Graduate Degrees* is designed to help you find colleges that offer what you want to study, where you want to study.

It is important to attend a college that has the major or majors of interest to you. A major (also called a field of study, or a program of study) is an academic field of specialization that students take the majority of courses in during their college studies. Most colleges expect students to take a broad range of courses before declaring a major.

Fields of study

If you already know what you want to study, go right to the list called "Majors" that begins on page 49 and find which colleges offer the major that interests you at the degree level you want. The majors are listed alphabetically, and the schools that offer a major are listed state by state. Some institutions listed here do not offer majors in the traditional sense but do provide in-depth specialization that approximates the course work usually required for a degree.

If you are still exploring options, browse through the list of "Majors by discipline." Here the majors are grouped under broad areas, or disciplines, of study. If you know the broad area in which you are interested— such as health or biological sciences—you can find the specific majors offered in each broad area. If you want to learn more about a specific major, consult "Brief descriptions of majors." The descriptions indicate the scope of the major and, where appropriate, the roles for which the major prepares an individual.

These descriptions are adapted from the Classification of Instructional Programs (CIP) 2000, published by the National Center for Education Statistics. These descriptions are generic and do not cor-

respond to any specific degree level; the scope of the major at a particular college may be different. You should read the college catalog to determine what a particular major is like at that school.

Levels of study

The levels at which colleges offer specific majors are designated by the following letters found after the college name:

C Certificate or diploma
A Associate degree
B Bachelor's degree
T Teacher certification
M Master's degree
D Doctoral degree
F First-professional degree
W Work beyond doctoral or first-professional degree

Undergraduate programs

Undergraduate programs vary in length and may lead to a certificate or diploma, an associate degree, a bachelor's degree, or teacher certification.

Certificate or diploma. These are nondegree offerings below the associate degree and are most often offered in technical and vocational fields of study. They generally lead to employment in an occupational field.

Associate. The associate of arts (A.A.) or associate of science (A.S.) degree is granted after completion of a program of study similar to the first two years of a four-year college curriculum. Students who earn an A.A. or A.S. often transfer to a four-year college or university where they complete the requirements for a bachelor's degree. The associate in applied science (A.A.S.) is awarded on completion of a technological or vocational program of study.

Bachelor's. Sometimes called baccalaureate degrees, these programs require four or five years of study. The bachelor of arts (B.A.) and bachelor of science (B.S.) are the most common baccalaureates, and both include general education courses, a major, and electives. The bachelor of science is more likely to be awarded in the sciences and for professional or technical fields of study. Bachelor of arts degrees are awarded more often in the humanities and arts. However, there are no absolute differences between the degrees, and policies concerning their award vary from college to college.

Teacher certification. *T* next to a major indicates the institution offers specific preparation for teacher certification. All institutions that prepare teachers are accredited by the state; each state sets its own certification standards. Students complete bachelor's degree requirements and state certification requirements; your college adviser will help you prepare a plan of study to meet those twin demands.

A program leading to teacher certification typically involves three types of courses:

- general liberal arts courses

- the major (such as elementary education or mathematics)

- professional education courses, including student teaching

In order to gain certification, most states require candidates to pass an achievement test in the field in which they plan to teach. At some colleges, students who have graduated with a major may complete teacher certification requirements in a fifth year of study.

Graduate programs

Graduate programs vary in length and lead to a master's degree, a doctorate, or a first-professional degree.

Master's. Master of arts (M.A.) and master of science (M.S.) programs lead to the first graduate degrees in the liberal arts and sciences. They usually take one to two academic years of study to complete. There are other master's degrees offered, such as the M.B.A. (master of business administration), M.L.S. (master of library science), and M.S.W. (master of social work). See also "Work beyond the doctorate or first-professional degree."

Doctorate. The doctorate degree may be the doctor of philosophy (Ph.D.), awarded in many of the humanities, arts, and sciences, or another degree such as the doctor of education (Ed.D.), or doctor of public health (D.P.H.). Doctorate programs usually consist of course work and independent research culminating in a dissertation or other formal presentation of the results of independent study.

First-professional. First-professional programs are those recognized by the U.S. Department of Education. They require completion of academic prerequisites to become licensed in a recognized profession, at least two years of previous college-level study prior to entering the program, and the total registered time equals at least six academic years. First-professional degrees are awarded in the following fields:

Chiropractic	D.C., D.C.M.
Dentistry	D.D.S., D.M.D.
Divinity/Ministry	B.D., M.Div.
Law	L.L.B., J.D.
Medicine	M.D.
Optometry	O.D.
Osteopathic medicine	D.O.
Pharmacy	B.Pharm, PharmD.
Podiatry	Pod.D., D.P., D.P.M.
Rabbinical/Talmudic studies	M.H.L., Rav.
Veterinary medicine	D.V.M.

Work beyond the doctorate or first-professional degree. Work beyond the doctorate or first-professional degree is advanced graduate study usually consisting of research or other independent pursuits. In some fields, the master's degree is the next highest degree awarded after completion of the first-professional degree. The degrees *M* or *D* listed in this book in the fields of dental specialties, medical specialties, and juridical science are awarded after the first-professional degree has been earned.

Special academic programs. There are 61 special academic programs listed in this section. These programs are described in the glossary. For each program, there is a state-by-state listing of colleges that offer that option.

Colleges in this book

Colleges are listed by state by their characterization of themselves as:

- two-year

- two-year upper division

- three-year

- four-year

- five-year

- graduate

Two-year colleges offer associate degrees and certificates or diplomas. Two-year upper-division institutions and colleges offering three or more years of study usually grant bachelor's degrees. Many of these colleges also offer degrees at the graduate and associate levels. Each college's address is included.

Glossary of special programs

Accelerated program. A program of study completed in less time than is usually required, most often by attending in summer or by carrying extra courses during the regular academic term. Completion of a bachelor's degree program in three years is an example of acceleration.

Combined bachelor's/graduate program. A program to which students are accepted for study at both the undergraduate and graduate levels. The program usually can be completed in less time than two individual programs.

Combined liberal arts/career program. A program of study in which a student typically completes three years of study in a liberal arts field followed by two years of professional/technical study (for example, engineering) at the end of which the student is awarded bachelor of arts and bachelor of science degrees. The combination is sometimes referred to as a 3 + 2 program.

Cooperative education. Also called work-study, this program alternates between semesters (or other periods) of full-time study and full-time employment in related work. Students are paid for their work at the prevailing rate. Five years are required to complete a bachelor's degree program under the cooperative plan, but graduates have the advantage of having completed about a year's practical experience in addition to their studies.

Distance learning. Courses that are broadcast via public or cable stations or the Internet that are viewed in the home (or on campus equipment) for credit.

Double major. Any program of study in which a student completes the requirements of two majors concurrently.

Dual enrollment. A program that lets you enroll in college courses for credit while still enrolled in high school.

ESL program. English as a Second Language is one of the special study options offered on many campuses to help international students improve their English skills.

External degree. A program in which students earn credits toward a college degree through independent study, college courses, proficiency examinations, and personal experience. External degree programs require minimal or no classroom attendance.

Honors program. Any special program for students offering the opportunity for educational enrichment, independent study, acceleration, or some combination of these.

Independent study. An arrangement that allows students to complete some of their college program by studying independently instead of attending scheduled classes and completing group assignments. Typically, students plan programs of study in consultation with a faculty adviser or committee to whom they may report periodically and submit a final report for evaluation.

Internship. Any short-term, supervised work experience, usually related to a student's major field, for which the student earns academic credit. The work can be full- or part-time, on or off campus, paid or unpaid. Student teaching and apprenticeships are examples of internships.

Semester at sea. A program for credit, usually for students with majors in oceanography or marine-related fields, in which students live for part of a semester on a ship, frequently a research vessel. Academic courses are generally taken in conjunction with the sea experience or at separate times during the semester.

Student-designed major. A program that allows a student to construct a major field of study not formally offered by the college. Often nontraditional and interdisciplinary in nature, the major is developed by the student with the approval of a designated college officer or committee.

Study abroad. Any arrangement by which a student completes part of the college program—typically the junior year but frequently only a semester or a summer—studying in another country. A college may operate a campus abroad or it may have a cooperative agreement with some other American college or an institution of the other country.

Teacher certification. A program designed to prepare students to meet the requirements for certification as teachers in elementary and secondary schools.

United Nations semester. A program in which students generally take courses at a college in the New York City metropolitan area while participating in an internship program at the United Nations.

Urban semester. A program for credit in which students of diverse majors spend a semester in a major city, such as Philadelphia, Chicago, New York, Denver, or San Francisco, experiencing the complexities of an urban center through course work, seminars, and/or internships related to their major.

Visiting/exchange student. Any arrangement between a student and a college that permits study for a semester or more at another college without extending the amount of time required for a degree.

Washington semester. A program in which students participate in an internship program with a government agency or department in the Washington, D.C., metropolitan area. Students earn field service credit for their work and frequently take courses at area colleges.

Weekend college. A program that allows students to take a complete course of study and attend classes only on weekends. These programs are generally restricted to a few areas of study at a college and require more than the traditional number of years to complete.

Majors by discipline

Agricultural business/sciences

Agribusiness operations
Agricultural business
Agricultural business technology
Agricultural communications
Agricultural economics
Agricultural education services
Agricultural equipment technology
Agricultural mechanization
Agricultural power machinery operation
Agricultural production
Agricultural supplies
Agricultural/food products processing
Agriculture, general
Agronomy/crop science
Animal breeding
Animal health
Animal husbandry
Animal nutrition
Animal sciences
Animal training
Aquaculture
Crop production
Dairy husbandry
Dairy science
Dog/pet/animal grooming
Equestrian studies
Farm/ranch management
Floriculture
Food science
Food technology/processing
Greenhouse operations
Horse husbandry/equine science
Horticultural operations
Horticultural science
International agriculture
Landscaping/grounds-keeping
Livestock management
Nursery operations
Ornamental horticulture
Plant breeding
Plant protection/pest management
Plant sciences
Poultry science
Range science
Soil chemistry/physics
Soil microbiology
Soil science
Taxidermy
Turf management

Architecture

Architectural history/criticism
Architectural technology
Architecture
Environmental design
Interior architecture
Landscape architecture
Urban/community/regional planning

Area/ethnic/cultural studies

African studies
African-American studies
American studies
Asian studies
Asian-American studies
Balkans studies
Baltic studies
Canadian studies
Caribbean studies
Central Asian studies
Central/Middle/Eastern European studies
Chinese studies
Commonwealth studies
East Asian studies
European studies
French studies
Gay/lesbian studies
German studies
Hispanic-American studies
Italian studies
Japanese studies
Korean studies
Latin American studies
Native American studies
Near/Middle Eastern studies
Pacific area/rim studies
Polish studies
Regional studies
Russian/Slavic studies
Scandinavian studies
Slavic studies
South Asian studies
Southeast Asian studies
Spanish/Iberian studies
Tibetan studies
Ukraine studies
Western European studies
Women's studies

Biological/biomedical sciences

Anatomy
Animal behavior/ethology
Animal genetics
Animal physiology
Aquatic biology/limnology
Bacteriology
Biochemistry
Biochemistry/biophysics and molecular biology
Bioinformatics
Biological immunology
Biology
Biomedical sciences
Biometrics
Biophysics
Biostatistics
Biotechnology
Botany
Cardiovascular science
Cell physiology
Cellular biology/histology
Cellular/anatomical biology
Cellular/molecular biology
Conservation biology
Developmental biology/embryology
Ecology
Endocrinology
Entomology
Environmental biology
Environmental toxicology
Epidemiology
Evolutionary biology
Exercise physiology
Genetics
Human/medical genetics
Marine biology
Microbial/eukaryotic genetics
Microbiology
Molecular biochemistry
Molecular biology
Molecular biophysics
Molecular genetics
Molecular pharmacology
Molecular physiology
Molecular toxicology

Mycology
Neuroanatomy
Neurobiology/physiology
Neuropharmacology
Oncology
Parasitology
Pathology, human/animal
Pharmacology
Pharmacology/toxicology
Photobiology
Physiology
Plant genetics
Plant molecular biology
Plant pathology
Plant physiology
Population biology
Radiation biology
Reproductive biology
Structural biology
Systematic biology
Toxicology
Virology
Vision science
Wildlife biology
Zoology

Business
Accounting
Accounting technology/
  bookkeeping
Accounting/business
  management
Accounting/finance
Actuarial science
Administrative/secretarial
  services
Apparel/accessories
  marketing
Auctioneering
Auditing
Banking/financial
  services
Business administration/
  management
Business communications
Business statistics
Business/commerce
Business/managerial
  economics

Construction management
Credit management
Customer service
  management
Customer service support
Electronic commerce
Entrepreneurial studies
Executive assistant
Fashion merchandizing
Fashion modeling
Finance
Financial planning
Franchise operations
Hospitality
  administration/
  management
Hospitality/recreation
  marketing
Hotel/motel
  administration/
  management
Human resources
  development
Human resources
  management
Information resources
  management
Insurance
International business
International finance
International marketing
Investments/securities
Knowledge management
Labor studies
Labor/industrial relations
Logistics/materials
  management
Management information
  systems
Management science
Marketing management
Marketing research
Merchandising/buying
  operations
Nonprofit/public
  organization
  management
Office management

Office technology/data
  entry
Office/clerical services
Operations management
Organizational behavior
  studies
Personal/financial
  services marketing
Public finance
Purchasing/procurement/
  contracts
Real estate
Receptionist
Resort management
Restaurant/food services
  management
Retailing
Sales/distribution
Selling/sales operations
Small business
  administration/
  management
Special products
  marketing
Taxation
Tourism promotion
Tourism/travel
  management
Tourism/travel services
Traffic/customs/
  transportation clerk
Transportation
  management
Vehicle parts/accessories
  marketing
Warehousing/inventory
  management

Communications
Advertising
Broadcast journalism
Communications
Digital media
Health communications
Journalism
Media studies
Organizational
  communication
Photojournalism

Political communications
Public relations
Publishing
Radio/television

Communications technologies
Animation/video
  graphics/special effects
Communications
  technology
Computer typography
Desktop publishing
Graphic communications
Graphic/printing
  production
Photographic/film/video
  technology
Platemaker/imager
Printing management
Printing press operator
Radio/television
  broadcasting
Recording arts

Computer/information sciences
Artificial
  intelligence/robotics
Computer graphics
Computer networking/
  telecommunications
Computer programming,
  general
Computer programming,
  specific applications
Computer science
Computer systems
  analysis
Computer/information
  sciences
Computer/systems
  security
Data entry/applications
Data processing
  technology
Database design/
  management
Information
  sciences/studies

Information technology
LAN/WAN management
System administration
Vendor/product
 certification
Web page/multimedia
 design
Web/multimedia
 management
Word processing

Construction trades
Blasting
Building inspection
Building/property
 maintenance
Carpentry
Concrete finishing
Construction management
Construction trades
Drywall installation
Electrician
Glazier
Lineworker
Masonry
Metal building assembly
Painting/wall covering
Pipefitting
Plumbing
Power/electrical
 transmission
Roofing
Well drilling

Education
Adult literacy instruction
Adult/continuing
 education
Adult/continuing
 education
 administration
Agricultural teacher
 education
Art teacher education
Bilingual/bicultural
 education
Biology teacher education
Business teacher
 education

Chemistry teacher
 education
College counseling
Community/junior
 college administration
Comparative/international
 education
Computer education
Counselor education
Curriculum/instruction
Drama/dance teacher
 education
Driver/safety education
Early childhood education
Early childhood special
 education
Education
Education of autistic
Education of blind/
 visually handicapped
Education of brain
 injured
Education of deaf/
 hearing impaired
Education of
 developmentally
 delayed
Education of emotionally
 handicapped
Education of gifted/
 talented
Education of learning
 disabled
Education of mentally
 handicapped
Education of multiple
 handicapped
Education of physically
 handicapped
Education of speech
 impaired
Educational
 assessment/testing
Educational
 evaluation/research
Educational leadership/
 adminstration

Educational
 statistics/research
 methods
Educational supervision
Elementary education
Elementary/middle school
 administration
English teacher education
ESL teacher education
Family/consumer sciences
 education
Foreign language teacher
 education
French teacher education
Geography teacher
 education
German teacher education
Health occupations
 teacher education
Health teacher education
Higher education
 administration
History teacher education
Instructional media
Junior high education
Kindergarten/preschool
 education
Latin teacher education
Mathematics teacher
 education
Montessori teacher
 education
Multicultural education
Music teacher education
Native American
 education
Physical education
Physics teacher education
Psychology teacher
 education
Reading teacher
 education
Sales/marketing
 education
School librarian
 education
Science teacher education
Secondary education

Secondary school
 administration
Social science teacher
 education
Social studies teacher
 education
Social/philosophical
 foundations of
 education
Spanish teacher education
Special education
Special education
 administration
Speech teacher education
Superintendency
Teacher assistance
Teacher education,
 multiple levels
Technology/industrial arts
 education
Trade/industrial education
Urban education
Vocational/technical
 education
Waldorf/Steiner teacher
 education

Engineering
Aeronautical/aerospace
 engineering
Agricultural/biological
 engineering
Architectural engineering
Biomedical engineering
Ceramic sciences/
 engineering
Chemical engineering
Civil engineering
Computer engineering
Computer hardware
 engineering
Construction engineering
Electrical/
 communications
 engineering
Engineering
Engineering mechanics
Engineering physics

Engineering science

Environmental engineering

Forest engineering

Geological engineering

Geotechnical engineering

Industrial engineering

Manufacturing engineering

Marine engineering/naval architecture

Materials engineering

Materials science

Mechanical engineering

Metallurgical engineering

Mining/mineral engineering

Nuclear engineering

Ocean engineering

Operations research

Petroleum engineering

Polymer/plastics engineering

Software engineering

Structural engineering

Surveying engineering

Systems engineering

Textile sciences/ engineering

Transportation/highway engineering

Water resource engineering

Engineering technologies

Aeronautical/aerospace engineering technology

Architectural drafting/CAD/CADD

Architectural engineering technology

Automotive engineering technology

Biomedical technology

CAD/CADD drafting/design technology

Civil engineering drafting/CAD/CADD

Civil engineering technology

Computer engineering technology

Computer hardware technology

Computer software technology

Computer systems technology

Construction/building technologies

Drafting and design technology

Electrical engineering technologies

Electrical/electronics drafting/CAD/CADD

Electromechanical technology

Energy systems technology

Engineering/industrial management

Environmental engineering technology

Hazardous materials information systems

Hazardous materials technology

Heating/air conditioning/ refrigeration technology

Hydraulics technology

Industrial safety technology

Industrial technology

Instrumentation technology

Laser/optical technology

Manufacturing technologies

Mechanical drafting/CAD/CADD

Mechanical engineering technology

Metallurgical technology

Mining technology

Nuclear engineering technology

Occupational safety/health technology

Petroleum technology

Plastics engineering technology

Quality control technology

Robotics technology

Solar energy technology

Surveying technology

Telecommunications technology

Water quality/treatment/ recycling technology

English language/ literature

American literature (Canadian)

American literature (U.S.)

Creative writing

English

English composition

English language/ literature

English literature (British)

Speech/rhetorical studies

Technical/business writing

Family/consumer sciences

Adult development/aging

Apparel/textile manufacture

Apparel/textile marketing

Child care management

Child care service

Child development

Clothing/apparel/textiles

Consumer economics

Consumer merchandising

Consumer services/ advocacy

Facilities/event planning

Family resource management studies

Family systems

Family/community services

Family/consumer business sciences

Family/consumer sciences/home economics

Fashion/fabric consultant

Food/nutrition studies

Home furnishings

Housing/human environments

Human development/ family studies

Human nutrition

Human sciences communication

Institutional food production

Textile science

Work/family studies

Foreign languages/ literatures

African languages

Albanian

American sign language (ASL)

Ancient Greek

Ancient Near Eastern/Biblical languages

Arabic

Australian/Oceanic/ Pacific languages

Bahasa Indonesian/Malay languages

Baltic languages

Bengali

Bulgarian

Burmese

Catalan

Celtic languages

Chinese

Classics

Comparative literature

Czech
Danish
Dutch/Flemish
East Asian languages
Filipino/Tagalog
Finnish/related languages
Foreign languages/
 literatures
French
German
Germanic languages
Hebrew
Hindi
Hungarian/Magyar
Iranian/Persian languages
Italian
Japanese
Khmer/Cambodian
Korean
Language interpretation/
 translation
Lao/Laotian
Latin
Linguistics
Modern Greek
Mongolian
Native American
 languages
Norwegian
Polish
Portuguese
Punjabi
Romance languages
Romanian
Russian
Sanskrit/classical Indian
 languages
Scandinavian languages
Semitic languages
Serbo-Croatian
Sign language
 interpretation
Sign language linguistics
Slavic languages

Slovak
South Asian languages
Southeast Asian
 languages
Spanish
Swedish
Tamil
Thai
Tibetan
Turkish
Ukrainian
Urdu
Vietnamese

**Health
professions/clinical
sciences**
Acupuncture
Adult health nursing
Anesthesiologist assistant
Aromatherapy
Art therapy
Asian bodywork therapy
Assistive technology/
 rehabilitation
 engineering
Athletic training
Audiology/hearing
 sciences
Audiology/speech
 pathology
Ayurvedic medicine
Bioethics/medical ethics
Blood bank technology
Cardiopulmonary
 technology
Cardiovascular
 technology
Chiropractic (D.C.)
Chiropractic assistant
Clinical laboratory
 science
Clinical nurse specialist
Clinical nutrition
Clinical pastoral
 counseling
Clinical/medical
 laboratory assistant

Clinical/medical
 laboratory technology
Clinical/medical social
 work
Communication disorders
Community health
 services
Community health/
 preventative medicine
Critical care nursing
Cytogenetics/clinical
 genetics technology
Cytotechnology
Dance therapy
Dental assistant
Dental clinical services
Dental hygiene
Dental laboratory
 technology
Dentistry (D.D.S.,
 D.M.D)
Diagnostic medical
 sonography
Dietetic technician
Dietetics
Dietician assistant
Electrocardiograph
 technology
Electroencephalograph
 technology
Emergency care attendant
 (EMT ambulance)
Emergency medical
 technology (EMT
 paramedic)
Environmental health
Family practice nurse/
 nurse practitioner
Gene therapy
Genetic counseling
Health aide
Health care
 administration
Health management/
 clinical assistant
Health physics/
 radiologic health

Health services
Health services
 administration
Health unit coordinator
Health unit manager
Hematology technology
Herbalism
Histologic assistant
Histologic technology
Home health attendant
Homeopathic medicine
Hospital/health care
 facilities administra-
 tion
Hypnotherapy
International public
 health
Kinesiotherapy
Licensed midwifery
Licensed practical nursing
Marriage/family therapy
Massage therapy
Maternal/child health
Maternal/child health
 nursing
Medical administrative
 assistant
Medical claims examiner
Medical illustrating
Medical informatics
Medical insurance coding
 specialist
Medical insurance
 specialist
Medical office
 administration
Medical office assistant
Medical office computer
 specialist
Medical radiologic
 technology/radiation
 therapy
Medical receptionist
Medical records
 administration
Medical records
 technology
Medical scientist

Medical staff services technology
Medical transcription
Medical/clinical assistant
Medication aide
Medicinal/pharmaceutical chemistry
Medicine (M.D.)
Mental health counseling
Mental health services technology
Movement therapy
Music therapy
Naturopathic medicine
Nuclear medical technology
Nurse anesthetist
Nurse midwifery
Nursing (R.N.)
Nursing administration
Nursing assistant
Nursing science
Occupational health/industrial hygiene
Occupational therapy
Occupational therapy assistant
Occupational/ environmental health nursing
Ophthalmic laboratory technology
Ophthalmic technology
Opticianry/ophthalmic dispensing
Optometric assistant
Optometry (O.D.)
Orthoptics
Orthotics/prosthetics
Osteopathic medicine (D.O.)
Pathology assistant
Pediatric nursing
Perfusion technology
Pharmacy (PharmD.)
Pharmacy assistant
Phlebotomy

Physical therapy
Physical therapy assistant
Physician assistant
Podiatry (D.P.M.)
Polarity therapy
Predentistry
Premedicine
Prenursing
Preoperative/surgical nursing
Prepharmacy
Preveterinary
Psychiatric nursing
Psychoanalysis
Public health
Public health education
Public health nursing
Radiation protection/health physics technology
Radiologic technology/medical imaging
Recreational therapy
Reiki
Renal/dialysis technology
Respiratory therapy
Respiratory therapy assistant
Somatic bodywork
Speech pathology
Substance abuse counseling
Surgical technology
Traditional Chinese medicine/herbology
Veterinary assistant
Veterinary medicine (D.V.M.)
Vocational rehabilitation counseling
Yoga teacher/therapy

History
American history (U.S.)
Asian history
Canadian history
European history

History
History of science/ technology
Public history/archives

Legal studies
Court reporting
Law (J.D.)
Legal administrative assistance
Legal studies
Paralegal/legal assistance
Prelaw

Liberal arts/ humanities
Humanities
Liberal arts/sciences
Library assistance
Library science

Mathematics
Algebra/number theory
Analysis/functional analysis
Applied mathematics
Computational mathematics
Geometry
Mathematical statistics/probability
Mathematics
Statistics
Topology/foundations

Mechanic/repair technologies
Aircraft mechanics
Aircraft powerplant technology
Alternative fuel vehicle technology
Appliance installation and repair
Auto body repair
Automotive technology
Avionics maintenance/ technology
Bicycle mechanics
Business machine repair

Communications systems installation/repair
Computer installation and repair
Diesel mechanics
Electronics/electrical equipment repair
Engine machinist
Gunsmithing
Heating/air conditioning/ refrigeration maintenance
Heavy equipment maintenance
Industrial electronics technology
Industrial equipment maintenance/repair
Locksmithing
Marine maintenance/ fitter/ship repair
Mechanics/repairers, general
Medium/heavy vehicle technology
Motorcycle maintenance
Musical instrument fabrication/repair
Parts/warehousing operations
Security system installation/repair/ inspection
Small engine mechanics
Vehicle emissions inspection/maintenance
Watch/jewelrymaking

Military
Military technologies

Multi/interdisciplinary studies
Accounting/computer science
Ancient studies
Behavioral sciences

Biological/physical
    sciences
Biopsychology
Classical/ancient
    Mediterranean/Near
    Eastern studies
Cognitive science
Cultural resource
    management
Gerontology
Global studies
Historic preservation
Holocaust studies
Intercultural/diversity
    studies
Mathematics/computer
    science
Medieval/renaissance
    studies
Museum studies
Natural sciences
Neuroscience
Nutritional sciences
Peace/conflict studies
Science/technology/
    society
Systems science/theory

Natural resources/ conservation

Environmental science
Environmental studies
Fishing and fisheries
Forest management
Forest resources
    production
Forest sciences/biology
Forest technology
Forestry
Land use planning
Natural resource
    economics
Natural resources
    management/policy
Natural resources/
    conservation, general
Urban forestry

Water, wetlands, and
    marine management
Wildlife/wilderness
    management
Wood science/pulp/paper
    technology

Parks/recreation/ fitness studies

Exercise sciences
Health/physical fitness
Parks, recreation, and
    leisure studies
Parks/recreational/leisure
    facilities management
Sports/fitness
    administration

Personal/culinary service

Aesthetician/skin care
Baking/pastry arts
Barbering
Bartending
Chef training
Cosmetic services
Cosmetology
Culinary arts/related
    services
Electrolysis
Facial treatment
Food preparation
Food service
Funeral direction
Funeral services/mortuary
    science
Hair styling
Institutional food service
Make-up artist
Manicurist
Meat cutting
Mortuary science/
    embalming
Permanent cosmetics/
    tattooing
Restaurant/catering
    management
Salon management

Philosophy/religion

Buddhist studies
Christian studies
Ethics
Hindu studies
Islamic studies
Jewish/Judaic studies
Logic
Philosophy
Philosophy/religion
Religion/religious studies

Physical sciences

Acoustics
Analytical chemistry
Astronomy
Astrophysics
Atmospheric
    physics/dynamics
Atmospheric sciences
Atomic/molecular physics
Chemical physics
Chemistry
Climatology
Geochemistry
Geochemistry/petrology
Geology/earth science
Geophysics/seismology
Hydrology/water
    resources science
Inorganic chemistry
Meteorology
Nuclear physics
Oceanography
Optics
Organic chemistry
Paleontology
Particle physics
Physical sciences
Physical/theoretical
    chemistry
Physics
Planetary sciences
Plasma/high-temperature
    physics
Polymer chemistry

Solid-state/
    low-temperature
    physics
Theoretical/mathematical
    physics

Precision production trades

Boilermaking
Cabinetmaking/
    millwright
Furniture design/
    manufacturing
Ironworking
Machine shop technology
Machine tool technology
Precision production
    trades, general
Sheet metal technology
Shoe/leather repair
Tool and die technology
Upholstery
Welding technology
Woodworking

Psychology

Clinical child psychology
Clinical psychology
Cognitive psychology/
    psycholinguistics
Community psychology
Comparative psychology
Counseling psychology
Developmental/child
    psychology
Educational psychology
Environmental
    psychology
Experimental psychology
Family psychology
Forensic psychology
Geropsychology
Health/medical
    psychology
Industrial/organizational
    psychology
Personality psychology

Psychobiology/
physiological
psychology
Psychology
Psychometrics/
quantitative psychology
Psychopharmacology
School psychology
Social psychology

Public administration
Community
organization/advocacy
Human services
Public administration
Public policy analysis
Public services
Social work
Youth services

Science technologies
Biotechnology
Chemical technology
Industrial radiologic
technology
Nuclear power technology
Science technologies

Security/protective
services
Correctional facilities
administration
Corrections
Criminal justice studies
Criminalistics/criminal
science
Fire protection/safety
technology
Fire services
administration
Firefighting/fire science
Forensic science
Juvenile corrections
Law enforcement
administration
Police science
Protective services

Security services
management
Security/loss prevention

Social sciences
American
government/politics
Anthropology
Applied economics
Archaeology
Canadian government/
politics
Cartography
Criminology
Demography/population
studies
Development economics
Econometrics/quantitative
economics
Economics
Geography
International economics
International relations
Physical anthropology
Political science/
government
Social sciences
Sociology
Urban studies

Theological studies
Bible studies
Divinity/ministry (B.Div.,
M.Div.)
Missionary studies
Pastoral counseling
Pre-ministerial studies
Rabbinical studies
(M.H.L., Rav.)
Religious education
Religious/sacred music
Talmudic studies
Theology/religious
vocations
Theological studies
Youth ministry

Transportation/
materials moving
Air traffic control
Air transportation
Airline/commercial pilot
Aviation management
Commercial fishing
Flight attendant
Flight instructor
Heavy/earthmoving
equipment operation
Marine science/Merchant
Marine
Mobile crane operation
Transportation
Truck/bus/commercial
vehicle operation
Underwater diving

Visual/performing
arts
Acting
Art
Art history/criticism/
conservation
Arts management
Ballet
Ceramics
Cinematography/film/
video production
Commercial photography
Commercial/advertising
art
Conducting
Crafts/folk art/artisanry
Dance
Design/visual
communications
Directing/theatrical
production
Drama/theater arts
Drawing
Fashion/apparel design
Fiber arts
Film/cinema studies
Fine/studio arts

Graphic design
Illustration
Industrial design
Interior design
Jazz studies
Metal/jewelry arts
Multimedia
Music
Music history/literature
Music management
Music pedagogy
Music performance
Music theory/composition
Musicology/
ethnomusicology
Painting
Photography
Piano/organ
Playwriting/screenwriting
Printmaking
Sculpture
Theater arts management
Theater design/
technology
Theater history/criticism
Violin/viola/guitar/
stringed instruments
Visual/performing arts
Voice/opera

Brief descriptions of majors

Accounting. Includes instruction in various types of accounting, legal considerations, auditing, report procedures, planning and consulting, research methods, and professional standards and ethics.

Accounting technology/bookkeeping. Prepares students to provide technical administrative support to financial management personnel.

Accounting/business management. Aids students in becoming accountants and business managers.

Accounting/computer science. A program that combines accounting with computer science and/or computer studies.

Accounting/finance. Trains individuals to function as accountants and financial managers.

Acoustics. Investigates the properties and behavior of sound waves under different conditions.

Acting. Prepares students to impart ideas and feelings through naturalistic and believable behavior in imaginary circumstances.

Actuarial science. Highlights the mathematical and statistical analysis of risk and its applications to insurance and other business management problems.

Acupuncture. Readies individuals to practice pulse diagnosis, acupuncture point selection, and needle insertion to treat health imbalances.

Administrative/secretarial services. Describes the duties of administrative assistants and/or secretaries and stenographers.

Adult development/aging. Investigates aging populations and the needs of older individuals in family and institutional settings.

Adult health nursing. Informs registered nurses how to provide general care for adult patients.

Adult literacy instruction. Prepares students to serve as instructors and mentors for adults in literacy programs in school, institutional, community, and private settings.

Adult/continuing education. Prepares students to instruct adult students in various types of educational programs.

Adult/continuing education administration. Readies individuals to serve the basic educational needs of undereducated adults or the needs of adults seeking further instruction.

Advertising. Focuses on commercial messages intended to promote and sell products.

Aeronautical/aerospace engineering. Highlights the design, development, and operational evaluation of aircraft, space vehicles, and their systems.

Aeronautical/aerospace engineering technology. Covers the development, manufacturing, and testing of aircraft, spacecraft, and their systems.

Aesthetician/skin care. Prepares individuals to cleanse, depilate, massage, and beautify the human body.

African languages. Focuses on one or more of the languages originating in Africa.

African studies. Explores the history, society, politics, culture, and economics of Africa.

African-American studies. Investigates the history, society, politics, culture, and economics of the North American peoples descended from Africa.

Agribusiness operations. Investigates the management of agricultural businesses and agriculturally related operations within diversified corporations.

Agricultural business. Focuses on the organization, operation, and management of agricultural enterprises.

Agricultural business technology. Explores the operation of agricultural office equipment, software, and information systems.

Agricultural communications. Prepares students to develop, produce, and transmit agricultural information.

Agricultural economics. The analysis of resource allocation, productivity, investments, and trends in the agricultural sector.

Agricultural education services. Features the provision of referral, consulting, technical assistance, and educational services to gardeners, farmers, ranchers, and agribusinesses.

Agricultural equipment technology. Provides instruction in the maintenance and repair of specialized farm, ranch, and agribusiness power equipment and vehicles.

Agricultural mechanization. Readies students to sell, select, and service agricultural or agribusiness technical equipment and facilities.

Agricultural power machinery operation. Highlights the operation of specialized farm, ranch, and agribusiness power equipment.

Agricultural production. Focuses on the general planning, economics, and use of facilities, natural resources, labor, and capital to produce plant and animal products.

Agricultural supplies. Highlights the purchasing, marketing, and selling of agricultural products.

Agricultural teacher education. Prepares students to teach vocational agricultural programs at various educational levels.

Agricultural/biological engineering. The study of systems used to produce, process, and store agricultural products; and the improvement of agricultural methods and biological systems.

Agricultural/food products processing. Readies individuals to receive, inspect, process, and package agricultural products in the form of human consumables.

Agriculture, general. The study of agricultural research and production.

Agronomy/crop science. The study of the chemical, physical, and biological relationships of crops and soils.

Air traffic control. Prepares students to manage and control air traffic, usually with additional training at the FAA Flight Control Center in a cooperative education program.

Air transportation. The study of aviation, including in-flight and ground support operations.

Aircraft mechanics. Prepares individuals to repair all aircraft components other than engines, propellers, avionics, and instruments.

Aircraft powerplant technology. Prepares students to repair, service, and maintain all types of aircraft power plant and related systems.

Airline/commercial pilot. Focuses on the flying and/or navigation of commercial fixed-wing aircraft.

Albanian. Features the Albanian language and its Ghegg and Tosk dialects.

Algebra/number theory. Prepares students to express quantities by means of symbols, vectors, matrices, equations, and integer properties.

Alternative fuel vehicle technology. Describes the maintenance of alternative fuel vehicles and the conversion of standard vehicles to AFV status.

American government/politics. Features the behavior of the United States and its political institutions.

American history (U.S.). Focuses on the development of American society, culture, and institutions.

American literature (Canadian). Focuses on Canadian literature from its origins to the present.

American literature (U.S.). Features the literature of the United States from the Colonial Era to the present.

American sign language (ASL). Focuses on American Sign Language as a medium of communication for deaf individuals and deaf culture.

American studies. The study of the history, society, politics, culture, and economics of the United States.

Analysis/functional analysis. Defines the properties of equations, multivariate solutions, functions, and dynamic systems.

Analytical chemistry. Prepares students to analyze and describe the composition of matter.

Anatomy. Highlights organs, tissues, and whole bodies together with their cellular and structural components.

Ancient Greek. Highlights the Greek language and literature from its origins through the fall of the Byzantine Empire, as a secular and/or theological subject.

Ancient Near Eastern/Biblical languages. The study of the extinct Semitic and/or Non-Semitic languages spoken in the ancient Near East, including those used to write historical Jewish and Christian religious texts.

Ancient studies. Focuses on Western and non-Western cultures and related topics in the periods of pre-history and antiquity.

Anesthesiologist assistant. Trains students to assist anesthesiologists and nurses in developing and implementing patient anesthesia care plans.

Animal behavior/ethology. Highlights the psychological and neurological processes of animals.

Animal breeding. Focuses on the improvement of agricultural animal health and the development of new animal breeds.

Animal genetics. Features animal genetics from the experimental, comparative, veterinary, and medical viewpoints.

Animal health. Investigates the prevention and control of diseases in agricultural animals.

Animal husbandry. Features livestock selection, breeding, processing, and marketing.

Animal nutrition. Focuses on nutrition as related to animal health, and on the production of improved animal products.

Animal physiology. The study of function, structure, and regulation within animal species, with comparative applications to humans.

Animal sciences. Describes the breeding and husbandry of agricultural animals; and the production and distribution of agricultural animal products.

Animal training. Prepares individuals to teach and exercise animals for leisure, sport, show, and professional purposes.

Animation/video graphics/special effects. Prepares individuals to communicate simulated real-world content through the manipulation of film, video, photographs, digital copy, and soundtracks.

Anthropology. Describes human beings, their antecedents, and their cultural behavior and institutions in comparative perspective.

Apparel/accessories marketing. Prepares students to perform operations connected with the distribution and sale of apparel and accessories.

Apparel/textile manufacture. A program that focuses on the design, development, and production of textile products and related processes and systems.

Apparel/textile marketing. Trains students to apply marketing research and management to the products of the apparel and textile industries.

Appliance installation and repair. Readies students to mend, install, and fix major gas, electric, and microwave appliances.

Applied economics. Applies economics to the study of particular industries, activities, or the exploitation of particular resources.

Applied mathematics. Readies individuals to find solutions to functional problems in fields such as engineering and the applied sciences.

Aquaculture. Prepares students to culture, propagate, harvest, and market domesticated fish, shellfish, and marine plants.

Aquatic biology/limnology. Highlights the ecology and behavior of microbes, plants, and animals inhabiting inland fresh waters.

Arabic. The study of the language, literature, and culture of Arabic-speaking peoples.

Archaeology. Explores societies via the excavation, analysis, and interpretation of their artifactual and human remains.

Architectural drafting/CAD/CADD. Highlights the technical skills used to develop working drawings and electronic simulations for architectural and related construction projects.

Architectural engineering. Features the materials, systems, and methods used to construct buildings for human habitation or other purposes.

Architectural engineering technology. Prepares students to support architects, engineers, and planners engaged in designing and developing buildings and urban complexes.

Architectural history/criticism. Focuses on the aesthetic, technical, and social development of the built environment and the architectural profession.

Architectural technology. Prepares students to assist architects in developing plans and in performing office services.

Architecture. Includes instruction in architectural design, history, and theory; building structures; site planning; and construction.

Architecture/related programs. Trains individuals to create, adapt, alter, preserve, and control human surroundings and habitations.

Area studies. A program that studies the areas, regions, and countries of the world; defined minority groups; and collective gender experience issues.

Aromatherapy. Readies individuals to provide therapeutic care through the preparation and application of essential oils.

Art. An introductory study and appreciation of the visual arts.

Art history/criticism/conservation. Focuses on the development of art as social and intellectual phenomenon, the analysis of art, and art conservation.

Art teacher education. Readies individuals to provide art and art appreciation programs at various educational levels.

Art therapy. Describes the use of drawings to assess, treat, and rehabilitate individuals with disorders.

Artificial intelligence/robotics. Focuses on the simulation by computers of human learning and reasoning.

Arts management. Trains individuals to organize and manage art organizations and facilities.

Asian bodywork therapy. Readies students to provide relief and improved health through the traditional bodywork therapies of Asia.

Asian history. Features the development of the societies, cultures, and institutions of the Asian continent.

Asian studies. Studies the history, society, politics, culture, and economics of the Asian continent.

Asian-American studies. Describes the history, society, politics, culture, and economics of Asian population groups who have immigrated to the United States and Canada.

Assistive technology/rehabilitation engineering. Features the design and implementation of technological interventions and systems to promote patient rehabilitation and function.

Astronomy. Focuses on the planetary, galactic, and stellar phenomena occurring in outer space.

Astrophysics. Highlights the characteristics of stars, star systems and clusters, and stellar life cycles.

Athletic training. Highlights the prevention and treatment of sports injuries.

Atmospheric physics/dynamics. Features the processes governing the behavior of atmospheric, terrestrial, and solar phenomena.

Atmospheric sciences. Investigates the earth's atmosphere and its effect on terrestrial weather, and on related environment and climate problems.

Atomic/molecular physics. Investigates the behavior of matter-energy phenomena at the atomic and molecular levels.

Auctioneering. Trains individuals for careers as auctioneers and auction managers and for meeting state licensing requirements.

Audiology/hearing sciences. Trains students to diagnose hearing loss, advise patients how to use their remaining hearing, and select and fit hearing aids.

Audiology/speech pathology. An integrated program that prepares individuals as audiologists and speech-language pathologists.

Auditing. Prepares individuals to evaluate organizational financial and operational activities, ensure regulatory compliance, safeguard assets, and promote resource allocation.

Australian/Oceanic/Pacific languages. Features the languages spoken by the Melanesian, Micronesian, and Polynesian peoples.

Auto body repair. Prepares individuals to repair, reconstruct, and finish automobile bodies, fenders, and external features.

Automotive engineering technology. Prepares students to aid in the development, manufacture, and testing of self-propelled ground vehicles and their systems.

Automotive technology. Describes the servicing and maintenance of all types of automobiles.

Aviation management. Emphasizes the management of aviation industry operations and services.

Avionics maintenance/technology. Trains individuals to mend aircraft operating, control, and electronic systems.

Ayurvedic medicine. Trains students to use dietary, lifestyle, spiritual, pharmacological, and physical therapies to remove imbalances and to restore health.

Bacteriology. Features bacteria that are significant factors in causing human disease.

Bahasa Indonesian/Malay languages. Highlights the modern Bahasa Malay and Bahasa Indonesian languages.

Baking/pastry arts. Describes bread and pastry making, decorating, marketing, and counter display and service.

Balkans studies. Focuses on the history, society, politics, culture, and economics of the Balkan Peninsula.

Ballet. Trains individuals to interpret classical dance choreography.

Baltic languages. Highlights the languages of the Baltic peoples and the relationship of Baltic literature to comparative linguistics and Indo-European origins.

Baltic studies. Studies the history, society, politics, culture, and economics of the peoples of the Baltic Sea coastlands.

Banking/financial services. Describes a variety of customer services in banks, insurance agencies, and savings and loan companies.

Barbering. Focuses on facial shaving, hair cutting, styling art, massage, hairpiece fitting, equipment operation, and safety.

Bartending. Readies students to mix beverages and manage bars, lounges, and beverage services operations.

Behavioral sciences. Studies problems of human individual and social growth and behavior.

Bengali. Features the Bengali language (Bangla) as spoken in India and Bangladesh.

Bible studies. The study of the Christian and/or Jewish Bible, with an emphasis on interpreting the messages contained therein.

Bicycle mechanics. Readies individuals to maintain bicycles and other human-powered vehicles.

Bilingual/bicultural education. Focuses on the design and provision of teaching to bilingual/bicultural children or adults.

Biochemistry. Focuses on living systems, their chemical substances and pathways, and information transfer systems.

Biochemistry/biophysics and molecular biology. Describes the structure, function, and behavior of biological systems at molecular levels and their influence on biological activity.

Bioethics/medical ethics. A course of study that analyzes health care issues, clinical decision-making, and research procedures.

Bioinformatics. Readies individuals to research biological, biomedical, and biotechnological issues, using computer technologies.

Biological immunology. Describes the biological origination and development of disease and its effect on humans.

Biological/physical sciences. A program that is either a general synthesis of the biological and physical sciences, or a specialization which draws from the biological and physical sciences.

Biology. Introductory study of living organisms and their relations to their natural environments.

Biology teacher education. Trains individuals to teach biology to students at various educational levels.

Biomedical engineering. Highlights the development of health systems and products.

Biomedical sciences. The scientific study of biological issues related to health and medicine.

Biomedical technology. Readies students to assist engineers engaged in developing biological or medical systems and products.

Biometrics. Studies problems in the biological sciences and related fields in agriculture and natural resources.

Biophysics. Highlights the workings of biological processes and assemblies.

Biopsychology. Highlights linkages between biochemical and biophysical activity to central nervous system functioning.

Biostatistics. Prepares students to apply statistics to biomedical research and clinical, health, and industrial issues related to humans.

Biotechnology. Prepares students to apply scientific principles and skills in support of biologists in research, industrial, and government settings.

Blasting. Prepares students to apply technical knowledge in using a variety of explosive materials to aid in the construction process.

Blood bank technology. Prepares individuals to administer blood testing procedures, process blood donations, and support other personnel administering transfusion therapy.

Boilermaking. Trains individuals to make and repair steam boiler components.

Botany. The study of plants, related organisms, and plant habitats and ecosystem relations.

Broadcast journalism. Prepares students to report, produce, and deliver news via radio, television, and video/film media.

Buddhist studies. Explores the Buddhist faith; along with its intellectual, cultural, social, and ritual developments.

Building inspection. The study of industrial, labor, and governmental standards to the oversight of construction projects and the maintenance of completed buildings.

Building/property maintenance. Prepares individuals to keep a building functioning and service a variety of structures.

Bulgarian. Focuses on the Bulgarian language and its applications in varied settings.

Burmese. The study of the Burmese language and its use in literature.

Business administration/management. Prepares students to plan, organize, direct, and control the functions of a firm or organization.

Business communications. Highlights the duties of organizational composers, editors, and proofreaders of business communications.

Business machine repair. Prepares individuals to sustain a variety of office machinery.

Business statistics. Features the description, analysis, and forecasting of business data.

Business teacher education. Prepares individuals to teach vocational business programs.

Business/commerce. The general study of business, business organization, and accounting as used in profit-making and nonprofit public and private institutions and agencies.

Business/managerial economics. Focuses on the analysis of the organization and operation of business enterprises.

Cabinetmaking/millwright. Prepares students to set up, operate, and repair woodworking machinery; and use it to design and fabricate wooden items.

CAD/CADD drafting/design technology. Prepares individuals to create graphic representations and simulations in support of engineering projects.

Canadian government/politics. Explores Canadian political institutions and behavior.

Canadian history. The study of the society, culture, and institutions of Canada.

Canadian studies. Describes the history, society, politics, culture, and economics of the Canadian people.

Cardiopulmonary technology. Readies individuals, under the supervision of physicians and nurses, to perform cardiovascular and pulmonary procedures.

Cardiovascular science. Highlights the heart, vascular system, and blood; and the disorders associated with the cardiovascular system.

Cardiovascular technology. Describes testing procedures used to aid in diagnoses and treatments.

Caribbean studies. Explores the history, society, politics, culture, and economics of the major islands and archipelagoes of the Caribbean Sea.

Carpentry. Prepares students to lay out, fabricate, install, and repair wooden structures and fixtures using hand and power tools.

Cartography. Describes map-making through the use of mathematical and computer techniques.

Catalan. The study of the Catalan language and its use in varied settings.

Cell physiology. Features the physiological processes, communications, and behavior of cells in the context of whole organisms.

Cellular biology/histology. Features the structure, function, and regulation of cells as individual units and as components of larger systems.

Cellular/anatomical biology. Describes cell structure and function and the cell as a biological system in plants and animals.

Cellular/molecular biology. Emphasizes the study of cells, cellular systems, and cell structure and function.

Celtic languages. A program that focuses on the historical and modern languages spoken by the Celtic peoples of the British Isles, Continental Europe, and Asia Minor.

Central Asian studies. Focuses on the history, society, politics, culture, and economics of Inner/Central Asia.

Central/Middle/Eastern European studies. Highlights the Balkans, Belarus, Czech Republic, Hungary, Poland, Romania, Russia, Slovakia, and the Ukraine.

Ceramic sciences/engineering. Prepares students to design and evaluate nonmetallic materials.

Ceramics. Studies the production of artwork out of clay and similar materials.

Chef training. Includes instruction in recipe and menu planning, cooking, training, resources management, and food presentation.

Chemical engineering. The study of systems employing chemical processes and the analysis of chemical problems such as corrosion, pollution, and energy loss.

Chemical physics. Combines the disciplines of physical chemistry and atomic/molecular physics to study structural phenomena.

Chemical technology. Prepares students to aid chemical and biochemical research and industrial operations.

Chemistry. Investigates the composition and behavior of matter, the processes of chemical change, and the laboratory simulation of these phenomena.

Chemistry teacher education. Prepares individuals to teach chemistry.

Child care management. Prepares individuals to plan, design, and manage facilities that meet children's developmental needs.

Child care service. Includes instruction in child development, nutrition, recreation, activities supervision, child abuse prevention, and parent-child relationships.

Child development. Features the intellectual, social, emotional, and biological development of children and the planning of related human services.

Chinese. Features the Chinese language and its associated dialects and literature.

Chinese studies. Investigates the history, society, politics, culture, and economics of present-day China.

Chiropractic (D.C.). Readies students to apply noninvasive treatments and spinal adjustments to alleviate problems caused by vertebral misalignments.

Chiropractic assistant. Prepares students to assist chiropractors by providing patient management, examinations, and treatment services.

Christian studies. Features the teachings of Jesus Christ and the subsequent movements and institutions based on Christianity.

Cinematography/film/video production. Focuses on the transmittal of dramatic information through the making and producing of films and videos.

Civil engineering. Investigates the design, development, and evaluation of structural, load-bearing, transportation, water resource, and material control systems.

Civil engineering drafting/CAD/CADD. Features the technical skills necessary to develop working drawings and electronic simulations in support of civil engineers and geological engineers.

Civil engineering technology. Trains individuals to assist civil engineers engaged in designing and executing public works projects.

Classical/ancient Mediterranean/Near Eastern studies. Features the cultures, environment, and history of the Near East, Europe, and Mediterranean basin.

Classics. Focuses on the Greek and Latin languages and literatures.

Climatology. Describes the characteristics of atmospheric elements and processes in predictive, current, and historical contexts.

Clinical child psychology. Emphasizes the developmental processes of children and associated disorders.

Clinical laboratory science. Readies students to conduct medical tests and research, manage laboratories, and consult with physicians and researchers.

Clinical nurse specialist. Trains registered nurses to deliver direct patient care in clinical settings.

Clinical nutrition. Readies students to manage nutrition programs as part of clinical therapies; and oversee health care facility food services.

Clinical pastoral counseling. Prepares students to respond to the emotional and spiritual needs of patients in emergencies and other situations.

Clinical psychology. Describes the analysis, diagnosis, and clinical treatment of psychological disorders and behavioral pathologies.

Clinical/medical laboratory assistant. Prepares students to assist laboratory teams by performing tests, phlebotomy, and other duties.

Clinical/medical laboratory technology. Trains individuals to engage in routine medical laboratory procedures and tests and to record and analyze data.

Clinical/medical social work. Describes the professional practice of social work in hospitals and other health care facilities and organizations.

Clothing/apparel/textiles. Highlights the development, distribution, and use of textile products in terms of the consumer's needs.

Cognitive psychology/psycholinguistics. Studies the processes of learning, thinking, and associated information systems.

Cognitive science. An interdisciplinary study of the mind and the nature of intelligence.

College counseling. Studies the provision of counseling and administrative services to students in postsecondary educational institutions and adult education facilities.

Commercial fishing. Prepares students to function as commercial fishermen or fishing operations supervisors.

Commercial photography. Focuses on transmitting ideas by recording images via photography.

Commercial/advertising art. Prepares students to communicate information to audiences via illustrations and other media.

Commonwealth studies. Covers the history, society, politics, culture, and economics of the countries that comprise the British Empire.

Communication disorders. The study of speech, language, hearing, and cognitive communication problems caused by disease, injury, or disability.

Communications. Explores human communication in a variety of formats, media, and contexts.

Communications systems installation/repair. Prepares students to assemble, operate, and fix one- and two- way communications equipment.

Communications technology. Prepares individuals to function within communications industries.

Community health services. Readies students to link health care and related social services with affected recipient communities.

Community health/preventative medicine. Prepares individuals to plan and manage health services in local community settings.

Community organization/advocacy. Prepares individuals to provide services to communities, organize communities for social action, and serve as community liaisons to public agencies.

Community psychology. Trains students to analyze social problems and implement intervention strategies for addressing these problems.

Community/junior college administration. Focuses on administration at community and junior colleges and related postsecondary systems.

Comparative literature. The study of the literatures of different societies and linguistic groups from a comparative perspective.

Comparative psychology. Focuses on the behavior of group members and the relationship of those behaviors to the group's evolutionary origins.

Comparative/international education. A program that compares educational practices and institutions within different countries, states, and societies.

Computational mathematics. Prepares students to apply mathematics to the theory, architecture, and design of computers, computational techniques, and algorithms.

Computer education. A program that prepares individuals to teach computer curricula.

Computer engineering. Prepares individuals to design and develop computer systems and to analyze specific problems related to computer applications.

Computer engineering technology. Trains students to support computer engineers that design and develop computer systems and installations.

Computer graphics. Studies the software and hardware used to represent, display, and manipulate topological, two-, and three-dimensional objects on a computer screen.

Computer hardware engineering. Readies students to design, develop, and evaluate computer hardware.

Computer hardware technology. Highlights the design of computer hardware and peripheral systems.

Computer installation and repair. Highlights the application of technical skills to maintain computers.

Computer networking/telecommunications. Analyzes the management of linked computer systems, peripherals, and software to maximize efficiency and productivity.

Computer programming, general. Studies the applications of software design and programming to software installation and maintenance.

Computer programming, specific applications. Prepares individuals to devise solutions for problems presented by software users.

Computer science. Focuses on computers, computing problems and solutions, and the design of computer systems and user interfaces.

Computer software technology. Prepares students to aid in developing, implementing, and evaluating computer software and program applications.

Computer systems analysis. Trains students to design and implement large-scale computer applications and networking systems.

Computer systems technology. Includes instruction in basic computer design and architecture, programming, maintenance and inspection, and problem diagnosis and repair.

Computer typography. Prepares students to execute page formats, layouts, and text composition; and to make typographical selections using computer programs.

Computer/information sciences. Focuses on computing, computer science, and information science as part of an interdisciplinary program.

Computer/systems security. Readies students to assess the security needs of computer systems, recommend solutions, and manage security devices and procedures.

Concrete finishing. Trains individuals to prepare, construct, and finish buildings using masonry mixtures.

Conducting. Prepares students to lead bands, choirs, orchestras, and other ensembles in performance.

Conservation biology. Specifies conservation issues that result from advancing human social, economic, and industrial pressures.

Construction engineering. Includes instruction in civil engineering, site analysis, geology, materials, contracting, project management, and graphic communications.

Construction management. Readies students to coordinate the construction process from concept development through project completion on timely and economic bases.

Construction trades. Focuses on the building, inspecting, and maintenance of structures.

Construction/building technologies. Focuses on working with engineering contractors to construct buildings and related structures.

Consumer economics. Prepares students to apply economic theories to consumer behavior and individual and family consumption of goods and services.

Consumer merchandising. Highlights product and service promotion from the consumer's perspective.

Consumer services/advocacy. Features the techniques needed to protect consumers from unsafe, unreliable, and/or unhealthy products and services.

Correctional facilities administration. Trains students to provide management services for institutional facilities that house and rehabilitate prisoners.

Corrections. The study of correctional science in preparation for becoming a corrections officer in an incarceration facility.

Cosmetic services. Describes hair cutting and styling, facial treatments, esthetics, sanitation and safety, and labor laws.

Cosmetology. Prepares grooming technicians to teach their specializations in schools of cosmetology and barbering.

Counseling psychology. Highlights the provision of therapeutic services to individuals and groups experiencing psychological problems and symptoms.

Counselor education. Prepares individuals to support student development and to organize guidance services within educational institutions.

Court reporting. Readies students to record examinations, testimony, judicial orders, and other proceedings via print or electronic methods.

Crafts/folk art/artisanry. Features the aesthetics and techniques for designing objects in the handcraft or folk art traditions.

Creative writing. Describes the composition of literary forms such as the short story, poetry, and the novel.

Credit management. Includes instruction in how to perform credit, collateral, and loan processing operations.

Criminal justice studies. Focuses on the criminal justice system, its components and processes, and its legal and public policy contexts.

Criminalistics/criminal science. Highlights the reconstruction of crimes and the analysis of physical evidence.

Criminology. Highlights crime as a sociopathological phenomenon, the behavior of criminals, and the social institutions developed to respond to crime.

Critical care nursing. Readies students to provide specialized care to patients with life-threatening problems.

Crop production. Prepares individuals to cultivate grain, fiber, forage, oilseed, fruits and nuts, vegetables, and other domesticated plant products.

Culinary arts/related services. Includes instruction in cooking techniques, equipment operation, sanitation and safety, and regulations.

Cultural resource management. Readies students to preserve and protect cultural heritage sites and artifacts.

Curriculum/instruction. Includes instruction in curriculum theory, design, planning, and evaluation, as well as instructional material design and evaluation.

Customer service management. Prepares students to monitor customer service performance and manage frontline customer support services.

Customer service support. Trains individuals to assist customers with inquiries and problems in call centers, help desks, teleservice centers, and online.

Cytogenetics/clinical genetics technology. Readies students to analyze human chromosomes for the research and diagnosis of genetic diseases, organ transplants, and cancer treatments.

Cytotechnology. Explores the change in body cells that may indicate the early development of cancers and other diseases.

Czech. Explores the languages, literatures, and cultures of the Czech people.

Dairy husbandry. Highlights the management, selection, and care of dairy animals and associated dairy farm facilities.

Dairy science. Prepares students to produce and manage dairy animals and products.

Dance. Explores the cultural effects of dance and prepares students to perform in one or more of the dance disciplines.

Dance therapy. A course of study that applies creative dance movement to promote client rehabilitation and physical, emotional, and mental health.

Danish. Features the Danish language as used in Denmark and Greenland.

Data entry/applications. Prepares individuals to perform basic data and text entry using varied software products.

Data processing technology. Describes the use of computers and software packages for text processing, number processing, graphics, and database management.

Database design/management. Prepares individuals to link data sets to create complex searchable databases and use analytical search tools.

Demography/population studies. Emphasizes population models, population phenomena, and related problems of social structure and behavior.

Dental assistant. Focuses on the provision of patient care, preparation for procedures, and the completion of office functions under the supervision of dental professionals.

Dental clinical services. Generally prepares dentists in one or more of the oral sciences and advanced/graduate dentistry specialties.

Dental hygiene. Prepares individuals to clean teeth; provide oral health education; identify oral pathologies; and manage dental hygiene practices.

Dental laboratory technology. Trains students, under the supervision of dentists, to design and construct dental prostheses.

Dentistry (D.D.S., D.M.D.). Prepares students to evaluate, diagnosis, prevent, and treat oral cavity conditions.

Design/visual communications. Focuses on effectively communicating information to business and consumer audiences.

Desktop publishing. Trains students to design the layout and typography of printed electronic and textual products.

Development economics. Defines economic development and its application to the problems of specific countries and regions.

Developmental biology/embryology. The scientific study of the development and growth of animals and human beings.

Developmental/child psychology. The study of the psychological growth and development of individuals from infancy through adulthood.

Diagnostic medical sonography. Features the utilization of medical ultrasound techniques to gather data used to diagnose a variety of conditions and diseases.

Diesel mechanics. Trains individuals to preserve diesel engines in vehicles, as well as stationary diesel engines in electrical generators.

Dietetic technician. Prepares individuals to implement nutritional and dietetic plans; and provide direct client services.

Dietetics. A program that trains students to design and manage effective nutrition programs in a variety of settings.

Dietician assistant. Trains students to assist in planning, preparing, and serving meals to individuals with specific dietary needs.

Digital media. Readies individuals to develop, use, and regulate communication technologies using computers.

Directing/theatrical production. Readies individuals to manage the planning, design, preparation, and production of theatrical entertainment programs.

Divinity/ministry (B.Div., M.Div.). Prepares individuals for ordination as ministers or priests in any of the Christian religious traditions.

Dog/pet/animal grooming. Studies the provision of cosmetic services for pets, show animals, work animals, and animal athletes.

Drafting and design technology. Features the application of technical skills to create working drawings and computer simulations for a variety of applications.

Drama/dance teacher education. A program that prepares students to teach components of drama and/or dance.

Drama/theater arts. Focuses on the general study of dramatic works and their performance.

Drawing. Highlights the expression of emotions, ideas, or inner visions through lines made on a surface.

Driver/safety education. The study of driver and safety education curricula.

Drywall installation. Describes how to install, tape, and plaster drywall installations in interior and exterior construction jobs.

Dutch/Flemish. Highlights the Dutch language as used in the Netherlands, Flemish-speaking Belgium, and Suriname.

Early childhood education. Readies individuals to teach all relevant subject matter to students ranging in age from infancy through eight years.

Early childhood special education. A program that specifies teaching to infant and pre-school age children with special learning needs.

East Asian languages. Highlights one or more of the Sino-Tibetan, Japanese, and Korean languages of East Asia.

Ecology. Prepares students to relate small-scale biological systems, such as organisms, to complex and whole systems.

Econometrics/quantitative economics. Prepares students for the mathematical and statistical analysis of economic phenomena.

Economics. Highlights the production, conservation, and allocation of resources in conditions of scarcity.

Education. Covers learning and teaching, educational psychology, educational activities, and the social foundations of education.

Education of autistic. Prepares students to plan and implement educational services for children or adults who are autistic.

Education of blind/visually handicapped. Readies individuals to provide services for children or adults with visual disabilities.

Education of brain injured. Highlights educational services for students who are recovering from brain injuries that affect their cognitive, perceptive, and motor functions.

Education of deaf/hearing impaired. Includes instruction in impairment identification, developing education plans, counseling, and applicable laws.

Education of developmentally delayed. Readies individuals to create services for students who exhibit slow social, physical, cognitive, or emotional growth patterns.

Education of emotionally handicapped. Highlights the educational challenges faced by individuals affected by emotional conditions.

Education of gifted/talented. Identifies the educational opportunities available to individuals exhibiting exceptional intellectual or artistic talent, maturity, or social leadership skills.

Education of learning disabled. Characterizes various learning disabilities and the programs designed to address them.

Education of mentally handicapped. Characterizes mental disabilities that adversely affect educational performance.

Education of multiple handicapped. Prepares students to design and provide educational services for individuals with multiple disabilities.

Education of physically handicapped. Describes orthopedic and other health impairments which affect students and their educational performance.

Education of speech impaired. Features educational services for children or adults with speech impairments.

Educational assessment/testing. Prepares students to design, implement, and evaluate tests, and to assess teaching tools, strategies, and curricula.

Educational evaluation/research. Highlights procedures for generating information about educational programs, personnel and methods, and the analysis of such information for planning purposes.

Educational leadership/adminstration. Describes the techniques of administering a wide variety of schools and prepares individuals as general administrators and supervisors.

Educational psychology. Features learning environments and their effects on behavior and the effects of non-school experience on the educational process.

Educational statistics/research methods. The application of statistics to the analysis of educational research problems; and the development of technical designs for research studies.

Educational supervision. Includes instruction in staffing and organization, personnel relations, and administrative duties related to management.

Electrical engineering technologies. Includes instruction in electrical circuitry, prototype testing, systems analysis and maintenance, instrument calibration, and report preparation.

Electrical/communications engineering. Trains students to design electrical and electronic communications systems and to analyze problems such as reception and amplification.

Electrical/electronics drafting/CAD/CADD. Readies students to design working schematics and representations in support of electrical/electronic engineers and computer engineers.

Electrician. Prepares students to install, operate, maintain, and repair electric systems, as well as DC and AC motors, controls, and electrical distribution panels.

Electrocardiograph technology. Readies individuals to administer EKG and ECG examinations, and to report results to the treatment team.

Electroencephalograph technology. Prepares students, under the supervision of a physician, to study and record electrical activity in the brain and nervous system.

Electrolysis. Describes the process of hair removal from the human scalp, face, and body using specialized needle probes.

Electromechanical technology. Prepares individuals to support engineers engaged in developing and testing automated, servomechanical, and other electromechanical systems.

Electronic commerce. Trains individuals to manage, supervise, and market electronic operations, products, and services provided on the Internet.

Electronics/electrical equipment repair. The study of the operation, maintenance, and repair of electrical and electronic equipment.

Elementary education. Readies individuals to teach subject matter to students in grades kindergarten through grade eight.

Elementary/middle school administration. Features educational administration at the elementary and middle school levels.

Emergency care attendant (EMT ambulance). Readies individuals to transport patients and operate emergency equipment.

Emergency medical technology (EMT paramedic). Prepares students, under physician supervision, to recognize, assess, and manage emergencies; and to supervise ambulance personnel.

Endocrinology. Emphasizes the role of endocrine substances in bodily processes.

Energy systems technology. Readies students to support engineers engaged in the development of energy-efficient systems or monitoring energy use.

Engine machinist. Focuses on the construction of automotive and commercial vehicle engines.

Engineering. Prepares individuals to solve a wide variety of practical problems in industry, social organizations, and commerce.

Engineering mechanics. Investigates the behavior of structures, forces, and materials in engineering problems.

Engineering physics. Prepares individuals to apply the principles of physics to the analysis of engineering problems.

Engineering science. Features the analysis and evaluation of engineering problems.

Engineering technology. A program that readies individuals to apply basic engineering principles and technical skills in support of engineers engaged in a wide variety of projects.

Engineering/industrial management. Covers the planning and operational management of industrial and manufacturing operations.

English. A general program that covers the structure and use of the English language and dialects, speech, writing, and various aspects of the literatures and cultures of the English-speaking peoples.

English composition. Investigates English vocabulary, grammar, morphology, syntax and semantics; and the techniques used to express ideas in written forms.

English language/literature. Explores the English language, including its history and structure; and the literature and culture of English-speaking peoples.

English literature (British). Highlights the literature composed by the peoples of the British Commonwealth.

English teacher education. Studies the teaching of English grammar, composition, and literature programs.

Entomology. The scientific study of insects.

Entrepreneurial studies. Prepares students to perform development, marketing, and management functions associated with owning a business.

Environmental biology. Focuses on living populations in relation to changing environmental processes.

Environmental design. The study of total environments and living systems, both indoor and outdoor.

Environmental engineering. Includes instruction in pollution control, waste and hazardous material disposal, health and safety protection, and conservation.

Environmental engineering technology. Investigates the development and use of indoor and outdoor environmental pollution control systems.

Environmental health. The study of environmental factors affecting human health.

Environmental psychology. Investigates ways in which to improve the behavioral interactions between human beings and the environment.

Environmental science. Highlights the environment and the solution of environmental problems.

Environmental studies. Studies environment-related issues using a combination of approaches.

Environmental toxicology. Focuses on toxic chemical exposure, the management of toxins, and the development of protective measures.

Epidemiology. Studies the distribution and prevention of disease across populations.

Equestrian studies. Readies students to care for horses and equipment; ride and drive horses; and manage and train horses and riders.

ESL teacher education. Studies the principles and practice of teaching English to students who are not proficient in the language or who do not speak, read, or write English.

Ethics. Investigates the theory of moral good and its application to various theoretical and practical problems.

European history. Highlights the development of European society, culture, and institutions.

European studies. Focuses on the history, society, politics, culture, and economics of the European Continent.

Evolutionary biology. Describes the emergence and changes of organisms over time.

Executive assistant. Trains individuals to function as special assistants and/or personal secretaries for business executives and top management.

Exercise physiology. Explores the processes involved in physical or motor activity.

Exercise sciences. Focuses on the anatomy, physiology, biochemistry, and biophysics of human movement; and applications to exercise and therapeutic rehabilitation.

Experimental psychology. Investigates behavior under experimental conditions and analyzes controlled behavioral responses.

Facial treatment. Studies massage and face and scalp treatments.

Facilities/event planning. Describes strategic workplace and facility planning and the preparation necessary to become facility and event managers and workplace consultants.

Family practice nurse/nurse practitioner. Readies registered nurses to provide independent general care for family groups and individuals.

Family psychology. Readies students to provide therapeutic, evaluative, and research services to families and individuals in the family unit context.

Family resource management studies. Includes instruction in financial goal-setting and management; preventing and resolving financial difficulties; and the use of relevant public resources.

Family systems. Highlights the family in its development and its significance as a system that impacts individuals and society.

Family/community services. Focuses on the development and implementation of support services for individuals, families, and localities.

Family/consumer business sciences. Investigates the relationship between the economy and the consuming individual and family.

Family/consumer sciences education. Highlights the relationship between people and aspects of their environment, such as food and clothing.

Family/consumer sciences/home economics. Studies the development of individuals in various settings and how they relate to their physical, social, emotional, and intellectual environments.

Farm/ranch management. Prepares individuals to manage farms, ranches, or similar enterprises.

Fashion merchandizing. Readies students to promote product lines/brands and organize promotional campaigns to attract retailer interest, wholesale purchasing, and supply contracts.

Fashion modeling. Highlights the display of fashion and accessories products in wholesale and retail settings.

Fashion/apparel design. Trains students to design and manage commercial apparel, accessories, and fashion development projects.

Fashion/fabric consultant. Readies individuals to assist in fashion selection, style coordination, sales, fabric selection, clothing specifications, and purchasing.

Fiber arts. Readies students to construct designs from woven or nonwoven fabrics and fibrous materials.

Filipino/Tagalog. Emphasizes the modern Filipino/Tagalog language as used in the Philippines.

Film/cinema studies. The study of film/video arts, as well as the basic principles of filmmaking and film production.

Finance. Readies students to plan, manage, and analyze the financial aspects and performance of business enterprises or banking institutions.

Financial planning. Prepares individuals to plan and manage the financial interests and growth of individuals and institutions.

Fine/studio arts. Prepares individuals to function as creative artists in the visual and plastic media.

Finnish/related languages. A program that focuses on Finnish languages such as Estonian, Karelian, and Sami.

Fire protection/safety technology. Studies the application of fire prevention and control skills to loss limitation, substance removal, and fire investigations.

Fire services administration. Prepares students to structure, manage, direct, and control fire departments, prevention services, and inspection and investigation offices.

Firefighting/fire science. Readies individuals to perform the duties of fire fighters.

Fishing and fisheries. Prepares individuals to produce non-domesticated fish and shellfish populations and manage fishing and product processing.

Flight attendant. Readies students to perform a variety of personal services conducive to the safety and comfort of airline passengers during flight.

Flight instructor. Focuses on the training of pilots or navigators to fly and/or navigate commercial aircraft.

Floriculture. Explores the operation and management of florist enterprises, supply and delivery services, and flower catering services.

Food preparation. Prepares students to serve under the supervision of food service professionals as kitchen support staff and food preparation workers.

Food science. Studies the conversion of raw agricultural products into processed forms suitable for human consumption.

Food service. Includes instruction in table and counter services, dining room operations, personnel supervision, business math, and safety and sanitation.

Food technology/processing. Describes the manufacturing, packaging, storage, and distribution technologies and processes for food products.

Food/nutrition studies. A general program that focuses on the role of foods and nutrition in human health and wellness.

Foreign language teacher education. Instructs individuals how to teach foreign languages other than French, German, or Spanish.

Foreign languages/literatures. A program that studies multiple foreign languages at the basic/elementary level.

Forensic psychology. Prepares individuals to assist the criminal justice and civil legal systems with the provision of clinical, counseling, school, and neuropsychological skills.

Forensic science. Trains students to apply physical, biomedical, and social sciences to analyze physical evidence, human testimony, and criminal suspects.

Forest engineering. Highlights the mechanical devices and processes used for efficient forest management, timber production, and related systems.

Forest management. Prepares individuals for the management of forest lands and related resources.

Forest resources production. Prepares students to perform technical and managerial functions as they relate to the production, harvesting, and processing of forest resources.

Forest sciences/biology. The study of environmental factors affecting forests and the growth and management of forest resources.

Forest technology. Readies individuals to assist foresters in the management and production of forest resources.

Forestry. Features the management and development of forest areas for varied purposes.

Franchise operations. Trains individuals to manage and operate franchises.

French. The study of the language and literature of French-speaking peoples, including related dialects and creoles.

French studies. Describes the history, society, politics, culture, and economics of France.

French teacher education. Describes how to teach French language programs.

Funeral direction. Prepares individuals for professional licensure as managers of funeral homes and cemeteries.

Funeral services/mortuary science. Describes the basic elements of mortuary science, the funeral service business, and counseling.

Furniture design/manufacturing. Readies individuals to design furniture projects; assemble, finish, and repair furniture articles; and use hand and power tools.

Gay/lesbian studies. The study of homosexuality and the public policies and legal issues surrounding the gay and lesbian community.

Gene therapy. Describes the treatment of diseases and inherited abnormalities through the modification of gene expression.

Genetic counseling. Readies students to counsel patients and families concerning inherited genetic disorders and diseases.

Genetics. The study of biological inheritance in organisms.

Geochemistry. Investigates the properties and behavior of the substances forming, and formed by, geomorphological processes of the earth and other planets.

Geochemistry/petrology. Explores the igneous, metamorphic, and hydrothermal processes within the earth and their resulting deposits.

Geography. Highlights the spatial distribution and interrelationships of people, natural resources, and plant and animal life.

Geography teacher education. Describes teaching aspects of historical, political, cultural, economic, and/or physical geography.

Geological engineering. Prepares students to analyze and evaluate engineering problems.

Geology/earth science. The scientific study of the earth, the forces acting upon it, and the behavior of the materials comprising it.

Geometry. Features the characteristics of points, lines, angles, surfaces, and solids.

Geophysics/seismology. The scientific study of the physics of solids and its application to the study of the earth and other planets.

Geotechnical engineering. Explores the systems used to manipulate and control surface and subsurface features at or incorporated into structural sites.

German. Highlights the German language as used in Austria, Germany, and Switzerland.

German studies. Focuses on the history, society, politics, culture, and economics of the Germanic peoples.

German teacher education. Prepares students to teach German language programs at various educational levels.

Germanic languages. A general program that focuses on one or more of the Germanic languages of Western, Central, and Northern Europe.

Gerontology. Investigates the aging process and aged human populations.

Geropsychology. Investigates the psychology of aging populations, with reference to growth and decline across the life span.

Glazier. Readies individuals to install and repair fixtures, sheets, windows, and skylights made of glass or plexiglass.

Global studies. Investigates global and international issues from the perspective of the social sciences and social services.

Graphic communications. Studies the manufacture and distribution of graphic communications products.

Graphic design. Readies students to use artistic techniques to develop and execute conceptual interpretations to authors' and designers' specifications.

Graphic/printing production. The study of commercial and industrial graphic communications jobs.

Greenhouse operations. Investigates the production and storage of plant species in controlled indoor environments for sale or research purposes.

Gunsmithing. Highlights the making and modification of firearms according to blueprints or customer specifications, using specialized tools and machines.

Hair styling. Readies individuals to shampoo, style, and set hair, and apply hair cosmetics and wigs.

Hazardous materials information systems. Readies individuals to implement, monitor, and enforce hazardous materials management and removal.

Hazardous materials technology. Focuses on basic engineering principles to aid in identifying and disposing of hazardous materials.

Health aide. Readies individuals to provide supervised care to patients, and/or perform maintenance and general assistance in health care facilities.

Health care administration. Readies individuals to develop, plan, and manage health care operations and services within health care facilities.

Health communications. Explores how people understand health and illness and the media's role in shaping health care messages.

Health management/clinical assistant. Prepares individuals to perform office services and clinical specialties.

Health occupations teacher education. Trains students to teach specific vocational health occupations programs.

Health physics/radiologic health. A program of study that applies nuclear science and engineering physics to diagnostic, treatment, and therapeutic processes, and to public health protection.

Health services. Prepares for entry into specialized training programs or for concentrations in the allied health area.

Health services administration. Readies students to plan and manage health services delivery systems in the public and private sectors.

Health teacher education. Prepares individuals to educate students about health-related topics.

Health unit coordinator. Readies individuals to perform administrative and reception duties in a patient care unit.

Health unit manager. Prepares students to supervise and coordinate the operations of patient care units.

Health/medical psychology. Features health, illness, and recovery, from the perspective that these phenomena arise from a combination of physical, behavioral, and social conditions.

Health/physical fitness. Readies students to promote physical fitness and athletic prowess, and to accomplish related research and service goals.

Heating/air conditioning/refrigeration maintenance. Describes the maintenance of heating, air conditioning, and refrigeration systems.

Heating/air conditioning/refrigeration technology. Focuses on supporting professionals that develop and install air conditioning, refrigeration, and heating systems.

Heavy equipment maintenance. Trains individuals to repair and overhaul heavy equipment.

Heavy/earthmoving equipment operation. Highlights the operation and maintenance of heavy equipment.

Hebrew. Explores the Hebrew language in either pre-modern or modern forms.

Hematology technology. Readies students, under the supervision of a laboratory scientist or physician, to perform tests and analyze blood samples.

Herbalism. A program that utilizes herbal medicines to prevent and cure illnesses and temporary physical disorders.

Higher education administration. Prepares students to become administrators in four-year colleges, universities, and higher education systems.

Hindi. Explores the Hindi language as spoken in India.

Hindu studies. A program that defines the philosophies, religious history, and cultural and social manifestations of Hinduism.

Hispanic-American studies. The study of the Hispanic American immigrant populations within the United States and Canada.

Histologic assistant. Readies individuals to process tissue samples and perform routine histologic procedures and tests.

Histologic technology. Trains students to identify tissue and cell components and relate these findings to physiological functions and to the detection and diagnoses of diseases.

Historic preservation. Studies the process of saving and restoring old structures for contemporary use.

History. The study and interpretation of the past.

History of science/technology. Describes the historical evolution of scientific theories and science applications and technologies.

History teacher education. Prepares students how to teach history programs at various educational levels.

Holocaust studies. Investigates acts of genocide in human history with particular reference to twentieth century genocides.

Home furnishings. Includes instruction in selecting, purchasing, designing, and decorating home furnishings; floral design; accessory construction; textiles; and upholstery.

Home health attendant. Highlights the provision of support services for homebound disabled, recovering, or elderly people.

Homeopathic medicine. Features a system that uses natural substances in highly diluted forms to mimic symptoms of illness and trigger autoimmune responses.

Horse husbandry/equine science. Trains students in the care and maintenance of horses and of horse farms, stables, and tracks.

Horticultural operations. Describes the production of domesticated plants, shrubs, flowers, trees, and groundcover; and the management of horticultural services.

Horticultural science. Prepares individuals to cultivate garden and ornamental plants, such as fruits, vegetables, and flowers.

Hospital/health care facilities administration. Prepares students to manage hospitals, clinics, nursing homes, and other health care facilities.

Hospitality administration/management. Prepares students to serve as general managers of hospitality operations.

Hospitality/recreation marketing. Focuses on the provision of marketing services in the hospitality and leisure fields.

Hotel/motel administration/management. Prepares individuals to oversee operations and facilities that provide lodging services to travelers.

Housing/human environments. The study of the behavioral, social, economic, functional, and aesthetic aspects of housing, interiors, and other environments.

Human development/family studies. Studies human development and behavioral characteristics of the individual within the context of the family.

Human nutrition. Highlights the relationships between food consumption and human development and health.

Human resources development. Readies students to manage and evaluate programs to improve individual productivity, employability and job satisfaction, and organizational effectiveness.

Human resources management. Prepares students to manage the development of human capital in organizations.

Human sciences communication. Focuses on communication of human sciences subject matter to a variety of audiences through print and non-print media.

Human services. Explores the provision of human and social services to individuals and communities.

Human/medical genetics. Describes human genetics as they relate to diagnosis, genetic engineering and therapy, transplantation, and diseases and their defense.

Humanities. Combined studies in the humanities, emphasizing languages, literatures, art, music, philosophy, and religion.

Hungarian/Magyar. The study of the language, literature, and culture of Hungarian-speaking peoples.

Hydraulics technology. Includes instruction in hydraulics principles, pipeline and pumping systems, operational testing, and inspection and maintenance procedures.

Hydrology/water resources science. The study of the circulation, distribution, and the chemical and physical properties of waters.

Hypnotherapy. Trains students to reduce pain, resolve emotional conflicts, and enhance communications through trance induction.

Illustration. Highlights artistic techniques to develop concept interpretations to specifications.

Industrial design. Readies individuals to convey information through the forms, shapes, and packaging of manufactured products.

Industrial electronics technology. Trains individuals to assemble, manage, and service industrial electrical/electronic equipment.

Industrial engineering. Prepares students to design systems for managing industrial production processes.

Industrial equipment maintenance/repair. Readies students to fix and sustain the operation of industrial machinery and equipment.

Industrial radiologic technology. Focuses on the operation of industrial and research testing equipment using radioisotopes.

Industrial safety technology. Prepares students to support engineers in implementing and enforcing industrial safety standards.

Industrial technology. Includes instruction in organizational behavior, industrial planning, computer applications, and report and presentation preparation.

Industrial/organizational psychology. Describes individual and group behavior in institutional settings; and applications to related problems of industrial and organizational settings.

Information resources management. Prepares students to plan, manage, and evaluate information services in organizations.

Information sciences/studies. Focuses on the process of information collection, transmission, and utilization in traditional and electronic forms.

Information technology. Highlights the design of technological information systems, as solutions to business, research, and communications support needs.

Inorganic chemistry. Covers elements and their compounds, other than the hydrocarbons and their derivatives.

Institutional food production. Focuses on the management of institutional food service operations.

Institutional food service. Provides instruction in the production and service used in institutional food establishments.

Instructional media. Focuses on the techniques of creating instructional products and educational resources in various media formats.

Instrumentation technology. Readies students to apply basic engineering principles in support of engineers engaged in developing measurement systems and procedures.

Insurance. Trains individuals to manage risk in organizational settings and provide insurance and risk-aversion services to businesses and individuals.

Intercultural/diversity studies. Emphasizes the promotion of cooperation between majority and minority groups; and the leadership of diverse groups and issues.

Interior architecture. Analyzes the processes and techniques of designing living, work, and leisure environments.

Interior design. Readies individuals to plan, design, equip and furnish interior spaces.

International agriculture. Studies the problems of global food production and distribution and the agricultural systems of other countries.

International business. Trains individuals to oversee international business operations.

International economics. Prepares individuals to analyze international commercial behavior and trade policy.

International finance. Trains students to manage international financial operations and related currency transactions.

International marketing. Readies students to perform marketing techniques for enterprises engaged in exporting or importing goods and services in world markets.

International public health. Describes health problems in low- and middle-income countries and regions.

International relations. The study of international politics and institutions, and the conduct of diplomacy and foreign policy.

Investments/securities. A program that prepares students to oversee assets placed in capital markets.

Iranian/Persian languages. A program that focuses on the languages used in ancient, medieval, and modern Iran.

Ironworking. Readies individuals to make and install ornamental and reinforcing metal structures and supports.

Islamic studies. The study of the history, culture, and interpretation of the Islamic faith.

Italian. Explores the Italian language and its applications in varied settings.

Italian studies. Highlights the history, society, politics, culture, and economics of modern Italy.

Japanese. The study of Japanese literature, language, and dialects, and their applications to business, science/technology, and other settings.

Japanese studies. Features the history, society, politics, culture, and economics of Japan.

Jazz studies. Studies the performance and composition of jazz.

Jewish/Judaic studies. Focuses on the history, culture, and religion of the Jewish people.

Journalism. Focuses on gathering, processing, and delivering news.

Junior high education. Trains individuals to guide students in the middle, intermediate, or junior high grades.

Juvenile corrections. Studies the provision of correction services to underage minor populations.

Khmer/Cambodian. Focuses on the Khmer language as spoken in Cambodia.

Kindergarten/preschool education. Trains individuals to instruct students ranging in age from three to six years, in settings prior to beginning regular elementary school.

Kinesiotherapy. Readies individuals to treat the effects of disease, injury, and congenital disorders through exercise and education.

Knowledge management. The study of knowledge management in government agencies and corporations for the purpose of supporting stated goals and objectives.

Korean. Describes Korean literature, language, and dialects.

Korean studies. Analyzes the history, society, politics, culture, and economics of Korea.

Labor studies. Highlights work, labor organization, policy, and movements from the perspective of the social sciences and history.

Labor/industrial relations. The study of employee-management interactions and the management of issues regarding working conditions and worker benefit packages.

LAN/WAN management. A program that prepares students to oversee and regulate organizational computer systems and performance requirements.

Land use planning. Focuses on how land can be preserved, developed, and used for maximum social, economic, and environmental benefit.

Landscape architecture. Includes instruction in geology and hydrology; soils, groundcovers, and horticultural elements; site planning; and landscape design.

Landscaping/groundskeeping. Describes the maintenance of ornamental and recreational plants and related conceptual designs.

Language interpretation/translation. Highlights the interpretation and/or translation of documents and data files, either from English or (Canadian) French into another language or vice versa.

Lao/Laotian. Highlights the Laotian language, dialects, and literature.

Laser/optical technology. Readies individuals to aid engineers engaged in developing and using lasers and other optical instruments for commercial or research purposes.

Latin. Features the Latin language and literature and its current ecclesiastical usage.

Latin American studies. Features the history, society, politics, culture, and economics of the North and South American Continents outside Canada and the United States.

Latin teacher education. A program that prepares individuals to teach Latin at various grade levels.

Law (J.D.). Preparation for the independent practice of law, taking bar examinations, and advanced research in jurisprudence.

Law enforcement administration. Prepares students to structure, manage, and control criminal justice agencies, including police departments and private protection services.

Legal administrative assistance. Instruction includes legal terminology, research, and documentation; software applications; and office procedures.

Legal studies. Describes the theory, history, and application of the rules of conduct by which societal relations are formally structured and adjudicated.

Liberal arts/sciences. A program that is a structured combination of the arts, sciences, and humanities, emphasizing breadth of study.

Library assistance. Includes instruction in library operation and services; acquisition, storage, and display systems; and material retrieval.

Library science. Prepares individuals to facilitate the use of information collections in print, audiovisual, and electronic formats.

Licensed midwifery. Readies individuals to provide for prenatal, natural birth, and immediate postpartum care to pregnant women.

Licensed practical nursing. Prepares students, under the direction of a registered nurse, physician, or dentist, to assist in providing general nursing care.

Lineworker. Describes how to install, operate, maintain, and repair electric power cables; erect and construct pole and tower lines; and install underground cables.

Linguistics. The study of language, language development, and the relationships among languages and language groups.

Livestock management. Readies individuals to produce and manage livestock animals and meat products.

Locksmithing. Prepares students to open locks; make keys; enter and change lock and safe combinations; and install and repair safes.

Logic. The systematic study of valid inference, argument, and sound reasoning.

Logistics/materials management. Prepares individuals to coordinate all logistical functions within an enterprise.

Machine shop technology. Trains students to make and modify metal parts used in manufacturing, repair, or design activities.

Machine tool technology. Prepares individuals to manufacture, assemble, test, and repair parts, mechanisms, and machines.

Make-up artist. Prepares students to apply cosmetics and perform specialized makeovers including wig work, masking, and costuming.

Management information systems. Readies individuals to manage data systems for processing and retrieving internal business information, to select systems, and to train personnel.

Management science. Highlights the application of mathematical modeling, programming, forecasting, and operations techniques to the analysis of business organization and performance problems.

Manicurist. Readies students to shape fingernails and toenails, remove unwanted skin, and apply polish and cosmetics to nails.

Manufacturing engineering. Includes instruction in the design, development, and implementation of manufacturing systems.

Manufacturing technologies. Covers the basic engineering principles used to the identify and resolve production problems in the manufacturing process.

Marine biology. Emphasizes marine organisms and their interactions with the physical environment.

Marine engineering/naval architecture. Prepares individuals to design vessels operating on or under the water; and analyzes related engineering problems.

Marine maintenance/fitter/ship repair. Prepares students to repair mechanical devices; repair vessel components; maintain sails; and repair and balance propeller and drive shafts.

Marine science/Merchant Marine. Prepares individuals to serve as captains, executive officers, engineers, and ranking mates on commercially licensed vessels.

Marketing management. Prepares students to develop consumer audiences and move products from producers to consumers.

Marketing research. A program that readies individuals to describe consumer behavior patterns and market environments to marketing managers.

Marriage/family therapy. Trains individuals to diagnose mental and emotional disorders within marriages and family systems, and to apply short- and long-term therapeutic strategies.

Masonry. Focuses on the laying or setting of brick, concrete block, hard tile, and marble, using hand tools.

Massage therapy. Prepares individuals to apply manual techniques for manipulating skin, muscles, and connective tissues.

Materials engineering. Highlights the evaluation of materials used in manufacturing; the synthesis of new materials; and analysis of materials requirements.

Materials science. Focuses on the analysis and evaluation of the characteristics and behavior of solids.

Maternal/child health. Emphasizes health issues affecting women, children, and families.

Maternal/child health nursing. Informs registered nurses how to provide prenatal care to pregnant women and to mothers and their newborn infants.

Mathematical statistics/probability. Focuses on the mathematical theory underlying the use of statistical methods.

Mathematics. A general program that analyzes quantities, magnitudes, forms, and their relationships, using symbolic logic and language.

Mathematics teacher education. Prepares individuals to teach mathematical subjects.

Mathematics/computer science. A program with a general synthesis of mathematics and computer science, or a specialization which draws from mathematics and computer science.

Meat cutting. Prepares individuals to receive, cut, and package animal meat products in commercial establishments.

Mechanical drafting/CAD/CADD. Trains individuals to prepare working drawings and electronic simulations in support of mechanical and industrial engineers.

Mechanical engineering. Focuses on the physical systems used in manufacturing and the integration of computers and remote control with operating systems.

Mechanical engineering technology. Investigates the design and development of projects involving mechanical systems.

Mechanics/repairers, general. Emphasizes the application of technical skills in the adjustment, maintenance, part replacement, and repair of tools, equipment, and machines.

Media studies. Analyzes the criticism of media, how people understand media, and the roles of media in transforming culture.

Medical administrative assistant. Prepares students to provide administrative assistance to physicians and other health professionals.

Medical claims examiner. Readies students to perform specialized functions related to insurance operations and their regulation.

Medical illustrating. Focuses on the creation of visual materials to facilitate educational, research, and clinical purposes.

Medical informatics. Prepares individuals to apply computer science to medical research and clinical support; and to develop advanced imaging, database, and decision systems.

Medical insurance coding specialist. Trains students to conduct data entry, classification, and record-keeping procedures related to medical insurance documentation.

Medical insurance specialist. Covers the management of insurance operations in a medical office, facility, or organization.

Medical office administration. Focuses on the management of business functions in a medical or clinical office.

Medical office assistant. Features the execution of administrative duties in an office environment.

Medical office computer specialist. Readies individuals to install, maintain, and upgrade medical software and associated hardware.

Medical radiologic technology/radiation therapy. Readies students to administer prescribed radiation treatments, manage patients, and maintain pertinent records.

Medical receptionist. Readies students to provide customer service, visitor reception, and patient services.

Medical records administration. Readies individuals to prepare, design, and manage the use of medical records and related information systems.

Medical records technology. Trains individuals to classify, construct, and secure medical records, under the supervision of health information administrators.

Medical scientist. Prepares graduated physicians as research scientists in various areas.

Medical staff services technology. Prepares individuals to execute compliance services for health care facilities and organizations.

Medical transcription. Prepares students to execute verbatim medical minutes, reports, and orders.

Medical/clinical assistant. Readies students to support physicians by providing assistance during patient consultations and examinations.

Medication aide. Prepares students to administer prescribed medications, report patient reactions, and perform emergency and recording duties.

Medicinal/pharmaceutical chemistry. A course of study that explores the properties of compounds intended for medicinal applications, and the development of related research methods.

Medicine (M.D.). Highlights the prevention, diagnosis, and treatment of illnesses and injuries of the human body.

Medieval/renaissance studies. Explores the Medieval and Renaissance periods in Europe from the perspective of the humanities and social sciences.

Medium/heavy vehicle technology. Highlights the specialized maintenance of commercial and industrial vehicles.

Mental health counseling. Trains students to evaluate, refer, and counsel people to prevent or mediate personal conflicts and emotional crises.

Mental health services technology. Prepares individuals to assist psychiatrists, psychologists, and nurses in patient care and treatment.

Merchandising/buying operations. Prepares students to function as professional buyers of resale products and product lines for stores, chains, and other retail enterprises.

Metal building assembly. Highlights the construction of metal structures using prefabricated framing and siding components.

Metal/jewelry arts. Trains individuals to fashion artwork from gems and other stones and precious metals.

Metallurgical engineering. Covers the metal components of structural, power, transmission, and moving systems, and the analysis of engineering problems.

Metallurgical technology. Trains students to support metallurgists engaged in developing and using industrial metals and manufacturing processes.

Meteorology. Readies students to predict atmospheric motion and climate change.

Microbial/eukaryotic genetics. Emphasizes the genetics of viruses, infectious agents, bacteria, and multi-celled organisms.

Microbiology. The study of small organisms, including bacteria and viruses, as distinguished from the cellular material of larger organisms.

Military technologies. Prepares individuals for various responsibilities in the armed services and related national security organizations.

Mining technology. Prepares individuals to support engineers engaged in the development and operation of mines and related mineral processing facilities.

Mining/mineral engineering. Studies the evaluation of mineral extraction and refining systems, including open shaft mines and prospecting equipment.

Missionary studies. The theory and practice of religious outreach, social service, and proselytization.

Mobile crane operation. Readies students to hoist and swing loads via rotating machinery that is driver operated.

Modern Greek. A program that focuses on the development and use of the Greek language.

Molecular biochemistry. Describes the chemical processes of living organisms at the molecular level.

Molecular biology. Investigates the molecular processes that transmit genetic information and energy, and processes such as development, growth, and aging.

Molecular biophysics. Applies physics principles to the study of living cells and organisms at the molecular level.

Molecular genetics. Covers the molecular structure and processes that regulate gene expression, information transfer, replication, and stability.

Molecular pharmacology. Highlights characteristics of drugs and their interaction with, and effects on, biological structures and processes.

Molecular physiology. Focuses on the scientific study of biochemical communications and processes at the subcellular level.

Molecular toxicology. Describes the interaction of toxic agents with biological systems at the molecular and cellular levels.

Mongolian. Features the language and literature, both oral and written, of the Mongolian-speaking peoples.

Montessori teacher education. Highlights the pedagogical principles and methods developed by Maria Montessori and her followers.

Mortuary science/embalming. Includes instruction in embalming, restorative art, laws and regulations, and special services required by specific religious communities.

Motorcycle maintenance. Prepares students to fix motorcycles and other similarly powered vehicles.

Movement therapy. Prepares individuals to promote body awareness and optimal mental and physical functioning.

Multicultural education. Highlights the design and implementation of instructional and advising services for culturally diverse learning populations.

Multimedia. Prepares students to display ideas in either two or three dimensions, through the simultaneous use of a variety of materials and media.

Museum studies. Prepares individuals to develop, conserve, and retrieve artifacts, exhibits, and collections in museums and galleries.

Music. An introductory study and appreciation of music and the performing arts.

Music history/literature. Highlights the evolution of music, the development of musical instruments, and the analysis and criticism of musical literature.

Music management. Explores the organization and management of music operations, facilities, and personnel.

Music pedagogy. Studies the provision of musical instruction and tutoring to clients in private and institutional settings.

Music performance. Prepares individuals to master musical instruments and become solo and/or ensemble performers.

Music teacher education. Prepares individuals to teach music and music appreciation.

Music theory/composition. The study of creating and arranging music.

Music therapy. Highlights the utilization of music to address patients' physical, psychological, cognitive, emotional, and social needs.

Musical instrument fabrication/repair. Describes the fabrication, repair, maintenance, and tuning of musical instruments.

Musicology/ethnomusicology. The study of the forms, methods, and functions of music in Western and non-Western societies and cultures.

Mycology. The study of various fungi and their relationship to diseases as well as to useful drug products.

Native American education. Prepares individuals to provide teaching and administrative services to American Indian, Alaska Native, and Hawaiian Native students that attend Tribal/First Nation schools.

Native American languages. A program that focuses on the languages native to the Western Hemisphere, with an emphasis on American Indian languages.

Native American studies. Highlights the history, society, politics, culture, and economics of the American Indian, Aleut, Inuit, and Hawaiian peoples.

Natural resource economics. The analysis of issues such as pollution, land use planning, waste disposal, and conservation policies.

Natural resources management/policy. Readies students to plan, manage, and evaluate programs to protect and regulate natural habitats and resources.

Natural resources/conservation, general. Focuses on the natural environment and its conservation, use, and improvement.

Natural sciences. A combined or undifferentiated focus on one or more of the physical and biological sciences.

Naturopathic medicine. Describes an approach that combines medical knowledge with noninvasive therapies and emphasizes disease prevention, wellness, and self-healing.

Near/Middle Eastern studies. Covers the history, society, politics, culture, and economics of North Africa, Southwestern Asia, Asia Minor, and the Arabian Peninsula.

Neuroanatomy. Focuses on the scientific study of the structure and function of the brain and central nervous system.

Neurobiology/physiology. Describes the neural functions and control of physiological systems in animals and humans.

Neuropharmacology. Focuses on drugs that modify brain function, the human body, and behavior, and the development of treatment therapies.

Neuroscience. Highlights aspects of the brain and nervous system.

Nonprofit/public organization management. Readies individuals to manage the business affairs of foundations, educational institutions, associations, public agencies, or governmental operations.

Norwegian. The study of the language and related dialects of the Norwegian-speaking peoples.

Nuclear engineering. Focuses on systems for controlling and manipulating nuclear energy and the analysis of related engineering problems.

Nuclear engineering technology. Readies individuals to support engineers operating nuclear facilities and engaged in nuclear applications and safety procedures.

Nuclear medical technology. Features the employment of nuclides in evaluations and therapeutic applications, while monitoring for patient health and safety.

Nuclear physics. The scientific study of the properties and behavior of atomic nuclei.

Nuclear power technology. Readies individuals to support engineers in the running of nuclear reactors, and in nuclear materials processing and disposal.

Nurse anesthetist. Teaches registered nurses how to administer anesthetics and provide care for patients before, during, and after anesthesia.

Nurse midwifery. Readies registered nurses to independently deliver babies and treat mothers in the prenatal, delivery, and post-delivery periods.

Nursery operations. Studies the management of plant farms, nurseries, and facilities that develop domesticated plant products for propagation, harvesting, and transplantation.

Nursing (R.N.). The study of the techniques and procedures for promoting health and providing care for sick individuals.

Nursing administration. Prepares registered nurses to manage nursing personnel and services in hospitals and other health agencies.

Nursing assistant. Readies individuals, under the training and supervision of a registered nurse or licensed practitioner, to provide nursing-related services to patients.

Nursing science. The study of clinical practices, research methodologies, and the administration of complex nursing services.

Nutritional sciences. Focuses on the utilization of food for human growth and metabolism in both normal and dysfunctional states.

Occupational health/industrial hygiene. Trains students to monitor and evaluate health and related safety standards in the workplace.

Occupational safety/health technology. Features the maintenance of job-related health and safety standards.

Occupational therapy. Prepares students to maximize patient independence and health through a mix of skills, motivation, environmental adaptations, and assistive technologies.

Occupational therapy assistant. Focuses on aiding occupational therapists by providing assistance during examinations and treatments and by keeping patient records.

Occupational/environmental health nursing. A program that prepares registered nurses to deliver nursing services to worker populations in clinical settings and at job sites.

Ocean engineering. Describes how to plan, design, and evaluate systems that monitor, control, and operate within ocean environments.

Oceanography. Features the chemical components, mechanisms, and movement of ocean waters and their interactions with terrestrial and atmospheric phenomena.

Office management. A program that prepares students to supervise and manage the operations and personnel of business offices and management-level divisions.

Office technology/data entry. Readies students to support businesses by using computer equipment for administrative purposes.

Office/clerical services. Prepares individuals, under the supervision of office managers, administrative assistants, and secretaries, to provide administrative support.

Oncology. Features the genetics, onset, and composition of cancer cells, as well as cancer behaviors and treatments.

Operations management. Readies students to direct the development, production, and manufacturing functions of an organization.

Operations research. Focuses on the development and application of simulation models to solve problems involving operational systems that are subject to human intervention.

Ophthalmic laboratory technology. Prepares individuals, under the supervision of an ophthalmologist or optometrist, to make corrective lenses and eyewear.

Ophthalmic technology. Prepares students to aid ophthalmologists and optometrists in examining and treating patients with vision disorders and eye diseases.

Opticianry/ophthalmic dispensing. Trains students to fit corrective eyewear, assist patients in selecting appropriate frames, and prepare work orders for ophthalmic technicians.

Optics. Covers light energy and its structure, properties, and behavior under different conditions.

Optometric assistant. Readies individuals to assist in providing patient care, administer examinations and treatments, and perform office functions.

Optometry (O.D.). Focuses on the techniques for examining, diagnosing, and treating conditions of the visual system.

Organic chemistry. Investigates the properties and behavior of hydrocarbon compounds and their derivatives.

Organizational behavior studies. Focuses on the scientific study of the behavior and motivations of individuals functioning in organized groups and its application to business and industrial settings.

Organizational communication. Includes instruction in group relations; decision-making and conflict management; and human interaction with computer technology.

Ornamental horticulture. Prepares students to breed, grow, and utilize ornamental plant varieties for commercial and aesthetic purposes.

Orthoptics. Readies students to analyze, evaluate, and treat specific disorders of vision, eye movement, and alignment in children and adults.

Orthotics/prosthetics. Features the techniques used to design and fit orthoses and prostheses for patients with disabling conditions or limb deformity.

Osteopathic medicine (D.O.). A program that involves a combination of medical and osteopathic principles, and describes the relationship of the musculoskeletal system to general health.

Pacific area/rim studies. Describes the history, society, politics, culture, and economics of Australia, New Zealand, and the Pacific Islands.

Painting. Readies individuals to impart ideas through the application of paints and chemical color substances to canvases.

Painting/wall covering. Prepares students to finish structural surfaces by applying protective or decorative coating materials, such as paint and wallpaper.

Paleontology. Features the reconstruction and analysis of ancient and extinct life forms, ecosystems, and geologic processes.

Paralegal/legal assistance. Prepares students to perform research, drafting, investigatory, record-keeping, and administrative functions under the supervision of an attorney or court.

Parasitology. Focuses on organisms that live on or within host organisms; and the role of parasites in causing injury, disease, and environmental damage.

Parks, recreation and leisure studies. Investigates the practices involved in the provision of recreational facilities and services to the general public.

Parks/recreational/leisure facilities management. Prepares students to develop and manage park facilities and other recreational and leisure facilities.

Particle physics. Studies the basic elements of subatomic matter and energy, and the forces governing their fundamental processes.

Parts/warehousing operations. Prepares students to maintain inventory control, care for inventory, and make minor repairs to warehouse equipment.

Pastoral counseling. Prepares ordained clergy to provide non-clinical pastoral counseling.

Pathology assistant. Trains individuals to help pathologists by performing autopsies, obtaining and preparing surgical specimens, and writing autopsy reports.

Pathology, human/animal. The scientific study of tissue injury and disease, including death and disease infestation and transfer.

Peace/conflict studies. Emphasizes the origins, resolution, and prevention of international and intergroup conflicts.

Pediatric nursing. Prepares registered nurses to provide care for children from infancy through adolescence.

Perfusion technology. Trains individuals to operate equipment that supports or replaces a patient's own respiratory or circulatory system.

Permanent cosmetics/tattooing. Focuses on the application of markings, color, and cosmetic products to the body for aesthetic or clinical purposes.

Personal/culinary services. Focuses on professional services related to cosmetology, funeral services, and food service.

Personal/financial services marketing. Prepares students to perform marketing and operational tasks associated with the provision of personal and financial services.

Personality psychology. Focuses on characteristics that set the individual apart from other individuals and on how others respond to that individual.

Petroleum engineering. Readies students to develop systems for locating, extracting, processing, and refining crude oil and natural gas.

Petroleum technology. Readies individuals to assist professionals in the development and operation of oil and natural gas extraction and processing facilities.

Pharmacology. Emphasizes the interactions of drugs on organisms and their various uses.

Pharmacology/toxicology. The study of pharmacological and toxicological issues in biology and the biomedical sciences.

Pharmacy (PharmD.). Trains students to prepare and dispense medications, manage pharmacy practices, and counsel patients.

Pharmacy assistant. Describes the preparation of medications, the provision of related services to patients, and the management of pharmacological and clinical operations.

Philosophy. Focuses on ideas and their structure, including arguments and investigations about abstract and real phenomena.

Philosophy/religion. Covers logical inquiry, organized belief systems, and practices.

Phlebotomy. Trains students to draw blood samples from patients using a variety of intrusive procedures.

Photobiology. Focuses on the effects of light on organisms, the ability of organisms to manufacture light, and the uses of light in biological research.

Photographic/film/video technology. Readies students to operate and maintain camera and lighting equipment; and produce finished still, video, and film products.

Photography. Describes the creation of images on photographic film, plates, and digital images.

Photojournalism. Describes the use of still and motion photography in journalism.

Physical anthropology. Features the adaptations, variability, and the evolution of human beings and their living and fossil relatives.

Physical education. Readies students to coach sports and/or teach physical education programs.

Physical sciences. The study of the topics, concepts, processes, and interrelationships of physical phenomena.

Physical therapy. Readies individuals to alleviate physical and functional impairments and limitations caused by injury or disease through the use of therapeutic interventions.

Physical therapy assistant. Trains individuals to support physical therapists by providing assistance during patient examinations, treatment, and monitoring.

Physical/theoretical chemistry. Investigates the properties of matter and the relation of force to the chemical structure and behavior of molecules.

Physician assistant. Prepares students, under the supervision of a physician, to practice medicine.

Physics. The study of matter and energy, and the formulation and testing of the laws governing their behavior.

Physics teacher education. Focuses on the teaching of physics curricula.

Physiology. The study of human behavior, including functions such as respiration, circulation, digestion, excretion, and reproduction.

Piano/organ. Readies students to develop the skills necessary to master the piano or organ, and to perform art as solo, ensemble, and/or accompanist performers.

Pipefitting. Focuses on the design, installation, and testing of piping systems and automatic fire and exposure protections systems.

Planetary sciences. The scientific study of planets, small objects, and related gravitational systems.

Plant breeding. Studies the improvement of agricultural plant health and populations and the development of new plant varieties.

Plant genetics. Highlights the relation of botanical research, comparative genetics, ecology, and evolutionary studies to the genetics of plants and fungi.

Plant molecular biology. Explores molecular structures, functions, and processes specific to plants and plant substances.

Plant pathology. Highlights plant diseases, plant health, and the development of disease control mechanisms.

Plant physiology. Investigates plants, plant-environment interaction, and plant life cycles and processes.

Plant protection/pest management. Prepares students to control animal and weed infestation; prevent/reduce economic loss; and control environmental pollution related to pest control measures.

Plant sciences. Highlights the breeding, cultivation, and production of plants and the processing and distribution of agricultural plant products.

Plasma/high-temperature physics. Highlights the properties and behavior of matter at high temperatures.

Plastics engineering technology. Includes instruction in the use of industrial polymers, plastics manufacturing and equipment, and design and operational testing procedures.

Platemaker/imager. Readies students to prepare film, digital data, and surfaces to reproduce printed or graphic images.

Playwriting/screenwriting. Describes the composition of written works for the theater and/or film.

Plumbing. Trains students to install and maintain piping fixtures and systems in home and business environments.

Podiatry (D.P.M.). Highlights the prevention, diagnosis, and treatment of diseases and injuries to the foot and lower extremities.

Polarity therapy. Includes instruction in energy-based anatomy and physiology; polarity processing, bodywork, and yoga; and energetic nutrition, evaluation, and assessment.

Police science. Prepares individuals to perform the duties of police and public security officers.

Polish. Highlights the Polish language and its use in literature.

Polish studies. Covers the history, society, politics, culture, and economics of Poland.

Political communications. Readies individuals to function as members of political and public affairs organizations, political campaign staffs, and related media entities.

Political science/government. A general program that focuses on the study of political institutions and behavior.

Polymer chemistry. The study of synthesized macromolecules and their interactions with other substances.

Polymer/plastics engineering. Describes the construction of industrial materials, the design of lightweight structural components, and the use of polymers.

Population biology. Investigates natural history, life cycle behavior, and ecosystem dynamics of single and multi-species communities and the causes of diversity among such populations.

Portuguese. Focuses on the Portuguese language and related dialects.

Poultry science. Prepares students for the production and management of poultry animals and products.

Power/electrical transmission. Features the installation of indoor and outdoor residential, commercial, and industrial electrical systems and associated power transmission lines.

Pre-ministerial studies. Readies students to enter a seminary or other religious ordination program, or a related religious vocation.

Precision production trades, general. A program that prepares individuals to apply technical knowledge in creating products using precision crafting and technical illustration.

Predentistry. Prepares individuals for advanced study in dentistry.

Prelaw. A four-year program, in virtually any major, that prepares individuals for admission to a professional law program.

Premedicine. Readies students for admission to a professional program in medicine, osteopathic medicine, or podiatric medicine.

Prenursing. Prepares individuals for advanced study in nursing.

Preoperative/surgical nursing. Readies registered nurses to provide care to surgery patients and to provide tableside assistance to surgeons.

Prepharmacy. Prepares individuals for entrance to a professional program in pharmacy.

Preveterinary. Readies students for admission to a professional program in veterinary medicine.

Printing management. Analyzes the application of managerial skills to printing operations from design through finished product.

Printing press operator. The application of technical skills to set up, operate, and maintain printing presses.

Printmaking. Prepares individuals to render art concepts onto surfaces and transfer images, via ink or dyes, onto paper or fabric.

Protective services. Focuses on the principles and procedures for providing police, fire, and other safety services, and on managing penal institutions.

Psychiatric nursing. Describes the provision of nursing care to patients with mental, emotional, or behavioral disorders.

Psychoanalysis. Readies individuals to provide psychoanalytic counseling to individuals and groups.

Psychobiology/physiological psychology. Covers the bases of psychological functioning and their application to experimental and therapeutic research.

Psychology. The study of individual and collective behavior, the bases of behavior, and the analysis and treatment of behavior problems and disorders.

Psychology teacher education. A program that prepares students to teach general psychology at the secondary school level.

Psychometrics/quantitative psychology. Explores psychological test construction and validation procedures; problems associated with behavior measurement; and quantitative methods used in research design.

Psychopharmacology. Describes the behavioral effects of drugs, nutrients, and chemicals in laboratory and clinical settings.

Public administration. Trains students to serve as managers in the executive arm of local, state, and federal government.

Public finance. Readies individuals to tend to the financial assets and budgets of public sector organizations.

Public health. Prepares individuals to plan, manage, and evaluate public health care services.

Public health education. A program of study that promotes preventive health measures and the education of targeted populations on health issues.

Public health nursing. Prepares individuals, under the supervision of a public health agency, to provide nursing services for groups or communities.

Public history/archives. A program that applies history and administrative skills to the recording of public events and the management of related historical resources.

Public policy analysis. The study of public policy issues and decision processes.

Public relations. Prepares students to manage the media image of an organization and communicate with clients and the general public.

Public services. Prepares individuals to analyze, manage, and deliver public services.

Publishing. Describes the creation, publishing, and distribution of books and other texts.

Punjabi. Focuses on the Punjabi language as spoken in India and Pakistan.

Purchasing/procurement/contracts. Readies individuals to manage the process of contracting goods and services for an organization.

Quality control technology. Highlights the maintenance of manufacturing and construction standards.

Rabbinical studies (M.H.L., Rav.). A program that prepares individuals for ordination as rabbis.

Radiation biology. Emphasizes the effects of radiation on organisms and biological systems.

Radiation protection/health physics technology. Prepares students to monitor and control radiation exposure and implement preventive measures in health care, work, and natural environments.

Radio/television. Highlights the planning, production, and distribution of audio and video programs.

Radio/television broadcasting. Describes the creation of radio and television programs.

Radiologic technology/medical imaging. Focuses on the provision of medical imaging services to patients and health care professionals.

Range science. Studies rangelands, arid regions, and grasslands, and the principles of managing such resources for maximum benefit and environmental balance.

Reading teacher education. Describes how to diagnose reading difficulties and teach reading programs.

Real estate. Prepares individuals to develop, buy, sell, appraise, and manage real property.

Receptionist. Prepares students to perform frontline public relations duties for a business, organization, or answering service.

Recording arts. Prepares individuals to produce sound recordings as finished products or as components of other media productions.

Recreational therapy. Trains students to organize and direct recreational activities designed to promote health for patients who suffer from disabling conditions.

Regional studies. The study of the defined geographic subregions and subcultures within countries and societies.

Reiki. Highlights the manipulation of the body's energy field to increase healing energy.

Religion/religious studies. Explores the nature of religious beliefs and specific religious and quasi-religious systems.

Religious education. Prepares individuals to provide religious educational services to members of faith communities.

Religious/sacred music. Highlights the history, theory, composition, and performance of music for religious or sacred purposes.

Renal/dialysis technology. Trains individuals to administer hemodialysis treatments to patients with renal failure.

Reproductive biology. The study of reproductive processes in animals and human beings.

Resort management. Emphasizes the planning, management, and marketing of comprehensive vacation facilities, services, and products.

Respiratory therapy. Trains individuals to assist in developing care plans, administering procedures, supervising personnel, maintaining records, and consulting with other health care team members.

Respiratory therapy assistant. Highlights the administration of general respiratory care procedures under the supervision of respiratory therapists.

Restaurant/catering management. Readies individuals to plan, supervise, and manage food and beverage service operations, restaurant facilities, and catering services.

Restaurant/food services management. Trains students to manage restaurants, food services in hospitality establishments, chains and franchises, and restaurant suppliers.

Retailing. Readies individuals to perform operations associated with retail sales in a variety of settings.

Robotics technology. Prepares individuals to aid engineers and other professionals engaged in developing and using robots.

Romance languages. A general curriculum that focuses on the Romance languages of Western, Central, and Southern Europe.

Romanian. Highlights the Romanian language and related dialects.

Roofing. Readies individuals to prepare, install, and maintain exterior roofing materials and roofs.

Russian. The study of the languages, literatures, and cultures of Russian-speaking peoples.

Russian/Slavic studies. Focuses on the history, society, politics, culture, and economics of the Russian Federation.

Sales/distribution. Studies the process and techniques of direct wholesale and retail buying and selling operations and introduces individuals to related careers.

Sales/marketing education. Investigates the teaching of vocational marketing operations and/or marketing and distributive education programs.

Salon management. Trains individuals to manage beauty parlors, shops, and specialized salons.

Sanskrit/classical Indian languages. The study of Sanskrit and related ancient and classical Indo-Aryan languages.

Scandinavian languages. A program that characterizes one or more of the languages, literatures, and linguistics of the Scandinavian peoples.

Scandinavian studies. Studies the history, society, politics, culture, and economics of Northern Europe.

School librarian education. Prepares students to serve as librarians and media specialists in elementary and secondary schools.

School psychology. Prepares individuals to treat and diagnose student behavioral problems.

Science teacher education. Prepares students to teach general science subjects or a combination of biology and physical science.

Science technologies. Prepares individuals to apply scientific skills in support of scientific research and development.

Science/technology/society. Covers the relationship, ramifications, and ethical dimensions of science and technology to public policy.

Sculpture. Features the use of clay, plaster, wood, stone, and metal to create three-dimensional works of art.

Secondary education. Readies individuals to teach a comprehensive curriculum or specific subject matter to students in the secondary grades.

Secondary school administration. Covers educational administration at the junior high, secondary, or senior high school levels.

Security services management. Readies individuals to plan, manage, and supervise services providing private security protection for people and property.

Security system installation/repair/inspection. Prepares individuals to install and repair household, business, and industrial security devices.

Security/loss prevention. Focuses on the performance of routine inspection, patrol, and crime prevention services for private clients.

Selling/sales operations. Focuses on the promotion of products and services to potential customers.

Semitic languages. Focuses on the Semitic languages of Western Asia, North Africa, and Europe.

Serbo-Croatian. Covers the Serbian and/or Croatian languages, either separately or considered as related derivatives of a common ancestor language.

Sheet metal technology. Focuses on the forming, shaping, bending, and folding of metal, including the creation of new products, using hand tools and machines.

Shoe/leather repair. Readies students to replace, mend, refinish, and dye leather goods and footwear.

Sign language interpretation. Includes instruction in American Sign Language, expressive nuances, cross-cultural communications, and slang and colloquialisms.

Sign language linguistics. Explores American Sign Language as a mode of communication within the deaf community and in relation to spoken and written languages.

Slavic languages. A general program that focuses on one or more of the Slavic languages of Central and Eastern Europe.

Slavic studies. Analyzes the history, society, politics, culture, and economics of the Slavic peoples.

Slovak. The study of the Slovak language, dialects, and literature.

Small business administration/management. A program that prepares individuals to develop and manage independent small businesses.

Small engine mechanics. Readies students to service small internal-combustion engines used on portable power equipment.

Social psychology. Explores individual behavior in group contexts, group behavior, and associated phenomena.

Social science teacher education. Studies the teaching of specific social science subjects and programs.

Social sciences. The study of human social behavior and institutions using any of the methodologies common to the social sciences and/or history.

Social studies teacher education. Prepares students to teach general social studies programs.

Social work. Studies the provision of basic support services for vulnerable individuals and groups.

Social/philosophical foundations of education. Studies education as a social and cultural institution, and the educational process as an object of humanistic inquiry.

Sociology. The systematic study of human social institutions and social relationships.

Software engineering. Prepares individuals to implement, validate, and maintain computer software systems using a variety of computer languages.

Soil chemistry/physics. The analysis of the nature, properties, conservation, and management of soils.

Soil microbiology. The study of the organismic properties of soils, soil-plant and soil-animal interactions, and the biological components and effects of soil management strategies.

Soil science. The scientific classification of soils, soil properties, and their relationship to agricultural crops.

Solar energy technology. Highlights the development of solar-powered energy systems.

Solid-state/low-temperature physics. Focuses on solids and related states of matter at low energy levels, including liquids and dense gases.

Somatic bodywork. A course of study that encourages physical and emotional balance through the provision of skilled touch principles and techniques.

South Asian languages. Features one or more of the languages, literatures, and linguistics of the peoples speaking the languages of the Indian subcontinent.

South Asian studies. Analyzes the history, society, politics, culture, and economics of Afghanistan, India, the Maldives, Burma, Pakistan, and Sri Lanka.

Southeast Asian languages. Focuses on one or more of the modern or historical languages spoken or originating in mainland Southeast Asia.

Southeast Asian studies. Covers the history, society, politics, culture, and economics of the peoples of Southeast Asia.

Spanish. Features the language, literature, and culture of Spanish-speaking peoples.

Spanish teacher education. Readies individuals to teach the language, literature, and culture of Spanish-speaking peoples.

Spanish/Iberian studies. Analyzes the history, society, politics, culture, and economics of the peoples of the Iberian Peninsula.

Special education. Describes the design and provision of educational services to children or adults with special learning needs.

Special education administration. Highlights the planning, supervision, and management of programs for exceptional students and their parents.

Special products marketing. Trains individuals to execute marketing and sales operations connected with the promotion of special products, including floristry, food, and home and office products.

Speech pathology. Readies individuals to evaluate patients' speaking capabilities and develop rehabilitative solutions in consultation with related professionals.

Speech teacher education. Prepares students to teach speech and language arts at various educational levels.

Speech/rhetorical studies. Studies interpersonal communication from the scientific/behavioral and humanistic perspectives.

Sports/fitness administration. Highlights the organization, administration, and management of athletic programs and teams, fitness/rehabilitation facilities, and sport recreation services.

Statistics. A study of the theory and proofs that form the basis of probability and inference.

Structural biology. The scientific study of molecular components and how they are organized into cells and tissues.

Structural engineering. Studies the design, analysis, and structural problems of load-bearing structures such as roads, bridges, and dams.

Substance abuse counseling. Focuses on intervention techniques and therapeutic services for persons suffering from addiction.

Superintendency. Prepares students to lead and manage multi-school educational systems and school districts.

Surgical technology. Prepares students to maintain, monitor, and enforce the sterile field and aseptic technique by surgical personnel.

Surveying engineering. Readies individuals to determine the location, elevations, and alignment of natural and man-made topographic features.

Surveying technology. Trains students to determine, plan, and position land tracts and water boundaries, and to prepare related maps, charts, and reports.

Swedish. Focuses on the Swedish language as used in Sweden and Finland.

System administration. Trains individuals to control the system configurations and manage the computer operations of a specific site or network hub.

Systematic biology. Features the patterns of origin, maintenance, diversification, distribution, and extinction of species.

Systems engineering. Trains individuals to design, develop, and evaluate systems solutions to a wide variety of engineering problems.

Systems science/theory. Focuses on the solution of problems using data from the natural, social, technological, behavioral, and life sciences.

Talmudic studies. Prepares students for advanced Talmudic scholarship and entry to ordination programs and conventional graduate and professional schools.

Tamil. The study of Tamil and its related dialects as spoken in South India and Sri Lanka.

Taxation. Prepares students to provide tax advice and management services to individuals and corporations.

Taxidermy. Trains individuals to reproduce life-like representations of living animals for permanent display and to manage taxidermy businesses.

Teacher assistance. Readies individuals to assist teachers in regular classroom settings or instruct and supervise special student populations.

Teacher education, multiple levels. Prepares individuals to teach students at more than one educational level.

Technical/business writing. The study of the methods and skills needed for writing and editing scientific, technical, and business papers.

Technology/industrial arts education. Trains students to guide technology education/industrial arts programs at various levels.

Telecommunications technology. Focuses on the design and implementation of telecommunications systems.

Textile science. Investigates the properties and processing of fibers, yarns, whole fabrics, dyes, and finishes.

Textile sciences/engineering. Focuses on systems that test and manufacture fiber products and the development of new and improved fibers, textiles, and their uses.

Thai. Features the Thai languages and their use in business settings.

Theater arts management. Trains students to manage theatres and production corporations.

Theater design/technology. Prepares students to communicate dramatic information, ideas, moods, and feelings through technical theatre methods.

Theater history/criticism. Studies the literature, history, and analysis of theatrical productions and theater methods and organization.

Theological studies. The study of the beliefs and doctrines of a particular religious faith from the point of view of that faith.

Theology/religious vocations. Programs that focus on the study of particular theologies and prepares individuals for the professional practice of religious vocations.

Theoretical/mathematical physics. Prepares individuals to formulate and evaluate the physical laws governing matter-energy phenomena and to analyze experimental designs and results.

Tibetan. Focuses on the Tibetan language.

Tibetan studies. Describes the history, society, politics, culture, and economics of Tibet.

Tool and die technology. Prepares individuals to operate tools and make instruments used to form metal parts.

Topology/foundations. Investigates geometric configurations under conditions of continuous transformations.

Tourism promotion. Trains students to perform marketing and sales operations connected with the promotion of tourism in a variety of settings.

Tourism/travel management. Readies individuals to manage travel-related enterprises and conventions and/or tour services.

Tourism/travel services. Features the provision of retail services to hotel and motel clients and customers in a variety of settings.

Toxicology. The study of toxic substances; their interaction with organisms; and their prevention, management, and counteraction.

Trade/industrial education. Prepares students to teach specific vocational trades and industries programs.

Traditional Chinese medicine/herbology. Highlights the use of natural products and prescribed medical formulae to treat health imbalances.

Traffic/customs/transportation clerk. Prepares students to manage revenue-based transportation services and assist in the control of fleet-based traffic for businesses.

Transportation. A program that prepares individuals to apply technical skills to perform services that facilitate the movement of people or materials.

Transportation management. Readies students to coordinate physical transportation operations, networks, and systems.

Transportation/highway engineering. Focuses on the development of systems for the physical movement of people, materials, and information.

Truck/bus/commercial vehicle operation. Trains individuals to drive trucks and buses, delivery vehicles, and for-hire vehicles.

Turf management. Readies individuals to develop, plant, and manage grassed areas and produce and store turf used for transplantation.

Turkish. A program that focuses on the Turkish language in either or both of its pre-modern and modern variants.

Ukraine studies. Relates the history, society, politics, culture, and economics of the Ukraine.

Ukrainian. Focuses on the Ukrainian language and its applications in varied settings.

Underwater diving. Prepares students to function as professional deep-water or scuba divers, diving instructors, or support personnel.

Upholstery. Highlights the installation of springs, padding, covering, and finishing on furniture, seats, caskets, mattresses, and bedsprings.

Urban education. Describes issues specific to the educational needs of populations located in metropolitan areas and inner cities.

Urban forestry. Studies the development, care, and maintenance of trees that are near areas of dense human habitation.

Urban studies. Emphasizes urban institutions and the forces influencing urban social and political life.

Urban/community/regional planning. The application of planning, analysis, and architecture to the development and improvement of urban areas.

Urdu. Highlights the Urdu language as spoken in Pakistan, India, and Afghanistan.

Vehicle emissions inspection/maintenance. Prepares individuals to test and service all vehicle emission systems in accordance with relevant laws and regulations.

Vehicle parts/accessories marketing. Prepares individuals to distribute and sell replacement parts and other supplies in the automotive, marine, and aviation industries.

Vendor/product certification. Studies the installation, customization, and maintenance of software products and/or processes.

Veterinary assistant. Readies students to aid animal specialists by executing patient care, clinical assistance, and owner communication.

Veterinary medicine (D.V.M.). Trains students to diagnose, treat, and manage animal health care and to prevent and manage zoonosis.

Vietnamese. The study of the language, literature, and culture of Vietnamese-speaking peoples.

Violin/viola/guitar/stringed instruments. Prepares students to master a stringed instrument.

Virology. Emphasizes viruses that inhabit living cells in parasitical relationships and their role in disease.

Vision science. The study of vision, visual processes, clinical research, and forms of treatment.

Visual/performing arts. Highlights the visual and performing arts, and prepares individuals in any of the visual artistic media or performing disciplines.

Vocational rehabilitation counseling. Prepares students to counsel disabled individuals in order for them to have fulfilling and productive lives.

Vocational/technical education. Readies individuals to teach vocational technical education programs to students.

Voice/opera. Trains individuals to master the human voice and perform in concerts, choirs, or operas.

Waldorf/Steiner teacher education. Features the pedagogical principles and methods developed by Rudolf Steiner and his followers.

Warehousing/inventory management. Readies individuals to support warehouse operations, inventory control, parts identification, and counter services for customers.

Watch/jewelrymaking. Readies individuals to mend and maintain time-measuring devices and jewelry items.

Water quality/treatment/recycling technology. Prepares individuals to support engineers engaged in the origination and use of water storage, waterpower, and wastewater treatment systems.

Water resource engineering. Describes systems for collecting, storing, moving, conserving, and controlling surface- and groundwater.

Water, wetlands, and marine management. Investigates the development, conservation, and management of freshwater and saltwater environments.

Web page/multimedia design. Readies students to produce and publish documents, images, graphics, sound, and multimedia projects on the World Wide Web.

Web/multimedia management. Covers the development and maintenance of Web servers and Web pages at Web sites.

Welding technology. A program that prepares individuals to apply technical knowledge and skills to join or cut metal surfaces.

Well drilling. Readies individuals to operate well-drilling equipment; locate, drill, and construct wells; and test and monitor wells.

Western European studies. Covers the history, society, politics, culture, and economics of historical Western Europe.

Wildlife biology. A program that applies biological principles to the study of vertebrate wildlife and habitats in remote and urban areas.

Wildlife/wilderness management. Describes the conservation and management of wilderness areas and the management of wildlife reservations and zoological facilities.

Women's studies. Focuses on the history, society, politics, culture, and economics of women in North America and the world.

Wood science/pulp/paper technology. Describes the behavior of wood and the development of processes for converting wood into paper and other products.

Woodworking. Trains students to shape, mark, saw, carve, sand, and repair wooden products, and to use a variety of hand and power tools.

Word processing. Highlights typing, table construction, and document formatting on personal computers.

Work/family studies. Focuses on family and consumer science concepts and the various career paths open to interested students.

Yoga teacher/therapy. Trains students to provide spiritual and physical Yoga therapy in private, institutional, and clinical settings.

Youth ministry. Studies the provision of spiritual counseling and leadership services to children, adolescents, and young adults.

Youth services. Readies students to plan, manage, and implement social services for children, youth, and families.

Zoology. Emphasizes the anatomy, structure, and behavior of animals.

Majors

Accounting

Alabama

Alabama Agricultural and Mechanical
University *B*
Alabama Southern Community
College *A*
Alabama State University *B, M*
Athens State University *B*
Auburn University *B, M*
Auburn University at Montgomery *B*
Birmingham-Southern College *B*
Bishop State Community College *A*
Calhoun Community College *A*
Chattahoochee Valley Community
College *A*
Faulkner University *B*
Harry M. Ayers State Technical
College *C, A*
Huntingdon College *B*
J. F. Drake State Technical College *C, A*
Jacksonville State University *B*
Lawson State Community College *A*
Miles College *B*
Northeast Alabama Community
College *A*
Oakwood College *A, B*
Samford University *B, M*
South University *A*
Southern Union State Community
College *A*
Spring Hill College *B, M*
Talladega College *B*
Trenholm State Technical College *A*
Troy State University *B*
Troy State University in Montgomery *B*
Tuskegee University *B*
University of Alabama *B, M, D*
University of Alabama
Birmingham *B, M*
Huntsville *B, M*
University of Mobile *B*
University of Montevallo *B*
University of North Alabama *B*
University of South Alabama *B, M*
University of West Alabama *B*
Virginia College *C, A*
Wallace Community College: Sparks
Campus *A*
Wallace State Community College at
Hanceville *A*

Alaska

Charter College *C, A*
University of Alaska
Anchorage *A, B*
Fairbanks *B*
Southeast *C, B*

Arizona

Arizona State University *B, M*
Central Arizona College *C, A*
DeVry University
Phoenix *M*
Eastern Arizona College *C*
Gateway Community College *C, A*
Glendale Community College *A*
International Institute of the Americas
Phoenix *C, A, B*
Tucson *C, A, B*
Northern Arizona University *B*
Paradise Valley Community
College *C, A*
Phoenix College *A*

Pima Community College *C, A*
Prescott College *B*
Rio Salado College *C, A*
Scottsdale Community College *C, A*
University of Arizona *B, M*
University of Phoenix *C, B, M*
Yavapai College *C, A*

Arkansas

Arkansas State University *B*
Arkansas State University
Beebe *C*
Arkansas Tech University *B*
Black River Technical College *A*
Harding University *B*
Henderson State University *B*
Hendrix College *B, M*
John Brown University *B*
Lyon College *B*
Northwest Arkansas Community
College *A*
Ouachita Baptist University *B*
Pulaski Technical College *C*
South Arkansas Community College *C*
Southeast Arkansas College *C*
Southern Arkansas University *B*
University of Arkansas *B, M*
University of Arkansas
Community College at Batesville *A*
Fort Smith *B*
Little Rock *B*
Monticello *B*
Pine Bluff *B*
University of Central Arkansas *B, M*
University of the Ozarks *B*

California

Azusa Pacific University *B*
Bakersfield College *A*
Barstow College *C, A*
Cabrillo College *C, A*
California State Polytechnic University:
Pomona *B*
California State University
Bakersfield *B*
Chico *B, M*
Dominguez Hills *B*
Fresno *B*
Fullerton *B, M*
Hayward *B, M*
Long Beach *B*
Los Angeles *B, M*
Northridge *M*
Sacramento *M*
Stanislaus *B*
Cerritos Community College *A*
Chabot College *A*
Chapman University *B*
Citrus College *C*
Claremont McKenna College *B*
Coastline Community College *C, A*
College of Alameda *A*
College of Marin: Kentfield *A*
College of the Canyons *C, A*
College of the Sequoias *C, A*
College of the Siskiyous *C, A*
Columbia College *C*
Concordia University *B*
Cuyamaca College *C, A*
De Anza College *C, A*
DeVry University
Fremont *B*
Long Beach *M*
Pomona *M*
West Hills *M*
Diablo Valley College *C*
East Los Angeles College *A*
Foothill College *C, A*
Fresno Pacific University *B*
Gavilan Community College *C*
Glendale Community College *C, A*
Golden Gate University *C, B, M*
Golden West College *C, A*
Heald College
Milpitas *C, A*
Irvine Valley College *C, A*

La Sierra University *B, M*
Laney College *C, A*
Las Positas College *C*
Long Beach City College *C, A*
Los Angeles Harbor College *C, A*
Los Angeles Pierce College *C, A*
Los Angeles Southwest College *A*
Los Angeles Trade and Technical
College *C, A*
Los Medanos College *C, A*
Loyola Marymount University *B*
MTI College of Business and
Technology *C*
Marymount College *B*
Master's College *B*
MiraCosta College *C, A*
Modesto Junior College *C, A*
Monterey Peninsula College *C, A*
Moorpark College *C, A*
Mount St. Mary's College *A, B*
Mount San Antonio College *C, A*
Napa Valley College *A*
National University *C, B, M*
Ohlone College *C, A*
Orange Coast College *C, A*
Pacific Union College *B*
Palomar College *C, A*
Pepperdine University *B*
Point Loma Nazarene University *B*
Reedley College *C, A*
Riverside Community College *C, A*
St. Mary's College of California *B*
San Diego City College *C, A*
San Diego Mesa College *C, A*
San Diego State University *C, B, M*
San Francisco State University *B, M*
San Joaquin Delta College *A*
San Jose State University *B, M*
Santa Barbara City College *C, A*
Santa Clara University *B*
Santa Monica College *A*
Santa Rosa Junior College *C*
Santiago Canyon College *A*
Shasta College *A*
Sierra College *A*
Southwestern College *C, A*
Taft College *C, A*
University of California
Santa Cruz *B*
University of La Verne *B*
University of Redlands *B*
University of San Diego *B*
University of San Francisco *B*
University of Southern
California *B, M, D*
Vanguard University of Southern
California *B*
Ventura College *C, A*
West Valley College *A*
Woodbury University *B*
Yuba Community College District *C, A*

Colorado

Arapahoe Community College *A*
Blair Junior College *A*
Colorado Christian University *B*
Colorado Mountain College
Alpine Campus *C, A*
Spring Valley Campus *C, A*
Timberline Campus *C, A*
Colorado State University *B*
Colorado State University
Pueblo *B*
Community College of Aurora *C, A*
Fort Lewis College *B*
Front Range Community College *C, A*
Mesa State College *B*
Metropolitan State College of Denver *B*
Morgan Community College *A*
National American University
Denver *A, B*
Parks College *A*
Red Rocks Community College *C, A*
Regis University *B*
Trinidad State Junior College *A*

University of Colorado
Boulder *B, M*
Colorado Springs *B*
Denver *M*
University of Denver *B, M*

Connecticut

Albertus Magnus College *B*
Asnuntuck Community College *A*
Briarwood College *A*
Capital Community College *C, A*
Central Connecticut State University *B*
Eastern Connecticut State
University *B, M*
Fairfield University *B*
Gateway Community College *A*
Gibbs College *C*
Housatonic Community College *A*
Manchester Community College *C, A*
Middlesex Community College *A*
Mitchell College *A*
Naugatuck Valley Community
College *C, A*
Northwestern Connecticut Community
College *A*
Norwalk Community College *A*
Quinebaug Valley Community College *A*
Quinnipiac University *B, M*
Sacred Heart University *B*
Southern Connecticut State University *B*
Teikyo Post University *A, B*
Three Rivers Community College *C, A*
Tunxis Community College *C, A*
University of Bridgeport *B, M*
University of Connecticut *B, M*
University of Hartford *B, M*
University of New Haven *B, M*
Western Connecticut State University *B*

Delaware

Delaware State University *B*
Delaware Technical and Community
College
Owens Campus *C, A*
Stanton/Wilmington Campus *C, A*
Terry Campus *C, A*
Goldey-Beacom College *A, B*
University of Delaware *B, M*
Wilmington College *B*

District of Columbia

American University *B, M*
Catholic University of America *B, M*
Gallaudet University *B*
George Washington University *B, M, D*
Georgetown University *B*
Howard University *B*
Strayer University *C, A, B, M*
University of the District of Columbia *B*

Florida

Barry University *B*
Bethune-Cookman College *B*
Broward Community College *C, A*
Daytona Beach Community
College *C, A*
DeVry University
Miramar *M*
Orlando *M*
Edward Waters College *B*
Flagler College *B*
Florida Agricultural and Mechanical
University *B*
Florida Atlantic University *B, M*
Florida Gulf Coast University *C, B, M*
Florida Institute of Technology *M*
Florida International University *B, M*
Florida Metropolitan University
Melbourne Campus *A, B*
Orlando College North *A, B*
Tampa College *A, B*
Tampa College Lakeland *B*
Florida National College *A*
Florida Southern College *B*
Florida State University *B, M*
Gulf Coast Community College *C, A*
Hillsborough Community College *C, A*

Indian River Community College *C, A*
Institute of Career Education *C*
International College *A, B*
Jacksonville University *B, M*
Jones College *A, B*
Lake City Community College *C*
Lake-Sumter Community College *C*
Manatee Community College *A*
Miami-Dade Community College *C, A*
Northwood University
    Florida Campus *A, B*
Nova Southeastern University *B, M*
Okaloosa-Walton Community
    College *C, A*
Palm Beach Community College *A*
Pensacola Junior College *C, A*
Polk Community College *A*
St. Leo University *B*
St. Petersburg College *C, A*
St. Thomas University *B, M*
Santa Fe Community College *C, A*
South Florida Community College *C, A*
Southeastern College of the Assemblies
    of God *B*
Southwest Florida College *C, A*
Stetson University *B, M*
Tallahassee Community College *A*
University of Central Florida *B, M*
University of Florida *B, M*
University of Miami *C, B, M, D*
University of North Florida *B, M*
University of South Florida *B, M*
University of Tampa *B*
University of West Florida *B, M*
Valencia Community College *A*
Webber International University *A, B, M*
Webster College: Holiday *A*

Georgia

Abraham Baldwin Agricultural
    College *A*
Albany State University *B*
Augusta State University *B*
Bainbridge College *A*
Berry College *B*
Brenau University *B*
Brewton-Parker College *B*
Central Georgia Technical College *C*
Chattahoochee Technical College *C, A*
Clark Atlanta University *B, M*
Clayton College and State University *B*
Coastal Georgia Community College *A*
Columbus State University *B*
Columbus Technical College *C, A*
Darton College *C, A*
DeKalb Technical College *C, A*
DeVry University
    Atlanta *M*
Emory University *B*
Fort Valley State University *B*
Gainesville College *A*
Georgia College and State
    University *B, M*
Georgia Military College *A*
Georgia Southern University *B, M*
Georgia Southwestern State
    University *A, B, M*
Georgia State University *B, M, D*
Griffin Technical College *A*
Kennesaw State University *B, M*
LaGrange College *B*
Macon State College *B*
Mercer University *B, M*
Middle Georgia College *A*
Morehouse College *B*
Morris Brown College *B*
North Georgia College & State
    University *B*
Northwestern Technical College *A*
Oglethorpe University *B*
Reinhardt College *B*
Savannah State University *B*
Savannah Technical College *A*
Shorter College *B*
South Georgia College *A*
South University *A*

State University of West Georgia *B, M*
Thomas University *B*
University of Georgia *B, M*
Valdosta State University *B, M*
Waycross College *A*
West Georgia Technical College *A*

Hawaii

Brigham Young University-Hawaii *B*
Chaminade University of Honolulu *B*
Hawaii Business College *A*
Hawaii Pacific University *A, B*
Heald College
    Honolulu *A*
University of Hawaii
    Hawaii Community College *A*
    Hilo *B*
    Kauai Community College *C, A*
    Leeward Community College *A*
    Manoa *B, M*
    Maui Community College *A*
    West Oahu *B*

Idaho

Albertson College of Idaho *B*
Boise State University *B, M*
Brigham Young University - Idaho *B*
College of Southern Idaho *A*
Eastern Idaho Technical College *C, A*
Idaho State University *B*
Northwest Nazarene University *B*
University of Idaho *B, M*

Illinois

Augustana College *B*
Aurora University *B*
Benedictine University *B*
Black Hawk College
    East Campus *C, A*
Blackburn College *B*
Bradley University *B, M*
Carl Sandburg College *C, A*
Chicago State University *B*
City Colleges of Chicago
    Harold Washington College *C, A*
    Kennedy-King College *C, A*
    Malcolm X College *C, A*
    Olive-Harvey College *C, A*
    Wright College *C, A*
College of DuPage *C, A*
College of Lake County *C, A*
Concordia University *B*
Danville Area Community College *C, A*
De Paul University *B, M*
Dominican University *B, M*
Eastern Illinois University *B*
Elgin Community College *C, A*
Elmhurst College *B, M*
Eureka College *B*
Gem City College *C, A*
Governors State University *B, M*
Greenville College *B*
Illinois Central College *C, A*
Illinois College *B*
Illinois Eastern Community Colleges
    Olney Central College *A*
Illinois Institute of Technology *M*
Illinois State University *B, M*
Illinois Wesleyan University *B*
John A. Logan College *C, A*
John Wood Community College *C, A*
Joliet Junior College *C, A*
Judson College *B*
Kankakee Community College *C, A*
Kishwaukee College *C, A*
Lewis University *B*
Lewis and Clark Community College *A*
Lincoln College *B*
Lincoln Land Community College *A*
Loyola University of Chicago *B, M*
MacMurray College *B*
McKendree College *B*
Midstate College *A*
Millikin University *B*
Monmouth College *B, T*
Moraine Valley Community College *C*

National-Louis University *C, B*
North Central College *B*
North Park University *B*
Northeastern Illinois University *B, M*
Northern Illinois University *B, M*
Northwestern Business College *A*
Northwestern University *C, D*
Oakton Community College *A*
Olivet Nazarene University *B*
Parkland College *C, A*
Prairie State College *C*
Quincy University *B*
Richland Community College *A*
Robert Morris College: Chicago *C, A*
Rock Valley College *C, A*
Rockford Business College *C, A*
Rockford College *B*
Roosevelt University *B, M*
St. Augustine College *C, A*
St. Xavier University *C, B*
Sauk Valley Community College *C, A*
Shawnee Community College *A*
South Suburban College of Cook
    County *A*
Southern Illinois University
    Carbondale *B, M*
Southern Illinois University
    Edwardsville *B, M*
Southwestern Illinois College *A*
Trinity Christian College *B*
Trinity International University *B*
Triton College *C, A*
University of Chicago *M, D*
University of Illinois
    Chicago *B, M*
    Springfield *B, M*
    Urbana-Champaign *B, M, D*
University of St. Francis *B*
Waubonsee Community College *C, A*
Western Illinois University *B, M*
William Rainey Harper College *C, A*

Indiana

Anderson University *B, M*
Ball State University *B*
Bethel College *B*
Butler University *B*
Calumet College of St. Joseph *C, A, B*
Commonwealth Business College:
    Michigan City *A*
Franklin College *B*
Goshen College *B*
Huntington College *B*
Indiana Business College *C, A*
Indiana Business College
    Anderson *A*
    Columbus *C, A*
    Evansville *C, A*
    Fort Wayne *A*
    Lafayette *C, A*
    Marion *A*
    Muncie *C, A*
    Terre Haute *C, A*
Indiana Institute of Technology *A, B*
Indiana State University *B*
Indiana University
    Bloomington *B, M*
    East *A, B*
    Kokomo *B*
    Northwest *M*
    South Bend *M*
    Southeast *B*
Indiana University-Purdue University
    Fort Wayne *B*
Indiana University-Purdue University
    Indianapolis *M*
Indiana Wesleyan University *A, B*
International Business College *C, A*
Ivy Tech State College
    Northcentral *A*
Manchester College *A, B, M*
Marian College *A, B*
Martin University *B*
Michiana College *C, A*
Michiana College: Fort Wayne *A*
Oakland City University *A*

Purdue University *B*
Purdue University
    Calumet
    North Central Campus *A, B*
St. Joseph's College *B*
Saint Mary's College *B*
St. Mary-of-the-Woods College *A, B*
Sawyer College *C, A*
Sawyer College: Merrillville *A*
Taylor University *B*
Tri-State University *A, B*
University of Evansville *B*
University of Indianapolis *B, M*
University of Notre Dame *B, M*
University of St. Francis *A, B*
University of Southern Indiana *C, B, M*
Valparaiso University *B*
Vincennes University *A*

Iowa

American Institute of Business *C, A*
Briar Cliff University *B*
Buena Vista University *B*
Central College *B*
Clarke College *B*
Coe College *B*
Des Moines Area Community
    College *C, A*
Dordt College *B*
Drake University *B, M*
Ellsworth Community College *A*
Franciscan University *B*
Graceland University *B*
Grand View College *B*
Hamilton College *C, A*
Hamilton College
    Cedar Falls *C, A*
    Cedar Rapids *A*
    Mason City *A*
Hawkeye Community College *C, A*
Indian Hills Community College *C*
Iowa Central Community College *A*
Iowa State University *B, M*
Iowa Wesleyan College *B*
Kaplan College *C, A*
Kirkwood Community College *C, A*
Loras College *B*
Luther College *B*
Marshalltown Community College *C, A*
Morningside College *B*
Mount Mercy College *B*
Muscatine Community College *A*
North Iowa Area Community College *A*
Northeast Iowa Community
    College *C, A*
Northwest Iowa Community College *A*
Northwestern College *B*
St. Ambrose University *B, M*
Scott Community College *A*
Simpson College *B*
Southeastern Community College
    North Campus *A*
Southwestern Community College *A*
University of Dubuque *A, B*
University of Iowa *B, M, D*
University of Northern Iowa *B, M*
Upper Iowa University *B*
Waldorf College *A*
Wartburg College *B*
Western Iowa Tech Community
    College *C, A*
William Penn University *B*

Kansas

Allen County Community College *A*
Baker University *B*
Barton County Community College *A*
Benedictine College *A, B*
Bethany College *B*
Butler County Community College *A*
Central Christian College *A, B*
Dodge City Community College *C*
Donnelly College *A*
Emporia State University *B*
Fort Hays State University *B*
Fort Scott Community College *A*

Friends University *B*
Haskell Indian Nations University *A*
Hutchinson Community College *A*
Independence Community College *A*
Johnson County Community College *A*
Kansas City Kansas Community
  College *A*
Kansas State University *A, B, M*
Kansas Wesleyan University *A, B*
Labette Community College *A*
McPherson College *B*
MidAmerica Nazarene University *B*
Newman University *B*
Pittsburg State University *B, M*
Pratt Community College *C, A*
St. Mary College *B*
Seward County Community
  College *C, A*
Tabor College *M*
University of Kansas *B, M*
Washburn University of Topeka *B, M*
Wichita State University *B, M*

Kentucky

Asbury College *B*
Bellarmine University *B*
Brescia University *C, B*
Campbellsville University *A, B*
Cumberland College *B*
Georgetown College *B*
Jefferson Community College *A*
Kentucky Wesleyan College *B*
Madisonville Community College *A*
Maysville Community College *C, A*
Morehead State University *B*
Murray State University *B*
National College of Business &
  Technology
    Danville *C, A*
    Florence *C, A*
    Lexington *C, A*
    Pikeville *C, A*
    Richmond *C, A*
Paducah Community College *A*
Paducah Technical College *C*
Prestonsburg Community College *A*
Spalding University *B*
Spencerian College *A*
Sullivan University *C, A, B*
Thomas More College *C, A, B*
Transylvania University *B*
Union College *A, B*
University of Kentucky *B, M*
University of Louisville *B*

Louisiana

Centenary College of Louisiana *B*
Delgado Community College *A*
Dillard University *B*
Grambling State University *B*
Louisiana College *B*
Louisiana State University
  Shreveport *B*
Louisiana State University and
  Agricultural and Mechanical
  College *B, M, D*
Louisiana Tech University *B, M*
Loyola University New Orleans *B*
McNeese State University *B*
Nicholls State University *B*
Northwestern State University *B*
Nunez Community College *C, A*
Our Lady of Holy Cross College *B*
Southeastern Louisiana University *B*
Southern University
  New Orleans *B*
  Shreveport *A*
Southern University and Agricultural and
  Mechanical College *B, M*
Tulane University *B*
University of Louisiana at Lafayette *B*
University of Louisiana at Monroe *B*
University of New Orleans *B, M*
Xavier University of Louisiana *B*

Maine

Andover College *A*
Beal College *A*
Central Maine Technical College *A*
Husson College *A, B*
St. Joseph's College *B*
Thomas College *A, B*
University of Maine *B*
University of Maine
  Machias *A, B*
  Presque Isle *B*
University of Southern Maine *B, M*

Maryland

Allegany College *A*
Anne Arundel Community College *C, A*
Bowie State University *B*
Carroll Community College *C, A*
Cecil Community College *A*
Chesapeake College *C, A*
Columbia Union College *A, B*
Community College of Baltimore County
  Catonsville *C, A*
  Dundalk *C, A*
  Essex *C, A*
Frederick Community College *A*
Frostburg State University *B*
Harford Community College *C, A*
Loyola College in Maryland *B*
Montgomery College
  Rockville Campus *A*
Morgan State University *B*
Mount St. Mary's College *B*
Salisbury University *B*
Towson University *B*
University of Baltimore *B, M*
University of Maryland
  College Park *B*
  University College *C, B, M*
Villa Julie College *A, B*
Wor-Wic Community College *C, A*

Massachusetts

American International College *B, M*
Anna Maria College *B*
Assumption College *B*
Atlantic Union College *A, B*
Babson College *B*
Bay State College *A*
Becker College *C, A, B*
Bentley College *B, M*
Boston College *B*
Boston University *B*
Bridgewater State College *C, B*
Bunker Hill Community College *C*
Cape Cod Community College *A*
Elms College *B*
Fisher College *A*
Fitchburg State College *B, M*
Gordon College *B*
Greenfield Community College *C, A*
Lasell College *B*
Marian Court College *C, A*
Massachusetts Bay Community
  College *C, A*
Massachusetts College of Liberal Arts *B*
Massasoit Community College *C, A*
Merrimack College *B*
Mount Ida College *A*
Mount Wachusett Community College *C*
Newbury College *C, A, B*
Nichols College *B*
Northeastern University *A, B, M*
Quinsigamond Community College *C*
Roxbury Community College *A*
Springfield Technical Community
  College *A*
Stonehill College *C, B, M*
Suffolk University *C, B, M*
University of Massachusetts
  Amherst *B, M*
  Dartmouth *B*
Western New England College *B, M*
Westfield State College *B*

Michigan

Adrian College *B*
Alma College *B*
Alpena Community College *A*
Andrews University *B*
Aquinas College *B, T*
Baker College
  of Auburn Hills *A, B*
  of Cadillac *C, A, B*
  of Clinton Township *C, A, B*
  of Jackson *C, A, B*
  of Muskegon *C, A, B*
  of Owosso *A, B*
  of Port Huron *C, A, B*
Bay de Noc Community College *C, A*
Calvin College *B*
Central Michigan University *B*
Cleary University *A, B*
Cornerstone University *B*
Davenport University
  Eastern Region *A, B, M*
  Midland *C, A*
Davenport University - Western
  Region *A, B*
Eastern Michigan University *B, M*
Ferris State University *B, M*
Finlandia University *B*
Glen Oaks Community College *C*
Gogebic Community College *A*
Grace Bible College *B*
Grand Rapids Community College *A*
Grand Valley State University *B, M*
Hillsdale College *B*
Hope College *B*
Jackson Community College *C, A*
Kellogg Community College *C, A*
Kettering University *B*
Kirtland Community College *A*
Lansing Community College *A*
Macomb Community College *C, A*
Madonna University *B, M*
Marygrove College *C, A, B*
Michigan State University *B, M, D*
Mid Michigan Community College *A*
Monroe County Community
  College *C, A*
Montcalm Community College *A*
Mott Community College *A*
Muskegon Community College *A*
North Central Michigan College *C, A*
Northern Michigan University *B*
Northwestern Michigan College *A*
Northwood University *A, B*
Oakland Community College *C, A*
Oakland University *B, M*
Saginaw Valley State University *B, M*
St. Clair County Community College *A*
Schoolcraft College *C, A*
Siena Heights University *A, B*
Southwestern Michigan College *A*
Spring Arbor University *B*
University of Michigan *M*
University of Michigan
  Flint *B*
Walsh College of Accountancy and
  Business Administration *B, M*
Washtenaw Community College *C, A*
Wayne State University *C, B, M*
West Shore Community College *A*
Western Michigan University *B, M*

Minnesota

Academy College *C, A*
Alexandria Technical College *C, A*
Anoka-Ramsey Community College *A*
Augsburg College *B*
Bemidji State University *B*
Bethel College *B*
Central Lakes College *A*
Century Community and Technical
  College *C, A*
College of St. Benedict *B*
College of St. Catherine *B*
College of St. Scholastica *B*
Concordia College: Moorhead *B*

Concordia University: St. Paul *B*
Dakota County Technical College *C*
Fergus Falls Community College *A*
Globe College *C, A, B*
Gustavus Adolphus College *B*
Hennepin Technical College *C, A*
Inver Hills Community College *C, A*
Itasca Community College *C, A*
Lake Superior College: A Community
  and Technical College *C, A*
Metropolitan State University *B*
Minneapolis Community and Technical
  College *C, A*
Minnesota School of Business *C, A*
Minnesota State College - Southeast
  Technical *C, A*
Minnesota State University
  Mankato *B*
  Moorhead *B*
National American University
  St. Paul *B*
North Hennepin Community College *A*
Northland Community & Technical
  College *C, A*
Northwestern College *B*
Pine Technical College *C*
Rasmussen College
  Mankato *C, A*
  Minnetonka *C, A*
  St. Cloud *C, A*
Ridgewater College: A Community and
  Technical College *C, A*
Riverland Community College: A
  Technical and Community College *A*
Rochester Community and Technical
  College *C, A*
St. Cloud State University *B, M*
St. Cloud Technical College *C, A*
St. John's University *B*
St. Mary's University of Minnesota *B*
St. Paul College - A Community and
  Technical College *C, A*
South Central Technical College *A*
Southwest State University *A, B*
University of Minnesota
  Crookston *A, B*
  Duluth *B*
  Twin Cities *C, B*
University of St. Thomas *C, B, M*
Vermilion Community College *A*
Winona State University *B*

Mississippi

Alcorn State University *B*
Delta State University *B*
Itawamba Community College *A*
Mary Holmes College *A*
Millsaps College *B, M*
Mississippi College *C, B, M*
Mississippi Gulf Coast Community
  College
  Perkinston *A*
Mississippi State University *B, M*
Mississippi University for Women *B*
Mississippi Valley State University *B*
Northwest Mississippi Community
  College *A*
University of Mississippi *B, M, D*
University of Southern Mississippi *B, M*

Missouri

Avila University *B*
Blue River Community College *A*
Central Methodist College *A, B*
Central Missouri State University *B, M*
College of the Ozarks *B*
Culver-Stockton College *B*
DeVry University
  Kansas City *M*
Drury University *B*
East Central College *C, A*
Evangel University *A, B*
Hannibal-LaGrange College *B*
Harris Stowe State College *B*
Hickey College *C, A*
Lincoln University *B*

Lindenwood University *B, M*
Longview Community College *C, A*
Maple Woods Community College *C, A*
Maryville University of Saint Louis *B, M*
Missouri Baptist University *B*
Missouri Southern State College *A, B*
Missouri Valley College *B*
Missouri Western State College *B*
National American University
  Kansas City *A, B*
North Central Missouri College *C, A*
Northwest Missouri State
  University *B, M*
Ozarks Technical Community College *A*
Penn Valley Community College *C, A*
Rockhurst University *C, B*
St. Charles Community College *C, A*
St. Louis Community College
    St. Louis Community College at
      Florissant Valley *C*
    St. Louis Community College at
      Forest Park *C, A*
    St. Louis Community College at
      Meramec *C, A*
St. Louis University *B, M*
Southeast Missouri State
  University *B, M*
Southwest Baptist University *A, B*
Southwest Missouri State
  University *B, M*
Southwest Missouri State University:
  West Plains Campus *C*
Springfield College *A*
Stephens College *B*
Three Rivers Community College *A*
Truman State University *B, M*
University of Missouri
  Columbia *B, M, D*
  Kansas City *B, M*
  St. Louis *B, M*
Washington University in St. Louis *B, M*
Webster University *C, B*
Westminster College *B*
William Jewell College *B*
William Woods University *B*

Montana

Carroll College *B*
Flathead Valley Community
  College *C, A*
Montana State University
  Billings *C, A*
  Billings College of
    Technology *C, A*
  Bozeman *M*
Montana Tech of the University of
  Montana *A, B*
Rocky Mountain College *B*
University of Great Falls *B*
University of Montana-Missoula *A, M, D*

Nebraska

Bellevue University *B, M*
Central Community College *C, A*
College of Saint Mary *A*
Concordia University *B*
Creighton University *B*
Doane College *B*
Hastings College *B*
Lincoln School of Commerce *A*
Metropolitan Community College *C, A*
Mid Plains Community College
  Area *C, A*
Midland Lutheran College *A, B*
Nebraska College of Business *A*
Northeast Community College *A*
Southeast Community College
  Lincoln Campus *A*
Union College *A, B*
University of Nebraska
  Lincoln *B, M*
  Omaha *B, M*
Western Nebraska Community
  College *C, A*
York College *A, B*

Nevada

Community College of Southern
  Nevada *A*
Great Basin College *C*
Morrison University *A, B*
Truckee Meadows Community
  College *A*
University of Nevada
  Las Vegas *B, M*
  Reno *B, M*
Western Nevada Community
  College *C, A*

New Hampshire

Franklin Pierce College *B*
Hesser College *C, A, B*
New England College *B*
New Hampshire Community Technical
  College
    Berlin *A*
    Claremont *A*
    Laconia *C, A*
    Manchester *C, A*
    Nashua *C, A*
    Stratham *C, A*
New Hampshire Technical Institute *C, A*
Plymouth State College *B*
St. Anselm College *B*
Southern New Hampshire
  University *C, A, B, M*
University of New Hampshire *B, M*

New Jersey

Atlantic Cape Community College *C, A*
Bergen Community College *A*
Berkeley College *A, B*
Bloomfield College *B*
Brookdale Community College *A*
Burlington County College *C, A*
Caldwell College *B, M*
Camden County College *A*
Centenary College *B, M*
The College of New Jersey *B, M*
College of St. Elizabeth *C*
Cumberland County College *C, A*
Essex County College *C, A*
Fairleigh Dickinson University
  College at Florham *B, M*
  Metropolitan Campus *B, M*
Georgian Court College *B*
Gloucester County College *C, A*
Hudson County Community College *A*
Kean University *B, M*
Mercer County Community College *A*
Middlesex County College *A*
Monmouth University *B*
New Jersey City University *M*
Ocean County College *C*
Passaic County Community College *A*
Ramapo College of New Jersey *B*
Raritan Valley Community College *A*
Rider University *B, M*
Rowan University *B*
Rutgers, The State University of New
  Jersey
    Camden Regional Campus *B, M*
    New Brunswick Regional
      Campus *B, M*
    Newark Regional Campus *B, M*
St. Peter's College *B, M*
Salem Community College *A*
Seton Hall University *B, M*
Sussex County Community College *C, A*
Thomas Edison State College *C, A, B*
Warren County Community College *C, A*
William Paterson University of New
  Jersey *B*

New Mexico

Albuquerque Technical-Vocational
  Institute *C, A*
Clovis Community College *A*
College of Santa Fe *B*
College of the Southwest *B*
Eastern New Mexico University *B*

Eastern New Mexico University: Roswell
  Campus *C*
Luna Community College *A*
National American University *C, A, B*
New Mexico Highlands University *B*
New Mexico Junior College *A*
New Mexico State University *B, M*
San Juan College *A*
Santa Fe Community College *A*
Southwestern Indian Polytechnic
  Institute *A*
University of New Mexico *M*
Western New Mexico University *B*

New York

Adelphi University *B, M*
Adirondack Community College *A*
Alfred University *B*
Berkeley College *A, B*
Berkeley College of New York City *A, B*
Briarcliffe College *C*
Broome Community College *A*
Bryant & Stratton Business Institute
  Albany *A*
  Rochester *A*
  Syracuse *C, A*
Canisius College *B, M*
Cayuga County Community
  College *C, A*
Cazenovia College *A*
City University of New York
  Baruch College *B, M, D*
  Borough of Manhattan Community
    College *A*
  Bronx Community College *A*
  Brooklyn College *B, M*
  College of Staten Island *B*
  Hostos Community College *A*
  Hunter College *B*
  Kingsborough Community
    College *A*
  La Guardia Community College *A*
  Medgar Evers College *B*
  Queens College *B, M*
  Queensborough Community
    College *A*
  York College *B*
Clarkson University *B*
Clinton Community College *A*
Concordia College *B*
Corning Community College *C, A*
D'Youville College *B*
Daemen College *C, B*
Dominican College of Blauvelt *B*
Dowling College *B*
Dutchess Community College *A*
Elmira Business Institute *C, A*
Elmira College *B*
Excelsior College *B*
Finger Lakes Community College *A*
Fordham University *B, M*
Fulton-Montgomery Community
  College *A*
Genesee Community College *C, A*
Hartwick College *B*
Hilbert College *A, B*
Hofstra University *B, M*
Houghton College *B*
Hudson Valley Community College *C, A*
Iona College *B*
Ithaca College *B*
Jamestown Business College *A*
Jamestown Community College *A*
Jefferson Community College *C, A*
Keuka College *B*
Le Moyne College *B*
Long Island Business Institute *A*
Long Island University
  C. W. Post Campus *B, M*
  Southampton College *B*
Manhattan College *B*
Maria College *A*
Marist College *B*
Marymount Manhattan College *B*
Mercy College *C, B*
Mildred Elley *C*

Molloy College *B*
Monroe College *A, B*
Monroe Community College *A*
Mount St. Mary College *C, B*
Nassau Community College *A*
Nazareth College of Rochester *B*
New York Institute of Technology *A, B*
New York University *A, B, M, D*
Niagara County Community
  College *C, A*
Niagara University *B*
Nyack College *B*
Olean Business Institute *A*
Onondaga Community College *A*
Orange County Community College *A*
Pace University *C, B, M*
Pace University:
  Pleasantville/Briarcliff *C, B, M*
Plaza College *A*
Roberts Wesleyan College *B*
Rochester Business Institute *A*
Rochester Institute of
  Technology *C, A, B, M*
Rockland Community College *A*
St. Bonaventure University *B*
St. John Fisher College *B*
St. John's University *C, A, B, M*
St. Joseph's College *B*
St. Joseph's College: Suffolk Campus *B*
State University of New York
  Albany *B, M*
  Binghamton *B, M*
  Buffalo *M, D*
  College at Brockport *B*
  College at Fredonia *B*
  College at Geneseo *B*
  College at Old Westbury *B*
  College at Oneonta *B*
  College at Plattsburgh *B*
  College of Agriculture and
    Technology at Cobleskill *A*
  College of Agriculture and
    Technology at Morrisville *A*
  College of Technology at Alfred *A*
  College of Technology at Canton *A*
  College of Technology at Delhi *A*
  Farmingdale *C*
  Institute of Technology at
    Utica/Rome *B, M*
  New Paltz *B, M*
  Oswego *B, M*
Suffolk County Community College *A*
Syracuse University *B, M*
Tompkins-Cortland Community
  College *C, A*
Touro College *C, A, B, M*
Ulster County Community College *A*
Utica College *B*
Utica School of Commerce *C, A*
Wagner College *B, M*
Westchester Business Institute *C, A*
Westchester Community College *C, A*
Yeshiva University *B*

North Carolina

Alamance Community College *C, A*
Appalachian State University *B, M*
Asheville Buncombe Technical
  Community College *A*
Barton College *B*
Beaufort County Community College *A*
Belmont Abbey College *B*
Bennett College *B*
Caldwell Community College and
  Technical Institute *A*
Campbell University *B*
Catawba College *B*
Catawba Valley Community
  College *C, A*
Central Carolina Community College *A*
Central Piedmont Community College *A*
Cleveland Community College *A*
Craven Community College *A*
Davidson County Community
  College *C, A*

Durham Technical Community
 College *A*
East Carolina University *B, M*
Edgecombe Community College *A*
Elizabeth City State University *B*
Fayetteville State University *B*
Fayetteville Technical Community
 College *A*
Forsyth Technical Community College *A*
Gardner-Webb University *B*
Gaston College *A*
Greensboro College *B*
Guilford College *B*
Guilford Technical Community
 College *C, A*
Halifax Community College *A*
Haywood Community College *C, A*
High Point University *B*
James Sprunt Community College *A*
Johnson C. Smith University *B*
Johnston Community College *A*
King's College *C, A*
Lenoir Community College *A*
Lenoir-Rhyne College *B*
Livingstone College *B*
Mars Hill College *B*
Mayland Community College *A*
Meredith College *B*
Methodist College *B*
Miller-Motte Technical College *C, A*
Mitchell Community College *A*
Montgomery Community College *A*
Mount Olive College *A, B*
Nash Community College *A*
North Carolina Agricultural and
 Technical State University *B*
North Carolina Central University *B*
North Carolina State University *B, M*
North Carolina Wesleyan College *B*
Pamlico Community College *A*
Pfeiffer University *B*
Piedmont Community College *A*
Pitt Community College *C, A*
Queens University of Charlotte *B*
Randolph Community College *A*
Richmond Community College *C, A*
Roanoke-Chowan Community
 College *C*
Rockingham Community College *A*
Rowan-Cabarrus Community
 College *C, A*
St. Augustine's College *B*
Salem College *B*
Sampson Community College *A*
Sandhills Community College *C, A*
South College *A*
South Piedmont Community
 College *C, A*
Southwestern Community College *C, A*
Stanly Community College *A*
Surry Community College *C, A*
Tri-County Community College *A*
University of North Carolina
 Asheville *B*
 Chapel Hill *M*
 Charlotte *B, M*
 Greensboro *B, M*
 Pembroke *B*
 Wilmington *B, M*
Vance-Granville Community College *A*
Wake Forest University *B, M*
Wake Technical Community College *A*
Wayne Community College *A*
Western Carolina University *B, M*
Western Piedmont Community
 College *C, A*
Wilson Technical Community College *A*
Wingate University *B*
Winston-Salem State University *B*

North Dakota
Aaker's Business College *C, A*
Dickinson State University *B*
Jamestown College *B*
Lake Region State College *A*
Minot State University *B*

Minot State University: Bottineau
 Campus *A*
North Dakota State University *B*
University of Mary *A, B*
University of North Dakota *B*

Ohio
Ashland University *B*
Baldwin-Wallace College *B, M*
Bluffton College *B*
Bohecker's Business College *A*
Bowling Green State University *B, M*
Bowling Green State University:
 Firelands College *C, A*
Bradford School *C, A*
Bryant & Stratton College
 Cleveland West *C, A*
 Willoughby Hills *A*
Case Western Reserve
 University *B, M, D*
Cedarville University *B*
Central Ohio Technical College *A*
Central State University *B*
Cincinnati State Technical and
 Community College *A*
Circleville Bible College *A*
Clark State Community College *C, A*
Cleveland State University *B, M*
College of Mount St. Joseph *A, B*
Columbus State Community
 College *A*
Cuyahoga Community College
 Eastern Campus *A*
 Metropolitan Campus *A*
 Western Campus *A*
David N. Myers College *B*
Davis College *A*
DeVry University
 Columbus *M*
Defiance College *A, B*
Edison State Community College *C, A*
Franciscan University of
 Steubenville *A, B*
Franklin University *A, B*
Gallipolis Career College *A*
Heidelberg College *B*
James A. Rhodes State College *A*
Jefferson Community College *A*
John Carroll University *B*
Kent State University *C, A, B, M, D*
Kent State University
 Ashtabula Regional Campus *A*
 Salem Regional Campus *A*
 Stark Campus *B*
 Trumbull Campus *A*
 Tuscarawas Campus *A*
Lake Erie College *B*
Lakeland Community College *C, A*
Lorain County Community College *C, A*
Malone College *B*
Marietta College *B*
Marion Technical College *C, A*
Miami University
 Hamilton Campus *C, A*
 Middletown Campus *C, A*
 Oxford Campus *B, M*
Miami-Jacobs College *A*
Mount Union College *B*
Mount Vernon Nazarene University *B*
Muskingum Area Technical College *C, A*
Muskingum College *B*
North Central State College *A*
Northwest State Community
 College *C, A*
Notre Dame College *C, B*
Ohio Business College *C, A*
Ohio Business College: Sandusky *C, A*
Ohio Dominican College *A*
Ohio Northern University *B*
Ohio State University
 Columbus Campus *B, M, D*
Ohio University *A, B, M*
Ohio Valley College of Technology *A*
Ohio Wesleyan University *B*
Otterbein College *B*
Shawnee State University *A*

Sinclair Community College *A*
Southeastern Business College *A*
Southeastern Business College:
 Lancaster *A*
Southwestern College of Business *A*
Stark State College of Technology *A*
Technology Education College *A*
Tiffin University *A, B*
Trumbull Business College *A*
University of Akron *B, M*
University of Cincinnati *B, D*
University of Dayton *B*
University of Findlay *A, B*
University of Northwestern Ohio *A, B*
University of Rio Grande *A, B*
University of Toledo *A, B, M*
Urbana University *B*
Ursuline College *B*
Walsh University *A, B*
Washington State Community College *A*
Wilmington College *B*
Wittenberg University *B*
Wright State University *B*
Wright State University: Lake Campus *A*
Xavier University *B, M*
Youngstown State University *A, B, M*

Oklahoma
Bacone College *A*
Cameron University *B*
Carl Albert State College *C, A*
East Central University *B*
Eastern Oklahoma State College *A*
Langston University *B*
Northeastern Oklahoma Agricultural and
 Mechanical College *C, A*
Northeastern State University *B, M*
Northern Oklahoma College *A*
Northwestern Oklahoma State
 University *B*
Oklahoma Baptist University *B*
Oklahoma Christian University of
 Science and Arts *B*
Oklahoma City University *B, M*
Oklahoma Panhandle State University *B*
Oklahoma State University *B, M*
Oklahoma State University
 Oklahoma City *A*
 Okmulgee *A*
Oklahoma Wesleyan University *B*
Oral Roberts University *B*
Redlands Community College *A*
Rogers State University *A*
Rose State College *A*
St. Gregory's University *A, B*
Southeastern Oklahoma State
 University *B*
Southern Nazarene University *B*
Southwestern Oklahoma State
 University *B*
Tulsa Community College *A*
University of Central Oklahoma *B*
University of Oklahoma *B, M*
University of Tulsa *B, M*

Oregon
Central Oregon Community College *A*
Chemeketa Community College *A*
Clackamas Community College *C, A*
Clatsop Community College *A*
Eastern Oregon University *B*
George Fox University *B*
Lane Community College *C, A*
Linfield College *B*
Mount Hood Community College *C, A*
Oregon Institute of Technology *B*
Oregon State University *C*
Pioneer Pacific College *A*
Portland Community College *C, A*
Portland State University *C, B*
Southern Oregon University *B*
Southwestern Oregon Community
 College *C, A*
Treasure Valley Community College *C*
Umpqua Community College *A*
University of Oregon *B, M, D*

University of Portland *B*
Warner Pacific College *C*
Western Baptist College *B*
Western Business College *A*

Pennsylvania
Academy of Medical Arts and
 Business *C, A*
Albright College *B*
Allentown Business School *A*
Arcadia University *B*
Bloomsburg University of
 Pennsylvania *B, M*
Bradford School: Pittsburgh *C, A*
Bucknell University *B, M*
Bucks County Community College *A*
Cabrini College *B*
California University of
 Pennsylvania *A, B*
Cambria County Area Community
 College *A*
Cambria-Rowe Business College *C, A*
Cambria-Rowe Business College:
 Indiana *A*
Carlow College *B*
Carnegie Mellon University *D*
Cedar Crest College *C, B*
Central Pennsylvania College *A*
Chatham College *B*
Chestnut Hill College *A, B*
Cheyney University of Pennsylvania *B*
Churchman Business School *A*
Commonwealth Technical Institute *A*
Community College of Philadelphia *A*
Consolidated School of Business
 Lancaster *A*
 York *A*
DeSales University *B*
DeVry University
 Ft. Washington *M*
Delaware Valley College *B*
Drexel University *B, M*
DuBois Business College *C, A*
DuBois Business College
 Oil City *A*
Duquesne University *B*
Education Direct: Center for Degree
 Studies *A*
Elizabethtown College *C, A, B*
Erie Business Center *A*
Geneva College *B*
Grove City College *B*
Gwynedd-Mercy College *A, B*
Harrisburg Area Community
 College *C, A*
Holy Family University *B*
ICM School of Business & Medical
 Careers *A*
Immaculata University *C, A, B*
Indiana University of Pennsylvania *B*
Juniata College *B*
Keystone College *A, B*
King's College *A, B*
Kutztown University of Pennsylvania *B*
La Roche College *B*
La Salle University *A, B*
Lackawanna College *A*
Lebanon Valley College of
 Pennsylvania *C, A, B*
Lehigh Carbon Community College *C, A*
Lehigh University *B, M*
Lincoln University *B*
Lock Haven University of
 Pennsylvania *B*
Luzerne County Community
 College *C, A*
Lycoming College *B*
Manor College *A*
Marywood University *B*
McCann School of Business
 Pottsville *A*
 Sunbury *A*
Mercyhurst College *C, A, B*
Messiah College *B*
Montgomery County Community
 College *C, A*

Moravian College *B*
Mount Aloysius College *A, B*
Muhlenberg College *B*
Neumann College *C, B*
Newport Business Institute *A*
PJA School *C, A*
Penn State
  Abington *B*
  Altoona *B*
  Beaver *B*
  Delaware County *B*
  Dubois *B*
  Erie, The Behrend College *B*
  Fayette *B*
  Harrisburg *B*
  Hazleton *B*
  Lehigh Valley *B*
  McKeesport *B*
  Mont Alto *B*
  New Kensington *B*
  Schuylkill - Capital College *B*
  Shenango *B*
  University Park *B*
  Wilkes-Barre *B*
  Worthington Scranton *B*
  York *B*
Pennsylvania College of Technology *B*
Philadelphia University *C, A, B, M*
Pittsburgh Technical Institute: Boyd
  School Division *A*
Point Park College *C, A, B*
Reading Area Community College *C, A*
Robert Morris University *B, M*
Rosemont College *B*
St. Joseph's University *A, B, M*
St. Vincent College *C, B, M*
Schuylkill Institute of Business &
  Technology *A*
Seton Hill University *B*
Shippensburg University of
  Pennsylvania *B*
Slippery Rock University of
  Pennsylvania *B, M*
South Hills School of Business &
  Technology *C, A*
South Hills School of Business and
  Technology *A*
Temple University *B, M, D*
Thiel College *A, B*
University of Pennsylvania *B, M, D*
University of Pittsburgh *C, B*
University of Pittsburgh
  Greensburg *B*
  Johnstown *B*
  Titusville *A*
University of Scranton *B, M*
Villanova University *B, M*
Washington and Jefferson College *A, B*
Waynesburg College *B*
West Chester University of
  Pennsylvania *B, M*
Westmoreland County Community
  College *A*
Widener University *B, M*
Wilkes University *B*
Wilson College *A, B*
York College of Pennsylvania *B*

Puerto Rico

Atlantic College *A, B*
Bayamon Central University *B, M*
Columbia College *A*
Huertas Junior College *A*
Inter American University of Puerto Rico
  Barranquitas Campus *A, B*
  Bayamon Campus *A, B*
  Fajardo Campus *A, B*
  Guayama Campus *A, B*
  Metropolitan Campus *A, B, M*
  San German Campus *B, M*
Pontifical Catholic University of Puerto
  Rico *B, M*
Technological College of San Juan *C, A*
Turabo University *A, B, M*
Universidad Metropolitana *B, M*
Universidad del Este *C, A, B*

University of Puerto Rico
  Cayey University College *B*
  Humacao *A, B*
  Mayaguez Campus *B*
  Ponce *B*
  Rio Piedras Campus *B, M*
  Utuado *A, B*
University of the Sacred Heart *B*

Rhode Island

Bryant College *B, M*
Community College of Rhode
  Island *C, A*
Rhode Island College *B*
Roger Williams University *B*
Salve Regina University *B*
University of Rhode Island *B, M*

South Carolina

Aiken Technical College *C, A*
Anderson College *B*
Benedict College *B*
Central Carolina Technical College *A*
Charleston Southern University *B, M*
Clemson University *B, M*
Coastal Carolina University *B*
College of Charleston *B, M*
Columbia College *B*
Converse College *B*
Florence-Darlington Technical College *A*
Forrest Junior College *A*
Francis Marion University *B*
Furman University *B*
Limestone College *B*
Midlands Technical College *C, A*
Northeastern Technical College *A*
Orangeburg-Calhoun Technical
  College *C, A*
Piedmont Technical College *C*
Presbyterian College *B*
South Carolina State University *B*
Southern Wesleyan University *B*
Spartanburg Technical College *A*
Technical College of the
  Lowcountry *C, A*
Tri-County Technical College *A*
Trident Technical College *A*
University of South Carolina *B, M*
University of South Carolina
  Aiken *B*
Voorhees College *B*
Wofford College *B*
York Technical College *C, A*

South Dakota

Augustana College *B*
Black Hills State University *B*
Dakota Wesleyan University *B*
Kilian Community College *A*
Mount Marty College *A, B*
Northern State University *B*
Sinte Gleska University *A*
Southeast Technical Institute *A*
University of Sioux Falls *B*
University of South Dakota *B, M*
Western Dakota Technical Institute *A*

Tennessee

Belmont University *B, M*
Bethel College *B*
Carson-Newman College *B*
Chattanooga State Technical Community
  College *A*
Christian Brothers University *B*
Columbia State Community College *A*
Draughons Junior College of Business:
  Nashville *A*
Draughons Junior College: Clarksville *A*
East Tennessee State University *B, M*
Freed-Hardeman University *B*
Jackson State Community College *A*
Lambuth University *B*
Lee University *B*
Middle Tennessee State University *B, M*
Miller-Motte Technical College *A*
Northeast State Technical Community
  College *C*

Rhodes College *M*
Roane State Community College *A*
South College *A*
Southern Adventist University *A, B, M*
Southwest Tennessee Community
  College *C, A*
Tennessee State University *A, B*
Tennessee Technological University *B*
Tennessee Wesleyan College *B*
Trevecca Nazarene University *B*
Tusculum College *B*
Union University *B, T*
University of Memphis *B, M*
University of Tennessee
  Chattanooga *M*
  Knoxville *B, M*
  Martin *B, M*
Walters State Community College *A*

Texas

Abilene Christian University *B, M*
Alvin Community College *A*
Amarillo College *C, A*
Amberton University *B*
Angelina College *A*
Angelo State University *B, M*
Austin Community College *C, A*
Baylor University *B, M*
Blinn College *A*
Brazosport College *A*
Brookhaven College *A*
Cisco Junior College *A*
Coastal Bend College *A*
College of the Mainland *A*
Dallas Baptist University *B, M*
Del Mar College *A*
East Texas Baptist University *B*
Eastfield College *C, A*
El Centro College *C, A*
El Paso Community College *C, A*
Frank Phillips College *C, A*
Galveston College *C, A*
Grayson County College *C, A*
Hallmark Institute of Technology *A*
Hardin-Simmons University *B*
Houston Baptist University *B, M*
Houston Community College
  System *C, A*
Howard College *C, A*
Howard Payne University *B*
Huston-Tillotson College *B*
Kilgore College *C, A*
Lamar State College at Orange *C, A*
Lamar State College at Port Arthur *C, A*
Lamar University *B*
Laredo Community College *C, A*
LeTourneau University *B*
Lee College *C, A*
Lon Morris College *A*
Lubbock Christian University *B*
MTI College of Business and
  Technology *A*
MTI College of Business and
  Technology *A*
McLennan Community College *C, A*
McMurry University *B*
Midland College *C, A*
Midwestern State University *B, M*
Mountain View College *A*
North Harris Montgomery Community
  College District *C, A*
North Lake College *A*
Northeast Texas Community
  College *C, A*
Northwood University: Texas
  Campus *A, B*
Our Lady of the Lake University of San
  Antonio *B*
Palo Alto College *A*
Paris Junior College *A*
Prairie View A&M University *B*
Rice University *M*
Richland College *A*
St. Edward's University *C, B*
St. Mary's University *B, M*
St. Philip's College *A*

Sam Houston State University *B*
San Antonio College *A*
San Jacinto College
  Central Campus *C*
Schreiner University *B*
South Plains College *A*
South Texas Community College *C, A*
Southern Methodist University *B, M*
Southwest Texas State University *B, M*
Southwestern Adventist University *B*
Southwestern Assemblies of God
  University *B*
Southwestern University *B*
Stephen F. Austin State University *B, M*
Sul Ross State University *B*
Tarleton State University *B*
Tarrant County College *A*
Texas A&M International
  University *B, M*
Texas A&M University *B, M, D*
Texas A&M University
  Commerce *B, M*
  Corpus Christi *B, M*
  Kingsville *B, M*
  Texarkana *B, M*
Texas Christian University *B, M*
Texas Lutheran University *B*
Texas Southern University *B, M*
Texas State Technical College
  West Texas *C, A*
Texas Tech University *B, M*
Texas Wesleyan University *B, M*
Texas Woman's University *B*
Trinity University *B, M*
Trinity Valley Community College *C, A*
University of Houston *B, M, D*
University of Houston
  Clear Lake *B, M*
  Downtown *B*
  Victoria *B*
University of Mary Hardin-Baylor *B*
University of North Texas *B, M, D*
University of St. Thomas *B, M*
University of Texas
  Arlington *B, M, D*
  Austin *B, M, D*
  Brownsville *B*
  Dallas *B, M, D*
  El Paso *B, M*
  Pan American *B*
  San Antonio *B, M, D*
  Tyler *B*
  of the Permian Basin *B, M*
West Texas A&M University *B, M*
Western Texas College *C, A*
Wiley College *B*

Utah

Brigham Young University *B, M*
College of Eastern Utah *C*
Dixie State College of Utah *A*
LDS Business College *C, A*
Salt Lake Community College *C, A*
Snow College *A*
Southern Utah University *B, M*
University of Utah *B, M*
Utah State University *B, M*
Utah Valley State College *C, A, B*
Weber State University *B, M*
Westminster College *B*

Vermont

Castleton State College *B*
Champlain College *C, A, B*
College of St. Joseph in Vermont *A, B*
Johnson State College *C, A, B*
Lyndon State College *B*
Norwich University *B*
St. Michael's College *B*
Vermont Technical College *A*

Virginia

Averett University *B*
Blue Ridge Community College *A*
Bluefield College *B*
Bryant & Stratton College *A*

College of William and Mary *M*
Danville Community College *A*
DeVry University
    Crystal City *M*
ECPI College of Technology *C, A*
ECPI Technical College: Roanoke *A*
Eastern Mennonite University *B*
Ferrum College *B*
George Mason University *B, M*
Hampton University *B*
J. Sargeant Reynolds Community
    College *C, A*
James Madison University *B, M*
Liberty University *B*
Longwood University *B*
Lynchburg College *B*
Marymount University *C, B*
Mountain Empire Community College *A*
National College of Business &
    Technology
        Bluefield *C, A*
        Charlottesville *A*
        Danville *C, A*
        Harrisonburg *C, A*
        Lynchburg *C, A*
        Martinsville *C, A*
        Roanoke *C, A, B*
Norfolk State University *B*
Old Dominion University *B, M*
Piedmont Virginia Community
    College *A*
Radford University *B*
Randolph-Macon College *B*
Rappahannock Community College *C, A*
Southwest Virginia Community
    College *A*
Thomas Nelson Community College *A*
University of Richmond *B*
University of Virginia *M*
University of Virginia's College at
    Wise *B*
Virginia Commonwealth
    University *B, M*
Virginia Highlands Community
    College *C, A*
Virginia Polytechnic Institute and State
    University *B, M*
Virginia State University *B*
Virginia Union University *B*
Virginia Western Community College *A*
Washington and Lee University *B*

Washington
Bellevue Community College *C, A*
Central Washington University *B, M*
Centralia College *C*
Clover Park Technical College *A*
DeVry University
    Seattle *M*
Eastern Washington University *B*
Edmonds Community College *C, A*
Everett Community College *C, A*
Gonzaga University *B*
Grays Harbor College *C, A*
Green River Community College *C, A*
Lake Washington Technical College *C, A*
Lower Columbia College *C, A*
Olympic College *C, A*
Pacific Lutheran University *B*
Peninsula College *A*
Renton Technical College *C, A*
St. Martin's College *B*
Seattle Central Community College *C, A*
Seattle Pacific University *B*
Seattle University *B, M*
South Seattle Community College *C, A*
Spokane Community College *A*
Spokane Falls Community College *A*
University of Washington *B, M*
Walla Walla College *B*
Walla Walla Community College *C, A*
Washington State University *B, M*
Western Washington University *B*
Whitworth College *B*

West Virginia
Alderson-Broaddus College *B*
Bethany College *B*
Bluefield State College *B*
Concord College *B*
Davis and Elkins College *A, B*
Fairmont State College *A, B*
Huntington Junior College *A*
Marshall University *B*
Mountain State College *A*
Mountain State University *A, B*
Ohio Valley College *B*
Potomac State College of West Virginia
    University *A*
Salem International University *M*
Shepherd College *A, B*
Southern West Virginia Community and
    Technical College *A*
University of Charleston *A, B*
Valley College of Technology *C*
West Liberty State College *B*
West Virginia Business College *A, D*
West Virginia Junior College *A*
West Virginia Northern Community
    College *A*
West Virginia State College *A, B*
West Virginia University *B, M*
West Virginia Wesleyan College *B*
Wheeling Jesuit University *B, M*

Wisconsin
Blackhawk Technical College *A*
Bryant & Stratton College *A*
Cardinal Stritch University *B*
Carroll College *B*
Carthage College *B*
Chippewa Valley Technical College *A*
Concordia University Wisconsin *B*
Edgewood College *B, M*
Fox Valley Technical College *C, A*
Lakeland College *B*
Lakeshore Technical College *A*
Marian College of Fond du Lac *B*
Marquette University *B*
Mid-State Technical College *C, A*
Milwaukee Area Technical College *A*
Moraine Park Technical College *C, A*
Mount Mary College *B*
Nicolet Area Technical College *A*
St. Norbert College *B*
Silver Lake College *B*
University of Wisconsin
        Eau Claire *B*
        Green Bay *B*
        La Crosse *B*
        Madison *B, M, D*
        Milwaukee *B*
        Oshkosh *B*
        Parkside *B*
        Platteville *B*
        River Falls *B*
        Stevens Point *B*
        Superior *B*
        Whitewater *B, M*
Viterbo University *B*
Waukesha County Technical College *A*
Western Wisconsin Technical College *A*
Wisconsin Indianhead Technical
    College *A*

Wyoming
Casper College *C, A*
Central Wyoming College *C, A*
Eastern Wyoming College *A*
Laramie County Community
    College *C, A*
Sheridan College *A*
University of Wyoming *B, M*
Western Wyoming Community
    College *C, A*

Alabama
Douglas MacArthur State Technical
    College *A*
Jefferson State Community College *C, A*
Northwest-Shoals Community
    College *C, A*

Alaska
University of Alaska
    Fairbanks *C, A*

California
Foothill College *C*
Santa Barbara City College *C, A*
Southwestern College *C*

Colorado
Red Rocks Community College *C, A*

Georgia
Albany Technical College *C*
Atlanta Metropolitan College *A*
Southwest Georgia Technical
    College *C, A*

Illinois
Black Hawk College *C, A*
College of DuPage *C, A*
College of Lake County *C, A*
Illinois Eastern Community Colleges
    Wabash Valley College *A*
Kaskaskia College *C, A*
McHenry County College *C, A*

Indiana
Indiana University
    Southeast *A, B*
Ivy Tech State College
    Bloomington *A*
    Central Indiana *A*
    Columbus *C, A*
    Eastcentral *C, A*
    Kokomo *C, A*
    Lafayette *C, A*
    Northcentral *C, A*
    Northeast *A*
    Northwest *C, A*
    Southcentral *C, A*
    Southeast *C, A*
    Southwest *C, A*
    Wabash Valley *C, A*
    Whitewater *C, A*

Iowa
Hamilton College
    Cedar Rapids *C*
Indian Hills Community College *C*
North Iowa Area Community College *C*

Kentucky
Somerset Community College *C*

Maryland
College of Southern Maryland *C, A*
Hagerstown Community College *A*

Michigan
Baker College
    of Muskegon *C*
    of Port Huron *C*
Ferris State University *A*
Northwestern Michigan College *A*

Minnesota
Hennepin Technical College *C, A*
Minneapolis Community and Technical
    College *A*
Normandale Community College *A*

Missouri
Moberly Area Community College *A*

Nevada
Western Nevada Community College *A*

New Jersey
Union County College *A*

New Mexico
Albuquerque Technical-Vocational
    Institute *C*
Santa Fe Community College *C*
Southwestern Indian Polytechnic
    Institute *A*

New York
Dutchess Community College *C*
Mohawk Valley Community
    College *C, A*
State University of New York
        College of Agriculture and
            Technology at Morrisville *A*

North Carolina
Cape Fear Community College *A*
Coastal Carolina Community College *A*
Martin Community College *C, A*
Wilkes Community College *C, A*

North Dakota
Lake Region State College *C, A*

Ohio
Hocking Technical College *C, A*
Miami University
    Oxford Campus *C, A*
North Central State College *C*
Owens Community College
    Findlay Campus *C, A*
    Toledo *C, A*
Southern State Community College *A*
University of Akron *A*
University of Cincinnati
    Clermont College *C, A*
    Raymond Walters College *C, A*
Youngstown State University *A*

Oklahoma
Rose State College *A*

Oregon
Blue Mountain Community College *C, A*
Linn-Benton Community College *A*

Pennsylvania
Butler County Community College *C, A*
Community College of Allegheny
    County *C, A*
Community College of Beaver County *A*
Consolidated School of Business
        Lancaster *A*
        York *A*
Delaware County Community
    College *C, A*
Douglas School of Business *C*
Montgomery County Community
    College *C, A*
Newport Business Institute *A*
Northampton County Area Community
    College *C, A*
Pennsylvania College of
    Technology *A, T*

Rhode Island
Bryant College *B*

South Carolina
York Technical College *C*

South Dakota
Southeast Technical Institute *C*

Tennessee
Cleveland State Community College *C*
Pellissippi State Technical Community
    College *A*

Texas
St. Philip's College *C, A*
Tyler Junior College *C, A*

Washington
Bellevue Community College *C, A*
Clark College *C, A*
Clover Park Technical College *C, A*

Edmonds Community College *C, A*
Walla Walla Community College *C, A*
Wenatchee Valley College *C, A*

Wisconsin
Marquette University *C*

Accounting/business management

California
California State University
Sacramento *M*
Claremont McKenna College *B*

Indiana
Grace College *B*

Kansas
Central Christian College *A, B*
Tabor College *B*

Massachusetts
Cape Cod Community College *A*

Michigan
Baker College
of Muskegon *B*

New York
Rochester Institute of Technology *B, M*
State University of New York
Buffalo *M*
College of Agriculture and
Technology at Morrisville *A*

Ohio
Miami University
Hamilton Campus *C*

Oregon
Western Baptist College *B*

Pennsylvania
Newport Business Institute *A*
Peirce College *A, B*

Texas
Baylor University *B*

Vermont
Champlain College *A, B*

Virginia
Rappahannock Community College *C, A*

Wisconsin
University of Wisconsin
Superior *B*

Accounting/computer science

Arizona
Paradise Valley Community College *C*

New York
Schenectady County Community
College *A*

Accounting/finance

Florida
Palm Beach Atlantic University *B*

Indiana
St. Joseph's College *B*

Iowa
American Institute of Business *A*
Maharishi University of
Management *C, M*

Kentucky
Jefferson Community College *A*

Maine
University of Southern Maine *B*

Michigan
Kettering University *B*

New Hampshire
Franklin Pierce College *B*

New York
Rochester Institute of Technology *M*
State University of New York
Buffalo *M*
College of Agriculture and
Technology at Morrisville *A*

Ohio
Hondros College *A*
Tiffin University *B*

Oregon
Western Baptist College *B*

Pennsylvania
Franklin & Marshall College *B*

Tennessee
Milligan College *B*

Washington
Bellevue Community College *B*

Wisconsin
University of Wisconsin
Superior *B*

Acoustics

North Carolina
Guilford Technical Community
College *A*

Pennsylvania
Penn State
University Park *M, D*

Acting

California
California Institute of the Arts *C, B, M*
California State University
Fullerton *B*
Grossmont Community College *C, A*

Connecticut
University of Connecticut *B*

Florida
University of West Florida *B*

Iowa
Drake University *B*
University of Northern Iowa *B*

Kansas
Central Christian College *A, B*

Maine
University of Southern Maine *B*

Massachusetts
Boston University *B, M*

New Hampshire
Franklin Pierce College *B*

New Mexico
College of Santa Fe *B*

New York
Bard College *B*
Ithaca College *B*
New York University *M*

Ohio
University of Akron *B*

Pennsylvania
Northampton County Area Community
College *A*

Penn State
Abington *B*
Altoona *B*
Beaver *B*
Berks *B*
Delaware County *B*
Dubois *B*
Fayette *B*
Hazleton *B*
Lehigh Valley *B*
McKeesport *B*
Mont Alto *B*
New Kensington *B*
Shenango *B*
York *B*

South Carolina
Coker College *B*

Utah
Brigham Young University *B*

Virginia
Old Dominion University *B*

Washington
Cornish College of the Arts *B*

Actuarial science

Connecticut
Central Connecticut State University *B*
University of Connecticut *B, D*
University of Hartford *B*

Florida
Florida State University *B*
University of Central Florida *B*

Georgia
Georgia State University *B, M*

Illinois
Bradley University *B*
Illinois Central College *A*
North Central College *B*
Roosevelt University *B*
St. Xavier University *B*
University of Illinois
Urbana-Champaign *B*
University of St. Francis *B*

Indiana
Ball State University *B, M*
Butler University *B*
Indiana University
Northwest *B*
South Bend *B*
Valparaiso University *B*
Vincennes University *A*

Iowa
Buena Vista University *B*
Drake University *B*
Northwestern College *B*
University of Iowa *B, M*

Kansas
Tabor College *B*
Washburn University of Topeka *A, B*

Kentucky
Bellarmine University *B*

Maryland
Frostburg State University *B*

Massachusetts
Boston University *M*

Michigan
Central Michigan University *B*
Eastern Michigan University *B*
Ferris State University *B*
University of Michigan
Flint *B*

Minnesota
University of Minnesota
Twin Cities *B*

University of St. Thomas *B*

Missouri
Central Missouri State University *B*
Maryville University of Saint Louis *B*
Missouri Valley College *B*

Nebraska
University of Nebraska
Kearney *B*
Lincoln *B, M*

New Jersey
Rider University *B*
St. Peter's College *A, B, M*

New York
City University of New York
Baruch College *B*
Hofstra University *B*
New York University *B*
St. John's University *B, M*
State University of New York
Albany *B*
Utica College *B*

North Carolina
North Carolina Central University *B*

North Dakota
Jamestown College *B*
North Dakota State University *B*

Ohio
Ohio State University
Columbus Campus *B*
Ohio University *B*

Oklahoma
University of Central Oklahoma *B*

Pennsylvania
Harrisburg Area Community College *A*
Lebanon Valley College of
Pennsylvania *B*
Lincoln University *B*
Lycoming College *B*
Mercyhurst College *B*
Penn State
Abington *B*
Altoona *B*
Beaver *B*
Berks *B*
Delaware County *B*
Dubois *B*
Fayette *B*
Hazleton *B*
Lehigh Valley *B*
McKeesport *B*
Mont Alto *B*
New Kensington *B*
Schuylkill - Capital College *B*
Shenango *B*
University Park *B*
Wilkes-Barre *B*
Worthington Scranton *B*
York *B*
Temple University *B, M*
Thiel College *B*
University of Pennsylvania *B*

Rhode Island
Bryant College *B*

Tennessee
Southern Adventist University *B*

Utah
Brigham Young University *B*

Wisconsin
Carroll College *B*
University of Wisconsin
Madison *M*

Acupuncture

Connecticut
University of Bridgeport *M*

Nevada
Community College of Southern
Nevada *A*

Pennsylvania
Duquesne University *M, D*

Washington
Bastyr University *B, M*

Administrative/secretarial services

Alabama
Alabama Southern Community
College *A*
Alabama State University *B*
Bishop State Community College *A*
Central Alabama Community
College *C, A*
Chattahoochee Valley Community
College *A*
Douglas MacArthur State Technical
College *A*
Enterprise State Junior College *C, A*
Faulkner University *A*
Gadsden State Community College *C, A*
George C. Wallace State Community
College
Dothan *C, A*
J. F. Drake State Technical College *C, A*
James H. Faulkner State Community
College *C, A*
Jefferson State Community College *C, A*
Lawson State Community College *A*
Northeast Alabama Community
College *A*
Northwest-Shoals Community College *A*
Reid State Technical College *C*
Snead State Community College *C*
Trenholm State Technical College *A*

Alaska
University of Alaska
Fairbanks *C, A*
Southeast *A*

Arizona
Arizona Western College *C, A*
Central Arizona College *C, A*
Cochise College *C, A*
Eastern Arizona College *C, A*
Gateway Community College *C, A*
Glendale Community College *C, A*
International Institute of the Americas
Phoenix *C, A, B*
Tucson *C, A, B*
Paradise Valley Community
College *C, A*
Pima Community College *C, A*
Scottsdale Community College *A*
South Mountain Community College *A*
Yavapai College *C, A*

Arkansas
Arkansas State University *C, A, B*
Arkansas State University
Beebe *C, A*
Mountain Home *C, A*
East Arkansas Community College *A*
Henderson State University *A*
Mississippi County Community
College *A*
North Arkansas College *C, A*
Northwest Arkansas Community
College *A*
Philander Smith College *B*
Rich Mountain Community College *C, A*
South Arkansas Community
College *C, A*
Southeast Arkansas College *C*
University of Arkansas
Community College at Batesville *A*
Fort Smith *C, A*
Monticello *B*
University of Central Arkansas *A, B*

California
Antelope Valley College *C, A*
Bakersfield College *A*
Barstow College *C, A*
Cerritos Community College *A*
Cerro Coso Community College *A*
Chabot College *C, A*
Citrus College *C*
Coastline Community College *C*
College of Alameda *C, A*
College of the Canyons *C, A*
College of the Redwoods *A*
College of the Sequoias *C, A*
College of the Siskiyous *C, A*
Columbia College *A*
Contra Costa College *C, A*
De Anza College *C, A*
Diablo Valley College *C*
East Los Angeles College *A*
Glendale Community College *C, A*
Golden West College *C, A*
Grossmont Community College *C, A*
Imperial Valley College *C, A*
Laney College *C, A*
Long Beach City College *C, A*
Los Angeles Harbor College *C, A*
Los Angeles Southwest College *A*
Los Angeles Trade and Technical
College *C, A*
MTI College of Business and
Technology *C*
MiraCosta College *C, A*
Modesto Junior College *C, A*
Moorpark College *C, A*
Mount San Antonio College *C, A*
Napa Valley College *C, A*
Ohlone College *C, A*
Orange Coast College *C, A*
Pacific Union College *A*
Palomar College *C, A*
Riverside Community College *C, A*
San Diego City College *C, A*
San Joaquin Delta College *A*
Santa Barbara City College *C, A*
Santa Rosa Junior College *C*
Shasta College *C, A*
Sierra College *C, A*
Southwestern College *C, A*
Taft College *A*
Ventura College *C, A*
Victor Valley College *C, A*
West Valley College *C, A*
Yuba Community College District *C, A*

Colorado
Arapahoe Community College *C, A*
Community College of Aurora *A*
IntelliTec College, Grand Junction *C, A*
Otero Junior College *A*
Red Rocks Community College *A*

Connecticut
Asnuntuck Community College *A*
Briarwood College *C, A*
Capital Community College *C, A*
Gateway Community College *C, A*
Gibbs College *C, A*
Housatonic Community College *C, A*
Manchester Community College *C, A*
Middlesex Community College *A*
Naugatuck Valley Community
College *C, A*
Northwestern Connecticut Community
College *C, A*
Quinebaug Valley Community
College *C, A*
Tunxis Community College *C, A*

Delaware
Delaware Technical and Community
College
Owens Campus *C, A*
Stanton/Wilmington Campus *C, A*
Terry Campus *C, A*

District of Columbia
University of the District of Columbia *A*

Florida
Broward Community College *C*
Hobe Sound Bible College *A*
Indian River Community College *A*
Lake City Community College *C, A*
Manatee Community College *A*
Miami-Dade Community College *C, A*
New England Institute of Technology *A*
Pensacola Junior College *A*
Polk Community College *A*
Santa Fe Community College *A*
Seminole Community College *A*
South Florida Community College *C*
Tallahassee Community College *C, A*
Valencia Community College *C, A*

Georgia
Albany State University *B*
Athens Technical College *C, A*
Atlanta Metropolitan College *A*
Bainbridge College *A*
Chattahoochee Technical College *A*
Coastal Georgia Community
College *C, A*
Columbus Technical College *C, A*
Dalton State College *C, A*
Darton College *A*
DeKalb Technical College *C*
Floyd College *A*
Gainesville College *A*
Griffin Technical College *A*
Savannah Technical College *A*
South Georgia College *A*
Southwest Georgia Technical
College *C, A*
University of Georgia *A*
West Georgia Technical College *A*

Hawaii
University of Hawaii
Hawaii Community College *C, A*

Idaho
Boise State University *A*
Eastern Idaho Technical College *C, A*
Idaho State University *C, A*
Lewis-Clark State College *A*
North Idaho College *A*
University of Idaho *B*

Illinois
Black Hawk College *C, A*
Black Hawk College
East Campus *C, A*
Carl Sandburg College *C, A*
City Colleges of Chicago
Harold Washington College *C, A*
Kennedy-King College *C, A*
Malcolm X College *C, A*
Olive-Harvey College *C, A*
Wright College *C, A*
College of DuPage *C, A*
College of Lake County *C, A*
Danville Area Community College *C, A*
East-West University *A*
Elgin Community College *C, A*
Gem City College *A*
Heartland Community College *C, A*
Illinois Central College *C, A*
Illinois Eastern Community Colleges
Frontier Community College *C, A*
Lincoln Trail College *C, A*
Olney Central College *C, A*
Wabash Valley College *C, A*
John Wood Community College *C, A*
Joliet Junior College *C, A*
Kankakee Community College *A*
Kaskaskia College *C*
Lake Land College *A*
Lincoln Land Community College *C, A*
McHenry County College *C, A*
Midstate College *A*
Moraine Valley Community
College *C, A*
Northwestern Business College *A*
Oakton Community College *C*
Parkland College *C, A*

Prairie State College *C, A*
Rend Lake College *C, A*
Robert Morris College: Chicago *C, A*
Rock Valley College *C, A*
St. Augustine College *C, A*
Sauk Valley Community College *C, A*
South Suburban College of Cook
County *C, A*
Southeastern Illinois College *C, A*
Triton College *C, A*
Waubonsee Community College *C, A*
William Rainey Harper College *C, A*

Indiana
Ball State University *B*
Bethel College *A*
Indiana Business College *C, A*
Indiana Business College
Anderson *A*
Columbus *C, A*
Evansville *C, A*
Fort Wayne *A*
Lafayette *C, A*
Marion *A*
Muncie *C, A*
Terre Haute *C, A*
Indiana State University *A*
International Business College *C, A*
Michiana College *A*
Oakland City University *C, A*
Professional Careers Institute *A*
Sawyer College *C, A*
University of Southern Indiana *A*
Vincennes University *A*

Iowa
American Institute of Business *A*
Clinton Community College *C, A*
Des Moines Area Community
College *C, A*
Ellsworth Community College *A*
Faith Baptist Bible College and
Theological Seminary *A*
Hamilton College *A*
Hamilton College
Cedar Falls *A*
Cedar Rapids *A*
Mason City *A*
Hawkeye Community College *C*
Indian Hills Community College *C*
Iowa Central Community College *A*
Iowa Lakes Community College *C*
Iowa Western Community College *A*
Kaplan College *A*
Kirkwood Community College *C, A*
Marshalltown Community College *A*
Muscatine Community College *C, A*
North Iowa Area Community
College *C, A*
Northeast Iowa Community College *C*
Northwest Iowa Community College *C*
Northwestern College *A*
Scott Community College *C, A*
Southeastern Community College
North Campus *C, A*
South Campus *A*
Southwestern Community College *C, A*
Western Iowa Tech Community
College *C*

Kansas
Allen County Community College *A*
Barton County Community College *C, A*
Central Christian College *A*
Fort Hays State University *A*
Fort Scott Community College *C, A*
Garden City Community College *C*
Haskell Indian Nations University *A*
Hutchinson Community College *C, A*
Independence Community College *A*
Johnson County Community
College *C, A*
Kansas City Kansas Community
College *C, A*
Seward County Community
College *C, A*

Tabor College *A, B*

Kentucky

Cumberland College *B*
Daymar College *C, A*
Elizabethtown Community College *A*
Henderson Community College *A*
Hopkinsville Community College *C, A*
Jefferson Community College *A*
Lexington Community College *A*
Lindsey Wilson College *A*
Madisonville Community College *A*
Murray State University *C, A*
National College of Business &
    Technology
    Danville *C, A*
    Florence *C, A*
    Lexington *C, A*
    Pikeville *C, A*
    Richmond *C, A*
Paducah Community College *A*
Paducah Technical College *C*
Prestonsburg Community College *A*
St. Catharine College *C, A*
Somerset Community College *C*
Southeast Community College *A*
Sullivan University *C, A*

Louisiana

Delgado Community College *C, A*
Louisiana College *B*
Louisiana State University
    Eunice *C, A*
Northwestern State University *A*
Southeastern Louisiana University *A*
Southern University
    New Orleans *A, B*
    Shreveport *A*
University of Louisiana at Monroe *A*

Maine

Andover College *C, A*
Beal College *C, A*
Thomas College *A*

Maryland

Allegany College *A*
Carroll Community College *C, A*
Cecil Community College *A*
Chesapeake College *C, A*
College of Southern Maryland *C*
Community College of Baltimore County
    Catonsville *C, A*
    Dundalk *C, A*
    Essex *C, A*
Harford Community College *C, A*
Villa Julie College *A*
Wor-Wic Community College *C, A*

Massachusetts

Bay State College *A*
Benjamin Franklin Institute of
    Technology *C*
Cape Cod Community College *C, A*
Greenfield Community College *C, A*
Katharine Gibbs School *A*
Marian Court College *C, A*
Massasoit Community College *C, A*
Quinsigamond Community College *A*
Roxbury Community College *A*
Springfield Technical Community
    College *A*

Michigan

Baker College
    of Auburn Hills *C, A*
    of Cadillac *A*
    of Clinton Township *C, A, B*
    of Jackson *C, A*
    of Muskegon *C, A, B*
    of Owosso *A, B*
    of Port Huron *C, A, B*
Bay de Noc Community College *A*
Central Michigan University *B*
Cleary University *A*

Davenport University
    Eastern Region *C, A*
    Midland *A*
Davenport University - Western
    Region *A*
Eastern Michigan University *B*
Ferris State University *A*
Glen Oaks Community College *C*
Gogebic Community College *A*
Grand Rapids Community College *C, A*
Kellogg Community College *C, A*
Kirtland Community College *A*
Lansing Community College *A*
Macomb Community College *C, A*
Mid Michigan Community College *A*
Monroe County Community
    College *A*
Montcalm Community College *A*
Mott Community College *C, A*
Muskegon Community College *C, A*
North Central Michigan College *A*
Northern Michigan University *C, A, B*
Northwestern Michigan College *C*
St. Clair County Community
    College *C, A*
Schoolcraft College *C, A*
Southwestern Michigan College *C, A*
Washtenaw Community College *C, A*
West Shore Community College *A*

Minnesota

Alexandria Technical College *C*
Anoka-Ramsey Community College *A*
Century Community and Technical
    College *C, A*
Dakota County Technical College *C*
Globe College *C, A*
Hibbing Community College: A
    Technical and Community College *A*
Inver Hills Community College *C, A*
Itasca Community College *C*
Lake Superior College: A Community
    and Technical College *C, A*
Mesabi Range Community and Technical
    College *A*
Minneapolis Community and Technical
    College *C, A*
Minnesota State College - Southeast
    Technical *C, A*
North Hennepin Community College *A*
Northland Community & Technical
    College *C, A*
Rasmussen College
    Mankato *C*
    Minnetonka *C, A*
    St. Cloud *C*
Ridgewater College: A Community and
    Technical College *C*
Riverland Community College: A
    Technical and Community
    College *C, A*
Rochester Community and Technical
    College *C, A*
St. Cloud Technical College *C, A*
St. Paul College - A Community and
    Technical College *C, A*
South Central Technical College *A*
Winona State University *B, T*

Mississippi

Alcorn State University *B*
Holmes Community College *C, A*
Itawamba Community College *A*
Mary Holmes College *A*
Mississippi Gulf Coast Community
    College
    Perkinston *C, A*

Missouri

Baptist Bible College *A, B*
Blue River Community College *C*
Central Missouri State University *A*
Crowder College *C, A*
East Central College *C, A*
Hickey College *C, A*
Jefferson College *A*

Longview Community College *C, A*
Maple Woods Community College *C, A*
Patricia Stevens College *C*
Penn Valley Community College *C, A*
St. Charles Community College *C, A*
St. Louis Community College
    St. Louis Community College at
        Florissant Valley *C, A*
    St. Louis Community College at
        Forest Park *C, A*
    St. Louis Community College at
        Meramec *C, A*
Southeast Missouri State University *C, B*
Southwest Baptist University *A*
Springfield College *A*
Three Rivers Community College *A*

Montana

Dawson Community College *C, A*
Flathead Valley Community College *C*
Miles Community College *A*
Montana State University
    Billings *C, A*
    Billings College of Technology *A*
Montana Tech of the University of
    Montana *A*
Salish Kootenai College *C, A*
University of Montana-Missoula *C, A*
University of Montana: Western *A*

Nebraska

Central Community College *C, A*
Lincoln School of Commerce *C, A*
Metropolitan Community College *C, A*
Midland Lutheran College *A*
Nebraska Indian Community College *A*
Northeast Community College *A*
Western Nebraska Community
    College *C, A*
York College *A*

Nevada

Community College of Southern
    Nevada *A*
Great Basin College *C, A*
Las Vegas College *A*
Morrison University *C, A, B*
Truckee Meadows Community
    College *A*

New Hampshire

New Hampshire Community Technical
    College
    Laconia *C*
    Manchester *C, A*
    Stratham *C, A*

New Jersey

Bergen Community College *C, A*
Berkeley College *C*
Brookdale Community College *C, A*
Camden County College *C*
County College of Morris *A*
Cumberland County College *C, A*
Essex County College *A*
Gloucester County College *A*
Hudson County Community
    College *C, A*
Mercer County Community College *C, A*
Ocean County College *C*
Passaic County Community
    College *C, A*
Salem Community College *C, A*
Sussex County Community College *C*
Thomas Edison State College *A*
Union County College *A*
Warren County Community College *C*

New Mexico

Albuquerque Technical-Vocational
    Institute *C, A*
Clovis Community College *C, A*
Dona Ana Branch Community College of
    New Mexico State University *C, A*
Eastern New Mexico University: Roswell
    Campus *C, A*
New Mexico Junior College *C, A*

New Mexico State University
    Alamogordo *C, A*
San Juan College *C, A*
Santa Fe Community College *C, A*
Western New Mexico University *C, A*

New York

Adirondack Community College *C, A*
Berkeley College *C*
Berkeley College of New York City *C*
Briarcliffe College *C, A*
Bryant & Stratton Business Institute
    Albany *C, A*
    Rochester *A*
    Syracuse *C, A*
Cayuga County Community College *C*
City University of New York
    Borough of Manhattan Community
        College *A*
    Bronx Community College *A*
    Hostos Community College *A*
    La Guardia Community College *A*
    Queensborough Community
        College *A*
Clinton Community College *C, A*
Concordia College *A*
Corning Community College *C, A*
Dutchess Community College *A*
Erie Community College
    City Campus *A*
    North Campus *A*
    South Campus *A*
Finger Lakes Community College *C, A*
Fulton-Montgomery Community
    College *A*
Genesee Community College *C, A*
Hofstra University *B*
Hudson Valley Community College *A*
Jamestown Business College *C, A*
Katharine Gibbs School
    Melville *A*
Long Island Business Institute *C, A*
Mildred Elley *C*
Mohawk Valley Community
    College *C, A*
Monroe College *A*
Monroe Community College *C, A*
Nassau Community College *A*
Niagara County Community College *A*
Olean Business Institute *C, A*
Onondaga Community College *C, A*
Orange County Community
    College *C, A*
Rochester Business Institute *A*
Rockland Community College *A*
St. John's University *B*
State University of New York
    College of Agriculture and
        Technology at Morrisville *A*
    College of Technology at Alfred *A*
    College of Technology at Canton *A*
    College of Technology at Delhi *A*
Suffolk County Community
    College *C, A*
Tompkins-Cortland Community
    College *C, A*
Trocaire College *A*
Utica School of Commerce *C, A*
Villa Maria College of Buffalo *A*
Westchester Business Institute *C, A*
Westchester Community College *C, A*

North Carolina

Alamance Community College *A*
Asheville Buncombe Technical
    Community College *A*
Beaufort County Community College *A*
Blue Ridge Community College *C, A*
Brunswick Community College *A*
Caldwell Community College and
    Technical Institute *C, A*
Cape Fear Community College *A*
Carteret Community College *A*
Catawba Valley Community
    College *C, A*
Central Carolina Community College *A*

Central Piedmont Community College *A*
Cleveland Community College *C, A*
Coastal Carolina Community College *A*
College of the Albemarle *A*
Craven Community College *C*
Durham Technical Community
 College *C, A*
Edgecombe Community College *A*
Fayetteville State University *A*
Fayetteville Technical Community
 College *A*
Gaston College *A*
Haywood Community College *C, A*
James Sprunt Community College *A*
Johnston Community College *A*
King's College *C, A*
Lenoir Community College *A*
Mayland Community College *A*
Mitchell Community College *C, A*
Montgomery Community College *C, A*
Nash Community College *A*
Piedmont Community College *A*
Pitt Community College *C, A*
Randolph Community College *A*
Richmond Community College *C, A*
Roanoke-Chowan Community College *A*
Sampson Community College *A*
Sandhills Community College *A*
South College *C, A*
South Piedmont Community
 College *C, A*
Southwestern Community College *A*
Stanly Community College *A*
Surry Community College *A*
Tri-County Community College *A*
Vance-Granville Community College *A*
Wake Technical Community College *A*
Wayne Community College *A*
Western Piedmont Community
 College *C, A*

North Dakota

Bismarck State College *C, A*
Dickinson State University *A, B*
Lake Region State College *C, A*
Mayville State University *A, B*
Minot State University: Bottineau
 Campus *A*
North Dakota State College of Science *A*
Trinity Bible College *A, B*
Williston State College *C, A*

Ohio

Bowling Green State University:
 Firelands College *A*
Bryant & Stratton College
 Cleveland West *C, A*
 Willoughby Hills *A*
Central Ohio Technical College *C, A*
Cincinnati State Technical and
 Community College *A*
Clark State Community College *C, A*
Columbus State Community College *A*
Cuyahoga Community College
 Eastern Campus *A*
 Metropolitan Campus *C, A*
 Western Campus *C, A*
David N. Myers College *A, B*
Davis College *A*
Gallipolis Career College *A*
God's Bible School and College *A*
Hocking Technical College *A*
James A. Rhodes State College *A*
Jefferson Community College *C, A*
Kent State University *C, A*
Kent State University
 Salem Regional Campus *A*
 Trumbull Campus *A*
 Tuscarawas Campus *A*
Lakeland Community College *C, A*
Miami University
 Middletown Campus *C, A*
 Oxford Campus *C*
Miami-Jacobs College *A*
Muskingum Area Technical College *C, A*
North Central State College *A*

Northwest State Community
 College *C, A*
Ohio Business College *C, A*
Ohio Business College: Sandusky *C, A*
Ohio University
 Chillicothe Campus *A*
Ohio Valley College of Technology *C, A*
Owens Community College
 Findlay Campus *C, A*
 Toledo *C, A*
RETS Tech Center *C*
Sinclair Community College *C, A*
Southeastern Business College *A*
Southeastern Business College:
 Lancaster *A*
Southern State Community College *A*
Southwestern College of Business *A*
Stark State College of Technology *A*
Stautzenberger College *C, A*
University of Akron *C, A*
University of Cincinnati
 Clermont College *C, A*
 Raymond Walters College *A*
University of Northwestern Ohio *A*
University of Rio Grande *C*
University of Toledo *A*
Wright State University: Lake Campus *A*
Youngstown State University *A, B*

Oklahoma

Carl Albert State College *A*
East Central University *B*
Eastern Oklahoma State College *A*
Langston University *B*
Murray State College *A*
Northeastern Oklahoma Agricultural and
 Mechanical College *C, A*
Oklahoma State University
 Okmulgee *A*
Oklahoma Wesleyan University *A*
Redlands Community College *A*
Rose State College *C, A*
Tulsa Community College *C, A*
Western Oklahoma State College *A*

Oregon

Blue Mountain Community College *C, A*
Central Oregon Community
 College *C, A*
Chemeketa Community College *A*
Clackamas Community College *C*
Lane Community College *A*
Linn-Benton Community College *A*
Mount Hood Community College *C, A*
Oregon Institute of Technology *A*
Portland Community College *C, A*
Rogue Community College *C*
Southwestern Oregon Community
 College *A*
Umpqua Community College *C, A*

Pennsylvania

Academy of Medical Arts and
 Business *A*
Allentown Business School *A*
Baptist Bible College of
 Pennsylvania *A, B*
Bradford School: Pittsburgh *C, A*
Bucks County Community College *A*
Cambria County Area Community
 College *A*
Cambria-Rowe Business College *C, A*
Cambria-Rowe Business College:
 Indiana *A*
Career Training Academy:
 Monroeville *C*
Central Pennsylvania College *A*
Community College of Allegheny
 County *C, A*
Community College of Philadelphia *A*
Consolidated School of Business
 Lancaster *C, A*
 York *C, A*
Delaware County Community College *C*
Douglas School of Business *C*
DuBois Business College *C, A*

DuBois Business College
 Oil City *A*
Erie Business Center *A*
Harrisburg Area Community College *A*
ICM School of Business & Medical
 Careers *A*
Lackawanna College *A*
Lancaster Bible College *A*
Lehigh Carbon Community College *C, A*
Luzerne County Community
 College *C, A*
McCann School of Business
 Pottsville *A*
 Sunbury *A*
Mercyhurst College *C, A*
Montgomery County Community
 College *C, A*
Newport Business Institute *A*
Northampton County Area Community
 College *C, A*
Pennsylvania College of Technology *A*
Pennsylvania Institute of Technology *A*
Reading Area Community College *C, A*
Schuylkill Institute of Business &
 Technology *C, A*
South Hills School of Business &
 Technology *C, A*
South Hills School of Business and
 Technology *A*
Westmoreland County Community
 College *C, A*

Puerto Rico

Atlantic College *A, B*
Bayamon Central University *A, B*
Columbia College *A*
Huertas Junior College *A*
Humacao Community College *A*
ICPR Junior College *A*
Inter American University of Puerto Rico
 Barranquitas Campus *A, B*
 Bayamon Campus *A, B*
 Fajardo Campus *A, B*
 Guayama Campus *A, B*
 Metropolitan Campus *A, B*
 San German Campus *A, B*
Pontifical Catholic University of Puerto
 Rico *A, B*
Technological College of San Juan *C, A*
Turabo University *A, B*
Universidad del Este *A, B*
University of Puerto Rico
 Carolina Regional College *A*
 Cayey University College *A, B*
 Humacao *A, B*
 Mayaguez Campus *B*
 Ponce *A, B*
 Rio Piedras Campus *B*
 Utuado *A, B*
University of the Sacred Heart *B*

Rhode Island

Community College of Rhode
 Island *C, A*

South Carolina

Aiken Technical College *C, A*
Central Carolina Technical College *C, A*
Denmark Technical College *C*
Florence-Darlington Technical
 College *C, A*
Forrest Junior College *A*
Horry-Georgetown Technical College *A*
Midlands Technical College *C, A*
Northeastern Technical College *C, A*
Orangeburg-Calhoun Technical
 College *A*
Piedmont Technical College *C, A*
Technical College of the
 Lowcountry *C, A*
Tri-County Technical College *C, A*
Trident Technical College *A*
University of South Carolina
 Lancaster *A*
Williamsburg Technical College *C, A*
York Technical College *C, A*

South Dakota

Black Hills State University *A*
Kilian Community College *A*
Northern State University *A*
Western Dakota Technical Institute *C*

Tennessee

Cleveland State Community
 College *C, A*
Columbia State Community College *A*
Draughons Junior College: Clarksville *A*
Jackson State Community College *A*
Northeast State Technical Community
 College *C, A*
Pellissippi State Technical Community
 College *A*
Roane State Community College *C, A*
South College *C*
Southwest Tennessee Community
 College *A*
Tennessee State University *A, B*
Volunteer State Community College *A*
Walters State Community College *A*

Texas

Alvin Community College *C, A*
Amarillo College *C, A*
Angelina College *C, A*
Austin Community College *C, A*
Blinn College *C*
Brazosport College *C, A*
Cedar Valley College *A*
Central Texas College *C, A*
Coastal Bend College *C, A*
College of the Mainland *C, A*
Collin County Community College
 District *C, A*
Del Mar College *C, A*
Eastfield College *C, A*
El Centro College *C, A*
El Paso Community College *C, A*
Frank Phillips College *C, A*
Galveston College *C, A*
Grayson County College *A*
Hallmark Institute of Technology *A*
Hill College *C, A*
Houston Community College
 System *C, A*
Lamar State College at Orange *C, A*
Lamar State College at Port Arthur *C, A*
Laredo Community College *A*
Lee College *C, A*
MTI College of Business and
 Technology *C, A*
MTI College of Business and
 Technology *C, A*
McLennan Community College *C*
Midland College *C, A*
Mountain View College *A*
North Central Texas College *A*
North Harris Montgomery Community
 College District *C, A*
North Lake College *A*
Northeast Texas Community
 College *C, A*
Palo Alto College *C, A*
Panola College *C, A*
Paris Junior College *A*
Ranger College *C, A*
Richland College *A*
St. Philip's College *C, A*
San Antonio College *A*
San Jacinto College
 Central Campus *C, A*
South Plains College *A*
South Texas Community College *C*
Southwest Texas Junior College *A*
Southwestern Adventist University *A, B*
Sul Ross State University *B*
Tarleton State University *B, T*
Tarrant County College *A*
Temple College *C, A*
Texarkana College *C, A*
Texas State Technical College
 West Texas *C, A*
Texas Woman's University *B*

Trinity Valley Community College *C, A*
Tyler Junior College *C, A*
Victoria College *C, A*
Western Texas College *C, A*

Utah
College of Eastern Utah *C, A*
LDS Business College *C, A*
Salt Lake Community College *C*
Utah State University *A, B*
Utah Valley State College *C, A*
Weber State University *A, B*

Vermont
Vermont Technical College *A*

Virginia
Blue Ridge Community College *C, A*
Bryant & Stratton College *A*
ECPI College of Technology *C, A*
ECPI Technical College: Roanoke *A*
J. Sargeant Reynolds Community
  College *C, A*
National College of Business &
  Technology
    Bluefield *C, A*
    Charlottesville *C, A*
    Danville *C, A*
    Harrisonburg *C, A*
    Lynchburg *C, A*
    Martinsville *C, A*
    Roanoke *A*
Paul D. Camp Community College *A*
Southside Virginia Community
  College *A*
Southwest Virginia Community
  College *C, A*
Virginia Commonwealth University *B*
Virginia Highlands Community
  College *A*
Virginia Intermont College *B*
Virginia Western Community College *A*

Washington
Bellevue Community College *C, A*
Clover Park Technical College *C*
Edmonds Community College *C*
Everett Community College *C, A*
Grays Harbor College *C, A*
Lake Washington Technical College *C, A*
Lower Columbia College *C, A*
North Seattle Community College *C, A*
Peninsula College *A*
Renton Technical College *C, A*
Seattle Central Community College *C, A*
South Seattle Community College *C, A*
Spokane Community College *C, A*
Spokane Falls Community College *A*
Walla Walla Community College *C, A*

West Virginia
Concord College *A*
Fairmont State College *A*
Glenville State College *A*
Huntington Junior College *C, A*
Mountain State College *A*
Mountain State University *C, A*
Potomac State College of West Virginia
  University *A*
Southern West Virginia Community and
  Technical College *C, A*
Valley College of Technology *C*
West Virginia Business College *A*
West Virginia Business College *A, D*
West Virginia Northern Community
  College *C, A*
West Virginia State College *A*
West Virginia University at
  Parkersburg *C, A*

Wisconsin
Blackhawk Technical College *C, A*
Bryant & Stratton College *A*
Chippewa Valley Technical College *A*
Fox Valley Technical College *A*
Lakeshore Technical College *A*
Maranatha Baptist Bible College *A, B*

Mid-State Technical College *C, A*
Milwaukee Area Technical College *A*
Moraine Park Technical College *C, A*
Nicolet Area Technical College *A*
Western Wisconsin Technical College *A*
Wisconsin Indianhead Technical
  College *C, A*

Wyoming
Central Wyoming College *C, A*
Eastern Wyoming College *A*
Laramie County Community
  College *C, A*
Sheridan College *C, A*
Western Wyoming Community
  College *C, A*

Adult development/aging

Florida
University of West Florida *M*

Pennsylvania
Penn State
  Wilkes-Barre *B*

Texas
Texas Tech University *B*

Adult health nursing

Connecticut
Western Connecticut State University *M*

Indiana
Indiana University-Purdue University
  Indianapolis *M*

Michigan
Madonna University *M*

Missouri
Maryville University of Saint Louis *D*
Webster University *B*

New York
Mount St. Mary College *M*
Pace University *C, M*
Pace University:
  Pleasantville/Briarcliff *C, M*
State University of New York
  Buffalo *M*
    Health Science Center at Stony
    Brook *M*
  Stony Brook *M*

Ohio
Case Western Reserve University *M*
Kent State University *C*
Youngstown State University *M*

Pennsylvania
Pennsylvania College of Technology *B*
University of Pennsylvania *C, M*

South Carolina
Medical University of South Carolina *M*

Texas
University of Texas
  Pan American *B, M*

Adult/continuing education

Alabama
Auburn University *B*
Troy State University in Montgomery *M*
University of West Alabama *M*

Arizona
University of Phoenix *M*

Arkansas
University of Arkansas *M, D*
University of Arkansas
  Little Rock *M*

California
College of the Sequoias *A*
Patten University *B*
San Diego State University *M*
San Francisco State University *M*
Whittier College *T*

Delaware
Delaware State University *M*

District of Columbia
George Washington University *M*

Florida
Florida Agricultural and Mechanical
  University *M*
Florida International University *M, D*
University of South Florida *M*

Georgia
Georgia State University *B, M, D*
University of Georgia *M, D*

Idaho
University of Idaho *M*

Illinois
National-Louis University *M, D*
Northeastern Illinois University *B, M*
University of St. Francis *M*

Indiana
Ball State University *M*
Indiana University-Purdue University
  Indianapolis *M*
Martin University *B*

Iowa
Loras College *M*
University of Iowa *M, D*
Vennard College *B*

Kansas
Kansas State University *M, D*

Kentucky
Morehead State University *M*

Maine
University of Southern Maine *M*

Maryland
Coppin State College *M*

Massachusetts
Boston University *M, T*

Michigan
Northern Michigan University *B, M*
University of Michigan *M*

Minnesota
Capella University *M, D*
Ridgewater College: A Community and
  Technical College *A*
University of Minnesota
  Twin Cities *M*

Missouri
Central Missouri State University *M, T*
University of Missouri
  Kansas City *M*
  St. Louis *M*

Nebraska
University of Nebraska
  Lincoln *M*

Nevada
University of Nevada
  Las Vegas *B, M*

New Mexico
University of New Mexico *M*

New York
Elmira College *M*
State University of New York
  College at Buffalo *M*
Syracuse University *M, D*

North Carolina
North Carolina Agricultural and
  Technical State University *M*
North Carolina State University *M*
University of North Carolina
  Greensboro *M*

Ohio
Cleveland State University *M, D*
Ohio University *M*

Oklahoma
Oklahoma State University *M, D*
University of Central Oklahoma *M*
University of Oklahoma *M, D*

Oregon
Oregon State University *M*
Portland State University *D*

Pennsylvania
Cheyney University of Pennsylvania *M*
Indiana University of Pennsylvania *M*
Penn State
  Lehigh Valley *B*
  University Park *M, D*
Temple University *M*

South Carolina
Francis Marion University *B, M*
University of South Carolina *M*

Texas
Southwest Texas State University *M*
Texas A&M University *B, M, D*
Texas A&M University
  Commerce *M*
University of North Texas *M, D*
University of Texas
  Tyler *M*

Virginia
James Madison University *M*
Virginia Commonwealth University *M*

Washington
Eastern Washington University *M*
Seattle University *M*
Western Washington University *M*

Wisconsin
University of Wisconsin
  Madison *M, D*

Adult/continuing education administration

Alaska
University of Alaska
  Anchorage *M*

Arizona
University of Phoenix *M*

Arkansas
Arkansas State University *M, T*
University of Arkansas *D*

California
San Francisco State University *M*

Florida
Florida State University *M, D*
Nova Southeastern University *D*

Illinois
De Paul University *M*
Northern Illinois University *M, D*

Indiana
Ball State University *D, T*
Purdue University
  Calumet *B, T*

Iowa
Drake University *B, M*
Iowa State University *M, D*
University of Iowa *M, D*

Kansas

Newman University *M*

Maine

University of Southern Maine *M*

Maryland

Coppin State College *M*

Massachusetts

Lesley University *M, T*
Suffolk University *M*

Michigan

Central Michigan University *M*
Grand Valley State University *M*
Michigan State University *M, D*

Mississippi

University of Southern Mississippi *M*

Missouri

University of Missouri
    Columbia *M, D*

New Hampshire

University of New Hampshire *M*

New York

Cornell University *B*
Fordham University *M, D*
State University of New York
    College at Buffalo *M*

North Carolina

East Carolina University *M*
North Carolina Agricultural and
    Technical State University *M*
North Carolina State University *M, D*

Ohio

Laura and Alvin Siegal College of Judaic
    Studies *M*
Ohio State University
    Columbus Campus *M*
Wittenberg University *B*

Oklahoma

Oklahoma State University *M, D*
University of Oklahoma *M, D*

Oregon

Oregon State University *M*

Pennsylvania

Penn State
    Abington *B*
    Altoona *B*
    Beaver *B*
    Berks *B*
    Delaware County *B*
    Dubois *B*
    Fayette *B*
    Hazleton *B*
    McKeesport *B*
    Mont Alto *B*
    New Kensington *B*
    Schuylkill - Capital College *B*
    Shenango *B*
    University Park *B, M, D*
    Wilkes-Barre *B*
    Worthington Scranton *B*
    York *B*
University of Pennsylvania *M*

South Carolina

University of South Carolina *M*

South Dakota

University of South Dakota *M, D*

Tennessee

Tusculum College *M*

Texas

Southwest Texas State University *M, T*
Texas A&M University
    Kingsville *M*
University of Texas
    San Antonio *D*
University of the Incarnate Word *M*

Washington

Seattle University *B*

West Virginia

Marshall University *B, M*

Wisconsin

University of Wisconsin
    Madison *M, D*

Advertising

Alabama

University of Alabama *B, M*

Arizona

Northern Arizona University *B*

Arkansas

Harding University *B*
University of Arkansas
    Little Rock *B*

California

Academy of Art College *C, A, B, M*
Art Center College of Design *B*
California State University
    Fullerton *B, M*
    Hayward *B*
Chapman University *B*
Irvine Valley College *A*
Long Beach City College *C, A*
Los Angeles Southwest College *A*
Mount San Antonio College *A*
Orange Coast College *A*
Palomar College *C, A*
Pepperdine University *B*
San Diego State University *B, M*
San Jose State University *B*

Colorado

Art Institute
    of Colorado *B*
Colorado State University
    Pueblo *B*
Trinidad State Junior College *A*
University of Denver *M*

Connecticut

Middlesex Community College *C*
Quinnipiac University *B*

Delaware

Delaware Technical and Community
    College
    Terry Campus *A*

District of Columbia

University of the District of Columbia *A*

Florida

Barry University *B*
Florida Southern College *B*
Florida State University *B*
Gulf Coast Community College *A*
Manatee Community College *A*
Northwood University
    Florida Campus *A, B*
University of Central Florida *B*
University of Florida *B*
University of Miami *B*
University of West Florida *B*

Georgia

Clark Atlanta University *B*
University of Georgia *B*
Wesleyan College *B*

Hawaii

Hawaii Pacific University *B*

Idaho

Brigham Young University - Idaho *B*
Idaho State University *B*

Illinois

American Academy of Art *B*
Bradley University *B*
Columbia College Chicago *B*

Concordia University *B*
Danville Area Community College *A*
Illinois Institute of Art *B*
Northwestern University *M*
Oakton Community College *C*
University of Illinois
    Urbana-Champaign *B, M*
University of St. Francis *B*

Indiana

Ball State University *B*
Vincennes University *A*

Iowa

Clarke College *B*
Drake University *B*
Iowa Lakes Community College *A*
Iowa State University *B*
Morningside College *B*
St. Ambrose University *B*

Kansas

Independence Community College *A*
Pittsburg State University *B*
University of Kansas *B*

Kentucky

Murray State University *B, M*
University of Kentucky *B*

Louisiana

Louisiana College *B*

Maine

New England School of
    Communications *A, B*

Maryland

Montgomery College
    Rockville Campus *C, A*

Massachusetts

Babson College *B*
Boston University *B, M*
Emerson College *B, M*
Mount Ida College *A*
Suffolk University *M*
Western New England College *B*

Michigan

Bay de Noc Community College *C*
Central Michigan University *B*
Ferris State University *C, B*
Grand Valley State University *B*
Lansing Community College *A*
Michigan State University *B, M*
North Central Michigan College *C*
Northwood University *A, B*
Schoolcraft College *A*
Western Michigan University *B*

Minnesota

Concordia College: Moorhead *B*
Hennepin Technical College *C, A*
Metropolitan State University *B*
Minnesota State University
    Moorhead *B*
St. Cloud State University *B*
St. Cloud Technical College *C, A*
Winona State University *B*

Mississippi

University of Southern Mississippi *B*

Missouri

Drury University *B*
St. Louis Community College
    St. Louis Community College at
    Florissant Valley *A*
Southeast Missouri State University *B*
Stephens College *B*
Washington University in St. Louis *B*
Webster University *A, B*
Westminster College *B*
William Woods University *B*

Nebraska

Hastings College *B*
Northeast Community College *A*

University of Nebraska
    Kearney *B*
    Lincoln *B*

Nevada

University of Nevada
    Reno *B*

New Hampshire

Franklin Pierce College *B*
New England College *B*
Southern New Hampshire University *B*

New Jersey

Rider University *B*
Rowan University *B*
Thomas Edison State College *B*
Union County College *C*

New Mexico

Santa Fe Community College *A*

New York

City University of New York
    Baruch College *B, M*
    City College *B*
Fashion Institute of Technology *A, B*
Iona College *B*
Marist College *B*
Medaille College *B*
Mohawk Valley Community
    College *C, A*
Monroe Community College *A*
New York Institute of Technology *B*
Onondaga Community College *A*
Pace University *B*
School of Visual Arts *B*
Syracuse University *B, M*

North Carolina

Alamance Community College *C*
Appalachian State University *B*
Campbell University *B*
Central Piedmont Community College *A*
Guilford Technical Community
    College *A*
Halifax Community College *A*

North Dakota

Minot State University: Bottineau
    Campus *C, A*

Ohio

Columbus College of Art and Design *B*
Kent State University *B*
Kent State University
    Stark Campus *B*
Marietta College *B*
Ohio University *B*
University of Findlay *B*
Xavier University *A, B*
Youngstown State University *B*

Oklahoma

Oklahoma Christian University of
    Science and Arts *B*
Oklahoma City University *B*
Southeastern Oklahoma State
    University *B*
University of Central Oklahoma *B*
University of Oklahoma *B*

Oregon

University of Oregon *B, M*

Pennsylvania

California University of Pennsylvania *B*
Marywood University *B*
Mercyhurst College *B*
Oakbridge Academy of Arts *A*

Penn State
  Abington *B*
  Altoona *B*
  Beaver *B*
  Berks *B*
  Delaware County *B*
  Dubois *B*
  Fayette *B*
  Hazleton *B*
  Lehigh Valley *B*
  McKeesport *B*
  Mont Alto *B*
  New Kensington *B*
  Schuylkill - Capital College *B*
  Shenango *B*
  University Park *B*
  Wilkes-Barre *B*
  Worthington Scranton *B*
Point Park College *B*
Waynesburg College *B*

Puerto Rico
University of Puerto Rico
  Carolina Regional College *A, B*
University of the Sacred Heart *B, M*

South Carolina
University of South Carolina *B*

South Dakota
Southeast Technical Institute *A*

Tennessee
Chattanooga State Technical Community
  College *A*
Southern Adventist University *B*
Union University *B*
University of Tennessee
  Knoxville *B*

Texas
Amarillo College *A*
Lamar University *B*
Northwood University: Texas
  Campus *A, B*
Palo Alto College *A*
Sam Houston State University *B*
Southern Methodist University *B*
Southwest Texas State University *B*
Texas A&M University
  Commerce *B*
Texas Christian University *B, M*
Texas Tech University *B*
University of Houston *B*
University of North Texas *B*
University of Texas
  Arlington *B*
  Austin *B, M, D*
West Texas A&M University *B*

Utah
Brigham Young University *B*
Southern Utah University *B*

Virginia
Hampton University *B*

Washington
Everett Community College *C, A*
Seattle Central Community College *C, A*
Washington State University *B*

West Virginia
Bethany College *B*
Concord College *B*
West Virginia State College *C, A*
West Virginia University *B*

Wisconsin
Marquette University *B, M*

Aeronautical/aerospace engineering

Alabama
Auburn University *B, M, D*
Tuskegee University *B*
University of Alabama *B, M*

Arizona
Arizona State University *B, M, D*
Embry-Riddle Aeronautical University:
  Prescott Campus *B*
University of Arizona *B, M, D*

California
California Institute of
  Technology *B, M, D*
California Polytechnic State University:
  San Luis Obispo *B, M*
California State Polytechnic University:
  Pomona *B*
California State University
  Long Beach *B, M*
  Northridge *M*
Northrop-Rice Aviation Institute of
  Technology *A, B*
San Diego State University *B, M*
San Jose State University *B, M*
Stanford University *M, D*
University of California
  Davis *B*
  Irvine *B*
  Los Angeles *B, M, D*
  San Diego *B, M, D*
University of Southern
  California *B, M, D*

Colorado
United States Air Force Academy *B*
University of Colorado
  Boulder *B, M, D*
  Colorado Springs *M*

Delaware
University of Delaware *B*

District of Columbia
George Washington University *M, D*

Florida
Embry-Riddle Aeronautical
  University *B, M*
Florida Institute of Technology *B, M, D*
University of Central Florida *B, M*
University of Florida *B, M, D*
University of Miami *B*

Georgia
Georgia Institute of Technology *B, M, D*

Hawaii
University of Hawaii
  Honolulu Community College *A*

Illinois
Illinois Institute of Technology *B*
University of Illinois
  Urbana-Champaign *B, M, D*

Indiana
Purdue University *B, M, D*
University of Notre Dame *B, M, D*

Iowa
Iowa State University *B, M, D*

Kansas
University of Kansas *B, M, D*
Wichita State University *B, M, D*

Maryland
Johns Hopkins University *M*
United States Naval Academy *B*
University of Maryland
  College Park *B, M, D*

Massachusetts
Boston University *B, M, D*
Massachusetts Institute of
  Technology *B, M, D*

Michigan
University of Michigan *B, M, D*
Western Michigan University *B*

Minnesota
University of Minnesota
  Twin Cities *B, M, D*

Mississippi
Mississippi State University *B, M*

Missouri
St. Louis University *B, M*
University of Missouri
  Rolla *B, M, D*

New York
City University of New York
  Bronx Community College *A*
Clarkson University *B*
Cornell University *M, D*
Rensselaer Polytechnic Institute *B, M, D*
Rochester Institute of Technology *B*
State University of New York
  Buffalo *B, M, D*
Syracuse University *B, M, D*
United States Military Academy *B*

North Carolina
North Carolina State University *B, M, D*

North Dakota
North Dakota State University *B*

Ohio
Case Western Reserve
  University *B, M, D*
Kent State University *C, B*
Kent State University
  Stark Campus *B*
Ohio State University
  Columbus Campus *B, M, D*
University of Cincinnati *B, M, D*
University of Dayton *M, D*

Oklahoma
Oklahoma State University *B*
Southeastern Oklahoma State
  University *B*
University of Oklahoma *B, M, D*

Pennsylvania
Gettysburg College *B*
Lock Haven University of
  Pennsylvania *B*
Penn State
  Abington *B*
  Altoona *B*
  Beaver *B*
  Berks *B*
  Delaware County *B*
  Dubois *B*
  Fayette *B*
  Hazleton *B*
  Lehigh Valley *B*
  McKeesport *B*
  Mont Alto *B*
  New Kensington *B*
  Schuylkill - Capital College *B*
  Shenango *B*
  University Park *B, M, D*
  Wilkes-Barre *B*
  Worthington Scranton *B*
  York *B*

Tennessee
University of Tennessee
  Knoxville *B, M, D*

Texas
Alvin Community College *A*
Laredo Community College *A*
LeTourneau University *B*
Rice University *M, D*
Texas A&M University *B, M, D*
University of Houston *M, D*
University of Texas
  Arlington *B, M, D*
  Austin *B, M, D*

Utah
Utah State University *B*

Virginia
University of Virginia *B, M, D*
Virginia Polytechnic Institute and State
  University *B, M, D*

Washington
University of Washington *B, M, D*

West Virginia
West Virginia University *B, M, D*

Aeronautical/aerospace engineering technology

Alabama
Calhoun Community College *A*

Arizona
Gateway Community College *A*

California
Antelope Valley College *C, A*
Northrop-Rice Aviation Institute of
  Technology *A, B*

Florida
Embry-Riddle Aeronautical University *B*

Georgia
Middle Georgia College *A*

Maryland
Capitol College *B*

Massachusetts
Northeastern University *B*

Michigan
Western Michigan University *B*

Missouri
St. Louis University *B*

New York
New York Institute of Technology *B*

Ohio
Kent State University *B, M, D*

Pennsylvania
Community College of Beaver County *A*

Aesthetician/skin care

Florida
Indian River Community College *C*

Minnesota
Minnesota State College - Southeast
  Technical *C*
St. Paul College - A Community and
  Technical College *C, A*

North Carolina
Carteret Community College *C*
Davidson County Community College *C*

Texas
Lamar State College at Port Arthur *C*

Washington
Clover Park Technical College *C*
Renton Technical College *C*

African languages

Indiana
Indiana University
  Bloomington *B*

African studies

California
Palomar College *C*
San Diego City College *A*
San Diego Mesa College *A*
San Francisco State University *B*
Stanford University *B*
University of California
  Los Angeles *M*

Connecticut
Connecticut College *B*
Trinity College *B*
Yale University *B, M*

District of Columbia
Howard University *B, M, D*

Florida
Barry University *C*
Manatee Community College *A*

Georgia
Clark Atlanta University *M, D*
Emory University *B*
Oxford College of Emory University *B*

Illinois
University of Illinois
    Urbana-Champaign *M*

Indiana
Earlham College *B*
Martin University *B*

Iowa
Luther College *B*
University of Iowa *B, M*

Kansas
University of Kansas *B*

Louisiana
Dillard University *B*

Maine
Bowdoin College *B*

Maryland
Washington College *B*

Massachusetts
Amherst College *B*
Brandeis University *B*
College of the Holy Cross *B*
Hampshire College *B*
Harvard College *B*
Mount Holyoke College *B*
Tufts University *M*
Wellesley College *B*

Michigan
Lansing Community College *A*
Oakland University *B*
University of Michigan *B*

Minnesota
Carleton College *B*
University of Minnesota
    Twin Cities *B*

Missouri
Washington University in St. Louis *B*

New Hampshire
Dartmouth College *B*

New Jersey
Rutgers, The State University of New
    Jersey
    New Brunswick Regional
        Campus *B*
    Newark Regional Campus *B*
William Paterson University of New
    Jersey *B*

New York
Bard College *B*
Barnard College *B*
City University of New York
    Brooklyn College *B*
    Queens College *B*
Colgate University *B*
Columbia University
    Columbia College *B*
Cornell University *B, M*
Fordham University *B*
Hobart and William Smith Colleges *B*
Hofstra University *B*
Nassau Community College *A*
St. Lawrence University *B*

Sarah Lawrence College *B*
State University of New York
    Binghamton *B*
Vassar College *B*

North Carolina
Shaw University *B*

Ohio
Antioch College *B*
Bowling Green State University *B*
College of Wooster *B*
Kent State University
    Stark Campus *B*
Oberlin College *B*
Ohio State University
    Columbus Campus *B, M*
Ohio University *B, M*
University of Akron *C*

Oregon
Portland State University *B*

Pennsylvania
Bryn Mawr College *B*
Franklin & Marshall College *B*
Lehigh University *B*
Penn State
    University Park *C*
University of Pennsylvania *B*
University of Pittsburgh *C*

Rhode Island
Brown University *B*

South Carolina
Claflin University *B*

Tennessee
Walters State Community College *A*

Vermont
Marlboro College *B*

Washington
University of Washington *A*

Alabama
Talladega College *B*
University of Alabama
    Birmingham *B*

Arizona
Arizona State University *B*

California
California State University
    Dominguez Hills *B*
    Fresno *B*
    Fullerton *B*
    Hayward *B*
    Long Beach *C, B*
    Los Angeles *B*
    Northridge *B*
Claremont McKenna College *B*
College of Alameda *A*
Contra Costa College *A*
De Anza College *C, A*
East Los Angeles College *A*
Laney College *A*
Los Angeles Southwest College *A*
Loyola Marymount University *B*
Pitzer College *B*
Pomona College *B*
San Diego City College *A*
San Diego Mesa College *A*
San Diego State University *B*
San Francisco State University *B*
San Jose State University *B*
Santa Barbara City College *A*
Scripps College *B*
Sonoma State University *B*
Southwestern College *A*
Stanford University *B*

University of California
    Berkeley *B, D*
    Davis *B*
    Irvine *B*
    Los Angeles *B, M*
    Riverside *B*
    Santa Barbara *B*
University of Southern California *B*
Ventura College *A*

Colorado
Fort Lewis College *B*
Metropolitan State College of Denver *B*
University of Northern Colorado *B*

Connecticut
Trinity College *B*
Wesleyan University *B*
Yale University *B, M, D*

District of Columbia
Howard University *B*

Florida
Florida Agricultural and Mechanical
    University *B*
Florida International University *M*
Polk Community College *A*
University of Miami *B*
University of South Florida *B*

Georgia
Clark Atlanta University *M*
Emory University *B, M, D*
Georgia State University *B*
Mercer University *B*
Morehouse College *B*
Morris Brown College *B*
Oxford College of Emory University *B*
University of Georgia *B*

Illinois
Chicago State University *B*
City Colleges of Chicago
    Kennedy-King College *A*
    Olive-Harvey College *A*
De Paul University *B*
Dominican University *B*
Eastern Illinois University *B*
Knox College *B*
Northwestern University *B*
Roosevelt University *B*
University of Illinois
    Chicago *B*
Western Illinois University *B*

Indiana
Earlham College *B*
Indiana State University *B*
Indiana University
    Bloomington *B, M*
    Northwest *B*
Martin University *B*
Purdue University *B*

Iowa
Coe College *B*
Luther College *B*
University of Iowa *B, M*

Kansas
University of Kansas *B*

Kentucky
University of Louisville *B*

Maine
Bates College *B*
Bowdoin College *B*
Colby College *B*

Maryland
Morgan State University *B, M, D*
University of Maryland
    Baltimore County *B*
    College Park *C, B*

Massachusetts
Amherst College *B*
Boston University *M*

Brandeis University *B*
College of the Holy Cross *B*
Hampshire College *B*
Harvard College *B*
Mount Holyoke College *B*
Simmons College *B*
Simon's Rock College of Bard *B*
Smith College *B*
Tufts University *B*
University of Massachusetts
    Amherst *B, M, D*
    Boston *B*
Wellesley College *B*

Michigan
Eastern Michigan University *B*
Michigan State University *B*
University of Michigan *B*
University of Michigan
    Flint *B*
Wayne State University *B*
Western Michigan University *B*

Minnesota
Carleton College *B*
University of Minnesota
    Twin Cities *B*

Missouri
Washington University in St. Louis *B*

Nebraska
University of Nebraska
    Omaha *B*

New Hampshire
Dartmouth College *B*

New Jersey
Monmouth University *C*
Rowan University *B*
Rutgers, The State University of New
    Jersey
    Camden Regional Campus *B*
    New Brunswick Regional
        Campus *B*
    Newark Regional Campus *B*
Seton Hall University *B*
William Paterson University of New
    Jersey *B*

New Mexico
University of New Mexico *B*

New York
Bard College *B*
City University of New York
    Brooklyn College *B*
    City College *B*
    College of Staten Island *B*
    Hunter College *B*
    York College *B*
Colgate University *B*
Columbia University
    Columbia College *B*
Cornell University *B, M*
Eugene Lang College/New School
    University *B*
Fordham University *B*
Hamilton College *B*
Hobart and William Smith Colleges *B*
Metropolitan College of New York *A, B*
New York University *B, M*
Sarah Lawrence College *B*
State University of New York
    Albany *B, M*
    Binghamton *B*
    Buffalo *B, M*
    College at Brockport *B*
    College at Cortland *B*
    College at Geneseo *B*
    College at Oneonta *B*
    New Paltz *B*
    Stony Brook *B*
Syracuse University *B*
University of Rochester *B*
Wells College *B*

North Carolina

Duke University *B*
St. Augustine's College *B*
University of North Carolina
    Chapel Hill *B*
    Charlotte *B*

Ohio

Antioch College *B*
College of Wooster *B*
Denison University *B*
Kent State University *B*
Miami University
    Oxford Campus *B*
Oberlin College *B*
Ohio State University
    Columbus Campus *B, M*
Ohio University *B*
Ohio Wesleyan University *B*
Owens Community College
    Findlay Campus *A*
    Toledo *A*
Sinclair Community College *A*
University of Cincinnati *B*
University of Toledo *B*
Wright State University *B*
Youngstown State University *B*

Oklahoma

University of Oklahoma *B*

Pennsylvania

Franklin & Marshall College *B*
Gettysburg College *B*
Lincoln University *B*
Penn State
    Abington *B*
    Altoona *B*
    Beaver *B*
    Berks *B*
    Delaware County *B*
    Dubois *B*
    Erie, The Behrend College *B*
    Fayette *B*
    Hazleton *B*
    Lehigh Valley *B*
    McKeesport *B*
    Mont Alto *B*
    New Kensington *B*
    Schuylkill - Capital College *B*
    Shenango *B*
    University Park *C, B*
    Wilkes-Barre *B*
    Worthington Scranton *B*
    York *B*
Temple University *B, M, D*
University of Pennsylvania *B*
University of Pittsburgh *B*

Rhode Island

Brown University *B*
Rhode Island College *B*
University of Rhode Island *B*

South Carolina

Claflin University *B*
University of South Carolina *B*

Tennessee

American Baptist College of ABT
    Seminary *A, B*
University of Memphis *B*
University of Tennessee
    Knoxville *B*
Vanderbilt University *B*

Texas

Southern Methodist University *B*
Texas Southern University *B*

Utah

Weber State University *B*

Vermont

Goddard College *B*
Marlboro College *B*

Virginia

College of William and Mary *B*

University of Virginia *B*

Washington

University of Washington *B*

Wisconsin

Marquette University *B*
University of Wisconsin
    Madison *B, M*

Agribusiness operations

Alabama

Alabama Agricultural and Mechanical
    University *M*
Wallace State Community College at
    Hanceville *C, A*

Arizona

Eastern Arizona College *A*

Arkansas

Arkansas State University *B*
Arkansas Tech University *A*
University of Arkansas *B*

California

Bakersfield College *A*
College of the Redwoods *A*
College of the Sequoias *A*
San Joaquin Delta College *C, A*
Santa Rosa Junior College *C, A*
Shasta College *C, A*
Ventura College *C, A*

Delaware

Delaware Technical and Community
    College
    Owens Campus *C, A*
University of Delaware *B*

Florida

Florida Agricultural and Mechanical
    University *B*
Miami-Dade Community College *A*
South Florida Community College *A*

Georgia

South Georgia College *A*

Hawaii

University of Hawaii
    Hilo *B*

Idaho

Brigham Young University - Idaho *A*

Illinois

Danville Area Community College *A*
Illinois State University *B, M*
Kishwaukee College *A*
Lincoln Land Community College *A*
Parkland College *A*

Indiana

Vincennes University *A*

Iowa

Des Moines Area Community College *C*
Dordt College *B*
Iowa State University *B*
Iowa Western Community College *A*
North Iowa Area Community College *A*

Kansas

Dodge City Community College *C, A*
Fort Scott Community College *A*
McPherson College *B*
MidAmerica Nazarene University *B*

Kentucky

Berea College *B*
Morehead State University *A*
Murray State University *B*

Michigan

Michigan State University *B*

Minnesota

Ridgewater College: A Community and
    Technical College *A*
Southwest State University *C, A, B*
University of Minnesota
    Crookston *B*

Mississippi

Mississippi State University *B*
Northwest Mississippi Community
    College *A*

Missouri

College of the Ozarks *B*
Crowder College *A*
Mineral Area College *C, A*
North Central Missouri College *C, A*
Southeast Missouri State University *B*

Nebraska

Nebraska College of Technical
    Agriculture *A*
Northeast Community College *A*
Southeast Community College
    Beatrice Campus *A*

New Mexico

Eastern New Mexico University *B*
Southwestern Indian Polytechnic
    Institute *A*

New York

Cornell University *B*
State University of New York
    College of Agriculture and
        Technology at Morrisville *A*

North Carolina

North Carolina State University *B*
Wayne Community College *A*

North Dakota

Bismarck State College *A*
Dickinson State University *C, A*
North Dakota State College of Science *A*

Ohio

Clark State Community College *A*
Wilmington College *B*

Oklahoma

Northern Oklahoma College *A*
Oklahoma Panhandle State University *B*
Oklahoma State University *B*
Redlands Community College *A*

Oregon

Chemeketa Community College *A*

Pennsylvania

Delaware Valley College *B*
Penn State
    Abington *B*
    Altoona *B*
    Beaver *B*
    Berks *B*
    Delaware County *B*
    Dubois *B*
    Erie, The Behrend College *B*
    Fayette *B*
    Hazleton *B*
    Lehigh Valley *B*
    McKeesport *B*
    Mont Alto *B*
    New Kensington *B*
    Schuylkill - Capital College *B*
    Shenango *B*
    University Park *B*
    Worthington Scranton *B*
    York *B*

Puerto Rico

University of Puerto Rico
    Mayaguez Campus *B*

South Carolina

Clemson University *B*
South Carolina State University *B, M*

South Dakota

Western Dakota Technical Institute *A*

Tennessee

Middle Tennessee State University *B*
Tennessee Technological University *B*
University of Tennessee
    Martin *M*

Texas

Abilene Christian University *B*
Palo Alto College *C, A*
Sam Houston State University *B, M*
Southwest Texas Junior College *A*
Southwest Texas State University *B*
Stephen F. Austin State University *B*
Sul Ross State University *B, M*
Tarleton State University *B*
Texarkana College *A*
Texas A&M University *B, M*
Texas A&M University
    Kingsville *B*
West Texas A&M University *B, M*

Utah

Brigham Young University *B*
Snow College *C, A*
Utah State University *M*

Vermont

Vermont Technical College *A*

Wisconsin

Fox Valley Technical College *A*
University of Wisconsin
    Madison *B*
    Platteville *B*

Wyoming

Casper College *A*
Eastern Wyoming College *A*
University of Wyoming *B*

Agricultural business

Alabama

Central Alabama Community College *A*
Enterprise State Junior College *A*
James H. Faulkner State Community
    College *A*
Jefferson State Community College *C, A*
Northeast Alabama Community
    College *A*
Northwest-Shoals Community College *C*

Arizona

Arizona Western College *A*
Central Arizona College *C, A*
Yavapai College *C, A*

Arkansas

Arkansas State University
    Beebe *A*
Southern Arkansas University *B*

California

California Polytechnic State University:
    San Luis Obispo *B*
California State Polytechnic University:
    Pomona *B*
California State University
    Chico *B*
    Fresno *B*
College of the Redwoods *C*
Imperial Valley College *C, A*
Los Angeles Pierce College *C, A*
MiraCosta College *C, A*
Modesto Junior College *A*
Mount San Antonio College *A*
Reedley College *C, A*
San Joaquin Delta College *A*
Santa Rosa Junior College *C*
Shasta College *A*
University of California
    Davis *B*
Yuba Community College District *C, A*

Colorado
Colorado State University *B*
Fort Lewis College *B*

Delaware
Delaware State University *B*
University of Delaware *B*

Florida
Florida Southern College *B*
Hillsborough Community College *C, A*

Georgia
Abraham Baldwin Agricultural
    College *A*
Gainesville College *C*
South Georgia College *A*
University of Georgia *B*

Idaho
College of Southern Idaho *C, A*
University of Idaho *B*

Illinois
Black Hawk College *A*
Black Hawk College
    East Campus *C, A*
Carl Sandburg College *A*
Illinois Central College *A*
Illinois Eastern Community Colleges
    Wabash Valley College *C, A*
John A. Logan College *A*
John Wood Community College *A*
Kaskaskia College *C, A*
Kishwaukee College *C, A*
Lake Land College *C*
Lewis and Clark Community
    College *C, A*
Lincoln Land Community College *A*
Parkland College *C, A*
Rend Lake College *A*
Richland Community College *A*
Shawnee Community College *A*

Indiana
Vincennes University *A*

Iowa
Des Moines Area Community College *A*
Dordt College *B*
Ellsworth Community College *C, A*
Hawkeye Community College *A*
Iowa Western Community College *A*
Marshalltown Community College *A*
North Iowa Area Community College *A*
Northeast Iowa Community College *A*
Northwestern College *B*
Southeastern Community College
    North Campus *A*
Southwestern Community College *A*
Waldorf College *A*

Kansas
Central Christian College *A*
Dodge City Community College *A*
Fort Hays State University *B*
Fort Scott Community College *A*
Garden City Community College *A*
Hutchinson Community College *C, A*
Independence Community College *A*
Kansas State University *B, M*
MidAmerica Nazarene University *B*
Pratt Community College *C, A*
Seward County Community College *A*
Tabor College *B*

Kentucky
Henderson Community College *C*
Murray State University *B*

Louisiana
Louisiana State University and
    Agricultural and Mechanical
    College *B*
Louisiana Tech University *B*
Nicholls State University *B*
University of Louisiana at Monroe *B*

Maine
University of Maine *B*

Maryland
Community College of Baltimore County
    Catonsville *A*
    Dundalk *A*
    Essex *A*
University of Maryland
    College Park *B*

Michigan
Andrews University *A, B*
Michigan State University *C, B*

Minnesota
Northland Community & Technical
    College *A*
Ridgewater College: A Community and
    Technical College *C, A*
Southwest State University *C*
University of Minnesota
    Crookston *B*
    Twin Cities *B*

Mississippi
Alcorn State University *B*
Itawamba Community College *A*
Mississippi State University *M*

Missouri
Central Missouri State University *B*
College of the Ozarks *B*
Mineral Area College *C, A*
Missouri Valley College *B*
Northwest Missouri State University *B*
Southeast Missouri State University *B*
Southwest Missouri State University *B*
Southwest Missouri State University:
    West Plains Campus *A*
Three Rivers Community College *A*
University of Missouri
    Columbia *B*

Montana
Dawson Community College *C, A*
Miles Community College *A*
Montana State University
    Bozeman *B*
Rocky Mountain College *B*

Nebraska
Central Community College *C, A*
Nebraska College of Technical
    Agriculture *A*
Northeast Community College *A*
Southeast Community College
    Beatrice Campus *A*
University of Nebraska
    Kearney *B*
    Lincoln *B*

New Hampshire
University of New Hampshire *B*

New Jersey
County College of Morris *A*

New Mexico
New Mexico State University *B*

New York
Cornell University *B*
State University of New York
    College of Agriculture and
        Technology at Cobleskill *A, B*
    College of Agriculture and
        Technology at Morrisville *A*
    College of Technology at Alfred *A*

North Carolina
James Sprunt Community College *A*
North Carolina Agricultural and
    Technical State University *B*
North Carolina State University *B*
Surry Community College *C, A*

North Dakota
Dickinson State University *A, B*
Lake Region State College *C, A*

North Dakota State College of Science *A*
North Dakota State University *B*

Ohio
Ohio State University
    Columbus Campus *A, B*
Owens Community College
    Findlay Campus *C, A*
    Toledo *C, A*
University of Northwestern Ohio *C, A*
Wilmington College *B*

Oklahoma
Eastern Oklahoma State College *A*
Langston University *B*
Northwestern Oklahoma State
    University *B*
Oklahoma Panhandle State University *B*
Oklahoma State University *B*
Redlands Community College *A*
Rogers State University *A*

Oregon
Blue Mountain Community College *A*
Chemeketa Community College *C*
Eastern Oregon University *B*
Linn-Benton Community College *A*
Oregon State University *B*
Treasure Valley Community College *A*

Pennsylvania
Penn State
    Abington *A*
    Altoona *A*
    Beaver *A*
    Berks *A*
    Delaware County *A*
    Dubois *A*
    Erie, The Behrend College *A*
    Fayette *A*
    Hazleton *A*
    Lehigh Valley *A*
    McKeesport *A*
    Mont Alto *A*
    New Kensington *A*
    Schuylkill - Capital College *A*
    Shenango *A*
    University Park *C, A*
    Wilkes-Barre *A, B*
    Worthington Scranton *A*
    York *A*

Puerto Rico
University of Puerto Rico
    Mayaguez Campus *B*

South Dakota
South Dakota State University *B*
Western Dakota Technical Institute *A*

Tennessee
Columbia State Community College *A*
Freed-Hardeman University *B*
Jackson State Community College *A*
University of Tennessee
    Martin *B*

Texas
Cisco Junior College *A*
Del Mar College *A*
Frank Phillips College *C*
Hill College *A*
Howard College *A*
Lubbock Christian University *B*
South Plains College *A*
Southwest Texas Junior College *A*
Tarleton State University *B*
Texas A&M University *B, M*
Texas A&M University
    Commerce *M*
    Kingsville *B, M*
Texas Tech University *B*
Trinity Valley Community College *A*
West Texas A&M University *B, M*

Utah
Brigham Young University *B*
Snow College *A*
Southern Utah University *B*

Utah State University *B*

Vermont
Vermont Technical College *A*

Virginia
Ferrum College *B*

Washington
Spokane Community College *A*
Walla Walla Community College *C, A*
Washington State University *B, M*
Wenatchee Valley College *C*

West Virginia
West Virginia University *B*

Wisconsin
Fox Valley Technical College *A*
Mid-State Technical College *C*
Moraine Park Technical College *C*
University of Wisconsin
    Madison *B*
    River Falls *B*

Wyoming
Central Wyoming College *A*
Laramie County Community College *A*
Sheridan College *C, A*

Agricultural business technology

Florida
Indian River Community College *A*

Kentucky
Henderson Community College *A*

New York
State University of New York
    College of Agriculture and
        Technology at Morrisville *A*

Washington
Edmonds Community College *C, A*

Wisconsin
Western Wisconsin Technical College *A*

Agricultural communications

Alabama
Auburn University *B*

Kansas
Kansas State University *B*

Missouri
University of Missouri
    Columbia *B*

Nebraska
University of Nebraska
    Lincoln *B*

Oklahoma
Oklahoma State University *B*

Texas
Texas A&M University
    Commerce *B*
Texas Tech University *B*

Wyoming
University of Wyoming *B*

Agricultural economics

Alabama
Alabama Agricultural and Mechanical
    University *B*
Auburn University *B, M, D*
Tuskegee University *M*

Arizona
University of Arizona *B, M*

Arkansas
University of Arkansas *M*

California
San Joaquin Delta College *A*
University of California
    Berkeley *D*
    Davis *B, M, D*

Colorado
Colorado State University *B, M, D*

Connecticut
University of Connecticut *B, M, D*

Delaware
University of Delaware *B, M*

Florida
University of Florida *B, M, D*

Georgia
University of Georgia *B, M, D*

Hawaii
University of Hawaii
    Manoa *B, M, D*

Idaho
University of Idaho *B, M*

Illinois
Southern Illinois University
    Carbondale *B, M*
University of Illinois
    Urbana-Champaign *B, M, D*

Indiana
Purdue University *B, M, D*

Iowa
Iowa State University *M, D*

Kansas
Garden City Community College *A*
Kansas State University *B, M, D*
Seward County Community College *A*

Kentucky
University of Kentucky *B, M, D*

Louisiana
Louisiana State University and
    Agricultural and Mechanical
    College *M, D*
Southern University and Agricultural and
    Mechanical College *B*

Maine
University of Maine *B, M*

Maryland
University of Maryland
    College Park *B, M, D*

Michigan
Michigan State University *B, M, D*

Minnesota
Northland Community & Technical
    College *A*
Ridgewater College: A Community and
    Technical College *A*
Southwest State University *C*
University of Minnesota
    Twin Cities *B, M, D*

Mississippi
Alcorn State University *B*
Mississippi State University *B, M, D*
Northwest Mississippi Community
    College *A*

Missouri
Central Missouri State University *B*
Truman State University *B*
University of Missouri
    Columbia *B, M, D*

Nebraska
University of Nebraska
    Lincoln *B, M, D*

Nevada
University of Nevada
    Reno *B, M*

New Jersey
Rutgers, The State University of New
    Jersey
        New Brunswick Regional
        Campus *M*

New Mexico
New Mexico State University *M*

New York
Cornell University *M*

North Carolina
North Carolina Agricultural and
    Technical State University *M*
North Carolina State University *B, M*

North Dakota
North Dakota State University *B, M*

Ohio
Ohio State University
    Columbus Campus *B, M, D*
Southern State Community College *A*

Oklahoma
Eastern Oklahoma State College *A*
Langston University *B*
Oklahoma State University *B, M, D*

Oregon
Eastern Oregon University *B*
Oregon State University *B, M, D*

Pennsylvania
Penn State
    University Park *B, M*

Puerto Rico
University of Puerto Rico
    Mayaguez Campus *B, M*

South Carolina
Clemson University *B, M, D*

South Dakota
South Dakota State University *B*

Tennessee
University of Tennessee
    Knoxville *M, D*

Texas
Prairie View A&M University *M*
Tarleton State University *B*
Texas A&M University *B, M, D*
Texas A&M University
    Commerce *B, M*
Texas Tech University *B, M, D*

Utah
Utah State University *B, M*

Vermont
Sterling College *B*
University of Vermont *B, M*

Virginia
Virginia Polytechnic Institute and State
    University *B, M, D*

Washington
Washington State University *B, M, D*

West Virginia
West Virginia University *B, M, D*

Wisconsin
University of Wisconsin
    Madison *B, M, D*
    Platteville *B*

Wyoming
University of Wyoming *M*

Agricultural education services

Illinois
University of Illinois
    Urbana-Champaign *M*

Iowa
Iowa State University *B*

Pennsylvania
Penn State
    Abington *B*
    Beaver *B*
    Berks *B*
    Delaware County *B*
    Dubois *B*
    Erie, The Behrend College *B*
    Fayette *B*
    Hazleton *B*
    Lehigh Valley *B*
    McKeesport *B*
    Mont Alto *B*
    New Kensington *B*
    Schuylkill - Capital College *B*
    Shenango *B*
    University Park *C, B, M, D*
    Worthington Scranton *B*
    York *B*

Agricultural equipment technology

Illinois
Black Hawk College *C, A*

New York
State University of New York
    College of Agriculture and
    Technology at Morrisville *A*

Ohio
Owens Community College
    Toledo *A*

Pennsylvania
Penn State
    Abington *B*
    Altoona *B*
    Beaver *B*
    Berks *B*
    Delaware County *B*
    Dubois *B*
    Erie, The Behrend College *B*
    Fayette *B*
    Hazleton *B*
    Lehigh Valley *B*
    McKeesport *B*
    Mont Alto *B*
    New Kensington *B*
    Schuylkill - Capital College *B*
    Shenango *B*
    University Park *B*
    Wilkes-Barre *B*
    Worthington Scranton *B*
    York *B*

Washington
Walla Walla Community College *C, A*

Agricultural mechanization

California
Yuba Community College District *A*

Illinois
Black Hawk College *C, A*
Rend Lake College *C, A*
University of Illinois
    Urbana-Champaign *B*

New York
State University of New York
    College of Agriculture and
    Technology at Morrisville *A*

North Carolina
Beaufort County Community
    College *C, A*

Texas
Sam Houston State University *B, M*
Stephen F. Austin State University *B*
Tarleton State University *A*

Washington
Walla Walla Community College *A*

Agricultural power machinery operation

Georgia
Southwest Georgia Technical College *A*

New York
State University of New York
    College of Agriculture and
    Technology at Morrisville *A*

North Dakota
North Dakota State College of Science *A*

Agricultural production

Arizona
Arizona Western College *A*

Hawaii
University of Hawaii
    Manoa *B*

Illinois
Black Hawk College *A*
Illinois Eastern Community Colleges
    Wabash Valley College *A*
Rend Lake College *C, A*

Kansas
Barton County Community College *C, A*
Cloud County Community College *A*

Missouri
Crowder College *A*

Ohio
Wilmington College *B*

Oregon
Blue Mountain Community College *A*

Texas
Stephen F. Austin State University *B*
Texas A&M University *B*

Washington
Wenatchee Valley College *C, A*

Agricultural supplies

Arizona
Glendale Community College *A*

California
Modesto Junior College *A*

Illinois
Carl Sandburg College *C*
John Wood Community College *C*
Joliet Junior College *C, A*
Kishwaukee College *A*

Iowa
Iowa Lakes Community College *A*
Kirkwood Community College *C, A*
Muscatine Community College *A*
Southeastern Community College
    North Campus *A*
Western Iowa Tech Community
    College *C*

Michigan
St. Clair County Community
    College *C, A*

North Dakota
North Dakota State College of Science *A*

Texas
Sul Ross State University *C, A*

Wisconsin
Fox Valley Technical College *A*

Agricultural teacher education

Arizona
Prescott College *T*
University of Arizona *B, M*

Arkansas
Arkansas State University *B, M, T*
Southern Arkansas University *B, T*
University of Arkansas *B, M*
University of Arkansas
   Pine Bluff *B, T*

California
California Polytechnic State University:
   San Luis Obispo *B, T*
California State Polytechnic University:
   Pomona *T*
California State University
   Chico *T*
   Fresno *M*
University of California
   Davis *T*

Colorado
Colorado State University *B, T*

Connecticut
University of Connecticut *B, T*

Delaware
University of Delaware *B, T*

Florida
University of Florida *B, M, D*

Georgia
Fort Valley State University *B, T*
University of Georgia *B, M*

Idaho
University of Idaho *B, M, T*

Illinois
University of Illinois
   Urbana-Champaign *B, M, T*

Indiana
Purdue University *B*

Iowa
Ellsworth Community College *A*
Iowa State University *B, M, D, T*

Kansas
Fort Scott Community College *A*
Kansas State University *B*
Wichita State University *T*

Kentucky
Morehead State University *B*
Murray State University *B, T*

Louisiana
Southern University and Agricultural and
   Mechanical College *B*

Minnesota
University of Minnesota
   Crookston *B*
   Twin Cities *B, M, T*

Mississippi
Mississippi State University *B, M, T*

Missouri
Central Missouri State University *B, T*
Northwest Missouri State
   University *B, M, T*
Southwest Missouri State University *B*

University of Missouri
   Columbia *B*

Montana
Miles Community College *A*
Montana State University
   Bozeman *B, M*

Nebraska
University of Nebraska
   Lincoln *B, M*

Nevada
University of Nevada
   Reno *B*

New Mexico
Eastern New Mexico University *B*
New Mexico State University *B, M*

New York
Cornell University *B, T*
State University of New York
   Oswego *B*

North Carolina
North Carolina Agricultural and
   Technical State University *B, M, T*
North Carolina State University *M, T*

North Dakota
North Dakota State University *B, M, T*

Ohio
Ohio State University
   Columbus Campus *B, M, D*
Wilmington College *B*

Oklahoma
East Central University *B*
Eastern Oklahoma State College *A*
Oklahoma Panhandle State University *B*
Oklahoma State University *B, M, D, T*

Oregon
Oregon State University *M*

Pennsylvania
Delaware Valley College *T*
Penn State
   University Park *B, M, D*

Puerto Rico
University of Puerto Rico
   Mayaguez Campus *B, M*

South Carolina
Clemson University *B, M*

South Dakota
South Dakota State University *B, M*

Tennessee
Tennessee Technological University *B, T*
University of Tennessee
   Knoxville *B, M, T*
   Martin *B, T*

Texas
Laredo Community College *A*
Lubbock Christian University *B, T*
Prairie View A&M University *M*
Sam Houston State University *M, T*
Southwest Texas State University *M, T*
Stephen F. Austin State University *T*
Tarleton State University *B, M, T*
Texas A&M University *M, D*
Texas A&M University
   Commerce *M, T*
   Kingsville *B, M*
Texas Tech University *M, D*
West Texas A&M University *T*

Utah
Utah State University *B*

Washington
Washington State University *B, T*

West Virginia
West Virginia University *B, M, T*

Wisconsin
University of Wisconsin
   Madison *B, M, T*
   Platteville *B, T*
   River Falls *B, M, T*

Wyoming
University of Wyoming *B*

Agricultural/biological engineering

Arizona
University of Arizona *B, M, D*

Arkansas
Arkansas State University *B*
University of Arkansas *B, M*

California
California State Polytechnic University:
   Pomona *B*
Imperial Valley College *C, A*
University of California
   Davis *B, M, D*

Colorado
Colorado State University *B, M, D*

Delaware
University of Delaware *B*

Florida
Florida Agricultural and Mechanical
   University *B*
University of Florida *B, M, D*

Georgia
Abraham Baldwin Agricultural
   College *A*
Fort Valley State University *B*
University of Georgia *B, M, D*

Hawaii
University of Hawaii
   Manoa *B, M*

Idaho
University of Idaho *B, M, D*

Illinois
Illinois Central College *A*
Judson College *B*
Parkland College *A*
University of Illinois
   Urbana-Champaign *B, M, D*

Indiana
Purdue University *B, M, D*

Iowa
Iowa State University *B, M, D*

Kansas
Kansas State University *B, M, D*

Kentucky
University of Kentucky *B, M, D*

Louisiana
Louisiana State University and
   Agricultural and Mechanical
   College *M*

Maine
University of Maine *B, M*

Michigan
Michigan State University *B, M, D*

Minnesota
University of Minnesota
   Twin Cities *B, M, D*

Mississippi
Mississippi State University *B*

Missouri
University of Missouri
   Columbia *B, M, D*

Nebraska
University of Nebraska
   Lincoln *B, M*

New York
Cornell University *B, M, D*
State University of New York
   College of Agriculture and
     Technology at Cobleskill *A, B*

North Carolina
North Carolina Agricultural and
   Technical State University *B*
North Carolina State University *B, M, D*

North Dakota
North Dakota State University *B, M*

Ohio
Ohio State University
   Columbus Campus *B, M, D*

Oklahoma
Oklahoma State University *B, M, D*

Oregon
Oregon State University *M, D*

Pennsylvania
Lock Haven University of
   Pennsylvania *B*
Penn State
   Abington *B*
   Altoona *B*
   Beaver *B*
   Berks *B*
   Delaware County *B*
   Dubois *B*
   Fayette *B*
   Hazleton *B*
   Lehigh Valley *B*
   McKeesport *B*
   Mont Alto *B*
   New Kensington *B*
   Schuylkill - Capital College *B*
   Shenango *B*
   University Park *B, M, D*
   Worthington Scranton *B*
   York *B*

South Carolina
Clemson University *B, M, D*

South Dakota
South Dakota State University *B, M*

Tennessee
University of Tennessee
   Knoxville *B, M, D*

Texas
Laredo Community College *A*
Texas A&M University *B*

Utah
Utah State University *B, M, D*

Washington
Washington State University *B*

Wisconsin
University of Wisconsin
   Madison *B, M, D*
   River Falls *B*

Agricultural/food products processing

Illinois
Black Hawk College *C*

Indiana
Vincennes University *A*

Oklahoma
Eastern Oklahoma State College *A*

Pennsylvania
Penn State
   Wilkes-Barre *B*

Washington
Wenatchee Valley College *A*

Agriculture, general

Alabama
Auburn University *B*
James H. Faulkner State Community
College *A*

Arizona
Arizona Western College *C, A*

Arkansas
Arkansas State University *B, M*
University of Arkansas
Community College at Hope *A*

California
California State University
Fresno *B*
Napa Valley College *C, A*
Shasta College *A*
Sierra College *C, A*

Connecticut
University of Connecticut *B, M, D*

Florida
Florida Southern College *B*
Pensacola Junior College *A*
Polk Community College *A*
South Florida Community College *A*

Georgia
Andrew College *A*
Gainesville College *C*
Middle Georgia College *A*
South Georgia College *C, A*

Hawaii
University of Hawaii
Hawaii Community College *C, A*
Maui Community College *A*

Illinois
Illinois Valley Community College *A*
John Wood Community College *A*
Joliet Junior College *C, A*
Lake Land College *A*
Lincoln Land Community College *A*
Parkland College *A*
Richland Community College *A*
Southern Illinois University
Carbondale *B, M*
University of Illinois
Urbana-Champaign *B*
Western Illinois University *A*

Indiana
Vincennes University *A*

Iowa
Iowa Western Community College *C, A*
Maharishi University of Management *B*
North Iowa Area Community College *A*
Southeastern Community College
North Campus *A*

Kansas
Barton County Community College *A*
Garden City Community College *A*
MidAmerica Nazarene University *A, B*
Pratt Community College *C, A*
Seward County Community College *A*

Kentucky
Hopkinsville Community College *C, A*
Murray State University *B*

Louisiana
University of Louisiana at Lafayette *B*

Michigan
Michigan State University *C, B, M, D*

Minnesota
Minnesota West Community and
Technical College: Worthington
Campus *A*

Ridgewater College: A Community and
Technical College *C, A*
South Central Technical College *A*
University of Minnesota
Crookston *B*

Mississippi
Alcorn State University *B*

Missouri
Central Missouri State University *B, M*
Lindenwood University *B*
University of Missouri
Columbia *B*

Nebraska
Nebraska College of Technical
Agriculture *A*
Northeast Community College *A*
University of Nebraska
Lincoln *B*
Western Nebraska Community
College *A*

New Jersey
Cumberland County College *C, A*

New Mexico
Mesalands Community College *C, A*
Western New Mexico University *A*

New York
Cornell University *B*
State University of New York
College of Agriculture and
Technology at Cobleskill *A*
College of Agriculture and
Technology at Morrisville *A*

North Dakota
North Dakota State University *B*

Ohio
Ohio State University
Agricultural Technical Institute *A*

Oklahoma
Cameron University *B*
Eastern Oklahoma State College *A*
Northeastern Oklahoma Agricultural and
Mechanical College *A*
Oklahoma Panhandle State University *A*
Oklahoma State University *M*
Redlands Community College *A*

Oregon
Oregon State University *B, M*
Treasure Valley Community College *A*

South Dakota
South Dakota State University *B*
Western Dakota Technical Institute *A*

Tennessee
Roane State Community College *A*

Texas
Brazosport College *A*
Howard College *A*
Kilgore College *A*
Laredo Community College *A*
Lubbock Christian University *A, B*
Northeast Texas Community College *A*
Sam Houston State University *B, M*
Southwest Texas Junior College *A*
Stephen F. Austin State University *B, M*
Tarleton State University *B, M*
Texas Tech University *M*
Tyler Junior College *C, A*
West Texas A&M University *B, M*
Wharton County Junior College *A*

Utah
Brigham Young University *B*

Vermont
University of Vermont *B, M*

Wisconsin
Chippewa Valley Technical College *A*
Milwaukee Area Technical College *A*

University of Wisconsin
Platteville *M*
Western Wisconsin Technical College *C*

Wyoming
Sheridan College *A*

Agronomy/crop science

Alabama
Auburn University *B, M, D*

Arizona
Prescott College *B, M*

Arkansas
University of Arkansas *B, M, D*

California
California State Polytechnic University:
Pomona *B*
California State University
Chico *B*
Fresno *B, M*
Modesto Junior College *A*
San Joaquin Delta College *A*
Sierra College *C, A*
University of California
Davis *B, M*
Ventura College *C, A*

Colorado
Colorado State University *B, M, D*

Connecticut
University of Connecticut *B*

Delaware
University of Delaware *B*

Florida
Florida Agricultural and Mechanical
University *B*
University of Florida *M, D*

Georgia
University of Georgia *B, M, D*

Hawaii
University of Hawaii
Hilo *B*

Idaho
Brigham Young University - Idaho *B*
University of Idaho *B*

Illinois
Richland Community College *A*
University of Illinois
Urbana-Champaign *B, M, D*

Indiana
Purdue University *A, B, M, D*

Iowa
Des Moines Area Community College *C*
Iowa State University *B, M*

Kansas
Garden City Community College *A*
Kansas State University *B, M, D*
McPherson College *B*

Kentucky
Murray State University *B*
University of Kentucky *B, M, D*

Louisiana
Louisiana State University and
Agricultural and Mechanical
College *M, D*

Michigan
Michigan State University *B, M, D*

Minnesota
Ridgewater College: A Community and
Technical College *C, A*
Southwest State University *B*

University of Minnesota
Crookston *B*
Twin Cities *M, D*

Mississippi
Alcorn State University *B*
Mississippi State University *B, M, D*

Missouri
College of the Ozarks *B*
Northwest Missouri State University *B*
Southeast Missouri State University *B*
Southwest Missouri State University *B*
Truman State University *B*
University of Missouri
Columbia *M, D*

Nebraska
Northeast Community College *A*
University of Nebraska
Lincoln *B, M, D*

New Hampshire
University of New Hampshire *B*

New Mexico
New Mexico State University *B, M, D*
Southwestern Indian Polytechnic
Institute *A*

New York
Cornell University *B*
State University of New York
College of Agriculture and
Technology at Cobleskill *A*
College of Technology at Alfred *A*

North Carolina
North Carolina State University *B, M, D*

North Dakota
North Dakota State University *B, M, D*

Ohio
Ohio State University
Agricultural Technical Institute *A*
Columbus Campus *B*
Wilmington College *B*

Oklahoma
Cameron University *B*
Eastern Oklahoma State College *A*
Oklahoma Panhandle State University *B*
Oklahoma State University *B, M, D*

Oregon
Eastern Oregon University *B*
Oregon State University *B, M, D*
Treasure Valley Community College *A*

Pennsylvania
Delaware Valley College *B*
Penn State
Abington *B*
Altoona *B*
Beaver *B*
Berks *B*
Delaware County *B*
Dubois *B*
Erie, The Behrend College *B*
Fayette *B*
Hazleton *B*
Lehigh Valley *B*
McKeesport *B*
Mont Alto *B*
New Kensington *B*
Schuylkill - Capital College *B*
Shenango *B*
University Park *C, B, M, D*
Wilkes-Barre *B*
Worthington Scranton *B*
York *B*

Puerto Rico
University of Puerto Rico
Mayaguez Campus *B, M*

South Carolina
Clemson University *M, D*

South Dakota
South Dakota State University *B, M, D*

Tennessee
Tennessee Technological University *B*
University of Tennessee
Martin *B*

Texas
Stephen F. Austin State University *B*
Tarleton State University *B*
Texas A&M University *B, M, D*
Texas A&M University
Commerce *M*
Kingsville *M*
Texas Tech University *B, D*

Utah
Brigham Young University *B, M*
Utah State University *B*

Virginia
Virginia Polytechnic Institute and State
University *B, M, D*

Washington
Washington State University *B, M, D*

Wisconsin
Chippewa Valley Technical College *A*
University of Wisconsin
Madison *B, M, D*
Platteville *B*
River Falls *B*

Wyoming
University of Wyoming *M, D*

Air traffic control

Alabama
Community College of the Air Force *A*

Alaska
University of Alaska
Anchorage *A, B*

California
Mount San Antonio College *A*

Colorado
Metropolitan State College of Denver *B*

Connecticut
Gateway Community College *A*

Florida
Embry-Riddle Aeronautical University *B*

Michigan
Western Michigan University *B*

Minnesota
Inver Hills Community College *A*
Minneapolis Community and Technical
College *C*

Missouri
St. Louis Community College
St. Louis Community College at
Meramec *A*

New Hampshire
Daniel Webster College *B*

New Jersey
Thomas Edison State College *A, B*

New York
College of Aeronautics *C*

North Dakota
University of North Dakota *B*

Pennsylvania
Community College of Beaver
County *C, A*
Geneva College *A*

Air transportation

Alabama
Community College of the Air Force *A*

Alaska
University of Alaska
Anchorage *A, B*

Arizona
Cochise College *A*
Embry-Riddle Aeronautical University:
Prescott Campus *B, M*

California
Chabot College *A*
Glendale Community College *C*
Long Beach City College *C, A*
Mount San Antonio College *A*
Northrop-Rice Aviation Institute of
Technology *A, B*
Orange Coast College *C, A*
Pacific Union College *B*
Palomar College *C, A*
San Diego Mesa College *C*
Santa Rosa Junior College *C*

Colorado
Arapahoe Community College *C*
Metropolitan State College of Denver *B*

Connecticut
Three Rivers Community College *A*
University of New Haven *B*

Delaware
Delaware State University *B*
Wilmington College *B*

District of Columbia
University of the District of
Columbia *A, B*

Florida
Broward Community College *A*
Embry Riddle Aeronautical
University-Extended Campus *B*
Embry-Riddle Aeronautical
University *A, B, M*
Florida Institute of Technology *B, M*
Jacksonville University *B*
Miami-Dade Community College *A*
Palm Beach Community College *A*

Illinois
Lewis University *A, B*
Lincoln Land Community College *A*
Midstate College *C*
Southern Illinois University
Carbondale *A*
Springfield College in Illinois *A*
University of Illinois
Urbana-Champaign *C*

Indiana
American Trans Air Aviation Training
Academy *A*
Indiana State University *A*
Purdue University *A, B*

Iowa
Indian Hills Community College *A*
Iowa Central Community College *A*
Iowa Lakes Community College *A*
University of Dubuque *B*

Kansas
Central Christian College *A*
Cloud County Community College *A*
Hesston College *A*
Kansas State University *A, B*

Louisiana
Louisiana Tech University *B*
University of Louisiana at Monroe *B*

Maryland
Community College of Baltimore County
Catonsville *C, A*
Dundalk *C, A*
Essex *C, A*

Michigan
Andrews University *B*
Cornerstone University *A, B*
Lansing Community College *A*
Northwestern Michigan College *A*
Oakland Community College *A*
Western Michigan University *B*

Minnesota
Academy College *A*
Vermilion Community College *A*

Mississippi
Delta State University *B, M*

Missouri
College of the Ozarks *B*
St. Louis Community College
St. Louis Community College at
Meramec *C*
St. Louis University *B*

Nebraska
University of Nebraska
Kearney *B*
Omaha *B*

New Hampshire
Daniel Webster College *A, B*

New Jersey
County College of Morris *A*
Cumberland County College *A*
Mercer County Community College *A*
Raritan Valley Community College *A*
Thomas Edison State College *A, B*

New Mexico
Eastern New Mexico University: Roswell
Campus *A*
San Juan College *A*

New York
Dowling College *B*
Schenectady County Community
College *A*

North Dakota
North Dakota State University *M*
University of North Dakota *B, M*

Ohio
Cuyahoga Community College
Eastern Campus *A*
Kent State University *B*

Oklahoma
Oklahoma City Community College *A*
Oklahoma State University *B*
Rose State College *A*
Southeastern Oklahoma State
University *B*
University of Oklahoma *B*
Western Oklahoma State College *A*

Oregon
Lane Community College *A*
Mount Hood Community College *A*

Pennsylvania
Geneva College *A*
Lehigh Carbon Community College *A*
Luzerne County Community College *A*

Puerto Rico
Inter American University of Puerto Rico
Bayamon Campus *B*

Tennessee
Middle Tennessee State University *B*

Texas
Baylor University *B*
LeTourneau University *B*
Palo Alto College *A*

Texas Southern University *B*
Texas State Technical College
Waco *C, A*

Utah
Utah Valley State College *A*
Westminster College *B*

Virginia
Averett University *B*

Washington
Central Washington University *B*
Green River Community College *A*

West Virginia
Fairmont State College *B*
Mountain State University *A*

Wisconsin
Concordia University Wisconsin *B*

Wyoming
Casper College *A*

Aircraft mechanics

Alabama
Community College of the Air Force *A*

Alaska
University of Alaska
Anchorage *C, A, B*
Fairbanks *C, A*

Arizona
Cochise College *A*
Pima Community College *C, A*

Arkansas
Northwest Arkansas Community
College *A*
Pulaski Technical College *A*
Southern Arkansas University Tech *C*

California
Antelope Valley College *C, A*
College of Alameda *C, A*
Foothill College *C, A*
Gavilan Community College *C, A*
Glendale Community College *C, A*
Mount San Antonio College *A*
Northrop-Rice Aviation Institute of
Technology *A, B*
Orange Coast College *C, A*
Reedley College *C*
Shasta College *C, A*

Connecticut
Housatonic Community College *A*
Quinebaug Valley Community College *A*

Georgia
Central Georgia Technical College *C*
Clayton College and State University *A*
Georgia Southwestern State University *A*
Middle Georgia College *A*

Hawaii
University of Hawaii
Honolulu Community College *C, A*

Idaho
Idaho State University *C, A*

Illinois
Lewis University *C, A, B*
Lincoln Land Community College *A*
Moody Bible Institute *B*
Rock Valley College *A*
Southwestern Illinois College *C, A*

Indiana
American Trans Air Aviation Training
Academy *A*
Ivy Tech State College
Wabash Valley *A*
Vincennes University *A*

Iowa
Hawkeye Community College *A*
Indian Hills Community College *A*
Iowa Western Community College *A*

Kansas
Kansas State University *A*
Pratt Community College *A*

Maryland
Chesapeake College *C, A*

Michigan
Lansing Community College *A*
Northern Michigan University *A*
Oakland Community College *A*
Southwestern Michigan College *C, A*
Wayne County Community College *C*

Minnesota
Minneapolis Community and Technical
    College *C*
Minnesota State College - Southeast
    Technical *C, A*
Northland Community & Technical
    College *C, A*

Missouri
College of the Ozarks *B*
Maple Woods Community College *C, A*

Nebraska
Western Nebraska Community
    College *C, A*

New Hampshire
New Hampshire Community Technical
    College
        Nashua *A*

New Jersey
Cumberland County College *A*
Mercer County Community College *A*
Thomas Edison State College *A, B*

New Mexico
Eastern New Mexico University: Roswell
    Campus *A*

New York
College of Aeronautics *A, B*
Mohawk Valley Community College *A*
State University of New York
    Farmingdale *C, A*

North Carolina
Guilford Technical Community
    College *A*
Wayne Community College *A*

Ohio
Cincinnati State Technical and
    Community College *C, A*
Columbus State Community College *A*
Cuyahoga Community College
    Western Campus *A*

Oklahoma
Southeastern Oklahoma State
    University *B*

Oregon
Lane Community College *C, A*
Portland Community College *C, A*

Pennsylvania
Lehigh Carbon Community College *A*
Pittsburgh Institute of Aeronautics *A*

South Carolina
Trident Technical College *A*

Texas
Amarillo College *C, A*
Houston Community College System *C*
LeTourneau University *B*
St. Philip's College *C, A*
Tarrant County College *C, A*
Texas State Technical College
    Waco *C, A*
    West Texas *C, A*

Utah
Salt Lake Community College *C, A*
Utah State University *A, B*

Virginia
Hampton University *A*

Washington
South Seattle Community College *C, A*
Spokane Community College *A*

Wisconsin
Blackhawk Technical College *C*
Fox Valley Technical College *C*

Aircraft powerplant technology

Arkansas
Southern Arkansas University Tech *C, A*

California
Antelope Valley College *C*
Long Beach City College *C, A*
Northrop-Rice Aviation Institute of
    Technology *A, B*

Florida
Embry-Riddle Aeronautical University *A*

Kentucky
Somerset Community College *C, A*

Maryland
Frederick Community College *C, A*

Michigan
Oakland Community College *A*

New Jersey
Thomas Edison State College *A, B, M*

New York
College of Aeronautics *C, A, B*

Pennsylvania
Pennsylvania College of
    Technology *C, A*

Texas
Hallmark Institute of Aeronautics *C, A*
St. Philip's College *C, A*

Washington
Clover Park Technical College *C, A*
Everett Community College *A*
South Seattle Community College *C, A*

Wisconsin
Fox Valley Technical College *A*

Airline/commercial pilot

Alaska
University of Alaska
    Fairbanks *A*

Arizona
Embry-Riddle Aeronautical University:
    Prescott Campus *B*

Arkansas
Henderson State University *B*

California
Northrop-Rice Aviation Institute of
    Technology *A, B*

Florida
Embry Riddle Aeronautical
    University-Extended Campus *A, B, M*
Embry-Riddle Aeronautical
    University *B, M*

Illinois
Kaskaskia College *C, A*
Southern Illinois University
    Carbondale *A*
Waubonsee Community College *A*

Indiana
Vincennes University *A*

Iowa
Indian Hills Community College *A*

Michigan
Baker College
    of Muskegon *A*
Northwestern Michigan College *A*
Western Michigan University *B*

Minnesota
Academy College *A*

Missouri
St. Louis University *B*

New Jersey
Thomas Edison State College *A, B*

New Mexico
San Juan College *C, A*

New York
Jamestown Community College *A*
Mohawk Valley Community
    College *C, A*

North Carolina
Lenoir Community College *C, A*

North Dakota
Williston State College *A*

Ohio
Bowling Green State University *B*
Cincinnati State Technical and
    Community College *C*
Kent State University *B*

Oklahoma
Oklahoma State University *B*

Oregon
Portland Community College *C*

Pennsylvania
Community College of Allegheny
    County *A*

Puerto Rico
Inter American University of Puerto Rico
    Bayamon Campus *B*

Texas
Tarleton State University *B*

Utah
Utah Valley State College *B*

Washington
Clover Park Technical College *A*
Northwest Aviation College *C, A*

Wisconsin
Fox Valley Technical College *A*

Algebra/number theory

Georgia
Georgia Institute of Technology *B*

Alternative fuel vehicle technology

California
Long Beach City College *C, A*

American government/ politics

Arizona
Northern Arizona University *B*

California
Chapman University *B*

Florida
University of West Florida *B*

New York
State University of New York
    Buffalo *M, D*
Wells College *B*

Ohio
University of Akron *B*

Pennsylvania
La Salle University *B*

South Carolina
Wofford College *B*

Texas
Texas A&M University *D*

American history (U.S.)

California
Chapman University *B*
Pitzer College *B*

Michigan
Calvin College *B*

New York
Bard College *B*
Columbia University
    Columbia College *B*
Sarah Lawrence College *B*
State University of New York
    Buffalo *M, D*

North Carolina
Western Carolina University *M*

Pennsylvania
La Salle University *B*

American literature (Canadian)

Indiana
Bethel College *C*

American literature (U.S.)

California
California State University
    Bakersfield *B, M*
    Hayward *B*
Pitzer College *B*
San Joaquin Delta College *A*
University of California
    San Diego *B, M, D*
    Santa Cruz *B*
University of Southern California *B*
Whittier College *B*

District of Columbia
George Washington University *M, D*

Florida
Eckerd College *B*
Miami-Dade Community College *A*
New College of Florida *B*

Idaho
Boise State University *B*

Illinois
Illinois Valley Community College *A*
Lincoln College *A*
Lincoln Land Community College *A*
Richland Community College *A*

Indiana
Indiana University-Purdue University
    Fort Wayne *B*
Purdue University
    Calumet *B*
University of Evansville *B*

Iowa
University of Iowa *B, M, T*

Kansas
Independence Community College *A*

Maine
Bowdoin College *B*

Maryland
Johns Hopkins University *D*

Massachusetts
Assumption College *B*
Clark University *M*
Hampshire College *B*
Harvard College *B*
Simmons College *B*
Tufts University *B, M, D*

Michigan
Lansing Community College *A*
Michigan State University *B, M, D*

Minnesota
Concordia College: Moorhead *B*
St. Cloud State University *B*

Missouri
Washington University in St.
Louis *B, M, D*

Montana
Miles Community College *A*

New Jersey
Rowan University *B*
Stevens Institute of Technology *B*

New York
Bard College *B*
City University of New York
Baruch College *B*
Brooklyn College *B*
Hunter College *M*
Columbia University
Columbia College *B*
Eugene Lang College/New School
University *B*
New York University *B, M, D*
St. Lawrence University *B*
Sarah Lawrence College *B*
State University of New York
Buffalo *M, D*
Purchase *B*
United States Military Academy *B*

Ohio
College of Wooster *B*
Miami University
Oxford Campus *B*
Wittenberg University *B*

Pennsylvania
California University of Pennsylvania *B*
Gettysburg College *B*
Holy Family University *B, T*
Immaculata University *B*
La Salle University *B*
Penn State
Harrisburg *B*
University of Pittsburgh
Johnstown *B*
West Chester University of
Pennsylvania *B*

Rhode Island
Brown University *B, M, D*

Texas
Texas A&M University
Commerce *B*
University of North Texas *D*

Utah
University of Utah *M, D*

Vermont
Bennington College *B*
Castleton State College *B*
Marlboro College *B*

Middlebury College *B*

Virginia
Longwood University *B, M, T*

Washington
Everett Community College *A*

West Virginia
Concord College *B*

Wisconsin
Lawrence University *B*
Marquette University *M, D*

American sign language (ASL)

California
Antelope Valley College *C, A*
Ohlone College *C, A*
San Diego Mesa College *C, A*

District of Columbia
Gallaudet University *B*

Indiana
Goshen College *B*
Indiana University-Purdue University
Indianapolis *B*
Vincennes University *A*

Missouri
William Woods University *B*

New Jersey
Union County College *C, A*

New York
Keuka College *B*

North Carolina
Gardner-Webb University *B*

Tennessee
Maryville College *B*

Texas
North Harris Montgomery Community
College District *C*

American studies

Alabama
Faulkner University *B*
Huntingdon College *B*
University of Alabama *B, M*

Arkansas
Harding University *B*
University of Arkansas *B*

California
California State University
Chico *B*
Fullerton *B, M*
San Bernardino *B*
Chapman University *B*
Claremont McKenna College *B*
Foothill College *C, A*
Mills College *B*
Mount St. Mary's College *B*
Occidental College *B*
Pepperdine University *M*
Pitzer College *B*
Pomona College *B*
San Diego State University *B*
San Francisco State University *B*
Scripps College *B*
Stanford University *B*
University of California
Berkeley *B*
Davis *B*
Los Angeles *B*
Santa Cruz *B*
University of Southern California *B*

Colorado
Fort Lewis College *B*

Connecticut
Central Connecticut State University *C*
Connecticut College *B*
Fairfield University *B, M*
St. Joseph College *B*
Trinity College *B, M*
Wesleyan University *B*
Western Connecticut State University *B*
Yale University *B, M, D*

District of Columbia
American University *B*
George Washington University *B, M, D*
Georgetown University *B*
Trinity College *B*

Florida
Eckerd College *B*
Florida State University *B, M*
Manatee Community College *A*
Miami-Dade Community College *A*
Stetson University *B*
University of Miami *B, M, D*
University of South Florida *B, M*
University of Tampa *B*

Georgia
Emory University *M, D*
Oglethorpe University *B*
Oxford College of Emory University *B*
Wesleyan College *B*

Hawaii
University of Hawaii
Manoa *B, M, D*
West Oahu *B*

Idaho
Idaho State University *B*
University of Idaho *B*

Illinois
De Paul University *B*
Dominican University *B*
Elmhurst College *B*
Knox College *B*
Lake Forest College *B*
Lewis University *B*
Millikin University *B*
Northwestern University *B*
Roosevelt University *B*

Indiana
Franklin College *B*
Indiana University
Bloomington *D*
Indiana University-Purdue University
Fort Wayne *C*
University of Notre Dame *B, M*
Valparaiso University *B*
Vincennes University *A*

Iowa
Coe College *B*
University of Iowa *B, M, D*
University of Northern Iowa *B*
Upper Iowa University *B*

Kansas
University of Kansas *B, M, D*

Kentucky
Lindsey Wilson College *B*

Louisiana
Tulane University *B*

Maine
Bates College *B*
Colby College *B*
University of New England *B*
University of Southern Maine *M*

Maryland
Goucher College *B*
Howard Community College *A*
Johns Hopkins University *B*
University of Maryland
Baltimore County *B*
College Park *B, M, D*

Washington College *B*

Massachusetts
Amherst College *B*
Boston College *M*
Boston University *B, M, D*
Brandeis University *B, M, D*
Elms College *B*
Emmanuel College *B*
Hampshire College *B*
Harvard College *B*
Mount Holyoke College *B*
Pine Manor College *B*
Smith College *B*
Stonehill College *B*
Tufts University *B, M*
University of Massachusetts
Boston *B, M*
Lowell *B*
Wellesley College *B*
Wheaton College *B*
Williams College *B*

Michigan
Hillsdale College *B*
Siena Heights University *B*
University of Michigan *B, M, D*
University of Michigan
Dearborn *B*
Wayne State University *B*
Western Michigan University *B*

Minnesota
Carleton College *B*
Minnesota State University
Moorhead *B*
St. Cloud State University *B*
St. Olaf College *B*
University of Minnesota
Twin Cities *B, M, D*

Mississippi
University of Southern Mississippi *B*

Missouri
St. Louis University *B, M, D*
Southeast Missouri State University *B*
University of Missouri
Kansas City *B*
Washington University in St. Louis *B, M*

Nebraska
Creighton University *B*
Midland Lutheran College *B*

New Hampshire
Franklin Pierce College *B*
Keene State College *B*
Southern New Hampshire University *B*

New Jersey
Bergen Community College *C*
College of St. Elizabeth *B*
Ramapo College of New Jersey *B*
Rider University *B*
Rowan University *B*
Rutgers, The State University of New
Jersey
New Brunswick Regional
Campus *B*
Newark Regional Campus *B*
St. Peter's College *B*

New Mexico
University of New Mexico *B, M, D*

New York
Bard College *B*
Barnard College *B*
City University of New York
Brooklyn College *B*
College of Staten Island *B*
Queens College *B*
College of New Rochelle *B*
Columbia University
Columbia College *B*
Cornell University *B*
Dominican College of Blauvelt *B*
Elmira College *B*

Eugene Lang College/New School
University *B*
Fordham University *B*
Fulton-Montgomery Community
College *A*
Hamilton College *B*
Hobart and William Smith Colleges *B*
Hofstra University *B*
Manhattanville College *B*
Marist College *B*
Marymount College of Fordham
University *B*
Nazareth College of Rochester *B*
New York University *B, M, D*
St. John Fisher College *B*
St. John's University *B*
Sarah Lawrence College *B*
Skidmore College *B*
State University of New York
Buffalo *B, M, D*
College at Fredonia *B*
College at Geneseo *B*
College at Old Westbury *B*
Oswego *B*
Stony Brook *B*
Syracuse University *B*
Union College *B*
Vassar College *B*
Wells College *B*

North Carolina
High Point University *B*
Meredith College *B*
Montreat College *B*
Salem College *B*
University of North Carolina
Chapel Hill *B*
Pembroke *B*
Wingate University *B*

Ohio
Antioch College *B*
Ashland University *B*
Bowling Green State University *B, M, D*
Case Western Reserve University *B*
Cedarville University *B*
Kent State University *B*
Kent State University
Stark Campus *B*
Kenyon College *B*
Miami University
Oxford Campus *B*
Mount Union College *B*
Mount Vernon Nazarene University *B*
Oberlin College *B*
University of Dayton *B*
University of Rio Grande *B*
University of Toledo *B*
Ursuline College *B*
Wittenberg University *B*
Youngstown State University *B*

Oklahoma
Northeastern State University *M*
Oklahoma State University *B*
Southern Nazarene University *B*

Oregon
Oregon State University *B*
Reed College *B*
Warner Pacific College *B*
Willamette University *B*

Pennsylvania
Albright College *B*
Bucks County Community College *A*
Cabrini College *B*
California University of Pennsylvania *B*
Dickinson College *B*
Franklin & Marshall College *B*
Gettysburg College *B*
Lafayette College *B*
Lebanon Valley College of
Pennsylvania *B*
Lehigh University *B, M*
Lycoming College *B*
Muhlenberg College *B*

Penn State
Abington *B*
Altoona *B*
Beaver *B*
Berks *B*
Delaware County *B*
Dubois *B*
Erie, The Behrend College *B*
Fayette *B*
Harrisburg *B, M*
Hazleton *B*
Lehigh Valley *B*
McKeesport *B*
Mont Alto *B*
New Kensington *B*
Schuylkill - Capital College *B*
Shenango *B*
University Park *B*
Wilkes-Barre *B*
Worthington Scranton *B*
York *B*
Temple University *B*
University of Pennsylvania *D*
University of Pittsburgh
Bradford *B*
Greensburg *B*
Johnstown *B*
West Chester University of
Pennsylvania *B*

Rhode Island
Brown University *B, M, D*
Roger Williams University *B*
Salve Regina University *B*

South Carolina
Claflin University *B*
Erskine College *B*

Tennessee
King College *B, T*
Tennessee Wesleyan College *B*
University of Tennessee
Knoxville *B*
Vanderbilt University *B*

Texas
Austin College *B*
Baylor University *B, M*
Our Lady of the Lake University of San
Antonio *B*
Southwest Texas State University *B*
Southwestern University *B*
Texas A&M University *B*
University of Dallas *M*
University of Texas
Austin *B, M, D*
Dallas *B*
San Antonio *B*

Utah
Brigham Young University *B*
University of Utah *M, D*
Utah State University *B, M*

Vermont
Bennington College *B*
College of St. Joseph in Vermont *B*
Goddard College *B*
Marlboro College *B*
Middlebury College *B*
St. Michael's College *B*

Virginia
College of William and Mary *B, M, D*
Mary Washington College *B*
Randolph-Macon Woman's College *B*
Shenandoah University *B*
University of Richmond *B*
Virginia Wesleyan College *B*

Washington
Washington State University *B, M, D*
Western Washington University *B*
Whitworth College *B*

Wisconsin
Edgewood College *B, T*

Wyoming
University of Wyoming *B, M*

Analytical chemistry

Florida
Florida State University *M, D*

Georgia
Clark Atlanta University *M, D*

Illinois
Governors State University *M*
Illinois Institute of Technology *M*
Loyola University of Chicago *M, D*

Iowa
Iowa State University *M, D*

Massachusetts
Harvard College *B*
Massachusetts College of Pharmacy and
Health Sciences *M, D*
Tufts University *M, D*

Montana
University of Montana-Missoula *M, D*

New Jersey
Stevens Institute of Technology *M, D*

New York
Sarah Lawrence College *B*
State University of New York
Buffalo *M, D*
College of Environmental Science
and Forestry *M, D*

Pennsylvania
Mercyhurst College *B*

Texas
University of North Texas *M, D*

Utah
University of Utah *M, D*

Wisconsin
Marquette University *M, D*
University of Wisconsin
La Crosse *B*
Madison *M*

Anatomy

Alabama
Auburn University *M*

Arizona
University of Arizona *M, D*

Arkansas
University of Arkansas
for Medical Sciences *M, D*

California
California State University
Fresno *B*
Loma Linda University *M, D*
Los Angeles Pierce College *C*
University of California
Irvine *D*
Los Angeles *M, D*

Colorado
Colorado State University *M, D*

District of Columbia
Georgetown University *D*
Howard University *M, D*

Florida
Barry University *M*
Broward Community College *A*

Georgia
Medical College of Georgia *M, D*
University of Georgia *M*

Hawaii
University of Hawaii
Manoa *M, D*

Illinois
Loyola University of Chicago *M, D*
Northwestern University *M, D*
Rush University *M, D*
University of Illinois
Chicago *M, D*

Indiana
Indiana University
Bloomington *M, D*
Indiana University-Purdue University
Indianapolis *M, D*

Iowa
University of Iowa *M, D*

Kansas
University of Kansas Medical
Center *M, D*

Kentucky
University of Kentucky: College of
Medicine *D*

Louisiana
Tulane University *M, D*

Maryland
Johns Hopkins University *D*
University of Maryland
Baltimore *M, D*

Massachusetts
Boston University *M, D*
Hampshire College *B*
Tufts University *D*

Michigan
Michigan State University *M, D*
University of Michigan *M, D*
Wayne State University *M, D*

Minnesota
Minnesota State University
Mankato *B*
University of Minnesota
Twin Cities *M*

Mississippi
University of Mississippi Medical
Center *M, D*

Missouri
St. Louis University *M, D*

Nebraska
Creighton University *M*
University of Nebraska
Medical Center *D*

New York
State University of New York
Buffalo *M, D*
Health Science Center at Stony
Brook *D*
Upstate Medical University *M, D*
University of Rochester *M*
Yeshiva University *M, D*

North Carolina
Duke University *B, M, D*

North Dakota
University of North Dakota *M, D*

Ohio
Case Western Reserve University *M, D*
Ohio State University
Columbus Campus *M, D*
University of Cincinnati *D*
Wright State University *M*

Oregon
Oregon Health Sciences University *M, D*

Puerto Rico
University of Puerto Rico
Medical Sciences Campus *M, D*

South Dakota
University of South Dakota *M, D*

Tennessee
University of Tennessee
    Knoxville *M, D*
University of Tennessee Health Science
    Center *M, D*

Texas
Texas A&M University *M, D*
University of Texas
    Houston Health Science
        Center *M, D*

Utah
Brigham Young University *M, D*

Vermont
University of Vermont *M, D*

Virginia
Virginia Commonwealth
    University *M, D*

Washington
Eastern Washington University *B*

Wisconsin
University of Wisconsin
    Madison *M, D*

Ancient Greek

Alabama
Samford University *B*

California
Master's College *B*
Santa Clara University *B*
University of California
    Berkeley *B, M*
    Davis *B*
    Los Angeles *B, M*
    Santa Cruz *B*

Connecticut
Yale University *B*

District of Columbia
Howard University *B*

Florida
Florida State University *B, M*

Georgia
Oxford College of Emory University *B*
University of Georgia *B, M*

Illinois
Augustana College *B*
Concordia University *B*
Loyola University of Chicago *B*
Monmouth College *B*
Moody Bible Institute *B*
North Central College *B*
Rockford College *B*
Trinity International University *M*
University of Chicago *B*

Indiana
Butler University *B*
DePauw University *B*
Indiana University
    Bloomington *B, M, D*
University of Notre Dame *B*
Wabash College *B*

Iowa
University of Iowa *B, M*

Kentucky
Asbury College *B*

Louisiana
Tulane University *B, M*

Maryland
Washington Bible College *M*

Massachusetts
Amherst College *B*
Boston College *B, M*
Boston University *B*
Brandeis University *B*
Harvard College *B*
Mount Holyoke College *B*
Smith College *B*
Tufts University *B*
Wellesley College *B*

Michigan
Calvin College *B*
Grand Valley State University *B*
University of Michigan *B, M, D, T*

Minnesota
Carleton College *B*
Macalester College *B*
St. Olaf College *B*
University of Minnesota
    Twin Cities *B, M, D*
University of St. Thomas *B*

Missouri
St. Louis University *B*
Washington University in St. Louis *B, M*

Nebraska
Creighton University *B*
University of Nebraska
    Lincoln *B*

New Hampshire
University of New Hampshire *B*

New York
Bard College *B*
City University of New York
    Brooklyn College *B*
    Hunter College *B*
    Queens College *B*
Columbia University
    Columbia College *B*
Elmira College *B*
Fordham University *B, M, D*
Hamilton College *B*
New York University *B*
Syracuse University *M*
Vassar College *B*

North Carolina
Duke University *B*
Wake Forest University *B*

Ohio
John Carroll University *B*
Kenyon College *B*
Miami University
    Oxford Campus *B*
Oberlin College *B*
Ohio State University
    Columbus Campus *M, D*
Ohio University *B*
University of Akron *B*
Wright State University *B*

Oregon
Multnomah Bible College *B*
University of Oregon *B*

Pennsylvania
Bryn Mawr College *B, M, D*
Dickinson College *B*
Duquesne University *B*
Franklin & Marshall College *B*
Haverford College *B*
Swarthmore College *B*
University of Scranton *B*

Rhode Island
Brown University *B*

South Carolina
Furman University *B*

Tennessee
University of Tennessee
    Knoxville *B*

Texas
Baylor University *B*
Rice University *B*
University of Dallas *B*
University of Texas
    Austin *B*

Vermont
Marlboro College *B*
University of Vermont *B, M*

Virginia
College of William and Mary *B*
Hampden-Sydney College *B*
Randolph-Macon College *B*
Randolph-Macon Woman's College *B*
Sweet Briar College *B*
University of Richmond *B*

Washington
University of Washington *B*

Wisconsin
Lawrence University *B, T*
University of Wisconsin
    Madison *B, M*

Ancient Near Eastern/ Biblical languages

California
Scripps College *B*
University of California
    Berkeley *B*

Colorado
Naropa University *M*

Connecticut
Yale University *B, M, D*

Delaware
University of Delaware *B*

District of Columbia
Catholic University of America *M, D*

Illinois
University of Chicago *B, M, D*
University of Illinois
    Chicago *B*
Wheaton College *B*

Maryland
Mount St. Mary's College *B*

Massachusetts
Brandeis University *B, M*
Harvard College *B*

Michigan
Calvin College *B*
Hope College *B*
University of Michigan *B*

Missouri
St. Louis University *B*

Montana
Carroll College *B*

New York
Columbia University
    Columbia College *B*
New York University *B*
State University of New York
    Binghamton *B*

North Dakota
North Dakota State University *B*

Ohio
Ohio Wesleyan University *B*

Pennsylvania
La Salle University *B*

Texas
Austin College *B*

Utah
Brigham Young University *B*

Washington
University of Washington *M*

Wisconsin
Lawrence University *B*

Ancient studies

Connecticut
Wesleyan University *B*

Minnesota
St. Olaf College *B*

Missouri
Southwest Missouri State University *B*

New Hampshire
Dartmouth College *B*

New York
Barnard College *B*
Columbia University
    Columbia College *B*

Rhode Island
Brown University *B*

Texas
University of Texas
    Austin *B*

Anesthesiologist assistant

Ohio
Case Western Reserve University *M*

Animal breeding

California
Modesto Junior College *A*

Illinois
John Wood Community College *C, A*
Kishwaukee College *C, A*

Iowa
Iowa State University *M, D*

Nebraska
Southeast Community College
    Beatrice Campus *A*

New York
Cornell University *B, M, D*

Ohio
Lake Erie College *B*

Oklahoma
Oklahoma State University *M, D*

Texas
Tarleton State University *B*
Texas A&M University *M, D*

Animal health

California
California State University
    Fresno *B*
Los Angeles Pierce College *A*
San Diego Mesa College *A*

Colorado
Colorado Mountain College
    Spring Valley Campus *A*

Nebraska
Nebraska College of Technical
    Agriculture *A*
University of Nebraska
    Lincoln *M*

New York
Cornell University *B*

Ohio
Cuyahoga Community College
　　Eastern Campus *A*

Oklahoma
Oklahoma State University *M*

Texas
Sul Ross State University *A, B*

Utah
Brigham Young University *B*

Animal husbandry

California
Santa Rosa Junior College *C*

Connecticut
University of Connecticut *A*

Illinois
Black Hawk College *C, A*
John Wood Community College *C, A*

Iowa
Ellsworth Community College *C*

New York
State University of New York
　　College of Agriculture and
　　Technology at Morrisville *A, B*

North Carolina
James Sprunt Community College *A*

Oregon
Blue Mountain Community College *A*

Texas
Tarleton State University *A*
Texas A&M University *B*
Texas Tech University *B*

Animal nutrition

Georgia
University of Georgia *D*

Illinois
Joliet Junior College *C*

Iowa
Iowa State University *M, D*

New York
Cornell University *B, M, D*

North Carolina
North Carolina State University *M, D*

Oklahoma
Oklahoma State University *D*

Texas
Texas A&M University *M, D*

Animal physiology

Illinois
University of Illinois
　　Urbana-Champaign *B, M, D*

Texas
Southwest Texas State University *B*

Animal sciences

Alabama
Auburn University *B, M, D*
Northeast Alabama Community
　　College *A*
Tuskegee University *B, M*

Arizona
University of Arizona *B, M, D*

Arkansas
Arkansas State University *B*
University of Arkansas *B, M, D*

California
Bakersfield College *A*
California Polytechnic State University:
　　San Luis Obispo *B*
California State Polytechnic University:
　　Pomona *B, M*
California State University
　　Chico *B*
　　Fresno *B, M*
College of the Redwoods *C, A*
College of the Sequoias *C*
College of the Siskiyous *A*
Los Angeles Pierce College *C, A*
Modesto Junior College *A*
Moorpark College *C, A*
Mount San Antonio College *C, A*
Reedley College *C*
San Joaquin Delta College *C, A*
Santa Rosa Junior College *C*
Sierra College *C, A*
University of California
　　Davis *B, M, D*
Ventura College *C, A*
Yuba Community College District *C*

Colorado
Colorado State University *B, M, D*
University of Denver *B*

Connecticut
University of Connecticut *A, B, M, D*

Delaware
University of Delaware *B, M, D*

Florida
Florida Agricultural and Mechanical
　　University *B*
South Florida Community College *A*
University of Florida *B, M, D*

Georgia
Abraham Baldwin Agricultural
　　College *A*
Berry College *B*
Fort Valley State University *B, M*
University of Georgia *B, M, D*

Hawaii
University of Hawaii
　　Hilo *B*
　　Manoa *B, M*

Idaho
Brigham Young University - Idaho *A, B*
University of Idaho *B, M*

Illinois
Black Hawk College
　　East Campus *C*
Southern Illinois University
　　Carbondale *B, M*
University of Illinois
　　Urbana-Champaign *B, M, D*

Indiana
Purdue University *B, M, D*

Iowa
Des Moines Area Community College *C*
Dordt College *B*
Hawkeye Community College *A*
Iowa State University *B, M, D*
Waldorf College *A*

Kansas
Butler County Community College *A*
Central Christian College *A*
Fort Scott Community College *A*
Garden City Community College *A*
Kansas State University *B, M, D*
McPherson College *B*
Pratt Community College *A*

Seward County Community College *A*

Kentucky
Murray State University *B*
University of Kentucky *B, M, D*

Louisiana
Louisiana State University and
　　Agricultural and Mechanical
　　College *B, M, D*
Louisiana Tech University *B*

Maine
University of Maine *B, M*

Maryland
University of Maryland
　　College Park *B, M, D*

Massachusetts
Becker College *A, B*
Berkshire Community College *C*
Hampshire College *B*
Mount Ida College *A, B*
University of Massachusetts
　　Amherst *B, M, D*

Michigan
Andrews University *B*
Michigan State University *C, B, M, D*

Minnesota
Globe College *A*
South Central Technical College *A*
University of Minnesota
　　Crookston *B*
　　Twin Cities *B, M, D*

Mississippi
Alcorn State University *B*
Mississippi State University *B*
Northwest Mississippi Community
　　College *A*

Missouri
College of the Ozarks *B*
Northwest Missouri State University *B*
Southeast Missouri State University *B*
Southwest Missouri State University *B*
Truman State University *B*
University of Missouri
　　Columbia *B, M, D*

Montana
Montana State University
　　Bozeman *B, M*

Nebraska
Northeast Community College *A*
University of Nebraska
　　Lincoln *B, M, D*

Nevada
University of Nevada
　　Reno *B, M*

New Hampshire
University of New
　　Hampshire *A, B, M, D*

New Jersey
Rutgers, The State University of New
　　Jersey
　　New Brunswick Regional
　　　Campus *B, M, D*

New Mexico
New Mexico State University *B, M, D*

New York
Cornell University *B, M, D*
Medaille College *A*
State University of New York
　　College of Agriculture and
　　　Technology at Cobleskill *A, B*
　　College of Agriculture and
　　　Technology at Morrisville *A, B*
　　College of Environmental Science
　　　and Forestry *B, M, D*
　　College of Technology at Alfred *A*
　　College of Technology at Delhi *A*

North Carolina
James Sprunt Community College *A*
North Carolina Agricultural and
　　Technical State University *B, M*
North Carolina State University *B, M, D*
Sampson Community College *C*

North Dakota
North Dakota State University *B, M, D*

Ohio
Ohio State University
　　Columbus Campus *B, M, D*
Wilmington College *B*

Oklahoma
Cameron University *B*
Eastern Oklahoma State College *A*
Langston University *B*
Oklahoma Panhandle State University *B*
Oklahoma State University *B, M*

Oregon
Linn-Benton Community College *A*
Oregon State University *B, M, D*
Treasure Valley Community College *A*

Pennsylvania
Delaware Valley College *B*
Penn State
　　Abington *B*
　　Altoona *B*
　　Beaver *B*
　　Berks *B*
　　Delaware County *B*
　　Dubois *B*
　　Erie, The Behrend College *B*
　　Fayette *B*
　　Hazleton *B*
　　Lehigh Valley *B*
　　McKeesport *B*
　　Mont Alto *B*
　　New Kensington *B*
　　Schuylkill - Capital College *B*
　　Shenango *B*
　　University Park *C, B, M, D*
　　Wilkes-Barre *B*
　　Worthington Scranton *B*
　　York *B*

Puerto Rico
University of Puerto Rico
　　Mayaguez Campus *B, M*
　　Utuado *A*

Rhode Island
University of Rhode Island *B*

South Carolina
Clemson University *B*

South Dakota
South Dakota State University *B, M, D*

Tennessee
Middle Tennessee State University *B*
Tennessee State University *B, M*
Tennessee Technological University *B*
University of Tennessee
　　Knoxville *B, M, D*
　　Martin *B*

Texas
Abilene Christian University *B*
Angelo State University *B, M*
Central Texas College *C*
Cisco Junior College *A*
Lubbock Christian University *B*
Palo Alto College *C, A*
Prairie View A&M University *M*
Sam Houston State University *B*
Southwest Texas State University *B*
Stephen F. Austin State University *B*
Sul Ross State University *B, M*
Tarleton State University *B*
Texas A&M University *B, M, D*
Texas A&M University
　　Commerce *B, M*
　　Kingsville *B, M*

Texas Tech University *B, M, D*
West Texas A&M University *B, M*
Western Texas College *A*

Utah
Brigham Young University *B, M*
Snow College *A*
Utah State University *B, M, D*

Vermont
University of Vermont *B, M, D*

Virginia
Blue Ridge Community College *C, A*
Virginia Polytechnic Institute and State
   University *B, M, D*

Washington
Everett Community College *A*
Washington State University *B, M, D*

West Virginia
West Virginia University *B, M*

Wisconsin
Chippewa Valley Technical College *A*
University of Wisconsin
   Madison *B, M, D*
   Platteville *B*
   River Falls *B*

Wyoming
Casper College *A*
Central Wyoming College *A*
Eastern Wyoming College *A*
Sheridan College *A*

Animation/video graphics/ special effects

Arizona
Collins College *A, B*

California
Art Center College of Design *B, M*
Art Institute of California - San
   Francisco *B*
California Institute of the Arts *C, B, M*
Long Beach City College *C*
Otis College of Art and Design *B*
Santa Rosa Junior College *C*
Silicon Valley College
   Emeryville *C, A, B*
Westwood College of Technology
   Inland Empire *B*

Florida
Full Sail Real World Education *A*
Miami-Dade Community College *A*

Georgia
Savannah College of Art and
   Design *B, M*

Illinois
City Colleges of Chicago
   Kennedy-King College *C*
Oakton Community College *C*

Indiana
University of St. Francis *B*

Minnesota
Academy College *C, A*
Art Institutes International
   Minnesota *B*

New Jersey
Bergen Community College *C*
Bloomfield College *B*

New York
Marist College *B*
Rochester Institute of Technology *B, M*

Ohio
Kent State University *A*
North Central State College *A*
University of Cincinnati
   Raymond Walters College *C*

Washington State Community College *A*

Pennsylvania
Art Institute
   of Philadelphia *A, B*
Bradley Academy for the Visual Arts *A*
Bucks County Community College *C*
Douglas School of Business *A*

Vermont
Burlington College *B*

Virginia
Art Institute
   of Washington *B*

Anthropology

Alabama
Auburn University *B*
University of Alabama *B, M*
University of Alabama
   Birmingham *B, M*
University of South Alabama *B*

Alaska
University of Alaska
   Anchorage *B, M*
   Fairbanks *B, M, D*

Arizona
Arizona State University *B, M, D*
Cochise College *A*
Eastern Arizona College *A*
Northern Arizona University *B, M*
Pima Community College *A*
Prescott College *B*
University of Arizona *B, M, D*

Arkansas
Hendrix College *B*
University of Arkansas *B, M*

California
Bakersfield College *A*
Biola University *B*
Cabrillo College *A*
California State Polytechnic University:
   Pomona *A*
California State University
   Bakersfield *B*
   Chico *B, M*
   Dominguez Hills *B*
   Fresno *B*
   Fullerton *B, M*
   Hayward *B, M*
   Long Beach *B, M*
   Los Angeles *B, M*
   Monterey Bay *B*
   Northridge *B*
   Sacramento *B, M*
   San Bernardino *B*
   Stanislaus *B*
Cerritos Community College *A*
College of Alameda *A*
Copper Mountain College *A*
De Anza College *A*
East Los Angeles College *A*
Foothill College *A*
Gavilan Community College *A*
Glendale Community College *A*
Golden West College *A*
Humboldt State University *B*
Imperial Valley College *A*
Irvine Valley College *A*
Los Angeles Pierce College *C*
Los Medanos College *A*
Mills College *B*
Monterey Peninsula College *A*
Occidental College *B*
Ohlone College *C*
Orange Coast College *A*
Pitzer College *B*
Pomona College *B*
St. Mary's College of California *B*
San Diego City College *A*
San Diego Mesa College *A*

San Diego State University *B, M*
San Francisco State University *B, M*
San Joaquin Delta College *A*
San Jose State University *B*
Santa Barbara City College *A*
Santa Clara University *B*
Santa Rosa Junior College *A*
Santiago Canyon College *A*
Scripps College *B*
Sonoma State University *B, M*
Southwestern College *A*
Stanford University *B, M, D*
University of California
   Berkeley *B, D*
   Davis *B, M, D*
   Irvine *B*
   Los Angeles *B, M, D*
   Riverside *B, M, D*
   San Diego *B, D*
   Santa Barbara *B, M, D*
   Santa Cruz *B, D*
University of La Verne *B*
University of Redlands *B*
University of San Diego *B*
University of Southern
   California *B, M, D*
Vanguard University of Southern
   California *B*
Ventura College *A*
Whittier College *B*

Colorado
Colorado College *B*
Colorado State University *B, M*
Fort Lewis College *B*
Metropolitan State College of
   Denver *B, T*
University of Colorado
   Boulder *B, M, D*
   Colorado Springs *B*
   Denver *B, M*
University of Denver *B, M*

Connecticut
Central Connecticut State University *B*
Connecticut College *B*
Trinity College *B*
University of Connecticut *B, M, D*
Wesleyan University *B, M*
Western Connecticut State University *B*
Yale University *B, M, D*

Delaware
University of Delaware *B*

District of Columbia
American University *C, B, M, D*
Catholic University of America *B, M, D*
George Washington University *B, M*
Georgetown University *B*
Howard University *B*
University of the District of Columbia *B*

Florida
Broward Community College *A*
Eckerd College *B*
Florida Atlantic University *B, M*
Florida State University *B, M, D*
Gulf Coast Community College *A*
Indian River Community College *A*
Manatee Community College *A*
Miami-Dade Community College *A*
New College of Florida *B*
Palm Beach Community College *A*
Rollins College *B*
Santa Fe Community College *A*
South Florida Community College *A*
University of Central Florida *B*
University of Florida *B, M, D*
University of Miami *B*
University of North Florida *B*
University of South Florida *B, M, D*
University of West Florida *B*

Georgia
Agnes Scott College *B*
Berry College *B*

East Georgia College *A*
Emory University *B, D*
Gainesville College *A*
Georgia Perimeter College *A*
Georgia Southern University *B*
Georgia State University *B, M*
Oxford College of Emory University *B*
State University of West Georgia *B*
Thomas University *B*
University of Georgia *B, M, D*
Valdosta State University *B*

Hawaii
Hawaii Pacific University *C, B*
University of Hawaii
   Hilo *B*
   Manoa *B, M, D*
   West Oahu *B*

Idaho
Albertson College of Idaho *B*
Boise State University *B*
College of Southern Idaho *A*
Idaho State University *B, M*
North Idaho College *A*
University of Idaho *B, M*

Illinois
Benedictine University *T*
Black Hawk College
   East Campus *A*
Chicago State University *B*
Illinois State University *B*
Judson College *B*
Knox College *B*
Lake Forest College *B*
Lincoln Land Community College *A*
Loyola University of Chicago *B*
National-Louis University *B*
North Park University *B*
Northeastern Illinois University *B*
Northern Illinois University *B, M*
Northwestern University *B, M, D*
Parkland College *A*
Richland Community College *A*
Rockford College *B*
South Suburban College of Cook
   County *A*
Southern Illinois University
   Carbondale *B, M, D*
Southern Illinois University
   Edwardsville *B*
Southwestern Illinois College *A*
Triton College *A*
University of Chicago *B, M, D*
University of Illinois
   Chicago *B, M, D*
   Urbana-Champaign *B, M, D*
Wheaton College *B*

Indiana
Ball State University *B, M*
Butler University *B*
DePauw University *B*
Earlham College *B*
Goshen College *B*
Hanover College *B*
Indiana State University *B, T*
Indiana University
   Bloomington *B, M, D*
Indiana University-Purdue University
   Fort Wayne *B*
Indiana University-Purdue University
   Indianapolis *B*
University of Evansville *B*
University of Indianapolis *B*
University of Notre Dame *B*
Vincennes University *A*

Iowa
Cornell College *B, T*
Drake University *B*
Grinnell College *B*
Iowa State University *B, M*
Luther College *B*
University of Iowa *B, M, D, T*
University of Northern Iowa *B*

Kansas
Barton County Community College *A*
Kansas State University *B*
University of Kansas *B, M, D*
Washburn University of Topeka *B*
Wichita State University *B, M*

Kentucky
Centre College *B*
University of Kentucky *B, M, D*
University of Louisville *B*

Louisiana
Grambling State University *B*
Louisiana State University and
   Agricultural and Mechanical
   College *B, M*
Northwestern State University *B*
Tulane University *B, M, D*
University of Louisiana at Lafayette *B*
University of New Orleans *B*

Maine
Bates College *B*
Bowdoin College *B*
Colby College *B*
University of Maine *B*
University of Maine
   Farmington *B*
University of Southern Maine *B*

Maryland
Community College of Baltimore County
   Catonsville *A*
   Dundalk *A*
   Essex *A*
Howard Community College *A*
Johns Hopkins University *B, M, D*
St. Mary's College of Maryland *B*
University of Maryland
   Baltimore County *B*
   College Park *B, M*
Washington College *B*

Massachusetts
Amherst College *B*
Boston University *B, M, D*
Brandeis University *B, M, D*
Bridgewater State College *B*
Hampshire College *B*
Harvard College *B*
Massachusetts Institute of Technology *B*
Mount Holyoke College *B*
Northeastern University *B, M*
Smith College *B*
Tufts University *B*
University of Massachusetts
   Amherst *B, M, D*
   Boston *B*
Wellesley College *B*
Wheaton College *B*
Williams College *B*

Michigan
Adrian College *A*
Alma College *B, T*
Central Michigan University *B, T*
Eastern Michigan University *B*
Grand Valley State University *B*
Kalamazoo College *B, T*
Kellogg Community College *A*
Lansing Community College *A*
Michigan State University *B, M, D*
Oakland University *B*
University of Michigan *B, M, D, T*
University of Michigan
   Dearborn *B*
   Flint *B*
Wayne State University *B, M, D*
Western Michigan University *B, M*

Minnesota
Bethel College *B*
Carleton College *B*
Gustavus Adolphus College *B*
Hamline University *B*
Macalester College *B*

Minnesota State University
   Mankato *B*
   Moorhead *B*
St. Cloud State University *B*
University of Minnesota
   Duluth *B*
   Twin Cities *B, M, D*

Mississippi
Millsaps College *B*
Mississippi State University *B*
University of Mississippi *B, M*
University of Southern Mississippi *B, M*

Missouri
Southeast Missouri State University *B*
Southwest Missouri State University *B*
University of Missouri
   Columbia *B, M, D*
   St. Louis *B*
Washington University in St.
   Louis *B, M, D*
Webster University *B*
Westminster College *B*

Montana
Montana State University
   Bozeman *B*
Rocky Mountain College *B, T*
University of Montana-Missoula *B, M*

Nebraska
Creighton University *B*
University of Nebraska
   Lincoln *B, M*
Western Nebraska Community
   College *A*

Nevada
Great Basin College *A*
Truckee Meadows Community
   College *C, A*
University of Nevada
   Las Vegas *B, M, D*
   Reno *B, M, D*

New Hampshire
Dartmouth College *B*
Franklin Pierce College *B*
University of New Hampshire *B*

New Jersey
Drew University *B*
Monmouth University *B*
Montclair State University *B, M*
Princeton University *B, M, D*
Richard Stockton College of New
   Jersey *B*
Rowan University *B*
Rutgers, The State University of New
   Jersey
   New Brunswick Regional
      Campus *B, M, D*
   Newark Regional Campus *B*
Seton Hall University *B*
Thomas Edison State College *B*
William Paterson University of New
   Jersey *B*

New Mexico
Eastern New Mexico University *B, M*
New Mexico Highlands University *B*
New Mexico State University *B, M*
San Juan College *A*
University of New Mexico *B, M, D*

New York
Adelphi University *B*
Bard College *B*
Barnard College *B*
City University of New York
   Brooklyn College *B*
   City College *B, M*
   College of Staten Island *B*
   Hunter College *B, M*
   Queens College *B*
   York College *B*
Colgate University *B*

Columbia University
   Columbia College *B*
Cornell University *B, M, D*
Dowling College *B*
Elmira College *B*
Eugene Lang College/New School
   University *B*
Fordham University *B*
Hamilton College *B*
Hartwick College *B*
Hobart and William Smith Colleges *B*
Hofstra University *B*
Ithaca College *B*
Nazareth College of Rochester *B*
New York University *B, M, D*
St. John Fisher College *B*
St. John's University *B*
St. Lawrence University *B*
Sarah Lawrence College *B*
Skidmore College *B*
State University of New York
   Albany *B, M, D*
   Binghamton *B, M, D*
   Buffalo *B, M, D*
   College at Brockport *B*
   College at Buffalo *B*
   College at Cortland *B*
   College at Geneseo *B, T*
   College at Oneonta *B*
   College at Plattsburgh *B*
   College at Potsdam *B*
   New Paltz *B*
   Oswego *B*
   Purchase *B*
   Stony Brook *B, M, D*
Syracuse University *B, M, D*
Union College *B*
University of Rochester *B*
Utica College *B*
Vassar College *B*
Wagner College *A*
Wells College *B*

North Carolina
Appalachian State University *B*
Belmont Abbey College *B*
Davidson College *B*
Duke University *B, M, D*
East Carolina University *B, M*
Elon University *B*
North Carolina State University *B*
North Carolina Wesleyan College *B*
University of North Carolina
   Chapel Hill *B, M, D*
   Charlotte *B*
   Greensboro *B*
   Wilmington *B*
Wake Forest University *B, M*
Warren Wilson College *B*
Western Carolina University *B*

North Dakota
North Dakota State University *B, M*
University of North Dakota *B*

Ohio
Case Western Reserve
   University *B, M, D*
Cleveland State University *B, M*
Denison University *B*
Franciscan University of Steubenville *B*
Heidelberg College *B*
Kent State University *B, M*
Kent State University
   Stark Campus *B*
Kenyon College *B*
Miami University
   Middletown Campus *A*
   Oxford Campus *B*
Oberlin College *B*
Ohio State University
   Columbus Campus *B, M, D*
Ohio University *B*
Ohio Wesleyan University *B*
University of Akron *B*
University of Cincinnati *B, M*

University of Toledo *B*
Wright State University *B*
Youngstown State University *B*

Oklahoma
Oklahoma Baptist University *B*
University of Oklahoma *B, M, D*
University of Tulsa *B, M*

Oregon
Central Oregon Community College *A*
Chemeketa Community College *A*
Eastern Oregon University *B, T*
Lewis & Clark College *B*
Linfield College *B*
Linn-Benton Community College *A*
Oregon State University *B, M*
Portland State University *B, M, D*
Reed College *B*
Southern Oregon University *B*
University of Oregon *B, M, D*
Warner Pacific College *B*
Western Oregon University *B*
Willamette University *B*

Pennsylvania
Albright College *B*
Bloomsburg University of
   Pennsylvania *B*
Bryn Mawr College *B*
Bucknell University *B*
California University of Pennsylvania *B*
Delaware County Community College *A*
Dickinson College *B*
Drexel University *B*
Edinboro University of Pennsylvania *B*
Elizabethtown College *B*
Franklin & Marshall College *B*
Gettysburg College *B*
Haverford College *B, T*
Indiana University of Pennsylvania *B*
Juniata College *B*
Kutztown University of Pennsylvania *B*
Lafayette College *B*
Lehigh University *B*
Lock Haven University of
   Pennsylvania *B*
Lycoming College *B*
Mercyhurst College *B*
Millersville University of
   Pennsylvania *B*
Muhlenberg College *B*
Penn State
   Abington *B*
   Altoona *B*
   Beaver *B*
   Berks *B*
   Delaware County *B*
   Dubois *B*
   Fayette *B*
   Hazleton *B*
   Lehigh Valley *B*
   McKeesport *B*
   Mont Alto *B*
   New Kensington *B*
   Schuylkill - Capital College *B*
   Shenango *B*
   University Park *B, M, D*
   Wilkes-Barre *B*
   Worthington Scranton *B*
   York *B*
St. Vincent College *B*
Slippery Rock University of
   Pennsylvania *B, T*
Swarthmore College *B*
Temple University *B, M, D*
University of Pennsylvania *A, B, M, D*
University of Pittsburgh *B, M, D*
University of Pittsburgh
   Greensburg *B*
West Chester University of
   Pennsylvania *B*
Widener University *B*

Puerto Rico
Inter American University of Puerto Rico
   Metropolitan Campus *B*

University of Puerto Rico
Rio Piedras Campus *B*

Rhode Island
Brown University *B, M, D*
Rhode Island College *B*
Roger Williams University *B*
Salve Regina University *B*
University of Rhode Island *B*

South Carolina
College of Charleston *B*
University of South Carolina *B, M*

South Dakota
University of South Dakota *B*

Tennessee
Middle Tennessee State University *B*
Rhodes College *B*
University of Memphis *B, M*
University of Tennessee
Knoxville *B, M, D*
Vanderbilt University *B, M, D*

Texas
Austin Community College *A*
Baylor University *B*
Galveston College *A*
Midland College *A*
Rice University *B, M, D*
Southern Methodist University *B, M, D*
Southwest Texas State University *B*
Southwestern University *B*
Texas A&M University *B, M, D*
Texas A&M University
Commerce *B*
Kingsville *B*
Texas Christian University *B*
Texas Tech University *B, M*
Trinity University *B*
University of Houston *B, M*
University of Houston
Clear Lake *B*
University of North Texas *B*
University of Texas
Arlington *B, M*
Austin *B, M, D*
El Paso *B*
Pan American *B*
San Antonio *B, M*

Utah
Brigham Young University *B, M*
Snow College *A*
University of Utah *B, M, D*
Utah State University *B*

Vermont
Bennington College *B*
Johnson State College *B*
Marlboro College *B*
St. Michael's College *B*
University of Vermont *B*

Virginia
College of William and Mary *B, M, D*
Emory & Henry College *B*
George Mason University *B*
James Madison University *B*
Longwood University *B, T*
Mary Washington College *B*
Radford University *B*
Sweet Briar College *B*
University of Virginia *B, M, D*
University of Virginia's College at
Wise *T*
Washington and Lee University *B*

Washington
Central Washington University *B*
Centralia College *A*
Eastern Washington University *B*
Everett Community College *A*
Lower Columbia College *A*
Olympic College *A*
Pacific Lutheran University *B*
University of Washington *B, M, D*
Washington State University *B, M, D*

Western Washington University *B, M, T*
Whitman College *B*

Wisconsin
Beloit College *B*
Lawrence University *B, T*
Marquette University *B, T*
Ripon College *B*
University of Wisconsin
Madison *B, M, D*
Milwaukee *B, M, D*
Oshkosh *B*
Parkside *T*
River Falls *T*

Wyoming
Casper College *A*
Laramie County Community College *A*
University of Wyoming *B, M, D*
Western Wyoming Community
College *A*

Apparel/accessories marketing

Texas
Sam Houston State University *B*

Washington
Art Institute of Seattle *A*

Apparel/textile manufacture

Alabama
Lawson State Community College *C*

Georgia
Southern Polytechnic State University *B*

Iowa
Iowa State University *B*

Oklahoma
Oklahoma State University *B, M*

Washington
Washington State University *B, M, D*

Apparel/textile marketing

Iowa
Iowa State University *B*

North Carolina
North Carolina State University *B*

Pennsylvania
Philadelphia University *B, M*

Appliance installation and repair

Kentucky
Somerset Community College *C*

Minnesota
St. Paul College - A Community and
Technical College *C*

Texas
Del Mar College *C, A*

Applied economics

Alaska
University of Alaska
Fairbanks *M*

District of Columbia
American University *C*

Indiana
St. Joseph's College *B*

Iowa
University of Northern Iowa *B*

Michigan
Western Michigan University *M, D*

Minnesota
College of St. Scholastica *B*

Mississippi
Mississippi State University *D*

New Hampshire
Plymouth State College *B*

New York
Hofstra University *B*
State University of New York
Buffalo *M*

North Carolina
East Carolina University *M*

Ohio
Bowling Green State University *B*
University of Dayton *B*

Pennsylvania
Allegheny College *B*
Penn State
Schuylkill - Capital College *B*
University Park *B*
Wilkes-Barre *B*
Worthington Scranton *B*
York *B*

Wisconsin
Marquette University *M*

Applied mathematics

Alabama
Auburn University *B, M*
Oakwood College *B*
University of Alabama *M, D*
University of Alabama
Birmingham *D*
Huntsville *D*

Alaska
University of Alaska
Fairbanks *B, M*

Arizona
Arizona State University *B*
University of Arizona *M, D*

Arkansas
University of Arkansas
Little Rock *B, M*
Pine Bluff *B*

California
California Institute of Technology *B, D*
California State Polytechnic University:
Pomona *B*
California State University
Chico *B*
Fullerton *B, M*
Hayward *B, M*
Long Beach *B, M, D*
Los Angeles *B, M*
Northridge *B, M*
Harvey Mudd College *B*
Mount St. Mary's College *B*
Ohlone College *C*
San Diego City College *A*
San Diego State University *B, M*
San Francisco State University *B*
San Jose State University *B*
Santa Clara University *M*
University of California
Berkeley *B, D*
Davis *M, D*
Los Angeles *B*
Riverside *B, M*
San Diego *B, M*
Santa Barbara *B, M*
Santa Cruz *B, M, D*

University of Southern California *M, D*

Colorado
Colorado School of Mines *B*
University of Colorado
Boulder *B, M, D*
Colorado Springs *M*
Denver *B, M, D*

Connecticut
University of Connecticut *B*
Yale University *B, M, D*

District of Columbia
American University *B*
George Washington University *B, M*

Florida
Florida Atlantic University *M*
Florida Institute of Technology *B, M, D*
Florida International University *B, M*
Florida State University *B, M, D*
University of Central Florida *M, D*
University of North Florida *M*
University of West Florida *B, M*

Georgia
Armstrong Atlantic State University *B, T*
Columbus State University *B*
Georgia Institute of Technology *M*
Georgia State University *B, M, D*
University of Georgia *M*
Valdosta State University *B*

Hawaii
Hawaii Pacific University *B*

Idaho
University of Idaho *B*

Illinois
Elgin Community College *A*
Illinois Valley Community College *A*
Millikin University *B, T*
National-Louis University *B*
North Central College *B*
North Park University *B*
Northeastern Illinois University *M*
Northwestern University *B, M, D*
University of Chicago *B*
University of Illinois
Urbana-Champaign *M*

Indiana
Goshen College *B*
Indiana University
South Bend *B*
Indiana University-Purdue University
Fort Wayne *M*
Oakland City University *B*
Purdue University
Calumet *B, M*
St. Joseph's College *B*
Saint Mary's College *B, T*
University of Evansville *B*
University of Notre Dame *M*

Iowa
Grand View College *B*
Iowa State University *M, D*
University of Iowa *D*

Kansas
Independence Community College *A*

Kentucky
Asbury College *B*
Brescia University *B*
Paducah Technical College *A*
University of Kentucky *M*

Louisiana
Louisiana College *B*
Nicholls State University *M*
Tulane University *M*

Maryland
Johns Hopkins University *B, M, D*
Loyola College in Maryland *B*
Towson University *M*

University of Maryland
  Baltimore County *M, D*
  College Park *M, D*

Massachusetts
Clark University *B*
Hampshire College *B*
Harvard College *B*
Massachusetts Institute of Technology *D*
Tufts University *B, M*
University of Massachusetts
  Amherst *M*
  Boston *B*
  Lowell *A, B*
Worcester Polytechnic Institute *B, M*

Michigan
Ferris State University *B*
Kettering University *B*
Lansing Community College *A*
Michigan State University *B, M, D*
Northern Michigan University *B*
Oakland University *M, D*
University of Michigan *B, M, D*
Wayne State University *M*
Western Michigan University *B, M*

Minnesota
Concordia College: Moorhead *B*
Metropolitan State University *B*
Minnesota State University
  Moorhead *B*
University of Minnesota
  Duluth *M*
Winona State University *B*

Mississippi
Mississippi State University *D*

Missouri
Central Methodist College *A*
Maryville University of Saint Louis *B*
St. Louis University *B*
Truman State University *B*
University of Missouri
  Columbia *M*
  Rolla *B, M*
  St. Louis *B, D*
Washington University in St. Louis *B*

Montana
Montana Tech of the University of
  Montana *B*
University of Montana: Western *B*

Nebraska
Creighton University *B*

Nevada
University of Nevada
  Las Vegas *B*

New Hampshire
Keene State College *B*
University of New Hampshire *B*

New Jersey
Bloomfield College *B*
New Jersey Institute of Technology *B, M*
Princeton University *M, D*
Rutgers, The State University of New
  Jersey
  Newark Regional Campus *B*
Stevens Institute of Technology *B, M*

New Mexico
New Mexico Institute of Mining and
  Technology *B, M*

New York
Adelphi University *M*
Barnard College *B*
City University of New York
  Baruch College *M*
  Brooklyn College *B, M*
  Hunter College *M*
  Queens College *B*
Clarkson University *B*

Columbia University
  Fu Foundation School of
    Engineering and Applied
    Science *B, M, D*
Cornell University *D*
Hofstra University *B, M*
Long Island University
  C. W. Post Campus *M*
New York University *M*
Rensselaer Polytechnic Institute *M*
Rochester Institute of
  Technology *A, B, M*
State University of New York
  Albany *B*
  Farmingdale *A, B*
  Institute of Technology at
    Utica/Rome *B*
  Oswego *B*
  Stony Brook *B, M, D*
University of Rochester *B, M*

North Carolina
Elizabeth City State University *B*
Johnson C. Smith University *B*
North Carolina Agricultural and
  Technical State University *M*
North Carolina State University *B, M, D*
St. Augustine's College *B*
University of North Carolina
  Chapel Hill *B*
  Charlotte *D*
Western Carolina University *M*

North Dakota
Jamestown College *B*

Ohio
Bowling Green State University *M*
Case Western Reserve
  University *B, M, D*
Kent State University *B, M, D*
Kent State University
  Stark Campus *B*
Ohio State University
  Columbus Campus *M, D*
Ohio University *B*
University of Akron *B, M*
University of Dayton *B*
Wright State University *M*

Oklahoma
East Central University *B*
University of Central Oklahoma *B, M*
University of Tulsa *B*

Oregon
Blue Mountain Community College *A*
University of Oregon *M, D*

Pennsylvania
California University of Pennsylvania *B*
Geneva College *B*
Indiana University of Pennsylvania *B*
La Roche College *B*
La Salle University *B, T*
Lehigh University *M, D*
Penn State
  Harrisburg *B*
Robert Morris University *B*
University of Pittsburgh *B, M*
University of Pittsburgh
  Bradford *B*
  Greensburg *B*

Puerto Rico
Inter American University of Puerto Rico
  San German Campus *B*
Turabo University *B*
Universidad Metropolitana *B*
University of Puerto Rico
  Mayaguez Campus *M*

Rhode Island
Brown University *B, M, D*
Salve Regina University *B*
University of Rhode Island *D*

South Carolina
Charleston Southern University *B*

Coastal Carolina University *B*
University of South Carolina *M*
University of South Carolina
  Aiken *B*

South Dakota
University of Sioux Falls *B*

Tennessee
Bethel College *B*
University of Tennessee
  Chattanooga *B*

Texas
Baylor University *B*
Lamar University *B*
Rice University *B, M, D*
Southern Methodist University *M*
Southwest Texas State University *B*
Southwestern Adventist University *B*
Texas A&M University *B*
University of Houston *B, M*
University of Houston
  Downtown *B*
University of Texas
  Arlington *D*
  Austin *M, D*
  Dallas *B, M, D*
  El Paso *B*

Utah
Utah State University *D*
Weber State University *B*

Vermont
Bennington College *B*

Virginia
Averett University *B*
Hampden-Sydney College *B*
Hampton University *M*
Longwood University *B, T*
Mary Baldwin College *B*
Old Dominion University *M, D*
Radford University *M*
University of Virginia *B, M, D*
University of Virginia's College at
  Wise *T*

Washington
Seattle University *B*
University of Washington *B, M, D*
Western Washington University *B*
Whitworth College *B*

West Virginia
Alderson-Broaddus College *B*
West Virginia State College *B*

Wisconsin
University of Wisconsin
  Milwaukee *B*
  Stout *B*

Aquaculture

Maine
University of New England *B*

New York
State University of New York
  College of Agriculture and
    Technology at Morrisville *A*

Texas
Texas A&M University *B*

West Virginia
Bluefield State College *A*

Aquatic biology/limnology

Arizona
Northern Arizona University *B*

California
University of California
  Santa Barbara *B*

Rhode Island
Brown University *B*

Texas
Southwest Texas State
  University *B, M, T*
Texas A&M University
  Galveston *B*

Wisconsin
University of Wisconsin
  Superior *B*

Arabic

California
Grossmont Community College *C, A*
University of California
  Los Angeles *B*

District of Columbia
Catholic University of America *M, D*
George Washington University *B*
Georgetown University *B, M, D*

Florida
University of Miami *B*

Georgia
Oxford College of Emory University *B*

Illinois
University of Chicago *B*

Indiana
University of Notre Dame *B*

Maine
University of Southern Maine *B*

Maryland
Johns Hopkins University *B*

Massachusetts
Harvard College *B*
Simon's Rock College of Bard *B*

Michigan
University of Michigan *B, M*

Minnesota
University of Minnesota
  Twin Cities *M*

Missouri
Washington University in St. Louis *B, M*

New Hampshire
Dartmouth College *B*

New York
State University of New York
  Binghamton *B*

Ohio
Ohio State University
  Columbus Campus *B*

Texas
University of Texas
  Austin *B, M, D*

Utah
Brigham Young University *B, M*

Washington
University of Washington *B*

Archaeology

Arizona
Pima Community College *C, A*

California
California State University
  Hayward *B*
  Stanislaus *B*
Imperial Valley College *C*
Palomar College *C, A*

University of California
  Berkeley *M, D*
  Los Angeles *M, D*
  San Diego *B*
  Santa Cruz *D*

Connecticut
Norwalk Community College *C*
Wesleyan University *B*
Yale University *B, M*

District of Columbia
George Washington University *B*

Florida
Gulf Coast Community College *A*

Illinois
Illinois State University *M*
Richland Community College *A*
Southwestern Illinois College *A*
Wheaton College *B*

Indiana
Ball State University *M*
Indiana University
  Bloomington *D*
University of Evansville *B*
University of Indianapolis *B*

Maine
Bowdoin College *B*

Massachusetts
Boston University *B, M, D*
Bridgewater State College *B*
Harvard College *B*
Tufts University *B*
Wellesley College *B*

Michigan
Michigan Technological University *M*
University of Michigan *M, D*

Minnesota
Hamline University *B*
University of Minnesota
  Twin Cities *M, D*

Missouri
Maryville University of Saint Louis *B*
Washington University in St.
  Louis *B, M, D*

New Hampshire
Franklin Pierce College *B*

New York
Bard College *B*
City University of New York
  Hunter College *B*
Columbia University
  Columbia College *B*
Cornell University *B, M*
Hamilton College *B*
New York University *M*
State University of New York
  Albany *B, M*
  Buffalo *M, D*
  College at Potsdam *B*

North Carolina
Appalachian State University *B*

Ohio
College of Wooster *B*
Oberlin College *B*
University of Cincinnati *M, D*

Pennsylvania
Bryn Mawr College *B, M, D*
Haverford College *B*
Lycoming College *B*
Mercyhurst College *B*
University of Pennsylvania *D*

Rhode Island
Brown University *B, M, D*

Tennessee
Southern Adventist University *B*

Texas
Baylor University *B*
Texas A&M University *D*
University of Texas
  Austin *B*

Utah
Weber State University *C, A*

Virginia
Washington and Lee University *B*

Washington
Western Washington University *B*

Wisconsin
University of Wisconsin
  La Crosse *B*

Architectural drafting/CAD/CADD

California
Long Beach City College *C, A*
Santa Rosa Junior College *C*
Shasta College *C, A*
Westwood College of Technology
  Inland Empire *A*

Florida
Indian River Community College *A*
New England Institute of Technology *A*
Palm Beach Community College *C*

Illinois
Kaskaskia College *C*

Indiana
Indiana State University *A*
Vincennes University *A*

Kansas
Central Christian College *A*

Maryland
Wor-Wic Community College *C*

Michigan
Baker College
  of Muskegon *A*

Minnesota
Hennepin Technical College *C, A*
Northwest Technical Institute *A*

Missouri
Jefferson College *C, A*

New York
Mohawk Valley Community College *C*
State University of New York
  College of Agriculture and
    Technology at Morrisville *A*

North Dakota
North Dakota State College of Science *A*

Ohio
Central Ohio Technical College *A*
Owens Community College
  Toledo *C*

Oklahoma
Platt College
  Tulsa *C*

Pennsylvania
Butler County Community College *A*
Community College of Allegheny
  County *A*
Delaware County Community
  College *C, A*
Montgomery County Community
  College *C, A*

Utah
Dixie State College of Utah *C, A*
Utah Valley State College *A*

Architectural engineering

Alabama
Auburn University *B, M*

Alaska
University of Alaska
  Anchorage *A*

California
East Los Angeles College *A*
San Joaquin Delta College *A*
University of Southern California *M*

Colorado
University of Colorado
  Boulder *B*

Connecticut
Norwalk Community College *A*

District of Columbia
University of the District of Columbia *A*

Florida
Miami-Dade Community College *A*
University of Miami *B, M*

Hawaii
University of Hawaii
  Honolulu Community College *A*

Illinois
City Colleges of Chicago
  Olive-Harvey College *C, A*
Dominican University *B*
Illinois Institute of Technology *B*
Lincoln Land Community College *A*
Parkland College *A*

Kansas
Central Christian College *A*
Independence Community College *A*
Kansas State University *B, M*
University of Kansas *B, M*

Kentucky
Louisville Technical Institute *A*

Massachusetts
Harvard College *B*
Tufts University *B*

Mississippi
Holmes Community College *A*

Missouri
University of Missouri
  Rolla *B*

Nebraska
University of Nebraska
  Lincoln *B*

New York
State University of New York
  College of Agriculture and
    Technology at Morrisville *A*

North Carolina
Guilford Technical Community
  College *C, A*
North Carolina Agricultural and
  Technical State University *B, M*

Ohio
Columbus State Community College *A*
Stark State College of Technology *A*

Oklahoma
Oklahoma State University *B, M*
Platt College
  Tulsa *C*

Pennsylvania
Drexel University *B*
Lock Haven University of
  Pennsylvania *B*

Penn State
  Abington *B*
  Altoona *B*
  Beaver *B*
  Berks *B*
  Delaware County *B*
  Dubois *B*
  Fayette *B*
  Hazleton *B*
  Lehigh Valley *B*
  McKeesport *B*
  Mont Alto *B*
  New Kensington *B*
  Schuylkill - Capital College *B*
  Shenango *B*
  University Park *B, M, D*
  Wilkes-Barre *B*
  Worthington Scranton *B*
  York *B*

Tennessee
Tennessee State University *B*

Texas
Laredo Community College *A*
University of Texas
  Austin *B, M*

Vermont
Vermont Technical College *A*

Virginia
Virginia Western Community
  College *C, A*

Wisconsin
Milwaukee Area Technical College *A*
Milwaukee School of Engineering *B*

Wyoming
University of Wyoming *B*

Architectural engineering technology

Alabama
Lawson State Community College *C, A*
Northeast Alabama Community
  College *A*

Alaska
University of Alaska
  Anchorage *A*

California
Chabot College *A*
College of the Sequoias *A*
Contra Costa College *A*
Cuyamaca College *A*
Diablo Valley College *C*
East Los Angeles College *A*
Golden West College *C, A*
Laney College *C, A*
Long Beach City College *C, A*
Los Angeles Harbor College *C, A*
Los Angeles Trade and Technical
  College *C, A*
Modesto Junior College *C, A*
Mount San Antonio College *C, A*
Orange Coast College *C, A*
San Joaquin Delta College *C, A*
Santa Monica College *C, A*
Sierra College *C, A*
Ventura College *A*

Colorado
Arapahoe Community College *C, A*
Front Range Community College *C, A*

Connecticut
Capital Community College *A*
Norwalk Community College *A*
Three Rivers Community College *C, A*
University of Hartford *B*

Delaware

Delaware Technical and Community
College
Owens Campus *A*
Stanton/Wilmington Campus *A*
Terry Campus *A*

Florida

Daytona Beach Community College *A*
Gulf Coast Community College *A*
Hillsborough Community College *A*
Miami-Dade Community College *A*
St. Petersburg College *A*
Seminole Community College *A*

Hawaii

University of Hawaii
Hawaii Community College *C*

Idaho

Brigham Young University - Idaho *A*

Illinois

Joliet Junior College *C, A*
Lincoln Land Community College *A*
Morrison Institute of Technology *A*
Oakton Community College *A*
Southern Illinois University
Carbondale *B*
William Rainey Harper College *C, A*

Indiana

Indiana State University *B*
Indiana University-Purdue University
Fort Wayne *A*
Indiana University-Purdue University
Indianapolis *A, B*
Purdue University *A, B*
Purdue University
North Central Campus *A*

Iowa

Iowa Western Community College *A*
University of Northern Iowa *B*
Western Iowa Tech Community
College *A*

Kansas

Central Christian College *A*
Fort Scott Community College *A*
Independence Community College *A*

Kentucky

Lexington Community College *A*
Louisville Technical Institute *A*

Louisiana

Delgado Community College *A*
Louisiana State University and
Agricultural and Mechanical
College *B*

Maryland

Montgomery College
Rockville Campus *A*

Massachusetts

Benjamin Franklin Institute of
Technology *A*
Fitchburg State College *B*
Massasoit Community College *A*
Wentworth Institute of Technology *A, B*

Michigan

Andrews University *A*
Baker College
of Auburn Hills *A*
of Muskegon *A*
of Owosso *A*
Ferris State University *A*
Monroe County Community
College *C, A*
Mott Community College *A*
Oakland Community College *A*

Minnesota

Anoka-Ramsey Community College *A*
Dakota County Technical College *C, A*
Lake Superior College: A Community
and Technical College *C, A*

St. Cloud Technical College *C, A*

Mississippi

University of Southern Mississippi *B*

Missouri

Central Missouri State University *A, B*
Mineral Area College *C, A*
St. Louis Community College
St. Louis Community College at
Meramec *A*
Washington University in St. Louis *B*

Nebraska

Southeast Community College
Lincoln Campus *A*

Nevada

Truckee Meadows Community
College *C, A*

New Hampshire

Keene State College *B*
New Hampshire Technical Institute *A*

New Jersey

Essex County College *A*
Mercer County Community College *C, A*
Thomas Edison State College *A, B*

New Mexico

Eastern New Mexico University: Roswell
Campus *A*

New York

Dutchess Community College *A*
Erie Community College
South Campus *A*
Finger Lakes Community College *A*
Institute of Design and Construction *A*
New York Institute of Technology *A, B*
Orange County Community College *A*
State University of New York
College of Agriculture and
Technology at Morrisville *A*
College of Technology at
Alfred *A, B*
College of Technology at Delhi *A*
Farmingdale *A*
Suffolk County Community College *A*

North Carolina

Cape Fear Community College *A*
Catawba Valley Community College *A*
Central Carolina Community College *A*
Central Piedmont Community College *A*
Coastal Carolina Community College *A*
Durham Technical Community
College *C, A*
Forsyth Technical Community College *A*
Gaston College *A*
Nash Community College *A*
Pitt Community College *A*
Sandhills Community College *A*
Wake Technical Community
College *C, A*
Wilkes Community College *C, A*

North Dakota

North Dakota State College of Science *A*

Ohio

Cincinnati State Technical and
Community College *A*
Columbus State Community College *A*
Cuyahoga Community College
Eastern Campus *A*
Metropolitan Campus *A*
Lakeland Community College *C*
Owens Community College
Findlay Campus *A*
Toledo *A*
Sinclair Community College *A*
Stark State College of Technology *A*
Technology Education College *A*

Oklahoma

Northeastern Oklahoma Agricultural and
Mechanical College *C, A*

Oklahoma State University
Oklahoma City *A*

Oregon

Mount Hood Community College *C, A*

Pennsylvania

Cambria County Area Community
College *A*
Community College of Philadelphia *A*
Delaware County Community College *A*
Harrisburg Area Community
College *C, A*
Northampton County Area Community
College *A*
Penn State
Fayette *A*
Worthington Scranton *A*
Pennsylvania College of Technology *A*
Pennsylvania Institute of Technology *A*

South Carolina

Midlands Technical College *C, A*
Spartanburg Technical College *A*
Trident Technical College *C, A*

South Dakota

Southeast Technical Institute *A*

Tennessee

Southwest Tennessee Community
College *A*

Texas

Del Mar College *A*
Midland College *A*
Tarrant County College *C, A*
Texas Tech University *B*
University of Houston *B*

Vermont

Vermont Technical College *A, B*

Virginia

J. Sargeant Reynolds Community
College *C, A*
Norfolk State University *A*
Virginia Western Community
College *C, A*

Washington

Clover Park Technical College *A*
Lake Washington Technical College *C, A*
Spokane Community College *A*
Spokane Falls Community College *C, A*

West Virginia

Bluefield State College *A, B*
Fairmont State College *A, B*

Wisconsin

Waukesha County Technical College *A*
Wisconsin Indianhead Technical
College *A*

Architectural history/ criticism

Georgia

Savannah College of Art and
Design *B, M*

Kansas

University of Kansas *B*

New York

Syracuse University *B*

Ohio

Kent State University *C*

Rhode Island

Brown University *B, M, D*

Virginia

University of Virginia *B, M, D*

Architectural technology

Florida

University of Miami *M*

Illinois

Rend Lake College *C, A*

Iowa

Des Moines Area Community
College *C, A*

Massachusetts

Benjamin Franklin Institute of
Technology *C, A*
Springfield Technical Community
College *C*

Michigan

Grand Rapids Community College *A*

New York

New York Institute of Technology *B*
State University of New York
College of Agriculture and
Technology at Morrisville *A*

North Carolina

College of the Albemarle *C, A*
Nash Community College *A*
Roanoke-Chowan Community College *A*
Sandhills Community College *A*

North Dakota

North Dakota State College of Science *A*

Ohio

Sinclair Community College *A*

Texas

North Harris Montgomery Community
College District *C, A*

West Virginia

Bluefield State College *A*

Architecture

Alabama

Auburn University *B*
Tuskegee University *B*

Arizona

Arizona State University *B, M, D*
Pima Community College *C*
University of Arizona *B, M*

Arkansas

University of Arkansas *B*

California

Academy of Art College *M*
California Polytechnic State University:
San Luis Obispo *B, M*
California State Polytechnic University:
Pomona *B, M*
Chabot College *A*
Los Angeles Harbor College *A*
Los Angeles Pierce College *C, A*
Los Angeles Trade and Technical
College *C, A*
Riverside Community College *C, A*
Southern California Institute of
Architecture *B, M*
University of California
Berkeley *B, M, D*
Los Angeles *M, D*
University of Southern California *B, M*
Woodbury University *B*
Yuba Community College District *C*

Colorado

University of Colorado
Denver *M*

Connecticut

Connecticut College *B*
Yale University *B, M*

District of Columbia
Catholic University of America *B, M*
Howard University *B*
University of the District of Columbia *B*

Florida
Broward Community College *A*
Florida Agricultural and Mechanical
University *B, M*
Florida Atlantic University *B*
Florida International University *B, M*
Indian River Community College *A*
Santa Fe Community College *A*
Seminole Community College *A*
University of Florida *B, M, D*
University of Miami *B, M*
University of South Florida *M*

Georgia
Georgia Institute of Technology *B, M, D*
Morehouse College *B*
Savannah College of Art and
Design *B, M*
Southern Polytechnic State University *B*

Hawaii
University of Hawaii
Manoa *D*

Idaho
University of Idaho *B, M*

Illinois
Illinois Institute of Technology *B, M, D*
Lincoln Land Community College *A*
Southern Illinois University
Carbondale *B*
Triton College *A*
University of Illinois
Chicago *M*
Urbana-Champaign *B, M, D*

Indiana
Ball State University *B, M*
Goshen College *B*
University of Notre Dame *B, M*

Iowa
Iowa State University *B, M*

Kansas
Central Christian College *A*
Kansas State University *B, M*
University of Kansas *B, M*

Kentucky
University of Kentucky *B*

Louisiana
Louisiana State University and
Agricultural and Mechanical
College *B, M*
Louisiana Tech University *B*
Southern University and Agricultural and
Mechanical College *B*
Tulane University *B*
University of Louisiana at Lafayette *M*

Maine
University of Maine
Augusta *A, B*

Maryland
Howard Community College *A*
Morgan State University *M*
University of Maryland
College Park *B, M*

Massachusetts
Boston Architectural Center *B, M*
Massachusetts Institute of
Technology *B, M, D*
Northeastern University *B, M*
Wellesley College *B*
Wentworth Institute of Technology *B*

Michigan
Andrews University *B*
Eastern Michigan University *B*
Lawrence Technological University *B, M*

University of Michigan *B, M, D*
Western Michigan University *B*

Minnesota
Northwest Technical Institute *A*
University of Minnesota
Twin Cities *B, M*

Mississippi
Mississippi State University *B, M*

Missouri
Drury University *B*
Washington University in St. Louis *B, M*

Montana
Montana State University
Bozeman *M*

Nebraska
University of Nebraska
Lincoln *B, M*

Nevada
Truckee Meadows Community
College *A*
University of Nevada
Las Vegas *B, M*

New Jersey
Brookdale Community College *A*
New Jersey Institute of Technology *B, M*
Princeton University *B, M, D*

New Mexico
University of New Mexico *B, M*

New York
Barnard College *B*
City University of New York
City College *B*
Columbia University
Columbia College *B*
Cooper Union for the Advancement of
Science and Art *B*
Cornell University *B, M*
Hobart and William Smith Colleges *B*
New York Institute of
Technology *A, B, M*
Parsons School of Design *B, M*
Pratt Institute *B, M*
Rensselaer Polytechnic Institute *B, M*
State University of New York
Buffalo *B, M*
Syracuse University *B, M*

North Carolina
Central Carolina Community College *A*
Central Piedmont Community
College *C, A*
Guilford Technical Community
College *C, A*
Nash Community College *A*
North Carolina State University *B, M*
University of North Carolina
Charlotte *B, M*
Wake Technical Community
College *C, A*

North Dakota
North Dakota State University *B*

Ohio
Kent State University *B, M*
Miami University
Oxford Campus *M*
Ohio State University
Columbus Campus *B, M*
University of Cincinnati *B, M*

Oklahoma
Oklahoma State University *B, M*
Oklahoma State University
Oklahoma City *A*
University of Oklahoma *B, M*

Oregon
Chemeketa Community College *A*
Portland State University *B*
University of Oregon *B, M*

Pennsylvania
Carnegie Mellon University *B, M, D*
Drexel University *B*
Harrisburg Area Community College *A*
Lehigh University *B*
Penn State
University Park *B, M*
Philadelphia University *B*
Temple University *B*
University of Pennsylvania *C, B, M, D*

Puerto Rico
Inter American University of Puerto Rico
San German Campus *B*
Universidad Politecnica de Puerto
Rico *B*
University of Puerto Rico
Rio Piedras Campus *M*

Rhode Island
Rhode Island School of Design *B, M*
Roger Williams University *B*

South Carolina
Clemson University *B, M*

Tennessee
Tennessee State University *B*
University of Memphis *B*
University of Tennessee
Knoxville *B, M*

Texas
Baylor University *B*
Brazosport College *A*
El Paso Community College *A*
Laredo Community College *A*
Palo Alto College *A*
Prairie View A&M University *B, M*
Rice University *B, M, D*
Texas A&M University *M, D*
Texas Tech University *B, M*
University of Houston *B, M*
University of Texas
Arlington *B, M*
Austin *B, M*
San Antonio *B, M*

Utah
University of Utah *B, M*

Vermont
Bennington College *B*
Norwich University *M*

Virginia
Hampton University *B*
University of Virginia *B, M*
Virginia Polytechnic Institute and State
University *B, M*

Washington
University of Washington *B, M*
Washington State University *B, M*

Wisconsin
Milwaukee Area Technical College *A*
University of Wisconsin
Milwaukee *B, M, D*

Architecture/related programs

Alabama
Northeast Alabama Community
College *A*

Arizona
High-Tech Institute *A*
Phoenix College *C*
Yavapai College *C, A*

California
East Los Angeles College *A*
Glendale Community College *C, A*
Golden West College *C, A*
Los Angeles Harbor College *A*

Los Angeles Trade and Technical
College *C, A*
MiraCosta College *C, A*
Modesto Junior College *C, A*
San Diego Mesa College *C, A*
San Joaquin Delta College *C*
Santa Rosa Junior College *C*
Silicon Valley College
Emeryville *C, A*
University of California
Irvine *B, M, D*
University of San Francisco *B*
Yuba Community College District *C*

Connecticut
Norwalk Community College *A*
Three Rivers Community College *C, A*

Florida
Art Institute
of Fort Lauderdale *C, B*
Broward Community College *A*
Miami-Dade Community College *C, A*
Okaloosa-Walton Community
College *C, A*
Polk Community College *A*
South Florida Community College *A*
Tallahassee Community College *A*
University of Miami *M*

Georgia
Floyd College *A*
Georgia Institute of Technology *B, M*

Illinois
City Colleges of Chicago
Wright College *C, A*
Illinois Eastern Community Colleges
Lincoln Trail College *A*
Kishwaukee College *A*
Oakton Community College *C, A*
University of Illinois
Chicago *B*
William Rainey Harper College *A*

Indiana
Ball State University *B*
Vincennes University *A*

Iowa
Cornell College *B*
Des Moines Area Community
College *C, A*

Kansas
Central Christian College *A*
Garden City Community College *A*
Independence Community College *C, A*
Seward County Community College *A*

Kentucky
Louisville Technical Institute *A*
Spencerian College: Lexington *C, A*

Louisiana
Tulane University *M*
University of Louisiana at Lafayette *B*

Maine
Central Maine Technical College *A*

Massachusetts
Benjamin Franklin Institute of
Technology *C, A*
Smith College *B*
Wentworth Institute of Technology *B*

Michigan
Baker College
of Owosso *A*
Ferris State University *A*
Lawrence Technological University *B*
Monroe County Community
College *C, A*
Northern Michigan University *A*
St. Clair County Community College *A*
Washtenaw Community College *A*

Minnesota
Hennepin Technical College *C, A*

Minneapolis Community and Technical
College *C*
Northland Community & Technical
College *C, A*
South Central Technical College *A*

Missouri
Washington University in St. Louis *B, M*

Nebraska
Northeast Community College *A*
Vatterott College *A*

New Hampshire
Keene State College *B*
University of New Hampshire *A*

New Jersey
Essex County College *A*

New York
Cornell University *B*
Genesee Community College *A*
Island Drafting and Technical Institute *A*
New York Institute of Technology *A, B*
Onondaga Community College *A*
State University of New York
Buffalo *B, M*
College of Agriculture and
Technology at Morrisville *A*
College of Technology at
Alfred *A, B*
Maritime College *B*

North Carolina
Durham Technical Community
College *C, A*
Fayetteville Technical Community
College *A*
Guilford Technical Community
College *C, A*
Wake Technical Community
College *C, A*

Ohio
Central Ohio Technical College *C, A*
Columbus State Community College *A*
Stark State College of Technology *A*

Oklahoma
Oklahoma State University *B, M*
Oklahoma State University
Oklahoma City *C, A*
Platt College
Tulsa *C*

Pennsylvania
Lehigh University *B*
Philadelphia University *B*

Puerto Rico
Turabo University *C*

South Dakota
Southeast Technical Institute *A*

Texas
El Paso Community College *A*

Utah
Salt Lake Community College *A*

Vermont
Bennington College *M*
Norwich University *B*

Washington
Washington State University *B*

Wisconsin
Milwaukee Area Technical College *A*

Area studies

Alaska
University of Alaska
Fairbanks *B, M*

Arizona
Northern Arizona University *B*

Prescott College *B, M*

Arkansas
Arkansas State University *D*

California
Azusa Pacific University *B*
Biola University *B, M, D*
California State University
Chico *B*
Fullerton *B*
Sacramento *B*
Chabot College *A*
Grossmont Community College *A*
Mount San Jacinto College *C, A*
Pitzer College *B*
Pomona College *B*
San Francisco State University *M*
Santa Barbara City College *A*
University of California
Irvine *B, M, D*
Santa Cruz *B*
Whittier College *B*

Colorado
United States Air Force Academy *B*
University of Colorado
Boulder *B*

Connecticut
Trinity College *B*
University of Connecticut *M*

Delaware
University of Delaware *M*

District of Columbia
Gallaudet University *C, B, M*

Florida
Eckerd College *B*
Polk Community College *A*
Schiller International University *B*
South Florida Community College *A*
University of West Florida *B*

Georgia
Wesleyan College *B*

Hawaii
Hawaii Pacific University *B*
University of Hawaii
Manoa *B*

Idaho
Boise State University *B*

Illinois
Columbia College Chicago *B*
Lake Forest College *B*
Loyola University of Chicago *C*
Northeastern Illinois University *B, M*

Indiana
Earlham College *B*
Indiana University
Bloomington *M, D*
Indiana University-Purdue University
Fort Wayne *C*
Manchester College *B*
Valparaiso University *M*

Iowa
Cornell College *B*

Kansas
Wichita State University *B*

Louisiana
Louisiana State University and
Agricultural and Mechanical
College *A*

Maine
University of New England *B*
University of Southern Maine *B, M*

Maryland
Baltimore Hebrew University *A, B, M, D*
Towson University *B*
Washington College *B*

Massachusetts
Amherst College *B*
Boston College *B*
Boston University *B, M*
Brandeis University *B, M, D*
Hampshire College *B*
Harvard College *B*
Hebrew College *B, M*
Mount Holyoke College *B*
Northeastern University *B*
Simon's Rock College of Bard *B*
Tufts University *M*

Minnesota
Bethel College *B*
Hamline University *B*
Metropolitan State University *B*
Minnesota State University
Mankato *B*

Mississippi
University of Mississippi *B*

Missouri
University of Missouri
Columbia *B*
Washington University in St. Louis *B*

New Mexico
New Mexico Highlands University *M*

New York
Bard College *B*
Barnard College *B*
City University of New York
Hunter College *B*
Columbia University
Columbia College *B*
Cornell University *B*
Eugene Lang College/New School
University *B*
Iona College *B*
Pratt Institute *B*
St. John's University *M*
Sarah Lawrence College *B*
Skidmore College *B*
State University of New York
Empire State College *A, B*

North Carolina
Appalachian State University *M*
East Carolina University *M*
University of North Carolina
Greensboro *B*

Ohio
Antioch College *B*
Kent State University *B*
University of Cincinnati
Raymond Walters College *C*
University of Dayton *B*
Youngstown State University *B*

Oklahoma
University of Oklahoma *B*

Oregon
Central Oregon Community College *A*
Northwest Christian College *B*
Pacific University *B*

Pennsylvania
Bryn Mawr College *B*
Chatham College *B*
Dickinson College *B*
Gettysburg College *B*
Immaculata University *C, D*
Penn State
University Park *C*
Seton Hill University *B*
Swarthmore College *B*
University of Pennsylvania *B, M*

Rhode Island
Brown University *B*

South Carolina
Columbia International University *B*
Wofford College *B*

South Dakota
Sinte Gleska University *B*
University of South Dakota *B*

Tennessee
Maryville College *B*

Texas
University of Texas
Austin *B*
San Antonio *D*

Vermont
Burlington College *B*
Goddard College *B, M*
Marlboro College *B*
University of Vermont *B*

Virginia
Emory & Henry College *B*
George Mason University *D*
University of Richmond *B*

Washington
Seattle University *B*
University of Washington *A*
Washington State University *B*

Wisconsin
St. Norbert College *B*

Art

Alabama
Alabama Agricultural and Mechanical
University *B*
Alabama State University *B, T*
Athens State University *B*
Auburn University at Montgomery *B*
Birmingham-Southern College *B, T*
Huntingdon College *B, T*
Jacksonville State University *B*
James H. Faulkner State Community
College *A*
Judson College *B*
Northeast Alabama Community
College *A*
Northwest-Shoals Community College *A*
Samford University *B*
Stillman College *B*
Troy State University *B*
University of Alabama
Huntsville *B*
University of Mobile *B, T*
University of Montevallo *B, T*
University of South Alabama *B*
Wallace State Community College at
Hanceville *A*

Alaska
University of Alaska
Anchorage *B*
Fairbanks *B, M*
Southeast *B*

Arizona
Arizona State University *M*
Central Arizona College *A*
Eastern Arizona College *A*
Northern Arizona University *B*
Phoenix College *A*
Pima Community College *A*
South Mountain Community College *A*
University of Arizona *M*

Arkansas
Arkansas State University *B, M*
Arkansas Tech University *B*
Black River Technical College *A*
Harding University *B*
Henderson State University *B*
Hendrix College *B*
Lyon College *B*
Southern Arkansas University *B*
University of Arkansas *B, M*

University of Arkansas
  Little Rock *B, M*
  Monticello *B*
  Pine Bluff *B*
University of Central Arkansas *B*
University of the Ozarks *B*

California
Art Center College of Design *B*
Azusa Pacific University *B*
Cabrillo College *A*
California Baptist University *B*
California Institute of the Arts *C, B, M*
California State Polytechnic University:
  Pomona *B*
California State University
  Bakersfield *B*
  Chico *B, M*
  Fresno *B, M*
  Fullerton *B*
  Hayward *B*
  Long Beach *B, M*
  Los Angeles *B*
  Monterey Bay *B*
  Northridge *B, M*
  Sacramento *B, M*
  San Bernardino *B*
  Stanislaus *B*
Cerritos Community College *A*
Cerro Coso Community College *A*
Chabot College *A*
Chapman University *B*
Citrus College *A*
Claremont McKenna College *B*
College of the Sequoias *A*
Columbia College *A*
Concordia University *B*
Copper Mountain College *A*
De Anza College *A*
East Los Angeles College *A*
Foothill College *C, A*
Gavilan Community College *A*
Golden West College *A*
Humboldt State University *B*
Imperial Valley College *A*
Irvine Valley College *A*
La Sierra University *B*
Laney College *A*
Long Beach City College *A*
Los Angeles Harbor College *A*
Los Angeles Southwest College *A*
Loyola Marymount University *B*
Mills College *B*
MiraCosta College *A*
Modesto Junior College *A*
Monterey Peninsula College *A*
Mount San Jacinto College *A*
Occidental College *B*
Orange Coast College *A*
Otis College of Art and Design *B, M*
Pacific Union College *B*
Palomar College *C, A*
Pepperdine University *B*
Pitzer College *B*
Point Loma Nazarene University *B*
Pomona College *B*
Reedley College *A*
St. Mary's College of California *B*
San Diego Mesa College *C, A*
San Diego State University *B, M*
San Francisco State University *B*
San Jose State University *M*
Santa Barbara City College *A*
Santa Rosa Junior College *C, A*
Shasta College *A*
Sierra College *C, A*
Southwestern College *A*
Stanford University *B, M, D*
Taft College *C, A*
University of California
  Irvine *B, M*
  Los Angeles *B, M*
  Santa Barbara *B*
  Santa Cruz *B*
University of La Verne *B*
University of Redlands *B*

University of San Diego *B*
University of San Francisco *B*
University of Southern California *B*
University of the Pacific *B*
Victor Valley College *A*
Vista Community College *A*
West Valley College *A*
Whittier College *B*
Yuba Community College District *A*

Colorado
Colorado Mountain College
  Alpine Campus *A*
  Spring Valley Campus *A*
  Timberline Campus *A*
Colorado State University *B*
Colorado State University
  Pueblo *B, T*
Fort Lewis College *B*
Metropolitan State College of Denver *B*
Morgan Community College *A*
Red Rocks Community College *A*
University of Denver *B*
University of Northern Colorado *B, M, T*

Connecticut
Albertus Magnus College *B*
Central Connecticut State University *B*
Eastern Connecticut State University *B*
Naugatuck Valley Community College *A*
Norwalk Community College *A*
Sacred Heart University *B*
Southern Connecticut State
  University *B, M*
Trinity College *B*
University of Connecticut *B*
University of Hartford *M*
University of New Haven *B*
Western Connecticut State University *B*
Yale University *B*

Delaware
Delaware State University *B*
University of Delaware *B*

District of Columbia
American University *B*
Catholic University of America *B, M, T*
Corcoran College of Art and Design *B*
Georgetown University *B*
Howard University *B, M*

Florida
Barry University *B*
Broward Community College *A*
Eckerd College *B*
Florida Atlantic University *B*
Florida Southern College *B*
Florida State University *B, M*
Gulf Coast Community College *A*
Hillsborough Community College *A*
Indian River Community College *A*
Jacksonville University *B, M*
New College of Florida *B*
Okaloosa-Walton Community College *A*
Palm Beach Atlantic University *B, T*
Pensacola Junior College *A*
Polk Community College *A*
Rollins College *B*
South Florida Community College *A*
Stetson University *B*
University of Central Florida *B*
University of Miami *B, M*
University of North Florida *B*
University of South Florida *B, M*
University of Tampa *B*
University of West Florida *B*

Georgia
Agnes Scott College *B*
Armstrong Atlantic State University *B*
Atlanta College of Art *B*
Atlanta Metropolitan College *A*
Berry College *B*
Brenau University *B*
Clark Atlanta University *B*
Clayton College and State University *A*

Columbus State University *B*
East Georgia College *A*
Georgia College and State University *B*
Georgia Perimeter College *A*
Georgia Southern University *B*
Georgia Southwestern State University *B*
Gordon College *A*
LaGrange College *B*
Macon State College *A*
Mercer University *B*
Middle Georgia College *A*
Morris Brown College *B*
North Georgia College & State
  University *B*
Oglethorpe University *B*
Piedmont College *B*
Reinhardt College *A*
State University of West Georgia *B*
University of Georgia *B, M, D*
Young Harris College *A*

Hawaii
Brigham Young University-Hawaii *B*
University of Hawaii
  Hilo *B*
  Manoa *B*

Idaho
Albertson College of Idaho *B*
Boise State University *B, M*
Brigham Young University - Idaho *B*
College of Southern Idaho *A*
Idaho State University *A, B, M*
University of Idaho *B*

Illinois
Augustana College *B*
Black Hawk College
  East Campus *A*
Blackburn College *B, T*
Bradley University *B*
Chicago State University *B*
City Colleges of Chicago
  Harold Washington College *A*
College of DuPage *A*
College of Lake County *A*
Columbia College Chicago *B*
Concordia University *B, T*
Dominican University *B*
Eastern Illinois University *B, M, T*
Elgin Community College *A*
Elmhurst College *B, T*
Eureka College *B*
Governors State University *B, M*
Greenville College *B, T*
Illinois College *B*
Illinois Institute of Art *B*
Illinois State University *B, M, T*
Illinois Valley Community College *A*
Illinois Wesleyan University *B*
John A. Logan College *A*
John Wood Community College *A*
Joliet Junior College *A*
Judson College *B*
Kankakee Community College *A*
Kishwaukee College *A*
Knox College *B*
Lewis University *B, T*
Lincoln College *A*
Loyola University of Chicago *B*
MacMurray College *B*
McHenry County College *A*
McKendree College *B, T*
Monmouth College *B, T*
North Central College *B*
North Park University *B*
Northeastern Illinois University *B*
Northern Illinois University *B, M*
Northwestern University *B, M*
Olivet Nazarene University *B, T*
Parkland College *A*
Rend Lake College *A*
Richland Community College *A*
Rockford College *B*
Sauk Valley Community College *A*

South Suburban College of Cook
  County *C*
Southern Illinois University
  Carbondale *C, B*
Southern Illinois University
  Edwardsville *B, T*
Southwestern Illinois College *A*
Spoon River College *A*
Springfield College in Illinois *A*
Trinity Christian College *B*
Trinity International University *M*
Triton College *A*
University of Illinois
  Springfield *B*
Waubonsee Community College *A*
Western Illinois University *B*
Wheaton College *B*
William Rainey Harper College *A*

Indiana
Ball State University *B, M*
Bethel College *B*
Earlham College *B*
Goshen College *B*
Grace College *B*
Huntington College *B*
Indiana State University *B, M, T*
Indiana University
  Northwest *B*
  South Bend *B*
  Southeast *B*
Manchester College *A, B, T*
Marian College *A, B, T*
Oakland City University *B*
Purdue University *B, M*
St. Joseph's College *B*
Saint Mary's College *B*
St. Mary-of-the-Woods College *B*
Taylor University *B*
University of Evansville *B*
University of Indianapolis *B, M*
University of St. Francis *B*
University of Southern Indiana *B*
Valparaiso University *B*
Vincennes University *A*
Wabash College *B*

Iowa
Briar Cliff University *B*
Buena Vista University *B, T*
Central College *B, T*
Clarke College *A, B, T*
Coe College *B*
Cornell College *B, T*
Dordt College *B*
Drake University *B*
Ellsworth Community College *A*
Grand View College *B*
Grinnell College *B*
Iowa State University *B*
Luther College *B*
Maharishi University of Management *B*
Morningside College *B*
Mount Mercy College *B*
North Iowa Area Community College *A*
Northwestern College *B, T*
Simpson College *B*
University of Iowa *B, M, T*
University of Northern Iowa *B, M*
Upper Iowa University *B*
Waldorf College *A, B*
Wartburg College *B, T*

Kansas
Allen County Community College *A*
Barton County Community College *A*
Bethany College *B, T*
Bethel College *B*
Butler County Community College *A*
Central Christian College *A, B*
Dodge City Community College *A*
Emporia State University *B*
Fort Hays State University *B*
Friends University *B*
Garden City Community College *A*
Independence Community College *A*

Kansas State University *B, M*
McPherson College *B, T*
Newman University *B*
Ottawa University *B, T*
Pittsburg State University *B, M, T*
St. Mary College *B*
Seward County Community College *A*
Sterling College *B*
Washburn University of Topeka *B*
Wichita State University *B, M, T*

Kentucky

Bellarmine University *B, T*
Berea College *B, T*
Brescia University *B*
Campbellsville University *B*
Centre College *B*
Cumberland College *B, T*
Kentucky Wesleyan College *B, T*
Lindsey Wilson College *B*
Murray State University *B, M*
Pikeville College *B*

Louisiana

Centenary College of Louisiana *B, T*
Delgado Community College *A*
Dillard University *B*
Grambling State University *B*
Louisiana State University
    Shreveport *B*
Louisiana Tech University *B, M*
Loyola University New Orleans *B*
McNeese State University *B*
Nicholls State University *B*
Northwestern State University *B, M*
Southeastern Louisiana University *B*
Tulane University *M*
University of Louisiana at Lafayette *B*
University of Louisiana at Monroe *B*
Xavier University of Louisiana *B*

Maine

Bates College *B*
Colby College *B*
Maine College of Art *B*
University of Maine
    Augusta *A, B*
    Farmington *B*
    Presque Isle *A, B*
University of Southern Maine *B*

Maryland

Allegany College *A*
College of Notre Dame of Maryland *B*
College of Southern Maryland *A*
Frederick Community College *A*
Goucher College *B*
Hood College *B*
Howard Community College *A*
Loyola College in Maryland *B*
McDaniel College *B*
St. Mary's College of Maryland *B*
Towson University *B*
University of Maryland
    Baltimore County *B*
Washington College *B*

Massachusetts

Anna Maria College *B*
Art Institute of Boston at Lesley
    University *M*
Berkshire Community College *A*
Brandeis University *B*
Bridgewater State College *B*
Clark University *B*
Framingham State College *M*
Gordon College *B*
Hampshire College *B*
Harvard College *B*
Lesley University *B, M*
Massachusetts Bay Community
    College *C*
Montserrat College of Art *B*
Mount Holyoke College *B*
Mount Ida College *A, B*
Mount Wachusett Community College *A*
Northeastern University *A, B*

Regis College *B*
School of the Museum of Fine Arts *B, M*
Simon's Rock College of Bard *B*
Smith College *B, M*
Springfield College *B*
University of Massachusetts
    Boston *B*
Westfield State College *B*

Michigan

Adrian College *A, B, T*
Alma College *B, T*
Andrews University *B*
Calvin College *B, T*
Central Michigan University *B, M*
Concordia University *B, T*
Eastern Michigan University *B, M, T*
Ferris State University *B*
Finlandia University *B*
Gogebic Community College *A*
Grand Valley State University *B*
Hillsdale College *B*
Kalamazoo College *B, T*
Kellogg Community College *C, A*
Lansing Community College *A*
Madonna University *C, B, T*
Marygrove College *B, T*
Michigan State University *B, M*
Northern Michigan University *B, T*
Northwestern Michigan College *A*
Oakland Community College *A*
Saginaw Valley State University *B*
Siena Heights University *A, B*
Spring Arbor University *B*
University of Michigan *B, M*
Wayne State University *B, M*
Western Michigan University *B, M*

Minnesota

Augsburg College *B*
Bemidji State University *B*
Bethel College *B*
College of St. Benedict *B*
Concordia College: Moorhead *B*
Concordia University: St. Paul *B*
Gustavus Adolphus College *B*
Minnesota State University
    Mankato *B, M, T*
Northland Community & Technical
    College *A*
Ridgewater College: A Community and
    Technical College *A*
St. Cloud State University *B, M*
St. John's University *B*
St. Olaf College *B*
Southwest State University *B, T*
University of Minnesota
    Duluth *B, M*
    Twin Cities *M, D*
Winona State University *B*

Mississippi

Itawamba Community College *A*
Mississippi College *B, M, T*

Missouri

Central Missouri State University *B, M*
College of the Ozarks *B*
Columbia College *B*
Crowder College *A*
Culver-Stockton College *B, T*
Drury University *B, T*
East Central College *A*
Fontbonne College *B, M, T*
Hannibal-LaGrange College *B*
Lincoln University *B*
Lindenwood University *M*
Missouri Valley College *B*
Missouri Western State College *B*
Northwest Missouri State University *B*
Southeast Missouri State
    University *B, M*
Southwest Baptist University *B*
Southwest Missouri State University *B*
Truman State University *B*

University of Missouri
    Columbia *B, M*
    Kansas City *B, M*
Washington University in St. Louis *B*
Webster University *B, M*
William Jewell College *B*
William Woods University *B, T*

Montana

Carroll College *A*
Montana State University
    Billings *B*
    Bozeman *B*
Rocky Mountain College *B*
University of Great Falls *B*
University of Montana-Missoula *B, M*
University of Montana: Western *B, T*

Nebraska

Bellevue University *B*
Chadron State College *B*
Creighton University *B*
Dana College *B*
Doane College *B*
Hastings College *B, T*
Midland Lutheran College *B, T*
Nebraska Wesleyan University *B*
Northeast Community College *A*
Peru State College *B*
Union College *A*
University of Nebraska
    Kearney *B, M, T*
    Lincoln *B*
    Omaha *B*
Wayne State College *B, M, T*
Western Nebraska Community
    College *A*
York College *A, T*

Nevada

Community College of Southern
    Nevada *A*
Great Basin College *A*
University of Nevada
    Las Vegas *B, M*
    Reno *B*

New Hampshire

Franklin Pierce College *B*
Keene State College *B*
New England College *B*
Plymouth State College *B*
St. Anselm College *B*

New Jersey

Brookdale Community College *A*
Caldwell College *B*
The College of New Jersey *B*
College of St. Elizabeth *B, T*
Drew University *B*
Essex County College *A*
Fairleigh Dickinson University
    College at Florham *B*
Felician College *B*
Georgian Court College *B, T*
Gloucester County College *A*
Kean University *B*
Monmouth University *B*
Montclair State University *B, M, T*
New Jersey City University *B, T*
Ocean County College *A*
Ramapo College of New Jersey *B*
Richard Stockton College of New
    Jersey *B*
Rider University *B*
Rowan University *B, T*
Rutgers, The State University of New
    Jersey
        Camden Regional Campus *B, T*
        New Brunswick Regional
            Campus *B*
        Newark Regional Campus *B, T*
Sussex County Community College *A*
Thomas Edison State College *B*
William Paterson University of New
    Jersey *B*

New Mexico

Eastern New Mexico University *A, B*
New Mexico State University *B, M*
New Mexico State University
    Alamogordo *A*
San Juan College *A*
Santa Fe Community College *A*
Southwestern Indian Polytechnic
    Institute *C*
University of New Mexico *B, M*

New York

Adirondack Community College *A*
Bard College *B, M, D*
Cayuga County Community College *A*
City University of New York
    Brooklyn College *M*
    City College *B*
    College of Staten Island *B*
    Kingsborough Community
        College *A*
    Queensborough Community
        College *A*
Colgate University *B*
Daemen College *B*
Dowling College *B, T*
Elmira College *B*
Fashion Institute of Technology *A*
Fordham University *B*
Fulton-Montgomery Community
    College *A*
Hartwick College *B*
Houghton College *B*
Ithaca College *B*
Long Island University
    C. W. Post Campus *B, M*
    Southampton College *B*
Marist College *B*
Mohawk Valley Community College *A*
Molloy College *B*
Nazareth College of Rochester *B, T*
Onondaga Community College *A*
Pace University *B*
Pace University:
    Pleasantville/Briarcliff *B*
Parsons School of Design *C, A, B, T*
Pratt Institute *B, M*
St. John's University *B*
Sarah Lawrence College *B*
School of Visual Arts *B, M*
State University of New York
    Albany *B, M*
    Binghamton *B*
    Buffalo *M*
    College at Brockport *B*
    College at Fredonia *B*
    College at Plattsburgh *B*
    College at Potsdam *B*
    New Paltz *B*
    Oswego *B*
Vassar College *B*
Wells College *B*
Westchester Community College *A*

North Carolina

Appalachian State University *B*
Brevard College *A, B*
Caldwell Community College and
    Technical Institute *A*
College of the Albemarle *A*
Davidson College *B*
East Carolina University *B, M*
Elizabeth City State University *B*
Elon University *B*
Guilford College *B*
High Point University *B*
Louisburg College *A*
Mars Hill College *B, T*
Methodist College *B*
North Carolina Agricultural and
    Technical State University *B, T*
North Carolina Central University *B*
St. Andrews Presbyterian College *B*
St. Augustine's College *B*
Sandhills Community College *A*
Southeastern Community College *A*

University of North Carolina
   Asheville *B, T*
   Charlotte *B*
   Greensboro *B, M, T*
Warren Wilson College *B*
Western Carolina University *B*
Wingate University *B*
Winston-Salem State University *B*

North Dakota
Dickinson State University *B, T*
Minot State University *B*
Minot State University: Bottineau
   Campus *A*
North Dakota State University *B*
University of North Dakota *B, M*
Valley City State University *B*

Ohio
Ashland University *A*
Baldwin-Wallace College *B*
Bluffton College *B*
Bowling Green State University *B, M*
Central State University *B*
Cleveland State University *B, T*
College of Mount St. Joseph *A, B, T*
Defiance College *B, T*
Kent State University
   Stark Campus *B*
Kenyon College *B*
Lourdes College *A, B*
Malone College *B*
Miami University
   Oxford Campus *B, M, T*
Mount Union College *B*
Mount Vernon Nazarene University *B*
Muskingum College *B*
Ohio Dominican College *B, T*
Ohio Northern University *B*
Ohio State University
   Columbus Campus *B, M*
Ohio University *B, M*
Otterbein College *B*
University of Findlay *B*
University of Rio Grande *A, B, T*
University of Toledo *A, B*
Virginia Marti College of Art and
   Design *A*
Wilmington College *B*
Wittenberg University *B*
Wright State University *B*
Youngstown State University *B*

Oklahoma
Bacone College *A*
Cameron University *B*
Carl Albert State College *A*
East Central University *B, T*
Langston University *B*
Northeastern Oklahoma Agricultural and
   Mechanical College *A*
Northeastern State University *B*
Northern Oklahoma College *A*
Oklahoma Baptist University *B, T*
Oklahoma Christian University of
   Science and Arts *B*
Oklahoma City University *B*
Oklahoma Panhandle State University *B*
Oklahoma State University *B*
Oral Roberts University *B*
Redlands Community College *A*
Rose State College *A*
Seminole State College *A*
Southeastern Oklahoma State
   University *B*
University of Central Oklahoma *B*
University of Oklahoma *M*
University of Science and Arts of
   Oklahoma *B, T*
University of Tulsa *B, M*
Western Oklahoma State College *A*

Oregon
Chemeketa Community College *A*
George Fox University *B*
Lewis & Clark College *B*
Linfield College *B*

Linn-Benton Community College *A*
Marylhurst University *C, B*
Oregon State University *B*
Pacific University *B*
Portland State University *B*
Southern Oregon University *B, T*
University of Oregon *B*
Western Oregon University *B*
Willamette University *B*

Pennsylvania
Allegheny College *B*
Bucknell University *B*
Carlow College *B*
Carnegie Mellon University *B, M*
Cedar Crest College *B*
Cheyney University of Pennsylvania *B*
Community College of Allegheny
   County *A*
Community College of Philadelphia *A*
Edinboro University of Pennsylvania *M*
Elizabethtown College *B*
Gettysburg College *B*
Harrisburg Area Community College *A*
Holy Family University *B*
Indiana University of Pennsylvania *B*
Keystone College *A*
Kutztown University of
   Pennsylvania *B, M, T*
Lehigh Carbon Community College *C*
Lehigh University *B*
Lock Haven University of
   Pennsylvania *B*
Lycoming College *B*
Marywood University *C*
Mercyhurst College *B*
Millersville University of
   Pennsylvania *B, T*
Montgomery County Community
   College *A*
Moravian College *B, T*
Penn State
   Abington *B*
   Altoona *B*
   Beaver *B*
   Berks *B*
   Delaware County *B*
   Dubois *B*
   Fayette *B*
   Hazleton *B*
   Lehigh Valley *B*
   McKeesport *B*
   Mont Alto *B*
   New Kensington *B*
   Shenango *B*
   University Park *B, M*
   Wilkes-Barre *B*
   Worthington Scranton *B*
   York *B*
Shippensburg University of
   Pennsylvania *B*
Slippery Rock University of
   Pennsylvania *B*
Temple University *B*
Thiel College *B*
University of Pennsylvania *A, B, M*
Washington and Jefferson College *A*
Waynesburg College *B*
York College of Pennsylvania *B*

Puerto Rico
University of Puerto Rico
   Mayaguez Campus *B*
   Rio Piedras Campus *B*

Rhode Island
Community College of Rhode Island *A*
Providence College *B*
University of Rhode Island *B*

South Carolina
Anderson College *B, T*
Benedict College *B*
Claflin University *B*
Coker College *B*
Columbia College *B*
Francis Marion University *B*

Furman University *B, T*
Lander University *B*
Newberry College *B*
North Greenville College *A*
Presbyterian College *B*
University of South Carolina
   Lancaster *A*
Winthrop University *B*

South Dakota
Augustana College *B*
Black Hills State University *B*
Dakota Wesleyan University *B*
Northern State University *B*
South Dakota State University *B*
University of Sioux Falls *B*
University of South Dakota *B, M*

Tennessee
Austin Peay State University *B*
Belmont University *B, T*
Carson-Newman College *B, T*
Columbia State Community College *A*
Fisk University *B*
Freed-Hardeman University *B, T*
Jackson State Community College *A*
Lambuth University *B*
Maryville College *B*
Memphis College of Art *B, M*
Middle Tennessee State University *B*
Milligan College *B*
Rhodes College *B*
Roane State Community College *A*
Southern Adventist University *B*
Tennessee Technological University *T*
Union University *B, T*
University of Memphis *B, M*
University of Tennessee
   Chattanooga *B, T*
   Knoxville *B, M*
   Martin *B*
Walters State Community College *A*

Texas
Abilene Christian University *B*
Alvin Community College *A*
Amarillo College *A*
Angelina College *A*
Angelo State University *B, T*
Austin College *B*
Austin Community College *A*
Baylor University *B*
Brazosport College *A*
Central Texas College *A*
Cisco Junior College *A*
Clarendon College *A*
Dallas Baptist University *B*
Del Mar College *A*
El Paso Community College *A*
Galveston College *A*
Grayson County College *A*
Hardin-Simmons University *B*
Hill College *A*
Howard College *A*
Howard Payne University *B, T*
Kilgore College *A*
Lamar University *B*
Laredo Community College *A*
Lon Morris College *A*
Lubbock Christian University *T*
McMurry University *B, T*
Midland College *A*
Midwestern State University *B*
Mountain View College *C, A*
Northeast Texas Community College *A*
Odessa College *A*
Our Lady of the Lake University of San
   Antonio *B*
Palo Alto College *A*
Panola College *A*
Rice University *B*
St. Philip's College *A*
Sam Houston State University *B, M*
Schreiner University *B*
Southwest Texas State University *B, T*
Southwestern University *B, T*

Stephen F. Austin State
   University *B, M, T*
Sul Ross State University *B, M*
Tarleton State University *B*
Temple College *A*
Texas A&M University
   Commerce *B, M*
   Corpus Christi *T*
Texas Christian University *T*
Texas College *B*
Texas Lutheran University *B*
Texas Southern University *B, M*
Texas Tech University *B, M, D*
Texas Wesleyan University *B*
Texas Woman's University *M, T*
Trinity University *B*
Trinity Valley Community College *A*
Tyler Junior College *A*
University of Houston *B*
University of Houston
   Clear Lake *B*
University of Mary Hardin-Baylor *B, T*
University of Texas
   Arlington *B*
   Austin *B*
   El Paso *B, M*
   Pan American *B, T*
   San Antonio *B, M*
   Tyler *B, M*
   of the Permian Basin *B*
University of the Incarnate Word *B*
Wayland Baptist University *B*
West Texas A&M University *B, M*
Western Texas College *A*
Wharton County Junior College *A*

Utah
Brigham Young University *B*
Dixie State College of Utah *A*
Snow College *A*
Southern Utah University *B, T*
University of Utah *B, M*
Utah State University *B, M*
Weber State University *D*
Westminster College *B*

Vermont
Bennington College *B, M, T*
Castleton State College *B*
Green Mountain College *B*
Johnson State College *B*
Marlboro College *B*
St. Michael's College *B*

Virginia
Averett University *B, T*
Bluefield College *B*
Bridgewater College *B*
Eastern Mennonite University *B*
Emory & Henry College *B, T*
Ferrum College *B*
George Mason University *B*
Hampton University *B*
James Madison University *B, M, T*
Longwood University *B, T*
Lynchburg College *B*
Mary Baldwin College *B*
Marymount University *B*
Norfolk State University *B*
Old Dominion University *B*
Radford University *B, M*
Roanoke College *B, T*
University of Virginia *B*
University of Virginia's College at
   Wise *B, T*
Virginia Intermont College *B*
Virginia Polytechnic Institute and State
   University *B*
Virginia Union University *B*
Virginia Wesleyan College *B*

Washington
Central Washington University *B, M*
Cornish College of the Arts *B*
Eastern Washington University *B, M, T*
Everett Community College *A*
Lower Columbia College *A*

North Seattle Community College *C, A*
Olympic College *A*
Pacific Lutheran University *B*
Seattle Pacific University *B*
Seattle University *B*
University of Puget Sound *B, T*
University of Washington *B, M*
Walla Walla College *B*
Washington State University *B, M*
Western Washington University *B, T*
Whitworth College *B, T*

West Virginia
Bethany College *B*
Concord College *B*
Davis and Elkins College *B*
Marshall University *B*
Shepherd College *B*
University of Charleston *B*
West Virginia University *B, M, T*

Wisconsin
Alverno College *B*
Cardinal Stritch University *B*
Carroll College *B*
Carthage College *B*
Concordia University Wisconsin *B*
Edgewood College *B*
Lakeland College *B*
Lawrence University *B*
Marian College of Fond du Lac *B*
Mount Mary College *B*
Northland College *B, T*
Ripon College *B, T*
St. Norbert College *B, T*
Silver Lake College *B*
University of Wisconsin
　　Eau Claire *B*
　　Green Bay *B*
　　La Crosse *B*
　　Madison *B, M*
　　Milwaukee *B, M, D*
　　Oshkosh *B*
　　Parkside *B, T*
　　Platteville *B*
　　River Falls *B*
　　Stevens Point *B*
　　Superior *B*
　　Whitewater *B, T*
Viterbo University *B*
Wisconsin Lutheran College *B*

Wyoming
Casper College *A*
Central Wyoming College *C, A*
Eastern Wyoming College *A*
Sheridan College *A*
University of Wyoming *B*
Western Wyoming Community
　College *A*

Art history/criticism/ conservation

Alabama
Birmingham-Southern College *B*
Chattahoochee Valley Community
　College *A*
University of Alabama *B, M*
University of Alabama
　　Birmingham *M*

Arizona
Arizona State University *D*
Northern Arizona University *B*
University of Arizona *B, M, D*

Arkansas
University of Arkansas
　　Little Rock *B*

California
Art Center College of Design *M*
California College of Arts and Crafts *M*
California State Polytechnic University:
　Pomona *B*

California State University
　Chico *B, M*
　Dominguez Hills *B*
　Fullerton *M*
　Hayward *B*
　Long Beach *B, M*
　Northridge *B, M*
　Stanislaus *B*
Chapman University *B*
De Anza College *C, A*
Dominican University of California *B*
Foothill College *C, A*
Gavilan Community College *A*
Grossmont Community College *A*
Los Angeles Southwest College *A*
Loyola Marymount University *B*
Mills College *B*
MiraCosta College *A*
Occidental College *B*
Ohlone College *C*
Pitzer College *B*
Pomona College *B*
San Diego City College *A*
San Diego State University *B, M*
San Francisco State University *M*
San Jose State University *B, M*
Santa Barbara City College *A*
Santa Clara University *B*
Scripps College *B*
Sonoma State University *B*
University of California
　Berkeley *M, D*
　Davis *B, M*
　Irvine *B, M*
　Los Angeles *B, M, D*
　Riverside *B, M*
　San Diego *B*
　Santa Barbara *B, M, D*
University of La Verne *B*
University of Redlands *B*
University of San Francisco *B*
University of Southern
　California *B, M, D*
University of the Pacific *B*
Whittier College *B*

Colorado
Colorado College *B*
Colorado State University *B*
University of Denver *B, M*

Connecticut
Albertus Magnus College *B*
Connecticut College *B*
Fairfield University *B*
St. Joseph College *B*
Southern Connecticut State
　University *B, M*
Trinity College *B*
University of Connecticut *B*
University of Hartford *B*
Wesleyan University *B*
Yale University *B, M, D*

Delaware
University of Delaware *B, M, D*

District of Columbia
American University *B, M*
Catholic University of America *B*
Gallaudet University *B*
George Washington University *B, M, D*
Georgetown University *B*
Howard University *B, M*
Trinity College *B*

Florida
Florida International University *B*
Florida State University *B, M, D*
Jacksonville University *B*
Palm Beach Community College *A*
Polk Community College *A*
Rollins College *B*
South Florida Community College *A*
University of Florida *B, M*
University of Miami *B, M*
University of South Florida *M*

University of West Florida *B*

Georgia
Berry College *B*
Emory University *B, M, D*
Georgia State University *M*
Oxford College of Emory University *B*
Savannah College of Art and
　Design *B, M*
University of Georgia *B, M*
Wesleyan College *B*

Hawaii
University of Hawaii
　　Manoa *M*

Illinois
Augustana College *B*
Bradley University *B*
De Paul University *B*
Dominican University *B*
Governors State University *B, M*
Illinois Valley Community College *A*
Knox College *B*
Lake Forest College *B*
Lincoln College *A*
Loyola University of Chicago *B*
North Park University *B*
Northern Illinois University *B*
Northwestern University *B, M, D*
Principia College *B*
Richland Community College *A*
Rockford College *B*
Roosevelt University *B*
Sauk Valley Community College *A*
School of the Art Institute of Chicago *M*
University of Chicago *B, M, D*
University of Illinois
　Chicago *B, M, D*
　Urbana-Champaign *B, M, D*

Indiana
DePauw University *B*
Hanover College *B*
Indiana University
　　Bloomington *B, M, D*
Indiana University-Purdue University
　Indianapolis *B*
Indiana Wesleyan University *B*
Marian College *B, T*
University of Evansville *B*
University of Notre Dame *B, M*

Iowa
Clarke College *A, B, T*
Drake University *B*
Loras College *B*
University of Iowa *B, M, D*
University of Northern Iowa *B*

Kansas
Baker University *B*
University of Kansas *B, M, D*
Washburn University of Topeka *B*
Wichita State University *B*

Kentucky
Thomas More College *A*
University of Kentucky *B, M*
University of Louisville *B, M, D*

Louisiana
Grambling State University *B*
Louisiana State University and
　Agricultural and Mechanical
　College *M*
Tulane University *B*
University of New Orleans *B*

Maine
Bowdoin College *B*
Colby College *B*
University of Maine *B*
University of Southern Maine *B*

Maryland
College of Notre Dame of Maryland *B*
Johns Hopkins University *B, M, D*
McDaniel College *B*

Montgomery College
　Rockville Campus *A*
University of Maryland
　College Park *B, M, D*

Massachusetts
Boston College *B*
Boston University *B, M, D*
Brandeis University *B*
Clark University *B*
College of the Holy Cross *B*
Framingham State College *B*
Hampshire College *B*
Harvard College *B*
Massachusetts College of Art *B*
Massachusetts College of Liberal Arts *B*
Northeastern University *B*
Simmons College *B*
Simon's Rock College of Bard *B*
Smith College *B*
Tufts University *B, M*
University of Massachusetts
　　Amherst *B, M*
　　Dartmouth *B*
Wellesley College *B*
Wheaton College *B*
Williams College *B, M*

Michigan
Andrews University *B*
Aquinas College *B*
Calvin College *B*
Eastern Michigan University *B*
Ferris State University *B*
Hope College *B*
Kalamazoo College *B*
Madonna University *C*
Michigan State University *B, M*
Oakland University *B*
University of Michigan *B, M, D*
Wayne State University *B, M*
Western Michigan University *B*

Minnesota
Augsburg College *B*
Bethel College *B*
Carleton College *B*
College of St. Benedict *B*
College of St. Catherine *B*
Concordia College: Moorhead *B*
Gustavus Adolphus College *B*
Hamline University *B*
Macalester College *B*
Minnesota State University
　　Mankato *B*
　　Moorhead *B*
St. Cloud State University *B*
St. Olaf College *B*
University of Minnesota
　　Duluth *B*
　　Morris *B*
　　Twin Cities *B, M, D*
University of St. Thomas *B, M*

Mississippi
Millsaps College *B, T*
University of Mississippi *B, M, T*

Missouri
Drury University *B*
Kansas City Art Institute *B*
Lindenwood University *B, M*
St. Louis University *B*
Truman State University *B*
University of Missouri
　　Kansas City *B, M*
　　St. Louis *B*
Washington University in St.
　Louis *B, M, D*

Montana
University of Montana-Missoula *B, M*

Nebraska
Bellevue University *B*
Hastings College *B*

University of Nebraska
Kearney *B*
Lincoln *B*
Omaha *B*

Nevada
University of Nevada
Reno *B*

New Hampshire
Dartmouth College *B*
Franklin Pierce College *B*
New England College *B*
University of New Hampshire *B*

New Jersey
Caldwell College *C*
Drew University *B*
Georgian Court College *B*
Kean University *B*
Monmouth University *B*
Princeton University *B, M, D*
Rowan University *B*
Rutgers, The State University of New
Jersey
New Brunswick Regional
Campus *B, M, D*
Seton Hall University *B*

New Mexico
College of Santa Fe *B*
University of New Mexico *B, M, D*

New York
Adelphi University *B*
Alfred University *B*
Bard College *B, M*
Barnard College *B*
Canisius College *B*
City University of New York
Brooklyn College *B, M*
City College *B, M*
Hunter College *B, M*
Queens College *B, M*
York College *B*
Colgate University *B*
College of New Rochelle *B, T*
Columbia University
Columbia College *B*
Cornell University *B, D*
Fordham University *B*
Hamilton College *B*
Hartwick College *B*
Hobart and William Smith Colleges *B*
Hofstra University *B*
Ithaca College *B*
Long Island University
C. W. Post Campus *B, M*
Manhattanville College *B*
Marist College *B*
Marymount College of Fordham
University *B*
Nazareth College of Rochester *B*
New York University *B, M, D*
Pace University *B*
Pace University:
Pleasantville/Briarcliff *B*
Parsons School of Design *M*
Pratt Institute *B, M*
Sarah Lawrence College *B*
Skidmore College *B*
State University of New York
Binghamton *B, M, D*
Buffalo *B, M*
College at Buffalo *B, M*
College at Fredonia *B*
College at Geneseo *B*
College at Oneonta *B*
College at Plattsburgh *B*
College at Potsdam *B*
New Paltz *B, M*
Purchase *B, M*
Stony Brook *B, M, D*
Syracuse University *B, M*
University of Rochester *B*
Wells College *B*

North Carolina
Duke University *B, D*
East Carolina University *B*
Meredith College *B*
Queens University of Charlotte *B*
Salem College *B*
University of North Carolina
Chapel Hill *B, M, D*
Greensboro *B*
Wilmington *B*
Wake Forest University *B*

Ohio
Art Academy of Cincinnati *B*
Baldwin-Wallace College *B*
Bowling Green State University *B, M*
Case Western Reserve
University *B, M, D*
College of Wooster *B*
Denison University *B*
Hiram College *B*
John Carroll University *B*
Kent State University *B, M*
Kenyon College *B*
Lourdes College *A, B*
Miami University
Oxford Campus *B*
Notre Dame College *B*
Oberlin College *B*
Ohio State University
Columbus Campus *B, M, D*
Ohio University *B, M*
Ohio Wesleyan University *B*
University of Akron *B*
University of Cincinnati *C, B, M*
University of Dayton *B*
University of Toledo *B*
Ursuline College *B*
Virginia Marti College of Art and
Design *A*
Wittenberg University *B*
Wright State University *B*
Youngstown State University *B*

Oklahoma
Oklahoma City University *M*
St. Gregory's University *A*
University of Oklahoma *B, M*
University of Tulsa *B*

Oregon
Portland State University *B*
Reed College *B*
University of Oregon *M, D*
Willamette University *B*

Pennsylvania
Allegheny College *B*
Arcadia University *B*
Bloomsburg University of
Pennsylvania *B, M*
Bryn Mawr College *B, M, D*
Bucknell University *B*
California University of Pennsylvania *B*
Carlow College *B*
Chatham College *B*
Chestnut Hill College *A, B*
Duquesne University *B*
Edinboro University of Pennsylvania *B*
Franklin & Marshall College *B*
Gettysburg College *B*
Haverford College *B*
Immaculata University *A*
Juniata College *B*
La Salle University *B*
Lycoming College *B*
Marywood University *C, B*
Messiah College *B*
Moravian College *B*
Muhlenberg College *B*

Penn State
Abington *B*
Altoona *B*
Beaver *B*
Berks *B*
Delaware County *B*
Dubois *B*
Fayette *B*
Hazleton *B*
Lehigh Valley *B*
McKeesport *B*
Mont Alto *B*
New Kensington *B*
Schuylkill - Capital College *B*
Shenango *B*
University Park *B, M, D*
Wilkes-Barre *B*
Worthington Scranton *B*
York *B*
Rosemont College *B*
St. Vincent College *B*
Seton Hill University *B*
Swarthmore College *B*
Temple University *B, M, D*
University of Pennsylvania *B, M, D*
University of Pittsburgh *B, M, D*
Villanova University *B*
Washington and Jefferson College *B*

Puerto Rico
University of Puerto Rico
Mayaguez Campus *B*
Rio Piedras Campus *B*

Rhode Island
Brown University *B, M, D*
Rhode Island College *B*
Roger Williams University *B*
Salve Regina University *B*
University of Rhode Island *B*

South Carolina
College of Charleston *B*
Converse College *B*
Furman University *B*
University of South Carolina *B, M*
Winthrop University *B*
Wofford College *B*

Tennessee
Lambuth University *B*
Southern Adventist University *B*
Tennessee State University *B*
University of Memphis *B, M*
University of Tennessee
Knoxville *B*

Texas
Baylor University *B*
Lamar University *M*
Lon Morris College *A*
Rice University *B, M*
Southern Methodist University *B, M*
Southwest Texas State University *B*
Southwestern University *B*
Stephen F. Austin State University *B*
Texas A&M University
Commerce *M, D*
Texas Christian University *B, M*
Texas Tech University *B*
Texas Woman's University *B, M*
Trinity University *B*
University of Dallas *B*
University of Houston *B*
University of North Texas *B, M*
University of Texas
Arlington *B*
Austin *B, M, D*

Utah
Brigham Young University *B, M*
Dixie State College of Utah *A*
University of Utah *B, M*

Vermont
Marlboro College *B*
Middlebury College *B*
University of Vermont *B*

Virginia
George Mason University *B*
Hollins University *B*
James Madison University *B*
Longwood University *B*
Mary Baldwin College *B*
Mary Washington College *B*
Old Dominion University *B*
Randolph-Macon College *B*
Randolph-Macon Woman's College *B*
Sweet Briar College *B*
University of Richmond *B*
University of Virginia *M, D*
Virginia Commonwealth
University *B, M, D*
Washington and Lee University *B*

Washington
Eastern Washington University *B*
Seattle University *B*
University of Washington *B, M, D*
Western Washington University *B*
Whitman College *B*

Wisconsin
Beloit College *B*
Lawrence University *B, T*
University of Wisconsin
Madison *B, M, D*
Milwaukee *B, M*
Superior *B*
Whitewater *B, T*

Art teacher education

Alabama
Alabama Agricultural and Mechanical
University *M*
Alabama State University *B*
Birmingham-Southern College *B, T*
Huntingdon College *B, T*
University of Alabama
Birmingham *M*
University of North Alabama *B*

Arizona
Arizona State University *B, T*
Eastern Arizona College *A*
Northern Arizona University *B, T*
Prescott College *B, M, T*
University of Arizona *B, M*

Arkansas
Arkansas State University *B, T*
Arkansas Tech University *B*
Harding University *B, M, T*
Henderson State University *B, M, T*
Ouachita Baptist University *B, T*
Southern Arkansas University *B, T*
University of Arkansas
Monticello *B*
Pine Bluff *B, T*
University of Central Arkansas *T*
University of the Ozarks *T*
Williams Baptist College *B*

California
Azusa Pacific University *B, T*
California Baptist University *T*
California State Polytechnic University:
Pomona *T*
California State University
Bakersfield *B, T*
Chico *T*
Dominguez Hills *T*
Fullerton *B, T*
Long Beach *B, T*
Northridge *B, T*
San Bernardino *T*
Cuesta College *C, A*
Humboldt State University *T*
Mount St. Mary's College *T*
Occidental College *T*
San Diego State University *B, T*
San Francisco State University *B, T*
San Jose State University *T*

Sonoma State University *T*
University of San Francisco *M*
University of the Pacific *T*
Vista Community College *A*

Colorado

Colorado State University *T*
Colorado State University
   Pueblo *T*
Fort Lewis College *T*
Metropolitan State College of
   Denver *B, T*
Rocky Mountain College of Art &
   Design *B*
University of Colorado
   Boulder *T*
University of Denver *B*

Connecticut

Central Connecticut State
   University *B, M, T*
Southern Connecticut State
   University *B, M, T*

Delaware

Delaware State University *B*

District of Columbia

Gallaudet University *B, T*
George Washington University *M, T*
Howard University *B*
Trinity College *M*
University of the District of Columbia *B*

Florida

Flagler College *B*
Florida Agricultural and Mechanical
   University *B, M*
Florida Atlantic University *M*
Florida International University *B, M, T*
Florida Southern College *B*
Florida State University *B, M, D, T*
Jacksonville University *B, M, T*
Palm Beach Atlantic University *B, T*
Palm Beach Community College *A*
Pensacola Junior College *A*
Stetson University *B, T*
University of Central Florida *B, M*
University of Florida *B, M*
University of Miami *M*
University of North Florida *B*
University of South Florida *B, M*
University of West Florida *B*

Georgia

Armstrong Atlantic State
   University *B, M, T*
Berry College *B*
Brenau University *B*
Clark Atlanta University *B*
Columbus State University *B, M*
Gainesville College *A*
Georgia College and State
   University *B, T*
Georgia Southern University *B, M, T*
Georgia Southwestern State
   University *B, M, T*
Georgia State University *B, M*
LaGrange College *B*
Mercer University *T*
North Georgia College & State
   University *B, M*
Piedmont College *M, T*
Shorter College *B*
State University of West Georgia *M*
University of Georgia *B, M, D, T*
Valdosta State University *B, M*
Young Harris College *A*

Hawaii

Brigham Young University-Hawaii *B, T*
University of Hawaii
   Manoa *B, T*

Idaho

Boise State University *B, M, T*
Brigham Young University - Idaho *T*
Northwest Nazarene University *B*

University of Idaho *B, T*

Illinois

Augustana College *B, T*
Blackburn College *B, T*
Chicago State University *B*
City Colleges of Chicago
   Olive-Harvey College *A*
Columbia College Chicago *M*
Dominican University *T*
Elmhurst College *B*
Greenville College *B, T*
Illinois College *T*
John A. Logan College *A*
Kankakee Community College *A*
Lewis University *T*
Lincoln College *A*
Loyola University of Chicago *T*
McKendree College *B, T*
Monmouth College *B, T*
Moraine Valley Community College *A*
North Central College *B, T*
North Park University *T*
Northern Illinois University *B, M, T*
Northwestern University *B, T*
Olivet Nazarene University *B, T*
Parkland College *A*
Quincy University *B, T*
Rockford College *T*
St. Xavier University *B, T*
Sauk Valley Community College *A*
School of the Art Institute of
   Chicago *B, M*
Trinity Christian College *B, T*
University of Illinois
   Chicago *B*
   Urbana-Champaign *B, M, D, T*
Waubonsee Community College *A*
Wheaton College *T*

Indiana

Anderson University *B, T*
Ball State University *B*
Calumet College of St. Joseph *B, T*
Goshen College *B*
Grace College *B*
Huntington College *B*
Indiana State University *B, T*
Indiana University
   Bloomington *B, M*
Indiana University-Purdue University
   Indianapolis *B, M, T*
Indiana Wesleyan University *B, T*
Oakland City University *B*
St. Joseph's College *B*
Saint Mary's College *T*
St. Mary-of-the-Woods College *B*
Taylor University *B, T*
University of Evansville *B*
University of Indianapolis *B, M, T*
University of St. Francis *B*
University of Southern Indiana *T*
Vincennes University *A*

Iowa

Briar Cliff University *B*
Buena Vista University *B, T*
Central College *T*
Clarke College *B, T*
Cornell College *B, T*
Dordt College *B*
Drake University *T*
Graceland University *T*
Grand View College *B, T*
Iowa State University *T*
Iowa Wesleyan College *B*
Loras College *B*
Luther College *B*
Maharishi University of Management *T*
Morningside College *B*
Mount Mercy College *T*
Northwestern College *T*
St. Ambrose University *B, T*
Simpson College *B*
University of Iowa *B, M, D, T*
Upper Iowa University *T*

Wartburg College *B, T*

Kansas

Baker University *B, T*
Bethany College *B*
Bethel College *T*
Emporia State University *B, T*
Fort Scott Community College *A*
Friends University *B*
Garden City Community College *A*
Independence Community College *A*
Kansas State University *B, T*
Kansas Wesleyan University *B, T*
McPherson College *B, T*
Ottawa University *B, T*
Pittsburg State University *B, T*
University of Kansas *B, M, T*
Wichita State University *B, M*

Kentucky

Asbury College *B, T*
Bellarmine University *B, T*
Berea College *B, T*
Brescia University *B, T*
Campbellsville University *B*
Cumberland College *B, T*
Kentucky Wesleyan College *T*
Morehead State University *M*
Murray State University *B, T*
Spalding University *B*
Thomas More College *B*
University of Kentucky *B, M*

Louisiana

Centenary College of Louisiana *B, T*
Grambling State University *B*
Louisiana College *B*
Louisiana State University
   Shreveport *B*
Louisiana Tech University *B*
McNeese State University *T*
Nicholls State University *B*
Northwestern State University *B*
Southeastern Louisiana University *B*
University of Louisiana at Monroe *B*
Xavier University of Louisiana *B, T*

Maine

Maine College of Art *T*
University of Maine *B*
University of New England *B*
University of Southern Maine *B, T*

Maryland

College of Notre Dame of Maryland *T*
Community College of Baltimore County
   Catonsville *A*
   Dundalk *A*
   Essex *A*
Maryland Institute College of
   Art *B, M, T*
Montgomery College
   Rockville Campus *A*
Mount St. Mary's College *T*
St. Mary's College of Maryland *T*
Salisbury University *T*
Towson University *B, M, T*
University of Maryland
   College Park *B*

Massachusetts

Anna Maria College *B, T*
Art Institute of Boston at Lesley
   University *B, M*
Boston University *B, M*
Bridgewater State College *M, T*
Fitchburg State College *M*
Framingham State College *T*
Lesley University *M, T*
Massachusetts College of Art *B, M*
Montserrat College of Art *T*
Northeastern University *B*
School of the Museum of Fine
   Arts *B, M, T*
Springfield College *B*
Tufts University *M, T*

University of Massachusetts
   Dartmouth *B, M, T*
Westfield State College *B, T*

Michigan

Adrian College *B, T*
Alma College *T*
Andrews University *M*
Aquinas College *B, T*
Calvin College *B*
Central Michigan University *B, M*
Concordia University *B, T*
Eastern Michigan University *B, M, T*
Gogebic Community College *A*
Grand Valley State University *T*
Hope College *T*
Kellogg Community College *A*
Lansing Community College *A*
Madonna University *T*
Northern Michigan University *B, M, T*
University of Michigan *B*
University of Michigan
   Dearborn *B*
   Flint *B, T*
Wayne State University *B, M, T*
Western Michigan University *B*

Minnesota

Augsburg College *T*
Bemidji State University *T*
Bethel College *B*
College of St. Benedict *B, T*
College of St. Catherine *B, M, T*
Concordia College: Moorhead *B, T*
Concordia University: St. Paul *B, T*
Gustavus Adolphus College *T*
Hamline University *B*
Minnesota State University
   Mankato *B, M, T*
   Moorhead *B, M, T*
Northwestern College *B*
Ridgewater College: A Community and
   Technical College *A*
St. John's University *B, T*
St. Olaf College *T*
Southwest State University *B, T*
University of Minnesota
   Duluth *B*
   Twin Cities *B, M, T*
Vermilion Community College *A*
Winona State University *B, T*

Mississippi

Coahoma Community College *A*
Delta State University *T*
Itawamba Community College *A*
Mississippi College *B, M*
Mississippi Gulf Coast Community
   College
   Perkinston *A*
Mississippi University for Women *B, T*
Northwest Mississippi Community
   College *A*
University of Mississippi *B, M, T*
University of Southern Mississippi *M*

Missouri

Avila University *B, T*
Central Missouri State University *B, T*
College of the Ozarks *B, T*
Columbia College *T*
Culver-Stockton College *B, T*
Evangel University *B, T*
Hannibal-LaGrange College *B*
Lincoln University *T*
Lindenwood University *B, M*
Maryville University of Saint
   Louis *B, M, T*
Missouri Southern State College *B, T*
Missouri Western State College *B*
Northwest Missouri State
   University *B, M, T*
Southeast Missouri State University *B, T*
Southwest Baptist University *B, T*
Southwest Missouri State University *B*
Truman State University *M, T*

University of Missouri
Columbia *B*
Washington University in St.
Louis *B, M, T*
William Woods University *B, T*

Montana
Montana State University
Billings *B, T*
Rocky Mountain College *B, T*
University of Montana-Missoula *B, T*
University of Montana: Western *B, T*

Nebraska
Chadron State College *B*
Concordia University *B, T*
Creighton University *T*
Dana College *B*
Doane College *T*
Hastings College *B, M, T*
Midland Lutheran College *B, T*
Nebraska Wesleyan University *T*
Peru State College *B, T*
Union College *T*
University of Nebraska
Kearney *B, M, T*
Lincoln *B, T*
Western Nebraska Community
College *A*

Nevada
University of Nevada
Reno *B*

New Hampshire
Chester College of New England *T*
Colby-Sawyer College *B, T*
New England College *B*
Plymouth State College *B, T*
University of New Hampshire *B, T*

New Jersey
Bloomfield College *B*
Caldwell College *T*
The College of New Jersey *B, T*
College of St. Elizabeth *T*
Cumberland County College *A*
Georgian Court College *T*
Kean University *B, M*
Monmouth University *B, T*
New Jersey City University *M, T*
Richard Stockton College of New
Jersey *B*
Rowan University *B, M*
Seton Hall University *B*
William Paterson University of New
Jersey *T*

New Mexico
New Mexico Highlands University *B*
University of New Mexico *B, M*
Western New Mexico University *B*

New York
Adelphi University *B, M*
Alfred University *M, T*
City University of New York
Brooklyn College *B*
City College *B, T*
Hunter College *M*
Queens College *B, M, T*
College of New Rochelle *B, M, T*
Daemen College *B, T*
Dowling College *B*
Elmira College *B, T*
Eugene Lang College/New School
University *T*
Fordham University *T*
Fulton-Montgomery Community
College *A*
Hofstra University *B, M, T*
Long Island University
C. W. Post Campus *B, M, T*
Southampton College *B, T*
Manhattanville College *M, T*
Marymount College of Fordham
University *B, T*
Marymount Manhattan College *B, T*

Molloy College *B*
Nazareth College of Rochester *B, M, T*
New York Institute of Technology *B, T*
New York University *D, T*
Pace University *M, T*
Pace University:
Pleasantville/Briarcliff *M, T*
Pratt Institute *B, M*
Roberts Wesleyan College *B, T*
Rochester Institute of Technology *M*
St. John's University *B, T*
St. Lawrence University *T*
School of Visual Arts *B, T*
State University of New York
College at Buffalo *B, M, T*
New Paltz *B, M, T*
Oswego *M*
Syracuse University *B, M, T*

North Carolina
Appalachian State University *B, M, T*
Barton College *B, T*
East Carolina University *B, M*
Greensboro College *B, T*
Guilford Technical Community
College *A*
High Point University *B, T*
Lenoir Community College *A*
Lenoir-Rhyne College *B, T*
Mars Hill College *B, T*
Meredith College *B, T*
Methodist College *B, T*
North Carolina Central University *B*
University of North Carolina
Charlotte *B*
Greensboro *B*
Pembroke *B, M, T*
Western Carolina University *B, T*
Wingate University *B, T*
Winston-Salem State University *B*

North Dakota
Dickinson State University *B, T*
Minot State University *B*
University of North Dakota *B, T*
Valley City State University *B, T*

Ohio
Art Academy of Cincinnati *M*
Ashland University *B, T*
Baldwin-Wallace College *B*
Bluffton College *B*
Bowling Green State University *B*
Case Western Reserve University *B, M*
Central State University *B*
College of Mount St. Joseph *B, T*
Defiance College *B, T*
Hiram College *T*
Kent State University *B, M*
Kent State University
Stark Campus *B*
Malone College *B*
Miami University
Oxford Campus *B, M, T*
Mount Union College *T*
Mount Vernon Nazarene University *B, T*
Notre Dame College *T*
Ohio Dominican College *B, T*
Ohio Northern University *T*
Ohio State University
Columbus Campus *B, M, D*
Ohio University *B, T*
Ohio Wesleyan University *B*
Otterbein College *B*
University of Akron *B, T*
University of Cincinnati *B, M, T*
University of Dayton *B, M, T*
University of Findlay *B, T*
University of Rio Grande *B, T*
University of Toledo *B, M, T*
Ursuline College *B, T*
Wittenberg University *B*
Wright State University *B, M, T*
Xavier University *M*
Youngstown State University *B, M, T*

Oklahoma
Cameron University *B, T*
Eastern Oklahoma State College *A*
Northeastern State University *B*
Oklahoma Baptist University *B, T*
Oklahoma Christian University of
Science and Arts *B, T*
Oklahoma City University *B*
Oral Roberts University *B, T*
Southeastern Oklahoma State
University *B, T*
Southwestern Oklahoma State
University *B, M, T*
University of Central Oklahoma *B*
University of Tulsa *M, T*

Oregon
Linfield College *T*
Portland State University *T*
Southern Oregon University *T*

Pennsylvania
Albright College *B, T*
Arcadia University *B, M, T*
Carlow College *B, M, T*
Indiana University of Pennsylvania *B, T*
Keystone College *B*
Lincoln University *B, T*
Lycoming College *T*
Marywood University *B, M*
Mercyhurst College *T*
Messiah College *B, T*
Millersville University of
Pennsylvania *B, M, T*
Moravian College *B, T*
Penn State
Abington *B*
Altoona *B*
Beaver *B*
Berks *B*
Delaware County *B*
Dubois *B*
Fayette *B*
Hazleton *B*
Lehigh Valley *B*
McKeesport *B*
Mont Alto *B*
New Kensington *B*
Schuylkill - Capital College *B*
Shenango *B*
University Park *B, M, D*
Wilkes-Barre *B*
Worthington Scranton *B*
York *B*
St. Vincent College *B*
Seton Hill University *B, T*
Temple University *B, M*
Washington and Jefferson College *T*
Wilkes University *T*

Puerto Rico
Escuela de Artes Plasticas de Puerto
Rico *B*
Inter American University of Puerto Rico
San German Campus *B*
Pontifical Catholic University of Puerto
Rico *B, T*
University of Puerto Rico
Mayaguez Campus *T*

Rhode Island
Rhode Island College *B, M*
Rhode Island School of Design *M, T*

South Carolina
Anderson College *B, T*
Claflin University *B*
Coker College *B, T*
Columbia College *B*
Converse College *T*
Francis Marion University *B*
Furman University *T*
Lander University *B*
Limestone College *B*
South Carolina State University *B, T*
University of South Carolina *B, M*
Williamsburg Technical College *A*

Winthrop University *M, T*

South Dakota
Augustana College *B, T*
Black Hills State University *B, T*
Dakota State University *B, T*
Dakota Wesleyan University *B, T*
Northern State University *B, T*
South Dakota State University *B*
University of Sioux Falls *B*
University of South Dakota *T*

Tennessee
Belmont University *B, M, T*
Bethel College *B*
Freed-Hardeman University *B, T*
Lambuth University *B, T*
Maryville College *B*
Middle Tennessee State University *B*
Roane State Community College *A*
Southern Adventist University *B*
Tennessee Technological University *T*
Tusculum College *B, T*
Union University *B, T*
University of Tennessee
Chattanooga *B*
Knoxville *B, T*
Martin *B, T*

Texas
Abilene Christian University *B, T*
Baylor University *B, T*
Del Mar College *A*
Hardin-Simmons University *B, T*
Houston Baptist University *B*
Howard Payne University *B, T*
Kilgore College *A*
Lamar University *T*
Laredo Community College *A*
Lubbock Christian University *B*
McMurry University *T*
Southwest Texas State University *B, T*
Southwestern University *T*
Tarleton State University *B, T*
Texas A&M University
Commerce *T*
Corpus Christi *T*
Kingsville *B, M*
Texas Christian University *B, T*
Texas Tech University *M*
Texas Wesleyan University *T*
Texas Woman's University *M*
University of Dallas *B, T*
University of Houston *M, T*
University of Houston
Clear Lake *T*
University of Mary Hardin-Baylor *T*
University of North Texas *B, M, D, T*
University of Texas
Arlington *T*
Austin *M*
Pan American *B, T*
San Antonio *T*
West Texas A&M University *T*

Utah
Brigham Young University *B, M*
Southern Utah University *B, T*
University of Utah *B*
Weber State University *B*

Vermont
Bennington College *B, M, T*
Castleton State College *B, T*
Goddard College *B*
Johnson State College *B*
St. Michael's College *B, M, T*
University of Vermont *B*

Virginia
Averett University *B, M, T*
Bluefield College *T*
Bridgewater College *T*
Eastern Mennonite University *T*
Hollins University *T*
Longwood University *B, T*

Virginia Commonwealth
University *B, M*
Virginia Intermont College *B, T*
Virginia Wesleyan College *B, T*

Washington
Central Washington University *B, T*
Eastern Washington University *B*
Pacific Lutheran University *T*
Seattle Pacific University *B, T*
Western Washington University *B, M, T*
Whitworth College *B, T*

West Virginia
Concord College *B, T*
Fairmont State College *B*
Shepherd College *T*
West Liberty State College *B*
West Virginia State College *B*
West Virginia University *T*
West Virginia Wesleyan College *B*

Wisconsin
Alverno College *B, T*
Beloit College *B, T*
Carroll College *B, T*
Edgewood College *B, T*
Lawrence University *T*
Marian College of Fond du Lac *B, T*
Mount Mary College *B, T*
St. Norbert College *T*
Silver Lake College *B, T*
University of Wisconsin
Green Bay *T*
La Crosse *B, T*
Madison *B, M, T*
Milwaukee *B, M*
Parkside *T*
Platteville *B*
River Falls *B, T*
Stout *B, T*
Superior *B, T*
Whitewater *B*
Viterbo University *B, T*

Art therapy

Alabama
Spring Hill College *B*

Arkansas
Harding University *B*
University of Central Arkansas *B*

Colorado
Naropa University *M*

Connecticut
Albertus Magnus College *B, M*

District of Columbia
George Washington University *M*

Florida
University of Tampa *C*

Illinois
Millikin University *B*
School of the Art Institute of Chicago *M*
Southern Illinois University
Edwardsville *M*
University of Illinois
Chicago *M*

Indiana
St. Mary-of-the-Woods College *M*
University of Indianapolis *B*

Iowa
Grand View College *C*

Kansas
Emporia State University *M*
Pittsburg State University *B*

Kentucky
University of Louisville *M*

Massachusetts
Anna Maria College *B*
Emmanuel College *B*
Endicott College *B*
Lesley University *B, M, D, T*
Springfield College *B, M*

Michigan
Adrian College *B*
Andrews University *B*
Marygrove College *B*

Missouri
Avila University *B*

New Jersey
Caldwell College *C, M*

New York
College of New Rochelle *B, M, T*
Hofstra University *M, T*
Long Island University
C. W. Post Campus *B, M*
Nazareth College of Rochester *M*
New York University *M*
Pratt Institute *M*
Russell Sage College *B*

Ohio
Bowling Green State University *B*
Ursuline College *M*

Oregon
Marylhurst University *M*

Pennsylvania
Arcadia University *B*
Cedar Crest College *B*
Drexel University *M*
Marywood University *C, A, B, M*
Mercyhurst College *B*
Seton Hill University *B, M*

South Carolina
Converse College *B*

Tennessee
Southern Adventist University *B*

Texas
University of Houston
Clear Lake *C*

Vermont
Burlington College *B*
Norwich University *M*

Wisconsin
Alverno College *B, T*
Edgewood College *B*
Marian College of Fond du Lac *B*
Mount Mary College *B, M*
University of Wisconsin
Superior *B, M*

Artificial intelligence/ robotics

Nevada
Western Nevada Community College *A*

Pennsylvania
Carnegie Mellon University *M, D*

Arts management

Alabama
Spring Hill College *B*

Arizona
Northern Arizona University *B*

California
California State University
Dominguez Hills *M*
Hayward *B*
Golden Gate University *M*
Santa Rosa Junior College *C*

University of San Francisco *B*

Delaware
Delaware State University *B*

District of Columbia
American University *C, B, M*
Howard University *B*

Florida
Florida State University *M*

Georgia
Brenau University *B*
Georgia College and State University *B*

Illinois
Benedictine University *B*
Columbia College Chicago *B, M*
Elmhurst College *B*
Millikin University *B*
Quincy University *B*
Roosevelt University *B, M*
School of the Art Institute of Chicago *M*

Indiana
Butler University *B*
Indiana University
Bloomington *M*

Iowa
Buena Vista University *B*
Luther College *B*
Upper Iowa University *B*
Waldorf College *B*
Wartburg College *B*

Kansas
Kansas Wesleyan University *B*

Kentucky
Bellarmine University *B*
University of Kentucky *B*

Louisiana
Dillard University *B*
Southeastern Louisiana University *B*
University of New Orleans *M*

Maine
University of Southern Maine *B*

Maryland
Goucher College *M*

Massachusetts
Simmons College *B*

Michigan
Adrian College *B*
Aquinas College *B*
Bay de Noc Community College *C*
Eastern Michigan University *B*
University of Michigan *M*

Minnesota
St. Mary's University of Minnesota *M*

Missouri
Culver-Stockton College *B*
Drury University *B*
Webster University *M*

Nebraska
Bellevue University *B*
Creighton University *B*

New Hampshire
Franklin Pierce College *B*

New Mexico
College of Santa Fe *B*

New York
City University of New York
Baruch College *B*
Concordia College *B*
Ithaca College *B*
Long Island University
C. W. Post Campus *B*
Marymount Manhattan College *C*
New York University *M*
Pratt Institute *M*

State University of New York
Buffalo *M*
Purchase *C*
Wagner College *B*

North Carolina
Bennett College *B*
Catawba College *B*
Pfeiffer University *B*
Salem College *B*
University of North Carolina
Charlotte *B*
Pembroke *B*

Ohio
Baldwin-Wallace College *B*
Notre Dame College *B*
University of Cincinnati *M*
University of Findlay *B*
Wright State University *B*

Oklahoma
Oklahoma City University *B, M*
University of Tulsa *B*

Oregon
University of Oregon *M*

Pennsylvania
Carnegie Mellon University *M*
Chatham College *B*
Drexel University *M*
Gettysburg College *B*
Marywood University *B*
Mercyhurst College *B*
Point Park College *B*
Seton Hill University *B*
University of Pennsylvania *M*
Waynesburg College *B*

Puerto Rico
Turabo University *M*

South Carolina
College of Charleston *B*

South Dakota
University of South Dakota *B*

Texas
El Paso Community College *C*
Southern Methodist University *M*
Texas A&M University
Commerce *B*
Texas Tech University *M*

Utah
Southern Utah University *M*

Vermont
Green Mountain College *B*

Virginia
Mary Baldwin College *B*
Randolph-Macon College *B*
Shenandoah University *B, M*

West Virginia
University of Charleston *B*

Wisconsin
University of Wisconsin
Madison *M*
Stevens Point *B*
Viterbo University *B*

Asian bodywork therapy

Pennsylvania
Academy of Medical Arts and
Business *C, A*

Asian history

New York
Bard College *B*
Sarah Lawrence College *B*

Asian studies

Alabama
Samford University *B*
University of Alabama *B*

Arizona
Pima Community College *A*

California
Cabrillo College *A*
California State University
   Chico *B*
   Long Beach *M*
   Sacramento *B*
Claremont McKenna College *B*
Laney College *A*
Loyola Marymount University *B*
Occidental College *B*
Pepperdine University *B*
Pitzer College *B*
Pomona College *B*
San Diego State University *B, M*
San Francisco State University *B, M*
Scripps College *B*
University of California
   Berkeley *B, M, D*
   Los Angeles *B, M*
   Riverside *B*
   Santa Barbara *B, M*
University of Redlands *B*
University of San Francisco *M*

Colorado
Colorado College *B*
University of Colorado
   Boulder *B*

Connecticut
Trinity College *B*

Florida
Florida International University *B*
Florida State University *B, M*
Miami-Dade Community College *A*
University of Florida *B*
University of West Florida *B, T*

Georgia
Emory University *B*
Oxford College of Emory University *B*

Hawaii
University of Hawaii
   Manoa *B, M*
   West Oahu *B*

Illinois
Augustana College *B*
Lake Forest College *B*
Northwestern University *B*
University of Illinois
   Urbana-Champaign *B, M, D*

Indiana
Earlham College *B*
Indiana University
   Bloomington *M, D*

Iowa
University of Iowa *B, M*
University of Northern Iowa *B*

Louisiana
Tulane University *B*

Maine
Bowdoin College *B*

Maryland
Johns Hopkins University *B*
University of Maryland
   University College *B*

Massachusetts
Amherst College *B*
College of the Holy Cross *B*
Hampshire College *B*
Harvard College *B*

Mount Holyoke College *B*
Simon's Rock College of Bard *B*
Smith College *B*
Tufts University *B*
Wellesley College *B*
Wheaton College *B*
Williams College *B*

Michigan
University of Michigan *B*
Wayne State University *B*

Minnesota
Carleton College *B*
Hamline University *B*
Macalester College *B*
St. Olaf College *B*

Missouri
Washington University in St. Louis *B*

Montana
University of Montana-Missoula *B*

Nevada
University of Nevada
   Las Vegas *B*

New Hampshire
Dartmouth College *B*

New Jersey
Seton Hall University *B, M*

New Mexico
University of New Mexico *B*

New York
Bard College *B*
City University of New York
   City College *B*
Colgate University *B*
Columbia University
   Columbia College *B*
Cornell University *B, M*
Hamilton College *B*
Hobart and William Smith Colleges *B*
Hofstra University *B*
Manhattanville College *B*
St. Lawrence University *B*
Sarah Lawrence College *B*
Skidmore College *B*
State University of New York
   Albany *B*
   New Paltz *B*
Vassar College *B*

North Carolina
Duke University *B*
St. Andrews Presbyterian College *B*
University of North Carolina
   Chapel Hill *B*

Ohio
Antioch College *B*
Bowling Green State University *B*
Case Western Reserve University *B*
Ohio University *B*
University of Cincinnati *B*
University of Findlay *B*
University of Toledo *B*

Oklahoma
Oklahoma City University *B*
University of Oklahoma *B*

Oregon
University of Oregon *B, M*

Pennsylvania
Gettysburg College *B*
Lehigh University *B*
Rosemont College *B*
Swarthmore College *B*
Temple University *B*
University of Pittsburgh *C*

Rhode Island
Brown University *B*

South Carolina
Furman University *B*

Tennessee
University of Tennessee
   Knoxville *B*

Texas
Baylor University *B*
Rice University *B*
Southwest Texas State University *B*
Trinity University *B*
University of Texas
   Austin *B, M, D*

Utah
Brigham Young University *B*
University of Utah *B*
Utah State University *B*

Vermont
Marlboro College *B*
University of Vermont *B*

Virginia
Mary Baldwin College *B*

Washington
Central Washington University *B*
Everett Community College *C, A*
Gonzaga University *B*
South Seattle Community College *A*
University of Puget Sound *B*
University of Washington *A, B*
Washington State University *B*
Whitman College *B*

Wisconsin
Lawrence University *B*
University of Wisconsin
   Madison *B*

Asian-American studies

California
California State University
   Fullerton *B*
   Hayward *B*
   Long Beach *C*
Claremont McKenna College *B*
De Anza College *C, A*
Pitzer College *B*
Pomona College *B*
San Francisco State University *B, M*
Scripps College *B*
Southwestern College *A*
University of California
   Berkeley *B*
   Irvine *B*
   Los Angeles *B, M*
   Riverside *B*
University of Southern California *B*

Colorado
University of Denver *B*

Georgia
Oxford College of Emory University *B*

Massachusetts
Hampshire College *B*
Harvard College *B*

New York
City University of New York
   Hunter College *B*
Columbia University
   Columbia College *B*
Sarah Lawrence College *B*

Pennsylvania
Gettysburg College *B*

Washington
University of Washington *B*

Astronomy

Arizona
Northern Arizona University *B*
University of Arizona *B, M, D*

California
California Institute of Technology *B, D*
De Anza College *A*
Gavilan Community College *A*
Golden West College *A*
Orange Coast College *A*
Palomar College *C, A*
Pomona College *B*
San Diego State University *B*
San Francisco State University *B*
San Joaquin Delta College *A*
Southwestern College *A*
University of California
   Los Angeles *M, D*
   Santa Cruz *D*
University of Southern
   California *B, M, D*

Colorado
University of Colorado
   Boulder *B*

Connecticut
Connecticut College *B*
Wesleyan University *B, M*
Yale University *B, M, D*

Delaware
University of Delaware *B*

District of Columbia
Howard University *M, D*

Florida
Florida Institute of Technology *B*
Polk Community College *A*
Santa Fe Community College *A*
South Florida Community College *A*
University of Florida *B, M, D*

Georgia
Georgia State University *D*
Oxford College of Emory University *B*
University of Georgia *B*
Valdosta State University *B*
Young Harris College *A*

Hawaii
University of Hawaii
   Hilo *B*
   Manoa *M, D*

Idaho
North Idaho College *A*

Illinois
Illinois Valley Community College *A*
Kishwaukee College *A*
Northwestern University *B, D*
Parkland College *A*
South Suburban College of Cook
   County *A*
Southwestern Illinois College *A*
University of Chicago *M, D*
University of Illinois
   Urbana-Champaign *B, M, D*

Indiana
Ball State University *B*
Indiana University
   Bloomington *B, M, D*

Iowa
Drake University *B*
University of Iowa *B, M*

Kansas
Benedictine College *B*
Central Christian College *A*
University of Kansas *B*

Maryland
Johns Hopkins University *B, D*

University of Maryland
   College Park *B, M, D*

Massachusetts
Amherst College *B*
Boston University *B, M, D*
Hampshire College *B*
Harvard College *B*
Mount Holyoke College *B*
Smith College *B*
Tufts University *B*
University of Massachusetts
   Amherst *B, M, D*
Wellesley College *B*
Wheaton College *B*
Williams College *B*

Michigan
Bay de Noc Community College *A*
Central Michigan University *B*
University of Michigan *B, M, D*

Minnesota
Minnesota State University
   Mankato *B*
University of Minnesota
   Twin Cities *B*
Vermilion Community College *A*

Nebraska
University of Nebraska
   Lincoln *M, D*

New Hampshire
Dartmouth College *B*

New Jersey
Middlesex County College *A*

New Mexico
New Mexico State University *M, D*

New York
Barnard College *B*
Colgate University *B*
Columbia University
   Columbia College *B*
Cornell University *B, M, D*
Sarah Lawrence College *B*
State University of New York
   Stony Brook *B*
Suffolk County Community College *A*
University of Rochester *B, M, D*
Vassar College *B*

Ohio
Case Western Reserve
   University *B, M, D*
Mount Union College *B*
Ohio Northern University *B*
Ohio State University
   Columbus Campus *B, M, D*
Ohio University *B*
Ohio Wesleyan University *B*
University of Toledo *B*
Wilmington College *B*
Youngstown State University *B*

Oklahoma
Tulsa Community College *A*
University of Oklahoma *B*

Pennsylvania
Bryn Mawr College *B*
Franklin & Marshall College *B*
Gettysburg College *B*
Haverford College *B*
Lycoming College *B*

Penn State
   Abington *B*
   Altoona *B*
   Beaver *B*
   Berks *B*
   Delaware County *B*
   Dubois *B*
   Fayette *B*
   Hazleton *B*
   Lehigh Valley *B*
   McKeesport *B*
   Mont Alto *B*
   New Kensington *B*
   Schuylkill - Capital College *B*
   Shenango *B*
   University Park *B, M, D*
   Wilkes-Barre *B*
   Worthington Scranton *B*
   York *B*
Swarthmore College *B*
University of Pittsburgh *M, D*
Villanova University *B*
West Chester University of
   Pennsylvania *B*

Tennessee
Vanderbilt University *M*

Texas
Austin Community College *A*
Lon Morris College *A*
Rice University *B, M, D*
University of Texas
   Austin *B, M, D*

Utah
Brigham Young University *B*
Snow College *A*

Vermont
Bennington College *B*
Marlboro College *B*

Virginia
University of Virginia *B, M, D*

Washington
Everett Community College *A*
Lower Columbia College *A*
University of Washington *B, M, D*
Whitman College *B*

Wisconsin
University of Wisconsin
   Madison *B, M, D*

Astrophysics

California
San Francisco State University *B*
University of California
   Berkeley *B, D*
   Los Angeles *B*
   Santa Cruz *B, D*

Colorado
University of Colorado
   Boulder *M, D*

Connecticut
Connecticut College *B*
Yale University *B*

Florida
Florida Institute of Technology *B*

Georgia
Agnes Scott College *B*

Illinois
Northwestern University *B*
University of Chicago *M, D*

Indiana
Indiana University
   Bloomington *B*

Iowa
Iowa State University *M, D*

University of Iowa *M, D*

Massachusetts
Boston University *B*
Harvard College *B*
Smith College *B*
Tufts University *M, D*
Williams College *B*

Michigan
Michigan State University *B, M, D*
University of Michigan *B*

Minnesota
University of Minnesota
   Twin Cities *B, M, D*

New Jersey
Princeton University *B, M, D*

New Mexico
New Mexico Institute of Mining and
   Technology *B, M, D*
University of New Mexico *B*

New York
Colgate University *B*
Columbia University
   Columbia College *B*

Oklahoma
University of Oklahoma *B*

Oregon
University of Oregon *M, D*

Pennsylvania
Franklin & Marshall College *B*
Lehigh University *B*
Penn State
   Schuylkill - Capital College *B*
   University Park *B, M, D*
Swarthmore College *B*
Villanova University *B*

Texas
Rice University *B, M, D*
Texas Christian University *B*
University of North Texas *M*

Vermont
Marlboro College *B*

Washington
University of Washington *B*

Wisconsin
University of Wisconsin
   Madison *B, M, D*

Athletic training

Alabama
Huntingdon College *C, B*
Northwest-Shoals Community College *A*
Samford University *B*
Troy State University *B*
University of Alabama *B*
University of Mobile *B*
University of West Alabama *B*
Wallace State Community College at
   Hanceville *A*

Arizona
Northern Arizona University *B*

Arkansas
Harding University *B*
Henderson State University *B*
John Brown University *B*
Southern Arkansas University *B*
University of Arkansas
   Monticello *B*

California
California State Polytechnic University:
   Pomona *B*

California State University
   Chico *C*
   Hayward *B*
   Northridge *M*
   Sacramento *B*
   Stanislaus *B*
Christian Heritage College *B*
Concordia University *B*
Diablo Valley College *A*
Foothill College *C, A*
Fresno Pacific University *B*
Grossmont Community College *C, A*
Hope International University *B*
Master's College *B*
Orange Coast College *C, A*
Pepperdine University *B*
Point Loma Nazarene University *B*
San Francisco State University *B*
Santa Barbara City College *C, A*
Santa Rosa Junior College *C*
University of the Pacific *B*
Whittier College *B*

Colorado
Colorado State University
   Pueblo *B*
Fort Lewis College *B*

Connecticut
Central Connecticut State University *B*
Mitchell College *A*
Quinnipiac University *B*
Sacred Heart University *B*

Delaware
University of Delaware *B*

Florida
Barry University *B, M*
Broward Community College *A*
Florida Southern College *B*
Florida State University *C*
Stetson University *B*
University of Tampa *B*
University of West Florida *B, M*

Georgia
Abraham Baldwin Agricultural
   College *A*
Emmanuel College *B*
Georgia Southern University *B*
Georgia State University *M*
North Georgia College & State
   University *B*
Valdosta State University *B*

Hawaii
University of Hawaii
   Manoa *B, M*

Idaho
Boise State University *B, M*
University of Idaho *B*

Illinois
Illinois Valley Community College *A*
Lewis University *B*
McKendree College *B*
Millikin University *B*
North Central College *B*
Olivet Nazarene University *B*
Quincy University *B*
Rockford College *B*
St. Xavier University *C*
Sauk Valley Community College *A*
Trinity International University *B*
Triton College *C*

Indiana
Anderson University *B*
Ball State University *B*
DePauw University *B*
Grace College *B*
Indiana State University *B, M*
Indiana Wesleyan University *B*
Taylor University *B*
University of Evansville *B*
University of Indianapolis *B*
Valparaiso University *B*

Vincennes University *A*

Iowa
Coe College *B*
Dordt College *B*
Ellsworth Community College *A*
Graceland University *B*
Loras College *B*
Luther College *B*
North Iowa Area Community College *A*
Northwestern College *C*
St. Ambrose University *B*
Simpson College *B*
University of Iowa *B, M*
Upper Iowa University *B*

Kansas
Barton County Community College *A*
Benedictine College *C, B*
Bethel College *B*
Central Christian College *A*
Dodge City Community College *A*
Emporia State University *B*
Garden City Community College *A*
Seward County Community College *A*
Sterling College *B*
Tabor College *B*
University of Kansas *B*
Washburn University of Topeka *B*

Kentucky
Campbellsville University *B*
Murray State University *C*

Louisiana
Louisiana College *B*
Southeastern Louisiana University *B*

Maine
University of New England *B*
University of Southern Maine *R*

Maryland
Community College of Baltimore County
    Catonsville *A*
    Dundalk *A*
    Essex *A*
Howard Community College *A*
Salisbury University *B*
Towson University *B*

Massachusetts
Boston University *B*
Dean College *A*
Endicott College *B*
Lasell College *B*
Merrimack College *B*
Northeastern University *B*
Springfield College *B, M*
Westfield State College *B*

Michigan
Aquinas College *B*
Calvin College *B*
Central Michigan University *B*
Eastern Michigan University *B*
Hope College *B*
Northern Michigan University *B*
University of Michigan *B, D*

Minnesota
Bethel College *B*
College of St. Scholastica *C*
Gustavus Adolphus College *B*
Hamline University *B*
Minnesota State University
    Mankato *B*
Northland Community & Technical
    College *A*
Ridgewater College: A Community and
    Technical College *A*
Winona State University *B*

Mississippi
Delta State University *B*

Missouri
Central Methodist College *B*
Culver-Stockton College *B*

Lindenwood University *B, M*
Missouri Baptist University *B*
Southeast Missouri State University *B*
Southwest Baptist University *B*
Southwest Missouri State University *B*
Westminster College *B*
William Woods University *B*

Montana
Rocky Mountain College *B*
University of Montana-Missoula *B*

Nebraska
Midland Lutheran College *B*
Nebraska Wesleyan University *B*
University of Nebraska
    Lincoln *B*

Nevada
University of Nevada
    Las Vegas *B*

New Hampshire
Colby-Sawyer College *B*
Keene State College *B*
New England College *B*
Plymouth State College *B, M, D*
University of New Hampshire *B*

New Jersey
Rowan University *B*

New Mexico
New Mexico Junior College *A*
New Mexico State University *B*

New York
Alfred University *B*
Canisius College *B*
Concordia College *B*
Dominican College of Blauvelt *B*
Finger Lakes Community College *A*
Hofstra University *B*
Ithaca College *B*
Marist College *B*
Russell Sage College *B*
State University of New York
    College at Brockport *B*

North Carolina
Appalachian State University *B*
Barton College *B*
Campbell University *B*
Catawba College *B*
Chowan College *B*
East Carolina University *B*
Elon University *B*
Gardner-Webb University *B*
Greensboro College *B*
Guilford College *B*
High Point University *B*
Lenoir-Rhyne College *B*
Louisburg College *A*
Mars Hill College *B*
Methodist College *B*
North Carolina Central University *B*
Pfeiffer University *B*
St. Andrews Presbyterian College *B*
Shaw University *B*
University of North Carolina
    Charlotte *B*
    Pembroke *B*
    Wilmington *B*
Wingate University *B*

North Dakota
Mayville State University *B*
North Dakota State University *B*
University of Mary *B*
University of North Dakota *B*

Ohio
Ashland University *B*
Baldwin-Wallace College *B*
Bowling Green State University *B*
Cedarville University *B*
College of Mount St. Joseph *B*
Defiance College *C, B*
Heidelberg College *B*

Kent State University *B*
Lorain County Community College *A*
Marietta College *B*
Miami University
    Oxford Campus *B*
Mount Union College *B*
Ohio Northern University *B*
Ohio University *B, M*
Otterbein College *B*
Shawnee State University *B*
University of Findlay *B*
Urbana University *B*
Youngstown State University *B*

Oklahoma
East Central University *B*
Northeastern Oklahoma Agricultural and
    Mechanical College *A*
Northeastern State University *B*
Oklahoma Baptist University *B*
Oklahoma City University *B*
Oklahoma State University *B*
Redlands Community College *A*
Rose State College *A*
St. Gregory's University *B*
Southern Nazarene University *B*
Southwestern Oklahoma State
    University *B*
University of Tulsa *B*

Oregon
Concordia University *B*
George Fox University *B*
Linfield College *B*
Southern Oregon University *B*

Pennsylvania
California University of
    Pennsylvania *B, M*
Carlow College *B*
Duquesne University *B*
East Stroudsburg University of
    Pennsylvania *B*
King's College *B*
Lock Haven University of
    Pennsylvania *B*
Marywood University *B*
Mercyhurst College *B*
Messiah College *B*
University of Pittsburgh
    Bradford *B*
Waynesburg College *B*
West Chester University of
    Pennsylvania *B, M*

Puerto Rico
University of Puerto Rico
    Mayaguez Campus *B*
    Ponce *B*

South Carolina
Anderson College *B*
Charleston Southern University *C*
Erskine College *B*
Lander University *B*
Limestone College *B*

South Dakota
Augustana College *B*
Dakota Wesleyan University *B*
Mount Marty College *B*
South Dakota State University *B*

Tennessee
Bryan College *B*
Carson-Newman College *B*
Lambuth University *B*
Middle Tennessee State University *B*
Tennessee Wesleyan College *B*
Tusculum College *B*
Union University *B*
University of Tennessee
    Chattanooga *M*
    Martin *B*

Texas
Angelo State University *B*
East Texas Baptist University *B*

Hardin-Simmons University *B*
Howard College *A*
Howard Payne University *B*
Lubbock Christian University *B*
McMurry University *T*
South Plains College *A*
Southwest Texas State University *B, T*
Texas A&M University
    Commerce *B*
Texas Lutheran University *B*
Texas Tech University *M*
Texas Wesleyan University *B*
Texas Woman's University *M*
University of Texas
    Arlington *B*

Utah
Brigham Young University *M*
Weber State University *B*

Vermont
Castleton State College *B*
Johnson State College *B*
Lyndon State College *C, B*
Norwich University *B*

Virginia
Averett University *B*
Bluefield College *B*
Bridgewater College *B*
College of Health Sciences *B*
Emory & Henry College *B*
Liberty University *B*
Longwood University *B*
Lynchburg College *B*
Marymount University *B*
Roanoke College *B*
Shenandoah University *M*

Washington
Centralia College *A*
Eastern Washington University *B*
Pacific Lutheran University *R*
Spokane Falls Community College *A*
Washington State University *B*
Western Washington University *B*
Whitworth College *B*

West Virginia
Alderson-Broaddus College *B*
Salem International University *B*
University of Charleston *B*
West Virginia University *B, T*
West Virginia Wesleyan College *B*

Wisconsin
Carroll College *B*
Carthage College *B*
Concordia University Wisconsin *B*
Marquette University *B*
University of Wisconsin
    Eau Claire *B*
    La Crosse *B*
    Madison *C*
    Stevens Point *B*

Atmospheric physics/ dynamics

New Mexico
New Mexico Institute of Mining and
    Technology *B, M, D*

Pennsylvania
Drexel University *B, M, D*

Atmospheric sciences

Alabama
Community College of the Air Force *A*
University of Alabama
    Huntsville *M, D*
University of South Alabama *B*

Alaska
University of Alaska
  Fairbanks *M, D*

Arizona
University of Arizona *B, M, D*

California
California State University
  Chico *B*
San Jose State University *M*
University of California
  Davis *B, M, D*
  Los Angeles *B, M, D*

Colorado
Colorado State University *M, D*
Metropolitan State College of Denver *B*
United States Air Force Academy *B*

Connecticut
Western Connecticut State University *B*

Delaware
University of Delaware *D*

Florida
Embry-Riddle Aeronautical University *B*
Florida State University *C, B, M, D*
Gulf Coast Community College *A*
Miami-Dade Community College *A*
Polk Community College *A*
South Florida Community College *A*
University of Miami *B, M, D*

Hawaii
University of Hawaii
  Manoa *B, M, D*

Illinois
Northern Illinois University *B*
Parkland College *A*
University of Illinois
  Urbana-Champaign *M, D*

Indiana
Purdue University *B, M, D*
Valparaiso University *B*

Iowa
Iowa State University *B, M, D*

Kansas
University of Kansas *B*

Louisiana
University of Louisiana at Monroe *B*

Maryland
Johns Hopkins University *B*
University of Maryland
  College Park *M, D*

Massachusetts
Harvard College *B*
Massachusetts Institute of Technology *D*

Michigan
University of Michigan *B, M, D*

Minnesota
St. Cloud State University *B*

Missouri
St. Louis University *B, M, D*
University of Missouri
  Columbia *B, M, D*

Nebraska
Creighton University *B, M*
University of Nebraska
  Lincoln *B*

Nevada
University of Nevada
  Reno *M, D*

New Hampshire
Plymouth State College *B*

New Jersey
Princeton University *M, D*

Rutgers, The State University of New
  Jersey
    New Brunswick Regional
      Campus *B*

New York
Cornell University *B*
State University of New York
  Albany *B, M, D*
  College at Brockport *B*
  College at Oneonta *B*
  Maritime College *B*
  Oswego *B*
  Stony Brook *B*

North Carolina
North Carolina State University *B*
University of North Carolina
  Asheville *B*

North Dakota
University of North Dakota *B*

Ohio
Ohio State University
  Columbus Campus *M, D*
Ohio University *B*
Shawnee State University *B*

Oklahoma
University of Oklahoma *B, M, D*

Oregon
Oregon State University *M, D*

Pennsylvania
California University of Pennsylvania *B*
Geneva College *B*
Millersville University of
  Pennsylvania *B*
Penn State
  Abington *B*
  Altoona *B*
  Beaver *B*
  Berks *B*
  Delaware County *B*
  Dubois *B*
  Fayette *B*
  Hazleton *B*
  Lehigh Valley *B*
  McKeesport *B*
  Mont Alto *B*
  New Kensington *B*
  Shenango *B*
  University Park *B, M, D*
  Worthington Scranton *B*
  York *B*

South Dakota
South Dakota School of Mines and
  Technology *M, D*

Texas
Texas A&M University *B, M, D*
Texas Tech University *M*

Utah
University of Utah *B, M, D*

Vermont
Lyndon State College *B*

Washington
Everett Community College *A*
University of Washington *B, M, D*

Wisconsin
Northland College *B*
University of Wisconsin
  Madison *B, M, D*

Wyoming
University of Wyoming *M, D*

Atomic/molecular physics

California
San Diego State University *B*

University of California
  San Diego *B*

District of Columbia
Catholic University of America *B*

Florida
Florida State University *M, D*

Illinois
University of Illinois
  Urbana-Champaign *D*

Kentucky
Centre College *B*

Maine
Bowdoin College *B*

Massachusetts
Harvard College *B*

Minnesota
St. Mary's University of Minnesota *B*
University of Minnesota
  Twin Cities *M, D*

Mississippi
Mississippi College *B*

Nevada
University of Nevada
  Reno *D*

New York
Columbia University
  Columbia College *B*

Ohio
College of Wooster *B*
Kent State University *M, D*
Ohio State University
  Columbus Campus *M, D*
University of Akron *B*

Tennessee
Maryville College *B*

Texas
Rice University *B*
University of North Texas *M, D*

Virginia
Norfolk State University *M*

Wisconsin
Marquette University *M, D*
University of Wisconsin
  Madison *M, D*

Audiology/hearing sciences

Alabama
University of Alabama *M*
University of Montevallo *B, M, T*

Arkansas
Arkansas State University
  Mountain Home *A*

California
California State University
  Chico *C*
San Diego State University *M*

Colorado
University of Northern Colorado *B, M*

District of Columbia
Gallaudet University *D*

Florida
Nova Southeastern University *D*
University of Florida *D*
University of South Florida *D*

Idaho
Idaho State University *M*

Illinois
Northwestern University *B, M, D*

Rush University *D*
Sauk Valley Community College *A*

Indiana
Ball State University *M*
Indiana University
  Bloomington *B*
Indiana University-Purdue University
  Fort Wayne *B*

Iowa
University of Iowa *B*
University of Northern Iowa *M*

Kansas
University of Kansas *D*
University of Kansas Medical
  Center *M, D*

Kentucky
Murray State University *M*

Maryland
University of Maryland
  College Park *D*

Massachusetts
Boston University *M, D*
Emerson College *B, M*
Northeastern University *M*

Michigan
Central Michigan University *M, D*
Wayne State University *M*

Minnesota
Minnesota State University
  Moorhead *B*

Mississippi
University of Southern Mississippi *B*

Missouri
Washington University in St. Louis *M, D*

New Jersey
Camden County College *C*
The College of New Jersey *M*
Seton Hall University *D*

New York
City University of New York
  Hunter College *M*
Hofstra University *M*
State University of New York
  Buffalo *M, D*
  College at Plattsburgh *B, M*
  New Paltz *B, M*
Syracuse University *M, D*

North Carolina
University of North Carolina
  Chapel Hill *M, D*

Ohio
Cleveland State University *B, M*
Kent State University *M, D, T*
Kent State University
  Stark Campus *B*
Ohio State University
  Columbus Campus *B, M, D*
Ohio University *B*

Oklahoma
University of Oklahoma *D*

Oregon
Portland State University *B, M*

Pennsylvania
California University of Pennsylvania *M*
La Salle University *B, M*

Puerto Rico
University of Puerto Rico
  Medical Sciences Campus *M*

Rhode Island
University of Rhode Island *M*

South Dakota
Northern State University *B, T*

Tennessee
University of Memphis *D*
University of Tennessee
    Knoxville *B, M, D*

Texas
Lamar University *M*
Stephen F. Austin State University *B, T*
Texas Tech University *B*
University of Houston *M*
University of North Texas *M*
University of Texas
    Dallas *D*
    Tyler *B*

Utah
Brigham Young University *B*
University of Utah *B, M*

Virginia
James Madison University *M*

Washington
University of Washington *M, D*

Wyoming
University of Wyoming *M*

Audiology/speech pathology

Alabama
Auburn University *B, M*
University of Alabama *B*
University of South Alabama *B, M, D*

Arizona
Arizona State University *M*

Arkansas
Arkansas State University *B*
University of Arkansas *B, M*
University of Arkansas
    Little Rock *B, M*
    for Medical Sciences *M*
University of Central Arkansas *B, M*

California
California State University
    Fullerton *B, M*
    Hayward *B, M*
    Los Angeles *B, M*
    Northridge *M*
    Sacramento *B, M*
Loma Linda University *C, B*
San Francisco State University *B, M*
San Jose State University *B, M*
University of California
    Santa Barbara *B, M, D*
University of Redlands *B, M*
University of the Pacific *B*

Connecticut
Southern Connecticut State University *M*
University of Connecticut *M, D*

District of Columbia
Gallaudet University *M*
George Washington University *B, M*
University of the District of Columbia *M*

Florida
Florida Atlantic University *M*
Florida International University *M*
Florida State University *B, M, D*
Polk Community College *A*
South Florida Community College *A*
University of Central Florida *B, M*
University of Florida *B, M, D*
University of South Florida *B, M*

Hawaii
University of Hawaii
    Manoa *B, M*

Idaho
College of Southern Idaho *A*
Idaho State University *B*
North Idaho College *A*

Illinois
Augustana College *B*
Illinois State University *B, M, T*
Northwestern University *B, D*
Southern Illinois University
    Edwardsville *B, M*
University of Illinois
    Urbana-Champaign *B, M, D*

Indiana
Ball State University *B*
Indiana State University *B, M*
Indiana University
    Bloomington *B, M, D*
Purdue University *B, M, D*

Iowa
University of Iowa *M, D*

Kansas
Fort Hays State University *M*
Wichita State University *B, M, D*

Kentucky
Brescia University *B*
University of Kentucky *B, M*
University of Louisville *M*

Louisiana
Louisiana State University
    Shreveport *B*
Louisiana State University and
    Agricultural and Mechanical
    College *B, M, D*
Louisiana Tech University *B, M*
Southern University and Agricultural and
    Mechanical College *B*
University of Louisiana at
    Lafayette *B, M*
University of Louisiana at Monroe *B, M*
Xavier University of Louisiana *B*

Maine
University of Maine *B, M*

Maryland
Loyola College in Maryland *B, M*
Towson University *B, M, D*

Massachusetts
Boston University *M, D*
Elms College *B*
Emerson College *B*
Northeastern University *B*

Michigan
Andrews University *B*
Calvin College *B*
Central Michigan University *B, T*
Michigan State University *B, M, D*
University of Michigan *B*
Western Michigan University *B, M*

Minnesota
Minnesota State University
    Moorhead *B, M*
St. Cloud State University *B*
University of Minnesota
    Twin Cities *B*

Mississippi
Delta State University *B*
University of Mississippi *B, M*
University of Southern Mississippi *B, M*

Missouri
Central Missouri State University *M*
Fontbonne College *B, M*
St. Louis University *B, M*
Southwest Missouri State
    University *B, M*
University of Missouri
    Columbia *B, M*
Washington University in St. Louis *M*

Nebraska
University of Nebraska
    Lincoln *B, M*

Nevada
University of Nevada
    Reno *B, M*

New Hampshire
University of New Hampshire *M*

New Jersey
Richard Stockton College of New
    Jersey *B*
William Paterson University of New
    Jersey *M*

New Mexico
Eastern New Mexico University *B, M*
University of New Mexico *B, M*

New York
Adelphi University *B, M, D*
City University of New York
    Brooklyn College *B, M*
    Queens College *B, M*
Elmira College *B*
Hofstra University *B, M*
Ithaca College *B, T*
Long Island University
    C. W. Post Campus *B*
Marymount Manhattan College *B*
Mercy College *B*
Molloy College *B*
New York University *M, D*
Pace University *B*
St. John's University *B, M*
State University of New York
    Buffalo *B, M, D, T*
    College at Cortland *B, M*
    College at Fredonia *B, M, T*
    College at Geneseo *B, T*
    College at Plattsburgh *B, M*
    New Paltz *B, M*
Syracuse University *B, M, D*
Yeshiva University *B*

North Carolina
Appalachian State University *B*
East Carolina University *B, M, D*
Guilford Technical Community
    College *A*
North Carolina Central University *M*
Randolph Community College *A*
Shaw University *B*
University of North Carolina
    Chapel Hill *M, D*
    Greensboro *B, M*

North Dakota
University of North Dakota *B, D*

Ohio
College of Wooster *B*
Kent State University *B*
Kent State University
    Stark Campus *B*
Miami University
    Oxford Campus *B, M, T*
Ohio State University
    Columbus Campus *B, M, D*
Ohio University *M, D*
University of Akron *B, M*
University of Cincinnati *B, M, D*

Oklahoma
Northeastern State University *B, M*
University of Central Oklahoma *B*

Oregon
University of Oregon *B, M, D*

Pennsylvania
California University of
    Pennsylvania *B, M*
East Stroudsburg University of
    Pennsylvania *B, M*
Indiana University of Pennsylvania *M*
La Salle University *B, M*
Marywood University *B, M*
Penn State
    University Park *B, M*
Temple University *B, M, D*

Thiel College *B*
University of Pittsburgh *B, M, D*
West Chester University of
    Pennsylvania *B, M*

Puerto Rico
Inter American University of Puerto Rico
    Barranquitas Campus *B*

South Carolina
South Carolina State University *B, M*
University of South Carolina *D*

South Dakota
Augustana College *B*
Northern State University *B, T*

Tennessee
East Tennessee State University *M*
Tennessee State University *B*
University of Memphis *M, D*
Vanderbilt University *M, D*

Texas
Abilene Christian University *B*
Baylor University *M*
Hardin-Simmons University *B*
Howard College *C, A*
Lamar University *B*
Southwest Texas State University *B, M*
Stephen F. Austin State University *B*
Texas Christian University *B, M, T*
Texas Woman's University *B*
University of Houston *B, M*
University of North Texas *B, M*
University of Texas
    Dallas *B, M*
    El Paso *B, M*

Utah
Brigham Young University *M*
University of Utah *B, M, D*
Utah State University *B, M, D*

Vermont
University of Vermont *M*

Virginia
Hampton University *B, M*
Old Dominion University *B, M*
Radford University *M*
University of Virginia *B, M*

Washington
Eastern Washington University *B*
University of Washington *B, M, D*
Western Washington University *B, M*

West Virginia
Marshall University *M*
West Virginia University *B, M*

Wisconsin
Marquette University *B*
University of Wisconsin
    Madison *B, M, D*
    Stevens Point *B, M, T*
    Whitewater *M*

Wyoming
University of Wyoming *B, M*

Auditing

Ohio
Bowling Green State University *B*

Australian/Oceanic/Pacific languages

Hawaii
University of Hawaii
    Hilo *M*

Auto body repair

Alabama

Alabama Southern Community
  College *A*
Bevill State Community College *A*
Bishop State Community College *C*
Gadsden State Community College *C*
George C. Wallace State Community
  College
    Dothan *C, A*
    Selma *C*
Harry M. Ayers State Technical
  College *C*
Lawson State Community College *C, A*
Northwest-Shoals Community College *C*
Reid State Technical College *C*
Shelton State Community College *C, A*
Wallace Community College: Sparks
  Campus *C*
Wallace State Community College at
  Hanceville *C, A*

Arizona

Arizona Western College *C*
Central Arizona College *C*

Arkansas

North Arkansas College *C*
Pulaski Technical College *C*
University of Arkansas
  Cossatot Community College of the
    C

California

Antelope Valley College *C, A*
Cerritos Community College *A*
Cerro Coso Community College *C, A*
Chabot College *A*
Citrus College *C, A*
College of Marin: Kentfield *C, A*
Columbia College *C*
Contra Costa College *C, A*
Cuesta College *C, A*
East Los Angeles College *C*
Gavilan Community College *C*
Golden West College *C, A*
Imperial Valley College *C, A*
Long Beach City College *C, A*
Los Angeles Pierce College *C, A*
Los Angeles Trade and Technical
  College *C, A*
MiraCosta College *C, A*
Modesto Junior College *C, A*
Mount San Jacinto College *C*
Palomar College *C, A*
Riverside Community College *C, A*
Santa Monica College *C, A*
Santa Rosa Junior College *C*
Yuba Community College District *C*

Colorado

Arapahoe Community College *C*
Mesa State College *C, A*
Morgan Community College *A*
Red Rocks Community College *C, A*
Trinidad State Junior College *C, A*

Florida

Daytona Beach Community College *C*
Hillsborough Community College *C*
Palm Beach Community College *C*
South Florida Community College *C*

Georgia

Albany Technical College *C*
Athens Technical College *C*
Central Georgia Technical College *C*
Columbus Technical College *C*
Dalton State College *C, A*
Floyd College *A*
Georgia Southwestern State University *A*
Middle Georgia College *A*

Hawaii

University of Hawaii
  Hawaii Community College *C, A*
  Honolulu Community College *A*
  Kauai Community College *C, A*
  Maui Community College *A*

Idaho

Boise State University *C, A*
College of Southern Idaho *C, A*
Idaho State University *C, A*
Lewis-Clark State College *C, A*
North Idaho College *C, A*

Illinois

Black Hawk College *C, A*
Carl Sandburg College *C, A*
City Colleges of Chicago
  Kennedy-King College *C*
College of Lake County *C*
Illinois Eastern Community Colleges
  Olney Central College *A*
John A. Logan College *A*
Joliet Junior College *C, A*
Kaskaskia College *A*
Kishwaukee College *C, A*
Lake Land College *C*
Parkland College *C*
Prairie State College *C*
Waubonsee Community College *C, A*

Indiana

Vincennes University *A*

Iowa

Des Moines Area Community
  College *C, A*
Hawkeye Community College *C*
Indian Hills Community College *C, A*
Iowa Lakes Community College *C*
Kirkwood Community College *C*
Northeast Iowa Community College *C*
Northwest Iowa Community College *C*
Scott Community College *A*
Southeastern Community College
  North Campus *C*
Southwestern Community College *C*
Western Iowa Tech Community
  College *C, A*

Kansas

Butler County Community College *C, A*
Hutchinson Community College *C, A*

Kentucky

Maysville Community College *C, A*
Somerset Community College *C*

Maryland

Harford Community College *C*

Michigan

Alpena Community College *C*
Bay de Noc Community College *C*
Ferris State University *A*
Kirtland Community College *C*
Mott Community College *A*
Northern Michigan University *C*
Oakland Community College *C*
Washtenaw Community College *C, A*

Minnesota

Central Lakes College *C, A*
Century Community and Technical
  College *C, A*
Dakota County Technical College *C, A*
Hennepin Technical College *C, A*
Inver Hills Community College *A*
Lake Superior College: A Community
  and Technical College *C*
Minnesota State College - Southeast
  Technical *C, A*
Northland Community & Technical
  College *C, A*
Ridgewater College: A Community and
  Technical College *C*
Riverland Community College: A
  Technical and Community College *C*

St. Cloud Technical College *C, A*
St. Paul College - A Community and
  Technical College *C*
South Central Technical College *A*

Mississippi

Coahoma Community College *C*
Itawamba Community College *C*
Mississippi Gulf Coast Community
  College
    Perkinston *C*
Northwest Mississippi Community
  College *C*
Pearl River Community College *C, A*

Missouri

Crowder College *C*
North Central Missouri College *A*
Ozarks Technical Community
  College *C, A*
Ranken Technical College *A*

Montana

Montana State University
  Billings *C, A*
    Billings College of Technology *C*
Montana Tech of the University of
  Montana *A*

Nebraska

Central Community College *C, A*
Metropolitan Community College *C, A*
Mid Plains Community College
  Area *C, A*
Northeast Community College *A*
Southeast Community College
  Milford Campus *A*
Western Nebraska Community
  College *C, A*

New Hampshire

New Hampshire Community Technical
  College
    Nashua *A*

New Mexico

Albuquerque Technical-Vocational
  Institute *C*
San Juan College *C, A*

New York

Erie Community College
  South Campus *A*
State University of New York
  College of Agriculture and
    Technology at Morrisville *A*
  College of Technology at Alfred *A*

North Carolina

Blue Ridge Community College *C*
Caldwell Community College and
  Technical Institute *C*
Cape Fear Community College *C*
Cleveland Community College *C*
Coastal Carolina Community College *C*
Craven Community College *C*
Edgecombe Community College *C*
Fayetteville Technical Community
  College *C*
Forsyth Technical Community College *C*
Guilford Technical Community
  College *C*
Haywood Community College *C*
Isothermal Community College *C, A*
Mayland Community College *C*
Montgomery Community College *C*
Randolph Community College *C*
Sandhills Community College *C*
South Piedmont Community College *C*
Stanly Community College *C*
Surry Community College *C*
Tri-County Community College *C*
Wilkes Community College *C*

North Dakota

Bismarck State College *C, A*
North Dakota State College of
  Science *C, A*

Ohio

Owens Community College
  Toledo *C, A*

Oklahoma

Oklahoma State University
  Okmulgee *A*
Western Oklahoma State College *A*

Oregon

Clackamas Community College *C, A*
Lane Community College *C, A*
Linn-Benton Community College *C*
Portland Community College *C, A*

Pennsylvania

Commonwealth Technical Institute *C*
Delaware County Community College *C*
Pennsylvania College of
  Technology *C, A*

South Dakota

Southeast Technical Institute *A*
Western Dakota Technical Institute *C*

Tennessee

Chattanooga State Technical Community
  College *C*
Nashville Auto-Diesel College *C, A*

Texas

Amarillo College *C*
Central Texas College *C, A*
Del Mar College *C*
Eastfield College *C, A*
Grayson County College *C*
Hill College *C, A*
Houston Community College System *C*
Howard College *C*
Kilgore College *C, A*
St. Philip's College *C, A*
South Plains College *C, A*
Tarrant County College *C, A*
Texarkana College *C*
Texas State Technical College
  Waco *C, A*
  West Texas *C*
Trinity Valley Community College *C*

Utah

Dixie State College of Utah *C, A*
Salt Lake Community College *C, A*
Utah Valley State College *C, A*
Weber State University *C, A*

Virginia

Danville Community College *C*

Washington

Clover Park Technical College *C*
Green River Community College *C, A*
Lake Washington Technical College *C, A*
Lower Columbia College *C, A*
Renton Technical College *C, A*
South Seattle Community College *C, A*
Spokane Community College *A*
Walla Walla Community College *C, A*

Wisconsin

Chippewa Valley Technical College *C*
Fox Valley Technical College *C*
Lakeshore Technical College *C*
Mid-State Technical College *C*
Milwaukee Area Technical College *C*
Moraine Park Technical College *C*
Waukesha County Technical College *C*
Wisconsin Indianhead Technical
  College *C*

Wyoming

Laramie County Community
  College *C, A*

Automotive engineering technology

California

Santa Barbara City College *C, A*

Taft College *C, A*

Illinois
Southern Illinois University
 Carbondale *B*

Kentucky
Jefferson Community College *A*

Massachusetts
Benjamin Franklin Institute of
 Technology *A, B*

Michigan
Grand Rapids Community College *A*
Western Michigan University *B*

Minnesota
Hennepin Technical College *C, A*

Missouri
Central Missouri State University *A*

New Mexico
Santa Fe Community College *C*

New York
Rochester Institute of Technology *B*
State University of New York
 College of Agriculture and
 Technology at
 Morrisville *C, A, B*
 College of Technology at
 Canton *C, A*

North Carolina
Pitt Community College *A*

North Dakota
North Dakota State College of Science *A*

Ohio
Sinclair Community College *C, A*
University of Akron *A*

Pennsylvania
Community College of Allegheny
 County *C, A*
Montgomery County Community
 College *C, A*
Northampton County Area Community
 College *C, A*
Pennsylvania College of
 Technology *C, A, B*

Wisconsin
Milwaukee Area Technical College *A*

Automotive technology

Alabama
Bishop State Community College *C*
Douglas MacArthur State Technical
 College *C*
Gadsden State Community College *C*
George C. Wallace State Community
 College
 Selma *C*
J. F. Drake State Technical College *C*
Northwest-Shoals Community College *C*
Shelton State Community College *C*
Wallace Community College: Sparks
 Campus *C*
Wallace State Community College at
 Hanceville *C, A*

Alaska
University of Alaska
 Anchorage *C, A*
 Fairbanks *C*
 Southeast *C, A*

Arizona
Arizona Automotive Institute *C, A*
Arizona Western College *A*
Central Arizona College *C, A*
Eastern Arizona College *C, A*
Gateway Community College *C, A*
Glendale Community College *C, A*
Pima Community College *C, A*

Yavapai College *C, A*

Arkansas
Arkansas State University *A*
North Arkansas College *C*
Ozarka College *C, A*
University of Arkansas
 Cossatot Community College of the
 A
 Fort Smith *C, A*

California
Antelope Valley College *C, A*
Bakersfield College *A*
Chabot College *C, A*
Citrus College *C, A*
Columbia College *A*
Copper Mountain College *C, A*
Don Bosco Technical Institute *A*
East Los Angeles College *C, A*
Golden West College *C, A*
Long Beach City College *C, A*
Los Angeles Harbor College *C, A*
Los Angeles Pierce College *C, A*
MiraCosta College *C, A*
Modesto Junior College *C, A*
Mount San Jacinto College *C, A*
Riverside Community College *C, A*
Santa Barbara City College *C, A*
Santa Rosa Junior College *C*
Santiago Canyon College *A*
Shasta College *C, A*
Sierra College *C, A*
Southwestern College *C, A*
Taft College *C, A*
Ventura College *C, A*
Victor Valley College *C, A*
Yuba Community College District *C, A*

Colorado
Arapahoe Community College *C, A*
Front Range Community College *C, A*
Mesa State College *C, A*
Morgan Community College *C, A*
Otero Junior College *C*
Red Rocks Community College *C, A*
Trinidad State Junior College *C, A*

Connecticut
Gateway Community College *A*
Naugatuck Valley Community
 College *C, A*

Florida
Broward Community College *A*
Indian River Community College *C, A*
New England Institute of Technology *A*
Palm Beach Community College *C, A*
Pensacola Junior College *A*
Seminole Community College *C, A*
South Florida Community College *C*

Georgia
Albany Technical College *C*
Athens Technical College *C*
Chattahoochee Technical College *C, A*
Columbus Technical College *C*
DeKalb Technical College *A*
Middle Georgia College *A*
Savannah Technical College *A*
Southwest Georgia Technical College *C*
Waycross College *A*
West Georgia Technical College *C*

Hawaii
University of Hawaii
 Hawaii Community College *C, A*
 Honolulu Community College *A*
 Kauai Community College *C, A*
 Maui Community College *A*

Idaho
Boise State University *C, A*
Brigham Young University - Idaho *A*
College of Southern Idaho *C, A*
Eastern Idaho Technical College *C, A*
Idaho State University *C, A*
North Idaho College *C, A*

Illinois
Black Hawk College *C, A*
Black Hawk College
 East Campus *C, A*
City Colleges of Chicago
 Kennedy-King College *C, A*
College of DuPage *C, A*
College of Lake County *C, A*
Elgin Community College *C, A*
John A. Logan College *C, A*
Kankakee Community College *C, A*
Kaskaskia College *C, A*
Kishwaukee College *C, A*
Lewis and Clark Community College *A*
McHenry County College *C, A*
Moraine Valley Community
 College *C, A*
Oakton Community College *C, A*
Parkland College *A*
Prairie State College *C, A*
Rend Lake College *C, A*
Richland Community College *A*
Rock Valley College *C, A*
Southern Illinois University
 Carbondale *B*
Spoon River College *A*
Triton College *C, A*
Waubonsee Community College *C, A*

Indiana
Ivy Tech State College
 Central Indiana *A*
 Columbus *A*
 Eastcentral *C, A*
 Kokomo *C, A*
 Lafayette *C, A*
 Northcentral *A*
 Northeast *C, A*
 Northwest *A*
 Southcentral *C, A*
 Southwest *A*
 Wabash Valley *C, A*
 Whitewater *A*
Vincennes University *A*

Iowa
Des Moines Area Community
 College *C, A*
Indian Hills Community College *A*
Iowa Central Community College *A*
Iowa Lakes Community College *C*
Kirkwood Community College *C, A*
North Iowa Area Community College *A*
Northeast Iowa Community
 College *C, A*
Northwest Iowa Community College *A*
Scott Community College *A*
Western Iowa Tech Community
 College *C, A*

Kansas
Barton County Community College *C, A*
Butler County Community College *C, A*
Hutchinson Community College *C, A*
Johnson County Community
 College *C, A*
McPherson College *A*
North Central Kansas Technical
 College *A*
Pittsburg State University *C, A, B*

Kentucky
Hazard Community College *A*
Maysville Community College *C, A*
Somerset Community College *C*

Louisiana
Delgado Community College *C, A*

Maine
Central Maine Technical College *A*

Maryland
Allegany College *C, A*
Community College of Baltimore County
 Catonsville *C, A*
 Dundalk *C, A*
 Essex *C, A*

Harford Community College *C*
Montgomery College
 Rockville Campus *C*

Massachusetts
Benjamin Franklin Institute of
 Technology *A, B*
Mount Wachusett Community
 College *C, A*
Quinsigamond Community College *C, A*

Michigan
Alpena Community College *C, A*
Baker College
 of Owosso *C, A*
Bay de Noc Community College *C, A*
Ferris State University *A*
Glen Oaks Community College *C*
Gogebic Community College *C, A*
Grand Rapids Community College *C*
Jackson Community College *C, A*
Kirtland Community College *C*
Macomb Community College *C, A*
Mid Michigan Community College *C*
Mott Community College *C, A*
Northern Michigan University *C, A*
Northwestern Michigan College *C, A*
Oakland Community College *C, A*
Southwestern Michigan College *C, A*
Wayne County Community College *C*

Minnesota
Anoka-Ramsey Community College *A*
Central Lakes College *C, A*
Century Community and Technical
 College *C, A*
Dakota County Technical College *C, A*
Hennepin Technical College *C, A*
Hibbing Community College: A
 Technical and Community College *C*
Lake Superior College: A Community
 and Technical College *C, A*
Mesabi Range Community and Technical
 College *C, A*
Minnesota State College - Southeast
 Technical *C*
Minnesota State University
 Mankato *B*
North Hennepin Community College *A*
Northland Community & Technical
 College *C, A*
Pine Technical College *C, A*
Ridgewater College: A Community and
 Technical College *C, A*
Riverland Community College: A
 Technical and Community College *C*
Rochester Community and Technical
 College *C*
St. Cloud Technical College *C, A*
St. Paul College - A Community and
 Technical College *C*
South Central Technical College *A*

Mississippi
Itawamba Community College *A*

Missouri
Central Missouri State University *A*
Crowder College *C, A*
Jefferson College *C, A*
Ozarks Technical Community
 College *C, A*
Ranken Technical College *A*
St. Louis Community College
 St. Louis Community College at
 Forest Park *C, A*

Montana
Dawson Community College *A*
Montana State University
 Billings *C, A*
 Billings College of
 Technology *C, A*
Montana Tech of the University of
 Montana *A*

Nebraska
Metropolitan Community College *C, A*

Mid Plains Community College
Area *C, A*
Northeast Community College *A*
Western Nebraska Community
College *C, A*

Nevada
Community College of Southern
Nevada *A*
Truckee Meadows Community
College *A*
Western Nevada Community
College *C, A*

New Hampshire
New Hampshire Community Technical
College
Berlin *C, A*
Laconia *A*
Manchester *C, A*
Nashua *A*
Stratham *C, A*

New Jersey
Brookdale Community College *C*
Burlington County College *A*
Gloucester County College *A*
Mercer County Community College *C, A*
Middlesex County College *A*
Sussex County Community College *C, A*

New Mexico
Albuquerque Technical-Vocational
Institute *C*
Clovis Community College *C, A*
Dona Ana Branch Community College of
New Mexico State University *C, A*
New Mexico Junior College *C, A*
San Juan College *C, A*
Santa Fe Community College *C*
Western New Mexico University *C, A*

New York
Corning Community College *C, A*
Erie Community College
South Campus *A*
Fulton-Montgomery Community
College *C, A*
Monroe Community College *A*
Onondaga Community College *A*
Rockland Community College *A*
State University of New York
College of Agriculture and
Technology at Morrisville *A*
College of Technology at Alfred *A*
College of Technology at
Canton *C, A*
Farmingdale *A*
Suffolk County Community College *A*
Westchester Community College *A*

North Carolina
Asheville Buncombe Technical
Community College *C, A*
Beaufort County Community College *A*
Bladen Community College *C*
Blue Ridge Community College *C*
Caldwell Community College and
Technical Institute *C*
Cape Fear Community College *A*
Catawba Valley Community
College *C, A*
Central Carolina Community College *A*
Coastal Carolina Community College *C*
Craven Community College *C, A*
Davidson County Community
College *C, A*
Durham Technical Community
College *A*
Fayetteville Technical Community
College *C, A*
Guilford Technical Community
College *C, A*
Haywood Community College *C, A*
Lenoir Community College *C, A*
Martin Community College *C, A*
Randolph Community College *A*

Rowan-Cabarrus Community College *C*
Sandhills Community College *C, A*
South Piedmont Community College *C*
Southwestern Community College *A*
Surry Community College *A*
Tri-County Community College *A*
Wilkes Community College *C, A*
Wilson Technical Community College *C*

North Dakota
Bismarck State College *C, A*
Lake Region State College *C, A*
North Dakota State College of
Science *C, A*
Williston State College *A*

Ohio
Cincinnati State Technical and
Community College *A*
Columbus State Community College *A*
Cuyahoga Community College
Eastern Campus *A*
Metropolitan Campus *A*
Western Campus *A*
Muskingum Area Technical College *A*
Owens Community College
Toledo *A*
Sinclair Community College *C, A*
Stark State College of Technology *A*
University of Cincinnati
Raymond Walters College *C, A*
University of Northwestern Ohio *C, A*
Washington State Community College *A*

Oklahoma
Oklahoma State University
Okmulgee *A*
Western Oklahoma State College *A*

Oregon
Blue Mountain Community College *A*
Central Oregon Community
College *C, A*
Chemeketa Community College *A*
Clackamas Community College *A*
Clatsop Community College *C*
Lane Community College *C, A*
Linn-Benton Community College *C, A*
Mount Hood Community College *A*
Portland Community College *C, A*
Rogue Community College *C, A*
Southwestern Oregon Community
College *A*

Pennsylvania
Delaware County Community College *C*
Lehigh Carbon Community College *C, A*
Luzerne County Community College *A*
New Castle School of Trades *A*

Puerto Rico
University of Puerto Rico
Carolina Regional College *A, B*

South Carolina
Aiken Technical College *A*
Florence-Darlington Technical
College *C, A*
Midlands Technical College *C, A*
Orangeburg-Calhoun Technical
College *A*
Piedmont Technical College *A*
Spartanburg Technical College *C, A*
Trident Technical College *C, A*
Williamsburg Technical College *C*
York Technical College *A*

South Dakota
Southeast Technical Institute *A*
Western Dakota Technical Institute *C, A*

Tennessee
Nashville Auto-Diesel College *C, A*
Northeast State Technical Community
College *C, A*
Southern Adventist University *C, A*
Southwest Tennessee Community
College *A*

Texas
Amarillo College *C, A*
Angelina College *C*
Austin Community College *C, A*
Brazosport College *C, A*
Central Texas College *C, A*
Del Mar College *A*
Eastfield College *C, A*
El Paso Community College *C*
Houston Community College
System *C, A*
Kilgore College *C, A*
Lamar State College at Port Arthur *C, A*
Laredo Community College *C*
Midland College *C, A*
North Harris Montgomery Community
College District *C, A*
Ranger College *C, A*
St. Philip's College *C, A*
South Plains College *C, A*
South Texas Community College *C, A*
Tarrant County College *C, A*
Temple College *C, A*
Texas State Technical College
Waco *A*
Trinity Valley Community College *C*
Tyler Junior College *C, A*

Utah
Dixie State College of Utah *C, A*
Salt Lake Community College *A*
Utah Valley State College *C, A*
Weber State University *C, A*

Vermont
Vermont Technical College *A*

Virginia
Blue Ridge Community College *C*
J. Sargeant Reynolds Community
College *C, A*
Southside Virginia Community
College *C*
Southwest Virginia Community
College *C*
Thomas Nelson Community
College *C, A*

Washington
Clark College *C, A*
Clover Park Technical College *C, A*
Grays Harbor College *A*
Lake Washington Technical College *C, A*
Olympic College *A*
Peninsula College *A*
Renton Technical College *C, A*
South Seattle Community College *C, A*
Spokane Falls Community College *C, A*
Walla Walla College *B*
Walla Walla Community College *C, A*
Wenatchee Valley College *C, A*

Wisconsin
Fox Valley Technical College *A*
Lakeshore Technical College *C*
Milwaukee Area Technical College *A*
Moraine Park Technical College *C*
Nicolet Area Technical College *A*
Waukesha County Technical College *A*
Western Wisconsin Technical College *A*

Wyoming
Casper College *C, A*
Central Wyoming College *C, A*
Western Wyoming Community
College *C, A*

Aviation management

Alabama
Auburn University *B*
Community College of the Air Force *A*

Alaska
University of Alaska
Anchorage *A, B*

California
College of Alameda *C, A*

Colorado
Metropolitan State College of Denver *B*

Connecticut
Naugatuck Valley Community College *A*

Delaware
Delaware State University *B*
Wilmington College *B*

Florida
Broward Community College *A*
Embry Riddle Aeronautical
University-Extended Campus *B, M*
Embry-Riddle Aeronautical University *B*
Everglades College *A, B*
Florida Institute of Technology *B, M*
Jacksonville University *B*
Miami-Dade Community College *A*

Hawaii
University of Hawaii
Honolulu Community College *A*

Illinois
Lewis University *C, B*
Lincoln Land Community College *A*
Quincy University *B*
Southern Illinois University
Carbondale *B*
University of Illinois
Urbana-Champaign *B*

Indiana
Indiana State University *B*
Vincennes University *A*

Iowa
University of Dubuque *B*

Kansas
Central Christian College *A*
Fort Scott Community College *A*

Louisiana
Louisiana Tech University *B*
Southern University
Shreveport *A*

Maryland
Community College of Baltimore County
Catonsville *C, A*
Dundalk *C, A*
Essex *C, A*

Massachusetts
Bridgewater State College *B*

Michigan
Baker College
of Muskegon *A, B*
Northern Michigan University *A*
Oakland Community College *A*
Western Michigan University *B*

Minnesota
Academy College *A*
Dakota County Technical College *C, A*
Inver Hills Community College *A*
Lake Superior College: A Community
and Technical College *A*
Minnesota State University
Mankato *B*
Northland Community & Technical
College *C, A*
Vermilion Community College *A*
Winona State University *A*

Missouri
Central Missouri State University *M*
St. Louis University *A, B*

Montana
Rocky Mountain College *B*

Nebraska
University of Nebraska
Omaha *B*

New Hampshire
Daniel Webster College *A, B*

New Jersey
Mercer County Community College *A*

New Mexico
Eastern New Mexico University: Roswell
Campus *C, A*

New York
College of Aeronautics *A, B*
Dowling College *B, M*
Schenectady County Community
College *A*
State University of New York
Farmingdale *B*

North Carolina
Caldwell Community College and
Technical Institute *A*
Guilford Technical Community
College *C, A*
Lenoir Community College *A*

North Dakota
North Dakota State University *B*
University of North Dakota *B*

Ohio
Bowling Green State University *B*
Ohio University *A, B*
Sinclair Community College *A*
University of Akron *A*

Oklahoma
Oklahoma State University *B*
Rose State College *A*
Southern Nazarene University *B*
Tulsa Community College *A*
Western Oklahoma State College *A*

Pennsylvania
Community College of Allegheny
County *A*
Community College of Beaver County *A*
Lehigh Carbon Community College *A*
Luzerne County Community College *A*
Marywood University *B*
Robert Morris University *B*

Puerto Rico
Inter American University of Puerto Rico
Bayamon Campus *B*

Tennessee
Middle Tennessee State University *M*

Texas
LeTourneau University *B*
Midland College *C*
Tarleton State University *B*
Texas Southern University *B*

Utah
Westminster College *B*

Virginia
Averett University *B*
Hampton University *B*

West Virginia
Fairmont State College *B*
Mountain State University *A*
Salem International University *B*

Avionics maintenance/ technology

Alabama
Bevill State Community College *C*

California
Northrop-Rice Aviation Institute of
Technology *A, B*

Georgia
Atlanta Metropolitan College *A*

Illinois
Lewis University *B*
Southern Illinois University
Carbondale *B*

Indiana
Ivy Tech State College
Wabash Valley *C*

Michigan
Lansing Community College *A*

Minnesota
Northland Community & Technical
College *A*

New York
College of Aeronautics *A, B*

Oklahoma
Tulsa Community College *A*

Pennsylvania
Pennsylvania College of
Technology *C, A, B*

Texas
Texas State Technical College
Waco *A*

Utah
Utah Valley State College *A*

Washington
Northwest Aviation College *A*
South Seattle Community College *C, A*

Wisconsin
Fox Valley Technical College *A*

Ayurvedic medicine

Iowa
Maharishi University of
Management *B, D*

Bacteriology

Alabama
Auburn University *B, M, D*
University of Alabama *B*
University of Alabama
Birmingham *D*

Arizona
Arizona State University *B, M, D*
Northern Arizona University *B*
University of Arizona *B, M, D*

Arkansas
University of Arkansas *B*
University of Arkansas
for Medical Sciences *M, D*

California
Bakersfield College *A*
California Polytechnic State University:
San Luis Obispo *B*
California State Polytechnic University:
Pomona *B*
California State University
Chico *B*
Dominguez Hills *B*
Fresno *B, M*
Long Beach *B, M*
Los Angeles *B, M*
Northridge *B*
Sacramento *B*
Stanislaus *B*
Cerritos Community College *A*
Loma Linda University *M, D*
Pitzer College *B*
San Diego State University *B, M*
San Francisco State University *B, M*
San Jose State University *M*
Stanford University *M, D*

University of California
Berkeley *D*
Davis *B, M, D*
Irvine *D*
Los Angeles *B, M, D*
Riverside *M, D*
San Diego *B*
Santa Barbara *B*
University of Southern California *M, D*

Colorado
Colorado State University *B, M, D*
University of Colorado
Health Sciences Center *D*

Connecticut
Southern Connecticut State University *B*
University of Connecticut *M, D*

District of Columbia
George Washington University *M, D*
Georgetown University *D*
Howard University *M, D*

Florida
University of Central Florida *B, M*
University of Florida *B, M, D*
University of South Florida *B, M*
University of West Florida *B*

Georgia
University of Georgia *B, M, D*

Hawaii
University of Hawaii
Manoa *B, M, D*

Idaho
Idaho State University *B, M*
University of Idaho *B, M, D*

Illinois
Chicago State University *B*
Finch University of Health Sciences/The
Chicago Medical School *M, D*
Loyola University of Chicago *M, D*
Northwestern University *M, D*
Southern Illinois University
Carbondale *B, M, D*
University of Chicago *M, D*
University of Illinois
Chicago *M, D*
Urbana-Champaign *B, M, D*

Indiana
Ball State University *B*
Indiana University
Bloomington *B, M, D*
Indiana University-Purdue University
Indianapolis *M, D*

Iowa
Iowa State University *B, M, D*
University of Iowa *B, M, D*

Kansas
Central Christian College *A*
Kansas State University *B, M, D*
University of Kansas Medical
Center *M, D*

Kentucky
University of Kentucky: College of
Medicine *D*
University of Louisville *M, D*

Louisiana
Nicholls State University *B*
Tulane University *M, D*
Xavier University of Louisiana *B*

Maine
University of Maine *B, M, D*

Maryland
Johns Hopkins University *D*
University of Maryland
Baltimore *M, D*
College Park *B, M, D*

Massachusetts
Boston University *M, D*
Hampshire College *B*
Tufts University *M, D*

Michigan
Michigan State University *B, M, D*
Northern Michigan University *B*
University of Michigan *B, M, D*
University of Michigan
Dearborn *B*

Minnesota
Minnesota State University
Mankato *B, M, T*
St. Cloud State University *B*
University of Minnesota
Duluth *M*
Twin Cities *B, M, D*

Mississippi
Mississippi State University *B*
Mississippi University for Women *B*
University of Mississippi Medical
Center *M, D*

Missouri
Missouri Southern State College *B*
University of Missouri
Columbia *B, M, D*
Washington University in St. Louis *D*

Montana
Montana State University
Bozeman *B, M, D*
University of Great Falls *B*
University of Montana-Missoula *B, M, D*

Nebraska
Creighton University *M, D*
University of Nebraska
Medical Center *M, D*

Nevada
University of Nevada
Reno *M, D*

New Hampshire
University of New Hampshire *B, M, D*

New Jersey
Rowan University *B*
Rutgers, The State University of New
Jersey
New Brunswick Regional
Campus *B, M, D*
Seton Hall University *M*

New Mexico
New Mexico State University *B*

New York
Cornell University *B, M, D*
Long Island University
C. W. Post Campus *M*
New York University *M, D*
State University of New York
Buffalo *M, D*
College of Environmental Science
and Forestry *B, M, D*
Health Science Center at Stony
Brook *D*
Stony Brook *D*
Upstate Medical University *M, D*
University of Rochester *B, M, D*
Wagner College *B, M*
Yeshiva University *M, D*

North Carolina
Duke University *M, D*
East Carolina University *D*
North Carolina State University *B, M, D*
University of North Carolina
Chapel Hill *M, D*
Wake Forest University *B*

North Dakota
North Dakota State University *B, M*
University of North Dakota *M, D*

Ohio

Bowling Green State University *B*
Case Western Reserve University *D*
Miami University
    Oxford Campus *B, M, D*
Ohio State University
    Columbus Campus *B, M, D*
Ohio University *B, M, D*
Ohio Wesleyan University *B*
University of Akron *B*
University of Cincinnati *M, D*
Wilmington College *B*
Wright State University *M*

Oklahoma

Eastern Oklahoma State College *A*
Oklahoma State University *M*
University of Oklahoma *B, M, D*

Oregon

Oregon Health Sciences University *M, D*
Oregon State University *B, M, D*

Pennsylvania

Drexel University *M, D*
Juniata College *B*
Penn State
    Abington *B*
    Altoona *B*
    Beaver *B*
    Berks *B*
    Delaware County *B*
    Dubois *B*
    Fayette *B*
    Hazleton *B*
    McKeesport *B*
    Mont Alto *B*
    New Kensington *B*
    Schuylkill - Capital College *B*
    Shenango *B*
    University Park *C, B*
    Wilkes-Barre *B*
    Worthington Scranton *B*
    York *B*
University of Pittsburgh *B*
University of the Sciences in
    Philadelphia *B*
West Chester University of
    Pennsylvania *B*

Puerto Rico

Inter American University of Puerto Rico
    Bayamon Campus *B*
    San German Campus *B*
University of Puerto Rico
    Humacao *B*
    Mayaguez Campus *B*
    Medical Sciences Campus *M, D*

Rhode Island

University of Rhode Island *B, M, D*

South Carolina

Clemson University *B, M, D*
Medical University of South
    Carolina *M, D*

South Dakota

South Dakota State University *B, M*
University of South Dakota *M, D*

Tennessee

University of Memphis *B*
University of Tennessee
    Knoxville *B, M, D*
University of Tennessee Health Science
    Center *M, D*
Vanderbilt University *M, D*

Texas

Laredo Community College *A*
Southwest Texas State University *B, T*
Texas A&M University *B, M, D*
Texas Tech University *B, M*
University of North Texas *M, D*

University of Texas
    Arlington *B*
    El Paso *B*
    Health Science Center at San
      Antonio *M, D*
    Houston Health Science
      Center *M, D*
    Southwestern Medical Center at
      Dallas *M, D*

Utah

Brigham Young University *B, M, D*
Snow College *A*
Weber State University *B*

Vermont

Bennington College *B*
University of Vermont *B, M, D*

Virginia

University of Virginia *D*
Virginia Commonwealth
    University *M, D*

Washington

Eastern Washington University *B*
University of Washington *B, D*
Washington State University *B, M, D*

West Virginia

West Liberty State College *B*

Wisconsin

Marquette University *M, D*
University of Wisconsin
    La Crosse *B*
    Madison *B, M, D*
    Oshkosh *B, M*

Wyoming

Sheridan College *A*

Baking/pastry arts

Alaska

University of Alaska
    Fairbanks *C*

California

California Culinary Academy *C*
Grossmont Community College *C, A*
Long Beach City College *C, A*
Santa Rosa Junior College *C*

Florida

New England Institute of Technology *A*

Illinois

Moraine Valley Community College *C*

Indiana

Vincennes University *C*

Michigan

Baker College
    of Muskegon *C*
Grand Rapids Community College *C*
Mott Community College *C*
Oakland Community College *C*

Minnesota

St. Paul College - A Community and
    Technical College *C*

New Jersey

Hudson County Community College *C*

New Mexico

Albuquerque Technical-Vocational
    Institute *C*

New York

Mohawk Valley Community College *A*

North Dakota

North Dakota State College of Science *A*

Pennsylvania

Bucks County Community College *A*
Pennsylvania College of Technology *A*

Texas

Del Mar College *C*
Houston Community College System *C*

Washington

Art Institute of Seattle *C*
Clark College *C, A*
Renton Technical College *C*
Seattle Central Community College *C, A*
South Seattle Community College *C, A*

Wisconsin

Fox Valley Technical College *A*
Milwaukee Area Technical College *A*

Banking/financial services

Alabama

Alabama Southern Community
    College *A*
George C. Wallace State Community
    College
      Selma *C*
Jefferson State Community College *C, A*
Northeast Alabama Community
    College *A*
University of South Alabama *B*
Wallace State Community College at
    Hanceville *A*

Arizona

Gateway Community College *A*
Phoenix College *A*
Pima Community College *C, A*
Rio Salado College *A*

Arkansas

Northwest Arkansas Community
    College *A*

California

Cabrillo College *A*
California State University
    Bakersfield *B*
    Dominguez Hills *B*
    Northridge *B*
Cerritos Community College *A*
Chabot College *A*
Imperial Valley College *C, A*
Laney College *C, A*
Los Angeles Pierce College *C*
Los Angeles Southwest College *A*
Mount San Antonio College *C, A*
Palomar College *C, A*
San Francisco State University *B*
San Joaquin Delta College *C*
Santa Barbara City College *A*
Shasta College *C*

Colorado

Arapahoe Community College *C, A*
Community College of Aurora *C, A*

Connecticut

Housatonic Community College *C*
Sacred Heart University *A*

Delaware

Delaware Technical and Community
    College
      Owens Campus *A*
      Stanton/Wilmington Campus *A*
      Terry Campus *C, A*

Florida

Daytona Beach Community College *A*
Gulf Coast Community College *A*
Lake-Sumter Community College *A*
Miami-Dade Community College *A*
Northwood University
    Florida Campus *A, B*
Okaloosa-Walton Community College *A*
Pensacola Junior College *A*
Polk Community College *A*
Santa Fe Community College *A*
Schiller International University *B*
Seminole Community College *A*

South Florida Community College *A*
Tallahassee Community College *A*
University of Miami *M*
University of North Florida *B*
University of West Florida *B*

Georgia

Mercer University *M*
South Georgia College *A*

Hawaii

Hawaii Pacific University *B*

Illinois

Black Hawk College *C, A*
Carl Sandburg College *A*
City Colleges of Chicago
    Harold Washington College *C, A*
De Paul University *B*
Illinois Central College *C, A*
Illinois Eastern Community Colleges
    Lincoln Trail College *C, A*
John A. Logan College *A*
Lewis and Clark Community College *A*
Prairie State College *C*
Sauk Valley Community College *C*
Southwestern Illinois College *A*
Waubonsee Community College *C, A*
William Rainey Harper College *C, A*

Indiana

Manchester College *B*
University of Evansville *A*
University of Indianapolis *A*
Vincennes University *A*

Iowa

American Institute of Business *A*
North Iowa Area Community College *A*
Northeast Iowa Community College *A*

Kansas

Dodge City Community College *C, A*
Seward County Community College *C*
Washburn University of Topeka *A*

Kentucky

Elizabethtown Community College *A*
Hopkinsville Community College *A*
Paducah Community College *A*
Southeast Community College *A*

Louisiana

Louisiana College *B*
Southern University
    Shreveport *A*

Maine

Husson College *B*

Maryland

Frederick Community College *C, A*
Hagerstown Community College *A*

Massachusetts

Berkshire Community College *A*
Massachusetts Bay Community
    College *C*
Suffolk University *B, M*

Michigan

Central Michigan University *B*
Ferris State University *B*
Mid Michigan Community College *A*
Monroe County Community
    College *C, A*
Northwood University *A, B*

Minnesota

Alexandria Technical College *C, A*
Minnesota State University
    Mankato *B*
University of Minnesota
    Twin Cities *C*

Mississippi

Mississippi Gulf Coast Community
    College
      Perkinston *A*

Missouri
East Central College *C*
St. Louis Community College
St. Louis Community College at
Florissant Valley *A*
St. Louis Community College at
Forest Park *A*
St. Louis Community College at
Meramec *A*
Southeast Missouri State University *B*

Nebraska
University of Nebraska
Omaha *B*

Nevada
Community College of Southern
Nevada *A*
Western Nevada Community
College *C, A*

New Jersey
Bergen Community College *A*
Camden County College *A*
St. Peter's College *B*

New Mexico
Albuquerque Technical-Vocational
Institute *C, A*
Clovis Community College *A*
Eastern New Mexico University: Roswell
Campus *C, A*
New Mexico Junior College *A*
New Mexico State University
Alamogordo *C*
San Juan College *A*

New York
Adirondack Community College *A*
Dominican College of Blauvelt *B*
Finger Lakes Community College *A*
Fordham University *M*
Hilbert College *A*
Mohawk Valley Community
College *C, A*
Monroe Community College *A*
New York University *C*
Onondaga Community College *A*
Pace University *A*
Pace University:
Pleasantville/Briarcliff *A*
Suffolk County Community College *C*

North Carolina
Alamance Community College *A*
Appalachian State University *B*
Fayetteville Technical Community
College *A*
Isothermal Community College *A*
Johnson C. Smith University *B*
Montgomery Community College *A*
North Carolina Central University *B*
Southeastern Community College *A*

North Dakota
North Dakota State College of Science *A*

Ohio
Cuyahoga Community College
Western Campus *A*
Defiance College *B*
Hondros College *A*
Jefferson Community College *A*
Kent State University *C, A*
Kent State University
Trumbull Campus *A*
Lorain County Community College *A*
Shawnee State University *A*
Sinclair Community College *A*
University of Akron *A*
University of Cincinnati
Raymond Walters College *C*

Oklahoma
Oklahoma City Community College *C*

Oregon
Southwestern Oregon Community
College *C, A*

University of Oregon *M, D*

Pennsylvania
Bucks County Community College *A*
California University of Pennsylvania *B*
Community College of Allegheny
County *C, A*
Delaware County Community
College *C, A*
La Salle University *A, B*
Lackawanna College *A*
Lebanon Valley College of
Pennsylvania *C*
Luzerne County Community College *A*
Northampton County Area Community
College *A*
Penn State
Delaware County *B*
Pennsylvania College of Technology *A*
Point Park College *A*
Reading Area Community College *C, A*
Westmoreland County Community
College *A*

Puerto Rico
Universidad Metropolitana *C, B*
University of Puerto Rico
Rio Piedras Campus *B*

Rhode Island
Providence College *B*

Texas
College of the Mainland *A*
Houston Community College
System *C, A*
Northeast Texas Community
College *C, A*
Northwood University: Texas
Campus *A, B*
Palo Alto College *A*
Texarkana College *C*
Texas Southern University *B*
University of North Texas *B, M, D*
University of Texas
Arlington *B, D*

Utah
Salt Lake Community College *C, A*

Virginia
Hampton University *B*
Southwest Virginia Community
College *C*
University of Richmond *C*
Virginia Western Community College *A*

Washington
Clover Park Technical College *C*
Gonzaga University *B*
Renton Technical College *C*
Spokane Community College *C, A*
Spokane Falls Community College *C, A*

West Virginia
Fairmont State College *A, B*
Mountain State University *A*
Southern West Virginia Community and
Technical College *A*
West Liberty State College *B*
West Virginia Northern Community
College *A*
West Virginia State College *A, B*

Wisconsin
Fox Valley Technical College *A*
Milwaukee Area Technical College *A*
University of Wisconsin
Whitewater *M*

Wyoming
Sheridan College *A*
Western Wyoming Community
College *C, A*

Barbering

Alabama
Calhoun Community College *C*
Douglas MacArthur State Technical
College *C*
Lawson State Community College *C*
Shelton State Community College *C*

Florida
Indian River Community College *C*
Pensacola Junior College *C*

Indiana
Ivy Tech State College
Wabash Valley *C*

Minnesota
Minneapolis Community and Technical
College *C*

New Mexico
San Juan College *A*

Washington
Olympic College *C, A*
Renton Technical College *C*

Wisconsin
Fox Valley Technical College *C*
Milwaukee Area Technical College *A*

Bartending

Puerto Rico
Universidad del Este *C*

Wisconsin
Milwaukee Area Technical College *A*

Behavioral sciences

Alabama
Athens State University *B*
University of Alabama *B, M*

Arizona
Northern Arizona University *B*
Prescott College *B, M*

California
California Baptist University *B*
California State Polytechnic University:
Pomona *B*
California State University
Bakersfield *M*
Monterey Bay *B*
Concordia University *B*
La Sierra University *B*
MiraCosta College *A*
Pacific Union College *B*
San Diego City College *A*
University of California
Davis *D*
San Diego *B*
University of La Verne *B*

Colorado
Metropolitan State College of Denver *B*
United States Air Force Academy *B*
University of Colorado
Denver *D*

Connecticut
Northwestern Connecticut Community
College *A*
University of Connecticut *M, D*

Delaware
Wilmington College *B*

Illinois
National-Louis University *B*
Southeastern Illinois College *A*

Indiana
Indiana University
Kokomo *B*

Iowa
Cornell College *B*
Ellsworth Community College *A*

Kansas
Garden City Community College *A*
Sterling College *B*

Maine
University of Maine
Machias *B*
Presque Isle *B*
University of Southern Maine *B*

Maryland
Johns Hopkins University *B*

Massachusetts
Cape Cod Community College *A*
Hampshire College *B*
Harvard College *B*
Simon's Rock College of Bard *B*

Michigan
Grand Valley State University *B*
Spring Arbor University *B*
University of Michigan
Dearborn *B*

Minnesota
College of St. Scholastica *B*

Missouri
Evangel University *M*

Nebraska
Concordia University *B*
Northeast Community College *A*

New Hampshire
College for Lifelong Learning *A, B*

New Jersey
Drew University *B*

New York
City University of New York
John Jay College of Criminal
Justice *F*
Concordia College *B*
Fulton-Montgomery Community
College *A*
Polytechnic University *M*
State University of New York
Health Science Center at
Brooklyn *D*

North Dakota
Dickinson State University *B, T*

Ohio
Kent State University *M, D*
Ursuline College *B*
Wright State University *M*

Oklahoma
St. Gregory's University *B*
Seminole State College *A*
Southern Nazarene University *B*

Pennsylvania
Franklin & Marshall College *B*
Gettysburg College *B*
Mount Aloysius College *A, B*
Penn State
Berks *B*
Point Park College *B*
Widener University *B*
York College of Pennsylvania *B*

South Dakota
Dakota Wesleyan University *B*
Mount Marty College *B*

Tennessee
King College *B, T*
Tennessee Wesleyan College *B*

Texas
South Plains College *A*
South Texas Community College *A*
University of Houston
    Clear Lake *B, M*

Utah
Southern Utah University *B*

Vermont
Green Mountain College *B*

Wisconsin
Beloit College *B*
Mount Mary College *B*
University of Wisconsin
    Madison *B*

Bible studies

Alabama
Faulkner University *B*
Heritage Christian University *A, B*
Oakwood College *A*
Southeastern Bible College *A, B, T*
Southern Christian University *B, M*

Alaska
Alaska Bible College *C, A, B*

Arizona
Southwestern College *C, A, B*

Arkansas
Central Baptist College *B*
Harding University *B, M*
Ouachita Baptist University *B*
Williams Baptist College *B*

California
Azusa Pacific University *B, M*
Bethesda Christian University *B, M*
Biola University *B, M*
Christian Heritage College *B*
Fresno Pacific University *B*
Hope International University *C, A, B*
LIFE Pacific College *A, B*
Master's College *C, B*
Pacific Union College *A*
Patten University *C, A*
San Jose Christian College *C, A, B*
Simpson College *C, A, B*
Vanguard University of Southern
    California *B, M*

Colorado
Colorado Christian University *B*
Nazarene Bible College *A, B*

District of Columbia
Catholic University of America *M, D*

Florida
Baptist College of Florida *B*
Florida Christian College *A, B*
Florida College *B*
Hobe Sound Bible College *C, A, B*
Southeastern College of the Assemblies
    of God *B*
Warner Southern College *B*

Georgia
Beulah Heights Bible College *C, A, B*
Covenant College *A, B*
Emmanuel College *B*
Toccoa Falls College *B*

Idaho
Boise Bible College *C, A, B*

Illinois
Judson College *B*
Lincoln Christian College and
    Seminary *A, B, M*
Moody Bible Institute *B, M*
North Park University *B*
Olivet Nazarene University *B*
Trinity International
    University *C, B, M, D*

Wheaton College *C, B*

Indiana
Anderson University *B, M*
Bethel College *A, B*
Grace College *A, B*
Huntington College *B*
Indiana Wesleyan University *A, B*
Taylor University *B*
Taylor University: Fort Wayne *B*
University of Evansville *B*

Iowa
Briar Cliff University *A, B*
Emmaus Bible College *C, A, B*
Faith Baptist Bible College and
    Theological Seminary *C, A, B, M*
Waldorf College *A*

Kansas
Barclay College *A, B*
Central Christian College *A, B*
Fort Scott Community College *A*
Tabor College *B*

Kentucky
Asbury College *B*
Campbellsville University *B*
Clear Creek Baptist Bible
    College *C, A, B*
Kentucky Christian College *B*
Mid-Continent College *C, B*
St. Catharine College *C, A*

Louisiana
New Orleans Baptist Theological
    Seminary: School of Christian
    Education *A, B*

Maryland
Washington Bible College *C, A, B, M, T*

Massachusetts
Boston College *M*
Boston University *M, D*

Michigan
Calvin College *B*
Cornerstone University *C, A, B, M*
Grace Bible College *A, B*
Reformed Bible College *A, B*
William Tyndale College *C, A*

Minnesota
Bethel College *B*
Concordia University: St. Paul *B*
Crossroads College *A*
Crown College *C, A, B*
North Central University *C*
Northwestern College *C, A, B*
Oak Hills Christian College *C, B*

Mississippi
Blue Mountain College *B*
Magnolia Bible College *B*
Wesley College *B*

Missouri
Calvary Bible College *C, A, B, M*
Central Bible College *A, B*
Central Christian College of the
    Bible *C, A*
Evangel University *B*
Global University *A, B, M*
Hannibal-LaGrange College *B*
Ozark Christian College *C, A, B*
St. Louis Christian College *B*
Southwest Baptist University *B*

Nebraska
Grace University *C, A, B, M*
Nebraska Christian College *B*
York College *A, B*

New Jersey
Drew University *M, D*
Somerset Christian College *A*

New York
Houghton College *B*

North Carolina
Montreat College *B*
Piedmont Baptist College *A, B*
Roanoke Bible College *A, B*
Southeastern Baptist Theological
    Seminary *A, B*

North Dakota
Trinity Bible College *A, B*

Ohio
Ashland University *B*
Cedarville University *C*
Cincinnati Bible College and
    Seminary *B, M*
God's Bible School and College *A*
Laura and Alvin Siegal College of Judaic
    Studies *B*
Malone College *B*
Pontifical College Josephinum *M*
Rosedale Bible College *C, A*

Oklahoma
Oklahoma Baptist University *B*
Oklahoma Christian University of
    Science and Arts *B*
Oklahoma City University *B*
Oklahoma Wesleyan University *A, B*
Oral Roberts University *B, M*
Southwestern Christian University *B*

Oregon
Eugene Bible College *C, B*
George Fox University *B, M*
Multnomah Bible College *B, M*
Western Baptist College *B*

Pennsylvania
Baptist Bible College of Pennsylvania *C*
Geneva College *A, B*
Lancaster Bible College *C, A, B, M*
Messiah College *B*
Philadelphia Biblical
    University *C, A, B, M*
Valley Forge Christian College *C, A, B*

Puerto Rico
Bayamon Central University *M*

Rhode Island
Zion Bible Institute *C, B*

South Carolina
Charleston Southern University *B*
Columbia International
    University *C, A, B*
Erskine College *M*

Tennessee
American Baptist College of ABT
    Seminary *A, B*
Bryan College *B*
Crichton College *C, B*
Freed-Hardeman University *B, M*
Johnson Bible College *C, A, B, M*
King College *B*
Lee University *B*
Southern Adventist University *A*
Tennessee Wesleyan College *B*
Trevecca Nazarene University *M*
Union University *C, A, B*

Texas
Abilene Christian University *B, M*
Arlington Baptist College *C, B*
Austin Graduate School of Theology *B*
Dallas Baptist University *A, B*
Dallas Christian College *B*
East Texas Baptist University *B*
Hardin-Simmons University *B*
Howard Payne University *B*
Lubbock Christian University *B, M*
San Jacinto College
    Central Campus *A*
Southwestern Assemblies of God
    University *B*

Virginia
Bluefield College *B*

Eastern Mennonite University *C, A, B*

Washington
Northwest College *B*
Trinity Lutheran College *C, A, B*

West Virginia
Appalachian Bible College *C, A, B*
Ohio Valley College *A, B*

Wisconsin
Maranatha Baptist Bible College *B, M*

Bilingual/bicultural education

Arizona
Northern Arizona University *M, T*
Prescott College *B, M*
University of Arizona *M*
University of Phoenix *M*

California
California State Polytechnic University:
    Pomona *B, M*
California State University
    Bakersfield *M*
    Chico *T*
    Fullerton *M*
    Hayward *T*
    Long Beach *T*
    Monterey Bay *M*
    Northridge *M*
    Sacramento *B, M, T*
    San Marcos *T*
    Stanislaus *B*
Cerritos Community College *A*
Contra Costa College *A*
Fresno Pacific University *M, T*
Imperial Valley College *A*
Loyola Marymount University *M*
National University *C, M, T*
San Diego City College *A*
San Diego State University *M*
San Francisco State University *M, T*
University of California
    Irvine *T*
    Los Angeles *M, D*
    Riverside *T*
    San Diego *M*
    Santa Cruz *M*
University of La Verne *T*
University of San Diego *M, T*
University of San Francisco *M, D, T*
University of Southern California *T*
University of the Pacific *T*
Ventura College *A*

Colorado
Colorado Mountain College
    Spring Valley Campus *A*
    Timberline Campus *A*
Fort Lewis College *T*

Connecticut
Fairfield University *M, T*
Southern Connecticut State University *M*

Delaware
University of Delaware *M*

Florida
Florida State University *B, M, D*

Idaho
Boise State University *B, T*
College of Southern Idaho *A*
Lewis-Clark State College *T*

Illinois
Chicago State University *M, T*
Columbia College Chicago *M*
Monmouth College *T*
Northeastern Illinois University *B, M*
Sauk Valley Community College *A*
Western Illinois University *B*

Indiana
Ball State University *T*

Kansas
Emporia State University *T*

Kentucky
Murray State University *B*

Maryland
University of Maryland
    Baltimore County *D*

Massachusetts
Boston University *B, M, T*
Elms College *B, M, T*
Lesley University *M, T*
University of Massachusetts
    Boston *M*

Michigan
Calvin College *B, T*
Eastern Michigan University *B, T*
Saginaw Valley State University *T*
Wayne State University *M, T*

Minnesota
College of St. Scholastica *T*
University of Minnesota
    Twin Cities *M*
Winona State University *B, T*

New Jersey
Fairleigh Dickinson University
    Metropolitan Campus *M*
Georgian Court College *T*
Montclair State University *T*
New Jersey City University *T*
Rider University *B, T*
Seton Hall University *M*
William Paterson University of New
    Jersey *T*

New Mexico
College of the Southwest *B*
Santa Fe Community College *A*
Western New Mexico University *T*

New York
Adelphi University *M*
City University of New York
    Brooklyn College *B, M*
    City College *B, M, T*
    Hunter College *M, T*
    La Guardia Community College *A*
    Queens College *M*
    York College *T*
Hofstra University *M, T*
Long Island University
    C. W. Post Campus *M*
Marist College *T*
Mercy College *M*
New York University *M, D*
St. John's University *B, M, T*
State University of New York
    Albany *M*
    Buffalo *M, T*
    College at Brockport *M, T*
    College at Buffalo *T*
    College at Old Westbury *B, T*
    New Paltz *M, T*
Touro College *C*

Ohio
University of Findlay *B, M, T*

Oregon
Chemeketa Community College *A*
Eastern Oregon University *T*
Western Oregon University *T*

Pennsylvania
Immaculata University *M*
La Salle University *B, M*
Lebanon Valley College of
    Pennsylvania *B, T*
University of Pennsylvania *M*

Puerto Rico
Inter American University of Puerto Rico
    Metropolitan Campus *B, M*
Turabo University *M*
Universidad Metropolitana *B*
University of the Sacred Heart *B*

Rhode Island
Rhode Island College *B*

Texas
Del Mar College *A*
Laredo Community College *A*
McMurry University *T*
Richland College *A*
St. Edward's University *B, T*
Southern Methodist University *M*
Southwest Texas State University *M, T*
Sul Ross State University *M*
Texas A&M International
    University *B, M, T*
Texas A&M University
    Commerce *B*
    Corpus Christi *T*
    Kingsville *B, M, D*
Texas Christian University *B*
Texas Southern University *M*
Texas Tech University *M*
Texas Wesleyan University *B, M, T*
University of Houston *M, T*
University of Houston
    Clear Lake *T*
    Downtown *M*
University of North Texas *M*
University of Texas
    Arlington *T*
    Brownsville *M*
    Pan American *M, T*
    San Antonio *M*
    of the Permian Basin *M*
West Texas A&M University *T*

Utah
Weber State University *B*

Vermont
Bennington College *B, M, T*

Washington
Central Washington University *M, T*
Heritage College *B, M*
University of Washington *M*
Walla Walla Community College *A*
Washington State University *T*

Wisconsin
Marquette University *T*
Mount Mary College *B*

Biochemistry

Alabama
Auburn University *B*
Oakwood College *B*
Samford University *B*
Spring Hill College *B*
University of Alabama
    Birmingham *D*

Arizona
Arizona State University *B*
University of Arizona *B, M, D*

Arkansas
Harding University *B*
John Brown University *B*
University of Arkansas
    for Medical Sciences *M, D*

California
Azusa Pacific University *B*
Biola University *B*
California Institute of Technology *D*
California Polytechnic State University:
    San Luis Obispo *B*

California State University
    Bakersfield *B*
    Chico *B*
    Fullerton *B*
    Hayward *B, M*
    Long Beach *B, M*
    Los Angeles *B, M*
    Northridge *B*
Claremont McKenna College *B*
La Sierra University *B*
Loma Linda University *M, D*
Loyola Marymount University *B*
Mills College *C, B*
Mount St. Mary's College *B*
Occidental College *B*
Pacific Union College *B*
Pepperdine University *B*
Pitzer College *B*
Point Loma Nazarene University *B*
Pomona College *B*
St. Mary's College of California *B*
San Francisco State University *B, M*
Scripps College *B*
Stanford University *D*
University of California
    Berkeley *M, D*
    Davis *B, M, D*
    Los Angeles *B, M, D*
    Riverside *B, M, D*
    San Diego *B, D*
    Santa Barbara *B, M, D*
    Santa Cruz *B*
University of Redlands *B*
University of Southern
    California *B, M, D*
University of the Pacific *B*

Colorado
Colorado College *B*
Colorado State University *B, M, D*
Fort Lewis College *B*
Regis University *B*
United States Air Force Academy *B*
University of Colorado
    Boulder *B, M, D*
    Health Sciences Center *D*
University of Denver *B*

Connecticut
Connecticut College *B*
Quinnipiac University *B*
St. Joseph College *B, M, T*
Trinity College *B*
University of Connecticut *M, D*
Wesleyan University *B, D*
Yale University *B, M, D*

Delaware
University of Delaware *B, M, D*

District of Columbia
American University *B*
Catholic University of America *B*
George Washington University *M, D*
Georgetown University *B, D*
Howard University *M, D*
Trinity College *B*

Florida
Florida Institute of Technology *B*
Florida State University *B, M, D*
Pensacola Junior College *A*
Rollins College *B*
Stetson University *B*
University of Florida *M, D*
University of Miami *B*
University of Tampa *B*
University of West Florida *B*

Georgia
Agnes Scott College *B*
Berry College *B*
LaGrange College *B*
Medical College of Georgia *M, D*
Spelman College *B*
University of Georgia *B, M, D*

Hawaii
Brigham Young University-Hawaii *B*
University of Hawaii
    Manoa *M, D*

Idaho
Idaho State University *B*

Illinois
Benedictine University *B*
Bradley University *B*
Chicago State University *B*
Dominican University *B*
Illinois State University *B*
Knox College *B*
Lewis University *B*
Loyola University of Chicago *M, D*
Monmouth College *B*
North Central College *B*
Northwestern University *B, M, D*
Rockford College *B*
Rush University *D*
University of Chicago *M, D*
University of Illinois
    Chicago *B, M, D*
    Urbana-Champaign *B, M, D*

Indiana
Anderson University *B*
Indiana University
    Bloomington *B, M, D*
Indiana University-Purdue University
    Indianapolis *M, D*
Manchester College *B*
Purdue University *B, M, D*
St. Joseph's College *A, B*
University of Evansville *B*
University of Notre Dame *B, M, D*

Iowa
Coe College *B*
Cornell College *B*
Drake University *B*
Grinnell College *B*
Iowa State University *B, M, D*
Loras College *B*
Simpson College *B*
University of Iowa *B, M, D*
University of Northern Iowa *B*
Wartburg College *B*

Kansas
Benedictine College *B*
Kansas State University *B, M, D*
Newman University *B*
Southwestern College *B*
University of Kansas *B, M, D*
University of Kansas Medical
    Center *M, D*

Kentucky
Asbury College *B*
Centre College *B*
Murray State University *B*

Louisiana
Centenary College of Louisiana *B*
Louisiana State University
    Shreveport *B*
Louisiana State University and
    Agricultural and Mechanical
    College *B, M, D*
Tulane University *B*
Xavier University of Louisiana *B*

Maine
Bates College *B*
Bowdoin College *B*
Colby College *B*
University of Maine *B, M, D*
University of New England *B*

Maryland
Columbia Union College *B*
Hood College *B*
Johns Hopkins University *B, D*
McDaniel College *B*
Mount St. Mary's College *B*

St. Mary's College of Maryland *B*
University of Maryland
 Baltimore *M, D*
 Baltimore County *M, D*
 College Park *B, M, D*

Massachusetts
American International College *B*
Boston College *B*
Boston University *B, M, D*
Brandeis University *B, M, D*
Bridgewater State College *B*
Clark University *B*
Hampshire College *B*
Harvard College *B*
Merrimack College *B*
Mount Holyoke College *B*
Northeastern University *B*
Regis College *B*
Simmons College *B*
Smith College *B*
Stonehill College *B*
Suffolk University *B*
Tufts University *D*
University of Massachusetts
 Boston *B*
Wellesley College *B*
Wheaton College *B*
Worcester Polytechnic Institute *B, M*

Michigan
Alma College *B*
Andrews University *B*
Calvin College *B*
Eastern Michigan University *B*
Grand Valley State University *B*
Hope College *B*
Madonna University *B*
Michigan State University *B, M, D*
Northern Michigan University *B, M*
Oakland University *B*
Saginaw Valley State University *B*
Spring Arbor University *B*
University of Michigan *B, M*
University of Michigan
 Dearborn *B*
Wayne State University *M, D*
Western Michigan University *B*

Minnesota
Bethel College *B*
College of St. Benedict *B*
College of St. Catherine *B*
College of St. Scholastica *B*
Concordia University: St. Paul *B*
Gustavus Adolphus College *B*
Minnesota State University
 Mankato *B*
St. John's University *B*
University of Minnesota
 Duluth *B*
 Twin Cities *B, M, D*
University of St. Thomas *B*

Mississippi
Mississippi College *B*
Mississippi State University *B, M*
University of Mississippi *B*
University of Mississippi Medical
 Center *M, D*

Missouri
Missouri Western State College *B*
St. Louis University *D*
University of Missouri
 Columbia *B, M, D*
 Rolla *B*
Washington University in St. Louis *B, D*
William Jewell College *B*

Montana
Montana State University
 Bozeman *M, D*
University of Montana-Missoula *M, D*

Nebraska
Nebraska Wesleyan University *B*
Union College *B*

University of Nebraska
 Lincoln *B, M, D*

Nevada
University of Nevada
 Reno *B, M, D*

New Hampshire
Dartmouth College *B, M, D*
St. Anselm College *B*
University of New Hampshire *B, M, D*

New Jersey
Bloomfield College *B*
College of St. Elizabeth *B*
Drew University *B*
Fairleigh Dickinson University
 Metropolitan Campus *B*
Georgian Court College *B*
Montclair State University *B*
Ramapo College of New Jersey *B*
Richard Stockton College of New
 Jersey *B*
Rider University *B*
Rowan University *B*
Rutgers, The State University of New
 Jersey
 New Brunswick Regional
  Campus *B, M, D*
St. Peter's College *B*
Seton Hall University *B*
Stevens Institute of Technology *B, M, D*

New Mexico
New Mexico Institute of Mining and
 Technology *B, M*
New Mexico State University *B*
University of New Mexico *B*

New York
Adelphi University *B*
Bard College *B*
Barnard College *B*
Canisius College *B*
City University of New York
 Brooklyn College *B, M*
 City College *B, M, D*
 College of Staten Island *B*
 Hunter College *B, M*
 Queens College *B, M*
Colgate University *B*
College of Mount St. Vincent *B*
Columbia University
 Columbia College *B*
Cornell University *B, M, D*
Daemen College *B*
Elmira College *B*
Hamilton College *B*
Hartwick College *B*
Hobart and William Smith Colleges *B*
Hofstra University *B*
Iona College *B*
Ithaca College *B*
Keuka College *B*
Le Moyne College *B*
Manhattan College *B, T*
Manhattanville College *B*
Marist College *B*
Nazareth College of Rochester *B*
New York University *B, M, D*
Niagara University *B*
Pace University *B*
Pace University:
 Pleasantville/Briarcliff *B*
Rensselaer Polytechnic Institute *B, M*
Roberts Wesleyan College *B*
Rochester Institute of Technology *B*
Russell Sage College *B*
St. Bonaventure University *B*
St. Lawrence University *B*
Sarah Lawrence College *B*
Skidmore College *B*

State University of New York
 Albany *B, M, D*
 Binghamton *B*
 Buffalo *B, M, D*
 College at Fredonia *B*
 College at Geneseo *B*
 College at Plattsburgh *B*
 College of Environmental Science
  and Forestry *B, M, D*
 Health Science Center at
  Brooklyn *D*
 Stony Brook *B*
 Upstate Medical University *M, D*
Syracuse University *B*
Union College *B*
University of Rochester *B, M, D*
Vassar College *B*
Wagner College *B*
Wells College *B*
Yeshiva University *M, D*

North Carolina
Campbell University *B*
Duke University *M, D*
East Carolina University *B, D*
North Carolina State University *B, M, D*
Queens University of Charlotte *B*
University of North Carolina
 Greensboro *B*
Wake Forest University *D*

North Dakota
Jamestown College *B*
North Dakota State University *M, D*
University of North Dakota *M, D*

Ohio
Case Western Reserve
 University *B, M, D*
College of Mount St. Joseph *B*
College of Wooster *B*
Denison University *B*
Kent State University
 Stark Campus *B*
Kenyon College *B*
Marietta College *B*
Miami University
 Oxford Campus *B*
Notre Dame College *B*
Oberlin College *B*
Ohio Northern University *B*
Ohio State University
 Columbus Campus *B, M, D*
Ohio University *B*
Ohio Wesleyan University *B*
Otterbein College *B*
University of Cincinnati *D*
University of Dayton *B*
Wilmington College *B*
Wittenberg University *B*
Wright State University *M*

Oklahoma
Oklahoma Baptist University *B*
Oklahoma Christian University of
 Science and Arts *B*
Oklahoma City University *B*
Oklahoma State University *B, M, D*
Oral Roberts University *B*
Southern Nazarene University *B*
University of Oklahoma *B, M, D*
University of Tulsa *B*

Oregon
Lewis & Clark College *B*
Oregon Health Sciences University *M, D*
Oregon State University *B, M, D*
Portland State University *B*
Reed College *B*
University of Oregon *B*

Pennsylvania
Albright College *B*
Allegheny College *B*
Carnegie Mellon University *D*
Cedar Crest College *B*
Chatham College *B*

Chestnut Hill College *B*
Dickinson College *B*
Drexel University *B*
Duquesne University *B*
East Stroudsburg University of
 Pennsylvania *B*
Elizabethtown College *B*
Franklin & Marshall College *B*
Gettysburg College *B*
Grove City College *B*
Holy Family University *B*
Immaculata University *B*
Indiana University of Pennsylvania *B*
Juniata College *B*
La Salle University *B*
Lafayette College *B*
Lebanon Valley College of
 Pennsylvania *B*
Lehigh University *B*
Mercyhurst College *B*
Messiah College *B*
Muhlenberg College *B*
Penn State
 Abington *B*
 Altoona *B*
 Beaver *B*
 Berks *B*
 Delaware County *B*
 Dubois *B*
 Fayette *B*
 Hazleton *B*
 Lehigh Valley *B*
 McKeesport *B*
 Mont Alto *B*
 New Kensington *B*
 Schuylkill - Capital College *B*
 Shenango *B*
 University Park *B, M, D*
 Wilkes-Barre *B*
 Worthington Scranton *B*
 York *B*
Philadelphia University *B*
Rosemont College *B*
St. Vincent College *B*
Seton Hill University *B*
Swarthmore College *B*
Temple University *B*
University of Pennsylvania *B, D*
University of Scranton *B, M*
University of the Sciences in
 Philadelphia *B, M, D*
Washington and Jefferson College *B*
West Chester University of
 Pennsylvania *B*
Wilkes University *B*

Puerto Rico
University of Puerto Rico
 Medical Sciences Campus *M, D*

Rhode Island
Brown University *B, M, D*
University of Rhode Island *M, D*

South Carolina
Clemson University *B, M, D*
College of Charleston *B*
Converse College *B*
Medical University of South
 Carolina *M, D*

South Dakota
South Dakota State University *B*
University of South Dakota *M, D*

Tennessee
Freed-Hardeman University *B*
King College *B*
Lee University *B*
Maryville College *B*
Southern Adventist University *B*
Tennessee State University *B*
Tennessee Technological University *B*
University of Tennessee
 Knoxville *B, M, D*
University of Tennessee Health Science
 Center *M, D*

Vanderbilt University *D*

Texas
Abilene Christian University *B*
Angelo State University *B*
Austin College *B*
Baylor University *B*
Hardin-Simmons University *B*
Houston Baptist University *B*
McMurry University *B*
Rice University *B, M, D*
St. Edward's University *B*
St. Mary's University *B*
Schreiner University *B*
Southern Methodist University *B*
Southwest Texas State University *B, M*
Texas A&M University *B, M, D*
Texas Christian University *B*
Texas Tech University *B*
Texas Wesleyan University *B*
Trinity University *B*
University of Dallas *B*
University of Houston *B, M, D*
University of North Texas *B, M, D*
University of Texas
  Arlington *B*
  Austin *B, M, D*
  Dallas *B*
  Health Science Center at San
    Antonio *M, D*
  Houston Health Science
    Center *M, D*
  Southwestern Medical Center at
    Dallas *M, D*

Utah
Brigham Young University *B, M, D*
University of Utah *M, D*
Utah State University *M, D*

Vermont
Bennington College *B*
Marlboro College *B*
Middlebury College *B*
Norwich University *B*
St. Michael's College *B*
University of Vermont *B, M, D*

Virginia
Averett University *B*
Eastern Mennonite University *B*
Hampden-Sydney College *B*
Mary Baldwin College *B*
Old Dominion University *B*
Roanoke College *B*
Sweet Briar College *B*
University of Richmond *B*
University of Virginia *D*
Virginia Commonwealth
  University *M, D*
Virginia Polytechnic Institute and State
  University *B, M*

Washington
Eastern Washington University *B*
Gonzaga University *B*
Seattle Pacific University *B*
Seattle University *B*
University of Washington *B, M, D*
Walla Walla College *B*
Washington State University *B, M, D*
Western Washington University *B*

West Virginia
Bethany College *B*
West Virginia University *B, M, D*

Wisconsin
Beloit College *B*
Carroll College *B*
Lawrence University *B, T*
Marquette University *B*
Ripon College *B*
University of Wisconsin
  Eau Claire *B*
  Madison *B, M, D*
Viterbo University *B*
Wisconsin Lutheran College *B*

Biochemistry/biophysics and molecular biology

California
University of California
  Irvine *M*

Colorado
University of Colorado
  Health Sciences Center *D*

Florida
University of Central Florida *D*

Illinois
Finch University of Health Sciences/The
  Chicago Medical School *M, D*

Iowa
University of Iowa *M, D*

Louisiana
Centenary College of Louisiana *B*

Maine
University of New England *B*

Massachusetts
University of Massachusetts
  Amherst *B, M, D*

Michigan
Saginaw Valley State University *B*

Nebraska
Nebraska Wesleyan University *B*
University of Nebraska
  Medical Center *M, D*

New Hampshire
Dartmouth College *B*

Ohio
College of Wooster *B*

Washington
Whitman College *B*

Wisconsin
Lawrence University *B*

Bioethics/medical ethics

California
Loma Linda University *M*

Ohio
Case Western Reserve University *M, D*

Bioinformatics

California
University of Southern California *M, D*

Georgia
Georgia Institute of Technology *M*

Indiana
Indiana University-Purdue University
  Indianapolis *M*

Maryland
Morgan State University *M*

Nebraska
University of Nebraska
  Medical Center *M*

New Jersey
Ramapo College of New Jersey *B*

New York
Canisius College *B*
Rochester Institute of Technology *B*
State University of New York
  Buffalo *M*

Pennsylvania
Chatham College *M*

University of the Sciences in
  Philadelphia *M*

Puerto Rico
Inter American University of Puerto Rico
  Bayamon Campus *B*

South Carolina
Medical University of South
  Carolina *M, D*

Texas
Baylor University *B*

Biological immunology

California
Stanford University *D*
University of California
  Berkeley *M, D*
  Davis *M, D*
  Los Angeles *M, D*

Colorado
University of Colorado
  Health Sciences Center *M*

Florida
University of Miami *M, D*

Illinois
Rush University *D*
University of Chicago *M, D*

Iowa
University of Iowa *D*

Maine
University of Southern Maine *M*

Michigan
University of Michigan *D*

Missouri
Washington University in St. Louis *D*

New York
Cornell University *B, M, D*
State University of New York
  Health Science Center at
    Brooklyn *D*
Yeshiva University *M, D*

North Carolina
North Carolina State University *M, D*

Ohio
Ohio State University
  Columbus Campus *M, D*

Texas
University of North Texas *M*
University of Texas
  Southwestern Medical Center at
    Dallas *M, D*

Utah
Brigham Young University *M*

Washington
University of Washington *M, D*

Biological/physical sciences

Alabama
Faulkner University *B*
Talladega College *B*
University of Alabama *B*
University of Alabama
  Birmingham *B*
University of South Alabama *M, D*

Alaska
University of Alaska
  Anchorage *B*
  Fairbanks *B, M*

Arizona
Arizona State University *M*

Central Arizona College *A*
Northern Arizona University *B*
Prescott College *B, M*

Arkansas
Southern Arkansas University *B*
University of Arkansas
  Little Rock *B*
University of Central Arkansas *B*

California
Cerro Coso Community College *C, A*
Citrus College *A*
College of the Canyons *A*
College of the Sequoias *A*
College of the Siskiyous *A*
Glendale Community College *A*
Golden West College *A*
Harvey Mudd College *B*
Laney College *A*
Loyola Marymount University *B*
Master's College *B*
National University *B*
Ohlone College *A*
Pitzer College *B*
Santa Monica College *A*
University of California
  Los Angeles *M, D*
  Santa Barbara *B*
University of La Verne *B*
University of the Pacific *B*

Colorado
Colorado Mountain College
  Alpine Campus *A*
  Spring Valley Campus *A*
  Timberline Campus *A*
Morgan Community College *A*
University of Colorado
  Denver *M*
University of Denver *B*

District of Columbia
Trinity College *B*

Florida
Florida Southern College *B*
Palm Beach Community College *A*
Polk Community College *A*
South Florida Community College *A*
University of North Florida *B*
University of South Florida *B*
University of West Florida *B*

Georgia
Atlanta Metropolitan College *A*
Spelman College *B*
University of Georgia *B*
Young Harris College *A*

Idaho
Lewis-Clark State College *B*
Northwest Nazarene University *B*

Illinois
Black Hawk College *A*
College of DuPage *A*
College of Lake County *A*
Heartland Community College *A*
John A. Logan College *A*
Kankakee Community College *A*
Kaskaskia College *A*
Kishwaukee College *A*
Lake Forest College *A*
Lincoln Land Community College *A*
McHenry County College *A*
Moraine Valley Community College *A*
National-Louis University *B*
North Central College *B, T*
Northwestern University *B*
Olivet Nazarene University *B, T*
Parkland College *A*
Prairie State College *A*
Rend Lake College *A*
St. Xavier University *B*
Shawnee Community College *A*
Southern Illinois University
  Carbondale *D*

Triton College *A*
Waubonsee Community College *A*

Indiana
Indiana University
  Bloomington *M*
  East *B*
  Kokomo *B*
Purdue University *B*
Taylor University *B*
University of Southern Indiana *B, T*
Valparaiso University *A*

Iowa
Briar Cliff University *B*
Clarke College *B*
Grinnell College *B*
St. Ambrose University *B*
University of Northern Iowa *B, M*
William Penn University *B*

Kansas
Benedictine College *B, T*
Central Christian College *A*
Fort Hays State University *B*
Pratt Community College *A*
Seward County Community College *A*
Tabor College *B*
University of Kansas *B*
University of Kansas Medical
  Center *M, D*

Kentucky
Alice Lloyd College *B*
Berea College *T*
Brescia University *B*
St. Catharine College *A*

Louisiana
Delgado Community College *A*
Louisiana College *B*
Louisiana State University and
  Agricultural and Mechanical
  College *M*
Our Lady of Holy Cross College *B*

Maine
University of Maine *B, M*

Maryland
Cecil Community College *C, A*
College of Southern Maryland *A*
Johns Hopkins University *B, D*
Montgomery College
  Rockville Campus *A*
St. Mary's College of Maryland *B*
Towson University *B*
Villa Julie College *B*
Washington College *B*

Massachusetts
Anna Maria College *B*
Berkshire Community College *A*
Elms College *B*
Hampshire College *B*
Harvard College *B*
Springfield College *B*
University of Massachusetts
  Amherst *B*
Wellesley College *B*
Wheaton College *B*
Worcester Polytechnic Institute *B, M, D*

Michigan
Andrews University *B, M*
Concordia University *B, T*
Eastern Michigan University *B, M*
Grand Valley State University *B*
Hope College *B*
Lansing Community College *A*
Michigan State University *B, M*
Northern Michigan University *B, T*
Saginaw Valley State University *B*

Minnesota
College of St. Benedict *B*
Concordia University: St. Paul *B*
Minnesota State University
  Mankato *B*

St. John's University *B*
University of Minnesota
  Twin Cities *B*
Winona State University *B, T*

Mississippi
Delta State University *B, M*
Mary Holmes College *A*
Mississippi State University *B*

Missouri
Maryville University of Saint Louis *B*
Missouri Valley College *B*
St. Louis Community College
  St. Louis Community College at
    Meramec *A*
Southeast Missouri State
  University *B, M*
Southwest Missouri State University *M*
Washington University in St.
  Louis *B, M, D*

Montana
Carroll College *B*
Montana Tech of the University of
  Montana *B*

Nebraska
Nebraska Wesleyan University *B*
University of Nebraska
  Omaha *B*

New Hampshire
Keene State College *B*
St. Anselm College *B*

New Jersey
Drew University *B*
Fairleigh Dickinson University
  Metropolitan Campus *B, M*
Gloucester County College *A*
Rutgers, The State University of New
  Jersey
  Camden Regional Campus *B*
St. Peter's College *B*

New York
Adelphi University *B*
Alfred University *B*
City University of New York
  Baruch College *B*
  Brooklyn College *B, M*
  Queens College *B*
Colgate University *B*
College of New Rochelle *B*
Corning Community College *A*
Fulton-Montgomery Community
  College *A*
Hofstra University *B*
Le Moyne College *B*
North Country Community College *A*
Paul Smith's College *B*
Rensselaer Polytechnic Institute *B, M, D*
Roberts Wesleyan College *B*
Sarah Lawrence College *B*
State University of New York
  Buffalo *M, D*
  College at Potsdam *B, T*
  College of Agriculture and
    Technology at Cobleskill *A*
  College of Environmental Science
    and Forestry *B, M, D*
  College of Technology at Alfred *A*
  Empire State College *A, B*
Touro College *B*
Union College *B, M*

North Carolina
Chowan College *B*
Mars Hill College *B*
North Carolina Central University *B*
Southeastern Community College *A*
Wayne Community College *A*

North Dakota
North Dakota State University *B*
University of Mary *B*

Ohio
Bowling Green State University:
  Firelands College *A*
Clark State Community College *A*
Defiance College *B, T*
Heidelberg College *B*
Jefferson Community College *A*
Kent State University *B*
Lorain County Community College *A*
Lourdes College *A, B*
Urbana University *B*
Ursuline College *B*
Walsh University *B*
Wittenberg University *B*
Wright State University *D*
Xavier University *B*
Youngstown State University *B*

Oklahoma
Bacone College *A*
Eastern Oklahoma State College *A*
Northeastern Oklahoma Agricultural and
  Mechanical College *A*
Oklahoma City University *B*
Oklahoma Panhandle State University *B*

Oregon
Linn-Benton Community College *A*
Oregon State University *B*
Portland State University *B, M*
Reed College *B*
Southern Oregon University *B*
Western Oregon University *B*

Pennsylvania
Arcadia University *B*
Bloomsburg University of
  Pennsylvania *B, T*
California University of Pennsylvania *B*
Community College of Beaver County *A*
Delaware County Community College *A*
Drexel University *B*
East Stroudsburg University of
  Pennsylvania *B, M*
Edinboro University of Pennsylvania *B*
Gettysburg College *B*
Indiana University of Pennsylvania *B*
Juniata College *B*
King's College *B, T*
Kutztown University of
  Pennsylvania *B, T*
La Salle University *B*
Lehigh University *B*
Lock Haven University of
  Pennsylvania *B*
Luzerne County Community College *A*
Penn State
  Abington *B*
  Altoona *A, B*
  Beaver *A, B*
  Berks *B*
  Delaware County *B*
  Dubois *A, B*
  Fayette *B*
  Hazleton *B*
  Lehigh Valley *B*
  McKeesport *A, B*
  Mont Alto *B*
  New Kensington *A, B*
  Schuylkill - Capital College *A, B*
  Shenango *A, B*
  University Park *B*
  Wilkes-Barre *B*
  Worthington Scranton *B*
  York *B*
Philadelphia University *B*
University of Pittsburgh *B*
Villanova University *A, B*

Puerto Rico
Bayamon Central University *B*
University of Puerto Rico
  Carolina Regional College *A*

Rhode Island
Brown University *B*
Community College of Rhode Island *A*

Ohio
South Carolina
Charleston Southern University *B*
Midlands Technical College *C*
North Greenville College *B*

South Dakota
Black Hills State University *B*

Tennessee
Bethel College *B*
Christian Brothers University *B*
Middle Tennessee State University *B*
Tennessee State University *B*

Texas
Angelo State University *B, T*
Central Texas College *A*
College of the Mainland *A*
Galveston College *A*
Hill College *A*
North Central Texas College *A*
Palo Alto College *A*
San Antonio College *A*
Stephen F. Austin State University *M*
Texas A&M University *B*
Texas A&M University
  Commerce *B, M*
Texas Christian University *B, M*
Texas Tech University *B*
University of Houston
  Downtown *B*
University of Texas
  Arlington *M*
  Austin *M, D*
  Dallas *M*
  El Paso *B*
  Houston Health Science
    Center *M, D*
  Medical Branch at Galveston *M*
  Pan American *M*
  San Antonio *B*
Wayland Baptist University *M*

Utah
Salt Lake Community College *A*

Vermont
Bennington College *B*
Castleton State College *B*
Lyndon State College *B*
Marlboro College *B*

Virginia
Averett University *B*
College of Health Sciences *B*
College of William and Mary *M, D*
Danville Community College *A*
J. Sargeant Reynolds Community
  College *A*
Mary Baldwin College *B*
Paul D. Camp Community College *A*
Southside Virginia Community
  College *A*
University of Virginia *M*
Virginia Highlands Community
  College *A*
Virginia Intermont College *B*
Virginia Polytechnic Institute and State
  University *M, D*
Virginia Western Community College *A*

Washington
Centralia College *A*
Pacific Lutheran University *C, B*
Seattle University *B*
University of Puget Sound *B, T*
University of Washington *M, D*
Washington State University *B*
Western Washington University *B*

West Virginia
Bluefield State College *A, B*
Mountain State University *B*

Wisconsin
Lawrence University *B, T*
Mount Mary College *B*
Northland College *B, T*

St. Norbert College *B*
University of Wisconsin
   Green Bay *B*
   Madison *M*
   River Falls *B, T*
   Stevens Point *B, T*
   Superior *B*

Wyoming

Laramie County Community College *A*

Biology

Alabama

Alabama Agricultural and Mechanical
   University *B, M*
Alabama State University *B, M*
Athens State University *B*
Auburn University *B*
Auburn University at Montgomery *B*
Birmingham-Southern College *B, T*
Chattahoochee Valley Community
   College *A*
Faulkner University *B*
Huntingdon College *B, T*
Jacksonville State University *B, M*
James H. Faulkner State Community
   College *A*
Judson College *B*
Lawson State Community College *A*
Miles College *B*
Northeast Alabama Community
   College *A*
Oakwood College *B*
Samford University *B*
Southern Union State Community
   College *A*
Spring Hill College *B, T*
Stillman College *B*
Talladega College *B*
Troy State University *B*
Troy State University Dothan *B, T*
Tuskegee University *B, M, T*
University of Alabama *B, M, D*
University of Alabama
   Birmingham *B, M, D*
   Huntsville *B, M*
University of Mobile *B, T*
University of Montevallo *B, T*
University of North Alabama *B*
University of South Alabama *B, M*
University of West Alabama *B, T*

Alaska

University of Alaska
   Anchorage *B, M*
   Fairbanks *B, M, D*
   Southeast *B*

Arizona

Arizona State University *B, M, D*
Arizona Western College *A*
Central Arizona College *A*
Cochise College *A*
Eastern Arizona College *A*
Northern Arizona University *B, M, D, T*
Prescott College *B, M*
South Mountain Community College *A*
University of Arizona *B*

Arkansas

Arkansas State University *B, M*
Arkansas State University
   Beebe *A*
Arkansas Tech University *B*
Harding University *B*
Henderson State University *B*
Hendrix College *B*
John Brown University *B*
Lyon College *B*
Ouachita Baptist University *B*
Philander Smith College *B*
Phillips Community College of the
   University of Arkansas *A*
Southern Arkansas University *B*
University of Arkansas *B, M, D*

University of Arkansas
   Fort Smith *A*
   Little Rock *B, M*
   Monticello *B*
   Pine Bluff *B*
University of Central Arkansas *B, M*
University of the Ozarks *B*
Williams Baptist College *B*

California

Antelope Valley College *A*
Azusa Pacific University *B*
Bakersfield College *A*
Barstow College *A*
Biola University *B*
Cabrillo College *A*
California Baptist University *B*
California Institute of Technology *B, D*
California Polytechnic State University:
   San Luis Obispo *B, M*
California State Polytechnic University:
   Pomona *B, M*
California State University
   Bakersfield *B*
   Chico *B, M*
   Dominguez Hills *B, M*
   Fresno *B, M*
   Fullerton *B, M*
   Hayward *B, M*
   Long Beach *B, M*
   Los Angeles *B, M*
   Northridge *B, M*
   Sacramento *B, M*
   San Bernardino *B, M*
   San Marcos *B*
   Stanislaus *B*
Cerritos Community College *A*
Chabot College *A*
Chapman University *B*
Christian Heritage College *B*
Claremont McKenna College *B*
College of Alameda *A*
College of Marin: Kentfield *A*
College of the Siskiyous *A*
Columbia College *A*
Concordia University *B*
Contra Costa College *A*
Cuesta College *C, A*
De Anza College *A*
Dominican University of California *B*
Feather River College *A*
Foothill College *A*
Gavilan Community College *A*
Glendale Community College *A*
Golden West College *A*
Grossmont Community College *A*
Harvey Mudd College *B*
Holy Names College *B*
Humboldt State University *B, M*
Irvine Valley College *A*
La Sierra University *B*
Las Positas College *A*
Loma Linda University *M, D*
Long Beach City College *A*
Los Angeles Pierce College *C*
Los Angeles Southwest College *A*
Los Medanos College *A*
Loyola Marymount University *B, M*
Marymount College *A*
Master's College *B*
Mills College *B*
MiraCosta College *A*
Monterey Peninsula College *A*
Moorpark College *A*
Mount St. Mary's College *B*
Mount San Antonio College *A*
Occidental College *B, M*
Ohlone College *C, A*
Orange Coast College *A*
Pacific Union College *B*
Palomar College *C, A*
Pepperdine University *B*
Pitzer College *B*
Point Loma Nazarene University *B*
Pomona College *B*
Reedley College *A*

St. Mary's College of California *B*
San Diego City College *A*
San Diego Mesa College *C, A*
San Diego State University *B, M, D*
San Francisco State University *B, M*
San Joaquin Delta College *A*
San Jose State University *B, M*
Santa Barbara City College *A*
Santa Clara University *B*
Santa Monica College *A*
Santiago Canyon College *A*
Scripps College *B*
Sierra College *A*
Sonoma State University *B, M*
Southwestern College *A*
Stanford University *B, M, D*
University of California
   Berkeley *B, M*
   Davis *B*
   Irvine *B, M, D*
   Los Angeles *B, M, D*
   Riverside *B, M, D*
   San Diego *B, D*
   Santa Barbara *B, M, D*
   Santa Cruz *B, D*
University of La Verne *B*
University of Redlands *B*
University of San Diego *B*
University of San Francisco *B, M*
University of Southern
   California *B, M, D*
University of the Pacific *B, M*
Vanguard University of Southern
   California *B*
Ventura College *C, A*
West Valley College *A*
Whittier College *B, M*

Colorado

Colorado Christian University *B*
Colorado College *B*
Colorado Mountain College
   Alpine Campus *A*
   Spring Valley Campus *A*
   Timberline Campus *A*
Colorado State University
   Pueblo *B, T*
Fort Lewis College *B*
Mesa State College *A, B*
Metropolitan State College of
   Denver *B, T*
Otero Junior College *A*
Red Rocks Community College *A*
Regis University *B*
Trinidad State Junior College *A*
United States Air Force Academy *B*
University of Colorado
   Colorado Springs *B*
   Denver *B, M*
University of Denver *B, M, D*
University of Northern
   Colorado *B, M, D, T*

Connecticut

Albertus Magnus College *B*
Central Connecticut State
   University *B, M, T*
Connecticut College *B*
Eastern Connecticut State University *B*
Fairfield University *B*
Quinnipiac University *B*
Sacred Heart University *B*
St. Joseph College *B, M, T*
Southern Connecticut State
   University *B, M, T*
Teikyo Post University *B*
Trinity College *B*
University of Bridgeport *B*
University of Connecticut *B, M*
University of Hartford *B, M*
University of New Haven *A, B*
Wesleyan University *B, D*
Western Connecticut State
   University *B, M*
Yale University *B, M, D*

Delaware

Delaware State University *B, M*
University of Delaware *B, M, D*

District of Columbia

American University *B, M*
Catholic University of America *B, T*
Gallaudet University *B*
George Washington University *B, M, D*
Georgetown University *B, M, D*
Howard University *B, M, D*
Trinity College *B*
University of the District of
   Columbia *B, T*

Florida

Barry University *B, M, T*
Bethune-Cookman College *B*
Broward Community College *A*
Chipola Junior College *A*
Eckerd College *B*
Edward Waters College *B*
Florida Agricultural and Mechanical
   University *B, M*
Florida Atlantic University *B, M*
Florida Institute of Technology *B, D*
Florida International University *B, M, D*
Florida Southern College *B*
Florida State University *B, M, D*
Gulf Coast Community College *A*
Indian River Community College *A*
Jacksonville University *B, M, D*
Manatee Community College *A*
Miami-Dade Community College *A*
New College of Florida *B*
Nova Southeastern University *B*
Okaloosa-Walton Community College *A*
Palm Beach Atlantic University *B, T*
Palm Beach Community College *A*
Pensacola Junior College *A*
Polk Community College *A*
Rollins College *B*
St. Leo University *B*
St. Thomas University *B*
South Florida Community College *A*
Southeastern College of the Assemblies
   of God *B*
Stetson University *B*
University of Central Florida *C, B, M*
University of Miami *B, M, D*
University of North Florida *B*
University of South Florida *B, M, D*
University of Tampa *A, B, T*
University of West Florida *B, M*
Warner Southern College *B*

Georgia

Abraham Baldwin Agricultural
   College *A*
Agnes Scott College *B*
Albany State University *B*
Armstrong Atlantic State University *B, T*
Atlanta Metropolitan College *A*
Augusta State University *B*
Berry College *B, T*
Brenau University *B*
Brewton-Parker College *B*
Clark Atlanta University *B, M, D*
Clayton College and State University *A*
Coastal Georgia Community College *A*
Columbus State University *B*
Covenant College *B*
Darton College *A*
East Georgia College *A*
Emory University *B, D*
Floyd College *A*
Fort Valley State University *B*
Georgia College and State
   University *B, M*
Georgia Institute of Technology *B, M, D*
Georgia Military College *A*
Georgia Perimeter College *A*
Georgia Southern University *B, M*
Georgia Southwestern State University *B*
Georgia State University *B, M, D*
Gordon College *A*

Kennesaw State University *B*
LaGrange College *B*
Life University *B*
Macon State College *A*
Mercer University *B*
Middle Georgia College *A*
Morehouse College *B*
Morris Brown College *B*
North Georgia College & State
   University *B*
Oglethorpe University *B*
Oxford College of Emory University *B*
Paine College *B*
Piedmont College *B*
Reinhardt College *B*
Savannah State University *B*
Shorter College *B*
South Georgia College *A*
Southern Polytechnic State University *B*
Spelman College *B*
State University of West Georgia *B, M*
Thomas University *B*
University of Georgia *B*
Valdosta State University *B*
Waycross College *A*
Wesleyan College *B*
Young Harris College *A*

Hawaii

Brigham Young University-Hawaii *B*
Chaminade University of Honolulu *B*
Hawaii Pacific University *B*
University of Hawaii
   Hilo *B*
   Manoa *B*

Idaho

Albertson College of Idaho *B*
Boise State University *B, M, T*
Brigham Young University - Idaho *A, B*
College of Southern Idaho *A*
Idaho State University *A, B, M, D*
Lewis-Clark State College *B*
North Idaho College *A*
Northwest Nazarene University *B*
University of Idaho *B, M*

Illinois

Augustana College *B*
Aurora University *B*
Benedictine University *B, T*
Black Hawk College
   East Campus *A*
Blackburn College *B*
Bradley University *B, M, T*
Chicago State University *B, T*
City Colleges of Chicago
   Harold Washington College *A*
   Kennedy-King College *C*
   Malcolm X College *A*
   Olive-Harvey College *A*
Concordia University *B, T*
Danville Area Community College *A*
De Paul University *B, M, T*
Dominican University *B*
Eastern Illinois University *B, M, T*
Elmhurst College *B, T*
Eureka College *B, T*
Governors State University *B, T*
Greenville College *B, T*
Illinois College *B*
Illinois Institute of Technology *B, M, D*
Illinois State University *B, M, D, T*
Illinois Valley Community College *A*
Illinois Wesleyan University *B*
John A. Logan College *A*
Joliet Junior College *A*
Judson College *B*
Kankakee Community College *A*
Knox College *B*
Lake Forest College *B*
Lewis University *B, T*
Lewis and Clark Community College *A*
Lincoln College *B*
Lincoln Land Community College *A*
Loyola University of Chicago *B, M*

MacMurray College *B, T*
McKendree College *B, T*
Millikin University *B, T*
Monmouth College *B, T*
National-Louis University *B*
North Central College *B, T*
North Park University *B*
Northeastern Illinois University *B, M*
Northern Illinois University *B, M, D, T*
Northwestern University *B, M, D*
Olivet Nazarene University *B, T*
Parkland College *A*
Principia College *B, T*
Quincy University *B, T*
Richland Community College *A*
Rockford College *B*
Roosevelt University *B, M*
St. Xavier University *B*
Sauk Valley Community College *A*
South Suburban College of Cook
   County *A*
Southern Illinois University
   Carbondale *B, M*
Southern Illinois University
   Edwardsville *B, M, T*
Southwestern Illinois College *A*
Trinity Christian College *B, T*
Trinity International University *B*
Triton College *A*
University of Illinois
   Chicago *B, M, D*
   Springfield *B, M*
   Urbana-Champaign *B, M, D*
University of St. Francis *B*
Western Illinois University *B, M*
Wheaton College *B*

Indiana

Ancilla College *A*
Anderson University *B*
Ball State University *B, M*
Bethel College *A, B*
Butler University *B*
DePauw University *B*
Earlham College *B*
Franklin College *B*
Goshen College *B*
Grace College *B*
Hanover College *B*
Huntington College *B*
Indiana State University *B, M, D, T*
Indiana University
   Bloomington *B, M*
   East *B*
   Kokomo *B*
   Northwest *B*
   South Bend *A, B*
   Southeast *B*
Indiana University-Purdue University
   Fort Wayne *A, B, M, T*
Indiana University-Purdue University
   Indianapolis *B, M*
Indiana Wesleyan University *A, B*
Manchester College *B, T*
Marian College *B, T*
Martin University *B*
Oakland City University *B*
Purdue University *B, M, D*
Purdue University
   Calumet *B, M*
   North Central Campus *A, B*
Rose-Hulman Institute of Technology *B*
St. Joseph's College *B*
Saint Mary's College *B, T*
St. Mary-of-the-Woods College *B*
Taylor University *B*
Tri-State University *B*
University of Evansville *B*
University of Indianapolis *B, M*
University of Notre Dame *B, M, D*
University of St. Francis *B*
University of Southern Indiana *B, T*
Valparaiso University *A, B*
Vincennes University *A*
Wabash College *B*

Iowa

Briar Cliff University *B*
Buena Vista University *B, T*
Central College *B, T*
Clarke College *B, T*
Coe College *B*
Cornell College *B, T*
Dordt College *B*
Drake University *B*
Ellsworth Community College *A*
Franciscan University *B*
Graceland University *B, T*
Grand View College *B*
Grinnell College *B*
Hawkeye Community College *A*
Iowa State University *B*
Iowa Wesleyan College *B*
Iowa Western Community College *A*
Loras College *B*
Luther College *B*
Maharishi University of Management *B*
Marshalltown Community College *A*
Morningside College *B*
Mount Mercy College *B, T*
North Iowa Area Community College *A*
Northwestern College *B, T*
St. Ambrose University *B*
Simpson College *B*
University of Dubuque *B*
University of Iowa *B, M, D, T*
University of Northern Iowa *B, M*
Upper Iowa University *B*
Waldorf College *A*
Wartburg College *B, T*
William Penn University *B*

Kansas

Allen County Community College *A*
Baker University *B, T*
Barton County Community College *A*
Benedictine College *B, T*
Bethany College *B, T*
Bethel College *B*
Central Christian College *A*
Cloud County Community College *A*
Dodge City Community College *A*
Donnelly College *A*
Emporia State University *B, M*
Fort Hays State University *B, M*
Friends University *B*
Garden City Community College *A*
Hutchinson Community College *A*
Independence Community College *A*
Kansas City Kansas Community
   College *A*
Kansas State University *B, M, D*
Kansas Wesleyan University *B, T*
Labette Community College *A*
McPherson College *B, T*
MidAmerica Nazarene University *B*
Newman University *B*
Ottawa University *B*
Pittsburg State University *B, M, T*
Pratt Community College *A*
St. Mary College *B*
Seward County Community College *A*
Southwestern College *B*
Sterling College *B*
Tabor College *B*
University of Kansas *B, M, D*
Washburn University of Topeka *B*
Wichita State University *B, M*

Kentucky

Alice Lloyd College *B*
Asbury College *B, T*
Bellarmine University *B, T*
Berea College *B, T*
Brescia University *B*
Campbellsville University *B*
Centre College *B*
Cumberland College *B, T*
Georgetown College *B*
Kentucky Wesleyan College *B, T*
Lindsey Wilson College *A, B, T*
Morehead State University *B, M, T*

Murray State University *B, M, T*
Pikeville College *B, T*
Spalding University *B*
Thomas More College *A, B*
Transylvania University *B*
Union College *B*
University of Kentucky *B, M, D*
University of Louisville *B, M*

Louisiana

Centenary College of Louisiana *B, T*
Dillard University *B*
Grambling State University *B*
Louisiana College *B*
Louisiana State University and
   Agricultural and Mechanical
   College *B, M, D*
Louisiana Tech University *B, M*
Loyola University New Orleans *B*
McNeese State University *B*
Nicholls State University *B*
Northwestern State University *B*
Our Lady of Holy Cross College *B, T*
Southeastern Louisiana University *B, M*
Southern University
   New Orleans *B*
   Shreveport *A*
Southern University and Agricultural and
   Mechanical College *B, M*
University of Louisiana at
   Lafayette *B, M*
University of Louisiana at Monroe *B, M*
University of New Orleans *B, M*
Xavier University of Louisiana *B*

Maine

Bates College *B, T*
Bowdoin College *B*
Colby College *B*
Husson College *B*
Maine Maritime Academy *T*
St. Joseph's College *B*
University of Maine *B, M, D*
University of Maine
   Augusta *B*
   Farmington *B*
   Machias *B, T*
   Presque Isle *B*
University of New England *B*
University of Southern Maine *B*

Maryland

Allegany College *A*
Bowie State University *B*
Cecil Community College *A*
College of Notre Dame of Maryland *B*
College of Southern Maryland *A*
Columbia Union College *B*
Community College of Baltimore County
   Essex *A*
Coppin State College *B*
Frederick Community College *A*
Frostburg State University *B, T*
Goucher College *B*
Harford Community College *A*
Hood College *B, T*
Johns Hopkins University *B, M, D*
Loyola College in Maryland *B*
McDaniel College *B*
Morgan State University *B*
Mount St. Mary's College *B*
St. Mary's College of Maryland *B*
Salisbury University *B, T*
Towson University *B, M, T*
University of Maryland
   Baltimore County *B, M, D*
   College Park *B, M, D*
Villa Julie College *A, B*
Washington College *B, T*

Massachusetts

American International College *B*
Amherst College *B*
Anna Maria College *B, M*
Assumption College *B*
Atlantic Union College *B*
Bay Path College *B*

Becker College *B*
Berkshire Community College *A*
Boston College *B, M, D*
Boston University *B, M, D*
Brandeis University *B*
Bridgewater State College *B, M*
Clark University *B, M, D*
College of the Holy Cross *B*
Elms College *B*
Emmanuel College *B*
Fitchburg State College *B, M*
Framingham State College *B, M*
Gordon College *B*
Hampshire College *B*
Harvard College *B, T*
Massachusetts College of Liberal Arts *B*
Massachusetts Institute of
 Technology *B, D*
Merrimack College *B*
Mount Holyoke College *B*
Northeastern University *A, B, M, D*
Pine Manor College *A, B*
Regis College *B*
Salem State College *B*
Simmons College *B*
Simon's Rock College of Bard *B*
Smith College *B, M, D*
Springfield College *B*
Springfield Technical Community
 College *A*
Stonehill College *B*
Suffolk University *B*
Tufts University *B, M, D*
University of Massachusetts
 Amherst *B, M, D*
 Boston *B, M*
 Dartmouth *B, M*
 Lowell *B, M*
Wellesley College *B*
Western New England College *B, T*
Westfield State College *B*
Wheaton College *B*
Williams College *B*
Worcester Polytechnic Institute *B, M*

Michigan
Adrian College *A, B, T*
Alma College *B, T*
Andrews University *B, M*
Aquinas College *B, T*
Calvin College *B, T*
Central Michigan University *B, M*
Concordia University *B, T*
Cornerstone University *B, T*
Eastern Michigan University *B, M*
Ferris State University *B*
Gogebic Community College *A*
Grand Valley State University *B, M*
Hillsdale College *B*
Hope College *B*
Kalamazoo College *B, T*
Kellogg Community College *A*
Lansing Community College *A*
Macomb Community College *A*
Madonna University *C, B, T*
Marygrove College *B, T*
Michigan State University *B, M*
Michigan Technological
 University *B, M, D, T*
Mid Michigan Community College *A*
Northern Michigan University *B, M, T*
Northwestern Michigan College *A*
Oakland University *B, M, T*
Saginaw Valley State University *B*
Siena Heights University *A, B*
Spring Arbor University *B*
University of Michigan *B, M, D, T*
University of Michigan
 Dearborn *B*
 Flint *B, M, T*
Wayne State University *B, M, D*
Western Michigan University *B, M, D*

Minnesota
Augsburg College *B*
Bemidji State University *B, M*

Bethany Lutheran College *B*
Bethel College *B*
Carleton College *B*
College of St. Benedict *B*
College of St. Catherine *B*
College of St. Scholastica *B*
Concordia College: Moorhead *B*
Concordia University: St. Paul *B*
Gustavus Adolphus College *B*
Hamline University *B*
Macalester College *B, T*
Metropolitan State University *B*
Minnesota State University
 Mankato *B, M, T*
 Moorhead *B*
Northland Community & Technical
 College *A*
Northwestern College *B*
Ridgewater College: A Community and
 Technical College *A*
St. Cloud State University *B, M*
St. John's University *B*
St. Mary's University of Minnesota *B*
St. Olaf College *B*
Southwest State University *B, T*
University of Minnesota
 Duluth *B, M*
 Morris *B*
 Twin Cities *B*
University of St. Thomas *B*
Vermilion Community College *A*
Winona State University *B, T*

Mississippi
Alcorn State University *B, M*
Blue Mountain College *B*
Delta State University *B, T*
Mary Holmes College *A*
Millsaps College *B, T*
Mississippi College *B, M, T*
Mississippi Gulf Coast Community
 College
 Perkinston *A*
Mississippi State University *B, M, D*
Mississippi University for Women *B, T*
Mississippi Valley State University *B*
Rust College *B*
University of Mississippi *B, M, D, T*
University of Southern
 Mississippi *B, M, D*

Missouri
Avila University *B*
Central Methodist College *B*
Central Missouri State University *B, M*
College of the Ozarks *B*
Columbia College *B*
Crowder College *A*
Culver-Stockton College *B, T*
Drury University *B*
East Central College *A*
Evangel University *B*
Fontbonne College *B*
Hannibal-LaGrange College *B, T*
Lincoln University *B*
Lindenwood University *B*
Maryville University of Saint Louis *B*
Mineral Area College *A*
Missouri Baptist University *B, T*
Missouri Southern State College *B, T*
Missouri Valley College *B*
Missouri Western State College *B, T*
Northwest Missouri State
 University *B, M*
Rockhurst University *B*
St. Louis Community College
 St. Louis Community College at
  Florissant Valley *A*
 St. Louis Community College at
  Forest Park *A*
St. Louis University *B, M, D*
Southeast Missouri State
 University *B, M*
Southwest Baptist University *B*
Southwest Missouri State
 University *B, M*

Stephens College *B*
Three Rivers Community College *A*
Truman State University *B, M*
University of Missouri
 Columbia *B, M, D*
 Kansas City *B, M*
 Rolla *B*
 St. Louis *B, M, D*
Washington University in St.
 Louis *B, M, D*
Webster University *B*
Westminster College *B*
William Jewell College *B, T*
William Woods University *B, T*

Montana
Carroll College *B, T*
Miles Community College *A*
Montana State University
 Billings *B*
 Bozeman *B, M, D*
Montana Tech of the University of
 Montana *B*
Rocky Mountain College *B, T*
University of Great Falls *B*
University of Montana-Missoula *B, M, D*
University of Montana: Western *B*

Nebraska
Bellevue University *B*
Chadron State College *B*
College of Saint Mary *B, T*
Concordia University *B, T*
Creighton University *B*
Dana College *B*
Doane College *B*
Hastings College *B*
Midland Lutheran College *B, T*
Nebraska Wesleyan University *B*
Northeast Community College *A*
Union College *B*
University of Nebraska
 Kearney *B, M, T*
 Lincoln *B, M, D*
 Omaha *B, M*
Wayne State College *B, T*
Western Nebraska Community
 College *A*
York College *B*

Nevada
Community College of Southern
 Nevada *A*
University of Nevada
 Las Vegas *B, M, D*
 Reno *B, M, D*
Western Nevada Community College *A*

New Hampshire
Colby-Sawyer College *B, T*
Dartmouth College *B, M, D, T*
Franklin Pierce College *B*
Keene State College *B, T*
New England College *B, T*
Plymouth State College *B*
Rivier College *B, M, T*
St. Anselm College *B, T*
Thomas More College of Liberal Arts *B*
University of New Hampshire *B, M, D*
University of New Hampshire at
 Manchester *A*

New Jersey
Atlantic Cape Community College *A*
Bloomfield College *B*
Caldwell College *B*
Centenary College *B*
The College of New Jersey *B, T*
College of St. Elizabeth *B, T*
Drew University *B*
Essex County College *A*
Fairleigh Dickinson University
 College at Florham *B, M*
 Metropolitan Campus *B, M*
Felician College *B*
Georgian Court College *B, M, T*
Gloucester County College *A*

Kean University *B*
Monmouth University *B*
Montclair State University *B, M, T*
New Jersey City University *B*
New Jersey Institute of
 Technology *B, M, D*
Ramapo College of New Jersey *B*
Raritan Valley Community College *A*
Richard Stockton College of New
 Jersey *B*
Rider University *B*
Rowan University *B*
Rutgers, The State University of New
 Jersey
 Camden Regional Campus *B, M, T*
 New Brunswick Regional
  Campus *B, T*
 Newark Regional
  Campus *B, M, D, T*
St. Peter's College *B*
Salem Community College *A*
Seton Hall University *B, M*
Sussex County Community College *A*
Thomas Edison State College *A, B*
Union County College *A*
Warren County Community College *A*
William Paterson University of New
 Jersey *B, M*

New Mexico
College of the Southwest *B*
Eastern New Mexico University *B, M*
New Mexico Highlands University *B*
New Mexico Institute of Mining and
 Technology *B, M*
New Mexico Junior College *A*
New Mexico State University *B, M, D*
San Juan College *A*
Santa Fe Community College *A*
University of New Mexico *B, M, D*
Western New Mexico University *B*

New York
Adelphi University *B, M*
Adirondack Community College *A*
Alfred University *B*
Bard College *B*
Barnard College *B*
Canisius College *B*
City University of New York
 Baruch College *B*
 Brooklyn College *B, M*
 City College *B, M, D, T*
 College of Staten Island *B, M, T*
 Hunter College *B, M*
 Kingsborough Community
  College *A*
 Medgar Evers College *A, B*
 Queens College *B, M*
 Queensborough Community
  College *A*
 York College *B*
Clarkson University *B*
Colgate University *B*
College of Mount St. Vincent *B, T*
College of New Rochelle *B, T*
Columbia University
 Columbia College *B*
Concordia College *B, T*
Cornell University *B*
D'Youville College *B*
Daemen College *B*
Dominican College of Blauvelt *B*
Dowling College *B, T*
Elmira College *B, T*
Excelsior College *B*
Fordham University *B, M, D*
Fulton-Montgomery Community
 College *A*
Hamilton College *B*
Hartwick College *B, T*
Hobart and William Smith Colleges *B*
Hofstra University *B, M*
Houghton College *B*
Iona College *B*
Ithaca College *B, T*

Keuka College *B*
Le Moyne College *B*
Long Island University
    C. W. Post Campus *B, M*
    Southampton College *B*
Manhattan College *B*
Manhattanville College *B*
Marist College *B, T*
Marymount College of Fordham
    University *B, T*
Marymount Manhattan College *B*
Medaille College *B*
Mercy College *B*
Molloy College *B*
Monroe Community College *A*
Mount St. Mary College *B, T*
Nazareth College of Rochester *B*
New York Institute of Technology *B*
New York University *B, M, D*
Niagara University *B*
Pace University *B*
Pace University:
    Pleasantville/Briarcliff *B*
Paul Smith's College *B*
Rensselaer Polytechnic Institute *B, M, D*
Roberts Wesleyan College *B*
Rochester Institute of Technology *A, B*
Russell Sage College *B*
St. Bonaventure University *B, T*
St. John Fisher College *B*
St. John's University *B, M, D*
St. Joseph's College *B*
St. Joseph's College: Suffolk
    Campus *B, T*
St. Lawrence University *B, T*
Sarah Lawrence College *B*
Skidmore College *B*
State University of New York
    Albany *B, M, D*
    Binghamton *B, M, D*
    Buffalo *B, M, D*
    College at Brockport *B, M, T*
    College at Buffalo *B, M*
    College at Cortland *B*
    College at Fredonia *B, M, T*
    College at Geneseo *B, M, T*
    College at Old Westbury *B, T*
    College at Oneonta *B, M*
    College at Plattsburgh *B, M*
    College at Potsdam *B, T*
    College of Agriculture and
        Technology at Morrisville *A*
    College of Environmental Science
        and Forestry *B, M, D*
    College of Technology at Canton *A*
    New Paltz *B, M, T*
    Oswego *B*
    Purchase *B*
    Stony Brook *B, M*
Suffolk County Community College *A*
Syracuse University *B, M, D*
Touro College *B*
Union College *B*
University of Rochester *B, M, D*
Utica College *B*
Vassar College *B*
Wagner College *B, T*
Wells College *B*
Yeshiva University *B*

North Carolina
Appalachian State University *B, M*
Barber-Scotia College *B*
Barton College *B*
Belmont Abbey College *B*
Bennett College *B*
Campbell University *B, T*
Catawba College *B, T*
Chowan College *B*
Davidson College *B*
Duke University *B*
East Carolina University *B, M*
Elizabeth City State University *B*
Elon University *B*
Fayetteville State University *B*
Gardner-Webb University *B*

Greensboro College *B*
Guilford College *B*
Guilford Technical Community
    College *A*
High Point University *B*
Johnson C. Smith University *B*
Lees-McRae College *B*
Lenoir-Rhyne College *B*
Livingstone College *B*
Louisburg College *A*
Mars Hill College *B, T*
Meredith College *B*
Methodist College *A, B, T*
Montreat College *B*
Mount Olive College *A, B*
North Carolina Agricultural and
    Technical State University *B, M*
North Carolina Central University *B, M*
North Carolina State University *B*
North Carolina Wesleyan College *B*
Peace College *B*
Pfeiffer University *B*
Queens University of Charlotte *B*
St. Andrews Presbyterian College *B*
St. Augustine's College *B*
Salem College *B*
Sandhills Community College *A*
Shaw University *B*
University of North Carolina
    Asheville *B, T*
    Chapel Hill *B, M, D*
    Charlotte *B, M, D*
    Greensboro *B, M, T*
    Pembroke *B*
    Wilmington *B, M*
Wake Forest University *B, M, D*
Warren Wilson College *B*
Western Carolina University *B, M*
Wingate University *B*
Winston-Salem State University *B*

North Dakota
Dickinson State University *B, T*
Jamestown College *B*
Mayville State University *B, T*
Minot State University *B*
Minot State University: Bottineau
    Campus *A*
North Dakota State University *B, M, T*
University of Mary *B*
University of North Dakota *B, M, D, T*
Valley City State University *B*

Ohio
Antioch College *B*
Ashland University *B*
Baldwin-Wallace College *B, T*
Bluffton College *B*
Bowling Green State University *B, M, D*
Case Western Reserve
    University *B, M, D*
Cedarville University *B, T*
Central State University *B*
Cincinnati State Technical and
    Community College *A*
College of Mount St. Joseph *B, T*
College of Wooster *B*
Defiance College *B, T*
Denison University *B*
Franciscan University of Steubenville *B*
Heidelberg College *B*
Hiram College *B*
Jefferson Community College *A*
John Carroll University *B, M*
Kent State University *B, M, D, T*
Kent State University
    Stark Campus *B*
Kenyon College *B*
Lake Erie College *B*
Lorain County Community College *A*
Lourdes College *A, B*
Malone College *B*
Marietta College *B*
Miami University
    Oxford Campus *B, T*
Mount Union College *B*

Mount Vernon Nazarene University *B*
Muskingum College *B*
Notre Dame College *B, T*
Oberlin College *B*
Ohio Dominican College *B, T*
Ohio Northern University *B*
Ohio State University
    Columbus Campus *B, M, D*
Ohio University *B*
Ohio Wesleyan University *B*
Otterbein College *B*
Owens Community College
    Toledo *A*
Shawnee State University *B*
Sinclair Community College *A*
University of Akron *B, M*
University of Cincinnati *B, M, D, T*
University of Cincinnati
    Clermont College *A*
    Raymond Walters College *A*
University of Dayton *B, M, D*
University of Findlay *B*
University of Rio Grande *A, B, T*
University of Toledo *A, B, M, D*
Ursuline College *B*
Walsh University *B*
Wilmington College *B*
Wittenberg University *B*
Wright State University *B, M*
Wright State University: Lake Campus *A*
Xavier University *B*
Youngstown State University *B, M*

Oklahoma
Bacone College *A*
Cameron University *B*
Carl Albert State College *A*
East Central University *B*
Eastern Oklahoma State College *A*
Langston University *B*
Northeastern Oklahoma Agricultural and
    Mechanical College *A*
Northeastern State University *B*
Northern Oklahoma College *A*
Northwestern Oklahoma State
    University *B*
Oklahoma Baptist University *B, T*
Oklahoma Christian University of
    Science and Arts *B*
Oklahoma City Community College *A*
Oklahoma City University *B*
Oklahoma Panhandle State University *B*
Oklahoma State University *B*
Oklahoma Wesleyan University *A, B*
Oral Roberts University *B*
Redlands Community College *A*
Rogers State University *A*
Rose State College *A*
St. Gregory's University *A, B*
Southeastern Oklahoma State
    University *B*
Southern Nazarene University *B*
Southwestern Oklahoma State
    University *B*
University of Central Oklahoma *B, M*
University of Science and Arts of
    Oklahoma *B*
University of Tulsa *B, M, D*
Western Oklahoma State College *A*

Oregon
Central Oregon Community College *A*
Chemeketa Community College *A*
Concordia University *B, T*
Eastern Oregon University *B, T*
George Fox University *B*
Lewis & Clark College *B*
Linfield College *B*
Linn-Benton Community College *A*
Oregon State University *B*
Pacific University *B*
Portland State University *B, M*
Reed College *B*
Southern Oregon University *B, T*
University of Oregon *B, M, D*
University of Portland *B, T*

Warner Pacific College *B, T*
Western Oregon University *B*
Willamette University *B*

Pennsylvania
Albright College *B, T*
Allegheny College *B*
Arcadia University *B*
Bloomsburg University of
    Pennsylvania *B, M, T*
Bryn Athyn College of the New
    Church *B*
Bryn Mawr College *B, M, D*
Bucknell University *B, M*
Bucks County Community College *A*
Butler County Community College *A*
Cabrini College *B*
California University of
    Pennsylvania *B, M*
Carlow College *B, T*
Carnegie Mellon University *B, M, D*
Cedar Crest College *B*
Chatham College *B, M*
Chestnut Hill College *A, B*
Cheyney University of Pennsylvania *B*
Community College of Allegheny
    County *A*
DeSales University *B*
Delaware Valley College *B*
Dickinson College *B*
Drexel University *B, M, D*
Duquesne University *B, M*
East Stroudsburg University of
    Pennsylvania *B, M*
Edinboro University of
    Pennsylvania *B, M, T*
Elizabethtown College *B*
Franklin & Marshall College *B*
Geneva College *B*
Gettysburg College *B*
Grove City College *B*
Gwynedd-Mercy College *B*
Harrisburg Area Community College *A*
Haverford College *B*
Holy Family University *B, T*
Immaculata University *B*
Indiana University of
    Pennsylvania *B, M, T*
Juniata College *B*
Keystone College *A, B*
King's College *B, T*
Kutztown University of
    Pennsylvania *B, T*
La Roche College *B*
La Salle University *B, T*
Lafayette College *B*
Lebanon Valley College of
    Pennsylvania *B, T*
Lehigh University *B*
Lincoln University *B*
Lock Haven University of
    Pennsylvania *B*
Lycoming College *B*
Marywood University *B*
Mercyhurst College *B*
Messiah College *B*
Millersville University of
    Pennsylvania *B, M, T*
Montgomery County Community
    College *A*
Moravian College *B, T*
Muhlenberg College *B, T*
Neumann College *B, T*
Northampton County Area Community
    College *A*

Penn State
    Abington *B*
    Altoona *B*
    Beaver *B*
    Berks *B*
    Delaware County *B*
    Dubois *B*
    Erie, The Behrend College *B*
    Fayette *B*
    Hazleton *B*
    Lehigh Valley *B*
    McKeesport *B*
    Mont Alto *B*
    New Kensington *B*
    Schuylkill - Capital College *B*
    Shenango *B*
    University Park *B, M, D*
    Wilkes-Barre *B*
    Worthington Scranton *B*
    York *B*
Pennsylvania College of Technology *A*
Philadelphia University *B*
Point Park College *B*
Reading Area Community College *A*
Rosemont College *B*
St. Joseph's University *A, B, M*
St. Vincent College *B*
Seton Hill University *B, T*
Shippensburg University of
    Pennsylvania *B, M, T*
Slippery Rock University of
    Pennsylvania *B, M, T*
Swarthmore College *B*
Temple University *B, M, D*
Thiel College *B*
University of Pennsylvania *C, B, M, D*
University of Pittsburgh *B, M, D*
University of Pittsburgh
    Bradford *B*
    Greensburg *B*
    Johnstown *B*
University of Scranton *B, T*
University of the Sciences in
    Philadelphia *B*
Villanova University *B, M*
Washington and Jefferson College *B*
Waynesburg College *B*
West Chester University of
    Pennsylvania *B, M*
Widener University *B*
Wilkes University *B*
Wilson College *B*
York College of Pennsylvania *A, B, T*

Puerto Rico

Bayamon Central University *B*
Inter American University of Puerto Rico
    Barranquitas Campus *B*
    Bayamon Campus *B*
    Guayama Campus *B*
    Metropolitan Campus *B*
    San German Campus *B*
Pontifical Catholic University of Puerto
    Rico *B*
Turabo University *B*
Universidad Metropolitana *B*
University of Puerto Rico
    Bayamon University College *B*
    Cayey University College *B*
    Humacao *B*
    Mayaguez Campus *B, M*
    Medical Sciences Campus *D*
    Ponce *A*
    Rio Piedras Campus *B, M, D*
University of the Sacred Heart *B*

Rhode Island

Brown University *B, M, D*
Rhode Island College *B, M*
Roger Williams University *B*
Salve Regina University *B*
University of Rhode Island *B*

South Carolina

Anderson College *B, T*
Benedict College *B*

Charleston Southern University *B*
The Citadel *B*
Claflin University *B*
Clemson University *B*
Coastal Carolina University *B*
Coker College *B*
College of Charleston *B, T*
Columbia College *B*
Converse College *B*
Erskine College *B, T*
Francis Marion University *B*
Furman University *B, T*
Lander University *B*
Limestone College *B*
Morris College *B*
Newberry College *B, T*
Presbyterian College *B, T*
South Carolina State University *B*
Southern Wesleyan University *B, T*
University of South Carolina *B, M, D*
University of South Carolina
    Aiken *B*
    Spartanburg *B*
Voorhees College *B*
Winthrop University *B, M*
Wofford College *B, T*

South Dakota

Augustana College *B, T*
Black Hills State University *B*
Dakota State University *B*
Dakota Wesleyan University *B*
Mount Marty College *B*
Northern State University *B*
Sinte Gleska University *A*
South Dakota State University *B, M*
University of Sioux Falls *B*
University of South Dakota *B, M, D*

Tennessee

Austin Peay State University *B, M*
Belmont University *B, T*
Bethel College *B, T*
Bryan College *B, T*
Carson-Newman College *B, T*
Christian Brothers University *B*
Columbia State Community College *A*
Crichton College *B*
Dyersburg State Community College *A*
East Tennessee State University *B, M*
Fisk University *B, M*
Freed-Hardeman University *B, T*
Jackson State Community College *A*
King College *B, T*
Lambuth University *B*
Lane College *B*
Maryville College *B, T*
Middle Tennessee State University *B, M*
Milligan College *B, T*
Rhodes College *B, T*
Roane State Community College *A*
Southern Adventist University *B*
Tennessee State University *B, M*
Tennessee Technological
    University *B, M, T*
Tennessee Wesleyan College *B, T*
Trevecca Nazarene University *B*
Tusculum College *B*
Union University *B, T*
University of Memphis *B, M, D*
University of Tennessee
    Chattanooga *B*
    Knoxville *B*
    Martin *B*
Walters State Community College *A*

Texas

Abilene Christian University *B*
Alvin Community College *A*
Amarillo College *A*
Angelina College *A*
Angelo State University *B, M, T*
Austin College *B*
Austin Community College *A*
Baylor University *B, M, D*
Blinn College *A*

Brazosport College *A*
Cedar Valley College *A*
Central Texas College *A*
Cisco Junior College *A*
Clarendon College *A*
Coastal Bend College *A*
College of the Mainland *A*
Concordia University at Austin *B*
Dallas Baptist University *B*
Del Mar College *A*
East Texas Baptist University *B*
El Paso Community College *A*
Frank Phillips College *A*
Galveston College *A*
Grayson County College *A*
Hardin-Simmons University *B*
Hill College *A*
Houston Baptist University *B*
Howard College *A*
Howard Payne University *B, T*
Huston-Tillotson College *B*
Jarvis Christian College *B*
Kilgore College *A*
Lamar University *B, M*
Laredo Community College *A*
LeTourneau University *B*
Lon Morris College *A*
Lubbock Christian University *B, T*
McMurry University *B, T*
Midland College *A*
Midwestern State University *B, M*
Northeast Texas Community College *A*
Odessa College *A*
Our Lady of the Lake University of San
    Antonio *B*
Palo Alto College *A*
Panola College *A*
Paris Junior College *A*
Paul Quinn College *B*
Prairie View A&M University *B, M*
Rice University *B, M, D*
St. Edward's University *B, T*
St. Mary's University *B*
St. Philip's College *A*
Sam Houston State University *B, M*
Schreiner University *B, T*
South Plains College *A*
Southern Methodist University *B, M, D*
Southwest Texas State
    University *B, M, T*
Southwestern Adventist University *B, T*
Southwestern University *B, T*
Stephen F. Austin State
    University *B, M, T*
Sul Ross State University *B, M, T*
Tarleton State University *B, M*
Temple College *A*
Texas A&M International
    University *B*
Texas A&M University *B, M, D*
Texas A&M University
    Commerce *B, M*
    Corpus Christi *B, M, T*
    Kingsville *B, M*
    Texarkana *T*
Texas Christian University *B, M, T*
Texas College *B*
Texas Lutheran University *B*
Texas Southern University *B, M*
Texas Tech University *B, M, D*
Texas Wesleyan University *B*
Texas Woman's University *B, M, T*
Trinity University *B*
Trinity Valley Community College *A*
Tyler Junior College *A*
University of Dallas *B*
University of Houston *B, M, D*
University of Houston
    Clear Lake *B*
    Downtown *B*
    Victoria *B*
University of Mary Hardin-Baylor *B, T*
University of North Texas *B, M, D*
University of St. Thomas *B*

University of Texas
    Arlington *B, M*
    Austin *B, M, D*
    Brownsville *B, M*
    Dallas *B*
    El Paso *B, M, D*
    Pan American *B, M, T*
    San Antonio *B, M*
    Tyler *B, M*
    of the Permian Basin *B, M*
University of the Incarnate Word *B, M*
Wayland Baptist University *B, T*
West Texas A&M University *B, M*
Western Texas College *A*
Wharton County Junior College *A*
Wiley College *B*

Utah

Brigham Young University *B*
Dixie State College of Utah *A*
Salt Lake Community College *A*
Snow College *A*
Southern Utah University *B, T*
University of Utah *B, M, D*
Utah State University *B, M, D*
Utah Valley State College *B*
Westminster College *B*

Vermont

Bennington College *B*
Castleton State College *B*
Goddard College *B*
Green Mountain College *B*
Johnson State College *B*
Marlboro College *B*
Middlebury College *B*
Norwich University *B*
St. Michael's College *B*
University of Vermont *B, M, D*

Virginia

Averett University *B, T*
Bluefield College *B*
Bridgewater College *B*
College of William and Mary *B, M*
Eastern Mennonite University *B*
Emory & Henry College *B, T*
Ferrum College *B*
George Mason University *B, M*
Hampden-Sydney College *B*
Hampton University *B, M*
Hollins University *B*
James Madison University *B, M, T*
Liberty University *B, T*
Longwood University *B, T*
Lynchburg College *B*
Mary Baldwin College *B*
Mary Washington College *B*
Marymount University *B*
Norfolk State University *B*
Old Dominion University *B, M*
Radford University *B*
Randolph-Macon College *B*
Randolph-Macon Woman's College *B*
Roanoke College *B, T*
Shenandoah University *B*
Sweet Briar College *B*
University of Richmond *B, M, T*
University of Virginia *B, M, D*
University of Virginia's College at
    Wise *B, T*
Virginia Commonwealth
    University *B, M*
Virginia Intermont College *B*
Virginia Military Institute *B*
Virginia Polytechnic Institute and State
    University *B, M, D, T*
Virginia State University *B, M*
Virginia Union University *B*
Virginia Wesleyan College *B*
Washington and Lee University *B*

Washington

Central Washington University *B, M*
Centralia College *A*
Eastern Washington University *B, M, T*
Everett Community College *A*

Gonzaga University *B*
Heritage College *B*
Lower Columbia College *A*
Northwest College *T*
Olympic College *A*
Pacific Lutheran University *B*
St. Martin's College *B*
Seattle Pacific University *B*
Seattle University *B*
University of Puget Sound *B, T*
University of Washington *B*
Walla Walla College *B, M*
Washington State University *B, M*
Western Washington University *B, M, T*
Whitman College *B*
Whitworth College *B, T*

West Virginia

Alderson-Broaddus College *B*
Bethany College *B*
Concord College *B*
Davis and Elkins College *B*
Fairmont State College *B*
Glenville State College *B*
Marshall University *B, M*
Potomac State College of West Virginia
  University *A*
Salem International University *B*
Shepherd College *B, T*
University of Charleston *B*
West Liberty State College *B*
West Virginia State College *B*
West Virginia University *B, M, D, T*
West Virginia University Institute of
  Technology *B*
West Virginia Wesleyan College *B*
Wheeling Jesuit University *B*

Wisconsin

Alverno College *B, T*
Beloit College *B, T*
Cardinal Stritch University *B*
Carroll College *B*
Carthage College *B, T*
Concordia University Wisconsin *B*
Edgewood College *B*
Lakeland College *B*
Lawrence University *B, T*
Marian College of Fond du Lac *B*
Marquette University *B, M, D*
Mount Mary College *B*
Northland College *B*
Ripon College *B*
St. Norbert College *B, T*
Silver Lake College *B, T*
University of Wisconsin
  Eau Claire *B, M*
  Green Bay *B*
  La Crosse *B*
  Madison *B, T*
  Milwaukee *B, M, D*
  Oshkosh *B*
  Parkside *B*
  Platteville *B, T*
  River Falls *B*
  Stevens Point *B, M*
  Superior *B*
  Whitewater *B, T*
Viterbo University *B, T*
Wisconsin Lutheran College *B*

Wyoming

Casper College *A*
Central Wyoming College *A*
Eastern Wyoming College *A*
Laramie County Community College *A*
Sheridan College *A*
University of Wyoming *B*
Western Wyoming Community
  College *A*

Biology teacher education

Alabama

Athens State University *B*

Birmingham-Southern College *T*
Faulkner University *B*
Judson College *B*
Oakwood College *B*
Talladega College *T*
Tuskegee University *B*

Arizona

Arizona State University *B, T*
Northern Arizona University *B, M, T*
Prescott College *B, M, T*
University of Arizona *B, M*

Arkansas

Arkansas State University *B, M, T*
Arkansas Tech University *B*
Harding University *B, M, T*
Henderson State University *B, M, T*
John Brown University *B, T*
Ouachita Baptist University *B, T*
Philander Smith College *B*
Southern Arkansas University *B, T*
University of Central Arkansas *T*
University of the Ozarks *B, T*

California

California State Polytechnic University:
  Pomona *T*
California State University
  Chico *T*
  Long Beach *T*
  San Bernardino *T*
Concordia University *B*
Humboldt State University *T*
Loyola Marymount University *M*
Master's College *T*
Pacific Union College *T*
San Diego State University *B, T*
San Francisco State University *B, T*
University of the Pacific *T*

Colorado

Colorado State University *T*
Colorado State University
  Pueblo *T*
Fort Lewis College *T*
Regis University *B, T*

Connecticut

Central Connecticut State University *B*
Fairfield University *T*
Quinnipiac University *B, M*
Sacred Heart University *T*
St. Joseph College *T*
Southern Connecticut State
  University *B, M, T*

Delaware

Delaware State University *B, M*
University of Delaware *B, T*

District of Columbia

Catholic University of America *B*

Florida

Barry University *T*
Bethune-Cookman College *B, T*
Florida Agricultural and Mechanical
  University *T*
Florida Institute of Technology *B*
Gulf Coast Community College *A*
St. Thomas University *B, T*
Southeastern College of the Assemblies
  of God *B, T*
Stetson University *B, T*
University of Tampa *T*
University of West Florida *B, T*

Georgia

Agnes Scott College *T*
Armstrong Atlantic State University *T*
Atlanta Metropolitan College *A*
Brewton-Parker College *B*
Columbus State University *B, M*
Covenant College *B*
Georgia College and State
  University *M, T*
Georgia Southern University *B*

North Georgia College & State
  University *B, M*
State University of West Georgia *B*

Hawaii

Brigham Young University-Hawaii *B, T*
University of Hawaii
  Manoa *B, T*

Idaho

Boise State University *T*
Brigham Young University - Idaho *T*
Northwest Nazarene University *B*
University of Idaho *T*

Illinois

Augustana College *B, T*
Benedictine University *T*
Blackburn College *B, T*
Chicago State University *B, T*
Concordia University *B, T*
Dominican University *T*
Eastern Illinois University *B, T*
Elmhurst College *B*
Eureka College *T*
Governors State University *B, T*
Greenville College *B*
Illinois College *T*
Lake Land College *A*
Lewis University *T*
Loyola University of Chicago *T*
MacMurray College *B, T*
McKendree College *B, T*
North Central College *B, T*
North Park University *T*
Northwestern University *B, T*
Olivet Nazarene University *B, T*
Quincy University *T*
Rockford College *T*
Roosevelt University *B*
St. Xavier University *B*
Sauk Valley Community College *A*
Trinity Christian College *B, T*
Trinity International University *B, T*
University of Illinois
  Chicago *B*
  Urbana-Champaign *M, T*
University of St. Francis *T*
Wheaton College *T*

Indiana

Ball State University *T*
Butler University *T*
Franklin College *B, T*
Goshen College *B*
Grace College *B*
Huntington College *B*
Indiana University
  Bloomington *B, T*
  Northwest *B*
  South Bend *B, T*
  Southeast *B*
Indiana University-Purdue University
  Fort Wayne *B, T*
Indiana Wesleyan University *T*
Manchester College *B, T*
Purdue University
  Calumet *B*
Saint Mary's College *T*
St. Mary-of-the-Woods College *B*
Taylor University *B, T*
University of Evansville *B*
University of Indianapolis *B, T*
University of Southern Indiana *T*
Valparaiso University *B*
Vincennes University *A*

Iowa

Buena Vista University *B, T*
Central College *T*
Clarke College *B, T*
Cornell College *B*
Dordt College *B*
Drake University *M*
Ellsworth Community College *A*
Franciscan University *B, D*
Graceland University *T*

Grand View College *B, T*
Iowa State University *T*
Iowa Wesleyan College *B*
Loras College *T*
Luther College *B*
Maharishi University of Management *T*
Morningside College *B*
Mount Mercy College *B*
Northwestern College *T*
St. Ambrose University *B, T*
University of Iowa *B, T*
Upper Iowa University *B, T*
Wartburg College *T*
William Penn University *B*

Kansas

Baker University *T*
Benedictine College *B, T*
Bethany College *B*
Bethel College *T*
Central Christian College *A, B*
Emporia State University *B, T*
Independence Community College *A*
McPherson College *B, T*
MidAmerica Nazarene University *B, T*
Newman University *T*
Ottawa University *T*
Pittsburg State University *B, T*
St. Mary College *T*
Sterling College *T*
Tabor College *B, T*
University of Kansas *B, T*

Kentucky

Alice Lloyd College *B*
Bellarmine University *B, M, T*
Campbellsville University *B*
Cumberland College *B, T*
Kentucky Wesleyan College *T*
Murray State University *B, M, T*
Pikeville College *B, T*
Thomas More College *B*
Union College *M*

Louisiana

Centenary College of Louisiana *B, T*
Louisiana State University
  Shreveport *T*
McNeese State University *T*
Nicholls State University *B*
Northwestern State University *B*
Southern University and Agricultural and
  Mechanical College *B*
Xavier University of Louisiana *B, T*

Maine

College of the Atlantic *B, T*
Husson College *B, T*
St. Joseph's College *B*
University of Maine *B*
University of Maine
  Farmington *B, T*
  Machias *T*
  Presque Isle *B*
University of New England *B, T*
University of Southern Maine *T*

Maryland

Coppin State College *B, T*
St. Mary's College of Maryland *T*
Salisbury University *T*
Washington College *T*

Massachusetts

American International College *B, M*
Assumption College *T*
Bridgewater State College *M, T*
Elms College *T*
Fitchburg State College *B, M, T*
Framingham State College *B, T*
Harvard College *T*
Merrimack College *T*
Northeastern University *M*
Tufts University *T*
University of Massachusetts
  Dartmouth *T*
Western New England College *T*

Westfield State College *B, M, T*

Michigan
Alma College *T*
Andrews University *M, T*
Calvin College *B*
Central Michigan University *B, M*
Concordia University *B, T*
Cornerstone University *B*
Eastern Michigan University *B, T*
Grand Valley State University *M, T*
Hope College *T*
Michigan Technological University *T*
Northern Michigan University *B, M, T*
University of Michigan
    Flint *T*
Western Michigan University *B*

Minnesota
Augsburg College *T*
Bemidji State University *T*
Bethel College *B*
College of St. Catherine *T*
College of St. Scholastica *T*
Concordia College: Moorhead *B, T*
Concordia University: St. Paul *B, T*
Gustavus Adolphus College *T*
Minnesota State University
    Mankato *B, M, T*
    Moorhead *B, T*
Northland Community & Technical
    College *A*
St. Cloud State University *M, T*
St. Mary's University of Minnesota *B*
St. Olaf College *T*
Southwest State University *B, T*
University of Minnesota
    Morris *T*
University of St. Thomas *B, T*
Vermilion Community College *A*
Winona State University *B, T*

Mississippi
Blue Mountain College *B*
Delta State University *B*
Itawamba Community College *A*
Mississippi College *B, M*
Mississippi State University *T*
Mississippi Valley State University *B, T*
Rust College *B*
University of Mississippi *B, T*

Missouri
Avila University *B, T*
Central Methodist College *B*
Central Missouri State University *B, T*
College of the Ozarks *B, T*
Lincoln University *B, T*
Lindenwood University *M*
Maryville University of Saint
    Louis *B, M, T*
Missouri Baptist University *T*
Missouri Southern State College *B, T*
Missouri Valley College *T*
Northwest Missouri State
    University *B, T*
Rockhurst University *B*
Southwest Missouri State University *B*
Truman State University *M, T*
University of Missouri
    Columbia *B*
    St. Louis *B*
Washington University in St.
    Louis *B, M, T*
William Woods University *T*

Montana
Montana State University
    Billings *B, T*
Rocky Mountain College *B, T*
University of Montana-Missoula *B, M, T*
University of Montana: Western *B, T*

Nebraska
Bellevue University *B*
Chadron State College *B*
College of Saint Mary *B, T*

Concordia University *B, T*
Creighton University *T*
Dana College *B*
Doane College *T*
Hastings College *B, M, T*
Midland Lutheran College *B, T*
Nebraska Wesleyan University *T*
Peru State College *B, T*
Union College *T*
University of Nebraska
    Kearney *B*
    Lincoln *B, T*
York College *B*

New Hampshire
Colby-Sawyer College *B, T*
Franklin Pierce College *T*
Keene State College *B, T*
New England College *B, T*
Plymouth State College *T*
Rivier College *B, T*
St. Anselm College *T*
University of New Hampshire *T*

New Jersey
Bloomfield College *B*
The College of New Jersey *B, T*
Georgian Court College *T*
Monmouth University *B, T*
Richard Stockton College of New
    Jersey *B*
Rowan University *T*
St. Peter's College *T*
William Paterson University of New
    Jersey *T*

New Mexico
New Mexico Institute of Mining and
    Technology *M*
Western New Mexico University *B*

New York
Adelphi University *M*
Alfred University *M, T*
Canisius College *B, M, T*
City University of New York
    Brooklyn College *B*
    City College *B*
    College of Staten Island *M*
    Hunter College *B, M, T*
    Queens College *M, T*
Colgate University *M*
D'Youville College *B, M, T*
Daemen College *B, T*
Dowling College *B*
Elmira College *B, T*
Fordham University *M, T*
Hofstra University *B, M*
Houghton College *B, T*
Ithaca College *B, T*
Keuka College *B, T*
Long Island University
    C. W. Post Campus *B, M, T*
    Southampton College *T*
Manhattan College *B, T*
Marist College *B*
Marymount College of Fordham
    University *B, T*
Marymount Manhattan College *B, T*
Mercy College *T*
Molloy College *B*
Nazareth College of Rochester *T*
New York Institute of Technology *B, T*
New York University *B, M, T*
Niagara University *B, T*
Pace University *B, M, T*
Pace University:
    Pleasantville/Briarcliff *B, M, T*
Roberts Wesleyan College *B, T*
St. John Fisher College *B, T*
St. John's University *B, M, T*
St. Joseph's College: Suffolk
    Campus *B, T*
St. Lawrence University *T*

State University of New York
    Albany *B, T*
    Binghamton *M*
    Buffalo *M, T*
    College at Brockport *M, T*
    College at Buffalo *B, M*
    College at Cortland *B, M*
    College at Fredonia *B, M, T*
    College at Geneseo *B, M, T*
    College at Old Westbury *B*
    College at Oneonta *B, T*
    College at Plattsburgh *B, M*
    College at Potsdam *B, M, T*
    College of Environmental Science
      and Forestry *B, T*
    New Paltz *B, M, T*
    Oswego *B, M*
    Stony Brook *T*
Syracuse University *B, M, T*
Vassar College *T*
Wagner College *T*
Wells College *T*

North Carolina
Campbell University *B, T*
Gardner-Webb University *B*
Greensboro College *B, T*
Guilford Technical Community
    College *A*
Lenoir Community College *A*
Louisburg College *A*
Mars Hill College *T*
Meredith College *T*
Methodist College *A, B, T*
North Carolina Agricultural and
    Technical State University *B, T*
St. Augustine's College *B*
Sandhills Community College *A*
Shaw University *B, T*
University of North Carolina
    Greensboro *B, M, T*
    Pembroke *B, T*
    Wilmington *B*
Wake Forest University *M, T*
Western Carolina University *M, T*
Wingate University *B, T*

North Dakota
Dickinson State University *B, T*
Jamestown College *B*
Mayville State University *B, T*
Minot State University *B*
North Dakota State University *B, T*
University of Mary *B*
University of North Dakota *B, T*
Valley City State University *B, T*

Ohio
Ashland University *B*
Baldwin-Wallace College *T*
Bluffton College *B*
Bowling Green State University *B, M*
Case Western Reserve University *T*
Cedarville University *B, T*
College of Mount St. Joseph *T*
Defiance College *B, T*
Hiram College *T*
John Carroll University *T*
Kent State University *B, T*
Kent State University
    Stark Campus *B*
Malone College *B*
Miami University
    Oxford Campus *B, M, T*
Mount Union College *T*
Mount Vernon Nazarene University *T*
Ohio Dominican College *B, T*
Ohio Northern University *B*
Otterbein College *B*
Shawnee State University *B*
University of Akron *B, T*
University of Dayton *B, M, T*
University of Findlay *B, T*
University of Rio Grande *B, T*
University of Toledo *T*
Urbana University *B*

Wilmington College *B*
Xavier University *B, M*
Youngstown State University *B, M*

Oklahoma
Cameron University *B*
East Central University *T*
Eastern Oklahoma State College *A*
Northeastern State University *B*
Oklahoma Baptist University *B, T*
Oklahoma State University *M*
Southern Nazarene University *B*
University of Central Oklahoma *B*
University of Tulsa *T*

Oregon
Concordia University *B, M, T*
George Fox University *T*
Linfield College *T*
Oregon State University *M*
Portland State University *T*
Southern Oregon University *T*
University of Portland *T*
Western Baptist College *B*
Western Oregon University *T*

Pennsylvania
Albright College *T*
Bryn Athyn College of the New
    Church *B*
Cabrini College *B, T*
California University of
    Pennsylvania *B, T*
Carlow College *T*
Chatham College *M*
DeSales University *T*
Delaware Valley College *T*
Dickinson College *T*
Duquesne University *B, M, T*
Elizabethtown College *T*
Geneva College *B, T*
Gettysburg College *T*
Grove City College *B, T*
Gwynedd-Mercy College *T*
Holy Family University *B, M, T*
Juniata College *B, T*
King's College *T*
La Roche College *B*
La Salle University *B, T*
Lebanon Valley College of
    Pennsylvania *B, T*
Lock Haven University of
    Pennsylvania *B, T*
Lycoming College *T*
Marywood University *B*
Mercyhurst College *B*
Messiah College *T*
Moravian College *T*
Point Park College *B*
St. Vincent College *T*
Seton Hill University *B, T*
Slippery Rock University of
    Pennsylvania *M, T*
Thiel College *B*
University of Pittsburgh
    Johnstown *B, T*
Villanova University *T*
Washington and Jefferson College *T*
Waynesburg College *B, T*
Widener University *T*
Wilkes University *M, T*
Wilson College *T*
York College of Pennsylvania *B, T*

Puerto Rico
Inter American University of Puerto Rico
    Barranquitas Campus *B*
    Fajardo Campus *B, T*
    Metropolitan Campus *B*
    San German Campus *B*
Pontifical Catholic University of Puerto
    Rico *B, T*
Turabo University *B*
Universidad Metropolitana *B*

Rhode Island
Rhode Island College *B*

Salve Regina University *B*

South Carolina
Anderson College *B, T*
The Citadel *M*
Claflin University *B*
Coker College *B, T*
Columbia College *B*
Francis Marion University *B, T*
Furman University *T*
Limestone College *B*
Morris College *B, T*
South Carolina State University *B, T*
Southern Wesleyan University *B, T*
Wofford College *T*

South Dakota
Augustana College *B, T*
Black Hills State University *B, T*
Dakota State University *B, T*
Dakota Wesleyan University *B, T*
Mount Marty College *B*
South Dakota State University *B*
University of Sioux Falls *T*
University of South Dakota *T*

Tennessee
Belmont University *T*
Bryan College *T*
Christian Brothers University *B, M, T*
Crichton College *C, B*
Freed-Hardeman University *B, T*
King College *T*
Lambuth University *T*
Lane College *B*
Maryville College *B, T*
Middle Tennessee State University *M, T*
Southern Adventist University *B*
Tennessee Technological University *T*
Tennessee Wesleyan College *B, T*
Trevecca Nazarene University *B, T*
Union University *B, T*
University of Tennessee
    Martin *B, T*

Texas
Abilene Christian University *B, T*
Baylor University *B, T*
Del Mar College *A*
East Texas Baptist University *B*
Hardin-Simmons University *B, T*
Houston Baptist University *T*
Howard Payne University *B, T*
Jarvis Christian College *B*
Kilgore College *A*
Lamar University *T*
Laredo Community College *A*
Lubbock Christian University *B, T*
McMurry University *T*
St. Mary's University *T*
Schreiner University *T*
Southwest Texas State University *M, T*
Tarleton State University *M, T*
Texas A&M International
    University *B, T*
Texas A&M University
    Commerce *B*
    Kingsville *T*
Texas Christian University *T*
Texas Wesleyan University *B, T*
University of Dallas *T*
University of Houston *T*
University of Houston
    Clear Lake *T*
University of Mary Hardin-Baylor *T*
University of Texas
    Arlington *T*
    San Antonio *T*
West Texas A&M University *T*

Utah
Brigham Young University *B, M*
Southern Utah University *B, T*
University of Utah *B*
Utah State University *B*
Utah Valley State College *B*
Weber State University *B*

Vermont
Bennington College *B, M, T*
Castleton State College *B, T*
Johnson State College *B*
St. Michael's College *T*

Virginia
Averett University *B, M, T*
Bluefield College *T*
Bridgewater College *T*
Eastern Mennonite University *T*
Hampton University *M*
Hollins University *T*
Liberty University *B*
Longwood University *B, T*
Radford University *T*
University of Virginia's College at
    Wise *T*
Virginia Intermont College *B, T*
Virginia Wesleyan College *T*

Washington
Central Washington University *B, T*
Heritage College *B*
Seattle Pacific University *B*
University of Washington *M, T*
Washington State University *T*
Western Washington University *B, T*
Whitworth College *B, T*

West Virginia
Alderson-Broaddus College *T*
Concord College *B, T*
Fairmont State College *B*
Salem International University *T*
Shepherd College *T*
University of Charleston *B*
West Liberty State College *B*
Wheeling Jesuit University *T*

Wisconsin
Carroll College *B, T*
Carthage College *T*
Edgewood College *B*
Lakeland College *T*
Lawrence University *T*
Marian College of Fond du Lac *B, T*
Mount Mary College *B, T*
Northland College *T*
St. Norbert College *T*
Silver Lake College *T*
University of Wisconsin
    Green Bay *T*
    La Crosse *B, T*
    Parkside *T*
    Platteville *B*
    River Falls *T*
    Superior *B, T*
    Whitewater *B*
Viterbo University *B, T*

Biomedical engineering

Alabama
University of Alabama
    Birmingham *B, M, D*

Arizona
Arizona State University *B, M, D*
University of Arizona *M, D*

Arkansas
University of Arkansas
    for Medical Sciences *A*

California
California State University
    Long Beach *B*
    Sacramento *M*
Napa Valley College *C, A*
University of California
    Berkeley *B, D*
    Davis *B, M, D*
    Irvine *B, M, D*
    Los Angeles *M, D*
    San Diego *B, M, D*

University of Southern
    California *B, M, D*

Connecticut
Trinity College *B*
University of Connecticut *B, M, D*
University of Hartford *B*
Yale University *B*

Delaware
University of Delaware *B, M, D*

District of Columbia
Catholic University of America *B, M, D*
George Washington University *B*

Florida
Florida International University *B, M*
Florida State University *B, M, D*
University of Florida *M, D*
University of Miami *B, M, D*
University of South Florida *M*

Georgia
Georgia Institute of Technology *M, D*
Mercer University *B, M*
University of Georgia *B, M*

Idaho
University of Idaho *B, M, D*

Illinois
Northwestern University *B, M, D*
University of Illinois
    Chicago *B, M, D*
    Urbana-Champaign *B*

Indiana
Indiana University-Purdue University
    Indianapolis *M*
Rose-Hulman Institute of Technology *M*

Iowa
Iowa State University *M, D*
University of Iowa *B, M, D*

Kentucky
University of Kentucky *M, D*

Louisiana
Louisiana State University and
    Agricultural and Mechanical
    College *B*
Louisiana Tech University *C, B, D*
Tulane University *B, M, D*

Maryland
Johns Hopkins University *B, M, D*

Massachusetts
Boston University *B, M, D*
Harvard College *B*
Massachusetts Institute of
    Technology *M, D*
Smith College *B*
Tufts University *M*
Western New England College *B*
Worcester Polytechnic Institute *B, M, D*

Michigan
Michigan State University *B*
Michigan Technological University *B*
Schoolcraft College *A*
University of Michigan *M, D*
Wayne State University *M, D*

Minnesota
University of Minnesota
    Twin Cities *M, D*

Mississippi
Mississippi State University *B, M*

Missouri
St. Louis University *B*
University of Missouri
    Columbia *B, M, D*
Washington University in St.
    Louis *B, M, D*

Nebraska
University of Nebraska
    Lincoln *B*

Nevada
University of Nevada
    Reno *M, D*

New Hampshire
Dartmouth College *B*

New Jersey
Fairleigh Dickinson University
    Metropolitan Campus *M*
New Jersey Institute of
    Technology *B, M, D*
Rutgers, The State University of New
    Jersey
    Camden Regional Campus *B*
    New Brunswick Regional
        Campus *B, M, D*
    Newark Regional Campus *B*
Stevens Institute of Technology *B*

New York
City University of New York
    City College *B, M, D*
Columbia University
    Fu Foundation School of
        Engineering and Applied
        Science *B, M, D*
Hofstra University *B*
New York Institute of Technology *B*
Polytechnic University *M*
Rensselaer Polytechnic Institute *B, M, D*
Rochester Institute of Technology *B*
State University of New York
    Buffalo *M, D*
    Stony Brook *B, M, D*
Syracuse University *B, M, D*
Touro College *C*
University of Rochester *B, M, D*

North Carolina
Duke University *B, M, D*
North Carolina State University *B*

North Dakota
North Dakota State University *B*

Ohio
Case Western Reserve
    University *B, M, D*
Ohio State University
    Columbus Campus *M, D*
University of Akron *C, B, M*
University of Toledo *B, M*
Wright State University *B, M*

Oklahoma
Oral Roberts University *B*
University of Central Oklahoma *B*

Oregon
Oregon State University *B*

Pennsylvania
Carnegie Mellon University *B, M, D*
Cedar Crest College *B*
Drexel University *M, D*
Gettysburg College *B*
Lehigh University *B*
Lock Haven University of
    Pennsylvania *B*

Penn State
  Abington *B*
  Altoona *B*
  Beaver *B*
  Berks *B*
  Delaware County *B*
  Dubois *B*
  Fayette *B*
  Hazleton *B*
  Lehigh Valley *B*
  McKeesport *B*
  Mont Alto *B*
  New Kensington *B*
  Schuylkill - Capital College *B*
  Shenango *B*
  University Park *B, M, D*
  Wilkes-Barre *B*
  Worthington Scranton *B*
  York *B*
Pennsylvania College of Technology *A*
Temple University *B, M*
University of Pennsylvania *B, M, D*
University of Pittsburgh *B, M, D*

Rhode Island
Brown University *B, M*
University of Rhode Island *B*

South Carolina
Clemson University *M, D*

Tennessee
University of Memphis *M, D*
University of Tennessee Health Science
  Center *M, D*
Vanderbilt University *B, M, D*

Texas
Rice University *B, M, D*
Texas A&M University *B, M, D*
University of Houston *M, D*
University of Texas
  Arlington *M, D*
  Austin *B, M, D*
  Southwestern Medical Center at
    Dallas *M, D*

Utah
University of Utah *B, M, D*

Vermont
University of Vermont *M*

Virginia
University of Virginia *M, D*
Virginia Commonwealth
  University *B, M, D*
Virginia Polytechnic Institute and State
  University *B, M, D*

Washington
University of Washington *B, M, D*
Walla Walla College *B*

Wisconsin
Marquette University *B, M, D*
Milwaukee Area Technical College *A*
Milwaukee School of Engineering *B*
University of Wisconsin
  Madison *B, M, D*

Biomedical sciences

Alabama
Northwest-Shoals Community College *A*

Arkansas
North Arkansas College *A*

California
California State University
  Hayward *B*
Cerritos Community College *A*
East Los Angeles College *C*
San Francisco State University *M*
University of California
  Riverside *B, M, D*
  San Diego *M, D*

Connecticut
Quinnipiac University *B*
University of Connecticut *M, D*

Florida
Barry University *M*
Hillsborough Community College *A*
Nova Southeastern University *M*

Idaho
University of Idaho *B*

Illinois
Chicago State University *M*
South Suburban College of Cook
  County *C, A*

Indiana
Indiana University-Purdue University
  Indianapolis *M, D*

Maine
University of Maine *B*

Maryland
Hood College *M*
Howard Community College *C, A*
Johns Hopkins University *B, M*

Massachusetts
Benjamin Franklin Institute of
  Technology *A*
Berkshire Community College *A*
University of Massachusetts
  Lowell *D, T*
Worcester Polytechnic Institute *M, D*

Michigan
University of Michigan *B*

Nebraska
Creighton University *M, D*

Nevada
Western Nevada Community College *A*

New Jersey
Rutgers, The State University of New
  Jersey
    Camden Regional Campus *B*
University of Medicine and Dentistry of
  New Jersey
    School of Health Related
      Professions *M, D*

New York
Touro College *C*

Ohio
Antioch College *B*
Kent State University *B, M, D*
Otterbein College *B*
Ursuline College *B*
Wright State University *D*

Pennsylvania
Delaware County Community
  College *C, A*
Drexel University *M, D*
Lock Haven University of
  Pennsylvania *B*

Puerto Rico
Inter American University of Puerto Rico
  Bayamon Campus *B*
  Metropolitan Campus *B*

Rhode Island
Salve Regina University *B*

South Carolina
Medical University of South Carolina *M*

South Dakota
Southeast Technical Institute *A*

Texas
Baylor University *M, D*
St. Philip's College *A*
Texas A&M University *B*
Texas A&M University
  Galveston *B*

University of Mary Hardin-Baylor *B*

Vermont
Norwich University *B*

Virginia
College of Health Sciences *A, B*
Old Dominion University *D*

West Virginia
Marshall University *M, D*
Ohio Valley College *A*
Shepherd College *A*

Biomedical technology

Alabama
Jefferson State Community College *C, A*

Arkansas
Phillips Community College of the
  University of Arkansas *C, A*

California
Santa Barbara City College *C, A*

Florida
Florida Hospital College of Health
  Sciences *C*

Indiana
Indiana University-Purdue University
  Indianapolis *A*

Iowa
Western Iowa Tech Community
  College *A*

Louisiana
Delgado Community College *A*

Maryland
Howard Community College *C, A*
Montgomery College
  Rockville Campus *A*

Massachusetts
Benjamin Franklin Institute of
  Technology *A*
Quinsigamond Community College *C*
Worcester Polytechnic Institute *B, M, D*

Missouri
Washington University in St. Louis *B*

New Jersey
Thomas Edison State College *A, B*

New York
Erie Community College
  South Campus *A*

North Carolina
Stanly Community College *A*
University of North Carolina
  Pembroke *B*
Wilkes Community College *A*

Ohio
Cuyahoga Community College
  Eastern Campus *A*
Kettering College of Medical Arts *A*
Owens Community College
  Toledo *C, A*

Pennsylvania
Delaware County Community College *C*
Edinboro University of Pennsylvania *A*
Penn State
  Altoona *A*
  Beaver *A*
  Berks *A*
  Dubois *A*
  Fayette *A*
  Hazleton *A*
  New Kensington *A*
  Schuylkill - Capital College *A*
  Shenango *A*
  Wilkes-Barre *C*
  York *A*

Pennsylvania College of Technology *A*

South Carolina
York Technical College *C*

South Dakota
Southeast Technical Institute *A*

Texas
St. Philip's College *A*
Texas Southern University *B*

Virginia
ECPI College of Technology *C, A*

Wisconsin
Milwaukee Area Technical College *A*
Western Wisconsin Technical College *A*

Biometrics

California
University of California
  Santa Cruz *B*
University of Southern California *M, D*

Colorado
University of Colorado
  Health Sciences Center *M, D*

Michigan
University of Michigan *B, M*

Nebraska
University of Nebraska
  Lincoln *M*

New York
Cornell University *B, M, D*
State University of New York
  Albany *M, D*
  College of Environmental Science
    and Forestry *M, D*

North Carolina
Duke University *M*
East Carolina University *D*
University of North Carolina
  Chapel Hill *M, D*

South Carolina
Medical University of South
  Carolina *M, D*

Texas
University of Texas
  Arlington *D*
  Houston Health Science
    Center *M, D*

Wisconsin
University of Wisconsin
  Madison *M*

Biophysics

California
California Institute of Technology *D*
La Sierra University *B*
Pacific Union College *B*
Pitzer College *B*
Stanford University *M, D*
University of California
  Berkeley *D*
  Davis *D*
  Riverside *D*
  San Diego *B, M, D*
University of Southern California *M, D*

Colorado
University of Colorado
  Health Sciences Center *M, D*

Connecticut
University of Connecticut *B, M, D*

Hawaii
University of Hawaii
  Manoa *M, D*

Illinois
Finch University of Health Sciences/The
Chicago Medical School *M, D*
Illinois Institute of Technology *B, M, D*
Loyola University of Chicago *D*
Northwestern University *B*
University of Chicago *M, D*
University of Illinois
Urbana-Champaign *B, M, D*

Indiana
Indiana University-Purdue University
Indianapolis *M, D*
University of Notre Dame *M*
University of Southern Indiana *B, T*

Iowa
Iowa State University *B, M, D*
University of Iowa *M, D*

Louisiana
Centenary College of Louisiana *B*

Maryland
Johns Hopkins University *B, M, D*
University of Maryland
Baltimore *M, D*

Massachusetts
Boston University *M, D*
Brandeis University *M, D*
Hampshire College *B*
Harvard College *B*
Suffolk University *B*
Tufts University *D*

Michigan
Andrews University *B*
Michigan State University *B*
Oakland University *D*
University of Michigan *B, D*

Minnesota
Minnesota State University
Mankato *M*
St. Mary's University of Minnesota *B*
University of Minnesota
Twin Cities *M, D*

Missouri
University of Missouri
Rolla *B*
Washington University in St. Louis *B, D*

New York
City University of New York
Brooklyn College *B, M*
Columbia University
Columbia College *B*
Rensselaer Polytechnic Institute *B, M*
St. Lawrence University *B*
State University of New York
Albany *D*
Buffalo *B, M, D*
College at Geneseo *B*
Syracuse University *D*
University of Rochester *M, D*
Yeshiva University *M, D*

North Carolina
East Carolina University *D*

Ohio
Case Western Reserve University *D*
Ohio State University
Columbus Campus *M, D*
University of Akron *B*
Wittenberg University *B*

Oklahoma
Oklahoma City University *B*
Southwestern Oklahoma State
University *B*

Oregon
Oregon State University *B, M, D*

Pennsylvania
Carnegie Mellon University *D*
Temple University *B*

University of Scranton *B*

Rhode Island
Brown University *B, M, D*

Tennessee
King College *B*
Southern Adventist University *B*
University of Tennessee Health Science
Center *M, D*
Vanderbilt University *D*

Texas
Texas A&M University *M*
University of Houston *B*
University of Texas
Houston Health Science
Center *M, D*
Southwestern Medical Center at
Dallas *M, D*

Virginia
Hampden-Sydney College *B*
University of Virginia *D*

Washington
University of Washington *M, D*
Walla Walla College *B*

Wisconsin
University of Wisconsin
Madison *M, D*

Biopsychology

California
University of California
Santa Barbara *B*
Santa Cruz *B*

Colorado
University of Denver *B*

Connecticut
Quinnipiac University *B*

Illinois
Monmouth College *B*
University of Chicago *M, D*

Indiana
Earlham College *B*

Iowa
Morningside College *B*

Massachusetts
Hampshire College *B*

Michigan
Grand Valley State University *B*
University of Michigan *B*

Missouri
Washington University in St. Louis *B*

Nebraska
Nebraska Wesleyan University *B*

New Jersey
Rider University *B*

New York
Barnard College *B*
Hamilton College *B*
Long Island University
Southampton College *B*
Rochester Institute of Technology *B*
Russell Sage College *B*
State University of New York
Albany *D*
New Paltz *B*
Vassar College *B*

Ohio
Wittenberg University *B*

Pennsylvania
Bucknell University *B, M*
Carnegie Mellon University *B*
Franklin & Marshall College *B*

Philadelphia University *B*
Wilson College *B*

Texas
University of North Texas *M*

Vermont
Bennington College *B*

Virginia
College of William and Mary *B*

Wisconsin
Ripon College *B*

Biostatistics

Alabama
University of Alabama
Birmingham *M, D*

California
Loma Linda University *M*
University of California
Berkeley *M, D*
Los Angeles *M, D*
University of Southern California *M, D*

District of Columbia
George Washington University *D*
Georgetown University *M*

Hawaii
University of Hawaii
Manoa *D*

Iowa
University of Iowa *M, D*

Louisiana
Tulane University *M, D*

Massachusetts
Boston University *M, D*
University of Massachusetts
Boston *B*

Michigan
University of Michigan *M, D*
Western Michigan University *M*

Minnesota
University of Minnesota
Twin Cities *B, M, D*

New York
Cornell University *B*
State University of New York
Albany *M, D*
Buffalo *M*
College of Environmental Science
and Forestry *M, D*

North Carolina
University of North Carolina
Chapel Hill *B, M, D*

Ohio
Case Western Reserve University *M, D*
Ohio State University
Columbus Campus *D*

Oklahoma
University of Oklahoma *M, D*

Pennsylvania
University of Pennsylvania *M, D*

Puerto Rico
University of Puerto Rico
Medical Sciences Campus *M*

South Carolina
Medical University of South
Carolina *M, D*

Texas
Southwestern Adventist University *B*

Vermont
University of Vermont *M*

Virginia
Virginia Commonwealth
University *M, D*

Washington
University of Washington *M, D*

Biotechnology

Alabama
Auburn University *B*

California
De Anza College *C, A*
Foothill College *C, A*
MiraCosta College *C, A*
San Diego City College *A*
Santa Barbara City College *A*
University of California
Davis *B*

Colorado
Community College of Aurora *C*

Connecticut
Quinnipiac University *B*
University of New Haven *A, B*

Delaware
Delaware Technical and Community
College
Stanton/Wilmington Campus *A*

Iowa
Ellsworth Community College *A*
Indian Hills Community College *A*

Maryland
Frederick Community College *A*
Villa Julie College *C, B*

Massachusetts
Fitchburg State College *B*
Massachusetts Bay Community
College *A*

Minnesota
St. Cloud State University *B*

Nebraska
Central Community College *C, A*
Southeast Community College
Beatrice Campus *A*

New Hampshire
New Hampshire Community Technical
College
Manchester *A*
University of New Hampshire *B*

New Jersey
County College of Morris *A*
Mercer County Community College *A*
Middlesex County College *A*
Rutgers, The State University of New
Jersey
New Brunswick Regional
Campus *B*
University of Medicine and Dentistry of
New Jersey
School of Health Related
Professions *C, D, T*

New York
Finger Lakes Community College *A*
Manhattan College *M*
Monroe Community College *A*
Rochester Institute of Technology *B*
State University of New York
College of Agriculture and
Technology at Cobleskill *A*
College of Technology at Alfred *A*

Ohio
Lakeland Community College *A*
Washington State Community College *A*

Oregon
Portland Community College *A*

Pennsylvania
Lackawanna College *A*
Marywood University *B*
Penn State
  Abington *B*
  Altoona *B*
  Beaver *B*
  Berks *B*
  Delaware County *B*
  Dubois *B*
  Fayette *B*
  Hazleton *B*
  Lehigh Valley *B*
  McKeesport *B*
  Mont Alto *B*
  New Kensington *B*
  Schuylkill - Capital College *B*
  Shenango *B*
  University Park *B*
  Wilkes-Barre *B*
  Worthington Scranton *B*
  York *B*

Texas
Austin Community College *C, A*
Collin County Community College
  District *C, A*
Houston Community College
  System *C, A*
North Harris Montgomery Community
  College District *A*
Texas State Technical College
  West Texas *A*
Texas Tech University *M*

Utah
Utah Valley State College *A*
Weber State University *C, A*

Vermont
Vermont Technical College *A*

West Virginia
Salem International University *B, M*

Wisconsin
Marquette University *B*

Blood bank technology

California
Ohlone College *C*

Illinois
Illinois Central College *C*

Massachusetts
Massasoit Community College *C*

New Mexico
Albuquerque Technical-Vocational
  Institute *C*

New York
Dutchess Community College *C*

North Carolina
Duke University *C*

Ohio
Lakeland Community College *C*

South Dakota
Southeast Technical Institute *C*
Western Dakota Technical Institute *C*

Wisconsin
Chippewa Valley Technical College *C*
Mid-State Technical College *C*

Boilermaking

Georgia
West Georgia Technical College *C*

Indiana
Ivy Tech State College
  Northwest *C*

Pennsylvania
Pennsylvania College of Technology *C*

Wisconsin
Western Wisconsin Technical College *C*

Botany

Alabama
Auburn University *B, M, D*

Alaska
University of Alaska
  Fairbanks *M*

Arizona
Arizona State University *B, M, D*
Northern Arizona University *B*

Arkansas
Arkansas State University *B*
Arkansas State University
  Beebe *A*

California
California State Polytechnic University:
  Pomona *B*
California State University
  Chico *M*
  Long Beach *B*
  Stanislaus *B*
Cerritos Community College *A*
Citrus College *A*
Humboldt State University *B*
San Francisco State University *B*
San Joaquin Delta College *A*
San Jose State University *B*
University of California
  Davis *B, M, D*
  Riverside *B, M, D*
Ventura College *A*

Colorado
Colorado State University *B, M, D*

Connecticut
Connecticut College *B, M*
Southern Connecticut State University *B*
University of Connecticut *M, D*

District of Columbia
George Washington University *M, D*

Florida
Pensacola Junior College *A*
Santa Fe Community College *A*
University of Florida *B, M, D*

Georgia
Georgia Military College *A*
Oxford College of Emory University *B*
University of Georgia *B, M, D*

Hawaii
University of Hawaii
  Manoa *B, M, D*

Idaho
College of Southern Idaho *A*
Idaho State University *B*
North Idaho College *A*
University of Idaho *B, M, D*

Illinois
St. Xavier University *B*
Southern Illinois University
  Carbondale *B, M, D*
University of Illinois
  Urbana-Champaign *B, M, D*

Indiana
Ball State University *B*
Indiana University
  Bloomington *M, D*
Purdue University *B, M, D*
Vincennes University *A*

Iowa
Iowa State University *B, M, D*
Marshalltown Community College *A*

Kansas
Independence Community College *A*
Pratt Community College *A*
University of Kansas *M, D*

Maine
College of the Atlantic *B*
University of Maine *B, M, D*

Massachusetts
Hampshire College *B*
Harvard College *B*
University of Massachusetts
  Amherst *M, D*

Michigan
Andrews University *B*
Michigan State University *B, M, D*
Northern Michigan University *B*
University of Michigan *B, M, D*

Minnesota
Minnesota State University
  Mankato *B*
St. Cloud State University *B*

Mississippi
Mary Holmes College *A*

Missouri
East Central College *A*
Mineral Area College *A*
Northwest Missouri State University *B*
Southeast Missouri State University *B*
Washington University in St. Louis *D*

Montana
University of Great Falls *B*
University of Montana-Missoula *B*

New Hampshire
University of New Hampshire *M, D*

New Jersey
Rowan University *B*
Rutgers, The State University of New
Jersey
  Newark Regional Campus *B*

New Mexico
Western New Mexico University *B*

New York
Cornell University *M, D*
State University of New York
  College of Environmental Science
  and Forestry *B, M, D*

North Carolina
Duke University *M, D*
Mars Hill College *B*
North Carolina State University *M, D*

North Dakota
North Dakota State University *B, M, D*

Ohio
Kent State University *B, M*
Kent State University
  Stark Campus *B*
Miami University
  Oxford Campus *B, M, D*
Ohio University *B, M, D*
Ohio Wesleyan University *B*
University of Akron *B*
Wittenberg University *B*

Oklahoma
Oklahoma State University *B, M*
Southeastern Oklahoma State
  University *B*
University of Oklahoma *B, M, D*

Oregon
Oregon State University *B*

Pennsylvania
California University of Pennsylvania *B*
Juniata College *B*

South Carolina
Clemson University *M*

Tennessee
University of Tennessee
  Knoxville *B, M, D*

Texas
Hill College *A*
Laredo Community College *A*
Southwest Texas State University *B, T*
Texas A&M University *B, M, D*
University of North Texas *M*
University of Texas
  Austin *B, M, D*

Utah
Brigham Young University *B, M, D*
Snow College *A*
Southern Utah University *B*
Utah State University *B, M*
Weber State University *B*

Vermont
Marlboro College *B*
University of Vermont *B, M, D*

Washington
Centralia College *A*
Eastern Washington University *B*
University of Washington *B, M, D*
Washington State University *M, D*
Western Washington University *B*

Wisconsin
Lawrence University *B*
University of Wisconsin
  Madison *B, M, D*
  Superior *B*

Wyoming
University of Wyoming *B, M, D*

Broadcast journalism

Alabama
Auburn University *R*
Trenholm State Technical College *A*
Troy State University *B*
University of Alabama *B, M*
University of Montevallo *B*

Arizona
Arizona Western College *A*
Northern Arizona University *B*
Pima Community College *C, A*
University of Arizona *B, M*

Arkansas
Arkansas State University *B, M*
Harding University *B*
John Brown University *A, B*
University of Arkansas
  Little Rock *B*

California
Bakersfield College *A*
Biola University *B*
California State University
  Bakersfield *B*
  Fullerton *B, M*
  Hayward *B*
  Long Beach *B*
  Los Angeles *B*
  Northridge *B, M*
Chabot College *A*
College of Marin: Kentfield *A*
College of the Canyons *C, A*
Cuesta College *C, A*
Foothill College *C, A*
Glendale Community College *A*
Golden West College *C, A*
Grossmont Community College *C, A*
Laney College *C, A*
Long Beach City College *C, A*
Master's College *B*
Modesto Junior College *C, A*
Moorpark College *C, A*
Mount San Antonio College *C, A*
Ohlone College *C, A*

Orange Coast College *C, A*
Pepperdine University *B*
San Diego City College *A*
San Diego State University *B, M*
San Francisco State University *B, M*
San Joaquin Delta College *A*
San Jose State University *A*
Santa Rosa Junior College *C*
Southwestern College *C, A*
University of Southern California *B, M*
Vanguard University of Southern
    California *B*

Colorado
Art Institute
    of Colorado *A*
Colorado State University
    Pueblo *B*
Metropolitan State College of Denver *B*

Connecticut
Briarwood College *A*
Middlesex Community College *C, A*
Quinnipiac University *B*

Delaware
Delaware State University *B*

District of Columbia
American University *B, M*
Gallaudet University *B*
Howard University *B*

Florida
Broward Community College *A*
Florida Agricultural and Mechanical
    University *B*
Florida State University *B*
Gulf Coast Community College *A*
Hillsborough Community College *A*
Manatee Community College *A*
Miami-Dade Community College *C, A*
Palm Beach Community College *A*
Polk Community College *A*
South Florida Community College *A*
University of Miami *B, M*
University of West Florida *B*

Georgia
Clark Atlanta University *B*
Toccoa Falls College *B*

Hawaii
University of Hawaii
    Leeward Community College *C, A*

Idaho
Boise State University *A*
Brigham Young University - Idaho *B*
Lewis-Clark State College *A*

Illinois
Bradley University *B*
Chicago State University *B*
City Colleges of Chicago
    Kennedy-King College *C, A*
Columbia College Chicago
Governors State University *B, M*
Illinois Central College *A*
Illinois Eastern Community Colleges
    Wabash Valley College *A*
Lake Land College *A*
Lewis University *B*
Lewis and Clark Community College *A*
North Central College *B*
Northwestern University *B, M, D*
Olivet Nazarene University *B*
Parkland College *A*
Quincy University *B*
South Suburban College of Cook
    County *A*
Southern Illinois University
    Carbondale *B, M*
University of Illinois
    Urbana-Champaign *B*
University of St. Francis *B*

Indiana
Ball State University *B*

Butler University *B*
Huntington College *B*
Indiana State University *B, M*
Manchester College *A, B*
Purdue University
    Calumet *B*
Taylor University *B*
University of Indianapolis *B*
Valparaiso University *B*
Vincennes University *A*

Iowa
Buena Vista University *B*
Dordt College *B*
Drake University *B*
Grand View College *B*
Iowa Central Community College *A*
Iowa Wesleyan College *B*
Morningside College *B*
St. Ambrose University *B*
University of Iowa *B, M, D*
Waldorf College *A, B*
Wartburg College *B*

Kansas
Central Christian College *A, B*
Dodge City Community College *C, A*
Hutchinson Community College *A*
Independence Community College *A*
Pittsburg State University *B*
University of Kansas *B*

Kentucky
Campbellsville University *B*
Murray State University *B*
University of Kentucky *B*

Louisiana
Louisiana College *B*
University of Louisiana at Monroe *B*

Maine
New England School of
    Communications *C, A, B*
St. Joseph's College *B*
University of Southern Maine *B*

Maryland
Columbia Union College *B*
Frederick Community College *C*
Montgomery College
    Rockville Campus *A*
Morgan State University *B*

Massachusetts
Ai The New England Institute of Art and
    Design *A*
Boston University *B, M*
Dean College *A*
Emerson College *B*
Hampshire College *B*
Massachusetts College of Liberal Arts *B*
Mount Wachusett Community College *A*
Newbury College *A*
Northeastern University *B*
Suffolk University *B*
Westfield State College *B*

Michigan
Bay de Noc Community College *C*
Central Michigan University *B, M*
Cornerstone University *A*
Grand Valley State University *B*
Lansing Community College *A*
Macomb Community College *C, A*
Michigan State University *B, M*
Northern Michigan University *B*
Oakland Community College *A*
St. Clair County Community College *A*
Schoolcraft College *A*
University of Michigan *M*
Wayne State University *B*
Western Michigan University *B*

Minnesota
Bethel College *B*
Brown College *A*
Concordia College: Moorhead *B*

Lake Superior College: A Community
    and Technical College *C*
Minnesota State University
    Moorhead *B*
North Central University *B*
Northland Community & Technical
    College *C, A*
St. Cloud State University *B*
Southwest State University *B*
Winona State University *B*

Mississippi
Coahoma Community College *A*
Itawamba Community College *A*
Mississippi University for Women *B*
Northwest Mississippi Community
    College *A*
Rust College *B*
University of Mississippi *B*
University of Southern Mississippi *B*

Missouri
Central Missouri State University *B*
College of the Ozarks *B*
Drury University *B*
Evangel University *A, B*
Lindenwood University *B, M*
Northwest Missouri State University *B*
St. Louis Community College
    St. Louis Community College at
    Florissant Valley *A*
Southeast Missouri State University *B*
Southwest Missouri State University *B*
Stephens College *B*
Webster University *B*
William Jewell College *B*
William Woods University *B*

Montana
University of Montana-Missoula *B, M*

Nebraska
Central Community College *C, A*
Grace University *B*
Hastings College *B*
Northeast Community College *A*
Southeast Community College
    Beatrice Campus *A*
University of Nebraska
    Kearney *B*
    Lincoln *B*

New Hampshire
Franklin Pierce College *B*
Hesser College *C, A*
Rivier College *B*

New Jersey
Cumberland County College *A*
Essex County College *A*
Montclair State University *A*
Rowan University *B*

New Mexico
Eastern New Mexico University *B*

New York
Adirondack Community College *C, A*
Cayuga County Community College *A*
City University of New York
    Brooklyn College *B, M*
    Kingsborough Community
    College *A*
Finger Lakes Community College *A*
Fulton-Montgomery Community
    College *A*
Hofstra University *B*
Ithaca College *B*
Long Island University
    C. W. Post Campus *B*
Manhattan College *B*
Marist College *B*
Medaille College *B*
Mercy College *B*
Nassau Community College *A*
New York Institute of Technology *B*
New York University *B*
Onondaga Community College *A*

St. John Fisher College *B*
State University of New York
    College at Brockport *B*
    College at Buffalo *B*
    College at Cortland *B*
    College at Fredonia *B*
    New Paltz *B*
    Oswego *B*
Suffolk County Community College *A*
Syracuse University *B, M*
Tompkins-Cortland Community
    College *A*

North Carolina
Appalachian State University *B*
Campbell University *B*
Central Carolina Community College *A*
East Carolina University *B*
Elon University *B*
Gardner-Webb University *B*
Gaston College *A*
Isothermal Community College *A*
North Carolina Agricultural and
    Technical State University *B*
North Carolina State University *B*
University of North Carolina
    Greensboro *B, M*
    Pembroke *B*

North Dakota
Minot State University *B*
North Dakota State University *B*

Ohio
Bowling Green State University *B*
Cedarville University *B*
Central State University *B*
Kent State University *B*
Kent State University
    Stark Campus *B*
Marietta College *B*
Mount Vernon Nazarene University *B*
Ohio Northern University *B*
Ohio University *A, B, M, D*
Otterbein College *B*
University of Cincinnati *M, T*
University of Dayton *B*
University of Findlay *B*
Washington State Community College *A*
Xavier University *A, B*
Youngstown State University *B*

Oklahoma
Cameron University *B*
East Central University *B*
Langston University *B*
Northeastern Oklahoma Agricultural and
    Mechanical College *A*
Northern Oklahoma College *A*
Northwestern Oklahoma State
    University *B*
Oklahoma Baptist University *B*
Oklahoma Christian University of
    Science and Arts *B*
Oklahoma City Community College *A*
Oklahoma City University *B*
Oklahoma State University *B*
Rogers State University *A*
Rose State College *A*
Southeastern Oklahoma State
    University *B*
University of Central Oklahoma *B*
University of Oklahoma *B*

Oregon
Lane Community College *C, A*
Mount Hood Community College *A*
University of Oregon *B, M*

Pennsylvania
Bucks County Community College *A*
California University of Pennsylvania *B*
Edinboro University of Pennsylvania *B*
La Salle University *B*
Lehigh Carbon Community College *A*
Marywood University *B*
Mercyhurst College *B*

Pennsylvania College of Technology *A*
Point Park College *B*
Waynesburg College *B*
York College of Pennsylvania *A, B*

South Carolina
Morris College *B*
North Greenville College *B*
Tri-County Technical College *A*
Trident Technical College *A*

Tennessee
Belmont University *B*
Draughons Junior College of Business:
   Nashville *A*
Southern Adventist University *B*
Trevecca Nazarene University *A*
Union University *B*
University of Tennessee
   Knoxville *B*

Texas
Alvin Community College *C, A*
Amarillo College *A*
Austin Community College *C, A*
Baylor University *B*
Central Texas College *C, A*
Del Mar College *A*
Hardin-Simmons University *B*
Laredo Community College *A*
Midland College *A*
Odessa College *A*
San Antonio College *A*
South Plains College *A*
Southern Methodist University *B, M*
Southwestern Adventist University *B*
Texas A&M University
   Commerce *B*
Texas Christian University *B, M*
Texas Southern University *B*
Texas Wesleyan University *B*
University of Houston *B*
University of North Texas *B, M*
University of Texas
   Arlington *B*
   Pan American *B*

Utah
Brigham Young University *B*
Dixie State College of Utah *A*
Salt Lake Community College *A*
Weber State University *B*

Vermont
Castleton State College *A, B*
Lyndon State College *B*

Virginia
Hampton University *B*
Mary Baldwin College *B*
Southwest Virginia Community
   College *C*
Virginia Western Community College *A*

Washington
Centralia College *A*
Eastern Washington University *B*
Gonzaga University *B*
Green River Community College *C*
Pacific Lutheran University *B*
Washington State University *B*

West Virginia
Alderson-Broaddus College *B*
Bethany College *B*
Concord College *B*
Mountain State University *A*
West Virginia University *B*

Wisconsin
Concordia University Wisconsin *B*
Marquette University *B, M*
University of Wisconsin
   Madison *B, M, D*
   Oshkosh *B*
   Superior *B, M*
   Whitewater *B*

Building inspection

Nevada
Western Nevada Community College *A*

New York
State University of New York
   College of Agriculture and
      Technology at Morrisville *A*

Oregon
Portland Community College *C, A*

Utah
Utah Valley State College *C, A*

Washington
Edmonds Community College *C*

Building/property maintenance

Alabama
Northwest-Shoals Community College *C*

Arizona
Arizona State University *B, M*
Eastern Arizona College *C*
Gateway Community College *C, A*
Pima Community College *C, A*
Yavapai College *C, A*

Arkansas
John Brown University *A, B*

California
California Polytechnic State University:
   San Luis Obispo *B*
California State University
   Fresno *B*
Chabot College *A*
College of the Redwoods *C, A*
College of the Sequoias *C, A*
Diablo Valley College *C*
Feather River College *C, A*
Laney College *C, A*
Los Angeles Trade and Technical
   College *C, A*
Modesto Junior College *C, A*
Orange Coast College *C, A*
Palomar College *C, A*
Riverside Community College *C, A*
San Francisco State University *C*
San Joaquin Delta College *C, A*
Santa Monica College *A*
Sierra College *A*
Southwestern College *C, A*
Ventura College *C, A*
West Valley College *C, A*

Colorado
Arapahoe Community College *C, A*

Delaware
Delaware Technical and Community
   College
      Terry Campus *A*

Florida
Miami-Dade Community College *A*
Palm Beach Community College *C, A*
Pensacola Junior College *A*
Santa Fe Community College *A*
South Florida Community College *C*
Tallahassee Community College *A*

Georgia
DeKalb Technical College *C*

Illinois
College of DuPage *A*
Oakton Community College *A*
Parkland College *A*
Rend Lake College *C*
South Suburban College of Cook
   County *A*
Southwestern Illinois College *C, A*
Triton College *C, A*

Indiana
Ivy Tech State College
   Bloomington *C, A*
   Central Indiana *C, A*
   Columbus *C, A*
   Eastcentral *C, A*
   Kokomo *C, A*
   Lafayette *C, A*
   Northcentral *C, A*
   Northeast *C, A*
   Northwest *C, A*
   Southcentral *C, A*
   Southwest *C, A*
   Wabash Valley *C, A*
   Whitewater *C, A*
Oakland City University *C*
Vincennes University *A*

Iowa
Indian Hills Community College *A*
Iowa Lakes Community College *C*
Kirkwood Community College *C, A*
Southeastern Community College
   North Campus *A*

Kansas
Hutchinson Community College *C, A*

Louisiana
Delgado Community College *A*

Maine
Central Maine Technical College *C, A*

Maryland
Montgomery College
   Rockville Campus *A*

Massachusetts
Cape Cod Community College *C*
Wentworth Institute of Technology *A, B*

Michigan
Ferris State University *C, B*
Gogebic Community College *A*
Lansing Community College *C, A*
Macomb Community College *C*
Northern Michigan University *C, A, B*
Oakland Community College *C, A*
Washtenaw Community College *C, A*

Minnesota
Hennepin Technical College *C, A*
Inver Hills Community College *A*
Minnesota State University
   Mankato *B*
Rochester Community and Technical
   College *C*
University of Minnesota
   Twin Cities *B*

Missouri
Longview Community College *C, A*
North Central Missouri College *C, A*
St. Louis Community College
   St. Louis Community College at
      Forest Park *A*

Montana
Miles Community College *A*
University of Montana-Missoula *C, A*

Nebraska
Central Community College *C*
Metropolitan Community College *C, A*
Mid Plains Community College
   Area *A*
Northeast Community College *A*

Nevada
Truckee Meadows Community
   College *A*
Western Nevada Community College *A*

New Hampshire
New Hampshire Community Technical
   College
      Manchester *A*

New Jersey
Raritan Valley Community College *A*

New Mexico
Albuquerque Technical-Vocational
   Institute *C, A*

New York
Erie Community College
   City Campus *A*
Fulton-Montgomery Community
   College *A*
Hudson Valley Community College *A*
Institute of Design and Construction *A*
Mohawk Valley Community College *A*
Orange County Community College *C*
State University of New York
   College of Agriculture and
      Technology at Morrisville *A*
   College of Environmental Science
      and Forestry *B*
   College of Technology at Alfred *A*
   College of Technology at Canton *C*
Suffolk County Community College *A*
Tompkins-Cortland Community
   College *C, A*

North Carolina
Blue Ridge Community College *C*
Guilford Technical Community
   College *A*
Haywood Community College *C, A*
Pitt Community College *A*
Surry Community College *C*
Western Piedmont Community
   College *C, A*
Wilkes Community College *C, A*

North Dakota
North Dakota State College of Science *A*

Ohio
Columbus State Community College *A*
Jefferson Community College *A*

Oklahoma
Oklahoma State University *B*
Oklahoma State University
   Okmulgee *A*
University of Central Oklahoma *B*
University of Oklahoma *B, M*

Oregon
Chemeketa Community College *C, A*
Lane Community College *C, A*

Pennsylvania
Community College of Allegheny
   County *C, A*
Delaware County Community
   College *C, A*
Luzerne County Community
   College *C, A*
Penn State
   University Park *C*
Westmoreland County Community
   College *C*
Williamson Free School of Mechanical
   Trades *A*

Puerto Rico
Technological College of San Juan *C*

South Carolina
Aiken Technical College *C*
Denmark Technical College *C*
Technical College of the Lowcountry *C*
Trident Technical College *C*

Tennessee
Southwest Tennessee Community
   College *A*

Texas
Del Mar College *C, A*
Houston Community College System *C*
Laredo Community College *C*
North Lake College *C*
Odessa College *C, A*
St. Philip's College *A*

Texas A&M University
    Commerce *B*
Texas State Technical College
    Waco *A*
Tyler Junior College *A*

Utah

Snow College *C, A*
Southern Utah University *B*
Utah Valley State College *A*
Weber State University *A, B*

Vermont

Vermont Technical College *A*

Washington

Olympic College *C, A*
Spokane Falls Community College *C*

Wisconsin

University of Wisconsin
    Platteville *B*
Western Wisconsin Technical College *C*

Wyoming

Casper College *C, A*

Business administration/ management

Alabama

Alabama Agricultural and Mechanical
    University *B, M*
Alabama State University *B*
Andrew Jackson University *M*
Athens State University *B*
Auburn University *B, M, D*
Auburn University at Montgomery *B*
Bevill State Community College *A*
Birmingham-Southern College *M*
Bishop State Community College *A*
Calhoun Community College *C, A*
Central Alabama Community College *A*
Chattahoochee Valley Community
    College *A*
Columbia Southern University *B, M*
Concordia College *B*
Enterprise State Junior College *A*
Faulkner University *A, B*
George C. Wallace State Community
    College
        Selma *C, A*
Huntingdon College *B*
Jacksonville State University *B, M*
James H. Faulkner State Community
    College *A*
Judson College *B*
Lawson State Community College *A*
Miles College *B*
Northeast Alabama Community
    College *A*
Northwest-Shoals Community College *A*
Oakwood College *B*
Remington College
    Southeast College of Technology *A*
Samford University *B, M*
Snead State Community College *A*
South University *A, B*
Spring Hill College *A, B, M*
Stillman College *B*
Talladega College *B*
Troy State University *B, M*
Troy State University Dothan *B, M*
Troy State University in
    Montgomery *B, M*
Tuskegee University *B*
University of Alabama *B, M, D*
University of Alabama
    Birmingham *B, M*
    Huntsville *B, M*
University of Mobile *B*
University of Montevallo *B*
University of North Alabama *B, M*
University of South Alabama *B, M*
University of West Alabama *B*
Virginia College *C, A*

Alaska

Alaska Pacific University *A, B, M*
Charter College *C, A, B*
Sheldon Jackson College *B*
University of Alaska
    Anchorage *C, A, B, M*
    Fairbanks *C, A, B, M*
    Southeast *A*

Arizona

Arizona State University *B, M, D*
Arizona Western College *A*
Central Arizona College *C, A*
Cochise College *A*
DeVry University
    Phoenix *B, M*
Eastern Arizona College *A*
Estrella Mountain Community College *A*
International Institute of the Americas
    Tucson *A*
Northern Arizona University *B, M*
Phoenix College *C, A*
Pima Community College *C, A*
Prescott College *B, M*
Rio Salado College *C, A*
South Mountain Community
    College *C, A*
Southwestern College *A*
University of Arizona *M, D*
University of Phoenix *A, B, M*
Yavapai College *C, A*

Arkansas

Arkansas Baptist College *B*
Arkansas State University *B, M*
Arkansas State University
    Beebe *A*
Arkansas Tech University *B*
Black River Technical College *A*
Central Baptist College *A*
East Arkansas Community College *A*
Harding University *B, M*
Henderson State University *B, M*
John Brown University *B*
Lyon College *B*
Northwest Arkansas Community
    College *A*
Ouachita Baptist University *B*
Ouachita Technical College *C, A*
Ozarka College *A*
Philander Smith College *B*
Phillips Community College of the
    University of Arkansas *A*
South Arkansas Community College *A*
Southeast Arkansas College *C*
Southern Arkansas University *B*
University of Arkansas *B, M, D*
University of Arkansas
    Community College at Batesville *A*
    Cossatot Community College of the
        C, A
    Fort Smith *C, A, B*
    Little Rock *B, M*
    Monticello *B*
    Pine Bluff *B*
University of Central Arkansas *B, M*
University of the Ozarks *B*

California

Antelope Valley College *C, A*
Azusa Pacific University *B, M*
Bakersfield College *A*
Barstow College *C, A*
Biola University *B*
Cabrillo College *A*
California Baptist University *B, M*
California Maritime Academy *B*
California Polytechnic State University:
    San Luis Obispo *B*
California State Polytechnic University:
    Pomona *B, M*

California State University
    Bakersfield *B, M*
    Chico *B, M*
    Dominguez Hills *B, M*
    Fresno *B, M*
    Fullerton *B, M*
    Hayward *B, M*
    Long Beach *M*
    Los Angeles *B, M*
    Monterey Bay *B*
    Northridge *B, M*
    San Bernardino *B, M*
    San Marcos *B, M*
    Stanislaus *B, M*
Cerritos Community College *A*
Cerro Coso Community College *C, A*
Chapman University *B, M*
Christian Heritage College *B*
Citrus College *C*
Claremont McKenna College *B*
Coastline Community College *C, A*
Coleman College *B, M*
College of Alameda *A*
College of the Canyons *C, A*
College of the Siskiyous *C, A*
Columbia College *C, A*
Concordia University *B, M*
Copper Mountain College *A*
Cuyamaca College *C, A*
De Anza College *C, A*
DeVry University
    Fremont *B, M*
    Long Beach *B, M*
    Pomona *B*
    West Hills *B, M*
Diablo Valley College *C*
Dominican University of California *M*
East Los Angeles College *A*
Feather River College *C, A*
Foothill College *C, A*
Fresno Pacific University *M*
Golden Gate University *A, B, M, D*
Golden West College *C, A*
Grossmont Community College *C, A*
Heald College
    Milpitas *C, A*
Holy Names College *B, M*
Hope International University *B, M*
Humboldt State University *B, M*
Imperial Valley College *A*
Irvine Valley College *C, A*
John F. Kennedy University *B, M*
La Sierra University *B, M*
Long Beach City College *C, A*
Los Angeles Harbor College *C, A*
Los Angeles Pierce College *C, A*
Los Angeles Southwest College *A*
Los Angeles Trade and Technical
    College *A*
Loyola Marymount University *B, M*
MTI College of Business and
    Technology *C, A*
Marymount College *A*
Master's College *B*
Menlo College *B*
MiraCosta College *C, A*
Modesto Junior College *A*
Monterey Peninsula College *A*
Moorpark College *C, A*
Mount St. Mary's College *B*
Mount San Antonio College *C, A*
Mount San Jacinto College *C, A*
National University *B, M*
Northwestern Polytechnic University *M*
Ohlone College *C, A*
Pacific States University *B, M*
Pacific Union College *B*
Palomar College *A*
Patten University *B*
Pepperdine University *B, M*
Point Loma Nazarene University *B*
Riverside Community College *C, A*
St. Mary's College of California *B, M*
San Diego City College *A*
San Diego Mesa College *C, A*

San Diego State University *C, B, M*
San Francisco State University *M*
San Joaquin Delta College *C, A*
San Jose State University *B, M*
Santa Barbara City College *C, A*
Santa Clara University *M*
Santa Monica College *C, A*
Santa Rosa Junior College *A*
Santiago Canyon College *A*
Shasta College *A*
Sierra College *C, A*
Silicon Valley College
    Emeryville *C*
Simpson College *B*
Sonoma State University *B, M*
Southwestern College *A*
Stanford University *M, D*
Taft College *A*
University of California
    Berkeley *B, M, D*
    Davis *M*
    Irvine *M, D*
    Los Angeles *M, D*
    Riverside *B, M*
    Santa Cruz *B*
University of La Verne *B, M*
University of Redlands *B, M*
University of San Diego *B, M*
University of San Francisco *B, M*
University of Southern
    California *B, M, D*
University of the Pacific *B, M*
Vanguard University of Southern
    California *B*
Ventura College *A*
Victor Valley College *C, A*
Vista Community College *C, A*
West Valley College *C, A*
Woodbury University *B, M*
Yuba Community College District *C, A*

Colorado

Arapahoe Community College *C, A*
Blair Junior College *A*
Colorado Christian University *B*
Colorado Mountain College
    Alpine Campus *A*
    Spring Valley Campus *C, A*
    Timberline Campus *A*
Colorado State University *B, M*
Colorado State University
    Pueblo *M*
Colorado Technical University *B, M, D*
Community College of Aurora *C, A*
DeVry University
    Denver *B*
DeVry University: Colorado Springs *B*
Fort Lewis College *B*
Front Range Community College *A*
Jones International University *B, M*
Mesa State College *B, M*
Metropolitan State College of Denver *B*
National American University
    Denver *A, B*
Otero Junior College *A*
Parks College *A*
Red Rocks Community College *C, A*
Regis University *B, M*
Trinidad State Junior College *A*
University of Colorado
    Boulder *B, M, D*
    Colorado Springs *B, M*
    Denver *B, M*
University of Denver *M*
University of Northern Colorado *B*

Connecticut

Albertus Magnus College *C, A, B, M*
Asnuntuck Community College *A*
Briarwood College *A*
Capital Community College *C, A*
Central Connecticut State University *B*
Fairfield University *B, M*
Gateway Community College *A*
Housatonic Community College *A*

International College of Hospitality
   Management *C, A*
Manchester Community College *A*
Middlesex Community College *A*
Mitchell College *A, B*
Naugatuck Valley Community
   College *C, A*
Northwestern Connecticut Community
   College *A*
Norwalk Community College *A*
Quinebaug Valley Community
   College *C, A*
Quinnipiac University *B, M*
St. Joseph College *B*
Southern Connecticut State
   University *B, M*
Teikyo Post University *A, B*
Three Rivers Community College *C, A*
Tunxis Community College *C, A*
University of Bridgeport *C, A, M*
University of Connecticut *C, B*
University of Hartford *B, M*
University of New Haven *A, B, M*
Western Connecticut State University *B*
Yale University *M, D*

Delaware

Delaware State University *M*
Delaware Technical and Community
   College
      Owens Campus *C, A*
      Terry Campus *C, A*
Goldey-Beacom College *A, B, M*
University of Delaware *B, M*
Wilmington College *M*

District of Columbia

American University *B, M*
Gallaudet University *B*
George Washington University *B, M, D*
Georgetown University *B, M*
Howard University *B, M*
Strayer University *C, A, B, M*
Trinity College *B, M*
University of the District of
   Columbia *B, M*

Florida

Barry University *B, M*
Bethune-Cookman College *B*
Broward Community College *A*
Carlos Albizu University *M*
Chipola Junior College *A*
Daytona Beach Community College *A*
DeVry University
      Miramar *B, M*
      Orlando *B, M*
Eckerd College *B*
Edward Waters College *B*
Embry Riddle Aeronautical
   University-Extended Campus *A, B, M*
Embry-Riddle Aeronautical
   University *A, B, M*
Everglades College *B*
Flagler College *B*
Florida Agricultural and Mechanical
   University *B, M*
Florida Atlantic University *B, M, D*
Florida Gulf Coast University *B, M*
Florida Institute of Technology *B, M*
Florida International University *B, M, D*
Florida Keys Community College *A*
Florida Metropolitan University
      Melbourne Campus *A, B, M*
      Orlando College North *A, B, M*
      Orlando College South *A, B, M*
      Tampa College *A, B, M*
      Tampa College Lakeland *B*
Florida National College *A*
Florida Southern College *B*
Florida State University *B, M, D*
Florida Technical College *C, A*
Florida Technical College
      Deland *A*
      Jacksonville *C, A*
Gulf Coast Community College *A*

Herzing College
   Orlando *A*
Hillsborough Community College *A*
Indian River Community College *A*
International College *A, B, M*
Jacksonville University *B, M*
Jones College *A, B*
Lake City Community College *A*
Lake-Sumter Community College *C, A*
Manatee Community College *A*
Miami-Dade Community College *A*
New England Institute of Technology *A*
Northwood University
   Florida Campus *A, B*
Nova Southeastern University *B, M, D*
Okaloosa-Walton Community
   College *C, A*
Palm Beach Atlantic University *M*
Palm Beach Community College *A*
Pasco-Hernando Community
   College *C, A*
Pensacola Junior College *A*
Polk Community College *A*
Rollins College *M*
St. Petersburg College *A*
St. Thomas University *B, M*
Santa Fe Community College *A*
Schiller International University *A, B*
South Florida Community College *A*
Southeastern College of the Assemblies
   of God *B*
Southwest Florida College *A*
Stetson University *B, M*
Tallahassee Community College *A*
Tampa Technical Institute *A*
University of Central Florida *B, M, D*
University of Miami *B, M, D*
University of North Florida *B*
University of South Florida *B, M, D*
University of Tampa *B, M*
University of West Florida *M*
Valencia Community College *C, A*
Warner Southern College *B*
Webber International University *A, B, M*
Webster College *C, A*
Webster College: Holiday *A*

Georgia

Abraham Baldwin Agricultural
   College *A*
Albany State University *B, M*
Atlanta Metropolitan College *A*
Augusta State University *B, M*
Bauder College *A*
Berry College *B, M*
Brewton-Parker College *B*
Clark Atlanta University *B, M, D*
Clayton College and State
   University *A, B*
Columbus Technical College *C, A*
Dalton State College *A*
Darton College *A*
DeVry University
      Alpharetta *B, M*
      Atlanta *B, M*
East Georgia College *A*
Emmanuel College *A, B*
Emory University *B*
Fort Valley State University *B*
Gainesville College *A*
Georgia College and State University *B*
Georgia Institute of Technology *B, M, D*
Georgia Military College *A*
Georgia Perimeter College *A*
Georgia Southern University *B, M*
Georgia Southwestern State
   University *B, M*
Georgia State University *B, M, D*
Gordon College *A*
Griffin Technical College *A*
Herzing College *A, B*
Kennesaw State University *B, M*
LaGrange College *B, M*
Life University *B*
Macon State College *C, A, B*
Mercer University *B, M*

Middle Georgia College *A*
Morehouse College *B*
Morris Brown College *B*
North Georgia College & State
   University *B*
Oglethorpe University *M*
Paine College *B*
Piedmont College *B, M*
Reinhardt College *A, B*
Shorter College *B*
South Georgia College *A*
South University *A, B*
Southwest Georgia Technical
   College *C, A*
State University of West Georgia *B, M*
Toccoa Falls College *B*
University of Georgia *B, M, D*
Valdosta State University *A, B, M*
Waycross College *A*
Wesleyan College *B, M*
West Georgia Technical College *A*

Hawaii

Brigham Young University-Hawaii *B*
Chaminade University of Honolulu *M*
Hawaii Pacific University *A, B, M*
Heald College
   Honolulu *B*
University of Hawaii
   Hilo *B*
   Manoa *B, M*
   West Oahu *B*

Idaho

Albertson College of Idaho *B*
Boise State University *M*
Brigham Young University - Idaho *B*
Idaho State University *A, B, M*
Lewis-Clark State College *B*
North Idaho College *A*
Northwest Nazarene University *B, M*

Illinois

Augustana College *B*
Aurora University *M*
Benedictine University *A, M*
Black Hawk College *A*
Blackburn College *B*
Bradley University *M*
Carl Sandburg College *A*
Chicago State University *B*
City Colleges of Chicago
      Harold Washington College *A*
      Kennedy-King College *A*
      Malcolm X College *A*
      Olive-Harvey College *A*
      Wright College *C, A*
College of DuPage *C, A*
College of Lake County *C, A*
College of Office Technology *A*
Columbia College Chicago *A*
De Paul University *B, M*
DeVry University
      Addison *B*
      Chicago *B*
      Tinley Park *B, M*
Dominican University *B, M*
East-West University *B*
Eastern Illinois University *M*
Elgin Community College *C, A*
Elmhurst College *C, B*
Eureka College *B*
Gem City College *C, A*
Governors State University *B, M*
Greenville College *B*
Heartland Community College *C*
Illinois Central College *A*
Illinois Institute of Technology *M*
Illinois State University *M*
Illinois Wesleyan University *B*
John A. Logan College *A*
John Wood Community College *C, A*
Joliet Junior College *A*
Judson College *B*
Kankakee Community College *C, A*
Kaskaskia College *C, A*

Kendall College *A, B*
Lake Forest Graduate School of
   Management *M*
Lewis University *B, M*
Lewis and Clark Community College *A*
Lincoln Christian College and
   Seminary *B*
Lincoln College *A*
Lincoln Land Community College *C, A*
Loyola University of Chicago *C, B, M*
MacMurray College *A, B*
McHenry County College *C, A*
McKendree College *B*
Midstate College *A*
Millikin University *B*
Monmouth College *B, T*
Moraine Valley Community College *A*
National-Louis University *C, B, M*
North Central College *M*
North Park University *B, M*
Northeastern Illinois University *B, M*
Northern Illinois University *M*
Northwestern Business College *A*
Northwestern University *M, D*
Oakton Community College *A*
Olivet Nazarene University *B, M*
Parkland College *A*
Principia College *B*
Quincy University *B, M*
Rend Lake College *C, A*
Robert Morris College: Chicago *C, A, B*
Rock Valley College *C, A*
Rockford Business College *C, A*
Rockford College *B, M*
Roosevelt University *B, M*
St. Augustine College *A*
St. Xavier University *M*
Sauk Valley Community College *C, A*
Southeastern Illinois College *A*
Southern Illinois University
   Carbondale *M*
Southern Illinois University
   Edwardsville *M*
Southwestern Illinois College *A*
Springfield College in Illinois *A*
Trinity Christian College *B*
Triton College *C, A*
University of Illinois
      Chicago *M, D*
      Springfield *B, M*
      Urbana-Champaign *M*
University of St. Francis *B, M*
Waubonsee Community College *C, A*
Western Illinois University *M*

Indiana

Anderson University *B, M*
Ball State University *A, B, M*
Bethel College *B, M*
Butler University *B, M*
Commonwealth Business College:
   Michigan City *A*
Earlham College *B*
Goshen College *B*
Grace College *B*
Hanover College *B*
Huntington College *A, B*
Indiana Business College *A*
Indiana Business College
      Anderson *C, A*
      Columbus *C, A*
      Evansville *C, A*
      Fort Wayne *C, A*
      Lafayette *C, A*
      Marion *C, A*
      Muncie *C, A*
      Terre Haute *C, A*
Indiana State University *B, M*
Indiana University
      Bloomington *B, M, D*
      East *A, B*
      Kokomo *A, B, M*
      South Bend *B, M*
Indiana University-Purdue University
   Fort Wayne *A, M*
Indiana Wesleyan University *A, B*

International Business College:
  Indianapolis *C, A*
Ivy Tech State College
  Central Indiana *A*
  Columbus *A*
  Eastcentral *C, A*
  Kokomo *C, A*
  Lafayette *A*
  Northcentral *C, A*
  Northeast *A*
  Northwest *C, A*
  Southcentral *C, A*
  Southeast *C, A*
  Southwest *A*
  Wabash Valley *A*
  Whitewater *A*
Manchester College *A, B*
Michiana College: Fort Wayne *A*
Oakland City University *A*
Professional Careers Institute *C, A*
Purdue University *B, M, D*
Purdue University
  Calumet *B, M*
St. Joseph's College *B*
Saint Mary's College *B*
St. Mary-of-the-Woods College *B*
Sawyer College: Merrillville *C, A*
Taylor University *A*
Taylor University: Fort Wayne *A, B*
Tri-State University *A, B*
University of Evansville *B*
University of Indianapolis *A, B*
University of Notre Dame *M*
University of St. Francis *M*
University of Southern Indiana *B*
Valparaiso University *B*
Vincennes University *A*

Iowa

American Institute of Business *A*
Briar Cliff University *B*
Buena Vista University *B*
Central College *B, T*
Clarke College *A, B, M*
Coe College *B*
Des Moines Area Community College *A*
Drake University *M*
Franciscan University *B*
Graceland University *B*
Grand View College *B*
Hamilton College *C, A*
Hamilton College
  Cedar Falls *A*
  Cedar Rapids *A, B*
Indian Hills Community College *A*
Iowa Central Community College *A*
Iowa State University *B, M*
Iowa Wesleyan College *B*
Kaplan College *C, A, B*
Kirkwood Community College *C, A*
Loras College *B*
Luther College *B*
Maharishi University of
  Management *A, B*
Marshalltown Community College *A*
Morningside College *B*
Mount Mercy College *B*
North Iowa Area Community College *A*
Northeast Iowa Community College *A*
Northwest Iowa Community College *A*
Northwestern College *B*
St. Ambrose University *B, M, D*
Simpson College *B*
University of Dubuque *A, B, M*
University of Northern Iowa *B, M*
Upper Iowa University *A, B, M*
Waldorf College *A, B*
Wartburg College *B*
Western Iowa Tech Community
  College *A*
William Penn University *B*

Kansas

Allen County Community College *A*
Barclay College *B*
Benedictine College *A, B, M*

Bethany College *B*
Bethel College *B*
Butler County Community College *C, A*
Central Christian College *A, B*
Cloud County Community College *C, A*
Emporia State University *B, M*
Fort Hays State University *B, M*
Fort Scott Community College *C, A*
Friends University *B, M*
Haskell Indian Nations University *A, B*
Independence Community College *A*
Johnson County Community College *A*
Kansas City Kansas Community
  College *A*
Kansas State University *B, M*
Labette Community College *A*
McPherson College *B*
MidAmerica Nazarene University *B, M*
Newman University *B, M*
Ottawa University *B*
Pittsburg State University *M*
Pratt Community College *C, A*
St. Mary College *B*
Seward County Community College *A*
Southwestern College *B, M*
Sterling College *B*
Tabor College *B*
University of Kansas *M*
Washburn University of Topeka *B, M*
Wichita State University *B, M*

Kentucky

Alice Lloyd College *B*
Beckfield College *A*
Bellarmine University *B, M*
Campbellsville University *A, B*
Cumberland College *B, T*
Daymar College *C, A*
Daymar College
  Louisville *C*
Elizabethtown Community College *A*
Georgetown College *B*
Henderson Community College *A*
Hopkinsville Community College *A*
Jefferson Community College *A*
Kentucky Christian College *B*
Lexington Community College *A*
Lindsey Wilson College *A, B*
Madisonville Community College *A*
Maysville Community College *C, A*
Mid-Continent College *B*
Morehead State University *B*
Murray State University *A, B, M*
National College of Business &
  Technology
    Danville *C, A*
    Florence *A*
    Lexington *C, A*
    Pikeville *C, A*
    Richmond *C, A*
Paducah Community College *A*
Pikeville College *A, B*
St. Catharine College *A*
Somerset Community College *A*
Southeast Community College *A*
Southern Ohio College
  Fort Mitchell *C, A*
Spencerian College *A*
Sullivan University *C, A, B, M*
Union College *A, B*
University of Louisville *B*

Louisiana

American School of Business *C*
Centenary College of Louisiana *B, M*
Delgado Community College *C, A*
Dillard University *B*
Grantham University *A, B*
Herzing College *A, B*
Louisiana College *B*
Louisiana State University
  Shreveport *B, M*
Louisiana State University and
  Agricultural and Mechanical
  College *B, M, D*
Louisiana Tech University *B, M, D*

Loyola University New Orleans *B, M*
McNeese State University *B, M*
Nicholls State University *A, B, M*
Northwestern State University *A, B*
Nunez Community College *A*
Our Lady of Holy Cross College *B*
Remington College *B*
Southeastern Louisiana University *B, M*
Southern University
  New Orleans *B*
  Shreveport *A*
Southern University and Agricultural and
  Mechanical College *B*
Tulane University *B*
University of Louisiana at
  Lafayette *B, M*
University of Louisiana at Monroe *B, M*
University of New Orleans *B, M*
Xavier University of Louisiana *B*

Maine

Andover College *A*
Beal College *C, A*
Central Maine Technical College *A*
Husson College *A, B, M*
Maine Maritime Academy *B*
St. Joseph's College *B*
Thomas College *B, M*
University of Maine *B, M*
University of Maine
  Augusta *A, B*
  Machias *B*
  Presque Isle *B*
University of New England *B*
University of Southern Maine *C, B, M*

Maryland

Allegany College *A*
Bowie State University *B, M*
Capitol College *B*
Cecil Community College *A*
Chesapeake College *C*
College of Southern Maryland *C, A*
Columbia Union College *B*
Community College of Baltimore County
  Catonsville *C, A*
  Dundalk *C, A*
  Essex *C, A*
Frederick Community College *A*
Frostburg State University *B, M*
Goucher College *B*
Hagerstown Community College *C, A*
Harford Community College *C, A*
Hood College *B, M*
Howard Community College *C, A*
Johns Hopkins University *M*
Loyola College in Maryland *M*
McDaniel College *B*
Montgomery College
  Rockville Campus *C, A*
Morgan State University *B, M*
Mount St. Mary's College *M*
Salisbury University *B, M*
Sojourner-Douglass College *B*
Towson University *B*
University of Baltimore *B, M*
University of Maryland
  College Park *B, M*
  University College *C, B, M*
Villa Julie College *C, A, B*
Wor-Wic Community College *C, A*

Massachusetts

American International College *A, B, M*
Anna Maria College *A, B, M*
Assumption College *M*
Atlantic Union College *B*
Babson College *B, M*
Bay State College *A*
Becker College *A, B*
Bentley College *A, B, M*
Berkshire Community College *A*
Boston College *B, M*
Boston University *B, M, D*
Bridgewater State College *B*
Bunker Hill Community College *A*

Cape Cod Community College *A*
Clark University *B, M*
Dean College *A*
Elms College *B*
Emmanuel College *B*
Endicott College *A, B, M*
Fisher College *C, A, B*
Fitchburg State College *B, M*
Framingham State College *B, M*
Gordon College *B*
Greenfield Community College *A*
Katharine Gibbs School *A*
Lasell College *B*
Lesley University *B, M*
Marian Court College *C, A*
Massachusetts Bay Community
  College *C, A*
Massachusetts College of Liberal Arts *B*
Massasoit Community College *A*
Merrimack College *A, B*
Mount Ida College *A, B*
Mount Wachusett Community
  College *C, A*
Newbury College *A, B*
Nichols College *A, B, M*
Northeastern University *A*
Pine Manor College *A, B*
Quinsigamond Community College *A*
Regis College *M*
Roxbury Community College *A*
Salem State College *B, M*
Simmons College *B, M*
Springfield College *B*
Springfield Technical Community
  College *A*
Stonehill College *C, B*
Suffolk University *B, M*
University of Massachusetts
  Amherst *B, M, D*
  Boston *B, M*
  Dartmouth *B, M*
  Lowell *B, M*
Urban College of Boston *C*
Western New England College *B, M*
Westfield State College *B*
Worcester Polytechnic Institute *B, M*

Michigan

Adrian College *A, B, T*
Alma College *B*
Alpena Community College *A*
Andrews University *B, M*
Aquinas College *B, M, T*
Baker College
  of Auburn Hills *A, B, M*
  of Cadillac *A, B*
  of Clinton Township *A, B, M*
  of Jackson *A*
  of Muskegon *A, B*
  of Owosso *A, B*
  of Port Huron *A, B*
Bay de Noc Community College *C, A*
Calvin College *B*
Central Michigan University *B, M*
Cleary University *A, B, M*
Concordia University *B, M*
Cornerstone University *B*
Davenport University
  Eastern Region *A, B*
  Midland *A, B*
Davenport University - Western
  Region *A, B*
Eastern Michigan University *B, M, T*
Ferris State University *A, B*
Finlandia University *B*
Glen Oaks Community College *C*
Gogebic Community College *A*
Grand Rapids Community College *A*
Grand Valley State University *B, M*
Hillsdale College *B*
Hope College *B*
Jackson Community College *C, A*
Kellogg Community College *C, A*
Kettering University *B*
Kirtland Community College *A*
Lansing Community College *A*

Lawrence Technological University *B, M*
Macomb Community College *C, A*
Madonna University *A, B, M*
Marygrove College *B*
Michigan State University *B, M, D*
Michigan Technological
   University *B, M, T*
Mid Michigan Community College *A*
Monroe County Community
   College *C, A*
Montcalm Community College *A*
North Central Michigan College *C, A*
Northern Michigan University *B*
Northwestern Michigan College *A*
Northwood University *A, B, M*
Oakland Community College *A*
Oakland University *C, M*
Saginaw Valley State University *B, M*
St. Clair County Community College *A*
Schoolcraft College *A*
Southwestern Michigan College *C, A*
Spring Arbor University *B, M*
University of Michigan *B, M, D*
University of Michigan
   Dearborn *B, M*
   Flint *B, M*
Walsh College of Accountancy and
   Business Administration *B*
Washtenaw Community College *C, A*
Western Michigan University *B, M*
William Tyndale College *B*

Minnesota

Academy College *C, A, B*
Alexandria Technical College *C, A*
Anoka-Ramsey Community College *A*
Augsburg College *B*
Bemidji State University *B*
Bethany Lutheran College *B*
Bethel College *B*
Capella University *M*
Central Lakes College *A*
Century Community and Technical
   College *A*
College of St. Benedict *B*
College of St. Catherine *B, M*
College of St. Scholastica *B, M*
Concordia College: Moorhead *B*
Crown College *A, B*
Globe College *C, A, B*
Hamline University *B*
Hibbing Community College: A
   Technical and Community College *A*
Inver Hills Community College *A*
Itasca Community College *A*
Metropolitan State University *B, M*
Minneapolis Community and Technical
   College *C, A*
Minnesota School of Business *C, A*
Minnesota School of Business: Brooklyn
   Center *C, A*
Minnesota State College - Southeast
   Technical *C, A*
Minnesota State University
   Mankato *B, M*
   Moorhead *B, M*
National American University
   St. Paul *B*
North Central University *B*
North Hennepin Community College *A*
Northwestern College *B*
Rasmussen College
   Mankato *C, A*
   Minnetonka *C, A*
   St. Cloud *C, A*
Rochester Community and Technical
   College *C, A*
St. Cloud State University *B, M*
St. Cloud Technical College *C, A*
St. John's University *B*
St. Mary's University of Minnesota *B, M*
Southwest State University *A, B, M*

University of Minnesota
   Crookston *A, B*
   Duluth *B, M*
   Morris *B*
   Twin Cities *C, B, M, D*
University of St. Thomas *B, M*
Vermilion Community College *A*
Winona State University *B, M*

Mississippi

Alcorn State University *B, M*
Antonelli College
   Jackson *C, A*
Blue Mountain College *B*
Delta State University *B, M*
Holmes Community College *A*
Mary Holmes College *A*
Millsaps College *B, M*
Mississippi College *B, M, T*
Mississippi Gulf Coast Community
   College
   Perkinston *A*
Mississippi State University *B, M, D*
Mississippi University for Women *B*
Mississippi Valley State University *B*
Northwest Mississippi Community
   College *A*
Pearl River Community College *A*
Rust College *B*
University of Mississippi *B, M, D*
University of Southern Mississippi *B, M*

Missouri

Avila University *B, M*
Blue River Community College *A*
Central Methodist College *B*
Central Missouri State University *B, M*
College of the Ozarks *B*
Columbia College *A, B, M*
ConCorde Career Institute *A*
Culver-Stockton College *B*
DeVry University
   Kansas City *B, M*
Drury University *B, M*
East Central College *A*
Evangel University *B*
Fontbonne College *B, M*
Hannibal-LaGrange College *B*
Harris Stowe State College *B*
Lincoln University *B, M*
Lindenwood University *B, M*
Longview Community College *A*
Maple Woods Community College *C, A*
Maryville University of Saint Louis *B, M*
Missouri Baptist University *C, A, B*
Missouri College *C*
Missouri Southern State College *B*
Missouri Valley College *B*
Missouri Western State College *A, B*
National American University
   Kansas City *A, B*
North Central Missouri College *C, A*
Northwest Missouri State University *M*
Ozarks Technical Community
   College *C, A*
Penn Valley Community College *C, A*
Rockhurst University *B, M*
St. Charles Community College *C, A*
St. Louis Community College
   St. Louis Community College at
      Florissant Valley *A*
St. Louis University *B, M, D*
Sanford-Brown College *C, A, B*
Southeast Missouri State
   University *B, M*
Southwest Baptist University *B, M*
Southwest Missouri State
   University *B, M*
Springfield College *A, B*
Stephens College *B, M*
Truman State University *B*
University of Missouri
   Columbia *B*
   Rolla *B*
   St. Louis *M*

Washington University in St.
   Louis *B, M, D*
Webster University *B, M*
Westminster College *B*
William Jewell College *B*
William Woods University *B, M*

Montana

Carroll College *B*
Miles Community College *A*
Montana State University
   Billings *A, B*
Montana Tech of the University of
   Montana *A, B*
Rocky Mountain College *B*
University of Great Falls *B*
University of Montana-Missoula *B, M*
University of Montana: Western *A*

Nebraska

Bellevue University *B, M*
Central Community College *C, A*
Chadron State College *B, M*
Clarkson College *B, M*
College of Saint Mary *C, A, B*
Concordia University *B, T*
Dana College *B*
Doane College *B, M*
Hastings College *B*
Lincoln School of Commerce *A*
Metropolitan Community College *A*
Mid Plains Community College
   Area *C, A*
Midland Lutheran College *B*
Nebraska College of Business *A*
Nebraska Wesleyan University *B*
Northeast Community College *A*
Peru State College *B*
Southeast Community College
   Beatrice Campus *A*
   Lincoln Campus *A*
Union College *A, B*
University of Nebraska
   Kearney *B, M*
   Lincoln *B, M, D*
   Omaha *M*
Vatterott College
   Dodge Campus *C, A*
Wayne State College *B, M, T*
Western Nebraska Community
   College *C, A*
York College *A, B*

Nevada

Career College of Northern Nevada *C, A*
Community College of Southern
   Nevada *C, A*
Great Basin College *C, A*
Heritage College *C*
Las Vegas College *A*
Morrison University *A, B, M*
Sierra Nevada College *B*
Truckee Meadows Community
   College *A*
University of Nevada
   Las Vegas *M*
   Reno *M*
Western Nevada Community College *A*

New Hampshire

Colby-Sawyer College *B*
Dartmouth College *M*
Franklin Pierce College *B, M*
Hesser College *C, A, B*
New England College *B*
New Hampshire Community Technical
   College
   Berlin *C, A*
   Laconia *C, A*
   Manchester *C, A*
   Nashua *A*
   Stratham *C, A*
New Hampshire Technical Institute *A*
Plymouth State College *B, M*
Rivier College *A, B, M*
Southern New Hampshire
   University *A, B, M*

University of New Hampshire *A, B*
University of New Hampshire at
   Manchester *A, B*

New Jersey

Atlantic Cape Community College *A*
Berkeley College *A, B*
Bloomfield College *B*
Brookdale Community College *A*
Burlington County College *A*
Caldwell College *B, M*
Camden County College *A*
Centenary College *B, M*
The College of New Jersey *B*
College of St. Elizabeth *C, B, M*
County College of Morris *A*
Cumberland County College *A*
DeVry College of Technology *A*
Essex County College *A*
Fairleigh Dickinson University
   College at Florham *B, M*
   Metropolitan Campus *B, M*
Felician College *B*
Georgian Court College *B, M*
Gloucester County College *A*
Hudson County Community College *A*
Kean University *B*
Mercer County Community College *C, A*
Middlesex County College *A*
Monmouth University *M*
Montclair State University *B, M*
New Jersey City University *B*
New Jersey Institute of Technology *B, M*
Ocean County College *A*
Passaic County Community College *C*
Ramapo College of New Jersey *B, M*
Raritan Valley Community College *C*
Richard Stockton College of New
   Jersey *M*
Rider University *A, B, M*
Rowan University *M*
Rutgers, The State University of New
   Jersey
   Camden Regional Campus *B, M*
   New Brunswick Regional
      Campus *B, M, D*
   Newark Regional Campus *B, M, D*
St. Peter's College *A, B, M*
Salem Community College *A*
Seton Hall University *B, M*
Stevens Institute of Technology *M*
Sussex County Community College *A*
Union County College *A*
William Paterson University of New
   Jersey *B*

New Mexico

Albuquerque Technical-Vocational
   Institute *C, A*
Clovis Community College *A*
College of the Southwest *B*
Dona Ana Branch Community College of
   New Mexico State University *C, A*
Eastern New Mexico University *B, M*
Luna Community College *A*
Mesalands Community College *A*
Metropolitan College of Court
   Reporting *B*
National American University *A, B*
New Mexico Highlands University *B, M*
New Mexico Institute of Mining and
   Technology *A, B*
New Mexico Junior College *A*
New Mexico State University *M, D*
San Juan College *A*
Santa Fe Community College *C, A*
Southwestern Indian Polytechnic
   Institute *A*
University of New Mexico *B, M*
Western New Mexico University *B, M*

New York

Adelphi University *B, M*
Adirondack Community College *A*
Alfred University *B, M*
Berkeley College *A, B*

Berkeley College of New York City *A, B*
Briarcliffe College *A, B*
Bryant & Stratton Business Institute
    Albany *A*
    Rochester *A*
    Syracuse *C, A*
Canisius College *M*
Cayuga County Community College *A*
Cazenovia College *A, B*
City University of New York
    Baruch College *B, M*
    Borough of Manhattan Community
      College *A*
    Brooklyn College *B*
    College of Staten Island *B*
    Kingsborough Community
      College *A*
    La Guardia Community College *A*
    Queensborough Community
      College *A*
    York College *B*
Clarkson University *B, M*
Clinton Community College *A*
College of Mount St. Vincent *B*
Concordia College *A, B*
Corning Community College *A*
D'Youville College *B*
Daemen College *B*
DeVry Institute of Technology
    New York *B*
Dominican College of Blauvelt *B*
Dowling College *C, B, M*
Dutchess Community College *A*
Elmira College *B*
Erie Community College
    City Campus *A*
    North Campus *A*
    South Campus *A*
Finger Lakes Community College *A*
Fordham University *B, M*
Fulton-Montgomery Community
    College *A*
Genesee Community College *A*
Globe Institute of Technology *C, A*
Hartwick College *B*
Hilbert College *A, B*
Hofstra University *B, M*
Hudson Valley Community College *A*
Iona College *B*
Ithaca College *B, M*
Jamestown Business College *A*
Jamestown Community College *A*
Jefferson Community College *C, A*
Katharine Gibbs School
    Melville *A*
Keuka College *B*
Le Moyne College *B, M*
Long Island Business Institute *A*
Long Island University
    C. W. Post Campus *B, M*
    Southampton College *B*
Manhattan College *M*
Manhattanville College *B*
Maria College *A*
Marist College *B, M*
Marymount College of Fordham
    University *B*
Marymount Manhattan College *B*
Medaille College *B, M*
Mercy College *B*
Metropolitan College of New York *B, M*
Mildred Elley *C, A*
Mohawk Valley Community College *A*
Molloy College *B*
Monroe College *A, B*
Mount St. Mary College *C, B, M*
Nassau Community College *C, A*
New York Institute of
    Technology *C, A, B, M*
New York University *B, M, D*
Niagara County Community College *A*
Niagara University *M*
North Country Community College *A*
Nyack College *A, B*
Orange County Community College *A*

Pace University *B, M, D*
Pace University:
    Pleasantville/Briarcliff *C, B, M, D*
Paul Smith's College *A, B*
Plaza College *A*
Rensselaer Polytechnic Institute *B, M, D*
Roberts Wesleyan College *B*
Rochester Business Institute *A*
Rochester Institute of
    Technology *A, B, M*
Rockland Community College *A*
Russell Sage College *B*
Sage College of Albany *A, B*
St. Bonaventure University *M*
St. John Fisher College *B, M*
St. John's University *C, A, B, M*
St. Joseph's College *B*
St. Joseph's College: Suffolk Campus *B*
State University of New York
    Albany *B, M*
    Binghamton *M*
    Buffalo *B, M, D*
    College at Brockport *B*
    College at Buffalo *B*
    College at Fredonia *B*
    College at Geneseo *B*
    College at Old Westbury *B*
    College at Plattsburgh *B*
    College at Potsdam *B*
    College of Agriculture and
      Technology at Cobleskill *A*
    College of Agriculture and
      Technology at Morrisville *A*
    College of Technology at Alfred *A*
    College of Technology at Canton *A*
    College of Technology at
      Delhi *A, B*
    Empire State College *M*
    Farmingdale *C, A*
    Institute of Technology at
      Utica/Rome *B, M*
    Maritime College *B*
    New Paltz *B, M*
    Oswego *B, M*
    Stony Brook *M*
Suffolk County Community College *A*
Syracuse University *B, M, D*
Tompkins-Cortland Community
    College *C, A*
Touro College *A, B*
Trocaire College *A*
Ulster County Community College *A*
Union College *M*
United States Military Academy *B*
University of Rochester *M, D*
Utica College *B*
Utica School of Commerce *A*
Villa Maria College of Buffalo *A*
Wagner College *B, M*
Westchester Business Institute *C, A*
Westchester Community College *A*
Yeshiva University *B*

North Carolina
Alamance Community College *C, A*
Appalachian State University *M*
Asheville Buncombe Technical
    Community College *A*
Barber-Scotia College *B*
Barton College *B*
Beaufort County Community College *A*
Belmont Abbey College *B*
Bennett College *B*
Bladen Community College *C, A*
Brunswick Community College *A*
Caldwell Community College and
    Technical Institute *A*
Campbell University *B, M*
Cape Fear Community College *C, A*
Catawba College *B*
Catawba Valley Community
    College *C, A*
Central Carolina Community College *A*
Central Piedmont Community College *A*
Chowan College *B*
Cleveland Community College *C, A*

Coastal Carolina Community College *A*
College of the Albemarle *A*
Craven Community College *A*
Davidson County Community
    College *C, A*
Duke University *M, D*
Durham Technical Community
    College *A*
East Carolina University *B, M*
Edgecombe Community College *A*
Elizabeth City State University *B*
Fayetteville State University *B, M*
Fayetteville Technical Community
    College *A*
Forsyth Technical Community College *A*
Gardner-Webb University *B, M*
Gaston College *A*
Guilford College *B*
Guilford Technical Community
    College *C, A*
Halifax Community College *A*
Haywood Community College *C, A*
High Point University *M*
Isothermal Community College *C, A*
James Sprunt Community College *A*
John Wesley College *B*
Johnson C. Smith University *B*
Johnston Community College *A*
Lees-McRae College *B*
Lenoir Community College *C, A*
Livingstone College *B*
Louisburg College *A*
Mars Hill College *B*
Martin Community College *C, A*
Mayland Community College *A*
Meredith College *B, M*
Methodist College *A, B*
Miller-Motte Technical College *A*
Mitchell Community College *A*
Montgomery Community College *C, A*
Montreat College *B, M*
Mount Olive College *A, B*
Nash Community College *A*
North Carolina Agricultural and
    Technical State University *B*
North Carolina Central University *B, M*
North Carolina State University *B, M*
North Carolina Wesleyan College *B*
Pamlico Community College *A*
Peace College *B*
Pfeiffer University *B, M*
Piedmont Community College *A*
Pitt Community College *C, A*
Queens University of Charlotte *B, M*
Randolph Community College *A*
Richmond Community College *C, A*
Roanoke-Chowan Community College *A*
Rockingham Community College *A*
Rowan-Cabarrus Community
    College *C, A*
St. Andrews Presbyterian College *B*
St. Augustine's College *B*
Salem College *B*
Sampson Community College *A*
Sandhills Community College *A*
Shaw University *A, B*
South College *A*
South Piedmont Community
    College *C, A*
Southeastern Community College *A*
Southwestern Community College *C, A*
Stanly Community College *A*
Surry Community College *C, A*
Tri-County Community College *A*
University of North Carolina
    Asheville *B*
    Chapel Hill *B, M, D*
    Charlotte *B, M*
    Greensboro *B, M*
    Pembroke *B, M*
    Wilmington *B, M*
Vance-Granville Community College *A*
Wake Forest University *M*
Warren Wilson College *B*
Wayne Community College *A*

Western Carolina University *B, M*
Western Piedmont Community
    College *C, A*
Wilkes Community College *C, A*
Wilson Technical Community
    College *C, A*
Wingate University *M*
Winston-Salem State University *B*

North Dakota
Aaker's Business College *C*
Dickinson State University *B*
Jamestown College *B*
Lake Region State College *C, A*
Mayville State University *B*
Minot State University *B, M*
Minot State University: Bottineau
    Campus *C, A*
North Dakota State College of Science *A*
North Dakota State University *B, M*
University of Mary *A, B, M*
University of North Dakota *B, M*
Valley City State University *B*

Ohio
AEC Southern Ohio College
    Findlay *A*
Antioch College *B*
Ashland University *C, B, M*
Baldwin-Wallace College *B, M*
Bluffton College *B*
Bohecker's Business College *A*
Bowling Green State University *M*
Bowling Green State University:
    Firelands College *C, A*
Case Western Reserve
    University *B, M, D*
Cedarville University *B*
Central Ohio Technical College *A*
Central State University *B*
Chatfield College *A*
Cincinnati State Technical and
    Community College *A*
Cleveland State University *M, D*
College of Mount St. Joseph *A, B*
Columbus State Community
    College *C, A*
Cuyahoga Community College
    Eastern Campus *A*
    Metropolitan Campus *A*
David N. Myers College *B, M*
Davis College *A*
DeVry University
    Columbus *B, M*
Defiance College *A, B, M*
Edison State Community College *A*
Franciscan University of
    Steubenville *A, B, M*
Gallipolis Career College *A*
Heidelberg College *B, M*
Hiram College *B*
James A. Rhodes State College *A*
Jefferson Community College *C, A*
John Carroll University *B, M*
Kent State University *B, M, D*
Kent State University
    Salem Regional Campus *A, B*
    Stark Campus *B*
    Trumbull Campus *A*
    Tuscarawas Campus *A, B*
Lake Erie College *B, M*
Lakeland Community College *C, A*
Lourdes College *C, A, B*
Malone College *B, M*
Miami University
    Hamilton Campus *A*
    Middletown Campus *C, A*
    Oxford Campus *B, M*
Mount Union College *B*
Mount Vernon Nazarene University *A, B*
Muskingum Area Technical College *C, A*
North Central State College *A*
Northwest State Community College *A*
Notre Dame College *C, A, B*
Ohio Business College *A*
Ohio Business College: Sandusky *A*

Ohio Dominican College *C, A, B, M*
Ohio Northern University *B*
Ohio State University
 Columbus Campus *M, D*
Ohio University *A, B, M*
Ohio University
 Chillicothe Campus *A, B*
 Southern Campus at Ironton *A, B*
Otterbein College *B*
Owens Community College
 Findlay Campus *A*
 Toledo *A*
Sinclair Community College *A*
Southeastern Business College *A*
Southeastern Business College:
 Lancaster *A*
Southern State Community College *A*
Southwestern College of Business *A*
Stark State College of Technology *A*
Tiffin University *A, B, M*
Trumbull Business College *C, A*
University of Akron *C, B, M*
University of Cincinnati *C, A, B, M, D*
University of Cincinnati
 Clermont College *A*
 Raymond Walters College *A*
University of Dayton *B, M*
University of Findlay *B, M*
University of Northwestern Ohio *A, B*
University of Rio Grande *A, B*
University of Toledo *A, B, M, D*
Ursuline College *B*
Walsh University *A, B, M*
Washington State Community College *A*
Wilmington College *B*
Wittenberg University *B*
Wright State University *B, M*
Wright State University: Lake Campus *A*
Xavier University *A, B, M*
Youngstown State University *A, B, M*

Oklahoma

Bacone College *A, B*
Cameron University *B, M*
Carl Albert State College *A*
East Central University *B*
Eastern Oklahoma State College *A*
Langston University *B*
Murray State College *A*
Northeastern Oklahoma Agricultural and
 Mechanical College *A*
Northeastern State University *B, M*
Northern Oklahoma College *A*
Northwestern Oklahoma State
 University *B*
Oklahoma Baptist University *B*
Oklahoma Christian University of
 Science and Arts *B, M*
Oklahoma City University *B, M*
Oklahoma Panhandle State
 University *A, B*
Oklahoma State University *B, M, D*
Oklahoma State University
 Okmulgee *A*
Oklahoma Wesleyan University *B*
Oral Roberts University *B, M*
Redlands Community College *A*
Rogers State University *A*
Rose State College *C, A*
St. Gregory's University *A*
Seminole State College *A*
Southeastern Oklahoma State
 University *B, M*
Southern Nazarene University *A, B, M*
Southwestern Oklahoma State
 University *B, M*
Tulsa Community College *A*
University of Central Oklahoma *B, M*
University of Oklahoma *B, M, D*
University of Tulsa *M*
Western Oklahoma State College *A*

Oregon

Blue Mountain Community College *A*
Central Oregon Community College *A*
Chemeketa Community College *A*

Clatsop Community College *A*
Concordia University *B*
Eastern Oregon University *B*
George Fox University *B, M*
Lane Community College *C*
Linn-Benton Community College *A*
Marylhurst University *B, M*
Northwest Christian College *B, M*
Oregon Institute of Technology *B*
Oregon State University *B, M*
Pacific University *B*
Pioneer Pacific College *A*
Portland Community College *A*
Portland State University *B, D*
Rogue Community College *C, A*
Southern Oregon University *B*
Southwestern Oregon Community
 College *A*
Treasure Valley Community College *A*
University of Oregon *B, M, D*
University of Portland *B, M*
Warner Pacific College *B*
Western Baptist College *A, B*
Western Business College *C, A*
Willamette University *M*

Pennsylvania

Academy of Medical Arts and
 Business *C, A*
Albright College *B*
Allentown Business School *A*
Arcadia University *C, B*
Bloomsburg University of
 Pennsylvania *B, M*
Bucknell University *B*
Bucks County Community College *A*
Butler County Community College *C, A*
Cabrini College *B*
California University of
 Pennsylvania *A, B, M*
Cambria County Area Community
 College *A*
Cambria-Rowe Business College *A*
Carlow College *B*
Carnegie Mellon University *B, M, D*
Cedar Crest College *B*
Chatham College *B, M*
Chestnut Hill College *C, A, B*
Cheyney University of Pennsylvania *B*
Churchman Business School *A*
Community College of Allegheny
 County *C, A*
Community College of Beaver County *A*
Community College of Philadelphia *C, A*
Consolidated School of Business
 Lancaster *A*
 York *A*
DeSales University *B, M*
DeVry University
 Ft. Washington *B, M*
Delaware County Community College *A*
Delaware Valley College *B*
Douglas School of Business *A*
Drexel University *M, D*
DuBois Business College *A*
Duquesne University *M*
East Stroudsburg University of
 Pennsylvania *B*
Edinboro University of
 Pennsylvania *A, B*
Elizabethtown College *C, A, B*
Franklin & Marshall College *B*
Geneva College *A, B, M*
Gettysburg College *B*
Grove City College *B*
Gwynedd-Mercy College *A, B*
Harrisburg Area Community
 College *C, A*
Holy Family University *C, B*
ICM School of Business & Medical
 Careers *A*
Immaculata University *B, M*
Indiana University of
 Pennsylvania *A, B, M*
Information Computer Systems
 Institute *C, A*

Juniata College *B*
Keystone College *A*
King's College *A, B*
Kutztown University of
 Pennsylvania *B, M*
La Roche College *C, B*
La Salle University *A, B, M*
Lackawanna College *A*
Lebanon Valley College of
 Pennsylvania *A, B, M*
Lehigh Carbon Community College *C, A*
Lehigh University *M*
Lincoln University *B*
Luzerne County Community College *A*
Lycoming College *B*
Manor College *A*
Marywood University *B, M*
McCann School of Business
 Pottsville *A*
Mercyhurst College *B*
Messiah College *B*
Metropolitan Career Center *C, A*
Millersville University of
 Pennsylvania *B, M*
Montgomery County Community
 College *C, A*
Moravian College *B, M*
Mount Aloysius College *A, B*
Muhlenberg College *B*
Neumann College *C, B*
Newport Business Institute *A*
Newport Business Institute *A*
Northampton County Area Community
 College *A*
Orleans Technical Institute - Center City
 Campus *A*
Peirce College *A, B*
Penn State
 Abington *B*
 Altoona *B*
 Beaver *B*
 Berks *B*
 Delaware County *B*
 Dubois *B*
 Erie, The Behrend College *B, M*
 Fayette *B*
 Harrisburg *C, B, M*
 Hazleton *B*
 Lehigh Valley *B*
 McKeesport *B*
 Mont Alto *B*
 New Kensington *A, B*
 Schuylkill - Capital College *A, B*
 University Park *C, B, M, D*
 Wilkes-Barre *A, B*
 Worthington Scranton *B*
 York *B*
Pennsylvania College of
 Technology *A, B*
Pennsylvania Institute of Technology *A*
Philadelphia Biblical University *B*
Philadelphia University *A, B, M*
Pittsburgh Technical Institute: Boyd
 School Division *A*
Point Park College *C, A, B, M*
Reading Area Community College *A*
Robert Morris University *B, M*
Rosemont College *B, M*
St. Joseph's University *A, B, M*
St. Vincent College *C, B*
Seton Hill University *B, M*
Shippensburg University of
 Pennsylvania *B*
Slippery Rock University of
 Pennsylvania *B*
South Hills School of Business &
 Technology *A*
South Hills School of Business and
 Technology *A*
Temple University *B, M, D*
Thiel College *B*
University of
 Pennsylvania *C, A, B, M, D*
University of Pittsburgh *M, D*

University of Pittsburgh
 Bradford *B*
 Greensburg *B*
University of Scranton *A, B, M*
University of the Sciences in
 Philadelphia *M*
Valley Forge Christian College *B*
Villanova University *B, M*
Washington and Jefferson College *A, B*
Waynesburg College *B, M*
West Chester University of
 Pennsylvania *B, M*
Western School of Health and Business
 Careers *C, A*
Westmoreland County Community
 College *C, A*
Widener University *A, B, M*
Wilkes University *B, M*
Wilson College *A, B*
York College of Pennsylvania *B, M*

Puerto Rico

Atlantic College *A, B*
Bayamon Central University *B, M*
Columbia College *A, B, M*
Huertas Junior College *A*
Humacao Community College *A*
ICPR Junior College *C, A*
Inter American University of Puerto Rico
 Barranquitas Campus *A, B*
 Bayamon Campus *A, B*
 Fajardo Campus *B*
 Guayama Campus *A, B*
 Metropolitan Campus *A, B, M*
 San German Campus *A, B, M*
Pontifical Catholic University of Puerto
 Rico *B, M, D*
Turabo University *A, B, M*
Universidad Metropolitana *B, M*
Universidad Politecnica de Puerto
 Rico *B, M*
Universidad del Este *C, A, B*
University of Puerto Rico
 Bayamon University College *A, B*
 Carolina Regional College *B*
 Cayey University College *B*
 Humacao *A, B*
 Mayaguez Campus *B, M*
 Ponce *A, B*
 Rio Piedras Campus *B, M*
 Utuado *B*
University of the Sacred Heart *B*

Rhode Island

Bryant College *B, M*
Community College of Rhode
 Island *C, A*
Providence College *C, A*
Rhode Island College *B*
Roger Williams University *B*
Salve Regina University *A, B, M*
University of Rhode Island *B*

South Carolina

Aiken Technical College *C, A*
Anderson College *B*
Benedict College *B*
Charleston Southern University *B, M*
The Citadel *B, M*
Claflin University *B, M*
Clemson University *B, M*
Coastal Carolina University *B*
Coker College *B*
College of Charleston *B*
Columbia College *B*
Erskine College *B*
Florence-Darlington Technical
 College *C*
Forrest Junior College *A*
Francis Marion University *B, M*
Furman University *B*
Lander University *B*
Limestone College *A, B*
Midlands Technical College *A*
Morris College *B*
Newberry College *B*

North Greenville College *B*
Northeastern Technical College *A*
Piedmont Technical College *C*
Presbyterian College *B*
South Carolina State University *B*
Southern Wesleyan University *B, M*
Spartanburg Technical College *A*
Technical College of the Lowcountry *C*
Tri-County Technical College *C, A*
Trident Technical College *A*
University of South Carolina *B, M, D*
University of South Carolina
   Aiken *B*
   Lancaster *A*
   Spartanburg *B*
Voorhees College *B*
Winthrop University *B, M*
York Technical College *A*

South Dakota

Augustana College *B*
Black Hills State University *B*
Dakota State University *A, B, T*
Kilian Community College *A*
Mount Marty College *A, B*
Northern State University *A, B*
Sinte Gleska University *A, B*
Southeast Technical Institute *A*
University of Sioux Falls *A, B*
University of South Dakota *B, M*

Tennessee

American Baptist College of ABT
   Seminary *A, B*
Aquinas College *A, B*
Austin Peay State University *A*
Belmont University *M*
Bethel College *B*
Bryan College *B*
Carson-Newman College *B*
Christian Brothers University *B, M*
Cleveland State Community College *A*
Columbia State Community College *C*
Crichton College *B*
Draughons Junior College of Business:
   Nashville *A*
Draughons Junior College: Clarksville *A*
Dyersburg State Community College *A*
East Tennessee State University *B, M*
Fisk University *B*
Freed-Hardeman University *B*
Jackson State Community College *A*
King College *B*
Lambuth University *B*
Lee University *B*
Maryville College *B*
Middle Tennessee State
   University *C, B, M*
Miller-Motte Technical College *A*
Milligan College *B*
Northeast State Technical Community
   College *A*
Pellissippi State Technical Community
   College *A*
Remington College
   Southeast College of Technology *A*
Rhodes College *B*
Roane State Community College *A*
South College *A, B*
Southern Adventist University *B, M*
Southwest Tennessee Community
   College *A*
Tennessee State University *B, M*
Tennessee Wesleyan College *B*
Trevecca Nazarene University *B, M*
Tusculum College *B, M*
Union University *B, M*
University of Memphis *B, M, D*
University of Tennessee
   Chattanooga *B, M*
   Knoxville *B, M, D*
   Martin *B*
Vanderbilt University *D*
Volunteer State Community College *A*

Texas

Alvin Community College *A*
Amberton University *B, M*
Angelina College *C, A*
Angelo State University *B, M*
Austin Business College *C, A*
Austin Community College *C, A*
Baylor University *B, M*
Border Institute of Technology *A*
Brazosport College *C, A*
Brookhaven College *A*
Central Texas College *C, A*
Coastal Bend College *A*
College of the Mainland *A*
Collin County Community College
   District *C, A*
Concordia University at Austin *B*
Dallas Baptist University *A, B, M*
Dallas Christian College *B*
DeVry University
   Irving *B, M*
Del Mar College *A*
East Texas Baptist University *B*
Eastfield College *A*
El Centro College *C, A*
El Paso Community College *C, A*
Frank Phillips College *A*
Galveston College *C, A*
Hallmark Institute of Technology *A*
Hardin-Simmons University *B, M*
Hill College *A*
Houston Baptist University *B, M*
Houston Community College
   System *C, A*
Howard Payne University *B*
Huston-Tillotson College *B*
Jarvis Christian College *B*
Kilgore College *C, A*
Lamar State College at Orange *C*
Lamar State College at Port Arthur *A*
Lamar University *B*
LeTourneau University *B, M*
Lee College *C, A*
MTI College of Business and
   Technology *C, A*
MTI College of Business and
   Technology *C, A*
McMurry University *B*
Midland College *C, A*
Midwestern State University *B, M*
North Harris Montgomery Community
   College District *C, A*
North Lake College *A*
Northeast Texas Community
   College *C, A*
Northwood University: Texas
   Campus *A, B*
Odessa College *C, A*
Our Lady of the Lake University of San
   Antonio *B, M*
Palo Alto College *A*
Paris Junior College *A*
Prairie View A&M University *B, M*
Remington College
   Dallas *A*
Rice University *M, D*
Richland College *A*
St. Edward's University *B, M, T*
St. Mary's University *M*
St. Philip's College *C, A*
Sam Houston State University *B, M*
San Antonio College *A*
Schreiner University *B*
South Plains College *A*
South Texas Community College *A*
Southwest Texas State University *B, M*
Southwestern Adventist University *B, M*
Southwestern Assemblies of God
   University *A, B*
Stephen F. Austin State University *B, M*
Sul Ross State University *B, M*
Tarleton State University *B, M*
Tarrant County College *C, A*
Texarkana College *C, A*

Texas A&M International
   University *B, M*
Texas A&M University *M, D*
Texas A&M University
   Commerce *B, M*
   Corpus Christi *B, M*
   Galveston *B*
   Kingsville *M*
   Texarkana *B, M*
Texas Christian University *B, M, T*
Texas College *B*
Texas Lutheran University *B*
Texas Southern University *M*
Texas Tech University *B, M, D*
Texas Wesleyan University *B, M*
Texas Woman's University *B, M, T*
Trinity University *B*
Trinity Valley Community College *A*
Tyler Junior College *C, A*
University of Dallas *B, M*
University of Houston *M, D*
University of Houston
   Clear Lake *B, M*
   Downtown *B*
   Victoria *B, T*
University of Mary Hardin-Baylor *B, M*
University of North Texas *B, M*
University of St. Thomas *B, M*
University of Texas
   Arlington *B, M, D*
   Austin *B, M, D*
   Brownsville *B, M*
   Dallas *M, D*
   El Paso *B, M*
   Pan American *M, D*
   San Antonio *B, M*
   Tyler *B, M*
   of the Permian Basin *B, M*
University of the Incarnate Word *B, M*
Victoria College *C, A*
Wayland Baptist University *A, B, M*
West Texas A&M University *B, M*
Western Texas College *A*
Wharton County Junior College *A*
Wiley College *B*

Utah

Brigham Young University *B, M*
College of Eastern Utah *A*
Dixie State College of Utah *A, B*
LDS Business College *A*
Salt Lake Community College *C, A*
Snow College *A*
Southern Utah University *B, M*
University of Utah *M, D*
Utah Career College *C*
Utah State University *B, M*
Weber State University *B*
Westminster College *B, M*

Vermont

Castleton State College *B*
Champlain College *C, A, B*
College of St. Joseph in Vermont *A, B*
Goddard College *B*
Green Mountain College *B*
Johnson State College *A, B*
Lyndon State College *A, B*
Norwich University *B, M*
St. Michael's College *B, M*
Southern Vermont College *B*
University of Vermont *B, M*
Vermont Technical College *A*

Virginia

Averett University *A, B, M*
Blue Ridge Community College *A*
Bluefield College *B*
Bridgewater College *B*
Bryant & Stratton College *A, B*
College of William and Mary *B, M*
Danville Community College *A*
DeVry University
   Crystal City *B, M*
Eastern Mennonite University *B, M*
Eastern Shore Community College *A*

Emory & Henry College *B*
Ferrum College *B*
George Mason University *B, M*
Hampton University *B, M*
J. Sargeant Reynolds Community
   College *C, A*
James Madison University *B, M*
Liberty University *B, M*
Longwood University *B*
Lynchburg College *B, M*
Mary Baldwin College *B*
Mary Washington College *B*
Marymount University *C, B, M*
Mountain Empire Community College *A*
National College of Business &
   Technology
   Bluefield *C, A*
   Charlottesville *C, A*
   Danville *C, A*
   Harrisonburg *C, A*
   Lynchburg *C, A*
   Martinsville *C, A*
   Roanoke *C, A, B*
Old Dominion University *B, M, D*
Paul D. Camp Community College *A*
Piedmont Virginia Community
   College *A*
Radford University *B, M*
Rappahannock Community College *A*
Roanoke College *B*
Shenandoah University *B, M*
Southside Virginia Community
   College *A*
Southwest Virginia Community
   College *A*
Thomas Nelson Community College *A*
University of Richmond *B, M*
University of Virginia *M, D*
University of Virginia's College at
   Wise *B*
Virginia Commonwealth
   University *B, M, D*
Virginia Highlands Community
   College *A*
Virginia Intermont College *B*
Virginia Polytechnic Institute and State
   University *M*
Virginia State University *B*
Virginia Union University *B*
Virginia Wesleyan College *B*
Virginia Western Community College *A*
Washington and Lee University *B*

Washington

Bellevue Community College *C, A*
Central Washington University *B*
Centralia College *A*
Clark College *C, A*
DeVry University
   Seattle *B, M*
Eastern Washington University *B, M*
Edmonds Community College *C, A*
Everett Community College *C, A*
Gonzaga University *B, M*
Grays Harbor College *C, A*
Henry Cogswell College *B*
Heritage College *C, B*
Lower Columbia College *A*
Northwest College *B*
Pacific Lutheran University *B, M*
Peninsula College *A*
St. Martin's College *B, M*
Seattle Pacific University *B, M*
Seattle University *B, M*
Spokane Community College *C, A*
Spokane Falls Community College *C, A*
University of Puget Sound *B*
University of Washington *B, M, D*
Walla Walla College *B*
Walla Walla Community College *A*
Washington State University *B, M, D*
Wenatchee Valley College *C, A*
Western Washington University *B, M*
Whitworth College *B*

West Virginia

Alderson-Broaddus College *A, B*
Bluefield State College *B*
Concord College *B*
Davis and Elkins College *A, B*
Fairmont State College *B*
Glenville State College *B*
International Academy of Design and
 Technology *A*
Marshall University *B*
Mountain State University *C, A, B*
Ohio Valley College *B*
Potomac State College of West Virginia
 University *A*
Salem International University *A, B*
Shepherd College *A, B*
University of Charleston *A, B, M*
Valley College of Technology *A*
West Liberty State College *B*
West Virginia Business College *A*
West Virginia Business College *A*
West Virginia Northern Community
 College *A*
West Virginia State College *A, B*
West Virginia University *B*
West Virginia University Institute of
 Technology *A, B*
West Virginia University at
 Parkersburg *B*
West Virginia Wesleyan College *B, M*
Wheeling Jesuit University *B*

Wisconsin

Beloit College *B*
Cardinal Stritch University *B, M*
Carroll College *B*
Carthage College *B*
Concordia University Wisconsin *B*
Edgewood College *B, M*
Lac Courte Oreilles Ojibwa Community
 College *A*
Lakeland College *B, M*
Lakeshore Technical College *A*
Maranatha Baptist Bible College *B*
Marian College of Fond du Lac *B, M*
Marquette University *B, M*
Milwaukee Area Technical College *A*
Mount Mary College *B*
Nicolet Area Technical College *A*
Northland College *B*
Ripon College *B*
St. Norbert College *B*
Silver Lake College *B*
University of Wisconsin
 Eau Claire *B, M*
 Green Bay *B*
 La Crosse *B, M*
 Madison *B, M, D*
 Milwaukee *M*
 Oshkosh *M*
 Parkside *B, M*
 Platteville *B*
 River Falls *B*
 Stevens Point *B*
 Stout *B*
 Superior *B*
 Whitewater *B, M*
Viterbo University *B*
Western Wisconsin Technical College *A*
Wisconsin Indianhead Technical
 College *A*

Wyoming

Casper College *A*
Central Wyoming College *A*
Eastern Wyoming College *A*
Laramie County Community College *A*
Sheridan College *A*
University of Wyoming *B, M*

Business communications

Arkansas

Harding University *B*

California

Chapman University *B*
Foothill College *C*
Golden Gate University *C*
Holy Names College *B*
Ohlone College *C*
Pepperdine University *B*
Point Loma Nazarene University *B*

Colorado

Jones International University *C, B, M*

Connecticut

Quinnipiac University *B*

District of Columbia

University of the District of Columbia *A*

Florida

Barry University *M*
Eckerd College *B*
Florida State University *B*
Gulf Coast Community College *A*

Georgia

South Georgia College *A*

Hawaii

Hawaii Pacific University *B*

Illinois

Roosevelt University *B, M*
Trinity Christian College *B*
Waubonsee Community College *C*

Indiana

St. Mary-of-the-Woods College *B*

Iowa

Franciscan University *B*
Morningside College *B*

Kansas

MidAmerica Nazarene University *B*

Maine

University of Maine
 Presque Isle *B*

Maryland

Cecil Community College *A*
Johns Hopkins University *M*
Villa Julie College *A, B*

Massachusetts

American International College *B*
Babson College *B*
Bentley College *B, M*
Emerson College *B, M*
Massachusetts College of Liberal Arts *B*
Nichols College *B*
Suffolk University *M*

Michigan

Aquinas College *B*
Calvin College *B*
Central Michigan University *B*
Macomb Community College *C*

Minnesota

University of St. Thomas *C, B, M*

Mississippi

Mississippi College *B*

Missouri

Rockhurst University *B*

Montana

University of Montana: Western *B*

Nebraska

Creighton University *B*
Hastings College *B*

New Jersey

College of St. Elizabeth *C*

New York

City University of New York
 Baruch College *B*
Metropolitan College of New York *B*
St. Bonaventure University *M*

North Carolina

Campbell University *B*

North Dakota

University of Mary *B*

Ohio

College of Mount St. Joseph *B*
Marietta College *B*
Ohio Dominican College *B*
Stark State College of Technology *A*
University of Dayton *B*
Urbana University *B*

Oklahoma

University of Central Oklahoma *B*

Oregon

Marylhurst University *B, M*
Western Baptist College *B*

Pennsylvania

Carlow College *B*
Chestnut Hill College *C, A, B*
Community College of Beaver County *C*
Grove City College *B*
La Salle University *B*
Marywood University *C*
Montgomery County Community
 College *C, A*
Point Park College *B*
Rosemont College *B*
Thiel College *B*

Puerto Rico

Pontifical Catholic University of Puerto
 Rico *B*

South Carolina

Forrest Junior College *A*

South Dakota

Augustana College *B*

Tennessee

Maryville College *B*

Texas

Houston Community College
 System *C, A*
Southwestern Adventist University *B*
University of Houston *B*

Vermont

Champlain College *A, B*

Virginia

Thomas Nelson Community College *C*

Business machine repair

California

Yuba Community College District *C*

New York

College of Aeronautics *C, A, B*

Pennsylvania

Community College of Allegheny
 County *A*

Washington

Clover Park Technical College *C, A*

Business statistics

Florida

University of Miami *M*
University of West Florida *B*

Georgia

South Georgia College *A*

Kansas

Fort Scott Community College *A*

Massachusetts

Babson College *B*

Michigan

Western Michigan University *B*

Minnesota

Winona State University *A*

New York

Manhattan College *B*
Rochester Institute of Technology *B, M*

Ohio

Bowling Green State University *B, M*
Cleveland State University *B*

Pennsylvania

La Salle University *B*
Temple University *B, M, D*

Puerto Rico

University of Puerto Rico
 Rio Piedras Campus *B*

Tennessee

University of Tennessee
 Knoxville *B, M*

Texas

Baylor University *B*
University of Houston *B, M, D*
University of Texas
 Arlington *D*

Utah

Brigham Young University *B*

Business teacher education

Alabama

Alabama Agricultural and Mechanical
 University *B, M*
Chattahoochee Valley Community
 College *A*
James H. Faulkner State Community
 College *A*
Oakwood College *B*

Arizona

Arizona State University *B, T*
Eastern Arizona College *A*
Prescott College *T*

Arkansas

Arkansas State University *B, M, T*
Arkansas Tech University *B*
Henderson State University *B, T*
Ouachita Baptist University *B, T*
Philander Smith College *B*
Southern Arkansas University *B, T*
University of Arkansas
 Monticello *B*
 Pine Bluff *B, T*
University of Central Arkansas *B, M, T*
University of the Ozarks *B, T*

California

Azusa Pacific University *B, T*
California Baptist University *T*
California State Polytechnic University:
 Pomona *T*
California State University
 Bakersfield *B, T*
 Chico *T*
 Dominguez Hills *T*
 Fullerton *T*
 Northridge *B, T*
Fresno Pacific University *T*
Humboldt State University *T*
Mount St. Mary's College *T*
San Jose State University *T*

Colorado

Colorado State University *T*

Connecticut

Central Connecticut State
 University *B, M, T*
Sacred Heart University *T*

Delaware

Delaware State University *B*

District of Columbia

University of the District of Columbia *B*

Florida

Bethune-Cookman College *B, T*
Florida Agricultural and Mechanical
    University *B, M*
University of Central Florida *B, M*
University of South Florida *B, M*

Georgia

Albany State University *M*
Armstrong Atlantic State University *B, T*
Clark Atlanta University *B*
Darton College *A*
East Georgia College *A*
Emmanuel College *B*
Georgia Southern University *B, M*
Georgia Southwestern State
    University *B, M*
South Georgia College *A*
State University of West Georgia *B, M*
University of Georgia *B, M, T*
Valdosta State University *B, M*

Hawaii

Brigham Young University-Hawaii *B, T*
University of Hawaii
    Manoa *B, T*

Idaho

Boise State University *B*
North Idaho College *A*
University of Idaho *B, M, T*

Illinois

Benedictine University *T*
Chicago State University *B*
Illinois State University *B, T*
McKendree College *B, T*
National-Louis University *C*
Northern Illinois University *M*
Parkland College *A*
Trinity Christian College *B, T*

Indiana

Ball State University *B, M, T*
Bethel College *B*
Goshen College *B*
Grace College *B*
Huntington College *B*
Indiana State University *B, T*
Indiana Wesleyan University *B*
Oakland City University *B*
Saint Mary's College *T*
University of Indianapolis *B, T*
University of St. Francis *B*
University of Southern Indiana *B, T*

Iowa

Buena Vista University *B, T*
Central College *T*
Dordt College *B*
Drake University *M, T*
Ellsworth Community College *A*
Grand View College *B, T*
Maharishi University of Management *T*
Morningside College *B*
Mount Mercy College *T*
Northwestern College *T*
St. Ambrose University *B, T*
University of Northern Iowa *B, M*
Upper Iowa University *T*
William Penn University *B*

Kansas

Baker University *T*
Bethany College *B*
Butler County Community College *A*
Central Christian College *A, B*
Emporia State University *B, M, T*
Fort Hays State University *B, T*
Garden City Community College *A*
Labette Community College *A*
McPherson College *B, T*

MidAmerica Nazarene University *B, T*
Tabor College *B, T*
Washburn University of Topeka *B*

Kentucky

Cumberland College *B, T*
Morehead State University *B*
Murray State University *B, T*
Spalding University *B*
Thomas More College *B*
Union College *B*

Louisiana

Grambling State University *B*
Louisiana College *B*
McNeese State University *T*
Nicholls State University *B*
Northwestern State University *B*
Our Lady of Holy Cross College *B*
Southern University and Agricultural and
    Mechanical College *B*

Maine

Husson College *B, T*
Thomas College *B*
University of Maine
    Machias *B*

Maryland

Frostburg State University *B, T*
Montgomery College
    Rockville Campus *A*
Morgan State University *B, M*

Massachusetts

American International College *T*
Suffolk University *B, M, T*
University of Massachusetts
    Dartmouth *T*
Westfield State College *B, T*

Michigan

Central Michigan University *B, M*
Eastern Michigan University *B, M, T*
Ferris State University *B*
Michigan Technological University *T*
Northern Michigan University *B, T*
Siena Heights University *B, T*
University of Michigan
    Dearborn *B*
Western Michigan University *B*

Minnesota

College of St. Catherine *B*
Concordia College: Moorhead *B, T*
Minnesota State University
    Mankato *B, M, T*
Northland Community & Technical
    College *A*
Ridgewater College: A Community and
    Technical College *A*
University of Minnesota
    Twin Cities *B, M, T*
Vermilion Community College *A*
Winona State University *B, M, T*

Mississippi

Blue Mountain College *B*
Coahoma Community College *A*
Delta State University *B*
Itawamba Community College *A*
Mary Holmes College *A*
Mississippi College *B, M*
Mississippi Gulf Coast Community
    College
    Perkinston *A*
Mississippi State University *B, T*
Northwest Mississippi Community
    College *A*
Rust College *B*
University of Mississippi *T*
University of Southern Mississippi *B*

Missouri

Avila University *B, T*
Central Missouri State
    University *B, M, T*
College of the Ozarks *B, T*
Columbia College *T*

Evangel University *B, T*
Hannibal-LaGrange College *B*
Lincoln University *B, T*
Lindenwood University *B, M*
Missouri Baptist University *B, T*
Missouri Southern State College *B, T*
Northwest Missouri State
    University *B, M, T*
Rockhurst University *B*
Southeast Missouri State
    University *B, M, T*
Southwest Baptist University *T*
Southwest Missouri State University *B*
University of Missouri
    Columbia *B*
    St. Louis *T*

Montana

Miles Community College *A*
Montana State University
    Billings *B, T*
University of Montana-Missoula *B, T*
University of Montana: Western *B, T*

Nebraska

Chadron State College *B, M*
Concordia University *B, T*
Dana College *B*
Doane College *B*
Hastings College *B, M, T*
Midland Lutheran College *B, T*
Northeast Community College *A*
Union College *T*
University of Nebraska
    Kearney *B, M, T*
    Lincoln *B, T*
    Omaha *B, T*
York College *B, T*

Nevada

University of Nevada
    Reno *B*

New Hampshire

Southern New Hampshire
    University *B, M*

New Jersey

Monmouth University *T*
Montclair State University *B, M, T*
Rider University *B, M, T*
Rowan University *T*
St. Peter's College *T*

New Mexico

Eastern New Mexico University *B*
Western New Mexico University *B*

New York

Alfred University *M, T*
Concordia College *B, T*
D'Youville College *B, M, T*
Daemen College *B, T*
Dowling College *B*
Fulton-Montgomery Community
    College *A*
Hofstra University *B, M, T*
Le Moyne College *T*
Molloy College *B*
Nazareth College of Rochester *B, M, T*
New York Institute of Technology *B, T*
New York University *M, D*
Niagara University *B, T*
Pace University *B, M, T*
Pace University:
    Pleasantville/Briarcliff *B, M, T*
St. Bonaventure University *T*
State University of New York
    College at Buffalo *B, M, T*
    Oswego *B*
Utica College *B*

North Carolina

Appalachian State University *B, M, T*
East Carolina University *B*
Elizabeth City State University *B, T*
Fayetteville State University *B, T*

Guilford Technical Community
    College *A*
Lenoir-Rhyne College *B, T*
North Carolina Agricultural and
    Technical State University *B, T*
North Carolina Central University *M*
North Carolina State University *T*
St. Augustine's College *B*
University of North Carolina
    Greensboro *M, T*

North Dakota

Dickinson State University *B, T*
Mayville State University *B, T*
Minot State University *B*
Minot State University: Bottineau
    Campus *A*
University of North Dakota *B, M, T*
Valley City State University *B, T*

Ohio

Ashland University *B, M, T*
Baldwin-Wallace College *T*
Bluffton College *B*
Bowling Green State University *B, M*
College of Mount St. Joseph *T*
Defiance College *B, T*
Kent State University *B*
Kent State University
    Stark Campus *B*
Mount Union College *T*
Mount Vernon Nazarene University *B, T*
Ohio University *B, T*
University of Akron *B, T*
University of Findlay *B, T*
University of Rio Grande *B, T*
University of Toledo *B, M, T*
Wright State University *B, M, T*
Xavier University *M*
Youngstown State University *B, M*

Oklahoma

East Central University *B*
Eastern Oklahoma State College *A*
Langston University *B*
Northwestern Oklahoma State
    University *B, T*
Oklahoma City University *B*
Oklahoma Panhandle State University *B*
Oklahoma Wesleyan University *B*
Oral Roberts University *B, T*
Southeastern Oklahoma State
    University *B, T*
Southern Nazarene University *B*
Southwestern Oklahoma State
    University *T*
University of Central Oklahoma *B*

Oregon

Concordia University *B, M, T*
Oregon State University *M*
Portland State University *T*
Western Baptist College *B*

Pennsylvania

Bloomsburg University of
    Pennsylvania *B, T*
Community College of Philadelphia *A*
Delaware Valley College *T*
Gwynedd-Mercy College *B, T*
Indiana University of
    Pennsylvania *B, M, T*
Mercyhurst College *T*
Reading Area Community College *A*
Robert Morris University *B, M, T*
St. Joseph's University *B, M*
St. Vincent College *B*
Temple University *B*

Puerto Rico

Inter American University of Puerto Rico
    Metropolitan Campus *M*
    San German Campus *M*
Pontifical Catholic University of Puerto
    Rico *B, T*
University of Puerto Rico
    Mayaguez Campus *T*

South Carolina

Coker College *B*
South Carolina State University *B, T*
University of South Carolina *M*

South Dakota

Black Hills State University *B*
Dakota State University *B, T*
Dakota Wesleyan University *B, T*
Northern State University *B, T*

Tennessee

Draughons Junior College of Business:
  Nashville *A*
Lane College *B*
Lee University *B*
Middle Tennessee State
  University *B, M, T*
Roane State Community College *A*
Union University *B, T*
University of Tennessee
    Knoxville *B, T*
    Martin *B, T*

Texas

Abilene Christian University *B, T*
Baylor University *B, T*
Houston Baptist University *T*
Howard Payne University *B, T*
Jarvis Christian College *B*
Lamar University *T*
Laredo Community College *A*
LeTourneau University *B*
Lubbock Christian University *B, T*
McMurry University *T*
St. Mary's University *B, T*
Southwestern Adventist University *B*
Tarleton State University *B, T*
Texas A&M University
    Commerce *T*
    Corpus Christi *T*
    Kingsville *T*
Texas Christian University *T*
Texas Tech University *M*
Texas Wesleyan University *B, T*
University of Mary Hardin-Baylor *T*
University of North Texas *M, T*
West Texas A&M University *T*

Utah

Snow College *C, A*
Southern Utah University *B, T*
Utah State University *B, M, D*
Utah Valley State College *B*
Weber State University *B*

Virginia

Bluefield College *B, T*
James Madison University *B, T*
Norfolk State University *B*
Shenandoah University *C*
University of Virginia's College at
  Wise *T*
Virginia Intermont College *B, T*
Virginia State University *B*

Washington

Central Washington University *B, M, T*
Eastern Washington University *B, M, T*
Renton Technical College *C, A*
Walla Walla College *B*

West Virginia

Concord College *B, T*
Fairmont State College *B*

Wisconsin

Concordia University Wisconsin *B, T*
Edgewood College *B, T*
Lakeland College *B*
Maranatha Baptist Bible College *B*
Marian College of Fond du Lac *T*
Mount Mary College *B, T*
Northland College *T*
University of Wisconsin
    Superior *B, T*
    Whitewater *B, T*
Viterbo University *B, T*

Wyoming

Eastern Wyoming College *A*

Business/commerce

Alabama

Alabama Agricultural and Mechanical
  University *B*
Alabama Southern Community
  College *A*
Andrew Jackson University *B*
Auburn University at Montgomery *B, M*
Birmingham-Southern College *B*
Central Alabama Community
  College *C, A*
Enterprise State Junior College *A*
Faulkner University *B*
Huntingdon College *B*
Jacksonville State University *B*
Jefferson State Community College *C, A*
Judson College *B*
Northeast Alabama Community
  College *A*
Reid State Technical College *C*
Shelton State Community College *C, A*
Talladega College *B*
Troy State University *B*
Troy State University in
  Montgomery *A, B, M*
University of Mobile *B, M*
University of Montevallo *B*
University of South Alabama *B*
Wallace State Community College at
  Hanceville *A*

Alaska

University of Alaska
    Anchorage *C, A*
    Southeast *B*

Arizona

American Indian College of the
  Assemblies of God *A*
Arizona Western College *A*
Central Arizona College *A*
Gateway Community College *A*
Glendale Community College *C, A*
International Institute of the Americas
    Tucson *C, A, B*
Paradise Valley Community
  College *A*
Phoenix College *A*
Prescott College *B, M*
Rio Salado College *C, A*
Scottsdale Community College *C, A*
University of Arizona *B*

Arkansas

Arkansas State University
    Beebe *A*
    Mountain Home *A*
Mississippi County Community
  College *C, A*
North Arkansas College *A*
Phillips Community College of the
  University of Arkansas *A*
Pulaski Technical College *A*
South Arkansas Community College *A*
Southeast Arkansas College *C, A*
Southern Arkansas University *A*
University of Arkansas *B*
University of Arkansas
    Community College at
      Batesville *C, A*
    Community College at Hope *C, A*
    Fort Smith *C, A*
    Little Rock *B*
    Monticello *B*
University of Central Arkansas *B*
Williams Baptist College *B*

California

Antelope Valley College *C, A*
Azusa Pacific University *B*
Barstow College *C, A*

Bethany College *B*
Cabrillo College *C, A*
California Polytechnic State University:
  San Luis Obispo *M*
California State University
    Bakersfield *B*
    Dominguez Hills *B*
    Fresno *B, M*
    Fullerton *M*
    Hayward *B*
    Long Beach *B*
    Los Angeles *B, M*
    Monterey Bay *B*
    Sacramento *B, M*
    Stanislaus *B*
Cerritos Community College *A*
Chabot College *A*
Citrus College *A*
Coastline Community College *C, A*
College of Alameda *C, A*
College of Marin: Kentfield *A*
College of the Redwoods *A*
College of the Sequoias *A*
Columbia College *A*
Concordia University *B*
Cuesta College *C, A*
Dominican University of California *B*
Foundation College of San Diego *C, A*
Fresno Pacific University *B*
Gavilan Community College *C, A*
Glendale Community College *A*
Golden Gate University *B, M*
Golden West College *C, A*
Grossmont Community College *C, A*
Humboldt State University *B*
Irvine Valley College *A*
John F. Kennedy University *C*
Laney College *C, A*
Long Beach City College *C, A*
Los Angeles Harbor College *C, A*
Los Angeles Pierce College *C, A*
Los Angeles Southwest College *A*
Los Angeles Trade and Technical
  College *A*
Loyola Marymount University *B, M*
Master's College *B*
Mills College *B*
Modesto Junior College *A*
Monterey Peninsula College *A*
Mount St. Mary's College *B*
Mount San Antonio College *A*
Napa Valley College *A*
National Hispanic University *B*
National University *B, M*
Ohlone College *A*
Orange Coast College *C, A*
Pacific Union College *B*
Palomar College *A*
Riverside Community College *C, A*
St. Mary's College of California *B, M*
San Diego City College *C, A*
San Diego Mesa College *C, A*
San Joaquin Delta College *C, A*
Santa Barbara Business College *C, A*
Santa Barbara Business College
    Bakersfield *C, A*
    Santa Maria *C, A*
Santa Barbara City College *C, A*
Santa Monica College *C, A*
Shasta College *A*
Sierra College *C, A*
Taft College *A*
University of La Verne *B*
University of Redlands *A*
University of San Diego *M*
University of San Francisco *B*
Vanguard University of Southern
  California *B*
Ventura College *C, A*
Victor Valley College *A*
West Valley College *A*
Whittier College *B*

Colorado

Colorado Mountain College
    Alpine Campus *C, A*
    Spring Valley Campus *C, A*
    Timberline Campus *C, A*
Colorado State University
    Pueblo *B*
Community College of Aurora *C, A*
Jones International University *C, B, M*
Morgan Community College *A*
Red Rocks Community College *A*
Regis University *B*
Trinidad State Junior College *A*
University of Denver *B, M*

Connecticut

Briarwood College *A*
Eastern Connecticut State University *B*
Gibbs College *C, A*
Housatonic Community College *C, A*
Quinnipiac University *B, M*
Sacred Heart University *A, B*
Teikyo Post University *A, B*
University of Bridgeport *B, M*
University of Connecticut *B, M, D*
Western Connecticut State University *M*

Delaware

Delaware Technical and Community
  College
    Owens Campus *C, A*
    Stanton/Wilmington Campus *C, A*
    Terry Campus *C, A*
Goldey-Beacom College *M*
Wilmington College *B*

District of Columbia

American University *B, M*
Catholic University of America *B*
Gallaudet University *B*

Florida

Broward Community College *A*
Carlos Albizu University *B*
Flagler College *B*
Florida Institute of Technology *B*
Florida Metropolitan University
    Orlando College North *A, B*
    Tampa College *A, B*
Florida Southern College *B, M*
Herzing College
    Orlando *A*
Hillsborough Community College *A*
International College *B*
Jacksonville University *B*
Lake City Community College *A*
Manatee Community College *A*
Nova Southeastern University *B*
Okaloosa-Walton Community College *A*
Palm Beach Community College *A*
Pensacola Junior College *A*
Polk Community College *A*
St. Leo University *A, B, M*
St. Thomas University *M*
Schiller International University *B*
South Florida Community College *A*
Tallahassee Community College *A*
University of Central Florida *B, M*
University of Florida *B, M, D*
University of North Florida *M*
University of South Florida *B, M*
Webber International University *A, B*

Georgia

Agnes Scott College *B*
Andrew College *A*
Atlanta Metropolitan College *A*
Bainbridge College *A*
Brewton-Parker College *B*
Central Georgia Technical College *A*
Chattahoochee Technical College *A*
Clayton College and State University *B*
Columbus State University *B*
Covenant College *B*
Dalton State College *A*
Darton College *C, A*
Emory University *B*

Floyd College *A*
Fort Valley State University *B*
Gainesville College *A*
Georgia College and State
   University *B, M*
Georgia Military College *A*
Georgia Perimeter College *A*
Georgia Southwestern State University *B*
LaGrange College *B*
Life University *B*
Macon State College *C, A, B*
Oxford College of Emory University *B*
Paine College *B*
Reinhardt College *B*
South Georgia College *C, A*
Thomas University *A, B, M*
Truett-McConnell College *A*
University of Georgia *B*
Waycross College *C*
Young Harris College *A*

Hawaii

Chaminade University of Honolulu *A, B*
Hawaii Business College *A*
Hawaii Pacific University *A, B*
University of Hawaii
   Hilo *B*
   Manoa *B*
   Maui Community College *C, A*

Idaho

College of Southern Idaho *A*
ITT Technical Institute
   Boise *B*
Idaho State University *A*
Lewis-Clark State College *B*

Illinois

Augustana College *B*
Aurora University *B*
Benedictine University *B, T*
Black Hawk College
   East Campus *A*
Bradley University *B*
City Colleges of Chicago
   Malcolm X College *A*
   Olive-Harvey College *C, A*
   Richard J. Daley College *C, A*
Concordia University *B*
De Paul University *B, M*
DeVry University
   Chicago *B*
Eastern Illinois University *B*
Elmhurst College *B*
Eureka College *B*
Gem City College *A*
Greenville College *B*
Illinois Central College *A*
Illinois College *B*
Illinois Institute of Technology *M, D*
Illinois State University *B*
John Wood Community College *A*
Judson College *B*
Kishwaukee College *A*
Lake Forest College *B*
Lake Land College *A*
Lewis University *B*
Lewis and Clark Community College *A*
Lincoln College *A*
Lincoln Land Community College *A*
McKendree College *B*
Midstate College *A*
Moraine Valley Community
   College *C, A*
North Central College *B*
North Park University *B, M*
Northeastern Illinois University *B*
Northern Illinois University *B*
Northwestern University *C, M, D*
Olivet Nazarene University *A, B*
Parkland College *A*
Quincy University *B*
Richland Community College *A*
Rock Valley College *C, A*
Rockford Business College *C, A*
Rockford College *B*

Roosevelt University *B, M*
St. Augustine College *A*
St. Xavier University *B*
Sauk Valley Community College *A*
Shawnee Community College *A*
South Suburban College of Cook
   County *A*
Southern Illinois University
   Carbondale *B, D*
Southern Illinois University
   Edwardsville *B*
Southwestern Illinois College *A*
Spoon River College *A*
Springfield College in Illinois *A*
Trinity Christian College *B*
Trinity International University *B*
University of Chicago *M, D*
University of Illinois
   Chicago *B*
   Springfield *B*
   Urbana-Champaign *B, M, D*
University of St. Francis *B*
Western Illinois University *B*
William Rainey Harper College *C, A*

Indiana

Ancilla College *A*
Anderson University *A*
Ball State University *B*
Bethel College *A*
Calumet College of St. Joseph *C, A, B*
Franklin College *B*
Goshen College *B*
Grace College *B*
Huntington College *B*
Indiana Institute of Technology *A, B, M*
Indiana University
   Bloomington *C, B, M, D*
   Kokomo *A, B, M*
   Northwest *A, B, M*
   South Bend *A, B, M*
   Southeast *A, B, M*
Indiana University-Purdue University
   Fort Wayne *B*
Indiana University-Purdue University
   Indianapolis *C, B, M*
International Business College *B*
Manchester College *A, B*
Marian College *A, B*
Martin University *B*
Oakland City University *A, B*
Purdue University
   Calumet *A, B*
   North Central Campus *C, A, B*
St. Mary-of-the-Woods College *A, B*
University of Indianapolis *A, B*
University of Notre Dame *B*
University of St. Francis *B*
University of Southern Indiana *B, M*
Valparaiso University *B*
Vincennes University *A*

Iowa

American Institute of Business *C, A*
Briar Cliff University *B*
Buena Vista University *B*
Coe College *B*
Des Moines Area Community College *A*
Dordt College *A, B*
Drake University *B*
Ellsworth Community College *A*
Franciscan University *B*
Grand View College *B*
Hawkeye Community College *A*
Iowa Wesleyan College *B*
Loras College *B*
Luther College *B*
Marshalltown Community College *A*
Mount Mercy College *B*
North Iowa Area Community College *A*
Northeast Iowa Community College *A*
St. Ambrose University *B*
Southeastern Community College
   North Campus *A*
   South Campus *A*
Southwestern Community College *A*

University of Northern Iowa *B*
Upper Iowa University *A, B*
Waldorf College *B*

Kansas

Baker University *B, T*
Barclay College *B*
Barton County Community College *A*
Central Christian College *A, B*
Cloud County Community College *A*
Dodge City Community College *A*
Donnelly College *A*
Fort Hays State University *B*
Fort Scott Community College *A*
Garden City Community College *A*
Haskell Indian Nations University *A*
Hesston College *A*
Highland Community College *A*
Hutchinson Community College *A*
Independence Community College *A*
Kansas City Kansas Community
   College *A*
Kansas State University *B*
Kansas Wesleyan University *A, B, M*
McPherson College *T*
MidAmerica Nazarene
   University *A, B, M*
Pittsburg State University *B*
St. Mary College *B*
Seward County Community
   College *C, A*
Southwestern College *B*
University of Kansas *B, M, D*
Washburn University of Topeka *B*

Kentucky

Asbury College *B*
Berea College *B*
Brescia University *A, B, M*
Campbellsville University *A, B*
Kentucky Wesleyan College *B*
Maysville Community College *C, A*
Morehead State University *M*
Murray State University *B*
St. Catharine College *A*
Spalding University *A, B*
Thomas More College *C, A, B, M*
Transylvania University *B*
University of Kentucky *B, M, D*
University of Louisville *M*

Louisiana

Louisiana College *B*
Louisiana State University
   Eunice *A*
Loyola University New Orleans *B, M*
Nicholls State University *B*
Tulane University *C, A*

Maine

Husson College *B, M*
Maine Maritime Academy *B, M*
St. Joseph's College *A*
Thomas College *A*
University of Maine *B*
University of Maine
   Machias *A, B*
   Presque Isle *B*
University of New England *B*
University of Southern Maine *B, M*

Maryland

Allegany College *C, A*
Anne Arundel Community College *C, A*
Bowie State University *B*
Carroll Community College *A*
Cecil Community College *C, A*
Chesapeake College *A*
College of Notre Dame of Maryland *B*
College of Southern Maryland *A*
Community College of Baltimore County
   Catonsville *C, A*
   Dundalk *C, A*
   Essex *C, A*
Hagerstown Community College *A*
Harford Community College *A*
Johns Hopkins University *B, M*

Loyola College in Maryland *B*
Morgan State University *B*
Mount St. Mary's College *B, T*
University of Baltimore *B, M*
University of Maryland
   College Park *B*
   University College *M, D*
Washington College *B*
Wor-Wic Community College *A*

Massachusetts

American International College *B, M*
Anna Maria College *B, M*
Assumption College *B*
Babson College *B*
Bay Path College *B*
Becker College *C, A, B*
Berkshire Community College *A*
Bridgewater State College *B*
Clark University *B, M*
Dean College *C, A*
Fitchburg State College *C*
Greenfield Community College *A*
Hampshire College *B*
Lasell College *M*
Massachusetts Institute of
   Technology *B, M, D*
Merrimack College *B*
Nichols College *M*
Northeastern University *A, B, M*
Regis College *B*
Springfield Technical Community
   College *A*
Suffolk University *B, M*
University of Massachusetts
   Lowell *A*
Western New England College *B*
Westfield State College *B*

Michigan

Andrews University *A*
Baker College
   of Auburn Hills *B*
   of Cadillac *A*
   of Jackson *B*
   of Muskegon *A*
   of Owosso *A*
   of Port Huron *A, B*
Bay de Noc Community College *C*
Calvin College *B*
Central Michigan University *B*
Concordia University *B*
Davenport University
   Midland *A*
Davenport University - Western
   Region *A, B*
Eastern Michigan University *B*
Ferris State University *A, B*
Finlandia University *B*
Glen Oaks Community College *A*
Gogebic Community College *C, A*
Grace Bible College *A, B*
Grand Rapids Community College *C, A*
Hillsdale College *B*
Jackson Community College *C, A*
Kettering University *B*
Kirtland Community College *C*
Lansing Community College *A*
Macomb Community College *C, A*
Madonna University *C, A, B*
Marygrove College *A, B*
Michigan Technological University *A*
Mott Community College *A*
North Central Michigan College *C, A*
Northern Michigan University *A, B, T*
Northwestern Michigan College *A*
Oakland University *B*
Saginaw Valley State University *B*
St. Clair County Community
   College *C, A*
Schoolcraft College *C, A*
Siena Heights University *A, B*
Southwestern Michigan College *C, A*
Walsh College of Accountancy and
   Business Administration *B*
Wayne State University *B, M*

West Shore Community College *A*
Western Michigan University *B*

Minnesota

Augsburg College *B*
Bethel College *B*
Brown College *B*
Capella University *B, M, D*
Concordia College: Moorhead *B*
Crown College *A, B*
Gustavus Adolphus College *B*
Lakeland Medical-Dental Academy *A*
Mesabi Range Community and Technical
College *A*
Minneapolis Community and Technical
College *C, A*
Minnesota State University
Mankato *B*
Moorhead *B*
Minnesota West Community and
Technical College: Worthington
Campus *A*
National American University
St. Paul *A, B*
Normandale Community College *C, A*
Northland Community & Technical
College *A*
Pine Technical College *A*
Rasmussen College
Mankato *A*
Ridgewater College: A Community and
Technical College *A*
Rochester Community and Technical
College *A*
St. Cloud State University *B*
Vermilion Community College *A*
Winona State University *B, M*

Mississippi

Blue Mountain College *B*
Coahoma Community College *A*
Delta State University *B*
Itawamba Community College *A*
Mary Holmes College *A*
Mississippi Gulf Coast Community
College
Perkinston *A*
University of Mississippi *B*

Missouri

Blue River Community College *A*
Central Methodist College *A*
College of the Ozarks *B*
Crowder College *C, A*
Drury University *B*
East Central College *C, A*
Evangel University *B*
Hannibal-LaGrange College *B*
Harris Stowe State College *B*
Jefferson College *A*
Lindenwood University *M*
Longview Community College *A*
Maple Woods Community College *A*
Maryville University of Saint Louis *B, M*
Mineral Area College *C, A*
Missouri Southern State College *A, B*
Northwest Missouri State University *B*
Penn Valley Community College *A*
Rockhurst University *B*
St. Louis Community College
St. Louis Community College at
Forest Park *A*
St. Louis Community College at
Meramec *C, A*
Southeast Missouri State University *B*
Southwest Baptist University *A*
Southwest Missouri State University *B*
Southwest Missouri State University:
West Plains Campus *A*
University of Missouri
Columbia *B, M, D*
Kansas City *B, M*
Rolla *B*
St. Louis *B*
Washington University in St. Louis *B*
Webster University *B, M, D*

Montana

Carroll College *A*
Dawson Community College *A*
Flathead Valley Community
College *A*
Fort Belknap College *A*
Miles Community College *A*
Montana State University
Billings *C, A, B*
Bozeman *B*
Montana Tech of the University of
Montana *A, B*
Rocky Mountain College *B*
University of Montana-Missoula *B, M*
University of Montana: Western *A, B, T*

Nebraska

Bellevue University *B, M*
Clarkson College *B, M*
Creighton University *M*
Hastings College *B*
Little Priest Tribal College *A*
Metropolitan Community College *A*
Mid Plains Community College
Area *C, A*
Midland Lutheran College *B, T*
Nebraska Indian Community College *A*
Nebraska Wesleyan University *B*
Northeast Community College *A*
Southeast Community College
Beatrice Campus *A*
University of Nebraska
Omaha *B*
Western Nebraska Community
College *C, A*

Nevada

Community College of Southern
Nevada *A*
Great Basin College *A*
Truckee Meadows Community
College *C, A*
University of Nevada
Reno *B*
Western Nevada Community
College *C, A*

New Hampshire

College for Lifelong Learning *A*
Daniel Webster College *B*
Franklin Pierce College *B*
Hesser College *A*
Keene State College *B*
New Hampshire Community Technical
College
Berlin *A*
Claremont *A*
Stratham *C, A*
Plymouth State College *M*
St. Anselm College *B*
Southern New Hampshire University *B*
University of New Hampshire *B, M*

New Jersey

Berkeley College *B*
Bloomfield College *B*
Brookdale Community College *A*
Burlington County College *A*
The College of New Jersey *B*
Essex County College *C, A*
Felician College *B*
Gloucester County College *A*
Mercer County Community College *C, A*
Ocean County College *A*
Passaic County Community
College *C, A*
Raritan Valley Community College *C*
Richard Stockton College of New
Jersey *B*
Rowan University *B, T*
St. Peter's College *C*
Salem Community College *A*
Stevens Institute of Technology *B*
Thomas Edison State College *A, B, M*
Union County College *A*
Warren County Community College *C, A*

New Mexico

Clovis Community College *A*
College of Santa Fe *A, B, M*
Eastern New Mexico University: Roswell
Campus *C, A*
Luna Community College *A*
New Mexico Junior College *A*
New Mexico State University *A, B*
New Mexico State University
Alamogordo *A*
Southwestern Indian Polytechnic
Institute *A*
Western New Mexico University *B, M*

New York

Adelphi University *B*
Adirondack Community College *A*
Berkeley College *B*
Berkeley College of New York City *B*
Cayuga County Community
College *C, A*
City University of New York
Baruch College *B, M*
Bronx Community College *A*
City College *B*
College of Staten Island *A, B*
Hostos Community College *A*
Medgar Evers College *A, B*
Queensborough Community
College *A*
College of Aeronautics *B*
College of Mount St. Vincent *A, B*
College of New Rochelle *B, T*
Concordia College *B*
Cornell University *D*
D'Youville College *B*
Excelsior College *A, B*
Finger Lakes Community College *A*
Fordham University *B, M*
Fulton-Montgomery Community
College *A*
Hofstra University *B, M*
Houghton College *B*
Hudson Valley Community College *A*
Iona College *M*
Ithaca College *B, M*
Long Island University
Southampton College *B*
Manhattan College *B*
Maria College *A*
Marymount College of Fordham
University *A, B*
Medaille College *B*
Mercy College *C*
Metropolitan College of New York *B, M*
Monroe Community College *A*
Nazareth College of Rochester *B, M*
New York University *A, B, M, D*
Niagara County Community College *A*
Niagara University *A, B*
North Country Community College *A*
Olean Business Institute *C, A*
Onondaga Community College *A*
Orange County Community College *A*
Pace University *C, A, B*
Pace University:
Pleasantville/Briarcliff *C, A, B*
Paul Smith's College *B*
Roberts Wesleyan College *B*
Rochester Institute of
Technology *A, B, M*
Rockland Community College *A*
St. John's University *A*
St. Joseph's College *C, B*
St. Joseph's College: Suffolk Campus *C*
Schenectady County Community
College *A*
Skidmore College *B*

State University of New York
Albany *B, M*
College at Buffalo *B*
College at Cortland *B*
College at Geneseo *B*
College at Plattsburgh *B*
College of Agriculture and
Technology at Cobleskill *A*
College of Agriculture and
Technology at Morrisville *A*
Empire State College *A, B*
Institute of Technology at
Utica/Rome *B, M*
Maritime College *B*
Purchase *C*
Suffolk County Community College *A*
Syracuse University *B*
Tompkins-Cortland Community
College *A*
Touro College *A, B*
Ulster County Community College *C, A*
Utica School of Commerce *A*
Wells College *B*
Westchester Community College *C*

North Carolina

Alamance Community College *C, A*
Appalachian State University *B*
Blue Ridge Community College *A*
Brevard College *B*
Campbell University *A, B, M*
Carteret Community College *A*
Fayetteville Technical Community
College *A*
Gardner-Webb University *B, M*
Johnson C. Smith University *B*
Lenoir-Rhyne College *B, M*
Louisburg College *A*
Mars Hill College *B*
North Carolina Agricultural and
Technical State University *B*
Pfeiffer University *B*
Piedmont Community College *A*
Queens University of Charlotte *B*
St. Andrews Presbyterian College *B*
Surry Community College *A*
Wake Forest University *B*
Wake Technical Community College *A*
Wayne Community College *A*
Wingate University *B*

North Dakota

Bismarck State College *A*
Dickinson State University *B*
Mayville State University *A*
North Dakota State College of Science *A*
Trinity Bible College *A, B*

Ohio

Ashland University *A, B, M*
Bluffton College *B*
Bowling Green State University *B*
Bowling Green State University:
Firelands College *A*
Bryant & Stratton College
Cleveland West *A*
Willoughby Hills *A*
Circleville Bible College *A*
Clark State Community College *A*
Cuyahoga Community College
Eastern Campus *A*
Metropolitan Campus *A*
Western Campus *A*
David N. Myers College *B*
Davis College *A*
Defiance College *A, B, T*
Franklin University *A, B, M*
James A. Rhodes State College *A*
Jefferson Community College *C, A*
Kent State University *C, A*
Kent State University
Ashtabula Regional Campus *C, A*
East Liverpool Regional Campus *A*
Stark Campus *B*
Trumbull Campus *A*
Lorain County Community College *A*

Lourdes College C, A, B
Marion Technical College C, A
Miami University
   Middletown Campus A
   Oxford Campus B
Muskingum College B
North Central State College A
Northwest State Community College A
Ohio State University
   Columbus Campus B, M, D
   Lima Campus B
Ohio University B
Ohio University
   Lancaster Campus A
   Zanesville Campus B
Ohio Valley College of Technology A
Otterbein College B
Shawnee State University B
Sinclair Community College C, A
Southern State Community College A
Southwestern College of Business
   Vine Street Campus A
Stark State College of Technology A
Tiffin University A
Union Institute & University B
University of Cincinnati
   Clermont College C, A
   Raymond Walters College C, A
University of Dayton B
University of Findlay A, B
University of Toledo A, B
Urbana University A, B
Walsh University A, B
Washington State Community College A
Wright State University M
Wright State University: Lake
   Campus C, A
Xavier University A, B
Youngstown State University A, B, M

Oklahoma

Bacone College A
Carl Albert State College A
East Central University B
Eastern Oklahoma State College A
Northeastern Oklahoma Agricultural and
   Mechanical College A
Northeastern State University B
Northern Oklahoma College A
Oklahoma Baptist University B
Oklahoma Christian University of
   Science and Arts B, M
Oklahoma City Community College A
Oklahoma City University B, M
Oklahoma State University B, M, D
Oklahoma State University
   Okmulgee A
Oklahoma Wesleyan University B
Rogers State University A
Rose State College C, A
St. Gregory's University A, B
Southern Nazarene University B, M
Southwestern Oklahoma State
   University B, M
Tulsa Community College A
University of Central Oklahoma B
University of Science and Arts of
   Oklahoma B, T
Western Oklahoma State College A

Oregon

Concordia University B
Eastern Oregon University B, T
George Fox University B
Linfield College B
Marylhurst University B, M
Mount Hood Community College C, A
Portland Community College A
Portland State University B, M
Rogue Community College C, A
Southern Oregon University B
Umpqua Community College A
University of Oregon B, M, D
Western Baptist College B
Western Oregon University B

Pennsylvania

Academy of Medical Arts and
   Business C, A
Arcadia University B
Bucks County Community College A
Cambria-Rowe Business College A
Career Training Academy C
Carlow College B
Community College of Philadelphia A
DeSales University B, M
Delaware Valley College A
Drexel University B
DuBois Business College A
Duquesne University B
Education Direct: Center for Degree
   Studies A
Harrisburg Area Community College C
Immaculata University C
Indiana University of Pennsylvania M
Juniata College B
Keystone College A, B
La Salle University B
Lackawanna College A
Lebanon Valley College of
   Pennsylvania C
Lehigh University B
Manor College A
Marywood University C
Mercyhurst College A, B
Montgomery County Community
   College C, A
Northampton County Area Community
   College A
PJA School A
Penn Commercial, Inc. A
Penn State
   Abington A, B
   Altoona A, B
   Beaver A, B
   Berks A, B
   Delaware County A, B
   Dubois A, B
   Erie, The Behrend College A
   Fayette A, B
   Harrisburg C, A
   Hazleton A, B
   Lehigh Valley A, B
   McKeesport A, B
   Mont Alto A, B
   New Kensington B
   Schuylkill - Capital College A, B
   Shenango A, B
   University Park C, A
   Worthington Scranton A, B
   York A, B
Philadelphia University B, M
Reading Area Community College C, A
Rosemont College B
St. Joseph's University A, B, M
Seton Hill University B
Shippensburg University of
   Pennsylvania M, T
South Hills School of Business &
   Technology A
Temple University B, M
University of Pittsburgh B
University of Pittsburgh
   Johnstown C, B
   Titusville A
Waynesburg College A, B
West Chester University of
   Pennsylvania M
Wilson College B
York College of Pennsylvania A, B

Puerto Rico

Bayamon Central University A, B, M
Huertas Junior College A
ICPR Junior College A
Inter American University of Puerto Rico
   Barranquitas Campus B
   Fajardo Campus A, B
Pontifical Catholic University of Puerto
   Rico B, M
Universidad Metropolitana B

Universidad Politecnica de Puerto
   Rico B
Universidad del Este C, A, B
University of Puerto Rico
   Bayamon University College A, B
   Cayey University College B
   Mayaguez Campus M
   Rio Piedras Campus B, M

Rhode Island

Bryant College M
Community College of Rhode Island A
Providence College C, A
Rhode Island College B
University of Rhode Island M, D

South Carolina

Charleston Southern University B, M
Converse College A
Denmark Technical College A
Forrest Junior College A
Midlands Technical College C
North Greenville College B
Orangeburg-Calhoun Technical
   College A
Piedmont Technical College C, A
Southern Wesleyan University A
Technical College of the
   Lowcountry C, A
Trident Technical College A
University of South Carolina
   Aiken B
Williamsburg Technical College A
York Technical College A

South Dakota

Augustana College B
Black Hills State University B
Dakota State University A, B
Dakota Wesleyan University A, B
Northern State University B
Sinte Gleska University A
University of Sioux Falls M

Tennessee

Austin Peay State University B
Belmont University B
Bryan College A, B
Carson-Newman College B, T
Christian Brothers University B
Columbia State Community College A
Freed-Hardeman University B
Lambuth University B
Lane College B
Lee University B
Roane State Community College A
Southwest Tennessee Community
   College A
Tennessee Technological
   University B, M
University of Tennessee
   Knoxville B
   Martin M
Walters State Community College A

Texas

Amarillo College C, A
Amberton University B, M
Angelina College C, A
Austin College B
Austin Community College A
Baylor University B
Blinn College A
Brazosport College A
Cedar Valley College A
Central Texas College C, A
Cisco Junior College C, A
Clarendon College A
Coastal Bend College A
College of the Mainland A
Concordia University at Austin B
Dallas Baptist University B
East Texas Baptist University B
Eastfield College A
El Paso Community College C, A
Frank Phillips College C, A
Grayson County College A

Hallmark Institute of Technology A
Howard College C, A
Howard Payne University B, T
Kilgore College C, A
Lamar State College at Orange A
Lamar University B, M
Laredo Community College A
LeTourneau University B
Lon Morris College A
Lubbock Christian University B, T
McLennan Community College C, A
McMurry University B
Midland College C, A
Midwestern State University B
North Central Texas College A
North Harris Montgomery Community
   College District A
Odessa College A
Our Lady of the Lake University of San
   Antonio M
Panola College A
Paris Junior College A
St. Mary's University B
Sam Houston State University B
San Jacinto College
   Central Campus C, A
South Plains College C
Southern Methodist University B, M
Southwestern Assemblies of God
   University A, B
Southwestern University B
Stephen F. Austin State University B
Sul Ross State University B
Tarleton State University B, T
Tarrant County College A
Temple College C, A
Texarkana College A
Texas A&M University
   Commerce B, M
   Kingsville B
   Texarkana B
Texas Christian University M
Texas Lutheran University B
Texas Southern University B
Tyler Junior College A
University of Houston M, D
University of Houston
   Clear Lake B
   Downtown B
   Victoria M
University of Mary Hardin-Baylor B
University of North Texas B, M, D
University of Texas
   Austin B, D
   Brownsville B
   Dallas B, M
   El Paso M
   Pan American B, M
   San Antonio M
   Tyler B
University of the Incarnate Word B, M
West Texas A&M University B
Western Texas College A

Utah

Brigham Young University B
Dixie State College of Utah A
LDS Business College A
Salt Lake Community College A
Snow College C, A
University of Utah B, M, D
Utah State University B
Utah Valley State College C, A, B
Westminster College B

Vermont

Castleton State College A, B
Champlain College C, A, B
College of St. Joseph in Vermont B
Community College of Vermont C, A
Johnson State College B
Southern Vermont College A
Vermont Technical College A

Virginia

Averett University B

Blue Ridge Community College *C*
Bluefield College *B*
Danville Community College *A*
George Mason University *B*
Hollins University *B*
J. Sargeant Reynolds Community
  College *A*
Longwood University *B*
Marymount University *M*
Mountain Empire Community College *A*
Norfolk State University *B*
Piedmont Virginia Community
  College *C, A*
Richard Bland College *A*
Shenandoah University *C*
Southwest Virginia Community
  College *A*
Tidewater Tech *A*
University of Virginia *B*
Virginia Commonwealth University *M*
Virginia Polytechnic Institute and State
  University *D*
Virginia Wesleyan College *B*
Virginia Western Community College *A*

Washington

Everett Community College *C, A*
Henry Cogswell College *B*
Heritage College *C, B*
Lower Columbia College *C, A*
North Seattle Community College *A*
Northwest College *B*
Olympic College *C, A*
South Seattle Community College *A*
Spokane Community College *C, A*
Spokane Falls Community College *C, A*
Walla Walla College *A*
Western Washington University *B*

West Virginia

Alderson-Broaddus College *A, B*
Bethany College *B*
Bluefield State College *A*
Concord College *B*
Davis and Elkins College *A, B*
Eastern West Virginia Community and
  Technical College *A*
Fairmont State College *A, B*
Glenville State College *A*
Huntington Junior College *A*
Marshall University *M*
Mountain State University *A, B*
Potomac State College of West Virginia
  University *A*
Southern West Virginia Community and
  Technical College *A*
Valley College of Technology *A*
West Liberty State College *B*
West Virginia Northern Community
  College *A*
West Virginia State College *A, B*
West Virginia University *M*
West Virginia University Institute of
  Technology *B*
Wheeling Jesuit University *M*

Wisconsin

Bryant & Stratton College *A*
Cardinal Stritch University *A, B*
Carthage College *B*
Chippewa Valley Technical College *A*
Concordia University Wisconsin *B*
Edgewood College *B, M*
Fox Valley Technical College *A*
Marian College of Fond du Lac *B, M*
Mid-State Technical College *A*
Milwaukee School of Engineering *B, M*
Northland College *B*
St. Norbert College *B*

University of Wisconsin
  Eau Claire *B*
  Green Bay *B*
  La Crosse *B*
  Madison *B, M, D*
  Parkside *B*
  Platteville *B*
  Richland *C*
  Superior *B*
Viterbo University *B*
Western Wisconsin Technical College *A*

Wyoming

Casper College *A*
Central Wyoming College *A*
Eastern Wyoming College *A*
Laramie County Community College *A*
Sheridan College *A*
Western Wyoming Community
  College *A*

Business/managerial economics

Alabama

Alabama State University *B*
Auburn University *B, M*
Auburn University at Montgomery *B*
Huntingdon College *B*
Jacksonville State University *B*
Talladega College *B*
University of Alabama *B, M, D*
University of Alabama
  Birmingham *B*
University of North Alabama *B*

Alaska

University of Alaska
  Fairbanks *B*

Arizona

Northern Arizona University *B*
University of Arizona *B*

Arkansas

Arkansas State University *B*
Hendrix College *B*
University of Arkansas *B*
University of Arkansas
  Little Rock *B*
University of Central Arkansas *B*

California

Barstow College *A*
California Institute of Technology *B*
California Polytechnic State University:
  San Luis Obispo *B, M*
California State University
  Fullerton *B*
  Hayward *B, M*
  Long Beach *B*
  Northridge *B*
Chapman University *B*
Claremont McKenna College *B*
College of the Redwoods *A*
East Los Angeles College *A*
Mills College *B*
San Joaquin Delta College *A*
Santa Clara University *B*
Santiago Canyon College *A*
University of California
  Los Angeles *B*
  Riverside *B*
  Santa Barbara *B, M, D*
  Santa Cruz *B*
University of La Verne *B*
University of Redlands *B*
University of San Diego *B*
Ventura College *A*

Colorado

University of Denver *B*

Connecticut

Albertus Magnus College *B*
Quinnipiac University *B*
Southern Connecticut State University *B*

University of New Haven *B*

Delaware

University of Delaware *M, D*

Florida

Barry University *B*
Florida Agricultural and Mechanical
  University *B*
Jacksonville University *B*
Stetson University *B*
University of Central Florida *B, M*
University of Miami *B, M, D*
University of North Florida *B*
University of South Florida *B, M*
University of Tampa *B*
University of West Florida *B*

Georgia

Berry College *B*
Clark Atlanta University *B*
Columbus State University *B*
Georgia College and State University *B*
Georgia Institute of Technology *B, M*
Georgia Southern University *B*
Georgia State University *M*
Kennesaw State University *B, M*
Mercer University *B*
Morehouse College *B*
Oglethorpe University *B*
Shorter College *B*
South Georgia College *A*
State University of West Georgia *B*
University of Georgia *B, M, D*
Valdosta State University *B*

Hawaii

Hawaii Pacific University *A, B*

Idaho

Boise State University *B*
University of Idaho *B*

Illinois

Benedictine University *B*
Bradley University *B*
De Paul University *B, M*
Lewis University *B*
Loyola University of Chicago *B*
Millikin University *B*
Monmouth College *B, T*
North Central College *B*
Northwestern University *M, D*
Rockford College *B*
Roosevelt University *B*
Southern Illinois University
  Carbondale *B*
Southern Illinois University
  Edwardsville *B*
University of Chicago *M, D*
Western Illinois University *B*
Wheaton College *B*

Indiana

Anderson University *B*
Huntington College *B*
Indiana University-Purdue University
  Fort Wayne *B*
Indiana Wesleyan University *B*
Taylor University *B*
University of Evansville *B*
University of Indianapolis *B*

Iowa

Buena Vista University *B*
Drake University *B*
Luther College *B*
North Iowa Area Community
  College *C, A*
Northwestern College *B*
Simpson College *B*
University of Iowa *B, D*

Kansas

Bethany College *B*
Central Christian College *A, B*
Fort Scott Community College *A*
Washburn University of Topeka *B*

Kentucky

Morehead State University *B*
Murray State University *B*
University of Kentucky *B*
University of Louisville *B*

Louisiana

Grambling State University *B*
Louisiana State University
  Shreveport *B*
Louisiana State University and
  Agricultural and Mechanical
  College *B*
Louisiana Tech University *B*
Loyola University New Orleans *B*
Nicholls State University *B*
Southern University
  New Orleans *B*
Southern University and Agricultural and
  Mechanical College *B*
University of Louisiana at Lafayette *B*
University of Louisiana at Monroe *B*
University of New Orleans *B, M, D*

Maine

Husson College *B*
St. Joseph's College *B*
University of Maine *B*
University of Maine
  Farmington *B*

Maryland

Allegany College *C, A*
University of Baltimore *B*

Massachusetts

American International College *B*
Babson College *B*
Bentley College *B*
Boston College *B*
Gordon College *B*
Nichols College *B*
Stonehill College *B*
Suffolk University *M*

Michigan

Andrews University *B, M*
Eastern Michigan University *B*
Grand Valley State University *B*
Michigan Technological
  University *B, M, T*
Northwood University *A, B*
Saginaw Valley State University *B, M*
Spring Arbor University *B*
Western Michigan University *B*

Minnesota

Winona State University *B*

Mississippi

Mississippi State University *B, M*
University of Mississippi *B, M, D*
University of Southern Mississippi *B, M*

Missouri

Lincoln University *B*
Northwest Missouri State University *B*
St. Louis University *B, D*
Southeast Missouri State University *B*
Washington University in St. Louis *B*
William Jewell College *B*
William Woods University *B*

Montana

Carroll College *B*
Montana State University
  Billings *T*
Rocky Mountain College *B*

Nebraska

Hastings College *B*
University of Nebraska
  Lincoln *B*
  Omaha *B, M*

Nevada

University of Nevada
  Las Vegas *B, M*
  Reno *B, M*

New Hampshire
St. Anselm College *B*
Southern New Hampshire University *B*

New Jersey
Bloomfield College *B*
Fairleigh Dickinson University
    College at Florham *B, M*
    Metropolitan Campus *B, M*
Monmouth University *B*
Rider University *B*
St. Peter's College *B*
Seton Hall University *B*
William Paterson University of New
    Jersey *B*

New Mexico
Eastern New Mexico University *B*
New Mexico State University *B, M*
Western New Mexico University *B*

New York
Canisius College *B*
City University of New York
    Baruch College *B*
    Brooklyn College *B*
    Hunter College *B, M*
Dominican College of Blauvelt *B*
Elmira College *B*
Fordham University *B, M*
Hofstra University *B*
Ithaca College *B*
Manhattan College *B*
Marist College *B*
Metropolitan College of New York *B*
New York University *B, M, D*
Pace University *C, B, M*
Pace University:
    Pleasantville/Briarcliff *C, B, M*
State University of New York
    Buffalo *D*
    College at Oneonta *B, M*
    College at Potsdam *B*
Touro College *B*
Utica College *B*
Wagner College *B*

North Carolina
Appalachian State University *B*
Barton College *B*
Greensboro College *B*
Meredith College *B*
North Carolina Agricultural and
    Technical State University *B*
North Carolina State University *B*
University of North Carolina
    Charlotte *B, M*
    Greensboro *B, M*
    Wilmington *B*
Winston-Salem State University *B*

North Dakota
University of North Dakota *B*

Ohio
Cleveland State University *B*
College of Wooster *B*
David N. Myers College *B*
Kent State University *B, M, D*
Kent State University
    Stark Campus *B*
Miami University
    Oxford Campus *B*
Muskingum College *B*
Notre Dame College *B*
Ohio State University
    Columbus Campus *B*
Ohio University *B*
Ohio Wesleyan University *B*
Otterbein College *B*
Tiffin University *B*
University of Dayton *B*
Wittenberg University *B*
Wright State University *B, M*
Xavier University *B, M*
Youngstown State University *B*

Oklahoma
East Central University *B*
Oklahoma City University *B, M*
Oklahoma State University *B*
Tulsa Community College *A*
University of Central Oklahoma *B*
University of Oklahoma *B*

Oregon
Eastern Oregon University *B*
George Fox University *B*

Pennsylvania
Bloomsburg University of
    Pennsylvania *B*
California University of Pennsylvania *B*
Carnegie Mellon University *B, D*
Drexel University *B*
Grove City College *B*
Immaculata University *B*
La Salle University *B*
Lehigh University *B, M, D*
Messiah College *B*
Penn State
    Abington *B*
    Altoona *B*
    Beaver *B*
    Berks *B*
    Delaware County *B*
    Dubois *B*
    Erie, The Behrend College *B*
    Fayette *B*
    Hazleton *B*
    Lehigh Valley *B*
    McKeesport *B*
    Mont Alto *B*
    New Kensington *B*
    Schuylkill - Capital College *B*
    Shenango *B*
    University Park *C, B*
    Wilkes-Barre *B*
    Worthington Scranton *B*
    York *B*
Robert Morris University *B*
Rosemont College *B*
Seton Hill University *B*
University of Pittsburgh
    Johnstown *B*
Villanova University *B*
West Chester University of
    Pennsylvania *B, M*
Widener University *B*
York College of Pennsylvania *B*

Puerto Rico
Inter American University of Puerto Rico
    Bayamon Campus *B*
Pontifical Catholic University of Puerto
    Rico *B*
Universidad Metropolitana *B*
University of Puerto Rico
    Bayamon University College *A, B*
    Rio Piedras Campus *B, M*

Rhode Island
Providence College *B*
Rhode Island College *B*

South Carolina
Forrest Junior College *A*
Francis Marion University *B*
Limestone College *B*
South Carolina State University *B*
University of South Carolina *B*
University of South Carolina
    Aiken *B*
Wofford College *B*

South Dakota
Northern State University *A*
University of South Dakota *B*

Tennessee
Belmont University *B*
Carson-Newman College *B*
East Tennessee State University *B*
Middle Tennessee State University *B*
Rhodes College *B*

Tennessee State University *B*
Tennessee Technological University *B*
Union University *B*
University of Memphis *B*
University of Tennessee
    Knoxville *M, D*
    Martin *B*

Texas
Baylor University *B, M*
Dallas Baptist University *B*
Hardin-Simmons University *B*
Houston Baptist University *B*
Lamar University *B*
McMurry University *B*
Midland College *A*
Sam Houston State University *B*
Southwest Texas State University *B*
Stephen F. Austin State University *B*
Texas A&M International University *B*
Texas A&M University
    Commerce *B*
    Kingsville *B*
Tyler Junior College *A*
University of Houston *B*
University of Mary Hardin-Baylor *B*
University of North Texas *B*
University of Texas
    Arlington *B, D*
    El Paso *B, M*
    Pan American *B*
    San Antonio *B, M*
    Tyler *B*
    of the Permian Basin *B*
West Texas A&M University *B*

Utah
Snow College *C, A*
Southern Utah University *B*
Utah Valley State College *B*
Weber State University *B*
Westminster College *B*

Virginia
Hampden-Sydney College *B*
Hampton University *B*
James Madison University *B*
Mary Baldwin College *B*
Old Dominion University *B*
Randolph-Macon College *B*
Southwest Virginia Community
    College *A*
Virginia Commonwealth
    University *B, M*
Virginia Polytechnic Institute and State
    University *B*
Virginia State University *B, M*

Washington
Gonzaga University *B*
Olympic College *A*
Seattle Pacific University *B*
Seattle University *B*
Washington State University *B*

West Virginia
Concord College *B*
Marshall University *B*
Potomac State College of West Virginia
    University *A*
West Liberty State College *B*
West Virginia University *B, M, D*

Wisconsin
Beloit College *B*
Marquette University *B*
University of Wisconsin
    Superior *B*
    Whitewater *B*
Wisconsin Lutheran College *B*

Wyoming
University of Wyoming *B, M, D*

Alabama
Harry M. Ayers State Technical
    College *C*
Lawson State Community College *C*
Northwest-Shoals Community College *C*

California
Long Beach City College *C, A*

Florida
Palm Beach Community College *C*

Indiana
Ivy Tech State College
    Central Indiana *C, A*
    Northcentral *A*
    Northwest *C, A*
    Southcentral *C, A*
    Southwest *C, A*

Minnesota
Minneapolis Community and Technical
    College *C, A*
Minnesota State College - Southeast
    Technical *C*
St. Paul College - A Community and
    Technical College *C*

North Carolina
Fayetteville Technical Community
    College *C*
Tri-County Community College *C*

Utah
Utah Valley State College *C, A*

Wisconsin
Milwaukee Area Technical College *C*

CAD/CADD drafting/design technology

Alabama
Northwest-Shoals Community College *A*

Alaska
University of Alaska
    Fairbanks *C*

Arkansas
University of Arkansas
    Fort Smith *C, A*

California
ITT Technical Institute
    San Bernardino *A, B*
Ohlone College *A*
Taft College *A*

Connecticut
Naugatuck Valley Community
    College *C, A*

Florida
ITT Technical Institute
    Ft. Lauderdale *A*
    Maitland *A*

Georgia
Southwest Georgia Technical College *C*

Illinois
Heartland Community College *C, A*

Indiana
ITT Technical Institute
    Fort Wayne *A*
    Indianapolis *A*

Iowa
Hamilton Technical College *A*

Kentucky
Hopkinsville Community College *C*

Maryland
Community College of Baltimore County
Catonsville *C, A*
Dundalk *C, A*

Massachusetts
ITT Technical Institute
Norwood *A*

Michigan
Baker College
of Muskegon *A*
ITT Technical Institute
Troy *A*
Mott Community College *C, A*

Minnesota
Minnesota State College - Southeast
Technical *C, A*

Missouri
ITT Technical Institute
Earth City *A*
Missouri Southern State College *C, A, B*
Ozarks Technical Community
College *C, A*

New York
College of Aeronautics *B*
Niagara County Community
College *C, A*
State University of New York
College of Agriculture and
Technology at Morrisville *A*
College of Technology at Canton *C*

Ohio
Bryant & Stratton College *A*
Central Ohio Technical College *C, A*
ITT Technical Institute
Dayton *A*
Youngstown *A*
Owens Community College
Findlay Campus *A*
Toledo *A*
University of Cincinnati
Clermont College *A*
Youngstown State University *A*

Oklahoma
Northeastern Oklahoma Agricultural and
Mechanical College *C, A*
Platt College
Tulsa *C*

Pennsylvania
Community College of Allegheny
County *A*
Delaware County Community
College *C, A*
ITT Technical Institute
Bensalem *A*

South Carolina
York Technical College *A*

Tennessee
Pellissippi State Technical Community
College *A*

Texas
Collin County Community College
District *C, A*
Eastfield College *C, A*
ITT Technical Institute
Austin *A*
Houston North *A*
Sam Houston State University *B*

Utah
ITT Technical Institute
Murray *A*

Virginia
Norfolk State University *B*
Piedmont Virginia Community
College *C, A*
Thomas Nelson Community College *A*

Washington
Clark College *C*
Everett Community College *C, A*
ITT Technical Institute
Seattle *A*
Renton Technical College *C*

Wisconsin
ITT Technical Institute
Green Bay *A*

Canadian history

Missouri
Truman State University *D*

Canadian studies

Indiana
Franklin College *B*

New York
St. Lawrence University *B*
State University of New York
College at Plattsburgh *B*

Ohio
University of Akron *C*

Vermont
Marlboro College *B*
University of Vermont *B*

Washington
University of Washington *B*

Cardiopulmonary technology

North Carolina
Johnston Community College *C, A*

Cardiovascular science

New York
Long Island University
C. W. Post Campus *M*

Ohio
Case Western Reserve University *M*

South Carolina
Medical University of South Carolina *D*

Cardiovascular technology

Alabama
Community College of the Air Force *A*

Arkansas
University of Arkansas
for Medical Sciences *A*

California
Grossmont Community College *C, A*
Orange Coast College *C, A*

Florida
Barry University *B*
Broward Community College *A*
Hillsborough Community College *C*

Illinois
Benedictine University *M*
William Rainey Harper College *A*

Indiana
Indiana University-Purdue University
Indianapolis *C*

Louisiana
Southern University
Shreveport *A*

Maryland
Howard Community College *C, A*

Minnesota
St. Cloud Technical College *C, A*

Nebraska
Nebraska Methodist College of Nursing
and Allied Health *A, B*

New York
Molloy College *A*

North Carolina
Caldwell Community College and
Technical Institute *C, A*
Central Piedmont Community College *A*

Ohio
Cuyahoga Community College
Eastern Campus *C, A*
Western Campus *C, A*
University of Toledo *A*

Pennsylvania
Community College of Allegheny
County *A*
Gwynedd-Mercy College *A*
Lackawanna College *A*
Pennsylvania College of Technology *B*

South Carolina
Medical University of South Carolina *B*
University of South Carolina *B*

South Dakota
Southeast Technical Institute *A*

Tennessee
Northeast State Technical Community
College *A*

Texas
El Centro College *A*

Washington
Spokane Community College *A*

Caribbean studies

California
Pitzer College *B*

Florida
Florida State University *B*
Rollins College *B*

Georgia
Emory University *B*

Maryland
Johns Hopkins University *B*

Michigan
University of Michigan *B*

New Hampshire
Dartmouth College *B*

New Jersey
Rutgers, The State University of New
Jersey
New Brunswick Regional
Campus *B*
Newark Regional Campus *B*
William Paterson University of New
Jersey *B*

New York
City University of New York
Brooklyn College *B*
City College *B*
Hofstra University *B*
New York University *M*
State University of New York
Albany *B, M*
Binghamton *B*
Buffalo *M*

Carpentry

Alabama
Alabama Southern Community
College *A*
Bishop State Community College *C*
Central Alabama Community College *C*
Gadsden State Community College *C*
Harry M. Ayers State Technical
College *C*
Lawson State Community College *C*
Northwest-Shoals Community College *C*
Reid State Technical College *C*
Shelton State Community College *C*
Southern Union State Community
College *A*
Wallace Community College: Sparks
Campus *C*

Alaska
University of Alaska
Southeast *A*

Arizona
Central Arizona College *C*
Eastern Arizona College *C*
Gateway Community College *C, A*

Arkansas
North Arkansas College *C*

California
Bakersfield College *A*
College of the Sequoias *C, A*
Feather River College *C, A*
Laney College *C, A*
Long Beach City College *C, A*
Los Angeles Trade and Technical
College *C, A*
Palomar College *C, A*
San Joaquin Delta College *C, A*
Santa Rosa Junior College *C*
Santiago Canyon College *A*
Shasta College *A*
Sierra College *C, A*
Victor Valley College *A*

Colorado
Arapahoe Community College *C*
Community College of Aurora *A*
Red Rocks Community College *C, A*
Trinidad State Junior College *C*

Florida
Indian River Community College *C*
Lake-Sumter Community College *C*
Palm Beach Community College *C*
South Florida Community College *C*

Georgia
Albany Technical College *C*
Columbus Technical College *C*
West Georgia Technical College *C*

Hawaii
University of Hawaii
Hawaii Community College *C, A*
Honolulu Community College *C, A*
Kauai Community College *C, A*
Maui Community College *A*

Idaho
Idaho State University *A*
North Idaho College *C, A*

Illinois
Black Hawk College *C, A*
John A. Logan College *A*
Southwestern Illinois College *C, A*
Triton College *C, A*

Indiana

Ivy Tech State College
  Central Indiana *C, A*
  Eastcentral *C, A*
  Kokomo *C*
  Lafayette *A*
  Northcentral *A*
  Northeast *C*
  Northwest *C, A*
  Southcentral *C, A*
  Southwest *C, A*
  Wabash Valley *C, A*
Oakland City University *C*
Vincennes University *A*

Iowa

Des Moines Area Community College *A*
Ellsworth Community College *C, A*
Indian Hills Community College *C*
Iowa Central Community College *C*
Kirkwood Community College *C*
Northeast Iowa Community College *C*
Northwest Iowa Community College *C*
Southwestern Community College *C*
Western Iowa Tech Community
  College *C*

Kansas

Hutchinson Community College *C, A*

Kentucky

Somerset Community College *C*

Louisiana

Delgado Community College *C*
Nunez Community College *C*

Maryland

Cecil Community College *C, A*

Michigan

Bay de Noc Community College *C*
Davenport University
  Midland *C, A*
Lansing Community College *C, A*
Northern Michigan University *C*
Oakland Community College *C, A*

Minnesota

Alexandria Technical College *C*
Hennepin Technical College *C, A*
Lake Superior College: A Community
  and Technical College *C, A*
Mesabi Range Community and Technical
  College *A*
Minneapolis Community and Technical
  College *C*
Minnesota State College - Southeast
  Technical *C, A*
Ridgewater College: A Community and
  Technical College *C*
Riverland Community College: A
  Technical and Community College *C*
Rochester Community and Technical
  College *C*
St. Cloud Technical College *C*
St. Paul College - A Community and
  Technical College *C*

Mississippi

Coahoma Community College *C*
Mississippi Gulf Coast Community
  College
    Perkinston *C*
Pearl River Community College *C, A*

Missouri

Ranken Technical College *A*
St. Louis Community College
  St. Louis Community College at
    Forest Park *A*

Montana

Miles Community College *A*
Salish Kootenai College *C*

Nebraska

Central Community College *C*

Mid Plains Community College
  Area *C, A*
Nebraska Indian Community College *A*

Nevada

Truckee Meadows Community
  College *C, A*
Western Nevada Community College *A*

New Mexico

Albuquerque Technical-Vocational
  Institute *C*
San Juan College *C, A*

New York

Fulton-Montgomery Community
  College *A*
Hudson Valley Community College *A*
Mohawk Valley Community College *C*
State University of New York
  College of Agriculture and
    Technology at Morrisville *A*
  College of Technology at Alfred *A*
  College of Technology at
    Delhi *C, A*

North Carolina

Alamance Community College *C*
Asheville Buncombe Technical
  Community College *C*
Bladen Community College *C*
Blue Ridge Community College *C*
Cape Fear Community College *C*
Cleveland Community College *C*
College of the Albemarle *C*
Davidson County Community College *C*
Fayetteville Technical Community
  College *C*
Forsyth Technical Community College *C*
Guilford Technical Community
  College *C*
Piedmont Community College *C*
Rowan-Cabarrus Community College *C*
Vance-Granville Community College *C*

North Dakota

Bismarck State College *C, A*
North Dakota State College of Science *A*

Oklahoma

Rose State College *A*

Oregon

Clackamas Community College *C*
Linn-Benton Community College *A*

Pennsylvania

Community College of Allegheny
  County *C*
Delaware County Community College *C*
Pennsylvania College of Technology *C*
Williamson Free School of Mechanical
  Trades *C*

Puerto Rico

Inter American University of Puerto Rico
  San German Campus *C*

South Carolina

Technical College of the Lowcountry *C*

South Dakota

Western Dakota Technical Institute *C*

Texas

Austin Community College *C*
Houston Community College System *C*
Howard College *C*
Laredo Community College *C*
North Lake College *A*
Odessa College *C, A*
Paris Junior College *A*
St. Philip's College *A*

Utah

College of Eastern Utah *C, A*
Salt Lake Community College *C, A*
Southern Utah University *A*
Utah Valley State College *A*

Virginia

J. Sargeant Reynolds Community
  College *C*

Washington

Edmonds Community College *C*
Grays Harbor College *C, A*
Green River Community College *A*
Renton Technical College *C*
Seattle Central Community College *C, A*
Spokane Community College *C, A*
Walla Walla Community College *C, A*
Wenatchee Valley College *C*

Wisconsin

Chippewa Valley Technical College *C*
Lac Courte Oreilles Ojibwa Community
  College *C*
Milwaukee Area Technical College *C*
Western Wisconsin Technical College *C*
Wisconsin Indianhead Technical
  College *C*

Cartography

California

California State University
  Long Beach *C*

Missouri

Southwest Missouri State University *B*

Montana

University of Montana-Missoula *B, M*

Nevada

Western Nevada Community College *A*

Ohio

Ohio University *B*
University of Akron *C, B*

Oklahoma

East Central University *B*

Pennsylvania

Penn State
  Schuylkill - Capital College *B*

Texas

Houston Community College
  System *C, A*
Southwest Texas State University *B, M*
Temple College *C, A*
Texas A&M University *B*

Cell physiology

Kansas

University of Kansas *M, D*

Ohio

Case Western Reserve University *D*

Cellular biology/histology

Alabama

Huntingdon College *B*
University of Alabama
  Birmingham *D*

Arizona

Northern Arizona University *B*
University of Arizona *B*

Arkansas

University of Arkansas *M, D*

California

California Institute of Technology *D*
California State University
  Fresno *B*
  Long Beach *B*
  Northridge *B*
Pomona College *B*
San Francisco State University *B, M*
Stanford University *D*

University of California
  Davis *B, D*
  Irvine *D*
  Los Angeles *B, M, D*
  Riverside *M, D*
  San Diego *B*
  Santa Barbara *B, M, D*
  Santa Cruz *B*
University of Southern California *M, D*

Colorado

Fort Lewis College *B*

Connecticut

Connecticut College *B*
Quinnipiac University *M*
University of Connecticut *B, M, D*
Yale University *M, D*

District of Columbia

Catholic University of America *M, D*
Georgetown University *D*

Florida

University of Miami *D*

Georgia

Medical College of Georgia *D*
University of Georgia *B, M, D*

Illinois

Loyola University of Chicago *M, D*
Northwestern University *B, M, D*
University of Chicago *M, D*
University of Illinois
  Urbana-Champaign *B, D*

Indiana

Ball State University *B*
University of Indianapolis *B*

Iowa

Iowa State University *M, D*
University of Iowa *M, D*

Louisiana

Tulane University *B, M, D*

Maine

Colby College *B*
University of Maine *B, M, D*

Maryland

University of Maryland
  Baltimore *M, D*
  Baltimore County *D*
  College Park *M, D*

Massachusetts

Boston University *D*
Brandeis University *M, D*
Bridgewater State College *B*
Hampshire College *B*
Harvard College *B*
Tufts University *D*

Michigan

University of Michigan *B, M, D*

Minnesota

Southwest State University *B*
University of Minnesota
  Duluth *B*
  Twin Cities *B, M, D*
Winona State University *B*

Missouri

Southwest Missouri State
  University *B, M*
University of Missouri
  Kansas City *M*
Washington University in St. Louis *D*

Nevada

University of Nevada
  Reno *M, D*

New Hampshire

Dartmouth College *B*
University of New Hampshire *B*

New Jersey
Rowan University *B*
Rutgers, The State University of New
Jersey
New Brunswick Regional
Campus *B, M, D*

New York
Bard College *B*
New York University *M, D*
State University of New York
Albany *M, D*
Buffalo *M, D*
College at Plattsburgh *B*
College of Environmental Science
and Forestry *B, M, D*
University of Rochester *B*
Yeshiva University *M, D*

North Carolina
Duke University *M, D*
East Carolina University *D*
Methodist College *A, B*
University of North Carolina
Chapel Hill *M, D*

North Dakota
North Dakota State University *D*

Ohio
Case Western Reserve University *D*
Kent State University *M, D*
Ohio State University
Columbus Campus *M, D*
Ohio University *B*

Oklahoma
Northeastern State University *B*
University of Oklahoma *D*

Oregon
Oregon Health Sciences University *M, D*

Pennsylvania
Juniata College *B*
Lock Haven University of
Pennsylvania *B*
Temple University *M*
University of Pennsylvania *D*
University of the Sciences in
Philadelphia *M*
West Chester University of
Pennsylvania *B*

Rhode Island
Brown University *B, M, D*

South Carolina
Medical University of South
Carolina *M, D*

Tennessee
Vanderbilt University *M, D*

Texas
Texas A&M University *B*
Texas A&M University
Commerce *B*
University of Texas
Health Science Center at San
Antonio *M, D*
Houston Health Science
Center *M, D*
Medical Branch at Galveston *M, D*
San Antonio *D*

Utah
Brigham Young University *M, D*

Vermont
Bennington College *B*
Johnson State College *B*
Marlboro College *B*
University of Vermont *M, D*

Virginia
Marymount University *B*
University of Virginia *D*

Washington
University of Washington *M, D*

Western Washington University *B*

Wisconsin
Beloit College *B*
Marquette University *D, T*
University of Wisconsin
Madison *M*
Superior *B*

Cellular/anatomical biology

California
University of Southern California *M, D*

Colorado
University of Colorado
Health Sciences Center *D*

Illinois
Finch University of Health Sciences/The
Chicago Medical School *M, D*

Iowa
University of Iowa *M, D*

Nebraska
University of Nebraska
Medical Center *M, D*

New York
State University of New York
Buffalo *M, D*

Texas
University of Texas
Houston Health Science
Center *M, D*

Cellular/molecular biology

California
University of California
Riverside *M, D*
University of Southern California *M, D*

Colorado
University of Colorado
Boulder *B, M, D*

Florida
Florida Institute of Technology *M*
University of Florida *M, D*

Hawaii
University of Hawaii
Manoa *M, D*

Illinois
Finch University of Health Sciences/The
Chicago Medical School *D*
University of Illinois
Urbana-Champaign *B, D*

Indiana
Indiana University
Bloomington *D*

Iowa
Drake University *B*

Kansas
University of Kansas *B, M*

Maryland
University of Maryland
College Park *M, D*

Massachusetts
University of Massachusetts
Amherst *M, D*

Michigan
Grand Valley State University *B*
Michigan State University *M, D*

Missouri
St. Louis University *M, D*

Montana
University of Montana-Missoula *B*

New York
State University of New York
Buffalo *M, D*
Stony Brook *D*

Ohio
Kent State University *M, D*

Oregon
Oregon State University *D*

Pennsylvania
Bucknell University *B*
Drexel University *M, D*

Puerto Rico
Universidad Metropolitana *B*

Texas
Texas A&M University *B*
Texas Tech University *B*
University of Texas
Austin *M, D*
Dallas *B, M, D*
Houston Health Science
Center *M, D*

Vermont
University of Vermont *M, D*

Wisconsin
Beloit College *B*

Central/Middle/Eastern European studies

California
California State University
Fullerton *B*

Connecticut
Connecticut College *B*
Wesleyan University *B*

Florida
Florida State University *B, M*

Georgia
Emory University *B*
Oxford College of Emory University *B*

Iowa
University of Iowa *B*

Massachusetts
Amherst College *B*
Harvard College *B*
Tufts University *B, M*
Wellesley College *B*

Michigan
University of Michigan *B*

Minnesota
Augsburg College *B*
Hamline University *B*

New Jersey
Rutgers, The State University of New
Jersey
New Brunswick Regional
Campus *B*

New York
Bard College *B*
Columbia University
Columbia College *B*
State University of New York
Albany *B*

Ohio
Ohio State University
Columbus Campus *B, M*

Oregon
Portland State University *B*

Pennsylvania
California University of Pennsylvania *B*
La Salle University *B, M*
University of Pittsburgh *C*

Utah
Brigham Young University *B*

Vermont
Marlboro College *B*
Middlebury College *B*
University of Vermont *B*

Washington
University of Washington *B*

Ceramic sciences/ engineering

Missouri
University of Missouri
Rolla *B, M, D*

New Jersey
Rutgers, The State University of New
Jersey
Camden Regional Campus *B*
New Brunswick Regional
Campus *B, M, D*
Newark Regional Campus *B*

New Mexico
New Mexico Institute of Mining and
Technology *B*

New York
Alfred University *B, M, D*

Ohio
Ohio State University
Columbus Campus *B*

Pennsylvania
Lock Haven University of
Pennsylvania *B*

South Carolina
Clemson University *B, M, D*

Washington
University of Washington *B*

Ceramics

Arizona
Arizona State University *B, M*

California
California College of Arts and
Crafts *B, M*
California State University
Fullerton *B, M*
Hayward *B*
Long Beach *B, M*
Northridge *B, M*
Chabot College *A*
De Anza College *C, A*
Glendale Community College *C*
Grossmont Community College *A*
Laney College *A*
Monterey Peninsula College *A*
Ohlone College *C*
Palomar College *A*
Santa Rosa Junior College *C*
Ventura College *A*

Colorado
Colorado State University *B*

Connecticut
University of Hartford *B, M*

District of Columbia
George Washington University *M*

Florida
University of Miami *B*

Georgia
LaGrange College *B*
University of Georgia *B*

Illinois
Lincoln College *A*

Richland Community College *A*
Rockford College *B*
School of the Art Institute of
Chicago *B, M*

Indiana
Ball State University *B*
Vincennes University *A*

Iowa
University of Iowa *B, M*

Kansas
Allen County Community College *A*
Pratt Community College *A*
Seward County Community College *A*
University of Kansas *B, M*

Maine
Maine College of Art *B*

Maryland
Maryland Institute College of Art *B*

Massachusetts
Art Institute of Boston at Lesley
University *A, B*
Massachusetts College of Art *B, M*
School of the Museum of Fine Arts *B, M*
Simon's Rock College of Bard *B*
University of Massachusetts
Dartmouth *B, M*

Michigan
Aquinas College *B*
College for Creative Studies *B*
Finlandia University *B*
Grand Valley State University *B*
Northern Michigan University *B*
Oakland Community College *C, A*
Siena Heights University *B*
University of Michigan *B*

Minnesota
Minnesota State University
Mankato *B*
Moorhead *B*

Missouri
Kansas City Art Institute *B*
Lindenwood University *M*
Washington University in St. Louis *B, M*

New Jersey
Rowan University *B*

New York
Alfred University *B*
Hofstra University *B*
Parsons School of Design *C, A, B, T*
Pratt Institute *B, M*
Rochester Institute of
Technology *A, B, M*
State University of New York
College at Fredonia *B*
College at Potsdam *B*
New Paltz *B, M*
Syracuse University *B, M*

North Carolina
Haywood Community College *A*

North Dakota
University of North Dakota *M*

Ohio
Bowling Green State University *B, M*
Cleveland Institute of Art *B*
Columbus College of Art and Design *B*
Ohio State University
Columbus Campus *B*
Ohio University *B, M*
Shawnee State University *B*
Sinclair Community College *C*
University of Akron *B*
University of Findlay *B*
Wittenberg University *B*

Oklahoma
University of Oklahoma *B*

Oregon
University of Oregon *B, M*

Pennsylvania
Arcadia University *B*
Immaculata University *A*
Marywood University *C, B, M*
Mercyhurst College *B*
Seton Hill University *B*
Temple University *B, M*

Puerto Rico
Inter American University of Puerto Rico
San German Campus *B, M*

Rhode Island
Providence College *B*
Rhode Island College *B*
Rhode Island School of Design *B, M*

Tennessee
Memphis College of Art *B, M*
Tennessee Technological University *B*

Texas
McMurry University *B*
Sam Houston State University *M*
Texas A&M University
Commerce *B, M*
Texas Woman's University *B, M*
University of Dallas *M, T*
University of Houston *B, M*
University of North Texas *B, M*
University of Texas
Arlington *B*
El Paso *B*
San Antonio *B, M*
Western Texas College *A*

Utah
Brigham Young University *B, M*
Dixie State College of Utah *A*

Vermont
Bennington College *B, M*
Marlboro College *B*

Washington
University of Washington *B, M*
Western Washington University *B*

West Virginia
West Virginia State College *B*
West Virginia Wesleyan College *B*

Wisconsin
University of Wisconsin
Madison *B*

Chef training

Alaska
University of Alaska
Fairbanks *C, A*

Arizona
Estrella Mountain Community
College *C, A*

California
Art Institute
of California - Orange County *A*
Santa Rosa Junior College *C*

Florida
New England Institute of Technology *A*

Illinois
Black Hawk College *C*
City Colleges of Chicago
Kennedy-King College *C*
College of DuPage *C, A*
College of Lake County *C, A*
Kaskaskia College *C, A*
Rend Lake College *C, A*

Kentucky
Jefferson Community College *A*

Maryland
Allegany College *A*

Michigan
Baker College
of Muskegon *A*
Grand Rapids Community College *A*
Mott Community College *A*
Northern Michigan University *C*
Northwestern Michigan College *A*
Oakland Community College *A*

Minnesota
Art Institutes International
Minnesota *C, A*
Hennepin Technical College *C, A*
St. Paul College - A Community and
Technical College *C, A*

New Jersey
Hudson County Community College *A*

New Mexico
Albuquerque Technical-Vocational
Institute *C, A*

New York
Erie Community College
City Campus *A*
Schenectady County Community
College *C*

Ohio
Hocking Technical College *A*
University of Akron *C, A*

Pennsylvania
Community College of Allegheny
County *C, A*
Community College of Beaver
County *C, A*
Indiana University of Pennsylvania *C*
Northampton County Area Community
College *C, A*
Pennsylvania College of
Technology *C, A*

Puerto Rico
Universidad del Este *C*

Texas
Austin Community College *C, A*
Houston Community College System *C*
Odessa College *C*
St. Philip's College *C, A*

Washington
Clark College *C, A*
Edmonds Community College *C, A*
Seattle Central Community College *C, A*
South Seattle Community College *C, A*

Wisconsin
Fox Valley Technical College *A*
Milwaukee Area Technical College *A*

Chemical engineering

Alabama
Auburn University *B, M, D*
Northeast Alabama Community
College *A*
Tuskegee University *B*
University of Alabama *B, M, D*
University of Alabama
Huntsville *B, M*
University of South Alabama *B, M*

Arizona
Arizona State University *B, M, D*
University of Arizona *B, M, D*

Arkansas
University of Arkansas *B, M*

California
California Institute of
Technology *B, M, D*

California State Polytechnic University:
Pomona *B*
California State University
Long Beach *B*
Northridge *B, M*
San Jose State University *B, M*
Stanford University *B, M, D*
University of California
Berkeley *B, M, D*
Davis *B*
Irvine *B, M, D*
Los Angeles *B, M, D*
Riverside *B, M, D*
San Diego *B, M, D*
Santa Barbara *B, M, D*
University of Southern
California *B, M, D*

Colorado
Colorado School of Mines *B, M, D*
Colorado State University *B, M, D*
National Technological University *M*
University of Colorado
Boulder *B, M, D*

Connecticut
Fairfield University *B*
University of Connecticut *B, M, D*
University of Hartford *B*
University of New Haven *A, B*
Yale University *B, M, D*

Delaware
University of Delaware *B, M, D*

District of Columbia
Howard University *B, M*

Florida
Florida Agricultural and Mechanical
University *B, M, D*
Florida Institute of Technology *B, M, D*
Florida International University *B*
Florida State University *B, M, D*
Miami-Dade Community College *A*
Pensacola Junior College *A*
University of Florida *B, M, D*
University of South Florida *B, M, D*

Georgia
Georgia Institute of Technology *B, M, D*
Southern Polytechnic State University *M*

Idaho
Brigham Young University - Idaho *A*
North Idaho College *A*
University of Idaho *B, M, D*

Illinois
Dominican University *B*
Illinois Institute of Technology *B, M, D*
Northwestern University *B, M, D*
University of Illinois
Chicago *B, M, D*
Urbana-Champaign *B, M, D*

Indiana
Purdue University *B, M, D*
Rose-Hulman Institute of
Technology *B, M*
Tri-State University *B*
University of Notre Dame *B, M, D*
Vincennes University *A*

Iowa
Iowa State University *B, M, D*
University of Iowa *B, M, D*

Kansas
Independence Community College *A*
Kansas State University *B, M, D*
University of Kansas *B, M, D*

Kentucky
University of Kentucky *B, M, D*
University of Louisville *B, M, D*

Louisiana
Louisiana State University and
   Agricultural and Mechanical
   College *B, M, D*
Louisiana Tech University *B*
Tulane University *B, M, D*
University of Louisiana at
   Lafayette *B, M*

Maine
University of Maine *B, M, D*

Maryland
Johns Hopkins University *B, M, D*
University of Maryland
   Baltimore County *B, M, D*
   College Park *B, M, D*

Massachusetts
Harvard College *B*
Massachusetts Institute of
   Technology *B, M, D*
Northeastern University *B, M, D*
Smith College *B*
Tufts University *B, M, D*
University of Massachusetts
   Amherst *B, M, D*
   Lowell *B, M*
Worcester Polytechnic Institute *B, M, D*

Michigan
Calvin College *B*
Michigan State University *B, M, D*
Michigan Technological
   University *B, M, D, T*
University of Michigan *B, M, D*
Wayne State University *B, M, D*
Western Michigan University *B*

Minnesota
University of Minnesota
   Duluth *B*
   Twin Cities *B, M, D*
Vermilion Community College *A*
Winona State University *B*

Mississippi
Mississippi State University *B, M, D*
University of Mississippi *B*

Missouri
University of Missouri
   Columbia *B, M, D*
   Rolla *B, M, D*
Washington University in St.
   Louis *B, M, D*

Montana
Montana State University
   Bozeman *B, M*

Nebraska
University of Nebraska
   Lincoln *B, M*

Nevada
University of Nevada
   Reno *B, M, D*

New Hampshire
University of New Hampshire *B, M, D*

New Jersey
Essex County College *A*
New Jersey Institute of
   Technology *B, M, D*
Princeton University *B, M, D*
Rowan University *B*
Rutgers, The State University of New
   Jersey
   Camden Regional Campus *B*
   New Brunswick Regional
      Campus *B, M, D*
   Newark Regional Campus *B*
Stevens Institute of Technology *B, M, D*

New Mexico
New Mexico Institute of Mining and
   Technology *B*
New Mexico State University *B, M*

University of New Mexico *B, M*

New York
City University of New York
   Bronx Community College *A*
   City College *B, M, D*
Clarkson University *B, M, D*
Columbia University
   Fu Foundation School of
      Engineering and Applied
      Science *B, M, D*
Cornell University *B, M, D*
Finger Lakes Community College *A*
Manhattan College *B, M*
New York University *B*
Polytechnic University *B, M, D*
Rensselaer Polytechnic Institute *B, M, D*
State University of New York
   Buffalo *B, M, D*
   College of Environmental Science
      and Forestry *B, M, D*
   Stony Brook *B*
Syracuse University *B, M, D*
United States Military Academy *B*
University of Rochester *B, M*

North Carolina
Cape Fear Community College *A*
Elon University *B*
North Carolina Agricultural and
   Technical State University *B*
North Carolina State University *B, M, D*

North Dakota
University of North Dakota *B, M*

Ohio
Case Western Reserve
   University *B, M, D*
Cleveland State University *B, M, D*
Ohio State University
   Columbus Campus *B, M, D*
Ohio University *B, M, D*
University of Akron *C, B, M, D*
University of Cincinnati *B, M, D*
University of Dayton *B, M*
University of Toledo *B, M*
Youngstown State University *B, M*

Oklahoma
Oklahoma State University *B, M, D*
University of Oklahoma *B, M, D*
University of Tulsa *B, M, D*

Oregon
Oregon State University *B, M, D*

Pennsylvania
Bucknell University *B, M*
Carnegie Mellon University *B, M, D*
Drexel University *B, M, D*
Geneva College *B*
Gettysburg College *B*
Lafayette College *B*
Lehigh University *B, M, D*
Lock Haven University of
   Pennsylvania *B*
Penn State
   Abington *B*
   Altoona *B*
   Beaver *B*
   Berks *B*
   Delaware County *B*
   Dubois *B*
   Fayette *B*
   Hazleton *B*
   Lehigh Valley *B*
   McKeesport *B*
   Mont Alto *B*
   New Kensington *B*
   Schuylkill - Capital College *B*
   Shenango *B*
   University Park *B, M, D*
   Wilkes-Barre *B*
   Worthington Scranton *B*
   York *B*
University of Pennsylvania *B, M, D*
University of Pittsburgh *B, M, D*

Villanova University *B, M*
Widener University *B, M*

Puerto Rico
University of Puerto Rico
   Mayaguez Campus *B, M, D*
   Ponce *A*

Rhode Island
Brown University *B, M, D*
University of Rhode Island *B, M, D*

South Carolina
Clemson University *B, M, D*
University of South Carolina *B, M, D*

South Dakota
South Dakota School of Mines and
   Technology *B, M*

Tennessee
Christian Brothers University *B*
Tennessee Technological
   University *B, M, D*
University of Tennessee
   Knoxville *B, M, D*
Vanderbilt University *B, M, D*

Texas
Houston Baptist University *B*
Kilgore College *A*
Lamar University *B*
Prairie View A&M University *B*
Rice University *B, M, D*
Texas A&M University *B, M, D*
Texas A&M University
   Kingsville *B, M*
Texas Tech University *B, M, D*
University of Houston *B, M, D*
University of Texas
   Austin *B, M, D*

Utah
Brigham Young University *B, M, D*
Snow College *A*
Southern Utah University *A*
University of Utah *B, M, D*

Virginia
Hampton University *B*
University of Virginia *B, M, D*
Virginia Commonwealth University *B*
Virginia Polytechnic Institute and State
   University *B, M, D*
Washington and Lee University *B*

Washington
Lower Columbia College *A*
University of Washington *B, M, D*
Washington State University *B, M, D*

West Virginia
West Virginia University *B, M, D*
West Virginia University Institute of
   Technology *B*

Wisconsin
University of Wisconsin
   Madison *B, M, D*

Wyoming
University of Wyoming *B, M, D*

Chemical physics

Colorado
University of Colorado
   Boulder *D*

Indiana
University of Notre Dame *M*

Michigan
Saginaw Valley State University *B*

Rhode Island
Brown University *B*

Tennessee
Maryville College *B*

Union University *B*

Utah
University of Utah *M, D*

Chemical technology

California
Ohlone College *C*

Florida
Pensacola Junior College *A*

Illinois
College of Lake County *A*

Indiana
Indiana University-Purdue University
   Fort Wayne *A*

Maryland
Community College of Baltimore County
   Catonsville *A*
   Dundalk *A*
   Essex *A*

Michigan
Grand Rapids Community College *A*
Lawrence Technological University *A*

New York
Mohawk Valley Community College *A*

Ohio
University of Akron *A*

Pennsylvania
Community College of Allegheny
   County *A*
Delaware County Community College *C*

Puerto Rico
University of Puerto Rico
   Humacao *A*

Rhode Island
Community College of Rhode
   Island *C, A*

Texas
Houston Community College
   System *C, A*

Washington
Edmonds Community College *A*

Chemistry

Alabama
Alabama Agricultural and Mechanical
   University *B*
Alabama State University *B*
Athens State University *B*
Auburn University *B, M, D*
Birmingham-Southern College *B, T*
Chattahoochee Valley Community
   College *A*
Huntingdon College *B, T*
Jacksonville State University *B*
James H. Faulkner State Community
   College *A*
Judson College *B*
Miles College *B*
Northeast Alabama Community
   College *A*
Oakwood College *B*
Samford University *B*
Southern Union State Community
   College *A*
Spring Hill College *B, T*
Talladega College *B*
Troy State University *B*
Tuskegee University *B, M*
University of Alabama *B, M, D*
University of Alabama
   Birmingham *B, M, D*
   Huntsville *B, M*
University of Mobile *B, T*

University of Montevallo B, T
University of North Alabama B
University of South Alabama B
University of West Alabama B, T

Alaska
University of Alaska
   Anchorage B
   Fairbanks B, M

Arizona
Arizona State University B, M, D
Arizona Western College A
Central Arizona College A
Cochise College A
Eastern Arizona College A
Northern Arizona University B, M, T
Phoenix College A
South Mountain Community College A
University of Arizona B, M, D

Arkansas
Arkansas State University B, M
Arkansas Tech University B
Harding University B
Henderson State University B
Hendrix College B
John Brown University B
Lyon College B
Ouachita Baptist University B
Philander Smith College B
Phillips Community College of the
   University of Arkansas A
Southern Arkansas University B
University of Arkansas B, M, D
University of Arkansas
   Little Rock B, M
   Monticello B
   Pine Bluff B
University of Central Arkansas B
University of the Ozarks B

California
Azusa Pacific University B
Bakersfield College A
Cabrillo College A
California Institute of Technology B, D
California Polytechnic State University:
   San Luis Obispo B, M
California State Polytechnic University:
   Pomona B, M
California State University
   Bakersfield B
   Chico C, B
   Dominguez Hills B
   Fresno B, M
   Fullerton B, M
   Hayward B, M
   Long Beach B, M
   Los Angeles B, M
   Northridge B, M
   Sacramento B, M
   San Bernardino B
   San Marcos B
   Stanislaus B
Cerritos Community College A
Chapman University B
Citrus College A
Claremont McKenna College B
College of the Siskiyous A
Columbia College A
Contra Costa College A
Cuesta College C, A
De Anza College A
East Los Angeles College A
Foothill College A
Gavilan Community College A
Glendale Community College A
Golden West College A
Grossmont Community College C, A
Harvey Mudd College B
Humboldt State University B
Irvine Valley College A
La Sierra University B
Las Positas College A
Los Angeles Southwest College A
Los Medanos College A

Loyola Marymount University B
Mills College B
MiraCosta College A
Monterey Peninsula College A
Moorpark College A
Mount St. Mary's College B
Occidental College B
Orange Coast College A
Pacific Union College B
Palomar College C, A
Pepperdine University B
Pitzer College B
Point Loma Nazarene University B
Pomona College B
St. Mary's College of California B
San Diego City College A
San Diego Mesa College C, A
San Diego State University B, M, D
San Francisco State University B, M
San Joaquin Delta College A
San Jose State University B, M
Santa Barbara City College A
Santa Clara University B
Santa Monica College A
Santa Rosa Junior College A
Santiago Canyon College A
Scripps College B
Sierra College A
Sonoma State University B
Southwestern College A
Stanford University B, M, D
University of California
   Berkeley B, D
   Davis B, M, D
   Irvine B, M, D
   Los Angeles B, M, D
   Riverside B, M, D
   San Diego B, D
   Santa Barbara B, M, D
   Santa Cruz B, M, D
University of La Verne B
University of Redlands B
University of San Diego B
University of San Francisco B, M
University of Southern
   California B, M, D
University of the Pacific B, M, D
Vanguard University of Southern
   California B
Ventura College A
West Valley College A
Whittier College B

Colorado
Colorado College B
Colorado Mountain College
   Spring Valley Campus A
Colorado School of Mines B, M, D
Colorado State University B, M, D
Colorado State University
   Pueblo B, T
Fort Lewis College B
Metropolitan State College of Denver B
Otero Junior College A
Red Rocks Community College A
Regis University B
Trinidad State Junior College A
United States Air Force Academy B
University of Colorado
   Boulder B, M, D
   Colorado Springs B
   Denver B, M
University of Denver B, M, D
University of Northern
   Colorado B, M, D, T

Connecticut
Albertus Magnus College B
Central Connecticut State University B
Connecticut College B
Fairfield University B
Quinnipiac University B
Sacred Heart University B, M
St. Joseph College B, M, T
Southern Connecticut State
   University B, M

Trinity College B
University of Connecticut B, M, D
University of Hartford B
University of New Haven A, B
Wesleyan University B, M, D
Western Connecticut State University B
Yale University B, M, D

Delaware
Delaware State University B, M
University of Delaware B, M, D

District of Columbia
American University B, M, D
Catholic University of
   America B, M, D, T
Gallaudet University B
George Washington University B, M, D
Georgetown University B, M, D
Howard University B, M, D
Trinity College B
University of the District of Columbia B

Florida
Barry University B
Bethune-Cookman College B
Broward Community College A
Eckerd College B
Florida Agricultural and Mechanical
   University B, M
Florida Atlantic University B, M, D
Florida Institute of Technology B, M, D
Florida International University B, M, D
Florida Southern College B
Florida State University B, M, D
Gulf Coast Community College A
Indian River Community College A
Jacksonville University B
Manatee Community College A
Miami-Dade Community College A
New College of Florida B
Okaloosa-Walton Community College A
Palm Beach Community College A
Pensacola Junior College A
Polk Community College A
Rollins College B
St. Thomas University B
Santa Fe Community College A
South Florida Community College A
Stetson University B
University of Central Florida B, M
University of Florida B, M, D
University of Miami B, M, D
University of North Florida B
University of South Florida B, M, D
University of Tampa A, B, T
University of West Florida B

Georgia
Abraham Baldwin Agricultural
   College A
Agnes Scott College B
Albany State University B
Armstrong Atlantic State University B, T
Atlanta Metropolitan College A
Augusta State University B
Berry College B, T
Clark Atlanta University B, M, D
Clayton College and State University A
Columbus State University B
Covenant College B
Dalton State College A
Darton College A
East Georgia College A
Emory University B, D
Floyd College A
Fort Valley State University B
Gainesville College A
Georgia College and State University B
Georgia Institute of Technology B, M, D
Georgia Perimeter College A
Georgia Southern University B
Georgia Southwestern State University B
Georgia State University B, M, D
Gordon College A
Kennesaw State University B
LaGrange College B

Macon State College A
Mercer University B
Middle Georgia College A
Morehouse College B
Morris Brown College B
North Georgia College & State
   University B
Oglethorpe University B
Oxford College of Emory University B
Paine College B
Piedmont College B
Savannah State University B
Shorter College B
South Georgia College A
Spelman College B
State University of West Georgia B
University of Georgia B, M, D
Valdosta State University B
Waycross College A
Wesleyan College B
Young Harris College A

Hawaii
Brigham Young University-Hawaii B
University of Hawaii
   Hilo B
   Manoa B, M, D

Idaho
Albertson College of Idaho B
Boise State University B, T
Brigham Young University - Idaho A
College of Southern Idaho A
Idaho State University A, B, M
Lewis-Clark State College B
North Idaho College A
Northwest Nazarene University B
University of Idaho B, M, D

Illinois
Augustana College B, T
Aurora University B
Benedictine University B, T
Black Hawk College
   East Campus A
Blackburn College B
Bradley University B, M, T
Chicago State University B, T
City Colleges of Chicago
   Harold Washington College A
   Kennedy-King College A
   Olive-Harvey College A
Concordia University B, T
Danville Area Community College A
De Paul University B, M, T
Dominican University B
Eastern Illinois University B, M, T
Elmhurst College B, T
Eureka College B
Governors State University B, T
Greenville College B, T
Illinois Central College A
Illinois College B
Illinois Institute of Technology B, M, D
Illinois State University B, M, T
Illinois Valley Community College A
Illinois Wesleyan University B
John A. Logan College A
Joliet Junior College A
Judson College B
Kishwaukee College A
Knox College B
Lake Forest College B
Lewis University B, T
Lincoln College A
Lincoln Land Community College A
Loyola University of Chicago B, M, D
MacMurray College B
McKendree College B
Millikin University B, T
Monmouth College B
North Central College B, T
North Park University B
Northeastern Illinois University B, M
Northern Illinois University B, M, D, T
Northwestern University B, M, D

Olivet Nazarene University *B, T*
Parkland College *A*
Principia College *B*
Quincy University *B*
Rockford College *B*
Roosevelt University *B*
St. Xavier University *B*
Sauk Valley Community College *A*
South Suburban College of Cook
County *A*
Southern Illinois University
Carbondale *B, M, D*
Southern Illinois University
Edwardsville *B, M, T*
Southwestern Illinois College *A*
Trinity Christian College *B, T*
Trinity International University *B*
Triton College *A*
University of Chicago *B, M, D*
University of Illinois
Chicago *B, M, D*
Springfield *B*
Urbana-Champaign *B, M, D*
Western Illinois University *B, M*
Wheaton College *B, T*

Indiana

Ancilla College *A*
Anderson University *B*
Ball State University *B, M*
Bethel College *A, B*
Butler University *B*
DePauw University *B*
Earlham College *B*
Franklin College *B*
Goshen College *B*
Grace College *B*
Hanover College *B*
Huntington College *B*
Indiana State University *B, M, T*
Indiana University
Bloomington *B, M, D*
Kokomo *B*
Northwest *B*
South Bend *A, B*
Southeast *B*
Indiana University-Purdue University
Fort Wayne *A, B, M, T*
Indiana University-Purdue University
Indianapolis *A, B, M*
Indiana Wesleyan University *A, B*
Manchester College *B, T*
Marian College *B, T*
Purdue University *B, M, D*
Purdue University
Calumet *B*
Rose-Hulman Institute of Technology *B*
St. Joseph's College *B*
Saint Mary's College *B, T*
Taylor University *B*
Tri-State University *B*
University of Evansville *B*
University of Indianapolis *A, B*
University of Notre Dame *B, M, D*
University of St. Francis *B*
University of Southern Indiana *B, T*
Valparaiso University *B*
Vincennes University *A*
Wabash College *B*

Iowa

Briar Cliff University *B*
Buena Vista University *B, T*
Central College *B, T*
Clarke College *B, T*
Coe College *B*
Cornell College *B, T*
Dordt College *B*
Drake University *B*
Ellsworth Community College *A*
Franciscan University *T*
Graceland University *B, T*
Grinnell College *B*
Iowa State University *B, M, D*
Iowa Wesleyan College *B*
Loras College *B*

Luther College *B*
Maharishi University of Management *B*
Morningside College *B*
North Iowa Area Community College *A*
Northwestern College *B, T*
St. Ambrose University *B*
Simpson College *B*
University of Iowa *B, M, D, T*
University of Northern Iowa *B, M*
Upper Iowa University *B*
Waldorf College *A*
Wartburg College *B, T*

Kansas

Allen County Community College *A*
Baker University *B, T*
Barton County Community College *A*
Benedictine College *B*
Bethany College *B, T*
Bethel College *B*
Butler County Community College *A*
Central Christian College *A*
Dodge City Community College *A*
Emporia State University *B*
Fort Hays State University *B*
Fort Scott Community College *A*
Friends University *B*
Garden City Community College *A*
Independence Community College *A*
Kansas City Kansas Community
College *A*
Kansas State University *B, M, D*
Kansas Wesleyan University *B, T*
McPherson College *B, T*
MidAmerica Nazarene University *B*
Newman University *B*
Pittsburg State University *B, M, T*
Pratt Community College *A*
St. Mary College *B*
Seward County Community College *A*
Southwestern College *B*
Tabor College *B*
University of Kansas *B, M, D*
Washburn University of Topeka *B*
Wichita State University *B, M, D, T*

Kentucky

Asbury College *B*
Bellarmine University *B, T*
Berea College *B, T*
Brescia University *B*
Campbellsville University *B*
Centre College *B*
Cumberland College *B, T*
Georgetown College *B, T*
Kentucky Wesleyan College *B, T*
Lindsey Wilson College *A*
Morehead State University *B*
Murray State University *B, M, T*
Pikeville College *B*
Thomas More College *A, B*
Transylvania University *B*
Union College *B*
University of Kentucky *B, M, D*
University of Louisville *B, M, D*

Louisiana

Centenary College of Louisiana *B, T*
Dillard University *B*
Grambling State University *B*
Louisiana College *B*
Louisiana State University
Shreveport *B*
Louisiana State University and
Agricultural and Mechanical
College *B, M, D*
Louisiana Tech University *B, M*
Loyola University New Orleans *B*
McNeese State University *B, M*
Nicholls State University *B*
Northwestern State University *B*
Our Lady of Holy Cross College *T*
Southeastern Louisiana University *B*
Southern University
New Orleans *B*
Shreveport *A*

Southern University and Agricultural and
Mechanical College *B, M*
Tulane University *B, M, D*
University of Louisiana at Lafayette *B*
University of Louisiana at Monroe *B, M*
University of New Orleans *B, M, D*
Xavier University of Louisiana *B*

Maine

Bates College *B*
Bowdoin College *B*
Colby College *B*
St. Joseph's College *B*
University of Maine *B, M, D*
University of New England *B*
University of Southern Maine *B*

Maryland

Allegany College *A*
Cecil Community College *A*
College of Notre Dame of Maryland *B*
Columbia Union College *B*
Community College of Baltimore County
Catonsville *A*
Dundalk *A*
Essex *A*
Coppin State College *B*
Frederick Community College *A*
Frostburg State University *B, T*
Goucher College *B*
Harford Community College *A*
Hood College *B, T*
Johns Hopkins University *B, M, D*
Loyola College in Maryland *B*
McDaniel College *B*
Morgan State University *B*
Mount St. Mary's College *B*
St. Mary's College of Maryland *B*
Salisbury University *B, T*
Towson University *B*
United States Naval Academy *B*
University of Maryland
Baltimore County *B, M, D*
College Park *B, M, D*
Villa Julie College *A, B*
Washington College *B*

Massachusetts

American International College *B*
Amherst College *B*
Assumption College *B*
Berkshire Community College *A*
Boston College *B, M, D*
Boston University *B, M, D*
Brandeis University *B, M, D*
Bridgewater State College *B, M*
Bunker Hill Community College *A*
Clark University *B, M, D*
College of the Holy Cross *B*
Elms College *B*
Emmanuel College *B*
Framingham State College *B*
Gordon College *B*
Hampshire College *B*
Harvard College *B*
Massachusetts College of Liberal Arts *B*
Massachusetts College of Pharmacy and
Health Sciences *B, M*
Massachusetts Institute of
Technology *B, D*
Merrimack College *B*
Mount Holyoke College *B*
Northeastern University *B, M, D*
Salem State College *B*
Simmons College *B*
Simon's Rock College of Bard *B*
Smith College *B*
Springfield Technical Community
College *A*
Stonehill College *B*
Suffolk University *B*
Tufts University *B*

University of Massachusetts
Amherst *B, M, D*
Boston *B, M*
Dartmouth *B, M*
Lowell *B, M, D*
Wellesley College *B*
Western New England College *B, T*
Wheaton College *B*
Williams College *B*
Worcester Polytechnic Institute *B, M, D*

Michigan

Adrian College *A, B, T*
Alma College *B, T*
Andrews University *B*
Aquinas College *B, T*
Calvin College *B, T*
Central Michigan University *B, M, T*
Eastern Michigan University *B*
Ferris State University *B*
Gogebic Community College *A*
Grand Valley State University *B*
Hillsdale College *B*
Hope College *B*
Kalamazoo College *B, T*
Kellogg Community College *A*
Kettering University *B*
Lansing Community College *A*
Lawrence Technological University *B*
Macomb Community College *A*
Madonna University *B, T*
Marygrove College *B, T*
Michigan State University *B, M, D*
Michigan Technological
University *B, M, D, T*
Mid Michigan Community College *A*
Northern Michigan University *A, B, M*
Oakland University *B, M, T*
Saginaw Valley State University *B*
Siena Heights University *A, B*
Spring Arbor University *B*
University of Michigan *B, M, D, T*
University of Michigan
Dearborn *B*
Flint *B, T*
Wayne State University *B, M, D*
Western Michigan University *B, M, D*

Minnesota

Augsburg College *B*
Bemidji State University *B, M*
Bethany Lutheran College *B*
Bethel College *B*
Carleton College *B*
College of St. Benedict *B*
College of St. Catherine *B*
College of St. Scholastica *B*
Concordia College: Moorhead *B*
Gustavus Adolphus College *B*
Hamline University *B*
Macalester College *B, T*
Minnesota State University
Mankato *B, M, T*
Moorhead *B*
Ridgewater College: A Community and
Technical College *A*
St. Cloud State University *B*
St. John's University *B*
St. Mary's University of Minnesota *B*
St. Olaf College *B*
Southwest State University *B*
University of Minnesota
Duluth *B, M*
Morris *B*
Twin Cities *B, M, D*
University of St. Thomas *B*
Vermilion Community College *A*
Winona State University *B*

Mississippi

Alcorn State University *B*
Blue Mountain College *B*
Delta State University *B, T*
Itawamba Community College *A*
Mary Holmes College *A*
Millsaps College *B, T*

Mississippi College *B, M*
Mississippi State University *B, M, D*
Mississippi University for Women *B, T*
Mississippi Valley State University *B*
Rust College *B*
University of Mississippi *B, M, D, T*
University of Southern
   Mississippi *B, M, D*

Missouri

Avila University *B*
Central Methodist College *A, B*
Central Missouri State University *B*
College of the Ozarks *B*
Columbia College *B*
Crowder College *A*
Culver-Stockton College *B*
Drury University *B, T*
East Central College *A*
Evangel University *B*
Lincoln University *B*
Lindenwood University *B*
Maryville University of Saint Louis *B*
Missouri Baptist University *B, T*
Missouri Southern State College *B, T*
Missouri Western State College *B, T*
Northwest Missouri State University *B*
Rockhurst University *B*
St. Louis Community College
   St. Louis Community College at
     Florissant Valley *A*
   St. Louis Community College at
     Forest Park *A*
St. Louis University *B, M*
Southeast Missouri State University *B*
Southwest Baptist University *B*
Southwest Missouri State
   University *B, M*
Three Rivers Community College *A*
Truman State University *B*
University of Missouri
   Columbia *B, M, D*
   Kansas City *B, M*
   Rolla *B, M, D, T*
   St. Louis *B, M, D*
Washington University in St.
   Louis *B, M, D*
Westminster College *B*
William Jewell College *B, T*

Montana

Carroll College *B, T*
Montana State University
   Billings *B, T*
   Bozeman *B, M, D*
Montana Tech of the University of
   Montana *B*
Rocky Mountain College *B, T*
University of Montana-Missoula *B, M, D*
University of Montana: Western *B*

Nebraska

Chadron State College *B*
College of Saint Mary *B, T*
Concordia University *B, T*
Creighton University *B*
Dana College *B*
Doane College *B*
Hastings College *B*
Midland Lutheran College *B, T*
Nebraska Wesleyan University *B*
Northeast Community College *A*
Union College *B*
University of Nebraska
   Kearney *B, T*
   Lincoln *B, M, D*
   Omaha *B*
Wayne State College *B, T*
Western Nebraska Community
   College *A*

Nevada

Great Basin College *A*
University of Nevada
   Las Vegas *B, M*
   Reno *B, M, D*

New Hampshire

Dartmouth College *B, M, D, T*
Keene State College *B*
Plymouth State College *B*
St. Anselm College *B, T*
University of New Hampshire *B, M, D*

New Jersey

Atlantic Cape Community College *A*
Bloomfield College *B*
Caldwell College *B*
The College of New Jersey *B, T*
College of St. Elizabeth *B, T*
Drew University *B*
Essex County College *A*
Fairleigh Dickinson University
   College at Florham *B, M*
   Metropolitan Campus *B*
Georgian Court College *B, T*
Gloucester County College *A*
Hudson County Community College *A*
Kean University *B*
Middlesex County College *A*
Monmouth University *B*
Montclair State University *B, M*
New Jersey City University *B*
New Jersey Institute of
   Technology *B, M, D*
Princeton University *B, M, D*
Ramapo College of New Jersey *B*
Raritan Valley Community College *A*
Richard Stockton College of New
   Jersey *B*
Rider University *B*
Rowan University *B*
Rutgers, The State University of New
   Jersey
     Camden Regional Campus *B, M, T*
     New Brunswick Regional
       Campus *B, M, D*
     Newark Regional Campus *B, M, D*
St. Peter's College *B*
Salem Community College *A*
Seton Hall University *B, M, D, T*
Stevens Institute of Technology *B, M, D*
Sussex County Community College *A*
Thomas Edison State College *A, B*
Union County College *A*
Warren County Community College *A*
William Paterson University of New
   Jersey *B*

New Mexico

Eastern New Mexico University *B, M*
New Mexico Highlands University *B, M*
New Mexico Institute of Mining and
   Technology *B, M, D*
New Mexico Junior College *A*
New Mexico State University *B, M, D*
San Juan College *A*
University of New Mexico *B, M, D*
Western New Mexico University *B*

New York

Adelphi University *B*
Adirondack Community College *A*
Alfred University *B*
Bard College *B*
Barnard College *B*
Canisius College *B*
City University of New York
   Brooklyn College *B, M*
   City College *B, M, D, T*
   College of Staten Island *B, T*
   Hunter College *B*
   Kingsborough Community
     College *A*
   Queens College *B, M*
   Queensborough Community
     College *A*
   York College *B*
Clarkson University *B, M, D*
Colgate University *B*
College of Mount St. Vincent *B, T*
College of New Rochelle *B, T*

Columbia University
   Columbia College *B*
Cornell University *B, D*
Elmira College *B, T*
Excelsior College *B*
Finger Lakes Community College *A*
Fordham University *B, M, D*
Hamilton College *B*
Hartwick College *B, T*
Hobart and William Smith Colleges *B*
Hofstra University *B*
Houghton College *B*
Hudson Valley Community College *A*
Iona College *B*
Ithaca College *B, T*
Le Moyne College *B*
Long Island University
   C. W. Post Campus *B*
   Southampton College *B*
Manhattan College *B*
Manhattanville College *B*
Marist College *B, T*
Marymount College of Fordham
   University *B*
Monroe Community College *A*
Mount St. Mary College *B, T*
Nazareth College of Rochester *B*
New York Institute of Technology *B*
New York University *B, M, D*
Niagara University *B*
Pace University *B*
Pace University:
   Pleasantville/Briarcliff *B*
Polytechnic University *B, M, D*
Rensselaer Polytechnic Institute *B, M, D*
Roberts Wesleyan College *B*
Rochester Institute of
   Technology *A, B, M*
Russell Sage College *B*
St. Bonaventure University *B, T*
St. John Fisher College *B*
St. John's University *B, M*
St. Joseph's College *B*
St. Lawrence University *B, T*
Sarah Lawrence College *B*
Skidmore College *B*
State University of New York
   Albany *B, M, D*
   Binghamton *B, M, D*
   Buffalo *B, M, D*
   College at Brockport *B, T*
   College at Buffalo *B, M*
   College at Cortland *B*
   College at Fredonia *B, M, T*
   College at Geneseo *B, T*
   College at Old Westbury *B, T*
   College at Oneonta *B*
   College at Plattsburgh *B*
   College at Potsdam *B, T*
   College of Agriculture and
     Technology at Morrisville *A*
   College of Environmental Science
     and Forestry *B, M, D*
   College of Technology at Alfred *A*
   New Paltz *B, M, T*
   Oswego *B, M*
   Purchase *B*
   Stony Brook *B, M, D, T*
Suffolk County Community College *A*
Syracuse University *B, M, D*
Touro College *B*
Union College *B*
United States Military Academy *B*
University of Rochester *B, M, D*
Utica College *B*
Vassar College *B*
Wagner College *B, T*
Wells College *B*
Yeshiva University *B*

North Carolina

Appalachian State University *B, M*
Barton College *B*
Bennett College *B*
Campbell University *B*
Catawba College *B, T*

Davidson College *B*
Duke University *B, M, D*
East Carolina University *B, M*
Elizabeth City State University *B*
Elon University *B*
Fayetteville State University *B*
Gardner-Webb University *B*
Greensboro College *B*
Guilford College *B*
Guilford Technical Community
   College *A*
High Point University *B*
Johnson C. Smith University *B*
Lenoir-Rhyne College *B*
Livingstone College *B*
Louisburg College *A*
Mars Hill College *B, T*
Meredith College *B*
Methodist College *A, B, T*
North Carolina Agricultural and
   Technical State University *B, M*
North Carolina Central University *B, M*
North Carolina State University *B, M, D*
North Carolina Wesleyan College *B*
Pfeiffer University *B*
St. Andrews Presbyterian College *B*
St. Augustine's College *B*
Salem College *B*
Shaw University *B*
University of North Carolina
   Asheville *B, T*
   Chapel Hill *B, M, D*
   Charlotte *B, M*
   Greensboro *B, M, T*
   Pembroke *B*
   Wilmington *B, M*
Wake Forest University *B, M, D*
Warren Wilson College *B*
Western Carolina University *B, M*
Wingate University *B*
Winston-Salem State University *B*

North Dakota

Dickinson State University *B, T*
Jamestown College *B*
Mayville State University *B, T*
Minot State University *B*
Minot State University: Bottineau
   Campus *A*
North Dakota State
   University *B, M, D, T*
University of North Dakota *B, M, D, T*
Valley City State University *B*

Ohio

Antioch College *B*
Ashland University *B*
Baldwin-Wallace College *B, T*
Bluffton College *B*
Bowling Green State University *B, M, D*
Case Western Reserve
   University *B, M, D*
Cedarville University *B, T*
Central State University *B*
Cleveland State University *B, M, D, T*
College of Mount St. Joseph *B, T*
College of Wooster *B*
Defiance College *B, T*
Denison University *B*
Franciscan University of Steubenville *B*
Heidelberg College *B*
Hiram College *B*
Jefferson Community College *A*
John Carroll University *B, M*
Kent State University *B, M, D, T*
Kent State University
   Stark Campus *B*
Kenyon College *B*
Lake Erie College *B*
Lorain County Community College *A*
Lourdes College *A, B*
Malone College *B*
Marietta College *B*
Miami University
   Middletown Campus *A*
   Oxford Campus *B, M, D, T*

Mount Union College *B*
Mount Vernon Nazarene University *B*
Muskingum College *B*
Notre Dame College *B, T*
Oberlin College *B*
Ohio Dominican College *A, B, T*
Ohio Northern University *B*
Ohio State University
  Columbus Campus *B, M, D*
Ohio University *B, M, D*
Ohio Wesleyan University *B*
Otterbein College *B*
Shawnee State University *B*
Sinclair Community College *A*
University of Akron *B, M, D*
University of Cincinnati *B, M, D*
University of Cincinnati
  Clermont College *A*
  Raymond Walters College *A*
University of Dayton *B, M*
University of Rio Grande *A, B, T*
University of Toledo *A, B, M, D*
Walsh University *B*
Wilmington College *B*
Wittenberg University *B*
Wright State University *B, M*
Wright State University: Lake Campus *A*
Xavier University *B*
Youngstown State University *B, M*

Oklahoma

Bacone College *A*
Cameron University *B*
East Central University *B, T*
Eastern Oklahoma State College *A*
Langston University *B*
Northeastern State University *B*
Northern Oklahoma College *A*
Northwestern Oklahoma State
  University *B*
Oklahoma Baptist University *B, T*
Oklahoma Christian University of
  Science and Arts *B*
Oklahoma City Community College *A*
Oklahoma City University *B*
Oklahoma Panhandle State University *B*
Oklahoma State University *B, M, D*
Oklahoma Wesleyan University *A, B*
Oral Roberts University *B*
Redlands Community College *A*
Rose State College *A*
Southeastern Oklahoma State
  University *B*
Southern Nazarene University *B*
Southwestern Oklahoma State
  University *B*
Tulsa Community College *A*
University of Central Oklahoma *B*
University of Oklahoma *B, M, D*
University of Science and Arts of
  Oklahoma *B*
University of Tulsa *B, M*

Oregon

Central Oregon Community College *A*
Chemeketa Community College *A*
Concordia University *B*
Eastern Oregon University *B, T*
George Fox University *B*
Lewis & Clark College *B*
Linfield College *B*
Linn-Benton Community College *A*
Oregon State University *B, M, D*
Pacific University *B*
Portland State University *B, M*
Reed College *B*
Southern Oregon University *B*
University of Oregon *B, M, D*
University of Portland *B*
Western Oregon University *B*
Willamette University *B*

Pennsylvania

Albright College *B, T*
Allegheny College *B*
Arcadia University *B*

Bloomsburg University of
  Pennsylvania *B, T*
Bryn Mawr College *B, M, D*
Bucknell University *B, M*
Bucks County Community College *A*
Cabrini College *B*
California University of Pennsylvania *B*
Carlow College *B*
Carnegie Mellon University *B, M, D*
Cedar Crest College *B*
Chatham College *B*
Chestnut Hill College *A, B*
Cheyney University of Pennsylvania *B*
Community College of Allegheny
  County *A*
DeSales University *B*
Delaware Valley College *B*
Dickinson College *B*
Drexel University *B, M, D*
Duquesne University *B, M, D*
East Stroudsburg University of
  Pennsylvania *B*
Edinboro University of
  Pennsylvania *B, T*
Elizabethtown College *B*
Franklin & Marshall College *B*
Geneva College *B, T*
Gettysburg College *B*
Grove City College *B*
Harrisburg Area Community College *A*
Haverford College *B, T*
Holy Family University *B, T*
Immaculata University *B*
Indiana University of
  Pennsylvania *B, M, T*
Juniata College *B*
King's College *B, T*
Kutztown University of
  Pennsylvania *B, T*
La Roche College *B*
La Salle University *B*
Lafayette College *B*
Lebanon Valley College of
  Pennsylvania *B, T*
Lehigh University *B, M, D*
Lincoln University *B*
Lock Haven University of
  Pennsylvania *B*
Lycoming College *B*
Mercyhurst College *B*
Messiah College *B*
Millersville University of
  Pennsylvania *B, T*
Moravian College *B, T*
Muhlenberg College *B, T*
Northampton County Area Community
  College *A*
Penn State
  Abington *B*
  Altoona *B*
  Beaver *B*
  Berks *B*
  Delaware County *B*
  Dubois *B*
  Erie, The Behrend College *B*
  Fayette *B*
  Hazleton *B*
  Lehigh Valley *B*
  McKeesport *B*
  Mont Alto *B*
  New Kensington *B*
  Schuylkill - Capital College *B*
  University Park *B, M, D*
  Wilkes-Barre *B*
  Worthington Scranton *B*
  York *B*
Philadelphia University *B*
Reading Area Community College *A*
Rosemont College *B*
St. Joseph's University *A, B, M*
St. Vincent College *B*
Seton Hill University *B, T*
Shippensburg University of
  Pennsylvania *B, T*

Slippery Rock University of
  Pennsylvania *B, M, T*
Swarthmore College *B*
Temple University *B, M, D*
Thiel College *B*
University of Pennsylvania *B, M, D*
University of Pittsburgh *B, M, D*
University of Pittsburgh
  Bradford *B*
  Johnstown *B*
University of Scranton *B, M, T*
University of the Sciences in
  Philadelphia *B, M, D*
Villanova University *B, M, D*
Washington and Jefferson College *B*
Waynesburg College *B*
West Chester University of
  Pennsylvania *B, M*
Widener University *B*
Wilkes University *B*
Wilson College *B*
York College of Pennsylvania *A, B*

Puerto Rico

Bayamon Central University *B*
Inter American University of Puerto Rico
  Bayamon Campus *A*
  Metropolitan Campus *B*
  San German Campus *B*
Pontifical Catholic University of Puerto
  Rico *B, M*
Turabo University *B*
Universidad Metropolitana *B*
University of Puerto Rico
  Cayey University College *B*
  Mayaguez Campus *B, M*
  Rio Piedras Campus *B, M, D*
University of the Sacred Heart *B*

Rhode Island

Brown University *B, M, D*
Providence College *M*
Rhode Island College *B*
Roger Williams University *B*
Salve Regina University *B*
University of Rhode Island *B, M, D*

South Carolina

Benedict College *B*
Charleston Southern University *B*
The Citadel *B*
Claflin University *B*
Clemson University *B, M, D*
Coastal Carolina University *B*
Coker College *B*
College of Charleston *B, T*
Columbia College *B*
Converse College *B*
Erskine College *B*
Francis Marion University *B*
Furman University *B, M, T*
Lander University *B*
Limestone College *B*
Newberry College *B*
Presbyterian College *B, T*
South Carolina State University *B*
Southern Wesleyan University *B*
University of South Carolina *B, M, D*
University of South Carolina
  Aiken *B*
  Spartanburg *B*
Winthrop University *B*
Wofford College *B, T*

South Dakota

Augustana College *B, T*
Black Hills State University *B*
Dakota State University *B*
Mount Marty College *B*
Northern State University *B*
South Dakota School of Mines and
  Technology *B*
South Dakota State University *B, M, D*
University of Sioux Falls *B*
University of South Dakota *B, M*

Tennessee

Austin Peay State University *B*
Belmont University *B, T*
Bethel College *B*
Carson-Newman College *B, T*
Christian Brothers University *B*
Columbia State Community College *A*
Crichton College *B*
East Tennessee State University *B, M*
Fisk University *B, M*
Freed-Hardeman University *B*
King College *B, T*
Lambuth University *B*
Lane College *B*
Lee University *B*
Maryville College *B, T*
Middle Tennessee State
  University *B, M, D*
Milligan College *B*
Rhodes College *B*
Roane State Community College *A*
Southern Adventist University *B*
Tennessee State University *B, M*
Tennessee Technological
  University *B, M, T*
Tennessee Wesleyan College *B, T*
Trevecca Nazarene University *B*
Union University *B, T*
University of Memphis *B, M, D*
University of Tennessee
  Chattanooga *B*
  Knoxville *B, M, D*
  Martin *B*
Vanderbilt University *B, M, D*

Texas

Abilene Christian University *B*
Amarillo College *A*
Angelo State University *B, T*
Austin College *B*
Austin Community College *A*
Baylor University *B, M, D*
Blinn College *A*
Brazosport College *A*
Central Texas College *A*
Cisco Junior College *A*
Clarendon College *A*
Coastal Bend College *A*
College of the Mainland *A*
Del Mar College *A*
East Texas Baptist University *B*
El Paso Community College *A*
Frank Phillips College *A*
Galveston College *A*
Grayson County College *A*
Hardin-Simmons University *B*
Hill College *A*
Houston Baptist University *B*
Howard College *A*
Howard Payne University *B, T*
Huston-Tillotson College *B*
Jarvis Christian College *B*
Kilgore College *A*
Lamar University *B, M*
Laredo Community College *A*
LeTourneau University *B*
Lon Morris College *A*
Lubbock Christian University *B, T*
McMurry University *B, T*
Midland College *A*
Midwestern State University *B*
Northeast Texas Community College *A*
Odessa College *A*
Our Lady of the Lake University of San
  Antonio *B*
Palo Alto College *A*
Panola College *A*
Paris Junior College *A*
Prairie View A&M University *B, M*
Rice University *B, M, D*
St. Edward's University *B, T*
St. Mary's University *B*
St. Philip's College *A*
Sam Houston State University *B, M*
Schreiner University *B*

South Plains College *A*
Southern Methodist University *B, M*
Southwest Texas State
    University *B, M, T*
Southwestern Adventist University *B, T*
Southwestern University *B, T*
Stephen F. Austin State
    University *B, M, T*
Sul Ross State University *B*
Tarleton State University *B, T*
Texas A&M International University *B*
Texas A&M University *B, M, D*
Texas A&M University
    Commerce *B, M*
    Corpus Christi *B, T*
    Kingsville *B, M*
Texas Christian University *B, M, D, T*
Texas Lutheran University *B*
Texas Southern University *B, M*
Texas Tech University *B, M, D*
Texas Wesleyan University *B*
Texas Woman's University *B, M, T*
Trinity University *B*
Trinity Valley Community College *A*
Tyler Junior College *A*
University of Dallas *B*
University of Houston *B, M, D*
University of Houston
    Clear Lake *B, M*
    Downtown *B*
University of Mary Hardin-Baylor *B, T*
University of North Texas *B, M, D*
University of St. Thomas *B*
University of Texas
    Arlington *B, M, D*
    Austin *B, M, D*
    Dallas *B, M, D*
    El Paso *B, M*
    Pan American *B, T*
    San Antonio *B, M*
    Tyler *B*
    of the Permian Basin *B*
University of the Incarnate Word *B*
Wayland Baptist University *B, T*
West Texas A&M University *B, M, T*
Wharton County Junior College *A*
Wiley College *B*

Utah

Brigham Young University *B, M, D*
Dixie State College of Utah *A*
Salt Lake Community College *A*
Snow College *A*
Southern Utah University *B, T*
University of Utah *B, M, D*
Utah State University *B, M, D*
Utah Valley State College *B*
Weber State University *B*
Westminster College *B*

Vermont

Bennington College *B*
Castleton State College *A*
Marlboro College *B*
Middlebury College *B*
Norwich University *B*
St. Michael's College *B*
University of Vermont *B, M, D*

Virginia

Averett University *B, T*
Bluefield College *B*
Bridgewater College *B*
College of William and Mary *B, M*
Eastern Mennonite University *B*
Emory & Henry College *B, T*
Ferrum College *B*
George Mason University *B, M*
Hampden-Sydney College *B*
Hampton University *B, M*
Hollins University *B*
James Madison University *B, T*
Longwood University *B, T*
Lynchburg College *B*
Mary Baldwin College *B*
Mary Washington College *B*

Norfolk State University *B*
Old Dominion University *B, M*
Radford University *B*
Randolph-Macon College *B*
Randolph-Macon Woman's College *B*
Roanoke College *B, T*
Shenandoah University *B*
Sweet Briar College *B*
University of Richmond *B, T*
University of Virginia *B, M, D*
University of Virginia's College at
    Wise *B, T*
Virginia Commonwealth
    University *B, M, D*
Virginia Military Institute *B*
Virginia Polytechnic Institute and State
    University *B, M, D, T*
Virginia State University *B*
Virginia Union University *B*
Virginia Wesleyan College *B*
Washington and Lee University *B*

Washington

Central Washington University *B, M*
Centralia College *A*
Eastern Washington University *B, T*
Everett Community College *A*
Gonzaga University *B*
Lower Columbia College *A*
Olympic College *A*
Pacific Lutheran University *B*
St. Martin's College *B*
Seattle Pacific University *B*
Seattle University *B*
University of Puget Sound *B, T*
University of Washington *B, M, D*
Walla Walla College *B*
Washington State University *B, M, D*
Western Washington University *B, M, T*
Whitman College *B*
Whitworth College *B, T*

West Virginia

Alderson-Broaddus College *B*
Bethany College *B*
Concord College *B*
Davis and Elkins College *B*
Fairmont State College *B*
Glenville State College *B*
Marshall University *B, M*
Potomac State College of West Virginia
    University *A*
Shepherd College *B*
University of Charleston *B*
West Liberty State College *B*
West Virginia State College *B*
West Virginia University *B, M, D, T*
West Virginia University Institute of
    Technology *B*
West Virginia Wesleyan College *B*
Wheeling Jesuit University *B*

Wisconsin

Alverno College *B, T*
Beloit College *B*
Cardinal Stritch University *B*
Carroll College *B*
Carthage College *B, T*
Edgewood College *B*
Lakeland College *B*
Lawrence University *B, T*
Marian College of Fond du Lac *B*
Marquette University *B, M, D, T*
Mount Mary College *B*
Northland College *B*
Ripon College *B, T*
St. Norbert College *B, T*

University of Wisconsin
    Eau Claire *B*
    Green Bay *B*
    La Crosse *B*
    Madison *B, M, D*
    Milwaukee *B, M, D*
    Oshkosh *B*
    Parkside *B*
    Platteville *B, T*
    River Falls *B*
    Stevens Point *B, T*
    Superior *B, T*
    Whitewater *B, T*
Viterbo University *B, T*
Wisconsin Lutheran College *B*

Wyoming

Casper College *A*
Laramie County Community College *A*
University of Wyoming *B, M, D*
Western Wyoming Community
    College *A*

Chemistry teacher education

Alabama

Athens State University *B*
Birmingham-Southern College *T*
Faulkner University *B*
Huntingdon College *T*
Judson College *B*
Oakwood College *B*
Talladega College *T*

Arizona

Arizona State University *B, T*
Prescott College *T*
University of Arizona *B, M*

Arkansas

Arkansas State University *B, M, T*
Arkansas Tech University *B*
Harding University *B, T*
John Brown University *B, T*
Ouachita Baptist University *B, T*
Southern Arkansas University *B, T*
University of Central Arkansas *T*
University of the Ozarks *B, T*

California

Azusa Pacific University *T*
California State Polytechnic University:
    Pomona *T*
California State University
    Long Beach *T*
    San Bernardino *T*
San Diego State University *B, T*
San Francisco State University *B, T*
University of the Pacific *T*

Colorado

Colorado State University *T*
Colorado State University
    Pueblo *T*
Fort Lewis College *T*
Regis University *B, T*

Connecticut

Central Connecticut State University *B*
Fairfield University *T*
Quinnipiac University *B, M*
Sacred Heart University *T*
St. Joseph College *T*
Southern Connecticut State
    University *B, M, T*

Delaware

University of Delaware *B, T*

District of Columbia

Catholic University of America *B*

Florida

Bethune-Cookman College *B, T*
Florida Agricultural and Mechanical
    University *T*

Florida Institute of Technology *B*
Gulf Coast Community College *A*
St. Thomas University *B, T*
Stetson University *B*
University of West Florida *B, T*

Georgia

Agnes Scott College *T*
Armstrong Atlantic State University *T*
Columbus State University *B*
Georgia Southern University *B*
North Georgia College & State
    University *B*
State University of West Georgia *T*

Hawaii

University of Hawaii
    Manoa *B, T*

Idaho

Boise State University *T*
Brigham Young University - Idaho *T*
Northwest Nazarene University *B*
University of Idaho *T*

Illinois

Augustana College *B, T*
Benedictine University *T*
Chicago State University *B, T*
Concordia University *B, T*
Dominican University *T*
Elmhurst College *B*
Governors State University *B, T*
Greenville College *B*
Illinois College *T*
Judson College *B, T*
Lewis University *T*
Loyola University of Chicago *T*
North Central College *B, T*
North Park University *T*
Northwestern University *B, T*
Olivet Nazarene University *B, T*
Rockford College *T*
Roosevelt University *B*
Sauk Valley Community College *A*
Trinity Christian College *B, T*
University of Illinois
    Chicago *B*
    Urbana-Champaign *M, T*
Wheaton College *T*

Indiana

Ball State University *T*
Butler University *T*
Franklin College *B, T*
Goshen College *B*
Huntington College *B*
Indiana University
    Bloomington *B, T*
    Northwest *B*
    South Bend *B, T*
Indiana University-Purdue University
    Fort Wayne *B, T*
Indiana Wesleyan University *T*
Manchester College *B, T*
Purdue University
    Calumet *B*
Saint Mary's College *T*
Taylor University *B, T*
University of Evansville *B*
University of Indianapolis *B, T*
University of St. Francis *T*
University of Southern Indiana *T*
Valparaiso University *B*
Vincennes University *A*

Iowa

Buena Vista University *B, T*
Central College *T*
Clarke College *B, T*
Cornell College *B, T*
Dordt College *B*
Drake University *M, T*
Ellsworth Community College *A*
Franciscan University *B, D*
Graceland University *T*
Grand View College *B, T*

Iowa State University *T*
Iowa Wesleyan College *B*
Loras College *T*
Luther College *B*
Maharishi University of Management *T*
Morningside College *B*
Northwestern College *T*
St. Ambrose University *B, T*
University of Iowa *B, T*
Upper Iowa University *B, T*
Wartburg College *T*
William Penn University *B*

Kansas
Baker University *T*
Benedictine College *B, T*
Bethany College *B*
Bethel College *T*
Central Christian College *A, B*
Emporia State University *T*
Garden City Community College *A*
Independence Community College *A*
McPherson College *B, T*
MidAmerica Nazarene University *B, T*
Ottawa University *T*
Pittsburg State University *B, T*
St. Mary College *T*
Sterling College *T*
Tabor College *B, T*
University of Kansas *B, T*

Kentucky
Bellarmine University *B, M, T*
Campbellsville University *B*
Cumberland College *B, T*
Murray State University *B, M, T*
Thomas More College *B*
Union College *M*

Louisiana
Centenary College of Louisiana *B, T*
Louisiana State University
 Shreveport *B*
McNeese State University *T*
Nicholls State University *B*
Northwestern State University *B*
Our Lady of Holy Cross College *T*
Southern University and Agricultural and
 Mechanical College *B*
Xavier University of Louisiana *B, T*

Maine
St. Joseph's College *B*
University of Maine *B*
University of New England *B, T*
University of Southern Maine *T*

Maryland
Coppin State College *B, T*
St. Mary's College of Maryland *T*
Salisbury University *T*

Massachusetts
Assumption College *T*
Boston University *B*
Bridgewater State College *M, T*
Elms College *T*
Framingham State College *B, T*
Harvard College *T*
Merrimack College *T*
Northeastern University *M*
Salem State College *M*
Tufts University *T*
University of Massachusetts
 Dartmouth *T*
Western New England College *T*
Westfield State College *M, T*

Michigan
Alma College *T*
Calvin College *B*
Central Michigan University *B, M*
Eastern Michigan University *B, T*
Grand Valley State University *M, T*
Hope College *T*
Michigan State University *B*
Michigan Technological University *T*
Northern Michigan University *B, M, T*

University of Michigan
 Flint *T*
Western Michigan University *B*

Minnesota
Augsburg College *T*
Bethel College *B*
College of St. Scholastica *T*
Concordia College: Moorhead *B, T*
Gustavus Adolphus College *T*
Minnesota State University
 Mankato *B, T*
 Moorhead *B, T*
St. Cloud State University *T*
St. Mary's University of Minnesota *B*
St. Olaf College *T*
Southwest State University *B, T*
University of Minnesota
 Morris *T*
University of St. Thomas *B, T*
Vermilion Community College *A*
Winona State University *B, T*

Mississippi
Blue Mountain College *B*
Delta State University *T*
Itawamba Community College *A*
Mississippi College *B, M*
Mississippi State University *T*
University of Mississippi *B, T*

Missouri
Avila University *B, T*
Central Methodist College *B*
Central Missouri State University *B, T*
College of the Ozarks *B, T*
Lincoln University *B, T*
Lindenwood University *M*
Maryville University of Saint
 Louis *B, M, T*
Missouri Baptist University *T*
Missouri Southern State College *B, T*
Northwest Missouri State
 University *B, T*
Rockhurst University *B*
Southwest Missouri State University *B*
Truman State University *M, T*
University of Missouri
 Columbia *B*
 St. Louis *T*
Washington University in St.
 Louis *B, M, T*

Montana
Montana State University
 Billings *B, T*
Montana Tech of the University of
 Montana *T*
Rocky Mountain College *B, T*
University of Montana-Missoula *M, T*
University of Montana: Western *B, T*

Nebraska
Chadron State College *B*
College of Saint Mary *B, T*
Concordia University *B, T*
Creighton University *B, T*
Dana College *B*
Doane College *T*
Hastings College *B, M, T*
Midland Lutheran College *B, T*
Nebraska Wesleyan University *T*
Peru State College *T*
Union College *T*
University of Nebraska
 Kearney *B*
 Lincoln *T*

New Hampshire
Keene State College *B, T*
St. Anselm College *T*
University of New Hampshire *T*

New Jersey
The College of New Jersey *B, T*
Monmouth University *B, T*
Rowan University *T*
St. Peter's College *T*

New Mexico
New Mexico Institute of Mining and
 Technology *M*
Western New Mexico University *B*

New York
Adelphi University *M*
Alfred University *M, T*
Canisius College *B, M, T*
City University of New York
 Brooklyn College *B*
 City College *B*
 College of Staten Island *T*
 Hunter College *B, M, T*
 Queens College *M, T*
Colgate University *M*
D'Youville College *M, T*
Dowling College *B*
Elmira College *B, T*
Fordham University *M, T*
Hofstra University *B, M*
Houghton College *B, T*
Ithaca College *B, T*
Long Island University
 C. W. Post Campus *B, T*
Manhattan College *T*
Marymount College of Fordham
 University *B, T*
Nazareth College of Rochester *T*
New York Institute of Technology *B, T*
New York University *B, M, T*
Niagara University *B, T*
Pace University *B, M, T*
Pace University:
 Pleasantville/Briarcliff *B, M, T*
Roberts Wesleyan College *B, T*
St. John Fisher College *B, T*
St. John's University *B, M, T*
St. Lawrence University *T*
State University of New York
 Albany *B, T*
 Binghamton *M*
 Buffalo *M, T*
 College at Brockport *M, T*
 College at Buffalo *B, M*
 College at Cortland *B, M*
 College at Fredonia *B, M, T*
 College at Geneseo *B, M, T*
 College at Old Westbury *B*
 College at Oneonta *B, T*
 College at Plattsburgh *B, M*
 College at Potsdam *B, M, T*
 College of Environmental Science
 and Forestry *B, T*
 New Paltz *B, M, T*
 Oswego *B, M*
 Stony Brook *T*
Syracuse University *B, M, T*
Vassar College *T*
Wagner College *T*
Wells College *T*

North Carolina
Catawba College *T*
Gardner-Webb University *B*
Guilford Technical Community
 College *A*
Lenoir Community College *A*
Louisburg College *A*
Mars Hill College *T*
Meredith College *T*
Methodist College *A, B, T*
North Carolina Agricultural and
 Technical State University *B, T*
North Carolina Central University *B, M*
Sandhills Community College *A*
University of North Carolina
 Charlotte *B*
 Greensboro *B, M, T*
 Wilmington *B*
Wake Forest University *M, T*

North Dakota
Dickinson State University *B, T*
Jamestown College *B*
Mayville State University *B, T*

Minot State University *B*
North Dakota State University *B, T*
University of North Dakota *B, T*
Valley City State University *B, T*

Ohio
Ashland University *B, T*
Baldwin-Wallace College *T*
Bluffton College *B*
Bowling Green State University *B, M*
Case Western Reserve University *T*
College of Mount St. Joseph *T*
Defiance College *B, T*
Hiram College *T*
John Carroll University *T*
Kent State University *B, T*
Kent State University
 Stark Campus *B*
Malone College *B*
Miami University
 Oxford Campus *B, T*
Mount Union College *T*
Ohio Dominican College *B, T*
Ohio Northern University *B*
Otterbein College *B*
Shawnee State University *B*
University of Akron *B, T*
University of Dayton *B, M, T*
University of Findlay *T*
University of Rio Grande *B, T*
University of Toledo *T*
Wilmington College *B*
Xavier University *B, M*
Youngstown State University *B, M*

Oklahoma
Cameron University *B*
East Central University *T*
Eastern Oklahoma State College *A*
Northeastern State University *T*
Oklahoma Baptist University *B, T*
Oklahoma State University *M*
Southern Nazarene University *B*
University of Central Oklahoma *B*
University of Tulsa *B, T*

Oregon
Concordia University *B, M, T*
George Fox University *T*
Linfield College *T*
Oregon State University *M*
Portland State University *T*
University of Portland *T*
Western Oregon University *T*

Pennsylvania
Albright College *T*
Cabrini College *B, T*
California University of
 Pennsylvania *B, T*
Carlow College *T*
Chatham College *M*
DeSales University *T*
Delaware Valley College *T*
Dickinson College *T*
Duquesne University *B, M, T*
Elizabethtown College *T*
Geneva College *B, T*
Gettysburg College *T*
Grove City College *B, T*
Holy Family University *B, M, T*
Juniata College *B, T*
King's College *T*
La Roche College *B*
La Salle University *B, T*
Lebanon Valley College of
 Pennsylvania *B, T*
Lock Haven University of
 Pennsylvania *B, T*
Lycoming College *T*
Mercyhurst College *B*
Messiah College *T*
Moravian College *T*
St. Vincent College *T*
Seton Hill University *B, T*
Slippery Rock University of
 Pennsylvania *M, T*

Thiel College *B*
University of Pittsburgh
    Johnstown *B, T*
Villanova University *T*
Washington and Jefferson College *T*
Waynesburg College *B, T*
Widener University *T*
Wilkes University *M, T*
Wilson College *T*

Puerto Rico

Inter American University of Puerto Rico
    Metropolitan Campus *B*
    San German Campus *B*
Pontifical Catholic University of Puerto
    Rico *B, T*

Rhode Island

Rhode Island College *B*
Salve Regina University *B*

South Carolina

Coker College *B, T*
Columbia College *B*
Francis Marion University *B, T*
Furman University *T*
South Carolina State University *B, T*
Wofford College *T*

South Dakota

Black Hills State University *B, T*
Dakota State University *B, T*
Mount Marty College *B*
South Dakota State University *B*
University of Sioux Falls *T*

Tennessee

Belmont University *T*
Christian Brothers University *B, M, T*
Crichton College *C, B*
King College *T*
Lambuth University *T*
Lane College *B*
Maryville College *B, T*
Southern Adventist University *B*
Tennessee Technological University *T*
Tennessee Wesleyan College *B, T*
Trevecca Nazarene University *B, T*
Union University *B, T*
University of Tennessee
    Martin *B, T*

Texas

Abilene Christian University *B, T*
Baylor University *B, T*
Hardin-Simmons University *B, T*
Houston Baptist University *T*
Howard Payne University *B, T*
Kilgore College *A*
Lamar University *T*
Laredo Community College *A*
Lubbock Christian University *B, T*
McMurry University *T*
St. Mary's University *T*
Southwest Texas State University *M, T*
Tarleton State University *T*
Texas A&M University
    Commerce *B*
    Kingsville *T*
Texas Christian University *T*
Texas Wesleyan University *B, T*
University of Dallas *T*
University of Houston *T*
University of Houston
    Clear Lake *T*
University of Mary Hardin-Baylor *T*
University of Texas
    Arlington *T*
    San Antonio *T*
West Texas A&M University *T*

Utah

Brigham Young University *B*
Southern Utah University *B, T*
University of Utah *B*
Utah State University *B*
Weber State University *B*

Vermont

Bennington College *B, M, T*
Castleton State College *B, T*
St. Michael's College *T*

Virginia

Averett University *B, M, T*
Bluefield College *T*
Bridgewater College *T*
Eastern Mennonite University *T*
Hampton University *M*
Hollins University *T*
Longwood University *B, T*
Radford University *T*
University of Virginia's College at
    Wise *T*
Virginia Wesleyan College *T*

Washington

Central Washington University *B, T*
Heritage College *B*
Washington State University *T*
Whitworth College *B, T*

West Virginia

Alderson-Broaddus College *T*
Concord College *B, T*
Fairmont State College *B*
Salem International University *T*
Shepherd College *T*
West Liberty State College *B*
Wheeling Jesuit University *T*

Wisconsin

Alverno College *T*
Carroll College *B, T*
Carthage College *T*
Edgewood College *B*
Lakeland College *T*
Lawrence University *T*
Marian College of Fond du Lac *B, T*
Marquette University *B*
Mount Mary College *B, T*
Northland College *T*
St. Norbert College *T*
University of Wisconsin
    Green Bay *T*
    La Crosse *B, T*
    Platteville *B*
    River Falls *T*
    Superior *B, T*
Viterbo University *B, T*

Child care management

Alabama

Calhoun Community College *C, A*
Gadsden State Community College *C*
Harry M. Ayers State Technical
    College *C, A*
Jefferson State Community College *C, A*
Northwest-Shoals Community College *C*
Reid State Technical College *C*
Snead State Community College *C, A*
Trenholm State Technical College *C*
Wallace State Community College at
    Hanceville *A*

Alaska

University of Alaska
    Anchorage *C, A*
    Southeast *C, A*

Arizona

Arizona Western College *C, A*
Eastern Arizona College *C, A*
Glendale Community College *C, A*
Phoenix College *C, A*
Pima Community College *C, A*
Scottsdale Community College *A*

Arkansas

East Arkansas Community College *A*
Henderson State University *A*
Pulaski Technical College *C, A*
South Arkansas Community College *A*
Southeast Arkansas College *A*

University of Arkansas
    Cossatot Community College of the
    C
University of Central Arkansas *A*

California

Antelope Valley College *C, A*
Barstow College *C, A*
Cabrillo College *C, A*
California State University
    Bakersfield *B*
    Long Beach *C*
    Northridge *B*
    Sacramento *B*
Cerro Coso Community College *C, A*
Chabot College *A*
Citrus College *C*
College of the Canyons *C, A*
College of the Sequoias *C, A*
College of the Siskiyous *C, A*
Cuyamaca College *C, A*
Diablo Valley College *C*
Feather River College *C, A*
Foothill College *C*
Glendale Community College *A*
Grossmont Community College *C, A*
Imperial Valley College *C, A*
Las Positas College *C, A*
Long Beach City College *C, A*
Los Angeles Harbor College *C, A*
Los Angeles Southwest College *C, A*
Los Medanos College *C, A*
MiraCosta College *C, A*
Modesto Junior College *C, A*
Moorpark College *C, A*
Ohlone College *C, A*
Orange Coast College *C, A*
Palomar College *C, A*
Reedley College *C*
San Diego City College *C, A*
San Joaquin Delta College *C, A*
Santa Barbara City College *C, A*
Santa Rosa Junior College *C*
Shasta College *C, A*
Sierra College *A*
Southwestern College *C, A*
University of La Verne *B*
Ventura College *C, A*
West Valley College *C, A*

Colorado

Arapahoe Community College *C*
Community College of Aurora *C, A*
Front Range Community College *C, A*

Connecticut

Briarwood College *C, A*
Gateway Community College *C*
Housatonic Community College *C, A*
Mitchell College *A*

Delaware

Delaware Technical and Community
    College
    Owens Campus *C, A*
    Stanton/Wilmington Campus *C, A*
    Terry Campus *C, A*
University of Delaware *B, T*

District of Columbia

Gallaudet University *B*

Florida

Broward Community College *A*
Chipola Junior College *C, A*
Daytona Beach Community
    College *C, A*
Hillsborough Community College *C, A*
Indian River Community College *C*
Miami-Dade Community College *C*
Okaloosa-Walton Community
    College *C, A*
Palm Beach Community College *A*
Pensacola Junior College *A*
Polk Community College *A*
Santa Fe Community College *A*
Seminole Community College *A*

South Florida Community College *A*

Georgia

Abraham Baldwin Agricultural
    College *A*
Athens Technical College *C*
Chattahoochee Technical College *C, A*
Darton College *A*
Fort Valley State University *B*
Gainesville College *A*
Macon State College *A*
Spelman College *B*
Waycross College *A*

Hawaii

University of Hawaii
    Honolulu Community College *C, A*

Idaho

Boise State University *C, A*
Idaho State University *C, A*
Lewis-Clark State College *C, A*

Illinois

Carl Sandburg College *A*
City Colleges of Chicago
    Harold Washington College *C*
    Malcolm X College *C, A*
    Olive-Harvey College *C, A*
College of DuPage *C, A*
College of Lake County *C, A*
Elgin Community College *C*
Illinois Central College *A*
Illinois Eastern Community Colleges
    Wabash Valley College *A*
Illinois Valley Community College *C, A*
John Wood Community College *A*
Kishwaukee College *A*
Lake Land College *C, A*
Lewis and Clark Community College *A*
Moraine Valley Community College *A*
Parkland College *C, A*
Prairie State College *C, A*
Rock Valley College *C, A*
Sauk Valley Community College *A*
South Suburban College of Cook
    County *C*
Southeastern Illinois College *A*
Southwestern Illinois College *C, A*
Triton College *C, A*
William Rainey Harper College *C, A*

Indiana

Ivy Tech State College
    Lafayette *A*
Vincennes University *A*

Iowa

Des Moines Area Community
    College *C, A*
Hawkeye Community College *A*
Indian Hills Community College *C, A*
Iowa Western Community College *A*
Kirkwood Community College *C, A*
Marshalltown Community College *C, A*
Muscatine Community College *C*
Northeast Iowa Community College *C*
Southeastern Community College
    North Campus *A*
Western Iowa Tech Community
    College *A*

Kansas

Allen County Community College *C*
Barton County Community College *C, A*
Butler County Community College *C, A*
Central Christian College *A, B*
Cloud County Community College *C, A*
Dodge City Community College *C, A*
Garden City Community College *A*
Hutchinson Community College *C, A*
Independence Community College *C, A*
Johnson County Community College *A*
Kansas City Kansas Community
    College *C, A*
Pittsburg State University *B*

Kentucky

Hopkinsville Community College *C, A*
Jefferson Community College *A*
Murray State University *A*
St. Catharine College *C, A*
Somerset Community College *C*
Sullivan University *C*

Louisiana

Nicholls State University *A*
Southern University
　　Shreveport *A*
University of Louisiana at Monroe *A*

Maine

Andover College *C, A*

Maryland

Anne Arundel Community College *A*
Carroll Community College *C, A*
Chesapeake College *C, A*
College of Southern Maryland *C, A*
Community College of Baltimore County
　　Catonsville *C, A*
　　Dundalk *C, A*
　　Essex *C, A*
Frederick Community College *A*
Hagerstown Community College *A*
Montgomery College
　　Rockville Campus *C, A*
Villa Julie College *A*
Wor-Wic Community College *C, A*

Massachusetts

Berkshire Community College *C*
Fisher College *A*
Massachusetts Bay Community
　　College *C, A*
Massasoit Community College *C*
Mount Wachusett Community
　　College *C, A*

Michigan

Baker College
　　of Muskegon *C*
　　of Owosso *A*
Bay de Noc Community College *A*
Central Michigan University *B*
Ferris State University *A*
Glen Oaks Community College *C, A*
Gogebic Community College *C*
Grand Rapids Community College *A*
Kellogg Community College *C, A*
Lansing Community College *A*
Macomb Community College *A*
Mid Michigan Community College *C, A*
Monroe County Community College *A*
Montcalm Community College *C, A*
Mott Community College *A*
Oakland Community College *A*
St. Clair County Community College *A*
Schoolcraft College *C, A*
Southwestern Michigan College *A*
Wayne County Community College *C*

Minnesota

Alexandria Technical College *C*
Anoka-Ramsey Community College *A*
Central Lakes College *C*
Concordia University: St. Paul *C, B*
Inver Hills Community College *A*
Minneapolis Community and Technical
　　College *C, A*
Minnesota State College - Southeast
　　Technical *C, A*
Pine Technical College *C*
Rasmussen College
　　St. Cloud *C, A*
Rochester Community and Technical
　　College *C, A*
St. Cloud Technical College *C, A*
St. Paul College - A Community and
　　Technical College *C, A*

Mississippi

Itawamba Community College *A*
Mary Holmes College *A*

Mississippi Gulf Coast Community
　　College
　　Perkinston *C*

Missouri

Central Missouri State University *A*
College of the Ozarks *B*
Mineral Area College *C*
Moberly Area Community College *C, A*
Northwest Missouri State University *C*
Penn Valley Community College *C, A*
St. Louis Community College
　　St. Louis Community College at
　　　Florissant Valley *A*
　　St. Louis Community College at
　　　Forest Park *A*
Southeast Missouri State University *A*
Southwest Missouri State University:
　　West Plains Campus *C, A*

Montana

Dawson Community College *C*

Nebraska

Central Community College *C, A*
Metropolitan Community College *C, A*
Mid Plains Community College
　　Area *C, A*
Northeast Community College *C, A*
Southeast Community College
　　Lincoln Campus *A*
Wayne State College *B*

Nevada

Truckee Meadows Community
　　College *C, A*
Western Nevada Community
　　College *C, A*

New Hampshire

New Hampshire Community Technical
　　College
　　Claremont *C*
　　Laconia *C*
　　Nashua *C*
　　Stratham *C, A*

New Jersey

Atlantic Cape Community College *A*
County College of Morris *C*
Hudson County Community
　　College *C, A*
Ocean County College *A*

New Mexico

Albuquerque Technical-Vocational
　　Institute *C, A*
Dona Ana Branch Community College of
　　New Mexico State University *C*
Eastern New Mexico University *A*
Eastern New Mexico University: Roswell
　　Campus *C, A*
San Juan College *C*

New York

Broome Community College *C, A*
City University of New York
　　College of Staten Island *A*
　　La Guardia Community College *A*
Dutchess Community College *C, A*
Erie Community College
　　City Campus *A*
Genesee Community College *C*
Hudson Valley Community College *A*
Jamestown Community College *C*
Medaille College *B*
Nassau Community College *A*
Orange County Community College *A*
Rockland Community College *C*
State University of New York
　　College at Plattsburgh *B*
　　College of Agriculture and
　　　Technology at Cobleskill *A*
Tompkins-Cortland Community
　　College *A*
Utica College *B*
Westchester Community College *C, A*

North Carolina

Asheville Buncombe Technical
　　Community College *C, A*
Beaufort County Community College *C*
Blue Ridge Community College *A*
Cape Fear Community College *C, A*
Carteret Community College *C*
Central Carolina Community
　　College *C, A*
Central Piedmont Community College *A*
Cleveland Community College *C, A*
Coastal Carolina Community
　　College *C, A*
Craven Community College *C, A*
Edgecombe Community College *A*
Halifax Community College *C*
Haywood Community College *C, A*
James Sprunt Community College *C, A*
Johnston Community College *C, A*
Lenoir Community College *C, A*
Mayland Community College *C*
Montgomery Community College *C, A*
Nash Community College *A*
Randolph Community College *A*
Richmond Community College *C, A*
Roanoke Bible College *C, A*
Roanoke-Chowan Community College *A*
Sandhills Community College *A*
South Piedmont Community
　　College *C, A*
Southeastern Community College *A*
Southwestern Community College *A*
Stanly Community College *A*
Vance-Granville Community
　　College *C, A*
Wayne Community College *A*
Western Piedmont Community
　　College *C, A*
Wilkes Community College *C, A*
Wilson Technical Community
　　College *C, A*

North Dakota

Lake Region State College *C, A*
Mayville State University *A*
North Dakota State University *B*

Ohio

Cuyahoga Community College
　　Eastern Campus *A*
　　Metropolitan Campus *A*
　　Western Campus *A*
Edison State Community College *A*
Hocking Technical College *C, A*
Jefferson Community College *C, A*
Kent State University *T*
Lakeland Community College *A*
Lourdes College *A, B*
Mount Vernon Nazarene University *A*
Muskingum Area Technical College *A*
North Central State College *C*
Ohio University *A, B*
Sinclair Community College *C, A*
University of Cincinnati
　　Clermont College *C, A*
University of Toledo *C*
Youngstown State University *A, B*

Oklahoma

Eastern Oklahoma State College *A*
Murray State College *A*
Oklahoma City Community
　　College *A*
Oklahoma State University *B*
Oklahoma State University
　　Oklahoma City *A*
Redlands Community College *A*
Rose State College *A*
Tulsa Community College *C, A*
Western Oklahoma State College *A*

Oregon

Central Oregon Community College *C*
Chemeketa Community College *A*
Clatsop Community College *C*
Lane Community College *C, A*
Linn-Benton Community College *C, A*

Portland Community College *C, A*
Rogue Community College *C*
Southwestern Oregon Community
　　College *C, A*

Pennsylvania

Academy of Medical Arts and
　　Business *A*
Butler County Community College *A*
Cambria County Area Community
　　College *C*
Central Pennsylvania College *A*
Chestnut Hill College *C, A, B*
Community College of Philadelphia *A*
Harrisburg Area Community College *C*
Keystone College *C, A*
Lehigh Carbon Community College *C, A*
Luzerne County Community College *A*
Montgomery County Community
　　College *C*
Northampton County Area Community
　　College *C, A*
Penn State
　　University Park *C*
Pennsylvania College of Technology *A*
Reading Area Community College *C, A*
Seton Hill University *C, B*
Western School of Health and Business
　　Careers *A*
Westmoreland County Community
　　College *C, A*

Puerto Rico

University of Puerto Rico
　　Rio Piedras Campus *B*

South Carolina

Aiken Technical College *C*
Denmark Technical College *C*
Florence-Darlington Technical
　　College *C*
Forrest Junior College *C, A*
Midlands Technical College *C*
Northeastern Technical College *C*
Orangeburg-Calhoun Technical
　　College *C*
Piedmont Technical College *C*
South Carolina State University *B*
Technical College of the
　　Lowcountry *C, A*
Tri-County Technical College *C*
Trident Technical College *C, A*

South Dakota

Kilian Community College *C, A*

Tennessee

Belmont University *B*
Northeast State Technical Community
　　College *C*
Southwest Tennessee Community
　　College *A*
Trevecca Nazarene University *A*
Walters State Community College *C, A*

Texas

Alvin Community College *C, A*
Amarillo College *C, A*
Austin Community College *C, A*
Blinn College *C, A*
Brazosport College *C, A*
Central Texas College *C, A*
Coastal Bend College *C, A*
College of the Mainland *A*
Del Mar College *C, A*
El Paso Community College *C, A*
Houston Community College
　　System *C, A*
Howard College *C*
Kilgore College *C, A*
Lamar State College at Port Arthur *C, A*
Laredo Community College *C, A*
McLennan Community College *C, A*
Midland College *C, A*
North Harris Montgomery Community
　　College District *C, A*
Odessa College *C, A*

St. Philip's College *C, A*
San Antonio College *C, A*
San Jacinto College
   Central Campus *C*
South Plains College *C, A*
South Texas Community College *C, A*
Tarrant County College *C, A*
Temple College *C, A*
Trinity Valley Community College *C, A*
Tyler Junior College *C, A*
University of North Texas *B*

Utah
College of Eastern Utah *A*
Dixie State College of Utah *A*
Salt Lake Community College *C, A*
Snow College *A*
Weber State University *A*

Vermont
Southern Vermont College *A*

Virginia
Danville Community College *C*
J. Sargeant Reynolds Community
   College *C, A*
Southwest Virginia Community
   College *C*
Thomas Nelson Community College *C*
Virginia Polytechnic Institute and State
   University *B*
Virginia Western Community College *A*

Washington
Centralia College *C, A*
Edmonds Community College *C, A*
Lake Washington Technical College *C, A*
North Seattle Community College *C, A*
Peninsula College *A*
Renton Technical College *C*
Spokane Falls Community College *C*
Walla Walla Community College *C*

West Virginia
Fairmont State College *A*
West Virginia Northern Community
   College *C*

Wisconsin
Blackhawk Technical College *C*
Fox Valley Technical College *A*
Lakeshore Technical College *C*
Mid-State Technical College *C*
Milwaukee Area Technical College *C*
Moraine Park Technical College *C, A*
Nicolet Area Technical College *C, A*
Waukesha County Technical College *A*
Western Wisconsin Technical College *A*
Wisconsin Indianhead Technical
   College *A*

Wyoming
Central Wyoming College *A*
University of Wyoming *C*

Child care service

Arkansas
South Arkansas Community
   College *C, A*

California
Antelope Valley College *C, A*
Foothill College *C*
Santa Rosa Junior College *C*
Southwestern College *C, A*
Taft College *C*

Florida
Palm Beach Community College *C*

Georgia
Southwest Georgia Technical
   College *C, A*

Illinois
McHenry County College *C, A*
Waubonsee Community College *C, A*

Kansas
Kansas City Kansas Community
   College *C, A*

Kentucky
Hopkinsville Community College *C*
Jefferson Community College *A*
Somerset Community College *C, A*

Massachusetts
Cape Cod Community College *C*

Michigan
Baker College
   of Muskegon *C*
   of Port Huron *C*
Northern Michigan University *A*

Minnesota
Ridgewater College: A Community and
   Technical College *C*

New Mexico
Santa Fe Community College *C*

North Carolina
Carteret Community College *C, A*
James Sprunt Community College *C*

North Dakota
Lake Region State College *A*

Ohio
North Central State College *C*

Oklahoma
Northeastern Oklahoma Agricultural and
   Mechanical College *C, A*

Wisconsin
Fox Valley Technical College *C*

Child development

Alabama
Calhoun Community College *A*
Lawson State Community College *C*
Shelton State Community College *C*

Arizona
Prescott College *B, M*

California
Antelope Valley College *A*
California State University
   Fresno *B*
   Sacramento *B*
Foothill College *C, A*
Grossmont Community College *C, A*
Long Beach City College *C, A*
San Diego Mesa College *C, A*
Santa Rosa Junior College *C*
Southwestern College *C, A*
Taft College *C*

Colorado
Red Rocks Community College *C, A*

Connecticut
St. Joseph College *B*

Florida
Eckerd College *B*
Gulf Coast Community College *C*
Indian River Community College *C*
Miami-Dade Community College *A*
Nova Southeastern University *D*

Illinois
City Colleges of Chicago
   Kennedy-King College *A*
Rend Lake College *C, A*

Indiana
Earlham College *B*

Ivy Tech State College
   Bloomington *C, A*
   Central Indiana *C, A*
   Columbus *C, A*
   Eastcentral *C, A*
   Kokomo *C, A*
   Lafayette *C, A*
   Northcentral *C, A*
   Northeast *C, A*
   Northwest *C, A*
   Southcentral *C, A*
   Southeast *C, A*
   Southwest *C, A*
   Wabash Valley *C, A*
   Whitewater *C, A*

Michigan
Grand Rapids Community College *A*
Madonna University *A, B*
Michigan State University *B*
Oakland Community College *A*
Western Michigan University *B*

Minnesota
Hennepin Technical College *C, A*
South Central Technical College *A*

Missouri
Central Missouri State University *A, B*
Fontbonne College *B*
Ozarks Technical Community
   College *C, A*

Nebraska
University of Nebraska
   Omaha *B*

New Jersey
Thomas Edison State College *A, B*

New York
State University of New York
   College at Oneonta *B*

North Carolina
Beaufort County Community
   College *C, A*
Campbell University *B*
Carteret Community College *A*
East Carolina University *B*
Meredith College *B*

North Dakota
North Dakota State University *B, M*

Ohio
Bowling Green State University *B*
Northwest State Community College *A*
Ohio University *M*
University of Akron *B, M*
Youngstown State University *A*

Oklahoma
Rose State College *A*

Pennsylvania
Community College of Allegheny
   County *C, A*
Seton Hill University *B*

South Carolina
York Technical College *C*

Tennessee
Cleveland State Community College *A*
Dyersburg State Community
   College *C, A*
Northeast State Technical Community
   College *C, A*

Texas
Collin County Community College
   District *C, A*
Del Mar College *C, A*
Eastfield College *C, A*
Texas Tech University *B*
University of Houston *B*
University of Texas
   Arlington *B*
Wharton County Junior College *C, A*

Washington
Eastern Washington University *B, M*

Chinese

California
Cabrillo College *A*
Claremont McKenna College *B*
Monterey Institute of International
   Studies *C*
National Hispanic University *C, B*
Pitzer College *B*
Pomona College *B*
San Francisco State University *B, M*
San Jose State University *B*
Scripps College *B*
Stanford University *B, M, D*
University of California
   Berkeley *B, M, D*
   Davis *B*
   Irvine *B*
   Los Angeles *B*
   Riverside *B*
   Santa Barbara *B*
   Santa Cruz *B*
University of Southern California *M, D*

Colorado
University of Colorado
   Boulder *B, M*

Connecticut
Connecticut College *B*
Fairfield University *B*
Trinity College *B*
Yale University *B*

District of Columbia
George Washington University *B*
Georgetown University *B*

Hawaii
University of Hawaii
   Manoa *B, M, D*

Indiana
Indiana University
   Bloomington *M, D*
University of Notre Dame *B*

Iowa
Grinnell College *B*
University of Iowa *B, T*

Maine
Bates College *B*

Maryland
Johns Hopkins University *B*
University of Maryland
   College Park *B*

Massachusetts
Harvard College *B*
Simon's Rock College of Bard *B*
Tufts University *B*
University of Massachusetts
   Amherst *B, M*
Wellesley College *B*
Williams College *B*

Michigan
University of Michigan *M, D*

Minnesota
Augsburg College *B*
University of Minnesota
   Twin Cities *B, M, D*

Missouri
Washington University in St.
   Louis *B, M, D*

New Hampshire
Dartmouth College *B*

New Jersey
Rutgers, The State University of New
Jersey
New Brunswick Regional
Campus *B*
Seton Hall University *T*

New York
Bard College *B*
City University of New York
Hunter College *B*
Columbia University
Columbia College *B*
Cornell University *B*
Hamilton College *B*
State University of New York
Albany *B*

Ohio
Kent State University *B, M*
Ohio State University
Columbus Campus *B*

Oregon
Pacific University *B*
Portland State University *B*
Reed College *B*
University of Oregon *B*

Pennsylvania
Haverford College *T*
Lincoln University *B*
Swarthmore College *B*
University of Pittsburgh *B, M*

Texas
Trinity University *B*

Utah
Brigham Young University *B, M*
University of Utah *B*

Vermont
Bennington College *B, M, T*
Marlboro College *B*
Middlebury College *B*

Washington
Central Washington University *B*
Pacific Lutheran University *B*
University of Puget Sound *T*
University of Washington *B*

Wisconsin
Lawrence University *B*
University of Wisconsin
Madison *B, M, D*

Chinese studies

New York
Columbia University
Columbia College *B*
St. John's University *B, M*

Washington
University of Washington *B*

Wisconsin
Lawrence University *B*

Chiropractic (D.C.)

California
Cleveland Chiropractic College of Los
Angeles *F*
Life Chiropractic College West *F*
Los Angeles College of Chiropractic *F*
Palmer College of Chiropractic-West *F*

Connecticut
University of Bridgeport College of
Chiropractic *F*

Georgia
Life College *F*

Illinois
National University of Health Sciences *F*

Iowa
Palmer College of Chiropractic *F*

Minnesota
Northwestern College of Chiropractic *F*

Missouri
Cleveland Chiropractic College of
Kansas City *F*
Logan College of Chiropractic *F*

New York
New York Chiropractic College *F*

Oregon
Western States Chiropractic College *F*

South Carolina
Sherman College of Straight
Chiropractic *F*

Texas
Parker College of Chiropractic *F*
Texas Chiropractic College *F*

Christian studies

Arkansas
Harding University *B, M*

California
California Baptist University *B*
Vanguard University of Southern
California *B*

Illinois
Trinity International University *M*

Indiana
University of Notre Dame *M*

Iowa
St. Ambrose University *C*

Kansas
Southwestern College *B*

Kentucky
Lindsey Wilson College *B*

Missouri
Lindenwood University *B*

Nebraska
Creighton University *M*

Ohio
University of Dayton *C*
Ursuline College *B*

Oregon
Eugene Bible College *B*

Texas
Baylor University *M*
East Texas Baptist University *B*
University of St. Thomas *B*

Wisconsin
Maranatha Baptist Bible College *C*

Cinematography/film/video production

Arizona
Art Institute
of Phoenix *A*
Scottsdale Community College *A*
Yavapai College *C*

California
Academy of Art College *C, A, B, M*
Antelope Valley College *C, A*
Art Center College of Design *B, M*
Art Institute
of California: Los Angeles *A*
Biola University *B*

California College of Arts and
Crafts *B, M*
California Institute of the Arts *C, B, M*
California State University
Long Beach *B*
Chapman University *B, M*
Cogswell Polytechnical College *B*
De Anza College *C, A*
Grossmont Community College *C, A*
Loyola Marymount University *B*
Master's College *B*
Modesto Junior College *A*
Moorpark College *A*
Orange Coast College *A*
Pacific Union College *B*
Pitzer College *B*
University of California
Los Angeles *M, D*
Santa Barbara *B*
University of Southern California *B, M*
Vanguard University of Southern
California *B*

Colorado
Art Institute
of Colorado *A*
Red Rocks Community College *C, A*

Connecticut
University of Hartford *B*

District of Columbia
American University *M*

Florida
Florida Atlantic University *C*
Florida Metropolitan University
Melbourne Campus *A*
Orlando College North *A*
Florida State University *B, M*
Full Sail Real World Education *A*
Miami-Dade Community College *A*
Palm Beach Community College *A*
University of Central Florida *B*
University of Miami *B*
Valencia Community College *A*

Georgia
Art Institute
of Atlanta *A, B*
Atlanta College of Art *B*
Savannah College of Art and
Design *B, M*

Illinois
Columbia College Chicago *B, M*
School of the Art Institute of
Chicago *B, M*
University of Illinois
Chicago *M*

Iowa
University of Iowa *B, M*

Louisiana
Centenary College of Louisiana *B*

Maine
New England School of
Communications *C, A, B*
University of Southern Maine *B*

Maryland
Howard Community College *A*
University of Maryland
Baltimore County *B*
Villa Julie College *A, B*

Massachusetts
Boston University *B, M*
Emerson College *B*
Fitchburg State College *B*
Hampshire College *B*
Harvard College *B*
Massachusetts College of Art *B, M*
School of the Museum of Fine Arts *B, M*
Simon's Rock College of Bard *B*
Suffolk University *B*

Michigan
College for Creative Studies *B*
Lansing Community College *A*
Northern Michigan University *B*

Minnesota
Minneapolis Community and Technical
College *C, A*
Minnesota State University
Moorhead *B*

Missouri
Kansas City Art Institute *B*
Webster University *B*

Montana
Montana State University
Bozeman *B*
University of Montana-Missoula *M*

New Jersey
Bloomfield College *B*
Cumberland County College *A*
Fairleigh Dickinson University
College at Florham *B*

New York
Bard College *B, M*
City University of New York
Brooklyn College *M*
City College *B, M*
Hunter College *M*
Hofstra University *B*
Ithaca College *B*
New York University *B, M*
Pratt Institute *B*
Rochester Institute of
Technology *A, B, M*
St. John's University *A, B*
Sarah Lawrence College *B*
School of Visual Arts *B*
State University of New York
Buffalo *M*
Purchase *B*
Syracuse University *B, M*

North Carolina
Cape Fear Community College *A*
Guilford Technical Community
College *A*
North Carolina School of the Arts *B*
St. Augustine's College *B*
University of North Carolina
Wilmington *B*

Ohio
Antioch College *B*
Columbus College of Art and Design *B*
Ohio University *B, M*
University of Findlay *B*

Oklahoma
University of Oklahoma *B*

Oregon
Portland Community College *C*

Pennsylvania
Art Institute
of Philadelphia *A, B*
of Pittsburgh *A*
Bucks County Community College *A*
Drexel University *B*
La Salle University *B*

Penn State
Abington *B*
Altoona *B*
Beaver *B*
Berks *B*
Delaware County *B*
Dubois *B*
Fayette *B*
Hazleton *B*
Lehigh Valley *B*
McKeesport *B*
Mont Alto *B*
New Kensington *B*
Schuylkill - Capital College *B*
Shenango *B*
University Park *B, M*
Wilkes-Barre *B*
Worthington Scranton *B*
York *B*
Point Park College *B*

Rhode Island
Rhode Island School of Design *B*

South Carolina
Trident Technical College *C*

Tennessee
Pellissippi State Technical Community
College *A*
Southern Adventist University *B*

Texas
El Paso Community College *C, A*
North Lake College *A*
South Plains College *A*
Texas State Technical College
Waco *A*

Vermont
Bennington College *B*
Burlington College *C, B*
Champlain College *C, A, B*
Marlboro College *B*
Middlebury College *B*

Virginia
J. Sargeant Reynolds Community
College *C*

Washington
Art Institute of Seattle *A*
Cornish College of the Arts *B*
Olympic College *A*

Wisconsin
Milwaukee Area Technical College *A*
University of Wisconsin
Madison *B*
Oshkosh *B*

Civil engineering

Alabama
Alabama Agricultural and Mechanical
University *B*
Alabama Southern Community
College *A*
Auburn University *B, M, D*
University of Alabama *M, D*
University of Alabama
Birmingham *B, M, D*
Huntsville *B, M*
University of South Alabama *B*

Alaska
University of Alaska
Anchorage *B, M*
Fairbanks *B, M*

Arizona
Arizona State University *B, M, D*
Central Arizona College *A*
Northern Arizona University *B*
University of Arizona *B, M, D*

Arkansas
University of Arkansas *B, M*

California
California Institute of
Technology *B, M, D*
California Polytechnic State University:
San Luis Obispo *B*
California State Polytechnic University:
Pomona *B*
California State University
Chico *B*
Fresno *B, M*
Fullerton *B, M*
Long Beach *B, M*
Los Angeles *B, M*
Northridge *B, M*
Sacramento *B, M*
Diablo Valley College *C*
East Los Angeles College *A*
Loyola Marymount University *B, M*
San Diego State University *B, M*
San Francisco State University *B*
San Joaquin Delta College *C*
San Jose State University *B, M*
Santa Clara University *B, M*
Shasta College *A*
Stanford University *B, M, D*
University of California
Berkeley *B, M, D*
Davis *B*
Irvine *B, M, D*
Los Angeles *B, M, D*
University of Southern
California *B, M, D*
University of the Pacific *B*

Colorado
Colorado State University *B, M, D*
United States Air Force Academy *B*
University of Colorado
Boulder *B, M, D*
Denver *B, M, D*

Connecticut
United States Coast Guard Academy *B*
University of Connecticut *B, M, D*
University of Hartford *B, M*
University of New Haven *A, B*

Delaware
University of Delaware *B, M, D*

District of Columbia
Catholic University of America *B, M, D*
George Washington University *B, M, D*
Howard University *B, M*
University of the District of
Columbia *A, B*

Florida
Broward Community College *A*
Embry-Riddle Aeronautical University *B*
Florida Agricultural and Mechanical
University *B, M*
Florida Atlantic University *B, M*
Florida Institute of Technology *B, M, D*
Florida International University *B, M, D*
Florida State University *B, M, D*
Manatee Community College *A*
Miami-Dade Community College *A*
Pensacola Junior College *A*
South Florida Community College *A*
Tallahassee Community College *A*
University of Central Florida *C, B, M, D*
University of Florida *B, M, D*
University of Miami *B, M, D*
University of North Florida *B*
University of South Florida *B, M, D*

Georgia
Armstrong Atlantic State University *A*
Georgia Institute of Technology *B, M, D*
Middle Georgia College *A*

Hawaii
University of Hawaii
Manoa *B, M, D*

Idaho
Boise State University *B*

Brigham Young University - Idaho *A*
College of Southern Idaho *A*
Idaho State University *B*
Lewis-Clark State College *A*
North Idaho College *A*
University of Idaho *B, M, D*

Illinois
Bradley University *B, M*
Dominican University *B*
Illinois Institute of Technology *B, M, D*
Lake Land College *A*
Lincoln Land Community College *A*
Northwestern University *B, M, D*
Parkland College *A*
Sauk Valley Community College *A*
Southern Illinois University
Carbondale *B, M*
Southern Illinois University
Edwardsville *B, M*
University of Illinois
Chicago *B, M, D*
Urbana-Champaign *B, M, D*

Indiana
Indiana Institute of Technology *B*
Purdue University *B, M, D*
Purdue University
Calumet *A*
Rose-Hulman Institute of Technology *B*
Tri-State University *B*
University of Evansville *B*
University of Notre Dame *B, M, D*
Valparaiso University *B*
Vincennes University *A*

Iowa
Iowa State University *B, M, D*
University of Iowa *B, M, D*

Kansas
Fort Scott Community College *A*
Independence Community College *A*
Kansas State University *B, M, D*
University of Kansas *B, M, D*

Kentucky
University of Kentucky *B, M, D*
University of Louisville *B, M, D*

Louisiana
Louisiana State University and
Agricultural and Mechanical
College *B, M, D*
Louisiana Tech University *B*
Southern University and Agricultural and
Mechanical College *B*
Tulane University *B, M, D*
University of Louisiana at
Lafayette *B, M*
University of New Orleans *B*

Maine
University of Maine *B, M, D*

Maryland
Johns Hopkins University *B, M, D*
Montgomery College
Rockville Campus *A*
Morgan State University *B*
University of Maryland
Baltimore County *M, D*
College Park *B, M, D*

Massachusetts
Massachusetts Institute of
Technology *B, M, D*
Merrimack College *B*
Northeastern University *B, M, D*
Smith College *B*
Tufts University *B, M*
University of Massachusetts
Amherst *B, M, D*
Dartmouth *B*
Lowell *B, M*
Worcester Polytechnic Institute *B, M, D*

Michigan
Calvin College *B*

Lawrence Technological University *B, M*
Michigan State University *B, M, D*
Michigan Technological
University *B, M, D, T*
University of Michigan *B, M, D*
Wayne State University *B, M, D*
Western Michigan University *B*

Minnesota
Minnesota State University
Mankato *B*
St. Cloud Technical College *C, A*
University of Minnesota
Twin Cities *C, B, M, D*
Vermilion Community College *A*

Mississippi
Mississippi State University *B, M*
University of Mississippi *B*

Missouri
East Central College *A*
University of Missouri
Columbia *B, M, D*
Kansas City *B, M*
Rolla *B, M, D*
St. Louis *B*
Washington University in St.
Louis *B, M, D*

Montana
Carroll College *B*
Montana State University
Bozeman *B, M*
Montana Tech of the University of
Montana *B*

Nebraska
Southeast Community College
Milford Campus *A*
University of Nebraska
Lincoln *B, M*
Omaha *B*

Nevada
University of Nevada
Las Vegas *B, M, D*
Reno *B, M, D*

New Hampshire
New England College *A, B*
University of New Hampshire *B, M, D*

New Jersey
Essex County College *A*
Middlesex County College *A*
New Jersey Institute of
Technology *B, M, D*
Ocean County College *C*
Princeton University *B, M, D*
Rowan University *B*
Rutgers, The State University of New
Jersey
Camden Regional Campus *B*
New Brunswick Regional
Campus *B, M, D*
Newark Regional Campus *B*
Stevens Institute of Technology *B, M, D*

New Mexico
New Mexico State University *B, M*
University of New Mexico *B, M*

New York
City University of New York
City College *B, M, D*
College of Staten Island *A*
Clarkson University *B, M, D*
Columbia University
Fu Foundation School of
Engineering and Applied
Science *B, M, D*
Cornell University *B*
Hofstra University *B*
Manhattan College *B, M*
New York University *B*
Polytechnic University *B, M, D*
Rensselaer Polytechnic Institute *B, M, D*

State University of New York
Buffalo *B, M, D*
College of Environmental Science
and Forestry *B, M, D*
Syracuse University *B, M, D*
United States Military Academy *B*

North Carolina
Central Carolina Community College *A*
Duke University *B, M, D*
Fayetteville Technical Community
College *A*
Guilford Technical Community
College *C, A*
Johnston Community College *A*
North Carolina Agricultural and
Technical State University *B*
North Carolina State University *B, M, D*
University of North Carolina
Charlotte *B, M*
Western Piedmont Community
College *A*

North Dakota
North Dakota State University *B, M*
University of North Dakota *B, M*

Ohio
Case Western Reserve
University *B, M, D*
Cleveland State University *B, M, D*
Columbus State Community College *A*
Ohio Northern University *B*
Ohio State University
Columbus Campus *B, M, D*
Ohio University *B, M*
Stark State College of Technology *A*
University of Akron *B, M, D*
University of Cincinnati *B, M, D*
University of Dayton *B, M*
University of Toledo *B, M*
Youngstown State University *B, M*

Oklahoma
Oklahoma State University *B, M, D*
Oklahoma State University
Oklahoma City *A*
Okmulgee *B*
University of Oklahoma *B, M, D*

Oregon
Oregon Institute of Technology *B*
Oregon State University *B, M, D*
Portland State University *B, M, D*
University of Portland *B, M*

Pennsylvania
Bucknell University *B, M*
Drexel University *B, M, D*
Gettysburg College *B*
Lafayette College *B*
Lehigh University *B, M, D*
Lock Haven University of
Pennsylvania *B*
Messiah College *B*
Penn State
Abington *B*
Altoona *B*
Beaver *B*
Berks *B*
Delaware County *B*
Dubois *B*
Fayette *B*
Hazleton *B*
Lehigh Valley *B*
McKeesport *B*
Mont Alto *B*
New Kensington *B*
Schuylkill - Capital College *B*
Shenango *B*
University Park *B, M, D*
Wilkes-Barre *B*
Worthington Scranton *B*
York *B*
Temple University *B, M*
University of Pennsylvania *B*
University of Pittsburgh *C, B, M, D*

Villanova University *B, M*
Widener University *B, M*

Puerto Rico
Universidad Politecnica de Puerto
Rico *B, M*
University of Puerto Rico
Mayaguez Campus *B, M, D*
Ponce *A*

Rhode Island
Brown University *B*
University of Rhode Island *B, M, D*

South Carolina
The Citadel *B*
Clemson University *B, M, D*
University of South Carolina *B, M, D*

South Dakota
South Dakota School of Mines and
Technology *B, M*
South Dakota State University *B*

Tennessee
Chattanooga State Technical Community
College *A*
Christian Brothers University *B*
Tennessee State University *B*
Tennessee Technological
University *B, M, D*
University of Memphis *B, M*
University of Tennessee
Knoxville *B, M, D*
Vanderbilt University *B, M, D*

Texas
Houston Baptist University *B*
Kilgore College *A*
Lamar University *B*
Prairie View A&M University *B*
Rice University *B, M, D*
Texas A&M University *B, M, D*
Texas A&M University
Kingsville *B, M*
Texas Tech University *B, M, D*
University of Houston *B, M, D*
University of Texas
Arlington *B, M, D*
Austin *B, M, D*
El Paso *B, M*
San Antonio *B, M*
University of the Incarnate Word *B*

Utah
Brigham Young University *B, M, D*
Salt Lake Community College *A*
Snow College *A*
University of Utah *B, M, D*
Utah State University *C, B, M, D*

Vermont
Norwich University *B*
University of Vermont *B, M, D*
Vermont Technical College *A*

Virginia
George Mason University *B, M*
Old Dominion University *B*
University of Virginia *B, M, D*
Virginia Military Institute *B*
Virginia Polytechnic Institute and State
University *B, M, D*
Virginia Western Community College *A*

Washington
Centralia College *A*
Gonzaga University *B*
St. Martin's College *B, M*
Seattle University *B*
University of Washington *B, M, D*
Walla Walla College *B*
Washington State University *B, M, D*

West Virginia
Potomac State College of West Virginia
University *A*
West Virginia University *B, M, D*

West Virginia University Institute of
Technology *B*

Wisconsin
Chippewa Valley Technical College *A*
Marquette University *B, M, D*
Milwaukee Area Technical College *A*
University of Wisconsin
Madison *B, M, D*
Milwaukee *B*
Platteville *B*

Wyoming
University of Wyoming *B, M, D*

Civil engineering drafting/ CAD/CADD

California
Santa Rosa Junior College *C*

Illinois
Parkland College *C*

Kentucky
Somerset Community College *C*

North Dakota
North Dakota State College of Science *A*

Ohio
Central Ohio Technical College *A*

Oklahoma
Platt College
Tulsa *C*

Pennsylvania
Community College of Allegheny
County *C*

Texas
Tyler Junior College *C, A*

Washington
Centralia College *A*

Civil engineering technology

Alabama
Alabama Agricultural and Mechanical
University *B*
Bishop State Community College *A*
Gadsden State Community College *C, A*

Arizona
Eastern Arizona College *A*
Phoenix College *A*

Arkansas
University of Arkansas
Little Rock *A, B*

California
California State University
Fresno *B*
Long Beach *B*
Chabot College *C*
San Joaquin Delta College *C*
Santa Rosa Junior College *C, A*
Shasta College *C, A*
Ventura College *A*

Colorado
Colorado State University
Pueblo *B*
Metropolitan State College of Denver *B*
Trinidad State Junior College *C, A*

Connecticut
Capital Community College *A*
Central Connecticut State University *B*
Three Rivers Community College *A*

Delaware
Delaware State University *B*

Delaware Technical and Community
College
Owens Campus *A*
Stanton/Wilmington Campus *A*
Terry Campus *C, A*

Florida
Broward Community College *A*
Daytona Beach Community College *A*
Florida Agricultural and Mechanical
University *B*
Gulf Coast Community College *A*
Indian River Community College *A*
Manatee Community College *A*
Miami-Dade Community College *A*
Pensacola Junior College *A*
Polk Community College *A*
South Florida Community College *A*
Tallahassee Community College *A*
Valencia Community College *A*

Georgia
Georgia Southern University *B*
Macon State College *A*
Middle Georgia College *A*
Savannah State University *B*
Southern Polytechnic State University *B*

Idaho
Idaho State University *A*
Lewis-Clark State College *A*

Illinois
Black Hawk College *A*
Bradley University *B*
College of Lake County *C, A*
Morrison Institute of Technology *A*
Parkland College *C*

Indiana
Indiana University-Purdue University
Fort Wayne *A*
Indiana University-Purdue University
Indianapolis *A*
Purdue University
North Central Campus *A*
Vincennes University *A*

Iowa
Des Moines Area Community College *A*
Hawkeye Community College *A*
Iowa Western Community College *A*

Kansas
Cloud County Community College *A*
Independence Community College *A*
Johnson County Community College *A*
Kansas State University *A*
Washburn University of Topeka *A*

Kentucky
Murray State University *A, B*

Louisiana
Delgado Community College *A*
Louisiana Tech University *B*
University of New Orleans *B, M*

Maine
Central Maine Technical College *A*
University of Maine *B*

Maryland
Community College of Baltimore County
Catonsville *C, A*
Dundalk *C, A*
Essex *C, A*
Montgomery College
Rockville Campus *A*

Massachusetts
Merrimack College *B*
Northeastern University *A, B*
Quinsigamond Community College *A*
Springfield Technical Community
College *A*
University of Massachusetts
Lowell *A, B*
Wentworth Institute of Technology *A, B*

Michigan

Ferris State University *C, A*
Lansing Community College *A*
Macomb Community College *C, A*
Michigan Technological University *A*

Minnesota

Lake Superior College: A Community
and Technical College *A*
Rochester Community and Technical
College *A*
St. Cloud Technical College *C, A*
South Central Technical College *A*

Mississippi

Northwest Mississippi Community
College *C, A*

Missouri

Lincoln University *B*
Mineral Area College *C, A*
Missouri Western State College *A, B*
St. Louis Community College
St. Louis Community College at
Florissant Valley *A*
Three Rivers Community College *A*
Washington University in St. Louis *B*

Montana

Montana Tech of the University of
Montana *A*

Nebraska

Metropolitan Community College *C, A*
Southeast Community College
Milford Campus *A*
University of Nebraska
Omaha *B*

New Hampshire

New Hampshire Technical Institute *A*
University of New Hampshire *A, B*

New Jersey

Essex County College *A*
Fairleigh Dickinson University
Metropolitan Campus *B*
Gloucester County College *C, A*
Mercer County Community College *A*
Middlesex County College *A*
Ocean County College *A*
Thomas Edison State College *A, B*
Union County College *A*

New York

Broome Community College *A*
City University of New York
College of Staten Island *A*
Columbia University
Fu Foundation School of
Engineering and Applied
Science *B*
Erie Community College
North Campus *A*
Hudson Valley Community College *A*
Mohawk Valley Community College *A*
Monroe Community College *C, A*
Nassau Community College *A*
Rochester Institute of Technology *B*
State University of New York
College of Technology at Alfred *A*
College of Technology at Canton *A*
Institute of Technology at
Utica/Rome *B*
Westchester Community College *A*

North Carolina

Asheville Buncombe Technical
Community College *A*
Central Carolina Community College *A*
Central Piedmont Community College *A*
Fayetteville Technical Community
College *A*
Gaston College *A*
Guilford Technical Community
College *C, A*
Sandhills Community College *A*

University of North Carolina
Charlotte *B*
Wake Technical Community College *A*

North Dakota

North Dakota State College of Science *A*

Ohio

Cincinnati State Technical and
Community College *A*
Clark State Community College *A*
Columbus State Community College *A*
Lakeland Community College *A*
Sinclair Community College *A*
Stark State College of Technology *A*
University of Toledo *C, A, B*
Youngstown State University *A, B*

Oklahoma

Oklahoma State University
Oklahoma City *A*
Okmulgee *A*
Tulsa Community College *C, A*

Oregon

Blue Mountain Community College *A*
Chemeketa Community College *A*
Linn-Benton Community College *C*
Mount Hood Community College *A*
Portland Community College *C, A*
Umpqua Community College *A*

Pennsylvania

Butler County Community College *A*
Community College of Allegheny
County *A*
Education Direct: Center for Degree
Studies *A*
Penn State
Harrisburg *B*
Pennsylvania College of
Technology *A, B*
Pennsylvania Institute of Technology *A*
Point Park College *A, B*
Temple University *A*
University of Pittsburgh
Johnstown *B*

Puerto Rico

University of Puerto Rico
Bayamon University College *A*
Ponce *A*

South Carolina

Central Carolina Technical College *A*
Florence-Darlington Technical College *A*
Francis Marion University *B*
Horry-Georgetown Technical College *A*
Midlands Technical College *A*
South Carolina State University *B*
Spartanburg Technical College *A*
Trident Technical College *C, A*

South Dakota

Southeast Technical Institute *A*

Tennessee

Pellissippi State Technical Community
College *A*
Southwest Tennessee Community
College *A*

Texas

Kilgore College *A*
Laredo Community College *A*
San Antonio College *A*
Texas Southern University *B*
University of Houston *B*
University of Houston
Downtown *B*

Vermont

Vermont Technical College *A*

Virginia

J. Sargeant Reynolds Community
College *A*
Virginia Western Community College *A*

Washington

Centralia College *A*
South Seattle Community College *A*
Spokane Community College *A*
Walla Walla Community College *C, A*

West Virginia

Bluefield State College *A, B*
Fairmont State College *A, B*
West Virginia University Institute of
Technology *A*

Wisconsin

Chippewa Valley Technical College *A*
Mid-State Technical College *A*
Moraine Park Technical College *A*

Classical/ancient Mediterranean/Near Eastern studies

Kansas

University of Kansas *B*

Maine

Colby College *B*

New Hampshire

Dartmouth College *B*

New York

Columbia University
Columbia College *B*

Pennsylvania

Dickinson College *B*

Classics

Alabama

Samford University *B*
University of Alabama *B*

Arizona

University of Arizona *B, M*

Arkansas

University of Arkansas *B*

California

California State University
Long Beach *B*
Claremont McKenna College *B*
Loyola Marymount University *B*
Pitzer College *B*
Pomona College *B*
St. Mary's College of California *B*
San Diego State University *B*
San Francisco State University *B, M*
Santa Clara University *B*
Scripps College *B*
Stanford University *B, M, D*
University of California
Berkeley *B, M, D*
Davis *B, M*
Irvine *B, M, D*
Los Angeles *M, D*
Riverside *B, M, D*
San Diego *B*
Santa Barbara *B, M, D*
Santa Cruz *B*
University of Southern
California *B, M, D*
University of the Pacific *B*

Colorado

Colorado College *B*
University of Colorado
Boulder *B, M, D*

Connecticut

Albertus Magnus College *B*
Connecticut College *B*
Trinity College *B*
University of Connecticut *B*
Wesleyan University *B*
Yale University *B, M, D*

Delaware

University of Delaware *B*

District of Columbia

Catholic University of America *B, M*
George Washington University *B*
Georgetown University *B*
Howard University *B*

Florida

Florida State University *B, M, D*
New College of Florida *B*
Rollins College *B*
University of Florida *B, M*
University of Miami *B*
University of South Florida *B, M*

Georgia

Agnes Scott College *B*
Emory University *B*
Georgia State University *B*
Mercer University *B*
Oxford College of Emory University *B*
University of Georgia *B, M*

Hawaii

University of Hawaii
Manoa *B, M*

Idaho

University of Idaho *B*

Illinois

Augustana College *B, T*
Knox College *B*
Loyola University of Chicago *B, M, D*
Monmouth College *B, T*
North Central College *B*
Northwestern University *B, M, D*
Rockford College *B*
Southern Illinois University
Carbondale *B*
University of Chicago *B, M, D*
University of Illinois
Chicago *B*
Urbana-Champaign *B, M*

Indiana

Ball State University *B*
DePauw University *B*
Earlham College *B*
Hanover College *B*
University of Evansville *B*
University of Notre Dame *B*
Valparaiso University *B*
Wabash College *B*

Iowa

Coe College *B*
Cornell College *B*
Grinnell College *B*
Loras College *B*
Luther College *B*
University of Iowa *B, M, D*

Kansas

University of Kansas *B, M*

Kentucky

Asbury College *B*
Centre College *B*
University of Kentucky *B, M*

Louisiana

Centenary College of Louisiana *B*
Louisiana College *B*
Loyola University New Orleans *B*
Tulane University *B*

Maine

Bowdoin College *B*
Colby College *B*
University of Southern Maine *B*

Maryland

College of Notre Dame of Maryland *B*
Johns Hopkins University *B, M, D*
Loyola College in Maryland *B*

University of Maryland
  Baltimore County *B*
  College Park *B, M*

Massachusetts
Amherst College *B*
Assumption College *B*
Boston College *B*
Boston University *B, M, D*
Clark University *B*
College of the Holy Cross *B*
Harvard College *B*
Hellenic College/Holy Cross *B*
Mount Holyoke College *B*
Smith College *B*
Tufts University *B, M*
University of Massachusetts
  Amherst *B, M*
  Boston *B*
Wellesley College *B*
Wheaton College *B*
Williams College *B*

Michigan
Calvin College *B*
Grand Valley State University *B*
Hillsdale College *B*
Hope College *B*
Kalamazoo College *B*
University of Michigan *B, M, D*
Wayne State University *B, M*

Minnesota
Carleton College *B*
College of St. Benedict *B*
Concordia College: Moorhead *B*
Gustavus Adolphus College *B*
Macalester College *B*
St. John's University *B*
St. Olaf College *B*
University of Minnesota
  Twin Cities *B, M, D*
University of St. Thomas *B*

Mississippi
Millsaps College *B, T*
University of Mississippi *B, M*

Missouri
St. Louis University *B*
Truman State University *B*
University of Missouri
  Columbia *B, M, D*
Washington University in St. Louis *B, M*

Montana
University of Montana-Missoula *B*

Nebraska
Creighton University *B*
University of Nebraska
  Lincoln *B, M*

New Hampshire
Dartmouth College *B*
St. Anselm College *C, B*
University of New Hampshire *B*

New Jersey
Drew University *B*
Montclair State University *B*
Princeton University *B, M, D*
Richard Stockton College of New
  Jersey *B*
Rutgers, The State University of New
  Jersey
    New Brunswick Regional
      Campus *B, M, D*
St. Peter's College *B*
Seton Hall University *B*

New Mexico
University of New Mexico *B*

New York
Bard College *B*
Barnard College *B*

City University of New York
  Brooklyn College *B, M*
  Hunter College *B*
  Queens College *B*
Colgate University *B*
College of New Rochelle *B, T*
Columbia University
  Columbia College *B*
Cornell University *B, M, D*
Elmira College *B*
Fordham University *B, M, D*
Hamilton College *B*
Hobart and William Smith Colleges *B*
Hofstra University *B*
Manhattanville College *B*
New York University *B, M, D*
St. Bonaventure University *B*
Sarah Lawrence College *B*
Skidmore College *B*
State University of New York
  Albany *B, M*
  Binghamton *B*
  Buffalo *B, M, D*
Syracuse University *B, M*
Union College *B*
Yeshiva University *B*

North Carolina
Davidson College *B*
Duke University *B, M, D*
Lenoir-Rhyne College *B*
University of North Carolina
  Asheville *B, T*
  Chapel Hill *B, M, D*
  Greensboro *B*
Wake Forest University *B*

North Dakota
University of North Dakota *B*

Ohio
Bowling Green State University *B*
Case Western Reserve University *B*
College of Wooster *B*
Denison University *B*
Franciscan University of Steubenville *B*
Hiram College *B*
Kent State University *B*
Kenyon College *B*
Miami University
  Oxford Campus *B*
Oberlin College *B*
Ohio State University
  Columbus Campus *B, M, D*
Ohio University *B*
Ohio Wesleyan University *B*
University of Akron *B*
University of Cincinnati *B, M, D*
University of Toledo *M*
Wright State University *B*
Xavier University *B*

Oklahoma
University of Oklahoma *B*
University of Tulsa *B*

Oregon
Reed College *B*
University of Oregon *B, M*
Willamette University *B*

Pennsylvania
Bryn Mawr College *B, M, D*
Bucknell University *B*
Dickinson College *B*
Duquesne University *B*
Franklin & Marshall College *B*
Gettysburg College *B*
Haverford College *B*
La Salle University *B*
Lehigh University *B*
Moravian College *B*

Penn State
  Abington *B*
  Altoona *B*
  Beaver *B*
  Berks *B*
  Delaware County *B*
  Dubois *B*
  Fayette *B*
  Hazleton *B*
  Lehigh Valley *B*
  McKeesport *B*
  Mont Alto *B*
  New Kensington *B*
  Schuylkill - Capital College *B*
  Shenango *B*
  University Park *B*
  Wilkes-Barre *B*
  Worthington Scranton *B*
  York *B*
Swarthmore College *B*
Temple University *B*
University of Pennsylvania *B, M, D*
University of Pittsburgh *B, M, D*
University of Scranton *B*
Villanova University *B, M*

Rhode Island
Brown University *B, M, D*
University of Rhode Island *B*

South Carolina
College of Charleston *B, T*
University of South Carolina *B*

Tennessee
Rhodes College *B, T*
University of Tennessee
  Chattanooga *B*
  Knoxville *B*
Vanderbilt University *B, M, D*

Texas
Austin College *B*
Baylor University *B*
Rice University *B*
Southwestern University *B*
Texas Tech University *B, M*
Trinity University *B*
University of Dallas *B*
University of Houston *B*
University of Texas
  Arlington *B*
  Austin *B, M, D*
  San Antonio *B*

Utah
Brigham Young University *B*
University of Utah *B*

Vermont
Marlboro College *B*
Middlebury College *B*
St. Michael's College *B*
University of Vermont *B, M*

Virginia
Christendom College *B*
College of William and Mary *B*
Hampden-Sydney College *B*
Hollins University *B*
Mary Washington College *B*
Randolph-Macon College *B*
Randolph-Macon Woman's College *B*
Sweet Briar College *B*
University of Richmond *B, T*
University of Virginia *B, M, D*
Washington and Lee University *B*

Washington
Pacific Lutheran University *B*
Seattle Pacific University *B*
University of Puget Sound *B*
University of Washington *B, M, D*
Washington State University *B*
Whitman College *B*

West Virginia
Huntington Junior College *C, A*

Wisconsin
Beloit College *B*
Lawrence University *B, T*
Marquette University *B*
Ripon College *B*
University of Wisconsin
  Madison *B, M, D*
  Milwaukee *B*

| Clinical child psychology |

Kansas
University of Kansas *D*

New York
St. John's University *D*
State University of New York
  Buffalo *M*

Ohio
Case Western Reserve University *D*

Pennsylvania
Marywood University *M*

| Clinical laboratory science |

Alabama
Central Alabama Community College *A*
Enterprise State Junior College *A*
James H. Faulkner State Community
  College *A*
Tuskegee University *B*
University of Alabama
  Birmingham *B, M*
University of South Alabama *B*

Arizona
Arizona State University *B*
Phoenix College *A*
University of Arizona *B, M*

Arkansas
Arkansas State University *A, B*
Arkansas Tech University *B*
Henderson State University *B*
John Brown University *B*
University of Arkansas
  for Medical Sciences *B*

California
California State University
  Bakersfield *B*
  Dominguez Hills *M*
Loma Linda University *A, B*
San Francisco State University *B*

Connecticut
Central Connecticut State University *B*
University of Connecticut *B*
University of Hartford *B*
University of New Haven *B*
Western Connecticut State University *B*

Delaware
University of Delaware *B*

District of Columbia
Catholic University of America *B*
Howard University *B*

Florida
Barry University *B*
Bethune-Cookman College *B*
Florida Gulf Coast University *B*
Manatee Community College *A*
Okaloosa-Walton Community College *A*
St. Leo University *B*
South Florida Community College *A*
Stetson University *B*
University of Central Florida *B*
University of South Florida *B*

Georgia
Armstrong Atlantic State University *B*
Augusta State University *B*
Clayton College and State University *A*

Georgia Southern University *B*
Georgia State University *B*
Oglethorpe University *B*
Savannah State University *B*

Hawaii
University of Hawaii
    Manoa *B*

Idaho
Idaho State University *B*

Illinois
Aurora University *B*
Benedictine University *B*
Bradley University *B*
De Paul University *B*
Eastern Illinois University *B*
Finch University of Health Sciences/The
    Chicago Medical School *M*
Illinois College *B*
Illinois State University *B*
National-Louis University *B*
North Park University *B*
Northern Illinois University *B*
Parkland College *A*
Quincy University *B*
Rush University *M*
Springfield College in Illinois *A*
University of Illinois
    Chicago *B, M*
    Springfield *B*
Western Illinois University *B*

Indiana
Indiana State University *B*
Indiana University
    Southeast *B*
Indiana University-Purdue University
    Fort Wayne *B*
Indiana University-Purdue University
    Indianapolis *B*
Manchester College *B*
Purdue University *B*
Purdue University
    Calumet *B*
St. Joseph's College *B*

Iowa
Dordt College *B*
Graceland University *B*
Simpson College *B*
University of Iowa *B*
Wartburg College *B*

Kansas
Barton County Community College *A*
University of Kansas Medical Center *B*
Wichita State University *B*

Kentucky
Bellarmine University *C, B, M*
Cumberland College *B*
Hazard Community College *A*
Madisonville Community College *A*
Murray State University *B*
Spalding University *B*
University of Kentucky *B, M, D*
University of Louisville *B*

Louisiana
Louisiana State University
    Alexandria *A*
Louisiana Tech University *B*
McNeese State University *B*
Northwestern State University *B*
University of Louisiana at Monroe *B*
University of New Orleans *B*

Maine
University of Maine *B, M*
University of New England *B*

Maryland
Johns Hopkins University *B*
Salisbury University *B*

Massachusetts
American International College *B*

Fitchburg State College *B*
Laboure College *C, A*
Northeastern University *A, B*
Salem State College *B*
Springfield College *B*
Stonehill College *B*
University of Massachusetts
    Amherst *B*
    Boston *B*
    Dartmouth *B*
    Lowell *B, M*

Michigan
Andrews University *B, M*
Central Michigan University *B*
Eastern Michigan University *B*
Ferris State University *B*
Gogebic Community College *A*
Grand Valley State University *B*
Lansing Community College *A*
Michigan State University *B, M*
Michigan Technological University *B*
Northern Michigan University *C, A, B*
Oakland University *B*
Saginaw Valley State University *B*
University of Michigan
    Flint *B*
Wayne State University *C, B, M*

Minnesota
Bemidji State University *B*
College of St. Catherine *B*
Concordia College: Moorhead *B*
Minnesota State University
    Mankato *B*
    Moorhead *B*
St. Cloud State University *B*
St. Mary's University of Minnesota *B*

Mississippi
Alcorn State University *B*
Mississippi Gulf Coast Community
    College
    Perkinston *A*
Mississippi State University *B*
University of Mississippi *B*
University of Mississippi Medical
    Center *B*
University of Southern Mississippi *B, M*

Missouri
Culver-Stockton College *B*
Lindenwood University *B*
Maryville University of Saint Louis *B*
Northwest Missouri State University *B*
Rockhurst University *B*
St. Louis Community College
    St. Louis Community College at
        Forest Park *A*
St. Louis University *B*
Southeast Missouri State University *B*
Southwest Missouri State University *B*
University of Missouri
    St. Louis *B*
William Jewell College *B*

Montana
University of Montana-Missoula *B*

Nebraska
University of Nebraska
    Medical Center *B*

Nevada
University of Nevada
    Las Vegas *B*

New Jersey
College of St. Elizabeth *B*
Fairleigh Dickinson University
    College at Florham *B*
    Metropolitan Campus *B, M*
Felician College *B*
Kean University *B*
Monmouth University *B*
Ramapo College of New Jersey *B*

Rutgers, The State University of New
    Jersey
    Newark Regional Campus *B*
St. Peter's College *B*
Thomas Edison State College *A, B*
University of Medicine and Dentistry of
    New Jersey
    School of Health Related
        Professions *B*

New Mexico
Eastern New Mexico University *B*

New York
Canisius College *B*
City University of New York
    College of Staten Island *B*
Elmira College *B*
Hudson Valley Community College *A*
Iona College *B*
Keuka College *B*
Long Island University
    C. W. Post Campus *B*
Mercy College *B*
Mount St. Mary College *B*
Nassau Community College *A*
Orange County Community College *A*
Pace University *B*
Pace University:
    Pleasantville/Briarcliff *B*
State University of New York
    Buffalo *M*
    College at Plattsburgh *B*
    Health Science Center at Stony
        Brook *B*
    Stony Brook *B*
    Upstate Medical University *B*
Westchester Community College *A*

North Carolina
Catawba College *B*
Durham Technical Community
    College *A*
East Carolina University *B*
High Point University *B*
University of North Carolina
    Chapel Hill *B*
    Charlotte *B*
    Greensboro *B*
    Pembroke *B*
    Wilmington *B*
Western Carolina University *B*
Winston-Salem State University *B*

North Dakota
Jamestown College *B*
Minot State University *B*
North Dakota State University *B*
University of Mary *B*
University of North Dakota *B, M*

Ohio
Bowling Green State University *B*
Cincinnati State Technical and
    Community College *A*
College of Mount St. Joseph *B*
Malone College *B*
Miami University
    Oxford Campus *B*
Ohio University *B*
University of Akron *B*
University of Cincinnati *B*
University of Rio Grande *B*
University of Toledo *A, B*
Walsh University *B*
Wright State University *B*
Youngstown State University *B*

Oklahoma
Oklahoma Christian University of
    Science and Arts *B*
Oklahoma Panhandle State University *B*
Oral Roberts University *B*
University of Central Oklahoma *B*
University of Science and Arts of
    Oklahoma *B*

Pennsylvania
Bloomsburg University of
    Pennsylvania *B*
Cabrini College *B*
Cheyney University of Pennsylvania *B*
Drexel University *A, B*
Elizabethtown College *B*
Gwynedd-Mercy College *B*
Indiana University of Pennsylvania *B*
Keystone College *A*
King's College *B*
Kutztown University of Pennsylvania *B*
Lock Haven University of
    Pennsylvania *B*
Marywood University *B*
Mercyhurst College *B*
Reading Area Community College *A*
Seton Hill University *B*
University of Pittsburgh *B*
University of Scranton *B*
Wilkes University *B*

Puerto Rico
Inter American University of Puerto Rico
    Metropolitan Campus *B*
    San German Campus *C, B*
Pontifical Catholic University of Puerto
    Rico *B*
University of Puerto Rico
    Medical Sciences Campus *B, M*

Rhode Island
Rhode Island College *B*
Salve Regina University *B*
University of Rhode Island *B, M*

South Carolina
Clemson University *B*
Coker College *B*
Lander University *B*
Medical University of South Carolina *B*
Winthrop University *B*

South Dakota
Augustana College *B*
Mount Marty College *B*
Northern State University *B*
University of South Dakota *B*

Tennessee
Austin Peay State University *B*
Carson-Newman College *B*
King College *B*
Southern Adventist University *B*
Tusculum College *B*
University of Tennessee
    Knoxville *B*

Texas
Amarillo College *A*
Angelo State University *B*
Baylor University *B*
Del Mar College *A*
Grayson County College *A*
Lamar University *B*
Midwestern State University *B*
Odessa College *A*
Prairie View A&M University *B*
St. Mary's University *B*
Sam Houston State University *B*
San Jacinto College
    Central Campus *A*
Southwest Texas State University *B*
Stephen F. Austin State University *B*
Tarleton State University *B*
Texas A&M University
    Corpus Christi *B*
Texas Southern University *B*
Texas State Technical College
    Waco *A*
Texas Woman's University *B*
University of Houston *B*
University of Mary Hardin-Baylor *B*
University of North Texas *B*

University of Texas
Arlington *B*
Austin *B*
El Paso *B*
Health Science Center at San Antonio *B*
Medical Branch at Galveston *B*
Pan American *B*
San Antonio *B*
Southwestern Medical Center at Dallas *B*
Tyler *B*
University of the Incarnate Word *B*
West Texas A&M University *B*

Utah
Brigham Young University *B*
Snow College *A*
University of Utah *B, M*
Utah State University *B*
Weber State University *B*

Vermont
University of Vermont *B, M*

Virginia
Averett University *B*
Bridgewater College *B*
George Mason University *B*
Mary Baldwin College *B*
Norfolk State University *B*
Old Dominion University *B*
Roanoke College *B*
Virginia Commonwealth University *B, M*

Washington
University of Washington *B, M*

West Virginia
Concord College *B*
Marshall University *B*
West Liberty State College *B*
West Virginia University *B, M*

Wisconsin
Marian College of Fond du Lac *B*
Marquette University *B*
St. Norbert College *B*
University of Wisconsin
Madison *B*
Milwaukee *B, M*
Stevens Point *B*

Clinical nurse specialist

Michigan
Saginaw Valley State University *M*

Minnesota
College of St. Scholastica *M*

Ohio
Ursuline College *M*

Clinical nutrition

California
California State Polytechnic University: Pomona *B, M*

New Jersey
University of Medicine and Dentistry of New Jersey
School of Health Related Professions *D*

North Carolina
East Carolina University *B*
Meredith College *C*

Ohio
University of Akron *B, M*

Oklahoma
University of Oklahoma *B, M*

Pennsylvania
Marywood University *C, B*
Messiah College *B*

Clinical pastoral counseling

New York
New York Institute of Technology *M*

Clinical psychology

Alabama
Alabama Agricultural and Mechanical University *M*
Auburn University *M, D*
University of Alabama *D*

Alaska
University of Alaska
Anchorage *M*

California
Antioch Southern California
Los Angeles *M*
Santa Barbara *M*
Azusa Pacific University *M, D*
Biola University *M, D*
California State University
Bakersfield *M*
Chico *M*
Fullerton *M*
Hayward *M*
Stanislaus *M*
John F. Kennedy University *M*
La Sierra University *B*
Loma Linda University *D*
Pepperdine University *B, M*
San Diego State University *M, D*
San Francisco State University *M*
San Jose State University *M*
University of California
Los Angeles *M, D*
Santa Cruz *B*
University of La Verne *D*
University of Southern California *M, D*

Colorado
University of Denver *M, D*

Connecticut
University of Hartford *M, D*

Delaware
University of Delaware *M, D*

District of Columbia
American University *D*
Catholic University of America *M, D*
Gallaudet University *D*
George Washington University *D*
University of the District of Columbia *M*

Florida
Carlos Albizu University *D*
Florida Institute of Technology *D*
Florida State University *M, D*
Nova Southeastern University *D*
University of Central Florida *M*
University of South Florida *M*

Georgia
Emory University *D*

Idaho
Idaho State University *D*

Illinois
Adler School of Professional Psychology *D*
Benedictine University *M*
De Paul University *M, D*
Eastern Illinois University *M*
Finch University of Health Sciences/The Chicago Medical School *D*
Loyola University of Chicago *M, D*
Northwestern University *M, D*

Roosevelt University *B, M, D*
Wheaton College *M, D*

Indiana
Indiana State University *D*
Indiana University
Bloomington *D*
Indiana University-Purdue University Indianapolis *M*
Purdue University
Calumet *B*
University of Evansville *B*
University of Indianapolis *M, D*
Valparaiso University *M*

Iowa
Loras College *M*
University of Iowa *D*
Upper Iowa University *B*

Kansas
Pittsburg State University *M*
University of Kansas *D*
Washburn University of Topeka *M*

Kentucky
Morehead State University *M*
Murray State University *M*
Spalding University *M, D*
University of Kentucky *M, D*
University of Louisville *M, D*

Louisiana
Northwestern State University *M*

Maine
Husson College *B*
University of Maine *D*

Maryland
Bowie State University *M*
Loyola College in Maryland *M, D*

Massachusetts
American International College *M*
Bridgewater State College *B*
Clark University *M, D*
Suffolk University *M, D*
Tufts University *B*
University of Massachusetts
Boston *D*
Dartmouth *M*
Westfield State College *M*

Michigan
Central Michigan University *M, D*
Madonna University *M*
University of Michigan
Flint *M*
Western Michigan University *M, D*

Minnesota
Capella University *M, D*
Minnesota State University
Mankato *M*

Missouri
Evangel University *M*
University of Missouri
Columbia *M, D*
Washington University in St. Louis *M, D*

New Hampshire
Keene State College *B*

New Jersey
Fairleigh Dickinson University
College at Florham *M*
Metropolitan Campus *D*
Rutgers, The State University of New Jersey
New Brunswick Regional Campus *D*
Seton Hall University *D*

New York
Adelphi University *M, D*
Bard College *B*

City University of New York
Brooklyn College *B*
City College *D*
Queens College *M*
Fordham University *M, D*
Long Island University
C. W. Post Campus *M, D*
New York University *D*
Pace University *M*
Rochester Institute of Technology *B*
St. John's University *D*
State University of New York
Albany *M, D*
Binghamton *D*
Buffalo *D*
Stony Brook *D*
Syracuse University *M, D*
University of Rochester *D*
Yeshiva University *D*

North Carolina
Duke University *D*
East Carolina University *M*
University of North Carolina
Charlotte *M*
Western Carolina University *M*

Ohio
Bowling Green State University *M, D*
Case Western Reserve University *D*
Kent State University *M, D*
Ohio University *M, D*
University of Dayton *M*
Wright State University *D*
Xavier University *D*

Oklahoma
University of Tulsa *M, D*

Oregon
George Fox University *M, D*
Pacific University *M, D*

Pennsylvania
Bryn Mawr College *M, D*
Chestnut Hill College *M, D*
Duquesne University *D*
Edinboro University of Pennsylvania *M*
Immaculata University *D*
Indiana University of Pennsylvania *D*
La Salle University *B, D*
Marywood University *B, M, D*
Millersville University of Pennsylvania *M*
Moravian College *B*
Penn State
Harrisburg *M*
Temple University *M, D*
University of Pennsylvania *D*
West Chester University of Pennsylvania *M*
Widener University *D*

Puerto Rico
Inter American University of Puerto Rico Metropolitan Campus *M*
Pontifical Catholic University of Puerto Rico *B, M, D*
University of Puerto Rico
Rio Piedras Campus *M, D*

Rhode Island
University of Rhode Island *D*

South Carolina
Francis Marion University *M*
University of South Carolina *M, D*
University of South Carolina
Aiken *M*

South Dakota
University of South Dakota *D*

Tennessee
University of Tennessee
Knoxville *B*
Vanderbilt University *M, D*

Texas

Abilene Christian University *M*
Baylor University *M, D*
Houston Baptist University *M*
Midwestern State University *M*
Our Lady of the Lake University of San
    Antonio *M*
St. Mary's University *M*
Sam Houston State University *M, D*
Southern Methodist University *M*
Texas A&M University *D*
Texas Tech University *D*
University of Houston *M, D*
University of Houston
    Clear Lake *M*
University of North Texas *M, D*
University of Texas
    El Paso *M*
    Southwestern Medical Center at
        Dallas *M, D*
    Tyler *M*
    of the Permian Basin *M*

Utah

Brigham Young University *B, D*

Vermont

College of St. Joseph in Vermont *M*
Marlboro College *B*
St. Michael's College *M*

Virginia

Averett University *B*
College of William and Mary *D*
Norfolk State University *D*
Old Dominion University *D*
University of Virginia *D*
Virginia Commonwealth
    University *M, D*

Washington

Eastern Washington University *M*
Seattle Pacific University *D*
University of Washington *D*

West Virginia

Marshall University *D*

Wisconsin

Marquette University *M, D*

Clinical/medical laboratory assistant

Alabama

Northwest-Shoals Community College *A*

Alaska

University of Alaska
    Fairbanks *C*

California

California State University
    Chico *B*
De Anza College *C*

Delaware

Delaware Technical and Community
    College
    Owens Campus *C, A*

Florida

Broward Community College *A*
Lake City Community College *A*

Georgia

Atlanta Metropolitan College *A*
Clayton College and State University *A*

Idaho

North Idaho College *A*

Illinois

Midstate College *C*
Oakton Community College *A*
Southwestern Illinois College *A*

Indiana

University of St. Francis *A*

Iowa

Northeast Iowa Community College *A*

Kansas

Seward County Community College *A*

Kentucky

Somerset Community College *A*
Southeast Community College *A*

Maine

University of New England *B*

Massachusetts

Bunker Hill Community College *C*

Michigan

Baker College
    of Owosso *A*
Monroe County Community College *C*
Northern Michigan University *C*
Oakland Community College *A*

Minnesota

College of St. Catherine *C*
Lake Superior College: A Community
    and Technical College *A*
Minnesota State University
    Mankato *B*
South Central Technical College *A*

Nevada

Community College of Southern
    Nevada *A*

New Jersey

Sussex County Community College *A*

New Mexico

New Mexico Junior College *A*
New Mexico State University
    Alamogordo *A*

New York

Elmira Business Institute *C, A*
Marist College *B*
Mohawk Valley Community College *C*
State University of New York
    College of Agriculture and
        Technology at Cobleskill *A*

North Carolina

Alamance Community College *A*
Fayetteville Technical Community
    College *C*
Guilford Technical Community
    College *A*
Mars Hill College *B*
North Carolina State University *B*
Western Piedmont Community
    College *A*

Ohio

Cincinnati State Technical and
    Community College *C, A*
Columbus State Community College *A*
Jefferson Community College *A*
Shawnee State University *A*
Stark State College of Technology *A*
Washington State Community College *A*
Youngstown State University *A*

Oklahoma

Rose State College *A*
Tulsa Community College *A*

Pennsylvania

California University of Pennsylvania *B*
Penn State
    Schuylkill - Capital College *A*
Western School of Health and Business
    Careers *A*

South Carolina

Aiken Technical College *C*
Forrest Junior College *C, A*
Orangeburg-Calhoun Technical
    College *C, A*

Tennessee

Northeast State Technical Community
    College *A*
Roane State Community College *A*

Texas

Austin Community College *A*
Central Texas College *C, A*
El Paso Community College *C*
Tarrant County College *C*
Tyler Junior College *A*

Virginia

Virginia Highlands Community
    College *A*

Washington

Clover Park Technical College *C*
Wenatchee Valley College *A*

Wisconsin

Chippewa Valley Technical College *A*
Lakeshore Technical College *C*

Clinical/medical laboratory technology

Alabama

Faulkner University *A*
Gadsden State Community College *A*
Harry M. Ayers State Technical
    College *C*
James H. Faulkner State Community
    College *A*
Jefferson State Community College *A*
Northwest-Shoals Community College *A*
Wallace State Community College at
    Hanceville *A*

Alaska

University of Alaska
    Anchorage *A*

Arkansas

North Arkansas College *A*
South Arkansas Community College *A*
Southern Arkansas University *B*
University of Central Arkansas *B*

California

California State University
    Bakersfield *B*
    Dominguez Hills *B*
    Hayward *B*
Chabot College *A*
De Anza College *C*
Los Angeles Southwest College *A*
Mount St. Mary's College *B*

Colorado

Arapahoe Community College *C, A*
Colorado State University
    Pueblo *B*

Connecticut

Central Connecticut State University *B*
Housatonic Community College *A*
Manchester Community College *A*
University of Connecticut *B*

Delaware

Delaware Technical and Community
    College
    Owens Campus *C, A*
    Stanton/Wilmington Campus *A*
University of Delaware *B*

District of Columbia

George Washington University *A*

Florida

Broward Community College *A*
Florida Atlantic University *B*
Indian River Community College *A*
Jacksonville University *B*
Lake City Community College *A*
Manatee Community College *A*
Miami-Dade Community College *A*

Palm Beach Community College *A*
Polk Community College *A*
St. Petersburg College *A*
University of West Florida *B*
Valencia Community College *A*

Georgia

Clayton College and State University *A*
Coastal Georgia Community College *A*
Dalton State College *A*
Darton College *C, A*
DeKalb Technical College *C*
Macon State College *A*
Medical College of Georgia *C, B*
Mercer University *B*
Southwest Georgia Technical College *A*
Waycross College *A*

Illinois

Blackburn College *B*
City Colleges of Chicago
    Malcolm X College *A*
College of Lake County *C, A*
Elgin Community College *C, A*
Finch University of Health Sciences/The
    Chicago Medical School *B*
Illinois Central College *A*
John Wood Community College *A*
Kankakee Community College *A*
McKendree College *B*
Moraine Valley Community College *A*
Rend Lake College *A*
Roosevelt University *B*
Rush University *B*
Southeastern Illinois College *A*
Southwestern Illinois College *A*
University of St. Francis *B*

Indiana

Goshen College *B*
Indiana University
    East *A*
    Northwest *A*
Indiana University-Purdue University
    Fort Wayne *B*
Ivy Tech State College
    Northcentral *A*
    Wabash Valley *A*
Purdue University
    North Central Campus *A*

Iowa

Des Moines Area Community College *A*
Dordt College *B*
Hawkeye Community College *A*
Iowa Central Community College *A*
Morningside College *B*
Mount Mercy College *B*
Northeast Iowa Community College *A*
Northwestern College *B*
Scott Community College *A*
Western Iowa Tech Community
    College *A*

Kansas

Barton County Community College *C, A*
Central Christian College *A*
Kansas State University *B*
Seward County Community College *A*
Tabor College *B*
Washburn University of Topeka *B*

Kentucky

Brescia University *B*
Henderson Community College *A*
Madisonville Community College *A*
Murray State University *B*
Somerset Community College *C, A*
Thomas More College *B*

Louisiana

Delgado Community College *A*
Louisiana College *B*
Southern University
    New Orleans *B*
    Shreveport *A*

Maine

Central Maine Technical College *A*
University of Maine
    Augusta *A*
    Presque Isle *A*
University of New England *B*

Maryland

Allegany College *A*
Community College of Baltimore County
    Catonsville *A*
    Dundalk *A*
    Essex *A*
Howard Community College *A*

Massachusetts

American International College *B*
Fitchburg State College *B*
Massachusetts College of Liberal Arts *B*
Mount Wachusett Community College *A*
Northeastern University *B*
Springfield College *B*
Springfield Technical Community
    College *A*

Michigan

Baker College
    of Owosso *A*
    of Port Huron *A*
Ferris State University *A*
Kellogg Community College *A*
Madonna University *C, A, B*
Northern Michigan University *A*
Saginaw Valley State University *B*

Minnesota

Alexandria Technical College *C, A*
Fergus Falls Community College *A*
Hibbing Community College: A
    Technical and Community College *A*
Lake Superior College: A Community
    and Technical College *A*
Minnesota State University
    Mankato *B*
    Moorhead *B*
Rochester Community and Technical
    College *A*
St. Paul College - A Community and
    Technical College *A*
South Central Technical College *A*
Winona State University *B*

Mississippi

Blue Mountain College *B*
Mississippi Gulf Coast Community
    College
    Perkinston *A*
Mississippi State University *B*

Missouri

Avila University *B*
Evangel University *B*
Lincoln University *B*
Missouri Southern State College *A*
Missouri Western State College *B*
Southwest Baptist University *B*
Three Rivers Community College *A*
Truman State University *B*
University of Missouri
    Kansas City *B*

Montana

University of Montana-Missoula *A*

Nebraska

Central Community College *C, A*
College of Saint Mary *B*
Dana College *B*
Mid Plains Community College Area *A*
Southeast Community College
    Lincoln Campus *A*

Nevada

Community College of Southern
    Nevada *A*
Western Nevada Community College *A*

New Hampshire

New Hampshire Community Technical
    College
    Claremont *A*
University of New Hampshire *B*

New Jersey

Bergen Community College *A*
Bloomfield College *B*
Brookdale Community College *A*
Caldwell College *B*
Camden County College *A*
County College of Morris *A*
Felician College *A*
Mercer County Community College *A*
Middlesex County College *A*
Ocean County College *A*
Rutgers, The State University of New
    Jersey
    New Brunswick Regional
        Campus *A*
    Newark Regional Campus *B*
University of Medicine and Dentistry of
    New Jersey
    School of Health Related
        Professions *A*

New Mexico

Albuquerque Technical-Vocational
    Institute *A*
Luna Community College *A*
New Mexico Junior College *A*
New Mexico State University
    Alamogordo *A*
University of New Mexico *B*
Western New Mexico University *B*

New York

Alfred University *B*
Broome Community College *A*
City University of New York
    Bronx Community College *A*
    College of Staten Island *A*
    Hunter College *B*
    Queensborough Community
        College *A*
    York College *B*
Clinton Community College *A*
Dutchess Community College *A*
Erie Community College
    North Campus *A*
Fulton-Montgomery Community
    College *A*
Hudson Valley Community College *A*
Jamestown Community College *A*
Marist College *B*
Orange County Community College *A*
St. John's University *B*
State University of New York
    Buffalo *B*
    College at Brockport *B*
    College at Fredonia *B*
    College of Agriculture and
        Technology at Morrisville *A*
    College of Technology at Alfred *A*
    Farmingdale *A*
    Oswego *B*
Westchester Community College *A*

North Carolina

Alamance Community College *A*
Appalachian State University *B*
Asheville Buncombe Technical
    Community College *A*
Beaufort County Community College *A*
Bennett College *B*
Coastal Carolina Community College *A*
Davidson County Community College *A*
Halifax Community College *A*
Salem College *B*
Sandhills Community College *A*
Southeastern Community College *A*
Southwestern Community College *A*
Wake Forest University *A*
Wake Technical Community College *A*

North Dakota

Bismarck State College *A*

Ohio

Baldwin-Wallace College *B*
Clark State Community College *A*
Columbus State Community College *A*
Cuyahoga Community College
    Eastern Campus *C, A*
    Metropolitan Campus *C, A*
Defiance College *B*
Jefferson Community College *A*
Kent State University *A, B*
Lakeland Community College *C, A*
Lorain County Community College *A*
Marion Technical College *A*
Muskingum Area Technical College *A*
Muskingum College *B*
Notre Dame College *B*
Ohio State University
    Columbus Campus *B*
Shawnee State University *B*
University of Cincinnati
    Raymond Walters College *C, A*
University of Rio Grande *A*
Xavier University *B*
Youngstown State University *A*

Oklahoma

Cameron University *B*
Northeastern Oklahoma Agricultural and
    Mechanical College *A*
Northeastern State University *B*
Oklahoma State University *B*
Rose State College *A*
Seminole State College *A*
Southeastern Oklahoma State
    University *B*
Southern Nazarene University *B*
Southwestern Oklahoma State
    University *B*
Tulsa Community College *A*

Oregon

Oregon Health Sciences University *B*
Oregon State University *B*
Portland Community College *A*

Pennsylvania

Bloomsburg University of
    Pennsylvania *B*
California University of Pennsylvania *B*
Community College of Allegheny
    County *A*
Community College of Philadelphia *A*
DeSales University *B*
Delaware County Community College *C*
Edinboro University of Pennsylvania *B*
Harrisburg Area Community College *A*
Holy Family University *B*
Lebanon Valley College of
    Pennsylvania *B*
Lehigh Carbon Community College *C*
Lock Haven University of
    Pennsylvania *B*
Montgomery County Community
    College *A*
Neumann College *C, B*
Penn State
    Dubois *A*
    Hazleton *A*
    New Kensington *A*
Slippery Rock University of
    Pennsylvania *B*
Thiel College *B*
University of the Sciences in
    Philadelphia *B*
Western School of Health and Business
    Careers *A*
York College of Pennsylvania *B*

Puerto Rico

University of Puerto Rico
    Medical Sciences Campus *C, B*
University of the Sacred Heart *C, B*

Rhode Island

Community College of Rhode Island *A*
Rhode Island College *B*
Salve Regina University *B*

South Carolina

Central Carolina Technical College *C*
Erskine College *B*
Florence-Darlington Technical College *A*
Forrest Junior College *C, A*
Midlands Technical College *C, A*
Orangeburg-Calhoun Technical
    College *A*
Tri-County Technical College *A*
Trident Technical College *A*
York Technical College *A*

South Dakota

Augustana College *B*
Dakota State University *A*

Tennessee

Columbia State Community College *A*
Jackson State Community College *A*
Roane State Community College *A*
Southwest Tennessee Community
    College *A*
Trevecca Nazarene University *B*
Union University *B*
University of Tennessee Health Science
    Center *B*

Texas

Amarillo College *A*
Angelina College *A*
Austin Community College *A*
Central Texas College *A*
Clarendon College *A*
Del Mar College *C, A*
East Texas Baptist University *B*
El Centro College *A*
El Paso Community College *A*
Galveston College *C*
Houston Community College System *A*
Kilgore College *A*
Laredo Community College *C, A*
Lubbock Christian University *B*
McLennan Community College *A*
McMurry University *B*
St. Philip's College *A*
Southwestern Adventist University *B*
Temple College *A*
Victoria College *A*
Wharton County Junior College *A*

Utah

Dixie State College of Utah *C*
Salt Lake Community College *A*
Weber State University *A*

Virginia

Bluefield College *A*
Eastern Mennonite University *B*
Emory & Henry College *B*
Ferrum College *B*
J. Sargeant Reynolds Community
    College *A*
Radford University *B*
Southside Virginia Community
    College *A*
University of Virginia's College at
    Wise *B*

Washington

Olympic College *A*
Seattle University *B*
Spokane Community College *A*
Spokane Falls Community College *A*

West Virginia

Alderson-Broaddus College *B*
Fairmont State College *A*
Marshall University *A*
Southern West Virginia Community and
    Technical College *A*
West Virginia Northern Community
    College *A*

Wisconsin
Carroll College *B*
Chippewa Valley Technical College *A*
Milwaukee Area Technical College *A*
University of Wisconsin
La Crosse *B*
Madison *B*
Oshkosh *B*
Western Wisconsin Technical College *A*

Clinical/medical social work

Alabama
Southern Union State Community
College *A*

Arkansas
Arkansas Tech University *B*

California
California State University
Fresno *B, M*
East Los Angeles College *C*
Loma Linda University *M*

Maine
University of New England *M*
University of Southern Maine *M*

Maryland
Johns Hopkins University *M, D*
University of Maryland
Baltimore *M, D*

Mississippi
University of Southern Mississippi *M*

Montana
Dawson Community College *A*

Nebraska
Central Community College *C, A*

New Mexico
New Mexico Highlands University *M*

Pennsylvania
Slippery Rock University of
Pennsylvania *B*
University of Pittsburgh *C*

South Dakota
University of South Dakota *B*

Texas
Baylor University *B*

Wisconsin
Concordia University Wisconsin *B*

Clothing/apparel/textiles

Alabama
Auburn University *B, M, D*
University of Alabama *B*

Arkansas
University of Arkansas *B*
University of Central Arkansas *B*

California
Antelope Valley College *C, A*
California State Polytechnic University:
Pomona *B*
California State University
Long Beach *B*
Northridge *B*
Cerritos Community College *A*
Chabot College *A*
Glendale Community College *A*
Los Angeles Trade and Technical
College *C, A*
Modesto Junior College *A*
Mount San Antonio College *A*
San Francisco State University *B*
Santa Rosa Junior College *C*

University of California
Davis *B, M*

Colorado
Colorado State University *B, M*

Delaware
Delaware State University *B*

Florida
Florida State University *B, M*

Georgia
Georgia Southern University *B*
Middle Georgia College *A*
University of Georgia *B, M, D*

Hawaii
University of Hawaii
Manoa *B*

Idaho
University of Idaho *B*

Illinois
Joliet Junior College *A*
Northern Illinois University *B*
Southern Illinois University
Carbondale *B*

Indiana
Indiana State University *B*
Indiana University
Bloomington *B, M*
Purdue University *B, M, D*
Vincennes University *A*

Iowa
Ellsworth Community College *A*
Iowa State University *B, M, D*
University of Northern Iowa *B*

Kansas
Kansas State University *B, M*
Pittsburg State University *B*

Kentucky
Murray State University *B*

Louisiana
University of Louisiana at Lafayette *B*

Massachusetts
Fisher College *A*
Framingham State College *B*
Lasell College *B*

Michigan
Eastern Michigan University *M*
Marygrove College *A, B*
Michigan State University *B, M*
Western Michigan University *B*

Minnesota
Concordia College: Moorhead *B*
Minnesota State University
Mankato *B, M*
University of Minnesota
Twin Cities *B*

Mississippi
Mississippi University for Women *B*
University of Southern Mississippi *B*

Missouri
Central Missouri State University *B*
College of the Ozarks *B*
Fontbonne College *B*
Southeast Missouri State University *B*
Southwest Missouri State University *B*
Stephens College *B*
University of Missouri
Columbia *B, M*

Nebraska
University of Nebraska
Kearney *B*
Lincoln *B, M*

New Mexico
New Mexico State University *B*

New York
Cornell University *B, M*
Fashion Institute of Technology *A*
Marymount College of Fordham
University *B*
State University of New York
College at Buffalo *B*
College at Oneonta *B*
Syracuse University *B, M*

North Carolina
Appalachian State University *B*
Bennett College *B*
East Carolina University *B*
North Carolina Agricultural and
Technical State University *B*
North Carolina State University *B*
University of North Carolina
Greensboro *B, M, D*

North Dakota
North Dakota State University *B*

Ohio
Bluffton College *B*
Kent State University *B*
Miami University
Oxford Campus *M*
Ohio State University
Columbus Campus *B, M, D*
Ohio University *B*
University of Akron *B, M*
Youngstown State University *B*

Oklahoma
East Central University *B*
Langston University *B*
Northeastern State University *B*
Oklahoma State University *B, M*
University of Central Oklahoma *B, M*

Oregon
Art Institute
of Portland *A, B*
Oregon State University *B*

Pennsylvania
Albright College *B*
Cheyney University of Pennsylvania *B*
Immaculata University *B*
Mercyhurst College *B*
Philadelphia University *B, M*

Rhode Island
University of Rhode Island *B, M*

South Carolina
Tri-County Technical College *A*

Tennessee
Carson-Newman College *B*
Lambuth University *B*
Middle Tennessee State University *B*
Southwest Tennessee Community
College *C*
Tennessee State University *B*
Tennessee Technological University *B*
University of Tennessee
Knoxville *B*

Texas
Baylor University *B*
Lamar University *B*
Texas A&M University
Kingsville *B*
Texas Christian University *B*
Texas Southern University *M*
Texas Tech University *B*
Texas Woman's University *B, M, D*
University of North Texas *B, M*
University of Texas
Austin *B*

Utah
Salt Lake Community College *C*
Snow College *A*
Utah State University *B*

Virginia
Virginia Polytechnic Institute and State
University *B, M, D*

Washington
Seattle Pacific University *B*
Washington State University *B, M*

West Virginia
Fairmont State College *A*
West Virginia University *B*

Wisconsin
University of Wisconsin
Madison *B, M*
Stout *B*

Cognitive psychology/ psycholinguistics

California
University of California
Berkeley *B*
Los Angeles *B*
San Diego *B, D*
Santa Cruz *B, D*
University of Southern California *M, D*

Connecticut
University of Connecticut *B*
Yale University *B*

Delaware
University of Delaware *M, D*

District of Columbia
George Washington University *D*

Florida
Florida State University *M, D*

Georgia
Emory University *D*
University of Georgia *B*

Illinois
Loyola University of Chicago *B, M*
Northwestern University *B*

Iowa
University of Iowa *D*

Kansas
University of Kansas *D*

Louisiana
Tulane University *B*

Maryland
Johns Hopkins University *B, D*

Massachusetts
Hampshire College *B*
Harvard College *B*
Massachusetts Institute of Technology *B*
Simon's Rock College of Bard *B*
Tufts University *B, M, D*
Wellesley College *B*

Michigan
University of Michigan *B*

Missouri
Washington University in St. Louis *B*

New Jersey
Kean University *M*

New York
Sarah Lawrence College *B*
State University of New York
Albany *M, D*
Binghamton *D*
Buffalo *D*
University of Rochester *B, M, D*

Oregon
George Fox University *B*

Pennsylvania
Carnegie Mellon University *B*

Temple University *D*
West Chester University of
Pennsylvania *B*

Rhode Island
Brown University *B, M, D*

Tennessee
Vanderbilt University *B*

Texas
University of Texas
Dallas *B, M*

Vermont
Marlboro College *B*

Virginia
Averett University *B*

Cognitive science

Colorado
University of Colorado
Boulder *D*

Louisiana
University of Louisiana at Lafayette *D*

Massachusetts
Massachusetts Institute of Technology *D*

New York
State University of New York
Buffalo *M, D*

Rhode Island
Brown University *B, M, D*

Texas
University of Texas
Dallas *D*

Wisconsin
Lawrence University *B*

College counseling

Arkansas
Arkansas State University *M*
Arkansas Tech University *M*
University of Central Arkansas *M*

California
University of Southern California *M*

Colorado
Colorado State University
Pueblo *M*
University of Northern Colorado *D*

Connecticut
Central Connecticut State University *M*
Southern Connecticut State University *M*

Delaware
University of Delaware *M*

Florida
University of Florida *M, D*

Illinois
Loyola University of Chicago *M*
Western Illinois University *M*

Indiana
Indiana State University *M*
Indiana University
Bloomington *M*

Iowa
Iowa State University *T*
St. Ambrose University *M, T*
University of Northern Iowa *M*

Louisiana
Nicholls State University *M*

Maine
University of Southern Maine *M*

Maryland
Johns Hopkins University *M*

Massachusetts
Northeastern University *M*
Springfield College *M*

Michigan
Michigan State University *M*
Western Michigan University *D*

Minnesota
Minnesota State University
Mankato *M*

New Hampshire
Rivier College *M*

New Jersey
The College of New Jersey *M*

New York
Fordham University *M, D*
Long Island University
C. W. Post Campus *M*
St. Bonaventure University *M*
State University of New York
Buffalo *M*

North Carolina
University of North Carolina
Charlotte *M*
Greensboro *M, D*
Western Carolina University *M*

Ohio
Bowling Green State University *M*
Miami University
Oxford Campus *M*
Ohio State University
Columbus Campus *M, D*
University of Dayton *M*
Youngstown State University *M*

Oklahoma
Oklahoma State University *M, D*

Pennsylvania
Indiana University of Pennsylvania *M*
Kutztown University of
Pennsylvania *B, M*
Lehigh University *M, D*
Shippensburg University of
Pennsylvania *M*
Villanova University *M*

Puerto Rico
Inter American University of Puerto Rico
Metropolitan Campus *M*
Universidad del Este *M*

South Carolina
University of South Carolina *M*

Vermont
Johnson State College *M*

Virginia
Longwood University *M*

Washington
Seattle University *M*
Walla Walla College *M*

Commercial photography

California
Academy of Art College *C, A, B, M*
Art Center College of Design *B*
California State University
Fullerton *C*
East Los Angeles College *C*
Long Beach City College *C, A*
Modesto Junior College *A*
Otis College of Art and Design *B*
Santa Monica College *A*
Ventura College *C, A*

Colorado
Art Institute
of Colorado *A*
Colorado Mountain College
Spring Valley Campus *A*

Connecticut
Paier College of Art *C, A*

Florida
Art Institute
of Fort Lauderdale *C*

Georgia
Art Institute
of Atlanta *A*
Atlanta College of Art *B*

Illinois
College of DuPage *C, A*
Judson College *B*
Prairie State College *C, A*

Iowa
Hawkeye Community College *A*

Louisiana
Tulane University *B, M*

Maryland
Community College of Baltimore County
Catonsville *A*
Dundalk *A*
Essex *A*
Harford Community College *C*
Montgomery College
Rockville Campus *A*

Michigan
College for Creative Studies *B*
Washtenaw Community College *A*

Minnesota
Ridgewater College: A Community and
Technical College *C, A*

Nebraska
Metropolitan Community College *A*

Nevada
Community College of Southern
Nevada *A*

New Jersey
Middlesex County College *A*

New York
City University of New York
La Guardia Community
College *C, A*
Fashion Institute of Technology *A*
Mohawk Valley Community College *A*
Parsons School of Design *C, A, B, T*
Pratt Institute *B*
Rochester Institute of Technology *B, M*
Rockland Community College *A*
School of Visual Arts *B*
Syracuse University *B*

North Carolina
Alamance Community College *C*
Randolph Community College *A*

Ohio
Antonelli College *A*
Cuyahoga Community College
Eastern Campus *A*
Ohio Institute of Photography and
Technology *A*
Sinclair Community College *C*

Oklahoma
University of Central Oklahoma *B*

Pennsylvania
Antonelli Institute of Art and
Photography *A*
Community College of Philadelphia *A*
Oakbridge Academy of Arts *A*

Tennessee
Memphis College of Art *B*

Nossi College of Art *A*

Texas
Amarillo College *A*
Austin Community College *C, A*
El Paso Community College *A*
Houston Community College
System *C, A*
Kilgore College *C, A*
Midland College *A*
North Central Texas College *A*
Odessa College *C, A*
Texas A&M University
Commerce *B*

Utah
Brigham Young University *B*

Virginia
Virginia Intermont College *B*

Washington
Art Institute of Seattle *A*
Seattle Central Community College *A*
Spokane Falls Community College *C, A*

Commercial/advertising art

Alabama
Alabama State University *B*
Calhoun Community College *A*
James H. Faulkner State Community
College *C, A*
Oakwood College *A*
Samford University *B*

Arizona
Arizona State University *B*
Art Institute
of Phoenix *A, B*
Collins College *A, B*
Eastern Arizona College *A*
Glendale Community College *C, A*
Phoenix College *C, A*
Pima Community College *C, A*
Yavapai College *C, A*

Arkansas
Arkansas State University *B, M*
John Brown University *B*
Northwest Arkansas Community
College *A*
Ouachita Baptist University *B*
South Arkansas Community College *A*
Southern Arkansas University Tech *C, A*

California
Academy of Art College *C, A, B, M*
Art Center College of Design *B, M*
Art Institute
of California *A, B*
of California - Orange County *A, B*
of California: Los Angeles *A, B*
Art Institute of California - San
Francisco *A, B*
Biola University *B*
California College of Arts and
Crafts *B, M*
California Institute of the Arts *C, B, M*
California Polytechnic State University:
San Luis Obispo *B*
California State Polytechnic University:
Pomona *B*
California State University
Fresno *B*
Fullerton *B*
Hayward *B*
Long Beach *B*
Northridge *B*
Sacramento *B*
Cerro Coso Community College *C*
Chabot College *A*
Chapman University *B*
Citrus College *C*
College of the Canyons *C, A*
College of the Redwoods *C, A*
College of the Sequoias *C, A*

De Anza College *C, A*
Fashion Institute of Design and
    Merchandising *A*
Foothill College *C, A*
Glendale Community College *C, A*
Golden West College *C, A*
La Sierra University *B*
Laney College *C, A*
Las Positas College *A*
Long Beach City College *C, A*
Los Angeles Pierce College *C, A*
Los Angeles Southwest College *A*
Los Angeles Trade and Technical
    College *A*
Los Medanos College *C, A*
MiraCosta College *C, A*
Modesto Junior College *C, A*
Moorpark College *C, A*
Ohlone College *C, A*
Orange Coast College *C, A*
Otis College of Art and Design *B*
Pacific Union College *A*
Palomar College *C, A*
Platt College
    Newport Beach *C, A*
    Ontario *C, A*
Point Loma Nazarene University *B*
Riverside Community College *C, A*
San Diego City College *C, A*
Santa Barbara City College *C, A*
Santa Monica College *A*
Santa Rosa Junior College *C, A*
Santiago Canyon College *A*
Shasta College *A*
Southwestern College *A*
Taft College *C*
University of the Pacific *B*
Ventura College *C*
Westwood College of Technology
    Inland Empire *A*
Woodbury University *B*

Colorado

Arapahoe Community College *C, A*
Art Institute
    of Colorado *A, B*
Colorado Mountain College
    Spring Valley Campus *C, A*
Colorado State University *B*
Platt College
    Aurora *C, A, B*
Red Rocks Community College *A*
Rocky Mountain College of Art &
    Design *B*
Trinidad State Junior College *C, A*
University of Denver *B*
Westwood College of Technology
    South *A, B*

Connecticut

Albertus Magnus College *B*
Housatonic Community College *C, A*
Manchester Community College *C, A*
Mitchell College *A*
Northwestern Connecticut Community
    College *C, A*
Norwalk Community College *C, A*
Paier College of Art *C, B*
Quinebaug Valley Community College *C*
Sacred Heart University *B*
Tunxis Community College *C, A*
University of Bridgeport *B*
University of Hartford *B*
University of New Haven *C, A, B*
Western Connecticut State University *B*

Delaware

University of Delaware *B*

District of Columbia

American University *B*
Corcoran College of Art and Design *B*
Gallaudet University *B*
George Washington University *M*

Florida

Art Institute
    of Fort Lauderdale *C, A, B*
Daytona Beach Community College *A*
Flagler College *B*
Florida Agricultural and Mechanical
    University *B*
Florida Keys Community College *A*
Florida Metropolitan University
    Orlando College North *A*
    Tampa College *A*
Florida Southern College *B*
Florida State University *B, M*
Indian River Community College *A*
International Academy of Design and
    Technology *A*
Jacksonville University *B*
Lake-Sumter Community College *A*
Manatee Community College *A*
Miami-Dade Community College *A*
Okaloosa-Walton Community
    College *C, A*
Palm Beach Community College *A*
Pensacola Junior College *A*
Ringling School of Art and Design *B*
St. Petersburg College *A*
Santa Fe Community College *A*
Tampa Technical Institute *A*
University of Florida *B*
University of Miami *C, B*
University of Tampa *B*
Valencia Community College *A*

Georgia

Art Institute
    of Atlanta *A, B*
Atlanta College of Art *B*
Bauder College *A*
Brenau University *B*
Darton College *A*
LaGrange College *B*
Savannah College of Art and
    Design *B, M*
University of Georgia *B*

Hawaii

University of Hawaii
    Honolulu Community College *C, A*

Idaho

Boise State University *B*
College of Southern Idaho *A*
Lewis-Clark State College *C, A*
North Idaho College *A*
Northwest Nazarene University *B*

Illinois

American Academy of Art *B*
Chicago State University *B*
City Colleges of Chicago
    Harold Washington College *A*
    Kennedy-King College *C, A*
Columbia College Chicago *B*
Dominican University *B*
Illinois Institute of Art *A, B*
Illinois Institute of Art *B*
International Academy of Design and
    Technology *A, B*
Judson College *B*
Lewis University *B*
Millikin University *B*
North Park University *B*
Oakton Community College *A*
Parkland College *A*
Rend Lake College *C, A*
Robert Morris College: Chicago *C, A*
Sauk Valley Community College *A*
Southern Illinois University
    Carbondale *A*
Trinity Christian College *B*
Triton College *C, A*
University of Illinois
    Chicago *B, M*
    Urbana-Champaign *B*

Indiana

Anderson University *B*

Ball State University *B*
Goshen College *B*
Grace College *B*
Huntington College *B*
Indiana University
    Bloomington *B, M*
Indiana University-Purdue University
    Fort Wayne *A, B*
International Business College *C, A*
Marian College *B*
Oakland City University *B*
University of Evansville *B*
University of Indianapolis *B*
University of St. Francis *A, B*
Vincennes University *A*

Iowa

Buena Vista University *B*
Clarke College *B*
Des Moines Area Community College *A*
Dordt College *B*
Drake University *B*
Ellsworth Community College *A*
Graceland University *B*
Grand View College *B*
Hawkeye Community College *A*
Iowa State University *B, M*
Morningside College *B*
Mount Mercy College *B*
St. Ambrose University *B*
Simpson College *B*
University of Dubuque *B*
Upper Iowa University *B*
Wartburg College *B*

Kansas

Cloud County Community College *A*
Haskell Indian Nations University *C*
Johnson County Community College *A*
Labette Community College *A*
Pittsburg State University *B*
Pratt Community College *A*
Tabor College *B*
University of Kansas *B*
Wichita State University *B*

Kentucky

Brescia University *B*
Jefferson Community College *A*
Louisville Technical Institute *A*
Murray State University *B*
Spencerian College: Lexington *A*

Louisiana

Delgado Community College *A*
Dryades YMCA School of Commerce *B*
Louisiana College *B*
Louisiana Tech University *B*
Loyola University New Orleans *B*

Maine

Maine College of Art *B*
University of Maine
    Augusta *A*

Maryland

Anne Arundel Community College *C, A*
Carroll Community College *C, A*
College of Southern Maryland *C*
Community College of Baltimore County
    Catonsville *C, A*
    Dundalk *C, A*
    Essex *C, A*
Frostburg State University *B*
Howard Community College *A*
Maryland College of Art and
    Design *C, A*
Montgomery College
    Rockville Campus *A*
University of Baltimore *M*
University of Maryland
    Baltimore County *B*
Villa Julie College *A*

Massachusetts

Ai The New England Institute of Art and
    Design *A, B*

Art Institute of Boston at Lesley
    University *C, B*
Becker College *C, A, B*
Boston University *B, M*
Bridgewater State College *B*
Cape Cod Community College *A*
Fitchburg State College *B*
Greenfield Community College *A*
Lasell College *B*
Massachusetts College of Art *B, M*
Massasoit Community College *A*
Montserrat College of Art *B*
Mount Ida College *A, B*
Newbury College *A, B*
Northeastern University *A, B*
Quinsigamond Community College *A*
Salem State College *B*
Simmons College *B*
Springfield Technical Community
    College *A*
Suffolk University *C, B*
University of Massachusetts
    Dartmouth *B, M*
Westfield State College *B*

Michigan

Alma College *B*
Andrews University *B*
Baker College
    of Auburn Hills *A*
    of Clinton Township *A*
    of Muskegon *A*
    of Owosso *A*
    of Port Huron *A*
Central Michigan University *B*
College for Creative Studies *B*
Ferris State University *C, A, B*
Finlandia University *B*
Gogebic Community College *A*
Grand Rapids Community College *A*
Grand Valley State University *B*
Kellogg Community College *A*
Lansing Community College *A*
Macomb Community College *C, A*
Madonna University *A, B*
Marygrove College *C*
Mid Michigan Community College *A*
Mott Community College *A*
Muskegon Community College *C, A*
Northern Michigan University *B*
Northwestern Michigan College *A*
Oakland Community College *C, A*
St. Clair County Community College *A*
Schoolcraft College *A*
Siena Heights University *B*
University of Michigan *B*
Western Michigan University *B*

Minnesota

Academy College *C, A*
Alexandria Technical College *C, A*
Art Institutes International
    Minnesota *A, B*
Bemidji State University *B*
Central Lakes College *C*
College of Visual Arts *B*
Dakota County Technical College *C, A*
Globe College *C, A*
Inver Hills Community College *A*
Mesabi Range Community and Technical
    College *C*
Minneapolis Community and Technical
    College *C, A*
Minnesota State University
    Mankato *B, M, T*
    Moorhead *B*
North Hennepin Community College *A*
Northwestern College *B*
Rochester Community and Technical
    College *C, A*
St. Cloud State University *B*
St. Cloud Technical College *C*
St. Mary's University of Minnesota *B*
St. Paul College - A Community and
    Technical College *C*
South Central Technical College *A*

University of Minnesota
Duluth *B*
Twin Cities *C, B*
Winona State University *B*

Mississippi
Mississippi College *B*
Mississippi Gulf Coast Community
College
Perkinston *A*
Mississippi University for Women *B*
Northwest Mississippi Community
College *A*

Missouri
Avila University *B*
Central Missouri State University *B*
College of the Ozarks *B*
Drury University *B*
Hickey College *C*
Kansas City Art Institute *B*
Lindenwood University *B*
Maryville University of Saint Louis *B*
Missouri Western State College *B*
Penn Valley Community College *A*
St. Charles Community College *A*
St. Louis Community College
St. Louis Community College at
Florissant Valley *A*
St. Louis Community College at
Meramec *A*
Southwest Baptist University *B*
Stephens College *B*
Truman State University *B*
University of Missouri
St. Louis *B*
Washington University in St. Louis *B, M*
Webster University *B*
William Woods University *B*

Montana
University of Montana: Western *A*

Nebraska
Bellevue University *B*
Central Community College *C, A*
Concordia University *B*
Creighton University *B*
Dana College *B*
Doane College *B*
Metropolitan Community College *A*
Midland Lutheran College *B*
Nebraska Indian Community College *A*
Southeast Community College
Milford Campus *A*
Union College *A, B*
University of Nebraska
Kearney *B*
Wayne State College *B*

Nevada
Community College of Southern
Nevada *A*
Western Nevada Community
College *C, A*

New Hampshire
Chester College of New England *B*
Colby-Sawyer College *B*
Franklin Pierce College *B*
Hesser College *C, A*
Keene State College *B*
New Hampshire Community Technical
College
Berlin *C, A*
Laconia *C, A*
Manchester *C, A*
Plymouth State College *B*
Rivier College *B*

New Jersey
Bergen Community College *C, A*
Bloomfield College *B*
Centenary College *B*
The College of New Jersey *B*
County College of Morris *A*
Cumberland County College *A*
Essex County College *A*

Felician College *B*
Gloucester County College *C, A*
Mercer County Community College *A*
Middlesex County College *A*
Monmouth University *B*
Ocean County College *C*
Rowan University *B*
Seton Hall University *B*
Sussex County Community College *C, A*

New Mexico
Art Center Design College *B*
Clovis Community College *A*
New Mexico Highlands University *B*
New Mexico Junior College *C, A*
New Mexico State University
Alamogordo *C, A*
San Juan College *A*

New York
Adelphi University *B*
Alfred University *B*
Briarcliffe College *A*
City University of New York
Bronx Community College *A*
City College *B*
Kingsborough Community
College *A*
Daemen College *B*
Dutchess Community College *A*
Eugene Lang College/New School
University *A*
Fashion Institute of Technology *A, B*
Finger Lakes Community College *A*
Fulton-Montgomery Community
College *A*
Genesee Community College *A*
Long Island University
C. W. Post Campus *B*
Southampton College *B*
Marymount Manhattan College *C*
Mohawk Valley Community
College *C, A*
Monroe Community College *A*
Nassau Community College *A*
New York Institute of Technology *B*
New York University *M*
Onondaga Community College *A*
Pace University *C, A*
Pace University:
Pleasantville/Briarcliff *C, A*
Parsons School of Design *C, A, B, T*
Pratt Institute *A, B, M*
Roberts Wesleyan College *B*
Rochester Institute of
Technology *A, B, M*
Rockland Community College *C, A*
Sage College of Albany *A*
St. John's University *B*
School of Visual Arts *B, M*
State University of New York
Buffalo *M*
College at Buffalo *B*
College at Fredonia *B*
College of Agriculture and
Technology at Cobleskill *A*
Farmingdale *C, A*
New Paltz *B*
Oswego *B*
Purchase *B*
Suffolk County Community College *A*
Syracuse University *B, M*
Tompkins-Cortland Community
College *A*
Ulster County Community College *C, A*
Villa Maria College of Buffalo *A*
Westchester Business Institute *C, A*
Westchester Community College *C*

North Carolina
Campbell University *B*
Catawba Valley Community College *A*
Central Piedmont Community College *A*
Chowan College *B*
Gaston College *C*

Guilford Technical Community
College *C, A*
Halifax Community College *A*
Isothermal Community College *A*
James Sprunt Community College *C, A*
Johnston Community College *A*
King's College *A, D*
Lenoir Community College *C, A*
Meredith College *B*
North Carolina State University *B, M*
Pitt Community College *A*
Randolph Community College *A*
South Piedmont Community College *A*
Southwestern Community College *A*
Surry Community College *A*

North Dakota
Bismarck State College *C, A*

Ohio
Antonelli College *A*
Art Academy of Cincinnati *A, B*
Ashland University *B*
Bradford School *C*
Clark State Community College *A*
Cleveland Institute of Art *B*
College of Art Advertising *A*
College of Mount St. Joseph *C, A, B*
Columbus College of Art and Design *B*
Cuyahoga Community College
Eastern Campus *A*
Metropolitan Campus *A*
Western Campus *A*
Davis College *C, A*
Defiance College *B*
Edison State Community College *A*
Kent State University *B, M*
Lakeland Community College *A*
Marietta College *B*
Ohio Dominican College *B, T*
Ohio Institute of Photography and
Technology *C, A*
Ohio Northern University *B*
Ohio University *B*
Sinclair Community College *A*
University of Akron *A*
University of Cincinnati *B*
University of Cincinnati
Raymond Walters College *C, A*
University of Dayton *B*
University of Findlay *B*
Virginia Marti College of Art and
Design *A*
Wilmington College *B*
Wittenberg University *B*
Youngstown State University *B*

Oklahoma
Northeastern State University *B*
Oklahoma City Community College *A*
Oklahoma State University *B*
Oklahoma State University
Oklahoma City *A*
Okmulgee *A*
Oral Roberts University *B*
Platt College *C*
Redlands Community College *C*
Rogers State University *C, A*
Rose State College *A*
Southwestern Oklahoma State
University *B*
University of Central Oklahoma *B*

Oregon
Art Institute
of Portland *A, B*
Lane Community College *C, A*
Linn-Benton Community College *A*
Mount Hood Community College *A*
Pacific Northwest College of Art *C, B*
Portland Community College *A*
Portland State University *B*

Pennsylvania
Allentown Business School *C*
Antonelli Institute of Art and
Photography *A*

Arcadia University *C, B*
Art Institute
of Philadelphia *A, B*
of Pittsburgh *A*
Bradford School: Pittsburgh *C, A*
Bradley Academy for the Visual Arts *A*
Bucks County Community College *A*
Butler County Community College *A*
Cabrini College *B*
California University of Pennsylvania *B*
Carlow College *B*
Community College of Allegheny
County *C, A*
Community College of Philadelphia *A*
Delaware County Community College *A*
Douglas School of Business *A*
Drexel University *B*
Harrisburg Area Community
College *C, A*
Keystone College *A*
Kutztown University of Pennsylvania *B*
La Roche College *B*
Lehigh Carbon Community College *A*
Luzerne County Community
College *C, A*
Montgomery County Community
College *A*
Moravian College *B*
Northampton County Area Community
College *A*
Oakbridge Academy of Arts *A*
Penn State
University Park *B*
Pennsylvania College of
Technology *A, B*
Philadelphia University *B*
Pittsburgh Technical Institute: Boyd
School Division *A*
Seton Hill University *C, B*
Temple University *B, M*
Waynesburg College *B*
Westmoreland County Community
College *A*
York College of Pennsylvania *B*

Puerto Rico
Atlantic College *A, B*
Inter American University of Puerto Rico
San German Campus *B*
University of Puerto Rico
Carolina Regional College *A, B*

Rhode Island
Rhode Island School of Design *C, B, M*
Salve Regina University *B*

South Carolina
Anderson College *B*
Clemson University *B*
Coker College *B*
Midlands Technical College *A*
Piedmont Technical College *C*
Trident Technical College *A*

South Dakota
Black Hills State University *B*
Northern State University *A*
South Dakota State University *B*
Southeast Technical Institute *A*

Tennessee
Belmont University *B*
Chattanooga State Technical Community
College *A*
Jackson State Community College *A*
Lambuth University *B*
Memphis College of Art *B*
Nossi College of Art *A*
O'More College of Design *B*
Roane State Community College *C, A*
Southern Adventist University *A, B*
Southwest Tennessee Community
College *A*
University of Tennessee
Knoxville *B*
Martin *B*

Texas

Abilene Christian University *B*
Amarillo College *C, A*
Austin Community College *C, A*
Brookhaven College *A*
Coastal Bend College *A*
Collin County Community College
    District *C, A*
El Paso Community College *A*
Grayson County College *C, A*
Hill College *A*
Houston Community College
    System *C, A*
Kilgore College *C, A*
Lamar University *B*
Midland College *A*
St. Edward's University *B, T*
Sam Houston State University *B*
San Antonio College *A*
San Jacinto College
    Central Campus *A*
Schreiner University *B*
South Plains College *A*
Southwest Texas State University *B*
Stephen F. Austin State University *M*
Texas A&M University
    Commerce *B, M*
Texas Christian University *B*
Texas State Technical College
    Waco *C, A*
Texas Tech University *B*
Texas Woman's University *B, M*
Tyler Junior College *C, A*
University of Houston *B, M*
University of North Texas *B, M*
University of the Incarnate Word *B*
West Texas A&M University *B*

Utah

Brigham Young University *B*
Salt Lake Community College *C, A*
Southern Utah University *B*
Utah Valley State College *A*
Weber State University *B*

Vermont

Castleton State College *B*
Champlain College *C, A, B*
Lyndon State College *A, B*

Virginia

Hampton University *B*
Longwood University *B*
Mary Baldwin College *B*
Marymount University *B*
Thomas Nelson Community College *A*
Virginia Intermont College *A, B*
Virginia Western Community College *A*

Washington

Art Institute of Seattle *C, A*
Central Washington University *B*
Centralia College *A*
Cornish College of the Arts *B*
Eastern Washington University *B*
Everett Community College *A*
Henry Cogswell College *B*
Pacific Lutheran University *B*
Spokane Falls Community College *C, A*
University of Washington *B, M*

West Virginia

Concord College *B*
Fairmont State College *B*
Shepherd College *A*
West Liberty State College *B*
West Virginia State College *B*
West Virginia Wesleyan College *B*

Wisconsin

Cardinal Stritch University *B*
Carroll College *B*
Carthage College *B*
Concordia University Wisconsin *B*
Edgewood College *B*
Milwaukee Area Technical College *A*
Milwaukee Institute of Art & Design *B*

Mount Mary College *B*
Silver Lake College *A*
University of Wisconsin
    Madison *B*
    Platteville *B*
    Stout *B*
Viterbo University *B*

Wyoming

Laramie County Community College *A*

Communication disorders

Alabama

Auburn University *B, M*

Arizona

Arizona State University *B, D*
University of Arizona *B, M, D*

Arkansas

Harding University *B*
Ouachita Baptist University *B*

California

Biola University
California State University
    Chico *B, M*
    Fresno *B, M*
San Diego State University *B, M, D*
University of the Pacific *B, M*

Colorado

University of Colorado
    Boulder *B, M, D*

District of Columbia

Howard University *M, D*

Georgia

University of Georgia *B, M, D*

Illinois

Eastern Illinois University *B, M*
Northern Illinois University *B, M*
Northwestern University *M*
Southern Illinois University
    Carbondale *B, M, D*
Western Illinois University *B, M*

Kansas

Kansas State University *B*
University of Kansas *B*

Kentucky

Murray State University *B, M*

Louisiana

Nicholls State University *B*
Southeastern Louisiana University *M*

Maine

University of Maine *B, M*

Massachusetts

Boston University *B, M*
Bridgewater State College *B, M*
Emerson College *B, M, D*
University of Massachusetts
    Amherst *B, M, D*

Michigan

Calvin College *B*
Northern Michigan University *B, M*
Wayne State University *B, M, D*

Minnesota

Minnesota State University
    Mankato *B, M*
St. Cloud State University *B, M*
University of Minnesota
    Duluth *B, M*
    Twin Cities *M, D*

Missouri

Rockhurst University *B, M*
Southeast Missouri State
    University *B, M*
Truman State University *B, M*

University of Missouri
    Columbia *M, D*

New Hampshire

University of New Hampshire *B, M*

New Jersey

Montclair State University *M*

New York

Nazareth College of Rochester *B*
Pace University *B*
Pace University:
    Pleasantville/Briarcliff *B*
State University of New York
    Buffalo *M, D*
    College at Fredonia *B*
    New Paltz *B, M*
Syracuse University *B*

North Carolina

Western Carolina University *B, M*

North Dakota

Minot State University *B, M*

Ohio

Baldwin-Wallace College *B*
Bowling Green State University *B, M, D*
Case Western Reserve
    University *B, M, D*
University of Akron *B*

Oklahoma

University of Oklahoma *B, M, D*

Pennsylvania

Edinboro University of Pennsylvania *B*
West Chester University of
    Pennsylvania *M*

Rhode Island

University of Rhode Island *B*

South Carolina

Medical University of South Carolina *M*
Winthrop University *B*

South Dakota

Augustana College *B*
University of South Dakota *B, M*

Texas

Baylor University *B, M*
Our Lady of the Lake University of San
    Antonio *B, M*
Southwest Texas State University *B, M*
University of Houston *B*
University of Texas
    Austin *B, M, D*
    Dallas *D*
    Pan American *B, M*
West Texas A&M University *B, M*

Vermont

University of Vermont *B, M*

Virginia

Hampton University *B*
Radford University *B, M*

Washington

Eastern Washington University *B, M*

Wisconsin

University of Wisconsin
    Eau Claire *B, M*
    Madison *B, M, D*
    Milwaukee *B, M*
    River Falls *B, M*

Communications

Alabama

Alabama State University *B*
Andrew Jackson University *B*
Auburn University at Montgomery *B*
Enterprise State Junior College *A*
Huntingdon College *B*
Jacksonville State University *B*

Miles College *B*
Oakwood College *B*
Southern Union State Community
    College *A*
Spring Hill College *B*
University of Alabama
    Birmingham *B*
University of Mobile *B*
University of Montevallo *M*
University of South Alabama *B, M*

Alaska

University of Alaska
    Fairbanks *B, M*
    Southeast *B*

Arizona

Arizona State University *B, M, D*
Cochise College *A*
Northern Arizona University *B*
Phoenix College *A*
Prescott College *B, M*
South Mountain Community College *C*
University of Arizona *B, M, D*

Arkansas

Harding University *B*
Ouachita Baptist University *B*
Southern Arkansas University *B*
University of Arkansas *B, M*
University of Arkansas
    Fort Smith *A*
    Little Rock *B, M*
    Pine Bluff *B*
University of the Ozarks *B*

California

Azusa Pacific University *B*
Barstow College *A*
Biola University *B*
California Baptist University *B*
California State Polytechnic University:
    Pomona *B*
California State University
    Bakersfield *B*
    Chico *B, M*
    Dominguez Hills *B*
    Fresno *B, M*
    Fullerton *B, M*
    Hayward *B*
    Monterey Bay *B*
    Northridge *M*
    Sacramento *B, M*
    San Bernardino *B*
    San Marcos *B*
    Stanislaus *B*
Chapman University *B*
Christian Heritage College *B*
College of Marin: Kentfield *A*
College of the Sequoias *A*
College of the Siskiyous *C, A*
Concordia University *B*
Cuesta College *C, A*
De Anza College *A*
Dominican University of California *B*
Fashion Institute of Design and
    Merchandising *A*
Foothill College *C, A*
Fresno Pacific University *B*
Gavilan Community College *A*
La Sierra University *B*
Loyola Marymount University *B, M*
Marymount College *A*
Master's College *B*
Menlo College *B*
Mills College *B*
MiraCosta College *A*
Modesto Junior College *C, A*
Monterey Peninsula College *A*
Moorpark College *A*
Pacific Union College *B*
Pepperdine University *B, M*
Point Loma Nazarene University *B*
St. Mary's College of California *B*
San Diego State University *B, M, D*
Santa Barbara City College *A*
Santa Clara University *B*

Santa Rosa Junior College *C*
Santiago Canyon College *A*
Shasta College *A*
Sierra College *A*
Simpson College *B*
Sonoma State University *B*
Southwestern College *A*
Stanford University *B, M, D*
University of California
    Los Angeles *B*
    San Diego *B, M, D*
    Santa Barbara *B, M, D*
University of La Verne *B*
University of San Diego *B*
University of San Francisco *B*
University of Southern
  California *B, M, D*
University of the Pacific *B*
Vanguard University of Southern
  California *B*
Ventura College *A*

Colorado

Art Institute
  of Colorado *B*
Colorado Christian University *B*
Colorado State University
  Pueblo *B*
Fort Lewis College *B*
Jones International University *C, B, M*
Metropolitan State College of Denver *B*
Red Rocks Community College *A*
Regis University *B*
University of Colorado
  Boulder *B, M, D*
  Colorado Springs *B, M*
  Denver *B, M*
University of Denver *B, M, D*
University of Northern Colorado *B, M, T*

Connecticut

Albertus Magnus College *B*
Asnuntuck Community College *A*
Briarwood College *A*
Central Connecticut State University *B*
Eastern Connecticut State University *B*
Fairfield University *B*
Middlesex Community College *A*
Quinnipiac University *B, M*
Sacred Heart University *B*
Southern Connecticut State University *B*
Tunxis Community College *C*
University of Bridgeport *B*
University of Connecticut *B, M, D*
University of Hartford *B, M*
University of New Haven *A, B*
Western Connecticut State University *B*

Delaware

University of Delaware *B, M*
Wilmington College *B*

District of Columbia

American University *B*
Catholic University of America *B*
Gallaudet University *B*
George Washington University *B*
Howard University *B, M, D*
Trinity College *B*

Florida

Barry University *B, M*
Eckerd College *B*
Edward Waters College *B*
Embry-Riddle Aeronautical University *B*
Flagler College *B*
Florida Institute of Technology *B, M*
Florida International University *B, M*
Florida Southern College *B*
Florida State University *B, M, D*
Gulf Coast Community College *A*
Jacksonville University *B*
Lake City Community College *A*
Palm Beach Atlantic University *B*
Pensacola Junior College *A*
Polk Community College *A*
Rollins College *M*

St. Thomas University *B*
Seminole Community College *A*
South Florida Community College *A*
Southeastern College of the Assemblies
  of God *B*
Stetson University *B*
University of Central Florida *B, M*
University of Florida *M, D*
University of Miami *B, M, D*
University of North Florida *B*
University of South Florida *B, M*
University of Tampa *B*
University of West Florida *B, M*
Warner Southern College *B*

Georgia

Abraham Baldwin Agricultural
  College *A*
Albany Technical College *A*
Andrew College *A*
Augusta State University *B*
Berry College *B*
Brewton-Parker College *B*
Clark Atlanta University *B*
Columbus State University *B*
Emmanuel College *B*
Floyd College *A*
Georgia Southern University *B*
Georgia State University *M*
Kennesaw State University *B*
Macon State College *B*
Mercer University *B, M*
Oglethorpe University *B*
Reinhardt College *B*
Savannah State University *B*
Shorter College *B*
South Georgia College *A*
Valdosta State University *B*
Wesleyan College *B*
Young Harris College *A*

Hawaii

Brigham Young University-Hawaii *A*
Chaminade University of Honolulu *B*
Hawaii Pacific University *B, M*
University of Hawaii
  Hilo *B*
  Manoa *B, M, D*

Idaho

Boise State University *B, T*
Brigham Young University - Idaho *B*
College of Southern Idaho *A*
Idaho State University *A, B, M*
Lewis-Clark State College *B*
North Idaho College *A*
University of Idaho *B*

Illinois

Augustana College *B*
Aurora University *B*
Benedictine University *B*
Blackburn College *B*
Bradley University *B*
Concordia University *B*
Danville Area Community College *A*
De Paul University *B, M*
Dominican University *B*
Elmhurst College *B*
Eureka College *B*
Governors State University *B, M*
Illinois State University *M*
Illinois Valley Community College *A*
John Wood Community College *A*
Judson College *B*
Kishwaukee College *A*
Lake Forest College *B*
Lewis University *B*
Lincoln College *A*
Lincoln Land Community College *A*
Loyola University of Chicago *C, B, T*
McKendree College *B*
Millikin University *B*
Monmouth College *B, T*
Moody Bible Institute *B*
North Central College *B*
North Park University *B*

Northwestern University *C, B, M, D*
Olivet Nazarene University *B*
Parkland College *A*
Quincy University *B*
Roosevelt University *B*
St. Xavier University *B*
Sauk Valley Community College *A*
Southwestern Illinois College *A*
Trinity Christian College *B*
Trinity International University *B*
University of Illinois
  Springfield *B, M*
  Urbana-Champaign *D*
University of St. Francis *B*
Western Illinois University *B*

Indiana

Bethel College *B*
Butler University *B*
Calumet College of St. Joseph *B*
DePauw University *B*
Goshen College *B*
Grace College *B*
Hanover College *B*
Indiana State University *B, M*
Indiana University
  Bloomington *B, M, D*
  East *B*
  Kokomo *B*
  Southeast *B*
Indiana University-Purdue University
  Fort Wayne *B, M, T*
Indiana University-Purdue University
  Indianapolis *B, M*
Indiana Wesleyan University *A, B*
Manchester College *B, T*
Marian College *B*
Martin University *B*
Purdue University *B, M, D*
Purdue University
  Calumet *B, M*
  North Central Campus *C*
St. Joseph's College *B*
Saint Mary's College *B*
Taylor University *B*
Tri-State University *A, B*
University of Evansville *B*
University of Indianapolis *B*
University of St. Francis *B*
University of Southern Indiana *A, B*
Valparaiso University *C, A, B*
Vincennes University *A*

Iowa

Buena Vista University *B*
Central College *B*
Clarke College *B*
Coe College *B*
Dordt College *B*
Drake University *B*
Ellsworth Community College *A*
Franciscan University *B*
Grand View College *C, B*
Iowa Wesleyan College *B*
Loras College *B*
Luther College *B*
Morningside College *B*
Mount Mercy College *B*
Northwestern College *B*
St. Ambrose University *B*
Simpson College *B*
University of Dubuque *B, M*
University of Iowa *B, M, D, T*
University of Northern Iowa *B, M*
Upper Iowa University *B*
Waldorf College *A, B*
Wartburg College *B*
William Penn University *B*

Kansas

Baker University *B*
Barton County Community College *A*
Bethany College *B*
Bethel College *B*
Central Christian College *A, B*
Cloud County Community College *A*

Emporia State University *B*
Fort Hays State University *B, M*
Fort Scott Community College *A*
Friends University *B*
Garden City Community College *A*
Haskell Indian Nations University *A*
Hutchinson Community College *A*
Independence Community College *A*
Kansas State University *B, M*
Kansas Wesleyan University *B, T*
McPherson College *B*
MidAmerica Nazarene University *B, T*
Newman University *B*
Ottawa University *B*
Pittsburg State University *B, M, T*
Pratt Community College *A*
St. Mary College *B*
Seward County Community College *A*
Southwestern College *B*
Sterling College *B*
Tabor College *B*
Washburn University of Topeka *B*
Wichita State University *B, M*

Kentucky

Bellarmine University *B*
Campbellsville University *B*
Cumberland College *B, T*
Henderson Community College *A*
Kentucky Mountain Bible College *B*
Kentucky Wesleyan College *B*
Lindsey Wilson College *B*
Morehead State University *B, M*
Murray State University *B, M*
Paducah Community College *A*
Pikeville College *B*
Spalding University *B*
Thomas More College *A, B*
Union College *B*
University of Kentucky *B, M, D*
University of Louisville *B*

Louisiana

Centenary College of Louisiana *B*
Dillard University *B*
Louisiana College *B*
Loyola University New Orleans *B, M*
Southeastern Louisiana University *B*
Tulane University *B*
University of Louisiana at
  Lafayette *B, M*
University of Louisiana at Monroe *M*
University of New Orleans *B, M*
Xavier University of Louisiana *B*

Maine

New England School of
  Communications *C, A, B*
St. Joseph's College *B*
Thomas College *B*
University of Maine *B*
University of Southern Maine *B*

Maryland

Allegany College *A*
Bowie State University *M*
College of Notre Dame of Maryland *B*
College of Southern Maryland *A*
Columbia Union College *B*
Community College of Baltimore County
  Catonsville *A*
  Dundalk *A*
  Essex *A*
Coppin State College *B*
Frederick Community College *A*
Frostburg State University *B*
Goucher College *B*
Hood College *B*
Loyola College in Maryland *B*
McDaniel College *B*
Salisbury University *B*
Towson University *B, M*
University of Baltimore *B*
University of Maryland
  College Park *M, D*
  University College *C, B*
Villa Julie College *A*

Massachusetts

American International College *B*
Becker College *B*
Berkshire Community College *A*
Boston College *B*
Boston University *B, M*
Bridgewater State College *B, M*
Bunker Hill Community College *A*
Cape Cod Community College *A*
Clark University *B, M*
Dean College *A*
Elms College *B*
Emerson College *B, M*
Emmanuel College *B*
Endicott College *B*
Fisher College *A*
Fitchburg State College *C, B, M*
Framingham State College *B*
Gordon College *B*
Hampshire College *B*
Lasell College *B*
Massachusetts Bay Community
    College *C, A*
Merrimack College *B*
Mount Ida College *A*
Newbury College *A, B*
Northeastern University *B*
Pine Manor College *B*
Regis College *B*
Salem State College *B*
Simmons College *B, M*
Stonehill College *B*
Suffolk University *B, M*
University of Massachusetts
    Amherst *B, M, D*
Western New England College *B*
Westfield State College *B*

Michigan

Adrian College *A, B, T*
Alma College *B*
Andrews University *B, M*
Aquinas College *B, T*
Baker College
    of Jackson *A*
Bay de Noc Community College *C*
Calvin College *B*
Concordia University *B*
Grand Valley State University *B, M*
Hope College *B*
Lansing Community College *A*
Lawrence Technological
    University *C, B, M*
Macomb Community College *C, A*
Madonna University *A, B, T*
Michigan State University *B, M, D*
Northern Michigan University *B*
Northwestern Michigan College *A*
Oakland University *B*
Saginaw Valley State University *B*
Schoolcraft College *A*
Siena Heights University *B*
Spring Arbor University *B*
University of Michigan *B, M, D*
University of Michigan
    Dearborn *B*
    Flint *B, T*
Wayne State University *B, M, D*
Western Michigan University *B, M*
William Tyndale College *B*

Minnesota

Augsburg College *B*
Bethany Lutheran College *B*
Bethel College *B, M*
Brown College *B*
College of St. Catherine *B*
College of St. Scholastica *B*
Concordia College: Moorhead *B*
Concordia University: St. Paul *B*
Gustavus Adolphus College *B*
Hamline University *B*
Lake Superior College: A Community
    and Technical College *C*
Macalester College *B*
Metropolitan State University *B*

Minnesota State University
    Mankato *B, M*
    Moorhead *B*
Northland Community & Technical
    College *A*
Northwestern College *B*
Ridgewater College: A Community and
    Technical College *A*
St. Cloud State University *B, M*
Southwest State University *B*
University of Minnesota
    Duluth *B*
    Morris *B*
University of St. Thomas *B*
Vermilion Community College *A*
Winona State University *B*

Mississippi

Mary Holmes College *A*
Mississippi College *B, M*
Mississippi Gulf Coast Community
    College
    Perkinston *A*
Mississippi State University *B*
Mississippi University for Women *B*
Mississippi Valley State University *B*
University of Southern
    Mississippi *B, M, D*

Missouri

Avila University *B*
Central Methodist College *B*
Central Missouri State University *B, M*
College of the Ozarks *B*
Drury University *B, M*
East Central College *A*
Evangel University *A, B*
Fontbonne College *B*
Hannibal-LaGrange College *B*
Lindenwood University *B, M*
Maryville University of Saint Louis *B*
Mineral Area College *A*
Missouri Baptist University *B*
Missouri Southern State College *B*
Missouri Valley College *B*
Missouri Western State College *T*
Northwest Missouri State University *B*
Rockhurst University *B*
St. Louis Community College
    St. Louis Community College at
        Florissant Valley *A*
    St. Louis Community College at
        Forest Park *A*
    St. Louis Community College at
        Meramec *A*
St. Louis University *B, M*
Southeast Missouri State University *B*
Southwest Baptist University *B*
Southwest Missouri State
    University *B, M*
Stephens College *B*
University of Missouri
    Columbia *B, M, D*
    Kansas City *B, M*
    St. Louis *B*
Webster University *B, M*
William Woods University *B*

Montana

Carroll College *A, B, T*
Miles Community College *A*
Montana State University
    Billings *B*
Montana Tech of the University of
    Montana *B, M*
Rocky Mountain College *B*
University of Montana-Missoula *B, M*

Nebraska

Bellevue University *B, M*
College of Saint Mary *A, B*
Concordia University *B*
Dana College *B*
Doane College *B*
Hastings College *B*
Midland Lutheran College *B*
Nebraska Wesleyan University *B*

University of Nebraska
    Kearney *B*
    Lincoln *B, M, D*
    Omaha *B, M*
Wayne State College *B, M, T*
York College *B*

Nevada

Community College of Southern
    Nevada *A*
University of Nevada
    Las Vegas *B, M*
    Reno *B, M*

New Hampshire

Colby-Sawyer College *B*
Franklin Pierce College *B*
Keene State College *B*
New England College *B*
Plymouth State College *B*
Rivier College *B*
Southern New Hampshire University *B*
University of New Hampshire *B*
University of New Hampshire at
    Manchester *B*

New Jersey

Bloomfield College *B*
Burlington County College *A*
Caldwell College *B*
Centenary College *B*
The College of New Jersey *B*
College of St. Elizabeth *B*
Fairleigh Dickinson University
    College at Florham *B*
    Metropolitan Campus *B*
Gloucester County College *A*
Kean University *B*
Middlesex County College *A*
Monmouth University *B, M*
New Jersey City University *B*
Passaic County Community College *A*
Ramapo College of New Jersey *A*
Raritan Valley Community College *A*
Richard Stockton College of New
    Jersey *B*
Rider University *B*
Rowan University *B*
Rutgers, The State University of New
    Jersey
    New Brunswick Regional
        Campus *B, M, D*
St. Peter's College *B*
Seton Hall University *B, M*
Thomas Edison State College *B*
Union County College *A*
William Paterson University of New
    Jersey *B, M*

New Mexico

Eastern New Mexico University *B, M*
New Mexico Highlands University *B*
New Mexico Junior College *A*
New Mexico State University *B, M*
San Juan College *A*

New York

Adelphi University *B*
Adirondack Community College *C, A*
Alfred University *B*
Broome Community College *A*
Canisius College *B*
City University of New York
    Baruch College *B, M*
    Brooklyn College *B*
    City College *B*
    College of Staten Island *B*
    Hunter College *M*
    Queens College *B, M*
College of Mount St. Vincent *B*
College of New Rochelle *B, M, T*
Cornell University *B, M, D*
Dutchess Community College *A*
Erie Community College
    South Campus *A*
Excelsior College *B*
Fashion Institute of Technology *A*

Finger Lakes Community College *A*
Fordham University *B, M*
Fulton-Montgomery Community
    College *A*
Genesee Community College *A*
Hamilton College *B*
Hofstra University *B*
Houghton College *B*
Iona College *B, M*
Ithaca College *B, M*
Jamestown Community College *A*
Keuka College *B*
Le Moyne College *B*
Long Island University
    Southampton College *B*
Manhattan College *B*
Manhattanville College *B*
Marist College *B*
Marymount College of Fordham
    University *B*
Marymount Manhattan College *B*
Medaille College *B*
Metropolitan College of New York *A, B*
Mohawk Valley Community College *C*
Molloy College *B*
Monroe Community College *A*
Mount St. Mary College *B, T*
Nassau Community College *A*
New York Institute of Technology *B*
New York University *B, M, D*
Niagara County Community College *A*
Niagara University *B*
Nyack College *B*
Orange County Community College *A*
Pace University *B*
Pace University:
    Pleasantville/Briarcliff *B*
Polytechnic University *C*
Rensselaer Polytechnic Institute *B, M, D*
Roberts Wesleyan College *B*
Rochester Institute of
    Technology *A, B, M*
Rockland Community College *A*
Russell Sage College *B*
Sage College of Albany *A*
St. John Fisher College *B*
St. John's University *B*
St. Joseph's College: Suffolk Campus *B*
State University of New York
    Albany *B, M*
    Buffalo *B, M, D*
    College at Brockport *B, M*
    College at Buffalo *B*
    College at Fredonia *B*
    College at Geneseo *B*
    College at Old Westbury *B*
    College at Oneonta *B*
    College at Plattsburgh *B*
    New Paltz *B*
    Oswego *B*
    Purchase *B*
Suffolk County Community College *A*
Syracuse University *B, M*
Tompkins-Cortland Community
    College *A*
Touro College *B*
Ulster County Community College *A*
Westchester Community College *A*

North Carolina

Appalachian State University *B*
Belmont Abbey College *B*
Bennett College *B*
Catawba College *B*
Chowan College *A*
East Carolina University *B*
Elon University *B*
Gardner-Webb University *B*
Guilford Technical Community
    College *A*
Johnson C. Smith University *B*
Lees-McRae College *B*
Lenoir-Rhyne College *B*
Louisburg College *A*
Mars Hill College *B*
Meredith College *B, T*

Methodist College *A, B*
Mount Olive College *B*
North Carolina Agricultural and
   Technical State University *B*
North Carolina State University *B*
Peace College *B*
Pfeiffer University *B*
Queens University of Charlotte *B*
St. Augustine's College *B*
Salem College *B*
University of North Carolina
   Chapel Hill *B, M, D*
   Charlotte *B, M*
   Pembroke *B*
Wake Forest University *B, M*
Western Carolina University *B*
Wingate University *B*
Winston-Salem State University *B*

North Dakota

Dickinson State University *B, T*
Jamestown College *B*
North Dakota State University *B, M, D*
University of Mary *B*
University of North Dakota *B, M, D*

Ohio

Antioch College *B*
Ashland University *C, B*
Baldwin-Wallace College *B*
Bluffton College *B*
Bowling Green State University *B, M, D*
Cedarville University *B*
Cleveland State University *B, M*
College of Mount St. Joseph *A, B, T*
College of Wooster *B*
Defiance College *B*
Denison University *B*
Franciscan University of Steubenville *B*
Heidelberg College *B*
Hiram College *B*
International College of
   Broadcasting *C, A*
John Carroll University *B, M*
Kent State University
   Stark Campus *B*
Lake Erie College *B*
Malone College *B*
Marietta College *B*
Miami University
   Middletown Campus *A*
   Oxford Campus *B, T*
Mount Union College *B, T*
Mount Vernon Nazarene University *B*
Notre Dame College *B, T*
Ohio Dominican College *C, B*
Ohio Northern University *B*
Ohio State University
   Columbus Campus *B, D*
Ohio University *B*
Ohio University
   Southern Campus at Ironton *A*
Otterbein College *B*
Shawnee State University *A*
Sinclair Community College *A*
Tiffin University *B*
Union Institute & University *B*
University of Akron *B, M*
University of Cincinnati *B, M, T*
University of Cincinnati
   Raymond Walters College *A*
University of Dayton *B, M*
University of Findlay *B*
University of Rio Grande *A, B*
University of Toledo *A, B*
Urbana University *B*
Walsh University *A, B*
Wilmington College *B*
Wright State University *B*
Wright State University: Lake Campus *A*
Youngstown State University *B*

Oklahoma

Cameron University *B*
East Central University *B*
Langston University *B*

Northeastern Oklahoma Agricultural and
   Mechanical College *A*
Northeastern State University *M*
Oklahoma Baptist University *B*
Oklahoma Christian University of
   Science and Arts *B, T*
Oklahoma City University *B*
Oklahoma State University *B, M*
Oklahoma Wesleyan University *B*
Oral Roberts University *B*
Southeastern Oklahoma State
   University *B*
Southern Nazarene University *A, B*
Southwestern Oklahoma State
   University *B*
University of Central Oklahoma *B*
University of Oklahoma *B, M, D*
University of Science and Arts of
   Oklahoma *B*
University of Tulsa *B*

Oregon

Central Oregon Community College *A*
George Fox University *B*
Lewis & Clark College *B*
Linfield College *B*
Marylhurst University *B*
Multnomah Bible College *B*
Northwest Christian College *B*
Oregon Institute of Technology *A, B*
Pacific University *B*
Pioneer Pacific College *A*
Portland Community College *C*
Southern Oregon University *B*
University of Portland *B, M*
Western Baptist College *B*

Pennsylvania

Albright College *B*
Allegheny College *B*
Arcadia University *C, B*
Baptist Bible College of Pennsylvania *B*
Bloomsburg University of
   Pennsylvania *B, M, T*
Bucks County Community College *A*
Cabrini College *B*
California University of
   Pennsylvania *B, M*
Carlow College *B, T*
Cedar Crest College *B*
Central Pennsylvania College *A*
Chatham College *B*
Cheyney University of
   Pennsylvania *B, T*
DeSales University *B*
Delaware County Community College *A*
Drexel University *B*
Duquesne University *B, M*
East Stroudsburg University of
   Pennsylvania *B, T*
Edinboro University of
   Pennsylvania *B, M*
Elizabethtown College *C, B*
Geneva College *B, T*
Gettysburg College *B*
Grove City College *B*
Holy Family University *B*
Immaculata University *A, B*
Indiana University of Pennsylvania *B*
Juniata College *B*
Keystone College *A, B*
King's College *B*
Kutztown University of
   Pennsylvania *B, M*
La Roche College *B*
La Salle University *A, B, M*
Lebanon Valley College of
   Pennsylvania *C*
Lincoln University *B*
Lock Haven University of
   Pennsylvania *B*
Lycoming College *B*
Marywood University *A, B, M*
Mercyhurst College *B*
Messiah College *B*

Millersville University of
   Pennsylvania *B*
Montgomery County Community
   College *A*
Muhlenberg College *B*
Neumann College *B*
Penn State
   Erie, The Behrend College *B*
   Harrisburg *B*
   University Park *B, M, D*
Point Park College *B*
Robert Morris University *B, M*
Rosemont College *B*
St. Vincent College *B*
Seton Hill University *B*
Shippensburg University of
   Pennsylvania *M*
Slippery Rock University of
   Pennsylvania *B*
Temple University *B, M, D*
Thiel College *B*
University of Pittsburgh *B*
University of Pittsburgh
   Greensburg *B*
   Johnstown *B*
University of Scranton *B, T*
Villanova University *B*
Waynesburg College *B*
West Chester University of
   Pennsylvania *B, M*
Widener University *B*
Wilkes University *B*
Wilson College *A, B*
York College of Pennsylvania *A, B*

Puerto Rico

Inter American University of Puerto Rico
   Bayamon Campus *A, B*
Pontifical Catholic University of Puerto
   Rico *B*
Turabo University *B*
Universidad Metropolitana *B*
University of Puerto Rico
   Rio Piedras Campus *B, M*
University of the Sacred Heart *B*

Rhode Island

Bryant College *B*
Providence College *B*
Rhode Island College *B*
Roger Williams University *B*
University of Rhode Island *B*

South Carolina

Anderson College *B*
Clemson University *B, M*
Coker College *B*
College of Charleston *B*
Columbia International University *B*
Furman University *B*
Newberry College *B*
North Greenville College *B*
University of South Carolina
   Aiken *B*
   Spartanburg *B*

South Dakota

Augustana College *B*
Dakota Wesleyan University *B*
South Dakota State University *B, M*

Tennessee

Belmont University *B*
Bryan College *B*
Carson-Newman College *B*
East Tennessee State University *M*
Freed-Hardeman University *B*
Jackson State Community College *A*
Lambuth University *B*
Lane College *B*
Lee University *B*
Milligan College *B*
Roane State Community College *A*
Tennessee State University *B*
Tennessee Technological University *B*
Trevecca Nazarene University *B*
Union University *B, T*

University of Memphis *B, M, D*
University of Tennessee
   Chattanooga *B*
   Knoxville *M, D*
Vanderbilt University *B*

Texas

Abilene Christian University *B*
Amarillo College *A*
Angelo State University *B, M, T*
Austin College *B*
Baylor University *B, M*
Blinn College *A*
Brazosport College *A*
Cisco Junior College *A*
Coastal Bend College *A*
Concordia University at Austin *B*
Dallas Baptist University *B*
El Paso Community College *A*
Hardin-Simmons University *B*
Hill College *A*
Houston Baptist University *B*
Howard Payne University *B, T*
Kilgore College *A*
Lamar University *B*
Laredo Community College *A*
McLennan Community College *A*
McMurry University *B, T*
Midland College *A*
Our Lady of the Lake University of San
   Antonio *B*
Palo Alto College *A*
Panola College *A*
Prairie View A&M University *B*
St. Edward's University *B*
St. Mary's University *B, M, T*
South Plains College *A*
Southern Methodist University *B*
Southwestern Adventist University *B*
Southwestern Assemblies of God
   University *B*
Southwestern University *B, T*
Stephen F. Austin State
   University *B, M, T*
Sul Ross State University *B*
Tarleton State University *B*
Texas A&M International University *B*
Texas A&M University
   Commerce *B*
   Corpus Christi *B*
   Kingsville *B*
Texas Christian University *B, M, T*
Texas Lutheran University *B*
Texas Southern University *B, M*
Texas Wesleyan University *B*
Trinity University *B*
Trinity Valley Community College *A*
University of Houston *B, M*
University of Houston
   Clear Lake *B*
   Victoria *B*
University of Mary Hardin-Baylor *B*
University of North Texas *B, M*
University of St. Thomas *B*
University of Texas
   Arlington *B*
   Austin *B*
   El Paso *M*
   Pan American *A, B, T*
   of the Permian Basin *B*
University of the Incarnate Word *B, M*
West Texas A&M University *M*

Utah

Brigham Young University *B, M*
Dixie State College of Utah *A*
Salt Lake Community College *A*
Southern Utah University *B*
University of Utah *B, M, D*
Utah Valley State College *A*
Westminster College *B, M*

Vermont

Bennington College *B*
Castleton State College *A, B*
Champlain College *A, B*

College of St. Joseph in Vermont *B*
Green Mountain College *B*
Lyndon State College *A, B*
Norwich University *B*
Southern Vermont College *B*

Virginia
Bridgewater College *B*
Eastern Mennonite University *B*
Emory & Henry College *B*
Hollins University *B*
James Madison University *B*
Liberty University *B*
Longwood University *B*
Lynchburg College *B*
Mary Baldwin College *B*
Marymount University *B*
Norfolk State University *D*
Radford University *B, M*
Randolph-Macon Woman's College *B*
Shenandoah University *B*
Thomas Nelson Community College *C*
University of Virginia's College at
     Wise *B*
Virginia Polytechnic Institute and State
     University *B*
Virginia Wesleyan College *B*

Washington
Central Washington University *B*
Clark College *A*
Eastern Washington University *B, M*
Edmonds Community College *C*
Everett Community College *A*
Grays Harbor College *A*
Green River Community College *C*
Lower Columbia College *A*
Northwest College *B*
Pacific Lutheran University *B*
Seattle Central Community College *A*
Seattle Pacific University *B*
Seattle University *B*
University of Puget Sound *B, T*
University of Washington *B, M, D*
Walla Walla College *B*
Washington State University *B, M*
Western Washington University *B*
Whitworth College *B*

West Virginia
Alderson-Broaddus College *B*
Bethany College *B*
Concord College *B*
Davis and Elkins College *B*
Fairmont State College *B*
Salem International University *A, B*
Shepherd College *B*
West Liberty State College *B*
West Virginia State College *A, B*
West Virginia University *B, M*
West Virginia Wesleyan College *B*

Wisconsin
Alverno College *B, T*
Cardinal Stritch University *B*
Carroll College *B*
Carthage College *B*
Concordia University Wisconsin *B*
Marian College of Fond du Lac *B*
Marquette University *B, M*
Milwaukee School of Engineering *B*
Moraine Park Technical College *A*
Mount Mary College *B*
Ripon College *B*
St. Norbert College *B*
University of Wisconsin
     Eau Claire *B*
     Green Bay *B*
     La Crosse *B*
     Madison *B, M, D*
     Milwaukee *B, M*
     Oshkosh *B*
     Parkside *B, T*
     Platteville *B*
     Stevens Point *B, M*
     Superior *B, M*
     Whitewater *B, M*

Wisconsin Lutheran College *B*

Wyoming
Casper College *A*
Eastern Wyoming College *A*
Sheridan College *A*
University of Wyoming *B, M*
Western Wyoming Community
     College *A*

Communications systems installation/repair

Alabama
Douglas MacArthur State Technical
     College *A*

Illinois
College of DuPage *A*

Iowa
Western Iowa Tech Community
     College *C*

Maryland
Community College of Baltimore County
     Dundalk *C*

Massachusetts
Springfield Technical Community
     College *A*

Michigan
Northern Michigan University *A*

Minnesota
Dakota County Technical College *C, A*
St. Paul College - A Community and
     Technical College *C*

New York
College of Aeronautics *A, B*
Erie Community College
     South Campus *A*

Ohio
University of Cincinnati
     Raymond Walters College *C, A*

Texas
St. Philip's College *C, A*

Virginia
ECPI Technical College: Roanoke *A*

Communications technology

Alabama
Alabama Agricultural and Mechanical
     University *B*
Calhoun Community College *A*
Community College of the Air Force *A*
Gadsden State Community College *A*

Arizona
Glendale Community College *C, A*

California
Bakersfield College *A*
Barstow College *C*
Chabot College *C, A*
College of the Canyons *C, A*
Diablo Valley College *C*
Golden Gate University *C, B*
Laney College *C, A*
Long Beach City College *C, A*
Los Angeles Southwest College *A*
Los Angeles Trade and Technical
     College *C, A*
Moorpark College *A*
Mount San Antonio College *C, A*
Napa Valley College *C, A*
Palomar College *C, A*
San Diego City College *A*
San Diego State University *M*
Santa Barbara City College *C, A*
Santa Monica College *A*

Southwestern College *A*
Ventura College *A*

Colorado
Arapahoe Community College *C*
Art Institute
     of Colorado *A*
Jones International University *C, B*
University of Denver *M*

Connecticut
Manchester Community College *C*
Naugatuck Valley Community College *C*
Norwalk Community College *A*

Delaware
Wilmington College *A, B*

Florida
Florida State University *M*
Florida Technical College *A*
Miami-Dade Community College *A*
Pensacola Junior College *A*
Seminole Community College *A*

Georgia
Clark Atlanta University *B*
University of Georgia *B*
Valdosta State University *B*

Illinois
College of DuPage *C, A*
Columbia College Chicago *B*
Governors State University *M*
John Wood Community College *A*
Lewis University *B*
Northwestern University *M*
Parkland College *C*
Southwestern Illinois College *C, A*
Waubonsee Community College *C*

Indiana
Ball State University *B, M*
Indiana University-Purdue University
     Indianapolis *A*
Ivy Tech State College
     Northcentral *A*
Martin University *B*
St. Mary-of-the-Woods College *B*

Iowa
Iowa Central Community College *A*
Kirkwood Community College *A*
Marshalltown Community College *A*
Scott Community College *A*
Waldorf College *A, B*

Kansas
Hutchinson Community College *A*
Kansas City Kansas Community
     College *C, A*

Kentucky
Asbury College *B*
Murray State University *B, M*

Maine
New England School of
     Communications *A, B*

Maryland
Anne Arundel Community College *C*
Bowie State University *B*
Community College of Baltimore County
     Dundalk *A*
     Essex *A*
Frederick Community College *A*
Harford Community College *A*
Villa Julie College *B*

Massachusetts
Ai The New England Institute of Art and
     Design *A*
Berkshire Community College *A*
Lesley University *B*
Mount Wachusett Community College *A*
Newbury College *A*
Northeastern University *A*

Michigan
Andrews University *B*
Eastern Michigan University *B*
Ferris State University *A, B*
Kellogg Community College *A*
Lansing Community College *A*
Mott Community College *C, A*
Oakland Community College *A*
Saginaw Valley State University *M*
Schoolcraft College *A*

Minnesota
Academy College *A*
Century Community and Technical
     College *C, A*
Dakota County Technical College *C*
Hennepin Technical College *C, A*
Inver Hills Community College *A*
Rochester Community and Technical
     College *C, A*
St. Cloud Technical College *C, A*
St. Mary's University of Minnesota *B, M*
Winona State University *B*

Mississippi
Northwest Mississippi Community
     College *A*

Missouri
Evangel University *B*
Penn Valley Community College *C*
Ranken Technical College *A*

Montana
Miles Community College *A*
Montana Tech of the University of
     Montana *A, B*

Nebraska
Central Community College *C, A*
Hastings College *B*

New Hampshire
New Hampshire Technical Institute *C, A*

New Jersey
Bergen Community College *C*
Brookdale Community College *A*
County College of Morris *A*
Mercer County Community College *A*
Ocean County College *A*
Rowan University *B*

New Mexico
San Juan College *A*

New York
Canisius College *B*
Cayuga County Community College *A*
City University of New York
     Borough of Manhattan Community
          College *A*
     Queensborough Community
          College *A*
Fulton-Montgomery Community
     College *A*
Genesee Community College *A*
Monroe Community College *A*
New York Institute of
     Technology *C, A, M*
New York University *B, M, D*
Rochester Institute of Technology *B, M*
St. John's University *B*
State University of New York
     College at Plattsburgh *B*
     Institute of Technology at
          Utica/Rome *B*
Suffolk County Community College *A*

North Carolina
Belmont Abbey College *B*
Chowan College *B*
Cleveland Community College *C, A*
Wilkes Community College *C, A*

North Dakota
Minot State University *B*

Ohio
Bowling Green State University:
    Firelands College *A*
Cedarville University *B*
Columbus State Community College *A*
Cuyahoga Community College
    Eastern Campus *A*
    Metropolitan Campus *A*
    Western Campus *A*
Kent State University *B*
University of Findlay *B*

Oklahoma
Langston University *B*
Oklahoma State University *M*
Oklahoma State University
    Oklahoma City *A*
Rogers State University *A*
Southern Nazarene University *B*
Tulsa Community College *A*

Oregon
Lane Community College *C, A*
Portland Community College *C*

Pennsylvania
California University of Pennsylvania *B*
Cheyney University of Pennsylvania *B*
Community College of Allegheny
    County *A*
Community College of Beaver County *A*
Delaware County Community College *A*
East Stroudsburg University of
    Pennsylvania *A, B*
Immaculata University *A*
Lebanon Valley College of
    Pennsylvania *B*
Luzerne County Community College *A*
Philadelphia University *M*
Point Park College *B*
St. Vincent College *B*
Westmoreland County Community
    College *A*

Puerto Rico
Inter American University of Puerto Rico
    Bayamon Campus *A*
University of Puerto Rico
    Humacao *A*

Rhode Island
Salve Regina University *B*

South Carolina
Trident Technical College *C, A*

Tennessee
Southern Adventist University *A, B*
Tennessee Technological University *B*
Trevecca Nazarene University *B*

Texas
Abilene Christian University *B*
Amarillo College *A*
Coastal Bend College *A*
Eastfield College *C, A*
El Paso Community College *A*
North Harris Montgomery Community
    College District *C, A*
Richland College *A*
St. Philip's College *A*
Tarrant County College *C, A*
Texas A&M University
    Commerce *M*
Texas State Technical College
    Waco *A*
    West Texas *A*
University of Houston *M*

Utah
Dixie State College of Utah *A*

Vermont
Lyndon State College *B*

Virginia
ECPI College of Technology *C, A*
ECPI Technical College: Roanoke *A*
George Mason University *M*

J. Sargeant Reynolds Community
    College *C*
Virginia Western Community College *A*

Washington
Eastern Washington University *B*
Edmonds Community College *A*
Spokane Falls Community College *A*
University of Washington *M*

West Virginia
Bluefield State College *A*
Shepherd College *A*
Southern West Virginia Community and
    Technical College *A*
West Virginia State College *A*

Wisconsin
Milwaukee Area Technical College *A*
University of Wisconsin
    Superior *B, M*
Western Wisconsin Technical College *A*

Wyoming
Central Wyoming College *A*

Community health services

Arkansas
University of Arkansas *M*

Connecticut
Western Connecticut State University *B*

Illinois
McHenry County College *C*
University of Illinois
    Urbana-Champaign *B, M, D*

Indiana
Indiana State University *B*
Indiana University-Purdue University
    Fort Wayne *B*

Michigan
Michigan State University *B, M*

New York
Erie Community College
    City Campus *A*

Ohio
Youngstown State University *B*

Pennsylvania
Seton Hill University *B*

Rhode Island
Brown University *B*

Tennessee
Southern Adventist University *M*

Texas
Stephen F. Austin State University *B*
University of Texas
    Austin *B*
    Houston Health Science
        Center *M, D*

Utah
Utah Valley State College *A*

Virginia
Old Dominion University *B*

Washington
Edmonds Community College *C, A*

Community health/ preventative medicine

Arkansas
Arkansas State University *B*

Indiana
Indiana University-Purdue University
    Indianapolis *M*

Iowa
University of Iowa *M, D*

Maine
University of Maine
    Farmington *B*

Massachusetts
University of Massachusetts
    Amherst *M, D*

New Jersey
Thomas Edison State College *B*

New York
Hofstra University *B*

North Dakota
North Dakota State University *B*
University of North Dakota *B*

Ohio
Youngstown State University *B*

Texas
University of Texas
    Houston Health Science
        Center *M, D*

Virginia
Old Dominion University *M*

Community organization/ advocacy

Alabama
Alabama State University *B*
Samford University *A*

Alaska
University of Alaska
    Fairbanks *A, B, M*

Arizona
Prescott College *B*

Arkansas
Southern Arkansas University *B*
University of Central Arkansas *M*

California
California State University
    Dominguez Hills *B*
Los Angeles Trade and Technical
    College *C, A*
National University *M*
University of California
    Davis *M*

Connecticut
Manchester Community College *C, A*
University of Hartford *B*

Florida
St. Leo University *B*

Georgia
Mercer University *B*

Hawaii
University of Hawaii
    Honolulu Community College *C, A*

Illinois
Lincoln Land Community College *A*
Loyola University of Chicago *M*
North Park University *M*
Triton College *A*
University of Illinois
    Urbana-Champaign *M, D*
Western Illinois University *M*

Indiana
Martin University *M*

Iowa
Iowa Central Community College *A*
Kirkwood Community College *A*
Marshalltown Community College *A*

Kentucky
Henderson Community College *A*
Murray State University *M*

Maryland
College of Notre Dame of Maryland *B*

Massachusetts
Brandeis University *M*
Massasoit Community College *A*
Springfield College *B, M*
University of Massachusetts
    Boston *B*

Michigan
Aquinas College *B*
Central Michigan University *B*
Madonna University *C*
University of Michigan *D*

Minnesota
Bemidji State University *B*
Capella University *M, D*
Concordia University: St. Paul *B*
Winona State University *B*

Mississippi
Delta State University *M*

Missouri
Rockhurst University *B*

Montana
University of Montana-Missoula *C*

Nebraska
University of Nebraska
    Omaha *B*

New Hampshire
University of New Hampshire *A*

New Jersey
Salem Community College *A*
Thomas Edison State College *A, B*

New Mexico
University of New Mexico *A, B*

New York
City University of New York
    Brooklyn College *B*
Cornell University *B*
Dominican College of Blauvelt *C*
Erie Community College
    City Campus *C*
    North Campus *C*
    South Campus *C*
Genesee Community College *A*
Hudson Valley Community College *A*
Metropolitan College of New York *A, B*
Mohawk Valley Community College *A*
Pace University *B, M*
Pace University:
    Pleasantville/Briarcliff *B, M*
State University of New York
    Empire State College *A, B*
Suffolk County Community College *A*
Ulster County Community College *A*

North Carolina
St. Augustine's College *B*

Ohio
University of Akron *A*
University of Cincinnati *M*
University of Findlay *A*
Urbana University *B*

Oklahoma
East Central University *B, M*

Oregon
Chemeketa Community College *A*
Clackamas Community College *A*
Lane Community College *A*

Pennsylvania
California University of Pennsylvania *A*
Marywood University *B*
Mercyhurst College *C*

St. Joseph's University *M*

Rhode Island
Providence College *C, B*

South Dakota
Black Hills State University *B*
Northern State University *B*

Tennessee
Cleveland State Community College *A*
University of Tennessee
    Chattanooga *B*

Texas
Abilene Christian University *M*
Texas A&M University *B*
University of North Texas *M*

Vermont
Goddard College *B*
Woodbury College *C*

Virginia
Emory & Henry College *B*
J. Sargeant Reynolds Community
    College *A*

Washington
Western Washington University *B*

Wisconsin
Alverno College *B*
Western Wisconsin Technical College *A*

Community psychology

Alabama
Troy State University *M*
Troy State University Dothan *M*

Alaska
University of Alaska
    Fairbanks *M*

California
University of La Verne *D*

Connecticut
Southern Connecticut State University *M*
University of New Haven *B, M*

Delaware
Wilmington College *M*

District of Columbia
Catholic University of America *M*
George Washington University *M*

Florida
Florida Agricultural and Mechanical
    University *M*

Illinois
Northwestern University *B*
Roosevelt University *M*

Kansas
Pittsburg State University *B*
St. Mary College *B*

Maine
University of New England *B*

Maryland
Johns Hopkins University *M*

Massachusetts
Hampshire College *B*

Michigan
Northern Michigan University *B*
Western Michigan University *D*

Minnesota
St. Cloud State University *M*

Montana
Montana State University
    Billings *B*

New Jersey
Fairleigh Dickinson University
    College at Florham *M*

New York
College of New Rochelle *M*
Hofstra University *M, D, T*
Metropolitan College of New York *A, B*
New York Institute of Technology *B*
New York University *D*
Pace University:
    Pleasantville/Briarcliff *B*

Ohio
Kent State University *M*
University of Akron *M*

Oregon
Western Baptist College *B*

Pennsylvania
Holy Family University *B*
Penn State
    Harrisburg *M*
Seton Hill University *B*

Puerto Rico
University of Puerto Rico
    Rio Piedras Campus *M*

South Carolina
Clemson University *M*
Francis Marion University *M*

Tennessee
Southern Adventist University *M*
Vanderbilt University *D*

Texas
Lamar University *M*
St. Mary's University *M, D*

Vermont
Burlington College *B*

Virginia
Norfolk State University *M*

West Virginia
Fairmont State College *B*
Salem International University *A*

Community/junior college administration

Arkansas
Arkansas State University *M, T*

California
University of Southern California *T*

Illinois
Chicago State University *M*
Northeastern Illinois University *M*

Indiana
Ball State University *M, D*

Iowa
University of Iowa *M, D*

Kansas
Pittsburg State University *M*

Massachusetts
Springfield College *D*

Michigan
Central Michigan University *M*

Minnesota
University of Minnesota
    Twin Cities *M*

Mississippi
Alcorn State University *M*
Mississippi State University *M, D*

New Jersey
Rowan University *M*

North Carolina
North Carolina State University *M, D*
Western Carolina University *M*

Oklahoma
Northeastern State University *M*

South Carolina
Clemson University *M*

Texas
Texas A&M University
    Commerce *M, D*

Virginia
Old Dominion University *D*

Washington
University of Washington *M, D*

Comparative literature

Arizona
Prescott College *B, M*
University of Arizona *M, D*

Arkansas
University of Arkansas *M, D*

California
California State University
    Fullerton *B, M*
    Long Beach *B*
    Northridge *B*
Chapman University *M*
Fresno Pacific University *B*
Glendale Community College *A*
Mills College *B, M*
Occidental College *B*
San Francisco State University *B, M*
Southwestern College *A*
Stanford University *B, M, D*
University of California
    Berkeley *B, M, D*
    Davis *B, M, D*
    Irvine *B, M, D*
    Los Angeles *M, D*
    Riverside *B, M, D*
    San Diego *M, D*
    Santa Barbara *B, M, D*
    Santa Cruz *B*
University of La Verne *B*
University of Southern
    California *B, M, D*
Whittier College *B*

Colorado
Colorado College *B*
University of Colorado
    Boulder *M, D*

Connecticut
Trinity College *B*
University of Connecticut *M, D*
Yale University *B, M, D*

Delaware
University of Delaware *B*

District of Columbia
Catholic University of America *M, D*
Georgetown University *B*

Florida
Eckerd College *B*

Georgia
Emory University *B, D*
Oxford College of Emory University *B*
University of Georgia *B, M, D*

Hawaii
Hawaii Pacific University *B*

Illinois
Illinois Valley Community College *A*
McKendree College *B*
Northeastern Illinois University *M*
Northwestern University *B, M, D*
Parkland College *A*

Roosevelt University *B, M*
University of Chicago *M, D*

Indiana
Earlham College *B*
Indiana University
    Bloomington *B, M, D*
Manchester College *A*
University of Notre Dame *D*

Iowa
Graceland University *B*
Loras College *B*
University of Iowa *B, M, D*

Louisiana
Louisiana State University and
    Agricultural and Mechanical
    College *M, D*

Maine
University of Southern Maine *B*

Maryland
Johns Hopkins University *B, D*
University of Maryland
    College Park *M, D*

Massachusetts
Brandeis University *B*
Clark University *B*
College of the Holy Cross *B*
Hampshire College *B*
Harvard College *B*
Massachusetts College of Liberal Arts *B*
Simmons College *B, M*
Simon's Rock College of Bard *B*
Smith College *B*
Tufts University *B, M, D*
University of Massachusetts
    Amherst *B, M, D*
Wellesley College *B*
Williams College *B*

Michigan
Central Michigan University *M*
Hillsdale College *B*
Michigan State University *M*
University of Michigan *B, M, D*
Wayne State University *M*

Minnesota
University of Minnesota
    Twin Cities *B, M, D*
University of St. Thomas *B*

Missouri
Washington University in St.
    Louis *B, M, D*

Nebraska
Wayne State College *B*

New Hampshire
Dartmouth College *B, M*

New Jersey
Princeton University *B, M, D*
Ramapo College of New Jersey *B*
Rutgers, The State University of New
    Jersey
    New Brunswick Regional
        Campus *B, M, D*

New Mexico
University of New Mexico *B, M*

New York
Bard College *B*
Barnard College *B*
City University of New York
    Baruch College *B*
    Brooklyn College *B*
    City College *B*
    Hunter College *B*
    Queens College *B*
Columbia University
    Columbia College *B*
Cornell University *B, D*

Eugene Lang College/New School
University *B*
Fordham University *B*
Hamilton College *B*
Hobart and William Smith Colleges *B*
Hofstra University *B*
Long Island University
C. W. Post Campus *B*
Southampton College *B*
New York University *B, M, D*
Sarah Lawrence College *B*
State University of New York
Binghamton *B, M, D*
Buffalo *B, M, D*
College at Geneseo *B*
Stony Brook *B*
Syracuse University *B*
University of Rochester *B, M*
Wells College *B*

North Carolina
Duke University *M, D*
University of North Carolina
Chapel Hill *B, M, D*

North Dakota
North Dakota State University *M*

Ohio
Case Western Reserve University *B, M*
Cleveland State University *T*
College of Wooster *B*
Miami University
Oxford Campus *B*
Oberlin College *B*
Ohio State University
Columbus Campus *B, M*
Ohio Wesleyan University *B*
Otterbein College *B*
University of Cincinnati *B, M, D, T*
Wittenberg University *B*

Oklahoma
East Central University *B*
University of Central Oklahoma *B, M*

Oregon
Chemeketa Community College *A*
Reed College *B*
University of Oregon *B, M, D*
Willamette University *B*

Pennsylvania
Bryn Mawr College *B*
Duquesne University *B*
Gettysburg College *B*
Haverford College *B, T*
Immaculata University *B*
La Salle University *B*
Penn State
Abington *B*
Altoona *B*
Beaver *B*
Berks *B*
Delaware County *B*
Dubois *B*
Fayette *B*
Hazleton *B*
Lehigh Valley *B*
McKeesport *B*
Mont Alto *B*
New Kensington *B*
Schuylkill - Capital College *B*
Shenango *B*
University Park *C, B, M, D*
Wilkes-Barre *B*
Worthington Scranton *B*
York *B*
Swarthmore College *B*
University of Pennsylvania *B, D*
West Chester University of
Pennsylvania *B*

Puerto Rico
University of Puerto Rico
Mayaguez Campus *B*
Rio Piedras Campus *B, M*

Rhode Island
Brown University *B, M, D*
University of Rhode Island *B*

South Carolina
University of South Carolina *M, D*

Tennessee
University of Tennessee
Knoxville *B*
Vanderbilt University *M, D*

Texas
Cisco Junior College *A*
St. Edward's University *B, T*
Texas A&M University *M*
University of North Texas *B*
University of Texas
Arlington *D*
Austin *M, D*
El Paso *B, M*

Utah
Brigham Young University *B, M*

Vermont
Bennington College *B*
Burlington College *B*
Johnson State College *B*
Marlboro College *B*

Virginia
Lynchburg College *B*
University of Virginia *B*

Washington
Eastern Washington University *B, M*
Everett Community College *A*
Gonzaga University *B*
Pacific Lutheran University *B*
University of Washington *B, M, D*

West Virginia
Alderson-Broaddus College *B*

Wisconsin
Beloit College *B*
University of Wisconsin
Madison *B, M, D*
Milwaukee *B*

Comparative/international education

California
University of Southern California *M*

District of Columbia
George Washington University *M*
Howard University *M*

Florida
Florida International University *M*
Florida State University *M, D*

Illinois
Loyola University of Chicago *M, D*

Indiana
Indiana University
Bloomington *M*

Massachusetts
Boston University *M*
Endicott College *M*

New Jersey
The College of New Jersey *M*

New York
New York University *D*
State University of New York
Albany *M, D*
Buffalo *M, D*

Ohio
Ohio State University
Columbus Campus *M*

Virginia
University of Virginia *M, D*

Computational mathematics

Georgia
Georgia Institute of Technology *M*

Indiana
Indiana University-Purdue University
Fort Wayne *B*

Michigan
Hillsdale College *B*
Kettering University *B*
Michigan State University *B*

New Hampshire
Keene State College *B*

New Jersey
Stevens Institute of Technology *B*

New York
Long Island University
C. W. Post Campus *M*
Rochester Institute of Technology *B*

Washington
Seattle Pacific University *B*

Computer education

Arkansas
John Brown University *B*
University of Central Arkansas *T*

California
California State University
Sacramento *T*
Fresno Pacific University *M*
National University *M*
San Diego State University *B, T*

Connecticut
Western Connecticut State University *M*

District of Columbia
Trinity College *M*

Florida
Barry University *M*
Florida Institute of Technology *B, M*
Nova Southeastern University *M*
Stetson University *B, T*

Georgia
Atlanta Metropolitan College *A*
Emmanuel College *B*

Illinois
Concordia University *B, M, T*
De Paul University *T*
Illinois Institute of Technology *M*
University of Illinois
Urbana-Champaign *B, T*

Indiana
Ball State University *T*
Goshen College *B*
Indiana Wesleyan University *T*
University of Evansville *T*
University of Indianapolis *T*
Vincennes University *A*

Iowa
Clarke College *B, T*
Loras College *T*
Morningside College *M*

Kansas
Emporia State University *T*
Independence Community College *A*
McPherson College *B, T*
Ottawa University *T*
Pittsburg State University *B, T*
St. Mary College *T*

Kentucky
Bellarmine University *T*
Cumberland College *T*

Spalding University *M*
Thomas More College *B*

Louisiana
Xavier University of Louisiana *M*

Maine
Thomas College *M*

Massachusetts
Lesley University *M, T*

Michigan
Central Michigan University *B*
Eastern Michigan University *B, T*
Grand Valley State University *T*
Michigan Technological University *T*
Northern Michigan University *B, T*

Minnesota
Minnesota State University
Mankato *B, T*
University of Minnesota
Morris *T*
Vermilion Community College *A*

Mississippi
Mississippi College *B, M*
Mississippi State University *T*

Missouri
Northwest Missouri State
University *M, T*
Webster University *M*

Montana
Montana State University
Billings *M, T*
Montana Tech of the University of
Montana *T*
University of Montana: Western *T*

Nebraska
College of Saint Mary *B, T*
Concordia University *B, T*
Doane College *B*
Hastings College *M*
Peru State College *B, T*
Union College *T*
University of Nebraska
Lincoln *B, T*

Nevada
University of Nevada
Las Vegas *B*

New Hampshire
Southern New Hampshire University *C*
University of New Hampshire *T*

New Jersey
Monmouth University *T*
Rowan University *T*
St. Peter's College *M, T*

New Mexico
New Mexico Institute of Mining and
Technology *M*

New York
College of Mount St. Vincent *T*
Long Island University
C. W. Post Campus *M*
Manhattan College *B, T*
Nazareth College of Rochester *M*
Pace University *C, B, T*
Pace University:
Pleasantville/Briarcliff *C, B, T*
State University of New York
College at Buffalo *M*
College at Plattsburgh *B, M*

North Carolina
University of North Carolina
Greensboro *B, T*

North Dakota
Dickinson State University *B, T*

Ohio
Ashland University *M, T*
Baldwin-Wallace College *T*

Bluffton College *B*
Mount Union College *T*
University of Akron *B, T*
University of Dayton *M*
Youngstown State University *B, T*

Oklahoma

Eastern Oklahoma State College *A*
Southwestern Oklahoma State
    University *T*
University of Central Oklahoma *B*

Oregon

Western Oregon University *T*

Pennsylvania

California University of Pennsylvania *M*
Philadelphia University *M*
University of Pennsylvania *M*

South Dakota

Dakota State University *B, M, D, T*

Texas

Abilene Christian University *B, T*
Baylor University *B, T*
Hardin-Simmons University *B, T*
Lamar University *T*
Laredo Community College *A*
Lubbock Christian University *B, T*
McMurry University *T*
St. Mary's University *T*
Tarleton State University *T*
Texas A&M University
    Commerce *M, T*
    Corpus Christi *T*
Texas Christian University *B, T*
University of Houston *T*
University of Houston
    Clear Lake *T*
University of Mary Hardin-Baylor *T*
University of North Texas *M*
University of Texas
    San Antonio *T*
West Texas A&M University *T*

Vermont

St. Michael's College *M, T*

Virginia

Bridgewater College *T*
Hollins University *T*
Shenandoah University *C, M*

Washington

Gonzaga University *M*
Heritage College *B*
Whitworth College *B, T*

Wisconsin

Cardinal Stritch University *M*
Lawrence University *T*
Northland College *T*
St. Norbert College *T*
Silver Lake College *T*
University of Wisconsin
    La Crosse *B, T*
    Whitewater *B, T*
Viterbo University *B, T*

Computer engineering

Alabama

Auburn University *B, M, D*
University of Alabama
    Birmingham *D*
    Huntsville *B, M, D*
University of South Alabama *B*

Alaska

University of Alaska
    Fairbanks *M*

Arizona

Arizona State University *B*
Embry-Riddle Aeronautical University:
    Prescott Campus *B*
Northern Arizona University *B*

University of Arizona *B*

Arkansas

Harding University *B*
University of Arkansas *B, M*

California

California Institute of Technology *B*
California Polytechnic State University:
    San Luis Obispo *B*
California State Polytechnic University:
    Pomona *B*
California State University
    Chico *B, M*
    Fresno *B*
    Long Beach *B, M*
    Northridge *B, M*
    Sacramento *B*
Coleman College *A, B*
De Anza College *A*
San Diego State University *B*
San Jose State University *B, M*
Santa Barbara City College *A*
Santa Clara University *B, M, D*
Sonoma State University *M*
University of California
    Davis *B*
    Irvine *B, M, D*
    Los Angeles *B*
    Riverside *B*
    San Diego *B, M, D*
    Santa Barbara *M, D*
    Santa Cruz *B, M, D*
University of Southern
    California *B, M, D*
University of the Pacific *B*

Colorado

Colorado Technical University *B, M*
DeVry University
    Denver *B*
Jones International University *B*
National Technological University *M*
United States Air Force Academy *B*
University of Colorado
    Boulder *B*
    Colorado Springs *B*
University of Denver *B, M*

Connecticut

Fairfield University *B, M*
University of Bridgeport *B, M*
University of Connecticut *B, M, D*
University of Hartford *B*

Delaware

University of Delaware *B*

District of Columbia

Catholic University of America *B*
George Washington University *B, M, D*

Florida

Broward Community College *A*
Daytona Beach Community College *A*
Embry-Riddle Aeronautical University *B*
Florida Atlantic University *B, M, D*
Florida Institute of Technology *B, M, D*
Florida International University *B, M*
Florida State University *B*
Hillsborough Community College *A*
Manatee Community College *A*
Pensacola Junior College *A*
South Florida Community College *A*
Southwest Florida College *A*
University of Central Florida *C, B, M, D*
University of Florida *B, M, D*
University of Miami *B*
University of South Florida *B, M, D*
University of West Florida *B*

Georgia

DeKalb Technical College *A*
Georgia Institute of Technology *B*
Mercer University *B, M*
Middle Georgia College *A*

Hawaii

University of Hawaii
    Honolulu Community College *A*

Idaho

Brigham Young University - Idaho *B*
College of Southern Idaho *A*
University of Idaho *B, M*

Illinois

Dominican University *B*
Illinois Institute of Technology *B, M*
Northwestern University *B, D*
Southern Illinois University
    Carbondale *B*
Southern Illinois University
    Edwardsville *B*
University of Illinois
    Chicago *B, M, D*
    Urbana-Champaign *B*

Indiana

Indiana Institute of Technology *B*
Indiana University-Purdue University
    Indianapolis *B*
Purdue University *B*
Purdue University
    Calumet *B*
Rose-Hulman Institute of Technology *B*
Taylor University *B*
University of Evansville *B*
University of Notre Dame *B, M, D*
Valparaiso University *B*

Iowa

Graceland University *B*
Iowa State University *B, M, D*
University of Iowa *B, M, D*

Kansas

Kansas State University *B*
University of Kansas *B, M*
Wichita State University *B*

Kentucky

Bellarmine University *B*
University of Louisville *B, M, D*

Louisiana

Grantham University *A, B*
Louisiana State University and
    Agricultural and Mechanical
    College *B*
Tulane University *B, M, D*
University of Louisiana at
    Lafayette *B, M, D*
Xavier University of Louisiana *B*

Maine

University of Maine *B*

Maryland

Capitol College *A, B*
Johns Hopkins University *B, M, D*
Loyola College in Maryland *M*
University of Maryland
    Baltimore County *B*
    College Park *B*

Massachusetts

Boston University *B, M, D*
Franklin W. Olin College of
    Engineering *B*
Harvard College *B*
Merrimack College *B*
Northeastern University *B, M, D*
Smith College *B*
Stonehill College *B*
Suffolk University *B*
Tufts University *B, M, D*
University of Massachusetts
    Amherst *B, M, D*
    Dartmouth *B, M*
    Lowell *M*

Michigan

Eastern Michigan University *B*
Kettering University *B*
Lawrence Technological University *B*

Michigan State University *B*
Michigan Technological University *B*
Oakland University *B, M*
University of Michigan *B, M, D*
University of Michigan
    Dearborn *M*
Wayne State University *M, D*
Western Michigan University *B, M*

Minnesota

Mesabi Range Community and Technical
    College *A*
Minnesota State University
    Mankato *B*
University of Minnesota
    Duluth *B*
    Twin Cities *B, M*

Mississippi

Mississippi State University *B, M, D*

Missouri

Missouri Technical School *A, B*
St. Louis University *B*
University of Missouri
    Columbia *B, M, D*
    Rolla *B, M, D*
Washington University in St.
    Louis *B, M, D*

Montana

Montana State University
    Bozeman *B*
Montana Tech of the University of
    Montana *B*

Nebraska

University of Nebraska
    Lincoln *B*
    Omaha *B*

Nevada

University of Nevada
    Las Vegas *B*
    Reno *M, D*

New Hampshire

University of New Hampshire *B, M, D*

New Jersey

The College of New Jersey *B*
Fairleigh Dickinson University
    Metropolitan Campus *M*
New Jersey Institute of
    Technology *B, M, D*
Princeton University *B, M, D*
Stevens Institute of Technology *B, M, D*

New Mexico

New Mexico State University
    Alamogordo *A*
University of New Mexico *B*

New York

City University of New York
    City College *B, M*
    Queensborough Community
    College *A*
Clarkson University *B*
Columbia University
    Fu Foundation School of
    Engineering and Applied
    Science *B, M, D*
Hofstra University *B*
Manhattan College *M*
Marist College *B*
New York Institute of Technology *B*
New York University *B*
Onondaga Community College *A*
Polytechnic University *B, M*
Rensselaer Polytechnic Institute *B, M, D*
Rochester Institute of Technology *B, M*
State University of New York
    Binghamton *B, M*
    Buffalo *B, M, D*
    College of Agriculture and
    Technology at Morrisville *A*
    New Paltz *B, M*
    Stony Brook *B*

Syracuse University *B, M, D*
United States Military Academy *B*

North Carolina
Central Carolina Community College *A*
Elon University *B*
Haywood Community College *A*
Johnson C. Smith University *B*
North Carolina State University *B, M, D*
Southwestern Community College *A*
Stanly Community College *A*
Surry Community College *A*
University of North Carolina
Charlotte *B*

North Dakota
North Dakota State University *B, M, D*

Ohio
Case Western Reserve
University *B, M, D*
Cedarville University *B*
Cuyahoga Community College
Eastern Campus *A*
Ohio Northern University *B*
Ohio State University
Columbus Campus *B*
Ohio University *B*
University of Akron *B*
University of Cincinnati *B, M, D*
University of Dayton *B*
University of Toledo *B*
Wright State University *B, M, D*
Youngstown State University *B*

Oklahoma
Oklahoma Christian University of
Science and Arts *B*
Oklahoma State University *B, M, D*
Oklahoma State University
Oklahoma City *A*
Oral Roberts University *B*
University of Oklahoma *B*

Oregon
Oregon State University *B, M, D*
Portland State University *B*
University of Portland *B*

Pennsylvania
Bucknell University *B*
Drexel University *B, M*
Elizabethtown College *B*
Gettysburg College *B*
ICM School of Business & Medical
Careers *A*
Lehigh University *B, M*
Lock Haven University of
Pennsylvania *B*
Montgomery County Community
College *C*
Penn State
Abington *B*
Altoona *B*
Beaver *B*
Berks *B*
Delaware County *B*
Dubois *B*
Erie, The Behrend College *B*
Hazleton *B*
Lehigh Valley *B*
McKeesport *B*
Mont Alto *B*
New Kensington *B*
Schuylkill - Capital College *B*
Shenango *B*
University Park *B*
Wilkes-Barre *B*
Worthington Scranton *B*
York *B*
University of Pennsylvania *B*
University of Pittsburgh *B*
University of Scranton *M*
Villanova University *B, M*
Widener University *M*

Puerto Rico
University of Puerto Rico
Mayaguez Campus *B, M, D*
Ponce *A*

Rhode Island
Brown University *B*
Roger Williams University *B*
University of Rhode Island *B*

South Carolina
Clemson University *B, M, D*
University of South Carolina *B, M, D*

South Dakota
South Dakota School of Mines and
Technology *B, M*

Tennessee
Christian Brothers University *B*
Tennessee Technological
University *B, M, D*
University of Memphis *B*
Vanderbilt University *B*

Texas
Amarillo College *A*
LeTourneau University *B*
Rice University *B, M, D*
St. Mary's University *B, M*
Southern Methodist University *B, M, D*
Texas A&M University *B, M, D*
Texas A&M University
Kingsville *B, M*
Texas Tech University *B*
University of Houston *B*
University of Houston
Clear Lake *B, M*
University of Texas
Arlington *B, M, D*
Dallas *B, M, D*
El Paso *M, D*
San Antonio *B, M*

Utah
Brigham Young University *B*
Salt Lake Community College *A*
University of Utah *B, M, D*
Utah State University *B*

Vermont
Vermont Technical College *A, B*

Virginia
George Mason University *M*
Hampton University *B*
Old Dominion University *B*
University of Virginia *B*
Virginia Polytechnic Institute and State
University *B, M, D*
Virginia State University *B*

Washington
Eastern Washington University *B*
Gonzaga University *B*
Pacific Lutheran University *B*
Seattle Pacific University *B*
Seattle University *M*
University of Washington *B, M*
Walla Walla College *B*
Washington State University *B*

West Virginia
West Virginia University *B, D*

Wisconsin
Marquette University *B, M*
Milwaukee School of Engineering *B*
University of Wisconsin
Madison *B, M, D*

Wyoming
University of Wyoming *B*

Computer engineering technology

Arizona
DeVry University
Phoenix *B*

California
DeVry University
Fremont *B*
Long Beach *B*
Pomona *B*
West Hills *B*

Colorado
DeVry University
Denver *B*

Connecticut
University of Hartford *B*

Florida
DeVry University
Miramar *B*

Georgia
DeVry University
Alpharetta *B*
Atlanta *B*
Middle Georgia College *A*
Southern Polytechnic State University *B*

Illinois
DeVry University
Addison *B*
Chicago *B*
Tinley Park *B*

Indiana
Indiana State University *B*
Indiana University-Purdue University
Indianapolis *A*

Kansas
Kansas State University *A*

Kentucky
Louisville Technical Institute *A*

Louisiana
Grantham University *A, B*
Nunez Community College *C, A*

Massachusetts
Benjamin Franklin Institute of
Technology *A*
Quinsigamond Community College *A*
Springfield Technical Community
College *A*
Wentworth Institute of Technology *A, B*

Michigan
Northern Michigan University *C*
Oakland Community College *C*

Minnesota
Globe College *C, A, B*

Missouri
DeVry University
Kansas City *B*

New Hampshire
New Hampshire Technical Institute *C, A*

New York
DeVry Institute of Technology
New York *B*
Rochester Institute of Technology *B*

North Carolina
Fayetteville Technical Community
College *C, A*
Nash Community College *A*
Sandhills Community College *C, A*

Ohio
DeVry University
Columbus *B*
North Central State College *A*
Ohio University *A*

Shawnee State University *C, A, B*
University of Dayton *B*

Pennsylvania
DeVry University
Ft. Washington *B*
Penn State
New Kensington *A*

Rhode Island
Community College of Rhode Island *A*

South Carolina
York Technical College *A*

Tennessee
University of Memphis *B*

Texas
Clarendon College *C, A*
Houston Community College
System *C, A*

Vermont
Vermont Technical College *A*

Washington
DeVry University
Seattle *B*

Computer graphics

Alabama
Huntingdon College *B*
James H. Faulkner State Community
College *C, A*

Arizona
Arizona Western College *A*
Estrella Mountain Community College *C*
Phoenix College *A*

Arkansas
South Arkansas Community College *A*

California
Antelope Valley College *C, A*
Art Institute
of California - Orange County *A, B*
of California: Los Angeles *A, B*
Art Institute of California - San
Francisco *B*
California Institute of the Arts *B, M*
California State University
Monterey Bay *B*
College of the Canyons *C, A*
College of the Siskiyous *C*
Foothill College *C, A*
Gavilan Community College *C, A*
Golden West College *C*
Los Angeles Southwest College *C, A*
MiraCosta College *C, A*
Modesto Junior College *C, A*
Ohlone College *C, A*
Orange Coast College *C, A*
Otis College of Art and Design *B*
Pacific Union College *B*
Platt College
Newport Beach *C, A*
Ontario *C, A*
Santa Barbara City College *C*
Santa Rosa Junior College *C*
Silicon Valley College
Emeryville *A, B*

Colorado
Art Institute
of Colorado *A*
Colorado Technical University *C*
Morgan Community College *C*

Connecticut
Norwalk Community College *C*
Quinnipiac University *B*
Tunxis Community College *C, A*

Florida
Broward Community College *A*
Full Sail Real World Education *A*

Herzing College
  Orlando *C*
Hillsborough Community College *A*
Indian River Community College *A*
Jacksonville University *B*
Okaloosa-Walton Community
  College *C, A*
Polk Community College *A*
Seminole Community College *A*
Southwest Florida College *A*
Tallahassee Community College *A*
University of Tampa *B*

Georgia
Atlanta College of Art *B*
Savannah College of Art and
  Design *B, M*

Hawaii
Hawaii Business College *C*
University of Hawaii
  Honolulu Community College *A*

Idaho
College of Southern Idaho *C, A*
Lewis-Clark State College *C*

Illinois
American Academy of Art *B*
Columbia College Chicago *B*
Dominican University *B*
Elgin Community College *C, A*
Greenville College *B*
Illinois Institute of Art *B*
International Academy of Design and
  Technology *A*
Lewis University *B*
Parkland College *A*
Richland Community College *A*
Triton College *C, A*

Indiana
Indiana University-Purdue University
  Indianapolis *A, B*
Purdue University *A, B*
Taylor University *B*
Vincennes University *A*

Iowa
Des Moines Area Community College *A*
Ellsworth Community College *A*
North Iowa Area Community College *A*
University of Dubuque *B, M*

Kansas
Pittsburg State University *B*
Seward County Community
  College *C, A*

Kentucky
Louisville Technical Institute *A*
Spencerian College: Lexington *A*

Maryland
Carroll Community College *C, A*
Community College of Baltimore County
  Catonsville *A*
  Dundalk *A*
  Essex *A*
Frederick Community College *C*
Howard Community College *A*
Montgomery College
  Rockville Campus *A*

Massachusetts
Becker College *B*
Berkshire Community College *C, A*
Hampshire College *B*
Harvard College *B*
Mount Wachusett Community College *A*
Newbury College *A*
Springfield College *B*

Michigan
Baker College
  of Auburn Hills *A*
  of Muskegon *A*
  of Owosso *A, B*
  of Port Huron *C, A*

College for Creative Studies *A*
Jackson Community College *C, A*
Mott Community College *A*
Northern Michigan University *B*
Washtenaw Community College *C, A*

Minnesota
Academy College *C, A*
Art Institutes International
  Minnesota *A, B*
Capella University *C, B, M*
Globe College *C, A*
Hennepin Technical College *C, A*
Pine Technical College *A*
St. Cloud Technical College *C, A*
South Central Technical College *A*

Missouri
Missouri Technical School *B*
St. Charles Community College *A*
St. Louis University *B*

Montana
Miles Community College *A*
University of Great Falls *B*

Nevada
Community College of Southern
  Nevada *C, A*
Sierra Nevada College *B*

New Hampshire
Franklin Pierce College *B*

New Jersey
Bloomfield College *B*
Burlington County College *A*
Camden County College *A*
Cumberland County College *C*
Essex County College *C*
Gloucester County College *C, A*
Middlesex County College *A*
Salem Community College *A*
Sussex County Community College *C, A*

New Mexico
Dona Ana Branch Community College of
  New Mexico State University *A*
New Mexico Junior College *A*
San Juan College *A*

New York
Briarcliffe College *C*
College of Aeronautics *B*
Corning Community College *C, A*
Island Drafting and Technical
  Institute *C, A*
Jamestown Community College *C*
Marist College *B*
Mercy College *B*
New York Institute of Technology *B*
North Country Community College *C*
Pratt Institute *B, M*
Rochester Institute of Technology *B, M*
Rockland Community College *A*
State University of New York
  Buffalo *M, D*
  College at Oneonta *B*
  College of Technology at Alfred *A*
Suffolk County Community College *A*
Syracuse University *B, M*
Westchester Business Institute *C, A*

North Carolina
Alamance Community College *C*
Campbell University *B*
Central Piedmont Community College *A*
Guilford Technical Community
  College *C*
Wake Technical Community College *A*
Western Piedmont Community
  College *C*

Ohio
Art Institute of Cincinnati *A*
Columbus State Community College *A*
Davis College *A*
Edison State Community College *A*
Kent State University *A*

Kent State University
  Ashtabula Regional Campus *C*
  Tuscarawas Campus *B*
Ohio Institute of Photography and
  Technology *A*
Ohio Northern University *B*
Stark State College of Technology *A*
University of Cincinnati
  Raymond Walters College *C, A*
Washington State Community College *A*

Oklahoma
Oklahoma State University
  Okmulgee *A*

Pennsylvania
Arcadia University *C*
Bucks County Community College *A*
CHI Institute *C, A*
Douglas School of Business *A*
La Salle University *B*
Pittsburgh Technical Institute: Boyd
  School Division *A*

South Carolina
Aiken Technical College *C*

South Dakota
Dakota State University *B*

Tennessee
Memphis College of Art *B, M*

Texas
Amarillo College *C, A*
Central Texas College *C*
Midland College *C, A*
Trinity Valley Community College *C, A*
University of Mary Hardin-Baylor *B*

Utah
College of Eastern Utah *C, A*
Dixie State College of Utah *C, A, B*

Vermont
Bennington College *B*
Champlain College *C, A, B*

Virginia
Thomas Nelson Community College *A*

Washington
Bellevue Community College *C, A*
Everett Community College *A*
Green River Community College *C*
South Seattle Community
  College *C, A, T*
Spokane Falls Community College *A*
Walla Walla College *A, B*

Wisconsin
Milwaukee Area Technical College *A*
Mount Mary College *B*

Computer hardware engineering

New York
Marist College *B*
State University of New York
  Buffalo *M, D*
  College of Agriculture and
  Technology at Morrisville *A*

Computer hardware technology

Arizona
South Mountain Community College *C*

Arkansas
Rich Mountain Community College *A*

Florida
Florida National College *A*

Illinois
Heartland Community College *C, A*

Iowa
Kaplan College *C*
Western Iowa Tech Community
  College *A*

Massachusetts
Benjamin Franklin Institute of
  Technology *A*

Michigan
Baker College
  of Muskegon *C*
Oakland Community College *C, A*

Minnesota
Globe College *C, A, B*

Mississippi
Pearl River Community College *C*

Missouri
St. Louis Community College
  St. Louis Community College at
  Florissant Valley *A*

New York
State University of New York
  College of Agriculture and
  Technology at Morrisville *A*
  College of Technology at Canton *C*

North Dakota
North Dakota State College of Science *A*

Ohio
Lakeland Community College *C*
Miami University
  Hamilton Campus *C*

Pennsylvania
Bucks County Community College *C*
Pennsylvania College of Technology *A*

South Carolina
York Technical College *C*

South Dakota
Southeast Technical Institute *C, A*

Texas
MTI College of Business and
  Technology *C, A*
St. Philip's College *C, A*

Virginia
ECPI College of Technology *C, A*
ECPI Technical College: Roanoke *A*

Computer installation and repair

Alaska
University of Alaska
  Fairbanks *C, A*

Arkansas
South Arkansas Community College *C*
Southern Arkansas University Tech *C*
University of Arkansas
  Fort Smith *C*

California
College of the Canyons *C*

Florida
Miami-Dade Community College *C*
New England Institute of Technology *A*

Illinois
College of Lake County *C, A*
Illinois Eastern Community Colleges
  Frontier Community College *C*
  Lincoln Trail College *C*
  Olney Central College *C*
  Wabash Valley College *C*
Waubonsee Community College *C*

Kentucky
Louisville Technical Institute *A*

Louisiana
Delgado Community College *C, A*

Massachusetts
Cape Cod Community College *C*

Michigan
Baker College
of Muskegon *C*
Montcalm Community College *C, A*

Ohio
Cincinnati State Technical and
Community College *C*
Davis College *C*

Pennsylvania
Northampton County Area Community
College *C, A*

Puerto Rico
Huertas Junior College *C*

South Carolina
York Technical College *C*

Texas
Temple College *C, A*
Western Texas College *C*

Virginia
ECPI College of Technology *C, A*
ECPI Technical College: Roanoke *A*

Washington
Walla Walla Community College *A*

Computer networking/telecommunications

Alabama
Community College of the Air Force *A*
Herzing College *A*

Arizona
Glendale Community College *C, A*
Pima Community College *C, A*
University of Phoenix *C, B*

Arkansas
University of Arkansas
Fort Smith *C, A*

California
California State University
Hayward *C, B, M*
Coastline Community College *C*
DeVry University
Fremont *B*
Golden Gate University *C, B, M*
ITT Technical Institute
San Bernardino *B*
Irvine Valley College *C, A*
National University *M*

Colorado
Arapahoe Community College *C, A*
Blair Junior College *C, A*
Colorado Mountain College
Spring Valley Campus *A*
Colorado Technical University *C*
Front Range Community College *C*
Parks College *C, A*
Remington College
Colorado Springs *A*

Connecticut
Gibbs College *C*
Manchester Community College *A*
Naugatuck Valley Community College *C*

Florida
Florida Metropolitan University
Orlando College South *A*
Florida Technical College
Auburndale *A*
Deland *A*
ITT Technical Institute
Maitland *B*
Pasco-Hernando Community College *A*

St. Petersburg College *C, A*
Seminole Community College *C, A*
Tallahassee Community College *C, A*
University of West Florida *B*

Georgia
Gordon College *A*
South Georgia College *C*
Southwest Georgia Technical
College *C, A*
West Georgia Technical College *C, A*

Hawaii
Remington College
Honolulu *A*

Idaho
Eastern Idaho Technical College *C, A*

Illinois
Aurora University *B*
College of Lake County *C, A*
De Paul University *B*
Elgin Community College *C*
Illinois State University *B*
Kaskaskia College *A*
Lake Land College *A*
McHenry County College *C*
Moraine Valley Community
College *C, A*
Roosevelt University *M*
Sauk Valley Community College *C*
Waubonsee Community College *C*

Indiana
Ancilla College *C, A*
ITT Technical Institute
Fort Wayne *A*
Indianapolis *A*
Indiana University-Purdue University
Fort Wayne *A, B*
Vincennes University *A*

Iowa
Des Moines Area Community College *A*
Iowa Central Community College *A*
Marshalltown Community College *A*
North Iowa Area Community College *A*
Northeast Iowa Community College *A*

Kansas
Cloud County Community College *A*
Johnson County Community College *A*
Kansas State University *B*

Kentucky
Daymar College *A*

Maryland
Carroll Community College *C, A*
Howard Community College *C, A*
Morgan State University *B*
University of Maryland
University College *M*

Massachusetts
Benjamin Franklin Institute of
Technology *C*
Cape Cod Community College *C, A*
Katharine Gibbs School *A*
Massasoit Community College *C*

Michigan
Alpena Community College *A*
Baker College
of Cadillac *A*
of Clinton Township *A*
of Muskegon *C, A*
of Owosso *A*
of Port Huron *C, A*
Calvin College *B*
Grand Rapids Community College *C*
Kettering University *B*
Lansing Community College *A*
Macomb Community College *C, A*
Walsh College of Accountancy and
Business Administration *M*

Minnesota
Alexandria Technical College *C, A*

Capella University *M, D*
Central Lakes College *C, A*
High-Tech Institute *A*
Minnesota State College - Southeast
Technical *C, A*
Rochester Community and Technical
College *C*
St. Cloud Technical College *C, A*
University of Minnesota
Twin Cities *B*

Mississippi
Northwest Mississippi Community
College *A*

Missouri
DeVry University
Kansas City *B*
Mineral Area College *C, A*
Vatterott College: Sunset Hills *A*
Webster University *M*

Montana
Montana Tech of the University of
Montana *C, A*

Nebraska
Nebraska College of Business *C, A*
University of Nebraska
Kearney *B*
Vatterott College *A*

New Hampshire
Franklin Pierce College *B*
New Hampshire Community Technical
College
Nashua *C, A*

New Jersey
Berkeley College *A*
Cumberland County College *C, A*
Georgian Court College *B*
Mercer County Community College *C, A*
Ocean County College *C*
Stevens Institute of Technology *M, D*

New York
City University of New York
Borough of Manhattan Community
College *A*
Hudson Valley Community College *A*
Iona College *M*
Niagara County Community College *A*
Onondaga Community College *A*
Polytechnic University *M*
State University of New York
Buffalo *M, D*
College of Agriculture and
Technology at Cobleskill *A*
Syracuse University *M*
Tompkins-Cortland Community
College *A*

North Carolina
Barton College *B*
Beaufort County Community College *A*
Central Carolina Community College *A*
Cleveland Community College *C, A*
College of the Albemarle *A*
Craven Community College *A*
Edgecombe Community College *A*
Fayetteville Technical Community
College *A*
Guilford Technical Community
College *C, A*
Haywood Community College *C, A*
Montgomery Community College *A*
Pitt Community College *C, A*
Randolph Community College *A*
Richmond Community College *C, A*
South Piedmont Community
College *C, A*
Southwestern Community College *A*

North Dakota
Bismarck State College *A*
Lake Region State College *C, A*

Ohio
Cincinnati State Technical and
Community College *A*
Davis College *A*
Hocking Technical College *A*
James A. Rhodes State College *A*
Kent State University *C*
Miami-Jacobs College *C, A*
Owens Community College
Findlay Campus *A*
Stark State College of Technology *A*
Stautzenberger College *C, A*

Oklahoma
Northeastern State University *B*
Oklahoma State University
Okmulgee *A*
Rose State College *A*
Southern Nazarene University *B*
University of Oklahoma *M*

Oregon
Clatsop Community College *A*
Portland Community College *C*

Pennsylvania
Allentown Business School *A*
Bucks County Community College *A*
Community College of Allegheny
County *C*
Community College of Beaver County *A*
Community College of Philadelphia *A*
Delaware County Community College *A*
Holy Family University *M*
Keystone College *B*
Pennsylvania College of Technology *B*
Reading Area Community College *A*
South Hills School of Business &
Technology *C*
Waynesburg College *B*

South Carolina
Midlands Technical College *C*
York Technical College *C*

South Dakota
Northern State University *A*
Southeast Technical Institute *A*

Tennessee
Tusculum College *B*

Texas
Austin Community College *A*
Central Texas College *C, A*
Eastfield College *C, A*
ITT Technical Institute
Houston North *A*
Remington College
Houston *A*
Texas Tech University *M*
University of Dallas *M*

Utah
ITT Technical Institute
Murray *A*
Weber State University *C, A, B*

Vermont
Champlain College *C, A, B*

Virginia
DeVry University
Crystal City *B*
ECPI College of Technology *C, A*
ECPI Technical College: Roanoke *A*
Hampton University *B*
J. Sargeant Reynolds Community
College *C*
Mountain Empire Community College *A*
Thomas Nelson Community College *A*

Washington
Bellevue Community College *C, A*
Centralia College *C, A*
Clark College *C, A*
Clover Park Technical College *C, A*
Everett Community College *A*

ITT Technical Institute
   Seattle *B*
Renton Technical College *C, A*
Seattle Pacific University *B*
Wenatchee Valley College *C, A*

West Virginia

Davis and Elkins College *C*
Fairmont State College *A*
Glenville State College *A*
International Academy of Design and
   Technology *C*
Mountain State University *B*

Wisconsin

ITT Technical Institute
   Green Bay *B*
University of Wisconsin
   Stout *B*
Western Wisconsin Technical College *A*

Wyoming

Eastern Wyoming College *A*

Computer programming, general

Alabama

Calhoun Community College *A*
Enterprise State Junior College *C*
ITT Technical Institute
   Birmingham *A*
J. F. Drake State Technical College *A*
Northwest-Shoals Community College *A*
Wallace Community College: Sparks
   Campus *A*
Wallace State Community College at
   Hanceville *A*

Arizona

Central Arizona College *C, A*
Eastern Arizona College *C*
High-Tech Institute *A*
ITT Technical Institute
   Phoenix *A*
   Tucson *A*
Pima Community College *C*
South Mountain Community College *C*
University of Phoenix *B*

Arkansas

ITT Technical Institute
   Little Rock *A*
Northwest Arkansas Community
   College *A*
South Arkansas Community College *A*
Southern Arkansas University Tech *C, A*
University of Arkansas
   Fort Smith *C, A, B*
   Little Rock *A*

California

Antelope Valley College *C, A*
Barstow College *C, A*
Cerritos Community College *A*
Chabot College *A*
Claremont McKenna College *B*
College of Marin: Kentfield *A*
College of the Canyons *A*
College of the Redwoods *C*
College of the Siskiyous *C*
Columbia College *A*
De Anza College *C, A*
East Los Angeles College *A*
Foothill College *C, A*
Gavilan Community College *C*
Grossmont Community College *C, A*

ITT Technical Institute
   Anaheim *A*
   Lathrop *A*
   Oxnard *A*
   Rancho Cordova *A*
   San Bernardino *A*
   San Diego *A*
   Sylmar *A*
   Torrance *A*
   West Covina *A*
Irvine Valley College *C, A*
Los Angeles Pierce College *C, A*
Los Angeles Southwest College *A*
MTI College of Business and
   Technology *C, A*
MiraCosta College *C, A*
Modesto Junior College *A*
Ohlone College *C, A*
Pacific Union College *B*
Riverside Community College *C, A*
San Diego Mesa College *C, A*
San Joaquin Delta College *C, A*
Santa Barbara City College *C*
Santa Monica College *C, A*
Santa Rosa Junior College *C*
Sierra College *A*
Sonoma State University *B*
Southwestern College *C, A*
Ventura College *A*
Victor Valley College *C*
West Valley College *C, A*
Westwood College of Technology *A*
Westwood College of Technology
   Los Angeles *A*

Colorado

Colorado State University
   Pueblo *B*
Colorado Technical University *C*
ITT Technical Institute
   Thornton *A*
Jones International University *C, B*
Red Rocks Community College *C, A*
Remington College
   Colorado Springs *A*
Trinidad State Junior College *A*
Westwood College of Technology
   South *A*

Connecticut

Asnuntuck Community College *C*
Capital Community College *C*
Naugatuck Valley Community College *A*
Northwestern Connecticut Community
   College *C, A*
Norwalk Community College *A*
Tunxis Community College *C*

Delaware

Delaware Technical and Community
   College
   Owens Campus *A*
   Stanton/Wilmington Campus *A*
   Terry Campus *A*

Florida

Art Institute
   of Fort Lauderdale *A, B*
Broward Community College *A*
Daytona Beach Community College *A*
Florida Keys Community College *A*
Florida Metropolitan University
   Tampa College *A, B*
Florida National College *A*
Florida Technical College *C*
Florida Technical College
   Deland *A*
Gulf Coast Community College *A*
Herzing College
   Orlando *A*
Hillsborough Community College *A*
ITT Technical Institute
   Ft. Lauderdale *A*
   Jacksonville *A*
   Maitland *A*
   Miami *A*
   Tampa *A*

Indian River Community College *A*
Lake City Community College *A*
Lake-Sumter Community College *A*
Manatee Community College *A*
New England Institute of Technology *A*
Okaloosa-Walton Community
   College *C, A*
Palm Beach Community College *A*
Pasco-Hernando Community College *A*
Pensacola Junior College *A*
Polk Community College *A*
Santa Fe Community College *A*
Seminole Community College *A*
Tallahassee Community College *C, A*
Valencia Community College *A*

Georgia

Abraham Baldwin Agricultural
   College *C*
Athens Technical College *C, A*
Atlanta Metropolitan College *A*
Columbus State University *A, B*
Darton College *A*
DeKalb Technical College *A*
Herzing College *A, B*
Kennesaw State University *B*
Macon State College *A, B*
Middle Georgia College *A*
Savannah Technical College *A*
South Georgia College *A*
Valdosta State University *B*
Waycross College *A*

Hawaii

Hawaii Business College *A*

Idaho

ITT Technical Institute
   Boise *A*
North Idaho College *A*

Illinois

Black Hawk College
   East Campus *A*
Blackburn College *B*
City Colleges of Chicago
   Olive-Harvey College *C, A*
Danville Area Community College *C, A*
Gem City College *A*
ITT Technical Institute
   Burr Ridge *A*
   Matteson *A*
   Mount Prospect *A*
Illinois Central College *A*
Illinois Valley Community College *C*
Joliet Junior College *A*
Lincoln Land Community College *C, A*
McKendree College *B*
Northwestern Business College *A*
Olivet Nazarene University *B*
Parkland College *A*
Prairie State College *A*
Richland Community College *A*
Rock Valley College *C*
Sauk Valley Community College *A*
South Suburban College of Cook
   County *C*
Southwestern Illinois College *A*
University of St. Francis *B*
Westwood College of Technology
   O'Hare *A*
William Rainey Harper College *C, A*

Indiana

Ancilla College *C, A*
ITT Technical Institute
   Fort Wayne *A*
   Indianapolis *A*
Indiana Business College *A*
Indiana Business College
   Evansville *A*
Indiana University
   East *A*
   South Bend *A*
   Southeast *A*
Purdue University
   Calumet *B*

St. Joseph's College *A*
Sawyer College: Merrillville *A*
Tri-State University *A*
University of Evansville *B*
Vincennes University *A*

Iowa

American Institute of Business *A*
Buena Vista University *B*
Des Moines Area Community College *A*
Ellsworth Community College *A*
Grand View College *B*
Hamilton College *A*
Hamilton College
   Cedar Falls *A*
Iowa Lakes Community College *A*
Iowa Western Community College *A*
Kaplan College *A*
Luther College *B*
Maharishi University of Management *C*
Northeast Iowa Community College *A*
Southeastern Community College
   North Campus *A*
Southwestern Community College *A*
Vatterott College *C, A*

Kansas

Cloud County Community College *A*
Donnelly College *C, A*
Fort Scott Community College *A*
Independence Community College *C, A*
Kansas City Kansas Community
   College *A*
Kansas State University *A, M*
Labette Community College *A*
McPherson College *B*
Seward County Community
   College *C, A*
Southwestern College *B*

Kentucky

Elizabethtown Community College *A*
Maysville Community College *C, A*
Murray State University *B*

Louisiana

Grambling State University *B*
Herzing College *A, B*
ITT Technical Institute
   St. Rose *A*
Louisiana College *B*

Maine

Andover College *C, A*
Husson College *A, B*
University of Southern Maine *B*

Maryland

College of Southern Maryland *A*
Columbia Union College *A*
Community College of Baltimore County
   Catonsville *A*
   Dundalk *A*
   Essex *A*
Harford Community College *C*
Montgomery College
   Rockville Campus *C, A*
University of Maryland
   University College *C*

Massachusetts

Benjamin Franklin Institute of
   Technology *A*
Berkshire Community College *C, A*
Clark University *B*
Fitchburg State College *C*
ITT Technical Institute
   Norwood *A*
   Woburn *A*
Massachusetts College of Liberal Arts *B*
Massasoit Community College *A*
Mount Wachusett Community College *A*
Newbury College *C, A*
Quinsigamond Community College *C, A*
Tufts University *B*
Wentworth Institute of Technology *C*

Michigan

Baker College
  of Auburn Hills *A*
  of Cadillac *A*
  of Clinton Township *A*
  of Jackson *A*
  of Muskegon *A*
  of Owosso *A*
  of Port Huron *A*
Calvin College *B*
Davenport University
  Eastern Region *A, B*
Ferris State University *C*
Gogebic Community College *A*
Grand Rapids Community College *C*
Grand Valley State University *B*
ITT Technical Institute
  Grand Rapids *A*
  Troy *A*
Jackson Community College *C, A*
Kellogg Community College *C, A*
Lansing Community College *A*
Macomb Community College *C, A*
Monroe County Community College *A*
Mott Community College *C*
Northern Michigan University *B*
Oakland Community College *C, A*
Schoolcraft College *A*
Southwestern Michigan College *A*
Washtenaw Community College *C, A*

Minnesota

Academy College *A*
Brown College *A*
Dakota County Technical College *C, A*
Globe College *C, A*
Hennepin Technical College *C, A*
Inver Hills Community College *A*
Lake Superior College: A Community
  and Technical College *C, A*
Mesabi Range Community and Technical
  College *C, A*
Minneapolis Community and Technical
  College *C, A*
National American University
  St. Paul *A, B*
Normandale Community College *A*
Pine Technical College *A*
St. Cloud Technical College *C, A*
St. Paul College - A Community and
  Technical College *C, A*
South Central Technical College *A*
Winona State University *B*

Mississippi

Holmes Community College *A*
Itawamba Community College *A*
Mary Holmes College *A*
Northwest Mississippi Community
  College *A*

Missouri

East Central College *C, A*
Hickey College *A*
ITT Technical Institute
  Arnold *A*
  Earth City *A*
Missouri Southern State College *C, A, B*
Missouri Technical School *A, B*
Moberly Area Community College *C, A*
St. Charles Community College *A*
St. Louis Community College
  St. Louis Community College at
    Florissant Valley *A*
  St. Louis Community College at
    Forest Park *A*
Southeast Missouri State University *B*

Montana

Montana Tech of the University of
  Montana *B*
University of Great Falls *B*

Nebraska

Creighton University *B*
ITT Technical Institute
  Omaha *A*

Lincoln School of Commerce *A*
Metropolitan Community College *A*
Midland Lutheran College *B*
Northeast Community College *A*
Peru State College *B*
Southeast Community College
  Milford Campus *A*
Western Nebraska Community
  College *A*

Nevada

Community College of Southern
  Nevada *A*
ITT Technical Institute
  Henderson *A*
Truckee Meadows Community
  College *A*
Western Nevada Community College *A*

New Hampshire

Daniel Webster College *C*
New Hampshire Community Technical
  College
  Laconia *C, A*
  Manchester *C*
  Stratham *C, A, D*

New Jersey

Atlantic Cape Community College *A*
Essex County College *A*
Middlesex County College *A*
Ocean County College *C*
Raritan Valley Community College *C, A*
St. Peter's College *C, A, B*
Salem Community College *C*
Union County College *C*

New Mexico

Clovis Community College *A*
ITT Technical Institute
  Albuquerque *A*
New Mexico Junior College *A*
Santa Fe Community College *C*

New York

Adirondack Community College *A*
Briarcliffe College *C*
Cayuga County Community College *C*
City University of New York
  Borough of Manhattan Community
    College *A*
  Brooklyn College *B*
  La Guardia Community College *A*
  Queensborough Community
    College *C, A*
Corning Community College *A*
Dominican College of Blauvelt *C*
Dutchess Community College *C*
Excelsior College *A, B*
Finger Lakes Community College *A*
Fulton-Montgomery Community
  College *A*
ITT Technical Institute
  Albany *A*
  Getzville *A*
  Liverpool *A*
Medaille College *B*
Mohawk Valley Community College *A*
Nassau Community College *A*
Pace University *C*
Pace University:
  Pleasantville/Briarcliff *C*
Rochester Business Institute *A*
Rochester Institute of Technology *A, B*
Rockland Community College *A*
Schenectady County Community
  College *C, A*
State University of New York
  Buffalo *M, D*
  College at Buffalo *B*
  College of Agriculture and
    Technology at Cobleskill *A*
  College of Agriculture and
    Technology at Morrisville *A*
  College of Technology at Canton *B*
  Farmingdale *A*
Utica School of Commerce *A*

Westchester Business Institute *C, A*

North Carolina

Alamance Community College *C, A*
Beaufort County Community
  College *C, A*
Belmont Abbey College *B*
Bladen Community College *C, A*
Blue Ridge Community College *A*
Brunswick Community College *A*
Caldwell Community College and
  Technical Institute *A*
Catawba Valley Community
  College *C, A*
Central Carolina Community College *A*
Central Piedmont Community College *A*
Cleveland Community College *C, A*
College of the Albemarle *A*
Davidson County Community
  College *C, A*
Durham Technical Community
  College *C, A*
Fayetteville Technical Community
  College *C, A*
Gaston College *C, A*
Guilford Technical Community
  College *C, A*
Isothermal Community College *C, A*
Johnston Community College *A*
Lenoir Community College *A*
Mayland Community College *C*
Mitchell Community College *C, A*
Piedmont Community College *A*
Rowan-Cabarrus Community
  College *C, A*
Sandhills Community College *C, A*
South Piedmont Community College *A*
Southwestern Community College *A*
Wake Technical Community
  College *C, A*
Wilson Technical Community College *A*
Winston-Salem State University *C*

North Dakota

Minot State University *C*

Ohio

Bowling Green State University:
  Firelands College *A*
Bradford School *C, A*
Cincinnati State Technical and
  Community College *A*
Cleveland Institute of Electronics *C*
Columbus State Community
  College *C, A*
Edison State Community College *C, A*
Hocking Technical College *A*
ITT Technical Institute
  Dayton *A*
  Norwood *A*
  Strongsville *A*
  Youngstown *A*
Kent State University
  Ashtabula Regional Campus *A*
  East Liverpool Regional Campus *A*
  Stark Campus *B*
  Trumbull Campus *A*
Lakeland Community College *C, A*
Marion Technical College *A*
Miami-Jacobs College *C, A*
North Central State College *A*
Northwest State Community College *A*
Ohio Business College: Sandusky *A*
Owens Community College
  Toledo *C, A*
Southern State Community College *A*
Stark State College of Technology *A*
Technology Education College *A*
Tiffin University *A*
University of Cincinnati
  Clermont College *A*
  Raymond Walters College *C, A*
Washington State Community College *A*
Youngstown State University *A, B*

Oklahoma

Eastern Oklahoma State College *A*

Northeastern Oklahoma Agricultural and
  Mechanical College *C, A*
Northwestern Oklahoma State
  University *B*
Oklahoma City Community College *A*
Oklahoma State University *B*
Oklahoma State University
  Okmulgee *A*
Rogers State University *C, A*
St. Gregory's University *A*
Tulsa Community College *C, A*
Vatterott College *C, A*
Western Oklahoma State College *A*

Oregon

Chemeketa Community College *A*
ITT Technical Institute
  Portland *A*
Lane Community College *A*
Southern Oregon University *B*

Pennsylvania

Academy of Medical Arts and
  Business *C, A*
Arcadia University *B*
Bradford School: Pittsburgh *A*
Bucks County Community College *C, A*
CHI Institute *C, A*
California University of
  Pennsylvania *A, B*
Cambria County Area Community
  College *A*
Community College of Allegheny
  County *C*
Delaware Valley College *C, A*
Gwynedd-Mercy College *A*
ICM School of Business & Medical
  Careers *A*
Keystone College *A*
La Salle University *A, B*
Mercyhurst College *C*
Montgomery County Community
  College *C, A*
Pittsburgh Technical Institute: Boyd
  School Division *A*
Reading Area Community College *A*
Temple University *B, M, D*
University of Pittsburgh
  Bradford *B*
Westmoreland County Community
  College *A*

Puerto Rico

Atlantic College *A*
Huertas Junior College *A*
Humacao Community College *A*
Pontifical Catholic University of Puerto
  Rico *A*
Universidad Metropolitana *C, A, B*
Universidad del Este *A*

Rhode Island

Community College of Rhode
  Island *C, A*

South Carolina

Aiken Technical College *C*
Central Carolina Technical College *A*
Charleston Southern University *B*
ITT Technical Institute
  Greenville *A*
Limestone College *A, B*
Midlands Technical College *C*
Orangeburg-Calhoun Technical
  College *A*
Piedmont Technical College *C*
Technical College of the
  Lowcountry *C, A*
Tri-County Technical College *A*
Trident Technical College *A*
York Technical College *A*

South Dakota

Southeast Technical Institute *A*

Tennessee

Chattanooga State Technical Community
  College *A*

ITT Technical Institute
Knoxville *A*
Memphis *A*
Nashville *A*
Northeast State Technical Community
College *C*
Roane State Community College *A*
Southern Adventist University *M*
Tennessee State University *B*

Texas

Alvin Community College *C, A*
Amarillo College *C, A*
Austin Community College *C, A*
Border Institute of Technology *A*
Brazosport College *C, A*
Brookhaven College *A*
Central Texas College *C, A*
Clarendon College *C*
Coastal Bend College *A*
College of the Mainland *A*
Collin County Community College
District *C, A*
Del Mar College *C, A*
Eastfield College *C, A*
El Centro College *C, A*
El Paso Community College *A*
Galveston College *C, A*
Grayson County College *A*
Hill College *A*
Houston Community College System *A*
ITT Technical Institute
Arlington *A*
Austin *A*
Houston *A*
Houston South *A*
San Antonio *A*
Kilgore College *A*
Laredo Community College *A*
LeTourneau University *B*
Lee College *C, A*
McLennan Community College *A*
Midland College *A*
North Lake College *C*
Northeast Texas Community College *A*
Odessa College *C, A*
Palo Alto College *A*
Remington College
Houston *A*
St. Philip's College *C, A*
San Antonio College *A*
Tarrant County College *C, A*
Temple College *C, A*
Texarkana College *C, A*
Texas State Technical College
Waco *A*
Trinity Valley Community College *C, A*
University of Texas
San Antonio *M*
Western Texas College *A*

Utah

ITT Technical Institute
Murray *A*
Salt Lake Community College *A*
Utah Career College *A*
Utah Valley State College *C*

Virginia

Blue Ridge Community College *A*
Danville Community College *A*
ECPI College of Technology *C, A*
ECPI Technical College: Roanoke *A*
ITT Technical Institute
Norfolk *A*
Richmond *A*
J. Sargeant Reynolds Community
College *C, A*
Piedmont Virginia Community
College *A*
Thomas Nelson Community
College *C, A*

Washington

Bellevue Community College *C, A*
Centralia College *A*
Clark College *A*

Clover Park Technical College *C, A*
Edmonds Community College *C, A*
Everett Community College *C, A*
ITT Technical Institute
Bothell *A*
Seattle *A*
Spokane *A*
North Seattle Community College *C, A*
Renton Technical College *A*
Seattle Central Community College *C, A*
South Seattle Community College *C, A*
Walla Walla College *A*

West Virginia

Huntington Junior College *A*
Potomac State College of West Virginia
University *A*
West Virginia State College *A*
West Virginia University Institute of
Technology *B*

Wisconsin

Blackhawk Technical College *A*
Chippewa Valley Technical College *A*
ITT Technical Institute
Green Bay *A*
Greenfield *A*
Mid-State Technical College *A*
Milwaukee Area Technical College *A*
Nicolet Area Technical College *A*
Silver Lake College *C*
Wisconsin Indianhead Technical
College *A*

Wyoming

Western Wyoming Community
College *A*

Computer programming, specific applications

Alabama

Calhoun Community College *A*
Enterprise State Junior College *A*
George C. Wallace State Community
College
Selma *A*
Northwest-Shoals Community
College *C, A*
Wallace Community College: Sparks
Campus *A*

Alaska

University of Alaska
Anchorage *A*

Arizona

Central Arizona College *A*
Collins College *A*
Estrella Mountain Community
College *C, A*
Gateway Community College *C*
Glendale Community College *C, A*
South Mountain Community College *C*

Arkansas

Henderson State University *B*
South Arkansas Community College *A*

California

Bakersfield College *A*
Barstow College *A*
Cerritos Community College *A*
Chabot College *A*
College of the Siskiyous *C, A*
Contra Costa College *A*
De Anza College *C, A*
Grossmont Community College *C, A*
Irvine Valley College *C, A*
Long Beach City College *C, A*
Los Angeles Harbor College *C, A*
Los Angeles Pierce College *C, A*
Los Angeles Southwest College *A*
MTI College of Business and
Technology *C, A*
Moorpark College *A*
Mount San Antonio College *C*

San Diego City College *C, A*
Shasta College *A*
Ventura College *A*
Westwood College of Technology
Inland Empire *A*

Colorado

National American University
Denver *A, B*
Westwood College of Technology
South *A*

Connecticut

Capital Community College *C*
Norwalk Community College *A*
Quinnipiac University *B*
Three Rivers Community College *A*
Tunxis Community College *C, A*

Florida

Gulf Coast Community College *A*
Indian River Community College *A*
Miami-Dade Community College *A*
Palm Beach Community College *A*
Pasco-Hernando Community College *A*
St. Petersburg College *C, A*
Seminole Community College *A*
South Florida Community College *A*
Valencia Community College *A*

Georgia

Abraham Baldwin Agricultural
College *A*
Atlanta Metropolitan College *A*
Chattahoochee Technical College *C, A*
Dalton State College *C, A*
Darton College *A*
Macon State College *A, B*
Middle Georgia College *A*
South Georgia College *A*

Idaho

Idaho State University *C, A*
North Idaho College *A*

Illinois

Black Hawk College *A*
City Colleges of Chicago
Wright College *C, A*
College of DuPage *C, A*
College of Lake County *C, A*
Elgin Community College *A*
Illinois Central College *A*
Illinois Valley Community College *A*
John Wood Community College *C, A*
Kankakee Community College *A*
Kaskaskia College *A*
Kishwaukee College *A*
McHenry County College *C, A*
Moraine Valley Community
College *C, A*
National-Louis University *C*
Northwestern Business College *A*
Parkland College *A*
Prairie State College *C, A*
Rend Lake College *A*
Robert Morris College: Chicago *C*
Sauk Valley Community College *C, A*
Southwestern Illinois College *C, A*
Triton College *C, A*
Waubonsee Community College *C, A*
William Rainey Harper College *C, A*

Indiana

Indiana Wesleyan University *A, B*
Professional Careers Institute *A*
Purdue University
North Central Campus *A*
Vincennes University *A*

Iowa

Des Moines Area Community College *A*
Indian Hills Community College *A*
Kirkwood Community College *A*
Luther College *B*
Northeast Iowa Community College *A*
Northwest Iowa Community College *C*
Scott Community College *A*

Southeastern Community College
North Campus *C*
Southwestern Community College *A*

Kansas

Central Christian College *A*
Fort Scott Community College *A*
Johnson County Community
College *C, A*
Seward County Community
College *C, A*

Kentucky

Paducah Community College *A*
Sullivan University *C*

Louisiana

Herzing College *A, B*
Southern University
New Orleans *A*
Shreveport *A*

Maine

Husson College *B*
University of Southern Maine *B*

Maryland

Community College of Baltimore County
Catonsville *C, A*
Dundalk *C, A*
Essex *C, A*
Frederick Community College *C, A*
Harford Community College *C*

Massachusetts

Berkshire Community College *A*
Cape Cod Community College *A*
Lasell College *B*
Roxbury Community College *A*

Michigan

Baker College
of Cadillac *A*
of Muskegon *A*
of Port Huron *A*
Gogebic Community College *A*
Grand Rapids Community College *A*
Jackson Community College *C, A*
Lansing Community College *A*
Mid Michigan Community College *A*
Monroe County Community
College *C, A*
Mott Community College *C*
Washtenaw Community College *C, A*
Western Michigan University *B*

Minnesota

Alexandria Technical College *C, A*
Dakota County Technical College *C, A*
Globe College *C, A*
Hennepin Technical College *C, A*
Minnesota State College - Southeast
Technical *C, A*
St. Cloud Technical College *C, A*
St. Paul College - A Community and
Technical College *C, A*
Winona State University *B*

Mississippi

Northwest Mississippi Community
College *A*
Pearl River Community College *A*

Missouri

East Central College *A*
Longview Community College *C, A*
Maple Woods Community College *C, A*
Mineral Area College *C, A*
St. Louis Community College
St. Louis Community College at
Florissant Valley *A*
St. Louis Community College at
Meramec *C, A*

Montana

Montana Tech of the University of
Montana *B*

Nebraska

Lincoln School of Commerce *A*

Vatterott College *A*

Nevada

Morrison University *A*

New Hampshire

New Hampshire Community Technical
  College
    Nashua *A*

New Jersey

Bergen Community College *A*
Burlington County College *C*
Camden County College *C*
Middlesex County College *C*
Passaic County Community
  College *C, A*
Sussex County Community College *A*

New Mexico

New Mexico Junior College *A*

New York

Fulton-Montgomery Community
  College *A*
Marist College *B*
Pace University:
  Pleasantville/Briarcliff *C*
State University of New York
  College of Agriculture and
    Technology at Cobleskill *A*
  College of Agriculture and
    Technology at Morrisville *A*
Westchester Business Institute *C, A*

North Carolina

Alamance Community College *A*
Asheville Buncombe Technical
  Community College *A*
Beaufort County Community
  College *C, A*
Brunswick Community College *C, A*
Caldwell Community College and
  Technical Institute *C, A*
Campbell University *A*
Central Carolina Community College *A*
Cleveland Community College *C, A*
College of the Albemarle *A*
Craven Community College *A*
Durham Technical Community
  College *C, A*
Fayetteville Technical Community
  College *C, A*
Forsyth Technical Community College *A*
Gaston College *A*
Guilford Technical Community
  College *A*
Haywood Community College *C, A*
James Sprunt Community College *C, A*
King's College *A*
Piedmont Community College *A*
Pitt Community College *C, A*
Sampson Community College *A*
Sandhills Community College *A*
South Piedmont Community
  College *C, A*
Stanly Community College *A*
Surry Community College *C, A*
Wake Technical Community
  College *C, A*
Wilkes Community College *C, A*
Wilson Technical Community College *A*

North Dakota

North Dakota State College of Science *A*

Ohio

Central Ohio Technical College *A*
Cincinnati State Technical and
  Community College *A*
Cuyahoga Community College
  Eastern Campus *A*
Jefferson Community College *C, A*
Kent State University *C, A*
Kent State University
  Stark Campus *B*
  Trumbull Campus *A*
Lorain County Community College *A*

Marion Technical College *C, A*
Miami University
  Middletown Campus *C, A*
Miami-Jacobs College *C, A*
North Central State College *A*
Sinclair Community College *C, A*
Southern State Community College *A*
Stark State College of Technology *A*
Trumbull Business College *A*
University of Cincinnati
  Raymond Walters College *A*
University of Northwestern Ohio *C, A*

Oklahoma

Oklahoma Baptist University *B*
Oklahoma State University
  Oklahoma City *A*
  Okmulgee *A*
St. Gregory's University *A*
Tulsa Community College *A*

Oregon

Chemeketa Community College *A*
Clatsop Community College *A*
George Fox University *B*
Southwestern Oregon Community
  College *A*

Pennsylvania

Allentown Business School *C, A*
Butler County Community College *A*
Community College of Allegheny
  County *C*
Community College of Beaver County *A*
Community College of Philadelphia *A*
Delaware County Community
  College *C, A*
Grove City College *B*
ICM School of Business & Medical
  Careers *A*
La Salle University *B, M*
Manor College *A*
Mount Aloysius College *A*
Peirce College *C, A, B*
Pennsylvania College of Technology *A*
South Hills School of Business &
  Technology *C*
York College of Pennsylvania *B*

Puerto Rico

ICPR Junior College *A*
Universidad del Este *A*

South Carolina

York Technical College *A*

South Dakota

Southeast Technical Institute *A*

Tennessee

Southwest Tennessee Community
  College *C*

Texas

Eastfield College *A*
Hill College *A*
Remington College
  Houston *A*
Richland College *A*
Tyler Junior College *A*

Utah

Southern Utah University *A*
Weber State University *C*

Virginia

Averett University *B*
ECPI College of Technology *C, A*
ECPI Technical College: Roanoke *A*

Washington

Peninsula College *A*
Renton Technical College *C, A*
Seattle Central Community College *C, A*
Spokane Community College *C, A*
Spokane Falls Community College *C*

West Virginia

Davis and Elkins College *B*
Mountain State College *A*

Potomac State College of West Virginia
  University *A*
Shepherd College *B*

Wisconsin

Chippewa Valley Technical College *A*
Fox Valley Technical College *A*
Milwaukee Area Technical College *A*
Moraine Park Technical College *A*
St. Norbert College *B*
Western Wisconsin Technical College *A*

Computer science

Alabama

Alabama State University *B*
American College of Computer and
  Information Sciences *B, M*
Auburn University *B*
Bevill State Community College *A*
Birmingham-Southern College *B*
Huntingdon College *B*
Lawson State Community College *C, A*
Northeast Alabama Community
  College *A*
Oakwood College *B*
Samford University *B*
Shelton State Community College *C*

Alaska

University of Alaska
  Anchorage *B*
  Fairbanks *B, M*

Arizona

Arizona State University *B, M, D*
Cochise College *A*
Embry-Riddle Aeronautical University:
  Prescott Campus *B*
Paradise Valley Community College *C*

Arkansas

Harding University *B*
Hendrix College *B*
John Brown University *B*
Lyon College *C*
Ouachita Baptist University *B*
Philander Smith College *B*
Phillips Community College of the
  University of Arkansas *A*
South Arkansas Community
  College *C, A*
Southern Arkansas University Tech *C, A*
University of Arkansas
  Fort Smith *A*
University of Central Arkansas *B, M*

California

Antelope Valley College *C, A*
Biola University *B*
California Institute of
  Technology *B, M, D*
California State Polytechnic University:
  Pomona *B, M*
California State University
  Bakersfield *B*
  Chico *B, M*
  Fresno *B, M*
  Fullerton *B, M*
  Hayward *B, M*
  Long Beach *B, M*
  Sacramento *B, M*
  San Bernardino *B, M*
  San Marcos *B, M*
Chabot College *A*
College of the Canyons *C, A*
College of the Sequoias *C, A*
College of the Siskiyous *A*
Columbia College *C*
Cuesta College *C, A*
De Anza College *A*
Don Bosco Technical Institute *A*
Feather River College *A*
Foothill College *A*
Fresno Pacific University *B*
Golden West College *C*

Grossmont Community College *C, A*
La Sierra University *B*
Las Positas College *A*
Los Angeles Pierce College *C, A*
Los Angeles Southwest College *C, A*
Los Angeles Trade and Technical
  College *C, A*
Los Medanos College *C*
Loyola Marymount University *M*
Master's College *B*
MiraCosta College *A*
Modesto Junior College *A*
Napa Valley College *C*
National University *B, M*
Pacific States University *B, M*
Pacific Union College *B*
Palomar College *C, A*
Pepperdine University *B*
Point Loma Nazarene University *B*
Pomona College *B*
Reedley College *A*
San Francisco State University *B, M*
San Joaquin Delta College *C, A*
San Jose State University *B, M*
Santa Barbara City College *C, A*
Santa Monica College *C*
Santa Rosa Junior College *C, A*
Santiago Canyon College *A*
Scripps College *B*
Sierra College *A*
Sonoma State University *B*
Southwestern College *C, A*
Stanford University *M, D*
Taft College *A*
University of California
  Berkeley *B, M, D*
  Los Angeles *B*
  Riverside *B, M, D*
  San Diego *B, M, D*
  Santa Cruz *B, M, D*
University of San Diego *B*
University of Southern
  California *B, M, D*
University of the Pacific *B*
Yuba Community College District *C, A*

Colorado

Colorado School of Mines *B*
Colorado Technical University *B, M, D*
Fort Lewis College *B*
IntelliTec College *A*
Jones International University *C, B*
Metropolitan State College of Denver *B*
Regis University *B*
Trinidad State Junior College *A*
United States Air Force Academy *B*
University of Colorado
  Boulder *B, M, D*
  Colorado Springs *B, M, D*
  Denver *B, M*

Connecticut

Connecticut College *B*
Fairfield University *B*
Quinnipiac University *B, M*
Trinity College *B*
University of Connecticut *B*

Delaware

Delaware State University *B*
Delaware Technical and Community
  College
  Terry Campus *A*

District of Columbia

American University *B, M*
Gallaudet University *B*
Georgetown University *B*
University of the District of
  Columbia *A, B*

Florida

Barry University *B*
Broward Community College *A*
Edward Waters College *B*
Embry-Riddle Aeronautical University *B*
Florida Institute of Technology *B, M, D*

Florida Southern College *B*
Florida State University *C, B, M, D*
Florida Technical College *A*
Gulf Coast Community College *A*
Hillsborough Community College *A*
Nova Southeastern University *B, M, D*
Pensacola Junior College *A*
St. Thomas University *B*
Seminole Community College *A*
Stetson University *B*
University of Miami *B, M*
University of West Florida *B, M*

Georgia
Atlanta Metropolitan College *A*
Berry College *B*
Clark Atlanta University *B, M*
Clayton College and State University *A*
Coastal Georgia Community College *A*
Columbus State University *A, B, M*
Emory University *B*
Georgia Perimeter College *A*
Georgia Southwestern State
   University *B, M*
Georgia State University *B, M*
Gordon College *A*
LaGrange College *B*
Macon State College *A*
Mercer University *B*
Middle Georgia College *A*
Morris Brown College *B*
Oxford College of Emory University *B*
Piedmont College *B*
Savannah State University *B*
State University of West Georgia *M*
Valdosta State University *B*
Young Harris College *A*

Hawaii
Brigham Young University-Hawaii *A, B*
Hawaii Pacific University *B*

Idaho
Boise State University *B, M*
Brigham Young University - Idaho *B*
College of Southern Idaho *A*
Idaho State University *B*
Lewis-Clark State College *B*

Illinois
Augustana College *B*
Benedictine University *B*
Concordia University *B*
Dominican University *B*
Elmhurst College *B*
Eureka College *B*
Governors State University *B, M*
Greenville College *B*
John Wood Community College *A*
Judson College *B*
Lake Forest College *B*
Lewis University *B*
Lewis and Clark Community College *A*
Lincoln College *A*
Loyola University of Chicago *C, B, M*
MacMurray College *B*
McKendree College *B*
Monmouth College *B*
North Central College *B, M*
Northwestern University *M, D*
Olivet Nazarene University *B*
Parkland College *A*
Principia College *B*
Quincy University *B*
Richland Community College *A*
Rockford College *B*
Roosevelt University *C, B, M*
St. Xavier University *B*
Southwestern Illinois College *C, A*
Triton College *A*
University of Chicago *M, D*
University of Illinois
   Urbana-Champaign *M*
Wheaton College *B*
William Rainey Harper College *A*

Indiana
Anderson University *B*
Bethel College *A*
DePauw University *B*
Earlham College *B*
Franklin College *B*
Goshen College *B*
Indiana Institute of Technology *B*
Indiana University-Purdue University
   Fort Wayne *A, B, M*
Manchester College *A, B*
Marian College *A, B, T*
Oakland City University *C, A, B*
Purdue University
   Calumet *B*
Rose-Hulman Institute of Technology *B*
Taylor University *B*
Taylor University: Fort Wayne *B*
Tri-State University *B*
University of Indianapolis *B*
Valparaiso University *B*
Vincennes University *A*

Iowa
Briar Cliff University *B*
Buena Vista University *B*
Clarke College *B*
Coe College *B*
Dordt College *B*
Drake University *B*
Ellsworth Community College *A*
Graceland University *B*
Grand View College *B*
Grinnell College *B*
Iowa Wesleyan College *B*
Loras College *B*
Luther College *B*
Maharishi University of Management *M*
Morningside College *B*
Mount Mercy College *B*
North Iowa Area Community College *A*
Northwestern College *B*
St. Ambrose University *B*
Simpson College *B*
University of Iowa *B, M, D*
University of Northern Iowa *B*

Kansas
Allen County Community College *A*
Baker University *B*
Barton County Community College *A*
Benedictine College *B*
Bethel College *B*
Butler County Community College *A*
Dodge City Community College *A*
Garden City Community College *A*
Kansas Wesleyan University *A, B, T*
McPherson College *T*
Pittsburg State University *B*
Seward County Community College *A*
Southwestern College *B*
Tabor College *B*

Kentucky
Bellarmine University *B*
Centre College *B*
Kentucky Wesleyan College *B*
Maysville Community College *C, A*
Murray State University *B*
National College of Business &
   Technology
   Danville *A*
   Florence *A*
   Lexington *A*
   Richmond *A*

Louisiana
Dillard University *B*
Grambling State University *B*
Grantham University *C, A, B*
Herzing College *C*
Louisiana State University
   Shreveport *A*
Louisiana State University and
   Agricultural and Mechanical
   College *B, D*
Louisiana Tech University *B, M*

McNeese State University *B*
Nicholls State University *B*
Nunez Community College *A*
Southeastern Louisiana University *B*
Southern University
   Shreveport *A*
Southern University and Agricultural and
   Mechanical College *B, M*
Tulane University *B, M, D*
University of Louisiana at
   Lafayette *B, M, D*
University of Louisiana at Monroe *B*
University of New Orleans *B, M*

Maine
Andover College *A*
Bowdoin College *B*
Colby College *B*
Thomas College *B*
University of Maine
   Farmington *B, T*
University of Southern Maine *B, M*

Maryland
Allegany College *A*
Bowie State University *B, M*
Capitol College *B, M*
College of Notre Dame of Maryland *B*
Columbia Union College *B*
Community College of Baltimore County
   Catonsville *A*
   Dundalk *A*
   Essex *A*
Coppin State College *B*
Frederick Community College *A*
Goucher College *B*
Harford Community College *A*
Hood College *B*
Howard Community College *A*
Johns Hopkins University *B, M*
Montgomery College
   Rockville Campus *A*
Morgan State University *B*
Mount St. Mary's College *B*
Salisbury University *B*
Towson University *B, M*
University of Maryland
   Baltimore County *B, M, D*
   University College *B*
Washington College *B*

Massachusetts
American International College *B*
Amherst College *B*
Atlantic Union College *B*
Berkshire Community College *A*
Boston College *B*
Bridgewater State College *B, M*
Bunker Hill Community College *C, A*
Cape Cod Community College *A*
Fitchburg State College *B, M*
Framingham State College *B*
Gordon College *B*
Hampshire College *B*
Harvard College *B*
Lasell College *B*
Massachusetts Bay Community
   College *A*
Massachusetts Institute of Technology *B*
Merrimack College *B*
Mount Holyoke College *B*
Newbury College *A, B*
Northeastern University *B, M, D*
Smith College *B*
Springfield Technical Community
   College *A*
Stonehill College *B*
Suffolk University *B*
Tufts University *B*
University of Massachusetts
   Amherst *B, M, D*
   Boston *M, D*
   Lowell *B, M, D*
Wellesley College *B*
Wentworth Institute of Technology *B*
Western New England College *B*

Westfield State College *B*
Wheaton College *B*
Williams College *B*
Worcester Polytechnic Institute *B, M, D*

Michigan
Alma College *B*
Baker College
   of Cadillac *B*
   of Clinton Township *B*
   of Muskegon *B*
   of Owosso *A, B*
   of Port Huron *A, B*
Calvin College *B*
Central Michigan University *B*
Cornerstone University *B*
Grand Valley State University *B*
Hillsdale College *B*
Kettering University *B*
Lawrence Technological University *B, M*
Madonna University *A, B, T*
Mid Michigan Community College *A*
Northern Michigan University *B*
Saginaw Valley State University *B*
University of Michigan *B, T*
University of Michigan
   Flint *B*
Washtenaw Community College *C, A*
Wayne State University *C*
Western Michigan University *B, M, D*

Minnesota
Academy College *B*
Bemidji State University *B*
Bethel College *B*
Carleton College *B*
College of St. Benedict *B*
Concordia College: Moorhead *B*
Gustavus Adolphus College *B*
Hamline University *B*
Lake Superior College: A Community
   and Technical College *A*
Metropolitan State University *B*
Minnesota State University
   Mankato *B, M*
   Moorhead *B*
Normandale Community College *A*
Ridgewater College: A Community and
   Technical College *A*
St. Cloud State University *B, M*
St. John's University *B*
St. Mary's University of Minnesota *B*
University of Minnesota
   Duluth *B, M*
   Morris *B*
   Twin Cities *C, B*
Winona State University *B*

Mississippi
Coahoma Community College *A*
Holmes Community College *A*
Itawamba Community College *A*
Millsaps College *B, T*
Mississippi College *B, M*
Rust College *B*

Missouri
Avila University *B*
Blue River Community College *A*
Central Methodist College *A, B*
College of the Ozarks *B*
Columbia College *B*
Drury University *B*
Lindenwood University *B*
Maryville University of Saint Louis *C, B*
Missouri Southern State College *A, B*
Missouri Technical School *B*
Northwest Missouri State University *B*
Southwest Baptist University *A, B*
University of Missouri
   Columbia *B, M, D*
   Rolla *B, M, D*
   St. Louis *B*
Washington University in St. Louis *B*
Webster University *B, M*
William Jewell College *B*

Montana

Carroll College *A, T*
Montana State University
    Bozeman *B, M, D*
Montana Tech of the University of
    Montana *B*
Rocky Mountain College *B*
University of Great Falls *B*
University of Montana-Missoula *B, M*

Nebraska

Concordia University *B, T*
Creighton University *A, B*
Dana College *B*
Doane College *B*
Hastings College *B*
Midland Lutheran College *B*
Nebraska Wesleyan University *B*
Peru State College *B*
Southeast Community College
    Beatrice Campus *A*
Union College *B*
University of Nebraska
    Lincoln *B, M, D*
    Omaha *B, M*
Western Nebraska Community
    College *A*

Nevada

Sierra Nevada College *B*
University of Nevada
    Las Vegas *B, M, D*
    Reno *B, M*

New Hampshire

Daniel Webster College *B*
Dartmouth College *B, M, D*
Franklin Pierce College *B*
Keene State College *B*
New Hampshire Community Technical
    College
    Nashua *C, A*
Rivier College *C, A, B, M*
St. Anselm College *B*
University of New Hampshire *B, M, D*

New Jersey

Burlington County College *A*
Caldwell College *B*
College of St. Elizabeth *B*
Cumberland County College *A*
Drew University *B*
Georgian Court College *B*
Gloucester County College *A*
Hudson County Community College *A*
New Jersey Institute of Technology *D*
Ocean County College *A*
Ramapo College of New Jersey *B*
Raritan Valley Community College *A*
Richard Stockton College of New
    Jersey *B*
Rowan University *B*
Rutgers, The State University of New
    Jersey
    Camden Regional Campus *B*
    New Brunswick Regional
        Campus *B*
    Newark Regional Campus *B*
St. Peter's College *B*
Stevens Institute of Technology *B, M, D*
Thomas Edison State College *C, A, B*
William Paterson University of New
    Jersey *B*

New Mexico

College of the Southwest *B*
Dona Ana Branch Community College of
    New Mexico State University *A*
New Mexico Institute of Mining and
    Technology *B, M, D*
New Mexico State University
    Alamogordo *C*
Southwestern Indian Polytechnic
    Institute *A*

New York

Adirondack Community College *A*

Alfred University *B*
Bard College *B*
Barnard College *B*
Canisius College *B*
Cayuga County Community College *A*
City University of New York
    Baruch College *B, M*
    Bronx Community College *A*
    City College *B*
    College of Staten Island *A, B, M, D*
    Kingsborough Community
        College *A*
    La Guardia Community College *A*
    Medgar Evers College *A*
    Queens College *B, M*
Clarkson University *B, M*
Clinton Community College *A*
Colgate University *B*
Columbia University
    Columbia College *B*
Corning Community College *A*
Dowling College *B*
Dutchess Community College *A*
Finger Lakes Community College *A*
Fulton-Montgomery Community
    College *A*
Hobart and William Smith Colleges *B*
Hofstra University *B, M*
Houghton College *B*
Iona College *B*
Ithaca College *B*
Jamestown Community College *A*
Jefferson Community College *A*
Long Island University
    C. W. Post Campus *B*
Manhattan College *B*
Marist College *B*
Medaille College *B*
Mercy College *B*
Molloy College *B*
Monroe Community College *A*
Mount St. Mary College *C, B, T*
Nassau Community College *A*
New York Institute of Technology *B*
New York University *B, M, D*
Niagara County Community College *A*
Niagara University *C, B*
Onondaga Community College *A*
Polytechnic University *B, M, D*
Rensselaer Polytechnic Institute *B, M, D*
Roberts Wesleyan College *B*
Rochester Institute of Technology *B, M*
Sage College of Albany *A*
St. Bonaventure University *B*
St. John Fisher College *B*
St. Joseph's College: Suffolk Campus *B*
St. Lawrence University *B*
Schenectady County Community
    College *A*
State University of New York
    Binghamton *B, M, D*
    Buffalo *B, M, D*
    College at Brockport *B*
    College at Oneonta *B*
    College at Plattsburgh *B*
    College of Agriculture and
        Technology at Cobleskill *A*
    College of Agriculture and
        Technology at Morrisville *A*
    College of Technology at Alfred *A*
    Farmingdale *A*
    New Paltz *B, M*
    Oswego *B*
    Stony Brook *B, M, D*
Suffolk County Community College *A*
Syracuse University *B, M*
Tompkins-Cortland Community
    College *A*
United States Military Academy *B*
Wagner College *B*
Wells College *B*
Westchester Business Institute *C, A*
Westchester Community College *A*
Yeshiva University *B*

North Carolina

Barber-Scotia College *B*
Campbell University *B*
East Carolina University *B, M*
Elon University *B*
High Point University *B*
Lees-McRae College *B*
Mars Hill College *B*
Meredith College *B*
Methodist College *A, B*
North Carolina State University *M, D*
St. Augustine's College *B*
Sandhills Community College *A*
Shaw University *B*
University of North Carolina
    Asheville *B*
    Charlotte *B, M*
    Greensboro *B*
    Pembroke *B*
    Wilmington *B*
Wake Forest University *B, M*
Western Carolina University *B*
Western Piedmont Community
    College *A*

North Dakota

Dickinson State University *B, T*
Jamestown College *B*
North Dakota State University *B, M, D*
University of North Dakota *B, M*

Ohio

Ashland University *B*
Baldwin-Wallace College *B*
Bluffton College *B*
Case Western Reserve University *B*
Cedarville University *B*
College of Mount St. Joseph *A, B*
Defiance College *A, B*
Franciscan University of Steubenville *B*
Heidelberg College *B*
Hiram College *B*
Jefferson Community College *A*
John Carroll University *B*
Kent State University *B, M, D*
Kent State University
    Stark Campus *B*
Malone College *B*
Marietta College *B*
Mount Union College *B*
Mount Vernon Nazarene University *B*
Muskingum Area Technical College *C, A*
Muskingum College *B*
Ohio Dominican College *B*
Ohio State University
    Columbus Campus *B, M, D*
Ohio University *B*
Ohio University
    Southern Campus at Ironton *A*
Ohio Wesleyan University *B*
Otterbein College *B*
Owens Community College
    Findlay Campus *A*
    Toledo *A*
RETS Tech Center *A*
Stark State College of Technology *A*
University of Dayton *B, M*
University of Findlay *A, B*
University of Rio Grande *A, B*
Virginia Marti College of Art and
    Design *A*
Wilmington College *B*
Xavier University *B*
Youngstown State University *C, B*

Oklahoma

Cameron University *B*
Carl Albert State College *A*
Eastern Oklahoma State College *A*
Murray State College *A*
Northeastern State University *B*
Oklahoma Baptist University *B*
Oklahoma Christian University of
    Science and Arts *B*
Oklahoma City Community College *A*
Oklahoma City University *B, M*

Oklahoma State University *B, M, D*
Oklahoma Wesleyan University *B*
Oral Roberts University *B*
Redlands Community College *A*
Seminole State College *A*
Southwestern Oklahoma State
    University *B*
University of Central Oklahoma *B*
University of Tulsa *B, M, D*
Western Oklahoma State College *A*

Oregon

Blue Mountain Community College *A*
Central Oregon Community College *A*
Eastern Oregon University *B*
George Fox University *B*
Lewis & Clark College *B*
Linfield College *B*
Oregon Institute of Technology *B*
Portland State University *B, M, D*
Southern Oregon University *B*
Southwestern Oregon Community
    College *A*
University of Portland *B*
Western Baptist College *B*
Willamette University *B*

Pennsylvania

Allegheny College *B*
Bryn Mawr College *B*
Bucks County Community College *A*
CHI Institute *C, A*
Carlow College *B*
Carnegie Mellon University *B, D*
Cedar Crest College *B*
Chestnut Hill College *C, A, B*
DeSales University *B*
Dickinson College *B*
Drexel University *B, M, D*
Duquesne University *B*
Elizabethtown College *B*
Erie Business Center *A*
Geneva College *B*
Gettysburg College *B*
King's College *B*
La Roche College *B*
La Salle University *B, M*
Lebanon Valley College of
    Pennsylvania *B*
Lehigh Carbon Community College *A*
Lehigh University *B, M, D*
Lock Haven University of
    Pennsylvania *B*
Messiah College *B*
Montgomery County Community
    College *A*
Moravian College *B*
Mount Aloysius College *A*
Muhlenberg College *B*
Penn State
    Abington *B*
    Altoona *B*
    Beaver *B*
    Berks *B*
    Delaware County *B*
    Dubois *B*
    Fayette *B*
    Harrisburg *B, M*
    Hazleton *B*
    McKeesport *B*
    Mont Alto *B*
    New Kensington *B*
    Shenango *B*
    Wilkes-Barre *B*
    Worthington Scranton *B*
    York *B*
Pennsylvania Institute of Technology *A*
Philadelphia University *C, B, M*
Seton Hill University *B*
University of Pittsburgh *B, M, D*
University of Pittsburgh
    Bradford *B*
Waynesburg College *A, B*
Westmoreland County Community
    College *C, A*
Widener University *B*

York College of Pennsylvania *B*

Puerto Rico

Atlantic College *A*
Huertas Junior College *A*
Inter American University of Puerto Rico
    Barranquitas Campus *A, B*
    Bayamon Campus *A, B*
    San German Campus *A, B*
Universidad Metropolitana *A, B*
University of Puerto Rico
    Mayaguez Campus *B, M*
    Rio Piedras Campus *B*
University of the Sacred Heart *B*

Rhode Island

Brown University *B, M, D*
Rhode Island College *B*
Roger Williams University *B*

South Carolina

Benedict College *B*
The Citadel *M*
Claflin University *B*
Clemson University *B, M*
Coker College *B*
College of Charleston *B*
Francis Marion University *B*
Furman University *B*
Presbyterian College *B*
Southern Wesleyan University *B*
Wofford College *B*

South Dakota

Augustana College *B*
Dakota State University *B, T*
Kilian Community College *A*
Sinte Gleska University *B*
South Dakota School of Mines and
    Technology *B, M*
South Dakota State University *B*
University of Sioux Falls *B*

Tennessee

Belmont University *B*
Bryan College *B*
Carson-Newman College *B*
Christian Brothers University *B*
Fisk University *B*
Freed-Hardeman University *B*
King College *B*
Lane College *B*
Middle Tennessee State University *B, M*
Milligan College *B*
Pellissippi State Technical Community
    College *A*
Rhodes College *B*
Roane State Community College *A*
Southern Adventist University *B*
Southwest Tennessee Community
    College *A*
Tennessee Technological University *B*
University of Memphis *B*
University of Tennessee
    Knoxville *B, M, D*
    Martin *B*

Texas

Abilene Christian University *B*
Alvin Community College *C, A*
Austin College *B*
Austin Community College *A*
Baylor University *B, M*
Central Texas College *C, A*
Coastal Bend College *A*
Concordia University at Austin *B*
Dallas Baptist University *B*
Del Mar College *A*
Eastfield College *C, A*
El Paso Community College *A*
Galveston College *A*
Hill College *C, A*
Huston-Tillotson College *B*
Laredo Community College *A*
LeTourneau University *B*
Lon Morris College *A*
McMurry University *B*

Panola College *A*
St. Edward's University *C, B, T*
St. Mary's University *B*
South Plains College *A*
Southern Methodist
    University *C, B, M, D*
Southwestern Adventist University *B*
Tarleton State University *B, T*
Texas A&M University *B, M, D*
Texas A&M University
    Commerce *B, M*
Texas College *B*
Texas Lutheran University *B*
Texas Southern University *B*
Texas State Technical College
    Waco *A*
Texas Tech University *M*
Texas Wesleyan University *B*
University of Houston
    Clear Lake *B, M*
University of Mary Hardin-Baylor *B*
University of Texas
    Arlington *B, M*
    Dallas *B, M, D*
    El Paso *M*
    Pan American *B, M, T*
Western Texas College *A*
Wiley College *B*

Utah

Brigham Young University *B, M, D*
Dixie State College of Utah *A, B*
Salt Lake Community College *A*
Snow College *A*
Southern Utah University *B*
University of Utah *B, M, D*
Utah Career College *C, A*
Utah Valley State College *C, A, B*
Weber State University *B*
Westminster College *B*

Vermont

Bennington College *B*
Lyndon State College *A*
Marlboro College *B*
Middlebury College *B*
Norwich University *B*
St. Michael's College *B*
University of Vermont *B, M*

Virginia

Bridgewater College *B*
Danville Community College *A*
ECPI College of Technology *C, A*
ECPI Technical College: Roanoke *A*
Eastern Mennonite University *B*
Emory & Henry College *B*
Ferrum College *B*
Hampton University *B, M*
Hollins University *B*
J. Sargeant Reynolds Community
    College *A*
Longwood University *B, T*
Mary Baldwin College *B*
Mary Washington College *B*
Marymount University *C, B, M*
National College of Business &
    Technology
    Bluefield *C, A*
    Charlottesville *C, A*
    Danville *C, A*
    Harrisonburg *C, A*
    Lynchburg *C, A*
    Martinsville *C, A*
    Roanoke *C, A*
Radford University *B*
Roanoke College *B*
Sweet Briar College *B*
Thomas Nelson Community College *A*
University of Richmond *B*
Virginia Military Institute *B*
Virginia State University *B*
Virginia Wesleyan College *B*
Virginia Western Community College *A*
Washington and Lee University *B*

Washington

Centralia College *A*
Eastern Washington University *B, M*
Everett Community College *A*
Gonzaga University *B*
Grays Harbor College *C*
Henry Cogswell College *B*
Lower Columbia College *A*
North Seattle Community College *C, A*
Olympic College *A*
Pacific Lutheran University *B*
Renton Technical College *C, A*
St. Martin's College *B*
Seattle University *B*
University of Puget Sound *B, T*
University of Washington *B*
Walla Walla College *B*
Walla Walla Community College *C, A*
Washington State University *B, M, D*
Whitworth College *B*

West Virginia

Alderson-Broaddus College *A, B*
Concord College *B*
Davis and Elkins College *B*
Fairmont State College *B*
Mountain State University *A, B*
Salem International University *B*
West Virginia University *B, M, D*
West Virginia University Institute of
    Technology *B*
West Virginia Wesleyan College *B*
Wheeling Jesuit University *B*

Wisconsin

Beloit College *B*
Cardinal Stritch University *A*
Carthage College *B*
Marquette University *B*
Mount Mary College *B*
Northland College *B*
Ripon College *B*
St. Norbert College *B*
Silver Lake College *B, T*
University of Wisconsin
    Green Bay *B*
    La Crosse *B, T*
    Milwaukee *B*
    Oshkosh *B*
    Parkside *B*
    Platteville *B*
    Superior *B*

Wyoming

Casper College *A*
University of Wyoming *B, M, D*
Western Wyoming Community
    College *A*

Computer software technology

Arizona

South Mountain Community
    College *C, A*

California

San Joaquin Delta College *C, A*

Florida

Palm Beach Community College *C*

Illinois

Heartland Community College *C, A*

Louisiana

Grantham University *A, B*

Minnesota

Globe College *C, A, B*

Missouri

Blue River Community College *A*

Montana

Montana Tech of the University of
    Montana *A*

Nebraska

Metropolitan Community College *A*

North Dakota

North Dakota State College of
    Science *C, A*

Texas

MTI College of Business and
    Technology *C, A*

Washington

North Seattle Community College *C*

Computer systems analysis

Alabama

James H. Faulkner State Community
    College *C, A*

Arizona

Gateway Community College *C, A*
Paradise Valley Community College *C*
Pima Community College *C, A*
South Mountain Community
    College *C, A*

Arkansas

Arkansas Tech University *B*
Rich Mountain Community College *C, A*
University of Arkansas *M*

California

Cerritos Community College *A*
College of Marin: Kentfield *A*
College of the Canyons *C, A*
De Anza College *C, A*
Glendale Community College *C*
Irvine Valley College *C, A*
MTI College of Business and
    Technology *C, A*
San Diego City College *A*
University of California
    San Diego *B, M, D*
    Santa Cruz *B, M, D*

Colorado

Art Institute
    of Colorado *A*
Colorado Mountain College
    Timberline Campus *A*
Colorado Technical University *B, M, D*
IntelliTec College *A*
Jones International University *C, A*

Connecticut

Norwalk Community College *A*

Delaware

Delaware Technical and Community
    College
    Owens Campus *A*
    Stanton/Wilmington Campus *A*
    Terry Campus *A*

Florida

Broward Community College *A*
Florida Technical College
    Deland *A*
Gulf Coast Community College *A*
Indian River Community College *A*
Palm Beach Community College *A*
Pasco-Hernando Community College *A*
Schiller International University *B*
Seminole Community College *A*
University of Miami *B*

Georgia

Georgia Southwestern State University *B*

Illinois

De Paul University *M*
Illinois Institute of Technology *M*
Parkland College *C, A*
William Rainey Harper College *A*

Indiana

Indiana Business College *C*

Indiana Business College
  Evansville *C*
  Fort Wayne *C*
  Lafayette *C*
  Muncie *C*
  Terre Haute *C, A*
Sawyer College: Merrillville *A*

Iowa
Des Moines Area Community College *A*
Hamilton College
  Cedar Rapids *C*
Marshalltown Community College *A*
Northeast Iowa Community College *A*
St. Ambrose University *B*
Vatterott College *C, A*

Kansas
Independence Community College *C, A*
Kansas State University *A*
Pittsburg State University *B*
Tabor College *B*

Kentucky
Daymar College *A*
Murray State University *B, M*

Louisiana
University of Louisiana at Lafayette *B*

Maine
Husson College *B*

Maryland
Frederick Community College *A*
University of Maryland
  University College *C*

Massachusetts
Clark University *B*
Harvard College *B*
Mount Ida College *A*
Northeastern University *M*
Wentworth Institute of Technology *C*

Michigan
Baker College
  of Muskegon *B*
Lansing Community College *A*
Northern Michigan University *B*
Saginaw Valley State University *B*

Minnesota
Hennepin Technical College *C, A*
Mesabi Range Community and Technical
  College *A*
Winona State University *B*

Missouri
Missouri Southern State College *B*
Missouri Technical School *B*
Rockhurst University *C, B*
St. Louis Community College
  St. Louis Community College at
    Florissant Valley *A*
  St. Louis Community College at
    Forest Park *A*

Montana
Montana Tech of the University of
  Montana *B*

New Hampshire
Hesser College *C, A*

New Mexico
Albuquerque Technical-Vocational
  Institute *C, A*
Clovis Community College *A*
San Juan College *A*

New York
City University of New York
  Baruch College *M*
Medaille College *B*
Rochester Institute of Technology *M*
State University of New York
  Buffalo *M, D*
  College of Agriculture and
    Technology at Cobleskill *A*

Westchester Business Institute *C, A*

North Carolina
Durham Technical Community
  College *C, A*
Mayland Community College *A*
Southeastern Community College *A*
Western Piedmont Community
  College *C, A*
Wilson Technical Community
  College *C, A*

Ohio
Cincinnati State Technical and
  Community College *A*
Jefferson Community College *A*
Kent State University
  Stark Campus *B*
Miami University
  Middletown Campus *A*
  Oxford Campus *B, M*
Southern State Community College *A*
Stark State College of Technology *A*
University of Akron *C, A*
University of Cincinnati *M*
University of Dayton *B*
University of Findlay *B*

Oklahoma
Eastern Oklahoma State College *A*
Oklahoma Baptist University *B*
Oklahoma City Community College *A*

Oregon
Lane Community College *A*

Pennsylvania
Academy of Medical Arts and
  Business *C, A*
Allentown Business School *C*
CHI Institute *C, A*
Drexel University *B*
Grove City College *B*
Keystone College *B*
Mercyhurst College *B*

Texas
El Paso Community College *A*
Kilgore College *C, A*
Remington College
  Houston *A*
Tarleton State University *B*
University of Houston *B*
University of North Texas *M*
University of Texas
  El Paso *B*

Utah
College of Eastern Utah *C, A*

Vermont
Champlain College *C, A, B*

Virginia
Blue Ridge Community College *C, A*
ECPI College of Technology *C, A*
ECPI Technical College: Roanoke *A*
Eastern Mennonite University *B*
Virginia Western Community College *C*

Washington
Grays Harbor College *C*
North Seattle Community College *C, A*
Renton Technical College *C*

West Virginia
Marshall University *B*

Wisconsin
Bryant & Stratton College *A*
Carthage College *B*
Lac Courte Oreilles Ojibwa Community
  College *A*
Lakeshore Technical College *A*
Mid-State Technical College *A*
University of Wisconsin
  Whitewater *B*

**Computer systems
technology**

Alabama
Herzing College *A, B*

Arizona
Northern Arizona University *B*

California
Cuyamaca College *C, A*
Sierra College *A*
Westwood College of Technology
  Inland Empire *A*

Florida
DeVry University
  Orlando *B*
University of Central Florida *B*

Illinois
Heartland Community College *C, A*
Waubonsee Community College *C*

Indiana
Indiana University-Purdue University
  Indianapolis *A, B*
University of Evansville *B*

Iowa
Hamilton College
  Cedar Falls *C*

Kansas
Barton County Community College *C, A*

Massachusetts
Benjamin Franklin Institute of
  Technology *A*
Newbury College *C, A*

Minnesota
Globe College *C, A, B*

Missouri
Blue River Community College *C*

New Hampshire
Hesser College *C, A*
New Hampshire Community Technical
  College
  Berlin *C, A*

New York
Erie Community College
  South Campus *A*
State University of New York
  College of Agriculture and
    Technology at Morrisville *A, B*

North Carolina
Cape Fear Community College *C, A*

Ohio
Kent State University *A*
Miami University
  Hamilton Campus *A*
Owens Community College
  Findlay Campus *C, A*
  Toledo *C, A*
University of Cincinnati
  Clermont College *C, A*

Oregon
Portland Community College *A*

Pennsylvania
Penn State
  University Park *C*

South Carolina
York Technical College *A*

Texas
DeVry University
  Irving *A*
Kilgore College *C*
MTI College of Business and
  Technology *A*

Virginia
ECPI College of Technology *C, A*
ECPI Technical College: Roanoke *A*

Washington
Edmonds Community College *C, A*

Wisconsin
Western Wisconsin Technical College *C*

Computer typography

Pennsylvania
Northampton County Area Community
  College *C*

Wisconsin
Milwaukee Area Technical College *A*

**Computer/information
sciences**

Alabama
Alabama Agricultural and Mechanical
  University *B, M*
Alabama Southern Community
  College *A*
American College of Computer and
  Information Sciences *B, M*
Athens State University *B*
Bevill State Community College *A*
Birmingham-Southern College *B*
Bishop State Community College *A*
Calhoun Community College *C, A*
Central Alabama Community
  College *C, A*
Chattahoochee Valley Community
  College *A*
Community College of the Air Force *A*
Douglas MacArthur State Technical
  College *A*
Enterprise State Junior College *A*
Faulkner University *A*
Gadsden State Community College *C, A*
George C. Wallace State Community
  College
  Dothan *C, A*
  Selma *C, A*
Harry M. Ayers State Technical
  College *C, A*
Herzing College *A, B*
Jacksonville State University *B*
James H. Faulkner State Community
  College *A*
Jefferson State Community College *C, A*
Northeast Alabama Community
  College *A*
Northwest-Shoals Community College *A*
Oakwood College *A, B*
Reid State Technical College *A*
Remington College
  Southeast College of Technology *A*
Shelton State Community College *C*
Snead State Community College *A*
Southern Union State Community
  College *A*
Spring Hill College *C, A, B*
Stillman College *B*
Talladega College *B*
Troy State University *B*
Troy State University Dothan *B*
Troy State University in
  Montgomery *A, B, M*
Tuskegee University *B*
University of Alabama *B, M, D*
University of Alabama
  Birmingham *B, M, D*
  Huntsville *B, M, D*
University of Mobile *B*
University of North Alabama *B*
University of South Alabama *B, M*
Virginia College *A*

Alaska

University of Alaska
Anchorage *B*
Southeast *C, A*

Arizona

Arizona Western College *C, A*
Central Arizona College *C, A*
Cochise College *A*
DeVry University
Phoenix *B*
Embry-Riddle Aeronautical University:
Prescott Campus *B*
Gateway Community College *C, A*
Glendale Community College *C*
High-Tech Institute *A*
International Institute of the Americas
Phoenix *C, A, B*
Tucson *C, A, B*
Northern Arizona University *B*
Paradise Valley Community
College *C, A*
Phoenix College *A*
Pima Community College *A*
Prescott College *B, M*
Rio Salado College *C, A*
Scottsdale Community College *C, A*
South Mountain Community
College *C, A*
University of Arizona *B, M, D*
University of Phoenix *B*
Yavapai College *C, A*

Arkansas

Arkansas State University *B, M*
Arkansas State University
Beebe *A*
Mountain Home *C*
Arkansas Tech University *B*
Harding University *B*
Henderson State University *B*
Northwest Arkansas Community
College *A*
Ouachita Technical College *A*
Pulaski Technical College *A*
Rich Mountain Community College *A*
South Arkansas Community College *A*
Southeast Arkansas College *C, A*
Southern Arkansas University *A*
University of Arkansas *B, M, D*
University of Arkansas
Community College at Batesville *A*
Cossatot Community College of the
A
Fort Smith *A, B*
Little Rock *B, M*
Pine Bluff *B*
University of Central Arkansas *B*
Williams Baptist College *B*

California

Antelope Valley College *C, A*
Azusa Pacific University *B*
Barstow College *C, A*
Cabrillo College *A*
California Polytechnic State University:
San Luis Obispo *B, M*
California State Polytechnic University:
Pomona *B, M*
California State University
Bakersfield *B*
Dominguez Hills *B, M*
Fresno *B, M*
Hayward *B, M*
Long Beach *B, M*
Los Angeles *B*
Monterey Bay *B*
Northridge *B, M*
Sacramento *B, M*
San Bernardino *B, M*
San Marcos *B*
Stanislaus *B*
Cerritos Community College *A*
Cerro Coso Community College *C, A*
Chabot College *A*
Chapman University *B*

Citrus College *C, A*
Claremont McKenna College *B*
Coastline Community College *C, A*
Coleman College *C, A, B, M*
College of Marin: Kentfield *A*
College of the Canyons *C, A*
College of the Redwoods *C, A*
College of the Sequoias *C*
College of the Siskiyous *A*
Columbia College *C, A*
Contra Costa College *A*
De Anza College *A*
Diablo Valley College *A*
East Los Angeles College *A*
Foothill College *C, A*
Fresno Pacific University *B*
Gavilan Community College *C, A*
Glendale Community College *C, A*
Golden Gate University *C, B, M*
Golden West College *A*
Grossmont Community College *C, A*
Harvey Mudd College *B*
ITT Technical Institute
San Bernardino *A*
Imperial Valley College *A*
Irvine Valley College *C, A*
Laney College *C, A*
Las Positas College *C, A*
Los Angeles Harbor College *C, A*
Los Angeles Pierce College *C, A*
Los Angeles Southwest College *A*
Los Angeles Trade and Technical
College *C, A*
Los Medanos College *C*
Loyola Marymount University *B, M*
Master's College *B*
Mills College *B, M*
MiraCosta College *C, A*
Modesto Junior College *A*
Monterey Peninsula College *C, A*
Moorpark College *A*
Mount San Jacinto College *A*
Napa Valley College *A*
National Hispanic University *B*
National University *M*
Orange Coast College *C, A*
Pacific States University *B, M*
Pacific Union College *B*
Palomar College *C, A*
Pepperdine University *B*
Pomona College *B*
Reedley College *A*
Riverside Community College *C, A*
San Diego City College *C, A*
San Diego State University *B, M*
San Francisco State University *B*
San Joaquin Delta College *C, A*
San Jose State University *B, M*
Santa Barbara City College *C, A*
Santa Monica College *C*
Shasta College *A*
Sierra College *A*
Southwestern College *C, A*
Stanford University *B, M, D*
Taft College *A*
University of California
Davis *B, M, D*
Irvine *B, M, D*
Los Angeles *B, M, D*
Riverside *B, M, D*
San Diego *B, M, D*
Santa Barbara *B*
Santa Cruz *B, M, D*
University of La Verne *B*
University of Redlands *B, M*
University of San Diego *B*
University of San Francisco *B, M*
University of Southern
California *B, M, D*
University of the Pacific *B*
Ventura College *C, A*
Vista Community College *C, A*
West Valley College *C, A*
Woodbury University *B*
Yuba Community College District *C, A*

Colorado

Blair Junior College *A*
Colorado Christian University *B*
Colorado School of Mines *B*
Colorado State University *B, M, D*
Colorado State University
Pueblo *B*
Colorado Technical University *B, M, D*
Community College of Aurora *C, A*
DeVry University
Denver *A*
IntelliTec College *A*
Jones International University *C, B*
Mesa State College *B*
Metropolitan State College of Denver *B*
National Technological University *M*
Otero Junior College *C, A*
Parks College *A*
Platt College
Aurora *A*
Red Rocks Community College *C, A*
Regis University *B*
Remington College
Colorado Springs *A*
Trinidad State Junior College *A*
United States Air Force Academy *B*
University of Colorado
Colorado Springs *B*
Denver *M*
University of Denver *B, M*

Connecticut

Asnuntuck Community College *A*
Capital Community College *A*
Central Connecticut State University *M*
Eastern Connecticut State University *B*
Fairfield University *A*
Housatonic Community College *C, A*
Mitchell College *A*
Naugatuck Valley Community College *A*
Norwalk Community College *A*
Quinebaug Valley Community
College *C, A*
Quinnipiac University *B, M*
Sacred Heart University *B, M*
Southern Connecticut State University *B*
Teikyo Post University *B*
Three Rivers Community College *A*
Trinity College *B*
Tunxis Community College *C*
University of Bridgeport *B, M*
University of Hartford *B*
University of New Haven *A, B, M*
Wesleyan University *B, M*
Western Connecticut State University *B*
Yale University *B, M, D*

Delaware

Delaware State University *B*
Delaware Technical and Community
College
Owens Campus *C, A*
Stanton/Wilmington Campus *A*
Terry Campus *A*
Goldey-Beacom College *A, B*
University of Delaware *B, M, D*

District of Columbia

Catholic University of America *B, M, D*
Gallaudet University *B*
George Washington University *B, M*
Potomac College *B*
Strayer University *C*
University of the District of
Columbia *C, A, B*

Florida

Barry University *T*
Bethune-Cookman College *B*
Broward Community College *A*
Chipola Junior College *A*
Cooper Career Institute *C, A*
Daytona Beach Community College *A*
Eckerd College *B*
Embry-Riddle Aeronautical University *B*
Florida Agricultural and Mechanical
University *B*

Florida Atlantic University *B, M, D*
Florida Gulf Coast University *B*
Florida International University *B, M, D*
Florida Metropolitan University
Melbourne Campus *A, B*
Orlando College North *A, B*
Tampa College *A, B*
Tampa College Lakeland *B*
Florida State University *B, M, D*
Florida Technical College *C, A*
Florida Technical College
Deland *A*
Jacksonville *C, A*
Full Sail Real World Education *A*
Gulf Coast Community College *A*
Hillsborough Community College *A*
Indian River Community College *A*
International College *A, B, M*
Jacksonville University *B*
Jones College *A, B*
Lake City Community College *A*
Manatee Community College *A*
Miami-Dade Community College *C, A*
Northwood University
Florida Campus *B*
Nova Southeastern University *B, M, D*
Okaloosa-Walton Community College *A*
Palm Beach Atlantic University *B*
Palm Beach Community College *A*
Pensacola Junior College *A*
Polk Community College *A*
Rollins College *B*
St. Petersburg College *C*
St. Thomas University *B*
Seminole Community College *A*
South Florida Community College *A*
Southwest Florida College *C, A*
Stetson University *B*
University of Central Florida *B, M, D*
University of Florida *B, M*
University of North Florida *B, M*
University of South Florida *B*
University of Tampa *A, B*
University of West Florida *B*
Webster College: Holiday *A*

Georgia

Abraham Baldwin Agricultural
College *A*
Albany State University *B*
Albany Technical College *A*
Armstrong Atlantic State
University *B, M*
Atlanta Metropolitan College *A*
Augusta State University *B*
Bainbridge College *C, A*
Central Georgia Technical College *C*
Chattahoochee Technical College *C, A*
Clark Atlanta University *B, M*
Clayton College and State University *B*
Columbus State University *B*
Covenant College *B*
Dalton State College *A, B*
Darton College *A*
DeKalb Technical College *C, A*
Emory University *M*
Floyd College *A*
Fort Valley State University *B*
Gainesville College *A*
Georgia College and State University *B*
Georgia Institute of Technology *B, M, D*
Georgia Southern University *B*
Georgia Southwestern State
University *A, B, M*
Georgia State University *B, M, D*
Griffin Technical College *A*
Kennesaw State University *B*
LaGrange College *B*
Macon State College *A*
Mercer University *B*
Middle Georgia College *A*
Morehouse College *B*
Morris Brown College *B*
North Georgia College & State
University *B*
Savannah State University *B*

Savannah Technical College *C, A*
Shorter College *B*
South Georgia College *A*
Southern Polytechnic State
    University *C, B, M*
Spelman College *B*
State University of West Georgia *B*
University of Georgia *B, M, D*
Valdosta State University *B*
Waycross College *A*
Wesleyan College *B*
West Georgia Technical College *A*
Young Harris College *A*

Hawaii
Brigham Young University-Hawaii *B*
Chaminade University of Honolulu *A, B*
Hawaii Business College *C, A*
Hawaii Pacific University *C, B*
Remington College
    Honolulu *A*
University of Hawaii
    Hilo *B*
    Honolulu Community College *A*
    Leeward Community College *C, A*
    Manoa *B, M, D*

Idaho
Boise State University *B, M, T*
Brigham Young University - Idaho *A, B*
Idaho State University *B, M*
North Idaho College *A*
Northwest Nazarene University *B*
University of Idaho *B, M, D*

Illinois
Aurora University *B*
Benedictine University *B*
Black Hawk College
    East Campus *A*
Blackburn College *B*
Bradley University *B, M*
Carl Sandburg College *A*
Chicago State University *B*
City Colleges of Chicago
    Harold Washington College *A*
    Kennedy-King College *C, A*
    Olive-Harvey College *C, A*
    Wright College *C, A*
Concordia University *B*
Danville Area Community College *A*
De Paul University *C, B, M, D*
Dominican University *B*
East-West University *A, B*
Eureka College *B*
Governors State University *B, M*
Greenville College *B*
Heartland Community College *A*
Illinois Central College *A*
Illinois College *B*
Illinois Eastern Community Colleges
    Frontier Community College *C, A*
    Lincoln Trail College *A*
Illinois Institute of Technology *C, M, D*
Illinois Valley Community College *A*
Illinois Wesleyan University *B*
John A. Logan College *A*
John Wood Community College *A*
Joliet Junior College *C, A*
Judson College *B*
Knox College *B*
Lake Land College *C, A*
Lewis University *B*
Lewis and Clark Community College *A*
Lincoln Land Community College *C, A*
MacMurray College *B*
McKendree College *B*
Monmouth College *B*
North Central College *B, M*
Northeastern Illinois University *B, M*
Northern Illinois University *B, M*
Northwestern Business College *A*
Northwestern University *C, B, M, D*
Oakton Community College *A*
Olivet Nazarene University *B*
Parkland College *C, A*

Quincy University *B*
Richland Community College *A*
Robert Morris College: Chicago *C, A, B*
Rock Valley College *A*
Rockford Business College *C, A*
Rockford College *B*
Roosevelt University *B, M*
St. Augustine College *C, A*
St. Xavier University *B*
Sauk Valley Community College *A*
South Suburban College of Cook
    County *C, A*
Southern Illinois University
    Carbondale *B, M*
Southern Illinois University
    Edwardsville *B, M*
Southwestern Illinois College *C, A*
Springfield College in Illinois *C*
Trinity Christian College *B*
Triton College *C, A*
University of Chicago *B*
University of Illinois
    Chicago *B, M, D*
    Springfield *B, M*
    Urbana-Champaign *B, M, D*
University of St. Francis *B*
Waubonsee Community College *A*
Western Illinois University *B, M*
William Rainey Harper College *A*

Indiana
Ball State University *B, M*
Bethel College *A*
Butler University *B*
Calumet College of St. Joseph *A*
Commonwealth Business College:
    Michigan City *C, A*
Franklin College *B*
Goshen College *B*
Grace College *B*
Hanover College *B*
Huntington College *B*
ITT Technical Institute
    Fort Wayne *A*
Indiana Business College *C, A*
Indiana Business College
    Columbus *C, A*
    Muncie *C, A*
    Terre Haute *C, A*
Indiana Institute of Technology *A, B*
Indiana State University *B*
Indiana University
    Bloomington *B, M, D*
    East *A*
    South Bend *B*
    Southeast *B*
Indiana University-Purdue University
    Fort Wayne *A, B*
Indiana University-Purdue University
    Indianapolis *B, M*
Indiana Wesleyan University *A, B*
International Business College *C, A*
International Business College:
    Indianapolis *C, A*
Ivy Tech State College
    Bloomington *A*
    Central Indiana *A*
    Columbus *A*
    Eastcentral *C, A*
    Kokomo *C, A*
    Lafayette *C, A*
    Northcentral *C, A*
    Northeast *C, A*
    Northwest *C, A*
    Southcentral *C, A*
    Southeast *C, A*
    Southwest *A*
    Wabash Valley *A*
    Whitewater *C, A*
Manchester College *A, B*
Michiana College *A*
Michiana College: Fort Wayne *A*
Oakland City University *C, A, B*
Professional Careers Institute *A*
Purdue University *B, M, D*

Purdue University
    Calumet *B*
St. Joseph's College *B*
St. Mary-of-the-Woods College *B*
Sawyer College *C, A*
Sawyer College: Merrillville *C, A*
Taylor University *B*
Taylor University: Fort Wayne *A*
Tri-State University *B*
University of Evansville *B*
University of Indianapolis *B*
University of Notre Dame *B*
University of Southern Indiana *C, B*
Valparaiso University *C, B*
Vincennes University *A*

Iowa
Briar Cliff University *B*
Buena Vista University *B*
Central College *B*
Clarke College *B*
Cornell College *B*
Des Moines Area Community
    College *C, A*
Dordt College *B*
Drake University *B*
Ellsworth Community College *A*
Emmaus Bible College *B*
Franciscan University *B*
Graceland University *B*
Grand View College *B*
Hamilton College *A*
Hamilton College
    Cedar Rapids *C, A, B*
Indian Hills Community College *C, A*
Iowa State University *B, M, D*
Iowa Wesleyan College *B*
Loras College *B*
Luther College *B*
Marshalltown Community College *C, A*
Morningside College *B*
Mount Mercy College *B*
Northeast Iowa Community College *C*
Northwestern College *B*
St. Ambrose University *C, B*
Simpson College *B*
Southwestern Community College *C*
University of Dubuque *B*
University of Iowa *B, M, D*
University of Northern Iowa *B, M*
Waldorf College *A, B*
Wartburg College *B*
William Penn University *B*

Kansas
Allen County Community College *A*
Butler County Community College *C, A*
Central Christian College *A*
Cloud County Community College *A*
Dodge City Community College *A*
Emporia State University *B*
Fort Hays State University *B*
Fort Scott Community College *C, A*
Friends University *B*
Garden City Community College *A*
Hesston College *A*
Hutchinson Community College *A*
Independence Community College *C, A*
Kansas City Kansas Community
    College *C, A*
Kansas State University *B, M, D*
Kansas Wesleyan University *A, B*
Labette Community College *A*
MidAmerica Nazarene University *B*
Pittsburg State University *B, T*
Pratt Community College *A*
Seward County Community
    College *C, A*
Southwestern College *B*
Sterling College *B*
Tabor College *B*
University of Kansas *B, M, D*
Washburn University of Topeka *A, B*
Wichita State University *B, M*

Kentucky
Beckfield College *C, A*
Bellarmine University *B*
Campbellsville University *C, A, B*
Cumberland College *B, T*
Daymar College *C, A*
Elizabethtown Community College *A*
Georgetown College *B*
Henderson Community College *C*
Jefferson Community College *A*
Lindsey Wilson College *A*
Maysville Community College *A*
Morehead State University *B*
Murray State University *B*
Paducah Community College *A*
RETS Institute of Technology *A*
St. Catharine College *A*
Somerset Community College *C, A*
Southeast Community College *A*
Southern Ohio College
    Fort Mitchell *A*
Southwestern College of Business *C, A*
Spalding University *B*
Sullivan University *A, B*
Thomas More College *C, A, B*
Transylvania University *B*
University of Kentucky *B, M, D*
University of Louisville *M*

Louisiana
Grantham University *C, A, B*
Herzing College *A, B*
Louisiana College *B*
Louisiana State University
    Eunice *A*
Loyola University New Orleans *B*
Our Lady of Holy Cross College *T*
Remington College *A*
Remington College
    Baton Rouge *A*
Southern University
    Shreveport *A*
Tulane University *B, M, D*
Xavier University of Louisiana *B*

Maine
Andover College *A*
St. Joseph's College *B*
Thomas College *A, B*
University of Maine *B, M, D*
University of Maine
    Augusta *A, B*
University of Southern Maine *B*

Maryland
Allegany College *A*
Anne Arundel Community College *C, A*
Bowie State University *B, M*
Carroll Community College *C, A*
Chesapeake College *A*
College of Notre Dame of Maryland *B*
Columbia Union College *B*
Community College of Baltimore County
    Catonsville *B*
    Dundalk *C, A*
    Essex *C, A*
Frederick Community College *A*
Frostburg State University *C, B, M*
Hagerstown Community College *A*
Harford Community College *C, A*
Hood College *M*
Johns Hopkins University *B, D*
Loyola College in Maryland *B*
Montgomery College
    Rockville Campus *A*
Morgan State University *B*
St. Mary's College of Maryland *B*
Towson University *B, M*
United States Naval Academy *B*
University of Baltimore *B, M*
University of Maryland
    Baltimore County *B, M, D*
    College Park *B, M, D*
    University College *C, B*
Villa Julie College *A, B*

Massachusetts

Assumption College *B*
Atlantic Union College *C, A, B*
Babson College *B*
Bay Path College *B*
Bay State College *A*
Becker College *C, A, B*
Benjamin Franklin Institute of
    Technology *C, A*
Berkshire Community College *C, A*
Boston College *B*
Boston University *B, M, D*
Brandeis University *B, M, D*
Cape Cod Community College *A*
Clark University *B*
Dean College *A*
Elms College *C, B*
Endicott College *A*
Fisher College *C, A*
Fitchburg State College *C, B*
Framingham State College *B*
Greenfield Community College *A*
Hampshire College *B*
Harvard College *B*
ITT Technical Institute
    Norwood *A*
Massachusetts Bay Community
    College *A*
Massachusetts College of Liberal Arts *B*
Massasoit Community College *C, A*
Merrimack College *A*
Mount Wachusett Community
    College *C, A*
Newbury College *A, B*
Northeastern University *B, M, D*
Regis College *B*
Roxbury Community College *C, A*
Salem State College *B*
Simmons College *B*
Springfield College *B*
Stonehill College *C*
Suffolk University *B, M*
Tufts University *B*
University of Massachusetts
    Boston *B*
    Dartmouth *B, M*
Urban College of Boston *C*
Wellesley College *B*
Wentworth Institute of Technology *B*
Western New England College *B*
Westfield State College *B*
Wheaton College *B*

Michigan

Alma College *B*
Alpena Community College *C, A*
Andrews University *B, M*
Aquinas College *B*
Baker College
    of Auburn Hills *A*
    of Cadillac *A*
    of Clinton Township *A, B*
    of Jackson *A*
    of Muskegon *B*
    of Owosso *A, B*
    of Port Huron *A, B*
Calvin College *B*
Central Michigan University *B, M*
Cornerstone University *B*
Davenport University
    Midland *C, A*
Davenport University - Western
    Region *A, B*
Eastern Michigan University *B, M*
Ferris State University *C, B*
Gogebic Community College *A*
Grand Rapids Community College *C, A*
Grand Valley State University *B*
Hope College *B*
ITT Technical Institute
    Troy *A*
Kalamazoo College *B*
Lansing Community College *A*
Macomb Community College *C, A*
Madonna University *C, A, B*

Marygrove College *C, B*
Michigan State University *B, M, D*
Michigan Technological
    University *B, M, T*
Monroe County Community
    College *C, A*
Montcalm Community College *A*
Mott Community College *A*
Muskegon Community College *C, A*
North Central Michigan College *C, A*
Northern Michigan University *A, B, T*
Northwood University *B*
Oakland Community College *C, A*
Oakland University *B, M*
Saginaw Valley State University *B, T*
Siena Heights University *A, B*
Southwestern Michigan College *C, A*
Spring Arbor University *B*
University of Michigan *B, M, D*
University of Michigan
    Dearborn *B*
Walsh College of Accountancy and
    Business Administration *B*
Washtenaw Community College *C, A*
Wayne State University *C, B, M, D*
Western Michigan University *B*

Minnesota

Academy College *C, A, B*
Augsburg College *B*
Bemidji State University *B, M*
Bethel College *B*
Capella University *B, M*
College of St. Catherine *B*
College of St. Scholastica *B*
Crown College *C, A, B*
Globe College *C, A, B*
Gustavus Adolphus College *B*
Hamline University *B*
Hennepin Technical College *C, A*
Hibbing Community College: A
    Technical and Community College *A*
Lake Superior College: A Community
    and Technical College *C, A*
Macalester College *B*
Mesabi Range Community and Technical
    College *C, A*
Minnesota State University
    Mankato *B, M*
    Moorhead *B*
Minnesota West Community and
    Technical College: Worthington
    Campus *A*
National American University
    St. Paul *A, B*
Normandale Community College *A*
North Hennepin Community College *A*
Northland Community & Technical
    College *A*
Rainy River Community College *C, A*
Rasmussen College
    St. Cloud *A*
Ridgewater College: A Community and
    Technical College *C, A*
Riverland Community College: A
    Technical and Community College *A*
Rochester Community and Technical
    College *C, A*
St. Cloud State University *B*
St. Cloud Technical College *C, A*
Southwest State University *B*
University of Minnesota
    Twin Cities *M, D*
University of St. Thomas *B*
Winona State University *B*

Mississippi

Alcorn State University *B, M*
Antonelli College
    Hattiesburg *C, A*
    Jackson *C, A*
Holmes Community College *C, A*
Itawamba Community College *A*
Mary Holmes College *A*
Mississippi College *B*

Mississippi Gulf Coast Community
    College
    Perkinston *A*
Mississippi State University *B, M, D*
Mississippi Valley State University *B*
Northwest Mississippi Community
    College *A*
University of Mississippi *B*
University of Southern Mississippi *B, M*

Missouri

Avila University *B*
Central Missouri State University *B*
College of the Ozarks *B*
Columbia College *A, B*
Crowder College *A*
Drury University *B*
East Central College *A*
Evangel University *B*
Fontbonne College *B*
Hannibal-LaGrange College *B*
Hickey College *C, A*
Jefferson College *C, A*
Lincoln University *A*
Lindenwood University *B*
Longview Community College *A*
Maple Woods Community College *A*
Mineral Area College *A*
Missouri Baptist University *B*
Missouri Southern State College *A, B*
Missouri Valley College *B*
Missouri Western State College *B*
North Central Missouri College *C, A*
Northwest Missouri State University *B*
Penn Valley Community College *C, A*
Ranken Technical College *A*
Rockhurst University *B*
St. Charles Community College *C, A*
St. Louis Community College
    St. Louis Community College at
        Florissant Valley *A*
    St. Louis Community College at
        Forest Park *A*
    St. Louis Community College at
        Meramec *C, A*
St. Louis University *B*
Sanford-Brown College *C, A*
Southeast Missouri State University *B*
Southwest Baptist University *B*
Southwest Missouri State University *B*
Southwest Missouri State University:
    West Plains Campus *A*
Springfield College *A*
Truman State University *B*
University of Missouri
    Columbia *B, M, D*
    Kansas City *B, M*
    Rolla *B, M, D*
    St. Louis *B*
Vatterott College: St. Joseph *A*
Vatterott College: Sunset Hills *A*
Washington University in St.
    Louis *B, M, D*
Webster University *B, M*
Westminster College *B*
William Woods University *B*

Montana

Dawson Community College *A*
Miles Community College *A*
Montana State University
    Billings *A*
    Billings College of
        Technology *A*
Montana Tech of the University of
    Montana *B*
Rocky Mountain College *B*
Salish Kootenai College *C, A*

Nebraska

Central Community College *C, A*
College of Saint Mary *C, A, B*
Doane College *B*
Little Priest Tribal College *A*
Metropolitan Community College *C*
Midland Lutheran College *B*

Nebraska Indian Community
    College *C, A*
Northeast Community College *A*
Peru State College *B*
Southeast Community College
    Beatrice Campus *A*
University of Nebraska
    Kearney *B*
    Omaha *B, M*
Wayne State College *B*
Western Nebraska Community
    College *A*

Nevada

Career College of Northern Nevada *C*
Great Basin College *C, A*
Morrison University *C, A*
Truckee Meadows Community
    College *A*
University of Nevada
    Reno *B*
Western Nevada Community College *A*

New Hampshire

College for Lifelong Learning *C, A, B*
Daniel Webster College *B*
Franklin Pierce College *B*
Hesser College *C, A*
Keene State College *A, B, M*
New England College *B*
New Hampshire Community Technical
    College
    Berlin *A*
    Laconia *C, A*
    Manchester *A*
    Nashua *C, A*
New Hampshire Technical Institute *C, A*
Plymouth State College *B*
Southern New Hampshire
    University *C, A, B, M*
University of New
    Hampshire *A, B, M, D*

New Jersey

Atlantic Cape Community College *A*
Bergen Community College *C*
Bloomfield College *B*
Brookdale Community College *A*
Caldwell College *C, B*
Camden County College *C, A*
Centenary College *B*
The College of New Jersey *B*
College of St. Elizabeth *C, B*
Essex County College *C, A*
Fairleigh Dickinson University
    College at Florham *B*
    Metropolitan Campus *B, M*
Felician College *B*
Gloucester County College *C, A*
Hudson County Community College *C*
Kean University *B*
Mercer County Community College *C*
Middlesex County College *A*
Monmouth University *C, B, M*
Montclair State University *B, M*
New Jersey City University *B*
New Jersey Institute of
    Technology *B, M, D*
Ocean County College *A*
Passaic County Community College *A*
Ramapo College of New Jersey *B*
Raritan Valley Community College *A*
Richard Stockton College of New
    Jersey *B*
Rider University *B*
Rowan University *B*
St. Peter's College *B*
Seton Hall University *B*
Stevens Institute of Technology *B, M, D*
Sussex County Community College *C, A*
Union County College *A*
Warren County Community College *C, A*
William Paterson University of New
    Jersey *B*

New Mexico

Clovis Community College *A*

College of Santa Fe *B*
Eastern New Mexico University *B*
Eastern New Mexico University: Roswell
  Campus *A*
Luna Community College *A*
Mesalands Community College *C, A*
New Mexico Highlands University *B*
New Mexico Institute of Mining and
  Technology *B, M, D*
New Mexico Junior College *C, A*
New Mexico State University *B, M, D*
San Juan College *A*
Santa Fe Community College *C, A*
Southwestern Indian Polytechnic
  Institute *A*
University of New Mexico *B, M, D*
Western New Mexico University *B*

New York

Adelphi University *B*
Adirondack Community College *A*
Alfred University *B*
Briarcliffe College *C, A*
Broome Community College *A*
Bryant & Stratton Business Institute
  Albany *A*
  Syracuse *C, A*
Cayuga County Community College *A*
City University of New York
  Baruch College *B, M*
  Brooklyn College *B, M*
  City College *B*
  College of Staten Island *A, B, M, D*
  Hunter College *B, M*
  John Jay College of Criminal
    Justice *B*
  La Guardia Community College *A*
  Medgar Evers College *A*
  Queensborough Community
    College *A*
Clinton Community College *A*
Colgate University *B*
College of Mount St. Vincent *B*
Columbia University
  Fu Foundation School of
    Engineering and Applied
    Science *B, M, D*
Cornell University *B, M, D*
Corning Community College *C, A*
Dominican College of Blauvelt *C, B*
Dowling College *B*
Dutchess Community College *C, A*
Erie Community College
  North Campus *A*
Excelsior College *B*
Finger Lakes Community College *C, A*
Fordham University *B*
Fulton-Montgomery Community
  College *A*
Globe Institute of Technology *C, A, B*
Hamilton College *B*
Hartwick College *B*
Hobart and William Smith Colleges *B*
Iona College *C, B, M*
Ithaca College *B*
Jamestown Business College *A*
Jamestown Community College *A*
Jefferson Community College *A*
Long Island Business Institute *C, A*
Long Island University
  C. W. Post Campus *B*
Manhattan College *B*
Manhattanville College *B*
Maria College *C, A*
Marist College *B*
Marymount College of Fordham
  University *B*
Marymount Manhattan College *C*
Medaille College *B*
Mercy College *C, B*
Mildred Elley *C, A*
Mohawk Valley Community College *A*
Monroe College *A, B*
Monroe Community College *A*
Mount St. Mary College *C, B, T*
Nassau Community College *A*

New York Institute of Technology *B, M*
New York University *B, M, D*
Niagara County Community College *A*
Niagara University *C, B*
Nyack College *B*
Olean Business Institute *A*
Onondaga Community College *A*
Orange County Community College *A*
Pace University *C, B, M, D*
Pace University:
  Pleasantville/Briarcliff *C, B, M, D*
Polytechnic University *B, M*
Rensselaer Polytechnic Institute *B, M, D*
Roberts Wesleyan College *B*
Rochester Institute of
  Technology *A, B, M*
Sage College of Albany *A, B*
St. Bonaventure University *B*
St. John Fisher College *B*
St. John's University *C, B*
Sarah Lawrence College *B*
Schenectady County Community
  College *A*
Skidmore College *B*
State University of New York
  Albany *B, M, D*
  Binghamton *B, M*
  Buffalo *B, M, D*
  College at Brockport *B, M*
  College at Buffalo *B*
  College at Fredonia *B*
  College at Geneseo *B*
  College at Old Westbury *B*
  College at Oneonta *B*
  College at Plattsburgh *B*
  College at Potsdam *B*
  College of Agriculture and
    Technology at Cobleskill *A*
  College of Agriculture and
    Technology at Morrisville *A*
  College of Technology at
    Alfred *A, B*
  College of Technology at
    Canton *A, B*
  Institute of Technology at
    Utica/Rome *B, M*
  Purchase *C*
Suffolk County Community
  College *C, A*
Syracuse University *B, M, D*
Tompkins-Cortland Community
  College *A*
Touro College *B*
Trocaire College *C, A*
Ulster County Community College *A*
Union College *B, M*
United States Military Academy *B*
University of Rochester *B, M, D*
Utica College *B*
Utica School of Commerce *A*
Vassar College *B*
Villa Maria College of Buffalo *A*
Westchester Business Institute *C, A*
Westchester Community College *A*
Yeshiva University *B*

North Carolina

Bennett College *B*
Bladen Community College *C, A*
Brunswick Community College *A*
Carteret Community College *C, A*
Catawba College *B*
Central Piedmont Community College *A*
College of the Albemarle *A*
Duke University *B, M, D*
Edgecombe Community College *A*
Elizabeth City State University *B*
Elon University *B*
Fayetteville State University *B*
Gardner-Webb University *B*
Guilford College *B*
Guilford Technical Community
  College *C, A*
Halifax Community College *C, A*
High Point University *B*
Johnson C. Smith University *B*

Lenoir-Rhyne College *B*
Livingstone College *B*
Louisburg College *A*
Meredith College *B*
Methodist College *A, B*
Miller-Motte Technical College *C, A*
Mount Olive College *B*
North Carolina Agricultural and
  Technical State University *B, M*
North Carolina Central University *B*
North Carolina State University *B*
Pfeiffer University *B*
St. Augustine's College *B*
Sampson Community College *A*
Sandhills Community College *C, A*
Shaw University *B*
South College *A*
South Piedmont Community College *A*
Southwestern Community College *A*
University of North Carolina
  Charlotte *M, D*
  Greensboro *B, M*
  Pembroke *B*
Wake Technical Community
  College *C, A*
Wilson Technical Community College *A*
Winston-Salem State University *B, M*

North Dakota

Jamestown College *B*
Lake Region State College *C, A*
Mayville State University *B*
Minot State University *B*
Minot State University: Bottineau
  Campus *A*
North Dakota State University *B*
University of North Dakota *B, M*
Valley City State University *B*
Williston State College *A*

Ohio

Antonelli College *A*
Bluffton College *B*
Bowling Green State University *B, M*
Bryant & Stratton College *A*
Bryant & Stratton College .
  Willoughby Hills *A*
Case Western Reserve
  University *B, M, D*
Cedarville University *B*
Central State University *B*
Cincinnati State Technical and
  Community College *A*
Cleveland State University *B, M*
College of Wooster *B*
Cuyahoga Community College
  Eastern Campus *A*
  Metropolitan Campus *A*
  Western Campus *A*
Defiance College *A, B*
Denison University *B*
Edison State Community College *C, A*
Franciscan University of Steubenville *B*
Franklin University *A, B, M*
Gallipolis Career College *A*
Heidelberg College *B*
Hiram College *B*
ITT Technical Institute
  Youngstown *A*
James A. Rhodes State College *A*
Jefferson Community College *A*
John Carroll University *B*
Kent State University
  East Liverpool Regional Campus *A*
  Salem Regional Campus *A*
  Stark Campus *B*
  Tuscarawas Campus *A*
Lorain County Community College *A*
Marietta College *B*
Marion Technical College *C, A*
Miami University
  Middletown Campus *A*
  Oxford Campus *C, A*
Miami-Jacobs College *C, A*
Mount Union College *B*
Mount Vernon Nazarene University *B*

Muskingum Area Technical College *A*
Muskingum College *B*
North Central State College *C, A*
Oberlin College *B*
Ohio State University
  Columbus Campus *B, M, D*
Ohio University *B*
Ohio Valley College of Technology *A*
Ohio Wesleyan University *B*
Owens Community College
  Findlay Campus *C, A*
  Toledo *C, A*
RETS Tech Center *A*
Shawnee State University *A*
Sinclair Community College *C, A*
Southeastern Business College *A*
Southeastern Business College:
  Lancaster *A*
Southwestern College of Business *C*
Stark State College of Technology *A*
Technology Education College *A*
Tiffin University *B*
Trumbull Business College *C, A*
University of Akron *B, M*
University of Cincinnati *B, M, T*
University of Cincinnati
  Clermont College *C*
  Raymond Walters College *A*
University of Dayton *B, M*
University of Findlay *A, B*
University of Northwestern Ohio *A*
University of Rio Grande *A, B*
University of Toledo *A, M*
Walsh University *A, B*
Wilmington College *B*
Wittenberg University *B*
Wright State University *B, M, D*
Youngstown State University *A, B*

Oklahoma

Bacone College *A*
Cameron University *A, B*
East Central University *B*
Eastern Oklahoma State College *C, A*
Langston University *B*
Murray State College *A*
Northeastern Oklahoma Agricultural and
  Mechanical College *A*
Northern Oklahoma College *A*
Northwestern Oklahoma State
  University *B*
Oklahoma Baptist University *B*
Oklahoma Christian University of
  Science and Arts *B*
Oklahoma City Community College *A*
Oklahoma City University *B, M*
Oklahoma Panhandle State
  University *A, B*
Oklahoma State University *B, M, D*
Oklahoma State University
  Okmulgee *A*
Oklahoma Wesleyan University *A, B*
Oral Roberts University *B*
Redlands Community College *A*
Rose State College *A*
St. Gregory's University *B*
Southeastern Oklahoma State
  University *B*
Southern Nazarene University *B*
Southwestern Oklahoma State
  University *B*
Tulsa Community College *C, A*
University of Central Oklahoma *B*
University of Oklahoma *B, M, D*
University of Science and Arts of
  Oklahoma *B*
University of Tulsa *B*
Vatterott College *C, A*
Western Oklahoma State College *A*

Oregon

Blue Mountain Community College *A*
Central Oregon Community College *A*
Chemeketa Community College *A*
Eastern Oregon University *B*
George Fox University *B*

185

Lewis & Clark College *B*
Linn-Benton Community College *A*
Mount Hood Community College *C, A*
Northwest Christian College *B*
Oregon State University *B, M, D*
Pacific University *B*
Pioneer Pacific College *A*
Rogue Community College *A*
Southern Oregon University *B*
University of Oregon *B, M, D*
Western Business College *C, A*
Western Oregon University *B*

Pennsylvania

Academy of Medical Arts and
    Business *C, A*
Albright College *B*
Arcadia University *C, B*
Bloomsburg University of
    Pennsylvania *B*
Bradford School: Pittsburgh *C*
Bucknell University *B*
Bucks County Community College *A*
Cabrini College *B*
California University of Pennsylvania *B*
Cambria County Area Community
    College *C, A*
Carnegie Mellon University *B, M, D*
Cedar Crest College *C, B*
Central Pennsylvania College *A*
Chatham College *B*
Chestnut Hill College *B*
Cheyney University of Pennsylvania *B*
Churchman Business School *C*
Commonwealth Technical Institute *A*
Community College of Philadelphia *A*
DeSales University *B, M*
Delaware County Community College *A*
Delaware Valley College *A, B*
Dickinson College *B*
Drexel University *M*
East Stroudsburg University of
    Pennsylvania *B, M*
Edinboro University of
    Pennsylvania *A, B, M*
Education Direct: Center for Degree
    Studies *A*
Gettysburg College *B*
Grove City College *B*
Gwynedd-Mercy College *B*
Harrisburg Area Community
    College *C, A*
Holy Family University *C, B*
ICM School of Business & Medical
    Careers *A*
ITT Technical Institute
    Bensalem *A*
Immaculata University *A, B*
Indiana University of Pennsylvania *B*
Information Computer Systems
    Institute *C, A*
Juniata College *B*
Keystone College *A, B*
King's College *A, B*
Kutztown University of
    Pennsylvania *B, M*
La Roche College *B*
La Salle University *B, M*
Lackawanna College *A*
Lafayette College *B*
Lehigh University *B, M, D*
Lincoln University *B*
Lock Haven University of
    Pennsylvania *B*
Luzerne County Community College *A*
Lycoming College *B*
Marywood University *B, M*
McCann School of Business
    Pottsville *C, A*
    Sunbury *C, A*
Metropolitan Career Center *C*
Millersville University of
    Pennsylvania *A, B*
Montgomery County Community
    College *A*
Moravian College *B*

Mount Aloysius College *B*
Neumann College *C, B*
Northampton County Area Community
    College *A*
PJA School *C*
Peirce College *C, A, B*
Penn State
    Harrisburg *C*
    Schuylkill - Capital College *A, B*
    University Park *C, B, M, D*
Pennsylvania College of Technology *A*
Philadelphia University *C, B*
Pittsburgh Technical Institute: Boyd
    School Division *A*
Point Park College *C, A, B*
Robert Morris University *B, M, D*
Rosemont College *M*
St. Joseph's University *A, B, M*
St. Vincent College *C, B*
Schuylkill Institute of Business &
    Technology *C, A*
Shippensburg University of
    Pennsylvania *B, M*
Slippery Rock University of
    Pennsylvania *B*
South Hills School of Business &
    Technology *A*
Swarthmore College *B*
Thiel College *B*
University of Pennsylvania *B, M, D*
University of Pittsburgh
    Johnstown *B*
University of Scranton *A, B*
University of the Sciences in
    Philadelphia *B*
Valley Forge Christian College *C*
Villanova University *B, M*
Waynesburg College *B*
West Chester University of
    Pennsylvania *B, M*
Western School of Health and Business
    Careers *C*
Widener University *B*
Wilkes University *B*
York College of Pennsylvania *B, M*

Puerto Rico

Bayamon Central University *A*
ICPR Junior College *A*
Inter American University of Puerto Rico
    Barranquitas Campus *A, B*
    Bayamon Campus *C, A, B*
    Fajardo Campus *A*
    Metropolitan Campus *B*
    San German Campus *B*
Technological College of San Juan *C, A*
Universidad Metropolitana *B*
Universidad del Este *C, B*
University of Puerto Rico
    Bayamon University College *A, B*
    Mayaguez Campus *B, M*
    Ponce *A, B*
    Rio Piedras Campus *B*

Rhode Island

Bryant College *B, M*
Providence College *B*
Roger Williams University *B*
University of Rhode Island *B, M*

South Carolina

Anderson College *B*
Benedict College *B*
The Citadel *B*
Claflin University *B*
Clemson University *B, M, D*
Coastal Carolina University *B*
College of Charleston *B*
Columbia College *B*
Converse College *B*
Denmark Technical College *C*
Forrest Junior College *C, A*
Francis Marion University *B*
Lander University *B*
Limestone College *A, B*
South Carolina State University *B*

Spartanburg Technical College *C, A*
Technical College of the
    Lowcountry *C, A*
Tri-County Technical College *C, A*
University of South Carolina *B, M, D*
University of South Carolina
    Spartanburg *B*
Voorhees College *B*
Williamsburg Technical College *C, A*
Winthrop University *B*
Wofford College *B*
York Technical College *C*

South Dakota

Black Hills State University *A*
Dakota State University *B, M*
Kilian Community College *C, A*
Mount Marty College *B*
South Dakota State University *B, T*
Southeast Technical Institute *A*
University of Sioux Falls *B*
University of South Dakota *B, M*

Tennessee

Austin Peay State University *B*
Carson-Newman College *B*
Columbia State Community College *A*
Draughons Junior College of Business:
    Nashville *A*
Draughons Junior College:
    Clarksville *C, A*
East Tennessee State University *B, M*
Jackson State Community College *A*
Lambuth University *B*
Maryville College *B*
Middle Tennessee State University *B*
Miller-Motte Technical College *C, A*
Milligan College *B*
Northeast State Technical Community
    College *C, A*
Remington College
    Southeast College of Technology *A*
Roane State Community College *A*
Southwest Tennessee Community
    College *A*
Tennessee State University *B*
Tennessee Technological University *B*
Tennessee Wesleyan College *B*
Trevecca Nazarene University *B*
Tusculum College *B*
Union University *B, T*
University of Tennessee
    Chattanooga *C, B, M*
    Knoxville *B, M, D*
Vanderbilt University *B, M, D*
Walters State Community College *C, A*

Texas

Abilene Christian University *B*
Amarillo College *C, A*
Angelina College *A*
Angelo State University *B, T*
Austin Community College *A*
Blinn College *A*
Brazosport College *A*
Cedar Valley College *A*
Central Texas College *C, A*
Cisco Junior College *C, A*
Clarendon College *A*
Coastal Bend College *A*
College of the Mainland *A*
Collin County Community College
    District *C, A*
Dallas Baptist University *B*
Del Mar College *A*
East Texas Baptist University *B*
Eastfield College *C, A*
El Centro College *A*
El Paso Community College *C, A*
Frank Phillips College *C, A*
Galveston College *A*
Grayson County College *C, A*
Hardin-Simmons University *B*
Hill College *C, A*
Houston Baptist University *B*

Houston Community College
    System *C, A*
Howard College *C, A*
Huston-Tillotson College *B*
ITT Technical Institute
    Austin *A*
    Houston North *A*
Jarvis Christian College *B*
Kilgore College *A*
Lamar State College at Orange *C, A*
Lamar State College at Port Arthur *C, A*
Lamar University *B*
Laredo Community College *A*
LeTourneau University *B*
Lee College *C, A*
Lubbock Christian University *B, T*
McLennan Community College *C, A*
McMurry University *B*
Midland College *A*
Midwestern State University *B, M*
Mountain View College *A*
North Central Texas College *A*
North Harris Montgomery Community
    College District *C, A*
North Lake College *A*
Northeast Texas Community
    College *C, A*
Northwood University: Texas Campus *B*
Palo Alto College *A*
Panola College *A*
Paul Quinn College *B*
Prairie View A&M University *B*
Ranger College *C, A*
Remington College
    Houston *A*
Rice University *B*
Richland College *A*
St. Edward's University *B, M, T*
St. Mary's University *B, M*
Sam Houston State University *B, M*
San Antonio College *C, A*
San Jacinto College
    Central Campus *C*
Schreiner University *B*
South Plains College *A*
Southern Methodist University *B, M, D*
Southwest Texas Junior College *A*
Southwest Texas State University *B, M*
Southwestern Adventist University *B*
Southwestern University *B, T*
Stephen F. Austin State
    University *B, M, T*
Sul Ross State University *B*
Tarleton State University *B, T*
Tarrant County College *C, A*
Temple College *C, A*
Texas A&M University *B, M, D*
Texas A&M University
    Commerce *B*
    Corpus Christi *B, M*
Texas Christian University *B, T*
Texas Lutheran University *B*
Texas Southern University *B*
Texas State Technical College
    Waco *A*
    West Texas *A*
Texas Tech University *B, M, D*
Texas Wesleyan University *B*
Texas Woman's University *B, T*
Trinity University *B*
Trinity Valley Community College *C, A*
Tyler Junior College *C, A*
University of Dallas *B*
University of Houston *B, M, D*
University of Houston
    Clear Lake *B, M*
    Downtown *B*
    Victoria *B, T*
University of Mary Hardin-Baylor *B*
University of North Texas *B, D*

University of Texas
Arlington *M, D*
Austin *B, M, D*
Dallas *B, M, D*
El Paso *B, M*
San Antonio *B, M, D*
Tyler *B, M*
of the Permian Basin *B*
West Texas A&M University *B*
Western Texas College *A*

Utah

Brigham Young University *B, M, D*
College of Eastern Utah *C*
ITT Technical Institute
Murray *A*
Salt Lake Community College *C, A*
Snow College *A*
Utah Career College *A*
Utah State University *B, M*
Weber State University *A, B*

Vermont

Bennington College *B*
Castleton State College *B*
Champlain College *A, B*
College of St, Joseph in Vermont *A, B*
Johnson State College *A, B*
Lyndon State College *A, B*
Marlboro College *B*
Norwich University *B*
University of Vermont *B, M*

Virginia

Blue Ridge Community College *C, A*
Bluefield College *B*
Bryant & Stratton College *A*
College of William and Mary *B, M, D*
Danville Community College *A*
ECPI College of Technology *C, A*
ECPI Technical College
Glen Allen *A*
ECPI Technical College: Roanoke *A*
Eastern Shore Community College *C, A*
Emory & Henry College *B*
George Mason University *B, M, D*
Hampton University *B*
J. Sargeant Reynolds Community
College *A*
James Madison University *B, M*
Liberty University *B*
Longwood University *B, T*
Lynchburg College *B*
Mary Baldwin College *B*
Marymount University *B*
Mountain Empire Community College *A*
National College of Business &
Technology
Lynchburg *A*
Norfolk State University *B*
Old Dominion University *B, M, D*
Paul D. Camp Community College *C, A*
Piedmont Virginia Community
College *C, A*
Radford University *B*
Randolph-Macon College *B*
Roanoke College *B*
Southside Virginia Community
College *C, A*
Southwest Virginia Community
College *A*
Thomas Nelson Community
College *C, A*
University of Virginia *B, M, D*
University of Virginia's College at
Wise *B*
Virginia Commonwealth
University *B, M*
Virginia Highlands Community
College *A*
Virginia Intermont College *B, T*
Virginia Polytechnic Institute and State
University *B, M, D*
Virginia Union University *B*
Virginia Western Community
College *C, A*

Washington and Lee University *B*

Washington

Bellevue Community College *C, A*
Central Washington University *B*
Centralia College *A*
Edmonds Community College *C, A*
Everett Community College *C, A*
Grays Harbor College *A*
Heritage College *C, A, B*
ITT Technical Institute
Seattle *A*
Lower Columbia College *A*
North Seattle Community College *C, A*
Pacific Lutheran University *B*
Peninsula College *A*
Renton Technical College *C*
St. Martin's College *B*
Seattle Central Community College *C, A*
Seattle Pacific University *B*
South Seattle Community College *C, A*
Spokane Falls Community College *C, A*
University of Puget Sound *B, T*
University of Washington *B, M, D*
Walla Walla College *B*
Walla Walla Community College *C, A*
Western Washington University *B*
Whitworth College *B*

West Virginia

Alderson-Broaddus College *B*
Bethany College *B*
Bluefield State College *A, B*
Concord College *B*
Fairmont State College *B*
Huntington Junior College *A*
International Academy of Design and
Technology *A*
Mountain State College *A*
Mountain State University *A, B*
Potomac State College of West Virginia
University *A*
Salem International University *A, B*
Shepherd College *B*
Southern West Virginia Community and
Technical College *A*
University of Charleston *A, B*
West Virginia Junior College:
Charleston *A*
West Virginia State College *A*
West Virginia University *M*
West Virginia University Institute of
Technology *B*
West Virginia University at
Parkersburg *A*
West Virginia Wesleyan College *B*

Wisconsin

Alverno College *B*
Carroll College *B*
Carthage College *B*
Chippewa Valley Technical College *A*
Edgewood College *B*
Fox Valley Technical College *C*
ITT Technical Institute
Green Bay *A*
Lac Courte Oreilles Ojibwa Community
College *C*
Lakeland College *B*
Lakeshore Technical College *A*
Lawrence University *B*
Marquette University *C, B*
Milwaukee Area Technical College *A*
Nicolet Area Technical College *A*
Northland College *B*
Ripon College *B*
St. Norbert College *B*
University of Wisconsin
Eau Claire *B*
Madison *B, M, D*
Milwaukee *M*
Parkside *M*
River Falls *B*
Stevens Point *B*
Superior *B*
Whitewater *B, T*

Waukesha County Technical College *A*
Wisconsin Indianhead Technical
College *C, A*

Wyoming

Central Wyoming College *A*
Sheridan College *A*
Western Wyoming Community
College *A*

Computer/systems security

Arizona

South Mountain Community
College *C, A*

California

ITT Technical Institute
San Bernardino *B*

Colorado

Colorado Technical University *C, M*

Florida

Florida State University *M*
ITT Technical Institute
Ft. Lauderdale *B*
Maitland *B*
St. Petersburg College *C, A*

Minnesota

Capella University *C, B, M*
Globe College *C, A, B*
Hennepin Technical College *C, A*
Hibbing Community College: A
Technical and Community College *A*

Missouri

Jefferson College *C, A*

New York

Jamestown Community College *A*
Rochester Institute of Technology *B*

North Carolina

Montreat College *B*

Puerto Rico

Atlantic College *B*

Texas

ITT Technical Institute
Houston North *A*

Utah

ITT Technical Institute
Murray *B*

Virginia

ECPI College of Technology *C, A*
ECPI Technical College: Roanoke *A*

Washington

Clover Park Technical College *A*
ITT Technical Institute
Seattle *B*

Conducting

Alabama

Alabama Agricultural and Mechanical
University *B*
Troy State University *M*

Alaska

University of Alaska
Fairbanks *M*

Arizona

University of Arizona *M*

California

Azusa Pacific University *M*
Bethesda Christian University *B, M*
California State University
Long Beach *B, M*
Chapman University *B*
San Diego State University *M*

San Francisco State University *M*
University of Southern California *M, D*

Connecticut

University of Hartford *M, D*

District of Columbia

Catholic University of America *M, D*
Howard University *B*

Florida

Florida State University *M*
University of Miami *M, D*

Illinois

Northwestern University *D*
Roosevelt University *B*

Indiana

American Conservatory of Music *M, D*
Butler University *M*
Indiana University
Bloomington *B*
Indiana University-Purdue University
Fort Wayne *T*

Iowa

University of Iowa *M*

Kansas

University of Kansas *M, D*

Kentucky

Campbellsville University *B*

Louisiana

Loyola University New Orleans *B, M*
University of New Orleans *M*

Maryland

Johns Hopkins University *B, M, D*
Johns Hopkins University: Peabody
Conservatory of Music *M, D*

Massachusetts

Boston Conservatory *M*
New England Conservatory of
Music *B, M, D*

Michigan

Calvin College *B*
Michigan State University *M*
University of Michigan *D*

Minnesota

Concordia College: Moorhead *B*

Mississippi

Mississippi College *M*

Missouri

Hannibal-LaGrange College *B*
University of Missouri
Kansas City *M, D*
Webster University *M*

New Jersey

Rider University *M*

New York

Bard College *B*
Eastman School of Music of the
University of Rochester *M, D*
Ithaca College *M*
Juilliard School *M*
Manhattan School of Music *M*
Mannes College of Music *B, M*
University of Rochester *M, D*

Ohio

Bowling Green State University *M*
Cleveland Institute of Music *B, M*
Kent State University *M*
Kent State University
Stark Campus *B*
Oberlin College *B, M*
Ohio University *M*
University of Cincinnati *B, M, D*

Oklahoma

University of Oklahoma *M, D*

Oregon
Portland State University *M*

Pennsylvania
Carnegie Mellon University *M*
Mercyhurst College *B*
Penn State
    University Park *M*
Temple University *M*

South Carolina
Columbia College *B*
University of South Carolina *M, D*

Texas
Arlington Baptist College *B*
Baylor University *M*
Concordia University at Austin *B*
Sam Houston State University *M*
Southern Methodist University *M*
Stephen F. Austin State University *M*
Texas Christian University *M*
Texas Tech University *D*
University of Houston *D*

Utah
Brigham Young University *M*
University of Utah *M*

Vermont
Bennington College *B*

Virginia
Shenandoah University *M*

Washington
University of Washington *M, D*

Wisconsin
University of Wisconsin
    Madison *B, M*

Conservation biology

Arizona
Arizona State University *B*

California
University of California
    Riverside *B*

New York
State University of New York
    Albany *B*
    College of Agriculture and
        Technology at Morrisville *A*

Pennsylvania
Cedar Crest College *B*

Construction engineering

California
California State University
    Chico *B*
University of Southern California *B, M*

Indiana
Vincennes University *A*

Iowa
Iowa State University *B*

Massachusetts
Worcester Polytechnic Institute *M*

New York
State University of New York
    Buffalo *M, D*
    College of Agriculture and
        Technology at Morrisville *A*
    College of Environmental Science
        and Forestry *B, M, D*

North Carolina
North Carolina State University *B*

North Dakota
North Dakota State University *B*

Oregon
Oregon State University *B*

Utah
Brigham Young University *B*

Construction management

Florida
University of Florida *M*

Kansas
University of Kansas *M*

Massachusetts
Wentworth Institute of Technology *A, B*

Mississippi
Mississippi State University *B*

New York
New York University *M*
Pratt Institute *B*
State University of New York
    College of Agriculture and
        Technology at Morrisville *A*

North Dakota
North Dakota State University *B*

Oklahoma
Oklahoma State University
    Oklahoma City *A*

Pennsylvania
Delaware County Community College *C*

Texas
St. Philip's College *A*

Virginia
Piedmont Virginia Community
    College *A*

Washington
University of Washington *B*

Wisconsin
Milwaukee School of Engineering *B*

Construction trades

Alabama
Shelton State Community College *C*

California
Foothill College *C*
Sierra College *C*

Colorado
Red Rocks Community College *C, A*

Illinois
Kaskaskia College *C*

Indiana
Vincennes University *A*

Iowa
North Iowa Area Community College *C*

New York
State University of New York
    College of Agriculture and
        Technology at Morrisville *A*

North Dakota
North Dakota State College of Science *A*

Pennsylvania
Community College of Allegheny
    County *C, A*

Utah
Utah Valley State College *C, A*

Washington
Clover Park Technical College *C*

Wisconsin
Fox Valley Technical College *A*

Wyoming
Sheridan College *A*

Construction/building technologies

Alabama
Community College of the Air Force *A*
Jefferson State Community College *C, A*
Lawson State Community College *C*
Northwest-Shoals Community College *C*
Shelton State Community College *C*
Tuskegee University *B*

Arizona
Northern Arizona University *B*

Arkansas
University of Arkansas
    Little Rock *B*

California
Antelope Valley College *C, A*
California State Polytechnic University:
    Pomona *B*
California State University
    Chico *B*
    Fresno *B*
    Long Beach *B*
College of the Redwoods *A*
College of the Sequoias *C, A*
Don Bosco Technical Institute *A*
Feather River College *C, A*
Los Angeles Pierce College *A*
Riverside Community College *C, A*
San Diego Mesa College *C, A*
San Joaquin Delta College *C*
Santa Rosa Junior College *C*
Shasta College *C, A*
Sierra College *A*

Colorado
Colorado State University *B*
Red Rocks Community College *C, A*
Trinidad State Junior College *A*

Connecticut
Central Connecticut State University *B*
Norwalk Community College *C, A*

Delaware
Delaware Technical and Community
    College
    Terry Campus *A*

Florida
Daytona Beach Community College *A*
Florida Agricultural and Mechanical
    University *B*
Florida International University *B*
Gulf Coast Community College *A*
Indian River Community College *A*
Manatee Community College *A*
Palm Beach Community College *A*
Pensacola Junior College *A*
Polk Community College *A*
St. Petersburg College *C, A*
Seminole Community College *A*
South Florida Community College *A*
Tallahassee Community College *A*
University of Florida *B*
University of North Florida *B*
University of West Florida *B*
Valencia Community College *A*

Georgia
Georgia Southern University *B*
Southern Polytechnic State
    University *C, B*

Idaho
Boise State University *B*
Brigham Young University - Idaho *A*
Idaho State University *C, A*

Illinois
College of Lake County *C, A*
Joliet Junior College *C, A*

Morrison Institute of Technology *A*
Oakton Community College *A*
Parkland College *A*
Rock Valley College *C, A*
South Suburban College of Cook
    County *C, A*
Southern Illinois University
    Edwardsville *B*
Southwestern Illinois College *C, A*
Triton College *C, A*

Indiana
Indiana University-Purdue University
    Fort Wayne *B*
Purdue University
    Calumet *B*
Tri-State University *A*
Vincennes University *A*

Iowa
Southeastern Community College
    North Campus *A*

Kansas
Kansas State University *B*
Pittsburg State University *B*

Kentucky
Murray State University *A*

Louisiana
Grambling State University *B*
University of Louisiana at Monroe *B*

Maryland
Community College of Baltimore County
    Catonsville *C, A*
    Dundalk *C, A*
    Essex *C, A*

Massachusetts
Cape Cod Community College *C*
Fitchburg State College *B*
Wentworth Institute of Technology *A, B*

Michigan
Alpena Community College *A*
Central Michigan University *B*
Lawrence Technological University *A*
Macomb Community College *C, A*
Mott Community College *A*
Northern Michigan University *C, B*
Washtenaw Community College *A*
Western Michigan University *B*

Minnesota
Hennepin Technical College *C, A*
Inver Hills Community College *A*
Lake Superior College: A Community
    and Technical College *C, A*
Minnesota State University
    Moorhead *B*
St. Cloud Technical College *C, A*

Missouri
Central Missouri State University *A, B*
Mineral Area College *C, A*
Ozarks Technical Community
    College *C, A*
Southwest Missouri State University *B*

Montana
Montana State University
    Bozeman *B*

Nebraska
Mid Plains Community College
    Area *C, A*
University of Nebraska
    Lincoln *B*
    Omaha *B*

Nevada
Great Basin College *A*
University of Nevada
    Las Vegas *B*

New Hampshire
New Hampshire Community Technical
College
Manchester *C, A*
University of New Hampshire *A*

New Jersey
Cumberland County College *C, A*
Essex County College *A*
Fairleigh Dickinson University
Metropolitan Campus *B*
Ocean County College *C*
Thomas Edison State College *B*

New Mexico
Santa Fe Community College *C, A*
Western New Mexico University *C, A*

New York
Dutchess Community College *A*
Fulton-Montgomery Community
College *A*
Monroe Community College *A*
Onondaga Community College *A*
State University of New York
College of Agriculture and
Technology at Morrisville *A*
College of Environmental Science
and Forestry *B*
College of Technology at
Alfred *A, B*
College of Technology at Canton *A*
College of Technology at Delhi *A*
Farmingdale *A, B*
Suffolk County Community College *A*
Tompkins-Cortland Community
College *A*

North Carolina
College of the Albemarle *C*
Guilford Technical Community
College *A*
Mitchell Community College *C, A*
Vance-Granville Community College *C*
Western Carolina University *B*
Western Piedmont Community
College *C, A*

North Dakota
North Dakota State College of Science *A*

Ohio
Bowling Green State University *B*
Cincinnati State Technical and
Community College *A*
Clark State Community College *A*
Columbus State Community College *A*
Jefferson Community College *A*
Lakeland Community College *C*
Ohio State University
Columbus Campus *C, B*
Owens Community College
Toledo *C, A*
Stark State College of Technology *A*
University of Akron *C, A, B*
University of Toledo *A, B*

Oklahoma
Oklahoma State University *B*
Oklahoma State University
Oklahoma City *C, A*
Okmulgee *A*
Western Oklahoma State College *A*

Oregon
Chemeketa Community College *A*
Clackamas Community College *C, A*
Lane Community College *C, A*
Portland Community College *C, A*
Rogue Community College *C*
Treasure Valley Community College *A*

Pennsylvania
Community College of Allegheny
County *C*
Community College of Philadelphia *A*
Delaware County Community College *A*

Harrisburg Area Community
College *C, A*
Lehigh Carbon Community College *A*
New Castle School of Trades *A*
Penn State
University Park *C*
Pennsylvania College of
Technology *A, B*

Puerto Rico
University of Puerto Rico
Bayamon University College *A*

South Carolina
Aiken Technical College *C*
Midlands Technical College *C*
Piedmont Technical College *C, A*
Technical College of the
Lowcountry *C, A*
Trident Technical College *C*

Texas
Brazosport College *C, A*
Houston Community College
System *C, A*
Howard College *C*
Midland College *C*
St. Philip's College *C, A*
Sam Houston State University *B*
Southwest Texas State University *B*
Tarleton State University *B*
Texas A&M University *B*
Texas A&M University
Commerce *B*
University of Houston *B*
University of North Texas *B*

Utah
Salt Lake Community College *C, A*

Vermont
Vermont Technical College *A*

Virginia
J. Sargeant Reynolds Community
College *C*
Norfolk State University *B*

Washington
Central Washington University *B*
Clark College *C, A*
Eastern Washington University *B*
Edmonds Community College *C, A*
Spokane Community College *C, A*
Washington State University *B*

West Virginia
Fairmont State College *A, B*

Wisconsin
University of Wisconsin
Stout *B*
Waukesha County Technical College *C*

Wyoming
Casper College *A*

Consumer economics

California
Long Beach City College *C, A*

Illinois
University of Illinois
Urbana-Champaign *B*

Louisiana
Southeastern Louisiana University *B*

Michigan
Western Michigan University *M*

Minnesota
Vermilion Community College *A*

Nebraska
University of Nebraska
Omaha *B*

Pennsylvania
Indiana University of Pennsylvania *B*

Tennessee
University of Memphis *B, M*

Virginia
Norfolk State University *B*

Consumer merchandising

Oregon
Oregon State University *B*

**Consumer services/
advocacy**

Florida
Pensacola Junior College *A*

**Correctional facilities
administration**

Arizona
Arizona Western College *C*

Connecticut
University of New Haven *B*

Michigan
Baker College
of Muskegon *C, A*
Northern Michigan University *A*

Virginia
Bluefield College *B*

Corrections

Arizona
Central Arizona College *C, A*
Eastern Arizona College *A*

California
California State University
Hayward *B*
Stanislaus *B*
College of the Redwoods *C*
Gavilan Community College *C, A*
Grossmont Community College *C, A*
Imperial Valley College *C, A*
Taft College *C, A*

Connecticut
Naugatuck Valley Community College *A*
University of New Haven *B*

Delaware
Wilmington College *M*

District of Columbia
University of the District of Columbia *A*

Florida
Gulf Coast Community College *C*
Hillsborough Community College *C*
Lake City Community College *C*
Palm Beach Community College *C*
St. Petersburg College *C*
South Florida Community College *C*
Valencia Community College *C*

Illinois
Bradley University *B*
City Colleges of Chicago
Harold Washington College *A*
Elgin Community College *A*
Heartland Community College *C, A*
Rend Lake College *C*
Triton College *C*

Indiana
Vincennes University *A*

Iowa
Simpson College *B*

Kansas
Kansas City Kansas Community
College *A*
Labette Community College *A*
Washburn University of Topeka *B*

Kentucky
Hopkinsville Community College *C*

Maryland
Community College of Baltimore County
Catonsville *C, A*
Dundalk *C, A*
Essex *C, A*
Hagerstown Community College *C*
University of Baltimore *C*

Massachusetts
Northeastern University *B*

Michigan
Alpena Community College *C, A*
Baker College
of Port Huron *C, A*
Ferris State University *M*
Glen Oaks Community College *C*
Gogebic Community College *C*
Grand Rapids Community College *A*
Kellogg Community College *C, A*
Kirtland Community College *C, A*
Marygrove College *C, A*
Northwestern Michigan College *C*
St. Clair County Community College *C*
Schoolcraft College *A*
Washtenaw Community College *A*

Minnesota
Lake Superior College: A Community
and Technical College *C*
Minnesota State University
Mankato *A*
Northland Community & Technical
College *A*
Winona State University *B*

Missouri
College of the Ozarks *B*
Longview Community College *C, A*
Penn Valley Community College *C, A*
St. Louis University *B*
Southeast Missouri State University *B*

Nevada
Community College of Southern
Nevada *A*
Truckee Meadows Community
College *A*
Western Nevada Community
College *C, A*

New Hampshire
College for Lifelong Learning *B*
Hesser College *C, A*

New Jersey
Burlington County College *C*
Middlesex County College *A*
Union County College *C*

New Mexico
New Mexico Junior College *C*
University of New Mexico *B*

New York
Cayuga County Community College *C*
Corning Community College *A*
Monroe Community College *C, A*
Westchester Community College *A*

Ohio
Clark State Community College *A*
Columbus State Community College *A*
Cuyahoga Community College
Eastern Campus *A*
Metropolitan Campus *A*
Western Campus *A*
Hocking Technical College *A*

James A. Rhodes State College *A*
Lakeland Community College *C, A*
Northwest State Community College *A*
Southern State Community College *A*
Tiffin University *B*
University of Akron *B*
Washington State Community College *A*
Xavier University *C, A*
Youngstown State University *A, B*

Oklahoma

Langston University *B*
Oklahoma Panhandle State University *A*
Western Oklahoma State College *A*

Oregon

Clackamas Community College *C, A*
Clatsop Community College *C*

Pennsylvania

Bucks County Community College *A*
Community College of Allegheny
  County *A*
ICM School of Business & Medical
  Careers *A*
University of Pittsburgh *B*
University of Pittsburgh
  Bradford *B*
York College of Pennsylvania *A, B*

Puerto Rico

Universidad Metropolitana *B*

Rhode Island

Community College of Rhode Island *A*

Texas

Alvin Community College *C*
Amarillo College *A*
Central Texas College *C*
Coastal Bend College *C, A*
El Paso Community College *C, A*
Hardin-Simmons University *B*
Lamar State College at Orange *C*
Southwest Texas State University *B*
Stephen F. Austin State University *B*
University of Texas
  Brownsville *B*
Western Texas College *A*

Utah

Weber State University *B*

Virginia

Mountain Empire Community College *A*
Southwest Virginia Community
  College *A*

Washington

Everett Community College *A*
Spokane Community College *C, A*
Walla Walla Community College *A*

West Virginia

Bluefield State College *A*
Glenville State College *A*

Wisconsin

Moraine Park Technical College *A*

Cosmetic services

Alabama

Alabama Southern Community
  College *A*
Bishop State Community College *C*
Calhoun Community College *C*
Douglas MacArthur State Technical
  College *C*
Gadsden State Community College *C*
George C. Wallace State Community
  College
  Dothan *C*
Harry M. Ayers State Technical
  College *C*
J. F. Drake State Technical College *C*
Northwest-Shoals Community College *C*
Reid State Technical College *C*

Shelton State Community College *C*
Wallace State Community College at
  Hanceville *C*

California

Citrus College *C, A*
College of the Sequoias *C, A*
College of the Siskiyous *C*
Contra Costa College *A*
Fashion Institute of Design and
  Merchandising *A*
Gavilan Community College *C, A*
Glendale Community College *A*
Golden West College *C, A*
Laney College *C, A*
Los Medanos College *C*
MiraCosta College *C, A*
Napa Valley College *C*
Riverside Community College *C, A*
Santa Barbara City College *C, A*
Santiago Canyon College *A*

Colorado

Trinidad State Junior College *C, A*

Florida

Daytona Beach Community College *C*
Indian River Community College *C*
Lake City Community College *C*
New England Institute of Technology *C*
Palm Beach Community College *C*
Pasco-Hernando Community College *C*
Pensacola Junior College *C*
South Florida Community College *C*

Georgia

Chattahoochee Technical College *C*
Columbus Technical College *C*
DeKalb Technical College *C*
Southwest Georgia Technical College *C*
Waycross College *A*

Hawaii

University of Hawaii
  Honolulu Community College *C, A*

Idaho

Idaho State University *C*

Illinois

College of DuPage *C, A*
Danville Area Community College *C, A*
Gem City College *C*
Illinois Eastern Community Colleges
  Olney Central College *C*
John A. Logan College *C, A*
Kaskaskia College *C*
Lake Land College *C*
Southwestern Illinois College *C*

Indiana

Vincennes University *A*

Iowa

Southeastern Community College
  North Campus *C*

Kansas

Garden City Community College *C*
Johnson County Community College *C*

Massachusetts

Greenfield Community College *C, A*
Springfield Technical Community
  College *C*

Michigan

Gogebic Community College *C*
Kirtland Community College *C*
Lansing Community College *A*
Montcalm Community College *C, A*
Mott Community College *C*
Northern Michigan University *C*

Minnesota

Century Community and Technical
  College *C*
Minneapolis Community and Technical
  College *C*

Minnesota State College - Southeast
  Technical *C, A*
Northland Community & Technical
  College *C*

Mississippi

Coahoma Community College *C*
Holmes Community College *C*
Mississippi Gulf Coast Community
  College
  Perkinston *C*
Pearl River Community College *C*

Montana

University of Montana-Missoula *C*

Nebraska

Western Nebraska Community
  College *C, A*

New Jersey

Ocean County College *C*

New Mexico

Albuquerque Technical-Vocational
  Institute *A*
New Mexico Junior College *C, A*
San Juan College *C*

North Carolina

Alamance Community College *C*
Beaufort County Community College *C*
Bladen Community College *C*
Blue Ridge Community College *C*
Brunswick Community College *C, A*
Caldwell Community College and
  Technical Institute *C*
Cape Fear Community College *C, A*
Carteret Community College *C*
Central Carolina Community College *A*
Cleveland Community College *C*
Coastal Carolina Community College *C*
College of the Albemarle *C*
Craven Community College *C*
Davidson County Community College *C*
Fayetteville Technical Community
  College *C*
Guilford Technical Community
  College *C, A*
Haywood Community College *C, A*
Isothermal Community College *C, A*
James Sprunt Community College *C, A*
Johnston Community College *C*
Martin Community College *C*
Mayland Community College *C, A*
Mitchell Community College *C*
Nash Community College *C*
Piedmont Community College *C, A*
Roanoke-Chowan Community
  College *C*
Rockingham Community College *C*
Sampson Community College *A*
Sandhills Community College *C, A*
Southeastern Community College *C*
Stanly Community College *C*
Vance-Granville Community College *C*
Wayne Community College *C*

Ohio

Lorain County Community College *A*

Oregon

Mount Hood Community College *A*
Umpqua Community College *A*

Pennsylvania

Butler County Community College *C*
Delaware County Community College *C*

South Carolina

Denmark Technical College *C*
Florence-Darlington Technical
  College *C*
Technical College of the
  Lowcountry *C, A*
Trident Technical College *C*

Texas

Central Texas College *C*

Del Mar College *C*
Frank Phillips College *C*
Grayson County College *A*
Houston Community College
  System *C, A*
Kilgore College *C*
Lamar State College at Port Arthur *C, A*
Lee College *A*
McLennan Community College *C*
North Harris Montgomery Community
  College District *C, A*
Northeast Texas Community
  College *C, A*
Odessa College *C, A*
Panola College *C*
Ranger College *C*
San Jacinto College
  Central Campus *C*
Texarkana College *C*
Trinity Valley Community College *C*

Utah

College of Eastern Utah *A*
Salt Lake Community College *A*

Washington

Clover Park Technical College *C*
Lake Washington Technical College *C*
Olympic College *C, A*
Renton Technical College *C*
South Seattle Community College *C, A*
Spokane Community College *C, A*
Walla Walla Community College *C, A*

Wisconsin

Chippewa Valley Technical College *C*
Mid-State Technical College *C*
Milwaukee Area Technical College *A*
Moraine Park Technical College *C*
Nicolet Area Technical College *C*
Wisconsin Indianhead Technical
  College *C*

Wyoming

Eastern Wyoming College *C, A*

Cosmetology

Alabama

Lawson State Community College *C*

California

Yuba Community College District *C, A*

Georgia

Savannah Technical College *C*
West Georgia Technical College *C*

Iowa

Southeastern Community College
  South Campus *C*

Kansas

Seward County Community
  College *C, A*

Kentucky

Somerset Community College *C*

Michigan

Oakland Community College *C, A*

North Carolina

Pamlico Community College *C*

Washington

Everett Community College *C*
Walla Walla Community College *A*

Counseling psychology

Alabama

Alabama Agricultural and Mechanical
  University *M*
Auburn University *D*
Samford University *B*
Troy State University *M*

Troy State University in Montgomery *M*
University of Alabama *M*
University of North Alabama *M*

Alaska
Alaska Pacific University *M*

Arizona
Northern Arizona University *M*
Prescott College *B, M*
Southwestern College *B*
University of Phoenix *M*

Arkansas
Arkansas State University *M*
Central Baptist College *B*
John Brown University *B*
University of Central Arkansas *M*

California
California Baptist University *M*
California State University
   Bakersfield *M*
   Chico *T*
   Fullerton *M*
   Hayward *M*
   Long Beach *M*
   Sacramento *M*
   Stanislaus *M*
Christian Heritage College *B*
Dominican University of California *M*
East Los Angeles College *A*
Holy Names College *M*
Hope International University *M*
John F. Kennedy University *M*
Loyola Marymount University *M*
Mount St. Mary's College *M*
National University *M, T*
Pacific Oaks College *M*
Santa Clara University *M*
University of California
   Santa Barbara *M, D*
University of La Verne *M*
University of Southern California *M, D*

Colorado
Colorado Christian University *M*
Naropa University *M*
University of Denver *M, D*
University of Northern Colorado *M, D*

Connecticut
Asnuntuck Community College *A*
Southern Connecticut State University *M*
University of Hartford *M*

Delaware
Wilmington College *M*

District of Columbia
George Washington University *M*
Howard University *M*

Florida
Barry University *M, D*
Carlos Albizu University *M*
Nova Southeastern University *M*
Palm Beach Atlantic University *M*
Rollins College *M*
St. Thomas University *M*
University of Florida *D*
University of Miami *M, D*
University of North Florida *M*
University of West Florida *M*

Georgia
Clark Atlanta University *M, D*
Georgia State University *D*
North Georgia College & State
   University *M*
Toccoa Falls College *B*
University of Georgia *D*
Valdosta State University *M*

Hawaii
Chaminade University of Honolulu *M*

Illinois
Adler School of Professional
   Psychology *M*

Blackburn College *B*
Chicago State University *M*
Governors State University *M*
Lewis University *M*
Loyola University of Chicago *M, D*
Northwestern University *B, M, D*
Olivet Nazarene University *M*
Roosevelt University *M*
St. Xavier University *M*
Trinity International University *M*
University of Illinois
   Springfield *M*

Indiana
Ball State University *M, D*
Grace College *M*
Indiana State University *M*
Indiana Wesleyan University *A, B, M*
Manchester College *B*
Martin University *B*
University of St. Francis *M*
Valparaiso University *M*

Iowa
Morningside College *B*
University of Iowa *D*

Kansas
Kansas Wesleyan University *B*
MidAmerica Nazarene University *M*
Newman University *B*
Pittsburg State University *B, M, T*
University of Kansas *M, D*

Kentucky
Kentucky Christian College *B*
Lindsey Wilson College *M*

Louisiana
Louisiana Tech University *D*
Nicholls State University *M*
Southern University and Agricultural and
   Mechanical College *M*

Maine
University of Maine *M, D*
University of New England *B*

Maryland
Allegany College *A*
Bowie State University *M*
Columbia Union College *B*
Coppin State College *B, M*
Frostburg State University *M*
Johns Hopkins University *M, D*
Loyola College in Maryland *M*
Towson University *T*
University of Baltimore *M*

Massachusetts
Anna Maria College *B, M*
Assumption College *M*
Boston University *D*
Clark University *M, D*
Emmanuel College *B*
Fitchburg State College *M*
Framingham State College *M*
Lesley University *B, M, T*
Northeastern University *M, D*
Salem State College *M*
Simon's Rock College of Bard *B*
Springfield College *M*
Suffolk University *M*
Tufts University *M*
Westfield State College *M*

Michigan
Finlandia University *B*
Michigan State University *M, D*
Western Michigan University *M, D*

Minnesota
Bethel College *M*
Capella University *M, D*
Crossroads College *B*
Minnesota State University
   Mankato *M*
St. Cloud State University *M*
St. Mary's University of Minnesota *M*

University of St. Thomas *M, D*

Mississippi
Mississippi College *M*
University of Southern Mississippi *M, D*

Missouri
Avila University *M*
Central Missouri State University *M*
Lindenwood University *M*
Northwest Missouri State University *M*
Ozark Christian College *B*
Southeast Missouri State University *M*
University of Missouri
   Columbia *M, D*
   Kansas City *M, D*
Webster University *M*

Montana
University of Great Falls *B, M*

Nebraska
Chadron State College *M*
Doane College *M*
Nebraska Indian Community College *A*
Wayne State College *B*

Nevada
University of Nevada
   Las Vegas *M*

New Hampshire
Rivier College *M*

New Jersey
Caldwell College *M*
Centenary College *M*
College of St. Elizabeth *M*
Georgian Court College *M*
Monmouth University *M*
New Jersey City University *M*
Rider University *M*
Seton Hall University *D*

New Mexico
New Mexico State University *D*

New York
City University of New York
   Brooklyn College *M*
College of New Rochelle *M*
Fordham University *M, D*
Marist College *M*
Mercy College *M*
Metropolitan College of New York *A, B*
New York University *D*
Pace University *M*
St. Bonaventure University *M*
State University of New York
   Albany *D*
   Buffalo *D*
   Oswego *M*

North Carolina
Appalachian State University *B, M*
Campbell University *M*
Gardner-Webb University *M*
John Wesley College *B*
Roanoke Bible College *B*

North Dakota
Trinity Bible College *B*
University of North Dakota *D*

Ohio
Circleville Bible College *B*
Franciscan University of Steubenville *M*
Heidelberg College *M*
John Carroll University *M*
University of Akron *M, D, T*
Walsh University *B, M*
Wright State University *M*

Oklahoma
East Central University *M*
Northeastern State University *M*
Northwestern Oklahoma State
   University *M*
Southeastern Oklahoma State
   University *M*

Southern Nazarene University *M*
University of Central Oklahoma *M*
University of Oklahoma *D*
University of Tulsa *M*

Oregon
George Fox University *M*
Lewis & Clark College *M*
Oregon State University *M, D*

Pennsylvania
Arcadia University *M*
Baptist Bible College of Pennsylvania *M*
Carlow College *M*
Chatham College *M*
Chestnut Hill College *B, M*
Geneva College *M*
Holy Family University *M*
Immaculata University *B, M, D*
Indiana University of Pennsylvania *M*
Kutztown University of
   Pennsylvania *B, M*
La Salle University *M*
Lancaster Bible College *M*
Marywood University *M*
Moravian College *B*
Penn State
   University Park *D*
Rosemont College *M*
Slippery Rock University of
   Pennsylvania *M*
Temple University *M, D*
University of Scranton *M*
Valley Forge Christian College *B*
Villanova University *M*
West Chester University of
   Pennsylvania *M*

Puerto Rico
Inter American University of Puerto Rico
   Metropolitan Campus *M, D*
   San German Campus *M, D*
Turabo University *M*

Rhode Island
Salve Regina University *M*

South Carolina
Coker College *B*
Columbia International University *M*
Limestone College *B*

South Dakota
Sinte Gleska University *B*

Tennessee
Freed-Hardeman University *M*
Johnson Bible College *M*
Lee University *B*
Southern Adventist University *M*
Trevecca Nazarene University *M*
University of Memphis *D*
University of Tennessee
   Knoxville *M*

Texas
Abilene Christian University *M*
Amberton University *M*
Angelo State University *M*
Dallas Baptist University *M*
Lamar University *M*
Midwestern State University *M*
Our Lady of the Lake University of San
   Antonio *M, D*
Prairie View A&M University *M*
St. Edward's University *M*
St. Mary's University *M, D*
Sam Houston State University *M*
Southern Methodist University *M*
Southwest Texas State University *M, T*
Stephen F. Austin State University *M*
Tarleton State University *B, M*
Texas A&M International University *M*
Texas A&M University *D*
Texas A&M University
   Commerce *B, M, D*
   Kingsville *M*
   Texarkana *M*

Texas Tech University *M, D*
Texas Woman's University *M, D*
University of Houston *D*
University of Houston
    Victoria *M*
University of Mary Hardin-Baylor *M*
University of North Texas *B, M, D*
University of Texas
    Tyler *M*
West Texas A&M University *M*

Vermont

Burlington College *B*
College of St. Joseph in Vermont *M*
Goddard College *M*
Johnson State College *M*
Marlboro College *B*

Virginia

Eastern Mennonite University *M*
Liberty University *M*
Longwood University *M*
Marymount University *M*

Washington

Central Washington University *M*
Eastern Washington University *M*
Gonzaga University *M*
Northwest College *B, M*
Pacific Lutheran University *M*
St. Martin's College *M*
Western Washington University *M*

West Virginia

West Virginia University *D*

Wisconsin

Marquette University *M, D*
University of Wisconsin
    Madison *M, D*
    Stout *M*
    Whitewater *M*

Counselor education

Alabama

Alabama Agricultural and Mechanical
    University *B, M*
Alabama State University *M*
Auburn University *M, D, T*
Auburn University at Montgomery *M*
Jacksonville State University *M*
Troy State University *M*
Troy State University in Montgomery *M*
University of Alabama
    Birmingham *M*
University of Montevallo *M*
University of North Alabama *M*
University of South Alabama *M, T*
University of West Alabama *M*

Alaska

University of Alaska
    Anchorage *M*
    Fairbanks *M*

Arizona

Arizona State University *M, D*
Northern Arizona University *M*
Prescott College *B, M*
University of Arizona *M, D*
University of Phoenix *M*

Arkansas

Arkansas State University *M, T*
Arkansas Tech University *M*
Harding University *B*
Henderson State University *M*
John Brown University *M*
Southern Arkansas University *M*
University of Arkansas *M, D, T*
University of Arkansas
    Little Rock *M*
University of Central Arkansas *M*

California

Azusa Pacific University *M*

California Polytechnic State University:
    San Luis Obispo *M*
California State University
    Bakersfield *M*
    Chico *T*
    Dominguez Hills *M*
    Fresno *M*
    Hayward *M, T*
    Long Beach *M*
    Northridge *M*
    Sacramento *M, T*
    San Bernardino *M*
    Stanislaus *M*
Chapman University *M, T*
Fresno Pacific University *M, T*
Humboldt State University *T*
La Sierra University *M*
Loyola Marymount University *M*
Mount St. Mary's College *M*
National University *M, T*
Point Loma Nazarene University *M*
St. Mary's College of California *M*
San Diego State University *M*
San Francisco State University *M*
San Jose State University *M*
Sonoma State University *M*
University of California
    Berkeley *T*
    Santa Barbara *M, D*
University of La Verne *M*
University of Redlands *M, T*
University of San Diego *M*
University of San Francisco *T*
University of Southern
    California *M, D, T*
Whittier College *M*

Colorado

Colorado State University
    Pueblo *M*
University of Colorado
    Colorado Springs *M*
    Denver *M*
University of Northern Colorado *M, D, T*

Connecticut

Central Connecticut State
    University *M, T*
Fairfield University *M*
St. Joseph College *M*
Southern Connecticut State University *M*
University of Bridgeport *M*
University of Hartford *M, T*
Western Connecticut State University *M*

Delaware

University of Delaware *M*
Wilmington College *M*

District of Columbia

Catholic University of America *M, D*
Gallaudet University *M*
George Washington University *M, D*
Howard University *M*
Trinity College *M*
University of the District of Columbia *M*

Florida

Barry University *M*
Carlos Albizu University *M*
Florida Agricultural and Mechanical
    University *M*
Florida Atlantic University *M*
Florida Gulf Coast University *M*
Florida International University *M*
Florida State University *M, D, T*
Nova Southeastern University *M*
St. Thomas University *M*
Stetson University *M*
University of Central Florida *M*
University of Florida *D*
University of North Florida *M*
University of South Florida *M*
University of West Florida *M*

Georgia

Albany State University *M*

Augusta State University *M*
Clark Atlanta University *M, D*
Columbus State University *M*
Fort Valley State University *M*
Georgia Southern University *M, T*
Georgia State University *D*
State University of West Georgia *M*
University of Georgia *M*

Hawaii

University of Hawaii
    Manoa *M*

Idaho

Boise State University *M, D*
Idaho State University *M, D*
Northwest Nazarene University *M*
University of Idaho *M*

Illinois

Bradley University *M*
Chicago State University *M*
Concordia University *M*
De Paul University *M*
Eastern Illinois University *M*
Governors State University *M*
Loyola University of Chicago *M, D*
Northeastern Illinois University *M*
Northern Illinois University *M, D*
Northwestern University *B*
Roosevelt University *M*
Western Illinois University *M*

Indiana

Ball State University *T*
Butler University *M*
Indiana State University *M, D*
Indiana University
    Bloomington *M, D*
    South Bend *M*
    Southeast *M*
Indiana University-Purdue University
    Fort Wayne *M*
Indiana University-Purdue University
    Indianapolis *M*
Purdue University *D, T*
Purdue University
    Calumet *M*
University of St. Francis *M*

Iowa

Buena Vista University *M*
Drake University *M*
Iowa State University *M, T*
Loras College *M*
University of Iowa *M, D*
University of Northern Iowa *M*

Kansas

Emporia State University *M*
Fort Hays State University *M*
Independence Community College *A*
Kansas State University *M, D*
Pittsburg State University *M*
Wichita State University *M*

Kentucky

Morehead State University *M*
Murray State University *M*
Spalding University *M*
University of Kentucky *M, D*
University of Louisville *M, D*

Louisiana

Louisiana State University and
    Agricultural and Mechanical
    College *M*
Louisiana Tech University *M*
Loyola University New Orleans *M*
McNeese State University *M, T*
Nicholls State University *M*
Our Lady of Holy Cross College *M*
Southeastern Louisiana University *M*
Southern University and Agricultural and
    Mechanical College *M*
University of Louisiana at Lafayette *M*
University of Louisiana at Monroe *M*
University of New Orleans *M, D*

Xavier University of Louisiana *M*

Maine

University of Maine *M, D*
University of Southern Maine *M*

Maryland

Bowie State University *M*
Frostburg State University *M*
Johns Hopkins University *M*
Loyola College in Maryland *M*
McDaniel College *M*
University of Maryland
    College Park *M, D*

Massachusetts

American International College *M*
Boston College *M, D*
Boston University *M, D, T*
Bridgewater State College *M, T*
Fitchburg State College *M, T*
Lesley University *M, T*
Northeastern University *M*
Salem State College *M*
Springfield College *M*
University of Massachusetts
    Boston *M*
Westfield State College *M*

Michigan

Andrews University *M, D*
Central Michigan University *M*
Eastern Michigan University *M*
Michigan State University *M, D*
Oakland University *M, D*
Siena Heights University *M*
Wayne State University *M, D*
Western Michigan University *M, D*

Minnesota

Minnesota State University
    Mankato *B, M*
    Moorhead *M*
St. Cloud State University *M*
Winona State University *M*

Mississippi

Delta State University *M*
Mississippi College *M*
Mississippi State University *M, T*
University of Southern Mississippi *B, M*

Missouri

Central Missouri State University *M*
Evangel University *M*
Lincoln University *M*
Lindenwood University *M*
Missouri Baptist University *M, T*
Northwest Missouri State
    University *M, T*
St. Louis University *M, D*
Southeast Missouri State University *M*
Southwest Missouri State University *M*
Stephens College *M*
Truman State University *M*
University of Missouri
    Columbia *M, D*
    Kansas City *M*
    St. Louis *M*

Montana

Montana State University
    Billings *M*
University of Montana-Missoula *M, D*

Nebraska

Chadron State College *M*
Creighton University *M*
University of Nebraska
    Kearney *M, T*
    Omaha *M*

Nevada

University of Nevada
    Las Vegas *M*
    Reno *M, D*

New Hampshire

Keene State College *M*

Plymouth State College *M*
Rivier College *M*
University of New Hampshire *M*

New Jersey
The College of New Jersey *M*
Kean University *M*
Monmouth University *M*
Montclair State University *M*
Rider University *M*
Rowan University *M*
Seton Hall University *M*
William Paterson University of New
    Jersey *M*

New Mexico
College of the Southwest *M*
Eastern New Mexico University *M*
New Mexico Highlands University *M*
New Mexico State University *M, D*
University of New Mexico *M, D, T*
Western New Mexico University *M*

New York
Alfred University *M*
Canisius College *M, T*
City University of New York
    Brooklyn College *M*
    College of Staten Island *M*
    Hunter College *M*
    Queens College *M*
College of New Rochelle *M*
Hofstra University *M, T*
Long Island University
    C. W. Post Campus *M*
Manhattan College *M*
Mercy College *M*
New York Institute of Technology *M*
New York University *M, D*
Niagara University *M*
Roberts Wesleyan College *M*
St. John's University *M, T*
St. Lawrence University *M*
State University of New York
    Albany *M*
    Buffalo *M, D, T*
    College at Brockport *M*
    College at Buffalo *M*
    College at Oneonta *M*
    College at Plattsburgh *M, T*
    Oswego *M*
Syracuse University *M, D*
University of Rochester *M*

North Carolina
Appalachian State University *M*
Campbell University *M*
East Carolina University *M*
Gardner-Webb University *M*
Lenoir-Rhyne College *M*
North Carolina Agricultural and
    Technical State University *M*
North Carolina Central University *M*
North Carolina State University *M, D*
University of North Carolina
    Chapel Hill *M*
    Charlotte *M, D*
    Greensboro *M, D*
    Pembroke *M, T*
Wake Forest University *M, T*
Western Carolina University *M*

North Dakota
North Dakota State University *M*
University of North Dakota *M, D*

Ohio
Bowling Green State University *M*
Cleveland State University *M, D*
Heidelberg College *M*
John Carroll University *M*
Kent State University *M, D*
Malone College *M*
Ohio State University
    Columbus Campus *M, D*
Ohio University *M, D*
University of Akron *B, M, D*

University of Cincinnati *M, D*
University of Dayton *M*
Wright State University *M*
Xavier University *M*
Youngstown State University *M*

Oklahoma
East Central University *M, T*
Northeastern State University *M*
Northwestern Oklahoma State
    University *M, T*
Oklahoma State University *M, D*
Southeastern Oklahoma State
    University *M, T*
Southwestern Oklahoma State
    University *M, T*
University of Central Oklahoma *M*
University of Oklahoma *M*

Oregon
Lewis & Clark College *M*
Northwest Christian College *M*
Oregon State University *M, D*
Portland State University *M, D, T*
University of Oregon *M, D*

Pennsylvania
Bucknell University *M*
California University of
    Pennsylvania *M, T*
Duquesne University *M, D, T*
Edinboro University of Pennsylvania *M*
Gwynedd-Mercy College *M*
Indiana University of Pennsylvania *M*
Kutztown University of
    Pennsylvania *B, M*
Lancaster Bible College *M*
Lehigh University *M, D*
Marywood University *M*
Millersville University of
    Pennsylvania *M*
Penn State
    University Park *M, D*
Philadelphia Biblical University *M*
Shippensburg University of
    Pennsylvania *M, T*
Slippery Rock University of
    Pennsylvania *M, T*
University of Pennsylvania *C, M, T*
University of Scranton *M*
Villanova University *M*
West Chester University of
    Pennsylvania *M*

Puerto Rico
Bayamon Central University *M*
Inter American University of Puerto Rico
    Metropolitan Campus *M*
    San German Campus *M*
Pontifical Catholic University of Puerto
    Rico *M*
Turabo University *M*
University of Puerto Rico
    Rio Piedras Campus *M, D*

Rhode Island
Rhode Island College *M*
University of Rhode Island *M*

South Carolina
The Citadel *M*
Clemson University *M*
South Carolina State University *M*
University of South Carolina *M, D*
Winthrop University *M, T*

South Dakota
Northern State University *M*
South Dakota State University *M*
University of South Dakota *M, D*

Tennessee
Austin Peay State University *M*
Carson-Newman College *M*
East Tennessee State University *M, T*
Freed-Hardeman University *M*
Middle Tennessee State University *M*
Tennessee State University *M*

Tennessee Technological University *M*
University of Memphis *M, D*
University of Tennessee
    Chattanooga *M*
    Knoxville *M*
    Martin *M*

Texas
Abilene Christian University *M, T*
Angelo State University *M*
Dallas Baptist University *M*
Hardin-Simmons University *M*
Houston Baptist University *B, M*
Lamar University *M*
Midwestern State University *M*
Our Lady of the Lake University of San
    Antonio *M*
Prairie View A&M University *M*
Sam Houston State University *M*
Southwest Texas State University *M, T*
Stephen F. Austin State University *M*
Sul Ross State University *M*
Tarleton State University *B, M, T*
Texas A&M International
    University *M, T*
Texas A&M University
    Corpus Christi *M, T*
    Kingsville *M*
Texas Christian University *M*
Texas Southern University *M, D*
Texas Tech University *M, D*
Texas Woman's University *M*
University of Houston *M*
University of Houston
    Clear Lake *M*
    Victoria *M*
University of Mary Hardin-Baylor *M*
University of North Texas *B, M, D, T*
University of Texas
    Brownsville *M*
    El Paso *M*
    Pan American *M*
    San Antonio *M*
    of the Permian Basin *M*
West Texas A&M University *M, T*

Utah
Brigham Young University *M, D*

Vermont
College of St. Joseph in Vermont *M*
Goddard College *M*
Johnson State College *M*
Lyndon State College *M*
University of Vermont *M*

Virginia
College of William and Mary *M, D*
George Mason University *M*
Hampton University *M*
James Madison University *M*
Longwood University *M*
Lynchburg College *M*
Marymount University *M*
Old Dominion University *M*
Radford University *M*
University of Virginia *M, D*
Virginia Commonwealth University *M*
Virginia State University *M*
Virginia Western Community College *A*

Washington
Central Washington University *M, T*
Eastern Washington University *M*
Gonzaga University *M*
Heritage College *M*
St. Martin's College *M*
Seattle Pacific University *M*
Seattle University *M*
University of Puget Sound *M*
Western Washington University *B, M*
Whitworth College *B, M, T*

West Virginia
Marshall University *B, M*
West Virginia University *M, T*

Wisconsin
Concordia University Wisconsin *M*
University of Wisconsin
    Madison *M, D*
    Oshkosh *M*
    Platteville *M*
    River Falls *M*
    Stout *M*
    Superior *M*
    Whitewater *M*

Court reporting

Alabama
Gadsden State Community College *A*
James H. Faulkner State Community
    College *A*
Prince Institute of Professional Studies *A*

Arizona
Gateway Community College *C, A*

California
Cerritos Community College *C, A*
Chabot College *A*
College of Marin: Kentfield *C, A*
College of the Redwoods *C*
San Diego State University *C*
Shasta College *C*
West Valley College *A*

Florida
Broward Community College *A*
Daytona Beach Community College *A*
Florida Metropolitan University
    Orlando College North *A*
Miami-Dade Community College *A*

Illinois
Illinois Central College *C, A*
Illinois Eastern Community Colleges
    Wabash Valley College *C*
Midstate College *A*
South Suburban College of Cook
    County *C, A*
Triton College *C, A*

Indiana
College of Court Reporting *A*

Iowa
American Institute of Business *A*
Kaplan College *A*

Maryland
Villa Julie College *A*

Massachusetts
Springfield Technical Community
    College *A*

Michigan
Central Michigan University *B*
Lansing Community College *A*
Oakland Community College *C, A*

Minnesota
Rasmussen College
    Mankato *A*
    Minnetonka *A*

Mississippi
Mississippi Gulf Coast Community
    College
    Perkinston *A*
Northwest Mississippi Community
    College *A*
University of Mississippi *B*

Missouri
Kansas City College of Legal
    Studies *C, B*
St. Louis Community College
    St. Louis Community College at
        Meramec *A*

Nevada
Las Vegas College *A*

Truckee Meadows Community
College *C*

New Mexico
Albuquerque Technical-Vocational
Institute *C, A*

New York
Long Island Business Institute *A*
Monroe Community College *C*
State University of New York
College of Technology at Alfred *A*

North Carolina
Lenoir Community College *A*

Ohio
Academy of Court Reporting *A*
Academy of Court Reporting
Akron *A*
Columbus *A*
Clark State Community College *A*
Cuyahoga Community College
Eastern Campus *A*
Metropolitan Campus *A*
Western Campus *A*
Stark State College of Technology *A*

Oklahoma
Metropolitan College *B*
Metropolitan College *B*
Rogers State University *A*
Rose State College *A*

Pennsylvania
Cambria County Area Community
College *A*
Community College of Allegheny
County *C, A*

South Carolina
Midlands Technical College *C, A*

Tennessee
Chattanooga State Technical Community
College *A*
Southwest Tennessee Community
College *A*

Texas
Alvin Community College *C, A*
Amarillo College *C, A*
Del Mar College *A*
El Paso Community College *A*
Houston Community College System *A*
Kilgore College *C, A*
Northwood University: Texas
Campus *A, B*
San Antonio College *C*

Washington
Green River Community College *A*

West Virginia
Huntington Junior College *A*

Wisconsin
Lakeshore Technical College *A*

Crafts/folk art/artisanry

Arizona
Prescott College *B, M*

California
California College of Arts and
Crafts *B, M*
California State University
Northridge *B*
College of the Siskiyous *A*
Palomar College *A*
San Joaquin Delta College *A*
Santiago Canyon College *A*

Georgia
North Georgia College & State
University *B*

Illinois
University of Illinois
Urbana-Champaign *B*

Indiana
Goshen College *B*
Indiana University-Purdue University
Fort Wayne *B*

Kansas
Allen County Community College *A*

Massachusetts
Bridgewater State College *B*
Merrimack College *B*

Michigan
College for Creative Studies *B*

New York
Fulton-Montgomery Community
College *A*
Rochester Institute of
Technology *A, B, M*

Ohio
Bowling Green State University *B*
Kent State University *B, M*
Kent State University
Stark Campus *B*
University of Akron *B*

Pennsylvania
Kutztown University of Pennsylvania *B*

Tennessee
Memphis College of Art *B*

Texas
University of North Texas *B, M*

Vermont
Goddard College *B*

Virginia
Southwest Virginia Community
College *C*
Virginia Commonwealth University *B*

Creative writing

Alabama
Huntingdon College *B*
University of Alabama *M*

Arizona
Arizona State University *M*
Prescott College *B, M*
University of Arizona *B, M*

Arkansas
Arkansas Tech University *B, T*
University of Arkansas *M*

California
Antioch Southern California
Los Angeles *M*
California College of Arts and Crafts *M*
California State University
Chico *M*
Long Beach *B, M*
Los Angeles *M*
Northridge *B*
Chapman University *M*
Foothill College *A*
Fresno Pacific University *B*
Grossmont Community College *C*
Mills College *M*
Otis College of Art and Design *M*
Pitzer College *B*
St. Mary's College of California *M*
San Diego State University *C, M*
San Francisco State University *M*
University of California
Irvine *M*
Riverside *B, M*
University of Redlands *B*
University of San Francisco *M*
University of Southern California *M*

Colorado
Colorado State University *M*
Naropa University *B, M*
University of Denver *M, D*

Connecticut
Albertus Magnus College *B*

District of Columbia
American University *M*

Florida
Eckerd College *B*
Florida International University *M*
University of Florida *M*
University of Miami *M*
University of Tampa *A, B*

Georgia
Emory University *B*
Georgia State University *M*

Idaho
Boise State University *M*
Brigham Young University - Idaho *M*
University of Idaho *M*

Illinois
Columbia College Chicago *B, M*
De Paul University *M*
Knox College *B*
Millikin University *B, T*
Roosevelt University *M*
School of the Art Institute of Chicago *M*
Southern Illinois University
Carbondale *M*
University of Illinois
Urbana-Champaign *M*

Indiana
Indiana University
Bloomington *M*
Indiana Wesleyan University *B*
Manchester College *A*
Saint Mary's College *B*
University of Evansville *B*

Iowa
Loras College *B*
University of Iowa *B, M*

Kansas
Wichita State University *M*

Louisiana
Louisiana State University and
Agricultural and Mechanical
College *M*
McNeese State University *M*

Maine
University of Maine
Farmington *B*
University of Southern Maine *M*

Maryland
Goucher College *M*
Johns Hopkins University *B, M*
University of Maryland
College Park *M*

Massachusetts
Boston University *M*
Brandeis University *B*
Emerson College *B, M*
Harvard College *B*
Lesley University *M*
Massachusetts College of Liberal Arts *B*
Massachusetts Institute of Technology *B*
Simon's Rock College of Bard *B*
University of Massachusetts
Amherst *M*

Michigan
Grand Valley State University *B*
Michigan State University *M*
Northern Michigan University *B, M*
Siena Heights University *B*
University of Michigan *M*
Western Michigan University *M*

Minnesota
Bethel College *B*
Concordia College: Moorhead *B*
Hamline University *M*
Minnesota State University
Mankato *B, M*
Moorhead *M*
University of Minnesota
Twin Cities *M*

Missouri
Drury University *B*
Rockhurst University *C*
Stephens College *B*
Washington University in St. Louis *M*

Montana
Carroll College *A, B*
Miles Community College *A*
University of Montana-Missoula *M*

Nebraska
University of Nebraska
Omaha *B*

Nevada
University of Nevada
Las Vegas *M*

New Hampshire
Chester College of New England *B*
New England College *B*
University of New Hampshire *M*

New Jersey
Fairleigh Dickinson University
College at Florham *M*

New Mexico
College of Santa Fe *B*
Institute of American Indian Arts *A, B*
New Mexico State University *M*

New York
Bard College *B, M*
City University of New York
Baruch College *B*
Brooklyn College *B, M*
City College *M*
Hunter College *B, M*
Columbia University
Columbia College *B, M*
Eugene Lang College/New School
University *B*
Hamilton College *B*
Hofstra University *B*
Houghton College *B*
Ithaca College *B*
Long Island University
Southampton College *B, M*
Medaille College *B*
New York University *M*
Pratt Institute *B*
Sarah Lawrence College *B, M*
State University of New York
Albany *D*
Buffalo *M, D*
Purchase *B*
Syracuse University *M*

North Carolina
St. Andrews Presbyterian College *B*
University of North Carolina
Greensboro *M, D*
Wilmington *B, M*
Warren Wilson College *M*

North Dakota
Dickinson State University *B*

Ohio
Ashland University *B*
Bowling Green State University *B, M*
Miami University
Oxford Campus *B*
Oberlin College *B*
Ohio Northern University *B*
Union Institute & University *M*
University of Cincinnati *M, D*

Oklahoma
Oklahoma Christian University of
    Science and Arts *B*
University of Central Oklahoma *M*

Oregon
Linfield College *B*
Oregon State University *M*
Pacific University *B*
Portland State University *M*
Reed College *B*
University of Oregon *M*

Pennsylvania
Carlow College *B*
Carnegie Mellon University *B*
Chatham College *M*
Geneva College *B*
Gettysburg College *B*
Seton Hill University *M*
Temple University *M*
University of Pittsburgh *C, B*
University of Pittsburgh
    Bradford *B*
    Johnstown *B*

Rhode Island
Brown University *M*
Roger Williams University *B*

South Carolina
Columbia College *B*
University of South Carolina *M*

Tennessee
University of Memphis *M*

Texas
Austin Community College *A*
St. Edward's University *B*
Southwest Texas State University *M, T*
University of Houston *M, D*
University of Texas
    Austin *M*
    El Paso *M*

Utah
University of Utah *M, D*

Vermont
Bennington College *M*
Burlington College *B*
Goddard College *B, M*
Green Mountain College *B*
Marlboro College *B*
Norwich University *M*
Southern Vermont College *B*

Virginia
George Mason University *M*
Hollins University *M*
Old Dominion University *M*
Randolph-Macon Woman's College *B*
Sweet Briar College *B*
University of Virginia *M*
Virginia Commonwealth University *M*

Washington
Eastern Washington University *M*
Everett Community College *A*
University of Washington *M*

West Virginia
Alderson-Broaddus College *B*
West Virginia University *M*

Wisconsin
Beloit College *B*
Cardinal Stritch University *B*
Lakeland College *B*
Northland College *B*
University of Wisconsin
    Whitewater *B, T*

Criminal justice studies

Alabama
Alabama State University *B*

Andrew Jackson University *B, M*
Athens State University *B*
Auburn University at Montgomery *B, M*
Central Alabama Community
    College *C, A*
Chattahoochee Valley Community
    College *C, A*
Community College of the Air Force *A*
Faulkner University *A, B*
Jacksonville State University *B, M*
Judson College *B*
Lawson State Community College *A*
Northwest-Shoals Community College *A*
Troy State University *B*
Troy State University Dothan *B*
University of Alabama *B, M*
University of South Alabama *B*

Alaska
University of Alaska
    Fairbanks *B*

Arizona
Arizona State University *B, M, D*
Arizona Western College *A*
Central Arizona College *A*
Estrella Mountain Community
    College *C, A*
Glendale Community College *C, A*
International Institute of the Americas
    Phoenix *A*
Northern Arizona University *B, M*
Pima Community College *A*
Scottsdale Community College *A*
University of Phoenix *B*

Arkansas
Arkansas State University
    Mountain Home *A*
Black River Technical College *A*
Southeast Arkansas College *A*
Southern Arkansas University *B*
University of Arkansas *B*
University of Arkansas
    Community College at Batesville *A*
    Fort Smith *B*
    Little Rock *B*
    Monticello *B*
    Pine Bluff *B*

California
California Baptist University *B*
California State University
    Bakersfield *B*
    Fullerton *B*
    Long Beach *B, M*
    Los Angeles *B, M*
    Sacramento *B, M*
    San Bernardino *B*
Citrus College *A*
College of the Redwoods *C*
Golden West College *C, A*
Modesto Junior College *A*
National University *B, M*
San Francisco State University *B*
Sierra College *A*
Southwestern College *A*
Taft College *A*
Ventura College *C, A*
West Valley College *A*
Yuba Community College District *A*

Colorado
Blair Junior College *A*
Colorado Mountain College
    Spring Valley Campus *A*
Community College of Aurora *A*
Metropolitan State College of Denver *B*
Red Rocks Community College *A*
Remington College
    Colorado Springs *A, B*
Trinidad State Junior College *A*

Connecticut
Albertus Magnus College *B*
Briarwood College *A*
Central Connecticut State University *M*

Quinnipiac University *B*
Three Rivers Community College *C, A*
University of Hartford *B*
University of New Haven *B, M*

Delaware
Delaware State University *B*
Delaware Technical and Community
    College
    Owens Campus *A*
    Terry Campus *A*
University of Delaware *B*
Wilmington College *B*

District of Columbia
American University *B, M, D*
George Washington University *B, M*

Florida
Barry University *B*
Bethune-Cookman College *B*
Broward Community College *A*
Florida Agricultural and Mechanical
    University *B*
Florida Atlantic University *B*
Florida Gulf Coast University *B*
Florida International University *B*
Florida Metropolitan University
    Tampa College *A, B*
    Tampa College Lakeland *B*
Florida Southern College *B*
Florida State University *B, M, D*
Gulf Coast Community College *A*
Hillsborough Community College *A*
Indian River Community College *A*
International College *B*
Lake City Community College *A*
Manatee Community College *A*
Miami-Dade Community College *C, A*
Okaloosa-Walton Community College *A*
Polk Community College *A*
St. Petersburg College *A*
St. Thomas University *B*
South Florida Community College *A*
Southwest Florida College *A*
Tallahassee Community College *A*
University of Central Florida *C, B, M*
University of Florida *B*
University of North Florida *B, M*
University of South Florida *B, M, D*
University of West Florida *B*

Georgia
Albany State University *A, B*
Albany Technical College *A*
Armstrong Atlantic State
    University *A, B, M*
Atlanta Metropolitan College *A*
Augusta State University *A, B*
Chattahoochee Technical College *C, A*
Clark Atlanta University *M*
Columbus State University *C, A, B*
Darton College *A*
East Georgia College *A*
Gainesville College *A*
Georgia Military College *A*
Georgia Southern University *B*
Georgia State University *M*
Gordon College *A*
Macon State College *A*
Middle Georgia College *C, A*
Piedmont College *B*
South Georgia College *A*
State University of West Georgia *B*
Thomas University *A, B*
University of Georgia *B*
West Georgia Technical College *C, A*
Young Harris College *A*

Hawaii
Remington College
    Honolulu *A, B*
University of Hawaii
    Hawaii Community College *A*
    Honolulu Community College *A*

Idaho
Idaho State University *A*
Lewis-Clark State College *B*
North Idaho College *A*
University of Idaho *B*

Illinois
Aurora University *B*
Blackburn College *B*
Carl Sandburg College *C*
Governors State University *B, M*
Illinois Central College *A*
Illinois State University *B, M*
John A. Logan College *C, A*
Lewis and Clark Community College *A*
Lincoln Land Community College *A*
Loyola University of Chicago *B, M*
McKendree College *B*
Northeastern Illinois University *B*
Olivet Nazarene University *B*
Parkland College *A*
Quincy University *B*
Richland Community College *A*
Rockford College *B*
Roosevelt University *B*
St. Xavier University *B*
Sauk Valley Community College *A*
South Suburban College of Cook
    County *C, A*
Southern Illinois University
    Edwardsville *B*
University of Illinois
    Chicago *B, M, D*
University of St. Francis *B*

Indiana
Ancilla College *A*
Anderson University *A, B*
Ball State University *A, B*
Grace College *B*
Indiana University
    Bloomington *B, M, D*
    East *A, B*
    Kokomo *A, B*
    Northwest *A, B*
    South Bend *A, B*
Indiana University-Purdue University
    Fort Wayne *A, B*
Indiana University-Purdue University
    Indianapolis *A, B*
Indiana Wesleyan University *A, B*
Ivy Tech State College
    Bloomington *A*
    Central Indiana *A*
    Eastcentral *A*
    Kokomo *A*
    Lafayette *A*
    Northcentral *A*
    Northwest *A*
    Southwest *A*
Manchester College *A*
Oakland City University *A, B*
St. Joseph's College *B*
Tri-State University *A, B*
University of Evansville *B*

Iowa
Briar Cliff University *B*
Buena Vista University *B*
Ellsworth Community College *A*
Graceland University *B*
Grand View College *B*
Iowa Wesleyan College *B*
Kaplan College *A*
Loras College *B*
St. Ambrose University *B, M, T*
Simpson College *B*
Southeastern Community College
    South Campus *A*
University of Dubuque *B*
Upper Iowa University *B*
William Penn University *B*

Kansas
Bethany College *B*
Bethel College *B*
Butler County Community College *A*

Central Christian College *A*
Fort Hays State University *B*
Kansas Wesleyan University *A, B*
Southwestern College *B*
Washburn University of Topeka *A, B*
Wichita State University *B, M*

Kentucky

Campbellsville University *A*
Elizabethtown Community College *A*
Hopkinsville Community College *C*
Lindsey Wilson College *B*
Murray State University *A, B*
Pikeville College *A, B*
Union College *B*

Louisiana

Grambling State University *B, M*
Louisiana State University
    Alexandria *A*
    Eunice *A*
    Shreveport *B*
Loyola University New Orleans *B, M*
Northwestern State University *B*
Southeastern Louisiana University *B*
Southern University and Agricultural and
    Mechanical College *B*
University of Louisiana at Lafayette *B*
University of Louisiana at Monroe *B, M*

Maine

Andover College *A*
Husson College *B*
Thomas College *B*
University of Maine
    Presque Isle *A*
University of Southern Maine *B*

Maryland

Allegany College *A*
Chesapeake College *A*
Frederick Community College *A*
Howard Community College *A*
Montgomery College
    Rockville Campus *A*
University of Baltimore *B, M*

Massachusetts

American International College *B, M*
Anna Maria College *B*
Bay Path College *B*
Becker College *A, B*
Berkshire Community College *A*
Bunker Hill Community College *C, A*
Cape Cod Community College *A*
Dean College *A*
Endicott College *B*
Fisher College *A*
Fitchburg State College *M*
Lasell College *B*
Mount Ida College *A, B*
Mount Wachusett Community
    College *C, A*
Nichols College *B*
Northeastern University *B*
Quinsigamond Community College *A*
Stonehill College *B*
Suffolk University *M*
University of Massachusetts
    Boston *B*
    Lowell *M*
Western New England College *B*
Westfield State College *B, M*

Michigan

Adrian College *A, B*
Calvin College *B*
Jackson Community College *C, A*
Kirtland Community College *A*
Lansing Community College *A*
Madonna University *C, A, B, M*
Michigan State University *B, M*
Montcalm Community College *C, A*
Northern Michigan University *A, B*
Saginaw Valley State University *B*
Schoolcraft College *A*
Siena Heights University *A, B*

Wayne State University *B, M*
Western Michigan University *B*

Minnesota

Bemidji State University *A, B*
Brown College *B*
Capella University *M, D*
Century Community and Technical
    College *A*
Concordia University: St. Paul *B*
Gustavus Adolphus College *B*
Hamline University *B*
Metropolitan State University *B*
Minneapolis Community and Technical
    College *A*
Minnesota State University
    Moorhead *B*
Normandale Community College *A*
Northland Community & Technical
    College *A*
Northwestern College *B*
Ridgewater College: A Community and
    Technical College *A*
Rochester Community and Technical
    College *A*
St. Cloud State University *B, M*
St. Mary's University of Minnesota *B*
Vermilion Community College *A*
Winona State University *B*

Mississippi

Alcorn State University *B*
Delta State University *B, M*
Itawamba Community College *A*
Mississippi Gulf Coast Community
    College
    Perkinston *A*
Mississippi Valley State University *B*
University of Southern
    Mississippi *B, M, D*

Missouri

Central Methodist College *B*
College of the Ozarks *B*
Drury University *M*
East Central College *A*
Evangel University *B*
Harris Stowe State College *B*
Lindenwood University *B*
Longview Community College *A*
Maple Woods Community College *A*
Mineral Area College *C, A*
Missouri Baptist University *B*
Missouri Western State College *B*
Moberly Area Community College *A*
North Central Missouri College *C, A*
Penn Valley Community College *A*
St. Louis Community College
    St. Louis Community College at
        Forest Park *C*
    St. Louis Community College at
        Meramec *A*
St. Louis University *B*
Southeast Missouri State
    University *B, M*
Southwest Missouri State University *B*
Truman State University *B*

Montana

University of Great Falls *A, B*

Nebraska

University of Nebraska
    Kearney *B*
    Omaha *A, B, M*
Wayne State College *B*
Western Nebraska Community
    College *A*

Nevada

Community College of Southern
    Nevada *C, A*
Truckee Meadows Community
    College *C, A*
Western Nevada Community
    College *C, A*

New Hampshire

College for Lifelong Learning *B*
Franklin Pierce College *B*
New England College *B*
Plymouth State College *B*
St. Anselm College *B*

New Jersey

Bloomfield College *B*
Caldwell College *B*
Centenary College *B*
College of St. Elizabeth *B*
Cumberland County College *A*
Essex County College *A*
Fairleigh Dickinson University
    Metropolitan Campus *A, B*
Hudson County Community College *A*
Monmouth University *B, M*
New Jersey City University *M*
Richard Stockton College of New
    Jersey *B*
Rowan University *B*
Rutgers, The State University of New
    Jersey
    Camden Regional Campus *B*
    Newark Regional Campus *B, M, D*
Seton Hall University *B*
Sussex County Community College *A*
Thomas Edison State College *A, B*
Union County College *A*
Warren County Community College *A*

New Mexico

Albuquerque Technical-Vocational
    Institute *A*
Clovis Community College *A*
College of the Southwest *B*
Eastern New Mexico University *B*
Eastern New Mexico University: Roswell
    Campus *A*
New Mexico Junior College *A*
New Mexico State University *A, B, M*
New Mexico State University
    Alamogordo *A*
Santa Fe Community College *A*
Western New Mexico University *B*

New York

Alfred University *B*
Broome Community College *C, A*
Canisius College *B*
Cayuga County Community
    College *C, A*
Cazenovia College *A*
City University of New York
    John Jay College of Criminal
        Justice *B, M, D*
Corning Community College *A*
Dutchess Community College *C, A*
Elmira College *B*
Excelsior College *B*
Finger Lakes Community College *C, A*
Fordham University *B, M, D*
Fulton-Montgomery Community
    College *C, A*
Hilbert College *A, B*
Jamestown Community College *A*
Long Island University
    C. W. Post Campus *B, M*
Marist College *B*
Medaille College *B*
Mercy College *C, B*
Molloy College *B*
Monroe Community College *A*
Niagara County Community College *A*
Niagara University *B, M*
North Country Community College *A*
Onondaga Community College *A*
Orange County Community College *A*
Rochester Institute of Technology *B*
Rockland Community College *A*
Russell Sage College *B*
Sage College of Albany *A, B*
St. John's University *M*
Schenectady County Community
    College *A*

State University of New York
    Albany *B, M, D*
    College at Brockport *B*
    College at Buffalo *B, M*
    College at Fredonia *B*
    College at Plattsburgh *B*
    College at Potsdam *B*
    College of Technology at
        Canton *A, B*
Tompkins-Cortland Community
    College *C, A*
Utica College *B*

North Carolina

Alamance Community College *A*
Appalachian State University *B*
Barton College *B*
Beaufort County Community
    College *C, A*
Belmont Abbey College *B*
Campbell University *B*
Carteret Community College *A*
Central Carolina Community College *A*
Cleveland Community College *C, A*
Davidson County Community College *A*
East Carolina University *B, M*
Edgecombe Community College *A*
Elon University *B*
Fayetteville State University *B*
Fayetteville Technical Community
    College *C, A*
Guilford College *B*
Haywood Community College *A*
High Point University *B*
Isothermal Community College *A*
Lees-McRae College *B*
Livingstone College *B*
Methodist College *A, B*
Montgomery Community College *A*
Mount Olive College *B*
North Carolina Central University *B, M*
North Carolina State University *B*
North Carolina Wesleyan College *B*
Pfeiffer University *B*
Piedmont Community College *A*
Roanoke-Chowan Community College *A*
Rowan-Cabarrus Community College *A*
St. Augustine's College *B*
Sandhills Community College *A*
Shaw University *A, B*
South Piedmont Community
    College *C, A*
Southwestern Community College *A*
Surry Community College *A*
University of North Carolina
    Charlotte *B, M*
    Pembroke *B*
    Wilmington *B*
Western Carolina University *B*
Western Piedmont Community
    College *A*
Wilkes Community College *C, A*
Wilson Technical Community College *A*

North Dakota

Bismarck State College *A*
Jamestown College *B*
Minot State University *B, M*
North Dakota State University *B, D*
University of Mary *B*
University of North Dakota *B, D*

Ohio

Baldwin-Wallace College *B*
Bowling Green State University *B*
Bowling Green State University:
    Firelands College *A*
Cedarville University *B*
Central Ohio Technical College *A*
Kent State University *A, B, M*
Kent State University
    Ashtabula Regional Campus *B*
    Stark Campus *B*
    Trumbull Campus *A*
Lourdes College *A, B*
Marion Technical College *A*

Mount Vernon Nazarene University *B*
North Central State College *A*
Northwest State Community College *A*
Ohio Dominican College *C, B*
Ohio Northern University *B*
Ohio University *B*
Ohio University
  Chillicothe Campus *B*
  Southern Campus at Ironton *B*
Owens Community College
  Findlay Campus *A*
  Toledo *A*
Sinclair Community College *A*
Tiffin University *B, M*
Union Institute & University *B*
University of Akron *B*
University of Cincinnati *B, M, D*
University of Cincinnati
  Clermont College *A*
  Raymond Walters College *A*
University of Dayton *B*
University of Toledo *B*
Urbana University *B*
Wilmington College *B*
Xavier University *A, B*
Youngstown State University *A, B, M*

Oklahoma
Cameron University *A, B*
Carl Albert State College *A*
East Central University *B*
Eastern Oklahoma State College *A*
Northeastern Oklahoma Agricultural and
  Mechanical College *A*
Northeastern State University *B, M*
Oklahoma City University *B*
Rogers State University *A*
Rose State College *A*
Southern Nazarene University *B*
Southwestern Oklahoma State
  University *B*
Tulsa Community College *A*

Oregon
Chemeketa Community College *C, A*
Clatsop Community College *A*
Lane Community College *A*
Linn-Benton Community College *A*
Pioneer Pacific College *A*
Portland Community College *A*
Portland State University *B, M*
Southern Oregon University *B*
Southwestern Oregon Community
  College *A*
Treasure Valley Community College *A*
Western Oregon University *B*

Pennsylvania
Allentown Business School *C*
Bloomsburg University of
  Pennsylvania *B*
Bucks County Community College *A*
CHI Institute *A*
DeSales University *B*
Edinboro University of Pennsylvania *B*
Elizabethtown College *B*
ICM School of Business & Medical
  Careers *A*
Juniata College *B*
Keystone College *A, B*
King's College *A, B*
Kutztown University of Pennsylvania *B*
La Roche College *B*
La Salle University *A, B*
Lackawanna College *A*
Lincoln University *B*
Lycoming College *B*
Marywood University *A, M*
Montgomery County Community
  College *A*
Moravian College *B*
Mount Aloysius College *A, B, M*
Neumann College *B*

Penn State
  Abington *B*
  Altoona *A, B*
  Beaver *B*
  Berks *B*
  Delaware County *B*
  Dubois *B*
  Fayette *B*
  Harrisburg *B*
  Hazleton *B*
  Lehigh Valley *B*
  McKeesport *B*
  Mont Alto *B*
  New Kensington *B*
  Schuylkill - Capital College *B*
  Shenango *B*
  University Park *B, M, D*
  Wilkes-Barre *B*
  Worthington Scranton *B*
  York *B*
Point Park College *B*
Shippensburg University of
  Pennsylvania *B, M*
Temple University *B, M, D*
Thiel College *B*
University of Scranton *A*
West Chester University of
  Pennsylvania *B, M*
Wilkes University *B*

Puerto Rico
Inter American University of Puerto Rico
  Fajardo Campus *B*
  Metropolitan Campus *B, M*
Turabo University *M*
Universidad del Este *B*

Rhode Island
Rhode Island College *B*
Roger Williams University *B, M*

South Carolina
Charleston Southern University *B, M*
Florence-Darlington Technical College *A*
Horry-Georgetown Technical College *A*
Limestone College *B*
Midlands Technical College *C, A*
Northeastern Technical College *C*
Orangeburg-Calhoun Technical
  College *A*
Piedmont Technical College *A*
Spartanburg Methodist College *A*
Technical College of the Lowcountry *A*
University of South Carolina
  Lancaster *A*
  Spartanburg *B*
Williamsburg Technical College *C*

South Dakota
Dakota Wesleyan University *A, B*
Kilian Community College *A*
University of South Dakota *B*

Tennessee
Lambuth University *B*
Lane College *B*
Tennessee State University *B, M*
University of Memphis *B, M*
University of Tennessee
  Knoxville *B*

Texas
Angelina College *A*
Angelo State University *B*
Blinn College *C, A*
Coastal Bend College *A*
Dallas Baptist University *B*
Del Mar College *A*
Eastfield College *C, A*
El Centro College *C, A*
El Paso Community College *A*
Galveston College *C, A*
Hill College *A*
Jarvis Christian College *B*
Kilgore College *C, A*
Lamar State College at Port Arthur *A*
Lamar University *B, M*

Laredo Community College *A*
Lon Morris College *A*
North Central Texas College *A*
North Harris Montgomery Community
  College District *A*
Our Lady of the Lake University of San
  Antonio *C*
Paul Quinn College *B*
Prairie View A&M University *B*
St. Edward's University *B, T*
St. Mary's University *B, M*
Sam Houston State University *B, D*
Southwest Texas State University *B, M*
Southwestern Adventist University *B*
Stephen F. Austin State University *B*
Sul Ross State University *B*
Tarleton State University *B, M*
Tarrant County College *A*
Temple College *A*
Texas A&M International
  University *B, M*
Texas A&M University
  Commerce *B*
  Texarkana *B*
Texas Christian University *B*
Texas Woman's University *B*
Tyler Junior College *A*
University of Houston
  Downtown *B, M*
University of Mary Hardin-Baylor *B*
University of North Texas *B*
University of Texas
  Arlington *B, M*
  El Paso *B*
  San Antonio *B*
  Tyler *B, M*
Wayland Baptist University *B*
West Texas A&M University *M*

Utah
Dixie State College of Utah *A*
Salt Lake Community College *A*
Southern Utah University *A, B*
Utah Valley State College *A*
Weber State University *A, B, M*

Vermont
Castleton State College *A, B*
Champlain College *A, B*
Norwich University *B*

Virginia
Averett University *B*
Bluefield College *B*
Ferrum College *B*
J. Sargeant Reynolds Community
  College *A*
Longwood University *B, M*
Mountain Empire Community College *A*
Radford University *B, M*
Rappahannock Community College *A*
Roanoke College *B*
University of Richmond *B*
University of Virginia's College at
  Wise *B*
Virginia State University *B*
Virginia Wesleyan College *B*
Virginia Western Community College *A*

Washington
Central Washington University *B*
Centralia College *A*
Crown College *A*
Gonzaga University *B*
Olympic College *A*
Peninsula College *A*
St. Martin's College *B*
Walla Walla Community College *A*

West Virginia
Bluefield State College *B*
Fairmont State College *B*
Marshall University *B, M*
Mountain State University *A, B*
Potomac State College of West Virginia
  University *A*
Salem International University *B*

Shepherd College *A*
West Liberty State College *B*
West Virginia State College *A, B*
Wheeling Jesuit University *B*

Wisconsin
Carroll College *B*
Carthage College *B*
Concordia University Wisconsin *B*
Edgewood College *B*
Fox Valley Technical College *A*
Marquette University *A, B, M*
Mid-State Technical College *A*
Mount Mary College *B*
Nicolet Area Technical College *A*
University of Wisconsin
  Eau Claire *B*
  Madison *B, M*
  Milwaukee *B, M*
  Parkside *B*
  Superior *B*
Viterbo University *B*

Wyoming
Eastern Wyoming College *A*
University of Wyoming *B*

Criminalistics/criminal science

Pennsylvania
Keystone College *A*

Criminology

Alabama
Alabama State University *M*
Auburn University *B*
Enterprise State Junior College *C*

Arizona
Central Arizona College *A*

Arkansas
Arkansas State University *B*

California
Bakersfield College *A*
California State Polytechnic University:
  Pomona *B*
California State University
  Bakersfield *B*
  Fresno *B, M*
  Stanislaus *B*
Chabot College *A*
Feather River College *A*
San Diego State University *M*
San Francisco State University *B*
San Jose State University *M*
University of California
  Irvine *B, D*
University of La Verne *B*

Colorado
Colorado State University
  Pueblo *B*
Regis University *B*
Trinidad State Junior College *A*

Connecticut
Central Connecticut State University *B*
Mitchell College *A, B*
Quinnipiac University *B*

Delaware
University of Delaware *M, D*

District of Columbia
Gallaudet University *B*

Florida
Florida State University *B, M, D*
Gulf Coast Community College *A*
Lake City Community College *A*
Manatee Community College *A*
Polk Community College *A*
St. Leo University *B*

St. Thomas University *B, M*
University of Miami *B*
University of Tampa *B*

Georgia
Clark Atlanta University *B*
Clayton College and State University *A*
Dalton State College *A*
Darton College *A*
East Georgia College *A*
South Georgia College *A*
Valdosta State University *B*

Hawaii
Chaminade University of Honolulu *A, B*

Illinois
Blackburn College *B*
Dominican University *B*
Kishwaukee College *A*
Roosevelt University *B*

Indiana
Ball State University *B*
Butler University *B*
Indiana State University *A, B, M*
Indiana Wesleyan University *B*
University of Evansville *B*
Valparaiso University *B*

Iowa
Ellsworth Community College *A*
North Iowa Area Community College *A*
University of Northern Iowa *B, M*
Upper Iowa University *B*

Kansas
Fort Scott Community College *A*
MidAmerica Nazarene University *B*

Louisiana
Dillard University *B*
Louisiana College *B*

Maine
Husson College *B*
University of Southern Maine *B*

Maryland
College of Notre Dame of Maryland *B*
Howard Community College *A*
Mount St. Mary's College *C*
University of Maryland
    College Park *B, M, D*
    University College *B*

Massachusetts
American International College *B, M*
Bridgewater State College *B*
Suffolk University *B, M*

Michigan
Central Michigan University *B*
Eastern Michigan University *B, M*
Western Michigan University *B, D*

Minnesota
Hamline University *B*
Minnesota State University
    Mankato *B*
Ridgewater College: A Community and
    Technical College *A*
St. Cloud State University *B, M*
University of Minnesota
    Duluth *B*
    Twin Cities *B*
University of St. Thomas *B*
Vermilion Community College *A*
Winona State University *B*

Missouri
College of the Ozarks *B*
Drury University *B*
Evangel University *B*
Lindenwood University *B*
University of Missouri
    St. Louis *B, M, D*

Montana
University of Montana-Missoula *B, M*

Nebraska
Midland Lutheran College *B*

Nevada
University of Nevada
    Reno *B*

New Jersey
The College of New Jersey *B*

New Mexico
New Mexico Highlands University *B*

New York
City University of New York
    John Jay College of Criminal
        Justice *B*
Iona College *B*
Keuka College *B*
Le Moyne College *B*
Medaille College *B*
Niagara University *B*
St. John's University *M*
St. Joseph's College *C*
St. Joseph's College: Suffolk Campus *C*
State University of New York
    College at Old Westbury *B*
Wagner College *M*

North Carolina
Barber-Scotia College *B*
Belmont Abbey College *B*
Chowan College *B*
North Carolina State University *B*

Ohio
Ohio State University
    Columbus Campus *B*
Ohio University *B*

Oklahoma
East Central University *B, M*
University of Oklahoma *B*

Oregon
Southern Oregon University *B*

Pennsylvania
Albright College *B*
DeSales University *T*
Indiana University of
    Pennsylvania *B, M, D*
La Salle University *B*
Marywood University *A, B*
Mercyhurst College *B*
Reading Area Community College *A*
St. Joseph's University *B, M*
University of Pennsylvania *D*
University of Pittsburgh
    Greensburg *B*

Puerto Rico
Pontifical Catholic University of Puerto
    Rico *B, M*
Turabo University *B*
Universidad del Este *A*

South Carolina
Coker College *B*

Texas
North Central Texas College *A*
Panola College *A*
South Plains College *A*
Texas A&M University
    Commerce *B*
University of Texas
    Dallas *B*
    of the Permian Basin *B*
Wharton County Junior College *A*

Utah
University of Utah *C*

Vermont
Castleton State College *B*

Virginia
Marymount University *B*
Old Dominion University *B*

Wisconsin
Marquette University *B*

Critical care nursing

Ohio
Case Western Reserve University *M*

Texas
Angelo State University *M*
Tyler Junior College *A*
University of Texas
    Arlington *M*

Crop production

Massachusetts
University of Massachusetts
    Amherst *A*

Michigan
Northwestern Michigan College *A*

Oregon
Blue Mountain Community College *A*

Pennsylvania
Delaware Valley College *B*

Texas
Texas Tech University *B*

Washington
Wenatchee Valley College *C*

Culinary arts/related services

Alabama
Bishop State Community College *C, A*
James H. Faulkner State Community
    College *C, A*
Trenholm State Technical College *A*

Alaska
University of Alaska
    Anchorage *A, B*
    Fairbanks *C, A*

Arizona
Arizona Western College *C*
Art Institute
    of Phoenix *A*
Central Arizona College *C, A*
Estrella Mountain Community
    College *C, A*
Pima Community College *C, A*
Scottsdale Community College *C, A*

Arkansas
North Arkansas College *C*
Ozarka College *C*

California
Art Institute
    of California: Los Angeles *A, B*
Bakersfield College *A*
California Culinary Academy *A*
Columbia College *A*
Diablo Valley College *C*
Glendale Community College *C, A*
Grossmont Community College *C, A*
Laney College *C, A*
Long Beach City College *C, A*
Los Angeles Trade and Technical
    College *C, A*
Modesto Junior College *C*
Orange Coast College *C, A*
San Diego Mesa College *C, A*
San Francisco State University *A*
San Joaquin Delta College *C, A*
Santa Barbara City College *C, A*
Santa Rosa Junior College *C*
Shasta College *C, A*

Colorado
Art Institute
    of Colorado *A, B*
Colorado Mountain College
    Timberline Campus *A*
Community College of Aurora *A*
Mesa State College *C, A*

Connecticut
Asnuntuck Community College *C, A*
International College of Hospitality
    Management *A*
Manchester Community College *C*
Naugatuck Valley Community
    College *C, A*
Norwalk Community College *C*

Delaware
Delaware Technical and Community
    College
        Stanton/Wilmington Campus *C, A*

District of Columbia
University of the District of Columbia *A*

Florida
Art Institute
    of Fort Lauderdale *C, A, B*
Gulf Coast Community College *A*
Indian River Community College *C*
Lake City Community College *C*
New England Institute of Technology *A*
Palm Beach Community College *C*
Pensacola Junior College *C, A*
Valencia Community College *A*

Georgia
Albany Technical College *A*
Art Institute
    of Atlanta *A*
Chattahoochee Technical College *C, A*
Georgia Southwestern State University *A*
Savannah Technical College *C*
West Georgia Technical College *C*

Hawaii
University of Hawaii
    Kauai Community College *C, A*

Idaho
Boise State University *C, A*
Brigham Young University - Idaho *A*
College of Southern Idaho *C, A*
Idaho State University *C, A*
North Idaho College *C*

Illinois
City Colleges of Chicago
    Malcolm X College *A*
College of DuPage *C, A*
College of Lake County *C*
Cooking & Hospitality Institute of
    Chicago *C, A*
Elgin Community College *C, A*
Joliet Junior College *C, A*
Kendall College *C, A*
Lincoln Land Community College *C, A*
Moraine Valley Community
    College *C, A*
Robert Morris College: Chicago *A*
Southwestern Illinois College *C, A*
Triton College *C, A*
William Rainey Harper College *C, A*

Indiana
Oakland City University *C, A*
Vincennes University *A*

Iowa
Des Moines Area Community College *A*
Iowa Western Community College *A*
Kirkwood Community College *C, A*
Scott Community College *A*

Kentucky
Jefferson Community College *C, A*
Paducah Community College *A*
Sullivan University *C, A*

Louisiana
Nicholls State University *A, B*
Nunez Community College *C, A*

Maine
Central Maine Technical College *C*

Maryland
Baltimore International College *C, A*
Frederick Community College *C, A*

Massachusetts
Berkshire Community College *C*
Bunker Hill Community College *C, A*
Cape Cod Community College *C*
Massasoit Community College *C, A*
Newbury College *C, A, B*

Michigan
Baker College
  of Muskegon *A, B*
Bay de Noc Community College *C*
Grand Rapids Community College *A*
Lansing Community College *A*
Macomb Community College *C, A*
Monroe County Community
  College *C, A*
Northern Michigan University *C, A, B*
Northwestern Michigan College *A*
Oakland Community College *A*
Schoolcraft College *C, A*
Washtenaw Community College *C, A*

Minnesota
Art Institutes International
  Minnesota *C, A*
Brown College *A*
Dakota County Technical College *A*
Hennepin Technical College *C, A*
Hibbing Community College: A
  Technical and Community College *A*
Metropolitan State University *B*
Minneapolis Community and Technical
  College *C, A*
St. Cloud Technical College *C*
South Central Technical College *A*

Mississippi
Mississippi University for Women *B*

Missouri
Ozarks Technical Community College *A*
St. Louis Community College
  St. Louis Community College at
    Florissant Valley *A*
  St. Louis Community College at
    Forest Park *A*

Montana
Montana State University
  Billings College of Technology *C*
University of Montana-Missoula *C, A*

Nebraska
Metropolitan Community College *C, A*
Southeast Community College
  Lincoln Campus *A*

Nevada
Community College of Southern
  Nevada *A*
University of Nevada
  Las Vegas *B*

New Hampshire
New Hampshire Community Technical
  College
  Berlin *C, A*
  Laconia *C, A*
Southern New Hampshire University *A*
University of New Hampshire *A*

New Jersey
Atlantic Cape Community College *A*
Bergen Community College *C, A*
Brookdale Community College *C, A*
Burlington County College *C*
Hudson County Community
  College *C, A*
Mercer County Community College *C, A*

Middlesex County College *C*

New Mexico
Albuquerque Technical-Vocational
  Institute *C*
Dona Ana Branch Community College of
  New Mexico State University *C*
Santa Fe Community College *A*
Southwestern Indian Polytechnic
  Institute *C*

New York
Adirondack Community College *C, A*
Culinary Institute of America *A, B*
Mohawk Valley Community College *C, A*
Monroe Community College *C, A*
New York Institute of Technology *A*
Niagara County Community College *A*
Onondaga Community College *C, A*
Paul Smith's College *C, A, B*
Rockland Community College *C*
Schenectady County Community
  College *C*
State University of New York
    College of Agriculture and
      Technology at Cobleskill *C, A*
    College of Technology at Alfred *A*
Suffolk County Community College *A*
Westchester Community College *A*

North Carolina
Alamance Community College *C, A*
Cape Fear Community College *C, A*
Central Piedmont Community College *A*
College of the Albemarle *C*
Guilford Technical Community
  College *C, A*
Lenoir Community College *C, A*
Nash Community College *A*
Piedmont Community College *C*
Sandhills Community College *A*
South Piedmont Community College *C*
Southwestern Community College *A*
Wake Technical Community College *A*

North Dakota
North Dakota State College of Science *A*

Ohio
Cincinnati State Technical and
  Community College *C, A*
Columbus State Community College *A*
Cuyahoga Community College
  Eastern Campus *A*
  Metropolitan Campus *A*
  Western Campus *A*
Muskingum Area Technical College *A*
Sinclair Community College *C, A*

Oklahoma
Oklahoma State University
  Okmulgee *A*

Oregon
Central Oregon Community College *C*
Lane Community College *C, A*
Linn-Benton Community College *A*
Portland Community College *C*
Southwestern Oregon Community
  College *C, A*

Pennsylvania
Academy of Medical Arts and
  Business *C, A*
Bucks County Community College *A*
Commonwealth Technical Institute *A*
Community College of Philadelphia *A*
Delaware Valley College *C, A*
Drexel University *B*
Harrisburg Area Community
  College *C, A*
Immaculata University *A, B*
Keystone College *A*
Lehigh Carbon Community College *A*
Mercyhurst College *C, A*
Pennsylvania College of
  Technology *C, A*
Pennsylvania Institute of Culinary Arts *A*

Reading Area Community College *A*
Westmoreland County Community
  College *C, A*

Puerto Rico
Universidad del Este *C*

South Carolina
Denmark Technical College *C*
Technical College of the Lowcountry *C*
Trident Technical College *C, A*

Tennessee
Walters State Community College *C, A*

Texas
Central Texas College *C, A*
Del Mar College *C, A*
El Centro College *C*
El Paso Community College *C, A*
Galveston College *C, A*
Odessa College *C*
St. Philip's College *C, A*
Trinity Valley Community College *C*

Utah
Salt Lake Community College *A*
Utah Valley State College *C, A*

Vermont
New England Culinary Institute *A, B*
New England Culinary Institute
  Essex Junction *A*

Virginia
Art Institute
  of Washington *A*
J. Sargeant Reynolds Community
  College *A*
Johnson & Wales University:
  Norfolk *C, A*
Virginia Intermont College *A*

Washington
Art Institute of Seattle *A*
Edmonds Community College *C, A*
Lake Washington Technical College *C, A*
North Seattle Community College *C, A*
Olympic College *C, A*
Renton Technical College *C, A*
Seattle Central Community College *C, A*
South Seattle Community College *C, A*
Spokane Community College *A*
Spokane Falls Community College *C*

West Virginia
Fairmont State College *A*
Mountain State University *A, B*
Shepherd College *A*
West Virginia Northern Community
  College *C, A*
West Virginia University Institute of
  Technology *A*

Wisconsin
Blackhawk Technical College *A*
Fox Valley Technical College *A*
Milwaukee Area Technical College *A*
Moraine Park Technical College *A*
Nicolet Area Technical College *A*
Waukesha County Technical College *A*

Wyoming
Sheridan College *A*

Curriculum/instruction

Alabama
Auburn University *D*

Alaska
University of Alaska
  Fairbanks *M*

Arizona
Arizona State University *M, D*
Northern Arizona University *M, D*
Prescott College *B, M*
University of Phoenix *M*

Arkansas
Arkansas State University *M, T*
Henderson State University *M*
University of Arkansas *D*
University of Arkansas
  Pine Bluff *B*

California
Azusa Pacific University *M*
California Polytechnic State University:
  San Luis Obispo *M*
California State Polytechnic University:
  Pomona *M*
California State University
  Bakersfield *M*
  Chico *M*
  Dominguez Hills *M*
  Fresno *M*
  Hayward *M*
  Los Angeles *M*
  Northridge *M*
  Sacramento *M*
Chapman University *M*
Concordia University *M*
Dominican University of California *M*
Fresno Pacific University *M*
Holy Names College *M*
La Sierra University *M, D*
National University *M*
Point Loma Nazarene University *M*
St. Mary's College of California *M*
San Diego State University *M*
Sonoma State University *M*
Stanford University *M, D*
University of California
  Riverside *M, D*
  San Diego *M*
  Santa Cruz *M*
University of Redlands *M*
University of San Diego *M*
University of San Francisco *D*
University of Southern California *M, D*
University of the Pacific *B, M, D*

Colorado
Colorado Christian University *M*
University of Colorado
  Boulder *M, D*
  Colorado Springs *M*
  Denver *M*
University of Denver *M, D*

Connecticut
Fairfield University *M*
University of Connecticut *M, D, T*
Western Connecticut State University *M*

Delaware
Delaware State University *M*
University of Delaware *M, D*

District of Columbia
Catholic University of America *D*
George Washington University *M, D*
Howard University *M*
Trinity College *M*

Florida
Barry University *M*
Florida Atlantic University *M, D*
Florida Gulf Coast University *M*
Florida International University *M, D*
Nova Southeastern University *M*
University of Central Florida *M, D*
University of Florida *M, D*
University of South Florida *B, M, D*
University of West Florida *M, D*

Georgia
Clark Atlanta University *M*
Columbus State University *M*
Covenant College *M*
Georgia Southern University *D*

Hawaii
University of Hawaii
  Manoa *D*

Idaho

Boise State University *M, D*
Northwest Nazarene University *M*
University of Idaho *M*

Illinois

Aurora University *D*
Benedictine University *M*
Bradley University *M*
Chicago State University *M, T*
Concordia University *M*
De Paul University *M*
Governors State University *M*
Illinois State University *M, D*
Loyola University of Chicago *M, D*
National-Louis University *M*
North Central College *M*
Northern Illinois University *M, D*
Northwestern University *M, D*
Olivet Nazarene University *M*
Quincy University *M*
St. Xavier University *M*
Southern Illinois University
   Carbondale *M*
University of Illinois
   Chicago *D*
University of St. Francis *M*

Indiana

Anderson University *M*
Ball State University *M, T*
Indiana State University *M, D*
Indiana University
   Bloomington *D*
Purdue University *D*
University of Indianapolis *M*
Valparaiso University *M*

Iowa

Buena Vista University *B*
Dordt College *M*
Drake University *B*
Iowa State University *M, D*
University of Iowa *M, D*

Kansas

Central Christian College *B*
Emporia State University *M*
Kansas State University *D*
Newman University *M*
Pittsburg State University *B, M*
St. Mary College *M*
University of Kansas *M, D*
Washburn University of Topeka *M*
Wichita State University *M*

Kentucky

Brescia University *M*
Campbellsville University *M*
Morehead State University *M*
Spalding University *M*
Union College *M*
University of Kentucky *M*

Louisiana

Grambling State University *D*
Louisiana State University and
   Agricultural and Mechanical
   College *D*
Louisiana Tech University *M, D*
Nicholls State University *M*
Our Lady of Holy Cross College *M*
Southeastern Louisiana University *M*
University of Louisiana at Lafayette *M*
University of Louisiana at Monroe *D*
University of New Orleans *M, D*

Maine

University of Southern Maine *M*

Maryland

Coppin State College *M*
Frostburg State University *M*
Hood College *M*
Loyola College in Maryland *M*
McDaniel College *M*

University of Maryland
   Baltimore County *T*
   College Park *M, D, T*
   University College *M*

Massachusetts

American International College *M*
Atlantic Union College *M*
Boston College *M, D*
Boston University *M, D*
Framingham State College *M*
Gordon College *M*
Lesley University *M*
Northeastern University *M*
Tufts University *M*
University of Massachusetts
   Lowell *M*

Michigan

Andrews University *M, D*
Calvin College *M, T*
Eastern Michigan University *M*
Michigan State University *M, D*
Wayne State University *D*

Minnesota

Bemidji State University *M*
Capella University *M, D*
College of St. Scholastica *M*
Minnesota State University
   Mankato *B, M, T*
   Moorhead *M*
St. Cloud State University *M*
University of Minnesota
   Twin Cities *M*
University of St. Thomas *M, D*
Winona State University *B, M, T*

Mississippi

Mississippi University for Women *M*
University of Mississippi *M*
University of Southern Mississippi *M*

Missouri

Central Missouri State University *M, T*
Lindenwood University *M*
Maryville University of Saint Louis *M, T*
Northwest Missouri State
   University *B, T*
St. Louis University *M, D*
University of Missouri
   Columbia *M, D*
   Kansas City *M*
   St. Louis *M*
Washington University in St. Louis *M*
William Woods University *M*

Montana

Montana State University
   Billings *B, M*
University of Montana-Missoula *M, D*

Nebraska

Concordia University *M*
Doane College *M*
University of Nebraska
   Kearney *M*
   Lincoln *M, D*

Nevada

University of Nevada
   Las Vegas *B, M, D, T*
   Reno *D*

New Hampshire

Keene State College *M*
Rivier College *M*
University of New Hampshire *D*

New Jersey

Caldwell College *M*
Rider University *M*
Rowan University *M*
Seton Hall University *M*

New Mexico

College of Santa Fe *M*
College of the Southwest *M*
New Mexico Highlands University *M*

New Mexico State University *D*
University of New Mexico *D, T*

New York

City University of New York
   Hunter College *M, T*
Fordham University *M, D*
Long Island University
   C. W. Post Campus *B, M, T*
Medaille College *M*
Mercy College *M*
New York University *D*
Pace University *M*
Pace University:
   Pleasantville/Briarcliff *M*
Roberts Wesleyan College *M*
St. John's University *D, T*
State University of New York
   Albany *M, D*
   College at Fredonia *M*
   College at Potsdam *M*
Syracuse University *M, D*
University of Rochester *M, D*

North Carolina

Appalachian State University *B*
Campbell University *M*
North Carolina State University *M, D*
Shaw University *M*
University of North Carolina
   Chapel Hill *D*
   Charlotte *M*
   Greensboro *D*
   Wilmington *M*

Ohio

Ashland University *M, T*
Bowling Green State University *B, M*
Cleveland State University *M*
John Carroll University *M*
Kent State University *M, D*
Kent State University
   Ashtabula Regional Campus *M*
Malone College *M*
Miami University
   Oxford Campus *M*
Mount Vernon Nazarene University *M*
Ohio State University
   Columbus Campus *M, D*
Ohio University *M, D*
Otterbein College *M*
University of Cincinnati *M, D*
University of Toledo *M, D*
Urbana University *M*
Wright State University *M*
Youngstown State University *M*

Oklahoma

Northeastern State University *M*
Oklahoma State University *M, D*
Oral Roberts University *M*
Southern Nazarene University *M*
University of Central Oklahoma *B*
University of Oklahoma *M, D*

Oregon

Concordia University *M*
George Fox University *M*
Portland State University *M, D*
Western Oregon University *M, T*

Pennsylvania

Bloomsburg University of
   Pennsylvania *M*
Bucknell University *M*
Community College of Philadelphia *A*
Duquesne University *D*
Immaculata University *M*
Lehigh University *D*
Lock Haven University of
   Pennsylvania *M*
Marywood University *M, D*
Neumann College *M, T*
Penn State
   Harrisburg *C, M*
   University Park *M, D*
Point Park College *M*

Robert Morris University *M*
Rosemont College *T*
St. Vincent College *M*
Shippensburg University of
   Pennsylvania *M*
Temple University *M*
University of Pennsylvania *M*

Puerto Rico

Inter American University of Puerto Rico
   Metropolitan Campus *D*
Pontifical Catholic University of Puerto
   Rico *M*
Turabo University *M*
Universidad Metropolitana *M*
Universidad del Este *M*
University of Puerto Rico
   Rio Piedras Campus *M, D*

Rhode Island

Rhode Island College *M*

South Carolina

Clemson University *D*
University of South Carolina *D*
Winthrop University *T*

South Dakota

Black Hills State University *M*
Northern State University *B*
South Dakota State University *M*
University of South Dakota *D*

Tennessee

Austin Peay State University *M*
Carson-Newman College *M*
Freed-Hardeman University *B, M, T*
Middle Tennessee State University *M, T*
Southern Adventist University *M*
Tennessee State University *M, D*
Tennessee Technological University *M*
Trevecca Nazarene University *M*
University of Memphis *M, D*
University of Tennessee
   Knoxville *M, D*
Vanderbilt University *M, D*

Texas

Angelo State University *M*
Baylor University *M, D*
Concordia University at Austin *M*
Midwestern State University *M*
Our Lady of the Lake University of San
   Antonio *M*
Prairie View A&M University *M*
Sam Houston State University *M*
Tarleton State University *B, T*
Texas A&M University *M, D*
Texas A&M University
   Commerce *D*
   Corpus Christi *M, T*
Texas Southern University *B, M, D*
Texas Tech University *M, D*
University of Houston *M, D, T*
University of Houston
   Clear Lake *M*
   Downtown *M*
University of North Texas *D*
University of Texas
   Arlington *M*
   Austin *M, D*
   El Paso *M*
   Pan American *T*
   San Antonio *M*
   Tyler *M*
Wayland Baptist University *M*
West Texas A&M University *M*

Utah

Southern Utah University *M*
Utah State University *B, M, D*

Vermont

Castleton State College *M, T*
Johnson State College *M*
Lyndon State College *M*
St. Michael's College *M*
University of Vermont *M, D*

Virginia
Averett University *M*
College of William and Mary *M*
Eastern Mennonite University *M*
George Mason University *M*
Longwood University *M*
Lynchburg College *M*
Radford University *M*
Randolph-Macon Woman's College *B*
University of Virginia *M, D*
Virginia Commonwealth University *M*
Virginia Polytechnic Institute and State
  University *M, D*
Virginia State University *M*

Washington
Eastern Washington University *M*
Gonzaga University *M*
Seattle Pacific University *M*
Seattle University *M*
University of Puget Sound *M*
University of Washington *D*
Walla Walla College *M*

West Virginia
West Virginia University *D*

Wisconsin
Concordia University Wisconsin *M*
Mount Mary College *M*
University of Wisconsin
  Madison *M, D*
  Milwaukee *M*
  Superior *M*

Customer service management

California
Santa Rosa Junior College *C*

Iowa
Maharishi University of
  Management *C, M*

Missouri
Penn Valley Community College *C*

New York
Rochester Institute of Technology *M*

Ohio
Hondros College *A*

Pennsylvania
Newport Business Institute *A*

Washington
Bellevue Community College *M*

Wisconsin
University of Wisconsin
  Stout *B*

Customer service support

Arizona
Paradise Valley Community
  College *C, A*
South Mountain Community
  College *C, A*

California
Santa Rosa Junior College *C*

Colorado
Colorado Technical University *A*

Missouri
Penn Valley Community College *A*

New Jersey
Bergen Community College *C*

North Carolina
Forsyth Technical Community College *C*

Ohio
Hondros College *A*

Pennsylvania
Newport Business Institute *A*

Washington
Clark College *C*
Clover Park Technical College *C*
Olympic College *C, A*

Wisconsin
Western Wisconsin Technical College *A*

Wyoming
Central Wyoming College *C*

Cytogenetics/clinical genetics technology

Alabama
Calhoun Community College *A*

Cytotechnology

Alabama
Community College of the Air Force *A*
Oakwood College *B*
University of Alabama
  Birmingham *B*

Arkansas
University of Arkansas
  for Medical Sciences *B*

California
California State University
  Dominguez Hills *M*
Loma Linda University *C, B*

Connecticut
University of Connecticut *B*

Florida
Barry University *B*

Illinois
Illinois College *B*
University of St. Francis *B*

Indiana
Indiana University
  Bloomington *B*
Indiana University-Purdue University
  Indianapolis *C, A, B*

Iowa
Franciscan University *B*
Luther College *B*

Kansas
University of Kansas Medical Center *B*

Kentucky
Bellarmine University *C, B*
University of Louisville *B*

Louisiana
Nicholls State University *C, B*

Massachusetts
American International College *B*

Michigan
Eastern Michigan University *B*
Northern Michigan University *B*

Minnesota
Minnesota State University
  Mankato *B, M*
  Moorhead *B*
St. Mary's University of Minnesota *B*
Winona State University *B*

Mississippi
University of Mississippi Medical
  Center *B*

Missouri
Rockhurst University *B*
University of Missouri
  St. Louis *B*

New Jersey
Bloomfield College *B*
College of St. Elizabeth *B*
Felician College *B*
St. Peter's College *B*
Thomas Edison State College *B*
University of Medicine and Dentistry of
  New Jersey
    School of Health Related
      Professions *B*

New York
St. John's University *B*
State University of New York
  College at Plattsburgh *B*
  Health Science Center at Stony
    Brook *B*
  Oswego *B*
  Stony Brook *B*
  Upstate Medical University *B*

North Carolina
Central Piedmont Community College *C*
University of North Carolina
  Chapel Hill *C*

North Dakota
University of North Dakota *B*

Ohio
Notre Dame College *B*
University of Akron *A, B*

Pennsylvania
Slippery Rock University of
  Pennsylvania *B*
Thiel College *B*

Puerto Rico
University of Puerto Rico
  Medical Sciences Campus *C*

Rhode Island
Salve Regina University *B*

South Carolina
Anderson College *B*
Medical University of South
  Carolina *B, M*

Tennessee
Southern Adventist University *A*
University of Tennessee Health Science
  Center *B*

Texas
Clarendon College *A*
University of North Texas *B*

West Virginia
Alderson-Broaddus College *B*
Marshall University *B*

Wisconsin
Edgewood College *B*
Marian College of Fond du Lac *B*

Czech

Texas
University of Texas
  Austin *B*

Dairy husbandry

New York
State University of New York
  College of Agriculture and
    Technology at Morrisville *A, B*

Dairy science

California
California Polytechnic State University:
  San Luis Obispo *B*

California State University
  Fresno *B*
College of the Sequoias *C*
Los Angeles Pierce College *C, A*
Modesto Junior College *A*

Florida
University of Florida *M*

Georgia
University of Georgia *B, M*

Idaho
University of Idaho *B*

Iowa
Iowa State University *B*
Northeast Iowa Community College *C*

Minnesota
Ridgewater College: A Community and
  Technical College *C*

Mississippi
Northwest Mississippi Community
  College *A*

Nebraska
Northeast Community College *C*

New Hampshire
University of New Hampshire *A, B*

New York
Cornell University *B*
State University of New York
  College of Agriculture and
    Technology at Cobleskill *A*
  College of Agriculture and
    Technology at Morrisville *A*
  College of Technology at Alfred *A*

Ohio
Ohio State University
  Agricultural Technical Institute *A*

Oregon
Linn-Benton Community College *A*

Pennsylvania
Delaware Valley College *B*

South Carolina
Clemson University *B, M*

South Dakota
South Dakota State University *B, M*

Texas
Texas A&M University *B, M, D*

Utah
Utah State University *C, B, M*

Vermont
Vermont Technical College *A*

Virginia
Virginia Polytechnic Institute and State
  University *B, M*

Wisconsin
Lakeshore Technical College *C*
University of Wisconsin
  Madison *B, M, D*
  River Falls *B*

Dance

Alabama
Birmingham-Southern College *B*
University of Alabama *B*

Arizona
Arizona State University *B, M*
Prescott College *B, M*
University of Arizona *B*

California
Cabrillo College *A*
California Institute of the Arts *C, B, M*

California State Polytechnic University:
Pomona *B*
California State University
Fresno *B*
Fullerton *B*
Hayward *B*
Long Beach *B, M*
Los Angeles *B*
Northridge *B*
Sacramento *B*
Chabot College *A*
Chapman University *B*
Claremont McKenna College *B*
Glendale Community College *C, A*
Golden West College *A*
Grossmont Community College *C, A*
Irvine Valley College *A*
Laney College *A*
Long Beach City College *A*
Loyola Marymount University *B*
Mills College *B, M*
MiraCosta College *A*
Monterey Peninsula College *A*
Mount San Jacinto College *A*
Orange Coast College *C, A*
Palomar College *C, A*
Pitzer College *B*
Pomona College *B*
St. Mary's College of California *B*
San Diego State University *B*
San Francisco State University *B*
San Jose State University *B, M*
Santa Monica College *A*
Santa Rosa Junior College *C*
Santiago Canyon College *A*
Scripps College *B*
Southwestern College *A*
University of California
Berkeley *B*
Irvine *B, M*
Los Angeles *M*
Riverside *B, M, D*
San Diego *B*
Santa Barbara *B*
Santa Cruz *C, B*

Colorado
Colorado College *B*
Colorado State University *B*
Naropa University *B*
University of Colorado
Boulder *B, M*

Connecticut
Connecticut College *B*
Naugatuck Valley Community
College *C, A*
Trinity College *B*
University of Hartford *B*
Wesleyan University *B*

District of Columbia
American University *C, M*
George Washington University *B*
Howard University *B*

Florida
Florida International University *B*
Florida State University *B, M*
Hillsborough Community College *A*
Indian River Community College *A*
Jacksonville University *B*
Miami-Dade Community College *A*
Okaloosa-Walton Community College *A*
Palm Beach Atlantic University *B*
Palm Beach Community College *A*
University of Florida *B*
University of Miami *B*
University of South Florida *B*

Georgia
Brenau University *B*
Emory University *B*
Oxford College of Emory University *B*

Hawaii
University of Hawaii
Manoa *B, M*

Idaho
University of Idaho *B*

Illinois
Columbia College Chicago *B*
Illinois Central College *A*
Lincoln College *A*
Northwestern University *B*
Rockford College *B*
Southern Illinois University
Edwardsville *B*
University of Illinois
Urbana-Champaign *B, M*

Indiana
Ball State University *B*
Butler University *B*
Indiana University
Bloomington *B, M*

Iowa
University of Iowa *B, M*

Kansas
Friends University *B*
University of Kansas *B*

Louisiana
Centenary College of Louisiana *B, T*

Maryland
College of Southern Maryland *A*
Frostburg State University *B*
Goucher College *B*
Howard Community College *A*
Montgomery College
Rockville Campus *A*
Towson University *B, T*
University of Maryland
Baltimore County *B*
College Park *B, M*

Massachusetts
Amherst College *B*
Boston Conservatory *B, M*
Cape Cod Community College *A*
Dean College *A, B*
Emerson College *B*
Hampshire College *B*
Mount Holyoke College *B*
Simon's Rock College of Bard *B*
Smith College *B, M*
Springfield College *B*
University of Massachusetts
Amherst *B*

Michigan
Alma College *B*
Central Michigan University *T*
Eastern Michigan University *B*
Hope College *B*
Lansing Community College *A*
Marygrove College *B, T*
Oakland University *B*
University of Michigan *B, M, T*
Wayne State University *B, T*
Western Michigan University *B*

Minnesota
Gustavus Adolphus College *B*
St. Olaf College *B*
University of Minnesota
Twin Cities *B*
Winona State University *A*

Mississippi
University of Southern Mississippi *B*

Missouri
Lindenwood University *B*
Southwest Missouri State University *B*
Stephens College *B*
University of Missouri
Kansas City *B*
Washington University in St. Louis *B*
Webster University *B*

Montana
University of Montana-Missoula *B*

Nebraska
University of Nebraska
Lincoln *B, M*

Nevada
University of Nevada
Las Vegas *B*

New Hampshire
Franklin Pierce College *B*

New Jersey
Middlesex County College *A*
Montclair State University *B*
Rowan University *B*
Rutgers, The State University of New
Jersey
New Brunswick Regional
Campus *B*

New Mexico
New Mexico State University *B*
Santa Fe Community College *A*
University of New Mexico *B*

New York
Adelphi University *B*
Bard College *B*
Barnard College *B*
City University of New York
Hunter College *B*
Queens College *B*
Queensborough Community
College *A*
Columbia University
Columbia College *B*
Cornell University *B*
Fordham University *B*
Hamilton College *B*
Hobart and William Smith Colleges *B*
Hofstra University *B*
Ithaca College *B*
Juilliard School *B*
Long Island University
C. W. Post Campus *B*
Manhattanville College *B*
Marymount Manhattan College *B*
New York University *B, M, D*
Sarah Lawrence College *B, M*
Skidmore College *B*
State University of New York
Buffalo *B*
College at Brockport *B, M, T*
College at Potsdam *B*
Purchase *B, M*
Wells College *B*

North Carolina
Duke University *C*
East Carolina University *B*
Elon University *B*
Louisburg College *A*
Meredith College *B, T*
North Carolina School of the Arts *B*
University of North Carolina
Charlotte *B, T*
Greensboro *B, M, T*

Ohio
Antioch College *B*
Baldwin-Wallace College *B*
Case Western Reserve University *M*
College of Wooster *B*
Denison University *B*
Kent State University *B*
Kenyon College *B*
Lake Erie College *B*
Oberlin College *B*
Ohio State University
Columbus Campus *B, M*
Ohio University *B*
Ohio Wesleyan University *B*
Sinclair Community College *C, A*
University of Akron *B*
University of Cincinnati *B*

Wittenberg University *B*
Wright State University *B*

Oklahoma
Oklahoma City University *B*
University of Central Oklahoma *B*
University of Oklahoma *B, M*

Oregon
Reed College *B*
University of Oregon *B, M*
Western Oregon University *B*

Pennsylvania
Cedar Crest College *B*
DeSales University *B*
Dickinson College *B*
La Roche College *B*
Mercyhurst College *B*
Muhlenberg College *B*
Point Park College *B*
Slippery Rock University of
Pennsylvania *B*
Swarthmore College *B*
Temple University *B, M, D*

Rhode Island
Roger Williams University *B*

South Carolina
Coker College *B*
Columbia College *B*
Winthrop University *B*

Tennessee
Columbia State Community College *C*
University of Tennessee
Martin *B*

Texas
Austin Community College *A*
Kilgore College *A*
Lamar University *B*
Midland College *A*
Sam Houston State University *B, M*
Southern Methodist University *B, M*
Southwest Texas State University *B, T*
Stephen F. Austin State University *B, T*
Texas Christian University *B, M, T*
Texas Tech University *B*
Texas Woman's University *B, M, D, T*
Tyler Junior College *A*
University of Houston *B*
University of North Texas *B*
University of Texas
Austin *B*
Pan American *B*
University of the Incarnate Word *B*
West Texas A&M University *B*

Utah
Brigham Young University *B, M*
Dixie State College of Utah *A*
Snow College *A*
Southern Utah University *B, T*
University of Utah *B, M*
Utah State University *B*
Utah Valley State College *A*
Weber State University *B*

Vermont
Bennington College *B, M, T*
Johnson State College *B*
Marlboro College *B*
Middlebury College *B*

Virginia
George Mason University *B, M*
Hollins University *B*
Longwood University *T*
Radford University *B*
Randolph-Macon Woman's College *B*
Shenandoah University *B, M*
Sweet Briar College *B*
Virginia Commonwealth University *B*
Virginia Intermont College *B*

Washington
Cornish College of the Arts *B*

University of Washington *B, M*

Wisconsin
University of Wisconsin
Madison *B, M*
Milwaukee *B*
Stevens Point *B*
Whitewater *B, T*

Wyoming
Casper College *A*
Western Wyoming Community
College *A*

Dance therapy

Colorado
Naropa University *B, M*

Illinois
Columbia College Chicago *M*

Massachusetts
Lesley University *M, D*

New York
Pratt Institute *M*

Pennsylvania
Cedar Crest College *B*
Drexel University *M*
Mercyhurst College *B*

South Carolina
Coker College *B*

Wisconsin
University of Wisconsin
Madison *B, M*

Danish

Washington
University of Washington *B*

Data entry/applications

Arizona
Estrella Mountain Community
College *C, A*
International Institute of the Americas
Phoenix *A*

Arkansas
East Arkansas Community College *C, A*
Mid-South Community College *C*

California
Glendale Community College *C*
MTI College of Business and
Technology *C*
Santa Rosa Junior College *C*

Connecticut
Manchester Community College *C, A*
Naugatuck Valley Community College *A*

Florida
Herzing College
Orlando *C*

Georgia
Middle Georgia College *A*
Southwest Georgia Technical
College *C, A*
West Georgia Technical College *C, A*

Illinois
Bradley University *B*
Richland Community College *A*

Indiana
Indiana Business College *A*
Professional Careers Institute *A*

Iowa
Des Moines Area Community College *C*

Hamilton College
Cedar Falls *C*
Western Iowa Tech Community
College *A*

Kansas
Central Christian College *A*
Seward County Community
College *C, A*

Kentucky
Jefferson Community College *A*

Maine
Central Maine Technical College *C, A*

Maryland
Community College of Baltimore County
Catonsville *C, A*
Dundalk *C, A*

Massachusetts
Newbury College *C, A*
Springfield Technical Community
College *C, A*

Michigan
Baker College
of Muskegon *A*

Minnesota
Normandale Community College *A*
Riverland Community College: A
Technical and Community College *C*

Missouri
St. Louis Community College
St. Louis Community College at
Meramec *C*

Nebraska
Metropolitan Community College *A*

New Hampshire
Hesser College *C, A*
New Hampshire Community Technical
College
Nashua *A*

New Jersey
Mercer County Community College *C*

New York
Pace University:
Pleasantville/Briarcliff *C*
Westchester Community College *C*

North Carolina
Beaufort County Community College *C*
Forsyth Technical Community
College *C, A*

North Dakota
North Dakota State College of
Science *C, A*

Ohio
Central Ohio Technical College *A*
Cuyahoga Community College
Western Campus *A*
Sinclair Community College *C*
University of Cincinnati
Clermont College *C, A*

Pennsylvania
Academy of Medical Arts and
Business *C, A*
Consolidated School of Business
Lancaster *A*
Delaware County Community
College *C, A*
Newport Business Institute *A*
PJA School *C*

South Carolina
York Technical College *C*

Tennessee
South College *C, A*
Trevecca Nazarene University *A*

Texas
St. Philip's College *C, A*
Temple College *C, A*

Virginia
ECPI College of Technology *C, A*
ECPI Technical College: Roanoke *A*

Washington
Clark College *C, A*
Edmonds Community College *C*
Walla Walla Community College *C, A*

West Virginia
Valley College of Technology *C*

Wisconsin
Western Wisconsin Technical College *A*

Data processing technology

Alabama
Chattahoochee Valley Community
College *A*
J. F. Drake State Technical College *A*
Northwest-Shoals Community
College *C, A*
Wallace State Community College at
Hanceville *A*

Arizona
Central Arizona College *A*
Eastern Arizona College *C*
Pima Community College *C*

Arkansas
Arkansas State University *B*
Central Baptist College *B*
University of Arkansas *B*
University of Central Arkansas *B*

California
Antelope Valley College *A*
Bakersfield College *A*
Barstow College *C*
Cabrillo College *A*
Cerritos Community College *A*
Chabot College *C, A*
Citrus College *A*
College of the Canyons *C, A*
College of the Redwoods *C*
Diablo Valley College *C, A*
Gavilan Community College *C*
Long Beach City College *C, A*
Monterey Peninsula College *C, A*
Mount San Antonio College *C, A*
Pacific Union College *B*
San Diego City College *C, A*
San Joaquin Delta College *A*
Santa Barbara City College *C, A*
Santa Monica College *C, A*
Sierra College *A*
Taft College *C*
Ventura College *A*
Victor Valley College *C*
Yuba Community College District *C*

Colorado
Colorado Mountain College
Alpine Campus *C*
Spring Valley Campus *C*
National American University
Denver *A*
Red Rocks Community College *C, A*

Connecticut
Norwalk Community College *A*
Three Rivers Community College *C*
University of New Haven *B*

Delaware
Delaware Technical and Community
College
Owens Campus *C, A*
Stanton/Wilmington Campus *A*
Terry Campus *A*

Florida
Broward Community College *A*
Florida Keys Community College *C*
Florida Metropolitan University
Orlando College North *A*
Florida Technical College *A*
Gulf Coast Community College *C*
Hillsborough Community College *C*
Indian River Community College *C*
Miami-Dade Community College *C*
Pasco-Hernando Community College *C*
Santa Fe Community College *A*
Seminole Community College *C, A*
Tallahassee Community College *C*

Georgia
Abraham Baldwin Agricultural
College *A*
Clayton College and State
University *C, A*
Columbus State University *C*
Dalton State College *C, A*
Darton College *A*
South Georgia College *C*

Hawaii
Hawaii Business College *C*
Hawaii Pacific University *A*

Idaho
Lewis-Clark State College *C*

Illinois
Black Hawk College *C*
Black Hawk College
East Campus *A*
Chicago State University *B*
City Colleges of Chicago
Harold Washington College *C, A*
Olive-Harvey College *C, A*
Kishwaukee College *C*
Lewis and Clark Community College *A*
Lincoln Land Community College *A*
Midstate College *A*
Oakton Community College *C, A*
Parkland College *A*
Rockford Business College *C, A*
Sauk Valley Community College *C, A*
Southwestern Illinois College *A*
Spoon River College *C, A*
Triton College *C, A*
William Rainey Harper College *C, A*

Indiana
Calumet College of St. Joseph *C*
Indiana University
Kokomo *B*
Northwest *C, A, B*
Purdue University *A, B*
Purdue University
North Central Campus *A*
Tri-State University *A*
University of Southern Indiana *B*
Vincennes University *A*

Iowa
Dordt College *A*
Ellsworth Community College *A*
Northeast Iowa Community College *A*
Southeastern Community College
North Campus *C, A*

Kansas
Barton County Community College *C, A*
Dodge City Community College *C, A*
Donnelly College *C, A*
Fort Scott Community College *A*
Haskell Indian Nations University *A*
Hutchinson Community College *C, A*
Independence Community College *C, A*
Kansas City Kansas Community
College *C, A*
Labette Community College *A*
Seward County Community
College *C, A*

Kentucky
Daymar College *C, A*

Henderson Community College *A*
Jefferson Community College *A*
Lexington Community College *A*
Maysville Community College *C, A*
Southeast Community College *A*
Thomas More College *A*

Louisiana
Delgado Community College *A*
ITI Technical College *A*
Louisiana State University
    Alexandria *A*
McNeese State University *A*

Maine
Andover College *C, A*
Husson College *A*

Maryland
Allegany College *C*
Cecil Community College *C, A*
Community College of Baltimore County
    Catonsville *C, A*
    Dundalk *C, A*
    Essex *C, A*

Massachusetts
Benjamin Franklin Institute of
    Technology *C*
Berkshire Community College *C, A*
Springfield Technical Community
    College *A*

Michigan
Baker College
    of Auburn Hills *A*
    of Clinton Township *A*
    of Jackson *A*
    of Muskegon *A*
    of Port Huron *A*
Bay de Noc Community College *C*
Davenport University
    Eastern Region *C*
Glen Oaks Community College *C*
Gogebic Community College *A*
Grand Rapids Community College *C, A*
Jackson Community College *C, A*
Lansing Community College *A*
Montcalm Community College *A*
Mott Community College *C*
Muskegon Community College *C, A*
Oakland Community College *C, A*
St. Clair County Community
    College *C, A*
Schoolcraft College *C*
Washtenaw Community College *C, A*
West Shore Community College *C, A*

Minnesota
Century Community and Technical
    College *A*
Hennepin Technical College *C, A*
Lake Superior College: A Community
    and Technical College *C*
Pine Technical College *C, A*
St. Cloud Technical College *C*
Winona State University *B*

Mississippi
Itawamba Community College *A*
Northwest Mississippi Community
    College *A*
Pearl River Community College *A*
University of Southern Mississippi *B*

Missouri
Central Missouri State University *B*
Missouri College *C*
St. Louis Community College
    St. Louis Community College at
        Florissant Valley *C, A*
    St. Louis Community College at
        Forest Park *C, A*
    St. Louis Community College at
        Meramec *C, A*
Springfield College *C, A*
Washington University in St. Louis *B*

Montana
Fort Belknap College *A*
Miles Community College *A*
Montana State University
    Billings *C, A*
Montana Tech of the University of
    Montana *A*
University of Montana-Missoula *A*

Nebraska
Northeast Community College *A*

Nevada
Community College of Southern
    Nevada *A*
Truckee Meadows Community
    College *A*
Western Nevada Community College *C*

New Hampshire
New Hampshire Community Technical
    College
    Laconia *C, A*
    Nashua *C, A*

New Jersey
Atlantic Cape Community College *A*
Burlington County College *C, A*
Essex County College *C*
Gloucester County College *C, A*
Hudson County Community
    College *C, A*
Rowan University *B*
St. Peter's College *A*
Union County College *C*

New Mexico
Albuquerque Technical-Vocational
    Institute *C, A*
Dona Ana Branch Community College of
    New Mexico State University *A*
New Mexico State University
    Alamogordo *C, A*
San Juan College *A*
Santa Fe Community College *C*

New York
Adirondack Community College *C, A*
Cayuga County Community
    College *C, A*
City University of New York
    Borough of Manhattan Community
        College *A*
    Bronx Community College *A*
    Hostos Community College *A*
    Kingsborough Community
        College *A*
    La Guardia Community College *A*
    Queensborough Community
        College *A*
Fulton-Montgomery Community
    College *A*
Genesee Community College *C*
Hudson Valley Community College *C, A*
Iona College *C*
Jamestown Business College *A*
New York Institute of Technology *C*
Onondaga Community College *C*
Orange County Community College *A*
Pace University *A*
Pace University:
    Pleasantville/Briarcliff *A*
Rockland Community College *C, A*
St. John's University *A*
State University of New York
    College of Agriculture and
        Technology at Cobleskill *A*
    College of Agriculture and
        Technology at Morrisville *C*
    College of Technology at Alfred *A*
    College of Technology at Delhi *C*
    Farmingdale *C, A*
    Purchase *C*
Tompkins-Cortland Community
    College *A*
Utica School of Commerce *A*
Westchester Business Institute *C, A*

North Carolina
Caldwell Community College and
    Technical Institute *A*
Lenoir Community College *C, A*
Western Piedmont Community
    College *C, A*

North Dakota
Lake Region State College *C, A*

Ohio
Cincinnati State Technical and
    Community College *A*
Davis College *A*
Jefferson Community College *C, A*
Miami-Jacobs College *A*
Mount Vernon Nazarene University *A*
Northwest State Community College *C*
Ohio Valley College of Technology *A*
RETS Tech Center *C*
Shawnee State University *A*
Stark State College of Technology *A*
University of Akron *C, A*
University of Toledo *A*
Washington State Community College *A*
Wright State University: Lake Campus *C*
Youngstown State University *A*

Oklahoma
Cameron University *A*
Oklahoma City Community College *A*

Oregon
Lane Community College *A*

Pennsylvania
Academy of Medical Arts and
    Business *C, A*
Bucks County Community College *A*
CHI Institute *C*
Consolidated School of Business
    Lancaster *C, A*
    York *C, A*
Harrisburg Area Community
    College *C, A*
Keystone College *C, A*
Mercyhurst College *C*
Montgomery County Community
    College *A*
Newport Business Institute *A*
Northampton County Area Community
    College *C, A*
Philadelphia University *A*
Reading Area Community College *A*
University of Pittsburgh
    Titusville *C*
Westmoreland County Community
    College *C, A*

Puerto Rico
Universidad del Este *A, B*

Rhode Island
Community College of Rhode Island *A*

South Carolina
Aiken Technical College *A*
Florence-Darlington Technical College *A*
Horry-Georgetown Technical
    College *C, A*
Midlands Technical College *C, A*
Northeastern Technical College *C, A*
Orangeburg-Calhoun Technical
    College *C, A*
Piedmont Technical College *C, A*
Spartanburg Technical College *A*
Technical College of the
    Lowcountry *C, A*
Tri-County Technical College *A*
Trident Technical College *C, A*
Williamsburg Technical College *C, A*

South Dakota
Sinte Gleska University *A*
Southeast Technical Institute *C*

Texas
Alvin Community College *C*
Angelina College *C, A*

Austin Community College *C*
Central Texas College *C, A*
Clarendon College *C*
Coastal Bend College *A*
Eastfield College *A*
El Centro College *A*
El Paso Community College *C*
Frank Phillips College *C*
Galveston College *C*
Hill College *C, A*
Howard College *C*
Lee College *C, A*
McLennan Community College *C, A*
Midland College *A*
North Central Texas College *A*
Paris Junior College *C, A*
St. Philip's College *A*
South Plains College *A*
Southwest Texas Junior College *A*
Stephen F. Austin State University *B*
Temple College *C, A*
Texarkana College *C, A*
Texas State Technical College
    Waco *C, A*
Trinity Valley Community College *A*
Tyler Junior College *C*
University of Texas
    El Paso *B*
Western Texas College *C, A*
Wharton County Junior College *A*

Utah
Dixie State College of Utah *A, B*
Salt Lake Community College *C*
Southern Utah University *A*

Virginia
ECPI College of Technology *C, A*
ECPI Technical College: Roanoke *A*
J. Sargeant Reynolds Community
    College *C, A*
Mountain Empire Community College *C*
Virginia Highlands Community
    College *A*

Washington
Bellevue Community College *C*
Centralia College *A*
Clover Park Technical College *C*
Edmonds Community College *A*
Lake Washington Technical College *C, A*
Lower Columbia College *C, A*
North Seattle Community College *C, A*
Peninsula College *A*
Renton Technical College *C*
Spokane Community College *C, A*
Walla Walla College *B*
Walla Walla Community College *C, A*

West Virginia
Potomac State College of West Virginia
    University *A*
West Virginia Northern Community
    College *C, A*

Wisconsin
Fox Valley Technical College *A*
Lakeshore Technical College *A*
Mid-State Technical College *A*
Milwaukee Area Technical College *A*
Moraine Park Technical College *A*
Western Wisconsin Technical College *A*
Wisconsin Indianhead Technical
    College *C*

Wyoming
Casper College *A*
Western Wyoming Community
    College *C, A*

**Database design/
management**

Arizona
University of Phoenix *B*

California

Foothill College *C, A*
San Joaquin Delta College *A*

Colorado

Colorado Technical University *C*
Jones International University *C, B*

Illinois

Parkland College *A*

Kansas

Kansas City Kansas Community
College *C, A*

Kentucky

Maysville Community College *C, A*

New York

State University of New York
Buffalo *M, D*
College of Agriculture and
Technology at Morrisville *B*

Ohio

University of Cincinnati
Clermont College *A*

Pennsylvania

La Salle University *B, M*
Newport Business Institute *A*

Washington

Bellevue Community College *A*
Clover Park Technical College *C*

West Virginia

Huntington Junior College *A*

Demography/population studies

California

University of California
Berkeley *M, D*
University of Southern California *M*

Colorado

University of Denver *M*

Florida

Florida State University *C, M*

Louisiana

Tulane University *M, D*

Massachusetts

Hampshire College *B*

Michigan

University of Michigan *D*

New York

State University of New York
Albany *B, M*

Ohio

Bowling Green State University *M*

Pennsylvania

Cambria County Area Community
College *A*
University of Pennsylvania *D*

Puerto Rico

University of Puerto Rico
Medical Sciences Campus *M*

Wisconsin

University of Wisconsin
Madison *M, D*

Dental assistant

Alabama

Calhoun Community College *C, A*
Community College of the Air Force *A*
James H. Faulkner State Community
College *C, A*
Northwest-Shoals Community College *A*

Trenholm State Technical College *A*
Wallace State Community College at
Hanceville *C, A*

Alaska

University of Alaska
Anchorage *C, A*
Fairbanks *C, A*

Arizona

Phoenix College *A*
Pima Community College *C*
Rio Salado College *C*

Arkansas

Pulaski Technical College *C*

California

Bakersfield College *A*
California State University
Dominguez Hills *B*
Cerritos Community College *C, A*
Citrus College *C, A*
College of Alameda *A*
College of the Redwoods *C*
Contra Costa College *A*
Diablo Valley College *C*
Foothill College *C, A*
Modesto Junior College *A*
Monterey Peninsula College *C, A*
Orange Coast College *C, A*
Palomar College *C, A*
Reedley College *C, A*
San Diego Mesa College *C, A*
Santa Rosa Junior College *C, A*

Colorado

Front Range Community College *C*
IntelliTec College, Grand Junction *C*

Connecticut

Briarwood College *C, A*
Tunxis Community College *C*

Florida

Broward Community College *C*
Daytona Beach Community College *C*
Gulf Coast Community College *C*
Indian River Community College *C*
New England Institute of Technology *C*
Palm Beach Community College *C*
Pasco-Hernando Community College *C*
Pensacola Junior College *C*
Santa Fe Community College *C*
South Florida Community College *C*
Tallahassee Community College *C*

Georgia

Albany Technical College *C*
Middle Georgia College *A*

Idaho

Boise State University *C*
College of Southern Idaho *C*
Eastern Idaho Technical College *C*

Illinois

Black Hawk College *C*
Elgin Community College *C*
Illinois Central College *C*
Illinois Valley Community College *C*
John A. Logan College *C*
Kaskaskia College *C*
Lewis and Clark Community College *C*
Midstate College *C*
Rock Valley College *C*

Indiana

Indiana University
Northwest *C*
South Bend *C*
Indiana University-Purdue University
Fort Wayne *C*
Indiana University-Purdue University
Indianapolis *C*

Ivy Tech State College
Columbus *C*
Eastcentral *C*
Kokomo *C*
Northeast *C*
Professional Careers Institute *C, A*
University of Southern Indiana *C, A*

Iowa

Des Moines Area Community College *C*
Hawkeye Community College *C*
Iowa Western Community College *C*
Kirkwood Community College *C, A*
Marshalltown Community College *C*
Northeast Iowa Community College *C*
Scott Community College *C*
Western Iowa Tech Community
College *C*

Kansas

Dodge City Community College *C, A*

Kentucky

Elizabethtown Community College *A*
Hazard Community College *A*

Maine

University of Maine
Augusta *C*

Maryland

Anne Arundel Community College *C, A*

Massachusetts

Berkshire Community College *A*
Massachusetts College of Pharmacy and
Health Sciences *C, A*
Massasoit Community College *C*
Mount Ida College *C, A*
Quinsigamond Community College *C*
Springfield Technical Community
College *C*

Michigan

Bay de Noc Community College *C*
Grand Rapids Community College *C, A*
Mott Community College *A*
Northwestern Michigan College *C, A*
Washtenaw Community College *C*
Wayne County Community College *C*

Minnesota

Century Community and Technical
College *C, A*
Dakota County Technical College *C*
Hennepin Technical College *C, A*
Hibbing Community College: A
Technical and Community College *A*
Minneapolis Community and Technical
College *C*
Rochester Community and Technical
College *C*
St. Cloud Technical College *C, A*
South Central Technical College *A*

Missouri

Missouri College *C*
Ozarks Technical Community College *C*
Penn Valley Community College *C, A*
St. Louis Community College
St. Louis Community College at
Forest Park *A*

Montana

Salish Kootenai College *A*

Nebraska

Central Community College *C, A*
Metropolitan Community College *C*
Mid Plains Community College Area *C*
Southeast Community College
Lincoln Campus *C*

Nevada

Truckee Meadows Community
College *C, A*

New Hampshire

New Hampshire Technical Institute *C*

New Jersey

Camden County College *C, A*
Essex County College *C*
Union County College *C*
University of Medicine and Dentistry of
New Jersey
School of Health Related
Professions *A*

New Mexico

Albuquerque Technical-Vocational
Institute *C*
San Juan College *C*
Santa Fe Community College *C*

New York

Monroe Community College *C*
New York University *C*
Niagara County Community College *C*

North Carolina

Alamance Community College *C*
Asheville Buncombe Technical
Community College *C*
Brunswick Community College *C*
Cape Fear Community College *C*
Central Piedmont Community College *C*
Coastal Carolina Community College *C*
Fayetteville Technical Community
College *C*
Guilford Technical Community
College *C*
Martin Community College *C*
Rowan-Cabarrus Community College *C*
University of North Carolina
Chapel Hill *C*
Wake Technical Community College *C*
Western Piedmont Community
College *C*
Wilkes Community College *C*

North Dakota

North Dakota State College of Science *C*

Ohio

Cuyahoga Community College
Eastern Campus *A*
Metropolitan Campus *C, A*
Western Campus *C, A*
James A. Rhodes State College *A*
Jefferson Community College *C, A*
Ohio Valley College of Technology *A*
Stautzenberger College *C, A*

Oklahoma

Platt College *C*
Platt College
Tulsa *C*
Rose State College *C, A*

Oregon

Blue Mountain Community College *C*
Central Oregon Community College *C*
Chemeketa Community College *C, A*
Lane Community College *C*
Linn-Benton Community College *C*
Portland Community College *C*

Pennsylvania

Academy of Medical Arts and
Business *C, A*
Career Training Academy *C*
Community College of Philadelphia *C*
Harrisburg Area Community College *C*
Luzerne County Community College *C*
Manor College *A*
Median School of Allied Health
Careers *C*
West Chester University of
Pennsylvania *B*
Westmoreland County Community
College *C*

Puerto Rico

Huertas Junior College *A*
University of Puerto Rico
Medical Sciences Campus *A*

Rhode Island
Community College of Rhode Island *C*

South Carolina
Aiken Technical College *C*
Florence-Darlington Technical
　College *C*
Horry-Georgetown Technical College *C*
Midlands Technical College *C, A*
Spartanburg Technical College *A*
Tri-County Technical College *C*
Trident Technical College *C*

Tennessee
Northeast State Technical Community
　College *C*
Roane State Community College *A*
Volunteer State Community College *C*

Texas
Amarillo College *C*
Del Mar College *C, A*
El Paso Community College *C, A*
Grayson County College *C*
Houston Community College System *C*
Lamar State College at Orange *C*
Lon Morris College *C*
Tarrant County College *C*
Texas State Technical College
　Waco *C*

Virginia
J. Sargeant Reynolds Community
　College *C*

Washington
Clover Park Technical College *C*
Lake Washington Technical College *C, A*
Renton Technical College *C*
Spokane Community College *C, A*

West Virginia
Huntington Junior College *C, A*

Wisconsin
Blackhawk Technical College *C*
Chippewa Valley Technical College *C*
Concordia University Wisconsin *C*
Fox Valley Technical College *C*
Lakeshore Technical College *C*
Moraine Park Technical College *C*
Waukesha County Technical College *C*
Western Wisconsin Technical College *C*

Wyoming
Sheridan College *C*
Western Wyoming Community
　College *A*

Dental clinical services

California
University of Southern California *D*

Connecticut
University of Connecticut *M*

Indiana
Indiana University-Purdue University
　Indianapolis *M, D*

Missouri
St. Louis University *B, M, D*

North Carolina
University of North Carolina
　Chapel Hill *M, D*

Ohio
Case Western Reserve University *M*

Pennsylvania
Temple University *T*

Tennessee
University of Tennessee
　Knoxville *B*

Dental hygiene

Alabama
Northwest-Shoals Community College *A*
Wallace State Community College at
　Hanceville *A*

Alaska
University of Alaska
　Anchorage *A*

Arizona
Northern Arizona University *B*
Phoenix College *A*
Pima Community College *A*
Rio Salado College *A*

Arkansas
University of Arkansas
　Fort Smith *A*
　for Medical Sciences *A, B*

California
Cabrillo College *C, A*
Cerritos Community College *C, A*
Chabot College *C, A*
Diablo Valley College *C*
Foothill College *A*
Loma Linda University *B*
Santa Rosa Junior College *C, A*
Southwestern College *A*
Taft College *A*
University of Southern California *B*

Colorado
University of Colorado
　Health Sciences Center *B*

Connecticut
Tunxis Community College *A*
University of Bridgeport *A, B*
University of New Haven *A, B*

Delaware
Delaware Technical and Community
　College
　　Stanton/Wilmington Campus *A*
　　Terry Campus *A*

District of Columbia
Howard University *C*

Florida
Broward Community College *A*
Gulf Coast Community College *A*
Indian River Community College *A*
Manatee Community College *A*
Miami-Dade Community College *A*
Palm Beach Community College *A*
Pasco-Hernando Community College *A*
Pensacola Junior College *A*
Polk Community College *A*
St. Petersburg College *A*
Santa Fe Community College *A*
South Florida Community College *A*
Tallahassee Community College *A*
Valencia Community College *A*

Georgia
Abraham Baldwin Agricultural
　College *A*
Armstrong Atlantic State University *A, B*
Athens Technical College *A*
Clayton College and State University *A*
Columbus Technical College *A*
Darton College *A*
Floyd College *A*
Gainesville College *A*
Georgia Perimeter College *A*
Gordon College *A*
Medical College of Georgia *B, M*
Middle Georgia College *A*
Valdosta State University *A*
Waycross College *A*

Hawaii
University of Hawaii
　Manoa *B*

Idaho
College of Southern Idaho *A*
Idaho State University *B*

Illinois
City Colleges of Chicago
　Kennedy-King College *A*
College of DuPage *A*
College of Lake County *A*
Illinois Central College *A*
John A. Logan College *A*
Lake Land College *A*
Lewis and Clark Community College *A*
Parkland College *A*
Prairie State College *A*
Southern Illinois University
　Carbondale *B*
William Rainey Harper College *A*

Indiana
Indiana University
　Bloomington *A, B*
　Northwest *A*
　South Bend *A*
Indiana University-Purdue University
　Fort Wayne *A*
Indiana University-Purdue University
　Indianapolis *A, B*
University of Southern Indiana *A, B*
Vincennes University *A*

Iowa
Des Moines Area Community College *A*
Hawkeye Community College *A*
Iowa Western Community College *A*
Kirkwood Community College *A*
Western Iowa Tech Community
　College *A*

Kansas
Johnson County Community College *A*
Seward County Community College *A*
Wichita State University *A, B*

Kentucky
Elizabethtown Community College *A*
Henderson Community College *C*
Lexington Community College *A*
Prestonsburg Community College *A*
University of Louisville *A, B*

Louisiana
Delgado Community College *A*
Southern University
　Shreveport *A*
University of Louisiana at Monroe *A, B*

Maine
University of Maine
　Augusta *A, B*
University of New England *A, B*

Maryland
Allegany College *A*
College of Southern Maryland *A*
University of Maryland
　Baltimore *B, M*
Villa Julie College *A*

Massachusetts
Cape Cod Community College *A*
Northeastern University *A, B*
Quinsigamond Community College *A*
Springfield Technical Community
　College *A*

Michigan
Baker College
　of Port Huron *A*
Ferris State University *A*
Grand Rapids Community College *A*
Kellogg Community College *A*
Lansing Community College *A*
Mott Community College *A*
Oakland Community College *C, A*
University of Michigan *B, M*

Minnesota
Century Community and Technical
　College *A*
Lake Superior College: A Community
　and Technical College *A*
Minnesota State University
　Mankato *B*
Normandale Community College *A*
Rochester Community and Technical
　College *A*
St. Cloud Technical College *A*
University of Minnesota
　Twin Cities *C, B*

Mississippi
University of Mississippi Medical
　Center *B*

Missouri
Missouri Southern State College *A*
Ozarks Technical Community College *A*
St. Louis Community College
　St. Louis Community College at
　　Forest Park *A*
University of Missouri
　Kansas City *B, M*

Nebraska
Central Community College *C, A*
University of Nebraska
　Medical Center *B*

Nevada
Community College of Southern
　Nevada *A*
Truckee Meadows Community
　College *A*

New Hampshire
New Hampshire Technical Institute *A*

New Jersey
Bergen Community College *A*
Brookdale Community College *A*
Camden County College *A*
Essex County College *A*
Middlesex County College *A*
Thomas Edison State College *B*
Union County College *A*
University of Medicine and Dentistry of
　New Jersey
　　School of Health Related
　　Professions *A, B*

New Mexico
San Juan College *A*
University of New Mexico *A, B*

New York
Broome Community College *A*
City University of New York
　Hostos Community College *A*
Erie Community College
　North Campus *A*
Hudson Valley Community College *A*
Monroe Community College *A*
New York University *A*
Onondaga Community College *A*
Orange County Community College *A*
State University of New York
　Farmingdale *A*

North Carolina
Asheville Buncombe Technical
　Community College *A*
Cape Fear Community College *A*
Catawba Valley Community College *A*
Central Piedmont Community College *A*
Coastal Carolina Community College *A*
Fayetteville Technical Community
　College *A*
Guilford Technical Community
　College *A*
University of North Carolina
　Chapel Hill *C, B*
Wayne Community College *A*
Wilkes Community College *A*

North Dakota
North Dakota State College of Science *A*

Ohio
Columbus State Community College *A*
Cuyahoga Community College
    Eastern Campus *A*
    Metropolitan Campus *A*
    Western Campus *A*
Lakeland Community College *A*
Lorain County Community College *A*
Ohio State University
    Columbus Campus *B*
Owens Community College
    Toledo *A*
Shawnee State University *A*
Sinclair Community College *A*
Stark State College of Technology *A*
University of Cincinnati
    Raymond Walters College *A*
Youngstown State University *A*

Oklahoma
Rose State College *A*
Tulsa Community College *A*
University of Oklahoma *B*

Oregon
Lane Community College *A*
Mount Hood Community College *A*
Oregon Health Sciences University *B*
Oregon Institute of Technology *A, B*
Portland Community College *A*

Pennsylvania
California University of Pennsylvania *B*
Community College of Philadelphia *A*
Harrisburg Area Community College *A*
Luzerne County Community College *A*
Manor College *A*
Montgomery County Community
    College *A*
Northampton County Area Community
    College *A*
Pennsylvania College of
    Technology *A, B*
University of Pittsburgh *C, B*
West Chester University of
    Pennsylvania *B*
Westmorland County Community
    College *A*

Puerto Rico
University of Puerto Rico
    Medical Sciences Campus *A*

Rhode Island
Community College of Rhode Island *A*
University of Rhode Island *B*

South Carolina
Central Carolina Technical College *C*
Florence-Darlington Technical College *A*
Horry-Georgetown Technical College *A*
Midlands Technical College *C, A*
Orangeburg-Calhoun Technical
    College *C*
Piedmont Technical College *C*
Tri-County Technical College *C*
Trident Technical College *C, A*
York Technical College *A*

South Dakota
University of South Dakota *A, B*

Tennessee
Chattanooga State Technical Community
    College *A*
Columbia State Community College *A*
East Tennessee State University *A, B*
Southern Adventist University *A*
Tennessee State University *A, B*
University of Tennessee
    Knoxville *B*
University of Tennessee Health Science
    Center *B*

Texas
Amarillo College *A*

Blinn College *C, A*
Coastal Bend College *A*
Collin County Community College
    District *A*
Del Mar College *A*
El Paso Community College *A*
Howard College *A*
Midwestern State University *B*
Northeast Texas Community College *A*
Tarrant County College *A*
Temple College *A*
Texas A&M University
    Baylor College of Dentistry *B, M*
Texas Woman's University *B*
Tyler Junior College *A*
University of Texas
    Health Science Center at San
        Antonio *B*
    Houston Health Science
        Center *C, B*
Wharton County Junior College *A*

Utah
Dixie State College of Utah *C, A*
Salt Lake Community College *A*
Utah Valley State College *A*
Weber State University *A, B*

Vermont
Vermont Technical College *A*

Virginia
Old Dominion University *B, M*
Virginia Commonwealth University *B*
Virginia Highlands Community
    College *A*
Virginia Western Community College *A*

Washington
Clark College *A*
Eastern Washington University *B*
Everett Community College *A*
Lake Washington Technical College *A*
University of Washington *B*

West Virginia
West Liberty State College *A, B*
West Virginia University *B, M*
West Virginia University Institute of
    Technology *A*

Wisconsin
Blackhawk Technical College *A*
Chippewa Valley Technical College *A*
Fox Valley Technical College *A*
Marquette University *B*
Milwaukee Area Technical College *A*
Waukesha County Technical College *A*
Western Wisconsin Technical College *A*

Wyoming
Laramie County Community College *A*
Sheridan College *A*
University of Wyoming *B*

Dental laboratory technology

Alabama
Community College of the Air Force *A*
Trenholm State Technical College *A*

Arizona
Pima Community College *A*

California
Diablo Valley College *C*
Riverside Community College *C, A*
San Diego Mesa College *A*

Florida
Florida National College *A*
Indian River Community College *A*

Georgia
Atlanta Metropolitan College *A*

Idaho
Idaho State University *A*

Illinois
Southern Illinois University
    Carbondale *A*

Indiana
Indiana University-Purdue University
    Fort Wayne *A*

Iowa
Kirkwood Community College *A*

Kentucky
Lexington Community College *A*

Louisiana
Delgado Community College *A*

Massachusetts
Boston University *B*

Michigan
Bay de Noc Community College *C*

Nevada
Western Nevada Community College *C*

New York
Erie Community College
    South Campus *A*
New York University *M*

North Carolina
Durham Technical Community
    College *C, A*

Ohio
Columbus State Community College *A*
Cuyahoga Community College
    Eastern Campus *C, A*
    Metropolitan Campus *C, A*
    Western Campus *C, A*

Oregon
Portland Community College *C, A*

Pennsylvania
Commonwealth Technical Institute *A*
Delaware County Community College *C*
West Chester University of
    Pennsylvania *B*

Tennessee
Northeast State Technical Community
    College *C, A*

Texas
Howard College *C, A*
University of Texas
    Health Science Center at San
        Antonio *B*

Virginia
J. Sargeant Reynolds Community
    College *C, A*

West Virginia
West Virginia State College *A*

Wisconsin
Milwaukee Area Technical College *A*

Dentistry (D.D.S., D.M.D.)

Alabama
University of Alabama at Birmingham:
    School of Dentistry *F*

California
Loma Linda University: School of
    Dentistry *F*
University of California Los Angeles:
    School of Dentistry *F*
University of California San Francisco:
    School of Dentistry *F*
University of Southern California: School
    of Dentistry *F*
University of the Pacific: School of
    Dentistry *F*

Colorado
University of Colorado Health Sciences
    Center: School of Dentistry *F*

Connecticut
University of Connecticut: School of
    Dentistry *F*

District of Columbia
Howard University: College of
    Dentistry *F*

Florida
University of Florida: College of
    Dentistry *F*

Georgia
Medical College of Georgia: School of
    Dentistry *F*

Illinois
Northwestern University: Dental
    School *F*
Southern Illinois University: School of
    Dentistry *F*
University of Illinois at Chicago: College
    of Dentistry *F*

Indiana
Indiana University School of Dentistry *F*

Iowa
University of Iowa College of
    Dentistry *F*

Kentucky
University of Kentucky: College of
    Dentistry *F*
University of Louisville: School of
    Dentistry *F*

Louisiana
Louisiana State University Health
    Sciences Center: School of Dentistry *F*

Maryland
University of Maryland at Baltimore:
    School of Dentistry *F*

Massachusetts
Boston University Goldman School of
    Dental Medicine *F*
Harvard School of Dental Medicine *F*
Tufts University: School of Dental
    Medicine *F*

Michigan
University of Detroit Mercy: School of
    Dentistry *F*
University of Michigan: School of
    Dentistry *F*

Minnesota
University of Minnesota Twin Cities:
    School of Dentistry *F*

Mississippi
University of Mississippi Medical
    Center: School of Dentistry *F*

Missouri
University of Missouri Kansas City:
    School of Dentistry *F*

Nebraska
Creighton University: School of
    Dentistry *F*
University of Nebraska Medical Center:
    College of Dentistry *F*

New Jersey
University of Medicine and Dentistry of
    New Jersey
        New Jersey Dental School *F*

New York
Columbia University
    School of Dental and Oral
        Surgery *F*
New York University: College of
    Dentistry *F*

State University of New York Health
Sciences Center at Stony Brook:
School of Dentistry *F*
State University of New York at Buffalo:
School of Dentistry *F*

North Carolina

University of North Carolina at Chapel
Hill: School of Dentistry *F*

Ohio

Case Western Reserve University: School
of Dentistry *F*
Ohio State University Columbus
Campus: College of Dentistry *F*

Oklahoma

University of Oklahoma Health Sciences
Center: College of Dentistry *F*

Oregon

Oregon Health Sciences University:
School of Dentistry *F*

Pennsylvania

Temple University: School of
Dentistry *F*
University of Pennsylvania: School of
Dental Medicine *F*
University of Pittsburgh: School of
Dental Medicine *F*

Puerto Rico

University of Puerto Rico Medical
Sciences Campus: School of
Dentistry *F*

South Carolina

Medical University of South Carolina:
College of Dental Medicine *F*

Tennessee

Meharry Medical College: School of
Dentistry *F*
University of Tennessee Memphis:
College of Dentistry *F*

Texas

Texas A&M University: Baylor College
of Dentistry *F*
University of Texas Health Science
Center: Dental School *F*
University of Texas Health Sciences
Center-Dental Branch *F*

Virginia

Virginia Commonwealth University:
School of Dentistry *F*

Washington

University of Washington: School of
Dentistry *F*

West Virginia

West Virginia University: School of
Dentistry *F*

Wisconsin

Marquette University: School of
Dentistry *F*

Design/visual communications

Alabama

Auburn University *B*

Arizona

Arizona State University *M*
Collins College *A*
Pima Community College *A*
Yavapai College *C*

Arkansas

John Brown University *B*

California

Academy of Art College *A, B, M*
Art Center College of Design *B, M*

Art Institute
of California: Los Angeles *A, B*
California State University
Chico *B*
Long Beach *B*
Sacramento *B*
Laney College *C, A*
Long Beach City College *A*
Mount San Antonio College *A*
Otis College of Art and Design *B*
San Diego State University *B*
University of California
Berkeley *M*
Davis *B*
Los Angeles *B, M*
Santa Cruz *C, B*
University of Southern California *M*
Westwood College of Technology *A, B*
Westwood College of Technology
Inland Empire *B*

Colorado

Art Institute
of Colorado *A, B*
Colorado Mountain College
Spring Valley Campus *A*
Front Range Community College *C*
Westwood College of Technology
South *B*

Connecticut

Central Connecticut State
University *B, M*
Northwestern Connecticut Community
College *A*
Paier College of Art *C, B*
Sacred Heart University *B*
University of Hartford *M*

District of Columbia

American University *B*
Howard University *B*

Florida

International Academy of Design and
Technology *A, B*
Jacksonville University *B*

Georgia

Atlanta College of Art *B*
DeKalb Technical College *C*

Idaho

Lewis-Clark State College *A, B*
University of Idaho *B*

Illinois

American Academy of Art *B*
Black Hawk College *A*
City Colleges of Chicago
Harold Washington College *A*
Wright College *C, A*
College of DuPage *C, A*
Columbia College Chicago *B*
Elgin Community College *C, A*
Illinois Institute of Art *B*
Illinois Institute of Technology *M, D*
International Academy of Design and
Technology *A, B*
Judson College *B*
Moraine Valley Community College *A*
Northwestern University *M*
Parkland College *A*
Prairie State College *A*
Robert Morris College: Chicago *A, B*
School of the Art Institute of
Chicago *B, M*
Southern Illinois University
Carbondale *B*
Waubonsee Community College *C, A*

Indiana

Ball State University *B*
Bethel College *A, B*
Indiana University-Purdue University
Indianapolis *M*
International Business College *C, A*

Ivy Tech State College
Central Indiana *A*
Columbus *A*
Kokomo *A*
Northcentral *A*
Southcentral *A*
Southwest *A*
Wabash Valley *A*
Purdue University *B*
University of Evansville *B*
University of Indianapolis *B*
University of Notre Dame *B, M*
Vincennes University *A*

Iowa

Dordt College *B*
Iowa State University *B, M*

Kansas

University of Kansas *B, M*

Louisiana

Delgado Community College *A*
Northwestern State University *B*

Maryland

Maryland College of Art and Design *A*
Maryland Institute College of Art *B*
Villa Julie College *B*

Massachusetts

Becker College *B*
Bunker Hill Community College *A*
Emmanuel College *B*
Endicott College *B*
Hampshire College *B*
Harvard College *B*
Katharine Gibbs School *A*
Lasell College *B*
Massachusetts College of Art *B, M*
Montserrat College of Art *B*
Northeastern University *A, B*
University of Massachusetts
Dartmouth *B, M*

Michigan

Andrews University *B*
Central Michigan University *B*
College for Creative Studies *B*
Ferris State University *B*
Finlandia University *B*
Northern Michigan University *B*
Saginaw Valley State University *B*
University of Michigan *B*

Minnesota

Brown College *A*
Central Lakes College *C*
College of Visual Arts *B*
University of Minnesota
Twin Cities *B*
Winona State University *B*

Missouri

Drury University *B*
Southwest Missouri State University *B*
Washington University in St. Louis *B, M*
William Woods University *B*

Nevada

Truckee Meadows Community
College *A*

New Hampshire

Franklin Pierce College *B*
Rivier College *A, B*

New Jersey

Bloomfield College *B*
Kean University *B*

New Mexico

New Mexico Highlands University *B*
New Mexico State University
Alamogordo *A*
Santa Fe Community College *C, A*

New York

Bryant & Stratton Business Institute
Rochester *A*

Cazenovia College *B*
City University of New York
Baruch College *B*
Daemen College *B*
Eugene Lang College/New School
University *B*
Hofstra University *B*
Parsons School of Design *C, A, B, M, T*
Pratt Institute *M*
Rochester Institute of Technology *A, B*
School of Visual Arts *B, M*
State University of New York
Farmingdale *B*

North Carolina

Duke University *B*
Mount Olive College *B*
North Carolina Central University *B*
Peace College *B*

Ohio

Art Institute of Cincinnati *A*
Bowling Green State University *B*
Edison State Community College *A*
Mount Union College *B*
Mount Vernon Nazarene University *B*
Northwest State Community College *A*
Ohio Institute of Photography and
Technology *A*
Ohio State University
Columbus Campus *B*
Ohio University *B*
University of Cincinnati *M*
University of Cincinnati
Raymond Walters College *A*
University of Dayton *B*
Virginia Marti College of Art and
Design *A*

Oklahoma

Oral Roberts University *B*
Rose State College *A*
University of Oklahoma *B, M*

Oregon

Chemeketa Community College *A*
Portland State University *B*

Pennsylvania

Allentown Business School *A*
Antonelli Institute of Art and
Photography *A*
Art Institute
of Philadelphia *A, B*
of Pittsburgh *A*
California University of Pennsylvania *A*
Carnegie Mellon University *B, M, D*
Chatham College *B*
Drexel University *B*
Harrisburg Area Community College *A*
Marywood University *C, B, M*
Oakbridge Academy of Arts *A*
Point Park College *B*
Robert Morris University *B*

Puerto Rico

Escuela de Artes Plasticas de Puerto
Rico *B*

South Carolina

Clemson University *B*
University of South Carolina
Spartanburg *B*
Winthrop University *M*

Tennessee

Memphis College of Art *B, M*

Texas

Amarillo College *C, A*
Howard Payne University *B*
Lubbock Christian University *B*
San Jacinto College
Central Campus *C*
South Plains College *A*
Texas A&M University
Commerce *B*
Texas Woman's University *B, M*

University of Texas
Austin *B, M*

Utah
Salt Lake Community College *A*
Utah Valley State College *C, A*
Weber State University *B*

Vermont
Bennington College *B*
Champlain College *C, A, B*

Virginia
Radford University *B*
Virginia Commonwealth
University *B, M*

Washington
Cornish College of the Arts *B*

West Virginia
Bethany College *B*
Fairmont State College *A*
Shepherd College *A*

Wisconsin
Carroll College *B*
Mount Mary College *B*
St. Norbert College *B*
University of Wisconsin
Madison *B*

Desktop publishing

Arkansas
Arkansas State University *B*
South Arkansas Community College *A*

California
Antelope Valley College *C*
Long Beach City College *C, A*
Ohlone College *A*
Silicon Valley College
Emeryville *C, A, B*

Connecticut
Manchester Community College *C*

Indiana
Vincennes University *A*

Iowa
Graceland University *B*
Maharishi University of Management *B*
Western Iowa Tech Community
College *A*

Maryland
Montgomery College
Rockville Campus *C, A*

Michigan
Baker College
of Muskegon *A*

Minnesota
Hennepin Technical College *C, A*
Minneapolis Community and Technical
College *C*
Riverland Community College: A
Technical and Community College *C*
St. Mary's University of Minnesota *B*
St. Paul College - A Community and
Technical College *C*

Nevada
Western Nevada Community College *C*

New York
Rochester Institute of Technology *B*

Ohio
Ohio University *B*
Sinclair Community College *C*
University of Cincinnati
Raymond Walters College *C*

Oregon
Portland Community College *C*

Pennsylvania
Chatham College *M*
La Salle University *B*
Marywood University *C*

Texas
Eastfield College *C, A*
Houston Community College System *C*

Vermont
Castleton State College *B*

Washington
Henry Cogswell College *B*

Wisconsin
Western Wisconsin Technical College *A*

Development economics

Alabama
Alabama Agricultural and Mechanical
University *M*

Arkansas
Arkansas State University *B*

Georgia
Covenant College *B*

Massachusetts
University of Massachusetts
Lowell *M*

Rhode Island
Brown University *B*

Virginia
Eastern Mennonite University *B*

**Developmental biology/
embryology**

Iowa
University of Iowa *M, D*

New York
University of Rochester *B*

Ohio
Case Western Reserve University *D*

**Developmental/child
psychology**

Arizona
South Mountain Community College *A*

Arkansas
University of Central Arkansas *B*

California
California State University
Bakersfield *B*
Hayward *M*
Sacramento *B*
Stanislaus *B*
St. Mary's College of California *B*
San Francisco State University *M*
San Jose State University *M*
University of California
Santa Cruz *B, D*
University of Southern California *M, D*

Connecticut
Connecticut College *B*
Mitchell College *B*

District of Columbia
Catholic University of America *M, D*
George Washington University *D*

Florida
Florida International University *D*

Georgia
University of Georgia *D*

Illinois
De Paul University *M*
Loyola University of Chicago *M, D*
National-Louis University *B*

Indiana
Purdue University
Calumet *B*

Iowa
University of Iowa *D*

Kansas
University of Kansas *B, M, D*

Kentucky
Lindsey Wilson College *M*

Maryland
Johns Hopkins University *M*
University of Maryland
Baltimore County *M, D*
College Park *M, D*

Massachusetts
Bay Path College *B*
Becker College *B*
Emmanuel College *B*
Fitchburg State College *B*
Hampshire College *B*
Harvard College *B*
Northeastern University *M*
Pine Manor College *B*
Simon's Rock College of Bard *B*
Suffolk University *B*
Tufts University *B, M, D*

Minnesota
Metropolitan State University *B*
St. Mary's University of Minnesota *M*
University of Minnesota
Twin Cities *B, M, D*

Montana
University of Montana-Missoula *M, D*

New Hampshire
Colby-Sawyer College *B*
Keene State College *B*
Southern New Hampshire University *B*

New Jersey
Gloucester County College *A*
Rowan University *M*

New York
Bard College *B*
Cornell University *B, M, D*
Fulton-Montgomery Community
College *A*
Metropolitan College of New York *A, B*
Sarah Lawrence College *B*
State University of New York
Albany *M, D*
Purchase *C*
University of Rochester *D*
Utica College *B*
Yeshiva University *D*

North Carolina
North Carolina State University *M*

Ohio
Bowling Green State University *M, D*
Case Western Reserve University *D*
University of Akron *T*

Oklahoma
Northeastern State University *B*
Redlands Community College *C*

Oregon
Warner Pacific College *B*

Pennsylvania
Duquesne University *D*
Moravian College *B*
Temple University *M, D*

Tennessee
Maryville College *B*

University of Tennessee
Knoxville *B*
Vanderbilt University *M, D*

Texas
Houston Baptist University *B*
University of Houston *M, D*
University of Texas
Dallas *M*
University of the Incarnate Word *M*

Vermont
Bennington College *B*
Marlboro College *B*

Virginia
Longwood University *B*
Radford University *M*

Washington
Eastern Washington University *B, M, T*
Western Washington University *B*

**Diagnostic medical
sonography**

Alabama
Northwest-Shoals Community College *A*
Wallace State Community College at
Hanceville *A*

Arizona
Gateway Community College *C, A*

California
Foothill College *C, A*
Loma Linda University *C*
Orange Coast College *C, A*

Colorado
Red Rocks Community College *C*

Connecticut
Gateway Community College *A*

Delaware
Delaware Technical and Community
College
Stanton/Wilmington Campus *A*

District of Columbia
George Washington University *B*

Florida
Barry University *B*
Broward Community College *A*
Florida Hospital College of Health
Sciences *C, A*
Hillsborough Community College *A*
Pensacola Junior College *C, A*
Polk Community College *A*
Valencia Community College *A*

Georgia
Athens Technical College *A*
Medical College of Georgia *C, B*
Southwest Georgia Technical College *C*

Illinois
City Colleges of Chicago
Wright College *A*
College of DuPage *C*
Kaskaskia College *C*
South Suburban College of Cook
County *C*
Triton College *A*

Indiana
Indiana University
Bloomington *B*

Iowa
Mercy College of Health Sciences *A*

Kansas
Fort Hays State University *B*
Newman University *B*
Washburn University of Topeka *C*

Louisiana
Delgado Community College *C*
Southern University
Shreveport *A*

Maryland
Montgomery College
Rockville Campus *A*

Massachusetts
Bunker Hill Community College *C*
Massasoit Community College *C*
Springfield Technical Community
College *A*

Michigan
Baker College
of Owosso *A*
of Port Huron *A*
Ferris State University *A*
Jackson Community College *C, A*
Lansing Community College *A*
Mott Community College *A*
Oakland Community College *C, A*

Minnesota
College of St. Catherine *A*
St. Cloud Technical College *C, A*

Mississippi
Itawamba Community College *A*

Missouri
Penn Valley Community College *C*
St. Louis Community College
St. Louis Community College at
Forest Park *C, A*

Nebraska
Nebraska Methodist College of Nursing
and Allied Health *A, B*
University of Nebraska
Medical Center *B*

New Hampshire
New Hampshire Technical Institute *C*

New Jersey
Bergen Community College *A*
Gloucester County College *A*
Thomas Edison State College *A, B*
University of Medicine and Dentistry of
New Jersey
School of Health Related
Professions *B*

New Mexico
Albuquerque Technical-Vocational
Institute *A*

New York
Hudson Valley Community College *C*
Rochester Institute of Technology *C, B*
State University of New York
Health Science Center at
Brooklyn *B*
Trocaire College *C*

North Carolina
Caldwell Community College and
Technical Institute *A*
Cape Fear Community College *C, A*
Forsyth Technical Community College *A*
Johnston Community College *C*
Pitt Community College *A*

Ohio
Central Ohio Technical College *C, A*
Cuyahoga Community College
Eastern Campus *A*
Western Campus *A*
Kent State University *A*
Kettering College of Medical Arts *C, A*

Oklahoma
University of Oklahoma *B*

Oregon
Oregon Health Sciences University *C*
Portland Community College *A*

Pennsylvania
Community College of Allegheny
County *C, A*
Keystone College *A*
Northampton County Area Community
College *C*
South Hills School of Business &
Technology *C, A*
Western School of Health and Business
Careers *A*

Puerto Rico
Universidad del Este *C, A*

Rhode Island
Community College of Rhode Island *C*

Tennessee
Volunteer State Community College *C*

Texas
Austin Community College *C, A*
Del Mar College *C, A*
El Centro College *C, A*
El Paso Community College *C*
Houston Community College System *C*
St. Philip's College *C*
Tyler Junior College *C, A*

Utah
Weber State University *B*

Virginia
Southwest Virginia Community
College *C*

Washington
Bellevue Community College *A*
Seattle University *B*
Wenatchee Valley College *A*

West Virginia
Mountain State University *A, B*

Wisconsin
Chippewa Valley Technical College *A*

Diesel mechanics

Alabama
Alabama Southern Community
College *A*
Bishop State Community College *C*
Douglas MacArthur State Technical
College *C*
Harry M. Ayers State Technical
College *C*
Shelton State Community College *C, A*
Wallace Community College: Sparks
Campus *C*
Wallace State Community College at
Hanceville *C, A*

Alaska
University of Alaska
Anchorage *C, A*
Southeast *C, A*

Arizona
Arizona Automotive Institute *C, A*
Central Arizona College *C, A*

California
Cerritos Community College *C*
Citrus College *C, A*
Golden West College *A*
Long Beach City College *C, A*
Los Angeles Trade and Technical
College *C, A*
Santa Rosa Junior College *C*
Shasta College *C, A*
Yuba Community College District *C*

Colorado
Trinidad State Junior College *C, A*

Georgia
Albany Technical College *C*
DeKalb Technical College *C*

Georgia Southwestern State University *A*

Hawaii
University of Hawaii
Hawaii Community College *C, A*
Honolulu Community College *C, A*

Idaho
College of Southern Idaho *C, A*
Eastern Idaho Technical College *C, A*
Idaho State University *C, A*
Lewis-Clark State College *C, A*
North Idaho College *C, A*

Illinois
Black Hawk College *C, A*
Black Hawk College
East Campus *C*
Danville Area Community College *A*
Illinois Eastern Community Colleges
Wabash Valley College *A*
John A. Logan College *C*
Kishwaukee College *C*
Parkland College *A*
Rend Lake College *A*
Sauk Valley Community College *A*
Southeastern Illinois College *C, A*

Indiana
Oakland City University *C, A*
Vincennes University *A*

Iowa
Des Moines Area Community
College *C, A*
Indian Hills Community College *A*
Kirkwood Community College *C, A*
Northeast Iowa Community College *C*
Northwest Iowa Community College *A*
Scott Community College *A*
Western Iowa Tech Community
College *C*

Kansas
North Central Kansas Technical
College *A*
Pittsburg State University *B*

Kentucky
Somerset Community College *C*

Massachusetts
Massasoit Community College *C, A*

Minnesota
Alexandria Technical College *C, A*
Central Lakes College *C*
Dakota County Technical College *C*
Hennepin Technical College *C, A*
Hibbing Community College: A
Technical and Community College *C*
Lake Superior College: A Community
and Technical College *C*
Riverland Community College: A
Technical and Community College *C*
St. Cloud Technical College *C, A*
St. Paul College - A Community and
Technical College *C*
South Central Technical College *C*

Mississippi
Itawamba Community College *C, A*

Missouri
Crowder College *C, A*
Ozarks Technical Community
College *C, A*
St. Louis Community College
St. Louis Community College at
Forest Park *C*

Montana
Montana State University
Billings *C, A*
Billings College of Technology *C*
University of Montana-Missoula *A*

Nebraska
Central Community College *C, A*

Mid Plains Community College
Area *A*
Nebraska College of Technical
Agriculture *A*
Northeast Community College *A*
Southeast Community College
Milford Campus *A*

Nevada
Great Basin College *C, A*
Truckee Meadows Community
College *A*

New Hampshire
New Hampshire Community Technical
College
Berlin *A*

New Mexico
Albuquerque Technical-Vocational
Institute *C*
San Juan College *C, A*

New York
State University of New York
College of Agriculture and
Technology at Cobleskill *A*
College of Agriculture and
Technology at Morrisville *A*
College of Technology at Alfred *A*

North Carolina
Cape Fear Community College *C*
Forsyth Technical Community College *C*
Guilford Technical Community
College *C, A*
Johnston Community College *C, A*
Wilkes Community College *C, A*
Wilson Technical Community College *C*

North Dakota
Lake Region State College *C, A*
North Dakota State College of
Science *C, A*
Williston State College *A*

Ohio
Owens Community College
Toledo *A*
University of Northwestern Ohio *C, A*
Washington State Community College *A*

Oklahoma
Oklahoma State University
Okmulgee *A*
Western Oklahoma State College *A*

Oregon
Lane Community College *C, A*
Linn-Benton Community College *C, A*
Portland Community College *C, A*
Rogue Community College *C, A*

Pennsylvania
Delaware County Community College *C*
Pennsylvania College of
Technology *C, A*

South Dakota
Southeast Technical Institute *A*
Western Dakota Technical Institute *C*

Tennessee
Nashville Auto-Diesel College *C, A*

Texas
Angelina College *C*
Central Texas College *C, A*
College of the Mainland *C, A*
Del Mar College *C, A*
Eastfield College *C, A*
Houston Community College System *C*
Kilgore College *C, A*
North Central Texas College *A*
Northeast Texas Community
College *C, A*
St. Philip's College *C, A*
South Plains College *C, A*
South Texas Community College *C, A*

Texas State Technical College
Waco *A*

Utah
College of Eastern Utah *A*
Dixie State College of Utah *C, A*
Salt Lake Community College *C, A*
Utah Valley State College *C, A*
Weber State University *A*

Virginia
J. Sargeant Reynolds Community
College *C*
Southside Virginia Community
College *C*
Southwest Virginia Community
College *C*

Washington
Centralia College *A*
Clark College *C, A*
Grays Harbor College *A*
Lake Washington Technical College *C, A*
Peninsula College *A*
Spokane Community College *A*

Wisconsin
Blackhawk Technical College *A*
Chippewa Valley Technical College *C*
Mid-State Technical College *C*
Western Wisconsin Technical College *A*

Wyoming
Casper College *C, A*
Sheridan College *C, A*

Dietetic technician

California
Long Beach City College *C, A*

Louisiana
University of Louisiana at Lafayette *B*

New Hampshire
University of New Hampshire *A*

Pennsylvania
Marywood University *C, B*

Texas
Tarleton State University *A*
University of Texas
Pan American *B*

Virginia
James Madison University *B*

Dietetics

Alabama
University of Alabama
Birmingham *M*

Arkansas
Harding University *B*
University of Central Arkansas *B*

California
California State Polytechnic University:
Pomona *B, M*
Loma Linda University *A, B*
University of California
Berkeley *B*

Connecticut
Briarwood College *A*

Florida
Palm Beach Community College *A*

Illinois
University of Illinois
Chicago *B, M, D*

Indiana
Indiana University-Purdue University
Indianapolis *M*

Louisiana
Louisiana State University and
Agricultural and Mechanical
College *B*
University of Louisiana at Lafayette *B*

Massachusetts
Laboure College *C, A*

Minnesota
Normandale Community College *A*

Missouri
University of Missouri
Columbia *B*

North Carolina
East Carolina University *B*

Ohio
Case Western Reserve
University *B, M, D*
James A. Rhodes State College *A*
Ohio State University
Columbus Campus *B, M*
University of Akron *B, M*

Oregon
Oregon Health Sciences University *C*

Pennsylvania
Mercyhurst College *B*

Texas
El Paso Community College *A*
Tarleton State University *B*

Washington
Bastyr University *B*

West Virginia
Marshall University *B*

Wisconsin
University of Wisconsin
Stout *B*

Dietician assistant

Indiana
Vincennes University *A*

Kansas
Barton County Community College *C, A*

Pennsylvania
Butler County Community College *A*
Community College of Allegheny
County *C, A*
Pennsylvania College of Technology *C*

Digital media

Arizona
Northern Arizona University *B*

Arkansas
Arkansas State University *B*
Harding University *B*
South Arkansas Community College *A*

California
Art Institute
of California - Orange County *A, B*
California State University
Chico *B*
Dominican University of California *B*
Grossmont Community College *C, A*
Long Beach City College *C*
National University *B*
Ohlone College *C, A*
Otis College of Art and Design *B*
Santa Barbara City College *C, A*
University of Southern California *B, M*
Vanguard University of Southern
California *B*
Westwood College of Technology
Inland Empire *A, B*

Colorado
Colorado Technical University *C*
Jones International University *C, B*

Connecticut
Manchester Community College *A*
Naugatuck Valley Community College *A*
Quinnipiac University *B*

District of Columbia
American University *B*

Florida
Florida Atlantic University *B*

Georgia
Georgia Institute of Technology *M*

Illinois
Bradley University *B*
Southern Illinois University
Carbondale *M*

Indiana
Indiana University
Bloomington *B, M*
Vincennes University *A*

Kansas
Southwestern College *B*

Maryland
Frederick Community College *C*
Howard Community College *A*

Massachusetts
Massachusetts Institute of
Technology *M, D*

Michigan
Calvin College *B*
College for Creative Studies *B*

Minnesota
Art Institutes International
Minnesota *A, B*
Hennepin Technical College *C, A*

Missouri
Ozarks Technical Community College *A*

New Jersey
Bloomfield College *C*
Sussex County Community College *C*

New York
Canisius College *B*
Long Island University
C. W. Post Campus *M*
Marist College *B*
New York University *B*
Rensselaer Polytechnic Institute *B*
Rochester Institute of Technology *B*
State University of New York
Buffalo *M, D*

Ohio
Bowling Green State University *B*
Denison University *B*
Franklin University *B*
Mount Union College *B*
North Central State College *A*
Ohio University
Zanesville Campus *A*
Sinclair Community College *C*
University of Cincinnati
Raymond Walters College *C, A*

Oklahoma
Rose State College *C, A*

Pennsylvania
Central Pennsylvania College *A*
La Salle University *B*
Marywood University *B*
Waynesburg College *B*

Tennessee
King College *B*
Union University *B*

Texas
Collin County Community College
District *C, A*
Del Mar College *A*
Sam Houston State University *B*
Texas A&M University
Commerce *B*

Vermont
Castleton State College *B*

Washington
Olympic College *A*

Directing/theatrical production

California
California Institute of the Arts *M*

Iowa
Drake University *B*

Maine
University of Southern Maine *B*

Massachusetts
Boston University *B, M*
Emerson College *B*

New York
Bard College *B*

Pennsylvania
Penn State
Abington *B*
Altoona *B*
Beaver *B*
Berks *B*
Delaware County *B*
Dubois *B*
Fayette *B*
Hazleton *B*
Lehigh Valley *B*
McKeesport *B*
Mont Alto *B*
New Kensington *B*
Shenango *B*
York *B*

Texas
Texas Christian University *B*
Texas Tech University *B, M*

Divinity/ministry (B.Div., M.Div.)

Alabama
Beeson Divinity School at Samford
University *F*
Southern Christian University *F*

California
American Baptist Seminary of the
West *F*
Azusa Pacific University: School of
Theology *F*
Church Divinity School of the Pacific *F*
Claremont School of Theology *F*
Dominican School of Philosophy and
Theology *F*
Franciscan School of Theology *F*
Fuller Theological Seminary *F*
Golden Gate Baptist Theological
Seminary *F*
International School of Theology *F*
Jesuit School of Theology at Berkeley:
Professional *F*
Mennonite Brethren Biblical Seminary *F*
Pacific Lutheran Theological
Seminary *F*
Pacific School of Religion *F*
St. John's Seminary *F*
St. Patrick's Seminary *F*
San Francisco Theological Seminary *F*
Starr King School for the Ministry *F*

Talbot School of Theology of Biola
University *F*
Westminster Theological Seminary in
California *F*

Colorado

Denver Conservative Baptist Seminary *F*
Iliff School of Theology *F*

Connecticut

Holy Apostles College and Seminary *F*
Yale University: Divinity School *F*

District of Columbia

Catholic University of America: School
of Theology *F*
Dominican House of Studies *F*
Howard University: Divinity School *F*
Washington Theological Union *F*
Wesley Theological Seminary *F*

Florida

St. Vincent De Paul Regional
Seminary *F*

Georgia

Candler School of Theology *F*
Columbia Theological Seminary *F*
Interdenominational Theological
Center *F*

Illinois

Bethany Theological Seminary *F*
Catholic Theological Union *F*
Chicago Theological Seminary *F*
Garrett-Evangelical Theological
Seminary *F*
Lincoln Christian Seminary *F*
Lutheran School of Theology at
Chicago *F*
McCormick Theological Seminary *F*
Meadville-Lombard Theological
School *F*
North Park Theological Seminary *F*
Northern Baptist Theological
Seminary *F*
Seabury-Western Theological
Seminary *F*
Trinity Evangelical Divinity School *F*
University of Chicago: Divinity
School *F*
University of St. Mary of the
Lake--Mundelein Seminary *F*

Indiana

Anderson University: School of
Theology *F*
Associated Mennonite Biblical
Seminary *F*
Bethel College *F*
Christian Theological Seminary *F*
Concordia Theological Seminary *F*
Earlham School of Religion *F*
St. Meinrad School of Theology *F*
University of Notre Dame: School of
Theology *F*

Iowa

Faith Baptist Theological Seminary *F*
University of Dubuque: School of
Theology *F*
Wartburg Theological Seminary *F*

Kansas

Central Baptist Theological Seminary *F*

Kentucky

Asbury Theological Seminary *F*
Lexington Theological Seminary *F*
Louisville Presbyterian Theological
Seminary *F*
Southern Baptist Theological
Seminary *F*

Louisiana

New Orleans Baptist Theological
Seminary *F*
Notre Dame Seminary School of
Theology *F*

Maine

Bangor Theological Seminary *F*

Maryland

Capital Bible Seminary *F*
Mount St. Mary's College: Seminary *F*
St. Mary's Seminary and University *F*

Massachusetts

Andover Newton Theological School *F*
Boston University: School of
Theology *F*
Episcopal Divinity School *F*
Gordon-Conwell Theological
Seminary *F*
Harvard University: Divinity School *F*
Holy Cross Greek Orthodox School of
Theology *F*
Pope John XXIII National Seminary *F*
St. John's Seminary *F*
Weston Jesuit School of Theology *F*

Michigan

Andrews University Seminary *F*
Calvin Theological Seminary *F*
Grand Rapids Baptist Seminary *F*
Sacred Heart Major Seminary *F*
Western Theological Seminary *F*

Minnesota

Bethel Theological Seminary *F*
Luther Seminary: Theological
Professions *F*
St. John's University: School of
Theology *F*
United Theological Seminary of the Twin
Cities *F*
University of St. Thomas: School of
Divinity *F*

Mississippi

Reformed Theological Seminary *F*
Wesley Biblical Seminary *F*

Missouri

Aquinas Institute of Theology *F*
Assemblies of God Theological
Seminary *F*
Concordia Seminary *F*
Covenant Theological Seminary *F*
Eden Theological Seminary *F*
Kenrick-Glennon Seminary *F*
Midwestern Baptist Theological
Seminary *F*
Nazarene Theological Seminary *F*
St. Paul School of Theology *F*

New Jersey

Drew University: School of Theology *F*
Immaculate Conception Seminary of
Seton Hall University *F*
New Brunswick Theological Seminary *F*
Princeton Theological Seminary *F*

New York

Alliance Theological Seminary *F*
Christ The King Seminary *F*
Colgate Rochester Divinity
School-Bexley Crozer Theological
Seminary *F*
General Theological Seminary *F*
New York Theological Seminary *F*
St. Bernard's Institute *F*
St. John's University *F*
St. Joseph's Seminary and College *F*
St. Vladimir's Orthodox Theological
Seminary *F*
Seminary of the Immaculate
Conception *F*
Union Theological Seminary:
Theological Professions *F*

North Carolina

Duke University: Divinity School *F*
Hood Theological Seminary *F*
Southeastern Baptist Theological
Seminary: Theological Professions *F*

Ohio

Ashland Theological Seminary *F*
Athenaeum of Ohio *F*
Methodist Theological School in Ohio *F*
Pontifical College Josephinum *F*
St. Mary Seminary *F*
Trinity Lutheran Seminary *F*
United Theological Seminary *F*
Winebrenner Seminary *F*

Oklahoma

Oral Roberts University: School of
Theology and Missions *F*
Phillips Theological Seminary *F*

Oregon

Mount Angel Seminary *F*
Multnomah Biblical Seminary *F*
Western Conservative Baptist
Seminary *F*
Western Evangelical Seminary *F*

Pennsylvania

Academy of the New Church *F*
Baptist Bible College and Seminary of
Pennsylvania *F*
Biblical Theological Seminary *F*
Eastern Baptist Theological Seminary *F*
Evangelical School of Theology *F*
Lancaster Theological Seminary *F*
Lutheran Theological Seminary at
Gettysburg *F*
Lutheran Theological Seminary at
Philadelphia *F*
Moravian Theological Seminary *F*
Pittsburgh Theological Seminary *F*
Reformed Presbyterian Theological
Seminary *F*
St. Charles Borromeo
Seminary-Overbrook *F*
St. Vincent Seminary *F*
Trinity Episcopal School for Ministry *F*
Westminster Theological Seminary *F*

Puerto Rico

Evangelical Seminary of Puerto Rico *F*

South Carolina

Columbia Biblical Seminary and
Graduate School of Missions *F*
Erskine Theological Seminary *F*
Lutheran Theological Southern
Seminary *F*

South Dakota

North American Baptist Seminary *F*

Tennessee

Church of God School of Theology *F*
Emmanuel School of Religion *F*
Harding University Graduate School of
Religion *F*
Memphis Theological Seminary *F*
Mid-America Baptist Theological
Seminary *F*
Temple Baptist Seminary: Theological
Professions *F*
University of the South: School of
Theology *F*
Vanderbilt University: The Divinity
School *F*

Texas

Abilene Christian University: College of
Biblical and Family Studies *F*
Austin Presbyterian Theological
Seminary *F*
Baptist Missionary Association
Theological Seminary *F*
Episcopal Theological Seminary of the
Southwest *F*
Houston Graduate School of Theology *F*
Oblate School of Theology *F*
Southern Methodist University: Perkins
School of Theology *F*
Southwestern Baptist Theological
Seminary: Theological Professions *F*

Texas Christian University: Brite
Divinity School *F*
University of St. Thomas: School of
Theology *F*

Virginia

Eastern Mennonite Seminary *F*
Liberty Baptist Theological Seminary *F*
Protestant Episcopal Theological
Seminary in Virginia *F*
Regent University: School of Divinity *F*
Union Theological Seminary in
Virginia *F*
Virginia Union University: School of
Theology *F*

Washington

Gonzaga University: Department of
Religious Studies *F*
Seattle University: School of Theology
and Ministry *F*

Wisconsin

Nashotah House *F*
Sacred Heart School of Theology *F*
St. Francis Seminary *F*

Drafting and design technology

Alabama

Bevill State Community College *A*
Bishop State Community College *A*
Calhoun Community College *C, A*
Central Alabama Community College *A*
Douglas MacArthur State Technical
College *A*
Faulkner University *A*
Gadsden State Community College *C*
George C. Wallace State Community
College
Dothan *C, A*
Selma *A*
Harry M. Ayers State Technical
College *C, A*
ITT Technical Institute
Birmingham *A*
J. F. Drake State Technical College *C, A*
Jefferson Davis Community College *C*
Lawson State Community College *C, A*
Northwest-Shoals Community
College *C, A*
Remington College
Southeast College of Technology *A*
Shelton State Community College *C, A*
Southern Union State Community
College *A*
Virginia College *A*
Wallace Community College: Sparks
Campus *A*
Wallace State Community College at
Hanceville *C, A*

Alaska

University of Alaska
Anchorage *C, A*

Arizona

Arizona Western College *C, A*
Central Arizona College *C*
Cochise College *A*
Eastern Arizona College *C, A*
Glendale Community College *C, A*
High-Tech Institute *A*
ITT Technical Institute
Phoenix *A*
Tucson *A*
Pima Community College *C, A*

Arkansas

Arkansas State University
Beebe *A*
East Arkansas Community College *C, A*
ITT Technical Institute
Little Rock *A*

Northwest Arkansas Community
College *A*
Phillips Community College of the
University of Arkansas *C, A*
Pulaski Technical College *C, A*
Southeast Arkansas College *C, A*
University of Arkansas
Cossatot Community College of the
C

California

Antelope Valley College *C, A*
Bakersfield College *A*
Barstow College *C*
Cabrillo College *C*
Cerritos Community College *A*
Cerro Coso Community College *C, A*
Chabot College *C, A*
Citrus College *C, A*
College of the Canyons *C, A*
College of the Redwoods *C, A*
College of the Sequoias *C, A*
Contra Costa College *C, A*
Cuyamaca College *A*
De Anza College *C, A*
Diablo Valley College *C*
Don Bosco Technical Institute *A*
East Los Angeles College *C*
Glendale Community College *C, A*
Golden West College *C, A*
ITT Technical Institute
Anaheim *A*
Lathrop *A*
Oxnard *A*
Rancho Cordova *A*
San Bernardino *A*
San Diego *A*
Sylmar *A*
Torrance *A*
West Covina *A*
Irvine Valley College *C, A*
Las Positas College *C, A*
Long Beach City College *C, A*
Los Angeles Harbor College *C, A*
Los Angeles Pierce College *C, A*
Los Angeles Southwest College *C, A*
Los Angeles Trade and Technical
College *C, A*
MiraCosta College *C, A*
Modesto Junior College *A*
Monterey Peninsula College *C, A*
Mount San Antonio College *C, A*
Napa Valley College *C, A*
Orange Coast College *C, A*
Palomar College *C, A*
Riverside Community College *C, A*
San Diego City College *C, A*
San Joaquin Delta College *A*
Santa Barbara City College *C, A*
Santa Monica College *C, A*
Santiago Canyon College *A*
Sierra College *C, A*
Southwestern College *C, A*
Ventura College *C, A*
West Valley College *C, A*
Westwood College of Technology
Inland Empire *A*

Colorado

Community College of Aurora *A*
Front Range Community College *C, A*
ITT Technical Institute
Thornton *A*
IntelliTec College *A*
IntelliTec College, Grand Junction *A*
Otero Junior College *C*
Red Rocks Community College *C, A*
Trinidad State Junior College *A*

Connecticut

Capital Community College *C*
Gateway Community College *C*
Gibbs College *C*
Three Rivers Community College *C, A*

Delaware

Delaware Technical and Community
College
Stanton/Wilmington Campus *A*

Florida

Daytona Beach Community College *A*
Florida Technical College
Auburndale *A*
Deland *A*
ITT Technical Institute
Ft. Lauderdale *A*
Jacksonville *A*
Maitland *A*
Miami *A*
Tampa *A*
New England Institute of Technology *A*
Okaloosa-Walton Community College *C*
Palm Beach Community College *A*
Santa Fe Community College *A*
Seminole Community College *C*
South Florida Community College *C, A*
Southwest Florida College *A*
Tallahassee Community College *C, A*
Valencia Community College *C, A*

Georgia

Athens Technical College *C*
Bainbridge College *C, A*
Central Georgia Technical College *C*
Chattahoochee Technical College *C*
Clayton College and State University *A*
Coastal Georgia Community
College *C, A*
Dalton State College *C, A*
Darton College *A*
DeKalb Technical College *C*
Georgia Southwestern State University *A*
Griffin Technical College *C*
Middle Georgia College *A*
Southwest Georgia Technical College *C*
West Georgia Technical College *C*

Hawaii

University of Hawaii
Hawaii Community College *A*
Honolulu Community College *A*
Maui Community College *A*

Idaho

Boise State University *A*
Brigham Young University - Idaho *A*
College of Southern Idaho *C, A*
ITT Technical Institute
Boise *A*
Idaho State University *C, A*
Lewis-Clark State College *A, B*
North Idaho College *C, A*

Illinois

Carl Sandburg College *C, A*
City Colleges of Chicago
Harold Washington College *C*
College of DuPage *C, A*
College of Lake County *C, A*
Danville Area Community College *C*
Heartland Community College *C, A*
ITT Technical Institute
Burr Ridge *A*
Matteson *A*
Mount Prospect *A*
Illinois Central College *C*
Illinois Eastern Community Colleges
Lincoln Trail College *A*
Illinois Valley Community College *A*
John A. Logan College *C, A*
John Wood Community College *A*
Joliet Junior College *C, A*
Kankakee Community College *C, A*
Kaskaskia College *C*
Kishwaukee College *A*
Lake Land College *A*
Lewis and Clark Community College *A*
Moraine Valley Community College *C*
Oakton Community College *A*
Prairie State College *C*
Rend Lake College *C*

Richland Community College *A*
Robert Morris College: Chicago *A*
Sauk Valley Community College *C, A*
Shawnee Community College *C, A*
South Suburban College of Cook
County *C, A*
Southwestern Illinois College *C, A*
Triton College *C, A*
Waubonsee Community College *C*
Westwood College of Technology
O'Hare *A*
William Rainey Harper College *C*

Indiana

ITT Technical Institute
Fort Wayne *A*
Indianapolis *A*
Indiana University-Purdue University
Indianapolis *A*
Oakland City University *C, A*
Purdue University *A, B*
Tri-State University *A, B*
Vincennes University *A*

Iowa

Clinton Community College *A*
Des Moines Area Community
College *C, A*
Hawkeye Community College *A*
Indian Hills Community College *A*
Iowa Central Community College *C, A*
Iowa Lakes Community College *A*
Kirkwood Community College *C, A*
Marshalltown Community College *A*
Northwest Iowa Community College *C*
Southeastern Community College
North Campus *C, A*
Southwestern Community College *C, A*
Vatterott College *C, A*

Kansas

Allen County Community College *A*
Butler County Community College *C, A*
Central Christian College *A*
Fort Scott Community College *A*
Garden City Community College *A*
Hutchinson Community College *A*
Independence Community College *C, A*
Johnson County Community
College *C, A*
Kansas City Kansas Community
College *C, A*

Kentucky

Hopkinsville Community College *C*
ITT Technical Institute
Louisville *A*
Louisville Technical Institute *C, A*
Madisonville Community College *A*
Murray State University *A*
Spencerian College: Lexington *C, A*

Louisiana

Grambling State University *B*
ITI Technical College *C, A*
ITT Technical Institute
St. Rose *A*
Nunez Community College *C, A*
Southern University
Shreveport *C*

Maine

Central Maine Technical College *A*

Maryland

Anne Arundel Community College *A*
Carroll Community College *C, A*
Chesapeake College *C, A*
College of Southern Maryland *C*
Community College of Baltimore County
Catonsville *C, A*
Dundalk *C, A*
Essex *C, A*
Frederick Community College *C*
Harford Community College *C*
Howard Community College *C, A*
Montgomery College
Rockville Campus *A*

Wor-Wic Community College *C, A*

Massachusetts

Benjamin Franklin Institute of
Technology *C*
Greenfield Community College *C*
ITT Technical Institute
Norwood *A*
Woburn *A*
Massachusetts Bay Community
College *C*
Roxbury Community College *A*
Springfield Technical Community
College *C*

Michigan

Alpena Community College *A*
Baker College
of Auburn Hills *A*
of Clinton Township *A*
of Muskegon *A*
of Owosso *A*
of Port Huron *A*
Bay de Noc Community College *A*
Ferris State University *A*
Glen Oaks Community College *C*
Gogebic Community College *A*
Grand Rapids Community College *C, A*
ITT Technical Institute
Grand Rapids *A*
Troy *A*
Jackson Community College *C, A*
Kellogg Community College *A*
Kirtland Community College *C*
Lansing Community College *A*
Macomb Community College *C, A*
Michigan Technological University *C*
Mid Michigan Community College *C*
Monroe County Community
College *C, A*
Montcalm Community College *C, A*
Muskegon Community College *C, A*
North Central Michigan College *C*
Northern Michigan University *B*
Northwestern Michigan College *A*
Oakland Community College *C, A*
St. Clair County Community
College *C, A*
Schoolcraft College *C, A*
Southwestern Michigan College *C, A*
Washtenaw Community College *C, A*

Minnesota

Alexandria Technical College *C, A*
Central Lakes College *C*
Century Community and Technical
College *C, A*
Hennepin Technical College *C, A*
Herzing College
Minneapolis Drafting School *A*
Lake Superior College: A Community
and Technical College *A*
Minneapolis Community and Technical
College *A*
Minnesota State College - Southeast
Technical *A*
Northland Community & Technical
College *C, A*
Northwest Technical Institute *A*
Ridgewater College: A Community and
Technical College *C, A*
Rochester Community and Technical
College *C, A*
St. Cloud Technical College *C, A*
St. Paul College - A Community and
Technical College *C, A*
South Central Technical College *A*

Mississippi

Holmes Community College *A*
Itawamba Community College *C*
Mississippi Gulf Coast Community
College
Perkinston *A*
Northwest Mississippi Community
College *A*
Pearl River Community College *A*

Missouri

Central Missouri State University *A, B*
East Central College *C, A*
ITT Technical Institute
　Arnold *A*
　Earth City *A*
Jefferson College *C, A*
Lincoln University *A*
Longview Community College *A*
Mineral Area College *A*
Missouri Southern State College *C, A, B*
Moberly Area Community College *C, A*
Penn Valley Community College *A*
St. Louis Community College
　St. Louis Community College at
　　Florissant Valley *C, A*
　St. Louis Community College at
　　Forest Park *A*
Southeast Missouri State University *C*
Southwest Missouri State University *B*
Southwest Missouri State University:
　West Plains Campus *A*
Three Rivers Community College *A*
Vatterott College: St. Joseph *A*
Vatterott College: Sunset Hills *A*

Montana

Montana State University
　Billings *C, A*
　Billings College of
　　Technology *C, A*
Montana Tech of the University of
　Montana *A*

Nebraska

Central Community College *C, A*
ITT Technical Institute
　Omaha *A*
Metropolitan Community College *C, A*
Northeast Community College *A*
Southeast Community College
　Lincoln Campus *A*
　Milford Campus *A*
Vatterott College *A*

Nevada

Community College of Southern
　Nevada *C, A*
ITT Technical Institute
　Henderson *A*
Truckee Meadows Community
　College *C, A*
Western Nevada Community
　College *C, A*

New Hampshire

Keene State College *A, B*
New Hampshire Community Technical
　College
　Berlin *C, A*
　Manchester *A*
　Nashua *C, A*
　Stratham *C, A*
University of New Hampshire *A*

New Jersey

Bergen Community College *C*
Brookdale Community College *C*
Burlington County College *C, A*
Camden County College *C, A*
County College of Morris *C*
Cumberland County College *C*
Gloucester County College *C, A*
Mercer County Community College *C*
Middlesex County College *C*
Ocean County College *C*
Thomas Edison State College *C, A, B*

New Mexico

Albuquerque Technical-Vocational
　Institute *C, A*
Clovis Community College *A*
Dona Ana Branch Community College of
　New Mexico State University *C, A*
Eastern New Mexico University: Roswell
　Campus *A*

ITT Technical Institute
　Albuquerque *A*
Luna Community College *A*
New Mexico Junior College *C, A*
New Mexico State University
　Alamogordo *C*
San Juan College *A*
Santa Fe Community College *A*
Southwestern Indian Polytechnic
　Institute *C*
Western New Mexico University *C, A*

New York

Adirondack Community College *C, A*
City University of New York
　Queensborough Community
　　College *A*
Corning Community College *C*
Dutchess Community College *C*
Genesee Community College *C, A*
Hudson Valley Community College *A*
ITT Technical Institute
　Albany *A*
　Getzville *A*
　Liverpool *A*
Institute of Design and Construction *A*
Island Drafting and Technical
　Institute *C, A*
Mohawk Valley Community
　College *C, A*
Onondaga Community College *C*
Orange County Community College *C*
State University of New York
　College of Technology at Alfred *A*
　College of Technology at Canton *C*
　College of Technology at
　　Delhi *C, A*
Suffolk County Community College *A*
Ulster County Community College *C, A*
Westchester Community College *C*

North Carolina

Alamance Community College *C, A*
Appalachian State University *B*
Asheville Buncombe Technical
　Community College *A*
Beaufort County Community College *A*
Blue Ridge Community College *C, A*
Caldwell Community College and
　Technical Institute *C, A*
Catawba Valley Community College *C*
Central Carolina Community College *A*
College of the Albemarle *C*
Durham Technical Community
　College *C, A*
Forsyth Technical Community College *A*
Gaston College *C*
Guilford Technical Community
　College *A*
Mitchell Community College *C, A*
Piedmont Community College *C*
Richmond Community College *C*
Rockingham Community College *C*
Rowan-Cabarrus Community College *A*
Sandhills Community College *C, A*
South Piedmont Community College *A*
Surry Community College *C, A*
Wake Technical Community
　College *C, A*
Wilson Technical Community College *A*

Ohio

AEC Southern Ohio College
　Findlay *A*
Cincinnati State Technical and
　Community College *A*
Clark State Community College *C, A*
Cuyahoga Community College
　Eastern Campus *A*
　Metropolitan Campus *C, A*
　Western Campus *C, A*
Edison State Community College *C*

ITT Technical Institute
　Dayton *A*
　Norwood *A*
　Strongsville *A*
　Youngstown *A*
James A. Rhodes State College *C*
Jefferson Community College *A*
Kent State University *A*
Kent State University
　Tuscarawas Campus *A*
Lakeland Community College *C*
Marion Technical College *C*
Miami University
　Hamilton Campus *C*
　Middletown Campus *C*
　Oxford Campus *C*
Muskingum Area Technical College *A*
North Central State College *C, A*
Northwest State Community College *A*
Owens Community College
　Toledo *A*
Shawnee State University *C, A*
Sinclair Community College *A*
Southern State Community College *A*
Technology Education College *C, A*
University of Akron *C, A*
University of Rio Grande *A*
University of Toledo *A*
Washington State Community College *A*
Wright State University: Lake
　Campus *C, A*
Youngstown State University *A*

Oklahoma

Cameron University *A*
Langston University *A*
Northern Oklahoma College *A*
Oklahoma City Community College *A*
Oklahoma State University
　Oklahoma City *A*
　Okmulgee *A*
Platt College *C*
Platt College
　Tulsa *C*
Redlands Community College *A*
Rose State College *A*
Tulsa Community College *A*
Western Oklahoma State College *A*

Oregon

Blue Mountain Community College *A*
Central Oregon Community
　College *C, A*
Chemeketa Community College *A*
Clackamas Community College *A*
Clatsop Community College *C*
ITT Technical Institute
　Portland *A*
Lane Community College *C, A*
Portland Community College *A*
Rogue Community College *A*
Treasure Valley Community
　College *C, A*

Pennsylvania

California University of
　Pennsylvania *A, B*
Commonwealth Technical Institute *A*
Community College of Allegheny
　County *A*
Community College of Beaver County *A*
Community College of Philadelphia *C, A*
Harrisburg Area Community College *C*
ITT Technical Institute
　Bensalem *A*
　Mechanicsburg *A*
　Monroeville *A*
　Pittsburgh *A*
Lehigh Carbon Community College *C, A*
Luzerne County Community
　College *C, A*
Northampton County Area Community
　College *A*
Penn State
　University Park *C*
Pennsylvania College of Technology *B*

Pittsburgh Technical Institute: Boyd
　School Division *A*
Westmoreland County Community
　College *A*

Puerto Rico

Turabo University *C*

South Carolina

Aiken Technical College *C*
Central Carolina Technical College *A*
Florence-Darlington Technical
　College *C, A*
Horry-Georgetown Technical College *C*
ITT Technical Institute
　Greenville *A*
Midlands Technical College *C, A*
Northeastern Technical College *C*
Orangeburg-Calhoun Technical
　College *A*
Piedmont Technical College *A*
Spartanburg Technical College *C*
Technical College of the Lowcountry *C*
Tri-County Technical College *C, A*
Trident Technical College *C*
Williamsburg Technical College *C, A*

South Dakota

Black Hills State University *A*
Southeast Technical Institute *A*
Western Dakota Technical Institute *A*

Tennessee

Chattanooga State Technical Community
　College *C*
ITT Technical Institute
　Knoxville *A*
　Memphis *A*
　Nashville *A*
Miller-Motte Technical College *A*
Northeast State Technical Community
　College *C, A*
Remington College
　Southeast College of Technology *A*

Texas

Alvin Community College *C, A*
Amarillo College *C, A*
Austin Community College *C, A*
Brazosport College *C, A*
Central Texas College *C, A*
Cisco Junior College *C, A*
Coastal Bend College *A*
College of the Mainland *A*
Del Mar College *C, A*
El Paso Community College *C, A*
Grayson County College *C, A*
Hill College *C, A*
Houston Community College
　System *C, A*
Howard College *C*
ITT Technical Institute
　Arlington *A*
　Austin *A*
　Houston *A*
　Houston North *A*
　Houston South *A*
　San Antonio *A*
Kilgore College *C, A*
LeTourneau University *A*
Lee College *C, A*
Midland College *A*
Mountain View College *A*
North Central Texas College *A*
Odessa College *C, A*
Paris Junior College *A*
Prairie View A&M University *B*
St. Philip's College *C, A*
San Antonio College *A*
San Jacinto College
　Central Campus *C, A*
South Plains College *C, A*
South Texas Community College *C*
Tarrant County College *C, A*
Temple College *C, A*
Texas Southern University *B*

Texas State Technical College
    Waco *C, A*
    West Texas *C, A*
Trinity Valley Community College *C, A*
Tyler Junior College *C, A*
Victoria College *C, A*
Wharton County Junior College *A*

Utah

College of Eastern Utah *C*
Dixie State College of Utah *C*
ITT Technical Institute
    Murray *A*
Salt Lake Community College *A*
Southern Utah University *A*
Utah State University *A*
Utah Valley State College *A*
Weber State University *A*

Virginia

Blue Ridge Community College *C*
Danville Community College *A*
Eastern Shore Community College *C*
ITT Technical Institute
    Norfolk *A*
    Richmond *A*
J. Sargeant Reynolds Community
    College *C*
Mountain Empire Community College *A*
Paul D. Camp Community College *C, A*
Southside Virginia Community
    College *A*
Southwest Virginia Community
    College *C*
Virginia Highlands Community
    College *C, A*
Virginia Western Community College *C*

Washington

Centralia College *C, A*
Green River Community College *A*
ITT Technical Institute
    Bothell *A*
    Seattle *A*
    Spokane *A*
Lake Washington Technical College *C, A*
North Seattle Community College *C, A*
Renton Technical College *C, A*
Seattle Central Community College *A*
South Seattle Community College *C, A*
Spokane Community College *C*
Spokane Falls Community College *C, A*
Walla Walla Community College *C*

West Virginia

Fairmont State College *B*
Southern West Virginia Community and
    Technical College *A*
West Virginia State College *A*
West Virginia University Institute of
    Technology *A*

Wisconsin

Blackhawk Technical College *A*
Chippewa Valley Technical College *A*
Fox Valley Technical College *A*
Herzing College *A, B*
ITT Technical Institute
    Green Bay *A*
    Greenfield *A*
Lakeshore Technical College *A*
Mid-State Technical College *C*
Milwaukee Area Technical College *C*
Moraine Park Technical College *C, A*
Waukesha County Technical
    College *C, A*
Wisconsin Indianhead Technical
    College *C*

Wyoming

Casper College *A*
Sheridan College *C, A*

Drama/dance teacher education

Alabama

Birmingham-Southern College *T*
Huntingdon College *T*

Arizona

Northern Arizona University *T*
Prescott College *T*
University of Arizona *B*

Arkansas

Ouachita Baptist University *B, T*
University of the Ozarks *B, T*

California

California State University
    Long Beach *T*
San Diego State University *B, T*
San Francisco State University *B, T*
University of the Pacific *T*

District of Columbia

Catholic University of America *B*
George Washington University *T*

Florida

Flagler College *B*
Jacksonville University *B*
Stetson University *B, T*
University of South Florida *B*

Georgia

Brenau University *B*
Columbus State University *B*
University of Georgia *B*

Hawaii

University of Hawaii
    Manoa *B, T*

Idaho

Brigham Young University - Idaho *T*

Illinois

Greenville College *B*
Loyola University of Chicago *T*
North Park University *T*
Rockford College *T*

Indiana

Anderson University *B, T*
Indiana University-Purdue University
    Fort Wayne *B, T*
University of Evansville *B*

Iowa

Buena Vista University *B, T*
Central College *T*
Clarke College *B, T*
Dordt College *B*
Drake University *B*
Graceland University *T*
Luther College *B*
Maharishi University of Management *T*
University of Iowa *T*

Kansas

Bethel College *T*
St. Mary College *T*
Southwestern College *B, T*

Louisiana

Centenary College of Louisiana *B, T*

Maryland

Community College of Baltimore County
    Catonsville *A*
    Dundalk *A*
    Essex *A*
St. Mary's College of Maryland *T*

Massachusetts

Boston University *B, M*
Bridgewater State College *B, T*
Emerson College *B, M*
Tufts University *T*

Michigan

Eastern Michigan University *B, T*
Hope College *T*

Minnesota

Minnesota State University
    Mankato *B, T*
St. Cloud State University *T*
Southwest State University *B, T*
Winona State University *B, T*

Missouri

Avila University *B, T*
Lindenwood University *M*
Washington University in St.
    Louis *B, M, T*
William Jewell College *T*

Montana

Montana State University
    Billings *T*
Rocky Mountain College *B, T*
University of Montana-Missoula *T*
University of Montana: Western *T*

Nebraska

Chadron State College *B*
Dana College *B*
Hastings College *B, T*
University of Nebraska
    Lincoln *B*
York College *T*

New Jersey

Rowan University *T*

New York

City University of New York
    Hunter College *B, T*
New York University *M, D*

North Carolina

East Carolina University *B*
Greensboro College *B, T*
Lees-McRae College *B, T*
Meredith College *B, T*
University of North Carolina
    Charlotte *B*
    Greensboro *B, M, T*

North Dakota

Dickinson State University *B, T*

Ohio

Ashland University *B, T*
Baldwin-Wallace College *T*
Bowling Green State University *B*
Kent State University *B, T*
Kent State University
    Stark Campus *B*
Miami University
    Oxford Campus *T*
Ohio State University
    Columbus Campus *M*
University of Akron *B, T*
University of Findlay *T*
Youngstown State University *B*

Oklahoma

East Central University *B, T*
Eastern Oklahoma State College *A*

Oregon

Portland State University *T*
University of Portland *T*

Pennsylvania

Marywood University *B*
Point Park College *B*

Rhode Island

Salve Regina University *B*

South Carolina

Columbia College *B*
Furman University *T*
South Carolina State University *B, T*

South Dakota

University of Sioux Falls *T*
University of South Dakota *T*

Texas

Abilene Christian University *B, T*
Baylor University *B, T*
East Texas Baptist University *B*
Howard Payne University *B, T*
Lamar University *T*
McMurry University *T*
Tarleton State University *T*
Texas A&M University
    Commerce *T*
    Kingsville *T*
Texas Christian University *T*
University of Dallas *T*
University of Houston *T*
West Texas A&M University *T*

Utah

Brigham Young University *B*
Southern Utah University *B, T*
University of Utah *B*
Weber State University *B*

Vermont

Bennington College *B, M, T*
Castleton State College *B, T*
Johnson State College *B*
St. Michael's College *T*

Virginia

Longwood University *T*
Virginia Highlands Community
    College *A*

Washington

Central Washington University *B, M, T*
Washington State University *T*
Western Washington University *B, T*
Whitworth College *B, T*

Wisconsin

Alverno College *T*
University of Wisconsin
    Green Bay *T*
    Whitewater *B*

Drama/theater arts

Alabama

Alabama State University *B*
Auburn University *B*
Birmingham-Southern College *B*
Chattahoochee Valley Community
    College *A*
Huntingdon College *B, T*
Jacksonville State University *B*
Northeast Alabama Community
    College *A*
Samford University *B*
Shelton State Community College *C, A*
Spring Hill College *B*
University of Alabama *B, M*
University of Alabama
    Birmingham *B*
University of Mobile *B*
University of Montevallo *B, T*
University of South Alabama *B*

Alaska

University of Alaska
    Anchorage *B*
    Fairbanks *B*

Arizona

Arizona State University *B, M, D*
Arizona Western College *A*
Central Arizona College *A*
Eastern Arizona College *A*
Northern Arizona University *B, T*
Pima Community College *A*
Prescott College *B, M*
University of Arizona *B, M*

Arkansas

Arkansas State University *B*
Harding University *B*
Henderson State University *B*
Hendrix College *B*

Lyon College *B*
Ouachita Baptist University *B*
Southern Arkansas University *B*
University of Arkansas *B, M*
University of Arkansas
   Little Rock *B*
University of the Ozarks *B*

California

Barstow College *A*
Bethany College *B*
Biola University *B*
California Institute of the Arts *C, B, M*
California State Polytechnic University:
  Pomona *B*
California State University
  Bakersfield *B*
  Chico *B*
  Dominguez Hills *B*
  Fresno *B*
  Fullerton *B, M*
  Hayward *B*
  Long Beach *B, M*
  Monterey Bay *B*
  Northridge *B, M*
  Sacramento *B, M*
  San Bernardino *B*
  Stanislaus *B*
Cerritos Community College *A*
Chabot College *A*
Chapman University *B*
Claremont McKenna College *B*
College of the Sequoias *A*
College of the Siskiyous *A*
Concordia University *B*
Contra Costa College *A*
East Los Angeles College *A*
Foothill College *A*
Fresno Pacific University *B*
Gavilan Community College *A*
Glendale Community College *C*
Golden West College *A*
Grossmont Community College *A*
Humboldt State University *B, M*
Irvine Valley College *A*
Laney College *C, A*
Las Positas College *A*
Long Beach City College *A*
Los Angeles Southwest College *A*
Loyola Marymount University *B*
MiraCosta College *A*
Modesto Junior College *A*
Monterey Peninsula College *A*
Moorpark College *A*
Mount San Jacinto College *A*
Occidental College *B*
Orange Coast College *A*
Palomar College *A*
Pepperdine University *B*
Pitzer College *B*
Point Loma Nazarene University *B*
Pomona College *B*
Reedley College *A*
St. Mary's College of California *B*
San Diego City College *A*
San Diego Mesa College *A*
San Diego State University *B*
San Francisco State University *B, M*
San Jose State University *B, M*
Santa Barbara City College *A*
Santa Clara University *B*
Santa Monica College *A*
Santa Rosa Junior College *C, A*
Scripps College *B*
Shasta College *C, A*
Sonoma State University *B*
Southwestern College *A*
Stanford University *B, M, D*

University of California
  Berkeley *B, D*
  Davis *B, M, D*
  Irvine *B, M, D*
  Los Angeles *B, M, D*
  Riverside *B*
  San Diego *B, M*
  Santa Barbara *B, M, D*
  Santa Cruz *C, B*
University of La Verne *B*
University of Redlands *B*
University of San Diego *M*
University of Southern California *B, M*
University of the Pacific *B*
Vanguard University of Southern
  California *B*
Ventura College *C, A*
West Valley College *A*
Whittier College *B, M*
Yuba Community College District *A*

Colorado

Colorado Christian University *B*
Colorado College *B*
Colorado Mountain College
  Spring Valley Campus *A*
Colorado State University *B*
Fort Lewis College *B*
Naropa University *B*
Otero Junior College *A*
Red Rocks Community College *A*
University of Colorado
  Boulder *B, M, D*
  Denver *B*
University of Denver *B*
University of Northern Colorado *B, T*

Connecticut

Albertus Magnus College *B*
Central Connecticut State University *B*
Connecticut College *B*
Fairfield University *B*
Southern Connecticut State University *B*
Trinity College *B*
University of Connecticut *B, M*
University of Hartford *B*
Wesleyan University *B*
Western Connecticut State University *B*
Yale University *B, M, D*

Delaware

Delaware State University *B*
University of Delaware *M*

District of Columbia

American University *B*
Catholic University of America *B, M, T*
Gallaudet University *B*
George Washington University *B, M*
University of the District of Columbia *B*

Florida

Barry University *B*
Broward Community College *A*
Chipola Junior College *A*
Eckerd College *B*
Flagler College *B*
Florida Agricultural and Mechanical
  University *B*
Florida Atlantic University *B, M*
Florida International University *B*
Florida Southern College *B*
Florida State University *B, M, D*
Gulf Coast Community College *A*
Indian River Community College *A*
Jacksonville University *B*
Miami-Dade Community College *A*
Okaloosa-Walton Community College *A*
Palm Beach Atlantic University *B, T*
Palm Beach Community College *A*
Pensacola Junior College *A*
Rollins College *B*
South Florida Community College *A*
Stetson University *B*
University of Central Florida *B, M*
University of Florida *B, M*
University of Miami *B*

University of South Florida *B*
University of West Florida *B*
Valencia Community College *A*

Georgia

Agnes Scott College *B*
Andrew College *A*
Armstrong Atlantic State University *B*
Berry College *B*
Brenau University *B*
Clark Atlanta University *B*
Columbus State University *B*
Darton College *A*
Emory University *B*
Gainesville College *A*
Georgia College and State University *B*
Georgia Perimeter College *A*
Georgia Southern University *B*
Georgia State University *B*
Gordon College *A*
LaGrange College *B*
Macon State College *B*
Middle Georgia College *A*
Morehouse College *B*
Oxford College of Emory University *B*
Piedmont College *B*
Savannah College of Art and
  Design *B, M*
Shorter College *B*
Spelman College *B*
State University of West Georgia *B*
University of Georgia *B, M, D*
Valdosta State University *B*
Young Harris College *A*

Hawaii

Brigham Young University-Hawaii *A*
University of Hawaii
  Manoa *B, M, D*

Idaho

Albertson College of Idaho *B*
Boise State University *B*
College of Southern Idaho *A*
Idaho State University *B, M*
University of Idaho *B, M*

Illinois

Augustana College *B*
Bradley University *B, T*
City Colleges of Chicago
  Harold Washington College *A*
  Kennedy-King College *C, A*
Columbia College Chicago *B*
De Paul University *B, M*
Dominican University *B*
Eastern Illinois University *B, T*
Elmhurst College *B*
Eureka College *B*
Illinois Central College *A*
Illinois State University *B, M, T*
Illinois Valley Community College *A*
Illinois Wesleyan University *B*
Judson College *B*
Kishwaukee College *A*
Knox College *B*
Lewis University *B, T*
Lincoln College *A*
Lincoln Land Community College *A*
Loyola University of Chicago *B*
MacMurray College *B*
Millikin University *B*
National-Louis University *B*
North Central College *B*
North Park University *B*
Northeastern Illinois University *M*
Northern Illinois University *B, M*
Northwestern University *B, M, D*
Parkland College *A*
Principia College *B*
Rockford College *B*
Roosevelt University *B, M*
Sauk Valley Community College *A*
South Suburban College of Cook
  County *A*
Southern Illinois University
  Carbondale *B, M*

Southern Illinois University
  Edwardsville *B*
Southwestern Illinois College *A*
Spoon River College *A*
Triton College *A*
University of Illinois
  Chicago *B, M*
  Urbana-Champaign *B, M, D*
Western Illinois University *B, M*

Indiana

Anderson University *B*
Ball State University *B*
Bethel College *B*
Butler University *B*
Earlham College *B*
Franklin College *B*
Goshen College *B*
Hanover College *B*
Indiana State University *B, T*
Indiana University
  Bloomington *B, M, D*
  Northwest *B*
  South Bend *B*
Indiana University-Purdue University
  Fort Wayne *B, T*
Purdue University *B, M*
Saint Mary's College *B*
Taylor University *B*
University of Evansville *B*
University of Indianapolis *B*
University of Notre Dame *B*
University of Southern Indiana *B*
Valparaiso University *B*
Vincennes University *A*
Wabash College *B*

Iowa

Briar Cliff University *B*
Buena Vista University *B, T*
Central College *B*
Clarke College *A, B, T*
Coe College *B*
Cornell College *B, T*
Dordt College *B*
Drake University *B, T*
Ellsworth Community College *A*
Graceland University *B, T*
Grand View College *B*
Grinnell College *B*
Maharishi University of Management *B*
Morningside College *B*
North Iowa Area Community College *A*
St. Ambrose University *B*
Simpson College *B*
University of Iowa *B, M, T*
University of Northern Iowa *B, M*
Waldorf College *A, B*
Wartburg College *B*

Kansas

Baker University *B, T*
Barton County Community College *A*
Benedictine College *B, T*
Bethel College *B*
Butler County Community College *A*
Central Christian College *A, B*
Emporia State University *B*
Friends University *B*
Garden City Community College *A*
Independence Community College *A*
Kansas City Kansas Community
  College *A*
Kansas State University *B*
Kansas Wesleyan University *B, T*
McPherson College *B, T*
Ottawa University *B, T*
Pittsburg State University *B*
Pratt Community College *A*
St. Mary College *B*
Seward County Community College *A*
Southwestern College *B*
Sterling College *B*
Tabor College *B*
University of Kansas *B, M, D*
Washburn University of Topeka *B*

Wichita State University *B*

Kentucky
Berea College *B*
Campbellsville University *B*
Centre College *B*
Cumberland College *B*
Georgetown College *B*
Morehead State University *B*
Murray State University *B, T*
Thomas More College *A, B*
Transylvania University *B*
Union College *B*
University of Kentucky *B, M*
University of Louisville *B, M*

Louisiana
Centenary College of Louisiana *B*
Dillard University *B*
Grambling State University *B*
Louisiana College *B*
Louisiana State University and
  Agricultural and Mechanical
  College *B, M, D*
Loyola University New Orleans *B*
McNeese State University *B*
Northwestern State University *B*
Southern University and Agricultural and
  Mechanical College *B*
Tulane University *B, M*
University of New Orleans *B, M*

Maine
Bates College *B*
Bowdoin College *B*
Colby College *B*
University of Maine *B, M*
University of Maine
  Farmington *B*
University of Southern Maine *B*

Maryland
College of Southern Maryland *A*
Community College of Baltimore County
  Catonsville *A*
  Dundalk *A*
  Essex *A*
Frederick Community College *A*
Frostburg State University *B*
Goucher College *B*
Howard Community College *A*
Johns Hopkins University *M*
McDaniel College *B*
Morgan State University *B*
St. Mary's College of Maryland *R*
Salisbury University *B*
Towson University *B, M*
University of Maryland
  Baltimore County *B*
  College Park *B, M, D*
Washington College *B*

Massachusetts
Amherst College *B*
Berkshire Community College *A*
Boston College *B*
Brandeis University *B, M*
Bridgewater State College *B*
Bunker Hill Community College *A*
Cape Cod Community College *A*
Clark University *B*
College of the Holy Cross *B*
Dean College *A*
Emerson College *B, M*
Fitchburg State College *B*
Hampshire College *B*
Massachusetts Bay Community
  College *A*
Massachusetts College of Liberal Arts *B*
Mount Holyoke College *B*
Northeastern University *B*
Pine Manor College *A*
Regis College *B*
Simon's Rock College of Bard *B*
Smith College *B*
Suffolk University *B*

University of Massachusetts
  Amherst *B, M*
  Boston *B*
Wellesley College *B*
Westfield State College *B*
Williams College *B*

Michigan
Adrian College *A, B*
Alma College *B*
Calvin College *B*
Central Michigan University *B*
Eastern Michigan University *B, M*
Grand Valley State University *B*
Hillsdale College *B*
Hope College *B*
Kalamazoo College *B, T*
Kellogg Community College *A*
Lansing Community College *A*
Michigan State University *B, M*
Mid Michigan Community College *A*
Northern Michigan University *B*
Northwestern Michigan College *A*
Saginaw Valley State University *B*
Schoolcraft College *A*
Siena Heights University *B*
University of Michigan *B, M, D, T*
University of Michigan
  Flint *B*
Wayne State University *B, M, D*
Western Michigan University *B*

Minnesota
Augsburg College *B*
Bemidji State University *B*
Bethany Lutheran College *B*
Bethel College *B*
College of St. Benedict *B*
College of St. Catherine *B*
Concordia College: Moorhead *B*
Concordia University: St. Paul *B*
Gustavus Adolphus College *B*
Hamline University *B*
Macalester College *B*
Metropolitan State University *B*
Minnesota State University
  Mankato *B, M*
  Moorhead *B*
North Central University *B*
Northwestern College *B*
St. Cloud State University *B*
St. John's University *B*
St. Mary's University of Minnesota *B*
St. Olaf College *B*
Southwest State University *B*
University of Minnesota
  Duluth *B*
  Morris *B*
  Twin Cities *B, M, D*
University of St. Thomas *B*
Vermilion Community College *A*
Winona State University *B*

Mississippi
Blue Mountain College *B*
Millsaps College *B, T*
Mississippi University for Women *B*
University of Mississippi *B, M*
University of Southern Mississippi *B, M*

Missouri
Avila University *B*
Central Methodist College *B*
Central Missouri State University *B, M*
College of the Ozarks *B*
Culver-Stockton College *B*
Drury University *B*
Evangel University *A, B*
Fontbonne College *B*
Hannibal-LaGrange College *B*
Lindenwood University *B*
Missouri Southern State College *B, T*
Missouri Valley College *B*
Northwest Missouri State University *B*
Rockhurst University *B*

St. Louis Community College
  St. Louis Community College at
    Florissant Valley *A*
St. Louis University *B*
Southeast Missouri State University *B*
Southwest Baptist University *B*
Southwest Missouri State
  University *B, M*
Stephens College *B*
Truman State University *B*
University of Missouri
  Columbia *B, M, D*
  Kansas City *B, M*
Washington University in St. Louis *B, M*
Webster University *B*
William Jewell College *B*
William Woods University *B, T*

Montana
Carroll College *B*
Montana State University
  Billings *B*
Rocky Mountain College *B*
University of Montana-Missoula *B, M*
University of Montana: Western *B*

Nebraska
Chadron State College *B*
Concordia University *B, T*
Creighton University *B*
Doane College *B*
Hastings College *B, T*
Midland Lutheran College *B, T*
Nebraska Wesleyan University *B*
Northeast Community College *A*
University of Nebraska
  Kearney *B, T*
  Lincoln *B, M*
  Omaha *B, M*
Wayne State College *B, T*

Nevada
Truckee Meadows Community
  College *C, A*
University of Nevada
  Las Vegas *B, M*
  Reno *B*

New Hampshire
Dartmouth College *B*
Franklin Pierce College *B*
Keene State College *B*
New England College *B*
Plymouth State College *B*
University of New Hampshire *B*

New Jersey
Bloomfield College *B*
Centenary College *B*
Cumberland County College *A*
Drew University *B*
Essex County College *A*
Fairleigh Dickinson University
  College at Florham *B*
  Metropolitan Campus *B*
Gloucester County College *A*
Kean University *B*
Middlesex County College *A*
Montclair State University *B, M*
Ocean County College *A*
Raritan Valley Community College *A*
Rider University *B*
Rowan University *B*
Rutgers, The State University of New
  Jersey
    Camden Regional Campus *B, T*
    New Brunswick Regional
      Campus *B, M*
    Newark Regional Campus *B*
Thomas Edison State College *B*

New Mexico
College of Santa Fe *B*
Eastern New Mexico University *B*
New Mexico State University *B*
San Juan College *A*
University of New Mexico *B, M*

New York
Adelphi University *B*
Adirondack Community College *A*
Alfred University *B*
Bard College *B*
Barnard College *B*
City University of New York
  Brooklyn College *B, M*
  City College *B*
  College of Staten Island *B*
  Hunter College *B, M*
  Queens College *B*
  Queensborough Community
    College *A*
  York College *B*
Colgate University *B*
Columbia University
  Columbia College *B*
Cornell University *B*
Dowling College *B*
Dutchess Community College *A*
Elmira College *B*
Finger Lakes Community College *A*
Fordham University *B*
Fulton-Montgomery Community
  College *A*
Genesee Community College *A*
Hamilton College *B*
Hartwick College *B*
Hobart and William Smith Colleges *B*
Hofstra University *B*
Ithaca College *B*
Juilliard School *B*
Le Moyne College *B*
Long Island University
  C. W. Post Campus *B, M*
Manhattanville College *B*
Marist College *B*
Marymount College of Fordham
  University *B*
Marymount Manhattan College *B*
Nazareth College of Rochester *B*
New York University *B, M, D*
Niagara University *B*
Pace University *B*
Pace University:
  Pleasantville/Briarcliff *B*
Rockland Community College *A*
Russell Sage College *B*
St. Lawrence University *B*
Sarah Lawrence College *B, M*
Skidmore College *B*
State University of New York
  Albany *B, M*
  Binghamton *B, M*
  College at Brockport *B*
  College at Buffalo *B*
  College at Fredonia *B*
  College at Geneseo *B*
  College at Oneonta *B*
  College at Plattsburgh *B*
  College at Potsdam *B*
  New Paltz *B*
  Oswego *B*
  Purchase *B*
  Stony Brook *B, M*
Suffolk County Community College *A*
Syracuse University *B, M*
Vassar College *B*
Wagner College *B*
Wells College *B*
Westchester Community College *A*

North Carolina
Barton College *B*
Campbell University *B*
Catawba College *B*
Chowan College *A*
College of the Albemarle *A*
Davidson College *B*
Duke University *B*
East Carolina University *B*
Elon University *B*
Fayetteville State University *B*
Greensboro College *B, T*

Guilford College *B*
Guilford Technical Community
  College *A*
High Point University *B*
Lees-McRae College *B, T*
Lenoir-Rhyne College *B, T*
Livingstone College *B*
Louisburg College *A*
Meredith College *B, T*
North Carolina Agricultural and
  Technical State University *B*
North Carolina Central University *B*
North Carolina School of the Arts *B*
North Carolina Wesleyan College *B*
Pfeiffer University *B*
Queens University of Charlotte *B*
Shaw University *B*
Southeastern Community College *A*
University of North Carolina
    Asheville *B, T*
    Chapel Hill *B, M*
    Charlotte *B, T*
    Greensboro *B, M*
    Wilmington *B*
Wake Forest University *B*
Western Carolina University *B*

North Dakota

Dickinson State University *B*
Jamestown College *B*
North Dakota State University *B*
Trinity Bible College *B*
University of North Dakota *B, M*

Ohio

Antioch College *B*
Ashland University *B*
Baldwin-Wallace College *B*
Bowling Green State University *B, M, D*
Case Western Reserve University *B, M*
Cleveland State University *B*
College of Wooster *B*
Denison University *B*
Hiram College *B, T*
Kent State University *B, M*
Kent State University
    Stark Campus *B*
Kenyon College *B*
Malone College *B*
Marietta College *B*
Miami University
    Oxford Campus *B, M*
Mount Union College *B*
Mount Vernon Nazarene University *B*
Muskingum College *B*
Oberlin College *B*
Ohio Northern University *B*
Ohio State University
    Columbus Campus *B, M, D*
Ohio University *B, M*
Ohio Wesleyan University *B*
Otterbein College *B*
Sinclair Community College *A*
University of Akron *B, M*
University of Cincinnati *B, M*
University of Dayton *B*
University of Findlay *B*
University of Toledo *B*
Wilmington College *B*
Wright State University *B*
Youngstown State University *B*

Oklahoma

Cameron University *B*
Carl Albert State College *A*
East Central University *B*
Eastern Oklahoma State College *A*
Northeastern Oklahoma Agricultural and
  Mechanical College *A*
Northeastern State University *B*
Northwestern Oklahoma State
  University *B*
Oklahoma Baptist University *B, T*
Oklahoma City University *B, M*
Oklahoma State University *B*
Oral Roberts University *B*

Rose State College *A*
St. Gregory's University *A, B*
Tulsa Community College *A*
University of Central Oklahoma *B*
University of Oklahoma *B, M*
University of Science and Arts of
  Oklahoma *B*
University of Tulsa *B*

Oregon

Concordia University *B*
Eastern Oregon University *B*
George Fox University *B*
Lewis & Clark College *B*
Linfield College *B*
Linn-Benton Community College *A*
Mount Hood Community College *A*
Pacific University *B*
Portland State University *B, M*
Reed College *B*
Southern Oregon University *B, T*
University of Oregon *B, M, D*
University of Portland *B, M*
Western Oregon University *B*
Willamette University *B*

Pennsylvania

Albright College *B*
Allegheny College *B*
Arcadia University *B*
Bloomsburg University of
  Pennsylvania *B*
Bucknell University *B*
Bucks County Community College *A*
California University of Pennsylvania *B*
Carnegie Mellon University *B, M*
Cedar Crest College *B*
Chatham College *B*
Cheyney University of Pennsylvania *B*
Community College of Allegheny
  County *A*
Community College of Philadelphia *A*
DeSales University *B*
Dickinson College *B*
Duquesne University *B*
East Stroudsburg University of
  Pennsylvania *B*
Edinboro University of Pennsylvania *B*
Franklin & Marshall College *B*
Gettysburg College *B*
Harrisburg Area Community College *A*
Indiana University of Pennsylvania *B*
King's College *B*
Kutztown University of Pennsylvania *B*
Lehigh University *B*
Lock Haven University of
  Pennsylvania *B*
Lycoming College *B*
Marywood University *B*
Messiah College *B*
Moravian College *B*
Muhlenberg College *B*
Penn State
    Abington *B*
    Altoona *B*
    Beaver *B*
    Berks *B*
    Delaware County *B*
    Dubois *B*
    Fayette *B*
    Hazleton *B*
    Lehigh Valley *B*
    McKeesport *B*
    Mont Alto *B*
    New Kensington *B*
    Schuylkill - Capital College *B*
    Shenango *B*
    University Park *B, M*
    Wilkes-Barre *B*
    Worthington Scranton *B*
Point Park College *B*
St. Vincent College *B*
Seton Hill University *B*
Slippery Rock University of
  Pennsylvania *B*
Swarthmore College *B*

Temple University *B, M*
University of Pennsylvania *B*
University of Pittsburgh *B, M, D*
University of Pittsburgh
  Johnstown *B*
University of Scranton *C, B*
Villanova University *M*
Washington and Jefferson College *A, B*
West Chester University of
  Pennsylvania *B*
Wilkes University *B*

Puerto Rico

University of Puerto Rico
  Rio Piedras Campus *B*
University of the Sacred Heart *B*

Rhode Island

Brown University *B, M, D*
Community College of Rhode Island *A*
Providence College *B*
Rhode Island College *B, M*
Roger Williams University *B*
Salve Regina University *B*
University of Rhode Island *B*

South Carolina

Anderson College *B*
Charleston Southern University *B*
Coastal Carolina University *B*
Coker College *B*
College of Charleston *B*
Converse College *B*
Francis Marion University *B*
Furman University *B, T*
Limestone College *B*
Newberry College *B*
North Greenville College *A*
Presbyterian College *B*
South Carolina State University *B*
University of South Carolina *B, M*
Winthrop University *B*

South Dakota

Augustana College *B*
University of Sioux Falls *B*
University of South Dakota *B, M*

Tennessee

Belmont University *B, T*
Bethel College *B*
Freed-Hardeman University *B, T*
Lambuth University *B*
Maryville College *B*
Middle Tennessee State University *B*
Milligan College *B*
Rhodes College *B*
Roane State Community College *A*
Tennessee State University *B*
Trevecca Nazarene University *B*
Union University *B, T*
University of Memphis *B, M*
University of Tennessee
    Chattanooga *B*
    Knoxville *B, M*
    Martin *B*
Vanderbilt University *B*
Walters State Community College *A*

Texas

Abilene Christian University *B*
Alvin Community College *A*
Amarillo College *A*
Angelina College *A*
Angelo State University *B, T*
Austin Community College *A*
Baylor University *B, M*
Brazosport College *A*
Cisco Junior College *A*
Clarendon College *A*
College of the Mainland *A*
Del Mar College *A*
East Texas Baptist University *B*
El Paso Community College *A*
Galveston College *A*
Grayson County College *A*
Hardin-Simmons University *B*

Howard College *A*
Howard Payne University *B, T*
Kilgore College *A*
Lamar University *B, M*
Laredo Community College *A*
Lee College *A*
Lon Morris College *A*
Lubbock Christian University *T*
McMurry University *B, T*
Midland College *A*
Midwestern State University *B*
Northeast Texas Community College *A*
Our Lady of the Lake University of San
  Antonio *B*
Panola College *A*
Paris Junior College *A*
Prairie View A&M University *B*
St. Edward's University *B, T*
St. Philip's College *A*
Sam Houston State University *B*
Schreiner University *B*
South Plains College *A*
Southern Methodist University *B, M*
Southwest Texas State
  University *B, M, T*
Southwestern University *B, T*
Stephen F. Austin State
  University *B, M, T*
Sul Ross State University *B*
Tarleton State University *B*
Texas A&M University *B*
Texas A&M University
    Commerce *B, M*
    Corpus Christi *T*
    Kingsville *B, T*
Texas Christian University *B, T*
Texas Lutheran University *B*
Texas Southern University *B*
Texas Tech University *B, M, D*
Texas Wesleyan University *B*
Texas Woman's University *B, M, T*
Trinity University *B*
Trinity Valley Community College *A*
Tyler Junior College *A*
University of Dallas *B*
University of Houston *B, M*
University of North Texas *B, M*
University of St. Thomas *B*
University of Texas
    Arlington *B*
    Austin *B, M, D*
    El Paso *B, M*
    Pan American *B, M, T*
    Tyler *B*
University of the Incarnate Word *B*
Wayland Baptist University *B, T*
West Texas A&M University *B, T*
Western Texas College *A*
Wharton County Junior College *A*

Utah

Brigham Young University *B, M, D*
Dixie State College of Utah *A*
Southern Utah University *B, T*
University of Utah *B, M, D*
Utah State University *B, M*
Utah Valley State College *A*
Weber State University *B*

Vermont

Bennington College *B, M, T*
Castleton State College *B*
Johnson State College *B*
Marlboro College *B*
Middlebury College *B*
St. Michael's College *B*
University of Vermont *B*

Virginia

Averett University *B, T*
Bluefield College *B*
College of William and Mary *B*
Eastern Mennonite University *B*
Emory & Henry College *B*
Ferrum College *B*
George Mason University *B*

Hampton University *B*
Hollins University *B*
James Madison University *B, T*
Longwood University *B, T*
Lynchburg College *B*
Mary Baldwin College *B*
Mary Washington College *B*
Old Dominion University *B*
Piedmont Virginia Community
   College *A*
Radford University *B*
Randolph-Macon College *B*
Randolph-Macon Woman's College *B*
Roanoke College *B, T*
Shenandoah University *B*
Sweet Briar College *B*
University of Richmond *B*
University of Virginia *B, M*
University of Virginia's College at
   Wise *B, T*
Virginia Commonwealth
   University *B, M*
Virginia Intermont College *B*
Virginia Polytechnic Institute and State
   University *B, M*
Virginia Union University *B*
Virginia Wesleyan College *B*
Washington and Lee University *B*

Washington
Central Washington University *B*
Centralia College *A*
Cornish College of the Arts *B*
Eastern Washington University *B*
Everett Community College *A*
Gonzaga University *B*
Lower Columbia College *A*
North Seattle Community College *C*
Northwest College *B*
Pacific Lutheran University *B*
St. Martin's College *B*
Seattle Pacific University *B*
Seattle University *B*
University of Puget Sound *B, T*
University of Washington *B, M, D*
Washington State University *B, M*
Western Washington University *B, M*
Whitman College *B*

West Virginia
Alderson-Broaddus College *B*
Bethany College *B*
Davis and Elkins College *B*
Fairmont State College *B*
West Virginia University *B, M*
West Virginia Wesleyan College *B*

Wisconsin
Beloit College *B*
Cardinal Stritch University *B*
Carroll College *B*
Carthage College *B, T*
Lakeland College *B*
Lawrence University *B, T*
Marquette University *B, T*
Ripon College *B, T*
University of Wisconsin
   Eau Claire *B*
   Green Bay *B*
   La Crosse *B*
   Madison *B, M, D*
   Milwaukee *B*
   Oshkosh *B*
   Parkside *B, T*
   Platteville *B*
   Stevens Point *B*
   Superior *B, M*
Viterbo University *B, T*
Wisconsin Lutheran College *B*

Wyoming
Casper College *A*
Central Wyoming College *A*
Laramie County Community College *A*
University of Wyoming *B*
Western Wyoming Community
   College *A*

Drawing

Alabama
Birmingham-Southern College *B*

Arizona
Arizona State University *B, M*

California
Academy of Art College *C, A, B, M*
Biola University *B*
California College of Arts and
   Crafts *B, M*
California State University
   Fullerton *B, M*
   Hayward *B*
   Long Beach *B, M*
   Northridge *B, M*
Chabot College *A*
Grossmont Community College *A*
Long Beach City College *A*
Monterey Peninsula College *A*
Ohlone College *C*
Otis College of Art and Design *B, M*
Santa Rosa Junior College *C*
University of San Francisco *B*

Colorado
Colorado State University *B*
Naropa University *B*

Connecticut
University of Hartford *B*

Georgia
Albany State University *B*
Atlanta College of Art *B*
Georgia State University *B, M*
LaGrange College *B*
University of Georgia *B*

Illinois
American Academy of Art *B*
City Colleges of Chicago
   Olive-Harvey College *A*
Lewis University *B*
Lincoln College *A*
Richland Community College *A*
Rockford College *B*
School of the Art Institute of
   Chicago *B, M*

Indiana
Ball State University *B*
Indiana University-Purdue University
   Fort Wayne *B*
Vincennes University *A*

Iowa
Drake University *B*
University of Iowa *B, M*

Kansas
Allen County Community College *A*
Central Christian College *A, B*
Pratt Community College *A*

Kentucky
Louisville Technical Institute *A*

Maine
University of Southern Maine *B*

Maryland
Maryland College of Art and Design *A*
Maryland Institute College of Art *B*

Massachusetts
Boston University *B*
Hampshire College *B*
Montserrat College of Art *B*
School of the Museum of Fine Arts *B, M*
Simon's Rock College of Bard *B*
University of Massachusetts
   Dartmouth *M*

Michigan
College for Creative Studies *B*
Finlandia University *B*

Lansing Community College *A*
Northern Michigan University *B*
Siena Heights University *B*
University of Michigan *B*

Minnesota
College of Visual Arts *B*
Minnesota State University
   Mankato *B*
   Moorhead *B*

Mississippi
Mississippi University for Women *B*

Missouri
Kansas City Art Institute *B*
Lindenwood University *B, M*
University of Missouri
   St. Louis *B*
Washington University in St. Louis *B, M*

New Hampshire
Rivier College *B*

New Jersey
Rowan University *B*

New York
Bard College *B*
City University of New York
   Brooklyn College *M*
Parsons School of Design *C, A, B, T*
Pratt Institute *B, M*
Rochester Institute of Technology *A, B*
Sarah Lawrence College *B*
School of Visual Arts *B, M*
State University of New York
   Albany *B, M*
   College at Fredonia *B*
   Purchase *B*

Ohio
Art Academy of Cincinnati *B*
Bowling Green State University *B, M*
Cleveland Institute of Art *B*
Ohio State University
   Columbus Campus *B*
Ohio University *B*
Shawnee State University *B*
University of Akron *B*
Wittenberg University *B*

Oregon
Pacific Northwest College of Art *B*
Portland State University *B*
University of Oregon *B, M*

Pennsylvania
Immaculata University *A*
Keystone College *A*
Mercyhurst College *B*
Oakbridge Academy of Arts *A*
Seton Hill University *B*

Puerto Rico
Inter American University of Puerto Rico
   San German Campus *B, M*
University of Puerto Rico
   Rio Piedras Campus *B*

Rhode Island
Providence College *B*
Rhode Island College *B*

South Carolina
Anderson College *B*

Tennessee
Carson-Newman College *B*
Tennessee Technological University *B*

Texas
Sam Houston State University *M*
Stephen F. Austin State University *M*
University of North Texas *B, M*
University of Texas
   El Paso *B*
   San Antonio *B, M*
Western Texas College *A*

Utah
Brigham Young University *B*
Dixie State College of Utah *A*

Vermont
Bennington College *B, M*
Burlington College *B*
Marlboro College *B*

Washington
Cornish College of the Arts *B*
North Seattle Community College *C*
Western Washington University *B*

West Virginia
Marshall University *M*
West Virginia State College *B*
West Virginia Wesleyan College *B*

Wisconsin
Milwaukee Institute of Art & Design *B*

Driver/safety education

Alabama
University of Montevallo *B, M, T*

Georgia
University of Georgia *M*

Iowa
Iowa State University *T*
William Penn University *B*

Kansas
Emporia State University *T*

Mississippi
Mississippi State University *T*

Missouri
Missouri Baptist University *T*
Missouri Western State College *T*

Nebraska
Peru State College *T*

New Hampshire
Keene State College *A*

North Carolina
North Carolina Agricultural and
   Technical State University *B, M, T*

Oklahoma
Southeastern Oklahoma State
   University *T*
Southwestern Oklahoma State
   University *T*
University of Central Oklahoma *B*

Pennsylvania
Lock Haven University of
   Pennsylvania *T*

South Dakota
Northern State University *T*

Texas
Lamar University *T*
Southwest Texas State University *T*
Texas A&M University
   Commerce *B*

Virginia
Bridgewater College *T*
University of Virginia's College at
   Wise *T*

West Virginia
Salem International University *T*
West Virginia University *T*

Dutch/Flemish

Iowa
Dordt College *B*

Michigan
Calvin College *B*

Early childhood education

Alabama

Alabama Agricultural and Mechanical University *B, M, T*
Alabama State University *A, B, M, T*
Athens State University *B*
Auburn University *B, M, D, T*
Birmingham-Southern College *B, T*
Bishop State Community College *C*
Calhoun Community College *A*
Concordia College *B*
Huntingdon College *B, T*
Jacksonville State University *B, M, T*
James H. Faulkner State Community College *A*
Lawson State Community College *A*
Northwest-Shoals Community College *A*
Samford University *B, M, T*
Shelton State Community College *C*
Spring Hill College *B, M*
Troy State University *B, M, T*
Troy State University Dothan *B, M, T*
Tuskegee University *B, T*
University of Alabama *B, M*
University of Alabama
    Birmingham *B, M, D, T*
University of Mobile *B, M, T*
University of Montevallo *B, M, T*
University of North Alabama *B, M*
University of South Alabama *B, M, T*
University of West Alabama *B, M, T*
Virginia College *A*

Alaska

University of Alaska
    Fairbanks *C, A*
    Southeast *C, A, M, T*

Arizona

Arizona State University *B*
Arizona Western College *C, A*
Central Arizona College *C, A*
Northern Arizona University *M, T*
Pima Community College *C, A*
Prescott College *B, M*
Scottsdale Community College *C, A*
South Mountain Community College *C, A*
University of Arizona *B, M*
Yavapai College *C, A*

Arkansas

Arkansas State University *B, M, T*
Arkansas Tech University *A, B*
Black River Technical College *A*
Harding University *B, T*
Henderson State University *B, M, T*
John Brown University *B*
Mississippi County Community College *A*
Ouachita Baptist University *B, T*
Ouachita Technical College *C, A*
Phillips Community College of the University of Arkansas *C, A*
Pulaski Technical College *A*
South Arkansas Community College *C, A*
Southern Arkansas University *B, T*
University of Arkansas
    Community College at Batesville *A*
    Little Rock *B, M*
    Monticello *B*
    Pine Bluff *B*
University of Central Arkansas *M, T*
University of the Ozarks *B, T*
Williams Baptist College *B*

California

Bethany College *A, B*
Bethesda Christian University *C, B*

California State University
    Bakersfield *B, M*
    Chico *B*
    Fresno *M*
    Long Beach *T*
    Northridge *M*
    Sacramento *B, M, T*
    Stanislaus *B*
Cerritos Community College *A*
Chabot College *C, A*
Christian Heritage College *B, T*
College of the Redwoods *C, A*
College of the Sequoias *C*
Concordia University *B*
Cuesta College *C, A*
De Anza College *C, A*
Diablo Valley College *C*
East Los Angeles College *C*
Foothill College *C, A*
Gavilan Community College *C*
Glendale Community College *C, A*
Imperial Valley College *C, A*
Irvine Valley College *C, A*
Long Beach City College *C*
Los Angeles Southwest College *A*
Marymount College *A*
Mills College *M, T*
MiraCosta College *C, A*
Mount St. Mary's College *A*
Mount San Jacinto College *C, A*
Napa Valley College *C, A*
Ohlone College *C, A*
Orange Coast College *C, A*
Pacific Oaks College *B, M*
Pacific Union College *A, B*
Palomar College *C, A*
Patten University *A, B*
Reedley College *C, A*
Riverside Community College *C, A*
San Francisco State University *T*
San Joaquin Delta College *C*
San Jose State University *M*
Santa Barbara City College *C, A*
Santa Rosa Junior College *C, A*
Shasta College *A*
Sierra College *C, A*
Sonoma State University *M, T*
Southwestern College *C, A*
Taft College *C, A*
University of California
    Santa Barbara *M*
University of La Verne *B, M, T*
Ventura College *C, A*
West Valley College *A*
Whittier College *B, T*
Yuba Community College District *C, A*

Colorado

Colorado Mountain College
    Alpine Campus *A*
Community College of Aurora *A*
Fort Lewis College *T*
Metropolitan State College of Denver *T*
Naropa University *B*
Otero Junior College *C, A*
Red Rocks Community College *A*
University of Colorado
    Denver *M*
University of Northern Colorado *M, T*

Connecticut

Asnuntuck Community College *C, A*
Capital Community College *C, A*
Central Connecticut State University *B, M*
Connecticut College *T*
Eastern Connecticut State University *B, M, T*
Gateway Community College *C, A*
Housatonic Community College *A*
Manchester Community College *A*
Mitchell College *A, B*
Naugatuck Valley Community College *C, A*
Northwestern Connecticut Community College *C, A*

Norwalk Community College *C, A*
Sacred Heart University *T*
St. Joseph College *M, T*
Teikyo Post University *C, A*
Three Rivers Community College *C, A*
Tunxis Community College *C, A*
University of Hartford *B, M*

Delaware

Delaware State University *B*
Delaware Technical and Community College
    Stanton/Wilmington Campus *C, A*
University of Delaware *B, T*
Wilmington College *A, B*

District of Columbia

Catholic University of America *B, M, T*
Gallaudet University *B, T*
George Washington University *M*
Howard University *M*
Trinity College *M, T*
University of the District of Columbia *B, T*

Florida

Barry University *B, M, T*
Broward Community College *A*
Florida Agricultural and Mechanical University *B*
Florida Atlantic University *M*
Florida Gulf Coast University *B*
Florida International University *M*
Florida Southern College *B*
Florida State University *C, B, M, D, T*
Indian River Community College *A*
Manatee Community College *A*
Miami-Dade Community College *C, A*
Nova Southeastern University *B*
Okaloosa-Walton Community College *A*
Palm Beach Community College *A*
Pensacola Junior College *A*
St. Petersburg College *A*
Santa Fe Community College *C, A*
Southeastern College of the Assemblies of God *B, T*
Tallahassee Community College *A*
University of Central Florida *B, M*
University of Florida *M*
University of Miami *M*
University of South Florida *B, M*
University of West Florida *B, M, T*

Georgia

Agnes Scott College *T*
Albany State University *B, M, T*
Albany Technical College *C, A*
Armstrong Atlantic State University *B*
Atlanta Metropolitan College *A*
Augusta State University *B, M*
Berry College *B, M, T*
Brenau University *B*
Brewton-Parker College *B*
Clark Atlanta University *B, M, D*
Columbus State University *B, M*
Columbus Technical College *C, A*
Covenant College *B, T*
DeKalb Technical College *C*
Gainesville College *A*
Georgia College and State University *B, M, T*
Georgia Southern University *B, M, T*
Georgia Southwestern State University *B, M, T*
Georgia State University *B, M, D*
Kennesaw State University *B, M*
LaGrange College *B*
Macon State College *A*
Middle Georgia College *A*
Morris Brown College *B*
North Georgia College & State University *B, M*
Northwestern Technical College *A*
Oglethorpe University *B, M, T*
Paine College *B*
Piedmont College *B, M, T*
Reinhardt College *B*

Savannah State University *B*
Savannah Technical College *C*
Spelman College *B, T*
Thomas University *B*
Toccoa Falls College *B, T*
University of Georgia *B, M, D, T*
Valdosta State University *B, M*
Wesleyan College *B, M, T*
West Georgia Technical College *C, A*

Hawaii

Chaminade University of Honolulu *B, T*
University of Hawaii
    Hawaii Community College *C, A*
    Honolulu Community College *C, A*
    Kauai Community College *C, A*
    Manoa *B, M, T*

Idaho

Boise State University *T*
Brigham Young University - Idaho *A*
College of Southern Idaho *A*
Idaho State University *B, T*
Lewis-Clark State College *C, A*
North Idaho College *A*

Illinois

Bradley University *B, T*
Chicago State University *B, M, T*
City Colleges of Chicago
    Harold Washington College *C, A*
    Kennedy-King College *A*
Columbia College Chicago *B*
Concordia University *B, M, T*
De Paul University *C, B, T*
Dominican University *B, T*
Eastern Illinois University *B*
Elmhurst College *B, M*
Governors State University *B, M, T*
Greenville College *B*
Heartland Community College *C, A*
Illinois College *B, T*
Illinois State University *B, T*
John A. Logan College *C, A*
Joliet Junior College *A*
Judson College *B, T*
Kankakee Community College *A*
Kendall College *C, A, T*
Kishwaukee College *A*
Lewis and Clark Community College *C, A*
Loyola University of Chicago *M, D, T*
National-Louis University *B, M, T*
North Park University *B, M*
Northeastern Illinois University *B*
Northern Illinois University *B, M, T*
Oakton Community College *A*
Olivet Nazarene University *B, T*
Parkland College *A*
Quincy University *M, T*
Roosevelt University *B, M*
St. Augustine College *C, A*
St. Xavier University *M*
Sauk Valley Community College *A*
South Suburban College of Cook County *A*
Southern Illinois University
    Carbondale *B*
Southern Illinois University
    Edwardsville *B*
Southwestern Illinois College *A*
Spoon River College *A*
Triton College *C, A*
University of Illinois
    Urbana-Champaign *B, M, D, T*
William Rainey Harper College *C, A*

Indiana

Ancilla College *C, A*
Ball State University *B, M, D, T*
Bethel College *A*
Butler University *B, T*
Indiana State University *B, M*
Indiana University
    Bloomington *B, T*
    South Bend *A*

Indiana University-Purdue University
Fort Wayne *A*
Indiana University-Purdue University
Indianapolis *A, B*
Indiana Wesleyan University *T*
Manchester College *A*
Marian College *B, T*
Martin University *B*
Purdue University *B, M*
Purdue University
Calumet *A*
St. Mary-of-the-Woods College *A, B, T*
Taylor University *A, T*
Taylor University: Fort Wayne *A*
Vincennes University *A*

Iowa

Central College *T*
Clarke College *B, M, T*
Des Moines Area Community
College *C, A*
Drake University *B, M*
Franciscan University *B, T*
Graceland University *T*
Iowa Lakes Community College *A*
Iowa State University *B, T*
Iowa Wesleyan College *B*
Loras College *B*
Luther College *B*
Mount Mercy College *T*
North Iowa Area Community College *A*
Northeast Iowa Community College *C*
Northwestern College *T*
St. Ambrose University *B, T*
Simpson College *B, T*
University of Iowa *M, D*
University of Northern Iowa *B, M*
Upper Iowa University *B, T*
Waldorf College *A*
Wartburg College *T*

Kansas

Benedictine College *T*
Bethel College *T*
Butler County Community College *A*
Central Christian College *A, B*
Donnelly College *C, A*
Emporia State University *M, T*
Fort Scott Community College *A*
Friends University *B*
Garden City Community College *A*
Hesston College *A*
Independence Community College *A*
Kansas City Kansas Community
College *C, A*
Kansas Wesleyan University *A*
Labette Community College *A*
McPherson College *B, T*
Pittsburg State University *B, T*
Pratt Community College *A*
Southwestern College *B, T*
Tabor College *B, T*
Washburn University of Topeka *A, B*

Kentucky

Campbellsville University *B*
Elizabethtown Community College *A*
Hazard Community College *A*
Henderson Community College *A*
Hopkinsville Community College *A*
Jefferson Community College *A*
Madisonville Community College *A*
Maysville Community College *A*
Morehead State University *B*
Murray State University *B*
Spalding University *B, M, T*
University of Kentucky *B*
University of Louisville *M*

Louisiana

Centenary College of Louisiana *B, T*
Delgado Community College *A*
Dillard University *B, T*
Grambling State University *B, M*
Louisiana State University
Alexandria *A*
Eunice *A*

Louisiana Tech University *B*
McNeese State University *A, B, T*
Nicholls State University *M*
Northwestern State University *B*
Nunez Community College *A*
Southern University
Shreveport *A*
Southern University and Agricultural and
Mechanical College *B*
University of Louisiana at Monroe *B*
Xavier University of Louisiana *B, T*

Maine

Andover College *C, A*
Central Maine Technical College *C, A*
University of Maine
Farmington *B, T*

Maryland

Allegany College *A*
Bowie State University *B, T*
Carroll Community College *C, A*
Chesapeake College *C*
College of Notre Dame of Maryland *B*
College of Southern Maryland *C, A*
Community College of Baltimore County
Catonsville *C, A*
Dundalk *C, A*
Essex *C, A*
Coppin State College *B*
Frederick Community College *A*
Frostburg State University *B, T*
Hood College *B*
Howard Community College *C, A*
Johns Hopkins University *M*
Montgomery College
Rockville Campus *A*
St. Mary's College of Maryland *T*
Salisbury University *B, T*
Towson University *B, M, T*
University of Maryland
College Park *B*
Villa Julie College *A, B, T*

Massachusetts

American International College *B, M*
Anna Maria College *B, M, T*
Atlantic Union College *B*
Bay Path College *B*
Bay State College *A*
Becker College *C, A, B, T*
Berkshire Community College *C, A*
Boston College *B, M, T*
Boston University *B, M, T*
Bridgewater State College *B, M, T*
Bunker Hill Community College *C, A*
Cape Cod Community College *C, A*
Dean College *A*
Elms College *B, M, T*
Endicott College *B*
Fisher College *C, A*
Fitchburg State College *B, M, T*
Framingham State College *B, M, T*
Gordon College *B*
Greenfield Community College *A*
Hampshire College *B*
Hebrew College *C*
Lasell College *B*
Lesley University *B, M, T*
Massachusetts College of Liberal Arts *T*
Mount Ida College *A, B, T*
Mount Wachusett Community
College *C, A*
Northeastern University *B*
Pine Manor College *T*
Quinsigamond Community College *C, A*
Roxbury Community College *A*
Salem State College *B, M*
Simmons College *B, M*
Springfield College *B, M, T*
Springfield Technical Community
College *A*
Tufts University *B, M, T*
Urban College of Boston *C, A*
Wellesley College *T*
Westfield State College *B, M, T*

Wheaton College *T*

Michigan

Adrian College *A, T*
Alma College *T*
Baker College
of Cadillac *A*
of Clinton Township *A*
of Muskegon *C, A*
of Port Huron *C, A*
Calvin College *B, T*
Central Michigan University *M*
Eastern Michigan University *B*
Ferris State University *A*
Glen Oaks Community College *C, A*
Gogebic Community College *A*
Grace Bible College *B*
Grand Valley State University *M*
Hillsdale College *B*
Madonna University *B, T*
Marygrove College *C, B, M, T*
Michigan State University *B, M*
Monroe County Community
College *C, A*
Mott Community College *C, A*
Muskegon Community College *C*
North Central Michigan College *C, A*
Northern Michigan University *A, B, T*
Oakland Community College *A*
Oakland University *M, D*
Saginaw Valley State University *M*
Spring Arbor University *T*
University of Michigan
Dearborn *B*
Flint *B, T*
Washtenaw Community College *C, A*
Wayne State University *M*
William Tyndale College *A*

Minnesota

Augsburg College *B, T*
Bethel College *B*
College of St. Catherine *B, T*
Concordia University: St. Paul *B, T*
Crown College *A, B, T*
Martin Luther College *B*
Minnesota State University
Mankato *M*
Moorhead *B, M, T*
Northwestern College *B*
St. Cloud State University *M*
St. Cloud Technical College *C, A*
St. Mary's University of Minnesota *B, M*
Southwest State University *B, T*
University of Minnesota
Crookston *B*
Duluth *B, T*
Twin Cities *B, M*
Winona State University *B, M, T*

Mississippi

Coahoma Community College *A*
Mary Holmes College *C, A*
Mississippi State University *T*
Mississippi Valley State University *B, T*
Rust College *A*
University of Mississippi *B*

Missouri

Central Methodist College *B*
Central Missouri State University *T*
Culver-Stockton College *T*
East Central College *A*
Evangel University *A, B, T*
Hannibal-LaGrange College *B*
Harris Stowe State College *B, T*
Jefferson College *A, B*
Lincoln University *A*
Lindenwood University *B*
Maryville University of Saint
Louis *B, M, T*
Mineral Area College *C*
Missouri Baptist University *B, T*
Missouri Southern State College *B, T*
Missouri Valley College *T*
North Central Missouri College *A*

Northwest Missouri State
University *B, M, T*
St. Charles Community College *C, A*
St. Louis Community College
St. Louis Community College at
Florissant Valley *A*
Southeast Missouri State University *B, T*
Southwest Baptist University *T*
Southwest Missouri State University *B*
Stephens College *B, T*
University of Missouri
Columbia *B*
Kansas City *M*
St. Louis *B, M, T*
Washington University in St. Louis *M*
William Jewell College *T*
William Woods University *T*

Montana

Dawson Community College *C, A*
Fort Belknap College *C*
Montana State University
Billings *A, M*
University of Great Falls *A, B*
University of Montana: Western *A*

Nebraska

College of Saint Mary *A, B, T*
Concordia University *B, M, T*
Hastings College *B, M, T*
Little Priest Tribal College *C*
Midland Lutheran College *B, T*
Nebraska Indian Community College *C*
Northeast Community College *C, A*
Peru State College *B, T*
University of Nebraska
Kearney *B, T*
Western Nebraska Community
College *A*

Nevada

Great Basin College *C, A*
Truckee Meadows Community
College *C, A*
University of Nevada
Las Vegas *B*

New Hampshire

College for Lifelong Learning *A, B*
Hesser College *C, A*
Keene State College *B, T*
New Hampshire Community Technical
College
Berlin *C, A*
Laconia *C, A*
Manchester *C, A, T*
Nashua *C, A*
New Hampshire Technical Institute *C, A*
Plymouth State College *B, T*
Rivier College *C, A, B, M, T*
University of New Hampshire *M*

New Jersey

Bergen Community College *A*
Brookdale Community College *C*
Caldwell College *T*
The College of New Jersey *B, T*
College of St. Elizabeth *T*
County College of Morris *A*
Cumberland County College *C, A*
Essex County College *A*
Gloucester County College *A*
Hudson County Community
College *C, A*
Kean University *B, M*
New Jersey City University *B, M*
Passaic County Community College *A*
Raritan Valley Community College *A*
Rider University *B*
Rowan University *B*
Rutgers, The State University of New
Jersey
Camden Regional Campus *T*
New Brunswick Regional
Campus *T*
Newark Regional Campus *T*
Salem Community College *C, A*

Seton Hall University *B, T*
Sussex County Community College *C, A*
Warren County Community College *C, A*
William Paterson University of New
    Jersey *T*

New Mexico

Eastern New Mexico University *B*
Luna Community College *A*
New Mexico Highlands University *B*
New Mexico State University *B*
New Mexico State University
    Alamogordo *A*
San Juan College *C, A*
Santa Fe Community College *A*
University of New Mexico *B*
Western New Mexico University *C, A*

New York

Adelphi University *M*
Barnard College *T*
Cayuga County Community College *A*
Cazenovia College *B*
City University of New York
    Borough of Manhattan Community
        College *A*
    Brooklyn College *B, M, T*
    City College *B, M, T*
    Hostos Community College *A*
    Hunter College *B, M, T*
    Kingsborough Community
        College *A*
    Queens College *B, M, T*
College of Mount St. Vincent *T*
Corning Community College *C, A*
D'Youville College *B, M, T*
Daemen College *B, T*
Dutchess Community College *C, A*
Eugene Lang College/New School
    University *T*
Fulton-Montgomery Community
    College *A*
Hofstra University *B, M, T*
Jamestown Community College *C*
Jefferson Community College *A*
Keuka College *B*
Long Island University
    C. W. Post Campus *B, M, T*
Manhattan College *B, T*
Manhattanville College *M, T*
Maria College *A*
Marymount Manhattan College *B, T*
Medaille College *B*
Mercy College *T*
Monroe Community College *C*
Nassau Community College *A*
Nazareth College of Rochester *M, T*
New York University *A, B, M, T*
Niagara University *B, T*
Onondaga Community College *C*
Pace University *A, B, M, T*
Pace University:
    Pleasantville/Briarcliff *A, B, M, T*
Roberts Wesleyan College *B, T*
St. Joseph's College *B, T*
St. Joseph's College: Suffolk
    Campus *B, M, T*
Sarah Lawrence College *M*
Schenectady County Community
    College *C, A*
State University of New York
    Buffalo *M*
    College at Brockport *B, M, T*
    College at Buffalo *B, T*
    College at Fredonia *B, T*
    College at Geneseo *T*
    College at Old Westbury *T*
    College at Oneonta *B, M, T*
    College at Plattsburgh *B*
    College at Potsdam *B*
    College of Agriculture and
        Technology at Cobleskill *A*
    College of Technology at Canton *A*
    New Paltz *M, T*
    Purchase *C*
Suffolk County Community College *A*

Syracuse University *B, M, T*
Tompkins-Cortland Community
    College *A*
Trocaire College *A*
Vassar College *T*
Villa Maria College of Buffalo *A*
Wagner College *B, T*
Westchester Community College *C, A*

North Carolina

Alamance Community College *C, A*
Appalachian State University *M*
Beaufort County Community College *A*
Bennett College *B*
Bladen Community College *C*
Brunswick Community College *C, A*
Caldwell Community College and
    Technical Institute *A*
Campbell University *M*
Catawba Valley Community
    College *C, A*
Central Carolina Community
    College *C, A*
Central Piedmont Community
    College *C, A*
College of the Albemarle *C, A*
Davidson County Community
    College *C, A*
Duke University *C*
Durham Technical Community
    College *C, A*
East Carolina University *B*
Edgecombe Community College *C, A*
Fayetteville Technical Community
    College *C, A*
Forsyth Technical Community College *A*
Gaston College *C, A*
Greensboro College *B, T*
Guilford Technical Community
    College *C, A*
Halifax Community College *A*
High Point University *B, T*
Isothermal Community College *A*
Johnson C. Smith University *B, T*
Lenoir Community College *C, A*
Lenoir-Rhyne College *B, M, T*
Louisburg College *A*
Martin Community College *C, A*
Mayland Community College *C, A*
Meredith College *T*
Mitchell Community College *A*
Montgomery Community College *C, A*
Nash Community College *A*
North Carolina Agricultural and
    Technical State University *B, T*
North Carolina Central University *B, T*
Pamlico Community College *C, A*
Piedmont Baptist College *A*
Pitt Community College *C, A*
Roanoke-Chowan Community College *A*
Rockingham Community College *C, A*
Rowan-Cabarrus Community College *A*
Salem College *M*
Sampson Community College *C, A*
Sandhills Community College *A*
Southwestern Community College *A*
Stanly Community College *C, A*
Surry Community College *C, A*
University of North Carolina
    Chapel Hill *B, M*
    Greensboro *B, M, D, T*
    Pembroke *B*
    Wilmington *B*
Vance-Granville Community
    College *C, A*
Wake Technical Community
    College *C, A*
Warren Wilson College *B, T*
Western Piedmont Community
    College *C, A*
Wilson Technical Community
    College *C, A*
Winston-Salem State University *B*

North Dakota

Dickinson State University *B, T*

Jamestown College *B*
Mayville State University *B, T*
University of Mary *B, M, T*
University of North Dakota *B, M, T*

Ohio

Antioch College *B*
Ashland University *B, M, T*
Baldwin-Wallace College *B*
Bluffton College *B*
Bowling Green State University *B*
Bowling Green State University:
    Firelands College *B*
Cedarville University *B, T*
Central Ohio Technical College *A*
Central State University *B*
Chatfield College *A*
Circleville Bible College *A*
Clark State Community College *A*
Cleveland State University *B*
College of Mount St. Joseph *A, B, T*
Columbus State Community College *A*
Cuyahoga Community College
    Eastern Campus *A*
    Metropolitan Campus *A*
    Western Campus *A*
Defiance College *B*
Edison State Community College *A*
Franciscan University of Steubenville *A*
Hiram College *T*
James A. Rhodes State College *C, A*
Jefferson Community College *C, A*
John Carroll University *M, T*
Kent State University *A, B, M*
Kent State University
    Ashtabula Regional Campus *A*
    Salem Regional Campus *A*
    Stark Campus *B*
Lakeland Community College *A*
Lorain County Community College *A*
Lourdes College *B*
Malone College *B*
Marietta College *B*
Miami University
    Oxford Campus *B*
Mount Union College *B, T*
Mount Vernon Nazarene University *B, T*
Muskingum College *B, T*
North Central State College *A*
Notre Dame College *B, T*
Ohio Dominican College *B, T*
Ohio Northern University *B, T*
Ohio State University
    Columbus Campus *M, D*
Ohio University *B, D, T*
Ohio University
    Chillicothe Campus *B*
    Zanesville Campus *B*
Ohio Wesleyan University *B*
Otterbein College *B*
Owens Community College
    Findlay Campus *A*
    Toledo *A*
Shawnee State University *B*
Southern State Community College *A*
Stark State College of Technology *A*
University of Akron *B, T*
University of Cincinnati *B, M, T*
University of Cincinnati
    Clermont College *A*
    Raymond Walters College *A*
University of Dayton *B, M, T*
University of Findlay *B*
University of Rio Grande *A, B*
University of Toledo *T*
Ursuline College *B, T*
Walsh University *B*
Wilmington College *B*
Wright State University *B, M, T*
Wright State University: Lake Campus *A*
Xavier University *A, B*
Youngstown State University *B, M*

Oklahoma

Cameron University *B*
Carl Albert State College *C*

East Central University *B, T*
Northeastern Oklahoma Agricultural and
    Mechanical College *C, A*
Northeastern State University *B, M*
Northwestern Oklahoma State
    University *B, T*
Oklahoma Baptist University *B, T*
Oklahoma Christian University of
    Science and Arts *B, T*
Oklahoma State University *B, M, D, T*
Oklahoma State University
    Oklahoma City *C, A*
Oral Roberts University *B, T*
Rose State College *A*
Southeastern Oklahoma State
    University *B, T*
Southern Nazarene University *B, M*
Southwestern Oklahoma State
    University *B, M, T*
University of Central Oklahoma *B, M*
University of Oklahoma *B, T*
University of Science and Arts of
    Oklahoma *B, T*

Oregon

Blue Mountain Community College *A*
Central Oregon Community College *A*
Chemeketa Community College *A*
Concordia University *B, M, T*
Eastern Oregon University *B, M*
Linfield College *T*
Mount Hood Community College *A*
Oregon State University *M*
Portland Community College *C, A*
Portland State University *T*
Umpqua Community College *C, A*
University of Portland *T*
Warner Pacific College *T*
Western Oregon University *M, T*
Willamette University *M*

Pennsylvania

Albright College *B, M, T*
Arcadia University *B, M, T*
Baptist Bible College of Pennsylvania *A*
Bloomsburg University of
    Pennsylvania *B, M, T*
Bucknell University *B, T*
Bucks County Community College *A*
Cabrini College *B, T*
California University of
    Pennsylvania *A, B, M, T*
Cambria County Area Community
    College *A*
Carlow College *B, M, T*
Cedar Crest College *C*
Chatham College *T*
Chestnut Hill College *B, M*
Cheyney University of
    Pennsylvania *B, T*
DeSales University *C, T*
Duquesne University *B, M, T*
East Stroudsburg University of
    Pennsylvania *B, T*
Edinboro University of
    Pennsylvania *A, B, T*
Elizabethtown College *B*
Grove City College *B*
Gwynedd-Mercy College *T*
Harrisburg Area Community College *A*
Holy Family University *B, T*
Immaculata University *T*
Indiana University of
    Pennsylvania *B, M, T*
Juniata College *B, T*
Keystone College *C, A, B*
King's College *B, T*
Kutztown University of
    Pennsylvania *B, T*
La Roche College *B*
La Salle University *B, M, T*
Lackawanna College *A*
Lancaster Bible College *A*
Lehigh Carbon Community College *A*
Lincoln University *B, M, T*

Lock Haven University of
Pennsylvania *B, T*
Manor College *A*
Marywood University *B, M*
Mercyhurst College *A, B*
Messiah College *B, T*
Millersville University of
Pennsylvania *M, T*
Montgomery County Community
College *A*
Mount Aloysius College *A, B*
Neumann College *B, T*
Philadelphia Biblical University *B, T*
Point Park College *A, B, T*
Reading Area Community College *A*
Rosemont College *T*
St. Vincent College *T*
Seton Hill University *T*
Slippery Rock University of
Pennsylvania *T*
Temple University *M*
University of Pittsburgh *T*
University of Scranton *B*
Valley Forge Christian College *A, B*
West Chester University of
Pennsylvania *B, T*
Widener University *B, M, T*
York College of Pennsylvania *C*

Puerto Rico

Bayamon Central University *B, M*
Inter American University of Puerto Rico
Barranquitas Campus *B*
Fajardo Campus *B, T*
Guayama Campus *B, M*
Metropolitan Campus *B*
San German Campus *B*
Pontifical Catholic University of Puerto
Rico *B, M*
Universidad Metropolitana *B*
Universidad del Este *B*
University of Puerto Rico
Bayamon University College *B*
Rio Piedras Campus *M*

Rhode Island

Community College of Rhode Island *A*
Rhode Island College *B, M*
Salve Regina University *B*

South Carolina

Anderson College *B, T*
Benedict College *B*
Charleston Southern University *M*
Clemson University *B, T*
Coastal Carolina University *B, M, T*
Coker College *B, T*
College of Charleston *M*
Columbia College *B, T*
Columbia International
University *B, M, T*
Converse College *B, M, T*
Erskine College *B, T*
Forrest Junior College *A*
Francis Marion University *B, M, T*
Furman University *M, T*
Lander University *B, T*
Morris College *B, T*
Newberry College *B, T*
North Greenville College *B, T*
Presbyterian College *B, T*
South Carolina State University *B, M*
Southern Wesleyan University *B, T*
Spartanburg Technical College *A*
University of South Carolina *M, D*
University of South Carolina
Aiken *B*
Spartanburg *B, M, T*
Voorhees College *B*
Williamsburg Technical College *C*
Winthrop University *B, T*
York Technical College *C, A*

South Dakota

Black Hills State University *B, T*
Northern State University *B, T*
South Dakota State University *B*

University of South Dakota *B*

Tennessee

Austin Peay State University *T*
Belmont University *B, T*
Carson-Newman College *B*
Chattanooga State Technical Community
College *A*
Columbia State Community
College *C, A*
East Tennessee State University *M, T*
Freed-Hardeman University *B, T*
Jackson State Community College *A*
Johnson Bible College *T*
Lee University *B, T*
Middle Tennessee State University *B, T*
Milligan College *B, T*
Roane State Community College *A*
Southern Adventist University *B*
Southwest Tennessee Community
College *A*
Tennessee State University *B*
Tennessee Technological
University *B, M, D, T*
Tusculum College *B, T*
Union University *B, T*
University of Memphis *T*
University of Tennessee
Knoxville *B, T*
Martin *B, T*
Vanderbilt University *B, M, D, T*
Walters State Community College *A*

Texas

Abilene Christian University *B, M, T*
Alvin Community College *C, A*
Baylor University *T*
Brookhaven College *A*
Concordia University at Austin *B, T*
Dallas Baptist University *B, M, T*
Del Mar College *A*
East Texas Baptist University *B*
Eastfield College *C*
Hardin-Simmons University *C, B, T*
Houston Baptist University *B*
Howard Payne University *T*
Jarvis Christian College *B*
Lamar University *B*
Laredo Community College *A*
LeTourneau University *B*
Lubbock Christian University *B*
McMurry University *T*
Sam Houston State University *M*
Southwest Texas State University *M, T*
Southwestern University *B*
Stephen F. Austin State University *M*
Tarleton State University *T*
Texas A&M International
University *B, M, T*
Texas A&M University
Commerce *B, M*
Corpus Christi *M, T*
Kingsville *M*
Texarkana *T*
Texas Christian University *B*
Texas College *A*
Texas Southern University *M*
Texas Tech University *M*
Texas Wesleyan University *B, M, T*
Texas Woman's University *M, D, T*
Trinity Valley Community College *C, A*
University of Houston *M, T*
University of Houston
Clear Lake *M, T*
University of Mary Hardin-Baylor *T*
University of North Texas *B, M, T*
University of Texas
Arlington *T*
Pan American *M, T*
San Antonio *T*
Tyler *M*
of the Permian Basin *M*
University of the Incarnate Word *B, M*
West Texas A&M University *T*
Western Texas College *C, A*

Utah

Brigham Young University *B*
College of Eastern Utah *A*
Dixie State College of Utah *A*
Southern Utah University *T*
Utah State University *B*
Utah Valley State College *B*
Weber State University *B*
Westminster College *B*

Vermont

Bennington College *B, M, T*
Champlain College *A, B*
College of St. Joseph in Vermont *B*
Goddard College *B*
Johnson State College *M*
Lyndon State College *B*
University of Vermont *B*

Virginia

Averett University *B*
Bluefield College *B*
Eastern Mennonite University *T*
Eastern Shore Community College *C*
Hollins University *T*
J. Sargeant Reynolds Community
College *C, A*
James Madison University *T*
Longwood University *B, T*
Norfolk State University *B, M*
Old Dominion University *M*
Paul D. Camp Community College *C*
Piedmont Virginia Community
College *C*
Radford University *T*
Southwest Virginia Community
College *A*
Thomas Nelson Community
College *C, A*
University of Richmond *B, T*
Virginia Western Community
College *C, A*

Washington

Central Washington University *B, T*
Centralia College *C, A*
Clark College *C, A*
Clover Park Technical College *C, A*
Eastern Washington University *M, T*
Everett Community College *A*
Grays Harbor College *C, A*
Green River Community College *A*
Heritage College *C, A, B*
North Seattle Community College *C, A*
Olympic College *C, A*
Renton Technical College *C, A*
Seattle Central Community College *C*
Spokane Falls Community College *A*
Trinity Lutheran College *B*
Walla Walla College *A*
Walla Walla Community College *C*
Washington State University *T*
Wenatchee Valley College *C, A*
Western Washington University *T*

West Virginia

Concord College *B, T*
Fairmont State College *B*
Glenville State College *B*
Shepherd College *T*
West Liberty State College *B*
West Virginia State College *B*
West Virginia University *T*

Wisconsin

Beloit College *T*
Carroll College *B*
Concordia University Wisconsin *B, T*
Edgewood College *B, T*
Lakeland College *B*
Maranatha Baptist Bible College *A, B*
Marian College of Fond du Lac *B, T*
Milwaukee Area Technical College *C*
Mount Mary College *B, T*
Nicolet Area Technical College *A*
Ripon College *T*
St. Norbert College *M, T*

Silver Lake College *B, T*
University of Wisconsin
Green Bay *T*
La Crosse *T*
Madison *B, T*
Oshkosh *M*
Parkside *T*
Platteville *B, T*
River Falls *T*
Stevens Point *B, T*
Stout *B, T*
Whitewater *B, T*
Viterbo University *T*

Wyoming

Casper College *A*
Central Wyoming College *A*
Sheridan College *C*
Western Wyoming Community
College *A*

Early childhood special education

Arkansas

Arkansas State University *M*
Harding University *B, M, T*

Iowa

Upper Iowa University *T*

Kansas

Tabor College *B, T*

Louisiana

Dillard University *B*

Maine

University of Maine
Farmington *B, T*

Massachusetts

Lesley University *B, M, T*

New York

Daemen College *B, T*
St. Joseph's College: Suffolk Campus *M*
State University of New York
Binghamton *M*
College at Brockport *M*

North Carolina

Fayetteville Technical Community
College *A*
Roanoke-Chowan Community College *A*

Ohio

University of Dayton *B, M, T*

Oregon

Portland State University *D*

Pennsylvania

La Salle University *B, M, T*
Marywood University *B, M*

Puerto Rico

Atlantic College *B*

Tennessee

Union University *B, T*

Washington

Trinity Lutheran College *B*

Wisconsin

University of Wisconsin
Superior *M*

East Asian languages

Arizona

Arizona State University *B, M*

Indiana

Indiana University
Bloomington *B*

Kansas
University of Kansas *B, M*

Massachusetts
Smith College *B*

Michigan
Michigan State University *B*

New York
Columbia University
    Columbia College *B*

Washington
University of Washington *B*

Wisconsin
Lawrence University *B*

East Asian studies

Arizona
University of Arizona *B, M, D*

California
Stanford University *B, M*
University of California
    Davis *B*
    Irvine *B, M, D*
    Los Angeles *B, M*
    Santa Cruz *B*
University of Southern
    California *B, M, D*

Colorado
Fort Lewis College *B*

Connecticut
Connecticut College *B*
Wesleyan University *B*
Yale University *B, M*

Florida
Eckerd College *B*

Illinois
De Paul University *B*
North Central College *B*
University of Chicago *M, D*

Indiana
DePauw University *B*
Indiana University
    Bloomington *B, M*
Valparaiso University *B*

Louisiana
Dillard University *B*

Maine
Bates College *B*
Colby College *B*

Maryland
Johns Hopkins University *B*
University of Maryland
    College Park *C*

Massachusetts
Boston University *B*
Hampshire College *B*
Harvard College *B*
Simmons College *B*
Tufts University *B, M*
Wellesley College *B*

Michigan
Oakland University *B*
University of Michigan *B, M*
Wayne State University *B*

Minnesota
Augsburg College *B*
Hamline University *B*
St. Cloud State University *B*
University of Minnesota
    Twin Cities *B, M*
University of St. Thomas *B*

Missouri
Washington University in St. Louis *B, M*

New Jersey
Princeton University *B, M, D*
Rutgers, The State University of New
    Jersey
        New Brunswick Regional
        Campus *B*

New York
City University of New York
    Queens College *B*
Columbia University
    Columbia College *B*
Cornell University *B, M, D*
Hamilton College *B*
New York University *B*
St. John's University *C, M*
Sarah Lawrence College *B*
State University of New York
    Albany *B*
United States Military Academy *B*

Ohio
College of Wooster *B*
Denison University *B*
Mount Vernon Nazarene University *B*
Oberlin College *B*
Ohio State University
    Columbus Campus *B, M*
Ohio Wesleyan University *B*
Wittenberg University *B*

Oregon
Lewis & Clark College *B*
Portland State University *B*
Willamette University *B*

Pennsylvania
Bryn Mawr College *B*
Bucknell University *B*
Dickinson College *B*
Gettysburg College *B*
Haverford College *B, T*
Penn State
    Abington *B*
    Altoona *B*
    Beaver *B*
    Berks *B*
    Delaware County *B*
    Dubois *B*
    Erie, The Behrend College *B*
    Fayette *B*
    Hazleton *B*
    Lehigh Valley *B*
    McKeesport *B*
    Mont Alto *B*
    New Kensington *B*
    Schuylkill - Capital College *B*
    Shenango *B*
    University Park *B*
    Wilkes-Barre *B*
    Worthington Scranton *B*
    York *B*
University of Pennsylvania *B, M, D*
University of Pittsburgh *C, M*

Rhode Island
Brown University *B*

Tennessee
Vanderbilt University *B*

Vermont
Marlboro College *B*
Middlebury College *B*

Virginia
College of William and Mary *B*
Emory & Henry College *B*
Mary Baldwin College *B*
University of Virginia *M*
Washington and Lee University *B*

Washington
Seattle University *B*
University of Washington *M*

Wisconsin
Lawrence University *B*

Ecology

Alabama
Tuskegee University *B, M*

Alaska
Sheldon Jackson College *B*

Arizona
Prescott College *B, M*
University of Arizona *B, M, D*

California
California Polytechnic State University:
    San Luis Obispo *B*
California State University
    Fresno *B*
Gavilan Community College *A*
Irvine Valley College *A*
Orange Coast College *A*
San Diego State University *B, M, D*
San Francisco State University *B, M*
University of California
    Davis *M, D*
    Los Angeles *B*
    San Diego *B*
    Santa Barbara *B, M, D*
    Santa Cruz *B, D*

Colorado
Colorado State University *M, D*
University of Colorado
    Boulder *B, M, D*
University of Denver *B*

Connecticut
University of Connecticut *B, M, D*
University of New Haven *B, M*
Wesleyan University *B, M*

Florida
Florida Institute of Technology *B, M*
Nova Southeastern University *M*
University of Florida *M, D*
University of Miami *B*

Georgia
Oxford College of Emory University *B*
State University of West Georgia *B*
University of Georgia *B, M, D*

Idaho
Idaho State University *B*

Illinois
Bradley University *B*
Greenville College *B*
University of Chicago *M, D*

Indiana
Indiana University
    Bloomington *M, D*

Iowa
Iowa State University *B, M, D*
Maharishi University of Management *B*
University of Dubuque *B*

Kentucky
Morehead State University *B*

Louisiana
McNeese State University *B, M*
Tulane University *B, M, D*

Maine
College of the Atlantic *B, M*
University of Maine *B, M, D*
University of Maine
    Machias *B*

Maryland
Frostburg State University *M*
Johns Hopkins University *B, M, D*
Towson University *B*
University of Maryland
    College Park *B*

Massachusetts
Berkshire Community College *A*

Boston University *B*
Hampshire College *B*
Harvard College *B*
Simon's Rock College of Bard *B*
Tufts University *B, M*

Michigan
Eastern Michigan University *B*
Michigan Technological University *B*
Northern Michigan University *B*
University of Michigan *B, M*
University of Michigan
    Dearborn *B*
    Flint *B*

Minnesota
Hamline University *B*
Minnesota State University
    Mankato *B, M, T*
St. Cloud State University *B*
Southwest State University *B*
University of Minnesota
    Twin Cities *B, M, D*

Missouri
Missouri Southern State College *B*
William Jewell College *B*

Montana
University of Montana-Missoula *M, D*

Nebraska
Western Nebraska Community
    College *A*

Nevada
Sierra Nevada College *B*

New Hampshire
Dartmouth College *B*
University of New Hampshire *B*

New Jersey
Princeton University *B, M, D*
Richard Stockton College of New
    Jersey *B*
Rutgers, The State University of New
    Jersey
        New Brunswick Regional
        Campus *M, D*

New York
Adelphi University *B*
Bard College *B*
College of New Rochelle *B*
Concordia College *B*
Cornell University *B, M, D*
Iona College *B*
New York Institute of Technology *M*
Pace University *B*
St. John's University *B*
State University of New York
    Albany *M*
    College of Environmental Science
        and Forestry *B, M, D*
    Purchase *B*
    Stony Brook *D*
University of Rochester *B*

North Carolina
Appalachian State University *B*
Brevard College *B*
North Carolina State University *M*
University of North Carolina
    Chapel Hill *M, D*

Ohio
Kent State University *M, D*
Ohio State University
    Columbus Campus *B, M, D*
University of Akron *B*

Oklahoma
Oklahoma State University *M, D*

Oregon
University of Oregon *M, D*

Pennsylvania
California University of Pennsylvania *B*

Carlow College *B*
East Stroudsburg University of
 Pennsylvania *B*
Juniata College *B*
Lock Haven University of
 Pennsylvania *B*
Penn State
 University Park *M, D*
Slippery Rock University of
 Pennsylvania *M*
University of Pittsburgh *B*
West Chester University of
 Pennsylvania *B*

South Dakota
Northern State University *B*

Tennessee
University of Tennessee
 Knoxville *M, D*

Texas
Baylor University *M*
Rice University *B*
University of North Texas *M, D*
University of Texas
 Austin *B*

Utah
Brigham Young University *M, D*
Dixie State College of Utah *A*
Utah State University *B, M, D*

Vermont
Bennington College *B*
Goddard College *B*
Marlboro College *B*
Sterling College *A, B*

Virginia
Averett University *B*
Lynchburg College *B*
Old Dominion University *D*

Washington
University of Washington *B, M, D*
Western Washington University *B*

Wisconsin
Lawrence University *B, T*
Marquette University *M, D*
Northland College *B*
University of Wisconsin
 Superior *B*

Econometrics/quantitative economics

Indiana
Anderson University *B*

Iowa
University of Northern Iowa *B*

Maine
Colby College *B*

Maryland
United States Naval Academy *B*

Ohio
Youngstown State University *B*

Economics

Alabama
Alabama State University *B*
Auburn University *B*
Birmingham-Southern College *B*
Jacksonville State University *B*
Lawson State Community College *A*
Talladega College *B*
Tuskegee University *B*
University of Alabama
 Birmingham *B*

Alaska
University of Alaska
 Anchorage *B*
 Fairbanks *B*

Arizona
Arizona State University *B, M, D*
Northern Arizona University *B*
University of Arizona *B, M, D*

Arkansas
Arkansas State University *B*
Arkansas Tech University *B*
Black River Technical College *A*
Harding University *B*
Hendrix College *B*
Lyon College *B*
University of Arkansas *B, M, D*
University of Arkansas
 Little Rock *B*
University of Central Arkansas *B*

California
Bakersfield College *A*
Cabrillo College *A*
California Institute of Technology *B*
California Polytechnic State University:
 San Luis Obispo *B*
California State Polytechnic University:
 Pomona *B, M.*
California State University
 Bakersfield *B*
 Chico *B*
 Dominguez Hills *B*
 Fresno *B, M*
 Fullerton *B, M*
 Hayward *B, M*
 Long Beach *B, M*
 Los Angeles *B, M*
 Northridge *B*
 Sacramento *B, M*
 San Bernardino *B*
 San Marcos *B*
 Stanislaus *B*
Cerritos Community College *A*
Chapman University *B*
Claremont McKenna College *B*
College of Alameda *A*
De Anza College *A*
East Los Angeles College *A*
Foothill College *A*
Gavilan Community College *A*
Glendale Community College *A*
Golden Gate University *B, M*
Golden West College *A*
Grossmont Community College *A*
Hope International University *C, M*
Humboldt State University *B*
Irvine Valley College *A*
Loyola Marymount University *B*
Marymount College *A*
MiraCosta College *A*
Monterey Peninsula College *A*
Occidental College *B*
Orange Coast College *A*
Palomar College *C, A*
Pepperdine University *B*
Pitzer College *B*
Point Loma Nazarene University *B*
Pomona College *B*
St. Mary's College of California *B*
San Diego State University *B, M*
San Francisco State University *B, M*
San Jose State University *B, M*
Santa Barbara City College *A*
Santa Clara University *B*
Santa Rosa Junior College *A*
Santiago Canyon College *A*
Scripps College *B*
Sonoma State University *B*
Southwestern College *A*
Stanford University *B, M, D*

University of California
 Berkeley *B, D*
 Davis *B, M, D*
 Irvine *B, M, D*
 Los Angeles *B, M, D*
 Riverside *B, M, D*
 San Diego *B, D*
 Santa Barbara *B, M, D*
 Santa Cruz *B, M, D*
University of La Verne *B*
University of Redlands *B*
University of San Diego *B*
University of San Francisco *B, M*
University of Southern
 California *B, M, D*
University of the Pacific *B*
Ventura College *A*

Colorado
Colorado College *B*
Colorado School of Mines *B, M, D*
Colorado State University *B, M, D*
Fort Lewis College *B*
Metropolitan State College of
 Denver *B, T*
Red Rocks Community College *A*
Regis University *B*
United States Air Force Academy *B*
University of Colorado
 Boulder *B, M, D*
 Colorado Springs *B*
 Denver *B, M*
University of Denver *B, M*
University of Northern Colorado *B*

Connecticut
Albertus Magnus College *B*
Central Connecticut State University *B*
Connecticut College *B*
Eastern Connecticut State University *B*
Fairfield University *B*
Quinnipiac University *B*
Sacred Heart University *B*
St. Joseph College *B*
Trinity College *B, M*
University of Connecticut *B, M, D*
University of Hartford *B*
University of New Haven *B*
Wesleyan University *B, M*
Western Connecticut State University *B*
Yale University *B, M, D*

Delaware
University of Delaware *B*

District of Columbia
American University *B, M, D*
Catholic University of America *B, M, D*
Gallaudet University *B*
George Washington University *B, M, D*
Georgetown University *B, D*
Howard University *B, M, D*
Strayer University *A, B*
Trinity College *B*
University of the District of Columbia *B*

Florida
Barry University *B*
Broward Community College *A*
Eckerd College *B*
Florida Agricultural and Mechanical
 University *B*
Florida Atlantic University *B, M*
Florida International University *B, M, D*
Florida Southern College *B*
Florida State University *B, M, D*
Gulf Coast Community College *A*
Indian River Community College *A*
Jacksonville University *B*
Miami-Dade Community College *A*
New College of Florida *B*
Polk Community College *A*
Rollins College *B*
Schiller International University *B*
South Florida Community College *A*
Stetson University *B*
University of Central Florida *B*

University of Florida *B, M, D*
University of North Florida *B*
University of South Florida *B*
University of Tampa *A, B*
University of West Florida *B*

Georgia
Agnes Scott College *B*
Armstrong Atlantic State University *B*
Berry College *B*
Clark Atlanta University *B, M*
Covenant College *B*
Dalton State College *A*
Emory University *B, D*
Fort Valley State University *B*
Georgia Southern University *B*
Georgia State University *B, M, D*
Kennesaw State University *B*
Mercer University *B*
Middle Georgia College *A*
Morehouse College *B*
Oglethorpe University *B*
Oxford College of Emory University *B*
South Georgia College *A*
Spelman College *B*
State University of West Georgia *B*
University of Georgia *B*
Valdosta State University *B*
Wesleyan College *B*

Hawaii
Hawaii Pacific University *B*
University of Hawaii
 Hilo *B*
 Manoa *B, M, D*
 West Oahu *B*

Idaho
Albertson College of Idaho *B*
Boise State University *B, T*
Brigham Young University - Idaho *B*
College of Southern Idaho *A*
Idaho State University *B*
University of Idaho *B, M*

Illinois
Augustana College *B*
Aurora University *B*
Benedictine University *B, T*
Black Hawk College
 East Campus *A*
Bradley University *B*
Chicago State University *B*
De Paul University *B, M*
Dominican University *B*
Eastern Illinois University *B, M*
Elmhurst College *B*
Illinois College *B*
Illinois State University *B, M*
Illinois Wesleyan University *B*
John A. Logan College *A*
John Wood Community College *A*
Kishwaukee College *A*
Knox College *B*
Lake Forest College *B*
Lake Land College *A*
Lewis University *B*
Lincoln College *A*
Lincoln Land Community College *A*
Loyola University of Chicago *B*
McKendree College *B*
Monmouth College *B, T*
National-Louis University *B*
North Central College *B*
North Park University *B*
Northeastern Illinois University *B*
Northern Illinois University *B, M, D*
Northwestern University *B, M, D*
Olivet Nazarene University *B*
Parkland College *A*
Principia College *B*
Richland Community College *A*
Rockford College *B*
Roosevelt University *B, M*
Sauk Valley Community College *A*
South Suburban College of Cook
 County *A*

Southern Illinois University
  Carbondale *B, M, D*
Southern Illinois University
  Edwardsville *B, M*
Southwestern Illinois College *A*
Triton College *A*
University of Chicago *B, M, D*
University of Illinois
  Chicago *B, M, D*
  Urbana-Champaign *B, M, D*
Waubonsee Community College *A*
Western Illinois University *B, M*
Wheaton College *B*

Indiana

Ball State University *B, M*
Butler University *B*
DePauw University *B*
Earlham College *B*
Franklin College *B*
Goshen College *B*
Hanover College *B*
Indiana State University *B, T*
Indiana University
  Bloomington *B, M, D*
  Northwest *B*
  South Bend *B*
  Southeast *B*
Indiana University-Purdue University
  Fort Wayne *B*
Indiana University-Purdue University
  Indianapolis *B, M*
Indiana Wesleyan University *A, B*
Manchester College *B*
Marian College *B*
Purdue University *M, D*
Rose-Hulman Institute of Technology *B*
St. Joseph's College *B*
Saint Mary's College *B*
Taylor University *B*
University of Evansville *B*
University of Indianapolis *B*
University of Notre Dame *B, M, D*
University of Southern Indiana *B*
Valparaiso University *B*
Vincennes University *A*
Wabash College *B*

Iowa

Buena Vista University *B, T*
Central College *B, T*
Coe College *B*
Cornell College *B, T*
Drake University *B*
Graceland University *B, T*
Grinnell College *B*
Iowa State University *B, M, D*
Loras College *B*
Luther College *B*
Northwestern College *B*
St. Ambrose University *B, T*
Simpson College *B*
University of Iowa *B, D, T*
University of Northern Iowa *B*
Waldorf College *A*
Wartburg College *B, T*

Kansas

Allen County Community College *A*
Baker University *B*
Barton County Community College *A*
Benedictine College *B, T*
Bethany College *B*
Butler County Community College *A*
Central Christian College *A, B*
Dodge City Community College *A*
Emporia State University *B, T*
Fort Hays State University *B*
Fort Scott Community College *A*
Independence Community College *A*
Kansas State University *B, M, D*
Pittsburg State University *B*
Seward County Community College *A*
University of Kansas *B, M, D*
Washburn University of Topeka *B*
Wichita State University *B, M*

Kentucky

Bellarmine University *B*
Berea College *B*
Campbellsville University *B*
Centre College *B*
Murray State University *B, M*
Thomas More College *A, B*
Transylvania University *B*
University of Kentucky *B, M, D*
University of Louisville *B*

Louisiana

Centenary College of Louisiana *B*
Dillard University *B*
Louisiana College *B*
Louisiana State University and
  Agricultural and Mechanical
  College *B, M, D*
Loyola University New Orleans *B*
Southern University
  New Orleans *B*
Tulane University *B, M, D*
University of New Orleans *B, D*

Maine

Bates College *B*
Bowdoin College *B*
Colby College *B*
University of Maine *B, M*
University of Maine
  Farmington *B*
University of Southern Maine *B*

Maryland

Allegany College *A*
Bowie State University *B*
College of Notre Dame of Maryland *B*
Community College of Baltimore County
  Catonsville *A*
  Dundalk *A*
  Essex *A*
Frederick Community College *A*
Frostburg State University *B*
Goucher College *B*
Hood College *B*
Johns Hopkins University *B, D*
Loyola College in Maryland *B*
McDaniel College *B*
Morgan State University *B, M*
Mount St. Mary's College *B*
St. Mary's College of Maryland *B*
Salisbury University *B*
Towson University *B*
United States Naval Academy *B*
University of Maryland
  Baltimore County *B, M*
  College Park *B, M, D*
Washington College *B*

Massachusetts

American International College *B*
Amherst College *B*
Assumption College *B*
Boston College *B, M, D*
Boston University *B, M, D*
Brandeis University *B, M, D*
Bridgewater State College *B*
Clark University *B, M, D*
College of the Holy Cross *B*
Fitchburg State College *B*
Framingham State College *B*
Gordon College *B*
Hampshire College *B*
Harvard University *B*
Massachusetts Institute of
  Technology *B, M, D*
Merrimack College *B*
Mount Holyoke College *B*
Nichols College *B*
Northeastern University *B, M, D*
Salem State College *B*
Simmons College *B*
Smith College *B*
Stonehill College *B*
Suffolk University *B, M*
Tufts University *B, M*

University of Massachusetts
  Amherst *B, M, D*
  Boston *B*
  Dartmouth *B*
  Lowell *B*
Wellesley College *B*
Western New England College *B*
Westfield State College *B*
Wheaton College *B*
Williams College *B, M*
Worcester Polytechnic Institute *B*

Michigan

Adrian College *A, B, T*
Alma College *B, T*
Andrews University *B*
Aquinas College *B, T*
Calvin College *B*
Central Michigan University *B, M, T*
Eastern Michigan University *B, M*
Grand Valley State University *B*
Hillsdale College *B*
Hope College *B*
Kalamazoo College *B, T*
Michigan State University *B, M, D*
Northern Michigan University *B, T*
Oakland University *B*
Saginaw Valley State University *B*
University of Michigan *B, M, D, T*
University of Michigan
  Dearborn *B*
  Flint *B, T*
Wayne State University *B, M, D*
Western Michigan University *B, M, D*

Minnesota

Augsburg College *B*
Bemidji State University *B*
Bethel College *B*
Carleton College *B*
College of St. Benedict *B*
College of St. Catherine *B*
Concordia College: Moorhead *B*
Gustavus Adolphus College *B*
Hamline University *B*
Macalester College *B*
Metropolitan State University *B*
Minnesota State University
  Mankato *B, M*
  Moorhead *B*
Ridgewater College: A Community and
  Technical College *A*
St. Cloud State University *B, M*
St. John's University *B*
St. Olaf College *B*
University of Minnesota
  Duluth *B*
  Morris *B*
  Twin Cities *B, M, D*
University of St. Thomas *B*
Winona State University *B*

Mississippi

Alcorn State University *B*
Itawamba Community College *A*
Mary Holmes College *A*
Millsaps College *B, T*
Mississippi State University *B, M*
University of Mississippi *B*

Missouri

Central Methodist College *B*
Central Missouri State University *B, M*
Drury University *B*
East Central College *A*
Lindenwood University *B*
Missouri Southern State College *B*
Missouri Valley College *B*
Missouri Western State College *B*
Northwest Missouri State University *B*
Rockhurst University *B*
St. Louis University *B, M*
Southeast Missouri State University *B*
Southwest Missouri State University *B*
Three Rivers Community College *A*
Truman State University *B*

University of Missouri
  Columbia *B, M, D*
  Kansas City *B, M*
  Rolla *B, T*
  St. Louis *B, M*
Washington University in St.
  Louis *B, M, D*
Webster University *B*
Westminster College *B*

Montana

Montana State University
  Bozeman *B, M*
Rocky Mountain College *B*
University of Montana-Missoula *B, M*

Nebraska

Creighton University *B*
Doane College *B*
Hastings College *B*
Midland Lutheran College *B*
Nebraska Wesleyan University *B*
University of Nebraska
  Kearney *B*
  Lincoln *B, M, D*
  Omaha *B, M*

New Hampshire

Dartmouth College *B*
Keene State College *B*
St. Anselm College *B*
Southern New Hampshire University *B*
University of New Hampshire *B, M, D*

New Jersey

Bloomfield College *B*
The College of New Jersey *B*
College of St. Elizabeth *B*
Drew University *B*
Fairleigh Dickinson University
  College at Florham *B*
  Metropolitan Campus *B*
Kean University *B*
Montclair State University *B*
New Jersey City University *B*
Princeton University *B, M, D*
Ramapo College of New Jersey *B*
Richard Stockton College of New
  Jersey *B*
Rider University *B*
Rowan University *B*
Rutgers, The State University of New
  Jersey
  Camden Regional Campus *B*
  New Brunswick Regional
    Campus *B, M, D*
  Newark Regional Campus *B*
St. Peter's College *B*
Seton Hall University *B*
Thomas Edison State College *B*
William Paterson University of New
  Jersey *B*

New Mexico

New Mexico State University *B*
San Juan College *A*
University of New Mexico *B, M, D*

New York

Adelphi University *B*
Alfred University *B*
Bard College *B*
Barnard College *B*
Canisius College *B*
City University of New York
  Baruch College *B, M*
  Brooklyn College *B, M*
  City College *B, M*
  College of Staten Island *B*
  Hunter College *B, M*
  Queens College *B, M*
  York College *B*
Clarkson University *B*
Colgate University *B*
College of Mount St. Vincent *B*
College of New Rochelle *B, T*

Columbia University
  Columbia College *B*
Cornell University *B, M, D*
Dominican College of Blauvelt *B*
Dowling College *B*
Elmira College *B*
Eugene Lang College/New School
  University *B*
Excelsior College *B*
Fordham University *B, M, D*
Hamilton College *B*
Hartwick College *B*
Hobart and William Smith Colleges *B*
Hofstra University *B*
Iona College *B, M*
Ithaca College *B*
Le Moyne College *B*
Long Island University
  C. W. Post Campus *B*
Manhattan College *B*
Manhattanville College *B*
Marist College *B*
Marymount College of Fordham
  University *B*
Nazareth College of Rochester *B*
New York Institute of Technology *B*
New York University *B, M, D*
Pace University *B*
Pace University:
  Pleasantville/Briarcliff *B, M*
Rensselaer Polytechnic Institute *B, M, D*
Rochester Institute of Technology *B*
St. John Fisher College *B*
St. John's University *C, B, M*
St. Lawrence University *B*
Sarah Lawrence College *B*
Skidmore College *B*
State University of New York
  Albany *B, M, D*
  Binghamton *B, M, D*
  Buffalo *B, M, D*
  College at Buffalo *B, M*
  College at Cortland *B*
  College at Fredonia *B*
  College at Geneseo *B, T*
  College at Oneonta *B*
  College at Plattsburgh *B*
  College at Potsdam *B*
  Empire State College *A, B*
  New Paltz *B*
  Oswego *B*
  Purchase *C, B*
  Stony Brook *B, M, D*
Suffolk County Community College *A*
Syracuse University *B, M, D*
Touro College *B*
Union College *B*
United States Military Academy *B*
University of Rochester *B, M, D*
Utica College *B*
Vassar College *B*
Wells College *B*
Yeshiva University *B*

North Carolina
Appalachian State University *B*
Belmont Abbey College *B*
Campbell University *B*
Davidson College *B*
Duke University *B, M, D*
East Carolina University *B*
Elon University *B*
Guilford College *B*
Johnson C. Smith University *B*
Lenoir-Rhyne College *B, T*
Meredith College *B*
North Carolina State University *B, M, D*
Pfeiffer University *B*
Salem College *B*
University of North Carolina
  Asheville *B, T*
  Chapel Hill *B, M, D*
  Charlotte *B*
  Greensboro *B, M, T*
  Wilmington *B*
Wake Forest University *B*

Warren Wilson College *B*
Wingate University *B*

North Dakota
Minot State University *B*
North Dakota State University *B*
University of North Dakota *B*

Ohio
Antioch College *B*
Ashland University *B*
Baldwin-Wallace College *B*
Bluffton College *B*
Bowling Green State University *B, M*
Case Western Reserve University *B*
Central State University *B*
Cleveland State University *B, M*
College of Wooster *B*
Denison University *B*
Franciscan University of Steubenville *B*
Heidelberg College *B*
Hiram College *B, T*
John Carroll University *B*
Kent State University *B, D*
Kent State University
  Stark Campus *B*
Kenyon College *B*
Marietta College *B*
Miami University
  Oxford Campus *B, M*
Mount Union College *B*
Muskingum College *B*
Notre Dame College *B, T*
Oberlin College *B*
Ohio Dominican College *B*
Ohio State University
  Columbus Campus *B, M, D*
Ohio University *B, M*
Ohio Wesleyan University *B*
Otterbein College *B*
University of Akron *B, M*
University of Cincinnati *C, B, M, D, T*
University of Cincinnati
  Raymond Walters College *A*
University of Dayton *B*
University of Findlay *B*
University of Rio Grande *B*
University of Toledo *B, M*
Wilmington College *B*
Wittenberg University *B*
Wright State University *B, M*
Xavier University *B*
Youngstown State University *B, M*

Oklahoma
Langston University *B*
Oklahoma City University *B*
Oklahoma State University *B, M, D*
Tulsa Community College *A*
University of Central Oklahoma *B, M*
University of Oklahoma *B, M, D*
University of Science and Arts of
  Oklahoma *B*
University of Tulsa *B*

Oregon
Central Oregon Community College *A*
Chemeketa Community College *A*
Lewis & Clark College *B*
Linfield College *B*
Linn-Benton Community College *A*
Oregon State University *B, M, D*
Pacific University *B*
Portland State University *B, M, D*
Reed College *B*
Southern Oregon University *B*
University of Oregon *B, M, D*
Western Oregon University *B*
Willamette University *B*

Pennsylvania
Albright College *B*
Allegheny College *B*
Bloomsburg University of
  Pennsylvania *B*
Bryn Mawr College *B*
Bucknell University *B*

California University of Pennsylvania *B*
Carnegie Mellon University *B, D*
Chatham College *B*
Chestnut Hill College *B*
Cheyney University of Pennsylvania *B*
Dickinson College *B*
East Stroudsburg University of
  Pennsylvania *B*
Edinboro University of Pennsylvania *B*
Elizabethtown College *B*
Franklin & Marshall College *B*
Gettysburg College *B*
Grove City College *B*
Haverford College *B, T*
Holy Family University *B*
Immaculata University *B*
Indiana University of Pennsylvania *B*
Juniata College *B*
King's College *B*
La Salle University *B*
Lafayette College *B*
Lebanon Valley College of
  Pennsylvania *B*
Lehigh University *B, M, D*
Lincoln University *B*
Lock Haven University of
  Pennsylvania *B*
Lycoming College *B*
Messiah College *B*
Millersville University of
  Pennsylvania *B, T*
Moravian College *B*
Muhlenberg College *B*
Penn State
  Abington *B*
  Altoona *B*
  Beaver *B*
  Berks *B*
  Delaware County *B*
  Dubois *B*
  Erie, The Behrend College *B*
  Fayette *B*
  Hazleton *B*
  Lehigh Valley *B*
  McKeesport *B*
  Mont Alto *B*
  New Kensington *B*
  Schuylkill - Capital College *B*
  Shenango *B*
  University Park *B, M, D*
  Wilkes-Barre *B*
  Worthington Scranton *B*
  York *B*
Robert Morris University *B*
Rosemont College *B*
St. Joseph's University *B*
St. Vincent College *B*
Seton Hill University *B*
Shippensburg University of
  Pennsylvania *B, T*
Slippery Rock University of
  Pennsylvania *B, T*
Swarthmore College *B*
Temple University *B, M, D*
University of Pennsylvania *B, D*
University of Pittsburgh *B, M, D*
University of Pittsburgh
  Bradford *B*
  Johnstown *B*
University of Scranton *B*
Villanova University *B*
Washington and Jefferson College *B*
Wilson College *B*
York College of Pennsylvania *B*

Puerto Rico
Turabo University *B*
University of Puerto Rico
  Cayey University College *B*
  Mayaguez Campus *B*
  Rio Piedras Campus *B, M*

Rhode Island
Brown University *B, M, D*
Bryant College *B*
Rhode Island College *B*

Salve Regina University *B*
University of Rhode Island *B, D*

South Carolina
Benedict College *B*
Charleston Southern University *B*
Clemson University *B, M*
College of Charleston *B*
Converse College *B*
Francis Marion University *B*
Furman University *B*
Presbyterian College *B*
University of South Carolina *B, M, D*
University of South Carolina
  Aiken *B*
Wofford College *B*

South Dakota
Augustana College *B, T*
Northern State University *B*
South Dakota State University *B, M, T*
University of South Dakota *B*

Tennessee
Belmont University *B*
Carson-Newman College *B*
Columbia State Community College *A*
East Tennessee State University *B*
Maryville College *B, T*
Middle Tennessee State
  University *B, M, D*
Rhodes College *B*
Roane State Community College *A*
Tennessee Technological University *B*
Union University *B, T*
University of Memphis *B, M*
University of Tennessee
  Chattanooga *B*
  Knoxville *B, M, D*
  Martin *B*
Vanderbilt University *B, M, D*

Texas
Austin College *B*
Austin Community College *A*
Baylor University *B, M*
Brazosport College *A*
Cisco Junior College *A*
College of the Mainland *A*
Galveston College *A*
Houston Baptist University *B*
Lamar University *B*
Laredo Community College *A*
Lon Morris College *A*
Midland College *A*
Midwestern State University *B*
Palo Alto College *A*
Rice University *B, M, D*
St. Edward's University *B, T*
St. Mary's University *M*
St. Philip's College *A*
Southern Methodist University *B, M, D*
Southwest Texas State University *B, T*
Southwestern University *B*
Stephen F. Austin State University *B*
Tarleton State University *B, T*
Texas A&M University *B, M, D*
Texas A&M University
  Commerce *B, M*
Texas Christian University *B, M, T*
Texas Lutheran University *B*
Texas Southern University *B*
Texas Tech University *B, M, D*
Texas Woman's University *B, T*
Trinity University *B*
University of Dallas *B, T*
University of Houston *B, M, D*
University of Mary Hardin-Baylor *B*
University of North Texas *B, M*
University of St. Thomas *B*
University of Texas
  Arlington *B, M*
  Austin *B, M, D*
  Dallas *B, M*
  El Paso *B, M*
  Tyler *B*
West Texas A&M University *B*

Western Texas College *A*

Utah

Brigham Young University *B, M*
Dixie State College of Utah *A*
Salt Lake Community College *A*
Snow College *A*
Southern Utah University *B*
University of Utah *B, M, D*
Utah State University *B, M, D*
Weber State University *B*

Vermont

Marlboro College *B*
Middlebury College *B*
Norwich University *B*
St. Michael's College *B*
University of Vermont *B*

Virginia

Bridgewater College *B*
College of William and Mary *B*
Eastern Mennonite University *B*
Emory & Henry College *B*
George Mason University *B, M, D*
Hampden-Sydney College *B*
Hollins University *B*
James Madison University *B*
Longwood University *B*
Lynchburg College *B*
Mary Baldwin College *B*
Mary Washington College *B*
Marymount University *B*
Norfolk State University *B*
Old Dominion University *B, M*
Radford University *B, M*
Randolph-Macon College *B*
Randolph-Macon Woman's College *B*
Roanoke College *B, T*
Sweet Briar College *B*
University of Richmond *B*
University of Virginia *B, M, D*
University of Virginia's College at Wise *B, T*
Virginia Military Institute *B*
Virginia Polytechnic Institute and State University *B, M, D*
Washington and Lee University *B*

Washington

Central Washington University *B*
Centralia College *A*
Eastern Washington University *B, T*
Everett Community College *A*
Gonzaga University *B*
Lower Columbia College *A*
Pacific Lutheran University *B*
Seattle Pacific University *B*
Seattle University *B, M*
University of Puget Sound *B, T*
University of Washington *B, M, D*
Washington State University *B, M, D*
Western Washington University *B, T*
Whitman College *B*
Whitworth College *B*

West Virginia

Bethany College *B*
Marshall University *B*
Potomac State College of West Virginia University *A*
Shepherd College *B*
West Virginia State College *B*
West Virginia University *B*
West Virginia Wesleyan College *B*

Wisconsin

Beloit College *B*
Carthage College *B, T*
Concordia University Wisconsin *B*
Edgewood College *B*
Lakeland College *B*
Lawrence University *B, T*
Marquette University *B, M*
Northland College *B, T*
Ripon College *B*
St. Norbert College *B, T*

University of Wisconsin
  Eau Claire *B*
  Green Bay *B*
  La Crosse *B, T*
  Madison *B, M, D*
  Milwaukee *B, M, D*
  Oshkosh *B*
  Parkside *B, T*
  Platteville *B*
  River Falls *B, T*
  Stevens Point *B, T*
  Superior *B*
  Whitewater *B, T*

Wyoming

Casper College *A*
Eastern Wyoming College *A*
Laramie County Community College *A*
Western Wyoming Community College *A*

Education

Alabama

Alabama Agricultural and Mechanical University *B, M*
Athens State University *B*
Birmingham-Southern College *B*
Bishop State Community College *A*
Calhoun Community College *A*
Central Alabama Community College *A*
Faulkner University *B*
Judson College *B*
Lawson State Community College *A*
Northwest-Shoals Community College *A*
Samford University *D*
Shelton State Community College *A*
Talladega College *B*
Troy State University *M*
Troy State University in Montgomery *M*
Tuskegee University *B, T*
University of Alabama
  Birmingham *D, T*
Wallace State Community College at Hanceville *A*

Alaska

Sheldon Jackson College *A*
University of Alaska
  Fairbanks *B, M, T*
  Southeast *M*

Arizona

Central Arizona College *C, A*
Cochise College *A*
Estrella Mountain Community College *A*
Gateway Community College *A*
Glendale Community College *A*
Northern Arizona University *B*
Phoenix College *A*
Prescott College *B, M, T*
Rio Salado College *C*
South Mountain Community College *A*
University of Arizona *M, D*

Arkansas

Central Baptist College *A*
Henderson State University *B, M, T*
John Brown University *B, M, T*
Ouachita Baptist University *B*
Philander Smith College *B*
Phillips Community College of the University of Arkansas *A*
South Arkansas Community College *A*
University of Arkansas *M*
University of Arkansas
  Community College at Hope *A*
  Cossatot Community College of the A
  Pine Bluff *B, M, T*
University of Central Arkansas *M*
University of the Ozarks *B*
Williams Baptist College *B*

California

Antioch Southern California
  Santa Barbara *M, T*
Azusa Pacific University *B, M, D*
Barstow College *C, A*
Bethany College *M*
Biola University *B, M, T*
California Baptist University *B, M*
California Polytechnic State University:
  San Luis Obispo *M*
California State Polytechnic University:
  Pomona *M*
California State University
  Bakersfield *M, T*
  Chico *M*
  Dominguez Hills *M*
  Fresno *B, M*
  Fullerton *M*
  Hayward *M*
  Los Angeles *M*
  Monterey Bay *B, M*
  Sacramento *B, M*
  San Bernardino *M*
  San Marcos *M*
  Stanislaus *M*
Cerro Coso Community College *A*
Chapman University *M*
Christian Heritage College *B*
College of the Siskiyous *A*
Columbia College *C*
Concordia University *B, T*
Feather River College *A*
Holy Names College *M*
John F. Kennedy University *M*
Laney College *A*
Los Angeles Southwest College *A*
Loyola Marymount University *M*
Master's College *B*
Mills College *B*
Napa Valley College *A*
National University *M, T*
Occidental College *T*
Pacific Union College *M*
Pepperdine University *B, M*
St. Mary's College of California *M*
San Diego State University *C, M, D, T*
Santa Rosa Junior College *A*
Simpson College *M, T*
Sonoma State University *M*
Southwestern College *A*
Stanford University *M, D*
Taft College *A*
University of California
  Berkeley *M, D*
  Davis *M, D, T*
  Irvine *M, T*
  Los Angeles *M, D*
  Riverside *M, D*
  Santa Barbara *M, D*
  Santa Cruz *M*
University of La Verne *B, M, T*
University of Redlands *M, T*
University of San Diego *B, M, D*
University of Southern
  California *B, M, D*
University of the Pacific *B*
Vanguard University of Southern
  California *M, T*
Ventura College *A*
Whittier College *B, M, T*

Colorado

Colorado Mountain College
  Alpine Campus *A*
  Spring Valley Campus *A*
  Timberline Campus *A*
Colorado State University
  Pueblo *B*
Fort Lewis College *T*
Jones International University *M*
Morgan Community College *A*
Naropa University *M*
National American University
  Denver *A*
Otero Junior College *A*

Regis University *B, M, T*
Trinidad State Junior College *A*
University of Colorado
  Colorado Springs *M*

Connecticut

Central Connecticut State
  University *B, M*
Eastern Connecticut State University *M*
Northwestern Connecticut Community
  College *C, A*
Sacred Heart University *M*
St. Joseph College *M, T*
Southern Connecticut State
  University *B, T*
Trinity College *B, T*
University of Connecticut *M, T*
University of New Haven *M*
Western Connecticut State University *M*

Delaware

Delaware State University *B*
University of Delaware *B, T*
Wilmington College *D*

District of Columbia

American University *D*
Catholic University of America *B, M*
Gallaudet University *B*
Howard University *M, D*
Trinity College *M*

Florida

Broward Community College *A*
Chipola Junior College *A*
Daytona Beach Community College *A*
Edward Waters College *B*
Flagler College *B*
Florida Southern College *B, T*
Hillsborough Community College *A*
Indian River Community College *A*
Jacksonville University *B*
Lake City Community College *A*
Manatee Community College *A*
Nova Southeastern University *B, M, D*
Okaloosa-Walton Community College *A*
Pensacola Junior College *A*
Polk Community College *A*
St. Leo University *M*
Stetson University *B, M*
University of Central Florida *B*
University of Miami *M, D*
University of South Florida *B, M, D*
University of Tampa *B*

Georgia

Abraham Baldwin Agricultural
  College *A*
Albany State University *B*
Andrew College *A*
Atlanta Metropolitan College *A*
Bainbridge College *A*
Brenau University *B*
Brewton-Parker College *B*
Clark Atlanta University *B*
Clayton College and State University *A*
Dalton State College *A*
Darton College *A*
Emory University *M, D*
Floyd College *A*
Gainesville College *A*
Georgia College and State University *M*
Georgia Military College *A*
Georgia Perimeter College *A*
Georgia Southwestern State
  University *M*
Gordon College *A*
Kennesaw State University *B*
LaGrange College *B, M*
Macon State College *A*
Morehouse College *B*
Oxford College of Emory University *B*
Reinhardt College *A*
South Georgia College *A*
Toccoa Falls College *B*
University of Georgia *M*
Valdosta State University *T*

Waycross College *A*
Young Harris College *A*

Hawaii

University of Hawaii
    Hilo *T*

Idaho

Albertson College of Idaho *M*
Boise State University *B, M*
Idaho State University *B, M, T*
Lewis-Clark State College *B, T*
North Idaho College *A*
University of Idaho *D*

Illinois

Augustana College *B*
Aurora University *M*
Blackburn College *B, T*
Chicago State University *B*
City Colleges of Chicago
    Kennedy-King College *A*
Columbia College Chicago *M*
Concordia University *B, T*
Danville Area Community College *A*
Dominican University *M*
Elmhurst College *B*
Governors State University *M*
Greenville College *B*
Illinois Valley Community College *A*
John Wood Community College *A*
Kankakee Community College *A*
Kishwaukee College *A*
Knox College *B*
Lake Forest College *B*
Lake Land College *A*
Lewis University *B*
Lewis and Clark Community College *A*
Lincoln College *A*
Lincoln Land Community College *A*
McKendree College *B, T*
Millikin University *B, T*
Monmouth College *B, T*
Moody Bible Institute *B*
Moraine Valley Community College *C*
National-Louis University *M*
North Central College *B, T*
North Park University *M*
Northern Illinois University *B*
Northwestern University *B, M, D*
Olivet Nazarene University *M*
Parkland College *A*
Quincy University *M*
Richland Community College *A*
Rockford College *B, M*
St. Xavier University *C, B, M*
Sauk Valley Community College *A*
South Suburban College of Cook
    County *A*
Southeastern Illinois College *A*
Southwestern Illinois College *A*
Trinity Christian College *B, T*
Trinity International University *D*
Triton College *A*
University of Chicago *M, D*
University of Illinois
    Urbana-Champaign *B, M, D*
University of St. Francis *B*
William Rainey Harper College *A*

Indiana

Anderson University *B*
Butler University *B*
Calumet College of St. Joseph *B, T*
Earlham College *B*
Goshen College *B*
Indiana University
    Bloomington *B, M, D, T*
    Southeast *B, T*
Manchester College *B, T*
Purdue University *B, M, D, T*
Purdue University
    Calumet *B, T*
St. Mary-of-the-Woods College *B*
University of Evansville *B*
University of Indianapolis *B*
University of Southern Indiana *A*

Valparaiso University *M*
Vincennes University *A*

Iowa

Buena Vista University *B, T*
Clarke College *B, M, T*
Coe College *B*
Cornell College *B, T*
Dordt College *B*
Drake University *B, D*
Ellsworth Community College *A*
Graceland University *M*
Grand View College *B*
Hawkeye Community College *A*
Iowa State University *M, D*
Iowa Wesleyan College *B*
Iowa Western Community College *A*
Loras College *B, M*
Luther College *B*
Marshalltown Community College *A*
Morningside College *B, M*
North Iowa Area Community College *A*
Northeast Iowa Community College *A*
Northwest Iowa Community College *C*
Northwestern College *B, T*
St. Ambrose University *B, T*
Simpson College *B*
Southwestern Community College *A*
University of Dubuque *M*
University of Northern Iowa *D*
Upper Iowa University *B*
Waldorf College *A*
William Penn University *B*

Kansas

Barton County Community College *A*
Bethany College *B, T*
Central Christian College *A, B*
Cloud County Community College *A*
Dodge City Community College *A*
Fort Scott Community College *A*
Friends University *M*
Garden City Community College *A*
Haskell Indian Nations University *B*
Highland Community College *A*
Hutchinson Community College *A*
Independence Community College *C, A*
Labette Community College *A*
McPherson College *B, T*
MidAmerica Nazarene University *M*
Pittsburg State University *B*
Pratt Community College *A*
St. Mary College *M*
Seward County Community College *A*
Southwestern College *B, M*
Tabor College *B, M, T*
Washburn University of Topeka *B*

Kentucky

Bellarmine University *B, M*
Berea College *B*
Campbellsville University *A, B*
Madisonville Community College *A*
Morehead State University *M*
Spalding University *B, M, T*
Thomas More College *B*

Louisiana

Centenary College of Louisiana *M*
Louisiana College *B*
Louisiana State University
    Shreveport *M*
Louisiana State University and
    Agricultural and Mechanical
    College *C, B, M*
McNeese State University *M*
Our Lady of Holy Cross College *M*
University of New Orleans *M*
Xavier University of Louisiana *B*

Maine

St. Joseph's College *B*
University of Maine *B, M*
University of Maine
    Machias *A*
    Presque Isle *B*
University of New England *B, M, T*

University of Southern Maine *B*

Maryland

Anne Arundel Community College *A*
Carroll Community College *A*
Chesapeake College *A*
College of Notre Dame of Maryland *M*
Columbia Union College *B*
Community College of Baltimore County
    Catonsville *A*
    Dundalk *A*
    Essex *A*
Coppin State College *B, M*
Frederick Community College *A*
Frostburg State University *C, M*
Hagerstown Community College *A*
Harford Community College *A*
Johns Hopkins University *M, D*
Loyola College in Maryland *M*
McDaniel College *M, T*
Montgomery College
    Rockville Campus *A*
Salisbury University *M*
University of Maryland
    Baltimore County *M, T*
Washington College *T*

Massachusetts

Anna Maria College *B, T*
Assumption College *B*
Becker College *A, B, T*
Berkshire Community College *C, A*
Boston University *B, M, D, T*
Bunker Hill Community College *C, A*
Cape Cod Community College *A*
Clark University *M*
Elms College *B, M*
Emmanuel College *B, M, T*
Fisher College *A*
Fitchburg State College *M, T*
Hampshire College *B*
Lesley University *B, M, D*
Massachusetts College of Liberal
    Arts *B, M, T*
Mount Ida College *A, B, T*
Northeastern University *B, M, T*
Salem State College *B, M*
Simmons College *B, M*
Smith College *B, M*
Springfield College *M*
Suffolk University *B, M, T*
Tufts University *M*
University of Massachusetts
    Amherst *B, M, D*
    Boston *D*
Western New England College *T*
Westfield State College *B, M, T*

Michigan

Adrian College *B*
Alpena Community College *A*
Andrews University *M, D*
Aquinas College *B, M*
Baker College
    of Auburn Hills *B*
Calvin College *B, M, T*
Cornerstone University *B*
Finlandia University *A, B*
Gogebic Community College *A*
Grand Valley State University *M, T*
Hillsdale College *B*
Kirtland Community College *A*
Lansing Community College *A*
Madonna University *B*
Michigan State University *M, D*
Northern Michigan University *M*
Northwestern Michigan College *A*
Oakland University *M, D*
Saginaw Valley State University *M*
St. Clair County Community College *A*
Spring Arbor University *M, T*
University of Michigan *M, D*
University of Michigan
    Dearborn *B, M, T*
    Flint *M*
West Shore Community College *A*

Minnesota

Augsburg College *M*
Bemidji State University *B, M*
Bethel College *B, M*
Capella University *M, D*
College of St. Benedict *B*
College of St. Catherine *B*
College of St. Scholastica *B*
Concordia College: Moorhead *B, T*
Concordia University: St. Paul *B, M*
Hamline University *B, M, D*
Itasca Community College *A*
Minneapolis Community and Technical
    College *A*
Minnesota State University
    Mankato *B, M*
    Moorhead *B, T*
North Hennepin Community College *A*
Northland Community & Technical
    College *A*
Ridgewater College: A Community and
    Technical College *A*
St. John's University *B*
St. Mary's University of
    Minnesota *M, D*
Southwest State University *M*
University of Minnesota
    Duluth *M*
    Morris *B, T*
    Twin Cities *M, D*
Vermilion Community College *A*
Winona State University *B, M, T*

Mississippi

Coahoma Community College *A*
Delta State University *D*
Mary Holmes College *A*
Mississippi Gulf Coast Community
    College
    Perkinston *A*
Mississippi State University *D*
Mississippi University for Women *B*
Northwest Mississippi Community
    College *A*
University of Mississippi *D*
University of Southern Mississippi *D*
Wesley College *C*

Missouri

Avila University *M, T*
Central Methodist College *M, T*
Columbia College *B, M*
Culver-Stockton College *B*
Drury University *B, M*
East Central College *A*
Evangel University *A, B, M*
Fontbonne College *B*
Hannibal-LaGrange College *B*
Lindenwood University *B, M*
Missouri Southern State College *B*
National American University
    Kansas City *A*
Rockhurst University *M*
St. Louis Christian College *B*
St. Louis Community College
    St. Louis Community College at
        Meramec *A*
Southeast Missouri State University *B*
Southwest Baptist University *M*
Stephens College *B*
Three Rivers Community College *A*
University of Missouri
    Columbia *B*
    Kansas City *B, M, D*
    Rolla *B*
    St. Louis *B, M, D*
Washington University in St.
    Louis *B, M, D, T*
Webster University *B, M, T*
William Woods University *B, T*

Montana

Miles Community College *A*
Montana State University
    Billings *B, M, T*
    Bozeman *M, D*

Rocky Mountain College *B, T*
University of Montana-Missoula *B, M, D*
University of Montana: Western *A, B, T*

Nebraska

Concordia University *B, M, T*
Dana College *B*
Doane College *M*
Little Priest Tribal College *A*
Midland Lutheran College *B, T*
Northeast Community College *A*
Peru State College *B, M, T*
Southeast Community College
    Beatrice Campus *A*
University of Nebraska
    Kearney *B, M, T*
    Lincoln *B*
Western Nebraska Community
  College *A*
York College *A, B, T*

New Hampshire

Franklin Pierce College *B*
Keene State College *B, T*
New Hampshire Technical Institute *A*
Rivier College *C, A, B, M, T*

New Jersey

Atlantic Cape Community College *A*
Brookdale Community College *A*
Burlington County College *A*
Caldwell College *B*
College of St. Elizabeth *M*
Essex County College *A*
Georgian Court College *M*
Gloucester County College *A*
Middlesex County College *A*
Monmouth University *B, M*
Montclair State University *M, D*
Richard Stockton College of New
  Jersey *T*
Rider University *B*
Rowan University *B, M*
Rutgers, The State University of New
  Jersey
    New Brunswick Regional
      Campus *M, D*
St. Peter's College *M*
Salem Community College *A*
Seton Hall University *M*
Warren County Community College *A*
William Paterson University of New
  Jersey *M*

New Mexico

College of Santa Fe *M*
Eastern New Mexico University *M*
New Mexico Junior College *A*
New Mexico State University *M*
New Mexico State University
  Alamogordo *A*
San Juan College *A*
Santa Fe Community College *A*
Western New Mexico University *B, M*

New York

Adelphi University *M*
Alfred University *B, M*
Barnard College *T*
Canisius College *M*
City University of New York
  Brooklyn College *B, M*
  Hunter College *B, M, T*
  Medgar Evers College *A*
  Queens College *M*
Colgate University *B, M*
College of Mount St. Vincent *B*
Columbia University
  Columbia College *B*
Concordia College *B*
Cornell University *B, M, D*
D'Youville College *B, T*
Dowling College *B*
Eugene Lang College/New School
  University *T*
Fordham University *T*

Fulton-Montgomery Community
  College *A*
Hofstra University *B*
Houghton College *B*
Iona College *M*
Manhattan College *B*
Manhattanville College *B, M*
Medaille College *B, T*
Mercy College *M*
Metropolitan College of New York *A, B*
Molloy College *B, M, T*
Nazareth College of Rochester *M, T*
New York Institute of Technology *A*
Niagara University *B, M, T*
Orange County Community College *A*
St. John Fisher College *B, M*
St. Joseph's College *B*
St. Joseph's College: Suffolk
  Campus *B, T*
St. Lawrence University *M*
State University of New York
  Buffalo *M*
  College at Brockport *M*
  College at Buffalo *B*
  College at Cortland *B*
  College at Fredonia *B, M, T*
  Empire State College *A, B*
  Oswego *M*
Touro College *M*
University of Rochester *M, D*
Utica College *M*
Villa Maria College of Buffalo *A*
Wagner College *B, M*
Yeshiva University *D*

North Carolina

Appalachian State University *B, D*
Barber-Scotia College *B*
Beaufort County Community College *A*
Belmont Abbey College *B*
Bladen Community College *A*
Campbell University *A, B, M, T*
Carteret Community College *A*
Central Carolina Community College *A*
Chowan College *B*
College of the Albemarle *A*
East Carolina University *M*
Elon University *B*
Gardner-Webb University *B, M*
Greensboro College *B, T*
Guilford Technical Community
  College *A*
Isothermal Community College *A*
James Sprunt Community College *A*
Lenoir Community College *A*
Livingstone College *B*
Louisburg College *A*
Mars Hill College *B, T*
Martin Community College *A*
Mayland Community College *C, A*
Methodist College *A, B*
Montgomery Community College *A*
Mount Olive College *A*
Nash Community College *A*
North Carolina Agricultural and
  Technical State University *B, T*
North Carolina State University *B, M, D*
Pamlico Community College *A*
Sampson Community College *A*
South Piedmont Community
  College *C, A*
Southwestern Community College *A*
University of North Carolina
  Asheville *T*
  Chapel Hill *M, D*
  Greensboro *M, D*
Vance-Granville Community College *A*
Wake Forest University *B*
Warren Wilson College *B, T*

North Dakota

Jamestown College *B*
Minot State University *A*
Minot State University: Bottineau
  Campus *A*
North Dakota State University *B*

University of Mary *B, M*
University of North Dakota *M*

Ohio

Antioch College *B*
Baldwin-Wallace College *B, M*
Bluffton College *B, M*
Bowling Green State University *B, M*
Cedarville University *B*
Central State University *M*
Circleville Bible College *B*
College of Mount St. Joseph *B*
Defiance College *B, M, T*
Denison University *B*
Edison State Community College *A*
Heidelberg College *M*
Hiram College *B*
Kent State University *B, M, D*
Kent State University
  Salem Regional Campus *M*
  Stark Campus *B*
  Trumbull Campus *A*
Lake Erie College *M*
Lourdes College *M*
Marietta College *B, M*
Mount Vernon Nazarene University *B*
Muskingum College *M*
Northwest State Community College *A*
Ohio Northern University *B*
Ohio State University
  Columbus Campus *M, D*
  Lima Campus *B, M, T*
Ohio University *M, D*
Ohio University
  Eastern Campus *M*
Ohio Wesleyan University *B*
Otterbein College *B*
Shawnee State University *B*
Union Institute & University *B, D*
University of Cincinnati
  Raymond Walters College *A*
University of Dayton *B, M*
University of Findlay *B, M*
University of Rio Grande *B, M, T*
University of Toledo *B*
Urbana University *B*
Ursuline College *B, T*
Walsh University *M*
Washington State Community College *A*
Wilmington College *B*
Wittenberg University *B, M*
Xavier University *B*
Youngstown State University *B, M*

Oklahoma

Bacone College *A*
Cameron University *B, M, T*
Langston University *B*
Northeastern State University *B, M*
Northwestern Oklahoma State
  University *B, M*
Oklahoma City Community College *A*
Oklahoma City University *B, M*
Oklahoma State University *B, M, D, T*
Oklahoma State University
  Oklahoma City *A*
  Okmulgee *A*
Oral Roberts University *M*
Redlands Community College *A*
St. Gregory's University *A, B*
Seminole State College *A*
Southeastern Oklahoma State
  University *B*
Southern Nazarene University *B*
Southwestern Oklahoma State
  University *M, T*
Tulsa Community College *A*
University of Central Oklahoma *B, M*
University of Tulsa *M*
Western Oklahoma State College *A*

Oregon

Central Oregon Community College *A*
Chemeketa Community College *C*
Concordia University *B, M, T*
Eastern Oregon University *B*

Lewis & Clark College *M*
Linfield College *T*
Linn-Benton Community College *C, A*
Oregon Institute of Technology *B*
Oregon State University *M, D*
Pacific University *B, M, T*
Portland State University *M*
Southern Oregon University *B, M, T*
Umpqua Community College *A*
University of Oregon *B*
University of Portland *M*
Warner Pacific College *T*
Western Baptist College *B*
Western Oregon University *B, M*

Pennsylvania

Arcadia University *B, M*
Baptist Bible College of Pennsylvania *M*
Bryn Athyn College of the New
  Church *A*
Bucknell University *B, M*
Bucks County Community College *A*
Cabrini College *B, M*
California University of
  Pennsylvania *A, B*
Community College of Philadelphia *A*
Geneva College *B, T*
Gratz College *C, M*
Grove City College *B*
Holy Family University *M*
Juniata College *B*
Keystone College *A*
Kutztown University of
  Pennsylvania *B, M*
La Salle University *B, M, T*
Lackawanna College *A*
Lehigh Carbon Community College *A*
Lehigh University *M, D*
Lincoln University *B, M*
Luzerne County Community College *A*
Marywood University *B*
Mercyhurst College *B*
Moravian College *M*
Neumann College *M, T*
Philadelphia Biblical University *M*
Point Park College *C, B*
Reading Area Community College *A*
St. Joseph's University *M*
St. Vincent College *T*
Swarthmore College *B*
University of Pennsylvania *C, M, D, T*
University of Pittsburgh *M, D, T*
University of Pittsburgh
  Greensburg *B*
Villanova University *M*
Washington and Jefferson College *B*
York College of Pennsylvania *B*

Puerto Rico

Inter American University of Puerto Rico
  Barranquitas Campus *B*
  Fajardo Campus *B*
  Guayama Campus *A, B*
  San German Campus *B*
Pontifical Catholic University of Puerto
  Rico *A, B, M*
Universidad Metropolitana *B, M*
Universidad del Este *B*
University of Puerto Rico
  Bayamon University College *A*
  Carolina Regional College *A*
  Ponce *A*
  Utuado *A, B*
University of the Sacred Heart *B*

Rhode Island

Brown University *B, M, T*
Community College of Rhode Island *A*
Providence College *B*
Rhode Island College *M*
University of Rhode Island *M, D*

South Carolina

Charleston Southern University *B, M*
The Citadel *T*
Coker College *B*
Columbia College *B, T*

Converse College *B, T*
Furman University *B*
Limestone College *B*
Northeastern Technical College *A*
Technical College of the Lowcountry *C*
University of South Carolina *D*
University of South Carolina
Aiken *B*

South Dakota

Dakota State University *B, T*
Dakota Wesleyan University *B, T*
Northern State University *B*
Sinte Gleska University *A, B, M*

Tennessee

American Baptist College of ABT
Seminary *B*
Austin Peay State University *M*
Belmont University *M*
Bethel College *M*
Bryan College *B*
Carson-Newman College *B, T*
Dyersburg State Community College *A*
Jackson State Community College *A*
Lambuth University *B*
Lee University *B, M*
Maryville College *B, T*
Milligan College *B, M*
Roane State Community College *A*
Southwest Tennessee Community
College *A*
Tennessee State University *B*
Tennessee Technological University *B*
Tennessee Wesleyan College *B, T*
Tusculum College *M*
Union University *B, M, T*
University of Tennessee
Knoxville *B, M, D*
Walters State Community College *A*

Texas

Amarillo College *A*
Angelina College *A*
Arlington Baptist College *B*
Baylor University *B, M*
Brazosport College *A*
Cedar Valley College *A*
Central Texas College *A*
Cisco Junior College *A*
Clarendon College *A*
Coastal Bend College *A*
Concordia University at Austin *B, M, T*
Dallas Baptist University *B, M, T*
Frank Phillips College *A*
Grayson County College *A*
Hill College *A*
Houston Baptist University *B, M*
Howard College *A*
Howard Payne University *B*
Huston-Tillotson College *B*
Jarvis Christian College *B*
Kilgore College *A*
Lamar State College at Orange *A*
Laredo Community College *A*
Lon Morris College *A*
Lubbock Christian University *B*
Midwestern State University *B*
Northeast Texas Community College *A*
Odessa College *A*
Our Lady of the Lake University of San
Antonio *M*
Panola College *A*
Paris Junior College *A*
St. Edward's University *B*
St. Philip's College *A*
Schreiner University *T*
South Plains College *A*
Southwest Texas Junior College *A*
Southwest Texas State University *M, T*
Southwestern Assemblies of God
University *A, M*
Southwestern University *B, T*
Tarleton State University *B, M, T*
Temple College *C, A*

Texas A&M University
Commerce *M, D*
Kingsville *B, M*
Texas Wesleyan University *B, T*
Trinity Valley Community College *A*
Tyler Junior College *A*
University of Dallas *B, T*
University of Houston
Clear Lake *B, M, T*
Victoria *B*
University of St. Thomas *M*
University of Texas
Arlington *M*
El Paso *M*
University of the Incarnate Word *B, M*
West Texas A&M University *M*
Western Texas College *A*

Utah

Brigham Young University *B, M*
Salt Lake Community College *A*
Snow College *A*
Southern Utah University *B, M*
Westminster College *B, M*

Vermont

Bennington College *B*
Castleton State College *M, T*
Champlain College *A, B*
College of St. Joseph in Vermont *M*
Community College of Vermont *C, A*
Goddard College *B*
Green Mountain College *B*
Johnson State College *B, M*
Lyndon State College *M*
Norwich University *M*
University of Vermont *B, M, D, T*

Virginia

Bluefield College *B*
Eastern Shore Community College *A*
George Mason University *D*
Hampton University *B*
Hollins University *M, T*
James Madison University *M*
Liberty University *B*
Longwood University *B, T*
Mary Baldwin College *M, T*
Mountain Empire Community College *A*
Norfolk State University *M*
Paul D. Camp Community College *A*
Piedmont Virginia Community
College *A*
Radford University *M*
Rappahannock Community College *A*
Shenandoah University *C, M*
Southside Virginia Community
College *A*
Southwest Virginia Community
College *A*
University of Richmond *T*
University of Virginia *M, D*
Virginia Commonwealth
University *M, D, T*
Virginia Highlands Community
College *A*
Virginia Polytechnic Institute and State
University *M, D*
Virginia Wesleyan College *T*
Virginia Western Community College *A*

Washington

Centralia College *A*
Eastern Washington University *B, T*
Edmonds Community College *C, A*
Everett Community College *A*
Gonzaga University *M*
Grays Harbor College *A*
Heritage College *B, M*
Lower Columbia College *A*
North Seattle Community College *C, A*
Olympic College *A*
Pacific Lutheran University *B, M*
St. Martin's College *M*
Seattle Central Community College *A*
Seattle University *B*
University of Washington *M, D, T*

Walla Walla College *B*
Washington State University *B, M, D, T*
Whitworth College *B, M, T*

West Virginia

Alderson-Broaddus College *B*
Bethany College *B*
Bluefield State College *A*
Concord College *B, T*
Davis and Elkins College *B*
Fairmont State College *B*
Marshall University *M*
Mountain State University *A*
Ohio Valley College *B*
Potomac State College of West Virginia
University *A*
Salem International University *M*
West Virginia State College *B*
West Virginia University *D*

Wisconsin

Alverno College *B, M*
Beloit College *B*
Cardinal Stritch University *B, M*
Carroll College *B, M*
Carthage College *B, M, T*
Concordia University Wisconsin *B*
Edgewood College *B, M, D*
Lakeland College *M*
Maranatha Baptist Bible College *B*
Marian College of Fond du Lac *B, M*
Marquette University *M, D*
Mount Mary College *B*
Ripon College *B*
St. Norbert College *T*
Silver Lake College *B, M*
University of Wisconsin
Green Bay *M*
Madison *M, D*
Milwaukee *B*
Platteville *M*
Stevens Point *M*
Stout *M*
Superior *M*
Whitewater *B, M, T*

Wyoming

Casper College *A*
Laramie County Community College *A*
Sheridan College *A*
University of Wyoming *M, D*
Western Wyoming Community
College *A*

Education of autistic

Kansas

University of Kansas *M, D*

Massachusetts

Emerson College *B, M*

North Carolina

University of North Carolina
Greensboro *M*

Ohio

Youngstown State University *B, M*

Puerto Rico

Bayamon Central University *M*

Education of blind/visually handicapped

Arizona

Prescott College *T*

Arkansas

University of Arkansas *B*
University of Arkansas
Little Rock *M*

California

San Francisco State University *T*

Florida

Florida State University *B, M, T*

Maryland

Johns Hopkins University *M*

Massachusetts

Boston College *M*

Michigan

Eastern Michigan University *B, T*
Western Michigan University *B, M*

Missouri

Lindenwood University *M*

New York

City University of New York
Hunter College *M, T*
Dominican College of Blauvelt *B, T*

North Carolina

Appalachian State University *M*

Ohio

Kent State University
Stark Campus *B*
Ohio State University
Columbus Campus *M, D*
University of Toledo *T*

Oklahoma

Northeastern State University *M*

Oregon

Portland State University *T*

Pennsylvania

Kutztown University of Pennsylvania *B*
University of Pittsburgh *T*

Puerto Rico

Inter American University of Puerto Rico
Barranquitas Campus *B*

West Virginia

West Virginia University *T*

Wisconsin

Silver Lake College *T*

Education of brain injured

California

California State University
Sacramento *B*

Louisiana

Dillard University *B*

Education of deaf/hearing impaired

Arizona

Prescott College *T*

Arkansas

University of Arkansas
Little Rock *M*

California

California State University
Fresno *B*
Los Angeles *M*
Northridge *M*
Stanislaus *B*
Ohlone College *A*
San Francisco State University *T*
San Jose State University *T*
University of Southern California *M, T*

Connecticut

Northwestern Connecticut Community
College *A*

District of Columbia

Gallaudet University *B, M, D*

Florida

Flagler College *B*

Georgia
Georgia State University *M*

Idaho
Idaho State University *M*

Illinois
MacMurray College *B, T*

Kansas
Central Christian College *A*
University of Kansas *M, D*
Wichita State University *T*

Louisiana
Southern University and Agricultural and
Mechanical College *B*

Maryland
McDaniel College *M*

Massachusetts
Boston College *M*
Boston University *B, M, T*
Elms College *B, M, T*
Emerson College *B, M*
Smith College *M*

Michigan
Calvin College *B, T*
Eastern Michigan University *B, T*
Grand Valley State University *M, T*

Mississippi
University of Southern Mississippi *B*

Missouri
Fontbonne College *B*
Washington University in St. Louis *M*

Nebraska
University of Nebraska
Lincoln *B, M, T*
Omaha *M*

New Jersey
The College of New Jersey *B, M, T*
Kean University *B*
William Paterson University of New
Jersey *M*

New York
Adelphi University *M*
Canisius College *M, T*
City University of New York
Brooklyn College *B, M*
Hunter College *M, T*
Elmira College *B, T*
Hofstra University *T*
Ithaca College *B, M, T*
Marymount Manhattan College *B, T*
Nazareth College of Rochester *T*
New York University *M, T*
Pace University *T*
Pace University:
Pleasantville/Briarcliff *B, T*
Rochester Institute of Technology *M*
State University of New York
College at Cortland *B, T*
New Paltz *B, M, T*

North Carolina
Barton College *B*
Lenoir-Rhyne College *B, M, T*
University of North Carolina
Greensboro *B*

North Dakota
Minot State University *B*

Ohio
Bowling Green State University *B*
Cincinnati State Technical and
Community College *A*
Kent State University
Stark Campus *B*
Ohio State University
Columbus Campus *M, D*
University of Cincinnati *M, D*
University of Toledo *T*

Oklahoma
University of Science and Arts of
Oklahoma *B, T*
University of Tulsa *B, T*

Oregon
Lewis & Clark College *M*
Western Oregon University *T*

Pennsylvania
Bloomsburg University of
Pennsylvania *M*
Indiana University of Pennsylvania *B*
Marywood University *B, M*
Rosemont College *T*
University of Pittsburgh *T*

South Carolina
Converse College *B, T*

South Dakota
Augustana College *B, M, T*

Tennessee
Lambuth University *B, T*
University of Tennessee
Knoxville *B, T*

Texas
Abilene Christian University *T*
Lamar University *M, D*
Texas Christian University *B, T*
Texas Woman's University *M, T*
University of the Incarnate Word *M*

Virginia
Hampton University *M*
Longwood University *M*

Washington
Spokane Falls Community College *A*

Wisconsin
University of Wisconsin
Milwaukee *T*

**Education of
developmentally delayed**

Iowa
Upper Iowa University *T*

Kansas
Tabor College *B*

New Jersey
William Paterson University of New
Jersey *T*

New York
College of New Rochelle *M, T*
St. Joseph's College: Suffolk Campus *M*
State University of New York
College at Brockport *M*

Ohio
University of Dayton *B, M, T*

Pennsylvania
La Salle University *B, M, T*

Wisconsin
University of Wisconsin
Superior *M*

**Education of emotionally
handicapped**

Arizona
Prescott College *T*

Arkansas
Arkansas State University *M, T*

California
California State University
Los Angeles *M*
Northridge *M*
Fresno Pacific University *M, T*

San Diego State University *M*
Sonoma State University *M*

District of Columbia
George Washington University *M, D*
Trinity College *M*

Florida
Florida International University *B, T*
Florida State University *B, M, T*
Nova Southeastern University *M*
University of South Florida *B, M*
University of West Florida *B, M, T*

Georgia
Columbus State University *B, M*
Georgia College and State
University *M, T*
North Georgia College & State
University *M*
State University of West Georgia *M*

Idaho
Lewis-Clark State College *T*

Illinois
Benedictine University *T*
Bradley University *B, T*
Chicago State University *M*
Greenville College *T*
MacMurray College *B, T*
National-Louis University *M*
Sauk Valley Community College *A*
Trinity Christian College *B, T*
University of St. Francis *B*

Indiana
Ball State University *T*
University of Evansville *B*
University of St. Francis *T*
Valparaiso University *M, T*

Iowa
Ellsworth Community College *A*
Loras College *B*

Kansas
Tabor College *B, T*
University of Kansas *M, D*
Wichita State University *T*

Louisiana
University of New Orleans *M*

Maine
University of Maine
Farmington *B, T*

Massachusetts
American International College *B, M*
Northeastern University *M*

Michigan
Central Michigan University *B, M*
Eastern Michigan University *B, M*
Grand Valley State University *M, T*
Hope College *B, T*
Saginaw Valley State University *T*
Western Michigan University *B*

Minnesota
Augsburg College *B, M*
Bethel College *M*
Minnesota State University
Mankato *M*
Moorhead *B, T*
University of St. Thomas *M*
Winona State University *B, T*

Mississippi
Mississippi State University *T*

Missouri
Avila University *B, T*
Harris Stowe State College *T*
Lindenwood University *M*
University of Missouri
Kansas City *M*

Nebraska
University of Nebraska
Omaha *B*

New Hampshire
Keene State College *M, T*
Rivier College *M*

New York
City University of New York
Brooklyn College *B, M*
City College *B, M, T*
Fordham University *M*
Manhattan College *M*
Nazareth College of Rochester *T*
New York University *M*
Pace University *B*
State University of New York
College at Buffalo *B, M*
New Paltz *M*

North Carolina
Appalachian State University *M*
East Carolina University *B*
Greensboro College *B, T*
North Carolina Central University *M*
University of North Carolina
Charlotte *M*
Greensboro *M*
Wilmington *B*

North Dakota
University of Mary *M*

Ohio
College of Mount St. Joseph *B, T*
Kent State University
Stark Campus *B*
University of Akron *B, T*
University of Cincinnati *M, D*
University of Findlay *T*
University of Toledo *T*
Walsh University *B*
Wright State University *M*
Youngstown State University *B, M*

Oklahoma
University of Central Oklahoma *B, M*

Pennsylvania
La Salle University *B, T*

Rhode Island
Rhode Island College *B, M*

South Carolina
Converse College *T*
Furman University *M, T*
South Carolina State University *B, T*
Southern Wesleyan University *B, T*

South Dakota
Augustana College *B, T*

Tennessee
Johnson Bible College *T*
Lambuth University *B, T*

Texas
Texas Woman's University *M*
West Texas A&M University *T*

Virginia
Eastern Mennonite University *T*
Longwood University *M*
Radford University *T*
University of Virginia's College at
Wise *T*

West Virginia
Fairmont State College *B*

Wisconsin
Silver Lake College *B, T*
University of Wisconsin
Oshkosh *M*

Education of gifted/talented

Arkansas
Arkansas State University *M, T*
Arkansas Tech University *M*
Southern Arkansas University *M*
University of Arkansas
    Little Rock *M*
University of Central Arkansas *M*

California
California State University
    Los Angeles *M*
    Northridge *M*
    Sacramento *M*
San Diego State University *M*

Delaware
Delaware State University *B*

Florida
Jacksonville University *B*
University of South Florida *M*

Georgia
Georgia State University *M*
University of Georgia *D*

Idaho
Lewis-Clark State College *T*

Illinois
Chicago State University *M*
Northeastern Illinois University *M*
Sauk Valley Community College *A*

Indiana
Ball State University *T*

Iowa
Buena Vista University *B*
University of Northern Iowa *M*

Kansas
Wichita State University *T*

Louisiana
University of Louisiana at Lafayette *M*

Maryland
Johns Hopkins University *M*

Michigan
Grand Valley State University *M*

Minnesota
Bethel College *M*
Minnesota State University
    Mankato *M*
University of St. Thomas *M*

Mississippi
Mississippi State University *T*
Mississippi University for Women *M*

Missouri
Drury University *B, M*
Harris Stowe State College *T*
Maryville University of Saint Louis *M, T*
University of Missouri
    Columbia *M, D*

Montana
University of Great Falls *B*

Nebraska
University of Nebraska
    Kearney *M, T*

New York
College of New Rochelle *M*
Hofstra University *M*
Manhattanville College *M, T*
St. Bonaventure University *M*

North Carolina
Catawba College *B, T*
University of North Carolina
    Charlotte *M*
    Greensboro *M*

Ohio
Ashland University *M, T*
Bowling Green State University *M*
Kent State University
    Stark Campus *B*
Ohio University *M*
Wright State University *M*
Youngstown State University *M*

Oklahoma
Northeastern State University *M*
Oklahoma City University *M*

Oregon
University of Oregon *M*

Pennsylvania
Bloomsburg University of
    Pennsylvania *M*
Chatham College *T*

South Carolina
Converse College *T*

Texas
Hardin-Simmons University *M*
Texas A&M International
    University *M, T*
University of Houston *M, T*
University of Texas
    Arlington *T*
    Pan American *M, T*

Vermont
Johnson State College *M*

Virginia
Norfolk State University *M*

Washington
Eastern Washington University *T*
Whitworth College *M*

West Virginia
Fairmont State College *B*
West Virginia State College *B*
West Virginia University *T*

Wisconsin
Carthage College *M*

Education of learning disabled

Arizona
Prescott College *T*
University of Phoenix *B*

Arkansas
University of Central Arkansas *M*

California
California State Polytechnic University:
    Pomona *T*
California State University
    Dominguez Hills *M, T*
    Long Beach *T*
    Los Angeles *M*
    Northridge *M*
Holy Names College *M*
San Jose State University *M*
Sonoma State University *M, T*
University of California
    Riverside *T*
University of San Francisco *T*

District of Columbia
American University *M*
Trinity College *M*

Florida
Bethune-Cookman College *B, T*
Flagler College *B*
Florida International University *B, T*
Florida Southern College *B*
Florida State University *B, M, T*
Jacksonville University *B, M, T*
Nova Southeastern University *M*
Palm Beach Atlantic University *B, T*

Stetson University *M*
University of Miami *M, D*
University of South Florida *B, M*
University of West Florida *B, M, T*

Georgia
Armstrong Atlantic State
    University *B, M, T*
Augusta State University *M*
Columbus State University *B, M*
Georgia College and State
    University *M, T*
Georgia State University *M*
Mercer University *B*
North Georgia College & State
    University *M*
State University of West Georgia *M*

Illinois
Benedictine University *T*
Bradley University *B, M*
Chicago State University *M*
Elmhurst College *B*
Greenville College *T*
MacMurray College *B, T*
National-Louis University *M*
Northwestern University *B, M, D*
Rockford College *M*
St. Xavier University *M*
Sauk Valley Community College *A*
Trinity Christian College *B, T*
University of St. Francis *B*

Indiana
Ball State University *T*
University of Evansville *B*
University of Indianapolis *T*
University of St. Francis *T*

Iowa
Iowa State University *T*
Morningside College *B, M*
Northwestern College *T*
University of Iowa *M*

Kansas
Bethany College *T*
Pittsburg State University *B*
Tabor College *B, T*
University of Kansas *M, D*
Washburn University of Topeka *M*
Wichita State University *T*

Kentucky
Brescia University *B, T*

Louisiana
University of New Orleans *M*

Maine
University of Maine
    Farmington *B, T*

Massachusetts
American International College *M, D*
Assumption College *M*

Michigan
Aquinas College *B*
Calvin College *M, T*
Central Michigan University *M*
Grand Valley State University *M, T*
Hope College *B, T*
Madonna University *B, M, T*
Michigan State University *B*
Northern Michigan University *M*
Saginaw Valley State University *B, M, T*

Minnesota
Minnesota State University
    Mankato *M*
    Moorhead *B, M, T*
University of Minnesota
    Duluth *T*
University of St. Thomas *M*
Winona State University *B, M, T*

Missouri
Avila University *B, T*
Culver-Stockton College *T*

Harris Stowe State College *T*
Northwest Missouri State
    University *B, M, T*
University of Missouri
    Columbia *M, D*
    Kansas City *M*
William Woods University *T*

Nebraska
University of Nebraska
    Kearney *B, M, T*

New Hampshire
Keene State College *M, T*
New England College *B, T*
Rivier College *M*

New Jersey
Fairleigh Dickinson University
    Metropolitan Campus *M*
Rowan University *M*
William Paterson University of New
    Jersey *M*

New York
City University of New York
    Brooklyn College *B, M, T*
    Hunter College *M, T*
Fordham University *M*
Manhattanville College *M, T*
Nazareth College of Rochester *T*
Pace University *B, T*
Pace University:
    Pleasantville/Briarcliff *B, T*
State University of New York
    College at Geneseo *M*
Syracuse University *M*

North Carolina
Appalachian State University *M*
Barton College *B*
East Carolina University *B, M*
Fayetteville State University *M*
Greensboro College *B, T*
Salem College *M, T*
University of North Carolina
    Chapel Hill *M*
    Charlotte *M*
    Pembroke *B, T*
    Wilmington *B*

North Dakota
Minot State University *M*
University of Mary *M*

Ohio
Ashland University *M, T*
Baldwin-Wallace College *B, M*
Bowling Green State University *B*
College of Mount St. Joseph *T*
Hiram College *T*
Kent State University
    Stark Campus *B*
Malone College *B, M*
Notre Dame College *M, T*
Ohio University *B, T*
University of Akron *B, T*
University of Cincinnati *M, D*
University of Dayton *B, M, T*
University of Findlay *B, T*
University of Toledo *T*
Wittenberg University *B*
Wright State University *B, M, T*
Youngstown State University *B, M*

Oklahoma
Northeastern State University *B*
Northwestern Oklahoma State
    University *B, T*
Oklahoma Baptist University *B, T*
Southwestern Oklahoma State
    University *B*
University of Central Oklahoma *B, M*
University of Oklahoma *B, T*

Oregon
University of Oregon *M, D*
University of Portland *T*
Western Oregon University *T*

Puerto Rico
Inter American University of Puerto Rico
    Metropolitan Campus *B*

Rhode Island
Rhode Island College *M*

South Carolina
Francis Marion University *M*
Furman University *M, T*
South Carolina State University *B, T*
Southern Wesleyan University *B, T*
University of South Carolina
    Spartanburg *B, T*

South Dakota
Augustana College *B, T*

Tennessee
Johnson Bible College *T*

Texas
Texas Woman's University *M*
West Texas A&M University *T*

Utah
Southern Utah University *B, T*

Vermont
St. Michael's College *M, T*

Virginia
Eastern Mennonite University *T*
Hampton University *M*
Longwood University *M*
Marymount University *M*
Radford University *T*
University of Virginia's College at
    Wise *T*

West Virginia
Bethany College *B*
Concord College *B, T*
West Virginia University *T*
West Virginia Wesleyan College *B*
Wheeling Jesuit University *T*

Wisconsin
Carthage College *B, T*
Silver Lake College *B, T*
University of Wisconsin
    Eau Claire *B, M*
    Madison *B, M, D, T*
    Oshkosh *M*
    Superior *M*
    Whitewater *B, T*

Education of mentally handicapped

Alabama
Tuskegee University *B, T*

Arizona
Prescott College *T*
University of Phoenix *B*

Arkansas
University of Central Arkansas *M*

California
California State University
    Northridge *M*
Fresno Pacific University *M, T*
San Francisco State University *T*
Sonoma State University *M*

Florida
Edward Waters College *B*
Flagler College *B*
Florida International University *B, T*
Florida State University *B, M, T*
Nova Southeastern University *M*
University of South Florida *B, M*
University of West Florida *B, M, T*

Georgia
Augusta State University *B, M*
Columbus State University *B, M*

Georgia College and State
    University *M, T*
North Georgia College & State
    University *B, M*
State University of West Georgia *B, M*

Idaho
Lewis-Clark State College *T*

Illinois
Bradley University *B, T*
Chicago State University *B, M*
Greenville College *T*
Sauk Valley Community College *A*
Trinity Christian College *B, T*

Indiana
Ball State University *T*
Manchester College *B, T*
University of Evansville *B*
Valparaiso University *M, T*

Iowa
Ellsworth Community College *A*
Iowa State University *T*
Loras College *B*
Morningside College *B, M*
Northwestern College *T*
University of Iowa *M*
University of Northern Iowa *B*

Kansas
Tabor College *B, T*
University of Kansas *M, D*
Wichita State University *T*

Kentucky
Brescia University *B*

Louisiana
Nicholls State University *M*
University of New Orleans *M*

Maine
University of Maine
    Farmington *B, T*

Massachusetts
American International College *B, M*

Michigan
Calvin College *B, T*
Central Michigan University *B*
Eastern Michigan University *B, T*
Grand Valley State University *M, T*
Northern Michigan University *B*
Western Michigan University *B*

Minnesota
Minnesota State University
    Mankato *M*
    Moorhead *B, T*
University of St. Thomas *M*
Winona State University *B, T*

Mississippi
Mississippi State University *T*

Missouri
Avila University *B, T*
Harris Stowe State College *T*
Lindenwood University *M*
Northwest Missouri State
    University *B, M, T*
University of Missouri
    Columbia *M, D*
William Woods University *T*

Nebraska
University of Nebraska
    Kearney *B, M, T*

New Hampshire
Keene State College *M, T*

New Jersey
William Paterson University of New
    Jersey *M*

New York
City University of New York
    Brooklyn College *B, M, T*
    City College *B, M, T*
Fordham University *M*
Hofstra University *T*
Manhattan College *M*
Nazareth College of Rochester *T*
State University of New York
    College at Buffalo *B, M*
    College at Geneseo *M, T*
    New Paltz *M*

North Carolina
Appalachian State University *M*
East Carolina University *B, M*
Greensboro College *B, T*
North Carolina Central University *M*
Shaw University *B, T*
University of North Carolina
    Charlotte *B, M*
    Greensboro *M*
    Pembroke *B, T*
    Wilmington *B*

North Dakota
Minot State University *B*
University of Mary *B*

Ohio
Bluffton College *B*
Bowling Green State University *B*
Hiram College *T*
Kent State University
    Stark Campus *B*
University of Cincinnati *M, D*
University of Dayton *B, M, T*
University of Findlay *T*
University of Toledo *T*
Walsh University *B*
Wright State University *B, M*
Youngstown State University *B*

Oklahoma
East Central University *B, T*
Northwestern Oklahoma State
    University *B, T*
Oklahoma Baptist University *B, T*
St. Gregory's University *A*
Southwestern Oklahoma State
    University *B*
University of Central Oklahoma *B, M*
University of Oklahoma *B, T*

Oregon
Western Oregon University *T*

Pennsylvania
California University of Pennsylvania *M*
Kutztown University of Pennsylvania *B*
La Salle University *B, T*
Slippery Rock University of
    Pennsylvania *B, T*
University of Pittsburgh *T*

Puerto Rico
Inter American University of Puerto Rico
    Metropolitan Campus *B*

Rhode Island
Rhode Island College *B, M*

South Carolina
Converse College *M, T*
Furman University *M, T*
South Carolina State University *B, T*
Southern Wesleyan University *B, T*

South Dakota
Augustana College *B, T*

Tennessee
Johnson Bible College *T*
Lambuth University *B, T*

Texas
Angelina College *A*
Texas A&M University
    Kingsville *M*
Texas Woman's University *M*

West Texas A&M University *T*

Virginia
Eastern Mennonite University *T*
Longwood University *M*
Radford University *T*
University of Virginia's College at
    Wise *T*

West Virginia
Alderson-Broaddus College *T*
Concord College *B, T*
Fairmont State College *B*
West Liberty State College *B*
West Virginia State College *B*
West Virginia University *T*

Wisconsin
Carthage College *B, T*
Silver Lake College *B, T*
University of Wisconsin
    Eau Claire *B, M*
    Oshkosh *M*

Education of multiple handicapped

Arkansas
Arkansas State University *M*

California
California State Polytechnic University:
    Pomona *T*
California State University
    Dominguez Hills *T*
    Long Beach *T*
    Los Angeles *M*
San Francisco State University *T*
San Jose State University *M, T*
Sonoma State University *M*

District of Columbia
Gallaudet University *B, M, T*

Florida
Flagler College *B*

Georgia
Georgia State University *M*

Idaho
Lewis-Clark State College *T*

Illinois
National-Louis University *M*
Sauk Valley Community College *A*

Indiana
Ball State University *T*
University of Evansville *B*

Iowa
Clarke College *M*
Iowa State University *T*
Loras College *M*
Morningside College *B, M*
Northwestern College *T*
University of Iowa *M*

Kansas
Tabor College *B, T*
University of Kansas *M, D*

Kentucky
Brescia University *B*

Maine
University of Maine *M*

Maryland
Johns Hopkins University *M*

Massachusetts
Boston College *M*

Minnesota
Minnesota State University
    Mankato *M*
Winona State University *B, T*

Mississippi
Mississippi State University *T*

Missouri
Lindenwood University *M*
Missouri Valley College *B, T*

Nebraska
University of Nebraska
Kearney *B, M, T*

New Jersey
Gloucester County College *A*

New York
City University of New York
Brooklyn College *B, M, T*
Hunter College *M, T*
Dominican College of Blauvelt *M*
Iona College *B, T*
Nazareth College of Rochester *T*
Syracuse University *M, D*

North Carolina
Appalachian State University *M*
University of North Carolina
Charlotte *M*
Greensboro *M*

North Dakota
Minot State University *M*

Ohio
Ashland University *M, T*
Bowling Green State University *B*
College of Mount St. Joseph *T*
Kent State University
Stark Campus *B*
Ohio Dominican College *B*
Ohio State University
Columbus Campus *M, D*
Ohio University *B, T*
Sinclair Community College *A*
University of Akron *B, T*
University of Dayton *M, T*
University of Findlay *T*
University of Toledo *T*
Walsh University *B*
Wright State University *B, M, T*
Youngstown State University *B*

Oklahoma
University of Central Oklahoma *M*

Oregon
Portland State University *T*
University of Oregon *M, D*
Western Oregon University *T*

Puerto Rico
Inter American University of Puerto Rico
Metropolitan Campus *B*

Rhode Island
Rhode Island College *B, M*

Tennessee
Johnson Bible College *T*
Lambuth University *B, T*

Virginia
Norfolk State University *M*
Radford University *T*
Virginia Commonwealth University *M*

West Virginia
West Virginia University *T*

Wisconsin
St. Norbert College *B*

Education of physically handicapped

Arkansas
University of Central Arkansas *B, M*

California
California State Polytechnic University:
Pomona *T*

California State University
Los Angeles *M*
Northridge *M*
Sacramento *T*
Fresno Pacific University *M, T*
San Francisco State University *T*
San Jose State University *T*

Florida
Flagler College *B*

Georgia
Georgia State University *M*

Idaho
Lewis-Clark State College *T*

Illinois
Sauk Valley Community College *A*

Indiana
Ball State University *T*

Iowa
Ellsworth Community College *A*

Louisiana
Louisiana College *B*

Maryland
Johns Hopkins University *M*

Massachusetts
Springfield College *M, T*

Michigan
Eastern Michigan University *B, T*
Western Michigan University *B*

Minnesota
University of St. Thomas *M*
Winona State University *B, T*

Missouri
Lindenwood University *M*

Nebraska
University of Nebraska
Kearney *B, M, T*

New Jersey
William Paterson University of New
Jersey *M*

New York
City University of New York
Brooklyn College *B, M, T*
State University of New York
College at Buffalo *B, M*

North Carolina
Appalachian State University *M*

North Dakota
University of Mary *B*

Ohio
Bluffton College *B*
Kent State University
Stark Campus *B*
Ohio State University
Columbus Campus *M, D*
University of Akron *B, M, T*
University of Cincinnati *M, D*
University of Toledo *T*
Wright State University *M*

Oklahoma
East Central University *B, T*

Oregon
Western Oregon University *T*

Pennsylvania
California University of Pennsylvania *M*
Cheyney University of Pennsylvania *T*
Indiana University of Pennsylvania *B*
La Salle University *B, T*
Slippery Rock University of
Pennsylvania *B, T*
University of Pittsburgh *T*

Puerto Rico
Pontifical Catholic University of Puerto
Rico *B*
University of Puerto Rico
Bayamon University College *A, B*

Rhode Island
Rhode Island College *B*

South Dakota
Augustana College *B, T*

Tennessee
Johnson Bible College *T*
Lambuth University *B, T*

Texas
Texas Woman's University *M*
West Texas A&M University *T*

Education of speech impaired

Alabama
Alabama Agricultural and Mechanical
University *B*

Alaska
Prince William Sound Community
College *A*

Arizona
Prescott College *T*

Arkansas
University of Central Arkansas *M*

California
California State University
Chico *T*
Long Beach *T*
Northridge *B, M*
San Francisco State University *B, M, T*
San Jose State University *T*
University of Redlands *B, M*
University of San Francisco *M*

Georgia
Armstrong Atlantic State
University *B, M, T*
Georgia State University *M*
Valdosta State University *B, M*

Illinois
Northwestern University *B*

Indiana
Ball State University *T*

Iowa
University of Iowa *M*

Kansas
Wichita State University *T*

Kentucky
Murray State University *B, M, T*

Louisiana
Louisiana Tech University *B*
Southeastern Louisiana University *B*
Southern University and Agricultural and
Mechanical College *B, M*

Massachusetts
Emerson College *B, M, D*

Michigan
Calvin College *B, T*
Eastern Michigan University *B, T*
Wayne State University *B, T*

Minnesota
Minnesota State University
Mankato *B, M*

Missouri
Fontbonne College *B, M*
Truman State University *B, M*

Nebraska
University of Nebraska
Kearney *B, M, T*
Lincoln *M*
Omaha *B, T*

New Jersey
Kean University *B, M*
William Paterson University of New
Jersey *M*

New Mexico
New Mexico State University *B*

New York
City University of New York
Brooklyn College *B, M, T*
Hunter College *M, T*
College of New Rochelle *M*
Elmira College *B, T*
Hofstra University *M, T*
Ithaca College *B, M, T*
Long Island University
C. W. Post Campus *B, M*
Mercy College *T*
Nazareth College of Rochester *M, T*
New York University *B, T*
Pace University *B*
Pace University:
Pleasantville/Briarcliff *B*
St. John's University *B, T*
State University of New York
College at Fredonia *B, M, T*
College at Geneseo *T*
New Paltz *B, M, T*

North Carolina
Appalachian State University *M*
University of North Carolina
Greensboro *M*

North Dakota
Minot State University *B, M*

Ohio
University of Toledo *B, M, T*

Oklahoma
University of Central Oklahoma *B*
University of Tulsa *B, T*

Oregon
Portland State University *T*

Pennsylvania
Bloomsburg University of
Pennsylvania *B, M, T*
Indiana University of Pennsylvania *B*
Kutztown University of Pennsylvania *B*
Marywood University *B*
West Chester University of
Pennsylvania *B, M, T*

Puerto Rico
Inter American University of Puerto Rico
Metropolitan Campus *B*
Pontifical Catholic University of Puerto
Rico *B*
Turabo University *B*

South Carolina
Columbia College *B*

South Dakota
Augustana College *B, T*

Tennessee
Lambuth University *B, T*

Texas
Baylor University *B*
El Paso Community College *A*
University of Texas
Pan American *T*

Virginia
Hampton University *M*

West Virginia
West Virginia University *T*

235

Wisconsin
University of Wisconsin
  Madison *B, M, D, T*
  River Falls *B, T*
  Whitewater *M*

Educational assessment/ testing

Alabama
Troy State University in Montgomery *M*

California
California State University
  Northridge *M*
Stanford University *M, D*

Colorado
Jones International University *M*

Delaware
University of Delaware *M, D*

Georgia
Georgia State University *M*
University of Georgia *M, D*

Indiana
Indiana University
  Bloomington *D*

Iowa
Iowa State University *M*
University of Iowa *M, D*

Kentucky
University of Louisville *D*

Louisiana
University of New Orleans *M*

Massachusetts
American International College *M*
Tufts University *M*

Michigan
Michigan State University *M, D*

New Mexico
College of the Southwest *M*

New York
Fordham University *M, D*
State University of New York
  Albany *M, D*
  Buffalo *M, D*
Syracuse University *M, D*

North Carolina
University of North Carolina
  Greensboro *M, D*

Ohio
Kent State University *M, D*
Ohio State University
  Columbus Campus *M, D*

Pennsylvania
University of Pennsylvania *M*

Texas
Sul Ross State University *M*
University of Texas
  Pan American *M*

Washington
University of Washington *M, D*

Educational evaluation/ research

California
California State University
  Fresno *M*
San Diego State University *M*
University of California
  Berkeley *T*

Colorado
Jones International University *M*

University of Colorado
  Boulder *D*

District of Columbia
Catholic University of America *D*

Florida
Florida State University *M, D*

Georgia
Clark Atlanta University *M*

Kentucky
University of Kentucky *M, D*

Massachusetts
Boston College *M, D*

Michigan
Michigan State University *D*
Wayne State University *M, D*
Western Michigan University *D*

Missouri
University of Missouri
  Kansas City *M*

New Jersey
Rowan University *M*

New York
Hofstra University *M*

North Carolina
North Carolina State University *M, D*
University of North Carolina
  Greensboro *M, D*

Ohio
Ohio University *M, D*
University of Dayton *M*
Youngstown State University *M*

Pennsylvania
Penn State
  University Park *M*

Puerto Rico
University of Puerto Rico
  Rio Piedras Campus *M*

South Carolina
University of South Carolina *M, D*

South Dakota
University of South Dakota *M, D*

Texas
University of the Incarnate Word *M*

Utah
Brigham Young University *M, D*

Educational leadership/ adminstration

Alabama
Alabama Agricultural and Mechanical
  University *M*
Alabama State University *M*
Auburn University *M, D*
Auburn University at Montgomery *M*
Community College of the Air
  Force *C, A*
Jacksonville State University *M, T*
Samford University *M, T*
Troy State University *M*
Troy State University Dothan *M*
Troy State University in Montgomery *M*
University of Alabama *M, D*
University of Alabama
  Birmingham *M, D, T*
University of Montevallo *M, T*
University of North Alabama *M*
University of South Alabama *M, T*
University of West Alabama *M*

Alaska
University of Alaska
  Anchorage *M, T*
  Fairbanks *T*

Arizona
Arizona State University *M, D*
Northern Arizona University *M, D*
Prescott College *B*
University of Arizona *M, D*
University of Phoenix *C, M*

Arkansas
Arkansas State University *D, T*
Harding University *M*
Henderson State University *M*
Southern Arkansas University *M*
University of Arkansas *M, D*
University of Arkansas
  Little Rock *M, D*
University of Central Arkansas *M*

California
Azusa Pacific University *M*
Barstow College *A*
Bethany College *M*
California Baptist University *M, T*
California Polytechnic State University:
  San Luis Obispo *M*
California State University
  Bakersfield *M*
  Chico *T*
  Dominguez Hills *M*
  Fresno *M, D*
  Fullerton *M*
  Hayward *M, T*
  Long Beach *M, T*
  Los Angeles *M*
  Northridge *M*
  Sacramento *M*
  San Bernardino *M*
  San Marcos *M*
  Stanislaus *M*
Chapman University *M, T*
Concordia University *M*
Fresno Pacific University *M*
La Sierra University *M, D*
Loyola Marymount University *M, T*
Mills College *D*
Mount St. Mary's College *M*
National University *M, T*
Pepperdine University *M, D*
Point Loma Nazarene University *M*
St. Mary's College of California *M*
San Diego State University *M*
San Francisco State University *T*
San Jose State University *M, T*
Santa Clara University *M*
Sonoma State University *M*
Stanford University *M, D*
University of California
  Berkeley *T*
  Irvine *D*
  Los Angeles *M, D*
  Riverside *M, D, T*
University of La Verne *C, M, D*
University of Redlands *M, T*
University of San Diego *M, D*
University of San Francisco *M, D, T*
University of Southern California *M, T*
University of the Pacific *M, D*
Whittier College *T*

Colorado
University of Colorado
  Denver *M, D*
University of Denver *M, D*
University of Northern Colorado *M, D, T*

Connecticut
Central Connecticut State
  University *M, D*
Fairfield University *M*
Sacred Heart University *M, T*
University of Bridgeport *D*
University of Connecticut *M, D*
University of Hartford *M, D, T*
University of New Haven *M*

Delaware
University of Delaware *M, D*
Wilmington College *M*

District of Columbia
American University *M, D*
Catholic University of America *M, D*
Gallaudet University *M*
George Washington University *M*
Howard University *M*
Trinity College *M*
University of the District of Columbia *M*

Florida
Barry University *M, D, T*
Florida Agricultural and Mechanical
  University *M, D*
Florida Atlantic University *M, D*
Florida Gulf Coast University *M*
Florida International University *M, D*
Florida State University *M, D*
Nova Southeastern University *M, D*
Stetson University *M*
University of Central Florida *M, D*
University of Florida *M, D*
University of North Florida *M, D*
University of South Florida *B, M, D*
University of West Florida *D*

Georgia
Albany State University *M*
Augusta State University *M*
Berry College *T*
Clark Atlanta University *M, D*
Columbus State University *M*
Covenant College *T*
Georgia College and State
  University *M, T*
Georgia Southern University *M, D, T*
Georgia State University *M, D*
State University of West Georgia *M*
University of Georgia *M, D*
Valdosta State University *M*

Hawaii
University of Hawaii
  Manoa *M, D*

Idaho
Idaho State University *D, T*
University of Idaho *B, M*

Illinois
Aurora University *D*
Benedictine University *M*
Bradley University *M*
Chicago State University *M*
Concordia University *M*
De Paul University *M*
Dominican University *M*
Eastern Illinois University *M*
Governors State University *M*
Illinois State University *M, D*
Lewis University *M*
Loyola University of Chicago *C, M, D*
National-Louis University *M*
North Central College *M*
Northeastern Illinois University *M*
Northern Illinois University *M, D*
Northwestern University *D*
Quincy University *M*
Roosevelt University *C, M, D*
St. Xavier University *M*
Southern Illinois University
  Carbondale *M, D*
Southern Illinois University
  Edwardsville *M*
University of Illinois
  Chicago *M, D*
  Urbana-Champaign *M, D, T*
University of St. Francis *B*
Western Illinois University *M*

Indiana
Ball State University *B, M, D, T*
Butler University *M*
Indiana State University *D*
Indiana University
  Bloomington *M, D*
Indiana University-Purdue University
  Fort Wayne *M*

Indiana University-Purdue University
  Indianapolis *M*
Purdue University *M, D, T*

Iowa
Buena Vista University *B, M*
Clarke College *M*
Drake University *M, D*
Iowa State University *M, D*
St. Ambrose University *M*
University of Iowa *M, D*
University of Northern Iowa *M*

Kansas
Benedictine College *M*
Emporia State University *M*
Friends University *M*
Kansas State University *M, D*
Newman University *M*
Pittsburg State University *M*
University of Kansas *M*
Wichita State University *M, D*

Kentucky
Murray State University *B, M, T*
Spalding University *M, D, T*
Union College *M*

Louisiana
Centenary College of Louisiana *M*
Grambling State University *D*
Louisiana State University and
  Agricultural and Mechanical
  College *M*
Louisiana Tech University *D*
McNeese State University *M, T*
Nicholls State University *M*
Northwestern State University *T*
Our Lady of Holy Cross College *M*
Southeastern Louisiana University *M*
Southern University and Agricultural and
  Mechanical College *M*
University of Louisiana at Lafayette *M*
University of Louisiana at Monroe *M, D*
University of New Orleans *M, D*

Maine
University of Maine *M, D*
University of Southern Maine *M*

Maryland
Bowie State University *M, D*
College of Notre Dame of Maryland *M*
Coppin State College *M*
Frostburg State University *M*
Hood College *M*
Loyola College in Maryland *M*
McDaniel College *M*
Morgan State University *M, D*
Salisbury University *M*
University of Maryland
  College Park *M, D, T*

Massachusetts
American International College *M*
Atlantic Union College *M*
Boston College *M, D*
Boston University *M, D*
Bridgewater State College *M, T*
Emmanuel College *M*
Fitchburg State College *M*
Framingham State College *M*
Lesley University *M, T*
Salem State College *M*
Springfield College *M*
Suffolk University *M*
University of Massachusetts
  Boston *M*
  Lowell *M, D*
Westfield State College *M*

Michigan
Andrews University *M, D*
Central Michigan University *M, D*
Eastern Michigan University *M, D*
Grand Valley State University *M*
Madonna University *M*
Marygrove College *M*

Northern Michigan University *M, D*
Oakland University *M, D*
Saginaw Valley State University *M*
University of Michigan
  Flint *M*
Wayne State University *D*
Western Michigan University *M, D, T*

Minnesota
Bemidji State University *M*
Capella University *M, D*
Minnesota State University
  Mankato *M*
  Moorhead *M*
St. Cloud State University *M, D, T*
St. Mary's University of Minnesota *M*
University of Minnesota
  Twin Cities *M, D*
University of St. Thomas *M, D*
Winona State University *M, T*

Mississippi
Delta State University *M*
Mississippi College *M*
Mississippi State University *M, T*
University of Mississippi *M, D*
University of Southern Mississippi *M*

Missouri
Central Missouri State University *M*
Lindenwood University *M*
Maryville University of Saint Louis *M, T*
Northwest Missouri State University *M*
St. Louis University *M, D*
Southeast Missouri State
  University *B, M*
Southwest Baptist University *M*
Southwest Missouri State University *M*
University of Missouri
  Columbia *M, D*
  Kansas City *M*
  St. Louis *M*
Webster University *T*
William Woods University *M*

Montana
University of Montana-Missoula *M, D*

Nebraska
Concordia University *M, T*
Doane College *M*
University of Nebraska
  Kearney *M*
  Omaha *M, D*

Nevada
University of Nevada
  Las Vegas *M, D*
  Reno *M, D*

New Hampshire
Keene State College *M*
Plymouth State College *T*
Rivier College *M*
University of New Hampshire *D*
University of New Hampshire at
  Manchester *M*

New Jersey
Caldwell College *M*
Centenary College *M*
The College of New Jersey *M*
College of St. Elizabeth *M*
Fairleigh Dickinson University
  Metropolitan Campus *M*
Georgian Court College *M*
Kean University *M*
Monmouth University *M*
Montclair State University *M*
New Jersey City University *C, M*
Rider University *M*
Rowan University *M, D*
St. Peter's College *M*
Seton Hall University *M, D*

New Mexico
College of the Southwest *M*
New Mexico Highlands University *M*
New Mexico State University *M, D*

University of New Mexico *M, D, T*
Western New Mexico University *M*

New York
Adelphi University *M*
Canisius College *M*
Cazenovia College *B*
City University of New York
  Baruch College *M*
  Brooklyn College *B, M, T*
  City College *M*
  College of Staten Island *T*
  Hunter College *C*
  Queens College *C*
College of New Rochelle *M*
Dowling College *C, D, T*
Fordham University *M, D*
Hofstra University *M, D, T*
Iona College *M*
Long Island University
  C. W. Post Campus *M*
Manhattan College *M*
Mercy College *M*
New York Institute of Technology *T*
New York University *M, D, T*
Niagara University *M*
Pace University *C, M*
Pace University:
  Pleasantville/Briarcliff *C, M*
St. Bonaventure University *M*
St. John Fisher College *M*
St. John's University *M, D, T*
St. Lawrence University *M*
State University of New York
  Albany *C, M, D*
  Binghamton *M, D*
  Buffalo *M, D, T*
  College at Brockport *M*
  College at Buffalo *C*
  College at Cortland *T*
  College at Fredonia *T*
  College at Plattsburgh *M, T*
  New Paltz *M, D*
  Oswego *M*
Syracuse University *M, D*
Touro College *C, M*
University of Rochester *M, D*

North Carolina
Campbell University *M*
East Carolina University *D, T*
Fayetteville State University *M*
Gardner-Webb University *M*
North Carolina Agricultural and
  Technical State University *M*
North Carolina Central University *M*
North Carolina State University *M, D*
University of North Carolina
  Chapel Hill *M*
  Charlotte *C, D*
  Greensboro *M, D*
  Wilmington *M*
Western Carolina University *D*

North Dakota
North Dakota State University *M*
University of Mary *M*
University of North Dakota *M, D*

Ohio
Ashland University *M, D, T*
Baldwin-Wallace College *M*
Bowling Green State University *M, D*
Cleveland State University *B, M, D*
Franciscan University of Steubenville *M*
John Carroll University *C, M*
Kent State University *M, D*
Laura and Alvin Siegal College of Judaic
  Studies *M*
Malone College *M*
Miami University
  Oxford Campus *D*
Ohio State University
  Columbus Campus *M, D*
Ohio University *M, D*
University of Akron *B, M, D*
University of Cincinnati *M, D*

University of Dayton *M, D, T*
University of Findlay *M*
University of Toledo *M, D, T*
Ursuline College *M*
Wright State University *M*
Xavier University *M*
Youngstown State University *M, D*

Oklahoma
East Central University *M, T*
Northeastern State University *M*
Northwestern Oklahoma State
  University *M*
Oklahoma State University *M, D*
Oral Roberts University *M*
Southeastern Oklahoma State
  University *M*
Southwestern Oklahoma State
  University *M, T*
University of Central Oklahoma *M*
University of Oklahoma *M, D, T*

Oregon
Concordia University *M*
George Fox University *M, D, T*
Lewis & Clark College *M*
Portland State University *D, T*
University of Oregon *M, D*

Pennsylvania
Arcadia University *M*
Bucknell University *M*
Carlow College *M*
Cheyney University of Pennsylvania *M*
Delaware Valley College *B*
Duquesne University *M, D*
Edinboro University of Pennsylvania *M*
Gratz College *C, M*
Immaculata University *M, D*
Indiana University of Pennsylvania *D*
Lehigh University *M, D*
Marywood University *M, D*
Penn State
  University Park *M, D*
Philadelphia Biblical University *M*
St. Joseph's University *M*
Slippery Rock University of
  Pennsylvania *C*
Temple University *M, D*
University of Pittsburgh *M, D*
University of Scranton *M*
Widener University *M, D*
York College of Pennsylvania *M*

Puerto Rico
Bayamon Central University *M*
Inter American University of Puerto Rico
  Metropolitan Campus *M, D*
  San German Campus *M, D*
Pontifical Catholic University of Puerto
  Rico *M*
Turabo University *M*
Universidad Metropolitana *M*
University of Puerto Rico
  Rio Piedras Campus *M, D*

Rhode Island
Rhode Island College *M*

South Carolina
Charleston Southern University *M*
The Citadel *M*
Clemson University *M*
Columbia International University *M*
Furman University *M*
South Carolina State University *D*
University of South Carolina *M, D*
Winthrop University *M, T*

South Dakota
South Dakota State University *M*
University of South Dakota *M, D*

Tennessee
Austin Peay State University *M*
East Tennessee State University *M, D, T*
Freed-Hardeman University *C*
Middle Tennessee State University *M, T*

Southern Adventist University *M*
Tennessee Technological University *M*
Trevecca Nazarene University *M, D*
University of Memphis *M, D*
University of Tennessee
    Chattanooga *M*
    Knoxville *M, D*

Texas
Abilene Christian University *M, T*
Angelo State University *M*
Baylor University *M, D*
Houston Baptist University *M*
Lamar University *M*
Lubbock Christian University *M*
Midwestern State University *M*
Prairie View A&M University *M*
St. Mary's University *M*
Sam Houston State University *D*
Schreiner University *M*
Southwest Texas State University *M, T*
Stephen F. Austin State University *M, D*
Sul Ross State University *M*
Tarleton State University *B, M, D, T*
Texas A&M International
    University *M, T*
Texas A&M University *M, D*
Texas A&M University
    Commerce *M, D*
    Corpus Christi *M, D, T*
    Kingsville *M*
Texas Christian University *M, T*
Texas Southern University *M, D*
Texas Tech University *M, D*
Texas Woman's University *M, T*
Trinity University *M*
University of Houston *M, D*
University of Houston
    Clear Lake *M*
    Victoria *M*
University of Mary Hardin-Baylor *M*
University of North Texas *M, D*
University of Texas
    Arlington *M*
    Austin *M, D*
    Brownsville *M*
    El Paso *M, D*
    Pan American *M, D*
    San Antonio *M, D*
    Tyler *M*
    of the Permian Basin *M*
West Texas A&M University *M, T*

Utah
Brigham Young University *M, D*
University of Utah *M, D*

Vermont
Castleton State College *M*
Goddard College *B*
Johnson State College *M*
St. Michael's College *M*
University of Vermont *M, D, T*

Virginia
College of William and Mary *M, D*
George Mason University *M*
Liberty University *M, D*
Longwood University *M*
Lynchburg College *M*
Old Dominion University *M*
Radford University *M*
Shenandoah University *D*
University of Virginia *M, D*
Virginia Commonwealth University *M*
Virginia State University *M, D*

Washington
Central Washington University *M, T*
Eastern Washington University *M*
Gonzaga University *M*
Heritage College *M*
Pacific Lutheran University *M*
Seattle University *M*
University of Washington *M, D*
Walla Walla College *M*
Washington State University *B, M, D*

Whitworth College *M*

West Virginia
West Virginia University *M, D*

Wisconsin
Concordia University Wisconsin *M*
Edgewood College *M*
Marian College of Fond du Lac *M*
University of Wisconsin
    Madison *M, D*
    Milwaukee *M, T*
    Superior *M*

Wyoming
University of Wyoming *C*

Educational psychology

Alabama
University of Alabama *M, D*

Arizona
Arizona State University *M, D*
Northern Arizona University *M, D*
Prescott College *B, M*
University of Arizona *M, D*

California
Azusa Pacific University *M*
California State University
    Dominguez Hills *T*
    Hayward *M, T*
    Long Beach *M*
    Northridge *M*
Chapman University *M, T*
Fresno Pacific University *M, T*
La Sierra University *M*
Loyola Marymount University *M*
St. Mary's College of California *M*
University of California
    Santa Barbara *M, D*
University of San Francisco *M, D*
University of Southern California *D, T*
University of the Pacific *M, D, T*

Colorado
University of Colorado
    Boulder *M, D*
    Denver *M*
University of Denver *M, D*
University of Northern Colorado *M, D*

Connecticut
Eastern Connecticut State University *M*
University of Connecticut *M, D, T*

Delaware
University of Delaware *B, M, T*

District of Columbia
Catholic University of America *D*
Howard University *M*

Florida
Florida State University *M, D*
University of Florida *M, D*

Georgia
Georgia State University *M, D*
University of Georgia *M, D*
Valdosta State University *M*

Hawaii
University of Hawaii
    Manoa *M, D*

Idaho
Idaho State University *M, D*

Illinois
Loyola University of Chicago *M, D*
National-Louis University *M, D*
Northern Illinois University *M, D*
Northwestern University *T*

Indiana
Indiana University
    Bloomington *M, D*

Iowa
Iowa State University *T*
University of Iowa *M, D*

Kansas
Fort Hays State University *M*
Kansas State University *D*
Pittsburg State University *A, B, D*
University of Kansas *M, D*
Wichita State University *M*

Kentucky
University of Kentucky *M, D*

Louisiana
Louisiana Tech University *M*
Nicholls State University *M*

Maryland
St. Mary's College of Maryland *B*

Massachusetts
American International College *B, M, D*
Boston College *D*
Mount Holyoke College *B*
Northeastern University *M*
Tufts University *M, T*

Michigan
Eastern Michigan University *M*
Michigan State University *M, D*
University of Michigan *D*
Wayne State University *M, D*

Minnesota
Capella University *M, D*
University of Minnesota
    Duluth *M*
    Twin Cities *M, D*

Mississippi
Alcorn State University *B*
Mississippi State University *B, M, D*
University of Mississippi *M, D*

Missouri
University of Missouri
    Columbia *M, D*

Nebraska
University of Nebraska
    Kearney *M*
    Lincoln *M, D*

Nevada
University of Nevada
    Las Vegas *M, D*

New Jersey
Kean University *M*
Montclair State University *M*
New Jersey City University *M*
Rowan University *M*
Rutgers, The State University of New
    Jersey
    New Brunswick Regional
        Campus *D*

New Mexico
University of New Mexico *M, D*

New York
City University of New York
    Brooklyn College *M*
Eugene Lang College/New School
    University *B*
Marist College *M*
New York University *M, D*
Rochester Institute of Technology *M*
State University of New York
    Albany *D*
    Buffalo *M, D*
    College at Plattsburgh *M, T*
Syracuse University *M, D*
Touro College *M*

North Carolina
University of North Carolina
    Chapel Hill *M*

Ohio
Bowling Green State University *M*
John Carroll University *M*
Kent State University *M, D*
Miami University
    Oxford Campus *M*
Ohio State University
    Columbus Campus *M, D*
University of Dayton *M*

Oklahoma
Northwestern Oklahoma State
    University *M*
Oklahoma State University *D*
University of Oklahoma *M, D*

Oregon
University of Oregon *M, D*

Pennsylvania
Edinboro University of Pennsylvania *M*
Indiana University of Pennsylvania *M*
Lehigh University *M, D*
Penn State
    University Park *M, D*
Temple University *M, D*
University of Pittsburgh *B, M, D*

Puerto Rico
Pontifical Catholic University of Puerto
    Rico *M*

Rhode Island
Rhode Island College *M*

South Dakota
University of South Dakota *M, D*

Tennessee
American Baptist College of ABT
    Seminary *B*
Tennessee State University *D*
Tennessee Technological
    University *M, D*
University of Memphis *M, D*
University of Tennessee
    Knoxville *M, D*
Vanderbilt University *M, D*

Texas
Baylor University *M, D*
Tarleton State University *B*
Texas A&M University *M, D*
Texas A&M University
    Commerce *M, D*
University of Houston *M, D*
University of Mary Hardin-Baylor *M*
University of North Texas *M, D*
University of Texas
    Austin *M, D*
    El Paso *M*
    Pan American *M*
    Tyler *M*

Utah
Brigham Young University *M, D*
University of Utah *M, D*

Virginia
College of William and Mary *M, D*
Marymount University *B*
Shenandoah University *B*
University of Virginia *M, D*
Virginia Polytechnic Institute and State
    University *D*

West Virginia
West Virginia University *M, D*

Wisconsin
Marquette University *M, D*
University of Wisconsin
    Eau Claire *M*
    Madison *M, D*
    Milwaukee *M*
    Whitewater *M*

Educational statistics/ research methods

Alabama
University of Alabama *D*

California
Stanford University *M, D*

Colorado
Jones International University *M*
University of Northern Colorado *M, D*

Connecticut
University of Connecticut *M*

Florida
Florida State University *M, D*
University of Florida *M, D*
University of Miami *M, D*

Georgia
Georgia State University *M, D*
University of Georgia *D*

Illinois
Loyola University of Chicago *M, D*

Iowa
University of Iowa *M, D*

Maryland
University of Maryland
    College Park *M, D, T*

New York
Fordham University *M, D*
State University of New York
    Albany *M, D*
    Buffalo *M, D*

North Carolina
North Carolina State University *B*
University of North Carolina
    Greensboro *M, D*

Ohio
Ohio State University
    Columbus Campus *M, D*
Ohio University *M, D*
University of Toledo *M*

Oklahoma
Oklahoma State University *M, D*

Pennsylvania
West Chester University of
    Pennsylvania *M*

Texas
University of North Texas *D*

Educational supervision

Alabama
University of Alabama *D*

Alaska
University of Alaska
    Anchorage *T*

Arkansas
University of Central Arkansas *M*

California
National University *M, T*
St. Mary's College of California *M*

Connecticut
Central Connecticut State University *M*
Fairfield University *M*

Delaware
University of Delaware *M, D*

District of Columbia
George Washington University *M*
Howard University *M*
University of the District of Columbia *M*

Florida
Stetson University *M*

Georgia
Clark Atlanta University *M, D*
Columbus State University *M*
Valdosta State University *M*

Idaho
Northwest Nazarene University *M*

Illinois
National-Louis University *D*
North Central College *M*
University of Illinois
    Chicago *M*
University of St. Francis *M*

Kansas
Wichita State University *T*

Kentucky
Murray State University *M, T*
Union College *M*
University of Louisville *D*

Louisiana
Centenary College of Louisiana *M*
Nicholls State University *M*
Xavier University of Louisiana *M*

Maine
University of Maine *M*

Maryland
Johns Hopkins University *M*
Morgan State University *M, D*

Massachusetts
American International College *M*
Springfield College *M*

Michigan
Central Michigan University *M, D*
Wayne State University *M*

Minnesota
Bethel College *M*
Minnesota State University
    Mankato *M*
Winona State University *M, T*

Missouri
Lindenwood University *M*

Nebraska
University of Nebraska
    Kearney *M*

New Hampshire
University of New Hampshire *M*

New Jersey
Georgian Court College *M*

New York
City University of New York
    Baruch College *M*
    Brooklyn College *M*
    Hunter College *C*
Fordham University *M, D*
Mercy College *M*
New York Institute of Technology *T*
State University of New York
    Albany *D*
    Buffalo *M, D*
    New Paltz *M*

North Carolina
Appalachian State University *M*
East Carolina University *M*
Fayetteville State University *M*
North Carolina Agricultural and
    Technical State University *M*
North Carolina Central University *M*
University of North Carolina
    Greensboro *M, D*
Western Carolina University *M*

Ohio
Baldwin-Wallace College *M*
John Carroll University *M*

Laura and Alvin Siegal College of Judaic
    Studies *M*
Otterbein College *M*
University of Akron *M*
University of Cincinnati *M, D*
University of Dayton *M, D*
University of Toledo *T*
Wright State University *M*
Youngstown State University *M, D*

Oklahoma
Northeastern State University *M*
Oklahoma State University *M, D*
University of Oklahoma *M, D*

Pennsylvania
Carlow College *M*
Lehigh University *M, D*
Marywood University *M*
St. Joseph's University *M*
Shippensburg University of
    Pennsylvania *T*
Villanova University *M*

Puerto Rico
Inter American University of Puerto Rico
    Metropolitan Campus *M*
Universidad del Este *M*

South Carolina
Clemson University *M*
Furman University *M*
Winthrop University *T*

Tennessee
Tennessee State University *M*
Tennessee Technological University *M*

Texas
Abilene Christian University *M, T*
Lamar University *M*
Our Lady of the Lake University of San
    Antonio *M*
Prairie View A&M University *M*
Sam Houston State University *M*
Southwestern Assemblies of God
    University *B*
Stephen F. Austin State University *M*
Sul Ross State University *M*
Tarleton State University *B, T*
Texas A&M International University *T*
Texas A&M University
    Commerce *D*
    Kingsville *M*
Texas Southern University *M*
Texas Tech University *M*
Texas Woman's University *M*
University of Houston
    Victoria *M*
University of North Texas *M*
University of Texas
    Brownsville *M*
    El Paso *M*
    Pan American *M*

Utah
Brigham Young University *D*

Vermont
Johnson State College *M*
St. Michael's College *M*

Virginia
Longwood University *M*
Radford University *M*

Washington
Central Washington University *M, T*
Eastern Washington University *M*
Seattle Pacific University *T*
Seattle University *D*
Washington State University *B, M, D*
Western Washington University *M*

Wisconsin
University of Wisconsin
    Oshkosh *M*
    River Falls *M*
    Superior *M*

Electrical engineering technologies

Alabama
Alabama Southern Community
    College *A*
Central Alabama Community College *A*
Community College of the Air Force *A*
Gadsden State Community College *C, A*
ITT Technical Institute
    Birmingham *A, B*
Jacksonville State University *B*
James H. Faulkner State Community
    College *C*
Lawson State Community College *C, A*
Northwest-Shoals Community College *A*
Reid State Technical College *A*
Shelton State Community College *C, A*
Wallace Community College: Sparks
    Campus *A*

Alaska
Prince William Sound Community
    College *C, A*
University of Alaska
    Anchorage *C, A, B*

Arizona
Central Arizona College *C, A*
Cochise College *A*
DeVry University
    Phoenix *A, B*
Glendale Community College *C, A*
ITT Technical Institute
    Phoenix *A, B*
    Tucson *A*
Pima Community College *C, A*

Arkansas
Arkansas State University *A*
Arkansas State University
    Beebe *A*
    Mountain Home *C, A*
Arkansas Tech University *C, A*
ITT Technical Institute
    Little Rock *A*
North Arkansas College *C, A*
Northwest Arkansas Community
    College *A*
Phillips Community College of the
    University of Arkansas *C*
Southern Arkansas University Tech *C*
University of Arkansas
    Little Rock *A, B*

California
Barstow College *C*
California State Polytechnic University:
    Pomona *B*
California State University
    Fresno *B*
    Long Beach *B*
Cerritos Community College *C, A*
Cerro Coso Community College *C, A*
Chabot College *A*
College of the Redwoods *C*
College of the Sequoias *C, A*
Cuyamaca College *A*
DeVry University
    Fremont *A, B*
    Long Beach *A, B*
    Pomona *A, B*
    West Hills *A, B*
Diablo Valley College *C*
Don Bosco Technical Institute *A*
Foothill College *C, A*
ITT Technical Institute
    Anaheim *A, B*
    Lathrop *A*
    Oxnard *A, B*
    Rancho Cordova *A, B*
    San Bernardino *A, B*
    San Diego *A, B*
    Sylmar *A*
    Torrance *A*
    West Covina *A*

Irvine Valley College C, A
Los Angeles Harbor College C, A
Los Angeles Southwest College C, A
Los Angeles Trade and Technical
   College C, A
Moorpark College C, A
Mount San Antonio College C, A
Napa Valley College C, A
Ohlone College A
Orange Coast College C, A
Riverside Community College C, A
San Diego City College C, A
San Joaquin Delta College C, A
Santa Barbara City College C, A
Santa Clara University C
Santa Monica College C, A
Santa Rosa Junior College C, A
Shasta College A
Sierra College C, A
Taft College A
University of California
   Riverside B
University of San Diego B
Ventura College A
West Valley College C, A
Yuba Community College District C, A

Colorado

Arapahoe Community College C, A
Colorado State University
   Pueblo B
Colorado Technical University A, B
Community College of Aurora A
DeVry University
   Denver A, B
DeVry University: Colorado Springs A
Front Range Community College C, A
ITT Technical Institute
   Thornton A, B
Mesa State College C, A
Metropolitan State College of Denver B
Red Rocks Community College C, A

Connecticut

Capital Community College A
Gateway Community College A
Naugatuck Valley Community College A
Northwestern Connecticut Community
   College C
Three Rivers Community College A
University of Hartford A, B

Delaware

Delaware State University B
Delaware Technical and Community
   College
   Owens Campus A
   Stanton/Wilmington Campus C, A
   Terry Campus A

District of Columbia

University of the District of Columbia A

Florida

Daytona Beach Community College A
DeVry University
   Miramar A, B
   Orlando A, B
Embry-Riddle Aeronautical University B
Florida Agricultural and Mechanical
   University B
Gulf Coast Community College A
Hillsborough Community College A
ITT Technical Institute
   Ft. Lauderdale A, B
   Jacksonville A, B
   Maitland A, B
   Miami A, B
   Tampa A, B
Indian River Community College A
Manatee Community College A
Miami-Dade Community College C, A
Okaloosa-Walton Community
   College C, A
Palm Beach Community College A
Pensacola Junior College A
Polk Community College A

St. Petersburg College A
Santa Fe Community College A
Seminole Community College A
South Florida Community College C, A
Tampa Technical Institute A, B
University of Central Florida B
University of West Florida B
Valencia Community College A

Georgia

Albany Technical College A
Athens Technical College A
Bainbridge College A
Chattahoochee Technical College A
Clayton College and State
   University C, A
Columbus Technical College A
DeKalb Technical College C, A
DeVry University
   Alpharetta A, B
   Atlanta A, B
Fort Valley State University A, B
Gainesville College A
Georgia Military College A
Georgia Southern University B
Georgia Southwestern State University A
Griffin Technical College A
Herzing College A
Macon State College A
Savannah State University B
Savannah Technical College A
Southern Polytechnic State University B

Hawaii

Heald College
   Honolulu A
University of Hawaii
   Hawaii Community College A
   Honolulu Community College C, A
   Kauai Community College C, A

Idaho

Brigham Young University - Idaho A
Eastern Idaho Technical College C, A
ITT Technical Institute
   Boise A, B
Idaho State University C, A
Lewis-Clark State College A

Illinois

Bradley University B
College of DuPage C, A
College of Lake County C, A
DeVry University
   Addison A, B
   Chicago A, B
   Tinley Park A, B
East-West University A, B
Elgin Community College C, A
Heartland Community College C, A
ITT Technical Institute
   Burr Ridge A
   Matteson A
   Mount Prospect A, B
Illinois Eastern Community Colleges
   Wabash Valley College A
Joliet Junior College C, A
Kaskaskia College C, A
Kishwaukee College C, A
Lincoln Land Community College C, A
McHenry County College C, A
Moraine Valley Community College C
Oakton Community College C, A
Parkland College C, A
Prairie State College C, A
Rend Lake College C
Rock Valley College C, A
Roosevelt University B
Shawnee Community College A
South Suburban College of Cook
   County C, A
Southern Illinois University
   Carbondale B, M
Waubonsee Community College C, A
William Rainey Harper College C, A

Indiana

ITT Technical Institute
   Fort Wayne A
   Indianapolis A, B
Indiana State University A, B
Indiana University-Purdue University
   Fort Wayne C, A, B
Indiana University-Purdue University
   Indianapolis A, B
Ivy Tech State College
   Bloomington A
   Central Indiana A
   Columbus A
   Eastcentral A
   Kokomo A
   Lafayette A
   Northcentral A
   Northeast A
   Northwest A
   Southcentral A
   Southeast A
   Southwest A
   Wabash Valley A
   Whitewater A
Oakland City University A
Purdue University A, B
Purdue University
   Calumet B
   North Central Campus A
Vincennes University A

Iowa

Clinton Community College A
Des Moines Area Community College A
Hamilton Technical College A, B
Hawkeye Community College A
Indian Hills Community College A
Iowa Western Community College A
Kirkwood Community College C, A
Northeast Iowa Community College A
Northwest Iowa Community College A
Southeastern Community College
   North Campus A
Southwestern Community College A
Western Iowa Tech Community
   College A

Kansas

Allen County Community College C
Johnson County Community College A
Kansas City Kansas Community
   College C, A
Kansas State University A, B
Pittsburg State University B
Washburn University of Topeka A
Wichita State University A

Kentucky

Henderson Community College A
Hopkinsville Community College C
ITT Technical Institute
   Louisville A
Jefferson Community College A
Lexington Community College A
Louisville Technical Institute A
Madisonville Community College A
Maysville Community College C, A
Murray State University A, B
Paducah Technical College A
RETS Institute of Technology A
Spencerian College: Lexington C, A

Louisiana

Delgado Community College A
Grambling State University B
Grantham University A, B
ITT Technical Institute
   St. Rose A
Louisiana Tech University B
Northwestern State University A, B
Remington College A
Southern University
   Shreveport A
Southern University and Agricultural and
   Mechanical College A, B
University of New Orleans B, M

Maine

University of Maine B
University of Southern Maine B

Maryland

Anne Arundel Community College C, A
Capitol College A, B
Cecil Community College C, A
Chesapeake College C
College of Southern Maryland C, A
Community College of Baltimore County
   Catonsville C, A
   Dundalk C, A
   Essex C, A
Harford Community College C, A
Howard Community College C, A
Montgomery College
   Rockville Campus A
Wor-Wic Community College C, A

Massachusetts

Benjamin Franklin Institute of
   Technology C, A
Berkshire Community College A
Bunker Hill Community College C, A
ITT Technical Institute
   Norwood A
   Woburn A
Massachusetts Bay Community
   College C, A
Massasoit Community College C, A
Mount Wachusett Community
   College C, A
Northeastern University A, B
Quinsigamond Community College A
Springfield Technical Community
   College C, A
University of Massachusetts
   Dartmouth B
   Lowell A, B
Wentworth Institute of Technology A, B

Michigan

Andrews University A
Baker College
   of Muskegon A
   of Owosso A
   of Port Huron C
Bay de Noc Community College C, A
Central Michigan University B
Davenport University
   Midland C, A
Ferris State University A, B
Glen Oaks Community College C
Grand Rapids Community College A
ITT Technical Institute
   Grand Rapids A
   Troy A
Jackson Community College C, A
Kellogg Community College C, A
Lansing Community College A
Lawrence Technological University A
Macomb Community College C, A
Michigan Technological University A, B
Monroe County Community College A
Montcalm Community College C, A
Mott Community College A
Muskegon Community College C, A
Northern Michigan University A, B
Northwestern Michigan College C, A
Oakland Community College C, A
St. Clair County Community
   College C, A
Schoolcraft College A
Southwestern Michigan College C, A
Washtenaw Community College A
Wayne County Community College C
Wayne State University B
West Shore Community College A

Minnesota

Anoka-Ramsey Community College A
Dakota County Technical College A
Hennepin Technical College C, A
Lake Superior College: A Community
   and Technical College C, A

Minnesota State College - Southeast
Technical *C, A*
Minnesota State University
Mankato *B*
North Hennepin Community College *A*
Ridgewater College: A Community and
Technical College *C, A*
Riverland Community College: A
Technical and Community College *A*
Rochester Community and Technical
College *C, A*
St. Cloud Technical College *C, A*
St. Paul College - A Community and
Technical College *C, A*
South Central Technical College *A*

Mississippi

Coahoma Community College *A*
Itawamba Community College *A*
Mississippi Gulf Coast Community
College
Perkinston *A*
Northwest Mississippi Community
College *A*
Pearl River Community College *C, A*
University of Southern Mississippi *B*

Missouri

Central Missouri State University *A, B*
Crowder College *C, A*
DeVry University
Kansas City *A, B*
East Central College *A*
ITT Technical Institute
Arnold *A*
Earth City *A, B*
Jefferson College *C, A*
Longview Community College *A*
Maple Woods Community College *C, A*
Mineral Area College *C, A*
Missouri Technical School *C, A*
Missouri Western State College *A, B*
Moberly Area Community College *C, A*
North Central Missouri College *A*
Ozarks Technical Community
College *C, A*
Penn Valley Community College *C, A*
Ranken Technical College *A*
St. Charles Community College *A*
St. Louis Community College
St. Louis Community College at
Florissant Valley *A*
St. Louis Community College at
Forest Park *A*
St. Louis Community College at
Meramec *A*
Southeast Missouri State University *C, B*
Southwest Missouri State University *B*

Montana

University of Montana-Missoula *A*

Nebraska

Central Community College *C, A*
ITT Technical Institute
Omaha *A*
Metropolitan Community College *C, A*
Mid Plains Community College
Area *C, A*
Northeast Community College *A*
Southeast Community College
Lincoln Campus *A*
University of Nebraska
Omaha *B*
Western Nebraska Community
College *C, A*

Nevada

Community College of Southern
Nevada *A*
Great Basin College *C*
ITT Technical Institute
Henderson *A*
Western Nevada Community
College *C, A*

New Hampshire

New Hampshire Community Technical
College
Manchester *A*
Nashua *A*
New Hampshire Technical Institute *C, A*
University of New Hampshire *B*
University of New Hampshire at
Manchester *B*

New Jersey

Bergen Community College *A*
Brookdale Community College *C, A*
Burlington County College *A*
Camden County College *A*
County College of Morris *A*
Cumberland County College *C, A*
DeVry College of Technology *A, B*
Essex County College *A*
Fairleigh Dickinson University
Metropolitan Campus *B*
Hudson County Community
College *C, A*
Mercer County Community College *C, A*
Middlesex County College *A*
Passaic County Community College *A*
Thomas Edison State College *A, B*

New Mexico

Albuquerque Technical-Vocational
Institute *C, A*
Dona Ana Branch Community College of
New Mexico State University *C, A*
ITT Technical Institute
Albuquerque *A, B*
New Mexico State University
Alamogordo *A*
San Juan College *A*
Santa Fe Community College *C, A*
Southwestern Indian Polytechnic
Institute *A*

New York

Adirondack Community College *A*
Briarcliffe College *C, A*
Broome Community College *A*
Cayuga County Community
College *C, A*
City University of New York
Bronx Community College *A*
College of Staten Island *A*
Queensborough Community
College *A*
Clinton Community College *A*
College of Aeronautics *A, B*
Corning Community College *A*
DeVry Institute of Technology
New York *A, B*
Dutchess Community College *A*
Erie Community College
North Campus *A*
Excelsior College *A, B*
Fulton-Montgomery Community
College *A*
Genesee Community College *A*
Hudson Valley Community College *A*
ITT Technical Institute
Albany *A*
Getzville *A*
Liverpool *A*
Island Drafting and Technical
Institute *C, A*
Jamestown Community College *A*
Mohawk Valley Community College *A*
Monroe Community College *C, A*
Nassau Community College *A*
New York Institute of
Technology *C, A, B*
Niagara County Community College *A*
Onondaga Community College *A*
Orange County Community College *A*
Rochester Institute of
Technology *A, B, M*
Rockland Community College *A*

State University of New York
College at Buffalo *B*
College of Agriculture and
Technology at Morrisville *A*
College of Technology at
Alfred *A, B*
College of Technology at Canton *A*
Farmingdale *C, A, B*
Institute of Technology at
Utica/Rome *B*
Suffolk County Community College *A*
Tompkins-Cortland Community
College *A*
Westchester Community College *A*

North Carolina

Asheville Buncombe Technical
Community College *A*
Beaufort County Community
College *C, A*
Bladen Community College *C, A*
Blue Ridge Community College *C, A*
Brunswick Community College *A*
Caldwell Community College and
Technical Institute *A*
Cape Fear Community College *C, A*
Catawba Valley Community College *A*
Central Carolina Community College *A*
Central Piedmont Community College *A*
Cleveland Community College *C, A*
College of the Albemarle *C, A*
Craven Community College *C, A*
Davidson County Community College *C*
Durham Technical Community
College *C, A*
East Carolina University *B*
Edgecombe Community College *C, A*
Fayetteville Technical Community
College *C, A*
Forsyth Technical Community College *A*
Guilford Technical Community
College *C, A*
Halifax Community College *A*
Haywood Community College *A*
Isothermal Community College *C, A*
James Sprunt Community College *C*
Johnston Community College *A*
Lenoir Community College *A*
Mitchell Community College *C, A*
Nash Community College *A*
Pamlico Community College *C, A*
Pitt Community College *A*
Randolph Community College *A*
Richmond Community College *A*
Rowan-Cabarrus Community College *A*
South Piedmont Community College *A*
Southeastern Community College *A*
Southwestern Community College *A*
Stanly Community College *A*
Surry Community College *C*
University of North Carolina
Charlotte *B*
Vance-Granville Community
College *C, A*
Wake Technical Community
College *C, A*
Western Carolina University *B*
Wilkes Community College *C, A*
Wilson Technical Community
College *C, A*

North Dakota

Bismarck State College *C, A*
North Dakota State College of Science *A*

Ohio

Bowling Green State University *B*
Bowling Green State University:
Firelands College *A*
Bryant & Stratton College *A, B*
Central Ohio Technical College *A*
Cincinnati State Technical and
Community College *A*
Clark State Community College *C*
Cleveland Institute of Electronics *C, A*
Cleveland State University *B*

Columbus State Community College *A*
Cuyahoga Community College
Eastern Campus *A*
Metropolitan Campus *A*
DeVry University
Columbus *A, B*
ETI Technical College of Niles *A*
Edison State Community College *A*
Hocking Technical College *A*
ITT Technical Institute
Dayton *A*
Norwood *A*
Strongsville *A*
Youngstown *A*
James A. Rhodes State College *A*
Jefferson Community College *A*
Kent State University *A, B*
Kent State University
Ashtabula Regional Campus *A*
Trumbull Campus *A*
Tuscarawas Campus *A, B*
Lakeland Community College *C, A*
Miami University
Hamilton Campus *A*
Middletown Campus *C, A, B*
Oxford Campus *A*
Muskingum Area Technical College *A*
North Central State College *A*
Northwest State Community
College *C, A*
Ohio University *A*
Owens Community College
Findlay Campus *A*
Toledo *A*
Shawnee State University *A, B*
Sinclair Community College *A*
Southern State Community College *A*
Stark State College of Technology *A*
University of Akron *C, A, B*
University of Cincinnati
Clermont College *A*
University of Dayton *B*
University of Toledo *B*
Washington State Community College *A*
Youngstown State University *A, B*

Oklahoma

Cameron University *A*
Northeastern Oklahoma Agricultural and
Mechanical College *C, A*
Oklahoma City Community College *A*
Oklahoma State University *B*
Oklahoma State University
Oklahoma City *C*
Okmulgee *A*
Redlands Community College *C, A*
Rogers State University *A*
Rose State College *C, A*
Southeastern Oklahoma State
University *B*
Tulsa Community College *C, A*

Oregon

Blue Mountain Community College *A*
Central Oregon Community College *C*
Chemeketa Community College *A*
Clackamas Community College *C, A*
ITT Technical Institute
Portland *A*
Lane Community College *A*
Linn-Benton Community College *A*
Oregon Institute of Technology *A, B*
Portland Community College *A*
Rogue Community College *C, A*

Pennsylvania

Butler County Community College *C, A*
CHI Institute *C, A*
California University of
Pennsylvania *A, B*
Community College of Allegheny
County *C, A*
Community College of Beaver County *A*
Community College of Philadelphia *C, A*
DeVry University
Ft. Washington *A, B*

Delaware County Community
College *C, A*
Education Direct: Center for Degree
Studies *A*
Electronic Institutes: Middletown *A*
Harrisburg Area Community
College *C, A*
ITT Technical Institute
Bensalem *A*
Mechanicsburg *A*
Monroeville *A*
Pittsburgh *A*
Lehigh Carbon Community College *C, A*
Luzerne County Community
College *C, A*
Montgomery County Community
College *C, A*
New Castle School of Trades *A*
Northampton County Area Community
College *C, A*
Penn State
Altoona *A*
Beaver *A*
Berks *A*
Dubois *A*
Erie, The Behrend College *A, B*
Fayette *A*
Harrisburg *B*
Hazleton *A*
New Kensington *A*
Schuylkill - Capital College *A*
University Park *C, B*
Wilkes-Barre *A*
York *A, B*
Pennsylvania College of
Technology *A, B*
Pennsylvania Institute of Technology *A*
Pittsburgh Institute of Aeronautics *A*
Pittsburgh Technical Institute: Boyd
School Division *A*
Point Park College *A, B*
Reading Area Community College *A*
South Hills School of Business &
Technology *A*
Temple University *A*
University of Pittsburgh
Johnstown *B*
Westmoreland County Community
College *A*

Puerto Rico

Humacao Community College *A*
Inter American University of Puerto Rico
Bayamon Campus *B*
San German Campus *B*
Technological College of San Juan *A*
University of Puerto Rico
Bayamon University College *A*
Humacao *A*

Rhode Island

Community College of Rhode
Island *C, A*

South Carolina

Aiken Technical College *A*
Florence-Darlington Technical College *A*
Francis Marion University *B*
ITT Technical Institute
Greenville *A*
Midlands Technical College *C, A*
Northeastern Technical College *C, A*
Orangeburg-Calhoun Technical
College *A*
Piedmont Technical College *A*
South Carolina State University *B*
Spartanburg Technical College *A*
Technical College of the Lowcountry *C*
Tri-County Technical College *A*
Trident Technical College *A*
York Technical College *A*

South Dakota

South Dakota State University *B*
Southeast Technical Institute *A*

Tennessee

Columbia State Community College *A*
Dyersburg State Community College *A*
ITT Technical Institute
Knoxville *A, B*
Memphis *A*
Nashville *A, B*
Northeast State Technical Community
College *C, A*
Pellissippi State Technical Community
College *A*
Remington College
Southeast College of Technology *A*
Southwest Tennessee Community
College *A*
University of Memphis *B*

Texas

Amarillo College *C, A*
Angelina College *C, A*
Austin Community College *C, A*
Brazosport College *C, A*
Brookhaven College *A*
College of the Mainland *A*
Collin County Community College
District *C, A*
DeVry University
Irving *A, B*
Del Mar College *A*
Eastfield College *C, A*
El Paso Community College *C, A*
Grayson County College *A*
Hill College *C, A*
Houston Community College System *A*
ITT Technical Institute
Arlington *A*
Austin *A*
Houston *A*
Houston North *A*
Houston South *A*
San Antonio *A*
Kilgore College *C, A*
Lamar State College at Port Arthur *C, A*
LeTourneau University *B*
Lee College *A*
Midland College *C, A*
Mountain View College *A*
North Central Texas College *A*
North Harris Montgomery Community
College District *A*
North Lake College *A*
Paris Junior College *A*
Prairie View A&M University *B*
Richland College *A*
St. Philip's College *A*
Sam Houston State University *B*
San Antonio College *C, A*
San Jacinto College
Central Campus *C*
Tarrant County College *C, A*
Texarkana College *C, A*
Texas A&M University *B*
Texas Southern University *B*
Texas State Technical College
Waco *C, A*
West Texas *C, A*
Texas Tech University *B*
Tyler Junior College *A*
University of Houston *B, M*
University of Houston
Downtown *B*
University of North Texas *A*
Victoria College *A*
Wharton County Junior College *A*

Utah

ITT Technical Institute
Murray *A, B*
Salt Lake Community College *A*
Snow College *A*
Utah State University *B*
Utah Valley State College *A, B*
Weber State University *A, B*

Vermont

Vermont Technical College *A*

Virginia

Blue Ridge Community College *A*
Danville Community College *C*
DeVry University
Crystal City *A, B*
ECPI College of Technology *C, A*
ECPI Technical College: Roanoke *A*
ITT Technical Institute
Norfolk *A*
Richmond *A*
J. Sargeant Reynolds Community
College *C, A*
Mountain Empire Community College *A*
Norfolk State University *B*
Paul D. Camp Community College *A*
Piedmont Virginia Community
College *A*
Rappahannock Community College *C, A*
Southside Virginia Community
College *C, A*
Thomas Nelson Community College *A*
Virginia Highlands Community
College *A*
Virginia Western Community
College *C, A*

Washington

Central Washington University *B*
Centralia College *A*
Clark College *A*
DeVry University
Seattle *A, B*
Eastern Washington University *B*
Edmonds Community College *C, A*
Green River Community College *A*
ITT Technical Institute
Bothell *A*
Seattle *A, B*
Spokane *A*
Lake Washington Technical College *C, A*
Lower Columbia College *A*
North Seattle Community College *C, A*
Olympic College *C, A*
Peninsula College *A*
Renton Technical College *C, A*
Spokane Community College *C, A*
Spokane Falls Community College *C, A*
Western Washington University *B*

West Virginia

Bluefield State College *A, B*
Corinthian Schools: National Institute of
Technology *A*
Fairmont State College *A, B*
Mountain State University *A*
Potomac State College of West Virginia
University *A*
Shepherd College *A*
West Virginia Northern Community
College *A*
West Virginia State College *A*
West Virginia University Institute of
Technology *A, B*
West Virginia University at
Parkersburg *A*

Wisconsin

Chippewa Valley Technical College *A*
Fox Valley Technical College *A*
Herzing College *A*
ITT Technical Institute
Green Bay *A, B*
Greenfield *A, B*
Lakeshore Technical College *A*
Mid-State Technical College *C, A*
Milwaukee Area Technical College *A*
Milwaukee School of Engineering *B*
Moraine Park Technical College *C*
Western Wisconsin Technical College *A*
Wisconsin Indianhead Technical
College *A*

Wyoming

Casper College *A*

Alabama

Alabama Southern Community
College *A*
Auburn University *B, M, D*
Lawson State Community College *A*
Northwest-Shoals Community
College *C, A*
Remington College
Southeast College of Technology *A*
Tuskegee University *B, M*
University of Alabama *B, M, D*
University of Alabama
Birmingham *B, M, D*
Huntsville *B, M, D*
University of South Alabama *B, M*
Wallace State Community College at
Hanceville *A*

Alaska

University of Alaska
Anchorage *B*
Fairbanks *B, M*

Arizona

Arizona State University *B, M, D*
Embry-Riddle Aeronautical University:
Prescott Campus *B*
High-Tech Institute *A*
Northern Arizona University *B*
University of Arizona *B, M, D*

Arkansas

Arkansas State University
Mountain Home *C, A*
Arkansas Tech University *B*
John Brown University *B*
University of Arkansas *B, M*
University of Arkansas
Fort Smith *B*

California

California Institute of
Technology *B, M, D*
California Polytechnic State University:
San Luis Obispo *B, M*
California State Polytechnic University:
Pomona *B, M*
California State University
Chico *B, M*
Fresno *B, M*
Fullerton *B, M*
Long Beach *B, M*
Los Angeles *B, M*
Northridge *B, M*
Sacramento *B, M*
Cogswell Polytechnical College *B*
College of the Redwoods *A*
Cuesta College *C, A*
De Anza College *A*
East Los Angeles College *A*
Los Angeles Harbor College *C, A*
Los Angeles Southwest College *C, A*
Loyola Marymount University *B, M*
Modesto Junior College *A*
Northwestern Polytechnic
University *B, M*
San Diego State University *B, M*
San Francisco State University *B*
San Jose State University *B, M*
Santa Clara University *C, B, M, D*
Santa Rosa Junior College *C*
Stanford University *B, M, D*
University of California
Berkeley *B, M, D*
Davis *B*
Irvine *B, M, D*
Los Angeles *B, M, D*
Riverside *B, M, D*
San Diego *B, M, D*
Santa Barbara *B, M, D*
Santa Cruz *B*
University of San Diego *B*

University of Southern
California *B, M, D*
University of the Pacific *B*

Colorado

Colorado State University *B, M, D*
Colorado Technical University *B, M*
IntelliTec College, Grand Junction *A*
National Technological University *M*
United States Air Force Academy *B*
University of Colorado
Boulder *B, M, D*
Colorado Springs *B, M, D*
Denver *B, M*
University of Denver *B, M*

Connecticut

Capital Community College *A*
Fairfield University *B*
Trinity College *B*
United States Coast Guard Academy *B*
University of Bridgeport *M*
University of Connecticut *B, M, D*
University of Hartford *B, M*
University of New Haven *A, B, M*
Yale University *B, M, D*

Delaware

University of Delaware *B, M, D*

District of Columbia

Catholic University of America *B, M, D*
George Washington University *B, M, D*
Howard University *B, M, D*
University of the District of Columbia *B*

Florida

Broward Community College *A*
Florida Agricultural and Mechanical
University *B, M, D*
Florida Atlantic University *B, M, D*
Florida Institute of Technology *B, M, D*
Florida International University *B, M, D*
Florida State University *B, M, D*
Florida Technical College *A*
Gulf Coast Community College *A*
Hillsborough Community College *C, A*
Jacksonville University *B*
Miami-Dade Community College *A*
Okaloosa-Walton Community College *A*
Palm Beach Community College *A*
Pensacola Junior College *A*
Polk Community College *A*
Seminole Community College *C, A*
South Florida Community College *C, A*
University of Central Florida *C, B, M, D*
University of Florida *B, M, D*
University of Miami *B, M, D*
University of North Florida *B*
University of South Florida *B, M, D*
University of West Florida *B*

Georgia

DeKalb Technical College *A*
Georgia Institute of Technology *B, M, D*
Mercer University *B, M*
Middle Georgia College *A*

Hawaii

University of Hawaii
Manoa *B, M, D*

Idaho

Boise State University *B*
Brigham Young University - Idaho *A*
College of Southern Idaho *A*
North Idaho College *A*
University of Idaho *B, M, D*

Illinois

Bradley University *B, M*
City Colleges of Chicago
Kennedy-King College *C*
Olive-Harvey College *C, A*
Dominican University *B*
Illinois Central College *A*
Illinois Institute of Technology *B, M, D*
Joliet Junior College *C, A*
Northern Illinois University *B, M*

Northwestern University *B, M, D*
Parkland College *A*
Sauk Valley Community College *C, A*
Southern Illinois University
Carbondale *B, M*
Southern Illinois University
Edwardsville *B, M*
University of Illinois
Chicago *B, M, D*
Urbana-Champaign *B, M, D*

Indiana

Indiana Institute of Technology *B*
Indiana University-Purdue University
Fort Wayne *B*
Indiana University-Purdue University
Indianapolis *B, M*
Purdue University *B, M, D*
Purdue University
Calumet *B*
Rose-Hulman Institute of
Technology *B, M*
Tri-State University *B*
University of Evansville *B*
University of Notre Dame *B, M, D*
Valparaiso University *B*
Vincennes University *A*

Iowa

Dordt College *B*
Iowa State University *B, M, D*
Maharishi University of
Management *B, M*
Northeast Iowa Community College *A*
Southeastern Community College
North Campus *A*
University of Iowa *B, M, D*

Kansas

Allen County Community College *C, A*
Kansas State University *B, M, D*
University of Kansas *B, M, D*
Wichita State University *B, M, D*

Kentucky

Jefferson Community College *A*
Lexington Community College *A*
Murray State University *B*
Paducah Technical College *A*
Spencerian College: Lexington *C, A*
University of Kentucky *B, M, D*
University of Louisville *B, M*

Louisiana

Grantham University *A, B*
Louisiana State University and
Agricultural and Mechanical
College *B, M, D*
Louisiana Tech University *B*
Southern University and Agricultural and
Mechanical College *B*
Tulane University *B, M, D*
University of Louisiana at Lafayette *B*
University of New Orleans *B*

Maine

University of Maine *B, M*
University of Southern Maine *B*

Maryland

Capitol College *A, B*
College of Southern Maryland *A*
Johns Hopkins University *B, M, D*
Loyola College in Maryland *B, M*
Morgan State University *B*
United States Naval Academy *B*
University of Maryland
Baltimore County *M, D*
College Park *B, M, D*

Massachusetts

Berkshire Community College *A*
Boston University *B, M, D*
Fitchburg State College *B*
Franklin W. Olin College of
Engineering *B*
Massachusetts Institute of
Technology *B, M, D*

Merrimack College *B*
Northeastern University *B, M, D*
Smith College *B*
Suffolk University *B*
Tufts University *B, M, D*
University of Massachusetts
Amherst *B*
Dartmouth *B, M, D*
Lowell *B, M, D*
Wentworth Institute of Technology *B*
Western New England College *B, M*
Worcester Polytechnic Institute *B, M, D*

Michigan

Baker College
of Muskegon *A*
Calvin College *B*
Grand Valley State University *B*
Kettering University *B*
Lawrence Technological University *B*
Michigan State University *B, M, D*
Michigan Technological
University *B, M, D, T*
Monroe County Community College *A*
Oakland University *B, M*
Saginaw Valley State University *B*
University of Michigan *B, M, D*
University of Michigan
Dearborn *B, M*
Wayne State University *B, M, D*
Western Michigan University *B, M*

Minnesota

Minnesota State University
Mankato *B, M*
Northland Community & Technical
College *A*
St. Cloud State University *B*
South Central Technical College *A*
University of Minnesota
Duluth *B*
Twin Cities *C, B, M, D*
University of St. Thomas *B*

Mississippi

Holmes Community College *A*
Itawamba Community College *A*
Mississippi State University *B, M, D*
University of Mississippi *B*

Missouri

East Central College *A*
Missouri Technical School *A, B*
Ozarks Technical Community College *A*
St. Louis University *A*
University of Missouri
Columbia *B, M, D*
Kansas City *B, M*
Rolla *B, M, D*
St. Louis *B*
Washington University in St.
Louis *B, M, D*

Montana

Montana State University
Bozeman *B, M*
Montana Tech of the University of
Montana *B*

Nebraska

Southeast Community College
Milford Campus *A*
University of Nebraska
Lincoln *B, M*
Omaha *B*

Nevada

Community College of Southern
Nevada *C, A*
University of Nevada
Las Vegas *B, M, D*
Reno *B, M, D*

New Hampshire

New Hampshire Community Technical
College
Nashua *A*
University of New Hampshire *B, M, D*

New Jersey

The College of New Jersey *B*
Essex County College *A*
Fairleigh Dickinson University
Metropolitan Campus *B, M*
Monmouth University *M*
New Jersey Institute of
Technology *B, M, D*
Ocean County College *C*
Princeton University *B, M, D*
Rowan University *B*
Rutgers, The State University of New
Jersey
Camden Regional Campus *B*
New Brunswick Regional
Campus *B, M, D*
Newark Regional Campus *B*
Stevens Institute of Technology *B, M, D*

New Mexico

Dona Ana Branch Community College of
New Mexico State University *C, A*
Luna Community College *A*
New Mexico Institute of Mining and
Technology *B*
New Mexico State University *B, M*
University of New Mexico *B, M*

New York

Alfred University *B, M*
Cayuga County Community College *A*
City University of New York
City College *B, M, D*
College of Staten Island *A*
Clarkson University *B, M, D*
Columbia University
Fu Foundation School of
Engineering and Applied
Science *B, M, D*
Cornell University *B, M, D*
Dutchess Community College *A*
Finger Lakes Community College *A*
Fulton-Montgomery Community
College *A*
Hofstra University *B*
Island Drafting and Technical
Institute *C, A*
Jamestown Community College *A*
Manhattan College *B, M*
New York Institute of Technology *B, M*
New York University *B*
Onondaga Community College *A*
Polytechnic University *B, M, D*
Rensselaer Polytechnic Institute *B, M, D*
Rochester Institute of Technology *B, M*
State University of New York
Binghamton *B, M, D*
Buffalo *B, M, D*
College of Agriculture and
Technology at Morrisville *A*
Maritime College *B*
New Paltz *B, M*
Stony Brook *B, M, D*
Suffolk County Community College *A*
Syracuse University *B, M, D*
Union College *B, M*
United States Military Academy *B*
University of Rochester *B, M, D*
Utica College *B*

North Carolina

Alamance Community College *A*
Appalachian State University *B*
Blue Ridge Community College *A*
College of the Albemarle *C*
Davidson County Community
College *C, A*
Duke University *B, M, D*
Durham Technical Community
College *C, A*
Guilford Technical Community
College *C, A*
Mayland Community College *A*
Mitchell Community College *C, A*
Nash Community College *A*

North Carolina Agricultural and
Technical State University *B, M, D*
North Carolina State University *B, M, D*
Pamlico Community College *C, A*
Richmond Community College *A*
Rockingham Community College *A*
Southwestern Community College *A*
Surry Community College *A*
University of North Carolina
Charlotte *B, M, D*
Vance-Granville Community
College *C, A*
Western Piedmont Community
College *C, A*

North Dakota

Lake Region State College *C, A*
North Dakota State University *B, M*
University of North Dakota *B, M*

Ohio

Bowling Green State University:
Firelands College *A*
Case Western Reserve
University *B, M, D*
Cedarville University *B*
Cleveland State University *B, M, D*
Columbus State Community College *A*
Edison State Community College *A*
Kent State University *A*
Kent State University
Ashtabula Regional Campus *A*
Trumbull Campus *A*
Lorain County Community College *C, A*
Marion Technical College *A*
Ohio Northern University *B*
Ohio State University
Columbus Campus *B, M, D*
Ohio University *B, M, D*
RETS Tech Center *C, A*
Stark State College of Technology *A*
University of Akron *B, M, D*
University of Cincinnati *B, M, D*
University of Dayton *B, M, D*
University of Toledo *B, M*
Washington State Community College *A*
Wright State University *B, M*
Youngstown State University *B, M*

Oklahoma

Oklahoma Christian University of
Science and Arts *B*
Oklahoma State University *B, M, D*
Oklahoma State University
Oklahoma City *A*
Okmulgee *A*
Oral Roberts University *B*
Rogers State University *A*
University of Oklahoma *B, M, D*
University of Tulsa *B, M*

Oregon

Chemeketa Community College *A*
George Fox University *B*
Oregon State University *B*
Portland State University *B, M, D*
University of Portland *B, M*

Pennsylvania

Bloomsburg University of
Pennsylvania *A, B*
Bucknell University *B, M*
Carnegie Mellon University *B, M, D*
Drexel University *B, M, D*
Gettysburg College *B*
Grove City College *B*
Lafayette College *B*
Lehigh Carbon Community College *A*
Lehigh University *B, M, D*
Lock Haven University of
Pennsylvania *B*

Penn State
Abington *B*
Altoona *B*
Berks *B*
Delaware County *B*
Dubois *B*
Erie, The Behrend College *B*
Harrisburg *B*
McKeesport *B*
Mont Alto *B*
New Kensington *B*
Schuylkill - Capital College *B*
Shenango *B*
University Park *B, M, D*
Wilkes-Barre *B*
Worthington Scranton *B*
York *B*
Pittsburgh Institute of Aeronautics *A*
Pittsburgh Technical Institute: Boyd
School Division *A*
Reading Area Community College *A*
Temple University *B, M*
University of Pennsylvania *B, M, D*
University of Pittsburgh *B, M, D*
University of Scranton *A, B*
Villanova University *B, M*
Widener University *B, M*
Wilkes University *B, M*

Puerto Rico

Columbia College *A*
Inter American University of Puerto Rico
Bayamon Campus *B*
Turabo University *B*
Universidad Politecnica de Puerto
Rico *B*
University of Puerto Rico
Mayaguez Campus *B, M*

Rhode Island

Brown University *B, M, D*
University of Rhode Island *B, M, D*

South Carolina

The Citadel *B*
Clemson University *B, M, D*
Horry-Georgetown Technical College *A*
Technical College of the
Lowcountry *C, A*
University of South Carolina *B, M, D*
Williamsburg Technical College *C, A*
York Technical College *C*

South Dakota

South Dakota School of Mines and
Technology *B, M*
South Dakota State University *B*

Tennessee

Christian Brothers University *B*
Columbia State Community College *C*
Tennessee State University *B*
Tennessee Technological
University *B, M, D*
Union University *B*
University of Memphis *B, M*
University of Tennessee
Knoxville *B, M, D*
Vanderbilt University *B, M, D*

Texas

Abilene Christian University *B*
Baylor University *B*
Del Mar College *A*
Eastfield College *C, A*
Hallmark Institute of Technology *C, A*
Houston Baptist University *B*
Lamar University *B*
Laredo Community College *A*
LeTourneau University *B*
Prairie View A&M University *B*
Remington College
Houston *A*
Rice University *B, M, D*
St. Mary's University *B, M*
Southern Methodist University *B, M, D*
Texas A&M University *B, M, D*

Texas A&M University
Kingsville *B, M*
Texas Tech University *B, M, D*
University of Houston *B, M, D*
University of Texas
Arlington *B, M, D*
Austin *B, M, D*
Dallas *B, M, D*
El Paso *B, M*
Pan American *B, M*
San Antonio *B, M, D*
Tyler *B*

Utah

Brigham Young University *B, M, D*
Salt Lake Community College *A*
Snow College *C, A*
University of Utah *B, M, D*
Utah State University *B, M, D*
Utah Valley State College *A*

Vermont

Norwich University *B*
University of Vermont *B, M, D*
Vermont Technical College *A*

Virginia

ECPI College of Technology *C, A*
ECPI Technical College: Roanoke *A*
George Mason University *B, M, D*
Hampton University *B*
Mountain Empire Community College *A*
Norfolk State University *B*
Old Dominion University *B*
Southwest Virginia Community
College *A*
Thomas Nelson Community College *A*
University of Virginia *B, M, D*
Virginia Commonwealth University *B*
Virginia Military Institute *B*
Virginia Polytechnic Institute and State
University *B, M, D*

Washington

Gonzaga University *B*
Henry Cogswell College *B*
Peninsula College *A*
Renton Technical College *C, A*
Seattle Pacific University *B*
Seattle University *B*
University of Washington *B, M, D*
Walla Walla College *B*
Washington State University *B, M, D*

West Virginia

Mountain State University *A*
Potomac State College of West Virginia
University *A*
West Virginia State College *A*
West Virginia University *B, M, D*
West Virginia University Institute of
Technology *B*

Wisconsin

Blackhawk Technical College *A*
Marquette University *B, M, D*
Milwaukee Area Technical College *A*
Milwaukee School of Engineering *B*
University of Wisconsin
Madison *B, M, D*
Milwaukee *B*
Platteville *B*

Wyoming

University of Wyoming *B, M, D*
Western Wyoming Community
College *C, A*

Electrical/electronics drafting/CAD/CADD

Florida

Miami-Dade Community College *C*
Palm Beach Community College *C*

Illinois

Kaskaskia College *C*

Oakton Community College *C, A*

Massachusetts

ITT Technical Institute
Norwood *A*

Ohio

Lakeland Community College *C, A*

Oklahoma

Platt College
Tulsa *C*

Texas

Collin County Community College
District *C, A*

Washington

ITT Technical Institute
Seattle *A*

Electrician

Alabama

Bishop State Community College *C*
Calhoun Community College *A*
Douglas MacArthur State Technical
College *A*
George C. Wallace State Community
College
Dothan *C, A*
Harry M. Ayers State Technical
College *A*
J. F. Drake State Technical College *C*
Lawson State Community College *C*
Shelton State Community College *C*
Wallace Community College: Sparks
Campus *A*

Arizona

Gateway Community College *C, A*

California

Foothill College *C*
Los Angeles Trade and Technical
College *C, A*
Modesto Junior College *C, A*
Santiago Canyon College *A*

Florida

Gulf Coast Community College *C*
Indian River Community College *C*
Palm Beach Community College *C*
Seminole Community College *C*
South Florida Community College *C*

Georgia

Bainbridge College *C, A*
Chattahoochee Technical College *C*
Southwest Georgia Technical College *C*
West Georgia Technical College *C*

Hawaii

University of Hawaii
Honolulu Community College *C, A*
Kauai Community College *C, A*

Idaho

Idaho State University *C*

Illinois

Black Hawk College *C*
College of Lake County *A*
Danville Area Community College *C*
Heartland Community College *A*
John Wood Community College *C, A*
Prairie State College *C, A*
Rend Lake College *A*
Richland Community College *A*
Sauk Valley Community College *C*
Southwestern Illinois College *C, A*
Waubonsee Community College *C, A*

Indiana
Ivy Tech State College
Central Indiana *C, A*
Eastcentral *C, A*
Kokomo *C, A*
Lafayette *C, A*
Northcentral *C, A*
Northeast *C, A*
Northwest *C, A*
Southcentral *C, A*
Southwest *C, A*
Wabash Valley *C, A*
Oakland City University *C*

Iowa
Iowa Central Community College *A*
Northwest Iowa Community College *A*
Western Iowa Tech Community
College *C*

Kansas
Pittsburg State University *C, A*

Kentucky
Somerset Community College *C*

Louisiana
Nunez Community College *C*

Massachusetts
Benjamin Franklin Institute of
Technology *C, A*

Michigan
Jackson Community College *C, A*
Kellogg Community College *C, A*
Macomb Community College *C*

Minnesota
Dakota County Technical College *C*
Hennepin Technical College *C, A*
Hibbing Community College: A
Technical and Community College *C*
Lake Superior College: A Community
and Technical College *C, A*
Minneapolis Community and Technical
College *C*
Ridgewater College: A Community and
Technical College *C*
Riverland Community College: A
Technical and Community College *C*
St. Cloud Technical College *C, A*
St. Paul College - A Community and
Technical College *C*

Mississippi
Itawamba Community College *A*

Missouri
St. Louis Community College
St. Louis Community College at
Forest Park *A*

Nebraska
Mid Plains Community College Area *C*
Northeast Community College *A*

Nevada
Western Nevada Community College *A*

New Hampshire
New Hampshire Community Technical
College
Laconia *C, A*

New Mexico
Albuquerque Technical-Vocational
Institute *C*
Dona Ana Branch Community College of
New Mexico State University *A*

New York
State University of New York
College of Technology at Canton *C*

North Carolina
Beaufort County Community College *C*
Bladen Community College *C*
Blue Ridge Community College *C*
Cape Fear Community College *C, A*
Cleveland Community College *C*

Coastal Carolina Community College *C*
Guilford Technical Community
College *C, A*
Haywood Community College *C, A*
Isothermal Community College *C, A*
Johnston Community College *C*
Martin Community College *C*
Montgomery Community College *C, A*
Pitt Community College *C, A*
Randolph Community College *C, A*
Rockingham Community College *C*
Southwestern Community College *C*
Tri-County Community College *A*
Vance-Granville Community College *C*
Wilkes Community College *A*
Wilson Technical Community College *C*

North Dakota
North Dakota State College of Science *A*

Oklahoma
Oklahoma State University
Okmulgee *A*

Oregon
Central Oregon Community College *C*
Chemeketa Community College *C*
Lane Community College *A*
Linn-Benton Community College *A*

Pennsylvania
CHI Institute *C*
Community College of Allegheny
County *A*
Delaware County Community College *C*
Luzerne County Community
College *C, A*
Pennsylvania College of
Technology *C, A*

Puerto Rico
Inter American University of Puerto Rico
San German Campus *C*

South Carolina
Technical College of the Lowcountry *C*
Trident Technical College *A*
Williamsburg Technical College *C, A*

South Dakota
Western Dakota Technical Institute *A*

Tennessee
Northeast State Technical Community
College *C, A*

Texas
Brazosport College *C, A*
Houston Community College System *C*
Laredo Community College *C*
St. Philip's College *C, A*
South Plains College *C*
Texas State Technical College
Waco *C*
Tyler Junior College *C, A*

Utah
Dixie State College of Utah *C*
Salt Lake Community College *C, A*
Southern Utah University *C*
Utah Valley State College *A*

Virginia
J. Sargeant Reynolds Community
College *C*
Paul D. Camp Community College *C*
Rappahannock Community College *C*
Southside Virginia Community
College *C*
Thomas Nelson Community College *C*
Virginia Highlands Community
College *C*

Washington
South Seattle Community College *C, A*

Wisconsin
Western Wisconsin Technical College *C*

Electrocardiograph technology

California
De Anza College *C*
East Los Angeles College *A*

Michigan
Baker College
of Auburn Hills *A*
of Muskegon *C*
of Port Huron *C*
Monroe County Community College *C*

Minnesota
North Hennepin Community College *A*

New York
Niagara County Community College *A*

Ohio
Cincinnati State Technical and
Community College *C*
Columbus State Community College *C*
Cuyahoga Community College
Eastern Campus *A*
Lakeland Community College *C*
Sinclair Community College *C*
University of Toledo *C*

South Carolina
Tri-County Technical College *C*

Texas
Austin Community College *C, A*

Virginia
Southwest Virginia Community
College *C*

Electroencephalograph technology

Arizona
Phoenix College *C*

California
Orange Coast College *C, A*

Illinois
Black Hawk College *A*

Iowa
Kirkwood Community College *A*

Maryland
Harford Community College *A*

North Carolina
Southwestern Community College *A*

Pennsylvania
Community College of Allegheny
County *C*

Wisconsin
Western Wisconsin Technical College *A*

Electrolysis

New Jersey
Union County College *C*

Electromechanical technology

California
Ohlone College *A*

Illinois
Black Hawk College *C, A*

Kentucky
Hopkinsville Community College *C*
Maysville Community College *C, A*

Maryland
Hagerstown Community College *C, A*

Massachusetts
ITT Technical Institute
Norwood *B*
Quinsigamond Community College *A*
Wentworth Institute of Technology *A*

Michigan
Michigan Technological University *A*
Northern Michigan University *A*
Oakland Community College *C, A*
Wayne State University *B*

Nebraska
Mid Plains Community College Area *A*

New Jersey
Union County College *A*

New Mexico
Albuquerque Technical-Vocational
Institute *C, A*

New York
Rochester Institute of Technology *B*

North Carolina
Cape Fear Community College *C*
Isothermal Community College *C, A*
Wilkes Community College *C, A*
Wilson Technical Community College *C*

Ohio
Central Ohio Technical College *A*
Sinclair Community College *A*
University of Akron *B*
University of Toledo *B*

Pennsylvania
Montgomery County Community
College *A*
Northampton County Area Community
College *A*
Penn State
University Park *C*
Pennsylvania College of Technology *A*

South Dakota
Southeast Technical Institute *A*

Tennessee
Cleveland State Community College *C*

Texas
Angelina College *C, A*

Virginia
Rappahannock Community College *C, A*

Wisconsin
Western Wisconsin Technical College *A*

Electronic commerce

Alabama
University of South Alabama *B*

California
Dominican University of California *B*
Foothill College *C*
National University *C, M*
University of San Francisco *M*
Westwood College of Technology
Inland Empire *B*

Colorado
Colorado Technical University *C, A, B*
Jones International University *C, B, M*
Red Rocks Community College *C*

District of Columbia
American University *B, M*

Georgia
Brenau University *B*

Illinois
International Academy of Design and
Technology *A*

Lewis University *C*
Moraine Valley Community College *C*

Indiana
Huntington College *B*
St. Mary-of-the-Woods College *B*

Iowa
North Iowa Area Community College *A*

Maryland
Howard Community College *C*

Massachusetts
Lesley University *B*
Nichols College *B*

Michigan
Cleary University *B*

Minnesota
Capella University *C, B*

Missouri
Maryville University of Saint Louis *B, M*

Nebraska
Bellevue University *B*
Creighton University *M*

New Hampshire
Hesser College *C, A*

New Jersey
Stevens Institute of Technology *B, M*

New York
State University of New York
  Buffalo *M*
Westchester Business Institute *A*
Westchester Community College *C*

North Carolina
Carteret Community College *C, A*
Cleveland Community College *A*
Fayetteville Technical Community
  College *A*
Lenoir Community College *A*
Sandhills Community College *A*

Ohio
Lakeland Community College *C, A*
Washington State Community College *A*

Oklahoma
Northwestern Oklahoma State
  University *B*

Oregon
Portland Community College *C*

Pennsylvania
Bucks County Community College *C*
Carnegie Mellon University *M*
Central Pennsylvania College *B*
DeSales University *B*
Holy Family University *B*
La Salle University *C*
Marywood University *C, M*
Messiah College *B*
Philadelphia University *B*
Wilkes University *B*

Rhode Island
Bryant College *M*

South Carolina
Southern Wesleyan University *B*

Tennessee
Pellissippi State Technical Community
  College *A*
University of Memphis *M*

Texas
Kilgore College *C, A*

Utah
LDS Business College *C*

Vermont
Castleton State College *B*
Champlain College *A, B*

Wyoming
University of Wyoming *M*

**Electronics/electrical
equipment repair**

Alabama
Alabama Southern Community
  College *C, A*
Bevill State Community College *A*
Bishop State Community College *A*
Community College of the Air Force *A*
George C. Wallace State Community
  College
    Dothan *C, A*
Harry M. Ayers State Technical
  College *C, A*
J. F. Drake State Technical College *C, A*
Northwest-Shoals Community College *C*
Reid State Technical College *A*
Wallace State Community College at
  Hanceville *C, A*

Alaska
University of Alaska
  Anchorage *C, A*

Arizona
Gateway Community College *A*
Pima Community College *C, A*

Arkansas
North Arkansas College *C*
Pulaski Technical College *C, A*
South Arkansas Community College *C*
Southeast Arkansas College *C, A*
University of Arkansas
    Community College at Batesville *A*
    Fort Smith *C, A*

California
Antelope Valley College *C, A*
Cerritos Community College *A*
Chabot College *A*
Citrus College *C, A*
Coastline Community College *C, A*
College of the Canyons *C, A*
College of the Redwoods *C*
College of the Sequoias *C, A*
East Los Angeles College *C*
Las Positas College *C, A*
Long Beach City College *C, A*
Los Angeles Harbor College *C, A*
Los Angeles Trade and Technical
  College *C, A*
Los Medanos College *C, A*
Modesto Junior College *C, A*
Mount San Antonio College *C, A*
Ohlone College *C, A*
Orange Coast College *C, A*
Palomar College *C, A*
Santa Barbara City College *C, A*
Sierra College *C, A*
Southwestern College *C, A*
Victor Valley College *C, A*
Yuba Community College District *C, A*

Colorado
Arapahoe Community College *C*
IntelliTec College *A*
Red Rocks Community College *C, A*

Connecticut
Gateway Community College *C*

Florida
Chipola Junior College *C*
Florida Technical College
    Deland *C*
Indian River Community College *C*
New England Institute of Technology *A*
Seminole Community College *C*

Georgia
Athens Technical College *C*
Chattahoochee Technical College *C*

Clayton College and State
  University *C, A*
Coastal Georgia Community
  College *C, A*
Dalton State College *C, A*
Darton College *A*
DeKalb Technical College *C*
Georgia Southwestern State University *A*
Macon State College *A*
Middle Georgia College *A*
Southwest Georgia Technical College *C*
Waycross College *A*
West Georgia Technical College *A*

Hawaii
University of Hawaii
    Hawaii Community College *A*
    Honolulu Community College *A*

Idaho
Boise State University *C, A*
College of Southern Idaho *C*
Idaho State University *C*
Lewis-Clark State College *C, A, B*

Illinois
City Colleges of Chicago
    Wright College *C, A*
College of DuPage *C, A*
College of Lake County *C, A*
Danville Area Community College *A*
Elgin Community College *C*
Heartland Community College *C*
Illinois Eastern Community Colleges
    Frontier Community College *C*
    Lincoln Trail College *C, A*
    Olney Central College *C*
    Wabash Valley College *C*
John A. Logan College *C, A*
John Wood Community College *A*
Joliet Junior College *C*
Kankakee Community College *C, A*
Lincoln Land Community College *C, A*
Prairie State College *C*
Richland Community College *A*
Sauk Valley Community College *C*
Southwestern Illinois College *C, A*
Spoon River College *A*
Triton College *C, A*
Waubonsee Community College *C*
William Rainey Harper College *C, A*

Indiana
Vincennes University *A*

Iowa
Des Moines Area Community College *A*
Hawkeye Community College *A*
Indian Hills Community College *C, A*
Kirkwood Community College *C, A*
Northeast Iowa Community College *A*
Southwestern Community College *C, A*

Kansas
Allen County Community College *A*
Butler County Community College *A*
Dodge City Community College *C, A*
Hutchinson Community College *A*
Johnson County Community
  College *C, A*
North Central Kansas Technical
  College *A*
Pittsburg State University *C, A*

Kentucky
Spencerian College: Lexington *C, A*

Louisiana
Delgado Community College *A*
ITI Technical College *C*
Nunez Community College *C, A*

Maine
Central Maine Technical College *A*

Maryland
Anne Arundel Community College *C, A*
Howard Community College *C, A*

Montgomery College
    Rockville Campus *A*

Massachusetts
Benjamin Franklin Institute of
  Technology *C*
Quinsigamond Community College *C, A*

Michigan
Baker College
    of Cadillac *A*
Bay de Noc Community College *C*
Glen Oaks Community College *C*
Grand Rapids Community College *C, A*
Jackson Community College *C, A*
Lansing Community College *A*
Macomb Community College *C, A*
Montcalm Community College *C, A*
Northern Michigan University *A*
Northwestern Michigan College *A*
Schoolcraft College *C*
Washtenaw Community College *A*

Minnesota
Alexandria Technical College *C, A*
Hennepin Technical College *C, A*
Lake Superior College: A Community
  and Technical College *C, A*
Minnesota State College - Southeast
  Technical *C, A*
Northland Community & Technical
  College *C, A*
Riverland Community College: A
  Technical and Community College *C*
St. Cloud Technical College *C, A*
St. Paul College - A Community and
  Technical College *C*
South Central Technical College *A*

Mississippi
Itawamba Community College *A*
Mississippi Gulf Coast Community
  College
    Perkinston *A*
Pearl River Community College *C*

Missouri
East Central College *C, A*
North Central Missouri College *A*
Ranken Technical College *A*
St. Charles Community College *A*
Vatterott College: Sunset Hills *A*

Montana
Miles Community College *C, A*

Nebraska
Metropolitan Community College *C*
Mid Plains Community College
    Area *C, A*
Northeast Community College *A*
Southeast Community College
    Milford Campus *A*

New Hampshire
New Hampshire Community Technical
  College
    Manchester *A*
    Nashua *A*

New Jersey
Raritan Valley Community College *A*
Thomas Edison State College *C, A*

New Mexico
Clovis Community College *C, A*
Dona Ana Branch Community College of
  New Mexico State University *C, A*
Eastern New Mexico University: Roswell
  Campus *C, A*
Western New Mexico University *A*

New York
College of Aeronautics *A, B*
Hudson Valley Community College *A*
Island Drafting and Technical
  Institute *C, A*
Mohawk Valley Community College *A*

State University of New York
  College of Agriculture and
    Technology at Morrisville *A*
  College of Technology at Alfred *A*
  College of Technology at Canton *C*

North Carolina
Alamance Community College *A*
Asheville Buncombe Technical
  Community College *C*
Bladen Community College *C, A*
Catawba Valley Community College *C*
Central Piedmont Community College *A*
Coastal Carolina Community
  College *C, A*
College of the Albemarle *C*
Davidson County Community
  College *C, A*
Durham Technical Community
  College *C, A*
Fayetteville Technical Community
  College *C, A*
Forsyth Technical Community College *C*
Gaston College *C*
Guilford Technical Community
  College *C, A*
Johnston Community College *C*
Lenoir Community College *C, A*
Piedmont Community College *C, A*
Pitt Community College *C, A*
Richmond Community College *C*
Rockingham Community College *A*
South Piedmont Community College *C*
Surry Community College *A*
Tri-County Community College *A*
Vance-Granville Community
  College *C, A*
Wake Technical Community
  College *C, A*
Wilson Technical Community
  College *C, A*

North Dakota
Bismarck State College *A*
Lake Region State College *A*
North Dakota State College of
  Science *C, A*

Ohio
Cleveland Institute of Electronics *C, A*
Columbus State Community College *A*
Edison State Community College *A*
Jefferson Community College *A*
North Central State College *A*
Ohio University *A*
Owens Community College
  Findlay Campus *C, A*
  Toledo *A*
Stark State College of Technology *A*

Oklahoma
Oklahoma State University
  Oklahoma City *C*
Rogers State University *A*
Tulsa Community College *A*
Western Oklahoma State College *A*

Oregon
Central Oregon Community
  College *C, A*
Clackamas Community College *C, A*
Lane Community College *A*
Linn-Benton Community College *A*
Mount Hood Community College *A*
Rogue Community College *A*
Southwestern Oregon Community
  College *A*

Pennsylvania
Community College of Allegheny
  County *A*
Lehigh Carbon Community College *A*
Luzerne County Community College *C*
Pittsburgh Institute of Aeronautics *A*

Puerto Rico
Huertas Junior College *C, A*
Technological College of San Juan *C*

South Carolina
Aiken Technical College *C*
Central Carolina Technical College *C*
Denmark Technical College *A*
Florence-Darlington Technical
  College *C*
Horry-Georgetown Technical College *A*
Midlands Technical College *C*
Northeastern Technical College *C*
Orangeburg-Calhoun Technical
  College *A*
Piedmont Technical College *C, A*
Technical College of the Lowcountry *C*
Tri-County Technical College *C*
Trident Technical College *C*
York Technical College *C, A*

South Dakota
Southeast Technical Institute *A*
Western Dakota Technical Institute *A*

Tennessee
Southwest Tennessee Community
  College *A*

Texas
Alvin Community College *C, A*
Amarillo College *C, A*
Austin Community College *C*
Central Texas College *C, A*
Collin County Community College
  District *C, A*
Del Mar College *C, A*
El Paso Community College *C, A*
Grayson County College *A*
Kilgore College *C, A*
Laredo Community College *C, A*
Lee College *C, A*
MTI College of Business and
  Technology *C*
MTI College of Business and
  Technology *C*
Midland College *A*
Odessa College *C, A*
St. Philip's College *C, A*
South Plains College *C, A*
Tarrant County College *C, A*
Temple College *C, A*
Texarkana College *C*
Texas State Technical College
  Waco *C, A*
  West Texas *C*

Utah
College of Eastern Utah *C*
Salt Lake Community College *C, A*
Southern Utah University *A*

Virginia
ECPI College of Technology *C, A*
ECPI Technical College: Roanoke *A*
Eastern Shore Community College *C, A*
Mountain Empire Community College *A*
Paul D. Camp Community College *A*
Southwest Virginia Community
  College *A*
Virginia Highlands Community
  College *C*

Washington
Centralia College *C, A*
Edmonds Community College *C*
Lower Columbia College *C*
North Seattle Community College *A*
Peninsula College *A*
Renton Technical College *C, A*
Spokane Community College *A*

West Virginia
West Virginia Northern Community
  College *A*

Wisconsin
Blackhawk Technical College *A*
Chippewa Valley Technical College *C, A*
Herzing College *A, B*
Lakeshore Technical College *C*
Mid-State Technical College *A*

Moraine Park Technical College *C, A*
Waukesha County Technical
  College *C, A*
Western Wisconsin Technical
  College *C, A*
Wisconsin Indianhead Technical
  College *C, A*

Wyoming
Western Wyoming Community
  College *C, A*

Elementary education

Alabama
Alabama Agricultural and Mechanical
  University *B, M*
Alabama State University *B, M, T*
Athens State University *B*
Auburn University *B, M, D, T*
Auburn University at Montgomery *B, M*
Birmingham-Southern College *B, T*
Calhoun Community College *A*
Chattahoochee Valley Community
  College *A*
Concordia College *B*
Faulkner University *B, T*
Huntingdon College *B, T*
Jacksonville State University *B, M, T*
James H. Faulkner State Community
  College *A*
Judson College *B*
Miles College *B*
Northeast Alabama Community
  College *B*
Northwest-Shoals Community College *A*
Oakwood College *B*
Samford University *B, M, T*
Southeastern Bible College *B, T*
Spring Hill College *B, M*
Stillman College *B, T*
Troy State University *B, M, T*
Troy State University Dothan *B, M, T*
Troy State University in Montgomery *M*
Tuskegee University *B, T*
University of Alabama *B, M, D*
University of Alabama
  Birmingham *B, M*
  Huntsville *B, T*
University of Mobile *B, M, T*
University of Montevallo *B, M, T*
University of North Alabama *B, M*
University of South Alabama *B, M, T*
University of West Alabama *B, M, T*

Alaska
Alaska Pacific University *B, M*
Sheldon Jackson College *B*
University of Alaska
  Anchorage *B, T*
  Fairbanks *M, T*
  Southeast *B, M, T*

Arizona
American Indian College of the
  Assemblies of God *B*
Arizona State University *B, M, D*
Arizona Western College *A*
Central Arizona College *A*
Eastern Arizona College *A*
Estrella Mountain Community College *A*
Gateway Community College *A*
Northern Arizona University *B, M*
Prescott College *B, M, T*
Southwestern College *B, T*
University of Arizona *B, M*
University of Phoenix *M*

Arkansas
Arkansas Baptist College *B*
Arkansas State University *B, M, T*
Arkansas Tech University *B, M*
Black River Technical College *A*
Harding University *B, M, T*
Henderson State University *B, M, T*
Hendrix College *T*

John Brown University *B*
Ouachita Baptist University *B, T*
Philander Smith College *B*
Phillips Community College of the
  University of Arkansas *A*
South Arkansas Community College *A*
Southern Arkansas University *B, M, T*
University of Arkansas *B, M, D*
University of Arkansas
  Fort Smith *A, B*
  Little Rock *B, M, T*
  Pine Bluff *M*
University of Central Arkansas *M, T*
Williams Baptist College *B*

California
Antioch Southern California
  Santa Barbara *C*
Azusa Pacific University *B, T*
Barstow College *C, A*
Biola University *B, T*
California Baptist University *T*
California Polytechnic State University:
  San Luis Obispo *T*
California State University
  Bakersfield *B, M*
  Chico *T*
  Dominguez Hills *M, T*
  Fullerton *T*
  Hayward *T*
  Long Beach *M, T*
  Los Angeles *M*
  Monterey Bay *B*
  Northridge *M*
  Sacramento *M, T*
  San Bernardino *T*
  San Marcos *T*
  Stanislaus *M*
Chapman University *T*
Christian Heritage College *B, T*
Concordia University *B, T*
Dominican University of California *T*
Fresno Pacific University *B, T*
Holy Names College *T*
Hope International University *B, T*
Humboldt State University *B, T*
Imperial Valley College *A*
La Sierra University *B, M*
Loyola Marymount University *M, T*
Master's College *B, T*
Mills College *T*
Mount St. Mary's College *B*
National University *T*
Occidental College *T*
Pacific Oaks College *T*
Pacific Union College *B, M, T*
Patten University *T*
Point Loma Nazarene University *T*
St. Mary's College of California *D*
San Diego State University *M, T*
San Francisco State University *M, T*
San Jose State University *M*
Simpson College *B, T*
Sonoma State University *M, T*
University of California
  Riverside *T*
  Santa Barbara *T*
  Santa Cruz *M*
University of La Verne *B, M, T*
University of Redlands *B, T*
University of San Francisco *T*
University of Southern California *T*
University of the Pacific *B, T*
Whittier College *T*

Colorado
Colorado College *M*
Colorado State University *T*
Colorado State University
  Pueblo *T*
Fort Lewis College *T*
Metropolitan State College of Denver *T*
Otero Junior College *A*
Regis University *B, T*

University of Colorado
  Boulder *T*
  Colorado Springs *T*
University of Northern Colorado *M, D, T*

Connecticut

Central Connecticut State
  University *B, M*
Connecticut College *M, T*
Eastern Connecticut State
  University *B, M, T*
Quinnipiac University *B, M*
Sacred Heart University *M, T*
St. Joseph College *M, T*
Southern Connecticut State
  University *B, M, T*
University of Bridgeport *M, T*
University of Connecticut *T*
University of Hartford *B, M*
University of New Haven *M*
Western Connecticut State
  University *B, M*

Delaware

Delaware State University *B*
University of Delaware *B, T*
Wilmington College *B, M*

District of Columbia

American University *B, M, T*
Catholic University of America *B, M, T*
Gallaudet University *B, T*
George Washington University *M*
Trinity College *M, T*
University of the District of
  Columbia *B, T*

Florida

Baptist College of Florida *B*
Barry University *B, M, T*
Bethune-Cookman College *B, T*
Broward Community College *A*
Carlos Albizu University *B, M*
Flagler College *B*
Florida Agricultural and Mechanical
  University *B, M*
Florida Atlantic University *B, M*
Florida Christian College *B*
Florida College *B*
Florida Gulf Coast University *B, M*
Florida International University *B, M, T*
Florida Southern College *B*
Florida State University *B, M, D, T*
Gulf Coast Community College *A*
Hillsborough Community College *A*
Hobe Sound Bible College *B, T*
Indian River Community College *A*
Jacksonville University *B, M, T*
Manatee Community College *A*
Miami-Dade Community College *A*
Nova Southeastern University *B, M*
Okaloosa-Walton Community College *A*
Palm Beach Atlantic University *B, M, T*
Palm Beach Community College *A*
Pensacola Junior College *A*
Rollins College *B, M, T*
St. Leo University *B*
St. Petersburg College *B*
St. Thomas University *B, M, T*
Southeastern College of the Assemblies
  of God *B, T*
Stetson University *B, M*
University of Central Florida *B, M*
University of Florida *B, M*
University of Miami *B, M*
University of North Florida *B, M*
University of South Florida *B, M*
University of Tampa *B, T*
University of West Florida *B, M, T*
Warner Southern College *B*

Georgia

Agnes Scott College *T*
Armstrong Atlantic State
  University *B, M, T*
Clark Atlanta University *B*
Columbus State University *B, M*

Covenant College *B, T*
Emmanuel College *B*
Emory University *B*
Fort Valley State University *B, M, T*
Gainesville College *A*
Georgia Southwestern State
  University *B, M, T*
Kennesaw State University *B, M*
LaGrange College *B*
Macon State College *A*
Mercer University *B, M, T*
Middle Georgia College *A*
Morehouse College *B*
North Georgia College & State
  University *B, M*
Oglethorpe University *B, M, T*
Piedmont College *B, M, T*
Reinhardt College *B*
Shorter College *B, T*
State University of West Georgia *B, M*
Thomas University *B*
Toccoa Falls College *B, T*
University of Georgia *D, T*
Valdosta State University *M*

Hawaii

Brigham Young University-Hawaii *B, T*
Chaminade University of
  Honolulu *B, M, T*
University of Hawaii
  Hilo *T*
  Manoa *B, M, T*

Idaho

Boise State University *B, T*
Brigham Young University - Idaho *B*
College of Southern Idaho *A*
Idaho State University *B, T*
Lewis-Clark State College *B, T*
North Idaho College *A*
Northwest Nazarene University *B*
University of Idaho *B, T*

Illinois

Augustana College *B, T*
Aurora University *B*
Benedictine University *B, T*
Black Hawk College
  East Campus *A*
Blackburn College *B, T*
Bradley University *B, T*
Chicago State University *B, M, T*
City Colleges of Chicago
  Harold Washington College *A*
  Kennedy-King College *A*
Columbia College Chicago *M*
Concordia University *B, T*
De Paul University *B, T*
Dominican University *T*
Eastern Illinois University *B, M*
Elmhurst College *B*
Eureka College *B*
Governors State University *B, T*
Greenville College *T*
Illinois Central College *A*
Illinois College *B, T*
Illinois State University *B, T*
Illinois Wesleyan University *B*
John A. Logan College *A*
Joliet Junior College *A*
Judson College *B, T*
Kankakee Community College *A*
Kendall College *A, B*
Kishwaukee College *A*
Knox College *T*
Lake Forest College *T*
Lewis University *B*
Lincoln College *A*
Lincoln Land Community College *A*
Loyola University of Chicago *B, T*
MacMurray College *B, T*
McKendree College *B, T*
Millikin University *B, T*
Monmouth College *B, T*
National-Louis University *B, M, T*
North Central College *B, T*

North Park University *B, M*
Northeastern Illinois University *B, M, T*
Northern Illinois University *B, M, T*
Olivet Nazarene University *B, M, T*
Parkland College *A*
Principia College *B, T*
Quincy University *B, T*
Rockford College *B, M*
Roosevelt University *B, M*
St. Xavier University *M*
Sauk Valley Community College *A*
Southern Illinois University
  Carbondale *B*
Southern Illinois University
  Edwardsville *B, M, T*
Southwestern Illinois College *A*
Springfield College in Illinois *A*
Trinity Christian College *B, T*
Trinity International University *B, T*
University of Illinois
  Chicago *B*
  Urbana-Champaign *B, M, D, T*
University of St. Francis *B, M, T*
Western Illinois University *B, M*
Wheaton College *B, T*

Indiana

Ancilla College *A*
Anderson University *B, T*
Ball State University *B, M, D, T*
Bethel College *B*
Butler University *B, M*
Calumet College of St. Joseph *B, T*
DePauw University *B*
Franklin College *B, T*
Goshen College *B, T*
Grace College *B*
Hanover College *B, T*
Huntington College *B*
Indiana State University *B, M, T*
Indiana University
  Bloomington *B, M, D, T*
  East *B*
  Kokomo *B, M*
  Northwest *B, M, T*
  South Bend *B, M, T*
  Southeast *B, M*
Indiana University-Purdue University
  Fort Wayne *B, M, T*
Indiana University-Purdue University
  Indianapolis *B, M, T*
Indiana Wesleyan University *B, M, T*
Manchester College *B, T*
Marian College *B*
Oakland City University *B*
Purdue University *B, M, D*
Purdue University
  Calumet *B, M, T*
  North Central Campus *B, M, T*
St. Joseph's College *B*
Saint Mary's College *B, T*
St. Mary-of-the-Woods College *B, T*
Taylor University *B, T*
Taylor University: Fort Wayne *B*
Tri-State University *B, T*
University of Evansville *B*
University of Indianapolis *B, M, T*
University of St. Francis *B, M*
University of Southern Indiana *B, M, T*
Valparaiso University *B, T*
Vincennes University *A*

Iowa

Briar Cliff University *B*
Buena Vista University *B, T*
Central College *B, T*
Clarke College *B, M, T*
Coe College *B*
Cornell College *B, T*
Dordt College *B, T*
Drake University *B, M*
Ellsworth Community College *A*
Emmaus Bible College *B*
Faith Baptist Bible College and
  Theological Seminary *B, T*
Franciscan University *B, T*

Graceland University *B, T*
Grand View College *B, T*
Grinnell College *T*
Iowa State University *B, M, T*
Iowa Wesleyan College *B*
Loras College *B*
Luther College *B*
Maharishi University of
  Management *B, M*
Marshalltown Community College *A*
Morningside College *B, M*
Mount Mercy College *B*
Northwestern College *B, T*
St. Ambrose University *B, T*
Simpson College *B, T*
University of Dubuque *B, T*
University of Iowa *B, M, D, T*
University of Northern Iowa *B, M*
Upper Iowa University *B, T*
Vennard College *B*
Waldorf College *B*
Wartburg College *B, T*
William Penn University *B*

Kansas

Baker University *B, T*
Barclay College *B*
Benedictine College *B, T*
Bethany College *B, T*
Bethel College *B, T*
Butler County Community College *A*
Central Christian College *A, B*
Dodge City Community College *A*
Donnelly College *A*
Emporia State University *B, M*
Fort Hays State University *B, M, T*
Fort Scott Community College *A*
Friends University *B, T*
Garden City Community College *A*
Haskell Indian Nations University *A, B*
Independence Community College *A*
Kansas City Kansas Community
  College *A*
Kansas State University *B, M, T*
Kansas Wesleyan University *B, T*
Labette Community College *A*
McPherson College *B*
MidAmerica Nazarene University *B, T*
Newman University *B, T*
Ottawa University *B, T*
Pittsburg State University *B, M, T*
Pratt Community College *A*
St. Mary College *B, T*
Southwestern College *B, M, T*
Sterling College *B*
Tabor College *B, T*
University of Kansas *B, T*
Washburn University of Topeka *B*
Wichita State University *B, M, T*

Kentucky

Alice Lloyd College *B*
Asbury College *B, T*
Bellarmine University *B, M, T*
Berea College *B, T*
Brescia University *B, T*
Campbellsville University *B*
Centre College *B, T*
Cumberland College *B, M, T*
Georgetown College *B, M*
Kentucky Christian College *B, T*
Kentucky Wesleyan College *B, T*
Lindsey Wilson College *B, T*
Mid-Continent College *B*
Morehead State University *B, M, T*
Murray State University *B, M, T*
Pikeville College *B, T*
Spalding University *B, M, T*
Thomas More College *B*
Transylvania University *B, T*
Union College *B, M, T*
University of Kentucky *B, M*
University of Louisville *M*

Louisiana

Centenary College of Louisiana *B, M, T*

Dillard University *B, T*
Grambling State University *B, M*
Louisiana College *B*
Louisiana State University
  Shreveport *B*
Louisiana State University and
  Agricultural and Mechanical
  College *B*
Louisiana Tech University *B*
Loyola University New Orleans *B, M*
McNeese State University *B, T*
Nicholls State University *B, M*
Northwestern State University *B*
Our Lady of Holy Cross College *B*
Southeastern Louisiana University *B*
Southern University
  New Orleans *B*
Southern University and Agricultural and
  Mechanical College *B, M*
University of Louisiana at Lafayette *B*
University of Louisiana at Monroe *B, M*
University of New Orleans *B*
Xavier University of Louisiana *B, T*

Maine

College of the Atlantic *B, T*
Husson College *B, T*
St. Joseph's College *B*
University of Maine *B, M*
University of Maine
  Farmington *B, T*
  Machias *B*
  Presque Isle *B*
University of New England *B, T*
University of Southern Maine *B, T*

Maryland

Allegany College *A*
Anne Arundel Community College *A*
Bowie State University *B, M, T*
Cecil Community College *A*
Chesapeake College *A*
College of Notre Dame of Maryland *B*
College of Southern Maryland *A*
Columbia Union College *B, T*
Community College of Baltimore County
  Catonsville *A*
  Dundalk *A*
  Essex *A*
Coppin State College *B*
Frostburg State University *B, M, T*
Goucher College *B, T*
Hagerstown Community College *A*
Howard Community College *A*
Johns Hopkins University *M*
Loyola College in Maryland *B, T*
McDaniel College *M, T*
Morgan State University *B, M, T*
Mount St. Mary's College *B, M, T*
St. Mary's College of Maryland *T*
Salisbury University *B, T*
Towson University *B, M, T*
University of Maryland
  College Park *B*
Villa Julie College *A, B, T*
Washington Bible College *B, T*
Washington College *T*
Wor-Wic Community College *A*

Massachusetts

American International College *B, M*
Anna Maria College *B, M, T*
Assumption College *B, T*
Atlantic Union College *B*
Bay Path College *B*
Becker College *A, B, T*
Boston College *B, M, T*
Boston University *B, M, T*
Bridgewater State College *B, M, T*
Clark University *M*
Elms College *B, M, T*
Emmanuel College *B, M, T*
Endicott College *B, M*
Fitchburg State College *B, M, T*
Framingham State College *B, M, T*
Gordon College *B*

Hampshire College *B*
Hellenic College/Holy Cross *B*
Lasell College *B*
Lesley University *B, M, T*
Massachusetts College of Liberal Arts *T*
Merrimack College *M, T*
Northeastern University *B, M*
Pine Manor College *T*
Regis College *M*
Salem State College *B, M*
Simmons College *B, M*
Smith College *M*
Springfield College *B, M, T*
Springfield Technical Community
  College *A*
Stonehill College *B*
Suffolk University *M, T*
Tufts University *M*
University of Massachusetts
  Boston *M*
  Dartmouth *T*
Wellesley College *T*
Western New England College *T*
Westfield State College *B, M, T*
Wheaton College *T*

Michigan

Adrian College *B, T*
Alma College *B, T*
Andrews University *B, M, T*
Aquinas College *B, T*
Baker College
  of Auburn Hills *B*
  of Muskegon *B*
  of Owosso *B*
Calvin College *B, T*
Central Michigan University *B, M*
Concordia University *B, T*
Cornerstone University *B*
Eastern Michigan University *B, M, T*
Ferris State University *A, B*
Finlandia University *B*
Gogebic Community College *A*
Grace Bible College *B*
Grand Valley State University *M, T*
Hillsdale College *B*
Hope College *B, T*
Kellogg Community College *A*
Lansing Community College *A*
Madonna University *B, T*
Marygrove College *T*
Michigan State University *B*
Mid Michigan Community College *A*
Northern Michigan University *B, M, T*
Oakland University *B*
Saginaw Valley State University *B, M*
Schoolcraft College *A*
Siena Heights University *B, M, T*
Spring Arbor University *T*
University of Michigan *B*
University of Michigan
  Dearborn *T*
  Flint *B, T*
Wayne State University *B, M, T*
Western Michigan University *B, M, T*

Minnesota

Augsburg College *B, T*
Bemidji State University *B, M, T*
Bethel College *B*
Capella University *M, D*
College of St. Benedict *B*
College of St. Catherine *B, M, T*
College of St. Scholastica *B, T*
Concordia College: Moorhead *B, T*
Concordia University: St. Paul *B, T*
Crown College *B, T*
Gustavus Adolphus College *B*
Hamline University *B, T*
Martin Luther College *B*
Minnesota State University
  Mankato *B, M, T*
  Moorhead *B, M, T*
North Central University *B*
Northland Community & Technical
  College *A*

Northwestern College *B*
Ridgewater College: A Community and
  Technical College *A*
St. Cloud State University *B, M, T*
St. John's University *B*
Southwest State University *B, T*
University of Minnesota
  Duluth *B, T*
  Morris *B*
  Twin Cities *B, M, T*
University of St. Thomas *B, M, T*
Vermilion Community College *A*
Winona State University *B, M, T*

Mississippi

Alcorn State University *B, M*
Blue Mountain College *B*
Coahoma Community College *A*
Delta State University *B, M*
Holmes Community College *A*
Itawamba Community College *A*
Mary Holmes College *A*
Millsaps College *B, T*
Mississippi College *B, M, T*
Mississippi Gulf Coast Community
  College
  Perkinston *A*
Mississippi State University *B, M, T*
Mississippi University for Women *B, T*
Mississippi Valley State
  University *B, M, T*
Northwest Mississippi Community
  College *A*
Rust College *B*
University of Mississippi *B, T*
University of Southern Mississippi *B*

Missouri

Avila University *B, T*
Baptist Bible College *B*
Calvary Bible College *B*
Central Methodist College *B*
Central Missouri State
  University *B, M, T*
College of the Ozarks *B, T*
Columbia College *T*
Crowder College *A*
Culver-Stockton College *B, T*
Drury University *B, T*
East Central College *A*
Evangel University *B, T*
Fontbonne College *B*
Hannibal-LaGrange College *B*
Harris Stowe State College *B, T*
Lincoln University *B, M*
Lindenwood University *B*
Maryville University of Saint
  Louis *B, M, T*
Mineral Area College *A*
Missouri Baptist University *B, T*
Missouri Southern State College *B, T*
Missouri Valley College *B, T*
Missouri Western State College *B*
Northwest Missouri State
  University *B, M, T*
Ozark Christian College *A*
Rockhurst University *B*
St. Louis Community College
  St. Louis Community College at
    Meramec *A*
Southeast Missouri State
  University *B, M, T*
Southwest Baptist University *B, T*
Southwest Missouri State
  University *B, M*
Stephens College *B, T*
Truman State University *M, T*
University of Missouri
  Columbia *B*
  Kansas City *B*
  St. Louis *B, M, T*
Washington University in St.
  Louis *B, M, T*
Westminster College *B, T*
William Jewell College *B, T*
William Woods University *B, T*

Montana

Carroll College *B*
Fort Belknap College *A*
Miles Community College *A*
Montana State University
  Billings *B, T*
  Bozeman *B*
Rocky Mountain College *B, T*
Salish Kootenai College *A*
University of Great Falls *B*
University of Montana-Missoula *B, M*
University of Montana: Western *B, T*

Nebraska

Chadron State College *B, M*
College of Saint Mary *B, T*
Concordia University *B, M, T*
Creighton University *B*
Dana College *B*
Doane College *B*
Grace University *A*
Hastings College *B, M, T*
Midland Lutheran College *B, T*
Nebraska Wesleyan University *B*
Northeast Community College *A*
Peru State College *B, T*
Union College *B, T*
University of Nebraska
  Kearney *B, M, T*
  Lincoln *B, T*
  Omaha *B, M, T*
Wayne State College *B, M*
Western Nebraska Community
  College *A*
York College *B, T*

Nevada

Great Basin College *A, B*
Sierra Nevada College *T*
Truckee Meadows Community
  College *A*
University of Nevada
  Las Vegas *B, T*
  Reno *B, M, T*

New Hampshire

Colby-Sawyer College *B, T*
Dartmouth College *T*
Franklin Pierce College *T*
Keene State College *B, T*
New England College *B, T*
Plymouth State College *B, M, T*
Rivier College *B, M, T*
University of New Hampshire *M*
University of New Hampshire at
  Manchester *M, T*

New Jersey

Bloomfield College *B*
Caldwell College *B, T*
Centenary College *T*
The College of New Jersey *B, M, T*
College of St. Elizabeth *B, T*
Essex County College *A*
Felician College *B, T*
Georgian Court College *B, T*
Kean University *B, M*
Monmouth University *M*
New Jersey City University *B, T*
Raritan Valley Community College *A*
Richard Stockton College of New
  Jersey *B*
Rider University *B, T*
Rowan University *B, M*
Rutgers, The State University of New
  Jersey
    Camden Regional Campus *T*
    New Brunswick Regional
      Campus *T*
    Newark Regional Campus *T*
St. Peter's College *B, T*
Seton Hall University *B, M, T*
Sussex County Community College *A*
William Paterson University of New
  Jersey *B, M, T*

New Mexico

Albuquerque Technical-Vocational
   Institute *A*
College of Santa Fe *B*
College of the Southwest *B, T*
Eastern New Mexico University *B*
New Mexico Highlands
   University *A, B, T*
New Mexico Junior College *A*
New Mexico State University *B*
University of New Mexico *B, M*
Western New Mexico University *B, M, T*

New York

Adelphi University *B, M, T*
Alfred University *B, M, T*
Barnard College *T*
Canisius College *B, M, T*
City University of New York
   Brooklyn College *B, M, T*
   City College *B, M, T*
   College of Staten Island *M*
   Hunter College *B, M, T*
   Kingsborough Community
     College *A*
   Medgar Evers College *B, T*
   Queens College *B, M, T*
   York College *T*
Colgate University *T*
College of Mount St. Vincent *T*
College of New Rochelle *M, T*
Concordia College *B, T*
Corning Community College *A*
D'Youville College *C, B, M, T*
Daemen College *B, T*
Dominican College of Blauvelt *B, T*
Dowling College *B, M, T*
Dutchess Community College *A*
Elmira College *B, M, T*
Eugene Lang College/New School
   University *T*
Fordham University *M, T*
Fulton-Montgomery Community
   College *A*
Hobart and William Smith Colleges *T*
Hofstra University *B, M, T*
Houghton College *B, T*
Iona College *B, M, T*
Jefferson Community College *A*
Le Moyne College *M, T*
Long Island University
   C. W. Post Campus *B, M, T*
   Southampton College *B, M, T*
Manhattan College *B, T*
Manhattanville College *M, T*
Marist College *B, T*
Marymount College of Fordham
   University *B, T*
Marymount Manhattan College *B, T*
Medaille College *B, M, T*
Mercy College *T*
Molloy College *B, M, T*
Mount St. Mary College *B, M*
Nazareth College of Rochester *B, M, T*
New York Institute of
   Technology *B, M, T*
New York University *B, M, D, T*
Niagara University *B, M, T*
Nyack College *B, M*
Orange County Community College *A*
Pace University *B, M, T*
Pace University:
   Pleasantville/Briarcliff *B, M, T*
Roberts Wesleyan College *B, T*
Rockland Community College *A*
Russell Sage College *B, T*
St. Bonaventure University *B, M*
St. John Fisher College *B, M, T*
St. John's University *B, M, T*
St. Joseph's College *B, T*
St. Joseph's College: Suffolk
   Campus *B, T*
Sarah Lawrence College *M*
Skidmore College *T*

State University of New York
   Binghamton *M*
   Buffalo *M, D, T*
   College at Brockport *B, M, T*
   College at Buffalo *B, M, T*
   College at Cortland *M*
   College at Fredonia *B, M, T*
   College at Geneseo *B, M, T*
   College at Old Westbury *B, T*
   College at Oneonta *B, M, T*
   College at Plattsburgh *B, M*
   College at Potsdam *B, M, T*
   New Paltz *B, M, T*
   Oswego *B, M, T*
Syracuse University *B, M, T*
Ulster County Community College *A*
University of Rochester *M*
Vassar College *T*
Wagner College *B, M, T*
Wells College *T*
Yeshiva University *B, M*

North Carolina

Appalachian State University *B, M, T*
Barber-Scotia College *B*
Barton College *B*
Belmont Abbey College *B*
Bennett College *B*
Campbell University *B, M, T*
Catawba College *B, M, T*
Chowan College *B, T*
East Carolina University *B, M*
Elizabeth City State University *B, T*
Elon University *B, M, T*
Fayetteville State University *M*
Gardner-Webb University *B, M*
Greensboro College *B, T*
Guilford College *B, T*
Guilford Technical Community
   College *A*
High Point University *B, T*
James Sprunt Community College *A*
John Wesley College *B*
Johnson C. Smith University *B, T*
Lees-McRae College *B, T*
Lenoir Community College *C, A*
Lenoir-Rhyne College *B, T*
Louisburg College *A*
Mars Hill College *B, T*
Martin Community College *A*
Meredith College *M, T*
Methodist College *A, B, T*
Montreat College *B, T*
North Carolina Agricultural and
   Technical State University *B, M, T*
North Carolina Central
   University *B, M, T*
North Carolina Wesleyan College *B*
Pfeiffer University *B, T*
Piedmont Baptist College *B*
Queens University of Charlotte *B, M, T*
St. Andrews Presbyterian College *B, T*
St. Augustine's College *B*
Salem College *M, T*
Sandhills Community College *A*
Shaw University *B, T*
Southeastern Community College *A*
University of North Carolina
   Asheville *T*
   Chapel Hill *B*
   Charlotte *B, M*
   Greensboro *B, M*
   Pembroke *B, T*
   Wilmington *B, M*
Wake Forest University *B*
Warren Wilson College *B, T*
Western Carolina University *B, M, T*
Wingate University *B, M, T*
Winston-Salem State University *B, M*

North Dakota

Dickinson State University *B, T*
Jamestown College *B*
Mayville State University *B, T*
Minot State University *B, M*

Minot State University: Bottineau
   Campus *A*
North Dakota State University *B, T*
Trinity Bible College *B, T*
University of Mary *B, M, T*
University of North Dakota *B, M, T*
Valley City State University *B, T*

Ohio

Baldwin-Wallace College *B*
Bluffton College *B*
Bowling Green State University *B, M*
Cedarville University *B*
Circleville Bible College *B*
Cleveland State University *B, T*
College of Mount St. Joseph *B, T*
College of Wooster *T*
Defiance College *B, T*
Franciscan University of
   Steubenville *B, M*
God's Bible School and College *B*
Heidelberg College *T*
Hiram College *B, T*
John Carroll University *B, M, T*
Kent State University *M, T*
Kent State University
   · Stark Campus *B*
Lake Erie College *B*
Lorain County Community College *A*
Lourdes College *B*
Marietta College *B*
Miami University
   Middletown Campus *B*
   Oxford Campus *B, M*
Mount Vernon Nazarene University *B, T*
Muskingum College *B, M, T*
Notre Dame College *B, T*
Ohio Northern University *B, T*
Ohio State University
   Columbus Campus *M, T*
Ohio University *B, M, D, T*
Ohio University
   Eastern Campus *B*
   Lancaster Campus *A*
   Southern Campus at Ironton *B, M*
Ohio Wesleyan University *B*
Otterbein College *B*
Owens Community College
   Findlay Campus *A*
   Toledo *A*
Sinclair Community College *A*
University of Akron *B, M, D, T*
University of Cincinnati *B, M, D, T*
University of Cincinnati
   Clermont College *A*
   Raymond Walters College *A*
University of Dayton *M*
University of Findlay *B, M, T*
University of Rio Grande *B, T*
University of Toledo *B, M, T*
Urbana University *B*
Walsh University *B*
Washington State Community College *A*
Wilmington College *B*
Wittenberg University *B*
Wright State University *B, M, T*
Wright State University: Lake
   Campus *A, B*
Xavier University *B, M*
Youngstown State University *B, M*

Oklahoma

Cameron University *B, T*
Carl Albert State College *A*
East Central University *B, M, T*
Eastern Oklahoma State College *A*
Langston University *B, M*
Murray State College *A*
Northeastern State University *B*
Northern Oklahoma College *A*
Northwestern Oklahoma State
   University *B, M, T*
Oklahoma Baptist University *B, T*
Oklahoma Christian University of
   Science and Arts *B, T*
Oklahoma City University *B, M*

Oklahoma Panhandle State University *B*
Oklahoma State University *B, M, D, T*
Oklahoma Wesleyan University *B, T*
Oral Roberts University *B, T*
Rogers State University *A*
Rose State College *A*
Seminole State College *A*
Southeastern Oklahoma State
   University *B, M, T*
Southern Nazarene University *B, M*
Southwestern Oklahoma State
   University *B, M, T*
University of Central Oklahoma *B, M*
University of Oklahoma *B, M, D, T*
University of Science and Arts of
   Oklahoma *B, T*
University of Tulsa *B, T*

Oregon

Chemeketa Community College *A*
Concordia University *B, M, T*
Eastern Oregon University *B, M*
George Fox University *B, T*
Lewis & Clark College *M*
Linfield College *B, T*
Linn-Benton Community College *A*
Northwest Christian College *B, T*
Oregon State University *M*
Portland State University *T*
Southern Oregon University *M, T*
University of Portland *B, M, T*
Warner Pacific College *T*
Western Baptist College *B*
Western Oregon University *B, T*
Willamette University *M*

Pennsylvania

Albright College *B, M, T*
Arcadia University *B, M, T*
Baptist Bible College of Pennsylvania *B*
Bloomsburg University of
   Pennsylvania *B, M, T*
Bucknell University *B, T*
Butler County Community College *A*
Cabrini College *B*
California University of
   Pennsylvania *B, M, T*
Carlow College *B, T*
Cedar Crest College *B, M, T*
Chatham College *M, T*
Chestnut Hill College *B, M*
Cheyney University of
   Pennsylvania *B, M, T*
Community College of Allegheny
   County *A*
DeSales University *B, M, T*
Duquesne University *B, M, T*
East Stroudsburg University of
   Pennsylvania *B, M, T*
Edinboro University of
   Pennsylvania *B, M, T*
Elizabethtown College *B*
Geneva College *B, T*
Gettysburg College *T*
Grove City College *B, T*
Gwynedd-Mercy College *B, T*
Harrisburg Area Community College *A*
Holy Family University *B, M, T*
Immaculata University *T*
Indiana University of
   Pennsylvania *B, M, D, T*
Juniata College *B, T*
Keystone College *B*
King's College *B, T*
Kutztown University of
   Pennsylvania *B, M, T*
La Roche College *B*
La Salle University *B, M, T*
Lancaster Bible College *B*
Lebanon Valley College of
   Pennsylvania *B, T*
Lehigh University *M, D*
Lincoln University *B, M, T*
Lock Haven University of
   Pennsylvania *B, T*
Lycoming College *T*

Manor College *A*
Marywood University *B, M*
Mercyhurst College *B, T*
Messiah College *B, T*
Millersville University of
   Pennsylvania *B, M, T*
Montgomery County Community
   College *A*
Moravian College *T*
Mount Aloysius College *B*
Muhlenberg College *T*
Neumann College *B, T*
Penn State
   Abington *B*
   Altoona *B*
   Beaver *B*
   Berks *B*
   Delaware County *B*
   Dubois *B*
   Fayette *B*
   Harrisburg *B*
   Hazleton *B*
   Lehigh Valley *B*
   McKeesport *B*
   Mont Alto *B*
   New Kensington *B*
   Schuylkill - Capital College *B*
   Shenango *B*
   University Park *B*
   Wilkes-Barre *B*
   Worthington Scranton *B*
   York *B*
Philadelphia Biblical University *B, T*
Point Park College *B, T*
Reading Area Community College *A*
Robert Morris University *B, T*
Rosemont College *T*
St. Joseph's University *B, M*
St. Vincent College *T*
Seton Hill University *M, T*
Shippensburg University of
   Pennsylvania *B, M, T*
Slippery Rock University of
   Pennsylvania *B, M, T*
Temple University *B, M*
Thiel College *T*
University of Pennsylvania *B, M*
University of Pittsburgh *T*
University of Pittsburgh
   Bradford *B, T*
   Johnstown *B, T*
University of Scranton *B, M*
Valley Forge Christian College *B*
Villanova University *B*
Washington and Jefferson College *T*
Waynesburg College *B, T*
West Chester University of
   Pennsylvania *B, M, T*
Widener University *B, M, T*
Wilkes University *B, M, T*
Wilson College *B*
York College of Pennsylvania *B, T*

Puerto Rico

Bayamon Central University *B, M*
Inter American University of Puerto Rico
   Barranquitas Campus *B*
   Fajardo Campus *B, T*
   Guayama Campus *B*
   Metropolitan Campus *B, M*
   San German Campus *B*
Pontifical Catholic University of Puerto
   Rico *B, T*
Turabo University *B*
Universidad Metropolitana *B*
University of Puerto Rico
   Cayey University College *B, T*
   Humacao *B*
   Ponce *B*
   Rio Piedras Campus *B, M*
University of the Sacred Heart *B*

Rhode Island

Rhode Island College *B, M, T*
Roger Williams University *B, M, T*
Salve Regina University *B*

University of Rhode Island *B*

South Carolina

Anderson College *B, T*
Benedict College *B*
Charleston Southern University *B, M*
Claflin University *B*
Clemson University *B, M, T*
Coastal Carolina University *B, M, T*
Coker College *B, T*
College of Charleston *B, M, T*
Columbia College *B, M, T*
Columbia International
   University *B, M, T*
Converse College *B, M, T*
Erskine College *B, T*
Francis Marion University *B, M*
Furman University *M, T*
Lander University *B, M, T*
Limestone College *B*
Morris College *B, T*
Newberry College *B, T*
North Greenville College *B, T*
Presbyterian College *B, T*
South Carolina State University *B, M*
Southern Wesleyan University *B, T*
University of South Carolina *M, D*
University of South Carolina
   Aiken *B, M, T*
   Spartanburg *B, M, T*
Voorhees College *B*
Winthrop University *B, M, T*

South Dakota

Augustana College *B, M, T*
Black Hills State University *B, T*
Dakota State University *B, T*
Dakota Wesleyan University *B, T*
Mount Marty College *B*
Northern State University *B, M, T*
Sinte Gleska University *B*
University of Sioux Falls *B, T*
University of South Dakota *B, M, T*

Tennessee

Aquinas College *B, T*
Austin Peay State University *M, T*
Belmont University *B, T*
Bethel College *B, T*
Bryan College *T*
Carson-Newman College *B, M, T*
Christian Brothers University *B, M, T*
Columbia State Community College *A*
Crichton College *C, B*
East Tennessee State University *M, T*
Fisk University *T*
Freed-Hardeman University *B, T*
Johnson Bible College *T*
King College *T*
Lambuth University *B, T*
Lane College *B*
Lee University *B, T*
Roane State Community College *A*
Southern Adventist University *B*
Tennessee State University *M, T*
Tennessee Technological
   University *M, T*
Tennessee Wesleyan College *B, T*
Trevecca Nazarene University *B, T*
Tusculum College *B, T*
Union University *B, T*
University of Tennessee
   Chattanooga *M*
   Knoxville *T*
   Martin *B, T*
Vanderbilt University *B, M, D, T*

Texas

Abilene Christian University *B, M, T*
Amarillo College *A*
Arlington Baptist College *B*
Austin College *M*
Baylor University *T*
Brazosport College *A*
Clarendon College *A*
Coastal Bend College *A*
College of the Mainland *A*

Concordia University at Austin *B, T*
Dallas Baptist University *B, M*
East Texas Baptist University *B*
El Centro College *C*
El Paso Community College *A*
Frank Phillips College *A*
Galveston College *A*
Grayson County College *A*
Hardin-Simmons University *B, T*
Houston Baptist University *B, M*
Howard Payne University *B, T*
Huston-Tillotson College *T*
Jarvis Christian College *B*
Lamar University *M, T*
Laredo Community College *A*
LeTourneau University *B*
Lubbock Christian University *B, M*
McMurry University *B*
Midwestern State University *B*
North Harris Montgomery Community
   College District *A*
Our Lady of the Lake University of San
   Antonio *T*
Paul Quinn College *B*
Prairie View A&M University *M*
St. Edward's University *T*
St. Mary's University *B, T*
Sam Houston State University *M*
Schreiner University *T*
Southern Methodist University *T*
Southwest Texas State University *M, T*
Southwestern Adventist University *B, M*
Southwestern Assemblies of God
   University *B*
Southwestern University *B, T*
Stephen F. Austin State University *M, T*
Sul Ross State University *B, M, T*
Tarleton State University *B, M, T*
Texas A&M International
   University *B, M, T*
Texas A&M University
   Commerce *B, M, D, T*
   Corpus Christi *M, T*
   Kingsville *B, M*
   Texarkana *M, T*
Texas Christian University *B, M, T*
Texas College *B*
Texas Lutheran University *B, T*
Texas Tech University *M*
Texas Wesleyan University *B, M, T*
Texas Woman's University *M*
Trinity University *B, M*
Trinity Valley Community College *A*
University of Dallas *B, T*
University of Houston *M, T*
University of Houston
   Downtown *M, T*
   Victoria *M*
University of Mary Hardin-Baylor *B, T*
University of North Texas *B, M, D, T*
University of St. Thomas *B*
University of Texas
   Arlington *T*
   Brownsville *M*
   Pan American *B, M, T*
   San Antonio *M, T*
   of the Permian Basin *M*
University of the Incarnate Word *B*
Wayland Baptist University *B, T*
West Texas A&M University *M, T*
Wharton County Junior College *A*
Wiley College *B*

Utah

Brigham Young University *B, M, D*
Dixie State College of Utah *A, B*
Salt Lake Community College *A*
Snow College *A*
Southern Utah University *B, T*
University of Utah *B, M, D*
Utah State University *B, M, D*
Utah Valley State College *B*
Weber State University *B, M*
Westminster College *B*

Vermont

Bennington College *B, M, T*
Castleton State College *B, M*
Champlain College *A, B*
College of St. Joseph in Vermont *B, M*
Goddard College *B*
Green Mountain College *B, T*
Johnson State College *B, M*
Lyndon State College *B*
Middlebury College *T*
Norwich University *T*
St. Michael's College *B, T*
University of Vermont *B*

Virginia

Averett University *B, M, T*
Bluefield College *B*
Bridgewater College *T*
College of William and Mary *T*
Eastern Mennonite University *T*
Hampton University *M*
Hollins University *T*
James Madison University *T*
Liberty University *B, M*
Longwood University *B, T*
Mary Baldwin College *T*
Mary Washington College *M*
Marymount University *M*
Old Dominion University *M*
Radford University *T*
Randolph-Macon College *T*
Randolph-Macon Woman's College *T*
Shenandoah University *C*
University of Richmond *T*
University of Virginia's College at
   Wise *T*
Virginia Intermont College *B, T*
Virginia Wesleyan College *T*

Washington

Central Washington University *B, M, T*
Eastern Washington University *B, M, T*
Evergreen State College *M*
Gonzaga University *T*
Northwest College *B*
Pacific Lutheran University *B*
St. Martin's College *B, T*
University of Washington *M, T*
Walla Walla College *B, T*
Western Washington University *M, T*
Whitworth College *B, M, T*

West Virginia

Alderson-Broaddus College *B*
Bethany College *B*
Bluefield State College *B*
Concord College *B, T*
Davis and Elkins College *B*
Fairmont State College *B*
Glenville State College *B*
Marshall University *B, M*
Mountain State University *A*
Ohio Valley College *B*
Potomac State College of West Virginia
   University *A*
Salem International University *B, T*
Shepherd College *B, T*
University of Charleston *B*
West Liberty State College *B*
West Virginia State College *B*
West Virginia University *M, T*
West Virginia University at
   Parkersburg *B*
West Virginia Wesleyan College *B*
Wheeling Jesuit University *T*

Wisconsin

Alverno College *B, T*
Beloit College *T*
Carroll College *B, T*
Carthage College *B, T*
Concordia University Wisconsin *B, T*
Edgewood College *B*
Lakeland College *B*
Lawrence University *T*
Maranatha Baptist Bible College *B*
Marian College of Fond du Lac *B, T*

Marquette University *B*
Mount Mary College *B, T*
Northland College *B, T*
Ripon College *T*
St. Norbert College *B, M, T*
Silver Lake College *B, T*
University of Wisconsin
Eau Claire *B, M*
Green Bay *B, T*
La Crosse *B, M, T*
Madison *B, T*
Oshkosh *B, M, T*
Parkside *T*
Platteville *B, T*
River Falls *B, M, T*
Stevens Point *B, M, T*
Superior *M*
Whitewater *B, T*
Viterbo University *B, M, T*
Wisconsin Lutheran College *B*

Wyoming
Casper College *A*
Central Wyoming College *A*
Eastern Wyoming College *A*
Laramie County Community College *A*
Sheridan College *A*
University of Wyoming *B*
Western Wyoming Community
College *A*

Elementary/middle school administration

Arkansas
Arkansas State University *M, T*
Arkansas Tech University *M*

Florida
University of West Florida *M*

Indiana
Indiana State University *M*

Kentucky
Murray State University *M, T*

Louisiana
Xavier University of Louisiana *M*

Massachusetts
Bridgewater State College *T*
Lesley University *M, T*

Michigan
Saginaw Valley State University *M*

Minnesota
Capella University *M, D*
Vermilion Community College *A*

Mississippi
Mississippi State University *D*

Missouri
University of Missouri
Columbia *M, D*

Nebraska
Creighton University *M*

New Jersey
College of St. Elizabeth *T*
William Paterson University of New
Jersey *M*

New York
St. Bonaventure University *M*
St. John Fisher College *M*
State University of New York
Buffalo *M, D, T*

North Carolina
East Carolina University *D*
University of North Carolina
Charlotte *M*
Western Carolina University *D*

Ohio
Baldwin-Wallace College *B*

University of Akron *B, T*
University of Dayton *M*
Youngstown State University *M*

Pennsylvania
Marywood University *M*

Puerto Rico
Turabo University *B*

South Dakota
University of South Dakota *M, D*

Texas
Southwest Texas State University *M*

Vermont
Castleton State College *D*
St. Michael's College *T*

Washington
Seattle Pacific University *T*
Seattle University *B*
University of Washington *M, T*

Wisconsin
Edgewood College *M*
University of Wisconsin
Superior *M*

Emergency care attendant (EMT ambulance)

California
Santa Rosa Junior College *C*

Florida
Pensacola Junior College *C*

Illinois
Southeastern Illinois College *C*

Indiana
University of St. Francis *C, A*
Vincennes University *A*

Iowa
Kirkwood Community College *A*
North Iowa Area Community College *C*

Kansas
Kansas City Kansas Community
College *A*

Massachusetts
Cape Cod Community College *C*

Michigan
Baker College
of Muskegon *C, A*

Nebraska
Nebraska Methodist College of Nursing
and Allied Health *C*

North Carolina
Carteret Community College *A*
Sandhills Community College *A*

Ohio
Lakeland Community College *C*

Oklahoma
Rose State College *A*

Texas
Howard College *C, A*
Tyler Junior College *C, A*

Virginia
Piedmont Virginia Community
College *A*

Wisconsin
Fox Valley Technical College *C*
Mid-State Technical College *C*

Emergency medical technology (EMT paramedic)

Alabama
Alabama Southern Community
College *A*
Bishop State Community College *C*
Calhoun Community College *C, A*
Central Alabama Community College *A*
Enterprise State Junior College *A*
Faulkner University *A*
Gadsden State Community College *A*
George C. Wallace State Community
College
Dothan *C, A*
James H. Faulkner State Community
College *A*
Lawson State Community College *C*
Lurleen B. Wallace Junior College *C, A*
Northeast Alabama Community
College *A*
Northwest-Shoals Community College *C*
Trenholm State Technical College *A*
University of Alabama
Birmingham *C*
University of South Alabama *C*
Wallace State Community College at
Hanceville *C, A*

Alaska
University of Alaska
Anchorage *A*

Arizona
Arizona Western College *C, A*
Central Arizona College *C, A*
Cochise College *A*
Eastern Arizona College *C, A*
Glendale Community College *C, A*
Phoenix College *C, A*
Pima Community College *C, A*
Scottsdale Community College *C, A*
Yavapai College *C*

Arkansas
Arkansas State University *A*
East Arkansas Community College *C, A*
North Arkansas College *A*
Northwest Arkansas Community
College *C, A*
Ozarka College *C*
South Arkansas Community
College *C, A*
Southeast Arkansas College *C, A*
Southern Arkansas University Tech *C, A*
University of Arkansas
Community College at Batesville *A*
Cossatot Community College of the
C
Fort Smith *C, A*
for Medical Sciences *C, A*

California
Bakersfield College *A*
Barstow College *C*
California State University
Chico *C*
College of the Canyons *C*
College of the Sequoias *C*
College of the Siskiyous *C, A*
Columbia College *C*
East Los Angeles College *C*
Foothill College *C*
Imperial Valley College *C*
Long Beach City College *C*
Los Medanos College *C, A*
Modesto Junior College *C*
Mount San Antonio College *C, A*
Palomar College *C, A*
San Joaquin Delta College *C, A*
Santa Barbara City College *C*
Santa Rosa Junior College *C, A*
Southwestern College *C, A*
Ventura College *A*
Victor Valley College *C, A*

Colorado
Arapahoe Community College *C, A*
Front Range Community College *C*
Morgan Community College *C*
Red Rocks Community College *C, A*

Connecticut
Capital Community College *C, A*
Naugatuck Valley Community College *C*
Three Rivers Community College *C*

Delaware
Delaware Technical and Community
College
Owens Campus *A*
Stanton/Wilmington Campus *A*
Terry Campus *A*

Florida
Broward Community College *C, A*
Daytona Beach Community
College *C, A*
Florida Keys Community College *C*
Gulf Coast Community College *C, A*
Hillsborough Community College *A*
Indian River Community College *C, A*
Lake City Community College *C, A*
Lake-Sumter Community College *A*
Miami-Dade Community College *A*
Palm Beach Community College *C, A*
Pasco-Hernando Community
College *C, A*
Pensacola Junior College *C, A*
Polk Community College *C*
St. Petersburg College *C, A*
Santa Fe Community College *C, A*
Seminole Community College *C, A*
South Florida Community College *C*
Tallahassee Community College *C, A*
Valencia Community College *C, A*

Georgia
Clayton College and State University *C*
Dalton State College *A*
Darton College *C, A*
DeKalb Technical College *C*
Floyd College *A*
Gainesville College *A*
Macon State College *A*
Southwest Georgia Technical College *C*
Valdosta State University *A*
Waycross College *A*
West Georgia Technical College *C*

Idaho
Brigham Young University - Idaho *A*
College of Southern Idaho *C*

Illinois
Black Hawk College *C*
City Colleges of Chicago
Malcolm X College *C, A*
College of DuPage *C, A*
College of Lake County *C*
Elgin Community College *C*
Heartland Community College *C*
Illinois Central College *C*
Illinois Eastern Community Colleges
Frontier Community College *C*
John A. Logan College *C*
John Wood Community College *A*
Kankakee Community College *C, A*
McHenry County College *C, A*
Moraine Valley Community College *C*
Parkland College *C*
Prairie State College *C*
Rend Lake College *C*
Richland Community College *C, A*
South Suburban College of Cook
County *C*
Southeastern Illinois College *C*
Southwestern Illinois College *C, A*
Waubonsee Community College *C*
William Rainey Harper College *C*

Indiana
Ball State University *A*

Indiana University
    Bloomington *A*
Indiana University-Purdue University
    Indianapolis *A*
Ivy Tech State College
    Kokomo *A*
    Southwest *A*
    Wabash Valley *A*
University of St. Francis *A*
Vincennes University *A*

Iowa
Hawkeye Community College *A*
Iowa Central Community College *C, A*
Kirkwood Community College *A*
North Iowa Area Community College *A*
Northeast Iowa Community College *A*
Northwest Iowa Community College *C*
Southeastern Community College
    North Campus *A*
Southwestern Community College *C*
Western Iowa Tech Community
    College *C, A*

Kansas
Allen County Community College *A*
Barton County Community College *C, A*
Cloud County Community College *C*
Dodge City Community College *C*
Hutchinson Community College *C, A*
Independence Community College *C, A*
Johnson County Community
    College *C, A*
Kansas City Kansas Community
    College *C, A*

Louisiana
Delgado Community College *A*
Nicholls State University *A*
Nunez Community College *C, A*

Maryland
Anne Arundel Community College *C, A*
Chesapeake College *C*
College of Southern Maryland *A*
Community College of Baltimore County
    Catonsville *C, A*
    Dundalk *C, A*
    Essex *C, A*
Frederick Community College *C, A*
Hagerstown Community College *C, A*
Howard Community College *C, A*
Wor-Wic Community College *C, A*

Massachusetts
Cape Cod Community College *C, A*
Greenfield Community College *C*
Massachusetts Bay Community
    College *C*
Northeastern University *A*
Quinsigamond Community College *C, A*
Springfield College *B*

Michigan
Baker College
    of Cadillac *C*
    of Clinton Township *C*
    of Muskegon *C, A*
Davenport University
    Midland *C, A*
Davenport University - Western
    Region *C, A*
Glen Oaks Community College *C*
Gogebic Community College *C*
Jackson Community College *C, A*
Kellogg Community College *C, A*
Lansing Community College *A*
Macomb Community College *C, A*
Mid Michigan Community College *A*
Montcalm Community College *C, A*
Mott Community College *A*
North Central Michigan College *A*
Oakland Community College *A*
Schoolcraft College *C*
Wayne County Community College *C*

Minnesota
Century Community and Technical
    College *C, A*
Hennepin Technical College *A*
Inver Hills Community College *A*
Lake Superior College: A Community
    and Technical College *C*
Mesabi Range Community and Technical
    College *C*
Rochester Community and Technical
    College *C, A*
St. Cloud Technical College *C, A*
South Central Technical College *A*
University of Minnesota
    Duluth *C*

Mississippi
Itawamba Community College *A*
Mississippi Gulf Coast Community
    College
    Perkinston *A*
University of Mississippi Medical
    Center *C*

Missouri
Crowder College *C*
East Central College *C, A*
Jefferson College *C, A*
Mineral Area College *C*
Missouri Southern State College *C*
Moberly Area Community College *C*
Ozarks Technical Community College *A*
Penn Valley Community College *A*
St. Louis Community College
    St. Louis Community College at
      Forest Park *A*
    St. Louis Community College at
      Meramec *A*
Southwest Baptist University *A*
Three Rivers Community College *C*

Montana
Montana State University
    Billings *C, A*
    Billings College of
      Technology *C, A*

Nebraska
Creighton University *C, A*
Nebraska Methodist College of Nursing
    and Allied Health *C, A*
Northeast Community College *A*

Nevada
Community College of Southern
    Nevada *A*
Western Nevada Community College *A*

New Hampshire
New Hampshire Technical Institute *A*

New Jersey
Essex County College *A*
Union County College *C*
University of Medicine and Dentistry of
    New Jersey
    School of Health Related
      Professions *C, A*

New Mexico
Dona Ana Branch Community College of
    New Mexico State University *C, A*
Eastern New Mexico University: Roswell
    Campus *C, A*
New Mexico Junior College *A*
New Mexico State University
    Alamogordo *C*
University of New Mexico *C*

New York
Broome Community College *A*
City University of New York
    Borough of Manhattan Community
      College *A*
    La Guardia Community College *A*
Corning Community College *A*
Dutchess Community College *C, A*

Erie Community College
    South Campus *C*
Finger Lakes Community College *C*
Fulton-Montgomery Community
    College *A*
Hudson Valley Community College *C*
Jefferson Community College *C, A*
Mohawk Valley Community College *A*
Rockland Community College *A*
Westchester Community College *C, A*

North Carolina
Asheville Buncombe Technical
    Community College *A*
Catawba Valley Community College *A*
Coastal Carolina Community College *A*
College of the Albemarle *A*
Davidson County Community College *A*
Fayetteville Technical Community
    College *C, A*
Gaston College *A*
Guilford Technical Community
    College *C, A*
Montgomery Community College *A*
Randolph Community College *A*
Rockingham Community College *A*
Sandhills Community College *A*
Southwestern Community College *A*
Tri-County Community College *C, A*
Wake Technical Community
    College *C, A*
Western Carolina University *B*
Wilson Technical Community College *A*

North Dakota
Bismarck State College *C, A*

Ohio
Central Ohio Technical College *A*
Cincinnati State Technical and
    Community College *C*
Clark State Community College *A*
Columbus State Community
    College *C, A*
Cuyahoga Community College
    Eastern Campus *A*
    Metropolitan Campus *A*
Hocking Technical College *C*
James A. Rhodes State College *A*
Jefferson Community College *C, A*
Lakeland Community College *C*
Lorain County Community College *C*
Shawnee State University *C, A*
Sinclair Community College *A*
Southern State Community College *C, A*
University of Cincinnati
    Clermont College *A*
    Raymond Walters College *C, A*
University of Toledo *C, A*
Youngstown State University *C, A*

Oklahoma
Oklahoma City Community
    College *C, A*
Redlands Community College *A*
Rose State College *A*
Western Oklahoma State College *A*

Oregon
Central Oregon Community College *A*
Chemeketa Community College *A*
Clackamas Community College *C*
Clatsop Community College *C*
Lane Community College *C, A*
Linn-Benton Community College *C*
Oregon Health Sciences University *C*
Portland Community College *C, A*
Rogue Community College *C, A*
Southwestern Oregon Community
    College *C*
Umpqua Community College *A*

Pennsylvania
California University of Pennsylvania *A*
Delaware County Community College *C*
Drexel University *A, B*

Harrisburg Area Community
    College *C, A*
Lackawanna College *C, A*
Lehigh Carbon Community College *C, A*
Luzerne County Community College *A*
Pennsylvania College of Technology *A*
University of Pittsburgh
    Johnstown *A*

Puerto Rico
Universidad Metropolitana *C*

South Carolina
Piedmont Technical College *C*

Tennessee
Jackson State Community College *C*
Northeast State Technical Community
    College *C*
Roane State Community College *A*
Southwest Tennessee Community
    College *C, A*
Volunteer State Community College *C*
Walters State Community College *C, A*

Texas
Alvin Community College *A*
Amarillo College *C, A*
Angelina College *C, A*
Austin Community College *C, A*
Blinn College *C*
Collin County Community College
    District *C, A*
Del Mar College *C, A*
El Centro College *C*
El Paso Community College *C*
Galveston College *C, A*
Grayson County College *C, A*
Houston Community College
    System *C, A*
Kilgore College *C, A*
Lamar State College at Orange *C, A*
Laredo Community College *A*
Lee College *C, A*
McLennan Community College *A*
Midland College *C*
North Central Texas College *A*
North Harris Montgomery Community
    College District *C, A*
Odessa College *C, A*
South Plains College *C, A*
South Texas Community College *C, A*
Tarrant County College *C, A*
Temple College *C, A*
Texarkana College *C, A*
Texas State Technical College
    West Texas *C*
Trinity Valley Community College *C*
Tyler Junior College *C, A*
University of North Texas *B*
Western Texas College *C, A*

Utah
Dixie State College of Utah *C, A*
Snow College *C, A*
Utah Valley State College *C*
Weber State University *A*

Virginia
College of Health Sciences *A*
Mountain Empire Community
    College *C, A*

Washington
North Seattle Community College *C*
Spokane Community College *C, A*
Spokane Falls Community College *C*

West Virginia
Mountain State University *A*
Shepherd College *A*

Wisconsin
Blackhawk Technical College *C*
Chippewa Valley Technical College *C*
Fox Valley Technical College *C*
Moraine Park Technical College *C*
Nicolet Area Technical College *C*
Western Wisconsin Technical College *C*

Wyoming

Central Wyoming College *C*
Sheridan College *C, A*

Endocrinology

Georgia

Medical College of Georgia *M, D*

Energy systems technology

Connecticut

Naugatuck Valley Community College *C*

Massachusetts

University of Massachusetts
Lowell *M*

Michigan

Alpena Community College *C*
Montcalm Community College *C*
Mott Community College *C*

New York

New York Institute of Technology *B*

Engineering

Alabama

Central Alabama Community College *A*
Chattahoochee Valley Community
College *A*
Lawson State Community College *A*
Northeast Alabama Community
College *A*
Shelton State Community College *A*
Snead State Community College *A*
University of Alabama
Huntsville *M*
Wallace State Community College at
Hanceville *A*

Alaska

University of Alaska
Anchorage *A*
Fairbanks *M, D*

Arizona

Arizona State University *M*
Arizona Western College *A*
Central Arizona College *A*
Embry-Riddle Aeronautical University:
Prescott Campus *B*
Gateway Community College *A*
High-Tech Institute *C, A*
Northern Arizona University *B*
Phoenix College *A*
University of Arizona *B*

Arkansas

Arkansas State University *B*
Arkansas Tech University *B*
John Brown University *B*
Phillips Community College of the
University of Arkansas *A*
University of Arkansas *M, D*
University of Arkansas
Fort Smith *A, B*

California

Antelope Valley College *C, A*
Biola University *B*
California Institute of Technology *B*
California Polytechnic State University:
San Luis Obispo *M*
California State Polytechnic University:
Pomona *M*
California State University
Long Beach *M*
Los Angeles *B*
Northridge *B, M*
Chabot College *A*
Citrus College *A*

College of the Sequoias *A*
College of the Siskiyous *C*
Contra Costa College *A*
De Anza College *A*
East Los Angeles College *A*
Foothill College *A*
Harvey Mudd College *B, M*
Imperial Valley College *A*
Long Beach City College *C, A*
Los Angeles Pierce College *A*
Los Angeles Southwest College *C, A*
Los Angeles Trade and Technical
College *C, A*
Modesto Junior College *A*
Mount San Antonio College *A*
Ohlone College *C*
Palomar College *A*
Pepperdine University *B*
Riverside Community College *C, A*
San Diego City College *C, A*
San Diego Mesa College *C, A*
San Francisco State University *M*
San Joaquin Delta College *A*
San Jose State University *M*
Santa Barbara City College *A*
Santa Clara University *C, B, M*
Santa Rosa Junior College *A*
Santiago Canyon College *A*
Scripps College *B*
Shasta College *A*
Sierra College *A*
Southwestern College *A*
Stanford University *B, M*
Taft College *A*
University of California
Davis *M, D*
Irvine *B, M, D*
Los Angeles *B, M, D*
Santa Barbara *B, M, D*
University of the Pacific *B*
Ventura College *C, A*
West Valley College *A*

Colorado

Colorado School of Mines *B*
Trinidad State Junior College *A*
United States Air Force Academy *B*
University of Colorado
Boulder *M*
Colorado Springs *M*
Denver *M*
University of Denver *B, D*

Connecticut

Fairfield University *B*
Norwalk Community College *A*
Trinity College *B*
University of Connecticut *M*
University of Hartford *B*
University of New Haven *M*

District of Columbia

George Washington University *B, M, D*

Florida

Barry University *B*
Broward Community College *A*
Chipola Junior College *A*
Daytona Beach Community College *A*
Embry-Riddle Aeronautical
University *B, M*
Florida Institute of Technology *B*
Gulf Coast Community College *A*
Hillsborough Community College *A*
Indian River Community College *A*
Manatee Community College *A*
Miami-Dade Community College *C*
Okaloosa-Walton Community College *A*
Palm Beach Atlantic University *A*
Palm Beach Community College *A*
Pensacola Junior College *A*
Polk Community College *A*
South Florida Community College *A*
Tallahassee Community College *A*
University of Central Florida *M*
University of South Florida *B, M, D*

Georgia

Andrew College *A*
Clark Atlanta University *B*
Dalton State College *A*
Darton College *A*
Gainesville College *A*
Georgia Military College *A*
Georgia Perimeter College *A*
Middle Georgia College *A*
Morehouse College *B*
Spelman College *B*
Young Harris College *A*

Idaho

Brigham Young University - Idaho *A*
Idaho State University *B*
Lewis-Clark State College *C*
North Idaho College *A*

Illinois

City Colleges of Chicago
Harold Washington College *A*
Olive-Harvey College *C, A*
College of DuPage *A*
College of Lake County *A*
Danville Area Community College *A*
Heartland Community College *A*
Illinois Central College *A*
Illinois College *B*
Illinois Institute of Technology *C, M, D*
Illinois Valley Community College *A*
John A. Logan College *A*
John Wood Community College *A*
Kankakee Community College *A*
Kaskaskia College *A*
Kishwaukee College *A*
Lake Land College *A*
Lincoln Land Community College *A*
MacMurray College *B*
McHenry County College *A*
Monmouth College *B*
Northwestern University *B*
Oakton Community College *A*
Olivet Nazarene University *B*
Parkland College *A*
Quincy University *B*
Rend Lake College *A*
Richland Community College *A*
Sauk Valley Community College *A*
South Suburban College of Cook
County *A*
Southern Illinois University
Carbondale *D*
Southwestern Illinois College *A*
Triton College *A*
University of Illinois
Urbana-Champaign *B, M*
Waubonsee Community College *A*
Wheaton College *B*
William Rainey Harper College *A*

Indiana

Bethel College *B*
Indiana University-Purdue University
Fort Wayne *B*
Indiana University-Purdue University
Indianapolis *B, M*
Purdue University *B, M, D*
Purdue University
Calumet *B, M*
University of Evansville *B*
University of Notre Dame *M*
University of Southern Indiana *B*
Vincennes University *A*

Iowa

Cornell College *B*
Dordt College *B*
Ellsworth Community College *A*
Hamilton College *A*
Iowa Wesleyan College *B*
Kirkwood Community College *A*
Marshalltown Community College *A*
North Iowa Area Community College *A*
Waldorf College *A*

Kansas

Barton County Community College *A*
Butler County Community College *A*
Central Christian College *A*
Cloud County Community College *A*
Dodge City Community College *A*
Fort Scott Community College *A*
Garden City Community College *A*
Hutchinson Community College *A*
Independence Community College *A*
Kansas City Kansas Community
College *A*
Pratt Community College *A*
Seward County Community College *A*
University of Kansas *B, M*

Kentucky

Brescia University *A*
Murray State University *B*

Louisiana

Louisiana Tech University *M, D*
McNeese State University *B, M*
Southern University and Agricultural and
Mechanical College *M*
Tulane University *B*

Maine

University of Maine *B, M*

Maryland

Allegany College *A*
Anne Arundel Community College *A*
College of Notre Dame of Maryland *B*
College of Southern Maryland *A*
Columbia Union College *A*
Community College of Baltimore County
Catonsville *A*
Dundalk *A*
Essex *A*
Frederick Community College *A*
Hagerstown Community College *A*
Harford Community College *A*
Howard Community College *A*
Johns Hopkins University *B*
Loyola College in Maryland *B, M*
Montgomery College
Rockville Campus *A*
Morgan State University *M, D*
United States Naval Academy *B*
University of Maryland
Baltimore County *B*
College Park *B, M*

Massachusetts

Berkshire Community College *C, A*
Boston University *B, M*
Cape Cod Community College *A*
Emmanuel College *B*
Franklin W. Olin College of
Engineering *B*
Harvard College *B*
Merrimack College *B*
Mount Ida College *A*
Northeastern University *B, M*
Quinsigamond Community College *A*
Smith College *B*
Springfield Technical Community
College *A*
Tufts University *B*
Wellesley College *B*

Michigan

Alpena Community College *A*
Andrews University *B*
Calvin College *B*
Ferris State University *A*
Gogebic Community College *A*
Hope College *B*
Kettering University *B*
Kirtland Community College *A*
Lansing Community College *A*
Michigan State University *B*
Michigan Technological
University *B, M, T*
Mid Michigan Community College *A*
Northwestern Michigan College *A*

Oakland Community College A
Schoolcraft College A
University of Michigan B, M, D
University of Michigan
    Dearborn B
Washtenaw Community College A

Minnesota
Anoka-Ramsey Community College A
Augsburg College B
Century Community and Technical
    College A
Itasca Community College A
Minnesota State University
    Mankato B, M
Normandale Community College A
Northland Community & Technical
    College A
Rochester Community and Technical
    College A
University of Minnesota
    Twin Cities C
Winona State University B

Mississippi
Holmes Community College A
Itawamba Community College A
Mary Holmes College A
Mississippi Gulf Coast Community
    College
    Perkinston A
Mississippi State University D
University of Mississippi B

Missouri
Blue River Community College A
Crowder College A
East Central College A
Hannibal-LaGrange College A
Jefferson College A
Longview Community College A
Maple Woods Community College A
Mineral Area College A
Missouri Southern State College A
Moberly Area Community College A
Penn Valley Community College A
St. Charles Community College A
St. Louis Community College
    St. Louis Community College at
      Florissant Valley A
    St. Louis Community College at
      Forest Park A
    St. Louis Community College at
      Meramec C, A
University of Missouri
    Columbia M
Washington University in St.
    Louis B, M, D

Montana
Miles Community College A
Montana State University
    Bozeman D
Montana Tech of the University of
    Montana A, B, M

Nebraska
Union College A
University of Nebraska
    Lincoln B, M, D
Western Nebraska Community
    College A

Nevada
Great Basin College A
University of Nevada
    Reno D
Western Nevada Community College A

New Hampshire
Dartmouth College M, D
St. Anselm College B
University of New Hampshire B

New Jersey
Brookdale Community College A
The College of New Jersey B
Cumberland County College A

Essex County College A
Gloucester County College A
New Jersey Institute of Technology M
Ocean County College A
Rowan University B, M
Stevens Institute of Technology B
Union County College A

New Mexico
Albuquerque Technical-Vocational
    Institute A
New Mexico Highlands University B
New Mexico Institute of Mining and
    Technology B
New Mexico Junior College A
New Mexico State University D
New Mexico State University
    Alamogordo A
San Juan College A
Santa Fe Community College A
University of New Mexico B, D

New York
Adirondack Community College A
Alfred University B
City University of New York
    Borough of Manhattan Community
      College A
    College of Staten Island A, B
Clarkson University B
Cooper Union for the Advancement of
    Science and Art B, M
Cornell University B
Erie Community College
    North Campus A
Finger Lakes Community College A
Fulton-Montgomery Community
    College A
Hudson Valley Community College A
Jamestown Community College A
Mohawk Valley Community College A
Nassau Community College A
Niagara University A
Orange County Community College A
Rensselaer Polytechnic Institute B, M, D
State University of New York
    Buffalo M, D
    College of Agriculture and
      Technology at Morrisville A
    College of Technology at Alfred A
    Maritime College B
    Oswego B
    Stony Brook B
Ulster County Community College A
University of Rochester B
Westchester Community College C, A
Yeshiva University B

North Carolina
Cleveland Community College A
Elon University B
Guilford Technical Community
    College A
Johnson C. Smith University B
Lenoir Community College A
Livingstone College B
Louisburg College A
North Carolina Agricultural and
    Technical State University M
North Carolina State University M
University of North Carolina
    Charlotte M
Western Piedmont Community
    College A

North Dakota
North Dakota State University B, M, D

Ohio
Baldwin-Wallace College B
Case Western Reserve University B, M
Edison State Community College A
Jefferson Community College A
Kent State University C, A, B, M
Lorain County Community College A
Muskingum College B
Oberlin College B

Ohio Northern University B
University of Akron B, M, D
University of Cincinnati B, M, D
University of Dayton B, M, D
University of Toledo B
Washington State Community College A
Wittenberg University B
Wright State University M
Youngstown State University B, M

Oklahoma
Eastern Oklahoma State College A
Oklahoma City Community College A
Oklahoma State University B, M, D
Oral Roberts University B
Redlands Community College A
Rose State College A
St. Gregory's University A
Southwestern Oklahoma State
    University B
Tulsa Community College A
University of Oklahoma B, M, D
Western Oklahoma State College A

Oregon
Chemeketa Community College A
George Fox University B
Linn-Benton Community College A
Southwestern Oregon Community
    College A

Pennsylvania
Arcadia University B
Bucks County Community College A
Butler County Community College A
Chatham College B
Community College of Philadelphia A
Delaware County Community College A
Dickinson College B
Drexel University M
Elizabethtown College B
Geneva College B
Gettysburg College B
Harrisburg Area Community College A
Lafayette College B
Lehigh Carbon Community College A
Lincoln University B
Lock Haven University of
    Pennsylvania B
Messiah College B
Northampton County Area Community
    College A
Pittsburgh Institute of Aeronautics A
Reading Area Community College A
St. Vincent College B
Seton Hill University B
Swarthmore College B
Temple University B, D
Thiel College B
University of Pittsburgh B, M
University of Pittsburgh
    Greensburg B
Washington and Jefferson College B
Widener University A, B
York College of Pennsylvania A

Puerto Rico
Turabo University B
University of Puerto Rico
    Mayaguez Campus B
    Ponce A

Rhode Island
Community College of Rhode Island A
Providence College B
Roger Williams University B

South Carolina
Presbyterian College B

South Dakota
South Dakota State University M

Tennessee
Columbia State Community College A
Jackson State Community College A
Maryville College B
Roane State Community College A

Southern Adventist University A
Tennessee State University B, M
University of Memphis M
University of Tennessee
    Chattanooga C, B, M
    Martin B
Walters State Community College A

Texas
Amarillo College A
Angelina College A
Austin Community College A
Baylor University B
Brazosport College A
Central Texas College A
Cisco Junior College A
Clarendon College A
Coastal Bend College A
College of the Mainland A
Del Mar College A
El Paso Community College A
Galveston College A
Grayson County College A
Hill College A
Houston Baptist University B
Kilgore College A
Lamar University M, D
Laredo Community College A
LeTourneau University B
Lubbock Christian University B
North Harris Montgomery Community
    College District A
Odessa College A
Palo Alto College A
Panola College A
Prairie View A&M University M
St. Mary's University M
St. Philip's College A
South Plains College A
Southern Methodist University B, M
Texas A&M University M, D
Texas A&M University
    Kingsville M
Texas Christian University B
Texas Tech University B, M, D
Trinity Valley Community College A
Tyler Junior College A
University of Houston M, D
University of Texas
    El Paso B, M
    Tyler M
Western Texas College A
Wharton County Junior College A

Utah
Dixie State College of Utah A
Salt Lake Community College A
Snow College A
Southern Utah University A, B
Utah State University B
Utah Valley State College A

Vermont
St. Michael's College B
University of Vermont B, M, D

Virginia
Danville Community College A
Emory & Henry College B
Hampton University B
J. Sargeant Reynolds Community
    College A
Mary Baldwin College B
Old Dominion University M, D
Piedmont Virginia Community
    College A
Southwest Virginia Community
    College A
Thomas Nelson Community College A
University of Virginia B
Virginia Western Community College A

Washington
Centralia College A
Everett Community College C, A
Gonzaga University B
Grays Harbor College A

Lower Columbia College *A*
South Seattle Community College *A*
University of Washington *B, M*
Walla Walla College *B*
Washington State University *M*
Whitworth College *B*

West Virginia
Marshall University *M*
Mountain State University *A*
West Virginia University *M, D*
West Virginia University at
    Parkersburg *A*

Wisconsin
Beloit College *B*
Milwaukee School of Engineering *M*
University of Wisconsin
    Madison *M*
    Milwaukee *M, D*

Wyoming
Casper College *A*
Laramie County Community College *A*
Sheridan College *A*
Western Wyoming Community
    College *A*

Engineering mechanics

Alabama
Alabama Southern Community
    College *A*
University of Alabama *M, D*

Arizona
Central Arizona College *A*
University of Arizona *M, D*

California
California State University
    Northridge *B, M*
East Los Angeles College *A*
University of California
    San Diego *B, M, D*

Colorado
Colorado School of Mines *M*
United States Air Force Academy *B*

Florida
University of Florida *M, D*

Georgia
Georgia Institute of Technology *M, D*

Idaho
Idaho State University *M*

Illinois
Northwestern University *M, D*
Parkland College *A*
University of Illinois
    Urbana-Champaign *B, M, D*

Indiana
Purdue University
    Calumet *B*

Iowa
Iowa State University *M, D*
Southeastern Community College
    North Campus *A*

Maryland
Johns Hopkins University *B, M, D*

Massachusetts
Boston University *M*
Smith College *B*

Michigan
Michigan State University *B, M, D*
Michigan Technological University *M, D*
Northern Michigan University *B*
University of Michigan *M*
Washtenaw Community College *A*

Minnesota
Winona State University *B*

Mississippi
Mississippi State University *M*

Missouri
East Central College *A*
University of Missouri
    Rolla *B, M, D*

Nebraska
University of Nebraska
    Lincoln *M*

New Mexico
New Mexico Institute of Mining and
    Technology *B, M*

New York
Columbia University
    Fu Foundation School of
    Engineering and Applied
    Science *B, M, D*
Hofstra University *B*
New York University *B*
Rensselaer Polytechnic Institute *B, M, D*
State University of New York
    College of Agriculture and
    Technology at Morrisville *A*

Ohio
Case Western Reserve University *M, D*
Cleveland State University *M*
Muskingum College *B*
Ohio State University
    Columbus Campus *M, D*
University of Cincinnati *B, M, D*
University of Dayton *M*

Pennsylvania
Gettysburg College *B*
Lehigh University *B*
Lock Haven University of
    Pennsylvania *B*
Penn State
    University Park *C, M*

South Carolina
Clemson University *M, D*

Texas
Texas A&M University *M, D*
University of Texas
    Arlington *M*
    Austin *M, D*

Virginia
University of Virginia *M*
Virginia Commonwealth University *B*
Virginia Polytechnic Institute and State
    University *M, D*

Wisconsin
University of Wisconsin
    Madison *B, M, D*
Waukesha County Technical College *A*

Engineering physics

Alabama
Samford University *B*

Arizona
Northern Arizona University *B*
University of Arizona *B*

Arkansas
Arkansas Tech University *B*
Ouachita Baptist University *B*
Southern Arkansas University *B*

California
California Institute of Technology *B*
Loyola Marymount University *B*
Point Loma Nazarene University *B*
Santa Clara University *B*
University of California
    Berkeley *B*
    San Diego *B, M, D*
University of the Pacific *B*

Colorado
Colorado School of Mines *B, M, D*
Fort Lewis College *B*
United States Air Force Academy *B*
University of Colorado
    Boulder *B*

Connecticut
Connecticut College *B*
University of Connecticut *B*
Yale University *B, M, D*

Florida
Embry-Riddle Aeronautical University *B*
Jacksonville University *B*

Idaho
Northwest Nazarene University *B*

Illinois
Augustana College *B*
Aurora University *B*
Bradley University *B*
Parkland College *A*
Sauk Valley Community College *A*
University of Illinois
    Chicago *B*
    Urbana-Champaign *B*

Indiana
Taylor University *B*
Vincennes University *A*

Iowa
Loras College *B*
Morningside College *B*
St. Ambrose University *B*
University of Northern Iowa *B*

Kansas
University of Kansas *B*

Kentucky
Murray State University *B, M*

Maine
University of Maine *B*

Maryland
Morgan State University *B*

Massachusetts
Bunker Hill Community College *A*
Harvard College *B*
Merrimack College *B*
Tufts University *B*
University of Massachusetts
    Boston *B*
Worcester Polytechnic Institute *B, M*

Michigan
Hope College *B*
Oakland University *B*
University of Michigan *B*

Minnesota
Bemidji State University *B*
Bethel College *B*
St. Mary's University of Minnesota *B*

Mississippi
Mississippi College *B*

Missouri
East Central College *A*
Southeast Missouri State University *B*
Southwest Missouri State University *B*
Washington University in St.
    Louis *B, M, D*

Nebraska
University of Nebraska
    Omaha *B*

Nevada
University of Nevada
    Reno *B*

New Hampshire
Dartmouth College *B*
St. Anselm College *B*

New Jersey
Stevens Institute of Technology *M, D*

New York
Barnard College *B*
Columbia University
    Fu Foundation School of
    Engineering and Applied
    Science *M, D*
Cornell University *B*
New York University *B*
Rensselaer Polytechnic Institute *B, M, D*
State University of New York
    Buffalo *B*
Syracuse University *B*
United States Military Academy *B*

North Carolina
Elon University *B*
North Carolina State University *B*

North Dakota
North Dakota State University *B*

Ohio
Case Western Reserve University *B*
John Carroll University *B*
Miami University
    Oxford Campus *B*
Ohio State University
    Columbus Campus *B*
University of Akron *B*
Wright State University *B*

Oklahoma
Northeastern State University *B*
Oklahoma Christian University of
    Science and Arts *B*
Oral Roberts University *B*
Southwestern Oklahoma State
    University *B*
University of Oklahoma *B, M, D*
University of Tulsa *B*

Oregon
Oregon State University *B*

Pennsylvania
Elizabethtown College *B*
Gettysburg College *B*
Juniata College *B*
Lehigh University *B*
Lock Haven University of
    Pennsylvania *B*
University of Pittsburgh *B*

Rhode Island
Brown University *B*
Providence College *B*

South Dakota
Augustana College *B*
South Dakota State University *B*

Tennessee
Christian Brothers University *B*
University of Tennessee
    Knoxville *B*

Texas
Abilene Christian University *B*
Northeast Texas Community College *A*
Texas A&M University *M*
Texas Tech University *B*

Utah
Weber State University *B*

Vermont
University of Vermont *M*

Virginia
University of Virginia *M, D*
Washington and Lee University *B*

West Virginia
West Virginia Wesleyan College *B*

Wisconsin
University of Wisconsin
    Platteville *B*

Engineering science

Arizona
Arizona State University *M, D*

California
California Institute of Technology *M, D*
California Polytechnic State University:
San Luis Obispo *B*
California State University
Fullerton *B*
Humboldt State University *B*
San Diego State University *D*
Stanford University *M*
University of California
Berkeley *B*
San Diego *B*

Colorado
Colorado State University *B*
United States Air Force Academy *B*

Connecticut
Gateway Community College *A*
Manchester Community College *A*
Norwalk Community College *A*
Tunxis Community College *A*
Yale University *B*

District of Columbia
George Washington University *M, D*

Florida
Manatee Community College *A*
University of Florida *B, M*
University of Miami *B*

Idaho
Idaho State University *D*

Illinois
Benedictine University *B*
Northwestern University *B, M, D*
Principia College *B*
South Suburban College of Cook
County *A*

Indiana
Manchester College *B*

Iowa
Iowa State University *B*
Wartburg College *B*

Kansas
Garden City Community College *A*

Louisiana
Louisiana State University and
Agricultural and Mechanical
College *M, D*
Tulane University *B*
University of New Orleans *B, M, D*

Maryland
Johns Hopkins University *B*
Loyola College in Maryland *B*

Massachusetts
Berkshire Community College *A*
Boston University *D*
Franklin W. Olin College of
Engineering *B*
Greenfield Community College *A*
Harvard College *B*
Merrimack College *A*
Smith College *B*
Tufts University *B*

Michigan
Glen Oaks Community College *A*
University of Michigan *B*
University of Michigan
Flint *B*
Washtenaw Community College *A*

Minnesota
Bethel College *B*

Mississippi
University of Mississippi *M, D*

Missouri
Washington University in St.
Louis *B, M, D*

Montana
Montana Tech of the University of
Montana *B, M*

Nebraska
Metropolitan Community College *A*

New Hampshire
Daniel Webster College *A*
Dartmouth College *B*

New Jersey
Camden County College *A*
The College of New Jersey *B*
County College of Morris *A*
Gloucester County College *A*
Hudson County Community College *A*
Middlesex County College *A*
New Jersey Institute of Technology *B, M*
Passaic County Community College *A*
Raritan Valley Community College *A*
Rutgers, The State University of New
Jersey
Camden Regional Campus *B*
New Brunswick Regional
Campus *B*

New Mexico
New Mexico Institute of Mining and
Technology *B, M*
University of New Mexico *B*

New York
Adirondack Community College *A*
Broome Community College *A*
City University of New York
Borough of Manhattan Community
College *A*
College of Staten Island *A, B*
Clarkson University *M, D*
Corning Community College *A*
Dutchess Community College *A*
Finger Lakes Community College *A*
Fulton-Montgomery Community
College *A*
Genesee Community College *A*
Hofstra University *B*
Hudson Valley Community College *A*
Jefferson Community College *A*
Monroe Community College *A*
Onondaga Community College *A*
Rensselaer Polytechnic Institute *B, M, D*
Rochester Institute of Technology *A*
State University of New York
Buffalo *M*
College of Agriculture and
Technology at Morrisville *A*
College of Technology at Alfred *A*
College of Technology at Canton *A*
College of Technology at Delhi *A*
Suffolk County Community College *A*
Tompkins-Cortland Community
College *A*
University of Rochester *B*
Westchester Community College *A*

Ohio
Case Western Reserve
University *B, M, D*
Franciscan University of Steubenville *B*
Jefferson Community College *A*
University of Cincinnati *M, D*
University of Toledo *M, D*
Wright State University *B, M*

Oklahoma
Oklahoma State University *B*

Pennsylvania
Gettysburg College *B*
Lock Haven University of
Pennsylvania *B*

Montgomery County Community
College *A*
Penn State
Abington *B*
Altoona *B*
Beaver *B*
Berks *B*
Delaware County *B*
Dubois *B*
Fayette *B*
Hazleton *B*
Lehigh Valley *B*
McKeesport *B*
Mont Alto *B*
New Kensington *B*
Schuylkill - Capital College *B*
Shenango *B*
University Park *B, M, D*
Wilkes-Barre *B*
Worthington Scranton *B*
York *B*

Tennessee
University of Tennessee
Knoxville *B, M, D*
Vanderbilt University *B*

Texas
Abilene Christian University *B*
St. Mary's University *B*
Trinity University *B*
University of Houston *M, D*

Virginia
George Mason University *M*
Virginia Polytechnic Institute and State
University *B*

Washington
Pacific Lutheran University *B*
Seattle Pacific University *B*
Washington State University *D*

Engineering technology

Arkansas
Arkansas State University *A, B*

California
ITT Technical Institute
San Bernardino *A, B*
Ohlone College *C*

Connecticut
University of Hartford *B*

Florida
ITT Technical Institute
Ft. Lauderdale *A*
Maitland *A, B*
South Florida Community College *A*

Georgia
Southern Polytechnic State University *M*

Idaho
Lewis-Clark State College *A*

Illinois
Southern Illinois University
Carbondale *B*

Indiana
University of Southern Indiana *B*
Vincennes University *A*

Kentucky
Hopkinsville Community College *C, A*
Murray State University *B, M*

Louisiana
University of New Orleans *M, D*

Massachusetts
Wentworth Institute of Technology *A, B*

Michigan
Grand Rapids Community College *A*
ITT Technical Institute
Troy *A*

Lawrence Technological University *B*
Michigan Technological University *A, B*

Minnesota
Itasca Community College *A*

Missouri
ITT Technical Institute
Earth City *A, B*

New Jersey
Bergen Community College *A*

New York
State University of New York
College of Agriculture and
Technology at Morrisville *A*

North Carolina
Cleveland Community College *A*

Ohio
ITT Technical Institute
Youngstown *A*
Kent State University *A*
University of Dayton *B*

Oklahoma
Oklahoma State University *B*
Oklahoma State University
Oklahoma City *A*

Pennsylvania
Community College of Allegheny
County *A*
ITT Technical Institute
Bensalem *A*
South Hills School of Business &
Technology *A*

Tennessee
University of Memphis *M*

Texas
ITT Technical Institute
Austin *A*
Houston North *A*
Southwest Texas State University *B*
Texas A&M University *B*
Texas Tech University *B*
University of Texas
Tyler *B*
West Texas A&M University *B, M*

Virginia
Old Dominion University *B*
Rappahannock Community College *A*

Washington
Edmonds Community College *C, A*
Everett Community College *A*
ITT Technical Institute
Seattle *A, B*

Wisconsin
ITT Technical Institute
Green Bay *A, B*
University of Wisconsin
Stout *B*

Engineering/industrial management

Arizona
Central Arizona College *A*
Gateway Community College *C*
University of Arizona *B*

Arkansas
East Arkansas Community College *C*

California
Claremont McKenna College *B*
Loyola Marymount University *M*
University of Southern California *M*
University of the Pacific *B*

Colorado
National Technological University *M*
University of Denver *M*

Connecticut

Naugatuck Valley Community College *A*

District of Columbia

Catholic University of America *M*
George Washington University *M, D*

Florida

Florida Institute of Technology *M*
Florida International University *M*
Hillsborough Community College *A*
Palm Beach Community College *A*
Polk Community College *A*
St. Petersburg College *A*
Tallahassee Community College *A*
University of Miami *M, D*
University of South Florida *M*

Georgia

Georgia Southern University *B, M*
Mercer University *B, M*
Southern Polytechnic State University *C*

Idaho

Idaho State University *B*
University of Idaho *M*

Illinois

Aurora University *B*
Bradley University *B*
Lincoln Land Community College *A*
Northern Illinois University *M*
Northwestern University *M*
Parkland College *C*
University of Illinois
     Chicago *B*

Indiana

Purdue University
     Calumet *B, T*
Rose-Hulman Institute of Technology *M*
Tri-State University *B*

Kansas

Fort Scott Community College *A*
Kansas State University *M*
University of Kansas *M*
Wichita State University *M*

Louisiana

Louisiana Tech University *M*
University of Louisiana at Lafayette *M*
University of New Orleans *C, M*

Maryland

Johns Hopkins University *M*
University of Maryland
     Baltimore County *M*

Massachusetts

Berkshire Community College *A*
University of Massachusetts
     Amherst *M*
Western New England College *M*
Worcester Polytechnic Institute *B, M*

Michigan

Baker College
     of Muskegon *B*
Kettering University *M*
Lawrence Technological University *B*
Oakland University *M*
University of Michigan
     Dearborn *M*
     Flint *B*
Wayne State University *M*
Western Michigan University *B, M*

Missouri

Longview Community College *A*
St. Louis University *B*
Southwest Missouri State University *B*
University of Missouri
     Rolla *B, M, D*

Montana

Montana State University
     Bozeman *M*

New Mexico

New Mexico Institute of Mining and
     Technology *M*

New York

College of Aeronautics *B*
Columbia University
     Fu Foundation School of
        Engineering and Applied
        Science *B*
Rensselaer Polytechnic Institute *B, M, D*
Rochester Institute of Technology *M*
Syracuse University *M*
United States Merchant Marine
     Academy *B*

North Carolina

Fayetteville Technical Community
     College *A*
Haywood Community College *A*
Mitchell Community College *A*
North Carolina Agricultural and
     Technical State University *B*
North Carolina State University *M, D*
Pitt Community College *C, A*
University of North Carolina
     Charlotte *M*

Ohio

David N. Myers College *B*
Edison State Community College *A*
Miami University
     Oxford Campus *B*
Northwest State Community College *A*
University of Dayton *B*

Oklahoma

Oklahoma State University *B, M, D*
University of Tulsa *M*

Oregon

Portland State University *M*
University of Portland *B*

Pennsylvania

Cheyney University of Pennsylvania *B*
Drexel University *M*
Grove City College *B*
Philadelphia University *M*
Robert Morris University *M*
York College of Pennsylvania *B*

Puerto Rico

Inter American University of Puerto Rico
     Bayamon Campus *B*
University of Puerto Rico
     Mayaguez Campus *M*

South Dakota

South Dakota State University *M*

Tennessee

Christian Brothers University *M*
University of Tennessee
     Chattanooga *B, M*
Vanderbilt University *M*

Texas

St. Mary's University *M*
Southern Methodist University *M, D*
Texas A&M University
     Kingsville *B, M*
University of Houston *B, M*
University of Texas
     Austin *M*

Utah

Utah Valley State College *B*

Vermont

University of Vermont *B*

Washington

St. Martin's College *M*
Washington State University *M*

Wisconsin

Marquette University *M*
University of Wisconsin
     Stout *B*

Alabama

Athens State University *B*
Auburn University *B, M, D, T*
Auburn University at Montgomery *B*
Birmingham-Southern College *B, T*
Calhoun Community College *A*
Faulkner University *B, T*
Huntingdon College *B, T*
Jacksonville State University *B, M*
James H. Faulkner State Community
     College *A*
Judson College *B*
Lawson State Community College *A*
Miles College *B*
Northeast Alabama Community
     College *A*
Oakwood College *B*
Stillman College *B*
Talladega College *B*
Troy State University *B*
Troy State University Dothan *B, T*
Tuskegee University *B*
University of Alabama *B, M, D*
University of Alabama
     Birmingham *B, M*
     Huntsville *B, M*
University of Mobile *B, T*
University of Montevallo *B, M, T*
University of North Alabama *B, M*
University of West Alabama *B, T*

Alaska

University of Alaska
     Anchorage *B, M*
     Southeast *B*

Arizona

Arizona Western College *A*
Cochise College *A*
Eastern Arizona College *A*
Northern Arizona University *B, M, T*
Prescott College *B, M*
South Mountain Community College *A*
University of Arizona *B, M, D*

Arkansas

Arkansas State University *B, M*
Arkansas State University
     Beebe *A*
Black River Technical College *A*
Harding University *B*
Henderson State University *B*
Hendrix College *B*
Lyon College *B*
Ouachita Baptist University *B*
Philander Smith College *B*
Phillips Community College of the
     University of Arkansas *A*
Southern Arkansas University *B*
University of Arkansas *B, M, D*
University of Arkansas
     Fort Smith *A*
     Little Rock *B*
     Monticello *B*
     Pine Bluff *B*
University of Central Arkansas *B*
University of the Ozarks *B, T*
Williams Baptist College *B*

California

Azusa Pacific University *B*
Bakersfield College *A*
Barstow College *A*
Bethany College *B*
Biola University *B*
Cabrillo College *A*
California Baptist University *B, M*
California Institute of Technology *B*
California Polytechnic State University:
     San Luis Obispo *B, M*

California State University
     Bakersfield *B, M*
     Chico *B, M*
     Dominguez Hills *B, M*
     Fresno *B, M*
     Fullerton *B, M*
     Hayward *B, M*
     Long Beach *B, M, T*
     Los Angeles *B*
     Monterey Bay *B*
     Northridge *B, M*
     Sacramento *B, M*
     San Bernardino *B*
     San Marcos *B*
     Stanislaus *B, M*
Cerritos Community College *A*
Chabot College *A*
Chapman University *B, M*
Christian Heritage College *B*
Citrus College *A*
Claremont McKenna College *B*
College of Alameda *A*
College of the Sequoias *A*
College of the Siskiyous *A*
Columbia College *A*
Concordia University *B*
Contra Costa College *A*
De Anza College *A*
Dominican University of California *B*
Feather River College *C, A*
Foothill College *A*
Fresno Pacific University *B*
Gavilan Community College *A*
Glendale Community College *A*
Golden West College *A*
Grossmont Community College *C, A*
Holy Names College *B*
Humboldt State University *B, M*
Imperial Valley College *A*
La Sierra University *B, M*
Laney College *A*
Long Beach City College *A*
Los Angeles Southwest College *A*
Loyola Marymount University *B, M*
Marymount College *A*
Master's College *B*
Mills College *B, M*
MiraCosta College *A*
Modesto Junior College *A*
Monterey Peninsula College *A*
Mount St. Mary's College *B*
Napa Valley College *A*
National University *B*
Occidental College *B*
Orange Coast College *A*
Pacific Union College *B*
Pepperdine University *B*
Pitzer College *B*
Pomona College *B*
Reedley College *A*
St. Mary's College of California *B*
San Diego City College *A*
San Diego State University *B, M*
San Francisco State University *B, M*
San Joaquin Delta College *A*
San Jose State University *B, M*
Santa Barbara City College *A*
Santa Monica College *A*
Santa Rosa Junior College *A*
Santiago Canyon College *A*
Scripps College *B*
Simpson College *B*
Sonoma State University *B, M*
Southwestern College *A*
Stanford University *B, M, D*
Taft College *A*
University of California
     Berkeley *B, D*
     Davis *B, M, D*
     Irvine *B, M, D*
     Los Angeles *B, M, D*
     Riverside *B, M, D*
     San Diego *B*
     Santa Barbara *B, M, D*
University of La Verne *B*

University of Redlands *B*
University of San Diego *B*
University of San Francisco *B*
University of Southern
 California *B, M, D*
University of the Pacific *B*
Ventura College *A*
West Valley College *A*
Whittier College *B*
Yuba Community College District *A*

Colorado
Colorado College *B*
Colorado Mountain College
 Alpine Campus *A*
 Spring Valley Campus *A*
 Timberline Campus *A*
Colorado State University *B, M*
Colorado State University
 Pueblo *B, T*
Fort Lewis College *B*
Mesa State College *A, B*
Metropolitan State College of
 Denver *B, T*
Red Rocks Community College *A*
Regis University *B*
United States Air Force Academy *B*
University of Colorado
 Colorado Springs *B*
 Denver *B, M*
University of Denver *B, M, D*
University of Northern Colorado *B, M, T*

Connecticut
Albertus Magnus College *B*
Connecticut College *B*
Eastern Connecticut State University *B*
Fairfield University *B*
Northwestern Connecticut Community
 College *A*
Quinnipiac University *B*
Sacred Heart University *B*
St. Joseph College *B, T*
Southern Connecticut State
 University *B, M*
Teikyo Post University *B*
Trinity College *B, M*
University of Bridgeport *B*
University of Connecticut *B, M, D*
University of Hartford *B*
University of New Haven *B*
Wesleyan University *B*
Western Connecticut State
 University *B, M*
Yale University *B, M, D*

Delaware
Delaware State University *B*
University of Delaware *B, M, D*

District of Columbia
American University *B, M*
Catholic University of
 America *B, M, D, T*
Gallaudet University *B*
George Washington University *B*
Howard University *B, M, D*
Trinity College *B*
University of the District of
 Columbia *A, B*

Florida
Bethune-Cookman College *B*
Broward Community College *A*
Flagler College *B*
Florida Agricultural and Mechanical
 University *B*
Florida Atlantic University *B, M*
Florida International University *B, M*
Florida Southern College *B*
Florida State University *C, B, M, D*
Gulf Coast Community College *A*
Indian River Community College *A*
Jacksonville University *B*
Manatee Community College *A*
Nova Southeastern University *B*
Palm Beach Atlantic University *B, T*

Palm Beach Community College *A*
Pensacola Junior College *A*
Polk Community College *A*
Rollins College *B*
St. Leo University *B*
St. Thomas University *B*
South Florida Community College *A*
Southeastern College of the Assemblies
 of God *B*
Stetson University *B, M*
University of Central Florida *C, B, M*
University of Florida *B, M, D*
University of Miami *B, M, D*
University of North Florida *B, M*
University of South Florida *B, M, D*
University of Tampa *A, B, T*
Warner Southern College *B*

Georgia
Abraham Baldwin Agricultural
 College *A*
Agnes Scott College *B*
Albany State University *B*
Armstrong Atlantic State University *B, T*
Atlanta Metropolitan College *A*
Augusta State University *B*
Bainbridge College *A*
Berry College *B, T*
Brenau University *B*
Brewton-Parker College *B*
Clark Atlanta University *B, M*
Clayton College and State University *A*
Columbus State University *B*
Covenant College *B*
Dalton State College *A*
Darton College *A*
East Georgia College *A*
Emmanuel College *B*
Floyd College *A*
Fort Valley State University *B*
Gainesville College *A*
Georgia College and State
 University *B, M*
Georgia Perimeter College *A*
Georgia Southwestern State University *B*
Georgia State University *B, M, D*
Gordon College *A*
Kennesaw State University *B*
LaGrange College *B*
Macon State College *A*
Mercer University *B*
Middle Georgia College *A*
Morehouse College *B*
Morris Brown College *B*
North Georgia College & State
 University *B*
Oglethorpe University *B*
Oxford College of Emory University *B*
Paine College *B*
Piedmont College *B*
Savannah State University *B*
Shorter College *B, T*
South Georgia College *A*
Spelman College *B*
Thomas University *B*
Toccoa Falls College *B*
University of Georgia *B, M, D*
Valdosta State University *B, M*
Waycross College *A*
Wesleyan College *B*
Young Harris College *A*

Hawaii
Brigham Young University-Hawaii *B*
Chaminade University of Honolulu *B*
Hawaii Pacific University *B*
University of Hawaii
 Hilo *B*
 Manoa *B, M, D*
 West Oahu *B*

Idaho
Albertson College of Idaho *B*
Boise State University *M, D*
Brigham Young University - Idaho *B*
College of Southern Idaho *A*

Idaho State University *A, B, M, D*
Lewis-Clark State College *B*
North Idaho College *A*
Northwest Nazarene University *B*
University of Idaho *B, M*

Illinois
Augustana College *B*
Aurora University *B*
Benedictine University *B, T*
Black Hawk College
 East Campus *A*
Blackburn College *B, T*
Chicago State University *B, M, T*
City Colleges of Chicago
 Harold Washington College *A*
 Kennedy-King College *A*
Concordia University *B*
De Paul University *B, M, T*
Dominican University *B*
Eastern Illinois University *B, M, T*
Elmhurst College *B, T*
Eureka College *B, T*
Governors State University *B, M, T*
Greenville College *B, T*
Illinois Central College *A*
Illinois College *B, T*
Illinois State University *B, M, D, T*
Illinois Valley Community College *A*
Illinois Wesleyan University *B*
Joliet Junior College *A*
Judson College *B*
Kishwaukee College *A*
Knox College *B*
Lake Forest College *B*
Lewis University *B, T*
Lewis and Clark Community College *A*
Lincoln College *A*
Lincoln Land Community College *A*
Loyola University of
 Chicago *C, B, M, D*
MacMurray College *B, T*
McKendree College *B, T*
Monmouth College *B, T*
National-Louis University *B*
North Central College *B, T*
North Park University *B*
Northeastern Illinois University *B, M*
Northern Illinois University *B, M, D, T*
Northwestern University *B, M, D*
Olivet Nazarene University *B, T*
Parkland College *A*
Principia College *B, T*
Quincy University *B, T*
Richland Community College *A*
Rockford College *B*
Roosevelt University *B, M*
St. Xavier University *C, B, M*
Sauk Valley Community College *A*
South Suburban College of Cook
 County *A*
Southern Illinois University
 Carbondale *B, M, D*
Southern Illinois University
 Edwardsville *B, M, T*
Southwestern Illinois College *A*
Spoon River College *A*
Trinity Christian College *B, T*
Trinity International University *B*
Triton College *A*
University of Chicago *B, M, D*
University of Illinois
 Chicago *B, M, D*
 Springfield *B, M*
University of St. Francis *B*
Wheaton College *B*
William Rainey Harper College *A*

Indiana
Ball State University *B, M, D, T*
Bethel College *B*
Butler University *B, M*
Calumet College of St. Joseph *A, B*
Earlham College *B*
Goshen College *B*
Grace College *B*

Hanover College *B*
Huntington College *B*
Indiana University
 Bloomington *B, M, D*
 East *B*
 Kokomo *B*
 Southeast *B*
Indiana University-Purdue University
 Fort Wayne *A, B, M, T*
Indiana University-Purdue University
 Indianapolis *B, M*
Indiana Wesleyan University *A, B*
Manchester College *B, T*
Marian College *B, T*
Martin University *B*
Oakland City University *B*
Purdue University *B, M, D*
Purdue University
 Calumet *B*
 North Central Campus *B*
Saint Mary's College *B, T*
St. Mary-of-the-Woods College *B*
Taylor University *B*
Taylor University: Fort Wayne *B*
University of Evansville *B*
University of Indianapolis *B, M*
University of St. Francis *B*
Valparaiso University *B, M*
Vincennes University *A*
Wabash College *B*

Iowa
Briar Cliff University *B*
Buena Vista University *B, T*
Central College *B, T*
Clarke College *A, B, T*
Coe College *B*
Cornell College *B, T*
Dordt College *B*
Drake University *B*
Ellsworth Community College *A*
Franciscan University *B, T*
Graceland University *T*
Grand View College *B*
Grinnell College *B*
Iowa State University *B, M, D*
Iowa Wesleyan College *B*
Loras College *B, M*
Luther College *B*
Maharishi University of Management *B*
Marshalltown Community College *A*
Morningside College *B*
Mount Mercy College *B, T*
North Iowa Area Community College *A*
Northwestern College *B, T*
St. Ambrose University *B, T*
Simpson College *B*
University of Dubuque *B*
University of Iowa *B, M, D, T*
University of Northern Iowa *B, M*
Upper Iowa University *B*
Waldorf College *A, B*
Wartburg College *B, T*
William Penn University *B*

Kansas
Baker University *B, T*
Benedictine College *B, T*
Bethany College *B*
Central Christian College *A*
Cloud County Community College *A*
Donnelly College *A*
Emporia State University *B, M*
Fort Hays State University *B, M*
Friends University *B*
Garden City Community College *A*
Haskell Indian Nations University *A*
Hutchinson Community College *A*
Independence Community College *A*
Kansas City Kansas Community
 College *A*
Kansas State University *B, M*
Kansas Wesleyan University *B, T*
Labette Community College *A*
McPherson College *B, T*
MidAmerica Nazarene University *B*

Newman University *B*
Ottawa University *B*
Pittsburg State University *B, M, T*
Pratt Community College *A*
St. Mary College *B*
Seward County Community College *A*
Southwestern College *B*
Sterling College *B*
Tabor College *B*
Washburn University of Topeka *B*
Wichita State University *B, M, T*

Kentucky

Alice Lloyd College *B*
Bellarmine University *B, T*
Berea College *B, T*
Brescia University *B*
Campbellsville University *B*
Centre College *B*
Cumberland College *B, T*
Georgetown College *B, T*
Kentucky Wesleyan College *B, T*
Lindsey Wilson College *A, B, T*
Mid-Continent College *B*
Murray State University *B, M, T*
Spalding University *B*
Thomas More College *A, B*
Transylvania University *B, T*
Union College *B*
University of Kentucky *B, M, D*
University of Louisville *B, M*

Louisiana

Centenary College of Louisiana *B, T*
Dillard University *B*
Grambling State University *B*
Louisiana College *B*
Louisiana State University
  Shreveport *B*
Louisiana Tech University *B, M*
Loyola University New Orleans *B*
McNeese State University *B, M*
Nicholls State University *B*
Northwestern State University *B, M*
Our Lady of Holy Cross College *B*
Southern University
  New Orleans *B*
Southern University and Agricultural and
  Mechanical College *B*
Tulane University *B, M, D*
University of Louisiana at Monroe *B, M*
University of New Orleans *B, M*
Xavier University of Louisiana *B*

Maine

Bates College *T*
Bowdoin College *B*
Colby College *B*
St. Joseph's College *B*
Thomas College *B*
University of Maine *B, M*
University of Maine
  Augusta *B*
  Farmington *B*
  Machias *B, T*
  Presque Isle *B*
University of New England *B*
University of Southern Maine *B*

Maryland

Allegany College *A*
Baltimore Hebrew University *A*
Bowie State University *B*
College of Notre Dame of Maryland *B*
Columbia Union College *B*
Community College of Baltimore County
  Catonsville *A*
  Dundalk *A*
  Essex *A*
Coppin State College *B*
Frederick Community College *A*
Frostburg State University *B, T*
Goucher College *B*
Hood College *B, T*
Howard Community College *A*
Johns Hopkins University *B, M, D*
Loyola College in Maryland *B*

McDaniel College *B*
Morgan State University *B, M*
Mount St. Mary's College *B, T*
Salisbury University *B, M, T*
Towson University *B*
United States Naval Academy *B*
University of Baltimore *B*
University of Maryland
  Baltimore County *B*
  University College *B*
Villa Julie College *B*
Washington College *B, M, T*

Massachusetts

American International College *B*
Amherst College *B*
Anna Maria College *B*
Assumption College *B*
Atlantic Union College *B*
Bentley College *B*
Boston College *B, M, D*
Boston University *B, M, D*
Brandeis University *B, M, D*
Bridgewater State College *B, M*
Bunker Hill Community College *A*
Clark University *B, M*
College of the Holy Cross *B*
Elms College *B*
Emmanuel College *B*
Fitchburg State College *B, M*
Framingham State College *B, M*
Hampshire College *B*
Harvard College *B, T*
Lesley University *B*
Massachusetts College of Liberal Arts *B*
Merrimack College *B*
Mount Holyoke College *B*
Nichols College *B*
Northeastern University *A, B, M, D*
Pine Manor College *A, B*
Regis College *B*
Roxbury Community College *A*
Salem State College *B, M*
Simmons College *B, M*
Simon's Rock College of Bard *B*
Smith College *B*
Springfield College *B*
Suffolk University *B*
Tufts University *B, M, D*
University of Massachusetts
  Boston *B, M*
  Lowell *B*
Wellesley College *B*
Western New England College *B*
Westfield State College *B, M, T*
Wheaton College *B*
Williams College *B*

Michigan

Adrian College *A, B, T*
Alma College *B, T*
Andrews University *B, M*
Aquinas College *B, T*
Calvin College *B, T*
Central Michigan University *B, M*
Concordia University *B, T*
Cornerstone University *B, T*
Eastern Michigan University *B*
Grand Valley State University *B*
Hillsdale College *B*
Hope College *B*
Kalamazoo College *B, T*
Kellogg Community College *C, A*
Lansing Community College *A*
Madonna University *A, B, T*
Marygrove College *B, T*
Michigan State University *B, M, D*
Northern Michigan University *B, M, T*
Oakland University *B, M, T*
Saginaw Valley State University *B*
Siena Heights University *B*
Spring Arbor University *B*
University of Michigan *B, M, D, T*
University of Michigan
  Dearborn *B*
  Flint *B, T*

Wayne State University *B, M, D*
Western Michigan University *B, M, D, T*
William Tyndale College *B*

Minnesota

Augsburg College *B*
Bemidji State University *B, M*
Bethel College *B*
Carleton College *B*
College of St. Benedict *B*
College of St. Catherine *B*
Concordia College: Moorhead *B, T*
Concordia University: St. Paul *B*
Crown College *B*
Gustavus Adolphus College *B*
Hamline University *B*
Macalester College *B, T*
Metropolitan State University *B*
Minnesota State University
  Mankato *B, M*
  Moorhead *B*
North Central University *B*
Northland Community & Technical
  College *A*
Northwestern College *B*
St. Cloud State University *B, M*
St. John's University *B*
St. Mary's University of Minnesota *B*
Southwest State University *B, T*
University of Minnesota
  Duluth *B, M*
  Morris *B*
  Twin Cities *B, M, D*
University of St. Thomas *B, M*
Vermilion Community College *A*
Winona State University *B, M*

Mississippi

Alcorn State University *B*
Blue Mountain College *B*
Delta State University *B, T*
Mary Holmes College *A*
Millsaps College *B, T*
Mississippi College *B, M*
Mississippi State University *B, M*
Mississippi University for Women *B, T*
Mississippi Valley State University *B*
Rust College *B*
University of Mississippi *B, M, D, T*
University of Southern
  Mississippi *B, M, D*

Missouri

Avila University *B*
Central Methodist College *A, B*
Central Missouri State University *B, M*
College of the Ozarks *B*
Columbia College *B*
Culver-Stockton College *B, T*
Drury University *B, T*
East Central College *A*
Evangel University *B, T*
Fontbonne College *B, T*
Hannibal-LaGrange College *B*
Lincoln University *B*
Lindenwood University *B*
Maryville University of Saint Louis *B*
Mineral Area College *A*
Missouri Baptist University *B, T*
Missouri Southern State College *B, T*
Missouri Valley College *B*
Missouri Western State College *B*
Northwest Missouri State
  University *B, M*
Rockhurst University *B*
St. Louis University *B, M, D*
Southeast Missouri State
  University *B, M*
Southwest Baptist University *B, T*
Southwest Missouri State
  University *B, M*
Stephens College *B*
Three Rivers Community College *A*
Truman State University *B, M*

University of Missouri
  Columbia *B, M, D*
  Kansas City *B, M*
  Rolla *B, T*
  St. Louis *B, M*
Washington University in St.
  Louis *B, M, D*
Webster University *C, B*
Westminster College *B*
William Jewell College *B, T*
William Woods University *B, T*

Montana

Carroll College *A, B, T*
Miles Community College *A*
Montana State University
  Billings *B*
  Bozeman *B, M*
Rocky Mountain College *B, T*
University of Great Falls *B*
University of Montana-Missoula *B, M*
University of Montana: Western *B*

Nebraska

Bellevue University *B*
Chadron State College *B*
College of Saint Mary *B, T*
Concordia University *B, T*
Creighton University *B, M*
Dana College *B*
Doane College *B*
Hastings College *B*
Little Priest Tribal College *A*
Midland Lutheran College *B, T*
Nebraska Wesleyan University *B*
Northeast Community College *A*
Peru State College *B, T*
Union College *B*
University of Nebraska
  Kearney *B, M, T*
  Lincoln *B, M, D*
Wayne State College *B, M, T*
Western Nebraska Community
  College *A*
York College *A, B, T*

Nevada

Community College of Southern
  Nevada *A*
Great Basin College *A*
Sierra Nevada College *B*
University of Nevada
  Las Vegas *B, M, D*
  Reno *B, M, D*

New Hampshire

Colby-Sawyer College *B, T*
Dartmouth College *B, T*
Franklin Pierce College *B*
Keene State College *B, T*
New England College *B, T*
New Hampshire Technical Institute *A*
Plymouth State College *B*
Rivier College *B, M, T*
Southern New Hampshire University *B*
Thomas More College of Liberal Arts *B*
University of New Hampshire *B, M, D*
University of New Hampshire at
  Manchester *B*

New Jersey

Bloomfield College *B*
Centenary College *B, M*
The College of New Jersey *B, M, T*
College of St. Elizabeth *B, T*
Drew University *B, M, D*
Fairleigh Dickinson University
  College at Florham *B*
  Metropolitan Campus *B, M*
Felician College *B, M*
Georgian Court College *B, T*
Gloucester County College *A*
Kean University *B*
Monmouth University *B*
Montclair State University *B, M, T*
New Jersey City University *B*
Passaic County Community College *A*

Richard Stockton College of New
   Jersey *B*
Rider University *B*
Rowan University *B*
Rutgers, The State University of New
   Jersey
      Camden Regional Campus *B, M, T*
      New Brunswick Regional
         Campus *B, M, D, T*
      Newark Regional Campus *B, M, T*
St. Peter's College *B*
Salem Community College *A*
Seton Hall University *B, M, T*
Stevens Institute of Technology *B*
Sussex County Community College *A*
Thomas Edison State College *B*
Warren County Community College *A*
William Paterson University of New
   Jersey *B, M*

New Mexico
College of the Southwest *B*
Eastern New Mexico University *B, M*
New Mexico Highlands University *B, M*
New Mexico State University *B, M*
San Juan College *A*
University of New Mexico *B, M, D*
Western New Mexico University *B*

New York
Alfred University *B*
Bard College *B*
Barnard College *B*
Canisius College *B*
Cazenovia College *B*
City University of New York
   Baruch College *B*
   Brooklyn College *B, M*
   City College *B, M, T*
   College of Staten Island *B, M, T*
   Hunter College *B, M*
   Queens College *B, M*
   York College *B*
Colgate University *B*
College of Mount St. Vincent *A, B, T*
College of New Rochelle *B, T*
Columbia University
   Columbia College *B*
Concordia College *B, T*
Cornell University *B, M, D, T*
D'Youville College *B*
Daemen College *B*
Dominican College of Blauvelt *B*
Dowling College *B, T*
Elmira College *B, T*
Eugene Lang College/New School
   University *B*
Excelsior College *B*
Fordham University *B, M, D*
Fulton-Montgomery Community
   College *A*
Hamilton College *B*
Hartwick College *B, T*
Hilbert College *B*
Hobart and William Smith Colleges *B*
Hofstra University *B*
Houghton College *B*
Iona College *B, M*
Ithaca College *B, T*
Keuka College *B*
Long Island University
   C. W. Post Campus *B, M*
   Southampton College *B*
Manhattanville College *B*
Marist College *B, T*
Marymount College of Fordham
   University *B, T*
Marymount Manhattan College *B*
Mercy College *B*
Molloy College *B*
Mount St. Mary College *B, T*
Nazareth College of Rochester *B*
New York Institute of Technology *B*
New York University *B, M, D*
Niagara University *B*
Nyack College *B*

Pace University *B*
Pace University:
   Pleasantville/Briarcliff *B*
Roberts Wesleyan College *B*
Russell Sage College *B*
St. Bonaventure University *B, T*
St. John Fisher College *B*
St. John's University *B, M, D*
St. Joseph's College *B, T*
St. Joseph's College: Suffolk
   Campus *B, T*
Sarah Lawrence College *B*
State University of New York
   Albany *B, M, D*
   Binghamton *B, M, D*
   Buffalo *B, M, D*
   College at Brockport *B, M, T*
   College at Buffalo *B, M*
   College at Cortland *B*
   College at Fredonia *B, M, T*
   College at Geneseo *B, T*
   College at Old Westbury *B*
   College at Oneonta *B*
   College at Plattsburgh *B, M*
   College at Potsdam *B, M, T*
   New Paltz *B, M, T*
   Oswego *B, M*
   Stony Brook *B, M, D, T*
Syracuse University *B, M, D*
Touro College *B*
United States Military Academy *B*
University of Rochester *B, M, D*
Utica College *B*
Vassar College *B*
Wagner College *B, T*
Wells College *B*
Yeshiva University *B, T*

North Carolina
Appalachian State University *B, M*
Barton College *B, T*
Belmont Abbey College *B*
Bennett College *B*
Brevard College *B*
Campbell University *B, T*
Catawba College *B, T*
Chowan College *B*
Davidson College *B*
Duke University *B, D*
Elizabeth City State University *B*
Elon University *B, T*
Fayetteville State University *B*
Gardner-Webb University *B*
Greensboro College *B, T*
Guilford College *B, T*
Guilford Technical Community
   College *A*
High Point University *B*
Johnson C. Smith University *B*
Lees-McRae College *B*
Lenoir-Rhyne College *B*
Livingstone College *B*
Louisburg College *A*
Mars Hill College *B, T*
Meredith College *B*
Montreat College *B*
Mount Olive College *B*
North Carolina Agricultural and
   Technical State University *B, M, T*
North Carolina Central University *B, M*
North Carolina State University *B, M*
North Carolina Wesleyan College *B*
Peace College *B*
Pfeiffer University *B*
Queens University of Charlotte *B*
St. Andrews Presbyterian College *B*
St. Augustine's College *B*
Salem College *B*
Shaw University *B*
University of North Carolina
   Asheville *B, T*
   Chapel Hill *B, M, D*
   Greensboro *B, M, D, T*
   Pembroke *B, M*
Wake Forest University *B, M*
Warren Wilson College *B*

Wingate University *B*
Winston-Salem State University *B*

North Dakota
Dickinson State University *B, T*
Jamestown College *B*
Mayville State University *B*
Minot State University *B*
Minot State University: Bottineau
   Campus *A*
North Dakota State University *B, M, T*
University of Mary *B*
University of North Dakota *B, M, D, T*
Valley City State University *B*

Ohio
Case Western Reserve
   University *B, M, D*
Cedarville University *B, T*
Central State University *B*
Cleveland State University *B, M, T*
College of Mount St. Joseph *B, T*
College of Wooster *B*
Defiance College *B, T*
Denison University *B*
Franciscan University of Steubenville *B*
Heidelberg College *B*
Hiram College *B*
John Carroll University *B, M*
Kent State University *B, M, D, T*
Kent State University
   Stark Campus *B*
Kenyon College *B*
Lake Erie College *B*
Lourdes College *A, B*
Marietta College *B*
Miami University
   Middletown Campus *A*
   Oxford Campus *B, M, D, T*
Mount Vernon Nazarene University *B*
Muskingum College *B*
Notre Dame College *B, T*
Oberlin College *B*
Ohio Dominican College *B, T*
Ohio Northern University *B*
Ohio State University
   Columbus Campus *B, M, D*
   Lima Campus *B*
Ohio University *B, M, D*
Ohio Wesleyan University *B*
Otterbein College *B*
Owens Community College
   Findlay Campus *A*
   Toledo *A*
Pontifical College Josephinum *B*
Shawnee State University *B*
Sinclair Community College *A*
University of Cincinnati *B, M, D, T*
University of Dayton *B, M*
University of Findlay *B*
University of Rio Grande *B, T*
University of Toledo *B, M, D*
Urbana University *B*
Walsh University *B*
Wilmington College *B*
Wittenberg University *B*
Wright State University *B, M*
Wright State University: Lake Campus *A*
Youngstown State University *B, M*

Oklahoma
Bacone College *A*
Cameron University *B, M*
Carl Albert State College *A*
East Central University *B*
Eastern Oklahoma State College *A*
Langston University *B*
Murray State College *A*
Northeastern Oklahoma Agricultural and
   Mechanical College *A*
Northeastern State University *B, M*
Northern Oklahoma College *A*
Northwestern Oklahoma State
   University *B*
Oklahoma Baptist University *B, T*

Oklahoma Christian University of
   Science and Arts *B, T*
Oklahoma City University *B*
Oklahoma Panhandle State University *B*
Oklahoma State University *B, M, D*
Oklahoma Wesleyan University *B*
Oral Roberts University *B*
Rogers State University *A*
Rose State College *A*
St. Gregory's University *A, B*
Southeastern Oklahoma State
   University *B*
Southern Nazarene University *B*
Southwestern Oklahoma State
   University *B*
Tulsa Community College *A*
University of Oklahoma *B, M, D*
University of Tulsa *B, M, D*
Western Oklahoma State College *A*

Oregon
Central Oregon Community College *A*
Chemeketa Community College *A*
Concordia University *B*
Eastern Oregon University *B, T*
Lewis & Clark College *B*
Linfield College *B*
Linn-Benton Community College *A*
Oregon State University *B, M*
Pacific University *B*
Portland State University *B, M*
Reed College *B*
Southern Oregon University *B, T*
University of Oregon *B, M, D*
University of Portland *B*
Warner Pacific College *B*
Western Baptist College *B*
Western Oregon University *B*
Willamette University *B*

Pennsylvania
Albright College *B, T*
Arcadia University *B, M*
Bloomsburg University of
   Pennsylvania *B, T*
Bryn Athyn College of the New
   Church *B*
Bryn Mawr College *B*
Bucknell University *B, M*
Cabrini College *B*
California University of
   Pennsylvania *B, M*
Carlow College *B, T*
Cedar Crest College *B*
Cheyney University of Pennsylvania *B*
DeSales University *B*
Dickinson College *B*
Drexel University *B*
East Stroudsburg University of
   Pennsylvania *B*
Franklin & Marshall College *B*
Geneva College *B, T*
Gettysburg College *B*
Grove City College *B*
Gwynedd-Mercy College *B*
Haverford College *B, T*
Holy Family University *B, T*
Immaculata University *B*
Juniata College *B*
King's College *B*
Kutztown University of
   Pennsylvania *B, M, T*
La Roche College *B*
La Salle University *B, T*
Lafayette College *B*
Lebanon Valley College of
   Pennsylvania *B, T*
Lehigh University *B, M, D*
Lincoln University *B*
Lock Haven University of
   Pennsylvania *B*
Marywood University *C, B*
Mercyhurst College *B*
Millersville University of
   Pennsylvania *B, M, T*
Moravian College *B, T*

Mount Aloysius College *B*
Muhlenberg College *B, T*
Neumann College *B, T*
Penn State
Abington *B*
Altoona *B*
Beaver *B*
Berks *B*
Delaware County *B*
Dubois *B*
Erie, The Behrend College *B*
Fayette *B*
Harrisburg *B*
Hazleton *B*
Lehigh Valley *B*
McKeesport *B*
Mont Alto *B*
New Kensington *B*
Schuylkill - Capital College *B*
Shenango *B*
University Park *B, M, D*
Wilkes-Barre *B*
Worthington Scranton *B*
York *B*
Point Park College *B*
Robert Morris University *B*
Rosemont College *B*
St. Joseph's University *B*
St. Vincent College *B*
Slippery Rock University of Pennsylvania *B, M, T*
Temple University *B, M, D*
Thiel College *B*
University of Pittsburgh *C, M, D*
University of Pittsburgh
Bradford *B*
Greensburg *B*
University of Scranton *B, T*
Villanova University *B, M*
Washington and Jefferson College *B*
Waynesburg College *B*
West Chester University of Pennsylvania *M*
Widener University *B*
Wilkes University *B*
Wilson College *B*
York College of Pennsylvania *B, T*

Puerto Rico
Bayamon Central University *B*
Inter American University of Puerto Rico
Metropolitan Campus *B*
San German Campus *B*
Pontifical Catholic University of Puerto Rico *B*
University of Puerto Rico
Cayey University College *B*
Mayaguez Campus *B*
Rio Piedras Campus *B, M, D*
University of the Sacred Heart *B*

Rhode Island
Brown University *B, M, D*
Rhode Island College *B, M*
Salve Regina University *B*
University of Rhode Island *B, M, D*

South Carolina
Anderson College *B, T*
Benedict College *B*
Charleston Southern University *B*
Clemson University *B, M*
Coastal Carolina University *B*
College of Charleston *B, M, T*
Columbia College *B*
Converse College *B*
Erskine College *B, T*
Francis Marion University *B*
Furman University *B, T*
Limestone College *B*
Morris College *B*
Newberry College *B, T*
Presbyterian College *B, T*
South Carolina State University *B*
Southern Wesleyan University *B, T*
University of South Carolina *B, M, D*
University of South Carolina
Aiken *B*
Spartanburg *B*
Voorhees College *B*
Winthrop University *B, M*
Wofford College *B, T*

South Dakota
Augustana College *B, T*
Black Hills State University *B*
Dakota State University *B*
Dakota Wesleyan University *B*
Mount Marty College *B*
Northern State University *B*
South Dakota State University *B, M*
University of Sioux Falls *B*
University of South Dakota *B, M, D*

Tennessee
Austin Peay State University *B, M*
Belmont University *B, T*
Bethel College *B, T*
Bryan College *B, T*
Carson-Newman College *B, T*
Christian Brothers University *B*
Crichton College *B*
East Tennessee State University *B, M, T*
Fisk University *B*
Freed-Hardeman University *B, T*
Jackson State Community College *A*
King College *B, T*
Lambuth University *B*
Lane College *B*
Lee University *B*
Maryville College *B, T*
Middle Tennessee State University *B, M, D*
Milligan College *B, T*
Roane State Community College *A*
Southern Adventist University *B*
Tennessee State University *B, M*
Tennessee Technological University *B, M, T*
Tennessee Wesleyan College *B, T*
Trevecca Nazarene University *B*
Tusculum College *B*
Union University *B, T*
University of Memphis *B, M, D*
University of Tennessee
Chattanooga *B, M, T*
Knoxville *B, M, D*
Martin *B*
Vanderbilt University *B, M, D*
Walters State Community College *A*

Texas
Abilene Christian University *B, M*
Amarillo College *A*
Angelina College *A*
Austin College *B*
Austin Community College *A*
Baylor University *B, M, D*
Blinn College *A*
Brazosport College *A*
Coastal Bend College *A*
Concordia University at Austin *B*
Dallas Baptist University *B*
Del Mar College *A*
East Texas Baptist University *B*
El Paso Community College *A*
Frank Phillips College *A*
Galveston College *A*
Hardin-Simmons University *B, M*
Hill College *A*
Houston Baptist University *B*
Howard College *A*
Howard Payne University *B, T*
Jarvis Christian College *B*
Kilgore College *A*
Lamar University *B, M*
Laredo Community College *A*
LeTourneau University *B*
Lon Morris College *A*
Lubbock Christian University *T*
McMurry University *B, T*
Midland College *A*
Midwestern State University *B, M*
Northeast Texas Community College *A*
Our Lady of the Lake University of San Antonio *B, M*
Palo Alto College *A*
Panola College *A*
Paris Junior College *A*
Prairie View A&M University *B, M*
Rice University *B, M, D*
St. Mary's University *B, M*
Schreiner University *B*
South Plains College *A*
Southern Methodist University *B, M*
Southwest Texas State University *B, M, T*
Southwestern Adventist University *B, T*
Southwestern University *B, T*
Stephen F. Austin State University *B, M, T*
Sul Ross State University *B, M, T*
Tarleton State University *B, M, T*
Texas A&M International University *B, M, T*
Texas A&M University
Commerce *B, M*
Corpus Christi *B, M, T*
Kingsville *B, M*
Texarkana *B, T*
Texas Christian University *B, M, D, T*
Texas College *B*
Texas Southern University *B, M*
Texas Tech University *B, M, D*
Texas Wesleyan University *B*
Texas Woman's University *B, M, T*
Trinity University *B*
Trinity Valley Community College *A*
Tyler Junior College *A*
University of Dallas *B, M, D*
University of Houston *B, M, D*
University of Houston
Clear Lake *B, M*
Downtown *B*
Victoria *B, T*
University of Mary Hardin-Baylor *B, T*
University of North Texas *B, M, D*
University of Texas
Arlington *B, M*
Brownsville *B, M*
El Paso *B, M*
Pan American *B, M, T*
San Antonio *B, M, D*
University of the Incarnate Word *B, M*
Wayland Baptist University *B, T*
Western Texas College *A*
Wharton County Junior College *A*
Wiley College *B*

Utah
Brigham Young University *B, M*
Dixie State College of Utah *A*
Snow College *A*
Southern Utah University *B, T*
Utah State University *B, M*
Weber State University *B*
Westminster College *B*

Vermont
Bennington College *B*
Burlington College *B*
Castleton State College *B*
College of St. Joseph in Vermont *B*
Goddard College *B*
Green Mountain College *B*
Johnson State College *B*
Lyndon State College *B*
Marlboro College *B*
Norwich University *B*
St. Michael's College *B*
Southern Vermont College *B*
University of Vermont *B, M*

Virginia
Averett University *B*
Bluefield College *B*
Christendom College *B*
College of William and Mary *B*
Emory & Henry College *B, T*
Ferrum College *B*
George Mason University *B*
Hampden-Sydney College *B*
Hampton University *B*
Hollins University *B*
James Madison University *B, M, T*
Liberty University *B, T*
Longwood University *B, M, T*
Mary Baldwin College *B*
Mary Washington College *B*
Marymount University *B, M*
Norfolk State University *B*
Radford University *B, M*
Randolph-Macon College *B*
Randolph-Macon Woman's College *B*
Roanoke College *B, T*
Sweet Briar College *B*
University of Richmond *B, M, T*
University of Virginia's College at Wise *B, T*
Virginia Commonwealth University *B, M*
Virginia Intermont College *B*
Virginia Military Institute *B*
Virginia Polytechnic Institute and State University *B, M, T*
Virginia State University *B, M*
Virginia Union University *B*
Virginia Wesleyan College *B*
Washington and Lee University *B*

Washington
Central Washington University *B, M*
Centralia College *A*
Eastern Washington University *B, M, T*
Everett Community College *A*
Gonzaga University *B, M*
Heritage College *B*
Lower Columbia College *A*
Northwest College *B*
Olympic College *A*
Pacific Lutheran University *B*
St. Martin's College *B*
Seattle Pacific University *B*
Seattle University *B*
University of Puget Sound *B, T*
University of Washington *B, M, D*
Walla Walla College *B*
Washington State University *B, M, D*
Western Washington University *B, M*
Whitman College *B*
Whitworth College *B, T*

West Virginia
Alderson-Broaddus College *B*
Bethany College *B*
Concord College *B*
Davis and Elkins College *B*
Fairmont State College *B*
Glenville State College *B*
Potomac State College of West Virginia University *A*
Shepherd College *B*
University of Charleston *B*
West Liberty State College *B*
West Virginia State College *B*
West Virginia University *B, M, D, T*
West Virginia Wesleyan College *B*
Wheeling Jesuit University *B*

Wisconsin
Alverno College *B, T*
Beloit College *B*
Cardinal Stritch University *B*
Carroll College *B*
Carthage College *B, T*
Concordia University Wisconsin *T*
Edgewood College *B*
Lakeland College *B*
Lawrence University *B, T*
Marian College of Fond du Lac *B, T*
Marquette University *B, M, D, T*
Mount Mary College *B*
Northland College *B*
Ripon College *B, T*

St. Norbert College *B, T*
Silver Lake College *B, T*
University of Wisconsin
Eau Claire *B, M*
Green Bay *B*
La Crosse *B*
Madison *B, M, D*
Milwaukee *B, M, D*
Oshkosh *B*
Parkside *B, T*
Platteville *B*
River Falls *B, M*
Stevens Point *B, M, T*
Superior *B*
Whitewater *B, T*
Viterbo University *B*
Wisconsin Lutheran College *B*

Wyoming
Casper College *A*
Eastern Wyoming College *A*
Laramie County Community College *A*
Sheridan College *A*
Western Wyoming Community
College *A*

English composition

Arizona
Prescott College *B, M*

Arkansas
John Brown University *B*
University of Central Arkansas *A*

California
California State University
Chico *C*
Long Beach *B*
Los Angeles *M*
San Bernardino *M*
Glendale Community College *A*
Humboldt State University *M*
Irvine Valley College *A*
Pitzer College *B*
San Diego State University *M*
San Francisco State University *C, M*
Stanford University *B*
University of California
San Diego *B*

Colorado
Colorado State University
Pueblo *B*
University of Colorado
Denver *B*

Connecticut
Quinnipiac University *B*
Southern Connecticut State University *M*
Western Connecticut State University *B*

Florida
Florida Southern College *B*
Polk Community College *A*
University of West Florida *B, M*

Idaho
Brigham Young University - Idaho *B*
Lewis-Clark State College *B*

Illinois
Aurora University *B*
East-West University *B*
Illinois State University *M*
Illinois Valley Community College *A*
Lincoln College *A*
National-Louis University *M*
Northeastern Illinois University *B, M*
Northwestern University *C*
Richland Community College *A*
Sauk Valley Community College *A*
University of Illinois
Urbana-Champaign *B*

Indiana
DePauw University *B*

Indiana University
Bloomington *B*
South Bend *A, B*
Indiana University-Purdue University
Fort Wayne *B*
Martin University *B*
Purdue University
Calumet *B*
University of Evansville *B*

Iowa
Drake University *B*
Graceland University *B, T*
Luther College *B*
University of Iowa *B*
Wartburg College *B*

Kansas
Butler County Community College *A*
Independence Community College *A*

Kentucky
University of Louisville *D*

Maine
University of Southern Maine *B*

Maryland
Johns Hopkins University *B, M*

Massachusetts
Emerson College *M*
Wheaton College *B*

Michigan
Eastern Michigan University *B*
Western Michigan University *B*

Minnesota
Concordia College: Moorhead *B*
Metropolitan State University *B*
St. Cloud State University *B*
Winona State University *B*

Missouri
William Woods University *B*

Montana
Miles Community College *A*

Nevada
University of Nevada
Reno *B*

New Jersey
Rowan University *B*

New York
Bard College *B*
Ithaca College *B*
Manhattan College *B*
Syracuse University *M, D*

North Dakota
North Dakota State University *M*

Ohio
Ohio Northern University *B*
Ohio State University
Columbus Campus *B*
Otterbein College *B*

Oklahoma
Oral Roberts University *B*
Redlands Community College *A*
University of Central Oklahoma *B, M*

Pennsylvania
Geneva College *B*
La Roche College *B*
La Salle University *B*
Penn State
Berks *B*
University of Pittsburgh
Greensburg *B*

Tennessee
Union University *B, T*
University of Tennessee
Knoxville *B*

Texas
Baylor University *B*
Huston-Tillotson College *B*
St. Edward's University *B, T*
St. Philip's College *A*
Texas A&M University
Commerce *B*
University of North Texas *B*

Utah
Snow College *A*

Vermont
Bennington College *B*
Burlington College *B*
Champlain College *B*
Marlboro College *B*

Virginia
University of Virginia's College at
Wise *T*

Washington
Eastern Washington University *M*
Everett Community College *A*

West Virginia
Concord College *B*

Wisconsin
Marquette University *B*

English language/literature

Alabama
Alabama Agricultural and Mechanical
University *B, M*
Alabama State University *B*
Northeast Alabama Community
College *A*
Samford University *B*
Spring Hill College *B, T*
Troy State University in Montgomery *B*
University of South Alabama *B, M*

Alaska
University of Alaska
Fairbanks *B, M*

Arizona
Arizona State University *B, M, D*

Arkansas
Arkansas Tech University *B, M*
University of Arkansas *B, M, D*
University of Arkansas
Fort Smith *B*
University of Central Arkansas *A, B*

California
California State Polytechnic University:
Pomona *B, M*
Chapman University *B*
Claremont McKenna College *B*
College of the Canyons *A*
Long Beach City College *A*
St. Mary's College of California *B*
Santa Barbara City College *A*
Santa Clara University *B*
University of La Verne *B*
Vanguard University of Southern
California *B*

Colorado
Colorado Christian University *B*
University of Colorado
Boulder *B, M, D*

Connecticut
Central Connecticut State
University *B, M*
Trinity College *B, M*
University of Connecticut *B, M, D*

District of Columbia
American University *B, M*
Georgetown University *B, M*

Florida
Barry University *B*
Florida Southern College *B*
Miami-Dade Community College *A*

Georgia
Columbus State University *B*
Georgia Southern University *B, M*
State University of West Georgia *B, M*

Illinois
Bradley University *B, M, T*
Millikin University *B, T*
Quincy University *B, T*
Southern Illinois University
Carbondale *B, M, D*
Trinity Christian College *B, T*
University of Illinois
Urbana-Champaign *B, M, D*
Western Illinois University *B, M*

Indiana
Ancilla College *A*
Anderson University *B*
Franklin College *B*
Indiana State University *B, M*
Indiana University
East *B*
Kokomo *B*
Northwest *A*
South Bend *B*
Southeast *B*
Indiana University-Purdue University
Indianapolis *B, M*
St. Joseph's College *B*
University of Notre Dame *B, M, D*
University of Southern Indiana *B*

Iowa
Loras College *B, M*
University of Northern Iowa *B, M*

Kansas
Barton County Community College *A*
Bethel College *B*
St. Mary College *B*
University of Kansas *B, M, D*

Kentucky
Asbury College *B, T*
Morehead State University *B, M*
Pikeville College *B, T*

Louisiana
Centenary College of Louisiana *B, T*
Louisiana State University and
Agricultural and Mechanical
College *B, M, D*
Loyola University New Orleans *B*
Southeastern Louisiana University *B, M*
University of Louisiana at
Lafayette *M, D, T*

Maine
Bates College *B, T*

Maryland
College of Notre Dame of Maryland *M*
St. Mary's College of Maryland *B*
University of Maryland
College Park *B, M, D*

Massachusetts
Gordon College *B*
Stonehill College *B*
University of Massachusetts
Amherst *B, M, D*
Dartmouth *B*

Michigan
Calvin College *B, T*
Hillsdale College *B*
Michigan State University *B, M, D*
Northern Michigan University *B, M*
Northwestern Michigan College *A*
Saginaw Valley State University *B*
Wayne State University *B, M, D*
Western Michigan University *B, M*

Minnesota
St. Mary's University of Minnesota *B*
St. Olaf College *B*

Mississippi
Alcorn State University *B*

Missouri
Fontbonne College *B*
Lindenwood University *B*
Southeast Missouri State
  University *B, M*
Washington University in St. Louis *B*

Nebraska
University of Nebraska
  Omaha *B, M*

New Hampshire
Plymouth State College *B*
St. Anselm College *B, T*

New Jersey
Bloomfield College *B*
Caldwell College *B*
The College of New Jersey *B, M*
Princeton University *B, M, D*

New Mexico
College of Santa Fe *A, B*

New York
Adelphi University *B, M*
City University of New York
  Hunter College *B, M*
Columbia University
  Columbia College *B*
Hofstra University *B*
Le Moyne College *B*
Medaille College *B*
Pace University:
  Pleasantville/Briarcliff *B*
Sarah Lawrence College *B*
Skidmore College *B*
State University of New York
  Buffalo *M, D*
  College of Agriculture and
    Technology at Morrisville *A*
  Stony Brook *B, M, D, T*
Union College *B*

North Carolina
Campbell University *B, T*
Catawba College *B*
East Carolina University *B, M*
University of North Carolina
  Charlotte *B, M*
  Wilmington *B, M*

North Dakota
Minot State University *B*

Ohio
Antioch College *B*
Ashland University *B*
Baldwin-Wallace College *B, T*
Bowling Green State University *B, M, D*
Malone College *B*
Ohio Northern University *B*
University of Akron *C, B, M*
University of Toledo *A, B, M, D*
Ursuline College *B*
Xavier University *A, B, M*
Youngstown State University *C, B, M*

Oklahoma
University of Science and Arts of
  Oklahoma *B, T*

Oregon
George Fox University *B*

Pennsylvania
Allegheny College *B*
Bryn Athyn College of the New
  Church *B*
Carnegie Mellon University *B, M*
Chestnut Hill College *B*
Delaware Valley College *B*
Duquesne University *B, M, D*

Edinboro University of
  Pennsylvania *B, T*
Elizabethtown College *B*
Geneva College *B*
Indiana University of
  Pennsylvania *B, M, D*
Juniata College *B*
Lincoln University *B*
Lycoming College *B*
Messiah College *B*
St. Vincent College *B*
Seton Hill University *B, T*
Shippensburg University of
  Pennsylvania *B*
Swarthmore College *B*
University of Pennsylvania *C, B, M, D*

Rhode Island
Bryant College *B*
Providence College *B*

South Carolina
Charleston Southern University *B*
The Citadel *B, M*
Coker College *B*
Lander University *B, T*

Tennessee
Rhodes College *B, T*

Texas
Angelo State University *B, M, T*
Clarendon College *A*
Sam Houston State University *B, M*
Texas A&M University *B, M, D*
Texas Lutheran University *B, T*
University of Houston
  Clear Lake *B, M*
University of St. Thomas *B*
University of Texas
  Arlington *B, M, D*
  Austin *B, M, D*
  Tyler *B, M*
  of the Permian Basin *B, M*
West Texas A&M University *B, M*

Utah
University of Utah *B, M, D*
Utah Valley State College *A, B*

Virginia
Averett University *B*
Bridgewater College *B*
Eastern Mennonite University *B*
Hampton University *B*
Old Dominion University *B, M*
Shenandoah University *B*
University of Virginia *B, M, D*

Washington
University of Washington *B*

West Virginia
Marshall University *B, M*

Wisconsin
Alverno College *B, T*
Edgewood College *B*
Lawrence University *B*
St. Norbert College *B, T*

Wyoming
Central Wyoming College *C, A*
University of Wyoming *B, M*

English literature (British)

California
California State University
  Bakersfield *B, M*
  Dominguez Hills *B, M*
  Hayward *B*
  Northridge *B*
Irvine Valley College *A*
Pitzer College *B*
Point Loma Nazarene University *B*
San Diego State University *M*
Stanford University *B*

University of California
  San Diego *B, M, D*
  Santa Cruz *B*
University of Redlands *B*
University of Southern California *B*
Whittier College *B*

Connecticut
Albertus Magnus College *B*

District of Columbia
Gallaudet University *B*
George Washington University *M, D*
Trinity College *B*

Florida
Eckerd College *B*
New College of Florida *B*
University of West Florida *M*

Idaho
Boise State University *B*

Illinois
Blackburn College *B*
Illinois Valley Community College *A*
North Central College *B*
Richland Community College *A*

Indiana
DePauw University *B*
Indiana University-Purdue University
  Fort Wayne *B*
University of Evansville *B*

Iowa
Drake University *B*
Marshalltown Community College *A*
University of Iowa *B, M, T*
Waldorf College *B*

Maine
Bowdoin College *B*

Maryland
Johns Hopkins University *D*

Massachusetts
Assumption College *B*
Clark University *M*
Fitchburg State College *B*
Hampshire College *B*
Harvard College *B*
Northeastern University *B*
Roxbury Community College *A*
Simmons College *B, M*
Simon's Rock College of Bard *B*
Tufts University *B, M, D*

Michigan
Eastern Michigan University *M*
University of Michigan *D*

Minnesota
Bethel College *B*
Concordia College: Moorhead *B*
St. Cloud State University *B*

Missouri
Washington University in St.
  Louis *B, M, D*

New Jersey
Rowan University *B*

New York
Bard College *B*
City University of New York
  Baruch College *B*
  Brooklyn College *B*
  Hunter College *B*
Columbia University
  Columbia College *B*
Elmira College *B, T*
Eugene Lang College/New School
  University *B*
Hamilton College *B*
Hofstra University *B, M*
Mercy College *B*
New York University *B, M, D*
St. Bonaventure University *M*

St. Lawrence University *B*
Sarah Lawrence College *B*
State University of New York
  Buffalo *M, D*
  Purchase *B*
United States Military Academy *B*

North Carolina
Campbell University *B, T*
Duke University *B*
Fayetteville State University *B*
North Carolina State University *B*

Ohio
College of Wooster *B*
Denison University *B*
Miami University
  Oxford Campus *B*
Mount Union College *B*
University of Cincinnati *B, M, D, T*

Oklahoma
Southeastern Oklahoma State
  University *B*

Oregon
Central Oregon Community College *A*
University of Oregon *B*

Pennsylvania
California University of Pennsylvania *B*
Gettysburg College *B*
Holy Family University *B, T*
Immaculata University *B*
La Salle University *B*
University of Pennsylvania *A, B, M, D*
University of Pittsburgh *B*
University of Pittsburgh
  Johnstown *B*
University of Scranton *M*
Waynesburg College *B*
West Chester University of
  Pennsylvania *B*

Rhode Island
Brown University *B, M, D*
Roger Williams University *B*

Texas
Texas A&M University
  Commerce *B*
University of North Texas *D*

Utah
Southern Utah University *B*
University of Utah *M, D*

Vermont
Bennington College *B*
Marlboro College *B*

Virginia
George Mason University *M*
Longwood University *B, M, T*
Randolph-Macon Woman's College *B*

Washington
Everett Community College *A*

West Virginia
Concord College *B*

Wisconsin
Lawrence University *B*
Marquette University *M, D*

English teacher education

Alabama
Athens State University *B*
Auburn University *B*
Birmingham-Southern College *T*
Faulkner University *B*
Huntingdon College *T*
Jacksonville State University *B, M*
Judson College *B*
Miles College *B*
Oakwood College *B*
Talladega College *T*

Troy State University Dothan *B, M*
University of Mobile *B, T*

Alaska

University of Alaska
  Anchorage *M*

Arizona

Arizona State University *B, T*
Northern Arizona University *B, T*
Prescott College *B, M, T*
University of Arizona *B, M, D*

Arkansas

Arkansas State University *B, M, T*
Arkansas Tech University *B, M*
Harding University *B, M, T*
Henderson State University *B, M, T*
John Brown University *B, T*
Ouachita Baptist University *B, T*
Philander Smith College *B*
Southern Arkansas University *B, T*
University of Arkansas *B*
University of Arkansas
  Monticello *B*
  Pine Bluff *B, M, T*
University of Central Arkansas *B, M, T*
University of the Ozarks *T*
Williams Baptist College *B*

California

Azusa Pacific University *T*
California Baptist University *T*
California Polytechnic State University:
  San Luis Obispo *B, T*
California State Polytechnic University:
  Pomona *T*
California State University
  Bakersfield *B, T*
  Chico *T*
  Dominguez Hills *T*
  Fullerton *T*
  Long Beach *T*
  Northridge *B, T*
  Sacramento *T*
  San Bernardino *T*
Christian Heritage College *B, T*
Concordia University *B, T*
Fresno Pacific University *B, T*
Hope International University *B*
Humboldt State University *T*
Los Angeles Southwest College *A*
Loyola Marymount University *M*
Master's College *T*
Mills College *T*
Mount St. Mary's College *T*
Occidental College *T*
Pacific Union College *T*
San Diego State University *B, T*
San Francisco State University *B, T*
San Jose State University *T*
Simpson College *B, T*
Sonoma State University *T*
University of San Francisco *T*
University of Southern California *T*
University of the Pacific *T*
Vanguard University of Southern
  California *M, T*

Colorado

Colorado State University *T*
Colorado State University
  Pueblo *T*
Fort Lewis College *T*
Metropolitan State College of Denver *T*
Regis University *B, T*
University of Colorado
  Boulder *T*
  Colorado Springs *T*

Connecticut

Central Connecticut State
  University *B, M*
Fairfield University *T*
Quinnipiac University *B, M*
Sacred Heart University *T*

Southern Connecticut State
  University *B, M, T*

Delaware

Delaware State University *B*
University of Delaware *B, T*

District of Columbia

Catholic University of America *B, M*
George Washington University *M, T*
Howard University *B*
Trinity College *M*

Florida

Barry University *T*
Bethune-Cookman College *B, T*
Flagler College *B*
Florida Agricultural and Mechanical
  University *B, M*
Florida Atlantic University *B*
Florida International University *B, M, T*
Florida State University *B, M, D, T*
Hobe Sound Bible College *B, T*
Nova Southeastern University *M*
Palm Beach Atlantic University *B, T*
St. Thomas University *B, T*
Southeastern College of the Assemblies
  of God *B, T*
Stetson University *B, T*
University of Central Florida *B, M*
University of Florida *M*
University of South Florida *B, M*
University of Tampa *B, T*
University of West Florida *B, T*
Warner Southern College *B*

Georgia

Agnes Scott College *M, T*
Albany State University *M*
Armstrong Atlantic State
  University *B, M, T*
Berry College *B*
Brewton-Parker College *B*
Clark Atlanta University *B*
Columbus State University *B, M*
Covenant College *B, T*
Emmanuel College *B*
Fort Valley State University *B, T*
Gainesville College *A*
Georgia College and State
  University *M, T*
Georgia Southern University *B, M, T*
Georgia Southwestern State
  University *B, M*
Georgia State University *M, D*
Kennesaw State University *B*
LaGrange College *T*
Mercer University *M, T*
North Georgia College & State
  University *B, M*
Piedmont College *T*
Shorter College *T*
State University of West Georgia *M*
Toccoa Falls College *B, T*
University of Georgia *B, M, T*
Valdosta State University *M, T*
Wesleyan College *T*

Hawaii

Brigham Young University-Hawaii *B*
University of Hawaii
  Manoa *B, T*

Idaho

Boise State University *M, T*
Brigham Young University - Idaho *T*
Lewis-Clark State College *B, T*
Northwest Nazarene University *B*

Illinois

Augustana College *B, T*
Benedictine University *T*
Blackburn College *B, T*
Chicago State University *B*
Columbia College Chicago *M*
Concordia University *B, T*
Dominican University *T*
Elmhurst College *B*

Eureka College *T*
Governors State University *B, M, T*
Greenville College *B, T*
Illinois College *T*
Judson College *B, T*
Lewis University *T*
Loyola University of Chicago *T*
MacMurray College *B, T*
McKendree College *B, T*
National-Louis University *M*
North Central College *B, T*
North Park University *T*
Northwestern University *B, T*
Olivet Nazarene University *B, T*
Quincy University *T*
Rockford College *T*
Roosevelt University *B*
St. Xavier University *M*
Sauk Valley Community College *A*
Trinity Christian College *B, T*
Trinity International University *B, T*
University of Illinois
  Chicago *B*
  Urbana-Champaign *B, M, T*
University of St. Francis *T*
Wheaton College *T*

Indiana

Anderson University *B, T*
Ball State University *T*
Bethel College *B*
Butler University *T*
Franklin College *B, T*
Goshen College *B*
Grace College *B*
Huntington College *B*
Indiana University
  Bloomington *B, T*
  Kokomo *T*
  Northwest *B*
  Southeast *B*
Indiana University-Purdue University
  Fort Wayne *B, M*
Indiana University-Purdue University
  Indianapolis *B, T*
Indiana Wesleyan University *B, T*
Manchester College *B, T*
Oakland City University *B*
Purdue University
  Calumet *B*
Saint Mary's College *T*
St. Mary-of-the-Woods College *B*
Taylor University *B, T*
Tri-State University *B, T*
University of Evansville *B*
University of Indianapolis *B, M, T*
University of St. Francis *B*
University of Southern Indiana *T*
Valparaiso University *B*
Vincennes University *A*

Iowa

Buena Vista University *B, T*
Central College *T*
Clarke College *B, T*
Cornell College *B, T*
Dordt College *B*
Drake University *T*
Faith Baptist Bible College and
  Theological Seminary *B*
Franciscan University *B, T*
Graceland University *T*
Grand View College *B, T*
Iowa State University *T*
Iowa Wesleyan College *B*
Loras College *T*
Luther College *B*
Maharishi University of Management *T*
Morningside College *B*
Mount Mercy College *T*
Northwestern College *T*
St. Ambrose University *B, T*
University of Iowa *B, M, T*
Upper Iowa University *T*
Wartburg College *T*
William Penn University *B*

Kansas

Baker University *T*
Benedictine College *T*
Bethany College *B*
Bethel College *T*
Emporia State University *B, T*
Fort Scott Community College *A*
Friends University *B*
Independence Community College *A*
Kansas Wesleyan University *B, T*
McPherson College *B, T*
MidAmerica Nazarene University *B, T*
Newman University *T*
Ottawa University *B, T*
Pittsburg State University *B, T*
St. Mary College *T*
Southwestern College *B, T*
Tabor College *B, T*
University of Kansas *B, T*
Washburn University of Topeka *B*

Kentucky

Alice Lloyd College *B*
Bellarmine University *B, M, T*
Campbellsville University *B*
Cumberland College *B, T*
Kentucky Wesleyan College *T*
Murray State University *B, M, T*
Pikeville College *B, T*
Thomas More College *B*
Union College *B*

Louisiana

Centenary College of Louisiana *B, T*
Grambling State University *B*
Louisiana College *B*
Louisiana State University
  Shreveport *B*
McNeese State University *T*
Nicholls State University *B*
Northwestern State University *B*
Our Lady of Holy Cross College *B*
Southeastern Louisiana University *B*
Southern University and Agricultural and
  Mechanical College *B*
University of Louisiana at Monroe *B*
University of New Orleans *B, M*
Xavier University of Louisiana *B, M, T*

Maine

St. Joseph's College *B*
University of Maine *B, M*
University of Maine
  Farmington *B, T*
  Machias *T*
  Presque Isle *B*
University of New England *B, T*
University of Southern Maine *T*

Maryland

Bowie State University *B, T*
College of Notre Dame of Maryland *T*
Columbia Union College *B*
Frostburg State University *B, T*
Mount St. Mary's College *T*
St. Mary's College of Maryland *T*
Salisbury University *T*
University of Maryland
  College Park *B*

Massachusetts

Assumption College *T*
Boston University *B, M, T*
Bridgewater State College *M, T*
Elms College *B, M, T*
Fitchburg State College *B, M, T*
Framingham State College *B, M, T*
Harvard College *T*
Lesley University *B, M*
Merrimack College *T*
Northeastern University *M*
Smith College *M*
Springfield College *T*
Tufts University *M, T*
University of Massachusetts
  Dartmouth *T*
Western New England College *T*

Westfield State College *B, T*

Michigan

Alma College *T*
Andrews University *M, T*
Calvin College *B*
Central Michigan University *B*
Concordia University *B, T*
Eastern Michigan University *B, T*
Ferris State University *B*
Grand Valley State University *M, T*
Hope College *T*
Lansing Community College *A*
Madonna University *T*
Michigan State University *M*
Michigan Technological University *T*
Northern Michigan University *B, M, T*
Saginaw Valley State University *T*
University of Michigan *B, D*
University of Michigan
  Flint *T*
Wayne State University *B, M, T*
Western Michigan University *B*

Minnesota

Augsburg College *T*
Bemidji State University *M, T*
Bethel College *B*
College of St. Benedict *T*
College of St. Catherine *B, T*
College of St. Scholastica *T*
Concordia College: Moorhead *B, T*
Crown College *B, T*
Gustavus Adolphus College *T*
Minnesota State University
  Mankato *B, M, T*
  Moorhead *B, T*
Northwestern College *B*
Ridgewater College: A Community and
  Technical College *A*
St. Cloud State University *M, T*
St. John's University *T*
St. Mary's University of Minnesota *B*
St. Olaf College *T*
University of Minnesota
  Duluth *B*
  Morris *T*
  Twin Cities *T*
University of St. Thomas *B, T*
Winona State University *B, M, T*

Mississippi

Blue Mountain College *B*
Coahoma Community College *A*
Delta State University *B, M*
Itawamba Community College *A*
Mississippi College *B, M*
Mississippi State University *T*
Mississippi Valley State University *B, T*
Rust College *B*
University of Mississippi *B, T*

Missouri

Central Missouri State
  University *B, M, T*
College of the Ozarks *B, T*
Columbia College *T*
Culver-Stockton College *T*
Evangel University *B, T*
Hannibal-LaGrange College *B*
Harris Stowe State College *T*
Lincoln University *B, T*
Maryville University of Saint
  Louis *B, M, T*
Missouri Baptist University *T*
Missouri Southern State College *B, T*
Missouri Valley College *T*
Missouri Western State College *B*
Northwest Missouri State
  University *B, M, T*
Rockhurst University *B*
Southeast Missouri State University *B, T*
Southwest Baptist University *T*
Southwest Missouri State University *B*
Truman State University *M, T*

University of Missouri
  Columbia *B*
  St. Louis *T*
William Jewell College *T*
William Woods University *B, T*

Montana

Montana State University
  Billings *B, T*
Rocky Mountain College *B, T*
University of Great Falls *B*
University of Montana-Missoula *B, T*
University of Montana: Western *B, T*

Nebraska

Chadron State College *B, M*
College of Saint Mary *B, T*
Concordia University *B, T*
Creighton University *T*
Dana College *B*
Doane College *T*
Hastings College *B, M, T*
Midland Lutheran College *B, T*
Nebraska Wesleyan University *T*
Peru State College *B, T*
Union College *T*
University of Nebraska
  Kearney *B, M, T*
  Lincoln *B, T*
York College *B, T*

Nevada

University of Nevada
  Reno *B*

New Hampshire

Colby-Sawyer College *B, T*
Franklin Pierce College *T*
Keene State College *T*
New England College *B, T*
Plymouth State College *M, T*
Rivier College *B, M, T*
St. Anselm College *T*
University of New Hampshire *B, T*
University of New Hampshire at
  Manchester *M*

New Jersey

Bloomfield College *B*
Caldwell College *T*
Centenary College *T*
The College of New Jersey *B, T*
College of St. Elizabeth *T*
Georgian Court College *T*
Monmouth University *B, T*
Richard Stockton College of New
  Jersey *B*
Rider University *B, T*
Rowan University *B, M*
Rutgers, The State University of New
  Jersey
    New Brunswick Regional
      Campus *T*
St. Peter's College *T*
William Paterson University of New
  Jersey *T*

New Mexico

College of Santa Fe *B*
College of the Southwest *B, T*
New Mexico Highlands University *B*

New York

Adelphi University *M*
Alfred University *M, T*
Canisius College *B, M, T*
City University of New York
  Brooklyn College *B, M*
  City College *B*
  College of Staten Island *T*
  Hunter College *B, M, T*
  Queens College *M, T*
Colgate University *T*
College of New Rochelle *T*
D'Youville College *B, M, T*
Daemen College *B, T*
Dominican College of Blauvelt *B, T*
Dowling College *B*

Elmira College *B, T*
Fordham University *M, T*
Hofstra University *B, M, T*
Houghton College *B, T*
Ithaca College *B, T*
Keuka College *B, T*
Le Moyne College *T*
Long Island University
  C. W. Post Campus *B, M, T*
  Southampton College *T*
Manhattan College *B, T*
Manhattanville College *M, T*
Marist College *B, T*
Marymount Manhattan College *B, T*
Mercy College *T*
Molloy College *B*
Nazareth College of Rochester *T*
New York Institute of Technology *B, T*
New York University *B, M, D, T*
Niagara University *B, T*
Pace University *B, M, T*
Pace University:
  Pleasantville/Briarcliff *B, M, T*
Roberts Wesleyan College *B, T*
St. Bonaventure University *M*
St. John Fisher College *B, M, T*
St. John's University *B, M, T*
St. Joseph's College: Suffolk
  Campus *B, T*
St. Lawrence University *T*
State University of New York
  Albany *B, M, T*
  Binghamton *M*
  Buffalo *M, D, T*
  College at Brockport *B, M, T*
  College at Buffalo *B, M*
  College at Cortland *B, M, T*
  College at Fredonia *B, M, T*
  College at Geneseo *B, M, T*
  College at Oneonta *B, T*
  College at Plattsburgh *B, M*
  College at Potsdam *B, M, T*
  New Paltz *B, M, T*
  Oswego *B, M*
  Stony Brook *T*
Syracuse University *B, M, D, T*
University of Rochester *M, D*
Utica College *B*
Vassar College *T*
Wells College *T*

North Carolina

Appalachian State University *B, M, T*
Belmont Abbey College *T*
Bennett College *B, T*
Campbell University *B, T*
Catawba College *T*
Chowan College *B, T*
Davidson College *T*
East Carolina University *B, M*
Elizabeth City State University *B, T*
Fayetteville State University *B, T*
Gardner-Webb University *B, M*
Greensboro College *B, T*
Guilford Technical Community
  College *A*
Johnson C. Smith University *B*
Lenoir Community College *A*
Lenoir-Rhyne College *B, T*
Livingstone College *T*
Louisburg College *A*
Mars Hill College *B, T*
Meredith College *T*
Methodist College *A, B, T*
Montreat College *T*
North Carolina Agricultural and
  Technical State University *B, M, T*
North Carolina Central University *B, M*
North Carolina State University *T*
Queens University of Charlotte *T*
St. Augustine's College *B*
Shaw University *B, T*

University of North Carolina
  Charlotte *B, M*
  Greensboro *B, M, T*
  Pembroke *B, M, T*
  Wilmington *B*
Wake Forest University *M, T*
Western Carolina University *B, M, T*
Wingate University *B, T*
Winston-Salem State University *B*

North Dakota

Dickinson State University *B, T*
Jamestown College *B*
Mayville State University *B, T*
Minot State University *B, M*
North Dakota State University *B, T*
University of Mary *B, T*
University of North Dakota *B, T*
Valley City State University *B, T*

Ohio

Ashland University *B, T*
Baldwin-Wallace College *T*
Bluffton College *B*
Bowling Green State University *B*
Case Western Reserve University *T*
Cedarville University *B, T*
Central State University *B*
College of Mount St. Joseph *T*
Defiance College *B, T*
Hiram College *T*
John Carroll University *T*
Kent State University *T*
Kent State University
  Stark Campus *T*
Malone College *B*
Miami University
  Oxford Campus *B, M, T*
Mount Union College *T*
Mount Vernon Nazarene University *B, T*
Ohio Dominican College *B, T*
Ohio Northern University *B, T*
Ohio University *B, T*
Otterbein College *B*
University of Akron *B, T*
University of Dayton *B, M, T*
University of Findlay *B*
University of Rio Grande *B, T*
University of Toledo *B, T*
Urbana University *B*
Ursuline College *B, T*
Walsh University *B*
Wilmington College *B*
Wittenberg University *B*
Wright State University *B, M, T*
Xavier University *M*
Youngstown State University *B, M*

Oklahoma

Cameron University *B, T*
East Central University *B, T*
Eastern Oklahoma State College *A*
Northeastern State University *B*
Northwestern Oklahoma State
  University *B, T*
Oklahoma Baptist University *B, T*
Oklahoma Christian University of
  Science and Arts *B, T*
Oklahoma City University *B*
Oklahoma Wesleyan University *B*
Oral Roberts University *B, T*
Southeastern Oklahoma State
  University *B, T*
Southern Nazarene University *B, M*
Southwestern Oklahoma State
  University *B, M, T*
University of Central Oklahoma *B*
University of Oklahoma *B*
University of Tulsa *T*

Oregon

Concordia University *B, M, T*
George Fox University *T*
Linfield College *T*
Oregon State University *M*
Portland State University *T*
Southern Oregon University *T*

University of Portland *T*
Warner Pacific College *T*
Western Baptist College *B*

Pennsylvania

Albright College *T*
Arcadia University *B, M, T*
Cabrini College *B, T*
California University of
    Pennsylvania *B, T*
Carlow College *T*
Chatham College *M*
DeSales University *M, T*
Delaware Valley College *T*
Dickinson College *T*
Duquesne University *B, T*
East Stroudsburg University of
    Pennsylvania *B, T*
Elizabethtown College *T*
Geneva College *B, T*
Gettysburg College *T*
Grove City College *B, T*
Gwynedd-Mercy College *T*
Holy Family University *B, T*
Immaculata University *T*
Indiana University of
    Pennsylvania *B, M, T*
Juniata College *B, T*
King's College *T*
La Roche College *B*
La Salle University *B, T*
Lebanon Valley College of
    Pennsylvania *B, T*
Lincoln University *B, T*
Lock Haven University of
    Pennsylvania *B, T*
Lycoming College *T*
Marywood University *B*
Mercyhurst College *B*
Messiah College *T*
Millersville University of
    Pennsylvania *B, M, T*
Moravian College *T*
Penn State
    Harrisburg *B*
Philadelphia Biblical University *B, T*
Point Park College *B*
Robert Morris University *T*
St. Joseph's University *B*
St. Vincent College *T*
Seton Hill University *B, T*
Slippery Rock University of
    Pennsylvania *B, T*
Temple University *B, M, T*
Thiel College *B*
University of Pennsylvania *M, D*
University of Pittsburgh
    Johnstown *B, T*
Villanova University *T*
Washington and Jefferson College *T*
Waynesburg College *T*
West Chester University of
    Pennsylvania *B, T*
Widener University *M, T*
Wilkes University *M, T*
Wilson College *T*
York College of Pennsylvania *B, T*

Puerto Rico

Bayamon Central University *B*
Inter American University of Puerto Rico
    Barranquitas Campus *B, T*
    Guayama Campus *B*
    Metropolitan Campus *B, M*
    San German Campus *B*
Pontifical Catholic University of Puerto
    Rico *B, T*
Turabo University *B, M*
Universidad Metropolitana *B*
University of Puerto Rico
    Mayaguez Campus *M*

Rhode Island

Rhode Island College *B, M*
Salve Regina University *B*

South Carolina

Anderson College *B, T*
Charleston Southern University *M, T*
Claflin University *B*
Coker College *B, T*
Columbia College *B*
Francis Marion University *B, T*
Furman University *T*
Limestone College *B*
Morris College *B, T*
South Carolina State University *B, T*
Southern Wesleyan University *B, T*
University of South Carolina
    Aiken *B, T*
Voorhees College *B*
Wofford College *T*

South Dakota

Augustana College *B, T*
Black Hills State University *B, T*
Dakota State University *B, T*
Dakota Wesleyan University *B, T*
Mount Marty College *B*
Northern State University *B, T*
South Dakota State University *B*
University of Sioux Falls *T*
University of South Dakota *B, T*

Tennessee

Belmont University *T*
Bethel College *B, T*
Bryan College *T*
Christian Brothers University *B, M, T*
Crichton College *C, B*
Freed-Hardeman University *B, T*
King College *T*
Lambuth University *T*
Lane College *B*
Lee University *B*
Maryville College *B, T*
Southern Adventist University *B*
Tennessee Technological University *B, T*
Tennessee Wesleyan College *B, T*
Trevecca Nazarene University *B, T*
Tusculum College *B, T*
Union University *B, T*
University of Tennessee
    Chattanooga *B, T*
    Knoxville *T*
    Martin *B, T*
Vanderbilt University *M, D*

Texas

Abilene Christian University *B, T*
Baylor University *B, T*
Del Mar College *A*
East Texas Baptist University *B*
Hardin-Simmons University *B, T*
Houston Baptist University *T*
Howard Payne University *B, T*
Jarvis Christian College *B*
Lamar University *T*
Laredo Community College *A*
LeTourneau University *B*
Lubbock Christian University *B, T*
McMurry University *T*
Prairie View A&M University *M*
St. Edward's University *B, T*
St. Mary's University *T*
Schreiner University *T*
Southwest Texas State University *T*
Tarleton State University *M, T*
Texas A&M International
    University *B, M, T*
Texas A&M University
    Commerce *D, T*
    Corpus Christi *T*
Texas Christian University *B, T*
Texas Lutheran University *B, T*
Texas Wesleyan University *B, M, T*
University of Dallas *T*
University of Houston *T*
University of Houston
    Clear Lake *T*
University of Mary Hardin-Baylor *T*

University of Texas
    Arlington *T*
    San Antonio *T*
West Texas A&M University *T*

Utah

Brigham Young University *B, M*
Southern Utah University *B, T*
University of Utah *B*
Utah Valley State College *B*
Weber State University *B*

Vermont

Bennington College *B, M, D, T*
Castleton State College *B, T*
College of St. Joseph in Vermont *B*
Goddard College *B*
Johnson State College *B*
Lyndon State College *B*
St. Michael's College *T*
University of Vermont *B*

Virginia

Averett University *B, M, T*
Bluefield College *T*
Bridgewater College *T*
Eastern Mennonite University *T*
Emory & Henry College *M*
Hampton University *M*
Hollins University *T*
Liberty University *B*
Longwood University *B, T*
Lynchburg College *M*
Radford University *T*
University of Virginia's College at
    Wise *T*
Virginia Intermont College *B, T*
Virginia Wesleyan College *T*

Washington

Central Washington University *B, M, T*
Northwest College *T*
Pacific Lutheran University *T*
Seattle Pacific University *B, T*
Washington State University *T*
Western Washington University *B, T*
Whitworth College *B, M, T*

West Virginia

Alderson-Broaddus College *T*
Concord College *B, T*
Fairmont State College *B*
Ohio Valley College *B*
Shepherd College *T*
West Liberty State College *B*
West Virginia State College *B*
West Virginia University *T*
West Virginia Wesleyan College *B*
Wheeling Jesuit University *T*

Wisconsin

Alverno College *B, T*
Carroll College *B, T*
Carthage College *T*
Edgewood College *B, T*
Lakeland College *T*
Lawrence University *T*
Maranatha Baptist Bible College *B*
Marian College of Fond du Lac *B, T*
Marquette University *B*
Mount Mary College *B, T*
Northland College *T*
St. Norbert College *T*
Silver Lake College *T*
University of Wisconsin
    Green Bay *T*
    La Crosse *B, T*
    Madison *M*
    Parkside *T*
    Platteville *B, T*
    River Falls *T*
    Superior *B, T*
    Whitewater *B*
Viterbo University *B, T*

Alabama

Auburn University *B, M, D*

Arizona

University of Arizona *M, D*

Arkansas

University of Arkansas *M, D*

California

California State University
    Stanislaus *B*
San Jose State University *B*
University of California
    Davis *B, M, D*
    Riverside *B, M, D*

Colorado

Colorado State University *M, D*

Connecticut

University of Connecticut *M, D*

Delaware

University of Delaware *B, M*

Florida

Florida Agricultural and Mechanical
    University *D*
University of Florida *B, M, D*

Georgia

University of Georgia *B, M, D*

Hawaii

University of Hawaii
    Manoa *B, M, D*

Idaho

University of Idaho *B, M, D*

Illinois

University of Illinois
    Urbana-Champaign *M, D*

Indiana

Purdue University *B, M, D*

Iowa

Iowa State University *B, M, D*

Kansas

Kansas State University *M, D*
University of Kansas *M, D*

Kentucky

University of Kentucky *M, D*

Louisiana

Louisiana State University and
    Agricultural and Mechanical
    College *M, D*

Maine

University of Maine *B, M*

Maryland

University of Maryland
    College Park *M, D*

Massachusetts

Harvard College *B*
University of Massachusetts
    Amherst *M, D*

Michigan

Michigan State University *B, M, D*

Minnesota

University of Minnesota
    Twin Cities *M, D*

Mississippi

Mississippi State University *M, D*

Missouri

University of Missouri
    Columbia *M, D*

Montana

Montana State University
Bozeman *M*

Nebraska

University of Nebraska
Lincoln *M, D*

New Jersey

Rutgers, The State University of New
Jersey
New Brunswick Regional
Campus *M, D*

New York

Cornell University *B, M, D*
State University of New York
College of Environmental Science
and Forestry *B, M, D*

North Carolina

North Carolina State University *B, M, D*

North Dakota

North Dakota State University *M, D*

Ohio

Ohio State University
Columbus Campus *B, M, D*

Oklahoma

Eastern Oklahoma State College *A*
Oklahoma State University *B, M, D*

Oregon

Chemeketa Community College *A*
Oregon State University *B, M, D*

Pennsylvania

Penn State
University Park *M, D*

South Carolina

Clemson University *M, D*

South Dakota

South Dakota State University *M*

Tennessee

University of Tennessee
Knoxville *M, D*

Texas

Texas A&M University *B, M, D*
Texas Tech University *M*

Utah

Brigham Young University *B, M, D*
Utah State University *B, M*

Virginia

Virginia Polytechnic Institute and State
University *M, D*

Washington

Washington State University *B, M, D*

Wisconsin

University of Wisconsin
Madison *B, M, D*

Wyoming

University of Wyoming *M, D*

Entrepreneurial studies

Alaska

University of Alaska
Anchorage *C, A, B*

Arizona

Eastern Arizona College *C, A*
Gateway Community College *C*
Rio Salado College *C*
University of Arizona *B*

California

Azusa Pacific University *M*
Cabrillo College *C, A*

California State University
Dominguez Hills *B*
Hayward *B, M*
Coastline Community College *A*
College of Alameda *C, A*
College of Marin: Kentfield *C, A*
Diablo Valley College *C*
Los Angeles Trade and Technical
College *A*
Los Medanos College *C, A*
Mount San Antonio College *C, A*
Mount San Jacinto College *C*
San Diego State University *M*
Santa Monica College *C, A*
Shasta College *A*
Southwestern College *C, A*
Yuba Community College District *C, A*

Colorado

Arapahoe Community College *A*

Connecticut

Quinnipiac University *B*

District of Columbia

Gallaudet University *B*
Trinity College *M*

Florida

Florida Keys Community College *C*
Palm Beach Atlantic University *B*
University of Miami *B*
Valencia Community College *C*

Georgia

Darton College *A*
Southern Polytechnic State
University *B, M*

Illinois

Black Hawk College *C, A*
College of Lake County *C*
De Paul University *M*
Elgin Community College *C*
Heartland Community College *C*
Kishwaukee College *C*
McHenry County College *C*
Moraine Valley Community College *A*
Northwestern Business College *A*
Northwestern University *M*
Parkland College *C*
Prairie State College *C*
Waubonsee Community College *C, A*
William Rainey Harper College *C, A*

Indiana

Grace College *B*
University of Southern Indiana *B*

Iowa

Indian Hills Community College *A*
Maharishi University of Management *C*

Kansas

Central Christian College *A, B*
Fort Scott Community College *A*
Pratt Community College *C, A*

Kentucky

St. Catharine College *A*

Louisiana

Southern University
Shreveport *A*

Maine

Maine Maritime Academy *A, B*
University of New England *B*

Maryland

Salisbury University *B*

Massachusetts

Boston University *B*
Northeastern University *B*
Springfield Technical Community
College *A*
Suffolk University *M*
University of Massachusetts
Lowell *B*

Michigan

Ferris State University *C, B*
Gogebic Community College *A*
Lansing Community College *C*
Mid Michigan Community College *A*
Montcalm Community College *C, A*
North Central Michigan College *C*
Oakland Community College *A*
Schoolcraft College *A*
Western Michigan University *B*

Minnesota

Alexandria Technical College *C*
St. Cloud Technical College *C, A*
University of St. Thomas *C, B, M*

Missouri

Missouri Valley College *A*
Three Rivers Community College *A*

Nebraska

University of Nebraska
Omaha *B*

Nevada

University of Nevada
Reno *B*

New Hampshire

University of New Hampshire *B*

New Jersey

Bergen Community College *C*
Burlington County College *C*
Mercer County Community College *C*
Stevens Institute of Technology *B*
Thomas Edison State College *A, B*
Warren County Community College *C, A*

New Mexico

Santa Fe Community College *A*

New York

Hofstra University *B*
Medaille College *C, B*
Mohawk Valley Community College *A*
Pace University *B*
Pace University:
Pleasantville/Briarcliff *B*
State University of New York
College of Technology at
Alfred *C, A*
Syracuse University *B*

Ohio

Baldwin-Wallace College *B*
Bowling Green State University:
Firelands College *C*
Cuyahoga Community College
Eastern Campus *A*
Metropolitan Campus *A*
Kent State University
Trumbull Campus *A*
Lakeland Community College *C*
University of Akron *C, A*
University of Findlay *B*
Xavier University *B, M*

Oklahoma

Rose State College *A*

Oregon

Portland Community College *C*
Southwestern Oregon Community
College *C*

Pennsylvania

Bucks County Community College *A*
Central Pennsylvania College *A, B*
Chatham College *B*
Community College of Allegheny
County *C, A*
Delaware County Community
College *C, A*
Drexel University *B*
Grove City College *B*
Messiah College *B*
Northampton County Area Community
College *C*
Reading Area Community College *C, A*

Seton Hill University *B*
Temple University *B*
West Chester University of
Pennsylvania *M*

Puerto Rico

ICPR Junior College *A*
Inter American University of Puerto Rico
San German Campus *D*
University of Puerto Rico
Rio Piedras Campus *B*

South Carolina

Florence-Darlington Technical College *A*
Morris College *B*
Voorhees College *B*

Tennessee

Southern Adventist University *M*
Tusculum College *B*

Texas

Baylor University *B*
Brookhaven College *A*
Galveston College *C, A*
Lubbock Christian University *B*
Midland College *C, A*
Palo Alto College *A*
Richland College *A*
St. Edward's University *B, T*
St. Mary's University *B*
Tarrant County College *A*
University of Houston *B*

Utah

LDS Business College *C*
Utah Valley State College *B*

Vermont

Lyndon State College *A, B*

Virginia

J. Sargeant Reynolds Community
College *C*

Washington

Lake Washington Technical College *C*
Washington State University *B*

West Virginia

Potomac State College of West Virginia
University *A*
Southern West Virginia Community and
Technical College *A*
West Virginia Wesleyan College *B*

Wisconsin

Fox Valley Technical College *C*
Moraine Park Technical College *C*
University of Wisconsin
Platteville *B*

Wyoming

University of Wyoming *B*

Environmental biology

Illinois

Chicago State University *B*

Iowa

Maharishi University of Management *B*

Kentucky

University of Louisville *M, D*

Louisiana

University of Louisiana at
Lafayette *B, D*

Maine

Colby College *B*
Maine Maritime Academy *T*

Maryland

Hood College *M*
Morgan State University *D*

Massachusetts
University of Massachusetts
Lowell *M*

Minnesota
St. Mary's University of Minnesota *B*

Missouri
Lindenwood University *B*

New Hampshire
Plymouth State College *B*

New York
Columbia University
Columbia College *B*
Marist College *B*

Ohio
Heidelberg College *B*
Mount Union College *B*
Ursuline College *B*
Wilmington College *B*

Wisconsin
Beloit College *B*
Lawrence University *B*
University of Wisconsin
Superior *B*

Environmental design

Alabama
Auburn University *B*

Arizona
Scottsdale Community College *C, A*
Yavapai College *C, A*

California
Art Center College of Design *B, M*
Otis College of Art and Design *B*
University of California
Los Angeles *M*

Colorado
Arapahoe Community College *C, A*
University of Colorado
Boulder *B*
Denver *M, D*

Connecticut
Yale University *M*

Georgia
Middle Georgia College *A*

Indiana
Ball State University *B*

Kansas
Kansas State University *M*

Maryland
Morgan State University *B*

Massachusetts
Hampshire College *B*
Massachusetts College of Art *B*
University of Massachusetts
Amherst *B*

Michigan
University of Michigan *B, M*

Minnesota
Northland Community & Technical
College *C, A*
University of Minnesota
Twin Cities *B*

Missouri
Ranken Technical College *A*
Washington University in St. Louis *M*

Montana
Montana State University
Bozeman *B*

New Mexico
University of New Mexico *B*

New York
Cornell University *B*
Parsons School of Design *B*
State University of New York
Buffalo *B*
College of Environmental Science
and Forestry *B, M*
Suffolk County Community College *A*

North Carolina
North Carolina State University *B*

North Dakota
North Dakota State University *B*

Ohio
Bowling Green State University *B*
Miami University
Oxford Campus *B*
Ohio State University
Columbus Campus *B*
Stark State College of Technology *A*

Oklahoma
University of Oklahoma *B*

Pennsylvania
University of Pennsylvania *B, M*

Puerto Rico
University of Puerto Rico
Rio Piedras Campus *B*

Texas
Texas A&M University *B*
University of Houston *B*

Virginia
Virginia Polytechnic Institute and State
University *D*

Environmental engineering

Alabama
University of Alabama
Birmingham *D*

Alaska
University of Alaska
Anchorage *M*
Fairbanks *M*

Arizona
University of Arizona *M, D*

Arkansas
Northwest Arkansas Community
College *A*
University of Arkansas *M*

California
Loyola Marymount University *M*
Santa Barbara City College *A*
University of California
Irvine *B, M*
Riverside *B, M, D*
University of Southern
California *B, M, D*

Colorado
United States Air Force Academy *B*
University of Colorado
Boulder *B*

Connecticut
University of Connecticut *B, M, D*
University of Hartford *M*
University of New Haven *M*
Yale University *B*

Delaware
University of Delaware *B*

Florida
Florida International University *M*
Hillsborough Community College *A*
University of Central Florida *C, B, M, D*
University of Florida *B, M, D*
University of Miami *B*
University of South Florida *M*

Georgia
Georgia Institute of Technology *M, D*
Mercer University *B, M*

Idaho
Idaho State University *M*
University of Idaho *M*

Illinois
Illinois Institute of Technology *B, M, D*
Northwestern University *B*
University of Illinois
Urbana-Champaign *M, D*

Indiana
Rose-Hulman Institute of Technology *M*
Taylor University *B*
University of Notre Dame *B*
Vincennes University *A*

Iowa
University of Iowa *M, D*

Kansas
University of Kansas *M, D*

Kentucky
Murray State University *B*

Louisiana
Louisiana State University and
Agricultural and Mechanical
College *B*
Tulane University *B*

Maine
University of Southern Maine *B*

Maryland
Johns Hopkins University *B, M, D*

Massachusetts
Harvard College *B*
Massachusetts Institute of Technology *B*
Smith College *B*
Suffolk University *B*
Tufts University *B, M*
University of Massachusetts
Amherst *M*
Wentworth Institute of Technology *B*

Michigan
Michigan State University *D*
Michigan Technological
University *B, M, D, T*
University of Michigan *B, M, D*
Wayne State University *C, M*

Missouri
University of Missouri
Rolla *M*
Washington University in St. Louis *M*

Montana
Montana State University
Bozeman *M*
Montana Tech of the University of
Montana *B, M*

Nebraska
University of Nebraska
Lincoln *M*

Nevada
University of Nevada
Reno *B, M, D*

New Hampshire
University of New Hampshire *B*

New Jersey
New Jersey Institute of
Technology *B, M, D*

New Mexico
Albuquerque Technical-Vocational
Institute *A*
New Mexico Institute of Mining and
Technology *B, M*
New Mexico State University *M*
University of New Mexico *M*

New York
Columbia University
Fu Foundation School of
Engineering and Applied
Science *B, M, D*
Hofstra University *B*
Manhattan College *B, M*
New York University *B*
Polytechnic University *M*
Rensselaer Polytechnic Institute *B*
State University of New York
College of Environmental Science
and Forestry *B, M*
Syracuse University *B, M*

North Dakota
North Dakota State University *M*

Ohio
Marietta College *B*
Ohio University *A*
Stark State College of Technology *A*
University of Findlay *B*

Oklahoma
Northeastern State University *B*
University of Oklahoma *B, M, D*

Oregon
Oregon State University *B*
University of Portland *B*

Pennsylvania
Drexel University *B, M, D*
Gettysburg College *B*
Lehigh University *B*
Penn State
Abington *B*
Altoona *B*
Beaver *B*
Berks *B*
Delaware County *B*
Dubois *B*
Harrisburg *B*
Hazleton *B*
Lehigh Valley *B*
Mont Alto *B*
New Kensington *B*
Schuylkill - Capital College *B*
Shenango *B*
University Park *B, M, D*
Wilkes-Barre *B*
Worthington Scranton *B*
York *B*
Temple University *B, M*
Villanova University *M*

Puerto Rico
Universidad Metropolitana *C*

South Carolina
Clemson University *M, D*

Tennessee
Christian Brothers University *B*
Vanderbilt University *M, D*

Texas
Lamar University *M*
Palo Alto College *C, A*
Rice University *B, M, D*
Southern Methodist University *B*
Texas Tech University *B, M*
University of Houston *M, D*
University of Texas
Arlington *M, D*
Austin *M*
El Paso *M, D*

Utah
University of Utah *M, D*
Utah State University *B*

Vermont
University of Vermont *B*

Virginia
Old Dominion University *B*

Washington
Seattle University *B*
University of Washington *B*
Washington State University *M*

West Virginia
West Virginia University *M, D*

Wisconsin
Milwaukee School of Engineering *M*

Wyoming
University of Wyoming *M*

Environmental engineering technology

Arkansas
Southern Arkansas University Tech *A*

Illinois
Black Hawk College *C*

Kansas
Kansas City Kansas Community
College *A*

Kentucky
Murray State University *A, B*

Maryland
College of Southern Maryland *C, A*
Community College of Baltimore County
Dundalk *C, A*
Essex *C, A*

Massachusetts
Wentworth Institute of Technology *A*

Michigan
Lansing Community College *A*

New Jersey
Thomas Edison State College *A, B*

New Mexico
Southwestern Indian Polytechnic
Institute *A*

New York
New York Institute of Technology *B*
Rochester Institute of Technology *B*
State University of New York
College of Technology at Canton *A*

North Carolina
East Carolina University *B*
Elon University *B*

Ohio
Ohio University
Chillicothe Campus *A, B*
Owens Community College
Toledo *A*
Shawnee State University *B*
Sinclair Community College *A*
University of Toledo *A*

Pennsylvania
Cambria County Area Community
College *A*
Community College of Allegheny
County *A*
Delaware County Community College *C*
Penn State
University Park *M*
Pennsylvania College of Technology *A*

Puerto Rico
Universidad Metropolitana *C*

Texas
Angelina College *C, A*
Austin Community College *C, A*
Collin County Community College
District *A*
Lamar State College at Orange *A*
Palo Alto College *C, A*

Utah
Utah Valley State College *A*

Washington
Clover Park Technical College *A*

Environmental health

Alabama
University of Alabama
Birmingham *D*

Arkansas
University of Arkansas
Cossatot Community College of the
A
Little Rock *B*
for Medical Sciences *M*

California
California State University
Fresno *B*
Hayward *B*
Las Positas College *C, A*
Loma Linda University *M*
San Diego State University *M*
San Jose State University *B*
University of California
Berkeley *M, D*
Los Angeles *M, D*
University of Southern California *M, D*

Colorado
Colorado State University *B, M, D*

Delaware
Delaware State University *B*

Florida
University of Miami *B*

Georgia
University of Georgia *B, M*

Idaho
Boise State University *B*

Illinois
Illinois State University *B*

Indiana
Indiana State University *B*

Iowa
Iowa Wesleyan College *B*
University of Iowa *M, D*

Kentucky
Murray State University *B, M*

Louisiana
Tulane University *M, D*

Maine
University of Southern Maine *B*

Maryland
University of Maryland
University College *C, M*

Massachusetts
Anna Maria College *M*
Boston University *M, D*

Michigan
Central Michigan University *B*
Ferris State University *A, B*
Oakland University *B*
University of Michigan *M, D*
University of Michigan
Flint *B*

Minnesota
University of Minnesota
Twin Cities *M, D*
Vermilion Community College *A*

Mississippi
Mississippi Valley State University *B, M*

Missouri
Crowder College *C, A*
Missouri Southern State College *B*

New Jersey
Richard Stockton College of New
Jersey *B*

New Mexico
New Mexico State University *B*

New York
City University of New York
Queensborough Community
College *A*
York College *B*
New York University *M, D*
State University of New York
Albany *M, D*
University of Rochester *M*

North Carolina
Durham Technical Community
College *C, A*
East Carolina University *B, M*
University of North Carolina
Chapel Hill *B*
Western Carolina University *B*

Ohio
Bowling Green State University *B*
Case Western Reserve University *M, D*
Ohio University *B*
University of Findlay *B*
Wright State University *B*

Oklahoma
East Central University *B*
University of Oklahoma *M, D*

Oregon
Oregon State University *B, M*

Pennsylvania
University of Pittsburgh *C, M, D*
West Chester University of
Pennsylvania *B*

Puerto Rico
University of Puerto Rico
Medical Sciences Campus *M*

South Carolina
University of South Carolina *M, D*

Tennessee
East Tennessee State University *B, M*
Roane State Community College *A*

Virginia
Old Dominion University *B*

Washington
University of Washington *B, M*

Wisconsin
University of Wisconsin
Eau Claire *B, M*

Environmental science

Alabama
Samford University *A, B*

Alaska
University of Alaska
Southeast *B*

Arizona
Arizona Western College *A*
Northern Arizona University *B*

California
Chapman University *B*
Claremont McKenna College *B*
Dominican University of California *B*
Santa Barbara City College *C, A*
Santa Clara University *B*
Scripps College *B*
University of California
Riverside *B, M, D*
University of La Verne *B*
University of Redlands *B*
University of San Francisco *B*

Colorado
Colorado College *B*
Mesa State College *B*

Connecticut
Trinity College *B*
University of Connecticut *B*
Yale University *M, D*

District of Columbia
American University *M*

Florida
Barry University *B*
Broward Community College *A*
Florida State University *B*
Miami-Dade Community College *A*
Nova Southeastern University *B, M*
Stetson University *B*
University of Miami *B*
University of Tampa *B*
University of West Florida *B*

Georgia
Piedmont College *B*

Illinois
Bradley University *B*
De Paul University *B*
Dominican University *B*
Illinois College *B*
Monmouth College *B*
University of Illinois
Urbana-Champaign *B, M, D*
Wheaton College *B*

Indiana
Huntington College *B*
Indiana University
Bloomington *B, M, D*
Martin University *B*
Taylor University *B*
University of Evansville *B*
University of Notre Dame *B*
University of St. Francis *B*
Valparaiso University *B*
Vincennes University *A*

Iowa
Drake University *B*
University of Iowa *B*
University of Northern Iowa *B, M*
Upper Iowa University *B*

Louisiana
Centenary College of Louisiana *B*

Maine
Bates College *B*
Bowdoin College *B*
Colby College *B*
University of Maine
Farmington *B*
University of Southern Maine *B*

Maryland
Hood College *B*
University of Maryland
College Park *B*

Massachusetts
Assumption College *B*
Cape Cod Community College *C, A*
Simmons College *B*
University of Massachusetts
Amherst *B*
Lowell *B*

Michigan
Calvin College *B*
Hope College *B*

Minnesota
College of St. Benedict *B*
St. John's University *B*

Missouri
Maryville University of Saint Louis *B*
North Central Missouri College *C, A*
Westminster College *B*

Nebraska
Bellevue University *B*
Creighton University *B*

New Hampshire
Franklin Pierce College *B*
New England College *B*
St. Anselm College *B*
University of New Hampshire *B*

New Jersey
Caldwell College *C*
Ramapo College of New Jersey *B*
Rider University *B*
William Paterson University of New
Jersey *B*

New Mexico
College of Santa Fe *B*

New York
Adelphi University *B, M*
Columbia University
Columbia College *B*
Long Island University
C. W. Post Campus *B*
Rochester Institute of Technology *B, M*
State University of New York
College at Brockport *B*
College of Agriculture and
Technology at Morrisville *A*
College of Environmental Science
and Forestry *B, M, D*
Stony Brook *M*
Suffolk County Community College *A*
University of Rochester *B*
Wells College *B*

North Carolina
Barton College *B*
Lenoir-Rhyne College *B*
Meredith College *B*
North Carolina State University *B*
Roanoke-Chowan Community College *A*
University of North Carolina
Chapel Hill *B, M, D*

Ohio
Ashland University *B*
Wright State University *M*

Oklahoma
Northeastern State University *B*
Rose State College *A*

Oregon
Oregon State University *B, M, D*
Willamette University *B*

Pennsylvania
Albright College *B*
Allegheny College *B*
Carlow College *B*
Chatham College *B*
Chestnut Hill College *B*
Juniata College *B*
Keystone College *A*
La Salle University *B*
Marywood University *B*
Messiah College *B*
Muhlenberg College *B*
Rosemont College *B*
University of the Sciences in
Philadelphia *B*

Puerto Rico
Inter American University of Puerto Rico
Bayamon Campus *B*
Turabo University *M*

Rhode Island
Brown University *B*

South Carolina
Lander University *B*

Texas
Lubbock Christian University *B*
Sam Houston State University *B*
Stephen F. Austin State University *B, M*

Texas A&M University *B*
University of Houston
Clear Lake *B, M*

Utah
Dixie State College of Utah *A*

Vermont
Castleton State College *B*
University of Vermont *B*

Virginia
Hampton University *B*
Sweet Briar College *B*
Virginia Wesleyan College *B*

Washington
Everett Community College *A*
Northwest College *B*
Washington State University *B, M*

West Virginia
Marshall University *B, M*

Wisconsin
Carthage College *B*

Environmental studies

Alabama
Birmingham-Southern College *B*
Northwest-Shoals Community College *A*

Alaska
Alaska Pacific University *B, M*
University of Alaska
Southeast *C, A*

Arizona
Prescott College *B, M*

Arkansas
Lyon College *B*
University of Arkansas *B, D*

California
California State University
Chico *B, M*
Fullerton *M*
Hayward *M*
Monterey Bay *B*
Sacramento *B*
Claremont McKenna College *B*
Feather River College *A*
National University *M*
Occidental College *B*
Pitzer College *B*
Pomona College *B*
Santa Clara University *B*
Santa Rosa Junior College *A*
Scripps College *B*
Sonoma State University *B*
Southwestern College *A*
University of California
Berkeley *B*
Irvine *M, D*
Los Angeles *D*
Riverside *B*
Santa Barbara *B*
Santa Cruz *B, D*
University of Redlands *B*
University of San Francisco *B, M*
University of Southern California *B*
University of the Pacific *B*

Colorado
Colorado Mountain College
Timberline Campus *A*
Metropolitan State College of Denver *B*
Naropa University *B, M*
University of Colorado
Boulder *B, M, D*

Connecticut
Connecticut College *B*
Teikyo Post University *B*
Wesleyan University *C*
Yale University *M, D*

District of Columbia
American University *C, B, M*
George Washington University *B, M*

Florida
Eckerd College *B*
Florida State University *B*
Indian River Community College *A*
International College *M*
New College of Florida *B*
Rollins College *B*
University of West Florida *B*

Georgia
Oxford College of Emory University *B*
Paine College *B*
Shorter College *B*

Hawaii
Chaminade University of Honolulu *B*
Hawaii Pacific University *B*

Illinois
Dominican University *B*
Elmhurst College *B*
Knox College *B*
Lake Forest College *B*
Lincoln College *A*
Northeastern Illinois University *B*
Olivet Nazarene University *B*
Roosevelt University *B*
University of Chicago *B*

Indiana
Earlham College *B*
Goshen College *B*
Indiana University-Purdue University
Indianapolis *M*
Manchester College *B*
Marian College *B, T*
St. Mary-of-the-Woods College *M*
University of Evansville *B*

Iowa
Central College *B*
Cornell College *B*
Dordt College *B*
Franciscan University *B*
Maharishi University of Management *B*
University of Dubuque *B*
University of Iowa *B*

Kansas
Friends University *M*
McPherson College *B*
Tabor College *A, B*
University of Kansas *B*

Kentucky
Maysville Community College *A*

Louisiana
University of New Orleans *B*
Xavier University of Louisiana *B*

Maine
Bates College *B*
Colby College *B*
College of the Atlantic *B, M*
St. Joseph's College *B*
University of Maine *B, M, D*
University of Maine
Machias *B*
Presque Isle *B*
University of New England *B*
University of Southern Maine *B*

Maryland
Johns Hopkins University *B*
Towson University *B*

Massachusetts
Berkshire Community College *A*
Boston University *B, M*
Cape Cod Community College *C, A*
Clark University *B*
Hampshire College *B*
Harvard College *B*
Lesley University *B*
Massachusetts College of Liberal Arts *B*

Mount Holyoke College *B*
Northeastern University *B*
Simon's Rock College of Bard *B*
Springfield College *B*
Wellesley College *B*
Worcester Polytechnic Institute *B*

Michigan
Aquinas College *B*
Northern Michigan University *B*
University of Michigan
Dearborn *B*

Minnesota
Bethel College *B*
Concordia College: Moorhead *B*
Gustavus Adolphus College *B*
Hamline University *B*
Macalester College *B*
Minnesota State University
Mankato *B, M*
St. Olaf College *B*
University of Minnesota
Duluth *B*
University of St. Thomas *B*
Vermilion Community College *A, B*
Winona State University *B*

Missouri
Drury University *B*
Maryville University of Saint
Louis *B, M, T*
St. Charles Community College *A*
Stephens College *B*
University of Missouri
Kansas City *B*
Washington University in St. Louis *B*
Westminster College *B*

Montana
Carroll College *B*
Montana State University
Billings *B*
Rocky Mountain College *B*
University of Montana: Western *B*

Nebraska
Dana College *B*
Doane College *B*
University of Nebraska
Lincoln *B*

Nevada
Truckee Meadows Community
College *A*
University of Nevada
Las Vegas *B*

New Hampshire
Dartmouth College *B*
Franklin Pierce College *B*
New Hampshire Community Technical
College
Berlin *A*
Plymouth State College *B*

New Jersey
Bloomfield College *B*
Caldwell College *C*
Ramapo College of New Jersey *B*
Richard Stockton College of New
Jersey *B*
Sussex County Community College *A*
Thomas Edison State College *B*
Warren County Community College *A*

New Mexico
New Mexico Institute of Mining and
Technology *B*

New York
Alfred University *B*
Bard College *M*
City University of New York
Queens College *B*
Colgate University *B*
College of New Rochelle *B*
Elmira College *B*
Finger Lakes Community College *A*

Fulton-Montgomery Community
College *A*
Hobart and William Smith Colleges *B*
Hudson Valley Community College *A*
Ithaca College *B*
Long Island University
C. W. Post Campus *B*
Marist College *B*
Pace University:
Pleasantville/Briarcliff *B, M*
Rensselaer Polytechnic Institute *M, D*
St. John's University *B*
St. Lawrence University *B*
Sarah Lawrence College *B*
Skidmore College *B*
State University of New York
Binghamton *B*
College at Brockport *B*
College at Fredonia *B*
College of Agriculture and
Technology at Cobleskill *A*
College of Agriculture and
Technology at Morrisville *A*
College of Environmental Science
and Forestry *B, M, D*
Maritime College *M*
Stony Brook *B*
Suffolk County Community College *A*
Syracuse University *B*
University of Rochester *B*
Vassar College *B*
Wells College *B*

North Carolina
Brevard College *B*
Elon University *B*
Guilford College *B*
Meredith College *B*
Montreat College *B*
North Carolina Central University *B*
Pfeiffer University *B*
University of North Carolina
Asheville *B*

Ohio
Antioch College *B*
Bowling Green State University *B*
Case Western Reserve University *B*
Cleveland State University *B*
Columbus State Community College *A*
Defiance College *B*
Hiram College *B*
John Carroll University *B*
Lake Erie College *B*
Lourdes College *B*
Marietta College *B*
Oberlin College *B*
Ohio Northern University *B*
Ohio University *C, M*
Ohio Wesleyan University *B*
Otterbein College *B*
University of Findlay *B*
University of Toledo *B*
Ursuline College *B*
Wittenberg University *B*
Youngstown State University *B*

Oklahoma
Eastern Oklahoma State College *A*
Oklahoma State University *B, M, D*
Southeastern Oklahoma State
University *B*
University of Tulsa *B*

Oregon
Lewis & Clark College *B*
Marylhurst University *B*
Southern Oregon University *B, M*
Southwestern Oregon Community
College *A*
University of Portland *B*

Pennsylvania
Albright College *B*
Allegheny College *B*
Arcadia University *B, M*
Bucknell University *B*

Cabrini College *B*
Chatham College *B*
Chestnut Hill College *B*
DeSales University *B*
Dickinson College *B*
Gettysburg College *B*
Grove City College *T*
Juniata College *B*
Keystone College *A*
Lackawanna College *A*
Neumann College *B*
Penn State
Altoona *B*
St. Vincent College *B*
Shippensburg University of
Pennsylvania *B*
Thiel College *B*
University of Pittsburgh
Bradford *B*
Johnstown *B*

Puerto Rico
Inter American University of Puerto Rico
San German Campus *M*
Pontifical Catholic University of Puerto
Rico *B*
Universidad Politecnica de Puerto
Rico *M*

Rhode Island
Brown University *B, M*

South Carolina
Charleston Southern University *B*
Furman University *B*

Tennessee
Maryville College *B*
Tusculum College *B*

Texas
Baylor University *M*
Lamar University *B*
Midland College *A*
Texas A&M University
Commerce *B*
Texas Southern University *B*
University of Houston
Clear Lake *B, M*
University of Texas
of the Permian Basin *B*
University of the Incarnate Word *B*

Utah
Salt Lake Community College *A*
University of Utah *B*
Utah State University *M*

Vermont
Bennington College *B*
Goddard College *B*
Green Mountain College *B*
Johnson State College *B*
Marlboro College *B*
Middlebury College *B*
St. Michael's College *B*
Southern Vermont College *B*
Sterling College *A, B*
University of Vermont *B*

Virginia
Averett University *B*
College of William and Mary *B*
Emory & Henry College *B*
Randolph-Macon College *B*
Randolph-Macon Woman's College *B*
Roanoke College *B*
Southwest Virginia Community
College *A*
Washington and Lee University *B*

Washington
Evergreen State College *M*
Western Washington University *B*
Whitman College *B*

West Virginia
Bethany College *B*
Davis and Elkins College *B*

Mountain State University *A, B*
Shepherd College *B*
West Virginia Wesleyan College *B*

Wisconsin
Lawrence University *B, T*
Northland College *B*
Ripon College *B*
University of Wisconsin
Green Bay *B, M*
Madison *B, M*
Richland *C*

Wyoming
University of Wyoming *A, B*

Environmental toxicology

California
University of California
Riverside *M, D*

Texas
Texas Tech University *M, D*

Washington
Eastern Washington University *B*

Epidemiology

Alabama
University of Alabama
Birmingham *D*

Arizona
University of Arizona *M, D*

California
Loma Linda University *M, D*
San Diego State University *M, D*
University of California
Berkeley *M, D*
Davis *M, D*
Los Angeles *M, D*
University of Southern California *D*

Connecticut
Yale University *M, D*

District of Columbia
George Washington University *D*

Georgia
Emory University *D*

Iowa
University of Iowa *M, D*

Louisiana
Tulane University *M, D*

Maryland
University of Maryland
Baltimore *M, D*

Massachusetts
Boston University *M, D*

Michigan
Michigan State University *M*
University of Michigan *M, D*

Minnesota
University of Minnesota
Twin Cities *M, D*

New York
State University of New York
Albany *B, M, D*
Buffalo *M, D*

North Carolina
University of North Carolina
Chapel Hill *M, D*

Ohio
Case Western Reserve University *M, D*

Oklahoma
University of Oklahoma *M, D*

Pennsylvania
University of Pennsylvania *M, D*
University of Pittsburgh *M, D*

Puerto Rico
University of Puerto Rico
Medical Sciences Campus *M*

South Carolina
Medical University of South
Carolina *M, D*
University of South Carolina *M, D*

Texas
Texas A&M University *M*
University of Texas
Houston Health Science
Center *M, D*

Washington
University of Washington *M*

Equestrian studies

Arizona
Scottsdale Community College *C, A*

California
Feather River College *C, A*
Los Angeles Pierce College *C, A*
Moorpark College *A*
Mount San Antonio College *C*
Santa Rosa Junior College *C, A*
Shasta College *C, A*
Sierra College *C, A*

Colorado
Colorado State University *B*

Connecticut
Teikyo Post University *C, A, B*

Idaho
College of Southern Idaho *A*

Illinois
Black Hawk College *A*
Black Hawk College
East Campus *C, A*
Parkland College *C, A*
South Suburban College of Cook
County *C*

Indiana
St. Mary-of-the-Woods College *A, B*

Iowa
Ellsworth Community College *A*
Kirkwood Community College *A*

Kansas
Dodge City Community College *C, A*

Kentucky
Murray State University *A, B*
University of Louisville *C, B*

Maine
University of Maine *C*

Massachusetts
Mount Ida College *A, B*
University of Massachusetts
Amherst *A*

Minnesota
University of Minnesota
Crookston *B*

Missouri
Truman State University *B*
William Woods University *B*

Montana
Dawson Community College *A*
Rocky Mountain College *B*

Nebraska
Nebraska College of Technical
Agriculture *A*

New Hampshire
University of New Hampshire *A, B*

New Jersey
Centenary College *A, B*

New York
Cazenovia College *C*
State University of New York
   College of Agriculture and
     Technology at Cobleskill *A*
   College of Agriculture and
     Technology at Morrisville *A, B*

North Carolina
Martin Community College *C, A*
St. Andrews Presbyterian College *B*

North Dakota
North Dakota State University *B*

Ohio
Hocking Technical College *C, A*
Lake Erie College *B*
Ohio State University
   Agricultural Technical Institute *A*
Ohio University *A*
Ohio University
   Southern Campus at Ironton *A*
Otterbein College *B*
University of Findlay *A, B*

Oklahoma
Northeastern Oklahoma Agricultural and
   Mechanical College *A*
Redlands Community College *A*

Oregon
Linn-Benton Community College *C, A*

Pennsylvania
Delaware Valley College *A, B*
Erie Business Center *A*
Wilson College *B*

Texas
Central Texas College *C*
Frank Phillips College *C, A*
North Central Texas College *A*
Sul Ross State University *B*
Tarleton State University *B*
West Texas A&M University *B*

Virginia
Averett University *B*
J. Sargeant Reynolds Community
   College *C*
Virginia Intermont College *B*

West Virginia
Salem International University *B*

Wyoming
Central Wyoming College *C, A*
Laramie County Community College *A*

ESL teacher education

Alabama
University of Alabama *M*
University of North Alabama *B*

Alaska
Alaska Bible College *B*

Arizona
Arizona State University *M*
Northern Arizona University *M*
University of Arizona *M, D*

Arkansas
University of Arkansas
   Little Rock *B*

California
Azusa Pacific University *M*

California State University
   Dominguez Hills *M*
   Fullerton *M, T*
   Hayward *M*
   Long Beach *T*
   Los Angeles *M*
College of Marin: Kentfield *C, A*
Fresno Pacific University *M*
Holy Names College *C, M*
Loyola Marymount University *M*
Master's College *B*
Monterey Institute of International
   Studies *M*
Ohlone College *C*
San Francisco State University *M*
San Jose State University *M*
University of California
   Los Angeles *M*
   San Diego *M*
University of San Francisco *M*
University of Southern California *M*
University of the Pacific *T*

Colorado
Fort Lewis College *T*

Connecticut
Central Connecticut State
   University *M, T*
Norwalk Community College *C*

Delaware
University of Delaware *B, M, T*

District of Columbia
American University *M, T*
Catholic University of America *B*
George Washington University *A*
Georgetown University *M*

Florida
Barry University *T*
Florida State University *C*
Nova Southeastern University *M*
Tallahassee Community College *C*
University of Central Florida *C, M*
University of Miami *B, M, D*
University of South Florida *D*

Georgia
Georgia State University *M*

Hawaii
Brigham Young University-Hawaii *B*
Hawaii Pacific University *B, M*
University of Hawaii
   Manoa *B, M, T*

Idaho
Boise State University *T*
Lewis-Clark State College *T*
University of Idaho *M*

Illinois
Lincoln Christian College and
   Seminary *C*
Moody Bible Institute *B*
Southern Illinois University
   Carbondale *M*
Southern Illinois University
   Edwardsville *M*
University of Illinois
   Urbana-Champaign *M*
Wheaton College *C*

Indiana
Ball State University *D, T*
Goshen College *B*
University of Evansville *T*

Iowa
Iowa State University *T*
Northwestern College *T*
University of Iowa *B, M, D, T*
University of Northern Iowa *B, M*
William Penn University *B*

Kansas
Emporia State University *T*
McPherson College *T*

Newman University *M*

Kentucky
Murray State University *B, M, T*

Maryland
University of Maryland
   Baltimore County *M*

Massachusetts
Boston University *M, T*
Elms College *B, M, T*
Framingham State College *M*
Salem State College *M*
Simmons College *B, M*
University of Massachusetts
   Boston *M*

Michigan
Andrews University *B, M, T*
Central Michigan University *M*
Michigan State University *M*

Minnesota
Bethel College *B*
Hamline University *B, M*
Minnesota State University
   Mankato *T*
   Moorhead *B, T*
Northwestern College *B*
University of Minnesota
   Duluth *T*
   Twin Cities *M, T*

Mississippi
University of Mississippi *M*

Missouri
Central Missouri State
   University *C, M, T*
Missouri Southern State College *B*

Montana
Carroll College *B*
University of Montana-Missoula *T*

Nebraska
Concordia University *B, T*
Doane College *B, T*
University of Nebraska
   Kearney *B, T*
   Lincoln *B*
   Omaha *C*

New Hampshire
Southern New Hampshire University *B*

New Jersey
The College of New Jersey *M, T*
Montclair State University *T*
New Jersey City University *T*
Rider University *B, T*
Rutgers, The State University of New
   Jersey
   Camden Regional Campus *T*
Seton Hall University *M*
William Paterson University of New
   Jersey *T*

New Mexico
College of Santa Fe *B*
Western New Mexico University *B*

New York
Adelphi University *M*
City University of New York
   Brooklyn College *B, M*
   Hunter College *M, T*
   Queens College *M, T*
College of New Rochelle *M, T*
Hofstra University *M, T*
Le Moyne College *T*
Long Island University
   C. W. Post Campus *M*
Manhattanville College *M*
Mercy College *T*
Nazareth College of Rochester *M*
New York University *M, D, T*
Nyack College *B*
St. John's University *M, T*

State University of New York
   Albany *M*
   Buffalo *M, T*
   College at Fredonia *M*
   New Paltz *M, T*
   Stony Brook *M, T*

North Carolina
Meredith College *M, T*
University of North Carolina
   Charlotte *M*

Ohio
Cedarville University *T*
Kent State University *T*
Ohio Dominican College *B, T*
Ohio State University
   Columbus Campus *M*
University of Akron *C*
University of Dayton *B, M, T*
University of Findlay *B, M, T*
University of Toledo *M, T*
Youngstown State University *C*

Oklahoma
Langston University *M*
Oklahoma Christian University of
   Science and Arts *B, T*
Oklahoma City University *M*
Oklahoma Wesleyan University *C*
Oral Roberts University *M*

Oregon
Eastern Oregon University *B, T*
Northwest Christian College *C*
Portland State University *M, T*
Southern Oregon University *T*
Western Oregon University *M, T*

Pennsylvania
Chatham College *M*
Marywood University *B*
Penn State
   University Park *M*
Temple University *M*
University of Pennsylvania *M, D*
University of Pittsburgh *C, T*
West Chester University of
   Pennsylvania *M*

Puerto Rico
Inter American University of Puerto Rico
   Fajardo Campus *B, T*
   Metropolitan Campus *B, M*
   San German Campus *B, M*
Pontifical Catholic University of Puerto
   Rico *B, M, T*
Turabo University *M*
University of Puerto Rico
   Humacao *B*

Rhode Island
Rhode Island College *M*

South Carolina
Columbia International University *C, A*

South Dakota
University of South Dakota *C*

Tennessee
Carson-Newman College *M*
Johnson Bible College *T*
Maryville College *B, T*
Tennessee Technological University *T*
Union University *B, T*

Texas
Houston Baptist University *B, T*
Lamar University *T*
McMurry University *T*
San Antonio College *C*
Texas A&M University
   Commerce *T*
   Corpus Christi *T*
Texas Wesleyan University *M*
University of Texas
   Arlington *T*
   San Antonio *M, T*

West Texas A&M University *T*

Utah
Brigham Young University *B, M, T*
Snow College *A*
University of Utah *C, T*
Utah State University *M*

Vermont
Bennington College *M*
St. Michael's College *T*

Virginia
Bridgewater College *T*
Eastern Mennonite University *T*
Liberty University *B*
Marymount University *M*
Shenandoah University *C*

Washington
Central Washington University *T*
Eastern Washington University *M, T*
Gonzaga University *M*
Northwest College *C, T*
Seattle Pacific University *M*
Seattle University *M*
University of Washington *B, T*
Washington State University *T*
Whitworth College *B, M, T*

West Virginia
Salem International University *T*

Wisconsin
St. Norbert College *T*
University of Wisconsin
River Falls *B, T*

Ethics

District of Columbia
American University *M*

Iowa
Drake University *B*

New York
Wells College *B*

Oklahoma
University of Oklahoma *B*

Oregon
Oregon State University *M*

Pennsylvania
Carnegie Mellon University *B*

Tennessee
Union University *B*

European history

California
Chapman University *B*

Iowa
University of Northern Iowa *B*

Michigan
Calvin College *B*

New York
Bard College *B*
Columbia University
Columbia College *B*
Sarah Lawrence College *B*
State University of New York
Buffalo *D*

European studies

Alabama
Huntingdon College *B*

California
Chapman University *B*
Claremont McKenna College *B*

Loyola Marymount University *B*
Pepperdine University *B*
Pitzer College *B*
St. Mary's College of California *B*
San Diego State University *B*
Scripps College *B*
University of California
Irvine *B*
Los Angeles *B*

Colorado
Fort Lewis College *B*

Connecticut
Connecticut College *B*
Yale University *B, M, D*

District of Columbia
George Washington University *B*

Florida
Rollins College *B*
Schiller International University *B*

Hawaii
University of Hawaii
West Oahu *B*

Indiana
Valparaiso University *B*

Iowa
University of Northern Iowa *B*

Kansas
University of Kansas *B*

Kentucky
Georgetown College *B*

Massachusetts
Amherst College *B*
Brandeis University *B*
Harvard College *B*
Mount Holyoke College *B*
Tufts University *B, M*
Wellesley College *B*

Michigan
Hillsdale College *B*

Minnesota
Hamline University *B*
University of Minnesota
Morris *B*
Twin Cities *B*

Mississippi
Millsaps College *B*

Missouri
Washington University in St. Louis *B, M*

Nebraska
University of Nebraska
Lincoln *B*

New Hampshire
University of New Hampshire *B*

New Mexico
University of New Mexico *B*

New York
Bard College *B*
Barnard College *B*
Canisius College *B*
Columbia University
Columbia College *B*
Cornell University *B*
Eugene Lang College/New School
University *B*
Hobart and William Smith Colleges *B*
Hofstra University *B*
New York University *B, M*
Sarah Lawrence College *B*

North Carolina
Queens University of Charlotte *B*

Ohio
Ohio University *B*
University of Toledo *B*

Wittenberg University *B*

Oklahoma
University of Oklahoma *B*

Oregon
Portland State University *B*
Willamette University *B*

Pennsylvania
California University of Pennsylvania *B*
Carnegie Mellon University *B*

Rhode Island
Brown University *B*

South Carolina
University of South Carolina *B*

Tennessee
Vanderbilt University *B*

Texas
Southern Methodist University *B*
Southwest Texas State University *B*
Trinity University *B*

Utah
Brigham Young University *B*

Vermont
Bennington College *B*
Goddard College *B*
Marlboro College *B*
Middlebury College *B*
University of Vermont *B*

Virginia
College of William and Mary *B*
Emory & Henry College *B*

Washington
Gonzaga University *B*
Seattle Pacific University *B*
University of Washington *B*

Evolutionary biology

California
San Diego State University *B*
University of California
Davis *B*
Los Angeles *B*
San Diego *B*

Colorado
University of Colorado
Boulder *B, M, D*

Connecticut
Yale University *B, M, D*

Florida
University of West Florida *B*

Illinois
University of Chicago *M, D*

Indiana
Indiana University
Bloomington *M, D*

Louisiana
Tulane University *B, M, D*

Massachusetts
Harvard College *B*
University of Massachusetts
Amherst *M, D*

Michigan
Michigan State University *D*

Missouri
Washington University in St. Louis *D*

New Hampshire
Dartmouth College *B*

New York
Cornell University *B, M, D*

Ohio
Case Western Reserve University *B*

Pennsylvania
Lehigh University *M, D*

Texas
Rice University *B*
University of Texas
Austin *M, D*

Washington
Western Washington University *B*

Wisconsin
Marquette University *M, D*

Executive assistant

California
Grossmont Community College *C, A*
Shasta College *A*

Georgia
West Georgia Technical College *A*

Illinois
John A. Logan College *A*
Kaskaskia College *A*
Robert Morris College: Chicago *C, A*

Indiana
Ivy Tech State College
Bloomington *C, A*
Central Indiana *C, A*
Columbus *C, A*
Eastcentral *C, A*
Kokomo *C, A*
Lafayette *C, A*
Northcentral *C, A*
Northeast *C, A*
Northwest *C, A*
Southcentral *C, A*
Southeast *C, A*
Southwest *C, A*
Wabash Valley *C, A*
Whitewater *C, A*

Iowa
Hawkeye Community College *A*
Western Iowa Tech Community
College *A*

Kentucky
Jefferson Community College *A*
Maysville Community College *C, A*
Somerset Community College *A*

Massachusetts
Cape Cod Community College *C, A*

Michigan
Grand Rapids Community College *A*
Montcalm Community College *A*
Mott Community College *C, A*
Northwestern Michigan College *C*

Missouri
Patricia Stevens College *C*

North Carolina
Cape Fear Community College *C, A*
Isothermal Community College *C, A*
Lenoir Community College *C, A*
Martin Community College *C, A*
Wilkes Community College *C, A*
Wilson Technical Community College *A*

North Dakota
Lake Region State College *C, A*
North Dakota State College of Science *A*

Ohio
University of Akron *A*
University of Cincinnati
Raymond Walters College *A*
Youngstown State University *A*

Pennsylvania
Consolidated School of Business
   Lancaster *A*
   York *A*
Douglas School of Business *A*
Newport Business Institute *A*
Northampton County Area Community
   College *A*

Puerto Rico
Universidad del Este *A, B*

Texas
Kilgore College *C, A*

Utah
LDS Business College *C, A*

Washington
Clark College *C, A*

Exercise physiology

Illinois
Finch University of Health Sciences/The
   Chicago Medical School *M*

Iowa
University of Iowa *M, D*

Kansas
Central Christian College *A, B*

Missouri
University of Missouri
   Columbia *M, D*

New York
State University of New York
   Buffalo *M*

Ohio
Kent State University *B*

Exercise sciences

Alabama
Auburn University *B*
Huntingdon College *B*
Jacksonville State University *B*
Samford University *B*
University of Alabama *D*

Alaska
University of Alaska
   Fairbanks *B*

Arizona
Arizona State University *B, M, D*
Arizona Western College *A*
Central Arizona College *C, A*
Northern Arizona University *B, M*

Arkansas
Arkansas State University *B, M, T*
Harding University *B*
John Brown University *B*
Southern Arkansas University *B*
University of Arkansas *M, D*
University of Central Arkansas *B, M*

California
California State University
   Chico *B*
   Fresno *A, B*
   Hayward *B, M*
   Sacramento *B*
Chapman University *B*
Concordia University *B*
Diablo Valley College *C, A*
Grossmont Community College *C, A*
La Sierra University *B*
MiraCosta College *C*
Occidental College *B*
Orange Coast College *C, A*
Point Loma Nazarene University *B*
St. Mary's College of California *B*
Santa Barbara City College *A*

Santiago Canyon College *A*
University of California
   Davis *B, M*
University of Southern
   California *B, M, D*
University of the Pacific *M*
Vanguard University of Southern
   California *B*

Colorado
Colorado State University *B, M*
Fort Lewis College *B*
Metropolitan State College of Denver *B*
University of Colorado
   Boulder *B, M, D*
University of Northern Colorado *B, T*

Connecticut
Central Connecticut State University *B*
Manchester Community College *A*
Southern Connecticut State
   University *B, M, T*

Delaware
University of Delaware *B, M, D*

District of Columbia
George Washington University *B, M*

Florida
Barry University *B, M*
Florida Atlantic University *B, M*
Florida International University *B, M*
Florida State University *B, M, D*
Miami-Dade Community College *A*
Polk Community College *A*
Santa Fe Community College *A*
South Florida Community College *A*
University of Florida *B, M, D*
University of Miami *B, M, D*
University of West Florida *B, M*
Warner Southern College *B*

Georgia
Columbus State University *B*
Darton College *A*
East Georgia College *A*
Emmanuel College *B*
Georgia Southern University *B, M*
Georgia State University *D*
North Georgia College & State
   University *B*
Valdosta State University *B*

Hawaii
Brigham Young University-Hawaii *B*
University of Hawaii
   Manoa *B*

Idaho
Albertson College of Idaho *B*
Boise State University *M*
Lewis-Clark State College *B, T*

Illinois
Concordia University *B*
Elmhurst College *B*
North Central College *B*
Northeastern Illinois University *M*
Olivet Nazarene University *B*
Sauk Valley Community College *A*
Trinity Christian College *B*
William Rainey Harper College *A*

Indiana
Anderson University *B*
DePauw University *B*
Huntington College *B*
Indiana University
   Bloomington *D*
University of Evansville *B*
University of Southern Indiana *B*
Valparaiso University *B*
Vincennes University *A*

Iowa
Buena Vista University *B*
Central College *B*
Clarke College *B*

Des Moines Area Community College *A*
Dordt College *B*
Iowa Wesleyan College *B*
Loras College *B*
North Iowa Area Community College *A*
Northwestern College *B*
University of Iowa *B, M, D*

Kansas
Barton County Community College *A*
Central Christian College *A, B*
Kansas City Kansas Community
   College *A*
Kansas State University *B, M*
Seward County Community College *A*
University of Kansas *B*
Washburn University of Topeka *B*

Kentucky
Alice Lloyd College *B*
Campbellsville University *B*
Morehead State University *B*
Murray State University *B*
Thomas More College *A*
University of Louisville *M*

Louisiana
Centenary College of Louisiana *B*
Tulane University *B*

Maine
University of Maine
   Farmington *C*
University of New England *B*
University of Southern Maine *B*

Maryland
Community College of Baltimore County
   Catonsville *A*
   Dundalk *A*
   Essex *A*
Frostburg State University *B*
Howard Community College *A*
Salisbury University *M*
Towson University *B*
University of Maryland
   College Park *B*

Massachusetts
Becker College *B*
Boston University *B, M*
Bridgewater State College *B*
Fitchburg State College *B*
Gordon College *B*
Hampshire College *B*
Lasell College *B*
Mount Ida College *A*
Northeastern University *M*
Smith College *M*
Springfield College *B, M*
University of Massachusetts
   Amherst *B, M, D*
   Lowell *B*
Westfield State College *B*

Michigan
Adrian College *B*
Alma College *B*
Calvin College *B*
Central Michigan University *M*
Cornerstone University *B*
Hope College *B*
Michigan State University *D*
Northern Michigan University *M*
Oakland Community College *C, A*
Oakland University *C, M*
University of Michigan *B, D*
Western Michigan University *B*

Minnesota
College of St. Scholastica *B, M*
Concordia College: Moorhead *B*
Dakota County Technical College *C, A*
Globe College *C, A*
Hamline University *B*
Minnesota State University
   Mankato *B, M, T*
Northwestern College *B*

St. Cloud State University *M*
St. Olaf College *B*
University of Minnesota
   Duluth *B*
Winona State University *B*

Mississippi
Mississippi University for Women *B*
University of Mississippi *B, M*

Missouri
Avila University *B*
Drury University *B*
Missouri Valley College *B*
St. Louis University *B*
Truman State University *B*

Montana
Rocky Mountain College *B*
University of Montana-Missoula *B, M*

Nebraska
Concordia University *B*
Creighton University *B*
Hastings College *B*
Nebraska Wesleyan University *B*
University of Nebraska
   Lincoln *B*

Nevada
University of Nevada
   Las Vegas *B, M*

New Hampshire
Colby-Sawyer College *B*
New England College *B*
New Hampshire Community Technical
   College
   Manchester *C, A*
University of New Hampshire *B*

New Jersey
Bergen Community College *C*
Gloucester County College *A*
Kean University *M*
Ocean County College *C*
Rutgers, The State University of New
   Jersey
   New Brunswick Regional
     Campus *B*
William Paterson University of New
   Jersey *B, T*

New York
City University of New York
   Kingsborough Community
     College *A*
Dutchess Community College *A*
Hofstra University *B*
Ithaca College *B, M*
Orange County Community College *A*
Skidmore College *B*
State University of New York
   Buffalo *B, M, D*
   College of Agriculture and
     Technology at Morrisville *A*
Syracuse University *B, M*

North Carolina
Appalachian State University *M*
Brevard College *B*
Campbell University *B, T*
Chowan College *B*
East Carolina University *B, M*
Elon University *B*
High Point University *B*
Louisburg College *A*
Meredith College *B*
Wake Forest University *B, M*

North Dakota
Mayville State University *B*
North Dakota State University *B*
University of Mary *B*

Ohio
Baldwin-Wallace College *B*
Bowling Green State University *B, M*
Cedarville University *B*

Cincinnati State Technical and
　Community College *C*
Defiance College *B*
Kent State University *B*
Kent State University
　Stark Campus *B*
Malone College *B*
Miami University
　Oxford Campus *B, M*
Mount Union College *B*
Mount Vernon Nazarene University *B*
Ohio Northern University *B*
Ohio State University
　Columbus Campus *B*
Ohio University *B, M*
Sinclair Community College *C*
University of Akron *C, B, M*
University of Findlay *B*
University of Toledo *B, M, D*
Youngstown State University *B*

Oklahoma
East Central University *B*
Northeastern State University *B*
Oklahoma Baptist University *B*
Oklahoma Wesleyan University *B*
Oral Roberts University *B*
Southern Nazarene University *B*
University of Tulsa *B*

Oregon
Central Oregon Community College *A*
Linfield College *B*
Oregon State University *M*
Pacific University *B*
University of Oregon *B, M, D*
Willamette University *B*

Pennsylvania
Bloomsburg University of
　Pennsylvania *M*
Cabrini College *B*
DeSales University *B*
East Stroudsburg University of
　Pennsylvania *B*
Immaculata University *B*
Marywood University *B, M*
Messiah College *B*
Penn State
　Abington *B*
　Altoona *B*
　Beaver *A, B*
　Berks *B*
　Delaware County *B*
　Dubois *B*
　Fayette *B*
　Hazleton *B*
　Lehigh Valley *B*
　McKeesport *B*
　Mont Alto *B*
　New Kensington *B*
　Schuylkill - Capital College *B*
　Shenango *B*
　University Park *B*
　Wilkes-Barre *B*
　Worthington Scranton *B*
　York *B*
Waynesburg College *B*
West Chester University of
　Pennsylvania *M*

Puerto Rico
Inter American University of Puerto Rico
　San German Campus *D*

South Carolina
Anderson College *B*
Coker College *B*
Erskine College *B, T*
Lander University *B*
University of South Carolina *B, M, D*
University of South Carolina
　Aiken *B*

South Dakota
Augustana College *B*
Black Hills State University *B*

Dakota Wesleyan University *B*
University of Sioux Falls *B*

Tennessee
Belmont University *B*
Bethel College *B*
Bryan College *B, T*
Middle Tennessee State University *M*
Southern Adventist University *B*
Tennessee Wesleyan College *B*
Union University *B*
University of Memphis *B, M*
University of Tennessee
　Chattanooga *B, M*
　Knoxville *B*

Texas
Angelo State University *B, T*
Blinn College *A*
Concordia University at Austin *B*
Hardin-Simmons University *B*
Howard Payne University *B*
LeTourneau University *B*
Lubbock Christian University *B*
McMurry University *B*
Midwestern State University *B, M*
St. Mary's University *B, T*
Schreiner University *B*
Southwest Texas State University *B*
Tarleton State University *B*
Texas Lutheran University *B*
Tyler Junior College *A*
University of Houston *B*
University of Texas
　Austin *M, D*
　Brownsville *B*
　Tyler *M*

Utah
University of Utah *B, M, D*
Weber State University *B*

Vermont
Castleton State College *B*
Johnson State College *B*

Virginia
Bluefield College *B*
Bridgewater College *B*
James Madison University *B, M, T*
Liberty University *B*
Longwood University *B*
Norfolk State University *B*

Washington
Bastyr University *B*
Centralia College *A*
Eastern Washington University *B*
Seattle Pacific University *B*
University of Puget Sound *B*
Washington State University *B, M*
Western Washington University *B*

West Virginia
Alderson-Broaddus College *B*
Davis and Elkins College *B*
Marshall University *M*
West Liberty State College *B*
West Virginia University *B, M*

Wisconsin
Carroll College *B*
Carthage College *B*
Lakeland College *B*
Ripon College *B*
University of Wisconsin
　Eau Claire *B*
　La Crosse *B, M*
　Milwaukee *B, M*

Wyoming
University of Wyoming *B, M*

Experimental psychology

California
California State University
　Stanislaus *B*
La Sierra University *B*
Pomona College *B*
San Francisco State University *M*
University of California
　Santa Cruz *B, D*

Connecticut
University of Connecticut *D*
University of Hartford *M*

District of Columbia
American University *D*
Catholic University of America *M, D*

Florida
Embry-Riddle Aeronautical
　University *B, M*
Florida Atlantic University *D*

Illinois
Blackburn College *B*
De Paul University *M, D*
Loyola University of Chicago *D*
Millikin University *B*

Indiana
University of Evansville *B*

Iowa
University of Iowa *D*

Kansas
Wichita State University *D*

Kentucky
University of Kentucky *M, D*
University of Louisville *M, D*

Maine
University of Maine *M, D*

Maryland
Johns Hopkins University *B*

Massachusetts
Harvard College *B*
Tufts University *B, M, D*

Michigan
Central Michigan University *D*
Northern Michigan University *B*
Western Michigan University *D*

Missouri
University of Missouri
　Columbia *M, D*

New Hampshire
Keene State College *B*

New Jersey
Fairleigh Dickinson University
　College at Florham *M*

New York
Adelphi University *D*
Bard College *B*
Fordham University *D*
Long Island University
　C. W. Post Campus *M*
New York University *D*
St. John's University *M*
Sarah Lawrence College *B*
State University of New York
　Buffalo *D*
　Stony Brook *D*
Syracuse University *M, D*

North Carolina
Duke University *M, D*
North Carolina State University *M*

Ohio
Bowling Green State University *M, D*
Case Western Reserve University *D*
Kent State University *M, D*

Ohio University *M, D*
University of Dayton *M*

Oklahoma
Northeastern State University *B*
University of Central Oklahoma *M*

Oregon
Oregon Health Sciences University *M, D*

Pennsylvania
Moravian College *B*
Temple University *M, D*

Rhode Island
University of Rhode Island *D*

South Carolina
University of South Carolina *B, M, D*

Texas
Southern Methodist University *M, D*
Texas Tech University *M, D*
University of Houston *M, D*
University of North Texas *M, D*
University of Texas
　Arlington *D*
　El Paso *M*
　of the Permian Basin *B*

Vermont
Goddard College *B*
Marlboro College *B*

Virginia
Longwood University *B*

Washington
Central Washington University *M*
Eastern Washington University *M*

Wisconsin
University of Wisconsin
　Madison *B, M, D*
　Oshkosh *M*

Facial treatment

Florida
Palm Beach Community College *C*

Texas
North Harris Montgomery Community
　College District *C*

Facilities/event planning

Massachusetts
Wentworth Institute of Technology *B*

North Dakota
North Dakota State University *B*

Utah
Brigham Young University *B*

Family practice nurse/ nurse practitioner

Alabama
University of Mobile *M*

California
Azusa Pacific University *B*
Holy Names College *M*
University of San Francisco *M*

Florida
Barry University *M*
University of Tampa *D*

Georgia
Medical College of Georgia *M*
North Georgia College & State
　University *M*

Illinois
Southern Illinois University
Edwardsville *M*

Indiana
Indiana University-Purdue University
Indianapolis *M*

Louisiana
Loyola University New Orleans *M*

Maine
University of Southern Maine *M*

Michigan
Grand Valley State University *M*
Madonna University *M*
Oakland University *M*
Saginaw Valley State University *M*

Missouri
Webster University *M*

New York
Dominican College of Blauvelt *M*
Pace University *M*
Pace University:
Pleasantville/Briarcliff *M*
St. John Fisher College *M*
State University of New York
Binghamton *M*
Buffalo *M*
Health Science Center at Stony
Brook *M*
Stony Brook *M*

North Carolina
University of North Carolina
Wilmington *M*
Western Carolina University *M*
Winston-Salem State University *M*

Ohio
Case Western Reserve University *M*
Ursuline College *M*

Oklahoma
University of Oklahoma *M*

Pennsylvania
Drexel University *M*
Duquesne University *M*
Millersville University of
Pennsylvania *M*
Widener University *M*

South Carolina
Medical University of South Carolina *M*

Tennessee
Southern Adventist University *M*

Texas
Baylor University *M*
Prairie View A&M University *M*
University of Texas
Arlington *M*
Medical Branch at Galveston *M*
Pan American *M*
West Texas A&M University *M*

Washington
Seattle Pacific University *M*

West Virginia
Marshall University *M*

Family psychology

Arkansas
John Brown University *B*

California
Pacific Oaks College *M*

Minnesota
Capella University *M, D*

Mississippi
Mississippi College *B*

Oklahoma
Oklahoma Baptist University *B*

Oregon
Western Baptist College *B*

Family resource management studies

Arizona
Arizona State University *B, M*

California
Antelope Valley College *C, A*
Long Beach City College *C, A*

Illinois
Bradley University *B*
Southern Illinois University
Carbondale *B*

Michigan
Michigan State University *B*

Missouri
University of Missouri
Columbia *B, M*

Nebraska
University of Nebraska
Omaha *B*

Ohio
Baldwin-Wallace College *B*
Ohio State University
Lima Campus *B*
University of Toledo *C*

Oregon
George Fox University *B*
Oregon State University *M, D*

Tennessee
Lambuth University *B*

Texas
Texas Tech University *B, M, D*

Utah
University of Utah *B, M*

Family systems

California
Azusa Pacific University *D*

Connecticut
University of Connecticut *D*

Florida
Florida State University *D*

Indiana
Anderson University *B*

Michigan
Michigan State University *M*
Western Michigan University *B*

Ohio
Ashland University *B*
University of Akron *C, B, M*

Pennsylvania
Community College of Allegheny
County *C*
DeSales University *B*

South Dakota
Kilian Community College *A*

Tennessee
Union University *B*

Texas
Abilene Christian University *B, M*
Texas Tech University *B*

Utah
Brigham Young University *B*

Family/community services

Arkansas
John Brown University *B*

California
California State University
Northridge *B*
Modesto Junior College *A*
Monterey Peninsula College *A*
Southwestern College *C*
University of California
Davis *M*
Yuba Community College District *C, A*

Delaware
University of Delaware *B, M, D*

Florida
University of Florida *B, M*

Illinois
College of Lake County *C*
Olivet Nazarene University *B, T*
Shawnee Community College *A*

Indiana
Goshen College *B*

Iowa
Ellsworth Community College *A*
Iowa State University *B*
University of Northern Iowa *B, M*

Kentucky
Murray State University *B*

Maine
University of Maine *B*

Maryland
University of Maryland
College Park *B, M, D*
Villa Julie College *B*

Massachusetts
Hampshire College *B*

Michigan
Adrian College *B, T*
Michigan State University *M*
Northern Michigan University *B*

Minnesota
Minnesota State University
Mankato *B, M, T*

Mississippi
University of Mississippi *B*

New Hampshire
University of New Hampshire *B*

New York
Marymount College of Fordham
University *T*
State University of New York
College at Plattsburgh *B*

North Carolina
North Carolina Agricultural and
Technical State University *B*
University of North Carolina
Greensboro *B, M, D, T*

North Dakota
North Dakota State University *B, M*

Ohio
Bowling Green State University *B*
James A. Rhodes State College *A*
Kent State University
Salem Regional Campus *A, B*
Ohio State University
Columbus Campus *B, M, D*
Ohio University *B, M*
Youngstown State University *B*

Oklahoma
Oklahoma Christian University of
Science and Arts *B*
Oklahoma State University *B, M*

Oregon
Warner Pacific College *B*

Pennsylvania
Messiah College *B*

Tennessee
Carson-Newman College *B, T*
Tennessee Technological University *B*
University of Tennessee
Knoxville *B, M*

Texas
Lamar University *B*
Our Lady of the Lake University of San
Antonio *M*
University of Houston *B*
University of Texas
Austin *B*

Utah
Brigham Young University *B, M, D*
Snow College *C, A*
University of Utah *B, M*
Utah Valley State College *C, A*

Vermont
University of Vermont *B, M*

Virginia
Liberty University *B*

West Virginia
Alderson-Broaddus College *B*
West Virginia University *B*

Wisconsin
University of Wisconsin
Madison *M, D*

Family/consumer business sciences

California
California State University
Northridge *B*
Point Loma Nazarene University *B*

Georgia
University of Georgia *B*

Illinois
Northern Illinois University *M*

Nebraska
University of Nebraska
Kearney *B*

South Carolina
South Carolina State University *B*

Texas
University of Houston *B*
University of North Texas *B*

Virginia
Virginia State University *B*

Family/consumer sciences education

Alabama
Jacksonville State University *B*
Northeast Alabama Community
College *A*
Oakwood College *B*

Arizona
Arizona State University *B, T*
Phoenix College *A*
University of Arizona *B*

Arkansas
Harding University *B, M, T*

Ouachita Baptist University *B, T*
University of Arkansas *B*
University of Arkansas
    Pine Bluff *B*
University of Central Arkansas *B, M, T*

California
California State Polytechnic University:
    Pomona *T*
California State University
    Dominguez Hills *T*
    Long Beach *B, T*
    Northridge *B, T*
    Sacramento *T*
Master's College *T*
San Francisco State University *B, M, T*

Colorado
Colorado State University *T*

Connecticut
St. Joseph College *T*

Delaware
University of Delaware *B, T*

District of Columbia
Gallaudet University *B, T*

Florida
Florida International University *B, M, T*
Florida State University *B, M, D*
Gulf Coast Community College *A*

Georgia
Fort Valley State University *B, T*
Georgia Southern University *B*
Middle Georgia College *A*
University of Georgia *B, M*

Hawaii
University of Hawaii
    Manoa *B, T*

Idaho
Brigham Young University - Idaho *T*
Idaho State University *B, T*
University of Idaho *T*

Illinois
Northern Illinois University *B*
Olivet Nazarene University *B, T*
Sauk Valley Community College *A*

Indiana
Ball State University *B*
Vincennes University *A*

Iowa
Ellsworth Community College *A*
Iowa State University *B, M, D, T*

Kansas
Kansas State University *B*
Pittsburg State University *B, T*

Kentucky
Berea College *B, T*
Morehead State University *B*
Murray State University *B, T*

Louisiana
Grambling State University *B*
McNeese State University *B, T*
Northwestern State University *B*

Massachusetts
Framingham State College *B, M, T*

Michigan
Eastern Michigan University *T*
Ferris State University *B*
Madonna University *T*
Michigan State University *B, M*
Northern Michigan University *B*
Western Michigan University *B*

Minnesota
College of St. Catherine *B, T*
Minnesota State University
    Mankato *B, M, T*

University of Minnesota
    Twin Cities *M, T*

Mississippi
Mississippi State University *T*
Northwest Mississippi Community
    College *A*

Missouri
Central Missouri State University *B*
College of the Ozarks *B*
Fontbonne College *B*
Northwest Missouri State
    University *B, T*
Southeast Missouri State
    University *B, M*
Southwest Missouri State University *B*

Nebraska
Chadron State College *B*
Concordia University *B, T*
University of Nebraska
    Kearney *B, T*

Nevada
University of Nevada
    Reno *B*

New Jersey
St. Peter's College *T*

New Mexico
New Mexico State University *B*
University of New Mexico *B*

New York
City University of New York
    Brooklyn College *B*
    Queens College *B, M, T*
Marymount College of Fordham
    University *B, T*
State University of New York
    College at Oneonta *B, T*

North Carolina
Appalachian State University *B, T*
Campbell University *B, T*
East Carolina University *B*
Meredith College *T*
North Carolina Agricultural and
    Technical State University *B, T*
North Carolina Central University *B, M*
University of North Carolina
    Greensboro *B, M, D, T*

North Dakota
North Dakota State University *B, M, T*

Ohio
Ashland University *B, T*
Bluffton College *B*
Bowling Green State University *B*
Kent State University *B, T*
Miami University
    Oxford Campus *M*
Mount Vernon Nazarene University *B, T*
Ohio State University
    Columbus Campus *M, D*
University of Akron *B, T*
Youngstown State University *B, M*

Oklahoma
East Central University *B*
Langston University *B*
Northeastern State University *B*
University of Central Oklahoma *B*

Oregon
George Fox University *T*
Oregon State University *M*

Pennsylvania
Immaculata University *T*
Indiana University of
    Pennsylvania *B, M, T*
Marywood University *B*
Seton Hill University *B, T*

Puerto Rico
Pontifical Catholic University of Puerto
    Rico *B, T*
University of Puerto Rico
    Rio Piedras Campus *B, M*

South Carolina
South Carolina State University *B, T*

South Dakota
South Dakota State University *B*

Tennessee
Carson-Newman College *B*
Tennessee Technological University *T*
University of Tennessee
    Knoxville *B, M, T*
    Martin *B, T*

Texas
Lamar University *T*
Laredo Community College *A*
Prairie View A&M University *M*
Sam Houston State University *M, T*
Texas A&M University
    Kingsville *B*
Texas Tech University *M, D*
University of Texas
    Tyler *M*
University of the Incarnate Word *B*

Utah
Brigham Young University *B*
Snow College *A*
Southern Utah University *B, T*
Utah State University *B*

Virginia
Bridgewater College *B*
Virginia Polytechnic Institute and State
    University *B, T*

Washington
Central Washington University *B, T*
Seattle Pacific University *B*
Washington State University *T*

West Virginia
Fairmont State College *B*
Shepherd College *T*

Wisconsin
Mount Mary College *T*
University of Wisconsin
    Madison *B, M, T*
    Stevens Point *B, T*
    Stout *B, M, T*

**Family/consumer sciences/
home economics**

Alabama
Alabama Agricultural and Mechanical
    University *B, M*
Jacksonville State University *B*
James H. Faulkner State Community
    College *A*
Northeast Alabama Community
    College *A*
Oakwood College *B*
University of Alabama *B, M*
University of Montevallo *B, T*
University of North Alabama *B*

Arizona
Phoenix College *A*
South Mountain Community College *A*

Arkansas
Harding University *B, T*
Henderson State University *B*
University of Arkansas *M*
University of Arkansas
    Pine Bluff *B*
University of Central Arkansas *B, M*

California
Antelope Valley College *A*

Bakersfield College *A*
Cabrillo College *C, A*
California State University
    Long Beach *B*
    Los Angeles *B, M*
    Northridge *B, M*
    Sacramento *B*
Cerritos Community College *A*
College of the Sequoias *A*
Glendale Community College *A*
Long Beach City College *C, A*
Master's College *B*
Modesto Junior College *A*
Monterey Peninsula College *A*
Moorpark College *A*
Mount San Antonio College *A*
Orange Coast College *A*
Riverside Community College *C, A*
San Francisco State University *B, M*
San Joaquin Delta College *A*
Santa Monica College *C, A*
Santiago Canyon College *A*
Shasta College *A*
Sierra College *A*
Ventura College *C, A*

Colorado
Colorado State University *B*

Connecticut
St. Joseph College *B, T*

Delaware
University of Delaware *B*

District of Columbia
Gallaudet University *B*
University of the District of Columbia *B*

Florida
Chipola Junior College *A*
Florida State University *B, D*
Gulf Coast Community College *A*
Okaloosa-Walton Community College *A*
Palm Beach Community College *A*
Polk Community College *A*

Georgia
Abraham Baldwin Agricultural
    College *A*
Clayton College and State University *A*
Dalton State College *A*
East Georgia College *A*
Fort Valley State University *B*
Life University *A*
University of Georgia *M*

Hawaii
University of Hawaii
    Manoa *B*

Idaho
Idaho State University *B*

Illinois
Eastern Illinois University *B, M, T*
Illinois Central College *A*
Illinois State University *B, M, T*
Illinois Valley Community College *A*
Kishwaukee College *A*
Lake Land College *A*
Olivet Nazarene University *B, T*
University of Illinois
    Urbana-Champaign *M*
Western Illinois University *B*

Indiana
Ball State University *B, M*
Indiana State University *B, M*
Purdue University *B, M, D*
Vincennes University *A*

Iowa
Ellsworth Community College *A*
Iowa State University *B, M*
Marshalltown Community College *A*
North Iowa Area Community College *A*

Kansas
Cloud County Community College *A*

Garden City Community College *A*
Hutchinson Community College *A*
Kansas State University *B, D*
Pittsburg State University *B, T*

Kentucky
Berea College *B, T*
Murray State University *B, M*
University of Kentucky *B*

Louisiana
Louisiana State University and
    Agricultural and Mechanical
    College *M, D*
Louisiana Tech University *M*
McNeese State University *B*
Nicholls State University *B*
Northwestern State University *B*
Southern University and Agricultural and
    Mechanical College *B*
University of Louisiana at Lafayette *M*
University of Louisiana at Monroe *B*

Massachusetts
Framingham State College *B, M*

Michigan
Central Michigan University *B, M*
Eastern Michigan University *M*
Ferris State University *B*
Lansing Community College *A*
Madonna University *B, T*
Michigan State University *B*

Minnesota
College of St. Catherine *B*
Concordia College: Moorhead *B*
Minnesota State University
    Mankato *B, M*
University of Minnesota
    Twin Cities *B, M, D*
Vermilion Community College *A*

Mississippi
Alcorn State University *B*
Delta State University *B*
Itawamba Community College *A*
Mississippi State University *B*
University of Southern Mississippi *B*

Missouri
Central Missouri State University *B*
College of the Ozarks *B*
East Central College *A*
Fontbonne College *B*
Southeast Missouri State
    University *B, M*
University of Missouri
    Columbia *D*

Montana
Miles Community College *A*
Montana State University
    Bozeman *B, M*

Nebraska
Central Community College *C, A*
Chadron State College *B*
Concordia University *B, T*
University of Nebraska
    Kearney *B*
    Lincoln *M, D*
    Omaha *B*
Wayne State College *B, T*

New Jersey
Montclair State University *B, M, T*

New Mexico
Eastern New Mexico University *B*
University of New Mexico *B, M, D*

New York
City University of New York
    Queens College *B, M*
Marymount College of Fordham
    University *B*
State University of New York
    College at Oneonta *B*

North Carolina
Appalachian State University *B, M*
Bennett College *B*
Campbell University *B*
Meredith College *B*
North Carolina Agricultural and
    Technical State University *B, T*
North Carolina Central University *B, M*
University of North Carolina
    Greensboro *B, M, T*

North Dakota
Minot State University: Bottineau
    Campus *A*

Ohio
Bluffton College *B*
Mount Vernon Nazarene University *A, B*
Ohio State University
    Columbus Campus *B*
University of Akron *B*
Youngstown State University *B*

Oklahoma
East Central University *B*
Langston University *B*
Northeastern State University *B*
Oklahoma State University *D*
Rose State College *A*
University of Central Oklahoma *B*

Oregon
Chemeketa Community College *A*
George Fox University *B*
Linn-Benton Community College *A*

Pennsylvania
Drexel University *M*
Immaculata University *A, B*
Indiana University of Pennsylvania *B*
University of Pittsburgh
    Titusville *A*

Puerto Rico
Pontifical Catholic University of Puerto
    Rico *B*
University of Puerto Rico
    Rio Piedras Campus *B, M*

South Carolina
South Carolina State University *B*

South Dakota
South Dakota State University *M*

Tennessee
East Tennessee State University *B, T*
Middle Tennessee State University *M*
Tennessee State University *B, M*
Tennessee Technological University *B, T*
University of Tennessee
    Chattanooga *B*
    Knoxville *B, M, D*
    Martin *B, M*

Texas
Baylor University *B*
Brazosport College *A*
Coastal Bend College *A*
Lamar State College at Port Arthur *A*
Lamar University *B, M*
Laredo Community College *A*
Panola College *A*
Prairie View A&M University *B, M*
Sam Houston State University *B, M*
South Plains College *A*
Southwest Texas State University *B, T*
Stephen F. Austin State University *B, M*
Tarleton State University *B, T*
Texas A&M University
    Kingsville *B, M*
Texas Tech University *B*
Texas Woman's University *B, T*
Tyler Junior College *A*
University of Houston *B*
University of Texas
    Austin *B*

Utah
Brigham Young University *B*
Snow College *A*
Southern Utah University *B, T*
Utah State University *M*

Vermont
University of Vermont *B, M*

Virginia
Bridgewater College *B*

Washington
Central Washington University *B, M*
Washington State University *B*

West Virginia
Fairmont State College *B*
Marshall University *B, M*
Shepherd College *B*
West Virginia University *B, M, T*

Wisconsin
University of Wisconsin
    Madison *B, M*

Wyoming
University of Wyoming *B, M*

Farm/ranch management

Arizona
Central Arizona College *C*

Colorado
Colorado State University *B*
Morgan Community College *C*
Otero Junior College *C*
Trinidad State Junior College *C*

Florida
University of Florida *B*

Georgia
Fort Valley State University *B*

Idaho
Boise State University *C*
Eastern Idaho Technical College *C, A*
Idaho State University *C, A*

Illinois
Lincoln Land Community College *A*

Indiana
Purdue University *B*

Iowa
Des Moines Area Community College *C*
Ellsworth Community College *C, A*
Hawkeye Community College *A*
Iowa State University *B*
North Iowa Area Community College *A*

Kansas
Allen County Community College *A*
Butler County Community College *A*
Dodge City Community College *C, A*
Fort Scott Community College *A*
Garden City Community College *A*
Hutchinson Community College *A*
McPherson College *B*
Pratt Community College *C, A*
Seward County Community College *A*

Maryland
Community College of Baltimore County
    Catonsville *C, A*
    Dundalk *C, A*
    Essex *C, A*

Michigan
Michigan State University *B*

Minnesota
Alexandria Technical College *C*
Northland Community & Technical
    College *C, A*
Ridgewater College: A Community and
    Technical College *C*

Riverland Community College: A
    Technical and Community College *A*
St. Cloud Technical College *C*
Southwest State University *C*
University of Minnesota
    Crookston *B*

Missouri
Crowder College *A*
North Central Missouri College *C, A*
Northwest Missouri State
    University *C, B*

Montana
Dawson Community College *A*
Miles Community College *A*

Nebraska
Central Community College *C, A*
Northeast Community College *A*

Nevada
University of Nevada
    Reno *B*

New York
Cornell University *B*
State University of New York
    College of Agriculture and
    Technology at Morrisville *A, B*

North Dakota
Dickinson State University *A*

Ohio
University of Findlay *B*
Wilmington College *B*

Oklahoma
Eastern Oklahoma State College *A*
Langston University *B*
Northeastern Oklahoma Agricultural and
    Mechanical College *C, A*
Oklahoma Panhandle State
    University *A, B*
Redlands Community College *C, A*

Oregon
Blue Mountain Community College *A*
Chemeketa Community College *C*
Treasure Valley Community College *A*

Pennsylvania
Erie Business Center *A*
Penn State
    University Park *C*

South Carolina
Clemson University *B*

South Dakota
Western Dakota Technical Institute *A*

Texas
Central Texas College *C, A*
Clarendon College *C, A*
Frank Phillips College *A*
North Central Texas College *A*
Northeast Texas Community College *C*
Southwest Texas Junior College *C, A*
Tarleton State University *B*
Texas A&M University *B*
Texas Christian University *C*
Trinity Valley Community College *C, A*
Tyler Junior College *C, A*
Wharton County Junior College *A*

Utah
Snow College *A*

Vermont
Vermont Technical College *A*

Virginia
Virginia Highlands Community
    College *C*

Wisconsin
Chippewa Valley Technical College *C*
Lakeshore Technical College *C*
Moraine Park Technical College *C*

Wyoming

Eastern Wyoming College *A*
Sheridan College *A*

Fashion merchandizing

Alabama

Lawson State Community College *C*
Wallace State Community College at
　Hanceville *A*

Arizona

Northern Arizona University *B*
Phoenix College *C*
Scottsdale Community College *C, A*

Arkansas

Harding University *B*
University of Central Arkansas *B*

California

California State Polytechnic University:
　Pomona *B*
California State University
　Long Beach *B*
College of Alameda *C, A*
Fashion Institute of Design and
　Merchandising *A*
Fashion Institute of Design and
　Merchandising
　　San Francisco *A*
Las Positas College *C*
Long Beach City College *C, A*
Los Angeles Trade and Technical
　College *C, A*
Marymount College *A*
Modesto Junior College *C, A*
Mount San Antonio College *C, A*
Orange Coast College *C, A*
Palomar College *C, A*
San Diego Mesa College *C, A*
San Francisco State University *B*
San Joaquin Delta College *C, A*
Santa Rosa Junior College *C*
Shasta College *A*
Sierra College *C, A*
Ventura College *C, A*
West Valley College *C, A*
Woodbury University *B*

Colorado

Colorado State University
　Pueblo *B*

Connecticut

Asnuntuck Community College *A*
Briarwood College *A*
Gateway Community College *A*
Tunxis Community College *C, A*
University of Bridgeport *A, B*

Delaware

University of Delaware *B*

District of Columbia

Howard University *B*
University of the District of Columbia *A*

Florida

Okaloosa-Walton Community College *A*
Santa Fe Community College *A*

Georgia

Abraham Baldwin Agricultural
　College *A*
Bauder College *A*
Brenau University *B*
Clark Atlanta University *B*
Middle Georgia College *C*
Morris Brown College *B*
University of Georgia *B*

Hawaii

University of Hawaii
　Honolulu Community College *C, A*

Illinois

Chicago State University *B*

College of DuPage *A*
Columbia College Chicago *B*
Dominican University *B*
Illinois Institute of Art *A, B*
Joliet Junior College *A*
Midstate College *A*
Olivet Nazarene University *B*
South Suburban College of Cook
　County *C, A*
Triton College *C*
University of Illinois
　　Urbana-Champaign *B*
William Rainey Harper College *C, A*

Indiana

Indiana Business College *A*
Vincennes University *A*

Iowa

Des Moines Area Community
　College *C, A*
Ellsworth Community College *C, A*
Kirkwood Community College *C, A*
North Iowa Area Community College *A*

Kansas

Pittsburg State University *B*
Seward County Community
　College *C, A*

Kentucky

Murray State University *B*

Louisiana

Dryades YMCA School of
　Commerce *A, B*
Louisiana State University and
　Agricultural and Mechanical
　College *B*

Massachusetts

Bay State College *A*
Fisher College *C, A*
Lasell College *B*
Massasoit Community College *C*
Mount Ida College *A, B*
Newbury College *A*

Michigan

Central Michigan University *B*
Eastern Michigan University *B*
Finlandia University *B*
Grand Rapids Community College *A*
Lansing Community College *A*
Madonna University *C, B*
Northwood University *A, B*

Minnesota

Alexandria Technical College *C, A*
College of St. Catherine *B*
Rasmussen College
　Mankato *A*
Ridgewater College: A Community and
　Technical College *C*

Mississippi

Delta State University *B*
Holmes Community College *A*
Mississippi Gulf Coast Community
　College
　　Perkinston *A*
Northwest Mississippi Community
　College *A*

Missouri

Central Missouri State University *A*
Lindenwood University *B*
Patricia Stevens College *C*
Penn Valley Community College *A*
St. Louis Community College
　St. Louis Community College at
　　Florissant Valley *A*
Southeast Missouri State University *B*
Stephens College *B*

Nebraska

Northeast Community College *A*

New Hampshire

Southern New Hampshire
　University *C, A, B*

New Jersey

Berkeley College *A*
Brookdale Community College *A*
Burlington County College *A*
Middlesex County College *A*

New Mexico

Dona Ana Branch Community College of
　New Mexico State University *A*

New York

Berkeley College *A*
Berkeley College of New York City *A*
City University of New York
　　Kingsborough Community
　　　College *A*
Fashion Institute of Technology *A, B*
Genesee Community College *A*
Laboratory Institute of
　Merchandising *A, B*
Monroe Community College *C, A*
Nassau Community College *A*
Parsons School of Design *A, B*
Pratt Institute *B*
State University of New York
　College at Buffalo *B*
　College at Oneonta *B*

North Carolina

Central Piedmont Community College *A*
Meredith College *B*

North Dakota

Lake Region State College *C, A*
North Dakota State University *B*

Ohio

Bowling Green State University *B*
Davis College *A*
Kent State University *B*
Mount Vernon Nazarene University *B*
University of Akron *A*
Ursuline College *B*
Virginia Marti College of Art and
　Design *A*
Youngstown State University *B*

Oklahoma

Northeastern State University *B*
Oklahoma State University *B*
Tulsa Community College *C, A*
University of Central Oklahoma *B*

Oregon

George Fox University *B*

Pennsylvania

Art Institute
　of Philadelphia *A*
　of Pittsburgh *A*
Bradley Academy for the Visual Arts *A*
Community College of Philadelphia *C, A*
ICM School of Business & Medical
　Careers *A*
Immaculata University *A, B*
Marywood University *C*
Mercyhurst College *B*
Philadelphia University *B*
Westmoreland County Community
　College *A*

Rhode Island

Community College of Rhode Island *A*
University of Rhode Island *B*

South Carolina

Midlands Technical College *C*
South Carolina State University *B*

South Dakota

South Dakota State University *B*

Tennessee

Draughons Junior College of Business:
　Nashville *A*
Lambuth University *B*

O'More College of Design *A, B*
University of Tennessee
　Martin *B*

Texas

Alvin Community College *C, A*
Austin Community College *C, A*
Border Institute of Technology *A*
Brookhaven College *A*
Cedar Valley College *A*
El Paso Community College *C, A*
Houston Community College
　System *C, A*
Laredo Community College *A*
Midland College *A*
Northwood University: Texas
　Campus *A, B*
Palo Alto College *C, A*
San Jacinto College
　Central Campus *C, A*
South Plains College *A*
Southwest Texas State University *B*
Stephen F. Austin State University *B*
Tarleton State University *B*
Tarrant County College *C, A*
Texarkana College *C, A*
Texas Woman's University *B*
University of North Texas *B*
University of the Incarnate Word *B*

Utah

Salt Lake Community College *C*
Utah State University *B*
Weber State University *A*

Virginia

J. Sargeant Reynolds Community
　College *A*
Marymount University *B*
Virginia Polytechnic Institute and State
　University *B*

Washington

Art Institute of Seattle *A*
Central Washington University *B*
Edmonds Community College *C, A*
Seattle Central Community College *A*
Spokane Falls Community College *A*

West Virginia

Fairmont State College *A*
Shepherd College *A*

Wisconsin

Milwaukee Area Technical College *A*
Mount Mary College *B*

Fashion/apparel design

Alabama

Wallace State Community College at
　Hanceville *A*

Arkansas

Harding University *B*

California

Academy of Art College *C, A, B, M*
Art Institute of California - San
　Francisco *A, B*
California College of Arts and Crafts *B*
Fashion Institute of Design and
　Merchandising *A*
Fashion Institute of Design and
　Merchandising
　　San Diego *C*
　　San Francisco *A*
Long Beach City College *C, A*
Los Angeles Southwest College *A*
Los Angeles Trade and Technical
　College *A*
Modesto Junior College *C, A*
Orange Coast College *C, A*
Otis College of Art and Design *B*
Palomar College *C, A*
San Joaquin Delta College *C, A*
Santa Rosa Junior College *C, A*

Santiago Canyon College *A*
Ventura College *C, A*
West Valley College *C, A*
Woodbury University *B*

Colorado
Art Institute
　of Colorado *A*

Connecticut
University of New Haven *A, B*

Delaware
University of Delaware *B*

Florida
Art Institute
　of Fort Lauderdale *A*
Florida State University *B, M*
International Academy of Design and
　Technology *A, B*
Manatee Community College *A*
Miami-Dade Community College *A*
Santa Fe Community College *A*

Georgia
Bauder College *A*
Savannah College of Art and
　Design *B, M*

Hawaii
University of Hawaii
　Honolulu Community College *C, A*

Illinois
Columbia College Chicago *B*
Dominican University *B*
Illinois Institute of Art *A, B*
International Academy of Design and
　Technology *A, B*
Sauk Valley Community College *A*
School of the Art Institute of Chicago *B*
William Rainey Harper College *C, A*

Indiana
Ball State University *B*
Vincennes University *A*

Iowa
Iowa State University *B*

Massachusetts
Bay State College *A*
Lasell College *B*
Massachusetts College of Art *B*
Mount Ida College *A, B*

Michigan
Adrian College *B*
Central Michigan University *B*
Finlandia University *B*

Minnesota
College of St. Catherine *B*
Minneapolis Community and Technical
　College *C, A*
University of Minnesota
　Twin Cities *B*

Missouri
Lindenwood University *B*
Stephens College *B*
Washington University in St. Louis *B, M*

New Jersey
Burlington County College *A*
Centenary College *B*

New Mexico
Santa Fe Community College *C*

New York
Eugene Lang College/New School
　University *B*
Fashion Institute of Technology *A, B*
Marist College *B*
Marymount College of Fordham
　University *B*
Parsons School of Design *A, B, T*
Pratt Institute *B*

State University of New York
　College at Buffalo *B*
Syracuse University *B, M*

North Carolina
Mars Hill College *B*
Meredith College *B*

Ohio
Bowling Green State University *B*
Columbus College of Art and Design *B*
Davis College *A*
Kent State University *B*
Ohio Institute of Photography and
　Technology *C, A*
Sinclair Community College *A*
University of Cincinnati *B*
Ursuline College *B*
Virginia Marti College of Art and
　Design *A*

Oklahoma
Oklahoma State University *B*

Oregon
Art Institute
　of Portland *A, B*
Oregon State University *B*

Pennsylvania
Art Institute
　of Philadelphia *A*
　of Pittsburgh *A*
Bradley Academy for the Visual Arts *A*
California University of Pennsylvania *A*
Drexel University *B, M*
Philadelphia University *C, B*

Puerto Rico
Pontifical Catholic University of Puerto
　Rico *A*

Texas
Baylor University *B*
El Centro College *A*
El Paso Community College *A*
Houston Community College
　System *C, A*
Texas Tech University *B*
Texas Woman's University *B, M*
University of North Texas *B, M*
University of the Incarnate Word *B*

Utah
Salt Lake Community College *C*

Virginia
Marymount University *B*
Virginia Commonwealth University *B*

Washington
Art Institute of Seattle *A*

Wisconsin
Mount Mary College *B*
University of Wisconsin
　Madison *B, M*
Waukesha County Technical College *A*

　　Fashion/fabric consultant

Wisconsin
Milwaukee Area Technical College *A*

　　Fiber arts

Arizona
Arizona State University *B, M*

California
Academy of Art College *C, A, B, M*
California College of Arts and
　Crafts *B, M*
California State University
　Long Beach *B, M*
University of California
　Davis *M*

Colorado
Colorado State University *B*

Georgia
Savannah College of Art and
　Design *B, M*
University of Georgia *B*

Illinois
School of the Art Institute of
　Chicago *B, M*

Indiana
Vincennes University *A*

Kansas
University of Kansas *B, M*

Maryland
Maryland Institute College of Art *B*

Massachusetts
Massachusetts College of Art *B, M*
University of Massachusetts
　Dartmouth *B, M*

Michigan
College for Creative Studies *B*
Finlandia University *B*
Northern Michigan University *B*
University of Michigan *B*

Minnesota
Minnesota State University
　Mankato *B*

Missouri
Kansas City Art Institute *B*
Lindenwood University *M*

New Jersey
Rowan University *B*

New York
Parsons School of Design *C, A, B, T*
State University of New York
　College at Buffalo *B*
Syracuse University *B, M*

North Carolina
Haywood Community College *A*
North Carolina State University *B*

Ohio
Bowling Green State University *B*
Cleveland Institute of Art *B*

Oregon
University of Oregon *B, M*

Pennsylvania
Marywood University *M*
Philadelphia University *A, B, M*
Temple University *B, M*

Rhode Island
Rhode Island College *B*
Rhode Island School of Design *B, M*

Tennessee
Memphis College of Art *B, M*
Tennessee Technological University *B*

Texas
Texas Woman's University *B, M*
University of North Texas *B, M*

Washington
University of Washington *B, M*
Western Washington University *B*

West Virginia
West Virginia State College *B*

Wisconsin
University of Wisconsin
　Madison *B*

　　Film/cinema studies

California
California Institute of the Arts *C, B, M*

Chapman University *B, M*
Long Beach City College *A*
Orange Coast College *A*
Palomar College *C, A*
Pitzer College *B*
San Francisco State University *B, M*
Santa Barbara City College *A*
University of California
　Berkeley *B*
　Irvine *B*
　Los Angeles *B*
　Santa Barbara *B*
　Santa Cruz *B*
University of Southern
　California *B, M, D*

Colorado
Colorado College *B*
University of Colorado
　Boulder *B*

Connecticut
Trinity College *B*
University of Hartford *B*
Wesleyan University *B*
Yale University *B*

District of Columbia
American University *B, M*
Howard University *M*

Florida
Tallahassee Community College *A*
University of Miami *B, M*

Georgia
Emory University *B, M*
Georgia State University *B*
Oxford College of Emory University *B*

Illinois
Columbia College Chicago *B*
Southern Illinois University
　Carbondale *B*

Indiana
Purdue University *B*

Iowa
Maharishi University of Management *B*
University of Iowa *B, M, D*

Kansas
Pittsburg State University *B*
Southwestern College *B*

Maine
New England School of
　Communications *C, A, B*

Maryland
Johns Hopkins University *B*

Massachusetts
Boston College *B*
Clark University *B*
Emerson College *B*
Hampshire College *B*
Harvard College *B*
Massachusetts College of Art *B, M*

Michigan
Calvin College *B*
Spring Arbor University *B*
University of Michigan *B*
Wayne State University *B*

Minnesota
Minnesota State University
　Moorhead *B*
University of Minnesota
　Twin Cities *B*

Missouri
Washington University in St. Louis *B*
Webster University *B*

Nebraska
University of Nebraska
　Lincoln *B*

Nevada

University of Nevada
    Las Vegas *B*

New Hampshire

Dartmouth College *B*
Keene State College *B*

New Jersey

Rowan University *B*

New Mexico

College of Santa Fe *B*
University of New Mexico *B*

New York

Bard College *B*
City University of New York
    Brooklyn College *B, M*
    City College *B, M*
    College of Staten Island *B, M*
    Hunter College *B*
    Queens College *B*
Columbia University
    Columbia College *B*
Fordham University *B*
Ithaca College *B*
Long Island University
    C. W. Post Campus *B*
Marist College *B*
New York University *B, M, D*
St. John's University *A, B*
Sarah Lawrence College *B*
School of Visual Arts *B*
State University of New York
    Binghamton *B*
    Stony Brook *B*
University of Rochester *B*
Vassar College *B*

North Carolina

University of North Carolina
    Greensboro *B, M*

Ohio

Bowling Green State University *B*
Denison University *B*
Oberlin College *B*
University of Toledo *B*
Wright State University *B*

Pennsylvania

DeSales University *B*
La Salle University *B*
Penn State
    Schuylkill - Capital College *B*
    University Park *B, M*
Temple University *B, M*
University of Pittsburgh *C, B*

Rhode Island

Rhode Island College *B*

South Carolina

University of South Carolina *B*

Tennessee

University of Tennessee
    Knoxville *B*

Texas

Southern Methodist University *B*

Utah

Brigham Young University *B, M, D*
University of Utah *B, M*

Vermont

Bennington College *B*
Burlington College *C, B*
Marlboro College *B*

Washington

Whitman College *B*

Wisconsin

University of Wisconsin
    Madison *B*
    Milwaukee *B*

Finance

Alabama

Alabama Agricultural and Mechanical
    University *B*
Alabama State University *B*
Auburn University *B*
Auburn University at Montgomery *B*
Birmingham-Southern College *B*
Huntingdon College *B*
Jacksonville State University *B*
James H. Faulkner State Community
    College *A*
Oakwood College *B*
Spring Hill College *B*
Talladega College *B*
Troy State University in Montgomery *B*
Tuskegee University *B*
University of Alabama *B, M, D*
University of Alabama
    Birmingham *B*
    Huntsville *B*
University of Montevallo *B*
University of North Alabama *B*
University of South Alabama *B*

Alaska

University of Alaska
    Anchorage *B*

Arizona

Arizona State University *B*
Northern Arizona University *B*
Scottsdale Community College *C*
University of Arizona *B*
University of Phoenix *C, B*

Arkansas

Arkansas State University *B*
East Arkansas Community College *A*
University of Arkansas *B*
University of Arkansas
    Little Rock *B*
University of Central Arkansas *B*

California

Azusa Pacific University *M*
California State Polytechnic University:
    Pomona *B*
California State University
    Chico *B*
    Fresno *B*
    Fullerton *B, M*
    Hayward *B, M*
    Long Beach *B*
    Los Angeles *B, M*
    Northridge *M*
    Sacramento *B*
    Stanislaus *B*
Golden Gate University *C, B, M*
La Sierra University *B, M*
Modesto Junior College *A*
National University *M*
Pacific Union College *B*
San Diego State University *B, M*
San Francisco State University *B*
San Joaquin Delta College *C*
San Jose State University *B*
Santa Barbara City College *C, A*
Santa Clara University *B*
Southwestern College *A*
University of San Francisco *B*
Vanguard University of Southern
    California *B*

Colorado

Colorado State University *B*
Colorado State University
    Pueblo *B*
Fort Lewis College *B*
Jones International University *B*
Metropolitan State College of Denver *B*
University of Colorado
    Boulder *B, M, D*
    Colorado Springs *B*
    Denver *M*

University of Denver *B, M*

Connecticut

Albertus Magnus College *B*
Central Connecticut State University *B*
Fairfield University *B, M*
Naugatuck Valley Community College *A*
Norwalk Community College *A*
Quinnipiac University *B, M*
Sacred Heart University *B*
Southern Connecticut State University *B*
Teikyo Post University *B*
Tunxis Community College *A*
University of Bridgeport *B, M*
University of Connecticut *B*
University of Hartford *B*
University of New Haven *B*
Western Connecticut State University *B*

Delaware

Delaware State University *B*
University of Delaware *B*
Wilmington College *B*

District of Columbia

American University *B, M*
Catholic University of America *B, M*
George Washington University *B, M*
Georgetown University *B*
Howard University *B*
University of the District of Columbia *B*

Florida

Barry University *C*
Broward Community College *A*
Florida Atlantic University *B*
Florida Gulf Coast University *B*
Florida International University *B, M*
Florida Southern College *B*
Florida State University *B, M*
Jacksonville University *B, M*
Palm Beach Community College *A*
St. Thomas University *B*
Stetson University *B*
University of Central Florida *B*
University of Florida *B, M*
University of Miami *B, M*
University of North Florida *B, M*
University of South Florida *B*
University of Tampa *B*
University of West Florida *B*
Webber International University *A, B*

Georgia

Augusta State University *B*
Berry College *B*
Clark Atlanta University *M*
Columbus State University *B*
Emory University *B*
Georgia Institute of Technology *M*
Georgia Southern University *B*
Georgia State University *B, M, D*
Kennesaw State University *M*
Mercer University *B, M*
Morehouse College *B*
North Georgia College & State
    University *B*
South Georgia College *A*
State University of West Georgia *B*
University of Georgia *B*
Valdosta State University *B*

Hawaii

Hawaii Pacific University *A, B*
University of Hawaii
    Hilo *B*
    Manoa *B*

Idaho

Boise State University *B*
Idaho State University *B*
University of Idaho *B*

Illinois

Augustana College *B*
Aurora University *B*
Benedictine University *B*
Bradley University *B*

Chicago State University *B*
Danville Area Community College *A*
De Paul University *B, M*
Eastern Illinois University *B*
Elmhurst College *B*
Eureka College *B*
Governors State University *B*
Illinois College *B*
Illinois Institute of Technology *M*
Illinois State University *B*
Lewis University *B*
Loyola University of Chicago *C, B*
MacMurray College *B*
Millikin University *B*
North Central College *B*
North Park University *B*
Northeastern Illinois University *B*
Northern Illinois University *B*
Northwestern University *D*
Olivet Nazarene University *B*
Quincy University *B*
Roosevelt University *B, M*
St. Xavier University *M*
South Suburban College of Cook
    County *C, A*
Southern Illinois University
    Carbondale *B*
University of Chicago *M, D*
University of Illinois
    Chicago *B*
    Urbana-Champaign *B, M, D*
University of St. Francis *B*
Western Illinois University *B*
William Rainey Harper College *C, A*

Indiana

Anderson University *B*
Ball State University *B*
Butler University *B*
Goshen College *B*
Indiana Institute of Technology *B*
Indiana State University *B*
Indiana University
    South Bend *A, B*
Indiana University-Purdue University
    Fort Wayne *B*
Indiana Wesleyan University *B*
Marian College *A, B*
Purdue University
    Calumet *B*
St. Joseph's College *B*
Saint Mary's College *B*
Taylor University *B*
University of Evansville *B*
University of Notre Dame *B*
University of Southern Indiana *B*
Valparaiso University *B*

Iowa

American Institute of Business *A*
Buena Vista University *B*
Clarke College *B*
Drake University *B*
Franciscan University *B*
Iowa State University *B*
Kirkwood Community College *A*
Loras College *B*
Northwestern College *B*
St. Ambrose University *B*
University of Iowa *B, D*
University of Northern Iowa *B*
Waldorf College *A, B*
Wartburg College *B*

Kansas

Central Christian College *A*
Hutchinson Community College *A*
Kansas State University *B*
McPherson College *B*
Pittsburg State University *B*
Seward County Community College *A*
Tabor College *B*
Wichita State University *B*

Kentucky

Beckfield College *A*
Madisonville Community College *A*

Morehead State University *B*
Murray State University *B*
Southeast Community College *A*
University of Kentucky *B*
University of Louisville *B*

Louisiana
Centenary College of Louisiana *B*
Dillard University *B*
Louisiana State University
    Shreveport *B*
Louisiana State University and
    Agricultural and Mechanical
    College *B, M, D*
Louisiana Tech University *B*
Loyola University New Orleans *B*
McNeese State University *B*
Nicholls State University *B*
Southeastern Louisiana University *B*
Southern University
    Shreveport *C, A*
Southern University and Agricultural and
    Mechanical College *B*
Tulane University *B*
University of Louisiana at Lafayette *B*
University of Louisiana at Monroe *B*
University of New Orleans *B*

Maine
Husson College *B*
Thomas College *B*
University of Maine *B*
University of Southern Maine *B, M*

Maryland
Bowie State University *B*
Cecil Community College *C, A*
College of Notre Dame of Maryland *B*
Johns Hopkins University *B, M*
Loyola College in Maryland *M*
Morgan State University *B, M*
University of Maryland
    College Park *B*

Massachusetts
American International College *B, M*
Babson College *B*
Bentley College *B, M*
Boston College *B, M, D*
Boston University *B, M*
Bridgewater State College *C, B*
Clark University *M*
Fitchburg State College *B*
Lasell College *B*
Massachusetts Bay Community
    College *C*
Massachusetts College of Liberal Arts *B*
Merrimack College *B*
Newbury College *A, B*
Nichols College *B*
Northeastern University *A, B, M*
Simmons College *B*
Springfield Technical Community
    College *A*
Stonehill College *B*
Suffolk University *B, M*
University of Massachusetts
    Amherst *B*
    Dartmouth *B*
Western New England College *B, M*
Westfield State College *B*

Michigan
Central Michigan University *B*
Davenport University
    Eastern Region *A, B*
Davenport University - Western
    Region *C*
Eastern Michigan University *B*
Ferris State University *B*
Glen Oaks Community College *C*
Grand Valley State University *B*
Hillsdale College *B*
Jackson Community College *C, A*
Michigan State University *B, M, D*
Northern Michigan University *B*
Oakland University *B*

Saginaw Valley State University *B, M*
University of Michigan
    Flint *B, M*
Walsh College of Accountancy and
    Business Administration *B, M*
Wayne State University *B*
Western Michigan University *B*

Minnesota
Academy College *A*
Augsburg College *B*
Bethel College *B*
Capella University *M*
Concordia University: St. Paul *B*
Metropolitan State University *B*
Minnesota State University
    Mankato *B*
    Moorhead *B*
Northwestern College *B*
St. Cloud State University *B*
St. Cloud Technical College *C, A*
University of St. Thomas *B*
Winona State University *B*

Mississippi
Delta State University *B*
Mississippi State University *B*
University of Mississippi *B*
University of Southern Mississippi *B*

Missouri
Avila University *B*
Central Missouri State University *B*
Culver-Stockton College *B*
Lindenwood University *B, M*
Mineral Area College *C, A*
Missouri Southern State College *B*
Missouri Western State College *B*
Northwest Missouri State University *B*
Rockhurst University *B*
St. Louis University *B, M*
Southeast Missouri State University *B*
Southwest Missouri State University *B*
University of Missouri
    Columbia *B*
    St. Louis *B*
Washington University in St. Louis *B, M*
Webster University *M*

Montana
Carroll College *B*
University of Montana-Missoula *B*

Nebraska
Creighton University *B*
Union College *B*
University of Nebraska
    Lincoln *B*
    Omaha *B*
York College *A, B*

Nevada
University of Nevada
    Las Vegas *B*
    Reno *B*

New Hampshire
Franklin Pierce College *B*
New England College *B*
St. Anselm College *B*
Southern New Hampshire University *B*
University of New Hampshire *B*

New Jersey
Bloomfield College *B*
The College of New Jersey *B*
Fairleigh Dickinson University
    College at Florham *M*
    Metropolitan Campus *M*
Gloucester County College *A*
Kean University *B*
Monmouth University *B*
Passaic County Community College *C*
Rider University *B*
Rowan University *B*

Rutgers, The State University of New
    Jersey
    Camden Regional Campus *B*
    New Brunswick Regional
        Campus *B*
    Newark Regional Campus *B*
St. Peter's College *A*
Seton Hall University *B*
Thomas Edison State College *C, A, B*
William Paterson University of New
    Jersey *B*

New Mexico
Eastern New Mexico University *B*
New Mexico Highlands University *B*
New Mexico State University *B*

New York
Adelphi University *B, M*
Canisius College *B*
City University of New York
    Baruch College *B, M, D*
Clarkson University *B*
Clinton Community College *C*
Concordia College *B*
Dominican College of Blauvelt *B*
Dowling College *C, B*
Excelsior College *B*
Fordham University *B, M*
Fulton-Montgomery Community
    College *A*
Globe Institute of Technology *C, A*
Hilbert College *B*
Hofstra University *B, M*
Hudson Valley Community College *A*
Iona College *B*
Ithaca College *B*
Long Island University
    C. W. Post Campus *B, M*
Manhattan College *B*
Manhattanville College *B*
Marist College *B*
New York Institute of
    Technology *C, B, M*
New York University *B, M, D*
Orange County Community College *A*
Pace University *B, M*
Pace University:
    Pleasantville/Briarcliff *B, M*
Rochester Institute of Technology *B, M*
St. Bonaventure University *B*
St. John Fisher College *B*
St. John's University *C, B, M*
State University of New York
    Albany *B, M*
    Buffalo *M*
    College at Fredonia *B*
    College at Old Westbury *B*
    College at Plattsburgh *B*
    College of Agriculture and
        Technology at Cobleskill *A*
    College of Technology at Alfred *A*
    Institute of Technology at
        Utica/Rome *B*
    New Paltz *B*
    Oswego *B*
Suffolk County Community College *A*
Syracuse University *B, M*
Ulster County Community College *C, A*
Wagner College *B*

North Carolina
Appalachian State University *B*
Catawba Valley Community
    College *C, A*
East Carolina University *B*
Elon University *B*
Forsyth Technical Community College *A*
Lenoir-Rhyne College *B*
Mars Hill College *B*
Meredith College *B*
North Carolina Agricultural and
    Technical State University *B*
Southwestern Community College *A*

University of North Carolina
    Charlotte *B*
    Greensboro *B*
    Wilmington *B*
Wake Forest University *B*
Western Carolina University *B*

North Dakota
Dickinson State University *B*
Minot State University *B*
North Dakota State College of Science *A*
University of North Dakota *B*

Ohio
Ashland University *B*
Baldwin-Wallace College *B*
Bowling Green State University *B, M*
Case Western Reserve University *M, D*
Cedarville University *B*
Central State University *B*
Cincinnati State Technical and
    Community College *A*
Cleveland State University *B, D*
David N. Myers College *B*
Defiance College *B*
Franklin University *B*
James A. Rhodes State College *A*
Jefferson Community College *C*
John Carroll University *B*
Kent State University *B, M*
Kent State University
    Stark Campus *B*
Miami University
    Middletown Campus *A*
    Oxford Campus *B, M*
Mount Vernon Nazarene University *B*
North Central State College *C*
Northwest State Community College *A*
Ohio State University
    Columbus Campus *B*
Ohio University *B*
Otterbein College *B*
Shawnee State University *A*
Tiffin University *B*
University of Akron *B, M*
University of Cincinnati *B, M, D*
University of Cincinnati
    Clermont College *C*
University of Dayton *B*
University of Findlay *A, B*
University of Rio Grande *B*
University of Toledo *B, M*
Walsh University *A, B*
Wright State University *M*
Xavier University *B, M*
Youngstown State University *A, B, M*

Oklahoma
East Central University *B*
Northeastern Oklahoma Agricultural and
    Mechanical College *C*
Northeastern State University *B*
Oklahoma Baptist University *B*
Oklahoma City Community
    College *C, A*
Oklahoma State University *B*
Oral Roberts University *B*
Rogers State University *C*
Southeastern Oklahoma State
    University *B*
Southern Nazarene University *B*
Tulsa Community College *C*
University of Central Oklahoma *B*
University of Oklahoma *B*
University of Tulsa *B, M*

Oregon
Chemeketa Community College *C*
Linfield College *B*
Portland State University *B, M*
University of Oregon *B*
University of Portland *B*

Pennsylvania
Albright College *B*
Arcadia University *B*
Bucks County Community College *A*

Cabrini College *B*
Carnegie Mellon University *D*
Central Pennsylvania College *A, B*
Chestnut Hill College *B*
DeSales University *B*
Drexel University *B, M*
Duquesne University *B*
Education Direct: Center for Degree Studies *A*
Holy Family University *B*
Immaculata University *B*
Indiana University of Pennsylvania *B*
Juniata College *B*
King's College *B*
Kutztown University of Pennsylvania *B*
La Roche College *B*
La Salle University *B*
Lehigh University *B*
Lincoln University *B*
Marywood University *M*
Mercyhurst College *B*
Penn State
   Abington *B*
   Altoona *B*
   Beaver *B*
   Berks *B*
   Dubois *B*
   Erie, The Behrend College *B*
   Fayette *B*
   Harrisburg *B*
   Hazleton *B*
   Lehigh Valley *B*
   McKeesport *B*
   Mont Alto *B*
   New Kensington *B*
   Schuylkill - Capital College *B*
   Shenango *B*
   University Park *B*
   Wilkes-Barre *B*
   Worthington Scranton *B*
   York *B*
Philadelphia University *B, M*
Robert Morris University *B*
St. Joseph's University *A, B, M*
St. Vincent College *B*
Seton Hill University *B*
Shippensburg University of Pennsylvania *B*
Temple University *B, M, D*
University of Pennsylvania *C, B, M, D*
University of Pittsburgh *B*
University of Pittsburgh Johnstown *B*
University of Scranton *B, M*
Villanova University *B*
Waynesburg College *B*
Widener University *B*
York College of Pennsylvania *B*

Puerto Rico
Inter American University of Puerto Rico
   Bayamon Campus *B*
   Metropolitan Campus *B, M*
   San German Campus *B, M*
Pontifical Catholic University of Puerto Rico *B*
University of Puerto Rico
   Bayamon University College *A, B*
   Mayaguez Campus *B, M*
   Ponce *B*
   Rio Piedras Campus *B, M, D*

Rhode Island
Bryant College *B, M*
Rhode Island College *B*
University of Rhode Island *B*

South Carolina
Anderson College *B*
Charleston Southern University *B, M*
Coastal Carolina University *B*
Converse College *B*
Francis Marion University *B*
University of South Carolina *B*
University of South Carolina Aiken *B*

Wofford College *B*

South Dakota
Northern State University *B*
Southeast Technical Institute *A*

Tennessee
Belmont University *B*
Christian Brothers University *B*
Cleveland State Community College *C*
East Tennessee State University *B*
Freed-Hardeman University *B*
Middle Tennessee State University *B*
Roane State Community College *A*
Southwest Tennessee Community College *A*
Tennessee Technological University *B*
Union University *B*
University of Memphis *B*
University of Tennessee
   Knoxville *B*
   Martin *B*

Texas
Amarillo College *A*
Angelo State University *B*
Austin Community College *C, A*
Baylor University *B*
Brazosport College *A*
Coastal Bend College *A*
Dallas Baptist University *B*
Del Mar College *C, A*
East Texas Baptist University *B*
El Paso Community College *A*
Hardin-Simmons University *B*
Houston Baptist University *B*
Lamar University *B*
Laredo Community College *C, A*
Lubbock Christian University *B*
McMurry University *B*
Midwestern State University *B*
Our Lady of the Lake University of San Antonio *M*
Prairie View A&M University *B*
St. Edward's University *B, T*
Sam Houston State University *B, M*
South Texas Community College *A*
Southern Methodist University *B*
Southwest Texas State University *B*
Stephen F. Austin State University *B*
Sul Ross State University *B*
Tarleton State University *B*
Texas A&M International University *B*
Texas A&M University *B, M, D*
Texas A&M University
   Corpus Christi *B*
   Kingsville *B*
   Texarkana *B*
Texas Christian University *B*
Texas Tech University *B*
Texas Wesleyan University *B*
Trinity University *B*
University of Dallas *M*
University of Houston *B, M, D*
University of Houston Clear Lake *B*
University of Mary Hardin-Baylor *B*
University of North Texas *B, M, D*
University of St. Thomas *B*
University of Texas
   Arlington *B*
   Austin *B, D*
   Brownsville *B*
   El Paso *B*
   Pan American *B*
   San Antonio *B, M, D*
   Tyler *B*
   of the Permian Basin *B*
West Texas A&M University *B, M*

Utah
Brigham Young University *B*
Southern Utah University *B*
University of Utah *B, M*
Utah State University *B*
Utah Valley State College *B*
Weber State University *B*

Westminster College *B*

Vermont
College of St. Joseph in Vermont *B*

Virginia
Averett University *B*
George Mason University *B*
Hampton University *B*
James Madison University *B*
Longwood University *B*
Marymount University *C, B*
Old Dominion University *B*
Radford University *B*
Virginia Highlands Community College *C*
Virginia Polytechnic Institute and State University *B*
Virginia Union University *B*

Washington
Seattle University *B, M*
University of Washington *B*
Walla Walla College *B*
Washington State University *B*
Western Washington University *B*

West Virginia
Bethany College *B*
Concord College *B*
Fairmont State College *A*
Marshall University *B*
University of Charleston *B*
West Virginia University *B*
West Virginia Wesleyan College *B*

Wisconsin
Concordia University Wisconsin *B*
Edgewood College *B, M*
Marian College of Fond du Lac *B*
Marquette University *B*
University of Wisconsin
   Eau Claire *B*
   La Crosse *B*
   Madison *M, D*
   Milwaukee *B*
   Oshkosh *B*
   Parkside *B*
   Platteville *B*
   Superior *B*
   Whitewater *B*
Western Wisconsin Technical College *A*

Wyoming
University of Wyoming *B, M*

Financial planning

California
Master's College *B*
San Diego State University *C, M*

Connecticut
Manchester Community College *C*
Naugatuck Valley Community College *C*

Florida
University of Miami *C*
University of West Florida *B*

Georgia
Georgia State University *M*

Illinois
De Paul University *M*
St. Xavier University *M*

Indiana
Taylor University *B*

Iowa
Des Moines Area Community College *C*
Morningside College *B*

Maryland
Howard Community College *C, A*
Villa Julie College *C*

Massachusetts
Bentley College *M*
Lasell College *B*
Merrimack College *C*

Michigan
Central Michigan University *B*
Cleary University *B*
Northern Michigan University *B*

Minnesota
Minnesota State University Mankato *B*

New Jersey
Seton Hall University *M*

New York
Medaille College *C, B*
Pace University *M*
Pace University: Pleasantville/Briarcliff *C, M*
State University of New York College of Technology at Alfred *B*

North Carolina
Guilford College *C*

Ohio
Defiance College *B*
Hondros College *A*
Kent State University Stark Campus *B*
Stark State College of Technology *A*
University of Akron *C, B*
Youngstown State University *B*

Pennsylvania
Marywood University *B*
Moravian College *C*
Penn State Harrisburg *C*
Widener University *M*

Rhode Island
Bryant College *B*

Texas
Angelo State University *B*
Baylor University *B*
University of Dallas *M*

Wisconsin
Fox Valley Technical College *C*
Waukesha County Technical College *A*

Fine/studio arts

Alabama
Auburn University *B*
Faulkner University *B*
Huntingdon College *B*
James H. Faulkner State Community College *A*
Northwest-Shoals Community College *A*
Spring Hill College *B*
Troy State University *B*
University of Alabama *B, M*
University of Alabama Birmingham *B*
University of North Alabama *B*

Alaska
University of Alaska Anchorage *B*

Arizona
Arizona State University *B*
Arizona Western College *A*
Cochise College *A*
Northern Arizona University *B*
Prescott College *B, M*
University of Arizona *B*

Arkansas
Harding University *B*
Henderson State University *B*
Ouachita Baptist University *B, T*
University of Arkansas *B*

University of Central Arkansas *B*
Williams Baptist College *B*

California
Academy of Art College *C, A, B, M*
Art Center College of Design *B, M*
Azusa Pacific University *B*
Barstow College *A*
Biola University *B*
Cabrillo College *A*
California Baptist University *B*
California Institute of the Arts *M*
California State Polytechnic University:
  Pomona *B*
California State University
    Chico *B, M*
    Fullerton *M*
    Hayward *B*
    Long Beach *B, M*
    Monterey Bay *B*
Chabot College *A*
Chapman University *B*
Citrus College *A*
College of Alameda *A*
College of Marin: Kentfield *A*
College of the Sequoias *A*
Dominican University of California *B*
Foothill College *C, A*
Gavilan Community College *A*
Golden West College *A*
Irvine Valley College *A*
John F. Kennedy University *M*
La Sierra University *B*
Las Positas College *A*
Los Angeles Pierce College *A*
Los Medanos College *A*
Marymount College *A*
Mills College *B*
Modesto Junior College *A*
Monterey Peninsula College *A*
Moorpark College *A*
Mount St. Mary's College *B*
National University *M*
Ohlone College *A*
Orange Coast College *A*
Otis College of Art and Design *B, M*
Pacific Union College *B*
Pepperdine University *B*
Pitzer College *B*
Pomona College *B*
San Diego City College *A*
San Diego Mesa College *A*
San Francisco State University *M*
San Joaquin Delta College *A*
Santa Barbara City College *C, A*
Santa Clara University *B*
Santa Monica College *A*
Scripps College *B*
Shasta College *A*
Sierra College *A*
Sonoma State University *B*
Stanford University *B*
University of California
    Berkeley *B, M*
    Davis *M*
    Irvine *B*
    Riverside *B*
    San Diego *B*
    Santa Barbara *B, M*
    Santa Cruz *B*
University of San Francisco *B*
University of Southern California *B, M*
University of the Pacific *B*
Ventura College *C, A*
Yuba Community College District *A*

Colorado
Colorado Christian University *B*
Colorado College *B*
Colorado Mountain College
    Alpine Campus *A*
Colorado State University *M*
Naropa University *B*

University of Colorado
    Boulder *B, M*
    Colorado Springs *B*
    Denver *B, M*
University of Denver *B, M*

Connecticut
Albertus Magnus College *B*
Asnuntuck Community College *A*
Capital Community College *C*
Central Connecticut State University *B*
Connecticut College *B*
Eastern Connecticut State University *B*
Fairfield University *B*
Housatonic Community College *A*
Middlesex Community College *A*
Mitchell College *A*
Naugatuck Valley Community College *C*
Northwestern Connecticut Community
    College *A*
Norwalk Community College *A*
Paier College of Art *C, B*
Quinebaug Valley Community College *A*
St. Joseph College *B*
Trinity College *B*
University of Connecticut *B, M*
University of Hartford *B, M*
Wesleyan University *B*
Western Connecticut State University *M*
Yale University *M*

Delaware
University of Delaware *B, M*

District of Columbia
American University *B*
Corcoran College of Art and Design *B*
Gallaudet University *B*
George Washington University *B*
Georgetown University *B*
University of the District of Columbia *B*

Florida
Eckerd College *B*
Flagler College *B*
Florida Atlantic University *M*
Florida International University *B, M*
Florida Southern College *B*
Florida State University *B, M*
Jacksonville University *B*
Miami-Dade Community College *A*
New College of Florida *B*
Palm Beach Community College *A*
Polk Community College *A*
Ringling School of Art and Design *B*
South Florida Community College *A*
Stetson University *B*
University of Central Florida *B*
University of Florida *M*
University of Miami *B*
University of North Florida *B*
University of Tampa *B, T*
University of West Florida *B*

Georgia
Abraham Baldwin Agricultural
    College *A*
Agnes Scott College *B*
Atlanta College of Art *B*
Brenau University *B*
Clark Atlanta University *B*
Gainesville College *A*
Georgia Southern University *M*
Georgia Southwestern State University *B*
Kennesaw State University *B*
Morehouse College *B*
Reinhardt College *B*
Shorter College *B*
Spelman College *B*
University of Georgia *B*
Wesleyan College *B*
Young Harris College *A*

Hawaii
Brigham Young University-Hawaii *B*
University of Hawaii
    Manoa *B, M*

Idaho
North Idaho College *A*
University of Idaho *M*

Illinois
American Academy of Art *B*
Augustana College *B*
Benedictine University *B*
Blackburn College *B, T*
Bradley University *B, M, T*
City Colleges of Chicago
    Kennedy-King College *A*
    Olive-Harvey College *A*
Columbia College Chicago *B*
Dominican University *B*
Illinois Central College *A*
Illinois State University *B, M*
Illinois Valley Community College *A*
Judson College *B*
Knox College *B*
Lake Forest College *B*
Lake Land College *A*
Lewis University *B*
Lewis and Clark Community College *A*
Lincoln College *A*
Lincoln Land Community College *A*
Loyola University of Chicago *B*
Millikin University *B, T*
Monmouth College *B*
National-Louis University *B*
North Central College *B*
North Park University *B*
Northeastern Illinois University *B*
Northern Illinois University *B, M*
Parkland College *A*
Principia College *B*
Rockford College *B*
St. Xavier University *B*
Sauk Valley Community College *A*
School of the Art Institute of
    Chicago *B, M*
South Suburban College of Cook
    County *A*
Southern Illinois University
    Carbondale *B, M*
Southern Illinois University
    Edwardsville *B, M*
Southwestern Illinois College *A*
Trinity Christian College *B*
University of Illinois
    Chicago *B, M*
    Urbana-Champaign *M*
Western Illinois University *B*
William Rainey Harper College *A*

Indiana
Ancilla College *A*
Anderson University *B*
Ball State University *B*
Calumet College of St. Joseph *C, B*
DePauw University *B*
Goshen College *B*
Hanover College *B*
Indiana University
    Bloomington *B, M*
    South Bend *B*
    Southeast *B*
Indiana University-Purdue University
    Fort Wayne *B*
Indiana University-Purdue University
    Indianapolis *B*
Indiana Wesleyan University *B*
Martin University *B*
Oakland City University *B*
St. Joseph's College *B*
Saint Mary's College *B*
University of Notre Dame *B, M*
University of St. Francis *M*
Valparaiso University *B*
Vincennes University *A*

Iowa
Clarke College *B*
Drake University *B*
Ellsworth Community College *A*
Franciscan University *B*

Graceland University *B, T*
Loras College *B*
Maharishi University of
    Management *B, M*
Marshalltown Community College *A*
Morningside College *B*
St. Ambrose University *B*
University of Iowa *B, M*
University of Northern Iowa *B, M*
Upper Iowa University *B*
William Penn University *B*

Kansas
Allen County Community College *A*
Baker University *B, T*
Fort Hays State University *M*
Independence Community College *A*
Kansas Wesleyan University *B, T*
Labette Community College *A*
Pittsburg State University *B*
Pratt Community College *A*
Seward County Community College *A*
University of Kansas *B, M*
Washburn University of Topeka *B*
Wichita State University *B, M*

Kentucky
Asbury College *B*
Berea College *B, T*
Campbellsville University *B*
Cumberland College *B, T*
Georgetown College *B, T*
Kentucky Wesleyan College *B*
Morehead State University *B, M*
Murray State University *B, M, T*
St. Catharine College *A*
Spalding University *B*
Transylvania University *B, T*
University of Louisville *B, M*

Louisiana
Centenary College of Louisiana *B*
Louisiana College *B*
Louisiana State University and
    Agricultural and Mechanical
    College *B, M*
Loyola University New Orleans *B*
Southern University and Agricultural and
    Mechanical College *B*
Tulane University *B*
University of New Orleans *B, M*

Maine
Colby College *B*
Maine College of Art *B, M*
University of Maine *B*
University of Maine
    Presque Isle *B*
University of Southern Maine *B*

Maryland
Bowie State University *B*
College of Notre Dame of Maryland *B*
Community College of Baltimore County
    Catonsville *A*
    Dundalk *A*
    Essex *A*
Frostburg State University *B, T*
Goucher College *B*
Howard Community College *A*
Loyola College in Maryland *B*
Maryland College of Art and
    Design *C, A*
Maryland Institute College of Art *B, M*
Montgomery College
    Rockville Campus *A*
Morgan State University *B*
Salisbury University *B*
Towson University *B*
University of Maryland
    Baltimore County *B*
    College Park *M, D*
Villa Julie College *A*

Massachusetts
Amherst College *B*
Anna Maria College *B*

Art Institute of Boston at Lesley
   University A, B, M
Atlantic Union College B
Berkshire Community College A
Boston College B
Boston University M
Brandeis University B
Bridgewater State College B
Bunker Hill Community College A
Clark University B
College of the Holy Cross B
Elms College B
Emmanuel College B
Framingham State College B
Hampshire College B
Harvard College B
Lesley University B, M
Massachusetts College of Art B, M
Massachusetts College of Liberal Arts B
Merrimack College B
Montserrat College of Art B
Northeastern University A, B
Quinsigamond Community College C
School of the Museum of Fine Arts B, M
Simon's Rock College of Bard B
Smith College .M
Springfield Technical Community
   College A
Stonehill College B
Suffolk University C, B
Tufts University B
University of Massachusetts
   Amherst B, M
   Dartmouth C, M
   Lowell B
Wellesley College B
Westfield State College B
Wheaton College B
Williams College B

Michigan
Andrews University B
Aquinas College B
Calvin College B
College for Creative Studies B
Ferris State University B
Finlandia University B
Grand Valley State University B
Hope College B
Marygrove College B
Michigan State University B, M
Monroe County Community College A
Northwestern Michigan College A
Oakland Community College A
St. Clair County Community College A
Schoolcraft College A
Siena Heights University B
University of Michigan B, M
University of Michigan
   Flint B
Western Michigan University M

Minnesota
Bethany Lutheran College B
Bethel College B
Carleton College B
College of St. Catherine B
College of Visual Arts B
Concordia College: Moorhead B
Hamline University B, M
Macalester College B
Minnesota State University
   Mankato B
   Moorhead M
Northland Community & Technical
   College A
Northwestern College B
Ridgewater College: A Community and
   Technical College A
St. Cloud State University B
St. Mary's University of Minnesota B
University of Minnesota
   Duluth B
   Morris B
Winona State University B

Mississippi
Millsaps College B, T
Mississippi State University M
Mississippi University for Women B
Mississippi Valley State University B
University of Southern Mississippi M

Missouri
Avila University B
Central Missouri State University B
College of the Ozarks B
Columbia College B
Drury University B, T
East Central College A
Evangel University B
Fontbonne College B, M, T
Hannibal-LaGrange College B
Lindenwood University B, M
Maryville University of Saint Louis B
Missouri Southern State College B, T
St. Louis Community College
   St. Louis Community College at
      Florissant Valley A
   St. Louis Community College at
      Forest Park A
   St. Louis Community College at
      Meramec A
St. Louis University B
Three Rivers Community College A
Truman State University B
University of Missouri
   Kansas City B, M
   St. Louis B
Washington University in St. Louis B, M
William Woods University B, T

Nebraska
Bellevue University B
College of Saint Mary B
Hastings College B
Metropolitan Community College A
Midland Lutheran College B
Union College B
University of Nebraska
   Kearney B, M, T
   Lincoln B, M

Nevada
Community College of Southern
   Nevada A
Sierra Nevada College B
University of Nevada
   Las Vegas B, M

New Hampshire
Colby-Sawyer College B, T
Dartmouth College B
Franklin Pierce College B
Keene State College B
New Hampshire Community Technical
   College
   Laconia A
Plymouth State College B
Rivier College B
University of New Hampshire B
University of New Hampshire at
   Manchester A

New Jersey
Atlantic Cape Community College A
Bloomfield College B
Brookdale Community College A
Caldwell College B
The College of New Jersey B, T
Essex County College A
Felician College B
Middlesex County College A
Monmouth University B
Montclair State University B, M
New Jersey City University B, M
Raritan Valley Community College A
Rider University B
Rowan University B
Rutgers, The State University of New
   Jersey
   New Brunswick Regional
      Campus M

St. Peter's College B
Sussex County Community College A
Warren County Community College A

New Mexico
Clovis Community College A
College of Santa Fe B
College of the Southwest B
Institute of American Indian Arts B
New Mexico Highlands University B
New Mexico Junior College A
New Mexico State University B, M
Western New Mexico University B

New York
Adelphi University B, M
Alfred University B
Bard College B, M
Cayuga County Community College A
Cazenovia College B
City University of New York
   Brooklyn College B, M
   City College B
   Hunter College B
   Kingsborough Community
      College A
   La Guardia Community College A
   Queens College B, M
Colgate University B
College of New Rochelle B, M, T
Columbia University
   Columbia College B
Cooper Union for the Advancement of
   Science and Art C, B
Cornell University B
Daemen College B
Eugene Lang College/New School
   University B
Fashion Institute of Technology A
Finger Lakes Community College A
Fordham University B
Fulton-Montgomery Community
   College A
Hamilton College B
Hobart and William Smith Colleges B
Hofstra University B
Houghton College B
Ithaca College B
Jamestown Community College A
Long Island University
   C. W. Post Campus M
   Southampton College B
Mannes College of Music B, M
Marist College B
Marymount College of Fordham
   University B, T
Marymount Manhattan College B
Monroe Community College A
Nassau Community College A
Nazareth College of Rochester B, T
New York Institute of Technology B
New York University B, M
Niagara County Community College A
Pace University A
Pace University:
   Pleasantville/Briarcliff A
Parsons School of Design C, A, B, T
Pratt Institute B, M
Rensselaer Polytechnic Institute B, M
Roberts Wesleyan College B
Rochester Institute of
   Technology A, B, M
Rockland Community College A
Sage College of Albany A
St. John's University B
St. Lawrence University B
Sarah Lawrence College B
School of Visual Arts B, M
Skidmore College B

State University of New York
   Albany B, M
   Binghamton B
   Buffalo B, M
   College at Brockport B, M
   College at Buffalo B
   College at Cortland B
   College at Fredonia B
   College at Geneseo B
   College at Oneonta B
   College at Plattsburgh B
   College at Potsdam B
   Empire State College A, B
   New Paltz B
   Oswego M
   Stony Brook B, M
Suffolk County Community College A
Syracuse University B, M
University of Rochester B
Vassar College B
Villa Maria College of Buffalo A
Wagner College B
Wells College B
Westchester Community College C, A

North Carolina
Appalachian State University B
Barton College B
Campbell University B
Central Piedmont Community College A
Chowan College B
East Carolina University B, M
Greensboro College B
Lenoir Community College A
Meredith College B
Methodist College B
Mitchell Community College A
Mount Olive College A, B
North Carolina Central University B
Queens University of Charlotte B
Randolph Community College A
Rockingham Community College A
Salem College B
University of North Carolina
   Chapel Hill B, M
   Charlotte B
   Greensboro B, T
   Pembroke B
   Wilmington B
Wake Forest University B
Western Carolina University B, M
Western Piedmont Community
   College A
Wingate University B

North Dakota
Dickinson State University B
Jamestown College B

Ohio
Antioch College B
Art Academy of Cincinnati B
Ashland University B
Baldwin-Wallace College B
Bowling Green State University M
College of Mount St. Joseph B
College of Wooster B
Columbus College of Art and Design B
Denison University B
Hiram College B, T
Kent State University B, M
Kent State University
   Stark Campus B
Kenyon College B
Lake Erie College B
Lorain County Community College A
Marietta College B
Notre Dame College B
Oberlin College B
Ohio Northern University B
Ohio State University
   Columbus Campus B, M
Ohio University B
Ohio Wesleyan University B
Shawnee State University B
Sinclair Community College A

University of Akron *B*
University of Cincinnati *C, B, M*
University of Dayton *B*
University of Findlay *B*
University of Rio Grande *B*
University of Toledo *B*
Ursuline College *B*
Xavier University *B*
Youngstown State University *B*

Oklahoma

Cameron University *B*
East Central University *B*
Oklahoma Baptist University *B*
Oklahoma City Community College *A*
Oklahoma State University *B*
Oral Roberts University *B*
University of Oklahoma *B*
University of Tulsa *M*

Oregon

Central Oregon Community College *A*
Eastern Oregon University *B*
Lewis & Clark College *B*
Marylhurst University *B*
Pacific Northwest College of Art *C, B*
Portland State University *B*
Reed College *B*
University of Oregon *B, M*
Willamette University *B*

Pennsylvania

Albright College *B*
Allegheny College *B*
Arcadia University *B*
Bloomsburg University of
    Pennsylvania *B, M*
Bryn Mawr College *B*
Bucknell University *B*
Bucks County Community College *A*
Cabrini College *B*
California University of Pennsylvania *B*
Carlow College *B*
Cedar Crest College *B*
Chatham College *B*
Chestnut Hill College *A, B*
Community College of Beaver County *A*
Dickinson College *B*
Duquesne University *B*
Franklin & Marshall College *B*
Gettysburg College *B*
Haverford College *B*
Immaculata University *C, A*
Juniata College *B*
Keystone College *A*
La Salle University *B*
Lafayette College *B*
Lehigh Carbon Community College *C, A*
Lincoln University *B*
Lock Haven University of
    Pennsylvania *B*
Marywood University *C, B*
Mercyhurst College *B*
Messiah College *B*
Moravian College *B*
Muhlenberg College *B*
Northampton County Area Community
    College *A*
St. Vincent College *B*
Seton Hill University *B*
Slippery Rock University of
    Pennsylvania *B*
Swarthmore College *B*
University of Pittsburgh *B*
West Chester University of
    Pennsylvania *B*
Wilson College *B*
York College of Pennsylvania *B*

Puerto Rico

Pontifical Catholic University of Puerto
    Rico *B*
University of Puerto Rico
    Rio Piedras Campus *B*

Rhode Island

Brown University *B*

Providence College *B*
Rhode Island College *B*
Roger Williams University *B*
Salve Regina University *B*

South Carolina

Anderson College *B*
Charleston Southern University *B*
Clemson University *B, M*
Coastal Carolina University *B*
Coker College *B*
College of Charleston *B*
Converse College *B*
Furman University *B*
Limestone College *B*
North Greenville College *A*
University of South Carolina
    Aiken *B*
Winthrop University *B*

South Dakota

Dakota State University *B*
University of South Dakota *B, M*

Tennessee

Bethel College *B*
East Tennessee State University *B, M, T*
Lambuth University *B*
Memphis College of Art *B, M*
Roane State Community College *A*
Tennessee Technological University *B*
University of Tennessee
    Knoxville *B*
Vanderbilt University *B*

Texas

Abilene Christian University *B*
Alvin Community College *A*
Angelo State University *B*
Baylor University *B*
Coastal Bend College *A*
College of the Mainland *A*
El Paso Community College *C*
Hardin-Simmons University *B*
Houston Baptist University *B*
Howard Payne University *B*
Lon Morris College *A*
Palo Alto College *A*
Paris Junior College *A*
Rice University *B, M*
St. Edward's University *B, T*
St. Philip's College *A*
Sam Houston State University *B, M*
South Texas Community College *A*
Southwest Texas State University *B, T*
Southwestern University *B*
Tarleton State University *B*
Texas A&M University
    Commerce *M*
    Corpus Christi *B*
    Kingsville *B, M, T*
Texas Christian University *B, M*
Texas Southern University *B, M*
Texas Tech University *B*
Texas Woman's University *B, M*
Tyler Junior College *A*
University of Dallas *B*
University of Houston *B, M*
University of North Texas *B, M, D*
University of St. Thomas *B*
University of Texas
    Arlington *B*
    Austin *B, M*
    El Paso *B, M*
    San Antonio *M*
West Texas A&M University *B, M*

Utah

Brigham Young University *M*
Utah State University *M*
Weber State University *B*

Vermont

Bennington College *B, M*
Burlington College *B*
Goddard College *B*
Green Mountain College *B*

Johnson State College *B, M*
Marlboro College *B*
Middlebury College *B*
St. Michael's College *B*
University of Vermont *B*

Virginia

Blue Ridge Community College *C*
College of William and Mary *B*
Ferrum College *B*
George Mason University *B*
Hampden-Sydney College *B*
Hollins University *B*
Longwood University *B, T*
Mary Baldwin College *B*
Mary Washington College *B*
Piedmont Virginia Community
    College *A*
Radford University *B, M*
Randolph-Macon College *B*
Randolph-Macon Woman's College *B*
Roanoke College *B*
Sweet Briar College *B*
Thomas Nelson Community College *A*
University of Richmond *B, T*
Virginia Commonwealth University *B*
Virginia Intermont College *B*
Virginia Wesleyan College *B*
Virginia Western Community College *A*
Washington and Lee University *B*

Washington

Central Washington University *B, M*
Centralia College *A*
Cornish College of the Arts *B*
Eastern Washington University *B*
Everett Community College *A*
Gonzaga University *B*
Lower Columbia College *A*
North Seattle Community College *C*
Pacific Lutheran University *B*
Seattle University *B*
Western Washington University *B*
Whitman College *B*

West Virginia

Bethany College *B*
Concord College *B*
West Virginia State College *A, B*

Wisconsin

Cardinal Stritch University *B*
Carroll College *B*
Carthage College *B*
Lawrence University *B, T*
Northland College *B*
University of Wisconsin
    Madison *M*
    Oshkosh *B*
    River Falls *B*
    Superior *B, M*
Viterbo University *B*

Wyoming

Laramie County Community College *A*

**Fire protection/safety
technology**

Alabama

Community College of the Air Force *A*
Lawson State Community College *C*
Shelton State Community College *C*

Alaska

University of Alaska
    Fairbanks *C, A*

Arizona

Cochise College *A*

California

Antelope Valley College *C, A*
Bakersfield College *A*
Barstow College *C, A*
College of the Canyons *C, A*
College of the Sequoias *C, A*

Columbia College *C, A*
Copper Mountain College *C*
Glendale Community College *C, A*
Long Beach City College *C, A*
Monterey Peninsula College *C, A*
Riverside Community College *C, A*
San Joaquin Delta College *C, A*
Santa Rosa Junior College *C*
Santiago Canyon College *A*
Shasta College *A*
Sierra College *C, A*
Victor Valley College *C, A*
Yuba Community College District *C, A*

Colorado

Arapahoe Community College *C*
Red Rocks Community College *A*

Connecticut

Capital Community College *A*
Naugatuck Valley Community College *A*
Norwalk Community College *A*
Three Rivers Community College *A*

Delaware

Delaware Technical and Community
    College
        Stanton/Wilmington Campus *A*

Florida

Gulf Coast Community College *A*
Indian River Community College *A*
Santa Fe Community College *A*
Valencia Community College *A*

Georgia

Georgia Perimeter College *A*
Savannah Technical College *A*

Hawaii

University of Hawaii
        Honolulu Community College *C, A*

Idaho

Boise State University *C*
College of Southern Idaho *A*
Idaho State University *A*

Illinois

College of DuPage *C, A*
College of Lake County *A*
Elgin Community College *C, A*
Illinois Central College *A*
Kankakee Community College *C*
Kishwaukee College *C, A*
Lincoln Land Community College *C, A*
Moraine Valley Community
    College *C, A*
Parkland College *C, A*
Prairie State College *C, A*
Waubonsee Community College *C, A*

Indiana

Vincennes University *A*

Kansas

Hutchinson Community College *A*
Kansas City Kansas Community
    College *C, A*

Kentucky

Jefferson Community College *C, A*

Louisiana

Delgado Community College *A*
Louisiana State University
    Eunice *C, A*

Maryland

Community College of Baltimore County
    Catonsville *C, A*
    Dundalk *C, A*
    Essex *C, A*
Montgomery College
    Rockville Campus *C, A*

Massachusetts

Berkshire Community College *A*
Bunker Hill Community College *A*
Cape Cod Community College *A*

Massasoit Community College *C*
Mount Wachusett Community College *A*
Springfield Technical Community
  College *A*

Michigan
Kellogg Community College *C, A*
Macomb Community College *C, A*
Mott Community College *A*

Mississippi
Mississippi Gulf Coast Community
  College
  Perkinston *A*

Missouri
East Central College *A*
Jefferson College *C, A*
Ozarks Technical Community College *A*
Penn Valley Community College *C, A*
St. Louis Community College
  St. Louis Community College at
    Florissant Valley *A*
  St. Louis Community College at
    Forest Park *C, A*

Montana
Montana State University
  Billings *A*

Nebraska
Southeast Community College
  Lincoln Campus *A*
University of Nebraska
  Lincoln *A*

Nevada
Community College of Southern
  Nevada *A*
Western Nevada Community
  College *C, A*

New Hampshire
New Hampshire Community Technical
  College
  Berlin *C, A*
  Laconia *A*

New Jersey
Camden County College *A*
Mercer County Community College *C, A*
Ocean County College *C, A*
Thomas Edison State College *A*
Union County College *C, A*

New Mexico
Albuquerque Technical-Vocational
  Institute *A*
Eastern New Mexico University: Roswell
  Campus *A*
San Juan College *A*

New York
City University of New York
  John Jay College of Criminal
    Justice *B, M*
Corning Community College *A*
Monroe Community College *A*
Onondaga Community College *C, A*
Rockland Community College *A*

North Carolina
Cleveland Community College *C, A*
Coastal Carolina Community
  College *C, A*
Gaston College *A*
Rockingham Community College *A*
Rowan-Cabarrus Community College *A*
Wilson Technical Community College *A*

Ohio
Cuyahoga Community College
  Eastern Campus *A*
  Metropolitan Campus *A*
Lorain County Community College *A*
Sinclair Community College *A*
University of Akron *C, A, B*

Oklahoma
Oklahoma State University *B*

Oklahoma State University
  Oklahoma City *C*
Tulsa Community College *A*

Oregon
Chemeketa Community College *A*
Portland Community College *C, A*
Rogue Community College *C, A*

Pennsylvania
Community College of Allegheny
  County *A*
Community College of Philadelphia *A*
Delaware County Community College *A*
Harrisburg Area Community
  College *C, A*
Luzerne County Community
  College *C, A*
Montgomery County Community
  College *C, A*
Westmoreland County Community
  College *C, A*

Rhode Island
Providence College *A*

Texas
Amarillo College *C, A*
College of the Mainland *A*
Collin County Community College
  District *C, A*
Del Mar College *A*
El Paso Community College *A*
Galveston College *C, A*
Houston Community College
  System *C, A*
Laredo Community College *A*
Midland College *A*
Odessa College *C, A*
San Antonio College *A*
San Jacinto College
  Central Campus *C, A*
South Plains College *C, A*
Tarrant County College *C, A*
Tyler Junior College *A*

Utah
Utah Valley State College *C, A*

Washington
Bellevue Community College *C, A*
Edmonds Community College *A*
Olympic College *C, A*
Spokane Falls Community College *C*

West Virginia
Shepherd College *A*

Wisconsin
Blackhawk Technical College *A*
Fox Valley Technical College *A*
Moraine Park Technical College *C*
Western Wisconsin Technical College *A*

Fire services administration

Alabama
Bishop State Community College *A*
Calhoun Community College *C*
Jefferson State Community College *A*
Northwest-Shoals Community College *A*
Shelton State Community College *C*

Alaska
University of Alaska
  Anchorage *A*

California
Cogswell Polytechnical College *B*

Connecticut
Gateway Community College *A*
Norwalk Community College *A*
University of New Haven *B, M*

District of Columbia
University of the District of
  Columbia *A, B*

Florida
Hillsborough Community College *C*
Miami-Dade Community College *A*
Palm Beach Community College *A*

Hawaii
University of Hawaii
  Honolulu Community College *A*

Illinois
Black Hawk College *A*
College of DuPage *C*
John Wood Community College *A*
Moraine Valley Community College *C*
Rend Lake College *C, A*
Southern Illinois University
  Carbondale *B*
Waubonsee Community College *C*

Iowa
Kirkwood Community College *C, A*

Kansas
Kansas City Kansas Community
  College *C, A*

Maryland
University of Maryland
  University College *C*

Massachusetts
Berkshire Community College *A*
Cape Cod Community College *C*
Salem State College *B*

New Hampshire
New Hampshire Community Technical
  College
  Laconia *A*

New York
City University of New York
  John Jay College of Criminal
    Justice *B*
Erie Community College
  South Campus *A*

North Carolina
University of North Carolina
  Charlotte *B*

Ohio
Sinclair Community College *C*

Oregon
Eastern Oregon University *B*
Western Oregon University *B*

Pennsylvania
Northampton County Area Community
  College *C, A*

Texas
Hill College *C, A*

Utah
Utah Valley State College *B*

Virginia
Hampton University *B*
Thomas Nelson Community College *A*

Washington
Bellevue Community College *A*
Edmonds Community College *C, A*
Olympic College *C, A*
Spokane Community College *A*
Wenatchee Valley College *A*

Firefighting/fire science

Alabama
Alabama Southern Community
  College *C, A*
Central Alabama Community
  College *C, A*
Chattahoochee Valley Community
  College *C, A*
Northwest-Shoals Community College *A*

Alaska
University of Alaska
  Fairbanks *C, A*

Arizona
Arizona Western College *C, A*
Central Arizona College *C, A*
Glendale Community College *C, A*
Phoenix College *C, A*
Pima Community College *C, A*
Scottsdale Community College *C, A*
Yavapai College *C, A*

Arkansas
Northwest Arkansas Community
  College *A*
Southeast Arkansas College *A*
Southern Arkansas University Tech *A*

California
Cabrillo College *A*
Chabot College *C, A*
College of the Sequoias *C*
College of the Siskiyous *C, A*
East Los Angeles College *C*
Imperial Valley College *C, A*
Las Positas College *A*
Los Angeles Harbor College *C, A*
Los Medanos College *C, A*
Modesto Junior College *A*
Mount San Antonio College *C, A*
Palomar College *C, A*
Santa Monica College *C, A*
Santa Rosa Junior College *C, A*
Sierra College *C, A*
Southwestern College *C, A*
Yuba Community College District *C*

Colorado
Arapahoe Community College *C*

District of Columbia
University of the District of Columbia *A*

Florida
Broward Community College *A*
Daytona Beach Community
  College *C, A*
Gulf Coast Community College *C, A*
Hillsborough Community College *C, A*
Indian River Community College *C*
Lake-Sumter Community College *A*
Manatee Community College *A*
Miami-Dade Community College *C*
Palm Beach Community College *C, A*
Pasco-Hernando Community College *C*
Pensacola Junior College *C, A*
Polk Community College *A*
St. Petersburg College *C, A*
Seminole Community College *C, A*
Valencia Community College *A*

Georgia
Albany Technical College *A*
West Georgia Technical College *C, A*

Hawaii
University of Hawaii
  Honolulu Community College *C, A*

Idaho
Eastern Idaho Technical College *C, A*

Illinois
Carl Sandburg College *C, A*
City Colleges of Chicago
  Harold Washington College *A*
College of DuPage *C*
Illinois Eastern Community Colleges
  Frontier Community College *C*
Illinois Valley Community College *A*
Joliet Junior College *C*
Kankakee Community College *C*
Kishwaukee College *C, A*
McHenry County College *C, A*
Moraine Valley Community College *C*
Oakton Community College *C, A*
Rend Lake College *C*
Richland Community College *A*

Rock Valley College *A*
South Suburban College of Cook
County *C, A*
Southeastern Illinois College *C*
Southwestern Illinois College *C, A*
Triton College *C, A*
Waubonsee Community College *C*
William Rainey Harper College *C, A*

Indiana
Vincennes University *A*

Iowa
Iowa Western Community College *A*
Kirkwood Community College *C, A*
Northeast Iowa Community College *A*

Kansas
Barton County Community College *C, A*
Butler County Community College *C, A*
Cloud County Community College *A*
Dodge City Community College *A*
Johnson County Community College *A*
Kansas City Kansas Community
College *C, A*
Labette Community College *C, A*

Kentucky
Somerset Community College *C, A*

Maryland
College of Southern Maryland *A*
Montgomery College
Rockville Campus *A*

Massachusetts
Berkshire Community College *A*
Cape Cod Community College *A*
Massasoit Community College *A*
Springfield Technical Community
College *C*

Michigan
Grand Rapids Community College *A*
Kellogg Community College *C*
Kirtland Community College *A*
Lansing Community College *A*
Macomb Community College *C, A*
Madonna University *C, A*
Mid Michigan Community College *A*
Oakland Community College *C, A*
Schoolcraft College *C, A*

Minnesota
Itasca Community College *A*
Lake Superior College: A Community
and Technical College *A*

Missouri
Three Rivers Community College *C*

Montana
Miles Community College *C*

Nebraska
Mid Plains Community College
Area *C, A*

Nevada
Community College of Southern
Nevada *A*
Great Basin College *A*
Truckee Meadows Community
College *C, A*

New Hampshire
New Hampshire Community Technical
College
Berlin *A*
Laconia *A*

New Jersey
Burlington County College *A*
Essex County College *A*
Middlesex County College *A*
Sussex County Community College *C, A*

New Mexico
Dona Ana Branch Community College of
New Mexico State University *A*
New Mexico Junior College *C*

New Mexico State University
Alamogordo *A*
San Juan College *A*

New York
Suffolk County Community College *A*

North Carolina
Alamance Community College *A*
Tri-County Community College *C*

Ohio
Columbus State Community College *A*
Hocking Technical College *A*
Lakeland Community College *C, A*
Owens Community College
Findlay Campus *C, A*
Toledo *C, A*
Sinclair Community College *C*
Stark State College of Technology *A*

Oklahoma
Oklahoma State University
Oklahoma City *A*
Western Oklahoma State College *A*

Oregon
Central Oregon Community College *A*
Chemeketa Community College *A*
Clatsop Community College *A*
Mount Hood Community College *C, A*
Southwestern Oregon Community
College *C, A*
Treasure Valley Community College *A*
Umpqua Community College *A*

Pennsylvania
Bucks County Community College *A*
Mercyhurst College *C*

Rhode Island
Community College of Rhode Island *A*
Providence College *A*

Tennessee
Southwest Tennessee Community
College *A*
Volunteer State Community College *C, A*

Texas
Austin Community College *C*
Blinn College *C, A*
Collin County Community College
District *C*
El Centro College *C*
Houston Community College System *C*
Midland College *A*
North Harris Montgomery Community
College District *C, A*
Odessa College *C, A*
South Plains College *A*
Tarrant County College *C, A*
Texas A&M University
Commerce *C*
Trinity Valley Community College *C, A*

Virginia
J. Sargeant Reynolds Community
College *C, A*
Southwest Virginia Community
College *C*
Virginia Highlands Community
College *C*
Virginia Western Community College *C*

Washington
Bellevue Community College *A*
Everett Community College *C, A*
Spokane Falls Community College *C, A*
Walla Walla Community College *A*
Wenatchee Valley College *A*

West Virginia
Mountain State University *A*

Wisconsin
Chippewa Valley Technical College *A*
Moraine Park Technical College *C*
Waukesha County Technical College *C*

Wyoming
Casper College *A*

Fishing and fisheries

Alabama
Auburn University *B, M, D*

Alaska
Sheldon Jackson College *B*
University of Alaska
Fairbanks *B, M, D*
Southeast *M*

Arkansas
University of Arkansas
Pine Bluff *B, M*

California
College of the Redwoods *C, A*
Feather River College *C, A*
Humboldt State University *B*
University of California
Davis *B*

Colorado
Colorado State University *B, M, D*
Trinidad State Junior College *C, A*

Delaware
Delaware State University *B*

Florida
Hillsborough Community College *C, A*
South Florida Community College *A*
University of Florida *M, D*

Georgia
University of Georgia *B*

Idaho
North Idaho College *A*
University of Idaho *B, M*

Illinois
Lake Land College *A*

Iowa
Iowa State University *M, D*

Kansas
Pittsburg State University *B*

Kentucky
Murray State University *B*

Louisiana
Louisiana State University and
Agricultural and Mechanical
College *M*

Maryland
Frostburg State University *B, M*

Michigan
Mid Michigan Community College *A*
University of Michigan *B, M*

Minnesota
University of Minnesota
Twin Cities *B, M, D*
Vermilion Community College *A*

Mississippi
Mississippi Gulf Coast Community
College
Perkinston *A*

Missouri
East Central College *A*
University of Missouri
Columbia *B, M, D*

Montana
Miles Community College *A*

Nebraska
University of Nebraska
Lincoln *B*

New Mexico
New Mexico State University *B*

New York
Cornell University *B*
Paul Smith's College *A*
State University of New York
College of Agriculture and
Technology at Cobleskill *A*
College of Agriculture and
Technology at Morrisville *A*
College of Environmental Science
and Forestry *B, M, D*

North Carolina
Brunswick Community College *A*
Haywood Community College *A*
North Carolina State University *B*

North Dakota
Minot State University: Bottineau
Campus *A*
North Dakota State University *B*

Ohio
Hocking Technical College *A*
Ohio State University
Columbus Campus *B*

Oklahoma
Southeastern Oklahoma State
University *B*

Oregon
Central Oregon Community College *A*
Mount Hood Community College *A*
Oregon State University *B, M, D*

Rhode Island
University of Rhode Island *B, M*

South Carolina
Clemson University *B, M*

South Dakota
South Dakota State University *B, M*

Tennessee
Roane State Community College *A*
Tennessee Technological University *B*
University of Tennessee
Knoxville *M*

Texas
Texas A&M University *B*
Texas A&M University
Galveston *B*
Texas Tech University *B, M, D*

Virginia
Virginia Polytechnic Institute and State
University *M, D*

Washington
Heritage College *C, A*
Peninsula College *A*
University of Washington *B, M, D*

West Virginia
West Virginia University *B*

Wisconsin
Northland College *B*
University of Wisconsin
Superior *B*

Flight attendant

California
Chabot College *A*
Mount San Antonio College *A*
Orange Coast College *C, A*
Travel University International *C*

Louisiana
University of Louisiana at Monroe *A*

New Jersey
Mercer County Community College *A*

North Carolina
Asheville Buncombe Technical
Community College *C, A*

Ohio
Cincinnati State Technical and
Community College *C*

Washington
Spokane Falls Community College *C*

Floriculture

California
Santa Rosa Junior College *C*

Georgia
Albany Technical College *C*

Minnesota
Hennepin Technical College *C, A*

New York
State University of New York
College of Agriculture and
Technology at Morrisville *A*

Oklahoma
Oklahoma State University
Oklahoma City *C*

Washington
Clover Park Technical College *C*

Food preparation

Alabama
Shelton State Community College *C*

California
Long Beach City College *C*
Santa Rosa Junior College *C*

Illinois
City Colleges of Chicago
Kennedy-King College *C*

Minnesota
Hennepin Technical College *A*

New Mexico
Southwestern Indian Polytechnic
Institute *C*

Ohio
Cincinnati State Technical and
Community College *A*

Washington
Art Institute of Seattle *C*
South Seattle Community College *C, A*

Wisconsin
Milwaukee Area Technical College *A*
Western Wisconsin Technical College *C*

Food science

Alabama
Trenholm State Technical College *A*

Arizona
Prescott College *B, M*

Arkansas
Mississippi County Community
College *A*
University of Arkansas *B, M, D*

California
California Polytechnic State University:
San Luis Obispo *B*
California State Polytechnic University:
Pomona *B*
California State University
Fresno *B, M*
Modesto Junior College *C, A*
Reedley College *C*
San Joaquin Delta College *A*
University of California
Davis *B, M, D*

Colorado
Colorado State University *B*

Delaware
University of Delaware *B, M*

Florida
Florida Agricultural and Mechanical
University *B*
University of Florida *B, M, D*

Georgia
University of Georgia *B, M, D*

Idaho
College of Southern Idaho *A*
University of Idaho *B, M*

Illinois
City Colleges of Chicago
Malcolm X College *C, A*
Illinois Institute of Technology *M*
University of Illinois
Urbana-Champaign *B, M, D*

Indiana
Purdue University *B, M, D*

Iowa
Iowa State University *M, D*

Kansas
Kansas State University *B, M, D*

Kentucky
Murray State University *B*
University of Kentucky *B*

Louisiana
Louisiana State University and
Agricultural and Mechanical
College *B, M, D*

Maine
University of Maine *B, M, D*

Maryland
University of Maryland
College Park *B, M, D*

Massachusetts
Berkshire Community College *C*
Framingham State College *B, M*
University of Massachusetts
Amherst *B, M, D*

Michigan
Michigan State University *B, M, D*

Minnesota
Minnesota State University
Mankato *B*
University of Minnesota
Twin Cities *B, M, D*

Mississippi
Mississippi State University *B, M, D*
Northwest Mississippi Community
College *A*

Missouri
University of Missouri
Columbia *B, M, D*

Nebraska
University of Nebraska
Lincoln *B, M, D*

New Hampshire
University of New Hampshire *B, M, D*

New Jersey
Rutgers, The State University of New
Jersey
New Brunswick Regional
Campus *B*

New York
Cornell University *B*
Fulton-Montgomery Community
College *A*

North Carolina
North Carolina State University *B, M, D*

North Dakota
North Dakota State University *B*

Ohio
Ohio State University
Columbus Campus *B, M, D*

Oklahoma
Eastern Oklahoma State College *A*
Oklahoma State University *M*

Oregon
Oregon State University *B, M, D*

Pennsylvania
Delaware Valley College *C, B*
Penn State
Abington *B*
Altoona *B*
Beaver *B*
Berks *B*
Delaware County *B*
Dubois *B*
Erie, The Behrend College *B*
Fayette *B*
Hazleton *B*
Lehigh Valley *B*
McKeesport *B*
Mont Alto *B*
New Kensington *B*
Schuylkill - Capital College *B*
Shenango *B*
University Park *B, M, D*
Wilkes-Barre *B*
Worthington Scranton *B*
York *B*

Puerto Rico
Inter American University of Puerto Rico
Barranquitas Campus *C*
University of Puerto Rico
Mayaguez Campus *M*
Utuado *A*

South Carolina
Clemson University *B, D*

Tennessee
University of Tennessee
Knoxville *B, M, D*

Texas
Sul Ross State University *B*
Texas A&M University *B, M, D*
Texas A&M University
Commerce *B*
Kingsville *B, M*
Texas Tech University *B, M*

Utah
Brigham Young University *B, M*
Snow College *A*
Utah State University *B, M, D*

Virginia
Virginia Polytechnic Institute and State
University *B, M*

Washington
Washington State University *M, D*

Wisconsin
University of Wisconsin
Madison *B, M, D*
River Falls *B*

Wyoming
University of Wyoming *M*

Food service

California
Santa Rosa Junior College *C*

Kentucky
Jefferson Community College *A*

Maryland
Montgomery College
Rockville Campus *A*

New York
Schenectady County Community
College *A*
State University of New York
College of Agriculture and
Technology at Morrisville *A*

Pennsylvania
Penn State
University Park *C*

Texas
Sam Houston State University *B*

Vermont
New England Culinary Institute
Essex Junction *A, B*

Wisconsin
Milwaukee Area Technical College *A*

Food technology/ processing

California
California State Polytechnic University:
Pomona *B*

Food/nutrition studies

Alabama
Auburn University *B*
Jacksonville State University *B*
Lawson State Community College *C*
Oakwood College *B*
Tuskegee University *B, M*
University of Alabama *B*
Wallace State Community College at
Hanceville *C, A*

Arizona
Central Arizona College *C*

Arkansas
University of Arkansas *B*

California
Antelope Valley College *A*
Bakersfield College *A*
California Polytechnic State University:
San Luis Obispo *B*
California State Polytechnic University:
Pomona *B*
California State University
Chico *B, M*
Fresno *B*
Long Beach *B, M*
Los Angeles *B*
Northridge *B*
Sacramento *B*
Chapman University *B, M*
College of the Sequoias *C*
Glendale Community College *A*
Modesto Junior College *A*
Ohlone College *C, A*
Orange Coast College *C, A*
Reedley College *C*
Riverside Community College *C, A*
San Diego State University *B*
San Joaquin Delta College *C, A*
San Jose State University *M*
Santa Rosa Junior College *C*
University of California
Davis *B*
Ventura College *A*

Colorado
Art Institute
of Colorado *A, B*
Colorado State University *B, M, D*

Connecticut
Gateway Community College *A*

St. Joseph College *B, M*
University of Bridgeport *M*
University of Connecticut *B*

Delaware
Delaware State University *B*
University of Delaware *B, M*

District of Columbia
Gallaudet University *B*
University of the District of Columbia *B*

Florida
Broward Community College *A*
Florida State University *B, M*
Hillsborough Community College *A*
Miami-Dade Community College *A*
Pensacola Junior College *C, A*
Polk Community College *A*

Georgia
Fort Valley State University *B*
Georgia Southern University *B*
Georgia State University *B, M*
University of Georgia *B, M, D*

Hawaii
University of Hawaii
      Hawaii Community College *C, A*

Idaho
Brigham Young University - Idaho *A*
Idaho State University *B*
University of Idaho *B*

Illinois
Dominican University *B*
Illinois Central College *A*
Loyola University of Chicago *C, B*
Northern Illinois University *B, M*
Rush University *M*
Shawnee Community College *C, A*
Southern Illinois University
      Carbondale *B, M*
University of Illinois
      Urbana-Champaign *B*
William Rainey Harper College *A*

Indiana
Ball State University *A, B*
Indiana State University *B*
Purdue University *B, M, D*
Purdue University
      North Central Campus *C*
Vincennes University *A*

Iowa
Des Moines Area Community College *C*
Iowa State University *B, M, D*
University of Northern Iowa *B*

Kansas
Kansas State University *B, M, D*

Kentucky
Murray State University *B*
Spalding University *T*
University of Kentucky *B, M*

Maine
University of Maine *B, M, D*

Maryland
Morgan State University *B*
University of Maryland
      College Park *B*

Massachusetts
Framingham State College *B, M*
Hampshire College *B*

Michigan
Andrews University *B, M*
Central Michigan University *B, M*
Madonna University *A, B*
Marygrove College *B*
Michigan State University *B, M*
Northern Michigan University *B*
Wayne State University *B, M, D*

Minnesota
College of St. Catherine *B*
Concordia College: Moorhead *B*
Minnesota State University
      Mankato *B, M, T*
University of Minnesota
      Crookston *A*
      Twin Cities *B*

Mississippi
Alcorn State University *B*
University of Southern
      Mississippi *B, M, D*

Missouri
College of the Ozarks *B*
Fontbonne College *B*
Northwest Missouri State University *B*
St. Louis Community College
      St. Louis Community College at
            Forest Park *C, A*
St. Louis University *M*
Southeast Missouri State University *B*
University of Missouri
      Columbia *B, M, D*

Nebraska
University of Nebraska
      Kearney *B*
      Lincoln *B, M*
      Omaha *B*
Wayne State College *B*

Nevada
University of Nevada
      Reno *B, M*

New Hampshire
University of New Hampshire *B*

New Jersey
College of St. Elizabeth *B, M*

New Mexico
New Mexico State University *B*
University of New Mexico *B, M*

New York
City University of New York
      Brooklyn College *B, M*
      Hunter College *B, M*
Cornell University *B, M, D*
Fulton-Montgomery Community
      College *C, A*
Long Island University
      C. W. Post Campus *B, M*
Marymount College of Fordham
      University *B*
New York University *B, M, D*
Rochester Institute of Technology *B*
Rockland Community College *A*
State University of New York
      Buffalo *M*
      College at Buffalo *B*
      College at Oneonta *B*
      College at Plattsburgh *B*
      College of Agriculture and
            Technology at Morrisville *A*
      Farmingdale *A*
Suffolk County Community College *A*
Syracuse University *B, M, D*
Westchester Community College *A*

North Carolina
Appalachian State University *B*
Bennett College *B*
Central Piedmont Community College *A*
East Carolina University *M*
Meredith College *B*
North Carolina Agricultural and
      Technical State University *B, M*
North Carolina Central University *B*
University of North Carolina
      Chapel Hill *B*
      Greensboro *B, M, D*

North Dakota
North Dakota State University *B*

Ohio
Ashland University *B*
Bluffton College *B*
Bowling Green State University *B, M*
Case Western Reserve
      University *B, M, D*
Hocking Technical College *A*
Kent State University *C, B, M*
Miami University
      Oxford Campus *B, M*
Ohio State University
      Columbus Campus *B, M, D*
Ohio University *B, M*
Sinclair Community College *C, A*
University of Akron *B, M*
University of Cincinnati *B, M*
University of Cincinnati
      Raymond Walters College *A*
University of Dayton *B*
Youngstown State University *A, B*

Oklahoma
Eastern Oklahoma State College *C*
Langston University *B*
Northeastern State University *B*
Oklahoma State University *B, M, D*
University of Central Oklahoma *B, M*

Oregon
George Fox University *B*
Oregon State University *B, M, D*

Pennsylvania
Cedar Crest College *B*
Cheyney University of Pennsylvania *B*
Harrisburg Area Community College *A*
Immaculata University *B, M, T*
Indiana University of Pennsylvania *B, M*
Marywood University *B, M*
Mercyhurst College *B*
Penn State
      Abington *B*
      Altoona *B*
      Beaver *B*
      Berks *B*
      Dubois *B*
      Fayette *B*
      Hazleton *B*
      Lehigh Valley *B*
      Mont Alto *B*
      New Kensington *B*
      Shenango *B*
      University Park *C, B, M, D*
      Worthington Scranton *B*
      York *B*
Pennsylvania College of Technology *A*
Seton Hill University *B*

Puerto Rico
University of Puerto Rico
      Rio Piedras Campus *B*

Rhode Island
University of Rhode Island *B, M, D*

South Carolina
South Carolina State University *B*
Winthrop University *B, M*

South Dakota
Mount Marty College *B*
South Dakota State University *B*

Tennessee
Carson-Newman College *B*
Lambuth University *B*
Middle Tennessee State University *B*
Southwest Tennessee Community
      College *A*
Tennessee State University *B*
Tennessee Technological University *B*
University of Memphis *M*
University of Tennessee
      Knoxville *B, M*

Texas
Abilene Christian University *B*
Baylor University *B*

Collin County Community College
      District *C*
Lamar University *B*
Palo Alto College *C, A*
Prairie View A&M University *B*
Sam Houston State University *B*
Southwest Texas State University *B*
Stephen F. Austin State University *B*
Texas A&M University *B*
Texas A&M University
      Kingsville *B*
Texas Christian University *B*
Texas Southern University *B, M*
Texas Tech University *B, M, D*
University of Houston *B*
University of Texas
      Austin *B, M*

Utah
Brigham Young University *B, M*
Dixie State College of Utah *A*
Snow College *A*
University of Utah *M*
Utah State University *B, M, D*

Vermont
University of Vermont *B, M*

Virginia
Bridgewater College *B*
Radford University *B*
Virginia Polytechnic Institute and State
      University *B, M, D*

Washington
Central Washington University *B*
Seattle Pacific University *B*
Washington State University *B*

West Virginia
Fairmont State College *A*
West Virginia University *B*

Wisconsin
University of Wisconsin
      Madison *B, M, D*
      Stevens Point *M*
Viterbo University *B*

Foreign language teacher education

Alabama
Auburn University *B*
Birmingham-Southern College *T*

Arizona
Arizona State University *B, T*
Northern Arizona University *T*
Prescott College *B, M, T*
University of Arizona *B, M*

Arkansas
Arkansas Tech University *B*
Harding University *B, M, T*
Ouachita Baptist University *B, T*
Southern Arkansas University *B, T*
University of Arkansas *B*
University of Central Arkansas *M, T*

California
Azusa Pacific University *T*
California Baptist University *T*
California State University
      Bakersfield *B, T*
      Chico *M*
      Long Beach *T*
      Northridge *B, T*
      Sacramento *T*
      San Bernardino *T*
Humboldt State University *T*
Los Angeles Southwest College *A*
Mount St. Mary's College *T*
Occidental College *T*
Pacific Union College *T*
San Diego State University *B, T*
San Francisco State University *B, T*

Sonoma State University *T*
University of Southern California *T*
University of the Pacific *T*

Colorado
Colorado State University *T*
Colorado State University
    Pueblo *T*
Metropolitan State College of Denver *T*
University of Colorado
    Boulder *T*

Connecticut
Central Connecticut State
    University *B, M, T*
Fairfield University *T*
Quinnipiac University *B, M*

Delaware
Delaware State University *B*
University of Delaware *B, T*

District of Columbia
George Washington University *M, T*

Florida
Flagler College *B*
Florida International University *B, M, T*
Florida State University *B, M, D, T*
Stetson University *B, T*
University of Central Florida *B*
University of Florida *M*
University of South Florida *B, M*

Georgia
Berry College *T*
Fort Valley State University *B, T*
Georgia Southwestern State
    University *B, M, T*
Kennesaw State University *B*
Mercer University *T*
North Georgia College & State
    University *M*
State University of West Georgia *M*
University of Georgia *B, M*

Hawaii
University of Hawaii
    Manoa *B, T*

Illinois
Augustana College *B, T*
North Park University *T*
Northwestern University *B, T*
Olivet Nazarene University *B, T*
Rockford College *T*
University of Illinois
    Chicago *B*
    Urbana-Champaign *B, M, T*

Indiana
Ball State University *T*
Butler University *T*
Goshen College *B*
Grace College *B*
Indiana University
    Bloomington *M, D, T*
Indiana University-Purdue University
    Indianapolis *M*
Manchester College *B, T*
Saint Mary's College *T*
St. Mary-of-the-Woods College *B*
University of Evansville *B*
University of Indianapolis *B, T*
University of Southern Indiana *T*
Valparaiso University *B*
Vincennes University *A*

Iowa
Clarke College *B, T*
Dordt College *B*
Graceland University *T*
Iowa State University *T*
Luther College *B*
Morningside College *B*
St. Ambrose University *B, T*
University of Iowa *B, M, D, T*

Kansas
Benedictine College *T*
Emporia State University *B, T*
McPherson College *B, T*
MidAmerica Nazarene University *B, T*
Pittsburg State University *B, T*
Southwestern College *B, T*
University of Kansas *B, T*
Washburn University of Topeka *B*

Kentucky
Kentucky Wesleyan College *T*
Murray State University *B, M, T*
University of Louisville *M*

Louisiana
Centenary College of Louisiana *B, T*
Louisiana College *B*
McNeese State University *T*
Nicholls State University *B*
University of Louisiana at Monroe *B*
University of New Orleans *B*

Maine
University of Maine *B*
University of Maine
    Presque Isle *B*
University of Southern Maine *T*

Maryland
College of Notre Dame of Maryland *T*
St. Mary's College of Maryland *T*
University of Maryland
    College Park *B*

Massachusetts
Assumption College *T*
Boston University *M, T*
Framingham State College *T*
Northeastern University *B*
Tufts University *M, T*
University of Massachusetts
    Dartmouth *T*

Michigan
Andrews University *M, T*
Northern Michigan University *B, T*
University of Michigan
    Dearborn *B*
Wayne State University *M, T*
Western Michigan University *B*

Minnesota
Bethel College *B*
College of St. Benedict *T*
College of St. Catherine *B*
Gustavus Adolphus College *T*
Minnesota State University
    Mankato *B, M, T*
St. John's University *T*
St. Mary's University of Minnesota *B*
St. Olaf College *T*
University of Minnesota
    Morris *T*
    Twin Cities *M*
University of St. Thomas *B, T*
Winona State University *B, T*

Mississippi
Blue Mountain College *B*
Delta State University *T*
Mississippi State University *T*
University of Mississippi *B, T*
University of Southern Mississippi *M*

Missouri
Central Methodist College *B*
Central Missouri State University *B, T*
College of the Ozarks *B, T*
Evangel University *B*
Missouri Southern State College *B, T*
Northwest Missouri State
    University *B, T*
Rockhurst University *B*
Southeast Missouri State University *B, T*
Truman State University *M, T*
University of Missouri
    Columbia *B*

William Jewell College *T*

Montana
Montana State University
    Billings *B, T*
University of Montana-Missoula *T*

Nebraska
Creighton University *T*
Dana College *B*
Doane College *B*
Hastings College *B, M, T*
Union College *T*
University of Nebraska
    Kearney *B, M, T*
    Lincoln *B, T*

Nevada
University of Nevada
    Reno *B*

New Hampshire
Keene State College *T*
Rivier College *B, M, T*
University of New Hampshire *T*

New Jersey
Caldwell College *T*
The College of New Jersey *B, T*
Monmouth University *B, T*
Richard Stockton College of New
    Jersey *A*
Rider University *B, T*
Rowan University *T*
Rutgers, The State University of New
    Jersey
    New Brunswick Regional
        Campus *T*
St. Peter's College *T*

New Mexico
New Mexico Highlands University *B*

New York
Adelphi University *M*
Canisius College *B, M, T*
City University of New York
    Brooklyn College *B, M*
    City College *B, T*
    College of Staten Island *T*
    Hunter College *B, M, T*
    Queens College *M, T*
College of Mount St. Vincent *T*
D'Youville College *M, T*
Dowling College *B*
Elmira College *B, T*
Fordham University *T*
Hofstra University *B, M, T*
Houghton College *B, T*
Ithaca College *B, T*
Le Moyne College *T*
Long Island University
    C. W. Post Campus *B, T*
Manhattan College *B, T*
Manhattanville College *M, T*
Mercy College *T*
Nazareth College of Rochester *T*
New York University *B, M, T*
Pace University *M, T*
Pace University:
    Pleasantville/Briarcliff *M, T*
St. Bonaventure University *T*
St. John Fisher College *T*
St. John's University *B, T*
St. Lawrence University *T*
State University of New York
    Albany *B, M, T*
    Buffalo *M, D, T*
    College at Buffalo *B, T*
    College at Cortland *B, M, T*
    College at Fredonia *B, T*
    College at Old Westbury *B, T*
    College at Oneonta *B, T*
    College at Plattsburgh *T*
    College at Potsdam *B, M*
    New Paltz *B, M, T*
University of Rochester *M*
Vassar College *T*

Wells College *T*
Yeshiva University *B*

North Carolina
Appalachian State University *B, M, T*
Davidson College *T*
Gardner-Webb University *B*
Lenoir-Rhyne College *B, T*
Meredith College *T*
Methodist College *A, B, T*
North Carolina Agricultural and
    Technical State University *B*
North Carolina Central University *B*
North Carolina State University *T*
University of North Carolina
    Greensboro *B, M, T*

North Dakota
Dickinson State University *B, T*
Minot State University *B*
University of North Dakota *B, T*

Ohio
Bowling Green State University *B*
Hiram College *T*
Kent State University *T*
Kent State University
    Stark Campus *B*
Laura and Alvin Siegal College of Judaic
    Studies *M*
Mount Union College *T*
Ohio Northern University *B*
Ohio State University
    Columbus Campus *M, D*
Ohio University *B, T*
Otterbein College *B*
University of Akron *B, T*
University of Dayton *B, M, T*
University of Toledo *T*
Wittenberg University *B*
Wright State University *B, T*
Youngstown State University *B, M, T*

Oklahoma
Oklahoma Baptist University *B, T*
Oklahoma City University *B, M*
Oral Roberts University *B, T*
Southeastern Oklahoma State
    University *B, T*
University of Central Oklahoma *B*
University of Oklahoma *B, T*
University of Tulsa *T*

Oregon
Linfield College *T*
University of Oregon *M, T*
University of Portland *T*
Western Oregon University *T*

Pennsylvania
DeSales University *B, T*
Dickinson College *T*
Duquesne University *B, T*
East Stroudsburg University of
    Pennsylvania *B, T*
Immaculata University *T*
King's College *T*
La Salle University *B, T*
Lincoln University *B, T*
Lock Haven University of
    Pennsylvania *B, T*
Lycoming College *T*
Marywood University *B*
Millersville University of
    Pennsylvania *B, M, T*
Moravian College *T*
St. Joseph's University *B*
St. Vincent College *T*
Seton Hill University *B, T*
Temple University *B, T*
Thiel College *B*
University of Pennsylvania *M*
Washington and Jefferson College *T*
West Chester University of
    Pennsylvania *B, M, T*
Widener University *M*

Rhode Island

Rhode Island College *B, M*

South Carolina

Charleston Southern University *B*
Columbia College *B*
Converse College *T*
Furman University *T*

South Dakota

Black Hills State University *B*
Northern State University *B, T*
University of South Dakota *B, T*

Tennessee

Lee University *B*
Middle Tennessee State University *M, T*
Tennessee Technological University *T*
Union University *B, T*
University of Tennessee
    Chattanooga *B, T*
    Knoxville *T*

Texas

Abilene Christian University *B, T*
Baylor University *B, T*
Houston Baptist University *T*
Lamar University *T*
Laredo Community College *A*
Texas Christian University *T*
University of Houston *M, T*
University of Texas
    Arlington *T*
    Austin *M, D*
West Texas A&M University *T*

Utah

Brigham Young University *B, M*
Southern Utah University *B*
University of Utah *B*

Vermont

Bennington College *B, M, T*
Castleton State College *B, T*
St. Michael's College *T*
University of Vermont *B*

Virginia

Longwood University *T*
Radford University *T*
University of Virginia's College at
    Wise *T*

Washington

Central Washington University *B*
Pacific Lutheran University *T*
Western Washington University *B, T*
Whitworth College *B, T*

West Virginia

Salem International University *T*
West Virginia University *T*
Wheeling Jesuit University *T*

Wisconsin

Carthage College *M, T*
Edgewood College *B*
Lawrence University *T*
Mount Mary College *B, T*
St. Norbert College *T*
University of Wisconsin
    La Crosse *B*
    Madison *M*
    Parkside *T*

Foreign languages/ literatures

Alabama

Auburn University at Montgomery *B*
Judson College *B*
Samford University *B*
University of Alabama
    Huntsville *B*
University of North Alabama *B*
University of South Alabama *B*

Alaska

University of Alaska
    Anchorage *B*
    Fairbanks *B*

Arizona

Cochise College *A*
Eastern Arizona College *A*
University of Arizona *B*

Arkansas

Arkansas Tech University *B*

California

Cabrillo College *A*
California State University
    Monterey Bay *B*
College of the Sequoias *A*
Glendale Community College *A*
Golden West College *A*
Imperial Valley College *A*
Long Beach City College *C, A*
Los Angeles Southwest College *A*
MiraCosta College *A*
Modesto Junior College *A*
Monterey Peninsula College *A*
Pitzer College *B*
Pomona College *B*
Reedley College *A*
St. Mary's College of California *B*
San Diego City College *A*
Santa Monica College *A*
Scripps College *B*
University of California
    Los Angeles *M, D*
    Riverside *B*
    San Diego *B*
West Valley College *A*
Whittier College *B*

Colorado

Colorado State University *M*
Colorado State University
    Pueblo *B*
Metropolitan State College of
    Denver *B, T*
University of Northern Colorado *M, T*

Connecticut

Central Connecticut State University *B*
Southern Connecticut State
    University *B, M*
Trinity College *B*
University of Hartford *B*

Delaware

University of Delaware *B, M*

District of Columbia

George Washington University *B*
Howard University *M*

Florida

Broward Community College *A*
Eckerd College *B*
Gulf Coast Community College *A*
Indian River Community College *A*
Miami-Dade Community College *A*
New College of Florida *B*
Polk Community College *A*
Rollins College *B*
South Florida Community College *A*
University of Central Florida *B*
University of Miami *M, D*
University of Tampa *A*

Georgia

Atlanta Metropolitan College *A*
Clark Atlanta University *B, M*
Georgia Perimeter College *A*
Gordon College *A*
Macon State College *A*
Middle Georgia College *A*
North Georgia College & State
    University *B, M*
Oxford College of Emory University *B*
South Georgia College *A*
University of Georgia *B, M, D*

Young Harris College *A*

Hawaii

University of Hawaii
    Manoa *B, D*

Idaho

College of Southern Idaho *A*
Idaho State University *A*
North Idaho College *A*
University of Idaho *B*

Illinois

City Colleges of Chicago
    Harold Washington College *A*
    Kennedy-King College *A*
    Olive-Harvey College *A*
De Paul University *T*
Eastern Illinois University *B, T*
Greenville College *B*
Illinois Central College *A*
Illinois State University *M*
Illinois Valley Community College *A*
Kishwaukee College *A*
Knox College *B*
Lincoln Land Community College *A*
Millikin University *B, T*
Northwestern University *B, T*
Olivet Nazarene University *B*
Principia College *B*
Rockford College *B*
Roosevelt University *B, M*
Sauk Valley Community College *A*
Southern Illinois University
    Carbondale *M*
Southern Illinois University
    Edwardsville *B*
Southwestern Illinois College *A*
Triton College *A*

Indiana

Earlham College *B*
Goshen College *B*
Grace College *B*
Indiana State University *B*
Indiana University
    Bloomington *B, M, D*
Manchester College *B, T*
Purdue University *B, M, D*
Purdue University
    Calumet *B*
University of Evansville *B*
Vincennes University *A*

Iowa

Cornell College *B*
Graceland University *B*
St. Ambrose University *B*
University of Northern Iowa *M*

Kansas

Barton County Community College *A*
Butler County Community College *A*
Cloud County Community College *A*
Emporia State University *B*
Fort Hays State University *B*
Hutchinson Community College *A*
Independence Community College *A*
Kansas City Kansas Community
    College *A*
Kansas State University *B, M*
Kansas Wesleyan University *B*
McPherson College *B, T*
MidAmerica Nazarene University *B*
Southwestern College *B*

Kentucky

Bellarmine University *B*
Kentucky Wesleyan College *B*
Murray State University *B, M*

Louisiana

Centenary College of Louisiana *B, T*
Dillard University *B*
Louisiana College *B*
University of Louisiana at Lafayette *B*

Maine

Bates College *T*

University of Maine *B*
University of Southern Maine *B*

Maryland

Frostburg State University *B*
St. Mary's College of Maryland *B*
University of Maryland
    Baltimore County *B*
    College Park *M*
Washington College *B*

Massachusetts

Assumption College *B*
Berkshire Community College *A*
Boston University *B*
Bunker Hill Community College *A*
Cape Cod Community College *A*
Clark University *B*
Gordon College *B*
Harvard College *B*
Massachusetts Institute of Technology *B*
Merrimack College *B*
Northeastern University *B*
Simon's Rock College of Bard *B*
Stonehill College *B*
Suffolk University *B*
Tufts University *B, M*
University of Massachusetts
    Lowell *B*
Wellesley College *B*

Michigan

Lansing Community College *A*
Northern Michigan University *T*
Oakland University *B*
Wayne State University *M, D*

Minnesota

Minnesota State University
    Mankato *B*
    Moorhead *B*
Northland Community & Technical
    College *A*
University of Minnesota
    Morris *B*
    Twin Cities *B*
Winona State University *B*

Mississippi

Delta State University *B*
Mississippi College *B*
Mississippi State University *B, M*
University of Southern Mississippi *B*

Missouri

Mineral Area College *A*
Three Rivers Community College *A*
University of Missouri
    Columbia *D*
    Kansas City *M*
Washington University in St.
    Louis *B, M, D*
Webster University *B*

Montana

Miles Community College *A*
Montana State University
    Billings *B*
    Bozeman *B*
University of Montana-Missoula *M*

Nebraska

Hastings College *B*
University of Nebraska
    Lincoln *M, D*

Nevada

University of Nevada
    Las Vegas *M*
    Reno *M*

New Jersey

Monmouth University *B*
Richard Stockton College of New
    Jersey *B*
Rowan University *B*
St. Peter's College *B*
Seton Hall University *B*
Thomas Edison State College *B*

New Mexico
New Mexico State University *B*
San Juan College *A*
University of New Mexico *B*

New York
Adelphi University *B*
Alfred University *B*
Bard College *B*
City University of New York
    City College *B, M*
    Hunter College *B*
College of Mount St. Vincent *M*
Cornell University *B*
Elmira College *B, T*
Eugene Lang College/New School
    University *B*
Excelsior College *B*
Hamilton College *B*
Iona College *B, M*
Ithaca College *B*
New York University *B, M, D*
Orange County Community College *A*
Pace University *B*
Pace University:
    Pleasantville/Briarcliff *B*
St. Joseph's College *B, T*
St. Lawrence University *B, T*
Sarah Lawrence College *B*
State University of New York
    College at Brockport *B*
    Purchase *B*
    Stony Brook *D*
Syracuse University *B, M, D*
Touro College *B*
Union College *B*
University of Rochester *B*
Wells College *B*

North Carolina
Elon University *B*
Gardner-Webb University *B*
High Point University *B*

North Dakota
University of North Dakota *B*

Ohio
Antioch College *B*
College of Wooster *B*
Kent State University
    Stark Campus *B*
Kenyon College *B*
Lake Erie College *B*
Laura and Alvin Siegal College of Judaic
    Studies *B, M*
University of Dayton *B*
Wright State University *B*
Youngstown State University *B*

Oklahoma
Oklahoma Baptist University *B, T*
Rose State College *A*

Oregon
Central Oregon Community College *A*
Chemeketa Community College *A*
Lewis & Clark College *B*
Linn-Benton Community College *A*
Pacific University *B*
Portland State University *M*
Southern Oregon University *B*
University of Oregon *B, M, D*

Pennsylvania
California University of Pennsylvania *B*
Community College of Allegheny
    County *A*
Duquesne University *B*
Immaculata University *B*
Juniata College *B*
La Salle University *B, T*
Lebanon Valley College of
    Pennsylvania *B, T*
Mercyhurst College *B*
Rosemont College *B*
Wilson College *B*
York College of Pennsylvania *A*

Puerto Rico
University of Puerto Rico
    Rio Piedras Campus *B*

South Carolina
Clemson University *B*
Converse College *B*
Newberry College *B*
University of South Carolina *M*
Winthrop University *B*

South Dakota
Augustana College *B*

Tennessee
Austin Peay State University *B*
East Tennessee State University *B, T*
King College *B*
Lambuth University *B*
Lee University *B*
Middle Tennessee State University *B*
Southern Adventist University *B*
University of Memphis *B*
University of Tennessee
    Knoxville *M, D*
Vanderbilt University *B, M, D*

Texas
Blinn College *A*
Brazosport College *A*
Central Texas College *A*
Del Mar College *A*
El Paso Community College *A*
Hill College *A*
Howard College *A*
Laredo Community College *A*
Lee College *A*
Midland College *A*
Odessa College *A*
Palo Alto College *A*
Panola College *A*
Paris Junior College *A*
St. Philip's College *A*
Southern Methodist University *B*
Texas A&M University *M*
Texas Tech University *M*
Tyler Junior College *A*
University of Texas
    Arlington *M*
    Austin *B, M, D*
    Tyler *B*
Western Texas College *A*

Utah
Brigham Young University *B*
Snow College *A*
Southern Utah University *B, T*
University of Utah *B, M, D*

Vermont
Bennington College *B, M, T*
Marlboro College *B*
St. Michael's College *B*
University of Vermont *B, M*

Virginia
George Mason University *B, M*
James Madison University *B, T*
Old Dominion University *B*
Radford University *B*
Sweet Briar College *B*
University of Virginia's College at
    Wise *B*
Virginia Commonwealth University *B*
Virginia Military Institute *B*
Virginia Polytechnic Institute and State
    University *B*
Virginia Wesleyan College *B*

Washington
Centralia College *A*
Everett Community College *A*
Olympic College *A*
Seattle University *B*
Washington State University *B, M*

West Virginia
Davis and Elkins College *B*

Marshall University *B*
West Virginia University *B, M*

Wisconsin
Beloit College *B*
Carthage College *B*
Ripon College *B, T*
University of Wisconsin
    Milwaukee *M*

Wyoming
Casper College *A*
Eastern Wyoming College *A*
Western Wyoming Community
    College *A*

Forensic psychology

Iowa
St. Ambrose University *B*

Massachusetts
Bay Path College *B*

New York
City University of New York
    John Jay College of Criminal
        Justice *M*

Ohio
Tiffin University *B, M*

Vermont
Castleton State College *B, M*

Forensic science

Alabama
University of Alabama
    Birmingham *M*

Arizona
Scottsdale Community College *C*

California
California State University
    Stanislaus *B*
Grossmont Community College *C, A*
Moorpark College *C, A*
National University *M*
Southwestern College *C*

Connecticut
Tunxis Community College *C*
University of New Haven *B, M*

District of Columbia
George Washington University *M*

Florida
Florida International University *M*
St. Petersburg College *C, A*
Santa Fe Community College *A*
South Florida Community College *A*
University of Central Florida *B*
University of Miami *B*

Hawaii
Chaminade University of Honolulu *B*

Illinois
University of Illinois
    Chicago *M*

Indiana
Indiana University
    Bloomington *M*

Iowa
Iowa Western Community College *C, A*

Kansas
Kansas City Kansas Community
    College *A*

Louisiana
Loyola University New Orleans *B*

Maryland
Anne Arundel Community College *C, A*

University of Baltimore *B*

Massachusetts
American International College *M*
Massachusetts Bay Community
    College *A*

Michigan
Macomb Community College *A*
Oakland Community College *C, A*

Minnesota
Hamline University *C*

Mississippi
University of Mississippi *B*

Missouri
College of the Ozarks *B*
Columbia College *B*

Nebraska
Nebraska Wesleyan University *C, M*

New Mexico
New Mexico State University
    Alamogordo *A*

New York
City University of New York
    John Jay College of Criminal
        Justice *B, M*
Hudson Valley Community College *A*
Russell Sage College *B*
State University of New York
    College at Buffalo *B*
Tompkins-Cortland Community
    College *A*

North Carolina
Guilford College *B*

North Dakota
University of North Dakota *B*

Ohio
Central Ohio Technical College *A*
Ohio Northern University *B*
Youngstown State University *C, B*

Oklahoma
University of Central Oklahoma *B, M*

Oregon
Treasure Valley Community College *A*

Pennsylvania
Butler County Community College *A*
Duquesne University *M*
Keystone College *B*
Waynesburg College *B*

Puerto Rico
University of Puerto Rico
    Ponce *B*

Texas
Baylor University *B*

Vermont
Champlain College *A, B*

Washington
Bellevue Community College *C*
Centralia College *C*
Eastern Washington University *M, D*

West Virginia
Marshall University *M*
Southern West Virginia Community and
    Technical College *C, A*

Wisconsin
Carroll College *B*

Forest engineering

New York
State University of New York
    College of Environmental Science
    and Forestry *B, M, D*

Oregon
Oregon State University *B, M, D*

Washington
University of Washington *B*

Forest management

Connecticut
Yale University *M*

Louisiana
Louisiana State University and
　Agricultural and Mechanical
　College *B*

Maryland
Allegany College *A*

Michigan
Michigan Technological University *C*

New York
State University of New York
　College of Agriculture and
　　Technology at Morrisville *A*

North Carolina
North Carolina State University *B*

Ohio
Hocking Technical College *A*

Oregon
Oregon State University *B*

Pennsylvania
Keystone College *A*
Penn State
　University Park *M, D*

Texas
Stephen F. Austin State University *B, M*
Texas A&M University *B*

Forest resources production

Alabama
Alabama Southern Community
　College *C, A*
Lurleen B. Wallace Junior College *A*
Northwest-Shoals Community College *C*

Florida
Pensacola Junior College *A*

Idaho
University of Idaho *B, M*

Iowa
Iowa State University *B, M, D*

Louisiana
Louisiana Tech University *B*

Maine
University of Maine *B*

Minnesota
University of Minnesota
　Twin Cities *B*
Vermilion Community College *A*

Mississippi
Mississippi State University *D*

New Hampshire
University of New Hampshire *A*

New York
Paul Smith's College *A*
State University of New York
　College of Environmental Science
　and Forestry *B, M, D*

North Carolina
Haywood Community College *C, A*
Montgomery Community College *A*
North Carolina State University *B*

Southeastern Community College *A*
Wayne Community College *A*

Oregon
Oregon State University *B, M, D*

Pennsylvania
Penn State
　Mont Alto *A*
　University Park *B*
Pennsylvania College of Technology *A*

South Carolina
Orangeburg-Calhoun Technical
　College *A*

Texas
Panola College *A*
Texarkana College *A*

Virginia
Mountain Empire Community College *C*
Virginia Polytechnic Institute and State
　University *B, M, D*

Washington
Green River Community College *A*
Spokane Community College *A*
University of Washington *B*

West Virginia
Glenville State College *A*

Wisconsin
University of Wisconsin
　Madison *B, M, D*

Forest sciences/biology

New York
State University of New York
　College of Agriculture and
　　Technology at Morrisville *A*

Oregon
Oregon State University *M, D*

Pennsylvania
Penn State
　Abington *B*
　Altoona *B*
　Beaver *B*
　Berks *B*
　Delaware County *B*
　Dubois *B*
　Erie, The Behrend College *B*
　Fayette *B*
　Hazleton *B*
　Lehigh Valley *B*
　McKeesport *B*
　Mont Alto *B*
　New Kensington *B*
　Schuylkill - Capital College *B*
　Shenango *B*
　University Park *B*
　Wilkes-Barre *B*
　Worthington Scranton *B*
　York *B*

Forest technology

California
Feather River College *C, A*

Colorado
Red Rocks Community College *C, A*

New York
State University of New York
　College of Agriculture and
　　Technology at Morrisville *A*
　College of Environmental Science
　and Forestry *A*

Pennsylvania
Keystone College *A*

Forestry

Alabama
Alabama Southern Community
　College *A*
Auburn University *B, M, D*
Chattahoochee Valley Community
　College *A*
James H. Faulkner State Community
　College *A*
Northeast Alabama Community
　College *A*
Northwest-Shoals Community College *C*
Tuskegee University *B*

Alaska
University of Alaska
　Fairbanks *B*

Arizona
Eastern Arizona College *A*
Northern Arizona University *B, M, D*

Arkansas
University of Arkansas
　Monticello *B, M*

California
Bakersfield College *A*
Citrus College *C*
College of the Redwoods *C, A*
Columbia College *C, A*
Feather River College *C, A*
Humboldt State University *B*
Modesto Junior College *C, A*
Mount San Antonio College *C, A*
Reedley College *A*
Sierra College *A*
University of California
　Berkeley *B, M, D*

Colorado
Colorado State University *B, M, D*

Connecticut
Yale University *M, D*

Florida
Gulf Coast Community College *A*
Lake City Community College *A*
Miami-Dade Community College *A*
Pensacola Junior College *A*
South Florida Community College *A*
University of Florida *B, M, D*

Georgia
Abraham Baldwin Agricultural
　College *A*
Albany Technical College *C, A*
Andrew College *A*
Clayton College and State University *A*
Dalton State College *A*
Darton College *A*
Gainesville College *A*
Gordon College *A*
Middle Georgia College *A*
University of Georgia *B, M, D*
Young Harris College *A*

Idaho
College of Southern Idaho *A*
North Idaho College *A*
University of Idaho *B, M*

Illinois
Illinois College *B*
Joliet Junior College *C*
Shawnee Community College *A*
Southern Illinois University
　Carbondale *B, M*
University of Illinois
　Urbana-Champaign *B, M*

Indiana
Purdue University *B, M, D*
Vincennes University *A*

Iowa
Cornell College *B*

Iowa State University *B, M, D*
Iowa Wesleyan College *B*
Marshalltown Community College *A*
Upper Iowa University *B*

Kansas
Barton County Community College *A*
Garden City Community College *A*
Hutchinson Community College *A*
Seward County Community College *A*
University of Kansas *M*

Kentucky
Hazard Community College *A*
University of Kentucky *B, M*

Louisiana
Louisiana State University and
　Agricultural and Mechanical
　College *M, D*
Louisiana Tech University *B*
Southern University and Agricultural and
　Mechanical College *B*
University of Louisiana at Monroe *C, A*

Maine
University of Maine *B, M, D*

Massachusetts
University of Massachusetts
　Amherst *B, M, D*

Michigan
Gogebic Community College *A*
Michigan State University *B, M, D*
Michigan Technological
　University *B, M, T*
University of Michigan *M*

Minnesota
Itasca Community College *A*
University of Minnesota
　Twin Cities *B, M, D*
Vermilion Community College *A*

Mississippi
Holmes Community College *A*
Itawamba Community College *A*
Mississippi Gulf Coast Community
　College
　Perkinston *A*
Mississippi State University *B, M*

Missouri
East Central College *A*
University of Missouri
　Columbia *B, M, D*

Montana
Miles Community College *A*
Salish Kootenai College *A*
University of Montana-Missoula *B, M, D*

Nebraska
University of Nebraska
　Lincoln *D*
Western Nebraska Community
　College *A*

Nevada
University of Nevada
　Reno *B*

New Hampshire
New Hampshire Community Technical
　College
　Berlin *A*
University of New Hampshire *B*

New Jersey
Thomas Edison State College *A, B*

New York
Fulton-Montgomery Community
　College *A*
Jamestown Community College *A*
Jefferson Community College *C*
Paul Smith's College *A*

State University of New York
    College of Agriculture and
      Technology at Morrisville *A*
    College of Environmental Science
      and Forestry *A, B, M, D*

North Carolina

Duke University *M, D*
Haywood Community College *C, A*
High Point University *B*
North Carolina State University *M, D*
Wake Forest University *B, M*

North Dakota

Minot State University: Bottineau
    Campus *C, A*
North Dakota State University *B*

Ohio

Hocking Technical College *A*
Miami University
    Oxford Campus *B, M*
Ohio State University
    Columbus Campus *B*

Oklahoma

Eastern Oklahoma State College *A*
Northeastern Oklahoma Agricultural and
    Mechanical College *A*
Oklahoma State University *B, M*

Oregon

Central Oregon Community College *A*
Chemeketa Community College *A*
Mount Hood Community College *C, A*
Oregon State University *M, D*
Southwestern Oregon Community
    College *C, A*

Pennsylvania

Elizabethtown College *B*
Gettysburg College *B*
Keystone College *C, A*
Lebanon Valley College of
    Pennsylvania *B*
Muhlenberg College *B*
Pennsylvania College of Technology *A*

South Carolina

Clemson University *B, M, D*
Horry-Georgetown Technical College *A*
Presbyterian College *B*

Tennessee

Roane State Community College *A*
University of Tennessee
    Knoxville *B, M*

Texas

Baylor University *B*
Panola College *C*
Stephen F. Austin State
    University *B, M, D*
Texas A&M University *B, M, D*

Utah

Dixie State College of Utah *A*
Snow College *A*
Utah State University *B, M, D*

Vermont

Sterling College *A, B*
University of Vermont *B, M*

Virginia

Mountain Empire Community
    College *C, A*
Virginia Polytechnic Institute and State
    University *B*

Washington

Edmonds Community College *C*
Heritage College *C, A*
Spokane Community College *A*
University of Washington *B, M, D*
Washington State University *B*

West Virginia

Potomac State College of West Virginia
    University *A*

West Virginia University *B, M, D*

Wisconsin

Beloit College *B*
Northland College *B*
University of Wisconsin
    Oshkosh *B*
    Stevens Point *B*

Wyoming

Casper College *A*

Franchise operations

Alabama

University of South Alabama *B*

Ohio

Ashland University *B*
University of Toledo *B*

French

Alabama

Alabama State University *B*
Auburn University *B, M*
Birmingham-Southern College *B, T*
Jacksonville State University *B*
Oakwood College *B*
Samford University *B*
Spring Hill College *T*
University of Alabama *B, M*
University of Alabama
    Birmingham *B*
University of Montevallo *B*

Alaska

University of Alaska
    Anchorage *B*

Arizona

Arizona State University *B, M*
Northern Arizona University *B, T*
University of Arizona *B, M, D*

Arkansas

Arkansas State University *B*
Harding University *B*
Hendrix College *B*
Ouachita Baptist University *B*
University of Arkansas *B, M*
University of Arkansas
    Little Rock *B*
University of Central Arkansas *B*

California

Cabrillo College *A*
California State University
    Chico *B*
    Dominguez Hills *B*
    Fresno *B*
    Fullerton *B, M*
    Hayward *B*
    Long Beach *B, M*
    Los Angeles *B, M*
    Northridge *B*
    Sacramento *B, M*
    San Bernardino *B*
    Stanislaus *B*
Cerritos Community College *A*
Chabot College *A*
Chapman University *B*
Citrus College *A*
Claremont McKenna College *B*
College of the Canyons *A*
College of the Sequoias *A*
De Anza College *A*
East Los Angeles College *C*
Foothill College *A*
Glendale Community College *A*
Golden West College *A*
Grossmont Community College *C, A*
Humboldt State University *B*
Imperial Valley College *A*
Irvine Valley College *A*
Los Angeles Pierce College *A*

Los Angeles Southwest College *A*
Loyola Marymount University *B*
Mills College *B*
MiraCosta College *A*
Modesto Junior College *A*
Monterey Institute of International
    Studies *C*
Mount St. Mary's College *B*
Occidental College *B*
Orange Coast College *A*
Pacific Union College *B*
Pepperdine University *B*
Pitzer College *B*
Pomona College *B*
St. Mary's College of California *B*
San Diego City College *A*
San Diego Mesa College *C, A*
San Diego State University *B, M*
San Francisco State University *B, M*
San Joaquin Delta College *A*
San Jose State University *B, M*
Santa Barbara City College *A*
Santa Clara University *B*
Santa Monica College *A*
Scripps College *B*
Sonoma State University *B*
Southwestern College *A*
Stanford University *B, M, D*
University of California
    Berkeley *B, M, D*
    Davis *B, M, D*
    Irvine *B, M, D*
    Los Angeles *B, M, D*
    Riverside *B, M, D*
    San Diego *B*
    Santa Barbara *B, M, D*
    Santa Cruz *B*
University of La Verne *B*
University of Redlands *B*
University of San Diego *B*
University of San Francisco *B*
University of Southern
    California *B, M, D*
University of the Pacific *B*
Ventura College *A*
Whittier College *B*

Colorado

Colorado State University *B*
Red Rocks Community College *A*
Regis University *B*
University of Colorado
    Boulder *B, M, D*
    Denver *B*
University of Denver *B, M*
University of Northern Colorado *B, T*

Connecticut

Albertus Magnus College *B*
Central Connecticut State
    University *B, M*
Connecticut College *B, M*
Fairfield University *B*
St. Joseph College *B, T*
Southern Connecticut State University *B*
Trinity College *B*
University of Connecticut *B, M, D*
University of Hartford *B*
Wesleyan University *B*
Yale University *B, M, D*

Delaware

Delaware State University *B*
University of Delaware *B, M, T*

District of Columbia

American University *B, M*
Catholic University of
    America *B, M, D, T*
Gallaudet University *B*
George Washington University *B*
Georgetown University *B*
Howard University *B, M, D*
Trinity College *B*
University of the District of Columbia *B*

Florida

Barry University *B*
Eckerd College *B*
Florida Agricultural and Mechanical
    University *B*
Florida Atlantic University *B, M*
Florida International University *B*
Florida State University *B, M, D*
Jacksonville University *B*
Manatee Community College *A*
New College of Florida *B*
Okaloosa-Walton Community College *A*
Polk Community College *A*
Rollins College *B*
Schiller International University *B*
South Florida Community College *A*
Stetson University *B*
University of Central Florida *B*
University of Florida *B, M*
University of Miami *B, M, D*
University of South Florida *B, M*

Georgia

Agnes Scott College *B*
Albany State University *B*
Augusta State University *B*
Berry College *B, T*
Clark Atlanta University *B, M*
Clayton College and State University *A*
Columbus State University *B*
Emory University *B, D*
Georgia College and State University *B*
Georgia Southern University *B*
Georgia Southwestern State University *B*
Georgia State University *B, M*
Kennesaw State University *B*
Mercer University *B*
Morehouse College *B*
Morris Brown College *B*
North Georgia College & State
    University *B*
Oxford College of Emory University *B*
Shorter College *B*
South Georgia College *A*
Spelman College *B*
State University of West Georgia *B*
University of Georgia *B, M*
Valdosta State University *B*
Young Harris College *A*

Hawaii

University of Hawaii
    Manoa *B, M*

Idaho

Boise State University *B*
Idaho State University *A, B*
University of Idaho *B, M*

Illinois

Augustana College *B, T*
Bradley University *B, T*
City Colleges of Chicago
    Harold Washington College *A*
De Paul University *B*
Dominican University *B*
Elmhurst College *B, T*
Illinois College *B, T*
Illinois State University *B, T*
Illinois Wesleyan University *B*
Kishwaukee College *A*
Knox College *B*
Lake Forest College *B*
Loyola University of Chicago *C, B*
MacMurray College *B*
Millikin University *B, T*
Monmouth College *B, T*
North Central College *B, T*
North Park University *B*
Northeastern Illinois University *B*
Northern Illinois University *B, M, T*
Northwestern University *B, M, D*
Parkland College *A*
Principia College *B, T*
Richland Community College *A*
Rockford College *B*
Sauk Valley Community College *A*

Southern Illinois University
Carbondale *B*
Southern Illinois University
Edwardsville *T*
Triton College *A*
University of Chicago *B*
University of Illinois
Chicago *B, M*
Urbana-Champaign *B, M, D*
Western Illinois University *B*
Wheaton College *B*

Indiana
Anderson University *B*
Ball State University *B, T*
Butler University *B*
DePauw University *B*
Earlham College *B*
Franklin College *B*
Grace College *B*
Hanover College *B*
Indiana State University *B, M*
Indiana University
Bloomington *B, M, D*
Northwest *A, B*
South Bend *B*
Southeast *B*
Indiana University-Purdue University
Fort Wayne *A, B, T*
Indiana University-Purdue University
Indianapolis *B*
Manchester College *B, T*
Marian College *B, T*
Purdue University
Calumet *B*
Saint Mary's College *B, T*
St. Mary-of-the-Woods College *B*
Taylor University *B*
University of Evansville *B*
University of Indianapolis *B*
University of Notre Dame *B, M*
University of Southern Indiana *B, T*
Valparaiso University *B*
Vincennes University *A*
Wabash College *B*

Iowa
Central College *B, T*
Clarke College *B, T*
Coe College *B*
Cornell College *B, T*
Grinnell College *B*
Iowa State University *B*
Loras College *B*
Luther College *B*
St. Ambrose University *B, T*
Simpson College *B*
University of Iowa *B, M, D, T*
University of Northern Iowa *B, M*
Wartburg College *B, T*

Kansas
Baker University *B, T*
Benedictine College *B, T*
Butler County Community College *A*
Independence Community College *A*
Pittsburg State University *B, T*
Pratt Community College *A*
University of Kansas *B, M, D*
Washburn University of Topeka *B*
Wichita State University *B*

Kentucky
Asbury College *B, T*
Berea College *B, T*
Centre College *B*
Georgetown College *B, T*
Morehead State University *B*
Murray State University *B, T*
Thomas More College *A*
Transylvania University *B, T*
University of Kentucky *B, M*
University of Louisville *B, M*

Louisiana
Centenary College of Louisiana *B, T*
Dillard University *B*

Grambling State University *B*
Louisiana College *B*
Louisiana State University
Shreveport *B*
Louisiana State University and
Agricultural and Mechanical
College *B, M, D*
Louisiana Tech University *B*
Loyola University New Orleans *B*
McNeese State University *B*
Nicholls State University *B*
Southeastern Louisiana University *B*
Southern University
New Orleans *B*
Southern University and Agricultural and
Mechanical College *B*
Tulane University *B, M, D*
University of Louisiana at
Lafayette *M, D*
University of Louisiana at Monroe *B*
University of New Orleans *B, M*
Xavier University of Louisiana *B*

Maine
Bates College *B*
Bowdoin College *B*
Colby College *B*
University of Maine *B, M*
University of Maine
Presque Isle *B*
University of Southern Maine *B*

Maryland
College of Notre Dame of Maryland *B*
Community College of Baltimore County
Catonsville *A*
Dundalk *A*
Essex *A*
Frostburg State University *T*
Goucher College *B*
Hood College *B, T*
Johns Hopkins University *B, M, D*
Loyola College in Maryland *B*
McDaniel College *B*
Mount St. Mary's College *B*
Salisbury University *B, T*
Towson University *B, T*
University of Maryland
Baltimore County *B*
College Park *B, M, D*
Washington College *B, T*

Massachusetts
Amherst College *B*
Assumption College *B*
Atlantic Union College *B*
Boston College *B, M, D*
Boston University *B, M, D*
Brandeis University *B*
Bridgewater State College *B*
Clark University *B*
College of the Holy Cross *B*
Framingham State College *B*
Gordon College *B*
Harvard College *B*
Mount Holyoke College *B*
Northeastern University *B*
Roxbury Community College *A*
Simmons College *B, M*
Simon's Rock College of Bard *B*
Smith College *B*
Suffolk University *B*
Tufts University *B, M*
University of Massachusetts
Amherst *B, M*
Boston *B*
Dartmouth *B*
Wellesley College *B*
Wheaton College *B*
Williams College *B*

Michigan
Adrian College *A, B, T*
Alma College *B, T*
Andrews University *B*
Aquinas College *B, T*
Calvin College *B, T*

Central Michigan University *B, T*
Eastern Michigan University *B, M*
Grand Valley State University *B*
Hillsdale College *B*
Hope College *B*
Kalamazoo College *B, T*
Lansing Community College *A*
Michigan State University *B, M, D*
Michigan Technological University *C*
Northern Michigan University *B, T*
Oakland University *B, T*
Saginaw Valley State University *B*
University of Michigan *B, M, D, T*
University of Michigan
Dearborn *B*
Flint *B, T*
Wayne State University *M*
Western Michigan University *B*

Minnesota
Augsburg College *B*
Bethel College *B*
Carleton College *B*
College of St. Benedict *B*
College of St. Catherine *B*
Concordia College: Moorhead *B, T*
Gustavus Adolphus College *B*
Hamline University *B*
Macalester College *B, T*
Minnesota State University
Mankato *B, M, T*
St. Cloud State University *B*
St. John's University *B*
St. Mary's University of Minnesota *B*
St. Olaf College *B*
University of Minnesota
Duluth *B, T*
Morris *B*
Twin Cities *B, M, D*
University of St. Thomas *B*
Winona State University *B*

Mississippi
Blue Mountain College *B*
Itawamba Community College *A*
Millsaps College *B, T*
Mississippi College *B*
Mississippi University for Women *T*
University of Mississippi *B, M, T*

Missouri
Central Methodist College *B*
Central Missouri State University *B, T*
College of the Ozarks *B*
Drury University *B, T*
East Central College *A*
Lindenwood University *B*
Missouri Southern State College *B*
Missouri Western State College *B, T*
Northwest Missouri State University *B*
Rockhurst University *B*
St. Louis University *B, M*
Southeast Missouri State University *B*
Southwest Missouri State University *B*
Truman State University *B*
University of Missouri
Columbia *B, M*
Kansas City *B*
St. Louis *B*
Washington University in St.
Louis *B, M, D*
Webster University *B*
Westminster College *B*
William Jewell College *B*

Montana
Carroll College *B, T*
University of Montana-Missoula *B, M*

Nebraska
Creighton University *B*
Doane College *B*
Nebraska Wesleyan University *B*
Union College *B*

University of Nebraska
Kearney *B, M, T*
Lincoln *B*
Omaha *B*
Western Nebraska Community
College *A*

Nevada
University of Nevada
Las Vegas *B*
Reno *B*

New Hampshire
Dartmouth College *B, T*
Keene State College *B, T*
Plymouth State College *B*
St. Anselm College *C, B, T*
University of New Hampshire *B*

New Jersey
Caldwell College *B*
Drew University *B*
Fairleigh Dickinson University
College at Florham *B*
Metropolitan Campus *B*
Georgian Court College *B, T*
Montclair State University *B, M, T*
Richard Stockton College of New
Jersey *B*
Rider University *B*
Rutgers, The State University of New
Jersey
Camden Regional Campus *B, T*
New Brunswick Regional
Campus *B, M, D, T*
Newark Regional Campus *B, T*
Seton Hall University *B, T*
William Paterson University of New
Jersey *B*

New Mexico
University of New Mexico *B, M, D*

New York
Adelphi University *B*
Alfred University *B*
Bard College *B*
Barnard College *B*
Canisius College *B*
City University of New York
Brooklyn College *B, M*
City College *B*
Hunter College *B, M*
Queens College *B, M*
York College *B*
Colgate University *B*
College of Mount St. Vincent *B, T*
College of New Rochelle *B, T*
Columbia University
Columbia College *B*
Cornell University *B, T*
Daemen College *B*
Elmira College *B, T*
Fordham University *B, M, D*
Hamilton College *B*
Hartwick College *B, T*
Hobart and William Smith Colleges *B*
Hofstra University *B*
Houghton College *B*
Iona College *B*
Ithaca College *B, T*
Le Moyne College *B*
Long Island University
C. W. Post Campus *B*
Manhattan College *B*
Marist College *B, T*
Marymount College of Fordham
University *B, T*
Molloy College *B*
Nazareth College of Rochester *B*
New York University *B, M, D*
Niagara University *B*
Orange County Community College *A*
Pace University *B*
Pace University:
Pleasantville/Briarcliff *B*
St. Bonaventure University *B*

St. John Fisher College *B*
St. John's University *B*
St. Lawrence University *B, T*
Sarah Lawrence College *B*
Skidmore College *B*
State University of New York
    Albany *B, M, D*
    Binghamton *B, M*
    Buffalo *B, M, D*
    College at Brockport *B, T*
    College at Buffalo *B*
    College at Cortland *B*
    College at Fredonia *B, T*
    College at Geneseo *B, T*
    College at Oneonta *B*
    College at Plattsburgh *B*
    College at Potsdam *B, T*
    New Paltz *B, T*
    Oswego *B*
    Stony Brook *B, M, T*
Syracuse University *B, M*
United States Military Academy *B*
University of Rochester *B, M*
Vassar College *B*
Wells College *B*
Yeshiva University *B*

North Carolina
Appalachian State University *B*
Campbell University *B*
Catawba College *B*
Davidson College *B*
Duke University *B, M, D*
East Carolina University *B*
Elon University *B*
Gardner-Webb University *B*
Greensboro College *B*
Guilford College *B, T*
High Point University *B*
Lenoir-Rhyne College *B*
Meredith College *B*
Methodist College *A, B, T*
North Carolina Agricultural and
   Technical State University *B, T*
North Carolina Central University *B*
North Carolina State University *B*
Queens University of Charlotte *B*
Salem College *B*
University of North Carolina
    Asheville *B, T*
    Chapel Hill *B*
    Charlotte *B*
    Greensboro *B, T*
    Wilmington *B*
Wake Forest University *B*
Western Carolina University *B*

North Dakota
Minot State University *B*
North Dakota State University *B, T*
University of North Dakota *B*

Ohio
Antioch College *B*
Ashland University *B*
Baldwin-Wallace College *B, T*
Bowling Green State University *B, M*
Case Western Reserve University *B, M*
Cleveland State University *B*
College of Wooster *B*
Denison University *B*
Franciscan University of Steubenville *B*
Hiram College *B, T*
John Carroll University *B*
Kent State University *B, M*
Kent State University
    Stark Campus *B*
Kenyon College *B*
Lake Erie College *B*
Lourdes College *A, B*
Marietta College *B*
Miami University
    Oxford Campus *B, M, T*
Mount Union College *B*
Muskingum College *B*
Oberlin College *B*

Ohio Northern University *B*
Ohio State University
    Columbus Campus *B, M, D*
Ohio University *B, M*
Ohio Wesleyan University *B*
Otterbein College *B*
University of Akron *B, M*
University of Cincinnati *B, M, D, T*
University of Dayton *B*
University of Toledo *B, M*
Walsh University *B*
Wittenberg University *B*
Wright State University *B*
Xavier University *A, B*
Youngstown State University *B*

Oklahoma
Oklahoma Baptist University *B, T*
Oklahoma City Community College *A*
Oklahoma City University *B*
Oklahoma State University *B*
Oral Roberts University *B*
Tulsa Community College *A*
University of Central Oklahoma *B*
University of Oklahoma *B, M, D*
University of Tulsa *B*

Oregon
Lewis & Clark College *B*
Linfield College *B*
Oregon State University *B*
Pacific University *B*
Portland State University *B, M*
Reed College *B*
University of Oregon *B, M*
University of Portland *T*
Western Oregon University *T*
Willamette University *B*

Pennsylvania
Albright College *B, T*
Allegheny College *B*
Bloomsburg University of
    Pennsylvania *B, T*
Bryn Mawr College *B, M*
Bucknell University *B*
Cabrini College *B*
California University of Pennsylvania *B*
Carnegie Mellon University *B*
Chatham College *B*
Chestnut Hill College *A, B*
Cheyney University of Pennsylvania *B*
Dickinson College *B*
East Stroudsburg University of
    Pennsylvania *B*
Elizabethtown College *B*
Franklin & Marshall College *B*
Gettysburg College *B*
Grove City College *B, T*
Haverford College *B, T*
Holy Family University *B, T*
Immaculata University *C, A, B*
Indiana University of Pennsylvania *B*
Juniata College *B*
King's College *B, T*
Kutztown University of
    Pennsylvania *B, T*
La Salle University *B, T*
Lafayette College *B*
Lebanon Valley College of
    Pennsylvania *B, T*
Lehigh University *B*
Lincoln University *B*
Lock Haven University of
    Pennsylvania *B*
Lycoming College *B*
Marywood University *B*
Mercyhurst College *B*
Messiah College *B*
Millersville University of
    Pennsylvania *B, M, T*
Moravian College *B, T*
Muhlenberg College *B, T*

Penn State
    Abington *B*
    Altoona *B*
    Beaver *B*
    Berks *B*
    Delaware County *B*
    Dubois *B*
    Fayette *B*
    Hazleton *B*
    Lehigh Valley *B*
    McKeesport *B*
    Mont Alto *B*
    New Kensington *B*
    Schuylkill - Capital College *B*
    Shenango *B*
    University Park *B, M, D*
    Wilkes-Barre *B*
    Worthington Scranton *B*
    York *B*
Rosemont College *B*
St. Joseph's University *B*
Seton Hill University *T*
Shippensburg University of
    Pennsylvania *B, T*
Slippery Rock University of
    Pennsylvania *B, T*
Swarthmore College *B*
Temple University *B*
Thiel College *B*
University of Pennsylvania *B*
University of Pittsburgh *B, M, D*
University of Scranton *B, T*
Villanova University *B*
Washington and Jefferson College *B*
West Chester University of
    Pennsylvania *B, M*
Widener University *B*
Wilkes University *B*

Puerto Rico
Pontifical Catholic University of Puerto
    Rico *B*
University of Puerto Rico
    Mayaguez Campus *B*
    Rio Piedras Campus *B*
University of the Sacred Heart *B*

Rhode Island
Brown University *B, M, D*
Rhode Island College *B, M*
Salve Regina University *B*
University of Rhode Island *B*

South Carolina
The Citadel *B*
Claflin University *B*
Clemson University *B*
Coker College *B*
College of Charleston *B, T*
Columbia College *B*
Converse College *B*
Erskine College *B*
Francis Marion University *B*
Furman University *B, T*
Newberry College *B*
Presbyterian College *B, T*
South Carolina State University *B*
University of South Carolina *B, M*
University of South Carolina
    Spartanburg *B*
Wofford College *B, T*

South Dakota
Augustana College *B, T*
Northern State University *B*
South Dakota State University *B*
University of South Dakota *B*

Tennessee
Belmont University *B, T*
Carson-Newman College *B, T*
King College *B, T*
Lane College *B*
Lee University *B*
Milligan College *B*
Rhodes College *B, T*
Southern Adventist University *B*

Tennessee State University *B*
Tennessee Technological University *B, T*
Union University *B, T*
University of Tennessee
    Chattanooga *B*
    Knoxville *B, M*
    Martin *B*
Vanderbilt University *B, M, D*

Texas
Angelo State University *B, T*
Austin College *B*
Austin Community College *A*
Baylor University *B*
Blinn College *A*
Cisco Junior College *A*
Coastal Bend College *A*
Hardin-Simmons University *B*
Houston Baptist University *B*
Kilgore College *A*
Lamar University *B*
Midland College *A*
Paris Junior College *A*
Rice University *B, M, D*
St. Mary's University *B*
Sam Houston State University *B*
South Plains College *A*
Southern Methodist University *B*
Southwest Texas State University *B, T*
Southwestern University *B, T*
Stephen F. Austin State University *B, T*
Texas A&M University *B*
Texas Christian University *B, T*
Texas Southern University *B*
Texas Tech University *B, M*
Trinity University *B*
Tyler Junior College *A*
University of Dallas *B*
University of Houston *B, M*
University of North Texas *B, M*
University of St. Thomas *B*
University of Texas
    Arlington *B, M*
    Austin *B, M, D*
    El Paso *B*
    San Antonio *B*

Utah
Brigham Young University *B, M*
Snow College *A*
Southern Utah University *B*
University of Utah *B, M, D*
Utah State University *B*
Weber State University *B*

Vermont
Bennington College *B, M, T*
Marlboro College *B*
Middlebury College *B, M, D*
St. Michael's College *B*
University of Vermont *B, M*

Virginia
Bridgewater College *B*
Christendom College *B*
College of William and Mary *B*
Eastern Mennonite University *B*
Emory & Henry College *B, T*
Ferrum College *B*
Hampden-Sydney College *B*
Hollins University *B*
Longwood University *B, T*
Lynchburg College *B*
Mary Baldwin College *B*
Mary Washington College *B*
Randolph-Macon College *B*
Randolph-Macon Woman's College *B*
Roanoke College *B, T*
Sweet Briar College *B*
University of Richmond *B, T*
University of Virginia *B, M, D*
University of Virginia's College at
    Wise *B, T*
Virginia Wesleyan College *B*
Washington and Lee University *B*

Washington

Central Washington University *B*
Centralia College *A*
Eastern Washington University *B, M, T*
Everett Community College *A*
Gonzaga University *B*
Pacific Lutheran University *B*
Seattle Pacific University *B*
Seattle University *B*
University of Puget Sound *B, T*
University of Washington *B*
Walla Walla College *B*
Washington State University *B*
Western Washington University *B, T*
Whitman College *B*
Whitworth College *B, T*

West Virginia

Bethany College *B*
Davis and Elkins College *B*
Fairmont State College *B*
Potomac State College of West Virginia
　University *A*
West Virginia University *T*
Wheeling Jesuit University *B*

Wisconsin

Beloit College *B*
Cardinal Stritch University *B*
Carthage College *B, T*
Edgewood College *B*
Lawrence University *B, T*
Marian College of Fond du Lac *T*
Marquette University *B*
Mount Mary College *B, T*
Ripon College *B, T*
St. Norbert College *B, T*
University of Wisconsin
　Eau Claire *B*
　Green Bay *B*
　La Crosse *B*
　Madison *B, M, D*
　Milwaukee *B*
　Oshkosh *B*
　Parkside *T*
　River Falls *B*
　Stevens Point *B, T*
　Whitewater *B, T*

Wyoming

Casper College *A*
University of Wyoming *B, M*

French studies

California

Scripps College *B*

Colorado

Colorado College *B*

District of Columbia

American University *B*

Iowa

University of Iowa *M, D*

Minnesota

Concordia College: Moorhead *B, T*

New Hampshire

University of New Hampshire *B*

New Jersey

William Paterson University of New
　Jersey *B*

New York

Bard College *B*
Columbia University
　Columbia College *B*
Sarah Lawrence College *B*

Ohio

Case Western Reserve University *B*

Rhode Island

Brown University *B, M, D*

Washington

University of Washington *B*

French teacher education

Alabama

Birmingham-Southern College *T*

Arizona

Arizona State University *B, T*
Prescott College *T*
University of Arizona *B, M*

Arkansas

Arkansas State University *B, T*
Ouachita Baptist University *B, T*
University of Central Arkansas *T*

California

California State University
　Chico *T*
　Long Beach *T*
　San Bernardino *T*
Humboldt State University *T*
Pacific Union College *T*
San Diego State University *B, T*
San Francisco State University *B, T*
San Jose State University *T*
University of the Pacific *T*

Colorado

Colorado State University *T*

Connecticut

Central Connecticut State University *B*
Fairfield University *T*

Delaware

Delaware State University *B*
University of Delaware *B, T*

Florida

Stetson University *B, T*

Georgia

Fort Valley State University *B, T*
Georgia Southern University *B, M*
Georgia Southwestern State
　University *B, M, T*
Kennesaw State University *B*
North Georgia College & State
　University *B*
Valdosta State University *T*

Hawaii

University of Hawaii
　Manoa *B, T*

Idaho

Boise State University *T*

Illinois

Augustana College *B, T*
Dominican University *T*
Elmhurst College *B*
Illinois College *T*
Loyola University of Chicago *T*
North Park University *T*
Northwestern University *B, T*
Rockford College *T*
Roosevelt University *B*
Sauk Valley Community College *A*
University of Illinois
　Chicago *B*
　Urbana-Champaign *B, M, T*
Wheaton College *T*

Indiana

Anderson University *B, T*
Ball State University *T*
Franklin College *B, T*
Grace College *B*
Indiana University
　Bloomington *B, T*
　Northwest *B*
　South Bend *B*
Indiana University-Purdue University
　Fort Wayne *T*

Indiana University-Purdue University
　Indianapolis *B, T*
Indiana Wesleyan University *T*
Manchester College *B, T*
Purdue University
　Calumet *B*
Saint Mary's College *T*
St. Mary-of-the-Woods College *B*
Taylor University *B, T*
University of Evansville *B*
University of Indianapolis *B, T*
University of Southern Indiana *T*
Valparaiso University *B*
Vincennes University *A*

Iowa

Central College *T*
Clarke College *B, T*
Cornell College *B, T*
Graceland University *T*
Iowa State University *T*
Loras College *T*
Luther College *B*
Northwestern College *T*
St. Ambrose University *B, T*
University of Iowa *B, D, T*
Wartburg College *T*

Kansas

Baker University *T*
Benedictine College *B, T*
Pittsburg State University *B, T*

Kentucky

Murray State University *B, M, T*

Louisiana

Centenary College of Louisiana *B, T*
Grambling State University *B*
Louisiana State University
　Shreveport *B*
Louisiana Tech University *B*
Southeastern Louisiana University *B*
Southern University and Agricultural and
　Mechanical College *B*

Maine

University of Maine *B*
University of Southern Maine *T*

Maryland

Salisbury University *T*
Towson University *T*
Washington College *T*

Massachusetts

Assumption College *T*
Elms College *T*
Framingham State College *B, T*
Harvard College *T*
Tufts University *T*
University of Massachusetts
　Dartmouth *T*

Michigan

Alma College *T*
Calvin College *B*
Central Michigan University *B*
Eastern Michigan University *B, T*
Grand Valley State University *T*
Hope College *T*
Northern Michigan University *B, M, T*
Saginaw Valley State University *T*
University of Michigan
　Flint *T*
Western Michigan University *B*

Minnesota

Augsburg College *T*
Bemidji State University *T*
Bethel College *B*
College of St. Benedict *T*
College of St. Catherine *T*
Concordia College: Moorhead *B, T*
Gustavus Adolphus College *T*
Minnesota State University
　Mankato *B, M, T*
St. Cloud State University *T*
St. John's University *T*

St. Mary's University of Minnesota *B*
St. Olaf College *T*
University of Minnesota
　Duluth *B*
　Morris *T*
University of St. Thomas *B, T*
Winona State University *B, T*

Mississippi

Blue Mountain College *B*
Itawamba Community College *A*
Mississippi College *B, T*
Mississippi State University *T*
University of Mississippi *B, T*

Missouri

Central Missouri State University *B, T*
College of the Ozarks *B, T*
Lindenwood University *M*
Missouri Southern State College *B, T*
Missouri Western State College *B*
Northwest Missouri State
　University *B, T*
Rockhurst University *B*
Southwest Missouri State University *B*
Truman State University *M, T*
University of Missouri
　Columbia *B*
　St. Louis *T*
Washington University in St.
　Louis *B, M, T*
William Jewell College *T*

Montana

Montana State University
　Billings *T*
University of Montana-Missoula *T*

Nebraska

Creighton University *T*
Doane College *T*
Nebraska Wesleyan University *T*
University of Nebraska
　Kearney *B*
　Lincoln *B, T*

New Hampshire

Keene State College *B, T*
Plymouth State College *T*
St. Anselm College *T*
University of New Hampshire *T*

New Jersey

Georgian Court College *T*
Monmouth University *B, T*
Richard Stockton College of New
　Jersey *B*
Rowan University *T*

New York

Alfred University *T*
Canisius College *B, M, T*
City University of New York
　Brooklyn College *B*
　City College *B*
　Hunter College *B, M, T*
　Queens College *M, T*
D'Youville College *M, T*
Daemen College *B, T*
Elmira College *B, T*
Fordham University *M, T*
Hofstra University *B, M*
Houghton College *B, T*
Ithaca College *B, T*
Long Island University
　C. W. Post Campus *B, T*
Manhattan College *B, T*
Marist College *B, T*
Marymount College of Fordham
　University *B, T*
Molloy College *B*
New York University *B, M, T*
Niagara University *B, T*
Pace University *B, M, T*
Pace University:
　Pleasantville/Briarcliff *B, M, T*
St. Bonaventure University *B*
St. John Fisher College *B, T*

St. John's University *B, M, T*
St. Lawrence University *T*
State University of New York
   Albany *B, M, T*
   Buffalo *T*
   College at Brockport *B, T*
   College at Buffalo *B*
   College at Cortland *B, M*
   College at Fredonia *B, T*
   College at Geneseo *B, M, T*
   College at Oneonta *B, T*
   College at Plattsburgh *B, M*
   College at Potsdam *B, T*
   New Paltz *B, M, T*
   Oswego *B*
   Stony Brook *T*
Vassar College *T*
Wells College *T*

North Carolina

Appalachian State University *M*
Campbell University *B, T*
Davidson College *T*
East Carolina University *B*
Gardner-Webb University *B*
Meredith College *T*
North Carolina Agricultural and
   Technical State University *B, T*
North Carolina Central University *B, M*
North Carolina State University *T*
Queens University of Charlotte *T*
Salem College *T*
University of North Carolina
   Charlotte *B*
   Greensboro *B, M, T*
   Wilmington *B*
Wake Forest University *M, T*

North Dakota

Minot State University *B*
North Dakota State University *B, T*
University of North Dakota *B, T*

Ohio

Ashland University *B, T*
Baldwin-Wallace College *T*
Bowling Green State University *B, M*
Case Western Reserve University *T*
Hiram College *T*
Kent State University *T*
Kent State University
   Stark Campus *B*
Miami University
   Oxford Campus *B, M, T*
Mount Union College *T*
Ohio Northern University *B*
Ohio University *B*
Otterbein College *B*
University of Akron *B, T*
University of Dayton *B, M, T*
University of Toledo *B, M, T*
Xavier University *M*
Youngstown State University *B, M, T*

Oklahoma

Northeastern State University *B*
Oklahoma Baptist University *B, T*
Oklahoma City University *B*
University of Central Oklahoma *B*
University of Tulsa *T*

Oregon

Linfield College *T*
Oregon State University *M*
Portland State University *T*
University of Portland *T*
Western Oregon University *T*

Pennsylvania

Albright College *T*
Cabrini College *B*
California University of
   Pennsylvania *B, T*
Dickinson College *T*
Duquesne University *B, T*
Gettysburg College *T*
Grove City College *B, T*

Holy Family University *B, M, T*
Juniata College *B, T*
King's College *T*
La Salle University *B, T*
Lebanon Valley College of
   Pennsylvania *B, T*
Lock Haven University of
   Pennsylvania *B, T*
Lycoming College *T*
Marywood University *B*
Messiah College *T*
Moravian College *T*
St. Vincent College *T*
Seton Hill University *T*
Slippery Rock University of
   Pennsylvania *B, T*
Villanova University *T*
Washington and Jefferson College *T*
Widener University *T*
Wilkes University *T*

Rhode Island

Rhode Island College *B*
Salve Regina University *B*

South Carolina

Columbia College *B*
Furman University *T*
South Carolina State University *B, T*
Wofford College *T*

South Dakota

Augustana College *B, T*
University of South Dakota *T*

Tennessee

Belmont University *T*
King College *T*
Southern Adventist University *B*
Tennessee Technological University *T*
Union University *B, T*
University of Tennessee
   Martin *B, T*

Texas

Baylor University *B, T*
Hardin-Simmons University *B, T*
Houston Baptist University *T*
Lamar University *T*
St. Mary's University *T*
San Antonio College *A*
Southwest Texas State University *M, T*
Texas A&M University
   Commerce *T*
   Kingsville *T*
Texas Christian University *T*
University of Dallas *T*
University of Houston *T*
University of Texas
   Arlington *T*
   San Antonio *T*

Utah

Brigham Young University *B*
Southern Utah University *B, T*
University of Utah *B*
Weber State University *B*

Vermont

Bennington College *B, M, T*
St. Michael's College *T*

Virginia

Bridgewater College *T*
Eastern Mennonite University *T*
Hollins University *T*
Longwood University *B, T*
Radford University *T*
University of Virginia's College at
   Wise *T*
Virginia Wesleyan College *T*

Washington

Central Washington University *B, T*
Eastern Washington University *M*
Pacific Lutheran University *B*
Whitworth College *B, T*

West Virginia

Wheeling Jesuit University *T*

Wisconsin

Carthage College *T*
Edgewood College *B*
Lawrence University *T*
Marquette University *B*
Mount Mary College *B, T*
St. Norbert College *T*
University of Wisconsin
   Green Bay *T*
   La Crosse *B, T*
   Parkside *T*
   River Falls *T*
   Whitewater *B*

Funeral direction

Indiana

Vincennes University *A*

Tennessee

John A. Gupton College *A*

Funeral services/mortuary science

Alabama

Bishop State Community College *A*
Jefferson State Community College *C, A*

Arkansas

Arkansas State University
   Mountain Home *A*
University of Arkansas
   Community College at Hope *A*

Colorado

Arapahoe Community College *A*

Connecticut

Briarwood College *A*

District of Columbia

University of the District of Columbia *A*

Florida

Miami-Dade Community College *A*
St. Petersburg College *A*

Georgia

Gupton Jones College of Funeral
   Service *C, A*

Illinois

Carl Sandburg College *A*
City Colleges of Chicago
   Malcolm X College *A*
Southern Illinois University
   Carbondale *B*

Indiana

Ivy Tech State College
   Northwest *A*
Mid-America College of Funeral
   Service *C, A*
Vincennes University *A*

Iowa

Marshalltown Community College *A*
North Iowa Area Community College *A*
Upper Iowa University *B*

Kansas

Barton County Community College *A*

Louisiana

Delgado Community College *A*

Maryland

Community College of Baltimore County
   Catonsville *C, A*
   Dundalk *C, A*
   Essex *C, A*

Massachusetts

Mount Ida College *A, B*

Michigan

Eastern Michigan University *B*
Ferris State University *B*
Gogebic Community College *A*
Schoolcraft College *A*
Wayne State University *B*

Minnesota

University of Minnesota
   Twin Cities *B*

Mississippi

University of Southern Mississippi *B*

Missouri

Lindenwood University *B*
St. Louis Community College
   St. Louis Community College at
     Forest Park *C, A*

New Jersey

Hudson County Community College *A*
Mercer County Community College *C, A*

New York

American Academy McAllister Institute
   of Funeral Service *C, A*
City University of New York
   La Guardia Community College *A*
Fulton-Montgomery Community
   College *A*
Hudson Valley Community College *A*
Nassau Community College *A*
St. John's University *A*
State University of New York
   College of Technology at
     Canton *A, B*

North Carolina

Edgecombe Community College *A*
Fayetteville Technical Community
   College *C, A*
Forsyth Technical Community College *C*

Ohio

Cincinnati College of Mortuary
   Science *A, B*

Oklahoma

University of Central Oklahoma *C, B*

Oregon

Mount Hood Community College *A*

Pennsylvania

Luzerne County Community College *A*
Northampton County Area Community
   College *A*
Point Park College *A, B*
Thiel College *B*

South Carolina

Florence-Darlington Technical College *A*
Piedmont Technical College *A*

Tennessee

John A. Gupton College *C, A*

Texas

Amarillo College *A*
Commonwealth Institute of Funeral
   Service *C, A*
Dallas Institute of Funeral Service *C, A*
San Antonio College *A*

Washington

Spokane Falls Community College *A*

Wisconsin

Milwaukee Area Technical College *A*

Furniture design/manufacturing

Georgia

Savannah College of Art and
   Design *B, M*

Michigan

Ferris State University *B*

New York
Rochester Institute of
Technology *A, B, M*
State University of New York
College of Agriculture and
Technology at Morrisville *A*

Gay/lesbian studies

Iowa
University of Iowa *C*

Maryland
University of Maryland
College Park *C*

Genetic counseling

California
University of California
Irvine *M*

Indiana
Martin University *B*

Iowa
Morningside College *B*

Louisiana
Louisiana State University
Alexandria *A*

Ohio
Case Western Reserve University *M*

Genetics

Alabama
University of Alabama
Birmingham *D*

Arizona
University of Arizona *M, D*

California
California Institute of Technology *D*
California State University
Stanislaus *B*
Stanford University *M, D*
University of California
Davis *B, M, D*
Los Angeles *M, D*
Riverside *D*

Connecticut
University of Connecticut *M, D*
Yale University *M, D*

District of Columbia
George Washington University *M, D*
Howard University *M, D*

Georgia
Oxford College of Emory University *B*
University of Georgia *B, M, D*

Hawaii
University of Hawaii
Manoa *M, D*

Illinois
University of Chicago *M, D*
University of Illinois
Chicago *D*

Indiana
Ball State University *B*
Indiana University
Bloomington *D*
Indiana University-Purdue University
Indianapolis *M, D*

Iowa
Iowa State University *B, M, D*
University of Iowa *D*

Kansas
Kansas State University *M, D*
University of Kansas *B*

Louisiana
Tulane University *M, D*

Maryland
Johns Hopkins University *D*
University of Maryland
Baltimore *M, D*

Massachusetts
Hampshire College *B*
Tufts University *M, D*

Michigan
Michigan State University *D*
University of Michigan *M, D*

Minnesota
Minnesota State University
Mankato *B*
St. Cloud State University *B*
University of Minnesota
Twin Cities *M, D*

Mississippi
Mississippi State University *M*

Missouri
Missouri Southern State College *B*
University of Missouri
Columbia *D*
Washington University in St. Louis *D*

New Hampshire
Dartmouth College *B, M, D*
University of New Hampshire *M, D*

New Jersey
Rutgers, The State University of New
Jersey
New Brunswick Regional
Campus *B*

New York
Cornell University *B, M, D*
Hofstra University *M*
State University of New York
Albany *D*
Buffalo *M, D*
College of Environmental Science
and Forestry *B, M, D*
Stony Brook *D*
University of Rochester *M, D*
Yeshiva University *M, D*

North Carolina
North Carolina State University *M, D*
University of North Carolina
Chapel Hill *M, D*
Wake Forest University *D*

Ohio
Case Western Reserve University *D*
Ohio State University
Columbus Campus *B, M, D*
Ohio Wesleyan University *B*
Wittenberg University *B*

Oregon
Oregon State University *M, D*
University of Oregon *M, D*

Pennsylvania
Cedar Crest College *B*
Penn State
University Park *M, D*
University of Pennsylvania *M, D*

South Carolina
Clemson University *B, M*

Texas
Texas A&M University *B, M, D*
University of Texas
Southwestern Medical Center at
Dallas *M, D*

Utah
Brigham Young University *M, D*
Dixie State College of Utah *A*

Vermont
Bennington College *B*
Marlboro College *B*

Virginia
Virginia Commonwealth
University *M, D*
Virginia Polytechnic Institute and State
University *D*

Washington
University of Washington *M, D*
Washington State University *B, M, D*

West Virginia
West Virginia University *M, D*

Wisconsin
Marquette University *M, D*
University of Wisconsin
Madison *M, D*

Geochemistry

Arizona
Northern Arizona University *B*

California
California Institute of Technology *B, D*
Pomona College *B*
San Diego State University *B*
San Francisco State University *B*
University of California
Los Angeles *M, D*

Colorado
Colorado School of Mines *M, D*

Maine
Bowdoin College *B*

Maryland
Johns Hopkins University *M, D*

Massachusetts
Bridgewater State College *B*
Hampshire College *B*
Harvard College *B*

Michigan
Grand Valley State University *B*
Hope College *B*

Missouri
University of Missouri
Rolla *B, M, D*

Montana
Montana Tech of the University of
Montana *M*

Nevada
University of Nevada
Reno *M, D*

New Mexico
New Mexico Institute of Mining and
Technology *M, D*

New York
Columbia University
Columbia College *B*
State University of New York
Albany *M, D*
College at Cortland *B*
College at Fredonia *B*
College at Geneseo *B*
Oswego *B*

Oregon
University of Oregon *M, D*

Rhode Island
Brown University *B*

Texas
University of Texas
Dallas *M, D*

Utah
Snow College *A*

Geography

Alabama
Auburn University *B*
Jacksonville State University *B*
Samford University *B*
University of Alabama *B, M*
University of North Alabama *B*
University of South Alabama *B*

Alaska
University of Alaska
Fairbanks *B*

Arizona
Arizona State University *B, M, D*
Northern Arizona University *B, M, T*
University of Arizona *B, M, D*

Arkansas
Arkansas State University *B*
University of Arkansas *B, M*
University of Central Arkansas *B*

California
Bakersfield College *A*
Cabrillo College *A*
California State Polytechnic University:
Pomona *B*
California State University
Chico *B, M*
Dominguez Hills *B*
Fresno *B, M*
Fullerton *B, M*
Hayward *B, M*
Long Beach *B, M*
Los Angeles *B, M*
Northridge *B*
Sacramento *B*
San Bernardino *B*
Stanislaus *B*
Cerritos Community College *A*
Chabot College *A*
College of Alameda *A*
Contra Costa College *A*
De Anza College *A*
East Los Angeles College *A*
Foothill College *A*
Gavilan Community College *A*
Grossmont Community College *A*
Humboldt State University *B*
Irvine Valley College *A*
Los Angeles Pierce College *C*
Los Angeles Southwest College *A*
MiraCosta College *A*
Ohlone College *C*
Orange Coast College *A*
San Diego City College *A*
San Diego State University *B, M, D*
San Francisco State University *B, M*
San Jose State University *B, M*
Santa Barbara City College *A*
Santa Rosa Junior College *A*
Santiago Canyon College *A*
Sonoma State University *B*
Southwestern College *A*
University of California
Berkeley *B, D*
Davis *B, M, D*
Los Angeles *B, M, D*
Santa Barbara *B, M, D*
University of Southern
California *B, M, D*
Ventura College *A*

Colorado
United States Air Force Academy *B*

University of Colorado
  Boulder *B, M, D*
  Colorado Springs *B, M*
  Denver *B*
University of Denver *B, M, D*
University of Northern Colorado *B, T*

Connecticut

Central Connecticut State
  University *B, M*
Southern Connecticut State University *B*
University of Connecticut *B, M, D*

Delaware

University of Delaware *B, M*

District of Columbia

George Washington University *B, M*
University of the District of Columbia *B*

Florida

Broward Community College *A*
Florida Atlantic University *B, M*
Florida International University *B*
Florida State University *B, M, D*
Jacksonville University *B*
Palm Beach Community College *A*
Polk Community College *A*
South Florida Community College *A*
Stetson University *B*
University of Florida *B, M, D*
University of Miami *B*
University of South Florida *B, M*
University of Tampa *A*
University of West Florida *B*

Georgia

Dalton State College *A*
Georgia Southern University *B*
Georgia State University *B, M*
State University of West Georgia *B, M*
University of Georgia *B, M, D*

Hawaii

University of Hawaii
  Hilo *B*
  Manoa *B, M, D*

Idaho

College of Southern Idaho *A*
University of Idaho *B, M, D*

Illinois

Augustana College *B, T*
Chicago State University *B, M, T*
Concordia University *B*
De Paul University *B, T*
Eastern Illinois University *B*
Elmhurst College *B, T*
Illinois State University *B, T*
Lincoln College *A*
Lincoln Land Community College *A*
Northeastern Illinois University *B, M*
Northern Illinois University *B, M*
Northwestern University *B*
Parkland College *A*
Richland Community College *A*
Roosevelt University *B*
South Suburban College of Cook
  County *A*
Southern Illinois University
  Carbondale *B, M, D*
Southern Illinois University
  Edwardsville *B, M*
Southwestern Illinois College *A*
Triton College *A*
University of Chicago *B, M*
University of Illinois
  Chicago *B, M*
  Urbana-Champaign *B, M, D*
Western Illinois University *B, M*

Indiana

Ball State University *B*
DePauw University *B*
Indiana State University *B, M, D, T*
Indiana University
  Bloomington *B, M, D*
  Southeast *B*

Indiana University-Purdue University
  Indianapolis *B, M*
Taylor University *B*
Valparaiso University *C, B*
Vincennes University *A*

Iowa

Graceland University *T*
North Iowa Area Community College *A*
University of Iowa *B, M, D, T*
University of Northern Iowa *B, M*

Kansas

Allen County Community College *A*
Benedictine College *T*
Kansas State University *B, M, D*
Pittsburg State University *B, T*
University of Kansas *B, M, D*

Kentucky

Morehead State University *B*
Murray State University *B, M, T*
University of Kentucky *B, M, D*
University of Louisville *B*

Louisiana

Grambling State University *B*
Louisiana State University
  Shreveport *B*
Louisiana State University and
  Agricultural and Mechanical
  College *B, M, D*
Louisiana Tech University *B*
Nicholls State University *A*
University of Louisiana at Monroe *B, M*
University of New Orleans *B, M*

Maine

University of Maine
  Farmington *B*
University of Southern Maine *B*

Maryland

Community College of Baltimore County
  Catonsville *A*
  Dundalk *A*
  Essex *A*
Frostburg State University *B*
Johns Hopkins University *B, M, D*
Salisbury University *B, T*
Towson University *B, M*
University of Maryland
  Baltimore County *B*
  College Park *B, M, D*

Massachusetts

Boston University *B, M, D*
Bridgewater State College *B*
Clark University *B, M, D*
Fitchburg State College *B*
Framingham State College *B*
Hampshire College *B*
Mount Holyoke College *B*
Salem State College *B, M*
University of Massachusetts
  Amherst *B, M*
  Boston *B*

Michigan

Aquinas College *B, T*
Calvin College *B, T*
Central Michigan University *B, T*
Eastern Michigan University *B, M*
Grand Valley State University *B*
Lansing Community College *A*
Michigan State University *B, M, D*
Northern Michigan University *B, T*
University of Michigan *B*
University of Michigan
  Flint *B*
Wayne State University *B, M*
Western Michigan University *B, M*

Minnesota

Bemidji State University *B*
Gustavus Adolphus College *B*
Macalester College *B*
Minnesota State University
  Mankato *B, M, T*

St. Cloud State University *B, M*
University of Minnesota
  Duluth *B*
  Twin Cities *B, M, D*
University of St. Thomas *B*
Vermilion Community College *A*
Winona State University *A*

Mississippi

University of Southern Mississippi *B, M*

Missouri

Central Missouri State University *B*
East Central College *A*
Northwest Missouri State University *B*
Southeast Missouri State University *B*
Southwest Missouri State University *B*
Three Rivers Community College *A*
University of Missouri
  Columbia *B, M*
  Kansas City *B*

Montana

Montana State University
  Billings *T*
University of Montana-Missoula *B, M*

Nebraska

Concordia University *B, T*
University of Nebraska
  Kearney *B, T*
  Lincoln *B, M, D*
  Omaha *B, M*
Wayne State College *B, T*
Western Nebraska Community
  College *A*

Nevada

University of Nevada
  Reno *B, M*

New Hampshire

Dartmouth College *B*
Keene State College *B*
Plymouth State College *B*
University of New Hampshire *B*

New Jersey

Montclair State University *B*
Rowan University *B*
Rutgers, The State University of New
  Jersey
    New Brunswick Regional
    Campus *B, M, D*
William Paterson University of New
  Jersey *B*

New Mexico

New Mexico State University *B, M*
University of New Mexico *B, M*

New York

City University of New York
  Hunter College *B, M*
Colgate University *B*
Erie Community College
  City Campus *C*
  North Campus *C*
  South Campus *C*
Excelsior College *B*
Hofstra University *B*
Long Island University
  C. W. Post Campus *B*
State University of New York
  Albany *B, M*
  Binghamton *B, M*
  Buffalo *B, M, D*
  College at Buffalo *B*
  College at Cortland *B*
  College at Geneseo *B, T*
  College at Oneonta *B*
  College at Plattsburgh *B*
  College at Potsdam *B*
  New Paltz *B*
Syracuse University *B, M, D*
United States Military Academy *B*
Vassar College *B*

North Carolina

Appalachian State University *B*
East Carolina University *B, M*
Fayetteville State University *B*
North Carolina Central University *B*
University of North Carolina
  Chapel Hill *B, M, D*
  Charlotte *B, M*
  Greensboro *B, M, T*
  Wilmington *B*

North Dakota

Minot State University *B*
University of North Dakota *B, M, T*

Ohio

Bowling Green State University *B*
Kent State University *B, M, D*
Kent State University
  Stark Campus *B*
Miami University
  Middletown Campus *A*
  Oxford Campus *B, M*
Ohio State University
  Columbus Campus *B, M, D*
Ohio University *B, M*
Ohio Wesleyan University *B*
Sinclair Community College *A*
University of Akron *B, M*
University of Cincinnati *B, M, D, T*
University of Toledo *C, B, M*
Wittenberg University *B*
Wright State University *B*
Youngstown State University *B*

Oklahoma

Langston University *B*
Northeastern State University *B*
Oklahoma State University *B, M*
Tulsa Community College *A*
University of Central Oklahoma *B*
University of Oklahoma *B, M, D*

Oregon

Central Oregon Community College *A*
Chemeketa Community College *A*
Linn-Benton Community College *A*
Oregon State University *B, M, D*
Portland State University *B, M*
Southern Oregon University *B*
University of Oregon *B, M, D*
Western Oregon University *B*

Pennsylvania

Bloomsburg University of
  Pennsylvania *B*
Bucknell University *B*
California University of
  Pennsylvania *B, M*
Cheyney University of Pennsylvania *B*
East Stroudsburg University of
  Pennsylvania *B*
Edinboro University of Pennsylvania *B*
Indiana University of Pennsylvania *B, M*
Kutztown University of Pennsylvania *B*
Lock Haven University of
  Pennsylvania *B, T*
Millersville University of
  Pennsylvania *B, T*
Penn State
  Abington *B*
  Altoona *B*
  Beaver *B*
  Berks *B*
  Delaware County *B*
  Dubois *B*
  Fayette *B*
  Hazleton *B*
  Lehigh Valley *B*
  McKeesport *B*
  Mont Alto *B*
  New Kensington *B*
  Shenango *B*
  University Park *B, M, D*
  Wilkes-Barre *B*
  Worthington Scranton *B*

Shippensburg University of
Pennsylvania *B, T*
Slippery Rock University of
Pennsylvania *B, T*
Temple University *M*
University of Pittsburgh *C*
University of Pittsburgh
Johnstown *B*
Villanova University *B*
West Chester University of
Pennsylvania *B, M*

Puerto Rico
University of Puerto Rico
Rio Piedras Campus *B*

Rhode Island
Rhode Island College *B*

South Carolina
Francis Marion University *B*
University of South Carolina *B, M, D*

South Dakota
South Dakota State University *B, M, T*

Tennessee
Columbia State Community College *A*
East Tennessee State University *B*
Southwest Tennessee Community
College *A*
University of Memphis *B, M*
University of Tennessee
Knoxville *B, M, D*
Martin *B*

Texas
Austin Community College *A*
Baylor University *B*
Del Mar College *A*
Galveston College *A*
Sam Houston State University *B*
Southwest Texas State
University *B, M, D, T*
Stephen F. Austin State University *B, T*
Texas A&M University *B, M, D*
Texas A&M University
Commerce *B, M*
Texas Tech University *B*
University of Houston
Clear Lake *B*
University of North Texas *B, M*
University of Texas
Arlington *T*
Austin *B, M, D*
Dallas *B, M*
San Antonio *B*
West Texas A&M University *B, T*
Western Texas College *A*

Utah
Brigham Young University *B, M*
Salt Lake Community College *A*
Snow College *A*
University of Utah *B, M, D*
Utah State University *B, M*
Weber State University *B*

Vermont
Middlebury College *B*
University of Vermont *B, M*

Virginia
Emory & Henry College *B*
George Mason University *B, M*
James Madison University *B, T*
Longwood University *T*
Mary Washington College *B*
Old Dominion University *B*
Radford University *B*
Virginia Polytechnic Institute and State
University *B, M*

Washington
Central Washington University *B*
Eastern Washington University *B, T*
Everett Community College *A*
University of Washington *B, M, D*
Western Washington University *B, M, T*

West Virginia
Concord College *B*
Marshall University *B, M*
West Virginia University *B, M, D*

Wisconsin
Carroll College *B*
Carthage College *B, T*
University of Wisconsin
Eau Claire *B*
La Crosse *B, T*
Madison *B, M, D*
Milwaukee *B, M, D*
Oshkosh *B*
Parkside *B, T*
Platteville *B, T*
River Falls *B, T*
Stevens Point *B, T*
Whitewater *B, T*

Wyoming
Casper College *A*
University of Wyoming *B, M*
Western Wyoming Community
College *A*

Geography teacher education

Kansas
Benedictine College *B, T*

Minnesota
Vermilion Community College *A*

New York
City University of New York
Hunter College *B, M, T*
State University of New York
Buffalo *M, T*

Ohio
Kent State University *T*

Utah
University of Utah *B*

Wisconsin
Carroll College *B, T*

Geological engineering

Alaska
University of Alaska
Fairbanks *B, M*

Arizona
University of Arizona *B*

California
University of Southern California *M*

Colorado
Colorado School of Mines *B, M, D*

Idaho
University of Idaho *B, M*

Illinois
University of Illinois
Chicago *D*

Massachusetts
Harvard College *B*

Michigan
Michigan Technological
University *B, M, D, T*

Minnesota
University of Minnesota
Twin Cities *B, M, D*

Mississippi
University of Mississippi *B*

Missouri
University of Missouri
Rolla *B, M, D*

Montana
Montana Tech of the University of
Montana *B, M*

Nevada
University of Nevada
Reno *B, M*

New Mexico
New Mexico State University *B*

New York
Columbia University
Fu Foundation School of
Engineering and Applied
Science *B, M, D*

North Dakota
University of North Dakota *B*

Oklahoma
University of Oklahoma *M, D*
University of Tulsa *B, M*

Pennsylvania
Drexel University *M*

South Dakota
South Dakota School of Mines and
Technology *B, M, D*

Texas
University of Texas
Austin *B*

Utah
University of Utah *B, M, D*

Wisconsin
University of Wisconsin
Madison *B, M, D*

Geology/earth science

Alabama
Auburn University *B, M*
University of Alabama *B, M, D*
University of North Alabama *B*
University of South Alabama *B*

Alaska
University of Alaska
Fairbanks *B, M, D*

Arizona
Arizona State University *B, M, D*
Arizona Western College *A*
Eastern Arizona College *A*
Northern Arizona University *B, M*
Prescott College *B, M*
University of Arizona *B, M, D*

Arkansas
Arkansas Tech University *B*
University of Arkansas *B, M*
University of Arkansas
Little Rock *B*

California
Bakersfield College *A*
California Institute of Technology *B, D*
California State Polytechnic University:
Pomona *B*
California State University
Bakersfield *B, M*
Chico *B, M*
Dominguez Hills *B*
Fresno *B, M*
Fullerton *B, M*
Hayward *B, M*
Long Beach *B, M*
Los Angeles *B, M*
Northridge *B, M*
Sacramento *B*
San Bernardino *B*
Stanislaus *B*
Cerritos Community College *A*
College of the Siskiyous *A*
De Anza College *A*

East Los Angeles College *A*
Foothill College *A*
Gavilan Community College *A*
Golden West College *A*
Grossmont Community College *A*
Humboldt State University *B*
Irvine Valley College *A*
Loma Linda University *B, M*
Los Angeles Southwest College *A*
MiraCosta College *A*
Moorpark College *A*
Occidental College *B*
Ohlone College *C*
Orange Coast College *A*
Palomar College *A*
Pomona College *B*
San Diego City College *A*
San Diego State University *B, D*
San Francisco State University *B, M*
San Joaquin Delta College *A*
San Jose State University *B, M*
Santa Barbara City College *A*
Santa Monica College *A*
Santiago Canyon College *A*
Scripps College *B*
Sierra College *A*
Sonoma State University *B*
Southwestern College *A*
Stanford University *B, M, D*
University of California
Davis *B, M, D*
Los Angeles *B, M, D*
Riverside *B*
Santa Barbara *B, M, D*
Santa Cruz *B, D*
University of Southern
California *B, M, D*
University of the Pacific *B*
Ventura College *A*
West Valley College *A*

Colorado
Colorado College *B*
Colorado Mountain College
Spring Valley Campus *A*
Colorado School of Mines *M, D*
Colorado State University *B, M, T*
Fort Lewis College *B*
Red Rocks Community College *A*
University of Colorado
Boulder *B, M, D*
Denver *B*

Connecticut
Eastern Connecticut State University *B*
University of Connecticut *B, M, D*
Wesleyan University *B*
Yale University *B, M, D*

Delaware
University of Delaware *B, M, D*

District of Columbia
George Washington University *B, M, D*

Florida
Florida Atlantic University *B, M*
Florida International University *B, M, D*
Florida State University *B, M, D*
Gulf Coast Community College *A*
Miami-Dade Community College *A*
Okaloosa-Walton Community College *A*
Pensacola Junior College *A*
South Florida Community College *A*
University of Florida *B, M, D*
University of Miami *B, M*
University of South Florida *B, M, D*

Georgia
Clayton College and State University *A*
Columbus State University *B*
East Georgia College *A*
Gainesville College *A*
Georgia Institute of Technology *B, M, D*
Georgia Perimeter College *A*
Georgia Southern University *B*
Georgia Southwestern State University *B*

Georgia State University *B, M*
Middle Georgia College *A*
State University of West Georgia *B*
University of Georgia *B, M, D*

Hawaii

University of Hawaii
    Hilo *B*
    Manoa *B*

Idaho

Boise State University *B, M*
Brigham Young University - Idaho *B*
College of Southern Idaho *A*
Idaho State University *A, B, M*
Lewis-Clark State College *B*
North Idaho College *A*
University of Idaho *B, M, D*

Illinois

Augustana College *B, T*
Bradley University *B, T*
Eastern Illinois University *B*
Illinois Central College *A*
Illinois State University *B*
Illinois Valley Community College *A*
Northern Illinois University *B, M, D*
Northwestern University *B, M, D*
Olivet Nazarene University *B*
Parkland College *A*
South Suburban College of Cook
    County *A*
Southern Illinois University
    Carbondale *B, M, D*
Triton College *A*
University of Illinois
    Chicago *B, M*
    Urbana-Champaign *B, M, D*
Western Illinois University *B*
Wheaton College *B, T*

Indiana

Ball State University *B, M*
DePauw University *B*
Earlham College *B*
Hanover College *B*
Indiana State University *B, M, T*
Indiana University
    Bloomington *B, M, D*
    Northwest *B*
Indiana University-Purdue University
    Fort Wayne *B*
Indiana University-Purdue University
    Indianapolis *B, M*
Purdue University *B, M, D*
Taylor University *B*
University of Notre Dame *B*
University of Southern Indiana *B*
Valparaiso University *B*
Vincennes University *A*

Iowa

Cornell College *B, T*
Iowa State University *B, M, D*
University of Iowa *B, M, D, T*
University of Northern Iowa *B*

Kansas

Fort Hays State University *B, M*
Kansas State University *B, M*
University of Kansas *B, M, D*
Wichita State University *B, M*

Kentucky

Morehead State University *B*
Murray State University *B, T*
University of Kentucky *B, M, D*

Louisiana

Centenary College of Louisiana *B*
Louisiana State University and
    Agricultural and Mechanical
    College *B, M, D*
Louisiana Tech University *B*
Tulane University *B, M, D*
University of Louisiana at
    Lafayette *B, M*
University of Louisiana at Monroe *B, M*

University of New Orleans *B, M*

Maine

Bates College *B*
Bowdoin College *B*
Colby College *B*
University of Maine *B, M, D*
University of Maine
    Presque Isle *B*
University of Southern Maine *B*

Maryland

Johns Hopkins University *B, M, D*
Salisbury University *B*
Towson University *B*
University of Maryland
    College Park *B, M, D*

Massachusetts

Amherst College *B*
Boston College *B, M*
Boston University *B, M, D*
Bridgewater State College *B*
Hampshire College *B*
Massachusetts Institute of
    Technology *B, M, D*
Mount Holyoke College *B*
Northeastern University *B*
Salem State College *B*
Smith College *B*
Tufts University *B*
University of Massachusetts
    Amherst *B, M, D*
Wellesley College *B*
Williams College *B*

Michigan

Calvin College *B, T*
Central Michigan University *B, T*
Eastern Michigan University *B*
Grand Valley State University *B*
Hope College *B*
Michigan State University *B, M, D*
Michigan Technological
    University *B, M, D, T*
University of Michigan *B, M*
Wayne State University *B, M*
Western Michigan University *B, M, D*

Minnesota

Bemidji State University *B*
Carleton College *B*
Gustavus Adolphus College *B*
Macalester College *B, T*
Ridgewater College: A Community and
    Technical College *A*
University of Minnesota
    Duluth *B, M*
    Morris *B*
    Twin Cities *B, M, D*
University of St. Thomas *B*
Vermilion Community College *A*
Winona State University *B*

Mississippi

Itawamba Community College *A*
Millsaps College *B, T*
Mississippi State University *B, M*
University of Mississippi *B*
University of Southern Mississippi *B, M*

Missouri

Central Missouri State University *B*
East Central College *A*
Northwest Missouri State University *B*
St. Louis University *B*
Southeast Missouri State University *B*
Southwest Missouri State University *B*
University of Missouri
    Columbia *B, M, D*
    Kansas City *B, M*
    Rolla *B, M, D*

Montana

Montana Tech of the University of
    Montana *M*
Rocky Mountain College *B*
University of Montana-Missoula *B, M, D*

University of Montana: Western *B*

Nebraska

University of Nebraska
    Lincoln *B, M, D*
    Omaha *B*

Nevada

Great Basin College *A*
University of Nevada
    Las Vegas *B, M, D*
    Reno *B, M, D*

New Hampshire

Dartmouth College *M, D*
Keene State College *B*

New Jersey

Fairleigh Dickinson University
    College at Florham *B*
Montclair State University *B, M, T*
New Jersey City University *B*
Princeton University *B, M, D*
Richard Stockton College of New
    Jersey *B*
Rider University *B*
Rutgers, The State University of New
    Jersey
      New Brunswick Regional
        Campus *B, M, D*
      Newark Regional Campus *B*

New Mexico

Eastern New Mexico University *B*
New Mexico Institute of Mining and
    Technology *B, M, D*
New Mexico State University *B, M*
San Juan College *A*
University of New Mexico *B, M, D*

New York

Adirondack Community College *A*
Alfred University *B*
City University of New York
    Brooklyn College *B, M*
    City College *B, M*
    Hunter College *B*
    Queens College *B, M*
    York College *B*
Colgate University *B*
Columbia University
    Columbia College *B*
Concordia College *B*
Cornell University *B, M, D*
Excelsior College *B*
Hamilton College *B*
Hartwick College *B*
Hobart and William Smith Colleges *B*
Hofstra University *B*
Long Island University
    C. W. Post Campus *B*
Pace University:
    Pleasantville/Briarcliff *B*
Rensselaer Polytechnic Institute *B, M, D*
St. Lawrence University *B, T*
Sarah Lawrence College *B*
Skidmore College *B*
State University of New York
    Albany *B, M, D*
    Binghamton *B, M, D*
    Buffalo *B, M, D*
    College at Brockport *B*
    College at Buffalo *B*
    College at Cortland *B*
    College at Fredonia *B, T*
    College at Geneseo *B, T*
    College at Oneonta *B*
    College at Plattsburgh *B*
    College at Potsdam *B*
    New Paltz *B, M, T*
    Oswego *B*
    Stony Brook *B, M, D*
Suffolk County Community College *A*
Syracuse University *B, M, D*
Union College *B*
University of Rochester *B, M, D*
Vassar College *B*

North Carolina

Duke University *B, M, D*
East Carolina University *B, M*
Elizabeth City State University *B*
Guilford College *B*
North Carolina State University *B*
University of North Carolina
    Chapel Hill *B, M, D*
    Charlotte *B*
    Wilmington *B, M*
Western Carolina University *B*

North Dakota

Minot State University *B*
North Dakota State University *B, T*
University of North Dakota *B, M, D, T*

Ohio

Antioch College *B*
Ashland University *B*
Bowling Green State University *B, M*
Case Western Reserve
    University *B, M, D*
Central State University *B*
Cleveland State University *B*
College of Mount St. Joseph *B*
College of Wooster *B*
Denison University *B*
Kent State University *B, M, D*
Kent State University
    Stark Campus *B*
Marietta College *B*
Miami University
    Oxford Campus *B, M, D*
Mount Union College *B*
Muskingum College *B*
Oberlin College *B*
Ohio State University
    Columbus Campus *B, M, D*
Ohio University *B, M*
Ohio Wesleyan University *B*
Sinclair Community College *A*
University of Akron *B, M*
University of Cincinnati *B, M, D, T*
University of Dayton *B*
University of Toledo *B, M*
Wilmington College *B*
Wittenberg University *B*
Wright State University *B, M*
Youngstown State University *B*

Oklahoma

Oklahoma State University *B, M*
Tulsa Community College *A*
University of Oklahoma *B, M, D*
University of Tulsa *B, M, D*

Oregon

Central Oregon Community College *A*
Chemeketa Community College *A*
Oregon State University *B, M, D*
Portland State University *B, M*
Southern Oregon University *B*
University of Oregon *B, M, D*

Pennsylvania

Allegheny College *B*
Bloomsburg University of
    Pennsylvania *B*
Bryn Mawr College *B, M, D*
Bucknell University *B*
California University of Pennsylvania *B*
Dickinson College *B*
Edinboro University of Pennsylvania *B*
Franklin & Marshall College *B*
Haverford College *B*
Indiana University of Pennsylvania *B*
Juniata College *B*
Kutztown University of Pennsylvania *B*
La Salle University *B*
Lafayette College *B*
Lock Haven University of
    Pennsylvania *B*
Mercyhurst College *B*
Millersville University of
    Pennsylvania *B*

Penn State
Abington *B*
Altoona *B*
Beaver *B*
Berks *B*
Delaware County *B*
Dubois *B*
Fayette *B*
Hazleton *B*
Lehigh Valley *B*
McKeesport *B*
Mont Alto *B*
New Kensington *B*
Schuylkill - Capital College *B*
Shenango *B*
University Park *B, M, D*
Worthington Scranton *B*
York *B*
Slippery Rock University of
Pennsylvania *B, M, T*
Temple University *B, M*
University of Pennsylvania *B, D*
University of Pittsburgh *B, M, D*
University of Pittsburgh
Bradford *B*
Johnstown *B*
West Chester University of
Pennsylvania *B*

Puerto Rico
University of Puerto Rico
Mayaguez Campus *B, M*

Rhode Island
Brown University *B, M, D*
University of Rhode Island *B*

South Carolina
Charleston Southern University *B*
Clemson University *B, M*
College of Charleston *B*
Furman University *B*
University of South Carolina *B, M, D*

South Dakota
South Dakota School of Mines and
Technology *B, M, D*

Tennessee
Austin Peay State University *B*
Middle Tennessee State University *B*
Tennessee Technological University *B*
University of Memphis *B, M*
University of Tennessee
Chattanooga *B*
Knoxville *B, M, D*
Martin *B*
Vanderbilt University *B, M*

Texas
Amarillo College *A*
Austin Community College *A*
Baylor University *B, M, D*
Central Texas College *A*
Coastal Bend College *A*
Del Mar College *A*
El Paso Community College *A*
Galveston College *A*
Grayson County College *A*
Hardin-Simmons University *B*
Hill College *A*
Lamar University *B*
Laredo Community College *A*
Midland College *A*
Midwestern State University *B*
Odessa College *A*
Palo Alto College *A*
Panola College *A*
Rice University *B, M, D*
St. Mary's University *B, T*
Sam Houston State University *B*
South Plains College *A*
Southern Methodist University *B, M, D*
Stephen F. Austin State University *B, M*
Sul Ross State University *B, M*
Tarleton State University *B*
Texas A&M University *B, M, D*

Texas A&M University
Commerce *B*
Corpus Christi *B, T*
Kingsville *B, M, T*
Texas Christian University *B, M*
Texas Tech University *B, M, D*
Trinity University *B*
Tyler Junior College *A*
University of Houston *B, M, D*
University of Texas
Arlington *B, M*
Austin *B, M, D*
Dallas *B, M, D*
El Paso *B, M, D*
San Antonio *B, M*
of the Permian Basin *B, M*
West Texas A&M University *B*
Western Texas College *A*

Utah
Brigham Young University *B, M*
Dixie State College of Utah *A*
Salt Lake Community College *A*
Snow College *A*
Southern Utah University *B*
University of Utah *B, M, D*
Utah State University *B, M*
Weber State University *B*

Vermont
Castleton State College *B*
Middlebury College *B*
Norwich University *B*
University of Vermont *B, M*

Virginia
College of William and Mary *B*
George Mason University *B*
James Madison University *B*
Mary Washington College *B*
Old Dominion University *M*
Radford University *B*
Virginia Polytechnic Institute and State
University *B, M, D*
Washington and Lee University *B*

Washington
Central Washington University *B, M*
Centralia College *A*
Eastern Washington University *B, M*
Everett Community College *A*
Olympic College *A*
University of Puget Sound *B, T*
University of Washington *B, M, D*
Washington State University *B, M, D*
Western Washington University *B, M, T*
Whitman College *B*

West Virginia
Marshall University *B*
Potomac State College of West Virginia
University *A*
West Virginia University *B, M, D*

Wisconsin
Beloit College *B*
Lawrence University *B, T*
Northland College *B*
St. Norbert College *B*
University of Wisconsin
Eau Claire *B*
Madison *B, M, D*
Milwaukee *B, M, D*
Oshkosh *B*
Parkside *B, T*
River Falls *B*

Wyoming
Casper College *A*
University of Wyoming *B, M, D*
Western Wyoming Community
College *A*

Geophysics/seismology

Alaska
University of Alaska
Fairbanks *M, D*

California
California Institute of Technology *B, D*
California State University
Northridge *B*
Occidental College *B*
San Diego State University *B, M*
San Francisco State University *B*
Stanford University *B, M, D*
University of California
Los Angeles *B, M, D*
Riverside *B*
Santa Barbara *B, M*
Santa Cruz *B, D*

Colorado
Colorado School of Mines *M, D*
University of Colorado
Boulder *D*

Connecticut
University of Connecticut *B, D*

Delaware
University of Delaware *B*

Hawaii
University of Hawaii
Manoa *B, M, D*

Idaho
Boise State University *B, M*
Idaho State University *M*
University of Idaho *M*

Illinois
Northwestern University *B, M, D*
University of Chicago *B, M, D*

Kansas
Kansas State University *B*

Louisiana
University of New Orleans *B*

Maine
Bowdoin College *B*

Maryland
Johns Hopkins University *B, M, D*

Massachusetts
Boston College *B, M*
Boston University *B*
Harvard College *B*
Massachusetts Institute of Technology *D*

Michigan
Eastern Michigan University *B*
Hope College *B*
Michigan Technological University *B, M*
Western Michigan University *B*

Minnesota
University of Minnesota
Twin Cities *B, M, D*

Missouri
St. Louis University *B, M, D*
University of Missouri
Rolla *B, M, D*

Montana
Montana Tech of the University of
Montana *M*

Nevada
University of Nevada
Reno *B, M, D*

New Mexico
New Mexico Institute of Mining and
Technology *B, M, D*

New York
Columbia University
Columbia College *B*
St. Lawrence University *B*
State University of New York
College at Fredonia *B*
College at Geneseo *B*

North Carolina
North Carolina State University *B*

Ohio
Ohio State University
Columbus Campus *B, M, D*
University of Akron *B, M*
Wright State University *D*

Oklahoma
University of Oklahoma *B, M*
University of Tulsa *B, M*

Oregon
Oregon State University *M, D*

Rhode Island
Brown University *B*

South Carolina
University of South Carolina *B*

Texas
Baylor University *B*
Rice University *B*
Southern Methodist University *B, M, D*
Texas A&M University *B, M, D*
Texas Tech University *B*
University of Houston *B*
University of Texas
Austin *B*
Dallas *M, D*
El Paso *B, M*

Utah
Snow College *A*
University of Utah *B, M, D*

Washington
University of Washington *M, D*
Western Washington University *B*

Wisconsin
Lawrence University *B*
University of Wisconsin
Madison *B, M, D*

Wyoming
University of Wyoming *M, D*

Geotechnical engineering

Alaska
University of Alaska
Fairbanks *B, M*

Michigan
Michigan Technological University *D*

German

Alabama
Auburn University *B*
Birmingham-Southern College *B, T*
Jacksonville State University *B*
Samford University *B*
University of Alabama *B, M*
University of Alabama
Birmingham *B*

Alaska
University of Alaska
Anchorage *B*

Arizona
Arizona State University *B, M*
Northern Arizona University *B, T*
University of Arizona *B, M*

Arkansas

Black River Technical College *A*
Hendrix College *B*
University of Arkansas *B, M*
University of Arkansas
    Little Rock *B*
University of Central Arkansas *B*

California

Bakersfield College *A*
Cabrillo College *A*
California State University
    Chico *B*
    Fullerton *B, M*
    Long Beach *B, M*
    Northridge *B*
    Sacramento *B, M*
Cerritos Community College *A*
Chabot College *A*
Citrus College *A*
Claremont McKenna College *B*
College of the Canyons *A*
De Anza College *A*
Foothill College *A*
Golden West College *A*
Grossmont Community College *C, A*
Humboldt State University *B*
Loyola Marymount University *B*
Mills College *B*
MiraCosta College *A*
Modesto Junior College *A*
Monterey Institute of International
    Studies *C*
Orange Coast College *A*
Pepperdine University *B*
Pitzer College *B*
Pomona College *B*
St. Mary's College of California *B*
San Diego State University *B*
San Francisco State University *B, M*
San Joaquin Delta College *A*
San Jose State University *B*
Santa Monica College *A*
Scripps College *B*
Sonoma State University *B*
Stanford University *B, M, D*
University of California
    Berkeley *B, M, D*
    Davis *B, M, D*
    Irvine *B, M, D*
    Los Angeles *B, M*
    Riverside *B, M, D*
    San Diego *B, M*
    Santa Barbara *B, M, D*
    Santa Cruz *B*
University of La Verne *B*
University of Redlands *B*
University of San Francisco *C*
University of Southern
    California *B, M, D*
University of the Pacific *B*
Ventura College *A*

Colorado

Colorado College *B*
Colorado State University *B*
Red Rocks Community College *A*
University of Colorado
    Boulder *B, M*
    Denver *B*
University of Denver *B, M*
University of Northern Colorado *B, T*

Connecticut

Central Connecticut State University *B*
Connecticut College *B*
Fairfield University *B*
Southern Connecticut State University *B*
Trinity College *B*
University of Connecticut *B, M, D*
University of Hartford *B*
Wesleyan University *B*
Yale University *B, M, D*

Delaware

University of Delaware *B, M, T*

District of Columbia

American University *B*
Catholic University of America *B, M, T*
George Washington University *B*
Georgetown University *B, M, D*
Howard University *B*

Florida

Eckerd College *B*
Florida Atlantic University *B, M*
Florida International University *B*
Florida State University *B, M*
Manatee Community College *A*
New College of Florida *B*
Schiller International University *B*
Stetson University *B*
University of Florida *B, M, D*
University of Miami *B*
University of South Florida *B*

Georgia

Agnes Scott College *B*
Berry College *B, T*
Clark Atlanta University *B*
Emory University *B*
Georgia Southern University *B*
Georgia State University *B, M*
Mercer University *B*
Morehouse College *B*
Oxford College of Emory University *B*
South Georgia College *A*
University of Georgia *B, M*

Hawaii

University of Hawaii
    Manoa *B, M*

Idaho

Boise State University *B*
Idaho State University *A, B*
University of Idaho *B, M*

Illinois

Augustana College *B, T*
Bradley University *B, T*
City Colleges of Chicago
    Harold Washington College *A*
De Paul University *B*
Elmhurst College *B, T*
Illinois College *B, T*
Illinois State University *B, T*
Illinois Wesleyan University *B*
Knox College *B*
Loyola University of Chicago *C, B*
North Central College *B, T*
Northern Illinois University *B, M, T*
Northwestern University *B, D*
Parkland College *A*
Principia College *B*
Richland Community College *A*
Rockford College *B*
Sauk Valley Community College *A*
Southern Illinois University
    Carbondale *B*
Southern Illinois University
    Edwardsville *T*
University of Chicago *B*
University of Illinois
    Chicago *B, M, D*
    Urbana-Champaign *B, M, D*
Wheaton College *B*

Indiana

Ball State University *B, T*
Butler University *B*
DePauw University *B*
Earlham College *B*
Grace College *B*
Hanover College *B*
Indiana State University *B*
Indiana University
    Bloomington *B, M, D*
    South Bend *B*
    Southeast *B*
Indiana University-Purdue University
    Fort Wayne *A, B, T*

Indiana University-Purdue University
    Indianapolis *B*
Manchester College *B, T*
University of Evansville *B*
University of Indianapolis *B*
University of Notre Dame *B, M*
University of Southern Indiana *B, T*
Valparaiso University *B*
Vincennes University *A*
Wabash College *B*

Iowa

Central College *B, T*
Coe College *B*
Cornell College *B, T*
Graceland University *B, T*
Grinnell College *B*
Iowa State University *B*
Loras College *B*
Luther College *B*
St. Ambrose University *B, T*
Simpson College *B*
University of Iowa *B, M, D, T*
University of Northern Iowa *B, M*
Waldorf College *A*
Wartburg College *B, T*

Kansas

Baker University *B, T*
Bethel College *B*
Kansas Wesleyan University *B*
Washburn University of Topeka *B*

Kentucky

Berea College *B, T*
Centre College *B*
Georgetown College *B, T*
Murray State University *B, T*
University of Kentucky *B, M*
University of Louisville *B, M*

Louisiana

Centenary College of Louisiana *B, T*
Dillard University *B*
Louisiana State University and
    Agricultural and Mechanical
    College *B*
Loyola University New Orleans *B*
Tulane University *B, M, D*
University of New Orleans *B*

Maine

Bates College *B*
Bowdoin College *B*
Colby College *B*
University of Maine *B*

Maryland

Community College of Baltimore County
    Catonsville *A*
    Dundalk *A*
    Essex *A*
Hood College *B*
Johns Hopkins University *B, M, D*
Loyola College in Maryland *B*
McDaniel College *B*
Mount St. Mary's College *B*
Towson University *B, T*
University of Maryland
    Baltimore County *B*
    College Park *B, M, D*
Washington College *B, T*

Massachusetts

Amherst College *B*
Boston College *B*
Boston University *B*
Brandeis University *B*
College of the Holy Cross *B*
Gordon College *B*
Harvard College *B*
Mount Holyoke College *B*
Northeastern University *B*
Simon's Rock College of Bard *B*
Smith College *B*
Tufts University *B, M*

University of Massachusetts
    Amherst *B, M, D*
    Boston *B*
Wellesley College *B*
Wheaton College *B*
Williams College *B*

Michigan

Adrian College *A, B, T*
Alma College *B, T*
Aquinas College *B, T*
Calvin College *B, T*
Central Michigan University *B, T*
Eastern Michigan University *B*
Grand Valley State University *B*
Hillsdale College *B*
Hope College *B*
Kalamazoo College *B, T*
Lansing Community College *A*
Michigan State University *B, M, D*
Michigan Technological University *C*
Northern Michigan University *T*
Oakland University *B, T*
University of Michigan *B, M, D, T*
Wayne State University *B, M*
Western Michigan University *B*

Minnesota

Augsburg College *B*
Bemidji State University *B*
Carleton College *B*
College of St. Benedict *B*
Concordia College: Moorhead *B, T*
Gustavus Adolphus College *B*
Hamline University *B*
Macalester College *B, T*
Minnesota State University
    Mankato *B, M, T*
St. Cloud State University *B*
St. John's University *B*
St. Olaf College *B*
University of Minnesota
    Duluth *B, T*
    Morris *B*
    Twin Cities *B, M, D*
University of St. Thomas *B*
Winona State University *B*

Mississippi

Millsaps College *B, T*
University of Mississippi *B, M*

Missouri

Central Missouri State University *B, T*
College of the Ozarks *B*
Drury University *B, T*
Missouri Southern State College *B*
Missouri Western State College *T*
St. Louis University *B*
Southeast Missouri State University *B*
Southwest Missouri State University *B*
Truman State University *B*
University of Missouri
    Columbia *B, M*
    Kansas City *B*
    St. Louis *B*
Washington University in St.
    Louis *B, M, D*
Webster University *B*

Montana

University of Montana-Missoula *B, M*

Nebraska

Creighton University *B*
Dana College *B*
Doane College *B*
Hastings College *B*
Nebraska Wesleyan University *B*
Union College *B*
University of Nebraska
    Kearney *B, M, T*
    Lincoln *B*
    Omaha *B*
Western Nebraska Community
    College *A*

Nevada
University of Nevada
 Las Vegas *B*
 Reno *B*

New Hampshire
Dartmouth College *B*
St. Anselm College *C*
University of New Hampshire *B*

New Jersey
Drew University *B*
Georgian Court College *T*
Princeton University *B, M, D*
Rider University *B*
Rutgers, The State University of New
 Jersey
 Camden Regional Campus *B, T*
 New Brunswick Regional
  Campus *B, M, D, T*
Seton Hall University *T*

New Mexico
University of New Mexico *B, M*

New York
Alfred University *B*
Bard College *B*
Barnard College *B*
Canisius College *B*
City University of New York
 Brooklyn College *B*
 Hunter College *B*
 Queens College *B*
Colgate University *B*
Columbia University
 Columbia College *B*
Cornell University *B, T*
Fordham University *B*
Hamilton College *B*
Hartwick College *B, T*
Hofstra University *B*
Ithaca College *B, T*
Long Island University
 C. W. Post Campus *B*
Nazareth College of Rochester *B*
New York University *B, M, D*
Orange County Community College *A*
Rensselaer Polytechnic Institute *B*
St. Lawrence University *B, T*
Sarah Lawrence College *B*
Skidmore College *B*
State University of New York
 Binghamton *B*
 Buffalo *B, M*
 New Paltz *B, T*
 Oswego *B*
 Stony Brook *B, M, T*
Syracuse University *B, M*
United States Military Academy *B*
University of Rochester *B, M*
Vassar College *B*
Wells College *B*

North Carolina
Davidson College *B*
Duke University *B, M*
East Carolina University *B*
Guilford College *B, T*
Lenoir-Rhyne College *B*
Methodist College *A*
Salem College *B*
University of North Carolina
 Asheville *B, T*
 Chapel Hill *B, M, D*
 Charlotte *B*
 Greensboro *B, T*
Wake Forest University *B*
Western Carolina University *B*

North Dakota
Minot State University *B*
University of North Dakota *B, T*

Ohio
Antioch College *B*
Baldwin-Wallace College *B, T*
Bowling Green State University *B, M*

Case Western Reserve University *B*
Cleveland State University *B*
College of Wooster *B*
Denison University *B*
Franciscan University of Steubenville *B*
Heidelberg College *B*
Hiram College *B, T*
John Carroll University *B*
Kent State University *B, M*
Kent State University
 Stark Campus *B*
Kenyon College *B*
Lake Erie College *B*
Miami University
 Oxford Campus *B, T*
Mount Union College *B*
Muskingum College *B*
Oberlin College *B*
Ohio Northern University *B*
Ohio State University
 Columbus Campus *B, M, D*
Ohio University *B, M*
Ohio Wesleyan University *B*
University of Akron *B*
University of Cincinnati *B, T*
University of Dayton *B*
University of Toledo *B, M*
Wittenberg University *B*
Wright State University *B*
Xavier University *A, B*

Oklahoma
Oklahoma Baptist University *B, T*
Oklahoma City University *B*
Oklahoma State University *B*
Oral Roberts University *B*
Tulsa Community College *A*
University of Central Oklahoma *B*
University of Oklahoma *B, M*
University of Tulsa *B*

Oregon
Lewis & Clark College *B*
Linfield College *B*
Oregon State University *B*
Pacific University *B*
Portland State University *B, M*
Reed College *B*
University of Oregon *B, M, D*
University of Portland *T*
Western Oregon University *T*
Willamette University *B*

Pennsylvania
Allegheny College *B*
Bloomsburg University of
 Pennsylvania *B*
Bryn Mawr College *B*
Bucknell University *B*
California University of Pennsylvania *B*
Carnegie Mellon University *B*
Dickinson College *B*
Edinboro University of
 Pennsylvania *B, T*
Elizabethtown College *B*
Franklin & Marshall College *B*
Gettysburg College *B*
Haverford College *B, T*
Immaculata University *C, A, B*
Indiana University of Pennsylvania *B*
Juniata College *B*
La Salle University *B*
Lafayette College *B*
Lebanon Valley College of
 Pennsylvania *B, T*
Lehigh University *B*
Lock Haven University of
 Pennsylvania *B, T*
Lycoming College *B*
Messiah College *B*
Millersville University of
 Pennsylvania *B, M, T*
Moravian College *B, T*
Muhlenberg College *B, T*

Penn State
 Abington *B*
 Altoona *B*
 Beaver *B*
 Berks *B*
 Delaware County *B*
 Dubois *B*
 Fayette *B*
 Hazleton *B*
 Lehigh Valley *B*
 McKeesport *B*
 Mont Alto *B*
 New Kensington *B*
 Schuylkill - Capital College *B*
 Shenango *B*
 University Park *B, M, D*
 Wilkes-Barre *B*
 Worthington Scranton *B*
 York *B*
Rosemont College *B*
St. Joseph's University *B*
Swarthmore College *B*
Temple University *B*
University of Pennsylvania *B, D*
University of Pittsburgh *C, B, M, D*
University of Scranton *B, T*
Villanova University *B*
Washington and Jefferson College *B*
West Chester University of
 Pennsylvania *B, M*
Wilkes University *B*

Rhode Island
Brown University *B, M, D*
University of Rhode Island *B*

South Carolina
The Citadel *B*
Clemson University *B*
College of Charleston *B, T*
Converse College *B*
Francis Marion University *B*
Furman University *B, T*
Newberry College *B*
Presbyterian College *B, T*
University of South Carolina *B, M*
Wofford College *B*

South Dakota
Augustana College *B, T*
Northern State University *B*
South Dakota State University *B*
University of South Dakota *B*

Tennessee
Belmont University *B*
Carson-Newman College *B, T*
Rhodes College *B, T*
Tennessee Technological University *B, T*
University of Tennessee
 Knoxville *M*
Vanderbilt University *B, M, D*

Texas
Angelo State University *B, T*
Austin College *B*
Austin Community College *A*
Baylor University *B*
Blinn College *A*
Coastal Bend College *A*
Hardin-Simmons University *B*
Kilgore College *A*
Paris Junior College *A*
Rice University *B, M, D*
St. Mary's University *B*
Sam Houston State University *B*
Southern Methodist University *B*
Southwest Texas State University *B, T*
Southwestern University *B*
Texas A&M University *B*
Texas A&M University
 Commerce *B*
Texas Tech University *B, M*
Trinity University *B*
University of Dallas *B*
University of Houston *B, M*
University of North Texas *B*

University of Texas
 Arlington *B, M*
 Austin *B*
 El Paso *B*
 San Antonio *B*

Utah
Brigham Young University *B, M*
Snow College *A*
Southern Utah University *B*
University of Utah *B, M, D*
Utah State University *B*
Weber State University *B*

Vermont
Bennington College *B, M, T*
Marlboro College *B*
Middlebury College *B, M, D*
University of Vermont *B, M*

Virginia
College of William and Mary *B*
Eastern Mennonite University *B*
Hampden-Sydney College *B*
Hollins University *B*
Longwood University *B, T*
Mary Baldwin College *B*
Mary Washington College *B*
Randolph-Macon College *B*
Sweet Briar College *B*
University of Richmond *B, T*
University of Virginia *B, M, D*
University of Virginia's College at
 Wise *B, T*
Virginia Wesleyan College *B*
Washington and Lee University *B*

Washington
Central Washington University *B*
Centralia College *A*
Eastern Washington University *B, T*
Everett Community College *A*
Gonzaga University *B*
Pacific Lutheran University *B*
Seattle Pacific University *B*
Seattle University *B*
University of Puget Sound *B, T*
University of Washington *B, M, D*
Walla Walla College *B*
Washington State University *B*
Western Washington University *B, T*
Whitman College *B*

West Virginia
Bethany College *B*
West Virginia University *T*

Wisconsin
Beloit College *B*
Carthage College *B, T*
Lakeland College *B*
Lawrence University *B, T*
Marquette University *B*
Ripon College *B, T*
St. Norbert College *B, T*
University of Wisconsin
 Eau Claire *B*
 Green Bay *B*
 La Crosse *B*
 Madison *B, M, D*
 Milwaukee *B*
 Oshkosh *B*
 Parkside *T*
 Platteville *B*
 River Falls *B*
 Stevens Point *B, T*
 Whitewater *B, T*

Wyoming
Casper College *A*
University of Wyoming *B, M*

German studies

California
Scripps College *B*

District of Columbia
American University *B*

Iowa
University of Iowa *M, D*

Massachusetts
College of the Holy Cross *B*

Minnesota
Concordia College: Moorhead *B, T*

New Hampshire
Dartmouth College *B*

New York
Bard College *B*
Columbia University
　Columbia College *B*
Manhattanville College *B*
Sarah Lawrence College *B*

Ohio
Case Western Reserve University *B*

Rhode Island
Brown University *B, M, D*

Texas
University of Houston *B*

Virginia
Randolph-Macon Woman's College *B*
Sweet Briar College *B*

Washington
University of Washington *B*

German teacher education

Alabama
Birmingham-Southern College *T*

Arizona
Arizona State University *B, T*
Prescott College *T*
University of Arizona *B, M*

California
California State University
　Chico *T*
　Long Beach *T*
Humboldt State University *T*
San Diego State University *B, T*
San Francisco State University *B, T*
San Jose State University *T*
University of the Pacific *T*

Colorado
Colorado State University *T*

Connecticut
Central Connecticut State University *B*
Fairfield University *T*

Delaware
University of Delaware *B, T*

Florida
Stetson University *B, T*

Georgia
Georgia Southern University *B, M*

Hawaii
University of Hawaii
　Manoa *B, T*

Idaho
Boise State University *T*

Illinois
Augustana College *B, T*
Elmhurst College *B*
Illinois College *T*
Loyola University of Chicago *T*
North Park University *T*
Northwestern University *B, T*
Rockford College *T*
Sauk Valley Community College *A*

University of Illinois
　Chicago *B*
　Urbana-Champaign *B, M, T*
Wheaton College *T*

Indiana
Ball State University *T*
Grace College *B*
Indiana University
　Bloomington *B, T*
　South Bend *B, T*
Indiana University-Purdue University
　Fort Wayne *B, T*
Indiana University-Purdue University
　Indianapolis *B, T*
Manchester College *B, T*
University of Evansville *B*
University of Indianapolis *T*
University of Southern Indiana *T*
Valparaiso University *B*

Iowa
Central College *T*
Cornell College *B, T*
Graceland University *T*
Iowa State University *T*
Loras College *T*
Luther College *B*
St. Ambrose University *T*
University of Iowa *B, T*
Wartburg College *T*

Kansas
Baker University *T*
Bethel College *T*

Kentucky
Murray State University *B, M, T*

Louisiana
Centenary College of Louisiana *B, T*

Maryland
Towson University *T*
Washington College *T*

Massachusetts
Harvard College *T*
Tufts University *T*

Michigan
Alma College *T*
Calvin College *B*
Central Michigan University *B*
Eastern Michigan University *B, T*
Grand Valley State University *T*
Hope College *T*
Northern Michigan University *B, M, T*

Minnesota
Augsburg College *T*
Bemidji State University *T*
College of St. Benedict *T*
Concordia College: Moorhead *B, T*
Gustavus Adolphus College *T*
Minnesota State University
　Mankato *B, M, T*
St. Cloud State University *T*
St. John's University *T*
St. Olaf College *T*
University of Minnesota
　Duluth *B*
　Morris *T*
University of St. Thomas *B, T*
Winona State University *B, T*

Mississippi
Mississippi State University *T*
University of Mississippi *B, T*

Missouri
Central Missouri State University *B, T*
College of the Ozarks *B, T*
Missouri Southern State College *B, T*
Southwest Missouri State University *B*
University of Missouri
　Columbia *B*
　St. Louis *T*

Washington University in St.
　Louis *B, M, T*

Montana
University of Montana-Missoula *T*

Nebraska
Creighton University *T*
Dana College *B*
Doane College *T*
Hastings College *B, M, T*
Midland Lutheran College *B, T*
Nebraska Wesleyan University *T*
University of Nebraska
　Kearney *T*
　Lincoln *B, T*

New Hampshire
University of New Hampshire *T*

New Jersey
Rider University *B*

New York
Canisius College *B, M, T*
City University of New York
　Hunter College *B, T*
　Queens College *T*
Fordham University *M, T*
Hofstra University *B, M*
Ithaca College *B, T*
New York University *B, M, T*
St. John Fisher College *B, T*
St. Lawrence University *T*
State University of New York
　Buffalo *T*
　New Paltz *B, T*
　Oswego *B*
　Stony Brook *T*
Vassar College *T*
Wells College *T*

North Carolina
East Carolina University *B*
University of North Carolina
　Charlotte *B*
　Greensboro *B, T*
Wake Forest University *M, T*
Western Carolina University *B, T*

North Dakota
Minot State University *B*
University of North Dakota *B, T*

Ohio
Baldwin-Wallace College *T*
Bowling Green State University *B, M*
Hiram College *T*
Kent State University *T*
Kent State University
　Stark Campus *B*
Miami University
　Oxford Campus *B, T*
Mount Union College *T*
Ohio University *B*
University of Akron *B, T*
University of Dayton *B, M, T*
University of Toledo *B, M, T*
Xavier University *M*

Oklahoma
Oklahoma Baptist University *B, T*
Oklahoma City University *B*
University of Central Oklahoma *B*
University of Tulsa *T*

Oregon
Eastern Oregon University *B, T*
Linfield College *T*
Oregon State University *M*
Portland State University *T*
University of Portland *T*
Western Oregon University *T*

Pennsylvania
California University of
　Pennsylvania *B, T*
Dickinson College *T*
Duquesne University *B, T*

Gettysburg College *T*
Juniata College *B, T*
La Salle University *B, T*
Lebanon Valley College of
　Pennsylvania *B, T*
Lock Haven University of
　Pennsylvania *B, T*
Lycoming College *T*
Messiah College *T*
Moravian College *T*
Villanova University *T*
Washington and Jefferson College *T*
Widener University *T*
Wilkes University *T*

South Carolina
Francis Marion University *B, T*
Furman University *T*

South Dakota
Augustana College *B, T*
South Dakota State University *B*
University of South Dakota *T*

Tennessee
Tennessee Technological University *T*
University of Tennessee
　Martin *B, T*

Texas
Baylor University *B, T*
Hardin-Simmons University *B, T*
Southwest Texas State University *M, T*
University of Dallas *T*
University of Houston *T*
University of Texas
　Arlington *T*
　San Antonio *T*

Utah
Brigham Young University *B*
Southern Utah University *B, T*
University of Utah *B*
Weber State University *B*

Vermont
Bennington College *B, M, T*
St. Michael's College *T*

Virginia
Eastern Mennonite University *T*
Hollins University *T*
Longwood University *B, T*
Radford University *T*

Washington
Central Washington University *B, T*
Pacific Lutheran University *B*
Western Washington University *B, T*
Whitworth College *T*

Wisconsin
Carthage College *T*
Lakeland College *B*
Lawrence University *T*
Marquette University *B*
St. Norbert College *T*
University of Wisconsin
　Green Bay *T*
　La Crosse *B, T*
　Madison *M*
　Parkside *T*
　Platteville *B, T*
　River Falls *T*
　Whitewater *B*

Germanic languages

Kansas
University of Kansas *B, M, D*

New York
Columbia University
　Columbia College *B*

Ohio
Ohio Northern University *B*

Texas
University of Texas
Austin *M, D*

Washington
University of Washington *B*

Gerontology

Alabama
Shelton State Community College *C*
Spring Hill College *C*
University of South Alabama *C*

Arizona
Phoenix College *C*
Pima Community College *C, A*
University of Arizona *M*
Yavapai College *C*

Arkansas
Arkansas State University *C*
University of Arkansas
Little Rock *A, M*
Pine Bluff *B*

California
California State University
Chico *C*
Dominguez Hills *B*
Long Beach *M*
Los Angeles *B*
Sacramento *B*
Coastline Community College *C*
MiraCosta College *A*
San Diego State University *B*
San Francisco State University *M*
San Jose State University *M*
University of La Verne *C, M*
University of Southern
California *B, M, D*

Colorado
Naropa University *M*
Red Rocks Community College *C*
University of Colorado
Colorado Springs *C*
University of Northern Colorado *B, M*

Connecticut
Manchester Community College *C*
Naugatuck Valley Community
College *C, A*
Norwalk Community College *C*
Quinnipiac University *B*
University of Connecticut *C*

Delaware
Delaware Technical and Community
College
Stanton/Wilmington Campus *A*

Florida
Bethune-Cookman College *B*
Florida State University *C, M*
South Florida Community College *A*
University of South Florida *B, M, D*

Georgia
Columbus State University *M*
North Georgia College & State
University *C*
State University of West Georgia *M*

Illinois
City Colleges of Chicago
Wright College *C, A*
Concordia University *M*
Dominican University *C, B*
Eastern Illinois University *M*
Kendall College *C, A, B*
McKendree College *B*
Northeastern Illinois University *M*
Roosevelt University *B, M*
Southern Illinois University
Carbondale *C*
Western Illinois University *M*

Indiana
Ancilla College *C*
Ball State University *M*
Indiana University
East *C*
Kokomo *B*
Manchester College *A*
Purdue University
Calumet *B*
St. Mary-of-the-Woods College *C, A*
Vincennes University *A*

Iowa
Briar Cliff University *C*

Kansas
Central Christian College *A*
University of Kansas *M, D*
Washburn University of Topeka *A, B*
Wichita State University *B, M*

Kentucky
Thomas More College *C, A*
University of Kentucky *D*

Louisiana
University of Louisiana at Monroe *M*
University of New Orleans *C*

Maryland
Sojourner-Douglass College *B*
Towson University *B, M*
University of Maryland
Baltimore County *M, D*
Villa Julie College *A*

Massachusetts
Cape Cod Community College *C*
College of the Holy Cross *B*
Hampshire College *B*
Stonehill College *C*
University of Massachusetts
Boston *B, D*
Dartmouth *C*

Michigan
Aquinas College *A*
Lansing Community College *A*
Madonna University *C, A, B*
Oakland Community College *C, A*
Siena Heights University *A*
University of Michigan *M, D*
Wayne County Community College *C*
Wayne State University *C*

Minnesota
Bethel College *M*
Minnesota State University
Mankato *M*
St. Cloud State University *M*
Winona State University *A*

Missouri
Central Missouri State University *M*
Lindenwood University *B, M*
St. Louis Community College
St. Louis Community College at
Forest Park *C*
Southwest Missouri State University *B*
University of Missouri
St. Louis *M*

Montana
Montana State University
Billings *A*

Nebraska
University of Nebraska
Omaha *C, B, M*

Nevada
University of Nevada
Las Vegas *C*

New Hampshire
New Hampshire Community Technical
College
Laconia *C, A*
Manchester *C, A*
Stratham *C, A*

New Hampshire Technical Institute *C*

New Jersey
College of St. Elizabeth *C*
Felician College *B*
Gloucester County College *C*
Ocean County College *A*
Thomas Edison State College *A, B*
Union County College *C, A*

New York
Alfred University *B*
Broome Community College *A*
City University of New York
Brooklyn College *B, M*
Hostos Community College *A*
La Guardia Community College *A*
York College *B*
College of New Rochelle *M*
Columbia University
School of Nursing *M*
Genesee Community College *C*
Hofstra University *M*
Ithaca College *C, B*
Long Island University
C. W. Post Campus *M*
Southampton College *M*
Marymount Manhattan College *C*
Mercy College *C*
New York Institute of Technology *M*
St. Joseph's College *C*
State University of New York
College at Oneonta *B*
Touro College *M*
Utica College *C, B*

North Carolina
Appalachian State University *M*
Barton College *C, B*
Shaw University *B*
University of North Carolina
Charlotte *M*
Winston-Salem State University *B*

Ohio
Bowling Green State University *B*
Case Western Reserve University *R*
College of Mount St. Joseph *A, B*
Columbus State Community College *A*
John Carroll University *B*
Kent State University
Stark Campus *B*
Lourdes College *C, A, B*
Miami University
Oxford Campus *M*
Ohio Dominican College *C, A*
Ohio University *C*
Sinclair Community College *C*
University of Akron *C*
University of Cincinnati
Clermont College *C*
University of Findlay *C*

Oklahoma
Rogers State University *A*

Oregon
Chemeketa Community College *A*
Marylhurst University *C, M*
Mount Hood Community College *C*
Oregon State University *C*
Portland Community College *C, A*

Pennsylvania
California University of
Pennsylvania *A, B*
Cedar Crest College *C*
Chestnut Hill College *C, A, B*
Community College of Philadelphia *C*
Duquesne University *M*
Gwynedd-Mercy College *C*
King's College *A, B*
La Roche College *C*
Lehigh Carbon Community College *A*
Lincoln University *C*
Marywood University *C*
Mercyhurst College *B*

Millersville University of
Pennsylvania *A*
Reading Area Community College *A*
Shippensburg University of
Pennsylvania *M*
University of Scranton *C, A, B*
West Chester University of
Pennsylvania *B, M*

Puerto Rico
Pontifical Catholic University of Puerto
Rico *A, B*
Universidad Metropolitana *B*
University of Puerto Rico
Medical Sciences Campus *C, M*

South Carolina
Coastal Carolina University *C*
Lander University *C*

Texas
Abilene Christian University *M*
Baylor University *M*
McLennan Community College *A*
Stephen F. Austin State University *B*
University of North Texas *B*
University of Texas
Houston Health Science Center *M*

Utah
University of Utah *C, M*
Weber State University *B*

Virginia
Lynchburg College *C*
Virginia Commonwealth University *M*

Washington
Central Washington University *B*
Edmonds Community College *C, A*
Heritage College *C*

West Virginia
Mountain State University *C, A*

Wisconsin
Mount Mary College *M*

Geropsychology

Pennsylvania
Marywood University *T*

Global studies

Alabama
Huntingdon College *B*

Arkansas
Harding University *B*
Southern Arkansas University *B*

California
California State University
Monterey Bay *B*
National University *B*
Sonoma State University *B*
University of California
Santa Barbara *B*

Colorado
University of Colorado
Boulder *B*

Connecticut
Sacred Heart University *B*

Georgia
Brenau University *B*

Illinois
Lewis University *B*

Indiana
Indiana University-Purdue University
Indianapolis *M*
Manchester College *B*

Iowa
University of Iowa *B*

Kansas
University of Kansas *B, M*

Maine
University of Southern Maine *B*

Massachusetts
Assumption College *B*
Berkshire Community College *A*
Bunker Hill Community College *C*
Cape Cod Community College *A*
Emmanuel College *B*
Hampshire College *B*
Lesley University *B*
Northeastern University *B*
Western New England College *B*

Missouri
Rockhurst University *B*

New York
Adelphi University *B*
D'Youville College *B*
Sage College of Albany *A*
St. Lawrence University *B*
Sarah Lawrence College *B*

North Carolina
Roanoke-Chowan Community College *A*
Wake Technical Community College *A*

Ohio
Baldwin-Wallace College *B*
Ohio University *C*
Wittenberg University *B*

Oklahoma
University of Tulsa *B*

Pennsylvania
Chatham College *B*
Gettysburg College *B*

South Carolina
Newberry College *B*
Piedmont Technical College *A*

Vermont
Bennington College *B*
Marlboro College *B*

Virginia
Randolph-Macon College *B*
Virginia Military Institute *B*

Washington
Pacific Lutheran University *B*

Wisconsin
Northland College *B*
Ripon College *B*
University of Wisconsin
Madison *B, M*

Graphic communications

California
Art Center College of Design *B, M*
Otis College of Art and Design *B*
Santa Rosa Junior College *C*
Santiago Canyon College *A*

District of Columbia
American University *B*

Florida
Miami-Dade Community College *A*

Illinois
City Colleges of Chicago
Kennedy-King College *C, A*

Indiana
Indiana State University *B*
St. Mary-of-the-Woods College *B*
Sawyer College: Merrillville *C, A*
Vincennes University *A*

Iowa
Briar Cliff University *B*

Kentucky
Somerset Community College *C*

Maryland
Montgomery College
Rockville Campus *C, A*

Michigan
Baker College
of Muskegon *A*
of Owosso *A, B*

Minnesota
Art Institutes International
Minnesota *A, B*
Brown College *A*
Hennepin Technical College *C, A*

Nebraska
Metropolitan Community College *C, A*

New York
Marist College *B*
New York University *M*
Rochester Institute of Technology *B, M*

Ohio
Kent State University *B*
University of Cincinnati
Raymond Walters College *C, A*

Pennsylvania
Delaware County Community College *C*

South Dakota
South Dakota State University *B*

Washington
Seattle Central Community College *C, A*

Wisconsin
Carroll College *B*
Edgewood College *B*
Milwaukee Area Technical College *A*

Graphic design

Arkansas
Harding University *B*
John Brown University *B*
University of Arkansas
Fort Smith *C, A*

California
Art Center College of Design *B, M*
Art Institute
of California - Orange County *A, B*
Bethesda Christian University *B*
California State University
Sacramento *B*
Fashion Institute of Design and
Merchandising
San Francisco *A*
Ohlone College *C, A*
Otis College of Art and Design *B*
Santa Barbara City College *C*
University of San Francisco *B*

Colorado
Rocky Mountain College of Art &
Design *B*
Westwood College of Technology
South *A, B*

Connecticut
University of Bridgeport *B*

District of Columbia
American University *B*

Georgia
Atlanta College of Art *B*
Brenau University *B*
Savannah College of Art and
Design *B, M*

Illinois
John A. Logan College *A*
Quincy University *B*

Indiana
Ivy Tech State College
Southwest *A*
University of St. Francis *B*
Vincennes University *A*

Kansas
Barton County Community College *A*
University of Kansas *B*

Maryland
Maryland Institute College of Art *B, M*

Massachusetts
Cape Cod Community College *A*

Michigan
Baker College
of Muskegon *A*
Finlandia University *B*
Jackson Community College *C, A*

Minnesota
Art Institutes International
Minnesota *A, B*
Northwestern College *B*
South Central Technical College *A*

Missouri
Ozarks Technical Community
College *C, A*

New York
City University of New York
City College *B*
Marist College *B*
Pratt Institute *B, M*
Rochester Institute of Technology *A, B*
State University of New York
Buffalo *M*
Syracuse University *B*

North Carolina
Fayetteville Technical Community
College *A*

Ohio
University of Akron *B*
Ursuline College *B*

Pennsylvania
Marywood University *M*
Oakbridge Academy of Arts *A*

Puerto Rico
Atlantic College *M*

Tennessee
Memphis College of Art *B*

Vermont
Champlain College *C, A, B*

Virginia
Art Institute
of Washington *A, B*

Washington
Cornish College of the Arts *B*

Wisconsin
Nicolet Area Technical College *A*
Western Wisconsin Technical College *A*

Graphic/printing production

Alabama
Alabama Agricultural and Mechanical
University *B*
Bishop State Community College *C*
J. F. Drake State Technical College *C, A*
Shelton State Community College *C*

Arizona
Pima Community College *A*

Arkansas
Arkansas State University *B*
Phillips Community College of the
University of Arkansas *A*

California
Antelope Valley College *C, A*
Bakersfield College *A*
California Polytechnic State University:
San Luis Obispo *B*
Don Bosco Technical Institute *A*
Fashion Institute of Design and
Merchandising *A*
Laney College *C, A*
Las Positas College *A*
Long Beach City College *A*
Los Angeles Trade and Technical
College *C, A*
Modesto Junior College *C, A*
Moorpark College *A*
Palomar College *C, A*
Riverside Community College *C, A*
San Joaquin Delta College *A*
Santa Barbara City College *C*
Ventura College *A*

Colorado
Community College of Aurora *A*

Connecticut
Gateway Community College *C*

District of Columbia
University of the District of
Columbia *A, B*

Florida
Indian River Community College *A*
Miami-Dade Community College *C, A*
Palm Beach Community College *A*
Tallahassee Community College *C*

Georgia
Art Institute
of Atlanta *A, B*
Chattahoochee Technical College *C*
Columbus Technical College *C*
Darton College *A*
DeKalb Technical College *C*
West Georgia Technical College *C*

Hawaii
University of Hawaii
Honolulu Community College *A*

Idaho
Idaho State University *C, A*
Lewis-Clark State College *A*

Illinois
College of DuPage *C, A*
College of Lake County *C*
Elgin Community College *C*
Kaskaskia College *C*
Moraine Valley Community College *C*
Parkland College *A*
Prairie State College *C*
Triton College *C, A*
Western Illinois University *B*

Indiana
Ball State University *A*
Sawyer College: Merrillville *C, A*
Vincennes University *A*

Iowa
Clinton Community College *A*
Des Moines Area Community
College *C, A*
Iowa Western Community College *A*
Kirkwood Community College *A*

Kansas
Fort Scott Community College *A*
Hutchinson Community College *C, A*
Pittsburg State University *B*

Kentucky
Murray State University *A*

Maine
Central Maine Technical College *A*

Maryland
Montgomery College
Rockville Campus *A*

Massachusetts
Massasoit Community College *C*

Michigan
Alpena Community College *C, A*
Andrews University *A, B*
Baker College
of Muskegon *A*
Bay de Noc Community College *C*
Gogebic Community College *C, A*
Grand Rapids Community College *A*
Lansing Community College *A*
Macomb Community College *C, A*
Muskegon Community College *A*
Oakland Community College *C, A*
Southwestern Michigan College *A*
Washtenaw Community College *A*

Minnesota
Art Institutes International
Minnesota *A, B*
Central Lakes College *C*
Dakota County Technical College *C, A*
Globe College *C, A*
Hennepin Technical College *C, A*
Mesabi Range Community and Technical
College *C, A*
St. Cloud Technical College *C*
South Central Technical College *A*

Mississippi
Northwest Mississippi Community
College *C, A*

Missouri
Central Missouri State University *A, B*
College of the Ozarks *B*
East Central College *C, A*
Evangel University *A*
Mineral Area College *A*
Moberly Area Community College *C, A*
Ozarks Technical Community
College *C, A*
St. Louis Community College
St. Louis Community College at
Florissant Valley *A*
St. Louis Community College at
Forest Park *A*
Southeast Missouri State University *C*

Montana
Miles Community College *A*

Nebraska
Central Community College *C, A*
Metropolitan Community College *C, A*
Southeast Community College
Lincoln Campus *C*

Nevada
Community College of Southern
Nevada *C, A*
Truckee Meadows Community
College *C*

New Hampshire
New Hampshire Community Technical
College
Berlin *C, A*
Laconia *C, A*

New Jersey
Bergen Community College *C*
Brookdale Community College *C, A*
Burlington County College *A*
Kean University *B, M*

New Mexico
Southwestern Indian Polytechnic
Institute *C, A*

New York
Erie Community College
South Campus *A*
Fulton-Montgomery Community
College *C, A*
Rochester Institute of
Technology *A, B, M*

North Carolina
Alamance Community College *C*
Appalachian State University *B*
Chowan College *A, B*
Forsyth Technical Community College *C*

Ohio
Cincinnati State Technical and
Community College *A*
Columbus State Community College *A*
Cuyahoga Community College
Eastern Campus *C*
Lourdes College *A*

Oklahoma
Northeastern State University *B*
Oklahoma State University
Okmulgee *A*

Oregon
Chemeketa Community College *A*
Mount Hood Community College *C, A*

Pennsylvania
Bradley Academy for the Visual Arts *C*
Bucks County Community College *A*
California University of
Pennsylvania *A, B*
Commonwealth Technical Institute *C*
Delaware County Community College *C*
Luzerne County Community College *A*
Montgomery County Community
College *A*
Pennsylvania College of
Technology *C, A*
Westmoreland County Community
College *A*

Puerto Rico
University of Puerto Rico
Carolina Regional College *A*

South Carolina
Midlands Technical College *C*
Trident Technical College *C*

South Dakota
Northern State University *A*
Southeast Technical Institute *A*

Texas
Angelina College *C, A*
Central Texas College *C, A*
College of the Mainland *C*
Eastfield College *C, A*
Houston Community College
System *C, A*
Lee College *C, A*
Midland College *A*
North Harris Montgomery Community
College District *C, A*
San Jacinto College
Central Campus *A*
South Plains College *A*
Southwest Texas State University *B*
Tarrant County College *A*
Texas A&M University
Commerce *B*
Texas State Technical College
Waco *C, A*
Tyler Junior College *C, A*

Utah
Dixie State College of Utah *C, A*
Salt Lake Community College *A*

Virginia
Danville Community College *A*
J. Sargeant Reynolds Community
College *C*
Virginia Intermont College *A*

Washington
Clark College *C, A*
Clover Park Technical College *C, A*
Edmonds Community College *C*
Lake Washington Technical College *C*
Seattle Central Community College *C, A*
Walla Walla College *C, A, B*

West Virginia
Fairmont State College *B*
West Virginia University Institute of
Technology *A*

Wisconsin
Fox Valley Technical College *C, A*
Lakeshore Technical College *C*
Milwaukee Area Technical College *A*
Moraine Park Technical College *C, A*
Waukesha County Technical College *A*

Greenhouse operations

California
Los Angeles Pierce College *C, A*
Yuba Community College District *C*

Georgia
Albany Technical College *C*

Illinois
College of DuPage *C*
Joliet Junior College *C, A*
Kishwaukee College *C, A*
Southwestern Illinois College *A*
Triton College *C, A*
William Rainey Harper College *C, A*

Iowa
Des Moines Area Community College *C*

Kentucky
Maysville Community College *C*

Maine
University of Maine *B*

Michigan
Bay de Noc Community College *C*

Minnesota
Rochester Community and Technical
College *C, A*
University of Minnesota
Crookston *B*

Nebraska
Central Community College *C*
Nebraska College of Technical
Agriculture *A*

New Hampshire
University of New Hampshire *A*

New York
State University of New York
College of Agriculture and
Technology at Cobleskill *A*
College of Agriculture and
Technology at Morrisville *A*

North Carolina
Alamance Community College *C*
Carteret Community College *C, A*
Johnston Community College *C*
Pitt Community College *C*

North Dakota
Minot State University: Bottineau
Campus *C, A*

Ohio
Ohio State University
Agricultural Technical Institute *A*
Columbus Campus *C*

Pennsylvania
Community College of Allegheny
County *C*
Westmoreland County Community
College *A*

South Dakota
Southeast Technical Institute *A*

Tennessee
Walters State Community College *A*

Texas
Western Texas College *C, A*

Vermont
Vermont Technical College *A*

Washington
Spokane Community College *A*

Wisconsin
Fox Valley Technical College *C*

Gunsmithing

Arizona
Yavapai College *C, A*

Hair styling

Alabama
Calhoun Community College *C*

Florida
New England Institute of Technology *C*

Minnesota
St. Paul College - A Community and
Technical College *C, A*

North Carolina
Lenoir Community College *C*
Surry Community College *A*

Hazardous materials information systems

Ohio
Ohio University *A*

Hazardous materials technology

Alabama
Central Alabama Community College *C*
James H. Faulkner State Community
College *A*

Arizona
Paradise Valley Community
College *C, A*

Florida
Pensacola Junior College *A*

Kansas
Barton County Community College *C, A*
Kansas City Kansas Community
College *A*

Ohio
University of Findlay *C, A, B, M*

Texas
Southern Methodist University *M*

Washington
Green River Community College *C, A*

Health aide

California
College of Alameda *C, A*

Colorado
Red Rocks Community College *C*

Illinois
McHenry County College *C*

Kansas

Barton County Community College *C*

Pennsylvania

Community College of Beaver County *A*

Washington

Edmonds Community College *C, A*

Health care administration

Alabama

Auburn University *B*
Community College of the Air Force *A*
University of Alabama *B*
University of Alabama
    Birmingham *M, D*

Alaska

University of Alaska
    Southeast *A*

Arizona

Arizona State University *M*
Gateway Community College *C, A*
University of Arizona *B*
University of Phoenix *M*

Arkansas

Arkansas State University *B*
Harding University *B*
University of Arkansas
    Little Rock *M*
University of Central Arkansas *A, B*

California

Barstow College *C*
California State University
    Bakersfield *M*
    Chico *B*
    Dominguez Hills *B*
    Fresno *B*
    Hayward *M*
    Northridge *M*
    San Bernardino *B, M*
Imperial Valley College *C, A*
Loma Linda University *M*
Mount St. Mary's College *B*
National University *C, B, M*
St. Mary's College of California *M*
San Jose State University *M*
University of La Verne *B, M*
University of San Francisco *M*
University of Southern California *M*

Colorado

Metropolitan State College of Denver *B*
University of Colorado
    Denver *M*
University of Denver *M*
University of Northern Colorado *B*

Connecticut

Quinnipiac University *B, M*
Sacred Heart University *M*
University of Connecticut *B*
University of New Haven *M*
Western Connecticut State University *M*

District of Columbia

George Washington University *M*
Georgetown University *M*

Florida

Barry University *C, B, M*
Broward Community College *A*
Florida Agricultural and Mechanical
    University *B*
Florida Atlantic University *C, B*
Florida Institute of Technology *M*
Florida International University *B, M*
Florida State University *C*
Pensacola Junior College *A*
Polk Community College *A*
South Florida Community College *A*
University of Central Florida *B*
University of Florida *M, D*
University of Miami *M*

University of North Florida *M*
University of South Florida *M*
University of Tampa *C, M*

Georgia

Armstrong Atlantic State
    University *B, M*
Columbus State University *B, M*
Georgia Institute of Technology *M*
Georgia Southern University *M*
Georgia State University *M, D*
Macon State College *B*
Medical College of Georgia *B*
Mercer University *M*

Hawaii

University of Hawaii
    Hawaii Community College *C*
    West Oahu *B*

Idaho

Idaho State University *B*

Illinois

Benedictine University *B*
Governors State University *B, M*
Illinois Central College *C, A*
Lewis University *M*
National-Louis University *B*
Northwestern University *M*
Roosevelt University *B, M*
Rush University *M*
University of St. Francis *M*
Western Illinois University *B*

Indiana

Calumet College of St. Joseph *B*
Goshen College *B*
Indiana University
    Bloomington *B*
    Northwest *B*
    South Bend *B*
Indiana University-Purdue University
    Fort Wayne *B*
Indiana University-Purdue University
    Indianapolis *B, M*
Purdue University
    North Central Campus *A*

Iowa

Des Moines Area Community College *A*
Franciscan University *B*
Indian Hills Community College *A*
Iowa Lakes Community College *A*
St. Ambrose University *M*
University of Osteopathic Medicine and
    Health Sciences
        Des Moines University -
        Osteopathic Medical Center *M*
Upper Iowa University *B*

Kansas

Friends University *B*
University of Kansas Medical Center *M*
Wichita State University *B*

Kentucky

University of Kentucky *B, M*

Louisiana

Tulane University *M, D*
University of Louisiana at Lafayette *M*
University of New Orleans *M*

Maine

St. Joseph's College *B, M*
University of New England *B*
University of Southern Maine *M*

Maryland

Columbia Union College *B*
University of Baltimore *B, M*

Massachusetts

Boston University *M*
Emmanuel College *B*
Framingham State College *M*
Newbury College *B*
Northeastern University *M*
Simmons College *M*

Springfield College *B, M*
Stonehill College *B*
University of Massachusetts
    Lowell *M*

Michigan

Baker College
    of Clinton Township *B*
    of Muskegon *B*
    of Owosso *B*
    of Port Huron *B*
Central Michigan University *M*
Concordia University *B*
Davenport University
    Eastern Region *B, M*
Davenport University - Western
    Region *B*
Eastern Michigan University *B*
Ferris State University *B*
Lansing Community College *A*
Madonna University *A, B, M*
Oakland Community College *A*
University of Michigan *M, D*
University of Michigan
    Dearborn *B*
    Flint *B, M*
Wayne State University *M*

Minnesota

Capella University *M, D*
Concordia College: Moorhead *B*
High-Tech Institute *A*
Minnesota State College - Southeast
    Technical *C*
Minnesota State University
    Mankato *B, M, T*
    Moorhead *M*
Ridgewater College: A Community and
    Technical College *C*
St. Mary's University of Minnesota *B, M*
University of Minnesota
    Crookston *B*
    Twin Cities *M*
University of St. Thomas *M*
Winona State University *B*

Mississippi

Mississippi College *M*
University of Mississippi *D*

Missouri

Avila University *M*
Lindenwood University *B*
Maryville University of Saint
    Louis *C, B, M*
St. Louis University *M, D*
Southwest Missouri State University *M*
University of Missouri
    Columbia *M*
Webster University *M*

Montana

Montana State University
    Billings *B, M*
University of Great Falls *B*

Nebraska

Bellevue University *M*
Central Community College *C, A*
Clarkson College *B*
Creighton University *B, M*

Nevada

University of Nevada
    Las Vegas *B*

New Hampshire

Rivier College *M*
University of New Hampshire *B, M*

New Jersey

College of St. Elizabeth *M*
Essex County College *A*
Seton Hall University *M*
Thomas Edison State College *A, B*
University of Medicine and Dentistry of
    New Jersey
        School of Health Related
        Professions *D*

New York

City University of New York
    Baruch College *M*
    Borough of Manhattan Community
        College *A*
    Brooklyn College *B, M*
D'Youville College *C, B, M*
Hofstra University *M*
Iona College *M*
Long Island University
    C. W. Post Campus *B, M*
New York University *A, M*
Rochester Institute of Technology *M*
St. Joseph's College *B*
State University of New York
    College at Fredonia *B*
    Health Science Center at Stony
        Brook *M*
    Institute of Technology at
        Utica/Rome *B, M*
    Stony Brook *M*

North Carolina

Duke University *M*
Pfeiffer University *B, M*
University of North Carolina
    Chapel Hill *B, M, D*
    Charlotte *M*

Ohio

Bohecker's Business College *A*
Bowling Green State University *B*
College of Mount St. Joseph *B*
David N. Myers College *C, B*
Franklin University *B*
Heidelberg College *B*
Kent State University *A, B*
Kent State University
    Stark Campus *B*
Ohio State University
    Columbus Campus *M*
Ohio University *B*
Shawnee State University *B*
University of Cincinnati *B, M*
University of Findlay *M*
University of Northwestern Ohio *B*
University of Rio Grande *B*
University of Toledo *M*
Wright State University *M*
Youngstown State University *M*

Oklahoma

Langston University *B*
Northeastern State University *B*
Oklahoma State University
    Oklahoma City *A*
Southwestern Oklahoma State
    University *B*
University of Oklahoma *M, D*

Oregon

Chemeketa Community College *C, A*
Concordia University *B*
Oregon State University *B, M*
Portland State University *M*
Rogue Community College *C*

Pennsylvania

Arcadia University *C, B*
Cambria County Area Community
    College *A*
Carnegie Mellon University *M*
Chestnut Hill College *C, A, B*
Drexel University *B*
Duquesne University *B, M*
Harrisburg Area Community College *A*
King's College *M*
Lebanon Valley College of
    Pennsylvania *C*
Manor College *C, A*
Marywood University *B, M*
Median School of Allied Health
    Careers *C*
Neumann College *C*
Penn State
    Harrisburg *B, M*
    University Park *B, M, D*

Philadelphia University C, B
Robert Morris University B
St. Joseph's University A, B, M
Temple University M
University of Pittsburgh M
University of Scranton C, A, B, M
West Chester University of
    Pennsylvania B, M
York College of Pennsylvania M

Puerto Rico
University of Puerto Rico
    Medical Sciences Campus M

Rhode Island
Providence College C, A
Salve Regina University M
University of Rhode Island B

South Carolina
Clemson University M
Medical University of South
    Carolina M, D
Tri-County Technical College C
University of South Carolina M

South Dakota
University of South Dakota B

Tennessee
Carson-Newman College B
Southern Adventist University B, M
Tennessee State University B
Tennessee Wesleyan College B
University of Tennessee
    Knoxville D

Texas
Baylor University M
Dallas Baptist University B
Galveston College A
Howard Payne University B
LeTourneau University M
Our Lady of the Lake University of San
    Antonio M
Southwest Texas State University B, M
Southwestern Adventist University B
Texas A&M University
    Commerce B
Texas Southern University B
Texas Woman's University M
Trinity University M
University of Houston
    Clear Lake B, M
University of Mary Hardin-Baylor M
University of North Texas M
University of Texas
    Arlington M
    Dallas M
    El Paso B
    Houston Health Science
        Center M, D
    Southwestern Medical Center at
        Dallas B

Utah
Weber State University B

Virginia
ECPI Technical College: Roanoke A
Mary Baldwin College B
Marymount University M
Norfolk State University B
Shenandoah University C
Virginia Commonwealth
    University M, D

Washington
Eastern Washington University B
University of Washington M
Washington State University M

West Virginia
Davis and Elkins College B
Fairmont State College B
Marshall University M
Mountain State University B
Wheeling Jesuit University B

Wisconsin
Cardinal Stritch University M
Mid-State Technical College C
University of Wisconsin
    Eau Claire B
    Madison M

Health communications

Massachusetts
Emerson College M

Pennsylvania
Juniata College B
Marywood University C, M

Health management/ clinical assistant

Alaska
University of Alaska
    Southeast C, A

Arizona
International Institute of the Americas
    Phoenix C, A, B
    Tucson A, B

California
Ohlone College C

North Carolina
Fayetteville Technical Community
    College C, A
Pitt Community College C

Pennsylvania
Consolidated School of Business
    Lancaster A
    York A

Health occupations teacher education

Alabama
Lawson State Community College A

Florida
Palm Beach Community College A

Georgia
Atlanta Metropolitan College A
Columbus State University M

Illinois
North Park University T
University of Illinois
    Chicago M

Iowa
University of Iowa B, T

Kansas
Emporia State University T

Kentucky
University of Louisville B, T

Maine
University of Maine
    Presque Isle B

Michigan
Saginaw Valley State University M

Minnesota
Gustavus Adolphus College T
Minnesota State University
    Mankato B
Winona State University B, M, T

New York
City University of New York
    Brooklyn College B
New York Institute of
    Technology A, B, T

State University of New York
    College at Brockport M
    College at Buffalo B, M
    Oswego B

North Carolina
North Carolina State University M
St. Augustine's College B

Ohio
Youngstown State University B, M

Pennsylvania
Lock Haven University of
    Pennsylvania B, T

Tennessee
Belmont University B, T

Texas
Kilgore College A
Southwest Texas State University M, T
Texas A&M University M, D
Texas A&M University
    Commerce M
University of Houston M, D

Wisconsin
University of Wisconsin
    La Crosse B, M, T

Health physics/radiologic health

Arkansas
University of Central Arkansas B

California
University of California
    Los Angeles M, D

Colorado
National Technological University M

Florida
Gulf Coast Community College A
University of Miami M

Georgia
Georgia Institute of Technology M

Illinois
Illinois Institute of Technology M
University of St. Francis B

Indiana
University of St. Francis A

Louisiana
Louisiana State University and
    Agricultural and Mechanical
    College M

Massachusetts
Massachusetts College of Pharmacy and
    Health Sciences B

Michigan
University of Michigan M
Wayne State University M

Nevada
University of Nevada
    Las Vegas B, M

New Jersey
Thomas Edison State College A, B

New York
Monroe Community College A

Ohio
Marion Technical College A

Oregon
Oregon State University B, M, D

Pennsylvania
Bloomsburg University of
    Pennsylvania B
University of Pittsburgh C

Puerto Rico
Universidad del Este C

Tennessee
Roane State Community College C

Texas
Texas A&M University B

Wisconsin
University of Wisconsin
    Madison M, D

Wyoming
Casper College A

Health services

Alabama
Central Alabama Community College A
Community College of the Air Force A
Wallace State Community College at
    Hanceville A

Arizona
Glendale Community College C
Pima Community College C
University of Phoenix B

Arkansas
University of Central Arkansas B

California
Los Angeles Trade and Technical
    College A
Mount San Antonio College C, A
Napa Valley College C, A
Ventura College A

Colorado
Community College of Aurora C

Connecticut
Naugatuck Valley Community
    College C, A
Norwalk Community College C

Florida
Daytona Beach Community College A
Gulf Coast Community College A
Hillsborough Community College A
Palm Beach Community College A
St. Petersburg College C, A
St. Thomas University M
Stetson University B

Georgia
Floyd College A
Macon State College B

Idaho
North Idaho College A

Illinois
City Colleges of Chicago
    Kennedy-King College A
Moraine Valley Community College C
South Suburban College of Cook
    County C
Southern Illinois University
    Carbondale B

Iowa
Marshalltown Community College C, A

Kansas
Washburn University of Topeka C, A, B

Louisiana
Southern University
    Shreveport A

Maine
University of Maine
    Augusta C

Maryland
Allegany College A
Anne Arundel Community College C, A

Community College of Baltimore County
  Catonsville *C, A*
  Dundalk *C, A*
  Essex *C, A*
Harford Community College *A*

Massachusetts
Berkshire Community College *C, A*
Lesley University *B*

Michigan
Kellogg Community College *A*
Madonna University *C, A, B*
Oakland Community College *A*
Wayne County Community College *C*

Minnesota
College of St. Scholastica *B*

Nebraska
Southeast Community College
  Lincoln Campus *A*
York College *A*

New Jersey
Essex County College *A*
Thomas Edison State College *B*

New York
City University of New York
  La Guardia Community College *A*
Dominican College of Blauvelt *B*
Dutchess Community College *A*
North Country Community College *C, A*
Orange County Community College *A*

North Carolina
Pitt Community College *A*
South Piedmont Community
  College *C, A*

Ohio
Baldwin-Wallace College *B*
Columbus State Community
  College *C, A*
Cuyahoga Community College
  Eastern Campus *A*
  Metropolitan Campus *A*
Muskingum Area Technical College *A*
North Central State College *A*
Ohio University
  Chillicothe Campus *A*
Sinclair Community College *A*
University of Toledo *M*
Urbana University *B*
Ursuline College *B*

Oklahoma
Oklahoma State University
  Oklahoma City *A*

Oregon
Mount Hood Community College *A*

Pennsylvania
Bucks County Community College *A*
Cedar Crest College *C*
Community College of Philadelphia *C*
Edinboro University of Pennsylvania *A*
Manor College *A*
Marywood University *B*
Montgomery County Community
  College *A*

Penn State
  Abington *B*
  Altoona *A*
  Beaver *B*
  Berks *B*
  Delaware County *B*
  Dubois *B*
  Fayette *B*
  Harrisburg *B, M*
  Hazleton *B*
  Lehigh Valley *A*
  McKeesport *B*
  Mont Alto *B*
  New Kensington *B*
  Schuylkill - Capital College *B*
  Shenango *B*
  Wilkes-Barre *B*
  Worthington Scranton *B*
  York *B*
Pennsylvania College of
  Technology *A, B*
Reading Area Community College *A*

Puerto Rico
Pontifical Catholic University of Puerto
  Rico *M*
University of Puerto Rico
  Cayey University College *B*

South Dakota
Kilian Community College *A*

Texas
Alvin Community College *C, A*
South Plains College *A*

Utah
Brigham Young University *B*

Vermont
Community College of Vermont *C, A*

Virginia
Blue Ridge Community College *A*
Old Dominion University *B*
Southwest Virginia Community
  College *A*
Virginia Western Community College *A*

Washington
Edmonds Community College *C, A*
Spokane Falls Community College *A*

West Virginia
Mountain State College *A*

Wisconsin
Moraine Park Technical College *A*

Wyoming
University of Wyoming *B*

**Health services
administration**

Colorado
Jones International University *M*
National American University
  Denver *B*

Florida
Nova Southeastern University *M*

Indiana
Indiana University-Purdue University
  Fort Wayne *B*
University of Evansville *B, M*
University of Southern Indiana *M*

Maine
University of New England *B*

Massachusetts
Elms College *B*
University of Massachusetts
  Amherst *M, D*

Missouri
Harris Stowe State College *B*

University of Missouri
  Columbia *B*

New Jersey
University of Medicine and Dentistry of
  New Jersey
  School of Health Related
    Professions *D*

New York
Molloy College *B*
Pace University:
  Pleasantville/Briarcliff *M*
Rochester Institute of Technology *M*
State University of New York
  Albany *M*

Ohio
Ursuline College *B*
Xavier University *M*

Pennsylvania
Arcadia University *B*
DeSales University *M*
Marywood University *M*

Texas
University of Texas
  Houston Health Science
    Center *M, D*

Health teacher education

Alabama
Alabama State University *B, T*
Auburn University *B*
Jacksonville State University *B*
Lawson State Community College *A*
Stillman College *B*
University of Alabama
  Birmingham *B, M, T*
University of South Alabama *B, M, T*

Arizona
Northern Arizona University *B*
Prescott College *T*
University of Arizona *B*

Arkansas
Arkansas State University *B, T*
Harding University *B, T*
Ouachita Baptist University *B, T*
University of Arkansas
  Little Rock *B*
University of Central Arkansas *B, M, T*

California
Azusa Pacific University *T*
California State University
  Chico *T*
  Dominguez Hills *T*
  Fullerton *T*
  Long Beach *M, T*
  Northridge *B, T*
  Sacramento *T*
  San Bernardino *T*
San Francisco State University *B, M, T*
San Jose State University *T*

Connecticut
Southern Connecticut State
  University *B, T*
Western Connecticut State University *B*

Delaware
Delaware State University *B*
University of Delaware *B, T*

District of Columbia
Howard University *B*
University of the District of Columbia *B*

Florida
Florida International University *B, M, T*
Florida State University *B, M*
Gulf Coast Community College *A*
Manatee Community College *A*
Nova Southeastern University *T*
Palm Beach Community College *A*

Tallahassee Community College *A*
University of West Florida *B, M, T*

Georgia
Armstrong Atlantic State
  University *B, M, T*
Augusta State University *M*
Clark Atlanta University *B*
Georgia College and State
  University *B, M, T*
Georgia Perimeter College *A*
Georgia Southwestern State
  University *B, M, T*
Kennesaw State University *B*
Medical College of Georgia *M*
Middle Georgia College *A*
Morris Brown College *B*
South Georgia College *A*
University of Georgia *M, D*
Valdosta State University *B*

Hawaii
University of Hawaii
  Manoa *B, T*

Idaho
Brigham Young University - Idaho *T*
Idaho State University *B, M, T*
Lewis-Clark State College *B, T*
Northwest Nazarene University *B*
University of Idaho *B*

Illinois
Chicago State University *B*
Eastern Illinois University *B, T*
Illinois State University *B, T*
McKendree College *T*
North Park University *T*
Northern Illinois University *B, T*
Olivet Nazarene University *B, T*
Sauk Valley Community College *A*
Southern Illinois University
  Carbondale *B, M, D*
Southern Illinois University
  Edwardsville *B, T*
Western Illinois University *B, M*

Indiana
Anderson University *B, T*
Ball State University *B*
Butler University *T*
Indiana State University *B, M, T*
Indiana University
  Bloomington *B, M, D, T*
Indiana University-Purdue University
  Indianapolis *B, M*
Indiana Wesleyan University *T*
Manchester College *B, T*
University of Evansville *T*
University of Indianapolis *T*
University of St. Francis *B*
Vincennes University *A*

Iowa
Central College *T*
Dordt College *B*
Drake University *T*
Graceland University *T*
Iowa State University *B, T*
Iowa Wesleyan College *B*
Northwestern College *T*
St. Ambrose University *B, T*
University of Iowa *T*
University of Northern Iowa *B, M*
Upper Iowa University *B, T*
Wartburg College *T*
William Penn University *B*

Kansas
Benedictine College *T*
Bethany College *B*
Bethel College *T*
Emporia State University *B, T*
Garden City Community College *A*
Independence Community College *A*
McPherson College *T*
MidAmerica Nazarene University *B, T*
Ottawa University *T*

Pittsburg State University *B, T*
Tabor College *B, T*
University of Kansas *B, T*
Washburn University of Topeka *B*
Wichita State University *T*

Kentucky
Campbellsville University *B*
Cumberland College *B, T*
Kentucky Wesleyan College *T*
Morehead State University *B*
Murray State University *B, T*
Union College *M*
University of Kentucky *B*

Louisiana
Centenary College of Louisiana *B, T*
Louisiana College *B*
Nicholls State University *B*

Maine
University of Maine
  Farmington *B, T*
  Presque Isle *B*

Maryland
Allegany College *A*
Community College of Baltimore County
  Catonsville *A*
  Dundalk *A*
  Essex *A*
Morgan State University *B*
Salisbury University *B, T*
University of Maryland
  College Park *B, M, D*

Massachusetts
Boston University *M, T*
Bridgewater State College *B, M, T*
Northeastern University *B*
Springfield College *B, M, T*
University of Massachusetts
  Lowell *B*
Westfield State College *B, T*

Michigan
Adrian College *B, T*
Alma College *T*
Central Michigan University *B, M*
Ferris State University *B*
Madonna University *T*
Michigan State University *M, D*
Northern Michigan University *B, M, T*
Wayne State University *B, M, T*
Western Michigan University *B*

Minnesota
Augsburg College *B, T*
Bemidji State University *T*
Bethel College *B*
Concordia College: Moorhead *B, T*
Gustavus Adolphus College *T*
Hamline University *B*
Minnesota State University
  Mankato *B, M, T*
  Moorhead *B, T*
Northland Community & Technical
  College *A*
Ridgewater College: A Community and
  Technical College *A*
Southwest State University *B, T*
University of Minnesota
  Duluth *B*
University of St. Thomas *B, T*
Vermilion Community College *A*
Winona State University *B, M, T*

Mississippi
Coahoma Community College *A*
Itawamba Community College *A*
Mary Holmes College *A*
Mississippi State University *T*
Mississippi University for Women *M*

Missouri
College of the Ozarks *T*
Culver-Stockton College *T*
Lindenwood University *B*
Missouri Baptist University *B, T*

Missouri Southern State College *B, T*
Northwest Missouri State
  University *B*
Southwest Baptist University *T*
Truman State University *M, T*

Montana
Montana State University
  Billings *B, T*
Rocky Mountain College *B, T*
University of Montana-Missoula *T*
University of Montana: Western *B, T*

Nebraska
Concordia University *B, T*
University of Nebraska
  Kearney *B, T*
  Lincoln *B, T*
  Omaha *B, T*

Nevada
University of Nevada
  Las Vegas *B*
  Reno *B*

New Hampshire
Plymouth State College *M, T*

New Jersey
Caldwell College *T*
The College of New Jersey *B, M*
Montclair State University *B, M, T*
Rowan University *B, T*
Seton Hall University *B, M, T*
Thomas Edison State College *B*
William Paterson University of New
  Jersey *B, T*

New Mexico
University of New Mexico *B, M, T*
Western New Mexico University *B*

New York
Adelphi University *M*
City University of New York
  Brooklyn College *B, M*
  Hunter College *B, T*
  York College *B, T*
College of Mount St. Vincent *B, T*
Corning Community College *A*
Fulton-Montgomery Community
  College *A*
Hofstra University *B, M, T*
Ithaca College *B, T*
Long Island University
  C. W. Post Campus *B, T*
Manhattan College *B, T*
New York University *M, D*
St. Bonaventure University *M*
State University of New York
  College at Brockport *B, M, T*
  College at Cortland *B, M, T*
  Oswego *T*
Syracuse University *B*

North Carolina
Appalachian State University *B, M, T*
East Carolina University *B, M*
Elon University *B, T*
Fayetteville State University *B, T*
Gardner-Webb University *B*
Guilford Technical Community
  College *A*
Johnson C. Smith University *B*
Lenoir Community College *A*
North Carolina Central University *B*
North Carolina State University *T*
University of North Carolina
  Greensboro *B, T*
  Pembroke *B, T*

North Dakota
Dickinson State University *B, T*
Mayville State University *B, T*
University of Mary *M*
Valley City State University *B, T*

Ohio
Ashland University *T*

Baldwin-Wallace College *B, T*
Bluffton College *B*
Bowling Green State University *B*
Cedarville University *T*
Central State University *B*
College of Mount St. Joseph *B, T*
Defiance College *B, T*
Kent State University *B, M, D, T*
Kent State University
  Stark Campus *B*
Malone College *B*
Miami University
  Oxford Campus *B, M, T*
Mount Union College *T*
Mount Vernon Nazarene University *B, T*
Ohio Northern University *B, T*
Ohio State University
  Columbus Campus *M, D*
Ohio University *B, T*
Ohio Wesleyan University *B*
Otterbein College *B*
University of Akron *B, T*
University of Cincinnati *B, M, T*
University of Findlay *B, T*
University of Rio Grande *B, T*
University of Toledo *B, M, T*
Wilmington College *B*
Youngstown State University *B, M, T*

Oklahoma
East Central University *T*
Eastern Oklahoma State College *A*
Northeastern State University *B*
Northwestern Oklahoma State
  University *B, T*
Oklahoma Baptist University *B, T*
Oklahoma City University *B*
Oklahoma State University *M*
Oral Roberts University *B, T*
Southeastern Oklahoma State
  University *B, M, T*
Southwestern Oklahoma State
  University *B, M, T*
University of Central Oklahoma *B*
University of Oklahoma *M*

Oregon
Chemeketa Community College *A*
Concordia University *B, M, T*
George Fox University *T*
Linfield College *T*
Oregon State University *M*
Portland State University *B, M, T*
University of Portland *T*
Western Oregon University *B, T*

Pennsylvania
Arcadia University *M*
Bucks County Community College *A*
Chatham College *D*
East Stroudsburg University of
  Pennsylvania *B, T*
Gettysburg College *T*
Immaculata University *M*
Lincoln University *B, T*
Lock Haven University of
  Pennsylvania *B, T*
Marywood University *B*
Penn State
  Harrisburg *M*
St. Joseph's University *M*
Slippery Rock University of
  Pennsylvania *B, T*
Temple University *B, M*
West Chester University of
  Pennsylvania *B, M, T*

Puerto Rico
Universidad del Este *B*

Rhode Island
Rhode Island College *B, M*

South Carolina
South Carolina State University *B, T*
University of South Carolina *M*

South Dakota
Dakota State University *B, T*
Mount Marty College *B*
University of Sioux Falls *B*
University of South Dakota *M*

Tennessee
Austin Peay State University *B, T*
Belmont University *T*
Bethel College *B*
Lambuth University *T*
Maryville College *B, T*
Middle Tennessee State University *B*
Tennessee Technological
  University *B, M, T*
Union University *T*
University of Tennessee
  Knoxville *M, D, T*
Vanderbilt University *M*

Texas
Angelina College *A*
Austin Community College *A*
Baylor University *B, M, T*
Brazosport College *A*
Del Mar College *A*
Kilgore College *A*
Lamar University *T*
Laredo Community College *A*
Prairie View A&M University *M*
Sam Houston State University *M, T*
Southwest Texas State University *M, T*
Texas A&M University *M, D*
Texas A&M University
  Commerce *M, T*
  Kingsville *B*
Texas Christian University *T*
Texas Southern University *M*
Texas Woman's University *D, T*
University of Houston *B, M*
University of Houston
  Clear Lake *T*
University of North Texas *B, M, T*
University of Texas
  Arlington *T*
  Austin *M, D*
  El Paso *M*
  Pan American *B, M, T*
  San Antonio *T*
  Tyler *M, T*
West Texas A&M University *M*

Utah
Brigham Young University *B*
Snow College *A*
University of Utah *B*
Utah State University *B*

Virginia
Averett University *B, T*
Bluefield College *T*
Eastern Mennonite University *T*
George Mason University *B, M*
Hampton University *B*
James Madison University *M, T*
Liberty University *B*
Longwood University *B, T*
Lynchburg College *B*
Radford University *B, T*
University of Virginia's College at
  Wise *T*
Virginia Commonwealth University *B*

Washington
Central Washington University *B, T*
Eastern Washington University *B, T*
Northwest College *T*
Pacific Lutheran University *T*
Renton Technical College *C, A*
Whitworth College *B, T*

West Virginia
Concord College *B*
Mountain State University *B*
Salem International University *T*
Shepherd College *B*
West Liberty State College *B*

West Virginia State College *B*
West Virginia University *T*
West Virginia Wesleyan College *B*

Wisconsin
Carroll College *B, T*
Ripon College *T*
University of Wisconsin
  La Crosse *B, M, T*
  Platteville *T*
  River Falls *T*
  Superior *T*

Wyoming
University of Wyoming *B*

Health unit coordinator

Florida
Pasco-Hernando Community College *C*
Pensacola Junior College *C*

Minnesota
Hennepin Technical College *C, A*
Minnesota State College - Southeast
  Technical *C*
St. Paul College - A Community and
  Technical College *C*

Mississippi
Mississippi Gulf Coast Community
  College
    Perkinston *C, A*

New Mexico
Albuquerque Technical-Vocational
  Institute *C*

North Carolina
Roanoke-Chowan Community
  College *C*

Pennsylvania
Career Training Academy:
  Monroeville *A*
Community College of Allegheny
  County *C*
Consolidated School of Business
  Lancaster *A*
  York *A*
Delaware County Community College *C*
Douglas School of Business *C*

Washington
Clover Park Technical College *C*
Spokane Community College *C, A*

Wisconsin
Mid-State Technical College *C*
Western Wisconsin Technical College *C*

Health unit manager

Pennsylvania
Delaware County Community
  College *C, A*

Health/medical psychology

Indiana
Indiana University-Purdue University
  Indianapolis *D*

Massachusetts
Massachusetts College of Pharmacy and
  Health Sciences *B*

Minnesota
Capella University *M, D*

Pennsylvania
University of the Sciences in
  Philadelphia *M*

Texas
Southwest Texas State University *M*

Washington
Bastyr University *B*

Health/physical fitness

Alabama
Chattahoochee Valley Community
  College *A*
Huntingdon College *B, T*
Lawson State Community College *A*
Northeast Alabama Community
  College *A*
Samford University *B*
University of Alabama *D*
University of Alabama
  Birmingham *D*

Arizona
Eastern Arizona College *A*
Northern Arizona University *B, M*
Pima Community College *C*
University of Arizona *M*

Arkansas
Arkansas State University *B*
John Brown University *B*
Ouachita Baptist University *B*
University of Arkansas *M*

California
Antelope Valley College *A*
California Baptist University *B*
California State Polytechnic University:
  Pomona *B, M*
California State University
  Chico *B, M*
  Fresno *A*
  Hayward *B, M*
  Long Beach *M*
  Sacramento *M*
  Stanislaus *B*
Citrus College *A*
College of the Canyons *A*
Columbia College *A*
Diablo Valley College *C, A*
East Los Angeles College *A*
Foothill College *C*
Humboldt State University *B*
Imperial Valley College *A*
Irvine Valley College *C, A*
La Sierra University *B*
Long Beach City College *A*
Modesto Junior College *A*
Palomar College *A*
Pepperdine University *B*
Point Loma Nazarene University *B*
St. Mary's College of California *B, M*
San Diego City College *C, A*
San Diego State University *M*
San Jose State University *B, M*
Santa Barbara City College *C, A*
Southwestern College *A*
University of San Francisco *B*
University of the Pacific *B, T*

Colorado
Colorado Mountain College
  Timberline Campus *A*
Fort Lewis College *B*
Mesa State College *B*
Trinidad State Junior College *A*

Connecticut
Central Connecticut State University *B*
Mitchell College *A*

Delaware
Delaware State University *B*
University of Delaware *B, M*

District of Columbia
American University *C, B, M*

Florida
Barry University *B*
Gulf Coast Community College *A*
Nova Southeastern University *B*

Palm Beach Community College *A*
University of West Florida *B, M*

Georgia
Armstrong Atlantic State University *B, T*
Brewton-Parker College *B*
Darton College *A*
East Georgia College *A*
Georgia Southern University *B*
Georgia State University *B, M*
Middle Georgia College *A*
North Georgia College & State
  University *B, M*
South Georgia College *A*
Valdosta State University *B*
Young Harris College *A*

Hawaii
Brigham Young University-Hawaii *B*
University of Hawaii
  Hilo *B*
  Manoa *B*

Idaho
Boise State University *B, M*
College of Southern Idaho *A*
North Idaho College *A*
Northwest Nazarene University *B*

Illinois
Chicago State University *B, M, T*
Elmhurst College *B*
Greenville College *B, T*
Illinois Valley Community College *A*
John Wood Community College *A*
Judson College *B, T*
Kishwaukee College *A*
Lincoln College *A*
McHenry County College *C*
Robert Morris College: Chicago *A*
South Suburban College of Cook
  County *A*
Southern Illinois University
  Edwardsville *B, M, T*
Southwestern Illinois College *A*
Trinity International University *B*
University of Illinois
  Chicago *B, M, D, T*
  Urbana-Champaign *B, M, D*
Waubonsee Community College *A*
Wheaton College *B*

Indiana
Anderson University *B*
Franklin College *B*
Goshen College *B*
Indiana Wesleyan University *B*
Taylor University *B*
Tri-State University *B*
University of Evansville *B*
Vincennes University *A*

Iowa
Cornell College *B, T*
Dordt College *B*
Ellsworth Community College *A*
Graceland University *B, T*
Iowa State University *B, M*
Iowa Wesleyan College *B*
Loras College *M*
Luther College *B*
Northwestern College *B, T*
St. Ambrose University *B*
University of Iowa *M*
Upper Iowa University *B*
William Penn University *B*

Kansas
Barton County Community College *A*
Benedictine College *B*
Bethel College *B*
Central Christian College *A, B*
Dodge City Community College *A*
Emporia State University *B*
Friends University *B*
Garden City Community College *A*
Kansas City Kansas Community
  College *A*

Kansas Wesleyan University *B, T*
McPherson College *B, T*
Ottawa University *B*
Pittsburg State University *B, M, T*
Seward County Community College *A*
Southwestern College *B*
Sterling College *B*
Tabor College *B*

Kentucky
Asbury College *B*
Campbellsville University *B*
Kentucky Wesleyan College *B, T*
Murray State University *B*
University of Kentucky *M, D*

Louisiana
Centenary College of Louisiana *B, T*
Louisiana College *B*
Louisiana State University
  Shreveport *B*
Louisiana Tech University *B*
Nicholls State University *B*
University of Louisiana at Monroe *B*

Maine
Husson College *B*
St. Joseph's College *B*
University of Maine
  Presque Isle *B*

Maryland
Anne Arundel Community College *A*
Chesapeake College *C*
Columbia Union College *B*
Community College of Baltimore County
  Catonsville *C, A*
  Dundalk *C, A*
  Essex *C, A*
Frostburg State University *B*
Howard Community College *A*
McDaniel College *B, M*

Massachusetts
Becker College *B*
Berkshire Community College *C*
Bridgewater State College *B, M*
Cape Cod Community College *A*
Dean College *A*
Greenfield Community College *C*
Mount Ida College *A*
Northeastern University *B*
Springfield College *B, M*
Westfield State College *B*

Michigan
Adrian College *B, T*
Alma College *T*
Aquinas College *B*
Calvin College *B, T*
Central Michigan University *B, M*
Eastern Michigan University *B, M*
Grand Valley State University *B*
Michigan State University *D*
Northern Michigan University *B, T*
Spring Arbor University *B*

Minnesota
Bemidji State University *B*
Bethel College *B*
Concordia College: Moorhead *B*
Concordia University: St. Paul *B*
Gustavus Adolphus College *B*
Hamline University *B*
Minnesota State University
  Mankato *B, T*
  Moorhead *B*
Ridgewater College: A Community and
  Technical College *A*
St. Cloud State University *B, M*
Southwest State University *B*
University of St. Thomas *B, M*
Winona State University *B, T*

Mississippi
Mississippi University for Women *B, T*
Mississippi Valley State University *B, T*
University of Mississippi *T*

University of Southern Mississippi *B*

Missouri
College of the Ozarks *B*
Culver-Stockton College *T*
East Central College *A*
Lindenwood University *B*
Missouri Southern State College *B, T*
Missouri Western State College *B, T*
St. Louis University *M, D*
Southeast Missouri State University *B*
Southwest Baptist University *B, T*
Southwest Missouri State University *M*
Three Rivers Community College *A*
Truman State University *B*
University of Missouri
　　Kansas City *B*

Montana
Miles Community College *A*
Rocky Mountain College *B, T*
University of Great Falls *B*
University of Montana-Missoula *B, M*

Nebraska
Concordia University *B, T*
Dana College *B*
Hastings College *B*
Nebraska Wesleyan University *B*
Northeast Community College *A*
Union College *B*
Wayne State College *B, T*
Western Nebraska Community
　　College *A*

Nevada
University of Nevada
　　Las Vegas *B*

New Hampshire
Hesser College *A*
Plymouth State College *B*

New Jersey
Camden County College *C*
County College of Morris *A*
Gloucester County College *A*
Middlesex County College *A*
Rowan University *B*
Salem Community College *A*

New Mexico
Albuquerque Technical-Vocational
　　Institute *C*
New Mexico Highlands University *B*
San Juan College *C, A*
Santa Fe Community College *C, A*

New York
City University of New York
　　Queens College *B*
Finger Lakes Community College *A*
Fulton-Montgomery Community
　　College *A*
Genesee Community College *A*
Ithaca College *B, M, T*
Long Island University
　　C. W. Post Campus *M*
Monroe Community College *A*
Nassau Community College *A*
Niagara County Community College *A*
State University of New York
　　College at Buffalo *B*
　　College of Agriculture and
　　　　Technology at Morrisville *A*
Suffolk County Community College *A*
Syracuse University *B*

North Carolina
Barton College *B*
Campbell University *B*
Catawba College *B*
Chowan College *B, T*
East Carolina University *B*
Elon University *B*
Greensboro College *B, T*
Lenoir-Rhyne College *B, T*
Mars Hill College *B*

North Carolina Agricultural and
　　Technical State University *B, T*
North Carolina Central University *B*
St. Augustine's College *B*
Shaw University *B*
University of North Carolina
　　Chapel Hill *B, M*
　　Charlotte *B*
　　Greensboro *M, D*
　　Wilmington *B*
Wake Forest University *B, M*

North Dakota
Dickinson State University *B, T*
Mayville State University *B*
Minot State University *B*
Minot State University: Bottineau
　　Campus *A*
North Dakota State University *B*
Valley City State University *B*

Ohio
Baldwin-Wallace College *B*
Bluffton College *B*
Cedarville University *B*
Cincinnati State Technical and
　　Community College *C*
Cleveland State University *M*
Defiance College *B, T*
Kent State University *B, M, D*
Kent State University
　　Stark Campus *B*
Malone College *B*
Miami University
　　Oxford Campus *B, T*
Mount Vernon Nazarene University *B, T*
Ohio Northern University *B*
Ohio State University
　　Columbus Campus *B, M, D*
Ohio University *B, M*
Otterbein College *B*
Shawnee State University *B*
Sinclair Community College *A*
University of Akron *B, M*
University of Dayton *B*
University of Findlay *B, T*
University of Rio Grande *B*
University of Toledo *B, D*
Youngstown State University *B*

Oklahoma
Cameron University *B*
Carl Albert State College *A*
East Central University *B, T*
Eastern Oklahoma State College *A*
Northeastern Oklahoma Agricultural and
　　Mechanical College *A*
Northeastern State University *B*
Northwestern Oklahoma State
　　University *B*
Oklahoma Baptist University *B, T*
Oklahoma Christian University of
　　Science and Arts *B*
Oklahoma City University *B*
Oklahoma Panhandle State University *B*
Oklahoma State University *B, M*
Oral Roberts University *B*
Rose State College *A*
Seminole State College *A*
University of Oklahoma *B, M, D*
University of Science and Arts of
　　Oklahoma *B, T*
Western Oklahoma State College *A*

Oregon
Blue Mountain Community College *A*
Central Oregon Community College *A*
Eastern Oregon University *B*
Lane Community College *C, A*
Linfield College *B*
Oregon State University *B, M, D*
Portland Community College *A*
Southern Oregon University *B, T*
Western Baptist College *B*

Pennsylvania
Bloomsburg University of
　　Pennsylvania *B*
Bucks County Community College *A*
Community College of Allegheny
　　County *A*
Edinboro University of Pennsylvania *B*
Indiana University of Pennsylvania *B, M*
Lincoln University *B*
Lock Haven University of
　　Pennsylvania *B*
Marywood University *B*
Neumann College *B*
Pennsylvania College of Technology *A*
Philadelphia Biblical University *B*
Slippery Rock University of
　　Pennsylvania *B, M, T*
West Chester University of
　　Pennsylvania *M*
Wilson College *B*

Puerto Rico
Universidad Metropolitana *B*
University of Puerto Rico
　　Mayaguez Campus *B*
University of the Sacred Heart *B*

South Carolina
Anderson College *B, T*
Benedict College *B*
Charleston Southern University *B*
Erskine College *B, T*
Furman University *B, M, T*
Limestone College *B*
Technical College of the Lowcountry *C*
University of South Carolina *M, D*
Voorhees College *B*

South Dakota
Augustana College *B, T*
Black Hills State University *B*
Dakota State University *B*
Northern State University *B*
South Dakota State University *B, M, T*

Tennessee
Austin Peay State University *B, M*
Belmont University *B, T*
Carson-Newman College *B, T*
Columbia State Community College *A*
East Tennessee State University *B, M, T*
Lambuth University *B*
Lee University *B*
Middle Tennessee State
　　University *B, M, D*
Milligan College *B, T*
Tennessee Wesleyan College *B, T*
Trevecca Nazarene University *B*
Tusculum College *B*
University of Tennessee
　　Knoxville *B, M, D*
　　Martin *B*
Walters State Community College *A*

Texas
Abilene Christian University *B*
Alvin Community College *A*
Amarillo College *A*
Angelo State University *B, M, T*
Austin Community College *C, A*
Baylor University *B*
Concordia University at Austin *T*
Del Mar College *A*
East Texas Baptist University *B*
El Paso Community College *A*
Hill College *A*
Houston Community College
　　System *C, A*
Howard College *A*
Kilgore College *A*
Lamar University *B, M*
LeTourneau University *B*
Lee College *A*
Lubbock Christian University *B*
Northeast Texas Community College *A*
Prairie View A&M University *B*
St. Edward's University *B, T*

St. Philip's College *A*
Sam Houston State University *B*
South Plains College *A*
Southwest Texas State
　　University *B, M, T*
Southwestern Adventist
　　University *A, B, T*
Stephen F. Austin State University *B, T*
Sul Ross State University *B, T*
Tarleton State University *B, D*
Texas A&M International
　　University *B, T*
Texas A&M University *B, M, D*
Texas A&M University
　　Commerce *B*
　　Corpus Christi *B*
Texas Christian University *B, M*
Texas Lutheran University *B, T*
Texas Southern University *B*
Texas Tech University *B, M*
Texas Wesleyan University *B, M*
Texas Woman's University *B, M, D, T*
Trinity Valley Community College *A*
Tyler Junior College *A*
University of Houston *B, M*
University of Houston
　　Clear Lake *B, M*
University of Mary Hardin-Baylor *B*
University of North Texas *B, M*
University of Texas
　　Arlington *B*
　　Austin *B*
　　El Paso *B, M*
　　Pan American *B, M, T*
　　San Antonio *B*
　　Tyler *B, M*
　　of the Permian Basin *B, M*
University of the Incarnate Word *B*
West Texas A&M University *B*
Western Texas College *A*

Utah
Brigham Young University *B, M*
University of Utah *B, M, D*
Weber State University *B*

Vermont
Castleton State College *B*
Johnson State College *B*

Virginia
Averett University *B*
Bridgewater College *B*
College of William and Mary *B*
Emory & Henry College *B, T*
George Mason University *B*
James Madison University *B, M, T*
Longwood University *B, T*
Lynchburg College *B*
University of Virginia's College at
　　Wise *T*
Virginia Intermont College *B, T*

Washington
Central Washington University *M*
Centralia College *A*
Eastern Washington University *B*
Grays Harbor College *C*
Pacific Lutheran University *B*
Seattle Pacific University *M*
Washington State University *B*
Western Washington University *B, T*
Whitworth College *B*

West Virginia
Shepherd College *T*
West Virginia University *B*
West Virginia Wesleyan College *B*

Wisconsin
University of Wisconsin
　　Platteville *B, T*
　　Stevens Point *B, T*

Heating/air conditioning/ refrigeration maintenance

Alabama

Bevill State Community College *A*
Calhoun Community College *C, A*
Community College of the Air Force *A*
George C. Wallace State Community
   College
      Selma *C*
J. F. Drake State Technical College *C*
Northwest-Shoals Community
   College *C, A*
Shelton State Community College *C, A*
Southern Union State Community
   College *A*
Wallace Community College: Sparks
   Campus *C*
Wallace State Community College at
   Hanceville *C, A*

Alaska

University of Alaska
     Anchorage *C, A*

Arizona

Arizona Western College *C, A*
Eastern Arizona College *C*
Gateway Community College *C, A*

Arkansas

North Arkansas College *C*
Pulaski Technical College *A*
Southeast Arkansas College *C*

California

Cerro Coso Community College *C, A*
Citrus College *A*
Foothill College *C*
Laney College *C, A*
Los Angeles Trade and Technical
   College *C, A*
Modesto Junior College *C, A*
Mount San Antonio College *C, A*
Orange Coast College *C, A*
Riverside Community College *C, A*
San Diego City College *C, A*
Santa Rosa Junior College *C*
Shasta College *C, A*
Southwestern College *C*

Colorado

Community College of Aurora *A*
IntelliTec College *C, A*
Red Rocks Community College *C, A*

Delaware

Delaware Technical and Community
   College
      Owens Campus *C, A*
      Stanton/Wilmington Campus *A*

District of Columbia

University of the District of Columbia *C*

Florida

Daytona Beach Community College *C*
Hillsborough Community College *A*
Indian River Community College *C, A*
Lake City Community College *C*
Miami-Dade Community College *A*
New England Institute of
   Technology *C, A*
Palm Beach Community College *C*
Santa Fe Community College *C*
Seminole Community College *C*
South Florida Community College *C*

Georgia

Athens Technical College *C*
Bainbridge College *C*
Central Georgia Technical College *C*
Chattahoochee Technical College *C*
Columbus Technical College *C*
Darton College *A*
DeKalb Technical College *C*
Georgia Southwestern State University *A*
Middle Georgia College *A*

Southwest Georgia Technical College *C*
Waycross College *A*

Hawaii

University of Hawaii
     Honolulu Community College *C, A*

Idaho

Boise State University *C, A*
College of Southern Idaho *C, A*
Lewis-Clark State College *C, A*
North Idaho College *C, A*

Illinois

Black Hawk College *C, A*
City Colleges of Chicago
     Kennedy-King College *C, A*
College of DuPage *C, A*
College of Lake County *C, A*
Elgin Community College *C, A*
Illinois Eastern Community Colleges
     Lincoln Trail College *C, A*
John A. Logan College *C*
Joliet Junior College *C*
Kankakee Community College *C, A*
Lake Land College *C*
Lincoln Land Community College *C*
Moraine Valley Community College *C*
Oakton Community College *C*
Prairie State College *C*
Rend Lake College *C, A*
Richland Community College *C*
Sauk Valley Community College *C, A*
Southwestern Illinois College *C, A*
Triton College *C, A*
Waubonsee Community College *C, A*
William Rainey Harper College *C, A*

Indiana

Ivy Tech State College
     Bloomington *A*
     Central Indiana *C, A*
     Columbus *C, A*
     Eastcentral *C, A*
     Kokomo *C, A*
     Lafayette *C, A*
     Northcentral *C, A*
     Northeast *C, A*
     Northwest *C, A*
     Southcentral *C, A*
     Southwest *C, A*
     Wabash Valley *C, A*
     Whitewater *C, A*
Oakland City University *C, A*

Iowa

Des Moines Area Community
   College *C, A*
Hawkeye Community College *C*
Indian Hills Community College *C*
Kirkwood Community College *C*
Marshalltown Community College *A*
North Iowa Area Community College *A*
Northeast Iowa Community College *C*
Scott Community College *A*
Western Iowa Tech Community
   College *C*

Kansas

Pittsburg State University *C, A*

Kentucky

Somerset Community College *C*

Louisiana

Delgado Community College *C*
ITI Technical College *C*
Nunez Community College *C, A*

Maryland

Cecil Community College *C, A*
Chesapeake College *C*
Community College of Baltimore County
     Catonsville *C, A*
     Dundalk *C, A*
     Essex *C, A*

Massachusetts

Springfield Technical Community
   College *C*

Michigan

Baker College
   of Owosso *C*
Grand Rapids Community College *C, A*
Jackson Community College *C, A*
Kellogg Community College *C, A*
Lansing Community College *A*
Macomb Community College *C, A*
Mid Michigan Community College *C, A*
Mott Community College *C, A*
Northern Michigan University *C, A*
Oakland Community College *C, A*
Washtenaw Community College *A*
Wayne County Community College *C*

Minnesota

Century Community and Technical
   College *C, A*
Hennepin Technical College *C, A*
Hibbing Community College: A
   Technical and Community College *C*
Minneapolis Community and Technical
   College *C, A*
Minnesota State College - Southeast
   Technical *C, A*
St. Cloud Technical College *C, A*
South Central Technical College *C, A*

Mississippi

Holmes Community College *A*
Itawamba Community College *C*
Mississippi Gulf Coast Community
   College
      Perkinston *C*
Northwest Mississippi Community
   College *C, A*
Pearl River Community College *C, A*

Missouri

East Central College *C, A*
Jefferson College *C, A*
Maple Woods Community College *C, A*
Ozarks Technical Community
   College *C, A*
Penn Valley Community College *C, A*
Ranken Technical College *A*
Vatterott College: Sunset Hills *A*

Montana

Montana State University
     Billings *A*
     Billings College of
       Technology *C, A*

Nebraska

Central Community College *C, A*
Metropolitan Community College *C, A*
Mid Plains Community College
   Area *C, A*
Northeast Community College *A*
Southeast Community College
     Milford Campus *A*
Vatterott College: Spring Valley *A*

Nevada

Community College of Southern
   Nevada *C, A*
Truckee Meadows Community
   College *C, A*
Western Nevada Community College *A*

New Hampshire

New Hampshire Community Technical
   College
     Manchester *C, A*

New Jersey

Raritan Valley Community College *A*

New Mexico

Albuquerque Technical-Vocational
   Institute *C*
Clovis Community College *C, A*
Dona Ana Branch Community College of
   New Mexico State University *C, A*

New York

Dutchess Community College *C*
Erie Community College
     North Campus *C*
Hudson Valley Community College *A*
Jamestown Community College *A*
Mohawk Valley Community College *C*
Monroe Community College *C, A*
State University of New York
     College of Technology at Alfred *A*
     College of Technology at Canton *C*
     College of Technology at
       Delhi *C, A*

North Carolina

Alamance Community College *C, A*
Asheville Buncombe Technical
   Community College *C, A*
Blue Ridge Community College *C*
Brunswick Community College *C*
Caldwell Community College and
   Technical Institute *C*
Cape Fear Community College *C*
Catawba Valley Community College *C*
Central Piedmont Community College *A*
Cleveland Community College *C*
Coastal Carolina Community College *C*
College of the Albemarle *C*
Craven Community College *C, A*
Davidson County Community College *C*
Forsyth Technical Community College *C*
Gaston College *C*
Guilford Technical Community
   College *C, A*
Johnston Community College *C, A*
Martin Community College *C, A*
Mitchell Community College *C*
Piedmont Community College *C*
Pitt Community College *C, A*
Roanoke-Chowan Community
   College *C*
Rockingham Community College *C*
Rowan-Cabarrus Community College *C*
South Piedmont Community
   College *C, A*
Southeastern Community College *C*
Southwestern Community College *C*
Surry Community College *A*
Tri-County Community College *C*
Vance-Granville Community College *C*
Wake Technical Community College *C*
Wilson Technical Community College *C*

North Dakota

Bismarck State College *C, A*
North Dakota State College of
   Science *C, A*

Ohio

Cincinnati State Technical and
   Community College *C, A*
Columbus State Community
   College *C, A*
ETI Technical College of Niles *C*
North Central State College *C, A*
Owens Community College
     Findlay Campus *C*
RETS Tech Center *C*
Sinclair Community College *C, A*
Stark State College of Technology *A*
University of Northwestern Ohio *C, A*
Washington State Community College *A*

Oklahoma

Oklahoma State University
     Okmulgee *A*
Rose State College *A*
Tulsa Community College *A*
Vatterott College *C, A*

Oregon

Lane Community College *C, A*
Linn-Benton Community College *C*
Portland Community College *C, A*

Pennsylvania

CHI Institute *C*

Cambria County Area Community
  College *A*
Community College of Allegheny
  County *C, A*
Dean Institute of Technology *A*
Delaware County Community College *C*
Lehigh Carbon Community College *C, A*
Northampton County Area Community
  College *C*
Pennsylvania College of
  Technology *A, B*
Reading Area Community College *C*
Westmoreland County Community
  College *A*

Puerto Rico

Huertas Junior College *C, A*

South Carolina

Aiken Technical College *C*
Central Carolina Technical College *C*
Florence-Darlington Technical
  College *C, A*
Horry-Georgetown Technical College *A*
Midlands Technical College *C, A*
Piedmont Technical College *C, A*
Spartanburg Technical College *C, A*
Technical College of the
  Lowcountry *C, A*
Tri-County Technical College *A*
Trident Technical College *C*
Williamsburg Technical College *C, A*
York Technical College *C, A*

South Dakota

Southeast Technical Institute *A*

Tennessee

Chattanooga State Technical Community
  College *C*
Northeast State Technical Community
  College *C*

Texas

Alvin Community College *A*
Austin Community College *C*
Brazosport College *C, A*
Cedar Valley College *A*
Central Texas College *C, A*
Coastal Bend College *C, A*
College of the Mainland *C, A*
Del Mar College *C, A*
Eastfield College *C, A*
El Paso Community College *C, A*
Frank Phillips College *C*
Grayson County College *C, A*
Hill College *C, A*
Houston Community College System *C*
Lamar State College at Port Arthur *C, A*
Laredo Community College *C*
Lee College *C, A*
Midland College *C, A*
North Harris Montgomery Community
  College District *C, A*
Odessa College *C, A*
Paris Junior College *A*
St. Philip's College *C, A*
South Plains College *C, A*
South Texas Community College *C, A*
Tarrant County College *C, A*
Texarkana College *C*
Texas State Technical College
  Waco *C, A*
  West Texas *C*
Trinity Valley Community College *C*
Tyler Junior College *C, A*
Western Texas College *C*
Wharton County Junior College *C*

Utah

Salt Lake Community College *C, A*
Utah Valley State College *C, A*

Virginia

Danville Community College *A*
Mountain Empire Community College *C*
Southside Virginia Community
  College *C*

Southwest Virginia Community
  College *C*
Thomas Nelson Community College *C*
Virginia Highlands Community
  College *C*
Virginia Western Community
  College *C, A*

Washington

Clover Park Technical College *C, A*
North Seattle Community College *A*
Renton Technical College *C, A*
Spokane Community College *A*
Spokane Falls Community College *C*
Walla Walla Community College *C, A*
Wenatchee Valley College *C, A*

West Virginia

West Virginia Northern Community
  College *A*

Wisconsin

Chippewa Valley Technical College *A*
Milwaukee Area Technical College *A*
Moraine Park Technical College *C*
Waukesha County Technical College *C*
Western Wisconsin Technical College *C*

Wyoming

Eastern Wyoming College *C*

Heating/air conditioning/ refrigeration technology

Alabama

Calhoun Community College *A*
Douglas MacArthur State Technical
  College *C*
Harry M. Ayers State Technical
  College *C, A*
Shelton State Community College *C, A*

California

Citrus College *C*
Long Beach City College *C, A*

Florida

Palm Beach Community College *C*

Idaho

Lewis-Clark State College *C, A*

Illinois

City Colleges of Chicago
  Kennedy-King College *C, A*
Oakton Community College *C*

Michigan

Grand Rapids Community College *A*
Jackson Community College *C, A*
Mott Community College *C, A*
Oakland Community College *C, A*

Minnesota

Hennepin Technical College *A*
Hibbing Community College: A
  Technical and Community College *C*
Minnesota State College - Southeast
  Technical *C, A*

New York

Mohawk Valley Community College *A*
State University of New York
  College of Technology at
    Canton *C, A*
Suffolk County Community College *A*

North Carolina

Fayetteville Technical Community
  College *C, A*
Roanoke-Chowan Community
  College *C*

North Dakota

North Dakota State College of Science *A*

Ohio

North Central State College *C, A*
Sinclair Community College *C*

Oklahoma

Rose State College *A*

Pennsylvania

Delaware County Community College *C*
Pennsylvania College of
  Technology *A, B*

Puerto Rico

Humacao Community College *A*

South Carolina

York Technical College *C, A*

South Dakota

Southeast Technical Institute *C, A*

Tennessee

Miller-Motte Technical College *C*
Northeast State Technical Community
  College *C*

Texas

Austin Community College *C, A*
St. Philip's College *C, A*

Wisconsin

Western Wisconsin Technical College *A*

Heavy equipment maintenance

Alabama

Shelton State Community College *C*

California

San Joaquin Delta College *C, A*

Georgia

Southwest Georgia Technical College *A*

Illinois

Rend Lake College *A*

Iowa

Northwest Iowa Community College *C*

Michigan

Ferris State University *A*

Minnesota

Dakota County Technical College *C, A*

New York

State University of New York
  College of Agriculture and
    Technology at Morrisville *A*

North Carolina

Wilson Technical Community College *C*

Oregon

Linn-Benton Community College *A*

Pennsylvania

Pennsylvania College of
  Technology *C, A*

Washington

Clover Park Technical College *C, A*

Heavy/earthmoving equipment operation

Florida

Indian River Community College *C*

Indiana

Ivy Tech State College
  Southwest *C, A*
  Wabash Valley *C, A*

North Carolina

Wilson Technical Community College *C*

Virginia

Southside Virginia Community
  College *C*

Hebrew

California

Master's College *B*
University of California
  Los Angeles *B*

Connecticut

Fairfield University *B*

District of Columbia

Catholic University of America *M, D*
George Washington University *B*

Illinois

Concordia University *B*
Moody Bible Institute *B*
Trinity International University *M*
University of Chicago *B*

Maryland

Baltimore Hebrew University *B, M, D*
Washington Bible College *M*

Massachusetts

Harvard College *B*

Michigan

University of Michigan *B*

Minnesota

Carleton College *B*
University of Minnesota
  Twin Cities *B*

Missouri

Washington University in St. Louis *B, M*

New Hampshire

Dartmouth College *B*

New York

City University of New York
  Brooklyn College *B*
  Hunter College *B*
  Queens College *B*
Cornell University *B*
Hofstra University *B*
New York University *B, M, D*
State University of New York
  Binghamton *B*
Touro College *B*
Yeshiva University *B*

Ohio

Laura and Alvin Siegal College of Judaic
  Studies *B, M*
Ohio State University
  Columbus Campus *B*

Oregon

University of Oregon *B*

Pennsylvania

Dickinson College *B*
Temple University *B*

Texas

University of Texas
  Austin *B, M, D*

Washington

University of Washington *B*

Wisconsin

University of Wisconsin
  Madison *B, M, D*
  Milwaukee *B*

Hematology technology

New Mexico

Albuquerque Technical-Vocational
  Institute *C*

New York

Westchester Community College *A*

Ohio

Columbus State Community College *C*

Pennsylvania
Academy of Medical Arts and
Business *C, A*

Texas
Clarendon College *A*

Utah
Utah Career College *C*

Herbalism

Washington
Bastyr University *B*

Higher education administration

Alabama
University of Alabama *M, D*

Alaska
University of Alaska
Anchorage *M, T*

Arizona
Arizona State University *M, D*
University of Arizona *M, D*

Arkansas
University of Arkansas *M, D*
University of Arkansas
Little Rock *M, D*

California
Azusa Pacific University *M, D*
San Jose State University *M*
University of Southern California *M*

Colorado
Colorado State University *M*
Jones International University *M*

Connecticut
University of Connecticut *M, D, T*

District of Columbia
George Washington University *M, D*

Florida
Barry University *M*
Florida International University *D*
Florida State University *M, D*
Nova Southeastern University *D*
University of Florida *D*
University of Miami *M, D*
University of South Florida *M*

Georgia
Georgia Southern University *M*
University of Georgia *D*

Illinois
Loyola University of Chicago *M, D*
North Central College *M*
Northeastern Illinois University *M*
Southern Illinois University
Carbondale *M, D*

Indiana
Ball State University *M, D*
Indiana University
Bloomington *D*
Purdue University *D*

Iowa
Iowa State University *M, D*
University of Iowa *M, D*

Kansas
Pittsburg State University *M*
University of Kansas *M*

Kentucky
University of Kentucky *M*
University of Louisville *M, T*

Maine
University of Maine *M, D*

University of Southern Maine *M*

Maryland
Morgan State University *D*

Massachusetts
Boston College *M, D*
Springfield College *D*
Suffolk University *M*

Michigan
Grand Valley State University *M*
Michigan State University *M, D*

Minnesota
Capella University *M, D*
Minnesota State University
Mankato *M*

Mississippi
University of Mississippi *M*
University of Southern Mississippi *D*

Missouri
Central Missouri State University *M*
St. Louis University *M, D*
Southeast Missouri State University *M*
University of Missouri
Columbia *D*

New Jersey
Rowan University *M*
Seton Hall University *D*

New York
Canisius College *M*
City University of New York
Baruch College *M*
Fordham University *M, D*
New York University *M, D*
St. Bonaventure University *M*
State University of New York
Albany *M, D*
Buffalo *M, D*
College at Brockport *M*
College at Buffalo *M*
New Paltz *D*
Syracuse University *M, D*
University of Rochester *M, D*

North Carolina
Fayetteville State University *M*
North Carolina State University *M, D*
University of North Carolina
Greensboro *M*

North Dakota
University of North Dakota *M, D*

Ohio
Bowling Green State University *D*
Kent State University *M, D*
Ohio State University
Columbus Campus *M, D*
University of Akron *M, D*
University of Toledo *M, D, T*
Wright State University *M*
Youngstown State University *M*

Oklahoma
Oklahoma State University *M, D*
University of Oklahoma *M, D*

Oregon
Portland State University *D*

Pennsylvania
Geneva College *B*
Marywood University *D*
Penn State
University Park *M, D*
University of Pennsylvania *M, D*
Villanova University *M*
Widener University *D*

Puerto Rico
Inter American University of Puerto Rico
Metropolitan Campus *M*
San German Campus *M*

South Dakota
University of South Dakota *M, D*

Tennessee
University of Memphis *D*
Vanderbilt University *M, D*

Texas
Dallas Baptist University *M*
Tarleton State University *D*
Texas A&M University
Commerce *M, D*
Kingsville *M, D*
Texas Southern University *D*
Texas Tech University *M, D*
University of Houston *M, D*
University of North Texas *D*
University of Texas
San Antonio *M*

Vermont
University of Vermont *M*

Virginia
University of Virginia *D*
Virginia Polytechnic Institute and State
University *M, D*

Washington
Seattle University *B*
University of Washington *M, D*
Washington State University *B, M, D*

Wisconsin
Concordia University Wisconsin *M*
University of Wisconsin
La Crosse *M*

Hispanic-American studies

Arizona
Arizona State University *B*
University of Arizona *B, M*

California
California State University
Fullerton *B*
Hayward *B*
Long Beach *B*
Cerritos Community College *A*
Contra Costa College *A*
De Anza College *C, A*
Loyola Marymount University *B*
Mills College *B*
Pitzer College *B*
San Diego Mesa College *A*
San Diego State University *B*
San Francisco State University *B*
Santa Barbara City College *A*
Scripps College *B*
Sonoma State University *B*
University of California
Berkeley *B*
Los Angeles *B*
Riverside *B*
Santa Barbara *B*
Santa Cruz *B*
University of San Diego *B*
Ventura College *A*

Colorado
Metropolitan State College of Denver *B*
University of Northern Colorado *B*

Connecticut
Connecticut College *B*

Illinois
University of Illinois
Chicago *M*

Indiana
Goshen College *B*

Maine
University of Southern Maine *B*

Maryland
Johns Hopkins University *B*

Massachusetts
Boston College *B*
Hampshire College *B*

Michigan
University of Michigan *B*
Wayne State University *B*

Minnesota
University of Minnesota
Twin Cities *B*

New Hampshire
Dartmouth College *B*

New Jersey
Rutgers, The State University of New
Jersey
New Brunswick Regional
Campus *B*
Newark Regional Campus *B*

New Mexico
Western New Mexico University *B*

New York
City University of New York
Brooklyn College *B*
Hunter College *B*
Columbia University
Columbia College *B*
Eugene Lang College/New School
University *B*
Hobart and William Smith Colleges *B*
Hofstra University *B*
Mount St. Mary College *B*
Sarah Lawrence College *B*
State University of New York
College at Oneonta *B*

Ohio
Pontifical College Josephinum *B*

Oregon
Portland State University *C*

Pennsylvania
Penn State
University Park *C*

Puerto Rico
Pontifical Catholic University of Puerto
Rico *B, M*

Rhode Island
Brown University *B, M, D*

Texas
Palo Alto College *A*
University of Texas
El Paso *B*
San Antonio *B, M*

Utah
Weber State University *B*

Washington
University of Washington *B*

Histologic assistant

Florida
Miami-Dade Community College *C*

Ohio
University of Akron *A*

Texas
Houston Community College System *A*

Histologic technology

Florida
Miami-Dade Community College *A*

Ohio
Lakeland Community College *C, A*

Texas
St. Philip's College *C*

Historic preservation

Delaware
Delaware State University *B*
University of Delaware *B, M*

District of Columbia
George Washington University *M*

Georgia
Georgia State University *M*
Savannah College of Art and
    Design *B, M*
University of Georgia *M*

Illinois
School of the Art Institute of Chicago *M*

Indiana
Ball State University *M*

Kentucky
University of Kentucky *M*

Maryland
Goucher College *B, M*
University of Maryland
    College Park *M*

Massachusetts
Boston University *M*
Harvard College *B*

Michigan
Eastern Michigan University *M*

New York
Cornell University *M*

North Carolina
Randolph Community College *C, A*

Ohio
Ursuline College *C, B*
Youngstown State University *C*

Oregon
University of Oregon *M*

Pennsylvania
Bucks County Community College *C*

Rhode Island
Roger Williams University *B*
Salve Regina University *B*

South Carolina
College of Charleston *B*

Texas
Texas Tech University *M*
University of Texas
    Austin *D*

Vermont
University of Vermont *M*

Virginia
Mary Washington College *B*

History

Alabama
Alabama State University *B*
Athens State University *B*
Auburn University *B, M, D*
Auburn University at Montgomery *B*
Birmingham-Southern College *B, T*
Community College of the Air Force *A*
Faulkner University *B*
Huntingdon College *B, T*
Jacksonville State University *B, M*
Judson College *B*
Lawson State Community College *A*
Northeast Alabama Community
    College *A*
Oakwood College *B*
Samford University *B*
Spring Hill College *B, T*
Stillman College *B*

Talladega College *B, T*
Troy State University *B*
Troy State University Dothan *B*
Troy State University in
    Montgomery *A, B*
Tuskegee University *B*
University of Alabama *B, M, D*
University of Alabama
    Birmingham *B, M*
    Huntsville *B, M*
University of Mobile *B, T*
University of Montevallo *B, T*
University of North Alabama *B*
University of South Alabama *B, M*
University of West Alabama *B, T*

Alaska
University of Alaska
    Anchorage *B*
    Fairbanks *B*

Arizona
Arizona State University *B, M, D*
Arizona Western College *A*
Cochise College *A*
Eastern Arizona College *A*
Northern Arizona University *B, M, D, T*
Prescott College *M*
South Mountain Community College *A*
University of Arizona *B, M, D*

Arkansas
Arkansas State University *B, M*
Arkansas State University
    Beebe *A*
Harding University *B*
Henderson State University *B*
Hendrix College *B*
John Brown University *B*
Lyon College *B*
Ouachita Baptist University *B*
Southern Arkansas University *B*
University of Arkansas *B, M, D*
University of Arkansas
    Little Rock *B, M*
    Monticello *B*
    Pine Bluff *B*
University of Central Arkansas *B, M*
University of the Ozarks *B*
Williams Baptist College *B*

California
Azusa Pacific University *B*
Bakersfield College *A*
Biola University *B*
Cabrillo College *A*
California Baptist University *B*
California Institute of Technology *B*
California Polytechnic State University:
    San Luis Obispo *B*
California State Polytechnic University:
    Pomona *B, M*
California State University
    Bakersfield *B, M*
    Chico *B, M*
    Dominguez Hills *B*
    Fresno *B, M*
    Fullerton *B, M*
    Hayward *B, M*
    Long Beach *B, M*
    Los Angeles *B, M*
    Northridge *B*
    Sacramento *B, M*
    San Bernardino *B*
    San Marcos *B*
    Stanislaus *B, M*
Cerritos Community College *A*
Chabot College *A*
Chapman University *B*
Christian Heritage College *B*
Claremont McKenna College *B*
College of Alameda *A*
Concordia University *B*
Contra Costa College *A*
De Anza College *A*
Dominican University of California *B*
East Los Angeles College *A*

Feather River College *A*
Foothill College *A*
Fresno Pacific University *B*
Gavilan Community College *A*
Glendale Community College *A*
Golden West College *A*
Grossmont Community College *A*
Holy Names College *B*
Humboldt State University *B*
Irvine Valley College *A*
La Sierra University *B*
Los Angeles Southwest College *A*
Loyola Marymount University *B, M*
Marymount College *A*
Master's College *B*
Mills College *B*
MiraCosta College *A*
Monterey Peninsula College *A*
Mount St. Mary's College *B*
Occidental College *B*
Orange Coast College *A*
Pacific Union College *B*
Pepperdine University *B, M*
Pitzer College *B*
Point Loma Nazarene University *B*
Pomona College *B*
St. Mary's College of California *B*
San Diego City College *A*
San Diego State University *B, M*
San Francisco State University *B, M*
San Jose State University *B, M*
Santa Barbara City College *A*
Santa Clara University *B*
Santa Monica College *A*
Santiago Canyon College *A*
Scripps College *B*
Simpson College *B*
Sonoma State University *B, M*
Southwestern College *A*
Stanford University *B, M, D*
University of California
    Berkeley *B, M, D*
    Davis *B, M, D*
    Irvine *B, M, D*
    Los Angeles *B, M, D*
    Riverside *B, M, D*
    San Diego *B, M, D*
    Santa Barbara *B, M, D*
    Santa Cruz *B, D*
University of La Verne *B*
University of Redlands *B*
University of San Diego *B, M*
University of San Francisco *B*
University of Southern
    California *B, M, D*
University of the Pacific *B*
Vanguard University of Southern
    California *B*
Ventura College *A*
West Valley College *A*
Whittier College *B*
Yuba Community College District *A*

Colorado
Colorado Christian University *B*
Colorado College *B*
Colorado State University *B, M, D*
Colorado State University
    Pueblo *B*
Mesa State College *B*
Metropolitan State College of
    Denver *B, T*
Otero Junior College *A*
Red Rocks Community College *A*
Regis University *B*
United States Air Force Academy *B*
University of Colorado
    Boulder *B, M, D*
    Colorado Springs *B, M*
    Denver *B, M*
University of Denver *B, M*
University of Northern Colorado *B, M, T*

Connecticut
Albertus Magnus College *B*

Central Connecticut State
    University *B, M*
Connecticut College *B*
Eastern Connecticut State University *B*
Fairfield University *B*
Quinnipiac University *B*
Sacred Heart University *B*
St. Joseph College *B, T*
Southern Connecticut State
    University *B, M*
Teikyo Post University *B*
Trinity College *B, M*
University of Connecticut *B, M, D*
University of Hartford *B*
University of New Haven *B*
Wesleyan University *B*
Western Connecticut State
    University *B, M*
Yale University *B, M, D*

Delaware
Delaware State University *B*
University of Delaware *B, M, D*

District of Columbia
American University *B, M, D*
Catholic University of
    America *B, M, D, T*
Gallaudet University *B*
George Washington University *B, M, D*
Georgetown University *B, D*
Howard University *B, M, D*
Trinity College *B*
University of the District of
    Columbia *A, B*

Florida
Barry University *B*
Bethune-Cookman College *B*
Broward Community College *A*
Eckerd College *B*
Edward Waters College *B*
Flagler College *B*
Florida Agricultural and Mechanical
    University *B*
Florida Atlantic University *B, M*
Florida International University *B, M, D*
Florida Southern College *B*
Florida State University *B, M, D*
Gulf Coast Community College *A*
Indian River Community College *A*
Jacksonville University *B*
Manatee Community College *A*
Miami-Dade Community College *A*
New College of Florida *B*
Palm Beach Atlantic University *B, T*
Palm Beach Community College *A*
Pensacola Junior College *A*
Polk Community College *A*
Rollins College *B*
St. Leo University *B*
St. Thomas University *B*
South Florida Community College *A*
Stetson University *B*
University of Central Florida *B, M*
University of Florida *B, M, D*
University of Miami *B, M, D*
University of North Florida *B, M*
University of South Florida *B, M*
University of Tampa *A, B*
University of West Florida *B, M*
Warner Southern College *B*

Georgia
Abraham Baldwin Agricultural
    College *A*
Agnes Scott College *B*
Albany State University *B*
Andrew College *A*
Armstrong Atlantic State
    University *B, M, T*
Atlanta Metropolitan College *A*
Augusta State University *B*
Bainbridge College *A*
Berry College *B, T*
Brenau University *B*
Brewton-Parker College *B*

Clark Atlanta University *B, M*
Clayton College and State University *A*
Columbus State University *B*
Covenant College *B*
Dalton State College *A*
Darton College *A*
East Georgia College *A*
Emmanuel College *B*
Emory University *B, M, D*
Gainesville College *A*
Georgia College and State
 University *B, M, T*
Georgia Perimeter College *A*
Georgia Southern University *B, M*
Georgia Southwestern State University *B*
Georgia State University *B, M, D*
Kennesaw State University *B*
LaGrange College *B*
Macon State College *A*
Mercer University *B*
Middle Georgia College *A*
Morehouse College *B*
Morris Brown College *B*
North Georgia College & State
 University *B*
Oglethorpe University *B*
Oxford College of Emory University *B*
Paine College *B*
Piedmont College *B*
Savannah State University *B*
Shorter College *B, T*
South Georgia College *A*
Spelman College *B*
State University of West Georgia *B, M*
Thomas University *B*
University of Georgia *B, M, D*
Valdosta State University *B, M*
Waycross College *A*
Wesleyan College *B*

Hawaii

Brigham Young University-Hawaii *B*
Chaminade University of Honolulu *B*
Hawaii Pacific University *B*
University of Hawaii
 Hilo *B*
 Manoa *B, M, D*
 West Oahu *B*

Idaho

Albertson College of Idaho *B*
Boise State University *B, M, T*
Brigham Young University - Idaho *B*
College of Southern Idaho *A*
Idaho State University *A, B*
Lewis-Clark State College *B*
North Idaho College *A*
Northwest Nazarene University *B*
University of Idaho *B, M, D*

Illinois

Augustana College *B, T*
Aurora University *B*
Benedictine University *B, T*
Black Hawk College
 East Campus *A*
Blackburn College *B, T*
Bradley University *B, T*
Chicago State University *B, M*
City Colleges of Chicago
 Kennedy-King College *A*
Concordia University *B*
Danville Area Community College *A*
De Paul University *B, M, T*
Dominican University *B*
Eastern Illinois University *B, M, T*
Elmhurst College *B, T*
Eureka College *B, T*
Illinois College *B*
Illinois State University *B, M, T*
Illinois Valley Community College *A*
Illinois Wesleyan University *B*
John A. Logan College *A*
John Wood Community College *A*
Joliet Junior College *A*
Judson College *B*

Kendall College *B*
Kishwaukee College *A*
Knox College *B*
Lake Forest College *B*
Lewis University *B, T*
Lewis and Clark Community College *A*
Lincoln College *A*
Lincoln Land Community College *A*
Loyola University of Chicago *B, M, D, T*
MacMurray College *B*
McKendree College *B*
Millikin University *B, T*
Monmouth College *B, T*
North Central College *B, T*
North Park University *B*
Northeastern Illinois University *B, M*
Northern Illinois University *B, M, D*
Northwestern University *B, M, D*
Olivet Nazarene University *B, T*
Parkland College *A*
Principia College *B, T*
Quincy University *B, T*
Richland Community College *A*
Rockford College *B*
Roosevelt University *B, M*
St. Xavier University *B*
Sauk Valley Community College *A*
South Suburban College of Cook
 County *A*
Southern Illinois University
 Carbondale *B, M, D*
Southern Illinois University
 Edwardsville *B, M, T*
Southwestern Illinois College *A*
Trinity Christian College *B, T*
Trinity International University *B*
Triton College *A*
University of Chicago *B, M, D*
University of Illinois
 Chicago *B, M, D*
 Springfield *B, M*
 Urbana-Champaign *B, M, D*
University of St. Francis *B*
Western Illinois University *B, M*
Wheaton College *B, T*

Indiana

Anderson University *B*
Ball State University *B, M*
Bethel College *B*
Butler University *B, M*
DePauw University *B*
Earlham College *B*
Franklin College *B*
Goshen College *B*
Hanover College *B*
Huntington College *B*
Indiana University
 Bloomington *B, M, D*
 East *B*
 Northwest *A, B*
 South Bend *A, B*
 Southeast *B*
Indiana University-Purdue University
 Fort Wayne *A, B*
Indiana University-Purdue University
 Indianapolis *B, M*
Indiana Wesleyan University *A, B*
Manchester College *B, T*
Marian College *B, T*
Martin University *B*
Oakland City University *A, B*
Purdue University *B, M, D*
Purdue University
 Calumet *B*
St. Joseph's College *B*
Saint Mary's College *B, T*
Taylor University *B*
University of Evansville *B*
University of Indianapolis *B, M*
University of Notre Dame *B, M, D*
University of St. Francis *B*
University of Southern Indiana *B*
Valparaiso University *B, M, D, T*
Vincennes University *A*
Wabash College *B*

Iowa

Briar Cliff University *B*
Buena Vista University *B, T*
Central College *B, T*
Clarke College *A, B, T*
Coe College *B*
Cornell College *B, T*
Dordt College *B*
Drake University *B*
Ellsworth Community College *A*
Franciscan University *T*
Graceland University *B, T*
Grand View College *B*
Grinnell College *B*
Iowa State University *B, M, D*
Iowa Wesleyan College *B*
Loras College *B*
Luther College *B*
Morningside College *B*
Mount Mercy College *B, T*
North Iowa Area Community College *A*
Northwestern College *B, T*
St. Ambrose University *B, T*
Simpson College *B*
University of Iowa *B, M, D, T*
University of Northern Iowa *B, M*
Waldorf College *A, B*
Wartburg College *B, T*
William Penn University *B*

Kansas

Allen County Community College *A*
Baker University *B, T*
Barton County Community College *A*
Benedictine College *B, T*
Bethany College *B, T*
Bethel College *B*
Butler County Community College *A*
Central Christian College *B*
Emporia State University *B, M*
Fort Hays State University *B, M*
Fort Scott Community College *A*
Friends University *B*
Independence Community College *A*
Kansas State University *B, M, D*
Kansas Wesleyan University *B, T*
Labette Community College *A*
McPherson College *B, T*
MidAmerica Nazarene University *B*
Newman University *B*
Ottawa University *B, T*
Pittsburg State University *B, M, T*
Pratt Community College *A*
St. Mary College *B*
Seward County Community College *A*
Southwestern College *B*
Sterling College *B*
Tabor College *B*
University of Kansas *B, M, D*
Washburn University of Topeka *B*
Wichita State University *B, M, T*

Kentucky

Alice Lloyd College *B*
Asbury College *B, T*
Bellarmine University *B, T*
Berea College *B, T*
Brescia University *B*
Campbellsville University *B*
Centre College *B*
Cumberland College *B, T*
Georgetown College *B, T*
Kentucky Christian College *B*
Kentucky Wesleyan College *B, T*
Lindsey Wilson College *B, T*
Morehead State University *B*
Murray State University *B, M, T*
Pikeville College *B*
Spalding University *B*
Thomas More College *A, B*
Transylvania University *B*
Union College *B*
University of Kentucky *B, M, D*
University of Louisville *B, M*

Louisiana

Centenary College of Louisiana *B, T*
Dillard University *B*
Grambling State University *B*
Louisiana College *B*
Louisiana State University
 Shreveport *B*
Louisiana State University and
 Agricultural and Mechanical
 College *B, M, D*
Louisiana Tech University *B, M*
Loyola University New Orleans *B*
McNeese State University *B*
Nicholls State University *B*
Northwestern State University *B, M*
Our Lady of Holy Cross College *B*
Southeastern Louisiana University *B, M*
Southern University
 New Orleans *B*
Southern University and Agricultural and
 Mechanical College *B, M*
Tulane University *B, M, D*
University of Louisiana at
 Lafayette *B, M*
University of Louisiana at Monroe *B, M*
University of New Orleans *B, M*
Xavier University of Louisiana *B*

Maine

Bates College *B*
Bowdoin College *B*
Colby College *B*
St. Joseph's College *B*
University of Maine *B, M, D*
University of Maine
 Farmington *B*
 Machias *B, T*
University of New England *B*
University of Southern Maine *B*

Maryland

Allegany College *A*
Bowie State University *B*
College of Notre Dame of Maryland *B*
Columbia Union College *B*
Community College of Baltimore County
 Essex *A*
Coppin State College *B*
Frederick Community College *A*
Frostburg State University *B*
Goucher College *B*
Hood College *B, T*
Johns Hopkins University *B, M, D*
Loyola College in Maryland *B*
McDaniel College *B*
Morgan State University *B, M, D*
Mount St. Mary's College *B*
St. Mary's College of Maryland *B*
Salisbury University *B, M, T*
Towson University *B*
United States Naval Academy *B*
University of Baltimore *B*
University of Maryland
 Baltimore County *B, M*
 College Park *B, M, D*
 University College *B*
Washington College *B, M, T*

Massachusetts

American International College *B*
Amherst College *B*
Anna Maria College *B*
Assumption College *B*
Atlantic Union College *B*
Bentley College *B*
Boston College *B, M, D*
Boston University *B, M, D*
Brandeis University *B, M, D*
Bridgewater State College *B, M*
Bunker Hill Community College *A*
Clark University *B, M, D*
College of the Holy Cross *B*
Elms College *B*
Emmanuel College *B*
Fitchburg State College *B, M*
Framingham State College *B, M*

Gordon College *B*
Hampshire College *B*
Harvard College *B*
Massachusetts College of Liberal Arts *B*
Massachusetts Institute of Technology *B*
Merrimack College *B*
Mount Holyoke College *B*
Nichols College *B*
Northeastern University *B, M, D*
Pine Manor College *A*
Regis College *B*
St. John's Seminary College *B*
Salem State College *B, M*
Simmons College *B*
Smith College *B*
Springfield College *B*
Stonehill College *B*
Suffolk University *B*
Tufts University *B, M, T*
University of Massachusetts
   Amherst *B, M, D*
   Boston *B, M*
   Dartmouth *B*
Wellesley College *B*
Western New England College *B*
Westfield State College *B, M*
Wheaton College *B*
Williams College *B*

Michigan

Adrian College *A, B, T*
Alma College *B, T*
Andrews University *B, M*
Aquinas College *B, T*
Calvin College *B, T*
Central Michigan University *B, M, D, T*
Cornerstone University *B, T*
Eastern Michigan University *B, M*
Ferris State University *B*
Grand Valley State University *B*
Hillsdale College *B*
Hope College *B*
Kalamazoo College *B, T*
Kellogg Community College *A*
Lansing Community College *A*
Madonna University *B*
Marygrove College *B, T*
Michigan State University *B, M, D*
Michigan Technological University *B*
Northern Michigan University *B, T*
Oakland University *B, M, T*
Saginaw Valley State University *B*
Siena Heights University *B*
Spring Arbor University *B*
University of Michigan *B, M, D, T*
University of Michigan
   Dearborn *B*
   Flint *B, T*
Wayne State University *B, M, D*
Western Michigan University *B, M, D*
William Tyndale College *B*

Minnesota

Augsburg College *B*
Bemidji State University *B*
Bethany Lutheran College *B*
Bethel College *B*
Carleton College *B*
College of St. Benedict *B*
College of St. Catherine *B*
College of St. Scholastica *B*
Concordia College: Moorhead *B*
Concordia University: St. Paul *B*
Crown College *B*
Gustavus Adolphus College *B*
Hamline University *B*
Macalester College *B*
Metropolitan State University *B*
Minnesota State University
   Mankato *B, M*
   Moorhead *B*
Northwestern College *B*
Ridgewater College: A Community and
   Technical College *A*
St. Cloud State University *B, M*
St. John's University *B*

St. Mary's University of Minnesota *B*
St. Olaf College *B*
Southwest State University *B*
University of Minnesota
   Duluth *B*
   Morris *B*
   Twin Cities *B, M, D*
University of St. Thomas *B*
Vermilion Community College *A*
Winona State University *B*

Mississippi

Alcorn State University *B*
Blue Mountain College *B*
Delta State University *B*
Itawamba Community College *A*
Millsaps College *B, T*
Mississippi College *B, M*
Mississippi State University *B, M, D*
Mississippi University for Women *B, T*
Mississippi Valley State University *B*
University of Mississippi *B, M, D, T*
University of Southern
   Mississippi *B, M, D*

Missouri

Avila University *B*
Central Methodist College *B*
Central Missouri State University *B, M*
College of the Ozarks *B*
Columbia College *B*
Crowder College *A*
Culver-Stockton College *B*
Drury University *B, T*
East Central College *A*
Evangel University *B*
Fontbonne College *B*
Hannibal-LaGrange College *B*
Lincoln University *B, M*
Lindenwood University *B*
Maryville University of Saint Louis *B*
Missouri Baptist University *B, T*
Missouri Southern State College *B, T*
Missouri Valley College *B*
Missouri Western State College *B, T*
Northwest Missouri State
   University *B, M*
Rockhurst University *B*
St. Louis University *B, M, D*
Southeast Missouri State
   University *B, M*
Southwest Baptist University *B*
Southwest Missouri State
   University *B, M*
Three Rivers Community College *A*
Truman State University *B, M*
University of Missouri
   Columbia *B, M, D*
   Kansas City *B, M*
   Rolla *B*
   St. Louis *B, M*
Washington University in St.
   Louis *B, M, D*
Webster University *B*
Westminster College *B*
William Jewell College *B*
William Woods University *B*

Montana

Carroll College *B, T*
Montana State University
   Billings *B*
   Bozeman *B, M*
Rocky Mountain College *B, T*
University of Great Falls *B*
University of Montana-Missoula *B, M*
University of Montana: Western *T*

Nebraska

Chadron State College *B, M*
Concordia University *B, T*
Creighton University *B*
Dana College *B*
Doane College *B*
Hastings College *B*
Midland Lutheran College *B, T*
Nebraska Wesleyan University *B*

Union College *B*
University of Nebraska
   Kearney *B, M, T*
   Lincoln *B, M, D*
   Omaha *B, M*
Wayne State College *B, M, T*
Western Nebraska Community
   College *A*
York College *A, B, T*

Nevada

Great Basin College *A*
Sierra Nevada College *B*
University of Nevada
   Las Vegas *B, M, D*
   Reno *B, M, D*

New Hampshire

Dartmouth College *B*
Franklin Pierce College *B*
Keene State College *B*
New England College *B*
Plymouth State College *B*
Rivier College *B*
St. Anselm College *B, T*
Southern New Hampshire University *B*
University of New Hampshire *B, M, D*
University of New Hampshire at
   Manchester *B*

New Jersey

Atlantic Cape Community College *A*
Bloomfield College *B*
Caldwell College *B*
Centenary College *B*
The College of New Jersey *B, T*
College of St. Elizabeth *B*
Drew University *B*
Fairleigh Dickinson University
   College at Florham *B*
   Metropolitan Campus *B, M*
Felician College *B*
Georgian Court College *B*
Gloucester County College *A*
Hudson County Community College *A*
Kean University *B*
Monmouth University *B, M*
Montclair State University *B*
New Jersey City University *B*
New Jersey Institute of Technology *B, M*
Princeton University *B, M, D*
Ramapo College of New Jersey *B*
Richard Stockton College of New
   Jersey *B*
Rider University *B*
Rowan University *B*
Rutgers, The State University of New
   Jersey
   Camden Regional Campus *B*
   New Brunswick Regional
      Campus *B, M, D*
   Newark Regional Campus *B*
St. Peter's College *B*
Salem Community College *A*
Seton Hall University *B, T*
Stevens Institute of Technology *B*
Thomas Edison State College *B*
William Paterson University of New
   Jersey *B*

New Mexico

College of the Southwest *B*
Eastern New Mexico University *B*
New Mexico Highlands University *B*
New Mexico State University *B, M*
San Juan College *A*
University of New Mexico *B, M, D*
Western New Mexico University *B*

New York

Adelphi University *B*
Adirondack Community College *A*
Alfred University *B*
Bard College *B*
Barnard College *B*
Canisius College *B*

City University of New York
   Baruch College *B*
   Brooklyn College *B, M*
   City College *B, M, T*
   College of Staten Island *B, M, T*
   Hunter College *B, M*
   Queens College *B, M*
   Queensborough Community
      College *A*
   York College *B*
Clarkson University *B*
Colgate University *B*
College of Mount St. Vincent *A, B, T*
College of New Rochelle *B, T*
Columbia University
   Columbia College *B*
Concordia College *B, T*
Cornell University *B, M, D*
D'Youville College *B*
Daemen College *B*
Dominican College of Blauvelt *B*
Dowling College *B*
Elmira College *B, T*
Eugene Lang College/New School
   University *B*
Excelsior College *B*
Fordham University *B, M, D*
Fulton-Montgomery Community
   College *A*
Hamilton College *B*
Hartwick College *B*
Hobart and William Smith Colleges *B*
Hofstra University *B*
Houghton College *B*
Iona College *B, M*
Ithaca College *B*
Le Moyne College *B*
Long Island University
   C. W. Post Campus *B, M*
   Southampton College *B*
Manhattan College *B*
Manhattanville College *B*
Marist College *B, T*
Marymount College of Fordham
   University *B*
Marymount Manhattan College *B*
Mercy College *B*
Molloy College *B*
Monroe Community College *A*
Mount St. Mary College *B, T*
Nazareth College of Rochester *B, T*
New York University *B, M, D*
Niagara University *B*
Nyack College *B*
Pace University *B*
Pace University:
   Pleasantville/Briarcliff *B*
Roberts Wesleyan College *B*
Russell Sage College *B*
St. Bonaventure University *B*
St. John Fisher College *B*
St. John's University *B, M, D*
St. Joseph's College *B*
St. Joseph's College: Suffolk
   Campus *B, T*
St. Lawrence University *B*
Sarah Lawrence College *B*
Skidmore College *B*
State University of New York
   Albany *B, M, D*
   Binghamton *B, M, D*
   Buffalo *B, M, D*
   College at Brockport *B, M, T*
   College at Buffalo *B, M*
   College at Cortland *B, M*
   College at Fredonia *B*
   College at Geneseo *B, T*
   College at Oneonta *B, M*
   College at Plattsburgh *B*
   College at Potsdam *B*
   Empire State College *A, B*
   New Paltz *B*
   Oswego *B, M*
   Purchase *B*
   Stony Brook *B, M, D*

Suffolk County Community College A
Syracuse University B, M, D
Touro College B
Union College B
United States Military Academy B
University of Rochester B, M, D
Utica College B
Vassar College B
Wagner College B
Wells College B
Yeshiva University B

North Carolina

Appalachian State University B, M
Barton College B
Belmont Abbey College B
Brevard College B
Campbell University B
Catawba College B, T
Chowan College B
Davidson College B
Duke University B, M, D
East Carolina University B, M
Elizabeth City State University B
Elon University B, T
Fayetteville State University B
Gardner-Webb University B
Greensboro College B, T
Guilford College B, T
Guilford Technical Community
    College A
High Point University B
Johnson C. Smith University B
Lees-McRae College B
Lenoir-Rhyne College B, T
Livingstone College B
Louisburg College A
Mars Hill College B, T
Meredith College B
Methodist College A, B
Montreat College A, B
Mount Olive College B
North Carolina Agricultural and
    Technical State University B, M, T
North Carolina Central University B, M
North Carolina State University B, M
North Carolina Wesleyan College B
Pfeiffer University B
Queens University of Charlotte B
St. Andrews Presbyterian College B
St. Augustine's College B
Salem College B
University of North Carolina
    Asheville B, T
    Chapel Hill B, M, D
    Charlotte B, M, T
    Greensboro B, M, T
    Pembroke B
    Wilmington B, M
Wake Forest University B, M
Warren Wilson College B
Western Carolina University B
Wingate University B
Winston-Salem State University B

North Dakota

Dickinson State University B, T
Jamestown College B
Minot State University B
Minot State University: Bottineau
    Campus A
North Dakota State University B, M, T
University of North Dakota B, M, D, T
Valley City State University B

Ohio

Antioch College B
Ashland University B
Baldwin-Wallace College B
Bluffton College B
Bowling Green State University B, M, D
Case Western Reserve
    University B, M, D
Cedarville University B
Central State University B
Cleveland State University B, M, T

College of Mount St. Joseph B, T
College of Wooster B
Defiance College B, T
Denison University B
Franciscan University of Steubenville B
Heidelberg College B
Hiram College B, T
John Carroll University B, M
Kent State University B, M, D
Kent State University
    Stark Campus B
Kenyon College B
Lake Erie College B
Lourdes College A, B
Malone College B
Marietta College B
Miami University
    Middletown Campus A
    Oxford Campus B, M
Mount Union College B
Mount Vernon Nazarene University B
Muskingum College B
Notre Dame College B, T
Oberlin College B
Ohio Dominican College B, T
Ohio Northern University B
Ohio State University
    Columbus Campus B, M, D
    Lima Campus B
Ohio University B, M, D
Ohio University
    Southern Campus at Ironton A
Ohio Wesleyan University B
Otterbein College B
Owens Community College
    Toledo A
Shawnee State University B
Sinclair Community College A
University of Akron B, M, D
University of Cincinnati B, M, D, T
University of Dayton B
University of Findlay B, T
University of Rio Grande A, B
University of Toledo B, M, D
Urbana University B
Ursuline College B
Walsh University B
Wilmington College B
Wittenberg University B
Wright State University B, M
Wright State University: Lake Campus A
Xavier University A, B, M
Youngstown State University B, M

Oklahoma

Bacone College A
Cameron University B, M
East Central University B
Eastern Oklahoma State College A
Langston University B
Murray State College A
Northeastern Oklahoma Agricultural and
    Mechanical College A
Northeastern State University B
Northwestern Oklahoma State
    University B
Oklahoma Baptist University B
Oklahoma Christian University of
    Science and Arts B
Oklahoma City Community College A
Oklahoma City University B
Oklahoma Panhandle State University B
Oklahoma State University B, M, D
Oklahoma Wesleyan University B
Oral Roberts University B
Redlands Community College A
Rogers State University A
Rose State College A
St. Gregory's University A, B
Southeastern Oklahoma State
    University B
Southern Nazarene University B
Southwestern Oklahoma State
    University B
Tulsa Community College A
University of Central Oklahoma B, M

University of Oklahoma B, M, D
University of Science and Arts of
    Oklahoma B
University of Tulsa B, M
Western Oklahoma State College A

Oregon

Central Oregon Community College A
Chemeketa Community College A
Eastern Oregon University B, T
George Fox University B, T
Lewis & Clark College B
Linfield College B
Linn-Benton Community College A
Multnomah Bible College B
Oregon State University B
Pacific University B
Portland State University B, M
Reed College B
Southern Oregon University B
University of Oregon B, M, D
University of Portland B
Warner Pacific College B
Western Baptist College B
Western Oregon University B
Willamette University B

Pennsylvania

Albright College B, T
Allegheny College B
Arcadia University B
Bloomsburg University of
    Pennsylvania B
Bryn Athyn College of the New
    Church A, B
Bryn Mawr College B
Bucknell University B
Cabrini College B
California University of Pennsylvania B
Carlow College B
Carnegie Mellon University B, M, D
Cedar Crest College B
Chatham College B
Chestnut Hill College B
DeSales University B, T
Dickinson College B
Drexel University B
Duquesne University B, M
East Stroudsburg University of
    Pennsylvania B, M
Edinboro University of Pennsylvania B
Elizabethtown College B
Franklin & Marshall College B
Geneva College B, T
Gettysburg College B
Grove City College B
Gwynedd-Mercy College B
Haverford College B, T
Holy Family University B, T
Immaculata University B
Indiana University of Pennsylvania B, M
Juniata College B
King's College B
Kutztown University of Pennsylvania B
La Roche College B
La Salle University B, T
Lafayette College B
Lebanon Valley College of
    Pennsylvania B, T
Lehigh University B, M, D
Lincoln University B
Lock Haven University of
    Pennsylvania B
Lycoming College B
Marywood University B
Mercyhurst College B
Messiah College B
Millersville University of
    Pennsylvania B, M, T
Moravian College B
Muhlenberg College B, T

Penn State
    Abington B
    Altoona B
    Beaver B
    Berks B
    Delaware County B
    Dubois B
    Erie, The Behrend College B
    Fayette B
    Hazleton B
    Lehigh Valley B
    McKeesport B
    Mont Alto B
    New Kensington B
    Schuylkill - Capital College B
    Shenango B
    University Park B, M, D
    Wilkes-Barre B
    Worthington Scranton B
Point Park College B
Rosemont College B
St. Joseph's University B
St. Vincent College B
Seton Hill University B, T
Shippensburg University of
    Pennsylvania B, M, T
Slippery Rock University of
    Pennsylvania B, M, T
Swarthmore College B
Temple University B, M, D
Thiel College B
University of
    Pennsylvania C, A, B, M, D
University of Pittsburgh B, M, D
University of Pittsburgh
    Bradford B
    Greensburg B
    Johnstown B
University of Scranton B, M
Villanova University B, M
Washington and Jefferson College B
Waynesburg College B
West Chester University of
    Pennsylvania B, M
Widener University B
Wilkes University B
Wilson College B
York College of Pennsylvania B

Puerto Rico

Inter American University of Puerto Rico
    Metropolitan Campus B
Pontifical Catholic University of Puerto
    Rico B
Turabo University B
University of Puerto Rico
    Mayaguez Campus B
    Rio Piedras Campus B, M, D
University of the Sacred Heart B

Rhode Island

Brown University B, M, D
Bryant College B
Providence College B, M, T
Rhode Island College B, M
Roger Williams University B
Salve Regina University B
University of Rhode Island B, M

South Carolina

Anderson College B, T
Benedict College B
Charleston Southern University B
The Citadel B, M
Claflin University B
Clemson University B, M
Coastal Carolina University B
Coker College B
College of Charleston B, M, T
Columbia College B
Converse College B
Erskine College B
Francis Marion University B
Furman University B, T
Lander University B, T
Limestone College B

Morris College *B*
Newberry College *B, T*
Presbyterian College *B, T*
South Carolina State University *B*
Southern Wesleyan University *B*
University of South Carolina *B, M, D*
University of South Carolina
    Aiken
    Spartanburg *B*
Winthrop University *B, M*
Wofford College *B*

South Dakota

Augustana College *B, T*
Black Hills State University *B*
Dakota Wesleyan University *B*
Mount Marty College *B*
Northern State University *B*
South Dakota State University *B*
University of Sioux Falls *B*
University of South Dakota *B, M*

Tennessee

Austin Peay State University *B*
Belmont University *B, T*
Bethel College *B*
Bryan College *B, T*
Carson-Newman College *B, T*
Christian Brothers University *B*
Columbia State Community College *A*
Crichton College *B*
East Tennessee State University *B, M*
Fisk University *B*
Freed-Hardeman University *B, T*
Jackson State Community College *A*
King College *B, T*
Lambuth University *B*
Lane College *B*
Lee University *B*
Maryville College *B, T*
Middle Tennessee State
  University *B, M, D*
Milligan College *B, T*
Rhodes College *B, T*
Roane State Community College *A*
Southern Adventist University *B*
Tennessee State University *B, M*
Tennessee Technological University *B, T*
Tennessee Wesleyan College *B*
Trevecca Nazarene University *B, T*
Tusculum College *B*
Union University *B, T*
University of Memphis *B, M, D*
University of Tennessee
    Chattanooga *B*
    Knoxville *B, M, D*
    Martin *B*
Vanderbilt University *B, M, D*

Texas

Abilene Christian University *B, M*
Angelo State University *B, M, T*
Austin College *B*
Austin Community College *A*
Baylor University *B, M*
Blinn College *A*
Brazosport College *A*
Cisco Junior College *A*
Clarendon College *A*
Coastal Bend College *A*
College of the Mainland *A*
Concordia University at Austin *B*
Dallas Baptist University *B*
Del Mar College *A*
East Texas Baptist University *B*
El Paso Community College *A*
Frank Phillips College *A*
Galveston College *A*
Hardin-Simmons University *B, M*
Houston Baptist University *B*
Howard Payne University *B, T*
Jarvis Christian College *B*
Kilgore College *A*
Lamar University *B, M*
Laredo Community College *A*
LeTourneau University *B*

Lon Morris College *A*
Lubbock Christian University *T*
McMurry University *B, T*
Midland College *A*
Midwestern State University *B, M*
Northeast Texas Community College *A*
Our Lady of the Lake University of San
  Antonio *B*
Palo Alto College *A*
Panola College *A*
Paris Junior College *A*
Prairie View A&M University *B*
Rice University *B, M, D*
St. Edward's University *B, T*
St. Mary's University *B, M*
St. Philip's College *A*
Sam Houston State University *B, M*
Schreiner University *B*
South Plains College *A*
Southern Methodist University *B, M, D*
Southwest Texas State
  University *B, M, T*
Southwestern Adventist University *B, T*
Southwestern University *B, T*
Stephen F. Austin State
  University *B, M, T*
Sul Ross State University *B, M, T*
Tarleton State University *B, M, T*
Texas A&M International
  University *B, M, T*
Texas A&M University *B, M, D*
Texas A&M University
    Commerce *B, M*
    Corpus Christi *B, T*
    Kingsville *B, M*
    Texarkana *B, T*
Texas Christian University *B, M, D, T*
Texas College *B*
Texas Lutheran University *B, T*
Texas Southern University *B, M*
Texas Tech University *B, M, D*
Texas Wesleyan University *B*
Texas Woman's University *B, M, T*
Trinity University *B*
Tyler Junior College *A*
University of Dallas *B*
University of Houston *B, M, D*
University of Houston
    Clear Lake *B, M*
    Downtown *B*
    Victoria *B, T*
University of Mary Hardin-Baylor *B, T*
University of North Texas *B, M, D*
University of St. Thomas *B*
University of Texas
    Arlington *B, M, D*
    Austin *B, M, D*
    Brownsville *B, M*
    Dallas
    El Paso *B, M, D*
    Pan American *B, M*
    San Antonio *B, M*
    Tyler *B, M*
    of the Permian Basin *B, M*
University of the Incarnate Word *B*
Wayland Baptist University *B, T*
West Texas A&M University *B, M, T*
Western Texas College *A*
Wharton County Junior College *A*
Wiley College *B*

Utah

Brigham Young University *B, M*
Dixie State College of Utah *A*
Salt Lake Community College *A*
Snow College *A*
Southern Utah University *B, T*
University of Utah *B, M, D*
Utah State University *B, M*
Utah Valley State College *A*
Weber State University *B*
Westminster College *B*

Vermont

Bennington College *B*
Burlington College *B*

Castleton State College *B*
College of St. Joseph in Vermont *B*
Goddard College *B*
Green Mountain College *B*
Johnson State College *B*
Marlboro College *B*
Middlebury College *B*
Norwich University *B*
St. Michael's College *B*
University of Vermont *B, M*

Virginia

Averett University *B, T*
Bluefield College *B*
Bridgewater College *B*
Christendom College *B*
College of William and Mary *B, M, D*
Eastern Mennonite University *B*
Emory & Henry College *B, T*
Ferrum College *B*
George Mason University *B, M*
Hampden-Sydney College *B*
Hampton University *B*
Hollins University *B*
James Madison University *B, M, T*
Liberty University *B, T*
Longwood University *B, T*
Lynchburg College *B*
Mary Baldwin College *B*
Mary Washington College *B*
Marymount University *B*
Norfolk State University *B*
Old Dominion University *B, M*
Radford University *B*
Randolph-Macon College *B*
Randolph-Macon Woman's College *B*
Roanoke College *B, T*
Shenandoah University *B*
Sweet Briar College *B*
University of Richmond *B, M, T*
University of Virginia *B, M, D*
University of Virginia's College at
  Wise *B, T*
Virginia Commonwealth
  University *B, M*
Virginia Intermont College *B*
Virginia Military Institute *B*
Virginia Polytechnic Institute and State
  University *B, M*
Virginia State University *B, M*
Virginia Union University *B*
Virginia Wesleyan College *B*
Washington and Lee University *B*

Washington

Central Washington University *B, M*
Centralia College *A*
Eastern Washington University *B, M, T*
Everett Community College *A*
Gonzaga University *B*
Lower Columbia College *A*
Northwest College *B, T*
Pacific Lutheran University *B*
St. Martin's College *B*
Seattle Pacific University *B*
Seattle University *B*
University of Puget Sound *B, T*
University of Washington *B, M, D*
Walla Walla College *B*
Washington State University *B, M, D*
Western Washington University *B, M, T*
Whitman College *B*
Whitworth College *B, T*

West Virginia

Alderson-Broaddus College *B*
Bethany College *B*
Concord College *B*
Davis and Elkins College *B*
Fairmont State College *B*
Glenville State College *B*
Marshall University *B, M*
Potomac State College of West Virginia
  University *A*
Shepherd College *B*
University of Charleston *B*

West Liberty State College *B*
West Virginia State College *B*
West Virginia University *B, M, D*
West Virginia University Institute of
  Technology *B*
West Virginia Wesleyan College *B*
Wheeling Jesuit University *B*

Wisconsin

Beloit College *B*
Cardinal Stritch University *B*
Carroll College *B*
Carthage College *B, T*
Concordia University Wisconsin *B, T*
Edgewood College *B*
Lakeland College *B*
Lawrence University *B, T*
Marian College of Fond du Lac *B*
Marquette University *B, M, D, T*
Mount Mary College *B*
Northland College *B, T*
Ripon College *B, T*
St. Norbert College *B, T*
Silver Lake College *B, T*
University of Wisconsin
    Eau Claire *B, M*
    Green Bay *B*
    La Crosse *B, T*
    Madison *B, M, D*
    Milwaukee *B, M*
    Oshkosh *B*
    Parkside *B, T*
    Platteville *B, T*
    River Falls *B*
    Stevens Point *B, M, T*
    Superior *B, T*
    Whitewater *B, T*
Wisconsin Lutheran College *B*

Wyoming

Casper College *A*
Eastern Wyoming College *A*
Laramie County Community College *A*
University of Wyoming *B, M*
Western Wyoming Community
  College *A*

History of science/ technology

Connecticut

Yale University *B, M, D*

Georgia

Georgia Institute of Technology *B, M, D*

Indiana

Indiana University
  Bloomington *M, D*

New York

City University of New York
  City College *B*

Ohio

Case Western Reserve University *B*

Oregon

Oregon State University *M, D*

History teacher education

Alabama

Athens State University *B*
Birmingham-Southern College *T*
Faulkner University *B*
Huntingdon College *T*
Judson College *B*
Oakwood College *B*
University of Mobile *B, T*

Arizona

Arizona State University *B, T*
Northern Arizona University *B, T*
Prescott College *T*
University of Arizona *B, M*

Arkansas

Harding University *B, M, T*
University of Central Arkansas *T*

California

Azusa Pacific University *T*
California State Polytechnic University:
   Pomona *T*
California State University
   Chico *T*
   San Bernardino *T*
Christian Heritage College *B, T*
Concordia University *B*
Loyola Marymount University *M*
Master's College *T*
Pacific Union College *T*
University of San Diego *M*
University of the Pacific *T*

Colorado

Colorado State University
   Pueblo *T*
Fort Lewis College *T*
Regis University *B, T*

Connecticut

Central Connecticut State University *B*
Fairfield University *T*
Quinnipiac University *B, M*
Sacred Heart University *T*
St. Joseph College *T*
Southern Connecticut State
   University *B, T*

Delaware

University of Delaware *B, T*

District of Columbia

Catholic University of America *B*

Florida

Barry University *T*
Flagler College *B*
Florida Agricultural and Mechanical
   University *T*
St. Thomas University *B, T*
Stetson University *B, T*
University of West Florida *B, T*

Georgia

Agnes Scott College *T*
Armstrong Atlantic State
   University *M, T*
Atlanta Metropolitan College *A*
Brewton-Parker College *B*
Columbus State University *B, M*
Covenant College *B, T*
Georgia Southern University *B*
Mercer University *M, T*
North Georgia College & State
   University *B, M*
Toccoa Falls College *B, T*
Valdosta State University *T*
Wesleyan College *T*

Hawaii

University of Hawaii
   Manoa *B, T*

Idaho

Boise State University *T*
Brigham Young University - Idaho *T*
Northwest Nazarene University *B*
University of Idaho *T*

Illinois

Augustana College *B, T*
Blackburn College *B, T*
Chicago State University *B, T*
Concordia University *B, T*
Dominican University *T*
Elmhurst College *B*
Eureka College *T*
Greenville College *B*
Illinois College *T*
John A. Logan College *A*
Lewis University *T*
MacMurray College *B, T*
McKendree College *B, T*

Monmouth College *B, T*
North Central College *B, T*
North Park University *T*
Northwestern University *B, T*
Olivet Nazarene University *B, T*
Quincy University *T*
Rockford College *T*
Roosevelt University *B*
St. Xavier University *B*
Sauk Valley Community College *A*
Trinity Christian College *B, T*
Trinity International University *B, T*
University of Illinois
   Chicago *B, M*
University of St. Francis *T*
Wheaton College *T*

Indiana

Ball State University *T*
Butler University *T*
Goshen College *B*
Indiana University-Purdue University
   Fort Wayne *B*
Manchester College *B, T*
Taylor University *B, T*
University of Indianapolis *B, M, T*
University of Southern Indiana *T*
Valparaiso University *B*
Vincennes University *A*

Iowa

Buena Vista University *B, T*
Central College *T*
Clarke College *B, T*
Cornell College *B, T*
Dordt College *B*
Drake University *M, T*
Ellsworth Community College *A*
Franciscan University *B, T*
Graceland University *T*
Grand View College *B, T*
Iowa State University *T*
Loras College *T*
Luther College *B*
Morningside College *B*
Mount Mercy College *T*
Northwestern College *T*
St. Ambrose University *B, T*
University of Iowa *B, T*
Upper Iowa University *B, T*
Wartburg College *B, T*
William Penn University *B*

Kansas

Baker University *T*
Benedictine College *B, T*
Bethany College *B*
Bethel College *T*
Central Christian College *A, B*
Emporia State University *T*
Garden City Community College *A*
Independence Community College *A*
McPherson College *B, T*
Ottawa University *T*
Pittsburg State University *B, T*
St. Mary College *T*
Sterling College *T*
Tabor College *B, T*

Kentucky

Bellarmine University *B, M, T*
Campbellsville University *B*
Cumberland College *B, T*
Kentucky Wesleyan College *T*
Murray State University *B, M, T*
Union College *M*

Louisiana

University of New Orleans *M*
Xavier University of Louisiana *M*

Maine

St. Joseph's College *B*
University of Maine *B*
University of Maine
   Machias *T*
   Presque Isle *B*

University of New England *B, T*
University of Southern Maine *T*

Maryland

Bowie State University *B, T*
College of Notre Dame of Maryland *T*
Salisbury University *T*
Washington College *T*

Massachusetts

American International College *B, M*
Assumption College *T*
Bridgewater State College *M, T*
Elms College *M, T*
Fitchburg State College *B, M, T*
Framingham State College *B, M, T*
Harvard College *T*
Merrimack College *T*
Northeastern University *M*
Salem State College *M*
Tufts University *T*
University of Massachusetts
   Dartmouth *T*
Western New England College *T*
Westfield State College *B, M, T*

Michigan

Alma College *T*
Andrews University *M, T*
Calvin College *B*
Central Michigan University *B*
Concordia University *B, T*
Eastern Michigan University *B, T*
Grand Valley State University *M, T*
Hope College *T*
Michigan State University *M*
Northern Michigan University *B, M, T*
Saginaw Valley State University *T*
University of Michigan
   Flint *T*
Western Michigan University *B*

Minnesota

Bemidji State University *T*
Bethel College *B*
Concordia College: Moorhead *B, T*
Concordia University: St. Paul *B, T*
Crown College *B, T*
Minnesota State University
   Mankato *B, M, T*
   Moorhead *B, T*
Northland Community & Technical
   College *A*
St. Cloud State University *M, T*
St. Olaf College *T*
University of Minnesota
   Morris *T*
Vermilion Community College *A*
Winona State University *B, T*

Mississippi

Itawamba Community College *A*
Mississippi College *B, M*

Missouri

Avila University *B, T*
College of the Ozarks *B, T*
Culver-Stockton College *T*
Maryville University of Saint
   Louis *B, T*
Missouri Baptist University *T*
Missouri Southern State College *B, T*
Northwest Missouri State
   University *M, T*
Southwest Baptist University *T*
Southwest Missouri State University *B*
Truman State University *M, T*
Washington University in St.
   Louis *B, M, T*

Montana

Montana State University
   Billings *B, T*
Rocky Mountain College *B, T*
University of Montana-Missoula *T*
University of Montana: Western *B, T*

Nebraska

Bellevue University *B*
Chadron State College *B*
Concordia University *B, T*
Creighton University *T*
Dana College *B*
Doane College *T*
Hastings College *B, M, T*
Midland Lutheran College *B, T*
Nebraska Wesleyan University *T*
Peru State College *B, T*
Union College *T*
University of Nebraska
   Kearney *B*
   Lincoln *B, T*
York College *B*

New Hampshire

Franklin Pierce College *T*
Keene State College *B, T*
Rivier College *B, T*
St. Anselm College *T*
University of New Hampshire *T*

New Jersey

Caldwell College *T*
The College of New Jersey *B, T*
Monmouth University *B, T*
Rider University *B*
Rowan University *T*
St. Peter's College *T*

New York

Canisius College *B, M, T*
City University of New York
   Brooklyn College *B*
   City College *B*
   Hunter College *B, T*
   Queens College *T*
D'Youville College *B, M, T*
Elmira College *B, T*
Fordham University *M, T*
Long Island University
   C. W. Post Campus *B, M, T*
Manhattan College *B, T*
Marist College *B, T*
Mercy College *T*
Molloy College *B*
Nazareth College of Rochester *T*
Pace University *B, T*
Pace University:
   Pleasantville/Briarcliff *B, T*
Roberts Wesleyan College *B, T*
St. John Fisher College *B, T*
St. Joseph's College: Suffolk
   Campus *B, T*
St. Lawrence University *T*
State University of New York
   Buffalo *M, D, T*
   College at Brockport *B, M, T*
   College at Geneseo *B, M, T*
   College at Oneonta *B, T*
   College at Plattsburgh *B, M*
   New Paltz *B, M, T*
   Oswego *B*
Vassar College *T*
Wells College *T*

North Carolina

Appalachian State University *M*
Campbell University *B, T*
East Carolina University *M*
Gardner-Webb University *B*
Lenoir Community College *A*
Louisburg College *A*
Mars Hill College *T*
Meredith College *T*
Montreat College *T*
North Carolina Agricultural and
   Technical State University *B, T*
North Carolina Central University *B, M*
North Carolina State University *T*
Queens University of Charlotte *T*
Sandhills Community College *A*

University of North Carolina
    Charlotte *B*
    Greensboro *B, M, T*
    Wilmington *B*
Wake Forest University *T*
Wingate University *B, T*

North Dakota

Dickinson State University *B, T*
Jamestown College *B*
Minot State University *B*
North Dakota State University *B, T*
University of North Dakota *B, T*
Valley City State University *B, T*

Ohio

Baldwin-Wallace College *T*
Bluffton College *B*
Bowling Green State University *B, M*
Case Western Reserve University *T*
Cedarville University *T*
College of Mount St. Joseph *T*
Defiance College *B, T*
Hiram College *T*
John Carroll University *T*
Kent State University *T*
Kent State University
    Stark Campus *B*
Miami University
    Oxford Campus *M, T*
Mount Union College *T*
Ohio Northern University *B*
Ohio University *B*
Otterbein College *B*
Shawnee State University *B*
University of Akron *B, T*
University of Dayton *B, M, T*
University of Findlay *B, T*
University of Rio Grande *B, T*
University of Toledo *M, T*
Wilmington College *B*
Xavier University *M*
Youngstown State University *B, M*

Oklahoma

Cameron University *B*
East Central University *B, T*
Eastern Oklahoma State College *A*
Oklahoma Baptist University *B, T*
Oklahoma City University *B*
Oklahoma State University *M*
Southern Nazarene University *B*
Southwestern Oklahoma State
    University *B, M, T*
University of Central Oklahoma *B*
University of Tulsa *T*

Oregon

Concordia University *B, M, T*
Linfield College *T*
University of Portland *T*
Warner Pacific College *T*
Western Baptist College *B*
Western Oregon University *T*

Pennsylvania

Albright College *T*
Bryn Athyn College of the New
    Church *B*
DeSales University *T*
Elizabethtown College *T*
Geneva College *B, T*
Gettysburg College *T*
Grove City College *B, T*
King's College *T*
La Salle University *B, T*
Lebanon Valley College of
    Pennsylvania *B, T*
Lock Haven University of
    Pennsylvania *B, T*
Lycoming College *T*
Mercyhurst College *T*
Moravian College *T*
St. Vincent College *T*
Slippery Rock University of
    Pennsylvania *B, T*
Thiel College *B*

Villanova University *T*
Washington and Jefferson College *T*
Waynesburg College *B, T*
Widener University *T*
Wilkes University *M*
York College of Pennsylvania *B, T*

Puerto Rico

Inter American University of Puerto Rico
    Metropolitan Campus *B*
    San German Campus *B*
Pontifical Catholic University of Puerto
    Rico *B, T*
Turabo University *B*
Universidad Metropolitana *B*

Rhode Island

Providence College *B*
Rhode Island College *B*
Salve Regina University *B*

South Carolina

Anderson College *B, T*
Coker College *B, T*
Columbia College *B*
Francis Marion University *B, T*
Lander University *B, T*
South Carolina State University *B, T*

South Dakota

Augustana College *B, T*
Black Hills State University *B, T*
Dakota State University *B, T*
Mount Marty College *B*
Northern State University *B, T*
South Dakota State University *B*
University of Sioux Falls *T*
University of South Dakota *B, T*

Tennessee

American Baptist College of ABT
    Seminary *B*
Belmont University *T*
Bethel College *B, T*
Bryan College *T*
Christian Brothers University *B, M, T*
Freed-Hardeman University *B, T*
King College *T*
Lambuth University *T*
Lane College *B*
Lee University *B*
Maryville College *B, T*
Southern Adventist University *B*
Tennessee Technological University *T*
Tennessee Wesleyan College *B, T*
Trevecca Nazarene University *B, T*
Tusculum College *B, T*
Union University *B, T*
University of Tennessee
    Martin *B, T*

Texas

Abilene Christian University *B, T*
Baylor University *B, T*
Del Mar College *A*
East Texas Baptist University *B*
Hardin-Simmons University *B, T*
Houston Baptist University *T*
Howard Payne University *B, T*
Jarvis Christian College *B*
Kilgore College *A*
Lamar University *T*
Laredo Community College *A*
Lubbock Christian University *B, T*
McMurry University *T*
St. Mary's University *T*
Schreiner University *T*
Southwest Texas State University *M, T*
Tarleton State University *T*
Texas A&M International
    University *B, T*
Texas A&M University
    Commerce *T*
    Corpus Christi *T*
    Kingsville *T*
Texas Christian University *T*
Texas Lutheran University *B, T*

Texas Wesleyan University *B, T*
University of Dallas *T*
University of Houston *T*
University of Houston
    Clear Lake *T*
University of Mary Hardin-Baylor *T*
University of Texas
    Arlington *T*
    San Antonio *T*
West Texas A&M University *T*

Utah

Brigham Young University *B*
Southern Utah University *B, T*
University of Utah *B*
Utah Valley State College *B*
Weber State University *B*

Vermont

Castleton State College *B, T*
College of St. Joseph in Vermont *B*
Johnson State College *B*

Virginia

Averett University *B, M, T*
Bluefield College *T*
Bridgewater College *T*
Hampton University *M*
Hollins University *T*
Liberty University *B*
Longwood University *B, T*
Radford University *T*
University of Virginia's College at
    Wise *T*
Virginia Intermont College *B, T*
Virginia Wesleyan College *T*

Washington

Central Washington University *B, T*
Heritage College *B*
Northwest College *T*
Washington State University *T*
Western Washington University *B, T*
Whitworth College *B, T*

West Virginia

Fairmont State College *B*
Wheeling Jesuit University *T*

Wisconsin

Alverno College *B, T*
Carroll College *B, T*
Carthage College *T*
Edgewood College *B*
Lakeland College *B, T*
Lawrence University *T*
Maranatha Baptist Bible College *B*
Marian College of Fond du Lac *B, T*
Marquette University *B*
Mount Mary College *B, T*
Northland College *T*
St. Norbert College *T*
University of Wisconsin
    Green Bay *T*
    La Crosse *B, T*
    Parkside *T*
    Platteville *B*
    River Falls *T*
    Superior *B, T*
    Whitewater *B*

Wyoming

Western Wyoming Community
    College *A*

Home furnishings

Alabama

Jefferson State Community College *A*

California

Antelope Valley College *A*

Michigan

Grand Rapids Community College *A*

Ohio

University of Akron *C, B*

Home health attendant

Alabama

Lawson State Community College *C*

Arizona

Eastern Arizona College *C*

Florida

Career Training Institute *C*

Illinois

McHenry County College *C*

Kansas

Barton County Community College *C*

Massachusetts

Cape Cod Community College *C*

Virginia

Eastern Shore Community College *C*

Washington

Olympic College *A*

Horse husbandry/equine science

California

Los Angeles Pierce College *C, A*
Santa Rosa Junior College *C, A*

Kentucky

University of Louisville *C, B*

New York

State University of New York
    College of Agriculture and
        Technology at Morrisville *A, B*

Ohio

Wilmington College *B*

Horticultural operations

Alabama

Calhoun Community College *C*
James H. Faulkner State Community
    College *C*
Northwest-Shoals Community College *C*
Trenholm State Technical College *A*
Wallace State Community College at
    Hanceville *C*

Arizona

Glendale Community College *C, A*

Arkansas

Mississippi County Community
    College *C, A*

California

Bakersfield College *A*
California Polytechnic State University:
    San Luis Obispo *B*
Diablo Valley College *C*
Los Angeles Pierce College *C, A*
Mount San Antonio College *C, A*
San Joaquin Delta College *A*
Santa Barbara City College *C, A*
Shasta College *C*
Ventura College *A*

Colorado

Front Range Community College *C, A*

Connecticut

Naugatuck Valley Community
    College *C, A*
University of Connecticut *A*

Delaware

Delaware Technical and Community
    College
        Owens Campus *C, A*

Florida

Florida Agricultural and Mechanical
University *B*

Georgia

Albany Technical College *C*
Darton College *A*
University of Georgia *B, M, D*

Idaho

Boise State University *C, A*
Brigham Young University - Idaho *B*

Illinois

Black Hawk College *C, A*
Black Hawk College
East Campus *C, A*
College of DuPage *C, A*
Illinois Central College *C, A*
Illinois Eastern Community Colleges
Wabash Valley College *A*
John Wood Community College *C, A*
Joliet Junior College *C, A*
Kaskaskia College *C, A*
Kishwaukee College *C, A*
McHenry County College *C, A*
Rend Lake College *C, A*
Richland Community College *A*
Shawnee Community College *C, A*
Southwestern Illinois College *C, A*
William Rainey Harper College *C, A*

Indiana

Vincennes University *A*

Iowa

Des Moines Area Community College *A*
Hawkeye Community College *A*
Iowa State University *B, M, D*

Kansas

Dodge City Community College *A*

Kentucky

Murray State University *A*
St. Catharine College *A*

Louisiana

Delgado Community College *C, A*

Maryland

Community College of Baltimore County
Catonsville *C, A*
Dundalk *C, A*
Essex *C, A*

Massachusetts

Becker College *C*
Cape Cod Community College *C*

Michigan

Andrews University *A, B*

Minnesota

Century Community and Technical
College *A*
Dakota County Technical College *C, A*
Pine Technical College *C*
University of Minnesota
Crookston *B*

Mississippi

Northwest Mississippi Community
College *A*

Missouri

College of the Ozarks *B*
Mineral Area College *C, A*
Southeast Missouri State University *B*

Nebraska

Central Community College *C, A*
Metropolitan Community College *C, A*
Nebraska College of Technical
Agriculture *A*
Northeast Community College *A*
University of Nebraska
Lincoln *D*

New Hampshire

University of New Hampshire *A*

New Jersey

Bergen Community College *A*

New York

Paul Smith's College *A*
State University of New York
College of Agriculture and
Technology at Cobleskill *A, B*
College of Agriculture and
Technology at Morrisville *A*
College of Technology at Delhi *A*
Suffolk County Community
College *C, A*

North Carolina

Alamance Community College *C, A*
Blue Ridge Community College *A*
Carteret Community College *C, A*
Edgecombe Community College *A*
Fayetteville Technical Community
College *C, A*
Forsyth Technical Community College *A*
Haywood Community College *C, A*
Johnston Community College *C*
Lenoir Community College *C, A*
Mayland Community College *C, A*
North Carolina State University *B*
Sampson Community College *A*
Surry Community College *A*
Tri-County Community College *C*
Western Piedmont Community
College *C, A*
Wilkes Community College *C, A*

North Dakota

Minot State University: Bottineau
Campus *C, A*
North Dakota State University *B, M*

Ohio

Clark State Community College *A*
Cuyahoga Community College
Eastern Campus *A*
Metropolitan Campus *A*
Western Campus *A*
Kent State University *A*
Kent State University
Salem Regional Campus *A*
Ohio State University
Columbus Campus *M, D*

Oklahoma

Bacone College *A*
Eastern Oklahoma State College *A*
Oklahoma State University *B, M*
Oklahoma State University
Oklahoma City *C, A*

Oregon

Linn-Benton Community College *C, A*
Mount Hood Community College *C, A*
Rogue Community College *C*

Pennsylvania

Community College of Allegheny
County *A*
Delaware County Community College *C*
Delaware Valley College *B*
Luzerne County Community
College *C, A*
Mercyhurst College *C*
Penn State
University Park *C*
Temple University *A*
Westmoreland County Community
College *A*
Williamson Free School of Mechanical
Trades *C, A*

Puerto Rico

University of Puerto Rico
Mayaguez Campus *M*

South Carolina

Clemson University *B, M*
Piedmont Technical College *C*
Technical College of the
Lowcountry *C, A*

Trident Technical College *C, A*

South Dakota

Southeast Technical Institute *A*

Tennessee

Jackson State Community College *C*
Southwest Tennessee Community
College *A*
Tennessee Technological University *B*

Texas

Central Texas College *C*
Houston Community College System *A*
Midland College *C*
Richland College *A*
Stephen F. Austin State University *B*
Tarleton State University *B*
Tarrant County College *C, A*
Texas A&M University *B, M, D*
Texas Tech University *B, M*
Trinity Valley Community College *C, A*
Western Texas College *C, A*

Utah

Salt Lake Community College *C*

Vermont

University of Vermont *B*
Vermont Technical College *A*

Virginia

J. Sargeant Reynolds Community
College *A*
Virginia Western Community College *A*

Washington

Clark College *A*
Edmonds Community College *C*
Lake Washington Technical College *C, A*
Spokane Community College *A*

Wisconsin

Fox Valley Technical College *A*

Horticultural science

Alabama

Auburn University *B, M, D*
Northwest-Shoals Community College *C*
Trenholm State Technical College *A*

Arizona

Cochise College *C*

Arkansas

University of Arkansas *B, M*

California

California State Polytechnic University:
Pomona *B*
California State University
Fresno *B*
Golden West College *C, A*
Los Angeles Pierce College *C, A*
Reedley College *C*
University of California
Davis *M*

Colorado

Colorado State University *B, M, D*

Connecticut

University of Connecticut *B*

Florida

Florida Agricultural and Mechanical
University *B*
Florida Southern College *B*
South Florida Community College *A*
University of Florida *B, M, D*

Georgia

Columbus Technical College *C, A*
Floyd College *A*
Fort Valley State University *A, B*
Gordon College *A*

Hawaii

University of Hawaii
Hilo *B*
Manoa *B, M, D*

Idaho

College of Southern Idaho *C, A*
University of Idaho *B*

Illinois

Black Hawk College
East Campus *C*
Danville Area Community College *A*
Kishwaukee College *A*
Richland Community College *A*
University of Illinois
Urbana-Champaign *B, M, D*
William Rainey Harper College *C, A*

Indiana

Purdue University *A, B, M, D*
Vincennes University *A*

Kansas

Kansas State University *B, M, D*

Kentucky

Maysville Community College *C, A*

Louisiana

Louisiana State University and
Agricultural and Mechanical
College *M, D*
Southeastern Louisiana University *B*

Maine

University of Maine *C, B, M*

Maryland

Howard Community College *A*

Massachusetts

Becker College *C*
Cape Cod Community College *C*

Michigan

Michigan State University *B, M, D*
St. Clair County Community
College *C, A*

Minnesota

Central Lakes College *C, A*
Rochester Community and Technical
College *A*
University of Minnesota
Twin Cities *M, D*

Mississippi

Mississippi State University *B, M, D*

Missouri

College of the Ozarks *B*
East Central College *C, A*
Northwest Missouri State University *B*
St. Louis Community College
St. Louis Community College at
Meramec *C, A*
Southeast Missouri State University *B*
Southwest Missouri State University *B*
University of Missouri
Columbia *M, D*

Montana

Montana State University
Bozeman *B*

Nebraska

Nebraska College of Technical
Agriculture *C, A*
Northeast Community College *A*
University of Nebraska
Lincoln *B, M*

New Hampshire

University of New Hampshire *A, B*

New Jersey

Thomas Edison State College *A, B*

New Mexico

New Mexico State University *B, M*

New York
City University of New York
    Bronx Community College *A*
Cornell University *M, D*
State University of New York
    College of Agriculture and
        Technology at Cobleskill *A, B*
    College of Agriculture and
        Technology at Morrisville *A*
    College of Technology at Delhi *A*

North Carolina
Alamance Community College *C, A*
Brunswick Community College *A*
Carteret Community College *C, A*
Catawba Valley Community
    College *C, A*
Central Piedmont Community
    College *C, A*
Johnston Community College *C*
North Carolina State University *B, M, D*
Rockingham Community College *C, A*

North Dakota
North Dakota State University *B, M*

Ohio
Kent State University
    Salem Regional Campus *A*
Ohio State University
    Columbus Campus *C*

Oklahoma
Cameron University *B*
Eastern Oklahoma State College *A*
Oklahoma State University *B, M*
Tulsa Community College *A*

Oregon
Central Oregon Community College *A*
Chemeketa Community College *A*
Oregon State University *B, M, D*

Pennsylvania
Delaware Valley College *B*
Penn State
    Abington *B*
    Altoona *B*
    Beaver *B*
    Berks *B*
    Delaware County *B*
    Dubois *B*
    Erie, The Behrend College *B*
    Fayette *B*
    Hazleton *B*
    Lehigh Valley *B*
    McKeesport *B*
    Mont Alto *B*
    New Kensington *B*
    Schuylkill - Capital College *B*
    University Park *B, M, D*
    Wilkes-Barre *B*
    Worthington Scranton *B*
    York *B*
Westmoreland County Community
    College *A*

Puerto Rico
University of Puerto Rico
    Mayaguez Campus *B, M*
    Utuado *A*

South Carolina
Clemson University *B, M*
Horry-Georgetown Technical College *A*
Spartanburg Technical College *A*
Trident Technical College *A*

South Dakota
South Dakota State University *B*

Tennessee
Jackson State Community College *C*
Tennessee Technological University *B*

Texas
Grayson County College *C*
Midland College *C*
Richland College *A*

Sam Houston State University *B*
Southwest Texas State University *B*
Stephen F. Austin State University *B*
Tarleton State University *B*
Texas A&M University *B, M, D*

Utah
Brigham Young University *B, M*
Salt Lake Community College *C*
Utah State University *B, M, D*

Vermont
Vermont Technical College *A*

Virginia
Ferrum College *B*
Virginia Polytechnic Institute and State
    University *B, M, D*
Virginia Western Community College *A*

Washington
Washington State University *B, M, D*

West Virginia
Potomac State College of West Virginia
    University *A*
West Virginia Northern Community
    College *A*
West Virginia University *B*

Wisconsin
Blackhawk Technical College *C*
Milwaukee Area Technical College *A*
University of Wisconsin
    Madison *B, M, D*
    River Falls *B*

Hospital/health care facilities administration

Arizona
University of Phoenix *B, M*

California
Loma Linda University *M*

Colorado
Jones International University *C, M*

Connecticut
Quinnipiac University *M*

Florida
Nova Southeastern University *B*
St. Leo University *B*
University of West Florida *M*

Illinois
College of DuPage *C, A*
Southern Illinois University
    Carbondale *B*

Indiana
Calumet College of St. Joseph *B*
Indiana University-Purdue University
    Fort Wayne *A*

Iowa
University of Iowa *M, D*
Upper Iowa University *B*

Maine
Husson College *M*

Maryland
Howard Community College *A*
University of Maryland
    University College *C, M*

Massachusetts
Newbury College *B*
Stonehill College *C*

Missouri
Washington University in St. Louis *M*

Nebraska
Bellevue University *B, M*

New Jersey
Thomas Edison State College *A, B*

University of Medicine and Dentistry of
    New Jersey
    School of Health Related
        Professions *D*

New York
New York University *M*
Pace University *M*
Pace University:
    Pleasantville/Briarcliff *C, M*
St. John's University *B*
State University of New York
    College of Technology at Canton *B*
Union College *M*

North Carolina
Carteret Community College *A*
Pitt Community College *C, A*

North Dakota
North Dakota State University *B*

Ohio
Ohio University *B*
Ursuline College *B*
Youngstown State University *B*

Pennsylvania
University of Pennsylvania *C, B, M, D*
Widener University *B, M*

Rhode Island
Providence College *C, A*

South Dakota
University of South Dakota *B*

Tennessee
University of Memphis *M*
University of Tennessee
    Knoxville *M*

Texas
Houston Baptist University *M*
Southwest Texas State University *B, M*
University of Houston
    Clear Lake *M*

Hospitality administration/ management

Alabama
James H. Faulkner State Community
    College *C, A*
Jefferson State Community College *C, A*
Tuskegee University *B*

Alaska
University of Alaska
    Anchorage *B*

Arizona
Arizona Western College *A*
Pima Community College *A*
Scottsdale Community College *C, A*

Arkansas
Arkansas Tech University *B*

California
California State Polytechnic University:
    Pomona *B*
College of the Redwoods *C, A*
Columbia College *C, A*
Diablo Valley College *C*
Golden Gate University *M*
Grossmont Community College *C, A*
MiraCosta College *C, A*
Monterey Peninsula College *A*
National University *C, A, B, M*
San Francisco State University *B*
San Jose State University *B*
Santa Rosa Junior College *C*
Travel University International *C, A*

Colorado
Arapahoe Community College *A*
Colorado Mountain College
    Alpine Campus *A*

Metropolitan State College of Denver *B*
University of Denver *B*

Connecticut
International College of Hospitality
    Management *C, A*
Norwalk Community College *A*
Three Rivers Community College *C, A*
University of New Haven *B, M*

Delaware
Delaware State University *B*
Delaware Technical and Community
    College
    Owens Campus *A*

District of Columbia
Howard University *B*

Florida
Broward Community College *A*
Daytona Beach Community College *A*
Florida International University *B, M*
Florida State University *B*
Hillsborough Community College *A*
Indian River Community College *A*
Lake-Sumter Community College *A*
Palm Beach Community College *A*
Polk Community College *A*
St. Thomas University *B*
South Florida Community College *A*
University of Central Florida *B, M*
Valencia Community College *A*
Webber International University *A, B, M*

Georgia
Abraham Baldwin Agricultural
    College *A*
Clark Atlanta University *B*
Morris Brown College *B*
Young Harris College *A*

Hawaii
Brigham Young University-Hawaii *B*
Heald College
    Honolulu *A*
University of Hawaii
    Kauai Community College *C, A*
    Manoa *B, M*

Illinois
City Colleges of Chicago
    Harold Washington College *C, A*
Lewis and Clark Community College *A*
Lincoln Land Community College *A*
Northwestern Business College *A*
Richland Community College *C, A*
Roosevelt University *C, B, M*
Southwestern Illinois College *C, A*
Triton College *C, A*
William Rainey Harper College *C, A*

Indiana
Indiana University-Purdue University
    Fort Wayne *A, B*
International Business College *C, A*
Ivy Tech State College
    Central Indiana *A*
    Northcentral *C*
    Northeast *A*
    Northwest *C, A*
Purdue University *A, B, M, D*
Vincennes University *A*

Iowa
Des Moines Area Community College *A*
University of Northern Iowa *B*

Kansas
Butler County Community College *A*
Seward County Community
    College *C, A*

Kentucky
University of Kentucky *B*

Louisiana
Delgado Community College *A*
Southern University
    Shreveport *A*

University of New Orleans *B*

Maine
Andover College *C, A*
Central Maine Technical College *A*
Husson College *M*
Thomas College *B*
University of Maine
    Machias *B*

Maryland
Allegany College *A*
Community College of Baltimore County
    Catonsville *A*
    Dundalk *A*
    Essex *A*
Frederick Community College *C, A*
Montgomery College
    Rockville Campus *C, A*
Morgan State University *B*
Sojourner-Douglass College *B*
Wor-Wic Community College *C, A*

Massachusetts
American International College *B*
Becker College *B*
Berkshire Community College *A*
Boston University *B*
Endicott College *B*
Katharine Gibbs School *A*
Lasell College *B*
Marian Court College *C, A*
Massachusetts Bay Community
    College *C, A*
Mount Ida College *A, B*
Newbury College *B*
Quinsigamond Community College *C*
Roxbury Community College *C*
University of Massachusetts
    Amherst *B, M*

Michigan
Baker College
    of Clinton Township *A*
Central Michigan University *B*
Eastern Michigan University *B*
Ferris State University *B*
Madonna University *B*

Minnesota
Metropolitan State University *B*
National American University
    St. Paul *B*
Normandale Community College *C, A*
Rasmussen College
    Mankato *A*
    Minnetonka *A*
Winona State University *B*

Mississippi
Delta State University *B*

Missouri
East Central College *C, A*
Harris Stowe State College *B*
Ozarks Technical Community College *A*
Springfield College *A*

Montana
Montana State University
    Billings College of Technology *C*

Nevada
Community College of Southern
    Nevada *A*
University of Nevada
    Las Vegas *B, M, D*

New Hampshire
New Hampshire Community Technical
    College
    Berlin *C, A*
New Hampshire Technical Institute *A*
Southern New Hampshire
    University *B, M*
University of New Hampshire *B*

New Jersey
Atlantic Cape Community College *C, A*

Essex County College *A*
Fairleigh Dickinson University
    College at Florham *M*
    Metropolitan Campus *M*
Gloucester County College *C, A*
Hudson County Community
    College *C, A*
Ocean County College *C*
Rutgers, The State University of New
    Jersey
    Camden Regional Campus *B*

New Mexico
Albuquerque Technical-Vocational
    Institute *C, A*
Dona Ana Branch Community College of
    New Mexico State University *A*

New York
Cornell University *B, M, D*
New York University *M*
Niagara University *B*
Paul Smith's College *B*
Rochester Institute of
    Technology *A, B, M*
Rockland Community College *A*
State University of New York
    College at Buffalo *B*
    College of Agriculture and
        Technology at Cobleskill *A*
    College of Agriculture and
        Technology at Morrisville *B*
Syracuse University *B*
Villa Maria College of Buffalo *A*

North Carolina
Barber-Scotia College *B*
Cape Fear Community College *A*
Central Piedmont Community College *A*
Methodist College *B*
University of North Carolina
    Greensboro *B*
Western Carolina University *B*

North Dakota
Bismarck State College *C, A*
North Dakota State University *B*

Ohio
Ashland University *C*
Bowling Green State University *B*
Central State University *B*
Columbus State Community
    College *C, A*
Cuyahoga Community College
    Eastern Campus *A*
    Metropolitan Campus *A*
    Western Campus *A*
Kent State University
    Stark Campus *B*
Lakeland Community College *C, A*
Ohio State University
    Columbus Campus *B*
    Lima Campus *B*
Owens Community College
    Toledo *A*
Stark State College of Technology *A*
Tiffin University *A, B*
University of Akron *C, A*
University of Findlay *B*
University of Toledo *B*
Youngstown State University *A, B*

Oklahoma
Oklahoma State University *M*
Tulsa Community College *A*

Oregon
Central Oregon Community College *A*
Chemeketa Community College *A*
Mount Hood Community College *C, A*
Southern Oregon University *B*

Pennsylvania
Bradford School: Pittsburgh *C, A*
Education Direct: Center for Degree
    Studies *A*
Marywood University *C, B*

Mercyhurst College *A, B*
Newport Business Institute *A*
Penn State
    Abington *B*
    Altoona *B*
    Beaver *A, B*
    Berks *A, B*
    Delaware County *B*
    Dubois *B*
    Fayette *B*
    Hazleton *B*
    Lehigh Valley *B*
    McKeesport *B*
    Mont Alto *B*
    New Kensington *B*
    Shenango *B*
    University Park *A, B, M, D*
Pittsburgh Technical Institute: Boyd
    School Division *A*
Robert Morris University *B*
Rosemont College *B*
Seton Hill University *B*
Temple University *B, M*
Widener University *B*

Puerto Rico
Universidad del Este *C, A*

South Carolina
Technical College of the Lowcountry *C*
University of South Carolina *B, M*

South Dakota
University of Sioux Falls *B*

Tennessee
Belmont University *B*

Texas
Austin Community College *C, A*
Central Texas College *C, A*
Collin County Community College
    District *C, A*
Galveston College *C*
Huston-Tillotson College *B*
Lamar State College at Port Arthur *C*
St. Philip's College *A*
Stephen F. Austin State University *B*
Tarrant County College *C, A*
Texas Tech University *D*
University of Dallas *M*
University of North Texas *B, M*

Utah
Utah Valley State College *C, A, B*

Vermont
Champlain College *A, B*
Johnson State College *B*
Southern Vermont College *A*

Virginia
J. Sargeant Reynolds Community
    College *A*
National College of Business &
    Technology
    Roanoke *C, A*
Southwest Virginia Community
    College *C*

Washington
North Seattle Community College *C*
South Seattle Community College *A*

West Virginia
Concord College *B*
Davis and Elkins College *B*
West Virginia Northern Community
    College *A*

Wisconsin
Fox Valley Technical College *A*
Lakeland College *B*
Milwaukee Area Technical College *A*
University of Wisconsin
    Stout *B, M*
Waukesha County Technical College *A*

Wyoming
Sheridan College *C, A*

Hospitality/recreation marketing

Arizona
Central Arizona College *A*

California
Glendale Community College *A*
Los Angeles Trade and Technical
    College *A*
Monterey Peninsula College *A*
Orange Coast College *C, A*
San Francisco State University *B*
Travel University International *C, A*

Colorado
Colorado Mountain College
    Alpine Campus *A*
Community College of Aurora *A*
Metropolitan State College of Denver *B*

Connecticut
International College of Hospitality
    Management *C, A*
Manchester Community College *C, A*
Norwalk Community College *A*

District of Columbia
Howard University *B*

Florida
Pensacola Junior College *A*
St. Petersburg College *C, A*
St. Thomas University *B*
Southwest Florida College *A*

Georgia
Floyd College *A*
Savannah State University *B*

Idaho
College of Southern Idaho *A*

Illinois
Lincoln Land Community College *C, A*
Midstate College *C, A*
Moraine Valley Community College *C*
Parkland College *C, A*
William Rainey Harper College *C, A*

Indiana
Vincennes University *A*

Kansas
Butler County Community College *C, A*

Louisiana
Northwestern State University *B*

Maine
Andover College *C, A*
Husson College *B*
University of Maine
    Machias *A, B*

Maryland
Allegany College *A*
Community College of Baltimore County
    Dundalk *A*
Montgomery College
    Rockville Campus *A*

Massachusetts
Bay State College *A*
Berkshire Community College *C, A*
Lasell College *B*
Quinsigamond Community College *C*
Roxbury Community College *A*

Michigan
Ferris State University *C, B*
Lansing Community College *A*
Siena Heights University *A, B*

Minnesota
University of Minnesota
    Crookston *A, B*

Mississippi
Northwest Mississippi Community
    College *A*

Missouri
East Central College *A*
Lindenwood University *B*

Montana
Montana State University
　Billings College of Technology *A*

Nevada
Community College of Southern
　Nevada *A*

New Hampshire
New Hampshire Community Technical
　College
　　Laconia *C, A*
New Hampshire Technical Institute *C, A*
University of New Hampshire *B*

New Jersey
Burlington County College *A*
Cumberland County College *A*

New York
Finger Lakes Community College *A*
Paul Smith's College *B*
Rochester Institute of Technology *M*
State University of New York
　College at Buffalo *B*
　College of Agriculture and
　　Technology at Cobleskill *A*
Tompkins-Cortland Community
　College *A*
Villa Maria College of Buffalo *A*

North Carolina
Wake Technical Community College *A*

Ohio
Columbus State Community College *A*
Ohio State University
　Columbus Campus *B*
University of Akron *A*
University of Findlay *B*
Youngstown State University *A, B*

Oklahoma
Oklahoma State University *M*
Oklahoma State University
　Okmulgee *A*
St. Gregory's University *B*
Tulsa Community College *A*

Oregon
Central Oregon Community College *A*

Pennsylvania
Allentown Business School *A*
Holy Family University *B*
Montgomery County Community
　College *A*
Newport Business Institute *A*
Pittsburgh Technical Institute: Boyd
　School Division *A*
Robert Morris University *B*

South Carolina
Technical College of the
　Lowcountry *C, A*

South Dakota
Sinte Gleska University *B*

Texas
Central Texas College *C*
El Paso Community College *C, A*
San Jacinto College
　Central Campus *A*

Vermont
Champlain College *A, B*
College of St. Joseph in Vermont *B*

Washington
Lake Washington Technical College *C, A*

West Virginia
Bluefield State College *A*
Concord College *B*
Mountain State College *A*
Mountain State University *B*

Wisconsin
Chippewa Valley Technical College *A*
Fox Valley Technical College *A*
Wisconsin Indianhead Technical
　College *C*

Hotel/motel administration/management

Arizona
Estrella Mountain Community
　College *C, A*
Northern Arizona University *B*

California
Long Beach City College *C, A*
San Diego Mesa College *C, A*
University of San Francisco *B*

Florida
Bethune-Cookman College *B*
Northwood University
　Florida Campus *A, B*

Georgia
Albany Technical College *C*
Georgia Southern University *B*

Illinois
Parkland College *C, A*

Indiana
Vincennes University *A*

Massachusetts
American International College *B*
Cape Cod Community College *A*

Michigan
Northwood University *A, B*
Oakland Community College *A*

Minnesota
University of Minnesota
　Crookston *A, B*

Missouri
Central Missouri State University *B*
Ozarks Technical Community College *A*
University of Missouri
　Columbia *B, M*

New Jersey
Thomas Edison State College *A, B*

New Mexico
Santa Fe Community College *A*

New York
Bryant & Stratton Business Institute
　Syracuse *A*
Erie Community College
　City Campus *A*
Mohawk Valley Community
　College *C, A*
New York Institute of Technology *B*
Rochester Institute of
　Technology *A, B, M*
State University of New York
　College at Plattsburgh *B*

North Carolina
Cape Fear Community College *C, A*
Carteret Community College *A*
East Carolina University *B*
Fayetteville Technical Community
　College *A*
Nash Community College *A*
Sandhills Community College *A*

North Dakota
North Dakota State University *B*

Ohio
Tiffin University *B*
University of Akron *C, A, B*

Oklahoma
Oklahoma State University *B*

Pennsylvania
Allentown Business School *A*
Montgomery County Community
　College *C, A*
Newport Business Institute *A*
Northampton County Area Community
　College *A*
Penn State
　Schuylkill - Capital College *B*
　Wilkes-Barre *B*
　Worthington Scranton *B*
　York *B*

Puerto Rico
Inter American University of Puerto Rico
　San German Campus *C*
Universidad del Este *A, B*

Tennessee
University of Memphis *B*

Texas
Del Mar College *C, A*
Houston Community College
　System *C, A*
Northwood University: Texas
　Campus *A, B*
Texas Tech University *B*

Utah
Utah Valley State College *B*

Vermont
Champlain College *A, B*

Virginia
James Madison University *B*

Housing/human environments

Alabama
Auburn University *B*

Arkansas
University of Arkansas *B*

California
California State University
　Northridge *B*
San Francisco State University *B*

Florida
Florida State University *B, M*
Okaloosa-Walton Community College *A*

Georgia
University of Georgia *B, M, D*

Illinois
Olivet Nazarene University *B*

Iowa
Iowa State University *B*
University of Northern Iowa *B*

Kentucky
Murray State University *B*

Michigan
Michigan State University *M, D*

Minnesota
Minnesota State University
　Mankato *B, M, T*
University of Minnesota
　Twin Cities *B*

Missouri
Southeast Missouri State University *B*
Southwest Missouri State University *B*
University of Missouri
　Columbia *B, M*

Nebraska
University of Nebraska
　Kearney *B*

Nevada
University of Nevada
　Reno *B*

New York
Cornell University *B, M, D*

North Carolina
Appalachian State University *B*
University of North Carolina
　Greensboro *B*

Ohio
Miami University
　Oxford Campus *B*

Oklahoma
Oklahoma State University *M, D*

Oregon
Oregon State University *B*

Tennessee
Tennessee Technological University *B*
University of Tennessee
　Knoxville *M*

Texas
Texas Christian University *B*
Texas Tech University *M*
University of North Texas *B*

Utah
Utah State University *B*

Virginia
Virginia Polytechnic Institute and State
　University *B, M, D*

Human development/family studies

Alabama
Auburn University *B, M, D*
Oakwood College *B*
Samford University *B*
University of Alabama *B*

Arizona
Arizona State University *D*
Central Arizona College *C, A*
Pima Community College *C, A*
University of Arizona *B*

Arkansas
University of Arkansas *B*
University of Arkansas
　Little Rock *M*
　Pine Bluff *B*

California
Azusa Pacific University *M*
California Polytechnic State University:
　San Luis Obispo *B*
California State University
　Bakersfield *B, M*
　Dominguez Hills *M*
　Northridge *B, M*
Christian Heritage College *B*
Hope International University *B*
Loma Linda University *M*
Loyola Marymount University *M*
Moorpark College *A*
Pacific Oaks College *B, M*
Point Loma Nazarene University *B*
San Diego State University *B, M*
University of California
　Davis *B, D*
University of La Verne *M*

Colorado
Colorado State University *B, M*

Connecticut
Mitchell College *A, B*
University of Connecticut *B, M, D*

Delaware
University of Delaware *B*

District of Columbia
University of the District of Columbia *B*

Florida
Florida State University *B, M, D*
Nova Southeastern University *D*
University of Florida *M, D*

Georgia
Fort Valley State University *B*
Georgia Southern University *B*
Middle Georgia College *A*
University of Georgia *B, M, D*

Hawaii
Hawaii Pacific University *B*

Idaho
University of Idaho *B*

Illinois
City Colleges of Chicago
    Harold Washington College *A*
Loyola University of Chicago *M*
Northern Illinois University *B, M*
Northwestern University *M*
University of Illinois
    Urbana-Champaign *B*

Indiana
Indiana State University *B*
Purdue University *B, M, D*
St. Mary-of-the-Woods College *C, A, B*

Iowa
Iowa State University *M, D*

Kansas
Friends University *M*
Kansas State University *B, M, T*

Kentucky
Murray State University *B*
University of Kentucky *M*

Louisiana
Grambling State University *A*
Louisiana State University and
    Agricultural and Mechanical
    College *B*
Louisiana Tech University *B*
University of Louisiana at Lafayette *B*
University of Louisiana at Monroe *M, D*

Maine
University of Maine *M*

Massachusetts
Hampshire College *B*
Hellenic College/Holy Cross *B*
Springfield College *M*

Michigan
Central Michigan University *B*
Concordia University *B*
Eastern Michigan University *B*
Kalamazoo College *B*
Kellogg Community College *C*
Michigan State University *M, D*
Northern Michigan University *B*
Spring Arbor University *B*
Wayne State University *B, M*
Western Michigan University *B*

Minnesota
Bethel College *B*
Concordia College: Moorhead *B*
Crown College *T*
Minnesota State University
    Mankato *B*
St. Mary's University of Minnesota *C, M*
St. Olaf College *B*
University of Minnesota
    Duluth *T*
    Twin Cities *B*

Mississippi
Mississippi University for Women *B, T*
University of Southern Mississippi *B*

Missouri
Central Missouri State University *B*
Missouri Baptist University *B*
Northwest Missouri State University *B*

Southeast Missouri State University *B*
Southwest Missouri State University *B*
University of Missouri
    Columbia *B, M*

Nebraska
Grace University *B*
University of Nebraska
    Kearney *B*
    Lincoln *M*
    Omaha *B*

Nevada
University of Nevada
    Reno *B, M*

New Hampshire
University of New Hampshire *B, M*

New Jersey
Kean University *M*
Seton Hall University *M, D*

New Mexico
New Mexico State University *B*

New York
Cornell University *B, M, D*
Fulton-Montgomery Community
    College *A*
New York Institute of Technology *C, M*
Nyack College *M*
State University of New York
    College at Oneonta *B*
Syracuse University *B, M, D*

North Carolina
Appalachian State University *B*
Campbell University *B*
East Carolina University *B, M*
North Carolina Agricultural and
    Technical State University *B*
North Carolina Central University *B*
University of North Carolina
    Charlotte *B*
    Greensboro *B, M, D*

Ohio
Bowling Green State University *B, M*
Kent State University *C, B, M, T*
Miami University
    Oxford Campus *B, M, T*
Northwest State Community College *A*
Ohio State University
    Columbus Campus *B, M, D*
Ohio University *B, M*
University of Akron *M*
University of Toledo *A*
Wright State University *M*
Youngstown State University *B*

Oklahoma
Langston University *B*
Northeastern State University *B*
Oklahoma Christian University of
    Science and Arts *B*
Oklahoma State University *B, M*
St. Gregory's University *A*
University of Central Oklahoma *B, M*

Oregon
Chemeketa Community College *A*
Clackamas Community College *C*
Oregon State University *B, M, D*
Southwestern Oregon Community
    College *A*

Pennsylvania
Indiana University of Pennsylvania *B*

Penn State
    Abington *B*
    Altoona *A, B*
    Beaver *B*
    Berks *B*
    Delaware County *A, B*
    Dubois *A, B*
    Fayette *A, B*
    Hazleton *B*
    Lehigh Valley *B*
    McKeesport *B*
    Mont Alto *A, B*
    New Kensington *A, B*
    Schuylkill - Capital College *A, B*
    Shenango *A, B*
    University Park *C, A, B, M, D*
    Worthington Scranton *A, B*
    York *A, B*
St. Joseph's University *M*

Rhode Island
Community College of Rhode
    Island *C, A*
University of Rhode Island *B, M*

South Carolina
Benedict College *B*
South Carolina State University *M*
Spartanburg Technical College *C*

South Dakota
South Dakota State University *B*

Tennessee
East Tennessee State University *B, T*
Freed-Hardeman University *B*
Lee University *B*
Northeast State Technical Community
    College *C, A*
Southern Adventist University *B*
Southwest Tennessee Community
    College *A*
Tennessee State University *B*
University of Tennessee
    Knoxville *M*
    Martin *B*
Vanderbilt University *B*

Texas
Angelina College *C, A*
Baylor University *B*
El Paso Community College *A*
Galveston College *A*
Southwest Texas State University *B, M*
Stephen F. Austin State University *B*
Texas A&M University
    Kingsville *B*
Texas Tech University *B, M, D*
Texas Woman's University *B, M, D*
University of Houston *B*
University of North Texas *B, M*
University of Texas
    Arlington *B*
    Austin *B, M, D*
    of the Permian Basin *B*

Utah
Brigham Young University *B, M, D*
University of Utah *B, M*
Utah State University *B, M, D*
Weber State University *B*

Vermont
Southern Vermont College *A*
University of Vermont *B, M*

Virginia
Radford University *B*
Virginia Commonwealth
    University *B, M*
Virginia Polytechnic Institute and State
    University *B, M, D*

Washington
Washington State University *B, M*

Wisconsin
Edgewood College *M*
Moraine Park Technical College *C, A*

University of Wisconsin
    Madison *B, M, D*
    Stout *B*

Wyoming
Eastern Wyoming College *A*

Human nutrition

Alabama
Samford University *B*

Connecticut
University of Bridgeport *M*

Maryland
University of Maryland
    College Park *B*

Massachusetts
University of Massachusetts
    Amherst *B*

Michigan
Northern Michigan University *B*

Missouri
University of Missouri
    Columbia *B, M*

New York
Rochester Institute of Technology *B*

North Carolina
Meredith College *M*

Ohio
Bowling Green State University *B*

Utah
Brigham Young University *B*

West Virginia
Marshall University *B*

Wisconsin
University of Wisconsin
    Stout *M*

Human resources development

California
California State University
    Sacramento *B, M*
University of San Francisco *M*

Colorado
Colorado Technical University *C*

Connecticut
University of Connecticut *B*

Georgia
West Georgia Technical College *C*

Illinois
Trinity International University *B*

Kansas
Southwestern College *B*

Maryland
McDaniel College *M*

Massachusetts
Lesley University *M*

North Carolina
Pitt Community College *C, A*

Ohio
Xavier University *M*

Oklahoma
University of Oklahoma *C*

Pennsylvania
Holy Family University *B, M*

Wisconsin
Fox Valley Technical College *A*

University of Wisconsin
Stout *M*

Human resources management

Alabama
Athens State University *B*
Auburn University *B*
Auburn University at Montgomery *B*
Birmingham-Southern College *B*
Community College of the Air Force *A*
Faulkner University *B, M*
Samford University *B*
Troy State University *M*
Troy State University Dothan *M*
Troy State University in
Montgomery *B, M*
Tuskegee University *M*

Arizona
DeVry University
Phoenix *M*
University of Arizona *B*
University of Phoenix *M*

Arkansas
Harding University *B*
University of Central Arkansas *B*

California
Antioch Southern California
Santa Barbara *M*
Azusa Pacific University *M*
California State Polytechnic University:
Pomona *B*
California State University
Chico *B*
Dominguez Hills *B*
Fresno *B*
Hayward *B, M*
Long Beach *B*
Los Angeles *B*
Northridge *B, M*
Sacramento *B, M*
Stanislaus *D*
Cerritos Community College *A*
Chapman University *M*
College of Marin: Kentfield *A*
DeVry University
Fremont *B*
Long Beach *M*
Pomona *B*
West Hills *B*
Dominican University of California *B*
Fresno Pacific University *B*
Holy Names College *B*
La Sierra University *M*
National University *B, M*
San Diego State University *M*
San Francisco State University *B*
San Jose State University *B*
Santa Rosa Junior College *C*
Simpson College *B*
Ventura College *A*
Yuba Community College District *A*

Colorado
Colorado Technical University *B, M*
University of Colorado
Boulder *B*
Colorado Springs *B*

Connecticut
Quinnipiac University *B*
University of New Haven *B*

Delaware
Delaware Technical and Community
College
Owens Campus *A*
Terry Campus *A*
Wilmington College *B, M*

District of Columbia
American University *B, M*
Catholic University of America *B, M*

George Washington University *D*
Trinity College *M*

Florida
Barry University *M*
DeVry University
Miramar *M*
Orlando *M*
Eckerd College *B*
Florida Atlantic University *B*
Florida Institute of Technology *M*
Florida International University *B*
Florida Southern College *B*
Florida State University *B*
Nova Southeastern University *M*
Polk Community College *A*
Rollins College *M*
St. Leo University *B*
St. Thomas University *M*
South Florida Community College *A*
University of Miami *B*
University of North Florida *M*
University of West Florida *B*

Georgia
DeVry University
Alpharetta *B*
Atlanta *M*
Georgia State University *B, M, D*
Kennesaw State University *M*
Macon State College *A, B*
Middle Georgia College *A*
University of Georgia *M*

Hawaii
Hawaii Pacific University *B, M*
University of Hawaii
Manoa *B, M*

Idaho
Boise State University *B*
Idaho State University *B, M*
University of Idaho *B*

Illinois
Benedictine University *M*
De Paul University *B, M*
DeVry University
Tinley Park *B*
Eastern Illinois University *B*
Governors State University *B*
Illinois Institute of Technology *M*
Kishwaukee College *A*
Lake Land College *A*
Lewis University *B*
Loyola University of Chicago *B, M*
Millikin University *B*
Moraine Valley Community College *A*
National-Louis University *M*
Northeastern Illinois University *B, M*
Northwestern University *M*
Rockford College *B*
Roosevelt University *B, M*
St. Xavier University *M*
Trinity Christian College *B*
Trinity International University *B, M*
Triton College *A*
Western Illinois University *B*
William Rainey Harper College *A*

Indiana
Bethel College *B*
Indiana Institute of Technology *B*
Indiana State University *B, M*
Oakland City University *B*
Purdue University
Calumet *B*
North Central Campus *C, A, B*
St. Mary-of-the-Woods College *B*
Taylor University *B*
University of Evansville *B*
University of St. Francis *B*

Iowa
Briar Cliff University *B*
Franciscan University *B*
Loras College *B*

Maharishi University of
Management *C, M, D*
Morningside College *B*
University of Iowa *B, D*
Vennard College *B*
Western Iowa Tech Community
College *A*

Kansas
Barton County Community College *C, A*
Central Christian College *A*
Friends University *B, M*
MidAmerica Nazarene University *B*
Pittsburg State University *B, M*
Southwestern College *B*
Tabor College *B*
Wichita State University *B*

Kentucky
Bellarmine University *C*

Louisiana
Louisiana Tech University *B*
Nicholls State University *B*
University of New Orleans *B*

Maine
Thomas College *B*
University of Maine
Augusta *C*

Maryland
Community College of Baltimore County
Catonsville *C*
Dundalk *C*
Essex *C*
Johns Hopkins University *B, M*
Towson University *M*
University of Baltimore *B*
University of Maryland
College Park *B*
University College *C, B*

Massachusetts
American International College *B, M*
Becker College *M*
Boston College *B*
Brandeis University *M*
Emerson College *M*
Emmanuel College *M*
Fitchburg State College *M*
Framingham State College *M*
Marian Court College *C, A*
Newbury College *A*
Nichols College *B*
Northeastern University *A, B*
Springfield College *M*

Michigan
Baker College
of Cadillac *A, B*
of Clinton Township *A, B*
of Muskegon *A, B*
of Owosso *A, B*
of Port Huron *A, B*
Central Michigan University *B, M*
Cleary University *B*
Davenport University - Western
Region *B*
Eastern Michigan University *B, M*
Ferris State University *B*
Grand Valley State University *B*
Lansing Community College *A*
Madonna University *M*
Marygrove College *M*
Michigan State University *B, M, D*
Oakland University *B, M*
Western Michigan University *B*

Minnesota
Capella University *B, M, D*
Crown College *B*
Inver Hills Community College *A*
Lake Superior College: A Community
and Technical College *C*
Metropolitan State University *B*
Minnesota State College - Southeast
Technical *C, A*

Minnesota State University
Mankato *B*
Normandale Community College *C*
St. Mary's University of Minnesota *B, M*
St. Paul College - A Community and
Technical College *C, A*
University of Minnesota
Twin Cities *B, M, D*
University of St. Thomas *B, M, D*
Winona State University *B*

Mississippi
University of Southern Mississippi *B*

Missouri
Central Missouri State University *B*
DeVry University
Kansas City *M*
Lindenwood University *B, M*
Northwest Missouri State University *B*
Rockhurst University *B*
St. Louis University *B*
Southeast Missouri State University *B*
Washington University in St. Louis *B, M*
Webster University *M*

Montana
Montana Tech of the University of
Montana *A*
University of Montana-Missoula *A*
University of Montana: Western *A*

Nebraska
Bellevue University *B*
Doane College *B*
Hastings College *B*
University of Nebraska
Omaha *B*
York College *A, B*

Nevada
University of Nevada
Las Vegas *B*
Reno *B*

New Hampshire
New Hampshire Technical Institute *A*
Rivier College *M*
Southern New Hampshire University *C*

New Jersey
Bloomfield College *B*
Fairleigh Dickinson University
College at Florham
Metropolitan Campus *M*
Rider University *B, M*
Rowan University *B*
Rutgers, The State University of New
Jersey
New Brunswick Regional
Campus *M*
Salem Community College *A*
Seton Hall University *M*
Thomas Edison State College *C, A, B*

New Mexico
Eastern New Mexico University *B*

New York
City University of New York
Baruch College *B, M*
Dominican College of Blauvelt *B*
Excelsior College *B*
Hofstra University *M*
Iona College *M*
Medaille College *C, B*
New York Institute of
Technology *C, B, M*
Pace University *B*
Pace University:
Pleasantville/Briarcliff *B*
Roberts Wesleyan College *B, M*
Rochester Institute of Technology *A, M*
St. John Fisher College *B, M*
St. Joseph's College *B*
St. Joseph's College: Suffolk
Campus *C, B*

State University of New York
    Albany *M*
    Buffalo *M, D*
    Oswego *B*
Suffolk County Community College *A*

North Carolina

Barton College *B*
Central Piedmont Community College *A*
Davidson County Community
    College *C, A*
Fayetteville Technical Community
    College *A*
Guilford Technical Community
    College *C, A*
High Point University *B*
Meredith College *B*
Mount Olive College *B*
North Carolina State University *B*
Peace College *B*
Stanly Community College *A*
University of North Carolina
    Chapel Hill *B*
Western Carolina University *M*

North Dakota

Valley City State University *B*

Ohio

Baldwin-Wallace College *B*
Bowling Green State University *B*
Central Ohio Technical College *A*
Columbus State Community College *A*
David N. Myers College *B*
DeVry University
    Columbus *B*
Defiance College *B*
Franklin University *B*
Lakeland Community College *C*
Lorain County Community College *A*
Lourdes College *B*
Marietta College *B*
Marion Technical College *A*
Miami University
    Oxford Campus *B*
Notre Dame College *B*
Ohio State University
    Columbus Campus *B, M, D*
Ohio University *B*
Tiffin University *B*
University of Akron *B, M*
University of Cincinnati *M*
University of Findlay *B*
University of Rio Grande *B*
University of Toledo *M*
Urbana University *B*
Ursuline College *B*
Wright State University *B*
Xavier University *B, M*
Youngstown State University *B*

Oklahoma

Langston University *B*
Northeastern State University *B*
Oklahoma State University *B*
Southwestern Oklahoma State
    University *B*
Tulsa Community College *C, A*
University of Central Oklahoma *B*

Oregon

George Fox University *B*
Portland State University *B*
University of Oregon *D*

Pennsylvania

Arcadia University *B*
Cabrini College *B*
California University of Pennsylvania *B*
Carlow College *B*
Cedar Crest College *C*
Chestnut Hill College *C, A, B*
Community College of Allegheny
    County *C, A*
Community College of Beaver County *A*
DeSales University *B*

DeVry University
    Ft. Washington *M*
Delaware County Community College *C*
Drexel University *B*
Holy Family University *B*
Indiana University of Pennsylvania *B*
Juniata College *B*
Keystone College *A, B*
King's College *A, B*
Kutztown University of Pennsylvania *B*
La Roche College *M*
La Salle University *B*
Lebanon Valley College of
    Pennsylvania *C*
Lincoln University *B*
Manor College *A*
Messiah College *B*
Moravian College *C*
Neumann College *C*
Penn State
    Harrisburg *C*
    University Park *C*
Point Park College *B*
Reading Area Community College *C, A*
Robert Morris University *B*
Rosemont College *B*
Seton Hill University *B*
University of Pennsylvania *M*
University of Scranton *B, M*
Villanova University *B*
West Chester University of
    Pennsylvania *M*
Widener University *B, M*

Puerto Rico

Bayamon Central University *B*
Inter American University of Puerto Rico
    Bayamon Campus *B*
    Guayama Campus *B*
    Metropolitan Campus *B, M, D*
    San German Campus *B, M*
Turabo University *M*
Universidad Metropolitana *B, M*
University of Puerto Rico
    Humacao *B*
    Mayaguez Campus *M*
    Rio Piedras Campus *B*
University of the Sacred Heart *M*

Rhode Island

Rhode Island College *B*

South Carolina

Anderson College *B*
Clemson University *M*
Forrest Junior College *A*
Limestone College *B*
Southern Wesleyan University *B*
University of South Carolina *M*
York Technical College *C*

Tennessee

Freed-Hardeman University *B*
Tennessee Wesleyan College *B*
University of Tennessee
    Knoxville *M, D*
Vanderbilt University *B, M, D*

Texas

Amberton University *M*
Baylor University *B*
DeVry University
    Irving *M*
Houston Baptist University *M*
Lamar University *B*
Our Lady of the Lake University of San
    Antonio *B*
St. Mary's University *B*
Sam Houston State University *B*
Tarleton State University *B, M*
Texas A&M University
    Commerce *B*
    Texarkana *B*
University of Dallas *M*
University of Houston *B*
University of Houston
    Clear Lake *M*

University of North Texas *B, M, D*
University of Texas
    Arlington *M*
    Austin *M*
    Pan American *B*
    San Antonio *B*

Utah

Salt Lake Community College *A*
Utah State University *B*
Weber State University *B*
Westminster College *B*

Vermont

Champlain College *A, B*

Virginia

Bluefield College *B*
DeVry University
    Crystal City *M*
Marymount University *C, B, M*
University of Richmond *C*

Washington

Clark College *C, A*
Clover Park Technical College *C*
DeVry University
    Seattle *B*
Eastern Washington University *B*
Edmonds Community College *C, A*
Pacific Lutheran University *B*
University of Washington *B*
Walla Walla College *B*
Washington State University *B*
Western Washington University *B*

West Virginia

Concord College *B*
Ohio Valley College *B*
University of Charleston *M*

Wisconsin

Cardinal Stritch University *C*
Carroll College *B*
Fox Valley Technical College *A*
Marian College of Fond du Lac *B*
Marquette University *B, M*
Mid-State Technical College *A*
Silver Lake College *B*
University of Wisconsin
    Madison *M*
    Milwaukee *B*
    Oshkosh *B*
    Parkside *B*
    Platteville *B*
    Whitewater *B*
Western Wisconsin Technical College *A*

Human sciences communication

Arizona

Arizona Western College *A*

California

Antelope Valley College *A*
California State University
    Sacramento *B*

Georgia

Middle Georgia College *A*

Louisiana

Southern University and Agricultural and
    Mechanical College *B*

Pennsylvania

Marywood University *B*

Texas

University of Houston *B*

Washington

Seattle Pacific University *B*

Human services

Alabama

Troy State University *B*
Troy State University in Montgomery *M*

Alaska

Alaska Pacific University *B*
Sheldon Jackson College *B*
University of Alaska
    Anchorage *A, B*
    Fairbanks *A*

Arizona

Pima Community College *C, A*
Prescott College *B, M*
University of Phoenix *B*

Arkansas

Henderson State University *B*

California

California State University
    Dominguez Hills *B*
    Fullerton *B*
    Monterey Bay *B*
    San Bernardino *B*
College of the Sequoias *C, A*
Columbia College *C*
Gavilan Community College *C*
Holy Names College *B*
Hope International University *B*
Long Beach City College *C, A*
Modesto Junior College *C, A*
Mount St. Mary's College *M*
Riverside Community College *C, A*
San Diego State University *C*
Santa Rosa Junior College *C*
Shasta College *C, A*
Southwestern College *A*
Yuba Community College District *A*

Colorado

Metropolitan State College of Denver *B*

Connecticut

Albertus Magnus College *B*
Asnuntuck Community College *C, A*
Housatonic Community College *A*
Middlesex Community College *A*
Mitchell College *A*
Naugatuck Valley Community
    College *C, A*
Northwestern Connecticut Community
    College *A*
Norwalk Community College *A*
Quinebaug Valley Community College *A*
Teikyo Post University *B*
Three Rivers Community College *A*
Tunxis Community College *C, A*
University of Bridgeport *B*

District of Columbia

George Washington University *B, M*

Florida

Beacon College *A, B*
Florida Atlantic University *C*
Florida Gulf Coast University *B*
Gulf Coast Community College *A*
Hillsborough Community College *A*
Indian River Community College *A*
Miami-Dade Community College *A*
Nova Southeastern University *M*
Palm Beach Community College *A*
Pasco-Hernando Community College *A*
Polk Community College *A*
St. Petersburg College *C, A*
St. Thomas University *B*

Georgia

Darton College *A*
Fort Valley State University *B*
LaGrange College *B*
Macon State College *B*

Hawaii

Hawaii Pacific University *B*

University of Hawaii
    Honolulu Community College *A*
    Maui Community College *A*

Idaho
College of Southern Idaho *C, A*
North Idaho College *A*

Illinois
Carl Sandburg College *C*
Danville Area Community College *A*
Elmhurst College *B*
Kendall College *A, B*
Lewis University *B*
Millikin University *B*
National-Louis University *B, M*
Oakton Community College *C*
Parkland College *A*
Quincy University *B*
Rock Valley College *C, A*
Roosevelt University *M*
Sauk Valley Community College *C, A*
South Suburban College of Cook
    County *A*
Southeastern Illinois College *A*
University of Illinois
    Springfield *M*

Indiana
Bethel College *B*
Calumet College of St. Joseph *B*
Indiana Institute of Technology *B*
Indiana University-Purdue University
    Fort Wayne *B*
St. Mary-of-the-Woods College *B*

Iowa
Des Moines Area Community College *A*
Ellsworth Community College *C, A*
Graceland University *B*
Grand View College *B*
Iowa Western Community College *A*
North Iowa Area Community College *A*
Northeast Iowa Community College *A*
Upper Iowa University *B*
Waldorf College *A*

Kansas
Independence Community College *A*
Ottawa University *B*
Washburn University of Topeka *C, A, B*

Kentucky
Elizabethtown Community College *A*
Hazard Community College *A*
Jefferson Community College *A*
Prestonsburg Community College *A*

Louisiana
Southern University
    Shreveport *A*

Maine
University of Maine
    Augusta *A, B*
    Machias *B*
    Presque Isle *B*

Maryland
Bowie State University *M*
Chesapeake College *C*
College of Southern Maryland *C, A*
Coppin State College *M*
Frederick Community College *A*
McDaniel College *M*
University of Baltimore *B, M*
University of Maryland
    Baltimore County *M, D*

Massachusetts
Becker College *C, B*
Berkshire Community College *A*
Bunker Hill Community College *A*
Cape Cod Community College *A*
Fitchburg State College *B*
Framingham State College *M*
Lasell College *B*
Lesley University *B*

Massachusetts Bay Community
    College *C, A*
Mount Ida College *A*
Simmons College *B*
Springfield College *B, M*
University of Massachusetts
    Boston *B, M*
Urban College of Boston *C, A*

Michigan
Adrian College *A, B*
Baker College
    of Auburn Hills *A*
    of Cadillac *A, B*
    of Clinton Township *A, B*
    of Jackson *A*
    of Muskegon *A, B*
    of Owosso *A, B*
Finlandia University *B*
Grace Bible College *A, B*
University of Michigan
    Flint *B*

Minnesota
Capella University *M, D*
Concordia University: St. Paul *B*
Inver Hills Community College *A*
Itasca Community College *A*
Mesabi Range Community and Technical
    College *A*
Metropolitan State University *B*
Minneapolis Community and Technical
    College *C, A*
Minnesota State University
    Mankato *B, M*
    Moorhead *M*
Northland Community & Technical
    College *A*
Pine Technical College *A*
Riverland Community College: A
    Technical and Community College *A*
Rochester Community and Technical
    College *C, A*
St. Mary's University of Minnesota *B*
South Central Technical College *A*
Winona State University *B*

Missouri
Central Methodist College *B*
Central Missouri State University *M*
Fontbonne College *B*
Hannibal-LaGrange College *B*
Lindenwood University *B*
Longview Community College *C, A*
Mineral Area College *C, A*
Missouri Baptist University *B*
North Central Missouri College *A*
St. Charles Community College *A*
Southeast Missouri State University *M*
Southwest Baptist University *B*
Southwest Missouri State University *M*

Montana
Flathead Valley Community College *A*
Fort Belknap College *A*
Miles Community College *A*
Salish Kootenai College *B*
University of Great Falls *M*

Nebraska
Bellevue University *B, M*
College of Saint Mary *B*
Doane College *B*
Hastings College *B*
Midland Lutheran College *B*
Western Nebraska Community
    College *A*

New Hampshire
Hesser College *C, A*
New Hampshire Community Technical
    College
      Berlin *C, A*
      Claremont *A*
      Laconia *C, A*
      Manchester *C, A*
      Nashua *C, A*

New Hampshire Technical Institute *C, A*

New Jersey
College of St. Elizabeth *M*
Essex County College *A*
Hudson County Community College *A*
Mercer County Community College *A*
Ocean County College *A*
Passaic County Community College *A*
Rider University *M*
Sussex County Community College *C, A*

New Mexico
San Juan College *C, A*
Santa Fe Community College *A*

New York
Broome Community College *A*
Cazenovia College *A*
City University of New York
    Borough of Manhattan Community
      College *A*
Clinton Community College *A*
Cornell University *B, M, D*
Corning Community College *A*
Finger Lakes Community College *A*
Fulton-Montgomery Community
    College *A*
Hilbert College *A, B*
Jamestown Community College *A*
Jefferson Community College *A*
Medaille College *C, B*
Metropolitan College of New York *A, B*
Monroe Community College *C, A*
Mount St. Mary College *B*
New York University *A*
Niagara County Community College *A*
Onondaga Community College *A*
Rockland Community College *A*
Russell Sage College *B*
State University of New York
    College of Technology at Alfred *A*
    Oswego *M*
Suffolk County Community College *A*
Tompkins-Cortland Community
    College *A*
Touro College *A*
Westchester Community College *C, A*

North Carolina
Beaufort County Community College *A*
Central Carolina Community College *A*
Edgecombe Community College *A*
Elon University *B*
Halifax Community College *A*
Lenoir Community College *A*
Mitchell Community College *A*
Montreat College *B*
South Piedmont Community
    College *C, A*
Wake Technical Community College *A*
Wayne Community College *A*
Wingate University *B*

Ohio
Baldwin-Wallace College *B*
Bowling Green State University:
    Firelands College *A*
Central Ohio Technical College *A*
Chatfield College *A*
Cincinnati State Technical and
    Community College *C*
David N. Myers College *B*
Edison State Community College *A*
John Carroll University *M*
Kent State University
    Ashtabula Regional Campus *A*
    Salem Regional Campus *A*
Lakeland Community College *C, A*
Marion Technical College *A*
Mount Vernon Nazarene University *B*
Ohio University *A*
Ohio University
    Zanesville Campus *B*
Sinclair Community College *A*
Southern State Community College *A*
Stark State College of Technology *A*

University of Cincinnati
    Clermont College *A*
Washington State Community College *A*

Oklahoma
East Central University *B*
Oklahoma State University
    Oklahoma City *A*

Oregon
Blue Mountain Community College *A*
Chemeketa Community College *A*

Pennsylvania
Geneva College *B*
Keystone College *A*
La Roche College *B*
Lackawanna College *A*
Lincoln University *B, M*
Montgomery County Community
    College *A*
St. Joseph's University *A*
University of Scranton *C, A, B*
Villanova University *B*
Waynesburg College *B*
Westmoreland County Community
    College *A*

Puerto Rico
Turabo University *M*

Rhode Island
University of Rhode Island *B*

South Carolina
Aiken Technical College *A*
Anderson College *B*
Denmark Technical College *A*
Horry-Georgetown Technical College *A*
Williamsburg Technical College *C*
York Technical College *C*

South Dakota
Sinte Gleska University *B*

Tennessee
Bethel College *B*
Tennessee Wesleyan College *B*

Texas
Austin Community College *C, A*
Eastfield College *C*
Laredo Community College *C, A*
McMurry University *B*
St. Edward's University *M*
San Antonio College *A*
South Plains College *A*
South Texas Community College *A*
Texas Southern University *B*
Texas Woman's University *B*
Tyler Junior College *C, A*

Utah
Salt Lake Community College *C*

Vermont
Burlington College *B*
Champlain College *A, B*
College of St. Joseph in Vermont *B*
Southern Vermont College *A*
Woodbury College *C, A, B*

Virginia
Blue Ridge Community College *A*
Southside Virginia Community
    College *A*
Southwest Virginia Community
    College *C*
Thomas Nelson Community College *A*
Virginia Highlands Community
    College *C, A*
Virginia Wesleyan College *B*
Virginia Western Community College *A*

Washington
Central Washington University *B*
Edmonds Community College *C, A*
Everett Community College *A*
Grays Harbor College *A*
Seattle Central Community College *A*

Western Washington University *B*

West Virginia
West Virginia Northern Community
College *C, A*

Wisconsin
Fox Valley Technical College *A*
Lac Courte Oreilles Ojibwa Community
College *A*
Marian College of Fond du Lac *B*
University of Wisconsin
Oshkosh *B*
Superior *M*

Wyoming
Central Wyoming College *A*

Human/medical genetics

Indiana
Indiana University-Purdue University
Indianapolis *M, D*

New York
State University of New York
Buffalo *M, D*

Pennsylvania
Cedar Crest College *B*
Drexel University *M, D*

Utah
University of Utah *D*

Humanities

Alabama
Spring Hill College *B*

Arizona
Arizona State University *B, M*
Central Arizona College *A*
Northern Arizona University *B*

Arkansas
Arkansas Tech University *B*

California
College of the Siskiyous *A*
Glendale Community College *A*
Holy Names College *B*
Marymount College *A*
Scripps College *B*
University of California
Irvine *B*
Riverside *B*

Colorado
University of Colorado
Boulder *B*
Denver *B*

Connecticut
University of Bridgeport *B*

Florida
Florida Institute of Technology *B*
Florida State University *B, M, D*
Nova Southeastern University *B*
Stetson University *B*
University of Central Florida *B*
University of South Florida *B*
University of West Florida *B*

Illinois
Black Hawk College *C*
College of Lake County *C*
McHenry County College *C*
Shimer College *B*
Trinity International University *B*

Indiana
Indiana State University *B, M*
Indiana University
East *B*
Kokomo *B*
South Bend *A*

St. Joseph's College *A*
St. Mary-of-the-Woods College *A, B*

Iowa
University of Northern Iowa *B*

Kansas
Tabor College *B*
University of Kansas *B*

Louisiana
Louisiana State University and
Agricultural and Mechanical
College *M*
Southeastern Louisiana University *B*

Maine
University of Southern Maine *B*

Maryland
Hood College *M*

Massachusetts
Newbury College *A*
University of Massachusetts
Amherst *B*

Michigan
Lawrence Technological University *B*
Michigan State University *B*

Minnesota
St. John's University *B*

Missouri
Moberly Area Community College *B*
St. Louis University *B*
Southeast Missouri State University *B*

New Hampshire
Chester College of New England *B*
Plymouth State College *B*

New Mexico
College of Santa Fe *M*

New York
Adelphi University *B*
Dutchess Community College *A*
Erie Community College
City Campus *A*
North Campus *A*
South Campus *A*
Mohawk Valley Community College *A*
Sarah Lawrence College *B*
State University of New York
Buffalo *M*
College of Agriculture and
Technology at Morrisville *A*
Stony Brook *B*
Wells College *B*

North Carolina
Fayetteville Technical Community
College *A*

Ohio
Franciscan University of Steubenville *B*
University of Toledo *B*
Ursuline College *B*
Xavier University *B, M*

Oklahoma
Oklahoma City University *B*

Oregon
Northwest Christian College *B*

Pennsylvania
Bryn Athyn College of the New
Church *A*
Bucks County Community College *A*
Butler County Community College *A*
Community College of Allegheny
County *A*
Community College of Beaver County *A*
East Stroudsburg University of
Pennsylvania *B*
Edinboro University of Pennsylvania *B*
Juniata College *B*
Keystone College *B*
Messiah College *B*

Montgomery County Community
College *C, A*
Penn State
Harrisburg *B, M*
University of Pennsylvania *B*

Rhode Island
Providence College *B*

South Carolina
Charleston Southern University *B*
Lander University *B*

Texas
Angelo State University *B, T*
Lubbock Christian University *B*
Stephen F. Austin State University *B*
University of Houston
Clear Lake *B, M*
Downtown *B*
University of Texas
Arlington *M*
Austin *B*

Utah
Brigham Young University *B, M*
Utah Valley State College *A*

Vermont
Burlington College *A, B*

Virginia
Old Dominion University *M*

West Virginia
Marshall University *B, M*

Wisconsin
St. Norbert College *B*

Wyoming
University of Wyoming *B*

Hydraulics technology

Kentucky
Hopkinsville Community College *C*

Maryland
Community College of Baltimore County
Catonsville *C, A*
Dundalk *C, A*
Essex *C, A*

Michigan
Lansing Community College *A*
Oakland Community College *C, A*

Minnesota
Hennepin Technical College *C, A*

Ohio
Owens Community College
Findlay Campus *C*
Toledo *C*

Washington
Spokane Community College *A*

Wisconsin
Milwaukee Area Technical College *A*

Hydrology/water resources science

Arizona
University of Arizona *B, M, D*

California
California State University
Chico *B, M*
Santiago Canyon College *A*

Illinois
Illinois State University *M*

Kansas
University of Kansas *M*

New Mexico
New Mexico Institute of Mining and
Technology *M, D*

North Carolina
North Carolina State University *B*

Oklahoma
Northeastern Oklahoma Agricultural and
Mechanical College *D*

Texas
Tarleton State University *B*
University of Texas
Austin *B*

Illustration

Arkansas
John Brown University *B*

California
Art Center College of Design *B*
California College of Arts and Crafts *B*
Otis College of Art and Design *B*
University of San Francisco *B*

Colorado
Rocky Mountain College of Art &
Design *B*

Connecticut
University of Bridgeport *B*

Georgia
Atlanta College of Art *B*
Savannah College of Art and
Design *B, M*

Kansas
University of Kansas *B*

Maryland
Maryland Institute College of Art *B*

Michigan
College for Creative Studies *B*
Finlandia University *B*

Minnesota
College of Visual Arts *B*

New Hampshire
Chester College of New England *B*

New York
Pratt Institute *B, M*
Rochester Institute of Technology *A, B*

Ohio
Art Academy of Cincinnati *B*
Cleveland Institute of Art *B*
Kent State University *B*
Ohio University *B*
Virginia Marti College of Art and
Design *A*

Pennsylvania
Marywood University *M*

Tennessee
Memphis College of Art *B*

Washington
Cornish College of the Arts *B*

Industrial design

Alabama
Auburn University *B, M*

Arizona
Arizona State University *B*
Yavapai College *C, A*

California
Academy of Art College *C, A, B, M*
Art Center College of Design *B, M*
California College of Arts and Crafts *B*

California State University
Long Beach *B, M*
Los Angeles Pierce College *C, A*
San Francisco State University *B*

Colorado
Art Institute
of Colorado *B*
Metropolitan State College of Denver *B*

Connecticut
University of Bridgeport *B*

Florida
Art Institute
of Fort Lauderdale *B*

Georgia
Georgia Institute of Technology *B*
Savannah College of Art and
Design *B, M*

Illinois
University of Illinois
Chicago *B, M*
Urbana-Champaign *B*

Indiana
ITT Technical Institute
Fort Wayne *B*
Oakland City University *A, B*
Purdue University *B*

Kansas
University of Kansas *B, M*

Louisiana
University of Louisiana at Lafayette *B*

Massachusetts
Massachusetts College of Art *B*
Wentworth Institute of Technology *A, B*

Michigan
College for Creative Studies *B*
Ferris State University *B*
Northern Michigan University *A*
Oakland Community College *A*
University of Michigan *B*
Western Michigan University *B*

Minnesota
St. Cloud Technical College *C, A*

Missouri
College of the Ozarks *B*

New Hampshire
University of New Hampshire *M*

New Jersey
Kean University *B*

New York
Pratt Institute *B, M*
Rochester Institute of
Technology *A, B, M*
Syracuse University *B, M*

North Carolina
North Carolina State University *M*

Ohio
Cleveland Institute of Art *B*
Columbus College of Art and Design *B*
Kent State University *B*
Notre Dame College *B*
Ohio State University
Columbus Campus *B, M*
University of Akron *A*
University of Cincinnati *B*

Pennsylvania
Art Institute
of Philadelphia *A, B*
of Pittsburgh *A*
California University of Pennsylvania *B*
Carnegie Mellon University *B*
Philadelphia University *B*

Puerto Rico
Escuela de Artes Plasticas de Puerto
Rico *B*

Rhode Island
Rhode Island School of Design *B, M*

South Carolina
Clemson University *B, M*

Texas
Border Institute of Technology *A*
Texas A&M University
Commerce *B*

Utah
Brigham Young University *B*

Virginia
Virginia Polytechnic Institute and State
University *B*

Washington
Art Institute of Seattle *A*
University of Washington *B, M*
Western Washington University *B*

Wisconsin
Milwaukee Institute of Art & Design *B*

Industrial electronics technology

Alabama
Douglas MacArthur State Technical
College *A*
Shelton State Community College *A*

Arkansas
Southern Arkansas University Tech *C*
University of Arkansas
Fort Smith *C, A*

California
Irvine Valley College *C*
Victor Valley College *A*

Illinois
College of DuPage *C, A*
College of Lake County *C, A*
Rend Lake College *A*

Kentucky
Somerset Community College *C, A*

Michigan
Oakland Community College *C, A*

Missouri
Crowder College *A*

North Carolina
Cleveland Community College *C*
Fayetteville Technical Community
College *C, A*

Pennsylvania
Lackawanna College *A*
Pennsylvania College of Technology *C*

South Carolina
Piedmont Technical College *C, A*

Virginia
ECPI Technical College: Roanoke *A*

Washington
Wenatchee Valley College *C, A*

Wisconsin
Western Wisconsin Technical College *C*

Industrial engineering

Alaska
University of Alaska
Fairbanks *B, M*

Arizona
Arizona State University *B, M, D*

California
California State Polytechnic University:
Pomona *B*

Florida
Florida State University *B, M, D*
University of Central Florida *B, M, D*

Georgia
Georgia Institute of Technology *B, M, D*

Illinois
Southern Illinois University
Edwardsville *B*
University of Illinois
Urbana-Champaign *B, M, D*

Indiana
Indiana Institute of Technology *B*

Iowa
St. Ambrose University *B*

Louisiana
Louisiana State University and
Agricultural and Mechanical
College *B, M*

Maryland
Morgan State University *B*

Massachusetts
University of Massachusetts
Amherst *B, M, D*
Western New England College *B*
Worcester Polytechnic Institute *B*

Michigan
Kettering University *B*
Northern Michigan University *B*

Mississippi
Mississippi State University *B, M*

Missouri
University of Missouri
Columbia *B, M, D*

New York
Hofstra University *B*
Rochester Institute of Technology *B, M*
State University of New York
Binghamton *B, M*
Buffalo *B, M, D*

North Carolina
North Carolina State University *B, M*

North Dakota
North Dakota State University *B, M*

Ohio
Youngstown State University *B*

Oklahoma
University of Tulsa *M*

Oregon
Oregon State University *B, M, D*

Pennsylvania
Penn State
Abington *B*
Altoona *B*
Beaver *B*
Berks *B*
Delaware County *B*
Dubois *B*
Fayette *B*
Hazleton *B*
Lehigh Valley *B*
McKeesport *B*
Mont Alto *B*
New Kensington *B*
Schuylkill - Capital College *B*
Shenango *B*
Wilkes-Barre *B*
Worthington Scranton *B*
York *B*

Puerto Rico
Inter American University of Puerto Rico
Bayamon Campus *B*
Turabo University *B*

South Dakota
South Dakota School of Mines and
Technology *B*

Texas
Texas A&M University *B, M, D*
Texas Tech University *B, M, D*
University of Texas
Arlington *B, M*
Austin *M, D*

Utah
Brigham Young University *B, M*

Washington
University of Washington *B*

Wisconsin
Milwaukee School of Engineering *B*

Industrial equipment maintenance/repair

Alabama
Alabama Southern Community
College *C, A*
Community College of the Air Force *A*
Gadsden State Community College *C, A*
Northwest-Shoals Community College *C*
Snead State Community College *C*
University of West Alabama *A*
Wallace Community College: Sparks
Campus *C*

Alaska
University of Alaska
Anchorage *C, A*

Arizona
Central Arizona College *A*

Arkansas
Arkansas Tech University *C, A*
Mississippi County Community
College *C, A*
North Arkansas College *C*
Phillips Community College of the
University of Arkansas *A*
Pulaski Technical College *C*
South Arkansas Community
College *C, A*
Southeast Arkansas College *C, A*
Southern Arkansas University Tech *C, A*
University of Arkansas
Community College at Batesville *A*
Fort Smith *C*
Monticello *A*

California
Cabrillo College *C, A*
Taft College *A*

Colorado
Red Rocks Community College *C*

Delaware
Delaware Technical and Community
College
Terry Campus *C, A*

Florida
Miami-Dade Community College *A*

Georgia
Athens Technical College *C*
Chattahoochee Technical College *C*
Coastal Georgia Community College *C*
Columbus Technical College *C*
Georgia Southwestern State University *A*
Middle Georgia College *A*
Southwest Georgia Technical College *C*
Waycross College *A*
West Georgia Technical College *A*

Idaho
Boise State University *C, A*
Lewis-Clark State College *A*
North Idaho College *A*

Illinois
Black Hawk College *C*
College of Lake County *C, A*
Danville Area Community College *A*
Heartland Community College *C, A*
Illinois Eastern Community Colleges
   Olney Central College *C, A*
   Wabash Valley College *C, A*
John Wood Community College *C, A*
Kankakee Community College *C, A*
Kaskaskia College *C, A*
Lake Land College *C*
Moraine Valley Community College *C*
Prairie State College *C*
Rend Lake College *C, A*
Richland Community College *A*
Southwestern Illinois College *C, A*
Triton College *C, A*
Waubonsee Community College *C, A*
William Rainey Harper College *C*

Indiana
Ivy Tech State College
   Bloomington *C, A*
   Central Indiana *C, A*
   Columbus *C, A*
   Eastcentral *C, A*
   Kokomo *C, A*
   Lafayette *C, A*
   Northcentral *C, A*
   Northeast *C, A*
   Northwest *C, A*
   Southcentral *C, A*
   Southeast *C, A*
   Southwest *C, A*
   Wabash Valley *C, A*
   Whitewater *A*
Vincennes University *A*

Iowa
Des Moines Area Community College *A*
Hawkeye Community College *C*
Marshalltown Community College *A*
Muscatine Community College *A*
Southeastern Community College
   South Campus *C*
Western Iowa Tech Community
   College *A*

Kansas
Haskell Indian Nations University *A*

Kentucky
Maysville Community College *C, A*
Somerset Community College *C, A*

Maryland
Community College of Baltimore County
   Catonsville *C, A*
   Dundalk *C, A*
   Essex *C, A*

Michigan
Davenport University
   Midland *C, A*
Grand Rapids Community College *C*
Jackson Community College *C*
Kellogg Community College *C, A*
Lansing Community College *A*
Macomb Community College *C*
Muskegon Community College *C*
Northern Michigan University *A*
Southwestern Michigan College *C, A*

Minnesota
Hennepin Technical College *C, A*
Inver Hills Community College *A*
Mesabi Range Community and Technical
   College *C*
Riverland Community College: A
   Technical and Community College *C*
St. Cloud Technical College *C*

St. Paul College - A Community and
   Technical College *C*

Missouri
Jefferson College *A*
Maple Woods Community College *A*
Ozarks Technical Community
   College *C, A*
Ranken Technical College *A*

Montana
University of Montana-Missoula *C*

Nebraska
Central Community College *C, A*
Metropolitan Community College *A*
Northeast Community College *A*
Southeast Community College
   Milford Campus *A*

Nevada
Great Basin College *A*

New Hampshire
New Hampshire Community Technical
   College
     Nashua *A*

New Jersey
Cumberland County College *A*

New York
State University of New York
   College of Agriculture and
     Technology at Cobleskill *A*

North Carolina
Alamance Community College *C, A*
Bladen Community College *C*
Blue Ridge Community College *C*
Brunswick Community College *C, A*
Caldwell Community College and
   Technical Institute *A*
Central Carolina Community College *A*
Craven Community College *A*
Davidson County Community College *C*
Durham Technical Community
   College *C*
Guilford Technical Community
   College *C, A*
Halifax Community College *C, A*
Mayland Community College *C*
Mitchell Community College *A*
Montgomery Community College *C, A*
Nash Community College *C*
Richmond Community College *C*
Roanoke-Chowan Community
   College *C*
Rockingham Community College *C*
Rowan-Cabarrus Community
   College *C, A*
Sampson Community College *C, A*
Vance-Granville Community College *C*
Wake Technical Community
   College *C, A*
Wilson Technical Community College *C*

Ohio
Jefferson Community College *A*
Owens Community College
   Findlay Campus *C*
   Toledo *C*
Stark State College of Technology *A*

Oregon
Blue Mountain Community College *A*
Chemeketa Community College *A*
Linn-Benton Community College *A*
Rogue Community College *C, A*

Pennsylvania
Pennsylvania College of
   Technology *C, A*
Reading Area Community College *A*
Westmoreland County Community
   College *A*

South Carolina
Aiken Technical College *C*
Central Carolina Technical College *C*

Spartanburg Technical College *A*
Tri-County Technical College *A*
Trident Technical College *C, A*
York Technical College *A*

South Dakota
Southeast Technical Institute *A*
Western Dakota Technical Institute *A*

Tennessee
Northeast State Technical Community
   College *C, A*
Southwest Tennessee Community
   College *A*

Texas
Amarillo College *C, A*
Eastfield College *A*
Grayson County College *A*
Houston Community College System *C*
Texarkana College *C*
Texas State Technical College
   Waco *C, A*

Utah
Utah Valley State College *C, A*
Weber State University *A*

Virginia
Piedmont Virginia Community
   College *C*
Southside Virginia Community
   College *C*
Southwest Virginia Community
   College *C*
Thomas Nelson Community College *C*
Virginia Highlands Community
   College *C*

Washington
Lake Washington Technical College *C*
Lower Columbia College *A*
Renton Technical College *C, A*
Spokane Community College *A*

West Virginia
West Virginia Northern Community
   College *C*

Wisconsin
Chippewa Valley Technical College *A*
Lakeshore Technical College *C*
Moraine Park Technical College *C*
Waukesha County Technical College *C*
Western Wisconsin Technical College *C*
Wisconsin Indianhead Technical
   College *C*

Wyoming
Western Wyoming Community
   College *C, A*

Industrial safety technology

Illinois
Southern Illinois University
   Carbondale *B*

North Carolina
East Carolina University *B, M*
Nash Community College *A*

Ohio
University of Akron *A, B*

Industrial technology

Alaska
University of Alaska
   Fairbanks *A*

Connecticut
Central Connecticut State University *B*

Georgia
Georgia Southern University *B*
Southern Polytechnic State University *B*

Illinois
Illinois State University *B, M*
Western Illinois University *B*

Indiana
Indiana State University *B, M*
Indiana University-Purdue University
   Fort Wayne *A, B*

Iowa
University of Northern Iowa *B, M, D*

Kentucky
Hopkinsville Community College *C, A*
Morehead State University *A, B, M*
Murray State University *B, M*

Louisiana
University of Louisiana at Lafayette *B*

Massachusetts
University of Massachusetts
   Lowell *B*

Michigan
Lawrence Technological University *B*
Mott Community College *A*

Minnesota
Hennepin Technical College *C, A*
St. Mary's University of Minnesota *B*

Missouri
North Central Missouri College *A*
Ozarks Technical Community
   College *C, A*

New Mexico
San Juan College *A*

New York
State University of New York
   College of Technology at Canton *A*

North Carolina
East Carolina University *B, M*
Roanoke-Chowan Community College *A*

North Dakota
North Dakota State University *M*
University of North Dakota *M*

Ohio
Kent State University *A, B*
Ohio Northern University *B*
Ohio University *B*

Pennsylvania
Butler County Community College *A*
Community College of Allegheny
   County *A*
Delaware County Community College *C*
Penn State
   Dubois *A*
   Wilkes-Barre *A*

Tennessee
Cleveland State Community College *A*
Jackson State Community College *A*

Texas
Houston Community College
   System *C, A*
Sam Houston State University *B, M*
Southwest Texas State University *M*
Texas Southern University *M*
University of Houston *B*
University of Texas
   Tyler *B, M*

Washington
Central Washington University *B*
Olympic College *C, A*

Industrial/organizational psychology

Alabama
Alabama Agricultural and Mechanical
   University *M*

Arkansas
University of Arkansas
  Little Rock *M*

California
Antioch Southern California
  Santa Barbara *M*
California State University
  Chico *M*
  Hayward *B*
  Long Beach *M*
  Sacramento *B*
John F. Kennedy University *M*
Pepperdine University *B*
Point Loma Nazarene University *B*
St. Mary's College of California *B, M*
San Diego State University *M*
San Francisco State University *M*

Connecticut
University of New Haven *M*

District of Columbia
George Washington University *D*

Florida
Carlos Albizu University *M*
Florida Institute of Technology *M, D*
University of Central Florida *M*
University of West Florida *M*

Georgia
Georgia Institute of Technology *B, M, D*

Illinois
Adler School of Professional
  Psychology *M*
De Paul University *B, M, D*
Elmhurst College *M*
Roosevelt University *M*
St. Xavier University *B*

Indiana
Purdue University
  Calumet *B*
University of Evansville *B*

Iowa
Morningside College *B*

Louisiana
Louisiana Tech University *M*

Maryland
University of Baltimore *M*

Massachusetts
Bridgewater State College *B*
Fitchburg State College *B*
Springfield College *M*

Michigan
Central Michigan University *M, D*

Minnesota
Capella University *M, D*
Minnesota State University
  Mankato *M*

Missouri
Washington University in St. Louis *B*
Webster University *M*

Nebraska
University of Nebraska
  Omaha *M*

New Jersey
Fairleigh Dickinson University
  College at Florham *M*
Rutgers, The State University of New
  Jersey
  New Brunswick Regional
  Campus *D*

New Mexico
College of Santa Fe *B*

New York
City University of New York
  Baruch College *B, M, D*
  Brooklyn College *B, M*

Hofstra University *M*
Ithaca College *B*
New York University *M, D*
State University of New York
  Albany *M, D*
  Buffalo *M, D*

North Carolina
High Point University *B*
University of North Carolina
  Charlotte *M*

Ohio
Bowling Green State University *M, D*
Ohio State University
  Columbus Campus *M, D*
Ohio University *M, D*
University of Akron *M, D*
Wright State University *M, D*

Oklahoma
Northeastern State University *B*
University of Tulsa *M, D*

Oregon
Western Baptist College *B*

Pennsylvania
Albright College *B*
California University of Pennsylvania *B*
Holy Family University *B*
La Salle University *B*
Lincoln University *B*
Marywood University *B*
Moravian College *B*
West Chester University of
  Pennsylvania *M*

Puerto Rico
Inter American University of Puerto Rico
  Metropolitan Campus *M, D*
  San German Campus *M, D*
University of Puerto Rico
  Rio Piedras Campus *M*

South Carolina
Clemson University *D*

Tennessee
Middle Tennessee State University *B*
University of Tennessee
  Knoxville *M, D*

Texas
Abilene Christian University *B*
Angelo State University *M*
Lamar University *M*
St. Mary's University *M*
Texas A&M University *D*
University of Houston *M, D*
University of North Texas *M*
University of the Incarnate Word *B*

Vermont
Champlain College *B*
Goddard College *M*

Virginia
Averett University *B*
Longwood University *B*
Marymount University *B*
Old Dominion University *D*

Wisconsin
University of Wisconsin
  Oshkosh *M*

Information resources management

Colorado
Colorado Technical University *B*

Indiana
Valparaiso University *B*

New York
State University of New York
  Buffalo *M, D*

North Carolina
Coastal Carolina Community
  College *C, A*

Pennsylvania
Penn State
  Shenango *B*

Utah
Westminster College *B*

Vermont
Champlain College *M*

Information sciences/ studies

Alabama
Alabama State University *B*
American College of Computer and
  Information Sciences *B, M*
Faulkner University *B*
Herzing College *A, B*
Northwest-Shoals Community College *A*
Oakwood College *B*
Prince Institute of Professional Studies *A*
Virginia College *C, A*

Alaska
Charter College *C, A, B*
University of Alaska
  Anchorage *A*

Arizona
Cochise College *A*
Collins College *A*
DeVry University
  Phoenix *B*
Eastern Arizona College *C, A*
Gateway Community College *C, A*
International Institute of the Americas
  Phoenix *C, A, B*
  Tucson *C, A, B*
Phoenix College *A*
Pima Community College *C*
Prescott College *B, M*
Scottsdale Community College *C, A*
South Mountain Community
  College *C, A*

Arkansas
Arkansas State University
  Mountain Home *A*
Arkansas Tech University *A, M*
Mid-South Community College *A*
Ozarka College *A*
Rich Mountain Community College *A*
University of Arkansas
  Fort Smith *A*
  Little Rock *B*
University of Central Arkansas *B*

California
Antelope Valley College *C, A*
Azusa Pacific University *B*
California Baptist University *B*
California State Polytechnic University:
  Pomona *B*
California State University
  Bakersfield *B*
  Chico *B*
  Fresno *B*
  Fullerton *B, M*
  Hayward *B, M*
  Long Beach *B*
  Los Angeles *B*
  Monterey Bay *B*
  Stanislaus *B*
Chabot College *A*
Chapman University *B*
Coleman College *M*
College of the Canyons *C, A*
College of the Siskiyous *C*

DeVry University
  Fremont *B*
  Long Beach *B*
  Pomona *B*
  West Hills *B*
Humboldt State University *B*
La Sierra University *B*
Laney College *A*
Los Angeles Harbor College *A*
Master's College *B*
Moorpark College *C, A*
National University *C, B*
Ohlone College *C, A*
Orange Coast College *C, A*
Pacific Union College *A, B*
Palomar College *C, A*
Platt College
  Ontario *C, A*
Reedley College *C, A*
San Diego City College *A*
San Diego State University *C, B, M*
San Joaquin Delta College *C*
Santa Monica College *C, A*
Santa Rosa Junior College *C*
Santiago Canyon College *A*
Sierra College *A*
Southwestern College *A*
Taft College *C, A*
University of California
  Berkeley *M, D*
  Riverside *B*
  San Diego *B*
  Santa Cruz *B*
University of Redlands *M*
University of San Francisco *B*
University of the Pacific *B*
Vanguard University of Southern
  California *B*
Ventura College *C, A*
Woodbury University *B*

Colorado
Colorado Mountain College
  Alpine Campus *A*
Colorado State University
  Pueblo *B*
Colorado Technical University *A, B, M*
Community College of Aurora *C, A*
DeVry University
  Denver *A, B*
DeVry University: Colorado
  Springs *A, B*
Fort Lewis College *B*
National American University
  Denver *A, B*
Regis University *M*
Remington College
  Colorado Springs *A*
University of Colorado
  Colorado Springs *B*
  Denver *M*
University of Denver *M*

Connecticut
Albertus Magnus College *C, A, B*
Central Connecticut State University *M*
Gateway Community College *C, A*
Manchester Community College *C, A*
Middlesex Community College *C, A*
Northwestern Connecticut Community
  College *A*
Norwalk Community College *C, A*
Sacred Heart University *M*
Three Rivers Community College *A*
University of Hartford *B*

Delaware
Delaware State University *B*
Delaware Technical and Community
  College
  Owens Campus *A*
  Stanton/Wilmington Campus *A*
  Terry Campus *A*

District of Columbia
American University *C, B, M*
Gallaudet University *B*

George Washington University *B, M*
Strayer University *A, B, M*

Florida

Barry University *C, B, M*
Bethune-Cookman College *B*
Broward Community College *A*
Cooper Career Institute *C, A*
Daytona Beach Community College *A*
DeVry University
   Miramar *B*
   Orlando *B*
Florida Institute of Technology *B, M*
Florida Metropolitan University
   Tampa College *A, B*
Florida State University *B*
Hillsborough Community College *A*
Jacksonville University *B*
Lake City Community College *A*
Miami-Dade Community College *C, A*
New England Institute of Technology *A*
Nova Southeastern University *D*
Palm Beach Community College *A*
Pensacola Junior College *A*
Polk Community College *A*
Rollins College *B*
St. Petersburg College *C*
Seminole Community College *A*
Tampa Technical Institute *A*
University of Miami *B, M*
University of South Florida *B*

Georgia

Atlanta Metropolitan College *A*
Brewton-Parker College *B*
Columbus State University *B*
Columbus Technical College *C*
Darton College *A*
DeVry University
   Alpharetta *B*
   Atlanta *B*
Emmanuel College *B*
Fort Valley State University *B*
Georgia Institute of Technology *M*
Georgia Military College *A*
Gordon College *A*
Griffin Technical College *A*
Herzing College *A, B*
Kennesaw State University *B, M*
Macon State College *B*
Mercer University *B*
Reinhardt College *B*
Savannah State University *B*
Southern Polytechnic State
   University *C, B, M*
University of Georgia *M*
Valdosta State University *B*

Hawaii

Brigham Young University-Hawaii *B*
Hawaii Pacific University *M*
University of Hawaii
   Honolulu Community College *A*

Idaho

Boise State University *B, M*
Idaho State University *B, M*
Lewis-Clark State College *C, A*

Illinois

Bradley University *B, M*
Chicago State University *B*
City Colleges of Chicago
   Harold Washington College *C, A*
Danville Area Community College *A*
De Paul University *C, B*
DeVry University
   Addison *B*
   Chicago *B*
   Tinley Park *B*
Dominican University *B, M*
Elmhurst College *B*
Illinois Valley Community College *A*
John Wood Community College *A*
Joliet Junior College *A*
Kendall College *C, B*
Lewis University *B*

National-Louis University *C, B*
Northwestern University *M*
Olivet Nazarene University *B*
Parkland College *A*
Rockford Business College *C, A*
Rockford College *B*
Roosevelt University *C, B, M*
Southeastern Illinois College *A*
Southwestern Illinois College *A*
Springfield College in Illinois *C*
Trinity Christian College *B*
University of St. Francis *B*
William Rainey Harper College *C, A*

Indiana

Anderson University *B*
Bethel College *B*
Goshen College *B*
ITT Technical Institute
   Indianapolis *A*
Indiana Business College *C*
Indiana Business College
   Columbus *C, A*
   Evansville *C*
   Lafayette *C*
   Muncie *C, A*
Indiana Institute of Technology *A, B*
Indiana University
   Kokomo *B*
Purdue University
   Calumet *A, B*
Taylor University *A*
University of Indianapolis *A, B*
Vincennes University *A*

Iowa

Briar Cliff University *B*
Buena Vista University *B*
Central College *B*
Des Moines Area Community College *A*
Dordt College *B*
Ellsworth Community College *C, A*
Graceland University *B*
Grand View College *C*
Hamilton College *A*
Hamilton College
   Mason City *A*
North Iowa Area Community College *A*
St. Ambrose University *B*
Simpson College *B*
Southeastern Community College
   South Campus *C*
Southwestern Community College *A*
University of Iowa *B, M, D*
University of Northern Iowa *B*
Waldorf College *A, B*
Wartburg College *B*

Kansas

Baker University *B*
Barton County Community College *A*
Central Christian College *A*
Emporia State University *B*
Independence Community College *C, A*
Kansas State University *B*
MidAmerica Nazarene University *B*
Newman University *A, B*
Pittsburg State University *B*
St. Mary College *B*
Southwestern College *B*

Kentucky

Daymar College *A*
Elizabethtown Community College *A*
Louisville Technical Institute *A*
Madisonville Community College *A*
Maysville Community College *C, A*
Murray State University *B*

Louisiana

Grambling State University *B*
Grantham University *A, B*
ITI Technical College *B*
Louisiana College *B*
Louisiana State University
   Shreveport *M*

Louisiana State University and
   Agricultural and Mechanical
   College *M*
Loyola University New Orleans *B*
Northwestern State University *A, B*
Nunez Community College *C, A*
Remington College
   Baton Rouge *A*
Tulane University *A, B*
Xavier University of Louisiana *B*

Maine

Husson College *A*
Thomas College *A, B*
University of Maine *M*
University of Maine
   Machias *A*

Maryland

Allegany College *A*
Bowie State University *M*
Cecil Community College *C, A*
Chesapeake College *C*
College of Southern Maryland *C, A*
Columbia Union College *B*
Community College of Baltimore County
   Catonsville *A*
   Essex *A*
Frederick Community College *A*
Frostburg State University *C*
Hood College *B, M*
Johns Hopkins University *B, M*
Montgomery College
   Rockville Campus *A*
Morgan State University *B*
TESST College of Technology *A*
TESST College of Technology
   Baltimore *C, A*
University of Maryland
   Baltimore County *C, B, M, D*
   University College *C, B, M*
Villa Julie College *C, B, M*

Massachusetts

American International College *B*
Assumption College *B*
Babson College *B*
Bentley College *B, M*
Berkshire Community College *C, A*
Boston College *B*
Bridgewater State College *C*
Bunker Hill Community College *A*
Cape Cod Community College *A*
Harvard College *B*
Massachusetts Bay Community
   College *C, A*
Massachusetts College of Liberal Arts *B*
Mount Wachusett Community College *C*
Northeastern University *M, D*
Springfield College *B*
Suffolk University *B*
Tufts University *B*
University of Massachusetts
   Lowell *A, B*
Wentworth Institute of Technology *A, B*
Westfield State College *B*

Michigan

Alpena Community College *C, A*
Andrews University *B*
Baker College
   of Auburn Hills *A*
   of Jackson *C*
   of Muskegon *B*
   of Owosso *A*
   of Port Huron *A, B*
Calvin College *B*
Central Michigan University *B, M*
Concordia University *B*
Davenport University
   Eastern Region *A, B*
Eastern Michigan University *B, M*
Ferris State University *B, M*
Grand Valley State University *B, M*
Lawrence Technological
   University *C, B, M, D*
Mott Community College *A*

Northwestern Michigan College *A*
Oakland Community College *A*
Schoolcraft College *A*
University of Michigan *M, D*
Washtenaw Community College *C, A*
Wayne State University *B*
William Tyndale College *B*

Minnesota

Anoka-Ramsey Community College *A*
Augsburg College *C*
Bethel College *B*
Brown College *A*
Capella University *B, M*
College of St. Catherine *B*
Concordia University: St. Paul *B*
Crown College *C, A, B*
Hennepin Technical College *C, A*
Metropolitan State University *B*
Minnesota State University
   Mankato *B, M*
National American University
   St. Paul *A*
Northland Community & Technical
   College *A*
Pine Technical College *A*
Rasmussen College
   St. Cloud *A*
St. Cloud Technical College *C, A*
St. Mary's University of Minnesota *B*
University of Minnesota
   Crookston *A, B*
   Twin Cities *C*
Winona State University *B*

Missouri

Central Missouri State University *M*
Culver-Stockton College *B*
DeVry University
   Kansas City *B*
Drury University *B*
Harris Stowe State College *B*
Lincoln University *B*
Lindenwood University *B*
Missouri College *C*
Missouri Southern State College *A, B*
Missouri Technical School *B*
Missouri Western State College *B*
National American University
   Kansas City *A, B*
Northwest Missouri State University *B*
Rockhurst University *B*
Southeast Missouri State University *B*
University of Missouri
   Kansas City *B*
   Rolla *M*
Washington University in St. Louis *B, M*
William Jewell College *B*

Montana

Montana Tech of the University of
   Montana *B*
Rocky Mountain College *B*
University of Montana: Western *A*

Nebraska

Chadron State College *B*
Doane College *B*
Lincoln School of Commerce *C, A*
Metropolitan Community College *A*
Nebraska College of Technical
   Agriculture *A*
Nebraska Wesleyan University *B*
Southeast Community College
   Lincoln Campus *C, A*
Union College *A, B*
University of Nebraska
   Kearney *B*
Wayne State College *B*

Nevada

Community College of Southern
   Nevada *A*

New Hampshire

Daniel Webster College *A, B*
Franklin Pierce College *B*

New Hampshire Community Technical
College
 Nashua *A*
 Stratham *C, A*

New Jersey

Burlington County College *C, A*
DeVry College of Technology *A*
Essex County College *C*
Mercer County Community College *C*
New Jersey Institute of
 Technology *B, M, D*
Ocean County College *C*
Ramapo College of New Jersey *B*
Rutgers, The State University of New
 Jersey
  Newark Regional Campus *B*
St. Peter's College *C, A, B*
Salem Community College *A*
Seton Hall University *M*
Stevens Institute of Technology *M, D*
Union County College *A*

New Mexico

Albuquerque Technical-Vocational
 Institute *C, A*
New Mexico Highlands University *B*
New Mexico State University
 Alamogordo *A*
San Juan College *A*

New York

Adirondack Community College *A*
Briarcliffe College *C*
Canisius College *B*
Cayuga County Community College *C*
City University of New York
 Baruch College *B*
 Brooklyn College *B, M*
 Medgar Evers College *B*
 Queensborough Community
  College *A*
Clarkson University *M*
Columbia University
 Fu Foundation School of
  Engineering and Applied
  Science *M, D*
DeVry Institute of Technology
 New York *B*
Dominican College of Blauvelt *B*
Erie Community College
 City Campus *A*
 North Campus *A*
 South Campus *A*
Excelsior College *B*
Finger Lakes Community College *C, A*
Fulton-Montgomery Community
 College *A*
Genesee Community College *A*
Hartwick College *B*
Hofstra University *B, M*
Island Drafting and Technical Institute *C*
Ithaca College *B*
Jefferson Community College *C, A*
Long Island University
 C. W. Post Campus *B, M*
Manhattan College *B*
Marist College *B, M*
Marymount College of Fordham
 University *B*
Medaille College *B*
Mercy College *B*
Mildred Elley *C, A*
Molloy College *B*
Mount St. Mary College *B*
Nazareth College of Rochester *B*
New York University *B, M, D*
Niagara University *C, B*
Pace University *C, A, B, M*
Pace University:
 Pleasantville/Briarcliff *C, B, M*
Plaza College *A*
Sage College of Albany *A*
St. John's University *C, B*

State University of New York
 Albany *B, M, D*
 College at Buffalo *B*
 College at Old Westbury *B*
 College of Agriculture and
  Technology at Cobleskill *A*
 Farmingdale *C, A*
 Institute of Technology at
  Utica/Rome *B*
 Oswego *B*
 Stony Brook *B*
Suffolk County Community
 College *C, A*
Syracuse University *B, M, D*
Tompkins-Cortland Community
 College *A*
United States Military Academy *B*
Westchester Business Institute *C, A*
Westchester Community College *C, A*

North Carolina

Alamance Community College *A*
Appalachian State University *B*
Beaufort County Community
 College *A*
Blue Ridge Community College *A*
Campbell University *B*
Catawba Valley Community College *A*
Central Carolina Community
 College *A*
Central Piedmont Community College *A*
Cleveland Community College *C, A*
Coastal Carolina Community College *A*
College of the Albemarle *A*
Davidson County Community
 College *C, A*
Durham Technical Community
 College *C, A*
Edgecombe Community College *A*
Elon University *B*
Fayetteville Technical Community
 College *A*
Guilford Technical Community
 College *C, A*
Lees-McRae College *B*
Lenoir-Rhyne College *B*
Martin Community College *C, A*
Mitchell Community College *C, A*
Montgomery Community College *A*
Nash Community College *A*
North Carolina Central University *M*
North Carolina Wesleyan College *B*
Queens University of Charlotte *B*
Richmond Community College *C, A*
Roanoke-Chowan Community College *A*
Rockingham Community College *A*
Rowan-Cabarrus Community
 College *C, A*
Sampson Community College *A*
Sandhills Community College *C, A*
South Piedmont Community College *A*
Stanly Community College *C, A*
Surry Community College *C, A*
Tri-County Community College *A*
University of North Carolina
 Chapel Hill *B, M*
Vance-Granville Community College *A*
Western Piedmont Community
 College *C, A*
Wilkes Community College *A*

North Dakota

Jamestown College *B*
Minot State University: Bottineau
 Campus *A*
North Dakota State College of Science *A*
University of Mary *B*

Ohio

Antonelli College *A*
Baldwin-Wallace College *B*
Bryant & Stratton College
 Cleveland West *A*
Case Western Reserve University *M, D*
Cincinnati State Technical and
 Community College *A*

Clark State Community College *C*
College of Mount St. Joseph *A, B*
Columbus State Community College *A*
David N. Myers College *C, B*
DeVry University
 Columbus *B*
Jefferson Community College *C, A*
Kent State University
 Stark Campus *B*
Lakeland Community College *C, A*
Lorain County Community College *A*
Marietta College *B*
Miami-Jacobs College *C, A*
Muskingum Area Technical College *A*
Notre Dame College *B*
Ohio Dominican College *B*
Ohio State University
 Columbus Campus *B*
Ohio University *B*
Shawnee State University *B*
Stark State College of Technology *A*
Stautzenberger College *C, A*
Tiffin University *B*
University of Cincinnati *M, D*
University of Dayton *B*
University of Findlay *B*
University of Toledo *A, B, M*
Urbana University *B*
Youngstown State University *A, B*

Oklahoma

Northwestern Oklahoma State
 University *B*
Oklahoma Baptist University *B*
Oklahoma Christian University of
 Science and Arts *B*
Oklahoma City University *M*
Oklahoma Panhandle State University *B*
Oklahoma State University *B*
Rogers State University *B*
Southeastern Oklahoma State
 University *B*
Southwestern Oklahoma State
 University *B*
University of Central Oklahoma *B*
Western Oklahoma State College *A*

Oregon

George Fox University *B*
Lane Community College *C*
Southwestern Oregon Community
 College *A*
Umpqua Community College *A*

Pennsylvania

Academy of Medical Arts and
 Business *C, A*
Albright College *B*
Bucks County Community College *A*
California University of
 Pennsylvania *A, B*
Carlow College *B*
Carnegie Mellon University *B, M*
Cedar Crest College *C, B*
Community College of Allegheny
 County *A*
DeVry University
 Ft. Washington *B*
Delaware County Community College *A*
Drexel University *B, M, D*
DuBois Business College
 Oil City *A*
Elizabethtown College *C, A, B*
Immaculata University *C, B*
Juniata College *B*
Keystone College *A, B*
La Salle University *A, B, M*
Lehigh Carbon Community College *C, A*
Lehigh University *B*
Lock Haven University of
 Pennsylvania *B*
Marywood University *M*
Messiah College *B*
Montgomery County Community
 College *C, A*
Moravian College *B*

Peirce College *C, A, B*
Penn State
 Abington *B*
 Altoona *A, B*
 Beaver *A, B*
 Berks *A, B*
 Delaware County *B*
 Dubois *A, B*
 Fayette *A, B*
 Harrisburg *C, B*
 Hazleton *A, B*
 Lehigh Valley *A, B*
 McKeesport *B*
 Mont Alto *A, B*
 New Kensington *A, B*
 Schuylkill - Capital College *A, B*
 Shenango *A, B*
 University Park *C, B*
 Wilkes-Barre *A, B*
 Worthington Scranton *A, B*
 York *A, B*
Philadelphia University *C, B*
Robert Morris University *B, M*
Shippensburg University of
 Pennsylvania *B*
Slippery Rock University of
 Pennsylvania *B*
Temple University *B, M*
Thiel College *A, B*
University of Pittsburgh *B, M, D*
University of Pittsburgh
 Bradford *A*
 Greensburg *B*
University of Scranton *C, B*
Villanova University *B*
Westmoreland County Community
 College *C*
Widener University *A, B*
Wilkes University *B*
York College of Pennsylvania *B, M*

Puerto Rico

Humacao Community College *A*
Inter American University of Puerto Rico
 Barranquitas Campus *B*
 Bayamon Campus *B*
 Metropolitan Campus *M*
Universidad Metropolitana *B*
University of Puerto Rico
 Mayaguez Campus *B*
University of the Sacred Heart *B*

Rhode Island

Bryant College *B, M*
Salve Regina University *B*

South Carolina

Charleston Southern University *B*
Claflin University *B*
Clemson University *B*
College of Charleston *B*
Forrest Junior College *C, A*
Orangeburg-Calhoun Technical
 College *C*
Spartanburg Methodist College *A*
Trident Technical College *A*
University of South Carolina
 Spartanburg *B*
Wofford College *C*

South Dakota

Dakota State University *A, B, M, D*
Southeast Technical Institute *C*

Tennessee

Belmont University *B, M*
Chattanooga State Technical Community
 College *C, A*
Dyersburg State Community
 College *C, A*
Lee University *B*
Middle Tennessee State University *B*
Tusculum College *B*
University of Tennessee
 Knoxville *M*
Walters State Community College *C, A*

Texas

Amarillo College *C, A*
Brookhaven College *A*
Central Texas College *C, A*
DeVry University
    Irving *B*
El Centro College *C, A*
El Paso Community College *C, A*
Frank Phillips College *C*
Galveston College *C, A*
Houston Baptist University *M*
Howard Payne University *B*
Lamar University *M*
Laredo Community College *A*
LeTourneau University *B*
Lee College *C, A*
Midland College *C, A*
Odessa College *A*
Palo Alto College *A*
Panola College *C, A*
St. Philip's College *A*
Southwestern Adventist
    University *A, B, T*
Tarleton State University *M*
Texas A&M University
    Commerce *B*
    Corpus Christi *B*
Texas Lutheran University *B*
Texas State Technical College
    Waco *C, A*
    West Texas *A*
Texas Wesleyan University *B*
Tyler Junior College *C, A*
University of Houston *B*
University of Houston
    Victoria *B*
University of Mary
    Hardin-Baylor *B, M, T*
University of North Texas *M, D*
University of Texas
    Pan American *B*
    San Antonio *M*
    of the Permian Basin *B*
Victoria College *C, A*

Utah

Brigham Young University *B*
College of Eastern Utah *C*
Salt Lake Community College *A*
Snow College *A*
Southern Utah University *A, B*
Utah State University *B, M*
Utah Valley State College *A, B*
Weber State University *B*
Westminster College *B, M*

Vermont

Champlain College *C, A, B*
College of St. Joseph in Vermont *B*
Johnson State College *A, B*
St. Michael's College *B*
University of Vermont *B*

Virginia

Averett University *B*
Blue Ridge Community College *A*
Danville Community College *C*
DeVry University
    Crystal City *B*
ECPI College of Technology *C, A*
ECPI Technical College: Roanoke *A*
Ferrum College *B*
George Mason University *M*
J. Sargeant Reynolds Community
    College *A*
James Madison University *B*
Mary Baldwin College *B*
Mountain Empire Community College *A*
Rappahannock Community College *A*
Roanoke College *B*
Shenandoah University *C*
Thomas Nelson Community
    College *C, A*
University of Richmond *C, A*
Virginia Commonwealth University *B*

Virginia Polytechnic Institute and State
    University *B, M*

Washington

Centralia College *A*
DeVry University
    Seattle *B*
Eastern Washington University *B*
Edmonds Community College *C*
Everett Community College *C, A*
Green River Community College *C, A*
North Seattle Community College *C, A*
Renton Technical College *C*
Seattle Central Community College *C, A*
South Seattle Community College *C, A*
Spokane Community College *A*
Spokane Falls Community College *A*
University of Washington *B*
Walla Walla College *B*
Walla Walla Community College *C, A*

West Virginia

Alderson-Broaddus College *B*
Eastern West Virginia Community and
    Technical College *A*
International Academy of Design and
    Technology *C*
Marshall University *M*
Mountain State University *B*
University of Charleston *A, B*
West Liberty State College *B*
West Virginia Junior College *A*
West Virginia Northern Community
    College *A*
West Virginia Wesleyan College *B*

Wisconsin

Bryant & Stratton College *A*
Carroll College *B*
Edgewood College *B*
Fox Valley Technical College *A*
Milwaukee Area Technical College *A*
Northland College *B*
Silver Lake College *B*
University of Wisconsin
    Green Bay *B*
    Madison *B, M, D*
    Superior *B*

Wyoming

Laramie County Community College *A*
Sheridan College *A*
Western Wyoming Community
    College *A*

Information technology

Alabama

American College of Computer and
    Information Sciences *B, M*
Northwest-Shoals Community College *A*
South University *A, B*

Arkansas

Harding University *B*
Phillips Community College of the
    University of Arkansas *A*
South Arkansas Community College *A*

California

Foothill College *C, A*
Holy Names College *B*
ITT Technical Institute
    San Bernardino *B*
National University *A*
Platt College
    Newport Beach *C, A*
Silicon Valley College
    Emeryville *C, A*

Colorado

Colorado Technical
    University *C, A, B, M*
Jones International University *C, B, M*

Florida

Florida International University *B*

Florida State University *B, M, D*
Herzing College
    Orlando *C, A*
ITT Technical Institute
    Ft. Lauderdale *B*
    Maitland *B*
Indian River Community College *A*
Miami-Dade Community College *A*
Pasco-Hernando Community College *A*
St. Petersburg College *C, A*
Schiller International University *A, B, M*
University of Central Florida *B*
University of South Florida *B*

Georgia

Armstrong Atlantic State University *B*
Middle Georgia College *A*
South University *A, B*

Illinois

DeVry University
    Addison *B*
    Chicago *B*
International Academy of Design and
    Technology *C, A*

Indiana

Ivy Tech State College
    Southwest *A*
Professional Careers Institute *A*

Iowa

American Institute of Business *A*
Hamilton College
    Cedar Falls *B*
Southeastern Community College
    South Campus *C, A*

Kansas

Seward County Community
    College *C, A*

Kentucky

Jefferson Community College *C, A*
Murray State University *B, M*

Maryland

Frederick Community College *C, A*
United States Naval Academy *B*

Massachusetts

Cape Cod Community College *A*
ITT Technical Institute
    Norwood *B*

Michigan

Grace Bible College *B*

Minnesota

Brown College *A, B*
Capella University *C, B, M*
Globe College *B*
Normandale Community College *A*
Winona State University *B*

Missouri

Lindenwood University *B*
Ozarks Technical Community
    College *C, A*
Sanford-Brown College *B*

Montana

Montana Tech of the University of
    Montana *B*

Nebraska

Mid Plains Community College Area *A*

Nevada

Western Nevada Community College *C*

New Hampshire

Franklin Pierce College *B*
Hesser College *C, A*
Plymouth State College *B*

New Jersey

Bloomfield College *B*

New Mexico

New Mexico Institute of Mining and
    Technology *B*

New York

D'Youville College *B*
Jamestown Community College *C*
Marist College *B*
Rensselaer Polytechnic Institute *B, M*
Rochester Institute of Technology *A, B*
St. Joseph's College: Suffolk Campus *B*
State University of New York
    College of Agriculture and
        Technology at Morrisville *A, B*
Suffolk County Community
    College *C, A*
Syracuse University *B, M, D*

North Carolina

Cape Fear Community College *C, A*
Carteret Community College *C, A*

Ohio

DeVry University
    Columbus *B*
Kent State University *B, M*
University of Cincinnati
    Clermont College *C, A*
    Raymond Walters College *C, A*
Youngstown State University *A, B*

Oklahoma

Northeastern Oklahoma Agricultural and
    Mechanical College *A*
Rogers State University *B*

Pennsylvania

Bradley Academy for the Visual Arts *C*
Carnegie Mellon University *M*
ICM School of Business & Medical
    Careers *A*
Keystone College *A, B*
La Roche College *B*
La Salle University *B*
Peirce College *C, A, B*
Penn State
    Delaware County *B*
    University Park *B, D*
    Wilkes-Barre *A, B*
Pennsylvania College of
    Technology *A, B*
Point Park College *A, B*
South Hills School of Business &
    Technology *C, A*
Washington and Jefferson College *A*
Waynesburg College *A, B*

Tennessee

Draughons Junior College of Business:
    Nashville *A*

Utah

Brigham Young University *B*
ITT Technical Institute
    Murray *B*
LDS Business College *C, A*

Vermont

Champlain College *M*
Vermont Technical College *A*

Washington

Crown College *B*
ITT Technical Institute
    Seattle *B*
Olympic College *C, A*
Seattle Central Community College *C, A*
University of Washington *B*

Wisconsin

ITT Technical Institute
    Green Bay *B*

Inorganic chemistry

Florida

Florida State University *M, D*

Georgia

Clark Atlanta University *M, D*

Illinois
Loyola University of Chicago *M, D*

Iowa
Iowa State University *M, D*

Kansas
Pratt Community College *A*

Maryland
Johns Hopkins University *B*

Massachusetts
Hampshire College *B*
Harvard College *B*
Tufts University *M, D*

Montana
University of Montana-Missoula *M, D*

New Jersey
Stevens Institute of Technology *M, D*

New York
Fordham University *M*
Sarah Lawrence College *B*
State University of New York
    Albany *D*
    Buffalo *M, D*

Oregon
University of Oregon *M, D*

Texas
University of North Texas *M, D*

Utah
University of Utah *M, D*

Vermont
Bennington College *B*

Wisconsin
Marquette University *M, D*

Institutional food production

Alabama
Enterprise State Junior College *A*
Gadsden State Community College *C*
Shelton State Community College *C*
Wallace State Community College at
    Hanceville *C, A*

Arizona
Arizona Western College *C*
Phoenix College *C, A*

Arkansas
Southeast Arkansas College *C*

California
Bakersfield College *A*
California State University
    Long Beach *C*
Cerritos Community College *A*
College of the Redwoods *C*
College of the Sequoias *C*
Contra Costa College *A*
Long Beach City College *C, A*
Los Angeles Trade and Technical
    College *C, A*
Modesto Junior College *C*
Ohlone College *C, A*
Orange Coast College *C*
Palomar College *C, A*
San Joaquin Delta College *A*
Santa Barbara City College *C, A*
Santa Rosa Junior College *C*
Shasta College *A*
Sierra College *C, A*

Colorado
Arapahoe Community College *C*
Art Institute
    of Colorado *A, B*
Front Range Community College *C, A*

Connecticut
Gateway Community College *C, A*
Manchester Community College *A*

Florida
Gulf Coast Community College *A*
Indian River Community College *C*
Pensacola Junior College *A*
Valencia Community College *A*

Georgia
Abraham Baldwin Agricultural
    College *A*
Darton College *A*

Hawaii
University of Hawaii
    Honolulu Community College *C, A*

Idaho
Idaho State University *C, A*

Illinois
City Colleges of Chicago
    Malcolm X College *A*
John Wood Community College *C*
William Rainey Harper College *C, A*

Indiana
Vincennes University *A*

Iowa
Des Moines Area Community College *C*
Indian Hills Community College *C, A*
Iowa Western Community College *A*
Kirkwood Community College *C, A*

Kansas
Johnson County Community
    College *C, A*

Kentucky
Murray State University *A*

Louisiana
Delgado Community College *A*
Grambling State University *B*

Maryland
Montgomery College
    Rockville Campus *C, A*

Michigan
Bay de Noc Community College *C*
Ferris State University *C, A*
Grand Rapids Community College *A*
Lansing Community College *A*
Northern Michigan University *A*
Oakland Community College *A*

Minnesota
Alexandria Technical College *C*

Mississippi
Mississippi Gulf Coast Community
    College
    Perkinston *C*

Missouri
Penn Valley Community College *C*
St. Louis Community College
    St. Louis Community College at
    Forest Park *A*

Nebraska
Central Community College *C, A*
Metropolitan Community College *C, A*
Southeast Community College
    Lincoln Campus *A*

Nevada
Truckee Meadows Community
    College *C, A*

New Mexico
Albuquerque Technical-Vocational
    Institute *C*
Southwestern Indian Polytechnic
    Institute *A*

New York
City University of New York
    La Guardia Community College *A*
Fulton-Montgomery Community
    College *A*
Mohawk Valley Community College *A*
Rockland Community College *A*
State University of New York
    College of Technology at Delhi *A*
Tompkins-Cortland Community
    College *A*
Westchester Community College *A*

North Carolina
Asheville Buncombe Technical
    Community College *A*
Cape Fear Community College *C, A*
James Sprunt Community College *C*
Johnston Community College *C*
Montgomery Community College *C*
Wilkes Community College *C, A*

North Dakota
North Dakota State College of Science *A*

Ohio
Cincinnati State Technical and
    Community College *C*
Sinclair Community College *C, A*

Pennsylvania
Bucks County Community College *A*
Cambria County Area Community
    College *A*
Community College of Allegheny
    County *C*
Community College of Philadelphia *C, A*
Harrisburg Area Community
    College *C, A*
Immaculata University *B*
Luzerne County Community
    College *C, A*
Montgomery County Community
    College *C, A*
Penn State
    University Park *A*
Pennsylvania College of Technology *A*
Westmoreland County Community
    College *A*

South Carolina
Horry-Georgetown Technical College *A*

Tennessee
Southwest Tennessee Community
    College *A*

Texas
El Paso Community College *A*
Hill College *A*
St. Philip's College *A*
San Jacinto College
    Central Campus *C, A*
Tarrant County College *A*
Texas State Technical College
    Waco *C, A*
Texas Woman's University *B, M*

Virginia
J. Sargeant Reynolds Community
    College *C, A*

Washington
North Seattle Community College *C*
Renton Technical College *C*

West Virginia
Fairmont State College *A*

Wisconsin
Blackhawk Technical College *A*
Fox Valley Technical College *C, A*
Waukesha County Technical College *C*
Wisconsin Indianhead Technical
    College *C*

Instructional media

Alabama
Alabama State University *M*
Auburn University *M, T*
Jacksonville State University *M*
Miles College *B*
University of South Alabama *M, D, T*

Arizona
Arizona State University *M, D*
University of Phoenix *M*

Arkansas
Arkansas Tech University *M*
Southern Arkansas University *M*
Southern Arkansas University Tech *A*
University of Arkansas *M*
University of Arkansas
    Little Rock *M*

California
California State University
    Chico *B, M*
National University *M*
San Diego State University *M*
San Francisco State University *M*
San Jose State University *M*
University of San Francisco *M*
University of Southern California *M*

Colorado
University of Northern Colorado *M, T*

Connecticut
Central Connecticut State University *M*
Fairfield University *M*
University of Connecticut *M, D, T*

District of Columbia
Gallaudet University *M*

Florida
Florida State University *M, D*
Nova Southeastern University *M*
University of Central Florida *M*

Georgia
Georgia College and State
    University *M, T*
Georgia Southern University *M, T*
Georgia State University *M, D*
State University of West Georgia *M*
University of Georgia *M, D, T*

Hawaii
University of Hawaii
    Manoa *M*

Idaho
Idaho State University *M*
University of Idaho *B*

Illinois
Illinois State University *D*
National-Louis University *M*
Northern Illinois University *M, D*
Southern Illinois University
    Edwardsville *M*
University of St. Francis *B*
Western Illinois University *B, M*

Indiana
Indiana State University *B, M, T*
Indiana University
    Bloomington *M, D, T*

Iowa
Clarke College *M*
Iowa State University *T*
Morningside College *M*
University of Northern Iowa *M*

Kansas
Emporia State University *M*

Kentucky
Asbury College *M, T*

Louisiana
McNeese State University *M*

Maryland
McDaniel College *M*
Towson University *M*
University of Maryland
University College *M*

Massachusetts
Boston University *M, T*
Bridgewater State College *M, T*
Lesley University *M, T*
University of Massachusetts
Boston *M*

Michigan
Wayne State University *M, D*

Minnesota
Capella University *M, D*
College of St. Scholastica *T*
Minnesota State University
Mankato *M*
St. Cloud State University *M*

Mississippi
University of Southern Mississippi *M*

Missouri
Southwest Missouri State University *M*
Webster University *M*

Nebraska
University of Nebraska
Omaha *B, T*

New Jersey
Georgian Court College *M*
Kean University *M*
Richard Stockton College of New
Jersey *M*
William Paterson University of New
Jersey *T*

New York
Rochester Institute of Technology *M*
State University of New York
Albany *M*
Buffalo *M, D, T*
College at Potsdam *M*
Syracuse University *M, D*

North Carolina
Appalachian State University *M*
East Carolina University *M*
North Carolina Agricultural and
Technical State University *M*
North Carolina Central University *M*
University of North Carolina
Charlotte *M*
Wilmington *M*
Western Carolina University *M*

Ohio
Baldwin-Wallace College *M*
John Carroll University *M*
Malone College *M*
Miami University
Oxford Campus *M*
Ohio Dominican College *B, T*
Ohio State University
Columbus Campus *M, D*
University of Akron *C*
University of Dayton *M*
University of Toledo *M*

Oklahoma
Northwestern Oklahoma State
University *M*
University of Central Oklahoma *B, M*
University of Oklahoma *M, D*

Oregon
Portland State University *M, T*
Western Oregon University *B*

Pennsylvania
Bloomsburg University of
Pennsylvania *M*

Chestnut Hill College *M*
Duquesne University *B, M, D*
Lehigh University *M, D*
Marywood University *M*
Penn State
University Park *B, M*
Seton Hill University *M*

Puerto Rico
Bayamon Central University *A, B*
University of the Sacred Heart *M*

South Dakota
University of South Dakota *M*

Tennessee
East Tennessee State University *M, T*
University of Tennessee
Chattanooga *T*

Texas
Prairie View A&M University *M*
Texas A&M University *M*
Texas A&M University
Corpus Christi *M, T*
Texas Tech University *M, D*
University of Houston *M, T*
University of Houston
Clear Lake *M*
University of North Texas *M*
University of Texas
Tyler *M*
West Texas A&M University *M*

Utah
Southern Utah University *M, T*
Utah State University *M, D*

Virginia
Longwood University *M*
Radford University *M*

Washington
Eastern Washington University *M*
Walla Walla College *M*

Instrumentation technology

Illinois
Kaskaskia College *C*
Moraine Valley Community
College *C, A*

New Mexico
Albuquerque Technical-Vocational
Institute *A*
San Juan College *A*

North Carolina
Cape Fear Community College *A*

North Dakota
Bismarck State College *C, A*

Ohio
University of Akron *B*

Pennsylvania
Butler County Community College *A*
Pennsylvania College of Technology *A*

Texas
Lamar State College at Port Arthur *A*
St. Philip's College *A*

Utah
Utah Valley State College *C*

Insurance

Alabama
Wallace State Community College at
Hanceville *A*

Arkansas
University of Central Arkansas *B*

California
Los Angeles Southwest College *A*
San Francisco State University *B*

Colorado
Community College of Aurora *C*

Connecticut
University of Connecticut *B*
University of Hartford *B, M*

District of Columbia
Howard University *B*

Florida
Daytona Beach Community College *C*
Florida International University *B*
Florida State University *B, M*
Miami-Dade Community College *C*
Okaloosa-Walton Community College *A*
Polk Community College *A*
South Florida Community College *A*
University of Florida *B, M*

Georgia
Georgia State University *B, M, D*
University of Georgia *B*

Illinois
Bradley University *B*
Heartland Community College *C*
Illinois State University *B*
Illinois Wesleyan University *B*
Roosevelt University *B*
William Rainey Harper College *C, A*

Indiana
Ball State University *B*
Martin University *B*

Iowa
Ellsworth Community College *A*
Northwest Iowa Community College *A*

Kansas
Hutchinson Community College *A*

Louisiana
University of Louisiana at Lafayette *B*

Michigan
Ferris State University *C*
Lansing Community College *A*
Oakland Community College *A*

Minnesota
Minnesota State University
Mankato *B*
St. Cloud State University *B*
University of Minnesota
Twin Cities *B*
University of St. Thomas *M*

Mississippi
Delta State University *B*
Mississippi State University *B*
University of Mississippi *B*

Missouri
Southwest Missouri State University *B*

New Jersey
Thomas Edison State College *A, B*

New York
Excelsior College *B*
Hudson Valley Community College *A*
Nassau Community College *C*
Onondaga Community College *A*
St. John's University *B, M*
Suffolk County Community College *A*

North Carolina
Appalachian State University *B*
Central Piedmont Community College *A*
Fayetteville Technical Community
College *A*

Ohio
Hondros College *C, A*
Ohio State University
Columbus Campus *B*

Oklahoma
Oklahoma City Community College *C*
Tulsa Community College *C, A*
University of Central Oklahoma *B*

Pennsylvania
Community College of Allegheny
County *C*
Delaware County Community College *C*
La Salle University *B*
Mercyhurst College *B*
Penn State
Abington *B*
Altoona *B*
Beaver *B*
Berks *B*
Delaware County *B*
Dubois *B*
Fayette *B*
Hazleton *B*
Lehigh Valley *B*
McKeesport *B*
Mont Alto *B*
New Kensington *B*
Schuylkill - Capital College *B*
Shenango *B*
University Park *B*
Wilkes-Barre *B*
Worthington Scranton *B*
York *B*
Temple University *B, M, D*
University of Pennsylvania *B, M, D*

South Carolina
University of South Carolina *B*

Tennessee
University of Memphis *B*

Texas
Baylor University *B*
University of North Texas *B, M, D*

Washington
Seattle University *B*
Washington State University *B*

Wisconsin
Chippewa Valley Technical College *C*
Fox Valley Technical College *A*
University of Wisconsin
La Crosse *B*
Madison *B, M, D*
Waukesha County Technical College *A*

Intercultural/diversity studies

Alabama
Spring Hill College *B*

California
Biola University *B*
Foothill College *A*

District of Columbia
American University *C*

Illinois
Trinity International University *D*

Indiana
Anderson University *M*
St. Mary-of-the-Woods College *B*

Iowa
Divine Word College *A, B*

Massachusetts
Lesley University *M*

Minnesota
St. Olaf College *B*

New Mexico
Santa Fe Community College *A*

New York
Bard College *B*

Ohio
Marietta College *B*

Tennessee
Union University *B, M*

Texas
University of Houston
    Clear Lake *M*
University of Texas
    San Antonio *M*

Interior architecture

Alabama
Auburn University *B*

Arizona
Arizona State University *B, M*
Glendale Community College *C*
Phoenix College *A*

California
California College of Arts and Crafts *B*
California State University
    Long Beach *B*
Woodbury University *B*

Colorado
University of Colorado
    Denver *M*

Connecticut
University of Bridgeport *B*
University of New Haven *A, B*

Florida
Palm Beach Community College *A*
Seminole Community College *A*

Illinois
Columbia College Chicago *M*
Harrington Institute of Interior
    Design *C, A, B*
Illinois Central College *A*
Illinois Institute of Art *B*
School of the Art Institute of Chicago *B*
Triton College *C, A*

Indiana
Indiana State University *B*

Iowa
Iowa State University *B, M*

Kansas
Central Christian College *A*
Kansas State University *B*

Louisiana
Delgado Community College *A*
Louisiana State University and
    Agricultural and Mechanical
    College *B*
Louisiana Tech University *B*
University of Louisiana at Lafayette *B*

Maryland
Community College of Baltimore County
    Catonsville *C, A*
    Dundalk *C, A*
    Essex *C, A*
Harford Community College *C, A*
Montgomery College
    Rockville Campus *C, A*

Massachusetts
Boston Architectural Center *B, M*
Pine Manor College *B*

Michigan
Central Michigan University *B*
Lansing Community College *A*
Lawrence Technological University *B*
Michigan State University *B*

Mississippi
University of Southern Mississippi *B*

Missouri
St. Louis Community College
    St. Louis Community College at
        Meramec *A*
Southeast Missouri State University *B*
Washington University in St. Louis *M*

Nebraska
Metropolitan Community College *A*

Nevada
University of Nevada
    Las Vegas *B*

New York
Cornell University *B*
Fashion Institute of Technology *A, B*
Onondaga Community College *A*
Parsons School of Design *B*
Suffolk County Community College *A*
Villa Maria College of Buffalo *A*

Ohio
Bowling Green State University *B*
Ohio State University
    Columbus Campus *B*

Oklahoma
University of Oklahoma *B*

Oregon
University of Oregon *B, M*

Pennsylvania
Indiana University of Pennsylvania *B*
La Roche College *B*
Northampton County Area Community
    College *A*
Philadelphia University *B*

Rhode Island
Rhode Island School of Design *B, M*

South Carolina
Converse College *B*

Texas
Lamar University *B*
St. Philip's College *C, A*
Sam Houston State University *B*
Southwest Texas State University *B*
Stephen F. Austin State University *B*
Texas A&M University
    Kingsville *B, M*
Texas Tech University *B*
University of Houston *B, M*
University of North Texas *B, M*
University of Texas
    Arlington *B*
    San Antonio *B*

Virginia
Longwood University *B*

Washington
Spokane Falls Community College *A*
Washington State University *B, M*

Wisconsin
University of Wisconsin
    Madison *M*

Interior design

Alabama
Samford University *B*
University of Alabama *B*
Virginia College *A*
Wallace State Community College at
    Hanceville *A*

Arizona
Arizona State University *M*
Art Institute
    of Phoenix *A*
Northern Arizona University *B*
Phoenix College *A*
Scottsdale Community College *A*

Arkansas
Harding University *B*

California
Academy of Art College *C, A, B, M*
Antelope Valley College *C, A*
Art Center College of Design *B, M*
Art Institute
    of California - Orange County *A, B*
Art Institute of California - San
    Francisco *B*
Bakersfield College *A*
California State University
    Chico *B*
    Fresno *B*
    Long Beach *B, M*
    Sacramento *B*
Cerritos Community College *A*
Contra Costa College *A*
Cuesta College *C, A*
Fashion Institute of Design and
    Merchandising *A*
Fashion Institute of Design and
    Merchandising
    San Francisco *A*
Las Positas College *C, A*
Long Beach City College *C, A*
Los Angeles Harbor College *A*
Marymount College *A*
Modesto Junior College *C, A*
Monterey Peninsula College *C, A*
Moorpark College *C, A*
Mount San Antonio College *C, A*
Ohlone College *C, A*
Orange Coast College *C, A*
Palomar College *C, A*
San Diego Mesa College *C, A*
San Diego State University *B*
San Joaquin Delta College *C, A*
San Jose State University *B*
Santa Barbara City College *C, A*
Santa Rosa Junior College *C*
Sierra College *C*
Ventura College *A*
West Valley College *C, A*
Westwood College of Technology
    Inland Empire *B*
Woodbury University *B*

Colorado
Arapahoe Community College *C, A*
Art Institute
    of Colorado *B*
Colorado State University *B*
Rocky Mountain College of Art &
    Design *B*
Westwood College of Technology
    South *B*

Connecticut
Paier College of Art *C, B*
University of New Haven *C, A, B*

Delaware
Delaware Technical and Community
    College
    Terry Campus *A*

District of Columbia
George Washington University *B, M*
Howard University *B*

Florida
Broward Community College *A*
Daytona Beach Community College *A*
Florida International University *B*
Florida State University *B, M*
Indian River Community College *A*
International Academy of Design and
    Technology *A, B*
Okaloosa-Walton Community College *A*
Palm Beach Community College *A*
Ringling School of Art and Design *B*
Seminole Community College *A*
University of Florida *B*

Georgia
Art Institute
    of Atlanta *B*
Bauder College *A*
Brenau University *B*
Georgia Southern University *B*
Middle Georgia College *A*
Savannah College of Art and
    Design *B, M*
University of Georgia *B*
Valdosta State University *B*

Hawaii
Chaminade University of Honolulu *B*

Idaho
Brigham Young University - Idaho *B*
University of Idaho *B*

Illinois
Columbia College Chicago *B, M*
Harrington Institute of Interior
    Design *C, A, B*
Illinois Institute of Art *A, B*
Illinois Institute of Art *B*
International Academy of Design and
    Technology *A*
Joliet Junior College *A*
Prairie State College *A*
Robert Morris College: Chicago *A*
Southern Illinois University
    Carbondale *B*
Triton College *C, A*
William Rainey Harper College *A*

Indiana
Indiana University
    Bloomington *B, M*
Indiana University-Purdue University
    Fort Wayne *A*
Indiana University-Purdue University
    Indianapolis *A*
Ivy Tech State College
    Northcentral *A*
    Southwest *A*
Purdue University *B*
Vincennes University *A*

Iowa
Hawkeye Community College *A*

Kansas
Kansas State University *B*
Pittsburg State University *B*
University of Kansas *B*

Kentucky
Berea College *B*
Louisville Technical Institute *C, A*
Murray State University *B*
University of Kentucky *B*
University of Louisville *B*

Louisiana
Dryades YMCA School of Commerce *B*
Northwestern State University *B*

Maryland
Anne Arundel Community College *C, A*
Community College of Baltimore County
    Catonsville *C, A*
    Dundalk *C, A*
    Essex *C, A*
Harford Community College *A*
Maryland Institute College of Art *C, B*
Montgomery College
    Rockville Campus *A*

Massachusetts
Atlantic Union College *B*
Bay Path College *C*
Becker College *C, A, B*
Endicott College *B*
Massachusetts Bay Community
    College *C*
Mount Ida College *A, B*
Newbury College *A, B*
Suffolk University *C, B, M*

University of Massachusetts
Amherst *B*
Wentworth Institute of Technology *A, B*

Michigan
Adrian College *A*
Baker College
of Auburn Hills *A*
of Cadillac *A*
of Clinton Township *A*
of Muskegon *A*
of Owosso *A*
Central Michigan University *B*
College for Creative Studies *B*
Eastern Michigan University *B*
Ferris State University *B*
Finlandia University *B*
Grand Rapids Community College *A*
Michigan State University *B, M*
Oakland Community College *A*
University of Michigan *B*
Western Michigan University *B*

Minnesota
Alexandria Technical College *C, A*
Art Institutes International
Minnesota *A, B*
Dakota County Technical College *C, A*
Minnesota State University
Mankato *B*
University of Minnesota
Twin Cities *B*

Mississippi
Mississippi College *B*
Mississippi Gulf Coast Community
College
Perkinston *A*
Mississippi University for Women *B*

Missouri
Central Missouri State University *B*
Maryville University of Saint Louis *B*
Patricia Stevens College *C, A*

New Hampshire
Hesser College *C, A*
New Hampshire Community Technical
College
Manchester *C*

New Jersey
Berkeley College *A*
Brookdale Community College *A*
Kean University *B*

New Mexico
Art Center Design College *A, B*
Santa Fe Community College *A*

New York
Broome Community College *C*
Cazenovia College *B*
Cornell University *B, M*
Dowling College *B*
Fashion Institute of Technology *A, B*
Institute of Design and Construction *A*
Marymount College of Fordham
University *C, B*
Monroe Community College *C, A*
Nassau Community College *C, A*
New York Institute of Technology *B*
New York School of Interior
Design *C, A, B, M*
Onondaga Community College *A*
Parsons School of Design *C, A, B, T*
Pratt Institute *B, M*
Rochester Institute of
Technology *A, B, M*
Sage College of Albany *A*
School of Visual Arts *B*
Suffolk County Community College *A*
Syracuse University *B, M*
Villa Maria College of Buffalo *A*

North Carolina
Cape Fear Community College *A*
Carteret Community College *A*
Central Piedmont Community College *A*

East Carolina University *B*
Halifax Community College *C, A*
High Point University *B*
Meredith College *B*
Randolph Community College *C, A*
Salem College *B*
University of North Carolina
Greensboro *B, M, T*
Western Carolina University *B*
Western Piedmont Community
College *C, A*

North Dakota
North Dakota State University *B*

Ohio
Antonelli College *A*
Cleveland Institute of Art *B*
College of Mount St. Joseph *C, A, B*
Columbus College of Art and Design *B*
Davis College *A*
Kent State University *B*
Ohio State University
Columbus Campus *B, M*
Ohio University *B*
Sinclair Community College *A*
University of Akron *B*
University of Cincinnati *B*
Ursuline College *B*
Virginia Marti College of Art and
Design *A*

Oklahoma
Oklahoma Christian University of
Science and Arts *B*
Oklahoma State University *B*
Tulsa Community College *C, A*
University of Central Oklahoma *B, M*

Oregon
Art Institute
of Portland *A, B*
Marylhurst University *B*
Oregon State University *B*
Portland Community College *C, A*

Pennsylvania
Arcadia University *B*
Art Institute
of Philadelphia *A, B*
of Pittsburgh *A*
Bradley Academy for the Visual Arts *A*
Drexel University *B, M*
Marywood University *C*
Mercyhurst College *B*
Northampton County Area Community
College *C*

Puerto Rico
University of Puerto Rico
Carolina Regional College *A*

Rhode Island
Rhode Island School of Design *C*

South Carolina
Anderson College *B*
Converse College *B*

South Dakota
South Dakota State University *B*

Tennessee
Carson-Newman College *B*
Freed-Hardeman University *B*
Lambuth University *B*
Middle Tennessee State University *B*
O'More College of Design *B*
Pellissippi State Technical Community
College *A*
University of Tennessee
Knoxville *B, M*
Martin *B*

Texas
Abilene Christian University *B*
Amarillo College *C, A*
Baylor University *B*

Collin County Community College
District *C, A*
El Centro College *C, A*
El Paso Community College *C, A*
Houston Community College
System *C, A*
North Harris Montgomery Community
College District *C, A*
St. Philip's College *C*
San Jacinto College
Central Campus *C*
Texas A&M University
Kingsville *B*
Tyler Junior College *A*
University of Houston *B*
University of North Texas *B, M*
University of Texas
Austin *B*
University of the Incarnate Word *B*

Utah
LDS Business College *C, A*
Salt Lake Community College *C*
Utah State University *B*
Weber State University *A*

Virginia
Art Institute
of Washington *B*
J. Sargeant Reynolds Community
College *C*
Marymount University *B, M*
Virginia Commonwealth University *B*

Washington
Art Institute of Seattle *C, A*
Bellevue Community College *A*
Clover Park Technical College *A*
Cornish College of the Arts *B*
Spokane Falls Community College *C, A*

West Virginia
Fairmont State College *A*
University of Charleston *B*

Wisconsin
Concordia University Wisconsin *B*
Fox Valley Technical College *A*
Milwaukee Area Technical College *A*
Milwaukee Institute of Art & Design *B*
Mount Mary College *B*
University of Wisconsin
Madison *B*
Stevens Point *B*
Waukesha County Technical College *A*
Western Wisconsin Technical College *A*

International agriculture

Virginia
Eastern Mennonite University *B*

International business

Alabama
Auburn University *B*
Birmingham-Southern College *B*
Huntingdon College *B*
Samford University *B*
Spring Hill College *B*

Arizona
Cochise College *A*
Gateway Community College *C, A*
Paradise Valley Community
College *C, A*
Pima Community College *A*
Rio Salado College *C, A*
Scottsdale Community College *C, A*
South Mountain Community
College *C, A*

Arkansas
Arkansas State University *B*
Harding University *B*
John Brown University *B*

Northwest Arkansas Community
College *A*
University of Arkansas *B*
University of Arkansas
Little Rock *B*
University of Central Arkansas *M*

California
Antioch Southern California
Santa Barbara *M*
Azusa Pacific University *M*
California State Polytechnic University:
Pomona *B*
California State University
Dominguez Hills *B*
Fresno *B*
Fullerton *B*
Hayward *B*
Long Beach *C, B*
Los Angeles *B, M*
Monterey Bay *B*
Sacramento *B*
Claremont McKenna College *B*
Coastline Community College *C*
Dominican University of California *B*
Foothill College *C, A*
Golden Gate University *C, B, M*
Grossmont Community College *C, A*
Monterey Institute of International
Studies *M*
Monterey Peninsula College *C, A*
Mount St. Mary's College *B*
National University *M*
Orange Coast College *C, A*
Pacific Union College *B*
Palomar College *C, A*
Pepperdine University *B, M*
St. Mary's College of California *B*
San Diego State University *B, M*
San Francisco State University *B*
San Jose State University *B*
Santa Rosa Junior College *C*
Southwestern College *C, A*
Travel University International *C, A*
University of La Verne *B*
University of San Diego *M*
University of San Francisco *B*
University of Southern California *M*
Vanguard University of Southern
California *B*
Vista Community College *C*

Colorado
Arapahoe Community College *C, A*
Fort Lewis College *B*
Jones International University *C, B, M*
University of Colorado
Boulder *B*
Denver *M*
University of Denver *B, M*

Connecticut
Albertus Magnus College *B*
Central Connecticut State
University *B, M*
Fairfield University *B*
Quinnipiac University *B*
Sacred Heart University *B*
Teikyo Post University *B*
University of Bridgeport *B, M*
University of New Haven *B*
Yale University *M*

Delaware
Goldey-Beacom College *B*

District of Columbia
American University *B, M*
George Washington University *B, M*
Georgetown University *B*
Howard University *B*

Florida
Barry University *C, B*
Bethune-Cookman College *B*
Broward Community College *A*
Eckerd College *B*

Florida Atlantic University *C, B, M*
Florida International University *B, M*
Florida Southern College *B, M*
Florida State University *B*
Jacksonville University *B, M*
Northwood University
    Florida Campus *A, B*
Nova Southeastern University *M, D*
Palm Beach Atlantic University *B*
Polk Community College *A*
Rollins College *B*
St. Thomas University *B, M*
Schiller International University *A, B, M*
South Florida Community College *A*
Stetson University *B*
University of Miami *C, M*
University of North Florida *B*
University of South Florida *B*
University of Tampa *B*
Webber International University *A, B*

Georgia

Georgia College and State University *B*
Georgia Southern University *B*
Georgia State University *M*
Kennesaw State University *M*
LaGrange College *B*
Mercer University *B, M*
Paine College *B*
Savannah State University *B*
University of Georgia *B, M*
Wesleyan College *B*

Hawaii

Brigham Young University-Hawaii *B*
Hawaii Pacific University *B*
Remington College
    Honolulu *A*
University of Hawaii
    Manoa *B, D*
    West Oahu *B*

Idaho

Albertson College of Idaho *B*
Boise State University *B*
Lewis-Clark State College *B*

Illinois

Augustana College *B*
Benedictine University *B*
Black Hawk College *C*
Bradley University *B*
City Colleges of Chicago
    Harold Washington College *A*
De Paul University *M*
Dominican University *B*
Elmhurst College *B*
Governors State University *B*
Illinois Central College *A*
Illinois State University *B*
Illinois Wesleyan University *B*
Judson College *B*
McHenry County College *C*
Millikin University *B*
Monmouth College *B*
North Central College *B*
North Park University *B*
Northwestern University *M*
Oakton Community College *C, A*
Olivet Nazarene University *B*
Parkland College *C*
Roosevelt University *B, M*
St. Xavier University *B, M*
Triton College *A*
William Rainey Harper College *C, A*

Indiana

Goshen College *B*
Grace College *B*
St. Joseph's College *B*
Saint Mary's College *B*
Taylor University *B*
Taylor University: Fort Wayne *B*
University of Evansville *B*
University of Indianapolis *B*
Valparaiso University *B*

Iowa

Buena Vista University *B*
Central College *B*
Clarke College *B*
Cornell College *B*
Drake University *B*
Graceland University *B*
Iowa State University *B*
Loras College *B*
Luther College *B*
St. Ambrose University *B*
Simpson College *B*
Wartburg College *B*

Kansas

Baker University *B*
Friends University *B*
McPherson College *B*
St. Mary College *B*
Wichita State University *B*

Kentucky

Murray State University *B*

Louisiana

Louisiana State University and
    Agricultural and Mechanical
    College *B*
Loyola University New Orleans *B*

Maine

Husson College *B*
Maine Maritime Academy *B*
St. Joseph's College *B*
Thomas College *B*

Maryland

College of Notre Dame of Maryland *B*
Frederick Community College *A*
Johns Hopkins University *M*
Loyola College in Maryland *M*
University of Baltimore *B, M*
University of Maryland
    University College *M*

Massachusetts

American International College *B*
Assumption College *B*
Babson College *B, M*
Bentley College *M*
Boston University *B*
Brandeis University *M*
Bunker Hill Community College *C*
Elms College *B*
Emerson College *M*
Fitchburg State College *B*
Hampshire College *B*
Lasell College *B*
Merrimack College *B*
Newbury College *A, B*
Northeastern University *B*
Suffolk University *B, M*

Michigan

Adrian College *B*
Alma College *B*
Aquinas College *B*
Baker College
    of Port Huron *B*
Central Michigan University *B, M*
Cornerstone University *B*
Davenport University
    Eastern Region *B*
Davenport University - Western
    Region *B*
Eastern Michigan University *B, M*
Ferris State University *C, B*
Finlandia University *B*
Grace Bible College *B*
Grand Valley State University *B*
Lansing Community College *A*
Madonna University *B, M*
Marygrove College *B*
Michigan Technological University *C*
Mott Community College *A*
Northwood University *A, B*
Oakland Community College *A*
Saginaw Valley State University *B*

Minnesota

Augsburg College *B*
Bethel College *B*
Capella University *M, D*
College of St. Catherine *B*
College of St. Scholastica *B*
Concordia College: Moorhead *B*
Gustavus Adolphus College *B*
Hamline University *B*
Metropolitan State University *B*
Minnesota State University
    Mankato *B*
    Moorhead *B*
National American University
    St. Paul *B*
Northwestern College *B*
St. Cloud State University *B*
St. Mary's University of Minnesota *B, M*
University of Minnesota
    Twin Cities *B*
University of St. Thomas *B, M*
Winona State University *A*

Mississippi

University of Mississippi *B*

Missouri

Avila University *B*
College of the Ozarks *B*
Drury University *B*
Lindenwood University *B*
Maryville University of Saint Louis *M*
Missouri Southern State College *B*
Northwest Missouri State University *B*
St. Louis Community College
    St. Louis Community College at
        Forest Park *A*
St. Louis University *B, M*
University of Missouri
    St. Louis *B, M*
Washington University in St. Louis *B*
Webster University *B, M*
William Jewell College *B*
William Woods University *B*

Montana

University of Montana-Missoula *B*

Nebraska

Creighton University *B*
Hastings College *B*
University of Nebraska
    Lincoln *B*

Nevada

University of Nevada
    Reno *B*

New Hampshire

Hesser College *C, A*
Southern New Hampshire
    University *B, M, D*
University of New Hampshire *B*

New Jersey

Berkeley College *A, B*
Caldwell College *B*
The College of New Jersey *B*
Fairleigh Dickinson University
    College at Florham *M*
    Metropolitan Campus *M*
Ramapo College of New Jersey *B*
Rider University *B*
St. Peter's College *A, B, M*
Seton Hall University *M*
Thomas Edison State College *A, B*

New Mexico

Albuquerque Technical-Vocational
    Institute *C, A*
New Mexico State University *B*

New York

Berkeley College *A, B*
Berkeley College of New York City *A, B*
Broome Community College *A*
Canisius College *B*

City University of New York
    Baruch College *M*
Concordia College *B*
D'Youville College *B, M*
Daemen College *M*
Dominican College of Blauvelt *B*
Dowling College *B*
Elmira College *B*
Excelsior College *B*
Fordham University *B, M*
Hofstra University *B, M*
Hudson Valley Community College *A*
Iona College *B, M*
Ithaca College *B*
Long Island University
    C. W. Post Campus *M*
Manhattan College *B*
Monroe Community College *A*
New York Institute of Technology *M*
New York University *B, M, D*
Pace University *C, B, M*
Pace University:
    Pleasantville/Briarcliff *C, B, M*
Rochester Institute of
    Technology *C, B, M*
St. John Fisher College *B*
St. John's University *M*
State University of New York
    Buffalo *M*
    College at Brockport *B*
    College at Plattsburgh *B*
    Farmingdale *C*
    New Paltz *B, M*
Tompkins-Cortland Community
    College *A*
Touro College *M*
Westchester Community College *A*

North Carolina

Belmont Abbey College *B*
Campbell University *B*
Central Piedmont Community College *A*
Elon University *B*
Gardner-Webb University *B*
High Point University *B, M*
Lenoir-Rhyne College *B*
Mars Hill College *B*
Meredith College *B*
North Carolina State University *B*
St. Andrews Presbyterian College *B*
Salem College *B*
University of North Carolina
    Charlotte *B*
    Greensboro *B*
Western Carolina University *B*

North Dakota

Minot State University *B*

Ohio

Baldwin-Wallace College *M*
Bowling Green State University *B*
Cedarville University *B*
Central State University *B*
Cincinnati State Technical and
    Community College *A*
Cleveland State University *B*
Kent State University *M, D*
Lake Erie College *B*
Lourdes College *B*
Marietta College *B*
Mount Union College *B*
Mount Vernon Nazarene University *B*
North Central State College *C*
Notre Dame College *B*
Ohio Dominican College *B*
Ohio Northern University *B*
Ohio State University
    Columbus Campus *B*
Ohio University *B*
Ohio Wesleyan University *B*
University of Akron *C, B, M*
University of Cincinnati *M, D*
University of Cincinnati
    Raymond Walters College *C*
University of Dayton *B*

University of Findlay *B*
University of Rio Grande *B*
University of Toledo *B, M*
Wittenberg University *B*
Wright State University *M*
Xavier University *B, M*

Oklahoma
Northeastern State University *B*
Oklahoma Baptist University *B*
Oklahoma City University *B, M*
Oklahoma State University *B*
Oral Roberts University *B*
University of Oklahoma *B*
University of Tulsa *B*

Oregon
Concordia University *B*
Linfield College *B*
Portland State University *C, M*
University of Portland *B*
Warner Pacific College *B*

Pennsylvania
Albright College *B*
Arcadia University *B*
California University of Pennsylvania *B*
Carlow College *B*
Cedar Crest College *C*
Chatham College *B*
Dickinson College *B*
Drexel University *B*
Duquesne University *B*
Elizabethtown College *B*
Grove City College *B*
Harrisburg Area Community College *C*
Holy Family University *B*
Immaculata University *B*
Indiana University of Pennsylvania *B*
Juniata College *B*
King's College *B*
Kutztown University of Pennsylvania *B*
La Roche College *B*
La Salle University *B*
Lebanon Valley College of
  Pennsylvania *B*
Luzerne County Community College *A*
Manor College *A*
Marywood University *B*
Messiah College *B*
Neumann College *B*
Penn State
  Abington *B*
  Altoona *B*
  Beaver *B*
  Berks *B*
  Delaware County *B*
  Dubois *B*
  Erie, The Behrend College *B*
  Fayette *B*
  Hazleton *B*
  Lehigh Valley *B*
  McKeesport *B*
  Mont Alto *B*
  New Kensington *B*
  Schuylkill - Capital College *B*
  Shenango *B*
  University Park *C, B*
  Wilkes-Barre *B*
  Worthington Scranton *B*
  York *B*
Philadelphia University *B, M*
Point Park College *M*
St. Joseph's University *M*
St. Vincent College *B*
Seton Hill University *B*
Temple University *B, M*
Thiel College *B*
University of Pittsburgh *C, M*
University of Scranton *B, M*
Washington and Jefferson College *B*
Waynesburg College *B*
Widener University *B*

Puerto Rico
Inter American University of Puerto Rico
  Metropolitan Campus *D*
  San German Campus *D*
Pontifical Catholic University of Puerto
  Rico *B*
University of Puerto Rico
  Humacao *B*
  Rio Piedras Campus *M, D*

Rhode Island
Rhode Island College *B*
Roger Williams University *B*
University of Rhode Island *B*

South Carolina
Clemson University *B*
Converse College *B*
North Greenville College *B*
University of South Carolina *M*
Wofford College *B*

South Dakota
Northern State University *B*

Tennessee
Maryville College *B*
Southern Adventist University *B*
Union University *B*
University of Memphis *B, M*
University of Tennessee
  Martin *B*

Texas
Angelo State University *B*
Austin Community College *C*
Baylor University *M*
El Paso Community College *C, A*
Houston Community College
  System *C, A*
LeTourneau University *B*
Midwestern State University *B*
Northwood University: Texas
  Campus *A, B*
Our Lady of the Lake University of San
  Antonio *M*
St. Edward's University *B, T*
St. Mary's University *B*
Sam Houston State University *B*
Southwestern Adventist University *B*
Stephen F. Austin State University *B*
Sul Ross State University *M*
Texas A&M International University *M*
Texas A&M University
  Kingsville *B*
  Texarkana *B*
Texas Christian University *B*
Texas Tech University *B, M*
Trinity University *B*
University of Dallas *M*
University of Houston *M*
University of Houston
  Downtown *B*
University of St. Thomas *M*
University of Texas
  Arlington *B*
  Dallas *B, M, D*
  Pan American *B, D*
  San Antonio *M*

Utah
Brigham Young University *B, M*
University of Utah *C*
Utah Valley State College *A, B*
Westminster College *B*

Vermont
Champlain College *A, B*

Virginia
Eastern Mennonite University *B*
James Madison University *B*
Lynchburg College *B*
Marymount University *C, B*

Washington
Edmonds Community College *A*
Gonzaga University *B*

North Seattle Community College *C*
Seattle University *B, M*
Spokane Falls Community College *A*
University of Washington *B*
Walla Walla College *B*
Washington State University *B*
Whitworth College *B, M*

West Virginia
Bethany College *B*
Davis and Elkins College *B*
Mountain State University *B*
Salem International University *M*
Wheeling Jesuit University *B*

Wisconsin
Alverno College *B*
Cardinal Stritch University *B*
Carthage College *B*
Lakeland College *B*
Marquette University *B*
Milwaukee School of Engineering *B*
St. Norbert College *B*
University of Wisconsin
  La Crosse *B*
  Madison *M*
  Superior *B*
Waukesha County Technical College *A*

International economics

District of Columbia
American University *C, M*

Georgia
State University of West Georgia *B*

Massachusetts
Assumption College *B*

Michigan
Madonna University *M*

Ohio
Youngstown State University *B*

Pennsylvania
La Salle University *B*
Penn State
  Shenango *B*

Tennessee
Carson-Newman College *B*

Wisconsin
St. Norbert College *B*

International finance

California
University of California
  Santa Cruz *B*

Colorado
University of Denver *M*

District of Columbia
American University *B, M*
Catholic University of America *B*

Hawaii
Hawaii Pacific University *C, B*

Illinois
Illinois Institute of Technology *M*

Maine
St. Joseph's College *B*

Maryland
Johns Hopkins University *M*

Massachusetts
Boston University *B, M*
Brandeis University *M, D*
Suffolk University *M*

Michigan
Ferris State University *C, B*

Madonna University *C, M*

Missouri
Washington University in St. Louis *B*

Nebraska
Union College *B*

New Jersey
William Paterson University of New
  Jersey *B*

New York
Pace University *M*
Pace University:
  Pleasantville/Briarcliff *M*

Ohio
University of Akron *B, M*

Oklahoma
Oklahoma Baptist University *B*

Pennsylvania
Penn State
  University Park *B*

Texas
Texas Tech University *B*
University of Dallas *M*

West Virginia
Bethany College *B*

Wisconsin
Lawrence University *B*

International marketing

Arkansas
John Brown University *B*
University of Central Arkansas *B*

California
Antioch Southern California
  Santa Barbara *M*
East Los Angeles College *A*
Travel University International *C, A*

Connecticut
Quinnipiac University *B, M*

District of Columbia
American University *B, M*

Florida
Broward Community College *A*
University of West Florida *B*

Idaho
Northwest Nazarene University *B*

Illinois
De Paul University *M*
Governors State University *B*
North Central College *B*
Roosevelt University *M*

Maine
Husson College *B*
St. Joseph's College *B*

Maryland
Montgomery College
  Rockville Campus *A*

Massachusetts
American International College *B*
Babson College *B*
Newbury College *A, B*

Michigan
Adrian College *B*
Central Michigan University *B*
Eastern Michigan University *B, M*
Finlandia University *B*
Hillsdale College *B*

Minnesota
Bethel College *B*
St. Paul College - A Community and
  Technical College *A*

Missouri

Lindenwood University *M*
Missouri Southern State College *B*
Northwest Missouri State University *B*

Nevada

University of Nevada
    Las Vegas *B*

New York

Pace University *B*
Pace University:
    Pleasantville/Briarcliff *C, B, M*
Rochester Institute of Technology *B*
State University of New York
    Buffalo *D*
    College at Brockport *B*
Wagner College *M*

Ohio

Muskingum College *B*
University of Akron *C, B, M*
University of Cincinnati
    Raymond Walters College *C*

Oklahoma

Oral Roberts University *B*

Pennsylvania

Community College of Philadelphia *A*
Holy Family University *B*
La Salle University *B*
Penn State
    Schuylkill - Capital College *B*
    University Park *B*
St. Joseph's University *B, M*
Waynesburg College *B*

Texas

Houston Community College System *C*
Texas Wesleyan University *B*

Utah

Brigham Young University *B*

Washington

Western Washington University *B*

International public health

Texas

University of Texas
    Houston Health Science
        Center *M, D*

International relations

Alabama

Samford University *B*
Spring Hill College *B*
Troy State University *M*
Troy State University Dothan *M*
University of Alabama *B*

Arizona

Northern Arizona University *B*

Arkansas

Hendrix College *B*
University of Arkansas *B*
University of Arkansas
    Little Rock *B*

California

Azusa Pacific University *B*
California State University
    Bakersfield *B*
    Chico *B*
    Fresno *M*
    Sacramento *B, M*
Chapman University *B*
Claremont McKenna College *B*
Dominican University of California *B*
Holy Names College *B*
Las Positas College *A*
Mills College *B*

Monterey Institute of International
    Studies *B, M*
Occidental College *B*
Pepperdine University *B*
Pitzer College *B*
Pomona College *B*
San Diego State University *B*
San Francisco State University *B, M*
Scripps College *B*
Stanford University *B, M*
University of California
    Davis *B*
    San Diego *D*
University of La Verne *B*
University of Redlands *B*
University of San Diego *B, M*
University of Southern
    California *B, M, D*
University of the Pacific *B*
Whittier College *B*

Colorado

University of Colorado
    Boulder *B*
University of Denver *B, M, D*

Connecticut

Connecticut College *B*
Fairfield University *B*
Trinity College *B*
University of Bridgeport *B*
University of Connecticut *M*
Yale University *M*

Delaware

University of Delaware *B, M*

District of Columbia

American University *B, M, D*
Catholic University of America *M*
George Washington University *B, M*
Georgetown University *B, M*
Trinity College *B*

Florida

Bethune-Cookman College *B*
Eckerd College *B*
Florida International University *B, M, D*
Florida State University *B, M*
Jacksonville University *B*
Miami-Dade Community College *A*
New College of Florida *B*
Palm Beach Community College *A*
Polk Community College *A*
Rollins College *B*
St. Leo University *B*
Schiller International University *B, M*
South Florida Community College *A*
Stetson University *B*
University of Florida *M, D*
University of Miami *B, M, D*
University of North Florida *B*
University of South Florida *B*

Georgia

Agnes Scott College *B*
Berry College *B*
Brenau University *B*
Clark Atlanta University *M, D*
Emory University *B*
Georgia Institute of Technology *B, M*
Georgia Southern University *B*
Kennesaw State University *B*
Morehouse College *B*
Oglethorpe University *B*
Oxford College of Emory University *B*
Southern Polytechnic State University *B*
State University of West Georgia *B*
Wesleyan College *B*

Hawaii

Chaminade University of Honolulu *B*
Hawaii Pacific University *B*

Idaho

Albertson College of Idaho *B*
Brigham Young University - Idaho *A*
Northwest Nazarene University *B*

Illinois

Bradley University *B*
De Paul University *B, M*
Dominican University *B*
Governors State University *M*
Illinois College *B*
Knox College *B*
Lake Forest College *B*
Loyola University of Chicago *C, B*
MacMurray College *B*
McKendree College *B*
Millikin University *B*
North Central College *B*
North Park University *B*
Northwestern University *B*
Roosevelt University *B*
St. Xavier University *B*
University of Chicago *B, M*
Wheaton College *B*

Indiana

Bethel College *B*
Butler University *B*
Indiana University
    Southeast *B*
St. Joseph's College *B*
University of Evansville *B*
Valparaiso University *B*

Iowa

Cornell College *B*
Drake University *B*
Iowa State University *B*
Loras College *B*
Simpson College *B*
University of Iowa *B*
Wartburg College *B*

Kentucky

Centre College *B*
Thomas More College *A, B*

Maine

Colby College *B*
University of Maine *B*
University of Maine
    Farmington *B*
University of Southern Maine *B*

Maryland

College of Notre Dame of Maryland *B*
Frostburg State University *B*
Goucher College *B*
Johns Hopkins University *B, M, D*
Mount St. Mary's College *B*
Washington College *B*

Massachusetts

American International College *B*
Boston University *B, M*
Bridgewater State College *B*
Clark University *B*
Elms College *B*
Gordon College *B*
Hampshire College *B*
Harvard College *B*
Mount Holyoke College *B*
Northeastern University *B*
Simmons College *B*
Stonehill College *B*
Tufts University *B, M, D*
Wellesley College *B*
Wheaton College *B*

Michigan

Adrian College *B*
Aquinas College *B*
Calvin College *B*
Central Michigan University *B*
Grand Valley State University *B*
Michigan State University *B*
Wayne State University *B*

Minnesota

Bethel College *B*
Carleton College *B*
College of St. Catherine *B*
Concordia College: Moorhead *B*

Hamline University *B*
Macalester College *B*
Minnesota State University
    Mankato *B*
St. Cloud State University *B*
University of Minnesota
    Twin Cities *B*
University of St. Thomas *B*
Winona State University *A*

Missouri

Lindenwood University *B*
Rockhurst University *B*
St. Louis University *B*
Southwest Missouri State University *M*
Stephens College *B*
Washington University in St. Louis *B, M*
Webster University *B, M*
Westminster College *B*
William Jewell College *B*

Montana

Carroll College *B*
University of Montana-Missoula *B*

Nebraska

Creighton University *B, M*
Doane College *B*
Hastings College *B*
Nebraska Wesleyan University *B*
University of Nebraska
    Kearney *B*
    Lincoln *B*
    Omaha *B*

Nevada

University of Nevada
    Reno *B*

New Hampshire

St. Anselm College *B*
University of New Hampshire *B*

New Jersey

The College of New Jersey *B*
Fairleigh Dickinson University
    Metropolitan Campus *B, M*
Felician College *B*
Rider University *B*
Seton Hall University *B, M*
William Paterson University of New
    Jersey *M*

New York

Bard College *B*
Canisius College *B*
City University of New York
    City College *B, M*
    College of Staten Island *B*
    Hunter College *B*
Colgate University *B*
Cornell University *M*
Elmira College *B*
Eugene Lang College/New School
    University *B*
Hamilton College *B*
Hobart and William Smith Colleges *B*
Houghton College *B*
Le Moyne College *B*
Long Island University
    C. W. Post Campus *B, M*
Marymount College of Fordham
    University *B*
Marymount Manhattan College *B*
New York University *B*
Sarah Lawrence College *B*
State University of New York
    College at Brockport *B*
    College at Cortland *B*
    College at Geneseo *B*
    New Paltz *B*
Syracuse University *B, M, D*
Vassar College *B*
Wells College *B*

North Carolina

Campbell University *B*
Duke University *M*

Elon University *B*
High Point University *B*
Lees-McRae College *B*
Meredith College *B*
St. Augustine's College *B*
Salem College *B*
Shaw University *B*
University of North Carolina
  Charlotte *B*

Ohio
Antioch College *B*
Bowling Green State University *B*
Case Western Reserve University *B*
College of Wooster *B*
Kent State University *B*
Kent State University
  Stark Campus *B*
Kenyon College *B*
Miami University
  Oxford Campus *B*
Muskingum College *B*
Ohio Northern University *B*
Ohio State University
  Columbus Campus *B*
Ohio Wesleyan University *B*
Otterbein College *B*
Shawnee State University *B*
University of Cincinnati *B*
University of Toledo *B*
Wittenberg University *B*
Wright State University *B*
Xavier University *B*

Oklahoma
Oral Roberts University *B*
University of Central Oklahoma *M*
University of Oklahoma *M*
University of Tulsa *B*

Oregon
George Fox University *B*
Lewis & Clark College *B*
Pacific University *B*
Portland State University *B*
Willamette University *B*

Pennsylvania
Allegheny College *B*
Bucknell University *B*
California University of Pennsylvania *B*
Dickinson College *B*
Gettysburg College *B*
Harrisburg Area Community College *A*
Immaculata University *B*
Indiana University of Pennsylvania *B*
Juniata College *B*
La Roche College *B*
La Salle University *B*
Lafayette College *B*
Lehigh University *B*
Lincoln University *B*
Muhlenberg College *B*
Penn State
  Abington *B*
  Altoona *B*
  Beaver *B*
  Berks *B*
  Delaware County *B*
  Dubois *B*
  Fayette *B*
  Hazleton *B*
  Lehigh Valley *B*
  McKeesport *B*
  Mont Alto *B*
  New Kensington *B*
  Schuylkill - Capital College *B*
  University Park *B*
  Wilkes-Barre *B*
  Worthington Scranton *B*
  York *B*
Point Park College *B*
St. Joseph's University *B*
Seton Hill University *B*
University of Pennsylvania *B*
University of Pittsburgh *M*
University of Scranton *B*

West Chester University of
  Pennsylvania *B*
Widener University *B*
Wilkes University *B*
Wilson College *B*
York College of Pennsylvania *B*

Rhode Island
Brown University *B*
Bryant College *B*
Salve Regina University *M*

South Carolina
University of South Carolina *B, M, D*

Tennessee
Lambuth University *B*
Middle Tennessee State University *B*
Rhodes College *B*
University of Memphis *B*
University of Tennessee
  Martin *B*

Texas
Angelo State University *M*
Austin College *B*
Baylor University *B, M*
St. Edward's University *B, T*
St. Mary's University *B, M*
Southern Methodist University *B*
Southwest Texas State University *B*
Southwestern Adventist University *B*
Southwestern University *B*
Texas A&M University *M, D*
Texas Christian University *B*
University of North Texas *M, D*
University of St. Thomas *B*
University of Texas
  Arlington *B, M*
Western Texas College *A*

Utah
Brigham Young University *B, M*

Vermont
Bennington College *B*
Marlboro College *B*
Middlebury College *B*
Norwich University *B*

Virginia
Bridgewater College *B*
College of William and Mary *B*
Ferrum College *B*
George Mason University *B, M*
James Madison University *B*
Lynchburg College *B*
Mary Baldwin College *B*
Mary Washington College *B*
Old Dominion University *B, M, D*
Randolph-Macon College *B*
Roanoke College *B*
Sweet Briar College *B*
University of Virginia *B, M, D*
Virginia Polytechnic Institute and State
  University *B*
Virginia Wesleyan College *B*

Washington
Eastern Washington University *B*
Gonzaga University *B*
Seattle University *B*
University of Washington *B, M*
Whitworth College *B*

West Virginia
Bethany College *B*
Marshall University *B*
West Virginia Wesleyan College *B*
Wheeling Jesuit University *B*

Wisconsin
Alverno College *B*
Beloit College *B*
Carroll College *B*
Edgewood College *B*
Marquette University *B, M*
University of Wisconsin
  Madison *B, M*

Wyoming
University of Wyoming *M*
Western Wyoming Community
  College *A*

Investments/securities

Florida
University of West Florida *B*

Illinois
Illinois Institute of Technology *M*
St. Xavier University *C, M*

Massachusetts
Babson College *B*

Minnesota
Minnesota State University
  Mankato *B*
University of St. Thomas *M*

New York
City University of New York
  Baruch College *M*
Pace University *M*
Pace University:
  Pleasantville/Briarcliff *M*
State University of New York
  Albany *B, M*

Pennsylvania
Duquesne University *B*

Wisconsin
University of Wisconsin
  Madison *B, M, D*
  Platteville *B*

Iranian/Persian languages

Texas
University of Texas
  Austin *B, M, D*

Ironworking

California
Foothill College *C*

Illinois
Waubonsee Community College *C*

Indiana
Ivy Tech State College
  Central Indiana *C, A*
  Lafayette *A*
  Northcentral *A*
  Northeast *C*
  Northwest *C, A*
  Southwest *C, A*
  Wabash Valley *C, A*

Minnesota
Hennepin Technical College *A*

Wisconsin
Western Wisconsin Technical College *C*

Islamic studies

California
University of California
  Los Angeles *M, D*

Massachusetts
Brandeis University *B*
Harvard College *B*

Michigan
University of Michigan *B*

Missouri
Washington University in St. Louis *B, M*

New York
Sarah Lawrence College *B*

Ohio
Ohio State University
  Columbus Campus *B*

Texas
University of Texas
  Austin *B*

Italian

Arizona
Arizona State University *B*
University of Arizona *B*

California
Cabrillo College *A*
California State University
  Long Beach *C*
Chabot College *A*
Claremont McKenna College *B*
East Los Angeles College *C*
Los Angeles Pierce College *A*
Loyola Marymount University *B*
Orange Coast College *A*
Pitzer College *B*
St. Mary's College of California *B*
San Diego City College *A*
San Francisco State University *B, M*
Santa Clara University *B*
Scripps College *B*
Stanford University *B, M, D*
University of California
  Berkeley *B, M, D*
  Davis *B*
  Los Angeles *B, M, D*
  San Diego *B*
  Santa Barbara *B*
  Santa Cruz *B, D*

Colorado
University of Colorado
  Boulder *B*
University of Denver *B*

Connecticut
Albertus Magnus College *B*
Central Connecticut State University *B*
Connecticut College *B*
Fairfield University *B*
Southern Connecticut State University *B*
Trinity College *B*
University of Connecticut *B, M, D*
University of Hartford *B*
Wesleyan University *B*
Yale University *B, M, D*

Delaware
University of Delaware *B, M, T*

District of Columbia
Catholic University of America *M, D*
George Washington University *B*
Georgetown University *B*

Florida
Florida International University *B*
Florida State University *B*
University of Miami *B*
University of South Florida *B*

Georgia
Emory University *B*
Oxford College of Emory University *B*
University of Georgia *B*

Illinois
De Paul University *B*
Dominican University *B*
Loyola University of Chicago *C, B*
Northwestern University *B, M, D*
Triton College *A*
University of Chicago *B*
University of Illinois
  Chicago *B*
  Urbana-Champaign *B, M, D*

Indiana

Indiana University
Bloomington *B, M, D*
University of Notre Dame *B, M*

Iowa

University of Iowa *B, T*

Louisiana

Tulane University *B*

Maryland

Johns Hopkins University *B, M, D*
University of Maryland
College Park *B*

Massachusetts

Boston College *B, M*
Boston University *B*
College of the Holy Cross *B*
Harvard College *B*
Mount Holyoke College *B*
Northeastern University *B*
Smith College *B, M*
Tufts University *B*
University of Massachusetts
Amherst *B, M*
Boston *B*
Wellesley College *B*

Michigan

University of Michigan *B, M, D*
Wayne State University *B, M*

Minnesota

University of Minnesota
Twin Cities *B, M*

Missouri

Washington University in St. Louis *B*

New Hampshire

Dartmouth College *B*

New Jersey

Montclair State University *B, T*
Princeton University *B, M, D*
Rutgers, The State University of New
Jersey
New Brunswick Regional
Campus *B, M, D, T*
Seton Hall University *B, T*

New York

Bard College *B*
Barnard College *B*
City University of New York
Brooklyn College *B*
Hunter College *B, M*
Queens College *B, M*
Columbia University
Columbia College *B*
Cornell University *B*
Fordham University *B*
Hofstra University *B*
Iona College *B*
Long Island University
C. W. Post Campus *B*
Nazareth College of Rochester *B*
New York University *B, M, D*
Pace University *C, B*
Pace University:
Pleasantville/Briarcliff *B*
St. John's University *B*
Sarah Lawrence College *B*
State University of New York
Albany *B*
Binghamton *B, M*
Buffalo *B*
College at Buffalo *B*
Stony Brook *B, M, T*
Syracuse University *B*
Vassar College *B*

North Carolina

Duke University *B*
University of North Carolina
Chapel Hill *B*
Greensboro *B*

Ohio

College of Wooster *B*
Lake Erie College *B*
Ohio State University
Columbus Campus *B, M, D*
Youngstown State University *B*

Oklahoma

Tulsa Community College *A*

Oregon

University of Oregon *B, M*

Pennsylvania

Bryn Mawr College *B*
Dickinson College *B*
Haverford College *B*
Immaculata University *C, B*
La Salle University *B, T*
Mercyhurst College *B*
Penn State
Abington *B*
Altoona *B*
Beaver *B*
Berks *B*
Delaware County *B*
Fayette *B*
Hazleton *B*
Lehigh Valley *B*
McKeesport *B*
Mont Alto *B*
New Kensington *B*
Schuylkill - Capital College *B*
Shenango *B*
University Park *B*
Wilkes-Barre *B*
Worthington Scranton *B*
York *B*
Rosemont College *B*
Temple University *B*
University of Pennsylvania *B*
University of Pittsburgh *B, M*

Rhode Island

Brown University *B, M, D*
Providence College *T*
University of Rhode Island *B*

South Carolina

University of South Carolina *B*

Tennessee

University of Tennessee
Knoxville *B*

Texas

University of Houston *B*
University of Texas
Austin *B*

Utah

Brigham Young University *B*

Vermont

Bennington College *B, M, T*
Marlboro College *B*
Middlebury College *B, M, D*

Virginia

Sweet Briar College *B*
University of Virginia *B, M*

Washington

Gonzaga University *B*
University of Washington *B*

Wisconsin

University of Wisconsin
Madison *B, M, D*
Milwaukee *B*

Italian studies

California

Scripps College *B*

Florida

Florida State University *M*

Massachusetts

Boston University *B*

New York

Bard College *B*
Columbia University
Columbia College *B*

Rhode Island

Brown University *B, M, D*

Vermont

Bennington College *B*

Virginia

Sweet Briar College *B*

Washington

University of Washington *B*

Japanese

Alaska

University of Alaska
Anchorage *B*
Fairbanks *B*

California

Cabrillo College *A*
California State University
Fullerton *B*
Long Beach *B*
Los Angeles *B*
Citrus College *A*
Claremont McKenna College *B*
Foothill College *C, A*
Grossmont Community College *C, A*
MiraCosta College *A*
Monterey Institute of International
Studies *C*
Orange Coast College *A*
Pitzer College *B*
Pomona College *B*
St. Mary's College of California *B*
San Diego State University *B*
San Francisco State University *B, M*
San Jose State University *B*
Scripps College *B*
Stanford University *B, M, D*
University of California
Berkeley *B, M, D*
Davis *B*
Irvine *B*
Los Angeles *B*
San Diego *B*
Santa Barbara *B*
Santa Cruz *B*
University of San Francisco *C*
University of Southern California *M, D*
University of the Pacific *B*

Colorado

University of Colorado
Boulder *B, M*

Connecticut

Connecticut College *B*
Fairfield University *B*
Trinity College *B*
Yale University *B*

District of Columbia

George Washington University *B*
Georgetown University *B*

Georgia

University of Georgia *B*

Hawaii

University of Hawaii
Hilo *B*
Manoa *B, M, D*

Illinois

City Colleges of Chicago
Harold Washington College *A*
Illinois Wesleyan University *B*
North Central College *B*

Parkland College *A*

Indiana

Indiana University
Bloomington *M, D*
University of Notre Dame *B*

Iowa

University of Iowa *B, T*

Kansas

Butler County Community College *A*

Louisiana

Dillard University *B*

Maine

Bates College *B*

Maryland

Johns Hopkins University *B*
University of Maryland
College Park *B*

Massachusetts

Harvard College *B*
Tufts University *B*
University of Massachusetts
Amherst *B, M*
Wellesley College *B*
Williams College *B*

Michigan

Aquinas College *B*
Eastern Michigan University *B*
University of Michigan *M, D*

Minnesota

Augsburg College *B*
Gustavus Adolphus College *B*
University of Minnesota
Twin Cities *B, M, D*
Winona State University *A*

Missouri

Washington University in St.
Louis *B, M, D*

Montana

University of Montana-Missoula *B*

New Hampshire

Dartmouth College *B*

New Jersey

Seton Hall University *T*

New York

Bard College *B*
Colgate University *B*
Columbia University
Columbia College *B*
Cornell University *B*
Hamilton College *B*
State University of New York
Albany *B*
University of Rochester *B*

Ohio

Antioch College *B*
Kent State University *B*
Mount Union College *B*
Ohio State University
Columbus Campus *B*
University of Findlay *B*

Oklahoma

Tulsa Community College *A*

Oregon

Pacific University *B*
Portland State University *B, T*
University of Oregon *B*
Willamette University *B*

Pennsylvania

Carnegie Mellon University *B*
Dickinson College *C*
Gettysburg College *B*

Penn State
  Abington *B*
  Altoona *B*
  Beaver *B*
  Berks *B*
  Delaware County *B*
  Dubois *B*
  Fayette *B*
  Hazleton *B*
  Lehigh Valley *B*
  McKeesport *B*
  Mont Alto *B*
  New Kensington *B*
  Schuylkill - Capital College *B*
  Shenango *B*
  University Park *C, B*
  Wilkes-Barre *B*
  Worthington Scranton *B*
  York *B*
University of Pittsburgh *B*

Texas
Austin Community College *A*

Utah
Brigham Young University *B, M*
Snow College *A*
University of Utah *B*

Vermont
Bennington College *B, M, T*
Middlebury College *B*

Washington
Central Washington University *B*
Everett Community College *A*
University of Puget Sound *T*
University of Washington *B*

West Virginia
Salem International University *B*

Wisconsin
Lawrence University *B*
University of Wisconsin
  Madison *B, M*

Japanese studies

Hawaii
University of Hawaii
  Hilo *A*

Louisiana
Dillard University *B*

Michigan
Hope College *B*

Minnesota
Gustavus Adolphus College *B*

Missouri
William Jewell College *B*

New York
Columbia University
  Columbia College *B*
Sarah Lawrence College *B*

Ohio
Case Western Reserve University *B*

Washington
University of Washington *B*

Wisconsin
Lawrence University *B*

Jazz studies

California
California Institute of the Arts *C, B, M*
California State University
  Long Beach *B, M*
University of Southern
  California *B, M, D*

Connecticut
University of Hartford *B*

District of Columbia
Howard University *B*

Florida
Florida State University *C, B, M*
Manatee Community College *A*
Palm Beach Community College *A*
Polk Community College *A*
University of Miami *B, M, D*
University of North Florida *B*
University of West Florida *B*

Illinois
Augustana College *B*
Columbia College Chicago *B*
Lincoln College *A*
North Central College *B*
Northwestern University *B*
Roosevelt University *B*

Indiana
American Conservatory of Music *A, B*
Indiana University
  Bloomington *B*

Iowa
University of Iowa *B*

Louisiana
Loyola University New Orleans *B, M*
Southern University and Agricultural and
  Mechanical College *A*
University of New Orleans *M*

Maine
University of Maine
  Augusta *A, B*
University of Southern Maine *B*

Massachusetts
Berklee College of Music *B*
Boston Conservatory *M*
New England Conservatory of
  Music *B, M, D*
Westfield State College *B*

Michigan
University of Michigan *B*
Western Michigan University *B*

Minnesota
University of Minnesota
  Duluth *B*

Missouri
Drury University *B*
University of Missouri
  Kansas City *B*
Webster University *M*

Nevada
University of Nevada
  Las Vegas *B*

New Jersey
Rowan University *B*
Rutgers, The State University of New
  Jersey
    Newark Regional Campus *M*
William Paterson University of New
  Jersey *B*

New York
Bard College *B*
City University of New York
  City College *B*
Eastman School of Music of the
  University of Rochester *B, M*
Eugene Lang College/New School
  University *B*
Ithaca College *B*
Juilliard School *B, D*
Manhattan School of Music *B, M*
Sarah Lawrence College *B*
State University of New York
  New Paltz *B*
University of Rochester *B, M, D*

Villa Maria College of Buffalo *A*

North Carolina
North Carolina Central University *B*

Ohio
Bowling Green State University *B*
Central State University *B*
Oberlin College *B, M*
Ohio State University
  Columbus Campus *B*
University of Cincinnati *B*
Youngstown State University *B*

Oregon
University of Oregon *M, D*

Pennsylvania
West Chester University of
  Pennsylvania *B*

Rhode Island
Community College of Rhode Island *A*

South Carolina
University of South Carolina *M*

Tennessee
University of Tennessee
  Martin *B*

Texas
Southwest Texas State University *B*
University of North Texas *B, M*

Utah
Brigham Young University *B*

Vermont
Bennington College *B, M*
Johnson State College *B*

Virginia
Shenandoah University *B*

Washington
Cornish College of the Arts *B*
Whitworth College *B*

Wisconsin
Lawrence University *B*
University of Wisconsin
  Madison *B, M*

Jewish/Judaic studies

Arizona
University of Arizona *B*

California
California State University
  Chico *B*
Scripps College *B*
University of California
  Berkeley *D*
  Los Angeles *B*
  San Diego *B, M*
University of Southern California *B*

Colorado
University of Denver *M*

Connecticut
Trinity College *B*
University of Connecticut *M*
University of Hartford *B*
Yale University *B*

District of Columbia
American University *B*
George Washington University *B*

Florida
Florida Atlantic University *B*
Talmudic College of Florida *B, M, D*
University of Florida *B*
University of Miami *B*

Georgia
Emory University *B*
Oxford College of Emory University *B*

Illinois
De Paul University *B*
Moody Bible Institute *B*

Indiana
Indiana University
  Bloomington *B*

Louisiana
Tulane University *B*

Maryland
Baltimore Hebrew University *B, M, D*
University of Maryland
  College Park *B*

Massachusetts
Hampshire College *B*
Harvard College *B*
Hebrew College *B, M, T*
Mount Holyoke College *B*
University of Massachusetts
  Amherst *B*
Wellesley College *B*

Michigan
University of Michigan *B*

Minnesota
University of Minnesota
  Twin Cities *B*

Missouri
University of Missouri
  Kansas City *B*
Washington University in St. Louis *B, M*

New Jersey
Rutgers, The State University of New
  Jersey
    New Brunswick Regional
      Campus *B*

New York
Bard College *B*
City University of New York
  Brooklyn College *B, M*
  City College *B*
  Hunter College *B*
  Queens College *B*
Hofstra University *B*
New York University *B, D*
Sarah Lawrence College *B*
State University of New York
  Albany *B*
  Binghamton *B*
Talmudical Institute of Upstate New
  York *B*
Touro College *B, M*
Vassar College *B*
Yeshiva University *A, B, M, D, T*

Ohio
Laura and Alvin Siegal College of Judaic
  Studies *B, M*
Oberlin College *B*
Ohio State University
  Columbus Campus *B*
University of Cincinnati *B*

Oregon
University of Oregon *B*

Pennsylvania
Dickinson College *B*
Gratz College *B, M*

Penn State
  Abington *B*
  Altoona *B*
  Beaver *B*
  Berks *B*
  Delaware County *B*
  Dubois *B*
  Fayette *B*
  Hazleton *B*
  Lehigh Valley *B*
  McKeesport *B*
  Mont Alto *B*
  New Kensington *B*
  Schuylkill - Capital College *B*
  Shenango *B*
  University Park *B*
  Worthington Scranton *B*
  York *B*
Temple University *B*
University of Pennsylvania *B*

Rhode Island

Brown University *B*

Vermont

Goddard College *B*

Washington

University of Washington *B*

Wisconsin

University of Wisconsin
  Madison *M, D*

Journalism

Alabama

Alabama Agricultural and Mechanical
  University *B*
Auburn University *B*
James H. Faulkner State Community
  College *A*
Samford University *B*
Spring Hill College *B*
Troy State University *B*
University of Alabama *B, M, D*

Alaska

University of Alaska
  Anchorage *B*
  Fairbanks *B*

Arizona

Arizona State University *B*
Central Arizona College *B*
Cochise College *A*
Northern Arizona University *B*
Pima Community College *A*
University of Arizona *B, M*

Arkansas

Arkansas State University *B, M*
Arkansas Tech University *B*
Harding University *B*
Henderson State University *B*
John Brown University *A, B*
Ouachita Baptist University *B, T*
University of Arkansas *B, M*
University of Arkansas
  Fort Smith *A*
  Little Rock *B, M*
University of Central Arkansas *B*

California

Azusa Pacific University *B*
Bakersfield College *A*
Cabrillo College *A*
California Baptist University *B*
California Polytechnic State University:
  San Luis Obispo *B*
California State Polytechnic University:
  Pomona *B*

California State University
  Chico *B*
  Dominguez Hills *B*
  Fresno *B, M*
  Fullerton *B, M*
  Hayward *B*
  Long Beach *B*
  Northridge *B, M*
  Sacramento *B*
Cerritos Community College *A*
Chabot College *A*
Chapman University *B*
College of the Canyons *C, A*
College of the Redwoods *C, A*
College of the Sequoias *A*
Cuesta College *C, A*
Diablo Valley College *C*
East Los Angeles College *A*
Gavilan Community College *A*
Glendale Community College *A*
Golden West College *C, A*
Grossmont Community College *C, A*
Humboldt State University *B*
Imperial Valley College *A*
Laney College *A*
Long Beach City College *C, A*
Los Angeles Pierce College *C, A*
Los Angeles Southwest College *A*
Los Angeles Trade and Technical
  College *C, A*
Los Medanos College *A*
Master's College *B*
Modesto Junior College *C, A*
Mount San Antonio College *A*
Ohlone College *C, A*
Pacific Union College *B*
Palomar College *C, A*
Pepperdine University *B*
Point Loma Nazarene University *B*
San Diego State University *B*
San Francisco State University *B*
San Joaquin Delta College *A*
San Jose State University *B, M*
Santa Monica College *A*
Santa Rosa Junior College *C*
Shasta College *C, A*
Sierra College *A*
Southwestern College *A*
Taft College *A*
University of California
  Berkeley *B, M*
University of La Verne *B*
University of Southern California *B, M*
Ventura College *C, A*
Yuba Community College District *C, A*

Colorado

Colorado Mountain College
  Alpine Campus *A*
Colorado State University *B, M*
Colorado State University
  Pueblo *B*
Jones International University *C, B, M*
Mesa State College *B*
Metropolitan State College of Denver *B*
Trinidad State Junior College *A*
University of Colorado
  Boulder *B, M*
University of Denver *B, M*
University of Northern Colorado *B*

Connecticut

Manchester Community College *A*
Norwalk Community College *A*
Quinnipiac University *B, M*
Southern Connecticut State University *B*
University of Bridgeport *B*
University of Connecticut *B*

Delaware

Delaware State University *B*
Delaware Technical and Community
  College
  Owens Campus *A*
University of Delaware *B*

District of Columbia

American University *B, M*
George Washington University *B*
Howard University *B*

Florida

Bethune-Cookman College *B*
Broward Community College *A*
Chipola Junior College *A*
Edward Waters College *B*
Florida Agricultural and Mechanical
  University *B, M*
Florida Southern College *B*
Gulf Coast Community College *A*
Hillsborough Community College *A*
Manatee Community College *A*
Miami-Dade Community College *A*
Palm Beach Community College *A*
Pensacola Junior College *A*
Polk Community College *A*
South Florida Community College *A*
University of Central Florida *B*
University of Florida *B*
University of Miami *B, M*
University of West Florida *B*

Georgia

Abraham Baldwin Agricultural
  College *A*
Albany State University *B*
Andrew College *A*
Clark Atlanta University *B*
Dalton State College *A*
Darton College *A*
Emory University *B*
Floyd College *A*
Fort Valley State University *B*
Gainesville College *A*
Georgia College and State University *B*
Georgia Perimeter College *A*
Georgia Southern University *B*
Georgia State University *B*
Macon State College *A*
Middle Georgia College *A*
Morris Brown College *B*
Paine College *B*
South Georgia College *A*
State University of West Georgia *B*
Toccoa Falls College *B*
University of Georgia *B, M*

Hawaii

Hawaii Pacific University *B*
University of Hawaii
  Manoa *B*

Idaho

Boise State University *B, T*
Brigham Young University - Idaho *B*
Idaho State University *B*
North Idaho College *A*
Northwest Nazarene University *B*
University of Idaho *B*

Illinois

Black Hawk College
  East Campus *A*
Bradley University *B*
City Colleges of Chicago
  Harold Washington College *A*
  Kennedy-King College *A*
College of DuPage *C*
Columbia College Chicago *B, M*
Danville Area Community College *A*
Dominican University *B*
Eastern Illinois University *B*
Governors State University *B, M*
Greenville College *B*
Illinois Central College *A*
Illinois State University *B*
Illinois Valley Community College *A*
John A. Logan College *A*
Judson College *B*
Kishwaukee College *A*
Lake Land College *A*
Lewis University *B*
Lewis and Clark Community College *A*

Lincoln College *A*
Lincoln Land Community College *A*
Loyola University of Chicago *C*
MacMurray College *B*
North Central College *B*
Northern Illinois University *B*
Northwestern University *B, M*
Olivet Nazarene University *B*
Parkland College *A*
Principia College *B*
Quincy University *B*
Richland Community College *A*
Roosevelt University *B, M*
Sauk Valley Community College *A*
South Suburban College of Cook
  County *A*
Southern Illinois University
  Carbondale *B, M, D*
Triton College *A*
University of Illinois
  Springfield *M*
  Urbana-Champaign *B, M*
University of St. Francis *B*
Western Illinois University *B*
William Rainey Harper College *A*

Indiana

Anderson University *B*
Ball State University *A, B, M, T*
Bethel College *A*
Butler University *B*
Calumet College of St. Joseph *B*
Franklin College *B*
Goshen College *B*
Huntington College *B*
Indiana State University *B*
Indiana University
  Bloomington *B, M, D, T*
  Southeast *A, B*
Indiana University-Purdue University
  Fort Wayne *B*
Indiana University-Purdue University
  Indianapolis *B*
Manchester College *B*
Purdue University
  Calumet *B*
St. Mary-of-the-Woods College *B*
Taylor University *B*
University of Indianapolis *B*
University of Southern Indiana *B*
Valparaiso University *B*
Vincennes University *A*

Iowa

Briar Cliff University *B*
Buena Vista University *B*
Clarke College *B*
Dordt College *B*
Drake University *B*
Grand View College *B*
Iowa State University *B, M*
Iowa Wesleyan College *B*
Loras College *B*
Marshalltown Community College *A*
Morningside College *B*
North Iowa Area Community College *A*
St. Ambrose University *B*
Simpson College *B*
University of Iowa *B, M, D, T*
Waldorf College *A, B*
Wartburg College *B, T*
William Penn University *B*

Kansas

Baker University *T*
Barton County Community College *A*
Benedictine College *B, T*
Butler County Community College *A*
Central Christian College *A, B*
Dodge City Community College *A*
Emporia State University *T*
Garden City Community College *A*
Haskell Indian Nations University *A*
Hutchinson Community College *A*
Independence Community College *A*

Kansas City Kansas Community
   College *A*
Kansas State University *B, M*
Labette Community College *A*
Pittsburg State University *B, T*
Pratt Community College *A*
Seward County Community College *A*
Tabor College *B*
University of Kansas *B, M*
Washburn University of Topeka *B*

Kentucky

Asbury College *B*
Campbellsville University *B*
Lindsey Wilson College *B*
Murray State University *B, M, T*
University of Kentucky *B*

Louisiana

Grambling State University *B, M*
Louisiana College *B*
Louisiana State University
   Shreveport *B*
Louisiana State University and
   Agricultural and Mechanical
   College *M*
Louisiana Tech University *B*
McNeese State University *B*
Nicholls State University *B*
Northwestern State University *B*
University of Louisiana at Lafayette *B*
University of Louisiana at Monroe *B*

Maine

St. Joseph's College *B*
University of Maine *B*
University of Southern Maine *B*

Maryland

Bowie State University *B*
College of Southern Maryland *C*
Columbia Union College *B*
Community College of Baltimore County
   Catonsville *A*
   Dundalk *A*
   Essex *A*
Coppin State College *B*
Towson University *B, M*
University of Maryland
   College Park *B, M, D*

Massachusetts

American International College *B*
Boston University *B, M*
Cape Cod Community College *A*
Dean College *A*
Emerson College *B, M*
Fitchburg State College *B*
Hampshire College *B*
Massachusetts College of Liberal Arts *B*
Massachusetts Institute of Technology *M*
Mount Ida College *B*
Newbury College *A*
Northeastern University *B, M*
Salem State College *B*
Suffolk University *B, M*
University of Massachusetts
   Amherst *B*
Westfield State College *B*

Michigan

Adrian College *B*
Andrews University *B*
Bay de Noc Community College *C*
Central Michigan University *B*
Eastern Michigan University *B*
Grand Valley State University *B*
Kellogg Community College *A*
Lansing Community College *A*
Madonna University *A, B*
Michigan State University *B, M, D*
Northern Michigan University *B*
Oakland Community College *A*
Oakland University *B*
St. Clair County Community College *A*
Schoolcraft College *A*
University of Michigan *B, M, D, T*

Wayne State University *B*
Western Michigan University *B*

Minnesota

Bemidji State University *B*
Bethel College *B*
Concordia College: Moorhead *B*
Minnesota State University
   Mankato *B*
   Moorhead *B*
North Central University *B*
Northland Community & Technical
   College *A*
Northwestern College *B*
Ridgewater College: A Community and
   Technical College *A*
St. Cloud State University *B*
St. Mary's University of Minnesota *B*
University of Minnesota
   Twin Cities *B, M, D*
University of St. Thomas *B*
Vermilion Community College *A*
Winona State University *B*

Mississippi

Alcorn State University *B*
Coahoma Community College *A*
Delta State University *B*
Itawamba Community College *A*
Mississippi College *B*
Mississippi University for Women *B*
Northwest Mississippi Community
   College *A*
Rust College *B*
University of Mississippi *B, M*
University of Southern Mississippi *B*

Missouri

Central Missouri State University *B, M*
College of the Ozarks *B*
Crowder College *A*
Culver-Stockton College *B*
Drury University *B*
East Central College *A*
Evangel University *A, B*
Lincoln University *B*
Lindenwood University *B, M*
Missouri Southern State College *B*
Missouri Western State College *B*
Northwest Missouri State University *B*
St. Louis Community College
   St. Louis Community College at
      Florissant Valley *A*
Southeast Missouri State University *B*
Southwest Missouri State University *B*
Stephens College *B*
Truman State University *B*
University of Missouri
   Columbia *B, M, D*
   Kansas City *B*
Washington University in St. Louis *B*
Webster University *B*
Westminster College *B*
William Woods University *B*

Montana

Miles Community College *A*
Montana State University
   Billings *B*
University of Montana-Missoula *B, M*

Nebraska

Central Community College *C, A*
Creighton University *A, B*
Doane College *B*
Grace University *B*
Hastings College *B, T*
Midland Lutheran College *B, T*
Northeast Community College *A*
Southeast Community College
   Beatrice Campus *A*
Union College *B*
University of Nebraska
   Kearney *B*
   Lincoln *B, M*
   Omaha *B*
Wayne State College *B, T*

Western Nebraska Community
   College *A*

Nevada

University of Nevada
   Reno *B, M*

New Hampshire

Franklin Pierce College *B*
Keene State College *B*
Rivier College *B*
University of New Hampshire *B*

New Jersey

The College of New Jersey *B*
Cumberland County College *A*
Essex County College *A*
Gloucester County College *A*
Middlesex County College *A*
Ocean County College *A*
Rider University *B*
Rowan University *B*
Rutgers, The State University of New
   Jersey
      New Brunswick Regional
         Campus *B*
      Newark Regional Campus *B*
Salem Community College *A*
Sussex County Community College *A*
Thomas Edison State College *B*

New Mexico

Eastern New Mexico University *B*
New Mexico Highlands University *B*
New Mexico State University *B*
University of New Mexico *B*

New York

City University of New York
   Baruch College *B, M*
   Brooklyn College *B*
   City College *B*
   Kingsborough Community
      College *A*
Fulton-Montgomery Community
   College *A*
Hobart and William Smith Colleges *B*
Hofstra University *B*
Iona College *B, M*
Ithaca College *B*
Long Island University
   C. W. Post Campus *B*
Manhattan College *B*
Marist College *B*
Marymount College of Fordham
   University *B*
Medaille College *B*
Mercy College *B*
Nassau Community College *A*
New York Institute of Technology *M*
New York University *B, M*
Pace University *B*
Pace University:
   Pleasantville/Briarcliff *B*
Polytechnic University *B, M*
St. Bonaventure University *B*
St. John Fisher College *B*
St. John's University *B*
State University of New York
   College at Brockport *B*
   College at Buffalo *B*
   College at Old Westbury *B*
   College at Plattsburgh *B*
   College of Agriculture and
      Technology at Morrisville *A*
   New Paltz *B*
   Oswego *B*
   Purchase *B*
Syracuse University *B, M, D*
Tompkins-Cortland Community
   College *A*
Utica College *B*

North Carolina

Appalachian State University *B*
Barber-Scotia College *B*
Bennett College *B*

Campbell University *B*
Elon University *B*
Gardner-Webb University *B*
North Carolina Agricultural and
   Technical State University *B*
North Carolina State University *B*
University of North Carolina
   Asheville *B*
   Greensboro *B*
   Pembroke *B*

North Dakota

North Dakota State University *B*

Ohio

Ashland University *B*
Bowling Green State University *B*
Central State University *B*
Defiance College *B*
Kent State University *B, M*
Kent State University
   Stark Campus *B*
Lorain County Community College *A*
Malone College *B*
Marietta College *B*
Miami University
   Oxford Campus *B, M*
Mount Union College *B*
Muskingum College *B*
Ohio Northern University *B*
Ohio State University
   Columbus Campus *B, M*
Ohio University *B, M, D*
Ohio University
   Southern Campus at Ironton *A*
Ohio Wesleyan University *B*
Otterbein College *B*
University of Cincinnati
   Raymond Walters College *C*
University of Dayton *B*
University of Findlay *B*
University of Rio Grande *B*
Wilmington College *B*
Wittenberg University *B*
Youngstown State University *B*

Oklahoma

Bacone College *A*
Cameron University *B*
Carl Albert State College *A*
East Central University *B*
Eastern Oklahoma State College *A*
Langston University *B*
Northeastern Oklahoma Agricultural and
   Mechanical College *A*
Northeastern State University *A*
Northern Oklahoma College *A*
Northwestern Oklahoma State
   University *B*
Oklahoma Baptist University *B*
Oklahoma Christian University of
   Science and Arts *B*
Oklahoma City Community College *A*
Oklahoma City University *B*
Oklahoma State University *B, M*
Rose State College *A*
St. Gregory's University *A, B*
Southeastern Oklahoma State
   University *B*
Southern Nazarene University *B*
Tulsa Community College *A*
University of Central Oklahoma *B*
University of Oklahoma *B, M*

Oregon

Chemeketa Community College *A*
Lane Community College *C, A*
Linfield College *B*
Linn-Benton Community College *A*
Mount Hood Community College *A*
Multnomah Bible College *B*
Pacific University *B*
Southern Oregon University *B*
Umpqua Community College *C*
University of Oregon *B, M*
Western Baptist College *B*

Pennsylvania

Bloomsburg University of
  Pennsylvania *B*
Bucks County Community College *A*
California University of Pennsylvania *B*
Community College of Allegheny
  County *A*
Delaware County Community College *A*
Duquesne University *B*
Edinboro University of Pennsylvania *B*
Harrisburg Area Community College *A*
Indiana University of Pennsylvania *B*
La Salle University *B*
Lehigh University *B*
Lincoln University *B*
Lock Haven University of
  Pennsylvania *B*
Luzerne County Community College *A*
Mercyhurst College *B*
Messiah College *B*
Northampton County Area Community
  College *A*
Penn State
  Abington *B*
  Altoona *B*
  Beaver *B*
  Berks *B*
  Delaware County *B*
  Dubois *B*
  Fayette *B*
  Hazleton *B*
  Lehigh Valley *B*
  McKeesport *B*
  Mont Alto *B*
  New Kensington *B*
  Schuylkill - Capital College *B*
  Shenango *B*
  University Park *B*
  Wilkes-Barre *B*
  Worthington Scranton *B*
  York *B*
Pennsylvania College of Technology *A*
Point Park College *A, B, M*
Seton Hill University *B*
Shippensburg University of
  Pennsylvania *B*
Temple University *B, M*
University of Pittsburgh
  Greensburg *B*
  Johnstown *B*
Waynesburg College *B*

Puerto Rico

Bayamon Central University *B*
Turabo University *B*
University of the Sacred Heart *B, M*

Rhode Island

University of Rhode Island *B*

South Carolina

Anderson College *B*
Claflin University *B*
Morris College *B*
North Greenville College *B*
University of South Carolina *B, M, D*
University of South Carolina
  Aiken *B*
Winthrop University *B*

South Dakota

Augustana College *B*
Black Hills State University *B*
Dakota Wesleyan University *B*
Mount Marty College *B*
South Dakota State University *B, M, T*
University of Sioux Falls *B*
University of South Dakota *B, M*

Tennessee

Austin Peay State University *B, M*
Belmont University *B*
Carson-Newman College *B*
Columbia State Community College *A*
East Tennessee State University *B*
Lee University *B*
Middle Tennessee State University *B, M*

Southern Adventist University *B*
Tennessee State University *B*
Tennessee Technological University *B*
Tusculum College *B*
Union University *B*
University of Memphis *B, M*
University of Tennessee
  Knoxville *B*
  Martin *B*

Texas

Abilene Christian University *B, M*
Amarillo College *A*
Angelina College *A*
Angelo State University *B, T*
Austin Community College *A*
Baylor University *B, M, T*
College of the Mainland *A*
Del Mar College *A*
El Paso Community College *A*
Hardin-Simmons University *B*
Hill College *C, A*
Houston Baptist University *B*
Howard College *A*
Jarvis Christian College *B*
Kilgore College *A*
Lee College *A*
Midland College *A*
Midwestern State University *B*
Northeast Texas Community College *A*
Palo Alto College *A*
Paris Junior College *A*
Sam Houston State University *B*
San Antonio College *A*
South Plains College *A*
Southern Methodist University *B*
Southwest Texas State
  University *B, M, T*
Southwestern Adventist University *B*
Stephen F. Austin State
  University *B, M, T*
Texas A&M University *B, M*
Texas A&M University
  Commerce *B*
Texas Christian University *B, M*
Texas Southern University *B*
Texas Tech University *B, M*
Texas Wesleyan University *B*
Texas Woman's University *B*
Trinity Valley Community College *A*
Tyler Junior College *A*
University of Houston *B, M*
University of Mary Hardin-Baylor *B*
University of North Texas *B, M*
University of Texas
  Arlington *B*
  Austin *B, M, D*
  El Paso *B*
  Pan American *B, T*
  San Antonio *B*
  Tyler *B*
Wayland Baptist University *B*
West Texas A&M University *B*
Western Texas College *A*
Wiley College *B*

Utah

Brigham Young University *B*
Dixie State College of Utah *A*
Salt Lake Community College *A*
Snow College *A*
Southern Utah University *B*
Utah State University *B, M*
Weber State University *B*

Vermont

Castleton State College *B*
College of St. Joseph in Vermont *B*
Johnson State College *B*
Lyndon State College *B*
St. Michael's College *B*

Virginia

Averett University *B*
Bluefield College *B*
Hampton University *B*
Liberty University *B*

Longwood University *B*
Norfolk State University *B*
Radford University *B*
Southwest Virginia Community
  College *C*
University of Richmond *B*
University of Virginia's College at
  Wise *B, T*
Virginia Commonwealth
  University *B, M*
Virginia Polytechnic Institute and State
  University *B*
Virginia State University *B*
Virginia Union University *B*
Washington and Lee University *B*

Washington

Central Washington University *B*
Centralia College *A*
Eastern Washington University *B*
Everett Community College *A*
Gonzaga University *B*
Olympic College *A*
Pacific Lutheran University *B*
Peninsula College *A*
Seattle University *B*
Walla Walla College *B*
Washington State University *B*
Western Washington University *B*
Whitworth College *B*

West Virginia

Bethany College *B*
Concord College *B*
Marshall University *B, M*
Potomac State College of West Virginia
  University *A*
University of Charleston *B*
West Virginia University *B, M, T*
West Virginia University at
  Parkersburg *A*

Wisconsin

Carroll College *B*
Marian College of Fond du Lac *B*
Marquette University *B, M, T*
University of Wisconsin
  Eau Claire *B*
  Madison *B, M, D*
  Milwaukee *B, M*
  Oshkosh *B*
  River Falls *B, T*
  Superior *B*
  Whitewater *B*

Wyoming

Casper College *A*
Laramie County Community College *A*
University of Wyoming *B*
Western Wyoming Community
  College *A*

Junior high education

Alabama

Athens State University *B*
Birmingham-Southern College *T*
Faulkner University *B, T*
Huntingdon College *B*
Troy State University Dothan *B, M, T*

Alaska

Alaska Pacific University *B, M*

Arkansas

Arkansas State University *B, T*
Arkansas Tech University *B*
Henderson State University *B, M, T*
John Brown University *B*
South Arkansas Community College *A*
Southern Arkansas University Tech *A*
University of Arkansas *B, M*
University of Arkansas
  Little Rock *B, M*
  Monticello *B*
  Pine Bluff *B*

University of Central Arkansas *B, M*
University of the Ozarks *B*

California

Azusa Pacific University *B, T*
California Baptist University *T*
California State University
  Bakersfield *B, M*
  Hayward *T*
  Long Beach *T*
  Northridge *M*
  San Marcos *T*
Christian Heritage College *B, T*
Mills College *T*
Mount St. Mary's College *B*
National University *T*
Occidental College *T*
St. Mary's College of California *T*
San Francisco State University *T*
Simpson College *B, T*
Sonoma State University *M*
University of California
  Riverside *T*
University of Redlands *B, T*
University of Southern California *T*
Whittier College *T*

Colorado

Fort Lewis College *T*
Regis University *B, T*
University of Northern Colorado *T*

Connecticut

Central Connecticut State University *T*
Eastern Connecticut State
  University *B, T*
Quinnipiac University *B, M*
St. Joseph College *T*

Delaware

Delaware State University *B*
University of Delaware *B, T*

Florida

Southeastern College of the Assemblies
  of God *B, T*
University of Florida *B*
University of North Florida *B*
University of West Florida *B, T*

Georgia

Albany State University *B, M*
Armstrong Atlantic State
  University *B, M, T*
Augusta State University *B, M*
Berry College *B, M, T*
Brenau University *B*
Clark Atlanta University *B*
Clayton College and State University *B*
Columbus State University *B, M*
Covenant College *B, T*
Emmanuel College *B*
Fort Valley State University *B, M, T*
Georgia College and State
  University *B, M, T*
Georgia Southern University *B, M, T*
Georgia Southwestern State
  University *B, M, T*
Georgia State University *B, M*
Kennesaw State University *B, M*
Mercer University *B, M, T*
Middle Georgia College *A*
Morehouse College *B*
North Georgia College & State
  University *B, M*
Oglethorpe University *B, M, T*
Paine College *B*
Piedmont College *B, T*
Reinhardt College *B*
Shorter College *B, T*
State University of West Georgia *B, M*
Thomas University *B*
Toccoa Falls College *B, T*
University of Georgia *B, M, D, T*
Valdosta State University *B, M*
Wesleyan College *B, M, T*

Idaho

Boise State University *T*
Northwest Nazarene University *B*

Illinois

Augustana College *B, T*
City Colleges of Chicago
    Kennedy-King College *A*
Dominican University *T*
Eastern Illinois University *B*
Eureka College *B*
Greenville College *T*
Illinois State University *B, T*
Judson College *B, T*
McKendree College *B, T*
Monmouth College *T*
North Park University *B, M*
Sauk Valley Community College *A*
Southwestern Illinois College *A*
Trinity Christian College *T*
University of St. Francis *M, T*

Indiana

Ball State University *M, T*
Butler University *B, M*
Earlham College *M*
Goshen College *B, T*
Indiana University
    Kokomo *T*
    Northwest *T*
Indiana Wesleyan University *B, M*
Manchester College *B, T*
St. Mary-of-the-Woods College *B*
Tri-State University *B, T*
University of Evansville *B*
University of Indianapolis *T*
Valparaiso University *B, T*
Vincennes University *A*

Iowa

Buena Vista University *M, T*
Central College *T*
Clarke College *B, M, T*
Cornell College *B, T*
Dordt College *B, T*
Ellsworth Community College *A*
Faith Baptist Bible College and
    Theological Seminary *B, T*
Franciscan University *B, T*
Graceland University *T*
Grand View College *B, T*
Iowa Wesleyan College *B*
Luther College *B*
Morningside College *B, M*
Mount Mercy College *T*
Northwestern College *T*
Simpson College *B, T*
University of Northern Iowa *B, M*
Upper Iowa University *B, T*

Kansas

Central Christian College *A, B*
Fort Scott Community College *A*
Friends University *B, T*
Garden City Community College *A*
Independence Community College *A*
McPherson College *B, T*
Newman University *B, T*
Ottawa University *T*
Pittsburg State University *B, T*
Tabor College *B, T*
University of Kansas *B, T*

Kentucky

Alice Lloyd College *B*
Asbury College *B, T*
Bellarmine University *B, M, T*
Berea College *B, T*
Brescia University *B, T*
Campbellsville University *B*
Cumberland College *B, M, T*
Kentucky Christian College *B, T*
Kentucky Wesleyan College *B, T*
Lindsey Wilson College *B, T*
Morehead State University *B, M, T*
Murray State University *B, M, T*
Pikeville College *B, T*

Spalding University *B, M, T*
Thomas More College *B*
Transylvania University *B, T*
Union College *B, M, T*
University of Kentucky *B, M*
University of Louisville *M, D*

Louisiana

Centenary College of Louisiana *B, T*
Louisiana College *B*
Nicholls State University *B*

Maine

University of Maine
    Farmington *B, T*
    Machias *B*
University of New England *T*
University of Southern Maine *T*

Maryland

Goucher College *M*
Morgan State University *M*
St. Mary's College of Maryland *T*

Massachusetts

American International College *B, M*
Assumption College *B, T*
Bridgewater State College *B, T*
Clark University *M*
Fitchburg State College *B, M, T*
Lesley University *B, M, T*
Massachusetts College of Liberal Arts *T*
Merrimack College *T*
Simmons College *B, M*
Tufts University *M, T*
Wellesley College *T*
Westfield State College *B, M, T*

Michigan

Adrian College *T*
Baker College
    of Auburn Hills *B*
    of Muskegon *B*
    of Owosso *B*
Calvin College *B, T*
Central Michigan University *M*
Cornerstone University *B*
Eastern Michigan University *M*
Grand Valley State University *T*
Madonna University *B, T*
Northern Michigan University *B, T*
Saginaw Valley State University *M*
Spring Arbor University *T*
Western Michigan University *M*

Minnesota

Bethel College *B*
Capella University *M, D*
College of St. Catherine *B*
College of St. Scholastica *T*
Concordia University: St. Paul *B, T*
Minnesota State University
    Mankato *B, T*
    Moorhead *B, T*
Northland Community & Technical
    College *A*
Ridgewater College: A Community and
    Technical College *A*
University of St. Thomas *B, T*
Vermilion Community College *A*
Winona State University *B, M, T*

Mississippi

Blue Mountain College *B*

Missouri

Avila University *B, T*
Central Methodist College *B*
Central Missouri State University *B, T*
College of the Ozarks *T*
Culver-Stockton College *T*
East Central College *A*
Evangel University *B, T*
Fontbonne College *B*
Harris Stowe State College *B, T*
Lindenwood University *B*
Maryville University of Saint
    Louis *B, M, T*

Missouri Baptist University *B, T*
Missouri Southern State College *B, T*
Missouri Valley College *T*
Missouri Western State College *B*
Northwest Missouri State
    University *B, M, T*
Ozark Christian College *A*
Rockhurst University *B*
Southeast Missouri State University *B*
Southwest Baptist University *B, T*
Southwest Missouri State University *B*
Truman State University *M, T*
University of Missouri
    Columbia *B*
    Kansas City *B*
    St. Louis *T*
Washington University in St.
    Louis *B, M, T*
Westminster College *B, T*
William Jewell College *T*
William Woods University *B, T*

Montana

Rocky Mountain College *B, T*
University of Great Falls *B*

Nebraska

Chadron State College *B*
College of Saint Mary *B, T*
Concordia University *B, T*
Midland Lutheran College *B, T*
Nebraska Wesleyan University *B*
Peru State College *B, T*
University of Nebraska
    Kearney *B, M, T*
    Lincoln *T*
York College *B, T*

New Hampshire

Franklin Pierce College *T*
Plymouth State College *T*

New Jersey

Caldwell College *T*
Centenary College *T*
The College of New Jersey *B, M, T*
Rowan University *B*
Rutgers, The State University of New
    Jersey
    Camden Regional Campus *T*
    New Brunswick Regional
        Campus *T*
    Newark Regional Campus *T*

New Mexico

New Mexico Junior College *A*
Western New Mexico University *B, M*

New York

Alfred University *T*
Barnard College *T*
Canisius College *B, M, T*
City University of New York
    Brooklyn College *B, M, T*
    Queens College *B, M, T*
College of Mount St. Vincent *T*
Concordia College *B, T*
D'Youville College *B, M*
Dowling College *B, M, T*
Dutchess Community College *A*
Elmira College *B, T*
Eugene Lang College/New School
    University *T*
Hofstra University *T*
Long Island University
    C. W. Post Campus *T*
Manhattan College *B, T*
Manhattanville College *M, T*
Marist College *T*
Marymount College of Fordham
    University *B, T*
Medaille College *B*
Mercy College *T*
Nazareth College of Rochester *T*
New York Institute of Technology *B, T*
St. John's University *B*
St. Joseph's College *B, T*

St. Joseph's College: Suffolk
    Campus *B, T*
State University of New York
    Buffalo *M, D, T*
    College at Cortland *M*
    College at Fredonia *T*
    College at Old Westbury *T*
    New Paltz *B, M, T*
Syracuse University *B, M, T*
Vassar College *T*
Wagner College *B, T*

North Carolina

Appalachian State University *B, M, T*
Barton College *B*
Bennett College *B*
Campbell University *B, M, T*
Catawba College *B, M, T*
East Carolina University *B, M*
Elizabeth City State University *B, T*
Elon University *B, M, T*
Fayetteville State University *B, M*
Gardner-Webb University *B*
Greensboro College *B, T*
High Point University *B, T*
Lenoir-Rhyne College *B, T*
Mars Hill College *B, T*
Meredith College *T*
Methodist College *A, B, T*
North Carolina Central University *B, M*
North Carolina State University *B*
North Carolina Wesleyan College *B*
University of North Carolina
    Asheville *T*
    Chapel Hill *B*
    Charlotte *B*
    Greensboro *B, M*
    Pembroke *B, M, T*
    Wilmington *B, M*
Warren Wilson College *B, T*
Western Carolina University *B, M, T*
Wingate University *B, T*
Winston-Salem State University *B*

North Dakota

Dickinson State University *B, T*
Mayville State University *B, T*
North Dakota State University *B, T*
University of North Dakota *B, T*

Ohio

Ashland University *B, T*
Baldwin-Wallace College *B*
Bluffton College *B*
Bowling Green State University *B*
Cedarville University *B, T*
Central State University *B*
College of Mount St. Joseph *B*
College of Wooster *T*
Defiance College *B, T*
Hiram College *T*
Kent State University *B*
Kent State University
    Stark Campus *B*
Lourdes College *B*
Malone College *B*
Marietta College *B*
Mount Union College *B, T*
Mount Vernon Nazarene University *B, T*
Notre Dame College *T*
Ohio Dominican College *B, T*
Ohio Northern University *B, T*
Ohio State University
    Columbus Campus *M*
Ohio University *B, D, T*
Ohio University
    Chillicothe Campus *B*
    Zanesville Campus *B*
Otterbein College *B*
University of Akron *B, M, T*
University of Cincinnati
    Clermont College *A*
    Raymond Walters College *A*
University of Dayton *B, M, T*
University of Findlay *B, T*
University of Rio Grande *B, T*

Urbana University *B*
Ursuline College *B, T*
Walsh University *B*
Wilmington College *B*
Wittenberg University *B*
Wright State University *M*
Xavier University *B*
Youngstown State University *B, M*

Oklahoma
Northwestern Oklahoma State
  University *T*
Oklahoma Christian University of
  Science and Arts *B, T*
Oklahoma State University *B, M, D, T*
Southeastern Oklahoma State
  University *T*
Southwestern Oklahoma State
  University *M, T*

Oregon
Concordia University *B, M, T*
Eastern Oregon University *B, M*
Lewis & Clark College *M*
Linfield College *T*
Portland State University *T*
Warner Pacific College *T*
Western Baptist College *B*
Western Oregon University *T*
Willamette University *M*

Pennsylvania
California University of
  Pennsylvania *A, B, T*
Cedar Crest College *B, T*
DeSales University *T*
Gettysburg College *T*
La Salle University *B, T*
Lock Haven University of
  Pennsylvania *B, T*
Reading Area Community College *A*
St. Vincent College *T*
Widener University *M*

Rhode Island
Rhode Island College *B, M*

South Carolina
Charleston Southern University *M*
Coastal Carolina University *B*
Columbia College *B*
University of South Carolina
  Aiken *B, T*
Winthrop University *M*

South Dakota
Black Hills State University *B, T*
Dakota State University *B, T*
Mount Marty College *B*

Tennessee
Austin Peay State University *T*
Belmont University *B, T*
Freed-Hardeman University *T*
Johnson Bible College *T*
King College *T*
Lambuth University *B, T*
Milligan College *B, T*
Tennessee Technological University *T*
Tennessee Wesleyan College *B, T*
Tusculum College *B, T*
Union University *B, T*
University of Tennessee
  Chattanooga *B*
  Knoxville *T*

Texas
Abilene Christian University *B, M, T*
Concordia University at Austin *B, T*
East Texas Baptist University *B*
Jarvis Christian College *B*
LeTourneau University *B*
Lubbock Christian University *B*
Schreiner University *T*
Texas A&M University
  Commerce *B*
  Kingsville *M*
Texas Lutheran University *B, T*

Trinity Valley Community College *A*
University of Texas
  Arlington *T*

Vermont
Castleton State College *B, M, T*
College of St. Joseph in Vermont *B*
Goddard College *B*
Johnson State College *B, M*
St. Michael's College *T*
University of Vermont *B*

Virginia
Averett University *M*
Bluefield College *B*
Eastern Mennonite University *T*
Hollins University *T*
Longwood University *B, T*
Mary Baldwin College *T*
Radford University *T*
Shenandoah University *C*
University of Richmond *B, T*
Virginia Wesleyan College *T*

Washington
Central Washington University *M*
Evergreen State College *M*
Northwest College *B*
University of Washington *M, T*
Whitworth College *B, M, T*

West Virginia
Alderson-Broaddus College *B*
Bluefield State College *B*
Fairmont State College *B*
Salem International University *T*
West Virginia State College *B*
Wheeling Jesuit University *T*

Wisconsin
Alverno College *B, T*
Beloit College *T*
Carroll College *B, T*
Carthage College *T*
Concordia University Wisconsin *B, T*
Edgewood College *B, T*
Marian College of Fond du Lac *B, T*
Marquette University *B*
Northland College *T*
Ripon College *T*
St. Norbert College *M, T*
Silver Lake College *T*
University of Wisconsin
  Green Bay *T*
  La Crosse *B, M, T*
  Parkside *T*
  Platteville *T*
  River Falls *T*
  Superior *M*
Viterbo University *B, M, T*

Wyoming
Western Wyoming Community
  College *A*

Juvenile corrections

Arizona
Arizona Western College *C*

California
Santa Rosa Junior College *C*

Connecticut
University of New Haven *B*

Florida
University of West Florida *B*

Indiana
Calumet College of St. Joseph *T*

Kansas
Kansas City Kansas Community
  College *C*

Nevada
Truckee Meadows Community
  College *A*

Oregon
Linn-Benton Community College *C*

Texas
Prairie View A&M University *M*

**Kindergarten/preschool
education**

Alabama
Samford University *B, M*

Arkansas
South Arkansas Community College *A*

Florida
Seminole Community College *C, A*
University of West Florida *B, M, T*

Illinois
De Paul University *B*
Waubonsee Community College *A*

Indiana
Indiana State University *B, M*

Iowa
University of Northern Iowa *B, M*
Upper Iowa University *B*

Kansas
Tabor College *B, T*

Maine
University of Maine
  Farmington *B, T*

Massachusetts
Cape Cod Community College *A*
Lesley University *B, M, T*
Stonehill College *B*

Michigan
Baker College
  of Muskegon *B*

Minnesota
Vermilion Community College *A*

New Jersey
William Paterson University of New
  Jersey *T*

New Mexico
Santa Fe Community College *A*

New York
City University of New York
  Hunter College *M, T*
Dutchess Community College *A*
Hofstra University *M*
St. Joseph's College: Suffolk
  Campus *B, T*
Sarah Lawrence College *M*

North Carolina
Meredith College *T*
Western Carolina University *B*

Ohio
Ashland University *B, M, T*
Shawnee State University *B*
University of Cincinnati
  Clermont College *C, A*
University of Dayton *B, M, T*
Youngstown State University *B*

Pennsylvania
Chestnut Hill College *B, M*
Seton Hill University *T*

Puerto Rico
Turabo University *B*

South Dakota
University of South Dakota *B*

Vermont
University of Vermont *B*

West Virginia
Marshall University *M*

Wisconsin
Edgewood College *B, T*

Kinesiotherapy

New York
State University of New York
  Buffalo *D*

Texas
University of Houston *B*

Knowledge management

Ohio
Kent State University *M*

Pennsylvania
Penn State
  York *B*

Texas
Texas A&M University *M, D*

Korean

Hawaii
University of Hawaii
  Manoa *B, M, D*

New York
Columbia University
  Columbia College *B*

Washington
University of Washington *B*

Korean studies

New York
Columbia University
  Columbia College *B*

Washington
University of Washington *B*

Labor studies

Indiana
Indiana University-Purdue University
  Fort Wayne *C, A, B*

New Jersey
Thomas Edison State College *C, B*

New York
Hofstra University *B*

Labor/industrial relations

Alabama
Wallace State Community College at
  Hanceville *A*

California
California State University
  Dominguez Hills *B*
Los Angeles Trade and Technical
  College *C, A*
Los Medanos College *C, A*
San Diego City College *A*
San Francisco State University *B*

Connecticut
University of Bridgeport *B, M*
University of New Haven *M*

Georgia
Georgia State University *M, D*
University of Georgia *B*

Illinois
Loyola University of Chicago *M*

Northwestern University *M*
Roosevelt University *B*
University of Illinois
    Springfield *B*
    Urbana-Champaign *M, D*

Indiana
Indiana University
    Bloomington *C, A, B*
    Kokomo *C, A, B*
    Northwest *C, A, B*
    South Bend *C, A, B*
    Southeast *A, B*
Indiana University-Purdue University
    Fort Wayne *C, A, B*
Indiana University-Purdue University
    Indianapolis *C, A, B*
Purdue University
    North Central Campus *A, B*

Iowa
Iowa State University *M*
University of Iowa *B, D*

Maine
University of Maine *B*

Maryland
Community College of Baltimore County
    Catonsville *C, A*
    Dundalk *C, A*
    Essex *C, A*

Massachusetts
University of Massachusetts
    Amherst *M*
    Boston *B*

Michigan
Michigan State University *M*
Wayne State University *M*

Minnesota
University of Minnesota
    Twin Cities *C, B, M, D*
Winona State University *B*

Missouri
Rockhurst University *B*

New Jersey
Rowan University *B*
Rutgers, The State University of New
    Jersey
    New Brunswick Regional
        Campus *B, M*
Seton Hall University *B*

New York
City University of New York
    Baruch College *B, M*
Cornell University *B, M, D*
Hofstra University *B*
Le Moyne College *B*
New York Institute of Technology *M*
New York University *B, M, D*
Onondaga Community College *A*
State University of New York
    College at Old Westbury *B*
    College at Potsdam *B*
    Empire State College *A, B, M*

Ohio
Bowling Green State University *B*
Case Western Reserve University *M, D*
Cincinnati State Technical and
    Community College *C*
Cleveland State University *B, M, D*
Lorain County Community College *A*
Sinclair Community College *C, A*
University of Akron *A*
Youngstown State University *A, B*

Oregon
University of Oregon *M*

Pennsylvania
Indiana University of Pennsylvania *M*
La Salle University *B*

Penn State
    Abington *B*
    Altoona *B*
    Beaver *B*
    Berks *B*
    Delaware County *B*
    Dubois *B*
    Fayette *B*
    Hazleton *B*
    Lehigh Valley *B*
    McKeesport *B*
    Mont Alto *B*
    New Kensington *B*
    Schuylkill - Capital College *B*
    Shenango *B*
    University Park *B, M*
    Wilkes-Barre *B*
    Worthington Scranton *B*
    York *B*
Temple University *B, M, D*

Puerto Rico
Inter American University of Puerto Rico
    Metropolitan Campus *M, D*
    San German Campus *D*
University of Puerto Rico
    Rio Piedras Campus *B*

Rhode Island
Community College of Rhode Island *A*
Providence College *C, A*
Rhode Island College *B*
University of Rhode Island *M*

Tennessee
Tennessee Technological University *B*

Texas
College of the Mainland *A*
San Antonio College *C*
University of North Texas *B, M, D*

Virginia
Norfolk State University *B*

Washington
Pacific Lutheran University *B*

West Virginia
Marshall University *M*
West Virginia University *M*

Wisconsin
Marquette University *C*
Milwaukee Area Technical College *A*
University of Wisconsin
    Madison *M, D*
    Milwaukee *M*

LAN/WAN management

Alabama
Herzing College *A, B*
ITT Technical Institute
    Birmingham *A*

Arizona
Arizona Western College *C*
Collins College *A, B*
Estrella Mountain Community
    College *C, A*

Arkansas
ITT Technical Institute
    Little Rock *A*
Phillips Community College of the
    University of Arkansas *C, A*
Rich Mountain Community College *A*
University of Arkansas
    Fort Smith *A, B*

California
Foothill College *C, A*
Grossmont Community College *C, A*
ITT Technical Institute
    San Bernardino *A*
Ohlone College *C, A*
San Diego Mesa College *C*

Santa Barbara City College *C*
Santa Rosa Junior College *C*
Westwood College of Technology
    Inland Empire *B*

Colorado
Blair Junior College *C, A*
Colorado Technical University *C*
National American University
    Denver *B*
Red Rocks Community College *C*
Westwood College of Technology
    South *B*

Florida
Cooper Career Institute *C*
Herzing College
    Orlando *C, A*
ITT Technical Institute
    Ft. Lauderdale *A, B*
    Maitland *A*
St. Petersburg College *C, A*

Illinois
Black Hawk College *C*
Moraine Valley Community College *A*
Oakton Community College *C*
Rend Lake College *A*
Robert Morris College: Chicago *C, A*
Southeastern Illinois College *A*

Indiana
ITT Technical Institute
    Fort Wayne *A*
Indiana University-Purdue University
    Fort Wayne *C*
Vincennes University *A*

Iowa
American Institute of Business *A*
Dordt College *B*
Hamilton College
    Cedar Falls *C*
Kirkwood Community College *C*
St. Ambrose University *B*
Southeastern Community College
    South Campus *A*

Kansas
Labette Community College *C, A*

Kentucky
Elizabethtown Community College *A*
Hopkinsville Community College *C, A*
Louisville Technical Institute *A*

Louisiana
Herzing College *C*
ITT Technical Institute
    St. Rose *A*
Remington College
    Baton Rouge *A*

Maine
Central Maine Technical College *A*

Massachusetts
Cape Cod Community College *A*
ITT Technical Institute
    Norwood *A*

Michigan
Alpena Community College *C, A*
Baker College
    of Muskegon *C, A*
ITT Technical Institute
    Troy *A*
Kettering University *B*

Minnesota
Capella University *C, B*
Globe College *C, A, B*
Itasca Community College *A*
Minneapolis Community and Technical
    College *C, A*
Rasmussen College
    St. Cloud *C, A*
Riverland Community College: A
    Technical and Community College *A*

Missouri
ITT Technical Institute
    Arnold *A*
Ozarks Technical Community College *A*
Ranken Technical College *A*

Montana
Montana Tech of the University of
    Montana *C, A*

Nebraska
ITT Technical Institute
    Omaha *A*

Nevada
ITT Technical Institute
    Henderson *A*

New Hampshire
Daniel Webster College *C*

New Mexico
New Mexico State University
    Alamogordo *C*
Santa Fe Community College *C*

New York
Jamestown Community College *C*
Rochester Institute of Technology *B*
State University of New York
    College of Agriculture and
        Technology at Morrisville *B*
Westchester Business Institute *A*
Westchester Community College *C, A*

North Carolina
Carteret Community College *C, A*
Davidson County Community
    College *C, A*
Miller-Motte Technical College *C, A*
Surry Community College *C, A*

North Dakota
Minot State University: Bottineau
    Campus *A*
North Dakota State College of
    Science *C, A*

Ohio
Davis College *A*
Hocking Technical College *A*
ITT Technical Institute
    Youngstown *A*
Lakeland Community College *A*
Northwest State Community College *A*
Owens Community College
    Findlay Campus *C, A*
    Toledo *C, A*
University of Findlay *B*

Oklahoma
Rose State College *A*

Oregon
Southwestern Oregon Community
    College *C*

Pennsylvania
Allentown Business School *C, A*
Consolidated School of Business
    York *A*
ITT Technical Institute
    Bensalem *A*
Keystone College *C, A, B*
Montgomery County Community
    College *C, A*
Peirce College *C, A, B*
Pennsylvania College of
    Technology *A, B*
South Hills School of Business &
    Technology *A*

Rhode Island
Community College of Rhode
    Island *C, A*

South Carolina
York Technical College *C*

South Dakota
Southeast Technical Institute *A*

Tennessee

ITT Technical Institute
    Memphis *A*
Northeast State Technical Community
    College *C*
South College *A*

Texas

Collin County Community College
    District *C, A*
Del Mar College *C, A*
ITT Technical Institute
    Austin *A*
    Houston North *A*
St. Philip's College *C, A*
Temple College *C, A*
Western Texas College *C*

Utah

LDS Business College *A*

Vermont

Champlain College *A, B*

Virginia

ECPI College of Technology *C, A*
ECPI Technical College: Roanoke *A*
Rappahannock Community College *C*

Washington

Centralia College *C, A*
Clover Park Technical College *C, A*
ITT Technical Institute
    Bothell *A*
    Seattle *A*
North Seattle Community College *C, A*
Northwest College *B*
South Seattle Community College *A*

Wisconsin

ITT Technical Institute
    Green Bay *A*
Milwaukee Area Technical College *A*
Western Wisconsin Technical College *A*

Land use planning

Georgia

Southern Polytechnic State University *C*

Louisiana

University of Louisiana at Lafayette *B*

Maine

University of Maine
    Farmington *B*

Texas

Southwest Texas State University *M*
Texas Tech University *B, D*

Landscape architecture

Alabama

Auburn University *B, M*

Arizona

Arizona State University *B*
University of Arizona *M, D*

Arkansas

University of Arkansas *B*
University of Arkansas
    Little Rock *A*

California

California State Polytechnic University:
    Pomona *B, M*
Diablo Valley College *C*
East Los Angeles College *A*
MiraCosta College *C, A*
Modesto Junior College *A*
San Diego Mesa College *C, A*
San Joaquin Delta College *C, A*
Santa Rosa Junior College *C*
Sierra College *C, A*
Southwestern College *C, A*

University of California
    Berkeley *B, M*
    Davis *B*
University of Southern California *M*
West Valley College *A*

Colorado

Colorado State University *B*
University of Colorado
    Denver *M*

Connecticut

University of Connecticut *B*

Florida

Broward Community College *A*
Florida Agricultural and Mechanical
    University *M*
Florida International University *M*
Lake City Community College *A*
University of Florida *B, M*

Georgia

University of Georgia *B, M*

Idaho

University of Idaho *B, M*

Illinois

Kishwaukee College *A*
University of Illinois
    Urbana-Champaign *B, M, D*

Indiana

Ball State University *B*
Purdue University *B*

Iowa

Iowa State University *B, M*

Kansas

Kansas State University *B, M*

Kentucky

Murray State University *A*
University of Kentucky *B*

Louisiana

Louisiana State University and
    Agricultural and Mechanical
    College *B, M*

Maine

University of Maine *B*

Maryland

Community College of Baltimore County
    Catonsville *C, A*
    Dundalk *C, A*
    Essex *C, A*
Morgan State University *M*
University of Maryland
    College Park *B*

Massachusetts

University of Massachusetts
    Amherst *B, M*

Michigan

Bay de Noc Community College *A*
Lansing Community College *A*
Michigan State University *B*
University of Michigan *M, D*

Minnesota

University of Minnesota
    Twin Cities *B, M*

Mississippi

Mississippi State University *B*

Missouri

Washington University in St. Louis *M*

Nevada

Truckee Meadows Community
    College *A*
University of Nevada
    Las Vegas *B*

New Jersey

Cumberland County College *C*

New Mexico

University of New Mexico *M*

New York

City University of New York
    City College *B*
Cornell University *B, M*
Monroe Community College *A*
Parsons School of Design *B*
State University of New York
    Buffalo *M*
    College of Agriculture and
        Technology at Morrisville *A*
    College of Environmental Science
        and Forestry *B, M*
    College of Technology at Delhi *A*

North Carolina

North Carolina Agricultural and
    Technical State University *B*
North Carolina State University *B, M*
Wake Technical Community College *A*

North Dakota

North Dakota State University *B*

Ohio

Columbus State Community College *A*
Ohio State University
    Columbus Campus *B, M*

Oklahoma

Oklahoma State University *B*
University of Oklahoma *M*

Oregon

Central Oregon Community College *A*
University of Oregon *B, M*

Pennsylvania

Keystone College *A*
Penn State
    University Park *B, M*
Temple University *B*
University of Pennsylvania *M*

Rhode Island

Rhode Island School of Design *B, M*
University of Rhode Island *B*

South Carolina

Clemson University *B*

Texas

Howard College *C*
Texas A&M University *B, M*
Texas Tech University *B, M*
University of Texas
    Arlington *M*

Utah

Utah State University *B, M*

Virginia

University of Virginia *M*
Virginia Polytechnic Institute and State
    University *B, M*

Washington

South Seattle Community College *C, A*
University of Washington *B, M*
Washington State University *B, M*

West Virginia

West Virginia University *B*

Wisconsin

University of Wisconsin
    Madison *M*

Landscaping/ groundskeeping

Alabama

James H. Faulkner State Community
    College *C, A*

Arkansas

University of Arkansas
    Little Rock *A*

California

Antelope Valley College *C, A*
California State Polytechnic University:
    Pomona *B*
College of the Redwoods *C*
College of the Sequoias *C, A*
Diablo Valley College *C*
Foothill College *C, A*
Los Angeles Pierce College *C, A*
MiraCosta College *C, A*
Modesto Junior College *C, A*
Mount San Antonio College *C*
San Joaquin Delta College *C*
Santa Barbara City College *C, A*
Santa Rosa Junior College *C*
Southwestern College *C, A*
Victor Valley College *C*
Yuba Community College District *C, A*

Colorado

Colorado State University *B*

Connecticut

Middlesex Community College *C*

Florida

Broward Community College *A*
Florida Agricultural and Mechanical
    University *B*
Gulf Coast Community College *A*
Lake City Community College *A*
Miami-Dade Community College *A*

Georgia

Albany Technical College *C*
Floyd College *A*
Gainesville College *C*
University of Georgia *B*
West Georgia Technical College *C*

Idaho

Brigham Young University - Idaho *A*

Illinois

College of DuPage *C*
College of Lake County *C, A*
Joliet Junior College *C, A*
Kishwaukee College *C, A*
McHenry County College *C*
Parkland College *A*
Southwestern Illinois College *A*
Triton College *C, A*
William Rainey Harper College *C, A*

Iowa

Iowa Lakes Community College *A*
Northeast Iowa Community College *A*
Western Iowa Tech Community
    College *C*

Kentucky

Maysville Community College *C*

Maine

University of Maine *B*
University of Maine
    Augusta *A*

Massachusetts

Springfield Technical Community
    College *C, A*
University of Massachusetts
    Amherst *A*

Michigan

Bay de Noc Community College *C*
Grand Rapids Community College *A*
Northwestern Michigan College *A*
Oakland Community College *C, A*

Minnesota

Anoka-Ramsey Community College *A*
Dakota County Technical College *C, A*
Hennepin Technical College *C, A*

Mississippi

Mississippi Gulf Coast Community
    College
    Perkinston *C*
Mississippi State University *B*

Nebraska
Central Community College *C*
Nebraska College of Technical
Agriculture *A*

Nevada
Community College of Southern
Nevada *A*

New Hampshire
New Hampshire Technical Institute *C*
University of New Hampshire *A*

New Jersey
Bergen Community College *C*

New Mexico
Albuquerque Technical-Vocational
Institute *C*
Dona Ana Branch Community College of
New Mexico State University *A*

New York
Finger Lakes Community College *C, A*
State University of New York
College of Agriculture and
Technology at Cobleskill *A*
College of Agriculture and
Technology at Morrisville *A*
College of Technology at Alfred *A*
College of Technology at Delhi *A*
Suffolk County Community
College *C, A*

North Carolina
Alamance Community College *C*
Blue Ridge Community College *C*
Cape Fear Community College *A*
North Carolina Agricultural and
Technical State University *B*
Sampson Community College *C*
Sandhills Community College *A*

North Dakota
Minot State University: Bottineau
Campus *A*

Ohio
Cincinnati State Technical and
Community College *A*
Clark State Community College *A*
Kent State University
Salem Regional Campus *A*
Ohio State University
Agricultural Technical Institute *A*
Columbus Campus *B*
Owens Community College
Toledo *A*

Oklahoma
Oklahoma State University *B*

Oregon
Central Oregon Community College *A*
Portland Community College *C, A*
Rogue Community College *C*

Pennsylvania
Community College of Allegheny
County *C, A*
Delaware Valley College *C*
Luzerne County Community
College *C, A*

Penn State
Abington *B*
Altoona *B*
Beaver *B*
Berks *B*
Delaware County *B*
Dubois *B*
Erie, The Behrend College *B*
Fayette *B*
Hazleton *B*
Lehigh Valley *B*
McKeesport *B*
Mont Alto *B*
New Kensington *B*
Schuylkill - Capital College *B*
Shenango *B*
University Park *C, B*
Wilkes-Barre *B*
Worthington Scranton *B*
York *B*
Temple University *A*
Williamson Free School of Mechanical
Trades *C*

South Carolina
Spartanburg Technical College *A*
Technical College of the Lowcountry *C*
Trident Technical College *C*

South Dakota
South Dakota State University *B*
Southeast Technical Institute *A*

Tennessee
Chattanooga State Technical Community
College *C*
Tennessee Technological University *B*
University of Tennessee
Martin *B*

Texas
Grayson County College *A*
Houston Community College System *C*
Palo Alto College *C, A*
Western Texas College *C, A*

Vermont
Vermont Technical College *A*

Virginia
J. Sargeant Reynolds Community
College *A*
Mountain Empire Community College *C*
Virginia Western Community College *A*

Washington
Clark College *C, A*
Clover Park Technical College *C, A*
Edmonds Community College *A*
South Seattle Community College *C, A*

Wisconsin
Milwaukee Area Technical College *A*

**Language interpretation/
translation**

Arizona
Pima Community College *C*

California
University of California
Santa Cruz *B*

District of Columbia
American University *C*

Florida
Barry University *C*
Gulf Coast Community College *A*
Miami-Dade Community College *C, A*

Georgia
East Georgia College *A*

Nebraska
University of Nebraska
Kearney *B*

New Jersey
Union County College *C*

New York
Bard College *B*
City University of New York
Brooklyn College *B*
New York University *M*

Ohio
Kent State University *M*
Kent State University
Stark Campus *B*
Wittenberg University *B*

Oklahoma
Oklahoma City Community College *A*

Oregon
Lewis & Clark College *B*

Pennsylvania
University of Pittsburgh *C*

Puerto Rico
University of Puerto Rico
Rio Piedras Campus *M*

South Carolina
College of Charleston *M*

Utah
Dixie State College of Utah *A*

Vermont
Bennington College *B, M, T*
Marlboro College *B*

Virginia
Shenandoah University *C*

Wisconsin
University of Wisconsin
Madison *B, M, D*

Laser/optical technology

Iowa
Indian Hills Community College *A*

New Mexico
Albuquerque Technical-Vocational
Institute *C, A*

Ohio
Kent State University *A*

Pennsylvania
Pennsylvania College of Technology *A*

South Dakota
Southeast Technical Institute *A*

Latin

Alabama
Samford University *B*

California
Loyola Marymount University *B, M*
Santa Clara University *B*
University of California
Berkeley *B, M*
Davis *B*
Los Angeles *B, M*
Santa Cruz *B*

Connecticut
Connecticut College *B*
Yale University *B*

Delaware
University of Delaware *B, M, T*

District of Columbia
Catholic University of America *B, M, T*
George Washington University *B*

Florida
Florida State University *B, M*

New College of Florida *B*
University of Florida *M*

Georgia
Emory University *B*
Oxford College of Emory University *B*
University of Georgia *B, M*

Idaho
Idaho State University *A*
University of Idaho *B*

Illinois
Augustana College *B, T*
Concordia University *B*
Loyola University of Chicago *B, M, T*
Monmouth College *B*
Rockford College *B*
University of Chicago *B*

Indiana
Butler University *B*
DePauw University *B*
Indiana University
Bloomington *B, M, D*
University of Notre Dame *B*
Wabash College *B*

Iowa
Cornell College *B, T*
Luther College *B*
University of Iowa *B, M, T*

Kansas
Wichita State University *B*

Kentucky
Asbury College *B, T*
Berea College *B, T*

Louisiana
Centenary College of Louisiana *B*
Louisiana State University and
Agricultural and Mechanical
College *B*
Tulane University *B, M*

Maine
University of Maine *B*

Maryland
Johns Hopkins University *B*
Loyola College in Maryland *B*
University of Maryland
College Park *B*

Massachusetts
Amherst College *B*
Boston College *B, M*
Boston University *B*
Brandeis University *B*
Harvard College *B*
Mount Holyoke College *B*
Simon's Rock College of Bard *B*
Smith College *B*
Tufts University *B*
Wellesley College *B*

Michigan
Aquinas College *B*
Calvin College *B, T*
Grand Valley State University *B*
Hope College *B*
Michigan State University *B, M*
University of Michigan *B, M, D, T*
Western Michigan University *B*

Minnesota
Carleton College *B*
Concordia College: Moorhead *B*
Macalester College *B*
St. Olaf College *B*
University of Minnesota
Twin Cities *B, M, D*
University of St. Thomas *B*

Missouri
Southwest Missouri State University *B*
Washington University in St. Louis *B, M*

Montana
University of Montana-Missoula *B*

Nebraska
Creighton University *B*
University of Nebraska
    Lincoln *B*

New Hampshire
St. Anselm College *T*
University of New Hampshire *B*

New Jersey
Montclair State University *B, T*
Seton Hall University *T*

New York
Bard College *B*
City University of New York
    Brooklyn College *B*
    Hunter College *B*
    Queens College *B*
Colgate University *B*
College of New Rochelle *B, T*
Columbia University
    Columbia College *B*
Cornell University *B, T*
Elmira College *B*
Fordham University *B, M, D*
Hamilton College *B*
Hobart and William Smith Colleges *B*
New York University *B*
St. Bonaventure University *B*
Sarah Lawrence College *B*
State University of New York
    Albany *B*
    Binghamton *B*
    Buffalo *B*
Syracuse University *B, M*
Vassar College *B*

North Carolina
Duke University *B*
University of North Carolina
    Greensboro *M*
Wake Forest University *B*

Ohio
Bowling Green State University *B*
College of Wooster *B*
John Carroll University *B*
Kent State University *B, M*
Kenyon College *B*
Miami University
    Oxford Campus *B, T*
Oberlin College *B*
Ohio State University
    Columbus Campus *M, D*
Ohio University *B, T*
University of Akron *B*
University of Cincinnati *B, T*
Wright State University *B*

Oregon
University of Oregon *B*

Pennsylvania
Bryn Mawr College *B, M, D*
Dickinson College *B*
Duquesne University *B*
Franklin & Marshall College *B*
Gettysburg College *B*
Haverford College *B, T*
Immaculata University *A, B*
La Salle University *B*
Swarthmore College *B*
University of Scranton *B, T*
West Chester University of
    Pennsylvania *B, M*

Puerto Rico
Pontifical Catholic University of Puerto
    Rico *B*

Rhode Island
Brown University *B*

South Carolina
Furman University *B, T*

Tennessee
Rhodes College *T*
University of Tennessee
    Chattanooga *B*
    Knoxville *B*
Vanderbilt University *M*

Texas
Austin College *B*
Austin Community College *A*
Baylor University *B*
Rice University *B*
Southwestern University *B, T*
University of Dallas *B, T*
University of Houston *B*
University of North Texas *B*
University of Texas
    Austin *B*

Vermont
Marlboro College *B*
St. Michael's College *B*
University of Vermont *B, M*

Virginia
College of William and Mary *B*
Hampden-Sydney College *B*
Mary Washington College *B*
Radford University *T*
Randolph-Macon College *B*
Randolph-Macon Woman's College *B*
Sweet Briar College *B*
University of Richmond *B, T*

Washington
Seattle Pacific University *B*
University of Washington *B*

Wisconsin
Lawrence University *B, T*
University of Wisconsin
    Madison *B, M*

Latin American studies

Alabama
Samford University *B*
University of Alabama *B, M*

Arizona
Prescott College *B, M*
University of Arizona *B, M*

California
California State University
    Chico *B*
    Fullerton *B*
    Hayward *B*
    Long Beach *C*
    Los Angeles *B, M*
    Monterey Bay *B*
Chapman University *B*
Claremont McKenna College *B*
De Anza College *C, A*
Laney College *A*
Los Angeles Pierce College *C, A*
Occidental College *B*
Pepperdine University *B*
Pitzer College *B*
Pomona College *B*
San Diego City College *A*
San Diego State University *B, M*
Scripps College *B*
Stanford University *M*
University of California
    Berkeley *B, M, D*
    Los Angeles *B, M*
    Riverside *B*
    San Diego *B, M*
    Santa Barbara *B, M*
    Santa Cruz *B*
University of Redlands *B*
University of San Francisco *M*
Whittier College *B*

Colorado
Fort Lewis College *B*

University of Denver *B*

Connecticut
Connecticut College *B*
Trinity College *B*
University of Connecticut *B*
Wesleyan University *B*
Yale University *B*

Delaware
University of Delaware *B*

District of Columbia
American University *B*
George Washington University *B, M*
Georgetown University *M*
Trinity College *B*

Florida
Flagler College *B*
Florida Atlantic University *C*
Florida International University *M*
Florida State University *B*
Manatee Community College *A*
Miami-Dade Community College *A*
Rollins College *B*
Stetson University *B*
University of Florida *M*
University of Miami *B, M*
University of South Florida *M*
University of Tampa *C*
University of West Florida *B*

Georgia
Emory University *B*
Oxford College of Emory University *B*

Idaho
University of Idaho *B*

Illinois
Blackburn College *B*
De Paul University *B*
Illinois Wesleyan University *B*
Lake Forest College *B*
University of Chicago *M*
University of Illinois
    Chicago *B*
    Urbana-Champaign *B, M*

Indiana
Earlham College *B*
Hanover College *B*
Indiana University
    Bloomington *M*

Iowa
Central College *B*
Cornell College *B*
Luther College *B*
University of Iowa *B*
University of Northern Iowa *B*

Kansas
University of Kansas *B, M*

Kentucky
University of Kentucky *B*

Louisiana
Tulane University *B, M, D*

Maine
Bowdoin College *B*
Colby College *B*

Maryland
Hood College *B*
Johns Hopkins University *B*
University of Maryland
    College Park *C*

Massachusetts
Amherst College *C*
Assumption College *B*
Boston University *B*
Brandeis University *B*
College of the Holy Cross *B*
Hampshire College *B*
Harvard College *B*
Mount Holyoke College *B*

Smith College *B*
Tufts University *B, M*
Wellesley College *B*

Michigan
Oakland University *B*
University of Michigan *B*

Minnesota
Carleton College *B*
Hamline University *B*
Macalester College *B*
St. Cloud State University *B*
St. Olaf College *B*
University of Minnesota
    Morris *B*
    Twin Cities *B*

Missouri
Washington University in St. Louis *B*

Nebraska
University of Nebraska
    Lincoln *B*

Nevada
University of Nevada
    Las Vegas *B*

New Hampshire
Dartmouth College *B*

New Jersey
Monmouth University *C*
Rutgers, The State University of New
    Jersey
    New Brunswick Regional
        Campus *B*
William Paterson University of New
    Jersey *B*

New Mexico
University of New Mexico *B, M, D*

New York
Adelphi University *B*
Bard College *B*
Barnard College *B*
City University of New York
    Brooklyn College *B*
    City College *B*
    Hunter College *B*
    Queens College *B*
Colgate University *B*
Columbia University
    Columbia College *B*
Cornell University *B*
Fordham University *B*
Hobart and William Smith Colleges *B*
Long Island University
    C. W. Post Campus *B*
New York University *B, M*
St. John's University *C*
Sarah Lawrence College *B*
State University of New York
    Albany *C, B, M*
    Binghamton *B*
    Buffalo *M*
    College at Plattsburgh *B*
    New Paltz *B*
Syracuse University *B*
United States Military Academy *B*
Vassar College *B*

North Carolina
Belmont Abbey College *B*
University of North Carolina
    Chapel Hill *B*
Wake Forest University *B*

Ohio
College of Wooster *B*
Denison University *B*
Kent State University *B*
Kent State University
    Stark Campus *B*
Oberlin College *B*
Ohio State University
    Columbus Campus *B*

Ohio University *B, M*
Pontifical College Josephinum *B*
University of Akron *C*
University of Cincinnati *B*
University of Toledo *B*

Oklahoma
University of Oklahoma *B*

Oregon
Oregon State University *C*
Portland State University *C, B*
Willamette University *B*

Pennsylvania
Albright College *B*
Bucknell University *B*
Dickinson College *C*
Gettysburg College *B*
Lock Haven University of
    Pennsylvania *B*
Penn State
    Abington *B*
    Altoona *B*
    Beaver *B*
    Berks *B*
    Delaware County *B*
    Dubois *B*
    Erie, The Behrend College *B*
    Fayette *B*
    Hazleton *B*
    Lehigh Valley *B*
    McKeesport *B*
    Mont Alto *B*
    New Kensington *B*
    Schuylkill - Capital College *B*
    Shenango *B*
    University Park *B*
    Wilkes-Barre *B*
    Worthington Scranton *B*
    York *B*
Temple University *B*
University of Pittsburgh *C*

Rhode Island
Brown University *B, M, D*
University of Rhode Island *B*

South Carolina
University of South Carolina *B*

Tennessee
Rhodes College *B*
University of Tennessee
    Knoxville *B*
Vanderbilt University *B, M*

Texas
Baylor University *B*
Palo Alto College *A*
Rice University *B*
St. Mary's University *B*
Southern Methodist University *B*
Texas A&M International University *B*
Texas Christian University *B*
Texas Tech University *B*
Trinity University *B*
University of Texas
    Austin *B, M, D*
    El Paso *B*
    Pan American *B*

Utah
Brigham Young University *B*

Vermont
Burlington College *B*
Goddard College *B*
Marlboro College *B*
Middlebury College *B*
University of Vermont *B*

Virginia
Mary Baldwin College *B*
University of Virginia *B*

Washington
Gonzaga University *B*
Seattle Pacific University *B*

University of Washington *B*
Western Washington University *B*

Wisconsin
Ripon College *B*
University of Wisconsin
    Eau Claire *B*
    Madison *B, M*

Latin teacher education

Indiana
Indiana University
    Bloomington *B, T*

Michigan
Hope College *B, T*

Missouri
Southwest Missouri State University *B*

Nebraska
Creighton University *B*

New York
City University of New York
    Hunter College *B, M, T*

Ohio
Bowling Green State University *B*
Kent State University *T*

Pennsylvania
Albright College *T*

Vermont
St. Michael's College *T*

Wisconsin
Lawrence University *T*

Law (J.D.)

Alabama
Samford University: Cumberland School
    of Law *F*
Thomas Goode Jones School of
    Law--Faulkner University *F*
University of Alabama: School of Law *F*

Arizona
Arizona State University: College of
    Law *F*
University of Arizona: College of Law *F*

Arkansas
University of Arkansas at Little Rock:
    School of Law *F*
University of Arkansas: School of Law *F*

California
California Western School of Law *F*
Golden Gate University: School of
    Law *F*
Humphreys College: School of Law *F*
John F. Kennedy University: School of
    Law *F*
Loyola Marymount University: School of
    Law *F*
McGeorge School of Law: University of
    the Pacific *F*
Pepperdine University: School of Law *F*
Santa Clara University: School of Law *F*
Southwestern University School of
    Law *F*
Stanford University: School of Law *F*
Thomas Jefferson School of Law *F*
University of California
    Hastings College of the Law *F*
University of California Berkeley: School
    of Law *F*
University of California Davis: School of
    Law *F*
University of California Los Angeles:
    School of Law *F*
University of La Verne College of Law at
    San Fernando Valley *F*

University of La Verne: School of Law *F*
University of San Diego: School of
    Law *F*
University of San Francisco: School of
    Law *F*
University of Southern California: Law
    School *F*
University of West Los Angeles: School
    of Law *F*
Western State University College of
    Law *F*
Whittier Law School *F*

Colorado
University of Colorado at Boulder:
    School of Law *F*
University of Denver: College of Law *F*

Connecticut
Quinnipiac College: School of Law *F*
University of Connecticut: School of
    Law *F*
Yale Law School *F*

Delaware
Widener University School of Law *F*

District of Columbia
American University: Washington
    College of Law *F*
Catholic University of America: School
    of Law *F*
George Washington University Law
    School *F*
Georgetown University: Law Center *F*
Howard University: School of Law *F*
University of the District of Columbia:
    School of Law *F*

Florida
Florida Coastal School of Law *F*
Florida State University: School of
    Law *F*
Nova Southeastern University: Shepard
    Broad Law Center *F*
St. Thomas University: School of Law *F*
Stetson University: College of Law *F*
University of Florida: College of Law *F*
University of Miami: School of Law *F*

Georgia
Emory University: School of Law *F*
Georgia State University: College of
    Law *F*
Mercer University: Walter F. George
    School of Law *F*
University of Georgia: School of Law *F*

Hawaii
University of Hawaii William S.
    Richardson: School of Law *F*

Idaho
University of Idaho: College of Law *F*

Illinois
Chicago-Kent College of Law, Illinois
    Institute of Technology *F*
De Paul University: College of Law *F*
John Marshall Law School *F*
John Marshall Law School *F*
Loyola University Chicago: School of
    Law *F*
Northern Illinois University: College of
    Law *F*
Northwestern University: School of
    Law *F*
Southern Illinois University at
    Carbondale: School of Law *F*
University of Chicago: School of Law *F*
University of Illinois at
    Urbana-Champaign: College of Law *F*

Indiana
Indiana University Bloomington: School
    of Law *F*
Indiana University Indianapolis: School
    of Law *F*

University of Notre Dame: School of
    Law *F*
Valparaiso University: School of Law *F*

Iowa
Drake University Law School *F*
University of Iowa: College of Law *F*

Kansas
University of Kansas: School of Law *F*
Washburn University School of Law *F*

Kentucky
Northern Kentucky University: Salmon P.
    Chase School of Law *F*
University of Kentucky: College of
    Law *F*
University of Louisville: School of
    Law *F*

Louisiana
Louisiana State University and
    Agricultural and Mechanical College:
    School of Law *F*
Loyola University: School of Law *F*
Southern University: Law Center *F*
Tulane University: School of Law *F*

Maine
University of Maine: School of Law *F*

Maryland
University of Baltimore: School of
    Law *F*
University of Maryland at Baltimore:
    School of Law *F*

Massachusetts
Boston College: Law School *F*
Boston University: School of Law *F*
Harvard University Law School *F*
New England School of Law *F*
Northeastern University: School of
    Law *F*
Suffolk University: Law School *F*
Western New England College: School of
    Law *F*

Michigan
Detroit College of Law *F*
Thomas M. Cooley Law School *F*
University of Detroit Mercy: School of
    Law *F*
University of Michigan: School of
    Law *F*
Wayne State University: School of
    Law *F*

Minnesota
Hamline University: School of Law *F*
University of Minnesota Twin Cities:
    School of Law *F*
William Mitchell College of Law: Law
    Professions *F*

Mississippi
Mississippi College: School of Law *F*
University of Mississippi: School of
    Law *F*

Missouri
St. Louis University: School of Law *F*
University of Missouri Columbia: School
    of Law *F*
University of Missouri Kansas City:
    School of Law *F*
Washington University: School of Law *F*

Montana
University of Montana: School of Law *F*

Nebraska
Creighton University: School of Law *F*
University of Nebraska Lincoln: College
    of Law *F*

New Hampshire
Franklin Pierce Law Center *F*

New Jersey

Rutgers, The State University of New Jersey
    Camden School of Law *F*
    Newark School of Law *F*
Seton Hall University: School of Law *F*

New Mexico

University of New Mexico: School of Law *F*

New York

Albany Law School of Union University *F*
Benjamin N. Cardozo School of Law *F*
Brooklyn Law School *F*
City University of New York School of Law at Queens College *F*
Columbia University School of Law *F*
Cornell University: School of Law *F*
Fordham University: School of Law *F*
Hofstra University: School of Law *F*
New York Law School *F*
New York University: School of Law *F*
Pace University Westchester: School of Law *F*
St. John's University: School of Law *F*
State University of New York at Buffalo: School of Law *F*
Syracuse University: College of Law *F*
Touro College: Jacob D. Fuchsberg Law Center *F*

North Carolina

Campbell University: Norman Adrian Wiggins School of Law *F*
Duke University: School of Law *F*
North Carolina Central University: School of Law *F*
University of North Carolina at Chapel Hill: School of Law *F*
Wake Forest University: School of Law *F*

North Dakota

University of North Dakota: School of Law *F*

Ohio

Capital University: School of Law *F*
Case Western Reserve University: School of Law *F*
Cleveland State University: College of Law *F*
Ohio Northern University: College of Law *F*
Ohio State University: College of Law *F*
University of Akron: School of Law *F*
University of Cincinnati: College of Law *F*
University of Dayton: School of Law *F*
University of Toledo: College of Law *F*

Oklahoma

Oklahoma City University: School of Law *F*
University of Oklahoma: College of Law *F*
University of Tulsa: College of Law *F*

Oregon

Lewis and Clark College: Northwestern School of Law *F*
University of Oregon: School of Law *F*
Willamette University: College of Law *F*

Pennsylvania

Dickinson School of Law *F*
Duquesne University: School of Law *F*
Temple University: School of Law *F*
University of Pennsylvania Law School *F*
University of Pittsburgh: School of Law *F*
Villanova University: School of Law *F*
Widener University School of Law *F*

Puerto Rico

Inter American University of Puerto Rico: School of Law *F*
Pontifical Catholic University of Puerto Rico: School of Law *F*
University of Puerto Rico Rio Piedras Campus: School of Law *F*

South Carolina

University of South Carolina: School of Law *F*

South Dakota

University of South Dakota: School of Law *F*

Tennessee

University of Memphis: School of Law *F*
University of Tennessee College of Law *F*
Vanderbilt University: School of Law *F*

Texas

Baylor University: School of Law *F*
St. Mary's University: School of Law *F*
South Texas College of Law *F*
Southern Methodist University: School of Law *F*
Texas Southern University: Thurgood Marshall School of Law *F*
Texas Tech University: School of Law *F*
University of Houston: Law Center *F*
University of Texas at Austin: School of Law *F*

Utah

Brigham Young University: School of Law *F*
University of Utah: College of Law *F*

Vermont

Vermont Law School *F*

Virginia

College of William and Mary: School of Law *F*
George Mason University: School of Law *F*
Regent University: School of Law *F*
University of Richmond: The T.C. Williams School of Law *F*
University of Virginia: School of Law *F*
Washington and Lee University: School of Law *F*

Washington

Gonzaga University: School of Law *F*
Seattle University: School of Law *F*
University of Washington: School of Law *F*

West Virginia

West Virginia University: College of Law *F*

Wisconsin

Marquette University: School of Law *F*
University of Wisconsin Madison: School of Law *F*

Wyoming

University of Wyoming: College of Law *F*

Law enforcement administration

Alabama

Bishop State Community College *A*
Columbia Southern University *B*
George C. Wallace State Community College
    Selma *A*
Jefferson Davis Community College *A*
Northwest-Shoals Community College *C*
Samford University *B*
Troy State University *M*

University of North Alabama *B, M*

Alaska

University of Alaska
    Fairbanks *M*
    Southeast *C*

Arizona

Arizona Western College *C*
Eastern Arizona College *A*
Pima Community College *C*
Scottsdale Community College *C, A*
University of Arizona *B*
Yavapai College *C, A*

Arkansas

East Arkansas Community College *C, A*
Northwest Arkansas Community College *A*
Ozarka College *A*

California

California State University
    Chico *B*
    Hayward *B*
    San Bernardino *M*
Citrus College *C, A*
College of the Canyons *C, A*
College of the Redwoods *C, A*
College of the Sequoias *C, A*
Copper Mountain College *C, A*
Cuesta College *C, A*
De Anza College *A*
Diablo Valley College *C*
Gavilan Community College *C*
Glendale Community College *A*
Golden West College *C, A*
Imperial Valley College *C, A*
Irvine Valley College *C, A*
Long Beach City College *C, A*
Modesto Junior College *A*
Monterey Peninsula College *C, A*
National University *B*
Ohlone College *C, A*
Palomar College *C, A*
San Diego State University *B, M*
San Jose State University *B, M*
Santa Barbara City College *C, A*
Santa Monica College *C, A*
Sonoma State University *B*
Southwestern College *C, A*
Victor Valley College *C, A*

Colorado

Arapahoe Community College *C, A*
Community College of Aurora *A*
Mesa State College *A*
Metropolitan State College of Denver *B*
Red Rocks Community College *C, A*
Trinidad State Junior College *A*
University of Colorado
    Denver *M*

Connecticut

Asnuntuck Community College *A*
Naugatuck Valley Community College *A*
Northwestern Connecticut Community College *A*
Norwalk Community College *A*
Tunxis Community College *C*
University of New Haven *B*
Western Connecticut State University *B, M*

Delaware

Delaware Technical and Community College
    Stanton/Wilmington Campus *A*

District of Columbia

George Washington University *M*
University of the District of Columbia *A*

Florida

Florida Atlantic University *M*
Florida International University *M*
Gulf Coast Community College *A*
Hillsborough Community College *A*
International College *M*

Lake City Community College *C*
Lake-Sumter Community College *A*
Okaloosa-Walton Community College *A*
Pasco-Hernando Community College *A*
Pensacola Junior College *A*
St. Petersburg College *C, A*
Seminole Community College *C, A*
South Florida Community College *A*
Tallahassee Community College *A*
Valencia Community College *A*

Georgia

Clayton College and State University *A*
Columbus State University *B, M*
Georgia College and State University *B, M*
Georgia Military College *A*
Griffin Technical College *A*
South Georgia College *A*

Hawaii

Chaminade University of Honolulu *M*
Hawaii Pacific University *A, B*
University of Hawaii
    Hawaii Community College *A*
    Honolulu Community College *A*

Idaho

Boise State University *A, B*
College of Southern Idaho *A*
Lewis-Clark State College *B*

Illinois

Aurora University *B*
Carl Sandburg College *A*
City Colleges of Chicago
    Harold Washington College *C, A*
Danville Area Community College *A*
Illinois Valley Community College *A*
Joliet Junior College *C, A*
Kaskaskia College *A*
Lewis University *M*
Lincoln College *A*
Lincoln Land Community College *C, A*
Rock Valley College *A*
Sauk Valley Community College *A*
Southeastern Illinois College *C*
Southern Illinois University
    Carbondale *B, M*
Triton College *C*
Waubonsee Community College *A*
Western Illinois University *B, M*

Indiana

Calumet College of St. Joseph *M*
Purdue University
    Calumet *B*
Taylor University: Fort Wayne *B*
University of Indianapolis *A, B*
Vincennes University *A*

Iowa

Des Moines Area Community College *A*
Ellsworth Community College *A*
Indian Hills Community College *A*
Iowa Lakes Community College *A*
Marshalltown Community College *A*
Southeastern Community College
    North Campus *A*
Western Iowa Tech Community College *A*

Kansas

Central Christian College *A, B*
Cloud County Community College *A*
Fort Scott Community College *A*
Garden City Community College *A*
Kansas City Kansas Community College *C, A*
Labette Community College *A*
Seward County Community College *A*

Kentucky

Campbellsville University *B*
Hopkinsville Community College *C*
Kentucky Wesleyan College *B*
Somerset Community College *A*
Thomas More College *A, B*

University of Louisville *B, M*

Louisiana

Southern University
    Shreveport *C, A*

Maine

Andover College *A*
Husson College *B*
Thomas College *B*
University of Maine
    Augusta *A, B*
    Presque Isle *A, B*

Maryland

Anne Arundel Community College *C, A*
Cecil Community College *C, A*
Community College of Baltimore County
    Catonsville *C, A*
    Dundalk *C, A*
    Essex *C, A*
Montgomery College
    Rockville Campus *A*
University of Baltimore *C*

Massachusetts

American International College *B, M*
Anna Maria College *M*
Becker College *B*
Berkshire Community College *A*
Boston University *M*
Cape Cod Community College *A*
Dean College *A*
Marian Court College *A*
Massachusetts Bay Community
    College *A*
Newbury College *A, B*
Northeastern University *M*
Salem State College *B*
Springfield College *B*
University of Massachusetts
    Lowell *B*
Western New England College *B, M*

Michigan

Alpena Community College *A*
Finlandia University *A*
Grand Valley State University *B, M*
Kirtland Community College *A*
Lansing Community College *A*
Mott Community College *C, A*
Muskegon Community College *A*
Northern Michigan University *A*
Northwestern Michigan College *A*
Oakland Community College *C, A*
St. Clair County Community
    College *C, A*
University of Michigan
    Flint *M*
Washtenaw Community College *A*
West Shore Community College *A*

Minnesota

Capella University *M, D*
Inver Hills Community College *A*
Minnesota State University
    Mankato *B*
Northland Community & Technical
    College *A*
St. Mary's University of Minnesota *B*
Southwest State University *B*
Vermilion Community College *A*
Winona State University *B*

Mississippi

Mississippi College *B, M*
Mississippi Valley State University *M*

Missouri

Blue River Community College *A*
Central Missouri State University *B, M*
College of the Ozarks *B*
Columbia College *A, B, M*
Hannibal-LaGrange College *B*
Jefferson College *A*
Lincoln University *A*
Lindenwood University *M*
Longview Community College *C, A*

Maple Woods Community College *C, A*
Missouri Southern State College *A, B*
Penn Valley Community College *C, A*
St. Charles Community College *A*
St. Louis Community College
    St. Louis Community College at
        Forest Park *C*
University of Missouri
    Kansas City *B, M*
Webster University *M*

Montana

Flathead Valley Community College *A*
University of Great Falls *M*

Nebraska

Bellevue University *B*
Peru State College *B*

Nevada

Great Basin College *A*
Truckee Meadows Community
    College *A*

New Hampshire

College for Lifelong Learning *B*
Hesser College *C, A, B*
New Hampshire Technical Institute *A*

New Jersey

The College of New Jersey *B*
Essex County College *A*
Kean University *B*
Middlesex County College *A*
Rutgers, The State University of New
    Jersey
        New Brunswick Regional
            Campus *B*

New Mexico

Western New Mexico University *C, B*

New York

City University of New York
    John Jay College of Criminal
        Justice *B*
Corning Community College *A*
Erie Community College
    City Campus *A*
    North Campus *A*
Genesee Community College *C, A*
Iona College *B, M*
Jefferson Community College *C, A*
Keuka College *B*
Mohawk Valley Community College *A*
Monroe Community College *C*
Nassau Community College *A*
New York Institute of Technology *B*
Pace University *B*
Pace University:
    Pleasantville/Briarcliff *B*
St. John's University *C, A, B, M*
State University of New York
    Farmingdale *C, A*

North Carolina

Alamance Community College *A*
Barton College *C*
Bladen Community College *A*
Catawba College *B*
College of the Albemarle *A*
Craven Community College *A*
Elizabeth City State University *B*
Fayetteville Technical Community
    College *C*
Forsyth Technical Community College *A*
Johnston Community College *A*
Rockingham Community College *A*
Wilson Technical Community College *C*

Ohio

Ashland University *A, B*
Bluffton College *B*
Central Ohio Technical College *A*
Clark State Community College *A*
Columbus State Community College *A*
Cuyahoga Community College
    Eastern Campus *A*
James A. Rhodes State College *A*

Kent State University
    Stark Campus *B*
Marion Technical College *A*
North Central State College *A*
Northwest State Community College *A*
Ohio Northern University *B*
Ohio University *A*
Tiffin University *A, B*
University of Akron *B*
University of Findlay *B*
Urbana University *B*
Washington State Community College *A*
Xavier University *M*
Youngstown State University *A, B, M*

Oklahoma

Eastern Oklahoma State College *A*
Northern Oklahoma College *A*
Oklahoma City University *M*
Redlands Community College *A*
Southeastern Oklahoma State
    University *B*
University of Central Oklahoma *M*

Oregon

Central Oregon Community College *A*
Chemeketa Community College *A*
Portland State University *B*
Southern Oregon University *B*
Treasure Valley Community College *A*

Pennsylvania

Chestnut Hill College *C, A, B*
Delaware Valley College *B*
Harrisburg Area Community College *A*
ICM School of Business & Medical
    Careers *A*
Lehigh Carbon Community College *A*
Marywood University *B, M*
Mercyhurst College *B, M*
Northampton County Area Community
    College *A*
Penn State
    Abington *B*
    Schuylkill - Capital College *B*
    University Park *B*
Reading Area Community College *A*
St. Vincent College *C*
University of Pittsburgh
    Greensburg *B*
    Titusville *C*
Villanova University *M*
Waynesburg College *B*

Puerto Rico

Inter American University of Puerto Rico
    Guayama Campus *B*
Universidad Metropolitana *B*
Universidad del Este *B*

Rhode Island

Salve Regina University *A, B, M*

South Carolina

Aiken Technical College *A*
Charleston Southern University *B*
The Citadel *B*
Morris College *B*
Technical College of the Lowcountry *A*
University of South Carolina *B, M*

Tennessee

Middle Tennessee State University *B, M*
Tennessee State University *M*
University of Tennessee
    Chattanooga *B, M*
    Martin *B*

Texas

Alvin Community College *C, A*
Central Texas College *C, A*
Collin County Community College
    District *C*
Concordia University at Austin *B*
Grayson County College *A*
Hill College *C, A*
Howard College *C*
Kilgore College *A*

McLennan Community College *C, A*
Midland College *A*
Sam Houston State University *M*
South Plains College *A*
Southwest Texas State University *B, M*
Sul Ross State University *M*
Texarkana College *A*
Texas A&M University
    Commerce *B*
Texas Southern University *B, M*
Trinity Valley Community College *C, A*
University of Texas
    of the Permian Basin *M*
West Texas A&M University *B*
Western Texas College *A*
Wharton County Junior College *A*

Utah

Utah Valley State College *B*

Virginia

Averett University *B*
Blue Ridge Community College *C*
Bluefield College *B*
Danville Community College *A*
Hampton University *B*
Mountain Empire Community College *A*
Rappahannock Community College *C*
Shenandoah University *B*
Thomas Nelson Community College *A*
Virginia Commonwealth
    University *B, M*
Virginia Wesleyan College *B*

Washington

Bellevue Community College *A*
Centralia College *A*
Everett Community College *A*
Lower Columbia College *A*
Olympic College *C, A*
Seattle University *B*
Spokane Community College *A*
Spokane Falls Community College *C, A*
Washington State University *B, M*

West Virginia

Fairmont State College *A, B*
Mountain State University *B, M*

Wisconsin

Lakeland College *B*
Marian College of Fond du Lac *B*
University of Wisconsin
    Platteville *B*

Wyoming

Central Wyoming College *A*
Western Wyoming Community
    College *A*

Legal administrative assistance

Alabama

George C. Wallace State Community
    College
        Dothan *C, A*
Harry M. Ayers State Technical
    College *C*
James H. Faulkner State Community
    College *A*
Lawson State Community College *A*
Northwest-Shoals Community College *C*
Samford University *C*
Trenholm State Technical College *A*
Wallace State Community College at
    Hanceville *A*

Arizona

Central Arizona College *C, A*
Cochise College *A*
Phoenix College *A*
Yavapai College *C, A*

Arkansas

Arkansas State University
    Mountain Home *C*

Pulaski Technical College *C*

California
Chabot College *A*
Coastline Community College *C*
College of the Redwoods *C, A*
Columbia College *C*
East Los Angeles College *A*
Glendale Community College *C, A*
Golden West College *C, A*
Las Positas College *C*
Long Beach City College *C, A*
Los Angeles Harbor College *C, A*
MTI College of Business and
    Technology *A*
Palomar College *C, A*
Platt College
    Ontario *C, A*
Riverside Community College *C, A*
Santa Rosa Junior College *C*
Shasta College *A*
Sierra College *C, A*
Southwestern College *C, A*
Ventura College *C, A*

Colorado
Blair Junior College *A*
Community College of Aurora *A*
Otero Junior College *A*
Red Rocks Community College *C, A*

Connecticut
Briarwood College *C, A*
Gateway Community College *A*
Gibbs College *C*
Middlesex Community College *A*
Naugatuck Valley Community College *A*
Northwestern Connecticut Community
    College *B*
Norwalk Community College *C, A*
Quinnipiac University *B*
Teikyo Post University *C, A, R*
Three Rivers Community College *A*
Tunxis Community College *C, A*

Florida
Broward Community College *A*
Cooper Career Institute *C*
Daytona Beach Community College *A*
Indian River Community College *A*
International College *B*
Miami-Dade Community College *A*
Nova Southeastern University *B*
Okaloosa-Walton Community College *A*
Pensacola Junior College *A*
St. Petersburg College *A*
Santa Fe Community College *A*
Seminole Community College *A*
University of West Florida *B*
Valencia Community College *A*

Georgia
Athens Technical College *C*
DeKalb Technical College *C*
Gainesville College *A*

Hawaii
Hawaii Business College *A*
Heald College
    Honolulu *A*

Idaho
Boise State University *A*
Idaho State University *C, A*
Lewis-Clark State College *A*
North Idaho College *A*

Illinois
College of DuPage *C, A*
Elgin Community College *C, A*
John Wood Community College *A*
Joliet Junior College *A*
Kankakee Community College *A*
Kishwaukee College *C*
Lake Land College *A*
McHenry County College *C*
Midstate College *C, A*
Moraine Valley Community College *C*

Robert Morris College: Chicago *C, A*
Rockford Business College *C, A*
Sauk Valley Community College *C, A*
Shawnee Community College *A*
William Rainey Harper College *C, A*

Indiana
Indiana Business College *A*
Indiana Business College
    Terre Haute *C*
Michiana College *A*
Professional Careers Institute *A*
Sawyer College *C, A*
Vincennes University *A*

Iowa
American Institute of Business *A*
Des Moines Area Community
    College *C, A*
Ellsworth Community College *A*
Hamilton College
    Cedar Falls *A*
Iowa Western Community College *A*
Kirkwood Community College *C, A*
North Iowa Area Community
    College *C, A*
Northeast Iowa Community College *A*
Western Iowa Tech Community
    College *A*

Kansas
Dodge City Community College *C, A*
Fort Scott Community College *A*
Independence Community College *C, A*
Labette Community College *A*
Pratt Community College *C, A*
Seward County Community
    College *C, A*
Washburn University of Topeka *C, A*

Kentucky
Daymar College *A*
National College of Business &
    Technology
    Lexington *A*
    Pikeville *A*
Sullivan University *C, A*

Maine
Andover College *C, A*
Beal College *A*

Maryland
Allegany College *C*
Community College of Baltimore County
    Catonsville *A*
    Dundalk *A*
    Essex *A*
Frederick Community College *C, A*
Howard Community College *C, A*
Villa Julie College *A*

Massachusetts
Atlantic Union College *A*
Bay State College *A*
Boston University *B*
Cape Cod Community College *C, A*
Marian Court College *C, A*
Massasoit Community College *A*
Quinsigamond Community College *A*
Roxbury Community College *A*

Michigan
Baker College
    of Auburn Hills *A*
    of Cadillac *A*
    of Jackson *A*
    of Owosso *A*
    of Port Huron *A*
Davenport University
    Eastern Region *A*
Davenport University - Western
    Region *A*
Gogebic Community College *A*
Grand Rapids Community College *A*
Kellogg Community College *A*
Kirtland Community College *A*
Lansing Community College *A*

Madonna University *C, A, B*
Mid Michigan Community College *A*
Monroe County Community
    College *C, A*
Mott Community College *C, A*
Muskegon Community College *A*
Northern Michigan University *A*
Northwestern Michigan College *C*
Oakland Community College *C, A*
St. Clair County Community College *A*

Minnesota
Alexandria Technical College *C, A*
Anoka-Ramsey Community College *A*
Fergus Falls Community College *C*
Globe College *C, A*
Hennepin Technical College *C, A*
Hibbing Community College: A
    Technical and Community College *A*
Inver Hills Community College *C, A*
Lake Superior College: A Community
    and Technical College *C, A*
Minnesota State College - Southeast
    Technical *C, A*
Rasmussen College
    Mankato *C*
    Minnetonka *C, A*
    St. Cloud *C*
Ridgewater College: A Community and
    Technical College *C, A*
Riverland Community College: A
    Technical and Community
    College *C, A*
Rochester Community and Technical
    College *A*
St. Cloud Technical College *C, A*
South Central Technical College *A*
Winona State University *B*

Mississippi
Northwest Mississippi Community
    College *A*
Pearl River Community College *C, A*

Missouri
East Central College *C, A*
Hickey College *C, A*
Longview Community College *C*
Maple Woods Community College *C*
Penn Valley Community College *C*
St. Louis Community College
    St. Louis Community College at
    Meramec *A*
Springfield College *A*

Montana
Flathead Valley Community College *A*
Miles Community College *A*
University of Montana-Missoula *A*

Nebraska
Lincoln School of Commerce *C, A*
Midland Lutheran College *A*
Northeast Community College *A*
Southeast Community College
    Beatrice Campus *A*

Nevada
Community College of Southern
    Nevada *C, A*
Great Basin College *C*
Morrison University *C, A*
Truckee Meadows Community
    College *A*

New Hampshire
New Hampshire Community Technical
    College
    Nashua *C*

New Jersey
Gloucester County College *A*
Warren County Community College *C*

New Mexico
Albuquerque Technical-Vocational
    Institute *A*
Clovis Community College *A*

Dona Ana Branch Community College of
    New Mexico State University *A*
New Mexico Junior College *C, A*
San Juan College *A*
Western New Mexico University *C, A*

New York
Briarcliffe College *A*
Bryant & Stratton Business Institute
    Albany *A*
    Rochester *A*
    Syracuse *A*
City University of New York
    Kingsborough Community
    College *A*
    La Guardia Community College *A*
Clinton Community College *C*
Dutchess Community College *C, A*
Elmira Business Institute *C, A*
Fulton-Montgomery Community
    College *A*
Genesee Community College *C*
Jamestown Business College *A*
Katharine Gibbs School
    Melville *A*
Long Island Business Institute *C*
Nassau Community College *A*
Olean Business Institute *C*
Rochester Business Institute *A*
State University of New York
    College of Technology at Delhi *A*
Trocaire College *A*
Ulster County Community College *C, A*
Utica School of Commerce *C, A*
Westchester Community College *A*

North Carolina
Alamance Community College *C, A*
Carteret Community College *A*
Central Carolina Community College *A*
Central Piedmont Community College *A*
Cleveland Community College *A*
Craven Community College *C, A*
Gaston College *A*
King's College *A*
Nash Community College *A*
Piedmont Community College *A*
Rockingham Community College *A*
South Piedmont Community
    College *C, A*
Wake Technical Community College *A*
Wayne Community College *A*
Western Piedmont Community
    College *C, A*

North Dakota
Bismarck State College *C, A*
Dickinson State University *A*
Lake Region State College *C, A*

Ohio
Academy of Court Reporting *C*
Academy of Court Reporting
    Akron *A*
    Columbus *C*
Bradford School *C, A*
Bryant & Stratton College
    Cleveland West *C, A*
Clark State Community College *A*
Columbus State Community College *A*
David N. Myers College *A, B*
Davis College *A*
ETI Technical College of Niles *A*
Edison State Community College *A*
James A. Rhodes State College *A*
Jefferson Community College *A*
Kent State University
    Trumbull Campus *A*
North Central State College *A*
Northwest State Community College *A*
Notre Dame College *C, B*
Ohio Business College: Sandusky *A*
Ohio University
    Chillicothe Campus *A*
Shawnee State University *A*
Sinclair Community College *A*
Southeastern Business College *A*

Southwestern College of Business *C*
Stark State College of Technology *A*
Stautzenberger College *A*
Trumbull Business College *A*
University of Akron *C, A*
University of Cincinnati
    Clermont College *C, A*
University of Northwestern Ohio *A*
University of Toledo *A, B*
Wright State University: Lake Campus *A*
Youngstown State University *A*

Oklahoma

Eastern Oklahoma State College *A*
Metropolitan College *A*
Northeastern Oklahoma Agricultural and
    Mechanical College *C, A*
Oklahoma State University
    Okmulgee *A*
Rose State College *A*
Tulsa Community College *C, A*

Oregon

Chemeketa Community College *A*
Clatsop Community College *A*
Lane Community College *A*
Linn-Benton Community College *A*
Mount Hood Community College *A*
Portland Community College *A*
Rogue Community College *C*
Southwestern Oregon Community
    College *C*
Treasure Valley Community College *A*
Umpqua Community College *A*

Pennsylvania

Bucks County Community College *A*
Butler County Community College *A*
Cambria-Rowe Business College *A*
Central Pennsylvania College *A*
Churchman Business School *A*
Consolidated School of Business
    Lancaster *C, A*
    York *C, A*
DuBois Business College *A*
DuBois Business College
    Oil City *A*
Erie Business Center *A*
Harrisburg Area Community College *A*
ICM School of Business & Medical
    Careers *A*
Lehigh Carbon Community College *A*
Luzerne County Community College *C*
Manor College *C, A*
Marywood University *C, A, B*
Mercyhurst College *C, A*
Newport Business Institute *A*
Northampton County Area Community
    College *C, A*
PJA School *C*
Penn State
    University Park *C*
Reading Area Community College *C, A*
South Hills School of Business &
    Technology *A*
South Hills School of Business and
    Technology *A*
Westmoreland County Community
    College *A*

Puerto Rico

Universidad Metropolitana *A, B*
Universidad del Este *C*
University of Puerto Rico
    Bayamon University College *A, B*

Rhode Island

Community College of Rhode
    Island *C, A*
Providence College *C, A, B*

South Carolina

Forrest Junior College *A*
York Technical College *C*

South Dakota

Western Dakota Technical Institute *C*

Tennessee

South College *C*

Texas

Alvin Community College *A*
Austin Community College *C, A*
Blinn College *C*
Brookhaven College *A*
Cedar Valley College *A*
Del Mar College *A*
Eastfield College *A*
El Centro College *C*
El Paso Community College *C*
Frank Phillips College *C, A*
Grayson County College *C*
Kilgore College *A*
Lamar State College at Port Arthur *A*
Laredo Community College *C*
McLennan Community College *A*
Midland College *C, A*
North Central Texas College *A*
North Harris Montgomery Community
    College District *C, A*
Northeast Texas Community
    College *C, A*
Richland College *A*
St. Philip's College *A*
San Antonio College *A*
South Plains College *A*
South Texas Community College *A*
Southwest Texas State University *M*
Texas A&M University
    Commerce *B*
Texas Wesleyan University *C*
Trinity Valley Community College *C, A*
Tyler Junior College *A*

Utah

LDS Business College *A*

Vermont

Burlington College *C*
Champlain College *C, A, B*

Virginia

Blue Ridge Community College *C*
Bryant & Stratton College *A*
Danville Community College *C*
J. Sargeant Reynolds Community
    College *C*
Mountain Empire Community College *A*
Rappahannock Community College *C*
Southwest Virginia Community
    College *C*
Tidewater Tech *D*
Virginia Highlands Community
    College *C, A*
Virginia Western Community College *A*

Washington

Centralia College *C, A*
Clark College *C, A*
Clover Park Technical College *C, A*
Edmonds Community College *A*
Everett Community College *C*
Grays Harbor College *C*
Green River Community College *A*
Lake Washington Technical College *C, A*
Lower Columbia College *A*
Olympic College *C, A*
Renton Technical College *C*
Spokane Community College *C, A*
Walla Walla Community College *C, A*
Wenatchee Valley College *C*

West Virginia

Bluefield State College *A*
Glenville State College *A*
Huntington Junior College *C, A*
Mountain State College *A*
Mountain State University *A*
Valley College of Technology *C*
West Virginia Business College *A*
West Virginia State College *A*
West Virginia University Institute of
    Technology *A*

Wisconsin

Blackhawk Technical College *A*
Bryant & Stratton College *A*
Fox Valley Technical College *A*
Milwaukee Area Technical College *A*
Moraine Park Technical College *A*

Wyoming

Western Wyoming Community
    College *C, A*

Legal studies

Alabama

Faulkner University *A*
South University *B*
University of Alabama *M, D*

Alaska

Charter College *C, A*

Arkansas

University of Arkansas *M*

California

California State University
    Chico *B*
    Long Beach *C*
Chapman University *B*
Claremont McKenna College *B*
Grossmont Community College *C, A*
MTI College of Business and
    Technology *C*
Mills College *B*
National University *B*
Pepperdine University *M*
St. Mary's College of California *B*
Santa Barbara City College *A*
Scripps College *B*
Stanford University *M, D*
Thomas Jefferson School of Law *D*
University of California
    Berkeley *B, M, D*
    Riverside *B*
    Santa Barbara *B*
    Santa Cruz *B*
University of La Verne *D*
University of San Diego *M*
University of Southern California *D*
University of West Los Angeles *D*
Western State University College of
    Law *D*

Colorado

United States Air Force Academy *B*
University of Denver *B*

Connecticut

Quinnipiac University *B, M*
University of Connecticut *M, D*
University of New Haven *B*
Yale University *M, D*

District of Columbia

American University *B, M*
Catholic University of America *M, D*
George Washington University *M, D*
Howard University *M*

Florida

Barry University *B, M, D*
Florida Agricultural and Mechanical
    University *D*
Gulf Coast Community College *A*
Manatee Community College *A*
Nova Southeastern University *B*
Palm Beach Atlantic University *B*
Southwest Florida College *A*
University of Central Florida *B*
University of Miami *B, M*
University of West Florida *B*

Georgia

Brenau University *B*
Georgia State University *D*
South University *B*
University of Georgia *M*

Hawaii

Hawaii Business College *C*

Idaho

Lewis-Clark State College *B*

Illinois

City Colleges of Chicago
    Harold Washington College *A*
    Olive-Harvey College *A*
Illinois Institute of Technology *M, D*
Illinois Valley Community College *A*
Loyola University of Chicago *M, D*
Roosevelt University *B*

Indiana

Indiana University
    Bloomington *M, D*
Indiana University-Purdue University
    Fort Wayne *B*
Indiana University-Purdue University
    Indianapolis *M, D*
Michiana College: Fort Wayne *A*
St. Mary-of-the-Woods College *C*
University of Evansville *B*

Iowa

Drake University *B*
University of Iowa *M*

Kansas

University of Kansas *D*

Kentucky

Daymar College
    Louisville *C*

Louisiana

Loyola University New Orleans *D*
Tulane University *M, D*

Maine

University of Southern Maine *M*

Maryland

College of Southern Maryland *A*
University of Baltimore *M*

Massachusetts

Bay Path College *B*
Becker College *B*
Boston University *M*
Bridgewater State College *B*
Elms College *B*
Fisher College *A*
Hampshire College *B*
Lasell College *B*
Mount Ida College *B*
Newbury College *B*
Northeastern University *M, D*
Suffolk University *A, B, D*
University of Massachusetts
    Amherst *B*
    Boston *B*
Worcester Polytechnic Institute *B*

Michigan

Grand Rapids Community College *A*
Grand Valley State University *B*
Wayne State University *M*

Minnesota

Hamline University *B, M*
Minnesota School of Business *A*
Minnesota School of Business: Brooklyn
    Center *A*
University of St. Thomas *D*
Winona State University *B*

Mississippi

Mississippi College *D*

Missouri

Northwest Missouri State University *B*
University of Missouri
    Columbia *M*
    Kansas City *M, D*
Webster University *B, M*
William Woods University *B*

Nebraska
University of Nebraska
Lincoln *M, D*

Nevada
Heritage College *A*
University of Nevada
Las Vegas *D*

New Hampshire
Hesser College *C, A*

New Jersey
Montclair State University *M*
Ramapo College of New Jersey *B*
Warren County Community College *A*

New Mexico
Albuquerque Technical-Vocational
Institute *C*
Clovis Community College *A*

New York
City University of New York
John Jay College of Criminal
Justice *B*
Cornell University *M*
Hofstra University *D*
Marymount College of Fordham
University *B*
Mildred Elley *C, A*
New York University *M, D*
Pace University:
Pleasantville/Briarcliff *M*
Sage College of Albany *A, B*
St. John's University *M, D*
State University of New York
College at Fredonia *B*
Syracuse University *D*
Touro College *M*
United States Military Academy *B*

North Carolina
Duke University *D*
King's College *A*
Livingstone College *B*
North Carolina Wesleyan College *B*

North Dakota
University of North Dakota *D*

Ohio
Academy of Court Reporting
Akron *C*
Franciscan University of Steubenville *B*
Ohio Dominican College *A*
RETS Tech Center *A*
University of Findlay *B*
University of Toledo *C, B, D*

Oklahoma
Metropolitan College *A, B*
University of Oklahoma *D*
University of Oklahoma: College of
Law *D*
University of Tulsa *B, D*

Oregon
Rogue Community College *A*
Western Business College *A*

Pennsylvania
Arcadia University *B*
DeSales University *B*
Dickinson College *C*
Pennsylvania College of
Technology *A, B*
Point Park College *B*
St. Joseph's University *A, B*
Temple University *B, M*
University of Pittsburgh *C, B*
University of Pittsburgh: School of
Law *D*
Villanova University *M*
Western School of Health and Business
Careers *C, A*
Widener University *M, D*
Widener University School of Law *D*
Wilson College *C, A, B*

Puerto Rico
Pontifical Catholic University of Puerto
Rico *B, M*
Universidad Metropolitana *C*
University of Puerto Rico
Rio Piedras Campus *M*

Tennessee
Draughons Junior College: Clarksville *A*
Jackson State Community College *A*
South College *B*
Vanderbilt University *D*

Texas
Baylor University *D*
Brazosport College *A*
Central Texas College *A*
Southern Methodist University *M, D*
Southwest Texas State University *M*
Texas Southern University *D*
Texas Tech University *D*
University of Houston *M, D*
University of Texas
Austin *M*

Utah
Brigham Young University *B*

Vermont
Burlington College *B*
Woodbury College *C, A, B*

Virginia
College of William and Mary *M*
George Mason University *M, D*

Washington
Edmonds Community College *C, A*
Gonzaga University *M*
Northwest College *C*
University of Washington *M, D*

West Virginia
Mountain State University *B*
West Virginia Junior College *A*
West Virginia University *M*

Wisconsin
University of Wisconsin
Superior *C, B*

Liberal arts/sciences

Alabama
Alabama Southern Community
College *A*
Athens State University *B*
Auburn University at Montgomery *B, M*
Bevill State Community College *A*
Bishop State Community College *A*
Calhoun Community College *A*
Central Alabama Community College *A*
Chattahoochee Valley Community
College *A*
Enterprise State Junior College *A*
Faulkner University *A, B*
Gadsden State Community College *A*
George C. Wallace State Community
College
Dothan *A*
Selma *A*
Huntingdon College *A, B*
Jacksonville State University *B, M*
James H. Faulkner State Community
College *A*
Jefferson Davis Community College *A*
Jefferson State Community College *A*
Lawson State Community College *A*
Lurleen B. Wallace Junior College *A*
Marion Military Institute *A*
Northeast Alabama Community
College *A*
Northwest-Shoals Community College *A*
Oakwood College *B*
Shelton State Community College *A*
Snead State Community College *A*
Spring Hill College *M*

Troy State University Dothan *A*
Troy State University in
Montgomery *A, B*
University of Mobile *A, B*
University of North Alabama *B*
Virginia College *A*
Wallace State Community College at
Hanceville *A*

Alaska
Alaska Pacific University *B*
Prince William Sound Community
College *A*
Sheldon Jackson College *B*
University of Alaska
Anchorage *B*
Fairbanks *A, B*
Southeast *A, B*

Arizona
Central Arizona College *A*
Cochise College *A*
Eastern Arizona College *A*
Estrella Mountain Community College *A*
Gateway Community College *A*
Northern Arizona University *B*
Paradise Valley Community College *A*
Phoenix College *A*
Pima Community College *C, A*
Prescott College *B, M*
South Mountain Community College *A*
University of Arizona *B*
Yavapai College *A*

Arkansas
Arkansas State University
Beebe *A*
Mountain Home *A*
Arkansas Tech University *M*
Crowley's Ridge College *A*
Harding University *B*
Henderson State University *M*
Hendrix College *B*
John Brown University *B*
Mississippi County Community
College *A*
North Arkansas College *A*
Northwest Arkansas Community
College *A*
Ouachita Technical College *A*
Ozarka College *A*
Phillips Community College of the
University of Arkansas *A*
Pulaski Technical College *A*
Rich Mountain Community College *A*
South Arkansas Community College *A*
Southeast Arkansas College *A*
Southern Arkansas University *A*
University of Arkansas
Community College at Batesville *A*
Community College at Hope *A*
Cossatot Community College of the
A
Fort Smith *A, B*
Little Rock *A, B*
Monticello *A*
Pine Bluff *B*
University of Central Arkansas *B*
Williams Baptist College *A, B*

California
Antelope Valley College *A*
Antioch Southern California
Los Angeles *B*
Santa Barbara *B*
Azusa Pacific University *B*
Bakersfield College *A*
Barstow College *A*
Bethany College *A, B, T*
Biola University *B*
Cabrillo College *A*
California Baptist University *B*
California Institute of Technology *B*
California Polytechnic State University:
San Luis Obispo *B*
California State Polytechnic University:
Pomona *B*

California State University
Bakersfield *B*
Chico *B*
Dominguez Hills *B, M*
Fullerton *B*
Hayward *B*
Long Beach *B*
Los Angeles *B*
Monterey Bay *B*
Northridge *B*
Sacramento *B*
San Bernardino *B*
San Marcos *B*
Stanislaus *B*
Cerritos Community College *A*
Cerro Coso Community College *A*
Chabot College *A*
Chapman University *B*
Citrus College *A*
Coastline Community College *A*
College of Alameda *A*
College of Marin: Kentfield *A*
College of the Canyons *A*
College of the Redwoods *A*
College of the Sequoias *A*
College of the Siskiyous *A*
Columbia College *A*
Concordia University *B*
Contra Costa College *A*
Cuesta College *A*
Cuyamaca College *A*
De Anza College *A*
Deep Springs College *A*
Diablo Valley College *A*
Dominican University of California *B, M*
Feather River College *A*
Foothill College *A*
Fresno Pacific University *A, B*
Gavilan Community College *A*
Glendale Community College *A*
Golden West College *A*
Grossmont Community College *A*
Holy Names College *B*
Hope International University *A*
Humboldt State University *B*
Imperial Valley College *A*
Irvine Valley College *A*
John F. Kennedy University *B*
La Sierra University *B*
Laney College *A*
Las Positas College *A*
Long Beach City College *A*
Los Angeles Harbor College *A*
Los Angeles Pierce College *A*
Los Angeles Southwest College *A*
Los Angeles Trade and Technical
College *A*
Los Medanos College *A*
Loyola Marymount University *B*
Marymount College *A*
Master's College *B*
Menlo College *B*
Mills College *B, M*
MiraCosta College *A*
Modesto Junior College *A*
Monterey Peninsula College *A*
Moorpark College *A*
Mount St. Mary's College *A*
Mount San Antonio College *A*
Mount San Jacinto College *A*
Napa Valley College *A*
National Hispanic University *C, A, B*
National University *A, B*
Occidental College *B*
Ohlone College *A*
Orange Coast College *A*
Palomar College *A*
Patten University *B*
Pepperdine University *B*
Pitzer College *B*
Point Loma Nazarene University *B*
Reedley College *A*
St. Mary's College of California *B, M*
San Diego City College *A*
San Diego Mesa College *C, A*

San Diego State University *B, M*
San Francisco State University *B, M*
San Joaquin Delta College *A*
San Jose State University *B*
Santa Barbara City College *A*
Santa Clara University *B*
Santa Monica College *A*
Santa Rosa Junior College *A*
Santiago Canyon College *A*
Sierra College *A*
Simpson College *A, B*
Sonoma State University *B*
Southwestern College *A*
Stanford University *B, M, D*
Taft College *A*
Thomas Aquinas College *B*
University of California
   Riverside *B*
   Santa Barbara *B*
University of La Verne *B*
University of Redlands *B*
University of San Diego *B*
University of San Francisco *B*
University of Southern
   California *B, M, D*
Vanguard University of Southern
   California *B*
Ventura College *A*
Victor Valley College *A*
West Valley College *A*
Whittier College *B*
Yuba Community College District *A*

Colorado

Arapahoe Community College *A*
Colorado Christian University *A, B*
Colorado College *B*
Colorado Mountain College
   Alpine Campus *A*
   Spring Valley Campus *A*
   Timberline Campus *A*
Colorado State University *B*
Fort Lewis College *B*
Front Range Community College *A*
Mesa State College *A, B*
Morgan Community College *A*
Otero Junior College *A*
Red Rocks Community College *A*
Regis University *M*
Trinidad State Junior College *A*
United States Air Force Academy *B*
University of Colorado
   Denver *B*
University of Denver *M*

Connecticut

Albertus Magnus College *A, B, M*
Asnuntuck Community College *A*
Briarwood College *A*
Capital Community College *A*
Charter Oak State College *A, B*
Connecticut College *B*
Eastern Connecticut State
   University *A, B*
Gateway Community College *A*
Housatonic Community College *A*
Manchester Community College *A*
Middlesex Community College *A*
Mitchell College *A, B*
Naugatuck Valley Community College *A*
Northwestern Connecticut Community
   College *A*
Norwalk Community College *A*
Quinebaug Valley Community College *A*
Sacred Heart University *A, B*
Southern Connecticut State
   University *A, B*
Teikyo Post University *A, B*
Three Rivers Community College *A*
Tunxis Community College *A*
University of Bridgeport *A, B*
University of Connecticut *B*
University of Hartford *A*
University of New Haven *A, B*
Wesleyan University *B, M*

Western Connecticut State
   University *A, B*
Yale University *B, M, D*

Delaware

University of Delaware *B, M, D*
Wilmington College *A, B*

District of Columbia

American University *A, B*
Catholic University of America *B*
George Washington University *B*
Georgetown University *B, M*
Strayer University *A*
Trinity College *B*

Florida

Barry University *B, M*
Beacon College *A, B*
Bethune-Cookman College *B*
Broward Community College *A*
Chipola Junior College *A*
Daytona Beach Community College *A*
Eckerd College *B*
Florida Agricultural and Mechanical
   University *A*
Florida Atlantic University *A, B, M*
Florida College *A, B*
Florida Gulf Coast University *A, B*
Florida International University *B*
Florida Keys Community College *A*
Florida Southern College *B*
Florida State University *A, B, M, D*
Gulf Coast Community College *A*
Hillsborough Community College *A*
Indian River Community College *A*
Jacksonville University *B*
Lake City Community College *A*
Lake-Sumter Community College *A*
Manatee Community College *A*
Miami-Dade Community College *A*
New College of Florida *B*
Nova Southeastern University *B*
Palm Beach Community College *A*
Pasco-Hernando Community College *A*
Pensacola Junior College *A*
Polk Community College *A*
St. Leo University *A*
St. Petersburg College *A*
St. Thomas University *B*
Santa Fe Community College *A*
Schiller International University *A*
Seminole Community College *A*
South Florida Community College *A*
Tallahassee Community College *A*
University of Central Florida *A, B, M*
University of Florida *A*
University of Miami *B, M*
University of North Florida *A, B*
University of South Florida *B, M*
University of Tampa *A, B*
University of West Florida *A, B*
Valencia Community College *A*
Warner Southern College *A*

Georgia

Abraham Baldwin Agricultural
   College *A*
Andrew College *A*
Atlanta Metropolitan College *A*
Augusta State University *A*
Bainbridge College *A*
Brenau University *B*
Clark Atlanta University *M, D*
Clayton College and State University *A*
Coastal Georgia Community College *A*
Columbus State University *A*
Dalton State College *A*
Darton College *A*
East Georgia College *A*
Emmanuel College *A*
Emory University *A*
Floyd College *A*
Fort Valley State University *A*
Gainesville College *A*
Georgia College and State University *B*
Georgia State University *M*

Gordon College *A*
LaGrange College *A*
Macon State College *A*
Mercer University *B*
Middle Georgia College *A*
Oglethorpe University *B*
Oxford College of Emory University *B*
Reinhardt College *A, B*
Shorter College *B*
South Georgia College *A*
Southern Polytechnic State
   University *A, B*
State University of West Georgia *B*
Thomas University *A, B*
Toccoa Falls College *A*
Truett-McConnell College *A*
University of Georgia *B*
Valdosta State University *B*
Waycross College *A*
Wesleyan College *B*
Young Harris College *A*

Hawaii

Chaminade University of Honolulu *A, B*
Hawaii Pacific University *B*
Hawaii Tokai International College *A*
University of Hawaii
   Hawaii Community College *A*
   Hilo *B*
   Honolulu Community College *A*
   Kauai Community College *A*
   Leeward Community College *C, A*
   West Oahu *B*

Idaho

Boise State University *B*
Brigham Young University - Idaho *A*
College of Southern Idaho *A*
Idaho State University *A, B*
Lewis-Clark State College *A, B*
North Idaho College *A*
Northwest Nazarene University *B*
University of Idaho *B*

Illinois

Augustana College *B*
Aurora University *B*
Black Hawk College *A*
Black Hawk College
   East Campus *A*
Bradley University *B, M*
City Colleges of Chicago
   Harold Washington College *A*
   Kennedy-King College *A*
   Malcolm X College *A*
   Olive-Harvey College *A*
   Richard J. Daley College *C, A*
   Wright College *A*
College of DuPage *A*
College of Lake County *C, A*
Columbia College Chicago *B*
Danville Area Community College *A*
De Paul University *B, M*
East-West University *A, B*
Eastern Illinois University *B*
Elgin Community College *A*
Elmhurst College *B*
Eureka College *B*
Governors State University *B*
Greenville College *B*
Heartland Community College *A*
Illinois Central College *A*
Illinois Eastern Community Colleges
   Frontier Community College *A*
   Lincoln Trail College *A*
   Olney Central College *A*
   Wabash Valley College *A*
Illinois State University *B*
John A. Logan College *A*
John Wood Community College *A*
Joliet Junior College *A*
Kankakee Community College *A*
Kaskaskia College *A*
Kendall College *B*
Kishwaukee College *A*
Lake Forest College *M*

Lake Land College *A*
Lewis University *B*
Lewis and Clark Community College *A*
Lincoln College *A*
Lincoln Land Community College *A*
Loyola University of Chicago *B, M*
McHenry County College *A*
Monmouth College *B*
Moraine Valley Community College *A*
National-Louis University *B*
North Central College *B, M*
North Park University *B*
Northeastern Illinois University *B*
Northern Illinois University *B*
Northwestern University *C, B, M*
Oakton Community College *A*
Olivet Nazarene University *B*
Parkland College *A*
Prairie State College *A*
Rend Lake College *A*
Richland Community College *A*
Rock Valley College *A*
Rockford College *B*
Roosevelt University *B, M*
St. Augustine College *A*
St. Xavier University *B, M*
Sauk Valley Community College *A*
Shawnee Community College *A*
Shimer College *B*
South Suburban College of Cook
   County *A*
Southeastern Illinois College *A*
Southern Illinois University
   Carbondale *B*
Southern Illinois University
   Edwardsville *B*
Southwestern Illinois College *A*
Spoon River College *A*
Springfield College in Illinois *A*
Triton College *A*
University of Chicago *B, M*
University of Illinois
   Chicago *B*
   Springfield *B, M*
   Urbana-Champaign *B*
University of St. Francis *B*
Waubonsee Community College *A*
Western Illinois University *B*
William Rainey Harper College *A*

Indiana

Ancilla College *A*
Ball State University *A, B*
Bethel College *A, B*
Butler University *A, B*
Calumet College of St. Joseph *A, B*
Goshen College *B*
Holy Cross College *A*
Indiana State University *A*
Indiana University
   Bloomington *A, B*
   East *A*
   Kokomo *A, B*
   Northwest *A*
   South Bend *A, M*
   Southeast *A, M*
Indiana University-Purdue University
   Fort Wayne *M*
Indiana University-Purdue University
   Indianapolis *A, B*
Ivy Tech State College
   Bloomington *C*
   Central Indiana *C, A*
   Columbus *C*
   Eastcentral *C, A*
   Kokomo *C*
   Lafayette *C, A*
   Northcentral *C*
   Northeast *C*
   Northwest *C, A*
   Southcentral *C*
   Southeast *C*
   Southwest *C, A*
   Wabash Valley *C*
   Whitewater *C*
Manchester College *B*

Marian College *A*
Martin University *B*
Oakland City University *A, B*
Purdue University *B*
Purdue University
　Calumet *B*
　North Central Campus *B*
Saint Mary's College *B*
Taylor University *A*
Taylor University: Fort Wayne *A*
University of Indianapolis *A*
University of Notre Dame *B*
University of St. Francis *B*
University of Southern Indiana *B, M*
Valparaiso University *B*
Vincennes University *A*
Wabash College *B*

Iowa
Briar Cliff University *A, B*
Central College *B*
Clarke College *A*
Clinton Community College *A*
Des Moines Area Community College *A*
Dordt College *B*
Ellsworth Community College *A*
Franciscan University *A, B*
Graceland University *B*
Grand View College *A, B*
Hawkeye Community College *A*
Indian Hills Community College *A*
Iowa Central Community College *A*
Iowa Lakes Community College *A*
Iowa State University *B*
Iowa Western Community College *A*
Kirkwood Community College *A*
Loras College *A, B*
Marshalltown Community College *A*
Mount Mercy College *B*
Muscatine Community College *A*
North Iowa Area Community College *A*
Northwest Iowa Community College *A*
Northwestern College *B*
Simpson College *B, T*
Southeastern Community College
　North Campus *A*
　South Campus *A*
Southwestern Community College *A*
University of Iowa *B*
University of Northern Iowa *B*
Upper Iowa University *A*
Waldorf College *A, B*
Western Iowa Tech Community
　College *A*
William Penn University *B*

Kansas
Barton County Community College *A*
Benedictine College *B*
Bethany College *B*
Butler County Community College *A*
Central Christian College *A, B*
Cloud County Community College *A*
Emporia State University *B*
Fort Scott Community College *A*
Friends University *A, B*
Garden City Community College *A*
Haskell Indian Nations University *A*
Hesston College *A*
Hutchinson Community College *A*
Independence Community College *A*
Johnson County Community College *A*
Kansas City Kansas Community
　College *A*
Kansas State University *B*
Labette Community College *A*
McPherson College *B*
MidAmerica Nazarene University *A*
Newman University *A, B*
Pittsburg State University *B*
Pratt Community College *A*
St. Mary College *A, B*
Seward County Community College *A*
Southwestern College *B*
Tabor College *A*
University of Kansas *B*

Washburn University of Topeka *A, B, M*
Wichita State University *A, B, M*

Kentucky
Bellarmine University *B*
Brescia University *B*
Campbellsville University *A*
Cumberland College *B*
Elizabethtown Community College *A*
Hazard Community College *A*
Henderson Community College *A*
Hopkinsville Community College *A*
Jefferson Community College *A*
Kentucky Christian College *B*
Lexington Community College *A*
Lindsey Wilson College *A, B*
Madisonville Community College *A*
Maysville Community College *A*
Murray State University *A, B*
Paducah Community College *A*
Prestonsburg Community College *A*
St. Catharine College *A*
Somerset Community College *A*
Southeast Community College *A*
Spalding University *B*
Thomas More College *A, B*
Transylvania University *B*
University of Louisville *B, M*

Louisiana
Centenary College of Louisiana *B*
Delgado Community College *A*
Grambling State University *M*
Louisiana College *B*
Louisiana State University
　Alexandria *A*
　Eunice *A*
　Shreveport *B, M*
Louisiana State University and
　Agricultural and Mechanical
　College *B*
Louisiana Tech University *A, B*
Loyola University New Orleans *B*
McNeese State University *A, B*
Nicholls State University *A, B*
Northwestern State University *A, B*
Nunez Community College *A*
Our Lady of Holy Cross College *B*
St. Joseph Seminary College *B*
Southern University
　Shreveport *A*
Tulane University *M*
University of Louisiana at Lafayette *B*
University of Louisiana at Monroe *A, B*
University of New Orleans *B, M*

Maine
Central Maine Technical College *A*
Husson College *B*
University of Maine *B, M*
University of Maine
　Augusta *A*
　Farmington *B*
　Machias *A*
　Presque Isle *A, B*
University of New England *B*
University of Southern Maine *A, B*

Maryland
Allegany College *A*
Anne Arundel Community College *A*
Carroll Community College *A*
Cecil Community College *A*
Chesapeake College *A*
College of Notre Dame of
　Maryland *B*
College of Southern Maryland *A*
Columbia Union College *A, B*
Community College of Baltimore County
　Catonsville *C, A*
　Dundalk *C, A*
　Essex *C, A*
Coppin State College *B*
Frederick Community College *A*
Frostburg State University *B, M*
Hagerstown Community College *A*
Harford Community College *A*

Howard Community College *A*
Johns Hopkins University *B, M, D*
Loyola College in Maryland *M*
McDaniel College *M*
Montgomery College
　Rockville Campus *A*
St. John's College *B, M*
Salisbury University *B*
Towson University *M*
University of Baltimore *B*
University of Maryland
　University College *A, B*
Villa Julie College *A, B*
Washington College *B*

Massachusetts
American International College *A, B*
Anna Maria College *B*
Atlantic Union College *B*
Bay Path College *A, B*
Becker College *A, B*
Bentley College *B*
Berkshire Community College *A*
Bunker Hill Community College *A*
Cape Cod Community College *A*
Clark University *B, M*
Dean College *A*
Elms College *B*
Emmanuel College *B*
Endicott College *A, B*
Fisher College *C, A*
Fitchburg State College *B*
Framingham State College *B*
Greenfield Community College *A*
Hampshire College *B*
Harvard College *B*
Hellenic College/Holy Cross *B*
Lasell College *B*
Lesley University *A, B, M*
Marian Court College *A*
Massachusetts Bay Community
　College *C, A*
Massachusetts College of Liberal Arts *B*
Massachusetts Institute of Technology *B*
Massasoit Community College *A*
Merrimack College *A, B*
Mount Ida College *A, B*
Mount Wachusett Community College *A*
Newbury College *A*
Northeastern University *A, B*
Pine Manor College *A*
Quinsigamond Community College *A*
Roxbury Community College *A*
St. John's Seminary College *B*
Simon's Rock College of Bard *A, B*
Springfield College *B*
Springfield Technical Community
　College *A*
Suffolk University *A, B*
Tufts University *B*
University of Massachusetts
　Dartmouth *B*
　Lowell *B*
Urban College of Boston *C, A*
Western New England College *A, B*
Westfield State College *B*
Wheaton College *B*
Worcester Polytechnic Institute *B*

Michigan
Alma College *B*
Alpena Community College *A*
Andrews University *A, B*
Aquinas College *A, B*
Bay de Noc Community College *A*
Calvin College *B*
Central Michigan University *B, M*
Concordia University *A*
Ferris State University *A*
Glen Oaks Community College *A*
Gogebic Community College *A*
Grand Rapids Community College *A*
Grand Valley State University *B*
Hillsdale College *B*
Jackson Community College *A*
Kellogg Community College *A*

Kirtland Community College *A*
Lansing Community College *A*
Macomb Community College *A*
Marygrove College *A, T*
Michigan State University *B, D*
Michigan Technological University *B*
Mid Michigan Community College *A*
Monroe County Community College *A*
Montcalm Community College *A*
North Central Michigan College *A*
Northern Michigan University *A, B, M*
Northwestern Michigan College *A*
Oakland Community College *A*
Oakland University *B, M*
St. Clair County Community College *A*
Schoolcraft College *A*
Siena Heights University *A, B*
Southwestern Michigan College *C, A*
Spring Arbor University *A*
University of Michigan *B*
University of Michigan
　Dearborn *B*
　Flint *B, M*
Washtenaw Community College *A*
Wayne County Community College *A*
West Shore Community College *A*
William Tyndale College *A*

Minnesota
Anoka-Ramsey Community College *A*
Augsburg College *B, M*
Bemidji State University *A, B*
Bethany Lutheran College *B*
Bethel College *A, B*
Central Lakes College *A*
Century Community and Technical
　College *A*
College of St. Benedict *B*
College of St. Scholastica *B*
Concordia College: Moorhead *B*
Concordia University: St. Paul *A, B*
Crossroads College *A*
Crown College *A, B*
Fergus Falls Community College *A*
Hamline University *M*
Hibbing Community College: A
　Technical and Community College *A*
Inver Hills Community College *A*
Itasca Community College *A*
Lake Superior College: A Community
　and Technical College *A*
Macalester College *B*
Mesabi Range Community and Technical
　College *A*
Metropolitan State University *B*
Minneapolis Community and Technical
　College *A*
Minnesota State University
　Mankato *A, B*
　Moorhead *A, B, M*
Minnesota West Community and
　Technical College: Worthington
　Campus *A*
Normandale Community College *A*
North Central University *A*
North Hennepin Community College *A*
Northland Community & Technical
　College *A*
Northwestern College *A*
Oak Hills Christian College *A*
Rainy River Community College *A*
Ridgewater College: A Community and
　Technical College *A*
Riverland Community College: A
　Technical and Community College *A*
Rochester Community and Technical
　College *A*
St. Cloud State University *A, B*
St. John's University *B*
St. Olaf College *B*
St. Paul College - A Community and
　Technical College *A*
Southwest State University *B*

University of Minnesota
  Duluth *M*
  Morris *B*
  Twin Cities *C, B*
Winona State University *A, B*

Mississippi

Alcorn State University *B*
Holmes Community College *A*
Itawamba Community College *A*
Mary Holmes College *A*
Millsaps College *B*
Mississippi Gulf Coast Community
  College
    Perkinston *A*
Mississippi State University *B*
Northwest Mississippi Community
  College *A*
Pearl River Community College *A*
University of Mississippi *B*
Wesley College *C*

Missouri

Avila University *B*
Blue River Community College *A*
Columbia College *A, B*
Conception Seminary College *B*
Cottey College *A*
Crowder College *A*
Drury University *B, M*
East Central College *A*
Evangel University *A*
Hannibal-LaGrange College *A, B*
Jefferson College *A*
Lincoln University *B*
Lindenwood University *B*
Longview Community College *A*
Maple Woods Community College *A*
Maryville University of Saint Louis *B*
Mineral Area College *A*
Missouri Southern State College *B*
Missouri Valley College *A, B*
Missouri Western State College *B*
Moberly Area Community College *A*
North Central Missouri College *A*
Northwest Missouri State University *B*
Ozarks Technical Community College *A*
Penn Valley Community College *A*
Rockhurst University *B*
St. Charles Community College *A*
St. Louis Christian College *A*
St. Louis Community College
  St. Louis Community College at
    Florissant Valley *A*
  St. Louis Community College at
    Forest Park *A*
  St. Louis Community College at
    Meramec *A*
St. Louis University *B*
Southeast Missouri State University *B*
Southwest Baptist University *A*
Southwest Missouri State University:
  West Plains Campus *A*
Stephens College *A, B*
Three Rivers Community College *A*
University of Missouri
  Columbia *B*
  Kansas City *B*
Washington University in St. Louis *B, M*
Webster University *B*
Wentworth Military Academy *C, A*

Montana

Dawson Community College *A*
Fort Belknap College *A*
Miles Community College *A*
Montana State University
  Billings *A, B*
Montana Tech of the University of
  Montana *B*
Rocky Mountain College *A*
Salish Kootenai College *A*
University of Montana-Missoula *A, B*
University of Montana: Western *A, B*

Nebraska

Bellevue University *B*

Central Community College *C, A*
Chadron State College *B, M*
College of Saint Mary *A, B*
Creighton University *M*
Dana College *B*
Grace University *B*
Hastings College *B*
Little Priest Tribal College *A*
Metropolitan Community College *A*
Mid Plains Community College
  Area *C, A*
Midland Lutheran College *B*
Nebraska Christian College *A*
Nebraska Indian Community College *A*
Northeast Community College *A*
Southeast Community College
  Beatrice Campus *A*
  Lincoln Campus *A*
Union College *B*
University of Nebraska
  Kearney *B*
  Lincoln *B*
  Omaha *B*
Western Nebraska Community
  College *A*

Nevada

Community College of Southern
  Nevada *A*
Great Basin College *B*
Sierra Nevada College *B*
University of Nevada
  Las Vegas *B, M*
Western Nevada Community College *A*

New Hampshire

Chester College of New England *A*
Colby-Sawyer College *A*
College for Lifelong Learning *A, B*
Daniel Webster College *A*
Dartmouth College *M*
Franklin Pierce College *B*
Hesser College *C, A*
Keene State College *A*
Magdalen College *A, B*
New Hampshire Community Technical
  College
    Berlin *A*
    Laconia *A*
    Manchester *A*
    Nashua *C, A*
New Hampshire Technical Institute *A*
Rivier College *A, B*
St. Anselm College *A*
Southern New Hampshire
  University *A, B*
University of New Hampshire *A*
University of New Hampshire at
  Manchester *A, B*

New Jersey

Assumption College for Sisters *A*
Bergen Community College *A*
Bloomfield College *B*
Brookdale Community College *A*
Burlington County College *A*
Caldwell College *M*
Camden County College *A*
Centenary College *A*
County College of Morris *A*
Cumberland County College *A*
Drew University *B*
Essex County College *A*
Fairleigh Dickinson University
  College at Florham *B*
  Metropolitan Campus *A, B*
Felician College *A, B*
Georgian Court College *B*
Gloucester County College *A*
Hudson County Community College *A*
Kean University *M*
Mercer County Community College *A*
Monmouth University *A, M*
Montclair State University *B*
Ocean County College *A*
Passaic County Community College *A*

Ramapo College of New Jersey *B, M*
Raritan Valley Community College *A*
Richard Stockton College of New
  Jersey *B*
Rider University *A, B*
Rowan University *B*
Rutgers, The State University of New
  Jersey
    Camden Regional Campus *B, M*
    Newark Regional Campus *M*
Salem Community College *A*
Seton Hall University *B*
Sussex County Community College *A*
Thomas Edison State College *A, B*
Union County College *C, A*
Warren County Community College *A*

New Mexico

Albuquerque Technical-Vocational
  Institute *A*
College of the Southwest *B*
Eastern New Mexico University *A, B*
Eastern New Mexico University: Roswell
  Campus *A*
New Mexico Junior College *A*
New Mexico Military Institute *A*
New Mexico State University
  Alamogordo *A*
St. John's College *B, M*
San Juan College *A*
Santa Fe Community College *A*
Southwestern Indian Polytechnic
  Institute *A*
University of New Mexico *B*
Western New Mexico University *B*

New York

Adelphi University *A*
Adirondack Community College *A*
Alfred University *B*
Bard College *B*
Broome Community College *A*
Canisius College *A, B*
Cayuga County Community College *A*
Cazenovia College *A, B*
City University of New York
  Baruch College *B*
  Borough of Manhattan Community
    College *A*
  Bronx Community College *A*
  Brooklyn College *M*
  College of Staten Island *A, B, M*
  Hostos Community College *A*
  Hunter College *B*
  Kingsborough Community
    College *A*
  La Guardia Community College *A*
  Medgar Evers College *A*
  Queensborough Community
    College *A*
  York College *B*
Clarkson University *B*
Clinton Community College *A*
Colgate University *B*
College of Mount St. Vincent *A, B*
College of New Rochelle: School of New
  Resources *B*
Concordia College *A, B*
Cornell University *B*
Corning Community College *A*
Daemen College *B*
Dominican College of Blauvelt *A, B*
Dowling College *B*
Dutchess Community College *A*
Erie Community College
  City Campus *A*
  North Campus *A*
  South Campus *A*
Eugene Lang College/New School
  University *B*
Excelsior College *A, B, M*
Finger Lakes Community College *A*
Fulton-Montgomery Community
  College *C, A*
Genesee Community College *A*
Hamilton College *B*

Hilbert College *A, B*
Houghton College *A*
Hudson Valley Community College *C*
Iona College *B*
Ithaca College *B*
Jamestown Community College *C, A*
Jefferson Community College *A*
Keuka College *B*
Long Island University
  C. W. Post Campus *A*
  Southampton College *B*
Manhattanville College *B, M*
Maria College *A*
Marist College *B*
Marymount College of Fordham
  University *A*
Marymount Manhattan College *B*
Medaille College *A, B*
Mercy College *C, A, B*
Mohawk Valley Community
  College *C, A*
Molloy College *A*
Monroe Community College *A*
Mount St. Mary College *B, T*
Nassau Community College *A*
New York University *A, B, M*
Niagara County Community College *A*
Niagara University *A*
North Country Community College *A*
Nyack College *A, B*
Onondaga Community College *A*
Orange County Community College *A*
Pace University *A, B*
Pace University:
  Pleasantville/Briarcliff *A, B*
Paul Smith's College *A*
Polytechnic University *B*
Rensselaer Polytechnic Institute *B*
Roberts Wesleyan College *B*
Rockland Community College *A*
Sage College of Albany *A*
St. John Fisher College *B*
St. John's University *A, B, M*
St. Joseph's College *B*
Sarah Lawrence College *B*
Schenectady County Community
  College *C, A*
Skidmore College *B, M*
State University of New York
  Albany *B, M, D*
  Buffalo *A, B, M*
  College at Brockport *M*
  College at Buffalo *B*
  College at Cortland *B*
  College at Old Westbury *B*
  College at Plattsburgh *B, M*
  College of Agriculture and
    Technology at Cobleskill *A*
  College of Agriculture and
    Technology at Morrisville *A*
  College of Technology at Alfred *A*
  College of Technology at Canton *A*
  College of Technology at Delhi *A*
  Empire State College *A, B, M*
  Farmingdale *A*
  Institute of Technology at
    Utica/Rome *B*
  Maritime College *B*
  New Paltz *B*
  Purchase *B*
Suffolk County Community College *A*
Syracuse University *D*
Tompkins-Cortland Community
  College *C, A*
Touro College *A, B*
Trocaire College *A*
Ulster County Community College *A*
Union College *B*
Utica College *B*
Vassar College *B*
Villa Maria College of Buffalo *A*
Wagner College *B*
Westchester Community College *A*

North Carolina

Alamance Community College *A*

Appalachian State University *B*
Asheville Buncombe Technical
  Community College *A*
Barton College *B*
Beaufort County Community College *A*
Belmont Abbey College *B*
Bennett College *B*
Bladen Community College *A*
Blue Ridge Community College *A*
Brevard College *A, B*
Brunswick Community College *A*
Caldwell Community College and
  Technical Institute *A*
Cape Fear Community College *A*
Carteret Community College *A*
Catawba Valley Community College *A*
Central Carolina Community College *A*
Central Piedmont Community College *A*
Chowan College *A, B*
Cleveland Community College *A*
Coastal Carolina Community College *A*
College of the Albemarle *A*
Craven Community College *A*
Davidson County Community College *A*
Duke University *M*
Durham Technical Community
  College *A*
East Carolina University *B*
Edgecombe Community College *A*
Fayetteville Technical Community
  College *A*
Forsyth Technical Community College *A*
Gaston College *C, A*
Guilford College *B*
Guilford Technical Community
  College *A*
Halifax Community College *A*
Haywood Community College *A*
Isothermal Community College *A*
James Sprunt Community College *C, A*
Johnson C. Smith University *B*
Johnston Community College *A*
Lees-McRae College *B*
Lenoir Community College *A*
Lenoir-Rhyne College *B*
Louisburg College *A*
Mars Hill College *B*
Martin Community College *A*
Mayland Community College *A*
Methodist College *A, B*
Mitchell Community College *A*
Montgomery Community College *A*
Montreat College *A, B*
Mount Olive College *A, B*
Nash Community College *A*
North Carolina School of the Arts *B*
North Carolina State University *B, M*
Peace College *A, B*
Piedmont Community College *A*
Pitt Community College *C, A*
Randolph Community College *A*
Richmond Community College *A*
Roanoke-Chowan Community College *A*
Rockingham Community College *A*
St. Andrews Presbyterian College *B*
Sandhills Community College *A*
Shaw University *B*
South Piedmont Community College *A*
Southeastern Community College *A*
Southwestern Community College *A*
Stanly Community College *A*
Surry Community College *A*
Tri-County Community College *C, A*
University of North Carolina
  Asheville *B, M*
  Chapel Hill *B*
  Charlotte *M*
  Greensboro *B, M*
  Wilmington *M*
Vance-Granville Community College *A*
Wake Forest University *M*
Wake Technical Community College *A*
Warren Wilson College *B*
Wayne Community College *A*
Western Carolina University *B*

Western Piedmont Community
  College *A*
Wilkes Community College *A*
Wilson Technical Community College *A*
Wingate University *B*
Winston-Salem State University *B*

North Dakota
Bismarck State College *A*
Dickinson State University *A, B, T*
Lake Region State College *A*
Mayville State University *B*
Minot State University *B*
Minot State University: Bottineau
  Campus *A*
North Dakota State College of Science *A*
North Dakota State University *B*
Trinity Bible College *A*
University of Mary *B*
University of North Dakota *B*
Valley City State University *B*
Williston State College *A*

Ohio
Antioch College *B*
Ashland University *A, B*
Bluffton College *B*
Bowling Green State University *B*
Bowling Green State University:
  Firelands College *A*
Chatfield College *A*
Cincinnati State Technical and
  Community College *A*
Clark State Community College *A*
Cleveland State University *B*
College of Mount St. Joseph *A, B*
Columbus State Community College *A*
Cuyahoga Community College
  Eastern Campus *A*
  Metropolitan Campus *A*
  Western Campus *A*
David N. Myers College *B*
Defiance College *B*
Edison State Community College *A*
Jefferson Community College *A*
John Carroll University *B, M*
Kent State University *A, B, M*
Kent State University
  Ashtabula Regional Campus *A, B*
  East Liverpool Regional Campus *A*
  Salem Regional Campus *A*
  Stark Campus *A, B*
  Trumbull Campus *A*
  Tuscarawas Campus *A, B*
Lakeland Community College *A*
Lorain County Community College *A*
Lourdes College *A, B*
Malone College *B*
Marietta College *A, M*
Miami University
  Hamilton Campus *A*
  Middletown Campus *A*
  Oxford Campus *B*
Mount Vernon Nazarene University *A*
Northwest State Community College *A*
Ohio Dominican College *C, A, B, T*
Ohio Northern University *B*
Ohio State University
  Columbus Campus *B, M*
  Lima Campus *A*
  Mansfield Campus *A*
  Marion Campus *A*
  Newark Campus *A*
Ohio University *A*
Ohio University
  Chillicothe Campus *A*
  Eastern Campus *A*
  Zanesville Campus *A*
Ohio Wesleyan University *B*
Owens Community College
  Findlay Campus *A*
  Toledo *A*
Pontifical College Josephinum *B*
Sinclair Community College *A*
Southern State Community College *A*
Stark State College of Technology *A*

Tiffin University *B*
Union Institute & University *B*
University of Cincinnati *B*
University of Cincinnati
  Clermont College *A*
  Raymond Walters College *A*
University of Dayton *B*
University of Findlay *A*
University of Rio Grande *A*
University of Toledo *B, M*
Urbana University *A, B*
Ursuline College *M*
Walsh University *A*
Washington State Community College *A*
Wilmington College *B*
Wittenberg University *B*
Wright State University *M*
Wright State University: Lake Campus *A*
Xavier University *A, B, M*
Youngstown State University *C, A*

Oklahoma
Bacone College *A*
Murray State College *A*
Northeastern Oklahoma Agricultural and
  Mechanical College *A*
Northeastern State University *B*
Northern Oklahoma College *A*
Oklahoma Baptist University *B*
Oklahoma Christian University of
  Science and Arts *B*
Oklahoma City Community College *A*
Oklahoma City University *B, M*
Oklahoma Panhandle State
  University *A, B*
Oral Roberts University *B*
Redlands Community College *A*
Rogers State University *A, D*
Rose State College *A*
St. Gregory's University *A, B*
Seminole State College *A*
University of Central Oklahoma *B*
University of Oklahoma *B, M*
University of Tulsa *B*
Western Oklahoma State College *A*

Oregon
Blue Mountain Community College *A*
Central Oregon Community College *A*
Chemeketa Community College *A*
Clackamas Community College *A*
Clatsop Community College *A*
Concordia University *A, B*
Eastern Oregon University *A, B*
Lane Community College *A*
Linn-Benton Community College *A*
Marylhurst University *B*
Oregon Institute of Technology *A*
Oregon State University *B*
Pacific University *B*
Portland Community College *A*
Portland State University *B*
Reed College *M*
Rogue Community College *A*
Southwestern Oregon Community
  College *A*
Treasure Valley Community College *A*
Umpqua Community College *A*
University of Oregon *B*
Warner Pacific College *B*
Western Baptist College *B*
Western Oregon University *A, B*
Willamette University *B*

Pennsylvania
Arcadia University *B, M*
Baptist Bible College of Pennsylvania *A*
Bloomsburg University of
  Pennsylvania *B*
Bryn Athyn College of the New
  Church *A*
Bucknell University *B*
Bucks County Community College *A*
Butler County Community College *A*
Cabrini College *B*
California University of Pennsylvania *B*

Cambria County Area Community
  College *A*
Carlow College *B*
Cedar Crest College *B*
Chatham College *M*
Community College of Allegheny
  County *A*
Community College of Beaver County *A*
Community College of Philadelphia *A*
DeSales University *B*
Delaware County Community College *A*
Drexel University *A, B*
Duquesne University *M*
East Stroudsburg University of
  Pennsylvania *B*
Edinboro University of
  Pennsylvania *A, B*
Geneva College *B*
Gettysburg College *B*
Gwynedd-Mercy College *A*
Harrisburg Area Community College *A*
Holy Family University *B*
Immaculata University *A, B*
Juniata College *B*
Keystone College *A*
Kutztown University of Pennsylvania *B*
La Roche College *B*
La Salle University *A, B*
Lackawanna College *A*
Lebanon Valley College of
  Pennsylvania *A, B*
Lehigh Carbon Community College *A*
Lehigh University *B*
Lock Haven University of
  Pennsylvania *B, M*
Luzerne County Community College *A*
Manor College *A*
Mercyhurst College *C, A*
Millersville University of
  Pennsylvania *A*
Montgomery County Community
  College *A*
Mount Aloysius College *A, B*
Muhlenberg College *B*
Neumann College *A, B*
Northampton County Area Community
  College *A*
Penn State
  Abington *A, B*
  Altoona *A, B*
  Beaver *A, B*
  Berks *A, B*
  Delaware County *A, B*
  Dubois *A, B*
  Erie, The Behrend College *A, B*
  Fayette *A, B*
  Harrisburg *B, M*
  Hazleton *A, B*
  Lehigh Valley *A, B*
  McKeesport *A, B*
  Mont Alto *A, B*
  New Kensington *A, B*
  Schuylkill - Capital College *A, B*
  Shenango *A, B*
  University Park *A, B*
  Wilkes-Barre *A, B*
  Worthington Scranton *A, B*
  York *A, B*
Pennsylvania College of Technology *A*
Point Park College *A, B*
Reading Area Community College *A*
Rosemont College *B, M*
St. Joseph's University *A, B*
St. Vincent College *B*
Temple University *A, B, M*
Thiel College *A*
University of Pennsylvania *B, M, D*
University of Pittsburgh *B*
University of Pittsburgh
  Bradford *B*
  Greensburg *B*
  Johnstown *B*
  Titusville *A*
Villanova University *A, B, M*
Waynesburg College *A*

West Chester University of
   Pennsylvania *B*
Westmoreland County Community
   College *A*
Widener University *A, B, M*
Wilkes University *B*
Wilson College *A*
York College of Pennsylvania *A, B*

Puerto Rico
Pontifical Catholic University of Puerto
   Rico *B*
Turabo University *B*
Universidad del Este *A*
University of Puerto Rico
   Bayamon University College *A*
   Carolina Regional College *A*
   Cayey University College *B*
   Ponce *A*
   Rio Piedras Campus *B*
   Utuado *A*

Rhode Island
Community College of Rhode Island *A*
Rhode Island College *B*
Salve Regina University *A, B, M, D*
University of Rhode Island *B*

South Carolina
Aiken Technical College *A*
Anderson College *B*
Central Carolina Technical College *A*
Charleston Southern University *A, B*
Coastal Carolina University *B*
Columbia College *B*
Columbia International University *A, B*
Converse College *M*
Denmark Technical College *A*
Florence-Darlington Technical College *A*
Lander University *B*
Limestone College *A, B*
Midlands Technical College *C, A*
Morris College *B*
North Greenville College *A, B*
Northeastern Technical College *A*
Orangeburg-Calhoun Technical
   College *A*
Piedmont Technical College *C, A*
Spartanburg Methodist College *A*
Technical College of the Lowcountry *A*
Tri-County Technical College *A*
Trident Technical College *A*
University of South Carolina *A, B*
University of South Carolina
   Lancaster *A*
   Salkehatchie Regional Campus *A*
   Sumter *A*
   Union *A*
Williamsburg Technical College *A*
Winthrop University *M*
Wofford College *B*
York Technical College *A*

South Dakota
Augustana College *B*
Dakota State University *A*
Dakota Wesleyan University *A*
Kilian Community College *A*
Northern State University *A*
Sinte Gleska University *A*
South Dakota State University *B*
University of Sioux Falls *B*
University of South Dakota *B, M*

Tennessee
American Baptist College of ABT
   Seminary *B*
Aquinas College *A*
Austin Peay State University *A*
Belmont University *B*
Bethel College *B*
Bryan College *A, B*
Carson-Newman College *B*
Chattanooga State Technical Community
   College *A*
Cleveland State Community
   College *C, A*

Columbia State Community College *A*
Crichton College *B*
Dyersburg State Community College *A*
East Tennessee State University *B, M*
Fisk University *B*
Freed-Hardeman University *B, T*
Jackson State Community College *A*
Lambuth University *B*
Lee University *B, M*
Milligan College *B*
Northeast State Technical Community
   College *A*
Pellissippi State Technical Community
   College *A*
Roane State Community College *A*
Southern Adventist University *A*
Southwest Tennessee Community
   College *A*
Tennessee State University *B*
Trevecca Nazarene University *A*
University of Memphis *M*
University of Tennessee
   Chattanooga *B*
Vanderbilt University *M*
Volunteer State Community College *A*
Walters State Community College *A*

Texas
Abilene Christian University *B, M*
Alvin Community College *A*
Amarillo College *A*
Amberton University *B*
Angelina College *A*
Angelo State University *B, T*
Austin Community College *A*
Blinn College *A*
Brazosport College *A*
Central Texas College *A*
Clarendon College *A*
Coastal Bend College *A*
College of Saint Thomas More *B*
College of the Mainland *A*
Concordia University at Austin *A, B*
Dallas Baptist University *A, B, M*
Dallas Christian College *B*
Del Mar College *A*
East Texas Baptist University *A*
Eastfield College *A*
El Centro College *A*
El Paso Community College *A*
Frank Phillips College *A*
Galveston College *A*
Grayson County College *A*
Hill College *C, A*
Houston Baptist University *M*
Howard College *A*
Howard Payne University *B*
Huston-Tillotson College *B*
Jacksonville College *A*
Kilgore College *A*
Lamar State College at Orange *A*
Lamar University *B*
Laredo Community College *A*
Lee College *A*
Lon Morris College *A*
Midland College *A*
North Harris Montgomery Community
   College District *A*
North Lake College *A*
Northeast Texas Community College *A*
Odessa College *A*
Our Lady of the Lake University of San
   Antonio *B*
Palo Alto College *A*
Panola College *A*
Paris Junior College *A*
Ranger College *A*
Richland College *A*
St. Edward's University *B, M*
St. Mary's University *B*
St. Philip's College *A*
San Antonio College *C, A*
Schreiner University *A, B*
South Plains College *A*
South Texas Community College *A*
Southern Methodist University *B, M*

Southwest Texas Junior College *A*
Southwestern Assemblies of God
   University *A*
Stephen F. Austin State University *B*
Tarleton State University *B, M*
Temple College *A*
Texarkana College *A*
Texas A&M University *B, M*
Texas A&M University
   Commerce *B*
   Texarkana *B*
Texas Christian University *B, M*
Texas Tech University *B*
Trinity Valley Community College *A*
Tyler Junior College *A*
University of Dallas *M*
University of Houston
   Clear Lake *B, M*
University of Mary Hardin-Baylor *B*
University of North Texas *B*
University of St. Thomas *B, M*
University of Texas
   Arlington *M, D*
   Austin *B*
   Brownsville *B*
   Dallas *B, M, D*
   Pan American *M*
   San Antonio *B*
   of the Permian Basin *B*
University of the Incarnate Word *B*
Victoria College *A*
Western Texas College *A*
Wharton County Junior College *A*

Utah
Brigham Young University *B, M*
College of Eastern Utah *A*
Salt Lake Community College *A*
Utah State University *A, B, M*
Weber State University *A, B*

Vermont
Bennington College *B, M*
Burlington College *A, B*
Castleton State College *A*
Champlain College *A, B*
College of St. Joseph in Vermont *A, B*
Community College of Vermont *A*
Goddard College *B*
Green Mountain College *B*
Johnson State College *A, B*
Landmark College *A*
Lyndon State College *A, B*
Marlboro College *B*
Middlebury College *B*
Norwich University *B*
Southern Vermont College *A, B*
University of Vermont *B*

Virginia
Averett University *A, B*
Blue Ridge Community College *A*
Bluefield College *B*
Bridgewater College *B*
Christendom College *A*
Danville Community College *A*
Eastern Mennonite University *B*
Eastern Shore Community College *A*
Ferrum College *B*
George Mason University *B*
Hampden-Sydney College *B*
Hampton University *B*
Hollins University *M*
J. Sargeant Reynolds Community
   College *A*
James Madison University *B*
Liberty University *B, T*
Longwood University *B, T*
Mary Baldwin College *B*
Mary Washington College *M*
Marymount University *A, B, M*
Mountain Empire Community College *A*
Paul D. Camp Community College *A*
Piedmont Virginia Community
   College *A*
Radford University *B*

Rappahannock Community College *A*
Richard Bland College *A*
Shenandoah University *B*
Southside Virginia Community
   College *A*
Southwest Virginia Community
   College *A*
Sweet Briar College *B*
Thomas Nelson Community College *A*
University of Richmond *C, A, M*
University of Virginia *B*
University of Virginia's College at
   Wise *B*
Virginia Commonwealth University *B*
Virginia Highlands Community
   College *A*
Virginia Intermont College *A, B*
Virginia Polytechnic Institute and State
   University *B*
Virginia State University *B*
Virginia Wesleyan College *B*
Virginia Western Community College *A*

Washington
Bellevue Community College *A*
Centralia College *A*
Clark College *A*
Eastern Washington University *B*
Edmonds Community College *A*
Everett Community College *A*
Evergreen State College *B*
Gonzaga University *B*
Grays Harbor College *A*
Green River Community College *A*
Heritage College *A, B*
Northwest College *A, B*
Peninsula College *A*
St. Martin's College *A, B*
Seattle Central Community College *A*
Seattle University *B*
South Seattle Community College *A*
Spokane Community College *A*
University of Washington *B*
Walla Walla College *B*
Walla Walla Community College *A*
Washington State University *B*
Wenatchee Valley College *A*
Western Washington University *B*
Whitworth College *B*

West Virginia
Alderson-Broaddus College *A, B*
Bluefield State College *A, B*
Concord College *B*
Fairmont State College *A*
Glenville State College *A, B*
Mountain State University *B*
Ohio Valley College *A, B*
Potomac State College of West Virginia
   University *A*
Salem International University *A, B*
Shepherd College *A*
Southern West Virginia Community and
   Technical College *A*
University of Charleston *A, B*
West Liberty State College *B*
West Virginia Northern Community
   College *A*
West Virginia State College *A, B*
West Virginia University *B, M*
West Virginia University Institute of
   Technology *A*
West Virginia University at
   Parkersburg *A*
West Virginia Wesleyan College *B*
Wheeling Jesuit University *B*

Wisconsin
Alverno College *A*
Beloit College *B*
Cardinal Stritch University *A*
Concordia University Wisconsin *B*
Edgewood College *A, B*
Lac Courte Oreilles Ojibwa Community
   College *A*
Lakeland College *A*

Lawrence University *B*
Marian College of Fond du Lac *B*
Milwaukee Area Technical College *A*
Moraine Park Technical College *A*
Nicolet Area Technical College *A*
Northland College *B*
St. Norbert College *B*
Silver Lake College *A*
University of Wisconsin
    Baraboo/Sauk County *A*
    Barron County *A*
    Eau Claire *A*
    Fond du Lac *A*
    Fox Valley *A*
    Green Bay *A, B*
    Manitowoc *A*
    Marathon County *A*
    Marinette *A*
    Milwaukee *B*
    Oshkosh *B*
    Parkside *B*
    Platteville *A*
    Richland *A*
    Rock County *A*
    Stevens Point *A, B*
    Superior *A, B*
    Washington County *A*
    Waukesha *A*
    Whitewater *A*
Viterbo University *B*

Wyoming

Casper College *A*
Eastern Wyoming College *A*
Laramie County Community College *A*
Sheridan College *A*
Western Wyoming Community
    College *A*

Library assistance

California

Barstow College *C*
Chabot College *A*
Citrus College *C, A*
College of the Canyons *C, A*
College of the Sequoias *C*
Cuesta College *C, A*
Foothill College *C, A*
Imperial Valley College *C*
Sierra College *A*

Connecticut

Capital Community College *A*
Three Rivers Community College *C*

Florida

Indian River Community College *A*

Illinois

Black Hawk College *C*
City Colleges of Chicago
    Wright College *C, A*
College of DuPage *A*
College of Lake County *C, A*
Illinois Central College *A*

Kansas

Central Christian College *A*
Seward County Community College *A*

Michigan

Bay de Noc Community College *C*
Oakland Community College *C, A*

New Mexico

Dona Ana Branch Community College of
    New Mexico State University *A*

Oklahoma

Rose State College *C, A*

Oregon

Portland Community College *C*

Pennsylvania

Northampton County Area Community
    College *C*

Washington

Lake Washington Technical College *C*

Library science

Alabama

University of Alabama *M, D*

Arizona

University of Arizona *M, D*

Arkansas

University of Central Arkansas *M*

California

Azusa Pacific University *M*
Cabrillo College *A*
Citrus College *A*
Diablo Valley College *C*
Los Angeles Harbor College *A*
Palomar College *C, A*
San Jose State University *M*
Santiago Canyon College *A*
Sierra College *A*
University of California
    Los Angeles *M, D*

Colorado

University of Colorado
    Denver *M*

Connecticut

Eastern Connecticut State University *B*
Southern Connecticut State
    University *B, M*

District of Columbia

Catholic University of America *M*

Florida

Florida State University *M, D*
Gulf Coast Community College *A*
South Florida Community College *A*
University of South Florida *M*

Georgia

Clark Atlanta University *M, D*
Valdosta State University *B*

Hawaii

University of Hawaii
    Manoa *M*

Idaho

College of Southern Idaho *A*

Illinois

Chicago State University *M*
Dominican University *M*
University of Illinois
    Urbana-Champaign *M, D*
University of St. Francis *C*

Indiana

Ball State University *B*
Indiana University
    Bloomington *M, D*
Indiana University-Purdue University
    Indianapolis *M*

Iowa

North Iowa Area Community College *A*
University of Iowa *M*
University of Northern Iowa *M*

Kansas

Allen County Community College *A*
Central Christian College *A*
Emporia State University *M, D*

Kentucky

University of Kentucky *M*

Louisiana

Louisiana State University and
    Agricultural and Mechanical
    College *C, M*
Our Lady of Holy Cross College *C*

Maine

University of Maine
    Augusta *A, B*

Maryland

University of Maryland
    College Park *M, D*

Massachusetts

Simmons College *M, D*

Michigan

Central Michigan University *B, M*
University of Michigan *M, D, T*
Wayne State University *C, M*

Minnesota

College of St. Catherine *B, M*
Minnesota State University
    Mankato *M*
St. Cloud State University *B, M*

Mississippi

Itawamba Community College *A*
University of Southern Mississippi *B, M*

Missouri

Central Missouri State University *M*
East Central College *A*
Harris Stowe State College *T*
Lindenwood University *M*
Missouri Baptist University *T*
Three Rivers Community College *A*
University of Missouri
    Columbia *M*

Montana

University of Montana: Western *T*

Nebraska

Chadron State College *B*
University of Nebraska
    Omaha *B*

New Jersey

Rowan University *M*
Rutgers, The State University of New
    Jersey
        New Brunswick Regional
        Campus *M, D*

New York

City University of New York
    Queens College *M*
Long Island University
    C. W. Post Campus *M*
Pratt Institute *M*
St. John's University *M*
State University of New York
    Albany *M*
    Buffalo *M, T*
Syracuse University *M*

North Carolina

Appalachian State University *M*
East Carolina University *M*
North Carolina Central University *M*
University of North Carolina
    Chapel Hill *C, M, D*
    Greensboro *M*

Ohio

Kent State University *M*
Miami University
    Oxford Campus *T*
University of Cincinnati
    Raymond Walters College *A*

Oklahoma

Northeastern State University *M*
Northwestern Oklahoma State
    University *M*
Tulsa Community College *A*
University of Oklahoma *B, M, T*

Pennsylvania

Drexel University *M*
Kutztown University of
    Pennsylvania *B, M, T*
Marywood University *C, D*

University of Pittsburgh *C, M, D*

Puerto Rico

Inter American University of Puerto Rico
    San German Campus *M*
University of Puerto Rico
    Rio Piedras Campus *M*

Rhode Island

University of Rhode Island *M*

South Carolina

University of South Carolina *M*

South Dakota

Black Hills State University *T*

Tennessee

Tennessee Technological University *M*
Trevecca Nazarene University *M*
Union University *T*
University of Tennessee
    Knoxville *M, T*

Texas

Brazosport College *A*
Sam Houston State University *M*
Texas A&M University
    Commerce *B, M*
Texas Woman's University *B, M, D*
University of Houston
    Clear Lake *M*
University of North Texas *B, M, D*
University of Texas
    Austin *M, D*

Virginia

Longwood University *M*
University of Virginia's College at
    Wise *T*

Washington

University of Washington *M*

West Virginia

Concord College *B, T*
Fairmont State College *B*

Wisconsin

University of Wisconsin
    Madison *M, D*
    Milwaukee *M*
    Superior *C*

Licensed midwifery

Florida

Miami-Dade Community College *A*

Illinois

Waubonsee Community College *C, A*

Indiana

Vincennes University *C*

Oregon

Central Oregon Community College *A*

Pennsylvania

Philadelphia University *M*

Licensed practical nursing

Alabama

Alabama Southern Community
    College *A*
Bevill State Community College *C*
Bishop State Community College *C*
Calhoun Community College *C*
Chattahoochee Valley Community
    College *C*
Douglas MacArthur State Technical
    College *C*
Gadsden State Community College *C*
George C. Wallace State Community
    College
        Selma *C*

Harry M. Ayers State Technical College *C*
J. F. Drake State Technical College *C*
Northwest-Shoals Community College *C*
Reid State Technical College *C*
Shelton State Community College *C*
Trenholm State Technical College *A*
Wallace Community College: Sparks Campus *C*
Wallace State Community College at Hanceville *C*

Arizona
Arizona Western College *C*
Central Arizona College *C*
Gateway Community College *C*
Phoenix College *C*
Scottsdale Community College *C*

Arkansas
Arkansas State University Mountain Home *C*
North Arkansas College *C*
Ouachita Technical College *C*
Ozarka College *C*
Phillips Community College of the University of Arkansas *C*
Pulaski Technical College *C*
Rich Mountain Community College *C*
South Arkansas Community College *C*
Southeast Arkansas College *C*
Southern Arkansas University Tech *C*
University of Arkansas
    Cossatot Community College of the *C*
    Fort Smith *C*

California
Antelope Valley College *C*
Bakersfield College *C*
Cabrillo College *A*
Cerritos Community College *A*
Cerro Coso Community College *C, A*
Citrus College *C, A*
College of the Canyons *A*
College of the Siskiyous *C, A*
Feather River College *C, A*
Gavilan Community College *C*
Glendale Community College *A*
Imperial Valley College *C, A*
Long Beach City College *C, A*
Los Angeles Trade and Technical College *A*
Los Medanos College *C*
MiraCosta College *C, A*
Modesto Junior College *A*
Mount San Jacinto College *C*
Riverside Community College *C, A*
Santa Barbara City College *C, A*
Santa Rosa Junior College *C, A*
Shasta College *C*
Sierra College *C, A*
Southwestern College *C, A*
Ventura College *A*

Colorado
Colorado Mountain College
    Spring Valley Campus *C*
Front Range Community College *C*
Otero Junior College *C*

Delaware
Delaware Technical and Community College
    Owens Campus *C*
    Terry Campus *C*

District of Columbia
George Washington University *C*

Florida
Chipola Junior College *C*
Daytona Beach Community College *C*
Indian River Community College *C*
Lake City Community College *C*
Palm Beach Community College *C*
Pasco-Hernando Community College *C*
Pensacola Junior College *C*

Santa Fe Community College *C*
Seminole Community College *C*
South Florida Community College *C*

Georgia
Athens Technical College *C*
Atlanta Metropolitan College *A*
Bainbridge College *C*
Central Georgia Technical College *C*
Chattahoochee Technical College *C*
Coastal Georgia Community College *C*
Columbus Technical College *C*
Darton College *A*
DeKalb Technical College *C*
Georgia Military College *A*
Middle Georgia College *A*
Southwest Georgia Technical College *C*
West Georgia Technical College *C*

Hawaii
University of Hawaii
    Hawaii Community College *C*
    Kauai Community College *C*

Idaho
Boise State University *C*
College of Southern Idaho *C*
Eastern Idaho Technical College *C*
Idaho State University *C*
Lewis-Clark State College *C*
North Idaho College *C*

Illinois
Black Hawk College *C*
Carl Sandburg College *C*
City Colleges of Chicago
    Kennedy-King College *C*
    Olive-Harvey College *C*
    Wright College *A*
Danville Area Community College *C*
Elgin Community College *C*
Heartland Community College *C*
Illinois Eastern Community Colleges
    Olney Central College *C*
Illinois Valley Community College *C*
John A. Logan College *C*
John Wood Community College *C*
Joliet Junior College *C*
Kankakee Community College *C*
Kaskaskia College *C*
Kishwaukee College *C*
Lake Land College *C*
Lewis and Clark Community College *A*
Parkland College *C*
Rend Lake College *C*
Richland Community College *C*
Sauk Valley Community College *C*
South Suburban College of Cook County *C*
Southeastern Illinois College *C*
Spoon River College *C*
Triton College *C*
William Rainey Harper College *C*

Indiana
Ivy Tech State College
    Bloomington *C*
    Central Indiana *C*
    Columbus *C*
    Eastcentral *C*
    Kokomo *C*
    Lafayette *C*
    Northcentral *C*
    Northeast *C*
    Northwest *C*
    Southcentral *C*
    Southeast *C*
    Southwest *C*
    Wabash Valley *C*
    Whitewater *C*
Vincennes University *A*

Iowa
Clinton Community College *C*
Des Moines Area Community College *C*
Ellsworth Community College *C*
Hawkeye Community College *C*

Indian Hills Community College *C*
Iowa Central Community College *C*
Iowa Lakes Community College *C*
Iowa Western Community College *C*
Kirkwood Community College *C*
Marshalltown Community College *C*
Muscatine Community College *C*
North Iowa Area Community College *A*
Northeast Iowa Community College *C*
Northwest Iowa Community College *C*
Scott Community College *C*
Southeastern Community College
    North Campus *C*
    South Campus *C*
Southwestern Community College *C*
Western Iowa Tech Community College *C*

Kansas
Barton County Community College *C*
Butler County Community College *C, A*
Dodge City Community College *C, A*
Fort Scott Community College *A*
Hutchinson Community College *C*
Johnson County Community College *C*
Labette Community College *C*
Pittsburg State University *B*
Pratt Community College *A*
Seward County Community College *C*

Kentucky
Hopkinsville Community College *C*
Maysville Community College *C, A*
Somerset Community College *C*
Spencerian College *C*

Louisiana
Delgado Community College *C*
Louisiana State University
    Eunice *A*
Nunez Community College *C, A*

Maryland
Anne Arundel Community College *C*
Cecil Community College *C*
College of Southern Maryland *C*
Frederick Community College *C*
Harford Community College *C*
Howard Community College *C*
Wor-Wic Community College *C*

Massachusetts
Berkshire Community College *C*
Greenfield Community College *C*
Quinsigamond Community College *C*
Roxbury Community College *C*

Michigan
Alpena Community College *C*
Bay de Noc Community College *C*
Davenport University
    Midland *C*
Glen Oaks Community College *C*
Gogebic Community College *C*
Grand Rapids Community College *C, A*
Jackson Community College *C*
Kellogg Community College *C*
Kirtland Community College *C*
Lansing Community College *A*
Mid Michigan Community College *C*
Montcalm Community College *C*
Mott Community College *A*
Muskegon Community College *A*
Northern Michigan University *C*
Northwestern Michigan College *C*
Oakland Community College *C*
St. Clair County Community College *C*
Schoolcraft College *C*
Southwestern Michigan College *C*

Minnesota
Alexandria Technical College *C*
Central Lakes College *C, A*
Dakota County Technical College *C*
Fergus Falls Community College *C*
Hennepin Technical College *C, A*
Itasca Community College *C*

Lake Superior College: A Community and Technical College *C*
Mesabi Range Community and Technical College *C*
Minneapolis Community and Technical College *C*
Minnesota State College - Southeast Technical *C*
Minnesota State University
    Mankato *B, M*
Minnesota West Community and Technical College: Worthington Campus *C*
Northland Community & Technical College *C*
Rainy River Community College *C*
Ridgewater College: A Community and Technical College *C*
Riverland Community College: A Technical and Community College *C*
Rochester Community and Technical College *C*
St. Cloud Technical College *C, A*
St. Paul College - A Community and Technical College *C*
South Central Technical College *A*

Mississippi
Coahoma Community College *C*
Itawamba Community College *C*
Mississippi Gulf Coast Community College
    Perkinston *C*
Pearl River Community College *C, A*

Missouri
Jefferson College *C*
Mineral Area College *A*
Moberly Area Community College *C*
North Central Missouri College *C*
Ozarks Technical Community College *C*
Penn Valley Community College *C*
St. Charles Community College *C*
Sanford-Brown College *C*

Montana
Montana State University
    Billings *C, A*
    Billings College of Technology *A*
University of Montana-Missoula *A*

Nebraska
Central Community College *C*
Metropolitan Community College *C*
Mid Plains Community College Area *C*
Nebraska College of Business *C*
Northeast Community College *C*
Southeast Community College
    Beatrice Campus *C*
    Lincoln Campus *C*
Western Nebraska Community College *C, A*

Nevada
Community College of Southern Nevada *C*
Western Nevada Community College *C*

New Hampshire
New Hampshire Community Technical College
    Claremont *C*

New Jersey
Raritan Valley Community College *A*
Salem Community College *C*
Union County College *C*

New Mexico
Albuquerque Technical-Vocational Institute *C*
Eastern New Mexico University: Roswell Campus *C*
New Mexico Junior College *C*
Western New Mexico University *A*

New York

City University of New York
    Hostos Community College *C*
    Medgar Evers College *C*
Iona College *C*
Niagara County Community College *C*
State University of New York
    College of Technology at Delhi *C*
Westchester Community College *C*

North Carolina

Alamance Community College *C*
Asheville Buncombe Technical
    Community College *C*
Beaufort County Community College *C*
Bladen Community College *C*
Brunswick Community College *C*
Cape Fear Community College *C*
Carteret Community College *C*
Central Carolina Community College *A*
Central Piedmont Community
    College *C, A*
Cleveland Community College *C*
Coastal Carolina Community College *C*
College of the Albemarle *C*
Craven Community College *C*
Durham Technical Community
    College *C*
Edgecombe Community College *C*
Fayetteville Technical Community
    College *C*
Forsyth Technical Community College *A*
Guilford Technical Community
    College *C*
Isothermal Community College *C*
James Sprunt Community College *C*
Lenoir Community College *C*
Mayland Community College *C*
Montgomery Community College *C*
Nash Community College *A*
Rockingham Community College *C*
Sampson Community College *A*
Sandhills Community College *C*
South Piedmont Community College *C*
Southeastern Community College *C, A*
Surry Community College *C*
Vance-Granville Community College *C*
Wayne Community College *A*
Wilson Technical Community
    College *C, A*

North Dakota

Bismarck State College *A*
Dickinson State University *A*
Lake Region State College *A*
North Dakota State College of Science *A*
Williston State College *A*

Ohio

Central Ohio Technical College *C*
Clark State Community College *C*
Hocking Technical College *C*
Jefferson Community College *C*
Lorain County Community College *C*
North Central State College *C*
Northwest State Community College *C*
Southern State Community College *C*

Oklahoma

Platt College *A*
Platt College
    Tulsa *A*

Oregon

Blue Mountain Community College *C*
Central Oregon Community College *C*
Chemeketa Community College *C*
Clackamas Community College *C*
Clatsop Community College *C*
Lane Community College *C*
Linn-Benton Community College *C*
Southwestern Oregon Community
    College *C*
Treasure Valley Community College *C*
Umpqua Community College *C*

Pennsylvania

Community College of Allegheny
    County *C*
Community College of Beaver County *C*
Harrisburg Area Community College *C*
Lehigh Carbon Community College *C*
Mercyhurst College *C*
Northampton County Area Community
    College *C*
Pennsylvania College of Technology *C*
Reading Area Community College *C, A*
Westmoreland County Community
    College *C*

Puerto Rico

Inter American University of Puerto Rico
    San German Campus *A*

Rhode Island

Community College of Rhode Island *C*

South Carolina

Aiken Technical College *C*
Central Carolina Technical College *C*
Florence-Darlington Technical
    College *C*
Horry-Georgetown Technical
    College *C, A*
Midlands Technical College *A*
Northeastern Technical College *C*
Orangeburg-Calhoun Technical
    College *C*
Piedmont Technical College *C*
Spartanburg Technical College *A*
Tri-County Technical College *C*
Trident Technical College *C*

South Dakota

Southeast Technical Institute *C, A*
Western Dakota Technical Institute *C*

Tennessee

Chattanooga State Technical Community
    College *C*
Tennessee State University *A*

Texas

Alvin Community College *C*
Amarillo College *C*
Angelina College *A*
Austin Community College *C*
Brazosport College *C*
Central Texas College *C*
Clarendon College *C, A*
Coastal Bend College *C*
College of the Mainland *A*
El Centro College *C*
El Paso Community College *C*
Frank Phillips College *C*
Galveston College *C*
Grayson County College *C*
Hill College *C, A*
Houston Community College System *C*
Howard College *C*
Kilgore College *C*
Lamar State College at Orange *C*
Lamar State College at Port Arthur *C*
McLennan Community College *C*
Midland College *C*
North Harris Montgomery Community
    College District *C*
Northeast Texas Community College *C*
Panola College *C*
Paris Junior College *A*
St. Philip's College *C*
Schreiner University *C*
South Plains College *C*
Southwest Texas Junior College *A*
Sul Ross State University *C*
Temple College *C*
Texas State Technical College
    West Texas *C*
Trinity Valley Community College *C*
Victoria College *C*
Western Texas College *C*
Wharton County Junior College *C*

Utah

Dixie State College of Utah *C*
Salt Lake Community College *C*
Southern Utah University *A*
Utah Valley State College *C*
Weber State University *C*

Vermont

Vermont Technical College *C*

Virginia

Danville Community College *C*
J. Sargeant Reynolds Community
    College *C*
Mountain Empire Community College *C*
Rappahannock Community College *C*
Southside Virginia Community
    College *C*
Virginia Western Community College *C*

Washington

Centralia College *C, A*
Clover Park Technical College *C*
Everett Community College *C*
Gonzaga University *M*
Grays Harbor College *C*
Green River Community College *C*
Lake Washington Technical College *C, A*
Lower Columbia College *A*
North Seattle Community College *C*
Olympic College *C, A*
Renton Technical College *C*
Spokane Community College *C*
Wenatchee Valley College *C*

Wisconsin

Chippewa Valley Technical College *C*
Fox Valley Technical College *C*
Milwaukee Area Technical College *C*
Moraine Park Technical College *C*
Waukesha County Technical College *C*

Wyoming

Sheridan College *C*
Western Wyoming Community
    College *C, A*

Lineworker

California

Santa Rosa Junior College *C*

Florida

South Florida Community College *C*

Indiana

Ivy Tech State College
    Lafayette *A*
    Northeast *C*

Iowa

Northwest Iowa Community
    College *C, A*
Western Iowa Tech Community
    College *A*

Michigan

Alpena Community College *C*

Minnesota

Dakota County Technical College *C*

North Carolina

Nash Community College *A*

North Dakota

Bismarck State College *C, A*

Washington

Clover Park Technical College *C*

Linguistics

Alaska

University of Alaska
    Fairbanks *B*

Arizona

Northern Arizona University *M, D*
University of Arizona *B, M, D*

Arkansas

University of Arkansas *M*

California

California State University
    Bakersfield *B*
    Chico *B*
    Dominguez Hills *B*
    Fresno *B, M*
    Fullerton *B, M*
    Northridge *B, M*
Foothill College *A*
Pitzer College *B*
Pomona College *B*
San Diego State University *B, M*
San Francisco State University *M*
San Jose State University *B, M*
Scripps College *B*
Stanford University *B, M, D*
University of California
    Berkeley *B, M, D*
    Davis *B, M*
    Irvine *B, M, D*
    Los Angeles *B, M, D*
    Riverside *B*
    San Diego *B, M, D*
    Santa Barbara *B, M, D*
    Santa Cruz *B, M, D*
University of Southern
    California *B, M, D*

Colorado

University of Colorado
    Boulder *B, M, D*

Connecticut

University of Connecticut *B, M, D*
Yale University *B, M, D*

Delaware

University of Delaware *M, D*

District of Columbia

Gallaudet University *M, D*
Georgetown University *B, M, D*

Florida

Florida Atlantic University *B, M*
Florida International University *M*
Florida State University *B, M, D*
South Florida Community College *A*
University of Florida *B, M, D*
University of South Florida *M*

Georgia

Morehouse College *B*
University of Georgia *B, M, D*

Hawaii

University of Hawaii
    Hilo *B*
    Manoa *M, D*

Illinois

Judson College *B*
Moody Bible Institute *B*
Northeastern Illinois University *M*
Northwestern University *B, M, D*
Southern Illinois University
    Carbondale *B, M*
University of Chicago *B, M, D*
University of Illinois
    Chicago *M*
    Urbana-Champaign *B, M, D*

Indiana

Ball State University *M*
Indiana University
    Bloomington *B, M, D*

Iowa

Central College *B*
Iowa State University *B*
University of Iowa *B, M, D*

Kansas
University of Kansas *B, M, D*

Kentucky
University of Kentucky *B*
University of Louisville *M*

Louisiana
Louisiana State University and
Agricultural and Mechanical
College *M, D*
Tulane University *B*

Maine
University of Southern Maine *B*

Maryland
University of Maryland
Baltimore County *B, M*
College Park *B, M, D*

Massachusetts
Boston College *B, M*
Boston University *B*
Brandeis University *B*
Hampshire College *B*
Harvard College *B*
Massachusetts Institute of
Technology *B, D*
Northeastern University *B*
University of Massachusetts
Amherst *B, M, D*
Wellesley College *B*

Michigan
Eastern Michigan University *B, M*
Michigan State University *B, M, D*
Oakland University *B, M*
University of Michigan *B, M, D*
Wayne State University *B, M*

Minnesota
Crown College *B*
Macalester College *B*
St. Cloud State University *B*
University of Minnesota
Twin Cities *B, M, D*

Mississippi
University of Mississippi *B*

Missouri
Central Missouri State University *M*
University of Missouri
Columbia *B*

Montana
University of Montana-Missoula *M*

New Hampshire
Dartmouth College *B*
University of New Hampshire *B*

New Jersey
Montclair State University *B, M*
Rutgers, The State University of New
Jersey
New Brunswick Regional
Campus *B, M, D*

New Mexico
University of New Mexico *B, M, D*

New York
Barnard College *B*
City University of New York
Brooklyn College *B*
Queens College *B, M*
Columbia University
Columbia College *B*
Cornell University *B, M, D*
New York University *B, M, D*
State University of New York
Albany *B*
Binghamton *B*
Buffalo *B, M, D*
Oswego *B*
Stony Brook *B, M, D*
Syracuse University *B, M*
University of Rochester *B, M*

North Carolina
University of North Carolina
Chapel Hill *B, M, D*

North Dakota
University of North Dakota *M*

Ohio
Antioch College *B*
Cleveland State University *B*
Miami University
Oxford Campus *B*
Ohio State University
Columbus Campus *B, M, D*
Ohio University *B, M*
University of Cincinnati *B*
University of Toledo *B*

Oklahoma
Oklahoma Wesleyan University *C*
University of Oklahoma *B*

Oregon
Portland State University *B, M*
Reed College *B*
University of Oregon *B, M, D*

Pennsylvania
Penn State
University Park *D*
Swarthmore College *B*
Temple University *B, M*
University of Pennsylvania *B, M, D*
University of Pittsburgh *B, M, D*

Puerto Rico
University of Puerto Rico
Rio Piedras Campus *M*

Rhode Island
Brown University *B*

South Carolina
University of South Carolina *M, D*

Tennessee
University of Tennessee
Knoxville *B*

Texas
Baylor University *B*
Rice University *B, M, D*
Texas Tech University *M*
University of Houston *M*
University of Texas
Arlington *M, D*
Austin *B, M, D*
El Paso *B, M*

Utah
Brigham Young University *B, M*
University of Utah *B, M, D*

Vermont
Marlboro College *B*

Virginia
College of William and Mary *B*
University of Virginia *M*

Washington
University of Washington *B, M, D*
Washington State University *B*
Western Washington University *B*

Wisconsin
Lawrence University *B*
University of Wisconsin
Madison *B, M, D*
Milwaukee *B*

Livestock management

New York
State University of New York
College of Agriculture and
Technology at Morrisville *A, B*

North Carolina
North Carolina State University *A*

Locksmithing

California
San Joaquin Delta College *C, A*

Logic

Pennsylvania
Carnegie Mellon University *B, M, D*

Logistics/materials management

Alabama
Auburn University *B*

Alaska
University of Alaska
Anchorage *B*

Arizona
South Mountain Community
College *C, A*

Arkansas
Southern Arkansas University Tech *C*
University of Arkansas *B, M*

California
California Maritime Academy *B*
California State University
Hayward *C, M*
Cerritos Community College *A*
Chabot College *A*
Golden Gate University *M*

Colorado
Arapahoe Community College *A*
Colorado Technical University *C, B, M*

Delaware
Wilmington College *M*

Florida
University of Miami *C*

Georgia
Georgia College and State University *M*
Georgia Institute of Technology *M*
Georgia Southern University *B*
West Georgia Technical College *C*

Illinois
Elmhurst College *B*
Heartland Community College *C*
Kishwaukee College *C*
Northwestern University *M*
Parkland College *C*
Prairie State College *C*
Rock Valley College *C, A*
Waubonsee Community College *C, A*
William Rainey Harper College *C, A*

Iowa
Iowa State University *B*

Kentucky
Cumberland College *B*

Maine
Maine Maritime Academy *B, M*

Maryland
University of Maryland
College Park *B*

Massachusetts
Northeastern University *B*
Springfield Technical Community
College *A*

Michigan
Central Michigan University *B*
Ferris State University *C*
Michigan State University *B, M, D*
Wayne State University *B*
Western Michigan University *B*

Minnesota
St. Paul College - A Community and
Technical College *C*

Missouri
University of Missouri
St. Louis *B*

Nevada
University of Nevada
Reno *B*

New Jersey
Thomas Edison State College *B*

North Carolina
South Piedmont Community College *A*

Ohio
Bowling Green State University *B*
Columbus State Community College *A*
John Carroll University *B*
Kent State University
Stark Campus *B*
Ohio State University
Columbus Campus *B*
Sinclair Community College *A*
University of Akron *C, A, B, M*
University of Toledo *A, M*
Wright State University *M*

Oregon
Portland State University *B*

Pennsylvania
Cambria County Area Community
College *A*
Duquesne University *B*
Mercyhurst College *C, A*
Penn State
Abington *B*
Altoona *B*
Beaver *B*
Berks *B*
Delaware County *B*
Dubois *B*
Fayette *B*
Hazleton *B*
Lehigh Valley *B*
McKeesport *B*
Mont Alto *B*
New Kensington *B*
Schuylkill - Capital College *B*
Shenango *B*
University Park *C, B*
Wilkes-Barre *B*
Worthington Scranton *B*
York *B*
Robert Morris University *B*

Puerto Rico
Turabo University *B, M*
University of Puerto Rico
Bayamon University College *B*

Tennessee
University of Memphis *B*
University of Tennessee
Knoxville *B*
Volunteer State Community College *C*

Texas
Houston Community College
System *C, A*
Palo Alto College *C, A*
Texas A&M International University *M*
Texas A&M University *M*
University of Texas
Arlington *M*

Utah
Salt Lake Community College *A*
Weber State University *B*

West Virginia
Mountain State University *B*

Wisconsin
Chippewa Valley Technical College *A*

Lac Courte Oreilles Ojibwa Community
College *A*
University of Wisconsin
Superior *C, B*

Machine shop technology

California
Long Beach City College *C, A*

Illinois
Black Hawk College *C*
College of Lake County *C, A*
Illinois Eastern Community Colleges
Wabash Valley College *C, A*
John A. Logan College *C, A*
Kaskaskia College *C*
McHenry County College *C*
Moraine Valley Community College *C*
Waubonsee Community College *C, A*

Indiana
Ivy Tech State College
Central Indiana *A*

Kentucky
Somerset Community College *C*

Louisiana
Delgado Community College *C, A*
Nunez Community College *C*

Michigan
Grand Rapids Community College *C, A*
Montcalm Community College *C*
Northwestern Michigan College *C*

Minnesota
Hennepin Technical College *A*

Missouri
Ranken Technical College *A*

New Mexico
Albuquerque Technical-Vocational
Institute *C*
San Juan College *C, A*

New York
Erie Community College
North Campus *A*
Mohawk Valley Community College *C*

North Carolina
Cape Fear Community College *C, A*
Fayetteville Technical Community
College *A*
Isothermal Community College *C, A*
Lenoir Community College *C, A*
Wilkes Community College *C, A*
Wilson Technical Community College *C*

Pennsylvania
Butler County Community College *C, A*
Community College of Allegheny
County *C*
Delaware County Community College *C*
Pennsylvania College of Technology *C*

South Carolina
Piedmont Technical College *C*

South Dakota
Southeast Technical Institute *A*

Texas
Houston Community College System *C*
St. Philip's College *A*

Washington
Renton Technical College *C, A*

Wisconsin
Western Wisconsin Technical College *A*

Machine tool technology

Alabama
Calhoun Community College *C, A*

Harry M. Ayers State Technical
College *C, A*
J. F. Drake State Technical College *C, A*
Northwest-Shoals Community College *A*

Arkansas
University of Arkansas
Fort Smith *C, A*

Illinois
Heartland Community College *C*
Waubonsee Community College *C*

Indiana
Ivy Tech State College
Bloomington *C, A*
Central Indiana *C, A*
Columbus *C, A*
Eastcentral *C, A*
Kokomo *C, A*
Lafayette *C, A*
Northcentral *C, A*
Northeast *C, A*
Northwest *C, A*
Southcentral *C, A*
Southwest *C, A*
Wabash Valley *C, A*
Whitewater *C, A*

Iowa
North Iowa Area Community College *C*
Northwest Iowa Community College *A*
Western Iowa Tech Community
College *A*

Michigan
Jackson Community College *C, A*
Kirtland Community College *C*
Northern Michigan University *A*
Oakland Community College *C, A*

Minnesota
Hennepin Technical College *C, A*
St. Paul College - A Community and
Technical College *C*

Missouri
Jefferson College *C, A*
Ozarks Technical Community
College *C, A*

Montana
Montana State University
Billings *C, A*

Nevada
Western Nevada Community
College *C, A*

North Carolina
Davidson County Community College *C*
Surry Community College *A*
Tri-County Community College *C*
Wilson Technical Community College *C*

North Dakota
North Dakota State College of
Science *C, A*

Ohio
Northwest State Community
College *C, A*
Owens Community College
Toledo *C*

Oregon
Linn-Benton Community College *C*

Pennsylvania
Butler County Community College *C*
Delaware County Community
College *C, A*
South Hills School of Business &
Technology *A*
Williamson Free School of Mechanical
Trades *C*

South Carolina
Piedmont Technical College *C, A*
York Technical College *C, A*

South Dakota
Southeast Technical Institute *A*

Texas
Angelina College *C, A*
Clarendon College *C*
Kilgore College *C, A*

Utah
Utah Valley State College *C, A*

Washington
Clark College *C, A*
Clover Park Technical College *C, A*

Wisconsin
Milwaukee Area Technical College *C*
Western Wisconsin Technical College *C*

Wyoming
Sheridan College *C, A*

Make-up artist

North Carolina
Carteret Community College *C*
Martin Community College *C*

Management information systems

Alabama
American College of Computer and
Information Sciences *B*
Auburn University *M*
Auburn University at Montgomery *B*
Central Alabama Community
College *C, A*
Community College of the Air Force *A*
Enterprise State Junior College *A*
Troy State University *B*
University of Alabama *B*
University of Alabama
Huntsville *B*
University of North Alabama *B*
University of West Alabama *B*
Virginia College *C*

Alaska
University of Alaska
Anchorage *B*
Southeast *C, A*

Arizona
Arizona State University *B*
Arizona Western College *C, A*
Central Arizona College *A*
Cochise College *A*
DeVry University
Phoenix *B*
Eastern Arizona College *C*
Glendale Community College *C, A*
Northern Arizona University *B, M*
Phoenix College *C, A*
Pima Community College *A*
Scottsdale Community College *C, A*
University of Arizona *B, M*
University of Phoenix *B*

Arkansas
Arkansas State University *C, A*
Arkansas State University
Beebe *C*
Black River Technical College *A*
East Arkansas Community College *A*
Henderson State University *B*
Mississippi County Community
College *A*
Pulaski Technical College *C, A*
Rich Mountain Community College *C, A*
Southern Arkansas University Tech *C*
University of Arkansas
Fort Smith *C, A*
Little Rock *B*
Monticello *B*
University of Central Arkansas *B*

California
Azusa Pacific University *B*
Bakersfield College *A*
Barstow College *A*
California State Polytechnic University:
Pomona *B*
California State University
Bakersfield *B*
Chico *C, B*
Dominguez Hills *B*
Fresno *B*
Fullerton *B, M*
Hayward *B, M*
Northridge *B*
Sacramento *B, M*
Stanislaus *B*
Chabot College *A*
Citrus College *A*
College of the Sequoias *C, A*
College of the Siskiyous *C, A*
Columbia College *C*
Concordia University *B*
DeVry University
Fremont *B*
Long Beach *M*
Pomona *B*
West Hills *B*
Gavilan Community College *C*
Hope International University *C*
Laney College *C, A*
Los Angeles Harbor College *C, A*
Los Angeles Southwest College *A*
Master's College *B*
Modesto Junior College *A*
Moorpark College *A*
Northwestern Polytechnic University *B*
Orange Coast College *C, A*
Pacific Union College *B*
Point Loma Nazarene University *B*
San Diego City College *C, A*
San Joaquin Delta College *A*
San Jose State University *B*
Shasta College *A*
Taft College *C, A*
University of California
Santa Cruz *B*
University of La Verne *B*
University of Redlands *B*
University of San Francisco *B*
Vanguard University of Southern
California *B*
Ventura College *A*

Colorado
Arapahoe Community College *C, A*
Colorado Christian University *B*
Colorado Mountain College
Alpine Campus *C, A*
Spring Valley Campus *A*
Timberline Campus *C*
Colorado State University *B*
Colorado Technical University *B, M*
Community College of Aurora *C, A*
Fort Lewis College *B*
Front Range Community College *C, A*
Jones International University *C, M*
National American University
Denver *B*
Red Rocks Community College *C, A*
University of Colorado
Boulder *M*
University of Denver *M*

Connecticut
Albertus Magnus College *C, A, B*
Central Connecticut State University *B*
Fairfield University *B*
Manchester Community College *C, A*
Northwestern Connecticut Community
College *C, A*
Norwalk Community College *A*
Quinnipiac University *B*
Three Rivers Community College *A*
University of Bridgeport *B, M*
University of Connecticut *B, M*
University of Hartford *B*

Western Connecticut State University *B*

Delaware

Delaware Technical and Community
  College
    Terry Campus *A*
Goldey-Beacom College *B*
University of Delaware *B*

District of Columbia

American University *B, M*
Gallaudet University *B*
George Washington University *B, M*
Howard University *B*
University of the District of Columbia *A*

Florida

Barry University *C, B*
DeVry University
    Miramar *M*
    Orlando *M*
Florida Atlantic University *B*
Florida Gulf Coast University *B*
Florida Institute of Technology *M*
Florida International University *B*
Florida Southern College *B*
Florida State University *B, M*
Indian River Community College *A*
Northwood University
    Florida Campus *A, B*
Nova Southeastern University *M*
Okaloosa-Walton Community
    College *C, A*
Palm Beach Community College *A*
Pensacola Junior College *A*
St. Leo University *B*
South Florida Community College *C, A*
Tallahassee Community College *A*
University of Central Florida *B, M*
University of Miami *M*
University of South Florida *B*
University of Tampa *A, B*
University of West Florida *B*
Valencia Community College *C*

Georgia

Albany State University *B*
Atlanta Metropolitan College *A*
Bainbridge College *C, A*
Clayton College and State University *B*
Coastal Georgia Community
    College *C, A*
Columbus State University *B*
Dalton State College *B*
Darton College *C, A*
DeVry University
    Alpharetta *B*
    Atlanta *M*
Georgia College and State University *M*
Georgia Southern University *B*
Georgia Southwestern State University *A*
Kennesaw State University *M*
Macon State College *B*
Mercer University *B, M*
Paine College *B*
Savannah Technical College *A*
South Georgia College *C, A*
State University of West Georgia *B*
Thomas University *B*
University of Georgia *B*
West Georgia Technical College *C*

Hawaii

Brigham Young University-Hawaii *B*
Hawaii Pacific University *B*
University of Hawaii
    Manoa *B*

Idaho

Boise State University *B, M*
Northwest Nazarene University *B*
University of Idaho *B*

Illinois

Augustana College *B*
Aurora University *B*
Benedictine University *M*
Blackburn College *B*

Bradley University *B*
Chicago State University *B*
City Colleges of Chicago
    Olive-Harvey College *C, A*
Danville Area Community College *C, A*
De Paul University *M*
DeVry University
    Tinley Park *B*
Eastern Illinois University *B*
Eureka College *B*
Governors State University *B, M*
Heartland Community College *C, A*
Illinois College *B*
Illinois State University *B, M*
Joliet Junior College *C*
Kishwaukee College *A*
Lewis University *B*
Loyola University of Chicago *C, B, M*
MacMurray College *B*
Millikin University *B*
Monmouth College *B*
North Central College *B, M*
Northern Illinois University *M*
Northwestern University *M*
Parkland College *C*
Richland Community College *A*
Robert Morris College: Chicago *C, A*
Rockford College *B*
Roosevelt University *M*
St. Augustine College *A*
St. Xavier University *M*
Sauk Valley Community College *A*
Southern Illinois University
    Edwardsville *B, M*
Southwestern Illinois College *C, A*
Trinity Christian College *B*
Triton College *C, A*
University of Illinois
    Chicago *B, M, D*
    Springfield *M*
University of St. Francis *B*
Western Illinois University *B*
William Rainey Harper College *C, A*

Indiana

Grace College *B*
Indiana Institute of Technology *A, B*
Indiana State University *B*
Indiana University
    East *B*
    South Bend *M*
    Southeast *M*
Indiana Wesleyan University *A*
Oakland City University *B*
St. Joseph's College *A, B*
Saint Mary's College *B*
Tri-State University *B*
University of Indianapolis *B*
University of Notre Dame *B*
University of Southern Indiana *A*
Vincennes University *A*

Iowa

Briar Cliff University *B*
Buena Vista University *B*
Central College *B*
Clarke College *B*
Des Moines Area Community College *A*
Drake University *B*
Iowa State University *B*
Loras College *B*
Luther College *B*
Morningside College *B*
North Iowa Area Community College *A*
Northeast Iowa Community College *A*
St. Ambrose University *B*
Southeastern Community College
    South Campus *C*
University of Iowa *B, D*
University of Northern Iowa *B*
Upper Iowa University *B*
William Penn University *B*

Kansas

Bethel College *B*
Dodge City Community College *C, A*

Fort Scott Community College *A*
Friends University *B, M*
Haskell Indian Nations University *A*
Hutchinson Community College *C, A*
Newman University *B*
Ottawa University *B*
Southwestern College *B*
Wichita State University *B*

Kentucky

Henderson Community College *A*
Hopkinsville Community College *A*
Madisonville Community College *A*
Morehead State University *A, B*
Murray State University *B*
Paducah Community College *A*
Prestonsburg Community College *A*
Southeast Community College *A*
University of Louisville *B*

Louisiana

Louisiana College *B*
Louisiana State University and
    Agricultural and Mechanical
    College *B*
Louisiana Tech University *B*
Nicholls State University *A, B*
University of New Orleans *B*

Maine

Husson College *B*
Thomas College *B*
University of Maine *B*
University of Southern Maine *B*

Maryland

Allegany College *C, A*
Bowie State University *B, M*
Capitol College *M*
Carroll Community College *C, A*
Chesapeake College *C, A*
College of Southern Maryland *C, A*
Hagerstown Community College *C, A*
Harford Community College *A*
Howard Community College *A*
Johns Hopkins University *B, M*
Mount St. Mary's College *B*
Salisbury University *B*
University of Baltimore *B, M*
University of Maryland
    University College *C, M*
Wor-Wic Community College *C, A*

Massachusetts

American International College *B*
Anna Maria College *B*
Babson College *B*
Berkshire Community College *A*
Boston College *B*
Boston University *B, M*
Bridgewater State College *B*
Bunker Hill Community College *C, A*
Greenfield Community College *C*
Lasell College *B*
Marian Court College *C, A*
Massasoit Community College *A*
Nichols College *B*
Northeastern University *A, B*
Roxbury Community College *A*
Simmons College *B*
Suffolk University *B*
University of Massachusetts
    Dartmouth *B*
Western New England College *B*
Worcester Polytechnic Institute *B, M*

Michigan

Alpena Community College *A*
Baker College
    of Muskegon *A*
    of Owosso *B*
    of Port Huron *B*
Calvin College *B*
Central Michigan University *B, M*
Cleary University *A, B*
Cornerstone University *B*

Davenport University
    Eastern Region *A, B, M*
Eastern Michigan University *B*
Grand Rapids Community College *C, A*
Kettering University *B*
Lansing Community College *A*
Michigan Technological University *C*
Montcalm Community College *A*
Northern Michigan University *A, B*
Northwestern Michigan College *C, A*
Northwood University *A, B*
Oakland University *B*
Spring Arbor University *B*
Walsh College of Accountancy and
    Business Administration *M*
Wayne State University *B*
West Shore Community College *A*
Western Michigan University *B*

Minnesota

Alexandria Technical College *C, A*
Augsburg College *B*
Century Community and Technical
    College *C, A*
College of St. Catherine *B*
Crown College *A*
Itasca Community College *A*
Metropolitan State University *C, B, M*
Minnesota State College - Southeast
    Technical *C, A*
Minnesota State University
    Mankato *B*
    Moorhead *B*
National American University
    St. Paul *A, B*
Northwestern College *B*
St. Cloud Technical College *C*
St. Paul College - A Community and
    Technical College *C, A*
University of Minnesota
    Crookston *A, B*
    Twin Cities *B*
University of St. Thomas *M*
Winona State University *B*

Mississippi

Delta State University *B*
Itawamba Community College *A*
Mississippi Gulf Coast Community
    College
    Perkinston *A*
Mississippi State University *B*
Northwest Mississippi Community
    College *A*
Pearl River Community College *A*
University of Mississippi *B*
University of Southern Mississippi *B*

Missouri

Avila University *B*
Central Methodist College *B*
Central Missouri State University *B*
DeVry University
    Kansas City *M*
Drury University *B*
East Central College *A*
Lindenwood University *B, M*
Maryville University of Saint Louis *B, M*
National American University
    Kansas City *A, B*
St. Louis Community College
    St. Louis Community College at
        Florissant Valley *C, A*
    St. Louis Community College at
        Meramec *A*
St. Louis University *B, M*
Southeast Missouri State University *B*
Southwest Missouri State
    University *B, M*
Three Rivers Community College *A*
University of Missouri
    Rolla *B*
    St. Louis *B, M, D*
Webster University *M*
Westminster College *B*
William Woods University *B*

Montana

Flathead Valley Community
College *C, A*
Montana State University
Billings *M*
Rocky Mountain College *B*
University of Montana-Missoula *B*

Nebraska

Bellevue University *B*
Concordia University *B*
Creighton University *B, M*
Doane College *B*
Metropolitan Community College *C, A*
Midland Lutheran College *B*
University of Nebraska
Omaha *B, M*

Nevada

Community College of Southern
Nevada *C, A*
Morrison University *A, B*
University of Nevada
Las Vegas *B*
Western Nevada Community College *A*

New Hampshire

Daniel Webster College *B*
Franklin Pierce College *B*
New England College *B*
New Hampshire Community Technical
College
Nashua *C*
Rivier College *A, B*
Southern New Hampshire University *B*
University of New Hampshire *B*

New Jersey

Atlantic Cape Community College *A*
Bergen Community College *A*
Bloomfield College *B*
Burlington County College *A*
Camden County College *A*
County College of Morris *A*
Cumberland County College *C, A*
Fairleigh Dickinson University
Metropolitan Campus *M*
Hudson County Community
College *C, A*
Mercer County Community College *C, A*
Passaic County Community
College *C, A*
Raritan Valley Community College *C*
Rowan University *B*
Rutgers, The State University of New
Jersey
New Brunswick Regional
Campus *B*
St. Peter's College *A, B, M*
Salem Community College *A*
Seton Hall University *B*
Stevens Institute of Technology *M, D*
Union County College *A*

New Mexico

Clovis Community College *A*
College of Santa Fe *B*
College of the Southwest *B*
Eastern New Mexico University *B*
National American University *C, A, B*
New Mexico Highlands University *B*
New Mexico State University
Alamogordo *C, A*
Santa Fe Community College *A*

New York

Canisius College *B*
City University of New York
Baruch College *B, M*
Bronx Community College *A*
Brooklyn College *B*
York College *B*
Clarkson University *B*
Dominican College of Blauvelt *B*
Dowling College *B*
Elmira College *B*
Excelsior College *B*

Fordham University *B, M*
Fulton-Montgomery Community
College *A*
Globe Institute of Technology *C, A*
Hilbert College *A*
Hofstra University *B, M*
Iona College *B, M*
Le Moyne College *B*
Long Island University
C. W. Post Campus *B, M*
Manhattan College *B*
Nassau Community College *A*
New York Institute of Technology *B, M*
Pace University *B, M*
Pace University:
Pleasantville/Briarcliff *B, M*
Polytechnic University *B, M*
Rochester Institute of
Technology *C, B, M*
Sage College of Albany *A*
St. John Fisher College *B*
State University of New York
Albany *B, M*
Buffalo *M, D*
College at Fredonia *B*
College of Technology at Alfred *A*
College of Technology at Delhi *A*
Tompkins-Cortland Community
College *A*
Touro College *B*
Utica School of Commerce *A*
Westchester Business Institute *C, A*

North Carolina

Appalachian State University *B*
Asheville Buncombe Technical
Community College *A*
Campbell University *A, B*
Catawba Valley Community
College *C, A*
Central Piedmont Community
College *C, A*
Craven Community College *A*
East Carolina University *B*
Elon University *B*
Fayetteville Technical Community
College *A*
Gardner Webb University *B*
Guilford Technical Community
College *C, A*
High Point University *B*
Isothermal Community College *A*
Lenoir Community College *C, A*
Lenoir-Rhyne College *B*
Martin Community College *C, A*
Methodist College *B*
Montgomery Community College *C, A*
Mount Olive College *B*
Nash Community College *A*
North Carolina State University *B*
Queens University of Charlotte *B*
Randolph Community College *A*
Richmond Community College *C, A*
Roanoke-Chowan Community College *A*
Stanly Community College *A*
University of North Carolina
Charlotte *B*
Greensboro *B, M*
Wilmington *B*
Western Carolina University *B*
Wilkes Community College *C, A*
Winston-Salem State University *B*

North Dakota

Dickinson State University *A, B*
Jamestown College *B*
Lake Region State College *C, A*
Minot State University *C, B*
North Dakota State University *B*
University of North Dakota *B*

Ohio

Ashland University *B*
Baldwin-Wallace College *B*
Bowling Green State University *B, M*
Case Western Reserve University *M, D*

Cedarville University *B*
Central State University *B*
Cincinnati State Technical and
Community College *A*
Cleveland State University *B, D*
Cuyahoga Community College
Eastern Campus *A*
Metropolitan Campus *A*
David N. Myers College *C, B*
DeVry University
Columbus *B*
Defiance College *B*
Franklin University *B*
James A. Rhodes State College *A*
Jefferson Community College *A*
Kent State University *B, M, D*
Kent State University
Stark Campus *B*
Lakeland Community College *A*
Lorain County Community College *A*
Miami University
Hamilton Campus *A*
Oxford Campus *B, M*
Mount Vernon Nazarene University *B*
Notre Dame College *C*
Ohio Dominican College *B*
Ohio State University
Columbus Campus *B*
Ohio University *B*
Ohio University
Chillicothe Campus *A*
Shawnee State University *B*
Stark State College of Technology *A*
Tiffin University *B*
University of Akron *C, A, B, M*
University of Cincinnati *B*
University of Cincinnati
Raymond Walters College *A*
University of Dayton *B*
University of Toledo *B*
Ursuline College *B*
Walsh University *B*
Wright State University *B, M*
Wright State University: Lake Campus *A*
Xavier University *C, B, M*
Youngstown State University *B*

Oklahoma

Eastern Oklahoma State College *A*
Northeastern State University *B*
Oklahoma Baptist University *B*
Oklahoma City University *B, M*
Oklahoma State University *B*
Oklahoma State University
Okmulgee *A*
Oral Roberts University *B*
Rogers State University *A*
Southwestern Oklahoma State
University *B*
Tulsa Community College *C, A*
University of Central Oklahoma *B*
University of Oklahoma *B, M*
University of Tulsa *B*

Oregon

Central Oregon Community College *A*
Chemeketa Community College *A*
Clatsop Community College *A*
George Fox University *B*
Oregon Institute of Technology *A*
Portland State University *B*
Southwestern Oregon Community
College *A*
University of Oregon *B, M, D*
Western Baptist College *B*

Pennsylvania

Arcadia University *C, B*
Cabrini College *B*
California University of
Pennsylvania *A, B*
Cambria-Rowe Business College:
Indiana *A*
Carlow College *B*
Carnegie Mellon University *M, D*
Chatham College *B*

Community College of Allegheny
County *C, A*
Community College of Beaver County *A*
DeSales University *B, M*
DeVry University
Ft. Washington *M*
Delaware County Community College *A*
Delaware Valley College *C, B*
Drexel University *B*
Duquesne University *B, M*
Harrisburg Area Community College *C*
Holy Family University *M*
Indiana University of Pennsylvania *B*
Juniata College *B*
Lackawanna College *A*
Luzerne County Community College *A*
Marywood University *M*
Montgomery County Community
College *A*
Penn State
Abington *B*
Altoona *B*
Beaver *B*
Berks *B*
Delaware County *B*
Dubois *B*
Erie, The Behrend College *B*
Fayette *B*
Harrisburg *B, M*
Hazleton *B*
Lehigh Valley *B*
McKeesport *B*
Mont Alto *B*
New Kensington *B*
Schuylkill - Capital College *B*
Shenango *B*
University Park *C, B*
Worthington Scranton *B*
York *B*
Pennsylvania College of
Technology *A, B*
Philadelphia University *A, B*
Reading Area Community College *A*
Robert Morris University *B, M*
St. Joseph's University *A, B, M*
Seton Hill University *B*
South Hills School of Business and
Technology *A*
Thiel College *A, B*
University of Pennsylvania *B, M*
University of Pittsburgh *M*
University of Pittsburgh
Greensburg *B*
Titusville *A*
Villanova University *B*
West Chester University of
Pennsylvania *M*
Widener University *B*
York College of Pennsylvania *B*

Puerto Rico

Bayamon Central University *A, B*
Columbia College *A*
Inter American University of Puerto Rico
Bayamon Campus *B*
Metropolitan Campus *B*
San German Campus *B, M*
Pontifical Catholic University of Puerto
Rico *B*
Turabo University *A, B*
Universidad Metropolitana *B*
Universidad del Este *A, B*
University of Puerto Rico
Mayaguez Campus *B*
Rio Piedras Campus *B*
University of the Sacred Heart *M*

Rhode Island

Rhode Island College *B, D*
University of Rhode Island *B*

South Carolina

Anderson College *B*
Charleston Southern University *B, M*
Francis Marion University *B*
Furman University *B*

South Dakota

Augustana College *B*
Dakota State University *B*
Northern State University *B*

Tennessee

Aquinas College *B*
Belmont University *B*
Bryan College *B*
Christian Brothers University *B*
Crichton College *B*
Middle Tennessee State University *B*
Southern Adventist University *B*
Southwest Tennessee Community
   College *A*
University of Memphis *B*
University of Tennessee
   Martin *B*

Texas

Alvin Community College *C*
Angelo State University *B*
Baylor University *B, M*
Brookhaven College *A*
Dallas Baptist University *B*
DeVry University
   Irving *M*
Eastfield College *A*
Kilgore College *C, A*
Lamar University *B*
LeTourneau University *B*
Midland College *A*
Midwestern State University *B*
Northwood University: Texas
   Campus *A, B*
Our Lady of the Lake University of San
   Antonio *B*
Panola College *A*
Prairie View A&M University *B*
Richland College *A*
St. Mary's University *M*
Sam Houston State University *B*
San Antonio College *A*
San Jacinto College
   Central Campus *A*
Schreiner University *B*
Southern Methodist University *B*
Southwest Texas Junior College *A*
Southwest Texas State University *B*
Southwestern Adventist
   University *C, A, B*
Tarleton State University *B, M*
Texarkana College *C, A*
Texas A&M International
   University *B, M*
Texas A&M University *M*
Texas A&M University
   Commerce *B*
   Corpus Christi *B*
   Kingsville *B*
   Texarkana *B*
Texas Tech University *B*
University of Dallas *M*
University of Houston *B, M, D*
University of Houston
   Clear Lake *B, M*
   Downtown *B*
University of Mary Hardin-Baylor *B*
University of North Texas *B, M, D*
University of St. Thomas *B, M*
University of Texas
   Arlington *B, M, D*
   Austin *B*
   Dallas *B, M, D*
   El Paso *B*
   San Antonio *B, M, D*
West Texas A&M University *B*

Utah

Brigham Young University *B, M*
Salt Lake Community College *C, A*
Southern Utah University *B*
University of Utah *C*
Utah Valley State College *A, B*
Weber State University *C, A, B*
Westminster College *B*

Vermont

Champlain College *M*
Johnson State College *A, B*

Virginia

Bridgewater College *B*
DeVry University
   Crystal City *M*
Hampton University *B*
Longwood University *B*
Marymount University *C, M*
Old Dominion University *B*
Radford University *B*
University of Virginia *M*
Virginia State University *B*
Virginia Union University *B*
Virginia Western Community College *A*

Washington

DeVry University
   Seattle *B*
Eastern Washington University *B*
Everett Community College *A*
Gonzaga University *B*
Pacific Lutheran University *B*
Seattle Pacific University *M*
Seattle University *B*
Spokane Community College *A*
Spokane Falls Community College *C, A*
University of Washington *B*
Washington State University *B*
Western Washington University *B*

West Virginia

Alderson-Broaddus College *B*
Fairmont State College *A, B*
Glenville State College *A*
International Academy of Design and
   Technology *A*
Ohio Valley College *B*
Potomac State College of West Virginia
   University *A*

Wisconsin

Cardinal Stritch University *C, B, M*
Edgewood College *B*
Lawrence University *B*
Marquette University *B*
Milwaukee School of Engineering *B*
University of Wisconsin
   Eau Claire *B*
   La Crosse *B*
   Madison *B, M*
   Milwaukee *B*
   Oshkosh *B*
   Parkside *B*
Viterbo University *B*
Waukesha County Technical College *A*

Wyoming

Central Wyoming College *A*
Eastern Wyoming College *A*
University of Wyoming *B*

Management science

Alabama

Central Alabama Community College *C*
Tuskegee University *B*
University of Alabama *B, M, D*

Alaska

University of Alaska
   Anchorage *M*
   Southeast *B*

Arizona

Arizona State University *M*
Phoenix College *C, A*

Arkansas

University of Arkansas *M*
University of Central Arkansas *B*

California

California State University
   Dominguez Hills *B*
   Fullerton *B, M*
   Hayward *M*
   Long Beach *B*
   Northridge *B, M*
Chabot College *A*
Coastline Community College *C, A*
Grossmont Community College *C, A*
Los Angeles Pierce College *C, A*
Master's College *B*
Palomar College *C, A*
San Diego City College *C, A*
San Francisco State University *B*
San Jose State University *B*
Santa Monica College *C, A*
University of California
   San Diego *B*
Ventura College *A*

Colorado

Colorado Christian University *B*
Colorado State University *B*
National American University
   Denver *A, B*
Regis University *M*
United States Air Force Academy *B*

Connecticut

Eastern Connecticut State University *B*
Quinnipiac University *B*
Southern Connecticut State University *B*
United States Coast Guard Academy *B*

Delaware

Goldey-Beacom College *A, B*

District of Columbia

Catholic University of America *B, M*
Potomac College *B*
University of the District of Columbia *A*

Florida

Broward Community College *A*
Florida Institute of Technology *M*
Florida State University *B, M*
Miami-Dade Community College *A*
Nova Southeastern University *B*
Palm Beach Atlantic University *B*
Pensacola Junior College *A*
Stetson University *B*
University of Florida *B, M*
University of Miami *B, M*
University of South Florida *B*

Georgia

Brenau University *B*
Emory University *B*
Georgia Institute of Technology *B*
Georgia Military College *A*
Georgia Southwestern State University *B*
Griffin Technical College *A*
Savannah State University *B*
West Georgia Technical College *A*

Illinois

Benedictine University *M*
Illinois Institute of Technology *D*
Illinois Valley Community College *A*
Lewis University *B*
Loyola University of Chicago *B*
Northeastern Illinois University *B*
Northwestern University *M, D*
Roosevelt University *B, M*
Shawnee Community College *A*
Southwestern Illinois College *A*
Trinity International University *B*

Indiana

Goshen College *B*
Indiana State University *B*
Indiana Wesleyan University *M*
Oakland City University *M*
Taylor University *B*
Taylor University: Fort Wayne *B*
Valparaiso University *B*

Iowa

Buena Vista University *B*
Drake University *B*
University of Iowa *B, M, D*

Kansas

St. Mary College *M*
Southwestern College *B*

Kentucky

Prestonsburg Community College *A*
University of Kentucky *B*

Louisiana

Louisiana State University and
   Agricultural and Mechanical
   College *M, D*
Louisiana Tech University *B*
Loyola University New Orleans *M*
Nicholls State University *B*
Xavier University of Louisiana *B*

Maryland

Cecil Community College *A*
College of Notre Dame of Maryland *M*
Community College of Baltimore County
   Catonsville *C*
   Dundalk *C*
   Essex *C*
Coppin State College *B*
Johns Hopkins University *M*
Montgomery College
   Rockville Campus *A*
University of Maryland
   College Park *B*
   University College *C*

Massachusetts

American International College *B, M*
Babson College *B*
Becker College *B*
Bridgewater State College *B*
Cape Cod Community College *A*
Massachusetts College of Liberal Arts *B*
Northeastern University *A, B*
Worcester Polytechnic Institute *B, M*

Michigan

Adrian College *B*
Baker College
   of Auburn Hills *A, B*
   of Clinton Township *A, B*
   of Muskegon *A, B*
Cornerstone University *B*
Davenport University
   Eastern Region *B*
Grand Valley State University *B*
Michigan State University *M*
Northern Michigan University *B*
Oakland Community College *A*
University of Michigan
   Dearborn *B*

Minnesota

Concordia University: St. Paul *B*
Minneapolis Community and Technical
   College *C, A*
Minnesota State University
   Mankato *B*
Riverland Community College: A
   Technical and Community College *A*
St. Mary's University of Minnesota *B*
Winona State University *B*

Missouri

Central Methodist College *B*
Missouri Southern State College *B*
Rockhurst University *B*
St. Louis University *B*
University of Missouri
   Columbia *B*

Montana

Rocky Mountain College *B*

Nebraska

Grace University *B*
Union College *B*

University of Nebraska
   Lincoln *B*
   Omaha *B*

New Hampshire
College for Lifelong Learning *B*
Hesser College *A*
New Hampshire Community Technical
  College
   Manchester *C, A*
Rivier College *A, B*

New Jersey
Bloomfield College *B*
Caldwell College *B, M*
Kean University *B, M*
Rider University *B*
Rowan University *B*
Rutgers, The State University of New
  Jersey
   New Brunswick Regional
    Campus *B*

New Mexico
New Mexico State University *B*

New York
Canisius College *B*
City University of New York
  Baruch College *D*
Hofstra University *B, M*
Iona College *M*
Olean Business Institute *A*
Pace University *B, M*
Pace University:
  Pleasantville/Briarcliff *B, M*
Polytechnic University *M*
Russell Sage College *B*
St. Bonaventure University *B*
St. John Fisher College *B*
State University of New York
  Albany *B, M*
  Binghamton *B, M, D*
  Buffalo *M, D*
  College at Cortland *B*
  College at Fredonia *B*
  New Paltz *B, M*
  Oswego *B*
Suffolk County Community
  College *C, A*

North Carolina
Alamance Community College *C, A*
North Carolina Central University *B*
St. Augustine's College *B*
Wake Forest University *B*

North Dakota
University of Mary *B, M*

Ohio
Case Western Reserve University *M*
Cincinnati State Technical and
  Community College *A*
David N. Myers College *A, B*
Franklin University *B*
Heidelberg College *B*
Kent State University *B*
Kent State University
  Stark Campus *B*
Miami University
  Oxford Campus *B, M*
Ohio Northern University *B*
Ohio University *B*
University of Akron *B, M*
University of Cincinnati *M, D*
University of Dayton *M*
Wilmington College *B*
Wright State University *B, M*
Wright State University: Lake Campus *C*

Oklahoma
Northeastern State University *B*
Oklahoma Baptist University *B*
Oklahoma Christian University of
  Science and Arts *B*
Oklahoma State University *B*

Oklahoma State University
  Oklahoma City *A*
Oral Roberts University *B, M*
Western Oklahoma State College *A*

Oregon
Chemeketa Community College *A*

Pennsylvania
Bucks County Community College *A*
Drexel University *M*
Duquesne University *B*
Gettysburg College *B*
Harrisburg Area Community College *A*
Kutztown University of Pennsylvania *B*
La Salle University *B*
Lock Haven University of
  Pennsylvania *B*
Marywood University *B, M*
Penn State
  Abington *B*
  Altoona *B*
  Beaver *B*
  Berks *B*
  Delaware County *B*
  Dubois *B*
  Fayette *B*
  Hazleton *B*
  Lehigh Valley *B*
  McKeesport *B*
  Mont Alto *B*
  New Kensington *B*
  Schuylkill - Capital College *B*
  Shenango *B*
  Worthington Scranton *B*
Rosemont College *B, M*
Shippensburg University of
  Pennsylvania *B*
University of Pennsylvania *B, M, D*
University of Scranton *B*
Widener University *M*

Puerto Rico
Bayamon Central University *B, M*
Inter American University of Puerto Rico
  Bayamon Campus *B*
  San German Campus *B*

South Carolina
Central Carolina Technical College *A*
Charleston Southern University *B, M*
Clemson University *D*
Southern Wesleyan University *M*
University of South Carolina *B*

Tennessee
Belmont University *B*
Chattanooga State Technical Community
  College *A*
Christian Brothers University *B*
Roane State Community College *A*
Southern Adventist University *B*
Tennessee Technological University *B*
Trevecca Nazarene University *B*
Union University *B*
University of Tennessee
  Knoxville *M, D*

Texas
Abilene Christian University *B*
El Paso Community College *C, A*
Hardin-Simmons University *B*
Midland College *C*
North Lake College *A*
Southern Methodist University *B*
Southwestern Adventist University *B*
Texas A&M University
  Kingsville *B*
Texas Wesleyan University *B*
Trinity University *B*
University of Mary Hardin-Baylor *B*
University of North Texas *M, D*
University of Texas
  El Paso *B*
  San Antonio *B, M*
University of the Incarnate Word *M*

Utah
Brigham Young University *B*

Vermont
Castleton State College *B*
College of St. Joseph in Vermont *B*

Virginia
Averett University *B*
Marymount University *B*
Southside Virginia Community
  College *C, A*
Thomas Nelson Community College *A*
Virginia Polytechnic Institute and State
  University *B*

Washington
Eastern Washington University *B*
Walla Walla College *B*

West Virginia
Fairmont State College *A, B*
Wheeling Jesuit University *B*

Wisconsin
Marquette University *C*
Northland College *B*
University of Wisconsin
  Green Bay *M*
  Milwaukee *D*

Wyoming
University of Wyoming *B*

Manicurist

Alabama
Lawson State Community College *C*

Florida
Indian River Community College *C*
Palm Beach Community College *C*
Pensacola Junior College *C*

Georgia
West Georgia Technical College *C*

Illinois
Kaskaskia College *C*

Minnesota
Minneapolis Community and Technical
  College *C*
Minnesota State College - Southeast
  Technical *C*
St. Paul College - A Community and
  Technical College *C*

North Carolina
Carteret Community College *C*
Davidson County Community College *C*
Lenoir Community College *C*
Martin Community College *C*
Roanoke-Chowan Community
  College *C*

Texas
Lamar State College at Port Arthur *C*
North Harris Montgomery Community
  College District *C*

Washington
Renton Technical College *C*

Wisconsin
Milwaukee Area Technical College *C*

Manufacturing engineering

Alabama
Auburn University *M*

California
California State Polytechnic University:
  Pomona *B*
Santa Clara University *C*

Connecticut
University of Connecticut *B*

Florida
University of Central Florida *B, M, D*
University of South Florida *B, M, D*

Illinois
Southern Illinois University
  Edwardsville *B*
University of Illinois
  Urbana-Champaign *B, M, D*

Kentucky
Maysville Community College *C, A*

Massachusetts
University of Massachusetts
  Amherst *M*
Worcester Polytechnic Institute *B, M, D*

Michigan
Grand Valley State University *B, M*
Kettering University *B, M*

New York
Hofstra University *B*
Rochester Institute of Technology *B, M*
State University of New York
  Buffalo *M, D*

North Dakota
North Dakota State University *B*

Oklahoma
Oklahoma State University *M*

Oregon
Oregon State University *B, M*
Portland State University *M*

Pennsylvania
Robert Morris University *B*

Puerto Rico
Turabo University *B*

Texas
Southwest Texas State University *B*
University of Texas
  Austin *M*

Utah
Brigham Young University *B*
Utah Valley State College *A*

Wisconsin
University of Wisconsin
  Stout *B*

Wyoming
Central Wyoming College *C*

Manufacturing technologies

Alabama
Jacksonville State University *B*
Northwest-Shoals Community College *C*
University of West Alabama *B*

Arizona
Central Arizona College *A*
Gateway Community College *C, A*
Yavapai College *A*

Arkansas
Arkansas State University
  Mountain Home *C, A*
Phillips Community College of the
  University of Arkansas *C, A*
University of Arkansas
  Fort Smith *B*

California
California State University
  Long Beach *B*
  Los Angeles *B*
Cerritos Community College *C, A*
College of the Sequoias *A*
Don Bosco Technical Institute *A*
Irvine Valley College *C, A*
Long Beach City College *C*

San Diego City College *C, A*
Santa Clara University *C*

Colorado

Mesa State College *C, A*
Red Rocks Community College *C, A*

Connecticut

Asnuntuck Community College *A*
Central Connecticut State University *B*
Gateway Community College *A*
Manchester Community College *A*
Naugatuck Valley Community
  College *C, A*
Three Rivers Community College *A*
Tunxis Community College *A*
University of New Haven *A*

Florida

Pensacola Junior College *A*
Polk Community College *A*
St. Petersburg College *A*
University of West Florida *B*

Georgia

Albany Technical College *A*
Georgia Southwestern State University *A*
Middle Georgia College *A*

Idaho

Brigham Young University - Idaho *A*

Illinois

Heartland Community College *C, A*
Illinois Eastern Community Colleges
  Wabash Valley College *A*
Illinois Institute of Technology *B*
Illinois State University *B, M*
John Wood Community College *C*
Kankakee Community College *A*
Kishwaukee College *C, A*
Morrison Institute of Technology *A*
Parkland College *C, A*
Rend Lake College *A*
Rock Valley College *C, A*
Sauk Valley Community College *A*
William Rainey Harper College *C, A*

Indiana

Ball State University *A*
Indiana State University *B, M*
Ivy Tech State College
  Bloomington *C, A*
  Central Indiana *C, A*
  Columbus *C, A*
  Eastcentral *C, A*
  Kokomo *C, A*
  Lafayette *C, A*
  Northcentral *C, A*
  Northeast *C, A*
  Northwest *C, A*
  Southcentral *C, A*
  Southeast *C, A*
  Southwest *C, A*
  Wabash Valley *C, A*
  Whitewater *A*
Vincennes University *A*

Iowa

Iowa Central Community College *A*
Northwest Iowa Community
  College *C, A*

Kansas

Pittsburg State University *B*

Kentucky

Morehead State University *A, B, M*
Murray State University *B*
St. Catharine College *A*

Louisiana

Southeastern Louisiana University *A, B*

Maine

University of Southern Maine *B, M*

Maryland

Chesapeake College *A*

Massachusetts

Northeastern University *B*
Quinsigamond Community College *C, A*
University of Massachusetts
  Lowell *M*

Michigan

Alpena Community College *A*
Eastern Michigan University *B*
Gogebic Community College *A*
Macomb Community College *C, A*
Michigan State University *B, M, D*
Mid Michigan Community College *A*
Monroe County Community
  College *C, A*
Mott Community College *A*
Oakland Community College *C, A*
St. Clair County Community College *A*
Wayne State University *B*

Minnesota

Hennepin Technical College *C, A*
Minnesota State University
  Mankato *B, M*
St. Cloud State University *B*
St. Paul College - A Community and
  Technical College *A*
University of St. Thomas *D*

Mississippi

Mississippi State University *B*

Missouri

Central Missouri State University *A*
Mineral Area College *C, A*
Missouri Southern State College *C*
Missouri Western State College *A*
Moberly Area Community College *C, A*
St. Louis Community College
  St. Louis Community College at
    Florissant Valley *A*

Montana

Montana Tech of the University of
  Montana *A*

Nebraska

University of Nebraska
  Lincoln *A, B, M*

New Hampshire

New Hampshire Community Technical
  College
  Berlin *A*
  Nashua *A*
New Hampshire Technical Institute *A*

New Jersey

Essex County College *A*
Middlesex County College *A*
Thomas Edison State College *A, B*
Union County College *A*

New York

Corning Community College *A*
Excelsior College *B*
Monroe Community College *A*
New York Institute of Technology *B*
Rochester Institute of Technology *B, M*
State University of New York
  College of Agriculture and
    Technology at Morrisville *A*
  College of Technology at Canton *A*
    Farmingdale *C, B*
Tompkins-Cortland Community
  College *A*

North Carolina

Central Carolina Community College *A*
Craven Community College *A*
Davidson County Community
  College *C, A*
Guilford Technical Community
  College *C, A*
Mitchell Community College *A*
Pitt Community College *C, A*
Randolph Community College *A*
Richmond Community College *A*
Rockingham Community College *C*

South Piedmont Community College *A*
University of North Carolina
  Charlotte *B*
Wake Technical Community College *A*
Western Carolina University *B, M*

Ohio

Bowling Green State University *B, M*
Bowling Green State University:
  Firelands College *A*
Cincinnati State Technical and
  Community College *C, A*
Clark State Community College *A*
Edison State Community College *A*
James A. Rhodes State College *C, A*
Jefferson Community College *A*
Kent State University *A, B*
Kent State University
  Ashtabula Regional Campus *C*
  Salem Regional Campus *A*
Lakeland Community College *C, A*
Miami University
  Hamilton Campus *C*
North Central State College *C*
Owens Community College
  Toledo *C, A*
Sinclair Community College *A*
Stark State College of Technology *A*
University of Dayton *B*
University of Rio Grande *A*
Wright State University: Lake Campus *A*

Oklahoma

Northeastern State University *B*
Oklahoma City Community College *A*
Oklahoma Panhandle State
  University *A, B*
Oklahoma State University
  Oklahoma City *A*
  Okmulgee *A*
Rogers State University *B*
Southwestern Oklahoma State
  University *B*
Western Oklahoma State College *A*

Oregon

Central Oregon Community
  College *C, A*
Portland Community College *C, A*

Pennsylvania

Butler County Community College *A*
Community College of Allegheny
  County *A*
Penn State
  Fayette *A*
  York *A*
Pennsylvania College of
  Technology *A, B*

South Carolina

Trident Technical College *C, A*
York Technical College *C*

Tennessee

Jackson State Community College *C*
Tennessee Technological University *B*
University of Memphis *B*
Walters State Community College *C, A*

Texas

Frank Phillips College *C, A*
Richland College *A*
Southern Methodist University *M*
Southwest Texas State University *B*
Tarleton State University *B*
Texas A&M University *B*
Texas A&M University
  Commerce *B*
University of Houston *B*

Utah

Salt Lake Community College *A*

Virginia

Danville Community College *A*
Mountain Empire Community College *A*
Thomas Nelson Community College *C*

Washington

Clark College *A*
Eastern Washington University *B*
Everett Community College *A*
Grays Harbor College *A*
Wenatchee Valley College *C, A*

West Virginia

Shepherd College *A*
West Virginia University at
  Parkersburg *A*

Marine biology

Alabama

Alabama State University *B*
Auburn University *B*
Samford University *B*
Spring Hill College *B*
Troy State University *B*
University of Alabama *B, M*
University of Mobile *B*
University of North Alabama *B*
University of South Alabama *M, D*
University of West Alabama *B*

Alaska

Sheldon Jackson College *B*
University of Alaska
  Fairbanks *M*
  Southeast *B*

California

California State University
  Fresno *M*
  Monterey Bay *B, M*
  Sacramento *M*
  Stanislaus *B, M*
College of the Redwoods *C*
Los Angeles Pierce College *C*
Mount San Antonio College *A*
San Diego State University *B*
San Francisco State University *B, M*
San Jose State University *B, M*
University of California
  Los Angeles *B*
  San Diego *D*
  Santa Barbara *B, M, D*
  Santa Cruz *B, M*
University of San Diego *B, M*
University of Southern
  California *B, M, D*

Connecticut

Mitchell College *A*
Southern Connecticut State University *B*
University of Connecticut *B*

Delaware

University of Delaware *M, D*

Florida

Barry University *B, T*
Eckerd College *B*
Florida Institute of Technology *B, M*
Florida International University *B*
Florida Keys Community College *A*
Gulf Coast Community College *A*
Jacksonville University *B*
Manatee Community College *A*
Nova Southeastern University *B, M*
Okaloosa-Walton Community College *A*
South Florida Community College *A*
Stetson University *B*
University of Miami *B, M, D*
University of Tampa *B*
University of West Florida *B*

Georgia

Oxford College of Emory University *B*
Savannah State University *B*
University of Georgia *M, D*

Hawaii

Hawaii Pacific University *B*

University of Hawaii
Hilo *B*
Manoa *B*

Indiana
Ball State University *B*

Kansas
Southwestern College *B*

Louisiana
Nicholls State University *B*

Maine
College of the Atlantic *B*
Maine Maritime Academy *B, T*
University of Maine *B, M, D*
University of Maine
Machias *B*
University of New England *B*

Maryland
University of Maryland
Baltimore *D*
Baltimore County *M, D*
College Park *M, D*

Massachusetts
Boston University *B*
Hampshire College *B*
Harvard College *B*
Northeastern University *B*
Salem State College *B*
Suffolk University *B*
University of Massachusetts
Lowell *M, D*

Minnesota
Bemidji State University *B*
St. Cloud State University *B*

Mississippi
University of Southern
Mississippi *B, M, D*

Missouri
Missouri Southern State College *B*

New Hampshire
University of New Hampshire *B*

New Jersey
Fairleigh Dickinson University
College at Florham *B*
Metropolitan Campus *B*
Richard Stockton College of New
Jersey *B*
Rider University *B*
Rutgers, The State University of New
Jersey
New Brunswick Regional
Campus *B*

New York
Hofstra University *B*
Long Island University
Southampton College *B*
Sarah Lawrence College *B*
State University of New York
College of Agriculture and
Technology at Morrisville *A*
College of Environmental Science
and Forestry *B*
Maritime College *M*

North Carolina
Brunswick Community College *A*
University of North Carolina
Wilmington *B, M*

Ohio
Ohio University *B*
Wittenberg University *B*

Oklahoma
Northeastern State University *B*

Oregon
University of Oregon *B, M, D*

Pennsylvania
East Stroudsburg University of
Pennsylvania *B*
Juniata College *B*
Waynesburg College *B*

Puerto Rico
University of Puerto Rico
Humacao *B*
Mayaguez Campus *B, M*

Rhode Island
Roger Williams University *B*
University of Rhode Island *B*

South Carolina
Coastal Carolina University *B, M*
College of Charleston *B, M*
Medical University of South Carolina *D*
University of South Carolina *B, M, D*

Texas
Galveston College *A*
Lamar University *B*
Laredo Community College *A*
Southwest Texas State University *B*
Texas A&M University *B*
Texas A&M University
Corpus Christi *M*
Galveston *B*

Utah
Dixie State College of Utah *A*
Utah State University *M, D*

Virginia
College of William and Mary *M, D*
Hampton University *B*

Washington
Olympic College *A*
University of Washington *B*
Western Washington University *B*

Wisconsin
Lawrence University *B, T*
University of Wisconsin
Superior *B*

Marine engineering/naval architecture

California
California Maritime Academy *B*
Santa Barbara City College *A*

Connecticut
United States Coast Guard Academy *B*

Florida
Gulf Coast Community College *A*

Louisiana
University of New Orleans *B*

Maine
Maine Maritime Academy *B*

Maryland
United States Naval Academy *B*

Michigan
University of Michigan *B, M, D*

New Jersey
Thomas Edison State College *A, B*

New York
State University of New York
Maritime College *B*
United States Merchant Marine
Academy *B*
Webb Institute *B*

Texas
Texas A&M University
Galveston *B*

Marine maintenance/fitter/ship repair

Kentucky
Louisville Technical Institute *C, A*

Minnesota
Hennepin Technical College *C, A*
South Central Technical College *A*

New Hampshire
New Hampshire Community Technical
College
Laconia *C, A*

New York
United States Merchant Marine
Academy *B*

North Carolina
Cape Fear Community College *C*
Carteret Community College *A*

Marine science/Merchant Marine

Maine
Maine Maritime Academy *B*

Michigan
Northwestern Michigan College *A*

New York
United States Merchant Marine
Academy *B*

Texas
Texas A&M University
Galveston *B*

Marketing management

Alabama
Alabama Agricultural and Mechanical
University *B*
Alabama State University *B*
Auburn University *B*
Auburn University at Montgomery *B*
Birmingham-Southern College *B*
Faulkner University *B*
Huntingdon College *B*
Jacksonville State University *B*
Spring Hill College *B*
University of Alabama *B, M, D*
University of Alabama
Birmingham *B*
Huntsville *B*
University of Mobile *B*
University of North Alabama *B*
University of South Alabama *B*

Alaska
University of Alaska
Anchorage *B*

Arizona
Phoenix College *C, A*
University of Arizona *B*
University of Phoenix *C, B, M*

Arkansas
Arkansas State University *B*
Harding University *B*
University of Arkansas *B*
University of Arkansas
Little Rock *B*
University of Central Arkansas *B*
University of the Ozarks *B*

California
California State Polytechnic University:
Pomona *B*
California State University
Chico *B*
Fresno *B*
Fullerton *B, M*

College of Alameda *C, A*
Concordia University *B*
De Anza College *C, A*
Fashion Institute of Design and
Merchandising *A*
Golden Gate University *B, M*
Grossmont Community College *C, A*
Los Angeles Pierce College *C, A*
Modesto Junior College *A*
National University *M*
Ohlone College *C, A*
Pacific Union College *B*
Riverside Community College *C, A*
San Diego State University *M*
Santa Barbara City College *C, A*
Santa Clara University *B*
Santiago Canyon College *A*
Southwestern College *C, A*
University of La Verne *B*
University of San Francisco *B*
Ventura College *A*
Yuba Community College District *C*

Colorado
Arapahoe Community College *C, A*
Community College of Aurora *A*
Metropolitan State College of Denver *B*
University of Colorado
Boulder *B, M*
Denver *M*
University of Denver *B, M*

Connecticut
Central Connecticut State University *B*
Fairfield University *B*
Middlesex Community College *A*
Northwestern Connecticut Community
College *A*
Norwalk Community College *A*
Quinnipiac University *B, M*
Southern Connecticut State University *B*
University of Bridgeport *B*
University of Connecticut *B*
University of New Haven *B*
Western Connecticut State University *B*

Delaware
Delaware State University *B*
Delaware Technical and Community
College
Owens Campus *C, A*
Stanton/Wilmington Campus *C, A*
Terry Campus *C, A*
Goldey-Beacom College *B*
Wilmington College *B*

District of Columbia
American University *B, M*
Georgetown University *B*
Strayer University *A*

Florida
Art Institute
of Fort Lauderdale *B*
Daytona Beach Community College *A*
Florida Atlantic University *B*
Florida International University *B*
Florida Metropolitan University
Orlando College North *A, B*
Tampa College *A, B*
Florida Southern College *B*
Florida State University *B, M*
Florida Technical College
Auburndale *A*
Gulf Coast Community College *A*
Jacksonville University *B, M*
Northwood University
Florida Campus *B*
Okaloosa-Walton Community
College *C, A*
Palm Beach Atlantic University *B*
Palm Beach Community College *A*
Pasco-Hernando Community College *A*
Polk Community College *A*
St. Petersburg College *A*
Santa Fe Community College *A*
Seminole Community College *C*

Stetson University *B*
University of Central Florida *B*
University of Florida *B, M*
University of Miami *B*
University of North Florida *B*
University of South Florida *B*
University of Tampa *B*
University of West Florida *B*
Webber International University *A, B*

Georgia

Albany State University *B*
Augusta State University *B*
Bauder College *A*
Berry College *B*
Brenau University *B*
Chattahoochee Technical College *C, A*
Clayton College and State
   University *C, A, B*
Coastal Georgia Community
   College *C, A*
Columbus State University *B*
Dalton State College *A*
DeKalb Technical College *A*
Emory University *B*
Fort Valley State University *B*
Georgia College and State University *B*
Georgia Southern University *B*
Georgia State University *B, M, D*
Kennesaw State University *B*
Mercer University *B, M*
Morehouse College *B*
North Georgia College & State
   University *B*
South Georgia College *A*
State University of West Georgia *B*
Thomas University *B*
University of Georgia *B*

Hawaii

Hawaii Pacific University *B*
University of Hawaii
   Hawaii Community College *C, A*
   Hilo *B*
   Manoa *B*
   West Oahu *B*

Idaho

Boise State University *B*
College of Southern Idaho *A*
Eastern Idaho Technical College *C, A*
Idaho State University *C, A*
Lewis-Clark State College *B*
University of Idaho *B*

Illinois

Augustana College *B*
Aurora University *B*
Benedictine University *B*
Blackburn College *B*
Bradley University *B*
College of DuPage *C*
Columbia College Chicago *B*
De Paul University *M*
Eastern Illinois University *B*
Elmhurst College *B*
Illinois Institute of Technology *M*
Illinois State University *B*
Loyola University of Chicago *C, B*
McKendree College *B*
Midstate College *C*
Millikin University *B*
North Central College *B*
North Park University *B*
Northwestern University *M, D*
Olivet Nazarene University *B*
Quincy University *B*
Rock Valley College *C, A*
Rockford Business College *C, A*
Rockford College *B*
Roosevelt University *B, M*
St. Xavier University *M*
Sauk Valley Community College *C, A*
South Suburban College of Cook
   County *C, A*
Southern Illinois University
   Carbondale *B*

Trinity Christian College *B*
Trinity International University *B*
Triton College *C, A*
University of Illinois
   Chicago *B*
University of St. Francis *B*
Waubonsee Community College *C, A*
Western Illinois University *B*
William Rainey Harper College *C, A*

Indiana

Anderson University *B*
Ball State University *B*
Butler University *B*
Goshen College *B*
Grace College *B*
Indiana Business College *A*
Indiana Business College
   Anderson *A*
   Columbus *A*
   Evansville *A*
   Fort Wayne *A*
   Marion *A*
   Muncie *A*
   Terre Haute *A*
Indiana Institute of Technology *B*
Indiana State University *B*
Indiana University
   Kokomo *B*
   South Bend *B*
Indiana University-Purdue University
   Fort Wayne *B*
Indiana Wesleyan University *B*
Marian College *B*
Purdue University
   North Central Campus *A*
St. Joseph's College *B*
Taylor University *B*
University of Evansville *B*
University of Notre Dame *B*
University of Southern Indiana *B*
Valparaiso University *B*
Vincennes University *A*

Iowa

American Institute of Business *A*
Buena Vista University *B*
Clarke College *B*
Des Moines Area Community College *A*
Drake University *B*
Franciscan University *B*
Hawkeye Community College *A*
Iowa State University *B*
Loras College *B*
Luther College *B*
Maharishi University of
   Management *C, M*
Morningside College *B*
Northeast Iowa Community College *A*
Northwest Iowa Community College *C*
Northwestern College *B*
St. Ambrose University *B*
Simpson College *B*
Southwestern Community College *A*
University of Iowa *B*
University of Northern Iowa *B*
Wartburg College *B*
William Penn University *B*

Kansas

Emporia State University *B*
Fort Hays State University *B*
Fort Scott Community College *A*
Kansas City Kansas Community
   College *A*
Newman University *B*
Pittsburg State University *M*
Tabor College *B*
Washburn University of Topeka *B*
Wichita State University *B*

Kentucky

Campbellsville University *B*
Hazard Community College *A*
Morehead State University *B*
Murray State University *B, M*
University of Kentucky *B*

University of Louisville *B*

Louisiana

Grambling State University *B*
Louisiana College *B*
Louisiana State University and
   Agricultural and Mechanical
   College *B, M, D*
Louisiana Tech University *B*
Loyola University New Orleans *B*
McNeese State University *B*
Nicholls State University *B*
Southeastern Louisiana University *B*
Southern University and Agricultural and
   Mechanical College *B*
University of Louisiana at Lafayette *B*
University of Louisiana at Monroe *B*
University of New Orleans *B*
Xavier University of Louisiana *B*

Maine

Husson College *B*
St. Joseph's College *B*
Thomas College *B*
University of Maine
   Machias *B*
University of Southern Maine *B, M*

Maryland

Allegany College *A*
Johns Hopkins University *M*
Morgan State University *B*
Salisbury University *B*
University of Baltimore *B, M*
University of Maryland
   College Park *B*
   University College *B*

Massachusetts

American International College *B, M*
Assumption College *B*
Babson College *B*
Becker College *B*
Boston University *B*
Bridgewater State College *B*
Cape Cod Community College *A*
Emerson College *M*
Fitchburg State College *B*
Greenfield Community College *C*
Lasell College *B, M*
Marian Court College *C, A*
Massasoit Community College *A*
Newbury College *A, B*
Nichols College *B*
Northeastern University *A, B*
Springfield Technical Community
   College *A*
Stonehill College *B*
Suffolk University *B, M*
University of Massachusetts
   Amherst *B*
   Dartmouth *B*
Western New England College *B*
Worcester Polytechnic Institute *M*

Michigan

Adrian College *B*
Baker College
   of Cadillac *A*
   of Muskegon *A, B*
   of Owosso *A, B*
   of Port Huron *A, B*
Central Michigan University *B*
Cleary University *B*
Davenport University
   Eastern Region *A, B*
Davenport University - Western
   Region *A, B*
Eastern Michigan University *B*
Ferris State University *C, B*
Finlandia University *B*
Grace Bible College *B*
Grand Rapids Community College *A*
Grand Valley State University *B*
Hillsdale College *B*
Kellogg Community College *C*
Kettering University *B*

Kirtland Community College *A*
Lansing Community College *A*
Macomb Community College *C, A*
Madonna University *B*
Michigan State University *B, M, D*
Mid Michigan Community College *A*
Muskegon Community College *A*
Northwood University *B*
Oakland University *B*
University of Michigan
   Flint *B*
Wayne State University *B*
West Shore Community College *A*
Western Michigan University *B*

Minnesota

Alexandria Technical College *C, A*
Anoka-Ramsey Community College *A*
Augsburg College *B*
Bethel College *B*
Century Community and Technical
   College *C, A*
Fergus Falls Community College *A*
Mesabi Range Community and Technical
   College *C, A*
Metropolitan State University *B*
Minneapolis Community and Technical
   College *C, A*
Minnesota State University
   Moorhead *B*
National American University
   St. Paul *B*
Normandale Community College *C, A*
Northwestern College *B*
Rasmussen College
   Minnetonka *A*
Riverland Community College: A
   Technical and Community College *A*
St. Cloud State University *B*
St. Mary's University of Minnesota *B*
University of Minnesota
   Crookston *B*
   Twin Cities *B*
University of St. Thomas *B, M*
Winona State University *B*

Mississippi

Delta State University *B*
Mississippi College *B*
Mississippi Gulf Coast Community
   College
   Perkinston *A*
Mississippi State University *B*
University of Mississippi *B*
University of Southern Mississippi *B, M*

Missouri

Central Missouri State University *B*
College of the Ozarks *B*
Harris Stowe State College *B*
Lindenwood University *B, M*
Maryville University of Saint Louis *B, M*
Mineral Area College *C, A*
Missouri Baptist University *B*
Missouri Southern State College *B*
Missouri Western State College *B*
Moberly Area Community College *C, A*
Rockhurst University *B*
St. Charles Community College *A*
St. Louis University *B*
Southeast Missouri State University *B*
Southwest Missouri State University *B*
Three Rivers Community College *A*
University of Missouri
   St. Louis *B*
Washington University in St. Louis *B, M*
Webster University *C, B, M*

Montana

Flathead Valley Community College *A*
Montana Tech of the University of
   Montana *B*
University of Montana-Missoula *A, B*

Nebraska

Bellevue University *B*
Creighton University *B*

Hastings College *B*
Lincoln School of Commerce *A*
Southeast Community College
  Lincoln Campus *A*
University of Nebraska
  Lincoln *B*
  Omaha *B*

Nevada
University of Nevada
  Las Vegas *B*
  Reno *B*
Western Nevada Community College *A*

New Hampshire
Franklin Pierce College *B*
Hesser College *A, B*
New Hampshire Community Technical
  College
  Manchester *C, A*
New Hampshire Technical Institute *A*
Plymouth State College *B*
Rivier College *M*
University of New Hampshire *A*

New Jersey
Brookdale Community College *A*
Caldwell College *B*
Camden County College *A*
The College of New Jersey *B*
College of St. Elizabeth *C*
Cumberland County College *A*
Fairleigh Dickinson University
  College at Florham *B*
  Metropolitan Campus *B*
Gloucester County College *A*
Kean University *B*
Monmouth University *B*
Passaic County Community College *A*
Richard Stockton College of New
  Jersey *B*
Rider University *B*
Rowan University *B*
Rutgers, The State University of New
  Jersey
  Camden Regional Campus *B*
  New Brunswick Regional
    Campus *B*
  Newark Regional Campus *B*
Seton Hall University *B*
Thomas Edison State College *C, A, B*

New Mexico
College of the Southwest *B*
Eastern New Mexico University *B*
New Mexico State University *B*
Western New Mexico University *B*

New York
Adirondack Community College *A*
Broome Community College *A*
Bryant & Stratton Business Institute
  Syracuse *A*
City University of New York
  Kingsborough Community
    College *A*
  York College *B*
Clarkson University *B*
Dominican College of Blauvelt *B*
Dowling College *B*
Elmira College *B*
Excelsior College *B*
Hofstra University *B, M*
Ithaca College *B*
Jamestown Business College *A*
Long Island University
  C. W. Post Campus *M*
  Southampton College *B*
Marist College *B, M*
Monroe Community College *A*
New York Institute of Technology *B*
Pace University *B, M*
Pace University:
  Pleasantville/Briarcliff *B, M*
Roberts Wesleyan College *B*
Rochester Institute of
  Technology *A, B, M*

Sage College of Albany *A*
St. John Fisher College *B*
State University of New York
  Albany *M*
  Buffalo *M, D*
  College at Old Westbury *B*
  College at Plattsburgh *B*
  College of Technology at Alfred *A*
Suffolk County Community
  College *C, A*
Touro College *B*
Westchester Community College *A*

North Carolina
East Carolina University *B*
Lenoir-Rhyne College *B*
Meredith College *B*
Methodist College *B*
North Carolina Agricultural and
  Technical State University
North Carolina State University *B*
Queens University of Charlotte *B*
Southwestern Community College *A*
University of North Carolina
  Charlotte *B*
  Wilmington *B*
Western Carolina University *B*

North Dakota
Minot State University *B*
Minot State University: Bottineau
  Campus *C, A*
University of North Dakota *B*
Williston State College *C, A*

Ohio
Ashland University *B*
Bowling Green State University:
  Firelands College *C*
Cedarville University *B*
Cincinnati State Technical and
  Community College *A*
Cleveland State University *B, M*
Cuyahoga Community College
  Eastern Campus *A*
  Western Campus *A*
David N. Myers College *B*
Davis College *A*
Defiance College *B*
Edison State Community College *A*
Franklin University *B*
James A. Rhodes State College *A*
Kent State University *B, D*
Kent State University
  Stark Campus *B*
Lakeland Community College *C*
Marion Technical College *C, A*
Miami University
  Oxford Campus *B, M*
Muskingum Area Technical College *A*
North Central State College *C*
Northwest State Community College *A*
Notre Dame College *C, B*
Ohio University *B*
Stark State College of Technology *A*
Tiffin University *B*
University of Akron *C, B, M*
University of Dayton *B*
University of Findlay *B*
University of Northwestern Ohio *A*
University of Toledo *B, M*
Urbana University *B*
Ursuline College *B*
Walsh University *A, B*
Washington State Community College *A*
Wilmington College *B*
Wright State University *B, M*
Xavier University *B, M*
Youngstown State University *A, B, M*

Oklahoma
East Central University *B*
Northeastern Oklahoma Agricultural and
  Mechanical College *C, A*
Northeastern State University *B*
Oklahoma Baptist University *B*
Oklahoma City University *B, M*

Oklahoma State University *B, M, D*
Oral Roberts University *B*
Southern Nazarene University *B*
University of Central Oklahoma *B*
University of Oklahoma *B*
University of Tulsa *B*

Oregon
Blue Mountain Community College *A*
Portland State University *B*
Southern Oregon University *B*
University of Portland *B*

Pennsylvania
Albright College *B*
Arcadia University *B*
Bucks County Community College *A*
California University of Pennsylvania *B*
Carnegie Mellon University *D*
Cedar Crest College *C*
Chatham College *B*
Chestnut Hill College *C, A, B*
Community College of Allegheny
  County *A*
Community College of Beaver County *A*
DeSales University *B*
Delaware Valley College *B*
Drexel University *B, M*
Duquesne University *B*
Education Direct: Center for Degree
  Studies *A*
Erie Business Center *A*
Grove City College *B*
Holy Family University *B*
Immaculata University *A*
Juniata College *B*
King's College *A, R*
Kutztown University of Pennsylvania *B*
La Roche College *B*
La Salle University *B*
Lebanon Valley College of
  Pennsylvania *C*
Lehigh University *B*
Manor College *A*
Marywood University *B*
Mercyhurst College *B*
Messiah College *B*
Montgomery County Community
  College *C, A*
Neumann College *B*
Peirce College *A*
Penn State
  Erie, The Behrend College *B*
  Schuylkill - Capital College *B*
  University Park *B*
  Worthington Scranton *B*
Philadelphia University *B*
Robert Morris University *B, M*
St. Joseph's University *A, B, M*
St. Vincent College *B*
Seton Hill University *B*
Shippensburg University of
  Pennsylvania *B*
South Hills School of Business &
  Technology *A*
Temple University *B, M, D*
University of Pittsburgh *B*
University of Scranton *B*
University of the Sciences in
  Philadelphia *B*
Villanova University *B*
York College of Pennsylvania *B*

Puerto Rico
Bayamon Central University *B, M*
ICPR Junior College *A*
Inter American University of Puerto Rico
  Metropolitan Campus *B, M*
  San German Campus *B, M*
Pontifical Catholic University of Puerto
  Rico *B*
Turabo University *B, M*
Universidad Metropolitana *B, M*
Universidad del Este *C, A, B*

University of Puerto Rico
  Bayamon University College *A, B*
  Mayaguez Campus *B, M*
  Ponce *B*
University of the Sacred Heart *M*

Rhode Island
Bryant College *B, M*
Community College of Rhode
  Island *C, A*
Providence College *A, B*
University of Rhode Island *B*

South Carolina
Anderson College *A*
Central Carolina Technical College *A*
Charleston Southern University *B, M*
Coastal Carolina University *B*
Forrest Junior College *A*
University of South Carolina *B*

South Dakota
Dakota State University *B*
Northern State University *B*
Western Dakota Technical Institute *A*

Tennessee
Belmont University *B*
Christian Brothers University *B*
East Tennessee State University *B*
Freed-Hardeman University *B*
Lambuth University *B*
Middle Tennessee State University *B*
Southern Adventist University *B*
Trevecca Nazarene University *B*
Union University *B*
University of Memphis *B*
University of Tennessee
  Martin *B*

Texas
Abilene Christian University *B*
Angelo State University *B*
Austin Community College *C, A*
Baylor University *B*
Brookhaven College *A*
College of the Mainland *A*
Dallas Baptist University *B, M*
East Texas Baptist University *B*
Galveston College *C, A*
Hardin-Simmons University *B*
Houston Baptist University *B*
Houston Community College
  System *C, A*
Howard Payne University *B*
Huston-Tillotson College *B*
Lamar University *B*
Laredo Community College *A*
LeTourneau University *B*
Lubbock Christian University *B*
McMurry University *B*
North Harris Montgomery Community
  College District *C, A*
Northwood University: Texas Campus *B*
Our Lady of the Lake University of San
  Antonio *B*
Prairie View A&M University *B*
St. Edward's University *B, T*
St. Mary's University *B*
Sam Houston State University *B*
Southern Methodist University *B*
Southwest Texas State University *B*
Stephen F. Austin State University *B*
Sul Ross State University *B*
Tarleton State University *B*
Texas A&M International University *B*
Texas A&M University *B, M, D*
Texas A&M University
  Commerce *B*
  Corpus Christi *B*
  Texarkana *B*
Texas Christian University *B*
Texas Southern University *B*
Texas Tech University *B*
Texas Woman's University *B*
Trinity University *B*
Tyler Junior College *C, A*

University of Houston *B, M, D*
University of Houston
    Clear Lake *B*
    Downtown *B*
University of Mary Hardin-Baylor *B*
University of North Texas *B, M, D*
University of St. Thomas *B*
University of Texas
    Arlington *B, D*
    Austin *B, D*
    Brownsville *B*
    Dallas *B, M, D*
    El Paso *B*
    San Antonio *B*
    Tyler *B*
University of the Incarnate Word *B*
West Texas A&M University *B*

Utah
Brigham Young University *B*
Southern Utah University *B*
University of Utah *B, M*
Utah State University *B*
Utah Valley State College *B*
Weber State University *B*
Westminster College *B*

Vermont
Castleton State College *B*
Champlain College *A, B*

Virginia
Averett University *B*
George Mason University *B*
Hampton University *B*
J. Sargeant Reynolds Community
   College *A*
James Madison University *B*
Longwood University *B*
Marymount University *C, B*
Old Dominion University *B*
Radford University *B*
Virginia Commonwealth University *B*
Virginia State University *B*

Washington
Bellevue Community College *C, A*
Centralia College *C*
Clover Park Technical College *C, A*
Eastern Washington University *B*
Edmonds Community College *C, A*
Green River Community College *A*
Seattle University *B*
Spokane Community College *C, A*
Spokane Falls Community College *C, A*
Washington State University *B*

West Virginia
Concord College *B*
Davis and Elkins College *B*
Glenville State College *B*
Marshall University *B*
University of Charleston *A, B*
West Virginia University *B*
West Virginia Wesleyan College *B*

Wisconsin
Cardinal Stritch University *C*
Carroll College *B*
Carthage College *B*
Lakeland College *B*
Lakeshore Technical College *A*
Mid-State Technical College *A*
Moraine Park Technical College *A*
Mount Mary College *B*
University of Wisconsin
    Eau Claire *B*
    Milwaukee *B*
    Superior *B*
Viterbo University *B*
Waukesha County Technical College *A*

Wyoming
University of Wyoming *B*
Western Wyoming Community
   College *A*

Marketing research

Alabama
Troy State University in Montgomery *B*

California
California State University
    Bakersfield *B*
    Northridge *M*

Florida
University of West Florida *B*

Georgia
University of Georgia *M*

Hawaii
University of Hawaii
    Hawaii Community College *C, A*

Idaho
Boise State University *B*

Illinois
Columbia College Chicago *B*
Southern Illinois University
    Edwardsville *M*

Indiana
Taylor University: Fort Wayne *B*

Kansas
Fort Hays State University *B*

Maine
Husson College *B*

Maryland
Johns Hopkins University *B, M*

Massachusetts
Boston University *B*
Emerson College *M*
Lasell College *M*
Mount Ida College *A*

Minnesota
Winona State University *B*

Missouri
Lindenwood University *M*
University of Missouri
    Columbia *B*

Nebraska
University of Nebraska
    Omaha *B*

New Jersey
Fairleigh Dickinson University
    College at Florham *M*
    Metropolitan Campus *M*

New York
Canisius College *B*
City University of New York
    Baruch College *M*
Fordham University *B, M*
Hofstra University *M*
Ithaca College *B*
Laboratory Institute of Merchandising *B*
State University of New York
    Buffalo *M, D*

North Dakota
Lake Region State College *C, A*

Ohio
Bowling Green State University *B*
Case Western Reserve University *M, D*
Defiance College *B*
Kent State University
    Stark Campus *B*
Tiffin University *B*
University of Toledo *B*
Wright State University *M*

Oklahoma
Oklahoma Christian University of
   Science and Arts *B*

Pennsylvania
La Salle University *B*
Penn State
    Abington *B*
    Altoona *B*
    Beaver *B*
    Berks *B*
    Delaware County *B*
    Dubois *B*
    Fayette *B*
    Harrisburg *B*
    Hazleton *B*
    Lehigh Valley *B*
    McKeesport *B*
    Mont Alto *B*
    New Kensington *B*
    Schuylkill - Capital College *B*
    Shenango *B*
    Wilkes-Barre *B*
    York *B*
University of Pennsylvania *C, B, M, D*

Texas
University of Texas
    Arlington *M*

Wisconsin
Edgewood College *B, M*

Marriage/family therapy

Arizona
Arizona State University *D*

Arkansas
Harding University *B, M*

California
Azusa Pacific University *M*
California State University
    Fresno *M*
Chapman University *M*
Mount St. Mary's College *M*
University of Southern
   California *B, M, D*

Florida
Nova Southeastern University *M, D*

Indiana
Indiana State University *M*

Michigan
Michigan State University *B, M*

Minnesota
Capella University *C, M, D*

New York
Hofstra University *M*

North Carolina
East Carolina University *B*

Ohio
University of Akron *M*

Oklahoma
Oklahoma Baptist University *M*

Pennsylvania
Seton Hill University *M*

Texas
Abilene Christian University *M*
Texas Tech University *M, D*
University of Houston
    Clear Lake *M*

Wisconsin
University of Wisconsin
   Stout *M*

Masonry

Alabama
Bishop State Community College *C*
Central Alabama Community College *C*

Gadsden State Community College *C*
Lawson State Community College *C*
Reid State Technical College *C*
Shelton State Community College *C*
Wallace Community College: Sparks
   Campus *C*

Arizona
Central Arizona College *C*
Cochise College *C*
Eastern Arizona College *C*
Gateway Community College *C, A*

California
Bakersfield College *A*
Palomar College *C, A*
Ventura College *A*

Colorado
Red Rocks Community College *C, A*

Florida
Lake-Sumter Community College *C*
Palm Beach Community College *C*

Illinois
Southwestern Illinois College *C, A*

Indiana
Ivy Tech State College
    Central Indiana *C, A*
    Columbus *C, A*
    Eastcentral *C, A*
    Kokomo *C*
    Lafayette *A*
    Northcentral *C, A*
    Northeast *C, A*
    Northwest *C, A*
    Southcentral *C, A*
    Southwest *C, A*
    Wabash Valley *C, A*
Oakland City University *C*

Iowa
Ellsworth Community College *C*
Kirkwood Community College *C*

Kentucky
Somerset Community College *C*

Maryland
Cecil Community College *C, A*

Michigan
Lansing Community College *A*
Oakland Community College *C*

Minnesota
Alexandria Technical College *C*
Dakota County Technical College *C, A*
Riverland Community College: A
   Technical and Community College *C*
St. Cloud Technical College *C*
St. Paul College - A Community and
   Technical College *C*

Mississippi
Pearl River Community College *C, A*

Nebraska
Mid Plains Community College Area *C*
Nebraska Indian Community College *C*

Nevada
Truckee Meadows Community
   College *C, A*
Western Nevada Community College *A*

New York
State University of New York
   College of Technology at Alfred *A*
   College of Technology at
    Delhi *C, A*

North Carolina
Blue Ridge Community College *C*
Davidson County Community College *C*
Fayetteville Technical Community
   College *C*
James Sprunt Community College *C*
Johnston Community College *C*

Piedmont Community College *C*
Southeastern Community College *C*
Southwestern Community College *C*
Tri-County Community College *C*

Oklahoma
Rose State College *A*

Pennsylvania
Delaware County Community College *C*
Pennsylvania College of Technology *A*
Williamson Free School of Mechanical
   Trades *C*

Texas
Howard College *C*
Trinity Valley Community College *C*

Wisconsin
Milwaukee Area Technical College *C*
Western Wisconsin Technical College *C*
Wisconsin Indianhead Technical
   College *C*

Massage therapy

Florida
Miami-Dade Community College *C*
Pensacola Junior College *C*

Illinois
Kaskaskia College *C*
Kishwaukee College *C*
Parkland College *C*
Rend Lake College *C*

Indiana
Indiana Business College
   Medical *C, A*
Professional Careers Institute *C, A*
Sawyer College *C, A*
Sawyer College: Merrillville *C, A*

Maryland
Allegany College *A*
Community College of Baltimore County
   Catonsville *A*
   Dundalk *A*
Howard Community College *A*

Massachusetts
Springfield Technical Community
   College *A*

Michigan
Baker College
   of Muskegon *C*
   of Port Huron *C, A*
Muskegon Community College *C*
Oakland Community College *C, A*

Minnesota
St. Paul College - A Community and
   Technical College *C, A*

New Hampshire
Hesser College *C*
New Hampshire Community Technical
   College
   Nashua *C*

New Jersey
Union County College *C*

New York
Finger Lakes Community College *A*
State University of New York
   College of Agriculture and
      Technology at Morrisville *A*

North Carolina
Carteret Community College *C, A*
Lenoir Community College *C, A*
Miller-Motte Technical College *C, A*
Sandhills Community College *C, A*

Ohio
Davis College *A*
Hocking Technical College *C*
Lakeland Community College *C*

North Central State College *C*
Ohio College of Massotherapy *C, A*

Pennsylvania
Academy of Medical Arts and
   Business *C, A*
Butler County Community College *C*
Community College of Allegheny
   County *C, A*

Rhode Island
Community College of Rhode
   Island *C, A*

Tennessee
Miller-Motte Technical College *C, A*
Roane State Community College *C*

Washington
Clover Park Technical College *C*
Renton Technical College *C*

Materials engineering

Alabama
Auburn University *B, M, D*
Tuskegee University *D*
University of Alabama *D*
University of Alabama
   Birmingham *B, M, D*

Arizona
Arizona State University *B, M*

California
California Polytechnic State University:
   San Luis Obispo *B*
California State Polytechnic University:
   Pomona *B*
California State University
   Long Beach *B*
   Northridge *B, M*
San Jose State University *B, M*
Stanford University *B, M, D*
University of California
   Berkeley *B, M, D*
   Davis *B*
   Irvine *M, D*
   Los Angeles *B, M, D*
   Santa Barbara *M, D*
University of Southern California *M*

Colorado
Colorado School of Mines *M*
University of Denver *D*

Connecticut
University of Connecticut *B, M, D*

Delaware
University of Delaware *M, D*

District of Columbia
George Washington University *M*
Howard University *M, D*

Florida
Florida International University *M*
Florida State University *B*
University of Central Florida *M, D*
University of Florida *B, M, D*

Georgia
Georgia Institute of Technology *B, M, D*

Illinois
Illinois Institute of Technology *B, M, D*
Northwestern University *B, M, D*
University of Illinois
   Chicago *M, D*

Indiana
Purdue University *B, M, D*

Iowa
Iowa State University *B, M, D*

Kentucky
University of Kentucky *B, M, D*

Maryland
Johns Hopkins University *B, M, D*
University of Maryland
   College Park *B, M, D*

Massachusetts
Massachusetts Institute of
   Technology *B, M, D*
Northeastern University *M*
Worcester Polytechnic Institute *M, D*

Michigan
Michigan Technological
   University *B, M, D, T*
University of Michigan *B, M, D*
Wayne State University *M, D*
Western Michigan University *B*

Minnesota
University of Minnesota
   Twin Cities *B, M, D*
Winona State University *B*

Missouri
Washington University in St. Louis *M, D*

Montana
Montana Tech of the University of
   Montana *B, M*

New Hampshire
University of New Hampshire *B*

New Jersey
New Jersey Institute of Technology *M, D*
Rowan University *B*
Stevens Institute of Technology *M, D*

New Mexico
New Mexico Institute of Mining and
   Technology *B, M, D*

New York
Alfred University *B, M*
Columbia University
   Fu Foundation School of
      Engineering and Applied
      Science *B, M, D*
Cornell University *B, M, D*
New York University *B*
Rensselaer Polytechnic Institute *B, M, D*
Rochester Institute of Technology *M*
State University of New York
   Binghamton *M, D*
   Buffalo *M, D*
   College of Environmental Science
      and Forestry *B, M, D*
Syracuse University *M*

North Carolina
North Carolina Agricultural and
   Technical State University *B*
North Carolina State University *B, M, D*

Ohio
Case Western Reserve
   University *B, M, D*
Ohio State University
   Columbus Campus *B, M, D*
University of Cincinnati *M, D*
University of Dayton *M, D*
Wright State University *B, M*

Oregon
Oregon State University *M*

Pennsylvania
Drexel University *B, M, D*
Lehigh University *B, M, D*

Penn State
   Abington *B*
   Altoona *B*
   Beaver *B*
   Berks *B*
   Delaware County *B*
   Dubois *B*
   Fayette *B*
   Hazleton *B*
   Lehigh Valley *B*
   McKeesport *B*
   Mont Alto *B*
   New Kensington *A, B*
   Shenango *B*
   University Park *M, D*
   Wilkes-Barre *B*
   Worthington Scranton *B*
   York *B*
University of Pennsylvania *B, M, D*
University of Pittsburgh *B, M, D*

Rhode Island
Brown University *B, M, D*

South Carolina
Clemson University *M, D*

South Dakota
South Dakota School of Mines and
   Technology *D*

Tennessee
Vanderbilt University *M, D*

Texas
Rice University *B, M, D*
Southern Methodist University *M*
University of Houston *M, D*
University of Texas
   Arlington *M, D*
   Austin *M, D*
   El Paso *M, D*

Utah
University of Utah *B, M, D*

Virginia
University of Virginia *M, D*
Virginia Polytechnic Institute and State
   University *B, M, D*

Washington
University of Washington *B, M, D*
Washington State University *B, M*

Wisconsin
University of Wisconsin
   Milwaukee *B*

Materials science

Alabama
Tuskegee University *D*
University of Alabama *D*
University of Alabama
   Birmingham *D*
   Huntsville *M, D*

Arizona
Arizona State University *M, D*
University of Arizona *B, M, D*

California
California Institute of Technology *M, D*
University of California
   Davis *B, M*
   Los Angeles *M, D*
   San Diego *M, D*
University of Southern California *M, D*

Colorado
Colorado School of Mines *M, D*
National Technological University *M*

Connecticut
University of Connecticut *M, D*

Idaho
University of Idaho *M, D*

Illinois
University of Illinois
   Urbana-Champaign *B, M, D*

Iowa
Iowa State University *M, D*

Maryland
Johns Hopkins University *B, M, D*

Massachusetts
Harvard College *B*

Michigan
Michigan State University *B, M, D*
University of Michigan *B, M, D*
Wayne State University *M, D*
Western Michigan University *M*

Minnesota
University of Minnesota
   Twin Cities *B, M, D*
Winona State University *B*

Missouri
Southwest Missouri State University *M*

Montana
Montana Tech of the University of
   Montana *B*

New Hampshire
University of New Hampshire *B*

New Jersey
Stevens Institute of Technology *M, D*

New York
Alfred University *B, M*
Columbia University
   Fu Foundation School of
      Engineering and Applied
      Science *B, M, D*
Polytechnic University *M*
Rochester Institute of Technology *M*
State University of New York
   Binghamton *M, D*
   Buffalo *M, D*
   Stony Brook *M, D*
University of Rochester *M, D*

North Carolina
North Carolina State University *B, M*
University of North Carolina
   Chapel Hill *M, D*

Ohio
Case Western Reserve
   University *B, M, D*
Hocking Technical College *A*
Ohio State University
   Columbus Campus *B, M, D*

Oregon
Oregon State University *M, D*

Pennsylvania
Carnegie Mellon University *B, M, D*
Lehigh University *B, M, D*
Temple University *B*

South Dakota
South Dakota School of Mines and
   Technology *D*

Tennessee
University of Tennessee
   Knoxville *B*

Texas
Southern Methodist University *M*
University of Texas
   El Paso *B, D*

Utah
Salt Lake Community College *A*

Vermont
University of Vermont *M, D*

Washington
University of Washington *B*
Washington State University *D*

Wisconsin
Marquette University *M, D*
University of Wisconsin
   Madison *M, D*

Maternal/child health

Indiana
Indiana University-Purdue University
   Indianapolis *M*

Maternal/child health nursing

Indiana
Indiana University-Purdue University
   Indianapolis *M*

Michigan
Wayne State University *M*

New Jersey
William Paterson University of New
   Jersey *T*

New York
City University of New York
   Hunter College *M*
Pace University:
   Pleasantville/Briarcliff *C, M*
State University of New York
   Buffalo *M*
   Health Science Center at Stony
      Brook *M*
   Stony Brook *M*

Ohio
Case Western Reserve University *M*

South Carolina
Medical University of South Carolina *M*

Mathematical statistics/ probability

Arizona
Northern Arizona University *B*

New York
Rochester Institute of Technology *B, M*

Mathematics

Alabama
Alabama Agricultural and Mechanical
   University *B*
Alabama State University *B, M*
Athens State University *B*
Auburn University *B, M, D, T*
Auburn University at Montgomery *B*
Birmingham-Southern College *B, T*
Calhoun Community College *A*
Chattahoochee Valley Community
   College *A*
Faulkner University *B*
Huntingdon College *B, T*
Jacksonville State University *B, M*
James H. Faulkner State Community
   College *A*
Judson College *B*
Lawson State Community College *A*
Miles College *B*
Northeast Alabama Community
   College *A*
Oakwood College *B*
Samford University *B*
Shelton State Community College *A*
Spring Hill College *B, T*
Stillman College *B*
Talladega College *B*
Troy State University *B*
Troy State University Dothan *B, T*
Troy State University in Montgomery *B*

Tuskegee University *B, T*
University of Alabama *B, M, D*
University of Alabama
   Birmingham *B, M*
   Huntsville *B, M*
University of Mobile *B, T*
University of Montevallo *B, T*
University of North Alabama *B*
University of South Alabama *M*
University of West Alabama *B, T*

Alaska
University of Alaska
   Anchorage *B*
   Fairbanks *B, M, D*
   Southeast *B*

Arizona
Arizona State University *B, M, D*
Arizona Western College *A*
Central Arizona College *A*
Eastern Arizona College *A*
Northern Arizona University *B, M, T*
South Mountain Community College *A*
University of Arizona *B, M, D*

Arkansas
Arkansas State University *B, M*
Arkansas State University
   Beebe *A*
Arkansas Tech University *B*
Black River Technical College *A*
Harding University *B*
Henderson State University *B*
Hendrix College *B*
John Brown University *B*
Lyon College *B*
Ouachita Baptist University *B*
Philander Smith College *B*
Phillips Community College of the
   University of Arkansas *A*
Southern Arkansas University *B*
University of Arkansas *B, M, D*
University of Arkansas
   Fort Smith *A*
   Little Rock *B*
   Monticello *B*
   Pine Bluff *B*
University of Central Arkansas *B, M*
University of the Ozarks *B*

California
Antelope Valley College *A*
Azusa Pacific University *B*
Bakersfield College *A*
Barstow College *A*
Biola University *B*
Cabrillo College *A*
California Baptist University *B*
California Institute of Technology *B, D*
California Polytechnic State University:
   San Luis Obispo *B, M*
California State Polytechnic University:
   Pomona *B, M*
California State University
   Bakersfield *B*
   Chico *B, M*
   Dominguez Hills *B*
   Fresno *B, M*
   Fullerton *B, M*
   Hayward *B, M*
   Long Beach *B, M*
   Los Angeles *B, M*
   Northridge *B, M*
   Sacramento *B, M*
   San Bernardino *B, M*
   San Marcos *B, M*
   Stanislaus *B*
Cerritos Community College *A*
Chabot College *A*
Chapman University *B*
Christian Heritage College *B*
Citrus College *A*
Claremont McKenna College *B*
College of Alameda *A*
College of Marin: Kentfield *A*
College of the Canyons *A*

College of the Sequoias *A*
College of the Siskiyous *A*
Columbia College *A*
Concordia University *B*
Contra Costa College *A*
Cuesta College *C, A*
De Anza College *A*
East Los Angeles College *C*
Feather River College *A*
Foothill College *A*
Fresno Pacific University *B*
Gavilan Community College *A*
Glendale Community College *A*
Golden West College *A*
Grossmont Community College *A*
Harvey Mudd College *B*
Humboldt State University *B*
Imperial Valley College *A*
Irvine Valley College *A*
La Sierra University *B*
Laney College *A*
Long Beach City College *A*
Los Angeles Pierce College *C*
Los Angeles Southwest College *A*
Los Medanos College *A*
Loyola Marymount University *B, M*
Marymount College *A*
Master's College *B*
Mills College *B*
MiraCosta College *A*
Modesto Junior College *A*
Monterey Peninsula College *A*
Moorpark College *A*
Mount St. Mary's College *B*
Mount San Jacinto College *A*
National University *B*
Occidental College *B*
Ohlone College *C*
Orange Coast College *A*
Pacific Union College *B*
Palomar College *A*
Pepperdine University *B*
Pitzer College *B*
Point Loma Nazarene University *B*
Pomona College *B*
Reedley College *A*
St. Mary's College of California *B*
San Diego City College *A*
San Diego Mesa College *C, A*
San Diego State University *B, M*
San Francisco State University *B, M*
San Joaquin Delta College *A*
San Jose State University *B, M*
Santa Barbara City College *A*
Santa Clara University *B*
Santa Monica College *A*
Santa Rosa Junior College *A*
Santiago Canyon College *A*
Scripps College *B*
Simpson College *B*
Sonoma State University *B*
Southwestern College *A*
Stanford University *B, M, D*
Taft College *A*
University of California
   Berkeley *B, M, D*
   Davis *B, M, D*
   Irvine *B, M, D*
   Los Angeles *B, M, D*
   Riverside *B, M, D*
   San Diego *B, M, D*
   Santa Barbara *B, M, D*
   Santa Cruz *B, M, D*
University of La Verne *B*
University of Redlands *B*
University of San Diego *B*
University of San Francisco *B*
University of Southern
   California *B, M, D*
University of the Pacific *B*
Vanguard University of Southern
   California *B*
Ventura College *A*
Victor Valley College *A*
West Valley College *A*

Whittier College *B*
Yuba Community College District *A*

Colorado

Colorado Christian University *B*
Colorado College *B*
Colorado Mountain College
    Alpine Campus *A*
    Timberline Campus *A*
Colorado School of Mines *M, D*
Colorado State University *B, M, D*
Colorado State University
    Pueblo *B, T*
Fort Lewis College *B*
Mesa State College *A, B*
Metropolitan State College of
    Denver *B, T*
Otero Junior College *A*
Regis University *B*
Trinidad State Junior College *A*
United States Air Force Academy *B*
University of Colorado
    Boulder *B, M, D*
    Colorado Springs *B*
    Denver *B*
University of Denver *B, M*
University of Northern Colorado *B, M, D*

Connecticut

Albertus Magnus College *B*
Central Connecticut State
    University *B, M*
Connecticut College *B*
Eastern Connecticut State University *B*
Fairfield University *B, M*
Manchester Community College *A*
Northwestern Connecticut Community
    College *A*
Norwalk Community College *A*
Quinnipiac University *B*
Sacred Heart University *B*
St. Joseph College *B, T*
Southern Connecticut State
    University *B, M*
Trinity College *B*
University of Bridgeport *B*
University of Connecticut *B, M, D*
University of Hartford *B*
University of New Haven *B*
Wesleyan University *B, M, D*
Western Connecticut State
    University *B, M*
Yale University *B, M, D*

Delaware

Delaware State University *B*
University of Delaware *B, M, D*

District of Columbia

American University *B, M*
Catholic University of America *B, T*
Gallaudet University *B*
George Washington University *B, M, D*
Georgetown University *B*
Howard University *B, M, D*
Trinity College *B*
University of the District of Columbia *B*

Florida

Barry University *B*
Bethune-Cookman College *B*
Broward Community College *A*
Chipola Junior College *A*
Eckerd College *B*
Edward Waters College *B*
Florida Agricultural and Mechanical
    University *B*
Florida Atlantic University *B, M, D*
Florida International University *B*
Florida Southern College *B*
Florida State University *B, M, D*
Gulf Coast Community College *A*
Indian River Community College *A*
Jacksonville University *B*
Lake City Community College *A*
Manatee Community College *A*
Miami-Dade Community College *A*

New College of Florida *B*
Okaloosa-Walton Community College *A*
Palm Beach Atlantic University *B, T*
Palm Beach Community College *A*
Pensacola Junior College *A*
Polk Community College *A*
Rollins College *B*
South Florida Community College *A*
Stetson University *B*
University of Central Florida *B*
University of Florida *B, M, D*
University of Miami *B, M, D*
University of North Florida *B*
University of South Florida *B, M, D*
University of Tampa *A, B, T*
University of West Florida *B, M*

Georgia

Abraham Baldwin Agricultural
    College *A*
Agnes Scott College *B*
Albany State University *B*
Andrew College *A*
Atlanta Metropolitan College *A*
Augusta State University *B*
Bainbridge College *A*
Berry College *B, T*
Brewton-Parker College *B*
Clark Atlanta University *B, M*
Clayton College and State University *A*
Coastal Georgia Community College *A*
Columbus State University *B*
Covenant College *B*
Dalton State College *A*
Darton College *A*
East Georgia College *A*
Emmanuel College *B*
Emory University *B, M, D*
Floyd College *A*
Fort Valley State University *B*
Gainesville College *A*
Georgia College and State University *B*
Georgia Institute of Technology *B, M, D*
Georgia Perimeter College *A*
Georgia Southern University *B, M*
Georgia Southwestern State University *B*
Georgia State University *B, M*
Gordon College *A*
Kennesaw State University *B*
LaGrange College *B*
Macon State College *A*
Mercer University *B*
Middle Georgia College *A*
Morehouse College *B*
Morris Brown College *B*
North Georgia College & State
    University *B*
Oglethorpe University *B*
Oxford College of Emory University *B*
Paine College *B*
Piedmont College *B*
Savannah State University *B*
Shorter College *B, T*
South Georgia College *A*
Southern Polytechnic State University *B*
Spelman College *B*
State University of West Georgia *B*
University of Georgia *B, M, D*
Valdosta State University *B*
Waycross College *A*
Wesleyan College *B, T*
Young Harris College *A*

Hawaii

Brigham Young University-Hawaii *B*
Hawaii Pacific University *A*
University of Hawaii
    Hilo *B*
    Manoa *B, M, D*

Idaho

Albertson College of Idaho *B*
Boise State University *B, T*
Brigham Young University - Idaho *B*
College of Southern Idaho *A*
Idaho State University *A, B, M, D*

Lewis-Clark State College *B, T*
North Idaho College *A*
Northwest Nazarene University *B*
University of Idaho *B, M, D*

Illinois

Augustana College *B, T*
Aurora University *B*
Benedictine University *B, T*
Black Hawk College
    East Campus *A*
Blackburn College *B, T*
Bradley University *B, T*
Chicago State University *B, M, T*
City Colleges of Chicago
    Harold Washington College *A*
    Kennedy-King College *A*
    Olive-Harvey College *A*
Concordia University *B, T*
Danville Area Community College *A*
De Paul University *B, M, T*
Dominican University *B*
East-West University *B*
Eastern Illinois University *B, M, T*
Elmhurst College *B, T*
Eureka College *B, T*
Greenville College *B, T*
Illinois Central College *A*
Illinois College *B, T*
Illinois State University *B, M, T*
Illinois Valley Community College *A*
Illinois Wesleyan University *B*
John A. Logan College *A*
John Wood Community College *A*
Joliet Junior College *A*
Judson College *B*
Kankakee Community College *A*
Kishwaukee College *A*
Knox College *B*
Lake Forest College *B*
Lake Land College *A*
Lewis University *B, T*
Lewis and Clark Community College *A*
Lincoln College *B*
Lincoln Land Community College *A*
Loyola University of Chicago *B, M*
MacMurray College *B, T*
McKendree College *B, T*
Millikin University *B, T*
Monmouth College *B, T*
National-Louis University *B*
North Central College *B, T*
North Park University *B*
Northeastern Illinois University *B, M*
Northern Illinois University *B, M, D, T*
Northwestern University *B, M, D*
Olivet Nazarene University *B, T*
Parkland College *A*
Principia College *B, T*
Richland Community College *A*
Rockford College *B*
Roosevelt University *B, M*
St. Xavier University *B*
Sauk Valley Community College *A*
South Suburban College of Cook
    County *A*
Southeastern Illinois College *A*
Southern Illinois University
    Carbondale *B, M, D*
Southern Illinois University
    Edwardsville *B, M, T*
Southwestern Illinois College *A*
Springfield College in Illinois *A*
Trinity Christian College *B, T*
Trinity International University *B*
Triton College *A*
University of Chicago *B, M, D*
University of Illinois
    Chicago *B, M, D*
    Springfield *B, M*
    Urbana-Champaign *B, M, D*
University of St. Francis *B*
Western Illinois University *B, M*
Wheaton College *B, T*
William Rainey Harper College *A*

Indiana

Ancilla College *A*
Anderson University *B*
Ball State University *B, M, T*
Bethel College *B*
Butler University *B*
DePauw University *B*
Earlham College *B*
Franklin College *B*
Goshen College *B*
Grace College *B*
Hanover College *B*
Huntington College *B*
Indiana State University *B, M*
Indiana University
    Bloomington *B, M, D*
    East *A*
    Kokomo *B*
    Northwest *B*
    South Bend *B*
    Southeast *B*
Indiana University-Purdue University
    Fort Wayne *A, B, M, T*
Indiana University-Purdue University
    Indianapolis *B, M*
Indiana Wesleyan University *B*
Manchester College *B, T*
Marian College *B, T*
Martin University *B*
Purdue University *B, M, D*
Purdue University
    Calumet *B, M*
Rose-Hulman Institute of Technology *B*
St. Joseph's College *B*
Saint Mary's College *B, T*
St. Mary-of-the-Woods College *B*
Taylor University *B*
Tri-State University *A, B*
University of Evansville *B*
University of Indianapolis *B*
University of Notre Dame *B, M, D*
University of Southern Indiana *B*
Valparaiso University *B*
Vincennes University *A*
Wabash College *B*

Iowa

Briar Cliff University *B*
Buena Vista University *B, T*
Central College *B, T*
Clarke College *B, T*
Coe College *B*
Cornell College *B, T*
Dordt College *B*
Drake University *B*
Ellsworth Community College *A*
Graceland University *B, T*
Grinnell College *B*
Iowa State University *B, M, D*
Iowa Wesleyan College *B*
Iowa Western Community College *A*
Loras College *B*
Luther College *B*
Maharishi University of Management *B*
Marshalltown Community College *A*
Morningside College *B*
Mount Mercy College *B, T*
North Iowa Area Community College *A*
Northwestern College *B*
St. Ambrose University *B*
Simpson College *B*
University of Iowa *B, M, D, T*
University of Northern Iowa *B, M*
Upper Iowa University *B*
Waldorf College *A*
Wartburg College *B, T*
William Penn University *B*

Kansas

Allen County Community College *A*
Baker University *B, T*
Barton County Community College *A*
Benedictine College *B, T*
Bethany College *B, T*
Bethel College *B*
Butler County Community College *A*

Central Christian College *A, B*
Cloud County Community College *A*
Dodge City Community College *A*
Donnelly College *A*
Emporia State University *B, M*
Fort Hays State University *B, M*
Friends University *B*
Garden City Community College *A*
Hutchinson Community College *A*
Independence Community College *A*
Kansas City Kansas Community
  College *A*
Kansas State University *B, M, D*
Kansas Wesleyan University *B, T*
McPherson College *B, T*
MidAmerica Nazarene University *B*
Newman University *B*
Ottawa University *B*
Pittsburg State University *B, M, T*
Pratt Community College *A*
St. Mary College *B*
Seward County Community College *A*
Southwestern College *B*
Sterling College *B*
Tabor College *B*
University of Kansas *B, M, D*
Washburn University of Topeka *B*
Wichita State University *B, M, D*

Kentucky

Asbury College *B, T*
Bellarmine University *B, T*
Berea College *B, T*
Campbellsville University *B*
Centre College *B*
Cumberland College *B, T*
Georgetown College *B*
Kentucky Christian College *B, T*
Kentucky Wesleyan College *B, T*
Lindsey Wilson College *B*
Morehead State University *B*
Murray State University *B, M, T*
Pikeville College *B, T*
St. Catharine College *A*
Spalding University *B*
Thomas More College *C, A, B*
Transylvania University *B*
Union College *B*
University of Kentucky *B, M, D*
University of Louisville *B, M*

Louisiana

Centenary College of Louisiana *B, T*
Dillard University *B*
Grambling State University *B*
Louisiana College *B*
Louisiana State University
  Shreveport *B*
Louisiana State University and
  Agricultural and Mechanical
  College *B, M, D*
Louisiana Tech University *B, M*
Loyola University New Orleans *B*
McNeese State University *B, M*
Nicholls State University *B*
Northwestern State University *B*
Southeastern Louisiana University *B*
Southern University
  New Orleans *B*
  Shreveport *A*
Southern University and Agricultural and
  Mechanical College *B, M, D*
Tulane University *B, M, D*
University of Louisiana at
  Lafayette *B, M, D*
University of Louisiana at Monroe *B*
University of New Orleans *B, M*
Xavier University of Louisiana *B*

Maine

Bates College *B, T*
Bowdoin College *B*
Colby College *B*
St. Joseph's College *B*
University of Maine *B, M*

University of Maine
  Farmington *B*
University of New England *B*
University of Southern Maine *B*

Maryland

Allegany College *A*
Anne Arundel Community College *A*
Bowie State University *B, M*
Cecil Community College *A*
College of Notre Dame of Maryland *B*
College of Southern Maryland *A*
Columbia Union College *B*
Community College of Baltimore County
  Catonsville *A*
  Dundalk *A*
  Essex *A*
Coppin State College *B*
Frederick Community College *A*
Frostburg State University *B*
Goucher College *B*
Harford Community College *A*
Hood College *B, T*
Howard Community College *A*
Johns Hopkins University *B, M, D*
Loyola College in Maryland *B*
McDaniel College *B*
Morgan State University *B, M*
Mount St. Mary's College *B, T*
St. Mary's College of Maryland *B*
Salisbury University *B, T*
Towson University *B, T*
United States Naval Academy *B*
University of Maryland
  Baltimore County *B*
  College Park *B, M, D*

Massachusetts

American International College *B*
Amherst College *B*
Assumption College *B*
Atlantic Union College *B*
Bentley College *B*
Berkshire Community College *A*
Boston College *B, M*
Boston University *B, M, D*
Brandeis University *B, M, D*
Bridgewater State College *B*
Bunker Hill Community College *A*
Cape Cod Community College *A*
Clark University *B*
College of the Holy Cross *B*
Elms College *B*
Emmanuel College *B*
Fitchburg State College *B*
Framingham State College *B*
Gordon College *B*
Hampshire College *B*
Harvard College *B, T*
Massachusetts College of Liberal Arts *B*
Massachusetts Institute of
  Technology *B, D*
Merrimack College *B*
Mount Holyoke College *B*
Nichols College *B*
Northeastern University *B, M, D*
Roxbury Community College *A*
Salem State College *B, M*
Simmons College *B*
Simon's Rock College of Bard *B*
Smith College *B*
Springfield College *B*
Springfield Technical Community
  College *A*
Stonehill College *B*
Suffolk University *B, T*
Tufts University *B, M, D*
University of Massachusetts
  Amherst *B, M, D*
  Boston *B*
  Dartmouth *B*
  Lowell *B, M*
Wellesley College *B*
Western New England College *B*
Westfield State College *B*
Wheaton College *B*

Williams College *B*
Worcester Polytechnic Institute *B, M, D*

Michigan

Adrian College *A, B, T*
Alma College *B, T*
Andrews University *B*
Aquinas College *B, T*
Calvin College *B, T*
Central Michigan University *B, M, D, T*
Concordia University *B, T*
Cornerstone University *B, T*
Eastern Michigan University *B, M*
Gogebic Community College *A*
Grand Valley State University *B*
Hillsdale College *B*
Hope College *B*
Kalamazoo College *B, T*
Kellogg Community College *A*
Lansing Community College *A*
Lawrence Technological University *B*
Macomb Community College *A*
Madonna University *B*
Marygrove College *B, T*
Michigan State University *B, M, D*
Michigan Technological
  University *B, M, D, T*
Mid Michigan Community College *A*
Northern Michigan University *B, T*
Northwestern Michigan College *A*
Oakland University *B, M*
Saginaw Valley State University *B*
Siena Heights University *A, B*
Spring Arbor University *B*
University of Michigan *B, M, D, T*
University of Michigan
  Dearborn *B, M*
  Flint *B, T*
Wayne State University *B, M, D*
West Shore Community College *A*
Western Michigan University *B, M, D*
William Tyndale College *B*

Minnesota

Augsburg College *B*
Bemidji State University *B*
Bethel College *B*
Carleton College *B*
College of St. Benedict *B*
College of St. Catherine *B*
College of St. Scholastica *B*
Concordia College: Moorhead *B*
Concordia University: St. Paul *B*
Gustavus Adolphus College *B*
Hamline University *B*
Macalester College *B, T*
Minnesota State University
  Mankato *B, M, T*
  Moorhead *B*
Northland Community & Technical
  College *A*
Northwestern College *B*
Ridgewater College: A Community and
  Technical College *A*
St. Cloud State University *B, M*
St. John's University *B*
St. Mary's University of Minnesota *B*
St. Olaf College *B*
Southwest State University *B, T*
University of Minnesota
  Duluth *B*
  Morris *B*
  Twin Cities *C, B, M, D*
University of St. Thomas *B*
Winona State University *B, T*

Mississippi

Alcorn State University *B*
Blue Mountain College *B*
Delta State University *B*
Holmes Community College *A*
Itawamba Community College *A*
Mary Holmes College *A*
Millsaps College *B, T*
Mississippi College *B, M, T*
Mississippi State University *B, M*

Mississippi University for Women *B, T*
Mississippi Valley State University *B*
Rust College *B*
University of Mississippi *B, M, D, T*
University of Southern Mississippi *B, M*

Missouri

Avila University *B*
Central Methodist College *B*
Central Missouri State University *B, M*
College of the Ozarks *B*
Crowder College *A*
Culver-Stockton College *B, T*
Drury University *B, T*
East Central College *A*
Evangel University *B, T*
Fontbonne College *B, T*
Hannibal-LaGrange College *B*
Lincoln University *B*
Lindenwood University *B*
Maryville University of Saint Louis *B*
Mineral Area College *A*
Missouri Baptist University *B, T*
Missouri Southern State College *B, T*
Missouri Valley College *B*
Missouri Western State College *B, T*
Northwest Missouri State University *B*
Rockhurst University *B*
St. Louis Community College
  St. Louis Community College at
    Florissant Valley *A*
  St. Louis Community College at
    Forest Park *A*
  St. Louis Community College at
    Meramec *A*
St. Louis University *B, M, D*
Southeast Missouri State
  University *B, M*
Southwest Baptist University *B, T*
Southwest Missouri State
  University *B, M*
Stephens College *B*
Three Rivers Community College *A*
Truman State University *B, M*
University of Missouri
  Columbia *B, M, D*
  Kansas City *B, M*
  Rolla *M, D, T*
  St. Louis *B, M*
Washington University in St.
  Louis *B, M, D*
Webster University *B*
Westminster College *B*
William Jewell College *B, T*
William Woods University *B, T*

Montana

Carroll College *B, T*
Miles Community College *A*
Montana State University
  Billings *B*
  Bozeman *B, M, D*
Montana Tech of the University of
  Montana *B*
Rocky Mountain College *B, T*
University of Great Falls *B*
University of Montana-Missoula *B, M, D*

Nebraska

Chadron State College *B*
College of Saint Mary *B, T*
Concordia University *B, T*
Creighton University *A, B, M*
Dana College *B*
Doane College *B*
Hastings College *B*
Little Priest Tribal College *A*
Midland Lutheran College *B, T*
Nebraska Wesleyan University *B*
Northeast Community College *A*
Peru State College *B*
Union College *B*
University of Nebraska
  Kearney *B, M, T*
  Lincoln *B, M, D*
  Omaha *B, M*

Wayne State College *B, M, T*
Western Nebraska Community
College *A*

Nevada

Great Basin College *A*
University of Nevada
Las Vegas *B, M*
Reno *B, M*
Western Nevada Community College *A*

New Hampshire

Dartmouth College *B, M, D*
Franklin Pierce College *B*
Keene State College *B, T*
New England College *B*
Plymouth State College *B*
Rivier College *B, M, T*
St. Anselm College *B, T*
University of New Hampshire *B, M, D*

New Jersey

Atlantic Cape Community College *A*
Caldwell College *B*
Centenary College *B*
The College of New Jersey *B, T*
College of St. Elizabeth *B, T*
Drew University *B*
Essex County College *A*
Fairleigh Dickinson University
College at Florham *B*
Metropolitan Campus *B*
Felician College *B*
Georgian Court College *B, M, T*
Gloucester County College *A*
Hudson County Community College *A*
Kean University *B, M*
Monmouth University *B*
Montclair State University *B, M, T*
New Jersey City University *B, M*
New Jersey Institute of Technology *D*
Passaic County Community College *A*
Princeton University *B, M, D*
Ramapo College of New Jersey *B*
Raritan Valley Community College *A*
Richard Stockton College of New
Jersey *B*
Rider University *B*
Rowan University *B, M*
Rutgers, The State University of New
Jersey
Camden Regional Campus *B, T*
New Brunswick Regional
Campus *B, M, D, T*
Newark Regional Campus *B, T*
St. Peter's College *B*
Salem Community College *A*
Seton Hall University *B, T*
Stevens Institute of Technology *M, D*
Sussex County Community College *A*
Thomas Edison State College *A, B*
William Paterson University of New
Jersey *B, T*

New Mexico

Clovis Community College *A*
College of the Southwest *B*
Eastern New Mexico University *B, M*
New Mexico Highlands University *B*
New Mexico Institute of Mining and
Technology *B, M*
New Mexico Junior College *A*
New Mexico State University *B, M, D*
San Juan College *A*
University of New Mexico *B, M, D*
Western New Mexico University *B*

New York

Adelphi University *B*
Adirondack Community College *A*
Alfred University *B*
Bard College *B*
Barnard College *B*
Canisius College *B*
Cayuga County Community College *A*

City University of New York
Baruch College *B*
Borough of Manhattan Community
College *A*
Brooklyn College *B, M*
City College *B, M, T*
College of Staten Island *B, T*
Hunter College *B, M*
Kingsborough Community
College *A*
Medgar Evers College *B*
Queens College *B, M*
York College *B*
Clarkson University *B, M, D*
Clinton Community College *A*
Colgate University *B*
College of Mount St. Vincent *B, T*
College of New Rochelle *B, T*
Columbia University
Columbia College *B*
Concordia College *B, T*
Cornell University *B, D*
Corning Community College *A*
Daemen College *B*
Dominican College of Blauvelt *B*
Dowling College *B, T*
Dutchess Community College *A*
Elmira College *B, T*
Excelsior College *B*
Fordham University *B, M, D*
Fulton-Montgomery Community
College *A*
Hamilton College *B*
Hartwick College *B, T*
Hobart and William Smith Colleges *B*
Hofstra University *B, M*
Houghton College *B*
Iona College *B, M*
Ithaca College *B, T*
Jefferson Community College *A*
Keuka College *B*
Le Moyne College *B*
Long Island University
C. W. Post Campus *B, M*
Manhattan College *B*
Manhattanville College *B*
Marist College *B, T*
Marymount College of Fordham
University *B, T*
Mercy College *B*
Molloy College *B*
Monroe Community College *A*
Mount St. Mary College *B, T*
Nassau Community College *A*
Nazareth College of Rochester *B*
New York University *B, M, D*
Niagara University *B*
Nyack College *B*
Orange County Community College *A*
Pace University *B*
Pace University:
Pleasantville/Briarcliff *B*
Polytechnic University *B, M, D*
Rensselaer Polytechnic Institute *B, M, D*
Roberts Wesleyan College *B*
Russell Sage College *B*
St. Bonaventure University *B, T*
St. John Fisher College *B*
St. John's University *B, M*
St. Joseph's College *B*
St. Joseph's College: Suffolk
Campus *B, T*
St. Lawrence University *B, T*
Sarah Lawrence College *B*
Skidmore College *B*

State University of New York
Albany *B, M, D*
Binghamton *B, M, D*
Buffalo *B, M, D*
College at Brockport *B, M, T*
College at Buffalo *B*
College at Cortland *B*
College at Fredonia *B, T*
College at Geneseo *B, T*
College at Old Westbury *B, T*
College at Oneonta *B*
College at Plattsburgh *B*
College at Potsdam *B, M, T*
College of Agriculture and
Technology at Cobleskill *A*
College of Agriculture and
Technology at Morrisville *A*
College of Technology at Alfred *A*
New Paltz *B, M, T*
Oswego *B*
Purchase *B*
Stony Brook *B, M, D, T*
Suffolk County Community College *A*
Syracuse University *B, M, D*
Touro College *B*
Ulster County Community College *A*
Union College *B*
United States Military Academy *B*
University of Rochester *B, M, D*
Utica College *B*
Vassar College *B*
Wagner College *B, T*
Wells College *B*
Yeshiva University *B, T*

North Carolina

Appalachian State University *B, M*
Barber-Scotia College *B*
Barton College *B*
Bennett College *B*
Brevard College *B*
Caldwell Community College and
Technical Institute *A*
Campbell University *B, T*
Catawba College *B*
Chowan College *B*
Davidson College *B*
Duke University *B*
East Carolina University *B, M*
Elizabeth City State University *B*
Elon University *B, T*
Fayetteville State University *B*
Gardner-Webb University *B*
Greensboro College *B, T*
Guilford College *B*
Guilford Technical Community
College *A*
High Point University *B*
Johnson C. Smith University *B*
Lees-McRae College *B*
Lenoir Community College *A*
Lenoir-Rhyne College *B, T*
Livingstone College *B*
Louisburg College *A*
Mars Hill College *B, T*
Meredith College *B, T*
Methodist College *B*
Montreat College *B*
Mount Olive College *B*
North Carolina Agricultural and
Technical State University *B, M, T*
North Carolina Central University *B, M*
North Carolina State University *B, M, D*
North Carolina Wesleyan College *B*
Pfeiffer University *B*
Queens University of Charlotte *B*
St. Andrews Presbyterian College *B*
St. Augustine's College *B*
Salem College *B*
Sandhills Community College *A*
Shaw University *B*

University of North Carolina
Asheville *B, T*
Chapel Hill *B, M, D*
Charlotte *B, M, T*
Greensboro *B, M, T*
Pembroke *B*
Wilmington *B, M*
Wake Forest University *B, M*
Warren Wilson College *B*
Western Carolina University *B*
Wingate University *B*
Winston-Salem State University *B*

North Dakota

Dickinson State University *B, T*
Jamestown College *B*
Mayville State University *B, T*
Minot State University *B*
Minot State University: Bottineau
Campus *A*
North Dakota State
University *B, M, D, T*
University of Mary *B*
University of North Dakota *B, M, T*
Valley City State University *B*

Ohio

Antioch College *B*
Ashland University *B*
Baldwin-Wallace College *B, T*
Bluffton College *B*
Bowling Green State University *B, M, D*
Case Western Reserve
University *B, M, D*
Cedarville University *B, T*
Central State University *B*
Cleveland State University *B, M, T*
College of Mount St. Joseph *B, T*
College of Wooster *B*
Defiance College *B, T*
Denison University *B*
Franciscan University of Steubenville *B*
Heidelberg College *B*
Hiram College *B, T*
John Carroll University *B, M, T*
Kent State University *B, M, D, T*
Kent State University
Stark Campus *B*
Kenyon College *B*
Lake Erie College *B*
Lorain County Community College *A*
Malone College *B*
Marietta College *B*
Miami University
Middletown Campus *A*
Oxford Campus *B, M, T*
Mount Union College *B*
Mount Vernon Nazarene University *B*
Muskingum College *B*
Notre Dame College *B, T*
Oberlin College *B*
Ohio Dominican College *B, T*
Ohio Northern University *B*
Ohio State University
Columbus Campus *B, M, D*
Ohio University *B, M, D*
Ohio Wesleyan University *B*
Otterbein College *B*
Owens Community College
Findlay Campus *A*
Toledo *A*
Shawnee State University *B*
Sinclair Community College *A*
University of Akron *B, M*
University of Cincinnati *B, M, D, T*
University of Dayton *B, M*
University of Findlay *B*
University of Rio Grande *A, B, T*
University of Toledo *B, M, D*
Urbana University *B*
Ursuline College *B*
Walsh University *B*
Washington State Community College *A*
Wilmington College *B*
Wittenberg University *B*
Wright State University *B, M*

Xavier University *B*
Youngstown State University *B, M*

Oklahoma

Bacone College *A*
Cameron University *B*
Carl Albert State College *A*
East Central University *B, T*
Eastern Oklahoma State College *A*
Langston University *B*
Murray State College *A*
Northeastern Oklahoma Agricultural and
　Mechanical College *A*
Northeastern State University *B*
Northern Oklahoma College *A*
Northwestern Oklahoma State
　University *B*
Oklahoma Baptist University *B, T*
Oklahoma Christian University of
　Science and Arts *B, T*
Oklahoma City Community College *A*
Oklahoma City University *B*
Oklahoma Panhandle State University *B*
Oklahoma State University *B, M, D*
Oklahoma Wesleyan University *A, B*
Oral Roberts University *B*
Redlands Community College *A*
Rogers State University *A*
Rose State College *A*
St. Gregory's University *A, B*
Seminole State College *A*
Southeastern Oklahoma State
　University *B*
Southern Nazarene University *B*
Southwestern Oklahoma State
　University *B*
Tulsa Community College *A*
University of Central Oklahoma *B*
University of Oklahoma *B, M, D*
University of Science and Arts of
　Oklahoma *B, T*
Western Oklahoma State College *A*

Oregon

Central Oregon Community College *A*
Chemeketa Community College *A*
Eastern Oregon University *B, T*
George Fox University *B*
Lewis & Clark College *B*
Linfield College *B*
Linn-Benton Community College *A*
Oregon State University *B, M, D*
Pacific University *B*
Portland State University *B, D*
Reed College *B*
Southern Oregon University *B, T*
University of Oregon *B, M, D*
University of Portland *B, T*
Warner Pacific College *A*
Western Baptist College *B*
Western Oregon University *B*
Willamette University *B*

Pennsylvania

Albright College *B, T*
Allegheny College *B*
Arcadia University *B*
Bloomsburg University of
　Pennsylvania *B, T*
Bryn Mawr College *B, M, D*
Bucknell University *B, M*
Bucks County Community College *A*
Butler County Community College *A*
Cabrini College *B*
California University of Pennsylvania *B*
Carlow College *B*
Carnegie Mellon University *B, M, D*
Cedar Crest College *B*
Chatham College *B*
Cheyney University of Pennsylvania *B*
Community College of Allegheny
　County *A*
Community College of Philadelphia *A*
DeSales University *B*
Delaware Valley College *B*
Dickinson College *B*

Drexel University *B, M, D*
Duquesne University *B*
East Stroudsburg University of
　Pennsylvania *B*
Edinboro University of
　Pennsylvania *B, T*
Elizabethtown College *B*
Franklin & Marshall College *B*
Geneva College *B, T*
Gettysburg College *B*
Grove City College *B*
Gwynedd-Mercy College *B*
Harrisburg Area Community College *A*
Haverford College *B, T*
Holy Family University *B, T*
Immaculata University *B*
Indiana University of Pennsylvania *B, M*
Juniata College *B*
King's College *B, T*
Kutztown University of
　Pennsylvania *B, M, T*
La Roche College *B*
La Salle University *B, T*
Lafayette College *B*
Lebanon Valley College of
　Pennsylvania *B, T*
Lehigh Carbon Community College *A*
Lehigh University *B, M, D*
Lincoln University *B, M*
Lock Haven University of
　Pennsylvania *B*
Luzerne County Community College *A*
Lycoming College *B*
Marywood University *B*
Mercyhurst College *B*
Messiah College *B*
Millersville University of
　Pennsylvania *B, M, T*
Montgomery County Community
　College *A*
Moravian College *B, T*
Mount Aloysius College *A, B*
Muhlenberg College *B, T*
Northampton County Area Community
　College *A*
Penn State
　Abington *B*
　Altoona *B*
　Beaver *B*
　Berks *B*
　Delaware County *B*
　Dubois *B*
　Erie, The Behrend College *B*
　Fayette *B*
　Harrisburg *B*
　Hazleton *B*
　Lehigh Valley *B*
　McKeesport *B*
　Mont Alto *B*
　New Kensington *B*
　Schuylkill - Capital College *B*
　Shenango *B*
　University Park *B, M, D*
　Wilkes-Barre *B*
　Worthington Scranton *B*
　York *B*
Rosemont College *B*
St. Joseph's University *B*
St. Vincent College *B*
Seton Hill University *B, T*
Shippensburg University of
　Pennsylvania *B, T*
Slippery Rock University of
　Pennsylvania *B, M, T*
Swarthmore College *B*
Temple University *B, M, D*
Thiel College *B*
University of Pennsylvania *B, M, D*
University of Pittsburgh *B, M, D*
University of Pittsburgh
　Johnstown *B*
University of Scranton *A, B, T*
Villanova University *B, M*
Washington and Jefferson College *B*
Waynesburg College *B*

West Chester University of
　Pennsylvania *B, M*
Widener University *B*
Wilkes University *B, M*
Wilson College *B*
York College of Pennsylvania *B, T*

Puerto Rico

Inter American University of Puerto Rico
　Bayamon Campus *B*
　Metropolitan Campus *B*
　San German Campus *B*
Pontifical Catholic University of Puerto
　Rico *B*
University of Puerto Rico
　Cayey University College *B*
　Mayaguez Campus *B, M*
　Ponce *B*
　Rio Piedras Campus *B, M*
University of the Sacred Heart *B*

Rhode Island

Brown University *B, M, D*
Providence College *M*
Rhode Island College *B, M*
Roger Williams University *B*
University of Rhode Island *B, M, D*

South Carolina

Anderson College *B, T*
Benedict College *B*
Charleston Southern University *B*
The Citadel *B*
Claflin University *B*
Clemson University *B, M, D*
Coker College *B*
College of Charleston *B, M, T*
Columbia College *B*
Converse College *B*
Erskine College *B, T*
Francis Marion University *B*
Furman University *B, T*
Lander University *B, T*
Limestone College *B*
Morris College *B*
Newberry College *B, T*
Presbyterian College *B, T*
South Carolina State University *B*
Southern Wesleyan University *B, T*
University of South Carolina *B, M, D*
University of South Carolina
　Spartanburg *B*
Voorhees College *B*
Winthrop University *B, M*
Wofford College *B, T*

South Dakota

Augustana College *B, T*
Black Hills State University *B*
Dakota State University *B*
Dakota Wesleyan University *B*
Mount Marty College *B*
Northern State University *B*
South Dakota School of Mines and
　Technology *B*
South Dakota State University *B, M*
University of Sioux Falls *B*
University of South Dakota *B, M*

Tennessee

Austin Peay State University *B*
Belmont University *B, T*
Bethel College *B*
Bryan College *B, T*
Carson-Newman College *B, T*
Christian Brothers University *B*
Columbia State Community College *A*
Dyersburg State Community College *A*
East Tennessee State University *B, M, T*
Fisk University *B*
Freed-Hardeman University *B, T*
Jackson State Community College *A*
King College *B*
Lambuth University *B*
Lane College *B*
Lee University *B*
Maryville College *B, T*

Middle Tennessee State University *B, M*
Milligan College *B, T*
Rhodes College *B, T*
Roane State Community College *A*
Southern Adventist University *B*
Tennessee State University *B, M*
Tennessee Technological
　University *B, M, T*
Tennessee Wesleyan College *B, T*
Trevecca Nazarene University *B*
Tusculum College *B*
Union University *B, T*
University of Memphis *B, M, D*
University of Tennessee
　Chattanooga *B, T*
　Knoxville *B, M, D*
　Martin *B*
Vanderbilt University *B, M, D*
Walters State Community College *A*

Texas

Abilene Christian University *B*
Alvin Community College *A*
Amarillo College *A*
Angelina College *A*
Angelo State University *B, T*
Austin College *B*
Austin Community College *A*
Baylor University *B, M, D*
Blinn College *A*
Brazosport College *A*
Cedar Valley College *A*
Central Texas College *A*
Cisco Junior College *A*
Clarendon College *A*
Coastal Bend College *A*
College of the Mainland *A*
Concordia University at Austin *T*
Dallas Baptist University *B*
Del Mar College *A*
East Texas Baptist University *B*
El Paso Community College *A*
Frank Phillips College *A*
Galveston College *A*
Grayson County College *A*
Hardin-Simmons University *B*
Hill College *A*
Houston Baptist University *B*
Howard College *A*
Howard Payne University *B, T*
Huston-Tillotson College *B*
Jarvis Christian College *B*
Kilgore College *A*
Lamar University *B, M*
Laredo Community College *A*
LeTourneau University *B*
Lee College *A*
Lon Morris College *A*
Lubbock Christian University *B, T*
McMurry University *B, T*
Midland College *A*
Midwestern State University *B*
Northeast Texas Community College *A*
Odessa College *A*
Our Lady of the Lake University of San
　Antonio *B*
Panola College *A*
Paris Junior College *A*
Prairie View A&M University *B, M*
Rice University *B, M, D*
St. Edward's University *B, T*
St. Mary's University *B*
St. Philip's College *A*
Sam Houston State University *B, M*
Schreiner University *B, T*
South Plains College *A*
Southern Methodist University *B, M, D*
Southwest Texas State
　University *B, M, T*
Southwestern Adventist University *B, T*
Southwestern University *B, T*
Stephen F. Austin State
　University *B, M, T*
Sul Ross State University *B*
Tarleton State University *B, M, T*

Texas A&M International
   University *B, M, T*
Texas A&M University *B, M, D*
Texas A&M University
   Commerce *B, M*
   Corpus Christi *B, M, T*
   Kingsville *B, M, T*
   Texarkana *B, T*
Texas Christian University *B, M, T*
Texas College *B*
Texas Lutheran University *B, T*
Texas Southern University *B, M*
Texas Tech University *B, M, D*
Texas Wesleyan University *B*
Texas Woman's University *B, M, T*
Trinity University *B*
Trinity Valley Community College *A*
Tyler Junior College *A*
University of Dallas *B*
University of Houston *B, M, D*
University of Houston
   Clear Lake *B, M*
   Victoria *B, T*
University of Mary Hardin-Baylor *B, T*
University of North Texas *B, M, D*
University of St. Thomas *B*
University of Texas
   Arlington *B, M*
   Austin *B, M, D*
   Brownsville *B*
   Dallas *B, M*
   El Paso *B, M*
   Pan American *B, M, T*
   San Antonio *B, M*
   Tyler *B, M*
   of the Permian Basin *B*
University of the Incarnate Word *B, M*
Wayland Baptist University *B, T*
West Texas A&M University *B, M*
Western Texas College *A*
Wharton County Junior College *A*
Wiley College *B*

Utah

Brigham Young University *B, M, D*
Dixie State College of Utah *A*
Snow College *A*
Southern Utah University *B, T*
University of Utah *B, M, D*
Utah State University *B, M*
Utah Valley State College *A, B*
Weber State University *B*
Westminster College *B*

Vermont

Bennington College *B*
Castleton State College *B*
Johnson State College *B*
Lyndon State College *B*
Marlboro College *B*
Middlebury College *B*
Norwich University *B*
St. Michael's College *B*
University of Vermont *B, M, D*

Virginia

Averett University *B, T*
Bluefield College *B*
Bridgewater College *B*
College of William and Mary *B*
Eastern Mennonite University *B*
Emory & Henry College *B, T*
Ferrum College *B*
George Mason University *B, M*
Hampden-Sydney College *B*
Hampton University *B, M*
James Madison University *B, T*
Liberty University *B, T*
Longwood University *B, T*
Lynchburg College *B*
Mary Baldwin College *B*
Mary Washington College *B*
Marymount University *B*
Mountain Empire Community College *A*
Norfolk State University *B*
Old Dominion University *B*

Radford University *B*
Randolph-Macon College *B*
Randolph-Macon Woman's College *B*
Roanoke College *B, T*
Shenandoah University *B*
Sweet Briar College *B*
University of Richmond *B, T*
University of Virginia *B, M, D*
University of Virginia's College at
   Wise *B, T*
Virginia Commonwealth
   University *B, M*
Virginia Intermont College *B, T*
Virginia Military Institute *B*
Virginia Polytechnic Institute and State
   University *B, M, D, T*
Virginia State University *B, M*
Virginia Union University *B*
Virginia Wesleyan College *B*
Washington and Lee University *B*

Washington

Central Washington University *B*
Centralia College *A*
Eastern Washington University *B, M, T*
Everett Community College *A*
Gonzaga University *B*
Heritage College *B*
Lower Columbia College *A*
Pacific Lutheran University *B*
St. Martin's College *B*
Seattle Pacific University *B*
Seattle University *B*
University of Puget Sound *B, T*
University of Washington *B, M, D*
Walla Walla College *B*
Washington State University *B, M, D*
Western Washington University *B, M, T*
Whitman College *B*
Whitworth College *B, T*

West Virginia

Bethany College *B*
Concord College *B*
Davis and Elkins College *B*
Fairmont State College *B*
Marshall University *B, M*
Potomac State College of West Virginia
   University *A*
Salem International University *B*
Shepherd College *B*
West Liberty State College *B*
West Virginia State College *B*
West Virginia University *B, M, D, T*
West Virginia University Institute of
   Technology *B*
West Virginia Wesleyan College *B*
Wheeling Jesuit University *B*

Wisconsin

Alverno College *B, T*
Beloit College *B*
Cardinal Stritch University *B*
Carroll College *B*
Carthage College *B, T*
Concordia University Wisconsin *B, T*
Edgewood College *B*
Lakeland College *B*
Lawrence University *B, T*
Marian College of Fond du Lac *B*
Marquette University *B, M, D, T*
Mount Mary College *B*
Northland College *B*
Ripon College *B, T*
St. Norbert College *B, T*
Silver Lake College *B, T*

University of Wisconsin
   Eau Claire *B, M*
   Green Bay *B*
   La Crosse *B*
   Madison *B, M, D*
   Milwaukee *B, M, D*
   Oshkosh *B*
   Parkside *B, T*
   Platteville *B, T*
   River Falls *B*
   Stevens Point *B, T*
   Superior *B, T*
   Whitewater *B, T*
Viterbo University *B, T*
Wisconsin Lutheran College *B*

Wyoming

Casper College *A*
Eastern Wyoming College *A*
Laramie County Community College *A*
Sheridan College *A*
University of Wyoming *B, M, D*
Western Wyoming Community
   College *A*

Mathematics teacher education

Alabama

Athens State University *B*
Auburn University *B*
Birmingham-Southern College *T*
Faulkner University *B, T*
Huntingdon College *T*
Jacksonville State University *B, M, T*
Judson College *B*
Miles College *B*
Oakwood College *B*
Talladega College *T*
Troy State University Dothan *B, M*
Tuskegee University *B*
University of Mobile *B, T*

Alaska

University of Alaska
   Fairbanks *M*

Arizona

Arizona State University *B, T*
Northern Arizona University *B, M, T*
Prescott College *B, M, T*
University of Arizona *B, M*

Arkansas

Arkansas State University *B, M, T*
Arkansas Tech University *B, M*
Harding University *B, M, T*
John Brown University *B, T*
Ouachita Baptist University *B, T*
Philander Smith College *B*
Southern Arkansas University *B, T*
University of Arkansas *M*
University of Arkansas
   Pine Bluff *B, M, T*
University of Central Arkansas *B, M, T*
University of the Ozarks *T*

California

Azusa Pacific University *T*
California Baptist University *T*
California State Polytechnic University:
   Pomona *T*
California State University
   Bakersfield *B, T*
   Chico *T*
   Dominguez Hills *M, T*
   Fullerton *T*
   Hayward *B, M*
   Long Beach *T*
   Northridge *B, T*
   Sacramento *T*
   San Bernardino *T*
Christian Heritage College *B, T*
Concordia University *B, T*
Cuesta College *A*
Fresno Pacific University *B, M, T*

Humboldt State University *T*
Los Angeles Southwest College *A*
Loyola Marymount University *M*
Master's College *T*
Mills College *T*
Mount St. Mary's College *T*
National University *B*
Occidental College *T*
Pacific Union College *T*
San Diego State University *B, M, T*
San Francisco State University *B, M, T*
San Jose State University *T*
Simpson College *B, T*
Sonoma State University *T*
University of California
   Berkeley *D*
   Irvine *M, T*
University of Southern California *T*
University of the Pacific *T*
Vanguard University of Southern
   California *M, T*

Colorado

Colorado State University *T*
Colorado State University
   Pueblo *T*
Fort Lewis College *T*
Metropolitan State College of Denver *T*
Regis University *B, T*
University of Colorado
   Boulder *T*
   Colorado Springs *T*
University of Northern Colorado *D, T*

Connecticut

Central Connecticut State
   University *B, M*
Fairfield University *T*
Quinnipiac University *B, M*
Sacred Heart University *T*
St. Joseph College *T*
Southern Connecticut State
   University *B, M, T*

Delaware

Delaware State University *B*
University of Delaware *B, T*

District of Columbia

American University *D*
Catholic University of America *B*
George Washington University *M, T*
University of the District of Columbia *M*

Florida

Barry University *T*
Bethune-Cookman College *B, T*
Broward Community College *A*
Edward Waters College *B*
Florida Agricultural and Mechanical
   University *B, M, T*
Florida Atlantic University *B*
Florida Institute of
   Technology *B, M, D, T*
Florida International University *B, M, T*
Florida State University *B, M, D, T*
Gulf Coast Community College *A*
Hobe Sound Bible College *B, T*
Nova Southeastern University *M*
Palm Beach Atlantic University *B, T*
St. Petersburg College *B*
South Florida Community College *A*
Southeastern College of the Assemblies
   of God *B, T*
Stetson University *B, T*
University of Central Florida *B, M*
University of Florida *M*
University of Miami *M, D*
University of North Florida *B, M*
University of South Florida *B, M*
University of Tampa *B, T*
University of West Florida *B, M, T*

Georgia

Agnes Scott College *T*
Albany State University *M*

Armstrong Atlantic State
University *B, M, T*
Brewton-Parker College *B*
Clark Atlanta University *B*
Columbus State University *B, M*
Covenant College *B, T*
Emmanuel College *B*
Fort Valley State University *B, T*
Gainesville College *A*
Georgia College and State
University *M, T*
Georgia Southern University *B, M, T*
Georgia Southwestern State
University *B, M*
Georgia State University *M, D*
Kennesaw State University *B*
LaGrange College *T*
Mercer University *M, T*
North Georgia College & State
University *B, M*
Piedmont College *M, T*
Shorter College *B, T*
State University of West Georgia *M*
University of Georgia *B, M, D, T*
Valdosta State University *M, T*
Wesleyan College *M, T*

Hawaii

Brigham Young University-Hawaii *B, T*
University of Hawaii
Manoa *B, T*

Idaho

Boise State University *T*
Brigham Young University - Idaho *T*
Lewis-Clark State College *B, T*
Northwest Nazarene University *B*

Illinois

Augustana College *B, T*
Benedictine University *T*
Blackburn College *B*
Chicago State University *B*
Concordia University *M*
De Paul University *M*
Dominican University *T*
Eastern Illinois University *M*
Elmhurst College *B*
Eureka College *T*
Greenville College *B, T*
Illinois College *T*
Illinois State University *D*
John A. Logan College *A*
Judson College *B, T*
Lake Land College *A*
Lewis University *T*
Loyola University of Chicago *T*
MacMurray College *B, T*
McKendree College *B, T*
National-Louis University *M*
North Central College *B, T*
North Park University *T*
Northeastern Illinois University *M*
Northwestern University *B, T*
Olivet Nazarene University *B, T*
Quincy University *T*
Rockford College *T*
Roosevelt University *B*
St. Xavier University *B, M, T*
Sauk Valley Community College *A*
Trinity Christian College *B, T*
Trinity International University *B, T*
University of Illinois
Chicago *B, M*
Urbana-Champaign *M, T*
University of St. Francis *T*
Wheaton College *T*

Indiana

Anderson University *B, T*
Ball State University *T*
Bethel College *B*
Butler University *T*
Franklin College *B, T*
Goshen College *B*
Grace College *B*
Huntington College *B*

Indiana University
Bloomington *B, T*
Northwest *B*
South Bend *B, T*
Southeast *B*
Indiana University-Purdue University
Fort Wayne *T*
Indiana Wesleyan University *B, T*
Manchester College *B, T*
Oakland City University *B*
Saint Mary's College *T*
St. Mary-of-the-Woods College *B*
Taylor University *B, T*
Tri-State University *B, T*
University of Evansville *B*
University of Indianapolis *B, T*
University of Southern Indiana *T*
Valparaiso University *B*
Vincennes University *A*

Iowa

Buena Vista University *B, T*
Central College *T*
Clarke College *B, T*
Cornell College *B, T*
Dordt College *B*
Drake University *B, M, T*
Ellsworth Community College *A*
Franciscan University *B, T*
Graceland University *T*
Grand View College *B, T*
Iowa State University *M, T*
Iowa Wesleyan College *B*
Loras College *T*
Luther College *B*
Maharishi University of Management *T*
Morningside College *B*
Mount Mercy College *T*
Northwestern College *T*
St. Ambrose University *B, T*
University of Iowa *B, M, D, T*
University of Northern Iowa *M*
Upper Iowa University *T*
Wartburg College *B, T*
William Penn University *B*

Kansas

Allen County Community College *A*
Baker University *T*
Benedictine College *T*
Bethany College *T*
Bethel College *T*
Emporia State University *B, T*
Fort Hays State University *M*
Fort Scott Community College *A*
Friends University *B*
Garden City Community College *A*
Independence Community College *A*
McPherson College *B, T*
MidAmerica Nazarene University *B, T*
Newman University *T*
Ottawa University *B, T*
Pittsburg State University *B, T*
St. Mary College *T*
Southwestern College *B, T*
Tabor College *B, T*
University of Kansas *B, T*
Washburn University of Topeka *B*

Kentucky

Bellarmine University *B, M, T*
Campbellsville University *B*
Cumberland College *B, T*
Kentucky Christian College *B*
Kentucky Wesleyan College *T*
Murray State University *B, M, T*
Pikeville College *B, T*
Thomas More College *B*
Union College *B*

Louisiana

Centenary College of Louisiana *B, T*
Louisiana College *B*
Louisiana State University
Shreveport *B*
Loyola University New Orleans *M*
McNeese State University *T*

Nicholls State University *B*
Northwestern State University *B*
Our Lady of Holy Cross College *B*
Southeastern Louisiana University *B*
Southern University and Agricultural and
Mechanical College *B*
University of Louisiana at Monroe *B*
University of New Orleans *B, M, D*
Xavier University of Louisiana *B, M, T*

Maine

St. Joseph's College *B*
University of Maine *B*
University of Maine
Farmington *B, T*
Presque Isle *T*
University of New England *T*
University of Southern Maine *T*

Maryland

Bowie State University *B, T*
College of Notre Dame of Maryland *T*
Columbia Union College *B*
Frostburg State University *B, T*
Johns Hopkins University *M*
Morgan State University *D*
Mount St. Mary's College *T*
St. Mary's College of Maryland *T*
Salisbury University *T*
Towson University *M, T*
University of Maryland
College Park *B*

Massachusetts

American International College *T*
Assumption College *T*
Boston University *B, M, T*
Bridgewater State College *M, T*
Elms College *M, T*
Fitchburg State College *B, M, T*
Framingham State College *B, M, T*
Harvard College *T*
Lesley University *B, M*
Merrimack College *T*
Northeastern University *B, M*
Springfield College *T*
Tufts University *M, T*
University of Massachusetts
Dartmouth *T*
Western New England College *T*
Westfield State College *B, M, T*
Worcester Polytechnic Institute *M*

Michigan

Alma College *T*
Andrews University *B*
Calvin College *B*
Central Michigan University *B, M*
Concordia University *B, T*
Cornerstone University *B*
Eastern Michigan University *B, T*
Ferris State University *B*
Grand Valley State University *M, T*
Hope College *T*
Lansing Community College *A*
Madonna University *B, T*
Michigan State University *D*
Michigan Technological University *T*
Northern Michigan University *B, M*
Saginaw Valley State University *T*
University of Michigan
Dearborn *B*
Flint *T*
Wayne State University *B, M, T*
Western Michigan University *B, M, D*

Minnesota

Augsburg College *T*
Bemidji State University *M, T*
Bethel College *B*
College of St. Benedict *T*
College of St. Catherine *B, T*
College of St. Scholastica *T*
Concordia College: Moorhead *B, T*
Concordia University: St. Paul *B, T*
Gustavus Adolphus College *T*

Minnesota State University
Mankato *B, M, T*
Moorhead *B, T*
Northland Community & Technical
College *A*
Northwestern College *B*
St. Cloud State University *M, T*
St. John's University *T*
St. Mary's University of Minnesota *B*
St. Olaf College *T*
Southwest State University *B, T*
University of Minnesota
Duluth *B*
Morris *T*
Twin Cities *B, M, T*
University of St. Thomas *B, T*
Vermilion Community College *A*
Winona State University *B, T*

Mississippi

Blue Mountain College *B*
Coahoma Community College *A*
Delta State University *B, M*
Itawamba Community College *A*
Mary Holmes College *A*
Mississippi College *B, M*
Mississippi Gulf Coast Community
College
Perkinston *A*
Mississippi State University *T*
Mississippi Valley State University *B, T*
Northwest Mississippi Community
College *A*
Rust College *B*
University of Mississippi *B, T*

Missouri

Avila University *B, T*
Central Missouri State
University *B, M, T*
College of the Ozarks *B, T*
Columbia College *T*
Culver-Stockton College *T*
Evangel University *B, T*
Hannibal-LaGrange College *B*
Harris Stowe State College *T*
Lincoln University *B, T*
Lindenwood University *B*
Maryville University of Saint
Louis *B, M, T*
Missouri Baptist University *T*
Missouri Southern State College *B, T*
Missouri Valley College *T*
Northwest Missouri State
University *B, M, T*
Rockhurst University *B*
Southeast Missouri State University *B, T*
Southwest Baptist University *T*
Southwest Missouri State University *B*
Truman State University *M, T*
University of Missouri
Columbia *B, M, D*
St. Louis *T*
Washington University in St.
Louis *B, M, T*
Webster University *M*
William Jewell College *T*
William Woods University *B, T*

Montana

Montana State University
Billings *B, M*
Montana Tech of the University of
Montana *T*
Rocky Mountain College *B, T*
University of Great Falls *B*
University of Montana-Missoula *B, M, T*
University of Montana: Western *B, T*

Nebraska

Chadron State College *B, M*
College of Saint Mary *B, T*
Concordia University *B, T*
Creighton University *T*
Dana College *B*
Doane College *T*
Hastings College *B, M, T*

Midland Lutheran College *B, T*
Nebraska Wesleyan University *T*
Peru State College *B, T*
Union College *T*
University of Nebraska
    Kearney *B, M, T*
    Lincoln *B, M, T*
    Omaha *M*
York College *B*

Nevada

University of Nevada
    Reno *B*

New Hampshire

Franklin Pierce College *T*
Keene State College *B, T*
New England College *B*
Plymouth State College *B, M, T*
Rivier College *B, T*
St. Anselm College *T*
University of New Hampshire *B, D, T*

New Jersey

Bloomfield College *B*
Caldwell College *T*
Centenary College *T*
The College of New Jersey *B, T*
College of St. Elizabeth *T*
Georgian Court College *T*
Kean University *M*
Monmouth University *B, T*
Montclair State University *D*
Richard Stockton College of New
    Jersey *B*
Rider University *B, T*
Rowan University *M, T*
Rutgers, The State University of New
    Jersey
    New Brunswick Regional
        Campus *D, T*
St. Peter's College *T*
William Paterson University of New
    Jersey *B, T*

New Mexico

College of the Southwest *B, T*
New Mexico Highlands University *B*
New Mexico Institute of Mining and
    Technology *B*
Western New Mexico University *B*

New York

Adelphi University *M*
Alfred University *M, T*
Canisius College *B, M, T*
City University of New York
    Brooklyn College *B, M*
    City College *B*
    College of Staten Island *M*
    Hunter College *B, M, T*
    Queens College *M, T*
Colgate University *M*
College of New Rochelle *T*
D'Youville College *M, T*
Daemen College *B, T*
Dominican College of Blauvelt *B, T*
Dowling College *B*
Elmira College *B, T*
Fordham University *T*
Hofstra University *B, M, T*
Houghton College *B, T*
Ithaca College *B, T*
Keuka College *B, T*
Le Moyne College *T*
Long Island University
    C. W. Post Campus *B, M, T*
Manhattan College *B, T*
Manhattanville College *M, T*
Marist College *B, T*
Marymount College of Fordham
    University *B, T*
Mercy College *T*
Molloy College *B*
Nazareth College of Rochester *T*
New York Institute of Technology *B, T*
New York University *B, M, D, T*

Niagara University *B, T*
Pace University *B, M, T*
Pace University:
    Pleasantville/Briarcliff *B, M, T*
Rensselaer Polytechnic Institute *B, T*
Roberts Wesleyan College *B, T*
St. Bonaventure University *M*
St. John Fisher College *B, M, T*
St. John's University *B, M, T*
St. Joseph's College *B, T*
St. Joseph's College: Suffolk
    Campus *B, T*
St. Lawrence University *T*
State University of New York
    Albany *B, M, T*
    Binghamton *M*
    Buffalo *M, D, T*
    College at Brockport *M*
    College at Buffalo *B, M, T*
    College at Cortland *B, M, T*
    College at Fredonia *B, M, T*
    College at Geneseo *B, M, T*
    College at Old Westbury *B*
    College at Oneonta *B, M, T*
    College at Plattsburgh *B, M*
    College at Potsdam *B, M, T*
    New Paltz *B, M, T*
    Oswego *B, M*
Syracuse University *B, M, D, T*
Tompkins-Cortland Community
    College *A*
Utica College *B*
Vassar College *T*
Wells College *T*

North Carolina

Appalachian State University *B, T*
Belmont Abbey College *T*
Bennett College *B, T*
Campbell University *B, T*
Catawba College *T*
Chowan College *B, T*
Davidson College *T*
East Carolina University *B, M*
Elizabeth City State University *B, T*
Elon University *B, T*
Fayetteville State University *B, T*
Gardner-Webb University *B*
Greensboro College *B, T*
Johnson C. Smith University *B*
Lenoir-Rhyne College *B, T*
Livingstone College *T*
Louisburg College *A*
Mars Hill College *T*
Meredith College *T*
Methodist College *A, B, T*
Montreat College *T*
North Carolina Agricultural and
    Technical State University *B, M, T*
North Carolina Central University *B, M*
North Carolina State University *M, D, T*
Queens University of Charlotte *T*
St. Augustine's College *B*
Shaw University *B, T*
University of North Carolina
    Charlotte *B, M*
    Greensboro *B, M, T*
    Pembroke *B, M, T*
    Wilmington *B*
Wake Forest University *M, T*
Western Carolina University *B, M, T*
Wingate University *B, T*
Winston-Salem State University *B*

North Dakota

Dickinson State University *B, T*
Jamestown College *B*
Mayville State University *B, T*
Minot State University *B, M*
North Dakota State
    University *B, M, D, T*
University of Mary *B*
University of North Dakota *B, T*
Valley City State University *B, T*

Ohio

Ashland University *B, T*
Baldwin-Wallace College *T*
Bluffton College *B*
Bowling Green State University *B, M*
Case Western Reserve University *T*
Cedarville University *B, T*
Central State University *B*
College of Mount St. Joseph *T*
Defiance College *B, T*
Hiram College *T*
John Carroll University *M*
Kent State University *M, T*
Kent State University
    Stark Campus *B*
Malone College *T*
Miami University
    Oxford Campus *B, M, T*
Mount Union College *T*
Mount Vernon Nazarene University *B, T*
Ohio Dominican College *B, T*
Ohio Northern University *B, T*
Ohio State University
    Columbus Campus *M, D*
Ohio University *B, M, D, T*
Otterbein College *B*
Shawnee State University *B*
University of Akron *B, T*
University of Dayton *B, M, T*
University of Findlay *B, T*
University of Rio Grande *B, T*
University of Toledo *B, M, T*
Urbana University *B*
Ursuline College *B, T*
Walsh University *B*
Wilmington College *B*
Wittenberg University *B*
Wright State University *B, M, T*
Xavier University *M*
Youngstown State University *B, M*

Oklahoma

Cameron University *B, T*
East Central University *B, T*
Eastern Oklahoma State College *A*
Langston University *B*
Northeastern State University *B*
Northwestern Oklahoma State
    University *B, T*
Oklahoma Baptist University *B, T*
Oklahoma Christian University of
    Science and Arts *B, T*
Oklahoma City University *B*
Oklahoma Wesleyan University *B*
Oral Roberts University *B, T*
Rogers State University *A*
Southeastern Oklahoma State
    University *B, T*
Southern Nazarene University *B*
Southwestern Oklahoma State
    University *B, M, T*
University of Central Oklahoma *B*
University of Oklahoma *B*
University of Tulsa *B, T*

Oregon

Concordia University *B, M, T*
George Fox University *T*
Linfield College *T*
Oregon State University *M, D*
Portland State University *D, T*
Southern Oregon University *T*
University of Portland *T*
Western Baptist College *B*
Western Oregon University *T*

Pennsylvania

Albright College *T*
Arcadia University *B, M, T*
Cabrini College *B, T*
California University of
    Pennsylvania *B, T*
Carlow College *T*
Chatham College *T*
Cheyney University of Pennsylvania *T*
DeSales University *M, T*

Delaware Valley College *T*
Dickinson College *T*
Duquesne University *B, M, T*
East Stroudsburg University of
    Pennsylvania *B, T*
Elizabethtown College *T*
Geneva College *B, T*
Gettysburg College *T*
Grove City College *B, T*
Gwynedd-Mercy College *T*
Holy Family University *B, M, T*
Immaculata University *T*
Indiana University of
    Pennsylvania *B, M, T*
Juniata College *B, T*
King's College *T*
La Roche College *B*
La Salle University *B, T*
Lebanon Valley College of
    Pennsylvania *B, T*
Lincoln University *B, T*
Lock Haven University of
    Pennsylvania *B, T*
Lycoming College *T*
Marywood University *B*
Mercyhurst College *B*
Messiah College *T*
Millersville University of
    Pennsylvania *B, M, T*
Moravian College *T*
Philadelphia Biblical University *B, T*
Point Park College *B*
Robert Morris University *T*
St. Joseph's University *B*
St. Vincent College *T*
Seton Hill University *B, T*
Slippery Rock University of
    Pennsylvania *M, T*
Temple University *B, M, T*
Thiel College *B*
University of Pennsylvania *M*
University of Pittsburgh *T*
University of Pittsburgh
    Johnstown *B, T*
Villanova University *T*
Washington and Jefferson College *T*
Waynesburg College *B, T*
West Chester University of
    Pennsylvania *B, M, T*
Widener University *T*
Wilkes University *M, T*
Wilson College *T*
York College of Pennsylvania *B, T*

Puerto Rico

Bayamon Central University *B*
Inter American University of Puerto Rico
    Barranquitas Campus *B*
    Metropolitan Campus *B, M*
    San German Campus *B*
Pontifical Catholic University of Puerto
    Rico *B, T*
Turabo University *B*
Universidad Metropolitana *B*
University of Puerto Rico
    Mayaguez Campus *B*

Rhode Island

Rhode Island College *B, M*
Salve Regina University *B*

South Carolina

Anderson College *B, T*
Charleston Southern University *B*
The Citadel *M*
Clemson University *B*
Coker College *B, T*
Columbia College *B*
Francis Marion University *B, T*
Furman University *T*
Limestone College *B*
Morris College *B, T*
South Carolina State University *B, T*
Southern Wesleyan University *B, T*
University of South Carolina
    Aiken *B, T*

Voorhees College *B*
Wofford College *T*

South Dakota
Augustana College *B, T*
Black Hills State University *B, T*
Dakota State University *B, T*
Dakota Wesleyan University *B, T*
Mount Marty College *B*
Northern State University *B, T*
South Dakota State University *B*
University of Sioux Falls *T*
University of South Dakota *B, T*

Tennessee
Belmont University *T*
Bryan College *T*
Christian Brothers University *B, M, T*
Freed-Hardeman University *B, T*
King College *T*
Lambuth University *T*
Lane College *B*
Lee University *B*
Maryville College *B, T*
Middle Tennessee State University *M, T*
Southern Adventist University *B*
Tennessee Technological University *T*
Trevecca Nazarene University *B, T*
Tusculum College *B, T*
Union University *B, T*
University of Tennessee
    Chattanooga *B, T*
    Martin *B, T*
Vanderbilt University *M, D*

Texas
Abilene Christian University *B, T*
Baylor University *B, T*
Del Mar College *A*
East Texas Baptist University *B*
Hardin-Simmons University *B, T*
Houston Baptist University *M, T*
Howard Payne University *B, T*
Jarvis Christian College *B*
Lamar University *T*
Laredo Community College *A*
LeTourneau University *B*
Lubbock Christian University *B, T*
McMurry University *T*
Prairie View A&M University *M*
St. Mary's University *T*
Schreiner University *T*
Southwest Texas State University *M, T*
Stephen F. Austin State University *M*
Tarleton State University *M, T*
Texas A&M International
    University *B, T*
Texas A&M University
    Commerce *T*
    Corpus Christi *T*
    Kingsville *T*
Texas Christian University *B, T*
Texas Lutheran University *B, T*
Texas Wesleyan University *B, T*
University of Dallas *T*
University of Houston *M, T*
University of Houston
    Clear Lake *T*
    Victoria *M*
University of Mary Hardin-Baylor *T*
University of Texas
    Arlington *T*
    Austin *M, D*
    Dallas *M*
    Pan American *T*
    San Antonio *M, T*
University of the Incarnate Word *D*
West Texas A&M University *T*

Utah
Brigham Young University *B, M*
Southern Utah University *B, T*
University of Utah *B, M*
Utah State University *B*
Utah Valley State College *B*
Weber State University *B*

Vermont
Bennington College *B, M, T*
Castleton State College *B, T*
Johnson State College *B*
St. Michael's College *T*
University of Vermont *B*

Virginia
Averett University *B, M, T*
Bluefield College *T*
Bridgewater College *T*
Eastern Mennonite University *T*
Hampton University *M*
Hollins University *T*
Liberty University *B*
Longwood University *B, T*
Radford University *T*
University of Virginia's College at
    Wise *T*
Virginia Wesleyan College *T*

Washington
Central Washington University *B, M, T*
Heritage College *B*
Pacific Lutheran University *T*
Seattle Pacific University *B, T*
Washington State University *T*
Western Washington University *B, T*
Whitworth College *B, T*

West Virginia
Alderson-Broaddus College *T*
Concord College *B, T*
Fairmont State College *B*
Ohio Valley College *B*
Salem International University *T*
Shepherd College *T*
West Liberty State College *B*
West Virginia State College *B*
West Virginia University *T*
West Virginia Wesleyan College *T*
Wheeling Jesuit University *T*

Wisconsin
Carroll College *B, T*
Carthage College *T*
Edgewood College *B*
Lakeland College *T*
Lawrence University *T*
Maranatha Baptist Bible College *B*
Marian College of Fond du Lac *B, T*
Marquette University *B*
Mount Mary College *B, T*
Northland College *T*
St. Norbert College *T*
Silver Lake College *T*
University of Wisconsin
    Green Bay *T*
    La Crosse *B, T*
    Madison *B, M, T*
    Oshkosh *M, T*
    Parkside *T*
    Platteville *B*
    River Falls *T*
    Superior *B, T*
    Whitewater *B*
Viterbo University *B, T*

Wyoming
Eastern Wyoming College *A*

Mathematics/computer science

Alabama
Birmingham-Southern College *B*
Oakwood College *B*

Arkansas
Philander Smith College *B*

California
Claremont McKenna College *B*
Mills College *C, B, M*
Pepperdine University *B*
Pomona College *B*
St. Mary's College of California *B*

Santa Clara University *B*
Stanford University *B*
University of California
    San Diego *B*
    Santa Cruz *B, M*

Colorado
Colorado College *B*
Colorado School of Mines *B*
Metropolitan State College of Denver *B*

Connecticut
Quinnipiac University *B*
Western Connecticut State University *B*
Yale University *B*

Delaware
Delaware State University *B*

District of Columbia
American University *M*

Florida
Polk Community College *A*
University of Tampa *B*
University of West Florida *B*

Georgia
Clark Atlanta University *B, M*
Emory University *B*
Oglethorpe University *B*
Paine College *B*
Piedmont College *B*

Illinois
Augustana College *B*
Dominican University *B*
Eastern Illinois University *B*
Loyola University of Chicago *B*
Parkland College *A*
Rockford College *B*
Roosevelt University *B*
Sauk Valley Community College *A*
Southeastern Illinois College *A*
University of Illinois
    Chicago *B, M*
    Urbana-Champaign *B*

Indiana
Anderson University *B*
Indiana University
    South Bend *M*
Indiana University-Purdue University
    Fort Wayne *B*
Manchester College *B*
Marian College *B, T*
Purdue University
    Calumet *B*
St. Joseph's College *B*
Saint Mary's College *B, T*
Taylor University *B*

Iowa
Central College *B, T*
Coe College *B*
Franciscan University *B*
Morningside College *B*

Kansas
Central Christian College *A*
Seward County Community College *A*
Tabor College *B*

Kentucky
Berea College *T*
Brescia University *B*

Louisiana
Southern University and Agricultural and
    Mechanical College *M*

Maine
Bowdoin College *B*
Colby College *B*
University of Maine
    Farmington *B, T*
University of Southern Maine *B*

Maryland
Cecil Community College *C, A*

Community College of Baltimore County
    Catonsville *A*
    Dundalk *A*
    Essex *A*
Washington College *B, T*

Massachusetts
Amherst College *B*
Boston University *B*
Clark University *B*
Hampshire College *B*
Harvard College *B*
Massachusetts Institute of Technology *B*
Merrimack College *B*
Salem State College *B*
Simon's Rock College of Bard *B*
Tufts University *B, M, D*
Wheaton College *B*

Michigan
Hillsdale College *B*
Lawrence Technological University *B*
Saginaw Valley State University *B*

Minnesota
Carleton College *B*
College of St. Benedict *B*
Concordia College: Moorhead *B*
Minnesota State University
    Mankato *M*
Northland Community & Technical
    College *A*
St. John's University *B*
St. Mary's University of Minnesota *B*
University of Minnesota
    Twin Cities *M, D*
Winona State University *B, T*

Mississippi
Mississippi College *M*

Missouri
Crowder College *A*
Stephens College *B*
Washington University in St.
    Louis *B, M, D*
William Jewell College *B*

Montana
University of Montana-Missoula *B*

Nebraska
Hastings College *B*

New Hampshire
Keene State College *B*
Rivier College *A, B*
St. Anselm College *B*

New Jersey
Cumberland County College *A*
Gloucester County College *A*

New York
Adirondack Community College *A*
Alfred University *B*
City University of New York
    Brooklyn College *B, M*
    College of Staten Island *B*
Colgate University *B*
Hobart and William Smith Colleges *B*
Hofstra University *B*
Marist College *B*
Onondaga Community College *A*
Pace University *B*
Pace University:
    Pleasantville/Briarcliff *B*
Rochester Institute of Technology *B*
St. Lawrence University *B*
Schenectady County Community
    College *A*
State University of New York
    Purchase *B*
Vassar College *B*

North Carolina
University of North Carolina
    Pembroke *B*
Wingate University *B*

Ohio

Antioch College *B*
College of Mount St. Joseph *B, T*
Defiance College *B, T*
Hiram College *B*
Jefferson Community College *A*
University of Akron *C, B, M*
Wittenberg University *B*
Youngstown State University *B*

Oklahoma

Oklahoma Baptist University *B*
Oklahoma Christian University of
   Science and Arts *B*

Oregon

Lewis & Clark College *B*
Southern Oregon University *B*
University of Oregon *B*
Western Oregon University *B*

Pennsylvania

Carnegie Mellon University *B*
Chestnut Hill College *B*
Dickinson College *B*
Duquesne University *M*
Gettysburg College *B*
Grove City College *B*
La Salle University *B*
Lock Haven University of
   Pennsylvania *B*
Mount Aloysius College *A, B*

Puerto Rico

Inter American University of Puerto Rico
   Bayamon Campus *B*
University of Puerto Rico
   Humacao *B*
   Mayaguez Campus *B, M*

Rhode Island

Brown University *B*

South Carolina

Charleston Southern University *B*
Claflin University *B*
Furman University *B*
Newberry College *B*
North Greenville College *B*
University of South Carolina
   Aiken *B*

Tennessee

Bryan College *B*
Christian Brothers University *B*
Maryville College *B*

Texas

Laredo Community College *A*
LeTourneau University *B*
McMurry University *B*
University of Houston
   Clear Lake *B, M*

Vermont

Bennington College *B*
Castleton State College *B*
Marlboro College *B*

Virginia

Averett University *B, T*
George Mason University *D*
Hampden-Sydney College *B*
Sweet Briar College *B*
University of Richmond *B*
Virginia Wesleyan College *B*

Washington

Gonzaga University *B*
Washington State University *B*

West Virginia

Bethany College *B*
Salem International University *B*

Wisconsin

Cardinal Stritch University *B*
Marquette University *B, M, D*
St. Norbert College *B*

University of Wisconsin
   Parkside *B*
   Superior *B*

Mechanical drafting/CAD/CADD

Alabama

Lawson State Community College *C, A*

California

Ohlone College *C*

Colorado

Westwood College of Technology
   South *A*

Florida

New England Institute of Technology *A*
Palm Beach Community College *C*

Illinois

City Colleges of Chicago
   Wright College *C, A*
Kaskaskia College *C*
Parkland College *C*
Waubonsee Community College *C, A*

Massachusetts

Benjamin Franklin Institute of
   Technology *A*

Michigan

Baker College
   of Muskegon *A*
Grand Rapids Community College *A*

Minnesota

Minnesota State College - Southeast
   Technical *C, A*
St. Paul College - A Community and
   Technical College *C, A*

New Mexico

Santa Fe Community College *C*

New York

Erie Community College
   South Campus *A*
Mohawk Valley Community College *C*

North Carolina

Davidson County Community College *C*

North Dakota

North Dakota State College of Science *A*

Ohio

Owens Community College
   Findlay Campus *C*
   Toledo *C*

Oklahoma

Platt College
   Tulsa *C*

Pennsylvania

Butler County Community College *A*
Community College of Allegheny
   County *A*
Montgomery County Community
   College *C, A*
Penn State
   University Park *C*
Pennsylvania College of
   Technology *C, A*

South Carolina

York Technical College *C, A*

South Dakota

Southeast Technical Institute *A*

Tennessee

Northeast State Technical Community
   College *C, A*

Utah

Dixie State College of Utah *C, A*

Washington

Centralia College *C*

Wisconsin

Fox Valley Technical College *A*
Milwaukee Area Technical College *A*
Western Wisconsin Technical College *A*

Mechanical engineering

Alabama

Alabama Agricultural and Mechanical
   University *B*
Auburn University *B, M, D*
Tuskegee University *B, M*
University of Alabama *B, M, D*
University of Alabama
   Birmingham *B, M, D*
   Huntsville *B, M, D*
University of South Alabama *B, M*

Alaska

University of Alaska
   Fairbanks *B, M*

Arizona

Arizona State University *B, M, D*
Central Arizona College *A*
Northern Arizona University *B*
University of Arizona *B, M, D*

Arkansas

Arkansas Tech University *B*
John Brown University *B*
University of Arkansas *B, M*
University of Arkansas
   Fort Smith *A, B*

California

California Institute of
   Technology *B, M, D*
California Maritime Academy *B*
California Polytechnic State University:
   San Luis Obispo *B*
California State Polytechnic University:
   Pomona *B*
California State University
   Chico *B*
   Fresno *B, M*
   Fullerton *B, M*
   Long Beach *B, M*
   Los Angeles *B, M*
   Northridge *B, M*
   Sacramento *B, M*
De Anza College *A*
Loyola Marymount University *B, M*
San Diego State University *B, M*
San Francisco State University *B*
San Jose State University *B, M*
Santa Clara University *C, B, M, D*
Stanford University *B, M, D*
University of California
   Berkeley *B, M, D*
   Davis *B*
   Irvine *B, M, D*
   Los Angeles *B, M, D*
   Riverside *B, M, D*
   San Diego *B, M, D*
   Santa Barbara *B, M, D*
University of Southern
   California *B, M, D*
University of the Pacific *B*

Colorado

Colorado State University *B, M, D*
National Technological University *M*
United States Air Force Academy *B*
University of Colorado
   Boulder *B, M, D*
   Colorado Springs *B, M*
   Denver *B, M*
University of Denver *B, M*

Connecticut

Fairfield University *B*
Trinity College *B*
United States Coast Guard Academy *B*

University of Bridgeport *M*
University of Connecticut *B, M, D*
University of Hartford *B, M*
University of New Haven *A, B, M*
Yale University *B, M, D*

Delaware

University of Delaware *B, M, D*

District of Columbia

Catholic University of America *B, M, D*
George Washington University *B, M*
Howard University *B, M, D*
University of the District of Columbia *B*

Florida

Florida Agricultural and Mechanical
   University *B, M, D*
Florida Atlantic University *B, M, D*
Florida Institute of Technology *B, M, D*
Florida International University *B, M, D*
Florida State University *B, M, D*
Jacksonville University *B*
University of Central Florida *C, B, M, D*
University of Florida *B, M, D*
University of Miami *B, M, D*
University of North Florida *B*
University of South Florida *B, M, D*

Georgia

Georgia Institute of Technology *B, M, D*
Mercer University *B, M*

Hawaii

University of Hawaii
   Manoa *B, M, D*

Idaho

Boise State University *B*
Brigham Young University - Idaho *B*
Idaho State University *B*
University of Idaho *B, M, D*

Illinois

Bradley University *B, M*
Dominican University *B*
Illinois Institute of Technology *B, M, D*
Northern Illinois University *B, M*
Northwestern University *B, M, D*
Parkland College *A*
Southern Illinois University
   Carbondale *B, M*
Southern Illinois University
   Edwardsville *B, M*
University of Illinois
   Chicago *B, M, D*
   Urbana-Champaign *B, M, D*

Indiana

Indiana Institute of Technology *B*
Indiana University-Purdue University
   Fort Wayne *B*
Indiana University-Purdue University
   Indianapolis *B, M*
Purdue University *B, M, D*
Purdue University
   Calumet *B, T*
Rose-Hulman Institute of
   Technology *B, M*
Tri-State University *B*
University of Evansville *B*
University of Notre Dame *B, M, D*
Valparaiso University *B*
Vincennes University *A*

Iowa

Dordt College *B*
Iowa State University *B, M, D*
University of Iowa *B, M, D*
William Penn University *B*

Kansas

Kansas State University *B, M, D*
University of Kansas *B, M, D*
Wichita State University *B, M, D*

Kentucky

University of Kentucky *B, M, D*
University of Louisville *B, M*

Louisiana

Louisiana State University and
Agricultural and Mechanical
College *B, M, D*
Louisiana Tech University *B*
Southern University and Agricultural and
Mechanical College *B*
Tulane University *B, M, D*
University of Louisiana at
Lafayette *B, M*
University of New Orleans *B*

Maine

University of Maine *B, M, D*

Maryland

Goucher College *B*
Johns Hopkins University *B, M, D*
United States Naval Academy *B*
University of Maryland
Baltimore County *C, B, M, D*
College Park *B, M, D*

Massachusetts

Boston University *B, M, D*
Franklin W. Olin College of
Engineering *B*
Harvard College *B*
Massachusetts Institute of
Technology *B, M, D*
Northeastern University *B, M, D*
Smith College *B*
Tufts University *B, M, D*
University of Massachusetts
Amherst *B, M, D*
Dartmouth *B, M*
Lowell *A, B, M, D*
Wentworth Institute of Technology *B*
Western New England College *B, M*
Worcester Polytechnic Institute *B, M, D*

Michigan

Calvin College *B*
Grand Valley State University *B, M*
Kettering University *B, M*
Lawrence Technological University *B*
Michigan State University *B, M, D*
Michigan Technological
University *B, M, D, T*
Oakland University *B, M, D*
Saginaw Valley State University *B*
University of Michigan *B, M, D*
University of Michigan
Dearborn *B, M*
Wayne State University *B, M, D*
Western Michigan University *B, M, D*

Minnesota

Minnesota State University
Mankato *B*
University of Minnesota
Duluth *B*
Twin Cities *C, B, M, D*
University of St. Thomas *B*
Winona State University *B*

Mississippi

Mississippi State University *B, M*
University of Mississippi *B*

Missouri

St. Louis University *B*
University of Missouri
Columbia *B, M, D*
Kansas City *B, M*
Rolla *B, M, D*
St. Louis *B*
Washington University in St.
Louis *B, M, D*

Montana

Montana State University
Bozeman *B, M*
Montana Tech of the University of
Montana *B*

Nebraska

University of Nebraska
Lincoln *B, M*
Omaha *B*

Nevada

University of Nevada
Las Vegas *B, M, D*
Reno *B, M, D*

New Hampshire

University of New Hampshire *B, M, D*

New Jersey

The College of New Jersey *B*
New Jersey Institute of
Technology *B, M, D*
Princeton University *B, M, D*
Rowan University *B*
Rutgers, The State University of New
Jersey
Camden Regional Campus *B*
New Brunswick Regional
Campus *B, M, D*
Newark Regional Campus *B*
Stevens Institute of Technology *B, M, D*

New Mexico

New Mexico Institute of Mining and
Technology *B*
New Mexico State University *B, M*
University of New Mexico *B, M*

New York

Alfred University *B, M*
City University of New York
City College *B, M, D*
Clarkson University *B, M, D*
Columbia University
Fu Foundation School of
Engineering and Applied
Science *B, M, D*
Cornell University *B, M, D*
Hofstra University *B*
Manhattan College *B, M*
New York Institute of Technology *B*
New York University *B*
Polytechnic University *B, M, D*
Rensselaer Polytechnic Institute *B, M, D*
Rochester Institute of Technology *B, M*
State University of New York
Binghamton *B, M, D*
Buffalo *B, M, D*
College of Environmental Science
and Forestry *B, M, D*
Maritime College *B*
Stony Brook *B, M, D*
Syracuse University *B, M, D*
Union College *B, M*
United States Military Academy *B*
University of Rochester *B, M, D*

North Carolina

Duke University *B, M, D*
North Carolina Agricultural and
Technical State University *B, M, D*
North Carolina State University *B, M, D*
University of North Carolina
Charlotte *B, M, D*
Western Piedmont Community
College *C, A*

North Dakota

North Dakota State University *B, M*
University of North Dakota *B, M*

Ohio

Case Western Reserve
University *B, M, D*
Cedarville University *B*
Cleveland State University *B, M, D*
Miami University
Oxford Campus *B*
Ohio Northern University *B*
Ohio State University
Columbus Campus *B, M, D*
Ohio University *B, M*
University of Akron *C, B, M, D*

University of Cincinnati *B, M, D*
University of Dayton *B, M, D*
University of Toledo *B, M*
Wright State University *B, M*
Youngstown State University *B, M*

Oklahoma

Oklahoma Christian University of
Science and Arts *B*
Oklahoma State University *B, M, D*
Oral Roberts University *B*
University of Oklahoma *B, M, D*
University of Tulsa *B, M, D*

Oregon

George Fox University *B*
Oregon Institute of Technology *B*
Oregon State University *B, M, D*
Portland State University *B, M, D*
University of Portland *B, M*

Pennsylvania

Bucknell University *B, M*
Carnegie Mellon University *B, M, D*
Drexel University *B, M, D*
Gettysburg College *B*
Grove City College *B*
Lafayette College *B*
Lehigh University *B, M, D*
Lock Haven University of
Pennsylvania *B*
Penn State
Abington *B*
Altoona *B*
Beaver *B*
Berks *B*
Delaware County *B*
Dubois *B*
Erie, The Behrend College *B*
Fayette *B*
Harrisburg *B*
Hazleton *B*
Lehigh Valley *B*
McKeesport *B*
Mont Alto *B*
New Kensington *B*
Schuylkill - Capital College *B*
Shenango *B*
University Park *B, M, D*
Wilkes-Barre *B*
Worthington Scranton *B*
York *B*
Temple University *B, M*
University of Pennsylvania *B, M, D*
University of Pittsburgh *B, M, D*
Villanova University *B, M*
Widener University *B, M*
Wilkes University *B*
York College of Pennsylvania *B*

Puerto Rico

Inter American University of Puerto Rico
Bayamon Campus *B*
Turabo University *B*
Universidad Politecnica de Puerto
Rico *B*
University of Puerto Rico
Mayaguez Campus *B, M*

Rhode Island

Brown University *B, M, D*
University of Rhode Island *B, M, D*

South Carolina

Clemson University *B, M, D*
University of South Carolina *B, M, D*

South Dakota

South Dakota School of Mines and
Technology *B, M*
South Dakota State University *B*

Tennessee

Chattanooga State Technical Community
College *A*
Christian Brothers University *B*
Tennessee Technological
University *B, M, D*

Union University *B*
University of Memphis *B, M*
University of Tennessee
Knoxville *B, M, D*
Vanderbilt University *B, M, D*

Texas

Baylor University *B*
Houston Baptist University *B*
Lamar University *B*
LeTourneau University *B*
Prairie View A&M University *B*
Rice University *B, M, D*
Southern Methodist University *B, M, D*
Texas A&M University *B, M, D*
Texas A&M University
Kingsville *B, M*
Texas Tech University *B, M, D*
University of Houston *B, M, D*
University of Texas
Arlington *B, M, D*
Austin *B, M, D*
El Paso *B, M*
Pan American *B, M*
San Antonio *B, M*
Tyler *B*

Utah

Brigham Young University *B, M, D*
University of Utah *B, M, D*
Utah State University *B, M, D*

Vermont

Norwich University *B*
University of Vermont *B, M, D*
Vermont Technical College *A*

Virginia

Old Dominion University *B*
University of Virginia *B, M, D*
Virginia Commonwealth University *B*
Virginia Military Institute *B*
Virginia Polytechnic Institute and State
University *B, M, D*

Washington

Gonzaga University *B*
Henry Cogswell College *B*
St. Martin's College *B*
Seattle University *B*
University of Washington *B, M, D*
Walla Walla College *B*
Washington State University *B, M, D*

West Virginia

West Virginia University *B, M, D*
West Virginia University Institute of
Technology *B*

Wisconsin

Marquette University *B, M, D*
Milwaukee School of Engineering *B*
University of Wisconsin
Madison *B, M, D*
Milwaukee *B, M, D*
Platteville *B*
Waukesha County Technical College *A*

Wyoming

University of Wyoming *B, M, D*

Mechanical engineering technology

Connecticut

Capital Community College *A*
Central Connecticut State University *B*
Naugatuck Valley Community College *A*

Florida

South Florida Community College *A*
University of Central Florida *B*

Georgia

Georgia Southern University *B*
Macon State College *A*
Southern Polytechnic State University *B*

Idaho
Lewis-Clark State College *C, A*

Illinois
College of Lake County *C, A*
McHenry County College *C, A*

Indiana
Indiana State University *B*
Indiana University-Purdue University
Fort Wayne *A, B*

Kentucky
Murray State University *A, B*

Louisiana
University of New Orleans *B, M*

Maryland
College of Southern Maryland *C*
Community College of Baltimore County
Catonsville *C, A*
Dundalk *C, A*
Essex *C, A*
Hagerstown Community College *A*

Massachusetts
Benjamin Franklin Institute of
Technology *A*
Wentworth Institute of Technology *A, B*

Michigan
Lawrence Technological University *A*
Mott Community College *A*
Saginaw Valley State University *M*

Minnesota
Hennepin Technical College *C, A*
Normandale Community College *C, A*

Missouri
St. Louis Community College
St. Louis Community College at
Florissant Valley *A*

New Jersey
Thomas Edison State College *A, B*
Union County College *A*

New York
Erie Community College
North Campus *A*
Mohawk Valley Community College *A*
New York Institute of Technology *A*
Niagara County Community College *A*
Rochester Institute of Technology *B*
State University of New York
College of Agriculture and
Technology at Morrisville *A*
College of Technology at Canton *A*

North Carolina
Cape Fear Community College *C, A*
Isothermal Community College *C, A*
Lenoir Community College *C, A*
University of North Carolina
Charlotte *B*
Wilson Technical Community College *A*

Ohio
Bowling Green State University *B*
Kent State University *A*
Lakeland Community College *C, A*
North Central State College *A*
Northwest State Community
College *C, A*
Owens Community College
Findlay Campus *A*
Toledo *A*
Sinclair Community College *A*
University of Akron *B, M*
University of Dayton *B*
University of Toledo *C, A, B*
Youngstown State University *A, B*

Oklahoma
Oklahoma Christian University of
Science and Arts *B*
Oklahoma State University *B*

Pennsylvania
Butler County Community College *A*
Delaware County Community College *A*
Montgomery County Community
College *A*
Penn State
Altoona *A*
Berks *A*
Dubois *A*
Fayette *A*
Hazleton *A*
New Kensington *A*
Shenango *A*
York *A*
Pennsylvania College of Technology *B*
University of Pittsburgh
Johnstown *B*
Williamson Free School of Mechanical
Trades *C*

Rhode Island
Community College of Rhode Island *A*

South Carolina
York Technical College *A*

Texas
Palo Alto College *C*
Texas Tech University *B*

Utah
Brigham Young University *M*

Washington
Central Washington University *B*
Clover Park Technical College *A*

Wisconsin
Milwaukee School of Engineering *B*

Mechanics/repairers, general

Alabama
Central Alabama Community College *C*
Enterprise State Junior College *A*
George C. Wallace State Community
College
Selma *A*

Alaska
University of Alaska
Anchorage *C, A*

Arkansas
Ouachita Technical College *C, A*
Pulaski Technical College *C*
Southeast Arkansas College *C*
University of Arkansas
Community College at
Batesville *C, A*
Community College at Hope *C*
Fort Smith *C*

California
Cerritos Community College *A*
College of the Canyons *A*
College of the Redwoods *C*
Columbia College *C*
Imperial Valley College *C, A*
Las Positas College *C*
Long Beach City College *C, A*
Modesto Junior College *C, A*
Palomar College *C, A*
Riverside Community College *C, A*
Shasta College *C, A*
Yuba Community College District *C, A*

Colorado
Otero Junior College *C*
Red Rocks Community College *C, A*

Connecticut
Gateway Community College *A*
Three Rivers Community College *A*

Florida
Chipola Junior College *C*

Seminole Community College *C*

Georgia
Columbus Technical College *C*
Georgia Southwestern State University *A*
Southwest Georgia Technical College *C*
West Georgia Technical College *A*

Hawaii
University of Hawaii
Honolulu Community College *C, A*

Idaho
Boise State University *C*
Eastern Idaho Technical College *C, A*
Idaho State University *C, A*
Lewis-Clark State College *C, A*
North Idaho College *C*

Illinois
Danville Area Community College *A*
Heartland Community College *C, A*
Kankakee Community College *C, A*
Moraine Valley Community
College *C, A*
Richland Community College *A*
Southwestern Illinois College *C, A*
Triton College *C*

Indiana
Ivy Tech State College
Northwest *C*
Lincoln Technical Institute *C, A*
Vincennes University *A*

Iowa
Des Moines Area Community
College *C, A*
Indian Hills Community College *A*
Iowa Western Community College *A*
Northwest Iowa Community
College *C, A*
Southeastern Community College
North Campus *A*

Kansas
Butler County Community College *C, A*

Kentucky
Maysville Community College *C, A*

Louisiana
Nunez Community College *C*

Maryland
Cecil Community College *C, A*

Massachusetts
Benjamin Franklin Institute of
Technology *A*

Michigan
Bay de Noc Community College *C, A*
Glen Oaks Community College *C*
Kirtland Community College *C, A*
Lansing Community College *A*
Macomb Community College *C*
Muskegon Community College *C, A*
Oakland Community College *C, A*
Southwestern Michigan College *C, A*

Minnesota
Hennepin Technical College *C, A*
Lake Superior College: A Community
and Technical College *C, A*
Mesabi Range Community and Technical
College *A*

Mississippi
Northwest Mississippi Community
College *C*

Missouri
North Central Missouri College *A*

Montana
Montana State University
Billings College of Technology *A*

Nebraska
Mid Plains Community College
Area *C, A*

Nebraska College of Technical
Agriculture *A*
Southeast Community College
Milford Campus *A*

New Jersey
Raritan Valley Community College *A*
Thomas Edison State College *A*

New Mexico
Luna Community College *C*
Mesalands Community College *C*

New York
State University of New York
College of Technology at Alfred *A*

North Carolina
Alamance Community College *C*
Forsyth Technical Community College *C*
James Sprunt Community College *C*
Johnston Community College *C*
Mayland Community College *C*
Rockingham Community College *A*
Sandhills Community College *C*

Ohio
Columbus State Community College *A*
Ohio Technical College *C, A*
Owens Community College
Findlay Campus *C, A*
Toledo *A*

Oklahoma
Oklahoma City Community College *A*

Oregon
Blue Mountain Community College *A*
Linn-Benton Community College *A*

Pennsylvania
Delaware County Community College *C*
Penn Commercial, Inc. *A*
Pennsylvania College of Technology *A*
Rosedale Technical Institute *C, A*

South Carolina
Central Carolina Technical College *C*
Tri-County Technical College *C*
Trident Technical College *C, A*
Williamsburg Technical College *C, A*
York Technical College *A*

South Dakota
Southeast Technical Institute *A*

Tennessee
Chattanooga State Technical Community
College *C*
Nashville Auto-Diesel College *C, A*
Northeast State Technical Community
College *C, A*
Southwest Tennessee Community
College *A*

Texas
Central Texas College *C, A*
Cisco Junior College *C, A*
Laredo Community College *C*
MTI College of Business and
Technology *C*
MTI College of Business and
Technology *C*
Texarkana College *C*
Texas Southern University *B*
Texas State Technical College
Waco *C, A*
Western Technical Institute *C, A*

Utah
Snow College *C, A*
Utah Career College *C*

Vermont
Community College of Vermont *A*

Virginia
ECPI College of Technology *C, A*
Virginia Highlands Community
College *C*
Virginia Western Community College *A*

Washington

Edmonds Community College *C, A*
Walla Walla Community College *C, A*

Wisconsin

Nicolet Area Technical College *C*
Western Wisconsin Technical College *C*

Wyoming

Casper College *C, A*
Western Wyoming Community
    College *C, A*

Media studies

Arizona

Arizona State University *B, M*

Arkansas

Arkansas Tech University *M*

California

Claremont McKenna College *B*
Foothill College *C, A*
University of San Francisco *B*
Yuba Community College District *C, A*

District of Columbia

American University *B*

Georgia

Brenau University *B*
Clark Atlanta University *B*
Piedmont College *B*

Hawaii

Hawaii Pacific University *M*

Idaho

Idaho State University *B*

Illinois

Principia College *B*
Robert Morris College: Chicago *C, A*
Southern Illinois University
    Carbondale *M, D*
Southern Illinois University
    Edwardsville *B, M*
University of Illinois
    Urbana-Champaign *B*
University of St. Francis *B*
Waubonsee Community College *A*

Indiana

Calumet College of St. Joseph *C, A, B*
Indiana University
    Bloomington *D*
    South Bend *B*
St. Joseph's College *B*
University of St. Francis *B*
Vincennes University *A*

Iowa

University of Iowa *D*

Kansas

Kansas State University *B*

Kentucky

Murray State University *B, M*

Louisiana

Centenary College of Louisiana *B*
Southern University and Agricultural and
    Mechanical College *B, M*
University of Louisiana at Lafayette *B*

Maine

University of Southern Maine *B*

Massachusetts

Cape Cod Community College *A*
Emerson College *B*
Massachusetts Institute of Technology *M*

Michigan

Calvin College *B*
Michigan State University *D*
Northern Michigan University *B*

Minnesota

Concordia College: Moorhead *B*
Metropolitan State University *B*
Winona State University *B*

Missouri

Lindenwood University *B*
Westminster College *B*

Nebraska

Doane College *B*

New Hampshire

Franklin Pierce College *B*

New Jersey

William Paterson University of New
    Jersey *M*

New York

Adirondack Community College *C, A*
City University of New York
    Hunter College *B*
Hofstra University *B*
Ithaca College *B*
Marist College *B*
Rochester Institute of Technology *M*
State University of New York
    Buffalo *M, D*
    College at Oneonta *B*
Syracuse University *D*
Tompkins-Cortland Community
    College *A*

North Carolina

Barton College *B*
Meredith College *B*
North Carolina State University *B*
Shaw University *B*
University of North Carolina
    Chapel Hill *B, M, D*

North Dakota

North Dakota State University *D*

Ohio

Bowling Green State University *D*
Lakeland Community College *C*
Ohio University *B*
University of Akron *B, M*
University of Cincinnati
    Raymond Walters College *C*
Washington State Community College *A*
Wilmington College *B*
Wright State University *B*

Oklahoma

Northeastern Oklahoma Agricultural and
    Mechanical College *A*
Oklahoma City University *B*
Oklahoma State University *M*

Pennsylvania

La Salle University *B*
Marywood University *M*
Penn State
    Abington *B*
    Altoona *B*
    Beaver *B*
    Berks *B*
    Delaware County *B*
    Dubois *B*
    Fayette *B*
    Hazleton *B*
    Lehigh Valley *B*
    McKeesport *B*
    Mont Alto *B*
    New Kensington *B*
    Schuylkill - Capital College *B*
    Shenango *B*
    University Park *B, M, D*
    Wilkes-Barre *B*
    Worthington Scranton *B*
Pennsylvania College of Technology *A*

South Carolina

Francis Marion University *B*
University of South Carolina *B, M*

South Dakota

University of South Dakota *B, M*

Tennessee

Belmont University *B*
Southern Adventist University *B*

Texas

Southwest Texas State University *B, M*
Texas Christian University *M*
University of Houston *B, M*

Utah

Brigham Young University *B*

Virginia

Hampton University *B*
Norfolk State University *M, D*

West Virginia

University of Charleston *B*

Wisconsin

Edgewood College *B, T*
University of Wisconsin
    Eau Claire *B*
    Superior *B*
Western Wisconsin Technical College *A*

Medical administrative assistant

Alabama

Harry M. Ayers State Technical
    College *C*
James H. Faulkner State Community
    College *A*
Lawson State Community College *C, A*
Northwest-Shoals Community College *C*

Alaska

University of Alaska
    Fairbanks *C*

Arizona

Central Arizona College *C, A*
Cochise College *A*
Gateway Community College *C*
International Institute of the Americas
    Phoenix *C, A, B*
    Tucson *C, A, B*
Yavapai College *C, A*

Arkansas

Arkansas State University
    Mountain Home *C*

California

Antelope Valley College *C, A*
Barstow College *C*
College of the Redwoods *C*
Columbia College *C*
De Anza College *C*
East Los Angeles College *C*
Gavilan Community College *C*
Glendale Community College *C, A*
Los Angeles Harbor College *C, A*
Mount San Antonio College *C, A*
Palomar College *C, A*
Riverside Community College *C, A*
Santa Rosa Junior College *C*
Shasta College *C*
Sierra College *C, A*
Ventura College *C, A*

Colorado

Blair Junior College *C, A*
Community College of Aurora *A*
Otero Junior College *A*
Parks College *A*
Red Rocks Community College *C, A*

Connecticut

Briarwood College *C, A*
Gateway Community College *A*
Gibbs College *C*
Middlesex Community College *A*
Naugatuck Valley Community College *A*

Quinebaug Valley Community College *C*
Three Rivers Community College *A*
Tunxis Community College *C, A*

Delaware

Delaware Technical and Community
    College
    Owens Campus *A*
    Stanton/Wilmington Campus *A*

Florida

Broward Community College *C*
Cooper Career Institute *C*
Daytona Beach Community College *A*
Florida Technical College
    Deland *A*
Indian River Community College *C*
Institute of Career Education *C*
Miami-Dade Community College *A*
Palm Beach Community College *C*
Pasco-Hernando Community College *C*
Santa Fe Community College *A*
Seminole Community College *C*
South Florida Community College *C*
Tallahassee Community College *C*
Valencia Community College *A*

Georgia

Chattahoochee Technical College *C*
Dalton State College *A*

Hawaii

Hawaii Business College *A*
Heald College
    Honolulu *A*

Idaho

Eastern Idaho Technical College *C, A*
Idaho State University *C, A*
Lewis-Clark State College *A*
North Idaho College *A*

Illinois

Black Hawk College *C, A*
College of Lake County *C*
Danville Area Community College *C, A*
Elgin Community College *A*
Illinois Eastern Community Colleges
    Olney Central College *C, A*
John A. Logan College *A*
John Wood Community College *A*
Joliet Junior College *A*
Kankakee Community College *A*
Midstate College *C, A*
Northwestern Business College *A*
Rockford Business College *C, A*
Sauk Valley Community College *C, A*
Shawnee Community College *A*
Waubonsee Community College *C*
William Rainey Harper College *C, A*

Indiana

Commonwealth Business College:
    Michigan City *C, A*
Indiana Business College *A*
International Business College *C, A*
Professional Careers Institute *C, A*
Sawyer College *C, A*
Vincennes University *A*

Iowa

American Institute of Business *A*
Des Moines Area Community
    College *C, A*
Dordt College *A*
Ellsworth Community College *A*
Hawkeye Community College *C*
Iowa Western Community College *A*
Kirkwood Community College *C, A*
Mercy College of Health Sciences *C*
North Iowa Area Community
    College *C, A*
Northeast Iowa Community College *A*
Southeastern Community College
    North Campus *C*
    South Campus *A*
Western Iowa Tech Community
    College *A*

Kansas

Central Christian College *A*
Independence Community College *C, A*
Labette Community College *A*
Pratt Community College *C, A*
Seward County Community
College *C, A*
Washburn University of Topeka *A*

Kentucky

Daymar College *C, A*
National College of Business &
Technology
Danville *A*
Florence *A*
Lexington *A*
Pikeville *A*
Richmond *A*
Somerset Community College *C, A*

Louisiana

Nunez Community College *A*

Maine

Andover College *C, A*
Beal College *A*

Maryland

Allegany College *A*
Community College of Baltimore County
Catonsville *A*
Dundalk *A*
Essex *A*
Villa Julie College *A*

Massachusetts

Bay State College *A*
Cape Cod Community College *C, A*
Marian Court College *C, A*
Mount Wachusett Community College *C*
Quinsigamond Community College *A*
Roxbury Community College *A*
Springfield Technical Community
College *A*

Michigan

Baker College
of Auburn Hills *C, A*
of Cadillac *A*
of Clinton Township *A*
of Jackson *C, A*
of Muskegon *C, A*
of Owosso *A*
of Port Huron *C, A*
Davenport University
Eastern Region *C, A*
Midland *A*
Davenport University - Western
Region *A*
Glen Oaks Community College *C*
Grand Rapids Community College *A*
Kellogg Community College *A*
Kirtland Community College *C, A*
Lansing Community College *A*
Macomb Community College *C, A*
Mid Michigan Community College *A*
Monroe County Community
College *C, A*
Montcalm Community College *C, A*
Mott Community College *C, A*
Muskegon Community College *A*
Northern Michigan University *A*
St. Clair County Community College *A*

Minnesota

Alexandria Technical College *C, A*
Anoka-Ramsey Community College *A*
Central Lakes College *C, A*
Century Community and Technical
College *C, A*
Fergus Falls Community College *C*
Hennepin Technical College *C, A*
Hibbing Community College: A
Technical and Community College *A*
Inver Hills Community College *C, A*
Itasca Community College *C*
Lake Superior College: A Community
and Technical College *C, A*

Minnesota State College - Southeast
Technical *C, A*
Northland Community & Technical
College *C, A*
Rasmussen College
Mankato *C*
Minnetonka *C, A*
St. Cloud *C*
Ridgewater College: A Community and
Technical College *C, A*
Riverland Community College: A
Technical and Community
College *C, A*
Rochester Community and Technical
College *C, A*
St. Cloud Technical College *C, A*
St. Paul College - A Community and
Technical College *C, A*
South Central Technical College *A*

Mississippi

Mississippi Gulf Coast Community
College
Perkinston *A*
Northwest Mississippi Community
College *A*
Pearl River Community College *A*

Missouri

East Central College *A*
Jefferson College *A*
Longview Community College *C*
Maple Woods Community College *C*
Northwest Missouri State University *C*
Penn Valley Community College *C*
Springfield College *C, A*
Vatterott College: St. Joseph *A*

Montana

Flathead Valley Community College *A*
Miles Community College *A*
Montana State University
Billings *A*
Billings College of Technology *A*
Montana Tech of the University of
Montana *A*
University of Montana-Missoula *A*

Nebraska

Lincoln School of Commerce *A*
Northeast Community College *A*
Southeast Community College
Beatrice Campus *A*
Vatterott College
Dodge Campus *A*

Nevada

Morrison University *C, A*
Truckee Meadows Community
College *A*
Western Nevada Community College *C*

New Hampshire

New Hampshire Community Technical
College
Claremont *C*
Laconia *C*
Manchester *C, A*

New Jersey

Essex County College *A*
Gloucester County College *C, A*
Mercer County Community College *C*
Sussex County Community College *C*

New Mexico

Clovis Community College *A*
Dona Ana Branch Community College of
New Mexico State University *A*
New Mexico State University
Alamogordo *C*
Western New Mexico University *C, A*

New York

Adirondack Community College *A*
Bryant & Stratton Business Institute
Syracuse *A*

City University of New York
Hostos Community College *A*
Kingsborough Community
College *A*
Clinton Community College *C*
Elmira Business Institute *C, A*
Fulton-Montgomery Community
College *A*
Genesee Community College *C*
Hudson Valley Community College *A*
Jamestown Business College *C, A*
Katharine Gibbs School
Melville *A*
Nassau Community College *A*
Olean Business Institute *C, A*
Rochester Business Institute *A*
Trocaire College *C*
Utica School of Commerce *C, A*

North Carolina

Alamance Community College *C, A*
Asheville Buncombe Technical
Community College *C*
Beaufort County Community College *A*
Blue Ridge Community College *C*
Caldwell Community College and
Technical Institute *C, A*
Central Carolina Community College *A*
Central Piedmont Community College *A*
Cleveland Community College *C, A*
College of the Albemarle *A*
Craven Community College *C, A*
Durham Technical Community
College *A*
Gaston College *A*
Guilford Technical Community
College *A*
Halifax Community College *A*
Johnston Community College *A*
King's College *A, D*
Lenoir Community College *A*
Martin Community College *C, A*
Mayland Community College *A*
Nash Community College *A*
Piedmont Community College *A*
Pitt Community College *C, A*
Rockingham Community College *A*
South Piedmont Community
College *C, A*
Wake Technical Community College *A*
Wayne Community College *A*

North Dakota

Dickinson State University *A*
Lake Region State College *A*
Minot State University: Bottineau
Campus *A*

Ohio

AEC Southern Ohio College
Findlay *A*
Bowling Green State University:
Firelands College *C*
Bryant & Stratton College
Cleveland West *C, A*
Central Ohio Technical College *A*
Columbus State Community College *A*
Davis College *A*
ETI Technical College of Niles *A*
Edison State Community College *A*
Gallipolis Career College *A*
Hocking Technical College *C*
James A. Rhodes State College *A*
Jefferson Community College *A*
Marion Technical College *A*
Miami-Jacobs College *A*
Northwest State Community College *A*
Ohio Business College *C, A*
Ohio Business College: Sandusky *C, A*
Ohio University
Chillicothe Campus *A*
Ohio Valley College of Technology *A*
Owens Community College
Findlay Campus *A*
Sinclair Community College *C*
Southeastern Business College *A*

Southeastern Business College:
Lancaster *A*
Southwestern College of Business *A*
Stautzenberger College *A*
Trumbull Business College *A*
University of Akron *A*
University of Cincinnati
Raymond Walters College *C, A*
University of Northwestern Ohio *A*
Wright State University: Lake Campus *A*
Youngstown State University *A*

Oklahoma

Eastern Oklahoma State College *A*
Northeastern Oklahoma Agricultural and
Mechanical College *C, A*
Oklahoma State University
Okmulgee *A*
Tulsa Community College *C, A*
Western Oklahoma State College *A*

Oregon

Blue Mountain Community College *C*
Chemeketa Community College *A*
Clackamas Community College *C*
Clatsop Community College *A*
Lane Community College *C*
Linn-Benton Community College *C, A*
Portland Community College *C*
Rogue Community College *C*
Southwestern Oregon Community
College *C*
Treasure Valley Community College *A*
Umpqua Community College *A*
Western Business College *A*

Pennsylvania

Academy of Medical Arts and
Business *C, A*
Allentown Business School *A*
Bucks County Community College *A*
Butler County Community College *A*
CHI Institute *C*
Cambria-Rowe Business College *C, A*
Cambria-Rowe Business College:
Indiana *A*
Career Training Academy *C, A*
Central Pennsylvania College *A*
Churchman Business School *A*
Commonwealth Technical Institute *A*
Community College of Allegheny
County *A*
Community College of Beaver County *A*
Consolidated School of Business
Lancaster *A*
York *A*
Douglas School of Business *A*
DuBois Business College *A*
DuBois Business College
Oil City *A*
Erie Business Center *C, A*
ICM School of Business & Medical
Careers *A*
Lackawanna College *A*
Lehigh Carbon Community College *A*
McCann School of Business
Sunbury *A*
Mercyhurst College *C, A*
Montgomery County Community
College *C, A*
Newport Business Institute *A*
Newport Business Institute *A*
Northampton County Area Community
College *C, A*
Pennsylvania College of
Technology *A, B*
Pennsylvania Institute of Technology *A*
Reading Area Community College *C, A*
Schuylkill Institute of Business &
Technology *C, A*
South Hills School of Business &
Technology *A*
South Hills School of Business and
Technology *A*
University of Pittsburgh
Titusville *C*

Westmoreland County Community
College *A*

Puerto Rico
Turabo University *C*
Universidad Metropolitana *A, B*
Universidad del Este *C, A*

Rhode Island
Community College of Rhode
Island *C, A*

South Carolina
Aiken Technical College *C*
Florence-Darlington Technical
College *A*
Forrest Junior College *A*
Orangeburg-Calhoun Technical
College *C*
Tri-County Technical College *C*
Trident Technical College *C*
Williamsburg Technical College *C*
York Technical College *C*

South Dakota
Kilian Community College *C, A*
Southeast Technical Institute *A*
Western Dakota Technical Institute *C*

Tennessee
Remington College
Southeast College of Technology *A*
Roane State Community College *C, A*

Texas
Alvin Community College *A*
Austin Community College *A*
Blinn College *C*
Central Texas College *C*
Coastal Bend College *A*
Del Mar College *C, A*
El Centro College *C*
El Paso Community College *C*
Frank Phillips College *C, A*
Galveston College *C, A*
Grayson County College *C*
Hallmark Institute of Technology *A*
Houston Community College
System *C, A*
Kilgore College *C*
Lamar State College at Port Arthur *C, A*
Laredo Community College *A*
McLennan Community College *C, A*
North Harris Montgomery Community
College District *C, A*
Northeast Texas Community
College *C, A*
St. Philip's College *A*
South Plains College *A*
Southwestern Adventist University *B*
Texas State Technical College
West Texas *C*
Tyler Junior College *C, A*

Utah
LDS Business College *A*
Salt Lake Community College *C*
Southern Utah University *C*

Virginia
ECPI College of Technology *C, A*
ECPI Technical College: Roanoke *A*
Mountain Empire Community College *A*
Tidewater Tech *D*
Virginia Western Community College *A*

Washington
Centralia College *C, A*
Clark College *A*
Edmonds Community College *C, A*
Everett Community College *C*
Grays Harbor College *C*
Green River Community College *A*
Lower Columbia College *A*
Peninsula College *A*
Renton Technical College *C*
Spokane Community College *C, A*
Walla Walla Community College *C, A*
Wenatchee Valley College *C*

West Virginia
Bluefield State College *C, A*
Glenville State College *A*
Mountain State University *A*
Potomac State College of West Virginia
University *A*
Valley College of Technology *C*
West Virginia Business College *A*
West Virginia Northern Community
College *C*
West Virginia State College *A*
West Virginia University Institute of
Technology *A*

Wisconsin
Blackhawk Technical College *C, A*
Bryant & Stratton College *C, A*
Chippewa Valley Technical College *C*
Fox Valley Technical College *C*
Lakeshore Technical College *A*
Milwaukee Area Technical College *A*
Moraine Park Technical College *C, A*
Waukesha County Technical College *C*

Wyoming
Western Wyoming Community
College *C, A*

Medical claims examiner

Indiana
Indiana Business College
Medical *A*

Medical illustrating

California
California State University
Long Beach *B*

Georgia
Clark Atlanta University *B*
Medical College of Georgia *M*

Illinois
University of Illinois
Chicago *M*

Iowa
Iowa State University *B*

Michigan
University of Michigan *M*

New York
Rochester Institute of Technology *B, M*

Ohio
Cleveland Institute of Art *B, M*

Pennsylvania
Arcadia University *B*

Texas
Texas Woman's University *B, M*
University of Texas
Southwestern Medical Center at
Dallas *M*

Wisconsin
Milwaukee Area Technical College *A*

Medical informatics

Alabama
University of Alabama
Birmingham *M*

Colorado
University of Colorado
Health Sciences Center *M*

Massachusetts
Massachusetts Bay Community
College *A, B*

Montana
Montana Tech of the University of
Montana *A, B*

New York
State University of New York
Buffalo *M*
Health Science Center at
Brooklyn *M*

Texas
Richland College *A*

Wisconsin
Milwaukee School of Engineering *M*

Medical insurance coding specialist

Arizona
International Institute of the Americas
Phoenix *C, A, B*
Tucson *C, A, B*

California
Santa Barbara City College *C*
Santa Rosa Junior College *C*

Colorado
Blair Junior College *C*

Florida
Herzing College
Orlando *C*
Miami-Dade Community College *C*
Palm Beach Community College *C*
Pasco-Hernando Community College *C*

Georgia
Albany Technical College *C*

Indiana
Indiana Business College
Medical *C*

Iowa
Mercy College of Health Sciences *C*

Massachusetts
Laboure College *C*

Michigan
Baker College
of Muskegon *C*
Gogebic Community College *A*

Minnesota
Minneapolis Community and Technical
College *C*
South Central Technical College *A*

North Dakota
North Dakota State College of Science *A*

Ohio
Lakeland Community College *C*

Pennsylvania
Consolidated School of Business
Lancaster *A*
York *A*
Newport Business Institute *A*
South Hills School of Business &
Technology *C*
University of Pittsburgh
Titusville *C*

Texas
Richland College *A*

Utah
LDS Business College *C*

Washington
Clark College *C*
Clover Park Technical College *C*
Everett Community College *C*
Renton Technical College *C*

West Virginia
Huntington Junior College *C, A*

Medical insurance specialist

California
Long Beach City College *C*
MTI College of Business and
Technology *C*
Santa Barbara City College *C*

Colorado
Blair Junior College *C*

Florida
Career Training Institute *A*
Herzing College
Orlando *C*
Palm Beach Community College *C*

Indiana
Indiana Business College
Medical *A*

Michigan
Baker College
of Muskegon *C*
of Port Huron *C, A*

Missouri
Sanford-Brown College *C*

Pennsylvania
Consolidated School of Business
Lancaster *A*
York *A*
Newport Business Institute *A*
South Hills School of Business &
Technology *C*

Puerto Rico
Inter American University of Puerto Rico
San German Campus *C*
Universidad Metropolitana *C*
Universidad del Este *C*

Medical office administration

California
MTI College of Business and
Technology *C*

Colorado
Blair Junior College *C*
Red Rocks Community College *C, A*

Florida
Herzing College
Orlando *C*

Illinois
College of Lake County *C, A*

Indiana
Indiana Business College
Medical *C*
Professional Careers Institute *C, A*
Sawyer College: Merrillville *C, A*

Iowa
Western Iowa Tech Community
College *A*

Louisiana
Nunez Community College *C, A*

Massachusetts
Springfield Technical Community
College *A*

Minnesota
Globe College *C, A*
Hennepin Technical College *C, A*

Nevada
Western Nevada Community College *C*

New Mexico
San Juan College *A*

New York
Erie Community College
North Campus *C, A*
Monroe College *A*

North Carolina
Beaufort County Community
College *C, A*
Carteret Community College *C, A*
Pitt Community College *C, A*
Surry Community College *C, A*
Western Piedmont Community
College *A*

North Dakota
North Dakota State College of Science *A*

Ohio
Miami University
Hamilton Campus *C*
University of Akron *A*
Youngstown State University *A*

Pennsylvania
Consolidated School of Business
Lancaster *A*
Douglas School of Business *A*
Newport Business Institute *A*
Pennsylvania Institute of Technology *C*
Pittsburgh Technical Institute: Boyd
School Division *A*

Puerto Rico
Universidad Metropolitana *A*

Tennessee
University of Tennessee
Knoxville *B*

Texas
Tyler Junior College *C, A*

Utah
LDS Business College *A*

Wisconsin
Western Wisconsin Technical College *C*

Medical office assistant

Arizona
International Institute of the Americas
Phoenix *C, A, B*
Tucson *C, A, B*

California
Antelope Valley College *C, A*
Feather River College *C*
Ohlone College *C*
San Joaquin Delta College *C*

Illinois
Southeastern Illinois College *A*

Michigan
Baker College
of Muskegon *A*

Minnesota
Hennepin Technical College *C*

Missouri
Crowder College *A*
North Central Missouri College *C, A*
Patricia Stevens College *A*

North Carolina
Pitt Community College *C*

North Dakota
North Dakota State College of
Science *C, A*

Ohio
Lakeland Community College *C*
University of Cincinnati
Raymond Walters College *A*

Oklahoma
Northeastern Oklahoma Agricultural and
Mechanical College *C, A*

Oregon
Linn-Benton Community College *C, A*

Pennsylvania
Consolidated School of Business
Lancaster *A*
Douglas School of Business *C*
Newport Business Institute *A*
Pittsburgh Technical Institute: Boyd
School Division *C*
St. Vincent College *B*
South Hills School of Business &
Technology *A*

Puerto Rico
Turabo University *C*

South Carolina
York Technical College *C*

Utah
LDS Business College *A*

Washington
Clover Park Technical College *C*
Olympic College *C, A*

Medical office computer specialist

California
MTI College of Business and
Technology *C*

Minnesota
Hennepin Technical College *C*

Pennsylvania
Consolidated School of Business
Lancaster *A*
York *A*
Newport Business Institute *A*
South Hills School of Business &
Technology *A*

South Carolina
York Technical College *C*

Medical radiologic technology/radiation therapy

Alabama
Central Alabama Community College *A*
Community College of the Air Force *A*
Faulkner University *A*
Gadsden State Community College *A*
George C. Wallace State Community
College
Dothan *A*
Jefferson State Community College *A*
Northwest-Shoals Community College *A*
University of Alabama
Birmingham *B*
University of South Alabama *C, B*
Wallace State Community College at
Hanceville *A*

Arizona
Gateway Community College *C, A*
Pima Community College *A*
Scottsdale Community College *A*

Arkansas
Arkansas State University *A, B*
North Arkansas College *A*
South Arkansas Community College *A*
Southeast Arkansas College *A*
University of Arkansas
Fort Smith *A*
for Medical Sciences *A, B*
University of Central Arkansas *B*

California
Bakersfield College *A*
Cabrillo College *C, A*

California State University
Long Beach *B*
Foothill College *C, A*
Loma Linda University *C, A, B*
Long Beach City College *C, A*
Moorpark College *C, A*
Mount San Antonio College *C, A*
Orange Coast College *C, A*
San Diego Mesa College *C, A*
San Diego State University *M*
San Joaquin Delta College *A*
Santa Barbara City College *A*
Santa Rosa Junior College *C, A*
Yuba Community College District *A*

Colorado
Mesa State College *A*

Connecticut
Capital Community College *A*
Gateway Community College *A*
Middlesex Community College *A*
Naugatuck Valley Community College *A*
University of Hartford *B*

Delaware
Delaware Technical and Community
College
Owens Campus *A*
Stanton/Wilmington Campus *A*

District of Columbia
George Washington University *C, A*
Georgetown University *M*
University of the District of Columbia *A*

Florida
Broward Community College *A*
Daytona Beach Community College *A*
Florida Hospital College of Health
Sciences *A*
Gulf Coast Community College *A*
Hillsborough Community College *C, A*
Indian River Community College *A*
Manatee Community College *A*
Miami-Dade Community College *A*
Palm Beach Community College *A*
Pasco-Hernando Community College *A*
Pensacola Junior College *A*
Polk Community College *A*
St. Petersburg College *A*
Santa Fe Community College *A*
South Florida Community College *A*
University of Central Florida *B*
Valencia Community College *A*

Georgia
Armstrong Atlantic State University *B*
Athens Technical College *A*
Coastal Georgia Community College *A*
Darton College *A*
Floyd College *A*
Medical College of Georgia *B, M*
Middle Georgia College *A*
Southwest Georgia Technical College *A*
Waycross College *A*
West Georgia Technical College *C*

Idaho
Boise State University *A, B*
Idaho State University *C, A*

Illinois
Black Hawk College *A*
City Colleges of Chicago
Malcolm X College *C, A*
Wright College *A*
College of DuPage *A*
College of Lake County *C, A*
Illinois Central College *A*
Illinois Eastern Community Colleges
Olney Central College *A*
Kankakee Community College *A*
Kaskaskia College *A*
Kishwaukee College *A*
Lincoln Land Community College *A*
Moraine Valley Community College *A*
National-Louis University *B*

Parkland College *A*
Sauk Valley Community College *A*
South Suburban College of Cook
County *C, A*
Southern Illinois University
Carbondale *A, B*
Southwestern Illinois College *A*
Triton College *A*
University of St. Francis *B*

Indiana
Ball State University *A*
Indiana University
Bloomington *B*
Kokomo *A*
South Bend *A*
Indiana University-Purdue University
Indianapolis *A, B*
Ivy Tech State College
Central Indiana *A*
Columbus *A*
Eastcentral *A*
Wabash Valley *A*
University of St. Francis *A*
University of Southern Indiana *A*

Iowa
Briar Cliff University *B*
Indian Hills Community College *A*
Iowa Central Community College *A*
Mercy College of Health Sciences *A*
Northeast Iowa Community College *A*
St. Luke's College *C, A*
Scott Community College *A*
Southeastern Community College
North Campus *A*

Kansas
Fort Hays State University *A*
Friends University *B*
Hutchinson Community College *A*
Johnson County Community College *A*
Newman University *A*
Washburn University of Topeka *C, A*

Kentucky
Hazard Community College *A*
Lexington Community College *A*
Madisonville Community College *A*
Morehead State University *A, B*
St. Catharine College *A*
Somerset Community College *C*
Southeast Community College *A*
Spencerian College *A*
University of Louisville *A*

Louisiana
Delgado Community College *A*
Louisiana State University
Eunice *A*
McNeese State University *B*
Northwestern State University *B*
Our Lady of Holy Cross College *B*
Southern University
Shreveport *A*
University of Louisiana at Monroe *B*

Maine
Central Maine Technical College *A*
St. Joseph's College *A, B*

Maryland
Allegany College *A*
Anne Arundel Community College *A*
Chesapeake College *A*
College of Notre Dame of Maryland *B*
Community College of Baltimore County
Catonsville *C, A*
Dundalk *C, A*
Essex *C, A*
Hagerstown Community College *A*
Montgomery College
Rockville Campus *A*
Wor-Wic Community College *A*

Massachusetts
Laboure College *A*

Massachusetts Bay Community
College A
Massachusetts College of Pharmacy and
Health Sciences B
Massasoit Community College A
Northeastern University A
Quinsigamond Community College A
Springfield Technical Community
College A
Suffolk University B

Michigan
Baker College
of Muskegon A
of Owosso A
Ferris State University A
Grand Rapids Community College A
Kellogg Community College A
Lansing Community College A
Marygrove College C, A
Mid Michigan Community College A
Montcalm Community College A
Mott Community College A
Oakland Community College A
University of Michigan
Flint A
Washtenaw Community College A
Wayne State University B

Minnesota
Century Community and Technical
College A
High-Tech Institute A
Lake Superior College: A Community
and Technical College A
Normandale Community College A
North Hennepin Community College A
Ridgewater College: A Community and
Technical College A
Riverland Community College: A
Technical and Community College A
Rochester Community and Technical
College A

Mississippi
Itawamba Community College A
Mississippi Gulf Coast Community
College
Perkinston A
University of Mississippi Medical
Center C

Missouri
Avila University B
Missouri Southern State College A
Penn Valley Community College A
St. Louis Community College
St. Louis Community College at
Forest Park A
Southwest Missouri State University B
University of Missouri
Columbia B

Nebraska
Clarkson College A, B
Northeast Community College A
Southeast Community College
Lincoln Campus A
University of Nebraska
Kearney B
Medical Center B
Western Nebraska Community
College A

Nevada
Truckee Meadows Community
College A
University of Nevada
Las Vegas C, B

New Hampshire
New Hampshire Technical Institute A

New Jersey
Bergen Community College A
Brookdale Community College A
Burlington County College A
County College of Morris A

Cumberland County College A
Essex County College A
Fairleigh Dickinson University
College at Florham A, B
Metropolitan Campus A, B
Mercer County Community College A
Passaic County Community College A
Union County College C, A
University of Medicine and Dentistry of
New Jersey
School of Health Related
Professions B

New Mexico
Clovis Community College A
Dona Ana Branch Community College of
New Mexico State University A
New Mexico Junior College A
University of New Mexico C, A, B

New York
Adirondack Community College A
Broome Community College A
City University of New York
Bronx Community College A
Hostos Community College A
Erie Community College
City Campus A
Hudson Valley Community College A
Iona College C, A
Long Island University
C. W. Post Campus B
Mohawk Valley Community College A
Nassau Community College A
North Country Community College A
Orange County Community College A
State University of New York
Oswego A
Trocaire College A
Westchester Community College A

North Carolina
Asheville Buncombe Technical
Community College A
Caldwell Community College and
Technical Institute A
Cape Fear Community College A
Carteret Community College A
Cleveland Community College A
Edgecombe Community College C, A
Forsyth Technical Community College A
Johnston Community College A
Pitt Community College A
Sandhills Community College A
Southwestern Community College A
University of North Carolina
Chapel Hill C, B
Vance-Granville Community College A
Wake Technical Community College A

North Dakota
Minot State University B
North Dakota State University B

Ohio
Central Ohio Technical College A
Columbus State Community College A
Cuyahoga Community College
Eastern Campus A
Western Campus A
James A. Rhodes State College C, A
Jefferson Community College A
Kent State University A
Kent State University
Salem Regional Campus A, B
Kettering College of Medical Arts A
Lakeland Community College C, A
Marion Technical College A
Miami University
Oxford Campus C
Muskingum Area Technical College A
North Central State College A
Ohio State University
Columbus Campus B
Owens Community College
Toledo A
Shawnee State University A

Sinclair Community College A
University of Akron A
University of Cincinnati
Raymond Walters College A
Washington State Community College A

Oklahoma
Bacone College A
Northern Oklahoma College A
Rose State College A
Tulsa Community College A
University of Oklahoma B
Western Oklahoma State College A

Oregon
Oregon Health Sciences University B
Oregon Institute of Technology B
Portland Community College A

Pennsylvania
Bloomsburg University of
Pennsylvania B
California University of Pennsylvania B
Community College of Allegheny
County C, A
Community College of Philadelphia A
Drexel University C, A
Harrisburg Area Community College A
Holy Family University A, B
Keystone College A
La Roche College A, B
Mount Aloysius College A, B
Northampton County Area Community
College A
Pennsylvania College of Technology A
Reading Area Community College A
Widener University A, B

Puerto Rico
Inter American University of Puerto Rico
Barranquitas Campus A
San German Campus A
Universidad del Este C, A, B
University of Puerto Rico
Medical Sciences Campus A

Rhode Island
Community College of Rhode
Island C, A
Rhode Island College B

South Carolina
Florence-Darlington Technical College A
Midlands Technical College C, A
Orangeburg-Calhoun Technical
College A
Piedmont Technical College A
Spartanburg Technical College A
Trident Technical College C, A
York Technical College A

South Dakota
Mount Marty College B

Tennessee
Austin Peay State University B
Chattanooga State Technical Community
College A
Columbia State Community College A
Jackson State Community College A
Roane State Community College A
Southwest Tennessee Community
College A
University of Tennessee
Knoxville B
Volunteer State Community College A

Texas
Amarillo College A
Angelina College A
Austin Community College C, A
Blinn College A
Del Mar College A
El Centro College A
El Paso Community College A
Galveston College C, A
Houston Community College System A
Kilgore College A
Laredo Community College A

McLennan Community College A
Midland College C, A
Midwestern State University A, B, M
Odessa College A
St. Philip's College C, A
San Jacinto College
Central Campus A
South Plains College A
South Texas Community College A
Southwest Texas State University B
Tarrant County College A
Tyler Junior College A
Wharton County Junior College A

Utah
Salt Lake Community College A
Weber State University A, B

Vermont
Champlain College C, A, B
University of Vermont B

Virginia
Averett University B
Southwest Virginia Community
College A
Virginia Highlands Community
College A
Virginia Western Community College A

Washington
Bellevue Community College A

West Virginia
Alderson-Broaddus College B
Bluefield State College A
Southern West Virginia Community and
Technical College A
University of Charleston B
West Virginia Northern Community
College A

Wisconsin
Blackhawk Technical College A
Chippewa Valley Technical College A
Concordia University Wisconsin B
Lakeshore Technical College A
Marian College of Fond du Lac B
Western Wisconsin Technical College A

Wyoming
Casper College A
Laramie County Community College A

Medical receptionist

California
Santa Rosa Junior College C

Michigan
Baker College
of Muskegon C
Jackson Community College C

Minnesota
Minnesota State College - Southeast
Technical C

Oregon
Linn-Benton Community College C

Pennsylvania
Consolidated School of Business
Lancaster C, A
York C, A
Douglas School of Business C
Newport Business Institute A

Washington
Clark College C
Everett Community College C

Medical records administration

Alabama
Alabama State University B

Shelton State Community College *C*
University of Alabama
    Birmingham *B*

Arkansas
Arkansas Tech University *B*

California
Barstow College *C*
Chabot College *C, A*
Loma Linda University *B*
Palomar College *C, A*
Santa Rosa Junior College *C*
Southwestern College *C, A*

Colorado
Blair Junior College *C*
IntelliTec College, Grand Junction *C*

Delaware
Delaware Technical and Community
    College
        Stanton/Wilmington Campus *C*

Florida
Broward Community College *A*
Cooper Career Institute *C*
Florida Agricultural and Mechanical
    University *B*
Florida International University *B*
Florida Technical College
    Auburndale *A*
Gulf Coast Community College *A*
Indian River Community College *A*
Miami-Dade Community College *A*
Pensacola Junior College *A*
Polk Community College *A*
St. Petersburg College *A*
South Florida Community College *A*
University of Central Florida *B*

Georgia
Clark Atlanta University *B*
Clayton College and State University *A*
Dalton State College *A*
Darton College *A*
Floyd College *A*
Macon State College *B*
Medical College of Georgia *B*
Middle Georgia College *A*

Hawaii
Hawaii Business College *C*

Idaho
Boise State University *A, B*

Illinois
Chicago State University *B*
Illinois State University *B*
University of Illinois
    Chicago *B*

Indiana
Indiana University
    Northwest *B*
Indiana University-Purdue University
    Indianapolis *B*
Michiana College: Fort Wayne *A*
Vincennes University *A*

Iowa
North Iowa Area Community College *A*
Northeast Iowa Community College *A*

Kansas
Barton County Community College *A*
Labette Community College *C*
Seward County Community College *C*
University of Kansas Medical Center *B*

Kentucky
Spencerian College *A*

Louisiana
Louisiana Tech University *B*
Southern University
    Shreveport *A*
University of Louisiana at Lafayette *B*

Maine
Andover College *A*

Massachusetts
Benjamin Franklin Institute of
    Technology *C*
Northeastern University *B*
Springfield College *B*

Michigan
Baker College
    of Auburn Hills *A*
    of Jackson *A*
Davenport University
    Eastern Region *B*
Ferris State University *C, B*
Gogebic Community College *A*
Washtenaw Community College *A*

Minnesota
College of St. Catherine *A*
College of St. Scholastica *B*
Globe College *C, A*
Hennepin Technical College *C*
Rasmussen College
    Minnetonka *A*

Mississippi
Itawamba Community College *A*
Mississippi Gulf Coast Community
    College
        Perkinston *A*
University of Mississippi Medical
    Center *A*

Missouri
St. Louis University *B*
Sanford-Brown College *C, A*
Springfield College *C*
Stephens College *B*

Nebraska
College of Saint Mary *A, B*

Nevada
Morrison University *A*

New Jersey
Kean University *B*

New Mexico
Albuquerque Technical-Vocational
    Institute *C*

New York
Elmira Business Institute *C, A*
Long Island University
    C. W. Post Campus *B*
Molloy College *A*
Monroe College *A*
Olean Business Institute *C, A*
State University of New York
    Institute of Technology at
    Utica/Rome *B*

North Carolina
Alamance Community College *A*
Central Piedmont Community College *A*
Durham Technical Community
    College *C, A*
East Carolina University *B*
Sandhills Community College *A*
Western Carolina University *B*

Ohio
Cuyahoga Community College
    Eastern Campus *A*
    Metropolitan Campus *C, A*
    Western Campus *A*
Ohio Business College: Sandusky *A*
Ohio State University
    Columbus Campus *B*

Oklahoma
Metropolitan College *C*
Southwestern Oklahoma State
    University *B*
Western Oklahoma State College *A*

Oregon
Chemeketa Community College *A*
Linn-Benton Community College *C, A*
Mount Hood Community College *A*
Portland Community College *A*

Pennsylvania
Academy of Medical Arts and
    Business *C, A*
Cambria County Area Community
    College *C*
Consolidated School of Business
    Lancaster *A*
Gwynedd-Mercy College *B*
Luzerne County Community College *A*
Mercyhurst College *C, A*
Newport Business Institute *A*
Pennsylvania College of Technology *A*
South Hills School of Business &
    Technology *C*
Temple University *B*
University of Pittsburgh *B*
Westmoreland County Community
    College *C*

Puerto Rico
Huertas Junior College *A*
Universidad del Este *A*

South Carolina
Forrest Junior College *C, A*

South Dakota
Dakota State University *B*

Tennessee
Chattanooga State Technical Community
    College *A*
Draughons Junior College of Business:
    Nashville *A*
Tennessee State University *B*
University of Tennessee Health Science
    Center *B*

Texas
El Centro College *A*
Howard College *C, A*
Laredo Community College *C*
St. Philip's College *A*
Southwest Texas State University *B*
Texas A&M University
    Commerce *B*
Texas Southern University *B*

Utah
LDS Business College *A*

Virginia
ECPI College of Technology *C, A*
ECPI Technical College: Roanoke *A*
Mountain Empire Community College *C*
Norfolk State University *B*

Washington
Renton Technical College *A*

Wisconsin
University of Wisconsin
    Milwaukee *B*

**Medical records
technology**

Alabama
Bishop State Community College *A*
Central Alabama Community College *A*
Chattahoochee Valley Community
    College *A*
Enterprise State Junior College *A*
Faulkner University *A*
Northwest-Shoals Community College *A*
Shelton State Community College *C*
Trenholm State Technical College *A*
Virginia College *A*
Wallace State Community College at
    Hanceville *A*

Arizona
Phoenix College *A*
Pima Community College *A*

Arkansas
North Arkansas College *C*

California
Cerritos Community College *A*
Chabot College *C, A*
East Los Angeles College *C*
Orange Coast College *C, A*
Santa Barbara City College *C*
Santa Rosa Junior College *C*
Southwestern College *C, A*
Ventura College *A*

Colorado
Arapahoe Community College *C, A*
Parks College *C, A*

Connecticut
Briarwood College *C, A*
Quinebaug Valley Community College *C*

Delaware
Delaware Technical and Community
    College
        Terry Campus *C*

Florida
Daytona Beach Community College *A*
Indian River Community College *A*
International College *A*
Lake-Sumter Community College *A*
Miami-Dade Community College *C*
Pasco-Hernando Community College *C*
Polk Community College *A*
St. Petersburg College *C, A*
Southwest Florida College *C*
Tallahassee Community College *C*

Georgia
Abraham Baldwin Agricultural
    College *A*
Atlanta Metropolitan College *A*
Bainbridge College *C*
Clark Atlanta University *B*
Dalton State College *A*
Darton College *A*
Macon State College *A*
Middle Georgia College *A*
Southwest Georgia Technical College *C*
West Georgia Technical College *C, A*

Idaho
Boise State University *A*
Idaho State University *C, A*

Illinois
Black Hawk College *C*
College of DuPage *A*
College of Lake County *A*
Gem City College *C*
Illinois Central College *A*
John A. Logan College *A*
Moraine Valley Community
    College *C, A*
Northwestern Business College *A*
Oakton Community College *A*
Rend Lake College *A*
Robert Morris College: Chicago *C, A*
Rock Valley College *C, A*
Shawnee Community College *C, A*
South Suburban College of Cook
    County *C*
Southeastern Illinois College *A*
Southwestern Illinois College *A*

Indiana
Indiana Business College
    Anderson *A*
    Columbus *A*
    Evansville *A*
    Fort Wayne *A*
    Marion *A*
    Medical *A*
    Muncie *A*
    Terre Haute *A*

Indiana University
   Bloomington *B*
   Northwest *A*
   Southeast *A*
Purdue University
   Calumet *C, A*
Vincennes University *A*

Iowa
Indian Hills Community College *A*
Kirkwood Community College *A*
Northeast Iowa Community College *A*
Northwest Iowa Community College *A*

Kansas
Central Christian College *A*
Dodge City Community College *C, A*
Hutchinson Community College *C, A*
Johnson County Community College *A*
Pittsburg State University *B*
Washburn University of Topeka *C, A*

Kentucky
Henderson Community College *C*
Hopkinsville Community College *C*
National College of Business &
   Technology
   Danville *C*
   Florence *C*
   Lexington *C*
   Pikeville *C*
   Richmond *C*

Louisiana
Delgado Community College *A*
Louisiana Tech University *A*
Southern University
   Shreveport *A*

Maine
Andover College *A*

Maryland
Chesapeake College *A*
Montgomery College
   Rockville Campus *A*

Massachusetts
Laboure College *C, A*
Springfield Technical Community
   College *C*

Michigan
Baker College
   of Auburn Hills *A*
   of Clinton Township *A*
   of Jackson *A*
   of Owosso *A*
   of Port Huron *A*
Bay de Noc Community College *C*
Ferris State University *A*
Gogebic Community College *A*
Schoolcraft College *A*

Minnesota
College of St. Catherine *C, A*
Hennepin Technical College *C*
Rasmussen College
   Mankato *A*
   Minnetonka *A*
   St. Cloud *A*
Ridgewater College: A Community and
   Technical College *A*
Riverland Community College: A
   Technical and Community College *A*
Rochester Community and Technical
   College *A*
St. Cloud Technical College *C*
St. Paul College - A Community and
   Technical College *C*

Mississippi
Itawamba Community College *A*

Missouri
Missouri Western State College *C, A*
Ozarks Technical Community
   College *C, A*
St. Charles Community College *A*

Nebraska
College of Saint Mary *C*
Mid Plains Community College Area *A*
Western Nebraska Community
   College *A*

Nevada
Academy of Healing Arts *A*
Community College of Southern
   Nevada *A*
Morrison University *A*
Truckee Meadows Community
   College *C*

New Hampshire
New Hampshire Community Technical
   College
      Manchester *C, A*
New Hampshire Technical Institute *C*

New Jersey
Burlington County College *A*
Cumberland County College *C*
Hudson County Community
   College *C, A*
Passaic County Community College *C*
Sussex County Community College *A*

New Mexico
Eastern New Mexico University: Roswell
   Campus *C, A*
San Juan College *C, A*

New York
Adirondack Community College *A*
Broome Community College *A*
Elmira Business Institute *C, A*
Erie Community College
   North Campus *A*
Fulton-Montgomery Community
   College *C, A*
Mohawk Valley Community College *A*
Monroe Community College *A*
Onondaga Community College *A*
Rockland Community College *A*
State University of New York
   College of Technology at Alfred *A*
Touro College *B*
Trocaire College *A*
Utica School of Commerce *A*

North Carolina
Brunswick Community College *A*
Catawba Valley Community College *A*
Central Piedmont Community
   College *C, A*
Davidson County Community
   College *C, A*
Edgecombe Community College *A*
Pitt Community College *C, A*
South Piedmont Community
   College *C, A*
Southwestern Community College *A*
Wake Technical Community College *A*

North Dakota
North Dakota State College of Science *A*
Williston State College *C, A*

Ohio
Bowling Green State University:
   Firelands College *A*
Cincinnati State Technical and
   Community College *A*
Columbus State Community College *A*
Cuyahoga Community College
   Eastern Campus *A*
   Metropolitan Campus *A*
   Western Campus *A*
Davis College *C*
Hocking Technical College *A*
Miami-Jacobs College *A*
Owens Community College
   Toledo *A*
Sinclair Community College *C, A*
Stark State College of Technology *A*

Oklahoma
East Central University *B*
Metropolitan College *A*
Rose State College *A*

Oregon
Blue Mountain Community College *C*
Central Oregon Community College *C*
Lane Community College *C*
Linn-Benton Community College *C*
Rogue Community College *C*

Pennsylvania
Academy of Medical Arts and
   Business *C, A*
Butler County Community College *C*
Community College of Allegheny
   County *C, A*
Community College of Philadelphia *A*
Delaware County Community College *C*
Gwynedd-Mercy College *A*
Lehigh Carbon Community College *C, A*
Mercyhurst College *C, A, B*
South Hills School of Business &
   Technology *A*
Western School of Health and Business
   Careers *A*

Puerto Rico
Huertas Junior College *A*
Inter American University of Puerto Rico
   Bayamon Campus *C*
   San German Campus *A*
Universidad del Este *A*

South Carolina
Florence-Darlington Technical College *A*
Forrest Junior College *C, A*
Midlands Technical College *C, A*
Piedmont Technical College *C*

South Dakota
Dakota State University *A*

Tennessee
Draughons Junior College: Clarksville *A*
Dyersburg State Community
   College *C, A*
Roane State Community College *A*
Tennessee State University *A*
University of Tennessee Health Science
   Center *B*
Volunteer State Community College *A*
Walters State Community College *C, A*

Texas
Amarillo College *A*
Austin Community College *C*
Central Texas College *C*
Cisco Junior College *C, A*
Coastal Bend College *A*
El Centro College *A*
El Paso Community College *C, A*
Galveston College *C, A*
Houston Community College
   System *C, A*
Howard College *C, A*
Lee College *C, A*
McLennan Community College *A*
Midland College *C, A*
Paris Junior College *A*
Richland College *A*
St. Philip's College *C, A*
South Plains College *A*
Tarrant County College *C, A*
Texas State Technical College
   West Texas *C, A*
Tyler Junior College *A*
Wharton County Junior College *A*

Utah
LDS Business College *C*
University of Utah *M, D*
Weber State University *A*

Virginia
ECPI College of Technology *C, A*
ECPI Technical College: Roanoke *A*

J. Sargeant Reynolds Community
   College *C*
National College of Business &
   Technology
   Bluefield *C*
   Charlottesville *C*
   Danville *C*
   Harrisonburg *C*
   Lynchburg *C*
   Martinsville *C*
   Roanoke *C*

Washington
Centralia College *A*
Clark College *C*
Renton Technical College *A*
Spokane Falls Community College *C, A*

West Virginia
Bluefield State College *A*
Fairmont State College *A*
Potomac State College of West Virginia
   University *A*

Wisconsin
Chippewa Valley Technical College *A*
Moraine Park Technical College *A*
Western Wisconsin Technical College *A*

Medical scientist

Colorado
University of Colorado
   Health Sciences Center *D*

Hawaii
University of Hawaii
   Manoa *M*

Missouri
Washington University in St. Louis *M*

New York
State University of New York
   Buffalo *D*

Ohio
Case Western Reserve University *M, D*

Pennsylvania
University of Pittsburgh *M*

South Dakota
University of South Dakota *D*

Utah
University of Utah *M, D*

Virginia
University of Virginia *M*

West Virginia
Marshall University *M, D*

Medical staff services technology

Indiana
St. Joseph's College *B*

Maryland
Morgan State University *B*

Missouri
Missouri Southern State College *A*

Wisconsin
Western Wisconsin Technical College *C*

Medical transcription

Alabama
Bevill State Community College *A*
George C. Wallace State Community
   College
   Dothan *C*

Prince Institute of Professional
  Studies *C, A*
Shelton State Community College *C*
Snead State Community College *C*
Wallace State Community College at
  Hanceville *C*

Arizona
Arizona Western College *C*
Central Arizona College *C, A*
Eastern Arizona College *C*
Gateway Community College *C, A*
International Institute of the Americas
    Phoenix *A*
    Tucson *A*
Phoenix College *A*

Arkansas
Arkansas State University
    Mountain Home *C, A*
Arkansas Tech University *C*
North Arkansas College *C*
Ozarka College *A*
Pulaski Technical College *C*
South Arkansas Community College *C*
Southeast Arkansas College *C*
University of Arkansas
    Cossatot Community College of the
    C

California
Chabot College *C*
Columbia College *C*
De Anza College *C*
Loma Linda University *C*
Modesto Junior College *C*
Ohlone College *C*
Riverside Community College *C, A*
Santa Rosa Junior College *C*
Shasta College *C*
Southwestern College *C, A*
Yuba Community College District *C, A*

Connecticut
Briarwood College *C*

Delaware
Delaware Technical and Community
  College
    Owens Campus *C, A*
    Stanton/Wilmington Campus *C*
    Terry Campus *C, A*

Florida
Cooper Career Institute *C*
Indian River Community College *A*
Lake City Community College *C*
Miami-Dade Community College *C*
Palm Beach Community College *C*
Pasco-Hernando Community College *C*
Polk Community College *A*
St. Petersburg College *C*
Seminole Community College *C*
Southwest Florida College *A*

Georgia
Albany Technical College *C*
Chattahoochee Technical College *C*
Dalton State College *A*
Southwest Georgia Technical College *C*
West Georgia Technical College *C*

Idaho
Lewis-Clark State College *A*
North Idaho College *A*

Illinois
Black Hawk College *C*
College of DuPage *C*
College of Lake County *C*
Danville Area Community College *A*
Elgin Community College *C, A*
Illinois Eastern Community Colleges
    Olney Central College *C*
John A. Logan College *C*
Kishwaukee College *C*
McHenry County College *C*
Midstate College *C*
Moraine Valley Community College *C*

Oakton Community College *C*
Parkland College *C*
Rend Lake College *C, A*
Rockford Business College *C, A*
Sauk Valley Community College *C*
South Suburban College of Cook
  County *C*
Southeastern Illinois College *C*
Waubonsee Community College *C*
William Rainey Harper College *C*

Indiana
College of Court Reporting *A*
Indiana Business College
    Columbus *C*
    Medical *C*
    Terre Haute *C*
Indiana University
    Southeast *C*
Michiana College *A*
Sawyer College *C*
Sawyer College: Merrillville *A*
Vincennes University *A*

Iowa
Des Moines Area Community College *C*
Hamilton College *C*
Hamilton College
    Cedar Rapids *C*
    Mason City *C*
Indian Hills Community College *C*
Kaplan College *A*
North Iowa Area Community College *A*
Northeast Iowa Community College *C*

Kentucky
National College of Business &
  Technology
    Danville *C*
    Florence *C*
    Lexington *C, D*
    Pikeville *C*
    Richmond *C*
Spencerian College *A*

Louisiana
Nunez Community College *C*

Maine
Andover College *A*
Beal College *C*
Central Maine Technical College *C*

Maryland
Allegany College *A*

Massachusetts
Marian Court College *C, A*
Springfield Technical Community
  College *C*

Michigan
Baker College
    of Cadillac *A*
    of Clinton Township *A*
    of Jackson *A*
    of Muskegon *A*
    of Port Huron *A*
Davenport University
    Midland *C*
Gogebic Community College *A*
Jackson Community College *C, A*
Mid Michigan Community College *A*
Mott Community College *C*
North Central Michigan College *C*
Oakland Community College *C, A*
Schoolcraft College *C*
Southwestern Michigan College *C*

Minnesota
Alexandria Technical College *C, A*
College of St. Catherine *C*
Hennepin Technical College *C*
Minneapolis Community and Technical
  College *C*
Minnesota State College - Southeast
  Technical *C*

Rasmussen College
    Minnetonka *C*
    St. Cloud *C, A*
St. Paul College - A Community and
  Technical College *C*
South Central Technical College *A*

Mississippi
Itawamba Community College *C*

Missouri
St. Charles Community College *A*
Springfield College *C*

Montana
Dawson Community College *A*
University of Montana-Missoula *A*

Nebraska
Metropolitan Community College *C*
Mid Plains Community College Area *C*

Nevada
Morrison University *A*

New Hampshire
New Hampshire Community Technical
  College
    Berlin *C*
    Manchester *C*
New Hampshire Technical Institute *C*

New Jersey
Gloucester County College *C*
Hudson County Community College *C*
Passaic County Community College *C*
Sussex County Community College *C*

New Mexico
Eastern New Mexico University: Roswell
  Campus *C*
San Juan College *C*

New York
Elmira Business Institute *C, A*
Long Island Business Institute *C*
State University of New York
    College of Technology at
    Alfred *C, A*
Trocaire College *C*

North Carolina
Alamance Community College *C*
Carteret Community College *C*
Durham Technical Community
  College *C*
Edgecombe Community College *C*
Guilford Technical Community
  College *C*
Sandhills Community College *C*
South College *C*
Western Piedmont Community
  College *C*

North Dakota
Minot State University: Bottineau
  Campus *C*
North Dakota State College of
  Science *C, A*
Williston State College *C, A*

Ohio
Cincinnati State Technical and
  Community College *C*
Columbus State Community College *C*
Davis College *C*
Marion Technical College *C*
Miami-Jacobs College *C, A*
Ohio Valley College of Technology *C*
Owens Community College
    Toledo *C*
Sinclair Community College *C*
Southern State Community College *C*
Stark State College of Technology *C*
Stautzenberger College *C*
University of Cincinnati
    Clermont College *C*
    Raymond Walters College *C, A*
Washington State Community College *A*

Oklahoma
Metropolitan College *C*
Metropolitan College *C*
Oklahoma State University
    Okmulgee *A*

Oregon
Central Oregon Community College *C*
Chemeketa Community College *A*
Linn-Benton Community College *C*
Southwestern Oregon Community
    College *C*

Pennsylvania
Academy of Medical Arts and
    Business *C, A*
Bucks County Community College *C*
Cambria-Rowe Business College *A*
Consolidated School of Business
    Lancaster *A*
    York *A*
Delaware County Community College *C*
Douglas School of Business *C*
Erie Business Center *A*
Lehigh Carbon Community College *C*
Mercyhurst College *C*
Newport Business Institute *A*
Northampton County Area Community
    College *C*
South Hills School of Business &
    Technology *C*
Westmoreland County Community
    College *A*
York College of Pennsylvania *C, A*

South Carolina
Aiken Technical College *C*
Florence-Darlington Technical
    College *C*
Forrest Junior College *C, A*
Tri-County Technical College *C*
York Technical College *C*

South Dakota
Southeast Technical Institute *A*
Western Dakota Technical Institute *A*

Tennessee
Dyersburg State Community College *C*
Roane State Community College *C*
South College *C*
Southwest Tennessee Community
    College *A*
Walters State Community College *C, A*

Texas
Central Texas College *C*
El Centro College *C*
Galveston College *C*
Houston Community College System *C*
Howard College *C*
Laredo Community College *C*
Lee College *C*
North Central Texas College *C*
St. Philip's College *C*
South Plains College *C*
South Texas Community College *C*
Texas State Technical College
    West Texas *C*
Tyler Junior College *C*

Utah
LDS Business College *C*
Southern Utah University *C*

Virginia
ECPI College of Technology *C, A*
ECPI Technical College: Roanoke *A*
J. Sargeant Reynolds Community
    College *C*
Mountain Empire Community College *A*

National College of Business &
Technology
  Bluefield *C*
  Charlottesville *C*
  Danville *C*
  Harrisonburg *C*
  Lynchburg *C*
  Martinsville *C*
  Roanoke *C*
Virginia Western Community College *C*

Washington
Clark College *C*
Clover Park Technical College *C*
Edmonds Community College *C*
Everett Community College *C*
Green River Community College *C*
Lake Washington Technical College *C*
Seattle Central Community College *C*
Spokane Community College *C*

West Virginia
Mountain State College *A*

Wisconsin
Chippewa Valley Technical College *C*
Fox Valley Technical College *C*
Lac Courte Oreilles Ojibwa Community
  College *C*
Mid-State Technical College *C*
Moraine Park Technical College *C*
Waukesha County Technical College *C*

Wyoming
Casper College *C, A*

Medical/clinical assistant

Alabama
Central Alabama Community College *A*
Community College of the Air Force *A*
Enterprise State Junior College *A*
Faulkner University *A*
George C. Wallace State Community
  College
    Dothan *C, A*
Northwest-Shoals Community College *A*
South University *A*
Trenholm State Technical College *A*
Virginia College *A*
Wallace State Community College at
  Hanceville *A*

Alaska
University of Alaska
    Anchorage *A*
    Fairbanks *A*

Arizona
Central Arizona College *C, A*
Eastern Arizona College *C*
International Institute of the Americas
    Phoenix *C, A, B*
    Tucson *C, A, B*

Arkansas
Arkansas State University
    Mountain Home *C*
Arkansas Tech University *A*
Southeast Arkansas College *A*

California
Antelope Valley College *C, A*
Barstow College *C*
Cabrillo College *C, A*
Cerritos Community College *C, A*
Chabot College *C, A*
Citrus College *C, A*
College of the Canyons *C*
College of the Redwoods *C*
Contra Costa College *A*
De Anza College *C, A*
East Los Angeles College *A*
Glendale Community College *A*
Long Beach City College *C, A*
Modesto Junior College *A*
Monterey Peninsula College *C, A*

Ohlone College *C, A*
Orange Coast College *C, A*
Palomar College *C, A*
Riverside Community College *C, A*
San Diego Mesa College *C, A*
Santa Rosa Junior College *C*
Santiago Canyon College *A*
Shasta College *C*
Silicon Valley College
    Emeryville *A*
Southwestern College *C*
Victor Valley College *C, A*
West Valley College *C, A*

Colorado
Blair Junior College *C, A*
IntelliTec College, Grand Junction *A*
Morgan Community College *C*
Parks College *A*

Connecticut
Briarwood College *C, A*
Capital Community College *C, A*
Northwestern Connecticut Community
  College *A*
Norwalk Community College *C*
Quinebaug Valley Community College *A*

Delaware
Delaware Technical and Community
  College
    Owens Campus *C, A*
    Stanton/Wilmington Campus *C, A*
    Terry Campus *C, A*

Florida
ATI Health Education Center *A*
Broward Community College *C*
Career Training Institute *A*
Cooper Career Institute *A*
Florida Metropolitan University
    Melbourne Campus *A*
    Tampa College *A*
    Tampa College Lakeland *A*
Florida National College *A*
Indian River Community College *C*
Institute of Career Education *C, A*
International College *A*
Jones College *A, B*
Miami-Dade Community College *C*
New England Institute of
  Technology *C, A*
Palm Beach Community College *C*
Pasco-Hernando Community College *C*
Seminole Community College *C*
Webster College: Holiday *A*

Georgia
Albany Technical College *C*
Athens Technical College *C*
Chattahoochee Technical College *C*
Clayton College and State University *A*
Columbus Technical College *C*
Dalton State College *A*
Darton College *A*
DeKalb Technical College *C*
Georgia Southwestern State University *A*
High Tech Institute
    High-Tech Institute: Atlanta *A*
Macon State College *A*
Middle Georgia College *A*
Northwestern Technical College *A*
South University *A*
Southwest Georgia Technical College *C*
West Georgia Technical College *C*

Hawaii
Hawaii Business College *C*
Heald College
    Honolulu *A*
Remington College
    Honolulu *A*

Idaho
College of Southern Idaho *C*
Eastern Idaho Technical College *C, A*
Idaho State University *A*
Lewis-Clark State College *A*

North Idaho College *A*

Illinois
Black Hawk College *C*
College of DuPage *C*
Gem City College *C*
Illinois Central College *C*
Midstate College *C*
Northwestern Business College *A*
Parkland College *C*
Robert Morris College: Chicago *C, A*
Rockford Business College *C, A*
South Suburban College of Cook
  County *C*
Southwestern Illinois College *C, A*
Waubonsee Community College *C*
William Rainey Harper College *C, A*

Indiana
Indiana Business College
    Columbus *A*
    Evansville *A*
    Medical *A*
    Terre Haute *A*
International Business College *C, A*
Ivy Tech State College
    Central Indiana *C, A*
    Columbus *C, A*
    Eastcentral *C, A*
    Kokomo *C, A*
    Lafayette *C, A*
    Northcentral *C, A*
    Northeast *C, A*
    Northwest *C, A*
    Southcentral *C, A*
    Southeast *C, A*
    Southwest *C, A*
    Wabash Valley *C, A*
    Whitewater *A*
Michiana College *A*
Michiana College: Fort Wayne *A*
Professional Careers Institute *C, A*
Sawyer College *A*
Sawyer College: Merrillville *A*

Iowa
Des Moines Area Community College *C*
Hamilton College *C, A*
Hamilton Technical College *C*
Iowa Central Community College *C, A*
Iowa Western Community College *C*
Kaplan College *C, A*
Kirkwood Community College *C, A*
Marshalltown Community College *C*
North Iowa Area Community College *C*
Southeastern Community College
    North Campus *A*

Kentucky
Daymar College *C, A*
National College of Business &
  Technology
    Danville *A*
    Florence *A*
    Lexington *A*
    Pikeville *A*
    Richmond *A*
Somerset Community College *C*
Southwestern College of Business *C, A*
Spencerian College *A*

Louisiana
Remington College *A*
Remington College
    Baton Rouge *C*
Southern University
    Shreveport *A*

Maine
Andover College *A*
Beal College *A*

Maryland
Allegany College *C, A*
Anne Arundel Community College *C, A*
College of Southern Maryland *C*
Villa Julie College *A*

Massachusetts
Bay State College *A*
Berkshire Community College *A*
Bunker Hill Community College *C*
Cape Cod Community College *C*
Massasoit Community College *C*
Newbury College *C*
Quinsigamond Community College *C, A*
Springfield Technical Community
  College *A*

Michigan
Alpena Community College *A*
Baker College
    of Auburn Hills *A*
    of Cadillac *A*
    of Clinton Township *A*
    of Jackson *A*
    of Muskegon *C, A*
    of Owosso *A*
    of Port Huron *A*
Bay de Noc Community College *C*
Davenport University
    Midland *A*
Davenport University - Western
    Region *A*
Glen Oaks Community College *C*
Jackson Community College *C, A*
Kirtland Community College *A*
Lansing Community College *A*
Macomb Community College *C, A*
Mid Michigan Community College *A*
Montcalm Community College *C*
Muskegon Community College *C*
North Central Michigan College *C*
Northwestern Michigan College *A*
Oakland Community College *C, A*
Schoolcraft College *C*

Minnesota
Century Community and Technical
  College *C*
Dakota County Technical College *C, A*
Globe College *C, A*
High-Tech Institute *A*
Lake Superior College: A Community
  and Technical College *C*
Rasmussen College
    Mankato *C, A*
Ridgewater College: A Community and
    Technical College *C*
Rochester Community and Technical
    College *C*

Missouri
Sanford-Brown College *C*
Springfield College *A*

Montana
Flathead Valley Community College *A*
Montana State University
    Billings *A*
University of Montana-Missoula *A*

Nebraska
Central Community College *C, A*
Lincoln School of Commerce *C, A*
Nebraska College of Business *C, A*
Nebraska Methodist College of Nursing
  and Allied Health *C*
Southeast Community College
    Lincoln Campus *C*
Vatterott College
    Dodge Campus *A*

Nevada
Las Vegas College *A*

New Hampshire
Hesser College *C, A*
New Hampshire Community Technical
  College
    Claremont *A*
    Manchester *C, A*

New Jersey
Bergen Community College *A*

Hudson County Community
College *C, A*
Ocean County College *A*
Sussex County Community College *C*

New Mexico
Eastern New Mexico University: Roswell
Campus *C, A*

New York
Broome Community College *A*
Bryant & Stratton Business Institute
Albany *A*
Syracuse *A*
City University of New York
Bronx Community College *A*
College of Staten Island *C*
Queensborough Community
College *C*
Elmira Business Institute *C, A*
Mildred Elley *C, A*
Mohawk Valley Community
College *C, A*
Niagara County Community College *A*
Rockland Community College *C, A*
State University of New York
College of Technology at Alfred *A*
Suffolk County Community College *A*
Trocaire College *A*

North Carolina
Brunswick Community College *A*
Carteret Community College *C*
Central Carolina Community College *A*
Central Piedmont Community College *A*
Davidson County Community
College *C, A*
Edgecombe Community College *A*
Forsyth Technical Community College *A*
Gaston College *A*
Guilford Technical Community
College *A*
Haywood Community College *C, A*
James Sprunt Community College *C, A*
Johnston Community College *A*
Lenoir Community College *A*
Martin Community College *C, A*
Miller-Motte Technical College *A*
Mitchell Community College *C*
Montgomery Community College *A*
Pamlico Community College *C*
Piedmont Community College *C*
Pitt Community College *A*
Richmond Community College *A*
South College *A*
South Piedmont Community
College *C, A*
Stanly Community College *C*
Tri-County Community College *A*
Vance-Granville Community College *A*
Wake Technical Community
College *C, A*
Wayne Community College *A*
Western Piedmont Community
College *C, A*
Wilkes Community College *C, A*

North Dakota
Minot State University: Bottineau
Campus *C, A*

Ohio
Bradford School *C*
Bryant & Stratton College
Cleveland West *A*
Cincinnati State Technical and
Community College *C, A*
Columbus State Community College *A*
Cuyahoga Community College
Eastern Campus *C, A*
Metropolitan Campus *C, A*
Western Campus *C, A*
Davis College *C, A*
ETI Technical College of Niles *C, A*
Hocking Technical College *C, A*
Jefferson Community College *C, A*
Lakeland Community College *C*

Lorain County Community College *C*
Marion Technical College *C*
Miami-Jacobs College *A*
Muskingum Area Technical College *C, A*
Ohio Institute of Photography and
Technology *A*
Ohio University *A*
Ohio Valley College of Technology *A*
RETS Tech Center *C, A*
Southern State Community College *A*
Southwestern College of Business *C*
Stark State College of Technology *A*
Stautzenberger College *C, A*
Technology Education College *C, A*
University of Akron *C, A*
University of Cincinnati
Raymond Walters College *A*
University of Northwestern Ohio *C, A*
University of Toledo *A*
Youngstown State University *C, A*

Oklahoma
Platt College
Tulsa *C*
Tulsa Community College *A*

Oregon
Central Oregon Community College *C*
Chemeketa Community College *C*
Clackamas Community College *C*
Clatsop Community College *A*
Linn-Benton Community College *A*
Mount Hood Community College *A*
Pioneer Pacific College *C, A*
Portland Community College *C*
Rogue Community College *C*
Southwestern Oregon Community
College *A*

Pennsylvania
Academy of Medical Arts and
Business *C, A*
Bradford School: Pittsburgh *C, A*
Bucks County Community College *A*
Butler County Community College *A*
CHI Institute *C*
Career Training Academy *C, A*
Career Training Academy:
Monroeville *C, A*
Central Pennsylvania College *A*
Community College of Allegheny
County *C, A*
Community College of Philadelphia *A*
Delaware County Community
College *C, A*
Douglas School of Business *A*
Erie Business Center *A*
Harrisburg Area Community College *A*
ICM School of Business & Medical
Careers *C, A*
Lehigh Carbon Community College *A*
McCann School of Business
Pottsville *C*
Sunbury *C*
Median School of Allied Health
Careers *C, A*
Mount Aloysius College *A*
Schuylkill Institute of Business &
Technology *C, A*

South Carolina
Central Carolina Technical College *C*
Forrest Junior College *C, A*
Midlands Technical College *A*
Piedmont Technical College *C*
Technical College of the Lowcountry *C*
Tri-County Technical College *C*
Trident Technical College *C*

Tennessee
Chattanooga State Technical Community
College *C*
Draughons Junior College of Business:
Nashville *A*
Draughons Junior College: Clarksville *A*
Miller-Motte Technical College *A*

Northeast State Technical Community
College *A*
South College *A*
Southwest Tennessee Community
College *C*

Texas
El Centro College *C*
El Paso Community College *C, A*
Houston Community College System *C*
Howard College *A*
Kilgore College *A*
Laredo Community College *A*
Remington College
Houston *C*
San Antonio College *A*
San Jacinto College
Central Campus *A*

Utah
LDS Business College *C*
Salt Lake Community College *C*
Utah Career College *C, A*

Virginia
Bryant & Stratton College *A*
National College of Business &
Technology
Bluefield *A*
Charlottesville *A*
Danville *A*
Harrisonburg *A*
Lynchburg *A*
Roanoke *A*

Washington
Clark College *C, A*
Clover Park Technical College *C*
Everett Community College *C, A*
Lake Washington Technical College *C, A*
Lower Columbia College *A*
North Seattle Community College *C, A*
Peninsula College *A*
Renton Technical College *C*
Spokane Falls Community College *C, A*
Wenatchee Valley College *C*

West Virginia
Bluefield State College *A*
Corinthian Schools: National Institute of
Technology *A*
Huntington Junior College *C, A*
Mountain State College *A*
Mountain State University *A*
West Virginia Junior College *A*
West Virginia Junior College:
Charleston *A*
West Virginia State College *A*

Wisconsin
Blackhawk Technical College *C*
Bryant & Stratton College *A*
Concordia University Wisconsin *C*
Lac Courte Oreilles Ojibwa Community
College *A*
Mid-State Technical College *C*
Nicolet Area Technical College *C, A*
Waukesha County Technical College *C*
Western Wisconsin Technical College *C*
Wisconsin Indianhead Technical
College *C*

Wyoming
Western Wyoming Community
College *A*

Medication aide

Kansas
Barton County Community College *C*

Kentucky
Maysville Community College *C*

Texas
Tyler Junior College *C*

Medicinal/pharmaceutical chemistry

Arizona
University of Arizona *M, D*

California
Loma Linda University *D*
University of California
San Diego *B*

Connecticut
University of Connecticut *M, D*

Illinois
University of Illinois
Chicago *M, D*

Indiana
Butler University *B, M*

Iowa
Drake University *B*
University of Iowa *M, D*

Kansas
University of Kansas *M, D*

Maryland
University of Maryland
Baltimore *M*

Massachusetts
Massachusetts College of Pharmacy and
Health Sciences *M, D*
Northeastern University *M*

Michigan
University of Michigan *B, M, D*

Minnesota
University of Minnesota
Twin Cities *M, D*

Mississippi
Mississippi College *B*
University of Mississippi *D*

Nebraska
Chadron State College *B*

New Jersey
Rutgers, The State University of New
Jersey
New Brunswick Regional
Campus *M, D*

New York
State University of New York
Buffalo *B, M, D*

North Carolina
Campbell University *B*
Livingstone College *B*

Ohio
Ohio Northern University *B*
Ohio State University
Columbus Campus *M, D*

Pennsylvania
Drexel University *M, D*
Duquesne University *M, D*
University of the Sciences in
Philadelphia *B, M, D*

Rhode Island
University of Rhode Island *M, D*

Tennessee
University of Tennessee Health Science
Center *M, D*

Texas
University of Houston *M*

Utah
University of Utah *M, D*

Washington
University of Washington *M, D*

Wisconsin

University of Wisconsin
  Madison *M, D*

Medicine (M.D.)

Alabama

University of Alabama at Birmingham:
  School of Medicine *F*
University of South Alabama: School of
  Medicine *F*

Arizona

University of Arizona: College of
  Medicine *F*

Arkansas

University of Arkansas for Medical
  Sciences: College of Medicine *F*

California

Loma Linda University: School of
  Medicine *F*
Stanford University: School of
  Medicine *F*
University of California Davis: School of
  Medicine *F*
University of California Irvine: College
  of Medicine *F*
University of California Los Angeles:
  School of Medicine *F*
University of California San Diego:
  School of Medicine *F*
University of California San Francisco:
  School of Medicine *F*
University of Southern California: School
  of Medicine *F*

Colorado

University of Colorado Health Sciences
  Center: School of Medicine *F*

Connecticut

University of Connecticut Health Center
  School of Medicine *F*
Yale University: School of Medicine *F*

District of Columbia

George Washington University: School of
  Medicine and Health Sciences *F*
Georgetown University: School of
  Medicine *F*
Howard University: School of
  Medicine *F*

Florida

University of Florida: School of
  Medicine *F*
University of Miami: School of
  Medicine *F*
University of South Florida: College of
  Medicine *F*

Georgia

Emory University: School of Medicine *F*
Medical College of Georgia: School of
  Medicine *F*
Mercer University: School of
  Medicine *F*
Morehouse School of Medicine *F*

Hawaii

University of Hawaii at Manoa: John A.
  Burns School of Medicine *F*

Illinois

Finch University of Health Sciences/The
  Chicago Medical School *F*
Loyola University Chicago: Stritch
  School of Medicine *F*
Northwestern University: School of
  Medicine *F*
Rush University: Rush Medical
  College *F*
Southern Illinois University: School of
  Medicine *F*
University of Chicago: Pritzker School of
  Medicine *F*

University of Illinois at Chicago: College
  of Medicine *F*

Indiana

Indiana University: School of
  Medicine *F*

Iowa

University of Iowa: College of
  Medicine *F*

Kansas

University of Kansas Medical Center:
  School of Medicine *F*

Kentucky

University of Kentucky: College of
  Medicine *F*
University of Louisville: School of
  Medicine *F*

Louisiana

Louisiana State University Health
  Sciences Center: School of
  Medicine *F*
Louisiana State University: School of
  Medicine *F*
Tulane University: School of Medicine *F*

Maryland

Johns Hopkins University: School of
  Medicine *F*
Uniformed Services University of the
  Health Sciences: School of
  Medicine *F*
University of Maryland at Baltimore:
  School of Medicine *F*

Massachusetts

Boston University: School of
  Medicine *F*
Harvard University: Harvard Medical
  School *F*
Tufts University: School of Medicine *F*
University of Massachusetts Medical
  School *F*

Michigan

Michigan State University: College of
  Human Medicine *F*
University of Michigan: School of
  Medicine *F*
Wayne State University: School of
  Medicine *F*

Minnesota

Mayo Medical School *F*
University of Minnesota Medical
  School *F*

Mississippi

University of Mississippi Medical
  Center: School of Medicine *F*

Missouri

St. Louis University: School of
  Medicine *F*
University of Missouri Columbia: School
  of Medicine *F*
University of Missouri Kansas City:
  School of Medicine *F*
Washington University: School of
  Medicine *F*

Nebraska

Creighton University: School of
  Medicine *F*
University of Nebraska Medical Center:
  College of Medicine *F*

Nevada

University of Nevada: School of
  Medicine *F*

New Hampshire

Dartmouth College: School of
  Medicine *F*

New Jersey

University of Medicine and Dentistry of
  New Jersey
    New Jersey Medical School *F*
    Robert Wood Johnson Medical
      School *F*
    Robert Wood Johnson Medical
      School at Camden *F*

New Mexico

University of New Mexico: School of
  Medicine *F*

New York

Albany Medical College: School of
  Medicine *F*
Albert Einstein College of Medicine *F*
Columbia University
    College of Physicians and
      Surgeons *F*
Cornell University Medical College *F*
Mount Sinai School of Medicine of City
  University of New York *F*
New York Medical College *F*
New York University: School of
  Medicine *F*
State University of New York Health
  Science Center at Brooklyn: School of
  Medicine *F*
State University of New York Health
  Science Center at Syracuse: School of
  Medicine *F*
State University of New York Health
  Sciences Center at Stony Brook:
  School of Medicine *F*
State University of New York at Buffalo:
  School of Medicine *F*
University of Rochester: School of
  Medicine and Dentistry *F*

North Carolina

Duke University: School of Medicine *F*
East Carolina University: School of
  Medicine *F*
University of North Carolina at Chapel
  Hill: School of Medicine *F*
Wake Forest University: Bowman Gray
  School of Medicine *F*

North Dakota

University of North Dakota: School of
  Medicine *F*

Ohio

Case Western Reserve University: School
  of Medicine *F*
Medical College of Ohio *F*
Northeastern Ohio Universities College
  of Medicine *F*
Ohio State University Columbus
  Campus: College of Medicine *F*
University of Cincinnati: College of
  Medicine *F*
Wright State University: School of
  Medicine *F*

Oklahoma

University of Oklahoma Health Sciences
  Center: College of Medicine *F*

Oregon

Oregon Health Sciences University:
  School of Medicine *F*

Pennsylvania

Jefferson Medical College of Thomas
  Jefferson University *F*
Medical College of Pennsylvania and
  Hahnemann University School of
  Medicine *F*
Pennsylvania State University College of
  Medicine *F*
Temple University: School of
  Medicine *F*
University of Pennsylvania: School of
  Medicine *F*
University of Pittsburgh: School of
  Medicine *F*

Puerto Rico

Ponce School of Medicine *F*
Universidad Central del Caribe: Medical
  School *F*
University of Puerto Rico Medical
  Sciences Campus: School of
  Medicine *F*

Rhode Island

Brown University: School of Medicine *F*

South Carolina

Medical University of South Carolina *F*
University of South Carolina: School of
  Medicine *F*

South Dakota

University of South Dakota: School of
  Medicine *F*

Tennessee

East Tennessee State University: James
  H. Quillen College of Medicine *F*
Meharry Medical College: School of
  Medicine *F*
University of Tennessee Memphis:
  College of Medicine *F*
Vanderbilt University: School of
  Medicine *F*

Texas

Baylor College of Medicine *F*
Texas A&M University: Health Science
  Center College of Medicine *F*
Texas Tech University Health Sciences
  Center: School of Medicine *F*
University of Texas
    Medical Branch at Galveston:
      School of Medicine *F*
University of Texas Health Science
  Center: Medical School *F*
University of Texas Southwestern
  Medical Center at Dallas Southwestern
  Medical School *F*
University of Texas-Houston Health
  Science Center *F*

Utah

University of Utah: School of
  Medicine *F*

Vermont

University of Vermont: College of
  Medicine *F*

Virginia

Eastern Virginia Medical School of the
  Medical College of Hampton Roads:
  Medical Professions *F*
University of Virginia: School of
  Medicine *F*
Virginia Commonwealth University:
  School of Medicine *F*

Washington

University of Washington: School of
  Medicine *F*

West Virginia

Marshall University: School of
  Medicine *F*
West Virginia University: School of
  Medicine *F*

Wisconsin

Medical College of Wisconsin: School of
  Medicine *F*
University of Wisconsin Madison: School
  of Medicine *F*

Medieval/renaissance studies

California

University of California
  Davis *B*
  Santa Barbara *B*

Connecticut
Connecticut College *B*
University of Connecticut *M, D*
Wesleyan University *B*
Yale University *B, M, D*

District of Columbia
Catholic University of America *B, M, D*
Georgetown University *B*

Florida
New College of Florida *B*

Georgia
Emory University *B*
Oxford College of Emory University *B*

Indiana
Hanover College *B*
University of Notre Dame *B, M, D*

Iowa
Cornell College *B*
University of Iowa *C*

Louisiana
Tulane University *B*

Maine
Bates College *B*

Massachusetts
Boston College *M*
College of the Holy Cross *B*
Hampshire College *B*
Harvard College *B*
Mount Holyoke College *B*
Smith College *B*
Wellesley College *B*

Michigan
University of Michigan *B*
Western Michigan University *M*

Minnesota
College of St. Benedict *B*
St. John's University *B*
St. Olaf College *B*

Missouri
Washington University in St. Louis *B*

Nebraska
University of Nebraska
    Lincoln *B*

New Hampshire
Plymouth State College *B*

New Jersey
Rutgers, The State University of New
  Jersey
    New Brunswick Regional
      Campus *B*

New York
Bard College *B*
Barnard College *B*
Columbia University
    Columbia College *B*
Cornell University *M, D*
New York University *B*
Sarah Lawrence College *B*
State University of New York
    Albany *B*
    Binghamton *B*
Syracuse University *B*
Vassar College *B*

North Carolina
Duke University *B*

Ohio
Ohio State University
    Columbus Campus *B*
Ohio Wesleyan University *B*
University of Toledo *B*

Pennsylvania
Dickinson College *B*
Gettysburg College *B*

Penn State
    Abington *B*
    Altoona *B*
    Beaver *B*
    Berks *B*
    Delaware County *B*
    Dubois *B*
    Fayette *B*
    Hazleton *B*
    Lehigh Valley *B*
    McKeesport *B*
    Mont Alto *B*
    New Kensington *B*
    Schuylkill - Capital College *B*
    Shenango *B*
    University Park *B*
    Wilkes-Barre *B*
    Worthington Scranton *B*
    York *B*
Swarthmore College *B*
University of Pittsburgh *C*

Rhode Island
Brown University *B*
Rhode Island College *B*

Tennessee
University of Tennessee
    Knoxville *B*

Texas
Southern Methodist University *B, M*
University of Texas
    Austin *D*

Vermont
Bennington College *B*
Marlboro College *B*

Virginia
College of William and Mary *B*
Washington and Lee University *B*

Wisconsin
University of Wisconsin
    Madison *M, D*

Medium/heavy vehicle technology

Minnesota
Hennepin Technical College *C, A*

Ohio
Owens Community College
    Toledo *C*

Mental health counseling

Indiana
University of St. Francis *M*

Kansas
Kansas City Kansas Community
    College *C, A*

Louisiana
Xavier University of Louisiana *M*

Massachusetts
Lesley University *C, M, T*

New York
New York Institute of Technology *M*
State University of New York
    Buffalo *M*

North Carolina
Gardner-Webb University *M*
Roanoke-Chowan Community College *A*

Ohio
Malone College *M*

Pennsylvania
Marywood University *M*

Mental health services technology

California
San Joaquin Delta College *A*
Santa Rosa Junior College *C, A*

Connecticut
Capital Community College *A*
Housatonic Community College *C, A*
Three Rivers Community College *A*

Delaware
Delaware Technical and Community
  College
    Owens Campus *C, A*
    Stanton/Wilmington Campus *C, A*
    Terry Campus *C, A*

Idaho
North Idaho College *A*

Illinois
College of DuPage *C*
Elgin Community College *C*
Illinois Eastern Community Colleges
    Frontier Community College *A*
    Lincoln Trail College *C*
    Olney Central College *C*
    Wabash Valley College *C*
Moraine Valley Community College *C*
Prairie State College *A*
Roosevelt University *M*
Waubonsee Community College *C*

Indiana
Indiana University-Purdue University
    Fort Wayne *B*
Ivy Tech State College
    Bloomington *A*
    Central Indiana *A*
    Columbus *A*
    Eastcentral *A*
    Kokomo *A*
    Lafayette *A*
    Northcentral *C, A*
    Northeast *A*
    Northwest *A*
    Southcentral *C, A*
    Southeast *C, A*
    Southwest *A*
    Wabash Valley *A*
    Whitewater *A*

Maine
University of Maine
    Machias *B*

Maryland
Allegany College *A*
Chesapeake College *C, A*
Community College of Baltimore County
    Catonsville *C, A*
    Dundalk *C, A*
    Essex *C, A*
Hagerstown Community College *C, A*

Massachusetts
Berkshire Community College *C*
Mount Wachusett Community
    College *C, A*
Springfield Technical Community
    College *A*

Michigan
Oakland Community College *A*

Missouri
Penn Valley Community College *A*

New Hampshire
New Hampshire Technical Institute *A*

New Mexico
San Juan College *A*

New York
Dutchess Community College *A*

State University of New York
    Buffalo *M*

North Carolina
Montgomery Community College *C, A*
Pitt Community College *A*
Richmond Community College *A*
Roanoke-Chowan Community College *A*
Southwestern Community College *A*
Wayne Community College *A*
Wilkes Community College *C, A*

North Dakota
North Dakota State College of Science *A*

Ohio
Columbus State Community
    College *C, A*
North Central State College *A*
Sinclair Community College *A*
University of Toledo *A*

Oregon
Rogue Community College *C*

Pennsylvania
Community College of Allegheny
    County *C, A*
Community College of Philadelphia *A*
Drexel University *B*
Luzerne County Community College *A*
Montgomery County Community
    College *C, A*
Pennsylvania College of
    Technology *A, B*
Westmoreland County Community
    College *C, A*

Rhode Island
Community College of Rhode Island *A*

Texas
Alvin Community College *C, A*
Angelina College *C, A*
Blinn College *C, A*
Del Mar College *C, A*
Eastfield College *C, A*
El Paso Community College *A*
Houston Community College
    System *C, A*
Laredo Community College *A*
McLennan Community College *C, A*
North Harris Montgomery Community
    College District *C, A*
St. Edward's University *B*
Tarrant County College *A*

Virginia
Virginia Western Community College *A*

Washington
Edmonds Community College *C, A*
Seattle Central Community College *A*

West Virginia
Mountain State College *A*

Merchandising/buying operations

Georgia
Middle Georgia College *A*

Illinois
International Academy of Design and
    Technology *A, B*

Pennsylvania
Albright College *B*
Marywood University *C*

Texas
Texas Tech University *B*
University of Houston *B*

Metal/jewelry arts

Arizona
Arizona State University *B*

California
California College of Arts and
Crafts *B, M*
California State University
Long Beach *B, M*
Northridge *M*
Monterey Peninsula College *A*
Palomar College *A*
Santa Rosa Junior College *C*
Santiago Canyon College *A*

Colorado
Colorado State University *B*

Connecticut
Middlesex Community College *A*

Georgia
Savannah College of Art and
Design *B, M*
University of Georgia *B*

Illinois
Gem City College *C*

Indiana
Ball State University *B*
University of Evansville *B*

Iowa
University of Iowa *B, M*

Kansas
University of Kansas *B, M*

Maine
Maine College of Art *B*

Massachusetts
Massachusetts College of Art *B, M*
School of the Museum of Fine Arts *B, M*
University of Massachusetts
Dartmouth *B, M*

Michigan
College for Creative Studies *B*
Grand Valley State University *B*
Northern Michigan University *B*
Siena Heights University *B*
University of Michigan *B*

Nevada
Sierra Nevada College *B*

New Jersey
Rowan University *B*

New York
Hofstra University *B*
Parsons School of Design *C, A, B, T*
Pratt Institute *B*
Rochester Institute of
Technology *A, B, M*
State University of New York
College at Buffalo *B*
New Paltz *B, M*

North Carolina
Haywood Community College *A*

Ohio
Bowling Green State University *B*
Cleveland Institute of Art *B*
University of Akron *B*

Oregon
University of Oregon *B, M*

Pennsylvania
Arcadia University *B*
Seton Hill University *B*
Temple University *B, M*

Rhode Island
Rhode Island College *B*
Rhode Island School of Design *B, M*

Tennessee
Memphis College of Art *B, M*

Texas
Paris Junior College *A*
Sam Houston State University *M*
Texas A&M University
Commerce *B*
Texas Woman's University *B, M*
University of Houston *B, M*
University of North Texas *B, M*
University of Texas
Arlington *B*
El Paso *B*
Western Texas College *A*

Washington
University of Washington *B, M*

Wisconsin
University of Wisconsin
Madison *B*

Metallurgical engineering

Alabama
University of Alabama *B, M, D*

California
California Polytechnic State University:
San Luis Obispo *B*

Colorado
Colorado School of Mines *B, M, D*

Connecticut
University of Connecticut *B, M, D*

Idaho
University of Idaho *B, M*

Illinois
Illinois Institute of Technology *B, M, D*
Parkland College *A*
University of Illinois
Urbana-Champaign *B*

Iowa
Northeast Iowa Community College *A*

Michigan
Michigan State University *M, D*
University of Michigan *B*

Missouri
University of Missouri
Rolla *B, M, D*

Montana
Montana Tech of the University of
Montana *B, M*

Nevada
University of Nevada
Reno *B, M, D*

New Mexico
New Mexico Institute of Mining and
Technology *B*

New York
Columbia University
Fu Foundation School of
Engineering and Applied
Science *B, M, D*

Ohio
Ohio State University
Columbus Campus *B*
University of Cincinnati *B, M, D*

Pennsylvania
Lock Haven University of
Pennsylvania *B*
Penn State
Schuylkill - Capital College *B*
University Park *B, M, D*
University of Pittsburgh *B, M, D*

South Dakota
South Dakota School of Mines and
Technology *B, M*

Tennessee
University of Tennessee
Knoxville *M, D*

Texas
University of Texas
El Paso *B*

Utah
University of Utah *B, M, D*

Washington
University of Washington *B*

Wisconsin
University of Wisconsin
Madison *M, D*

Metallurgical technology

California
Don Bosco Technical Institute *A*

Illinois
Moraine Valley Community College *C*

Michigan
Western Michigan University *B*

New York
Mohawk Valley Community College *C*

Pennsylvania
Penn State
Altoona *A*
Schuylkill - Capital College *A*

Texas
Kilgore College *C, A*

Meteorology

Florida
Florida Institute of Technology *B, M*

Massachusetts
Massachusetts Institute of
Technology *M, D*

New York
Suffolk County Community College *A*

North Carolina
North Carolina State University *B*

Pennsylvania
Millersville University of
Pennsylvania *B*
Penn State
Schuylkill - Capital College *B*
University Park *B, M, D*
Wilkes-Barre *B*

Microbiology

California
University of Southern California *M, D*

Florida
University of West Florida *B*

Georgia
Medical College of Georgia *M, D*

Kansas
University of Kansas *B, M, D*

Louisiana
University of Louisiana at Lafayette *B*

Massachusetts
University of Massachusetts
Amherst *B, M, D*

Michigan
Michigan State University *B, M, D*

New York
Bard College *B*
State University of New York
Buffalo *M, D*
Health Science Center at Stony
Brook *D*
Stony Brook *D*

Oklahoma
University of Oklahoma *D*

Pennsylvania
Duquesne University *B*
Penn State
Lehigh Valley *B*

Puerto Rico
Universidad del Este *B*

Texas
University of Texas
Austin *B, M, D*
Houston Health Science
Center *M, D*

Washington
University of Washington *B*

Wisconsin
Lawrence University *B*

Wyoming
University of Wyoming *B*

Military technologies

Arizona
Pima Community College *C*
University of Phoenix *A*

Colorado
Colorado Mountain College
Spring Valley Campus *A*

Georgia
Georgia Military College *A*

Hawaii
Hawaii Pacific University *C*

Iowa
Drake University *B*

Kansas
Barton County Community College *A*
Seward County Community College *A*
Washburn University of Topeka *C*

Missouri
Southwest Missouri State
University *B, M*

Nevada
Truckee Meadows Community
College *A*

Puerto Rico
University of Puerto Rico
Cayey University College *B*

South Carolina
Wofford College *C*

Utah
Weber State University *B*

Mining technology

Illinois
Rend Lake College *C, A*

Mining/mineral engineering

Alaska
University of Alaska
Fairbanks *B, M*

Arizona
University of Arizona *B, M, D*

Colorado
Colorado School of Mines *B, M, D*

Idaho
University of Idaho *B, M, D*

Illinois
Southern Illinois University
Carbondale *B, M*

Kentucky
University of Kentucky *B, M, D*

Michigan
Michigan Technological
University *C, B, M, D, T*

Missouri
University of Missouri
Rolla *B, M, D*

Montana
Montana Tech of the University of
Montana *B, M*

Nevada
University of Nevada
Reno *B, M*

New Mexico
New Mexico Institute of Mining and
Technology *B, M*

New York
Columbia University
Fu Foundation School of
Engineering and Applied
Science *B, M, D*

Oregon
Oregon State University *B*

Pennsylvania
Penn State
Berks *B*
Delaware County *B*
Dubois *B*
Fayette *B*
Lehigh Valley *B*
McKeesport *B*
Mont Alto *B*
New Kensington *B*
Schuylkill - Capital College *B*
Shenango *B*
University Park *B, M, D*
Wilkes-Barre *B*
Worthington Scranton *B*
York *B*
University of Pittsburgh *M*

South Dakota
South Dakota School of Mines and
Technology *B*

Utah
University of Utah *B, M, D*

Virginia
Virginia Polytechnic Institute and State
University *B, M, D*

West Virginia
West Virginia University *B, M, D*

Wisconsin
University of Wisconsin
Madison *B*

Missionary studies

Alabama
Southeastern Bible College *A, B, T*

Alaska
Alaska Bible College *B*

Arizona
Southwestern College *C, A, B*

Arkansas
Harding University *B, M*
John Brown University *B*
Ouachita Baptist University *B*
Williams Baptist College *B*

California
Bethany College *B*
Bethesda Christian University *B*
Biola University *D*
Christian Heritage College *B*
Fresno Pacific University *B*
Holy Names College *C, M*
Hope International University *A, B, M*
Master's College *B*
San Jose Christian College *C, B*
Simpson College *B, M*
Vanguard University of Southern
California *B*

Florida
Florida Christian College *B*
Hobe Sound Bible College *C, A, B*
Southeastern College of the Assemblies
of God *B*

Georgia
Covenant College *B*
Toccoa Falls College *B*

Idaho
Northwest Nazarene University *B*

Illinois
Lincoln Christian College and
Seminary *B, M*
Moody Bible Institute *B*
Trinity International University *M*
Wheaton College *M*

Indiana
Anderson University *M*
Taylor University *C*
Taylor University: Fort Wayne *B*

Iowa
Dordt College *B*
Emmaus Bible College *B*
Faith Baptist Bible College and
Theological Seminary *B*

Kansas
Barclay College *B*
Central Christian College *A, B*
MidAmerica Nazarene University *B*

Kentucky
Kentucky Mountain Bible College *B*
Mid-Continent College *C, B*

Michigan
Cornerstone University *B, M*
Grace Bible College *B*
Reformed Bible College *B*

Minnesota
Bethel College *B*
Concordia University: St. Paul *B*
Crossroads College *B*
Crown College *B, M*
Northwestern College *B*
Oak Hills Christian College *B*

Mississippi
Magnolia Bible College *B*
Wesley College *B*

Missouri
Baptist Bible College *B, M*

Calvary Bible College *B*
Central Bible College *A, B*
Evangel University *B*
Global University *B*
Ozark Christian College *B*
St. Louis Christian College *A, B*

Nebraska
Grace University *B*
Nebraska Christian College *A, B*

North Carolina
Piedmont Baptist College *B*
Roanoke Bible College *A, B*

North Dakota
Trinity Bible College *B*

Ohio
Ashland University *B*
Cedarville University *B*
Cincinnati Bible College and
Seminary *B*
Circleville Bible College *A, B*
God's Bible School and College *B*

Oklahoma
Oklahoma Baptist University *B*
Oklahoma Christian University of
Science and Arts *B*
Oklahoma Wesleyan University *B*
Oral Roberts University *B, M*
Southern Nazarene University *B*
Southwestern Christian University *B*

Oregon
Eugene Bible College *B*
George Fox University *B*
Multnomah Bible College *B*
Western Baptist College *B*

Pennsylvania
Baptist Bible College of Pennsylvania *B*
Lancaster Bible College *B*
Philadelphia Biblical University *B*
Valley Forge Christian College *B*

South Carolina
Columbia International University *B, M*

Tennessee
Freed-Hardeman University *B*
Lee University *B*
Milligan College *B*
Southern Adventist University *A*

Texas
Abilene Christian University *B, M*
Arlington Baptist College *B*
East Texas Baptist University *B*
Lubbock Christian University *B*
Southwestern Assemblies of God
University *B*

Washington
Northwest College *B*
Trinity Lutheran College *C, B*

Wisconsin
Maranatha Baptist Bible College *B*

Modern Greek

California
Loyola Marymount University *B*

Connecticut
Connecticut College *B*

District of Columbia
Catholic University of America *B, M, D*
Howard University *B*

Georgia
Oxford College of Emory University *B*

Iowa
Luther College *B*

Louisiana
Tulane University *B*

Maryland
Johns Hopkins University *B*

Massachusetts
Boston University *B*
Harvard College *B*

Michigan
Calvin College *B*
University of Michigan *B*

New Hampshire
University of New Hampshire *B*

New York
City University of New York
Brooklyn College *M*
Queens College *B*
Colgate University *B*
Columbia University
Columbia College *B*
Fordham University *B*
New York University *B*

Ohio
College of Wooster *B*
Ohio State University
Columbus Campus *B, M, D*

Pennsylvania
Gettysburg College *B*

Tennessee
Rhodes College *B*

Molecular biochemistry

California
California State University
Sacramento *B, M*

Colorado
University of Colorado
Health Sciences Center *D*

Illinois
Finch University of Health Sciences/The
Chicago Medical School *M, D*

New York
Clarkson University *B*

Wisconsin
Lawrence University *B*

Molecular biology

Alabama
Auburn University *B*

Arizona
Arizona State University *B, M, D*
Northern Arizona University *B*
University of Arizona *M, D*

Arkansas
University of Arkansas *M, D*

California
California Institute of Technology *D*
California State University
Fresno *B*
Long Beach *B*
Northridge *B*
Loma Linda University *M, D*
Los Angeles Southwest College *A*
Pomona College *B*
San Diego State University *M*
San Francisco State University *M*
San Jose State University *B*
Scripps College *B*
Stanford University *D*

University of California
  Berkeley *B, D*
  Davis *B*
  Irvine *D*
  Los Angeles *B, D*
  Riverside *M, D*
  San Diego *B*
  Santa Barbara *B, M, D*
  Santa Cruz *B*
University of Southern California *M, D*

Colorado
Colorado State University *M, D*
Fort Lewis College *B*
University of Colorado
  Health Sciences Center *D*
University of Denver *B*

Connecticut
Connecticut College *B*
Quinnipiac University *M*
University of Connecticut *B, M, D*
University of New Haven *M*
Wesleyan University *B, D*
Yale University *B, M, D*

District of Columbia
Georgetown University *D*

Florida
Florida Institute of Technology *B*
Stetson University *B*
University of Central Florida *B, M*
University of Tampa *B*
University of West Florida *B*

Georgia
Medical College of Georgia *D*

Idaho
University of Idaho *B*

Illinois
Benedictine University *B*
Bradley University *B*
Chicago State University *B*
Finch University of Health Sciences/The
  Chicago Medical School *D*
Loyola University of Chicago *M, D*
Northwestern University *B, M, D*
Southern Illinois University
  Carbondale *M, D*
University of Chicago *M, D*

Indiana
Ball State University *B*
Goshen College *B*
Indiana University
  Bloomington *D*

Iowa
Coe College *B*
Iowa State University *M, D*
University of Iowa *D*

Kansas
University of Kansas *B*

Kentucky
Centre College *B*

Louisiana
Tulane University *B*

Maine
Colby College *B*
University of Maine *B, M, D*
University of Southern Maine *D*

Maryland
Johns Hopkins University *M, D*
University of Maryland
  Baltimore *M, D*
  Baltimore County *M, D*
  College Park *M, D*

Massachusetts
Assumption College *B*
Boston University *B, M, D*
Brandeis University *M, D*
Bridgewater State College *B*

Clark University *B*
Hampshire College *B*
Harvard College *B*
Tufts University *M, D*

Michigan
Andrews University *B*
University of Michigan *B, M, D*
University of Michigan
  Flint *B*
Wayne State University *M, D*

Minnesota
University of Minnesota
  Duluth *B*
  Twin Cities *D*
Winona State University *B*

Mississippi
Mississippi State University *D*

Missouri
Northwest Missouri State University *B*
University of Missouri
  Kansas City *M*
Washington University in St. Louis *D*
William Jewell College *B*

Montana
Montana State University
  Bozeman *M, D*

Nevada
University of Nevada
  Reno *M, D*

New Hampshire
Dartmouth College *B*

New Jersey
Montclair State University *B*
Princeton University *B, M, D*
Richard Stockton College of New
  Jersey *B*
Rutgers, The State University of New
  Jersey
    New Brunswick Regional
    Campus *B*

New Mexico
New Mexico State University *M, D*

New York
Bard College *B*
Colgate University *B*
Hamilton College *B*
State University of New York
  Albany *B, M, D*
  Buffalo *M, D*
  College of Environmental Science
    and Forestry *M, D*
  Stony Brook *D*
University of Rochester *B*
Wells College *B*
Yeshiva University *M, D*

North Carolina
East Carolina University *M*
Meredith College *B*
Wake Forest University *M, D*
Winston-Salem State University *B*

North Dakota
North Dakota State University *D*

Ohio
Case Western Reserve University *D*
Kent State University *M, D*
Kenyon College *B*
Miami University
  Middletown Campus *A*
Muskingum College *B*
Ohio Northern University *B*
Ohio State University
  Columbus Campus *M, D*
Otterbein College *B*
University of Cincinnati *M, D*
Wittenberg University *B*

Oklahoma
Eastern Oklahoma State College *A*
Oklahoma State University *B, M*
University of Tulsa *D*

Oregon
Oregon Health Sciences University *M, D*
Oregon State University *D*
Reed College *B*
University of Oregon *M, D*

Pennsylvania
Chestnut Hill College *B*
Dickinson College *B*
Grove City College *B*
Juniata College *B*
Lehigh University *B, M, D*
University of Pittsburgh *B*
West Chester University of
  Pennsylvania *B*

Puerto Rico
Universidad Metropolitana *B*

Rhode Island
Brown University *B, M, D*

South Carolina
Medical University of South Carolina *D*

Tennessee
Vanderbilt University *B, M, D*

Texas
Texas A&M University *B*
Texas Lutheran University *B*
Texas Woman's University *D*
University of North Texas *M*
University of Texas
  Austin *B, M, D*
  Houston Health Science
    Center *M, D*

Utah
Brigham Young University *B, M, D*

Vermont
Bennington College *B*
Johnson State College *B*
Marlboro College *B*
Middlebury College *B*
University of Vermont *B, M, D*

Virginia
Hampton University *B*
Marymount University *B*
Sweet Briar College *B*
University of Richmond *B*

Washington
University of Washington *M, D*
Western Washington University *B*

West Virginia
Salem International University *B, M*

Wisconsin
Beloit College *B*
Marquette University *B, M, D*
University of Wisconsin
  Eau Claire *B*
  Madison *B, M, D*
  Parkside *B, M*
  Superior *B*

Wyoming
University of Wyoming *B, M, D*

Molecular genetics

New York
State University of New York
  Buffalo *M, D*
University of Rochester *B*

South Carolina
Medical University of South Carolina *D*

Texas
University of Texas
  Houston Health Science
    Center *M, D*

Molecular pharmacology

Illinois
Finch University of Health Sciences/The
  Chicago Medical School *M, D*

New York
State University of New York
  Buffalo *M, D*
  Stony Brook *D*

Ohio
Ohio Northern University *D*

South Carolina
Medical University of South Carolina *D*

Molecular physiology

Oklahoma
University of Oklahoma *M, D*

Wisconsin
University of Wisconsin
  Superior *B*

Montessori teacher education

Massachusetts
Endicott College *M*

Ohio
Xavier University *B, M*

Oklahoma
Oklahoma City University *B*

Mortuary science/ embalming

Florida
Miami-Dade Community College *C*

Kansas
Kansas City Kansas Community
  College *A*

New York
State University of New York
  College of Technology at
    Canton *A, B*

Motorcycle maintenance

Minnesota
Hennepin Technical College *C, A*

New York
State University of New York
  College of Technology at Canton *C*

North Carolina
Edgecombe Community College *C, A*

Texas
Austin Community College *C*

Movement therapy

California
Ohlone College *C*

Pennsylvania
Academy of Medical Arts and
  Business *C, A*

Multicultural education

Illinois
Trinity International University *D*

New Mexico
College of Santa Fe *M*

New York
College of New Rochelle *M*

Ohio
University of Akron *B, M*
Xavier University *M*

Oklahoma
Langston University *M*

South Dakota
Augustana College *B, M*

Texas
University of Houston
Clear Lake *M*

Washington
University of Washington *M, D*

Multimedia

Arizona
Arizona State University *B*
Arizona Western College *C, A*

California
Academy of Art College *C, A, B, M*
Antelope Valley College *C, A*
College of the Canyons *A*
College of the Sequoias *A*
Long Beach City College *A*
Ohlone College *C, A*
Santa Barbara City College *A*

Colorado
Art Institute
of Colorado *A*

Connecticut
Naugatuck Valley Community College *A*

Florida
Full Sail Real World Education *A*
University of Central Florida *B*

Georgia
Atlanta College of Art *B*
Augusta State University *B*
University of Georgia *B*

Illinois
American Academy of Art *B*
Columbia College Chicago *B*
Illinois Institute of Art *B*
International Academy of Design and
Technology *A, B*

Indiana
Indiana University
South Bend *B*

Iowa
St. Ambrose University *B*
University of Iowa *M*

Louisiana
Tulane University *C, B*

Maryland
Maryland Institute College of Art *B*

Massachusetts
Art Institute of Boston at Lesley
University *A, B*
Hampshire College *B*
Massachusetts College of Art *B, M*
School of the Museum of Fine Arts *B, M*
University of Massachusetts
Dartmouth *B*

Michigan
University of Michigan *B*

Minnesota
Art Institutes International
Minnesota *A, B*
Minnesota State University
Moorhead *B*

New Jersey
Bloomfield College *B*
Ramapo College of New Jersey *B*

New Mexico
College of Santa Fe *B*

New York
Bard College *B*
City University of New York
Borough of Manhattan Community
College *A*
Fulton-Montgomery Community
College *C, A*
Long Island University
C. W. Post Campus *M*
Medaille College *C*
Rochester Institute of Technology *B*

Ohio
Sinclair Community College *C*
University of Findlay *B*

Oregon
Pacific University *B*
Portland Community College *C*

Pennsylvania
Indiana University of Pennsylvania *B, M*

Puerto Rico
University of Puerto Rico
Rio Piedras Campus *B*

South Carolina
Benedict College *B*

Tennessee
Memphis College of Art *B, M*

Utah
Salt Lake Community College *A*

Vermont
Bennington College *B, M*

Washington
Art Institute of Seattle *A*
Western Washington University *B*

Wisconsin
University of Wisconsin
Milwaukee *B*

Museum studies

California
John F. Kennedy University *M*
San Francisco State University *M*
University of Southern California *M*

Colorado
University of Colorado
Boulder *M*

District of Columbia
George Washington University *M*

Florida
University of Florida *M*

Indiana
Earlham College *B*

Kansas
University of Kansas *M*

Massachusetts
Regis College *B*

Mississippi
University of Southern Mississippi *B*

Nebraska
University of Nebraska
Lincoln *M*

New Jersey
Seton Hall University *M*

New Mexico
Institute of American Indian Arts *A, B*

New York
City University of New York
City College *M*
Fashion Institute of Technology *M*
New York University *M*
State University of New York
College at Oneonta *M*
Syracuse University *M*

Oklahoma
University of Central Oklahoma *B, M*

Pennsylvania
Juniata College *B*

Tennessee
Tusculum College *B*

Texas
Baylor University *B, M*
Texas A&M University *B*
Texas Tech University *M*

Virginia
Randolph-Macon Woman's College *B*

Washington
University of Washington *C, M*

Wisconsin
University of Wisconsin
Madison *M, D*

Music

Alabama
Alabama Agricultural and Mechanical
University *B, M*
Alabama State University *B, T*
Birmingham-Southern College *B, T*
Calhoun Community College *C, A*
Chattahoochee Valley Community
College *A*
Community College of the Air Force *A*
Faulkner University *B*
Huntingdon College *B, T*
Jacksonville State University *B, M*
James H. Faulkner State Community
College *A*
Judson College *B*
Northeast Alabama Community
College *A*
Northwest-Shoals Community College *A*
Stillman College *B*
Talladega College *B*
University of Alabama *B, M, D*
University of Alabama
Birmingham *B*
Huntsville *B*
University of Mobile *B, T*
University of Montevallo *B, T*
University of North Alabama *B*
University of South Alabama *B*
Wallace State Community College at
Hanceville *A*

Alaska
University of Alaska
Anchorage *B*
Fairbanks *B, M*

Arizona
Arizona State University *B, M, D*
Arizona Western College *A*
Central Arizona College *A*
Eastern Arizona College *A*
Northern Arizona University *B, M, T*
Pima Community College *A*

South Mountain Community College *A*
University of Arizona *B*

Arkansas
Arkansas State University *B*
Arkansas Tech University *B*
Central Baptist College *A*
Harding University *B*
Henderson State University *B*
Hendrix College *B*
John Brown University *B*
Lyon College *B*
Ouachita Baptist University *B*
Philander Smith College *B*
University of Arkansas
Fort Smith *A, B*
Little Rock *B*
Monticello *B*
Pine Bluff *B*
University of Central Arkansas *B, M*
University of the Ozarks *B*

California
Antelope Valley College *C, A*
Azusa Pacific University *B, M*
Bakersfield College *A*
Barstow College *A*
Bethany College *A*
Bethesda Christian University *B, M*
Biola University *B*
Cabrillo College *A*
California Baptist University *B*
California Institute of the Arts *C, B*
California State Polytechnic University:
Pomona *B*
California State University
Bakersfield *B*
Chico *B, M*
Dominguez Hills *B*
Fresno *B, M*
Fullerton *B*
Hayward *B, M*
Long Beach *B, M*
Los Angeles *B, M*
Monterey Bay *B*
Northridge *B, M*
Sacramento *B, M*
San Bernardino *B*
Stanislaus *B*
Cerritos Community College *A*
Chabot College *A*
Chapman University *B*
Christian Heritage College *B*
Citrus College *A*
Claremont McKenna College *B*
College of Alameda *A*
College of Marin: Kentfield *A*
College of the Canyons *A*
College of the Sequoias *A*
College of the Siskiyous *A*
Columbia College *A*
Concordia University *B*
Contra Costa College *A*
De Anza College *A*
Dominican University of California *B*
East Los Angeles College *A*
Foothill College *C, A*
Fresno Pacific University *B*
Gavilan Community College *A*
Golden West College *A*
Grossmont Community College *A*
Holy Names College *B, M*
Humboldt State University *B*
Imperial Valley College *A*
Irvine Valley College *A*
La Sierra University *B*
Laney College *A*
Las Positas College *A*
Long Beach City College *A*
Los Angeles Pierce College *C, A*
Los Angeles Southwest College *A*
Los Medanos College *A*
Loyola Marymount University *B*
Marymount College *A*
Master's College *B*
Mills College *B, M*

MiraCosta College *A*
Modesto Junior College *A*
Monterey Peninsula College *A*
Moorpark College *A*
Mount St. Mary's College *B*
Mount San Jacinto College *A*
Occidental College *B*
Orange Coast College *A*
Pacific Union College *B*
Palomar College *A*
Pepperdine University *B*
Point Loma Nazarene University *B*
Pomona College *B*
Reedley College *A*
St. Mary's College of California *B*
San Diego City College *A*
San Diego Mesa College *A*
San Diego State University *M*
San Francisco State University *B, M*
San Joaquin Delta College *A*
San Jose Christian College *C, B*
San Jose State University *B, M*
Santa Barbara City College *A*
Santa Clara University *B*
Santa Monica College *A*
Santiago Canyon College *A*
Scripps College *B*
Shasta College *A*
Sonoma State University *B*
Southwestern College *A*
Stanford University *B, M, D*
University of California
   Berkeley *B, M, D*
   Davis *B, M, D*
   Irvine *B, M*
   Los Angeles *B, M, D*
   Riverside *B, M*
   San Diego *B, M, D*
   Santa Barbara *B, M, D*
   Santa Cruz *B*
University of La Verne *B*
University of Redlands *B, M*
University of San Diego *B*
University of Southern California *B*
University of the Pacific *B, M*
Vanguard University of Southern
   California *B*
Ventura College *C, A*
West Valley College *A*
Whittier College *B*
Yuba Community College District *A*

Colorado
Colorado Christian University *B*
Colorado College *B*
Colorado State University *B, M*
Colorado State University
   Pueblo *B, T*
Fort Lewis College *B*
Naropa University *B*
University of Colorado
   Boulder *B*
   Denver *B*
University of Denver *B*
University of Northern
   Colorado *B, M, D, T*

Connecticut
Central Connecticut State University *B*
Connecticut College *B, M*
Eastern Connecticut State University *B*
Fairfield University *B*
Manchester Community College *A*
Naugatuck Valley Community College *A*
Southern Connecticut State University *B*
Trinity College *B*
University of Bridgeport *B*
University of Connecticut *B, M, D*
University of Hartford *B*
University of New Haven *B*
Wesleyan University *B, M*
Western Connecticut State University *B*
Yale University *B, M, D*

Delaware
Delaware State University *B*

University of Delaware *B*

District of Columbia
American University *B*
Catholic University of America *B*
George Washington University *B*
Georgetown University *B*
Howard University *M*
University of the District of
   Columbia *A, B*

Florida
Barry University *B*
Bethune-Cookman College *B*
Broward Community College *A*
Chipola Junior College *A*
Daytona Beach Community College *A*
Eckerd College *B*
Florida Atlantic University *B, M*
Florida International University *B, M*
Florida Southern College *B*
Florida State University *B*
Gulf Coast Community College *A*
Hillsborough Community College *A*
Indian River Community College *A*
Jacksonville University *B*
Manatee Community College *A*
Miami-Dade Community College *A*
New College of Florida *B*
Okaloosa-Walton Community College *A*
Palm Beach Atlantic University *B, T*
Palm Beach Community College *A*
Pensacola Junior College *A*
Polk Community College *A*
Rollins College *B*
South Florida Community College *A*
Southeastern College of the Assemblies
   of God *B*
University of Central Florida *B*
University of Florida *B, M, D*
University of Miami *B, M, D*
University of North Florida *B*
University of Tampa *A, B, T*
University of West Florida *B*

Georgia
Abraham Baldwin Agricultural
   College *A*
Agnes Scott College *B*
Albany State University *B*
Armstrong Atlantic State University *B, T*
Atlanta Metropolitan College *A*
Augusta State University *B*
Berry College *B*
Brenau University *B*
Brewton-Parker College *B*
Clark Atlanta University *B*
Columbus State University *B, M*
Covenant College *B*
Darton College *A*
Emory University *B*
Georgia College and State University *B*
Georgia Perimeter College *A*
Georgia Southern University *B, M*
Georgia Southwestern State University *B*
Gordon College *A*
Kennesaw State University *B*
LaGrange College *B*
Macon State College *A*
Mercer University *B*
Middle Georgia College *A*
Morehouse College *B*
Morris Brown College *B*
North Georgia College & State
   University *B*
Oxford College of Emory University *B*
Piedmont College *B*
Reinhardt College *B*
Spelman College *B*
Thomas University *B*
Truett-McConnell College *A*
University of Georgia *B, M, D*
Valdosta State University *B*
Wesleyan College *B*
Young Harris College *A*

Hawaii
Brigham Young University-Hawaii *B*
University of Hawaii
   Hilo *B*
   Manoa *B, M, D*

Idaho
Albertson College of Idaho *B*
Brigham Young University - Idaho *A, B*
College of Southern Idaho *A*
Idaho State University *B*
North Idaho College *A*
Northwest Nazarene University *B*
University of Idaho *B, M*

Illinois
Augustana College *B*
Benedictine University *B*
Black Hawk College
   East Campus *A*
Blackburn College *B, T*
Bradley University *B*
Chicago State University *B*
City Colleges of Chicago
   Harold Washington College *A*
   Kennedy-King College *C*
   Olive-Harvey College *A*
College of DuPage *A*
College of Lake County *A*
Columbia College Chicago *B*
Concordia University *B, T*
De Paul University *B, M*
Eastern Illinois University *B, M, T*
Elmhurst College *B, T*
Greenville College *B, T*
Illinois Central College *A*
Illinois College *B*
Illinois Eastern Community Colleges
   Olney Central College *A*
   Wabash Valley College *A*
Illinois State University *B*
Illinois Valley Community College *A*
John A. Logan College *A*
John Wood Community College *A*
Joliet Junior College *A*
Judson College *B*
Kishwaukee College *A*
Knox College *B*
Lake Forest College *B*
Lewis University *B, T*
Lewis and Clark Community College *A*
Lincoln College *A*
Lincoln Land Community College *A*
Loyola University of Chicago *B*
MacMurray College *B*
McHenry County College *A*
McKendree College *B*
Millikin University *B*
Monmouth College *B*
North Central College *B, T*
North Park University *B*
Northeastern Illinois University *B, M*
Northern Illinois University *B, M*
Northwestern University *B, M, D*
Olivet Nazarene University *B, T*
Principia College *B*
Quincy University *B, T*
Richland Community College *A*
Roosevelt University *B*
St. Xavier University *B*
Sauk Valley Community College *A*
South Suburban College of Cook
   County *A*
Southern Illinois University
   Carbondale *B, M*
Southern Illinois University
   Edwardsville *B, M, T*
Southwestern Illinois College *A*
Trinity Christian College *B*
Trinity International University *B*
Triton College *A*
University of Chicago *B, M, D*
University of Illinois
   Chicago *B*
   Urbana-Champaign *B, M, D*
Waubonsee Community College *A*

Western Illinois University *B, M*
Wheaton College *B*
William Rainey Harper College *A*

Indiana
Bethel College *A, B*
Butler University *B*
DePauw University *B*
Earlham College *B*
Goshen College *B*
Hanover College *B*
Indiana State University *B, M, T*
Indiana University
   Bloomington *B, M, D*
   Southeast *B*
Indiana University-Purdue University
   Fort Wayne *B, T*
Indiana University-Purdue University
   Indianapolis *M*
Indiana Wesleyan University *B*
Manchester College *B, T*
Marian College *A, B, T*
Oakland City University *B*
St. Joseph's College *B*
Saint Mary's College *B*
St. Mary-of-the-Woods College *B*
Taylor University *B*
Taylor University: Fort Wayne *B*
University of Evansville *B*
University of Indianapolis *B*
University of Notre Dame *B, M*
Valparaiso University *B, M*
Vincennes University *A*
Wabash College *B*

Iowa
Briar Cliff University *B*
Buena Vista University *B, T*
Central College *B, T*
Clarke College *A, B, T*
Coe College *B*
Cornell College *B, T*
Dordt College *B*
Drake University *B*
Franciscan University *B, T*
Graceland University *B, T*
Grand View College *B*
Grinnell College *B*
Iowa State University *B*
Iowa Western Community College *A*
Loras College *B*
Luther College *B*
Marshalltown Community College *A*
Morningside College *B*
Mount Mercy College *B*
North Iowa Area Community College *A*
Northwestern College *B, T*
St. Ambrose University *B*
Simpson College *B*
University of Iowa *B, M, D, T*
University of Northern Iowa *B, M*
Vennard College *A*
Waldorf College *A, B*
Wartburg College *B, T*

Kansas
Allen County Community College *A*
Baker University *B, T*
Barton County Community College *A*
Benedictine College *B, T*
Bethany College *B, T*
Bethel College *B*
Butler County Community College *A*
Central Christian College *A, B*
Dodge City Community College *A*
Emporia State University *B, M*
Fort Hays State University *B, M*
Friends University *B*
Garden City Community College *A*
Hutchinson Community College *A*
Independence Community College *A*
Kansas City Kansas Community
   College *A*
Kansas State University *B, M*
Kansas Wesleyan University *T*
Labette Community College *A*

McPherson College *B, T*
MidAmerica Nazarene University *B*
Ottawa University *B, T*
Pittsburg State University *B, M, T*
Pratt Community College *A*
Seward County Community College *A*
Southwestern College *B*
Sterling College *B*
Tabor College *B*
University of Kansas *B, M, D*
Washburn University of Topeka *B*
Wichita State University *B, M*

Kentucky

Asbury College *B*
Bellarmine University *B*
Berea College *B, T*
Campbellsville University *B, M*
Centre College *B*
Cumberland College *B, T*
Georgetown College *B*
Morehead State University *B*
Murray State University *B, M*
Thomas More College *A*
Union College *B*
University of Kentucky *D*
University of Louisville *B*

Louisiana

Centenary College of Louisiana *B*
Delgado Community College *A*
Dillard University *B*
Louisiana College *B*
Louisiana State University and
    Agricultural and Mechanical
    College *B, D*
Louisiana Tech University *B*
Loyola University New Orleans *B, M*
Northwestern State University *B*
Southern University and Agricultural and
    Mechanical College *A*
Tulane University *B, M*
University of Louisiana at Monroe *B, M*
University of New Orleans *B, M*
Xavier University of Louisiana *B*

Maine

Bates College *B*
Bowdoin College *B*
Colby College *B*
University of Maine *B, M*
University of Maine
    Farmington *B*
University of Southern Maine *B*

Maryland

Anne Arundel Community College *C*
Bowie State University *B*
College of Notre Dame of Maryland *B*
College of Southern Maryland *A*
Columbia Union College *B*
Community College of Baltimore County
    Catonsville *A*
    Dundalk *A*
    Essex *A*
Frostburg State University *B*
Goucher College *B*
Hood College *B*
Howard Community College *A*
Johns Hopkins University *B, M, D*
McDaniel College *B*
Montgomery College
    Rockville Campus *A*
Morgan State University *B, M*
St. Mary's College of Maryland *B*
Salisbury University *B, T*
Towson University *B*
University of Maryland
    Baltimore County *B*
    College Park *B, M, D*
Washington Bible College *A, B*
Washington College *B*

Massachusetts

Amherst College *B*
Anna Maria College *B*
Atlantic Union College *B*

Berklee College of Music *B*
Berkshire Community College *A*
Boston College *B*
Brandeis University *B, M*
Bridgewater State College *B*
Bunker Hill Community College *A*
Cape Cod Community College *A*
College of the Holy Cross *B*
Gordon College *B*
Hampshire College *B*
Harvard College *B*
Massachusetts College of Liberal Arts *B*
Massachusetts Institute of Technology *B*
Mount Holyoke College *B*
New England Conservatory of
    Music *B, M*
Northeastern University *B*
Salem State College *B*
Simmons College *B*
Simon's Rock College of Bard *B*
Smith College *B, M*
Tufts University *B, M*
University of Massachusetts
    Amherst *B*
    Boston *B*
    Dartmouth *B*
Wellesley College *B*
Westfield State College *B*
Wheaton College *B*
Williams College *B*

Michigan

Adrian College *A, B, T*
Alma College *B, T*
Andrews University *B, M*
Calvin College *B, T*
Central Michigan University *B*
Concordia University *B, T*
Cornerstone University *B, T*
Eastern Michigan University *B, M*
Grace Bible College *A, B*
Grand Rapids Community College *A*
Grand Valley State University *B*
Hillsdale College *B*
Hope College *B*
Kalamazoo College *B, T*
Kellogg Community College *C, A*
Lansing Community College *A*
Madonna University *B*
Marygrove College *T*
Northern Michigan University *B, T*
Northwestern Michigan College *A*
Oakland University *B, M*
Saginaw Valley State University *B*
Schoolcraft College *A*
Siena Heights University *B*
Spring Arbor University *B*
University of Michigan *B*
University of Michigan
    Dearborn *B*
    Flint *B*
Wayne State University *B, M, T*
Western Michigan University *B, M*
William Tyndale College *B*

Minnesota

Augsburg College *B*
Bemidji State University *B*
Bethany Lutheran College *B*
Bethel College *B*
Carleton College *B*
College of St. Benedict *B*
College of St. Catherine *B*
Concordia College: Moorhead *B*
Concordia University: St. Paul *B*
Crossroads College *B*
Crown College *A, B*
Gustavus Adolphus College *B*
Hamline University *B*
Macalester College *B*
Minnesota State University
    Mankato *B, M, T*
    Moorhead *B, M*
Northland Community & Technical
    College *A*
Northwestern College *B*

Ridgewater College: A Community and
    Technical College *A*
St. Cloud State University *B, M*
St. John's University *B*
St. Mary's University of Minnesota *B*
St. Olaf College *B, T*
Southwest State University *B, T*
University of Minnesota
    Duluth *B*
    Morris *B*
    Twin Cities *B, M, D*
University of St. Thomas *B*
Winona State University *B, T*

Mississippi

Blue Mountain College *B*
Delta State University *B*
Itawamba Community College *A*
Mary Holmes College *A*
Millsaps College *B, T*
Mississippi College *B, M, T*
Mississippi University for Women *B*
Mississippi Valley State University *B*
Rust College *B*
University of Mississippi *B, M, D, T*
University of Southern Mississippi *B, M*

Missouri

Avila University *B*
Baptist Bible College *B*
Central Christian College of the Bible *B*
Central Methodist College *B*
Central Missouri State University *B, M*
College of the Ozarks *B*
Crowder College *A*
Culver-Stockton College *B, T*
Drury University *B, T*
East Central College *A*
Evangel University *A, B*
Lindenwood University *B, M*
Missouri Southern State College *B, T*
Missouri Western State College *B*
Northwest Missouri State University *B*
St. Louis Community College
    St. Louis Community College at
        Florissant Valley *A*
    St. Louis Community College at
        Forest Park *A*
    St. Louis Community College at
        Meramec *A*
St. Louis University *B*
Southeast Missouri State
    University *B, M*
Southwest Baptist University *B, T*
Southwest Missouri State
    University *B, M*
Three Rivers Community College *A*
Truman State University *B, M*
University of Missouri
    Columbia *B, M*
    Kansas City *B, M*
    St. Louis *B*
Washington University in St.
    Louis *B, M, D*
Webster University *B*
William Jewell College *B*

Montana

Montana State University
    Billings *B*
    Bozeman *B*
Rocky Mountain College *B*
University of Montana-Missoula *B, M*
University of Montana: Western *B, T*

Nebraska

Chadron State College *B*
Concordia University *B, T*
Creighton University *B*
Dana College *B*
Doane College *B*
Hastings College *B, T*
Midland Lutheran College *B, T*
Nebraska Wesleyan University *B*
Northeast Community College *A*
Peru State College *B*
Union College *B*

University of Nebraska
    Kearney *B, M, T*
    Lincoln *B, M, D*
    Omaha *B, M*
Wayne State College *B, T*
Western Nebraska Community
    College *A*

Nevada

Sierra Nevada College *B*
Truckee Meadows Community
    College *C, A*
University of Nevada
    Las Vegas *B, M*
    Reno *B, M*
Western Nevada Community College *A*

New Hampshire

Dartmouth College *B*
Franklin Pierce College *B*
Keene State College *B*
Plymouth State College *B*
University of New Hampshire *B, M*

New Jersey

Bloomfield College *B*
Caldwell College *B*
The College of New Jersey *B, M, T*
College of St. Elizabeth *B*
Cumberland County College *A*
Drew University *B*
Essex County College *A*
Georgian Court College *B, T*
Kean University *B*
Monmouth University *B*
Montclair State University *B, M*
New Jersey City University *B, T*
Princeton University *B, M, D*
Raritan Valley Community College *A*
Rider University *B, M*
Rowan University *B*
Rutgers, The State University of New
    Jersey
    Camden Regional Campus *B, T*
    New Brunswick Regional
        Campus *B, M, D*
    Newark Regional Campus *B, T*
Seton Hall University *B, T*
Thomas Edison State College *B*
William Paterson University of New
    Jersey *B*

New Mexico

College of Santa Fe *B*
Eastern New Mexico University *B, M*
New Mexico Highlands University *B*
New Mexico Junior College *A*
New Mexico State University *B, M*
San Juan College *A*
Western New Mexico University *B*

New York

Adelphi University *B*
Adirondack Community College *A*
Bard College *B, M*
Barnard College *B*
City University of New York
    Baruch College *B*
    Brooklyn College *B, M*
    City College *B, M*
    College of Staten Island *B*
    Hunter College *B, M*
    Kingsborough Community
        College *A*
    Queens College *B, M*
    York College *B*
Colgate University *B*
Columbia University
    Columbia College *B*
Concordia College *B*
Cornell University *B, M, D*
Dowling College *B, T*
Eastman School of Music of the
    University of Rochester *B*
Elmira College *B*
Excelsior College *B*
Finger Lakes Community College *A*

Fordham University *B*
Hamilton College *B*
Hartwick College *B*
Hobart and William Smith Colleges *B*
Hofstra University *B*
Houghton College *B*
Ithaca College *B, M, T*
Long Island University
    C. W. Post Campus *B, M*
Manhattanville College *B*
Mercy College *B*
Molloy College *B*
Nazareth College of Rochester *B, T*
New York University *B, M, D*
Niagara County Community College *A*
Nyack College *B*
Onondaga Community College *A*
Roberts Wesleyan College *B*
Rockland Community College *A*
St. Lawrence University *B*
Sarah Lawrence College *B*
Skidmore College *B*
State University of New York
    Albany *B*
    Binghamton *B*
    Buffalo *B, M, D, T*
    College at Buffalo *M*
    College at Fredonia *B*
    College at Oneonta *B*
    College at Plattsburgh *B*
    College at Potsdam *B, T*
    New Paltz *B*
    Oswego *B*
    Stony Brook *B, M, D*
Suffolk County Community College *A*
Syracuse University *B*
University of Rochester *B*
Vassar College *B*
Wells College *B*
Yeshiva University *B*

North Carolina

Appalachian State University *B*
Barber-Scotia College *B*
Bennett College *B*
Brevard College *A, B*
Caldwell Community College and
    Technical Institute *A*
Campbell University *B*
Catawba College *B, T*
Central Piedmont Community College *A*
Chowan College *B*
College of the Albemarle *A*
Davidson College *B*
Duke University *B*
Elizabeth City State University *B*
Elon University *B*
Gardner-Webb University *B*
Greensboro College *B, T*
Guilford College *B*
Lenoir-Rhyne College *B, T*
Livingstone College *B*
Mars Hill College *B, T*
Meredith College *B*
Methodist College *B*
Montreat College *B*
Mount Olive College *A, B*
North Carolina Agricultural and
    Technical State University *B, T*
North Carolina Central University *B*
Peace College *A*
Pfeiffer University *B*
Piedmont Baptist College *B*
Queens University of Charlotte *B*
Salem College *B*
Sandhills Community College *A*
Shaw University *B*
Southeastern Community College *A*
University of North Carolina
    Asheville *B*
    Chapel Hill *B*
    Charlotte *B*
    Pembroke *B*
    Wilmington *B*
Wake Forest University *B*
Western Carolina University *B, M*

Wingate University *B*
Winston-Salem State University *B*

North Dakota

Dickinson State University *B, T*
Jamestown College *B*
Minot State University: Bottineau
    Campus *A*
North Dakota State
    University *B, M, D, T*
Trinity Bible College *A, B*
University of Mary *B*
University of North Dakota *B, M, T*
Valley City State University *B*

Ohio

Antioch College *B*
Bluffton College *B*
Bowling Green State University *B*
Case Western Reserve
    University *B, M, D*
Cedarville University *B, T*
Central State University *B*
Cleveland State University *B, M, T*
College of Mount St. Joseph *B, T*
College of Wooster *B*
Denison University *B*
Heidelberg College *B*
Hiram College *B, T*
Kent State University *B, M, D*
Kent State University
    Stark Campus *B*
Kenyon College *B*
Lake Erie College *B*
Lorain County Community College *A*
Lourdes College *A*
Malone College *B*
Marietta College *B*
Miami University
    Oxford Campus *B, T*
Mount Union College *B*
Mount Vernon Nazarene University *B*
Muskingum College *B*
Oberlin College *B*
Ohio Northern University *B*
Ohio State University
    Columbus Campus *B, M, D*
Ohio Wesleyan University *B*
Otterbein College *B*
Owens Community College
    Toledo *A*
Shawnee State University *A*
Sinclair Community College *A*
University of Akron *B, M*
University of Cincinnati *B, M, D*
University of Dayton *B*
University of Rio Grande *B*
University of Toledo *B*
Wilmington College *B*
Wittenberg University *B*
Wright State University *B*
Xavier University *B*
Youngstown State University *B, M*

Oklahoma

Cameron University *B*
Carl Albert State College *A*
East Central University *B*
Eastern Oklahoma State College *A*
Langston University *B*
Northeastern Oklahoma Agricultural and
    Mechanical College *A*
Northeastern State University *B*
Northwestern Oklahoma State
    University *B*
Oklahoma Baptist University *B, T*
Oklahoma City Community College *A*
Oklahoma City University *B, M*
Oklahoma Panhandle State University *B*
Oklahoma State University *B*
Oral Roberts University *B*
Rose State College *A*
St. Gregory's University *A*
Southeastern Oklahoma State
    University *B*
Southern Nazarene University *B*

Southwestern Oklahoma State
    University *B, M*
Tulsa Community College *A*
University of Central Oklahoma *B*
University of Oklahoma *B, M*
University of Science and Arts of
    Oklahoma *B, T*
University of Tulsa *M*
Western Oklahoma State College *A*

Oregon

Chemeketa Community College *A*
Eastern Oregon University *B*
George Fox University *B*
Lewis & Clark College *B*
Linfield College *B*
Linn-Benton Community College *A*
Marylhurst University *B*
Mount Hood Community College *A*
Northwest Christian College *B*
Oregon State University *B*
Pacific University *B*
Portland State University *B, M*
Reed College *B*
Southern Oregon University *B, T*
University of Oregon *B, M*
University of Portland *B, M, T*
Warner Pacific College *B, T*
Western Baptist College *B*
Western Oregon University *B*

Pennsylvania

Albright College *B*
Allegheny College *B*
Bloomsburg University of
    Pennsylvania *B*
Bryn Mawr College *B*
Bucknell University *B*
Bucks County Community College *A*
Carnegie Mellon University *B, M*
Cedar Crest College *B*
Chatham College *B*
Chestnut Hill College *A, B*
Cheyney University of Pennsylvania *B*
Community College of Allegheny
    County *A*
Community College of Philadelphia *A*
Dickinson College *B*
Drexel University *B*
Edinboro University of
    Pennsylvania *B, T*
Elizabethtown College *B*
Franklin & Marshall College *B*
Geneva College *B, T*
Gettysburg College *B*
Grove City College *B*
Haverford College *B*
Immaculata University *B*
Indiana University of Pennsylvania *B, M*
Kutztown University of Pennsylvania *B*
La Salle University *B*
Lebanon Valley College of
    Pennsylvania *B, T*
Lehigh University *B*
Lincoln University *B*
Lock Haven University of
    Pennsylvania *B*
Lycoming College *B*
Marywood University *B*
Mercyhurst College *B*
Messiah College *B*
Millersville University of
    Pennsylvania *B, T*
Moravian College *B, T*
Muhlenberg College *B*
Penn State
    University Park *B*
Philadelphia Biblical University *B*
St. Vincent College *B*
Seton Hill University *B, T*
Slippery Rock University of
    Pennsylvania *B, T*
Swarthmore College *B*
Temple University *B*
University of Pennsylvania *B, D*
University of Pittsburgh *B, M, D*

Valley Forge Christian College *B*
Washington and Jefferson College *B*
West Chester University of
    Pennsylvania *B, M*
York College of Pennsylvania *B, T*

Puerto Rico

Conservatory of Music of Puerto Rico *B*
Inter American University of Puerto Rico
    Metropolitan Campus *A, B*
    San German Campus *B*
Pontifical Catholic University of Puerto
    Rico *B*
University of Puerto Rico
    Rio Piedras Campus *B*

Rhode Island

Brown University *B, M*
Community College of Rhode Island *A*
Providence College *B*
Rhode Island College *B*
Salve Regina University *B*
University of Rhode Island *B, M*

South Carolina

Anderson College *B, T*
Charleston Southern University *B*
Claflin University *B*
Coastal Carolina University *B*
Coker College *B, T*
College of Charleston *B*
Columbia College *B*
Converse College *B, M*
Erskine College *B, T*
Furman University *B, T*
Lander University *B, T*
Limestone College *B*
Newberry College *B*
North Greenville College *A, B*
Presbyterian College *B*
Southern Wesleyan University *B, T*
University of South Carolina *B*
Winthrop University *B, M*

South Dakota

Augustana College *B*
Black Hills State University *B*
Dakota State University *B*
Dakota Wesleyan University *B*
Mount Marty College *B*
Northern State University *B*
South Dakota State University *B*
University of Sioux Falls *B*
University of South Dakota *B*

Tennessee

Austin Peay State University *B, M*
Belmont University *B, T*
Bryan College *B*
Carson-Newman College *B, T*
Columbia State Community College *A*
East Tennessee State University *B, T*
Fisk University *B*
Freed-Hardeman University *B, T*
Jackson State Community College *A*
Lambuth University *B*
Lane College *B*
Maryville College *B, T*
Middle Tennessee State University *B, M*
Milligan College *B*
Rhodes College *B*
Roane State Community College *A*
Southern Adventist University *B*
Tennessee State University *B*
Tennessee Wesleyan College *B, T*
Trevecca Nazarene University *B*
Union University *B*
University of Memphis *B, M, D*
University of Tennessee
    Chattanooga *B, M, T*
    Knoxville *B, M*
    Martin *B*
Walters State Community College *A*

Texas

Abilene Christian University *B*
Amarillo College *A*

Angelo State University *B, T*
Arlington Baptist College *B*
Austin College *B*
Austin Community College *A*
Baylor University *B*
Blinn College *A*
Brazosport College *A*
Central Texas College *A*
Clarendon College *A*
Coastal Bend College *A*
College of the Mainland *A*
Dallas Baptist University *A, B*
Dallas Christian College *B*
East Texas Baptist University *B*
El Paso Community College *A*
Frank Phillips College *A*
Galveston College *A*
Grayson County College *A*
Hardin-Simmons University *B*
Hill College *A*
Houston Baptist University *B*
Howard College *A*
Howard Payne University *B, T*
Huston-Tillotson College *B*
Jarvis Christian College *B*
Kilgore College *A*
Lamar University *B, M*
Laredo Community College *A*
Lee College *A*
Lon Morris College *A*
Lubbock Christian University *B, T*
McMurry University *B, T*
Midland College *A*
Midwestern State University *B*
North Harris Montgomery Community
    College District *A*
Northeast Texas Community College *A*
Odessa College *A*
Our Lady of the Lake University of San
    Antonio *B*
Palo Alto College *A*
Panola College *A*
Paris Junior College *A*
Prairie View A&M University *B*
Rice University *B, M*
St. Mary's University *B, T*
St. Philip's College *A*
Sam Houston State University *B, M*
Schreiner University *B*
South Plains College *A*
Southern Methodist University *C, B, T*
Southwest Texas State
    University *B, M, T*
Southwestern Adventist University *B, T*
Southwestern Assemblies of God
    University *A*
Stephen F. Austin State
    University *B, M, T*
Sul Ross State University *B*
Tarleton State University *B*
Temple College *A*
Texas A&M University *B*
Texas A&M University
    Commerce *B, M*
    Corpus Christi *B, T*
    Kingsville *B, M*
Texas Christian University *B, T*
Texas College *B*
Texas Lutheran University *B*
Texas Southern University *B*
Texas Tech University *B, D*
Texas Wesleyan University *B*
Texas Woman's University *B, M, T*
Trinity University *B*
Trinity Valley Community College *A*
Tyler Junior College *A*
University of Houston *B, D*
University of North Texas *B, M*
University of St. Thomas *B*

University of Texas
    Arlington *B*
    Austin *B, M, D*
    El Paso *B*
    Pan American *B, M, T*
    San Antonio *B, M*
    Tyler *B*
University of the Incarnate Word *B*
Wayland Baptist University *B*
West Texas A&M University *B, M*
Western Texas College *A*
Wharton County Junior College *A*
Wiley College *B*

Utah
Brigham Young University *B, M*
Dixie State College of Utah *A*
Snow College *A*
Southern Utah University *B, T*
University of Utah *B, M, D*
Utah State University *B*
Utah Valley State College *A*
Weber State University *B*

Vermont
Bennington College *B, M*
Castleton State College *B*
Goddard College *B*
Johnson State College *B*
Marlboro College *B*
Middlebury College *B*
St. Michael's College *B*
University of Vermont *B*

Virginia
Averett University *B*
Bluefield College *B*
Bridgewater College *B*
College of William and Mary *B*
Eastern Mennonite University *B*
Emory & Henry College *B, T*
Hampton University *B*
Hollins University *B*
J. Sargeant Reynolds Community
    College *C, A*
Liberty University *B*
Longwood University *B, T*
Lynchburg College *B*
Mary Baldwin College *B*
Norfolk State University *B*
Radford University *B, M*
Randolph-Macon College *B*
Roanoke College *B, T*
Shenandoah University *B*
Sweet Briar College *B*
University of Richmond *B*
University of Virginia *B, M, D*
Virginia Polytechnic Institute and State
    University *B, T*
Virginia Union University *B*
Virginia Wesleyan College *B*
Washington and Lee University *B*

Washington
Central Washington University *B, M*
Centralia College *A*
Eastern Washington University *B, M, T*
Everett Community College *A*
Lower Columbia College *A*
North Seattle Community College *A*
Northwest College *B*
Olympic College *A*
Pacific Lutheran University *B*
St. Martin's College *B*
Seattle Pacific University *B*
University of Puget Sound *B*
University of Washington *B, M, D*
Walla Walla College *B*
Washington State University *B*
Western Washington University *B, M, T*
Whitman College *B*
Whitworth College *B, T*

West Virginia
Alderson-Broaddus College *B*
Bethany College *B*
Concord College *B*

Marshall University *M*
Potomac State College of West Virginia
    University *A*
Shepherd College *B*
University of Charleston *B*
West Virginia University *B, M, D, T*
West Virginia Wesleyan College *B*

Wisconsin
Alverno College *B*
Beloit College *B*
Carroll College *B*
Carthage College *B, T*
Edgewood College *B*
Lakeland College *B*
Lawrence University *B, T*
Marian College of Fond du Lac *B*
Northland College *B*
Ripon College *B, T*
St. Norbert College *B, T*
Silver Lake College *B*
University of Wisconsin
    Eau Claire *B*
    Green Bay *B*
    La Crosse *B*
    Madison *B, M, D*
    Milwaukee *B, M*
    Oshkosh *B*
    Parkside *B, T*
    Platteville *B*
    River Falls *B*
    Stevens Point *B*
    Superior *B, M, T*
    Whitewater *B, T*
Viterbo University *B, T*
Wisconsin Lutheran College *B*

Wyoming
Central Wyoming College *A*
Eastern Wyoming College *A*
Laramie County Community College *A*
Sheridan College *A*
University of Wyoming *B, M*
Western Wyoming Community
    College *A*

Music history/literature

Alabama
Birmingham-Southern College *B*

Arkansas
Ouachita Baptist University *B*

California
California State University
    Fullerton *M*
    Hayward *M*
    Long Beach *B*
    Northridge *B, M*
Foothill College *C*
Mills College *M*
Pepperdine University *B*
San Diego State University *M*
San Francisco State University *M*
University of California
    Santa Barbara *D*
University of Redlands *B*
University of Southern California *M, D*
University of the Pacific *B*
Whittier College *B*

Colorado
University of Colorado
    Boulder *D*
University of Denver *M*

Connecticut
Connecticut College *B*
University of Hartford *B, M*
Yale University *M, D*

District of Columbia
Catholic University of America *B, M, D*
Howard University *B*

Florida
Broward Community College *A*
Florida State University *B*
Polk Community College *A*
South Florida Community College *A*

Idaho
University of Idaho *B*

Illinois
Illinois State University *B, M, T*
Illinois Valley Community College *A*
Lincoln College *A*
North Park University *B*
Northwestern University *B, M, D*
Rockford College *B*
Roosevelt University *B*
University of Illinois
    Urbana-Champaign *B*
Wheaton College *B*

Indiana
American Conservatory of
    Music *B, M, D*
Ball State University *M, D*
Butler University *B, M*
St. Joseph's College *B*

Iowa
Luther College *B*
University of Iowa *B, M, D*
University of Northern Iowa *M*

Kansas
University of Kansas *B, M*

Kentucky
University of Kentucky *B, M, D*
University of Louisville *B, M, D*

Louisiana
University of New Orleans *B*

Maryland
Johns Hopkins University *B, M, D*
Johns Hopkins University: Peabody
    Conservatory of Music *M*

Massachusetts
Atlantic Union College *B*
Berkshire Community College *A*
Boston University *B, M, D*
Brandeis University *M, D*
Hampshire College *B*
Harvard College *B*
New England Conservatory of
    Music *B, M*
Northeastern University *B*
Simmons College *B*
Tufts University *B, M*
Wellesley College *B*

Michigan
Calvin College *B*
Central Michigan University *B, T*
Michigan State University *M, D*
Northern Michigan University *B, T*
University of Michigan *M, D*

Missouri
University of Missouri
    Kansas City *M*
Washington University in St.
    Louis *B, M, D*

New Hampshire
Keene State College *B*
University of New Hampshire *B*

New Jersey
Seton Hall University *B*

New York
Bard College *B*
City University of New York
    Hunter College *B, M*
    Queensborough Community
        College *A*
Eastman School of Music of the
    University of Rochester *M, D*

Hofstra University *B*
Nazareth College of Rochester *B*
Sarah Lawrence College *B*
State University of New York
 Buffalo *M, D*
 College at Fredonia *B*
 College at Potsdam *M*
 New Paltz *B*
Syracuse University *M*
University of Rochester *M, D*

North Carolina
University of North Carolina
 Chapel Hill *M, D*
 Greensboro *B, T*

Ohio
Baldwin-Wallace College *B*
Bowling Green State University *B, M*
Case Western Reserve University *M*
Cedarville University *B*
College of Wooster *B*
Oberlin College *B, M*
Ohio State University
 Columbus Campus *B*
Ohio University *B, M*
Otterbein College *B*
Sinclair Community College *A*
University of Akron *B, M*
University of Cincinnati *B, M*
Youngstown State University *B, M*

Oklahoma
University of Oklahoma *M*

Oregon
University of Oregon *M, D*

Pennsylvania
Bucknell University *B*
La Salle University *B*
Lafayette College *B*
Penn State
 University Park *M*
Swarthmore College *B*
Temple University *B, M*
West Chester University of
 Pennsylvania *B, M*

South Carolina
Furman University *B*
North Greenville College *A, B*
University of South Carolina *M*

South Dakota
University of South Dakota *M*

Texas
Baylor University *B, M*
Lon Morris College *A*
McMurry University *T*
Rice University *B, M*
Sam Houston State University *B*
Southern Methodist University *M*
Southwestern University *B*
Texas A&M University
 Commerce *B*
Texas Christian University *B*
Texas Lutheran University *B*
Texas Tech University *M*
University of Houston *M*
University of North Texas *B*
University of Texas
 Austin *B*

Utah
University of Utah *M*

Vermont
Bennington College *B, M*
Johnson State College *B*
Marlboro College *B*

Virginia
Mary Baldwin College *B*
Mary Washington College *B*
Randolph-Macon Woman's College *B*
University of Richmond *B*

Washington
University of Washington *B*
Western Washington University *B*

Wisconsin
Lawrence University *B, T*
University of Wisconsin
 La Crosse *B*
 Madison *B, M, D*
 Stevens Point *B*

Music management

Arkansas
Central Baptist College *B*

California
Bethesda Christian University *B, M*
Diablo Valley College *C*
Los Medanos College *C*
Point Loma Nazarene University *B*
University of Southern California *B*
University of the Pacific *B*

Connecticut
University of Hartford *B*
University of New Haven *B*

District of Columbia
Howard University *B*

Florida
Florida Southern College *B*
Jacksonville University *B*
University of Miami *B, M*

Idaho
Boise State University *B*
University of Idaho *B*

Illinois
Columbia College Chicago *B*
De Paul University *B*
Elmhurst College *B*
Lewis University *B*
Millikin University *B*
Quincy University *B*
Roosevelt University *B*

Indiana
Anderson University *B*
Butler University *B*
DePauw University *B*
Indiana University-Purdue University
 Indianapolis *M*
Taylor University *B*
University of Evansville *B*
Valparaiso University *B*

Iowa
Drake University *B*
Luther College *B*
Waldorf College *A, B*

Kansas
Benedictine College *B*
Central Christian College *A*
Labette Community College *A*
Tabor College *B*

Kentucky
Union College *B*

Louisiana
Dillard University *B*
Loyola University New Orleans *B*

Massachusetts
Berklee College of Music *B*
Northeastern University *B*

Michigan
Ferris State University *B*

Minnesota
Minnesota State University
 Mankato *B, M, T*
 Moorhead *B*
St. Mary's University of Minnesota *B*
Winona State University *B*

Missouri
College of the Ozarks *B*
Drury University *B*
University of Missouri
 St. Louis *B*

Nebraska
Northeast Community College *A*

New Hampshire
Franklin Pierce College *B*

New Jersey
Bloomfield College *B*
Monmouth University *B*
William Paterson University of New
 Jersey *B*

New York
City University of New York
 Baruch College *B*
Concordia College *B*
Hofstra University *B*
New York University *B*
State University of New York
 College at Fredonia *B*
 College at Oneonta *B, M*
 College at Potsdam *B*
Syracuse University *B*
Villa Maria College of Buffalo *A*

North Carolina
Chowan College *A*
St. Augustine's College *B*
Wingate University *B*
Winston-Salem State University *B*

Ohio
Baldwin-Wallace College *B*
Heidelberg College *B*
Ohio Northern University *B*
Otterbein College *B*
University of Rio Grande *B*

Oklahoma
Northern Oklahoma College *A*
Oklahoma City University *B*
Oklahoma State University *B*
Southwestern Oklahoma State
 University *B*

Oregon
Southern Oregon University *B*

Pennsylvania
Cheyney University of Pennsylvania *B*
Geneva College *B*
Grove City College *B*
Harrisburg Area Community College *A*
Waynesburg College *B*

South Carolina
South Carolina State University *B*

Tennessee
Belmont University *B*
Bryan College *B*
Middle Tennessee State University *B*
Trevecca Nazarene University *B*
University of Memphis *B*

Texas
Angelina College *A*
Collin County Community College
 District *C, A*
Houston Community College
 System *C, A*
University of Texas
 Arlington *B*
 San Antonio *B*
University of the Incarnate Word *B*

Vermont
Johnson State College *B*

Washington
Central Washington University *B*
Northwest College *B*
University of Puget Sound *B*

West Virginia
Davis and Elkins College *B*
University of Charleston *B*

Wisconsin
Marian College of Fond du Lac *B*

Music pedagogy

Illinois
Trinity International University *B*

Indiana
Butler University *B, M*
Goshen College *B*

Iowa
Drake University *B*

Minnesota
University of Minnesota
 Duluth *B*

New York
Ithaca College *M*

Oklahoma
Oklahoma State University *M*

Tennessee
Belmont University *B*
Bryan College *B*

Texas
Texas A&M University
 Commerce *B, M*
Texas Christian University *B, M*

Utah
Brigham Young University *B*
University of Utah *M*

Wisconsin
Alverno College *A*
Viterbo University *B*

Music performance

Alabama
Alabama Agricultural and Mechanical
 University *B, M*
Alabama State University *B, M*
Huntingdon College *B*
Samford University *B*
Talladega College *B*
University of Montevallo *B, M*

Alaska
University of Alaska
 Anchorage *B*
 Fairbanks *B, M*

Arizona
Arizona State University *B, M, D*
Northern Arizona University *B*
University of Arizona *B, M*

Arkansas
Arkansas State University *B, M*
Harding University *B*
Henderson State University *B*
Ouachita Baptist University *B*
University of Arkansas *B*
University of Central Arkansas *B, M*

California
Antelope Valley College *C*
Azusa Pacific University *B*
Bethesda Christian University *B, M*
Biola University *B*
California Institute of the Arts *C, B, M*

California State University
  Chico *B*
  Dominguez Hills *B*
  Fullerton *B, M*
  Hayward *M*
  Long Beach *B, M*
  Los Angeles *B*
  Northridge *B, M*
  Sacramento *B, M*
  Stanislaus *B*
Chabot College *A*
Chapman University *B*
Christian Heritage College *B*
Dominican University of California *B*
Foothill College *C*
Fresno Pacific University *B*
Gavilan Community College *A*
Golden West College *C, A*
Holy Names College *B, M*
Los Medanos College *C, A*
Master's College *B*
Mills College *M*
Mount St. Mary's College *B*
Pacific Union College *B*
San Diego State University *B, M*
San Francisco State University *B, M*
San Jose State University *B, M*
Sierra College *A*
Simpson College *B*
University of California
  Irvine *B, M*
  Los Angeles *M*
University of Redlands *B*
University of Southern
  California *B, M, D*
University of the Pacific *R*

Colorado
Colorado Christian University *B*
Colorado State University *B*
Fort Lewis College *B*
Metropolitan State College of Denver *B*
University of Colorado
  Boulder *B, M, D*
University of Denver *B, M*

Connecticut
University of Connecticut *D*
University of Hartford *B, M, D*
Yale University *M, D*

Delaware
University of Delaware *B, M*

District of Columbia
Catholic University of America *B, M, D*
George Washington University *M*

Florida
Florida Agricultural and Mechanical
  University *B*
Florida State University *C, B, M, D*
Hobe Sound Bible College *B*
Jacksonville University *B*
Polk Community College *A*
South Florida Community College *A*
Stetson University *B*
University of Central Florida *B*
University of Miami *B, M, D*
University of North Florida *B*
University of South Florida *B, M*
University of Tampa *B*
University of West Florida *B*

Georgia
Augusta State University *B*
Berry College *B*
Brenau University *B*
Brewton-Parker College *B*
Clayton College and State
  University *A, B*
Columbus State University *B, M*
Covenant College *B*
Emmanuel College *B*
Gainesville College *A*
Georgia College and State University *B*
Georgia Southern University *B*

Georgia Southwestern State University *B*
Georgia State University *B, M*
Kennesaw State University *B*
LaGrange College *B*
Mercer University *B*
Savannah State University *B*
State University of West Georgia *B, M*
Toccoa Falls College *B*
University of Georgia *B*
Valdosta State University *B*

Hawaii
Brigham Young University-Hawaii *B*
University of Hawaii
  Manoa *B, M*

Idaho
Boise State University *B, M*
Idaho State University *B*
North Idaho College *A*
Northwest Nazarene University *B*
University of Idaho *B*

Illinois
Augustana College *B*
Benedictine University *B*
Blackburn College *B, T*
Bradley University *B*
Columbia College Chicago *B*
Concordia University *B*
De Paul University *B, M*
Elmhurst College *C*
Eureka College *B*
Illinois State University *B*
Illinois Valley Community College *A*
Illinois Wesleyan University *B*
Judson College *B*
Lincoln College *A*
Millikin University *B*
Moody Bible Institute *B*
North Central College *B*
North Park University *B*
Northern Illinois University *M*
Northwestern University *C, B, D*
Olivet Nazarene University *B*
Parkland College *A*
Quincy University *B, T*
Roosevelt University *B, M*
Sauk Valley Community College *A*
Trinity Christian College *B*
Trinity International University *B*
University of Illinois
  Urbana-Champaign *B*
Wheaton College *B*

Indiana
American Conservatory of
  Music *C, A, B, M, D*
Anderson University *B*
Butler University *B, M*
DePauw University *B*
Goshen College *B*
Grace College *B*
Huntington College *B*
Indiana University
  Bloomington *B, M, D*
  South Bend *B, M*
Indiana University-Purdue University
  Fort Wayne *B*
Indiana Wesleyan University *B, T*
Manchester College *B*
Martin University *B*
Oakland City University *B*
Saint Mary's College *B*
St. Mary-of-the-Woods College *B*
Taylor University *B*
University of Evansville *B*
Valparaiso University *B, M*
Vincennes University *A*

Iowa
Coe College *B*
Cornell College *B*
Drake University *B*
Luther College *B*
Morningside College *B*
Simpson College *B*

Southwestern Community College *A*
University of Iowa *B, M, D*
University of Northern Iowa *B, M*
Waldorf College *A, B*
Wartburg College *B*

Kansas
Baker University *B*
Bethany College *B*
Central Christian College *A*
Friends University *B*
Kansas State University *B*
Kansas Wesleyan University *B*
McPherson College *B*
MidAmerica Nazarene University *B*
Pittsburg State University *B*
Seward County Community College *A*
University of Kansas *B, M, D*
Washburn University of Topeka *B*

Kentucky
Berea College *B, T*
Campbellsville University *B*
Kentucky Christian College *B, T*
Morehead State University *M*
Murray State University *B*
Transylvania University *B*
Union College *B*
University of Kentucky *B, M*
University of Louisville *B, M*

Louisiana
Centenary College of Louisiana *B, T*
Grambling State University *B*
Louisiana College *B*
Louisiana State University and
  Agricultural and Mechanical
  College *B, M, D*
Louisiana Tech University *B*
Loyola University New Orleans *B, M*
McNeese State University *B*
Northwestern State University *M*
Southeastern Louisiana University *B, M*
Southern University and Agricultural and
  Mechanical College *B*
University of Louisiana at
  Lafayette *B, M*
University of Louisiana at Monroe *B*
University of New Orleans *B, M*
Xavier University of Louisiana *B*

Maine
University of Maine *B, M*
University of Southern Maine *B*

Maryland
College of Notre Dame of Maryland *B*
Johns Hopkins University *B, M, D*
Johns Hopkins University: Peabody
  Conservatory of Music *B, M, D*
Salisbury University *B*
Towson University *M*
University of Maryland
  College Park *B*
Washington Bible College *A, B*

Massachusetts
Anna Maria College *B*
Berklee College of Music *B*
Berkshire Community College *A*
Boston Conservatory *B, M*
Boston University *B, M, D*
Brandeis University *M, D*
Gordon College *B*
Greenfield Community College *C*
Hampshire College *B*
New England Conservatory of
  Music *B, M, D*
Northeastern University *B*
Simmons College *B*
University of Massachusetts
  Amherst *B, M, D*
  Lowell *B, M*
Westfield State College *B*

Michigan
Andrews University *B, M*
Aquinas College *A*

Calvin College *B*
Central Michigan University *M, T*
Cornerstone University *B, T*
Eastern Michigan University *B, M*
Grace Bible College *B*
Hope College *B*
Lansing Community College *A*
Marygrove College *B*
Michigan State University *B, M, D*
Oakland University *B, M*
University of Michigan *B, M, D, T*
University of Michigan
  Flint *B*
Western Michigan University *B*
William Tyndale College *B*

Minnesota
Augsburg College *B*
Bethel College *B*
College of St. Catherine *B*
Concordia College: Moorhead *B*
Gustavus Adolphus College *B*
Hamline University *B*
Minnesota State University
  Mankato *B, M, T*
  Moorhead *B*
North Central University *B*
Northwestern College *B*
St. Mary's University of Minnesota *B*
St. Olaf College *B*
University of Minnesota
  Duluth *B, M*
  Twin Cities *B, M, D*
University of St. Thomas *B*
Winona State University *B*

Mississippi
Alcorn State University *B*
Millsaps College *B, T*
Mississippi College *B, M*
University of Southern Mississippi *D*

Missouri
Central Methodist College *B*
Drury University *B*
Evangel University *B*
Hannibal-LaGrange College *B*
Missouri Baptist University *B*
Southeast Missouri State University *B*
Southwest Missouri State University *B*
Truman State University *B*
University of Missouri
  Kansas City *B, M, D*
  St. Louis *B*
Webster University *M*
William Jewell College *B*

Montana
Rocky Mountain College *B*
University of Montana-Missoula *B, M*

Nebraska
Hastings College *B, T*
Nebraska Wesleyan University *B*
Northeast Community College *A*
Union College *B*
University of Nebraska
  Kearney *B*
  Omaha *B*

Nevada
University of Nevada
  Reno *B*

New Hampshire
Franklin Pierce College *B*
Keene State College *B*
University of New Hampshire *B*

New Jersey
Caldwell College *B*
Middlesex County College *A*
Montclair State University *B*
Rowan University *B*
Seton Hall University *B*
William Paterson University of New
  Jersey *B*

New Mexico
University of New Mexico *B, M*

New York
Bard College *B, M*
City University of New York
　Brooklyn College *B, M*
　City College *B, M*
　Hunter College *B, M*
　Queens College *B, M*
Concordia College *B*
Dutchess Community College *C*
Eastman School of Music of the
　University of Rochester *B, M, D*
Hofstra University *B*
Houghton College *B*
Ithaca College *B, M, T*
Jamestown Community College *A*
Juilliard School *B, M, D*
Manhattan School of Music *B, M, D*
Mannes College of Music *B, M*
Monroe Community College *A*
Nassau Community College *A*
Nazareth College of Rochester *B*
New York University *B, M, D*
Nyack College *B*
Sarah Lawrence College *B*
State University of New York
　Albany *B*
　Binghamton *B, M*
　Buffalo *B, M*
　College at Fredonia *B*
　College at Geneseo *B*
　College at Potsdam *B, M*
　New Paltz *B*
　Purchase *B, M*
　Stony Brook *M, D*
Syracuse University *B, M*
University of Rochester *M, D*
Villa Maria College of Buffalo *A*
Wagner College *B*
Westchester Community College *A*

North Carolina
Appalachian State University *B, M*
Catawba College *B*
Duke University *M*
East Carolina University *B, M*
Elon University *B*
Gardner-Webb University *B*
Greensboro College *B, T*
Lenoir-Rhyne College *B*
Mars Hill College *B*
Meredith College *B, M*
Methodist College *B*
North Carolina School of the Arts *B, M*
Peace College *B*
Queens University of Charlotte *B*
St. Augustine's College *B*
Salem College *B*
University of North Carolina
　Chapel Hill *B*
　Charlotte *B, T*
　Greensboro *B, M*
　Pembroke *B*
　Wilmington *B*
Western Carolina University *B*
Wingate University *B*

North Dakota
Jamestown College *B*
Minot State University *B*
North Dakota State University *B*
University of North Dakota *B*

Ohio
Ashland University *B*
Baldwin-Wallace College *B*
Bowling Green State University *B, M*
Cedarville University *B*
Cleveland Institute of Music *B, M, D*
College of Wooster *B*
Heidelberg College *B*
Kent State University *B*
Kent State University
　Stark Campus *B*

Miami University
　Oxford Campus *B, M*
Mount Union College *B*
Mount Vernon Nazarene University *B*
Ohio Northern University *B*
Ohio State University
　Columbus Campus *B*
Ohio University *B, M*
Ohio Wesleyan University *B*
Otterbein College *B*
Sinclair Community College *A*
University of Akron *B, M*
University of Cincinnati *B, M, D*
University of Dayton *B*
University of Toledo *M*
Wittenberg University *B*
Wright State University *B*
Youngstown State University *B, M*

Oklahoma
Langston University *B*
Northwestern Oklahoma State
　University *B*
Oklahoma Baptist University *B*
Oklahoma Christian University of
　Science and Arts *B*
Oklahoma City University *B, M*
Oklahoma State University *B*
Oral Roberts University *B*
Southwestern Oklahoma State
　University *B*
University of Central Oklahoma *B*
University of Tulsa *B*

Oregon
Lewis & Clark College *B*
Linfield College *B*
Pacific University *B*
Portland Community College *C, A*
Portland State University *B, M*
University of Oregon *B, M, D*
Western Baptist College *B*
Willamette University *B*

Pennsylvania
Bucknell University *B*
Carnegie Mellon University *B, M*
Community College of Philadelphia *A*
Curtis Institute of Music *C, B*
Duquesne University *B, M*
Gettysburg College *B*
Grove City College *B*
Indiana University of Pennsylvania *B*
Lebanon Valley College of
　Pennsylvania *B*
Lock Haven University of
　Pennsylvania *B*
Marywood University *B*
Mercyhurst College *B*
Moravian College *B*
Penn State
　University Park *B, M*
Philadelphia Biblical University *B*
St. Vincent College *B*
Seton Hill University *B*
Slippery Rock University of
　Pennsylvania *B*
Temple University *C, B, M, D*
Valley Forge Christian College *B*
West Chester University of
　Pennsylvania *B, M*
Wilkes University *B*
York College of Pennsylvania *B*

Puerto Rico
Conservatory of Music of Puerto
　Rico *B, T*
Inter American University of Puerto Rico
　San German Campus *B*

Rhode Island
Rhode Island College *B*
University of Rhode Island *B*

South Carolina
Anderson College *B, T*
Charleston Southern University *B*

Coker College *B, T*
Columbia International University *B*
Furman University *B*
North Greenville College *A, B*
University of South Carolina *M, D*

South Dakota
University of South Dakota *B, M*

Tennessee
Belmont University *B*
Bryan College *B*
Carson-Newman College *B*
Lambuth University *B*
Lee University *B*
Maryville College *B, T*
Roane State Community College *A*
Southern Adventist University *B*
Tennessee Technological University *B*
Union University *B*
Vanderbilt University *B*

Texas
Baylor University *B, M*
Del Mar College *A*
Hardin-Simmons University *B, M*
Houston Baptist University *B*
Houston Community College
　System *C, A*
Lon Morris College *A*
Midland College *A*
Prairie View A&M University *B*
Rice University *B, M*
Sam Houston State University *B, M*
Southern Methodist University *B, M*
Southwest Texas State University *B, M*
Southwestern University *B*
Stephen F. Austin State University *B, M*
Texas A&M University
　Commerce *B, M*
Texas Christian University *C, B, M*
Texas Lutheran University *B*
Texas Tech University *B, M, D*
Texas Woman's University *B, M*
Trinity University *B*
Tyler Junior College *A*
University of Houston *B, M, D*
University of Mary Hardin-Baylor *B, T*
University of North Texas *B, M, D*
University of Texas
　Arlington *T*
　Austin *B*
　El Paso *B, M*
　San Antonio *B, M*
West Texas A&M University *B, M*

Utah
University of Utah *M*
Weber State University *B*

Vermont
Bennington College *B, M*
Johnson State College *B*
Marlboro College *B*
University of Vermont *B*

Virginia
Averett University *B*
Bluefield College *B*
George Mason University *B, M*
Hampton University *B*
James Madison University *B, M, T*
Longwood University *B*
Mary Baldwin College *B*
Mary Washington College *B*
Norfolk State University *M*
Old Dominion University *B*
Piedmont Virginia Community
　College *A*
Randolph-Macon Woman's College *B*
Shenandoah University *B, M, D*
University of Richmond *B*
Virginia Commonwealth
　University *B, M*
Virginia State University *B*

Washington
Central Washington University *B*

Cornish College of the Arts *B*
Eastern Washington University *B, T*
Everett Community College *A*
Gonzaga University *B*
Pacific Lutheran University *B*
University of Puget Sound *B*
University of Washington *B, M, D*
Walla Walla College *B*
Washington State University *B, M*
Western Washington University *B*
Whitworth College *B, T*

West Virginia
Alderson-Broaddus College *B*

Wisconsin
Cardinal Stritch University *B*
Carthage College *B, T*
Lawrence University *B, T*
Maranatha Baptist Bible College *B*
Northland College *B, T*
University of Wisconsin
　La Crosse *B, T*
　Madison *B, M, D*
　Stevens Point *B*
　Superior *B, M*
Viterbo University *B*

Wyoming
Casper College *A*
University of Wyoming *B*

Music teacher education

Alabama
Alabama Agricultural and Mechanical
　University *B*
Alabama State University *B, M*
Auburn University *B, M, D, T*
Birmingham-Southern College *B, T*
Huntingdon College *B, T*
Jacksonville State University *B, M, T*
Judson College *B*
Oakwood College *B*
Samford University *B, M*
Shelton State Community College *A*
Talladega College *B*
University of Alabama *B, M, D*
University of Alabama
　Birmingham *T*
University of Mobile *B, T*
University of Montevallo *B, M, T*
University of North Alabama *B*

Alaska
University of Alaska
　Anchorage *B*
　Fairbanks *B*

Arizona
Arizona State University *B, M*
Northern Arizona University *B, T*
Prescott College *B, M, T*
South Mountain Community College *A*
University of Arizona *B, M, D*

Arkansas
Arkansas State University *B, M, T*
Arkansas Tech University *B*
Harding University *B, M, T*
John Brown University *B*
Ouachita Baptist University *B, T*
Southern Arkansas University *B, T*
University of Arkansas *M*
University of Arkansas
　Monticello *B*
University of Central Arkansas *M, T*
University of the Ozarks *T*
Williams Baptist College *B*

California
Azusa Pacific University *T*
Biola University *B, T*
California Baptist University *T*
California State Polytechnic University:
　Pomona *T*

California State University
    Bakersfield *B, T*
    Chico *T*
    Dominguez Hills *T*
    Fullerton *B, T*
    Hayward *M*
    Long Beach *M, T*
    Northridge *B, T*
    Sacramento *T*
    San Bernardino *T*
Chapman University *B*
Christian Heritage College *B, T*
Concordia University *B*
Fresno Pacific University *B, T*
Holy Names College *M*
Hope International University *B*
Humboldt State University *T*
La Sierra University *M*
Los Angeles Southwest College *A*
Master's College *T*
Mount St. Mary's College *T*
Occidental College *T*
Pacific Union College *B, T*
Pepperdine University *B*
San Francisco State University *B, T*
San Jose State University *T*
Simpson College *B, T*
Sonoma State University *T*
University of Redlands *B, T*
University of Southern
    California *B, M, D*
University of the Pacific *B, T*

Colorado
Colorado State University *T*
Colorado State University
    Pueblo *T*
Fort Lewis College *T*
Metropolitan State College of
    Denver *B, T*
University of Colorado
    Boulder *B, M, D, T*
University of Denver *M*
University of Northern Colorado *B, M, T*

Connecticut
Central Connecticut State
    University *B, M, T*
University of Connecticut *B*
University of Hartford *B, M, D*
Western Connecticut State
    University *B, M*

Delaware
Delaware State University *B*
University of Delaware *B, T*

District of Columbia
Catholic University of America *B, T*
George Washington University *M, T*
Howard University *B, M*

Florida
Baptist College of Florida *B*
Bethune-Cookman College *B, T*
Broward Community College *A*
Florida Agricultural and Mechanical
    University *B, T*
Florida Atlantic University *B*
Florida International University *B, M, T*
Florida Southern College *B*
Florida State University *B, M, D, T*
Hobe Sound Bible College *B, T*
Jacksonville University *B, M, T*
Manatee Community College *A*
Palm Beach Atlantic University *B*
Palm Beach Community College *A*
Pensacola Junior College *A*
South Florida Community College *A*
Southeastern College of the Assemblies
    of God *B, T*
Stetson University *B, T*
University of Central Florida *B, M*
University of Florida *B, M, D*
University of Miami *B, M, D, T*
University of North Florida *B, M*
University of South Florida *B, M*

University of Tampa *B, T*
University of West Florida *B, T*
Warner Southern College *B*

Georgia
Albany State University *M*
Armstrong Atlantic State
    University *B, M, T*
Augusta State University *B, M*
Berry College *B, T*
Brenau University *B*
Brewton-Parker College *B*
Clark Atlanta University *B*
Columbus State University *B, M*
Emmanuel College *B*
Fort Valley State University *B, T*
Gainesville College *A*
Georgia College and State University *B*
Georgia Southern University *B, M, T*
Georgia Southwestern State University *B*
Kennesaw State University *B*
Mercer University *B, T*
North Georgia College & State
    University *B, M*
Paine College *B*
Piedmont College *M, T*
Shorter College *B, T*
State University of West Georgia *B, M*
Thomas University *B*
Toccoa Falls College *B, T*
University of Georgia *B, M, D, T*
Valdosta State University *B, M*
Young Harris College *A*

Hawaii
University of Hawaii
    Manoa *B, T*

Idaho
Boise State University *B, T*
Brigham Young University - Idaho *T*
Idaho State University *B, T*
Northwest Nazarene University *B*
University of Idaho *B*

Illinois
Augustana College *B, T*
Benedictine University *B, T*
Blackburn College *B, T*
Bradley University *B, T*
Chicago State University *B*
College of Lake County *A*
Concordia University *B, M, T*
De Paul University *B, M, T*
Elmhurst College *B*
Eureka College *T*
Greenville College *B, T*
Illinois College *T*
Illinois Eastern Community Colleges
    Lincoln Trail College *A*
    Olney Central College *A*
Illinois State University *B, M, T*
Illinois Wesleyan University *B*
Judson College *B, T*
Loyola University of Chicago *T*
MacMurray College *B, T*
McKendree College *B, D, T*
Millikin University *B, T*
Monmouth College *B, T*
North Central College *B, T*
North Park University *T*
Northern Illinois University *M*
Northwestern University *B, M, D, T*
Olivet Nazarene University *B, T*
Quincy University *B, T*
Roosevelt University *B, M*
St. Xavier University *B*
Sauk Valley Community College *A*
Trinity Christian College *B, T*
Trinity International University *B, T*
University of Illinois
    Urbana-Champaign *B, M, D, T*
VanderCook College of Music *B, M, T*
Waubonsee Community College *A*
Wheaton College *B, T*

Indiana
Anderson University *B, T*
Ball State University *T*
Bethel College *B*
Butler University *B, M, T*
DePauw University *B*
Goshen College *B*
Grace College *B*
Huntington College *B*
Indiana University
    Bloomington *B, M, D, T*
    South Bend *B, T*
Indiana University-Purdue University
    Fort Wayne *B, T*
Indiana Wesleyan University *B, T*
Manchester College *B, T*
Oakland City University *B*
Saint Mary's College *T*
St. Mary-of-the-Woods College *B*
Taylor University *B, T*
University of Evansville *B*
University of Indianapolis *B, T*
Valparaiso University *B, M*
Vincennes University *A*

Iowa
Briar Cliff University *B*
Central College *B, T*
Clarke College *B, T*
Cornell College *B, T*
Dordt College *B*
Drake University *B*
Faith Baptist Bible College and
    Theological Seminary *B*
Franciscan University *B, T*
Graceland University *T*
Iowa State University *B, T*
Iowa Wesleyan College *B*
Loras College *B*
Luther College *B*
Morningside College *B*
Mount Mercy College *T*
Northwestern College *T*
St. Ambrose University *B, T*
Simpson College *B*
University of Iowa *B, M, D, T*
University of Northern Iowa *B, M*
Wartburg College *B, T*

Kansas
Allen County Community College *A*
Baker University *B, T*
Benedictine College *B, T*
Bethany College *B*
Bethel College *T*
Central Christian College *A, B*
Emporia State University *B, T*
Fort Hays State University *B*
Fort Scott Community College *A*
Friends University *B*
Garden City Community College *A*
Independence Community College *A*
Kansas State University *B, M, T*
Labette Community College *A*
McPherson College *B, T*
MidAmerica Nazarene University *B, T*
Ottawa University *B, T*
Pittsburg State University *B, T*
Southwestern College *B, T*
Sterling College *B*
Tabor College *B*
University of Kansas *B, M, D, T*
Washburn University of Topeka *B*
Wichita State University *B, M*

Kentucky
Asbury College *B, T*
Bellarmine University *B, T*
Berea College *B, T*
Campbellsville University *B, M*
Cumberland College *B, T*
Georgetown College *B*
Kentucky Christian College *B*
Kentucky Wesleyan College *T*
Morehead State University *B, M*
Murray State University *B, M, T*

Transylvania University *B, T*
Union College *B, M*
University of Kentucky *B, M*
University of Louisville *M*

Louisiana
Centenary College of Louisiana *B, T*
Grambling State University *B*
Louisiana College *B*
Louisiana State University and
    Agricultural and Mechanical
    College *B*
Louisiana Tech University *B*
Loyola University New Orleans *B, M*
McNeese State University *B, M, T*
Nicholls State University *B*
Northwestern State University *B*
Southeastern Louisiana University *B*
Southern University and Agricultural and
    Mechanical College *B*
University of Louisiana at Lafayette *B*
University of Louisiana at Monroe *B*
University of New Orleans *B*
Xavier University of Louisiana *B*

Maine
University of Maine *B*
University of Southern Maine *B, T*

Maryland
College of Notre Dame of Maryland *T*
Columbia Union College *B*
Community College of Baltimore County
    Catonsville *A*
    Dundalk *A*
    Essex *A*
Frostburg State University *B, T*
Johns Hopkins University *M*
Johns Hopkins University: Peabody
    Conservatory of Music *B, M*
Montgomery College
    Rockville Campus *A*
St. Mary's College of Maryland *T*
Salisbury University *T*
Towson University *B, M, T*
University of Maryland
    College Park *B*
Washington Bible College *B, T*

Massachusetts
Anna Maria College *B, T*
Berklee College of Music *B*
Boston Conservatory *B, M*
Boston University *B, M, D*
Bridgewater State College *T*
Gordon College *B*
New England Conservatory of Music *M*
Northeastern University *B*
Smith College *M*
Tufts University *M*
University of Massachusetts
    Dartmouth *T*
    Lowell *B, M*
Westfield State College *B, M, T*

Michigan
Adrian College *B, T*
Alma College *T*
Andrews University *M, T*
Aquinas College *B, T*
Calvin College *B*
Central Michigan University *B, M*
Concordia University *B, T*
Cornerstone University *B, T*
Eastern Michigan University *B, T*
Grace Bible College *B*
Grand Valley State University *B, T*
Hope College *B, T*
Lansing Community College *A*
Madonna University *B*
Michigan State University *B, M, D*
Northern Michigan University *B, T*
Oakland University *B*
Spring Arbor University *B*
University of Michigan *B, M, D, T*
University of Michigan
    Flint *B, T*

Western Michigan University *B, M*

Minnesota

Augsburg College *B, T*
Bemidji State University *T*
Bethel College *B*
College of St. Benedict *T*
College of St. Catherine *B, T*
College of St. Scholastica *T*
Concordia College: Moorhead *B, T*
Concordia University: St. Paul *B, T*
Crown College *B, T*
Gustavus Adolphus College *T*
Hamline University *B*
Minnesota State University
    Mankato *B, M, T*
    Moorhead *B, M, T*
Northland Community & Technical
    College *A*
Northwestern College *B*
Ridgewater College: A Community and
    Technical College *A*
St. Cloud State University *M, T*
St. John's University *T*
St. Mary's University of Minnesota *B*
St. Olaf College *B*
Southwest State University *B*
University of Minnesota
    Duluth *B*
    Morris *T*
    Twin Cities *B, M*
University of St. Thomas *B, M, T*
Winona State University *B, T*

Mississippi

Alcorn State University *B*
Blue Mountain College *B*
Coahoma Community College *A*
Delta State University *B, M*
Itawamba Community College *A*
Mississippi College *B, M*
Mississippi State University *B, T*
Mississippi University for Women *B, T*
Mississippi Valley State University *B, T*
Northwest Mississippi Community
    College *A*
University of Mississippi *B, T*
University of Southern
    Mississippi *B, M, D*

Missouri

Avila University *B, T*
Baptist Bible College *B*
Calvary Bible College *B*
Central Methodist College *B*
Central Missouri State
    University *B, M, T*
College of the Ozarks *B, T*
Culver-Stockton College *B, T*
Drury University *B, T*
Evangel University *B, T*
Hannibal-LaGrange College *B*
Lincoln University *B, T*
Lindenwood University *B, M*
Missouri Baptist University *B, T*
Missouri Southern State College *B, T*
Missouri Western State College *B*
Northwest Missouri State
    University *B, M, T*
Southeast Missouri State
    University *B, M, T*
Southwest Baptist University *B, T*
Southwest Missouri State University *B*
Truman State University *M, T*
University of Missouri
    Columbia *B, M, D*
    Kansas City *B, M*
    St. Louis *B, T*
Washington University in St. Louis *M*
Webster University *B, M*
William Jewell College *B, T*

Montana

Montana State University
    Billings *B, T*
    Bozeman *B*
Rocky Mountain College *B, T*

University of Montana-Missoula *B, M, T*
University of Montana: Western *B, T*

Nebraska

Chadron State College *B*
Concordia University *B, T*
Dana College *B*
Doane College *T*
Grace University *B*
Hastings College *B, M, T*
Midland Lutheran College *B, T*
Nebraska Wesleyan University *B*
Northeast Community College *A*
Peru State College *B, T*
Union College *T*
University of Nebraska
    Kearney *B, M, T*
    Lincoln *B, T*
    Omaha *B, T*
Western Nebraska Community
    College *A*
York College *B, T*

Nevada

University of Nevada
    Reno *B*

New Hampshire

Keene State College *B, T*
Plymouth State College *B, T*
University of New Hampshire *B, M, T*

New Jersey

Caldwell College *T*
The College of New Jersey *M, T*
Essex County College *A*
Georgian Court College *T*
Kean University *B*
Monmouth University *B, T*
New Jersey City University *M, D, T*
Rider University *B, M*
Rowan University *B*
William Paterson University of New
    Jersey *B, T*

New Mexico

Eastern New Mexico University *B*
New Mexico Highlands University *B*
New Mexico State University *B*
University of New Mexico *B*
Western New Mexico University *B*

New York

City University of New York
    Brooklyn College *B, M*
    City College *B, T*
    Hunter College *B, M, T*
    Queens College *M, T*
Concordia College *B, T*
Dowling College *B*
Eastman School of Music of the
    University of Rochester *B, M, D, T*
Fordham University *T*
Hartwick College *B, T*
Hofstra University *B, M, T*
Houghton College *B, T*
Ithaca College *B, M, T*
Long Island University
    C. W. Post Campus *B, M, T*
Manhattanville College *M, T*
Molloy College *B*
Monroe Community College *A*
Nazareth College of Rochester *B, M, T*
New York University *B, M, D, T*
Nyack College *B*
Roberts Wesleyan College *B, T*
State University of New York
    Buffalo *M, T*
    College at Fredonia *B, M, T*
    College at Potsdam *B, M, T*
Syracuse University *B, M, T*
University of Rochester *M, D*
Wagner College *T*
Wells College *T*

North Carolina

Appalachian State University *B, M, T*
Bennett College *B, T*

Campbell University *B, T*
Catawba College *B, T*
Chowan College *B*
East Carolina University *B, M*
Elizabeth City State University *B*
Elon University *B, T*
Fayetteville State University *B, T*
Gardner-Webb University *B*
Greensboro College *B, T*
Lenoir-Rhyne College *B, T*
Livingstone College *T*
Mars Hill College *B, T*
Meredith College *B, T*
Methodist College *A, B, T*
North Carolina Agricultural and
    Technical State University *B, T*
North Carolina Central University *B*
Pfeiffer University *B, T*
Piedmont Baptist College *B*
St. Augustine's College *B*
University of North Carolina
    Charlotte *B*
    Greensboro *B, M, D, T*
    Pembroke *B, T*
    Wilmington *B*
Western Carolina University *B, T*
Wingate University *B, T*
Winston-Salem State University *B*

North Dakota

Dickinson State University *B, T*
Jamestown College *B*
Minot State University *B, M*
North Dakota State
    University *B, M, D, T*
University of Mary *B*
University of North Dakota *B, T*
Valley City State University *B, T*

Ohio

Ashland University *B, T*
Baldwin-Wallace College *B, T*
Bluffton College *B*
Bowling Green State University *B, M*
Case Western Reserve
    University *B, M, D*
Cedarville University *B, T*
Central State University *B*
College of Mount St. Joseph *T*
College of Wooster *B*
God's Bible School and College *B*
Heidelberg College *B*
Hiram College *T*
Kent State University *B, M, D, T*
Kent State University
    Stark Campus *B*
Lorain County Community College *A*
Malone College *B*
Miami University
    Oxford Campus *B, M, T*
Mount Union College *B, T*
Mount Vernon Nazarene University *B, T*
Oberlin College *B, M*
Ohio Northern University *B*
Ohio State University
    Columbus Campus *B*
Ohio University *B, T*
Ohio Wesleyan University *B*
Otterbein College *B*
Sinclair Community College *A*
University of Akron *B, M, T*
University of Cincinnati *B, M, D, T*
University of Dayton *B, M, T*
University of Rio Grande *B, T*
University of Toledo *B, M, T*
Wittenberg University *B*
Wright State University *B, M, T*
Xavier University *B, M*
Youngstown State University *B, M, T*

Oklahoma

Cameron University *B, T*
East Central University *B*
Eastern Oklahoma State College *A*
Langston University *B*
Northeastern State University *B*

Northwestern Oklahoma State
    University *B, T*
Oklahoma Baptist University *B, T*
Oklahoma Christian University of
    Science and Arts *B, T*
Oklahoma City University *B*
Oklahoma Panhandle State University *B*
Oklahoma State University *B*
Oklahoma Wesleyan University *B*
Oral Roberts University *B, T*
Southeastern Oklahoma State
    University *B, M, T*
Southern Nazarene University *B*
Southwestern Oklahoma State
    University *B, M, T*
University of Central Oklahoma *B, M*
University of Oklahoma *B, M, D*
University of Tulsa *B, M, T*

Oregon

George Fox University *T*
Linfield College *B, T*
Oregon State University *M*
Portland State University *T*
Southern Oregon University *T*
University of Oregon *B, M, D, T*
University of Portland *B, M, T*
Warner Pacific College *B, T*
Western Baptist College *B*

Pennsylvania

Baptist Bible College of Pennsylvania *B*
Bucknell University *B, T*
Chestnut Hill College *A, B*
Duquesne University *B, M, T*
Elizabethtown College *T*
Geneva College *B, T*
Gettysburg College *B, T*
Gratz College *M*
Grove City College *B, T*
Immaculata University *T*
Indiana University of Pennsylvania *B, T*
Lancaster Bible College *B*
Lebanon Valley College of
    Pennsylvania *B, M, T*
Lincoln University *B, T*
Lycoming College *T*
Marywood University *B, M*
Mercyhurst College *B*
Messiah College *B, T*
Millersville University of
    Pennsylvania *B, T*
Moravian College *B, T*
Penn State
    University Park *B, M, D*
Philadelphia Biblical University *B, T*
St. Vincent College *B, T*
Seton Hill University *B, T*
Slippery Rock University of
    Pennsylvania *B, T*
Temple University *B, M, D, T*
Valley Forge Christian College *B*
West Chester University of
    Pennsylvania *B, M, T*
Wilkes University *B*
York College of Pennsylvania *B, T*

Puerto Rico

Inter American University of Puerto Rico
    San German Campus *B*
Pontifical Catholic University of Puerto
    Rico *B, T*

Rhode Island

Rhode Island College *B, M*
Salve Regina University *B*
University of Rhode Island *B*

South Carolina

Anderson College *B, T*
Charleston Southern University *B*
Claflin University *B*
Coker College *B, T*
Columbia College *B*
Converse College *T*
Erskine College *B, T*
Furman University *B, T*

Lander University *B*
Limestone College *B*
North Greenville College *B, T*
Presbyterian College *B, T*
South Carolina State University *B, T*
Southern Wesleyan University *B, T*
University of South Carolina *M, D*
Winthrop University *B, M, T*

South Dakota
Augustana College *B, T*
Black Hills State University *B, T*
Dakota State University *B, T*
Dakota Wesleyan University *B, T*
Mount Marty College *B*
Northern State University *B, T*
South Dakota State University *B*
University of Sioux Falls *B*
University of South Dakota *B, M, T*

Tennessee
Belmont University *M*
Bryan College *T*
Carson-Newman College *B*
East Tennessee State University *M, T*
Freed-Hardeman University *B, T*
Lambuth University *B, T*
Lane College *B*
Lee University *B*
Maryville College *B, T*
Milligan College *B*
Roane State Community College *A*
Southern Adventist University *B*
Tennessee Technological University *B, T*
Tennessee Wesleyan College *B, T*
Trevecca Nazarene University *B, T*
Union University *B, T*
University of Tennessee
    Chattanooga *B*
    Knoxville *B, T*
    Martin *B, T*

Texas
Abilene Christian University *B, T*
Amarillo College *A*
Arlington Baptist College *B*
Baylor University *B, M, T*
Dallas Baptist University *B*
Del Mar College *A*
East Texas Baptist University *B*
Hardin-Simmons University *B, M, T*
Houston Baptist University *B*
Howard Payne University *B, T*
Lamar University *M, T*
Laredo Community College *A*
Lubbock Christian University *B, T*
McMurry University *T*
Prairie View A&M University *M*
Sam Houston State University *M, T*
Schreiner University *T*
Southern Methodist University *B, M, T*
Southwest Texas State University *M, T*
Southwestern University *B, T*
Stephen F. Austin State University *B, M*
Tarleton State University *B, T*
Texas A&M University
    Commerce *M, T*
    Kingsville *B, M, T*
Texas Christian University *B, M, T*
Texas Lutheran University *B, T*
Texas Tech University *M*
Texas Wesleyan University *B, T*
Texas Woman's University *B, M*
University of Houston *M, D, T*
University of Mary Hardin-Baylor *B, T*
University of North Texas *M, D*
University of St. Thomas *B*
University of Texas
    Arlington *D*
    Austin *M, D*
    El Paso *M*
    Pan American *T*
    San Antonio *M, T*
University of the Incarnate Word *B*
Wayland Baptist University *B, T*
West Texas A&M University *T*

Utah
Brigham Young University *B, M*
Southern Utah University *B, T*
University of Utah *B*
Utah State University *B*
Weber State University *B*

Vermont
Bennington College *B, M, T*
Castleton State College *B, T*
Johnson State College *B*
University of Vermont *B*

Virginia
Bluefield College *B, T*
Bridgewater College *T*
Eastern Mennonite University *T*
Hampton University *M*
Hollins University *T*
James Madison University *T*
Liberty University *B*
Longwood University *B, T*
Radford University *T*
Shenandoah University *B, M, D*
Virginia Wesleyan College *T*

Washington
Central Washington University *B, T*
Eastern Washington University *B, M, T*
Gonzaga University *B, T*
Northwest College *T*
Pacific Lutheran University *T*
Seattle Pacific University *B, T*
University of Puget Sound *B*
University of Washington *B*
Walla Walla College *B*
Western Washington University *T*
Whitworth College *B, T*

West Virginia
Alderson-Broaddus College *B, T*
Concord College *B, T*
Fairmont State College *B*
Potomac State College of West Virginia
    University *A*
Shepherd College *T*
Univcrsity of Charleston *B*
West Liberty State College *B*
West Virginia State College *B*
West Virginia University *T*
West Virginia Wesleyan College *B*

Wisconsin
Alverno College *B, T*
Carroll College *B, T*
Carthage College *B, T*
Concordia University Wisconsin *B, T*
Edgewood College *B*
Lakeland College *T*
Lawrence University *B, T*
Maranatha Baptist Bible College *B*
Marian College of Fond du Lac *B, T*
Mount Mary College *B, T*
Northland College *T*
St. Norbert College *B, T*
Silver Lake College *B, M, T*
University of Wisconsin
    Green Bay *T*
    La Crosse *B, T*
    Madison *B, M, T*
    Milwaukee *B, T*
    Oshkosh *B, T*
    Parkside *T*
    River Falls *B, T*
    Stevens Point *B, M, T*
    Superior *B, T*
    Whitewater *B*
Viterbo University *B, T*

Wyoming
Casper College *A*
Eastern Wyoming College *A*
University of Wyoming *B*
Western Wyoming Community
    College *A*

Music theory/composition

Alabama
Birmingham-Southern College *B*
Huntingdon College *B*
Samford University *B*
University of Montevallo *B*

Alaska
University of Alaska
    Fairbanks *M*

Arizona
Arizona State University *B, M*
University of Arizona *M, D*

Arkansas
Henderson State University *B*
Ouachita Baptist University *B*

California
Azusa Pacific University *B, M*
Biola University *B*
California Institute of the Arts *C, B, M*
California State University
    Dominguez Hills *B*
    Fresno *B*
    Fullerton *B, M*
    Hayward *M*
    Long Beach *M*
    Northridge *B, M*
Chapman University *B*
Foothill College *C*
Fresno Pacific University *B*
Golden West College *C, A*
Master's College *B*
Mills College *M*
Mount St. Mary's College *B*
Ohlone College *C*
Pepperdine University *B*
San Diego State University *M*
San Francisco State University *M*
University of Redlands *B*
University of Southern
    California *B, M, D*
University of the Pacific *B*

Colorado
University of Denver *M*

Connecticut
Connecticut College *B*
University of Hartford *B, M, D*
Western Connecticut State University *B*
Yale University *M, D*

Delaware
University of Delaware *B*

District of Columbia
Catholic University of America *B, M, D*
Howard University *B*

Florida
Florida Southern College *B*
Florida State University *B, M, D*
Jacksonville University *B*
Manatee Community College *A*
Palm Beach Atlantic University *B*
Polk Community College *A*
Stetson University *B*
University of Miami *B, M, D*
University of Tampa *B*

Georgia
Clayton College and State University *B*
Columbus State University *B, M*
Georgia Southern University *B*
State University of West Georgia *B*
Toccoa Falls College *B*
University of Georgia *B*

Idaho
Boise State University *B*
North Idaho College *A*
Northwest Nazarene University *B*
University of Idaho *B*

Illinois
Bradley University *B*
Concordia University *B*
De Paul University *B, M*
Eureka College *B*
Lincoln College *A*
Moody Bible Institute *B*
Northwestern University *B, M, D*
Roosevelt University *B, M*
Trinity International University *B*
University of Illinois
    Urbana-Champaign *B*
Wheaton College *B*

Indiana
American Conservatory of
    Music *B, M, D*
Ball State University *B*
Butler University *B, M*
DePauw University *B*
Indiana University
    Bloomington *B, M, D*
Indiana Wesleyan University *B*
Valparaiso University *B*
Vincennes University *A*

Iowa
Coe College *B*
Luther College *B*
University of Iowa *B, M, D*
University of Northern Iowa *B, M*
Wartburg College *B*

Kansas
Central Christian College *A*
University of Kansas *B, M, D*

Kentucky
Campbellsville University *B*
University of Louisville *B, M*

Louisiana
Centenary College of Louisiana *B*
Louisiana College *B*
Loyola University New Orleans *B*
University of New Orleans *B, M*

Maine
University of Maine *M*

Maryland
College of Notre Dame of Maryland *B*
Johns Hopkins University *B, M, D*
Johns Hopkins University: Peabody
    Conservatory of Music *B, M, D*

Massachusetts
Berklee College of Music *B*
Boston Conservatory *B, M*
Boston University *B, M, D*
Hampshire College *B*
Harvard College *B*
New England Conservatory of
    Music *B, M*
Tufts University *B*
Westfield State College *B*

Michigan
Calvin College *B*
Central Michigan University *B*
Cornerstone University *B, T*
Lansing Community College *A*
Marygrove College *B*
Michigan State University *B, M, D*
Oakland University *B*
University of Michigan *B, M*
Western Michigan University *B*

Minnesota
College of St. Scholastica *B*
Hamline University *B*
Minnesota State University
    Mankato *B*
    Moorhead *B*
Rochester Community and Technical
    College *C, A*
St. Olaf College *B*

Mississippi

Mississippi College *B, M*
Mississippi University for Women *B*

Missouri

Drury University *B*
Southeast Missouri State University *B*
University of Missouri
    Kansas City *B, M, D*
Washington University in St. Louis *B*
Webster University *M*
William Jewell College *B*

Montana

University of Montana-Missoula *B, M*

Nebraska

University of Nebraska
    Omaha *B*

New Hampshire

Franklin Pierce College *B*
Keene State College *B*
University of New Hampshire *B*

New Jersey

Bloomfield College *B*
Rider University *B, M*
Rowan University *B*

New York

Bard College *B, M*
City University of New York
    Brooklyn College *B, M*
    City College *B, M*
    Hunter College *B, M*
    Queens College *B, M*
Eastman School of Music of the
    University of Rochester *B, M, D*
Hofstra University *B*
Houghton College *B*
Ithaca College *B, M*
Juilliard School *B, M, D*
Manhattan School of Music *B, M, D*
Mannes College of Music *B, M*
Nazareth College of Rochester *B*
New York University *B, M, D*
Nyack College *B*
Sarah Lawrence College *B*
State University of New York
    Albany *B*
    Buffalo *M, D*
    College at Fredonia *B*
    College at Potsdam *B, M*
    New Paltz *B*
    Purchase *B, M*
Syracuse University *B, M*
University of Rochester *B, M, D*

North Carolina

Appalachian State University *B*
Duke University *M*
East Carolina University *B, M*
Meredith College *B*
North Carolina School of the Arts *M*
University of North Carolina
    Greensboro *B, M*

Ohio

Ashland University *B*
Baldwin-Wallace College *B*
Bowling Green State University *B, M*
Cedarville University *B*
Cleveland Institute of Music *B, M, D*
College of Wooster *B*
Heidelberg College *B*
Kent State University *B, M, D*
Kent State University
    Stark Campus *B*
Miami University
    Oxford Campus *M*
Oberlin College *B*
Ohio Northern University *B*
Ohio State University
    Columbus Campus *B*
Ohio University *B, M*
Otterbein College *B*
University of Akron *B, M*

University of Cincinnati *B, M, D*
University of Dayton *B*
Youngstown State University *B, M*

Oklahoma

Oklahoma Baptist University *B*
Oklahoma City University *B*
Oral Roberts University *B*
Southwestern Oklahoma State
    University *B*
University of Oklahoma *M, D*
University of Tulsa *B*

Oregon

Linfield College *B*
University of Oregon *B, M, D*
Warner Pacific College *B*
Willamette University *B*

Pennsylvania

Bucknell University *B*
Carnegie Mellon University *B, M*
Curtis Institute of Music *C, B*
Duquesne University *B*
Mercyhurst College *B*
Moravian College *B*
Penn State
    University Park *M*
Philadelphia Biblical University *B*
Temple University *B, M, D*
West Chester University of
    Pennsylvania *B, M*

Puerto Rico

Conservatory of Music of Puerto Rico *B*

Rhode Island

University of Rhode Island *B*

South Carolina

Coker College *B, T*
Furman University *B*
North Greenville College *A, B*
University of South Carolina *M, D*

Tennessee

Belmont University *B*
Carson-Newman College *B*
Southern Adventist University *B*
Union University *B*
University of Tennessee
    Knoxville *B*
Vanderbilt University *B*

Texas

Baylor University *B, M*
Dallas Baptist University *B*
Del Mar College *A*
Hardin-Simmons University *B, M*
Houston Community College
    System *C, A*
Lon Morris College *A*
Rice University *B, M*
Sam Houston State University *B, M*
Southern Methodist University *B, M*
Texas A&M University
    Commerce *B, M*
Texas Christian University *B, M*
Texas Tech University *B, M, D*
Trinity University *B*
University of Houston *B, M, D*
University of North Texas *B, M, D*
University of Texas
    Arlington *T*
    Austin *B*
    El Paso *B*
    San Antonio *B*
West Texas A&M University *B*

Utah

Brigham Young University *M*
University of Utah *M, D*

Vermont

Bennington College *B, M*
Johnson State College *B*
Marlboro College *B*

Virginia

Randolph-Macon Woman's College *B*
Shenandoah University *B, M*
University of Richmond *B*
Virginia Union University *B*

Washington

Central Washington University *B*
Centralia College *A*
Cornish College of the Arts *B*
Eastern Washington University *B, M*
Pacific Lutheran University *B*
University of Washington *B, M*
Washington State University *B*
Western Washington University *B*

Wisconsin

Lawrence University *B, T*
University of Wisconsin
    La Crosse *B*
    Madison *B, M*
    Whitewater *B, T*

Wyoming

University of Wyoming *B*

Music therapy

Arizona

Arizona State University *B*

California

California State University
    Northridge *M*
Chapman University *B*
University of the Pacific *B*

Colorado

Colorado State University *B*
Naropa University *M*

District of Columbia

Howard University *B*

Florida

Florida State University *C, B, M*
Polk Community College *A*
South Florida Community College *A*
University of Miami *B, M*

Georgia

Georgia College and State University *B*
University of Georgia *B*

Indiana

Indiana University-Purdue University
    Fort Wayne *B*
St. Mary-of-the-Woods College *B, M*
University of Evansville *B*

Iowa

University of Iowa *B*
Wartburg College *B*

Kansas

Central Christian College *A*
University of Kansas *B, M*

Louisiana

Loyola University New Orleans *B, M*

Maryland

Howard Community College *A*

Massachusetts

Anna Maria College *B*
Berklee College of Music *B*
Lesley University *M, D*

Michigan

Eastern Michigan University *B, T*
Michigan State University *B, M*
Western Michigan University *B*

Minnesota

Augsburg College *B*
University of Minnesota
    Twin Cities *B*

Missouri

Maryville University of Saint Louis *B*
University of Missouri
    Kansas City *B, M*

New Jersey

Montclair State University *B*

New York

Molloy College *B*
Nazareth College of Rochester *B*
New York University *M, D*
State University of New York
    College at Fredonia *B*
    New Paltz *B*

North Carolina

East Carolina University *B, M*
Queens University of Charlotte *B*

Ohio

Baldwin-Wallace College *B*
College of Wooster *B*
Ohio University *B*
University of Dayton *B*

Oklahoma

Southwestern Oklahoma State
    University *B*

Pennsylvania

Drexel University *M*
Duquesne University *B*
Elizabethtown College *B*
Immaculata University *B, M*
Marywood University *C, A, B*
Mercyhurst College *B*
Slippery Rock University of
    Pennsylvania *B*
Temple University *B, M*

South Carolina

Charleston Southern University *C, B*

Tennessee

Tennessee Technological University *B*

Texas

Sam Houston State University *B*
Southern Methodist University *B, M*
Texas Woman's University *B, M*
University of the Incarnate Word *B*
West Texas A&M University *B*

Utah

Utah State University *B, M*

Virginia

Radford University *B*
Shenandoah University *C, B, M*

Wisconsin

Alverno College *B*
University of Wisconsin
    Eau Claire *B*
    Madison *M*
    Oshkosh *B*

Musical instrument fabrication/repair

Iowa

Western Iowa Tech Community
    College *A*

Minnesota

Minnesota State College - Southeast
    Technical *C, A*

Washington

Renton Technical College *C, A*

Musicology/ ethnomusicology

Arizona

University of Arizona *M*

California
San Diego State University *M*
University of California
    Los Angeles *B, M, D*

Colorado
University of Denver *B*

Connecticut
Wesleyan University *D*

Florida
Florida State University *M, D*
University of Miami *M*

Illinois
De Paul University *B, M*
Northwestern University *B, D*
Roosevelt University *M*

Indiana
Indiana University
    Bloomington *M, D*

Iowa
University of Iowa *M, D*

Kansas
University of Kansas *B*

Louisiana
Loyola University New Orleans *B*

Maryland
Johns Hopkins University *B, M, D*
University of Maryland
    College Park *M*

Massachusetts
Boston University *D*
Harvard College *R*
New England Conservatory of Music *M*
Tufts University *B*

Michigan
University of Michigan *M*
Western Michigan University *B*

Minnesota
Bethel College *M*

Missouri
Washington University in St. Louis *M, D*

New York
Eastman School of Music of the
    University of Rochester *M, D*
Sarah Lawrence College *B*
State University of New York
    Buffalo *D*
University of Rochester *M, D*

North Carolina
Duke University *M, D*

Ohio
Bowling Green State University *B*
Case Western Reserve University *D*
Kent State University *M, D*
University of Akron *B*
University of Cincinnati *D*

Pennsylvania
Gratz College *C, M*
Marywood University *M*
Penn State
    University Park *M*

Rhode Island
Brown University *B, M, D*

Texas
Sam Houston State University *M*
Texas A&M University
    Commerce *B*
Texas Christian University *M*
University of North Texas *M, D*

Utah
Brigham Young University *M, D*
University of Utah *M*

Washington
University of Washington *B*

Mycology

South Carolina
Medical University of South Carolina *D*

Native American studies

Arizona
Arizona State University *B*
Pima Community College *A*
Scottsdale Community College *C, A*
University of Arizona *M, D*

California
California State University
    Hayward *B*
    Long Beach *C*
De Anza College *C, A*
Grossmont Community College *A*
Humboldt State University *B*
Palomar College *C*
Santa Barbara City College *A*
University of California
    Berkeley *B*
    Davis *B*
    Los Angeles *M*
    Riverside *B*

Idaho
North Idaho College *A*

Indiana
Indiana University-Purdue University
    Fort Wayne *C*

Iowa
University of Iowa *C*

Kansas
Haskell Indian Nations University *B*
University of Kansas *M*

Massachusetts
Hampshire College *B*

Minnesota
Bemidji State University *B*
Itasca Community College *C, A*
Rainy River Community College *A*
University of Minnesota
    Duluth *B*
    Twin Cities *B*

Montana
Fort Belknap College *A*
Montana State University
    Bozeman *M*
Salish Kootenai College *C, A*
University of Montana-Missoula *B*

Nebraska
Creighton University *B*
Little Priest Tribal College *A*
Nebraska Indian Community College *A*

New Hampshire
Dartmouth College *B*

New Mexico
Institute of American Indian Arts *A*

New York
Colgate University *B*
Sarah Lawrence College *B*
State University of New York
    Buffalo *M*

North Carolina
University of North Carolina
    Pembroke *B*
Western Carolina University *M*

North Dakota
University of North Dakota *B*

Oklahoma
Bacone College *A*
Northeastern Oklahoma Agricultural and
    Mechanical College *A*
Northeastern State University *B*
Northern Oklahoma College *A*
University of Oklahoma *B*
University of Science and Arts of
    Oklahoma *B*

South Dakota
Black Hills State University *B*
University of South Dakota *B*

Texas
University of the Incarnate Word *B*

Utah
Weber State University *B*

Vermont
Goddard College *B*

Washington
University of Washington *B*

Wisconsin
Lac Courte Oreilles Ojibwa Community
    College *A*
Northland College *B*
University of Wisconsin
    Eau Claire *B*

Wyoming
Central Wyoming College *A*

Natural resource economics

Florida
Florida Institute of Technology *M*

Indiana
Taylor University *B*

Massachusetts
University of Massachusetts
    Amherst *B, M, D*

North Carolina
North Carolina State University *B*

Pennsylvania
Penn State
    University Park *B*

Texas
University of Texas
    Austin *B*

Natural resources management/policy

Alaska
University of Alaska
    Fairbanks *B, M*

Arizona
Prescott College *B, M*
University of Arizona *M, D*

Arkansas
Arkansas Tech University *B*

California
California State University
    Chico *B*
    Monterey Bay *B*
College of the Redwoods *C*
Columbia College *C, A*
Feather River College *C, A*
Humboldt State University *B, M*
Los Angeles Pierce College *C, A*
San Joaquin Delta College *C*
University of California
    Berkeley *B, M, D*
    Davis *B*
University of Redlands *B*

Colorado
Colorado Mountain College
    Timberline Campus *A*
Colorado State University *B*
University of Denver *M*

Connecticut
University of Connecticut *B, M, D*

Delaware
Delaware State University *B*
University of Delaware *B*

District of Columbia
American University *M*

Florida
Pensacola Junior College *A*
University of Miami *B*
University of West Florida *B*

Hawaii
University of Hawaii
    Manoa *B, M, D*

Idaho
University of Idaho *B, M, D*

Illinois
College of Lake County *C, A*
Illinois Institute of Technology *M*
Southern Illinois University
    Carbondale *D*
University of Illinois
    Urbana-Champaign *M*

Indiana
Ball State University *B*
Taylor University *B*
University of Evansville *B*

Iowa
Cornell College *B*
Drake University *B*
Hawkeye Community College *C, A*
Upper Iowa University *B*

Kansas
Garden City Community College *A*
Haskell Indian Nations University *A*

Maine
University of Maine *B, M, D*
University of Maine
    Farmington *B*

Maryland
University of Maryland
    College Park *B*

Massachusetts
Boston University *B*
Bridgewater State College *B*
Cape Cod Community College *C*
University of Massachusetts
    Amherst *B*

Michigan
Grand Valley State University *B*
University of Michigan *B, M, D*
University of Michigan
    Flint *B*

Minnesota
Central Lakes College *A*
Northland Community & Technical
    College *A*
St. Mary's University of Minnesota *C, M*
University of Minnesota
    Crookston *B*
University of St. Thomas *M*
Vermilion Community College *A*

Missouri
Missouri Southern State College *B*
Webster University *M*

Montana
Flathead Valley Community College *A*
Fort Belknap College *A*

Montana State University
  Bozeman *B, D*
University of Montana-Missoula *M*

Nebraska
Nebraska College of Technical
  Agriculture *C, A*
Nebraska Indian Community College *A*
University of Nebraska
  Lincoln *B*

Nevada
University of Nevada
  Las Vegas *B, M*
  Reno *B*

New Hampshire
New Hampshire Community Technical
  College
  Berlin *A*

New Jersey
Rutgers, The State University of New
  Jersey
  New Brunswick Regional
    Campus *B*
Stevens Institute of Technology *B*

New Mexico
College of Santa Fe *B*
New Mexico Highlands University *B, M*
Southwestern Indian Polytechnic
  Institute *A*

New York
Bard College *M*
Cornell University *B*
Finger Lakes Community College *A*
Fulton-Montgomery Community
  College *A*
Hofstra University *B*
Paul Smith's College *B*
Rensselaer Polytechnic Institute *M, D*
Rochester Institute of
  Technology *C, B, M*
State University of New York
  College of Agriculture and
    Technology at Morrisville *A*
  College of Environmental Science
    and Forestry *B, M, D*
  Purchase *C*

North Carolina
North Carolina State University *M*
Western Carolina University *B*

North Dakota
Minot State University: Bottineau
  Campus *A*
North Dakota State University *B, M, D*

Ohio
Bowling Green State University *B*
Heidelberg College *B*
Hocking Technical College *A*
Kent State University
  Trumbull Campus *A*
Muskingum Area Technical College *A*
Ohio State University
  Columbus Campus *B, M, D*
Otterbein College *B*
University of Findlay *M*

Oklahoma
Bacone College *A*
Northwestern Oklahoma State
  University *B*
Southeastern Oklahoma State
  University *B*

Oregon
Concordia University *B*
Mount Hood Community College *A*
Oregon State University *B*
Portland State University *M*
Treasure Valley Community College *A*

Pennsylvania
Keystone College *B*

Penn State
  Abington *B*
  Altoona *B*
  Beaver *B*
  Berks *B*
  Delaware County *B*
  Dubois *B*
  Erie, The Behrend College *B*
  Fayette *B*
  Hazleton *B*
  Lehigh Valley *B*
  McKeesport *B*
  Mont Alto *B*
  New Kensington *B*
  Schuylkill - Capital College *B*
  Shenango *B*
  University Park *B*
  Wilkes-Barre *B*
  Worthington Scranton *B*
  York *B*
St. Vincent College *B*

Puerto Rico
Turabo University *M*
Universidad Metropolitana *B, M*

Rhode Island
University of Rhode Island *B, M*

South Carolina
Central Carolina Technical College *A*
Medical University of South Carolina *M*

South Dakota
South Dakota State University *B*

Tennessee
University of Tennessee
  Martin *B*
Volunteer State Community College *A*

Texas
Hardin-Simmons University *M*
Sul Ross State University *B*
Texas A&M University *B*
Texas A&M University
  Galveston *B, M*

Utah
Brigham Young University *B, M*
Dixie State College of Utah *A*
Snow College *A*
Utah State University *M*

Vermont
Green Mountain College *B*
Johnson State College *B*
Southern Vermont College *A, B*
Sterling College *A, B*
University of Vermont *B, M, D*

Virginia
Virginia Polytechnic Institute and State
  University *B*

Washington
Central Washington University *M*
Grays Harbor College *A*
Heritage College *C, A*
University of Washington *M, D*
Washington State University *B*
Wenatchee Valley College *C*
Western Washington University *B, M*

Wisconsin
Milwaukee Area Technical College *A*
Northland College *B*
University of Wisconsin
  Green Bay *B*
  River Falls *B*

**Natural resources/
conservation, general**

Alabama
Auburn University *B*
Spring Hill College *B*
Tuskegee University *B, M*

University of Alabama
  Huntsville *C*
University of West Alabama *B*

Alaska
Alaska Pacific University *B, M*
Sheldon Jackson College *B*
University of Alaska
  Fairbanks *B, M*

Arizona
Prescott College *B, M*
University of Arizona *B*

Arkansas
Arkansas State University *D*
John Brown University *B*
South Arkansas Community
  College *C, A*
University of Arkansas *B*
University of Arkansas
  Pine Bluff *B*
University of Central Arkansas *B*
University of the Ozarks *B*

California
California Polytechnic State University:
  San Luis Obispo *B*
California State University
  Chico *B, M*
  Hayward *B*
  Monterey Bay *B*
  Sacramento *B*
  Stanislaus *B*
Columbia College *A*
Feather River College *C, A*
Fresno Pacific University *B*
Irvine Valley College *C, A*
Mills College *B*
Modesto Junior College *C, A*
Moorpark College *A*
Mount San Antonio College *A*
National University *M*
Ohlone College *C*
San Diego State University *C, B*
San Francisco State University *M*
San Joaquin Delta College *A*
San Jose State University *M*
Santa Rosa Junior College *C, A*
Sonoma State University *B*
University of California
  Berkeley *M*
  Davis *B*
  Irvine *M, D*
  Riverside *M, D*
  Santa Barbara *B*
  Santa Cruz *B, M, D*
Whittier College *B*

Colorado
Colorado College *B*
Colorado Mountain College
  Timberline Campus *A*
Metropolitan State College of Denver *B*
Trinidad State Junior College *A*
University of Colorado
  Denver *M*

Connecticut
Connecticut College *B*
Gateway Community College *A*
Middlesex Community College *A*
Sacred Heart University *B*
Teikyo Post University *B*
University of Connecticut *B, M, D*
University of New Haven *B, M*
Wesleyan University *B, M*

Delaware
University of Delaware *B*

District of Columbia
George Washington University *B*
Trinity College *B*
University of the District of Columbia *B*

Florida
Florida Atlantic University *C, M*
Florida Institute of Technology *B, M, D*

Florida International University *B, M*
Florida Southern College *B*
Gulf Coast Community College *A*
Jacksonville University *B*
Polk Community College *A*
St. Leo University *B*
Seminole Community College *A*
South Florida Community College *A*
University of Florida *B*
University of South Florida *B, M*

Georgia
Berry College *B*
Columbus State University *M*
Mercer University *B*
Shorter College *B*
State University of West Georgia *B*
Thomas University *B*
University of Georgia *M*
Valdosta State University *B*

Hawaii
Hawaii Pacific University *B*
University of Hawaii
  Manoa *B*

Idaho
College of Southern Idaho *A*
University of Idaho *B, M*

Illinois
Augustana College *B*
Aurora University *B*
De Paul University *B*
Illinois Central College *A*
Lewis University *B*
Lincoln College *A*
Loyola University of Chicago *C, B*
Monmouth College *B*
Northeastern Illinois University *B*
Northwestern University *B*
Principia College *B*
Southern Illinois University
  Edwardsville *B*
University of Illinois
  Springfield *M*
Wheaton College *B*

Indiana
Ball State University *M*
Bethel College *B*
Goshen College *B*
Indiana University
  Bloomington *B, M, D*
Manchester College *B*
Purdue University *B, M*
St. Joseph's College *B*
Tri-State University *B*
University of Indianapolis *B*
University of St. Francis *B*
Vincennes University *A*

Iowa
Briar Cliff University *B*
Central College *B*
Dordt College *B*
Ellsworth Community College *A*
Iowa State University *B*
Kirkwood Community College *A*
Muscatine Community College *A*
Northwestern College *B*
Simpson College *B*
University of Dubuque *B*
University of Iowa *B*
Upper Iowa University *B*

Kansas
Fort Scott Community College *A*
Haskell Indian Nations University *A, B*
Pittsburg State University *B*
Wichita State University *M*

Kentucky
Georgetown College *B*
Lexington Community College *A*
University of Kentucky *B*

Louisiana

Louisiana State University
    Shreveport *B*
Louisiana State University and
    Agricultural and Mechanical
    College *B, M*
Louisiana Tech University *B*
Southern University and Agricultural and
    Mechanical College *M*
Tulane University *B*
University of Louisiana at Lafayette *B*

Maine

College of the Atlantic *B*
University of Maine *M, D*
University of Maine
    Farmington *B*
    Machias *B, T*
    Presque Isle *B*
University of New England *B*
University of Southern Maine *B*

Maryland

Frostburg State University *B, M*
Harford Community College *C, A*
Howard Community College *A*
University of Maryland
    Baltimore County *B*
    College Park *B, M*
    University College *B*

Massachusetts

Anna Maria College *M*
Berkshire Community College *A*
Boston University *B, M*
Cape Cod Community College *C, A*
College of the Holy Cross *B*
Fitchburg State College *B*
Harvard College *B*
Merrimack College *B*
Roxbury Community College *A*
Simmons College *B*
Springfield College *B*
Suffolk University *A*
University of Massachusetts
    Amherst *B*
    Lowell *B*
Westfield State College *B*
Wheaton College *B*
Worcester Polytechnic Institute *B*

Michigan

Adrian College *A, B*
Aquinas College *B*
Gogebic Community College *A*
Lansing Community College *A*
Michigan State University *B, M, D*
Mid Michigan Community College *A*
Northern Michigan University *B*
Schoolcraft College *A*
University of Michigan *B, M, D*
University of Michigan
    Dearborn *B*
Western Michigan University *B*

Minnesota

Bemidji State University *B, M*
Bethel College *B*
Gustavus Adolphus College *B*
Itasca Community College *A*
Minnesota State University
    Mankato *B, M*
Rainy River Community College *A*
St. Cloud State University *B, M*
University of Minnesota
    Twin Cities *B, M, D*
University of St. Thomas *M*
Vermilion Community College *A*
Winona State University *B*

Missouri

Central Methodist College *B*
Maryville University of Saint Louis *B*
Missouri Southern State College *B*
St. Charles Community College *A*
St. Louis University *B*

Southeast Missouri State
    University *B, M*
Stephens College *B*
Washington University in St. Louis *B*
Westminster College *B*

Montana

Miles Community College *A*
Montana State University
    Billings *B*
    Bozeman *B, M*
Rocky Mountain College *B*
Salish Kootenai College *B*
University of Montana-Missoula *B, M*
University of Montana: Western *B*

Nebraska

Bellevue University *B*
Dana College *B*
Little Priest Tribal College *A*
Midland Lutheran College *B*
Southeast Community College
    Beatrice Campus *A*
University of Nebraska
    Lincoln *B, M*

Nevada

Great Basin College *A*
Sierra Nevada College *B*
University of Nevada
    Las Vegas *B, M, D*
    Reno *B, M*
Western Nevada Community College *A*

New Hampshire

Colby-Sawyer College *B*
Dartmouth College *B*
Franklin Pierce College *B*
Keene State College *B*
New England College *B*
University of New Hampshire *B, M, D*

New Jersey

Fairleigh Dickinson University
    Metropolitan Campus *B, M*
Montclair State University *M*
New Jersey Institute of
    Technology *B, M, D*
Ocean County College *A*
Raritan Valley Community College *A*
Richard Stockton College of New
    Jersey *B*
Rowan University *M*
Rutgers, The State University of New
    Jersey
        New Brunswick Regional
        Campus *B, M, D*
        Newark Regional Campus *B, M, D*
Thomas Edison State College *A, B*
William Paterson University of New
    Jersey *B*

New Mexico

College of Santa Fe *B*
College of the Southwest *B*
New Mexico Highlands University *B, M*
New Mexico Institute of Mining and
    Technology *B*
New Mexico State University *B*
San Juan College *C, A*
Southwestern Indian Polytechnic
    Institute *C*

New York

Barnard College *B*
Canisius College *M*
City University of New York
    Medgar Evers College *B*
    Queens College *B*
Colgate University *B*
Columbia University
    Columbia College *B*
Concordia College *B*
Cornell University *B, M, D*
Elmira College *B*
Finger Lakes Community College *C, A*
Fulton-Montgomery Community
    College *A*

Ithaca College *B*
Keuka College *B*
Long Island University
    C. W. Post Campus *B, M*
Marist College *B*
Molloy College *B*
Paul Smith's College *A, B*
Rensselaer Polytechnic Institute *B*
St. Bonaventure University *B*
State University of New York
    College at Brockport *B*
    College at Oneonta *B*
    College at Plattsburgh *B*
    College of Agriculture and
        Technology at Cobleskill *A*
    College of Agriculture and
        Technology at Morrisville *A*
    College of Environmental Science
        and Forestry *B, M, D*
    College of Technology at Alfred *A*
    College of Technology at Canton *B*
    Maritime College *B*
    Purchase *B*
Syracuse University *B*
Tompkins-Cortland Community
    College *A*
Trocaire College *A*
United States Military Academy *B*
Wells College *B*

North Carolina

Belmont Abbey College *B*
Blue Ridge Community College *C, A*
Cape Fear Community College *C, A*
Catawba College *B*
Duke University *B, M, D*
Elon University *B*
Guilford College *B*
Montreat College *B*
North Carolina Central University *B*
North Carolina State University *B*
North Carolina Wesleyan College *B*
Pamlico Community College *A*
Shaw University *B*
Southeastern Community College *A*
University of North Carolina
    Chapel Hill *B, M, D*
    Wilmington *B*
Wake Technical Community College *A*
Warren Wilson College *B*
Western Piedmont Community
    College *C, A*
Wilson Technical Community College *A*

Ohio

Antioch College *B*
Cleveland State University *B*
Columbus State Community College *A*
Defiance College *B*
Denison University *B*
Hocking Technical College *A*
Kent State University *B*
Kent State University
    Ashtabula Regional Campus *C, A*
    Stark Campus *B*
Lake Erie College *B*
Marietta College *B*
Miami University
    Oxford Campus *M*
Mount Vernon Nazarene University *B*
Muskingum College *B*
Ohio Northern University *B*
Ohio State University
    Agricultural Technical Institute *A*
    Columbus Campus *B, M, D*
Ohio University *B*
Otterbein College *B*
University of Cincinnati *M, D*
University of Findlay *A, B*
University of Rio Grande *B*
University of Toledo *B*
Youngstown State University *B*

Oklahoma

Eastern Oklahoma State College *A*
Northeastern State University *B*

Oklahoma State University *B, M, D*
St. Gregory's University *B*
Southeastern Oklahoma State
    University *B*
Southern Nazarene University *B*
University of Tulsa *B*

Oregon

Eastern Oregon University *B*
Marylhurst University *B*
Oregon Institute of Technology *B*
Oregon State University *B*
Portland State University *B, D*
University of Oregon *B, M*

Pennsylvania

Albright College *B*
Arcadia University *M*
Bryn Mawr College *B*
Bucks County Community College *A*
Cabrini College *B*
California University of Pennsylvania *B*
DeSales University *B*
Delaware Valley College *B*
Drexel University *B, M, D*
Edinboro University of Pennsylvania *B*
Elizabethtown College *B*
Gettysburg College *B*
Harrisburg Area Community College *A*
Immaculata University *B*
Keystone College *A*
King's College *B*
Kutztown University of Pennsylvania *B*
La Salle University *B*
Lehigh University *M, D*
Marywood University *B*
Penn State
    University Park *C, B*
Point Park College *B*
St. Joseph's University *B*
St. Vincent College *B*
Slippery Rock University of
    Pennsylvania *C, B*
Temple University *B*
Thiel College *B*
University of Pittsburgh
    Greensburg *B*
University of Scranton *B*
Waynesburg College *B*
Widener University *B*
Wilson College *B*

Puerto Rico

Bayamon Central University *B*
Inter American University of Puerto Rico
    Bayamon Campus *B*
Pontifical Catholic University of Puerto
    Rico *B*
Turabo University *M*
Universidad Metropolitana *A, B*
University of Puerto Rico
    Rio Piedras Campus *B*

Rhode Island

Roger Williams University *B*
University of Rhode Island *B, M, D*

South Carolina

Charleston Southern University *B*
College of Charleston *M*
Furman University *B*

South Dakota

Mount Marty College *B*
Sinte Gleska University *A*

Tennessee

Tennessee Technological
    University *B, D*
Tusculum College *B*
University of Tennessee
    Chattanooga *B, M*
    Martin *B*

Texas

Abilene Christian University *B*
Baylor University *B, M*
Coastal Bend College *A*

Concordia University at Austin *B*
Lamar University *B, M*
McMurry University *B*
Midland College *C, A*
Midwestern State University *B*
Southern Methodist University *B*
Southwest Texas State
    University *B, M, T*
Sul Ross State University *B*
Tarleton State University *M*
Texas A&M International University *B*
Texas A&M University *B, M*
Texas A&M University
    Commerce *B*
    Corpus Christi *B, M*
    Galveston *B*
Texas Southern University *B*
Texas Tech University *B*
University of Houston
    Clear Lake *B, M*
University of North Texas *M, D*
University of St. Thomas *B*
University of Texas
    San Antonio *M*
University of the Incarnate Word *B*
West Texas A&M University *B, M*

Utah

Brigham Young University *B*
Dixie State College of Utah *A*
Snow College *A*

Vermont

Bennington College *B*
Green Mountain College *B*
Johnson State College *B*
Marlboro College *B*
Norwich University *B*
Southern Vermont College *A, B*
Sterling College *A, B*
University of Vermont *B*

Virginia

Averett University *B*
Emory & Henry College *B*
Ferrum College *B*
Longwood University *M*
Mary Washington College *B*
Marymount University *B*
Mountain Empire Community College *A*
Roanoke College *B, T*
Shenandoah University *B*
Sweet Briar College *B*
University of Virginia *B, M, D*
University of Virginia's College at
    Wise *B*
Virginia Intermont College *B*
Virginia Polytechnic Institute and State
    University *B*

Washington

Everett Community College *A*
Evergreen State College *M*
Heritage College *B*
Seattle University *B*
University of Washington *B*
Washington State University *B, M, D*

West Virginia

Alderson-Broaddus College *B*
Davis and Elkins College *B*
Mountain State University *A*
Salem International University *B*
Shepherd College *B*
University of Charleston *B*
West Virginia Wesleyan College *B*
Wheeling Jesuit University *B*

Wisconsin

Carroll College *B*
Fox Valley Technical College *A*
Northland College *B*
St. Norbert College *B*

University of Wisconsin
    Green Bay *B, M*
    Madison *M, D*
    Platteville *B*
    River Falls *B*
    Stevens Point *B, T*

Wyoming

Central Wyoming College *A*
University of Wyoming *B*
Western Wyoming Community
    College *A*

Natural sciences

Alabama

Oakwood College *B*
University of Alabama
    Birmingham *B*

Alaska

University of Alaska
    Anchorage *B*

Arizona

Prescott College *B, M*

California

California State University
    Fresno *B*
Columbia College *A*
Loma Linda University *M, D*
Loyola Marymount University *B*
Master's College *B*
Ohlone College *A*
Pacific Union College *B*
Pepperdine University *B*
Pitzer College *B*
San Joaquin Delta College *A*
Santa Rosa Junior College *A*

Colorado

Colorado Mountain College
    Timberline Campus *A*

Florida

New College of Florida *B*
Polk Community College *A*
University of West Florida *B*

Georgia

Covenant College *B*
Oxford College of Emory University *B*
Reinhardt College *A*

Hawaii

University of Hawaii
    Hilo *B*

Idaho

College of Southern Idaho *A*
Lewis-Clark State College *B*

Illinois

Black Hawk College
    East Campus *A*
Concordia University *B, T*
Shimer College *B*
Southeastern Illinois College *A*

Indiana

Goshen College *B*
Tri-State University *A*

Iowa

Ellsworth Community College *A*
Northwestern College *T*
St. Ambrose University *B, T*

Kansas

Benedictine College *B*
Bethel College *B*
Central Christian College *A, B*
Garden City Community College *A*
Seward County Community College *A*
Tabor College *B*
Washburn University of Topeka *A*

Louisiana

Louisiana State University
    Eunice *A*

Maine

University of Maine *B, M, D*
University of Southern Maine *B*

Massachusetts

Cape Cod Community College *A*
Hampshire College *B*
Harvard College *B*
Lesley University *B*
Simon's Rock College of Bard *B*

Michigan

Calvin College *B*
Concordia University *B, T*
Madonna University *A, B*
Marygrove College *A, B, T*
Siena Heights University *A, B*

Minnesota

College of St. Benedict *B*
College of St. Scholastica *B*
St. John's University *B*

Missouri

Avila University *B*
Columbia College *B*
Missouri Western State College *B*
Stephens College *B*

Nebraska

Concordia University *B, T*
Hastings College *B, T*
Northeast Community College *A*
Peru State College *B*
York College *A*

New Hampshire

University of New Hampshire *B*

New Jersey

Thomas Edison State College *B*
Warren County Community College *A*

New Mexico

Clovis Community College *A*

New York

Alfred University *B*
City University of New York
    Brooklyn College *B, M*
Colgate University *B*
Daemen College *B*
Rensselaer Polytechnic Institute *M*
Roberts Wesleyan College *A*
State University of New York
    Buffalo *M*
    College at Geneseo *B, T*
    College at Plattsburgh *M, D*
    College at Potsdam *B, T*
    College of Agriculture and
        Technology at Cobleskill *A*
    College of Environmental Science
        and Forestry *B*

North Carolina

St. Augustine's College *B*
Western Piedmont Community
    College *A*

North Dakota

Dickinson State University *B, T*

Ohio

Case Western Reserve University *B*
Cleveland State University *T*
College of Mount St. Joseph *B*
Defiance College *B*
Kent State University *C*
Shawnee State University *B*
University of Findlay *B*
Walsh University *B*
Washington State Community College *A*
Xavier University *B*

Oklahoma

Bacone College *A*

Oklahoma State University *M*
St. Gregory's University *B*
University of Science and Arts of
    Oklahoma *B, T*

Oregon

Marylhurst University *B*
Warner Pacific College *B*
Western Oregon University *B*

Pennsylvania

Gettysburg College *B*
Lehigh Carbon Community College *A*
Lehigh University *B*
Lock Haven University of
    Pennsylvania *B*
University of Pittsburgh
    Titusville *A*

Puerto Rico

Bayamon Central University *B*
Pontifical Catholic University of Puerto
    Rico *B*
Turabo University *B*
Universidad Metropolitana *A, B*
Universidad del Este *A*
University of Puerto Rico
    Ponce *A*
    Rio Piedras Campus *B*
    Utuado *B*
University of the Sacred Heart *B*

South Carolina

Charleston Southern University *B, M*
University of South Carolina *M*

Tennessee

Christian Brothers University *B*

Texas

Lee College *A*
McMurry University *B, T*
Our Lady of the Lake University of San
    Antonio *B*
Tyler Junior College *A*

Vermont

Bennington College *B*
Castleton State College *B*
Sterling College *A, B*

Virginia

College of Health Sciences *A*
J. Sargeant Reynolds Community
    College *A*
Thomas Nelson Community College *A*
Virginia Union University *B*
Virginia Wesleyan College *B*
Virginia Western Community College *A*

Washington

Everett Community College *A*
University of Puget Sound *B*

West Virginia

Alderson-Broaddus College *A*

Wisconsin

Northland College *B*
Silver Lake College *T*

Wyoming

University of Wyoming *M*

Naturopathic medicine

Connecticut

University of Bridgeport *D*

Washington

Bastyr University *D*

Near/Middle Eastern studies

Arizona

University of Arizona *B, M, D*

Arkansas
University of Arkansas *B*

California
University of California
    Berkeley *B*

Connecticut
Trinity College *B*
University of Connecticut *B*

District of Columbia
George Washington University *B*
Georgetown University *M*

Georgia
Oxford College of Emory University *B*

Illinois
University of Chicago *M*

Maryland
Johns Hopkins University *B, M, D*

Massachusetts
College of the Holy Cross *B*
Harvard College *B*
Tufts University *B, M*
University of Massachusetts
    Amherst *B*

Michigan
University of Michigan *B, M, D*
William Tyndale College *B*

Minnesota
University of Minnesota
    Twin Cities *B*

Missouri
Washington University in St. Louis *B, M*

New Hampshire
Dartmouth College *B*

New Jersey
Princeton University *B, M, D*
Rutgers, The State University of New
    Jersey
        New Brunswick Regional
        Campus *B*

New York
Barnard College *B*
Columbia University
    Columbia College *B*
Cornell University *M, D*
Fordham University *B*
New York University *B, M, D*
Sarah Lawrence College *B*
United States Military Academy *B*

Ohio
College of Wooster *B*
Mount Vernon Nazarene University *B*
Oberlin College *B*
Ohio State University
    Columbus Campus *B*
University of Toledo *B*

Oregon
Portland State University *B*

Pennsylvania
Penn State
    University Park *C*

Rhode Island
Brown University *B*

Texas
Southwest Texas State University *B*
University of Texas
    Austin *B, M, D*

Utah
Brigham Young University *B*
University of Utah *B, M, D*

Vermont
Goddard College *B*
Marlboro College *B*

Virginia
Emory & Henry College *B*

Washington
University of Washington *M, D*

Neurobiology/physiology

California
University of California
    Irvine *B*
    Riverside *B, D*
University of Southern California *M, D*

Connecticut
University of Connecticut *B, M, D*
Yale University *M, D*

Indiana
Indiana University-Purdue University
    Indianapolis *M, D*

Iowa
University of Iowa *M, D*

Louisiana
Centenary College of Louisiana *B*

Maine
Colby College *B*

North Carolina
University of North Carolina
    Chapel Hill *D*

Pennsylvania
Drexel University *M*

South Carolina
Medical University of South Carolina *M*

Neuroscience

Alabama
University of Alabama
    Birmingham *D*

Arizona
University of Arizona *M, D*

California
California Institute of Technology *D*
Claremont McKenna College *B*
Pitzer College *B*
Pomona College *B*
Scripps College *B*
Stanford University *M, D*
University of California
    Berkeley *D*
    Davis *B, M, D*
    Los Angeles *B, D*
    Riverside *B, M, D*
    San Diego *B, M, D*
    Santa Cruz *B*
University of Southern California *M, D*

Colorado
Colorado College *B*
Regis University *B*
University of Colorado
    Health Sciences Center *D*

Connecticut
Connecticut College *B*
Trinity College *B*
University of Hartford *M*
Wesleyan University *B, M*
Yale University *M, D*

Delaware
University of Delaware *D*

District of Columbia
George Washington University *D*
Georgetown University *D*

Florida
Florida State University *D*
University of Miami *D*

Illinois
Finch University of Health Sciences/The
    Chicago Medical School *D*
Loyola University of Chicago *M, D*
Northwestern University *B, M, D*
Rush University *D*
University of Chicago *M, D*

Indiana
Indiana University
    Bloomington *D*

Iowa
Iowa State University *M, D*
University of Iowa *D*

Kansas
University of Kansas *M, D*

Louisiana
Centenary College of Louisiana *B*
Tulane University *M, D*

Maine
Bates College *B*
Bowdoin College *B*
Colby College *B*

Maryland
Johns Hopkins University *B, M, D*
University of Maryland
    Baltimore *M, D*
    Baltimore County *M, D*
    College Park *D*
Washington College *B*

Massachusetts
Amherst College *B*
Boston University *B, M, D*
Brandeis University *B, M, D*
Hampshire College *B*
Harvard College *B*
Massachusetts Institute of Technology *D*
Mount Holyoke College *B*
Northeastern University *B*
Smith College *B*
Tufts University *M, D*
University of Massachusetts
    Amherst *M, D*
Wellesley College *B*

Michigan
Michigan State University *D*
University of Michigan *M, D*

Minnesota
Macalester College *B*
University of Minnesota
    Twin Cities *D*

Missouri
St. Louis University *D*
University of Missouri
    Columbia *M, D*
Washington University in St. Louis *B, D*

New Hampshire
Dartmouth College *B*

New Jersey
Rutgers, The State University of New
    Jersey
        Newark Regional Campus *D*

New York
City University of New York
    College of Staten Island *D*
Colgate University *B*
Columbia University
    Columbia College *B*
Cornell University *B*
Hamilton College *B*
Manhattanville College *B*
New York University *B, M, D*
Skidmore College *B*
State University of New York
    Albany *M, D*
    Buffalo *M, D*
    Stony Brook *D*
Syracuse University *M, D*

University of Rochester *M, D*
Yeshiva University *M, D*

North Carolina
Duke University *B, M, D*

Ohio
Baldwin-Wallace College *B*
Bowling Green State University *B*
Case Western Reserve University *D*
Kent State University *M, D*
Kenyon College *B*
Muskingum College *B*
Oberlin College *B*
Ohio State University
    Columbus Campus *M*
Ohio Wesleyan University *B*

Oregon
University of Oregon *M, D*

Pennsylvania
Allegheny College *B*
Bryn Mawr College *M, D*
Cedar Crest College *B*
Chatham College *B*
Franklin & Marshall College *B*
King's College *B*
Lehigh University *B*
University of Pennsylvania *D*
University of Pittsburgh *B, M, D*
University of Scranton *B*

Rhode Island
Brown University *B, M, D*

South Carolina
Medical University of South
    Carolina *M, D*

Tennessee
University of Tennessee Health Science
    Center *D*

Texas
Rice University *B*
Texas Christian University *B*
University of Texas
    Austin *M, D*
    Dallas *B, D*
    Houston Health Science
        Center *M, D*
    Medical Branch at Galveston *D*
    San Antonio *M, D*
    Southwestern Medical Center at
        Dallas *M, D*

Utah
University of Utah *D*

Virginia
University of Virginia *D*
Washington and Lee University *B*

Washington
University of Washington *D*
Washington State University *B, M, D*

Wisconsin
Carthage College *B*
Lawrence University *B, T*
University of Wisconsin
    Madison *M, D*

Nonprofit/public organization management

Alabama
Birmingham-Southern College *M*

Arizona
DeVry University
    Phoenix *M*

California
California State University
    Hayward *C*

DeVry University
Fremont *M*
Long Beach *M*
Pomona *M*
West Hills *M*
Hope International University *C, M*

Colorado
Regis University *M*
University of Denver *M*

Connecticut
Central Connecticut State University *B*
Quinnipiac University *B, M*

Florida
DeVry University
Miramar *M*
Orlando *M*
Florida Atlantic University *C, M*

Georgia
DeVry University
Alpharetta *M*
Atlanta *M*
University of Georgia *M*

Illinois
DeVry University
Tinley Park *M*
Northwestern University *M*
Trinity International University *B*

Indiana
Huntington College *B*
Manchester College *A, B*
St. Mary-of-the-Woods College *B*

Kentucky
Bellarmine University *C*

Maryland
College of Notre Dame of
Maryland *B, M*

Massachusetts
Boston University *M*
Suffolk University *M*

Michigan
Andrews University *M*
Madonna University *M*
University of Michigan
Flint *M*
Western Michigan University *B*

Minnesota
Capella University *M, D*
Hamline University *M*
St. Mary's University of Minnesota *M*
University of St. Thomas *M*

Missouri
DeVry University
Kansas City *M*
Lindenwood University *M*
Rockhurst University *B*

New York
City University of New York
Baruch College *M*
New York University *M*
Pace University *B, M*
Pace University:
Pleasantville/Briarcliff *C, M*
State University of New York
College at Brockport *M*
Utica School of Commerce *A*

Ohio
Case Western Reserve University *M*
DeVry University
Columbus *M*
Franklin University *M*

Pennsylvania
Carlow College *B*
DeVry University
Ft. Washington *M*
La Salle University *B*

Penn State
University Park *C*
Philadelphia Biblical University *M*
Robert Morris University *M*

Puerto Rico
University of the Sacred Heart *M*

South Dakota
Dakota State University *C*

Tennessee
Austin Peay State University *B*
Crichton College *B*
East Tennessee State University *M*
Southern Adventist University *B, M*

Texas
Stephen F. Austin State University *B*
University of Texas
Dallas *D*

Virginia
DeVry University
Crystal City *M*

Washington
Crown College *B*
DeVry University
Seattle *M*
Seattle University *M*

West Virginia
Mountain State University *B*
Salem International University *B*

Wisconsin
University of Wisconsin
Madison *M*

Norwegian

Minnesota
St. Olaf College *B*

North Dakota
North Dakota State University *B, T*
University of North Dakota *B, T*

Washington
University of Washington *B*

Nuclear engineering

Arizona
University of Arizona *B, M, D*

California
University of California
Berkeley *B, M, D*
University of Southern California *M*

Florida
University of Florida *B, M, D*

Georgia
Georgia Institute of Technology *B, M, D*

Idaho
Idaho State University *M, D*
University of Idaho *M, D*

Illinois
University of Illinois
Urbana-Champaign *B, M, D*

Indiana
Purdue University *B, M, D*

Kansas
Kansas State University *B, M, D*

Maryland
University of Maryland
College Park *B, M, D*

Massachusetts
Massachusetts Institute of
Technology *B, M, D*

Michigan
University of Michigan *B, M, D*

Missouri
University of Missouri
Columbia *M, D*
Rolla *B, M, D*

New Mexico
University of New Mexico *B, M*

New York
Columbia University
Fu Foundation School of
Engineering and Applied
Science *M, D*
Cornell University *M, D*
Rensselaer Polytechnic Institute *B, M, D*
United States Military Academy *B*

North Carolina
North Carolina State University *B, M, D*

Ohio
Ohio State University
Columbus Campus *M, D*
University of Cincinnati *B, M, D*

Oregon
Oregon State University *B, M, D*

Pennsylvania
Gettysburg College *B*
Penn State
Abington *B*
Altoona *B*
Beaver *B*
Berks *B*
Delaware County *B*
Dubois *B*
Fayette *B*
Hazleton *B*
Lehigh Valley *B*
McKeesport *B*
Mont Alto *B*
New Kensington *B*
Schuylkill - Capital College *B*
Shenango *B*
University Park *B, M, D*
Wilkes-Barre *B*
Worthington Scranton *B*
York *B*

Tennessee
University of Tennessee
Knoxville *B, M, D*

Texas
Texas A&M University *B, M, D*

Utah
University of Utah *B, M, D*

Washington
University of Washington *M, D*

Wisconsin
University of Wisconsin
Madison *B, M, D*

Nuclear engineering technology

New Jersey
Thomas Edison State College *A, B*

Ohio
Lakeland Community College *A*

Nuclear medical technology

Alabama
Community College of the Air Force *A*
Enterprise State Junior College *A*
Faulkner University *A*
University of Alabama
Birmingham *B*

Arizona
Gateway Community College *C, A*

Arkansas
University of Arkansas
for Medical Sciences *B*
University of Central Arkansas *B*

California
California State University
Dominguez Hills *B*
Loma Linda University *C*

Connecticut
Gateway Community College *A*
Middlesex Community College *C, A*

Delaware
Delaware Technical and Community
College
Stanton/Wilmington Campus *A*

District of Columbia
George Washington University *C, A, B*

Florida
Barry University *B*
Broward Community College *A*
Florida Hospital College of Health
Sciences *B*
Hillsborough Community College *A*
Manatee Community College *A*
Polk Community College *A*
Santa Fe Community College *A*

Georgia
Dalton State College *A*
Medical College of Georgia *C*

Illinois
Benedictine University *B*
College of DuPage *C*
Roosevelt University *B*
Triton College *A*
University of St. Francis *B*

Indiana
Ball State University *A*
Indiana University
Bloomington *B*
Indiana University-Purdue University
Indianapolis *B*

Iowa
Mercy College of Health Sciences *C*
University of Iowa *B*

Kentucky
Jefferson Community College *A*
Lexington Community College *A*
University of Louisville *B*

Louisiana
Delgado Community College *C*

Maryland
Howard Community College *A*

Massachusetts
Laboure College *A*
Massachusetts College of Pharmacy and
Health Sciences *B*
Salem State College *B*
Springfield Technical Community
College *A*
Suffolk University *B*

Michigan
Aquinas College *B*
Ferris State University *A, B*
Lansing Community College *A*
Oakland Community College *A*

Minnesota
St. Cloud State University *B*
St. Mary's University of Minnesota *B*

Mississippi
University of Mississippi Medical
Center *C*

Missouri

St. Louis University *B*

University of Missouri
Columbia *B*

Nebraska

University of Nebraska
Medical Center *B*

Nevada

University of Nevada
Las Vegas *B*

New Jersey

Gloucester County College *A*

Thomas Edison State College *A, B*

Union County College *A*

University of Medicine and Dentistry of
New Jersey
School of Health Related
Professions *C, B*

New Mexico

University of New Mexico *C*

New York

City University of New York
Bronx Community College *A*

Hudson Valley Community College *C*

Long Island University
C. W. Post Campus *B*

Manhattan College *B*

Molloy College *A*

Rochester Institute of Technology *C, B*

State University of New York
Buffalo *B*

North Carolina

Caldwell Community College and
Technical Institute *A*

Forsyth Technical Community College *A*

Pitt Community College *A*

University of North Carolina
Chapel Hill *C*

Ohio

Kent State University *A*

Kettering College of Medical Arts *A*

Lorain County Community College *A*

Notre Dame College *B*

Owens Community College
Toledo *A*

University of Cincinnati *B*

University of Findlay *C, A, B*

Oklahoma

University of Oklahoma *B*

Oregon

Oregon Health Sciences University *C*

Pennsylvania

Cedar Crest College *C, B*

Community College of Allegheny
County *C, A*

Harrisburg Area Community College *A*

Indiana University of Pennsylvania *B*

York College of Pennsylvania *B*

Puerto Rico

University of Puerto Rico
Medical Sciences Campus *B*

South Carolina

Midlands Technical College *A*

South Dakota

Southeast Technical Institute *A*

Tennessee

Chattanooga State Technical Community
College *C*

Texas

Amarillo College *A*

El Paso Community College *C*

Galveston College *C, A*

Houston Community College
System *C, A*

University of Houston *B*

University of the Incarnate Word *B*

Utah

Weber State University *B*

Vermont

University of Vermont *B*

Virginia

J. Sargeant Reynolds Community
College *C*

Old Dominion University *B*

Washington

Bellevue Community College *A*

West Virginia

West Virginia State College *A*

Wheeling Jesuit University *B*

Wisconsin

University of Wisconsin
La Crosse *B*
Madison *B, M, D*

Nuclear physics

Illinois

Northwestern University *B, M, D*

Iowa

Iowa State University *M, D*

Texas

University of North Texas *M, D*

University of Texas
Arlington *M*

Nuclear power technology

Ohio

Lakeland Community College *A*

Texas

Texas A&M University *M*

Nurse anesthetist

Alabama

University of Alabama
Birmingham *M*

Arkansas

Arkansas State University *M*

California

California State University
Long Beach *M*

Samuel Merritt College *M*

University of California
Los Angeles *M*

University of Southern California *M*

Connecticut

Central Connecticut State University *M*

Florida

Barry University *M*

Georgia

Medical College of Georgia *M*

Illinois

Bradley University *M*

Rush University *M*

Southern Illinois University
Edwardsville *M*

Iowa

University of Iowa *M*

Kansas

Newman University *M*

University of Kansas Medical Center *M*

Kentucky

Murray State University *M*

Maine

University of New England *M*

Massachusetts

Northeastern University *M*

Michigan

Oakland University *M*

University of Michigan
Flint *M*

Wayne State University *M*

Minnesota

St. Mary's University of Minnesota *M*

University of Minnesota
Twin Cities *B*

Missouri

Southwest Missouri State University *M*

Webster University *M*

New York

Columbia University
School of Nursing *M*

State University of New York
Buffalo *M*

Ohio

Case Western Reserve University *M*

Ohio State University
Columbus Campus *M*

Youngstown State University *M*

Pennsylvania

California University of Pennsylvania *B*

Drexel University *M*

St. Joseph's University *M*

University of Pittsburgh *M*

Villanova University *M*

Puerto Rico

Pontifical Catholic University of Puerto
Rico *M*

University of Puerto Rico
Medical Sciences Campus *M*

South Carolina

Medical University of South Carolina *M*

University of South Carolina *M*

South Dakota

Mount Marty College *M*

Texas

Texas Wesleyan University *M*

University of Texas
Houston Health Science Center *M*

Virginia

Virginia Commonwealth University *M*

Washington

Gonzaga University *M*

Nurse midwifery

Colorado

University of Colorado
Health Sciences Center *M*

New Jersey

University of Medicine and Dentistry of
New Jersey
School of Health Related
Professions *M*

William Paterson University of New
Jersey *M*

New York

State University of New York
Health Science Center at Stony
Brook *M*
Stony Brook *M*

Ohio

Case Western Reserve University *M*

Pennsylvania

University of Pennsylvania *M*

South Carolina

Medical University of South Carolina *M*

Texas

University of Texas
Medical Branch at Galveston *M*

Wisconsin

Marquette University *M*

Nursery operations

California

College of the Redwoods *C*

Foothill College *C, A*

Los Angeles Pierce College *C*

MiraCosta College *C, A*

Modesto Junior College *C*

Santa Rosa Junior College *C*

Southwestern College *C, A*

Florida

South Florida Community College *C*

Georgia

Albany Technical College *C*

Illinois

College of DuPage *C*

Joliet Junior College *C, A*

Kishwaukee College *C, A*

Southwestern Illinois College *A*

William Rainey Harper College *C, A*

Iowa

Indian Hills Community College *C, A*

Kirkwood Community College *A*

Kansas

Dodge City Community College *C*

Kentucky

Maysville Community College *C*

Maine

University of Maine *B*

Michigan

Northwestern Michigan College *A*

Minnesota

Anoka-Ramsey Community College *A*

Hennepin Technical College *C, A*

Nebraska

Metropolitan Community College *C, A*

Nebraska College of Technical
Agriculture *A*

New Hampshire

University of New Hampshire *A*

New York

State University of New York
College of Agriculture and
Technology at Cobleskill *A*
College of Agriculture and
Technology at Morrisville *A*

North Dakota

Minot State University: Bottineau
Campus *A*

Ohio

Ohio State University
Agricultural Technical Institute *A*

Pennsylvania

Pennsylvania College of Technology *A*

South Dakota

Southeast Technical Institute *A*

Tennessee

Tennessee Technological University *B*

Texas

Western Texas College *C, A*

Washington

Clark College *C*

Edmonds Community College *A*

South Seattle Community College *C, A*

Spokane Community College *A*

Nursing (R.N.)

Alabama

Alabama Southern Community
College *A*
Auburn University *B*
Auburn University at Montgomery *B*
Bevill State Community College *A*
Bishop State Community College *A*
Calhoun Community College *A*
Chattahoochee Valley Community
College *A*
Gadsden State Community College *A*
Jacksonville State University *B, M*
Jefferson Davis Community College *A*
Jefferson State Community College *A*
Lawson State Community College *A*
Northeast Alabama Community
College *A*
Northwest-Shoals Community College *A*
Samford University *B, M*
Shelton State Community College *A*
Spring Hill College *B*
Troy State University *A, B, M*
University of Alabama *B*
University of Alabama
Birmingham *B, M, D*
Huntsville *B, M*
University of Mobile *A, B, M*
University of North Alabama *B*
University of South Alabama *B, M*
University of West Alabama *A*
Wallace Community College: Sparks
Campus *A*
Wallace State Community College at
Hanceville *A*

Alaska

University of Alaska
Anchorage *A, B, M*

Arizona

Arizona State University *B, M*
Arizona Western College *A*
Central Arizona College *C, A*
Cochise College *A*
Eastern Arizona College *A*
Gateway Community College *A*
Glendale Community College *A*
Northern Arizona University *B, M*
Phoenix College *A*
Pima Community College *A*
Scottsdale Community College *A*
University of Arizona *B*
Yavapai College *A*

Arkansas

Arkansas State University *A, B, M*
Arkansas State University
Mountain Home *A*
Arkansas Tech University *B*
East Arkansas Community College *A*
Harding University *B, M*
Henderson State University *B*
Mississippi County Community
College *A*
North Arkansas College *A*
Northwest Arkansas Community
College *A*
Phillips Community College of the
University of Arkansas *A*
Southeast Arkansas College *A*
Southern Arkansas University *A, B*
University of Arkansas *B*
University of Arkansas
Community College at Batesville *A*
Fort Smith *A, B*
Little Rock *A*
Monticello *A, B*
Pine Bluff *B*
for Medical Sciences *B, M*
University of Central Arkansas *B, M*

California

Antelope Valley College *A*
Azusa Pacific University *B*

Bakersfield College *A*
Biola University *B*
Cabrillo College *C, A*
California State University
Bakersfield *B*
Chico *B, M*
Dominguez Hills *B*
Fresno *B*
Fullerton *B*
Long Beach *B*
Northridge *B*
Stanislaus *B*
Cerritos Community College *A*
Chabot College *A*
College of the Canyons *A*
College of the Redwoods *C*
College of the Sequoias *A*
Contra Costa College *A*
Cuesta College *C, A*
De Anza College *A*
Dominican University of California *B, M*
East Los Angeles College *A*
Gavilan Community College *C, A*
Glendale Community College *C, A*
Golden West College *C, A*
Grossmont Community College *A*
Imperial Valley College *A*
Loma Linda University *A, B*
Long Beach City College *C, A*
Los Angeles Harbor College *A*
Los Angeles Pierce College *A*
Los Angeles Southwest College *A*
Los Medanos College *A*
Modesto Junior College *A*
Monterey Peninsula College *A*
Moorpark College *A*
Mount St. Mary's College *A, B*
Mount San Antonio College *C, A*
Mount San Jacinto College *A*
Napa Valley College *A*
Ohlone College *A*
Pacific Union College *A, B*
Palomar College *A*
Point Loma Nazarene University *B*
Riverside Community College *C, A*
Samuel Merritt College *B*
San Diego City College *A*
San Diego State University *B, M*
San Joaquin Delta College *C, A*
Santa Barbara City College *A*
Santa Monica College *A*
Santa Rosa Junior College *C, A*
Shasta College *C, A*
Sierra College *A*
Sonoma State University *B*
Southwestern College *A*
University of San Francisco *B, M*
Ventura College *C, A*
Victor Valley College *C, A*
Yuba Community College District *A*

Colorado

Arapahoe Community College *A*
Colorado Mountain College
Spring Valley Campus *A*
Colorado State University
Pueblo *B*
Front Range Community College *A*
Mesa State College *B*
Metropolitan State College of Denver *B*
Morgan Community College *A*
Otero Junior College *A*
University of Colorado
Colorado Springs *B*
Health Sciences Center *B, M, D*
University of Northern Colorado *B, M*

Connecticut

Capital Community College *A*
Central Connecticut State University *B*
Fairfield University *B, M*
Housatonic Community College *A*
Naugatuck Valley Community College *A*
Norwalk Community College *A*
Quinnipiac University *B, M*
St. Joseph College *B, M*

Southern Connecticut State University *B*
University of Connecticut *B, M, D*
University of Hartford *B*
Western Connecticut State University *B*
Yale University *M, D*

Delaware

Delaware State University *B*
Delaware Technical and Community
College
Owens Campus *A*
Stanton/Wilmington Campus *A*
Terry Campus *A*

District of Columbia

Catholic University of America *B*
Georgetown University *B, M*
University of the District of
Columbia *A, B*

Florida

Barry University *B*
Bethune-Cookman College *B*
Broward Community College *A*
Chipola Junior College *A*
Florida Agricultural and Mechanical
University *B, M*
Florida Atlantic University *B, M, D*
Florida Gulf Coast University *B, M*
Florida Hospital College of Health
Sciences *A, B*
Florida International University *B, M*
Florida Keys Community College *A*
Florida State University *B, M*
Gulf Coast Community College *A*
Hillsborough Community College *A*
Indian River Community College *A*
Jacksonville University *B*
Lake City Community College *A*
Lake-Sumter Community College *A*
Miami-Dade Community College *A*
Palm Beach Community College *A*
Pasco-Hernando Community College *A*
Pensacola Junior College *A*
Polk Community College *A*
St. Petersburg College *A*
Santa Fe Community College *A*
Seminole Community College *A*
South Florida Community College *A*
Tallahassee Community College *A*
University of Central Florida *C, B, M*
University of Florida *B, M, D*
University of Miami *B, M, D*
University of North Florida *B, M*
University of South Florida *B, M, D*
University of West Florida *B*
Valencia Community College *A*

Georgia

Albany State University *B, M*
Augusta State University *A*
Brenau University *B*
Coastal Georgia Community College *A*
Columbus State University *B*
Columbus Technical College *A*
Covenant College *B*
Dalton State College *A*
Darton College *A*
Floyd College *A*
Georgia College and State
University *B, M*
Georgia Perimeter College *A*
Georgia Southern University *B*
Georgia Southwestern State University *B*
Georgia State University *B, M, D*
Gordon College *A*
Kennesaw State University *B, M*
LaGrange College *B*
Macon State College *A, B*
Mercer University *B*
Middle Georgia College *A*
North Georgia College & State
University *A, B*
Piedmont College *B*
South Georgia College *A*
State University of West Georgia *B, M*
Thomas University *B*

Hawaii

Hawaii Pacific University *B, M*
University of Hawaii
Hawaii Community College *A*
Kauai Community College *A*
Manoa *B*

Idaho

Boise State University *A, B*
Brigham Young University - Idaho *A, B*
College of Southern Idaho *A*
Idaho State University *B*
Lewis-Clark State College *B*
North Idaho College *A*
Northwest Nazarene University *B*

Illinois

Aurora University *B*
Black Hawk College *A*
Blessing-Reiman College of Nursing *B*
Bradley University *B*
Carl Sandburg College *A*
Chicago State University *B*
City Colleges of Chicago
Kennedy-King College *A*
Malcolm X College *A*
College of DuPage *A*
College of Lake County *A*
Concordia University *B*
Danville Area Community College *A*
De Paul University *B*
Elgin Community College *A*
Heartland Community College *A*
Illinois Eastern Community Colleges
Olney Central College *A*
Illinois State University *B, M*
Illinois Valley Community College *A*
Illinois Wesleyan University *B*
John A. Logan College *A*
John Wood Community College *A*
Joliet Junior College *A*
Kankakee Community College *A*
Kaskaskia College *A*
Kishwaukee College *A*
Lake Land College *A*
Lakeview College of Nursing *B*
Lewis University *B*
Lewis and Clark Community College *A*
Millikin University *B*
Moraine Valley Community College *A*
North Park University *B*
Northern Illinois University *B*
Oakton Community College *A*
Parkland College *A*
Prairie State College *A*
Rend Lake College *A*
Richland Community College *A*
Rock Valley College *A*
Rockford College *B*
Rush University *B, M, D*
St. Xavier University *B*
Sauk Valley Community College *A*
South Suburban College of Cook
County *A*
Southeastern Illinois College *A*
Southern Illinois University
Edwardsville *B*
Southwestern Illinois College *A*
Trinity Christian College *B*
Triton College *A*
University of Illinois
Chicago *B*
University of St. Francis *B, M*
Waubonsee Community College *A*
West Suburban College of Nursing *B*
William Rainey Harper College *A*

Indiana

Anderson University *B*
Ball State University *B*
Bethel College *A, B*
Goshen College *B*
Indiana State University *A, B, M*

Indiana University
  Bloomington *B*
  Kokomo *A, B*
  Northwest *A, B*
  South Bend *A, B*
  Southeast *B*
Indiana University-Purdue University
  Fort Wayne *A, B*
Indiana University-Purdue University
  Indianapolis *A, B, M, D*
Ivy Tech State College
  Bloomington *A*
  Central Indiana *A*
  Eastcentral *A*
  Lafayette *A*
  Northcentral *A*
  Northwest *A*
  Southcentral *A*
  Southeast *A*
  Southwest *A*
  Whitewater *A*
Purdue University *B*
Purdue University
  Calumet *A, B*
Saint Mary's College *B*
University of Indianapolis *A, B*
University of St. Francis *A*
University of Southern Indiana *A, B, M*
Valparaiso University *B*
Vincennes University *A*

Iowa

Clinton Community College *A*
Coe College *B*
Des Moines Area Community College *A*
Dordt College *B*
Ellsworth Community College *A*
Graceland University *B*
Hawkeye Community College *A*
Indian Hills Community College *C, A*
Iowa Central Community College *A*
Iowa Wesleyan College *B*
Iowa Western Community College *A*
Kirkwood Community College *A*
Luther College *B*
Marshalltown Community College *A*
Mercy College of Health Sciences *C*
North Iowa Area Community College *A*
Northeast Iowa Community College *A*
St. Ambrose University *B*
St. Luke's College *A*
Scott Community College *A*
Southeastern Community College
  North Campus *A*
  South Campus *A*
Southwestern Community College *A*
University of Iowa *B*
Western Iowa Tech Community
  College *A*

Kansas

Baker University *B*
Barton County Community College *A*
Bethel College *B*
Butler County Community College *C, A*
Cloud County Community College *A*
Dodge City Community College *A*
Garden City Community College *A*
Hesston College *A*
Hutchinson Community College *A*
Johnson County Community College *A*
Kansas City Kansas Community
  College *A*
Kansas Wesleyan University *A*
Labette Community College *A*
MidAmerica Nazarene University *B*
Newman University *B*
North Central Kansas Technical
  College *A*
Pittsburg State University *B*
Pratt Community College *A*
Seward County Community College *A*
Southwestern College *B*
Washburn University of Topeka *B*

Kentucky

Bellarmine University *B, M*
Berea College *B*
Hazard Community College *A*
Hopkinsville Community College *A*
Jefferson Community College *A*
Madisonville Community College *A*
Maysville Community College *A*
Morehead State University *A, B*
Murray State University *B*
Pikeville College *A*
Prestonsburg Community College *A*
St. Catharine College *A*
Somerset Community College *A*
Southeast Community College *A*
Spalding University *B*
Spencerian College *A*
Thomas More College *B*
University of Louisville *B*

Louisiana

Delgado Community College *A*
Dillard University *B*
Grambling State University *B*
Louisiana Tech University *A*
Loyola University New Orleans *B, M*
McNeese State University *A, B*
Nicholls State University *A, B*
Northwestern State University *A, B*
Southeastern Louisiana University *B*
Southern University and Agricultural and
  Mechanical College *B, M*
University of Louisiana at Lafayette *B*
University of Louisiana at Monroe *B*

Maine

Central Maine Medical Center School of
  Nursing *A*
Central Maine Technical College *A*
Husson College *B*
St. Joseph's College *B*
University of Maine *B, M*
University of Maine
  Augusta *A*
University of New England *A, B*
University of Southern Maine *B, M*

Maryland

Allegany College *A*
Anne Arundel Community College *A*
Bowie State University *B, M*
Chesapeake College *A*
College of Southern Maryland *A*
Columbia Union College *B*
Community College of Baltimore County
  Catonsville *A*
  Dundalk *A*
  Essex *A*
Coppin State College *B*
Frederick Community College *A*
Hagerstown Community College *A*
Harford Community College *A*
Howard Community College *A*
Johns Hopkins University *M, D*
Montgomery College
  Rockville Campus *A*
Salisbury University *B*
University of Maryland
  Baltimore *B*
Wor-Wic Community College *A*

Massachusetts

American International College *B*
Atlantic Union College *B*
Becker College *A*
Berkshire Community College *A*
Boston College *B*
Bunker Hill Community College *A*
Cape Cod Community College *A*
Endicott College *B*
Fitchburg State College *B*
Greenfield Community College *A*
Laboure College *A*
Massachusetts Bay Community
  College *A, B*
Massasoit Community College *A*
Mount Wachusett Community College *A*

Northeastern University *B, M*
Quinsigamond Community College *A*
Regis College *A, B, M*
Salem State College *B*
Simmons College *B, M*
Springfield Technical Community
  College *A*
University of Massachusetts
  Amherst *B*
  Boston *B*
  Dartmouth *B*
  Lowell *B, M, D*

Michigan

Alpena Community College *A*
Baker College
  of Owosso *A*
Bay de Noc Community College *A*
Davenport University
  Midland *A*
Eastern Michigan University *B, M*
Ferris State University *A, B*
Finlandia University *A*
Glen Oaks Community College *A*
Gogebic Community College *A*
Grand Rapids Community College *A*
Grand Valley State University *B, M*
Hope College *B*
Jackson Community College *A*
Kellogg Community College *A*
Kirtland Community College *C, A*
Macomb Community College *A*
Madonna University *B, M*
Michigan State University *B, M*
Mid Michigan Community College *A*
Monroe County Community College *A*
Montcalm Community College *A*
Mott Community College *A*
Muskegon Community College *A*
North Central Michigan College *A*
Northern Michigan University *B*
Northwestern Michigan College *A*
Oakland Community College *A*
Oakland University *B*
Saginaw Valley State University *B*
St. Clair County Community College *A*
Schoolcraft College *A*
Southwestern Michigan College *A*
University of Michigan *B*
Washtenaw Community College *C, A*
Wayne County Community College *A*
Wayne State University *B, D*
West Shore Community College *A*

Minnesota

Anoka-Ramsey Community College *A*
Bethel College *B*
Century Community and Technical
  College *A*
College of St. Benedict *B*
College of St. Catherine *A, B*
College of St. Scholastica *B*
Concordia College: Moorhead *B*
Fergus Falls Community College *A*
Gustavus Adolphus College *B*
Hibbing Community College: A
  Technical and Community College *A*
Inver Hills Community College *A*
Lake Superior College: A Community
  and Technical College *A*
Minneapolis Community and Technical
  College *A*
Minnesota State College - Southeast
  Technical *A*
Minnesota State University
  Mankato *B, M*
Minnesota West Community and
  Technical College: Worthington
  Campus *A*
Normandale Community College *A*
North Hennepin Community College *A*
Northland Community & Technical
  College *A*
Ridgewater College: A Community and
  Technical College *A*

Riverland Community College: A
  Technical and Community College *A*
Rochester Community and Technical
  College *A*
St. Cloud State University *B*
St. John's University *B*
St. Olaf College *B*
South Central Technical College *A*
University of Minnesota
  Twin Cities *B, M, D*
Winona State University *B, M*

Mississippi

Alcorn State University *A, B*
Delta State University *B, M*
Itawamba Community College *A*
Mississippi College *B*
Mississippi Gulf Coast Community
  College
  Perkinston *A*
University of Southern Mississippi *B*

Missouri

Avila University *B*
Central Methodist College *B*
Central Missouri State University *B, M*
Crowder College *A*
Culver-Stockton College *B*
Deaconess College of Nursing *A, B*
East Central College *A*
Hannibal-LaGrange College *B*
Jefferson College *A*
Lincoln University *A, B*
Maple Woods Community College *A*
Mineral Area College *A*
Missouri Southern State College *B*
Missouri Western State College *B*
Moberly Area Community College *A*
North Central Missouri College *A*
Penn Valley Community College *A*
St. Charles Community College *A*
St. Louis University *B, M, D*
St. Luke's College *B*
Sanford-Brown College *A*
Southeast Missouri State
  University *B, M*
Southwest Baptist University *A*
Southwest Missouri State University:
  West Plains Campus *A*
Three Rivers Community College *A*
Truman State University *B*
William Jewell College *B*

Montana

Miles Community College *A*
Montana State University
  Bozeman *A, B*
Montana Tech of the University of
  Montana *A, B*
Salish Kootenai College *A, B*

Nebraska

Central Community College *C, A*
Clarkson College *B*
College of Saint Mary *A, B*
Creighton University *B*
Grace University *B*
Metropolitan Community College *A*
Mid Plains Community College Area *A*
Nebraska Methodist College of Nursing
  and Allied Health *B*
Southeast Community College
  Lincoln Campus *A*

Nevada

Community College of Southern
  Nevada *A*
Great Basin College *A*
Truckee Meadows Community
  College *A*
University of Nevada
  Las Vegas *B, M*
  Reno *B*
Western Nevada Community College *A*

New Hampshire

Colby-Sawyer College *B*

New Hampshire Community Technical
  College
    Berlin *A*
    Claremont *A*
    Manchester *A*
    Nashua *A*
    Stratham *A*
New Hampshire Technical Institute *A*
Rivier College *A, B*
St. Anselm College *B*
University of New Hampshire *B, M*
University of New Hampshire at
  Manchester *B*

New Jersey

Atlantic Cape Community College *A*
Bergen Community College *A*
Bloomfield College *B*
Brookdale Community College *A*
Burlington County College *A*
Camden County College *A*
The College of New Jersey *B*
County College of Morris *A*
Cumberland County College *A*
Fairleigh Dickinson University
  College at Florham *B*
Felician College *B*
Gloucester County College *A*
Mercer County Community College *A*
Middlesex County College *A*
Monmouth University *B, M*
Ocean County College *A*
Passaic County Community College *A*
Ramapo College of New Jersey *B, M*
Raritan Valley Community College *A*
Richard Stockton College of New
  Jersey *B, M*
Sussex County Community College *A*
Union County College *A*
Warren County Community College *A*
William Paterson University of New
  Jersey *B*

New Mexico

Albuquerque Technical-Vocational
  Institute *A*
Dona Ana Branch Community College of
  New Mexico State University *A*
Eastern New Mexico University *B*
New Mexico State University *B, M*
San Juan College *A*
Santa Fe Community College *A*
University of New Mexico *B, M*

New York

Adelphi University *B*
Adirondack Community College *A*
Broome Community College *A*
Cayuga County Community College *A*
City University of New York
  Borough of Manhattan Community
    College *A*
  Bronx Community College *A*
  College of Staten Island *B*
  Hostos Community College *A*
  Hunter College *B, M*
  Kingsborough Community
    College *A*
  Queensborough Community
    College *A*
  York College *B*
Clinton Community College *A*
Cochran School of Nursing-St. John's
  Riverside Hospital *A*
College of New Rochelle *B, M*
Concordia College *B*
Corning Community College *A*
D'Youville College *B, M*
Dominican College of Blauvelt *B*
Dutchess Community College *A*
Elmira College *B*
Erie Community College
  City Campus *A*
  North Campus *A*
Excelsior College *A, B, M*
Finger Lakes Community College *A*

Fulton-Montgomery Community
  College *A*
Genesee Community College *A*
Hartwick College *B*
Helene Fuld College of Nursing *A*
Hudson Valley Community College *A*
Jamestown Community College *A*
Jefferson Community College *A*
Keuka College *B*
Maria College *A*
Mercy College *B*
Mohawk Valley Community College *A*
Molloy College *B, M*
Monroe Community College *C, A*
Mount St. Mary College *B, M*
Nassau Community College *A*
New York Institute of Technology *B*
New York University *B, M*
Niagara County Community College *A*
Niagara University *B*
North Country Community College *A*
Pace University *B, M*
Pace University:
  Pleasantville/Briarcliff *B, M*
Phillips Beth Israel School of Nursing *A*
Roberts Wesleyan College *B*
Rockland Community College *A*
Russell Sage College *B*
St. Elizabeth College of Nursing *A*
St. John Fisher College *B*
St. Joseph's Hospital Health Center
  School of Nursing *A*
State University of New York
  Binghamton *B*
  Buffalo *B*
  College at Brockport *B*
  College at Plattsburgh *B*
  College of Agriculture and
    Technology at Morrisville *A*
  College of Technology at Alfred *A*
  College of Technology at Canton *A*
  College of Technology at Delhi *A*
  Farmingdale *A*
  Health Science Center at
    Brooklyn *B, M*
  Health Science Center at Stony
    Brook *B*
  Institute of Technology at
    Utica/Rome *B, M*
  Stony Brook *B*
  Upstate Medical University *B*
Suffolk County Community College *A*
Tompkins-Cortland Community
  College *A*
Trocaire College *A*
Ulster County Community College *A*
Utica College *B*
Wagner College *B*
Westchester Community College *A*

North Carolina

Alamance Community College *A*
Asheville Buncombe Technical
  Community College *A*
Barton College *B*
Beaufort County Community College *A*
Blue Ridge Community College *A*
Caldwell Community College and
  Technical Institute *A*
Cape Fear Community College *A*
Catawba Valley Community College *A*
Central Carolina Community College *A*
Cleveland Community College *A*
Coastal Carolina Community College *A*
College of the Albemarle *A*
Craven Community College *A*
Davidson County Community
  College *C, A*
Durham Technical Community
  College *A*
East Carolina University *B*
Edgecombe Community College *A*
Fayetteville Technical Community
  College *A*
Forsyth Technical Community College *A*
Gardner-Webb University *B, M*

Gaston College *A*
Guilford Technical Community
  College *A*
Halifax Community College *A*
Haywood Community College *A*
Isothermal Community College *A*
James Sprunt Community College *A*
Lenoir Community College *A*
Lenoir-Rhyne College *B*
Mayland Community College *A*
Mitchell Community College *A*
Nash Community College *A*
North Carolina Central University *B*
Piedmont Community College *A*
Pitt Community College *A*
Queens University of Charlotte *B*
Randolph Community College *A*
Richmond Community College *A*
Roanoke-Chowan Community
  College *C, A*
Rockingham Community College *A*
Rowan-Cabarrus Community College *A*
Sampson Community College *A*
Sandhills Community College *A*
Southeastern Community College *A*
Stanly Community College *A*
Surry Community College *A*
Tri-County Community College *A*
University of North Carolina
  Chapel Hill *B*
  Charlotte *B, M*
  Greensboro *C, B, M*
  Wilmington *B, M*
Vance-Granville Community College *A*
Wake Technical Community College *A*
Wayne Community College *A*
Western Carolina University *B*
Western Piedmont Community
  College *A*
Wilkes Community College *A*
Wilson Technical Community College *A*
Winston-Salem State University *B*

North Dakota

Dickinson State University *B*
Jamestown College *B*
Medcenter One College of Nursing *B*
Minot State University *B*
North Dakota State University *B, M*
University of North Dakota *B, M, D, T*

Ohio

Bowling Green State University *B*
Bowling Green State University:
  Firelands College *A*
Case Western Reserve University *B*
Cedarville University *B*
Central Ohio Technical College *A*
Cincinnati State Technical and
  Community College *A*
Clark State Community College *A*
Cleveland State University *B*
College of Mount St. Joseph *B*
Columbus State Community College *A*
Cuyahoga Community College
  Eastern Campus *A*
  Metropolitan Campus *A*
  Western Campus *A*
Edison State Community College *A*
Hocking Technical College *A*
James A. Rhodes State College *A*
Kent State University *A*
Kent State University
  Ashtabula Regional Campus *A*
  East Liverpool Regional Campus *A*
  Salem Regional Campus *A, B*
  Tuscarawas Campus *A, B*
Kettering College of Medical Arts *A*
Lakeland Community College *A*
Malone College *B*
Marion Technical College *A*
Miami University
  Hamilton Campus *A*
  Middletown Campus *A*
  Oxford Campus *B*
North Central State College *A*

Northwest State Community College *A*
Ohio University *A*
Ohio University
  Chillicothe Campus *A, B*
  Southern Campus at Ironton *B*
  Zanesville Campus *A*
Otterbein College *B*
Owens Community College
  Findlay Campus *A*
  Toledo *A*
Shawnee State University *A*
Southern State Community College *A*
Stark State College of Technology *A*
University of Akron *B, M, D*
University of Cincinnati *B*
University of Cincinnati
  Clermont College *A*
  Raymond Walters College *A*
University of Rio Grande *A, B*
University of Toledo *A, B*
Ursuline College *B*
Walsh University *B*
Washington State Community College *A*
Wright State University *B*
Youngstown State University *B*

Oklahoma

Bacone College *A, B*
Carl Albert State College *A*
Eastern Oklahoma State College *A*
Northeastern Oklahoma Agricultural and
  Mechanical College *A*
Northern Oklahoma College *A*
Northwestern Oklahoma State
  University *A*
Oklahoma Baptist University *B*
Oklahoma City Community College *A*
Oklahoma City University *B*
Oklahoma Panhandle State University *B*
Oklahoma State University
  Oklahoma City *A*
Oklahoma Wesleyan University *A*
Oral Roberts University *B*
Redlands Community College *A*
Seminole State College *A*
Southwestern Oklahoma State
  University *B*
University of Oklahoma *B, M*
University of Tulsa *B*
Western Oklahoma State College *A*

Oregon

Blue Mountain Community College *A*
Central Oregon Community College *A*
Chemeketa Community College *A*
Clackamas Community College *A*
Clatsop Community College *A*
Eastern Oregon University *B*
Lane Community College *A*
Linfield College *B*
Linn-Benton Community College *A*
Oregon Health Sciences University *B*
Rogue Community College *A*
Southern Oregon University *B*
Treasure Valley Community College *A*
Umpqua Community College *A*
University of Portland *B, M*

Pennsylvania

Bloomsburg University of
  Pennsylvania *B, M*
Bucks County Community College *A*
Butler County Community College *A*
Carlow College *B*
Community College of Allegheny
  County *A*
Community College of Beaver County *A*
Community College of Philadelphia *A*
Delaware County Community College *A*
Drexel University *B, M*
Duquesne University *B*
East Stroudsburg University of
  Pennsylvania *B*
Edinboro University of
  Pennsylvania *B, M*
Gettysburg College *B*

Gwynedd-Mercy College A
Harrisburg Area Community College A
Immaculata University B
Indiana University of Pennsylvania B, M
Kutztown University of Pennsylvania B
La Salle University B
Lehigh Carbon Community College A
Lock Haven University of
Pennsylvania A
Luzerne County Community College A
Marywood University B
Messiah College B
Montgomery County Community
College A
Moravian College B
Mount Aloysius College A
Neumann College B, M
Northampton County Area Community
College A
Penn State
Abington B
Altoona A, B
Beaver B
Berks B
Delaware County B
Dubois B
Fayette A, B
Harrisburg B
Hazleton B
Lehigh Valley B
Mont Alto A, B
New Kensington B
Schuylkill - Capital College B
Shenango B
University Park B, M, D
Wilkes-Barre B
Worthington Scranton A, B
York B
Pennsylvania College of Technology A
Reading Area Community College A
Seton Hill University B
Slippery Rock University of
Pennsylvania B, M
Temple University B, M
University of Pennsylvania C, B, M, D
University of Pittsburgh B
University of Pittsburgh
Bradford A, B
University of Scranton M
Villanova University B
Waynesburg College B
Westmoreland County Community
College A
Widener University M
Wilkes University B, M
York College of Pennsylvania B, M

Puerto Rico
Columbia College B
Inter American University of Puerto Rico
Barranquitas Campus A, B
Metropolitan Campus A, B
Turabo University B
Universidad Metropolitana A, B
University of Puerto Rico
Humacao A, B
Mayaguez Campus B
Medical Sciences Campus B
University of the Sacred Heart A, B

Rhode Island
Community College of Rhode Island A
University of Rhode Island B

South Carolina
Central Carolina Technical College A
Charleston Southern University C, B
Florence-Darlington Technical College A
Lander University B
Medical University of South
Carolina B, M, D
Midlands Technical College C, A
Northeastern Technical College C
Orangeburg-Calhoun Technical
College A
Piedmont Technical College C, A

Technical College of the Lowcountry A
Tri-County Technical College A
Trident Technical College A
University of South Carolina B
University of South Carolina
Aiken A, B
Lancaster A
Spartanburg A, B
York Technical College A

South Dakota
Augustana College B
Dakota Wesleyan University A
University of South Dakota A

Tennessee
Aquinas College A
Austin Peay State University B
Belmont University B
Carson-Newman College B
Cleveland State Community College A
Dyersburg State Community College A
East Tennessee State University B
Jackson State Community College A
King College B
Maryville College B
Middle Tennessee State University B
Milligan College B
Roane State Community College A
Southern Adventist University A
Southwest Tennessee Community
College A
Tennessee Technological University B
Tennessee Wesleyan College B
Union University B
University of Memphis B
University of Tennessee
Chattanooga C, B, M
Knoxville B
Martin B
University of Tennessee Health Science
Center M, D
Walters State Community College A

Texas
Abilene Christian University B
Alvin Community College C, A
Amarillo College A
Angelina College C, A
Baylor University B
Blinn College C, A
Brazosport College A
Central Texas College A
Clarendon College A
Coastal Bend College A
Collin County Community College
District A
Del Mar College A
East Texas Baptist University B
El Centro College C, A
El Paso Community College A
Galveston College C, A
Grayson County College A
Hardin-Simmons University B, M
Houston Baptist University A, B, M
Houston Community College System A
Howard College A
Kilgore College A
Lamar State College at Port Arthur A
Lamar University A, B, M
Laredo Community College A
North Central Texas College A
North Harris Montgomery Community
College District C, A
Northeast Texas Community College A
Odessa College A
Panola College A
Prairie View A&M University B, M
St. Philip's College A
San Jacinto College
Central Campus A
South Plains College A
Southwest Texas Junior College A
Southwestern Adventist University A, B
Stephen F. Austin State University B
Tarleton State University B

Tarrant County College A
Temple College A
Texas A&M International University B
Texas Christian University B, M
Texas Woman's University B, M
Trinity Valley Community College A
Tyler Junior College A
University of Mary Hardin-Baylor B
University of Texas
Arlington B, M
Austin B, M, D
El Paso B, M
Health Science Center at San
Antonio B
Houston Health Science Center B
Medical Branch at Galveston B
Tyler B
University of the Incarnate Word B, M
Victoria College A
West Texas A&M University B, M
Wharton County Junior College A

Utah
Brigham Young University B
Dixie State College of Utah A
Salt Lake Community College A
Snow College A
Southern Utah University B
University of Utah B, M, D
Utah Valley State College A, B
Weber State University A, B

Vermont
Castleton State College A
University of Vermont B, M
Vermont Technical College A

Virginia
Blue Ridge Community College A
College of Health Sciences A, B
Eastern Mennonite University B
George Mason University B, M, D
Hampton University B
J. Sargeant Reynolds Community
College A
James Madison University B
Marymount University A
Mountain Empire Community College A
Norfolk State University A, B
Old Dominion University B, M
Piedmont Virginia Community
College A
Radford University B, M
Rappahannock Community College A
Shenandoah University B
Southside Virginia Community
College A
Southwest Virginia Community
College A
University of Virginia B, M, D
Virginia Commonwealth University B
Virginia Highlands Community
College A
Virginia Western Community College A

Washington
Bellevue Community College A
Clark College A
Everett Community College C, A
Grays Harbor College A
Lower Columbia College A
Northwest College B
Olympic College C, A
Peninsula College A
Seattle Pacific University B
Seattle University B
Spokane Falls Community College A
University of Washington B
Walla Walla College B
Walla Walla Community College A
Washington State University B, M
Wenatchee Valley College A

West Virginia
Alderson-Broaddus College B
Bluefield State College A
Davis and Elkins College A

Fairmont State College A, B
Glenville State College B
Marshall University A, B
Mountain State University B
Shepherd University B
University of Charleston B
West Virginia Northern Community
College A
West Virginia Wesleyan College B

Wisconsin
Alverno College B
Bellin College of Nursing B
Beloit College B
Blackhawk Technical College A
Cardinal Stritch University A, B
Carroll College B
Chippewa Valley Technical College A
Columbia College of Nursing B
Concordia University Wisconsin B
Edgewood College B, M
Fox Valley Technical College A
Marian College of Fond du Lac B
Marquette University B, M
Mid-State Technical College A
Milwaukee Area Technical College A
Milwaukee School of Engineering B
Moraine Park Technical College A
Mount Mary College B
Nicolet Area Technical College A
University of Wisconsin
Eau Claire B, M
Madison B
Milwaukee B, M, D
Oshkosh B, M
Parkside B
Viterbo University B, M
Waukesha County Technical College A
Western Wisconsin Technical College A

Wyoming
Casper College A
Central Wyoming College A
Sheridan College A
University of Wyoming B, M
Western Wyoming Community
College C, A

Nursing administration

Alabama
University of Alabama M
University of Mobile M

California
Samuel Merritt College M
San Diego State University M
University of San Francisco M
University of Southern California M

Connecticut
Sacred Heart University M
Southern Connecticut State University M
University of Connecticut M
University of Hartford M

Florida
Barry University B, M, D
University of Tampa M, D

Georgia
Armstrong Atlantic State University M
Clayton College and State University B
Georgia College and State University B

Illinois
Bradley University M
Loyola University of Chicago M
North Park University M
St. Xavier University M
Southern Illinois University
Edwardsville M
University of Illinois
Chicago M

Indiana

Indiana University-Purdue University
  Fort Wayne *M*
Indiana University-Purdue University
  Indianapolis *M*
University of St. Francis *M*
Valparaiso University *M*

Iowa

University of Iowa *M, D*

Kentucky

Bellarmine University *M*

Louisiana

Northwestern State University *M*
Southern University and Agricultural and
  Mechanical College *D*

Maine

St. Joseph's College *M*
University of Southern Maine *M*

Maryland

University of Maryland
  Baltimore *M*

Massachusetts

Northeastern University *M*
Salem State College *M*
University of Massachusetts
  Boston *M*

Michigan

Andrews University *M*
Madonna University *M*
Northern Michigan University *M*
Saginaw Valley State University *M*
University of Michigan *M*
Wayne State University *M*

Minnesota

College of St. Scholastica *M*
Winona State University *M*

Mississippi

University of Southern Mississippi *M*

Missouri

Central Methodist College *B*

Nebraska

Clarkson College *M*

Nevada

University of Nevada
  Reno *M*

New Jersey

Kean University *M*
Seton Hall University *M*

New York

City University of New York
  Hunter College *M*
College of Mount St. Vincent *M*
College of New Rochelle *M*
Mount St. Mary College *M*
Pace University *M*
Pace University:
  Pleasantville/Briarcliff *M*
St. John Fisher College *M*
State University of New York
  Buffalo *M*
  Institute of Technology at
    Utica/Rome *M*
Wagner College *M*

Ohio

Ashland University *B*
Ohio University
  Chillicothe Campus *B*
Otterbein College *M*
Xavier University *M*
Youngstown State University *M*

Pennsylvania

Carlow College *M*
Duquesne University *M*
Marywood University *M*
Pennsylvania College of Technology *B*

Robert Morris University *B*
University of Pennsylvania *M*
Villanova University *M*
Widener University *M*

South Carolina

Medical University of South Carolina *M*
University of South Carolina *M*

Tennessee

Southern Adventist University *M*
Union University *M*

Texas

Abilene Christian University *M*
Baylor University *M*
Midwestern State University *M*
Texas A&M University
  Corpus Christi *M*
Texas Woman's University *M*
University of Texas
  Arlington *M*
  El Paso *M*
  Medical Branch at Galveston *M*
  Tyler *M*
West Texas A&M University *M*

Utah

Brigham Young University *B, M*

Virginia

George Mason University *M, D*
Marymount University *M*

Washington

Pacific Lutheran University *M*
Seattle Pacific University *M*

West Virginia

Mountain State University *M*
Wheeling Jesuit University *M*

Wisconsin

Mount Mary College *B*
University of Wisconsin
  Oshkosh *M*

Nursing assistant

Alabama

Alabama Southern Community
  College *A*
Bevill State Community College *C*
Bishop State Community College *C*
Gadsden State Community College *C*
George C. Wallace State Community
  College
    Selma *C*
Harry M. Ayers State Technical
  College *C*
Lawson State Community College *C*
Northwest-Shoals Community College *C*
Reid State Technical College *C*
Shelton State Community College *C*
Trenholm State Technical College *C*

Arizona

Arizona Western College *C*
Eastern Arizona College *C*
Gateway Community College *C*
Glendale Community College *C*
International Institute of the Americas
  Phoenix *C*
Phoenix College *C*
Scottsdale Community College *C*

Arkansas

Arkansas State University
  Mountain Home *C*
South Arkansas Community College *C*
Southeast Arkansas College *C*
Southern Arkansas University Tech *C*

California

College of the Canyons *C*
College of the Sequoias *C*
Copper Mountain College *C*
Gavilan Community College *C*

Imperial Valley College *C*
Long Beach City College *C*
MiraCosta College *C*
Modesto Junior College *A*
Santa Barbara City College *C*
Santa Rosa Junior College *C, A*
Shasta College *C*
Southwestern College *C*
Yuba Community College District *C*

Colorado

Arapahoe Community College *C*
Colorado Mountain College
  Alpine Campus *C*
  Spring Valley Campus *C*
  Timberline Campus *C*
Front Range Community College *C*
Morgan Community College *C*
Otero Junior College *C*
Red Rocks Community College *C*
Trinidad State Junior College *C*

Connecticut

Capital Community College *C*

Florida

Career Training Institute *C*
Daytona Beach Community College *C*
Florida National College *C*
Indian River Community College *C*
Lake City Community College *C*
Palm Beach Community College *C*
Pasco-Hernando Community College *C*
Pensacola Junior College *C*
Seminole Community College *C*
South Florida Community College *C*
Tallahassee Community College *C*

Georgia

Bainbridge College *C*
Coastal Georgia Community College *C*
Columbus Technical College *C*
South University *C*
Southwest Georgia Technical College *C*
West Georgia Technical College *C*

Hawaii

University of Hawaii
  Hawaii Community College *C*
  Kauai Community College *C*

Idaho

Eastern Idaho Technical College *C*
Lewis-Clark State College *C*

Illinois

Black Hawk College *C*
City Colleges of Chicago
  Harold Washington College *C*
  Kennedy-King College *C*
  Malcolm X College *C*
  Wright College *C*
College of DuPage *C*
College of Lake County *C*
Elgin Community College *C*
Heartland Community College *C*
Illinois Eastern Community Colleges
  Frontier Community College *C*
  Lincoln Trail College *C*
  Olney Central College *C*
  Wabash Valley College *C*
John A. Logan College *C*
John Wood Community College *C*
Kankakee Community College *C*
Kaskaskia College *C*
Kishwaukee College *C*
Lewis and Clark Community College *C*
McHenry County College *C*
Midstate College *C*
Parkland College *C*
Prairie State College *C*
Rend Lake College *C*
Richland Community College *C*
Rock Valley College *C*
Sauk Valley Community College *C*
South Suburban College of Cook
  County *C*
Southeastern Illinois College *C*

Southwestern Illinois College *C*
Spoon River College *C*
Triton College *C*
Waubonsee Community College *C*
William Rainey Harper College *C*

Iowa

Des Moines Area Community College *C*
Hawkeye Community College *C*
Mercy College of Health Sciences *C*
North Iowa Area Community College *C*
Northeast Iowa Community College *C*
Western Iowa Tech Community
  College *C*

Kansas

Allen County Community College *A*
Barton County Community College *C*
Cloud County Community College *C*
Dodge City Community College *C, A*
Independence Community College *C, A*
Johnson County Community College *C*

Kentucky

Hopkinsville Community College *C*

Louisiana

Nunez Community College *C*

Maine

Central Maine Medical Center School of
  Nursing *C*

Maryland

Anne Arundel Community College *C*
College of Southern Maryland *C*

Massachusetts

Becker College *C*
Berkshire Community College *C*
Cape Cod Community College *C*

Michigan

Gogebic Community College *C*
Kellogg Community College *C*
Montcalm Community College *C*
Southwestern Michigan College *C*
West Shore Community College *A*

Minnesota

Itasca Community College *C*
Lake Superior College: A Community
  and Technical College *C*
Mesabi Range Community and Technical
  College *C*
Minneapolis Community and Technical
  College *C*
Minnesota State College - Southeast
  Technical *C*
Ridgewater College: A Community and
  Technical College *C*
St. Cloud Technical College *C*
St. Paul College - A Community and
  Technical College *C*
South Central Technical College *C*

Mississippi

Itawamba Community College *C*
Mississippi Gulf Coast Community
  College
    Perkinston *C*
Northwest Mississippi Community
  College *C*

Missouri

Mineral Area College *C*
Moberly Area Community College *C*

Montana

Montana Tech of the University of
  Montana *C*

Nebraska

Central Community College *C, A*
Nebraska Methodist College of Nursing
  and Allied Health *C*
Northeast Community College *C*

New Jersey

Sussex County Community College *C*

New Mexico
Albuquerque Technical-Vocational
Institute *C*
Clovis Community College *C*
Dona Ana Branch Community College of
New Mexico State University *C*
Eastern New Mexico University: Roswell
Campus *C*

New York
St. Joseph's Hospital Health Center
School of Nursing *C*
Westchester Community College *C, A*

North Carolina
Beaufort County Community College *C*
Bladen Community College *C*
Brunswick Community College *C*
Carteret Community College *C*
Central Carolina Community College *C*
Central Piedmont Community College *C*
Coastal Carolina Community College *C*
College of the Albemarle *C*
Craven Community College *C*
Edgecombe Community College *C*
Fayetteville Technical Community
College *C*
Gaston College *C*
Halifax Community College *C*
Haywood Community College *C*
Mitchell Community College *C*
Nash Community College *C*
Richmond Community College *C*
Sampson Community College *C*
Sandhills Community College *C*
South Piedmont Community College *C*
Southeastern Community College *C, A*
Stanly Community College *C*
Tri-County Community College *C*
Vance-Granville Community College *C*
Wilson Technical Community College *C*

North Dakota
Lake Region State College *C*

Ohio
Central Ohio Technical College *C*
Cincinnati State Technical and
Community College *C*
Columbus State Community College *C*

Oregon
Central Oregon Community College *C*
Chemeketa Community College *C*
Linn-Benton Community College *C*
Rogue Community College *C*
Southwestern Oregon Community
College *C*
Umpqua Community College *C*

Pennsylvania
Community College of Allegheny
County *C*
Delaware County Community College *C*
Douglas School of Business *C*

South Carolina
Forrest Junior College *C*
Trident Technical College *C*
Williamsburg Technical College *C*
York Technical College *C*

South Dakota
Western Dakota Technical Institute *C*

Texas
Clarendon College *C*
El Centro College *C*
El Paso Community College *C*
Galveston College *C*
Howard College *C*
South Plains College *C*
Tarrant County College *C*

Utah
Dixie State College of Utah *C*
Southern Utah University *C*

Virginia
J. Sargeant Reynolds Community
College *C*
Mountain Empire Community College *C*
Rappahannock Community College *C*
Southside Virginia Community
College *C*
Virginia Western Community College *C*

Washington
Centralia College *C*
Clover Park Technical College *C*
Everett Community College *C*
Lake Washington Technical College *C*
Lower Columbia College *C, A*
Renton Technical College *C*
Wenatchee Valley College *C*

Wisconsin
Chippewa Valley Technical College *C*
Fox Valley Technical College *C*
Lakeshore Technical College *C*
Mid-State Technical College *C*
Moraine Park Technical College *C*
Nicolet Area Technical College *C*
Waukesha County Technical College *C*
Western Wisconsin Technical College *C*

Wyoming
Sheridan College *C*

Nursing science

Arizona
University of Phoenix *B, M*

California
California State University
Fullerton *M*

Connecticut
University of Connecticut *D*

Illinois
Bradley University *M*
De Paul University *M*
Lewis University *M*

Indiana
University of St. Francis *M*

Iowa
University of Iowa *M, D*

Maryland
University of Maryland
Baltimore *M, D*

Minnesota
Metropolitan State University *M*

Nebraska
University of Nebraska
Medical Center *M, D*

New Jersey
The College of New Jersey *M*
New Jersey Institute of Technology *B, M*
William Paterson University of New
Jersey *M*

New York
State University of New York
Binghamton *M, D*
Buffalo *D*

North Carolina
East Carolina University *D*
University of North Carolina
Chapel Hill *D*

Ohio
Case Western Reserve University *M*
Kent State University *D, T*
Xavier University *B*

Pennsylvania
Millersville University of
Pennsylvania *M*

South Carolina
Medical University of South Carolina *D*
University of South Carolina *D*

Texas
University of Texas
Medical Branch at Galveston *D*

Virginia
Hampton University *M, D*
Shenandoah University *M*

Nutritional sciences

Alabama
Auburn University *M, D*
Community College of the Air Force *A*
University of Alabama
Birmingham *D*

Arizona
University of Arizona *B, M, D*

Arkansas
University of Arkansas
for Medical Sciences *M*

California
California State University
San Bernardino *B*
Loma Linda University *M*
Pepperdine University *B*
University of California
Berkeley *B, M, D*
Davis *B, M, D*
University of Southern California *M, D*

Connecticut
University of Connecticut *B, M, D*
University of New Haven *B, M*

Delaware
University of Delaware *B, M*

District of Columbia
Howard University *B, M, D*

Florida
Florida State University *B, M*
Okaloosa-Walton Community College *A*
Polk Community College *A*

Georgia
Clark Atlanta University *B*

Hawaii
University of Hawaii
Manoa *B, M*

Illinois
Benedictine University *B*
Dominican University *B*
Finch University of Health Sciences/The
Chicago Medical School *M*
Rush University *M*
University of Chicago *M*
University of Illinois
Urbana-Champaign *M, D*

Kansas
University of Kansas Medical Center *M*

Kentucky
University of Kentucky *M, D*

Louisiana
Tulane University *M*

Maine
University of Maine *D*

Maryland
University of Maryland
College Park *M, D*

Massachusetts
Boston University *B, M, D*
Framingham State College *B, M*
Hampshire College *B*
Simmons College *B, M*
Tufts University *M, D*

University of Massachusetts
Amherst *M*

Michigan
University of Michigan *B, M, D*

Minnesota
College of St. Benedict *B*
St. John's University *B*
University of Minnesota
Twin Cities *B, M, D*

Mississippi
Mississippi State University *M, D*
University of Southern Mississippi *M*

Missouri
University of Missouri
Columbia *B, M, D*

Nebraska
University of Nebraska
Lincoln *M, D*

Nevada
University of Nevada
Las Vegas *B*

New Jersey
Rutgers, The State University of New
Jersey
New Brunswick Regional
Campus *B, M, D*

New York
City University of New York
Queens College *B*
Cornell University *B, M, D*
Hofstra University *B*
Ithaca College *B*
Long Island University
C. W. Post Campus *M*
Mohawk Valley Community College *A*
New York Institute of Technology *B, M*
Russell Sage College *B*
State University of New York
Buffalo *M*
College of Agriculture and
Technology at Morrisville *A*
Syracuse University *B*

North Carolina
North Carolina State University *B, M, D*
University of North Carolina
Chapel Hill *M, D*

Ohio
Case Western Reserve
University *B, M, D*
Notre Dame College *B*
Ohio State University
Columbus Campus *M*

Oklahoma
Oklahoma State University *B, M*
University of Oklahoma *B, M*

Pennsylvania
Drexel University *B, M, D*
Immaculata University *B*
La Salle University *B*

Puerto Rico
University of Puerto Rico
Medical Sciences Campus *M*

South Carolina
Clemson University *M, D*
South Carolina State University *M*

Texas
Texas A&M University *B, M, D*
Texas Woman's University *B, M, D*
University of Texas
Austin *D*
University of the Incarnate Word *B, M*

Utah
Brigham Young University *M*
Utah State University *M*

Vermont
University of Vermont *B, M*

Washington
Bastyr University *B, M*
University of Washington *M, D*
Washington State University *D*

Wisconsin
Mount Mary College *B, M*
University of Wisconsin
Green Bay *B*
Madison *M, D*

Occupational health/industrial hygiene

Alabama
James H. Faulkner State Community
College *C*

Arkansas
University of Arkansas
for Medical Sciences *M*
University of Central Arkansas *B*

California
California State University
Fresno *B*
San Diego State University *M*

Connecticut
University of New Haven *C, A, B, M*

Hawaii
University of Hawaii
Honolulu Community College *A*

Illinois
Illinois State University *B*

Iowa
University of Iowa *M, D*

Kentucky
Murray State University *B, M*

Maine
Central Maine Technical College *C, A*

Maryland
Community College of Baltimore County
Catonsville *C, A*
Dundalk *C, A*
Essex *C, A*

Massachusetts
University of Massachusetts
Lowell *M, D*

Michigan
Grand Valley State University *B*
Oakland University *C, B*
University of Michigan *M, D*
Wayne State University *M*

Mississippi
Itawamba Community College *A*

Missouri
Central Missouri State University *M*
Southwest Baptist University *A, B*

Montana
Montana Tech of the University of
Montana *B, M*

New York
Niagara County Community College *A*

North Carolina
Durham Technical Community
College *A*
East Carolina University *M*
North Carolina Agricultural and
Technical State University *B*
St. Augustine's College *B*

Ohio
Ohio University *B*
University of Findlay *B*

Oklahoma
University of Oklahoma *M, D*

Pennsylvania
Northampton County Area Community
College *A*
University of Pittsburgh *C, M*

Puerto Rico
Bayamon Central University *B*
University of Puerto Rico
Medical Sciences Campus *M*
University of the Sacred Heart *M*

Tennessee
Roane State Community College *C*

Texas
Laredo Community College *A*
North Central Texas College *A*

Washington
Central Washington University *B*

Occupational safety/health technology

Colorado
Red Rocks Community College *C*

Indiana
Ivy Tech State College
Central Indiana *A*
Northeast *A*
Northwest *A*
Wabash Valley *C, A*

Kentucky
Murray State University *B, M*

Louisiana
Delgado Community College *A*

Maryland
Community College of Baltimore County
Catonsville *C, A*
Dundalk *C, A*
Essex *C, A*

Michigan
Madonna University *C*

North Carolina
North Carolina Agricultural and
Technical State University *B*

Ohio
Owens Community College
Toledo *C*

Oklahoma
Oklahoma State University
Oklahoma City *A*

Pennsylvania
Indiana University of Pennsylvania *B, M*
Slippery Rock University of
Pennsylvania *B*

Texas
Angelina College *C*
Kilgore College *C, A*
Odessa College *C, A*
University of Texas
Tyler *B, M*

West Virginia
Marshall University *B, M*

Wisconsin
University of Wisconsin
Stout *M*

Occupational therapy

Alabama
Alabama State University *B*
Oakwood College *A*
Tuskegee University *B*

University of Alabama
Birmingham *M*
University of South Alabama *M*

Arkansas
South Arkansas Community College *A*
University of Central Arkansas *B, M*

California
Dominican University of California *B*
East Los Angeles College *C*
Grossmont Community College *A*
Loma Linda University *C, B, M*
Samuel Merritt College *M*
San Jose State University *B, M*
University of Southern
California *B, M, D*

Colorado
Colorado State University *M*

Connecticut
Quinnipiac University *C, B, M*
Sacred Heart University *M*
University of Hartford *B*

District of Columbia
Howard University *C, B*

Florida
Barry University *M*
Broward Community College *A*
Florida Gulf Coast University *B*
Florida International University *B, M*
Gulf Coast Community College *A*
Hillsborough Community College *A*
Nova Southeastern University *M, D*
South Florida Community College *A*
University of Florida *B, M*

Georgia
Andrew College *A*
Brenau University *B, M*
Dalton State College *A*
Gordon College *A*
Medical College of Georgia *B, M*

Idaho
College of Southern Idaho *A*
Idaho State University *M*

Illinois
Chicago State University *B*
City Colleges of Chicago
Wright College *A*
Dominican University *B*
Governors State University *M*
Illinois Central College *A*
Illinois College *B*
McKendree College *B*
North Park University *B*
Parkland College *A*
Rush University *M*
Southeastern Illinois College *A*
University of Illinois
Chicago *M*

Indiana
Indiana University-Purdue University
Indianapolis *B*
Manchester College *B*
University of Indianapolis *M*
University of Southern Indiana *B*
Vincennes University *A*

Iowa
St. Ambrose University *M*
Wartburg College *B*

Kansas
Newman University *B*
University of Kansas Medical
Center *B, M, D*

Kentucky
Murray State University *B, M*
Spalding University *B*

Louisiana
University of Louisiana at Monroe *B*

Maine
Husson College *M*
University of New England *M*
University of Southern Maine *M*

Maryland
Allegany College *A*
Towson University *B, M, D*

Massachusetts
American International College *B, M*
Bay Path College *B, M*
Boston University *B, M*
Quinsigamond Community College *A*
Springfield College *M*

Michigan
Calvin College *B*
Eastern Michigan University *B, M*
Grand Valley State University *M*
Saginaw Valley State University *B*
Schoolcraft College *A*
Wayne State University *B, M*
Western Michigan University *B, M*

Minnesota
College of St. Catherine *B, M*
College of St. Scholastica *M*
Gustavus Adolphus College *B*
Hamline University *B*
University of Minnesota
Twin Cities *B*

Mississippi
University of Mississippi Medical
Center *B*

Missouri
Avila University *B*
Drury University *B*
Maryville University of Saint Louis *M*
Rockhurst University *M*
St. Louis University *M*
University of Missouri
Columbia *B*
Washington University in St. Louis *M, D*

Nebraska
College of Saint Mary *B*
Creighton University *D*

New Hampshire
University of New Hampshire *B*

New Jersey
Kean University *B, M*
Richard Stockton College of New
Jersey *M*
Seton Hall University *M*

New Mexico
Eastern New Mexico University: Roswell
Campus *A*
University of New Mexico *B, M*
Western New Mexico University *A*

New York
City University of New York
York College *B*
D'Youville College *B, M*
Dominican College of Blauvelt *B, M*
Ithaca College *B, M*
Keuka College *B*
Mercy College *B*
New York Institute of Technology *B, M*
New York University *M, D*
Russell Sage College *B*
State University of New York
Buffalo *B, M*
Health Science Center at
Brooklyn *B*
Health Science Center at Stony
Brook *M*
Stony Brook *M*
Touro College *B, M*
Utica College *B, M*

North Carolina
East Carolina University *B, M*
Lenoir-Rhyne College *B*

Southwestern Community College *A*
University of North Carolina
Chapel Hill *A*
Winston-Salem State University *B*

North Dakota
University of Mary *M*
University of North Dakota *M*

Ohio
Cleveland State University *B*
Ohio State University
Columbus Campus *B, M*
Shawnee State University *B*
University of Findlay *M*
Wittenberg University *B*
Xavier University *C, B*

Oklahoma
University of Oklahoma *M*

Oregon
Pacific University *M*

Pennsylvania
Carlow College *B*
Chatham College *M*
Duquesne University *B, M*
Elizabethtown College *B, M*
ICM School of Business & Medical
Careers *A*
Keystone College *A*
Mount Aloysius College *B, M*
Penn State
Mont Alto *B*
Philadelphia University *M*
St. Vincent College *B*
Temple University *B, M*
University of Pittsburgh *B, M*
University of Scranton *B, M*
University of the Sciences in
Philadelphia *B, M*

Puerto Rico
University of Puerto Rico
Humacao *B*
Medical Sciences Campus *B*
Ponce *A*

South Carolina
Florence-Darlington Technical College *A*
Medical University of South Carolina *M*
Tri-County Technical College *C*

South Dakota
University of South Dakota *M*

Tennessee
Belmont University *M*
Milligan College *M*
University of Tennessee
Chattanooga *B*
University of Tennessee Health Science
Center *B*

Texas
Amarillo College *A*
Laredo Community College *A*
San Jacinto College
Central Campus *A*
South Texas Community College *A*
Texas Woman's University *C, M, D*
University of Texas
El Paso *B*
Health Science Center at San
Antonio *B*
Medical Branch at Galveston *B*
Pan American *B*
San Antonio *B*

Utah
University of Utah *B, M*

Virginia
College of Health Sciences *A, B*
J. Sargeant Reynolds Community
College *A*
Shenandoah University *M*
Virginia Commonwealth University *M*

Washington
Eastern Washington University *B*
University of Puget Sound *M*
University of Washington *B*

West Virginia
West Virginia University *M*

Wisconsin
Carthage College *B*
Concordia University Wisconsin *B, M*
Mount Mary College *B, M*
University of Wisconsin
La Crosse *B*
Madison *M*
Milwaukee *B*
Oshkosh *B*

Occupational therapy assistant

Alabama
Central Alabama Community College *A*
Enterprise State Junior College *A*
Faulkner University *A*
Northwest-Shoals Community College *A*
Wallace State Community College at
Hanceville *A*

Arkansas
South Arkansas Community College *A*

California
Loma Linda University *A*
Mount St. Mary's College *C, A*

Colorado
Arapahoe Community College *A*
Morgan Community College *A*

Connecticut
Briarwood College *A*
Manchester Community College *A*

Delaware
Delaware Technical and Community
College
Owens Campus *A*
Stanton/Wilmington Campus *A*

Florida
Florida Hospital College of Health
Sciences *A*
Hillsborough Community College *A*
Manatee Community College *A*
Palm Beach Community College *A*
Polk Community College *A*
Tallahassee Community College *C*

Georgia
Darton College *A*
Middle Georgia College *A*

Illinois
Black Hawk College *A*
City Colleges of Chicago
Wright College *A*
College of DuPage *A*
Illinois Central College *A*
John A. Logan College *A*
Lewis and Clark Community College *A*
Parkland College *A*
Rend Lake College *A*
South Suburban College of Cook
County *A*
Southeastern Illinois College *A*

Indiana
Ivy Tech State College
Central Indiana *A*
Michiana College *A*
Michiana College: Fort Wayne *A*
University of St. Francis *A*
University of Southern Indiana *A, M*

Iowa
Iowa Central Community College *A*
Kirkwood Community College *A*

Waldorf College *A*

Kansas
Johnson County Community College *A*
Kansas City Kansas Community
College *A*
Wichita State University *A*

Kentucky
Jefferson Community College *A*
Madisonville Community College *A*

Louisiana
Delgado Community College *A*
University of Louisiana at Monroe *A*

Maryland
Allegany College *A*
Community College of Baltimore County
Catonsville *A*
Dundalk *A*
Essex *A*

Massachusetts
Bay Path College *A*
Bay State College *A*
Greenfield Community College *A*
Massachusetts Bay Community
College *A*
Quinsigamond Community College *A*
Springfield Technical Community
College *A*

Michigan
Baker College
of Cadillac *A*
of Muskegon *A*
Grand Rapids Community College *A*
Macomb Community College *A*
Mott Community College *A*
Schoolcraft College *A*

Minnesota
Anoka-Ramsey Community College *A*
College of St. Catherine *A*
Lake Superior College: A Community
and Technical College *A*
Riverland Community College: A
Technical and Community College *A*

Missouri
Ozarks Technical Community College *A*
Penn Valley Community College *A*
St. Charles Community College *A*
St. Louis Community College
St. Louis Community College at
Meramec *A*

Nebraska
Clarkson College *A*

New Hampshire
New Hampshire Community Technical
College
Claremont *A*

New Jersey
Atlantic Cape Community College *A*

New Mexico
Eastern New Mexico University: Roswell
Campus *A*

New York
Adirondack Community College *A*
City University of New York
La Guardia Community College *A*
Erie Community College
North Campus *A*
Genesee Community College *A*
Jamestown Community College *A*
Maria College *A*
Orange County Community College *A*
Rockland Community College *A*
State University of New York
College of Technology at Canton *A*
Suffolk County Community College *A*
Touro College *A*

North Carolina
Cape Fear Community College *A*
Durham Technical Community
College *A*
Guilford Technical Community
College *A*
Pitt Community College *A*
Rockingham Community College *A*
Southwestern Community College *A*
Stanly Community College *A*

North Dakota
North Dakota State College of Science *A*

Ohio
Cincinnati State Technical and
Community College *A*
Cuyahoga Community College
Eastern Campus *A*
Metropolitan Campus *A*
Western Campus *A*
James A. Rhodes State College *A*
Kent State University *A*
Kent State University
East Liverpool Regional Campus *A*
Lourdes College *A*
Muskingum Area Technical College *A*
Owens Community College
Toledo *A*
Shawnee State University *A*
Sinclair Community College *A*
Stark State College of Technology *A*

Oklahoma
Oklahoma City Community College *A*
Tulsa Community College *A*

Oregon
Mount Hood Community College *A*

Pennsylvania
Community College of Allegheny
County *A*
ICM School of Business & Medical
Careers *A*
Lehigh Carbon Community College *A*
Mount Aloysius College *A*
Penn State
Berks *A*
Dubois *A*
Mont Alto *A*
Worthington Scranton *A*
Pennsylvania College of
Technology *A, B*

Puerto Rico
University of Puerto Rico
Humacao *A*
Ponce *A*

Rhode Island
Community College of Rhode Island *A*

South Carolina
Central Carolina Technical College *C*
Midlands Technical College *C*
Piedmont Technical College *C*
Tri-County Technical College *C*
Trident Technical College *A*

Tennessee
Cleveland State Community College *A*
Roane State Community College *A*
South College *A*

Texas
Amarillo College *A*
Austin Community College *A*
Del Mar College *A*
Houston Community College
System *C, A*
Laredo Community College *A*
North Central Texas College *A*
North Harris Montgomery Community
College District *A*
St. Philip's College *A*

Utah
Salt Lake Community College *A*

Virginia
College of Health Sciences *A*
J. Sargeant Reynolds Community
College *A*
Southwest Virginia Community
College *C*

Washington
Green River Community College *A*
Spokane Falls Community College *A*

West Virginia
Mountain State University *A*

Wisconsin
Fox Valley Technical College *A*
Milwaukee Area Technical College *A*
Western Wisconsin Technical College *A*
Wisconsin Indianhead Technical
College *A*

Wyoming
Casper College *A*

Occupational/ environmental health nursing

New Jersey
Thomas Edison State College *A*

Tennessee
University of Tennessee
Knoxville *B*

Ocean engineering

California
University of California
Berkeley *M, D*
San Diego *M, D*
University of Southern California *D*

Connecticut
University of Connecticut *M*

Florida
Florida Atlantic University *B, M, D*
Florida Institute of Technology *B, M, D*
University of Florida *M, D*

Hawaii
University of Hawaii
Manoa *M, D*

Maryland
United States Naval Academy *B*

Massachusetts
Massachusetts Institute of
Technology *B, M, D*

New Hampshire
University of New Hampshire *B, M*

New Jersey
Stevens Institute of Technology *M, D*

Oregon
Oregon State University *M*

Rhode Island
University of Rhode Island *B, M, D*

Texas
Texas A&M University *B, M, D*
Texas A&M University
Galveston *B*

Virginia
Virginia Polytechnic Institute and State
University *B, M*

Wisconsin
University of Wisconsin
Madison *M*

Oceanography

Alaska
University of Alaska
Fairbanks *M, D, T*

California
California State University
Monterey Bay *B*
Humboldt State University *B*
San Jose State University *B*
University of California
San Diego *D*
University of Southern California *M, D*

Connecticut
University of Connecticut *M, D*

Delaware
University of Delaware *M, D*

Florida
Eckerd College *B*
Florida Institute of Technology *B, M, D*
Florida State University *M, D*
Gulf Coast Community College *A*
Nova Southeastern University *D*
University of Miami *B, M, D*
University of South Florida *M, D*

Hawaii
Hawaii Pacific University *B*
University of Hawaii
Manoa *M, D*

Illinois
Illinois Valley Community College *A*

Louisiana
Louisiana State University and
Agricultural and Mechanical
College *M, D*

Maine
Maine Maritime Academy *B*
University of Maine *B, M, D*
University of New England *B*

Maryland
Johns Hopkins University *B, M, D*
United States Naval Academy *B*

Massachusetts
Massachusetts Institute of
Technology *M, D*

Michigan
Central Michigan University *B*
University of Michigan *B, M, D*

Mississippi
University of Southern Mississippi *M, D*

New Hampshire
University of New Hampshire *M, D*

New Jersey
Rider University *B*
Rutgers, The State University of New
Jersey
New Brunswick Regional
Campus *M, D*

New York
State University of New York
Maritime College *B*
Stony Brook *D*

North Carolina
Cape Fear Community College *A*
University of North Carolina
Chapel Hill *M, D*
Wilmington *B, M*

Oregon
Oregon State University *M, D*

Pennsylvania
California University of Pennsylvania *B*
Kutztown University of
Pennsylvania *B, T*

Millersville University of
Pennsylvania *B*
Penn State
University Park *C*

Rhode Island
University of Rhode Island *M, D*

Texas
Texas A&M University *M, D*
Texas A&M University
Galveston *B*

Virginia
Old Dominion University *B, M, D*

Washington
Everett Community College *A*
University of Washington *B, M, D*

Wisconsin
University of Wisconsin
Madison *M, D*

Office management

Alabama
Alabama Agricultural and Mechanical
University *B*
Alabama State University *B*
Community College of the Air Force *A*
Enterprise State Junior College *A*
Faulkner University *B*
Harry M. Ayers State Technical
College *C, A*
Lawson State Community College *A*
Northeast Alabama Community
College *A*
Northwest-Shoals Community
College *C, A*
Oakwood College *B*
Southern Union State Community
College *C, A*
Virginia College *C, A*
Wallace State Community College at
Hanceville *A*

Alaska
Prince William Sound Community
College *C, A*
University of Alaska
Fairbanks *A*

Arizona
Central Arizona College *A*
Cochise College *A*
Gateway Community College *A*
Rio Salado College *C, A*
South Mountain Community College *C*
Yavapai College *C, A*

Arkansas
Arkansas State University
Beebe *A*
Southern Arkansas University Tech *A*
University of Central Arkansas *A*

California
Barstow College *C, A*
Cerritos Community College *A*
Cerro Coso Community College *C, A*
Chabot College *A*
Citrus College *C, A*
Coastline Community College *C*
De Anza College *C*
Foothill College *C*
Glendale Community College *A*
Golden Gate University *C*
Golden West College *C, A*
Imperial Valley College *C, A*
Irvine Valley College *C, A*
Las Positas College *A*
Los Angeles Harbor College *C, A*
Los Medanos College *C, A*
MiraCosta College *C, A*
Modesto Junior College *C*
Moorpark College *A*

Napa Valley College *C*
Ohlone College *C, A*
Santa Barbara City College *C, A*
Santa Rosa Junior College *C*
Shasta College *C, A*
Southwestern College *C, A*
West Valley College *A*
Yuba Community College District *C*

Colorado
Mesa State College *A*
Red Rocks Community College *C*

Connecticut
Asnuntuck Community College *A*
Central Connecticut State University *B*
Gibbs College *C, A*
Norwalk Community College *C, A*
Quinebaug Valley Community College *A*
Quinnipiac University *B*

District of Columbia
University of the District of Columbia *B*

Florida
Daytona Beach Community College *A*
Herzing College
Orlando *C*
Hillsborough Community College *A*
Indian River Community College *A*
Jones College *A, B*
Miami-Dade Community College *C*
New England Institute of Technology *A*
Okaloosa-Walton Community
College *C, A*
Pasco-Hernando Community
College *C, A*
Pensacola Junior College *C, A*
Polk Community College *A*
South Florida Community College *C*
Valencia Community College *A*

Georgia
Atlanta Metropolitan College *A*
Chattahoochee Technical College *C, A*
Darton College *A*
Emmanuel College *A*
Fort Valley State University *B*
Georgia College and State University *B*
Macon State College *C*
South Georgia College *A*
State University of West Georgia *B*

Hawaii
Hawaii Business College *C*

Idaho
Boise State University *A*

Illinois
Black Hawk College *C*
College of DuPage *C, A*
Elgin Community College *C*
John A. Logan College *A*
Joliet Junior College *C, A*
Kaskaskia College *C*
Kishwaukee College *A*
Lincoln Christian College and
Seminary *A*
Lincoln Land Community College *A*
Midstate College *C*
Northwestern University *C*
Oakton Community College *C, A*
Sauk Valley Community College *A*
South Suburban College of Cook
County *C, A*
William Rainey Harper College *C, A*

Indiana
Indiana Business College *A*
Indiana State University *B*
University of Southern Indiana *B*
Vincennes University *A*

Iowa
Des Moines Area Community College *A*
Hawkeye Community College *A*
Iowa Central Community College *C, A*
Iowa Lakes Community College *A*

Northeast Iowa Community College A

Kansas
Allen County Community College A
Central Christian College A, B
Cloud County Community College C, A
Dodge City Community College C, A
Fort Hays State University B
Haskell Indian Nations University A
Kansas City Kansas Community
    College C, A
Pratt Community College C, A
Seward County Community
    College C, A
Tabor College B
Washburn University of Topeka A

Kentucky
Campbellsville University A, B
Daymar College A
Hopkinsville Community College A
Maysville Community College C, A
Murray State University B
National College of Business &
    Technology
        Lexington A
Paducah Technical College C

Louisiana
Louisiana College B
Nunez Community College A

Maine
Andover College A
Beal College A
Husson College A, B
University of Maine
    Augusta C
    Machias A, B

Maryland
Cecil Community College A
Community College of Baltimore County
    Catonsville A
    Dundalk A
    Essex A
Howard Community College C, A
Johns Hopkins University B
Villa Julie College A

Massachusetts
Bay State College A
Berkshire Community College A
Cape Cod Community College C, A
Fitchburg State College C
Massasoit Community College A
Roxbury Community College A
Springfield Technical Community
    College A

Michigan
Andrews University B
Baker College
    of Auburn Hills A
    of Cadillac A, B
    of Clinton Township B
    of Jackson C, A
    of Muskegon B
    of Owosso A, B
    of Port Huron A, B
Central Michigan University B
Cornerstone University B
Davenport University
    Eastern Region B
Davenport University - Western
    Region A
Eastern Michigan University B
Ferris State University B
Gogebic Community College A
Grand Rapids Community College A
Lansing Community College A
Michigan State University M
Mott Community College C, A
Northern Michigan University C
Oakland Community College A
Western Michigan University B

Minnesota
Alexandria Technical College C, A
Concordia College: Moorhead B
Inver Hills Community College A
Lake Superior College: A Community
    and Technical College C, A
Minnesota State College - Southeast
    Technical C, A
Normandale Community College A
North Hennepin Community College A
Rasmussen College
    Minnetonka C, A
    St. Cloud C, A
Winona State University B

Mississippi
Delta State University B
Mississippi University for Women B
Mississippi Valley State University B

Missouri
Central Missouri State University B
Evangel University A
Fontbonne College M
Lincoln University A, B
Longview Community College C, A
Maple Woods Community College C, A
Penn Valley Community College C, A
St. Louis Community College
    St. Louis Community College at
        Florissant Valley C
    St. Louis Community College at
        Meramec C
Southeast Missouri State University B
Southwest Baptist University A

Montana
Miles Community College A
University of Montana-Missoula A

Nebraska
Midland Lutheran College A, B
Union College A
University of Nebraska
    Kearney B
    Lincoln B

Nevada
Community College of Southern
    Nevada C, A
Great Basin College A
Morrison University A
Truckee Meadows Community
    College A
Western Nevada Community College A

New Hampshire
New Hampshire Community Technical
    College
        Laconia C
        Manchester C, A

New Jersey
Berkeley College A, B
Cumberland County College C, A
Gloucester County College C, A
Middlesex County College A
Raritan Valley Community College C
Rider University B
Salem Community College A
Thomas Edison State College C, A, B
Warren County Community College C

New Mexico
Clovis Community College C, A
Dona Ana Branch Community College of
    New Mexico State University C, A
Luna Community College A
New Mexico Junior College C, A
Western New Mexico University C, A

New York
Berkeley College A, B
Berkeley College of New York City A, B
Bryant & Stratton Business Institute
    Syracuse C, A

City University of New York
    Borough of Manhattan Community
        College A
    Kingsborough Community
        College A
    Queensborough Community
        College A
Clinton Community College A
Erie Community College
    City Campus A
    North Campus A
    South Campus A
Jamestown Business College C
Jefferson Community College A
Katharine Gibbs School
    Melville A
Mohawk Valley Community College C
Rochester Business Institute A
Rockland Community College C
St. Joseph's College: Suffolk Campus C
State University of New York
    College at Buffalo B, M
    College of Agriculture and
        Technology at Cobleskill A
    College of Agriculture and
        Technology at Morrisville A
Suffolk County Community College A
Trocaire College A
Westchester Business Institute C, A

North Carolina
Alamance Community College A
Central Piedmont Community
    College C, A
Fayetteville State University A, B
Halifax Community College A

North Dakota
Dickinson State University A, B
Lake Region State College C, A
North Dakota State College of Science A
Valley City State University B

Ohio
Bowling Green State University B
Bradford School C, A
Cincinnati State Technical and
    Community College A
Columbus State Community
    College C, A
Cuyahoga Community College
    Eastern Campus A
    Western Campus C, A
David N. Myers College A, B
Defiance College B
Edison State Community College A
James A. Rhodes State College A
Jefferson Community College C, A
Kent State University
    Ashtabula Regional Campus A
    Salem Regional Campus A
    Trumbull Campus A
    Tuscarawas Campus A
Miami University
    Hamilton Campus C
    Middletown Campus C, A
    Oxford Campus C, A
Miami-Jacobs College C, A
Mount Vernon Nazarene University A, B
Ohio University A
Ohio University
    Chillicothe Campus A
Owens Community College
    Findlay Campus C, A
    Toledo C, A
Shawnee State University A
Tiffin University B
University of Akron C
University of Cincinnati
    Clermont College C, A
    Raymond Walters College A
Youngstown State University A, B

Oklahoma
East Central University B
Eastern Oklahoma State College C
Northern Oklahoma College A

Oklahoma State University
    Oklahoma City C
Seminole State College A

Oregon
Chemeketa Community College C, A
Clackamas Community College C, A
Clatsop Community College A
Eugene Bible College C
Lane Community College C, A
Linn-Benton Community College C, A
Portland Community College A
Rogue Community College C, A
Southwestern Oregon Community
    College A
Umpqua Community College C
Western Business College A

Pennsylvania
Bucks County Community College A
Cheyney University of Pennsylvania B
Churchman Business School A
Community College of Beaver County A
Delaware County Community
    College C, A
Indiana University of Pennsylvania B
Lebanon Valley College of
    Pennsylvania C
Lehigh Carbon Community College A
Marywood University C
Reading Area Community College A
South Hills School of Business &
    Technology A
Widener University B

Puerto Rico
Inter American University of Puerto Rico
    Bayamon Campus A
Turabo University A, B
Universidad del Este B
University of Puerto Rico
    Cayey University College B
    Mayaguez Campus B

Rhode Island
Providence College C, A

South Carolina
Forrest Junior College A
Northeastern Technical College C
Technical College of the
    Lowcountry C, A
University of South Carolina B

South Dakota
Dakota State University A

Tennessee
Belmont University B
Lee University B
Middle Tennessee State University B
Pellissippi State Technical Community
    College C
Walters State Community College A

Texas
Brookhaven College A
Cedar Valley College A
Central Texas College C, A
College of the Mainland A
Eastfield College A
El Centro College A
Grayson County College A
Hallmark Institute of Technology C
Hill College C, A
Lamar University B
Laredo Community College C, A
North Lake College A
Palo Alto College C, A
Paris Junior College A
San Antonio College A
South Plains College C, A
Southwestern Adventist University A, B
Stephen F. Austin State University B
Sul Ross State University C, B
Tarleton State University B
Texas A&M University
    Commerce B

Texas Woman's University *B*
Tyler Junior College *A*
University of Houston
 Downtown *B*
University of North Texas *B*

Utah
College of Eastern Utah *C*
LDS Business College *A*
Salt Lake Community College *A*
Utah Valley State College *B*
Weber State University *B*

Vermont
Vermont Technical College *A*

Virginia
Blue Ridge Community College *C*
Mountain Empire Community College *A*
National College of Business &
 Technology
 Bluefield *A*
 Harrisonburg *A*
 Roanoke *A*
Norfolk State University *B*
Paul D. Camp Community College *A*
Radford University *B*
Thomas Nelson Community College *A*
Virginia Commonwealth University *B*
Virginia Highlands Community
 College *C, A*
Virginia Intermont College *B*

Washington
Bellevue Community College *C, A*
Central Washington University *B*
Clover Park Technical College *A*
Edmonds Community College *C, A*
Peninsula College *A*
Renton Technical College *C, A*
South Seattle Community College *C, A*
Spokane Community College *A*
Spokane Falls Community College *A*
Walla Walla Community College *A*
Wenatchee Valley College *A*

West Virginia
Concord College *A*
Davis and Elkins College *B*
Fairmont State College *B*
Mountain State University *A, B*
West Virginia Junior College:
 Charleston *A*
West Virginia University Institute of
 Technology *A*

Wisconsin
Blackhawk Technical College *A*
Lac Courte Oreilles Ojibwa Community
 College *A*
Maranatha Baptist Bible College *B*
Milwaukee Area Technical College *A*
Moraine Park Technical College *A*

Wyoming
Casper College *C, A*
Sheridan College *A*
Western Wyoming Community
 College *A*

Office technology/data entry

Alabama
James H. Faulkner State Community
 College *C, A*
Lawson State Community College *A*

Arizona
Central Arizona College *A*
Gateway Community College *C*
Paradise Valley Community
 College *C, A*
Phoenix College *C*
Scottsdale Community College *C*
South Mountain Community
 College *C, A*

Yavapai College *C, A*

Arkansas
Arkansas State University
 Beebe *A*
Phillips Community College of the
 University of Arkansas *A*
Southern Arkansas University Tech *C*

California
Bakersfield College *A*
Barstow College *C, A*
Cabrillo College *C, A*
Cerro Coso Community College *A*
Chabot College *C, A*
Coastline Community College *A*
College of the Redwoods *C, A*
College of the Sequoias *C*
Columbia College *C*
Diablo Valley College *A*
East Los Angeles College *C, A*
Gavilan Community College *C*
Golden West College *C, A*
Imperial Valley College *C, A*
Irvine Valley College *C, A*
Laney College *C, A*
Long Beach City College *C, A*
Los Angeles Harbor College *C, A*
Los Angeles Southwest College *A*
MTI College of Business and
 Technology *C*
MiraCosta College *C*
Ohlone College *C, A*
Orange Coast College *C, A*
Reedley College *C*
Riverside Community College *C, A*
San Diego City College *C, A*
San Joaquin Delta College *A*
Santa Barbara City College *C*
Santa Rosa Junior College *C*
Shasta College *C, A*
Sierra College *C, A*
West Valley College *C, A*

Colorado
Arapahoe Community College *C, A*
Community College of Aurora *A*
Morgan Community College *C*
Red Rocks Community College *C, A*

Connecticut
Briarwood College *C, A*
Gateway Community College *C*
Middlesex Community College *C*
Naugatuck Valley Community
 College *C, A*
Northwestern Connecticut Community
 College *C*
Norwalk Community College *C, A*
Quinebaug Valley Community
 College *C, A*
Three Rivers Community College *A*
Tunxis Community College *C*

Delaware
Delaware Technical and Community
 College
 Owens Campus *C, A*
 Stanton/Wilmington Campus *C, A*
 Terry Campus *C, A*

District of Columbia
University of the District of
 Columbia *C, A*

Florida
Daytona Beach Community
 College *C, A*
Indian River Community College *C*
Institute of Career Education *C*
Pasco-Hernando Community College *C*
St. Petersburg College *C, A*
Santa Fe Community College *A*
Tallahassee Community College *C*
Valencia Community College *C, A*

Georgia
Abraham Baldwin Agricultural
 College *A*
Dalton State College *C, A*
DeKalb Technical College *C*
Macon State College *C, B*
South Georgia College *A*
Southwest Georgia Technical College *C*
Valdosta State University *A, B*
West Georgia Technical College *C*

Hawaii
Hawaii Business College *C*

Illinois
Black Hawk College *C, A*
Black Hawk College
 East Campus *C, A*
City Colleges of Chicago
 Malcolm X College *C, A*
College of Lake County *C, A*
Danville Area Community College *C*
Elgin Community College *C*
Gem City College *C*
Heartland Community College *C*
Illinois Central College *C*
Illinois Eastern Community Colleges
 Frontier Community College *C, A*
 Lincoln Trail College *C, A*
 Olney Central College *C, A*
 Wabash Valley College *C, A*
John A. Logan College *C*
John Wood Community College *C*
Joliet Junior College *C, A*
Kankakee Community College *C*
Kaskaskia College *C, A*
Kishwaukee College *C*
Lake Land College *C*
Lincoln Land Community College *C, A*
McHenry County College *C*
Midstate College *C*
National-Louis University *C*
Parkland College *A*
Prairie State College *C*
Rend Lake College *C, A*
Sauk Valley Community College *A*
Shawnee Community College *C*
Southeastern Illinois College *A*
Triton College *C, A*
Waubonsee Community College *C, A*
William Rainey Harper College *C*

Indiana
Ancilla College *C, A*
College of Court Reporting *A*
Grace College *A*
Oakland City University *C, A*
Vincennes University *A*

Iowa
Des Moines Area Community College *C*
Ellsworth Community College *C, A*
Hawkeye Community College *C*
Kirkwood Community College *A*
Northeast Iowa Community College *C*
Western Iowa Tech Community
 College *A*

Kansas
Allen County Community College *C*
Central Christian College *A*
Fort Scott Community College *A*
Independence Community College *C, A*
Pratt Community College *C, A*
Seward County Community
 College *C, A*
Washburn University of Topeka *A*

Kentucky
Murray State University *A*
Paducah Community College *A*

Louisiana
Nunez Community College *C*
Southern University
 Shreveport *A*

Maine
Andover College *A*
Central Maine Technical College *C, A*
Husson College *A*

Maryland
Community College of Baltimore County
 Catonsville *C, A*
 Dundalk *C, A*
 Essex *C, A*
Villa Julie College *A*

Massachusetts
Benjamin Franklin Institute of
 Technology *C*
Mount Wachusett Community College *C*
Roxbury Community College *A*

Michigan
Baker College
 of Auburn Hills *A*
 of Muskegon *A*
 of Port Huron *A*
Cornerstone University *A*
Davenport University - Western
 Region *A*
Gogebic Community College *A*
Lansing Community College *A*
Macomb Community College *C, A*
Monroe County Community
 College *C, A*
Montcalm Community College *C, A*
Mott Community College *C, A*
North Central Michigan College *C*
Northwestern Michigan College *A*
St. Clair County Community College *A*
West Shore Community College *A*

Minnesota
Alexandria Technical College *C, A*
Hennepin Technical College *C, A*
Lake Superior College: A Community
 and Technical College *C*
Mesabi Range Community and Technical
 College *C, A*
Minneapolis Community and Technical
 College *A*
Minnesota State College - Southeast
 Technical *C*
Northland Community & Technical
 College *C*
Pine Technical College *C*
Rainy River Community College *A*
Riverland Community College: A
 Technical and Community College *C*
St. Cloud Technical College *C*
St. Paul College - A Community and
 Technical College *C, A*

Mississippi
Itawamba Community College *C*
Mary Holmes College *A*
Mississippi Gulf Coast Community
 College
 Perkinston *A*
Northwest Mississippi Community
 College *A*
Pearl River Community College *A*

Missouri
Baptist Bible College *A*
East Central College *C, A*
Longview Community College *C, A*
Maple Woods Community College *C, A*
North Central Missouri College *C, A*
Ozarks Technical Community
 College *C, A*
Penn Valley Community College *C, A*
St. Louis Community College
 St. Louis Community College at
 Florissant Valley *C, A*
 St. Louis Community College at
 Meramec *C, A*
Southwest Missouri State University:
 West Plains Campus *C*

Montana
Flathead Valley Community College *A*

Montana State University
   Billings *A*
University of Montana: Western *A*

Nevada

Great Basin College *C*
Las Vegas College *C*
Morrison University *C*
Truckee Meadows Community
   College *A*
Western Nevada Community
   College *C, A*

New Hampshire

New Hampshire Community Technical
   College
      Berlin *C*
      Nashua *C*

New Jersey

Berkeley College *C*
Camden County College *C*
County College of Morris *C*
Essex County College *A*
Gloucester County College *A*
Salem Community College *A*
Warren County Community College *C*

New Mexico

Clovis Community College *A*
New Mexico Junior College *C, A*
New Mexico State University
   Alamogordo *C*
Southwestern Indian Polytechnic
   Institute *C*

New York

Berkeley College of New York City *C*
Briarcliffe College *A*
City University of New York
   Bronx Community College *A*
   Hostos Community College *C*
   Medgar Evers College *A*
   Queensborough Community
      College *C*
Clinton Community College *C, A*
Dutchess Community College *C*
Fulton-Montgomery Community
   College *A*
Hudson Valley Community College *C, A*
Jamestown Community College *C*
Jefferson Community College *C, A*
Olean Business Institute *A*
Orange County Community
   College *C, A*
Pace University *C, A, B*
Pace University:
   Pleasantville/Briarcliff *C, A, B*
Plaza College *C*
Rochester Business Institute *A*
St. Joseph's College: Suffolk Campus *C*
State University of New York
   College of Agriculture and
      Technology at Morrisville *C, A*
   College of Technology at Alfred *A*
Suffolk County Community College *C*
Tompkins-Cortland Community
   College *A*
Trocaire College *C*
Ulster County Community College *A*
Westchester Business Institute *C, A*

North Carolina

Bladen Community College *A*
East Carolina University *B*
Halifax Community College *A*
Piedmont Community College *A*
South College *C*
Vance-Granville Community College *A*
Western Piedmont Community
   College *C, A*

North Dakota

Bismarck State College *C, A*
Minot State University *C*

Ohio

Ashland University *C, A*

Bowling Green State University:
   Firelands College *C*
Columbus State Community
   College *C, A*
Cuyahoga Community College
   Eastern Campus *C*
David N. Myers College *A, B*
Kent State University
   Ashtabula Regional Campus *A*
   Trumbull Campus *A*
Lorain County Community College *C*
Marion Technical College *C*
Miami University
   Middletown Campus *C*
Miami-Jacobs College *A*
Northwest State Community College *A*
Ohio Business College *C, A*
Sinclair Community College *C*
Southern State Community College *C*
Stark State College of Technology *A*
Stautzenberger College *C*
Trumbull Business College *A*
University of Akron *C, A*
University of Cincinnati
   Clermont College *C, A*
   Raymond Walters College *C*
University of Northwestern Ohio *C, A*
University of Toledo *A*
Youngstown State University *A*

Oklahoma

Bacone College *A*
Northeastern Oklahoma Agricultural and
   Mechanical College *A*
Oklahoma State University
   Oklahoma City *C*
Rogers State University *A*
St. Gregory's University *A*
Tulsa Community College *A*
Western Oklahoma State College *A*

Oregon

Chemeketa Community College *A*
Clatsop Community College *C, A*
Portland Community College *C, A*
Rogue Community College *C*
Treasure Valley Community College *C*

Pennsylvania

Academy of Medical Arts and
   Business *C, A*
Allentown Business School *C*
Bucks County Community College *C*
California University of Pennsylvania *A*
Churchman Business School *C*
Community College of Allegheny
   County *C*
Consolidated School of Business
   Lancaster *A*
   York *A*
Montgomery County Community
   College *A*
Newport Business Institute *A*
Pennsylvania College of Technology *A*
Reading Area Community College *C, A*
South Hills School of Business &
   Technology *C*

Puerto Rico

Huertas Junior College *C*
ICPR Junior College *C*
Turabo University *A*
Universidad Metropolitana *C*
Universidad del Este *A*

South Carolina

Aiken Technical College *C*
Central Carolina Technical College *C*
Denmark Technical College *C*
Florence-Darlington Technical
   College *C*
Forrest Junior College *A*
Horry-Georgetown Technical College *C*
Northeastern Technical College *C, A*
Orangeburg-Calhoun Technical
   College *C*
Tri-County Technical College *C*

Trident Technical College *C*
York Technical College *C*

Tennessee

Austin Peay State University *A*
Chattanooga State Technical Community
   College *C*
Southwest Tennessee Community
   College *C, A*

Texas

Alvin Community College *C*
Amarillo College *C*
Brookhaven College *A*
Cedar Valley College *A*
Central Texas College *C*
Coastal Bend College *A*
College of the Mainland *C, A*
Eastfield College *A*
El Centro College *C*
El Paso Community College *C*
Galveston College *C*
Grayson County College *A*
Hill College *C, A*
Laredo Community College *C, A*
McLennan Community College *C, A*
Midland College *A*
North Central Texas College *A*
North Lake College *A*
Palo Alto College *A*
Paris Junior College *A*
San Antonio College *C*
San Jacinto College
   Central Campus *A*
Southwest Texas Junior College *A*
Temple College *A*
Texas Wesleyan University *B*
Trinity Valley Community College *C, A*

Utah

Salt Lake Community College *A*
Utah Valley State College *A*

Virginia

Blue Ridge Community College *C*
ECPI College of Technology *C, A*
ECPI Technical College: Roanoke *A*
J. Sargeant Reynolds Community
   College *C*
Mountain Empire Community College *C*
Paul D. Camp Community College *C*
Virginia Western Community College *A*

Washington

Centralia College *C, A*
Clark College *C, A*
Green River Community College *C, A*
Lower Columbia College *C, A*
North Seattle Community College *A*
Olympic College *C, A*
Seattle Central Community College *C*
South Seattle Community College *A*
Spokane Community College *C, A*
Walla Walla Community College *C*

West Virginia

Fairmont State College *A*
Mountain State University *C*
Shepherd College *A*
West Virginia Northern Community
   College *C*
West Virginia University at
   Parkersburg *A*

Wisconsin

Blackhawk Technical College *C, A*
Chippewa Valley Technical College *A*
Fox Valley Technical College *C, A*
Lakeshore Technical College *A*
Mid-State Technical College *C, A*
Moraine Park Technical College *A*

Wyoming

Laramie County Community College *A*
Western Wyoming Community
   College *C, A*

Office/clerical services

Alabama

Gadsden State Community College *C*
George C. Wallace State Community
   College
      Selma *C*
James H. Faulkner State Community
   College *C*
Lawson State Community College *C*
Northwest-Shoals Community College *C*
Wallace Community College: Sparks
   Campus *A*
Wallace State Community College at
   Hanceville *C, A*

Alaska

University of Alaska
   Anchorage *C*
   Southeast *A*

Arizona

Cochise College *C, A*
Eastern Arizona College *C*
International Institute of the Americas
   Phoenix *C, A, B*
   Tucson *C, A, B*
Paradise Valley Community
   College *C, A*
Phoenix College *C*

Arkansas

East Arkansas Community College *C*
Pulaski Technical College *C*

California

Bakersfield College *A*
Barstow College *C, A*
Cerritos Community College *A*
Cerro Coso Community College *C, A*
Chabot College *A*
Citrus College *C, A*
Coastline Community College *C*
College of Alameda *A*
College of the Redwoods *C*
College of the Sequoias *C, A*
College of the Siskiyous *C, A*
Columbia College *C*
Contra Costa College *A*
East Los Angeles College *A*
Feather River College *C, A*
Gavilan Community College *C*
Golden West College *C, A*
Imperial Valley College *C, A*
Laney College *C, A*
Long Beach City College *C, A*
Los Angeles Harbor College *C, A*
Los Angeles Southwest College *A*
Los Angeles Trade and Technical
   College *C, A*
MTI College of Business and
   Technology *C*
MiraCosta College *C, A*
Modesto Junior College *C*
Monterey Peninsula College *C, A*
Mount St. Mary's College *A*
Mount San Antonio College *C, A*
Mount San Jacinto College *C*
Ohlone College *C, A*
Orange Coast College *C, A*
Palomar College *C, A*
Reedley College *C*
San Diego City College *C, A*
San Joaquin Delta College *C, A*
Santa Barbara City College *C*
Santa Monica College *C, A*
Santa Rosa Junior College *C*
Shasta College *A*
Sierra College *C, A*
Southwestern College *C, A*
Taft College *C, A*
Ventura College *C, A*
Vista Community College *C*
West Valley College *A*
Yuba Community College District *C*

Colorado
Trinidad State Junior College *C*

Connecticut
Briarwood College *C*
Gateway Community College *C, A*
Naugatuck Valley Community College *C*
Northwestern Connecticut Community
College *C*
Quinebaug Valley Community College *C*
Tunxis Community College *A*

Delaware
Delaware Technical and Community
College
Owens Campus *C, A*
Stanton/Wilmington Campus *A*

Florida
Broward Community College *A*
Gulf Coast Community College *C, A*
Herzing College
Orlando *C*
Hillsborough Community College *C*
Lake City Community College *C, A*
Miami-Dade Community College *A*
Pensacola Junior College *C*
Polk Community College *A*
Santa Fe Community College *A*
Seminole Community College *C*
Valencia Community College *C, A*

Georgia
Abraham Baldwin Agricultural
College *A*
Atlanta Metropolitan College *A*
Chattahoochee Technical College *C*
Clayton College and State
University *C, A*
Dalton State College *C, A*
Darton College *C*
Georgia Military College *A*
Macon State College *C, A*
South Georgia College *A*
Southwest Georgia Technical
College *C, A*

Hawaii
University of Hawaii
Kauai Community College *C, A*
Leeward Community College *C, A*

Idaho
Idaho State University *C, A*

Illinois
City Colleges of Chicago
Kennedy-King College *C*
Wright College *C*
Elgin Community College *C*
Gem City College *C*
Heartland Community College *C*
John A. Logan College *C*
Joliet Junior College *A*
Kankakee Community College *C*
Kaskaskia College *C*
Kishwaukee College *C, A*
Lake Land College *C*
Lewis and Clark Community College *A*
Midstate College *C*
Rockford Business College *C, A*
Sauk Valley Community College *C, A*
Southeastern Illinois College *C*
Southwestern Illinois College *C, A*
Waubonsee Community College *C*
William Rainey Harper College *C*

Indiana
Indiana Wesleyan University *A*
Purdue University
North Central Campus *A*
Sawyer College *C*
Vincennes University *A*

Iowa
Des Moines Area Community College *C*
Dordt College *A*
Ellsworth Community College *C, A*

Hawkeye Community College *C*
Iowa Lakes Community College *C*
Iowa Western Community College *C*
Marshalltown Community College *C*
North Iowa Area Community College *C*
Northeast Iowa Community College *C*
Southeastern Community College
North Campus *C, A*
South Campus *C*

Kansas
Allen County Community College *C*
Butler County Community College *C, A*
Independence Community College *C, A*
Kansas City Kansas Community
College *C, A*
Labette Community College *A*
Pratt Community College *C, A*
Seward County Community
College *C, A*
Washburn University of Topeka *C, A*

Kentucky
Cumberland College *A*
Daymar College *C, A*
Kentucky Christian College *A*
National College of Business &
Technology
Lexington *A*
Sullivan University *C*

Louisiana
Grambling State University *A*
Nunez Community College *C*

Maine
Andover College *C, A*
University of Maine
Machias *A, B*

Maryland
College of Southern Maryland *C*
Community College of Baltimore County
Catonsville *A*
Dundalk *A*
Essex *A*

Massachusetts
Berkshire Community College *A*
Cape Cod Community College *C, A*
Massasoit Community College *C*
Quinsigamond Community College *C, A*
Springfield Technical Community
College *C*

Michigan
Baker College
of Auburn Hills *C*
of Cadillac *C*
of Clinton Township *C*
of Jackson *C*
of Muskegon *C*
of Owosso *C, A*
of Port Huron *C*
Bay de Noc Community College *C*
Davenport University
Midland *C*
Glen Oaks Community College *C*
Grand Rapids Community College *C*
Kellogg Community College *C*
Kirtland Community College *C*
Mid Michigan Community College *C*
Monroe County Community
College *C, A*
North Central Michigan College *C, A*
St. Clair County Community
College *C, A*
Wayne County Community College *C*
West Shore Community College *C, A*

Minnesota
Alexandria Technical College *C*
Central Lakes College *C*
Fergus Falls Community College *C*
Hennepin Technical College *C, A*
Hibbing Community College: A
Technical and Community
College *C, A*

Itasca Community College *C*
Lake Superior College: A Community
and Technical College *C*
Minneapolis Community and Technical
College *C*
Minnesota State College - Southeast
Technical *C*
Normandale Community College *A*
Northland Community & Technical
College *C*
Pine Technical College *C*
Rainy River Community College *C*
Rasmussen College
Minnetonka *C, A*
Ridgewater College: A Community and
Technical College *C*
Rochester Community and Technical
College *C*
St. Cloud Technical College *C, A*
St. Paul College - A Community and
Technical College *C*
Winona State University *B*

Mississippi
Itawamba Community College *C, A*

Missouri
Crowder College *C, A*
Hannibal-LaGrange College *A*
Jefferson College *C*
Longview Community College *C*
Maple Woods Community College *C*
Mineral Area College *C, A*
Moberly Area Community College *C, A*
North Central Missouri College *C, A*
Penn Valley Community College *C*
St. Louis Community College
St. Louis Community College at
Meramec *A*
Three Rivers Community College *C*

Montana
Miles Community College *C, A*
Montana State University
Billings *C*
Montana Tech of the University of
Montana *A*

Nebraska
Lincoln School of Commerce *C*
Mid Plains Community College
Area *C, A*
Southeast Community College
Beatrice Campus *A*
Lincoln Campus *A*
University of Nebraska
Kearney *B*
Western Nebraska Community
College *C, A*

Nevada
Morrison University *C*
Western Nevada Community College *A*

New Hampshire
New Hampshire Community Technical
College
Claremont *C*

New Jersey
Essex County College *C*
Gloucester County College *C, A*
Raritan Valley Community College *C*
Salem Community College *C*
Sussex County Community College *C*

New Mexico
Dona Ana Branch Community College of
New Mexico State University *C*
New Mexico State University
Alamogordo *C*
Southwestern Indian Polytechnic
Institute *C*

New York
Adirondack Community College *C, A*
Corning Community College *C*

Erie Community College
City Campus *C*
North Campus *C*
South Campus *C*
Fulton-Montgomery Community
College *C*
Mohawk Valley Community College *C*
Niagara County Community
College *C, A*
North Country Community College *C, A*
Olean Business Institute *C*
Onondaga Community College *C, A*
Pace University:
Pleasantville/Briarcliff *A*
Plaza College *A*
Rochester Business Institute *A*
Schenectady County Community
College *C*
Trocaire College *C*
Utica School of Commerce *C*
Westchester Business Institute *C, A*
Westchester Community College *C, A*

North Carolina
Asheville Buncombe Technical
Community College *C, A*
Bladen Community College *C, A*
Carteret Community College *A*
Central Carolina Community College *A*
College of the Albemarle *A*
Forsyth Technical Community
College *C, A*
Gaston College *C*
Halifax Community College *A*
Johnston Community College *A*
Mayland Community College *C*
Pamlico Community College *A*
Rockingham Community College *A*
Sampson Community College *A*
South Piedmont Community
College *C, A*
Southeastern Community College *A*
Surry Community College *C, A*
Western Piedmont Community
College *C, A*
Wilson Technical Community College *C*

North Dakota
Lake Region State College *C, A*
Minot State University: Bottineau
Campus *C*
North Dakota State College of
Science *C, A*

Ohio
Bowling Green State University:
Firelands College *C*
Cincinnati State Technical and
Community College *A*
Columbus State Community
College *C*
Cuyahoga Community College
Eastern Campus *C*
Western Campus *C, A*
Davis College *C*
Edison State Community College *C*
Jefferson Community College *C*
Kent State University
Trumbull Campus *A*
Tuscarawas Campus *A*
Marion Technical College *C, A*
Miami University
Hamilton Campus *C, A*
Middletown Campus *C, A*
Miami-Jacobs College *C, A*
Northwest State Community College *C*
Ohio Valley College of Technology *A*
Southern State Community College *C*
Stark State College of Technology *C*
University of Akron *C*
University of Cincinnati
Raymond Walters College *C, A*
University of Findlay *A*
University of Northwestern Ohio *C*
University of Toledo *C*
Youngstown State University *A*

Oklahoma

Carl Albert State College *C*
Eastern Oklahoma State College *A*
Northeastern Oklahoma Agricultural and
   Mechanical College *C*
Oklahoma City Community College *A*
Redlands Community College *A*
Seminole State College *A*
Tulsa Community College *C*
Western Oklahoma State College *A*

Oregon

Blue Mountain Community College *C*
Central Oregon Community College *C*
Chemeketa Community College *C*
Clackamas Community College *C*
Clatsop Community College *C*
Lane Community College *C*
Linn-Benton Community College *C*
Rogue Community College *C*
Southwestern Oregon Community
   College *C*
Treasure Valley Community College *A*
Umpqua Community College *C*

Pennsylvania

Allentown Business School *C*
Bucks County Community College *C, A*
Butler County Community College *C*
Churchman Business School *C*
Community College of Philadelphia *C, A*
Consolidated School of Business
   Lancaster *C*
   York *C*
Lehigh Carbon Community College *A*
Mercyhurst College *C*
Montgomery County Community
   College *A*
Newport Business Institute *A*
Northampton County Area Community
   College *C*
Pennsylvania College of Technology *C*
Reading Area Community College *C, A*
South Hills School of Business &
   Technology *A*

Puerto Rico

Humacao Community College *C*
Inter American University of Puerto Rico
   Metropolitan Campus *A, B*
Pontifical Catholic University of Puerto
   Rico *A*
Universidad Metropolitana *C*
Universidad del Este *C, A*

Rhode Island

Community College of Rhode Island *C*

South Carolina

Aiken Technical College *C*
Florence-Darlington Technical
   College *C*
Forrest Junior College *A*
Northeastern Technical College *C, A*
Orangeburg-Calhoun Technical
   College *C*
Piedmont Technical College *C*
Technical College of the Lowcountry *C*
Tri-County Technical College *C*
Trident Technical College *C*
Williamsburg Technical College *C*
York Technical College *C*

South Dakota

Northern State University *C, A, B*
Sinte Gleska University *A*
Western Dakota Technical Institute *C*

Tennessee

Chattanooga State Technical Community
   College *A*
Roane State Community College *C, A*

Texas

Alvin Community College *C, A*
Amarillo College *A*
Austin Community College *C*
Blinn College *A*

Central Texas College *C*
Clarendon College *C, A*
Coastal Bend College *A*
College of the Mainland *A*
El Centro College *C*
El Paso Community College *C, A*
Galveston College *C, A*
Grayson County College *C, A*
Hallmark Institute of Technology *C*
Hill College *A*
Houston Community College System *C*
Howard College *C, A*
Kilgore College *C*
Laredo Community College *C, A*
Lee College *C, A*
MTI College of Business and
   Technology *C*
MTI College of Business and
   Technology *C*
McLennan Community College *C*
Midland College *C, A*
Mountain View College *C*
North Central Texas College *A*
Panola College *C*
San Antonio College *C, A*
South Plains College *C*
Tarrant County College *C*
Texarkana College *C, A*
Texas A&M University
   Commerce *B*
Texas Southern University *B*
Texas State Technical College
   West Texas *C, A*
Tyler Junior College *C*
Victoria College *C*

Utah

Dixie State College of Utah *C, A*
LDS Business College *C*

Virginia

ECPI College of Technology *C, A*
ECPI Technical College: Roanoke *C, A*
Eastern Shore Community College *C, A*
J. Sargeant Reynolds Community
   College *C*
Mountain Empire Community College *A*
Paul D. Camp Community College *C*
Piedmont Virginia Community
   College *C, A*
Southside Virginia Community
   College *C*

Washington

Centralia College *C, A*
Clark College *C*
Clover Park Technical College *C*
Everett Community College *C, A*
Green River Community College *C, A*
Lake Washington Technical College *C*
Lower Columbia College *A*
North Seattle Community College *C*
Renton Technical College *C, A*
Spokane Community College *C, A*
Spokane Falls Community College *C, A*
Walla Walla Community College *C, A*
Wenatchee Valley College *C*

West Virginia

Concord College *A*
Fairmont State College *C*
Valley College of Technology *C*

Wisconsin

Blackhawk Technical College *A*
Chippewa Valley Technical College *C*
Fox Valley Technical College *C*
Lakeshore Technical College *C*
Moraine Park Technical College *C*
Nicolet Area Technical College *C*
University of Wisconsin
   Whitewater *A*
Western Wisconsin Technical College *C*

Wyoming

Eastern Wyoming College *C*

Oncology

Arizona

University of Arizona *M, D*

Florida

University of South Florida *D*

New York

State University of New York
   Buffalo *M, D*

Texas

University of Texas
   Houston Health Science
   Center *M, D*

Operations management

Alabama

Alabama Southern Community
   College *A*
Auburn University *B*
Community College of the Air Force *A*
Lawson State Community College *A*
Remington College
   Southeast College of Technology *B*

Arizona

DeVry University
   Phoenix *B*
Eastern Arizona College *C*
Glendale Community College *A*
International Institute of the Americas
   Phoenix *A*
University of Arizona *B*

Arkansas

University of Arkansas *B, M*

California

California State Polytechnic University:
   Pomona *B*
California State University
   Fullerton *B*
   Hayward *M*
   Long Beach *B*
   Stanislaus *B*
Citrus College *C*
DeVry University
   Fremont *B*
   Long Beach *B*
   Pomona *B*
   West Hills *B*
Fashion Institute of Design and
   Merchandising *A*
Golden Gate University *M*
Laney College *C, A*
National University *B*
Palomar College *C, A*
San Diego City College *C, A*
San Diego State University *B, M*

Colorado

DeVry University: Colorado Springs *B*
Fort Lewis College *B*
University of Colorado
   Boulder *B*

Connecticut

Central Connecticut State University *M*
Naugatuck Valley Community College *C*

Delaware

University of Delaware *B*

District of Columbia

George Washington University *M*
Trinity College *B*

Florida

DeVry University
   Miramar *B*
Florida Southern College *B*
Florida State University *B*

Georgia

Dalton State College *B*

DeVry University
   Alpharetta *B*
   Atlanta *B*
Georgia Institute of Technology *B*
Georgia State University *D*
Kennesaw State University *M*
South Georgia College *A*

Hawaii

University of Hawaii
   Hawaii Community College *C, A*

Idaho

University of Idaho *B*

Illinois

Aurora University *B*
Benedictine University *M*
Carl Sandburg College *A*
De Paul University *B*
DeVry University
   Addison *B*
Illinois Institute of Technology *M*
Kishwaukee College *C, A*
Loyola University of Chicago *C, B*
McHenry County College *C, A*
Northern Illinois University *B*
Northwestern University *M*
Prairie State College *C, A*
Trinity Christian College *B*
University of Illinois
   Chicago *D*
Waubonsee Community College *C, A*
William Rainey Harper College *C, A*

Indiana

Indiana Institute of Technology *B*
Indiana State University *A, B*
Indiana University-Purdue University
   Fort Wayne *C, A, B*
Indiana University-Purdue University
   Indianapolis *A, B*
Purdue University *A, B*
Purdue University
   North Central Campus *C, A, B*
Tri-State University *B*
University of Southern Indiana *M*

Iowa

Iowa State University *B*

Kansas

Pratt Community College *C, A*

Kentucky

Daymar College *A*

Louisiana

Louisiana Tech University *A, B*
Nicholls State University *B*

Maryland

University of Maryland
   College Park *B*
   University College *C, M*

Massachusetts

Boston College *B*
Boston University *B*
Bridgewater State College *C*
Northeastern University *A, B*
Suffolk University *M*
Worcester Polytechnic Institute *B, M*

Michigan

Central Michigan University *B, M*
Ferris State University *C, B*
Kettering University *M*
Lawrence Technological University *M*
Macomb Community College *C, A*
Madonna University *C, M*
Michigan State University *B, M, D*
Michigan Technological University *M*
Oakland Community College *A*
Saginaw Valley State University *B*
University of Michigan
   Flint *B*
Western Michigan University *B*

Minnesota

Alexandria Technical College *C, A*
Metropolitan State University *B*
Minnesota State University
  Mankato *B*
Rasmussen College
  Minnetonka *C, A*
University of St. Thomas *B, M*
Winona State University *B*

Mississippi

Mississippi State University *B*

Missouri

DeVry University
  Kansas City *B*
Mineral Area College *C, A*
Missouri Baptist University *B*
Southeast Missouri State University *B*
University of Missouri
  St. Louis *B*
Washington University in St. Louis *B, M*
Webster University *M*

Nebraska

University of Nebraska
  Omaha *B*

Nevada

Truckee Meadows Community
  College *C*

New Hampshire

New Hampshire Community Technical
  College
  Nashua *C*

New Jersey

Cumberland County College *A*
Thomas Edison State College *C, A, B*
Warren County Community College *C*

New Mexico

Western New Mexico University *B*

New York

City University of New York
  Baruch College *B*
DeVry Institute of Technology
  New York *B*
Excelsior College *B*
Iona College *M*
New York University *M*
Pace University *B*
Pace University:
  Pleasantville/Briarcliff *B*
Polytechnic University *M*
State University of New York
  Buffalo *M*
Syracuse University *B, M*

North Carolina

Asheville Buncombe Technical
  Community College *A*
Central Piedmont Community College *A*
Cleveland Community College *A*
Durham Technical Community
  College *C, A*
Fayetteville Technical Community
  College *A*
Isothermal Community College *A*
Johnston Community College *A*
Mitchell Community College *A*
Pitt Community College *A*
Stanly Community College *A*
University of North Carolina
  Asheville *C, B*
  Charlotte *B*
Western Piedmont Community
  College *C, A*
Wilson Technical Community College *A*

Ohio

Bowling Green State University *B*
Bowling Green State University:
  Firelands College *C, A*
Case Western Reserve University *M, D*
Cuyahoga Community College
  Eastern Campus *C, A*

DeVry University
  Columbus *B*
Franklin University *B*
Kent State University *B*
Lakeland Community College *C*
Miami University
  Oxford Campus *B*
North Central State College *C, A*
Ohio State University
  Columbus Campus *B*
Ohio University *B*
Stark State College of Technology *A*
Tiffin University *B*
University of Cincinnati *B, M, D*
University of Cincinnati
  Raymond Walters College *C, A*
University of Toledo *M*
Wright State University *M*
Youngstown State University *B*

Oklahoma

East Central University *B*
University of Central Oklahoma *B*

Oregon

Chemeketa Community College *A*

Pennsylvania

Bucks County Community College *A*
Butler County Community College *C, A*
California University of Pennsylvania *B*
Cheyney University of Pennsylvania *B*
Community College of Philadelphia *A*
DeVry University
  Ft. Washington *B*
Delaware County Community College *A*
Drexel University *B*
Edinboro University of Pennsylvania *B*
Holy Family University *B*
La Salle University *B*
Lehigh Carbon Community College *A*
Penn State
  University Park *C, B*
Reading Area Community College *A*
Robert Morris University *B*
University of Pennsylvania *B, M*
University of Scranton *B, M*

Rhode Island

Bryant College *M*

South Carolina

Clemson University *B, M, D*

Tennessee

Tennessee Technological University *B*

Texas

Baylor University *B*
DeVry University
  Irving *B*
Del Mar College *C, A*
El Paso Community College *A*
Houston Community College
  System *C, A*
Kilgore College *C, A*
Lamar University *M*
LeTourneau University *B*
Odessa College *C*
Sam Houston State University *B*
Tarrant County College *A*
Texas A&M University *M*
Texas A&M University
  Commerce *B*
Texas State Technical College
  Waco *A*
  West Texas *C, A*
University of Houston *B, M, D*
University of North Texas *B, M, D*
University of Texas
  Arlington *M*
  San Antonio *B, M*
Wiley College *B*

Utah

Brigham Young University *B*
Utah State University *B*
Utah Valley State College *B*

Vermont

College of St. Joseph in Vermont *B*

Virginia

George Mason University *M*

Washington

Crown College *A, B*
DeVry University
  Seattle *B*
Eastern Washington University *B*
Seattle Central Community College *C*
Seattle University *B*
Western Washington University *B*

West Virginia

West Virginia Junior College *A*

Wisconsin

Blackhawk Technical College *A*
Chippewa Valley Technical College *A*
Marian College of Fond du Lac *B*
Mid-State Technical College *A*
University of Wisconsin
  Madison *M*
  Milwaukee *B*
  Oshkosh *B*
  Stout *B*
Western Wisconsin Technical College *A*
Wisconsin Indianhead Technical
  College *C*

Operations research

Alabama

University of Alabama
  Huntsville *M*

Arkansas

University of Arkansas
  Little Rock *B*

California

San Diego State University *M*
Stanford University *M, D*

Colorado

United States Air Force Academy *B*

Connecticut

Central Connecticut State University *B*
United States Coast Guard Academy *B*
University of New Haven *B, M*

Delaware

University of Delaware *B, M, D*

District of Columbia

George Washington University *M, D*

Florida

Florida Institute of Technology *M, D*

Indiana

Indiana University-Purdue University
  Fort Wayne *B, M*

Iowa

Iowa State University *M*

Kansas

Kansas State University *M*

Massachusetts

Massachusetts Institute of
  Technology *M, D*

Michigan

Michigan State University *M*

Minnesota

Bethel College *B*

Missouri

University of Missouri
  Rolla *M*

New Jersey

Princeton University *B, M, D*

Rutgers, The State University of New
  Jersey
  New Brunswick Regional
    Campus *M, D*

New York

City University of New York
  Baruch College *B, M*
  City College *B*
Columbia University
  Fu Foundation School of
    Engineering and Applied
    Science *B, M, D*
Rensselaer Polytechnic Institute *M*
St. John's University *C, M*
United States Military Academy *B*

Ohio

Case Western Reserve University *M, D*

Oregon

Oregon State University *M*

Pennsylvania

Carnegie Mellon University *B, D*
University of Pennsylvania *M, D*

Texas

Southern Methodist University *M, D*
Texas A&M University
  Commerce *B*

Utah

Utah State University *M*

Wisconsin

University of Wisconsin
  Madison *B*

Ophthalmic laboratory technology

Connecticut

Middlesex Community College *A*

Delaware

Delaware Technical and Community
  College
  Owens Campus *A*

Florida

Broward Community College *A*

Georgia

DeKalb Technical College *C, A*

Illinois

Triton College *C, A*

Indiana

Indiana University
  Bloomington *A*

Minnesota

St. Cloud Technical College *C, A*

New Mexico

New Mexico State University
  Alamogordo *C*

New York

Rochester Institute of Technology *C, A*

North Carolina

Caldwell Community College and
  Technical Institute *C*
Duke University *C*
Durham Technical Community
  College *C*

Ohio

AEC Southern Ohio College
  Findlay *A*
Lakeland Community College *C, A*

Oregon

Eastern Oregon University *B*

Puerto Rico

University of Puerto Rico
  Medical Sciences Campus *A*

Texas
Tyler Junior College *C, A*

Washington
Seattle Central Community College *C*

Ophthalmic technology

New York
Rochester Institute of Technology *A*

Opticianry/ophthalmic dispensing

California
University of California
    Berkeley *C, B, M, D*

Connecticut
Middlesex Community College *A*

Florida
Gulf Coast Community College *A*
Hillsborough Community College *C, A*
Miami-Dade Community College *A*
Polk Community College *A*

Georgia
DeKalb Technical College *C, A*

Indiana
Indiana University
    Bloomington *A*

Michigan
Bay de Noc Community College *C*
Ferris State University *A, D*

Minnesota
Anoka-Ramsey Community College *A*

Mississippi
Mississippi Gulf Coast Community
    College
        Perkinston *A*

Nevada
Community College of Southern
    Nevada *A*

New Jersey
Camden County College *A*
Essex County College *A*
Raritan Valley Community College *A*

New Mexico
Southwestern Indian Polytechnic
    Institute *C, A*

New York
Erie Community College
    North Campus *A*
Suffolk County Community College *A*

North Carolina
Durham Technical Community
    College *C, A*

Ohio
Cuyahoga Community College
    Eastern Campus *C, A*
    Metropolitan Campus *C, A*
    Western Campus *C, A*
Hocking Technical College *A*
Lakeland Community College *A*
Ohio State University
    Columbus Campus *M*
Stark State College of Technology *C*

Pennsylvania
Western School of Health and Business
    Careers *A*
Westmoreland County Community
    College *C, A*

South Carolina
Florence-Darlington Technical
    College *C*

Tennessee
Roane State Community College *A*
University of Tennessee
    Knoxville *B, M*

Texas
El Paso Community College *C, A*
Tyler Junior College *C*
University of Houston *B, D*

Virginia
J. Sargeant Reynolds Community
    College *A*
Thomas Nelson Community College *A*

Washington
Spokane Community College *C, A*

Optics

Alabama
University of Alabama
    Huntsville *B, D*

Arizona
University of Arizona *M, D*

California
Yuba Community College District *C*

Florida
University of Central Florida *M, D*

Indiana
Indiana University
    Bloomington *M, D*

Massachusetts
Tufts University *M, D*

Michigan
Saginaw Valley State University *B*

Missouri
University of Missouri
    St. Louis *M, D*

New Jersey
Stevens Institute of Technology *M, D*

New Mexico
University of New Mexico *D*

New York
Corning Community College *A*
Monroe Community College *A*
University of Rochester *B, M, D*

North Carolina
University of North Carolina
    Charlotte *M*

North Dakota
North Dakota State University *B*

Ohio
University of Dayton *M, D*

Pennsylvania
Albright College *B*
University of Pittsburgh *C*

Texas
University of North Texas *M*

Optometric assistant

District of Columbia
Georgetown University *C*

New Mexico
Southwestern Indian Polytechnic
    Institute *C*

Ohio
Owens Community College
    Toledo *A*

Optometry (O.D.)

Alabama
University of Alabama at Birmingham:
    School of Optometry *F*

California
Southern California College of
    Optometry *F*
University of California Berkeley: School
    of Optometry *F*

Florida
Nova Southeastern University Health
    Professions Division: College of
    Optometry *F*

Illinois
Illinois College of Optometry *F*

Indiana
Indiana University Bloomington: School
    of Optometry *F*

Massachusetts
New England College of Optometry *F*

Michigan
Ferris State University: College of
    Optometry *F*

Missouri
University of Missouri St. Louis: School
    of Optometry *F*

New York
State University of New York College of
    Optometry *F*

Ohio
Ohio State University Columbus
    Campus: College of Optometry *F*

Oklahoma
Northeastern State University: College of
    Optometry *F*

Oregon
Pacific University: School of
    Optometry *F*

Pennsylvania
Pennsylvania College of Optometry *F*

Puerto Rico
Inter American University of Puerto Rico
    School of Optometry *F*

Tennessee
Southern College of Optometry *F*

Texas
University of Houston: College of
    Optometry *F*

Organic chemistry

California
Pitzer College *B*

Florida
Florida State University *M, D*

Georgia
Clark Atlanta University *M, D*
Oxford College of Emory University *B*

Illinois
Loyola University of Chicago *M, D*

Iowa
Iowa State University *M, D*

Maryland
Johns Hopkins University *B*

Massachusetts
Hampshire College *B*
Harvard College *B*
Massachusetts College of Pharmacy and
    Health Sciences *M, D*

Tufts University *M, D*

Montana
University of Montana-Missoula *M, D*

New Jersey
Stevens Institute of Technology *M, D*

New York
Fordham University *M*
Sarah Lawrence College *B*
State University of New York
    Albany *D*
    Buffalo *M, D*
    College of Environmental Science
        and Forestry *M, D*

Oregon
University of Oregon *M, D*
University of Portland *B*

Texas
Texas A&M University
    Commerce *B*
University of North Texas *M, D*

Utah
University of Utah *M, D*

Vermont
Bennington College *B*
Marlboro College *B*

Wisconsin
Marquette University *M, D*
University of Wisconsin
    River Falls *B*

Organizational behavior studies

Arizona
Estrella Mountain Community
    College *C, A*
Paradise Valley Community
    College *C, A*
University of Phoenix *M*

Arkansas
Central Baptist College *B*

California
Antioch Southern California
    Santa Barbara *M*
California Baptist University *B*
Chapman University *M*
Claremont McKenna College *B*
Golden Gate University *B*
National University *B*
Pepperdine University *M*
Pitzer College *B*
St. Mary's College of California *M*
Santa Clara University *B*
Scripps College *B*
University of La Verne *M*
University of San Francisco *B*

Colorado
Colorado Technical University *C*
University of Colorado
    Denver *M*

Connecticut
Central Connecticut State University *M*
Eastern Connecticut State University *M*
University of Hartford *M*

District of Columbia
American University *M*
George Washington University *M*

Florida
Rollins College *M*
Warner Southern College *B*

Georgia
Covenant College *B*
Oglethorpe University *B*

Illinois
Benedictine University *B, M, D*
Greenville College *B*
Loyola University of Chicago *C, M*
North Park University *B*
Northwestern University *B, M, D*
Trinity Christian College *B*
Trinity International University *M, D*

Indiana
Calumet College of St. Joseph *B*
Indiana University
    Bloomington *D*
Indiana University-Purdue University
    Fort Wayne *A, B*
Oakland City University *B*

Iowa
St. Ambrose University *B*
University of Iowa *D*

Kentucky
Mid-Continent College *B*

Louisiana
Loyola University New Orleans *B*

Maine
University of New England *B*
University of Southern Maine *B*

Maryland
Columbia Union College *B*

Massachusetts
Boston College *D*
Boston University *B*
Emerson College *M*

Michigan
Eastern Michigan University *M*
Michigan State University *D*
Saginaw Valley State University *M*
University of Michigan
    Flint *B*
Wayne State University *B*

Minnesota
Bethel College *B*
Capella University *C, B*
Concordia University: St. Paul *B*

Missouri
Hannibal-LaGrange College *B*
Maryville University of Saint Louis *B*
St. Louis Community College
    St. Louis Community College at
    Forest Park *C, A*
St. Louis University *B*
University of Missouri
    St. Louis *B*
Washington University in St. Louis *M*

Nebraska
University of Nebraska
    Omaha *B*

New Jersey
Rider University *B*
Thomas Edison State College *B*

New York
City University of New York
    Baruch College *M, D*
New York University *B, M, D*
Polytechnic University *M*
State University of New York
    Albany *D*
    Buffalo *M, D*

North Carolina
High Point University *B*
Mount Olive College *B*

North Dakota
North Dakota State University *B*
University of North Dakota *B*

Ohio
Baldwin-Wallace College *B*
Bowling Green State University *M*

Case Western Reserve University *M, D*
College of Mount St. Joseph *M*
Denison University *B*
Lourdes College *M*
Miami University
    Oxford Campus *B*
Union Institute & University *D*
University of Findlay *M*
University of Toledo *B*

Oklahoma
Southeastern Oklahoma State
    University *B*

Oregon
University of Oregon *D*

Pennsylvania
Carnegie Mellon University *D*
Geneva College *M*
La Salle University *B*
Neumann College *M*
Penn State
    Harrisburg *B*
Rosemont College *B*
Shippensburg University of
    Pennsylvania *M*
Villanova University *M*

Puerto Rico
University of Puerto Rico
    Mayaguez Campus *B, M*

South Carolina
Converse College *B*

South Dakota
University of Sioux Falls *B*

Texas
St. Edward's University *M*
Southern Methodist University *B*
University of Houston *B*
University of North Texas *B, D*
University of Texas
    Dallas *B, M, D*
University of the Incarnate Word *A, B*

Utah
Brigham Young University *B, M*

Vermont
Champlain College *A, B*

Virginia
Eastern Mennonite University *B*
Marymount University *C, M*

Washington
Central Washington University *M*
Seattle Pacific University *B*
University of Washington *B*

Wisconsin
Carroll College *B*
Marquette University *B*
Silver Lake College *M*
University of Wisconsin
    Platteville *B*

Organizational communication

California
Ohlone College *C*

Colorado
Jones International University *C, M*

Florida
University of Miami *B*
University of West Florida *B*

Georgia
Toccoa Falls College *B*

Illinois
McKendree College *B*

Indiana
Indiana University
    Northwest *B*
Indiana University-Purdue University
    Fort Wayne *B*

Kansas
Tabor College *B*
University of Kansas *B*

Maryland
Bowie State University *M*

Massachusetts
Assumption College *B*

Michigan
Michigan Technological University *C*

Minnesota
College of St. Scholastica *B*

Nebraska
Creighton University *A, B*
Doane College *B*

New York
Canisius College *M*
Ithaca College *B*
Marist College *B*
State University of New York
    Buffalo *M, D*

North Carolina
Queens University of Charlotte *B*

Ohio
Marietta College *B*
Ohio Northern University *B*
Ohio University
    Chillicothe Campus *B*
    Zanesville Campus *B*
Xavier University *A, B*

Pennsylvania
Marywood University *C*

Rhode Island
Providence College *C, B*

Texas
Lubbock Christian University *B*

Washington
Northwest College *B*

Wisconsin
Carroll College *B*

Ornamental horticulture

Alabama
Northwest-Shoals Community College *C*

Arkansas
University of Arkansas *B*

California
Antelope Valley College *C, A*
Bakersfield College *A*
Cabrillo College *C, A*
California Polytechnic State University:
    San Luis Obispo *B*
California State Polytechnic University:
    Pomona *B*
Cerritos Community College *A*
College of the Sequoias *C, A*
Cuyamaca College *A*
Foothill College *C, A*
Las Positas College *C, A*
Long Beach City College *C, A*
Los Angeles Pierce College *C, A*
Modesto Junior College *A*
Monterey Peninsula College *C, A*
Moorpark College *A*
Mount San Antonio College *C*
Orange Coast College *C, A*
San Joaquin Delta College *C, A*
Santa Barbara City College *C, A*
Santa Rosa Junior College *C*

Shasta College *C, A*
Sierra College *C, A*
Ventura College *A*
Victor Valley College *C, A*
Yuba Community College District *C, A*

Delaware
University of Delaware *B, M*

Florida
Florida Agricultural and Mechanical
    University *B*
Florida Southern College *B*
Gulf Coast Community College *A*
Hillsborough Community College *C, A*
Palm Beach Community College *A*
Pensacola Junior College *A*
Santa Fe Community College *A*
Valencia Community College *A*

Georgia
Abraham Baldwin Agricultural
    College *A*
Albany Technical College *C*
Fort Valley State University *A*

Illinois
College of DuPage *C*
College of Lake County *C, A*
Joliet Junior College *C, A*
Kishwaukee College *C, A*
McHenry County College *C*
Triton College *C, A*
University of Illinois
    Urbana-Champaign *B*
William Rainey Harper College *C, A*

Iowa
Kirkwood Community College *C*

Kentucky
Murray State University *B*

Maine
University of Maine *B*

Maryland
University of Maryland
    College Park *B*

Massachusetts
University of Massachusetts
    Amherst *A*

Michigan
Ferris State University *A*
Wayne County Community College *C*

Mississippi
Mississippi Gulf Coast Community
    College
    Perkinston *A*

Missouri
St. Louis Community College
    St. Louis Community College at
    Meramec *C, A*

Nebraska
Central Community College *C*
Metropolitan Community College *C, A*
Nebraska College of Technical
    Agriculture *A*

Nevada
Community College of Southern
    Nevada *C, A*

New Hampshire
University of New Hampshire *A*

New Jersey
Brookdale Community College *C*
Cumberland County College *C, A*
Mercer County Community College *C, A*

New York
Cornell University *B*
Finger Lakes Community College *C, A*
Niagara County Community College *C*

State University of New York
  College of Agriculture and
    Technology at Cobleskill *A, B*
  College of Agriculture and
    Technology at Morrisville *A*
  College of Technology at Delhi *A*
  Farmingdale *C, A*
Suffolk County Community College *A*

North Carolina
Blue Ridge Community College *C*
Sampson Community College *A*

North Dakota
Minot State University: Bottineau
  Campus *A*

Ohio
Cincinnati State Technical and
  Community College *A*

Oklahoma
Eastern Oklahoma State College *A*

Oregon
Clackamas Community College *C, A*

Pennsylvania
Community College of Allegheny
  County *C*
Delaware Valley College *B*
Mercyhurst College *C*
Penn State
  University Park *C*
Pennsylvania College of Technology *A*

Puerto Rico
Inter American University of Puerto Rico
  Barranquitas Campus *A*

Tennessee
University of Tennessee
  Knoxville *B, M*
Walters State Community College *A*

Texas
Alvin Community College *C*
Grayson County College *C*
Houston Community College System *C*
Palo Alto College *A*
Tarleton State University *B*
Texarkana College *C*
Texas A&M University *B, M*
Western Texas College *C, A*

Utah
Utah State University *C, A, B*

Vermont
Vermont Technical College *A*

Virginia
J. Sargeant Reynolds Community
  College *C, A*

Washington
South Seattle Community College *C, A*
Spokane Community College *C*

Wisconsin
Blackhawk Technical College *C*
Fox Valley Technical College *C*

Orthotics/prosthetics

California
California State University
  Dominguez Hills *B*

Florida
Florida International University *B*

Massachusetts
Boston University *M, D*

Minnesota
Century Community and Technical
  College *C, A*

Nevada
Community College of Southern
  Nevada *A*

Pennsylvania
Median School of Allied Health
  Careers *A*

Texas
University of Texas
  Southwestern Medical Center at
    Dallas *B*

Washington
Spokane Falls Community College *A*
University of Washington *B*

Osteopathic medicine (D.O.)

California
Western University of Health Sciences *F*

Florida
Nova Southeastern University Health
  Professions Division: College of
  Osteopathic Medicine *F*

Illinois
Midwestern University: Chicago College
  of Osteopathic Medicine *F*

Iowa
Des Moines University - Osteopathic
  Medical Center *F*

Maine
University of New England: School of
  Osteopathic Medicine *F*

Michigan
Michigan State University: College of
  Osteopathic Medicine *F*

Missouri
Kirksville College of Osteopathic
  Medicine *F*
University of Health Sciences College of
  Osteopathic Medicine *F*

New Jersey
UMDNJ-School of Osteopathic
  Medicine *F*

New York
New York College of Osteopathic
  Medicine of New York Institute of
  Technology *F*

Ohio
Ohio University
  College of Osteopathic Medicine *F*

Oklahoma
Oklahoma State University: College of
  Osteopathic Medicine *F*

Pennsylvania
Lake Erie College of Osteopathic
  Medicine *F*
Philadelphia College of Osteopathic
  Medicine *F*

Texas
University of North Texas Health Science
  Center at Fort Worth: Osteopathic
  Medicine *F*

West Virginia
West Virginia School of Osteopathic
  Medicine *F*

Pacific area/rim studies

California
Loyola Marymount University *B*
University of California
  San Diego *M*

Hawaii
Brigham Young University-Hawaii *B*
University of Hawaii
  Manoa *M*
  West Oahu *B*

Missouri
Northwest Missouri State University *B*

Painting

Alabama
Birmingham-Southern College *B*

Arizona
Arizona State University *B, M*

Arkansas
Harding University *B*

California
Academy of Art College *C, A, B, M*
Art Center College of Design *B, M*
Biola University *B*
California College of Arts and
  Crafts *B, M*
California State University
  Fullerton *B, M*
  Hayward *B*
  Long Beach *B, M*
  Northridge *B, M*
  Stanislaus *B*
Chabot College *A*
De Anza College *C, A*
Grossmont Community College *A*
Monterey Peninsula College *A*
Ohlone College *C*
Otis College of Art and Design *B, M*
Palomar College *A*
San Diego State University *B*
Santa Rosa Junior College *C*
University of San Francisco *B*

Colorado
Colorado State University *B*
Naropa University *B*
Rocky Mountain College of Art &
  Design *B*

Connecticut
Paier College of Art *C, B*
Sacred Heart University *B*
University of Connecticut *B*
University of Hartford *B, M*

District of Columbia
American University *M*
George Washington University *M*

Florida
University of Miami *B*

Georgia
Atlanta College of Art *B*
LaGrange College *B*
Savannah College of Art and
  Design *B, M*
University of Georgia *B*

Idaho
Northwest Nazarene University *B*

Illinois
American Academy of Art *B*
City Colleges of Chicago
  Olive-Harvey College *A*
Lewis University *B*
Lincoln College *A*
Richland Community College *A*
Rockford College *B*
School of the Art Institute of
  Chicago *B, M*
University of Illinois
  Urbana-Champaign *B*

Indiana
Ball State University *B*

Indiana University-Purdue University
  Fort Wayne *B*
University of Evansville *B*
Vincennes University *A*

Iowa
Drake University *B*
University of Iowa *B, M*

Kansas
Allen County Community College *A*
Central Christian College *A, B*
Pratt Community College *A*
Seward County Community College *A*
University of Kansas *B, M*

Louisiana
Centenary College of Louisiana *B*

Maine
Maine College of Art *B*
University of Southern Maine *B*

Maryland
Maryland College of Art and Design *A*
Maryland Institute College of Art *B, M*

Massachusetts
Art Institute of Boston at Lesley
  University *A, B, M*
Boston University *B, M*
Emmanuel College *B*
Hampshire College *B*
Massachusetts College of Art *B, M*
Montserrat College of Art *B*
School of the Museum of Fine Arts *B, M*
Simon's Rock College of Bard *B*
University of Massachusetts
  Dartmouth *B, M*

Michigan
Aquinas College *B*
College for Creative Studies *B*
Ferris State University *B*
Finlandia University *B*
Grand Valley State University *B*
Lansing Community College *A*
Northern Michigan University *B*
Siena Heights University *B*
University of Michigan *B*
University of Michigan
  Dearborn *B*

Minnesota
College of Visual Arts *B*
Minnesota State University
  Mankato *B*
  Moorhead *B*

Mississippi
Mississippi University for Women *B*

Missouri
Kansas City Art Institute *B*
Lindenwood University *B, M*
University of Missouri
  St. Louis *B*
Washington University in St. Louis *B, M*

Nebraska
University of Nebraska
  Omaha *B*

New Hampshire
Rivier College *B*
University of New Hampshire *M*

New Jersey
Rowan University *B*

New Mexico
College of Santa Fe *B*

New York
Alfred University *B*
Bard College *B, M*
City University of New York
  Brooklyn College *M*
Hofstra University *B*
Parsons School of Design *C, A, B, M, T*
Pratt Institute *B, M*

Rochester Institute of
   Technology *A, B, M*
Sarah Lawrence College *B*
School of Visual Arts *B, M*
State University of New York
   Albany *B, M*
   Buffalo *M*
   College at Buffalo *B*
   College at Fredonia *B*
   College at Potsdam *B*
   New Paltz *B, M*
   Purchase *B, M*
Syracuse University *B, M*

Ohio

Art Academy of Cincinnati *B*
Bowling Green State University *B, M*
Cleveland Institute of Art *B*
Columbus College of Art and Design *B*
Ohio State University
   Columbus Campus *B*
Ohio University *B, M*
Shawnee State University *B*
University of Akron *B*
University of Findlay *B*
Wittenberg University *B*
Youngstown State University *B*

Oklahoma

University of Oklahoma *B*

Oregon

Pacific Northwest College of Art *B*
Portland State University *B, M*
University of Oregon *B, M*

Pennsylvania

Arcadia University *B*
Immaculata University *A*
Keystone College *A*
Marywood University *C, M*
Mercyhurst College *B*
Oakbridge Academy of Arts *A*
Seton Hill University *B*
Temple University *B, M*

Puerto Rico

Escuela de Artes Plasticas de Puerto
   Rico *B*
Inter American University of Puerto Rico
   San German Campus *B, M*
University of Puerto Rico
   Rio Piedras Campus *B*

Rhode Island

Providence College *B*
Rhode Island College *B*
Rhode Island School of Design *B, M*

South Carolina

Anderson College *B*

Tennessee

Carson-Newman College *B*
Memphis College of Art *B, M*
Tennessee Technological University *B*

Texas

McMurry University *B*
Sam Houston State University *M*
Stephen F. Austin State University *M*
Texas A&M University
   Commerce *B, M*
Texas Woman's University *B, M*
University of Dallas *M, T*
University of Houston *B, M*
University of North Texas *B, M*
University of Texas
   Arlington *B*
   El Paso *B*
   San Antonio *B, M*
Western Texas College *A*

Utah

Brigham Young University *B, M*
Dixie State College of Utah *A*

Vermont

Bennington College *B, M*

Burlington College *B*
Marlboro College *B*

Virginia

Virginia Commonwealth University *B*

Washington

Cornish College of the Arts *B*
North Seattle Community College *C*
University of Washington *B, M*
Western Washington University *B*

West Virginia

Alderson-Broaddus College *B*
West Virginia State College *B*
West Virginia Wesleyan College *B*

Wisconsin

Milwaukee Institute of Art & Design *B*
University of Wisconsin
   Madison *B*

Painting/wall covering

Indiana

Ivy Tech State College
   Central Indiana *C, A*
   Southwest *C, A*

Minnesota

St. Paul College - A Community and
   Technical College *C*

Oregon

Linn-Benton Community College *A*

Pennsylvania

Community College of Allegheny
   County *A*

Paleontology

Arkansas

University of Arkansas *D*

California

Loma Linda University *M*
San Diego State University *B*

Florida

University of Miami *B, M, D*

Louisiana

Tulane University *D*

Massachusetts

Harvard College *B*

Michigan

University of Michigan *B, M*

Ohio

Ohio State University
   Columbus Campus *M, D*

Pennsylvania

University of Pittsburgh *B*

South Dakota

South Dakota School of Mines and
   Technology *M*

Texas

Baylor University *B*

Washington

Western Washington University *B*

Paralegal/legal assistance

Alabama

Community College of the Air Force *A*
Enterprise State Junior College *A*
Gadsden State Community College *A*
Huntingdon College *A*
James H. Faulkner State Community
   College *A*

Northeast Alabama Community
   College *A*
Shelton State Community College *C*
South University *A*
Virginia College *C, A*
Wallace State Community College at
   Hanceville *A*

Alaska

University of Alaska
   Anchorage *C*
   Fairbanks *A*
   Southeast *A*

Arizona

Phoenix College *C, A*
Pima Community College *C, A*
Yavapai College *C, A*

Arkansas

Ouachita Technical College *A*
Pulaski Technical College *A*
Southeast Arkansas College *A*
University of Arkansas
   Fort Smith *A*

California

California State University
   Chico *C*
   Hayward *C*
Cerritos Community College *A*
Coastline Community College *C*
College of the Redwoods *C, A*
College of the Sequoias *A*
De Anza College *C, A*
Glendale Community College *A*
Imperial Valley College *C, A*
Los Angeles Southwest College *A*
MTI College of Business and
   Technology *A*
Mount San Antonio College *A*
Napa Valley College *C, A*
Palomar College *C, A*
Platt College
   Ontario *C, A*
St. Mary's College of California *C*
San Diego City College *A*
San Francisco State University *C*
Santiago Canyon College *A*
Shasta College *A*
Southwestern College *C, A*
University of San Diego *C*
University of West Los Angeles *B*
West Valley College *A*

Colorado

Arapahoe Community College *C, A*
Blair Junior College *A*
Community College of Aurora *C, A*
Front Range Community College *C*
Parks College *A*

Connecticut

Briarwood College *A*
Manchester Community College *C, A*
Naugatuck Valley Community College *A*
Norwalk Community College *C, A*
Quinnipiac University *B*
Sacred Heart University *A, B*
Teikyo Post University *C, A, B*
University of Hartford *C, A, B*
University of New Haven *C*

Delaware

Delaware Technical and Community
   College
   Owens Campus *C, A*

District of Columbia

George Washington University *C*
University of the District of Columbia *A*

Florida

Broward Community College *A*
Cooper Career Institute *A*
Daytona Beach Community College *A*

Florida Metropolitan University
   Orlando College North *A*
   Tampa College *A*
   Tampa College Lakeland *A*
Florida National College *A*
Gulf Coast Community College *A*
Hillsborough Community College *A*
Indian River Community College *A*
International College *A*
Jones College *A, B*
Lake-Sumter Community College *A*
Manatee Community College *A*
Miami-Dade Community College *A*
New England Institute of Technology *A*
Nova Southeastern University *B*
Okaloosa-Walton Community College *A*
Palm Beach Community College *A*
Pasco-Hernando Community College *A*
Pensacola Junior College *A*
Polk Community College *A*
Santa Fe Community College *A*
Seminole Community College *A*
South Florida Community College *A*
Tallahassee Community College *A*
Valencia Community College *A*

Georgia

Athens Technical College *A*
Atlanta Metropolitan College *C*
Augusta State University *C*
Darton College *C, A*
Floyd College *A*
Gainesville College *A*
Georgia College and State University *B*
South University *A*
Valdosta State University *B*

Idaho

Eastern Idaho Technical College *C, A*
Idaho State University *A*
Lewis-Clark State College *C, A, B*

Illinois

Black Hawk College
   East Campus *A*
Elgin Community College *C, A*
Gem City College *A*
Illinois Central College *C, A*
Midstate College *A*
Northwestern Business College *A*
Robert Morris College: Chicago *C, A*
Rock Valley College *C, A*
Rockford Business College *A*
Sauk Valley Community College *C*
South Suburban College of Cook
   County *C, A*
Southern Illinois University
   Carbondale *B*
Southwestern Illinois College *C, A*
University of Illinois
   Springfield *B*
William Rainey Harper College *A*

Indiana

Ball State University *A, B*
Calumet College of St. Joseph *C, A, B*
Commonwealth Business College:
   Michigan City *A*
Indiana Wesleyan University *A, B*
International Business College *C, A*
International Business College:
   Indianapolis *A*
Ivy Tech State College
   Bloomington *A*
   Central Indiana *A*
   Columbus *A*
   Eastcentral *A*
   Kokomo *A*
   Lafayette *A*
   Northeast *A*
   Northwest *A*
   Southcentral *A*
   Southeast *A*
   Southwest *A*
   Wabash Valley *A*
Michiana College: Fort Wayne *A*
Professional Careers Institute *A*

St. Mary-of-the-Woods College *C, A, B*
University of Evansville *B*
University of Indianapolis *A*
Vincennes University *A*

Iowa

Des Moines Area Community College *A*
Hamilton College
 Cedar Falls *A*
 Mason City *A*
Iowa Lakes Community College *A*
Iowa Western Community College *A*
Kaplan College *A*
Kirkwood Community College *A*
Northeast Iowa Community College *C*

Kansas

Central Christian College *A*
Cloud County Community College *C, A*
Hutchinson Community College *C, A*
Independence Community College *A*
Johnson County Community
 College *C, A*
Kansas City Kansas Community
 College *A*
Washburn University of Topeka *C, A*
Wichita State University *A*

Kentucky

Beckfield College *C, A*
Bellarmine University *C*
Daymar College *A*
Morehead State University *B*
Southwestern College of Business *C*
Sullivan University *C, A, B*
University of Louisville *A*

Louisiana

Grambling State University *C, A, B*
Herzing College *A*
Louisiana State University
 Eunice *A*
McNeese State University *A*
Nicholls State University *A*
Nunez Community College *A*
Southern University
 Shreveport *A*
Tulane University *C*

Maine

Andover College *C, A*
Beal College *C, A*
Husson College *A, B*
Thomas College *A*
University of Maine
 Augusta *C, A*

Maryland

Anne Arundel Community College *C, A*
Chesapeake College *C, A*
College of Southern Maryland *A*
Community College of Baltimore County
 Catonsville *A*
 Dundalk *A*
 Essex *A*
Frederick Community College *C, A*
Hagerstown Community College *C*
Harford Community College *A*
Montgomery College
 Rockville Campus *A*
Villa Julie College *A, B*

Massachusetts

Anna Maria College *C, A, B*
Atlantic Union College *C, A*
Bay Path College *C, A*
Bay State College *A*
Becker College *C, A*
Boston University *B*
Bunker Hill Community College *C*
Cape Cod Community College *C*
Elms College *C, A, B*
Massachusetts Bay Community
 College *C, A*
Massasoit Community College *A*
Merrimack College *A*
Mount Ida College *A*
Mount Wachusett Community College *C*

Newbury College *C, A, B*
Northeastern University *C*
Roxbury Community College *A*
Stonehill College *C*
Suffolk University *A, B*

Michigan

Baker College
 of Auburn Hills *A*
Bay de Noc Community College *C*
Davenport University
 Midland *A*
Davenport University - Western
 Region *C, A, B*
Eastern Michigan University *B*
Ferris State University *A*
Kellogg Community College *C, A*
Lansing Community College *A*
Macomb Community College *A*
Mott Community College *A*
North Central Michigan College *A*
Northern Michigan University *A*
Northwestern Michigan College *C*
Oakland Community College *C, A*
Southwestern Michigan College *A*

Minnesota

Globe College *C, A*
Hamline University *B*
Inver Hills Community College *A*
Minnesota State University
 Moorhead *B*
North Hennepin Community College *A*
Northland Community & Technical
 College *A*
Winona State University *B*

Mississippi

Itawamba Community College *A*
Mississippi College *C, B*
Mississippi Gulf Coast Community
 College
 Perkinston *A*
Mississippi University for Women *B*
Northwest Mississippi Community
 College *A*
University of Southern Mississippi *B*

Missouri

Avila University *C, B*
Hickey College *C, A*
Kansas City College of Legal Studies *A*
Maryville University of Saint Louis *B*
Mineral Area College *C, A*
Missouri Western State College *C, A*
Patricia Stevens College *A*
Penn Valley Community College *C, A*
Rockhurst University *C*
St. Louis Community College
 St. Louis Community College at
  Meramec *C, A*
Sanford-Brown College *A*
Springfield College *A*
Webster University *C, B*
William Jewell College *C*
William Woods University *A, B*

Montana

University of Montana-Missoula *A*

Nebraska

Central Community College *C, A*
College of Saint Mary *C, A, B*
Lincoln School of Commerce *C, A*
Metropolitan Community College *A*
Midland Lutheran College *B*
Nebraska College of Business *A*
Nebraska Indian Community College *A*
Northeast Community College *C, A*
University of Nebraska
 Omaha *B*

Nevada

Community College of Southern
 Nevada *C, A*
Las Vegas College *A*
Morrison University *A*

Truckee Meadows Community
 College *A*
Western Nevada Community College *A*

New Hampshire

College for Lifelong Learning *C*
Hesser College *C, A*
New Hampshire Community Technical
 College
 Laconia *C*
 Nashua *C, A*
New Hampshire Technical Institute *C, A*

New Jersey

Atlantic Cape Community College *A*
Bergen Community College *A*
Berkeley College *A*
Brookdale Community College *A*
Burlington County College *A*
Cumberland County College *A*
Essex County College *A*
Gloucester County College *C, A*
Hudson County Community College *A*
Mercer County Community College *C, A*
Middlesex County College *A*
Montclair State University *C*
Ocean County College *C*
Raritan Valley Community College *A*
Sussex County Community College *C, A*
Thomas Edison State College *A, B*
Warren County Community College *C, A*

New Mexico

Albuquerque Technical-Vocational
 Institute *A*
Dona Ana Branch Community College of
 New Mexico State University *A*
Eastern New Mexico University: Roswell
 Campus *A*
New Mexico Junior College *C, A*
New Mexico State University
 Alamogordo *C, A*
Santa Fe Community College *C, A*

New York

Berkeley College *A*
Berkeley College of New York City *A*
Broome Community College *C, A*
Bryant & Stratton Business Institute
 Albany *A*
City University of New York
 Bronx Community College *A*
 Hostos Community College *A*
 La Guardia Community College *A*
Corning Community College *A*
Dutchess Community College *C, A*
Elmira Business Institute *C, A*
Erie Community College
 City Campus *A*
Finger Lakes Community College *A*
Fulton-Montgomery Community
 College *C, A*
Genesee Community College *A*
Hilbert College *A, B*
Jefferson Community College *A*
Long Island University
 C. W. Post Campus *C*
Maria College *C, A*
Marist College *C*
Mercy College *B*
Mildred Elley *C, A*
Monroe Community College *C*
Nassau Community College *C, A*
New York University *C*
Olean Business Institute *C, A*
Rockland Community College *C, A*
St. John's University *C, A, B*
Suffolk County Community
 College *C, A*
Tompkins-Cortland Community
 College *A*
Westchester Community College *C, A*

North Carolina

Caldwell Community College and
 Technical Institute *A*
Cape Fear Community College *A*

Carteret Community College *A*
Central Carolina Community
 College *C, A*
Central Piedmont Community
 College *C, A*
Coastal Carolina Community College *A*
Davidson County Community
 College *C, A*
Durham Technical Community
 College *A*
Fayetteville Technical Community
 College *A*
Forsyth Technical Community College *A*
Gaston College *A*
Guilford Technical Community
 College *A*
Johnston Community College *A*
King's College *A*
Meredith College *C*
Pitt Community College *A*
Rockingham Community College *A*
Rowan-Cabarrus Community College *A*
South College *A*
South Piedmont Community College *A*
Southwestern Community College *A*
Surry Community College *A*
Western Piedmont Community
 College *C, A*
Wilkes Community College *A*
Wilson Technical Community College *A*

North Dakota

Lake Region State College *C, A*

Ohio

Academy of Court Reporting *B*
Academy of Court Reporting
 Columbus *A*
Bohecker's Business College *A*
Bradford School *A*
Bryant & Stratton College *A*
College of Mount St. Joseph *C, A, B*
Columbus State Community College *A*
Cuyahoga Community College
 Eastern Campus *C, A*
 Metropolitan Campus *C, A*
 Western Campus *C, A*
David N. Myers College *A, B*
ETI Technical College of Niles *A*
Edison State Community College *A*
James A. Rhodes State College *A*
Kent State University *C, A*
Kent State University
 East Liverpool Regional Campus *A*
 Trumbull Campus *C*
Lake Erie College *B*
Lakeland Community College *C, A*
Marion Technical College *A*
Muskingum Area Technical College *A*
North Central State College *A*
Northwest State Community College *A*
Ohio Business College: Sandusky *A*
RETS Tech Center *A*
Shawnee State University *A*
Sinclair Community College *A*
University of Akron *C, A*
University of Cincinnati
 Clermont College *C, A*
University of Findlay *C, A*
University of Northwestern Ohio *C, A*
University of Rio Grande *A*
University of Toledo *C, A, B*
Ursuline College *B*

Oklahoma

East Central University *B*
Metropolitan College *A*
Northeastern State University *B*
Oklahoma City University *C*
Oklahoma Wesleyan University *A*
Rogers State University *A*
Rose State College *A*
Tulsa Community College *A*

Oregon

Linn-Benton Community College *A*
Pioneer Pacific College *A*

Portland Community College *C, A*

Pennsylvania
Academy of Medical Arts and
   Business *C, A*
Allentown Business School *C*
Bradford School: Pittsburgh *A*
Bucks County Community College *C, A*
Career Training Academy *C*
Central Pennsylvania College *A*
Community College of Allegheny
   County *C, A*
Community College of Philadelphia *A*
Consolidated School of Business
   York *A*
Delaware County Community
   College *C, A*
Erie Business Center *A*
Harrisburg Area Community
   College *C, A*
Keystone College *C*
Lackawanna College *A*
Lehigh Carbon Community College *A*
Luzerne County Community College *A*
Manor College *C, A*
Marywood University *C, A, B*
McCann School of Business
   Pottsville *A*
   Sunbury *A*
Mount Aloysius College *A*
Northampton County Area Community
   College *A*
PJA School *C, A*
Peirce College *C, A, B*
Pennsylvania College of Technology *A*
Point Park College *A*
Schuylkill Institute of Business &
   Technology *A*
South Hills School of Business &
   Technology *C*
Western School of Health and Business
   Careers *A*
Westmoreland County Community
   College *C, A*
Widener University *C, A*

Puerto Rico
Turabo University *C*
Universidad del Este *A, B*

Rhode Island
Community College of Rhode Island *A*
Providence College *C, A*
Roger Williams University *B*

South Carolina
Aiken Technical College *C*
Central Carolina Technical College *A*
Florence-Darlington Technical College *A*
Forrest Junior College *C, A*
Horry-Georgetown Technical College *C*
Midlands Technical College *C, A*
Orangeburg-Calhoun Technical
   College *A*
Technical College of the Lowcountry *C*
Trident Technical College *C, A*
York Technical College *C*

South Dakota
Western Dakota Technical Institute *A*

Tennessee
Chattanooga State Technical Community
   College *A*
Cleveland State Community College *A*
Draughons Junior College of Business:
   Nashville *A*
Miller-Motte Technical College *A*
Pellissippi State Technical Community
   College *A*
Roane State Community College *A*
South College *A*
Southwest Tennessee Community
   College *A*
University of Tennessee
   Chattanooga *B*
Volunteer State Community College *A*

Walters State Community College *A*

Texas
Alvin Community College *C, A*
Angelina College *A*
Austin Community College *C, A*
Blinn College *C, A*
Brazosport College *A*
Central Texas College *A*
Collin County Community College
   District *C, A*
Del Mar College *A*
El Centro College *A*
El Paso Community College *C, A*
Grayson County College *A*
Houston Community College System *A*
Howard College *A*
Howard Payne University *B*
Kilgore College *C, A*
Lee College *A*
McLennan Community College *A*
Midland College *C, A*
North Central Texas College *A*
North Harris Montgomery Community
   College District *C, A*
Odessa College *C, A*
St. Philip's College *A*
San Antonio College *A*
South Plains College *A*
Southwest Texas State University *C*
Stephen F. Austin State University *B*
Tarrant County College *A*
Texas A&M University
   Commerce *B*
Texas Wesleyan University *B*
Texas Woman's University *B*
Trinity Valley Community College *C, A*
Tyler Junior College *A*
Victoria College *C, A*

Utah
Salt Lake Community College *A*
Southern Utah University *A*
Utah Valley State College *A, B*

Vermont
Burlington College *C*
Champlain College *C, A, B*
Woodbury College *B*

Virginia
Blue Ridge Community College *C*
Hampton University *C, B*
J. Sargeant Reynolds Community
   College *A*
Marymount University *C*
Mountain Empire Community College *A*
Thomas Nelson Community College *C*
Tidewater Tech *A*
University of Richmond *C, A*
Virginia Highlands Community
   College *C*
Virginia Intermont College *B*
Virginia Western Community College *A*

Washington
Clark College *C, A*
Crown College *A*
Edmonds Community College *C, A*
Lake Washington Technical College *C, A*
Lower Columbia College *A*
Renton Technical College *C, A*
Spokane Community College *C, A*
Spokane Falls Community College *C, A*

West Virginia
Bluefield State College *A*
Glenville State College *A*
Mountain State College *A*
Mountain State University *A*
Shepherd College *A*
West Virginia Business College *A*
West Virginia Business College *A*
West Virginia Junior College *A*

Wisconsin
Carthage College *C*
Chippewa Valley Technical College *A*

Concordia University Wisconsin *B*
Fox Valley Technical College *A*
Lakeshore Technical College *A*
Milwaukee Area Technical College *A*
University of Wisconsin
   Superior *C*
Western Wisconsin Technical College *A*
Wisconsin Indianhead Technical
   College *C*

Wyoming
Casper College *A*
Laramie County Community College *A*
Western Wyoming Community
   College *A*

Parasitology

Louisiana
Tulane University *M, D*

New York
New York University *M, D*

Pennsylvania
University of Pennsylvania *D*

Texas
Texas A&M University *M*

Wisconsin
University of Wisconsin
   Madison *M, D*

Parks, recreation and leisure studies

Alabama
Community College of the Air Force *A*
Huntingdon College *B*
Jacksonville State University *B*
University of North Alabama *B, M*
University of South Alabama *B*

Alaska
Sheldon Jackson College *B*
University of Alaska
   Southeast *C*

Arizona
Arizona State University *B, M*
Prescott College *B, M*

Arkansas
Arkansas Tech University *B*
Henderson State University *B*
University of Arkansas *B*
University of Arkansas
   Pine Bluff *B*

California
Bakersfield College *A*
California State University
   Chico *B, M*
   Hayward *B*
   Northridge *B, M*
   Sacramento *M*
Cerritos Community College *A*
Chabot College *A*
Glendale Community College *C, A*
Los Angeles Southwest College *A*
Modesto Junior College *A*
Mount San Antonio College *A*
Palomar College *C, A*
San Diego State University *B*
San Jose State University *B, M*
Santa Barbara City College *A*
Santa Monica College *C, A*
Santa Rosa Junior College *C, A*
Southwestern College *A*
Taft College *A*

Colorado
Colorado Mountain College
   Timberline Campus *A*
Colorado State University
   Pueblo *B*

Metropolitan State College of Denver *B*

Connecticut
Northwestern Connecticut Community
   College *A*
Norwalk Community College *C, A*
Southern Connecticut State
   University *B, M*

District of Columbia
Gallaudet University *M*
University of the District of
   Columbia *A, B*

Florida
Bethune-Cookman College *B*
Broward Community College *A*
Gulf Coast Community College *A*
Okaloosa-Walton Community College *A*
Palm Beach Community College *A*
Polk Community College *A*
South Florida Community College *A*
University of West Florida *B*

Georgia
Atlanta Metropolitan College *A*
Columbus State University *B, M*
East Georgia College *A*
Georgia College and State University *B*
Georgia Southern University *B*
Middle Georgia College *A*
Savannah State University *B*
Shorter College *A*
South Georgia College *A*

Hawaii
University of Hawaii
   Manoa *B*

Idaho
Brigham Young University - Idaho *B*
University of Idaho *B, M*

Illinois
Aurora University *B*
Moraine Valley Community College *A*
Southern Illinois University
   Carbondale *B, M*
University of Illinois
   Urbana-Champaign *B, M, D*
University of St. Francis *B*

Indiana
Franklin College *B*
Indiana Institute of Technology *A, B*
Indiana University
   Bloomington *B, M, D*
   Southeast *A*
Vincennes University *A*

Iowa
Dordt College *B*
Graceland University *B*
University of Dubuque *B*
University of Iowa *B, M*
University of Northern Iowa *B, M, D*
Waldorf College *A*

Kansas
Central Christian College *A*
Emporia State University *B*
Hutchinson Community College *A*
Kansas State University *B*
Seward County Community College *A*

Kentucky
Campbellsville University *B*
Georgetown College *B*
Murray State University *B*
Union College *B*

Louisiana
Grambling State University *B*
Southern University and Agricultural and
   Mechanical College *B, M*

Maine
University of Maine
   Machias *A, B*
   Presque Isle *A, B*

University of Southern Maine *B*

Maryland

Community College of Baltimore County
    Catonsville *C, A*
    Dundalk *C, A*
    Essex *C, A*
Frostburg State University *B, M*

Massachusetts

American International College *B*
Bridgewater State College *B*
Cape Cod Community College *A*
Gordon College *B*
Northeastern University *B*

Michigan

Calvin College *B*
Central Michigan University *B*
Grand Valley State University *B*
Michigan State University *B*
Northern Michigan University *B*
University of Michigan *B*
Wayne State University *B, M*
Western Michigan University *B*

Minnesota

Minnesota School of Business *C, A*
Minnesota State University
    Mankato *B*
Northland Community & Technical
    College *A*
Ridgewater College: A Community and
    Technical College *A*
St. Cloud State University *B*
University of Minnesota
    Duluth *B*
    Twin Cities *B, M*
Vermilion Community College *A*
Winona State University *B*

Mississippi

Alcorn State University *B*
Mississippi University for Women *R*
University of Mississippi *B*
University of Southern Mississippi *B, M*

Missouri

Blue River Community College *C*
Central Missouri State University *B*
Longview Community College *C*
Maple Woods Community College *C*
Northwest Missouri State University *B*
Penn Valley Community College *C*
Southeast Missouri State University *B*
Southwest Baptist University *B*
Southwest Missouri State University *B*
University of Missouri
    Columbia *B, M*

Montana

University of Montana: Western *A*

Nebraska

Chadron State College *B*
University of Nebraska
    Omaha *B*

Nevada

University of Nevada
    Las Vegas *B*
    Reno *B*

New Hampshire

Plymouth State College *B*

New Jersey

Thomas Edison State College *A, B*

New Mexico

Albuquerque Technical-Vocational
    Institute *C, A*
San Juan College *C*
Santa Fe Community College *A*
University of New Mexico *B, M, T*

New York

City University of New York
    Kingsborough Community
        College *A*

Dutchess Community College *A*
Houghton College *B*
Ithaca College *B, M*
State University of New York
    College at Brockport *B, M*
    College at Cortland *B*
    College of Agriculture and
        Technology at Morrisville *B*
Suffolk County Community College *A*
Ulster County Community College *A*

North Carolina

Barber-Scotia College *B*
Belmont Abbey College *B*
Brevard College *C, B*
Carteret Community College *A*
Catawba College *B*
Fayetteville Technical Community
    College *A*
Louisburg College *A*
Montreat College *A*
Mount Olive College *A, B*
North Carolina State University *B*
Shaw University *B*
Vance-Granville Community College *A*

North Dakota

North Dakota State University *B*

Ohio

Ashland University *B*
Bowling Green State University *B, M*
Central State University *B*
Malone College *B*
Ohio University *B*
University of Toledo *B, M*

Oklahoma

East Central University *B*
Oklahoma State University *B*
Southeastern Oklahoma State
    University *B*
Southwestern Oklahoma State
    University *B*

Oregon

Chemeketa Community College *A*
Oregon State University *B*

Pennsylvania

Butler County Community College *A*
Keystone College *B*
Lock Haven University of
    Pennsylvania *B*
Marywood University *B*
Messiah College *B*
Penn State
    Abington *B*
    Altoona *B*
    Beaver *B*
    Berks *B*
    Delaware County *B*
    Dubois *B*
    Fayette *B*
    Hazleton *B*
    Lehigh Valley *B*
    McKeesport *B*
    Mont Alto *B*
    New Kensington *B*
    Shenango *B*
    University Park *M, D*
    Wilkes-Barre *B*
    Worthington Scranton *B*
    York *B*
Temple University *B, M*
York College of Pennsylvania *B*

South Carolina

Erskine College *B*
Horry-Georgetown Technical College *A*
Newberry College *B*
Southern Wesleyan University *B*

South Dakota

Black Hills State University *B*
University of South Dakota *B*

Tennessee

Carson-Newman College *B*

Lambuth University *B*
Maryville College *B*
University of Tennessee
    Chattanooga *M*
    Knoxville *B, M*

Texas

Del Mar College *A*
Howard Payne University *B*
Rice University *B*
Southwest Texas State University *M, T*
Texas A&M University *B, M, D*
Texas Tech University *B*
University of Mary Hardin-Baylor *B*
University of North Texas *B, M*

Utah

Snow College *A*
University of Utah *B, M, D*
Utah State University *B*
Utah Valley State College *A*

Vermont

Green Mountain College *B*
Johnson State College *B*

Virginia

Ferrum College *B*
George Mason University *B*
Hampton University *B*
Marymount University *B*
Radford University *B, M*
Virginia Commonwealth
    University *B, M*
Virginia Wesleyan College *B*

Washington

Bellevue Community College *A*
Central Washington University *B*
Eastern Washington University *B*
Washington State University *B*
Western Washington University *B*

West Virginia

Alderson-Broaddus College *B*
Concord College *B*
Shepherd College *B*

Wisconsin

Carthage College *B*
Northland College *B*
University of Wisconsin
    Milwaukee *B*

**Parks/recreational/leisure
facilities management**

Alabama

Alabama State University *B*
Enterprise State Junior College *A*
James H. Faulkner State Community
    College *C, A*
Wallace State Community College at
    Hanceville *A*

Alaska

Alaska Pacific University *B*

Arizona

Northern Arizona University *B*
Prescott College *B, M*

Arkansas

Henderson State University *M*
University of Arkansas *M, D*
University of Arkansas
    Pine Bluff *B*

California

California Polytechnic State University:
    San Luis Obispo *B*
California State University
    Dominguez Hills *B*
    Fresno *A, B*
    Hayward *B*
    Long Beach *B, M*
    Sacramento *B, M*
College of the Sequoias *A*

Humboldt State University *B*
Mount San Antonio College *A*
Palomar College *C, A*
San Francisco State University *B, M*
Santa Rosa Junior College *C*
Ventura College *C, A*
West Valley College *C, A*

Colorado

Colorado State University *B, M, D*
University of Northern Colorado *B*

Connecticut

Northwestern Connecticut Community
    College *A*
University of Connecticut *B*

Delaware

Delaware State University *B*
University of Delaware *B*

District of Columbia

Gallaudet University *B*

Florida

Florida International University *B, M*
Florida State University *B, M*
Polk Community College *A*
Santa Fe Community College *A*
Tallahassee Community College *A*
University of Florida *B, M*

Georgia

Abraham Baldwin Agricultural
    College *A*
Georgia Southern University *M*
Georgia State University *B, M*
South Georgia College *A*
State University of West Georgia *B*
Thomas University *B*

Hawaii

University of Hawaii
    Hilo *B*

Idaho

Northwest Nazarene University *B*

Illinois

Aurora University *M*
Eastern Illinois University *B*
Illinois State University *B*
Moraine Valley Community College *A*
Western Illinois University *B, M*
William Rainey Harper College *C, A*

Indiana

Bethel College *B*
Huntington College *B*
Indiana Institute of Technology *A, B*
Indiana State University *B*
Indiana University
    Bloomington *B, M, D*
    Southeast *A*
Indiana Wesleyan University *B*
Vincennes University *A*

Iowa

Iowa Lakes Community College *A*
University of Iowa *B, M*
Upper Iowa University *B*
Waldorf College *A*

Kansas

Bethany College *B*
Central Christian College *A, B*
Fort Scott Community College *A*
Friends University *B*
Kansas State University *B*
Pittsburg State University *B*
University of Kansas *B*

Kentucky

Asbury College *B*
Morehead State University *B*
Murray State University *B, M*

Louisiana

Grambling State University *M*

Maine
Husson College B
University of Maine B, M
University of Maine
  Farmington C
  Machias A, B
  Presque Isle A, B

Maryland
Allegany College A
Community College of Baltimore County
  Catonsville C, A
  Dundalk C, A
  Essex C, A

Massachusetts
Greenfield Community College C
Springfield College B, M

Michigan
Bay de Noc Community College C
Central Michigan University B, M
Eastern Michigan University B
Ferris State University B
Gogebic Community College A
Lansing Community College A
Michigan State University B, M, D
Northern Michigan University B

Minnesota
Minnesota State University
  Mankato B
University of Minnesota
  Crookston B
Vermilion Community College A
Winona State University B

Mississippi
University of Mississippi M

Missouri
Central Methodist College B
Central Missouri State University B
College of the Ozarks B
Culver-Stockton College B
Hannibal-LaGrange College B
Mineral Area College A
Missouri Valley College B
Missouri Western State College B

Montana
University of Montana-Missoula B, M

Nebraska
University of Nebraska
  Kearney B
Wayne State College B

Nevada
Truckee Meadows Community
  College A
Western Nevada Community College A

New Hampshire
Franklin Pierce College B
New England College B
University of New Hampshire B

New Jersey
Kean University B
Montclair State University B

New York
Dutchess Community College A
Erie Community College
  South Campus A
Mohawk Valley Community College A
New York University M, D
North Country Community College A
Onondaga Community College A
Orange County Community College A
Paul Smith's College A, B
St. Joseph's College: Suffolk Campus B

State University of New York
  College at Brockport B, M
  College at Cortland M
  College of Agriculture and
    Technology at Cobleskill A
  College of Agriculture and
    Technology at Morrisville A
  College of Environmental Science
    and Forestry B, M
  College of Technology at Delhi A
Tompkins-Cortland Community
  College A

North Carolina
Appalachian State University B
Central Piedmont Community College A
East Carolina University B, M
Elon University B
Louisburg College A
Mars Hill College B
North Carolina Agricultural and
  Technical State University B
North Carolina Central University B
North Carolina State University M
Southeastern Community College A
University of North Carolina
  Chapel Hill B, M
  Greensboro B, M
  Pembroke B
  Wilmington B
Wayne Community College A
Western Carolina University B
Wingate University B

North Dakota
University of North Dakota B

Ohio
Ashland University B
Bluffton College B
Bowling Green State University B
Columbus State Community
  College C, A
Kent State University B
Kent State University
  Stark Campus B
Ohio State University
  Columbus Campus B
Ohio University B

Oklahoma
Eastern Oklahoma State College A
Oklahoma Baptist University B
Oklahoma State University B
Oral Roberts University B
Southwestern Oklahoma State
  University B

Oregon
Central Oregon Community College A

Pennsylvania
California University of Pennsylvania B
Cheyney University of Pennsylvania B
East Stroudsburg University of
  Pennsylvania B
Keystone College A
Lock Haven University of
  Pennsylvania B
Penn State
  Schuylkill - Capital College B
  University Park B
Slippery Rock University of
  Pennsylvania B, M
York College of Pennsylvania B

Puerto Rico
Universidad Metropolitana M
University of Puerto Rico
  Mayaguez Campus B

South Carolina
Clemson University B, M, D
Horry-Georgetown Technical College A
Morris College B
Technical College of the Lowcountry C

South Dakota
South Dakota State University B

Tennessee
Middle Tennessee State University B
University of Tennessee
  Martin B

Texas
Southwest Texas State
  University B, M, T
Texas A&M University B
Texas Wesleyan University B
University of North Texas B, M
University of Texas
  Pan American B
Western Texas College A

Utah
Brigham Young University B, M
Utah State University B, M, D

Vermont
College of St. Joseph in Vermont B
Green Mountain College B
Lyndon State College B

Virginia
Hampton University B
Old Dominion University B
Virginia Wesleyan College B

Washington
Eastern Washington University B
Spokane Community College A
Walla Walla Community College C, A
Washington State University B, M

West Virginia
Concord College B
Marshall University B
Mountain State University B
Potomac State College of West Virginia
  University A
West Virginia State College B
West Virginia University B, M

Wisconsin
Fox Valley Technical College A
University of Wisconsin
  La Crosse B, M
  Madison B, M

Wyoming
Central Wyoming College A
University of Wyoming B

Particle physics

Maryland
Johns Hopkins University B

Massachusetts
Harvard College B
Tufts University M, D

Wisconsin
University of Wisconsin
  Madison M, D

Pastoral counseling

Alabama
Southeastern Bible College A, B
Southern Christian University M, D
Spring Hill College M
University of Mobile B

Arkansas
Harding University M
Ouachita Baptist University B

California
Biola University M, D
Holy Names College M
Loyola Marymount University M
Master's College B, M
San Jose Christian College B
University of San Diego M

Colorado
Colorado Christian University M
Nazarene Bible College B

Florida
Baptist College of Florida B
Barry University M
Florida Christian College B
Southeastern College of the Assemblies
  of God B

Hawaii
Chaminade University of Honolulu M

Illinois
Lewis University M
Lincoln Christian College and
  Seminary B
Loyola University of Chicago M
Moody Bible Institute M
Olivet Nazarene University M
St. Xavier University C
Trinity International University M

Indiana
Huntington College M
Martin University M
Oakland City University M
St. Joseph's College C

Iowa
Loras College M
Vennard College B
Wartburg College B

Kansas
Central Christian College A, B
St. Mary College B

Kentucky
Kentucky Christian College B
Spalding University A, B, M

Maryland
Loyola College in Maryland M, D
Washington Bible College B

Massachusetts
Boston College M

Michigan
Marygrove College M

Minnesota
St. Mary's University of Minnesota B, M
University of St. Thomas M

Mississippi
Magnolia Bible College B
Wesley College B

Missouri
Baptist Bible College M
Calvary Bible College B, M
Central Christian College of the Bible B
Global University B

Nebraska
Grace University M
Union College B

New Jersey
Caldwell College M
Seton Hall University M

New York
Roberts Wesleyan College M

North Carolina
Gardner-Webb University M
John Wesley College B
Roanoke Bible College B
Southeastern Baptist Theological
  Seminary M

Ohio
Ashland University M, D
Circleville Bible College A, B
College of Mount St. Joseph B, M
Malone College B, M
University of Dayton M

Oklahoma
Oral Roberts University *B, M*
Southwestern Christian University *B*

Oregon
Eugene Bible College *B*
George Fox University *M*
Marylhurst University *C*
Northwest Christian College *B*
Western Baptist College *B*

Pennsylvania
Duquesne University *M*
La Salle University *M*
Lancaster Bible College *B*
Moravian College *M*
Neumann College *M*
Philadelphia Biblical University *B*
Valley Forge Christian College *B*

Puerto Rico
Bayamon Central University *M*

South Carolina
Charleston Southern University *B*
Erskine College *M*

Tennessee
American Baptist College of ABT
  Seminary *B*
Freed-Hardeman University *M*

Texas
Abilene Christian University *B, M, D*
Dallas Baptist University *B*
East Texas Baptist University *B*
Hardin-Simmons University *M*
Southwestern Assemblies of God
  University *B*
Texas Christian University *D*
University of Dallas *M*
University of St. Thomas *M*

Washington
Northwest College *B*
Seattle University *M*
University of Puget Sound *M*

Wisconsin
Maranatha Baptist Bible College *M*

Pathology assistant

Connecticut
Quinnipiac University *M*

Illinois
Finch University of Health Sciences/The
  Chicago Medical School *M*

Massachusetts
Boston University *M, D*

New York
St. John's University *B*

Pathology, human/animal

Alabama
Auburn University *M*
University of Alabama
  Birmingham *D*

Arizona
University of Arizona *M, D*

Arkansas
University of Arkansas
  for Medical Sciences *M*

California
University of California
  Davis *M, D*
  Los Angeles *M, D*
University of Southern California *M, D*

Colorado
Colorado State University *M, D*

University of Colorado
  Health Sciences Center *M, D*

Connecticut
University of Connecticut *B, M, D*
Yale University *M, D*

District of Columbia
Georgetown University *D*

Illinois
Finch University of Health Sciences/The
  Chicago Medical School *M, D*
Northwestern University *M*
University of Chicago *M, D*

Indiana
Indiana University
  Bloomington *M, D*
Indiana University-Purdue University
  Indianapolis *M, D*

Iowa
University of Iowa *M*

Kansas
Kansas State University *M, D*
University of Kansas Medical
  Center *M, D*

Maine
University of Maine *B, M*

Maryland
University of Maryland
  Baltimore *M, D*

Massachusetts
Boston University *D*
Tufts University *M, D*

Michigan
Michigan State University *M, D*
University of Michigan *D*
Wayne State University *D*

Mississippi
University of Mississippi Medical
  Center *M, D*

Missouri
St. Louis University *M, D*
University of Missouri
  Columbia *M, D*

Nebraska
University of Nebraska ·
  Medical Center *M, D*

New York
New York University *M, D*
State University of New York
  Buffalo *M, D*
  Health Science Center at Stony
    Brook *M, D*
University of Rochester *M, D*
Yeshiva University *M, D*

North Carolina
Duke University *M, D*
University of North Carolina
  Chapel Hill *M, D*

Ohio
Case Western Reserve University *M, D*
Ohio State University
  Columbus Campus *M, D*
University of Cincinnati *M, D*

Oklahoma
University of Oklahoma *M, D*

Pennsylvania
Drexel University *D*
Penn State
  University Park *M, D*
University of Pennsylvania *D*

South Carolina
Medical University of South
  Carolina *M, D*

Tennessee
University of Tennessee
  Knoxville *M, D*
University of Tennessee Health Science
  Center *M, D*
Vanderbilt University *M, D*

Texas
Texas A&M University *M, D*
University of Texas
  Houston Health Science
    Center *M, D*

Utah
University of Utah *B, M, D*

Vermont
University of Vermont *M*

Virginia
Virginia Commonwealth University *D*

Washington
University of Washington *M, D*

Wisconsin
University of Wisconsin
  Madison *M, D*

Peace/conflict studies

Arizona
Prescott College *B, M*

California
California State University
  Long Beach *C*
Chapman University *B*
University of California
  Berkeley *B*
University of La Verne *C*

Colorado
University of Denver *M*

District of Columbia
American University *M*
Georgetown University *B*

Florida
Florida Atlantic University *C*
Nova Southeastern University *M, D*

Georgia
Brenau University *B*
Middle Georgia College *T*
Oxford College of Emory University *T*

Illinois
Quincy University *B*

Indiana
DePauw University *B*
Earlham College *B*
Goshen College *B*
Indiana University-Purdue University
  Fort Wayne *C*
Manchester College *B*
University of Notre Dame *M*

Iowa
Clarke College *A, B*
St. Ambrose University *C*

Kansas
Bethel College *C, B*

Maryland
Salisbury University *B*

Massachusetts
Bay Path College *B*
Berkshire Community College *A*
College of the Holy Cross *B*
Hampshire College *B*
Tufts University *B*
University of Massachusetts
  Boston *M*
Wellesley College *B*

Michigan
Wayne State University *C, M*

Minnesota
College of St. Benedict *B*
Hamline University *B, M*
St. John's University *B*
University of St. Thomas *B*

Nebraska
Creighton University *B*

New Hampshire
New Hampshire Technical Institute *C*
University of New Hampshire *B*

New Jersey
Richard Stockton College of New
  Jersey *M*

New York
Colgate University *B*
Manhattan College *B*
Molloy College *B*

North Carolina
Guilford College *B*
University of North Carolina
  Chapel Hill *B*

Ohio
Antioch College *B*
Bluffton College *B*
Kent State University *B*
Ohio State University
  Columbus Campus *B*
Wilmington College *C*

Oklahoma
Oklahoma Panhandle State University *B*

Oregon
Oregon State University *C*

Pennsylvania
Arcadia University *M*
Elizabethtown College *B*
Gettysburg College *B*
Juniata College *B*
La Salle University *B*

Vermont
Bennington College *B*
Goddard College *B*
Marlboro College *B*
Norwich University *B*

Virginia
Eastern Mennonite University *B, M*
George Mason University *D*

Washington
University of Washington *B*
Whitworth College *B*

Wisconsin
Northland College *B*

Pediatric nursing

Georgia
Medical College of Georgia *M*

Indiana
Indiana University-Purdue University
  Indianapolis *M*

Maine
University of Southern Maine *B, M*

New York
City University of New York
  Hunter College *M*
State University of New York
  Buffalo *M*

Ohio
Case Western Reserve University *M*

South Carolina
Medical University of South Carolina *M*

Perfusion technology

Connecticut
Quinnipiac University *C*

Illinois
Rush University *B*

Massachusetts
Northeastern University *M*

New Jersey
Thomas Edison State College *B*

New York
State University of New York
    Upstate Medical University *B*

Pennsylvania
Drexel University *B*

Rhode Island
Community College of Rhode Island *C*

South Carolina
Medical University of South Carolina *B*

Wisconsin
Milwaukee School of Engineering *M*

Personal/culinary services

Alabama
Alabama Southern Community
    College *A*

California
Chabot College *A*
MiraCosta College *C*

Florida
Manatee Community College *A*
Palm Beach Community College *C*

Georgia
Central Georgia Technical College *A*

Indiana
Sawyer College: Merrillville *A*

Iowa
Northeast Iowa Community College *A*

Massachusetts
Berkshire Community College *C*

Michigan
Baker College
    of Muskegon *A, B*
Southwestern Michigan College *C*

North Carolina
Central Carolina Community College *A*
College of the Albemarle *C*
Piedmont Community College *A*

Oregon
Central Oregon Community
    College *C, A*

Pennsylvania
Career Training Academy:
    Monroeville *C*

Puerto Rico
Universidad del Este *C*

South Carolina
Denmark Technical College *C*
Forrest Junior College *A*

Tennessee
Roane State Community College *C*

Washington
Seattle Central Community College *C, A*

Wisconsin
Milwaukee Area Technical College *A*

Personal/financial services marketing

Kentucky
Murray State University *B, M*

New Jersey
Union County College *A*

New York
Mohawk Valley Community College *C*

Texas
University of Houston *B*

Personality psychology

New York
Bard College *B*

Petroleum engineering

Alaska
University of Alaska
    Fairbanks *B, M*

California
California State University
    Bakersfield *B*
Stanford University *B, M, D*
University of Southern
    California *B, M, D*

Colorado
Colorado School of Mines *B, M, D*

Kansas
University of Kansas *B, M, D*

Louisiana
Louisiana State University and
    Agricultural and Mechanical
    College *B, M, D*
University of Louisiana at Lafayette *B*

Missouri
University of Missouri
    Rolla *B, M, D*

Montana
Montana Tech of the University of
    Montana *B, M*

New Mexico
New Mexico Institute of Mining and
    Technology *B, M, D*

Ohio
Marietta College *B*

Oklahoma
University of Oklahoma *B, M, D*
University of Tulsa *B, M, D*

Pennsylvania
Penn State
    Abington *B*
    Altoona *B*
    Beaver *B*
    Berks *B*
    Delaware County *B*
    Dubois *B*
    Fayette *B*
    Hazleton *B*
    Lehigh Valley *B*
    McKeesport *B*
    Mont Alto *B*
    New Kensington *B*
    Schuylkill - Capital College *B*
    Shenango *B*
    University Park *B, M, D*
    Wilkes-Barre *B*
    Worthington Scranton *B*
    York *B*
University of Pittsburgh *M*

Texas
Laredo Community College *A*
Midland College *A*
Texas A&M University *B, M, D*
Texas A&M University
    Kingsville *B, M*
Texas Tech University *B, M, D*
University of Houston *M*
University of Texas
    Austin *B, M, D*

West Virginia
West Virginia University *B, M, D*

Wyoming
University of Wyoming *M, D*

Petroleum technology

California
Taft College *C, A*

Montana
Montana State University
    Billings *A*

Pennsylvania
University of Pittsburgh
    Bradford *B*

Texas
Odessa College *C*

Pharmacology

Alabama
Auburn University *M*
University of Alabama
    Birmingham *D*

Arizona
University of Arizona *M, D*

Arkansas
University of Arkansas
    for Medical Sciences *M, D*

California
Loma Linda University *M, D*
Stanford University *M, D*
University of California
    Davis *M, D*
    Irvine *M, D*
    Los Angeles *M, D*
    Santa Barbara *B*
University of Southern California *M, D*

Colorado
University of Colorado
    Health Sciences Center *D*

Connecticut
Yale University *M, D*

District of Columbia
George Washington University *M, D*
Georgetown University *D*
Howard University *M, D*

Florida
University of Miami *M, D*

Georgia
Medical College of Georgia *M, D*
University of Georgia *M, D*

Hawaii
University of Hawaii
    Manoa *M, D*

Illinois
Loyola University of Chicago *M, D*
Northwestern University *M*
Rush University *M, D*
Southern Illinois University
    Carbondale *M, D*
University of Chicago *M, D*

University of Illinois
    Chicago *M, D*

Indiana
Indiana University
    Bloomington *M, D*
Indiana University-Purdue University
    Indianapolis *M, D*

Iowa
University of Iowa *M, D*

Kansas
University of Kansas *M, D*
University of Kansas Medical
    Center *M, D*

Kentucky
University of Kentucky *D*
University of Louisville *M, D*

Louisiana
Tulane University *M, D*

Maryland
Johns Hopkins University *M, D*
University of Maryland
    Baltimore *M, D*

Massachusetts
Boston University *M, D*
Massachusetts College of Pharmacy and
    Health Sciences *M, D*
Tufts University *M*

Michigan
Michigan State University *M, D*
University of Michigan *M, D*
Wayne State University *M, D*

Minnesota
University of Minnesota
    Duluth *M*
    Twin Cities *M, D*

Mississippi
University of Mississippi Medical
    Center *M, D*

Missouri
St. Louis University *M, D*
University of Missouri
    Columbia *M, D*

Montana
University of Montana-Missoula *D*

Nebraska
Creighton University *M, D*
University of Nebraska
    Medical Center *M, D*

Nevada
University of Nevada
    Reno *M, D*

New Hampshire
Dartmouth College *M, D*

New York
New York University *M, D*
State University of New York
    Buffalo *M, D*
    Health Science Center at
        Brooklyn *M*
    Health Science Center at Stony
        Brook *B, M, D*
    Stony Brook *B, D*
    Upstate Medical University *D*
University of Rochester *M, D*
Yeshiva University *D*

North Carolina
University of North Carolina
    Chapel Hill *M, D*
Wake Forest University *D*

North Dakota
North Dakota State University *M, D*
University of North Dakota *M, D*

Ohio
Case Western Reserve University *D*
Kent State University *M, D*
Ohio State University
Columbus Campus *B, M, D*
University of Cincinnati *D*

Pennsylvania
University of Pennsylvania *D*
University of the Sciences in
Philadelphia *B, M, D*

Puerto Rico
University of Puerto Rico
Medical Sciences Campus *M, D*

Rhode Island
University of Rhode Island *M, D*

South Carolina
Medical University of South Carolina *D*

South Dakota
University of South Dakota *M, D*

Tennessee
University of Tennessee
Knoxville *M, D*
University of Tennessee Health Science
Center *M, D*
Vanderbilt University *D*

Texas
Texas A&M University *M, D*
University of Texas
Health Science Center at San
Antonio *M, D*
Houston Health Science
Center *M, D*

Vermont
University of Vermont *M, D*

Virginia
University of Virginia *D*
Virginia Commonwealth
University *M, D*

Washington
University of Washington *M, D*

Wisconsin
University of Wisconsin
Madison *M, D*

Pharmacology/toxicology

Kansas
University of Kansas *M, D*

Texas
University of Texas
Houston Health Science
Center *M, D*
Medical Branch at Galveston *M, D*

Utah
University of Utah *M, D*

Pharmacy (PharmD.)

Alabama
Auburn University: School of
Pharmacy *F*
Samford University: McWhorter School
of Pharmacy *F*

Arizona
University of Arizona: College of
Pharmacy *F*

Arkansas
University of Arkansas for Medical
Sciences: College of Pharmacy *F*

California
University of California San Francisco:
School of Pharmacy *F*

University of Southern California: School
of Pharmacy *F*
University of the Pacific: School of
Pharmacy *F*

Colorado
University of Colorado Health Sciences
Center: College of Pharmacy *F*

Connecticut
University of Connecticut: School of
Pharmacy *F*

District of Columbia
Howard University: School of
Pharmacy *F*

Florida
Florida Agricultural and Mechanical
University: School of Pharmacy *F*
Nova Southeastern University of the
Health Sciences: College of
Pharmacy *F*
University of Florida: College of
Pharmacy *F*

Georgia
Mercer University Southern School of
Pharmacy *F*
University of Georgia: College of
Pharmacy *F*

Idaho
Idaho State University: College of
Pharmacy *F*

Illinois
Midwestern University: Chicago College
of Pharmacy *F*
University of Illinois at Chicago: College
of Pharmacy *F*

Indiana
Butler University: College of
Pharmacy *F*
Purdue University: School of
Pharmacy *F*

Iowa
Drake University: College of
Pharmacy *F*
University of Iowa: College of
Pharmacy *F*

Louisiana
Northeast Louisiana University School of
Pharmacy *F*
Xavier University of Louisiana: College
of Pharmacy *F*

Maryland
University of Maryland at Baltimore:
School of Pharmacy *F*

Massachusetts
Massachusetts College of Pharmacy and
Allied Health Sciences: School of
Pharmacy *F*
Northeastern University: Bouve College
of Pharmacy and Health Sciences *F*

Michigan
Ferris State University College of
Pharmacy *F*
University of Michigan: College of
Pharmacy *F*
Wayne State University: College of
Pharmacy and Allied Health *F*

Mississippi
University of Mississippi: School of
Pharmacy *F*

Missouri
St. Louis College of Pharmacy *F*

Montana
University of Montana School of
Pharmacy and Allied Health
Sciences *F*

Nebraska
University of Nebraska Medical Center:
College of Pharmacy *F*

New Jersey
Rutgers, The State University of New
Jersey
College of Pharmacy *F*

New Mexico
University of New Mexico College of
Pharmacy *F*

New York
Albany College of Pharmacy *F*
Long Island University:Arnold and Marie
Schwartz College of Pharmacy and
Health Sciences *F*
St. John's University: College of
Pharmacy and Allied Health
Professions *F*
State University of New York at Buffalo:
School of Pharmacy *F*

North Carolina
Campbell University: School of
Pharmacy *F*
University of North Carolina at Chapel
Hill: School of Pharmacy *F*

North Dakota
North Dakota State University: College
of Pharmacy *F*

Ohio
Ohio Northern University: College of
Pharmacy *F*
Ohio State University Columbus
Campus: College of Pharmacy *F*
University of Cincinnati: College of
Pharmacy *F*
University of Toledo: College of
Pharmacy *F*

Oklahoma
Southwestern Oklahoma State University
School of Pharmacy *F*
University of Oklahoma College of
Pharmacy *F*

Oregon
Oregon State University: College of
Pharmacy *F*

Pennsylvania
Philadelphia College of Pharmacy and
Science: School of Pharmacy *F*
Temple University: School of
Pharmacy *F*
University of Pittsburgh: School of
Pharmacy *F*

Puerto Rico
University of Puerto Rico Medical
Sciences Campus: School of
Pharmacy *F*

Rhode Island
University of Rhode Island: College of
Pharmacy *F*

South Carolina
Medical University of South Carolina:
College of Pharmacy *F*
University of South Carolina: School of
Pharmacy *F*

South Dakota
South Dakota State University: College
of Pharmacy *F*

Tennessee
University of Tennessee Memphis:
College of Pharmacy *F*

Texas
Texas Southern University: College of
Pharmacy and Health Sciences *F*
University of Houston: College of
Pharmacy *F*

University of Texas at Austin: College of
Pharmacy *F*

Utah
University of Utah: College of
Pharmacy *F*

Washington
Washington State University: College of
Pharmacy *F*

West Virginia
West Virginia University: School of
Pharmacy *F*

Wisconsin
University of Wisconsin Madison: School
of Pharmacy *F*

Wyoming
University of Wyoming: School of
Pharmacy *F*

Pharmacy assistant

Alabama
Community College of the Air Force *A*

Arizona
Central Arizona College *A*
Pima Community College *C, A*

California
Foothill College *C, A*
Imperial Valley College *C*
Santa Rosa Junior College *C, A*
Silicon Valley College
Emeryville *A*

Colorado
Arapahoe Community College *C*
Front Range Community College *C*
Otero Junior College *A*

Connecticut
Gateway Community College *C, A*
Manchester Community College *A*

Florida
Manatee Community College *A*
Pensacola Junior College *C*
Southwest Florida College *A*

Georgia
Albany Technical College *C*
Darton College *A*
Macon State College *A*
Middle Georgia College *A*
Southwest Georgia Technical College *C*
West Georgia Technical College *C, A*

Idaho
College of Southern Idaho *A*
North Idaho College *A*

Illinois
Black Hawk College *C*
City Colleges of Chicago
Malcolm X College *C*
Richland Community College *C*
Rock Valley College *C*
South Suburban College of Cook
County *A*
William Rainey Harper College *C*

Indiana
Vincennes University *A*

Iowa
Clinton Community College *C*
Muscatine Community College *C*
Scott Community College *C, A*
Waldorf College *A*

Kansas
Labette Community College *C*

Kentucky

National College of Business &
Technology
Florence *C*
Richmond *C*

Louisiana

Delgado Community College *C*
Louisiana State University
Alexandria *C*

Maryland

Allegany College *C*
Anne Arundel Community College *A*

Michigan

Baker College
of Jackson *C, A*
of Muskegon *C, A*
Bay de Noc Community College *C*
Oakland Community College *C, A*
St. Clair County Community College *C*
Southwestern Michigan College *C*
Washtenaw Community College *C*
Wayne County Community College *C*

Minnesota

Century Community and Technical
College *C, A*
Lake Superior College: A Community
and Technical College *C*
Rochester Community and Technical
College *C*

Montana

University of Montana-Missoula *C*

New Jersey

County College of Morris *C*
Middlesex County College *A*

New Mexico

Albuquerque Technical-Vocational
Institute *C*

North Carolina

Cape Fear Community College *C*
Davidson County Community College *C*
Durham Technical Community
College *C*
Fayetteville Technical Community
College *C*
Southeastern Community College *C, A*

North Dakota

North Dakota State College of
Science *C, A*

Ohio

Cuyahoga Community College
Eastern Campus *C, A*
Metropolitan Campus *C, A*
Sinclair Community College *C*
University of Northwestern Ohio *C, A*

Oklahoma

Platt College
Tulsa *C*

Oregon

Linn-Benton Community College *C*
Southwestern Oregon Community
College *C*

Pennsylvania

Community College of Allegheny
County *C, A*
Harrisburg Area Community
College *C, A*
Mount Aloysius College *A*

Puerto Rico

Huertas Junior College *C, A*
Inter American University of Puerto Rico
San German Campus *C*
Universidad del Este *A*

South Carolina

Central Carolina Technical College *C*
Midlands Technical College *C, A*
Tri-County Technical College *C*

Trident Technical College *C*

South Dakota

Western Dakota Technical Institute *C*

Tennessee

Draughons Junior College of Business:
Nashville *A*
Southwest Tennessee Community
College *C*
Walters State Community College *C, A*

Texas

Amarillo College *C*
Angelina College *C*
Austin Community College *C*
El Paso Community College *C*
Houston Community College System *C*
Lamar State College at Orange *C*
Tarrant County College *C*
Texas Southern University *D*

Utah

Salt Lake Community College *C*

Vermont

Vermont Technical College *C, A*

Virginia

J. Sargeant Reynolds Community
College *C*
Mountain Empire Community College *C*

Washington

Clark College *C*
Clover Park Technical College *C*
Edmonds Community College *C*
Grays Harbor College *C*
North Seattle Community College *C, A*
Renton Technical College *C*
Spokane Community College *C, A*
Spokane Falls Community College *C*

Wisconsin

Lakeshore Technical College *C*
Mid-State Technical College *C*
Wisconsin Indianhead Technical
College *C*

Philosophy

Alabama

Auburn University *B*
Birmingham-Southern College *B*
Samford University *B*
Spring Hill College *B*
University of Alabama *B*
University of Alabama
Birmingham *B*
Huntsville *B*
University of South Alabama *B*

Alaska

University of Alaska
Fairbanks *B*

Arizona

Arizona State University *B, M, D*
Arizona Western College *A*
Northern Arizona University *B*
Prescott College *M*
University of Arizona *B, M, D*

Arkansas

Arkansas State University *B*
Hendrix College *B*
Ouachita Baptist University *B*
Philander Smith College *B*
University of Arkansas *B, M, D*
University of Arkansas
Little Rock *B*
University of Central Arkansas *B*

California

Azusa Pacific University *B*
Bakersfield College *A*
Biola University *B, M, D*
California Baptist University *B*

California State Polytechnic University:
Pomona *B*
California State University
Bakersfield *B*
Chico *B*
Dominguez Hills *B*
Fresno *B*
Fullerton *B*
Hayward *B*
Long Beach *B, M*
Los Angeles *B, M*
Northridge *B*
Sacramento *B*
San Bernardino *B*
Stanislaus *B*
Cerritos Community College *A*
Chabot College *A*
Chapman University *B*
Claremont McKenna College *B*
College of Alameda *A*
De Anza College *A*
Dominican School of Philosophy and
Theology *B, M*
East Los Angeles College *A*
Foothill College *A*
Gavilan Community College *A*
Glendale Community College *A*
Golden West College *A*
Grossmont Community College *A*
Holy Names College *B*
Humboldt State University *B*
Irvine Valley College *A*
Los Angeles Southwest College *A*
Loyola Marymount University *B*
Marymount College *A*
Mills College *B*
MiraCosta College *A*
Monterey Peninsula College *A*
Mount St. Mary's College *B*
Occidental College *B*
Orange Coast College *A*
Pepperdine University *B*
Pitzer College *B*
Point Loma Nazarene University *B*
Pomona College *B*
St. Mary's College of California *B*
San Diego City College *A*
San Diego Mesa College *C, A*
San Diego State University *B, M*
San Francisco State University *B, M*
San Jose State University *B, M*
Santa Barbara City College *A*
Santa Clara University *B*
Santiago Canyon College *A*
Scripps College *B*
Sonoma State University *B*
Southwestern College *A*
Stanford University *B, M, D*
University of California
Berkeley *B, D*
Davis *B, M, D*
Irvine *B, M, D*
Los Angeles *B, M, D*
Riverside *B, M, D*
San Diego *B, M, D*
Santa Barbara *B, M, D*
Santa Cruz *B, M, D*
University of La Verne *B*
University of Redlands *B*
University of San Diego *B*
University of San Francisco *B*
University of Southern
California *B, M, D*
University of the Pacific *B*
Ventura College *A*
Whittier College *B*

Colorado

Colorado College *B*
Colorado State University *B, M*
Fort Lewis College *B*
Metropolitan State College of Denver *B*
Regis University *B*
Trinidad State Junior College *A*

University of Colorado
Boulder *B, M, D*
Colorado Springs *B*
Denver *B*
University of Denver *B, M*
University of Northern Colorado *B*

Connecticut

Central Connecticut State University *B*
Connecticut College *B*
Fairfield University *B*
Holy Apostles College and
Seminary *B, M*
Sacred Heart University *B*
St. Joseph College *B, T*
Southern Connecticut State University *B*
Trinity College *B*
University of Connecticut *B, M, D*
University of Hartford *B*
Wesleyan University *B*
Yale University *B, M, D*

Delaware

University of Delaware *B*

District of Columbia

American University *B, M*
Catholic University of America *B, M, D*
Gallaudet University *B*
George Washington University *B*
Georgetown University *B, M, D*
Howard University *B, M*
University of the District of
Columbia *A, B*

Florida

Barry University *B*
Eckerd College *B*
Florida Agricultural and Mechanical
University *B*
Florida Atlantic University *B*
Florida Christian College *B*
Florida International University *B*
Florida Southern College *B*
Florida State University *B, M, D*
Gulf Coast Community College *A*
Indian River Community College *A*
Jacksonville University *B*
Miami-Dade Community College *A*
New College of Florida *B*
Palm Beach Community College *A*
Pensacola Junior College *A*
Rollins College *B*
St. John Vianney College Seminary *B*
South Florida Community College *A*
Stetson University *B*
University of Central Florida *B*
University of Florida *B, M, D*
University of Miami *B, M, D*
University of North Florida *B*
University of South Florida *B, M, D*
University of Tampa *A*
University of West Florida *B*

Georgia

Agnes Scott College *B*
Clark Atlanta University *B*
Clayton College and State University *A*
Covenant College *B*
Emory University *B, D*
Georgia Perimeter College *A*
Georgia Southern University *B*
Georgia State University *B, M*
Mercer University *B*
Middle Georgia College *A*
Morehouse College *B*
Oglethorpe University *B*
Oxford College of Emory University *B*
South Georgia College *A*
Spelman College *B*
State University of West Georgia *B*
University of Georgia *B, M, D*
Valdosta State University *B*
Wesleyan College *B*

Hawaii

University of Hawaii
Hilo *B*
Manoa *B, M, D*
West Oahu *B*

Idaho

Albertson College of Idaho *B*
Boise State University *B*
Idaho State University *B*
North Idaho College *A*
Northwest Nazarene University *B*
University of Idaho *B*

Illinois

Augustana College *B*
Aurora University *B*
Benedictine University *B*
Bradley University *B*
City Colleges of Chicago
Harold Washington College *A*
Olive-Harvey College *A*
Concordia University *B*
De Paul University *B, M, D*
Dominican University *B*
Eastern Illinois University *B*
Elmhurst College *B*
Greenville College *B*
Illinois College *B*
Illinois State University *B*
Illinois Wesleyan University *B*
Judson College *B*
Knox College *B*
Lake Forest College *B*
Lewis University *B*
Lincoln College *A*
Lincoln Land Community College *A*
Loyola University of Chicago *B, M, D*
MacMurray College *B*
McKendree College *B*
Millikin University *B*
North Central College *B*
North Park University *B*
Northeastern Illinois University *B*
Northern Illinois University *B, M*
Northwestern University *B, M, D*
Parkland College *A*
Principia College *B*
Richland Community College *A*
Rockford College *B*
Roosevelt University *B*
St. Xavier University *B*
Sauk Valley Community College *A*
South Suburban College of Cook
County *A*
Southern Illinois University
Carbondale *B, M, D*
Southern Illinois University
Edwardsville *B*
Southwestern Illinois College *A*
Trinity Christian College *B*
Trinity International University *B, D*
Triton College *A*
University of Chicago *B, M, D*
University of Illinois
Chicago *B, M, D*
Urbana-Champaign *B, M, D*
Waubonsee Community College *A*
Western Illinois University *B*
Wheaton College *B*
William Rainey Harper College *C, A*

Indiana

Anderson University *B*
Ball State University *B*
Bethel College *B*
Butler University *B*
DePauw University *B*
Earlham College *B*
Franklin College *B*
Hanover College *B*
Huntington College *B*
Indiana State University *B*

Indiana University
Bloomington *B, M, D*
Northwest *B*
South Bend *B*
Southeast *B*
Indiana University-Purdue University
Fort Wayne *B*
Indiana University-Purdue University
Indianapolis *B*
Indiana Wesleyan University *A, B*
Manchester College *B*
Marian College *B*
Purdue University *B, M, D*
Purdue University
Calumet *B*
St. Joseph's College *B*
Saint Mary's College *B*
Taylor University *B*
University of Evansville *B*
University of Indianapolis *B*
University of Notre Dame *B, M, D*
University of St. Francis *B*
University of Southern Indiana *B*
Valparaiso University *B*
Vincennes University *A*
Wabash College *B*

Iowa

Buena Vista University *B*
Central College *B*
Clarke College *A, B*
Coe College *B*
Cornell College *B*
Divine Word College *B*
Dordt College *B*
Drake University *B*
Grinnell College *B*
Iowa State University *B*
Loras College *B*
Luther College *B*
Morningside College *B*
Mount Mercy College *B*
Northwestern College *B*
St. Ambrose University *B*
Simpson College *B*
University of Dubuque *B*
University of Iowa *B, M, D*
University of Northern Iowa *B*
Wartburg College *B*

Kansas

Baker University *B*
Barton County Community College *A*
Benedictine College *B*
Fort Hays State University *B*
Kansas State University *B*
Tabor College *B*
University of Kansas *B, M, D*
Washburn University of Topeka *B*
Wichita State University *B*

Kentucky

Asbury College *B*
Bellarmine University *B*
Berea College *B*
Centre College *B*
Georgetown College *B*
Morehead State University *B*
Murray State University *B*
Thomas More College *A, B*
Transylvania University *B*
University of Kentucky *B, M, D*
University of Louisville *B, M*

Louisiana

Centenary College of Louisiana *B*
Louisiana State University and
Agricultural and Mechanical
College *B, M*
Loyola University New Orleans *B*
Tulane University *B, M, D*
University of Louisiana at Lafayette *B*
University of New Orleans *B, D*
Xavier University of Louisiana *B*

Maine

Bates College *B*

Bowdoin College *B*
Colby College *B*
St. Joseph's College *B*
University of Maine *B*
University of Southern Maine *B*

Maryland

College of Notre Dame of Maryland *B*
College of Southern Maryland *A*
Community College of Baltimore County
Catonsville *A*
Dundalk *A*
Essex *A*
Frederick Community College *A*
Frostburg State University *B*
Goucher College *B*
Harford Community College *A*
Hood College *B*
Johns Hopkins University *B, M, D*
Loyola College in Maryland *B*
McDaniel College *B*
Mount St. Mary's College *B*
St. Mary's College of Maryland *B*
Salisbury University *B*
University of Maryland
Baltimore County *B, M*
College Park *B, M, D*
Washington College *B*

Massachusetts

American International College *B*
Amherst College *B*
Assumption College *B*
Bentley College *B*
Boston College *B, M, D*
Boston University *B, M, D*
Brandeis University *B*
Bridgewater State College *B*
Cape Cod Community College *A*
Clark University *B*
College of the Holy Cross *B*
Gordon College *B*
Hampshire College *B*
Harvard University *B*
Massachusetts College of Liberal Arts *B*
Massachusetts Institute of
Technology *B, D*
Merrimack College *B*
Mount Holyoke College *B*
Northeastern University *B*
St. John's Seminary College *B*
Simmons College *B*
Simon's Rock College of Bard *B*
Smith College *B, D*
Stonehill College *B*
Suffolk University *B*
Tufts University *B, M*
University of Massachusetts
Amherst *B, M, D*
Boston *B*
Dartmouth *B*
Lowell *B*
Wellesley College *B*
Wheaton College *B*
Williams College *B*

Michigan

Alma College *B*
Aquinas College *B*
Calvin College *B*
Central Michigan University *B, T*
Eastern Michigan University *B*
Grand Valley State University *B*
Hillsdale College *B*
Hope College *B*
Kalamazoo College *B*
Kellogg Community College *A*
Lansing Community College *A*
Michigan State University *B, M, D*
Northern Michigan University *B*
Oakland University *B*
Sacred Heart Major Seminary *B*
Siena Heights University *B*
Spring Arbor University *B*
University of Michigan *B, M, D*

University of Michigan
Dearborn *B*
Flint *B*
Wayne State University *B, M, D*
Western Michigan University *B, M*

Minnesota

Augsburg College *B*
Bemidji State University *B*
Bethel College *B*
Carleton College *B*
College of St. Benedict *B*
College of St. Catherine *B*
Concordia College: Moorhead *B*
Gustavus Adolphus College *B*
Hamline University *B*
Macalester College *B*
Metropolitan State University *B*
Minnesota State University
Mankato *B*
Moorhead *B*
St. Cloud State University *B*
St. John's University *B*
St. Mary's University of Minnesota *B*
St. Olaf College *B*
Southwest State University *B*
University of Minnesota
Duluth *B*
Morris *B*
Twin Cities *B, M, D*
University of St. Thomas *B*
Winona State University *A*

Mississippi

Itawamba Community College *A*
Millsaps College *B, T*
Mississippi State University *B*
University of Mississippi *B, M*
University of Southern Mississippi *B, M*

Missouri

Central Methodist College *B*
Drury University *B*
East Central College *A*
Lindenwood University *B*
Northwest Missouri State University *B*
Rockhurst University *B*
St. Louis University *B, M, D*
Southeast Missouri State University *B*
Southwest Missouri State University *B*
Three Rivers Community College *A*
University of Missouri
Columbia *B, M, D*
Kansas City *B*
Rolla *B*
St. Louis *B*
Washington University in St.
Louis *B, M, D*
Webster University *B*
Westminster College *B*
William Jewell College *B*

Montana

Carroll College *B*
Montana State University
Bozeman *B*
University of Montana-Missoula *B, M*

Nebraska

Creighton University *B*
Doane College *B*
Hastings College *B*
Nebraska Wesleyan University *B*
University of Nebraska
Lincoln *B, M, D*
Omaha *B*

Nevada

Sierra Nevada College *B*
University of Nevada
Las Vegas *B*
Reno *B, M*

New Hampshire

Dartmouth College *B*
New England College *B*
Plymouth State College *B*
St. Anselm College *B*

Thomas More College of Liberal Arts *B*
University of New Hampshire *B*

New Jersey

Bloomfield College *B*
The College of New Jersey *B*
College of St. Elizabeth *B*
Drew University *B*
Fairleigh Dickinson University
    College at Florham *B*
    Metropolitan Campus *B*
Montclair State University *B*
Princeton University *B, M, D*
Richard Stockton College of New
   Jersey *B*
Rider University *B*
Rowan University *B*
Rutgers, The State University of New
   Jersey
    Camden Regional Campus *B*
    New Brunswick Regional
      Campus *B, M, D*
    Newark Regional Campus *B*
St. Peter's College *B*
Seton Hall University *B*
Stevens Institute of Technology *B*
Thomas Edison State College *B*
William Paterson University of New
   Jersey *B*

New Mexico

New Mexico State University *B*
San Juan College *A*
University of New Mexico *B, M, D*

New York

Adelphi University *B*
Alfred University *B*
Bard College *B*
Barnard College *B*
Canisius College *B*
City University of New York
    Baruch College *B*
    Brooklyn College *B*
    City College *B*
    College of Staten Island *B*
    Hunter College *B*
    Queens College *B, M*
    York College *B*
Colgate University *B*
College of Mount St. Vincent *B*
College of New Rochelle *B, T*
Columbia University
    Columbia College *B*
Cornell University *B, M, D*
D'Youville College *B*
Excelsior College *B*
Fordham University *B, M, D*
Hamilton College *B*
Hartwick College *B*
Hobart and William Smith Colleges *B*
Hofstra University *B*
Houghton College *B*
Iona College *B*
Ithaca College *B*
Le Moyne College *B*
Long Island University
   C. W. Post Campus *B*
Manhattan College *B*
Manhattanville College *B*
Metropolitan College of New York *A, B*
Molloy College *B*
Nazareth College of Rochester *B*
New York University *B, M, D*
Niagara University *B*
Nyack College *B*
Rensselaer Polytechnic Institute *B, M*
St. Bonaventure University *B*
St. John Fisher College *B*
St. John's University *B, M*
St. Lawrence University *B*
Sarah Lawrence College *B*
Skidmore College *B*

State University of New York
    Albany *B, M, D*
    Binghamton *B, M, D*
    Buffalo *B, M, D*
    College at Brockport *B*
    College at Buffalo *B*
    College at Cortland *B*
    College at Fredonia *B*
    College at Geneseo *B*
    College at Oneonta *B*
    College at Plattsburgh *B*
    College at Potsdam *B*
    New Paltz *B*
    Oswego *B*
    Purchase *B*
    Stony Brook *B, M, D*
Syracuse University *B, M, D*
Touro College *B*
Union College *B*
Union Theological Seminary:
   Theological Professions *D*
United States Military Academy *B*
University of Rochester *B, M, D*
Utica College *B*
Vassar College *B*
Wells College *B*
Yeshiva University *B*

North Carolina

Appalachian State University *B*
Belmont Abbey College *B*
Davidson College *B*
Duke University *B, M, D*
East Carolina University *B*
Elon University *B*
Guilford College *B*
High Point University *B*
Lenoir-Rhyne College *B*
Methodist College *A, B*
North Carolina State University *B*
St. Andrews Presbyterian College *B*
Salem College *B*
Southeastern Baptist Theological
   Seminary *M*
University of North Carolina
    Asheville *B*
    Chapel Hill *B, M, D*
    Charlotte *B*
    Greensboro *B*
Wake Forest University *B*
Western Carolina University *B*
Wingate University *B*

North Dakota

North Dakota State University *B*
University of North Dakota *B*

Ohio

Antioch College *B*
Ashland University *B*
Baldwin-Wallace College *B*
Bluffton College *B*
Bowling Green State University *B, M, D*
Case Western Reserve University *B*
Cedarville University *B*
Cleveland State University *B, M*
College of Wooster *B*
Defiance College *B*
Denison University *B*
Franciscan University of
   Steubenville *B, M*
Hiram College *B*
John Carroll University *B*
Kent State University *B, M*
Kent State University
   Stark Campus *B*
Kenyon College *B*
Lourdes College *A, B*
Malone College *B*
Marietta College *B*
Miami University
   Middletown Campus *A*
   Oxford Campus *B, M*
Mount Union College *B*
Mount Vernon Nazarene University *B*
Muskingum College *B*

Oberlin College *B*
Ohio Dominican College *B*
Ohio Northern University *B*
Ohio State University
   Columbus Campus *B, M, D*
Ohio University *B, M*
Ohio Wesleyan University *B*
Otterbein College *B*
Pontifical College Josephinum *B*
University of Akron *B, M*
University of Cincinnati *B, M, D*
University of Dayton *B, M*
University of Findlay *B*
University of Toledo *B, M*
Urbana University *B*
Ursuline College *B*
Walsh University *B*
Wittenberg University *B*
Wright State University *B*
Xavier University *B*
Youngstown State University *B*

Oklahoma

Oklahoma Baptist University *B*
Oklahoma City University *B*
Oklahoma State University *B, M*
Southern Nazarene University *B*
Tulsa Community College *A*
University of Central Oklahoma *B*
University of Oklahoma *B, M, D*
University of Tulsa *B*

Oregon

Chemeketa Community College *A*
Lewis & Clark College *B*
Linfield College *B*
Marylhurst University *B*
Oregon State University *B*
Pacific University *B*
Portland State University *B*
Reed College *B*
University of Oregon *B, M, D*
University of Portland *B*
Western Oregon University *B*
Willamette University *B*

Pennsylvania

Albright College *B*
Allegheny College *B*
Arcadia University *B*
Bloomsburg University of
   Pennsylvania *B*
Bryn Mawr College *B*
Bucknell University *B*
Cabrini College *B*
California University of Pennsylvania *B*
Carlow College *B*
Carnegie Mellon University *B, M*
Chatham College *B*
DeSales University *B*
Dickinson College *B*
Duquesne University *B, M, D*
East Stroudsburg University of
   Pennsylvania *B*
Edinboro University of Pennsylvania *B*
Elizabethtown College *B*
Franklin & Marshall College *B*
Geneva College *B*
Gettysburg College *B*
Grove City College *B*
Haverford College *B*
Holy Family University *B*
Indiana University of Pennsylvania *B*
King's College *B*
Kutztown University of Pennsylvania *B*
La Salle University *B*
Lafayette College *B*
Lebanon Valley College of
   Pennsylvania *B*
Lehigh University *B*
Lincoln University *B*
Lock Haven University of
   Pennsylvania *B*
Lycoming College *B*
Mercyhurst College *B*
Messiah College *B*

Millersville University of
   Pennsylvania *B*
Moravian College *B*
Muhlenberg College *B*
Penn State
    Altoona *B*
    Beaver *B*
    Dubois *B*
    Fayette *B*
    Lehigh Valley *B*
    McKeesport *B*
    Mont Alto *B*
    New Kensington *B*
    University Park *B, M, D*
    Worthington Scranton *B*
    York *B*
Rosemont College *B*
St. Charles Borromeo Seminary -
   Overbrook *B*
St. Joseph's University *B*
St. Vincent College *B*
Slippery Rock University of
   Pennsylvania *B*
Swarthmore College *B*
Temple University *B, M, D*
Thiel College *B*
University of Pennsylvania *B, M, D*
University of Pittsburgh *B, M, D*
University of Scranton *B*
Villanova University *B, M, D*
Washington and Jefferson College *B*
West Chester University of
   Pennsylvania *B, M*
Wilkes University *B*
York College of Pennsylvania *A*

Puerto Rico

Bayamon Central University *B*
Pontifical Catholic University of Puerto
   Rico *B*
University of Puerto Rico
    Mayaguez Campus *B*
    Rio Piedras Campus *B, M*

Rhode Island

Brown University *B, M, D*
Rhode Island College *B*
Roger Williams University *B*
Salve Regina University *B*
University of Rhode Island *B*

South Carolina

Clemson University *B*
Coastal Carolina University *B*
College of Charleston *B*
Erskine College *B*
Furman University *B*
University of South Carolina *B, M, D*
Winthrop University *B*
Wofford College *B*

South Dakota

Augustana College *B*
University of South Dakota *B*

Tennessee

Austin Peay State University *B*
Belmont University *B*
Carson-Newman College *B*
East Tennessee State University *B*
Freed-Hardeman University *B*
Middle Tennessee State University *B*
Rhodes College *B*
Union University *B*
University of Memphis *B, M, D*
University of Tennessee
    Knoxville *B, M, D*
    Martin *B*
Vanderbilt University *B, M, D*
Walters State Community College *A*

Texas

Austin College *B*
Baylor University *B, M, D*
Blinn College *A*
Dallas Baptist University *B*
Frank Phillips College *A*

Hardin-Simmons University *B*
Howard Payne University *B*
Laredo Community College *A*
Lon Morris College *A*
McMurry University *B*
Our Lady of the Lake University of San
 Antonio *B*
Rice University *B, M, D*
St. Edward's University *B*
St. Mary's University *B*
Sam Houston State University *B*
Schreiner University *B*
Southern Methodist University *B*
Southwest Texas State University *B, M*
Southwestern Baptist Theological
 Seminary: Theological Professions *D*
Southwestern University *B*
Texas A&M University *B, M, D*
Texas Christian University *B*
Texas Lutheran University *B*
Texas Tech University *B, M*
Trinity University *B*
University of Dallas *B, M, D*
University of Houston *B, M*
University of North Texas *B, M*
University of St. Thomas *B, M, D*
University of Texas
 Arlington *B*
 Austin *B, M, D*
 El Paso *B*
 Pan American *B*
 San Antonio *B*
University of the Incarnate Word *B*
Western Texas College *A*

Utah
Brigham Young University *B*
Dixie State College of Utah *A*
Southern Utah University *B*
University of Utah *B, M, D*
Utah State University *B*
Utah Valley State College *A, B*
Westminster College *B*

Vermont
Bennington College *B*
Burlington College *B*
Goddard College *B*
Green Mountain College *B*
Marlboro College *B*
Middlebury College *B*
St. Michael's College *B*
University of Vermont *B*

Virginia
Bluefield College *B*
Christendom College *B*
College of William and Mary *B*
Emory & Henry College *B*
Ferrum College *B*
George Mason University *B*
Hampden-Sydney College *B*
Hollins University *B*
Lynchburg College *B*
Mary Baldwin College *B*
Mary Washington College *B*
Marymount University *B*
Old Dominion University *B*
Randolph-Macon College *B*
Randolph-Macon Woman's College *B*
Roanoke College *B, T*
Sweet Briar College *B*
University of Richmond *B*
University of Virginia *B, M, D*
Virginia Commonwealth University *B*
Virginia Polytechnic Institute and State
 University *B, M*
Virginia Wesleyan College *B*
Washington and Lee University *B*

Washington
Central Washington University *B*
Centralia College *B*
Eastern Washington University *B*
Everett Community College *A*
Gonzaga University *B, M*
Lower Columbia College *A*

Pacific Lutheran University *B*
St. Martin's College *B*
Seattle Pacific University *B*
Seattle University *B*
University of Puget Sound *B*
University of Washington *B, M, D*
Washington State University *B*
Western Washington University *B*
Whitman College *B*
Whitworth College *B*

West Virginia
Bethany College *B*
West Virginia University *B*
West Virginia Wesleyan College *B*
Wheeling Jesuit University *B*

Wisconsin
Alverno College *B*
Carthage College *B*
Lakeland College *B*
Lawrence University *B, T*
Marquette University *B, M, D, T*
Mount Mary College *B*
Ripon College *B*
St. Norbert College *B*
University of Wisconsin
 Eau Claire *B*
 Green Bay *B*
 La Crosse *B*
 Madison *B, M, D*
 Milwaukee *B, M*
 Oshkosh *B*
 Parkside *B*
 Platteville *B*
 Stevens Point *B, T*

Wyoming
University of Wyoming *B, M*

Philosophy/religion

Alabama
Birmingham-Southern College *B*
Huntingdon College *B*
Samford University *B, M*
Stillman College *B*

Arizona
Prescott College *B, M*

Arkansas
Hendrix College *B*
Lyon College *B*
University of the Ozarks *B*

California
Bethany College *B*
Chapman University *B*
Holy Names College *B*
Point Loma Nazarene University *B*
Pomona College *B*
San Francisco State University *B*
University of La Verne *B*
University of San Francisco *B*

Colorado
Trinidad State Junior College *A*

Connecticut
Albertus Magnus College *B*
Holy Apostles College and Seminary *B*

Florida
Bethune-Cookman College *B*
Edward Waters College *B*
Flagler College *B*
New College of Florida *B*
Okaloosa-Walton Community College *A*
Palm Beach Atlantic University *B*
Polk Community College *A*
South Florida Community College *A*
Talmudic College of Florida *B, M, D*
University of West Florida *B*

Georgia
Andrew College *A*
Berry College *B*

Covenant College *B*
Oxford College of Emory University *B*
Paine College *B*
Piedmont College *B*
Toccoa Falls College *B*
Young Harris College *A*

Illinois
Eureka College *B*
Greenville College *B*
Illinois College *B*
Illinois Valley Community College *A*
Lewis University *B*
Lincoln Christian College and
 Seminary *M*
Lincoln College *A*
MacMurray College *B*
Monmouth College *B*
Olivet Nazarene University *B*
Trinity International University *M*

Indiana
Goshen College *B*
Indiana University
 Bloomington *B*
Manchester College *B*
St. Joseph's College *B*
University of Evansville *B*
University of Indianapolis *B*
University of Notre Dame *B*

Iowa
Buena Vista University *B*
Coe College *B*
Graceland University *B*
Morningside College *B*

Kansas
Baker University *B*
Benedictine College *B*
Butler County Community College *A*
Central Christian College *A, B*
Donnelly College *A*
Friends University *B*
McPherson College *B*
MidAmerica Nazarene University *B, T*
Seward County Community College *A*
Southwestern College *B*
Sterling College *B*
Tabor College *B*

Kentucky
Cumberland College *B*
Kentucky Wesleyan College *B*

Louisiana
Centenary College of Louisiana *B*
Dillard University *B*
Louisiana College *B*
Loyola University New Orleans *M*
St. Joseph Seminary College *B*

Maine
University of Maine
 Farmington *B*

Maryland
Columbia Union College *B*
Goucher College *B*
Johns Hopkins University *M, D*
Towson University *B*

Massachusetts
Boston University *B*
Hampshire College *B*
Harvard College *B*
Merrimack College *B*
Northeastern University *B*

Michigan
Adrian College *A, B*
Sacred Heart Major Seminary *B*
Spring Arbor University *B*

Minnesota
Northland Community & Technical
 College *A*

Missouri
College of the Ozarks *B*

Missouri Valley College *B*
Ozark Christian College *C, B*
Rockhurst University *B*
St. Louis Christian College *B*
Truman State University *B*
University of Missouri
 St. Louis *B*
Washington University in St.
 Louis *B, M, D*

Montana
Miles Community College *A*
Rocky Mountain College *B*

Nebraska
Hastings College *B*
Midland Lutheran College *B*

New Hampshire
University of New Hampshire *B*

New Jersey
The College of New Jersey *B*
Cumberland County College *A*
Kean University *B*
Rowan University *B*

New York
Bard College *B*
Colgate University *B*
Cornell University *B*
Elmira College *B*
Eugene Lang College/New School
 University *B*
Fordham University *M, D*
Houghton College *B*
Iona College *B*
Ithaca College *B*
Manhattan College *B*
Pace University:
 Pleasantville/Briarcliff *B*
Roberts Wesleyan College *B*
St. John's University *B, M*
Sarah Lawrence College *B*
State University of New York
 College at Old Westbury *B*
Wagner College *M*

North Carolina
Barton College *B*
Belmont Abbey College *B*
Campbell University *B*
Catawba College *B*
Louisburg College *A*
Methodist College *A, B*
North Carolina Wesleyan College *B*
Queens University of Charlotte *B*
Shaw University *B*
University of North Carolina
 Pembroke *B*
 Wilmington *B*

North Dakota
Jamestown College *B*

Ohio
Defiance College *B*
Heidelberg College *B*
Ohio Northern University *B*
Otterbein College *B*
Sinclair Community College *A*
Wilmington College *B*
Youngstown State University *B*

Oklahoma
Oklahoma City University *B*
Oklahoma Wesleyan University *B*

Oregon
Linn-Benton Community College *A*
Marylhurst University *B*

Pennsylvania
Gettysburg College *B*
La Salle University *B*
Millersville University of
 Pennsylvania *B*

Penn State
  Abington *B*
  Berks *B*
  Delaware County *B*
  Hazleton *B*
  Schuylkill - Capital College *B*
  Shenango *B*
  Wilkes-Barre *B*
Wilson College *B*

South Carolina
Benedict College *B*
Charleston Southern University *B*
Claflin University *B*
Coker College *B*
Erskine College *B*
Newberry College *B*
Presbyterian College *B*

South Dakota
Dakota Wesleyan University *B*
Mount Marty College *B*

Tennessee
Christian Brothers University *B*
Fisk University *B*
Union University *B*
University of Tennessee
    Chattanooga *B*

Texas
Lon Morris College *A*
Texas Wesleyan University *B*

Vermont
Burlington College *B*
Marlboro College *B*
University of Vermont *B*

Virginia
Bridgewater College *B*
Eastern Mennonite University *B*
Ferrum College *B*
Hampden-Sydney College *B*
James Madison University *B*
Radford University *B*
Roanoke College *B*
Virginia Wesleyan College *B*

Washington
Northwest College *B*

West Virginia
Alderson-Broaddus College *B*
Bethany College *B*
Davis and Elkins College *B*
West Virginia Wesleyan College *B*

Wisconsin
Beloit College *B*
Lawrence University *B*
Northland College *B*

Phlebotomy

Alaska
University of Alaska
    Fairbanks *C*

Arkansas
Phillips Community College of the
    University of Arkansas *A*
South Arkansas Community College *C*

California
Ohlone College *C*

Connecticut
Manchester Community College *C*
Quinebaug Valley Community College *C*

Florida
Miami-Dade Community College *C*

Georgia
Bainbridge College *C*

Illinois
City Colleges of Chicago
    Malcolm X College *C*

Finch University of Health Sciences/The
    Chicago Medical School *C*
Moraine Valley Community College *C*

Massachusetts
Massasoit Community College *C*

New York
Dutchess Community College *C*

North Carolina
Cape Fear Community College *C*
Davidson County Community College *C*
Johnston Community College *C*

North Dakota
Bismarck State College *C*

Ohio
Lakeland Community College *C*
Southwestern College of Business *C*

Oregon
Linn-Benton Community College *C*

Pennsylvania
Community College of Allegheny
    County *C*

Tennessee
Roane State Community College *C*

Texas
Tyler Junior College *C*

Utah
Dixie State College of Utah *C*

Washington
Clover Park Technical College *C*
Everett Community College *C*
Renton Technical College *C*

Wisconsin
Fox Valley Technical College *C*
Milwaukee Area Technical College *C*

Photographic/film/video technology

Alabama
Calhoun Community College *A*

California
Academy of Art College *C, A, B, M*
Santiago Canyon College *A*

Colorado
Colorado Mountain College
    Timberline Campus *A*

Kansas
Central Christian College *A, B*

Maryland
Frederick Community College *C*

Michigan
Grace Bible College *B*

Minnesota
Dakota County Technical College *C, A*
Hennepin Technical College *C, A*

New Mexico
New Mexico State University
    Alamogordo *C, A*

New York
Mohawk Valley Community College *C*
Rochester Institute of Technology *B*

North Carolina
Carteret Community College *C, A*

Ohio
Sinclair Community College *C*

Oklahoma
University of Tulsa *B*

Puerto Rico
Inter American University of Puerto Rico
    Bayamon Campus *C*

Vermont
Burlington College *B*

Washington
Seattle Central Community College *C, A*

Wisconsin
Milwaukee Area Technical College *A*

Photography

Alabama
Birmingham-Southern College *B*

Arizona
Arizona State University *B*
Northern Arizona University *B*
Prescott College *B, M*

California
Academy of Art College *C, A, B, M*
Antelope Valley College *C, A*
Art Center College of Design *B*
Bakersfield College *A*
California College of Arts and
    Crafts *B, M*
California Institute of the Arts *C, B, M*
California State University
    Fullerton *B, M*
    Hayward *B*
    Long Beach *B*
Cerritos Community College *A*
Chabot College *A*
Citrus College *C, A*
College of the Canyons *C, A*
College of the Siskiyous *A*
Columbia College *A*
De Anza College *A*
East Los Angeles College *A*
Foothill College *C, A*
Glendale Community College *C*
Golden West College *A*
Grossmont Community College *A*
Irvine Valley College *A*
Los Angeles Pierce College *A*
Los Angeles Southwest College *A*
Los Angeles Trade and Technical
    College *C, A*
Modesto Junior College *A*
Monterey Peninsula College *C, A*
Moorpark College *A*
Mount San Antonio College *C, A*
Mount San Jacinto College *A*
Ohlone College *C*
Orange Coast College *C, A*
Otis College of Art and Design *B, M*
Pacific Union College *A*
Palomar College *C, A*
Riverside Community College *C, A*
San Diego City College *C, A*
San Joaquin Delta College *A*
San Jose State University *M*
Santa Monica College *A*
Santa Rosa Junior College *C*
Sierra College *C, A*
Southwestern College *A*
University of California
    Santa Cruz *B*
Ventura College *C, A*
Yuba Community College District *C, A*

Colorado
Art Institute
    of Colorado *A*
Colorado Mountain College
    Spring Valley Campus *C, A*
Colorado State University *B*

Connecticut
Albertus Magnus College *B*
Paier College of Art *C, A*
University of Hartford *B, M*

District of Columbia
Corcoran College of Art and Design *B*
George Washington University *M*

Florida
Art Institute
    of Fort Lauderdale *A*
Barry University *C, B, M*
Daytona Beach Community College *A*
Palm Beach Community College *A*
Ringling School of Art and Design *B*
University of Miami *B*

Georgia
Atlanta College of Art *B*
LaGrange College *B*
Savannah College of Art and
    Design *B, M*
University of Georgia *B*

Idaho
Brigham Young University - Idaho *A*
College of Southern Idaho *A*

Illinois
City Colleges of Chicago
    Olive-Harvey College *A*
Columbia College Chicago *B, M*
Dominican University *B*
Judson College *B*
Lincoln College *A*
Prairie State College *C, A*
School of the Art Institute of
    Chicago *B, M*
Southern Illinois University
    Carbondale *B*
Southwestern Illinois College *A*
University of Illinois
    Chicago *B, M*
    Urbana-Champaign *B*

Indiana
Ball State University *B*
Indiana University-Purdue University
    Fort Wayne *B*
Purdue University *B*

Iowa
Iowa Lakes Community College *A*
Morningside College *B*
University of Iowa *M*

Kansas
Pittsburg State University *B*

Louisiana
Louisiana Tech University *B*

Maine
Maine College of Art *B*
University of Maine
    Augusta *A*

Maryland
Cecil Community College *C, A*
College of Notre Dame of Maryland *B*
Harford Community College *A*
Howard Community College *A*
Maryland Institute College of Art *B, M*
Montgomery College
    Rockville Campus *A*
University of Maryland
    Baltimore County *B*

Massachusetts
Art Institute of Boston at Lesley
    University *B*
Fitchburg State College *B*
Hampshire College *B*
Massachusetts College of Art *B, M*
Montserrat College of Art *B*
School of the Museum of Fine Arts *B, M*
Simon's Rock College of Bard *B*
University of Massachusetts
    Dartmouth *B, M*

Michigan
Andrews University *B*
College for Creative Studies *B*
Grand Valley State University *B*

Lansing Community College *A*
Mott Community College *A*
Northern Michigan University *B*
Oakland Community College *C, A*
Siena Heights University *B*
University of Michigan *B*
Washtenaw Community College *A*

Minnesota

College of Visual Arts *B*
Minneapolis Community and Technical College *C, A*
Ridgewater College: A Community and Technical College *C*

Missouri

Central Missouri State University *B*
Kansas City Art Institute *B*
St. Louis Community College
  St. Louis Community College at Forest Park *C, A*
  St. Louis Community College at Meramec *A*
University of Missouri
  St. Louis *B*
Washington University in St. Louis *B, M*
Webster University *B*

New Hampshire

Chester College of New England *B*
New England College *B*
Rivier College *B*

New Jersey

Brookdale Community College *A*
Camden County College *A*
Rowan University *B*
Thomas Edison State College *B*

New Mexico

College of Santa Fe *B*
New Mexico State University
  Alamogordo *C*

New York

Adirondack Community College *C, A*
Bard College *B, M*
City University of New York
  Queensborough Community College *C, A*
Fordham University *B*
Hofstra University *B*
Ithaca College *B*
Long Island University
  C. W. Post Campus *B*
Monroe Community College *A*
Nassau Community College *C*
New York University *B*
Onondaga Community College *A*
Parsons School of Design *C, A, B, T*
Pratt Institute *B, M*
Rochester Institute of Technology *A, B, M*
Rockland Community College *A*
Sage College of Albany *A*
St. John's University *B*
Sarah Lawrence College *B*
School of Visual Arts *B, M*
State University of New York
  Albany *B, M*
  Buffalo *M*
  College at Buffalo *B*
  College at Plattsburgh *B*
  College at Potsdam *B*
  New Paltz *B, M*
  Purchase *B*
Syracuse University *B, M*
Villa Maria College of Buffalo *A*

North Carolina

Carteret Community College *A*
Duke University *C*
Guilford Technical Community College *C*
Randolph Community College *A*

Ohio

Antioch College *B*

Antonelli College *A*
Art Academy of Cincinnati *B*
Bowling Green State University *B*
Clark State Community College *C*
Cleveland Institute of Art *B*
Columbus College of Art and Design *B*
Cuyahoga Community College
  Eastern Campus *A*
  Metropolitan Campus *A*
  Western Campus *A*
Ohio Institute of Photography and Technology *C, A*
Ohio State University
  Columbus Campus *B*
Ohio University *B, M*
Shawnee State University *B*
University of Akron *B*
University of Dayton *B*
Virginia Marti College of Art and Design *A*
Youngstown State University *B*

Oklahoma

Oklahoma State University
  Okmulgee *A*
University of Central Oklahoma *B*
University of Oklahoma *B*

Oregon

Linn-Benton Community College *A*
Pacific Northwest College of Art *B*

Pennsylvania

Antonelli Institute of Art and Photography *A*
Arcadia University *B*
Art Institute
  of Philadelphia *A*
  of Pittsburgh *A*
Drexel University *B*
Harrisburg Area Community College *C, A*
Marywood University *M*
Oakbridge Academy of Arts *A*
Temple University *B, M*
Westmoreland County Community College *A*

Puerto Rico

Inter American University of Puerto Rico
  San German Campus *B, M*

Rhode Island

Providence College *B*
Rhode Island School of Design *B, M*

South Carolina

Coker College *B*

Tennessee

Carson-Newman College *B*
Memphis College of Art *B, M*
Milligan College *B*
Pellissippi State Technical Community College *C*
Roane State Community College *A*

Texas

Amarillo College *A*
Austin Community College *C*
El Paso Community College *A*
St. Edward's University *B, T*
Sam Houston State University *B*
Texas A&M University
  Commerce *B*
Texas Woman's University *B, M*
Tyler Junior College *C*
University of Houston *B, M*
University of North Texas *B, M*
University of Texas
  San Antonio *B, M*
Western Texas College *A*

Utah

Brigham Young University *B*
Dixie State College of Utah *A*
Salt Lake Community College *A*
Weber State University *B*

Vermont

Bennington College *B, M*
Burlington College *B*
Marlboro College *B*

Virginia

J. Sargeant Reynolds Community College *C*
Southwest Virginia Community College *C*
Thomas Nelson Community College *A*
Virginia Commonwealth University *B*
Virginia Intermont College *B*

Washington

Cornish College of the Arts *B*
Everett Community College *A*
Seattle University *B*
University of Washington *B, M*

West Virginia

West Virginia State College *B*

Wisconsin

Cardinal Stritch University *B*
Carroll College *B*
Milwaukee Area Technical College *A*
Milwaukee Institute of Art & Design *B*

Wyoming

Casper College *A*
Western Wyoming Community College *A*

Photojournalism

California

Long Beach City College *C*

Colorado

Colorado Mountain College
  Timberline Campus *A*

Idaho

Idaho State University *B*

Minnesota

Winona State University *B*

New York

Rochester Institute of Technology *B*

North Carolina

Carteret Community College *A*

Texas

Texas A&M University
  Commerce *B*

Physical anthropology

Louisiana

Loyola University New Orleans *B*

New York

State University of New York
  Buffalo *M, D*

Ohio

Kent State University *B, M, D*

Physical education

Alabama

Alabama Agricultural and Mechanical University *B, M*
Alabama State University *B, M, T*
Athens State University *B*
Auburn University *B, M, D, T*
Chattahoochee Valley Community College *A*
Faulkner University *B, T*
Huntingdon College *B, T*
Jacksonville State University *B, M, T*
James H. Faulkner State Community College *A*
Lawson State Community College *A*

Oakwood College *B*
Samford University *B*
Southern Union State Community College *A*
Tuskegee University *B*
University of Alabama *B, M*
University of Alabama
  Birmingham *B, M, T*
University of Mobile *B, T*
University of Montevallo *B, M, T*
University of North Alabama *B*
University of South Alabama *B, M, T*
University of West Alabama *B, M, T*

Alaska

University of Alaska
  Anchorage *B*
  Fairbanks *B*

Arizona

Arizona State University *M, T*
Northern Arizona University *B, T*
Pima Community College *C*
Prescott College *B, M*
South Mountain Community College *A*
University of Arizona *B*

Arkansas

Arkansas State University *B, M, T*
Arkansas Tech University *B, M*
Harding University *B, M, T*
Henderson State University *M, T*
Hendrix College *B*
John Brown University *B, T*
Ouachita Baptist University *B, T*
Philander Smith College *B*
Southern Arkansas University *B, M, T*
University of Arkansas *M, D*
University of Arkansas
  Monticello *B*
  Pine Bluff *B, M, T*
University of Central Arkansas *B, M, T*
University of the Ozarks *B, T*
Williams Baptist College *B*

California

Azusa Pacific University *T*
Biola University *B, T*
California Baptist University *B, T*
California State Polytechnic University:
  Pomona *T*
California State University
  Bakersfield *B, T*
  Chico *B, M, T*
  Dominguez Hills *M, T*
  Fresno *B*
  Fullerton *B, M, T*
  Hayward *B, T*
  Long Beach *B, M, T*
  Los Angeles *B, M, T*
  Northridge *B, T*
  Sacramento *T*
  San Bernardino *B, T*
  Stanislaus *B, M*
Christian Heritage College *B, T*
College of the Sequoias *A*
College of the Siskiyous *A*
Columbia College *C*
Concordia University *B*
Cuesta College *C, A*
Diablo Valley College *C, A*
Fresno Pacific University *B, T*
Golden West College *A*
Humboldt State University *B, M, T*
Irvine Valley College *A*
Master's College *B, T*
Mount San Jacinto College *A*
Pacific Union College *B, T*
Pepperdine University *B*
Reedley College *A*
San Diego Mesa College *C, A*
San Diego State University *B*
San Francisco State University *B, M, T*
Santa Barbara City College *A*
Sonoma State University *M, T*
Southwestern College *A*
Taft College *A*

University of California
  Davis *M*
University of La Verne *B*
University of the Pacific *T*
Vanguard University of Southern
  California *M, T*
Yuba Community College District *A*

Colorado

Colorado State University *T*
Colorado State University
  Pueblo *T*
Fort Lewis College *T*
Metropolitan State College of Denver *T*
Regis University *B, T*
Trinidad State Junior College *A*
University of Northern Colorado *M, D, T*

Connecticut

Central Connecticut State
  University *B, M, T*
Eastern Connecticut State
  University *B, T*
Mitchell College *A*
Southern Connecticut State
  University *B, M, T*
University of Connecticut *B, M, D, T*

Delaware

Delaware State University *B*
University of Delaware *B, M, T*

District of Columbia

Gallaudet University *B, T*
George Washington University *A, B, M*
Howard University *B, M, T*
University of the District of Columbia *B*

Florida

Barry University *B*
Bethune-Cookman College *B, T*
Edward Waters College *B*
Florida Agricultural and Mechanical
  University *B, M, T*
Florida International University *B, M, T*
Florida Southern College *B*
Florida State University *B, M, D, T*
Hillsborough Community College *A*
Jacksonville University *B, M, T*
Miami-Dade Community College *A*
Palm Beach Atlantic University *B, T*
Palm Beach Community College *A*
Pensacola Junior College *A*
University of Central Florida *B, M*
University of Miami *M*
University of North Florida *B*
University of South Florida *B, M*
University of Tampa *B, T*
University of West Florida *B, M, T*
Valencia Community College *A*
Warner Southern College *B*

Georgia

Albany State University *B, M*
Armstrong Atlantic State University *B, T*
Augusta State University *B, M*
Berry College *B, T*
Clark Atlanta University *B*
Columbus State University *B*
Fort Valley State University *B, T*
Gainesville College *A*
Georgia College and State
  University *M, T*
Georgia Perimeter College *A*
Georgia Southern University *B, M, T*
Georgia Southwestern State
  University *B, M*
Georgia State University *B, M*
Kennesaw State University *B*
Morehouse College *B*
Morris Brown College *B*
North Georgia College & State
  University *B, M*
Reinhardt College *B*
South Georgia College *A*
State University of West Georgia *B, M*
University of Georgia *B, M, D, T*

Valdosta State University *B, M*
Waycross College *A*

Hawaii

Brigham Young University-Hawaii *B*
University of Hawaii
  Manoa *B, T*

Idaho

Albertson College of Idaho *B*
Boise State University *B, M, T*
College of Southern Idaho *A*
Idaho State University *B, M, T*
Lewis-Clark State College *B, T*
Northwest Nazarene University *B*
University of Idaho *B, M, T*

Illinois

Augustana College *B, T*
Aurora University *B*
Blackburn College *B, T*
Chicago State University *B, M*
Concordia University *B, T*
De Paul University *B, T*
Eastern Illinois University *B, M, T*
Elmhurst College *B*
Eureka College *T*
Greenville College *B, T*
Illinois Central College *A*
Illinois College *B, T*
Illinois State University *B, M, T*
John A. Logan College *A*
Judson College *B, T*
Kishwaukee College *A*
Lewis University *T*
MacMurray College *B, T*
McKendree College *B, T*
Millikin University *B, T*
Monmouth College *B, T*
North Central College *B, T*
North Park University *T*
Northeastern Illinois University *B*
Northern Illinois University *B, M, T*
Olivet Nazarene University *B, T*
Quincy University *B, T*
Rockford College *B, T*
Sauk Valley Community College *A*
Southern Illinois University
  Carbondale *B, M, D*
Trinity Christian College *B, T*
Trinity International University *B, T*
University of Illinois
  Urbana-Champaign *M, T*
Western Illinois University *B, M*

Indiana

Anderson University *B, T*
Ball State University *B, M*
Bethel College *B*
Butler University *T*
Franklin College *B, T*
Goshen College *B*
Grace College *B*
Hanover College *B, T*
Huntington College *B*
Indiana State University *B, M, T*
Indiana University
  Bloomington *B, M, D, T*
Indiana University-Purdue University
  Indianapolis *B, M*
Indiana Wesleyan University *B, T*
Manchester College *B, T*
Marian College *B, T*
Oakland City University *B*
Purdue University *B, M, D*
St. Joseph's College *B*
Taylor University *B, T*
Tri-State University *B, T*
University of Evansville *B*
University of Indianapolis *B, T*
University of St. Francis *C*
University of Southern Indiana *B, T*
Valparaiso University *B*
Vincennes University *A*

Iowa

Briar Cliff University *B*

Buena Vista University *B, T*
Central College *T*
Clarke College *B*
Cornell College *B, T*
Dordt College *B*
Ellsworth Community College *A*
Graceland University *T*
Iowa State University *T*
Iowa Wesleyan College *B*
Loras College *B, M*
Luther College *B*
Marshalltown Community College *A*
North Iowa Area Community College *A*
Northwestern College *T*
St. Ambrose University *B, T*
Simpson College *B, T*
University of Dubuque *B, T*
University of Iowa *M, D*
University of Northern Iowa *B, M*
Upper Iowa University *B, T*
Wartburg College *B, T*
William Penn University *B*

Kansas

Baker University *B, T*
Benedictine College *B, T*
Bethany College *B, T*
Bethel College *T*
Butler County Community College *A*
Central Christian College *A, B*
Emporia State University *B, M, T*
Fort Hays State University *B, M, T*
Fort Scott Community College *A*
Friends University *B*
Garden City Community College *A*
Independence Community College *A*
Kansas City Kansas Community
  College *A*
McPherson College *B, T*
MidAmerica Nazarene University *B, T*
Ottawa University *B, T*
Pittsburg State University *B, M, T*
Southwestern College *B, T*
Sterling College *T*
Tabor College *B, T*
University of Kansas *B, M, D, T*
Washburn University of Topeka *B*
Wichita State University *B, M*

Kentucky

Alice Lloyd College *B*
Asbury College *B, T*
Berea College *B, T*
Campbellsville University *B*
Cumberland College *B, T*
Kentucky Wesleyan College *T*
Lindsey Wilson College *B*
Morehead State University *B, M*
Murray State University *B, M, T*
St. Catharine College *A*
Transylvania University *B, T*
Union College *B*
University of Kentucky *B*
University of Louisville *M*

Louisiana

Centenary College of Louisiana *B, T*
Dillard University *B*
Grambling State University *B*
Louisiana College *B*
Louisiana State University
  Shreveport *B*
Louisiana State University and
  Agricultural and Mechanical
  College *B, M, D*
Louisiana Tech University *B, M*
McNeese State University *B, M, T*
Nicholls State University *B*
Northwestern State University *B, M*
Southeastern Louisiana University *B, M*
Southern University and Agricultural and
  Mechanical College *B*
University of Louisiana at Lafayette *B*
University of Louisiana at Monroe *B, M*
University of New Orleans *B, M*
Xavier University of Louisiana *B*

Maine

Husson College *B, T*
St. Joseph's College *B*
University of Maine *B, M*
University of Maine
  Presque Isle *B*

Maryland

Allegany College *A*
Columbia Union College *B*
Community College of Baltimore County
  Catonsville *C*
  Essex *C*
Frederick Community College *A*
Frostburg State University *B, M, T*
Montgomery College
  Rockville Campus *A*
Morgan State University *B, M*
Salisbury University *B, T*
Towson University *B, T*
University of Maryland
  College Park *B, M, D*

Massachusetts

Boston University *B, M, T*
Bridgewater State College *B, M, T*
Dean College *A*
Northeastern University *B*
Salem State College *B*
Springfield College *B, M, D, T*
University of Massachusetts
  Boston *B*
Westfield State College *B, M, T*

Michigan

Adrian College *B, T*
Alma College *T*
Andrews University *M, T*
Aquinas College *B, T*
Calvin College *B, T*
Central Michigan University *B, M*
Concordia University *B, T*
Cornerstone University *B, T*
Eastern Michigan University *B, M, T*
Grand Valley State University *B, T*
Hillsdale College *B*
Hope College *B, T*
Kellogg Community College *A*
Lansing Community College *A*
Michigan State University *B, M, D*
Mid Michigan Community College *A*
Northern Michigan University *B, T*
Saginaw Valley State University *B, T*
Schoolcraft College *A*
University of Michigan *B, M, D*
Wayne State University *B, M, T*
Western Michigan University *B, M*

Minnesota

Augsburg College *B, T*
Bemidji State University *M, T*
Bethel College *B*
College of St. Catherine *B, T*
Concordia College: Moorhead *B, T*
Concordia University: St. Paul *B, T*
Gustavus Adolphus College *T*
Hamline University *B*
Minnesota State University
  Mankato *B, M, T*
  Moorhead *B, T*
Northland Community & Technical
  College *A*
Northwestern College *B*
Ridgewater College: A Community and
  Technical College *A*
St. Cloud State University *M, T*
St. Olaf College *T*
Southwest State University *B, T*
University of Minnesota
  Duluth *B, T*
  Twin Cities *B, M, D, T*
University of St. Thomas *B, T*
Winona State University *B, M, T*

Mississippi

Alcorn State University *B*
Blue Mountain College *B*

Delta State University *B, M*
Itawamba Community College *A*
Mary Holmes College *A*
Mississippi State University *B, M, T*
Mississippi Valley State University *B, T*
Northwest Mississippi Community
 College *A*
University of Southern
 Mississippi *B, M, D*

Missouri

Central Methodist College *B*
Central Missouri State
 University *B, M, T*
College of the Ozarks *B, T*
Crowder College *A*
Culver-Stockton College *B, T*
Drury University *B, T*
Evangel University *B, T*
Hannibal-LaGrange College *B*
Lincoln University *B, T*
Lindenwood University *B*
Missouri Baptist University *B, T*
Missouri Southern State College *B, T*
Missouri Valley College *B*
Northwest Missouri State
 University *B, M, T*
Southeast Missouri State University *B, T*
Southwest Baptist University *B, T*
Southwest Missouri State University *B*
Truman State University *M, T*
University of Missouri
 Kansas City *B*
 St. Louis *B, M, T*
Westminster College *B, T*
William Woods University *B, T*

Montana

Carroll College *B, T*
Montana State University
 Billings *B, T*
Rocky Mountain College *B, T*
University of Montana-Missoula *B, M, T*
University of Montana: Western *B, T*

Nebraska

Bellevue University *B*
Chadron State College *B, M*
Concordia University *B, T*
Dana College *B*
Doane College *B, T*
Hastings College *B, M, T*
Midland Lutheran College *B, T*
Nebraska Wesleyan University *B*
Northeast Community College *A*
Peru State College *B, T*
Union College *T*
University of Nebraska
 Kearney *B, M, T*
 Lincoln *B, M, T*
 Omaha *B, M, T*
Wayne State College *B, M*
Western Nebraska Community
 College *A*
York College *B*

Nevada

University of Nevada
 Las Vegas *B*
 Reno *B, M*

New Hampshire

Keene State College *B, T*
New England College *B, T*
Plymouth State College *T*
University of New Hampshire *M, T*

New Jersey

The College of New Jersey *B, M, T*
Essex County College *A*
Gloucester County College *A*
Kean University *B*
Montclair State University *B, M, T*
Rowan University *B, M, T*
William Paterson University of New
 Jersey *B, T*

New Mexico

College of the Southwest *B, T*
Eastern New Mexico University *B, M*
New Mexico Highlands University *B, M*
New Mexico Junior College *A*
New Mexico State University *B*
University of New Mexico *B, M, D, T*
Western New Mexico University *B*

New York

Adelphi University *B, M*
Canisius College *B, M, T*
City University of New York
 Brooklyn College *B*
 Hunter College *B, T*
 Queens College *M, T*
 York College *B*
College of Mount St. Vincent *B, T*
Corning Community College *A*
Fulton-Montgomery Community
 College *A*
Hofstra University *B, M, T*
Houghton College *B, T*
Hudson Valley Community College *A*
Ithaca College *B, M, T*
Long Island University
 C. W. Post Campus *B, T*
Manhattan College *B, T*
Mohawk Valley Community College *C*
St. Bonaventure University *B, T*
State University of New York
 College at Brockport *B, M, T*
 College at Cortland *B, M, T*
 College of Technology at Delhi *A*
Syracuse University *B, M, T*

North Carolina

Appalachian State University *B, T*
Barton College *B, T*
Campbell University *B, M, T*
Catawba College *B, T*
Chowan College *B, T*
East Carolina University *B, M*
Elizabeth City State University *B*
Elon University *B, T*
Fayetteville State University *B, T*
Gardner-Webb University *B, M*
Greensboro College *B, T*
Guilford College *B, T*
Guilford Technical Community
 College *A*
High Point University *B, T*
Johnson C. Smith University *B*
Lees-McRae College *B, T*
Lenoir Community College *A*
Lenoir-Rhyne College *B, T*
Livingstone College *T*
Louisburg College *A*
Mars Hill College *B, T*
Meredith College *B, T*
Methodist College *A, B, T*
North Carolina Agricultural and
 Technical State University *B, M, T*
North Carolina Central University *B, M*
North Carolina Wesleyan College *B*
Pfeiffer University *B*
Piedmont Baptist College *B*
St. Andrews Presbyterian College *B, T*
St. Augustine's College *B*
University of North Carolina
 Greensboro *B, M, D, T*
 Pembroke *B, M, T*
 Wilmington *B*
Western Carolina University *B, M, T*
Wingate University *B, T*
Winston-Salem State University *B*

North Dakota

Dickinson State University *B, T*
Jamestown College *B*
Mayville State University *B, T*
Minot State University *B*
Minot State University: Bottineau
 Campus *A*
North Dakota State University *B, M, T*
University of Mary *B, T*

University of North Dakota *M, T*
Valley City State University *B, T*

Ohio

Ashland University *B, M, T*
Baldwin-Wallace College *B, T*
Bluffton College *B*
Bowling Green State University *B*
Cedarville University *B*
Central State University *B*
Cleveland State University *B, M, T*
College of Mount St. Joseph *B, T*
Defiance College *B, T*
Denison University *B*
Heidelberg College *B*
John Carroll University *B*
Kent State University *B, M, D, T*
Kent State University
 Stark Campus *B*
Malone College *B*
Miami University
 Oxford Campus *B, T*
Mount Union College *B, T*
Mount Vernon Nazarene University *B, T*
Ohio Northern University *B, T*
Ohio State University
 Columbus Campus *B, M, D*
Ohio University *B, T*
Ohio Wesleyan University *B*
Otterbein College *B*
Sinclair Community College *A*
University of Akron *B, M, T*
University of Dayton *B, M, T*
University of Findlay *B, T*
University of Rio Grande *A, B, T*
University of Toledo *B, M, T*
Walsh University *B*
Wilmington College *B*
Wright State University *B, M, T*
Xavier University *M*
Youngstown State University *B, M, T*

Oklahoma

Cameron University *B, T*
East Central University *B, T*
Eastern Oklahoma State College *A*
Langston University *B*
Northeastern State University *B*
Northern Oklahoma College *A*
Northwestern Oklahoma State
 University *B, T*
Oklahoma Baptist University *B, T*
Oklahoma Christian University of
 Science and Arts *B, T*
Oklahoma City University *B*
Oklahoma State University *M*
Oklahoma Wesleyan University *B*
Oral Roberts University *B, T*
Redlands Community College *A*
Southern Nazarene University *B*
Southwestern Oklahoma State
 University *B, M, T*
Tulsa Community College *A*
University of Central Oklahoma *B*
Western Oklahoma State College *A*

Oregon

Chemeketa Community College *A*
Concordia University *B, M, T*
George Fox University *T*
Linfield College *T*
Oregon State University *M*
University of Portland *T*
Warner Pacific College *B, T*
Western Baptist College *B*
Western Oregon University *B, T*

Pennsylvania

Baptist Bible College of Pennsylvania *B*
Bucks County Community College *A*
East Stroudsburg University of
 Pennsylvania *B, M, T*
Gettysburg College *T*
Indiana University of Pennsylvania *B, T*
Lancaster Bible College *B*
Lincoln University *B, T*

Lock Haven University of
 Pennsylvania *B, T*
Marywood University *B*
Messiah College *B, T*
Montgomery County Community
 College *A*
Philadelphia Biblical University *B, T*
Slippery Rock University of
 Pennsylvania *B, M, T*
Temple University *B, M, D, T*
University of Pittsburgh *B, M, D, T*
West Chester University of
 Pennsylvania *B, M, T*

Puerto Rico

Bayamon Central University *B*
Inter American University of Puerto Rico
 Guayama Campus *B*
 Metropolitan Campus *B, M*
 San German Campus *B, M*
Pontifical Catholic University of Puerto
 Rico *B, T*
Turabo University *B*
Universidad Metropolitana *B, M*
University of Puerto Rico
 Cayey University College *B, T*

Rhode Island

Rhode Island College *B*
University of Rhode Island *B, M*

South Carolina

Anderson College *B, T*
Charleston Southern University *B*
The Citadel *B, M, T*
Claflin University *B*
Coastal Carolina University *B*
Coker College *B, T*
College of Charleston *B, T*
Erskine College *B, T*
Furman University *T*
Lander University *B, T*
Limestone College *B*
Newberry College *B, T*
South Carolina State University *B, T*
Southern Wesleyan University *B, T*
University of South Carolina *B, M*
University of South Carolina
 Spartanburg *B, T*
Voorhees College *B*
Winthrop University *B, M, T*

South Dakota

Augustana College *B, T*
Black Hills State University *B, T*
Dakota State University *B, T*
Dakota Wesleyan University *B, T*
Mount Marty College *B*
Northern State University *B, T*
University of Sioux Falls *T*
University of South Dakota *B, M, T*

Tennessee

Bethel College *B*
Bryan College *T*
Carson-Newman College *B*
Freed-Hardeman University *B, T*
Lambuth University *B, T*
Lane College *B*
Lee University *B, T*
Maryville College *B, T*
Southern Adventist University *B*
Tennessee State University *B*
Tennessee Technological
 University *B, M, T*
Tennessee Wesleyan College *B, T*
Trevecca Nazarene University *B, T*
Tusculum College *B*
Union University *B, T*
University of Memphis *B*
University of Tennessee
 Knoxville *M, D*
 Martin *B, T*

Texas

Abilene Christian University *B, T*
Alvin Community College *A*

Amarillo College *A*
Angelina College *A*
Baylor University *B, T*
Dallas Baptist University *B, T*
Del Mar College *A*
East Texas Baptist University *B*
El Paso Community College *A*
Galveston College *A*
Hardin-Simmons University *B, M, T*
Houston Baptist University *B*
Howard Payne University *B, T*
Huston-Tillotson College *B*
Jarvis Christian College *B*
Lamar University *T*
Laredo Community College *A*
LeTourneau University *B*
Lubbock Christian University *B, T*
McMurry University *B, T*
Midland College *A*
Panola College *A*
Prairie View A&M University *M*
Sam Houston State University *M, T*
Schreiner University *T*
Southwest Texas State University *M, T*
Southwestern Adventist University *T*
Southwestern University *B, T*
Stephen F. Austin State University *M*
Sul Ross State University *M*
Tarleton State University *B, M, T*
Texas A&M International University *T*
Texas A&M University *M, D*
Texas A&M University
    Commerce *B, T*
    Corpus Christi *T*
    Kingsville *B, M*
Texas College *B*
Texas Lutheran University *B, T*
Texas Southern University *M*
Texas Wesleyan University *B, M, T*
University of Houston *B, M, D, T*
University of Mary Hardin-Baylor *B, T*
University of North Texas *B, M, T*
University of Texas
    Arlington *B, T*
    Austin *M, D*
    Pan American *B, M, T*
    San Antonio *M, T*
    of the Permian Basin *M*
University of the Incarnate Word *B, M*
Wayland Baptist University *B, T*
West Texas A&M University *T*
Wiley College *B*

Utah
Brigham Young University *B, M, D*
Dixie State College of Utah *A*
Snow College *A*
Southern Utah University *T*
Utah State University *B*
Weber State University *B*

Vermont
Castleton State College *B, T*
Johnson State College *B*
Lyndon State College *B*
Norwich University *B, T*
University of Vermont *B*

Virginia
Averett University *B, M, T*
Bluefield College *B, T*
Eastern Mennonite University *T*
Ferrum College *B*
George Mason University *B, M*
Hampton University *B*
Liberty University *B*
Longwood University *B, T*
Lynchburg College *B*
Old Dominion University *B, M*
Radford University *B, M, T*
Roanoke College *B, T*
Shenandoah University *B*
University of Richmond *T*
University of Virginia *B, M, D*
University of Virginia's College at
    Wise *T*

Virginia Commonwealth
    University *B, M*
Virginia Intermont College *B, T*
Virginia State University *B*

Washington
Central Washington University *B, M, T*
Eastern Washington University *B, M, T*
Gonzaga University *B, M, T*
Northwest College *B*
Pacific Lutheran University *T*
Seattle Pacific University *B, T*
Walla Walla College *B*
Washington State University *B*
Western Washington University *B, M, T*
Whitworth College *B, T*

West Virginia
Alderson-Broaddus College *T*
Bethany College *B*
Concord College *B, T*
Fairmont State College *B*
Marshall University *B, M*
Ohio Valley College *B*
Potomac State College of West Virginia
    University *A*
Salem International University *T*
Shepherd College *T*
West Liberty State College *B*
West Virginia State College *B*
West Virginia University *B, M, D, T*
West Virginia University Institute of
    Technology *A*
West Virginia Wesleyan College *B*

Wisconsin
Carroll College *B, T*
Carthage College *B, T*
Concordia University Wisconsin *B, T*
Maranatha Baptist Bible College *B*
Ripon College *T*
University of Wisconsin
    La Crosse *B, M, T*
    Madison *B, M, D, T*
    Oshkosh *B, T*
    River Falls *B, T*
    Stevens Point *B, T*
    Superior *B, T*
    Whitewater *B, T*

Wyoming
Casper College *A*
Eastern Wyoming College *A*
Laramie County Community College *A*
Sheridan College *A*
University of Wyoming *B*
Western Wyoming Community
    College *A*

Physical sciences

Arizona
South Mountain Community College *A*

Arkansas
Arkansas Tech University *B*

California
California State University
    Chico *B*
ITT Technical Institute
    Torrance *A*
Long Beach City College *A*
Ohlone College *C*
Taft College *A*

Connecticut
Three Rivers Community College *A*
University of Bridgeport *B*
University of New Haven *A*

Delaware
Delaware Technical and Community
    College
        Stanton/Wilmington Campus *A*

District of Columbia
University of the District of Columbia *A*

Illinois
College of Lake County *C, A*

Indiana
Ball State University *A*
ITT Technical Institute
    Indianapolis *A*
Taylor University *B*
Vincennes University *A*

Iowa
Loras College *B*

Kansas
Barton County Community College *A*
Cloud County Community College *A*
Emporia State University *B, M*

Kentucky
Alice Lloyd College *B*
Asbury College *B*

Maine
Bates College *T*

Maryland
United States Naval Academy *B*
University of Maryland
    College Park *B*

Massachusetts
Cape Cod Community College *A*
Westfield State College *B*

Michigan
Ferris State University *A*
Kellogg Community College *A*
Michigan State University *B, M*
Northwestern Michigan College *A*

Minnesota
Crown College *A, B*
Vermilion Community College *A*

Missouri
Crowder College *A*
Maple Woods Community College *C, A*

Nebraska
Concordia University *B, T*

Nevada
Western Nevada Community College *A*

New Jersey
Burlington County College *A*
County College of Morris *A*
Gloucester County College *C, A*
Union County College *A*

New York
Corning Community College *A*
Schenectady County Community
    College *A*
Westchester Community College *A*

Ohio
Mount Union College *T*
University of Dayton *B*
University of Toledo *A*
Youngstown State University *B, M*

Oklahoma
Northeastern Oklahoma Agricultural and
    Mechanical College *A*

Pennsylvania
Butler County Community College *A*
Community College of Philadelphia *A*
East Stroudsburg University of
    Pennsylvania *B*
Juniata College *B*
Lincoln University *B*
Millersville University of
    Pennsylvania *A*
Montgomery County Community
    College *A*
Pennsylvania College of Technology *A*

University of Pittsburgh
    Bradford *B*

Puerto Rico
University of Puerto Rico
    Humacao *A*

Rhode Island
Community College of Rhode
    Island *C, A*

South Carolina
Aiken Technical College *C*
Florence-Darlington Technical College *A*
Midlands Technical College *C*
Trident Technical College *A*

Tennessee
Jackson State Community College *A*
Southwest Tennessee Community
    College *A*
Union University *B*

Texas
Amarillo College *A*
Brazosport College *C, A*
Lee College *A*
Palo Alto College *A*
Texas A&M University *M*
Texas State Technical College
    Waco *A*

Utah
Brigham Young University *B*
Utah Valley State College *A*
Weber State University *C, A*

Vermont
St. Michael's College *B*
University of Vermont *M*

Washington
Edmonds Community College *A*

West Virginia
Marshall University *M*

Wyoming
Central Wyoming College *A*

Physical therapy

Alabama
Alabama State University *M*
Oakwood College *A*
University of Alabama
    Birmingham *M*
University of South Alabama *M*

Arizona
Northern Arizona University *M*

Arkansas
Arkansas State University *M*
Northwest Arkansas Community
    College *A*
University of Central Arkansas *M, D*

California
Azusa Pacific University *M, D*
California State University
    Fresno *B*
    Long Beach *M*
    Northridge *B*
    Sacramento *M*
Chapman University *D*
Loma Linda University *M, D*
Los Angeles Southwest College *A*
Mount San Antonio College *M, C, A*
Samuel Merritt College *M*
San Francisco State University *M*
University of Southern California *M, D*
University of the Pacific *M*
Whittier College *B*

Colorado
Regis University *D*
University of Colorado
    Health Sciences Center *M*

Connecticut

Quinnipiac University *B, M, D*
Sacred Heart University *M*
University of Connecticut *B, M*
University of Hartford *M*

Delaware

University of Delaware *M*

District of Columbia

Howard University *M*

Florida

Broward Community College *A*
Florida Agricultural and Mechanical
University *B*
Florida Gulf Coast University *M*
Florida International University *M*
Nova Southeastern University *M, D*
University of Central Florida *M*
University of Florida *M*
University of Miami *B, M, D*
University of North Florida *M*
University of South Florida *M*

Georgia

Armstrong Atlantic State
University *B, M*
Clark Atlanta University *B*
Dalton State College *A*
Floyd College *A*
Georgia State University *M*
Gordon College *A*
Medical College of Georgia *M*
North Georgia College & State
University *M*

Idaho

Idaho State University *M*

Illinois

Bradley University *M*
Finch University of Health Sciences/The
Chicago Medical School *M, D*
Governors State University *M*
Illinois Central College *A*
North Park University *B*
Northern Illinois University *B, M*
Northwestern University *M, D*
Rush University *M*
Trinity International University *B*
University of Illinois
Chicago *M, D*

Indiana

Indiana University-Purdue University
Indianapolis *B, M, D*
Manchester College *B*
University of Evansville *B, M*
University of Indianapolis *M, D*

Iowa

Buena Vista University *B*
Clarke College *M*
North Iowa Area Community College *A*
St. Ambrose University *M*
University of Iowa *M, D*
University of Osteopathic Medicine and
Health Sciences
Des Moines University -
Osteopathic Medical Center *D*

Kansas

Central Christian College *A*
Pratt Community College *A*
University of Kansas Medical
Center *M, D*
Wichita State University *M*

Kentucky

Bellarmine University *M*
University of Kentucky *B, M*

Maine

Husson College *M*
University of New England *M*

Maryland

University of Maryland
Baltimore *M, D*

Massachusetts

American International College *B, M*
Becker College *A*
Boston University *B, M, D*
Northeastern University *B, M*
Simmons College *B, M, D*
Springfield College *B, M*
University of Massachusetts
Lowell *M, D*

Michigan

Andrews University *M*
Central Michigan University *M*
Grand Valley State University *M*
Oakland University *B, M, D*
University of Michigan
Flint *M, D*
Wayne State University *M*

Minnesota

Bethel College *B*
College of St. Catherine *B, D*
College of St. Scholastica *M*
St. Mary's University of Minnesota *B*
University of Minnesota
Twin Cities *B, M*

Mississippi

Alcorn State University *B*
University of Mississippi Medical
Center *B*

Missouri

Avila University *B*
Drury University *B*
Maryville University of Saint Louis *M*
Rockhurst University *M*
St. Louis University *M*
Southwest Baptist University *M*
Southwest Missouri State University *M*
Truman State University *B*
University of Missouri
Columbia *M*
Washington University in St. Louis *M, D*

Montana

University of Montana-Missoula *M, D*

Nebraska

Creighton University *D*
University of Nebraska
Medical Center *M*

Nevada

University of Nevada
Las Vegas *M*

New Hampshire

New England College *B*

New Jersey

Kean University *B, M*
Richard Stockton College of New
Jersey *M*
Rutgers, The State University of New
Jersey
Camden Regional Campus *M*
University of Medicine and Dentistry of
New Jersey
School of Health Related
Professions *M, D*

New Mexico

Luna Community College *A*
University of New Mexico *B, M*

New York

City University of New York
College of Staten Island *B, M*
Hunter College *M*
Clarkson University *M*
Concordia College *B*
D'Youville College *C, B, M*
Daemen College *M, D*
Dominican College of Blauvelt *M*
Ithaca College *B, M*
Manhattan College *B*
Mercy College *B, M*
Mount St. Mary College *B*

Nazareth College of Rochester *B, M*
New York Institute of Technology *B, M*
New York University *M, D*
State University of New York
Buffalo *B*
Health Science Center at
Brooklyn *B*
Health Science Center at Stony
Brook *M, D*
Oswego *B*
Stony Brook *M, D*
Upstate Medical University *B, M*
Touro College *B, M*
Utica College *B, M*

North Carolina

Duke University *M*
East Carolina University *M*
Elon University *D*
Southwestern Community College *A*
University of North Carolina
Chapel Hill *M*
Western Carolina University *M*
Winston-Salem State University *M*

North Dakota

University of Mary *M*
University of North Dakota *B, D*

Ohio

Bowling Green State University *B*
Cleveland State University *M*
College of Mount St. Joseph *M*
Marion Technical College *A*
Ohio State University
Columbus Campus *B, M*
Ohio University *M*
University of Cincinnati
Raymond Walters College *A*
University of Findlay *M*
University of Toledo *B*
Walsh University *M*
Youngstown State University *M*

Oklahoma

Langston University *B*
Murray State College *A*
University of Oklahoma *B, M*

Oregon

Pacific University *M*
Rogue Community College *C*

Pennsylvania

Arcadia University *D*
Carlow College *B*
Chatham College *D*
Drexel University *B, M, D*
Duquesne University *B, D*
Elizabethtown College *B*
Lebanon Valley College of
Pennsylvania *B, M*
Mount Aloysius College *B, D*
Neumann College *M*
St. Vincent College *B*
Slippery Rock University of
Pennsylvania *D*
Temple University *M, D*
University of Pittsburgh *M, D*
University of Scranton *B, M*
University of the Sciences in
Philadelphia *B, M*
Widener University *M, D*

Puerto Rico

University of Puerto Rico
Medical Sciences Campus *B*

Rhode Island

University of Rhode Island *M*

South Carolina

Medical University of South Carolina *M*
University of South Carolina *D*

South Dakota

Augustana College *B*
University of South Dakota *M*

Tennessee

Belmont University *D*
Carson-Newman College *T*
Columbia State Community College *A*
East Tennessee State University *M*
University of Tennessee
Chattanooga *B, M*
University of Tennessee Health Science
Center *B, M*

Texas

Amarillo College *A*
Angelo State University *M*
Baylor University *M, D*
Blinn College *A*
Grayson County College *A*
Hardin-Simmons University *M, D*
McLennan Community College *A*
San Antonio College *A*
Southwest Texas State University *M*
Texas Woman's University *M, D*
University of Texas
El Paso *B*
Health Science Center at San
Antonio *B, M*
Medical Branch at Galveston *M*
San Antonio *B*
Southwestern Medical Center at
Dallas *M*

Utah

Brigham Young University *D*
University of Utah *B, M*

Vermont

University of Vermont *M*

Virginia

College of Health Sciences *A*
Marymount University *M*
Old Dominion University *D*
Shenandoah University *M*
Virginia Commonwealth University *M*

Washington

Eastern Washington University *M, D*
University of Puget Sound *M*
University of Washington *B, M*

West Virginia

West Virginia University *M*
Wheeling Jesuit University *M*

Wisconsin

Carroll College *M*
Concordia University Wisconsin *B, M*
Marquette University *M, D*
University of Wisconsin
La Crosse *M*
Madison *M*

Physical therapy assistant

Alabama

Bishop State Community College *A*
Central Alabama Community College *A*
Community College of the Air Force *A*
Enterprise State Junior College *A*
Faulkner University *A*
Jefferson State Community College *A*
Northwest-Shoals Community College *A*
South University *A*
Wallace State Community College at
Hanceville *A*

Arizona

Gateway Community College *C, A*

Arkansas

Arkansas State University *A*
Northwest Arkansas Community
College *A*
South Arkansas Community College *A*
University of Central Arkansas *A*

California

Cerritos Community College *A*
De Anza College *C*

Loma Linda University *A*
Mount St. Mary's College *C, A*
Ohlone College *A*
San Diego Mesa College *A*

Colorado
Arapahoe Community College *A*
Morgan Community College *A*

Connecticut
Capital Community College *A*
Housatonic Community College *A*
Manchester Community College *A*
Northwestern Connecticut Community
College *A*

Delaware
Delaware Technical and Community
College
Stanton/Wilmington Campus *A*

District of Columbia
George Washington University *C*

Florida
Broward Community College *A*
Gulf Coast Community College *A*
Indian River Community College *A*
Lake City Community College *A*
Manatee Community College *A*
Pasco-Hernando Community College *A*
Pensacola Junior College *A*
Polk Community College *A*
St. Petersburg College *A*
Seminole Community College *A*

Georgia
Athens Technical College *A*
Darton College *A*
Middle Georgia College *A*
South University *A*
Southwest Georgia Technical College *A*

Idaho
Idaho State University *A*
North Idaho College *A*

Illinois
Black Hawk College *A*
College of DuPage *A*
Elgin Community College *A*
Illinois Central College *A*
Kankakee Community College *A*
Kaskaskia College *A*
Lake Land College *A*
Oakton Community College *A*
Southern Illinois University
Carbondale *A*
Southwestern Illinois College *A*

Indiana
Ivy Tech State College
Eastcentral *A*
Kokomo *A*
Northeast *A*
Northwest *A*
Michiana College *A*
Purdue University
Calumet *A*
University of Evansville *A*
University of Indianapolis *A*
University of St. Francis *A*
Vincennes University *A*

Iowa
Indian Hills Community College *A*
Iowa Central Community College *A*
Kirkwood Community College *A*
North Iowa Area Community College *A*
Upper Iowa University *B*
Waldorf College *A*
Western Iowa Tech Community
College *A*

Kansas
Central Christian College *A*
Fort Hays State University *B*
Johnson County Community College *A*

Kansas City Kansas Community
College *A*
Washburn University of Topeka *A*
Wichita State University *A*

Kentucky
Hazard Community College *A*
Jefferson Community College *A*
Madisonville Community College *A*
Paducah Community College *A*
Somerset Community College *A*
Southeast Community College *A*

Louisiana
Delgado Community College *A*
Southern University
Shreveport *A*

Maryland
Allegany College *A*
Anne Arundel Community College *A*
Carroll Community College *A*
Chesapeake College *A*
College of Southern Maryland *A*
Community College of Baltimore County
Dundalk *C*
Howard Community College *A*
Montgomery College
Rockville Campus *A*

Massachusetts
Bay State College *A*
Becker College *A*
Berkshire Community College *A*
Cape Cod Community College *A*
Massachusetts Bay Community
College *A*
Mount Wachusett Community College *A*
Springfield Technical Community
College *A*

Michigan
Baker College
of Cadillac *A*
of Muskegon *A*
Bay de Noc Community College *C*
Finlandia University *A*
Kellogg Community College *A*
Macomb Community College *A*
Mott Community College *A*
Oakland Community College *A*
University of Michigan
Flint *B*

Minnesota
Anoka-Ramsey Community College *A*
College of St. Catherine *A*
Lake Superior College: A Community
and Technical College *A*
Riverland Community College: A
Technical and Community College *A*

Mississippi
Itawamba Community College *A*

Missouri
Missouri Western State College *A*
Ozarks Technical Community College *A*
Penn Valley Community College *A*
St. Louis Community College
St. Louis Community College at
Meramec *A*

Nebraska
Clarkson College *A*
Northeast Community College *A*

Nevada
Community College of Southern
Nevada *A*

New Hampshire
Hesser College *A*
New Hampshire Community Technical
College
Claremont *A*
Manchester *A*

New Jersey
Atlantic Cape Community College *A*

Essex County College *A*
Fairleigh Dickinson University
College at Florham *A*
Mercer County Community College *A*
Union County College *A*

New Mexico
San Juan College *A*

New York
Adirondack Community College *A*
Broome Community College *A*
City University of New York
Kingsborough Community
College *A*
La Guardia Community College *A*
Dutchess Community College *A*
Genesee Community College *A*
Maria College *A*
Nassau Community College *A*
New York University *A*
Niagara County Community College *A*
Onondaga Community College *A*
Orange County Community College *A*
State University of New York
College of Technology at Canton *A*
Suffolk County Community College *A*
Touro College *A*
Villa Maria College of Buffalo *A*

North Carolina
Caldwell Community College and
Technical Institute *A*
Central Piedmont Community College *A*
Fayetteville Technical Community
College *A*
Guilford Technical Community
College *A*
Martin Community College *A*

North Dakota
Williston State College *A*

Ohio
Clark State Community College *A*
Cuyahoga Community College
Eastern Campus *A*
Metropolitan Campus *A*
Western Campus *A*
Hocking Technical College *A*
James A. Rhodes State College *A*
Kent State University *A*
Kent State University
Ashtabula Regional Campus *A*
East Liverpool Regional Campus *A*
Lorain County Community College *A*
Marion Technical College *A*
Muskingum Area Technical College *A*
North Central State College *A*
Owens Community College
Toledo *A*
Shawnee State University *A*
Stark State College of Technology *A*
Washington State Community College *A*

Oklahoma
Carl Albert State College *A*
Northeastern Oklahoma Agricultural and
Mechanical College *A*
Oklahoma City Community College *A*
Tulsa Community College *A*

Oregon
Mount Hood Community College *A*

Pennsylvania
Academy of Medical Arts and
Business *C, A*
Butler County Community College *A*
Central Pennsylvania College *A*
Community College of Allegheny
County *A*
Lehigh Carbon Community College *A*
Mercyhurst College *A*
Mount Aloysius College *A*

Penn State
Dubois *A*
Hazleton *A*
Mont Alto *A*
Shenango *A*
University of Pittsburgh
Titusville *A*

Puerto Rico
University of Puerto Rico
Humacao *A*
Ponce *A*

Rhode Island
Community College of Rhode Island *A*

South Carolina
Aiken Technical College *C*
Central Carolina Technical College *C*
Florence-Darlington Technical
College *C, A*
Midlands Technical College *C, A*
Orangeburg-Calhoun Technical
College *C*
Piedmont Technical College *C*
Spartanburg Technical College *A*
Trident Technical College *A*

Tennessee
Chattanooga State Technical Community
College *A*
Jackson State Community College *A*
Roane State Community College *A*
South College *A*
Southwest Tennessee Community
College *A*
Volunteer State Community College *A*
Walters State Community College *A*

Texas
Amarillo College *A*
Austin Community College *A*
Del Mar College *A*
El Paso Community College *A*
Houston Community College System *A*
Howard College *A*
Kilgore College *A*
Laredo Community College *A*
North Harris Montgomery Community
College District *A*
Odessa College *A*
St. Philip's College *A*
Tarrant County College *A*
Wharton County Junior College *A*

Utah
Salt Lake Community College *A*

Virginia
College of Health Sciences *A*
Virginia Highlands Community
College *A*

Washington
Green River Community College *A*
Spokane Falls Community College *A*

West Virginia
Fairmont State College *A*
Mountain State University *A*

Wisconsin
Blackhawk Technical College *A*
Milwaukee Area Technical College *A*
Western Wisconsin Technical College *A*

Physical/theoretical chemistry

California
University of Southern California *D*

Florida
Florida State University *M, D*

Illinois
Loyola University of Chicago *M, D*

Iowa
Iowa State University *M, D*

Maryland
University of Maryland
 College Park *M, D*

Massachusetts
Harvard College *B*

Michigan
Michigan State University *B, M, D*
University of Michigan *M, D*

Montana
University of Montana-Missoula *M, D*

New Jersey
Stevens Institute of Technology *M, D*

New York
Fordham University *M*
Sarah Lawrence College *B*
State University of New York
 Albany *D*
 Buffalo *M, D*
 College of Environmental Science
  and Forestry *M, D*

Oregon
University of Oregon *M, D*

Pennsylvania
Lehigh University *M, D*

Puerto Rico
University of Puerto Rico
 Rio Piedras Campus *D*

Texas
Rice University *B, M, D*
University of North Texas *M, D*

Utah
University of Utah *M, D*

Vermont
Bennington College *B*

Wisconsin
Marquette University *M, D*

Physician assistant

Alabama
Northwest-Shoals Community College *A*
Oakwood College *A*
University of Alabama
 Birmingham *B*

California
California State University
 Dominguez Hills *B*
Loma Linda University *M*
Samuel Merritt College *M*

Colorado
Red Rocks Community College *C*
University of Colorado
 Health Sciences Center *M*

Connecticut
Quinnipiac University *B, M*

District of Columbia
George Washington University *C, B, M*
Howard University *C, B*

Florida
Barry University *M*
Nova Southeastern University *B*
University of Florida *B, M*

Georgia
Dalton State College *A*
Medical College of Georgia *B, M*
South University *B*

Idaho
Idaho State University *B*

Illinois
Finch University of Health Sciences/The
 Chicago Medical School *M*
Southern Illinois University
 Carbondale *A*
University of St. Francis *M*

Indiana
Butler University *B*
University of St. Francis *B*

Iowa
University of Iowa *M*
University of Osteopathic Medicine and
 Health Sciences
  Des Moines University -
  Osteopathic Medical Center *M*

Kansas
Wichita State University *B*

Kentucky
National College of Business &
 Technology
 Danville *A*
 Lexington *A*
 Pikeville *C*
University of Kentucky *M*

Maine
University of New England *M*

Massachusetts
Massachusetts College of Pharmacy and
 Health Sciences *M*
Northeastern University *M*
Simmons College *M, D*
Springfield College *B*
Western New England College *B, M*

Michigan
Central Michigan University *M*
Grand Valley State University *M*
Lansing Community College *A*
Wayne State University *M*
Western Michigan University *M*

Minnesota
Augsburg College *C, M*

Missouri
Rockhurst University *B*
St. Louis University *C, B, M*
Southwest Missouri State University *M*

Montana
Rocky Mountain College *B*

Nebraska
Union College *B*
University of Nebraska
 Medical Center *M*

New Jersey
Rutgers, The State University of New
 Jersey
  New Brunswick Regional
  Campus *B*
Seton Hall University *M*
University of Medicine and Dentistry of
 New Jersey
  School of Health Related
  Professions *B, M*

New Mexico
University of New Mexico *B*

New York
City University of New York
 City College *B*
 College of Staten Island *B*
D'Youville College *B*
Daemen College *M*
Hofstra University *B*
Hudson Valley Community College *A*
New York Institute of Technology *B*
Pace University *B*
Pace University:
 Pleasantville/Briarcliff *B*
Rochester Institute of Technology *B*

St. John's University *B*
State University of New York
 Health Science Center at
 Brooklyn *B*
 Health Science Center at Stony
 Brook *B*
 Stony Brook *B*
Touro College *B*
Wagner College *B*

North Carolina
Duke University *M*
East Carolina University *B*
High Point University *B*
Lenoir-Rhyne College *B*
Mars Hill College *B*
Methodist College *B, M*
Wake Forest University *M*

Ohio
Kettering College of Medical
 Arts *C, A, B*
Ohio Northern University *B*
University of Findlay *B*

Oklahoma
University of Oklahoma *M*

Oregon
Pacific University *M*

Pennsylvania
Arcadia University *M*
Carlow College *B*
Chatham College *M*
DeSales University *B, M*
Drexel University *B, M*
Duquesne University *B, M*
King's College *M*
Lock Haven University of
 Pennsylvania *M*
Marywood University *M*
Mount Aloysius College *B, M*
Philadelphia University *M*
Seton Hill University *B*
University of the Sciences in
 Philadelphia *B, M*

South Carolina
Medical University of South Carolina *B*

South Dakota
University of South Dakota *B*

Tennessee
Bethel College *A, M*
Carson-Newman College *T*
Trevecca Nazarene University *M*

Texas
San Antonio College *A*
University of Texas
 Health Science Center at San
 Antonio *B*
 Medical Branch at Galveston *M*
 Pan American *B*
 Southwestern Medical Center at
 Dallas *M*

Virginia
College of Health Sciences *B*
Shenandoah University *M*

Washington
University of Washington *B*

West Virginia
Alderson-Broaddus College *B, M*
Mountain State University *B, M*

Wisconsin
Marquette University *M*
University of Wisconsin
 La Crosse *B*
 Madison *B*

Physics

Alabama
Alabama Agricultural and Mechanical
 University *B, M*
Alabama State University *B*
Athens State University *B*
Auburn University *B, M, D, T*
Birmingham-Southern College *B, T*
Chattahoochee Valley Community
 College *A*
Jacksonville State University *B*
Northeast Alabama Community
 College *A*
Samford University *B*
Talladega College *B*
Tuskegee University *B*
University of Alabama *B, M, D*
University of Alabama
 Birmingham *B, M, D*
 Huntsville *B, M, D*
University of North Alabama *B*
University of South Alabama *B*

Alaska
University of Alaska
 Fairbanks *B, M, D*

Arizona
Arizona State University *B, M, D*
Arizona Western College *A*
Eastern Arizona College *A*
Northern Arizona University *B*
South Mountain Community College *A*
University of Arizona *B, M, D*

Arkansas
Arkansas State University *B*
Harding University *B*
Henderson State University *B*
Hendrix College *B*
Ouachita Baptist University *B*
Phillips Community College of the
 University of Arkansas *A*
University of Arkansas *B, M, D*
University of Arkansas
 Little Rock *B*
 Pine Bluff *B*
University of Central Arkansas *B*
University of the Ozarks *B*

California
Azusa Pacific University *B*
Bakersfield College *A*
Cabrillo College *A*
California Institute of Technology *B, D*
California Polytechnic State University:
 San Luis Obispo *B*
California State Polytechnic University:
 Pomona *B*
California State University
 Bakersfield *B*
 Chico *B*
 Dominguez Hills *B*
 Fresno *B, M*
 Fullerton *B, M*
 Hayward *B*
 Long Beach *B, M*
 Los Angeles *B, M*
 Northridge *B*
 Sacramento *B, M*
 San Bernardino *B*
 Stanislaus *B*
Cerritos Community College *A*
Chabot College *A*
Citrus College *A*
Claremont McKenna College *B*
College of the Siskiyous *A*
Columbia College *A*
Contra Costa College *A*
Cuesta College *C, A*
De Anza College *A*
East Los Angeles College *A*
Foothill College *A*
Glendale Community College *A*
Grossmont Community College *A*

Harvey Mudd College *B*
Humboldt State University *B*
Las Positas College *A*
Los Angeles Southwest College *A*
Loyola Marymount University *B*
MiraCosta College *A*
Monterey Peninsula College *A*
Moorpark College *A*
Occidental College *B*
Ohlone College *C*
Orange Coast College *A*
Pacific Union College *B*
Pitzer College *B*
Point Loma Nazarene University *B*
Pomona College *B*
St. Mary's College of California *B*
San Diego City College *A*
San Diego Mesa College *C, A*
San Diego State University *B, M*
San Francisco State University *B, M*
San Joaquin Delta College *A*
San Jose State University *B, M*
Santa Barbara City College *A*
Santa Clara University *B*
Santa Monica College *A*
Santa Rosa Junior College *A*
Santiago Canyon College *A*
Scripps College *B*
Sonoma State University *B*
Southwestern College *A*
Stanford University *B, M, D*
University of California
    Berkeley *B, D*
    Davis *B, M, D*
    Irvine *B, M, D*
    Los Angeles *B, M, D*
    Riverside *B, M, D*
    San Diego *B, M, D*
    Santa Barbara *B, M, D*
    Santa Cruz *B, M, D*
University of La Verne *B*
University of Redlands *B*
University of San Diego *B*
University of San Francisco *B*
University of Southern
    California *B, M, D*
University of the Pacific *B*
Ventura College *A*
West Valley College *A*
Whittier College *B*

Colorado

Colorado Christian University *B*
Colorado College *B*
Colorado School of Mines *M, D*
Colorado State University *B, M, D*
Colorado State University
    Pueblo *B, T*
Fort Lewis College *B*
Metropolitan State College of Denver *B*
Red Rocks Community College *A*
United States Air Force Academy *B*
University of Colorado
    Boulder *B, M, D*
    Colorado Springs *B*
    Denver *B*
University of Denver *B, M, D*
University of Northern Colorado *B, T*

Connecticut

Central Connecticut State University *B*
Connecticut College *B*
Fairfield University *B*
Southern Connecticut State University *B*
Trinity College *B*
University of Connecticut *B, M, D*
University of Hartford *B*
Wesleyan University *B, M, D*
Yale University *B, M, D*

Delaware

Delaware State University *B, M*
University of Delaware *B, M, D*

District of Columbia

American University *C, B*
Catholic University of America *B, M, D*

Gallaudet University *B*
George Washington University *B, M, D*
Georgetown University *B, D*
Howard University *B, M, D*
University of the District of Columbia *B*

Florida

Bethune-Cookman College *B*
Broward Community College *A*
Eckerd College *B*
Florida Agricultural and Mechanical
    University *B, M, D*
Florida Atlantic University *B, M, D*
Florida Institute of Technology *B, M, D*
Florida International University *B, M, D*
Florida Southern College *B*
Florida State University *B, M, D*
Gulf Coast Community College *A*
Indian River Community College *A*
Jacksonville University *B*
Manatee Community College *A*
Miami-Dade Community College *A*
New College of Florida *B*
Okaloosa-Walton Community College *A*
Palm Beach Community College *A*
Pensacola Junior College *A*
Polk Community College *A*
Rollins College *B*
South Florida Community College *A*
Stetson University *B*
University of Central Florida *B, M, D*
University of Florida *B, M, D*
University of Miami *B, M, D*
University of North Florida *B*
University of South Florida *B, M, D*
University of West Florida *B*

Georgia

Agnes Scott College *B*
Armstrong Atlantic State University *B*
Atlanta Metropolitan College *A*
Augusta State University *B*
Berry College *B, T*
Clark Atlanta University *B, M*
Clayton College and State University *A*
Covenant College *B*
Dalton State College *A*
Darton College *A*
Emory University *B, M, D*
Gainesville College *A*
Georgia Institute of Technology *B, M, D*
Georgia Perimeter College *A*
Georgia Southern University *B*
Georgia State University *B, M, D*
Macon State College *A*
Mercer University *B*
Middle Georgia College *A*
Morehouse College *B*
Morris Brown College *B*
North Georgia College & State
    University *B*
Oglethorpe University *B*
Oxford College of Emory University *B*
South Georgia College *A*
Southern Polytechnic State University *B*
Spelman College *B*
State University of West Georgia *B*
University of Georgia *B, M, D*
Valdosta State University *B*
Wesleyan College *B*
Young Harris College *A*

Hawaii

University of Hawaii
    Hilo *B*
    Manoa *B, M, D*

Idaho

Albertson College of Idaho *B*
Boise State University *B, T*
Brigham Young University - Idaho *B*
College of Southern Idaho *B*
Idaho State University *A, B, M*
North Idaho College *A*
Northwest Nazarene University *B*
University of Idaho *B, M, D*

Illinois

Augustana College *B, T*
Benedictine University *B, T*
Bradley University *B, T*
Chicago State University *B*
City Colleges of Chicago
    Harold Washington College *A*
    Kennedy-King College *A*
    Olive-Harvey College *A*
De Paul University *B, M, T*
Eastern Illinois University *B, T*
Elmhurst College *B, T*
Greenville College *B, T*
Illinois Central College *A*
Illinois College *B*
Illinois Institute of Technology *B, M, D*
Illinois State University *B, T*
Illinois Valley Community College *A*
Illinois Wesleyan University *B*
John A. Logan College *A*
John Wood Community College *A*
Judson College *B*
Kishwaukee College *A*
Knox College *B*
Lake Forest College *B*
Lewis University *B, T*
Lincoln College *A*
Lincoln Land Community College *A*
Loyola University of Chicago *B*
MacMurray College *B*
Millikin University *B*
Monmouth College *B, T*
North Central College *B, T*
North Park University *B*
Northeastern Illinois University *B, M*
Northern Illinois University *B, M, T*
Northwestern University *B, M, D*
Parkland College *A*
Principia College *B, T*
Roosevelt University *B*
Sauk Valley Community College *A*
South Suburban College of Cook
    County *A*
Southern Illinois University
    Carbondale *B, M*
Southern Illinois University
    Edwardsville *B, M*
Southwestern Illinois College *A*
Triton College *A*
University of Chicago *B, M, D*
University of Illinois
    Chicago *B, M, D*
    Urbana-Champaign *B, M, D*
Western Illinois University *B, M*
Wheaton College *B, T*

Indiana

Anderson University *B*
Ball State University *B, M*
Butler University *B*
DePauw University *B*
Earlham College *B*
Goshen College *B*
Grace College *B*
Hanover College *B*
Indiana State University *B, M, T*
Indiana University
    Bloomington *B, M, D*
    South Bend *B*
    Southeast *B*
Indiana University-Purdue University
    Fort Wayne *B, T*
Indiana University-Purdue University
    Indianapolis *B, M*
Manchester College *B, T*
Marian College *T*
Purdue University *B, M, D*
Purdue University
    Calumet *B*
Rose-Hulman Institute of Technology *B*
Taylor University *B*
University of Evansville *B*
University of Indianapolis *B*
University of Notre Dame *B, M, D*
Valparaiso University *B*

Vincennes University *A*
Wabash College *B*

Iowa

Buena Vista University *B, T*
Central College *B, T*
Coe College *B*
Cornell College *B, T*
Dordt College *B*
Drake University *B*
Ellsworth Community College *A*
Graceland University *T*
Grinnell College *B*
Iowa State University *B, M, D*
Luther College *B*
Maharishi University of Management *B*
Morningside College *B*
North Iowa Area Community College *A*
Northwestern College *T*
St. Ambrose University *B*
University of Iowa *B, M, D, T*
University of Northern Iowa *B, M*
Wartburg College *B*

Kansas

Allen County Community College *A*
Baker University *B*
Barton County Community College *A*
Benedictine College *B*
Bethel College *B*
Butler County Community College *A*
Central Christian College *A*
Emporia State University *B*
Fort Hays State University *B*
Fort Scott Community College *A*
Kansas City Kansas Community
    College *A*
Kansas State University *B, M, D*
Kansas Wesleyan University *B, T*
MidAmerica Nazarene University *B*
Pittsburg State University *B, M, T*
Pratt Community College *A*
Seward County Community College *A*
Southwestern College *B*
University of Kansas *B, M, D*
Washburn University of Topeka *B*
Wichita State University *B, M, T*

Kentucky

Berea College *B, T*
Campbellsville University *B*
Centre College *B*
Cumberland College *B, T*
Georgetown College *B*
Kentucky Wesleyan College *B, T*
Morehead State University *B*
Murray State University *B, M, T*
Thomas More College *A, B, T*
Transylvania University *B*
Union College *B*
University of Kentucky *B, M, D*
University of Louisville *B, M*

Louisiana

Centenary College of Louisiana *B, T*
Dillard University *B*
Grambling State University *B*
Louisiana State University
    Shreveport *B*
Louisiana State University and
    Agricultural and Mechanical
    College *B, M, D*
Louisiana Tech University *B, M*
Loyola University New Orleans *B*
McNeese State University *B*
Northwestern State University *B*
Southeastern Louisiana University *B*
Southern University
    New Orleans *B*
Southern University and Agricultural and
    Mechanical College *B, M*
Tulane University *B, M, D*
University of Louisiana at
    Lafayette *B, M*
University of Louisiana at Monroe *B*
University of New Orleans *B, M, D*
Xavier University of Louisiana *B*

Maine

Bates College *B*
Bowdoin College *B*
Colby College *B*
University of Maine *B, M, D*
University of Southern Maine *B*

Maryland

Allegany College *A*
Cecil Community College *A*
College of Notre Dame of Maryland *B*
Community College of Baltimore County
    Catonsville *A*
    Dundalk *A*
    Essex *A*
Frostburg State University *B, T*
Goucher College *B*
Harford Community College *A*
Johns Hopkins University *B, D*
Loyola College in Maryland *B*
McDaniel College *B*
Morgan State University *B*
St. Mary's College of Maryland *B*
Salisbury University *B*
Towson University *B*
United States Naval Academy *B*
University of Maryland
    Baltimore County *B, M, D*
    College Park *M, D*
Washington College *B*

Massachusetts

Amherst College *B*
Boston College *B, M, D*
Boston University *B, M, D*
Brandeis University *B, M, D*
Bridgewater State College *B*
Clark University *R, M, D*
College of the Holy Cross *B*
Gordon College *B*
Hampshire College *B*
Harvard College *B*
Massachusetts College of Liberal Arts *B*
Massachusetts Institute of
    Technology *B, M, D*
Merrimack College *B*
Mount Holyoke College *B*
Northeastern University *B, M, D*
Simon's Rock College of Bard *B*
Smith College *B*
Suffolk University *B*
Tufts University *B, M, D*
University of Massachusetts
    Amherst *B, M, D*
    Boston *B*
    Dartmouth *B, M*
    Lowell *B, M, D*
Wellesley College *B*
Wheaton College *B*
Williams College *B*
Worcester Polytechnic Institute *B, M, D*

Michigan

Adrian College *A, B, T*
Alma College *B, T*
Andrews University *B*
Aquinas College *B*
Calvin College *B, T*
Central Michigan University *B, M*
Eastern Michigan University *B, M*
Gogebic Community College *A*
Grand Valley State University *B*
Hillsdale College *B*
Hope College *B*
Kalamazoo College *B, T*
Kellogg Community College *A*
Kettering University *B*
Kirtland Community College *A*
Lawrence Technological University *B*
Michigan State University *B, M, D*
Michigan Technological
    University *B, M, D, T*
Northern Michigan University *B, T*
Oakland University *B, M, T*
Saginaw Valley State University *B*
University of Michigan *B, M, D, T*

University of Michigan
    Dearborn *B*
    Flint *B, T*
Wayne State University *B, M, D*
Western Michigan University *B, M, D*

Minnesota

Augsburg College *B*
Bemidji State University *B*
Bethel College *B*
Carleton College *B*
College of St. Benedict *B*
College of St. Catherine *B*
Concordia College: Moorhead *B*
Gustavus Adolphus College *B*
Hamline University *B*
Macalester College *B, T*
Minnesota State University
    Mankato *B, M, T*
    Moorhead *B*
St. Cloud State University *B*
St. John's University *B*
St. Mary's University of Minnesota *B*
St. Olaf College *B*
University of Minnesota
    Duluth *B, M*
    Morris *B*
    Twin Cities *B, M, D*
University of St. Thomas *B*
Vermilion Community College *A*
Winona State University *B*

Mississippi

Itawamba Community College *A*
Mary Holmes College *A*
Millsaps College *B, T*
Mississippi College *B*
Mississippi State University *B, M*
University of Mississippi *B, M, D, T*
University of Southern Mississippi *B, M*

Missouri

Central Methodist College *B*
Central Missouri State University *B*
Crowder College *A*
East Central College *A*
Lincoln University *B*
Missouri Southern State College *B, T*
Northwest Missouri State University *B*
Rockhurst University *B*
St. Louis Community College
    St. Louis Community College at
        Florissant Valley *A*
    St. Louis Community College at
        Forest Park *A*
St. Louis University *B*
Southeast Missouri State University *B*
Southwest Missouri State University *B*
Truman State University *B*
University of Missouri
    Columbia *B, M, D*
    Kansas City *B, M*
    Rolla *B, M, D, T*
    St. Louis *B, M, D*
Washington University in St.
    Louis *B, M, D*
Westminster College *B*
William Jewell College *B*

Montana

Montana State University
    Billings *T*
    Bozeman *B, M, D*
University of Montana-Missoula *B, M*

Nebraska

Chadron State College *B*
Creighton University *B, M*
Doane College *B*
Hastings College *B*
Nebraska Wesleyan University *B*
Northeast Community College *A*
Union College *B*
University of Nebraska
    Kearney *B, T*
    Lincoln *B, M, D*
    Omaha *B*

Western Nebraska Community
    College *A*

Nevada

Great Basin College *A*
University of Nevada
    Las Vegas *B, M, D*
    Reno *B, M, D*

New Hampshire

Dartmouth College *B, M, D, T*
St. Anselm College *B*
University of New Hampshire *B, M, D*

New Jersey

The College of New Jersey *B, T*
Drew University *B*
Georgian Court College *B*
Middlesex County College *B*
Montclair State University *B*
New Jersey City University *B*
New Jersey Institute of
    Technology *B, M, D*
Princeton University *B, M, D*
Ramapo College of New Jersey *B*
Richard Stockton College of New
    Jersey *B*
Rider University *B*
Rowan University *B*
Rutgers, The State University of New
    Jersey
    Camden Regional Campus *B, T*
    New Brunswick Regional
        Campus *B, M, D*
    Newark Regional Campus *B*
St. Peter's College *B*
Salem Community College *A*
Seton Hall University *B, T*
Stevens Institute of Technology *M, D*
Thomas Edison State College *A, B*

New Mexico

Eastern New Mexico University *B*
New Mexico Highlands University *B*
New Mexico Institute of Mining and
    Technology *B, M, D*
New Mexico Junior College *A*
New Mexico State University *B, M, D*
San Juan College *A*
University of New Mexico *B, M, D*

New York

Adelphi University *B*
Adirondack Community College *A*
Alfred University *B*
Bard College *B*
Barnard College *B*
Canisius College *B*
City University of New York
    Brooklyn College *B, M*
    City College *B, M, D, T*
    College of Staten Island *B, T*
    Hunter College *B*
    Kingsborough Community
        College *A*
    Queens College *B, M*
    York College *B*
Clarkson University *B, M, D*
Colgate University *B*
College of Mount St. Vincent *B*
College of New Rochelle *B, T*
Columbia University
    Columbia College *B*
Cornell University *B, M, D*
Excelsior College *B*
Fordham University *B, M, D*
Hamilton College *B*
Hartwick College *B, T*
Hobart and William Smith Colleges *B*
Hofstra University *B*
Houghton College *B*
Iona College *B*
Ithaca College *B, T*
Le Moyne College *B*
Long Island University
    C. W. Post Campus *B*
Manhattan College *B*

Manhattanville College *B*
Monroe Community College *A*
New York Institute of Technology *B*
New York University *B, M, D*
Pace University *B, T*
Pace University:
    Pleasantville/Briarcliff *B*
Polytechnic University *B*
Rensselaer Polytechnic Institute *B, M, D*
Roberts Wesleyan College *B*
Rochester Institute of Technology *A, B*
St. Bonaventure University *B, T*
St. John Fisher College *B*
St. John's University *B*
St. Lawrence University *B, T*
Sarah Lawrence College *B*
Skidmore College *B*
State University of New York
    Albany *B, M, D*
    Binghamton *B, M*
    Buffalo *B, M, D*
    College at Brockport *B, T*
    College at Buffalo *B*
    College at Cortland *B*
    College at Fredonia *B, T*
    College at Geneseo *B, T*
    College at Oneonta *B*
    College at Plattsburgh *B*
    College at Potsdam *B, T*
    College of Agriculture and
        Technology at Morrisville *A*
    New Paltz *B, T*
    Oswego *B*
    Stony Brook *B, M, D, T*
Suffolk County Community College *A*
Syracuse University *B, M, D*
Union College *B*
United States Military Academy *B*
University of Rochester *B, M, D*
Utica College *B*
Vassar College *B*
Wagner College *B, T*
Wells College *B*
Yeshiva University *B*

North Carolina

Appalachian State University *B*
Barber-Scotia College *B*
Davidson College *B*
Duke University *B, M, D*
East Carolina University *B, M*
Elizabeth City State University *B*
Elon University *B*
Guilford College *B*
Johnson C. Smith University *B*
Lenoir-Rhyne College *B*
North Carolina Agricultural and
    Technical State University *B, M, T*
North Carolina Central University *B*
North Carolina State University *B, M, D*
Shaw University *B*
University of North Carolina
    Asheville *B, T*
    Chapel Hill *B, M, D*
    Charlotte *B, M, T*
    Greensboro *B*
    Wilmington *B*
Wake Forest University *B, M, D*

North Dakota

Dickinson State University *T*
Minot State University *B*
North Dakota State
    University *B, M, D, T*
University of North Dakota *B, M, D, T*

Ohio

Antioch College *B*
Ashland University *B*
Baldwin-Wallace College *B, T*
Bluffton College *B*
Bowling Green State University *B, M*
Case Western Reserve
    University *B, M, D*
Cedarville University *B, T*
Cleveland State University *B, M, T*

473

College of Wooster *B*
Denison University *B*
Heidelberg College *B*
Hiram College *B*
Jefferson Community College *A*
John Carroll University *B, M*
Kent State University *B, M, D, T*
Kent State University
    Stark Campus *B*
Kenyon College *B*
Lorain County Community College *A*
Miami University
    Middletown Campus *A*
    Oxford Campus *B, M, T*
Mount Union College *B*
Muskingum College *B*
Oberlin College *B*
Ohio Northern University *B*
Ohio State University
    Columbus Campus *B, M, D*
Ohio University *B, M, D*
Ohio Wesleyan University *B*
Otterbein College *B*
Sinclair Community College *A*
University of Akron *B, M*
University of Cincinnati *B, M, D, T*
University of Dayton *B, M*
University of Rio Grande *B, T*
University of Toledo *B, M, D*
Wittenberg University *B*
Wright State University *B, M*
Xavier University *B*
Youngstown State University *B*

Oklahoma

Cameron University *B*
East Central University *B, T*
Eastern Oklahoma State College *A*
Northeastern State University *B*
Northern Oklahoma College *A*
Oklahoma Baptist University *B, T*
Oklahoma City Community College *A*
Oklahoma City University *B*
Oklahoma State University *B, M, D*
Oral Roberts University *B*
Rogers State University *A*
Rose State College *A*
Southeastern Oklahoma State
    University *B*
Southern Nazarene University *B*
Southwestern Oklahoma State
    University *B*
Tulsa Community College *A*
University of Central Oklahoma *B, M*
University of Oklahoma *B, M, D*
University of Science and Arts of
    Oklahoma *B*
University of Tulsa *B*

Oregon

Central Oregon Community College *A*
Chemeketa Community College *A*
Eastern Oregon University *B, T*
Lewis & Clark College *B*
Linfield College *B*
Linn-Benton Community College *A*
Oregon State University *B, M, D*
Pacific University *B*
Portland State University *B, M*
Reed College *B*
Southern Oregon University *B*
University of Oregon *B, M, D*
University of Portland *B*
Willamette University *B*

Pennsylvania

Albright College *B, T*
Allegheny College *B*
Bloomsburg University of
    Pennsylvania *B, T*
Bryn Mawr College *B, M, D*
Bucknell University *B*
California University of Pennsylvania *B*
Carnegie Mellon University *B, M, D*
Chatham College *B*

Community College of Allegheny
    County *A*
Dickinson College *B*
Drexel University *B, M, D*
Duquesne University *B*
East Stroudsburg University of
    Pennsylvania *B*
Edinboro University of
    Pennsylvania *B, T*
Elizabethtown College *B*
Franklin & Marshall College *B*
Geneva College *B, T*
Gettysburg College *B*
Grove City College *B*
Haverford College *B, T*
Immaculata University *A*
Indiana University of
    Pennsylvania *B, M, T*
Juniata College *B*
Kutztown University of
    Pennsylvania *B, T*
Lafayette College *B*
Lebanon Valley College of
    Pennsylvania *B, T*
Lehigh University *B, M, D*
Lincoln University *B*
Lock Haven University of
    Pennsylvania *B*
Lycoming College *B*
Mercyhurst College *B*
Messiah College *B*
Millersville University of
    Pennsylvania *B, T*
Moravian College *B, T*
Muhlenberg College *B, T*
Northampton County Area Community
    College *A*
Penn State
    Abington *B*
    Altoona *B*
    Beaver *B*
    Berks *B*
    Delaware County *B*
    Dubois *B*
    Erie, The Behrend College *B*
    Fayette *B*
    Hazleton *B*
    Lehigh Valley *B*
    McKeesport *B*
    Mont Alto *B*
    Schuylkill - Capital College *B*
    Shenango *B*
    University Park *B, M, D*
    Wilkes-Barre *B*
    Worthington Scranton *B*
    York *B*
St. Joseph's University *B*
St. Vincent College *B*
Seton Hill University *B, T*
Shippensburg University of
    Pennsylvania *B, T*
Slippery Rock University of
    Pennsylvania *B, M, T*
Swarthmore College *B*
Temple University *B, M, D*
Thiel College *B*
University of Pennsylvania *B, M, D*
University of Pittsburgh *B, M, D*
University of Scranton *B, T*
Villanova University *B*
Washington and Jefferson College *B*
West Chester University of
    Pennsylvania *B*
Widener University *B*
York College of Pennsylvania *A*

Puerto Rico

Pontifical Catholic University of Puerto
    Rico *B*
University of Puerto Rico
    Cayey University College *B*
    Mayaguez Campus *B, M*
    Ponce *A*
    Rio Piedras Campus *B, M*

Rhode Island

Brown University *B, M, D*
Rhode Island College *B*
University of Rhode Island *B, M, D*

South Carolina

Benedict College *B*
Charleston Southern University *B*
The Citadel *B*
Clemson University *B, M, D*
College of Charleston *B, T*
Erskine College *B*
Francis Marion University *B*
Furman University *B, T*
Presbyterian College *B*
South Carolina State University *B*
University of South Carolina *B, M, D*
Wofford College *B, T*

South Dakota

Augustana College *B, T*
South Dakota School of Mines and
    Technology *B*
South Dakota State University *B, M*
University of South Dakota *B, M*

Tennessee

Austin Peay State University *B*
Belmont University *B, T*
Christian Brothers University *B*
Columbia State Community College *A*
East Tennessee State University *B*
Fisk University *B, M*
King College *B, T*
Lane College *B*
Maryville College *T*
Middle Tennessee State University *B*
Rhodes College *B, T*
Roane State Community College *A*
Southern Adventist University *B*
Tennessee State University *B*
Tennessee Technological University *B, T*
Trevecca Nazarene University *B*
Union University *B, T*
University of Memphis *B, M*
University of Tennessee
    Chattanooga *B*
    Knoxville *B, M, D*
Vanderbilt University *B, M, D*

Texas

Abilene Christian University *B*
Amarillo College *A*
Angelina College *A*
Angelo State University *B, T*
Austin College *B*
Austin Community College *A*
Baylor University *B, M, D*
Blinn College *A*
Brazosport College *A*
Central Texas College *A*
Coastal Bend College *A*
Del Mar College *A*
El Paso Community College *A*
Frank Phillips College *A*
Galveston College *A*
Grayson County College *A*
Hardin-Simmons University *B*
Hill College *A*
Houston Baptist University *B*
Howard College *A*
Kilgore College *A*
Lamar University *B*
Laredo Community College *A*
Lon Morris College *A*
McMurry University *B*
Midland College *A*
Midwestern State University *B*
Panola College *A*
Paris Junior College *A*
Prairie View A&M University *B*
Rice University *B, M, D*
St. Mary's University *B*
Sam Houston State University *B, M*
South Plains College *A*
Southern Methodist University *B, M, D*

Southwest Texas State
    University *B, M, T*
Southwestern Adventist University *B, T*
Southwestern University *B, T*
Stephen F. Austin State
    University *B, M, T*
Tarleton State University *B*
Texas A&M University *B, M, D*
Texas A&M University
    Commerce *B, M*
    Kingsville *B, M*
Texas Christian University *B, M, D, T*
Texas Lutheran University *B*
Texas Tech University *B, M, D*
Trinity University *B*
Trinity Valley Community College *A*
Tyler Junior College *A*
University of Dallas *B*
University of Houston *B, M, D*
University of North Texas *B, M, D*
University of Texas
    Arlington *B, M, D*
    Austin *B, M, D*
    Dallas *B, M, D*
    El Paso *B, M*
    Pan American *B*
    San Antonio *B*
University of the Incarnate Word *B*
West Texas A&M University *B, T*
Western Texas College *A*
Wharton County Junior College *A*

Utah

Brigham Young University *B, M, D*
Dixie State College of Utah *A*
Salt Lake Community College *A*
Snow College *A*
University of Utah *B, M, D*
Utah State University *B, M, D*
Utah Valley State College *A, B*
Weber State University *B*
Westminster College *B*

Vermont

Bennington College *B*
Marlboro College *B*
Middlebury College *B*
Norwich University *B*
St. Michael's College *B*
University of Vermont *B, M*

Virginia

Bridgewater College *B*
College of William and Mary *B, M, D*
Emory & Henry College *B, T*
George Mason University *B*
Hampden-Sydney College *B*
Hampton University *B, M, D*
Hollins University *B*
James Madison University *B*
Longwood University *B, T*
Lynchburg College *B*
Mary Baldwin College *B*
Mary Washington College *B*
Norfolk State University *B*
Old Dominion University *B, M, D*
Randolph-Macon College *B*
Randolph-Macon Woman's College *B*
Roanoke College *B, T*
Sweet Briar College *B*
University of Richmond *B, T*
University of Virginia *B, M, D*
Virginia Commonwealth
    University *B, M*
Virginia Military Institute *B*
Virginia Polytechnic Institute and State
    University *B, M, D, T*
Virginia State University *B, M*
Washington and Lee University *B*

Washington

Central Washington University *B*
Centralia College *A*
Eastern Washington University *B, T*
Everett Community College *A*
Gonzaga University *B*
Olympic College *A*

Pacific Lutheran University *B*
Seattle Pacific University *B*
Seattle University *B*
University of Puget Sound *B, T*
University of Washington *B, M, D*
Walla Walla College *B*
Washington State University *B, M, D*
Western Washington University *B, T*
Whitman College *B*
Whitworth College *B, T*

West Virginia

Bethany College *B*
Marshall University *B*
Potomac State College of West Virginia
 University *A*
West Virginia State College *B*
West Virginia University *B, M, D, T*
West Virginia Wesleyan College *B*
Wheeling Jesuit University *B*

Wisconsin

Beloit College *B*
Carthage College *B, T*
Lawrence University *B, T*
Northland College *T*
St. Norbert College *B, T*
University of Wisconsin
 Eau Claire *B*
 Green Bay *B*
 La Crosse *B, T*
 Madison *B, M, D*
 Milwaukee *B, M, D*
 Oshkosh *B, M*
 Parkside *B, T*
 River Falls *B*
 Stevens Point *B, T*
 Whitewater *B, T*

Wyoming

Casper College *A*
University of Wyoming *B, M, D*
Western Wyoming Community
 College *A*

Physics teacher education

Alabama

Athens State University *B*
Birmingham-Southern College *T*

Arizona

Arizona State University *B, T*
Northern Arizona University *R, T*
Prescott College *T*
University of Arizona *B, M*

Arkansas

Arkansas State University *B, T*
Harding University *B, T*
Ouachita Baptist University *B, T*
Southern Arkansas University *B, T*
University of Central Arkansas *T*

California

Azusa Pacific University *T*
California State Polytechnic University:
 Pomona *T*
California State University
 San Bernardino *T*
San Francisco State University *B, T*
University of the Pacific *T*

Colorado

Colorado State University *T*
Colorado State University
 Pueblo *T*
Fort Lewis College *T*

Connecticut

Central Connecticut State University *B*
Southern Connecticut State
 University *B, T*

Delaware

Delaware State University *B, M*
University of Delaware *B, T*

Florida

Bethune-Cookman College *B, T*
Florida Agricultural and Mechanical
 University *T*
Florida Institute of Technology *B*
Gulf Coast Community College *A*
University of West Florida *B, T*

Georgia

Agnes Scott College *T*
Atlanta Metropolitan College *A*
Georgia Southern University *B*
State University of West Georgia *B*

Hawaii

University of Hawaii
 Manoa *B, T*

Idaho

Boise State University *T*
Brigham Young University - Idaho *T*
University of Idaho *T*

Illinois

Augustana College *B, T*
Benedictine University *T*
Elmhurst College *B*
Greenville College *B*
Illinois College *T*
Judson College *B, T*
Lewis University *T*
Loyola University of Chicago *T*
North Park University *T*
Northwestern University *B, T*
Sauk Valley Community College *A*
University of Illinois
 Chicago *B*
Wheaton College *T*

Indiana

Ball State University *T*
Butler University *T*
Goshen College *B*
Indiana University
 Bloomington *B, T*
 South Bend *B, T*
Indiana University-Purdue University
 Fort Wayne *B, T*
Manchester College *B, T*
Purdue University
 Calumet *B*
Taylor University *B, T*
University of Evansville *B*
University of Indianapolis *B, T*
University of Southern Indiana *T*
Valparaiso University *B*
Vincennes University *A*

Iowa

Buena Vista University *B, T*
Central College *T*
Cornell College *B, T*
Dordt College *B*
Drake University *T*
Ellsworth Community College *A*
Graceland University *T*
Grand View College *B, T*
Iowa State University *T*
Loras College *T*
Luther College *B*
Maharishi University of Management *T*
Morningside College *B*
Northwestern College *T*
St. Ambrose University *B, T*
University of Iowa *B, T*
Wartburg College *T*
William Penn University *B*

Kansas

Benedictine College *B, T*
Bethel College *T*
Emporia State University *T*
Garden City Community College *A*
Pittsburg State University *B, T*
University of Kansas *B, T*

Kentucky

Bellarmine University *B, M, T*

Campbellsville University *B*
Cumberland College *B, T*
Kentucky Wesleyan College *T*
Murray State University *B, M, T*
Thomas More College *B*
Union College *M*

Louisiana

Louisiana State University
 Shreveport *B*
McNeese State University *T*
Northwestern State University *B*
Southern University and Agricultural and
 Mechanical College *B*
University of New Orleans *B*

Maine

University of Southern Maine *T*

Maryland

St. Mary's College of Maryland *T*

Massachusetts

Bridgewater State College *M, T*
Harvard College *T*
Tufts University *T*
University of Massachusetts
 Dartmouth *T*

Michigan

Alma College *T*
Andrews University *M, T*
Calvin College *B*
Central Michigan University *B*
Eastern Michigan University *B, M, T*
Grand Valley State University *M, T*
Hope College *T*
Michigan Technological University *T*
Northern Michigan University *B, T*
University of Michigan
 Flint *T*
Western Michigan University *B*

Minnesota

Augsburg College *T*
Bethel College *B*
College of St. Catherine *T*
Concordia College: Moorhead *B, T*
Gustavus Adolphus College *T*
Minnesota State University
 Mankato *B, M, T*
 Moorhead *B, T*
St. Cloud State University *T*
St. Mary's University of Minnesota *B*
St. Olaf College *T*
University of Minnesota
 Morris *T*
University of St. Thomas *B, T*
Vermilion Community College *A*
Winona State University *B, T*

Mississippi

Itawamba Community College *A*
Mississippi College *B*
Mississippi State University *T*

Missouri

Central Methodist College *B*
Central Missouri State University *B, T*
Lincoln University *B, T*
Missouri Southern State College *B, T*
Northwest Missouri State
 University *B, T*
Rockhurst University *B*
Southwest Missouri State University *B*
Truman State University *M, T*
University of Missouri
 Columbia *B*
 St. Louis *T*
Washington University in St.
 Louis *B, M, T*

Montana

Montana State University
 Billings *B, T*
Montana Tech of the University of
 Montana *T*
Rocky Mountain College *T*
University of Montana-Missoula *T*

Nebraska

Chadron State College *B*
Concordia University *B, T*
Creighton University *T*
Doane College *T*
Hastings College *B, M, T*
Nebraska Wesleyan University *T*
Peru State College *B, T*
Union College *T*
University of Nebraska
 Kearney *B*
 Lincoln *B, T*

New Hampshire

University of New Hampshire *T*

New Jersey

The College of New Jersey *B, T*
St. Peter's College *T*

New Mexico

New Mexico Institute of Mining and
 Technology *M*

New York

Adelphi University *M*
Alfred University *M*
Canisius College *B, M, T*
City University of New York
 Brooklyn College *B*
 City College *B*
 Hunter College *B, D, T*
 Queens College *T*
Colgate University *M*
D'Youville College *M, T*
Fordham University *M, T*
Hofstra University *B, M*
Houghton College *B, T*
Ithaca College *B, T*
Long Island University
 C. W. Post Campus *B, T*
Manhattan College *B, T*
New York Institute of Technology *B, T*
New York University *B, M, T*
Pace University *B, T*
Pace University:
 Pleasantville/Briarcliff *B, T*
Roberts Wesleyan College *B, T*
St. John Fisher College *B, T*
St. John's University *B, M, T*
St. Lawrence University *T*
State University of New York
 Albany *B, M, T*
 Binghamton *M*
 Buffalo *T*
 College at Brockport *B, M, T*
 College at Buffalo *B*
 College at Cortland *B, M*
 College at Fredonia *B, T*
 College at Geneseo *B, M, T*
 College at Oneonta *B, T*
 College at Plattsburgh *B, M*
 College at Potsdam *B, M, T*
 New Paltz *B, T*
 Oswego *B, M*
 Stony Brook *T*
Syracuse University *B, M, T*
Vassar College *T*
Wagner College *T*
Wells College *T*

North Carolina

North Carolina Agricultural and
 Technical State University *B, T*
North Carolina Central University *B, M*
University of North Carolina
 Greensboro *B, M, T*
 Wilmington *B*
Wake Forest University *M, T*

North Dakota

Minot State University *B*
North Dakota State University *B, T*
University of North Dakota *T*

Ohio

Baldwin-Wallace College *T*
Bluffton College *B*

Bowling Green State University *B, M*
Case Western Reserve University *T*
Cedarville University *B, T*
Hiram College *T*
John Carroll University *T*
Kent State University *T*
Kent State University
    Stark Campus *B*
Malone College *B*
Miami University
    Oxford Campus *B, M, T*
Mount Union College *T*
Mount Vernon Nazarene University *B, T*
Ohio Dominican College *B, T*
Ohio Northern University *B*
Otterbein College *B*
University of Akron *B, T*
University of Dayton *B, M, T*
University of Rio Grande *B, T*
University of Toledo *M, T*
Xavier University *B*
Youngstown State University *B, M*

Oklahoma
East Central University *T*
Eastern Oklahoma State College *A*
Northeastern State University *T*
Oklahoma Baptist University *B, T*
Oklahoma State University *M*
University of Central Oklahoma *B*
University of Tulsa *T*

Oregon
Linfield College *T*
Oregon State University *M*
Portland State University *T*
University of Portland *T*

Pennsylvania
Albright College *T*
California University of
    Pennsylvania *B, T*
Chatham College *M*
Dickinson College *T*
Duquesne University *B, T*
Geneva College *B, T*
Gettysburg College *T*
Grove City College *B, T*
Juniata College *B, T*
Lebanon Valley College of
    Pennsylvania *B, T*
Lock Haven University of
    Pennsylvania *B, T*
Lycoming College *T*
Moravian College *T*
St. Vincent College *B, T*
Slippery Rock University of
    Pennsylvania *M, T*
Thiel College *B*
Villanova University *T*
Widener University *T*
Wilkes University *M, T*

Puerto Rico
Pontifical Catholic University of Puerto
    Rico *B, T*

Rhode Island
Rhode Island College *B*

South Carolina
Furman University *T*
Wofford College *T*

South Dakota
Augustana College *B, T*
Dakota State University *B, T*
South Dakota State University *B*
University of South Dakota *T*

Tennessee
Belmont University *T*
Christian Brothers University *B, M, T*
King College *T*
Maryville College *B, T*
Southern Adventist University *B*
Tennessee Technological University *T*

Texas
Abilene Christian University *B, T*
Baylor University *B, T*
Del Mar College *A*
Hardin-Simmons University *B, T*
Houston Baptist University *T*
Lamar University *T*
Laredo Community College *A*
St. Mary's University *T*
Tarleton State University *T*
Texas A&M University
    Commerce *T*
    Kingsville *T*
Texas Christian University *T*
University of Dallas *T*
University of Houston *T*
University of Houston
    Clear Lake *T*
University of Texas
    Arlington *T*
    San Antonio *T*
West Texas A&M University *T*

Utah
Brigham Young University *B*
Utah State University *B*
Weber State University *B*

Vermont
Castleton State College *B, T*

Virginia
Bridgewater College *T*
Hampton University *M*
Hollins University *T*
Longwood University *B, T*
Radford University *B, T*
Virginia Wesleyan College *T*

Washington
Central Washington University *T*
Washington State University *T*
Western Washington University *B, T*
Whitworth College *B, T*

West Virginia
Fairmont State College *B*
Wheeling Jesuit University *T*

Wisconsin
Carthage College *T*
Lawrence University *T*
Northland College *T*
St. Norbert College *T*
University of Wisconsin
    Green Bay *T*
    La Crosse *B, T*
    Parkside *T*
    River Falls *T*

Physiology

District of Columbia
Georgetown University *M, D*

Georgia
Medical College of Georgia *M, D*

Hawaii
University of Hawaii
    Manoa *M, D*

Illinois
Finch University of Health Sciences/The
    Chicago Medical School *M, D*
Southern Illinois University
    Carbondale *B, M, D*
University of Illinois
    Urbana-Champaign *B, M, D*

Indiana
Indiana University
    Bloomington *M, D*
Indiana University-Purdue University
    Indianapolis *M, D*

Iowa
University of Iowa *M, D*

Kansas
University of Kansas Medical
    Center *M, D*

Missouri
University of Missouri
    Columbia *M, D*

New York
State University of New York
    Buffalo *M, D*
    Health Science Center at Stony
        Brook *D*
    Stony Brook *D*

Ohio
University of Akron *B, M*

Oklahoma
Oklahoma State University *B*
University of Oklahoma *M, D*

Pennsylvania
Penn State
    University Park *M, D*

Texas
University of Texas
    Houston Health Science
        Center *M, D*

Utah
Brigham Young University *B*
University of Utah *D*

Virginia
University of Virginia *D*

Piano/organ

Alabama
Birmingham-Southern College *B*
Huntingdon College *B*
Samford University *B*

Arkansas
John Brown University *B*
Ouachita Baptist University *B*
University of Central Arkansas *B*

California
Bethesda Christian University *B, M*
California Institute of the Arts *C, B, M*
California State University
    Fullerton *B, M*
    Long Beach *B, M*
Master's College *B*
Ohlone College *C*
San Diego State University *M*
San Francisco State University *B*
University of Southern
    California *B, M, D*
University of the Pacific *B*

Connecticut
University of Hartford *B, M*

Delaware
University of Delaware *B*

District of Columbia
Catholic University of America *B, M, D*
Howard University *B*

Florida
Florida State University *B, M, D*
Hobe Sound Bible College *B*
Palm Beach Atlantic University *B*
Southeastern College of the Assemblies
    of God *B*
Stetson University *B*
University of Miami *B, M, D*

Georgia
Clayton College and State University *C*
Columbus State University *B, M*
Shorter College *B*

Hawaii
Brigham Young University-Hawaii *B*

Idaho
Brigham Young University - Idaho *A*

Illinois
Augustana College *B*
Benedictine University *B*
Blackburn College *B, T*
Judson College *B*
Lincoln College *A*
Millikin University *B*
Moody Bible Institute *B*
North Park University *B*
Northwestern University *B, D*
Olivet Nazarene University *B*
Roosevelt University *C, B, M*
Trinity Christian College *B*
Trinity International University *B*

Indiana
American Conservatory of
    Music *C, B, M, D*
Ancilla College *C*
Ball State University *B*
Butler University *B, M*
Goshen College *B*
Grace College *B*
Indiana University
    Bloomington *B*
Indiana University-Purdue University
    Fort Wayne *B*
Martin University *B*
Saint Mary's College *B*
University of Indianapolis *B*
Valparaiso University *M*
Vincennes University *A*

Iowa
Clarke College *B*
Dordt College *B*
Drake University *B*
Luther College *B*
Simpson College *B*
University of Iowa *B*
Waldorf College *B*

Kansas
Central Christian College *A*
MidAmerica Nazarene University *T*
Pittsburg State University *B*
Tabor College *B*
University of Kansas *B, M, D*

Kentucky
Campbellsville University *B*

Louisiana
Centenary College of Louisiana *B, T*
Loyola University New Orleans *B*
Nicholls State University *B*

Maine
University of Southern Maine *B*

Maryland
Columbia Union College *B*
Johns Hopkins University *B, M, D*
Johns Hopkins University: Peabody
    Conservatory of Music *B, M, D*
Washington Bible College *B*

Massachusetts
Anna Maria College *B*
Berklee College of Music *B*
Boston Conservatory *B, M*
Boston University *B, M, D*
New England Conservatory of
    Music *B, M, D*

Michigan
Calvin College *B*
Northwestern Michigan College *A*
Oakland University *B*
University of Michigan *B, M, T*

Minnesota
Bethel College *B*
Concordia College: Moorhead *B*

Minnesota State University
  Mankato *B, M, T*
  Moorhead *B*
Northwestern College *B*

Mississippi
Blue Mountain College *B*
Mississippi College *B*

Missouri
Drury University · *B*
Hannibal-LaGrange College *B*
University of Missouri
  Kansas City *B, M, D*
Webster University *M*

Nebraska
Concordia University *B, T*
Hastings College *B*

New Hampshire
University of New Hampshire *B*

New Jersey
Rider University *B, M*

New York
Bard College *B*
City University of New York
  City College *B*
Eastman School of Music of the
  University of Rochester *B, M, D*
Houghton College *B*
Ithaca College *B, M*
Juilliard School *B, M, D*
Manhattan School of Music *B, M, D*
Mannes College of Music *B, M*
New York University *B*
Roberts Wesleyan College *B*
Sarah Lawrence College *B*
State University of New York
  College at Fredonia *B*
  New Paltz *B, M*
Syracuse University *B, M*
University of Rochester *M, D*

North Carolina
Campbell University *B*
Gardner-Webb University *B*
Meredith College *B*
Wingate University *B*

Ohio
Baldwin-Wallace College *B*
Bowling Green State University *B, M*
Kent State University *B*
Kent State University
  Stark Campus *B*
Oberlin College *B, M*
Ohio State University
  Columbus Campus *B*
Ohio University *B*
University of Akron *B, M*
University of Cincinnati *B, M, D*
Youngstown State University *B, M*

Oklahoma
East Central University *B, T*
Northeastern State University *B*
Northwestern Oklahoma State
  University *B*
Oklahoma Baptist University *B*
Oklahoma Christian University of
  Science and Arts *B*
Oklahoma City University *B*
Oral Roberts University *B*
Southwestern Oklahoma State
  University *B*
University of Central Oklahoma *B*
University of Oklahoma *B, M, D*

Oregon
Western Baptist College *B*
Willamette University *B*

Pennsylvania
Carnegie Mellon University *B, M*
Gettysburg College *B*
Mercyhurst College *B*

Penn State
  University Park *M*
Temple University *B, M*
West Chester University of
  Pennsylvania *M*

Puerto Rico
Conservatory of Music of Puerto Rico *B*

South Carolina
Coker College *B*
Furman University *B*
North Greenville College *B*
South Carolina State University *B*
University of South Carolina *M, D*

Tennessee
Belmont University *B*
Bryan College *B*
Lambuth University *B*
Union University *B*
University of Tennessee
  Knoxville *B*
  Martin *B*

Texas
Abilene Christian University *B*
Angelina College *A*
Baylor University *M*
Concordia University at Austin *B*
Dallas Baptist University *B*
East Texas Baptist University *B*
Howard Payne University *B*
Lon Morris College *A*
McMurry University *B*
Prairie View A&M University *B*
Southern Methodist University *B, M*
Texas A&M University
  Commerce *B, M*
Texas Christian University *C, B, M*
Texas Tech University *D*
University of Mary Hardin-Baylor *B*
University of Texas
  Arlington *B*
  El Paso *B*

Utah
Brigham Young University *M*
Weber State University *B*

Vermont
Bennington College *B, M*
Johnson State College *B*

Virginia
Shenandoah University *B, M*
Virginia Union University *B*

Washington
Central Washington University *B*
Cornish College of the Arts *B*
Eastern Washington University *B*
University of Washington *B, M, D*
Whitworth College *B*

Wisconsin
Carthage College *B, T*
Lawrence University *B*
Maranatha Baptist Bible College *B*
University of Wisconsin
  Madison *B, M*

Pipefitting

Alabama
Bishop State Community College *C*
Gadsden State Community College *C*
Lawson State Community College *C*
Shelton State Community College *C*

Arizona
Central Arizona College *C*
Gateway Community College *C, A*

California
Bakersfield College *A*
Foothill College *C*

Los Angeles Trade and Technical
  College *C, A*
Modesto Junior College *C, A*
Orange Coast College *C, A*
Palomar College *C, A*
San Diego City College *C, A*
Santa Rosa Junior College *C*
Ventura College *A*

Colorado
Red Rocks Community College *C, A*

Florida
Palm Beach Community College *C*
Seminole Community College *C*
Tallahassee Community College *C*

Indiana
Ivy Tech State College
  Bloomington *A*
  Central Indiana *C, A*
  Columbus *C, A*
  Eastcentral *C, A*
  Kokomo *C, A*
  Lafayette *C, A*
  Northcentral *C, A*
  Northeast *C, A*
  Northwest *C, A*
  Southcentral *C, A*
  Southwest *C, A*
  Wabash Valley *C, A*
  Whitewater *C, A*
Oakland City University *C*

Iowa
Kirkwood Community College *C*
Northeast Iowa Community College *C*

Kentucky
Somerset Community College *C*

Michigan
Bay de Noc Community College *C*
Kellogg Community College *C, A*
Lansing Community College *A*
Macomb Community College *C*
Oakland Community College *C*

Minnesota
St. Cloud Technical College *C, A*
St. Paul College - A Community and
  Technical College *C*

Mississippi
Mississippi Gulf Coast Community
  College
  Perkinston *C, A*

Missouri
Ranken Technical College *C*
St. Louis Community College
  St. Louis Community College at
    Forest Park *A*

Nebraska
Nebraska Indian Community College *C*

Nevada
Truckee Meadows Community
  College *C, A*

New Mexico
Albuquerque Technical-Vocational
  Institute *C*

New York
State University of New York
  College of Technology at Alfred *A*
  College of Technology at Canton *C*
  College of Technology at
    Delhi *C, A*

North Carolina
Blue Ridge Community College *C*
Cleveland Community College *C*
Fayetteville Technical Community
  College *C*
Forsyth Technical Community College *C*
Johnston Community College *C*
Southeastern Community College *C*

Southwestern Community College *C*
Tri-County Community College *C*
Wake Technical Community College *C*

North Dakota
North Dakota State College of Science *C*

Ohio
Owens Community College
  Toledo *C*

Oklahoma
Oklahoma State University
  Okmulgee *A*
Rose State College *A*

Oregon
Central Oregon Community College *C*
Chemeketa Community College *C*
Linn-Benton Community College *A*
Rogue Community College *A*
Southwestern Oregon Community
  College *C, A*

Pennsylvania
Community College of Allegheny
  County *C*
Delaware County Community College *C*
Luzerne County Community
  College *C, A*
Pennsylvania College of Technology *C*

South Carolina
Denmark Technical College *C*

Texas
Brazosport College *C, A*
Frank Phillips College *C, A*
Howard College *C*
Lee College *A*
North Lake College *C*
St. Philip's College *C*

Utah
Dixie State College of Utah *C*
Southern Utah University *C*

Wisconsin
Chippewa Valley Technical College *C*

Planetary sciences

Alaska
University of Alaska
  Fairbanks *B*

Arizona
Northern Arizona University *B, T*
Prescott College *B, M*
University of Arizona *M, D*

Arkansas
University of Arkansas *B*

California
California Institute of Technology *B, D*
California State University
  Chico *B*
  Dominguez Hills *B*
  Los Angeles *B*
  Monterey Bay *B*
  Northridge *B*
  Stanislaus *B*
Cerritos Community College *A*
College of the Redwoods *C, A*
Columbia College *A*
Ohlone College *C*
Stanford University *B, M*
University of California
  Berkeley *B, M, D*
  Irvine *M, D*
  Los Angeles *B*
  San Diego *B, D*
  Santa Cruz *B, M, D*

Colorado
Colorado State University *B, M, D*
University of Northern Colorado *B, M, T*

Connecticut
Central Connecticut State
University *B, M*
Southern Connecticut State University *B*
Wesleyan University *B, M*
Western Connecticut State
University *B, M*

Delaware
University of Delaware *B, T*

Florida
Florida Institute of Technology *M*

Georgia
State University of West Georgia *B*

Idaho
Boise State University *B*
Lewis-Clark State College *B*
University of Idaho *M*

Illinois
Augustana College *B, T*
Black Hawk College
East Campus *A*
City Colleges of Chicago
Olive-Harvey College *A*
Concordia University *B*
Illinois Central College *A*
Illinois Valley Community College *A*
Northeastern Illinois University *B, M*
Northwestern University *B*
Parkland College *A*
Richland Community College *A*

Indiana
Ball State University *M*
DePauw University *B*
University of Indianapolis *B*
Vincennes University *A*

Iowa
Iowa State University *B, M, D*
University of Dubuque *B*

Kansas
Emporia State University *B*

Kentucky
Murray State University *B, T*

Louisiana
Tulane University *B*
University of New Orleans *M*

Maine
Colby College *B*

Maryland
Frostburg State University *B, T*
Johns Hopkins University *B, M, D*
Towson University *B*

Massachusetts
Boston University *B*
Bridgewater State College *B*
Fitchburg State College *B*
Hampshire College *B*
Harvard College *B*
Massachusetts Institute of
Technology *M, D*
Tufts University *T*
University of Massachusetts
Amherst *B*

Michigan
Adrian College *A, B, T*
Central Michigan University *B, T*
Eastern Michigan University *B*
Michigan State University *B*
Northern Michigan University *B, T*
University of Michigan *D*
University of Michigan
Flint *T*
Western Michigan University *B, M*

Minnesota
Minnesota State University
Mankato *M, T*
St. Cloud State University *B*

Winona State University *B, T*

Missouri
Central Missouri State University *B*
Southeast Missouri State
University *B, M*
University of Missouri
Kansas City *B*
Washington University in St.
Louis *B, M, D*

Montana
Montana State University
Bozeman *B, M*

Nebraska
Midland Lutheran College *T*
University of Nebraska
Kearney *B, T*

New Hampshire
Dartmouth College *B, M, D, T*
University of New Hampshire *B, M, D*

New Jersey
Kean University *B*
Rutgers, The State University of New
Jersey
Newark Regional Campus *T*
William Paterson University of New
Jersey *T*

New Mexico
University of New Mexico *B*

New York
Adelphi University *M*
Alfred University *T*
City University of New York
City College *B*
Hunter College *M, T*
Queens College *B*
Columbia University
Columbia College *B*
Sarah Lawrence College *B*
State University of New York
Albany *B*
College at Brockport *B, T*
College at Buffalo *B*
College at Cortland *B*
College at Fredonia *B*
College at Geneseo *T*
College at Oneonta *B, M*
College at Potsdam *T*
New Paltz *B*
Oswego *T*
Stony Brook *T*
Suffolk County Community College *A*

North Carolina
North Carolina Central University *M*
University of North Carolina
Charlotte *B, M, T*

North Dakota
Minot State University *B*
North Dakota State University *B, T*

Ohio
Ashland University *B, T*
Central State University *B*
Kent State University *B*
Mount Union College *T*
Muskingum College *B*
Ohio Dominican College *B, T*
Wilmington College *B*
Wittenberg University *B*
Wright State University *M*
Youngstown State University *B*

Oregon
Western Oregon University *B*

Pennsylvania
Bloomsburg University of
Pennsylvania *B, T*
California University of
Pennsylvania *B, M*
East Stroudsburg University of
Pennsylvania *B*

Edinboro University of
Pennsylvania *B, T*
La Salle University *B*
Lock Haven University of
Pennsylvania *B, T*
Millersville University of
Pennsylvania *B, M, T*
Penn State
Abington *B*
Altoona *B*
Beaver *B*
Berks *B*
Delaware County *B*
Dubois *B*
Fayette *B*
Hazleton *B*
Lehigh Valley *B*
McKeesport *B*
Mont Alto *B*
New Kensington *B*
Schuylkill - Capital College *B*
Shenango *B*
University Park *B, M, D*
Wilkes-Barre *B*
Worthington Scranton *B*
York *B*
Shippensburg University of
Pennsylvania *B, T*
Slippery Rock University of
Pennsylvania *B, M, T*
West Chester University of
Pennsylvania *B*
Wilkes University *B*

South Carolina
University of South Carolina *M*

South Dakota
University of South Dakota *B*

Tennessee
University of Memphis *D*

Texas
Baylor University *B, M*
Brazosport College *A*
College of the Mainland *A*
Lamar University *B*
Southwest Texas State University *T*
Stephen F. Austin State University *T*
Texas A&M University *B*
Texas A&M University
Commerce *B, M*
Corpus Christi *T*
University of Houston *B*
University of Texas
El Paso *B*
of the Permian Basin *B*
West Texas A&M University *T*

Utah
Brigham Young University *B, M*
Southern Utah University *B*

Virginia
George Mason University *B*

Washington
Central Washington University *B*
Centralia College *A*
Eastern Washington University *B, T*
Pacific Lutheran University *B*
University of Washington *B*

Wisconsin
Northland College *B, T*
University of Wisconsin
Green Bay *B*
Madison *B*
River Falls *B, T*

Plant breeding

Arizona
Prescott College *B, M*

California
University of California
Riverside *D*

Iowa
Iowa State University *M, D*

Minnesota
University of Minnesota
Twin Cities *M, D*

New York
Cornell University *B, M, D*

North Carolina
North Carolina State University *M, D*

Oklahoma
Oklahoma State University *M, D*

Texas
Texas A&M University *B, M, D*

Utah
Brigham Young University *B*

Plant genetics

California
University of California
Riverside *D*

Utah
Brigham Young University *B*

Plant pathology

Alabama
Auburn University *M, D*

Arkansas
University of Arkansas *M*

California
University of California
Davis *M, D*
Riverside *M, D*

Colorado
Colorado State University *M, D*

Delaware
University of Delaware *B*

Florida
University of Florida *M, D*
University of West Florida *B*

Georgia
University of Georgia *B, M, D*

Hawaii
University of Hawaii
Manoa *M, D*

Illinois
University of Illinois
Urbana-Champaign *M, D*

Indiana
Purdue University *B, M, D*

Iowa
Iowa State University *B, M, D*

Kansas
Kansas State University *M, D*

Kentucky
University of Kentucky *M, D*

Louisiana
Louisiana State University and
Agricultural and Mechanical
College *M, D*

Michigan
Michigan State University *B, M, D*

Minnesota
University of Minnesota
 Twin Cities *M, D*

Mississippi
Mississippi State University *M, D*

Missouri
University of Missouri
 Columbia *M, D*

Montana
Montana State University
 Bozeman *M*

New York
Cornell University *B, M, D*
State University of New York
 College of Environmental Science
 and Forestry *B, M, D*

North Carolina
North Carolina State University *M, D*

North Dakota
North Dakota State University *M, D*

Ohio
Ohio State University
 Columbus Campus *M, D*

Oklahoma
Oklahoma State University *M, D*

Oregon
Oregon State University *M, D*

Pennsylvania
Penn State
 University Park *M, D*

South Carolina
Clemson University *B, M, D*

Texas
Texas A&M University *M, D*

Virginia
Virginia Polytechnic Institute and State
 University *M, D*

Washington
Washington State University *M, D*

Wisconsin
University of Wisconsin
 Madison *B, M, D*

Plant physiology

Florida
University of West Florida *B*

Hawaii
University of Hawaii
 Manoa *M, D*

Iowa
Iowa State University *M, D*

Kentucky
University of Kentucky *D*

Missouri
Washington University in St. Louis *D*

Nebraska
Peru State College *B*

New Hampshire
University of New Hampshire *B*

New York
State University of New York
 Albany *D*
 College of Environmental Science
 and Forestry *B, M, D*

North Carolina
North Carolina State University *M, D*

North Dakota
North Dakota State University *D*

Oregon
Oregon State University *M, D*

Pennsylvania
Penn State
 University Park *M, D*

South Carolina
Charleston Southern University *B*
Clemson University *D*

Texas
Texas A&M University *M, D*

Vermont
Marlboro College *B*

Virginia
Virginia Polytechnic Institute and State
 University *M, D*

Washington
Washington State University *M, D*

Wisconsin
University of Wisconsin
 Madison *M, D*

Plant protection/pest management

Arkansas
University of Arkansas *B*

California
California State University
 Fresno *B*
College of the Sequoias *C*
San Joaquin Delta College *A*
University of California
 Davis *M*
 Riverside *M*
Ventura College *A*

Florida
Florida Agricultural and Mechanical
 University *B*

Georgia
University of Georgia *B, M*

Hawaii
University of Hawaii
 Hilo *B*

Idaho
University of Idaho *B*

Iowa
Iowa State University *B*
Southwestern Community College *A*

Mississippi
Mississippi State University *B, M*

Nebraska
University of Nebraska
 Lincoln *B*

New York
Cornell University *B, M*
State University of New York
 College of Environmental Science
 and Forestry *M, D*

North Carolina
North Carolina State University *A*

North Dakota
North Dakota State University *B, M, D*

Ohio
Ohio State University
 Columbus Campus *B*

Puerto Rico
University of Puerto Rico
 Mayaguez Campus *B, M*
 Utuado *A*

South Carolina
Clemson University *M*

Texas
Lubbock Christian University *B*
Texas A&M University *B, M*
Texas Tech University *B*
West Texas A&M University *B*

Utah
Snow College *A*

Washington
Washington State University *B, M*

Plant sciences

Alabama
Tuskegee University *B, M*

Arizona
Arizona Western College *A*
University of Arizona *B, M, D*

Arkansas
Arkansas State University *B*
University of Arkansas *D*

California
California Polytechnic State University:
 San Luis Obispo *B*
California State Polytechnic University:
 Pomona *M*
California State University
 Fresno *B, M*
College of the Redwoods *C, A*
College of the Sequoias *C*
College of the Siskiyous *A*
Modesto Junior College *A*
Reedley College *A*
San Joaquin Delta College *C, A*
Santa Rosa Junior College *C*
University of California
 Berkeley *B, D*
 Davis *B, M, D*
 Riverside *M*
 Santa Cruz *B*
Ventura College *A*
Yuba Community College District *C*

Connecticut
University of Connecticut *M, D*

Delaware
Delaware State University *B*
University of Delaware *B, M, D*

Florida
University of Florida *B, D*

Georgia
Abraham Baldwin Agricultural
 College *A*
Fort Valley State University *B*

Hawaii
University of Hawaii
 Manoa *B, M, D*

Idaho
University of Idaho *B, M, D*

Illinois
Southern Illinois University
 Carbondale *B, M*

Iowa
Dordt College *B*
Iowa State University *B*

Louisiana
Louisiana State University and
 Agricultural and Mechanical
 College *B*
Louisiana Tech University *B*

Maine
University of Maine *B, M, D*

Massachusetts
University of Massachusetts
 Amherst *B, M, D*

Michigan
Michigan State University *B, M, D*

Minnesota
Minnesota State University
 Mankato *B, M, T*

Mississippi
Northwest Mississippi Community
 College *A*

Missouri
Southwest Missouri State University *M*
University of Missouri
 Columbia *B*

Montana
Montana State University
 Bozeman *B, M, D*

New Hampshire
University of New Hampshire *B, M, D*

New Jersey
Mercer County Community College *A*
Rutgers, The State University of New
 Jersey
 New Brunswick Regional
 Campus *B*

New York
Cornell University *B*
State University of New York
 College of Agriculture and
 Technology at Cobleskill *A, B*
 College of Environmental Science
 and Forestry *M, D*

North Carolina
North Carolina Agricultural and
 Technical State University *B*
North Carolina State University *M, D*

North Dakota
North Dakota State University *M, D*

Ohio
Cuyahoga Community College
 Eastern Campus *A*
Ohio State University
 Agricultural Technical Institute *A*
 Columbus Campus *B, M*

Oklahoma
Oklahoma State University *D*

Oregon
Oregon State University *B, M*

South Carolina
Clemson University *B, M, D*

Tennessee
Middle Tennessee State University *B*
University of Tennessee
 Knoxville *B, M, D*

Texas
Lubbock Christian University *B*
Texas A&M University *B, M*
Texas A&M University
 Commerce *B*
 Kingsville *B, M*
West Texas A&M University *B, M*

Utah
Utah State University *M, D*

Vermont
University of Vermont *B, M, D*
Vermont Technical College *A*

Washington
Washington State University *B*

West Virginia
West Virginia University *B, M*

Wisconsin
University of Wisconsin
 River Falls *B*

Plasma/high-temperature physics

Wisconsin
University of Wisconsin
Madison *M, D*

Plastics engineering technology

California
Cerritos Community College *C, A*

Connecticut
Central Connecticut State University *B*
Naugatuck Valley Community
College *C, A*
Quinebaug Valley Community College *A*

Florida
St. Petersburg College *C*

Illinois
College of DuPage *C, A*
McHenry County College *C*

Michigan
Grand Rapids Community College *C, A*
Western Michigan University *B*

Minnesota
Hennepin Technical College *A*

New York
State University of New York
College of Agriculture and
Technology at Morrisville *A*

North Carolina
Davidson County Community
College *C, A*
Isothermal Community College *C, A*

Ohio
Kent State University *C, A*
Northwest State Community College *A*
Shawnee State University *C, A, B*
Sinclair Community College *C, A*

Pennsylvania
Northampton County Area Community
College *C*
Pennsylvania College of
Technology *A, B*

Texas
St. Philip's College *C*

Platemaker/imager

Pennsylvania
Pennsylvania College of Technology *A*

Wisconsin
Milwaukee Area Technical College *A*

Playwriting/screenwriting

California
California Institute of the Arts *M*
Otis College of Art and Design *M*
Pomona College *B*
University of Southern California *B, M*

Florida
University of South Florida *M*

Illinois
Columbia College Chicago *B*
De Paul University *B*

Iowa
University of Iowa *M*

Massachusetts
Emerson College *B, M*

Hampshire College *B*
Smith College *M*

Michigan
University of Michigan *B*

Minnesota
Metropolitan State University *B*
Minneapolis Community and Technical
College *A*

New Mexico
University of New Mexico *M*

New York
Bard College *B*
New York University *B, M*
Sarah Lawrence College *B, M*
State University of New York
Purchase *B*
Stony Brook *M*

Ohio
Ohio University *M*

Pennsylvania
Drexel University *B*

Texas
Texas Tech University *M*

Vermont
Bennington College *B, M*
Marlboro College *B*

Virginia
Hollins University *M*

Plumbing

Alabama
Lawson State Community College *C*

California
Foothill College *C*

Florida
Gulf Coast Community College *C*
Indian River Community College *C*
South Florida Community College *C*

Kentucky
Somerset Community College *C*

Minnesota
St. Paul College - A Community and
Technical College *C*

New York
State University of New York
College of Technology at Canton *C*

North Dakota
North Dakota State College of Science *C*

Pennsylvania
Community College of Allegheny
County *C*

Utah
Utah Valley State College *A*

Wisconsin
Western Wisconsin Technical College *C*

Podiatry (D.P.M.)

California
California College of Podiatric
Medicine *F*

Florida
Barry University: School of Graduate
Medical Sciences *F*

Illinois
Dr. William M. Scholl College of
Podiatric Medicine *F*

Iowa
University of Osteopathic Medicine and
Health Sciences: College of Podiatric
Medicine and Surgery *F*

New York
New York College of Podiatric
Medicine *F*

Ohio
Ohio College of Podiatric Medicine *F*

Pennsylvania
Pennsylvania College of Podiatric
Medicine *F*

Police science

Alabama
Central Alabama Community
College *C, A*
Enterprise State Junior College *A*
George C. Wallace State Community
College
Dothan *C*
Jefferson State Community College *C, A*
Wallace State Community College at
Hanceville *A*

Arizona
Central Arizona College *C*
Cochise College *A*
Eastern Arizona College *C, A*
Glendale Community College *C, A*
Phoenix College *A*
Pima Community College *C, A*
Scottsdale Community College *C*

Arkansas
Arkansas State University *A*
Mississippi County Community
College *C, A*
South Arkansas Community College *A*
University of Arkansas
Little Rock *A*

California
Bakersfield College *A*
Barstow College *C, A*
Cabrillo College *C, A*
California State University
Stanislaus *B*
Cerritos Community College *A*
Cerro Coso Community College *C, A*
Chabot College *A*
Citrus College *C*
College of the Redwoods *C*
College of the Siskiyous *A*
Contra Costa College *A*
East Los Angeles College *C, A*
Glendale Community College *A*
Grossmont Community College *C, A*
Irvine Valley College *C, A*
Los Angeles Harbor College *C, A*
MiraCosta College *C, A*
Modesto Junior College *A*
Moorpark College *A*
Mount San Antonio College *C, A*
Mount San Jacinto College *C, A*
Napa Valley College *C, A*
Palomar College *C, A*
San Joaquin Delta College *A*
Santa Monica College *A*
Santa Rosa Junior College *C, A*
Shasta College *A*
Sierra College *A*
Southwestern College *C*
Ventura College *A*
Yuba Community College District *A*

Colorado
Arapahoe Community College *C*
Colorado Mountain College
Spring Valley Campus *C*
Red Rocks Community College *C*
Trinidad State Junior College *A*

Connecticut
Housatonic Community College *C, A*
Three Rivers Community College *A*
University of New Haven *B*
Western Connecticut State University *B*

Florida
Daytona Beach Community
College *C, A*
Florida State University *C*
Hillsborough Community College *C*
Indian River Community College *C*
Lake City Community College *C*
Miami-Dade Community College *C*
Okaloosa-Walton Community College *C*
Palm Beach Community College *C*
Pasco-Hernando Community College *C*
Polk Community College *C, A*
St. Petersburg College *C, A*
Santa Fe Community College *C*
Seminole Community College *C*
South Florida Community College *C*
Tallahassee Community College *C*
Valencia Community College *C*

Georgia
Abraham Baldwin Agricultural
College *A*
Armstrong Atlantic State University *A*
Dalton State College *A*
Floyd College *A*
Macon State College *C*
Middle Georgia College *C, A*
South Georgia College *A*

Hawaii
University of Hawaii
Honolulu Community College *A*

Idaho
College of Southern Idaho *C, A*
Idaho State University *C*
North Idaho College *A*

Illinois
Black Hawk College *C, A*
City Colleges of Chicago
Harold Washington College *C, A*
Olive-Harvey College *C*
College of DuPage *C, A*
College of Lake County *C, A*
Elgin Community College *A*
Illinois Eastern Community Colleges
Frontier Community College *C*
Olney Central College *A*
Illinois Valley Community College *A*
John Wood Community College *A*
Kankakee Community College *A*
Kaskaskia College *C, A*
Kishwaukee College *C, A*
Lake Land College *A*
Lincoln College *A*
McHenry County College *A*
Moraine Valley Community College *A*
Oakton Community College *C, A*
Prairie State College *C, A*
Rend Lake College *C, A*
Richland Community College *A*
Sauk Valley Community College *A*
Southeastern Illinois College *C, A*
Southwestern Illinois College *C, A*
Triton College *A*
Waubonsee Community College *C, A*
William Rainey Harper College *C, A*

Indiana
Calumet College of St. Joseph *B, M*
Indiana Wesleyan University *A*
Vincennes University *A*

Iowa
Hawkeye Community College *A*
Iowa Central Community College *C, A*
Kirkwood Community College *C, A*
Marshalltown Community College *A*
North Iowa Area Community College *A*

Kansas

Allen County Community College *A*
Barton County Community College *C, A*
Butler County Community College *C, A*
Cloud County Community College *A*
Fort Scott Community College *A*
Garden City Community College *A*
Hutchinson Community College *C, A*
Johnson County Community
College *C, A*
Kansas City Kansas Community
College *C, A*
Seward County Community
College *C, A*
Washburn University of Topeka *B*

Kentucky

Madisonville Community College *A*
Prestonsburg Community College *A*
Somerset Community College *A*
Southeast Community College *A*

Louisiana

Delgado Community College *A*
Grambling State University *A*
Nicholls State University *A*
Northwestern State University *A*
Southeastern Louisiana University *A*
Southern University and Agricultural and
Mechanical College *A*
University of Louisiana at Monroe *A*

Maine

Andover College *A*
Beal College *A*

Maryland

Chesapeake College *C, A*
Community College of Baltimore County
Catonsville *C, A*
Dundalk *C, A*
Essex *C, A*
Frostburg State University *B*
Hagerstown Community College *C, A*
Harford Community College *A*
Montgomery College
Rockville Campus *A*
Wor-Wic Community College *C, A*

Massachusetts

American International College *B*
Becker College *B*
Greenfield Community College *A*
Massasoit Community College *A*
Northeastern University *A, B*
Springfield Technical Community
College *A*

Michigan

Grand Rapids Community College *A*
Kellogg Community College *A*
Kirtland Community College *C, A*
Lansing Community College *A*
Macomb Community College *C, A*
Michigan State University *B*
Mid Michigan Community College *A*
North Central Michigan College *C*
Northern Michigan University *C, B*
Northwestern Michigan College *A*
Oakland Community College *C, A*
Schoolcraft College *A*
Washtenaw Community College *A*

Minnesota

Alexandria Technical College *C, A*
Century Community and Technical
College *A*
Fergus Falls Community College *A*
Hibbing Community College: A
Technical and Community College *A*
Inver Hills Community College *A*
Metropolitan State University *C, B*
Minneapolis Community and Technical
College *C, A*
Minnesota State University
Mankato *B*
Normandale Community College *C, A*
North Hennepin Community College *A*

Northland Community & Technical
College *A*
Ridgewater College: A Community and
Technical College *A*
Riverland Community College: A
Technical and Community College *A*
Rochester Community and Technical
College *A*
St. Mary's University of Minnesota *B*
Vermilion Community College *A*
Winona State University *B*

Missouri

Blue River Community College *C, A*
College of the Ozarks *B*
Jefferson College *C, A*
Missouri Southern State College *C*
Missouri Western State College *A*
Moberly Area Community College *C*
Penn Valley Community College *C, A*
St. Louis Community College
St. Louis Community College at
Florissant Valley *A*
St. Louis Community College at
Meramec *C, A*
Southeast Missouri State University *B*
Southwest Missouri State University:
West Plains Campus *A*
Three Rivers Community College *A*

Montana

Dawson Community College *C, A*

Nebraska

Metropolitan Community College *A*
Northeast Community College *A*
University of Nebraska
Kearney *B*

Nevada

Community College of Southern
Nevada *C, A*
Great Basin College *A*
Truckee Meadows Community
College *A*
Western Nevada Community
College *C, A*

New Jersey

Bergen Community College *A*
Brookdale Community College *A*
Burlington County College *A*
Camden County College *A*
County College of Morris *A*
Cumberland County College *C, A*
Essex County College *A*
Gloucester County College *A*
Mercer County Community College *A*
Ocean County College *C, A*
Passaic County Community
College *C, A*
Rowan University *B*
Union County College *C, A*

New Mexico

New Mexico Junior College *A*
San Juan College *A*

New York

Adirondack Community College *A*
City University of New York
John Jay College of Criminal
Justice *A, B*
Erie Community College
North Campus *A*
Jamestown Community College *A*
Monroe Community College *A*
Orange County Community College *A*
Westchester Community College *A*

North Carolina

Asheville Buncombe Technical
Community College *C, A*
Brunswick Community College *C*
Cape Fear Community College *C, A*
Carteret Community College *C, A*
Catawba Valley Community College *C*
Central Piedmont Community College *A*

Cleveland Community College *C*
Coastal Carolina Community
College *C, A*
College of the Albemarle *C*
Craven Community College *C*
Davidson County Community College *C*
Durham Technical Community
College *C*
Gaston College *C*
Guilford Technical Community
College *A*
Halifax Community College *C*
Isothermal Community College *A*
Johnston Community College *C, A*
Lenoir Community College *C*
Mayland Community College *C*
Mitchell Community College *C, A*
Montgomery Community College *C, A*
Nash Community College *A*
Pfeiffer University *B*
Pitt Community College *A*
Randolph Community College *C, A*
Sampson Community College *C*
Sandhills Community College *C*
Southwestern Community College *C*
Stanly Community College *C, A*
Vance-Granville Community College *C*
Wake Technical Community College *A*
Wayne Community College *A*
Western Piedmont Community
College *C*
Wilkes Community College *C*
Wilson Technical Community College *C*

North Dakota

Lake Region State College *C, A*

Ohio

Columbus State Community College *A*
Cuyahoga Community College
Eastern Campus *A*
Metropolitan Campus *A*
Western Campus *A*
Hocking Technical College *A*
James A. Rhodes State College *A*
Jefferson Community College *A*
Kent State University
Stark Campus *B*
Trumbull Campus *A*
Lakeland Community College *C, A*
Lorain County Community College *A*
North Central State College *C, A*
Northwest State Community College *A*
Ohio Northern University *B*
Ohio University *A*
Ohio University
Chillicothe Campus *A*
Southern Campus at Ironton *A*
Zanesville Campus *A*
Owens Community College
Findlay Campus *A*
Toledo *A*
Sinclair Community College *A*
Southern State Community College *A*
University of Akron *C, A*
University of Toledo *A*
Youngstown State University *C, A*

Oklahoma

East Central University *B*
Langston University *B*
Northwestern Oklahoma State
University *B*
Oklahoma City University *B*
Oklahoma State University
Oklahoma City *A*
Tulsa Community College *A*
Western Oklahoma State College *A*

Oregon

Chemeketa Community College *A*
Clackamas Community College *A*
Lane Community College *C*
Rogue Community College *C, A*
Southern Oregon University *B*
Treasure Valley Community College *A*
Umpqua Community College *C*

Western Oregon University *B*

Pennsylvania

Bucks County Community College *A*
Butler County Community College *A*
Community College of Allegheny
County *A*
Community College of Philadelphia *C, A*
Delaware County Community
College *C, A*
Edinboro University of Pennsylvania *A*
Harrisburg Area Community
College *C, A*
ICM School of Business & Medical
Careers *A*
Lackawanna College *C*
Lehigh Carbon Community College *C, A*
Luzerne County Community
College *C, A*
Mercyhurst College *C, A, B*
Montgomery County Community
College *A*
Reading Area Community College *A*
Westmoreland County Community
College *A*
York College of Pennsylvania *A, B*

Rhode Island

Community College of Rhode Island *A*

South Dakota

Western Dakota Technical Institute *A*

Tennessee

Dyersburg State Community College *A*
Middle Tennessee State University *A*
Roane State Community College *C, A*
Southwest Tennessee Community
College *C, A*
Walters State Community College *C, A*

Texas

Alvin Community College *C, A*
Amarillo College *C, A*
Angelina College *C*
Austin Community College *C, A*
Brazosport College *C*
Central Texas College *C*
Coastal Bend College *A*
College of the Mainland *A*
Del Mar College *C, A*
Eastfield College *C*
El Centro College *C*
Grayson County College *A*
Hardin-Simmons University *B*
Hill College *C, A*
Houston Community College
System *C, A*
Kilgore College *C, A*
Lee College *A*
Midland College *A*
North Central Texas College *A*
Northeast Texas Community
College *C, A*
Odessa College *C, A*
St. Mary's University *M*
San Antonio College *A*
San Jacinto College
Central Campus *C, A*
Southwest Texas State University *B*
Stephen F. Austin State University *B*
Tarrant County College *C, A*
Temple College *C, A*
Tyler Junior College *C, A*
University of Texas
Brownsville *B*
Pan American *B*
Western Texas College *A*

Utah

Salt Lake Community College *C*
Weber State University *B*

Virginia

George Mason University *B*
Mountain Empire Community College *C*
Paul D. Camp Community College *A*

Southwest Virginia Community
   College *C*
Virginia Highlands Community
   College *A*
Virginia Western Community College *A*

Washington

Centralia College *A*
Green River Community College *A*
Spokane Community College *A*

West Virginia

Bluefield State College *A*
Fairmont State College *A*
West Virginia State College *B*

Wisconsin

Blackhawk Technical College *A*
Chippewa Valley Technical College *A*
Fox Valley Technical College *A*
Lakeshore Technical College *A*
Mid-State Technical College *A*
Moraine Park Technical College *A*
Nicolet Area Technical College *A*
University of Wisconsin
   Superior *A*
Waukesha County Technical College *A*
Western Wisconsin Technical College *A*

Wyoming

Casper College *A*
Eastern Wyoming College *A*
Laramie County Community College *A*
Sheridan College *A*

Polish studies

New York

Columbia University
   Columbia College *B*

Political communications

Florida

Florida State University *M*

Massachusetts

Emerson College *B, M*

New York

State University of New York
   Buffalo *M, D*

Ohio

Ohio University *C*

Tennessee

Bryan College *B*

Political science/ government

Alabama

Alabama Agricultural and Mechanical
   University *B*
Alabama State University *B*
Athens State University *B*
Auburn University *B*
Auburn University at Montgomery *B, M*
Birmingham-Southern College *B, T*
Huntingdon College *B*
Jacksonville State University *B, M*
Lawson State Community College *A*
Miles College *B*
Samford University *B*
Spring Hill College *B*
Troy State University *B*
Troy State University in Montgomery *B*
Tuskegee University *B*
University of Alabama *B, M, D*
University of Alabama
   Birmingham *B*
   Huntsville *B*
University of Mobile *B*
University of Montevallo *B, T*

University of North Alabama *B*
University of South Alabama *B*

Alaska

University of Alaska
   Anchorage *B*
   Fairbanks *B*
   Southeast *B*

Arizona

Arizona State University *B, M, D*
Arizona Western College *A*
Cochise College *A*
Eastern Arizona College *A*
Northern Arizona University *B, M, D*
Pima Community College *A*
South Mountain Community College *A*
University of Arizona *B, M, D*

Arkansas

Arkansas State University *B, M*
Harding University *B*
Henderson State University *B*
Hendrix College *B*
John Brown University *B*
Lyon College *B*
Ouachita Baptist University *B*
Philander Smith College *B*
Southern Arkansas University *B*
University of Arkansas *B, M*
University of Arkansas
   Little Rock *B*
   Monticello *B*
   Pine Bluff *B*
University of Central Arkansas *B*

California

Azusa Pacific University *B*
Bakersfield College *A*
Cabrillo College *A*
California Baptist University *B*
California Maritime Academy *B*
California Polytechnic State University:
   San Luis Obispo *B*
California State Polytechnic University:
   Pomona *A*
California State University
   Bakersfield *B*
   Chico *B, M*
   Dominguez Hills *B*
   Fresno *B*
   Fullerton *B, M*
   Hayward *B*
   Los Angeles *B, M*
   Northridge *B*
   Sacramento *B, M*
   San Bernardino *B, T*
   San Marcos *B*
   Stanislaus *B*
Cerritos Community College *A*
Chabot College *A*
Chapman University *B*
Claremont McKenna College *B*
College of Alameda *A*
Concordia University *B*
De Anza College *A*
Dominican University of California *B*
East Los Angeles College *A*
Foothill College *A*
Gavilan Community College *A*
Golden Gate University *C, B*
Golden West College *A*
Grossmont Community College *A*
Humboldt State University *B*
Irvine Valley College *A*
La Sierra University *B*
Los Angeles Southwest College *A*
Loyola Marymount University *B*
Master's College *B*
Mills College *B*
MiraCosta College *A*
Monterey Peninsula College *A*
Mount St. Mary's College *B*
Occidental College *B*
Orange Coast College *A*
Pepperdine University *B*
Pitzer College *B*

Point Loma Nazarene University *B*
Pomona College *B*
St. Mary's College of California *B*
San Diego City College *A*
San Diego State University *B, M*
San Francisco State University *B, M*
San Jose State University *B*
Santa Barbara City College *A*
Santa Clara University *B*
Santa Monica College *A*
Santa Rosa Junior College *A*
Santiago Canyon College *A*
Sonoma State University *B*
Southwestern College *A*
Stanford University *B, M, D*
University of California
   Berkeley *B, D*
   Davis *B, M, D*
   Irvine *B, D*
   Los Angeles *B, M, D*
   Riverside *B, M, D*
   San Diego *B, M, D*
   Santa Barbara *B, M, D*
   Santa Cruz *B, D*
University of La Verne *B*
University of Redlands *B*
University of San Diego *B*
University of San Francisco *B*
University of Southern
   California *M, D*
University of the Pacific *B*
Vanguard University of Southern
   California *B*
Ventura College *A*
Whittier College *B, M*

Colorado

Colorado College *B*
Colorado State University *B, M, D*
Colorado State University
   Pueblo *B*
Fort Lewis College *B*
Mesa State College *B*
Metropolitan State College of
   Denver *B, T*
Otero Junior College *A*
Red Rocks Community College *A*
Regis University *B*
United States Air Force Academy *B*
University of Colorado
   Boulder *B, M, D*
   Colorado Springs *B*
   Denver *B, M*
University of Denver *B*
University of Northern Colorado *B*

Connecticut

Albertus Magnus College *B*
Central Connecticut State University *B*
Connecticut College *B*
Eastern Connecticut State University *B*
Fairfield University *B*
Quinnipiac University *B*
Sacred Heart University *B*
Southern Connecticut State
   University *B, M*
Trinity College *B*
United States Coast Guard Academy *B*
University of Connecticut *B, M, D*
University of Hartford *B*
University of New Haven *B*
Wesleyan University *B*
Western Connecticut State University *B*
Yale University *B, M, D*

Delaware

Delaware State University *B*
University of Delaware *B, M, D*

District of Columbia

American University *B, M, D*
Catholic University of America *B, M, D*
Gallaudet University *B*
George Washington University *B, M, D*
Georgetown University *B, M, D*
Howard University *B, M, D*
Trinity College *B*

University of the District of Columbia *B*

Florida

Barry University *B*
Bethune-Cookman College *B*
Broward Community College *A*
Eckerd College *B*
Flagler College *B*
Florida Agricultural and Mechanical
   University *B*
Florida Atlantic University *B, M*
Florida International University *B, M, D*
Florida Southern College *B*
Florida State University *B, M, D*
Gulf Coast Community College *A*
Indian River Community College *A*
Jacksonville University *B*
Miami-Dade Community College *A*
New College of Florida *B*
Palm Beach Atlantic University *B, T*
Palm Beach Community College *A*
Polk Community College *A*
Rollins College *B*
St. Leo University *B*
St. Thomas University *B*
South Florida Community College *A*
Stetson University *B*
University of Central Florida *B, M*
University of Florida *B, M, D*
University of Miami *B*
University of North Florida *B*
University of South Florida *B, M*
University of Tampa *A, B*
University of West Florida *B*

Georgia

Agnes Scott College *B*
Albany State University *B*
Armstrong Atlantic State University *B, T*
Atlanta Metropolitan College *A*
Augusta State University *B*
Berry College *B, T*
Brenau University *B*
Brewton-Parker College *B*
Clark Atlanta University *B, M, D*
Clayton College and State University *A*
Columbus State University *B*
Dalton State College *A*
Darton College *A*
East Georgia College *A*
Emmanuel College *B*
Emory University *B, D*
Fort Valley State University *B*
Gainesville College *A*
Georgia College and State University *B*
Georgia Perimeter College *A*
Georgia Southern University *B, M*
Georgia Southwestern State University *B*
Georgia State University *B, M, D*
Gordon College *A*
Kennesaw State University *B*
LaGrange College *B*
Mercer University *B*
Middle Georgia College *A*
Morehouse College *B*
Morris Brown College *B*
North Georgia College & State
   University *B*
Oglethorpe University *B*
Oxford College of Emory University *B*
Piedmont College *B*
Savannah State University *B*
South Georgia College *A*
Spelman College *B*
State University of West Georgia *B*
University of Georgia *B, M, D*
Valdosta State University *B*
Waycross College *A*

Hawaii

Brigham Young University-Hawaii *B*
Chaminade University of Honolulu *B*
Hawaii Pacific University *B*

University of Hawaii
    Hilo *B*
    Manoa *B, M, D*
    West Oahu *B*

Idaho

Albertson College of Idaho *B*
Boise State University *B, T*
College of Southern Idaho *A*
Idaho State University *A, B, M, D*
North Idaho College *A*
Northwest Nazarene University *B*
University of Idaho *B, M, D*

Illinois

Augustana College *B, T*
Aurora University *B*
Benedictine University *B*
Black Hawk College
    East Campus *A*
Blackburn College *B*
Bradley University *B, T*
Chicago State University *B*
Concordia University *B*
Danville Area Community College *A*
De Paul University *B*
Dominican University *B*
Eastern Illinois University *B, M*
Elmhurst College *B, T*
Eureka College *B*
Governors State University *M*
Illinois College *B*
Illinois State University *B, M*
Illinois Valley Community College *A*
Illinois Wesleyan University *B*
John A. Logan College *A*
Joliet Junior College *A*
Judson College *B*
Kendall College *B*
Kishwaukee College *A*
Knox College *B*
Lake Forest College *B*
Lewis University *B*
Lewis and Clark Community College *A*
Lincoln Land Community College *A*
Loyola University of
    Chicago *C, B, M, D, T*
MacMurray College *B*
McKendree College *B*
Millikin University *B*
Monmouth College *B, T*
North Central College *B*
North Park University *B*
Northeastern Illinois University *B, M*
Northern Illinois University *B, M, D*
Northwestern University *B, M, D*
Olivet Nazarene University *B*
Parkland College *A*
Principia College *B*
Quincy University *B*
Richland Community College *A*
Rockford College *B*
Roosevelt University *B, M*
St. Xavier University *B*
Sauk Valley Community College *A*
South Suburban College of Cook
    County *A*
Southern Illinois University
    Carbondale *B, M, D*
Southern Illinois University
    Edwardsville *B*
Southwestern Illinois College *A*
Triton College *A*
University of Chicago *B, M, D*
University of Illinois
    Chicago *B, M, D*
    Springfield *B, M*
    Urbana-Champaign *B, M, D*
University of St. Francis *B*
Western Illinois University *B, M*
Wheaton College *B, T*

Indiana

Anderson University *B*
Ball State University *B, M*
Butler University *B*

DePauw University *B*
Earlham College *B*
Franklin College *B*
Goshen College *B*
Hanover College *B*
Indiana State University *B, M, T*
Indiana University
    Bloomington *B, M, D*
    Northwest *B*
    South Bend *B*
    Southeast *B*
Indiana University-Purdue University
    Fort Wayne *A, B*
Indiana University-Purdue University
    Indianapolis *B*
Indiana Wesleyan University *A, B*
Manchester College *B*
Marian College *B, T*
Martin University *B*
Purdue University *B, M, D*
Purdue University
    Calumet *B*
St. Joseph's College *B*
Saint Mary's College *B*
Taylor University *B*
University of Evansville *B*
University of Indianapolis *B*
University of Notre Dame *B, M, D*
University of Southern Indiana *B*
Valparaiso University *B*
Vincennes University *A*
Wabash College *B*

Iowa

Briar Cliff University *B*
Buena Vista University *B, T*
Central College *B, T*
Clarke College *A, B, T*
Coe College *B*
Cornell College *B, T*
Dordt College *B*
Drake University *B*
Graceland University *T*
Grand View College *B*
Grinnell College *B*
Iowa State University *B, M*
Loras College *B*
Luther College *B*
Morningside College *B*
North Iowa Area Community College *A*
Northwestern College *B*
St. Ambrose University *B, T*
Simpson College *B*
University of Iowa *B, M, D, T*
University of Northern Iowa *B, M*
Waldorf College *A, B*
Wartburg College *B, T*
William Penn University *B*

Kansas

Baker University *B, T*
Barton County Community College *A*
Benedictine College *B, T*
Butler County Community College *A*
Central Christian College *A*
Emporia State University *B, T*
Fort Hays State University *B, M*
Fort Scott Community College *A*
Friends University *B*
Independence Community College *A*
Kansas State University *B, M*
Labette Community College *A*
Ottawa University *B*
Pittsburg State University *B, T*
Pratt Community College *A*
St. Mary College *B*
University of Kansas *B, M, D*
Washburn University of Topeka *B*
Wichita State University *B, M, T*

Kentucky

Bellarmine University *B*
Berea College *B*
Campbellsville University *B*
Centre College *B*
Cumberland College *B, T*

Georgetown College *B, T*
Kentucky Wesleyan College *B, T*
Morehead State University *B*
Murray State University *B, T*
Thomas More College *A*
Transylvania University *B*
Union College *B*
University of Kentucky *B, M, D*
University of Louisville *B, M*

Louisiana

Centenary College of Louisiana *B, T*
Dillard University *B*
Grambling State University *B*
Louisiana College *B*
Louisiana State University
    Shreveport *B*
Louisiana State University and
    Agricultural and Mechanical
    College *B, M, D*
Louisiana Tech University *B*
Loyola University New Orleans *B*
McNeese State University *B*
Nicholls State University *B*
Northwestern State University *B*
Southeastern Louisiana University *B*
Southern University
    New Orleans *B*
Southern University and Agricultural and
    Mechanical College *B, M*
Tulane University *B, M, D*
University of Louisiana at Lafayette *B*
University of Louisiana at Monroe *B*
University of New Orleans *B, M, D*
Xavier University of Louisiana *B*

Maine

Bates College *B*
Bowdoin College *B*
Colby College *B*
University of Maine *B*
University of Maine
    Farmington *B*
    Presque Isle *B*
University of New England *B*
University of Southern Maine *B*

Maryland

Allegany College *A*
Bowie State University *B*
College of Notre Dame of Maryland *B*
Columbia Union College *B*
Community College of Baltimore County
    Catonsville *A*
    Dundalk *A*
    Essex *A*
Coppin State College *B*
Frederick Community College *A*
Frostburg State University *B*
Hood College *B*
Johns Hopkins University *B, M, D*
Loyola College in Maryland *B*
McDaniel College *B*
Morgan State University *B*
Mount St. Mary's College *B*
St. Mary's College of Maryland *B*
Salisbury University *B, T*
Towson University *B*
United States Naval Academy *B*
University of Baltimore *B*
University of Maryland
    Baltimore County *B*
    College Park *B, M, D*
Washington College *B*

Massachusetts

American International College *B*
Amherst College *B*
Assumption College *B*
Boston College *B, M, D*
Boston University *B, M, D*
Brandeis University *B, M, D*
Bridgewater State College *B*
Clark University *B*
College of the Holy Cross *B*
Emmanuel College *B*
Fitchburg State College *B*

Framingham State College *B*
Gordon College *B*
Hampshire College *B*
Harvard College *B*
Massachusetts Institute of
    Technology *B, M, D*
Merrimack College *B*
Mount Holyoke College *B*
Northeastern University *B, M*
Regis College *B*
Salem State College *B*
Simmons College *B*
Simon's Rock College of Bard *B*
Smith College *B*
Springfield College *B*
Stonehill College *B*
Suffolk University *B, M*
Tufts University *B*
University of Massachusetts
    Amherst *B, M, D*
    Boston *B*
    Dartmouth *B*
    Lowell *B*
Wellesley College *B*
Western New England College *B*
Westfield State College *B*
Wheaton College *B*
Williams College *B*

Michigan

Adrian College *A, B, T*
Alma College *B, T*
Andrews University *B*
Aquinas College *B, T*
Calvin College *B, T*
Central Michigan University *B, M, T*
Cornerstone University *B*
Eastern Michigan University *B*
Grand Valley State University *B*
Hillsdale College *B*
Hope College *B*
Kalamazoo College *B, T*
Kellogg Community College *A*
Lansing Community College *A*
Marygrove College *B, T*
Michigan State University *B, M, D*
Northern Michigan University *B, T*
Oakland University *B, T*
Saginaw Valley State University *B*
University of Michigan *B, M, D, T*
University of Michigan
    Dearborn *B*
    Flint *B, T*
Wayne State University *B, M, D*
Western Michigan University *B, M, D*

Minnesota

Augsburg College *B*
Bemidji State University *B*
Bethel College *B*
Carleton College *B*
College of St. Benedict *B*
College of St. Catherine *B*
Concordia College: Moorhead *B*
Concordia University: St. Paul *B*
Gustavus Adolphus College *B*
Hamline University *B*
Macalester College *B*
Minnesota State University
    Mankato *B, M*
    Moorhead *B*
Ridgewater College: A Community and
    Technical College *A*
St. Cloud State University *B*
St. John's University *B*
St. Mary's University of Minnesota *B*
St. Olaf College *B*
Southwest State University *B*
University of Minnesota
    Duluth *B*
    Morris *B*
    Twin Cities *B, M, D*
University of St. Thomas *B*
Vermilion Community College *A*
Winona State University *B*

Mississippi

Alcorn State University *B*
Delta State University *B*
Millsaps College *B, T*
Mississippi College *B, M*
Mississippi State University *B, M*
Mississippi University for Women *B*
Mississippi Valley State University *B*
Rust College *B*
University of Mississippi *B, M, D*
University of Southern Mississippi *B, M*

Missouri

Avila University *B*
Central Methodist College *B*
Central Missouri State University *B*
College of the Ozarks *B*
Columbia College *B*
Drury University *B, T*
East Central College *A*
Evangel University *B*
Lincoln University *B*
Lindenwood University *B*
Missouri Southern State College *B, T*
Missouri Valley College *B*
Missouri Western State College *B*
Northwest Missouri State University *B*
Rockhurst University *B*
St. Louis University *B*
Southeast Missouri State University *B*
Southwest Baptist University *B*
Southwest Missouri State University *B*
Stephens College *B*
Three Rivers Community College *A*
Truman State University *B*
University of Missouri
    Columbia *B, M, D*
    Kansas City *B, M*
    St. Louis *B, M, D*
Washington University in St.
    Louis *B, M, D*
Westminster College *B*
William Jewell College *B*
William Woods University *B*

Montana

Carroll College *B, T*
Montana State University
    Billings *T*
    Bozeman *B*
Rocky Mountain College *B, T*
University of Great Falls *B*
University of Montana-Missoula *B, M*

Nebraska

Creighton University *B*
Doane College *B*
Hastings College *B*
Nebraska Wesleyan University *B*
University of Nebraska
    Kearney *B, T*
    Lincoln *B, M, D*
    Omaha *B*
Wayne State College *B, T*
Western Nebraska Community
    College *A*

Nevada

University of Nevada
    Las Vegas *B, M*
    Reno *B, M, D*

New Hampshire

Dartmouth College *B*
Franklin Pierce College *B*
Keene State College *B*
New England College *B*
Plymouth State College *B*
Rivier College *B*
St. Anselm College *B, T*
Southern New Hampshire University *B*
Thomas More College of Liberal Arts *B*
University of New Hampshire *B, M*

New Jersey

Bloomfield College *B*
Caldwell College *B*

Centenary College *B*
The College of New Jersey *B*
Drew University *B*
Fairleigh Dickinson University
    College at Florham *B*
    Metropolitan Campus *B, M*
Gloucester County College *A*
Kean University *B*
Middlesex County College *A*
Monmouth University *B*
Montclair State University *B*
New Jersey City University *B*
Princeton University *B, M, D*
Ramapo College of New Jersey *B*
Richard Stockton College of New
    Jersey *B*
Rider University *B*
Rowan University *B*
Rutgers, The State University of New
    Jersey
        Camden Regional Campus *B*
        New Brunswick Regional
            Campus *B*
        Newark Regional Campus *B, M*
St. Peter's College *B*
Salem Community College *A*
Seton Hall University *B, T*
Thomas Edison State College *B*
William Paterson University of New
    Jersey *B*

New Mexico

College of Santa Fe *B*
Eastern New Mexico University *B*
New Mexico Highlands University *B*
New Mexico State University *B, M*
San Juan College *A*
University of New Mexico *B, M, D*

New York

Adelphi University *B*
Adirondack Community College *A*
Alfred University *B*
Bard College *B*
Barnard College *B*
Canisius College *B*
City University of New York
    Baruch College *B*
    Brooklyn College *B, M*
    City College *B*
    College of Staten Island *B*
    Hunter College *B*
    Queens College *B, M*
    Queensborough Community
        College *A*
    York College *B*
Clarkson University *B*
Colgate University *B*
College of New Rochelle *B, T*
Columbia University
    Columbia College *B*
Cornell University *B, D*
Daemen College *B*
Dowling College *B*
Elmira College *B*
Eugene Lang College/New School
    University *B*
Excelsior College *B*
Fordham University *B, M, D*
Fulton-Montgomery Community
    College *A*
Hamilton College *B*
Hartwick College *B*
Hobart and William Smith Colleges *B*
Hofstra University *B*
Houghton College *B*
Iona College *B*
Ithaca College *B*
Le Moyne College *B*
Long Island University
    C. W. Post Campus *B, M*
    Southampton College *B*
Manhattanville College *B*
Marist College *B*
Marymount College of Fordham
    University *B*

Marymount Manhattan College *B*
Medaille College *B*
Mercy College *B*
Molloy College *B*
Monroe Community College *A*
Mount St. Mary College *B*
Nazareth College of Rochester *B*
New York Institute of Technology *B*
New York University *B, M, D*
Niagara University *B*
Pace University *B, M*
Pace University:
    Pleasantville/Briarcliff *B, M*
Russell Sage College *B*
St. Bonaventure University *B*
St. John Fisher College *B*
St. John's University *B, M*
St. Joseph's College: Suffolk Campus *B*
St. Lawrence University *B*
Sarah Lawrence College *B*
Skidmore College *B*
State University of New York
    Albany *B, M, D*
    Binghamton *B, M, D*
    Buffalo *B, M, D*
    College at Brockport *B*
    College at Buffalo *B*
    College at Cortland *B*
    College at Fredonia *B*
    College at Geneseo *B, T*
    College at Oneonta *B*
    College at Plattsburgh *B*
    College at Potsdam *B*
    New Paltz *B*
    Oswego *B*
    Purchase *B*
    Stony Brook *B, M, D*
Suffolk County Community College *A*
Syracuse University *B, M, D*
Touro College *B*
Union College *B*
United States Military Academy *B*
University of Rochester *B, M, D*
Utica College *B*
Vassar College *B*
Wagner College *B*
Yeshiva University *B*

North Carolina

Appalachian State University *B, M*
Barber-Scotia College *B*
Barton College *B*
Belmont Abbey College *B*
Bennett College *B*
Campbell University *B*
Catawba College *B*
Davidson College *B*
Duke University *B, M, D*
East Carolina University *B*
Elizabeth City State University *B*
Elon University *B*
Fayetteville State University *B*
Gardner-Webb University *B*
Greensboro College *B*
Guilford College *B*
Guilford Technical Community
    College *A*
High Point University *B*
Johnson C. Smith University *B*
Lenoir-Rhyne College *B, T*
Livingstone College *B*
Mars Hill College *B*
Meredith College *B*
Methodist College *A, B*
North Carolina Agricultural and
    Technical State University *B*
North Carolina Central University *B*
North Carolina State University *B, M*
North Carolina Wesleyan College *B*
Queens University of Charlotte *B*
St. Andrews Presbyterian College *B*
St. Augustine's College *B*

University of North Carolina
    Asheville *B, T*
    Chapel Hill *B, M, D*
    Charlotte *B*
    Greensboro *B, M, T*
    Pembroke *B*
    Wilmington *B*
Wake Forest University *B*
Warren Wilson College *B*
Western Carolina University *B*
Winston-Salem State University *B*

North Dakota

Dickinson State University *B*
Jamestown College *B*
North Dakota State University *B*
University of North Dakota *B, M*

Ohio

Antioch College *B*
Ashland University *B*
Baldwin-Wallace College *B*
Bluffton College *B*
Bowling Green State University *B, M*
Case Western Reserve
    University *B, M, D*
Cedarville University *B*
Central State University *B*
Cleveland State University *B*
College of Wooster *B*
Denison University *B*
Franciscan University of Steubenville *B*
Heidelberg College *B*
Hiram College *B*
John Carroll University *B*
Kent State University *B, M, D*
Kent State University
    Stark Campus *B*
Kenyon College *B*
Malone College *B*
Marietta College *B*
Miami University
    Middletown Campus *A*
    Oxford Campus *B, M, D*
Mount Union College *B*
Muskingum College *B*
Notre Dame College *B, T*
Oberlin College *B*
Ohio Dominican College *B, T*
Ohio Northern University *B*
Ohio State University
    Columbus Campus *B, M, D*
Ohio University *B, M*
Ohio Wesleyan University *B*
Otterbein College *B*
University of Akron *C, B, M*
University of Cincinnati *B, M, D*
University of Dayton *B*
University of Findlay *B*
University of Rio Grande *A*
University of Toledo *A, B, M*
Urbana University *B*
Walsh University *B*
Wilmington College *B*
Wittenberg University *B*
Wright State University *B*
Xavier University *A, B*
Youngstown State University *B*

Oklahoma

Bacone College *A*
Cameron University *B*
East Central University *B*
Northeastern State University *B*
Northwestern Oklahoma State
    University *B*
Oklahoma Baptist University *B*
Oklahoma Christian University of
    Science and Arts *B*
Oklahoma City University *B*
Oklahoma State University *B, M*
Oklahoma Wesleyan University *B*
Oral Roberts University *B*
Rose State College *A*
St. Gregory's University *A, B*
Southern Nazarene University *B*

Southwestern Oklahoma State
  University *B*
Tulsa Community College *A*
University of Central Oklahoma *B, M*
University of Oklahoma *B, M, D*
University of Science and Arts of
  Oklahoma *B*
University of Tulsa *B*
Western Oklahoma State College *A*

Oregon

Chemeketa Community College *A*
Eastern Oregon University *B*
George Fox University *B*
Lewis & Clark College *B*
Linfield College *B*
Linn-Benton Community College *A*
Oregon State University *B*
Pacific University *B*
Portland State University *B, M*
Reed College *B*
Southern Oregon University *B*
University of Oregon *B, M, D*
University of Portland *B*
Western Oregon University *B*
Willamette University *B*

Pennsylvania

Albright College *B*
Allegheny College *R*
Arcadia University *B*
Bloomsburg University of
  Pennsylvania *B*
Bryn Mawr College *B*
Bucknell University *B*
Cabrini College *R*
California University of Pennsylvania *B*
Carnegie Mellon University *B*
Cedar Crest College *B*
Chatham College *B*
Chestnut Hill College *B*
Cheyney University of Pennsylvania *B*
DeSales University *B, T*
Dickinson College *B*
Duquesne University *B*
East Stroudsburg University of
  Pennsylvania *B, M*
Edinboro University of Pennsylvania *B*
Elizabethtown College *B*
Franklin & Marshall College *B*
Geneva College *B*
Gettysburg College *B*
Grove City College *B*
Haverford College *B, T*
Immaculata University *C, B*
Indiana University of Pennsylvania *B*
Juniata College *B*
King's College *B*
Kutztown University of Pennsylvania *B*
La Salle University *B*
Lafayette College *B*
Lebanon Valley College of
  Pennsylvania *B*
Lehigh University *B, M*
Lincoln University *B*
Lock Haven University of
  Pennsylvania *B*
Lycoming College *B*
Mercyhurst College *B*
Messiah College *B*
Millersville University of
  Pennsylvania *B, T*
Moravian College *B*
Muhlenberg College *B*
Neumann College *B, T*

Penn State
  Abington *B*
  Altoona *B*
  Beaver *B*
  Berks *B*
  Delaware County *B*
  Dubois *B*
  Erie, The Behrend College *B*
  Fayette *B*
  Hazleton *B*
  Lehigh Valley *B*
  McKeesport *B*
  Mont Alto *B*
  New Kensington *B*
  Schuylkill - Capital College *B*
  Shenango *B*
  University Park *B, M, D*
  Wilkes-Barre *B*
  Worthington Scranton *B*
  York *B*
Point Park College *B*
Rosemont College *B*
St. Joseph's University *B*
St. Vincent College *B*
Seton Hill University *B*
Shippensburg University of
  Pennsylvania *B, T*
Slippery Rock University of
  Pennsylvania *B, T*
Swarthmore College *B*
Temple University *B, M, D*
Thiel College *B*
University of Pennsylvania *B, M, D*
University of Pittsburgh *B, M, D*
University of Pittsburgh
  Bradford *B*
  Greensburg *R*
  Johnstown *B*
University of Scranton *A, B*
Villanova University *B, M*
Washington and Jefferson College *B*
Waynesburg College *B*
West Chester University of
  Pennsylvania *B*
Widener University *B*
Wilkes University *B*
Wilson College *B*
York College of Pennsylvania *B*

Puerto Rico

Inter American University of Puerto Rico
  Metropolitan Campus *B*
  San German Campus *B*
Pontifical Catholic University of Puerto
  Rico *B*
University of Puerto Rico
  Mayaguez Campus *B*
  Rio Piedras Campus *B*

Rhode Island

Brown University *B, M, D*
Rhode Island College *B*
Roger Williams University *B*
Salve Regina University *B*
University of Rhode Island *B, M*

South Carolina

Benedict College *B*
Charleston Southern University *B*
The Citadel *B*
Clemson University *B*
Coastal Carolina University *B*
Coker College *B*
College of Charleston *B, T*
Converse College *B*
Francis Marion University *B*
Furman University *B*
Lander University *B, T*
Morris College *B*
Newberry College *B*
Presbyterian College *B*
South Carolina State University *B*
University of South Carolina *B, M, D*
University of South Carolina
  Aiken *B*
  Spartanburg *B*

Voorhees College *B*
Winthrop University *B*

South Dakota

Augustana College *B, T*
Black Hills State University *B*
Northern State University *B*
South Dakota State University *B, T*
University of Sioux Falls *B*
University of South Dakota *B, M*

Tennessee

Austin Peay State University *B*
Belmont University *B, T*
Carson-Newman College *B, T*
East Tennessee State University *B*
Fisk University *B*
Jackson State Community College *A*
King College *B, T*
Lambuth University *B*
Lee University *B*
Maryville College *B, T*
Middle Tennessee State University *B*
Rhodes College *B*
Roane State Community College *A*
Tennessee State University *B*
Tennessee Technological University *B*
Trevecca Nazarene University *B, T*
Union University *B, T*
University of Memphis *B, M*
University of Tennessee
  Chattanooga *B*
  Knoxville *B, M, D*
  Martin *B*
Vanderbilt University *B, M, D*

Texas

Abilene Christian University *B, T*
Angelo State University *B, T*
Austin College *B*
Austin Community College *A*
Baylor University *B, M*
Brazosport College *A*
Coastal Bend College *A*
College of the Mainland *A*
Dallas Baptist University *B*
Del Mar College *A*
El Paso Community College *A*
Frank Phillips College *A*
Galveston College *A*
Hardin-Simmons University *B*
Houston Baptist University *B*
Howard Payne University *B, T*
Huston-Tillotson College *B*
Lamar University *B, M*
Laredo Community College *A*
LeTourneau University *B*
Lon Morris College *A*
McMurry University *B, T*
Midland College *A*
Midwestern State University *B, M*
Northeast Texas Community College *A*
Our Lady of the Lake University of San
  Antonio *B*
Palo Alto College *A*
Panola College *A*
Paris Junior College *A*
Prairie View A&M University *B*
Rice University *B, M, D*
St. Edward's University *B, T*
St. Mary's University *B, M, T*
St. Philip's College *A*
Sam Houston State University *B, M*
Schreiner University *B*
South Plains College *A*
Southern Methodist University *B*
Southwest Texas State
  University *B, M, T*
Southwestern University *B, T*
Stephen F. Austin State University *B, T*
Sul Ross State University *B, M*
Tarleton State University *B, M, T*
Texas A&M International
  University *B, M, T*
Texas A&M University *B, M, D*

Texas A&M University
  Commerce *B, M*
  Corpus Christi *B, T*
  Kingsville *B, M, T*
Texas Christian University *B, T*
Texas College *B*
Texas Lutheran University *B*
Texas Southern University *B*
Texas Tech University *B, M, D*
Texas Wesleyan University *B, T*
Texas Woman's University *B, M, T*
Trinity University *B*
University of Dallas *B, M, T*
University of Houston *B, M, D*
University of Houston
  Clear Lake *B*
  Downtown *B*
University of Mary Hardin-Baylor *B, T*
University of North Texas *B, M, D*
University of St. Thomas *B*
University of Texas
  Arlington *B, M*
  Austin *B, M, D*
  Brownsville *B*
  Dallas *B*
  El Paso *B, M*
  Pan American *B*
  San Antonio *B, M*
  Tyler *B, M*
  of the Permian Basin *B*
University of the Incarnate Word *B*
Wayland Baptist University *B*
West Texas A&M University *B, M, T*
Western Texas College *A*

Utah

Brigham Young University *B, M*
Dixie State College of Utah *A*
Snow College *A*
Southern Utah University *B*
University of Utah *B, M, D*
Utah State University *B, M*
Weber State University *B*
Westminster College *B*

Vermont

Bennington College *B*
College of St. Joseph in Vermont *B*
Johnson State College *B*
Marlboro College *B*
Middlebury College *B*
Norwich University *B*
St. Michael's College *B*
University of Vermont *B*

Virginia

Averett University *B*
Bridgewater College *B*
Christendom College *B*
College of William and Mary *B*
Emory & Henry College *B*
Ferrum College *B*
George Mason University *B*
Hampden-Sydney College *B*
Hampton University *B*
Hollins University *B*
James Madison University *B, T*
Liberty University *B*
Longwood University *B, T*
Lynchburg College *B*
Mary Baldwin College *B*
Mary Washington College *B*
Marymount University *B*
Norfolk State University *B*
Old Dominion University *B*
Radford University *B*
Randolph-Macon College *B*
Randolph-Macon Woman's College *B*
Roanoke College *B*
Sweet Briar College *B*
University of Richmond *B*
University of Virginia *B, M, D*
University of Virginia's College at
  Wise *B, T*
Virginia Commonwealth University *B*
Virginia Intermont College *B*

Virginia Polytechnic Institute and State
University *B, M*
Virginia State University *B*
Virginia Union University *B*
Virginia Wesleyan College *B*
Washington and Lee University *B*

Washington
Central Washington University *B*
Eastern Washington University *B, T*
Everett Community College *A*
Gonzaga University *B*
Lower Columbia College *A*
Olympic College *A*
Pacific Lutheran University *B*
St. Martin's College *B*
Seattle Pacific University *B*
Seattle University *B*
University of Puget Sound *B, T*
University of Washington *B, M, D*
Washington State University *B, M, D*
Western Washington University *B, M*
Whitman College *B*
Whitworth College *B*

West Virginia
Bethany College *B*
Concord College *B*
Davis and Elkins College *B*
Fairmont State College *B*
Marshall University *B, M*
Potomac State College of West Virginia
University *A*
Shepherd College *B*
University of Charleston *B*
West Liberty State College *B*
West Virginia State College *B*
West Virginia University *B, M, D*
West Virginia Wesleyan College *B*
Wheeling Jesuit University *B*

Wisconsin
Alverno College *B*
Beloit College *B*
Cardinal Stritch University *B*
Carroll College *B*
Carthage College *B*
Edgewood College *B*
Lawrence University *B, T*
Marian College of Fond du Lac *B*
Marquette University *B, M, T*
Ripon College *B*
St. Norbert College *B, T*
University of Wisconsin
Eau Claire *B*
Green Bay *B*
La Crosse *B, T*
Madison *B, M, D*
Milwaukee *B, M, D*
Oshkosh *B*
Parkside *B, T*
Platteville *B, T*
River Falls *B, T*
Stevens Point *B*
Superior *B*
Wisconsin Lutheran College *B*

Wyoming
Eastern Wyoming College *A*
Laramie County Community College *A*
Sheridan College *A*
University of Wyoming *B, M*
Western Wyoming Community
College *A*

Polymer chemistry

California
University of California
Davis *B*

Connecticut
University of Connecticut *M, D*

Georgia
Clark Atlanta University *M, D*

Georgia Institute of Technology *M*

Iowa
Loras College *B*

Massachusetts
Harvard College *B*
University of Massachusetts
Amherst *M, D*
Lowell *D*

Minnesota
Winona State University *B*

Mississippi
University of Southern
Mississippi *B, M, D*

New Jersey
Stevens Institute of Technology *M, D*

New York
City University of New York
College of Staten Island *D*
Rochester Institute of Technology *B*
State University of New York
College of Environmental Science
and Forestry *B, M, D*

North Carolina
North Carolina State University *M, D*

North Dakota
North Dakota State University *B, M, D*

Ohio
University of Akron *B, M, D*

Pennsylvania
Carnegie Mellon University *M*
Millersville University of
Pennsylvania *B*

Wisconsin
University of Wisconsin
River Falls *B*

Polymer/plastics engineering

California
University of Southern California *B*

Connecticut
Quinebaug Valley Community
College *C, A*

Georgia
Georgia Institute of Technology *M*

Hawaii
University of Hawaii
Honolulu Community College *C, A*

Massachusetts
Berkshire Community College *A*
Harvard College *B*
University of Massachusetts
Lowell *B, M, D*

Michigan
Eastern Michigan University *M*
Oakland Community College *A*
University of Michigan *M, D*
Wayne State University *C*

Minnesota
Winona State University *B*

Missouri
University of Missouri
Rolla *B*

New Jersey
Stevens Institute of Technology *M, D*

New York
Polytechnic University *M*
Rochester Institute of Technology *B*

State University of New York
Buffalo *M*
College of Agriculture and
Technology at Morrisville *A*

North Carolina
Wilson Technical Community College *A*

Ohio
Case Western Reserve
University *B, M, D*
Kent State University
Ashtabula Regional Campus *C, A*
University of Akron *C, B, M, D*

Pennsylvania
Lehigh University *M, D*

Tennessee
University of Tennessee
Knoxville *M, D*

Texas
Trinity Valley Community College *A*

Population biology

California
University of California
Riverside *D*

Colorado
University of Colorado
Boulder *B, M, D*

Maryland
University of Maryland
College Park *B*

Portuguese

California
Chabot College *A*
Santa Rosa Junior College *A*
University of California
Los Angeles *B, M*
Santa Barbara *B, M*

Connecticut
University of Connecticut *B*
Yale University *B, M, D*

District of Columbia
George Washington University *B*
Georgetown University *B*

Florida
Florida International University *B*
University of Florida *B*
University of Miami *B*

Illinois
University of Chicago *B*
University of Illinois
Urbana-Champaign *B, M, D*

Indiana
Indiana University
Bloomington *B, M, D*

Iowa
University of Iowa *B, T*

Louisiana
Tulane University *B, M, D*

Massachusetts
Harvard College *B*
Smith College *B*
University of Massachusetts
Amherst *B*
Dartmouth *B*

Minnesota
University of Minnesota
Twin Cities *B, M*

New Jersey
Rutgers, The State University of New
Jersey
New Brunswick Regional
Campus *B*

New Mexico
University of New Mexico *B, M*

New York
New York University *B, M, D*
United States Military Academy *B*

North Carolina
University of North Carolina
Chapel Hill *B*

Ohio
Ohio State University
Columbus Campus *B, M, D*

Pennsylvania
Dickinson College *C*

Rhode Island
Brown University *B, M, D*

Tennessee
University of Tennessee
Knoxville *B*
Vanderbilt University *D*

Texas
University of Texas
Austin *B, M, D*

Utah
Brigham Young University *B, M*

Wisconsin
University of Wisconsin
Madison *B, M, D*

Poultry science

Alabama
Auburn University *B, M, D*
Tuskegee University *B, M*

Arkansas
University of Arkansas *B, M, D*

California
California Polytechnic State University:
San Luis Obispo *B*
Modesto Junior College *A*

Delaware
Delaware Technical and Community
College
Owens Campus *C, A*

Florida
University of Florida *M*

Georgia
Abraham Baldwin Agricultural
College *A*
University of Georgia *B, M, D*

Minnesota
Ridgewater College: A Community and
Technical College *C*

Mississippi
Mississippi State University *B, M*
Northwest Mississippi Community
College *A*

Missouri
College of the Ozarks *B*
Crowder College *A*

North Carolina
James Sprunt Community College *C, A*
North Carolina State University *B, M*
Surry Community College *A*
Wayne Community College *A*

Ohio
Ohio State University
    Columbus Campus *M, D*

Oregon
Oregon State University *M, D*

Pennsylvania
Penn State
    University Park *C*

Puerto Rico
Inter American University of Puerto Rico
    Barranquitas Campus *C*

South Carolina
Clemson University *B*

Texas
Stephen F. Austin State University *B*
Texas A&M University *B, M, D*
Texas Tech University *C*

Utah
Snow College *A*

Power/electrical transmission

Alabama
Alabama Southern Community
    College *C, A*
Bevill State Community College *A*
Lawson State Community College *C*
Northwest-Shoals Community College *C*
Shelton State Community College *C, A*

Arizona
Gateway Community College *C, A*

Arkansas
Phillips Community College of the
    University of Arkansas *C*

California
Bakersfield College *A*
Chabot College *A*
Coastline Community College *C*
College of the Redwoods *C*
Foothill College *C*
Los Angeles Trade and Technical
    College *A*
Orange Coast College *C, A*
Palomar College *C, A*
San Diego City College *C, A*
San Joaquin Delta College *C, A*

Colorado
Community College of Aurora *A*
Mesa State College *C*
Red Rocks Community College *C, A*

Connecticut
Central Connecticut State University *B*

Florida
Palm Beach Community College *C*
South Florida Community College *C*

Georgia
Chattahoochee Technical College *C*
Clayton College and State University *A*
Darton College *A*

Hawaii
University of Hawaii
    Hawaii Community College *C, A*

Idaho
Boise State University *C*

Illinois
Illinois Eastern Community Colleges
    Lincoln Trail College *C*
Kishwaukee College *C*
Lincoln Land Community College *C*
Parkland College *C*
Sauk Valley Community College *C*
Southwestern Illinois College *C, A*

Indiana
Ivy Tech State College
    Columbus *C, A*
    Southwest *C*
Oakland City University *C*

Iowa
Kirkwood Community College *A*
Northeast Iowa Community College *A*
Northwest Iowa Community College *A*

Kansas
Allen County Community College *C*
Johnson County Community
    College *C, A*

Massachusetts
Benjamin Franklin Institute of
    Technology *C*

Michigan
Lansing Community College *A*
Macomb Community College *C*

Minnesota
St. Paul College - A Community and
    Technical College *C*

Mississippi
Mississippi Gulf Coast Community
    College
    Perkinston *C, A*
Pearl River Community College *A*

Montana
Miles Community College *A*

Nebraska
Central Community College *C, A*
Metropolitan Community College *C, A*
Nebraska Indian Community College *C*
Northeast Community College *A*

Nevada
Great Basin College *C*
Truckee Meadows Community
    College *C, A*

New Hampshire
New Hampshire Community Technical
    College
    Berlin *A*

New York
Mohawk Valley Community College *C*
State University of New York
    College of Technology at
    Delhi *C, A*

North Carolina
Durham Technical Community
    College *C*
James Sprunt Community College *C*
Mayland Community College *C*
Randolph Community College *C*
Richmond Community College *C*
Wake Technical Community
    College *C, A*

Ohio
Jefferson Community College *A*
Ohio State University
    Agricultural Technical Institute *A*

Oklahoma
Oklahoma State University
    Okmulgee *A*

Oregon
Rogue Community College *A*

Pennsylvania
Dean Institute of Technology *A*
Delaware County Community College *C*
Pennsylvania College of Technology *C*

South Carolina
Aiken Technical College *C*
Technical College of the Lowcountry *C*

South Dakota
Western Dakota Technical Institute *C, A*

Tennessee
Northeast State Technical Community
    College *A*
Walters State Community College *A*

Texas
Amarillo College *C, A*
Frank Phillips College *C, A*
Houston Community College System *C*
Laredo Community College *A*
North Lake College *A*
South Plains College *C, A*
Texarkana College *C*
Texas State Technical College
    Waco *A*

Utah
Salt Lake Community College *C, A*
Utah Valley State College *C, A*

Washington
Clover Park Technical College *C*
Olympic College *C, A*
Spokane Community College *A*

Wisconsin
Chippewa Valley Technical College *C*
Milwaukee Area Technical College *C*
Western Wisconsin Technical College *C*

Pre-ministerial studies

Connecticut
University of Hartford *B*

Florida
Florida State University *B*

Illinois
Trinity International University *B*

Indiana
Valparaiso University *B*

Iowa
Loras College *B*

Massachusetts
St. John's Seminary College *B*

Michigan
Adrian College *B*

Minnesota
St. John's University *B*
St. Mary's University of Minnesota *B*

Nebraska
Concordia University *B*

Pennsylvania
Juniata College *B*

Texas
Texas A&M University
    Commerce *B*
Texas Lutheran University *B*

Virginia
Shenandoah University *C*

Precision production trades, general

Alabama
Harry M. Ayers State Technical
    College *A*

California
Yuba Community College District *C, A*

Michigan
Ferris State University *A*
Grand Rapids Community College *A*

Minnesota
Dakota County Technical College *C*

Wisconsin
Western Wisconsin Technical College *A*

Predentistry

Alabama
Alabama Southern Community
    College *A*
Calhoun Community College *A*
Faulkner University *B*
Huntingdon College *B*
James H. Faulkner State Community
    College *A*
Northeast Alabama Community
    College *A*
Northwest-Shoals Community College *A*
Spring Hill College *B*

Arkansas
Harding University *B*
John Brown University *B*
Ouachita Baptist University *B*
University of Arkansas
    Fort Smith *A*
University of Central Arkansas *B*

California
Azusa Pacific University *B*
Bakersfield College *A*
California State University
    Chico *B*
Chabot College *A*
Chapman University *B*
Claremont McKenna College *B*
College of the Siskiyous *A*
Foothill College *A*
Golden West College *A*
Marymount College *B*
Master's College *B*
Monterey Peninsula College *A*
Mount St. Mary's College *B*
Pacific Union College *C*
Ventura College *A*
Whittier College *B*

Colorado
Otero Junior College *A*
Regis University *B*

Connecticut
Albertus Magnus College *B*
Quinnipiac University *B*
Southern Connecticut State University *B*
University of Hartford *B*
University of New Haven *B*

Delaware
University of Delaware *B*

Florida
Barry University *B*
Broward Community College *A*
Eckerd College *B*
Florida State University *B*
Gulf Coast Community College *A*
Indian River Community College *A*
Jacksonville University *B*
Miami-Dade Community College *A*
Okaloosa-Walton Community College *A*
Pensacola Junior College *A*
Santa Fe Community College *A*
University of Central Florida *B*
University of Miami *B*
University of Tampa *B*
University of West Florida *B*

Georgia
Abraham Baldwin Agricultural
    College *A*
Andrew College *A*
Columbus State University *B*
Darton College *A*
Georgia Institute of Technology *B*
Georgia Perimeter College *A*
Georgia Southwestern State University *B*
Kennesaw State University *B*
LaGrange College *B*
Macon State College *A*
Middle Georgia College *A*
Morehouse College *B*

North Georgia College & State
   University *B*
Oglethorpe University *B*
South Georgia College *A*
University of Georgia *B*
Young Harris College *A*

Idaho

Boise State University *B*
Brigham Young University - Idaho *B*
College of Southern Idaho *A*
North Idaho College *A*
Northwest Nazarene University *B*
University of Idaho *B*

Illinois

Augustana College *B*
Black Hawk College
   East Campus *A*
Blackburn College *B*
City Colleges of Chicago
   Harold Washington College *A*
   Kennedy-King College *A*
Dominican University *B*
Elmhurst College *B*
Eureka College *B*
Greenville College *B*
Illinois Central College *A*
Judson College *B*
Kankakee Community College *A*
Kishwaukee College *A*
Lewis and Clark Community College *A*
Lincoln Land Community College *A*
MacMurray College *B*
McKendree College *B*
Millikin University *B*
North Park University *B*
Parkland College *A*
Rockford College *B*
Roosevelt University *B*
Sauk Valley Community College *A*
Southeastern Illinois College *C*
Springfield College in Illinois *A*
University of Illinois
   Chicago *B*
University of St. Francis *B*

Indiana

Bethel College *B*
Goshen College *B*
Grace College *B*
Indiana University
   Kokomo *B*
Indiana University-Purdue University
   Fort Wayne *B*
Indiana Wesleyan University *B*
Manchester College *B*
St. Joseph's College *B*
St. Mary-of-the-Woods College *B*
University of Evansville *B*
University of Indianapolis *B*
University of St. Francis *B*
Vincennes University *A*

Iowa

Buena Vista University *B*
Clarke College *B*
Coe College *B*
Cornell College *B*
Dordt College *B*
Ellsworth Community College *A*
Iowa Wesleyan College *B*
Luther College *B*
Marshalltown Community College *A*
Morningside College *B*
North Iowa Area Community College *A*
Northwestern College *B*
Simpson College *B*
University of Iowa *B*
Upper Iowa University *B*
Waldorf College *A*

Kansas

Barton County Community College *A*
Kansas City Kansas Community
   College *A*
Kansas State University *B*

McPherson College *B*
Pittsburg State University *B*
Pratt Community College *A*
Seward County Community College *A*
Tabor College *B*
Washburn University of Topeka *B*

Kentucky

Bellarmine University *B*
Campbellsville University *B*
Centre College *B*
Cumberland College *B*
Murray State University *B*
Thomas More College *B*
Union College *B*

Louisiana

Centenary College of Louisiana *B*
Louisiana College *B*
Nicholls State University *B*
University of Louisiana at Monroe *B*

Maine

University of New England *B*
University of Southern Maine *B*

Maryland

Columbia Union College *B*
Community College of Baltimore County
   Catonsville *A*
   Dundalk *A*
   Essex *A*
Coppin State College *B*
Frostburg State University *B*
Howard Community College *A*
Montgomery College
   Rockville Campus *A*
Morgan State University *B*
University of Maryland
   Baltimore County *B*
Villa Julie College *B*

Massachusetts

American International College *B*
Cape Cod Community College *A*
Elms College *B*
Framingham State College *B*
Hampshire College *B*
Simmons College *B*
Springfield College *B*
Springfield Technical Community
   College *A*
University of Massachusetts
   Amherst *B*
Worcester Polytechnic Institute *B*

Michigan

Adrian College *B*
Alma College *B*
Calvin College *B*
Cornerstone University *B*
Eastern Michigan University *B*
Ferris State University *A*
Gogebic Community College *A*
Grand Valley State University *B*
Hillsdale College *B*
Kalamazoo College *B*
Kirtland Community College *A*
Lansing Community College *A*
Michigan Technological University *B*
Northern Michigan University *B*
Schoolcraft College *A*
Siena Heights University *A, B*

Minnesota

Bethel College *B*
College of St. Benedict *B*
College of St. Catherine *B*
Concordia College: Moorhead *B*
Gustavus Adolphus College *B*
Hamline University *B*
Minnesota State University
   Mankato *B*
   Moorhead *B*
St. Cloud State University *B*
St. John's University *B*

University of Minnesota
   Duluth *B*
   Twin Cities *B*
Vermilion Community College *A*
Winona State University *B*

Mississippi

Blue Mountain College *B*
Coahoma Community College *A*
Holmes Community College *A*
Itawamba Community College *A*
Mary Holmes College *A*

Missouri

Drury University *B*
East Central College *A*
Evangel University *B*
Lindenwood University *B*
Maryville University of Saint Louis *B*
Missouri Southern State College *A*
St. Louis Community College
   St. Louis Community College at
      Florissant Valley *A*
Stephens College *B*
Truman State University *B*
University of Missouri
   Rolla *B*
   St. Louis *B*
Washington University in St. Louis *B*

Montana

Montana Tech of the University of
   Montana *B*

Nebraska

Bellevue University *B*
College of Saint Mary *B*
Concordia University *B*
Dana College *B*
Hastings College *B*
Midland Lutheran College *B*
Northeast Community College *A*
University of Nebraska
   Lincoln *B*
Western Nebraska Community
   College *A*
York College *A*

Nevada

Sierra Nevada College *B*

New Hampshire

Franklin Pierce College *B*
Rivier College *B*
St. Anselm College *B*
University of New Hampshire *B*

New Jersey

Bloomfield College *B*
Georgian Court College *B*
Rowan University *B*
Rutgers, The State University of New
   Jersey
      Camden Regional Campus *B*
      New Brunswick Regional
         Campus *B*
      Newark Regional Campus *B*
Stevens Institute of Technology *B*
Sussex County Community College *A*

New Mexico

New Mexico Junior College *A*

New York

Alfred University *B*
Bard College *B*
City University of New York
   Brooklyn College *B*
   College of Staten Island *B*
   Queens College *B*
Colgate University *B*
D'Youville College *B*
Elmira College *B*
Fordham University *B*
Hobart and William Smith Colleges *B*
Houghton College *B*
Ithaca College *B*
Le Moyne College *B*

Long Island University
   C. W. Post Campus *B*
Manhattan College *B*
Marist College *B*
Molloy College *B*
New York University *B*
Paul Smith's College *B*
Rensselaer Polytechnic Institute *B*
Rochester Institute of Technology *B*
St. Joseph's College: Suffolk Campus *B*
Sarah Lawrence College *B*
State University of New York
   Albany *B*
   College at Brockport *B*
   College at Geneseo *B*
   College at Plattsburgh *B*
   College of Environmental Science
      and Forestry *B*
   New Paltz *B*
Syracuse University *B*
Touro College *B*
Wagner College *B*
Wells College *B*

North Carolina

Appalachian State University *B*
Barton College *B*
Belmont Abbey College *B*
Campbell University *B*
Carteret Community College *A*
Chowan College *B*
Elon University *B*
Lees-McRae College *B*
Livingstone College *B*
Mars Hill College *B*
Meredith College *B*
Methodist College *B*
Mitchell Community College *A*
North Carolina State University *B*
Pfeiffer University *B*
Queens University of Charlotte *B*
Sandhills Community College *A*
Wingate University *B*

North Dakota

Dickinson State University *B*
Mayville State University *B*
Valley City State University *B*

Ohio

Defiance College *B*
Heidelberg College *B*
John Carroll University *B*
Kent State University *B*
Kent State University
   Stark Campus *B*
Kettering College of Medical Arts *A*
Miami University
   Oxford Campus *B*
Mount Vernon Nazarene University *B*
Muskingum College *B*
Oberlin College *B*
Ohio Northern University *B*
Ohio University *B*
Ohio Wesleyan University *B*
Otterbein College *B*
University of Cincinnati *B*
University of Cincinnati
   Clermont College *A*
   Raymond Walters College *A*
University of Dayton *B*
University of Toledo *B*
Urbana University *B*
Walsh University *B*
Wittenberg University *B*
Youngstown State University *B*

Oklahoma

East Central University *B*
Eastern Oklahoma State College *A*
Northeastern Oklahoma Agricultural and
   Mechanical College *A*
Oklahoma Christian University of
   Science and Arts *B*
Oklahoma City University *B*
Oklahoma State University *B*
Redlands Community College *A*

Rose State College *A*

Oregon

Central Oregon Community College *A*
Chemeketa Community College *A*
Eastern Oregon University *B*
Linn-Benton Community College *A*
Southern Oregon University *B*
University of Portland *B*
Western Baptist College *B*

Pennsylvania

Albright College *B*
Allegheny College *B*
California University of Pennsylvania *B*
Elizabethtown College *B*
Gettysburg College *B*
Grove City College *B*
Holy Family University *B*
Immaculata University *B*
Juniata College *B*
La Salle University *B*
Lehigh University *B*
Lock Haven University of
  Pennsylvania *B*
Mercyhurst College *B*
Muhlenberg College *B*
Reading Area Community College *A*
St. Vincent College *B*
University of Pittsburgh
  Greensburg *B*
  Johnstown *B*
Villanova University *B*
Waynesburg College *B*
Wilkes University *B*
York College of Pennsylvania *B*

Puerto Rico

University of Puerto Rico
  Ponce *A*

Rhode Island

Rhode Island College *B*

South Carolina

Charleston Southern University *B*
College of Charleston *B*
Furman University *B*
North Greenville College *B*
Spartanburg Technical College *A*

South Dakota

Augustana College *B*
Dakota State University *B*
Dakota Wesleyan University *B*

Tennessee

Carson-Newman College *B*
Columbia State Community College *A*
Freed-Hardeman University *B*
Lambuth University *B*
Maryville College *B*
Roane State Community College *A*
Tennessee Technological University *B*
Tennessee Wesleyan College *B*
Union University *B*
University of Tennessee
  Knoxville *B*
  Martin *B*
Walters State Community College *A*

Texas

Abilene Christian University *B*
Amarillo College *A*
Angelina College *A*
Austin Community College *A*
Baylor University *B*
Coastal Bend College *A*
Concordia University at Austin *B*
Del Mar College *A*
El Paso Community College *A*
Galveston College *A*
Grayson County College *A*
Howard College *A*
Laredo Community College *A*
LeTourneau University *B*
Lon Morris College *A*
Lubbock Christian University *B*

McMurry University *B*
Midland College *A*
Midwestern State University *B*
Panola College *A*
Paris Junior College *A*
St. Edward's University *B*
St. Philip's College *A*
San Antonio College *A*
South Plains College *A*
Texas A&M University *B*
Texas A&M University
  Commerce *B*
Texas Christian University *B*
Texas Wesleyan University *B*
Trinity Valley Community College *A*
Tyler Junior College *A*
University of Texas
  Pan American *B*
Western Texas College *A*

Utah

Brigham Young University *B*
Snow College *A*
Southern Utah University *B*
University of Utah *B*
Utah State University *B*

Vermont

Castleton State College *B*

Virginia

College of Health Sciences *B*
Longwood University *B*
Mountain Empire Community College *A*
Virginia Intermont College *B*
Virginia Wesleyan College *B*

Washington

Centralia College *A*
Eastern Washington University *B*
Everett Community College *A*
Lower Columbia College *A*
St. Martin's College *B*
Seattle Pacific University *B*
Washington State University *B*

West Virginia

Alderson-Broaddus College *B*
Concord University *B*
Davis and Elkins College *B*
Potomac State College of West Virginia
  University *A*
West Virginia Wesleyan College *B*

Wisconsin

Carthage College *B*
Lawrence University *B*
Marian College of Fond du Lac *B*
Mount Mary College *B*
Northland College *B*
Ripon College *B*
St. Norbert College *B*
University of Wisconsin
  Madison *B*
  Milwaukee *B*
  Oshkosh *B*
  Parkside *B*

Wyoming

Casper College *A*
Eastern Wyoming College *A*
Western Wyoming Community
  College *A*

Prelaw

Alabama

Alabama Southern Community
  College *A*
Enterprise State Junior College *A*
Faulkner University *B*
Huntingdon College *B*
Lawson State Community College *A*
Northwest-Shoals Community College *A*
Shelton State Community College *A*
Talladega College *B*

Wallace State Community College at
  Hanceville *A*

Alaska

Alaska Pacific University *B*
University of Alaska
  Southeast *A*

Arizona

Arizona State University *B*
Eastern Arizona College *A*
Northern Arizona University *B*

Arkansas

John Brown University *B*
Ouachita Baptist University *B*
Phillips Community College of the
  University of Arkansas *A*

California

Bakersfield College *A*
Biola University *B*
California State University
  Bakersfield *B*
  Chico *B*
  Dominguez Hills *B*
  Stanislaus *B*
Chabot College *A*
Claremont McKenna College *B*
College of the Siskiyous *A*
Concordia University *B*
Foothill College *A*
Golden West College *A*
Marymount College *A*
Master's College *B*
MiraCosta College *A*
Mount St. Mary's College *B*
Pacific Union College *B*
San Diego City College *A*
San Joaquin Delta College *A*
University of California
  Riverside *B*
Ventura College *A*
Whittier College *B*

Colorado

Colorado Mountain College
  Spring Valley Campus *A*
  Timberline Campus *A*
Otero Junior College *A*
Regis University *B*
Trinidad State Junior College *A*

Connecticut

Albertus Magnus College *B*
Quinnipiac University *B*
Southern Connecticut State University *B*
Teikyo Post University *B*
Trinity College *B*
University of Hartford *B*

Delaware

University of Delaware *B*

Florida

Barry University *B*
Broward Community College *A*
Chipola Junior College *A*
Eckerd College *B*
Edward Waters College *B*
Florida State University *B*
Gulf Coast Community College *A*
Indian River Community College *A*
Jacksonville University *B*
Lake City Community College *A*
Manatee Community College *A*
Miami-Dade Community College *A*
Nova Southeastern University *B*
Pensacola Junior College *A*
St. Thomas University *B*
University of Central Florida *B*
University of Miami *B*
University of Tampa *B*
University of West Florida *B*
Webber International University *B*

Georgia

Abraham Baldwin Agricultural
  College *A*

Andrew College *A*
Coastal Georgia Community College *A*
Columbus State University *B*
Emmanuel College *B*
Kennesaw State University *B*
LaGrange College *B*
Middle Georgia College *A*
North Georgia College & State
  University *B*
Oglethorpe University *B*
South Georgia College *A*
State University of West Georgia *B*
Valdosta State University *B*
Young Harris College *A*

Hawaii

Chaminade University of Honolulu *B*

Idaho

Brigham Young University - Idaho *A*
College of Southern Idaho *A*
Lewis-Clark State College *B*
North Idaho College *A*
Northwest Nazarene University *B*

Illinois

Augustana College *B*
Aurora University *B*
Black Hawk College
  East Campus *A*
Blackburn College *B*
City Colleges of Chicago
  Harold Washington College *A*
  Kennedy-King College *A*
Danville Area Community College *A*
Elmhurst College *B*
Illinois Central College *A*
Illinois Institute of Technology *B*
John Wood Community College *A*
Judson College *B*
Kishwaukee College *A*
Lake Land College *A*
Lewis and Clark Community College *A*
Lincoln Land Community College *A*
McKendree College *B*
Millikin University *B*
Monmouth College *B*
North Central College *B*
Richland Community College *A*
Rockford College *B*
Roosevelt University *B*
St. Xavier University *B*
Sauk Valley Community College *A*
Southeastern Illinois College *A*
Southwestern Illinois College *A*
Springfield College in Illinois *A*
Trinity International University *B*
University of St. Francis *B*

Indiana

Anderson University *B*
Ball State University *B*
Goshen College *B*
Grace College *B*
Huntington College *B*
Indiana Wesleyan University *B*
Manchester College *B*
Marian College *B*
Purdue University
  Calumet *B*
St. Joseph's College *B*
St. Mary-of-the-Woods College *B*
Taylor University: Fort Wayne *B*
University of Evansville *B*
University of Indianapolis *B*
University of St. Francis *B*
Vincennes University *A*

Iowa

Briar Cliff University *B*
Buena Vista University *B*
Coe College *B*
Dordt College *B*
Ellsworth Community College *A*
Franciscan University *B*
Grand View College *B*
Hawkeye Community College *A*

Iowa Central Community College A
Iowa Wesleyan College B
Loras College B
Luther College B
Marshalltown Community College A
Mount Mercy College B
North Iowa Area Community College A
Simpson College B
University of Iowa B
Upper Iowa University B
Waldorf College A

Kansas

Barton County Community College A
Butler County Community College A
Central Christian College A
Dodge City Community College A
Garden City Community College A
Independence Community College A
Kansas City Kansas Community
   College A
Labette Community College A
McPherson College B
Pittsburg State University B
Pratt Community College A
Seward County Community College A
Tabor College B
Washburn University of Topeka B

Kentucky

Campbellsville University B
Centre College B
Lindsey Wilson College A
Murray State University B
Thomas More College A
Union College B

Louisiana

Centenary College of Louisiana B
Grambling State University B
Louisiana College B
University of Louisiana at Lafayette B
University of Louisiana at Monroe B
University of New Orleans B

Maine

University of Southern Maine B

Maryland

College of Notre Dame of Maryland B
Community College of Baltimore County
   Catonsville A
   Dundalk A
   Essex A
Frostburg State University B
Morgan State University B
University of Baltimore B
University of Maryland
   Baltimore County B
Villa Julie College B

Massachusetts

American International College B
Bay Path College B
Becker College B
Clark University B
Elms College B
Framingham State College B
Lasell College B
Newbury College B
Springfield College B

Michigan

Adrian College B
Alma College B
Aquinas College B
Bay de Noc Community College A
Calvin College B
Concordia University B
Cornerstone University B
Eastern Michigan University B
Ferris State University B
Gogebic Community College A
Hillsdale College B
Kalamazoo College B
Kellogg Community College A
Kirtland Community College A
Lansing Community College A

Madonna University B
Northern Michigan University B
Schoolcraft College A
Siena Heights University B
West Shore Community College A

Minnesota

Bethel College B
College of St. Benedict B
College of St. Catherine B
Concordia College: Moorhead B
Gustavus Adolphus College B
Minnesota State University
   Mankato B
   Moorhead B
Northland Community & Technical
   College A
Ridgewater College: A Community and
   Technical College A
St. Cloud State University B
St. John's University B
University of Minnesota
   Duluth B
   Twin Cities B
Vermilion Community College A
Winona State University B

Mississippi

Blue Mountain College B
Coahoma Community College A
Itawamba Community College A
Mary Holmes College A
Mississippi College B

Missouri

College of the Ozarks B
Evangel University B
Fontbonne College B
Hannibal-LaGrange College A
Lindenwood University B
Maryville University of Saint Louis B
Stephens College B
Three Rivers Community College A
Truman State University B
University of Missouri
   St. Louis B
Washington University in St. Louis B

Montana

Miles Community College A
Montana Tech of the University of
   Montana B

Nebraska

Bellevue University B
Concordia University B
Creighton University B
Dana College B
Midland Lutheran College B
Northeast Community College A
Southeast Community College
   Beatrice Campus A
University of Nebraska
   Lincoln B
Western Nebraska Community
   College A

New Hampshire

New England College B
Rivier College B
St. Anselm College B

New Jersey

Rowan University B
Rutgers, The State University of New
   Jersey
   Camden Regional Campus B
   New Brunswick Regional
      Campus B
   Newark Regional Campus B
Stevens Institute of Technology B
Warren County Community College A

New Mexico

New Mexico Highlands University B
New Mexico Junior College A

New York

Alfred University B

Bard College B
City University of New York
   Brooklyn College B
   City College B
   John Jay College of Criminal
      Justice B
College of New Rochelle B
Concordia College B
D'Youville College B
Elmira College B
Fordham University B
Hofstra University B
Ithaca College B
Keuka College B
Le Moyne College B
Long Island University
   C. W. Post Campus B
   Southampton College B
Manhattan College B
Marist College B
Metropolitan College of New York A, B
Molloy College B
Mount St. Mary College B
New York University B
Rensselaer Polytechnic Institute B
Rochester Institute of Technology B
Sarah Lawrence College B
State University of New York
   Albany M
   College at Fredonia B
   College at Geneseo B
   College at Plattsburgh B
   College of Environmental Science
      and Forestry B
   New Paltz B
   Oswego B
Syracuse University B
Wells College B

North Carolina

Appalachian State University B
Barber-Scotia College B
Barton College B
Belmont Abbey College B
Campbell University B
Catawba College B
Chowan College B
College of the Albemarle A
Elon University B
Gardner-Webb University B
Johnson C. Smith University B
Lenoir-Rhyne College B
Mars Hill College B
Methodist College B
Mitchell Community College A
North Carolina State University B
Pfeiffer University B
Queens University of Charlotte B
St. Andrews Presbyterian College B
St. Augustine's College B
Sandhills Community College A
University of North Carolina
   Pembroke B
Wingate University B

North Dakota

Dickinson State University B
Mayville State University B
North Dakota State University B
Valley City State University B

Ohio

Ashland University B
Bluffton College B
Bowling Green State University B
Cedarville University B
Defiance College B
Heidelberg College B
John Carroll University B
Kent State University
   Stark Campus B
Lake Erie College B
Lorain County Community College A
Miami University
   Oxford Campus B
Muskingum College B

Oberlin College B
Ohio University B
Ohio Wesleyan University B
Otterbein College B
University of Cincinnati
   Clermont College A
   Raymond Walters College A
University of Dayton B
University of Findlay B
University of Rio Grande B
University of Toledo B
Urbana University B
Ursuline College B
Walsh University B
Wilmington College B
Youngstown State University B

Oklahoma

Bacone College A
Carl Albert State College A
East Central University B
Eastern Oklahoma State College A
Langston University B
Northeastern Oklahoma Agricultural and
   Mechanical College A
Northern Oklahoma College A
Northwestern Oklahoma State
   University B
Oklahoma Christian University of
   Science and Arts B
Oklahoma City Community College A
Oklahoma City University B
Oklahoma State University B
Rogers State University A
St. Gregory's University B
Southern Nazarene University B

Oregon

Central Oregon Community College A
Chemeketa Community College A
Eastern Oregon University B
Linn-Benton Community College A
Southern Oregon University B
Western Baptist College B
Willamette University B

Pennsylvania

Allegheny College B
California University of Pennsylvania B
Dickinson College B
Elizabethtown College B
Gettysburg College B
Grove City College B
Holy Family University B
Juniata College B
La Salle University B
Lock Haven University of
   Pennsylvania B
Marywood University B
Mercyhurst College B
Mount Aloysius College B
Muhlenberg College B
Reading Area Community College A
St. Vincent College B
Seton Hill University B
University of Pittsburgh
   Johnstown B
Washington and Jefferson College B
Waynesburg College B
West Chester University of
   Pennsylvania B
Widener University B
York College of Pennsylvania B

Puerto Rico

Pontifical Catholic University of Puerto
   Rico B
University of Puerto Rico
   Rio Piedras Campus B

South Carolina

Charleston Southern University B
Clemson University B
Columbia College B
Furman University B
Lander University B
North Greenville College B

South Dakota
Dakota State University *B*
Dakota Wesleyan University *B*

Tennessee
Columbia State Community College *A*
Crichton College *B*
Lambuth University *B*
Maryville College *B*
Roane State Community College *A*
Tennessee Wesleyan College *B*
Tusculum College *B*
Union University *B*
University of Tennessee
  Knoxville *B*

Texas
Abilene Christian University *B*
Amarillo College *A*
Angelina College *A*
Baylor University *B*
Central Texas College *A*
Cisco Junior College *A*
Clarendon College *A*
Coastal Bend College *A*
Concordia University at Austin *B*
Galveston College *A*
Grayson County College *A*
Hill College *A*
Houston Baptist University *B*
Howard Payne University *B*
Jarvis Christian College *B*
Kilgore College *A*
LeTourneau University *B*
Lon Morris College *A*
Lubbock Christian University *B*
McMurry University *B*
Midland College *A*
Panola College *A*
Paris Junior College *A*
St. Edward's University *B*
Schreiner University *B*
Texas A&M University
  Commerce *B*
Texas Wesleyan University *B*
Trinity Valley Community College *A*
Tyler Junior College *A*
University of Houston
  Clear Lake *B*
West Texas A&M University *B*
Western Texas College *A*

Utah
Dixie State College of Utah *A*
Snow College *A*
Southern Utah University *B*
Utah State University *B*
Westminster College *B*

Vermont
Champlain College *B*
College of St. Joseph in Vermont *B*
Marlboro College *B*
Norwich University *B*
Southern Vermont College *B*

Virginia
Averett University *B*
Hampton University *B*
Longwood University *B*
Virginia Polytechnic Institute and State
  University *B*
Virginia Wesleyan College *B*

Washington
Centralia College *A*
Eastern Washington University *B*
Everett Community College *A*
Lower Columbia College *A*
Seattle Pacific University *B*
Spokane Community College *A*
Washington State University *B*

West Virginia
Alderson-Broaddus College *B*
Concord College *B*
Potomac State College of West Virginia
  University *A*

West Virginia Wesleyan College *B*

Wisconsin
Carthage College *B*
Concordia University Wisconsin *B*
Lawrence University *B*
Marian College of Fond du Lac *B*
Mount Mary College *B*
Northland College *B*
Ripon College *B*
St. Norbert College *B*
University of Wisconsin
  La Crosse *B*
  Madison *B*
  Milwaukee *B*
  Oshkosh *B*
  Parkside *B*
  Superior *B*
  Whitewater *B*

Wyoming
Casper College *A*
Central Wyoming College *A*
Laramie County Community College *A*
Western Wyoming Community
  College *A*

Premedicine

Alabama
Alabama Southern Community
  College *A*
Auburn University *B*
Calhoun Community College *A*
Faulkner University *B*
Huntingdon College *B*
James H. Faulkner State Community
  College *A*
Northeast Alabama Community
  College *A*
Northwest-Shoals Community College *A*
Spring Hill College *B*

Arizona
Arizona State University *B*
Eastern Arizona College *A*
Northern Arizona University *B*
Phoenix College *A*

Arkansas
Harding University *B*
John Brown University *B*
Ouachita Baptist University *B*
University of Arkansas *B*
University of Arkansas
  Fort Smith *A*
University of Central Arkansas *B*

California
Azusa Pacific University *B*
Bakersfield College *A*
California State University
  Chico *B*
Chabot College *A*
Chapman University *B*
Claremont McKenna College *B*
College of the Siskiyous *A*
Concordia University *B*
Dominican University of California *B*
Foothill College *A*
Fresno Pacific University *B*
Golden West College *A*
Marymount College *A*
Master's College *B*
Mills College *C*
MiraCosta College *A*
Monterey Peninsula College *A*
Mount St. Mary's College *B*
Pacific Union College *C*
Scripps College *C*
University of California
  Berkeley *M*
  Riverside *B*
Ventura College *A*
Whittier College *B*

Colorado
Otero Junior College *A*
Regis University *B*

Connecticut
Albertus Magnus College *B*
Quinnipiac University *B*
Southern Connecticut State University *B*
Trinity College *B*
University of New Haven *B*

Delaware
University of Delaware *B*

District of Columbia
George Washington University *A*

Florida
Barry University *B*
Broward Community College *A*
Chipola Junior College *A*
Eckerd College *B*
Florida Southern College *B*
Florida State University *B*
Gulf Coast Community College *A*
Hillsborough Community College *A*
Indian River Community College *A*
Jacksonville University *B*
Miami-Dade Community College *A*
Nova Southeastern University *B*
Okaloosa-Walton Community College *A*
Palm Beach Community College *A*
Pensacola Junior College *A*
St. Thomas University *B*
Santa Fe Community College *A*
University of Central Florida *B*
University of Miami *B*
University of Tampa *B*
University of West Florida *B*

Georgia
Abraham Baldwin Agricultural
  College *A*
Andrew College *A*
Clayton College and State University *A*
Columbus State University *B*
Darton College *A*
Floyd College *A*
Georgia Institute of Technology *B*
Georgia Perimeter College *A*
Georgia Southwestern State University *B*
Kennesaw State University *B*
LaGrange College *B*
Macon State College *A*
Middle Georgia College *A*
Morehouse College *B*
North Georgia College & State
  University *B*
Oglethorpe University *B*
South Georgia College *A*
State University of West Georgia *B*
University of Georgia *B*
Young Harris College *A*

Hawaii
Chaminade University of Honolulu *B*
Hawaii Pacific University *B*
University of Hawaii
  Hilo *B*

Idaho
Boise State University *B*
Brigham Young University - Idaho *B*
College of Southern Idaho *A*
Lewis-Clark State College *B*
North Idaho College *A*
Northwest Nazarene University *B*
University of Idaho *B*

Illinois
Augustana College *B*
Black Hawk College
  East Campus *A*
Blackburn College *B*
City Colleges of Chicago
  Harold Washington College *A*
  Kennedy-King College *A*
Dominican University *B*

Elmhurst College *B*
Eureka College *B*
Greenville College *B*
Illinois Central College *A*
Illinois Institute of Technology *B*
John A. Logan College *A*
Judson College *B*
Kankakee Community College *A*
Kishwaukee College *A*
Lake Land College *A*
Lewis and Clark Community College *A*
Lincoln Land Community College *A*
MacMurray College *B*
McKendree College *B*
Millikin University *B*
North Park University *B*
Northwestern University *B, D*
Parkland College *A*
Rockford College *B*
Roosevelt University *B*
St. Xavier University *B*
Sauk Valley Community College *A*
Southeastern Illinois College *C*
Southwestern Illinois College *A*
Springfield College in Illinois *A*
Trinity International University *B*
University of St. Francis *B*

Indiana
Ball State University *B*
Bethel College *B*
Earlham College *B*
Goshen College *B*
Grace College *B*
Huntington College *B*
Indiana University
  Kokomo *B*
Indiana University-Purdue University
  Fort Wayne *B*
Indiana University-Purdue University
  Indianapolis *M*
Indiana Wesleyan University *B*
Manchester College *B*
Purdue University *B*
Purdue University
  Calumet *B*
St. Joseph's College *B*
St. Mary-of-the-Woods College *B*
Taylor University *B*
Tri-State University *B*
University of Evansville *B*
University of Indianapolis *B*
University of Notre Dame *B*
University of St. Francis *B*
Vincennes University *A*

Iowa
Buena Vista University *B*
Clarke College *B*
Coe College *B*
Cornell College *B*
Dordt College *B*
Ellsworth Community College *A*
Franciscan University *B*
Grand View College *B*
Iowa Wesleyan College *B*
Luther College *B*
Marshalltown Community College *A*
Morningside College *B*
North Iowa Area Community College *A*
Northwestern College *B*
Simpson College *B*
University of Iowa *B*
Upper Iowa University *B*
Waldorf College *A*

Kansas
Barton County Community College *A*
Butler County Community College *A*
Central Christian College *A*
Dodge City Community College *A*
Kansas City Kansas Community
  College *A*
Kansas State University *B*
McPherson College *B*
Pittsburg State University *B*

Pratt Community College *A*
Seward County Community College *A*
Tabor College *B*
Washburn University of Topeka *B*

Kentucky

Bellarmine University *B*
Campbellsville University *B*
Centre College *B*
Cumberland College *B*
Lindsey Wilson College *A*
Murray State University *B*
Thomas More College *B*
Union College *B*

Louisiana

Centenary College of Louisiana *B*
Dillard University *B*
Louisiana College *B*
Nicholls State University *B*
University of Louisiana at Monroe *B*

Maine

University of New England *B*
University of Southern Maine *B*

Maryland

Columbia Union College *B*
Community College of Baltimore County
    Catonsville *A*
    Dundalk *A*
    Essex *A*
Frostburg State University *B*
Howard Community College *A*
Montgomery College
    Rockville Campus *A*
Morgan State University *B*
University of Maryland
    Baltimore County *B*
Villa Julie College *B*

Massachusetts

American International College *B*
Cape Cod Community College *A*
Elms College *B*
Framingham State College *B*
Hampshire College *B*
Harvard College *B*
Simmons College *B*
Simon's Rock College of Bard *B*
Springfield Technical Community
    College *A*
University of Massachusetts
    Amherst *B*
    Dartmouth *C*
Worcester Polytechnic Institute *B*

Michigan

Adrian College *B*
Alma College *B*
Aquinas College *B*
Calvin College *B*
Concordia University *B*
Cornerstone University *B*
Eastern Michigan University *B*
Gogebic Community College *A*
Grand Valley State University *B*
Hillsdale College *B*
Kalamazoo College *B*
Kellogg Community College *A*
Kirtland Community College *A*
Michigan State University *A, B, M*
Michigan Technological University *B*
Northern Michigan University *B*
Schoolcraft College *A*
Siena Heights University *B*
Washtenaw Community College *A*

Minnesota

Bethel College *B*
College of St. Benedict *B*
College of St. Catherine *B*
Concordia College: Moorhead *B*
Gustavus Adolphus College *B*
Hamline University *B*
Minnesota State University
    Mankato *B*
    Moorhead *B*

Rochester Community and Technical
    College *A*
St. Cloud State University *B*
St. John's University *B*
University of Minnesota
    Twin Cities *B*
Vermilion Community College *A*
Winona State University *B*

Mississippi

Blue Mountain College *B*
Coahoma Community College *A*
Holmes Community College *A*
Itawamba Community College *A*
Mary Holmes College *A*

Missouri

Avila University *B*
Drury University *B*
East Central College *A*
Evangel University *B*
Lindenwood University *B*
Maryville University of Saint Louis *B*
Missouri Southern State College *B*
St. Louis Community College
    St. Louis Community College at
        Florissant Valley *A*
Stephens College *B*
Three Rivers Community College *A*
Truman State University *B*
University of Missouri
    Rolla *B*
    St. Louis *B*
Washington University in St. Louis *B*

Montana

Montana Tech of the University of
    Montana *B*

Nebraska

Bellevue University *B*
College of Saint Mary *B*
Concordia University *B*
Creighton University *C*
Dana College *B*
Hastings College *B*
Midland Lutheran College *B*
Northeast Community College *A*
University of Nebraska
    Lincoln *B*
Western Nebraska Community
    College *A*
York College *A*

Nevada

Sierra Nevada College *B*

New Hampshire

Franklin Pierce College *B*
New England College *B*
Rivier College *B*
St. Anselm College *B*
University of New Hampshire *B*

New Jersey

Bloomfield College *B*
Essex County College *A*
Georgian Court College *B*
Rowan University *B*
Rutgers, The State University of New
    Jersey
    Camden Regional Campus *B*
    New Brunswick Regional
        Campus *B*
    Newark Regional Campus *B*
Stevens Institute of Technology *B*
Sussex County Community College *A*

New Mexico

New Mexico Junior College *A*
San Juan College *A*

New York

Albany College of Pharmacy *B*
Alfred University *B*
Bard College *B*

City University of New York
    Brooklyn College *B*
    City College *B*
    College of Staten Island *B*
    Queens College *B*
Colgate University *B*
Concordia College *B*
Cornell University *B*
D'Youville College *B*
Dowling College *C*
Elmira College *B*
Fordham University *B*
Hobart and William Smith Colleges *B*
Houghton College *B*
Ithaca College *B*
Le Moyne College *B*
Long Island University
    C. W. Post Campus *B*
    Southampton College *B*
Manhattan College *B*
Manhattanville College *B*
Marist College *B*
Marymount College of Fordham
    University *B*
Mercy College *B*
Molloy College *B*
New York Institute of Technology *B*
New York University *B*
Paul Smith's College *B*
Rensselaer Polytechnic Institute *B*
Rochester Institute of Technology *B*
St. Joseph's College: Suffolk Campus *B*
Sarah Lawrence College *B*
State University of New York
    Albany *B*
    College at Brockport *B*
    College at Geneseo *B*
    College at Plattsburgh *B*
    College of Environmental Science
        and Forestry *B*
    New Paltz *B*
Syracuse University *B*
Touro College *B*
Wagner College *B*
Wells College *B*
Yeshiva University *B*

North Carolina

Appalachian State University *B*
Barton College *B*
Belmont Abbey College *B*
Campbell University *B*
Carteret Community College *A*
Chowan College *B*
Elon University *B*
Lees-McRae College *B*
Lenoir-Rhyne College *B*
Louisburg College *A*
Mars Hill College *B*
Meredith College *B*
Methodist College *B*
Mitchell Community College *A*
North Carolina State University *B*
North Carolina Wesleyan College *B*
Pfeiffer University *B*
Queens University of Charlotte *B*
St. Andrews Presbyterian College *B*
St. Augustine's College *B*
Sandhills Community College *A*
Warren Wilson College *B*
Wingate University *B*

North Dakota

Dickinson State University *B*
Mayville State University *B*
University of North Dakota *B*
Valley City State University *B*

Ohio

Defiance College *B*
Heidelberg College *B*
John Carroll University *B*
Kent State University *B*
Kent State University
    Stark Campus *B*
Kettering College of Medical Arts *A*

Lorain County Community College *A*
Miami University
    Oxford Campus *B*
Mount Vernon Nazarene University *B*
Muskingum College *B*
Oberlin College *B*
Ohio Northern University *B*
Ohio University *B*
Ohio Wesleyan University *B*
Otterbein College *B*
Shawnee State University *B*
University of Akron *B*
University of Cincinnati *B*
University of Cincinnati
    Clermont College *A*
    Raymond Walters College *A*
University of Dayton *B*
University of Findlay *B*
University of Rio Grande *B*
University of Toledo *A, B*
Urbana University *B*
Ursuline College *B*
Walsh University *B*
Wittenberg University *B*
Youngstown State University *B*

Oklahoma

Carl Albert State College *A*
East Central University *B*
Eastern Oklahoma State College *A*
Northeastern Oklahoma Agricultural and
    Mechanical College *A*
Northern Oklahoma College *A*
Oklahoma Christian University of
    Science and Arts *B*
Oklahoma City University *B*
Oklahoma State University *B*
Redlands Community College *A*
Rogers State University *A*
Rose State College *A*

Oregon

Central Oregon Community College *A*
Chemeketa Community College *A*
Concordia University *B*
Eastern Oregon University *B*
Linn-Benton Community College *A*
Southern Oregon University *B*
University of Portland *B*
Western Baptist College *B*

Pennsylvania

Albright College *B*
Allegheny College *B*
Cabrini College *B*
California University of Pennsylvania *B*
East Stroudsburg University of
    Pennsylvania *B*
Elizabethtown College *B*
Gettysburg College *B*
Grove City College *B*
Gwynedd-Mercy College *B*
Holy Family University *B*
Immaculata University *B*
Juniata College *B*
La Salle University *B*
Lehigh University *B*
Lock Haven University of
    Pennsylvania *B*
Mercyhurst College *B*
Muhlenberg College *B*

Penn State
    Abington *B*
    Altoona *B*
    Beaver *B*
    Berks *B*
    Delaware County *B*
    Dubois *B*
    Fayette *B*
    Hazleton *B*
    Lehigh Valley *B*
    McKeesport *B*
    Mont Alto *B*
    New Kensington *B*
    Schuylkill - Capital College *B*
    Shenango *B*
    University Park *B*
    Wilkes-Barre *B*
    Worthington Scranton *B*
    York *B*
Philadelphia University *B*
Reading Area Community College *A*
St. Vincent College *B*
University of Pittsburgh
    Greensburg *B*
    Johnstown *B*
Villanova University *B*
Waynesburg College *B*
West Chester University of
    Pennsylvania *B*
Widener University *B*
Wilkes University *B*
York College of Pennsylvania *B*

Puerto Rico

Bayamon Central University *C*
University of Puerto Rico
    Mayaguez Campus *A*
    Medical Sciences Campus *C*
    Ponce *A*

Rhode Island

Rhode Island College *B*

South Carolina

Charleston Southern University *B*
Clemson University *B*
College of Charleston *B*
Denmark Technical College *C*
Furman University *B*
North Greenville College *B*

South Dakota

Augustana College *B*
Dakota State University *B*
Dakota Wesleyan University *B*

Tennessee

Carson-Newman College *B*
Columbia State Community College *A*
Fisk University *B*
Freed-Hardeman University *B*
Jackson State Community College *A*
Lambuth University *B*
Maryville College *B*
Roane State Community College *A*
Tennessee Technological University *B*
Tennessee Wesleyan College *B*
Tusculum College *B*
Union University *B*
University of Tennessee
    Knoxville *B*
    Martin *B*
Walters State Community College *A*

Texas

Abilene Christian University *B*
Amarillo College *A*
Angelina College *A*
Austin Community College *A*
Baylor University *B*
Central Texas College *A*
Coastal Bend College *A*
Concordia University at Austin *B*
Del Mar College *A*
El Paso Community College *A*
Galveston College *A*
Grayson County College *A*

Howard College *A*
Howard Payne University *B*
Jarvis Christian College *B*
Laredo Community College *A*
LeTourneau University *B*
Lon Morris College *A*
Lubbock Christian University *B*
McMurry University *B*
Midland College *A*
Midwestern State University *B*
Northeast Texas Community College *A*
Panola College *A*
Paris Junior College *A*
St. Edward's University *B*
St. Philip's College *A*
South Plains College *A*
Texas A&M University *B*
Texas A&M University
    Commerce *B*
Texas Christian University *B*
Texas Wesleyan University *B*
Trinity Valley Community College *A*
Tyler Junior College *A*
University of Mary Hardin-Baylor *B*
University of Texas
    Pan American *B*
Western Texas College *A*

Utah

Brigham Young University *B*
Snow College *A*
Southern Utah University *B*
University of Utah *B*
Utah State University *B*
Westminster College *B*

Vermont

Bennington College *C*
Castleton State College *B*
Johnson State College *B*

Virginia

Averett University *B*
College of Health Sciences *B*
Longwood University *B*
Mountain Empire Community College *A*
Virginia Intermont College *B*
Virginia Wesleyan College *B*

Washington

Centralia College *A*
Eastern Washington University *B*
Everett Community College *A*
Lower Columbia College *A*
St. Martin's College *B*
Seattle Pacific University *B*
Washington State University *B*

West Virginia

Alderson-Broaddus College *B*
Concord College *B*
Davis and Elkins College *B*
Mountain State University *B*
Potomac State College of West Virginia
    University *A*
West Virginia Wesleyan College *B*

Wisconsin

Carthage College *B*
Lawrence University *B*
Marian College of Fond du Lac *B*
Mount Mary College *B*
Northland College *B*
Ripon College *B*
St. Norbert College *B*
University of Wisconsin
    Madison *B*
    Milwaukee *B*
    Oshkosh *B*
    Parkside *B*
    Whitewater *B*

Wyoming

Casper College *A*
Eastern Wyoming College *A*
Western Wyoming Community
    College *A*

Prenursing

Alabama

Calhoun Community College *A*
James H. Faulkner State Community
    College *A*
Northeast Alabama Community
    College *A*
Northwest-Shoals Community
    College *C, A*
Trenholm State Technical College *C*

California

California State University
    Hayward *B*
Southwestern College *A*

Colorado

Red Rocks Community College *A*

Florida

Broward Community College *A*
Pensacola Junior College *A*

Georgia

Andrew College *A*
Middle Georgia College *A*
Young Harris College *A*

Illinois

Dominican University *B*
Eureka College *B*
Kishwaukee College *A*
Lewis and Clark Community College *A*
Sauk Valley Community College *A*
Springfield College in Illinois *A*
Trinity International University *A*

Indiana

Manchester College *A*
University of St. Francis *B*

Iowa

Dordt College *B*
Marshalltown Community College *A*
North Iowa Area Community College *A*
Simpson College *B*
University of Iowa *B*

Kansas

Barton County Community College *A*
Central Christian College *A*
Donnelly College *A*
Kansas City Kansas Community
    College *A*
Seward County Community College *A*
Tabor College *A*

Kentucky

Bellarmine University *B*
Campbellsville University *B*
Henderson Community College *C*

Maryland

College of Southern Maryland *C, A*
Frederick Community College *A*
Frostburg State University *B*
Mount St. Mary's College *B*
University of Maryland
    Baltimore County *A*
    College Park *B*

Massachusetts

Berkshire Community College *A*
Cape Cod Community College *A*

Michigan

Gogebic Community College *A*
Hillsdale College *B*
Washtenaw Community College *C*

Minnesota

Itasca Community College *A*

Mississippi

Coahoma Community College *A*

Missouri

College of the Ozarks *B*

Montana

Miles Community College *A*

Nebraska

Bellevue University *B*
Concordia University *B*
Western Nebraska Community
    College *A*

New Jersey

Bloomfield College *B*

New York

St. Joseph's College *B*
State University of New York
    College of Agriculture and
        Technology at Morrisville *A*
Villa Maria College of Buffalo *A*

North Carolina

Carteret Community College *A*
Chowan College *B*
Guilford Technical Community
    College *A*
Mayland Community College *C*
Sandhills Community College *A*

North Dakota

Mayville State University *B*
Minot State University: Bottineau
    Campus *A*
Valley City State University *B*

Ohio

Heidelberg College *B*
Kent State University
    Salem Regional Campus *A, B*
Miami University
    Hamilton Campus *A*
Muskingum College *B*
University of Cincinnati
    Clermont College *A*
University of Findlay *A*
Ursuline College *B*
Wittenberg University *B*

Oklahoma

Eastern Oklahoma State College *A*
Northeastern Oklahoma Agricultural and
    Mechanical College *A*
Northeastern State University *B*
Oklahoma Christian University of
    Science and Arts *B*
Rose State College *A*

Oregon

Chemeketa Community College *A*
Linn-Benton Community College *A*
Oregon Institute of Technology *A*

Pennsylvania

Allegheny College *B*
Juniata College *B*
Keystone College *A*
Marywood University *B*

South Carolina

Furman University *B*
North Greenville College *A*
Technical College of the Lowcountry *C*
Williamsburg Technical College *C*

Tennessee

Freed-Hardeman University *B*
Jackson State Community College *A*
Lambuth University *B*
Roane State Community College *A*

Texas

Del Mar College *A*
Lon Morris College *A*
St. Philip's College *A*
South Plains College *A*
Trinity Valley Community College *A*
Tyler Junior College *A*

Washington

Centralia College *A*
Spokane Falls Community College *A*

Wisconsin
Ripon College *B*

Preoperative/surgical nursing

California
De Anza College *C*
Holy Names College *B, M*
Loma Linda University *B, M*
National University *B*
Samuel Merritt College *C, M*
Sonoma State University *M*
University of California
    Los Angeles *M, D*
University of San Diego *B, M*
University of Southern California *M*

Colorado
University of Colorado
    Colorado Springs *M*

Connecticut
Quinnipiac University *M*
Sacred Heart University *B*

Delaware
Wilmington College *B*

Florida
Indian River Community College *C*
Pasco-Hernando Community College *C*
Polk Community College *C*
St. Petersburg College *B*
University of West Florida *B*

Georgia
Medical College of Georgia *B, M*
Valdosta State University *B*

Illinois
Benedictine University *B*
Governors State University *B*
Lewis University *M*
McKendree College *B*
Quincy University *B*
Rockford College *B*
St. Xavier University *M*
Southern Illinois University
    Edwardsville *M*
University of Illinois
    Chicago *M, D*
University of St. Francis *M*

Indiana
Ball State University *M*
Purdue University
    Calumet *B*
St. Joseph's College *B*
University of Indianapolis *B*
University of St. Francis *B*
Valparaiso University *B, M*

Iowa
Briar Cliff University *B*
Graceland University *B*
Hawkeye Community College *C*
Mercy College of Health Sciences *B*
St. Ambrose University *B*

Kansas
Emporia State University *B*
Kansas Wesleyan University *B*
Tabor College *B*
University of Kansas Medical
    Center *A, B, M*
Wichita State University *B, M*

Kentucky
Bellarmine University *B, M*
Murray State University *M*
Thomas More College *B*
University of Louisville *B, M*

Maine
Husson College *M*
University of Maine *M*
University of Southern Maine *B*

Maryland
Coppin State College *B*
University of Maryland
    Baltimore *B*

Massachusetts
American International College *B*
Berkshire Community College *A*
Elms College *B*
Emmanuel College *B*
Framingham State College *B*
Northeastern University *M*
Salem State College *M*
University of Massachusetts
    Dartmouth *M*

Michigan
Calvin College *B*
Davenport University
    Midland *B*
Wayne County Community College *A*
Wayne State University *M*

Minnesota
Bemidji State University *B*
Bethel College *M*
Metropolitan State University *B*
Minneapolis Community and Technical
    College *A*
Minnesota State University
    Mankato *B, M*
Winona State University *B, M*

Mississippi
Mississippi University for Women *T*

Missouri
Central Methodist College *B*
Drury University *B*
Maryville University of Saint Louis *B*
Missouri Baptist University *B*
Southwest Baptist University *B*
Southwest Missouri State University *B*
University of Missouri
    Columbia *B, M, D*
    Kansas City *B, M, D*

Nebraska
Clarkson College *B, M*
Creighton University *M*
Midland Lutheran College *B*
Nebraska Methodist College of Nursing
    and Allied Health *C, M*
Nebraska Wesleyan University *B, M*
Northeast Community College *A*
University of Nebraska
    Medical Center *B*

New Hampshire
Rivier College *B, M*

New Jersey
The College of New Jersey *B*
College of St. Elizabeth *B*
Ramapo College of New Jersey *B, M*
Richard Stockton College of New
    Jersey *B*
St. Peter's College *B, M*
Thomas Edison State College *B*

New York
College of Mount St. Vincent *B*
Columbia University
    School of Nursing *B, M, D*
D'Youville College *B, M*
Daemen College *C, B, M*
Dominican College of Blauvelt *B*
Long Island University
    C. W. Post Campus *B, M*
Molloy College *B, M*
Nazareth College of Rochester *M*
New York University *M, D*
Roberts Wesleyan College *B*
St. John Fisher College *B*
St. Joseph's College: Suffolk Campus *B*

State University of New York
    Buffalo *M, D*
    New Paltz *B, M*
    Upstate Medical University *M*

North Carolina
Queens University of Charlotte *B*
University of North Carolina
    Chapel Hill *M, D*

North Dakota
North Dakota State University *M*

Ohio
Case Western Reserve University *M*
Kent State University *B*
Kent State University
    Ashtabula Regional Campus *B*
Lourdes College *B*
Miami University
    Hamilton Campus *B*
    Middletown Campus *B*
Ohio University *B*
Ursuline College *B*

Oklahoma
Northeastern State University *B*
Rose State College *A*

Oregon
Eastern Oregon University *B*
Oregon Health Sciences University *M, D*
Southern Oregon University *B*

Pennsylvania
California University of Pennsylvania *B*
Community College of Allegheny
    County *C*
DeSales University *B, M*
Delaware County Community College *C*
Holy Family University *B, M*
La Salle University *M*
Mount Aloysius College *B*
University of Pittsburgh *M*
Westmoreland County Community
    College *C*

South Carolina
Medical University of South Carolina *M*
University of South Carolina *M*

Tennessee
Aquinas College *B*
Southern Adventist University *B*
Union University *B*
University of Tennessee
    Knoxville *B*

Texas
East Texas Baptist University *B*
Lamar State College at Orange *A*
Lee College *C*
Lubbock Christian University *B*
South Plains College *A*
Texas A&M International University *B*
Texas A&M University
    Corpus Christi *M*
University of Texas
    Health Science Center at San
    Antonio *M, D*
    Houston Health Science
    Center *M, D*
    Pan American *M*

Utah
Brigham Young University *M*
University of Utah *M*
Utah Valley State College *A, B*

Vermont
University of Vermont *C*

Virginia
College of Health Sciences *B*
J. Sargeant Reynolds Community
    College *C*
Marymount University *B*
University of Virginia's College at
    Wise *B*

Virginia Commonwealth
    University *M, D*

Washington
Gonzaga University *B, M*
Seattle Central Community College *C, A*

West Virginia
Wheeling Jesuit University *B*

Wisconsin
Cardinal Stritch University *M*
Marian College of Fond du Lac *B*
Mount Mary College *B*
University of Wisconsin
    Green Bay *B*
    Madison *M, D*
Viterbo University *B*

Prepharmacy

Alabama
Alabama Southern Community
    College *A*
Calhoun Community College *A*
Huntingdon College *B*
James H. Faulkner State Community
    College *A*
Northeast Alabama Community
    College *A*
Northwest-Shoals Community College *A*

Arizona
Eastern Arizona College *A*

Arkansas
Harding University *B*
John Brown University *B*
Ouachita Baptist University *B*
University of Arkansas
    Fort Smith *A*
University of Central Arkansas *B*

California
Bakersfield College *A*
Chabot College *A*
College of the Siskiyous *A*
Foothill College *A*
Golden West College *A*
Marymount College *A*
Monterey Peninsula College *A*
Ventura College *A*
Whittier College *B*

Colorado
Otero Junior College *A*

Connecticut
Albertus Magnus College *B*
Southern Connecticut State University *B*
University of Connecticut *B*

Delaware
University of Delaware *B*

Florida
Barry University *B*
Broward Community College *A*
Chipola Junior College *A*
Florida State University *B*
Gulf Coast Community College *A*
Indian River Community College *A*
Jacksonville University *B*
Miami-Dade Community College *A*
Okaloosa-Walton Community College *A*
Pensacola Junior College *A*
Santa Fe Community College *A*
University of Central Florida *B*
University of Miami *B*
University of West Florida *B*

Georgia
Abraham Baldwin Agricultural
    College *A*
Andrew College *A*
Clayton College and State University *A*
Columbus State University *B*
Darton College *A*

Emmanuel College *A*
Floyd College *A*
Georgia Perimeter College *A*
Georgia Southwestern State University *B*
Gordon College *A*
Kennesaw State University *B*
LaGrange College *A*
Macon State College *A*
Middle Georgia College *A*
North Georgia College & State
    University *B*
Oglethorpe University *B*
South Georgia College *A*
State University of West Georgia *B*
Young Harris College *A*

Idaho
Brigham Young University - Idaho *B*
College of Southern Idaho *A*
North Idaho College *A*

Illinois
Black Hawk College
    East Campus *A*
City Colleges of Chicago
    Harold Washington College *A*
    Kennedy-King College *A*
Dominican University *B*
Elmhurst College *B*
Illinois Central College *A*
John A. Logan College *A*
Kankakee Community College *A*
Kishwaukee College *A*
Lake Land College *A*
Lincoln Land Community College *A*
Millikin University *B*
North Park University *B*
Parkland College *A*
Rockford College *B*
Roosevelt University *B*
St. Xavier University *B*
Sauk Valley Community College *A*
Southeastern Illinois College *C*
Southwestern Illinois College *A*
Springfield College in Illinois *A*

Indiana
Ball State University *B*
Goshen College *B*
Grace College *B*
Indiana University
    Kokomo *B*
Indiana Wesleyan University *B*
Manchester College *B*
Purdue University
    Calumet *B*
St. Mary-of-the-Woods College *B*
University of Evansville *B*
University of St. Francis *B*
Vincennes University *A*

Iowa
Buena Vista University *B*
Clarke College *B*
Dordt College *B*
Ellsworth Community College *A*
Grand View College *B*
Iowa Central Community College *A*
Iowa Wesleyan College *B*
Luther College *B*
Marshalltown Community College *A*
Morningside College *B*
North Iowa Area Community College *A*
Simpson College *B*
University of Iowa *B*
Upper Iowa University *B*
Waldorf College *A*

Kansas
Barton County Community College *A*
Dodge City Community College *A*
Kansas City Kansas Community
    College *A*
McPherson College *B*
Pittsburg State University *B*
Pratt Community College *A*
Seward County Community College *A*

Tabor College *B*
Washburn University of Topeka *B*

Kentucky
Bellarmine University *B*
Campbellsville University *B*
Centre College *B*
Cumberland College *B*
Murray State University *B*
Thomas More College *B*
Union College *B*

Louisiana
Centenary College of Louisiana *B*
Louisiana College *B*
Nicholls State University *A*

Maine
University of New England *B*

Maryland
Allegany College *A*
Columbia Union College *B*
Community College of Baltimore County
    Catonsville *A*
    Dundalk *A*
    Essex *A*
Coppin State College *B*
Frederick Community College *A*
Frostburg State University *B*
Howard Community College *A*
Montgomery College
    Rockville Campus *A*
Morgan State University *B*
University of Maryland
    Baltimore County *B*
    College Park *B*
Villa Julie College *B*

Massachusetts
Cape Cod Community College *A*
Simmons College *B*
Western New England College *B*

Michigan
Adrian College *B*
Calvin College *B*
Eastern Michigan University *B*
Ferris State University *A*
Gogebic Community College *A*
Grand Valley State University *B*
Hillsdale College *B*
Kellogg Community College *A*
Kirtland Community College *A*
Michigan Technological University *B*
Mid Michigan Community College *A*
Northern Michigan University *B*
Schoolcraft College *A*
Siena Heights University *A, B*
West Shore Community College *A*

Minnesota
Bethel College *B*
College of St. Benedict *B*
College of St. Catherine *B*
Concordia College: Moorhead *B*
Minnesota State University
    Mankato *B*
    Moorhead *B*
St. Cloud State University *B*
St. John's University *B*
University of Minnesota
    Duluth *B*
    Twin Cities *B*
Winona State University *B*

Mississippi
Blue Mountain College *B*
Coahoma Community College *A*
Holmes Community College *A*
Itawamba Community College *A*
Mary Holmes College *A*
Mississippi Gulf Coast Community
    College
    Perkinston *A*

Missouri
East Central College *A*
Missouri Southern State College *A*

St. Louis Community College
    St. Louis Community College at
        Florissant Valley *A*
Stephens College *B*
Three Rivers Community College *A*
Truman State University *B*
University of Missouri
    St. Louis *B*
Washington University in St. Louis *B*

Montana
Montana Tech of the University of
    Montana *B*

Nebraska
Bellevue University *B*
College of Saint Mary *B*
Concordia University *B*
Dana College *B*
Hastings College *B*
Midland Lutheran College *B*
Northeast Community College *A*
University of Nebraska
    Lincoln *B*
Western Nebraska Community
    College *A*
York College *A*

New Jersey
Bloomfield College *B*
Rowan University *B*
Sussex County Community College *A*

New Mexico
New Mexico Junior College *A*

New York
Bard College *B*
City University of New York
    City College *B*
    Kingsborough Community
        College *A*
D'Youville College *B*
Fordham University *B*
Long Island University
    C. W. Post Campus *B*
Mercy College *B*
Rochester Institute of Technology *B*
State University of New York
    Albany *B*
    Buffalo *B*
    College at Geneseo *B*
    College at Plattsburgh *B*
    College of Environmental Science
        and Forestry *B*
Touro College *B*

North Carolina
Appalachian State University *B*
Barton College *B*
Belmont Abbey College *B*
Campbell University *B*
Carteret Community College *A*
Chowan College *B*
Fayetteville Technical Community
    College *C*
Lenoir-Rhyne College *B*
Livingstone College *B*
Louisburg College *A*
Mars Hill College *B*
Meredith College *B*
Methodist College *B*
Mitchell Community College *A*
North Carolina State University *B*
Queens University of Charlotte *B*
St. Andrews Presbyterian College *B*
Sandhills Community College *A*
Wingate University *B*

North Dakota
Dickinson State University *A*
Mayville State University *B*
Valley City State University *B*

Ohio
Lorain County Community College *A*
Mount Vernon Nazarene University *B*
Ohio University *B*

Otterbein College *B*
Shawnee State University *B*
University of Cincinnati *B*
University of Cincinnati
    Clermont College *A*
    Raymond Walters College *A*
Wittenberg University *B*
Youngstown State University *B*

Oklahoma
Carl Albert State College *A*
East Central University *B*
Eastern Oklahoma State College *A*
Northeastern Oklahoma Agricultural and
    Mechanical College *A*
Northern Oklahoma College *A*
Oklahoma Christian University of
    Science and Arts *A*
Oklahoma City University *B*
Oklahoma State University *B*
Redlands Community College *A*
Rose State College *A*

Oregon
Central Oregon Community College *A*
Chemeketa Community College *A*
Eastern Oregon University *B*
Linn-Benton Community College *A*
Southern Oregon University *B*
Western Baptist College *B*

Pennsylvania
Allegheny College *B*
California University of Pennsylvania *B*
East Stroudsburg University of
    Pennsylvania *B*
Gettysburg College *B*
Holy Family University *B*
Immaculata University *B*
Juniata College *B*
Lock Haven University of
    Pennsylvania *B*
Luzerne County Community College *A*
Mercyhurst College *B*
Reading Area Community College *A*
St. Vincent College *B*
University of Pittsburgh
    Greensburg *B*
Wilkes University *B*
York College of Pennsylvania *B*

Puerto Rico
University of Puerto Rico
    Ponce *A*

South Carolina
Aiken Technical College *C*
Charleston Southern University *B*
Clemson University *B*
Furman University *B*
North Greenville College *B*

South Dakota
Augustana College *B*
Dakota State University *B*
Dakota Wesleyan University *B*

Tennessee
Carson-Newman College *B*
Columbia State Community College *A*
Freed-Hardeman University *B*
Lambuth University *B*
Maryville College *B*
Roane State Community College *A*
Tennessee Technological University *B*
Tennessee Wesleyan College *B*
Tusculum College *B*
Union University *B*
University of Tennessee
    Knoxville *B*
    Martin *B*
Walters State Community College *A*

Texas
Abilene Christian University *B*
Amarillo College *A*
Angelina College *A*
Austin Community College *A*

Coastal Bend College *A*
Del Mar College *A*
El Paso Community College *A*
Grayson County College *A*
Laredo Community College *A*
LeTourneau University *B*
Lon Morris College *A*
Lubbock Christian University *B*
McMurry University *B*
Midland College *A*
Midwestern State University *B*
Panola College *A*
Paris Junior College *A*
San Antonio College *A*
South Plains College *A*
Texas A&M University
    Commerce *B*
Texas Southern University *B*
Trinity Valley Community College *A*
Tyler Junior College *A*
University of Houston *B*
Western Texas College *A*

Utah
Snow College *A*
Southern Utah University *B*
University of Utah *B*

Vermont
Castleton State College *B*

Virginia
Averett University *B*
College of Health Sciences *B*
Longwood University *B*
Mountain Empire Community College *A*
Virginia Intermont College *B*
Virginia Wesleyan College *B*

Washington
Centralia College *A*
Eastern Washington University *B*
Everett Community College *A*
Lower Columbia College *A*
St. Martin's College *B*

West Virginia
Alderson-Broaddus College *B*
Concord College *B*
Davis and Elkins College *A*
Potomac State College of West Virginia
    University *A*
West Virginia Wesleyan College *B*

Wisconsin
Carthage College *B*
Lawrence University *B*
Marian College of Fond du Lac *B*
Northland College *B*
Ripon College *B*
University of Wisconsin
    Madison *B*
    Milwaukee *B*
    Oshkosh *B*
    Whitewater *A*

Wyoming
Casper College *A*
Eastern Wyoming College *A*
Western Wyoming Community
    College *A*

Preveterinary

Alabama
Alabama Southern Community
    College *A*
Calhoun Community College *A*
Faulkner University *B*
Huntingdon College *B*
James H. Faulkner State Community
    College *A*
Northeast Alabama Community
    College *A*
Northwest-Shoals Community College *A*
Spring Hill College *B*

Arizona
Central Arizona College *A*
Northern Arizona University *B*
University of Arizona *B*

Arkansas
Harding University *B*
John Brown University *B*
Ouachita Baptist University *B*
University of Arkansas
    Fort Smith *A*
University of Central Arkansas *B*

California
Bakersfield College *A*
California State University
    Chico *B*
Chabot College *A*
Chapman University *B*
Claremont McKenna College *B*
College of the Siskiyous *A*
Foothill College *A*
Golden West College *A*
Los Angeles Pierce College *A*
Marymount College *A*
MiraCosta College *A*
Monterey Peninsula College *A*
Mount St. Mary's College *B*
Pacific Union College *C*
Ventura College *A*
Whittier College *B*

Colorado
Otero Junior College *A*
Regis University *B*

Connecticut
Albertus Magnus College *B*
Quinnipiac University *B*
Southern Connecticut State University *B*
University of New Haven *B*

Delaware
Delaware State University *B*
University of Delaware *B*

Florida
Barry University *B*
Broward Community College *A*
Chipola Junior College *A*
Eckerd College *B*
Florida State University *B*
Gulf Coast Community College *A*
Indian River Community College *A*
Jacksonville University *B*
Miami-Dade Community College *A*
Okaloosa-Walton Community College *A*
Pensacola Junior College *A*
St. Thomas University *B*
University of Central Florida *B*
University of Miami *B*
University of Tampa *B*
University of West Florida *B*

Georgia
Andrew College *A*
Columbus State University *B*
Floyd College *A*
Georgia Institute of Technology *B*
Georgia Southwestern State University *B*
Kennesaw State University *B*
LaGrange College *B*
Macon State College *A*
Middle Georgia College *A*
North Georgia College & State
    University *B*
Oglethorpe University *B*
University of Georgia *B*
Young Harris College *A*

Idaho
Boise State University *B*
Brigham Young University - Idaho *B*
College of Southern Idaho *A*
North Idaho College *A*
Northwest Nazarene University *B*

Illinois
Blackburn College *B*
Dominican University *B*
Eureka College *B*
Greenville College *B*
Illinois Central College *A*
John A. Logan College *A*
Kankakee Community College *A*
Kishwaukee College *A*
Lake Land College *A*
Lincoln Land Community College *A*
MacMurray College *B*
McKendree College *B*
Millikin University *B*
North Park University *B*
Parkland College *A*
Rockford College *B*
Roosevelt University *B*
St. Xavier University *B*
Sauk Valley Community College *A*
Southeastern Illinois College *C*
Southwestern Illinois College *A*
Springfield College in Illinois *A*
University of Illinois
    Urbana-Champaign *B*
University of St. Francis *B*

Indiana
Goshen College *B*
Grace College *B*
Indiana Wesleyan University *B*
Manchester College *B*
Purdue University
    Calumet *B*
St. Joseph's College *B*
St. Mary-of-the-Woods College *B*
University of Evansville *B*
University of Indianapolis *B*
University of St. Francis *B*
Vincennes University *A*

Iowa
Buena Vista University *B*
Clarke College *B*
Coe College *B*
Dordt College *B*
Ellsworth Community College *A*
Iowa Central Community College *A*
Iowa Wesleyan College *B*
Luther College *B*
Marshalltown Community College *A*
Morningside College *B*
North Iowa Area Community College *A*
Northwestern College *B*
Simpson College *B*
University of Iowa *B*
Upper Iowa University *B*

Kansas
Barton County Community College *A*
Central Christian College *A*
Dodge City Community College *A*
Kansas City Kansas Community
    College *A*
Kansas State University *B*
McPherson College *B*
Pittsburg State University *B*
Pratt Community College *A*
Seward County Community College *A*
Tabor College *B*
Washburn University of Topeka *B*

Kentucky
Campbellsville University *B*
Centre College *B*
Cumberland College *B*
Murray State University *B*
Thomas More College *B*
Union College *B*

Louisiana
Centenary College of Louisiana *B*
Louisiana College *B*
Nicholls State University *A*

Maine
University of New England *B*

University of Southern Maine *B*

Maryland
Columbia Union College *B*
Community College of Baltimore County
    Catonsville *A*
    Dundalk *A*
    Essex *A*
Frostburg State University *B*
Howard Community College *A*
University of Maryland
    Baltimore County *B*
    College Park *B*
Villa Julie College *B*

Massachusetts
American International College *B*
Becker College *B*
Elms College *B*
Framingham State College *B*
Hampshire College *B*
University of Massachusetts
    Amherst *B*
Worcester Polytechnic Institute *B*

Michigan
Adrian College *B*
Alma College *B*
Calvin College *B*
Cornerstone University *B*
Ferris State University *A*
Gogebic Community College *A*
Grand Valley State University *B*
Hillsdale College *B*
Kalamazoo College *B*
Kellogg Community College *A*
Kirtland Community College *A*
Michigan Technological University *B*
Northern Michigan University *B*
Oakland Community College *A*
Schoolcraft College *A*
Siena Heights University *A*

Minnesota
Bethel College *B*
College of St. Benedict *B*
College of St. Catherine *B*
Concordia College: Moorhead *B*
Gustavus Adolphus College *B*
Hamline University *B*
Minnesota State University
    Mankato *B*
    Moorhead *B*
St. Cloud State University *B*
St. John's University *B*
University of Minnesota
    Duluth *B*
    Twin Cities *B*
Vermilion Community College *A*
Winona State University *B*

Mississippi
Blue Mountain College *B*
Coahoma Community College *A*
Holmes Community College *A*
Itawamba Community College *A*
Mary Holmes College *A*

Missouri
Drury University *B*
East Central College *A*
Evangel University *B*
Lindenwood University *B*
Missouri Southern State College *A*
Northwest Missouri State University *B*
Stephens College *B*
Three Rivers Community College *A*
Truman State University *B*
University of Missouri
    St. Louis *B*
Washington University in St. Louis *B*

Montana
Montana Tech of the University of
    Montana *B*
University of Great Falls *B*

Nebraska

College of Saint Mary *B*
Concordia University *B*
Dana College *B*
Hastings College *B*
Midland Lutheran College *B*
Northeast Community College *A*
University of Nebraska
    Lincoln *B*
Vatterott College
    Dodge Campus *A*
Western Nebraska Community
    College *A*
York College *A*

Nevada

Sierra Nevada College *B*
University of Nevada
    Reno *B*

New Hampshire

Franklin Pierce College *B*
Rivier College *B*
University of New Hampshire *B*

New Jersey

Bloomfield College *B*
Georgian Court College *B*
Rowan University *B*

New York

Alfred University *B*
Bard College *B*
City University of New York
    City College *B*
    College of Staten Island *B*
Colgate University *B*
Cornell University *R*
D'Youville College *B*
Elmira College *B*
Fordham University *B*
Hobart and William Smith Colleges *R*
Houghton College *B*
Ithaca College *B*
Le Moyne College *B*
Long Island University
    C. W. Post Campus *B*
    Southampton College *R*
Manhattan College *B*
Marist College *B*
Mercy College *B*
Molloy College *B*
Paul Smith's College *B*
Rochester Institute of Technology *B*
St. Joseph's College: Suffolk Campus *B*
State University of New York
    Albany *B*
    College at Brockport *B*
    College at Geneseo *B*
    College at Plattsburgh *B*
    College of Environmental Science
        and Forestry *B*
    New Paltz *B*
Syracuse University *B*
Touro College *B*
Wells College *B*

North Carolina

Barton College *B*
Belmont Abbey College *B*
Campbell University *B*
Carteret Community College *A*
Chowan College *B*
Elon University *B*
Lees-McRae College *B*
Mars Hill College *B*
Meredith College *B*
Methodist College *B*
Mitchell Community College *A*
North Carolina State University *B*
Pfeiffer University *B*
Queens University of Charlotte *B*
St. Andrews Presbyterian College *B*
Sandhills Community College *A*
Warren Wilson College *B*
Wingate University *B*

North Dakota

Dickinson State University *B*
Mayville State University *B*
Minot State University: Bottineau
    Campus *A*
North Dakota State University *B*
Valley City State University *B*

Ohio

Defiance College *B*
Heidelberg College *B*
John Carroll University *B*
Lorain County Community College *A*
Mount Vernon Nazarene University *B*
Muskingum College *B*
Oberlin College *B*
Ohio Northern University *B*
Ohio University *B*
Ohio Wesleyan University *B*
Otterbein College *B*
Shawnee State University *B*
University of Cincinnati *B*
University of Cincinnati
    Clermont College *A*
    Raymond Walters College *A*
University of Findlay *B*
University of Toledo *B*
Ursuline College *B*
Walsh University *B*
Wittenberg University *B*
Youngstown State University *B*

Oklahoma

Carl Albert State College *A*
East Central University *B*
Eastern Oklahoma State College *A*
Langston University *B*
Murray State College *A*
Northeastern Oklahoma Agricultural and
    Mechanical College *A*
Oklahoma Christian University of
    Science and Arts *B*
Oklahoma City University *B*
Oklahoma State University *B*

Oregon

Eastern Oregon University *B*
Linn-Benton Community College *A*
Southern Oregon University *B*
University of Portland *B*
Western Baptist College *B*

Pennsylvania

Albright College *B*
Allegheny College *B*
California University of Pennsylvania *B*
Elizabethtown College *B*
Gettysburg College *B*
Grove City College *B*
Gwynedd-Mercy College *B*
Holy Family University *B*
Immaculata University *B*
Juniata College *B*
La Salle University *B*
Lock Haven University of
    Pennsylvania *B*
Mercyhurst College *B*
Muhlenberg College *B*
St. Vincent College *B*
University of Pittsburgh
    Greensburg *B*
    Johnstown *B*
Waynesburg College *B*
Widener University *B*
Wilkes University *B*
York College of Pennsylvania *B*

Puerto Rico

University of Puerto Rico
    Mayaguez Campus *C*

Rhode Island

Rhode Island College *B*

South Carolina

Clemson University *B*
Furman University *B*

South Dakota

Augustana College *B*
Dakota State University *B*
Dakota Wesleyan University *B*

Tennessee

Freed-Hardeman University *B*
Lambuth University *B*
Maryville College *B*
Roane State Community College *A*
Tennessee Technological University *B*
Tennessee Wesleyan College *B*
Union University *B*
University of Tennessee
    Knoxville *B*
    Martin *B*
Walters State Community College *A*

Texas

Abilene Christian University *B*
Amarillo College *A*
Angelina College *A*
Austin Community College *A*
Coastal Bend College *A*
Del Mar College *A*
El Paso Community College *A*
Galveston College *A*
Laredo Community College *A*
LeTourneau University *B*
Lon Morris College *A*
Lubbock Christian University *B*
McMurry University *B*
Midwestern State University *B*
Panola College *A*
Paris Junior College *A*
San Antonio College *A*
South Plains College *A*
Sul Ross State University *A*
Texas A&M University *B*
Texas A&M University
    Commerce *B*
Trinity Valley Community College *A*
Tyler Junior College *A*
Western Texas College *A*

Utah

Southern Utah University *B*
Utah State University *B, M*

Vermont

Bennington College *C*
Castleton State College *B*

Virginia

Averett University *B*
Longwood University *B*
Mountain Empire Community College *A*
Virginia Intermont College *B*
Virginia Wesleyan College *B*

Washington

Centralia College *A*
Eastern Washington University *B*
Everett Community College *A*
Lower Columbia College *A*
St. Martin's College *B*

West Virginia

Alderson-Broaddus College *B*
Concord College *B*
Davis and Elkins College *B*
Potomac State College of West Virginia
    University *A*
West Virginia Wesleyan College *B*

Wisconsin

Carthage College *B*
Lawrence University *B*
Marian College of Fond du Lac *B*
Mount Mary College *B*
Northland College *B*
Ripon College *B*
St. Norbert College *B*

University of Wisconsin
    Madison *B*
    Milwaukee *B*
    Oshkosh *B*
    Parkside *B*
    Whitewater *B*

Wyoming

Casper College *A*
Eastern Wyoming College *A*
Western Wyoming Community
    College *A*

Printing management

Georgia

Georgia Southern University *B*

Indiana

Indiana State University *B*

Kentucky

Somerset Community College *C*

New York

Rochester Institute of Technology *B, M*

Washington

Seattle Central Community College *C, A*

Wisconsin

University of Wisconsin
    Stout *B*

Printing press operator

Illinois

City Colleges of Chicago
    Kennedy-King College *A*

Indiana

Vincennes University *A*

Minnesota

Hennepin Technical College *A*

Ohio

Sinclair Community College *C*

Texas

Southwest Texas State University *B*

Wisconsin

Milwaukee Area Technical College *A*

Printmaking

Arizona

Arizona State University *B, M*

Arkansas

Phillips Community College of the
    University of Arkansas *C, A*

California

Academy of Art College *C, A, B, M*
California College of Arts and
    Crafts *B, M*
California State University
    Fullerton *B, M*
    Hayward *B*
    Long Beach *B, M*
    Northridge *B, M*
    Stanislaus *C*
De Anza College *C, A*
Long Beach City College *A*
Monterey Peninsula College *A*
Ohlone College *C*
Otis College of Art and Design *B, M*
Palomar College *A*
Santa Rosa Junior College *C*

Colorado

Colorado State University *B*

Connecticut

Capital Community College *C*

University of Hartford *B, M*

District of Columbia
American University *M*
George Washington University *M*

Florida
University of Miami *B*

Georgia
Atlanta College of Art *B*
University of Georgia *B*

Idaho
Lewis-Clark State College *C*

Illinois
Rockford College *B*
School of the Art Institute of
    Chicago *B, M*

Indiana
Ball State University *B*
Indiana University-Purdue University
    Fort Wayne *B*
Vincennes University *A*

Iowa
Drake University *B*
University of Iowa *B, M*

Kansas
University of Kansas *B, M*

Maine
Maine College of Art *B*

Maryland
Maryland Institute College of Art *B*

Massachusetts
Art Institute of Boston at Lesley
    University *A, B*
Emmanuel College *B*
Massachusetts College of Art *B, M*
Montserrat College of Art *B*
School of the Museum of Fine Arts *B, M*
Simon's Rock College of Bard *B*
University of Massachusetts
    Dartmouth *M*

Michigan
Aquinas College *B*
College for Creative Studies *B*
Ferris State University *B*
Grand Valley State University *B*
Northern Michigan University *B*
University of Michigan *B*

Minnesota
College of Visual Arts *B*
Minnesota State University
    Moorhead *B*

Mississippi
Mississippi University for Women *B*

Missouri
Kansas City Art Institute *B*
Lindenwood University *M*
University of Missouri
    St. Louis *B*
Washington University in St. Louis *B, M*

New Hampshire
New Hampshire Community Technical
    College
        Laconia *C*

New Jersey
Rowan University *B*

New Mexico
College of Santa Fe *B*

New York
Alfred University *B*
Bard College *B*
Parsons School of Design *C*
Pratt Institute *B, M*
Sarah Lawrence College *B*
School of Visual Arts *B, M*

State University of New York
    Buffalo *M*
    College at Buffalo *B*
    College at Fredonia *B*
    College at Potsdam *B*
    New Paltz *B, M*
    Purchase *B, M*
Syracuse University *B, M*

Ohio
Art Academy of Cincinnati *B*
Bowling Green State University *B*
Cleveland Institute of Art *B*
Columbus College of Art and Design *B*
Ohio State University
    Columbus Campus *B*
Ohio University *M*
University of Akron *B*
University of Findlay *B*
Wittenberg University *B*
Youngstown State University *B*

Oregon
Pacific Northwest College of Art *B*
Portland State University *B*
University of Oregon *B, M*

Pennsylvania
Arcadia University *B*
Immaculata University *A*
Marywood University *C, M*
Seton Hill University *B*
Temple University *B, M*

Puerto Rico
Escuela de Artes Plasticas de Puerto
    Rico *B*
Inter American University of Puerto Rico
    San German Campus *M*

Rhode Island
Providence College *B*
Rhode Island School of Design *B*

South Carolina
South Carolina State University *B*

Tennessee
Memphis College of Art *B, M*

Texas
Sam Houston State University *M*
Texas A&M University
    Commerce *B*
University of Dallas *M, T*
University of Houston *B, M*
University of North Texas *B, M*
University of Texas
    Arlington *B*
    El Paso *B*
    San Antonio *B, M*

Utah
Brigham Young University *B, M*
Dixie State College of Utah *A*

Vermont
Bennington College *B, M*

Washington
Cornish College of the Arts *B*
University of Washington *B, M*
Western Washington University *B*

West Virginia
West Virginia State College *B*

Wisconsin
Milwaukee Institute of Art & Design *B*
University of Wisconsin
    Madison *B*

Protective services

Arkansas
University of Arkansas
    Community College at Hope *A*

California
Bakersfield College *A*
Chabot College *A*
Citrus College *A*
San Joaquin Delta College *A*
Yuba Community College District *C, A*

Colorado
Blair Junior College *C*

Connecticut
Briarwood College *C*
Capital Community College *A*

Illinois
Illinois Central College *C, A*
Lewis University *B*
Moraine Valley Community
    College *A*
Richland Community College *A*

Indiana
Vincennes University *A*

Kansas
Hutchinson Community College *A*
Kansas City Kansas Community
    College *C, A*
Seward County Community
    College *C, A*

Louisiana
Louisiana State University
    Eunice *A*

Maryland
Montgomery College
    Rockville Campus *A*

Massachusetts
Northeastern University *B, M*

Michigan
Kirtland Community College *C*
Lansing Community College *A*
Madonna University *A, B*
Michigan State University *B, M*

Minnesota
Northland Community & Technical
    College *A*

Nevada
Truckee Meadows Community
    College *A*

New York
City University of New York
    John Jay College of Criminal
        Justice *A, B*
Hudson Valley Community College *A*
Iona College *M*
Mercy College *B*
Tompkins-Cortland Community
    College *A*

North Carolina
Alamance Community College *A*
Central Piedmont Community College *A*
Edgecombe Community College *A*
Fayetteville Technical Community
    College *A*
Nash Community College *A*

Ohio
Franklin University *B*
Ohio University *A*
Ohio University
    Chillicothe Campus *A*
Sinclair Community College *A*
Youngstown State University *C, A, B, M*

Oregon
Rogue Community College *A*

Pennsylvania
ICM School of Business & Medical
    Careers *A*
York College of Pennsylvania *B*

South Carolina
Aiken Technical College *A*
Trident Technical College *A*

Tennessee
Roane State Community College *A*

Texas
Central Texas College *A*
Hill College *C, A*
San Antonio College *A*
Texas A&M University
    Texarkana *B*

Virginia
Piedmont Virginia Community
    College *C, A*
Southside Virginia Community
    College *C, A*
Virginia Western Community College *A*

Washington
Centralia College *C, A*
Edmonds Community College *C*
Renton Technical College *C, A*
Walla Walla Community College *A*

Wisconsin
Chippewa Valley Technical College *A*
Milwaukee Area Technical College *A*

Wyoming
Sheridan College *A*

Psychiatric nursing

Illinois
Southern Illinois University
    Edwardsville *M*

Indiana
Indiana University-Purdue University
    Indianapolis *M*

Louisiana
Southeastern Louisiana University *M*

Maine
University of Southern Maine *B, M*

Michigan
University of Michigan
    Flint *M*
Wayne State University *M*

New York
City University of New York
    Hunter College *M*
Pace University *M*
Pace University:
    Pleasantville/Briarcliff *M*
State University of New York
    Buffalo *M*
    Health Science Center at Stony
        Brook *M*
    Stony Brook *M*

Ohio
Case Western Reserve University *M*

Pennsylvania
Drexel University *M*
University of Pennsylvania *C, M*

South Carolina
Medical University of South Carolina *M*

**Psychobiology/
physiological psychology**

California
La Sierra University *B*
Occidental College *B*
Pepperdine University *B*
San Francisco State University *M*

University of California
    Los Angeles *B*
    Riverside *B*
    Santa Barbara *B*
    Santa Cruz *B*
University of Southern California *B*

Colorado

University of Colorado
    Denver *B*

Connecticut

Quinnipiac University *B*
Wesleyan University *B*

Florida

Florida Atlantic University *B, D*
Florida State University *M, D*
University of Miami *B, D*

Georgia

Emory University *D*

Illinois

Loyola University of Chicago *D*
Northwestern University *B, M, D*

Indiana

University of Evansville *B*

Iowa

Luther College *B*

Kentucky

Centre College *B*

Maine

University of New England *B*

Massachusetts

Hampshire College *B*
Harvard College *B*
Pine Manor College *B*
Simmons College *B*
Wellesley College *B*
Wheaton College *B*

Missouri

Northwest Missouri State University *B*

Nebraska

York College *B*

New York

Hamilton College *B*
Long Island University
    Southampton College *B*
Medaille College *B*
Rochester Institute of Technology *B*
Sarah Lawrence College *B*
State University of New York
    Albany *M, D*
    Binghamton *B, D*
    New Paltz *B*
    Stony Brook *D*
Wagner College *B*

Ohio

Hiram College *B*
Oberlin College *B*

Oklahoma

University of Oklahoma *M, D*

Pennsylvania

Albright College *B*
Arcadia University *B*
Chatham College *B*
Holy Family University *B*
Lebanon Valley College of
    Pennsylvania *B*
Lincoln University *B*
Swarthmore College *B*
University of Pennsylvania *B*

Texas

Baylor University *B, M, D*
University of Houston *M, D*
University of Texas
    Tyler *M*

Utah

Utah Valley State College *A, B*

Virginia

Averett University *B*
College of William and Mary *B*
Lynchburg College *B*

Psychology

Alabama

Alabama Agricultural and Mechanical
    University *B*
Alabama State University *B*
Athens State University *B*
Auburn University *B, M, D*
Auburn University at Montgomery *B, M*
Birmingham-Southern College *B*
Faulkner University *B*
Huntingdon College *B*
Jacksonville State University *B, M*
Judson College *B*
Lawson State Community College *A*
Northeast Alabama Community
    College *A*
Oakwood College *B*
Samford University *B*
Spring Hill College *B*
Talladega College *B*
Troy State University *B*
Troy State University Dothan *B*
Troy State University in Montgomery *B*
Tuskegee University *B*
University of Alabama *B, M, D*
University of Alabama
    Birmingham *B, M, D*
    Huntsville *B, M*
University of Mobile *B*
University of Montevallo *B*
University of North Alabama *B*
University of South Alabama *B, M*
University of West Alabama *B*

Alaska

Alaska Pacific University *B*
University of Alaska
    Anchorage *B*
    Fairbanks *B*

Arizona

Arizona State University *B, M, D*
Arizona Western College *A*
Central Arizona College *A*
Cochise College *A*
Eastern Arizona College *A*
Estrella Mountain Community College *A*
Northern Arizona University *B, M*
Prescott College *B, M*
South Mountain Community College *A*
University of Arizona *B, M, D*

Arkansas

Arkansas State University *B*
Arkansas Tech University *B*
Harding University *B*
Henderson State University *B*
Hendrix College *B*
John Brown University *B*
Lyon College *B*
Ouachita Baptist University *B*
Philander Smith College *B*
Phillips Community College of the
    University of Arkansas *A*
Southern Arkansas University *B*
University of Arkansas *B, M, D*
University of Arkansas
    Fort Smith *A, B*
    Little Rock *B*
    Monticello *B*
    Pine Bluff *B*
University of Central Arkansas *B*
University of the Ozarks *B*
Williams Baptist College *B*

California

Antioch Southern California
    Los Angeles *M*
    Santa Barbara *M*
Azusa Pacific University *B*
Bakersfield College *A*
Barstow College *A*
Bethany College *B*
Biola University *B, M, D*
Cabrillo College *A*
California Baptist University *B*
California State Polytechnic University:
    Pomona *B, M*
California State University
    Bakersfield *B, M*
    Chico *B, M*
    Dominguez Hills *B*
    Fresno *B, M*
    Fullerton *B, M*
    Hayward *B*
    Long Beach *B, M*
    Los Angeles *B, M*
    Northridge *B*
    Sacramento *B, M*
    San Bernardino *B, M*
    San Marcos *B, M*
    Stanislaus *B, M*
Cerritos Community College *A*
Chabot College *A*
Chapman University *B*
Christian Heritage College *B*
Citrus College *A*
Claremont McKenna College *B*
College of Alameda *A*
Concordia University *B*
Contra Costa College *A*
De Anza College *A*
Dominican University of California *B*
East Los Angeles College *A*
Foothill College *A*
Fresno Pacific University *B*
Gavilan Community College *A*
Glendale Community College *A*
Golden Gate University *B, M*
Golden West College *A*
Holy Names College *B*
Hope International University *B*
Humboldt State University *B, M*
Imperial Valley College *A*
Irvine Valley College *A*
John F. Kennedy University *B, D*
La Sierra University *B*
Loma Linda University *M, D*
Los Angeles Harbor College *A*
Los Angeles Pierce College *C*
Los Angeles Southwest College *A*
Los Medanos College *A*
Loyola Marymount University *B*
Marymount College *A*
Mills College *B*
MiraCosta College *A*
Monterey Peninsula College *A*
Mount St. Mary's College *B*
National University *B*
Occidental College *B*
Orange Coast College *A*
Pacific Union College *B*
Pepperdine University *B, M, D*
Pitzer College *B*
Point Loma Nazarene University *B*
Pomona College *B*
St. Mary's College of California *B, M*
San Diego City College *A*
San Diego Mesa College *C, A*
San Diego State University *B, M*
San Francisco State University *B*
San Joaquin Delta College *A*
San Jose State University *B, M*
Santa Barbara City College *A*
Santa Clara University *B*
Santa Rosa Junior College *A*
Santiago Canyon College *A*
Scripps College *B*
Simpson College *B*
Sonoma State University *B, M*

Southwestern College *A*
Stanford University *B, M, D*
University of California
    Berkeley *B, D*
    Davis *B, D*
    Irvine *B, D*
    Los Angeles *B, M, D*
    Riverside *B, M, D*
    San Diego *B, M, D*
    Santa Barbara *B, M, D*
    Santa Cruz *B, D*
University of La Verne *B*
University of Redlands *B*
University of San Diego *B*
University of San Francisco *B*
University of Southern
    California *B, M, D*
University of the Pacific *B, M*
Vanguard University of Southern
    California *B*
Ventura College *A*
West Valley College *A*
Whittier College *B*

Colorado

Colorado Christian University *B*
Colorado College *B*
Colorado Mountain College
    Alpine Campus *A*
Colorado State University *B, M, D*
Colorado State University
    Pueblo *B, T*
Fort Lewis College *B*
Mesa State College *B*
Metropolitan State College of Denver *B*
Naropa University *B, M*
Otero Junior College *A*
Red Rocks Community College *A*
Regis University *B*
Trinidad State Junior College *A*
United States Air Force Academy *B*
University of Colorado
    Boulder *B, M, D*
    Colorado Springs *B, M*
    Denver *B, M*
University of Denver *B, M, D*
University of Northern Colorado *B, M*

Connecticut

Albertus Magnus College *B*
Central Connecticut State
    University *B, M*
Connecticut College *B, M*
Eastern Connecticut State University *B*
Fairfield University *B*
Mitchell College *B*
Quinnipiac University *B*
Sacred Heart University *B*
St. Joseph College *B*
Southern Connecticut State
    University *B, M*
Teikyo Post University *B*
Trinity College *B*
University of Connecticut *B, M, D*
University of Hartford *B, M*
University of New Haven *B*
Wesleyan University *B, M*
Western Connecticut State University *B*
Yale University *B, M, D*

Delaware

Delaware State University *B*
University of Delaware *B, M, D*
Wilmington College *B*

District of Columbia

American University *B, M, D*
Catholic University of America *B, M*
Gallaudet University *B*
George Washington University *B, M, D*
Georgetown University *B, D*
Howard University *B, M, D*
Trinity College *B*
University of the District of Columbia *B*

Florida

Barry University *B, M*

Bethune-Cookman College *B*
Broward Community College *A*
Carlos Albizu University *B, M, D*
Eckerd College *B*
Edward Waters College *B*
Flagler College *B*
Florida Agricultural and Mechanical
   University *B*
Florida Atlantic University *B, M*
Florida Institute of Technology *B, M*
Florida International University *B, M, D*
Florida Southern College *B*
Florida State University *B, M, D*
Gulf Coast Community College *A*
Indian River Community College *A*
Jacksonville University *B*
Manatee Community College *A*
Miami-Dade Community College *A*
New College of Florida *B*
Nova Southeastern University *B*
Palm Beach Atlantic University *B*
Palm Beach Community College *A*
Pensacola Junior College *A*
Polk Community College *A*
Rollins College *B*
St. Leo University *B*
St. Thomas University *B*
Schiller International University *B*
South Florida Community College *A*
Southeastern College of the Assemblies
   of God *B*
Stetson University *B*
University of Central Florida *B, D*
University of Florida *B, M, D*
University of Miami *B, M, D*
University of North Florida *B, M*
University of South Florida *B, M, D*
University of Tampa *A, B*
University of West Florida *B, M*
Warner Southern College *B*

Georgia

Abraham Baldwin Agricultural
   College *A*
Agnes Scott College *B*
Albany State University *B*
Andrew College *A*
Armstrong Atlantic State University *B*
Atlanta Metropolitan College *A*
Augusta State University *B, M*
Bainbridge College *A*
Berry College *B*
Brenau University *B*
Brewton-Parker College *B*
Clark Atlanta University *B*
Clayton College and State University *A*
Coastal Georgia Community College *A*
Columbus State University *B*
Covenant College *B*
Dalton State College *A*
Darton College *A*
East Georgia College *A*
Emmanuel College *B*
Emory University *B, D*
Floyd College *A*
Fort Valley State University *B*
Gainesville College *A*
Georgia College and State
   University *B, M*
Georgia Perimeter College *A*
Georgia Southern University *B, M*
Georgia Southwestern State University *B*
Georgia State University *B, M, D*
Gordon College *A*
Kennesaw State University *B*
LaGrange College *B*
Macon State College *A*
Mercer University *B*
Middle Georgia College *A*
Morehouse College *B*
Morris Brown College *B*
North Georgia College & State
   University *B*
Oglethorpe University *B*
Oxford College of Emory University *B*
Paine College *B*

Piedmont College *B*
Reinhardt College *B*
Shorter College *B*
South Georgia College *A*
Spelman College *B*
State University of West Georgia *B, M*
Thomas University *B*
University of Georgia *B, M, D*
Valdosta State University *B, M*
Waycross College *A*
Wesleyan College *B*
Young Harris College *A*

Hawaii

Brigham Young University-Hawaii *B*
Chaminade University of Honolulu *B*
Hawaii Pacific University *B*
University of Hawaii
   Hilo *B*
   Manoa *B, M, D*
   West Oahu *B*

Idaho

Albertson College of Idaho *B*
Boise State University *B*
Brigham Young University - Idaho *B*
College of Southern Idaho *A*
Idaho State University *B, M*
Lewis-Clark State College *B*
North Idaho College *A*
Northwest Nazarene University *B*
University of Idaho *B, M*

Illinois

Augustana College *B, T*
Aurora University *B*
Benedictine University *B*
Black Hawk College
   East Campus *A*
Blackburn College *B*
Bradley University *B, T*
Chicago State University *B*
City Colleges of Chicago
   Kennedy-King College *A*
Concordia University *B, M*
Danville Area Community College *A*
De Paul University *B, M*
Dominican University *B*
Eastern Illinois University *B, T*
Elmhurst College *B, T*
Eureka College *B*
Governors State University *B, M*
Greenville College *B*
Illinois College *B*
Illinois Institute of Technology *B, M, D*
Illinois State University *B, M*
Illinois Valley Community College *A*
Illinois Wesleyan University *B*
John A. Logan College *A*
John Wood Community College *A*
Joliet Junior College *A*
Judson College *B*
Kankakee Community College *A*
Kishwaukee College *A*
Knox College *B*
Lake Forest College *B*
Lake Land College *A*
Lewis University *B, T*
Lewis and Clark Community College *A*
Lincoln College *A*
Lincoln Land Community College *A*
Loyola University of Chicago *B, T*
MacMurray College *B*
McKendree College *B*
Millikin University *B*
Monmouth College *B, T*
National-Louis University *B, M*
North Central College *B*
North Park University *B*
Northeastern Illinois University *B*
Northern Illinois University *B, M, D*
Northwestern University *B, M, D*
Olivet Nazarene University *B, M*
Parkland College *A*
Quincy University *A, B*
Richland Community College *A*

Rockford College *B*
Roosevelt University *B, M*
St. Augustine College *A*
St. Xavier University *B*
Sauk Valley Community College *A*
South Suburban College of Cook
   County *A*
Southern Illinois University
   Carbondale *B, M, D*
Southern Illinois University
   Edwardsville *B, M*
Southwestern Illinois College *A*
Trinity Christian College *B*
Trinity International University *B, M*
Triton College *A*
University of Chicago *B, M, D*
University of Illinois
   Chicago *B, M, D*
   Springfield *B, M*
   Urbana-Champaign *B, M, D*
University of St. Francis *B*
Western Illinois University *B, M*
Wheaton College *B, T*
William Rainey Harper College *A*

Indiana

Anderson University *B*
Ball State University *B, M*
Bethel College *B*
Butler University *B*
Calumet College of St. Joseph *B*
DePauw University *B*
Earlham College *B*
Franklin College *B*
Goshen College *B*
Grace College *B*
Hanover College *B*
Huntington College *B*
Indiana State University *B, M*
Indiana University
   Bloomington *B, M, D*
   East *R*
   Kokomo *B*
   Northwest *B*
   South Bend *B, M*
   Southeast *B*
Indiana University-Purdue University
   Fort Wayne *A, B*
Indiana University-Purdue University
   Indianapolis *B, M*
Indiana Wesleyan University *B, T*
Manchester College *B*
Marian College *B, T*
Martin University *B*
Purdue University *B, M, D*
Purdue University
   Calumet *B*
St. Joseph's College *B*
Saint Mary's College *B*
St. Mary-of-the-Woods College *B*
Taylor University *B*
Taylor University: Fort Wayne *B*
Tri-State University *B*
University of Evansville *B*
University of Indianapolis *B*
University of Notre Dame *B, M, D*
University of St. Francis *B, M*
University of Southern Indiana *B*
Valparaiso University *B*
Vincennes University *A*
Wabash College *B*

Iowa

Briar Cliff University *B*
Buena Vista University *B*
Central College *B, T*
Clarke College *B, T*
Coe College *B*
Cornell College *B*
Dordt College *B*
Drake University *B*
Ellsworth Community College *A*
Franciscan University *B, T*
Graceland University *B, T*
Grand View College *B*
Grinnell College *B*

Iowa Central Community College *A*
Iowa State University *B, M, D*
Iowa Wesleyan College *B*
Iowa Western Community College *A*
Loras College *B, M*
Luther College *B*
Marshalltown Community College *A*
Morningside College *B*
Mount Mercy College *B*
North Iowa Area Community College *A*
Northwestern College *B, T*
St. Ambrose University *B, T*
Simpson College *B*
University of Dubuque *B*
University of Iowa *B, D, T*
University of Northern Iowa *B, M*
Upper Iowa University *B*
Vennard College *B*
Waldorf College *A*
Wartburg College *B, T*
William Penn University *B*

Kansas

Baker University *B, T*
Barclay College *B*
Barton County Community College *A*
Benedictine College *B*
Bethany College *B, T*
Bethel College *B*
Butler County Community College *A*
Central Christian College *A*
Cloud County Community College *A*
Emporia State University *B, M, T*
Fort Hays State University *B, M*
Fort Scott Community College *A*
Friends University *B*
Garden City Community College *A*
Hutchinson Community College *A*
Independence Community College *A*
Kansas City Kansas Community
   College *A*
Kansas State University *B, M, D*
Kansas Wesleyan University *B*
Labette Community College *A*
McPherson College *B, T*
MidAmerica Nazarene University *B, T*
Newman University *B*
Ottawa University *B*
Pittsburg State University *B, M, T*
Pratt Community College *A*
St. Mary College *B, M*
Seward County Community College *A*
Southwestern College *B*
Tabor College *B*
University of Kansas *B, M, D*
Washburn University of Topeka *B*
Wichita State University *B, M, D*

Kentucky

Asbury College *B*
Bellarmine University *B*
Berea College *B*
Brescia University *B*
Campbellsville University *B*
Centre College *B*
Cumberland College *B, T*
Georgetown College *B, T*
Kentucky Christian College *B*
Kentucky Wesleyan College *B*
Lindsey Wilson College *B*
Mid-Continent College *B*
Morehead State University *B, M*
Murray State University *B, M*
Pikeville College *B*
Spalding University *B*
Thomas More College *A, B*
Transylvania University *B*
Union College *B*
University of Kentucky *B*
University of Louisville *B, M*

Louisiana

Centenary College of Louisiana *B, T*
Dillard University *B*
Grambling State University *B*
Louisiana College *B*

Louisiana State University
   Shreveport *B*
Louisiana State University and
   Agricultural and Mechanical
   College *B, M, D*
Louisiana Tech University *B*
Loyola University New Orleans *B*
McNeese State University *B, M*
Nicholls State University *B*
Northwestern State University *B*
Southeastern Louisiana University *B, M*
Southern University
   New Orleans *B*
Southern University and Agricultural and
   Mechanical College *B*
Tulane University *B, M, D*
University of Louisiana at
   Lafayette *B, M*
University of Louisiana at Monroe *B, M*
University of New Orleans *B, M, D*
Xavier University of Louisiana *B*

Maine

Bates College *B*
Bowdoin College *B*
Colby College *B*
St. Joseph's College *B*
Thomas College *B*
University of Maine *B, M, D*
University of Maine
   Farmington *B*
   Machias *B*
   Presque Isle *B*
University of New England *B*
University of Southern Maine *B*

Maryland

Allegany College *A*
Bowie State University *B*
Chesapeake College *C, A*
College of Notre Dame of Maryland *B*
Columbia Union College *B*
Community College of Baltimore County
   Catonsville *A*
   Dundalk *A*
   Essex *A*
Coppin State College *B, M*
Frederick Community College *A*
Frostburg State University *C, B*
Goucher College *B*
Hood College *B*
Howard Community College *A*
Johns Hopkins University *B, M, D*
Loyola College in Maryland *B, M*
McDaniel College *B*
Morgan State University *B*
Mount St. Mary's College *B*
St. Mary's College of Maryland *B*
Salisbury University *B*
Towson University *B, M*
University of Baltimore *B, M, D*
University of Maryland
   Baltimore County *B, M, D*
   College Park *B, M, D*
   University College *B*
Villa Julie College *B*
Washington College *B, M*

Massachusetts

American International College *B, M*
Amherst College *B*
Anna Maria College *B, M*
Assumption College *B*
Atlantic Union College *B*
Bay Path College *B*
Becker College *A, B*
Berkshire Community College *A*
Boston College *B, D*
Boston University *B, M, D*
Brandeis University *B, M, D*
Bridgewater State College *B, M*
Bunker Hill Community College *A*
Cape Cod Community College *A*
Clark University *B, D*
College of the Holy Cross *B*
Elms College *B*

Emmanuel College *B*
Endicott College *B*
Fisher College *A*
Fitchburg State College *B*
Framingham State College *B*
Gordon College *B*
Hampshire College *B*
Harvard College *B*
Hellenic College/Holy Cross *B*
Lasell College *B*
Lesley University *B*
Massachusetts College of Liberal Arts *B*
Merrimack College *B*
Mount Holyoke College *B, M*
Newbury College *A, B*
Nichols College *B*
Northeastern University *B, M, D*
Pine Manor College *B*
Regis College *B*
St. John's Seminary College *B*
Salem State College *B*
Simmons College *B*
Simon's Rock College of Bard *B*
Smith College *B*
Springfield College *B*
Stonehill College *B*
Suffolk University *B, M*
Tufts University *B, M, D*
University of Massachusetts
   Amherst *B, M, D*
   Boston *B*
   Dartmouth *B, M*
   Lowell *B*
Wellesley College *B*
Western New England College *B*
Westfield State College *B, M*
Wheaton College *B*
Williams College *B*

Michigan

Adrian College *A, B, T*
Alma College *B, T*
Andrews University *B, M, D*
Aquinas College *B, T*
Calvin College *B, T*
Central Michigan University *B, M, T*
Concordia University *B, T*
Cornerstone University *B*
Eastern Michigan University *B, M*
Ferris State University *B*
Finlandia University *B*
Gogebic Community College *A*
Grand Valley State University *B, T*
Hillsdale College *B*
Hope College *B*
Kalamazoo College *B, T*
Kellogg Community College *A*
Lansing Community College *A*
Lawrence Technological University *B*
Madonna University *C, M*
Marygrove College *B*
Michigan State University *B, M, D*
Mid Michigan Community College *A*
Northern Michigan University *B, M*
Oakland University *B*
Saginaw Valley State University *B*
Siena Heights University *A, B*
Spring Arbor University *B*
University of Michigan *B, M, D, T*
University of Michigan
   Dearborn *B*
   Flint *B, T*
Wayne State University *B, M, D*
Western Michigan University *B*
William Tyndale College *B*

Minnesota

Augsburg College *B*
Bemidji State University *B*
Bethel College *B*
Capella University *M, D*
Carleton College *B*
College of St. Benedict *B*
College of St. Catherine *B*
College of St. Scholastica *B*
Concordia College: Moorhead *B*

Concordia University: St. Paul *B*
Crown College *A, B*
Gustavus Adolphus College *B*
Hamline University *B*
Itasca Community College *A*
Macalester College *B*
Metropolitan State University *B, M*
Minnesota State University
   Mankato *B, M*
   Moorhead *B*
North Central University *B*
Northland Community & Technical
   College *A*
Northwestern College *B*
Oak Hills Christian College *B*
Ridgewater College: A Community and
   Technical College *A*
St. Cloud State University *B, M*
St. John's University *B*
St. Mary's University of Minnesota *B*
St. Olaf College *B*
Southwest State University *B*
University of Minnesota
   Duluth *B*
   Morris *B*
   Twin Cities *B, M, D*
University of St. Thomas *B*
Vermilion Community College *A*
Winona State University *B*

Mississippi

Blue Mountain College *B*
Delta State University *B*
Itawamba Community College *A*
Mary Holmes College *A*
Millsaps College *B, T*
Mississippi College *B*
Mississippi Gulf Coast Community
   College
   Perkinston *A*
Mississippi State University *B, M*
Mississippi University for Women *B*
University of Mississippi *B, M, D*
University of Southern
   Mississippi *B, M, D*

Missouri

Avila University *B*
Central Methodist College *B*
Central Missouri State University *B, M*
College of the Ozarks *B*
Columbia College *B*
Crowder College *A*
Culver-Stockton College *B*
Drury University *B*
East Central College *A*
Evangel University *B, M*
Fontbonne College *B*
Hannibal-LaGrange College *B*
Jefferson College *C, A*
Lincoln University *B*
Lindenwood University *B*
Maryville University of Saint Louis *B*
Mineral Area College *A*
Missouri Baptist University *B*
Missouri Southern State College *B*
Missouri Valley College *B*
Missouri Western State College *B*
Northwest Missouri State University *B*
Rockhurst University *B*
St. Louis Community College
   St. Louis Community College at
      Florissant Valley *A*
   St. Louis Community College at
      Forest Park *A*
St. Louis University *B, M, D*
Southeast Missouri State University *B*
Southwest Baptist University *B*
Southwest Missouri State
   University *B, M*
Stephens College *B*
Three Rivers Community College *A*
Truman State University *B*

University of Missouri
   Columbia *B, M, D*
   Kansas City *B, M, D*
   Rolla *B, T*
   St. Louis *B, M, D*
Washington University in St.
   Louis *B, M, D*
Webster University *B*
Westminster College *B*
William Jewell College *B*
William Woods University *B*

Montana

Carroll College *B, T*
Miles Community College *A*
Montana State University
   Billings *A, B, M, T*
   Bozeman *B, M*
Rocky Mountain College *B, T*
University of Great Falls *B*
University of Montana-Missoula *B, M, D*

Nebraska

Bellevue University *B*
Chadron State College *B*
College of Saint Mary *B*
Concordia University *B*
Creighton University *B*
Dana College *B*
Doane College *B*
Hastings College *B, T*
Midland Lutheran College *B*
Nebraska Wesleyan University *B*
Northeast Community College *A*
Peru State College *B, T*
Southeast Community College
   Beatrice Campus *A*
Union College *B*
University of Nebraska
   Kearney *B, T*
   Lincoln *B, M, D*
   Omaha *B, M*
Wayne State College *B, T*
Western Nebraska Community
   College *A*
York College *A, B*

Nevada

Community College of Southern
   Nevada *A*
Sierra Nevada College *B*
University of Nevada
   Las Vegas *B, M, D*
   Reno *B, M, D*

New Hampshire

Colby-Sawyer College *B*
Dartmouth College *B, M, D*
Franklin Pierce College *B*
Hesser College *C, A*
Keene State College *B*
New England College *B*
Plymouth State College *B*
Rivier College *B*
St. Anselm College *B*
Southern New Hampshire University *B*
University of New Hampshire *B, M, D*
University of New Hampshire at
   Manchester *B*

New Jersey

Atlantic Cape Community College *A*
Bloomfield College *B*
Caldwell College *B*
Centenary College *B*
The College of New Jersey *B*
College of St. Elizabeth *B*
Drew University *B*
Fairleigh Dickinson University
   College at Florham *B*
   Metropolitan Campus *B, M*
Felician College *B*
Georgian Court College *B*
Gloucester County College *A*
Kean University *B, M*
Monmouth University *B*
Montclair State University *B, M, T*

New Jersey City University *B, M*
Ocean County College *A*
Passaic County Community College *A*
Princeton University *B, M, D*
Ramapo College of New Jersey *B*
Richard Stockton College of New
    Jersey *B*
Rider University *B*
Rowan University *B, M*
Rutgers, The State University of New
    Jersey
    Camden Regional Campus *B*
    New Brunswick Regional
        Campus *B, M, D*
    Newark Regional Campus *B, D*
St. Peter's College *B*
Salem Community College *A*
Seton Hall University *B, M*
Sussex County Community College *A*
Thomas Edison State College *B*
William Paterson University of New
    Jersey *B*

New Mexico

Clovis Community College *A*
College of Santa Fe *B*
College of the Southwest *B*
Eastern New Mexico University *A, B, M*
New Mexico Highlands University *B, M*
New Mexico Institute of Mining and
    Technology *B*
New Mexico Junior College *A*
New Mexico State University *B, M, D*
San Juan College *A*
University of New Mexico *B, M, D*
Western New Mexico University *B*

New York

Adelphi University *B, M*
Adirondack Community College *A*
Alfred University *B*
Bard College *B*
Barnard College *B*
Canisius College *B*
Cazenovia College *B*
City University of New York
    Baruch College *B*
    Brooklyn College *B, M*
    City College *B, M*
    College of Staten Island *B*
    Hunter College *B, M*
    John Jay College of Criminal
        Justice *B, M*
    Medgar Evers College *B*
    Queens College *B, M*
    Queensborough Community
        College *A*
    York College *B*
Clarkson University *B*
Colgate University *B*
College of Mount St. Vincent *A, B*
College of New Rochelle *B, T*
Columbia University
    Columbia College *B*
Concordia College *B*
Cornell University *B, D*
D'Youville College *B*
Daemen College *B*
Dominican College of Blauvelt *B*
Dowling College *B*
Elmira College *B*
Eugene Lang College/New School
    University *B*
Excelsior College *B*
Fordham University *B, M, D*
Fulton-Montgomery Community
    College *A*
Hamilton College *B*
Hartwick College *B*
Hilbert College *B*
Hobart and William Smith Colleges *B*
Hofstra University *B*
Houghton College *B*
Iona College *B*
Ithaca College *B*
Keuka College *B*

Le Moyne College *B*
Long Island University
    C. W. Post Campus *B, M*
    Southampton College *B*
Manhattan College *B*
Manhattanville College *B*
Marist College *B, M*
Marymount College of Fordham
    University *B*
Marymount Manhattan College *B*
Medaille College *B, M*
Mercy College *B, M*
Metropolitan College of New York *A, B*
Molloy College *B*
Mount St. Mary College *B, T*
Nazareth College of Rochester *B*
New York Institute of Technology *C, B*
New York University *B, M*
Niagara University *B*
Nyack College *B*
Pace University *B, M, D*
Pace University:
    Pleasantville/Briarcliff *B, M, D*
Rensselaer Polytechnic Institute *B, M*
Roberts Wesleyan College *B*
Rochester Institute of Technology *B*
Russell Sage College *B*
Sage College of Albany *B*
St. Bonaventure University *B*
St. John Fisher College *B*
St. John's University *B*
St. Joseph's College *B*
St. Joseph's College: Suffolk Campus *B*
St. Lawrence University *B*
Sarah Lawrence College *B, M*
Skidmore College *B*
State University of New York
    Albany *B, M, D*
    Binghamton *B, M*
    Buffalo *B, M*
    College at Brockport *B, M*
    College at Buffalo *B*
    College at Cortland *B, M*
    College at Fredonia *B*
    College at Geneseo *B, T*
    College at Old Westbury *B*
    College at Oneonta *B*
    College at Plattsburgh *B*
    College at Potsdam *B, T*
    College of Technology at Canton *A*
    Empire State College *A, B*
    Institute of Technology at
        Utica/Rome *B*
    New Paltz *B, M*
    Oswego *B*
    Purchase *B*
    Stony Brook *B, M*
Suffolk County Community College *A*
Syracuse University *B, M, D*
Touro College *B*
Union College *B*
United States Military Academy *B*
University of Rochester *B, M*
Utica College *B*
Vassar College *B*
Wagner College *B*
Wells College *B*
Yeshiva University *B, M, D*

North Carolina

Appalachian State University *B*
Barton College *B*
Belmont Abbey College *B*
Bennett College *B*
Campbell University *B*
Catawba College *B*
Chowan College *B*
Davidson College *B*
Duke University *B*
East Carolina University *B, M*
Elizabeth City State University *B*
Elon University *B*
Fayetteville State University *B*
Gardner-Webb University *B*
Gaston College *C*
Greensboro College *B*

Guilford College *B*
Guilford Technical Community
    College *A*
High Point University *B*
Johnson C. Smith University *B*
Lees-McRae College *B*
Lenoir Community College *A*
Lenoir-Rhyne College *B*
Livingstone College *B*
Louisburg College *A*
Mars Hill College *B*
Meredith College *B*
Methodist College *A, B*
Mount Olive College *B*
North Carolina Agricultural and
    Technical State University *B*
North Carolina Central University *B, M*
North Carolina State University *B, M, D*
North Carolina Wesleyan College *B*
Peace College *B*
Pfeiffer University *B*
Queens University of Charlotte *B*
St. Andrews Presbyterian College *B*
St. Augustine's College *B*
Salem College *B*
Sandhills Community College *A*
Shaw University *B*
University of North Carolina
    Asheville *B, T*
    Chapel Hill *B, M, D*
    Charlotte *B*
    Greensboro *B, M, D, T*
    Pembroke *B*
    Wilmington *B, M*
Wake Forest University *B, M*
Warren Wilson College *B*
Western Carolina University *B*
Wingate University *B*
Winston-Salem State University *B*

North Dakota

Dickinson State University *B*
Jamestown College *B*
Minot State University *B, T*
North Dakota State University *B, M, D*
University of Mary *B*
University of North Dakota *B, M, D*
Valley City State University *B*

Ohio

Ashland University *B*
Baldwin-Wallace College *B*
Bluffton College *B*
Bowling Green State University *B, M, D*
Case Western Reserve
    University *B, M, D*
Cedarville University *B*
Central State University *B*
Circleville Bible College *A, B*
Cleveland State University *B, M*
College of Mount St. Joseph *B*
College of Wooster *B*
Defiance College *B*
Denison University *B*
Franciscan University of Steubenville *B*
Heidelberg College *B, M*
Hiram College *B, T*
Jefferson Community College *A*
John Carroll University *B*
Kent State University *B, M, D*
Kent State University
    Stark Campus *B*
Kenyon College *B*
Lake Erie College *B*
Lorain County Community College *A*
Lourdes College *A, B*
Malone College *B*
Marietta College *B*
Miami University
    Middletown Campus *A*
    Oxford Campus *B, M, D*
Mount Union College *B*
Mount Vernon Nazarene University *B*
Muskingum College *B*
Notre Dame College *C, B, T*
Oberlin College *B*

Ohio Dominican College *B*
Ohio Northern University *B*
Ohio State University
    Columbus Campus *B, M, D*
    Lima Campus *B*
Ohio University *B*
Ohio University
    Southern Campus at Ironton *A*
Ohio Wesleyan University *B*
Otterbein College *B*
Owens Community College
    Findlay Campus *A*
    Toledo *A*
Shawnee State University *B*
Sinclair Community College *A*
Tiffin University *A, B*
Union Institute & University *B*
University of Akron *M*
University of Cincinnati *B, M, D*
University of Dayton *B, M*
University of Findlay *B*
University of Rio Grande *A, B*
University of Toledo *A, B, M, D*
Urbana University *B*
Ursuline College *B*
Walsh University *B*
Wilmington College *B*
Wittenberg University *B*
Wright State University *B*
Wright State University: Lake Campus *A*
Xavier University *A, B, M*
Youngstown State University *B*

Oklahoma

Bacone College *A*
Cameron University *B, M*
Carl Albert State College *A*
East Central University *B*
Eastern Oklahoma State College *A*
Langston University *B*
Northeastern Oklahoma Agricultural and
    Mechanical College *A*
Northeastern State University *B*
Northwestern Oklahoma State
    University *B*
Oklahoma Baptist University *B*
Oklahoma Christian University of
    Science and Arts *B*
Oklahoma City Community College *A*
Oklahoma City University *B*
Oklahoma Panhandle State University *B*
Oklahoma State University *B, M, D*
Oral Roberts University *B*
Redlands Community College *A*
Rose State College *A*
St. Gregory's University *A, B*
Southeastern Oklahoma State
    University *B*
Southern Nazarene University *B*
Southwestern Oklahoma State
    University *B, M*
Tulsa Community College *A*
University of Central Oklahoma *B*
University of Oklahoma *B, M, D*
University of Science and Arts of
    Oklahoma *B*
University of Tulsa *B*
Western Oklahoma State College *A*

Oregon

Central Oregon Community College *A*
Chemeketa Community College *A*
Concordia University *B*
Eastern Oregon University *B, T*
George Fox University *B, M*
Lewis & Clark College *B*
Linfield College *B*
Linn-Benton Community College *A*
Marylhurst University *B*
Northwest Christian College *B, M*
Oregon Institute of Technology *B*
Oregon State University *B*
Pacific University *B, M, D*
Portland State University *B, M, D*
Reed College *B*
Southern Oregon University *B, M*

University of Oregon *B, M, D*
University of Portland *B*
Warner Pacific College *B*
Western Baptist College *B*
Western Oregon University *B*
Willamette University *B*

Pennsylvania

Albright College *B*
Allegheny College *B*
Arcadia University *B*
Bloomsburg University of
    Pennsylvania *B*
Bryn Mawr College *B*
Bucknell University *B, M*
Bucks County Community College *A*
Butler County Community College *A*
Cabrini College *B*
California University of Pennsylvania *B*
Carlow College *B*
Carnegie Mellon University *B, M, D*
Cedar Crest College *B*
Chatham College *B*
Chestnut Hill College *A, B*
Cheyney University of Pennsylvania *B*
Community College of Allegheny
    County *A*
DeSales University *B*
Delaware County Community College *A*
Dickinson College *B*
Drexel University *B, M, D, T*
Duquesne University *B, M*
East Stroudsburg University of
    Pennsylvania *B*
Edinboro University of Pennsylvania *B*
Elizabethtown College *B*
Franklin & Marshall College *B*
Geneva College *B*
Gettysburg College *B*
Grove City College *B*
Gwynedd-Mercy College *B*
Harrisburg Area Community College *A*
Haverford College *B*
Holy Family University *B*
Immaculata University *B*
Indiana University of Pennsylvania *B*
Juniata College *B*
King's College *B*
Kutztown University of Pennsylvania *B*
La Roche College *B*
La Salle University *B, M, D*
Lafayette College *B*
Lebanon Valley College of
    Pennsylvania *B*
Lehigh University *B, M, D*
Lincoln University *B*
Lock Haven University of
    Pennsylvania *B*
Lycoming College *B*
Manor College *A*
Marywood University *B, M*
Mercyhurst College *B*
Messiah College *B*
Millersville University of
    Pennsylvania *B, M*
Moravian College *B*
Mount Aloysius College *B, M*
Muhlenberg College *B*
Neumann College *C, B*

Penn State
    Abington *B*
    Altoona *B*
    Beaver *B*
    Berks *B*
    Delaware County *B*
    Dubois *B*
    Erie, The Behrend College *B*
    Fayette *B*
    Harrisburg *B, M*
    Hazleton *B*
    Lehigh Valley *B*
    McKeesport *B*
    Mont Alto *B*
    New Kensington *B*
    Schuylkill - Capital College *B*
    Shenango *B*
    University Park *B, M, D*
    Wilkes-Barre *B*
    Worthington Scranton *B*
    York *B*
Philadelphia University *B*
Point Park College *B*
Reading Area Community College *A*
Rosemont College *B*
St. Joseph's University *B, M*
St. Vincent College *B*
Seton Hill University *B*
Shippensburg University of
    Pennsylvania *B, M*
Slippery Rock University of
    Pennsylvania *B*
Swarthmore College *B*
Temple University *B*
Thiel College *B*
University of Pennsylvania *B, D*
University of Pittsburgh *B, M, D*
University of Pittsburgh
    Bradford *B*
    Greensburg *B*
    Johnstown *B*
University of Scranton *B*
University of the Sciences in
    Philadelphia *B, M*
Villanova University *B, M*
Washington and Jefferson College *B*
Waynesburg College *B*
West Chester University of
    Pennsylvania *B, M*
Widener University *B*
Wilkes University *B*
Wilson College *B*
York College of Pennsylvania *B*

Puerto Rico

Bayamon Central University *B, M*
Inter American University of Puerto Rico
    Metropolitan Campus *B, M*
    San German Campus *B*
Pontifical Catholic University of Puerto
    Rico *B*
Turabo University *B*
Universidad Metropolitana *B*
University of Puerto Rico
    Cayey University College *B*
    Mayaguez Campus *B*
    Ponce *B*
    Rio Piedras Campus *B, M, D*
University of the Sacred Heart *B*

Rhode Island

Brown University *B, M, D*
Bryant College *B*
Rhode Island College *B, M*
Roger Williams University *B*
Salve Regina University *B*
University of Rhode Island *B*

South Carolina

Anderson College *B*
Charleston Southern University *B*
The Citadel *B, M*
Clemson University *B*
Coastal Carolina University *B*
Coker College *B*
College of Charleston *B*

Columbia College *B*
Columbia International University *B*
Converse College *B*
Erskine College *B*
Francis Marion University *B*
Furman University *B*
Lander University *B*
Limestone College *B*
Newberry College *B*
Presbyterian College *B, T*
South Carolina State University *B*
Southern Wesleyan University *B*
University of South Carolina
    Aiken *B*
    Spartanburg *B*
Winthrop University *B*
Wofford College *B*

South Dakota

Augustana College *B*
Black Hills State University *B*
Dakota Wesleyan University *M*
Northern State University *B*
South Dakota State University *B, T*
University of Sioux Falls *B*
University of South Dakota *B, M, D*

Tennessee

Austin Peay State University *B, M*
Belmont University *B, T*
Bethel College *B*
Bryan College *B, T*
Carson-Newman College *B*
Christian Brothers University *B*
Columbia State Community College *A*
Crichton College *B*
Dyersburg State Community College *A*
East Tennessee State University *B, M*
Fisk University *B, M*
Freed-Hardeman University *B*
Jackson State Community College *A*
King College *B*
Lambuth University *B*
Lee University *B*
Maryville College *B*
Middle Tennessee State University *B, M*
Milligan College *B*
Rhodes College *B*
Roane State Community College *A*
Southern Adventist University *B*
Tennessee State University *B, M*
Tennessee Technological University *B*
Tennessee Wesleyan College *B*
Trevecca Nazarene University *B*
Tusculum College *B*
Union University *B*
University of Memphis *B, M, D*
University of Tennessee
    Chattanooga *B, M*
    Knoxville *B, M, D*
    Martin *B*
Vanderbilt University *B, M, D*
Walters State Community College *A*

Texas

Abilene Christian University *B, M, T*
Amarillo College *A*
Angelo State University *B, M*
Austin College *B*
Austin Community College *A*
Baylor University *B*
Blinn College *A*
Brazosport College *A*
Cedar Valley College *A*
Cisco Junior College *A*
Clarendon College *A*
Coastal Bend College *A*
College of the Mainland *A*
Dallas Baptist University *B*
Dallas Christian College *B*
Del Mar College *A*
East Texas Baptist University *B*
El Paso Community College *A*
Frank Phillips College *A*
Galveston College *A*
Grayson County College *A*

Hardin-Simmons University *B, M*
Hill College *A*
Houston Baptist University *B*
Howard College *A*
Howard Payne University *B*
Kilgore College *A*
Lamar University *B*
Laredo Community College *A*
LeTourneau University *B*
Lon Morris College *A*
Lubbock Christian University *B*
McMurry University *B, T*
Midland College *A*
Midwestern State University *B, M*
Northeast Texas Community College *A*
Odessa College *A*
Our Lady of the Lake University of San
    Antonio *B*
Palo Alto College *A*
Panola College *A*
Paris Junior College *A*
Prairie View A&M University *B*
Rice University *B, M, D*
St. Edward's University *B, T*
St. Mary's University *B, M, T*
St. Philip's College *A*
Sam Houston State University *B, M*
Schreiner University *B*
South Plains College *A*
Southern Methodist University *B*
Southwest Texas State University *B, M*
Southwestern Adventist University *B, T*
Southwestern Assemblies of God
    University *A*
Southwestern University *B, T*
Stephen F. Austin State
    University *B, M, T*
Sul Ross State University *B*
Tarleton State University *B*
Texas A&M International
    University *B, M, T*
Texas A&M University *B, M, D*
Texas A&M University
    Commerce *B, M*
    Corpus Christi *B, M*
    Kingsville *B, M*
    Texarkana *B*
Texas Christian University *B, M, D, T*
Texas Lutheran University *B*
Texas Southern University *B, M*
Texas Tech University *B, M, D*
Texas Wesleyan University *B, T*
Texas Woman's University *B, M, T*
Trinity University *B*
Trinity Valley Community College *A*
Tyler Junior College *A*
University of Dallas *B, T*
University of Houston *B, M, D*
University of Houston
    Clear Lake *B, M*
    Downtown *B*
    Victoria *B*
University of Mary
    Hardin-Baylor *B, M, T*
University of North Texas *B, M, D*
University of St. Thomas *B*
University of Texas
    Arlington *B, M*
    Austin *B, M, D*
    Dallas *B*
    El Paso *B, M, D*
    Pan American *B, M, T*
    San Antonio *B, M*
    Tyler *B*
    of the Permian Basin *B*
University of the Incarnate Word *B*
Wayland Baptist University *B*
West Texas A&M University *B, M*
Western Texas College *A*
Wharton County Junior College *A*

Utah

Brigham Young University *B, M, D*
Dixie State College of Utah *A*
Snow College *A*
Southern Utah University *B, T*

University of Utah *B, M, D*
Utah State University *B, M, D*
Utah Valley State College *A, B*
Weber State University *B*
Westminster College *B*

Vermont
Bennington College *B*
Burlington College *B*
Castleton State College *B*
Champlain College *B*
College of St. Joseph in Vermont *B, M*
Goddard College *B, M*
Green Mountain College *B*
Johnson State College *B*
Lyndon State College *B*
Marlboro College *B*
Middlebury College *B*
Norwich University *B*
St. Michael's College *B*
Southern Vermont College *B*
University of Vermont *B, M, D*

Virginia
Averett University *B*
Bluefield College *B*
Bridgewater College *B*
College of William and Mary *B, M*
Eastern Mennonite University *B*
Emory & Henry College *B*
Ferrum College *B*
George Mason University *B, M, D*
Hampden-Sydney College *B*
Hampton University *B*
Hollins University *B*
James Madison University *B, M, D*
Liberty University *B*
Longwood University *B, T*
Lynchburg College *B*
Mary Baldwin College *B*
Mary Washington College *B*
Marymount University *B*
Norfolk State University *B*
Old Dominion University *B, M*
Radford University *B, M*
Randolph-Macon College *B*
Randolph-Macon Woman's College *B*
Roanoke College *B, T*
Shenandoah University *B*
Sweet Briar College *B*
University of Richmond *B, M*
University of Virginia *B, M, D*
University of Virginia's College at
  Wise *B*
Virginia Commonwealth
  University *B, M, D*
Virginia Intermont College *B*
Virginia Military Institute *B*
Virginia Polytechnic Institute and State
  University *B, M, D, T*
Virginia State University *B, M*
Virginia Union University *B*
Virginia Wesleyan College *B*
Washington and Lee University *B*

Washington
Central Washington University *B*
Centralia College *A*
Eastern Washington University *B, T*
Everett Community College *A*
Gonzaga University *B*
Heritage College *B*
Lower Columbia College *A*
Northwest College *B*
Olympic College *A*
Pacific Lutheran University *B*
St. Martin's College *B*
Seattle Pacific University *B*
Seattle University *B, M*
University of Puget Sound *B, T*
University of Washington *B, M, D*
Walla Walla College *B*
Washington State University *B, M, D*
Western Washington University *B, M, T*
Whitman College *B*
Whitworth College *B*

West Virginia
Alderson-Broaddus College *B*
Bethany College *B*
Concord College *B*
Davis and Elkins College *B*
Fairmont State College *B*
Marshall University *B, M*
Ohio Valley College *B*
Potomac State College of West Virginia
  University *A*
Shepherd College *B*
University of Charleston *B*
West Liberty State College *B*
West Virginia State College *B*
West Virginia University *B, M, D*
West Virginia Wesleyan College *B*
Wheeling Jesuit University *B*

Wisconsin
Alverno College *B, T*
Beloit College *B*
Cardinal Stritch University *B*
Carroll College *B*
Carthage College *B, T*
Concordia University Wisconsin *B*
Edgewood College *B*
Lakeland College *B, M*
Lawrence University *B, T*
Marian College of Fond du Lac *B*
Marquette University *B, T*
Mount Mary College *B*
Northland College *B*
Ripon College *B*
St. Norbert College *B, T*
Silver Lake College *B, T*
University of Wisconsin
  Eau Claire *B*
  Green Bay *B*
  La Crosse *B, T*
  Madison *B, M, D*
  Milwaukee *B, M, D*
  Oshkosh *B, M*
  Parkside *B*
  Platteville *B, T*
  River Falls *B, T*
  Stevens Point *B, T*
  Stout *B, M*
  Superior *B*
  Whitewater *B, T*
Viterbo University *B*
Wisconsin Lutheran College *B*

Wyoming
Casper College *A*
Central Wyoming College *A*
Eastern Wyoming College *A*
Laramie County Community College *A*
Sheridan College *A*
University of Wyoming *B, M, D*
Western Wyoming Community
  College *A*

Psychology teacher education

Indiana
Goshen College *B*

Iowa
Morningside College *B*
St. Ambrose University *B*

Kansas
Benedictine College *B, T*
Emporia State University *B, T*
Sterling College *T*

Pennsylvania
St. Vincent College *B*

Tennessee
Bryan College *T*

Texas
Texas Tech University *M, D*

Utah
University of Utah *B*

Psychometrics/quantitative psychology

Alabama
Alabama Agricultural and Mechanical
  University *M*

Arizona
University of Phoenix *M*

Kansas
University of Kansas *D*

Psychopharmacology

Florida
Nova Southeastern University *M*

Public administration

Alabama
Alabama State University *M*
Andrew Jackson University *M*
Auburn University *B, M, D*
Auburn University at Montgomery *M, D*
Huntingdon College *B*
Jacksonville State University *M*
Samford University *B*
Talladega College *B*
Troy State University *M*
Troy State University in Montgomery *M*
University of Alabama *M, D*
University of Alabama
  Birmingham *M*
  Huntsville *M*
University of South Alabama *M*

Alaska
University of Alaska
  Anchorage *M*
  Southeast *M*

Arizona
Arizona State University *M, D*
Northern Arizona University *M*
Rio Salado College *C, A*
Scottsdale Community College *C*
University of Arizona *B, M*

Arkansas
Arkansas State University *M*
Harding University *B*
Henderson State University *B*
University of Arkansas *B, M*
University of Arkansas
  Little Rock *M*
University of Central Arkansas *B*
University of the Ozarks *B*

California
California State Polytechnic University:
  Pomona *M*
California State University
  Bakersfield *B, M*
  Chico *B, M*
  Dominguez Hills *M*
  Fresno *B, M*
  Fullerton *B, M*
  Hayward *B, M*
  Long Beach *M*
  Los Angeles *B, M*
  Northridge *M*
  San Bernardino *M*
Golden Gate University *M, D*
Long Beach City College *C, A*
Monterey Institute of International
  Studies *M*
National University *M*
Palomar College *C, A*
San Francisco State University *M*
San Joaquin Delta College *A*

San Jose State University *M*
Sonoma State University *M*
University of California
  Los Angeles *M*
University of La Verne *B, M, D*
University of San Francisco *B, M*
University of Southern
  California *B, M, D*

Colorado
Red Rocks Community College *C, A*
University of Colorado
  Colorado Springs *M*
  Denver *M, D*
University of Denver *B, M*

Connecticut
Mitchell College *A*
Three Rivers Community College *A*
University of Connecticut *M*
University of New Haven *M*

Delaware
University of Delaware *M*
Wilmington College *M*

District of Columbia
American University *M, D*
Howard University *M*
University of the District of Columbia *M*

Florida
Barry University *C, B*
Florida Atlantic University *C, B, M, D*
Florida Gulf Coast University *M*
Florida International University *B, M, D*
Florida Metropolitan University
  Orlando College North *M*
Florida State University *C, M, D*
Miami-Dade Community College *A*
Nova Southeastern University *M, D*
Polk Community College *A*
South Florida Community College *A*
Tallahassee Community College *A*
University of Central Florida *C, B, M, D*
University of Miami *M, D*
University of North Florida *M*
University of South Florida *M*
University of West Florida *M*

Georgia
Albany State University *M*
Augusta State University *M*
Clark Atlanta University *M, D*
Columbus State University *M*
Darton College *A*
Georgia College and State University *M*
Georgia Southern University *M*
Georgia State University *M*
Kennesaw State University *M*
Macon State College *A*
Middle Georgia College *A*
North Georgia College & State
  University *M*
Piedmont College *M*
Savannah State University *M*
State University of West Georgia *M*
University of Georgia *M, D*
Valdosta State University *M*

Hawaii
Hawaii Pacific University *B*
University of Hawaii
  Hilo *B*
  Manoa *M*
  West Oahu *B*

Idaho
Boise State University *M*
Idaho State University *M*

Illinois
Augustana College *B*
Blackburn College *B*
De Paul University *M*
Governors State University *B, M*
Illinois Institute of Technology *M*
Lewis University *B*
Northern Illinois University *M*

Northwestern University *M*
Roosevelt University *C, M*
Southern Illinois University
  Carbondale *M*
Southern Illinois University
  Edwardsville *M*
University of Illinois
  Chicago *M, D*
  Springfield *M*
  Urbana-Champaign *M*

Indiana

Ball State University *M*
Indiana State University *M*
Indiana University
  Bloomington *A, B, M, D*
  Kokomo *B*
  Northwest *A, B, M*
  South Bend *A, B, M*
Indiana University-Purdue University
  Fort Wayne *C, A, B, M*
Indiana University-Purdue University
  Indianapolis *A, B, M*
University of Notre Dame *M*

Iowa

Buena Vista University *B*
Drake University *M*
Iowa State University *B, M*
St. Ambrose University *B*
University of Northern Iowa *B*

Kansas

Barton County Community College *A*
Fort Scott Community College *A*
Washburn University of Topeka *C, B*
Wichita State University *M*

Kentucky

Murray State University *M*
University of Kentucky *M, D*
University of Louisville *M*

Louisiana

Grambling State University *B, M*
Louisiana State University and
  Agricultural and Mechanical
  College *M*
Southern University and Agricultural and
  Mechanical College *M*
University of New Orleans *M*

Maine

University of Maine *B, M*
University of Maine
  Augusta *A, B*
University of Southern Maine *M, D*

Maryland

Bowie State University *B, M*
University of Baltimore *M, D*
University of Maryland
  College Park *M*

Massachusetts

American International College *B, M*
Bridgewater State College *B, M*
Clark University *B, M*
Mount Ida College *A, B*
Northeastern University *M*
Stonehill College *B*
Suffolk University *B, M*
University of Massachusetts
  Boston *B, M*

Michigan

Calvin College *B*
Central Michigan University *M*
Eastern Michigan University *B, M*
Ferris State University *C, B*
Grand Valley State University *B*
Michigan State University *B, M*
Northern Michigan University *B, M*
Oakland University *B, M*
Saginaw Valley State University *B*
University of Michigan *M, D*
University of Michigan
  Dearborn *B*
  Flint *B, M*

Wayne State University *B, M*
Western Michigan University *M, D*

Minnesota

Hamline University *B*
Metropolitan State University *B, M*
Minnesota State University
  Mankato *M*
  Moorhead *M*
St. Cloud State University *B*
St. Mary's University of Minnesota *B*
Southwest State University *B*
University of Minnesota
  Twin Cities *M*
Winona State University *B*

Mississippi

Mississippi State University *M, D*
Mississippi Valley State University *B*
University of Mississippi *B*

Missouri

Central Methodist College *A, B*
East Central College *A*
Lincoln University *B*
Lindenwood University *B*
Longview Community College *A*
Northwest Missouri State University *B*
St. Louis University *M*
Southwest Missouri State
  University *B, M*
University of Missouri
  Columbia *M*
  Kansas City *M*
  St. Louis *B, M*
Webster University *M*

Montana

Miles Community College *A*
Montana State University
  Bozeman *M*
University of Montana-Missoula *M*

Nebraska

Bellevue University *B*
Doane College *B*
Hastings College *B*
University of Nebraska
  Omaha *B, M, D*

Nevada

University of Nevada
  Las Vegas *M*
  Reno *M*

New Hampshire

Plymouth State College *B*
University of New Hampshire *M*

New Jersey

Bloomfield College *B*
The College of New Jersey *B*
County College of Morris *A*
Fairleigh Dickinson University
  Metropolitan Campus *M*
Kean University *B, M*
Princeton University *B, M, D*
Rider University *C*
Rutgers, The State University of New
  Jersey
  Camden Regional Campus *M*
  Newark Regional Campus *M, D*
Seton Hall University *M*
Thomas Edison State College *C, A, B*
William Paterson University of New
  Jersey *M*

New Mexico

College of Santa Fe *B*
San Juan College *A*
University of New Mexico *M*

New York

Alfred University *B*
City University of New York
  Baruch College *B, M*
  Hostos Community College *A*
  John Jay College of Criminal
    Justice *A, B*

Dowling College *M*
Fordham University *B, M*
Long Island University
  C. W. Post Campus *B, M*
Marist College *B, M*
New York University *M, D*
Pace University *M*
St. John's University *C, B*
State University of New York
  Albany *M, D*
  Binghamton *M*
  College at Brockport *M*
Syracuse University *M, D*
Wagner College *B*

North Carolina

Appalachian State University *M*
Campbell University *B*
East Carolina University *M*
Elon University *B*
Fayetteville State University *B*
Fayetteville Technical Community
  College *A*
North Carolina Central University *M*
North Carolina State University *M, D*
Shaw University *B*
University of North Carolina
  Chapel Hill *M*
  Charlotte *M*
Western Carolina University *M*
Winston-Salem State University *B*

North Dakota

University of North Dakota *B, M*

Ohio

Bowling Green State University *B, M*
Cedarville University *B*
Cleveland State University *M*
David N. Myers College *A, B*
Heidelberg College *B*
Kent State University *M*
Miami University
  Oxford Campus *B*
Ohio State University
  Columbus Campus *M, D*
Ohio University *B, M*
Sinclair Community College *A*
University of Akron *B, M*
University of Cincinnati *M*
University of Toledo *C, M*
Wright State University *B, M*
Youngstown State University *B*

Oklahoma

Northeastern State University *B*
University of Oklahoma *B, M*

Oregon

Portland State University *M, D*

Pennsylvania

California University of Pennsylvania *B*
Carnegie Mellon University *M, D*
Indiana University of Pennsylvania *M*
Juniata College *B*
Kutztown University of
  Pennsylvania *B, M*
La Salle University *B*
Lincoln University *B*
Marywood University *B, M*
Penn State
  Harrisburg *M, D*
Point Park College *A, B*
Reading Area Community College *A*
St. Joseph's University *B*
Shippensburg University of
  Pennsylvania *B, M*
Slippery Rock University of
  Pennsylvania *B, M*
University of Pennsylvania *M*
University of Pittsburgh *C, B, M*
Villanova University *M*
Widener University *M*
York College of Pennsylvania *B*

Puerto Rico

Bayamon Central University *B*

Inter American University of Puerto Rico
  Bayamon Campus *B*
  San German Campus *B*
Pontifical Catholic University of Puerto
  Rico *B, M, D*
Turabo University *A, B*
Universidad Metropolitana *B*
Universidad del Este *B*
University of Puerto Rico
  Rio Piedras Campus *M*

Rhode Island

Providence College *C*
Rhode Island College *B*
University of Rhode Island *M*

South Carolina

College of Charleston *M*
University of South Carolina *M*

South Dakota

University of South Dakota *M*

Tennessee

Tennessee State University *M, D*
University of Memphis *M*
University of Tennessee
  Chattanooga *M*
  Knoxville *B, M*
  Martin *B*

Texas

Abilene Christian University *B*
Angelo State University *M*
Baylor University *B, M*
Brazosport College *A*
College of the Mainland *A*
Del Mar College *A*
Lamar University *M*
Midwestern State University *M*
Our Lady of the Lake University of San
  Antonio *M*
St. Mary's University *M*
San Antonio College *A*
Southwest Texas State University *B, M*
Stephen F. Austin State University *B, M*
Sul Ross State University *M*
Tarrant County College *C, A*
Texas A&M International University *M*
Texas A&M University *M, D*
Texas Southern University *B, M*
Texas Tech University *M*
University of Houston *M*
University of Houston
  Clear Lake *M*
University of North Texas *B, M, D*
University of Texas
  Arlington *M, D*
  Dallas *M*
  El Paso *M*
  San Antonio *M*
  Tyler *M*
West Texas A&M University *B*

Utah

Brigham Young University *B, M*
University of Utah *C, M*

Vermont

University of Vermont *M*

Virginia

George Mason University *B, M, D*
James Madison University *B, M*
Old Dominion University *M*
Shenandoah University *C, B*
Thomas Nelson Community College *A*
University of Virginia's College at
  Wise *B*
Virginia Commonwealth
  University *M, D*
Virginia Polytechnic Institute and State
  University *M, D*
Virginia State University *B*

Washington

Eastern Washington University *M*
Evergreen State College *M*
Seattle University *B, M*

University of Washington *M*
Washington State University *B, M*

West Virginia

West Virginia University *M*

Wisconsin

Silver Lake College *B*
University of Wisconsin
    Green Bay *B*
    La Crosse *B*
    Madison *M*
    Milwaukee *M*
    Oshkosh *M*
    Stevens Point *B*
    Superior *B*

Wyoming

University of Wyoming *M*

Public finance

Alabama

Alabama Agricultural and Mechanical
    University *B*

California

National University *M*

Florida

University of West Florida *B*

Maine

Husson College *B*

Maryland

Morgan State University *B*

Massachusetts

Boston University *M*

New York

City University of New York
    Baruch College *M*

Ohio

Defiance College *B*
Youngstown State University *B*

Texas

Texas A&M University
    Commerce *B*
University of North Texas *B, M*

Washington

Eastern Washington University *B*

Public health

Alabama

University of Alabama
    Birmingham *M, D*

Alaska

University of Alaska
    Fairbanks *C, A*

Arizona

University of Arizona *M, D*

Arkansas

University of Central Arkansas *B*

California

California State University
    Chico *C*
    Fresno *M*
    Long Beach *M*
    Northridge *M*
Loma Linda University *B, M, D*
San Diego State University *M, D*
San Francisco State University *M*
San Jose State University *M*
University of California
    Berkeley *M, D*
    Los Angeles *M, D*
University of Southern
  California *B, M, D*

Colorado

University of Colorado
    Health Sciences Center *M*
University of Denver *M*

Connecticut

Southern Connecticut State
    University *B, M*
University of Connecticut *M*
Yale University *M, D*

Delaware

Delaware State University *B*

District of Columbia

George Washington University *M, D*
Trinity College *B*

Florida

Florida Agricultural and Mechanical
    University *M*
Florida International University *M*
Nova Southeastern University *M*
Palm Beach Community College *A*
University of Florida *M*
University of Miami *M, D*
University of North Florida *M*
University of South Florida *M, D*

Georgia

Fort Valley State University *M*
Mercer University *M*

Hawaii

University of Hawaii
    Manoa *M, D*

Idaho

Boise State University *M*
Idaho State University *M*

Illinois

Benedictine University *M*
Northern Illinois University *M*
Northwestern University *M*
St. Xavier University *M*
University of Illinois
    Chicago *M, D*
    Springfield *M*
    Urbana-Champaign *M*

Indiana

Indiana University
    Bloomington *B, M*
Indiana University-Purdue University
    Indianapolis *B, M*

Iowa

University of Iowa *M*
University of Osteopathic Medicine and
    Health Sciences
    Des Moines University -
      Osteopathic Medical Center *M*

Kansas

University of Kansas Medical Center *M*
Wichita State University *M*

Kentucky

Cumberland College *B*
University of Kentucky *M*

Louisiana

Tulane University *M, D*

Maine

University of Maine
    Presque Isle *B*
University of Southern Maine *M*

Maryland

Johns Hopkins University *B, M, D*
Morgan State University *M, D*

Massachusetts

Boston University *M, D*
Springfield College *B, M*
University of Massachusetts
    Amherst *M, D*

Michigan

Central Michigan University *B*
University of Michigan *M, D*

Minnesota

Minnesota State University
    Mankato *B, T*
    Moorhead *B*
University of Minnesota
    Twin Cities *M*

Mississippi

University of Southern Mississippi *B, M*

Missouri

East Central College *A*
St. Louis University *M*
Southwest Missouri State University *M*
University of Missouri
    Columbia *M*

Nebraska

University of Nebraska
    Omaha *M*

New Jersey

New Jersey Institute of Technology *M*
Richard Stockton College of New
  Jersey *B*
Rutgers, The State University of New
  Jersey
    New Brunswick Regional
      Campus *B*

New Mexico

New Mexico State University *M*
University of New Mexico *M*

New York

City University of New York
    Brooklyn College *M*
State University of New York
    Albany *M, D*
    Buffalo *M, D*
    Health Science Center at
      Brooklyn *M*
University of Rochester *M*

North Carolina

East Carolina University *M*
University of North Carolina
    Chapel Hill *M*
    Greensboro *M*

Ohio

Bowling Green State University *M*
Case Western Reserve University *M*
Kent State University *B, M*
Ohio State University
    Columbus Campus *M*
University of Akron *A*
Youngstown State University *M*

Oklahoma

Southwestern Oklahoma State
  University *B*
University of Oklahoma *M, D*

Oregon

Oregon Health Sciences University *M*
Oregon State University *M, D*
Portland State University *B, M*

Pennsylvania

Arcadia University *M*
Drexel University *M*
La Salle University *M*
Slippery Rock University of
  Pennsylvania *B, M*
Temple University *M*
University of Pittsburgh *M, D*
West Chester University of
  Pennsylvania *B, M*

Puerto Rico

University of Puerto Rico
    Medical Sciences Campus *M, D*

South Carolina

University of South Carolina *M, D*

Tennessee

East Tennessee State University *B, M*
University of Tennessee
    Knoxville *M*

Texas

University of Texas
    El Paso *M*
    Houston Health Science
      Center *M, D*
    Medical Branch at Galveston *M*

Utah

Snow College *A*
University of Utah *M*
Utah State University *B*

Virginia

Old Dominion University *M*
Virginia Commonwealth University *M*

Washington

University of Washington *B, M*

West Virginia

West Virginia University *M*

Wisconsin

University of Wisconsin
    La Crosse *M*
    Madison *M, D*

Public health education

Alabama

Northwest-Shoals Community College *A*

Arkansas

University of Central Arkansas *B*

California

California State University
    Chico *B, T*
    Long Beach *B, M*
Loma Linda University *B, M, D*
San Diego State University *M*
University of California
    Los Angeles *M*

Colorado

University of Northern Colorado *B, M*

Georgia

Armstrong Atlantic State University *M*
Darton College *A*
Georgia Southern University *B, M*

Kentucky

Cumberland College *B*

Louisiana

Dillard University *B*

Maine

University of Maine
    Farmington *B*
    Presque Isle *B*

Maryland

Johns Hopkins University *B*

Massachusetts

Boston University *M*
Springfield College *M*

Michigan

University of Michigan *M, D*
University of Michigan
    Flint *B, M*

Minnesota

Bethel College *B*
Minnesota State University
    Mankato *M*
University of St. Thomas *B*
Winona State University *B*

Nebraska

University of Nebraska
    Lincoln *B*

New Hampshire
Plymouth State College B

New Jersey
University of Medicine and Dentistry of New Jersey
  School of Health Related Professions M

New York
City University of New York
  Brooklyn College B, M
  Hunter College M
Ithaca College B

North Carolina
East Carolina University B, M
University of North Carolina
  Chapel Hill M, D
  Charlotte M

Ohio
Kent State University B, M
Malone College B
University of Toledo B, M, D
Youngstown State University B

Oklahoma
University of Oklahoma M, D

Oregon
Oregon State University B, M
Portland State University B, M

Pennsylvania
Drexel University M
Temple University D

Puerto Rico
University of Puerto Rico
  Medical Sciences Campus B, M

South Carolina
Coastal Carolina University B
University of South Carolina M, D

Tennessee
University of Tennessee
  Knoxville M

Texas
University of Texas
  Austin M, D

Utah
University of Utah B, M, D

Washington
Eastern Washington University B, T

Wisconsin
University of Wisconsin
  La Crosse B, M
  Madison B, M

Public health nursing

California
Holy Names College M

Illinois
Southern Illinois University
  Edwardsville M

Indiana
Indiana University-Purdue University
  Indianapolis M

Michigan
Wayne State University M

Minnesota
Augsburg College M

Missouri
Maryville University of Saint Louis C, B
St. Louis University M
Washington University in St. Louis M

New Jersey
William Paterson University of New Jersey B, M

New York
City University of New York
  Hunter College M

North Carolina
University of North Carolina
  Chapel Hill M

Ohio
Case Western Reserve University M
University of Akron M

Pennsylvania
Drexel University M
University of Pennsylvania M
Widener University M

South Carolina
Medical University of South Carolina M
University of South Carolina M

Public history/archives

California
Chapman University B

District of Columbia
American University M

Florida
University of West Florida M

North Carolina
East Carolina University B
Meredith College B

South Carolina
University of South Carolina M

Texas
McMurry University B
Texas Lutheran University B

Public policy analysis

Alabama
Huntingdon College B

Arkansas
University of Arkansas D

California
California State University
  Hayward B
Loma Linda University D
Pomona College B
Stanford University B
University of California
  Berkeley M, D
  Los Angeles M, D
  San Diego B
University of Southern California M, D

Colorado
University of Denver B

Connecticut
Three Rivers Community College A
Trinity College B, M

District of Columbia
American University M
George Washington University B, M, D
Georgetown University M

Florida
New College of Florida B
University of Miami B

Georgia
Georgia Institute of Technology B, M, D

Illinois
De Paul University B
Northwestern University B
Olivet Nazarene University B

University of Chicago M, D
University of Illinois
  Chicago D

Indiana
Indiana University
  Bloomington D
Indiana University-Purdue University
  Fort Wayne M

Iowa
University of Northern Iowa M

Louisiana
Southern University and Agricultural and Mechanical College M, D

Maine
University of Southern Maine M, D

Maryland
Johns Hopkins University B, M
St. Mary's College of Maryland B
University of Maryland
  Baltimore County M, D
  College Park M, D

Massachusetts
Brandeis University D
Simmons College B
University of Massachusetts
  Amherst M
  Boston D

Michigan
Michigan Technological University M
University of Michigan M, D

Minnesota
Winona State University B

Missouri
St. Louis University D

New Jersey
Bloomfield College B
New Jersey Institute of Technology M
Rutgers, The State University of New Jersey
  New Brunswick Regional Campus M, D
St. Peter's College A, B
William Paterson University of New Jersey M

New York
Cornell University B
Hamilton College B
Hobart and William Smith Colleges B
Ithaca College B
Rochester Institute of Technology B, M
Sarah Lawrence College B
State University of New York
  Albany M
  College of Environmental Science and Forestry B, M, D
Syracuse University B

North Carolina
Duke University B
University of North Carolina
  Chapel Hill B, D
  Charlotte D

Ohio
Ohio State University
  Columbus Campus M, D

Oregon
Oregon State University M

Pennsylvania
Carnegie Mellon University M, D
Chatham College B
Dickinson College B
Duquesne University M
Penn State
  Harrisburg B
  University Park B
St. Vincent College B
University of Pennsylvania B, M, D

University of Pittsburgh M

Rhode Island
Brown University B

South Carolina
Clemson University D

Tennessee
Vanderbilt University M

Texas
Rice University B
San Antonio College A
Southern Methodist University B
University of Houston
  Clear Lake B
University of Texas
  Austin M, D
  Dallas C, D

Virginia
College of William and Mary B, M
George Mason University D
Virginia Polytechnic Institute and State University B

Washington
Central Washington University B
University of Washington M

Wisconsin
Northland College B
University of Wisconsin
  Madison M
  Superior B
  Whitewater B, T

Public relations

Alabama
Auburn University B
Community College of the Air Force A
University of Alabama B

Arizona
Glendale Community College A
Northern Arizona University B
Scottsdale Community College C, A

Arkansas
Harding University B
John Brown University B

California
California State Polytechnic University:
  Pomona B
California State University
  Chico B
  Dominguez Hills B
  Fresno B
  Fullerton B, M
  Hayward B
  Long Beach B
  Los Angeles B
Chapman University B
College of Marin: Kentfield A
Golden Gate University M
Golden West College C, A
Long Beach City College C, A
Master's College B
Pacific Union College B
Pepperdine University B
San Diego State University B
San Jose State University B
University of Southern California B, M

Colorado
Colorado State University M
Colorado State University
  Pueblo B
University of Denver M

Connecticut
Manchester Community College C
Quinnipiac University B

Delaware
Delaware State University B

District of Columbia
American University *C, B, M*

Florida
Barry University *B*
Florida Agricultural and Mechanical
   University *B*
Florida Southern College *B*
Florida State University *B*
Gulf Coast Community College *A*
Indian River Community College *A*
Manatee Community College *A*
University of Florida *B*
University of Miami *B, M*
University of West Florida *B*

Georgia
Clark Atlanta University *B*
Fort Valley State University *B*
Georgia Southern University *B*
Shorter College *B*
Toccoa Falls College *B*
University of Georgia *B*
Valdosta State University *B*

Hawaii
Hawaii Pacific University *B*

Idaho
Brigham Young University - Idaho *B*
Idaho State University *B*
North Idaho College *A*

Illinois
Black Hawk College
   East Campus *A*
Bradley University *B*
Columbia College Chicago *B*
Greenville College *B*
Illinois State University *B*
Lewis University *B*
McKendree College *B*
Monmouth College *B*
North Central College *B*
Northwestern University *M*
Quincy University *B*
Roosevelt University *B*
Sauk Valley Community College *A*
University of St. Francis *B*

Indiana
Ball State University *B, M*
Huntington College *B*
Purdue University
   Calumet *B*
Taylor University: Fort Wayne *B*
Valparaiso University *B*
Vincennes University *A*

Iowa
Buena Vista University *B*
Clarke College *B*
Dordt College *B*
Drake University *B*
Loras College *B*
North Iowa Area Community College *A*
St. Ambrose University *B*
Simpson College *B*
University of Northern Iowa *B*
Waldorf College *A, B*
Wartburg College *B*
William Penn University *B*

Kansas
Fort Scott Community College *A*
Pittsburg State University *B*
Tabor College *B*

Kentucky
Campbellsville University *B*
Murray State University *B*

Louisiana
Southeastern Louisiana University *M*
University of Louisiana at Lafayette *B*

Maine
New England School of
   Communications *A, B*

University of Southern Maine *B*

Maryland
Villa Julie College *A*

Massachusetts
Boston University *B, M*
Cape Cod Community College *A*
Emerson College *B, M*
Massachusetts College of Liberal Arts *B*
Northeastern University *B*
Salem State College *B*
Simmons College *B*
Suffolk University *B, M*

Michigan
Andrews University *B*
Central Michigan University *B*
Eastern Michigan University *B*
Ferris State University *C, B*
Grand Valley State University *B*
Kellogg Community College *A*
Macomb Community College *C, A*
Michigan State University *M*
Northern Michigan University *B*
Wayne State University *B*
Western Michigan University *B*

Minnesota
Bethel College *B*
Concordia College: Moorhead *B*
Metropolitan State University *B*
Minnesota State University
   Mankato *B*
   Moorhead *B*
Northwestern College *B*
St. Cloud State University *B*
St. Cloud Technical College *C, A*
St. Mary's University of Minnesota *B*
Winona State University *B*

Mississippi
Alcorn State University *M*
Itawamba Community College *A*
Mississippi College *B, M*
Mississippi University for Women *B*
Northwest Mississippi Community
   College *A*
University of Southern Mississippi *M*

Missouri
Central Missouri State University *B*
College of the Ozarks *B*
Crowder College *A*
Drury University *B*
East Central College *A*
Lindenwood University *B, M*
Northwest Missouri State University *B*
Rockhurst University *B*
St. Louis Community College
   St. Louis Community College at
     Florissant Valley *A*
St. Louis University *B*
Southeast Missouri State University *B*
Stephens College *B*
University of Missouri
   Columbia *M*
Webster University *B, M*
William Jewell College *B*
William Woods University *B*

Montana
Carroll College *B*
Montana State University
   Billings *B, M*

Nebraska
Bellevue University *B*
Hastings College *B*
Midland Lutheran College *B*
Union College *B*

Nevada
University of Nevada
   Reno *B*

New Hampshire
Hesser College *C, A*
New England College *B*

Rivier College *B*

New Jersey
Rowan University *B, M*

New York
City University of New York
   City College *B*
Cornell University *B*
Hofstra University *B*
Iona College *B*
Long Island University
   C. W. Post Campus *B*
Marist College *B*
Medaille College *B*
Mount St. Mary College *C, B*
New York Institute of Technology *M*
Rochester Institute of Technology *C*
State University of New York
   Buffalo *M, D*
   College at Fredonia *B*
   New Paltz *B*
   Oswego *B*
Syracuse University *B, M*
Utica College *B*

North Carolina
Appalachian State University *B*
Campbell University *B*
Gardner-Webb University *B*
North Carolina Agricultural and
   Technical State University *B*
North Carolina State University *B*
University of North Carolina
   Pembroke *B*

North Dakota
North Dakota State University *B*

Ohio
Bowling Green State University *B*
Defiance College *B*
Heidelberg College *B*
Kent State University *B*
Kent State University
   Stark Campus *B*
Malone College *B*
Marietta College *B*
Ohio Dominican College *B*
Ohio Northern University *B*
Ohio State University
   Columbus Campus *B, M*
Ohio University *B*
Otterbein College *B*
University of Dayton *B*
University of Findlay *B*
University of Rio Grande *A, B*
Ursuline College *B*
Wilmington College *B*
Xavier University *A, B*
Youngstown State University *B*

Oklahoma
Cameron University *B*
Northern Oklahoma College *A*
Northwestern Oklahoma State
   University *B*
Oklahoma Baptist University *B*
Oklahoma Christian University of
   Science and Arts *B*
Oklahoma City University *B*
Southeastern Oklahoma State
   University *B*
University of Central Oklahoma *B*
University of Oklahoma *B*

Oregon
George Fox University *B*
Marylhurst University *C*
Southern Oregon University *B*
University of Oregon *B, M*

Pennsylvania
California University of Pennsylvania *B*
La Salle University *B*
Lebanon Valley College of
   Pennsylvania *C*
Marywood University *B*

Mercyhurst College *B*
Point Park College *B*
University of Pittsburgh
   Bradford *B*
   Greensburg *B*
York College of Pennsylvania *B*

Puerto Rico
University of the Sacred Heart *M*

Rhode Island
University of Rhode Island *B*

South Carolina
University of South Carolina *B*
Winthrop University *B*

Tennessee
Lambuth University *B*
Lee University *B*
Southern Adventist University *B*
Union University *B*
University of Tennessee
   Martin *B*

Texas
Hardin-Simmons University *B*
Howard Payne University *B*
Sam Houston State University *B*
Southern Methodist University *B*
Southwest Texas State University *B*
Texas A&M University
   Commerce *B*
Texas Tech University *B*
Texas Wesleyan University *B*
University of Houston *B, M*
University of North Texas *B*
University of Texas
   Arlington *B*
   Austin *B*
   San Antonio *B*

Utah
Brigham Young University *B*
Salt Lake Community College *A*
Southern Utah University *B*
Weber State University *B*

Vermont
Champlain College *A, B*

Virginia
Hampton University *B*
Mary Baldwin College *B*

Washington
Central Washington University *B*
Eastern Washington University *B*
Edmonds Community College *C*
Gonzaga University *B*
Pacific Lutheran University *B*
Seattle University *B*
Washington State University *B*

West Virginia
Bethany College *B*
Concord College *B*
West Virginia University *B*
West Virginia Wesleyan College *B*

Wisconsin
Cardinal Stritch University *B*
Carroll College *B*
Carthage College *B*
Marquette University *B*
Mount Mary College *B*
University of Wisconsin
   La Crosse *B*
   Whitewater *B*

Public services

Alabama
Alabama State University *M*
Central Alabama Community College *A*
Community College of the Air Force *A*
Huntingdon College *B*

Arizona
Northern Arizona University *B*
Pima Community College *C, A*
Prescott College *B, M*

Arkansas
Arkansas Tech University *B*
Henderson State University *B*
University of Central Arkansas *B*

California
California State University
    Bakersfield *B, M*
    Dominguez Hills *B*
    Hayward *M*
    Sacramento *B, M*
    Stanislaus *M*
Chabot College *A*
Citrus College *A*
Gavilan Community College *A*
Moorpark College *A*
Mount San Jacinto College *A*
San Diego State University *B, M*
Santiago Canyon College *A*
Southwestern College *A*
University of California
    Irvine *M*
    Riverside *B*
Ventura College *A*

Colorado
Red Rocks Community College *C, A*

Connecticut
Housatonic Community College *A*
Manchester Community College *C, A*
University of Connecticut *M*
University of New Haven *M*

District of Columbia
George Washington University *M, D*
Howard University *M*
Trinity College *B*
University of the District of Columbia *A*

Florida
Broward Community College *A*
Florida Atlantic University *C*
Manatee Community College *A*
Miami-Dade Community College *A*
Okaloosa-Walton Community College *A*
Polk Community College *A*

Georgia
Central Georgia Technical College *A*
Clark Atlanta University *D*
Darton College *A*
Kennesaw State University *B*
Macon State College *B*

Idaho
University of Idaho *M*

Illinois
Blackburn College *B*
De Paul University *M*
Roosevelt University *B, M*
Southern Illinois University
    Carbondale *M*

Indiana
Ball State University *A*
Indiana University
    Bloomington *B, M*
Indiana University-Purdue University
    Fort Wayne *A, B*
Indiana University-Purdue University
    Indianapolis *M*
Valparaiso University *C*

Iowa
Buena Vista University *B*

Kansas
Kansas State University *M*
University of Kansas *M*

Kentucky
Kentucky Wesleyan College *B*
Murray State University *M*

Louisiana
Louisiana College *B*
Southern University
    Shreveport *C, A*

Maine
University of Southern Maine *M, D*

Massachusetts
Brandeis University *M*
Clark University *B, M*
Framingham State College *M*
Mount Ida College *A, B*
Northeastern University *B, M*
Suffolk University *B, M*

Michigan
Grand Valley State University *M*
Lansing Community College *A*
Michigan State University *B, M*
Northern Michigan University *B, M*
Schoolcraft College *A*
University of Michigan
    Dearborn *B*
Western Michigan University *M, D*

Minnesota
Hamline University *M, D*
Metropolitan State University *B*
Minneapolis Community and Technical
    College *C, A*
Minnesota State University
    Mankato *M*
Northland Community & Technical
    College *A*
Winona State University *B*

Mississippi
Itawamba Community College *A*

Missouri
Central Missouri State University *M*
East Central College *A*
Evangel University *B*
Missouri Valley College *B*

Montana
Carroll College *B*
Miles Community College *A*

Nebraska
Bellevue University *B*
Doane College *B*
Hastings College *B*
University of Nebraska
    Omaha *B*

New Jersey
Caldwell College *C*

New Mexico
College of Santa Fe *B*
New Mexico Highlands University *M*
New Mexico State University *M*
Western New Mexico University *A, B*

New York
Alfred University *M*
City University of New York
    Baruch College *B, M*
    John Jay College of Criminal
        Justice *M*
    Medgar Evers College *A, B*
Cornell University *M*
Dominican College of Blauvelt *C*
Hudson Valley Community College *A*
Marist College *M*
Medaille College *A, B*
New York University *M*
State University of New York
    College at Brockport *M*

North Dakota
Bismarck State College *A*

Ohio
Cleveland State University *M*
Ohio Wesleyan University *B*
Sinclair Community College *A*
Union Institute & University *B*

University of Rio Grande *B*
University of Toledo *C*
Wright State University *B, M*
Youngstown State University *B*

Oklahoma
Oklahoma State University
    Oklahoma City *A*

Oregon
Western Oregon University *B*

Pennsylvania
Indiana University of Pennsylvania *B*
La Salle University *A, B*
Marywood University *B*
University of Pittsburgh *M*
Villanova University *M*
West Chester University of
    Pennsylvania *M*
Widener University *M, D*
York College of Pennsylvania *B*

Puerto Rico
Inter American University of Puerto Rico
    Bayamon Campus *B*
Turabo University *M*

Rhode Island
Providence College *C*

South Carolina
Clemson University *M*

South Dakota
University of South Dakota *M*

Tennessee
University of Tennessee
    Knoxville *B*

Texas
St. Edward's University *B*
Texas A&M University *M*
Texas A&M University
    Corpus Christi *M*
University of Texas
    El Paso *M*
    Pan American *M*

Utah
Snow College *A*

Vermont
Goddard College *B*
University of Vermont *B, M*
Woodbury College *C, A*

Virginia
University of Virginia's College at
    Wise *B*

Washington
Crown College *B*
Edmonds Community College *C*
Heritage College *B*
Olympic College *C, A*
Seattle University *B*

West Virginia
West Virginia University Institute of
    Technology *B*

Wisconsin
Marquette University *M*
University of Wisconsin
    Green Bay *B*

Wyoming
Laramie County Community College *C*

Publishing

California
Long Beach City College *C, A*

Illinois
Benedictine University *B*

Iowa
Drake University *B*

Massachusetts
Emerson College *B, M*

Minnesota
Hennepin Technical College *C, A*

Missouri
Webster University *C, B*

New York
New York University *M*
Pace University:
    Pleasantville/Briarcliff *M*
Rochester Institute of Technology *B, M*

Ohio
Youngstown State University *B*

Purchasing/procurement/contracts

Alabama
Athens State University *C*
Community College of the Air Force *A*
Miles College *B*

Arizona
Arizona State University *B*
DeVry University
    Phoenix *M*

California
California State University
    Hayward *C, B*
Coastline Community College *C*
De Anza College *C, A*
DeVry University
    Fremont *M*
    Long Beach *M*
    Pomona *M*
    West Hills *M*
Golden Gate University *M*
San Diego City College *C, A*
Sierra College *A*

Florida
DeVry University
    Miramar *M*
    Orlando *M*
Florida Institute of Technology *M*

Georgia
DeVry University
    Alpharetta *M*
    Atlanta *M*

Illinois
DeVry University
    Tinley Park *M*
Northwestern University *M*

Iowa
Des Moines Area Community College *C*
St. Ambrose University *C*

Kansas
Washburn University of Topeka *C, A*

Massachusetts
Northeastern University *A*
Suffolk University *M*

Michigan
Eastern Michigan University *B*
Kirtland Community College *C, A*
Michigan State University *B, M*

Minnesota
University of St. Thomas *M*

Missouri
DeVry University
    Kansas City *M*
Webster University *M*

Nebraska
Southeast Community College
    Lincoln Campus *A*

New Jersey
Thomas Edison State College *A, B*

New York
St. John's University *M*
Syracuse University *B*
Westchester Business Institute *C, A*

Ohio
Ashland University *B, M*
Cincinnati State Technical and
    Community College *A*
Columbus State Community College *A*
Cuyahoga Community College
    Eastern Campus *A*
    Western Campus *A*
DeVry University
    Columbus *M*
Miami University
    Oxford Campus *B*
North Central State College *C*
Sinclair Community College *C, A*
Youngstown State University *B*

Oklahoma
University of Central Oklahoma *B*

Pennsylvania
DeVry University
    Ft. Washington *M*
Mercyhurst College *C, A*
Penn State
    University Park *C*
St. Joseph's University *A, B*

South Carolina
Horry-Georgetown Technical
    College *C, A*

Texas
Brazosport College *A*
DeVry University
    Irving *M*
University of Dallas *M*
University of Houston
    Downtown *B*

Virginia
DeVry University
    Crystal City *M*
Shenandoah University *C*

Washington
DeVry University
    Seattle *M*

Wisconsin
Lakeshore Technical College *A*
University of Wisconsin
    Green Bay *A*

Quality control technology

Arkansas
East Arkansas Community College *C*

California
College of the Canyons *C, A*

Georgia
Southern Polytechnic State
    University *C, M*

Illinois
Heartland Community College *C*
Moraine Valley Community
    College *C, A*
Waubonsee Community College *C, A*

Indiana
Indiana University-Purdue University
    Fort Wayne *C*
Ivy Tech State College
    Lafayette *A*

Kentucky
Jefferson Community College *A*
Murray State University *B, M*

Maryland
Community College of Baltimore County
    Catonsville *C*
    Dundalk *C*
    Essex *C*

Michigan
Baker College
    of Muskegon *C, A*
Grand Rapids Community College *C, A*
Mott Community College *C, A*

Minnesota
Capella University *C, B*
Century Community and Technical
    College *C, A*

Missouri
Missouri Southern State College *C*

New Hampshire
Hesser College *C, A*

Ohio
Cincinnati State Technical and
    Community College *C*
Kent State University *C*
Northwest State Community
    College *C, A*
Owens Community College
    Findlay Campus *C, A*
    Toledo *C, A*

Pennsylvania
Community College of Allegheny
    County *A*
Northampton County Area Community
    College *C, A*
Penn State
    University Park *C*
Pennsylvania College of Technology *A*

Wisconsin
Marquette University *C*

Rabbinical studies (M.H.L., Rav.)

California
Hebrew Union College-Jewish Institute
    of Religion *F*

Colorado
Yeshiva Toras Chaim Talmudical
    Seminary *F*

Connecticut
Beth Benjamin Academy of
    Connecticut *F*

Illinois
Brisk Rabbinical College *F*
Hebrew Theological College *F*
Telshe Yeshiva-Chicago *F*

Maryland
Ner Israel Rabbinical College *F*

New York
Central Yeshiva Tomchei Tmimim
    Lubavitz *F*
Jewish Theological Seminary of
    America *F*
Kehilath Yakov Rabbinical Seminary *F*
Kol Yaakov Torah Center *F*
Mesivta Eastern Parkway Rabbinical
    Seminary *F*
Mesivta Tifereth Jerusalem of America *F*
Mirrer Yeshiva Central Institute *F*
Ohr Hameir Theological Seminary *F*
Ohr Somayach Institutions: School of
    Theology *F*
Rabbi Isaac Elchanan Theological
    Seminary *F*
Rabbinical College Beth Shraga *F*
Rabbinical College Bobover Yeshiva
    B'nei Zion *F*
Rabbinical Seminary M'Kor Chaim *F*

Sh'or Yoshuv Rabbinical College *F*
Yeshiva Karlin Stolin Beth Aron Y'Israel
    Rabbinical Institute *F*
Yeshiva of Nitra Rabbinical College *F*
Yeshivat Mikdash Melech *F*

Ohio
Hebrew Union College-Jewish Institute
    of Religion *F*

Radiation biology

California
University of California
    Irvine *M, D*

Colorado
Colorado State University *M, D*

District of Columbia
George Washington University *D*

Florida
Barry University *B*

Illinois
University of Chicago *M*

Iowa
University of Iowa *M, D*

Maine
University of Southern Maine *B*

Massachusetts
Suffolk University *B*
University of Massachusetts
    Lowell *M*

Ohio
University of Cincinnati *M*

Pennsylvania
Drexel University *M, D*

Texas
University of Texas
    Health Science Center at San
        Antonio *D*
    Southwestern Medical Center at
        Dallas *M, D*

Radiation protection/health physics technology

New Jersey
Thomas Edison State College *A, B*

Ohio
University of Cincinnati
    Raymond Walters College *A*

Radio/television

Alabama
Lawson State Community College *C, A*
Spring Hill College *B*

Arizona
Arizona State University *B*

Arkansas
Arkansas State University *B, M*

California
California State University
    Chico *B*
University of La Verne *B*

Florida
Barry University *B*
University of Central Florida *B*

Illinois
Bradley University *B*
Northwestern University *B, M, D*
Southern Illinois University
    Carbondale *M*

Western Illinois University *B, M*

Indiana
University of Southern Indiana *B*
Valparaiso University *B*

Iowa
University of Northern Iowa *B*

Michigan
Michigan State University *B, M*
Northern Michigan University *B*
Western Michigan University *B*

Minnesota
Northwestern College *A, B*

Nebraska
University of Nebraska
    Omaha *B*

New Hampshire
Franklin Pierce College *B*

New York
Ithaca College *B*
Marist College *B*
New York Institute of Technology *B*
New York University *B*
Syracuse University *B, M*

North Dakota
Minot State University *B*

Ohio
Ashland University *A, B*
Baldwin-Wallace College *B*
Xavier University *A, B*
Youngstown State University *B*

Oregon
George Fox University *B*

Pennsylvania
La Salle University *B*
Messiah College *B*
Temple University *B, M, D*

Texas
Southwest Texas State University *B*
Stephen F. Austin State University *B*
Texas Tech University *B*
University of Texas
    Austin *B, M, D*

Washington
Centralia College *A*

Radio/television broadcasting

Alabama
Jefferson State Community College *C, A*

Idaho
Lewis-Clark State College *A*

Illinois
Waubonsee Community College *C, A*

Indiana
Vincennes University *A*

Massachusetts
Springfield Technical Community
    College *A*

Ohio
North Central State College *A*

Pennsylvania
La Salle University *B*
Lebanon Valley College of
    Pennsylvania *B*
Marywood University *B, M*
Northampton County Area Community
    College *A*

South Carolina
York Technical College *C*

Texas
Houston Community College
    System *C, A*

Washington
Centralia College *A*
Clover Park Technical College *A*

Wisconsin
Milwaukee Area Technical College *A*

Radiologic technology/ medical imaging

Arkansas
South Arkansas Community College *A*

California
Foothill College *C, A*

Colorado
Red Rocks Community College *A*

Florida
Florida Hospital College of Health
    Sciences *C, B*

Georgia
Albany Technical College *C*

Idaho
Lewis-Clark State College *C, A*

Illinois
City Colleges of Chicago
    Wright College *A*
Richland Community College *A*

Indiana
Indiana University
    Northwest *A*
Indiana University-Purdue University
    Fort Wayne *A*
Indiana University-Purdue University
    Indianapolis *B*

Iowa
Allen College *A*

Kansas
Labette Community College *A*

Louisiana
Louisiana State University
    Alexandria *A*

Maryland
Howard Community College *A*

Massachusetts
Laboure College *C, A*

Michigan
Baker College
    of Muskegon *A*
Jackson Community College *C, A*
Oakland Community College *A*

Missouri
Sanford-Brown College *A*
University of Missouri
    Columbia *B*

Nebraska
Nebraska Methodist College of Nursing
    and Allied Health *A*
University of Nebraska
    Medical Center *B*

Nevada
Truckee Meadows Community
    College *A*

New Jersey
Thomas Edison State College *A, B*

New York
Niagara County Community College *A*

North Carolina
Carteret Community College *A*
Johnston Community College *A*

Lenoir Community College *A*

North Dakota
Jamestown College *B*
University of Mary *A, B*

Ohio
Kent State University *B*
North Central State College *A*
University of Cincinnati
    Raymond Walters College *A*
Xavier University *A*

Oklahoma
Rose State College *A*
University of Oklahoma *B*

Oregon
Linn-Benton Community College *C*

Pennsylvania
Keystone College *A*
Mount Aloysius College *A, B*
University of Pittsburgh
    Bradford *B*

South Carolina
Horry-Georgetown Technical College *A*
York Technical College *A*

Texas
Tyler Junior College *C, A*

Washington
Wenatchee Valley College *A*

Wisconsin
Nicolet Area Technical College *A*

Range science

Arizona
University of Arizona *M, D*

California
California State University
    Chico *B*
College of the Redwoods *C*
University of California
    Berkeley *M*
    Davis *B*

Colorado
Colorado State University *B, M, D*

Idaho
College of Southern Idaho *A*
University of Idaho *B, M*

Kansas
Pratt Community College *A*

Montana
Montana State University
    Bozeman *B*

Nebraska
Chadron State College *B*
University of Nebraska
    Lincoln *B*

Nevada
University of Nevada
    Reno *B*

New Mexico
New Mexico State University *B, M, D*

North Dakota
North Dakota State University *B, M, D*

Oklahoma
Northeastern Oklahoma Agricultural and
    Mechanical College *C, A*
Rogers State University *A*
Southeastern Oklahoma State
    University *B*

Oregon
Eastern Oregon University *B*
Oregon State University *B, M, D*

South Dakota
Sinte Gleska University *A*
South Dakota State University *B*

Texas
Abilene Christian University *B*
Frank Phillips College *A*
Sul Ross State University *B, M*
Tarleton State University *B*
Texas A&M University *B, M, D*
Texas A&M University
    Kingsville *B, M*
Texas Tech University *B, M, D*

Utah
Brigham Young University *B, M*
Utah State University *B, M, D*

Washington
Washington State University *B, M*

Wyoming
University of Wyoming *B, M, D*

Reading teacher education

Alabama
Alabama State University *M*
Auburn University *D, T*
University of Alabama *M, D*
University of South Alabama *M*

Arizona
University of Arizona *M, D*

Arkansas
Arkansas State University *M, T*
Harding University *B, M, T*
Southern Arkansas University *M*
University of Arkansas
    Little Rock *M*
University of Central Arkansas *M*

California
Azusa Pacific University *M, T*
California Polytechnic State University:
    San Luis Obispo *M*
California State University
    Bakersfield *M*
    Chico *M, T*
    Dominguez Hills *M*
    Fresno *M*
    Fullerton *M*
    Hayward *M, T*
    Long Beach *T*
    Los Angeles *M*
    Stanislaus *M*
Chapman University *M*
Fresno Pacific University *M*
Loyola Marymount University *M*
National University *M*
St. Mary's College of California *M, D*
San Francisco State University *M*
San Jose State University *T*
Sonoma State University *M, T*
University of California
    Berkeley *T*
University of La Verne *M*

Colorado
University of Northern Colorado *M, T*

Connecticut
Central Connecticut State
    University *M, T*
Eastern Connecticut State University *M*
University of New Haven *M*
Western Connecticut State University *M*

District of Columbia
Howard University *M*
Trinity College *M*
University of the District of Columbia *M*

Florida
Barry University *M*
Florida Agricultural and Mechanical
    University *T*

Florida Atlantic University *M*
Florida Gulf Coast University *M*
Florida International University *M*
Florida State University *M, D, T*
Nova Southeastern University *M*
University of Central Florida *M*
University of Florida *M*
University of Miami *M, D*
University of South Florida *M*
University of West Florida *M*

Georgia
Albany State University *M*
Clark Atlanta University *B*
Columbus State University *M*
Georgia Southern University *M, T*
Georgia Southwestern State
    University *B, M*
Georgia State University *M, D*
Mercer University *M*
State University of West Georgia *M*
University of Georgia *M, D*

Illinois
Chicago State University *M, T*
Concordia University *M*
De Paul University *M*
Governors State University *M*
Illinois State University *M, T*
Lewis University *M, T*
National-Louis University *M, D*
North Park University *T*
Northeastern Illinois University *M*
Northern Illinois University *M*
Rockford College *T*
Roosevelt University *M*
St. Xavier University *M*
Western Illinois University *M*

Indiana
Ball State University *M, D, T*
Butler University *M, T*
University of Evansville *T*
University of Indianapolis *T*
University of St. Francis *B, M*

Iowa
Buena Vista University *B, T*
Central College *T*
Clarke College *T*
Dordt College *B*
Drake University *M, T*
Franciscan University *B, T*
Graceland University *T*
Iowa State University *T*
Iowa Wesleyan College *T*
Luther College *B*
Morningside College *M*
Mount Mercy College *T*
Northwestern College *T*
St. Ambrose University *T*
University of Iowa *M*
University of Northern Iowa *B, M*
Upper Iowa University *B, T*
Wartburg College *T*

Kansas
Fort Scott Community College *A*
Garden City Community College *A*
Pittsburg State University *M*
Washburn University of Topeka *M*
Wichita State University *T*

Kentucky
Campbellsville University *B*
Cumberland College *M*
Kentucky Wesleyan College *T*
Murray State University *B, M, T*
St. Catharine College *A*
Spalding University *M*
Union College *M*
University of Louisville *M*

Louisiana
Centenary College of Louisiana *T*
Loyola University New Orleans *M*
McNeese State University *T*
Nicholls State University *M*

Northwestern State University *B*
University of Louisiana at Monroe *M*

Maine
University of Maine *M*
University of Southern Maine *M, T*

Maryland
Bowie State University *M*
Frostburg State University *M, T*
Johns Hopkins University *M*
Loyola College in Maryland *M*
McDaniel College *M*
Salisbury University *T*
Towson University *M, T*

Massachusetts
Boston College *M*
Boston University *M, T*
Bridgewater State College *M*
Elms College *M*
Endicott College *M*
Lesley University *M, T*
Northeastern University *M*
Salem State College *M*
Tufts University *M*
University of Massachusetts
    Lowell *M, D*
Westfield State College *M, T*

Michigan
Andrews University *M, T*
Aquinas College *B, T*
Calvin College *B, M, T*
Central Michigan University *M*
Eastern Michigan University *M*
Madonna University *M*
Marygrove College *M*
Michigan State University *M*
Oakland University *M, D*
Saginaw Valley State University *M*
Wayne State University *M, D*
Western Michigan University *M*

Minnesota
Bethel College *B*
Minnesota State University
    Moorhead *B, M, T*
St. Cloud State University *M, T*
University of St. Thomas *M*
Winona State University *B, M, T*

Mississippi
Mississippi State University *T*

Missouri
Central Missouri State University *M, T*
Evangel University *M*
Harris Stowe State College *T*
Lindenwood University *M*
Missouri Baptist University *T*
Missouri Southern State College *B, T*
Northwest Missouri State
    University *M, T*
Southwest Missouri State University *M*
University of Missouri
    Columbia *M, D*
    Kansas City *M*

Montana
Carroll College *T*
Montana State University
    Billings *M, T*
University of Montana: Western *T*

Nebraska
Chadron State College *M*
College of Saint Mary *B, T*
Concordia University *M*
Hastings College *M*
University of Nebraska
    Kearney *M, T*
    Omaha *M*
York College *B*

New Hampshire
Plymouth State College *M*
Rivier College *M*
University of New Hampshire *M, T*

New Jersey
The College of New Jersey *M, T*
Georgian Court College *T*
Kean University *M*
Monmouth University *M*
Montclair State University *M, T*
New Jersey City University *B*
Rider University *M, T*
Rowan University *M*
St. Peter's College *M, T*
William Paterson University of New
    Jersey *T*

New Mexico
Western New Mexico University *M*

New York
Adelphi University *M*
Alfred University *M*
Canisius College *M, T*
City University of New York
    Brooklyn College *B, M*
    Queens College *M*
College of New Rochelle *M*
Dowling College *M*
Hofstra University *M, D, T*
Long Island University
    C. W. Post Campus *B, M, T*
    Southampton College *M*
Manhattanville College *M, T*
Medaille College *M*
Mercy College *M*
Nazareth College of Rochester *M*
New York University *M, T*
Pace University *M, T*
Pace University:
    Pleasantville/Briarcliff *M, T*
St. Bonaventure University *M*
St. John's University *M, T*
State University of New York
    Albany *M, D*
    Binghamton *M*
    Buffalo *M, D, T*
    College at Brockport *M*
    College at Buffalo *B, M, T*
    College at Cortland *M*
    College at Fredonia *M*
    College at Geneseo *M, T*
    College at Oneonta *M, T*
    College at Plattsburgh *M*
    College at Potsdam *M*
    New Paltz *M, T*
    Oswego *M*
Syracuse University *M, D, T*

North Carolina
Appalachian State University *B, M, T*
Catawba College *T*
East Carolina University *M*
Mars Hill College *T*
Meredith College *M*
North Carolina Agricultural and
    Technical State University *M*
University of North Carolina
    Asheville *T*
    Charlotte *M*
    Pembroke *M, T*
    Wilmington *M*
Wingate University *B, T*

North Dakota
Dickinson State University *B, T*
University of Mary *M*
University of North Dakota *M*

Ohio
Ashland University *M, T*
Baldwin-Wallace College *M*
Bowling Green State University *M*
Hiram College *T*
John Carroll University *M, T*
Kent State University *M, T*
Kent State University
    Stark Campus *B*
Lake Erie College *M*
Malone College *M*

Miami University
    Oxford Campus *M*
Notre Dame College *M, T*
Ohio Northern University *T*
Ohio State University
    Columbus Campus *M, D*
Ohio University *D*
Otterbein College *M*
University of Akron *B, M, T*
University of Cincinnati *M*
University of Dayton *M, T*
University of Rio Grande *B, T*
Walsh University *B*
Wilmington College *M, T*
Wittenberg University *B*
Wright State University *M*
Xavier University *M*
Youngstown State University *M*

Oklahoma
Northeastern State University *M*
Northwestern Oklahoma State
    University *M*
Southeastern Oklahoma State
    University *M, T*
Southern Nazarene University *M*
University of Central Oklahoma *B, M*
University of Oklahoma *T*

Oregon
Portland State University *T*
University of Portland *T*
Warner Pacific College *T*
Western Oregon University *T*

Pennsylvania
Arcadia University *M*
Bloomsburg University of
    Pennsylvania *M*
Bucknell University *M, T*
Cabrini College *T*
California University of Pennsylvania *M*
Drexel University *B*
Duquesne University *M, T*
East Stroudsburg University of
    Pennsylvania *M*
Edinboro University of Pennsylvania *M*
Gwynedd-Mercy College *M*
Holy Family University *M*
Indiana University of Pennsylvania *M*
King's College *M*
Kutztown University of
    Pennsylvania *B, M, T*
Lincoln University *B, M, T*
Marywood University *M*
Millersville University of
    Pennsylvania *M, T*
St. Joseph's University *M*
Shippensburg University of
    Pennsylvania *M, T*
Slippery Rock University of
    Pennsylvania *M*
University of Pennsylvania *C, M, D, T*
University of Pittsburgh *T*
University of Scranton *M*
West Chester University of
    Pennsylvania *M*
Widener University *M*
York College of Pennsylvania *M*

Rhode Island
Rhode Island College *M*

South Carolina
The Citadel *M*
Clemson University *M*
University of South Carolina *M, D*
Winthrop University *M, T*

South Dakota
University of Sioux Falls *M*

Tennessee
Austin Peay State University *M*
East Tennessee State University *M, T*
Middle Tennessee State University *M*
Tennessee Technological
    University *M, D, T*

Vanderbilt University *M, D*

Texas
Abilene Christian University *B, M, T*
Angelo State University *M*
Baylor University *B, T*
Dallas Baptist University *T*
Del Mar College *A*
Hardin-Simmons University *B, M, T*
Houston Baptist University *M*
Jarvis Christian College *B*
Laredo Community College *A*
LeTourneau University *B*
McMurry University *T*
Prairie View A&M University *M*
St. Mary's University *B, M, T*
Sam Houston State University *M, T*
Southwest Texas State University *M, T*
Southwestern University *T*
Stephen F. Austin State University *M, T*
Sul Ross State University *M*
Texas A&M International
    University *B, M, T*
Texas A&M University
    Commerce *M, T*
    Corpus Christi *M, T*
    Kingsville *M, T*
Texas Christian University *T*
Texas Lutheran University *B, T*
Texas Tech University *M*
Texas Wesleyan University *B, M, T*
Texas Woman's University *M, D, T*
University of Houston *M, T*
University of Houston
    Clear Lake *M, T*
    Victoria *M*
University of Mary Hardin-Baylor *M, T*
University of North Texas *M, D*
University of Texas
    Arlington *T*
    Brownsville *M*
    El Paso *M*
    Pan American *M, T*
    San Antonio *T*
    Tyler *M*
    of the Permian Basin *M*
University of the Incarnate Word *M*
West Texas A&M University *M, T*

Utah
Brigham Young University *D*

Vermont
Castleton State College *M*
College of St. Joseph in Vermont *M*
Johnson State College *M*
St. Michael's College *M, T*
University of Vermont *M*

Virginia
Averett University *M*
James Madison University *T*
Longwood University *M, T*
Old Dominion University *M*
Radford University *M, T*
Virginia Commonwealth University *M*

Washington
Central Washington University *M, T*
Eastern Washington University *B, M, T*
Northwest College *M*
Pacific Lutheran University *M, T*
Walla Walla College *M*
Western Washington University *M*
Whitworth College *B, T*

West Virginia
Marshall University *M*
West Virginia University *M, T*

Wisconsin
Cardinal Stritch University *M*
Carthage College *M*
Mount Mary College *T*
Silver Lake College *T*

University of Wisconsin
    Eau Claire *M*
    La Crosse *M*
    Oshkosh *M*
    Platteville *T*
    River Falls *M, T*
    Superior *B, T*
Viterbo University *T*

Real estate

Alabama
Enterprise State Junior College *A*

Arizona
Arizona State University *B*
Glendale Community College *A*
Paradise Valley Community College *C*
Pima Community College *C, A*
Yavapai College *C*

Arkansas
Arkansas State University *B*

California
Antelope Valley College *C, A*
Bakersfield College *A*
Barstow College *C, A*
Cabrillo College *C, A*
California State Polytechnic University:
    Pomona *B*
California State University
    Dominguez Hills *B*
    Fresno *B*
    Hayward *B*
    Long Beach *B*
    Los Angeles *B*
    Northridge *B*
    Sacramento *B*
Cerritos Community College *C, A*
Chabot College *A*
Citrus College *C*
Coastline Community College *C, A*
College of Marin: Kentfield *C, A*
College of the Canyons *C, A*
College of the Redwoods *A*
College of the Sequoias *C, A*
Contra Costa College *C, A*
Cuesta College *C, A*
Cuyamaca College *A*
De Anza College *C, A*
Diablo Valley College *C*
East Los Angeles College *C, A*
Foothill College *C, A*
Glendale Community College *C, A*
Golden West College *C, A*
Imperial Valley College *C, A*
Irvine Valley College *C, A*
Long Beach City College *C, A*
Los Angeles Harbor College *A*
Los Angeles Southwest College *C, A*
Los Angeles Trade and Technical
    College *C, A*
Los Medanos College *C, A*
MiraCosta College *C, A*
Modesto Junior College *A*
Monterey Peninsula College *C, A*
Moorpark College *C, A*
Mount San Antonio College *C, A*
Mount San Jacinto College *C, A*
Napa Valley College *C, A*
Ohlone College *C, A*
Palomar College *C, A*
Riverside Community College *C, A*
San Diego City College *C, A*
San Diego Mesa College *C, A*
San Diego State University *M*
San Francisco State University *B*
San Joaquin Delta College *C, A*
Santa Barbara City College *C, A*
Santa Monica College *A*
Santa Rosa Junior College *C*
Shasta College *C*
Sierra College *C, A*
Southwestern College *C, A*

University of Southern California *M*
Ventura College *C, A*
Victor Valley College *C, A*
West Valley College *C, A*

Colorado
Arapahoe Community College *C*
Colorado Mountain College
    Spring Valley Campus *C, A*
    Timberline Campus *C, A*
Colorado State University *B*
University of Colorado
    Boulder *B, M*
University of Denver *B, M*

Connecticut
Manchester Community College *C*
University of Connecticut *B*

District of Columbia
American University *M*
George Washington University *M*

Florida
Florida Atlantic University *B*
Florida International University *B*
Florida State University *B*
Gulf Coast Community College *A*
Miami-Dade Community College *C*
Okaloosa-Walton Community College *A*
Polk Community College *A*
Seminole Community College *C*
South Florida Community College *C, A*
University of Florida *B, M*

Georgia
Georgia State University *B, M, D*
State University of West Georgia *B*
University of Georgia *B*

Hawaii
University of Hawaii
    Manoa *B*

Idaho
College of Southern Idaho *A*

Illinois
City Colleges of Chicago
    Kennedy-King College *C*
    Olive-Harvey College *C*
College of DuPage *C, A*
Danville Area Community College *C*
Illinois Central College *C, A*
Joliet Junior College *C*
Kankakee Community College *A*
Kishwaukee College *C*
Lewis and Clark Community College *A*
Lincoln Land Community College *A*
McHenry County College *C, A*
Northwestern University *M*
Oakton Community College *C, A*
Prairie State College *C*
Sauk Valley Community College *C*
South Suburban College of Cook
    County *C*
Southeastern Illinois College *C*
Southwestern Illinois College *C*
Triton College *C*
Waubonsee Community College *C*
William Rainey Harper College *C, A*

Indiana
Vincennes University *C*

Iowa
Des Moines Area Community College *C*
University of Northern Iowa *B*

Kansas
Dodge City Community College *C*

Kentucky
Elizabethtown Community College *A*
Jefferson Community College *A*
Madisonville Community College *A*
Morehead State University *B*
Paducah Community College *A*
Prestonsburg Community College *A*

Louisiana
Southern University
    New Orleans *A*
University of New Orleans *B*

Maine
University of Southern Maine *C*

Maryland
Community College of Baltimore County
    Catonsville *C, A*
    Dundalk *C, A*
    Essex *C, A*
Harford Community College *C*
Johns Hopkins University *M*

Massachusetts
Greenfield Community College *C*
Massachusetts Bay Community
    College *C*

Michigan
Eastern Michigan University *B*
Ferris State University *C, A, B*
Kirtland Community College *A*
Lansing Community College *A*
Western Michigan University *B*

Minnesota
Dakota County Technical College *C, A*
St. Cloud State University *B*
University of St. Thomas *B, M*

Mississippi
Mississippi State University *B*
University of Mississippi *B*

Missouri
Lindenwood University *M*
St. Louis Community College
    St. Louis Community College at
        Meramec *C, A*
University of Missouri
    Columbia *B*
Webster University *M*

Nebraska
Northeast Community College *A*
University of Nebraska
    Omaha *B*

Nevada
Community College of Southern
    Nevada *C, A*
Truckee Meadows Community
    College *A*
University of Nevada
    Las Vegas *B*
Western Nevada Community College *A*

New Hampshire
New Hampshire Community Technical
    College
    Laconia *C*
    Manchester *C*
New Hampshire Technical Institute *A*

New Jersey
Burlington County College *C*
Camden County College *C*
Gloucester County College *C*
Ocean County College *C*
Raritan Valley Community College *C, A*
Thomas Edison State College *A, B*

New Mexico
New Mexico Junior College *A*
San Juan College *C, A*

New York
City University of New York
    Baruch College *B*
Cornell University *M*
Hudson Valley Community College *A*
Nassau Community College *C*
New York University *B, M*
Orange County Community College *A*
St. John's University *B*
Suffolk County Community
    College *C, A*

Utica School of Commerce *C*

North Carolina
Alamance Community College *A*
Appalachian State University *B*
Asheville Buncombe Technical
    Community College *C*
Bladen Community College *A*
Blue Ridge Community College *C*
Cape Fear Community College *C*
Carteret Community College *C*
Central Carolina Community College *C*
Central Piedmont Community College *A*
Cleveland Community College *C*
College of the Albemarle *C*
Craven Community College *C*
Durham Technical Community
    College *C*
Fayetteville Technical Community
    College *C*
Forsyth Technical Community College *C*
Guilford Technical Community
    College *C*
Haywood Community College *C*
Isothermal Community College *C*
Rockingham Community College *C*
Sampson Community College *C*
Southwestern Community College *C*
Stanly Community College *C*
Surry Community College *C*
Tri-County Community College *C*
Wilson Technical Community College *C*

Ohio
Cincinnati State Technical and
    Community College *A*
Columbus State Community College *A*
Cuyahoga Community College
    Eastern Campus *A*
    Metropolitan Campus *A*
    Western Campus *A*
Edison State Community College *A*
Hocking Technical College *C*
Hondros College *C, A*
Jefferson Community College *C*
Kent State University
    Trumbull Campus *A*
Lakeland Community College *C*
Lorain County Community College *A*
Marion Technical College *A*
Miami University
    Hamilton Campus *A*
Northwest State Community College *C*
Ohio Business College: Sandusky *C*
Ohio State University
    Columbus Campus *B*
Shawnee State University *A*
Sinclair Community College *A*
Southern State Community College *A*
Stautzenberger College *C*
University of Akron *C, A*
University of Cincinnati *B, M*
University of Cincinnati
    Raymond Walters College *C, A*
University of Rio Grande *B*

Oklahoma
Oklahoma City Community College *A*
Tulsa Community College *A*
University of Central Oklahoma *B*
University of Oklahoma *B*

Oregon
Chemeketa Community College *A*
Clackamas Community College *C*
Lane Community College *C, A*
Marylhurst University *C, B*
Portland Community College *A*
Southwestern Oregon Community
    College *C*

Pennsylvania
Bucks County Community College *C*
Community College of Philadelphia *A*
Harrisburg Area Community College *A*
Immaculata University *A*
La Roche College *B*

Lehigh Carbon Community College *C, A*
Luzerne County Community College *A*
Montgomery County Community
    College *C, A*
Northampton County Area Community
    College *C*
Peirce College *B*
Penn State
    Abington *B*
    Altoona *B*
    Beaver *B*
    Berks *B*
    Delaware County *B*
    Dubois *B*
    Fayette *B*
    Hazleton *B*
    Lehigh Valley *B*
    McKeesport *B*
    Mont Alto *B*
    New Kensington *B*
    Schuylkill - Capital College *B*
    Shenango *B*
    University Park *B*
    Wilkes-Barre *B*
    Worthington Scranton *B*
    York *B*
Temple University *B, M*
University of Pennsylvania *B, M, D*
Westmoreland County Community
    College *C*

South Carolina
University of South Carolina *B*

Tennessee
University of Memphis *B*

Texas
Amarillo College *C, A*
Angelina College *C*
Angelo State University *B*
Austin Community College *C, A*
Baylor University *B*
Blinn College *C*
Central Texas College *C, A*
Coastal Bend College *A*
College of the Mainland *A*
Collin County Community College
    District *C, A*
Del Mar College *C*
El Paso Community College *C, A*
Grayson County College *C, A*
Hill College *A*
Houston Community College
    System *C, A*
Kilgore College *A*
Laredo Community College *C, A*
Lee College *C*
McLennan Community College *C, A*
Midland College *C, A*
North Lake College *A*
Northeast Texas Community College *A*
Panola College *C*
Paris Junior College *A*
Richland College *A*
San Antonio College *A*
San Jacinto College
    Central Campus *C, A*
South Plains College *C, A*
Southern Methodist University *B*
Tarrant County College *C, A*
Texarkana College *C*
Texas A&M University *M*
Texas Christian University *B*
Trinity Valley Community College *C*
Tyler Junior College *C*
University of North Texas *B, M*
University of Texas
    Arlington *B, M*

Utah
Salt Lake Community College *C*

Virginia
Eastern Shore Community College *C*
J. Sargeant Reynolds Community
    College *C*

Southwest Virginia Community
    College *C*
Virginia Western Community
    College *C, A*

Washington
Bellevue Community College *C, A*
Green River Community College *C, A*
North Seattle Community College *C, A*
Spokane Falls Community College *C*
Washington State University *B*

West Virginia
Fairmont State College *A*

Wisconsin
Chippewa Valley Technical College *C*
Fox Valley Technical College *C*
Milwaukee Area Technical College *A*
University of Wisconsin
    Madison *B, M*
    Milwaukee *B*
Waukesha County Technical College *A*

Wyoming
University of Wyoming *C*

Receptionist

California
Ohlone College *A*

Iowa
Hamilton College
    Cedar Rapids *C*

Michigan
Baker College
    of Muskegon *C*

Minnesota
Minneapolis Community and Technical
    College *C*
Minnesota State College - Southeast
    Technical *C*
South Central Technical College *C*

North Carolina
Lenoir Community College *C*

Ohio
Youngstown State University *A*

Pennsylvania
Consolidated School of Business
    Lancaster *C*
    York *C*
Newport Business Institute *A*

Utah
Utah Valley State College *C, A*

Washington
Centralia College *C, A*
Clark College *C*

West Virginia
Valley College of Technology *C*

Recording arts

Colorado
University of Colorado
    Denver *M*

District of Columbia
American University *B*

Florida
Full Sail Real World Education *A*

Illinois
Waubonsee Community College *C*

Indiana
Ball State University *B*
Indiana University
    Bloomington *A, B*

Minnesota
Hennepin Technical College *C, A*
Minneapolis Community and Technical
    College *A*

New Mexico
Santa Fe Community College *A*

New York
Finger Lakes Community College *A*
Ithaca College *B*

Ohio
Malone College *B*

Pennsylvania
Duquesne University *B*

Texas
Southwest Texas State University *B*

Recreational therapy

Arkansas
University of Central Arkansas *B*

California
California State University
    Chico *B*
    Hayward *B*
Santa Barbara City College *C, A*
Whittier College *B*

Connecticut
Gateway Community College *C*
Manchester Community College *C*
Middlesex Community College *C*
Northwestern Connecticut Community
    College *C, A*
Norwalk Community College *C, A*

District of Columbia
Gallaudet University *B*
Howard University *B*

Florida
Broward Community College *A*

Georgia
Morris Brown College *B*

Illinois
Moraine Valley Community College *A*
University of St. Francis *B*

Indiana
Indiana Institute of Technology *A, B*
Vincennes University *A*

Iowa
University of Iowa *B*

Kansas
Pittsburg State University *B*

Kentucky
Murray State University *B*

Maine
University of Southern Maine *A, B*

Massachusetts
Bay Path College *C*
Northeastern University *A, B*
Springfield College *B, M*

Michigan
Calvin College *B*

Minnesota
Minnesota State University
    Mankato *B*
Winona State University *B*

New Hampshire
University of New Hampshire *B*

New Jersey
Bergen Community College *A*

New York
Ithaca College *B*

Mercy College *B*
New York University *M, D*
Onondaga Community College *A*
St. Joseph's College: Suffolk Campus *B*
Utica College *B*

North Carolina
Carteret Community College *A*
Catawba College *B*
East Carolina University *B, M*
University of North Carolina
    Wilmington *B*
Vance-Granville Community College *A*
Western Carolina University *B*
Western Piedmont Community
    College *A*
Winston-Salem State University *B*

Ohio
Ashland University *B*
College of Mount St. Joseph *B*
Kent State University *B*
Ohio University *B*
University of Findlay *B*

Oregon
Rogue Community College *C*

Pennsylvania
Community College of Allegheny
    County *C*
Lincoln University *B*
Lock Haven University of
    Pennsylvania *B*
Messiah College *B*
Penn State
    University Park *C*
Temple University *B, M*
York College of Pennsylvania *B*

South Carolina
Coker College *B*

Texas
Austin Community College *C, A*

Utah
Brigham Young University *B*

Vermont
Green Mountain College *B*

Virginia
Longwood University *B*

Washington
Eastern Washington University *B*
Spokane Community College *C, A*

West Virginia
Alderson-Broaddus College *B*
West Virginia State College *B*

Wisconsin
Northland College *B*
University of Wisconsin
    La Crosse *B, M*

Regional studies

New Mexico
Santa Fe Community College *A*

New York
Columbia University
    Columbia College *B*

Pennsylvania
La Salle University *B*

Religion/religious studies

Alabama
Athens State University *B*
Auburn University *B*
Birmingham-Southern College *B*
Faulkner University *B*
Huntingdon College *B*

Judson College *B*
Oakwood College *B*
Samford University *A, B*
University of Alabama *B*
University of Mobile *B, M*
Wallace State Community College at
 Hanceville *C*

Arizona
Arizona State University *B, M*
Northern Arizona University *B*
Prescott College *M*
Southwestern College *C, B*
University of Arizona *B*

Arkansas
Hendrix College *B*
Ouachita Baptist University *A, B*
Philander Smith College *B*
University of Central Arkansas *B*

California
Azusa Pacific University *B*
Bethesda Christian University *B, M*
Biola University *B*
California Baptist University *B*
California State University
 Bakersfield *B*
 Chico *B*
 Fresno *B*
 Fullerton *B*
 Hayward *B*
 Long Beach *B, M*
 Northridge *B*
Chapman University *B*
Claremont McKenna College *B*
Concordia University *B*
Dominican University of California *B*
Holy Names College *B*
Hope International University *M*
Humboldt State University *B*
LIFE Pacific College *A, B*
La Sierra University *B, M*
Loma Linda University *M*
Los Angeles Pierce College *A*
Loyola Marymount University *B, M*
Marymount College *A*
Master's College *B*
Mount St. Mary's College *B, M*
Occidental College *B*
Orange Coast College *A*
Pacific Union College *B*
Patten University *A, B*
Pepperdine University *B, M*
Pitzer College *B*
Point Loma Nazarene University *M*
Pomona College *B*
Queen of the Holy Rosary College *C, A*
St. Mary's College of California *B*
San Diego State University *B*
San Jose Christian College *C, B*
San Jose State University *B*
Santa Clara University *B, M*
Scripps College *B*
Stanford University *B, M, D*
University of California
 Berkeley *B*
 Davis *B*
 Los Angeles *B*
 Riverside *B*
 San Diego *B*
 Santa Barbara *B, M, D*
 Santa Cruz *B, M, D*
University of La Verne *B*
University of Redlands *B*
University of San Diego *B*
University of Southern
 California *B, M, D*
University of the Pacific *B*
Vanguard University of Southern
 California *B*
Whittier College *B*

Colorado
Colorado College *B*
Naropa University *B, M*
Nazarene Bible College *A*

Regis University *B*
University of Colorado
 Boulder *B, M*
University of Denver *B*

Connecticut
Connecticut College *B*
Fairfield University *B*
Holy Apostles College and
 Seminary *A, B, M*
Sacred Heart University *B, M*
St. Joseph College *B, T*
Trinity College *B*
University of Bridgeport *B*
Wesleyan University *B*
Yale University *B, M, D*

District of Columbia
Catholic University of America *B, M, D*
George Washington University *B, M*
Georgetown University *B*
Howard University *M*

Florida
Broward Community College *A*
Eckerd College *B*
Florida Agricultural and Mechanical
 University *B*
Florida Christian College *B*
Florida College *B*
Florida International University *B, M*
Florida Southern College *B*
Florida State University *B, M, D*
Gulf Coast Community College *A*
Hobe Sound Bible College *B*
Miami-Dade Community College *A*
New College of Florida *B*
Palm Beach Atlantic University *B*
Pensacola Junior College *A*
Rollins College *B*
St. John Vianney College Seminary *B*
St. Thomas University *B, M*
South Florida Community College *A*
Southeastern College of the Assemblies
 of God *B*
Stetson University *B*
University of Florida *B, M*
University of Miami *B*
University of South Florida *B, M*
University of West Florida *B*

Georgia
Agnes Scott College *B*
Brewton-Parker College *A, B*
Clark Atlanta University *B*
Emory University *B, D*
Georgia State University *B*
LaGrange College *B*
Mercer University *B*
Morehouse College *B*
Morris Brown College *B*
Oxford College of Emory University *B*
Shorter College *B*
Spelman College *B*
University of Georgia *B, M*
Wesleyan College *B*

Hawaii
Chaminade University of Honolulu *B*
University of Hawaii
 Hilo *B*
 Manoa *B, M*

Idaho
Albertson College of Idaho *B*
Northwest Nazarene University *B*

Illinois
Augustana College *B*
Bradley University *B*
De Paul University *B*
Elmhurst College *B*
Greenville College *B*
Illinois College *B*
Illinois Wesleyan University *B*
Judson College *B*
Lewis University *B*

Lincoln Christian College and
 Seminary *C, A, B*
Lincoln College *A*
Loyola University of Chicago *B, M, D*
MacMurray College *B*
McKendree College *B*
Moody Bible Institute *B*
North Central College *B*
North Park University *B*
Northwestern University *B, M, D*
Olivet Nazarene University *B, M*
Principia College *B*
Quincy University *B*
St. Xavier University *B*
Springfield College in Illinois *A*
Trinity International University *M*
University of Chicago *M, D*
University of Illinois
 Urbana-Champaign *B*
Wheaton College *B*

Indiana
Anderson University *B*
Ball State University *B*
Bethel College *B*
Butler University *B*
Calumet College of St. Joseph *C, A, B*
DePauw University *B*
Earlham College *B*
Franklin College *B*
Indiana University
 Bloomington *B, M, D*
Indiana University-Purdue University
 Indianapolis *B*
Indiana Wesleyan University *A, B*
Manchester College *A, B*
Martin University *B*
Oakland City University *C, A, B*
Purdue University *B*
St. Joseph's College *B*
Saint Mary's College *B*
St. Mary-of-the-Woods College *B*
University of Evansville *B*
University of Indianapolis *B*
University of St. Francis *B*
Wabash College *B*

Iowa
Briar Cliff University *A, B*
Buena Vista University *B*
Central College *B*
Clarke College *A, B*
Coe College *B*
Cornell College *B*
Dordt College *B*
Drake University *B*
Faith Baptist Bible College and
 Theological Seminary *M*
Franciscan University *B*
Graceland University *B, M*
Grand View College *B*
Grinnell College *B*
Iowa State University *B*
Loras College *B*
Luther College *B*
Morningside College *B*
Mount Mercy College *B*
Northwestern College *B*
Simpson College *B*
University of Dubuque *B, M*
University of Iowa *B, M, D*
University of Northern Iowa *B*
Wartburg College *B*

Kansas
Baker University *B*
Barclay College *B*
Benedictine College *B*
Bethel College *B*
Central Christian College *A, B*
Kansas Wesleyan University *B*
MidAmerica Nazarene University *B, T*
Ottawa University *B*
Seward County Community College *A*
Tabor College *B*
University of Kansas *B, M*

Washburn University of Topeka *B*

Kentucky
Berea College *B*
Brescia University *A, B*
Campbellsville University *B*
Centre College *B*
Georgetown College *B*
Kentucky Mountain Bible College *A*
Lindsey Wilson College *A*
Pikeville College *B*
Spalding University *B, M*
Thomas More College *C, A, B*
Transylvania University *B*
Union College *B*

Louisiana
Centenary College of Louisiana *B*
Louisiana College *B*
Loyola University New Orleans *B, M*

Maine
Bates College *B*
Bowdoin College *B*
Colby College *B*
St. Joseph's College *B*

Maryland
College of Notre Dame of Maryland *B*
Columbia Union College *B*
Goucher College *B*
Hood College *B*
Loyola College in Maryland *B*
McDaniel College *B*
St. Mary's College of Maryland *B*

Massachusetts
Amherst College *B*
Assumption College *B*
Atlantic Union College *B*
Boston University *B, M, D*
College of the Holy Cross *B*
Elms College *B, M*
Hampshire College *B*
Harvard College *B*
Merrimack College *B*
Mount Holyoke College *B*
Smith College *B, M*
Stonehill College *B*
Tufts University *B*
Wellesley College *B*
Wheaton College *B*
Williams College *B*

Michigan
Adrian College *B, T*
Alma College *B*
Andrews University *B, M*
Aquinas College *B*
Calvin College *B, T*
Central Michigan University *B, T*
Concordia University *B*
Cornerstone University *B*
Hillsdale College *B*
Hope College *B*
Kalamazoo College *B*
Lansing Community College *A*
Madonna University *C, A, B*
Marygrove College *B*
Michigan State University *B*
Siena Heights University *B*
University of Michigan *B*
Western Michigan University *B, M, D*

Minnesota
Augsburg College *B*
Bethel College *B*
Carleton College *B*
College of St. Scholastica *B*
Concordia College: Moorhead *B*
Concordia University: St. Paul *B*
Gustavus Adolphus College *B*
Hamline University *B*
Macalester College *B*
St. Olaf College *B*
University of Minnesota
 Twin Cities *B*
University of St. Thomas *B*

Mississippi

Mary Holmes College *A*
Millsaps College *B, T*
Mississippi College *B*
Wesley College *B*

Missouri

Avila University *B*
Baptist Bible College *B*
Central Christian College of the Bible *B*
Central Methodist College *B*
Culver-Stockton College *B*
East Central College *A*
Hannibal-LaGrange College *B*
Lindenwood University *B*
Missouri Baptist University *A, B*
Southwest Baptist University *B*
Southwest Missouri State
    University *B, M*
University of Missouri
    Columbia *B, M*
Washington University in St. Louis *B, M*
Webster University *B*
Westminster College *B*
William Jewell College *B*

Montana

University of Great Falls *B*

Nebraska

Dana College *B*
Doane College *B*
Hastings College *B*
Midland Lutheran College *B*
Nebraska Wesleyan University *B*
Union College *B*
University of Nebraska
    Omaha *B*
York College *A, B, T*

New Hampshire

Dartmouth College *B*

New Jersey

Bloomfield College *B*
Drew University *B*
Felician College *C*
Georgian Court College *B*
Montclair State University *B*
Princeton University *B, M, D*
Rabbinical College of America *B*
Rowan University *B*
Rutgers, The State University of New
    Jersey
        New Brunswick Regional
            Campus *B*
St. Peter's College *B*
Seton Hall University *B, M*
Thomas Edison State College *B*

New Mexico

College of Santa Fe *B*
Eastern New Mexico University *B*
University of New Mexico *B*

New York

Bard College *B*
Barnard College *B*
Canisius College *B*
City University of New York
        Brooklyn College *B*
        Hunter College *B*
        Queens College *B*
Colgate University *B*
College of Mount St. Vincent *B*
College of New Rochelle *B, T*
Columbia University
        Columbia College *B*
Concordia College *A, B*
Cornell University *B*
Daemen College *B*
Fordham University *B, M, D*
Hamilton College *B*
Hartwick College *B*
Hobart and William Smith Colleges *B*
Houghton College *B*
Iona College *B*
Le Moyne College *B*

Manhattan College *B*
Manhattanville College *B*
Nazareth College of Rochester *B*
New York University *B, M*
Niagara University *B*
Nyack College *B*
St. John Fisher College *B*
St. John's University *C, B, M*
St. Lawrence University *B*
Sarah Lawrence College *B*
Skidmore College *B*
State University of New York
        Stony Brook *B*
Syracuse University *B, M, D*
University of Rochester *B*
Vassar College *B*
Wells College *B*

North Carolina

Appalachian State University *B*
Belmont Abbey College *B*
Brevard College *B*
Campbell University *B*
Catawba College *B*
Chowan College *B*
Davidson College *B*
Duke University *B, M, D*
Elon University *B*
Gardner-Webb University *B*
Greensboro College *B*
Guilford College *B*
High Point University *B*
Lees-McRae College *B*
Lenoir-Rhyne College *B*
Mars Hill College *B*
Meredith College *B*
Methodist College *A, B, T*
Montreat College *B*
Mount Olive College *A, B*
North Carolina State University *B*
North Carolina Wesleyan College *B*
Pfeiffer University *B*
Roanoke Bible College *C, A, B*
St. Andrews Presbyterian College *B*
Salem College *B*
University of North Carolina
        Chapel Hill *B, M, D*
        Charlotte *B, M*
        Greensboro *B*
Wake Forest University *B, M*
Wingate University *B*

North Dakota

University of Mary *B*
University of North Dakota *B*

Ohio

Antioch College *B*
Ashland University *B*
Baldwin-Wallace College *B*
Bluffton College *B*
Case Western Reserve University *B*
Circleville Bible College *A, B*
Cleveland State University *B*
College of Mount St. Joseph *B, M, T*
College of Wooster *B*
Defiance College *B*
Denison University *B*
Heidelberg College *B*
Hiram College *B*
John Carroll University *B, M, T*
Kenyon College *B*
Lourdes College *A, B*
Miami University
        Oxford Campus *B, M*
Mount Union College *B*
Mount Vernon Nazarene University *B*
Muskingum College *B*
Oberlin College *B*
Ohio Northern University *B*
Ohio State University
        Columbus Campus *B*
Ohio University *B*
Ohio Wesleyan University *B*
Otterbein College *B*
Pontifical College Josephinum *B*

University of Dayton *B*
University of Findlay *A, B*
Walsh University *B*
Wittenberg University *B*
Wright State University *B*
Youngstown State University *B*

Oklahoma

Bacone College *A*
Oklahoma Baptist University *B*
Oklahoma Christian University of
    Science and Arts *B*
Oklahoma City University *B, M*
St. Gregory's University *B*
Southern Nazarene University *B*
Southwestern Christian University *A, B*
University of Oklahoma *B*
University of Tulsa *B*

Oregon

Concordia University *B*
Eugene Bible College *B*
George Fox University *B*
Lewis & Clark College *B*
Linfield College *B*
Marylhurst University *B*
Reed College *B*
University of Oregon *B*
Warner Pacific College *A, B, M*
Western Baptist College *B*
Willamette University *B*

Pennsylvania

Albright College *B*
Allegheny College *B*
Baptist Bible College of Pennsylvania *B*
Bryn Athyn College of the New
    Church *B, M*
Bryn Mawr College *B*
Bucknell University *B*
Cabrini College *B*
Chestnut Hill College *C*
Dickinson College *B*
Elizabethtown College *B*
Franklin & Marshall College *B*
Gettysburg College *B*
Gratz College *B, M*
Grove City College *B*
Haverford College *B*
Holy Family University *B*
Immaculata University *B*
Indiana University of Pennsylvania *B*
La Roche College *B*
La Salle University *B, M*
Lafayette College *B*
Lebanon Valley College of
    Pennsylvania *B*
Lehigh University *B*
Lincoln University *B*
Lycoming College *B*
Marywood University *B*
Mercyhurst College *B*
Messiah College *B*
Moravian College *B*
Muhlenberg College *B*
Neumann College *B*
Penn State
        Abington *B*
        Altoona *B*
        Beaver *B*
        Berks *B*
        Delaware County *B*
        Dubois *B*
        Fayette *B*
        Hazleton *B*
        Lehigh Valley *B*
        McKeesport *B*
        Mont Alto *B*
        New Kensington *B*
        Schuylkill - Capital College *B*
        Shenango *B*
        University Park *B*
        Wilkes-Barre *B*
        Worthington Scranton *B*
        York *B*
Rosemont College *B*

St. Charles Borromeo Seminary -
    Overbrook *C*
St. Joseph's University *B*
Seton Hill University *C, B*
Swarthmore College *B*
Temple University *B, M, D*
Thiel College *B*
University of Pennsylvania *B, D*
University of Pittsburgh *B, M, D*
University of Scranton *B, M*
Villanova University *B, M*
West Chester University of
    Pennsylvania *B*

Puerto Rico

Bayamon Central University *B*
Pontifical Catholic University of Puerto
    Rico *M*

Rhode Island

Brown University *B, M, D*
Providence College *B*
Salve Regina University *B*

South Carolina

Anderson College *B*
Charleston Southern University *B*
College of Charleston *B*
Columbia College *B*
Converse College *B*
Erskine College *B*
Furman University *B*
North Greenville College *B*
Presbyterian College *B*
Southern Wesleyan University *B, M*
University of South Carolina *B, M*
Winthrop University *B*
Wofford College *B*

South Dakota

Augustana College *B*
University of Sioux Falls *B*

Tennessee

Belmont University *B, T*
Bryan College *B*
Carson-Newman College *B*
King College *B*
Lambuth University *B*
Lane College *B*
Maryville College *B*
Rhodes College *B*
Southern Adventist University *B, M*
Trevecca Nazarene University *B*
University of Tennessee
        Knoxville *B*
Vanderbilt University *B, M, D*

Texas

Amarillo College *A*
Arlington Baptist College *B*
Austin College *B*
Baylor University *B, M, D*
Concordia University at Austin *B, T*
Hardin-Simmons University *M*
Houston Baptist University *B, M*
Howard Payne University *B*
Jarvis Christian College *B*
LeTourneau University *B*
Lon Morris College *A*
McMurry University *B*
Our Lady of the Lake University of San
    Antonio *B*
Paul Quinn College *B*
Rice University *B, M, D*
St. Edward's University *B*
Schreiner University *B*
Southern Methodist University *B, M, D*
Southwestern Adventist University *B*
Southwestern University *B*
Texas Christian University *B*
Trinity University *B*
University of Dallas *B, M*
University of Mary Hardin-Baylor *B*
University of Texas
        Austin *B*
University of the Incarnate Word *B, M*

Wayland Baptist University *A, B, M*
Wiley College *B*

Vermont
Burlington College *B*
Goddard College *B*
Marlboro College *B*
Middlebury College *B*
St. Michael's College *B*
University of Vermont *B*

Virginia
Averett University *B*
Bluefield College *B*
College of William and Mary *B*
Emory & Henry College *B*
Ferrum College *B*
Hampden-Sydney College *B*
Hollins University *B*
Liberty University *A, B, M*
Lynchburg College *B*
Mary Baldwin College *B*
Mary Washington College *B*
Marymount University *B*
Randolph-Macon College *B*
Randolph-Macon Woman's College *B*
Roanoke College *B, T*
Shenandoah University *B*
Sweet Briar College *B*
University of Richmond *B*
University of Virginia *B, M, D*
Virginia Commonwealth University *B*
Virginia Intermont College *B*
Virginia Union University *B*
Virginia Wesleyan College *B*
Washington and Lee University *B*

Washington
Central Washington University *B*
Gonzaga University *B, M*
Pacific Lutheran University *B*
St. Martin's College *B*
Seattle University *B*
University of Puget Sound *B*
University of Washington *B, M*
Walla Walla College *B*
Washington State University *B*
Whitman College *B*
Whitworth College *B*

West Virginia
Alderson-Broaddus College *B*
Bethany College *B*
Ohio Valley College *B*
West Virginia Wesleyan College *B*
Wheeling Jesuit University *B, M*

Wisconsin
Alverno College *B, T*
Cardinal Stritch University *B, M*
Carroll College *B*
Carthage College *B*
Concordia University Wisconsin *B*
Edgewood College *B, M*
Lakeland College *B*
Lawrence University *B, T*
Marquette University *C, D*
Mount Mary College *B, T*
Northland College *B*
Ripon College *B*
St. Norbert College *B, T*
Silver Lake College *B, T*
University of Wisconsin
    Eau Claire *B*
    Madison *B, M*
    Oshkosh *B*
Viterbo University *B, T*

Religious education

Alabama
Faulkner University *B*
Oakwood College *B*
Southeastern Bible College *A, B, T*

Alaska
Alaska Bible College *B*

Arizona
Southwestern College *C, A, B*

Arkansas
Central Baptist College *A, B*
Harding University *B, M, T*
Ouachita Baptist University *B*
Williams Baptist College *B*

California
Azusa Pacific University *B, M, D*
Bethesda Christian University *B*
Biola University *B, M, D*
Concordia University *B, M*
Master's College *B*
Mount St. Mary's College *M*
Pacific Union College *B*
Patten University *B*
Point Loma Nazarene University *M*
San Jose Christian College *B*
Simpson College *B, M*
University of San Francisco *M*
Vanguard University of Southern
    California *B*

Colorado
Nazarene Bible College *A, B*

Connecticut
Holy Apostles College and Seminary *M*

District of Columbia
Catholic University of America *M, D*

Florida
Baptist College of Florida *A, B*
Florida Southern College *B*
St. Thomas University *B*
Southeastern College of the Assemblies
    of God *B*
Talmudic College of Florida *B, M, D*

Georgia
Toccoa Falls College *B*

Idaho
Boise Bible College *A, B*
Northwest Nazarene University *B*

Illinois
Concordia University *M*
Lincoln Christian College and
    Seminary *B, M*
Loyola University of Chicago *M*
Moody Bible Institute *B, T*
North Park University *M*
Olivet Nazarene University *B*
Trinity Christian College *B*
Trinity International University *B, M*
Wheaton College *C, B, M*

Indiana
Huntington College *B, M*
Indiana Wesleyan University *A, B*
Marian College *A, B*
Martin University *B*
St. Mary-of-the-Woods College *B*
Taylor University *B*
Taylor University: Fort Wayne *B*

Iowa
Faith Baptist Bible College and
    Theological Seminary *B*
Loras College *M*
Northwestern College *B*
Vennard College *B*
Wartburg College *B, T*

Kansas
Barclay College *C*
Central Christian College *A, B*
Kansas Wesleyan University *B*
MidAmerica Nazarene University *A, B*
Sterling College *B*

Kentucky
Asbury College *B*

Campbellsville University *B, M*
Cumberland College *B*
Kentucky Christian College *B*
Kentucky Mountain Bible College *B*
Mid-Continent College *C, B*
Union College *B*

Louisiana
Louisiana College *B*
Loyola University New Orleans *M*
New Orleans Baptist Theological
    Seminary: School of Christian
    Education *A, B*

Maryland
Baltimore Hebrew University *M, D*
Columbia Union College *B*
Washington Bible College *B*

Massachusetts
Boston College *M, D*

Michigan
Andrews University *B, M, D*
Aquinas College *A*
Concordia University *B, T*
Cornerstone University *A, B*
Grace Bible College *A, B*
Reformed Bible College *A, B*
William Tyndale College *B*

Minnesota
College of St. Benedict *B*
College of St. Scholastica *B*
Concordia University: St. Paul *B*
Crossroads College *B*
Crown College *C, B*
North Central University *B*
Northwestern College *B*
St. John's University *B*
University of St. Thomas *M*

Mississippi
Magnolia Bible College *B*
Wesley College *B*

Missouri
Baptist Bible College *B*
Calvary Bible College *A, B*
Central Bible College *A, B*
Central Christian College of the Bible *B*
Global University *B*
Hannibal-LaGrange College *B*
Missouri Baptist University *B*
Ozark Christian College *B*
St. Louis Christian College *B*
Southwest Baptist University *B*

Nebraska
Concordia University *B, T*
Grace University *B*
Nebraska Christian College *A, B*
Union College *B, T*
York College *A, B, T*

New Jersey
College of St. Elizabeth *C*
Felician College *M*
Seton Hall University *B, T*

New York
Concordia College *B*
Nyack College *B*

North Carolina
Campbell University *M*
Duke University *M*
Gardner-Webb University *B*
Livingstone College *B*
Methodist College *A, B, T*
Pfeiffer University *B, M*
Southeastern Baptist Theological
    Seminary *M*

North Dakota
Trinity Bible College *B*

Ohio
Ashland University *B, M, T*
Cedarville University *B*

Cincinnati Bible College and
    Seminary *B, M*
Circleville Bible College *A, B*
College of Mount St. Joseph *B, T*
Defiance College *B, T*
God's Bible School and College *B*
Laura and Alvin Siegal College of Judaic
    Studies *B, M*
Mount Vernon Nazarene University *B*
Muskingum College *B*
Notre Dame College *C*

Oklahoma
Oklahoma Baptist University *B*
Oklahoma Christian University of
    Science and Arts *B*
Oklahoma City University *M*
Oral Roberts University *B, M*
St. Gregory's University *A*
Southern Nazarene University *B*
Southwestern Christian University *B*

Oregon
Eugene Bible College *B*
George Fox University *B*
Multnomah Bible College *B*
University of Portland *T*

Pennsylvania
Duquesne University *M*
Gratz College *T*
Holy Family University *B*
Immaculata University *B*
La Roche College *C, B*
La Salle University *B, M*
Lancaster Bible College *B*
Manor College *C, A*
Marywood University *B*
Mercyhurst College *A, B*
Messiah College *B*
Philadelphia Biblical University *B, T*
St. Vincent College *B*
Thiel College *B*
Valley Forge Christian College *B*

Puerto Rico
Inter American University of Puerto Rico
    Metropolitan Campus *D*
Pontifical Catholic University of Puerto
    Rico *M*

Rhode Island
Providence College *A, B*

South Carolina
Columbia College *B*
Columbia International University *B, M*
Erskine College *B, M*
Morris College *B*
Presbyterian College *B*

South Dakota
Mount Marty College *B*

Tennessee
American Baptist College of ABT
    Seminary *B*
Bryan College *B*
Lee University *B*
Milligan College *B*
Southern Adventist University *B, M*
Tennessee Wesleyan College *B*

Texas
Abilene Christian University *M*
Arlington Baptist College *B*
Dallas Baptist University *A, B*
Dallas Christian College *B*
East Texas Baptist University *B*
Howard Payne University *B*
McMurry University *B*
Southern Methodist University *M*
Southwestern Assemblies of God
    University *B*
Texas Wesleyan University *B*
Wayland Baptist University *B*

Virginia
Averett University *B*

Liberty University *M*

Washington
Northwest College *B*
Seattle Pacific University *B*
Seattle University *M*
Trinity Lutheran College *C, A, B*

Wisconsin
Maranatha Baptist Bible College *A, B*
Marquette University *D, T*
Viterbo University *B*

Religious/sacred music

Alabama
Birmingham-Southern College *B*
Southeastern Bible College *A, B*

Arizona
Southwestern College *C, A, B*

Arkansas
Central Baptist College *B*
John Brown University *B*
Ouachita Baptist University *B*
Williams Baptist College *B*

California
Azusa Pacific University *B*
Bethesda Christian University *B*
California Baptist University *C*
Fresno Pacific University *B*
Hope International University *B, M*
Master's College *B*
Mount St. Mary's College *B*
Patten University *B*
San Jose Christian College *B*
Santa Clara University *M*
Simpson College *B*
University of Southern California *M, D*

Colorado
Nazarene Bible College *A, B*

Connecticut
Holy Apostles College and Seminary *M*

District of Columbia
Catholic University of America *M, D*

Florida.
Baptist College of Florida *A, B*
Florida Christian College *B*
Florida Southern College *B*
Florida State University *C*
Hobe Sound Bible College *C, B*
Jacksonville University *B*
Southeastern College of the Assemblies of God *B*
Warner Southern College *B*

Georgia
Andrew College *C*
Emory University *M*
LaGrange College *B*
Shorter College *B*
Toccoa Falls College *B*
University of Georgia *B*

Idaho
Boise Bible College *A, B*
Northwest Nazarene University *B*

Illinois
Concordia University *M*
Judson College *B*
Lincoln Christian College and Seminary *B*
Moody Bible Institute *B*
Northwestern University *B, M, D*
Olivet Nazarene University *B*
Trinity International University *B*

Indiana
Anderson University *B*
Bethel College *B*
Goshen College *B*
Indiana Wesleyan University *A, B*

Manchester College *B*
Oakland City University *B*
St. Joseph's College *C, A, B, M*
University of Evansville *B*

Iowa
Dordt College *B*
Drake University *C*
Faith Baptist Bible College and Theological Seminary *B*
Wartburg College *B*

Kansas
Central Christian College *A, B*
MidAmerica Nazarene University *A, B*

Kentucky
Campbellsville University *B, M*
Cumberland College *B*
Kentucky Christian College *B*
Kentucky Mountain Bible College *B*
Union College *B*

Louisiana
Centenary College of Louisiana *B*
Louisiana College *B*
Loyola University New Orleans *B*

Maryland
Washington Bible College *B*

Massachusetts
Boston University *D*
Hebrew College *C*

Michigan
Aquinas College *A, B*
Calvin College *B*
Concordia University *B*
Cornerstone University *B*
Grace Bible College *B*
Marygrove College *C*
Spring Arbor University *B*
William Tyndale College *B*

Minnesota
Bethel College *B*
College of St. Catherine *C*
Concordia University: St. Paul *B*
Crossroads College *B*
Gustavus Adolphus College *B*
North Central University *C, B*
St. John's University *M*
St. Olaf College *B*

Mississippi
Magnolia Bible College *B*
Mississippi College *B*

Missouri
Baptist Bible College *B*
Calvary Bible College *B*
Central Bible College *A, B*
Central Christian College of the Bible *B*
Evangel University *B*
Hannibal-LaGrange College *B*
Missouri Baptist University *B*
Ozark Christian College *C, B*
St. Louis Christian College *B*
Southwest Baptist University *B*

Nebraska
Concordia University *B*
Grace University *B*
Nebraska Christian College *A, B*

New Jersey
Rider University *B, M*
Seton Hall University *B*

New York
Concordia College *B*
Nyack College *B*

North Carolina
Campbell University *B, T*
Lenoir-Rhyne College *B*
North Carolina Central University *B*
Pfeiffer University *B*

Southeastern Baptist Theological Seminary *M*
Wingate University *B*

Ohio
Ashland University *M*
Cedarville University *B*
Cincinnati Bible College and Seminary *B*
Circleville Bible College *A, B*
God's Bible School and College *B*
Malone College *B*
Mount Vernon Nazarene University *A, B*
Wittenberg University *B*

Oklahoma
Oklahoma Baptist University *B*
Oklahoma Wesleyan University *B*
Oral Roberts University *B, M*
Southern Nazarene University *B*
Southwestern Christian University *B*
Southwestern Oklahoma State University *B*

Oregon
Eugene Bible College *B*
Multnomah Bible College *B*
Western Baptist College *B*

Pennsylvania
Baptist Bible College of Pennsylvania *B*
Duquesne University *M*
Gratz College *M*
Immaculata University *A*
Lancaster Bible College *B*
Marywood University *B, M*
Philadelphia Biblical University *B*
St. Charles Borromeo Seminary - Overbrook *C*
Seton Hill University *C, B*
Valley Forge Christian College *B*

South Carolina
Anderson College *B*
Charleston Southern University *B*
Columbia International University *B*
Erskine College *M*
North Greenville College *B*

South Dakota
Dakota Wesleyan University *B*

Tennessee
Belmont University *B*
Carson-Newman College *B*
Johnson Bible College *B*
Lambuth University *B*
Lee University *B, M*
Tennessee Wesleyan College *B*
Trevecca Nazarene University *B*
Union University *B*

Texas
Arlington Baptist College *B*
Baylor University *B, M*
Concordia University at Austin *B*
Dallas Baptist University *B*
Dallas Christian College *B*
Hardin-Simmons University *B, M*
Houston Baptist University *B*
Howard Payne University *B*
McMurry University *B*
Southern Methodist University *M*
Southwestern Assemblies of God University *B*
Southwestern Baptist Theological Seminary: Theological Professions *M*
Southwestern University *B*
Wayland Baptist University *B*

Virginia
Averett University *B*
Bluefield College *B*
Shenandoah University *C, B, M*

Washington
Northwest College *B*
Pacific Lutheran University *B*
Trinity Lutheran College *C, B*

West Virginia
Alderson-Broaddus College *B*

Renal/dialysis technology

Illinois
City Colleges of Chicago Malcolm X College *A*

North Carolina
Wilson Technical Community College *C*

Reproductive biology

Texas
University of Texas Houston Health Science Center *M, D*

Wyoming
University of Wyoming *M, D*

Resort management

Minnesota
University of Minnesota Crookston *B*

New York
Rochester Institute of Technology *A, B, M*
State University of New York College of Agriculture and Technology at Morrisville *B*

Ohio
Lourdes College *C*

Pennsylvania
Newport Business Institute *A*

Tennessee
University of Memphis *B*

Respiratory therapy

Alabama
Central Alabama Community College *A*
Enterprise State Junior College *A*
Faulkner University *A*
George C. Wallace State Community College Dothan *A*
Northwest-Shoals Community College *A*
Shelton State Community College *C, A*
University of Alabama Birmingham *B*
University of South Alabama *B*
Wallace State Community College at Hanceville *A*

Arizona
Gateway Community College *C, A*
Pima Community College *A*

Arkansas
Northwest Arkansas Community College *A*
Pulaski Technical College *A*
University of Arkansas Community College at Hope *A*
Fort Smith *A*
for Medical Sciences *C, A*
University of Central Arkansas *B*

California
Diablo Valley College *C*
East Los Angeles College *A*
Foothill College *C, A*
Grossmont Community College *A*
Los Angeles Southwest College *A*
Modesto Junior College *A*
Mount San Antonio College *C, A*
Napa Valley College *C, A*

Ohlone College *A*
Orange Coast College *C, A*
Santa Monica College *A*
Victor Valley College *C, A*

Colorado
Front Range Community College *A*

Connecticut
Manchester Community College *A*
Naugatuck Valley Community College *A*
Norwalk Community College *A*
Quinnipiac University *B*
University of Hartford *B*

Delaware
Delaware Technical and Community
College
Owens Campus *A*
Stanton/Wilmington Campus *A*

District of Columbia
University of the District of Columbia *A*

Florida
ATI Health Education Center *A*
Broward Community College *A*
Daytona Beach Community College *A*
Florida Agricultural and Mechanical
University *B*
Gulf Coast Community College *C, A*
Hillsborough Community College *A*
Indian River Community College *A*
Manatee Community College *A*
Miami-Dade Community College *A*
Palm Beach Community College *C, A*
Pensacola Junior College *A*
Polk Community College *A*
St. Petersburg College *A*
Santa Fe Community College *A*
Seminole Community College *A*
South Florida Community College *A*
Tallahassee Community College *A*
University of Central Florida *B*
Valencia Community College *A*

Georgia
Armstrong Atlantic State University *B*
Athens Technical College *C, A*
Darton College *A*
Floyd College *A*
Georgia State University *B*
Macon State College *A*
Medical College of Georgia *B, M*
Middle Georgia College *A*
Southwest Georgia Technical College *A*

Idaho
Boise State University *A, B*
College of Southern Idaho *A*

Illinois
Black Hawk College *A*
City Colleges of Chicago
Malcolm X College *A*
Olive-Harvey College *C*
College of DuPage *C, A*
Illinois Central College *C, A*
Kankakee Community College *A*
Kaskaskia College *C, A*
Lincoln Land Community College *A*
Moraine Valley Community College *A*
National-Louis University *B*
Parkland College *A*
Rock Valley College *A*
St. Augustine College *A*
Southern Illinois University
Carbondale *A*
Southwestern Illinois College *C, A*
Triton College *A*

Indiana
Ball State University *A*
Indiana University
Bloomington *B*
Northwest *A*
Indiana University-Purdue University
Indianapolis *A, B*

Ivy Tech State College
Central Indiana *A*
Lafayette *A*
Northcentral *C*
Northeast *C, A*
Northwest *A*
University of Southern Indiana *A*

Iowa
Des Moines Area Community College *A*
Hawkeye Community College *C*
Kirkwood Community College *A*
Northeast Iowa Community College *A*

Kansas
Johnson County Community
College *C, A*
Kansas City Kansas Community
College *A*
Labette Community College *A*
Newman University *A*
Seward County Community
College *C, A*
University of Kansas Medical Center *B*
Washburn University of Topeka *C, A*

Kentucky
Bellarmine University *C, B*
Jefferson Community College *A*
Lexington Community College *A*
Madisonville Community College *A*
Morehead State University *A*
St. Catharine College *A*
Somerset Community College *C*
Southeast Community College *A*
University of Louisville *B*

Louisiana
Delgado Community College *C, A*
Louisiana State University
Eunice *A*
Nicholls State University *C, A*
Our Lady of Holy Cross College *A, B*
Southern University
Shreveport *A*

Maryland
Allegany College *A*
Columbia Union College *A, B*
Community College of Baltimore County
Catonsville *A*
Dundalk *A*
Essex *A*
Frederick Community College *A*
Salisbury University *B*

Massachusetts
Berkshire Community College *A*
Massachusetts Bay Community
College *C, A*
Massasoit Community College *A*
Quinsigamond Community College *A*
Springfield Technical Community
College *A*

Michigan
Ferris State University *A*
Lansing Community College *A*
Macomb Community College *A*
Marygrove College *C, A*
Monroe County Community College *A*
Mott Community College *A*
Muskegon Community College *C, A*
Oakland Community College *A*
Washtenaw Community College *A*

Minnesota
College of St. Catherine *A*
Lake Superior College: A Community
and Technical College *A*
Rochester Community and Technical
College *A*
St. Paul College - A Community and
Technical College *A*

Mississippi
Itawamba Community College *A*

Mississippi Gulf Coast Community
College
Perkinston *C, A*
Northwest Mississippi Community
College *A*
Pearl River Community College *C, A*

Missouri
Hannibal-LaGrange College *A*
Missouri Southern State College *A*
Ozarks Technical Community College *A*
Penn Valley Community College *A*
St. Louis Community College
St. Louis Community College at
Forest Park *A*
Sanford-Brown College *A*
Southwest Missouri State University *B*
University of Missouri
Columbia *B*

Montana
University of Montana-Missoula *A*

Nebraska
Metropolitan Community College *C, A*
Midland Lutheran College *A, B*
Nebraska Methodist College of Nursing
and Allied Health *A, B*
Southeast Community College
Lincoln Campus *A*
University of Nebraska
Kearney *B*

New Hampshire
New Hampshire Community Technical
College
Claremont *A*

New Jersey
Atlantic Cape Community College *A*
Bergen Community College *A*
Brookdale Community College *A*
Camden County College *A*
County College of Morris *A*
Essex County College *C, A*
Gloucester County College *C, A*
Hudson County Community
College *C, A*
Mercer County Community College *A*
Middlesex County College *A*
Passaic County Community College *A*
Sussex County Community College *A*
Thomas Edison State College *A, B*
Union County College *A*
University of Medicine and Dentistry of
New Jersey
School of Health Related
Professions *A, B*

New Mexico
Albuquerque Technical-Vocational
Institute *A*
Dona Ana Branch Community College of
New Mexico State University *A*

New York
City University of New York
Borough of Manhattan Community
College *A*
Erie Community College
North Campus *A*
Genesee Community College *A*
Hudson Valley Community College *A*
Mohawk Valley Community College *A*
Molloy College *A*
Nassau Community College *A*
Onondaga Community College *C, A*
Rockland Community College *A*
State University of New York
Health Science Center at Stony
Brook *A*
Oswego *B*
Stony Brook *B*
Upstate Medical University *B*
Westchester Community College *A*

North Carolina
Carteret Community College *A*

Catawba Valley Community College *A*
Central Piedmont Community College *A*
Durham Technical Community
College *C, A*
Edgecombe Community College *C, A*
Fayetteville Technical Community
College *A*
Forsyth Technical Community College *A*
Guilford Technical Community
College *A*
Pitt Community College *A*
Rockingham Community College *A*
Sandhills Community College *A*
Southwestern Community College *A*
Stanly Community College *C, A*

North Dakota
North Dakota State University *B*
University of Mary *B*

Ohio
Bowling Green State University:
Firelands College *A*
Cincinnati State Technical and
Community College *A*
Columbus State Community College *A*
Cuyahoga Community College
Eastern Campus *A*
Western Campus *A*
James A. Rhodes State College *A*
Jefferson Community College *A*
Kettering College of Medical Arts *A, B*
Lakeland Community College *A*
North Central State College *A*
Ohio State University
Columbus Campus *B, M*
Shawnee State University *A*
Sinclair Community College *A*
Stark State College of Technology *A*
University of Akron *A*
University of Cincinnati
Clermont College *A*
University of Toledo *A*
Washington State Community College *A*
Youngstown State University *B*

Oklahoma
Northern Oklahoma College *A*
Rose State College *A*
Tulsa Community College *C, A*

Oregon
Lane Community College *A*
Mount Hood Community College *A*
Rogue Community College *C, A*

Pennsylvania
Community College of Allegheny
County *A*
Community College of Philadelphia *A*
Delaware County Community College *A*
Gwynedd-Mercy College *A*
Harrisburg Area Community College *A*
Indiana University of Pennsylvania *B*
La Roche College *B*
Lehigh Carbon Community College *A*
Luzerne County Community College *A*
Reading Area Community College *A*
University of Pittsburgh
Johnstown *A*
Western School of Health and Business
Careers *A*
York College of Pennsylvania *A, B*

Puerto Rico
Huertas Junior College *A*
Universidad Metropolitana *A, B*

Rhode Island
Community College of Rhode Island *A*

South Carolina
Florence-Darlington Technical
College *C, A*
Medical University of South Carolina *B*
Midlands Technical College *C, A*
Orangeburg-Calhoun Technical
College *C*

Piedmont Technical College *A*
Spartanburg Technical College *A*
Tri-County Technical College *C*
Trident Technical College *A*

South Dakota
Dakota State University *A, B*

Tennessee
Chattanooga State Technical Community
College *A*
Columbia State Community College *A*
Jackson State Community College *A*
Roane State Community College *A*
Volunteer State Community College *C*
Walters State Community College *C*

Texas
ATI-Career Training Center *A*
Alvin Community College *C, A*
Amarillo College *A*
Angelina College *A*
Collin County Community College
District *A*
Del Mar College *C, A*
El Centro College *C, A*
El Paso Community College *A*
Houston Community College
System *C, A*
Howard College *C, A*
McLennan Community College *A*
Midland College *A*
Midwestern State University *B*
North Harris Montgomery Community
College District *A*
Odessa College *A*
St. Philip's College *C, A*
San Jacinto College
Central Campus *A*
South Plains College *A*
Southwest Texas State University *B*
Tarrant County College *A*
Temple College *A*
Texas Southern University *B*
Tyler Junior College *A*
University of Texas
Health Science Center at San
Antonio *B*
Medical Branch at Galveston *B*
Victoria College *A*

Utah
Weber State University *A, B*

Vermont
Champlain College *C, A, B*

Virginia
College of Health Sciences *A, B*
J. Sargeant Reynolds Community
College *C, A*
Mountain Empire Community College *A*
Shenandoah University *A, B*
Southside Virginia Community
College *A*
Southwest Virginia Community
College *C*

Washington
Seattle Central Community College *A*
Spokane Community College *A*

West Virginia
Mountain State University *A, B*
West Virginia Northern Community
College *A*
West Virginia University Institute of
Technology *A*
Wheeling Jesuit University *B*

Wisconsin
Mid-State Technical College *A*
Milwaukee Area Technical College *A*
Western Wisconsin Technical College *A*

Respiratory therapy assistant

California
Foothill College *C, A*
Santa Rosa Junior College *C*

Indiana
Ivy Tech State College
Northcentral *C*

Kansas
Kansas City Kansas Community
College *A*

Kentucky
Jefferson Community College *A*

Maryland
Howard Community College *A*

Missouri
Sanford-Brown College *A*

North Carolina
Pitt Community College *A*

Oklahoma
Rose State College *A*

Tennessee
Walters State Community College *C, A*

Texas
Del Mar College *A*

Wisconsin
Mid-State Technical College *C*

Restaurant/catering management

Alabama
Shelton State Community College *C*

California
California Culinary Academy *A*
Grossmont Community College *C, A*
Long Beach City College *C, A*

Florida
Indian River Community College *A*
New England Institute of Technology *A*
Pensacola Junior College *C*

Illinois
Black Hawk College *A*
College of DuPage *C, A*
College of Lake County *C, A*
Moraine Valley Community
College *C, A*
Parkland College *A*
Richland Community College *C*
University of Illinois
Urbana-Champaign *B*

Indiana
Vincennes University *A*

Iowa
Des Moines Area Community College *A*

Massachusetts
Newbury College *C*

Michigan
Baker College
of Muskegon *C, A*
Ferris State University *A*
Grand Rapids Community College *A*

Minnesota
Hennepin Technical College *C, A*
South Central Technical College *A*
University of Minnesota
Crookston *B*

New Hampshire
New Hampshire Community Technical
College
Berlin *C, A*
University of New Hampshire *A, B*

New Jersey
Hudson County Community College *C*

New York
Erie Community College
North Campus *A*
Rochester Institute of
Technology *A, B, M*
Schenectady County Community
College *A*

North Carolina
Carteret Community College *A*

North Dakota
North Dakota State College of Science *A*

Ohio
Cincinnati State Technical and
Community College *A*
University of Akron *A*

Pennsylvania
Bucks County Community College *A*
Community College of Allegheny
County *C, A*
Keystone College *A*

Texas
Del Mar College *C, A*
St. Philip's College *C, A*

Utah
Utah Valley State College *B*

Washington
Clover Park Technical College *C*
South Seattle Community College *C, A*

West Virginia
Fairmont State College *A*

Wisconsin
Milwaukee Area Technical College *A*
Western Wisconsin Technical College *A*

Restaurant/food services management

Arizona
South Mountain Community College *C*

California
Long Beach City College *C, A*
University of San Francisco *B*

Georgia
Albany Technical College *C*

Illinois
John Wood Community College *A*
Parkland College *C, A*

Indiana
Indiana University-Purdue University
Indianapolis *A, B*
Vincennes University *A*

Massachusetts
American International College *B*

Michigan
Baker College
of Muskegon *A, B*
Oakland Community College *A*

Minnesota
South Central Technical College *A*
University of Minnesota
Crookston *A, B*

New Jersey
Thomas Edison State College *A, B*
Union County College *A*

New York
New York Institute of Technology *B*
Rochester Institute of
Technology *A, B, M*
State University of New York
College at Plattsburgh *B*
College of Agriculture and
Technology at Morrisville *A*

North Carolina
Cape Fear Community College *C, A*
Fayetteville Technical Community
College *C, A*
Sandhills Community College *A*

North Dakota
North Dakota State College of Science *A*
North Dakota State University *B*

Ohio
Owens Community College
Toledo *C, A*

Pennsylvania
Montgomery County Community
College *C, A*
Northampton County Area Community
College *A*
Penn State
Worthington Scranton *B*

Texas
Del Mar College *A*
Texas Tech University *B*

Vermont
Champlain College *A, B*

Washington
South Seattle Community College *C, A*

Wisconsin
Fox Valley Technical College *A*
Viterbo University *B*

Retailing

Alabama
Jefferson State Community College *C, A*
Virginia College *C, A*

Arizona
Scottsdale Community College *C, A*

Illinois
McHenry County College *C*
Robert Morris College: Chicago *A*

Missouri
Patricia Stevens College *A*

Ohio
Youngstown State University *B*

Pennsylvania
Butler County Community College *C, A*
Marywood University *B*
Newport Business Institute *A*
Pennsylvania College of Technology *C*

Utah
Dixie State College of Utah *C, A*

Washington
Clark College *A*

Robotics technology

Alabama
Jefferson State Community College *C, A*
Northwest-Shoals Community College *A*

Arkansas
Arkansas State University
Mountain Home *C*

California
Cerritos Community College *A*

ITT Technical Institute
West Covina *B*
Long Beach City College *C*
Orange Coast College *C*
University of California
San Diego *M, D*

Colorado
Colorado State University
Pueblo *B*
Red Rocks Community College *C*

Illinois
Black Hawk College *A*
College of DuPage *C, A*
Illinois Central College *C, A*
Oakton Community College *A*
Waubonsee Community College *C, A*
William Rainey Harper College *C*

Indiana
ITT Technical Institute
Fort Wayne *B*
Indianapolis *B*
Indiana State University *B*
Indiana University-Purdue University
Fort Wayne *C*
Indiana University-Purdue University
Indianapolis *A, B*
Ivy Tech State College
Columbus *A*
Eastcentral *A*
Lafayette *A*
Northcentral *A*
Northeast *C, A*
Northwest *C*
Southcentral *C, A*
Southeast *A*
Southwest *A*
Wabash Valley *A*
Whitewater *A*
Purdue University *A, B*
Purdue University
North Central Campus *A*
Vincennes University *A*

Iowa
Des Moines Area Community College *A*
Indian Hills Community College *A*
Southeastern Community College
North Campus *A*

Kentucky
Louisville Technical Institute *A*

Maine
Central Maine Technical College *C*

Maryland
Cecil Community College *C*

Michigan
Oakland Community College *C, A*

Minnesota
Mesabi Range Community and Technical
College *C, A*

New Hampshire
New Hampshire Community Technical
College
Nashua *A*

New York
State University of New York
College of Technology at Alfred *A*

North Carolina
Central Carolina Community College *A*
Forsyth Technical Community College *A*
Wake Technical Community College *A*

Ohio
James A. Rhodes State College *C*
Jefferson Community College *A*
Kent State University *C*
Kent State University
Ashtabula Regional Campus *C*
Lorain County Community College *A*
Sinclair Community College *A*

Oregon
ITT Technical Institute
Portland *B*

Pennsylvania
Community College of Allegheny
County *A*
Delaware County Community
College *C, A*
Electronic Institutes: Middletown *A*
Lehigh Carbon Community College *C, A*

South Carolina
Trident Technical College *A*

Texas
Hill College *A*
Texas State Technical College
West Texas *A*

Utah
Salt Lake Community College *A*
Utah Valley State College *A*

Virginia
ITT Technical Institute
Norfolk *B*

Washington
Spokane Community College *A*

Wisconsin
Blackhawk Technical College *A*
Chippewa Valley Technical College *A*

Romance languages

Alabama
Alabama State University *B*

Indiana
University of Notre Dame *B, M*

Louisiana
University of New Orleans *M*

Maine
Bowdoin College *B*

Maryland
University of Maryland
College Park *B*

Massachusetts
Mount Holyoke College *B*

Minnesota
Carleton College *B*

Missouri
University of Missouri
Columbia *D*

New York
City University of New York
Hunter College *B*
Manhattanville College *B*
State University of New York
Buffalo *M, D*

Pennsylvania
University of Pennsylvania *B, M, D*

Tennessee
University of Memphis *M*

Roofing

Washington
Clover Park Technical College *C*

Russian

Alabama
University of Alabama *B*

Alaska
University of Alaska
Anchorage *B*
Fairbanks *B, M*

Arizona
Arizona State University *B*
University of Arizona *B, M*

Arkansas
Ouachita Baptist University *B*

California
Cabrillo College *A*
California State University
Long Beach *C*
Claremont McKenna College *B*
De Anza College *A*
Grossmont Community College *C, A*
Monterey Institute of International
Studies *C*
Pitzer College *B*
Pomona College *B*
San Diego State University *B*
San Francisco State University *B, M*
Scripps College *B*
Stanford University *M*
University of California
Davis *B, M*
Los Angeles *B*
Riverside *B*
San Diego *B*
Santa Barbara *B*
Santa Cruz *B*
University of Southern
California *B, M, D*

Colorado
University of Colorado
Boulder *B*
University of Denver *B, M*

Connecticut
Connecticut College *B*
Fairfield University *B*
Trinity College *B*
Wesleyan University *B*
Yale University *B*

Delaware
University of Delaware *B, T*

District of Columbia
American University *B, M*
George Washington University *B*
Georgetown University *B*
Howard University *B*

Florida
Eckerd College *B*
Florida State University *B*
New College of Florida *B*
University of Florida *B*
University of Miami *B*
University of South Florida *B*

Georgia
Emory University *B*
Oxford College of Emory University *B*
University of Georgia *B*

Hawaii
University of Hawaii
Manoa *B, M*

Idaho
Idaho State University *A*

Illinois
Illinois Wesleyan University *B*
Knox College *B*
Northern Illinois University *B*
Parkland College *A*
Principia College *B*
Southern Illinois University
Carbondale *B*
University of Chicago *B, M, D*
University of Illinois
Chicago *B*
Urbana-Champaign *B*

Indiana
University of Notre Dame *B*

Iowa
Cornell College *B, T*
Grinnell College *B*
Iowa State University *B*
University of Iowa *B, T*
University of Northern Iowa *M*

Kansas
University of Kansas *B, M, D*

Kentucky
University of Kentucky *B*
University of Louisville *B*

Louisiana
Loyola University New Orleans *B*
Tulane University *B*

Maine
Bates College *B*
Bowdoin College *B*
Colby College *B*

Maryland
Goucher College *B*
Johns Hopkins University *B*
University of Maryland
Baltimore County *B*
College Park *B*

Massachusetts
Amherst College *B*
Boston College *B, M*
Boston University *B*
Brandeis University *B*
College of the Holy Cross *B*
Harvard College *B*
Mount Holyoke College *B*
Northeastern University *B*
Smith College *B*
Tufts University *B*
University of Massachusetts
Boston *B*
Wellesley College *B*
Wheaton College *B*
Williams College *B*

Michigan
Michigan State University *B, M, D*
Oakland University *B, T*
University of Michigan *B, M, T*
Wayne State University *B*

Minnesota
Augsburg College *B*
Carleton College *B*
Concordia College: Moorhead *B, T*
Gustavus Adolphus College *B*
Macalester College *B*
St. Cloud State University *B*
St. Olaf College *B*
University of Minnesota
Twin Cities *B*
University of St. Thomas *B*

Missouri
St. Louis University *B*
Truman State University *B*
University of Missouri
Columbia *B, M*
Washington University in St. Louis *B*

Montana
University of Montana-Missoula *B*

Nebraska
University of Nebraska
Lincoln *B*

New Hampshire
Dartmouth College *B*
University of New Hampshire *B*

New Jersey
Drew University *B*
Montclair State University *T*
Rider University *B*

Rutgers, The State University of New
Jersey
New Brunswick Regional
Campus *B, T*
Seton Hall University *T*

New Mexico
University of New Mexico *B*

New York
Bard College *B*
Barnard College *B*
City University of New York
Brooklyn College *B*
Hunter College *B*
Queens College *B*
Colgate University *B*
Columbia University
Columbia College *B*
Cornell University *B, T*
Fordham University *B, M*
Hamilton College *B*
Hobart and William Smith Colleges *B*
Hofstra University *B*
New York University *B*
Sarah Lawrence College *B*
State University of New York
Albany *C, B, M*
Buffalo *B*
Stony Brook *B, T*
Syracuse University *B*
United States Military Academy *B*
University of Rochester *B*
Vassar College *B*

North Carolina
Duke University *B, M*
Wake Forest University *B*

Ohio
Bowling Green State University *B*
Kent State University *B, M*
Miami University
Oxford Campus *B, T*
Oberlin College *B*
Ohio State University
Columbus Campus *B*
Ohio University *B*

Oklahoma
Oklahoma State University *B*
Tulsa Community College *A*
University of Oklahoma *B*

Oregon
Portland State University *B, T*
Reed College *B*
University of Oregon *B, M*

Pennsylvania
Bryn Mawr College *B, M, D*
Bucknell University *B*
California University of Pennsylvania *B*
Dickinson College *B*
Haverford College *B, T*
Immaculata University *A*
Juniata College *B*
Lafayette College *B*
Lincoln University *B*
Penn State
Abington *B*
Altoona *B*
Beaver *B*
Berks *B*
Delaware County *B*
Dubois *B*
Fayette *B*
Hazleton *B*
Lehigh Valley *B*
McKeesport *B*
Mont Alto *B*
New Kensington *B*
Schuylkill - Capital College *B*
Shenango *B*
University Park *B, M*
Wilkes-Barre *B*
Worthington Scranton *B*
York *B*

Swarthmore College *B*
Temple University *B*
University of Pennsylvania *B, D*
University of Pittsburgh *B*
Washington and Jefferson College *T*
West Chester University of
Pennsylvania *B*

South Carolina
University of South Carolina *B*

Tennessee
Rhodes College *B*
University of Tennessee
Knoxville *B*
Vanderbilt University *B*

Texas
Austin Community College *A*
Baylor University *B*
Rice University *B*
Southern Methodist University *B*
Texas A&M University *B*
Trinity University *B*
University of Texas
Arlington *B*
Austin *B*

Utah
Brigham Young University *B, M*
University of Utah *B*

Vermont
Middlebury College *B, M, D*
Norwich University *M*
University of Vermont *B*

Virginia
Ferrum College *B*

Washington
Central Washington University *B*
Everett Community College *A*
Seattle Pacific University *B*
University of Washington *B, M, D*
Washington State University *B*

West Virginia
West Virginia University *T*

Wisconsin
Beloit College *B, T*
Lawrence University *B, T*
University of Wisconsin
Madison *B, M, D*
Milwaukee *B*

Wyoming
University of Wyoming *B*

Russian/Slavic studies

Alaska
University of Alaska
Fairbanks *B*

California
California State University
Fullerton *B*
San Diego State University *B*
Stanford University *M*
University of California
Los Angeles *B*
Riverside *B*
San Diego *B*
Santa Cruz *B*

Colorado
Colorado College *B*
University of Colorado
Boulder *B*
University of Denver *B*

Connecticut
Connecticut College *B*
Trinity College *B*
University of Connecticut *B*
Wesleyan University *B*
Yale University *B, M*

District of Columbia
American University *B*
Georgetown University *M*

Florida
Eckerd College *B*
Florida State University *B, M*
Stetson University *B*

Georgia
Emory University *B*
Oxford College of Emory University *B*

Illinois
Knox College *B*
University of Chicago *M*
University of Illinois
Urbana-Champaign *B, M*

Indiana
DePauw University *B*
Indiana University
Bloomington *M*

Iowa
Cornell College *B*
University of Iowa *B*
University of Northern Iowa *B*

Kansas
University of Kansas *B, M*

Kentucky
University of Louisville *B*

Louisiana
Louisiana State University and
Agricultural and Mechanical
College *B*
Tulane University *B*

Maine
Colby College *B*
University of Southern Maine *B*

Maryland
University of Maryland
College Park *B*

Massachusetts
Boston College *M*
Boston University *B*
Hampshire College *B*
Harvard College *B*
Mount Holyoke College *B*
Tufts University *B*
University of Massachusetts
Amherst *B*
Wellesley College *B*
Wheaton College *B*

Michigan
Grand Valley State University *B*
Oakland University *B*
University of Michigan *B, M*

Minnesota
Carleton College *B*
Concordia College: Moorhead *B*
Gustavus Adolphus College *B*
Hamline University *B*
Macalester College *B*
St. Cloud State University *B*
St. Olaf College *B*
University of Minnesota
Twin Cities *B, M*
University of St. Thomas *B*

Missouri
Washington University in St. Louis *B*

New Hampshire
Dartmouth College *B*

New Jersey
Drew University *B*
Rutgers, The State University of New
Jersey
New Brunswick Regional
Campus *B*

New Mexico
University of New Mexico *B*

New York
Bard College *B*
Barnard College *B*
City University of New York
Brooklyn College *B*
Hunter College *B*
Colgate University *B*
Columbia University
Columbia College *B*
Cornell University *B, M, D*
Fordham University *B*
Hamilton College *B*
Hobart and William Smith Colleges *B*
New York University *M*
Sarah Lawrence College *B*
State University of New York
Albany *B, M*
Syracuse University *B*
United States Military Academy *B*
University of Rochester *B*

North Carolina
University of North Carolina
Chapel Hill *B, M*

Ohio
Bowling Green State University *B*
College of Wooster *B*
Kent State University *B*
Mount Vernon Nazarene University *B*
Oberlin College *B*
Ohio State University
Columbus Campus *B, M*
University of Akron *C*
Wittenberg University *B*

Oklahoma
University of Oklahoma *B*

Oregon
Oregon State University *C*

Pennsylvania
California University of Pennsylvania *B*
Carnegie Mellon University *B*
Dickinson College *B*
La Salle University *B*
Lehigh University *B*
Muhlenberg College *B*
Penn State
University Park *C*
University of Pittsburgh *C*

Tennessee
Rhodes College *B*
University of Tennessee
Knoxville *B*

Texas
Baylor University *B*
Rice University *B*
Southern Methodist University *B*
Southwest Texas State University *B*
Texas Tech University *B*
University of Houston *B*
University of Texas
Austin *B, M*

Vermont
Marlboro College *B*
Middlebury College *B*
University of Vermont *B*

Virginia
College of William and Mary *B*
George Mason University *B*
Randolph-Macon Woman's College *B*
Washington and Lee University *B*

Washington
University of Washington *B, M*

Wisconsin
Lawrence University *B*

Sales/distribution

Alabama
Gadsden State Community College *A*
Wallace State Community College at
    Hanceville *A*

Arkansas
Harding University *B*

California
Chabot College *A*
Citrus College *C*
College of the Sequoias *C, A*
Columbia College *C*
Diablo Valley College *C*
Fashion Institute of Design and
    Merchandising *A*
Golden West College *C, A*
Grossmont Community College *C, A*
Laney College *C, A*
Las Positas College *A*
Long Beach City College *C, A*
Santa Barbara City College *C, A*
Shasta College *A*
Sierra College *C, A*

Colorado
Community College of Aurora *C, A*
Front Range Community College *C*

Connecticut
Central Connecticut State University *B*
Gateway Community College *A*
Middlesex Community College *C*
University of New Haven *A, B*

Florida
Indian River Community College *A*
Palm Beach Community College *A*
Tallahassee Community College *A*

Georgia
Athens Technical College *C, A*
Middle Georgia College *A*
Savannah Technical College *A*

Hawaii
Hawaii Business College *C, A*

Idaho
College of Southern Idaho *C*
Lewis-Clark State College *C*

Illinois
Black Hawk College *C, A*
City Colleges of Chicago
    Wright College *C, A*
College of DuPage *C, A*
Elgin Community College *C, A*
Illinois Eastern Community Colleges
    Wabash Valley College *C*
John Wood Community College *C, A*
Joliet Junior College *C*
Kishwaukee College *C*
Lincoln Land Community College *A*
Moraine Valley Community College *A*
Robert Morris College: Chicago *A*
Southwestern Illinois College *A*
Triton College *C*
University of Illinois
    Urbana-Champaign *B*
University of St. Francis *B*
Waubonsee Community College *C, A*
William Rainey Harper College *C, A*

Indiana
International Business College *C, A*
Vincennes University *A*

Iowa
Des Moines Area Community
    College *C, A*
Iowa Western Community College *A*
Kirkwood Community College *C, A*
Muscatine Community College *C*
North Iowa Area Community College *A*
Northwest Iowa Community College *A*

Kansas
Allen County Community College *A*
Hutchinson Community College *C, A*
Johnson County Community College *A*
Seward County Community
    College *C, A*

Kentucky
Henderson Community College *C*
Madisonville Community College *A*
Maysville Community College *A*

Maine
Beal College *A*
Husson College *B*

Maryland
Harford Community College *C, A*
Howard Community College *C, A*
Montgomery College
    Rockville Campus *A*

Massachusetts
Babson College *B*
Bay State College *A*
Fisher College *C, A*
Mount Ida College *B*
Newbury College *A*
Roxbury Community College *A*
Simmons College *B*

Michigan
Bay de Noc College *C, A*
Davenport University - Western
    Region *A*
Eastern Michigan University *B*
Ferris State University *C, A, B*
Lansing Community College *A*
Madonna University *C, B*

Minnesota
Alexandria Technical College *C, A*
Dakota County Technical College *C, A*
Lake Superior College: A Community
    and Technical College *A*
Minnesota State College - Southeast
    Technical *C, A*
North Hennepin Community College *A*
Rasmussen College
    Mankato *A*
Ridgewater College: A Community and
    Technical College *A*
Rochester Community and Technical
    College *C, A*
St. Cloud Technical College *C, A*
University of Minnesota
    Twin Cities *B*

Missouri
Longview Community College *A*
Maple Woods Community College *A*
Penn Valley Community College *A*

Montana
University of Montana-Missoula *C*

Nevada
Community College of Southern
    Nevada *A*

New Hampshire
Southern New Hampshire University *B*

New Jersey
Atlantic Cape Community College *C*
Bergen Community College *A*
Burlington County College *A*
Camden County College *A*
Cumberland County College *C*
Gloucester County College *C, A*
Mercer County Community College *C*
Ocean County College *C*
Passaic County Community College *A*
Raritan Valley Community College *C*
Thomas Edison State College *A, B*

New Mexico
Clovis Community College *A*

New York
Bryant & Stratton Business Institute
    Syracuse *A*
City University of New York
    Baruch College *B, M*
Dutchess Community College *A*
Finger Lakes Community College *C, A*
Genesee Community College *A*
Jefferson Community College *C, A*
Keuka College *B*
Monroe Community College *C, A*
Nassau Community College *A*
New York Institute of Technology *C*
Onondaga Community College *A*
Orange County Community College *A*
Suffolk County Community College *A*
Syracuse University *B*
Tompkins-Cortland Community
    College *A*
Utica School of Commerce *A*
Westchester Community College *A*

North Carolina
Alamance Community College *C, A*
Asheville Buncombe Technical
    Community College *A*
Blue Ridge Community College *A*
Craven Community College *A*
Pitt Community College *C, A*
Wake Technical Community College *C*
Wayne Community College *A*
Western Piedmont Community
    College *C, A*
Wilkes Community College *C, A*

North Dakota
Bismarck State College *C, A*
Lake Region State College *C, A*

Ohio
Bryant & Stratton College
    Cleveland West *A*
Columbus State Community College *A*
Cuyahoga Community College
    Eastern Campus *A*
Edison State Community College *C, A*
Miami University
    Oxford Campus *B*
Muskingum Area Technical College *A*
Sinclair Community College *A*
Stark State College of Technology *A*
University of Akron *A*
University of Northwestern Ohio *C*
University of Toledo *A*
Wilmington College *B*
Youngstown State University *A, B, M*

Oklahoma
East Central University *B*

Oregon
Clackamas Community College *C, A*
Lane Community College *C*
Southwestern Oregon Community
    College *C, A*
Umpqua Community College *C*

Pennsylvania
Bradford School: Pittsburgh *C, A*
Bucks County Community College *A*
Central Pennsylvania College *A*
Commonwealth Technical Institute *C*
Community College of Philadelphia *C, A*
Delaware County Community College *A*
Harrisburg Area Community
    College *C, A*
Marywood University *C*
Montgomery County Community
    College *C*
Philadelphia University *B*
Pittsburgh Technical Institute: Boyd
    School Division *A*
Westmoreland County Community
    College *A*

Puerto Rico
Columbia College *A*

University of Puerto Rico
    Mayaguez Campus *B*

Rhode Island
Community College of Rhode
    Island *C, A*

South Carolina
Aiken Technical College *A*
Florence-Darlington Technical
    College *C, A*
Midlands Technical College *A*
University of South Carolina *B*

Texas
Alvin Community College *C, A*
Lamar University *B*
Laredo Community College *A*
Tarleton State University *B*
Tarrant County College *C, A*
University of Houston *B*

Utah
Weber State University *A*

Virginia
Virginia Union University *B*

Washington
Centralia College *C*
Lake Washington Technical College *C*
Walla Walla Community College *C, A*

West Virginia
Wheeling Jesuit University *B*

Wisconsin
Mid-State Technical College *A*
Milwaukee Area Technical College *A*
Moraine Park Technical College *C, A*
University of Wisconsin
    Stout *B*
Western Wisconsin Technical College *A*
Wisconsin Indianhead Technical
    College *C, A*

Sales/marketing education

Arkansas
University of Central Arkansas *A*

California
San Diego Mesa College *C, A*
San Diego State University *B, T*

Colorado
Colorado State University *T*

Florida
Gulf Coast Community College *A*
Palm Beach Community College *A*

Georgia
University of Georgia *B, M*

Hawaii
University of Hawaii
    Manoa *B, T*

Idaho
University of Idaho *B*

Illinois
Sauk Valley Community College *A*

Indiana
Ball State University *B, M*
Vincennes University *A*

Kansas
Independence Community College *A*

Louisiana
Northwestern State University *B*

Michigan
Central Michigan University *B*
Eastern Michigan University *B, T*
Western Michigan University *B*

Minnesota

Northland Community & Technical
    College *A*
Ridgewater College: A Community and
    Technical College *C*
University of Minnesota
    Twin Cities *B, M*

Mississippi

Northwest Mississippi Community
    College *A*

Nebraska

University of Nebraska
    Lincoln *B, T*
York College *T*

New Hampshire

Southern New Hampshire University *B*

New Jersey

Rider University *B, T*

New Mexico

College of the Southwest *B, T*
Eastern New Mexico University *B*

New York

Nazareth College of Rochester *T*
New York Institute of Technology *B, T*
State University of New York
    College at Buffalo *B, M, T*

North Carolina

Appalachian State University *B, T*
East Carolina University *B*
Guilford Technical Community
    College *A*
North Carolina State University *M, T*
University of North Carolina
    Greensboro *B, M, T*

North Dakota

University of North Dakota *B, T*

Ohio

Bowling Green State University *B*
Kent State University *B, T*
Ohio State University
    Columbus Campus *M, D*

Oklahoma

University of Central Oklahoma *B*

Oregon

Oregon State University *M*

Pennsylvania

Delaware Valley College *T*
Temple University *B, T*

South Carolina

Forrest Junior College *A*

South Dakota

Dakota State University *B, T*

Tennessee

Middle Tennessee State University *B*
University of Tennessee
    Knoxville *B, T*

Texas

University of North Texas *M*

Utah

Utah State University *B, M*

Washington

Eastern Washington University *B, M, T*

Wisconsin

University of Wisconsin
    Stout *B, T*
    Whitewater *B, T*

Wyoming

Laramie County Community College *A*

Scandinavian languages

California

University of California
    Berkeley *B, M, D*
    Los Angeles *B, M*

Illinois

Augustana College *B*
North Park University *B*
University of Chicago *B*

Iowa

Luther College *B*
Waldorf College *A*

Massachusetts

Harvard College *B*

Minnesota

Augsburg College *B*
Concordia College: Moorhead *B*
Gustavus Adolphus College *B*
University of Minnesota
    Twin Cities *B*

Texas

University of Texas
    Austin *B*

Washington

Pacific Lutheran University *B*
University of Washington *B, M, D*

Wisconsin

University of Wisconsin
    Madison *B, M, D*

Scandinavian studies

Iowa

Luther College *B*

Massachusetts

Harvard College *B*

Michigan

University of Michigan *B*

Minnesota

Augsburg College *B*
Concordia College: Moorhead *B*
Gustavus Adolphus College *B*
Minnesota State University
    Mankato *B*
University of Minnesota
    Twin Cities *M, D*

Vermont

Marlboro College *B*

Washington

Pacific Lutheran University *B*
University of Washington *B*

Wisconsin

University of Wisconsin
    Madison *B, M, D*

School librarian education

New York

Long Island University
    C. W. Post Campus *M*
State University of New York
    Buffalo *M*
Syracuse University *M*

School psychology

Alabama

Auburn University *M, D*
University of Alabama *M, D*

Arizona

Northern Arizona University *M*

Arkansas

University of Central Arkansas *M, D*

California

California State University
    Chico *M, T*
    Hayward *T*
    Long Beach *M*
    Los Angeles *M*
National University *M*
San Diego State University *M*
San Francisco State University *M*
San Jose State University *M*
Stanford University *D*
University of California
    Los Angeles *M, D*

Colorado

University of Northern Colorado *D, T*

Connecticut

Fairfield University *M, T*
University of Hartford *M*

District of Columbia

Gallaudet University *M*
Howard University *M*

Florida

Barry University *M*
Carlos Albizu University *M*
Florida Agricultural and Mechanical
    University *M*
Florida International University *M*
Nova Southeastern University *M*
University of Central Florida *M*
University of Florida *M, D*
University of South Florida *M, D*
University of West Florida *M*

Georgia

Georgia Southern University *M, T*
Georgia State University *M, D*
University of Georgia *M, D*
Valdosta State University *B*

Idaho

Idaho State University *D*

Illinois

Eastern Illinois University *M*
Governors State University *M*
Illinois State University *M, D, T*
Lewis University *M*
Loyola University of Chicago *M, D*
National-Louis University *M, D*
Western Illinois University *M*

Indiana

Ball State University *M, D*
Indiana State University *M*
Valparaiso University *M*

Iowa

University of Iowa *D*
University of Northern Iowa *M*

Kansas

Emporia State University *M*
Pittsburg State University *M*
University of Kansas *D*
Wichita State University *M*

Louisiana

Nicholls State University *M*

Maine

University of Southern Maine *M*

Massachusetts

American International College *B, M*
Northeastern University *M, D*
University of Massachusetts
    Amherst *D*
    Boston *M*

Michigan

Central Michigan University *M, D*
Northern Michigan University *B, M*
Wayne State University *M*
Western Michigan University *D, T*

Minnesota

Capella University *M, D*
Minnesota State University
    Mankato *M*
    Moorhead *M*

Missouri

Lindenwood University *M*
University of Missouri
    Columbia *M, D*

Montana

University of Montana-Missoula *M*

Nebraska

University of Nebraska
    Kearney *M*
    Omaha *M*

Nevada

University of Nevada
    Las Vegas *M*

New Hampshire

Rivier College *M*

New Jersey

Fairleigh Dickinson University
    Metropolitan Campus *M, D*
Kean University *M*
New Jersey City University *M*
Rider University *M, T*
Rowan University *M*
Rutgers, The State University of New
    Jersey
    New Brunswick Regional
        Campus *D*
Seton Hall University *M*

New York

Alfred University *M, D*
City University of New York
    Brooklyn College *M*
    Queens College *M*
College of New Rochelle *M*
Hofstra University *M, D, T*
Marist College *M*
New York University *D*
Pace University *C, M*
Pace University:
    Pleasantville/Briarcliff *C, M*
Roberts Wesleyan College *M*
Rochester Institute of Technology *M*
St. John's University *M, D*
State University of New York
    Albany *D*
    Buffalo *M, T*
    College at Plattsburgh *M*
    Oswego *M*
Syracuse University *D*
Touro College *B*
Yeshiva University *D*

North Carolina

East Carolina University *M*
North Carolina State University *M*
University of North Carolina
    Chapel Hill *M, D*
Western Carolina University *M*

North Dakota

Minot State University *M*

Ohio

Bowling Green State University *M*
John Carroll University *M*
Kent State University *M, D*
Miami University
    Oxford Campus *M*
University of Akron *M*
University of Cincinnati *M, D*
University of Dayton *M*
University of Toledo *M*
Wright State University *M*

Oklahoma

Northeastern State University *M*

Pennsylvania

Bucknell University *M*

Duquesne University *M, D*
Edinboro University of Pennsylvania *M*
Immaculata University *M*
Indiana University of Pennsylvania *D*
Lehigh University *M, D*
Millersville University of
　Pennsylvania *M*
Penn State
　University Park *M, D*
Temple University *M, D*

Puerto Rico

Inter American University of Puerto Rico
　Metropolitan Campus *M, D*
　San German Campus *M, D*

Rhode Island

Rhode Island College *M*
University of Rhode Island *M, D*

South Carolina

The Citadel *M*
Francis Marion University *M*
University of South Carolina *M, D*
Winthrop University *M, T*

South Dakota

University of South Dakota *D*

Tennessee

Southern Adventist University *M*
University of Memphis *M*

Texas

Abilene Christian University *M*
Houston Baptist University *M*
Our Lady of the Lake University of San
　Antonio *M*
Sam Houston State University *M*
Southwest Texas State University *M*
Stephen F. Austin State University *M*
Tarleton State University *B, M*
Texas A&M University *D*
Texas A&M University
　Texarkana *M*
Texas Woman's University *M, D*
Trinity University *M*
University of Houston
　Clear Lake *M*
University of Mary Hardin-Baylor *M*
University of North Texas *M*
University of Texas
　Tyler *M*

Virginia

College of William and Mary *M*
James Madison University *M, T*
Radford University *M*
Virginia Union University *B*

Washington

Central Washington University *M, T*
Eastern Washington University *M*
Seattle University *M*

Wisconsin

Marquette University *M, D*
University of Wisconsin
　La Crosse *M*
　Madison *M, D*
　River Falls *M*
　Stout *M*
　Superior *D*
　Whitewater *M*

Science teacher education

Alabama

Alabama State University *B*
Athens State University *B*
Auburn University *B*
Birmingham-Southern College *T*
Faulkner University *B*
Huntingdon College *T*
Jacksonville State University *B, M, T*
Judson College *B*
Miles College *B*

Oakwood College *B*
Samford University *B*
Talladega College *T*
Troy State University Dothan *B, M*
Tuskegee University *B, M*
University of Mobile *T*

Alaska

University of Alaska
　Fairbanks *M*

Arizona

Northern Arizona University *M*
Prescott College *B, M*
University of Arizona *B, M*

Arkansas

Arkansas Tech University *B*
Harding University *B, T*
Philander Smith College *B*
Southern Arkansas University *B, T*
University of Arkansas *B*
University of Arkansas
　Pine Bluff *B, M, T*
University of Central Arkansas *B, M, T*
University of the Ozarks *B, T*

California

Azusa Pacific University *T*
California State Polytechnic University:
　Pomona *T*
California State University
　Bakersfield *B, T*
　Chico *T*
　Dominguez Hills *T*
　Fullerton *M, T*
　Long Beach *T*
Concordia University *B*
Fresno Pacific University *M, T*
Humboldt State University *T*
Master's College *T*
Mills College *T*
Mount St. Mary's College *T*
San Diego State University *B, T*
San Francisco State University *B, T*
San Jose State University *T*
Sonoma State University *T*
University of California
　Berkeley *D*
University of Southern California *T*
University of the Pacific *T*

Colorado

Colorado State University *T*
Colorado State University
　Pueblo *T*
Fort Lewis College *T*
Metropolitan State College of Denver *T*
Regis University *B, T*
University of Colorado
　Boulder *T*
　Colorado Springs *T*

Connecticut

Central Connecticut State University *T*
Eastern Connecticut State University *M*
Fairfield University *T*
Quinnipiac University *B, M*
Sacred Heart University *T*
St. Joseph College *T*
Southern Connecticut State
　University *B, T*

Delaware

Delaware State University *B, M*
University of Delaware *B, T*

District of Columbia

George Washington University *M, T*

Florida

Broward Community College *A*
Florida Agricultural and Mechanical
　University *B, M, T*
Florida Atlantic University *B*
Florida Institute of
　Technology *B, M, D, T*
Florida International University *B, M, T*
Florida State University *B, M, D, T*

Gulf Coast Community College *A*
Nova Southeastern University *M*
Palm Beach Community College *A*
St. Petersburg College *B*
Southeastern College of the Assemblies
　of God *B, T*
University of Central Florida *B, M*
University of Florida *M*
University of North Florida *B, M*
University of South Florida *B, M*
Warner Southern College *B*

Georgia

Albany State University *B, M*
Armstrong Atlantic State
　University *B, M, T*
Clark Atlanta University *M*
Columbus State University *B, M*
Covenant College *B, T*
Gainesville College *A*
Georgia Southern University *M, T*
Georgia Southwestern State
　University *B, M*
Georgia State University *M, D*
Kennesaw State University *B*
LaGrange College *T*
Mercer University *M, T*
North Georgia College & State
　University *B, M*
Piedmont College *M, T*
State University of West Georgia *M*
University of Georgia *B, M, D, T*
Valdosta State University *M, T*
Wesleyan College *M*

Hawaii

Brigham Young University-Hawaii *B, T*
University of Hawaii
　Manoa *B, T*

Idaho

Boise State University *T*
Brigham Young University - Idaho *T*
Lewis-Clark State College *B, T*
Northwest Nazarene University *B*

Illinois

Augustana College *B, T*
Blackburn College *B, T*
Chicago State University *T*
Concordia University *B, T*
Eastern Illinois University *M*
Eureka College *T*
Greenville College *T*
Judson College *B, T*
Lewis University *T*
Monmouth College *B, T*
National-Louis University *M*
North Park University *T*
Northwestern University *B, T*
Olivet Nazarene University *B, T*
Sauk Valley Community College *A*
Southern Illinois University
　Edwardsville *B, T*
Trinity Christian College *B, T*
University of Illinois
　Urbana-Champaign *M, T*
University of St. Francis *T*

Indiana

Anderson University *B, T*
Ball State University *B, D, T*
Bethel College *B*
Butler University *T*
Calumet College of St. Joseph *B*
Goshen College *B*
Grace College *B*
Indiana State University *B, M, T*
Indiana University
　Bloomington *B, D, T*
　Kokomo *T*
　South Bend *B, T*
　Southeast *B*
Indiana University-Purdue University
　Fort Wayne *B*
Indiana Wesleyan University *B, T*
Manchester College *B, T*

Oakland City University *B*
Purdue University
　Calumet *B*
Saint Mary's College *T*
St. Mary-of-the-Woods College *B*
Taylor University *B, T*
Tri-State University *B, T*
University of Evansville *B*
University of Indianapolis *B, T*
University of Notre Dame *B*
University of St. Francis *B*
University of Southern Indiana *T*
Valparaiso University *B*
Vincennes University *A*

Iowa

Buena Vista University *T*
Central College *T*
Clarke College *B, T*
Cornell College *B, T*
Dordt College *B*
Drake University *M, T*
Ellsworth Community College *A*
Franciscan University *B, T*
Graceland University *T*
Grand View College *B, T*
Iowa State University *T*
Loras College *T*
Luther College *B*
Morningside College *B*
Mount Mercy College *T*
Northwestern College *T*
St. Ambrose University *B, T*
University of Iowa *B, M, D, T*
University of Northern Iowa *B, M*
Upper Iowa University *B*
Wartburg College *T*
William Penn University *B*

Kansas

Benedictine College *B, T*
Bethany College *T*
Bethel College *T*
Emporia State University *T*
Fort Scott Community College *A*
Friends University *B*
Garden City Community College *A*
Independence Community College *A*
Kansas Wesleyan University *T*
McPherson College *B, T*
MidAmerica Nazarene University *B, T*
Newman University *T*
Pittsburg State University *B, T*
Southwestern College *B, T*
Tabor College *B, T*
University of Kansas *B, T*
Washburn University of Topeka *B*

Kentucky

Campbellsville University *B*
Kentucky Wesleyan College *T*
Murray State University *B, M, T*
Spalding University *B*
Thomas More College *B*
Union College *B, M*
University of Kentucky *B*

Louisiana

Centenary College of Louisiana *B, T*
Grambling State University *M*
Louisiana College *B*
Louisiana State University
　Shreveport *B*
Nicholls State University *B*
Northwestern State University *B*
Our Lady of Holy Cross College *T*
Southeastern Louisiana University *B*
University of Louisiana at Monroe *B*
University of New Orleans *B, M*
Xavier University of Louisiana *B, T*

Maine

St. Joseph's College *B*
University of Maine *B, M*
University of Maine
　Farmington *B, T*
　Presque Isle *B*

University of New England *B, T*
University of Southern Maine *T*

Maryland

Bowie State University *B, T*
College of Notre Dame of Maryland *T*
Columbia Union College *B*
Johns Hopkins University *M*
Montgomery College
    Rockville Campus *A*
Morgan State University *D*
Towson University *T*
University of Maryland
    College Park *B*

Massachusetts

American International College *T*
Assumption College *T*
Boston University *B, M, T*
Bridgewater State College *M, T*
Fitchburg State College *M*
Framingham State College *T*
Lesley University *B, M*
Merrimack College *T*
Smith College *M*
Tufts University *M, T*
University of Massachusetts
    Lowell *D*
Westfield State College *B, M, T*

Michigan

Andrews University *M, T*
Aquinas College *B, T*
Calvin College *T*
Central Michigan University *B*
Concordia University *B, T*
Cornerstone University *B, T*
Eastern Michigan University *B, T*
Ferris State University *B*
Grand Valley State University *B, T*
Hope College *T*
Lansing Community College *A*
Lawrence Technological University *M*
Michigan Technological University *M, T*
Northern Michigan University *B, T*
Saginaw Valley State University *B, M*
University of Michigan *M*
University of Michigan
    Dearborn *B*
    Flint *T*
Wayne State University *B, M, T*
Western Michigan University *B, M, D*

Minnesota

Augsburg College *T*
Bemidji State University *T*
Bethel College *B*
College of St. Benedict *T*
College of St. Catherine *T*
College of St. Scholastica *T*
Concordia College: Moorhead *B, T*
Concordia University: St. Paul *B, T*
Gustavus Adolphus College *T*
Hamline University *B*
Minnesota State University
    Mankato *B, M, T*
    Moorhead *B, T*
Northland Community & Technical
    College *A*
Ridgewater College: A Community and
    Technical College *A*
St. Cloud State University *T*
St. John's University *T*
St. Mary's University of Minnesota *B*
St. Olaf College *T*
Southwest State University *B, T*
University of Minnesota
    Duluth *B*
    Morris *T*
    Twin Cities *M, T*
University of St. Thomas *B, T*
Vermilion Community College *A*
Winona State University *B, M, T*

Mississippi

Blue Mountain College *B*
Coahoma Community College *A*

Delta State University *T*
Itawamba Community College *A*
Mississippi College *B, M*
Mississippi Gulf Coast Community
    College
      Perkinston *A*
Mississippi State University *T*
Northwest Mississippi Community
    College *A*
University of Mississippi *B, T*
University of Southern Mississippi *M, D*

Missouri

Avila University *B, T*
Central Methodist College *B*
Central Missouri State University *B, T*
College of the Ozarks *B, T*
Culver-Stockton College *T*
Evangel University *B*
Hannibal-LaGrange College *B*
Harris Stowe State College *T*
Lincoln University *B, T*
Lindenwood University *M*
Missouri Baptist University *B, T*
Missouri Southern State College *B, T*
Missouri Valley College *T*
Northwest Missouri State University *T*
Rockhurst University *B*
Southeast Missouri State
    University *B, M, T*
Southwest Baptist University *T*
Southwest Missouri State University *B*
Truman State University *M, T*
University of Missouri
    Columbia *B, M, D*
Washington University in St.
    Louis *B, M, T*
Webster University *M*
William Jewell College *T*
William Woods University *B*

Montana

Montana State University
    Billings *B, T*
    Bozeman *M*
Montana Tech of the University of
    Montana *T*
Rocky Mountain College *B, T*
University of Great Falls *B*
University of Montana-Missoula *T*
University of Montana: Western *B, T*

Nebraska

Chadron State College *B, M*
College of Saint Mary *B, T*
Concordia University *B, T*
Dana College *B*
Doane College *B, T*
Hastings College *B, M, T*
Midland Lutheran College *B, T*
Nebraska Wesleyan University *B*
Peru State College *B, T*
University of Nebraska
    Kearney *B, M, T*
    Lincoln *B, T*
Wayne State College *B, M*

Nevada

University of Nevada
    Reno *B*

New Hampshire

Franklin Pierce College *T*
Keene State College *B, T*
New England College *B*
Plymouth State College *B, T*
Rivier College *B, T*
St. Anselm College *T*
University of New Hampshire *B, T*

New Jersey

Caldwell College *T*
Centenary College *T*
The College of New Jersey *M, T*
College of St. Elizabeth *T*
Monmouth University *B, T*
Ramapo College of New Jersey *M*

Richard Stockton College of New
    Jersey *B*
Rider University *B, T*
Rowan University *M, T*
Rutgers, The State University of New
    Jersey
      New Brunswick Regional
        Campus *T*
      Newark Regional Campus *T*
St. Peter's College *T*
William Paterson University of New
    Jersey *T*

New Mexico

College of Santa Fe *B*
College of the Southwest *B, T*
New Mexico Highlands University *B*
New Mexico Institute of Mining and
    Technology *M*
Western New Mexico University *B*

New York

Adelphi University *M*
Canisius College *B, M, T*
City University of New York
    Brooklyn College *B, M*
    City College *B, T*
    College of Staten Island *M*
    Queens College *M, T*
College of Mount St. Vincent *T*
College of New Rochelle *T*
Concordia College *T*
D'Youville College *M, T*
Dominican College of Blauvelt *B, T*
Dowling College *B*
Elmira College *T*
Fordham University *M, T*
Hofstra University *M, T*
Ithaca College *B, T*
Le Moyne College *T*
Long Island University
    C. W. Post Campus *B, T*
Manhattan College *B, T*
Manhattanville College *M, T*
Marist College *B*
Marymount College of Fordham
    University *B, T*
Mercy College *T*
Mount St. Mary College *B*
Nazareth College of Rochester *T*
New York Institute of Technology *B, T*
Pace University *B, M, T*
Pace University:
    Pleasantville/Briarcliff *B, M, T*
Rensselaer Polytechnic Institute *B, T*
Roberts Wesleyan College *B, T*
St. Bonaventure University *T*
St. John Fisher College *B, T*
St. John's University *B, T*
St. Joseph's College *B, T*
St. Joseph's College: Suffolk
    Campus *B, T*
St. Lawrence University *T*
State University of New York
    Albany *B, M, T*
    Buffalo *M, D, T*
    College at Brockport *M, T*
    College at Buffalo *B, M*
    College at Cortland *B, M, T*
    College at Geneseo *B, M, T*
    College at Oneonta *B, T*
    College at Plattsburgh *M*
    College at Potsdam *B, M, T*
    College of Environmental Science
      and Forestry *B, T*
    New Paltz *B, M, T*
    Oswego *B, M*
Syracuse University *B, M, D, T*
Tompkins-Cortland Community
    College *A*
Utica College *B*
Vassar College *T*
Wagner College *T*
Wells College *T*

North Carolina

Appalachian State University *B, T*
Belmont Abbey College *T*
Bennett College *B, T*
Catawba College *T*
East Carolina University *B, M*
Elizabeth City State University *B*
Elon University *B*
Forsyth Technical Community College *A*
Gardner-Webb University *B*
Lenoir-Rhyne College *B, T*
Livingstone College *T*
Louisburg College *A*
Mars Hill College *T*
Meredith College *T*
Montreat College *T*
North Carolina Central University *B, M*
North Carolina State University *M, D, T*
Sandhills Community College *A*
University of North Carolina
    Greensboro *M, T*
    Pembroke *B, M, T*
Wake Forest University *M, T*
Western Carolina University *B*

North Dakota

Dickinson State University *B, T*
Jamestown College *B*
Mayville State University *B, T*
Minot State University *B, M*
North Dakota State University *B, T*
University of North Dakota *B, T*
Valley City State University *B, T*

Ohio

Ashland University *B, T*
Baldwin-Wallace College *T*
Bluffton College *B*
Bowling Green State University *B, M*
Cedarville University *B, T*
Central State University *B*
College of Mount St. Joseph *T*
Defiance College *B, T*
Hiram College *T*
Kent State University *B, T*
Kent State University
    Stark Campus *B*
Malone College *B*
Miami University
    Oxford Campus *B, T*
Mount Union College *T*
Mount Vernon Nazarene University *B, T*
Ohio Dominican College *B, T*
Ohio Northern University *B, T*
Ohio State University
    Columbus Campus *M, D*
Ohio University *B, T*
Otterbein College *B*
Shawnee State University *B*
University of Akron *B, T*
University of Dayton *B, M, T*
University of Findlay *B, T*
University of Rio Grande *B, T*
University of Toledo *B, T*
Urbana University *B*
Ursuline College *B, T*
Walsh University *B*
Wilmington College *B*
Wittenberg University *B*
Wright State University *B, M, T*
Xavier University *B*
Youngstown State University *B, M*

Oklahoma

Cameron University *B, T*
East Central University *B*
Eastern Oklahoma State College *A*
Northeastern State University *B*
Northwestern Oklahoma State
    University *B, T*
Oklahoma Baptist University *B, T*
Oklahoma Christian University of
    Science and Arts *B, T*
Oklahoma City University *B*
Oklahoma State University *B, T*
Oklahoma Wesleyan University *B*

Oral Roberts University *B, T*
Southeastern Oklahoma State
    University *B, M, T*
Southern Nazarene University *B*
Southwestern Oklahoma State
    University *B, M, T*
University of Central Oklahoma *B*
University of Oklahoma *B, D, T*
University of Tulsa *T*

Oregon
Concordia University *B, M, T*
Eastern Oregon University *B*
Linfield College *T*
Oregon State University *M, D*
University of Portland *T*
Western Baptist College *B*
Western Oregon University *T*

Pennsylvania
Albright College *T*
Arcadia University *B, M, T*
Bloomsburg University of
    Pennsylvania *B, T*
California University of
    Pennsylvania *B, T*
Carlow College *T*
Cedar Crest College *B, T*
Cheyney University of Pennsylvania *T*
DeSales University *M, T*
Delaware Valley College *T*
Dickinson College *T*
Duquesne University *B, T*
East Stroudsburg University of
    Pennsylvania *B, M, T*
Elizabethtown College *T*
Gettysburg College *T*
Grove City College *T*
Holy Family University *B, T*
Immaculata University *T*
Indiana University of Pennsylvania *B, T*
Juniata College *B, T*
La Roche College *B*
La Salle University *B, T*
Lebanon Valley College of
    Pennsylvania *M*
Lincoln University *B, T*
Lock Haven University of
    Pennsylvania *B, T*
Lycoming College *T*
Marywood University *B*
Mercyhurst College *B*
Millersville University of
    Pennsylvania *B, T*
St. Joseph's University *B*
St. Vincent College *T*
Slippery Rock University of
    Pennsylvania *M*
Temple University *B, M, T*
Thiel College *B*
University of Pennsylvania *M*
University of Pittsburgh *T*
University of Pittsburgh
    Johnstown *B, T*
University of Scranton *T*
University of the Sciences in
    Philadelphia *T*
Villanova University *T*
Waynesburg College *B, T*
West Chester University of
    Pennsylvania *B, M, T*
Widener University *B, T*
Wilkes University *T*
York College of Pennsylvania *B, T*

Puerto Rico
Bayamon Central University *B*
Inter American University of Puerto Rico
    Metropolitan Campus *B, M*
    San German Campus *M*
Pontifical Catholic University of Puerto
    Rico *B, T*
Turabo University *B*
Universidad Metropolitana *B*
Universidad del Este *B*

University of Puerto Rico
    Cayey University College *T*

Rhode Island
Rhode Island College *B, M, T*

South Carolina
Anderson College *B, T*
Charleston Southern University *B, M*
Clemson University *B*
Converse College *T*
Furman University *T*
Lander University *M*
University of South Carolina
    Aiken *B, T*

South Dakota
Black Hills State University *B, T*
Dakota State University *B, T*
Dakota Wesleyan University *B, T*
Mount Marty College *B*
Northern State University *B, T*
University of South Dakota *B, T*

Tennessee
Belmont University *T*
Bethel College *B*
Freed-Hardeman University *B, T*
King College *T*
Lee University *B*
Tennessee Technological University *T*
Tennessee Wesleyan College *B, T*
Tusculum College *B, T*
Union University *B, T*
University of Tennessee
    Chattanooga *B, T*
    Knoxville *T*
    Martin *B, T*
Vanderbilt University *M, D*

Texas
Abilene Christian University *B, T*
Baylor University *B, T*
Dallas Baptist University *B, T*
Del Mar College *A*
East Texas Baptist University *B*
Hardin-Simmons University *B, T*
Howard Payne University *B, T*
Lamar University *T*
LeTourneau University *B*
Lubbock Christian University *B, T*
McMurry University *T*
Prairie View A&M University *M*
Stephen F. Austin State University *T*
Tarleton State University *B, T*
Texas A&M University
    Commerce *T*
    Kingsville *T*
Texas Christian University *B, T*
Texas Tech University *M*
Texas Woman's University *M*
University of Houston *M, T*
University of Houston
    Clear Lake *T*
University of Mary Hardin-Baylor *T*
University of Texas
    Arlington *T*
    Austin *M, D*
    San Antonio *T*
University of the Incarnate Word *D*
West Texas A&M University *T*

Utah
Brigham Young University *B, M*
Southern Utah University *B*
University of Utah *B, M*
Utah State University *B*
Utah Valley State College *B*
Weber State University *B*

Vermont
Bennington College *B, M, T*
Castleton State College *B, T*
Johnson State College *B*
Lyndon State College *B*
St. Michael's College *T*
University of Vermont *B*

Virginia
Averett University *M*
Bluefield College *B*
Eastern Shore Community College *A*
Liberty University *B*
Longwood University *B, T*
Radford University *T*
University of Virginia's College at
    Wise *T*
Virginia Wesleyan College *T*

Washington
Central Washington University *B, T*
Eastern Washington University *M*
Pacific Lutheran University *T*
Seattle Pacific University *B, T*
University of Washington *B*
Washington State University *T*
Western Washington University *B, M, T*
Whitworth College *B, T*

West Virginia
Alderson-Broaddus College *T*
Concord College *B, T*
Fairmont State College *B*
Ohio Valley College *B*
Salem International University *T*
Shepherd College *T*
University of Charleston *B*
West Liberty State College *B*
West Virginia State College *B*
West Virginia University *T*
Wheeling Jesuit University *M*

Wisconsin
Alverno College *T*
Beloit College *B*
Carroll College *T*
Carthage College *M, T*
Concordia University Wisconsin *B, T*
Edgewood College *B*
Lawrence University *T*
Maranatha Baptist Bible College *B*
Northland College *T*
Ripon College *T*
St. Norbert College *T*
Silver Lake College *T*
University of Wisconsin
    Eau Claire *B*
    Green Bay *T*
    La Crosse *B, T*
    Madison *B, T*
    Milwaukee *M*
    Oshkosh *B*
    Parkside *T*
    Platteville *B, T*
    River Falls *T*
    Superior *B, T*
    Whitewater *B, T*
Viterbo University *B, T*

Wyoming
Western Wyoming Community
    College *A*

Science technologies

Alabama
Athens State University *B*
Bishop State Community College *A*
Community College of the Air Force *A*
Snead State Community College *C*

Alaska
University of Alaska
    Fairbanks *A*
    Southeast *A*

Arizona
Arizona Western College *C, A*

Arkansas
Pulaski Technical College *A*

California
Bakersfield College *A*
Barstow College *A*

Cabrillo College *A*
Chabot College *A*
College of Alameda *A*
Grossmont Community College *C, A*
Los Angeles Harbor College *A*
Los Angeles Trade and Technical
    College *C, A*
Mount San Antonio College *A*
San Joaquin Delta College *A*
Victor Valley College *A*

Colorado
Red Rocks Community College *C, A*

Georgia
Abraham Baldwin Agricultural
    College *A*
Atlanta Metropolitan College *A*

Illinois
Black Hawk College
    East Campus *A*
Lake Land College *A*
Lincoln Land Community College *A*

Indiana
Butler University *B*

Kansas
Central Christian College *A*
Fort Scott Community College *A*
Johnson County Community College *A*

Louisiana
Southern University
    Shreveport *A*

Maryland
Chesapeake College *A*
College of Southern Maryland *A*
Harford Community College *A*

Massachusetts
Mount Wachusett Community College *A*

Michigan
Madonna University *A, B*
Mott Community College *C*
Oakland Community College *C, A*

Minnesota
North Hennepin Community College *A*

Missouri
St. Louis Community College
    St. Louis Community College at
        Forest Park *A*

Montana
Montana State University
    Billings College of Technology *A*

Nebraska
Central Community College *C, A*

New Mexico
New Mexico State University
    Alamogordo *A*

New York
Cornell University *M, D*
Corning Community College *A*
Jefferson Community College *A*
Niagara County Community College *A*
Rensselaer Polytechnic Institute *M, D*
Rochester Institute of
    Technology *B, M, D*
Rockland Community College *A*
State University of New York
    Institute of Technology at
        Utica/Rome *M*
Suffolk County Community College *A*

North Carolina
Alamance Community College *A*
Catawba College *B*
Isothermal Community College *A*

Ohio
Lorain County Community College *A*

Miami University
  Middletown Campus A
  Oxford Campus A
Ohio State University
  Agricultural Technical Institute A
Wittenberg University B

Oklahoma
Tulsa Community College A

Oregon
Chemeketa Community College A

Pennsylvania
Carlow College B
Community College of Allegheny
  County A
Delaware County Community
  College C, A
Lehigh University B
Reading Area Community College A

South Carolina
Clemson University B, M

Tennessee
Belmont University B
Volunteer State Community College A

Texas
Cisco Junior College A
College of the Mainland A
Hill College A
North Central Texas College A
Texas State Technical College
  Waco C, A
University of Mary Hardin-Baylor B

Virginia
Virginia Western Community College A

West Virginia
Ohio Valley College A

Wisconsin
University of Wisconsin
  Stout B

Science/technology/society

Alabama
Samford University A, B

California
Pitzer College B
Pomona College B
Scripps College B
Stanford University B
University of California
  Davis B

Connecticut
Wesleyan University B

District of Columbia
George Washington University M
Georgetown University B, M

Georgia
Georgia Institute of Technology B

Indiana
Butler University B
Indiana University
  Bloomington C, B, M
Indiana University-Purdue University
  Indianapolis A, B, M

Kentucky
Hazard Community College A

Maryland
Johns Hopkins University B

Massachusetts
Clark University B
Hampshire College B
Harvard College B

Massachusetts Institute of
  Technology B, D
Wellesley College B
Worcester Polytechnic Institute B

Michigan
Eastern Michigan University M
Michigan State University M

Minnesota
University of Minnesota
  Twin Cities M

Missouri
Washington University in St.
  Louis B, M, D

Montana
Montana Tech of the University of
  Montana B

Nevada
University of Nevada
  Reno B

New Jersey
New Jersey Institute of Technology B
Rutgers, The State University of New
  Jersey
    Newark Regional Campus B
Stevens Institute of Technology B

New York
Cornell University B
Eugene Lang College/New School
  University B
Rensselaer Polytechnic Institute B, M, D
Sarah Lawrence College B
State University of New York
  Buffalo M
Vassar College B

North Carolina
North Carolina State University M

Pennsylvania
Lehigh University B
Penn State
  University Park C
Slippery Rock University of
  Pennsylvania B

Vermont
Bennington College B

Virginia
James Madison University B, M
University of Virginia M

West Virginia
West Virginia University M, D

Sculpture

Alabama
Birmingham-Southern College B

Arizona
Arizona State University B, M

California
Academy of Art College C, A, B, M
Biola University B
California College of Arts and
  Crafts B, M
California State University
  Fullerton B, M
  Hayward B
  Long Beach B, M
  Northridge B, M
  Stanislaus B
Chabot College A
De Anza College C, A
Grossmont Community College A
Long Beach City College A
Monterey Peninsula College A
Ohlone College C
Otis College of Art and Design B, M
Palomar College A

San Diego State University B
Santa Rosa Junior College C

Colorado
Colorado State University B
Rocky Mountain College of Art &
  Design B

Connecticut
University of Hartford B, M

District of Columbia
American University M
George Washington University M

Florida
University of Miami B

Georgia
Atlanta College of Art B
LaGrange College B
University of Georgia B

Idaho
Northwest Nazarene University B

Illinois
Lincoln College A
Richland Community College A
Rockford College B
School of the Art Institute of
  Chicago B, M
University of Illinois
  Urbana-Champaign B

Indiana
Indiana University-Purdue University
  Fort Wayne B
University of Evansville B
Vincennes University A

Iowa
Drake University B
University of Iowa B, M

Kansas
University of Kansas B, M

Louisiana
Centenary College of Louisiana B

Maine
Maine College of Art B
University of Southern Maine B

Maryland
Maryland College of Art and Design A
Maryland Institute College of Art B, M

Massachusetts
Art Institute of Boston at Lesley
  University A, B
Boston University B, M
Hampshire College B
Massachusetts College of Art B, M
Montserrat College of Art B
School of the Museum of Fine Arts B, M
Simon's Rock College of Bard B
University of Massachusetts
  Dartmouth B, M

Michigan
Aquinas College B
College for Creative Studies B
Ferris State University B
Grand Valley State University B
Northern Michigan University B
Siena Heights University B
University of Michigan B

Minnesota
College of Visual Arts B
Minnesota State University
  Mankato B
  Moorhead B

Mississippi
Mississippi Gulf Coast Community
  College
    Perkinston A

Missouri
Kansas City Art Institute B
Lindenwood University M
Washington University in St. Louis B, M

New Jersey
Rowan University B

New Mexico
College of Santa Fe B

New York
Alfred University B
Bard College B, M
City University of New York
  Brooklyn College M
Parsons School of Design C, A, B, M, T
Pratt Institute B, M
Rochester Institute of
  Technology A, B, M
Sarah Lawrence College B
School of Visual Arts B, M
State University of New York
  Albany B, M
  Buffalo M
  College at Buffalo B
  College at Fredonia B
  College at Potsdam B
  New Paltz B, M
  Purchase B, M
Syracuse University B, M

Ohio
Art Academy of Cincinnati B
Bowling Green State University B
Cleveland Institute of Art B
Columbus College of Art and Design B
Ohio State University
  Columbus Campus B
Ohio University B, M
University of Akron B
University of Findlay B
Wittenberg University B

Oklahoma
University of Oklahoma B

Oregon
Pacific Northwest College of Art B
Portland State University B, M
University of Oregon B, M

Pennsylvania
Immaculata University A
Keystone College A
Marywood University C, M
Mercyhurst College B
Seton Hill University B
Temple University B, M

Puerto Rico
Escuela de Artes Plasticas de Puerto
  Rico B
Inter American University of Puerto Rico
  San German Campus B, M
University of Puerto Rico
  Rio Piedras Campus B

Rhode Island
Providence College B
Rhode Island College B
Rhode Island School of Design B, M

Tennessee
Memphis College of Art B, M
Tennessee Technological University B
Union University B
University of Tennessee
  Knoxville M

Texas
Sam Houston State University M
Stephen F. Austin State University M
Texas A&M University
  Commerce B, M
Texas Woman's University B, M
University of Dallas M, T
University of Houston B, M
University of North Texas B, M

University of Texas
Arlington *B*
El Paso *B*
San Antonio *B, M*
Western Texas College *A*

Utah

Brigham Young University *B, M*
Dixie State College of Utah *A*

Vermont

Bennington College *B, M*
Marlboro College *B*

Virginia

Virginia Commonwealth University *B*

Washington

Cornish College of the Arts *B*
Pacific Lutheran University *B*
University of Washington *B, M*
Western Washington University *B*

West Virginia

West Virginia State College *B*

Wisconsin

Milwaukee Institute of Art & Design *B*
University of Wisconsin
Madison *B*

Secondary education

Alabama

Alabama Agricultural and Mechanical
University *B, M*
Alabama State University *B, M, T*
Athens State University *B*
Auburn University *M, D, T*
Auburn University at Montgomery *B, M*
Birmingham-Southern College *T*
Calhoun Community College *A*
Chattahoochee Valley Community
College *A*
Faulkner University *B, T*
Huntingdon College *T*
Jacksonville State University *B, M, T*
Judson College *B*
Miles College *B*
Northeast Alabama Community
College *A*
Northwest-Shoals Community College *A*
Shelton State Community College *A*
Spring Hill College *B, M*
Troy State University *B, M, T*
Troy State University Dothan *B, M, T*
University of Alabama *B, M, D*
University of Alabama
Birmingham *B, M*
University of Montevallo *M, T*
University of North Alabama *B, M*
University of South Alabama *B, M, T*
University of West Alabama *B, M*

Alaska

Sheldon Jackson College *B*
University of Alaska
Anchorage *T*
Fairbanks *M, T*
Southeast *M, T*

Arizona

Arizona State University *B, D*
Arizona Western College *A*
Eastern Arizona College *A*
Estrella Mountain Community College *A*
Northern Arizona University *M, T*
Prescott College *B, M*
Southwestern College *B, T*
University of Arizona *B, M*
University of Phoenix *M*

Arkansas

Harding University *B, M, T*
Hendrix College *T*
John Brown University *B*
Ouachita Baptist University *B, T*

Philander Smith College *B*
South Arkansas Community College *A*
Southern Arkansas University *B, M, T*
University of Arkansas *M, D*
University of Arkansas
Little Rock *M*
Monticello *B, M*
University of Central Arkansas *T*
University of the Ozarks *B, T*
Williams Baptist College *B*

California

Azusa Pacific University *B, T*
Biola University *B, T*
California Baptist University *T*
California State Polytechnic University:
Pomona *T*
California State University
Bakersfield *B, M*
Dominguez Hills *M*
Fullerton *T*
Hayward *T*
Long Beach *M, T*
Los Angeles *M*
Northridge *M*
Sacramento *B, M, T*
San Marcos *T*
Stanislaus *M*
Chapman University *T*
Christian Heritage College *B, T*
Concordia University *B, T*
Dominican University of California *T*
Holy Names College *T*
Hope International University *B, T*
Humboldt State University *T*
La Sierra University *M*
Loyola Marymount University *M, T*
Master's College *B, T*
Mills College *T*
Mount St. Mary's College *B*
National University *T*
Occidental College *T*
Pacific Union College *B*
Point Loma Nazarene University *T*
St. Mary's College of California *D*
San Diego State University *M, T*
San Francisco State University *M, T*
San Jose State University *M*
Simpson College *B, T*
Sonoma State University *M*
Stanford University *M*
University of California
Riverside *T*
Santa Barbara *T*
Santa Cruz *M*
University of La Verne *B, M, T*
University of Redlands *B, T*
University of San Francisco *T*
University of Southern California *T*
University of the Pacific *B, T*
Whittier College *T*

Colorado

Colorado College *M*
Colorado State University *T*
Colorado State University
Pueblo *T*
Fort Lewis College *T*
Metropolitan State College of Denver *T*
Otero Junior College *A*
Regis University *B, T*
University of Colorado
Boulder *T*
Colorado Springs *T*
University of Denver *M*

Connecticut

Central Connecticut State University *B*
Connecticut College *M, T*
Fairfield University *M*
Quinnipiac University *B, M*
Sacred Heart University *T*
St. Joseph College *M, T*
Southern Connecticut State
University *B, M, T*
University of Bridgeport *M, T*

University of Connecticut *T*
University of Hartford *B, M*
University of New Haven *M*
Western Connecticut State
University *B, M*

Delaware

University of Delaware *B, M, T*

District of Columbia

American University *B, M, T*
Catholic University of America *B, M, T*
Gallaudet University *B, T*
George Washington University *M, T*
Howard University *M*
Trinity College *M*

Florida

Flagler College *B*
Florida Agricultural and Mechanical
University *M*
Florida Gulf Coast University *M*
Florida Southern College *B*
Hillsborough Community College *A*
Indian River Community College *A*
Jacksonville University *B, M, T*
Manatee Community College *A*
Miami-Dade Community College *A*
Okaloosa-Walton Community College *A*
Palm Beach Atlantic University *B, T*
Palm Beach Community College *A*
Rollins College *T*
St. Thomas University *B, T*
Southeastern College of the Assemblies
of God *B, T*
University of Miami *B, M*
University of North Florida *B, M*
University of Tampa *T*

Georgia

Agnes Scott College *T*
Armstrong Atlantic State
University *B, M*
Augusta State University *M*
Bainbridge College *A*
Berry College *B, M, T*
Brewton-Parker College *B*
Clark Atlanta University *B*
Columbus State University *B, M*
Covenant College *B, T*
Emmanuel College *B*
Emory University *B*
Fort Valley State University *B, T*
Gainesville College *A*
Georgia College and State
University *M, T*
Georgia Southwestern State
University *B, T*
Kennesaw State University *B*
LaGrange College *B*
Macon State College *A*
Mercer University *M*
Middle Georgia College *A*
Morehouse College *A*
North Georgia College & State
University *B, M*
Oglethorpe University *B, T*
Paine College *B, T*
Piedmont College *M, T*
State University of West Georgia *B, M*
Thomas University *B*
Toccoa Falls College *B, T*
Valdosta State University *B, M*

Hawaii

Brigham Young University-Hawaii *B, T*
Chaminade University of
Honolulu *B, M, T*
University of Hawaii
Hilo *A*
Manoa *B, M, T*

Idaho

Boise State University *T*
College of Southern Idaho *A*
Idaho State University *B, T*
Lewis-Clark State College *B, T*

North Idaho College *A*
Northwest Nazarene University *B*
University of Idaho *B, T*

Illinois

Augustana College *B, T*
Aurora University *B*
Benedictine University *T*
Black Hawk College
East Campus *A*
Blackburn College *B, T*
Chicago State University *B, M, T*
City Colleges of Chicago
Harold Washington College *A*
Columbia College Chicago *M*
Concordia University *B, T*
De Paul University *B, T*
Dominican University *T*
Elmhurst College *B*
Greenville College *T*
Illinois Central College *A*
Illinois Wesleyan University *B*
John A. Logan College *A*
Joliet Junior College *A*
Judson College *B, T*
Kankakee Community College *A*
Kishwaukee College *A*
Knox College *T*
Lake Forest College *T*
Lewis University *T*
Lincoln Christian College and
Seminary *B*
MacMurray College *B, T*
McKendree College *T*
Monmouth College *B, T*
National-Louis University *M, T*
North Central College *B, T*
North Park University *M, T*
Northeastern Illinois University *M*
Northern Illinois University *M*
Northwestern University *B, T*
Olivet Nazarene University *B, M, T*
Parkland College *A*
Principia College *T*
Quincy University *T*
Rockford College *M, T*
Roosevelt University *B, M*
St. Xavier University *B*
Sauk Valley Community College *A*
Southern Illinois University
Edwardsville *M, T*
Southwestern Illinois College *A*
Springfield College in Illinois *A*
Trinity Christian College *T*
Trinity International University *B, T*
University of Illinois
Urbana-Champaign *M, D*
Western Illinois University *M*
Wheaton College *M, T*

Indiana

Anderson University *T*
Ball State University *B, M, T*
Butler University *B, M*
Calumet College of St. Joseph *B, T*
Earlham College *M*
Goshen College *B, T*
Grace College *B*
Hanover College *T*
Indiana University
Bloomington *B, M, D, T*
East *B*
Kokomo *M*
Northwest *B, M, T*
South Bend *B, T*
Southeast *B, M*
Indiana University-Purdue University
Fort Wayne *B, M, T*
Indiana University-Purdue University
Indianapolis *B, M, T*
Indiana Wesleyan University *B, M*
Manchester College *B, T*
Marian College *T*
Purdue University
Calumet *B, M*
St. Joseph's College *B*

Saint Mary's College *T*
St. Mary-of-the-Woods College *B, T*
Taylor University *T*
University of Evansville *B*
University of Indianapolis *A, B, T*
University of St. Francis *B, M*
University of Southern Indiana *M, T*
Valparaiso University *B, T*
Vincennes University *A*
Wabash College *T*

Iowa

Briar Cliff University *B*
Buena Vista University *B, T*
Central College *T*
Clarke College *B, M, T*
Coe College *B*
Cornell College *B, T*
Dordt College *B, T*
Drake University *B, M*
Ellsworth Community College *A*
Faith Baptist Bible College and
    Theological Seminary *B*
Franciscan University *B, T*
Graceland University *T*
Grand View College *B, T*
Grinnell College *T*
Iowa State University *T*
Iowa Wesleyan College *B*
Loras College *B*
Luther College *B*
Maharishi University of
    Management *B, M*
Marshalltown Community College *A*
Morningside College *B*
Mount Mercy College *T*
North Iowa Area Community College *A*
Northwestern College *T*
St. Ambrose University *B, T*
Simpson College *B, T*
University of Iowa *B, M, D, T*
Upper Iowa University *B, T*
Vennard College *B*
Waldorf College *A*
Wartburg College *T*
William Penn University *B*

Kansas

Allen County Community College *A*
Benedictine College *B, T*
Bethany College *B, T*
Bethel College *T*
Butler County Community College *A*
Central Christian College *A, B*
Dodge City Community College *A*
Emporia State University *B, M, T*
Fort Hays State University *M*
Fort Scott Community College *A*
Friends University *B, T*
Garden City Community College *A*
Kansas City Kansas Community
    College *A*
Kansas State University *B, M, T*
Kansas Wesleyan University *B, T*
Labette Community College *A*
MidAmerica Nazarene University *B, T*
Newman University *B, T*
Pittsburg State University *B, M, T*
Pratt Community College *A*
Southwestern College *B, M, T*
Tabor College *B, T*
University of Kansas *B, T*
Washburn University of Topeka *B*
Wichita State University *B, T*

Kentucky

Alice Lloyd College *B*
Bellarmine University *B, M, T*
Campbellsville University *B*
Centre College *T*
Cumberland College *M, T*
Georgetown College *M*
Kentucky Wesleyan College *B, T*
Lindsey Wilson College *B, T*
Morehead State University *M*
Murray State University *M*

Spalding University *M, T*
Thomas More College *B*
Union College *B, M, T*
University of Kentucky *M*
University of Louisville *M*

Louisiana

Centenary College of Louisiana *B, M, T*
Dillard University *B, T*
Louisiana College *B*
Louisiana State University and
    Agricultural and Mechanical
    College *B*
Louisiana Tech University *B*
Loyola University New Orleans *M*
McNeese State University *B, T*
Nicholls State University *B, M*
Northwestern State University *B*
Our Lady of Holy Cross College *B*
Southern University
    New Orleans *B*
Southern University and Agricultural and
    Mechanical College *B, M*
University of Louisiana at Lafayette *B*
University of Louisiana at Monroe *M*
University of New Orleans *B*
Xavier University of Louisiana *M*

Maine

Bowdoin College *T*
St. Joseph's College *B*
University of Maine *B, M*
University of Maine
    Farmington *B, T*
    Machias *T*
    Presque Isle *B*
University of New England *B, T*
University of Southern Maine *T*

Maryland

Allegany College *A*
Anne Arundel Community College *A*
Bowie State University *M*
Cecil Community College *A*
Chesapeake College *A*
College of Notre Dame of
    Maryland *B, M*
College of Southern Maryland *A*
Columbia Union College *B, T*
Community College of Baltimore County
    Catonsville *A*
    Dundalk *A*
    Essex *A*
Coppin State College *B, T*
Frostburg State University *M*
Goucher College *T*
Harford Community College *A*
Hood College *T*
Howard Community College *A*
Johns Hopkins University *M*
McDaniel College *M, T*
Morgan State University *B, T*
St. Mary's College of Maryland *T*
Salisbury University *B*
Towson University *M, T*
University of Maryland
    Baltimore County *T*
    University College *M*
Washington College *T*
Wor-Wic Community College *A*

Massachusetts

American International College *B, M*
Amherst College *T*
Assumption College *B, T*
Atlantic Union College *B*
Boston College *B, M, T*
Clark University *M*
Elms College *B, M, T*
Emmanuel College *B, M, T*
Fitchburg State College *B, M, T*
Framingham State College *B, M, T*
Hampshire College *B*
Harvard College *T*
Lesley University *B, M, T*
Massachusetts College of Liberal Arts *T*
Merrimack College *T*

Nichols College *B*
Simmons College *B, M*
Smith College *M*
Springfield College *B, T*
Suffolk University *M, T*
Tufts University *M, T*
University of Massachusetts
    Boston *M*
    Dartmouth *T*
Wellesley College *T*
Western New England College *T*
Westfield State College *M, T*
Wheaton College *T*

Michigan

Adrian College *B*
Alma College *B, T*
Andrews University *M, T*
Baker College
    of Auburn Hills *B*
    of Muskegon *B*
    of Owosso *B*
Calvin College *B, T*
Central Michigan University *M*
Concordia University *B, T*
Cornerstone University *B*
Eastern Michigan University *B, M, T*
Ferris State University *A, M*
Gogebic Community College *A*
Grace Bible College *B*
Grand Valley State University *M, T*
Hillsdale College *B*
Hope College *B, T*
Kalamazoo College *T*
Kellogg Community College *A*
Lansing Community College *A*
Madonna University *B, T*
Marygrove College *T*
Michigan Technological University *T*
Mid Michigan Community College *A*
Northern Michigan University *B, M, T*
Saginaw Valley State University *M*
Siena Heights University *B, M, T*
Spring Arbor University *T*
University of Michigan *B*
University of Michigan
    Dearborn *B, T*
Wayne State University *M*

Minnesota

Augsburg College *B, T*
Bethel College *B*
Capella University *M, D*
College of St. Benedict *T*
College of St. Catherine *B, T*
College of St. Scholastica *B*
Concordia College: Moorhead *B, T*
Concordia University: St. Paul *B, T*
Crown College *B*
Gustavus Adolphus College *B*
Hamline University *B, T*
Minnesota State University
    Mankato *B, M, T*
    Moorhead *B, T*
North Central University *B*
Northland Community & Technical
    College *A*
Ridgewater College: A Community and
    Technical College *A*
St. Cloud State University *M, T*
St. John's University *T*
University of Minnesota
    Duluth *T*
    Morris *T*
University of St. Thomas *B, M, T*
Vermilion Community College *A*
Winona State University *B, M, T*

Mississippi

Alcorn State University *M*
Holmes Community College *A*
Itawamba Community College *A*
Mary Holmes College *A*
Millsaps College *T*
Mississippi College *B, M, T*

Mississippi Gulf Coast Community
    College
    Perkinston *A*
Mississippi State University *B, M, T*
Northwest Mississippi Community
    College *A*
University of Mississippi *B*
University of Southern Mississippi *M*

Missouri

Calvary Bible College *B*
Central Methodist College *B*
Central Missouri State
    University *B, M, T*
College of the Ozarks *B, T*
Columbia College *T*
Crowder College *A*
Culver-Stockton College *T*
Drury University *B, T*
East Central College *A*
Evangel University *B, T*
Hannibal-LaGrange College *B*
Harris Stowe State College *B, T*
Lincoln University *M*
Lindenwood University *B*
Maryville University of Saint
    Louis *B, M, T*
Missouri Baptist University *T*
Missouri Southern State College *B, T*
Missouri Valley College *B, T*
Ozark Christian College *A*
Rockhurst University *B*
St. Louis Community College
    St. Louis Community College at
    Meramec *A*
Southeast Missouri State
    University *B, M, T*
Southwest Baptist University *T*
Southwest Missouri State University *M*
Truman State University *M, T*
University of Missouri
    Columbia *B*
    Kansas City *B*
    Rolla *T*
    St. Louis *B, M, T*
Washington University in St.
    Louis *B, M, T*
Westminster College *B, T*
William Jewell College *T*
William Woods University *B, T*

Montana

Carroll College *B*
Miles Community College *A*
Montana State University
    Billings *B, M, T*
    Bozeman *B*
Montana Tech of the University of
    Montana *T*
Rocky Mountain College *B, T*
University of Great Falls *B*
University of Montana-Missoula *B, M*
University of Montana: Western *B, T*

Nebraska

Chadron State College *B, M*
College of Saint Mary *B, T*
Concordia University *B, T*
Dana College *B*
Doane College *T*
Hastings College *B, M, T*
Midland Lutheran College *B, T*
Nebraska Wesleyan University *T*
Northeast Community College *A*
Peru State College *B, T*
Union College *B, T*
University of Nebraska
    Kearney *B, M, T*
    Omaha *B, M, T*
Western Nebraska Community
    College *A*
York College *B, T*

Nevada

Sierra Nevada College *T*
Truckee Meadows Community
    College *A*

University of Nevada
  Las Vegas *B, T*
  Reno *M, T*

New Hampshire
Dartmouth College *T*
Franklin Pierce College *T*
Keene State College *B, T*
New England College *B, T*
Plymouth State College *M*
Rivier College *B, M, T*
St. Anselm College *T*
Southern New Hampshire University *B*
University of New Hampshire *M*
University of New Hampshire at
  Manchester *T*

New Jersey
Bloomfield College *B*
Caldwell College *T*
Centenary College *T*
The College of New Jersey *M, T*
College of St. Elizabeth *T*
Essex County College *A*
Richard Stockton College of New
  Jersey *B*
Rider University *B*
Rowan University *B, M*
Rutgers, The State University of New
  Jersey
    Camden Regional Campus *T*
    New Brunswick Regional
      Campus *T*
    Newark Regional Campus *T*
St. Peter's College *T*
Seton Hall University *B, M*
Sussex County Community College *A*

New Mexico
College of Santa Fe *B*
College of the Southwest *B, T*
New Mexico Highlands University *B, T*
New Mexico Institute of Mining and
  Technology *M*
New Mexico Junior College *A*
New Mexico State University *B*
University of New Mexico *B, M*
Western New Mexico University *B, M, T*

New York
Adelphi University *B, M, T*
Alfred University *M, T*
Barnard College *T*
Canisius College *B, M, T*
City University of New York
    Brooklyn College *B, M, T*
    City College *B, T*
    College of Staten Island *M*
    Hunter College *B, M, T*
    Queens College *B, M, T*
    York College *T*
Colgate University *M, T*
College of Mount St. Vincent *T*
College of New Rochelle *T*
Concordia College *B, T*
D'Youville College *B, M, T*
Dominican College of Blauvelt *B, T*
Dowling College *B, M, T*
Dutchess Community College *A*
Elmira College *B, M, T*
Eugene Lang College/New School
  University *T*
Fordham University *M, T*
Fulton-Montgomery Community
  College *A*
Hobart and William Smith Colleges *T*
Hofstra University *B, M*
Houghton College *B, T*
Iona College *B, M, T*
Ithaca College *B, M, T*
Le Moyne College *M, T*
Long Island University
    C. W. Post Campus *B, M, T*
    Southampton College *T*
Manhattan College *B, T*
Manhattanville College *M, T*
Marist College *B*

Marymount College of Fordham
  University *B, T*
Marymount Manhattan College *B, T*
Mercy College *T*
Molloy College *B, M, T*
Mount St. Mary College *B, M*
Nazareth College of Rochester *B, M, T*
New York University *B, M, T*
Niagara University *B, M, T*
Pace University *M, T*
Pace University:
  Pleasantville/Briarcliff *M, T*
St. Bonaventure University *M*
St. John Fisher College *B, M, T*
St. John's University *B, M, T*
St. Joseph's College *B, T*
St. Joseph's College: Suffolk
  Campus *B, T*
State University of New York
    Albany *B, M, T*
    Buffalo *M, D, T*
    College at Brockport *B, M, T*
    College at Buffalo *B, M, T*
    College at Cortland *B, M*
    College at Fredonia *B, M, T*
    College at Geneseo *T*
    College at Old Westbury *T*
    College at Plattsburgh *M*
    New Paltz *B, M, T*
    Oswego *B, M, T*
Suffolk County Community College *A*
Syracuse University *B, M, T*
Union College *M, T*
University of Rochester *T*
Vassar College *T*
Wagner College *B, T*
Wells College *T*
Yeshiva University *M*

North Carolina
Appalachian State University *B, M, T*
Belmont Abbey College *B*
Campbell University *M*
Catawba College *T*
Chowan College *B*
Davidson College *T*
Duke University *M*
Elon University *B, T*
Fayetteville State University *B*
Gardner-Webb University *B, M*
Greensboro College *T*
Guilford College *B, T*
High Point University *B*
James Sprunt Community College *A*
Johnson C. Smith University *B, T*
Louisburg College *A*
Mars Hill College *B, T*
Martin Community College *A*
Meredith College *T*
Methodist College *A, B, T*
Montreat College *T*
North Carolina Central University *M*
North Carolina State University *B*
North Carolina Wesleyan College *T*
Pfeiffer University *B, T*
Queens University of Charlotte *T*
St. Augustine's College *B*
Salem College *T*
Sandhills Community College *A*
Southeastern Community College *A*
University of North Carolina
    Asheville *T*
    Wilmington *M*
Warren Wilson College *B, T*

North Dakota
Dickinson State University *B, T*
Jamestown College *B*
Mayville State University *B, T*
Minot State University: Bottineau
  Campus *A*
North Dakota State University *B*
University of Mary *B, T*
University of North Dakota *B, M, T*
Valley City State University *B, T*

Ohio
Baldwin-Wallace College *B*
Bluffton College *B*
Bowling Green State University *B*
Cedarville University *T*
College of Mount St. Joseph *T*
College of Wooster *T*
Defiance College *B, T*
Heidelberg College *T*
Hiram College *T*
John Carroll University *M, T*
Kent State University *M*
Kent State University
    Stark Campus *B*
Lake Erie College *B*
Lorain County Community College *A*
Malone College *T*
Marietta College *B*
Miami University
    Oxford Campus *M*
Mount Union College *T*
Mount Vernon Nazarene University *B, T*
Muskingum College *B, M, T*
Notre Dame College *B, T*
Ohio Dominican College *B, T*
Ohio Northern University *B, T*
Ohio State University
    Columbus Campus *M*
Ohio University *B, M, D, T*
Ohio Wesleyan University *B*
Otterbein College *B*
Owens Community College
    Findlay Campus *A*
    Toledo *A*
Sinclair Community College *A*
University of Akron *B, M, D, T*
University of Cincinnati *B, M, D, T*
University of Cincinnati
    Clermont College *A*
    Raymond Walters College *A*
University of Dayton *B, M, T*
University of Findlay *B, T*
University of Rio Grande *B, T*
University of Toledo *B, M, T*
Urbana University *B*
Walsh University *B*
Washington State Community College *A*
Wilmington College *B*
Wittenberg University *B*
Wright State University *M*
Wright State University: Lake
  Campus *A, B*
Xavier University *M*
Youngstown State University *B, M*

Oklahoma
Cameron University *B, T*
Carl Albert State College *A*
East Central University *M, T*
Eastern Oklahoma State College *A*
Langston University *B*
Northeastern State University *B*
Northern Oklahoma College *A*
Northwestern Oklahoma State
  University *M*
Oklahoma Baptist University *B, T*
Oklahoma Christian University of
  Science and Arts *B, T*
Oklahoma City Community College *A*
Oklahoma City University *B, M*
Oklahoma State University *B, M, D, T*
Rogers State University *A*
Rose State College *A*
St. Gregory's University *B*
Southeastern Oklahoma State
  University *B, M, T*
Southern Nazarene University *B*
Southwestern Oklahoma State
  University *M, T*
University of Central Oklahoma *B, M*
University of Oklahoma *D*
University of Tulsa *B, T*

Oregon
Chemeketa Community College *A*
Concordia University *B, M, T*

Eastern Oregon University *B, M*
Lewis & Clark College *M*
Linfield College *T*
Linn-Benton Community College *A*
Oregon State University *M*
Portland State University *T*
Southern Oregon University *M, T*
University of Portland *B, M, T*
Warner Pacific College *T*
Western Baptist College *B*
Western Oregon University *B, M, T*
Willamette University *M*

Pennsylvania
Albright College *B, M, T*
Arcadia University *B, M, T*
Baptist Bible College of Pennsylvania *B*
Bryn Mawr College *T*
Bucknell University *B, T*
Butler County Community College *A*
Carlow College *T*
Cedar Crest College *B, M, T*
Chatham College *T*
DeSales University *M, T*
Delaware Valley College *B, T*
Dickinson College *T*
Duquesne University *B, M, T*
East Stroudsburg University of
  Pennsylvania *B, M, T*
Elizabethtown College *T*
Gettysburg College *T*
Grove City College *B*
Harrisburg Area Community College *A*
Holy Family University *B, M, T*
Immaculata University *T*
Juniata College *B, T*
King's College *T*
Kutztown University of
  Pennsylvania *B, M, T*
La Roche College *T*
La Salle University *B, M, T*
Lebanon Valley College of
  Pennsylvania *T*
Lehigh University *M*
Lincoln University *B, M, T*
Lock Haven University of
  Pennsylvania *B, T*
Lycoming College *T*
Marywood University *B*
Mercyhurst College *B*
Millersville University of
  Pennsylvania *B*
Montgomery County Community
  College *A*
Muhlenberg College *T*
Penn State
    Abington *B*
    Altoona *B*
    Beaver *B*
    Berks *B*
    Delaware County *B*
    Dubois *B*
    Fayette *B*
    Hazleton *B*
    Lehigh Valley *B*
    McKeesport *B*
    Mont Alto *B*
    New Kensington *B*
    Schuylkill - Capital College *B*
    Shenango *B*
    University Park *B*
    Wilkes-Barre *B*
    Worthington Scranton *B*
    York *B*
Point Park College *B*
Reading Area Community College *A*
Robert Morris University *B, T*
Rosemont College *T*
St. Joseph's University *B, M*
St. Vincent College *T*
Slippery Rock University of
  Pennsylvania *B, M*
Temple University *M*
Thiel College *T*
University of Pennsylvania *B*
University of Pittsburgh *T*

University of Pittsburgh
Bradford *B, T*
Johnstown *B, T*
University of Scranton *B, M*
Villanova University *B, M*
Washington and Jefferson College *T*
Waynesburg College *B, T*
West Chester University of
Pennsylvania *T*
Widener University *M*
Wilson College *T*
York College of Pennsylvania *B, T*

Puerto Rico
Bayamon Central University *B*
Inter American University of Puerto Rico
Barranquitas Campus *B*
Fajardo Campus *B, T*
Guayama Campus *B*
Metropolitan Campus *B*
San German Campus *B*
Pontifical Catholic University of Puerto
Rico *B*
Turabo University *B*
University of Puerto Rico
Cayey University College *B, T*
Rio Piedras Campus *B, M*
University of the Sacred Heart *B*

Rhode Island
Providence College *B*
Rhode Island College *B, M, T*
Roger Williams University *B, T*
Salve Regina University *B*
University of Rhode Island *B*

South Carolina
Anderson College *B, T*
Charleston Southern University *B, M*
The Citadel *B, M*
Clemson University *B, M, T*
Coastal Carolina University *B, M, T*
Converse College *M, T*
Erskine College *B, T*
Francis Marion University *B, M, T*
Furman University *M, T*
Limestone College *B*
Presbyterian College *B, T*
South Carolina State University *M*
University of South Carolina *M, D*
University of South Carolina
Aiken *B, T*
Spartanburg *B, T*
Winthrop University *M, T*
Wofford College *T*

South Dakota
Augustana College *B, M, T*
Black Hills State University *B, T*
Dakota State University *B, T*
Mount Marty College *B*
South Dakota State University *B*
University of Sioux Falls *B*
University of South Dakota *M, T*

Tennessee
Austin Peay State University *T*
Belmont University *B, T*
Bethel College *B, T*
Bryan College *T*
Carson-Newman College *B*
Christian Brothers University *B, M, T*
Crichton College *C, B*
East Tennessee State University *M, T*
Fisk University *T*
Freed-Hardeman University *B, T*
King College *T*
Lambuth University *B, T*
Lee University *B, T*
Rhodes College *T*
Roane State Community College *A*
Tennessee State University *B, M, T*
Tennessee Technological
University *B, M, T*
Tennessee Wesleyan College *B, T*
Trevecca Nazarene University *B, T*
Tusculum College *B, T*

Union University *B, T*
University of Tennessee
Chattanooga *B, M, T*
Knoxville *T*
Vanderbilt University *B, M, T*

Texas
Abilene Christian University *B, M, T*
Austin College *M*
Baylor University *T*
Brazosport College *A*
Coastal Bend College *A*
College of the Mainland *A*
Concordia University at Austin *B, T*
Dallas Baptist University *B, M*
East Texas Baptist University *B*
El Paso Community College *A*
Frank Phillips College *A*
Grayson County College *A*
Hardin-Simmons University *B, M, T*
Houston Baptist University *B, M*
Howard Payne University *T*
Huston-Tillotson College *T*
Jarvis Christian College *B*
Lamar University *M, T*
LeTourneau University *B*
Lubbock Christian University *B, M*
McMurry University *B*
Midwestern State University *B*
North Harris Montgomery Community
College District *A*
Our Lady of the Lake University of San
Antonio *T*
Paul Quinn College *B*
Rice University *M*
St. Edward's University *T*
Sam Houston State University *M, T*
Schreiner University *T*
Southern Methodist University *T*
Southwest Texas State University *M, T*
Southwestern Assemblies of God
University *B*
Southwestern University *T*
Stephen F. Austin State University *M*
Sul Ross State University *M*
Tarleton State University *M, T*
Texas A&M International
University *M, T*
Texas A&M University
Commerce *M, D, T*
Corpus Christi *M, T*
Kingsville *B, M*
Texarkana *M, T*
Texas Christian University *B, M, T*
Texas Lutheran University *T*
Texas Tech University *M*
Texas Wesleyan University *B, M, T*
Trinity University *M*
University of Dallas *B, T*
University of Houston *M, T*
University of Houston
Downtown *M, T*
Victoria *M*
University of Mary Hardin-Baylor *T*
University of North Texas *M, D*
University of St. Thomas *B*
University of Texas
Arlington *T*
Brownsville *M*
Pan American *B, M, T*
University of the Incarnate Word *B*
West Texas A&M University *T*
Wiley College *B*

Utah
Brigham Young University *B*
Dixie State College of Utah *A*
Snow College *A*
Southern Utah University *B*
Utah State University *B, M, D*
Utah Valley State College *B*
Weber State University *B*
Westminster College *B, T*

Vermont
Bennington College *B, M, T*

Castleton State College *B, M*
College of St. Joseph in Vermont *B*
Goddard College *B*
Green Mountain College *B, T*
Johnson State College *B, M*
Middlebury College *T*
Norwich University *T*
St. Michael's College *T*
University of Vermont *B*

Virginia
Averett University *B*
Bluefield College *B*
Bridgewater College *T*
College of William and Mary *T*
Eastern Mennonite University *T*
Hampton University *M*
Hollins University *T*
James Madison University *T*
Liberty University *B, M*
Longwood University *T*
Mary Baldwin College *T*
Mary Washington College *T*
Marymount University *M*
Old Dominion University *M*
Radford University *T*
Randolph-Macon College *T*
Randolph-Macon Woman's College *T*
University of Richmond *B, T*
University of Virginia's College at
Wise *T*
Virginia Polytechnic Institute and State
University *B*
Virginia Wesleyan College *T*

Washington
Central Washington University *M*
Eastern Washington University *M*
Evergreen State College *M*
Gonzaga University *T*
Northwest College *B*
Pacific Lutheran University *B*
St. Martin's College *B, T*
Seattle Pacific University *M*
University of Washington *M, T*
Walla Walla College *M*
Western Washington University *M*
Whitworth College *B, M, T*

West Virginia
Alderson-Broaddus College *B*
Davis and Elkins College *B*
Fairmont State College *B*
Glenville State College *B*
Marshall University *B, M*
Mountain State University *A*
Ohio Valley College *B*
Potomac State College of West Virginia
University *A*
Salem International University *B, T*
Shepherd College *B, T*
University of Charleston *B*
West Liberty State College *B*
West Virginia State College *B*
West Virginia University *M*
West Virginia Wesleyan College *B*
Wheeling Jesuit University *T*

Wisconsin
Alverno College *T*
Beloit College *T*
Carroll College *T*
Carthage College *T*
Concordia University Wisconsin *B, T*
Edgewood College *B, T*
Lawrence University *T*
Maranatha Baptist Bible College *B*
Marian College of Fond du Lac *B, T*
Marquette University *B*
Mount Mary College *B, T*
Northland College *T*
Ripon College *T*
St. Norbert College *M, T*

University of Wisconsin
Green Bay *T*
La Crosse *B, M, T*
Oshkosh *B, T*
Parkside *T*
Platteville *T*
River Falls *T*
Stevens Point *B, T*
Superior *T*
Whitewater *B, T*
Viterbo University *B, M, T*

Wyoming
Central Wyoming College *A*
Eastern Wyoming College *A*
Laramie County Community College *A*
Sheridan College *A*
University of Wyoming *B*
Western Wyoming Community
College *A*

Secondary school administration

Arkansas
Arkansas State University *M, T*

Illinois
Principia College *B*

Iowa
University of Dubuque *B*

Louisiana
Xavier University of Louisiana *M*

Massachusetts
Lesley University *M, T*

Michigan
Saginaw Valley State University *M*

Minnesota
Capella University *M, D*

Missouri
Crowder College *A*

Nebraska
Creighton University *M*

New Jersey
William Paterson University of New
Jersey *M*

New York
St. Bonaventure University *M*
St. John Fisher College *M*
State University of New York
Buffalo *M, D, T*

North Carolina
Western Carolina University *D*

Ohio
Baldwin-Wallace College *B*
University of Dayton *M*

Pennsylvania
Marywood University *M*

South Dakota
University of South Dakota *M, D*

Texas
Southwest Texas State University *M*

Vermont
Castleton State College *D*
St. Michael's College *T*

Washington
Seattle Pacific University *T*
University of Washington *M, T*

Wisconsin
University of Wisconsin
Superior *M*

Security services management

New York
St. John's University *B*

Security system installation/repair/inspection

Washington
Clover Park Technical College *C*

Security/loss prevention

California
De Anza College *C, A*
Grossmont Community College *C, A*
Palomar College *C, A*
Sierra College *A*

Connecticut
Naugatuck Valley Community College *A*

Florida
Broward Community College *A*
Florida State University *C*
Miami-Dade Community College *C*
St. Petersburg College *C, A*

Illinois
Black Hawk College *C*
Lewis University *B*
Lewis and Clark Community College *A*
Moraine Valley Community College *C*
Southwestern Illinois College *C, A*
Waubonsee Community College *C*
William Rainey Harper College *C*

Indiana
Vincennes University *A*

Kansas
Washburn University of Topeka *B*

Maryland
Community College of Baltimore County
    Catonsville *C, A*
    Dundalk *C, A*
    Essex *C, A*

Massachusetts
Marian Court College *C, A*
Northeastern University *A, B*

Michigan
Baker College
    of Muskegon *C*
Grand Valley State University *B*
Macomb Community College *C*
Schoolcraft College *C*

Minnesota
Winona State University *B*

Missouri
Central Missouri State University *M*
St. Louis Community College
    St. Louis Community College at
    Forest Park *C*

Nevada
Community College of Southern
    Nevada *A*

New Jersey
Essex County College *C*
New Jersey City University *B*

New Mexico
San Juan College *A*

New York
Dutchess Community College *C*
Long Island University
    C. W. Post Campus *M*
Nassau Community College *A*

Schenectady County Community
    College *A*

Ohio
Cuyahoga Community College
    Western Campus *A*
Lakeland Community College *C, A*
Ohio University *A*
Ohio University
    Zanesville Campus *A*
Owens Community College
    Toledo *A*
Youngstown State University *B*

Pennsylvania
ICM School of Business & Medical
    Careers *A*
York College of Pennsylvania *B*

Tennessee
Roane State Community College *A*

Texas
Hill College *A*

Washington
Clover Park Technical College *C*
Spokane Community College *A*

Wisconsin
Fox Valley Technical College *A*
Western Wisconsin Technical College *C*

Selling/sales operations

California
Santiago Canyon College *A*

Illinois
McHenry County College *C, A*
Robert Morris College: Chicago *A*

New Jersey
Bloomfield College *B*

New York
Mohawk Valley Community College *C*

Ohio
Hondros College *A*
Ohio University *C*
Owens Community College
    Findlay Campus *C*
    Toledo *C*

Pennsylvania
Pennsylvania College of Technology *C*
University of Pennsylvania *B, M*

Tennessee
University of Memphis *B*

Texas
Baylor University *B*

Utah
LDS Business College *C*

Washington
Clark College *C, A*
Spokane Community College *A*

Semitic languages

Illinois
Trinity International University *M*

Sheet metal technology

California
Foothill College *C*
Yuba Community College District *C, A*

Illinois
Black Hawk College *C*

Indiana
Ivy Tech State College
    Central Indiana *C, A*
    Lafayette *A*
    Northcentral *C, A*
    Northeast *C, A*
    Northwest *C, A*
    Southcentral *C, A*
    Southwest *C, A*
    Wabash Valley *C, A*

Minnesota
Hennepin Technical College *A*
St. Paul College - A Community and
    Technical College *C*

Montana
Montana State University
    Billings *C*

New Mexico
Albuquerque Technical-Vocational
    Institute *C*

Ohio
Northwest State Community
    College *C, A*

Pennsylvania
Community College of Allegheny
    County *C*

Texas
St. Philip's College *C*

Washington
Clover Park Technical College *C*

Wisconsin
Western Wisconsin Technical College *C*

Sign language interpretation

Arizona
Phoenix College *C, A*
Pima Community College *A*

Arkansas
University of Arkansas
    Little Rock *A, B*

California
College of the Sequoias *C*
Golden West College *C, A*
Los Angeles Pierce College *C, A*
Mount San Antonio College *C, A*
Palomar College *C, A*
Riverside Community College *C, A*
San Diego City College *C*
Vista Community College *C, A*

Colorado
Front Range Community College *A*

Connecticut
Northwestern Connecticut Community
    College *C, A*

Delaware
Delaware Technical and Community
    College
    Stanton/Wilmington Campus *A*

District of Columbia
Gallaudet University *M*

Florida
Hillsborough Community College *C, A*
Miami-Dade Community College *A*
St. Petersburg College *A*

Georgia
Floyd College *C, A*
Georgia Perimeter College *C, A*

Idaho
College of Southern Idaho *A*
Idaho State University *A, B*

Illinois
Columbia College Chicago *B*
Illinois Central College *C*
MacMurray College *C*
South Suburban College of Cook
    County *C*
Waubonsee Community College *C, A*
William Rainey Harper College *C, A*

Indiana
Bethel College *A, B*
Indiana University-Purdue University
    Indianapolis *B*
Vincennes University *A*

Iowa
Iowa Western Community College *A*
Kirkwood Community College *A*
Scott Community College *A*

Kansas
Johnson County Community College *A*

Louisiana
Delgado Community College *C, A*

Maryland
Community College of Baltimore County
    Catonsville *C, A*
    Dundalk *C, A*
    Essex *C, A*
Frederick Community College *C*

Massachusetts
Mount Wachusett Community
    College *C, A*
Northeastern University *B*

Michigan
Lansing Community College *A*
Madonna University *C, A, B*
Mott Community College *A*

Minnesota
College of St. Catherine *B*
St. Cloud Technical College *C*
St. Paul College - A Community and
    Technical College *C, A*

Mississippi
Itawamba Community College *A*

Missouri
Maple Woods Community College *A*
St. Louis Community College
    St. Louis Community College at
    Florissant Valley *A*

Nebraska
Metropolitan Community College *C*

New Hampshire
New Hampshire Community Technical
    College
    Nashua *C*
University of New Hampshire at
    Manchester *B*

New Jersey
Camden County College *A*

New Mexico
Santa Fe Community College *C, A*
University of New Mexico *B*

New York
Rochester Institute of Technology *A, B*
Suffolk County Community College *A*
University of Rochester *B*

North Carolina
Blue Ridge Community College *A*
Central Piedmont Community College *A*
Gardner-Webb University *B*
Randolph Community College *C, A*
Wilson Technical Community College *A*

Ohio
Cincinnati State Technical and
    Community College *A*

Columbus State Community
College *C, A*
Cuyahoga Community College
Eastern Campus *A*
Metropolitan Campus *A*
Western Campus *A*
Sinclair Community College *A*

Oklahoma
Oklahoma State University
Oklahoma City *C, A*
Tulsa Community College *C, A*

Oregon
Portland Community College *C, A*
Western Oregon University *B*

Pennsylvania
Bloomsburg University of
Pennsylvania *B*
Community College of Allegheny
County *C, A*
Community College of Philadelphia *C, A*
Mount Aloysius College *A, B*

South Dakota
Southeast Technical Institute *A*

Tennessee
Maryville College *B*

Texas
Austin Community College *C, A*
Blinn College *A*
Del Mar College *A*
Eastfield College *C, A*
El Paso Community College *C, A*
Houston Community College
System *C, A*
Howard College *C, A*
McLennan Community College *C, A*
Tarrant County College *A*
Tyler Junior College *C, A*
University of Dallas *T*

Utah
Salt Lake Community College *A*

Virginia
J. Sargeant Reynolds Community
College *C*

Washington
Seattle Central Community College *A*

West Virginia
Fairmont State College *A*

Wyoming
Sheridan College *A*

Sign language linguistics

Ohio
University of Akron *C*

Slavic languages

California
University of California
Santa Barbara *B*

Florida
Florida State University *M*

Illinois
University of Illinois
Urbana-Champaign *M, D*

Indiana
Indiana University
Bloomington *B, M, D*

Kansas
University of Kansas *B, M, D*

New Jersey
Princeton University *B, M, D*

New York
Columbia University
Columbia College *B*

Rhode Island
Brown University *B, M, D*

Texas
University of Texas
Austin *M, D*

Utah
Brigham Young University *B*

Virginia
University of Virginia *B, M, D*

Slavic studies

New York
Columbia University
Columbia College *B*

Rhode Island
Brown University *B, M, D*

Washington
University of Washington *B*

Slovak

New York
State University of New York
Stony Brook *M*

Small business administration/ management

Alaska
University of Alaska
Southeast *C*

California
Foothill College *C*
Ohlone College *C, A*
Santa Barbara City College *C, A*

Colorado
Colorado Technical University *C*
Jones International University *C, B, M*
Red Rocks Community College *C*

Florida
Pasco-Hernando Community College *C*
Valencia Community College *C*

Indiana
Huntington College *B*
Manchester College *A, B*

Kansas
Central Christian College *A, B*

Michigan
Baker College
of Muskegon *C, A*

Minnesota
Normandale Community College *C*

New Hampshire
Hesser College *C, A*

North Dakota
Lake Region State College *A*

Ohio
Lakeland Community College *C, A*
Miami University
Hamilton Campus *C*
Owens Community College
Findlay Campus *C*
Toledo *C*

Pennsylvania
Newport Business Institute *A*

Vermont
Champlain College *A, B*

Washington
Clark College *C*

West Virginia
Valley College of Technology *A*

Small engine mechanics

California
Los Medanos College *C, A*

Minnesota
Hennepin Technical College *C, A*

New Mexico
Albuquerque Technical-Vocational
Institute *C*

North Dakota
North Dakota State College of
Science *C, A*

Pennsylvania
Delaware County Community College *C*
Pennsylvania College of Technology *C*

Texas
Austin Community College *C*

Wisconsin
Nicolet Area Technical College *A*

Social psychology

Arizona
Prescott College *B*

California
Los Angeles Southwest College *A*
San Francisco State University *M*
University of California
Irvine *B*
Santa Cruz *B, D*

District of Columbia
George Washington University *D*

Florida
Florida Atlantic University *B*
South Florida Community College *A*

Illinois
Eureka College *B*
Lincoln College *A*
Loyola University of Chicago *B, M, D*
Northwestern University *B, M, D*

Indiana
Ball State University *M*
Purdue University
Calumet *B*

Iowa
University of Iowa *D*

Kansas
Pittsburg State University *M*
University of Kansas *D*

Louisiana
Our Lady of Holy Cross College *B*

Maryland
Johns Hopkins University *B*

Massachusetts
Hampshire College *B*
Harvard College *B*
Northeastern University *M*
Simon's Rock College of Bard *B*
Suffolk University *B*
Tufts University *B, M, D*
University of Massachusetts
Lowell *M*

Missouri
Maryville University of Saint Louis *B*

Northwest Missouri State University *B*
University of Missouri
Columbia *M, D*

Nevada
University of Nevada
Reno *B, D*

New Hampshire
Keene State College *B*

New York
Bard College *B*
Eugene Lang College/New School
University *B*
Fordham University *M, D*
New York University *D*
Sarah Lawrence College *B*
State University of New York
Albany *M, D*
Buffalo *D*
Syracuse University *M, D*
University of Rochester *D*

North Carolina
Duke University *M, D*

Ohio
Bowling Green State University *M, D*
Miami University
Oxford Campus *T*
Wright State University *M*

Oklahoma
St. Gregory's University *B*

Pennsylvania
California University of Pennsylvania *M*
Penn State
Abington *B*
Temple University *M, D*

Texas
Our Lady of the Lake University of San
Antonio *M*
University of Houston *M, D*
University of the Incarnate Word *B*

Utah
Brigham Young University *B*

Vermont
Bennington College *B*
Burlington College *B*
Marlboro College *B*

Virginia
Longwood University *B*
Marymount University *B*

Wisconsin
University of Wisconsin
Superior *M*

Social science teacher education

Alabama
Alabama State University *B*
Athens State University *B*
Auburn University *B*
Birmingham-Southern College *T*
Huntingdon College *T*
Jacksonville State University *B, M, T*
Judson College *B*
Miles College *B*
Oakwood College *B*
Samford University *B*
Troy State University Dothan *B, M*

Alaska
University of Alaska
Fairbanks *M*

Arizona
Prescott College *B, M, T*
University of Arizona *B, M*

Arkansas
Arkansas State University *B, M, T*

Henderson State University *B, M, T*
University of Arkansas *B*
University of Arkansas
 Pine Bluff *B, T*
University of Central Arkansas *T*

California

Azusa Pacific University *T*
California Baptist University *T*
California Polytechnic State University:
 San Luis Obispo *B, T*
California State Polytechnic University:
 Pomona *T*
California State University
 Bakersfield *B, T*
 Chico *T*
 Dominguez Hills *T*
 Long Beach *T*
 Northridge *B, T*
 Sacramento *T*
 San Bernardino *T*
Christian Heritage College *B, T*
Concordia University *B*
Fresno Pacific University *T*
Hope International University *B*
Humboldt State University *T*
Master's College *T*
Mills College *T*
Mount St. Mary's College *T*
Occidental College *T*
Pacific Union College *T*
San Diego State University *B, T*
San Francisco State University *B, T*
San Jose State University *T*
Simpson College *B, T*
Sonoma State University *T*
Taft College *A*
University of Redlands *T*
University of Southern California *T*
University of the Pacific *T*
Vanguard University of Southern
 California *M, T*

Colorado

Colorado State University
 Pueblo *T*
Metropolitan State College of Denver *T*

Connecticut

Central Connecticut State University *B*
St. Joseph College *T*
Southern Connecticut State
 University *B, T*

Delaware

University of Delaware *B*

District of Columbia

George Washington University *T*

Florida

Bethune-Cookman College *B, T*
Flagler College *B*
Florida Agricultural and Mechanical
 University *T*
Florida Atlantic University *B*
Florida International University *B, M, T*
Florida State University *B, M, D, T*
Palm Beach Community College *A*
St. Thomas University *B, T*
Stetson University *B, T*
University of Central Florida *B, M*
University of Florida *M*
University of South Florida *B, M*
University of Tampa *B, T*
Warner Southern College *B*

Georgia

Armstrong Atlantic State
 University *B, M, T*
Clark Atlanta University *B*
Columbus State University *B, M*
Emmanuel College *B*
Gainesville College *A*
Georgia College and State
 University *B, M, T*
Georgia Southern University *M, T*

Georgia Southwestern State
 University *B, M*
North Georgia College & State
 University *B, M*
Piedmont College *M, T*
State University of West Georgia *M*
University of Georgia *B, M, D, T*

Hawaii

Brigham Young University-Hawaii *B, T*
University of Hawaii
 Manoa *B, T*

Idaho

Boise State University *T*
Brigham Young University - Idaho *T*
Lewis-Clark State College *B, T*
Northwest Nazarene University *B*

Illinois

Augustana College *B, T*
Benedictine University *T*
Blackburn College *B, T*
Concordia University *B, T*
Dominican University *T*
Eastern Illinois University *B, T*
Lake Land College *A*
Lewis University *T*
McKendree College *B, T*
Millikin University *B, T*
North Park University *T*
Northwestern University *B, T*
Olivet Nazarene University *B, T*
Rockford College *T*
Roosevelt University *B*
St. Xavier University *B*
Sauk Valley Community College *A*
University of Illinois
 Chicago *B*
Wheaton College *T*

Indiana

Butler University *T*
Goshen College *B*
Manchester College *B, T*
Purdue University
 Calumet *B*
St. Mary-of-the-Woods College *B*
Taylor University *B, T*
University of Southern Indiana *T*
Valparaiso University *B*
Vincennes University *A*

Iowa

Buena Vista University *B, T*
Central College *T*
Clarke College *B, T*
Cornell College *B, T*
Dordt College *B*
Drake University *M, T*
Ellsworth Community College *A*
Franciscan University *B, T*
Grand View College *B, T*
Iowa State University *T*
Loras College *T*
Luther College *B*
Morningside College *B*
Mount Mercy College *T*
Northwestern College *T*
St. Ambrose University *B, T*
University of Northern Iowa *B*
Upper Iowa University *B, T*
Wartburg College *T*
William Penn University *B*

Kansas

Benedictine College *B, T*
Bethany College *B*
Central Christian College *A, B*
Emporia State University *B, M, T*
Fort Scott Community College *A*
Friends University *B*
Garden City Community College *A*
Independence Community College *A*
Newman University *T*
Pittsburg State University *B, T*
Tabor College *B, T*

Washburn University of Topeka *B*

Kentucky

Campbellsville University *B*
Murray State University *B, M, T*
Thomas More College *B*
Union College *M*

Louisiana

Grambling State University *B*
Northwestern State University *B*

Maine

University of Maine
 Farmington *B, T*
 Presque Isle *B*
University of New England *T*
University of Southern Maine *T*

Maryland

Frostburg State University *B, T*
Washington College *T*

Massachusetts

American International College *T*
Bridgewater State College *M, T*
Westfield State College *T*

Michigan

Adrian College *B, T*
Alma College *T*
Andrews University *B, M, T*
Aquinas College *B, T*
Central Michigan University *B*
Cornerstone University *B, T*
Eastern Michigan University *B, T*
Grand Valley State University *T*
Lansing Community College *A*
Michigan State University *B*
Michigan Technological University *T*
Northern Michigan University *B*
University of Michigan
 Flint *T*
Western Michigan University *R, M*

Minnesota

Bethel College *B*
College of St. Scholastica *B*
Concordia College: Moorhead *B, T*
Crown College *A*
Gustavus Adolphus College *T*
Minnesota State University
 Mankato *B, M, T*
St. Mary's University of Minnesota *B*
University of Minnesota
 Morris *T*
Winona State University *B, T*

Mississippi

Blue Mountain College *B*
Coahoma Community College *A*
Delta State University *B, M*
Mary Holmes College *A*
Mississippi College *B, M*
Mississippi State University *T*
Mississippi Valley State University *B, T*
Northwest Mississippi Community
 College *A*
Rust College *B*
University of Mississippi *B, T*

Missouri

Avila University *B, T*
Central Methodist College *B*
Evangel University *T*
Lincoln University *B, T*
Lindenwood University *M*
Missouri Baptist University *T*
Missouri Southern State College *B, T*
Northwest Missouri State
 University *B, T*
Southwest Baptist University *B, T*
University of Missouri
 St. Louis *T*
Washington University in St.
 Louis *B, M, T*
Webster University *M*
William Woods University *B, T*

Montana

Montana State University
 Billings *B, T*
University of Great Falls *B*
University of Montana-Missoula *T*

Nebraska

Chadron State College *B*
College of Saint Mary *B, T*
Concordia University *B, T*
Creighton University *T*
Dana College *B*
Doane College *B, T*
Hastings College *B, M, T*
Midland Lutheran College *B, T*
Nebraska Wesleyan University *B*
Peru State College *B, T*
Union College *T*
University of Nebraska
 Kearney *B, M, T*
 Lincoln *B, T*

Nevada

University of Nevada
 Reno *B*

New Hampshire

Keene State College *B, T*
New England College *B*
New Hampshire Community Technical
 College
 Stratham *A*
Plymouth State College *B, T*
Rivier College *B, T*
St. Anselm College *T*
University of New Hampshire *T*

New Jersey

The College of New Jersey *B, T*
Georgian Court College *T*
Rowan University *M*
St. Peter's College *T*

New Mexico

College of Santa Fe *B*
College of the Southwest *B, T*
Western New Mexico University *B*

New York

City University of New York
 Hunter College *B*
Dominican College of Blauvelt *B, T*
Dowling College *B*
Elmira College *B, T*
Fordham University *M, T*
Long Island University
 C. W. Post Campus *B, T*
Manhattan College *B, T*
Manhattanville College *M, T*
New York Institute of Technology *B, T*
Pace University *B*
Pace University:
 Pleasantville/Briarcliff *B*
Roberts Wesleyan College *B, T*
St. John Fisher College *B, T*
St. Joseph's College: Suffolk Campus *B*
State University of New York
 College at Brockport *M, T*
 College at Oneonta *B, T*
 College at Plattsburgh *B*
Tompkins-Cortland Community
 College *A*
Vassar College *T*
Wells College *T*

North Carolina

Appalachian State University *B, M, T*
Elon University *B, T*
Fayetteville State University *B, T*
Gardner-Webb University *B*
Guilford Technical Community
 College *A*
Johnson C. Smith University *B*
Lenoir Community College *A*
Mars Hill College *T*
North Carolina Agricultural and
 Technical State University *B, M, T*
Pfeiffer University *B*

Sandhills Community College *A*
University of North Carolina
   Greensboro *B, M, T*

North Dakota

Dickinson State University *B, T*
Mayville State University *B, T*
Minot State University *B*
North Dakota State University *B, T*
University of Mary *B*
Valley City State University *B, T*

Ohio

Bowling Green State University *B*
Defiance College *B, T*
Hiram College *T*
Kent State University *T*
Kent State University
   Stark Campus *B*
Miami University
   Oxford Campus *M*
Shawnee State University *B*
University of Akron *B, T*
University of Dayton *B, M, T*
University of Findlay *B, T*
University of Rio Grande *B, T*
University of Toledo *M*
Walsh University *B*
Wilmington College *B*
Wittenberg University *B*
Wright State University *M*
Xavier University *M*
Youngstown State University *B, M*

Oklahoma

Eastern Oklahoma State College *A*
Northwestern Oklahoma State
   University *B, T*
Oklahoma Baptist University *B, T*
Oklahoma State University *B, T*
Southwestern Oklahoma State
   University *B, M, T*
University of Tulsa *T*

Oregon

Eastern Oregon University *B*
Linfield College *T*
University of Portland *T*
Western Baptist College *B*

Pennsylvania

Elizabethtown College *T*
Grove City College *T*
Holy Family University *B, M, T*
Immaculata University *T*
La Salle University *B, T*
Lock Haven University of
   Pennsylvania *B, T*
Marywood University *B*
Mercyhurst College *B*
Point Park College *B*
Robert Morris University *B, T*
St. Vincent College *T*
Thiel College *B*
University of Pittsburgh
   Johnstown *B, T*
West Chester University of
   Pennsylvania *B, M, T*
Widener University *T*
Wilson College *T*

Puerto Rico

Inter American University of Puerto Rico
   Metropolitan Campus *B*
Turabo University *B*

South Carolina

Charleston Southern University *B, M*
The Citadel *M*
Converse College *T*
Lander University *T*
University of South Carolina
   Aiken *B, T*
Wofford College *T*

South Dakota

Black Hills State University *B, T*
Dakota Wesleyan University *B, T*

Mount Marty College *B*
Northern State University *B, T*
University of Sioux Falls *T*
University of South Dakota *B, T*

Tennessee

American Baptist College of ABT
   Seminary *B*
Belmont University *T*
Maryville College *B, T*
University of Tennessee
   Martin *B, T*

Texas

Abilene Christian University *B, T*
Baylor University *B, T*
Del Mar College *A*
Hardin-Simmons University *B, T*
Howard Payne University *B, T*
Kilgore College *A*
Lamar University *T*
LeTourneau University *B*
Southwest Texas State University *M, T*
Stephen F. Austin State University *T*
Texas A&M University
   Commerce *T*
Texas Christian University *T*
Texas Wesleyan University *B, M, T*
University of Mary Hardin-Baylor *T*
University of Texas
   San Antonio *T*

Utah

Brigham Young University *B*
Southern Utah University *B*
University of Utah *B*
Weber State University *B*

Vermont

Bennington College *B, M, T*
Castleton State College *B, T*
Johnson State College *B*
Lyndon State College *B*
University of Vermont *B*

Virginia

Averett University *M*
Eastern Mennonite University *T*
Liberty University *B*
Radford University *T*
University of Virginia's College at
   Wise *T*
Virginia Western Community College *A*

Washington

Central Washington University *B, T*
Eastern Washington University *B, M, T*
Pacific Lutheran University *T*
Seattle Pacific University *B, T*
Western Washington University *B*
Whitworth College *B, T*

West Virginia

West Liberty State College *B*

Wisconsin

Alverno College *B, T*
Carroll College *T*
Carthage College *M, T*
Edgewood College *B*
Lakeland College *B*
Lawrence University *T*
Marquette University *B, T*
Northland College *T*
Ripon College *T*
St. Norbert College *T*
Silver Lake College *T*
University of Wisconsin
   Green Bay *T*
   La Crosse *B, T*
   Madison *B, T*
   Oshkosh *B, T*
   Parkside *T*
   Platteville *B, T*
   River Falls *T*
   Superior *B, T*
   Whitewater *B, T*

Wyoming

Western Wyoming Community
   College *A*

Social sciences

Alabama

James H. Faulkner State Community
   College *A*
Samford University *A, B*
Southern Union State Community
   College *A*
Spring Hill College *T*
Troy State University *B*
Troy State University Dothan *B, T*
Troy State University in Montgomery *B*
University of Montevallo *B, T*
Virginia College *A*

Alaska

University of Alaska
   Southeast *B*

Arizona

Central Arizona College *A*
Prescott College *B, M*

Arkansas

Arkansas Baptist College *B*
Arkansas State University
   Beebe *A*
Harding University *B*
John Brown University *B*
Phillips Community College of the
   University of Arkansas *A*
University of Arkansas
   Fort Smith *A*
   Monticello *B*
University of Central Arkansas *M*
University of the Ozarks *B*

California

Azusa Pacific University *B*
Barstow College *A*
Bethany College *B*
Biola University *B*
Cabrillo College *A*
California Baptist University *B*
California Institute of Technology *B, D*
California Polytechnic State University:
   San Luis Obispo *B*
California State Polytechnic University:
   Pomona *B*
California State University
   Chico *B, M*
   Fullerton *B, M*
   Los Angeles *M*
   Monterey Bay *B*
   Sacramento *B, M*
   San Bernardino *B, M*
   San Marcos *B*
   Stanislaus *B*
Cerro Coso Community College *A*
Chabot College *A*
Christian Heritage College *B*
Citrus College *A*
College of Alameda *A*
College of the Canyons *A*
College of the Sequoias *A*
College of the Siskiyous *A*
Columbia College *A*
East Los Angeles College *A*
Feather River College *A*
Foothill College *A*
Fresno Pacific University *B*
Gavilan Community College *A*
Glendale Community College *A*
Golden West College *A*
Hope International University *B*
Humboldt State University *B, M*
Imperial Valley College *A*
Laney College *A*
Las Positas College *A*
Long Beach City College *A*
Marymount College *A*

Mills College *B*
MiraCosta College *A*
Modesto Junior College *A*
Moorpark College *A*
Mount St. Mary's College *B*
Mount San Jacinto College *A*
Napa Valley College *A*
Ohlone College *A*
Pacific Oaks College *B, M*
Pacific Union College *B*
Pitzer College *B*
Point Loma Nazarene University *B*
Pomona College *B*
Reedley College *A*
San Diego City College *A*
San Diego Mesa College *A*
San Diego State University *B*
San Francisco State University *B, M*
San Joaquin Delta College *A*
San Jose State University *M*
Santa Monica College *A*
Santiago Canyon College *A*
Simpson College *B*
Taft College *A*
University of California
   Berkeley *B*
   Irvine *B, M, D*
University of La Verne *B*
University of the Pacific *B, T*
Vanguard University of Southern
   California *B*
Ventura College *A*
West Valley College *A*
Yuba Community College District *A*

Colorado

Colorado Christian University *B*
Colorado Mountain College
   Alpine Campus *A*
   Spring Valley Campus *A*
   Timberline Campus *A*
Colorado State University
   Pueblo *B, T*
Fort Lewis College *B*
Mesa State College *B*
United States Air Force Academy *B*
University of Colorado
   Denver *M*
University of Denver *B*
University of Northern Colorado *B, M, T*

Connecticut

Albertus Magnus College *B*
Central Connecticut State
   University *B, M*
Connecticut College *B*
Eastern Connecticut State University *B*
Holy Apostles College and Seminary *B*
Northwestern Connecticut Community
   College *A*
Quinnipiac University *B*
St. Joseph College *B, T*
Trinity College *B*
University of Bridgeport *B*
Western Connecticut State University *B*

Florida

Flagler College *B*
Florida Agricultural and Mechanical
   University *M*
Florida Atlantic University *B*
Florida Southern College *B*
Florida State University *B, M*
New College of Florida *B*
Palm Beach Community College *A*
Polk Community College *A*
South Florida Community College *A*
Stetson University *B*
Tallahassee Community College *A*
University of Central Florida *B*
University of South Florida *B*
University of Tampa *B, T*
University of West Florida *B*
Warner Southern College *B*

Georgia

Abraham Baldwin Agricultural
College *A*
Andrew College *A*
Berry College *B, T*
Brewton-Parker College *B*
Clark Atlanta University *B*
Dalton State College *A*
Darton College *A*
Floyd College *A*
Georgia College and State University *B*
Georgia Southwestern State University *B*
Mercer University *B*
Piedmont College *B*
Shorter College *B, T*
South Georgia College *A*
Thomas University *B*
Wesleyan College *B*
Young Harris College *A*

Hawaii

Hawaii Pacific University *B*
University of Hawaii
West Oahu *B*

Idaho

Boise State University *A, B, T*
Lewis-Clark State College *B*
North Idaho College *A*
Northwest Nazarene University *B*

Illinois

Benedictine University *B, T*
City Colleges of Chicago
Harold Washington College *A*
Kennedy-King College *A*
Olive-Harvey College *A*
Richard J. Daley College *C, A*
De Paul University *B, T*
Dominican University *B*
Eastern Illinois University *T*
Governors State University *B*
Greenville College *B, T*
Illinois College *T*
Illinois Valley Community College *A*
Kankakee Community College *A*
Kendall College *B*
Kishwaukee College *A*
Lake Land College *A*
Lewis University *B*
Lincoln College *A*
McKendree College *B*
National-Louis University *B*
North Central College *T*
North Park University *B*
Northeastern Illinois University *B*
Northern Illinois University *T*
Northwestern University *T*
Olivet Nazarene University *B, T*
Principia College *B*
Richland Community College *A*
Rockford College *B*
Roosevelt University *B*
St. Augustine College *A*
St. Xavier University *B*
Sauk Valley Community College *A*
Shimer College *B*
Southern Illinois University
Carbondale *B*
Trinity International University *B*
Triton College *A*
University of Chicago *B*
Waubonsee Community College *A*
Wheaton College *T*
William Rainey Harper College *A*

Indiana

Bethel College *A, B*
Goshen College *B*
Indiana University
Bloomington *B, M*
Kokomo *B*
Indiana Wesleyan University *B*
Manchester College *B, T*
Martin University *B*
Oakland City University *A, B*
Purdue University *B, M*

Purdue University
Calumet *B*
St. Mary-of-the-Woods College *B*
Taylor University *B*
Tri-State University *A, B*
University of Southern Indiana *A, B*
Valparaiso University *A, M*
Vincennes University *A*

Iowa

Buena Vista University *B, T*
Dordt College *B*
Drake University *B*
Ellsworth Community College *A*
Franciscan University *B*
Graceland University *B*
Grand View College *B*
Luther College *B*
Marshalltown Community College *A*
Mount Mercy College *T*
North Iowa Area Community College *A*
Northwestern College *T*
Upper Iowa University *B*
Waldorf College *A, B*
Wartburg College *T*
William Penn University *B*

Kansas

Benedictine College *B, T*
Bethany College *B, T*
Central Christian College *A, B*
Cloud County Community College *A*
Dodge City Community College *A*
Donnelly College *A*
Emporia State University *B, M*
Fort Scott Community College *A*
Garden City Community College *A*
Hutchinson Community College *A*
Independence Community College *A*
Kansas City Kansas Community
College *A*
Kansas State University *B*
Labette Community College *A*
McPherson College *B*
MidAmerica Nazarene University *B*
Pittsburg State University *B, M, T*
Pratt Community College *A*
Seward County Community College *A*
Tabor College *B*

Kentucky

Alice Lloyd College *B*
Asbury College *B, T*
Brescia University *A, B*
Campbellsville University *A, B, M*
Lindsey Wilson College *A, B*
Mid-Continent College *B*
Morehead State University *B*
Pikeville College *B*
St. Catharine College *A*
Spalding University *B*
University of Kentucky *B*

Louisiana

Grambling State University *B, M*
Louisiana College *B*
Loyola University New Orleans *B*
Northwestern State University *B*
Nunez Community College *A*
Our Lady of Holy Cross College *B, T*
Southern University
New Orleans *B*
Shreveport *A*
Southern University and Agricultural and
Mechanical College *M*
Tulane University *B*

Maine

Bates College *T*
St. Joseph's College *B*
University of Maine
Augusta *B*
Farmington *B*
Presque Isle *B*
University of New England *B*
University of Southern Maine *B*

Maryland

Allegany College *A*
Cecil Community College *A*
Chesapeake College *A*
College of Southern Maryland *A*
Coppin State College *B*
Frostburg State University *B, T*
Howard Community College *A*
Johns Hopkins University *B, M*
Salisbury University *T*
Towson University *B*
University of Maryland
University College *B*

Massachusetts

Berkshire Community College *A*
Boston University *M*
Cape Cod Community College *A*
Hampshire College *B*
Harvard College *B*
Massachusetts Bay Community
College *A*
Northeastern University *B, M, D*
Simon's Rock College of Bard *B*
University of Massachusetts
Boston *B*
Worcester Polytechnic Institute *B*

Michigan

Adrian College *B, T*
Andrews University *B*
Aquinas College *B*
Calvin College *B*
Central Michigan University *B, M, T*
Concordia University *B, T*
Cornerstone University *B*
Eastern Michigan University *B, M*
Gogebic Community College *A*
Grand Valley State University *B*
Hope College *B*
Kalamazoo College *T*
Lansing Community College *A*
Madonna University *B*
Marygrove College *B*
Michigan State University *B, M, D*
Michigan Technological University *B, T*
Northern Michigan University *B, T*
Northwestern Michigan College *A*
Oakland University *B*
Siena Heights University *B*
Spring Arbor University *B*
University of Michigan *B, T*
University of Michigan
Flint *B, T*
Western Michigan University *B*
William Tyndale College *B*

Minnesota

Augsburg College *B*
Bemidji State University *B*
Bethany Lutheran College *B*
College of St. Benedict *B*
College of St. Catherine *B*
College of St. Scholastica *B*
Concordia University: St. Paul *B*
Hamline University *B*
Metropolitan State University *B*
Minnesota State University
Moorhead *B, T*
Northland Community & Technical
College *A*
Northwestern College *B*
Ridgewater College: A Community and
Technical College *A*
St. Cloud State University *B*
St. John's University *B*
St. Mary's University of Minnesota *B*
University of Minnesota
Morris *B*
University of St. Thomas *B*
Vermilion Community College *A*
Winona State University *B*

Mississippi

Blue Mountain College *B*
Delta State University *B*
Mary Holmes College *A*

Mississippi College *B, M, T*
Mississippi University for Women *B, T*
Rust College *B*

Missouri

Crowder College *A*
Culver-Stockton College *T*
East Central College *A*
Evangel University *A, B*
Lincoln University *M, D*
Mineral Area College *A*
Missouri Baptist University *B, T*
Missouri Southern State College *B, T*
Rockhurst University *B*
St. Louis Community College
St. Louis Community College at
Florissant Valley *A*
St. Louis Community College at
Forest Park *A*
St. Louis Community College at
Meramec *A*
St. Louis University *B*
Washington University in St. Louis *B*
Webster University *B*

Montana

Carroll College *B*
Miles Community College *A*
Rocky Mountain College *B, T*
University of Great Falls *B*
University of Montana: Western *B*

Nebraska

Bellevue University *B*
Chadron State College *B*
College of Saint Mary *B*
Concordia University *B, T*
Dana College *B*
Doane College *B*
Hastings College *B, T*
Midland Lutheran College *B, T*
Nebraska Wesleyan University *B*
Northeast Community College *A*
Peru State College *B, T*
Southeast Community College
Beatrice Campus *A*
Union College *B*
University of Nebraska
Kearney *B, M, T*
Wayne State College *B, M, T*
York College *A, T*

Nevada

Community College of Southern
Nevada *A*
Great Basin College *B*
Sierra Nevada College *B*

New Hampshire

Daniel Webster College *B*
Dartmouth College *T*
Franklin Pierce College *B*
Keene State College *B*
New Hampshire Technical Institute *A*
Plymouth State College *B*
Rivier College *B, T*
Southern New Hampshire University *B*

New Jersey

Atlantic Cape Community College *A*
Brookdale Community College *A*
Caldwell College *B*
Essex County College *A*
Felician College *B*
Monmouth University *B*
Montclair State University *M*
Raritan Valley Community College *A*
Rowan University *B, M*
St. Peter's College *A, B*
Salem Community College *A*
Sussex County Community College *A*
Thomas Edison State College *B*
Warren County Community College *A*

New Mexico

College of the Southwest *B*
Eastern New Mexico University *B*
New Mexico Junior College *A*

Western New Mexico University *B*

New York

Adelphi University *B*
Adirondack Community College *A*
Bard College *B*
Canisius College *A*
Cazenovia College *B*
City University of New York
    Queens College *B*
Clarkson University *B*
Colgate University *B*
Concordia College *B, T*
Cornell University *B*
Corning Community College *A*
Dominican College of Blauvelt *B*
Dowling College *B*
Elmira College *B, T*
Eugene Lang College/New School
    University *B*
Finger Lakes Community College *A*
Fulton-Montgomery Community
    College *A*
Hofstra University *B*
Hudson Valley Community College *A*
Iona College *B, M*
Ithaca College *B, T*
Jamestown Community College *A*
Keuka College *B*
Long Island University
    Southampton College *B*
Medaille College *B*
Metropolitan College of New York *A, B*
Monroe Community College *A*
Mount St. Mary College *B, T*
Nazareth College of Rochester *B*
New York Institute of Technology *B, M*
New York University *B*
Niagara County Community College *A*
Nyack College *B*
Pace University *B*
Pace University:
    Pleasantville/Briarcliff *B*
Roberts Wesleyan College *B*
Rockland Community College *A*
Sage College of Albany *A*
St. Bonaventure University *B*
St. John's University *A, B*
St. Joseph's College *B*
St. Joseph's College: Suffolk
    Campus *B, T*
Sarah Lawrence College *B*
Schenectady County Community
    College *A*
State University of New York
    Binghamton *M*
    Buffalo *B, M*
    College at Potsdam *T*
    College of Agriculture and
      Technology at Cobleskill *A*
    College of Agriculture and
      Technology at Morrisville *A*
    College of Technology at Alfred *A*
    College of Technology at Canton *A*
    College of Technology at Delhi *A*
    Empire State College *A, B*
    Stony Brook *B*
Suffolk County Community College *A*
Syracuse University *M, D*
Tompkins-Cortland Community
    College *A*
Touro College *B*
Ulster County Community College *A*
United States Military Academy *B*
Utica College *B*
Westchester Community College *A*

North Carolina

Appalachian State University *B*
Belmont Abbey College *B*
Elizabeth City State University *B*
Elon University *B*
Fayetteville State University *B*
Gardner-Webb University *B*
Johnson C. Smith University *B*
Lenoir-Rhyne College *B*

Livingstone College *B*
Louisburg College *A*
Meredith College *T*
North Carolina Agricultural and
    Technical State University *B, M, T*
North Carolina State University *B*
Sandhills Community College *A*
University of North Carolina
    Greensboro *M*
Western Carolina University *B*

North Dakota

Dickinson State University *B, T*
Mayville State University *B, T*
Minot State University *B*
Minot State University: Bottineau
    Campus *A*
North Dakota State University *B, M, T*
University of Mary *B*
University of North Dakota *B, T*
Valley City State University *B*

Ohio

Antioch College *B*
Bowling Green State University:
    Firelands College *A*
Cedarville University *B, T*
Cleveland State University *B, M*
Defiance College *B, T*
Heidelberg College *B*
Kent State University *B*
Lake Erie College *B*
Lorain County Community College *A*
Lourdes College *A, B*
Notre Dame College *B, T*
Ohio Dominican College *B, T*
Ohio Northern University *B*
Ohio State University
    Columbus Campus *B, M, D*
Ohio University *A, M*
Ohio University
    Southern Campus at Ironton *A*
Shawnee State University *A, B*
Stark State College of Technology *A*
Union Institute & University *B*
University of Akron *B*
University of Findlay *A, B*
University of Rio Grande *A, B, T*
University of Toledo *A*
Urbana University *B*
Wilmington College *B*
Wittenberg University *B*
Wright State University: Lake Campus *A*
Youngstown State University *B*

Oklahoma

Bacone College *A*
Carl Albert State College *A*
East Central University *B*
Eastern Oklahoma State College *A*
Langston University *B*
Northeastern Oklahoma Agricultural and
    Mechanical College *A*
Northern Oklahoma College *A*
Northwestern Oklahoma State
    University *B*
Oklahoma Baptist University *B, T*
Oklahoma Panhandle State University *B*
Oklahoma Wesleyan University *A, B*
Rogers State University *B*
Rose State College *A*
St. Gregory's University *A, B*
Seminole State College *A*
Southern Nazarene University *B*
Tulsa Community College *A*
University of Oklahoma *B, M, D*
University of Science and Arts of
    Oklahoma *T*
Western Oklahoma State College *A*

Oregon

Central Oregon Community College *A*
Concordia University *B*
Linn-Benton Community College *A*
Marylhurst University *B*
Northwest Christian College *B*
Portland State University *B, M*

Rogue Community College *A*
Southern Oregon University *B, T*
University of Oregon *B*
Warner Pacific College *A, B*
Western Baptist College *B*
Western Oregon University *B*

Pennsylvania

Bloomsburg University of
    Pennsylvania *B*
Bryn Athyn College of the New
    Church *A*
Bucks County Community College *A*
California University of
    Pennsylvania *B, M*
Cambria County Area Community
    College *A*
Carnegie Mellon University *B, M, D*
Chestnut Hill College *C, A, B*
Cheyney University of Pennsylvania *B*
Community College of Allegheny
    County *A*
Community College of Beaver County *A*
DeSales University *T*
Edinboro University of
    Pennsylvania *A, B, M*
Gettysburg College *B*
Harrisburg Area Community College *A*
Juniata College *B*
Kutztown University of
    Pennsylvania *B, M, T*
La Salle University *B, T*
Lehigh Carbon Community College *A*
Lehigh University *B, M, D*
Lock Haven University of
    Pennsylvania *B*
Luzerne County Community College *A*
Marywood University *B*
Montgomery County Community
    College *A*
Penn State
    University Park *M, D*
Point Park College *B*
Reading Area Community College *A*
Robert Morris University *B*
Rosemont College *B*
St. Joseph's University *B*
University of Pennsylvania *A, B, D*
University of Pittsburgh *B*
University of Pittsburgh
    Bradford *B*
    Greensburg *B*
    Johnstown *B*
University of Scranton *T*
Waynesburg College *B*
Widener University *B*
Wilson College *B*
York College of Pennsylvania *B*

Puerto Rico

Inter American University of Puerto Rico
    Metropolitan Campus *B*
Pontifical Catholic University of Puerto
    Rico *B*
Turabo University *A, B*
University of Puerto Rico
    Carolina Regional College *A*
    Cayey University College *B*
    Mayaguez Campus *B*
    Ponce *A*
    Rio Piedras Campus *B*
    Utuado *A*
University of the Sacred Heart *B*

Rhode Island

Rhode Island College *B*

South Carolina

Charleston Southern University *B*
Presbyterian College *B, T*
Southern Wesleyan University *B*
University of South Carolina *M*
Wofford College *T*

South Dakota

Augustana College *T*
Black Hills State University *B*

Dakota Wesleyan University *B*
Sinte Gleska University *A, B*
University of Sioux Falls *A, B*

Tennessee

American Baptist College of ABT
    Seminary *A, B*
Bethel College *B*
Dyersburg State Community College *A*
Freed-Hardeman University *B, T*
Lee University *B*
Northeast State Technical Community
    College *A*
Roane State Community College *A*
Tennessee State University *B*
Trevecca Nazarene University *B*
University of Tennessee
    Chattanooga *B*

Texas

Abilene Christian University *T*
Amarillo College *A*
Angelo State University *B, T*
Cedar Valley College *A*
Central Texas College *A*
Cisco Junior College *A*
Clarendon College *A*
College of the Mainland *A*
Concordia University at Austin *A, B*
East Texas Baptist University *A*
El Paso Community College *A*
Frank Phillips College *A*
Howard College *A*
Howard Payne University *B, T*
Huston-Tillotson College *B*
Laredo Community College *A*
Lon Morris College *A*
Lubbock Christian University *T*
McMurry University *T*
Midland College *A*
Odessa College *A*
Our Lady of the Lake University of San
    Antonio *B*
St. Edward's University *B, T*
Sam Houston State University *B, M*
Southern Methodist University *B*
Southwestern Adventist University *B*
Southwestern Assemblies of God
    University *A*
Southwestern University *B, T*
Stephen F. Austin State University *B*
Sul Ross State University *B, M, T*
Texas A&M International University *B*
Texas A&M University
    Commerce *B, M*
Texas Wesleyan University *B*
Trinity Valley Community College *A*
Tyler Junior College *A*
University of Houston
    Downtown *B*
University of Mary Hardin-Baylor *B*
University of North Texas *B*
Wayland Baptist University *A, B*
West Texas A&M University *B*
Western Texas College *A*

Utah

Brigham Young University *B*
Salt Lake Community College *A*
Snow College *A*
Southern Utah University *B, T*
University of Utah *B, M, D*
Utah State University *M*
Utah Valley State College *A*
Westminster College *B*

Vermont

Bennington College *B*
Burlington College *B*
Castleton State College *B*
Goddard College *B*
Johnson State College *B*
Lyndon State College *B*
Marlboro College *B*
University of Vermont *B, M*

Virginia

Averett University *B*
Bluefield College *B*
Eastern Mennonite University *B*
Ferrum College *B*
Hollins University *M*
J. Sargeant Reynolds Community
    College *A*
James Madison University *B, T*
Liberty University *B, T*
Lynchburg College *B*
Radford University *B*
Thomas Nelson Community College *A*
University of Virginia's College at
    Wise *T*
Virginia Wesleyan College *B*
Virginia Western Community College *A*

Washington

Central Washington University *B*
Centralia College *A*
Everett Community College *A*
Lower Columbia College *A*
Northwest College *T*
Pacific Lutheran University *B*
University of Washington *B*
Washington State University *B*
Whitworth College *B, T*

West Virginia

Alderson-Broaddus College *B*
Bluefield State College *B*
Marshall University *B, M*
Mountain State University *B*
University of Charleston *B*
West Liberty State College *B*
West Virginia University at
    Parkersburg *A*
West Virginia Wesleyan College *B*

Wisconsin

Alverno College *B, T*
Cardinal Stritch University *B*
Carthage College *B, T*
Edgewood College *B*
Mount Mary College *B*
Northland College *B, T*
Silver Lake College *B, T*
University of Wisconsin
    Milwaukee *B*
    Platteville *B*
    River Falls *B*
    Stevens Point *B, T*
    Superior *B*
    Whitewater *B*
Wisconsin Lutheran College *B*

Wyoming

Central Wyoming College *A*
Laramie County Community College *A*
Sheridan College *A*
University of Wyoming *B*
Western Wyoming Community
    College *A*

Social studies teacher education

Alabama

Athens State University *B*
Birmingham-Southern College *T*
Faulkner University *B, T*
Huntingdon College *T*
Judson College *B*
Lawson State Community College *A*
Miles College *B*
Talladega College *T*
University of Mobile *B, T*

Arizona

Arizona State University *B, T*
Prescott College *B, T*
University of Arizona *B, M*

Arkansas

Arkansas Tech University *B, M*

Harding University *B, M, T*
John Brown University *B, T*
Ouachita Baptist University *B, T*
Southern Arkansas University *B, T*
University of Arkansas *B*
University of Arkansas
    Monticello *B*
    Pine Bluff *B, M, T*
University of Central Arkansas *B, T*
Williams Baptist College *B*

California

Azusa Pacific University *T*
California State University
    Northridge *B, T*
Concordia University *B*
Master's College *T*
Mount St. Mary's College *T*
Occidental College *T*
University of San Francisco *T*
University of the Pacific *T*

Colorado

Colorado State University *T*
Colorado State University
    Pueblo *T*
Fort Lewis College *T*
Metropolitan State College of Denver *T*
Trinidad State Junior College *A*
University of Colorado
    Boulder *T*
    Colorado Springs *T*

Connecticut

Central Connecticut State
    University *B, T*
Fairfield University *T*
Quinnipiac University *B, M*
Sacred Heart University *T*
Southern Connecticut State
    University *B, T*

Delaware

Delaware State University *B*
University of Delaware *T*

District of Columbia

George Washington University *M, T*

Florida

Barry University *T*
Flagler College *B*
Florida Agricultural and Mechanical
    University *B, M*
Florida International University *B, M, T*
Gulf Coast Community College *A*
Nova Southeastern University *M*
Southeastern College of the Assemblies
    of God *B, T*
University of West Florida *B, T*

Georgia

Agnes Scott College *T*
Georgia State University *M, D*
Kennesaw State University *B*
LaGrange College *T*
Mercer University *M, T*
State University of West Georgia *M*
Valdosta State University *M, T*

Hawaii

University of Hawaii
    Manoa *B, T*

Idaho

Boise State University *T*
Brigham Young University - Idaho *T*

Illinois

Blackburn College *B, T*
Bradley University *B*
Chicago State University *T*
Concordia University *B, T*
Greenville College *B, T*
Illinois College *T*
Illinois State University *B, T*
John A. Logan College *A*
Kankakee Community College *A*
Lewis University *T*

Monmouth College *B, T*
North Park University *T*
Northwestern University *B, T*
Olivet Nazarene University *B, T*
Rockford College *T*
Sauk Valley Community College *A*
Trinity Christian College *B, T*
University of Illinois
    Urbana-Champaign *B, M, T*
University of St. Francis *T*

Indiana

Anderson University *B, T*
Ball State University *B, T*
Bethel College *B*
Butler University *T*
Franklin College *T*
Huntington College *B*
Indiana State University *B, M, T*
Indiana University
    Bloomington *B, M, T*
    Kokomo *T*
    Northwest *B*
    South Bend *B*
    Southeast *B*
Indiana University-Purdue University
    Fort Wayne *B*
Indiana University-Purdue University
    Indianapolis *B, T*
Indiana Wesleyan University *B, T*
Manchester College *B, T*
Oakland City University *B*
Purdue University
    Calumet *B*
Saint Mary's College *T*
St. Mary-of-the-Woods College *B*
Taylor University *B, T*
Tri-State University *B, T*
University of Evansville *B*
University of Indianapolis *B, T*
University of St. Francis *B*
University of Southern Indiana *T*
Valparaiso University *B*
Vincennes University *A*

Iowa

Buena Vista University *B, T*
Clarke College *B, T*
Cornell College *B, T*
Dordt College *B*
Drake University *M, T*
Ellsworth Community College *A*
Franciscan University *B, T*
Graceland University *T*
Grand View College *B, T*
Luther College *B*
Mount Mercy College *T*
Northwestern College *T*
St. Ambrose University *T*
University of Iowa *B, M, D, T*
Upper Iowa University *B, T*
Wartburg College *T*
William Penn University *B*

Kansas

Benedictine College *B, T*
Bethel College *T*
Central Christian College *A, B*
Fort Scott Community College *A*
Garden City Community College *A*
Independence Community College *A*
Kansas Wesleyan University *T*
McPherson College *B, T*
MidAmerica Nazarene University *B, T*
Pittsburg State University *B, T*
St. Mary College *T*
Tabor College *B, T*
University of Kansas *B, T*
Washburn University of Topeka *B*

Kentucky

Alice Lloyd College *B*
Bellarmine University *B, M, T*
Brescia University *B*
Campbellsville University *B*
Cumberland College *B, T*
Kentucky Wesleyan College *T*

Murray State University *B, M, T*
Pikeville College *B, T*
Spalding University *B*
Thomas More College *B*
Union College *B, M*

Louisiana

Centenary College of Louisiana *B, T*
Louisiana College *B*
Louisiana State University
    Shreveport *B*
McNeese State University *T*
Nicholls State University *B*
Our Lady of Holy Cross College *B, T*
Southeastern Louisiana University *B*
Southern University and Agricultural and
    Mechanical College *B*
University of Louisiana at Monroe *B*
University of New Orleans *B*
Xavier University of Louisiana *B*

Maine

Bowdoin College *T*
College of the Atlantic *B, T*
St. Joseph's College *T*
University of Maine *B, M*
University of Maine
    Presque Isle *B*
University of New England *T*
University of Southern Maine *T*

Maryland

College of Notre Dame of Maryland *T*
Montgomery College
    Rockville Campus *A*
Mount St. Mary's College *B, T*
St. Mary's College of Maryland *T*
Salisbury University *T*
University of Maryland
    College Park *B*

Massachusetts

American International College *T*
Assumption College *T*
Boston University *B, M, T*
Bridgewater State College *T*
Elms College *T*
Harvard College *T*
Lesley University *B*
Merrimack College *T*
Northeastern University *T*
Springfield College *T*
Tufts University *M, T*
University of Massachusetts
    Dartmouth *T*
Western New England College *T*
Westfield State College *B, M, T*

Michigan

Alma College *T*
Andrews University *B*
Calvin College *B*
Central Michigan University *B*
Concordia University *B, T*
Eastern Michigan University *B, T*
Grand Valley State University *T*
Hope College *T*
Northern Michigan University *B, T*
University of Michigan
    Dearborn *B*
    Flint *B, T*
Wayne State University *B, M, T*

Minnesota

Augsburg College *T*
Bemidji State University *M, T*
Bethel College *B*
College of St. Benedict *T*
College of St. Catherine *T*
College of St. Scholastica *T*
Concordia College: Moorhead *B, T*
Concordia University: St. Paul *B, T*
Crown College *B, T*
Gustavus Adolphus College *T*
Minnesota State University
    Mankato *B, M, T*
    Moorhead *B, T*

Northland Community & Technical
   College *A*
Northwestern College *B*
St. Cloud State University *T*
St. John's University *T*
St. Mary's University of Minnesota *B*
St. Olaf College *B*
Southwest State University *T*
University of Minnesota
   Duluth *B*
   Twin Cities *M, T*
University of St. Thomas *B, T*
Vermilion Community College *A*
Winona State University *B, T*

Mississippi

Itawamba Community College *A*
Mary Holmes College *A*
Mississippi College *B*
Mississippi State University *T*
Northwest Mississippi Community
   College *A*

Missouri

Central Missouri State
   University *B, M, T*
College of the Ozarks *B, T*
Columbia College *T*
Evangel University *B, T*
Hannibal-LaGrange College *B*
Harris Stowe State College *T*
Lindenwood University *M*
Missouri Baptist University *T*
Missouri Valley College *B, T*
Rockhurst University *B*
Southeast Missouri State
   University *B, M, T*
Truman State University *M, T*
University of Missouri
   Columbia *B, M, D*
Washington University in St.
   Louis *B, M, T*
William Jewell College *T*

Montana

Montana State University
   Billings *B, T*
Rocky Mountain College *B, T*
University of Montana-Missoula *T*
University of Montana: Western *B, T*

Nebraska

Creighton University *T*
Dana College *B*
Hastings College *B, M, T*
Midland Lutheran College *B, T*
Nebraska Wesleyan University *T*

Nevada

University of Nevada
   Reno *B*

New Hampshire

Colby-Sawyer College *B, T*
Franklin Pierce College *T*
New England College *B, T*
Rivier College *B, T*
Southern New Hampshire University *B*
University of New Hampshire *T*
University of New Hampshire at
   Manchester *M*

New Jersey

Bloomfield College *B*
Caldwell College *T*
Centenary College *T*
The College of New Jersey *B, T*
College of St. Elizabeth *T*
Ramapo College of New Jersey *M*
Richard Stockton College of New
   Jersey *B*
Rider University *B, T*
Rowan University *T*
Rutgers, The State University of New
   Jersey
      Camden Regional Campus *T*
      Newark Regional Campus *T*
St. Peter's College *T*

William Paterson University of New
   Jersey *T*

New Mexico

New Mexico Highlands University *B*
Western New Mexico University *B*

New York

Adelphi University *M*
Alfred University *M, T*
Canisius College *B, M, T*
City University of New York
   Brooklyn College *B, M*
   City College *B, T*
   College of Staten Island *M*
   Hunter College *B, M, T*
   Queens College *M, T*
Colgate University *M*
College of Mount St. Vincent *T*
College of New Rochelle *T*
D'Youville College *B, M, T*
Daemen College *B, T*
Dowling College *B*
Elmira College *B, T*
Fordham University *T*
Hofstra University *B, M, T*
Houghton College *B, T*
Ithaca College *B, T*
Keuka College *B, T*
Le Moyne College *T*
Long Island University
   C. W. Post Campus *M, T*
   Southampton College *T*
Manhattan College *B, T*
Manhattanville College *M, T*
Marist College *B, T*
Marymount College of Fordham
   University *B, T*
Marymount Manhattan College *B, T*
Mercy College *T*
Molloy College *B*
Mount St. Mary College *B*
Nazareth College of Rochester *T*
New York Institute of Technology *B, T*
New York University *B, M, T*
Niagara University *B, T*
Pace University *B, M, T*
Pace University:
   Pleasantville/Briarcliff *B, T*
Roberts Wesleyan College *B, T*
St. Bonaventure University *M, T*
St. John Fisher College *B, M, T*
St. John's University *B, M, T*
St. Joseph's College *B, T*
St. Joseph's College: Suffolk
   Campus *B, T*
St. Lawrence University *T*
State University of New York
   Albany *B, M, T*
   Binghamton *M*
   Buffalo *M, T*
   College at Brockport *M, T*
   College at Buffalo *B, M, T*
   College at Cortland *B, M, T*
   College at Fredonia *B, T*
   College at Geneseo *B, T*
   College at Plattsburgh *B, M*
   College at Potsdam *B, M, T*
   New Paltz *B, M, T*
   Oswego *B, M*
   Stony Brook *T*
Syracuse University *B, M, T*
Utica College *B*
Wagner College *T*
Wells College *T*

North Carolina

Appalachian State University *M*
Barton College *B, T*
Belmont Abbey College *T*
Campbell University *B, T*
Catawba College *T*
Davidson College *T*
East Carolina University *B*
Elizabeth City State University *B*
Greensboro College *T*

Lenoir-Rhyne College *B, T*
Livingstone College *T*
Mars Hill College *T*
Meredith College *T*
Methodist College *A, B, T*
North Carolina State University *B, T*
Queens University of Charlotte *T*
St. Augustine's College *B*
Sandhills Community College *A*
Shaw University *B, T*
University of North Carolina
   Greensboro *M*
   Pembroke *B, M, T*
Wake Forest University *T*
Western Carolina University *B, T*
Winston-Salem State University *B*

North Dakota

North Dakota State University *B, T*
University of North Dakota *B, T*

Ohio

Ashland University *B, T*
Baldwin-Wallace College *T*
Bluffton College *B*
Bowling Green State University *B*
Cedarville University *B, T*
Central State University *B*
College of Mount St. Joseph *T*
Defiance College *B, T*
Hiram College *T*
John Carroll University *T*
Kent State University *B, T*
Kent State University
   Stark Campus *B*
Lorain County Community College *A*
Malone College *B*
Miami University
   Oxford Campus *B, T*
Mount Union College *T*
Mount Vernon Nazarene University *B, T*
Ohio Dominican College *B, T*
Ohio Northern University *B, T*
Ohio State University
   Columbus Campus *M, D*
Ohio University *B, D, T*
Otterbein College *B*
University of Akron *B, T*
University of Dayton *B, M, T*
University of Findlay *B, T*
University of Toledo *B, T*
Urbana University *B*
Ursuline College *B, T*
Walsh University *B*
Wilmington College *B*
Wittenberg University *B*
Wright State University *B, T*
Youngstown State University *B, M*

Oklahoma

Cameron University *B, T*
East Central University *B*
Eastern Oklahoma State College *A*
Langston University *B*
Northeastern State University *B*
Oklahoma Baptist University *B, T*
Oklahoma Christian University of
   Science and Arts *B, T*
Oklahoma City University *B*
Oklahoma State University *B, T*
Oklahoma Wesleyan University *B*
Oral Roberts University *B*
Southeastern Oklahoma State
   University *B, M, T*
University of Central Oklahoma *B*
University of Oklahoma *B, T*
University of Tulsa *T*
Western Oklahoma State College *A*

Oregon

Concordia University *B, M, T*
Eastern Oregon University *B*
George Fox University *T*
Portland State University *T*
Southern Oregon University *T*
University of Portland *T*
Warner Pacific College *T*

Western Baptist College *B*
Western Oregon University *T*

Pennsylvania

Albright College *T*
Arcadia University *B, M, T*
Bloomsburg University of
   Pennsylvania *B, T*
Cabrini College *B, T*
California University of
   Pennsylvania *B, T*
Carlow College *B, T*
Chatham College *M*
Cheyney University of Pennsylvania *T*
DeSales University *T*
Dickinson College *T*
Duquesne University *B, T*
East Stroudsburg University of
   Pennsylvania *B, M, T*
Elizabethtown College *T*
Geneva College *T*
Gettysburg College *T*
Grove City College *B, T*
Gwynedd-Mercy College *T*
Holy Family University *B, M, T*
Indiana University of Pennsylvania *B, T*
Juniata College *B, T*
King's College *T*
La Salle University *B, T*
Lebanon Valley College of
   Pennsylvania *T*
Lincoln University *B, T*
Lock Haven University of
   Pennsylvania *B, T*
Lycoming College *T*
Messiah College *T*
Millersville University of
   Pennsylvania *B, T*
Penn State
   Harrisburg *B*
Philadelphia Biblical University *B, T*
Robert Morris University *T*
St. Joseph's University *B*
St. Vincent College *T*
Seton Hill University *T*
Slippery Rock University of
   Pennsylvania *T*
Temple University *B, T*
Thiel College *B*
University of Pennsylvania *M*
University of Pittsburgh *T*
University of Pittsburgh
   Johnstown *B, T*
Villanova University *T*
Waynesburg College *B, T*
Widener University *M*
Wilkes University *T*
York College of Pennsylvania *B, T*

Puerto Rico

Inter American University of Puerto Rico
   Barranquitas Campus *B, T*
   Fajardo Campus *B, T*
   Metropolitan Campus *B*
Pontifical Catholic University of Puerto
   Rico *B, T*

Rhode Island

Providence College *T*
Rhode Island College *B, M*

South Carolina

Anderson College *B, T*
Charleston Southern University *B, M*
Converse College *T*
Erskine College *B, T*
Francis Marion University *T*
Furman University *T*
Limestone College *B*
Morris College *B*
South Carolina State University *B, T*
University of South Carolina
   Aiken *B, T*

South Dakota

Augustana College *B, T*
Dakota State University *B, T*

Dakota Wesleyan University *B, T*

Tennessee
Belmont University *T*
Bryan College *T*
King College *T*
Lane College *B*
Tennessee Technological University *T*
University of Tennessee
    Chattanooga *B, T*
    Knoxville *T*
Vanderbilt University *B, M, D*

Texas
Abilene Christian University *B, T*
Baylor University *B, T*
Dallas Baptist University *T*
East Texas Baptist University *B*
Hardin-Simmons University *B, T*
Howard Payne University *T*
Lamar University *T*
LeTourneau University *B*
Lubbock Christian University *B, T*
McMurry University *T*
St. Edward's University *B, T*
St. Mary's University *B, T*
Texas A&M International
    University *B, T*
Texas A&M University
    Commerce *T*
    Corpus Christi *T*
    Kingsville *T*
Texas Christian University *B, T*
Texas Lutheran University *B, T*
Texas Wesleyan University *B*
University of Dallas *T*
University of Houston *M, T*
University of Houston
    Clear Lake *T*
University of Texas
    Arlington *T*
    San Antonio *T*
West Texas A&M University *T*

Utah
University of Utah *B*
Utah State University *B*
Weber State University *B*

Vermont
Bennington College *B, M, T*
Castleton State College *B, T*
College of St. Joseph in Vermont *B*
Goddard College *B*
Johnson State College *B*
St. Michael's College *T*

Virginia
Averett University *B, T*
Bluefield College *T*
Bridgewater College *T*
Hollins University *T*
Longwood University *B, T*
Old Dominion University *M*
University of Richmond *T*
University of Virginia's College at
    Wise *T*
Virginia Intermont College *B, T*
Virginia Wesleyan College *T*

Washington
Northwest College *T*
Pacific Lutheran University *T*
Washington State University *T*
Western Washington University *B, T*
Whitworth College *B, T*

West Virginia
Alderson-Broaddus College *T*
Concord College *B, T*
Fairmont State College *B*
Ohio Valley College *B*
Shepherd College *T*
University of Charleston *B*
West Virginia State College *B*
West Virginia University *T*
Wheeling Jesuit University *T*

Wisconsin
Alverno College *T*
Carroll College *T*
Carthage College *T*
Concordia University Wisconsin *B, T*
Marian College of Fond du Lac *B, T*
Mount Mary College *B, T*
Northland College *T*
Ripon College *T*
St. Norbert College *T*
University of Wisconsin
    Eau Claire *B*
    Green Bay *T*
    La Crosse *B, T*
    Platteville *B, T*
    River Falls *T*
Viterbo University *B, T*

Social work

Alabama
Alabama Agricultural and Mechanical
    University *B, M*
Alabama State University *B*
Auburn University *B*
Community College of the Air Force *A*
Jacksonville State University *B*
Lawson State Community College *A*
Miles College *B*
Oakwood College *B*
Shelton State Community College *A*
Talladega College *B*
Troy State University *B, M*
Tuskegee University *B*
University of Alabama *B, M, D*
University of Alabama
    Birmingham *B*
University of Montevallo *B*
University of North Alabama *B*

Alaska
University of Alaska
    Anchorage *B, M*
    Fairbanks *B*

Arizona
Arizona State University *B, M, D*
Cochise College *A*
Estrella Mountain Community College *A*
Northern Arizona University *B*

Arkansas
Arkansas State University *B*
Harding University *B*
Henderson State University *B, M*
Philander Smith College *B*
Southern Arkansas University *B*
University of Arkansas *B*
University of Arkansas
    Little Rock *B, M*
    Monticello *B*
    Pine Bluff *B*

California
Azusa Pacific University *B*
California State Polytechnic University:
    Pomona *B*
California State University
    Chico *B, M*
    Fresno *B, M*
    Hayward *B*
    Long Beach *B, M*
    Los Angeles *B, M*
    Sacramento *B, M*
    San Bernardino *M*
    Stanislaus *M*
Chapman University *B*
Fresno Pacific University *B*
Humboldt State University *B*
La Sierra University *B*
Loma Linda University *M, D*
Pacific Union College *B*
Point Loma Nazarene University *B*
San Diego State University *B, M*
San Francisco State University *B, M*

San Jose State University *B, M*
Southwestern College *A*
University of California
    Berkeley *B, M, D*
    Los Angeles *M, D*
University of Southern California *M, D*
Whittier College *B*

Colorado
Colorado State University *B, M*
Metropolitan State College of Denver *B*
University of Denver *M, D*

Connecticut
Asnuntuck Community College *A*
Capital Community College *C*
Central Connecticut State University *B*
Eastern Connecticut State University *B*
Naugatuck Valley Community
    College *C, A*
Sacred Heart University *B*
St. Joseph College *B*
Southern Connecticut State University *B*
University of Connecticut *M, D*
Western Connecticut State University *B*

Delaware
Delaware State University *B, M*

District of Columbia
Catholic University of America *B, M, D*
Gallaudet University *B, M*
Howard University *M, D*
University of the District of Columbia *B*

Florida
Barry University *B, M, D*
Broward Community College *A*
Florida Agricultural and Mechanical
    University *B, M*
Florida Atlantic University *B, M*
Florida Gulf Coast University *M*
Florida International University *B, M, D*
Florida State University *C, B, M, D*
Gulf Coast Community College *A*
Manatee Community College *A*
Miami-Dade Community College *A*
Palm Beach Community College *A*
Polk Community College *A*
St. Leo University *B*
South Florida Community College *A*
Southeastern College of the Assemblies
    of God *B*
University of Central Florida *B, M*
University of South Florida *B, M*
University of West Florida *B*
Warner Southern College *B*

Georgia
Albany State University *B*
Atlanta Metropolitan College *A*
Clark Atlanta University *B, M, D*
Darton College *A*
Fort Valley State University *B*
Gainesville College *A*
Georgia State University *B, M*
Gordon College *A*
Middle Georgia College *A*
Oglethorpe University *B*
Savannah State University *B, M*
Thomas University *B*
University of Georgia *B, M, D*
Valdosta State University *M*

Hawaii
Brigham Young University-Hawaii *B*
Hawaii Pacific University *B*
University of Hawaii
    Honolulu Community College *A*
    Manoa *B, M, D*

Idaho
Boise State University *B, M*
Idaho State University *B*
Lewis-Clark State College *B*
Northwest Nazarene University *B, M*

Illinois
Aurora University *B, M*

Bradley University *B*
City Colleges of Chicago
    Harold Washington College *A*
    Kennedy-King College *A*
College of DuPage *C, A*
College of Lake County *C, A*
Concordia University *B*
Dominican University *M*
Elgin Community College *C, A*
Governors State University *B, M*
Greenville College *B*
Illinois Eastern Community Colleges
    Wabash Valley College *A*
Illinois State University *B, M*
Illinois Valley Community College *A*
Judson College *B*
Kishwaukee College *A*
Lewis University *B*
Lincoln Land Community College *A*
Loyola University of Chicago *B, M, D*
MacMurray College *B*
Northeastern Illinois University *B*
Olivet Nazarene University *B*
Parkland College *A*
Quincy University *A, B*
Roosevelt University *B*
St. Augustine College *B*
Sauk Valley Community College *A*
South Suburban College of Cook
    County *C*
Southern Illinois University
    Carbondale *B, M*
Southern Illinois University
    Edwardsville *B, M*
Springfield College in Illinois *A*
Trinity Christian College *B*
University of Illinois
    Chicago *B, M, D*
    Springfield *B*
    Urbana-Champaign *M, D*
University of St. Francis *B*
Waubonsee Community College *C, A*
Western Illinois University *B*

Indiana
Anderson University *B*
Ball State University *B*
Goshen College *B*
Grace College *B*
Indiana State University *B*
Indiana University
    East *A, B*
Indiana University-Purdue University
    Indianapolis *B, M, D*
Indiana Wesleyan University *B*
Manchester College *B*
Purdue University
    Calumet *B*
St. Joseph's College *B*
Saint Mary's College *B*
Taylor University *B*
Taylor University: Fort Wayne *B*
University of Evansville *B*
University of Indianapolis *B*
University of St. Francis *B*
University of Southern Indiana *B, M*
Valparaiso University *B*
Vincennes University *A*

Iowa
Briar Cliff University *B*
Buena Vista University *B*
Clarke College *B*
Des Moines Area Community College *A*
Dordt College *B*
Ellsworth Community College *A*
Hawkeye Community College *A*
Iowa Western Community College *A*
Loras College *B*
Luther College *B*
North Iowa Area Community College *A*
Northwestern College *B*
St. Ambrose University *M*
University of Iowa *B, M, D*
University of Northern Iowa *B, M*
Waldorf College *A*

Wartburg College *B*

Kansas

Barton County Community College *A*
Bethany College *B*
Bethel College *B*
Butler County Community College *A*
Central Christian College *A*
Fort Hays State University *B*
Haskell Indian Nations University *A*
Independence Community College *A*
Kansas State University *B*
Newman University *M*
Pittsburg State University *B*
Seward County Community College *A*
University of Kansas *B, M, D*
Washburn University of Topeka *B, M*
Wichita State University *B*

Kentucky

Asbury College *B*
Brescia University *A, B*
Campbellsville University *B*
Cumberland College *B*
Henderson Community College *A*
Jefferson Community College *A*
Kentucky Christian College *B*
Morehead State University *B*
Murray State University *B, M*
St. Catharine College *A*
Spalding University *B, M*
University of Kentucky *B, M, D*
University of Louisville *M, D*

Louisiana

Dillard University *B*
Grambling State University *B, M*
Louisiana College *B*
Louisiana State University and
    Agricultural and Mechanical
    College *M, D*
Northwestern State University *B*
Southeastern Louisiana University *B*
Southern University
    New Orleans *B, M*
Southern University and Agricultural and
    Mechanical College *B*
Tulane University *M, D*
University of Louisiana at Monroe *B*

Maine

St. Joseph's College *B*
University of Maine *B, M*
University of Maine
    Augusta *A*
    Presque Isle *B*
University of New England *M*
University of Southern Maine *B, M*

Maryland

Allegany College *A*
Bowie State University *B, M*
Coppin State College *B*
Frostburg State University *B*
Hood College *B*
McDaniel College *B*
Salisbury University *B, M*
University of Maryland
    Baltimore *M, D*
    Baltimore County *B*

Massachusetts

Anna Maria College *B*
Atlantic Union College *B*
Berkshire Community College *A*
Boston College *M, D*
Boston University *M, D*
Bridgewater State College *B*
Dean College *A*
Elms College *B*
Gordon College *B*
Massachusetts College of Liberal Arts *B*
Northeastern University *B*
Regis College *B*
Salem State College *B, M*
Simmons College *M, D*
Smith College *M, D*

Springfield College *M*
Western New England College *B*
Westfield State College *B*

Michigan

Andrews University *B, M*
Bay de Noc Community College *C*
Calvin College *B*
Central Michigan University *B*
Cornerstone University *B*
Eastern Michigan University *B, M*
Ferris State University *B*
Glen Oaks Community College *C*
Gogebic Community College *A*
Grand Valley State University *B, M*
Hope College *B*
Kellogg Community College *A*
Lansing Community College *A*
Madonna University *B, M*
Marygrove College *B*
Michigan State University *B, M*
Mott Community College *A*
Northern Michigan University *B*
Oakland Community College *C, A*
Reformed Bible College *A, B*
Saginaw Valley State University *B*
Schoolcraft College *A*
Siena Heights University *A, B*
Spring Arbor University *B*
University of Michigan *M, D*
University of Michigan
    Flint *B*
Wayne State University *C, B, M*
Western Michigan University *B, M*

Minnesota

Alexandria Technical College *C, A*
Augsburg College *M*
Bemidji State University *B*
Bethel College *B*
Capella University *M, D*
Central Lakes College *C, A*
Century Community and Technical
    College *C, A*
College of St. Benedict *B*
College of St. Catherine *B, M*
College of St. Scholastica *B*
Concordia College: Moorhead *B*
Itasca Community College *A*
Metropolitan State University *B*
Minnesota State University
    Mankato *B*
    Moorhead *B*
Ridgewater College: A Community and
    Technical College *A*
St. Cloud State University *B, M*
St. Cloud Technical College *C, A*
St. John's University *B*
St. Olaf College *B*
Southwest State University *B*
University of Minnesota
    Duluth *M*
    Twin Cities *M, D*
University of St. Thomas *B, M*
Winona State University *B*

Mississippi

Delta State University *B, M*
Itawamba Community College *A*
Mississippi College *B*
Mississippi Gulf Coast Community
    College
    Perkinston *A*
Mississippi State University *B*
Mississippi Valley State University *B, M*
Rust College *B*
University of Mississippi *B*
University of Southern Mississippi *B, M*

Missouri

Avila University *B*
Central Missouri State University *B*
College of the Ozarks *B*
Columbia College *B*
East Central College *A*
Evangel University *A, B*
Lindenwood University *B*

Missouri Western State College *B*
St. Louis Community College
    St. Louis Community College at
        Meramec *A*
St. Louis University *B, M*
Southeast Missouri State University *B*
Southwest Missouri State
    University *B, M*
University of Missouri
    Columbia *B, M, D*
    Kansas City *M*
    St. Louis *B, M*
Washington University in St. Louis *M, D*
William Woods University *B*

Montana

Carroll College *B*
Miles Community College *A*
Salish Kootenai College *A*
University of Montana-Missoula *B, M*

Nebraska

Chadron State College *B*
Creighton University *B*
Dana College *B*
Metropolitan Community College *A*
Nebraska Wesleyan University *B*
Northeast Community College *A*
Union College *B*
University of Nebraska
    Kearney *B*
    Omaha *B, M*
Western Nebraska Community
    College *A*
York College *A*

Nevada

University of Nevada
    Las Vegas *B, M*
    Reno *B, M*

New Hampshire

Franklin Pierce College *B*
Keene State College *M*
New Hampshire Community Technical
    College
    Laconia *C, A*
Plymouth State College *B*
University of New Hampshire *B, M*
University of New Hampshire at
    Manchester *M*

New Jersey

Atlantic Cape Community College *A*
Brookdale Community College *A*
Camden County College *A*
Cumberland County College *A*
Essex County College *A*
Georgian Court College *B*
Kean University *B, M*
Monmouth University *B*
Ocean County College *C, A*
Ramapo College of New Jersey *B*
Richard Stockton College of New
    Jersey *B*
Rutgers, The State University of New
    Jersey
    Camden Regional Campus *B, M*
    New Brunswick Regional
        Campus *B, D*
    Newark Regional Campus *B*
Seton Hall University *B*

New Mexico

Eastern New Mexico University: Roswell
    Campus *A*
New Mexico Highlands University *B, M*
New Mexico State University *B, M*
New Mexico State University
    Alamogordo *A*
San Juan College *C, A*
Santa Fe Community College *A*
Western New Mexico University *B*

New York

Adelphi University *B, M, D*

City University of New York
    College of Staten Island *B*
    Hunter College *M*
    York College *B*
College of New Rochelle *B*
Concordia College *B, D*
Cornell University *B*
Daemen College *B*
Dominican College of Blauvelt *B*
Elmira College *B*
Fordham University *B, M, D*
Fulton-Montgomery Community
    College *A*
Hofstra University *M*
Hudson Valley Community College *A*
Keuka College *B*
Long Island University
    C. W. Post Campus *B*
Marist College *B*
Mercy College *B*
Metropolitan College of New York *A, B*
Molloy College *B*
Nazareth College of Rochester *B, M*
New York University *B, M, D*
Nyack College *B*
Roberts Wesleyan College *B, M*
Rochester Institute of Technology *B*
Skidmore College *B*
State University of New York
    Albany *B, M, D*
    Binghamton *M*
    Buffalo *M, D*
    College at Brockport *B, M*
    College at Buffalo *B*
    College at Fredonia *B*
    College at Plattsburgh *B*
    Health Science Center at Stony
        Brook *B, M, D*
    New Paltz *B, M, D*
    Stony Brook *B, M, D*
Syracuse University *B, M*
Ulster County Community College *A*
Yeshiva University *M, D*

North Carolina

Appalachian State University *B*
Asheville Buncombe Technical
    Community College *A*
Barton College *B*
Bennett College *B*
Campbell University *B*
East Carolina University *B, M*
Elizabeth City State University *B*
Gaston College *A*
Guilford Technical Community
    College *A*
Halifax Community College *A*
Johnson C. Smith University *B*
Lenoir Community College *C, A*
Livingstone College *B*
Louisburg College *A*
Mars Hill College *B*
Martin Community College *A*
Meredith College *B, T*
Methodist College *A, B*
North Carolina Agricultural and
    Technical State University *B, M*
North Carolina Central University *B*
North Carolina State University *B*
Piedmont Community College *A*
Richmond Community College *A*
Sandhills Community College *A*
Shaw University *B*
South Piedmont Community College *A*
University of North Carolina
    Chapel Hill *M, D*
    Charlotte *B, M*
    Greensboro *B, M*
    Pembroke *B*
    Wilmington *B*
Warren Wilson College *B*
Western Carolina University *B*

North Dakota

Minot State University *B*
University of Mary *B*

University of North Dakota *B, M*

Ohio

Ashland University *B*
Baldwin-Wallace College *B*
Bluffton College *B*
Bowling Green State University *B*
Case Western Reserve University *M, D*
Cedarville University *B*
Central Ohio Technical College *A*
Central State University *B*
Clark State Community College *A*
Cleveland State University *B, M*
College of Mount St. Joseph *B*
College of Wooster *B*
Defiance College *C, B*
Franciscan University of Steubenville *B*
Lorain County Community College *A*
Lourdes College *A, B*
Malone College *B*
Miami University
    Oxford Campus *B*
Mount Vernon Nazarene University *B*
Muskingum Area Technical College *A*
Northwest State Community College *A*
Ohio Dominican College *B*
Ohio State University
    Columbus Campus *B, M, D*
    Lima Campus *M*
Ohio University *B, M*
Ohio University
    Chillicothe Campus *A*
Sinclair Community College *A*
Union Institute & University *B*
University of Akron *B, M*
University of Cincinnati *B, M*
University of Cincinnati
    Clermont College *A*
    Raymond Walters College *A*
University of Findlay *B*
University of Rio Grande *A, B*
University of Toledo *A, B*
Ursuline College *B*
Wilmington College *B*
Wright State University *B*
Wright State University: Lake Campus *A*
Xavier University *B*
Youngstown State University *A, B, M*

Oklahoma

East Central University *B*
Northeastern Oklahoma Agricultural and
    Mechanical College *A*
Northeastern State University *B*
Northwestern Oklahoma State
    University *B*
Oklahoma Baptist University *B*
Oral Roberts University *B*
Southwestern Oklahoma State
    University *B*
University of Oklahoma *B, M*

Oregon

Chemeketa Community College *A*
Concordia University *B*
George Fox University *B*
Pacific University *B*
Portland State University *M, D*
Rogue Community College *A*
Southwestern Oregon Community
    College *A*
University of Portland *B*
Warner Pacific College *B*

Pennsylvania

Bloomsburg University of
    Pennsylvania *B*
Bryn Mawr College *M, D*
Bucks County Community College *A*
Cabrini College *B*
California University of Pennsylvania *B*
Carlow College *B*
Cedar Crest College *B*
Chatham College *B*
Community College of Allegheny
    County *C, A*
DeSales University *B*

Edinboro University of
    Pennsylvania *A, B, M*
Elizabethtown College *B*
Harrisburg Area Community College *A*
Holy Family University *B*
Immaculata University *B*
Juniata College *B*
Keystone College *A*
Kutztown University of
    Pennsylvania *C, B, M*
La Salle University *B*
Lehigh Carbon Community College *C, A*
Lock Haven University of
    Pennsylvania *B*
Marywood University *B, M, D*
Mercyhurst College *B*
Messiah College *B*
Millersville University of
    Pennsylvania *B*
Northampton County Area Community
    College *A*
Philadelphia Biblical University *B*
Reading Area Community College *A*
Seton Hill University *B*
Shippensburg University of
    Pennsylvania *B*
Slippery Rock University of
    Pennsylvania *B*
Temple University *B, M*
University of Pennsylvania *M, D*
University of Pittsburgh *C, B, M, D*
West Chester University of
    Pennsylvania *B, M*
Widener University *B, M*

Puerto Rico

Bayamon Central University *B*
Inter American University of Puerto Rico
    Metropolitan Campus *B, M*
Pontifical Catholic University of Puerto
    Rico *B, M, D*
Turabo University *B*
Universidad del Este *A, B*
University of Puerto Rico
    Humacao *B*
    Rio Piedras Campus *B, M*
University of the Sacred Heart *B*

Rhode Island

Community College of Rhode Island *A*
Providence College *B*
Rhode Island College *B, M*
Salve Regina University *B*

South Carolina

Aiken Technical College *A*
Benedict College *B*
Coker College *B*
Columbia College *B*
Florence-Darlington Technical College *A*
Limestone College *B*
Midlands Technical College *A*
Orangeburg-Calhoun Technical
    College *C*
Piedmont Technical College *A*
South Carolina State University *B*
University of South Carolina *M, D*
Winthrop University *B*

South Dakota

Augustana College *B*
Northern State University *B*
University of Sioux Falls *B*
University of South Dakota *B*

Tennessee

Austin Peay State University *B*
Belmont University *B, T*
East Tennessee State University *B, M*
Freed-Hardeman University *B*
Middle Tennessee State University *B*
Southern Adventist University *B*
Tennessee State University *B*
Trevecca Nazarene University *B*
Union University *B, T*
University of Memphis *B*

University of Tennessee
    Chattanooga *B*
    Knoxville *B, M, D*
    Martin *B*

Texas

Abilene Christian University *B*
Amarillo College *A*
Angelina College *A*
Austin Community College *A*
Baylor University *B, M*
Cisco Junior College *C, A*
College of the Mainland *A*
Del Mar College *A*
Eastfield College *C, A*
Galveston College *C, A*
Hardin-Simmons University *B*
Howard Payne University *B*
Lamar University *B*
Laredo Community College *A*
Lubbock Christian University *B*
Midland College *A*
Midwestern State University *B*
Our Lady of the Lake University of San
    Antonio *B, M*
Panola College *A*
Prairie View A&M University *B*
St. Edward's University *B*
Southwest Texas State University *B, M*
Southwestern Adventist University *B*
Stephen F. Austin State University *B, M*
Tarleton State University *B*
Temple College *A*
Texas A&M International University *B*
Texas A&M University
    Commerce *B, M*
Texas Christian University *B*
Texas College *B*
Texas Southern University *B*
Texas Tech University *B*
Texas Woman's University *B*
University of Houston *M, D*
University of Houston
    Clear Lake *B*
University of Mary Hardin-Baylor *B*
University of North Texas *B*
University of Texas
    Arlington *B, M, D*
    Austin *B, M, D*
    El Paso *B*
    Pan American *B, M*
West Texas A&M University *B*

Utah

Brigham Young University *B, M*
Dixie State College of Utah *A*
Salt Lake Community College *A*
Snow College *A*
University of Utah *M, D*
Utah State University *B*
Weber State University *B*

Vermont

Castleton State College *B*
Champlain College *A, B*
Goddard College *B*
Southern Vermont College *B*
University of Vermont *B, M*

Virginia

Eastern Mennonite University *B*
Ferrum College *B*
George Mason University *B*
James Madison University *B*
Longwood University *B*
Mary Baldwin College *B*
Mountain Empire Community College *A*
Norfolk State University *B, M, D*
Radford University *B, M*
Thomas Nelson Community College *A*
Virginia Commonwealth
    University *B, M, D*
Virginia Highlands Community
    College *C, A*
Virginia Intermont College *B*
Virginia State University *B*
Virginia Union University *B*

Washington

Eastern Washington University *B, M*
Edmonds Community College *C*
Heritage College *B*
Pacific Lutheran University *B*
Seattle University *B*
Trinity Lutheran College *C, B*
University of Washington *B, M, D*
Walla Walla College *B, M*
Washington State University *B*

West Virginia

Bethany College *B*
Concord College *B*
Fairmont State College *B*
Marshall University *B*
Mountain State University *B*
Potomac State College of West Virginia
    University *A*
Shepherd College *B*
West Virginia State College *A, B*
West Virginia University *B, M*

Wisconsin

Beloit College *B*
Carthage College *B*
Concordia University Wisconsin *B*
Marian College of Fond du Lac *B*
Marquette University *B*
Mount Mary College *B*
University of Wisconsin
    Eau Claire *B*
    Madison *B, M, D*
    Milwaukee *B, M*
    Oshkosh *B*
    River Falls *B*
    Superior *B*
    Whitewater *B, T*
Viterbo University *B*

Wyoming

Casper College *A*
Sheridan College *A*
University of Wyoming *B, M*

Social/philosophical foundations of education

Alabama

Troy State University *M*
Troy State University Dothan *M*

Arizona

Arizona State University *M*
University of Arizona *M, D*

California

California State University
    Long Beach *M*
    Los Angeles *M*
    Northridge *M*
Hope International University *M*
Stanford University *M, D*

Colorado

University of Colorado
    Boulder *M, D*

Connecticut

Central Connecticut State University *M*
University of Connecticut *D, T*

Florida

Florida Atlantic University *M*
Florida State University *M, D*
University of Florida *M, D*

Georgia

Georgia State University *M, D*
University of Georgia *M, D*

Hawaii

University of Hawaii
    Manoa *M, D*

Illinois

Loyola University of Chicago *M, D*
Northern Illinois University *M*

Northwestern University *B, M, D*
University of Illinois
    Urbana-Champaign *M, D*
Western Illinois University *M*

Indiana
Indiana University
    Bloomington *M, D*

Iowa
Iowa State University *M*
University of Iowa *M, D*
University of Northern Iowa *M*

Kansas
University of Kansas *M*

Kentucky
University of Kentucky *M*

Maryland
Loyola College in Maryland *M*

Massachusetts
Tufts University *M*

Michigan
Eastern Michigan University *M*

Minnesota
University of Minnesota
    Twin Cities *B, M*

Missouri
Washington University in St. Louis *B*

New Mexico
University of New Mexico *D*

New York
Eugene Lang College/New School
    University *B*
Fordham University *M*
Hofstra University *M, T*
New York University *M, D*
State University of New York
    Buffalo *D*
Syracuse University *M, D*

Ohio
Kent State University *M, D*
University of Akron *B, M, T*
University of Cincinnati *M, D*
University of Toledo *M, D*
Youngstown State University *M*

Oklahoma
University of Oklahoma *M, D*

Pennsylvania
Penn State
    University Park *M, D*
University of Pennsylvania *M*

South Carolina
University of South Carolina *D*

Texas
Texas Christian University *M*
Texas Southern University *D*
University of Houston *M, D*
University of Texas
    San Antonio *M*

Utah
University of Utah *M, D*

Washington
Eastern Washington University *M*
University of Washington *M, D*

Wisconsin
University of Wisconsin
    Milwaukee *M*
    Whitewater *M*

Sociology

Alabama
Alabama Agricultural and Mechanical
    University *B*

Alabama State University *B*
Athens State University *B*
Auburn University *B, M*
Auburn University at Montgomery *B*
Birmingham-Southern College *B*
Jacksonville State University *B*
Lawson State Community College *A*
Samford University *B*
Talladega College *B*
Troy State University Dothan *B*
Tuskegee University *B*
University of Alabama *B*
University of Alabama
    Birmingham *B, M*
    Huntsville *B*
University of Mobile *B*
University of Montevallo *B, T*
University of North Alabama *B*
University of South Alabama *B, M*
University of West Alabama *B*

Alaska
University of Alaska
    Anchorage *B*
    Fairbanks *B*

Arizona
Arizona State University *B, M, D*
Arizona Western College *A*
Eastern Arizona College *A*
Gateway Community College *A*
Northern Arizona University *B, M*
Pima Community College *A*
Prescott College *B, M*
South Mountain Community College *A*
University of Arizona *B, M, D*

Arkansas
Arkansas State University *B, M*
Arkansas State University
    Beebe *A*
Arkansas Tech University *B*
Henderson State University *B*
Hendrix College *B*
Ouachita Baptist University *B*
Philander Smith College *B*
Southern Arkansas University *B*
University of Arkansas *B, M*
University of Arkansas
    Little Rock *B*
    Pine Bluff *B*
University of Central Arkansas *B, M*
University of the Ozarks *B*

California
Azusa Pacific University *B*
Bakersfield College *A*
Biola University *B*
Cabrillo College *A*
California State Polytechnic University:
    Pomona *B*
California State University
    Bakersfield *B*
    Chico *B*
    Dominguez Hills *B*
    Fresno *B*
    Fullerton *B, M*
    Hayward *B, M*
    Long Beach *B*
    Los Angeles *B, M*
    Northridge *B*
    Sacramento *B, M*
    San Bernardino *B*
    San Marcos *B, M*
    Stanislaus *B*
Cerritos Community College *A*
Chabot College *A*
Chapman University *B*
College of Alameda *A*
Concordia University *B*
Contra Costa College *A*
De Anza College *A*
East Los Angeles College *A*
Foothill College *A*
Gavilan Community College *A*
Glendale Community College *A*
Golden West College *A*

Holy Names College *B*
Humboldt State University *B, M*
Irvine Valley College *A*
La Sierra University *B*
Las Positas College *A*
Los Angeles Southwest College *A*
Los Medanos College *A*
Loyola Marymount University *B*
Marymount College *A*
Mills College *B*
MiraCosta College *A*
Monterey Peninsula College *A*
Mount St. Mary's College *B*
Occidental College *B*
Ohlone College *C*
Orange Coast College *A*
Pepperdine University *B*
Pitzer College *B*
Point Loma Nazarene University *B*
Pomona College *B*
St. Mary's College of California *B*
San Diego Mesa College *A*
San Diego State University *B, M*
San Francisco State University *B*
San Jose State University *B, M*
Santa Barbara City College *A*
Santa Clara University *B*
Santa Rosa Junior College *A*
Santiago Canyon College *A*
Scripps College *B*
Sonoma State University *B*
Southwestern College *A*
Stanford University *B, M, D*
University of California
    Berkeley *B, D*
    Davis *B, M, D*
    Irvine *B, M, D*
    Los Angeles *B, M, D*
    Riverside *B, M, D*
    San Diego *B, M, D*
    Santa Barbara *B, M, D*
    Santa Cruz *B, D*
University of La Verne *B*
University of Redlands *B*
University of San Diego *B*
University of San Francisco *B*
University of Southern
    California *B, M, D*
University of the Pacific *B*
Vanguard University of Southern
    California *B*
Ventura College *A*
West Valley College *A*
Whittier College *B*

Colorado
Colorado College *B*
Colorado State University *B, M, D*
Colorado State University
    Pueblo *B*
Fort Lewis College *B*
Mesa State College *B*
Metropolitan State College of
    Denver *B, T*
Red Rocks Community College *A*
Regis University *B*
University of Colorado
    Boulder *B, M, D*
    Colorado Springs *B, M*
    Denver *B, M*
University of Denver *B, M*
University of Northern Colorado *B*

Connecticut
Albertus Magnus College *B*
Central Connecticut State University *B*
Connecticut College *B*
Eastern Connecticut State University *B*
Fairfield University *B*
Quinnipiac University *B*
Sacred Heart University *B*
St. Joseph College *B*
Southern Connecticut State
    University *B, M*
Teikyo Post University *B*
Trinity College *B*

University of Connecticut *B, M, D*
University of Hartford *B*
University of New Haven *B*
Wesleyan University *B*
Western Connecticut State University *B*
Yale University *B, M, D*

Delaware
Delaware State University *B*
University of Delaware *B, M, D*

District of Columbia
American University *B, M, D*
Catholic University of America *B, M, D*
Gallaudet University *B*
George Washington University *B, M*
Georgetown University *B*
Howard University *B, M, D*
Trinity College *B*
University of the District of Columbia *B*

Florida
Barry University *B*
Bethune-Cookman College *B*
Broward Community College *A*
Eckerd College *B*
Edward Waters College *B*
Flagler College *B*
Florida Agricultural and Mechanical
    University *B*
Florida Atlantic University *B, M*
Florida International University *B, M, D*
Florida Southern College *B*
Florida State University *B, M, D*
Gulf Coast Community College *A*
Indian River Community College *A*
Jacksonville University *B*
Miami-Dade Community College *A*
New College of Florida *B*
Palm Beach Community College *A*
Pensacola Junior College *A*
Polk Community College *A*
Rollins College *B*
St. Leo University *B*
St. Thomas University *B*
South Florida Community College *A*
Stetson University *B*
University of Central Florida *C, B, M*
University of Florida *B, M, D*
University of Miami *B, M, D*
University of North Florida *B*
University of South Florida *B, M*
University of Tampa *A, B*
University of West Florida *B*

Georgia
Abraham Baldwin Agricultural
    College *A*
Agnes Scott College *B*
Albany State University *B*
Andrew College *A*
Atlanta Metropolitan College *A*
Augusta State University *B*
Berry College *B*
Brewton-Parker College *B*
Clark Atlanta University *B, M*
Clayton College and State University *A*
Columbus State University *B*
Covenant College *B*
Dalton State College *A*
Darton College *A*
East Georgia College *A*
Emory University *B, D*
Fort Valley State University *B*
Gainesville College *A*
Georgia College and State University *B*
Georgia Perimeter College *A*
Georgia Southern University *B, M*
Georgia Southwestern State University *B*
Georgia State University *B, M, D*
Kennesaw State University *B*
LaGrange College *B*
Macon State College *A*
Mercer University *B*
Middle Georgia College *A*
Morehouse College *B*
Morris Brown College *B*

North Georgia College & State
  University *B*
Oglethorpe University *B*
Oxford College of Emory University *B*
Paine College *B*
Piedmont College *B*
Reinhardt College *B*
Savannah State University *B*
Shorter College *B*
South Georgia College *A*
Spelman College *B*
State University of West Georgia *B, M*
University of Georgia *B, M, D*
Valdosta State University *B, M*
Waycross College *A*
Wesleyan College *B*

Hawaii
Hawaii Pacific University *B*
University of Hawaii
  Hilo *B*
  Manoa *B, M, D*
  West Oahu *B*

Idaho
Albertson College of Idaho *B*
Boise State University *A, B, T*
Brigham Young University - Idaho *B*
College of Southern Idaho *A*
Idaho State University *B, M*
Lewis-Clark State College *B*
North Idaho College *A*
University of Idaho *B*

Illinois
Augustana College *B, T*
Aurora University *B*
Benedictine University *B, T*
Black Hawk College
  East Campus *A*
Bradley University *B, T*
Chicago State University *B*
Concordia University *B*
Danville Area Community College *A*
De Paul University *B, M*
Dominican University *B*
Eastern Illinois University *B*
Elmhurst College *B, T*
Greenville College *B*
Illinois College *B*
Illinois State University *B, M*
Illinois Valley Community College *A*
Illinois Wesleyan University *B*
John Wood Community College *A*
Joliet Junior College *A*
Judson College *B*
Kishwaukee College *A*
Knox College *B*
Lake Forest College *B*
Lewis University *B, T*
Lewis and Clark Community College *A*
Lincoln College *A*
Lincoln Land Community College *A*
Loyola University of Chicago *B, M, D, T*
McKendree College *B*
Millikin University *B*
Monmouth College *B, T*
North Central College *B*
North Park University *B*
Northeastern Illinois University *B*
Northern Illinois University *B, M*
Northwestern University *B, M, D*
Olivet Nazarene University *B*
Parkland College *A*
Richland Community College *A*
Rockford College *B*
Roosevelt University *B, M*
St. Xavier University *B*
Sauk Valley Community College *A*
Shimer College *B*
South Suburban College of Cook
  County *A*
Southern Illinois University
  Carbondale *B, M, D*
Southern Illinois University
  Edwardsville *B, M*

Southwestern Illinois College *A*
Trinity Christian College *B*
University of Chicago *B, M, D*
University of Illinois
  Chicago *B, M, D*
  Springfield *B, M*
  Urbana-Champaign *B, M, D*
Western Illinois University *B, M*
Wheaton College *B*

Indiana
Anderson University *B*
Ball State University *B*
Bethel College *B*
Butler University *B*
DePauw University *B*
Earlham College *B*
Franklin College *B*
Goshen College *B*
Grace College *B*
Hanover College *B*
Huntington College *B*
Indiana State University *B, M, T*
Indiana University
  Bloomington *B, M, D*
  East *B*
  Kokomo *B*
  Northwest *A, B*
  South Bend *B*
  Southeast *B*
Indiana University-Purdue University
  Fort Wayne *B, M*
Indiana University-Purdue University
  Indianapolis *B, M*
Indiana Wesleyan University *A, B*
Manchester College *B*
Marian College *B, T*
Martin University *B*
Purdue University *D, M, D*
Purdue University
  Calumet *B*
St. Joseph's College *B*
Saint Mary's College *B*
Taylor University *B*
University of Evansville *B*
University of Indianapolis *B, M*
University of Notre Dame *B, M, D*
University of Southern Indiana *B*
Valparaiso University *B*
Vincennes University *A*

Iowa
Briar Cliff University *B*
Central College *B, T*
Clarke College *A, B*
Coe College *B*
Cornell College *B, T*
Drake University *B*
Ellsworth Community College *A*
Franciscan University *T*
Graceland University *B, T*
Grinnell College *B*
Iowa State University *B, M, D*
Iowa Wesleyan College *B*
Loras College *B*
Luther College *B*
Mount Mercy College *B*
North Iowa Area Community College *A*
Northwestern College *B, T*
St. Ambrose University *B, T*
Simpson College *B*
University of Dubuque *B, T*
University of Iowa *B, M, D, T*
University of Northern Iowa *B, M*
Upper Iowa University *B*
Waldorf College *A*
Wartburg College *B, T*
William Penn University *B*

Kansas
Allen County Community College *A*
Baker University *B*
Barton County Community College *A*
Benedictine College *B*
Bethany College *B*
Central Christian College *A*

Dodge City Community College *A*
Emporia State University *B, T*
Fort Hays State University *B*
Fort Scott Community College *A*
Friends University *B*
Independence Community College *A*
Kansas State University *B, M, D*
Kansas Wesleyan University *B*
McPherson College *B, T*
MidAmerica Nazarene University *B*
Newman University *B*
Ottawa University *B*
Pittsburg State University *B, T*
Pratt Community College *A*
St. Mary College *B*
Seward County Community College *A*
Tabor College *B*
University of Kansas *B, M, D*
Washburn University of Topeka *B*
Wichita State University *B, M, T*

Kentucky
Asbury College *B*
Bellarmine University *B*
Berea College *B*
Campbellsville University *B*
Centre College *B*
Georgetown College *B, T*
Kentucky Wesleyan College *B*
Morehead State University *B, M*
Murray State University *B*
Pikeville College *B*
Spalding University *B*
Thomas More College *A, B*
Transylvania University *B*
Union College *B*
University of Kentucky *B, M, D*
University of Louisville *B, M*

Louisiana
Centenary College of Louisiana *B*
Dillard University *B*
Grambling State University *B*
Louisiana College *B*
Louisiana State University
  Shreveport *B*
Louisiana State University and
  Agricultural and Mechanical
  College *B, M, D*
Louisiana Tech University *B*
Loyola University New Orleans *B*
McNeese State University *B*
Nicholls State University *B*
Northwestern State University *B*
Southeastern Louisiana University *B, M*
Southern University
  New Orleans *B*
  Shreveport *A*
Southern University and Agricultural and
  Mechanical College *B, M*
Tulane University *B, M, D*
University of Louisiana at Lafayette *B*
University of Louisiana at Monroe *B*
University of New Orleans *B, M*
Xavier University of Louisiana *B*

Maine
Bates College *B*
Bowdoin College *B*
Colby College *B*
St. Joseph's College *B*
University of Maine *B*
University of Maine
  Presque Isle *B*
University of New England *B*
University of Southern Maine *B*

Maryland
Allegany College *A*
Bowie State University *B*
Community College of Baltimore County
  Essex *A*
Coppin State College *B*
Frederick Community College *A*
Frostburg State University *B*
Goucher College *B*
Harford Community College *A*

Hood College *B*
Johns Hopkins University *B, M, D*
Loyola College in Maryland *B*
McDaniel College *B*
Morgan State University *B, M*
Mount St. Mary's College *B*
St. Mary's College of Maryland *B*
Salisbury University *B*
Towson University *B*
University of Maryland
  Baltimore County *B, M*
  College Park *B, M, D*
Washington College *B*

Massachusetts
American International College *B*
Amherst College *B*
Assumption College *B*
Boston College *B, M, D*
Boston University *B, M, D*
Brandeis University *B, M, D*
Bridgewater State College *B*
Bunker Hill Community College *A*
Cape Cod Community College *A*
Clark University *B*
College of the Holy Cross *B*
Elms College *B*
Emmanuel College *B*
Fitchburg State College *B*
Framingham State College *B*
Gordon College *B*
Hampshire College *B*
Harvard College *B*
Lasell College *B*
Massachusetts College of Liberal Arts *B*
Merrimack College *B*
Mount Holyoke College *B*
Newbury College *A*
Northeastern University *B, M, D*
Regis College *B*
St. John's Seminary College *B*
Salem State College *B*
Simmons College *B*
Smith College *B*
Springfield College *B*
Stonehill College *B*
Suffolk University *B*
Tufts University *B*
University of Massachusetts
  Amherst *B, M, D*
  Boston *B, M*
  Dartmouth *B*
  Lowell *B*
Wellesley College *B*
Western New England College *B*
Westfield State College *B*
Wheaton College *B*
Williams College *B*

Michigan
Adrian College *B, T*
Alma College *B, T*
Andrews University *B*
Aquinas College *B, T*
Calvin College *B*
Central Michigan University *B, M*
Cornerstone University *B*
Eastern Michigan University *B, M*
Ferris State University *B*
Grand Valley State University *B*
Hillsdale College *B*
Hope College *B*
Kalamazoo College *B, T*
Kellogg Community College *A*
Lansing Community College *A*
Madonna University *B*
Michigan State University *B, M, D*
Mid Michigan Community College *A*
Northern Michigan University *B, T*
Oakland University *B, T*
Saginaw Valley State University *B*
Spring Arbor University *B*
University of Michigan *B, M, D, T*
University of Michigan
  Dearborn *B*
  Flint *B*

Wayne State University *B, M, D*
Western Michigan University *B, M, D*

Minnesota
Augsburg College *B*
Bemidji State University *B*
Bethel College *B*
Carleton College *B*
College of St. Benedict *B*
College of St. Catherine *B*
Concordia College: Moorhead *B*
Concordia University: St. Paul *B*
Gustavus Adolphus College *B*
Hamline University *B*
Macalester College *B*
Minnesota State University
    Mankato *B, M*
    Moorhead *B*
Ridgewater College: A Community and
    Technical College *A*
St. Cloud State University *B*
St. John's University *B*
St. Mary's University of Minnesota *B*
St. Olaf College *B*
Southwest State University *B*
University of Minnesota
    Duluth *B*
    Morris *B*
    Twin Cities *B, M, D*
University of St. Thomas *B*
Winona State University *B*

Mississippi
Alcorn State University *B*
Itawamba Community College *A*
Millsaps College *B, T*
Mississippi College *B*
Mississippi State University *B, M, D*
Mississippi Valley State University *B*
Rust College *B*
University of Mississippi *B, M*
University of Southern Mississippi *B*

Missouri
Avila University *B*
Central Methodist College *B*
Central Missouri State University *B, M*
College of the Ozarks *B*
Columbia College *B*
Culver-Stockton College *B*
Drury University *B*
East Central College *A*
Evangel University *B*
Lincoln University *B, M*
Lindenwood University *B*
Maryville University of Saint Louis *B*
Missouri Southern State College *B, T*
Missouri Valley College *B*
Northwest Missouri State University *B*
Rockhurst University *B*
St. Louis University *B*
Southeast Missouri State University *B*
Southwest Baptist University *B*
Southwest Missouri State University *B*
Three Rivers Community College *A*
Truman State University *B*
University of Missouri
    Columbia *B, M, D*
    Kansas City *B, M*
    St. Louis *B, M*
Webster University *B*
Westminster College *B*

Montana
Carroll College *B*
Montana State University
    Billings *B, T*
    Bozeman *B*
Rocky Mountain College *B, T*
University of Great Falls *B*
University of Montana-Missoula *B, M*

Nebraska
Bellevue University *B*
Chadron State College *B*
Creighton University *B*
Dana College *B*

Doane College *B*
Hastings College *B*
Midland Lutheran College *B*
Nebraska Wesleyan University *B*
Peru State College *B, T*
Southeast Community College
    Beatrice Campus *A*
University of Nebraska
    Kearney *B*
    Lincoln *B, M, D*
    Omaha *B*
Wayne State College *B, T*
Western Nebraska Community
    College *A*

Nevada
Great Basin College *A*
University of Nevada
    Las Vegas *B, M, D*
    Reno *B, M*

New Hampshire
Dartmouth College *B*
Franklin Pierce College *B*
Keene State College *B*
New England College *B*
Rivier College *B*
St. Anselm College *B*
University of New Hampshire *B, M, D*

New Jersey
Atlantic Cape Community College *A*
Bloomfield College *B*
Caldwell College *B*
Centenary College *B*
The College of New Jersey *B*
College of St. Elizabeth *B*
Drew University *B*
Fairleigh Dickinson University
    College at Florham *B*
    Metropolitan Campus *B*
Felician College *B*
Georgian Court College *B*
Gloucester County College *A*
Hudson County Community College *A*
Kean University *B*
Middlesex County College *A*
Montclair State University *B*
New Jersey City University *B*
Passaic County Community College *A*
Princeton University *B, M, D*
Ramapo College of New Jersey *B*
Richard Stockton College of New
    Jersey *B*
Rider University *B*
Rowan University *B*
Rutgers, The State University of New
    Jersey
    Camden Regional Campus *B*
    New Brunswick Regional
        Campus *B, M, D*
    Newark Regional Campus *B*
St. Peter's College *B*
Salem Community College *A*
Seton Hall University *B, T*
Thomas Edison State College *B*
William Paterson University of New
    Jersey *B, M*

New Mexico
Eastern New Mexico University *B*
New Mexico Highlands University *B*
New Mexico State University *B, M*
San Juan College *A*
University of New Mexico *B, M, D*
Western New Mexico University *B*

New York
Adelphi University *B*
Adirondack Community College *A*
Alfred University *B*
Bard College *B*
Barnard College *B*

City University of New York
    Baruch College *B*
    Brooklyn College *B, M*
    City College *B, M*
    College of Staten Island *B*
    Hunter College *B*
    Queens College *B, M*
    Queensborough Community
        College *A*
    York College *B*
Clarkson University *B*
Colgate University *B*
College of Mount St. Vincent *B*
College of New Rochelle *B, T*
Columbia University
    Columbia College *B*
Cornell University *B, M, D*
D'Youville College *B*
Dowling College *B*
Elmira College *B*
Eugene Lang College/New School
    University *B*
Excelsior College *B*
Fordham University *B, M, D*
Fulton-Montgomery Community
    College *A*
Hamilton College *B*
Hartwick College *B*
Hobart and William Smith Colleges *B*
Hofstra University *B*
Houghton College *B*
Iona College *B*
Ithaca College *B*
Keuka College *B*
Le Moyne College *B*
Long Island University
    C. W. Post Campus *B*
    Southampton College *B*
Manhattan College *B*
Manhattanville College *B*
Marymount College of Fordham
    University *B*
Marymount Manhattan College *B*
Mercy College *B*
Metropolitan College of New York *A, B*
Molloy College *B*
Mount St. Mary College *B, T*
Nazareth College of Rochester *B*
New York Institute of Technology *B*
New York University *B, M, D*
Niagara University *B*
Pace University *T*
Roberts Wesleyan College *B*
Russell Sage College *B*
St. Bonaventure University *B*
St. John Fisher College *B*
St. John's University *B, M*
St. Joseph's College *B*
St. Joseph's College: Suffolk Campus *B*
St. Lawrence University *B*
Sarah Lawrence College *B*
Skidmore College *B*
State University of New York
    Albany *B, M, D*
    Binghamton *B, M, D*
    Buffalo *B, M, D*
    College at Brockport *B*
    College at Buffalo *B*
    College at Cortland *B*
    College at Fredonia *B*
    College at Geneseo *B, T*
    College at Old Westbury *B*
    College at Oneonta *B*
    College at Plattsburgh *B*
    College at Potsdam *B*
    Institute of Technology at
        Utica/Rome *B, M*
    New Paltz *B, M*
    Oswego *B*
    Purchase *B*
    Stony Brook *B, M, D*
Syracuse University *B, M, D*
Touro College *B*
Union College *B*
United States Military Academy *B*

Utica College *B*
Vassar College *B*
Wagner College *B*
Wells College *B*
Yeshiva University *B*

North Carolina
Appalachian State University *B, M*
Barber-Scotia College *B*
Belmont Abbey College *B*
Bennett College *B*
Catawba College *B*
Davidson College *B*
Duke University *B, M, D*
East Carolina University *B, M*
Elizabeth City State University *B*
Elon University *B*
Fayetteville State University *B*
Gardner-Webb University *B*
Greensboro College *B*
Guilford College *B*
Guilford Technical Community
    College *A*
High Point University *B*
Johnson C. Smith University *B*
Lees-McRae College *B*
Lenoir-Rhyne College *B*
Livingstone College *B*
Louisburg College *A*
Mars Hill College *B, T*
Meredith College *B*
Methodist College *A, B*
North Carolina Agricultural and
    Technical State University *B*
North Carolina Central University *B, M*
North Carolina State University *B, M, D*
North Carolina Wesleyan College *B*
Pfeiffer University *B*
Queens University of Charlotte *B*
St. Augustine's College *B*
Salem College *B*
Shaw University *B*
University of North Carolina
    Asheville *B, T*
    Chapel Hill *B, M, D*
    Charlotte *B, M*
    Greensboro *B, M, T*
    Pembroke *B*
    Wilmington *B*
Wake Forest University *B*
Warren Wilson College *B*
Western Carolina University *B*
Wingate University *B*
Winston-Salem State University *B*

North Dakota
Minot State University *B*
North Dakota State University *B, T*
University of North Dakota *B, M*

Ohio
Ashland University *B*
Baldwin-Wallace College *B*
Bluffton College *B*
Bowling Green State University *B, M, D*
Case Western Reserve
    University *B, M, D*
Cedarville University *B*
Central State University *B*
Cleveland State University *B, M*
College of Mount St. Joseph *B*
College of Wooster *B*
Denison University *B*
Franciscan University of Steubenville *B*
Hiram College *B*
Jefferson Community College *A*
John Carroll University *B*
Kent State University *B, M, D*
Kent State University
    Stark Campus *B*
Kenyon College *B*
Lake Erie College *B*
Lourdes College *A, B*
Miami University
    Middletown Campus *A*
    Oxford Campus *B*

Mount Union College *B*
Mount Vernon Nazarene University *B*
Muskingum College *B*
Notre Dame College *B, T*
Oberlin College *B*
Ohio Dominican College *B, T*
Ohio Northern University *B*
Ohio State University
    Columbus Campus *B, M, D*
Ohio University *B, M*
Ohio Wesleyan University *B*
Otterbein College *B*
Owens Community College
    Findlay Campus *A*
    Toledo *A*
Shawnee State University *B*
Sinclair Community College *A*
University of Akron *B, M, D*
University of Cincinnati *B, M, D*
University of Dayton *B*
University of Findlay *B*
University of Rio Grande *A*
University of Toledo *B, M*
Urbana University *B*
Ursuline College *B*
Walsh University *B*
Wilmington College *B*
Wittenberg University *B*
Wright State University *B*
Wright State University: Lake Campus *A*
Xavier University *A, B*
Youngstown State University *B*

Oklahoma

Cameron University *B*
Carl Albert State College *A*
East Central University *B*
Eastern Oklahoma State College *A*
Langston University *B*
Northeastern Oklahoma Agricultural and
    Mechanical College *A*
Northeastern State University *B*
Northwestern Oklahoma State
    University *B*
Oklahoma Baptist University *B*
Oklahoma City Community College *A*
Oklahoma City University *B*
Oklahoma State University *B, M, D*
Rose State College *A*
Southeastern Oklahoma State
    University *B*
Southern Nazarene University *B*
Southwestern Oklahoma State
    University *B*
Tulsa Community College *A*
University of Central Oklahoma *B*
University of Oklahoma *B, M, D*
University of Science and Arts of
    Oklahoma *A*
University of Tulsa *B*
Western Oklahoma State College *A*

Oregon

Central Oregon Community College *A*
Chemeketa Community College *A*
Eastern Oregon University *B, T*
George Fox University *B*
Lewis & Clark College *B*
Linfield College *B*
Linn-Benton Community College *A*
Oregon State University *B*
Pacific University *B*
Portland State University *B, M, D*
Reed College *B*
Southern Oregon University *B*
University of Oregon *B, M, D*
University of Portland *B*
Warner Pacific College *B*
Western Oregon University *B*
Willamette University *B*

Pennsylvania

Albright College *B*
Arcadia University *B*
Bloomsburg University of
    Pennsylvania *B*

Bryn Mawr College *B*
Bucknell University *B*
Cabrini College *B*
California University of Pennsylvania *B*
Carlow College *B, T*
Cedar Crest College *B*
Chestnut Hill College *B*
Cheyney University of Pennsylvania *B*
Community College of Allegheny
    County *A*
Delaware County Community College *A*
Dickinson College *B*
Drexel University *B*
Duquesne University *B*
East Stroudsburg University of
    Pennsylvania *B*
Edinboro University of Pennsylvania *B*
Elizabethtown College *B*
Franklin & Marshall College *B*
Geneva College *B*
Gettysburg College *B*
Grove City College *B*
Gwynedd-Mercy College *B*
Haverford College *B, T*
Holy Family University *B*
Immaculata University *B*
Indiana University of Pennsylvania *B, M*
Juniata College *B*
King's College *B*
Kutztown University of Pennsylvania *B*
La Roche College *B*
La Salle University *B*
Lafayette College *B*
Lebanon Valley College of
    Pennsylvania *B*
Lehigh University *B, M*
Lincoln University *B*
Lock Haven University of
    Pennsylvania *B*
Lycoming College *B*
Marywood University *B*
Mercyhurst College *B*
Messiah College *B*
Millersville University of
    Pennsylvania *B, T*
Moravian College *B*
Muhlenberg College *B*
Penn State
    Abington *B*
    Altoona *B*
    Beaver *B*
    Berks *B*
    Delaware County *B*
    Dubois *B*
    Fayette *B*
    Harrisburg *B*
    Hazleton *B*
    Lehigh Valley *B*
    McKeesport *B*
    Mont Alto *B*
    New Kensington *B*
    Schuylkill - Capital College *B*
    Shenango *B*
    University Park *A, B, M, D*
    Wilkes-Barre *B*
    Worthington Scranton *B*
    York *B*
Rosemont College *B*
St. Joseph's University *B*
St. Vincent College *B*
Seton Hill University *B*
Shippensburg University of
    Pennsylvania *B, T*
Slippery Rock University of
    Pennsylvania *B, T*
Swarthmore College *B*
Temple University *B, M, D*
Thiel College *B*
University of Pennsylvania *A, B, M, D*
University of Pittsburgh *B, M, D*
University of Pittsburgh
    Bradford *B*
    Johnstown *B*
University of Scranton *A, B*
Villanova University *B*

Washington and Jefferson College *B*
Waynesburg College *B*
West Chester University of
    Pennsylvania *B*
Widener University *B*
Wilkes University *B*
Wilson College *B*
York College of Pennsylvania *B*

Puerto Rico

Inter American University of Puerto Rico
    Metropolitan Campus *B*
    San German Campus *B*
Pontifical Catholic University of Puerto
    Rico *B*
Turabo University *B*
Universidad Metropolitana *B*
University of Puerto Rico
    Cayey University College *B*
    Mayaguez Campus *B*
    Rio Piedras Campus *B, M*

Rhode Island

Brown University *B, M, D*
Rhode Island College *B*
Roger Williams University *B*
Salve Regina University *B*
University of Rhode Island *B*

South Carolina

Charleston Southern University *B*
Claflin University *B*
Clemson University *B, M*
Coastal Carolina University *B*
Coker College *B*
College of Charleston *B, T*
Converse College *B*
Francis Marion University *B*
Furman University *B*
Lander University *B*
Morris College *B*
Newberry College *B*
Presbyterian College *B*
South Carolina State University *B*
University of South Carolina *B, M, D*
University of South Carolina
    Aiken *B*
    Spartanburg *B*
Voorhees College *B*
Winthrop University *B*
Wofford College *B*

South Dakota

Augustana College *B, T*
Black Hills State University *B*
Dakota Wesleyan University *B*
Northern State University *B*
South Dakota State
    University *B, M, D, T*
University of Sioux Falls *B*
University of South Dakota *B, M*

Tennessee

Austin Peay State University *B*
Belmont University *B, T*
Carson-Newman College *B*
Columbia State Community College *A*
East Tennessee State University *B, M*
Fisk University *B*
Jackson State Community College *A*
Lambuth University *B*
Lane College *B*
Lee University *B*
Maryville College *B*
Middle Tennessee State University *B, M*
Milligan College *B*
Rhodes College *B*
Roane State Community College *A*
Tennessee State University *B*
Tennessee Technological University *B*
Union University *B, T*
University of Memphis *B, M*
University of Tennessee
    Chattanooga *B*
    Knoxville *B, M, D*
    Martin *B*
Vanderbilt University *B, M, D*

Texas

Abilene Christian University *B, T*
Angelo State University *B*
Austin College *B*
Austin Community College *A*
Baylor University *B, M, D*
Brazosport College *A*
Cisco Junior College *A*
Coastal Bend College *A*
College of the Mainland *A*
Dallas Baptist University *B*
Del Mar College *A*
East Texas Baptist University *B*
El Paso Community College *A*
Frank Phillips College *A*
Galveston College *A*
Grayson County College *A*
Hardin-Simmons University *B*
Houston Baptist University *B*
Howard Payne University *B*
Huston-Tillotson College *B*
Jarvis Christian College *B*
Kilgore College *A*
Lamar State College at Orange *A*
Lamar University *B*
Laredo Community College *A*
Lon Morris College *A*
McMurry University *B*
Midland College *A*
Midwestern State University *B*
Northeast Texas Community College *A*
Our Lady of the Lake University of San
    Antonio *B*
Palo Alto College *A*
Panola College *A*
Paris Junior College *A*
Prairie View A&M University *B, M*
Rice University *B*
St. Edward's University *B, T*
St. Mary's University *B, T*
St. Philip's College *A*
Sam Houston State University *B, M*
South Plains College *A*
Southern Methodist University *B*
Southwest Texas State
    University *B, M, T*
Southwestern University *B*
Stephen F. Austin State University *B, T*
Tarleton State University *B*
Texas A&M International
    University *B, M*
Texas A&M University *B, M, D*
Texas A&M University
    Commerce *B, M*
    Corpus Christi *B*
    Kingsville *B, M*
Texas Christian University *B*
Texas College *B*
Texas Lutheran University *B*
Texas Southern University *B, M*
Texas Tech University *B, M*
Texas Woman's University *B, M, D, T*
Trinity University *B*
Trinity Valley Community College *A*
Tyler Junior College *A*
University of Houston *B, M*
University of Houston
    Clear Lake *B, M*
    Downtown *B*
University of Mary Hardin-Baylor *B, T*
University of North Texas *B, M, D*
University of Texas
    Arlington *B, M, T*
    Austin *B, M, D*
    Brownsville *B*
    Dallas *B, M*
    El Paso *B, M*
    Pan American *B, M*
    San Antonio *B, M*
    Tyler *B, M*
    of the Permian Basin *B*
University of the Incarnate Word *B*
West Texas A&M University *B*
Western Texas College *A*
Wharton County Junior College *A*

Wiley College *B*

Utah
Brigham Young University *B, M, D*
Dixie State College of Utah *A*
Salt Lake Community College *A*
Snow College *A*
Southern Utah University *B*
University of Utah *B, M, D*
Utah State University *B, M, D*
Weber State University *B*
Westminster College *B*

Vermont
Castleton State College *B*
Johnson State College *B*
Marlboro College *B*
Middlebury College *B*
St. Michael's College *B*
University of Vermont *B*

Virginia
Averett University *B*
Bridgewater College *B*
College of William and Mary *B*
Eastern Mennonite University *B*
Emory & Henry College *B*
George Mason University *B, M*
Hampton University *B*
Hollins University *B*
James Madison University *B*
Longwood University *B, M, T*
Lynchburg College *B*
Mary Baldwin College *B*
Mary Washington College *B*
Marymount University *B*
Norfolk State University *B, M*
Old Dominion University *B, M*
Radford University *B*
Randolph-Macon College *B*
Randolph-Macon Woman's College *B*
Roanoke College *B, T*
Shenandoah University *B*
Sweet Briar College *B*
University of Richmond *B*
University of Virginia *B, M, D*
University of Virginia's College at
   Wise *B, T*
Virginia Commonwealth
   University *C, B, M*
Virginia Polytechnic Institute and State
   University *B, M, D*
Virginia State University *B*
Virginia Union University *B*
Virginia Wesleyan College *B*
Washington and Lee University *B*

Washington
Central Washington University *B*
Centralia College *A*
Eastern Washington University *B, T*
Everett Community College *A*
Gonzaga University *B*
Heritage College *B*
Lower Columbia College *A*
Olympic College *A*
Pacific Lutheran University *B*
Seattle Pacific University *B*
Seattle University *B*
University of Puget Sound *B, T*
University of Washington *B, M, D*
Walla Walla College *B*
Washington State University *B, M, D*
Western Washington University *B, T*
Whitman College *B*
Whitworth College *B*

West Virginia
Concord College *B*
Davis and Elkins College *B*
Fairmont State College *B*
Marshall University *B, M*
Potomac State College of West Virginia
   University *A*
Shepherd College *B*
West Liberty State College *B*
West Virginia State College *B*

West Virginia University *B, M*
West Virginia Wesleyan College *B*

Wisconsin
Beloit College *B*
Cardinal Stritch University *B*
Carroll College *B*
Carthage College *B, T*
Edgewood College *B*
Lakeland College *B*
Marquette University *B, T*
Northland College *B, T*
Ripon College *B*
St. Norbert College *B, T*
University of Wisconsin
   Eau Claire *B*
   La Crosse *B, T*
   Madison *B, M, D*
   Milwaukee *B, M*
   Oshkosh *B*
   Parkside *B, T*
   Platteville *B*
   River Falls *B, T*
   Stevens Point *B, T*
   Superior *B*
   Whitewater *B, T*
Viterbo University *B*

Wyoming
Casper College *A*
Eastern Wyoming College *A*
Laramie County Community College *A*
Sheridan College *A*
University of Wyoming *B, M*
Western Wyoming Community
   College *A*

Software engineering

Alabama
Auburn University *B, M*
University of Alabama
   Huntsville *C*

Arizona
Phoenix College *A*

California
California State University
   Hayward *B*
   Sacramento *M*
Cogswell Polytechnical College *B*
Diablo Valley College *C*
Foothill College *C, A*
National University *M*
Northwestern Polytechnic
   University *B, M*
Santa Clara University *C, M*

Colorado
Colorado Technical University *B, M, D*
National Technological University *M*

District of Columbia
Catholic University of America *M*
George Washington University *M*

Florida
Broward Community College *A*
Embry-Riddle Aeronautical
   University *M*
Florida Agricultural and Mechanical
   University *M*
Florida Institute of Technology *B, M*
Florida State University *B, M*
Hillsborough Community College *A*
Lake-Sumter Community College *A*
Seminole Community College *A*
Tallahassee Community College *A*

Georgia
Southern Polytechnic State
   University *C, B, M*

Iowa
University of Iowa *M*

Kansas
Southwestern College *B*

Maine
Thomas College *B*

Maryland
Capitol College *B*
Harford Community College *C*
University of Maryland
   University College *M*

Massachusetts
Berkshire Community College *A*
Fitchburg State College *C*
Northeastern University *M*

Michigan
Andrews University *M*
Oakland University *M*
University of Michigan
   Dearborn *M*

Minnesota
Globe College *C, A*
Lake Superior College: A Community
   and Technical College *C*
Riverland Community College: A
   Technical and Community College *A*
St. Paul College - A Community and
   Technical College *C, A*
University of St. Thomas *M*

Mississippi
Mississippi State University *B*
University of Southern Mississippi *D*

Missouri
Hickey College *C, A*
Missouri Technical School *A, B*

Montana
Carroll College *B*
Montana Tech of the University of
   Montana *B*

Nevada
Community College of Southern
   Nevada *C, A*
University of Nevada
   Las Vegas *B*

New Jersey
Essex County College *C*
Monmouth University *M*
Stevens Institute of Technology *B, M, D*

New York
Clarkson University *B*
Long Island University
   C. W. Post Campus *M*
Polytechnic University *C*
Rochester Institute of Technology *B*
State University of New York
   Buffalo *M, D*
   College of Agriculture and
      Technology at Morrisville *A*
Westchester Business Institute *C, A*

Ohio
Lorain County Community College *A*
Miami-Jacobs College *C, A*
Ohio Business College: Sandusky *A*
Stark State College of Technology *A*

Oklahoma
Oklahoma Baptist University *B*
Oklahoma State University
   Oklahoma City *C*

Oregon
Oregon Institute of Technology *A, B*
Oregon State University *M*
Portland Community College *C, A*
Portland State University *M*
University of Oregon *B*

Pennsylvania
Allegheny College *B*
Carnegie Mellon University *M*
Drexel University *M*

Marywood University *A*
Montgomery County Community
   College *C, A*
Robert Morris University *B*

South Carolina
Winthrop University *C*

Tennessee
Draughons Junior College of Business:
   Nashville *A*

Texas
Eastfield College *C, A*
Remington College
   Houston *A*
Southern Methodist University *M*
University of Houston
   Clear Lake *B*
University of Texas
   Dallas *B, D*

Vermont
Champlain College *A, B*

Virginia
J. Sargeant Reynolds Community
   College *C*

Washington
Grays Harbor College *C*
North Seattle Community College *C, A*
Seattle University *M*
South Seattle Community College *A*

Wisconsin
Carroll College *B, M*
Milwaukee School of Engineering *B*

Soil science

Alabama
Auburn University *B, M, D*
Tuskegee University *B, M*

Arizona
Prescott College *B, M*
University of Arizona *B, M, D*

California
California Polytechnic State University:
   San Luis Obispo *B*
California State Polytechnic University:
   Pomona *B*
Modesto Junior College *A*
San Joaquin Delta College *A*
University of California
   Berkeley *B*
   Davis *B, M, D*
   Riverside *M, D*
Ventura College *A*

Colorado
Colorado Mountain College
   Timberline Campus *A*

Delaware
Delaware State University *B*
University of Delaware *B, M, D*

Florida
University of Florida *B, M, D*

Georgia
University of Georgia *B*

Hawaii
University of Hawaii
   Hilo *B*
   Manoa *B, M, D*

Idaho
University of Idaho *B, M, D*

Iowa
Iowa State University *M, D*

Kentucky
University of Kentucky *D*

Maine
University of Maine *B, M*

Michigan
Michigan State University *B*

Minnesota
University of Minnesota
Crookston *B*
Twin Cities *M, D*

Missouri
University of Missouri
Columbia *B, M, D*

Nebraska
University of Nebraska
Lincoln *B*

New Hampshire
University of New Hampshire *B, M*

New Mexico
New Mexico State University *B*
Southwestern Indian Polytechnic
Institute *A*

New York
Cornell University *B*
State University of New York
College of Agriculture and
Technology at Cobleskill *A*
College of Environmental Science
and Forestry *M, D*

North Carolina
North Carolina State University *B, M, D*

North Dakota
North Dakota State University *B, M, D*

Ohio
Ohio State University
Agricultural Technical Institute *A*
Columbus Campus *D*

Oklahoma
Eastern Oklahoma State College *A*
Oklahoma State University *B, M, D*

Oregon
Eastern Oregon University *B*
Oregon State University *M, D*

Pennsylvania
Penn State
Abington *B*
Altoona *B*
Beaver *B*
Berks *B*
Delaware County *B*
Dubois *B*
Erie, The Behrend College *B*
Fayette *B*
Hazleton *B*
Lehigh Valley *B*
McKeesport *B*
Mont Alto *B*
New Kensington *B*
Schuylkill - Capital College *B*
Shenango *B*
University Park *B, M, D*
Wilkes-Barre *B*
Worthington Scranton *B*
York *B*

Puerto Rico
University of Puerto Rico
Mayaguez Campus *B, M*

South Carolina
Clemson University *B*

Tennessee
Middle Tennessee State University *B*
Tennessee Technological University *B*
University of Tennessee
Knoxville *B, M, D*

Texas
Prairie View A&M University *M*

Tarleton State University *B*
Texas A&M University *B, M, D*
Texas A&M University
Commerce *B*
Kingsville *M*
Texas Tech University *M*

Utah
Brigham Young University *B, M*
Utah State University *B, M, D*

Vermont
Sterling College *B*
University of Vermont *B, M, D*

Virginia
Mountain Empire Community College *A*
Virginia Polytechnic Institute and State
University *B, M, D*

Washington
Spokane Community College *A*
Washington State University *B, M, D*

West Virginia
West Virginia University *B*

Wisconsin
University of Wisconsin
Madison *B, M, D*
River Falls *B*
Stevens Point *B*

Wyoming
University of Wyoming *M, D*

Solar energy technology

Missouri
Crowder College *A*

Nevada
Truckee Meadows Community
College *C, A*

New Mexico
San Juan College *C, A*

Solid-state/
low-temperature physics

Illinois
Northwestern University *B, M, D*

Massachusetts
Tufts University *M, D*

New Jersey
Stevens Institute of Technology *M, D*

New York
State University of New York
Albany *M, D*

Texas
University of North Texas *M, D*

Wisconsin
University of Wisconsin
Madison *M, D*

Somatic bodywork

Tennessee
Roane State Community College *C*

South Asian languages

Illinois
Northwestern University *B*
University of Chicago *B*

Massachusetts
Harvard College *B*

Minnesota
University of Minnesota
Twin Cities *M, D*

New Hampshire
Dartmouth College *B*

Washington
University of Washington *B*

Wisconsin
University of Wisconsin
Madison *B, M, D*

South Asian studies

California
University of California
Santa Cruz *B*

Illinois
University of Chicago *M*

Massachusetts
Harvard College *B*

Michigan
Oakland University *B*
University of Michigan *B*

Minnesota
Hamline University *B*
University of Minnesota
Twin Cities *M, D*

New York
Sarah Lawrence College *B*

Ohio
College of Wooster *B*

Pennsylvania
University of Pennsylvania *B, M, D*

Rhode Island
Brown University *B*

Vermont
Marlboro College *B*

Virginia
Mary Baldwin College *B*

Washington
University of Washington *B, M*

Wisconsin
University of Wisconsin
Madison *B, M*

Southeast Asian languages

Washington
University of Washington *B*

Southeast Asian studies

California
University of California
Berkeley *B, M, D*
Los Angeles *B, D*
Santa Cruz *B*

Massachusetts
Hampshire College *B*
Harvard College *B*

Michigan
University of Michigan *B, M*

Minnesota
Hamline University *B*

Ohio
Ohio State University
Columbus Campus *M*
Ohio University *M*

Vermont
Marlboro College *B*

Virginia
Mary Baldwin College *B*

Washington
University of Washington *B*

Spanish

Alabama
Alabama State University *B*
Auburn University *B, M*
Birmingham-Southern College *B, T*
Huntingdon College *B*
Jacksonville State University *B*
Oakwood College *B*
Samford University *B*
Spring Hill College *B, T*
University of Alabama *B*
University of Alabama
Birmingham *B*
University of Montevallo *B*

Alaska
University of Alaska
Anchorage *B*

Arizona
Arizona State University *B, M, D*
Arizona Western College *A*
Cochise College *A*
Northern Arizona University *B, T*
Prescott College *B, M*
University of Arizona *B, M, D*

Arkansas
Arkansas State University *B*
Arkansas Tech University *M*
Harding University *B*
Henderson State University *B*
Hendrix College *B*
John Brown University *B*
Lyon College *B*
Ouachita Baptist University *B*
Southern Arkansas University *B*
University of Arkansas *B, M*
University of Arkansas
Little Rock *B*
University of Central Arkansas *B, M*

California
Azusa Pacific University *B*
Bakersfield College *A*
Biola University *B*
Cabrillo College *A*
California State Polytechnic University:
Pomona *B*
California State University
Bakersfield *B*
Chico *B*
Dominguez Hills *B*
Fresno *B, M*
Fullerton *B, M*
Hayward *B*
Long Beach *B, M*
Los Angeles *B, M*
Monterey Bay *B*
Northridge *B, M*
Sacramento *B, M*
San Bernardino *B*
San Marcos *B*
Stanislaus *B*
Cerritos Community College *A*
Chabot College *A*
Chapman University *B*
Citrus College *A*
Claremont McKenna College *B*
College of Alameda *A*
College of the Canyons *A*
College of the Siskiyous *A*
De Anza College *A*
Foothill College *A*
Fresno Pacific University *B*
Gavilan Community College *A*

Glendale Community College *A*
Golden West College *A*
Grossmont Community College *C, A*
Holy Names College *B*
Humboldt State University *B*
Imperial Valley College *A*
Irvine Valley College *A*
La Sierra University *B*
Long Beach City College *C, A*
Los Angeles Pierce College *A*
Los Angeles Southwest College *A*
Loyola Marymount University *B*
Mills College *B*
MiraCosta College *A*
Modesto Junior College *A*
Monterey Institute of International
   Studies *C*
Mount St. Mary's College *B*
Occidental College *B*
Orange Coast College *A*
Pacific Union College *B*
Pepperdine University *B*
Pitzer College *B*
Point Loma Nazarene University *B*
Pomona College *B*
St. Mary's College of California *B*
San Diego City College *A*
San Diego Mesa College *C, A*
San Diego State University *B, M*
San Francisco State University *B, M*
San Joaquin Delta College *A*
San Jose State University *B, M*
Santa Barbara City College *A*
Santa Clara University *B*
Santa Monica College *A*
Scripps College *B*
Sonoma State University *B*
Southwestern College *A*
Stanford University *B, M, D*
University of California
   Berkeley *B, M, D*
   Davis *B, M, D*
   Irvine *B, M, D*
   Los Angeles *B, M*
   Riverside *B, M, D*
   San Diego *B, M*
   Santa Barbara *B, M, D*
   Santa Cruz *B, D*
University of La Verne *B*
University of Redlands *B*
University of San Diego *B*
University of San Francisco *B*
University of Southern
   California *B, M, D*
University of the Pacific *B*
Vanguard University of Southern
   California *B*
Ventura College *A*
Whittier College *B*

Colorado

Colorado College *B*
Colorado State University *B*
Colorado State University
   Pueblo *B, T*
Fort Lewis College *B*
Mesa State College *B*
Metropolitan State College of
   Denver *B, T*
Red Rocks Community College *A*
Regis University *B*
Trinidad State Junior College *A*
University of Colorado
   Boulder *B, M, D*
   Colorado Springs *B*
   Denver *B*
University of Denver *B, M*
University of Northern Colorado *B, T*

Connecticut

Albertus Magnus College *B*
Central Connecticut State
   University *B, M*
Connecticut College *B*
Eastern Connecticut State University *B*
Fairfield University *B*

Quinnipiac University *B*
Sacred Heart University *B*
St. Joseph College *B, T*
Southern Connecticut State University *B*
Trinity College *B*
University of Connecticut *B, M, D*
University of Hartford *B*
Wesleyan University *B*
Western Connecticut State University *B*
Yale University *B, M, D*

Delaware

Delaware State University *B*
University of Delaware *B, M, T*

District of Columbia

American University *B, M*
Catholic University of
   America *B, M, D, T*
Gallaudet University *B*
George Washington University *B*
Georgetown University *B, M, D*
Howard University *B, M, D*
Trinity College *B*
University of the District of Columbia *B*

Florida

Barry University *B*
Eckerd College *B*
Flagler College *B*
Florida Agricultural and Mechanical
   University *B*
Florida Atlantic University *B, M*
Florida International University *B, M, D*
Florida Southern College *B*
Florida State University *B, M, D*
Jacksonville University *B*
Manatee Community College *A*
New College of Florida *B*
Okaloosa-Walton Community College *A*
Polk Community College *A*
Rollins College *B*
South Florida Community College *A*
Stetson University *B*
University of Central Florida *B, M*
University of Florida *B, M*
University of Miami *B, M, D*
University of North Florida *B*
University of South Florida *B, M*
University of Tampa *A, B*

Georgia

Agnes Scott College *B*
Albany State University *B*
Armstrong Atlantic State University *B, T*
Atlanta Metropolitan College *A*
Augusta State University *B*
Berry College *B, T*
Clark Atlanta University *B, M*
Clayton College and State University *A*
Emory University *B, D*
Georgia College and State University *B*
Georgia Southern University *B*
Georgia Southwestern State University *B*
Georgia State University *B, M*
Kennesaw State University *B*
LaGrange College *B*
Mercer University *B*
Morehouse College *B*
Morris Brown College *B*
North Georgia College & State
   University *B*
Oxford College of Emory University *B*
Piedmont College *B*
Shorter College *B*
South Georgia College *A*
Spelman College *B*
State University of West Georgia *B*
University of Georgia *B, M*
Valdosta State University *B*
Wesleyan College *B*
Young Harris College *A*

Hawaii

University of Hawaii
   Manoa *B, M*

Idaho

Albertson College of Idaho *B*
Boise State University *B*
Idaho State University *A, B*
Northwest Nazarene University *B*
University of Idaho *B, M*

Illinois

Augustana College *B, T*
Benedictine University *B, T*
Blackburn College *B*
Bradley University *B, T*
Chicago State University *B*
City Colleges of Chicago
   Harold Washington College *A*
De Paul University *B*
Dominican University *B*
Elmhurst College *B, T*
Greenville College *B*
Illinois College *B, T*
Illinois State University *B, T*
Illinois Wesleyan University *B*
John Wood Community College *A*
Kishwaukee College *A*
Knox College *B*
Lake Forest College *B*
Loyola University of Chicago *C, B, M*
MacMurray College *B, T*
Millikin University *B, T*
Monmouth College *B, T*
North Central College *B, T*
North Park University *B*
Northeastern Illinois University *B*
Northern Illinois University *B, M, T*
Northwestern University *B, M, D*
Olivet Nazarene University *B, T*
Parkland College *A*
Principia College *B, T*
Richland Community College *A*
Rockford College *B*
Roosevelt University *B, M*
St. Xavier University *B*
Sauk Valley Community College *A*
South Suburban College of Cook
   County *A*
Southern Illinois University
   Carbondale *B*
Southern Illinois University
   Edwardsville *T*
Trinity Christian College *B, T*
Triton College *A*
University of Chicago *B*
University of Illinois
   Chicago *B, D*
   Urbana-Champaign *B, M, D*
Western Illinois University *B*
Wheaton College *B*

Indiana

Anderson University *B*
Ball State University *B, M, T*
Butler University *B*
DePauw University *B*
Earlham College *B*
Franklin College *B*
Goshen College *B*
Grace College *B*
Hanover College *B*
Indiana State University *B, M*
Indiana University
   Bloomington *B, M, D*
   Northwest *A, B*
   South Bend *B*
   Southeast *B*
Indiana University-Purdue University
   Fort Wayne *A, B, T*
Indiana University-Purdue University
   Indianapolis *B*
Indiana Wesleyan University *B*
Manchester College *B, T*
Marian College *B, T*
Martin University *B*
Purdue University
   Calumet *B*
Saint Mary's College *B, T*
St. Mary-of-the-Woods College *B*

Taylor University *B*
University of Evansville *B*
University of Indianapolis *B*
University of Notre Dame *B, M*
University of Southern Indiana *B, T*
Valparaiso University *B*
Vincennes University *A*
Wabash College *B*

Iowa

Briar Cliff University *B*
Buena Vista University *B, T*
Central College *B, T*
Clarke College *B, T*
Coe College *B*
Cornell College *B, T*
Dordt College *B*
Graceland University *B, T*
Grinnell College *B*
Iowa State University *B*
Loras College *B*
Luther College *B*
Marshalltown Community College *A*
Morningside College *B*
Northwestern College *B, T*
St. Ambrose University *B, T*
Simpson College *B*
University of Iowa *B, M, D, T*
University of Northern Iowa *B, M*
Waldorf College *A*
Wartburg College *B, T*

Kansas

Baker University *B, T*
Benedictine College *B, T*
Bethel College *B*
Butler County Community College *A*
Friends University *B*
Independence Community College *A*
Kansas Wesleyan University *B, T*
McPherson College *B, T*
MidAmerica Nazarene University *B*
Pittsburg State University *B, T*
Southwestern College *B*
University of Kansas *B, M, D*
Washburn University of Topeka *B*
Wichita State University *B, M*

Kentucky

Asbury College *B, T*
Berea College *B, T*
Brescia University *B*
Centre College *B*
Georgetown College *B, T*
Morehead State University *B*
Murray State University *B, T*
Thomas More College *A*
Transylvania University *B, T*
University of Kentucky *B, M, D*
University of Louisville *B, M*

Louisiana

Centenary College of Louisiana *B, T*
Dillard University *B*
Grambling State University *B*
Louisiana State University
   Shreveport *B*
Louisiana State University and
   Agricultural and Mechanical
   College *B, M*
Louisiana Tech University *B*
Loyola University New Orleans *B*
McNeese State University *B*
Southeastern Louisiana University *B*
Southern University
   New Orleans *B*
Southern University and Agricultural and
   Mechanical College *B*
Tulane University *B, M, D*
University of Louisiana at Monroe *B*
University of New Orleans *B, M*
Xavier University of Louisiana *B*

Maine

Bates College *B*
Bowdoin College *B*
Colby College *B*

University of Maine *B*

Maryland

Allegany College *A*
College of Notre Dame of Maryland *B*
Community College of Baltimore County
 Catonsville *A*
 Dundalk *A*
 Essex *A*
Frostburg State University *T*
Goucher College *B*
Hood College *B, T*
Johns Hopkins University *B, M, D*
Loyola College in Maryland *B*
McDaniel College *B*
Mount St. Mary's College *B*
Salisbury University *B, T*
Towson University *B, T*
University of Maryland
 Baltimore County *B*
 College Park *B, M, D*
Washington College *B, T*

Massachusetts

American International College *B*
Amherst College *B*
Anna Maria College *B*
Assumption College *B*
Atlantic Union College *B*
Boston College *B, M, D*
Boston University *B, M, D*
Brandeis University *B*
Bridgewater State College *B, T*
Clark University *B*
College of the Holy Cross *B*
Elms College *B, M, T*
Emmanuel College *B*
Framingham State College *B*
Gordon College *B*
Harvard College *B*
Mount Holyoke College *B*
Northeastern University *B*
Regis College *B*
Salem State College *B*
Simmons College *B, M*
Simon's Rock College of Bard *B*
Smith College *B*
Tufts University *B*
University of Massachusetts
 Amherst *B, M, D*
 Boston *B*
 Dartmouth *B*
Wellesley College *B*
Wheaton College *B*
Williams College *B*

Michigan

Adrian College *A, B, T*
Alma College *B, T*
Andrews University *B*
Aquinas College *B, T*
Calvin College *B, T*
Central Michigan University *B, M, T*
Concordia University *B*
Eastern Michigan University *B, M*
Grand Valley State University *B*
Hillsdale College *B*
Hope College *B*
Kalamazoo College *B, T*
Lansing Community College *A*
Madonna University *B*
Michigan State University *B, M, D*
Michigan Technological University *C*
Northern Michigan University *B, T*
Oakland University *B, T*
Saginaw Valley State University *B*
Siena Heights University *B*
Spring Arbor University *B*
University of Michigan *B, M, D, T*
University of Michigan
 Dearborn *B*
 Flint *B, T*
Wayne State University *B, M*
Western Michigan University *B, M*

Minnesota

Augsburg College *B*

Bemidji State University *B*
Bethel College *B*
Carleton College *B*
College of St. Benedict *B*
College of St. Catherine *B*
Concordia College: Moorhead *B, T*
Gustavus Adolphus College *B*
Hamline University *B*
Macalester College *B, T*
Minnesota State University
 Mankato *B, M*
 Moorhead *B, M*
Northland Community & Technical
 College *A*
Northwestern College *B*
St. Cloud State University *B*
St. John's University *B*
St. Mary's University of Minnesota *B*
St. Olaf College *B*
Southwest State University *B*
University of Minnesota
 Duluth *B, T*
 Morris *B*
 Twin Cities *B, M, D*
University of St. Thomas *B*
Winona State University *B*

Mississippi

Blue Mountain College *B*
Itawamba Community College *A*
Millsaps College *B, T*
Mississippi College *B*
Mississippi University for Women *B, T*
University of Mississippi *B, M, T*

Missouri

Central Methodist College *B*
Central Missouri State University *B, T*
College of the Ozarks *B*
Crowder College *A*
Drury University *B, T*
East Central College *A*
Evangel University *B, T*
Lincoln University *B*
Lindenwood University *B*
Missouri Southern State College *B*
Missouri Western State College *B, T*
Northwest Missouri State University *B*
Rockhurst University *B*
St. Louis University *B, M*
Southeast Missouri State University *B*
Southwest Baptist University *B, T*
Southwest Missouri State University *B*
Stephens College *B*
Truman State University *B*
University of Missouri
 Columbia *B, M*
 Kansas City *B*
 St. Louis *B*
Washington University in St.
 Louis *B, M, D*
Webster University *B*
Westminster College *B*
William Jewell College *B*
William Woods University *B*

Montana

Carroll College *B, T*
Montana State University
 Billings *B*
University of Montana-Missoula *B, M*

Nebraska

Chadron State College *B*
Concordia University *B, T*
Creighton University *B*
Dana College *B*
Doane College *B*
Hastings College *B*
Midland Lutheran College *B*
Nebraska Wesleyan University *B*
Union College *B*
University of Nebraska
 Kearney *B, M, T*
 Lincoln *B*
 Omaha *B*
Wayne State College *B, T*

Western Nebraska Community
 College *A*

Nevada

University of Nevada
 Las Vegas *B, M*
 Reno *B*

New Hampshire

Dartmouth College *B, T*
Keene State College *B, T*
Plymouth State College *B*
Rivier College *B, M, T*
St. Anselm College *C, B, T*
University of New Hampshire *B, M*

New Jersey

Caldwell College *B*
The College of New Jersey *B*
College of St. Elizabeth *B, T*
Drew University *B*
Fairleigh Dickinson University
 College at Florham *B*
 Metropolitan Campus *B*
Georgian Court College *B, T*
Kean University *B*
Montclair State University *B, M, T*
New Jersey City University *B*
Princeton University *B, M, D*
Richard Stockton College of New
 Jersey *A*
Rider University *B*
Rowan University *B*
Rutgers, The State University of New
 Jersey
 Camden Regional Campus *B, T*
 New Brunswick Regional
  Campus *B, M, D, T*
 Newark Regional Campus *B, T*
St. Peter's College *B*
Seton Hall University *B, T*
William Paterson University of New
 Jersey *B*

New Mexico

Eastern New Mexico University *B*
New Mexico Highlands University *B*
New Mexico Junior College *A*
New Mexico State University *M*
Santa Fe Community College *A*
University of New Mexico *B, M, D*
Western New Mexico University *B*

New York

Adelphi University *B*
Alfred University *B*
Bard College *B*
Barnard College *B*
Canisius College *B*
City University of New York
 Baruch College *B*
 Brooklyn College *B, M*
 City College *B, M, T*
 College of Staten Island *B*
 Hunter College *B, M*
 Queens College *B, M*
 York College *B*
Colgate University *B*
College of Mount St. Vincent *B, T*
College of New Rochelle *B, T*
Columbia University
 Columbia College *B*
Cornell University *B, T*
Daemen College *B*
Elmira College *B, T*
Fordham University *B, M*
Hamilton College *B*
Hartwick College *B, T*
Hobart and William Smith Colleges *B*
Hofstra University *B*
Houghton College *B*
Iona College *B, M*
Ithaca College *B, T*
Le Moyne College *B*
Long Island University
 C. W. Post Campus *B, M*
Manhattan College *B*

Marist College *B, T*
Marymount College of Fordham
 University *B, T*
Mercy College *B*
Molloy College *B*
Mount St. Mary College *B*
Nazareth College of Rochester *B*
New York University *B, M, D*
Niagara University *B*
Orange County Community College *A*
Pace University *C, B*
Pace University:
 Pleasantville/Briarcliff *B*
Russell Sage College *B*
St. Bonaventure University *B*
St. John Fisher College *B*
St. John's University *B, M*
St. Lawrence University *B, T*
Sarah Lawrence College *B*
Skidmore College *B*
State University of New York
 Albany *B, M, D*
 Binghamton *B, M*
 Buffalo *B, M, D*
 College at Brockport *B, T*
 College at Buffalo *B*
 College at Cortland *B*
 College at Fredonia *B, T*
 College at Geneseo *B, T*
 College at Old Westbury *C, B, T*
 College at Oneonta *B*
 College at Plattsburgh *B*
 College at Potsdam *B, T*
 New Paltz *B, T*
 Oswego *B*
 Stony Brook *B, M, D, T*
Syracuse University *B, M*
United States Military Academy *B*
University of Rochester *B, M*
Vassar College *B*
Wagner College *B, M*
Wells College *B*

North Carolina

Appalachian State University *B*
Barton College *B, T*
Campbell University *B*
Catawba College *B*
Davidson College *B*
Duke University *B, M, D*
East Carolina University *B*
Elon University *B*
Gardner-Webb University *B*
Greensboro College *B, T*
Guilford College *B, T*
High Point University *B*
Lenoir-Rhyne College *B*
Mars Hill College *B*
Meredith College *B*
Methodist College *A, B, T*
North Carolina Central University *B*
North Carolina State University *B*
Peace College *B*
Queens University of Charlotte *B*
Salem College *B*
University of North Carolina
 Asheville *B, T*
 Chapel Hill *B*
 Charlotte *B, M*
 Greensboro *B, T*
 Wilmington *B*
Wake Forest University *B*
Western Carolina University *B*
Wingate University *B*
Winston-Salem State University *B*

North Dakota

Dickinson State University *B, T*
Minot State University *B*
North Dakota State University *B, T*
University of North Dakota *B*
Valley City State University *B*

Ohio

Antioch College *B*
Ashland University *B*

Baldwin-Wallace College *B, T*
Bluffton College *B*
Bowling Green State University *B, M*
Case Western Reserve University *B*
Cedarville University *B, T*
Cleveland State University *B, M*
College of Wooster *B*
Denison University *B*
Franciscan University of Steubenville *B*
Heidelberg College *B*
Hiram College *B, T*
John Carroll University *B*
Kent State University *B, M*
Kent State University
    Stark Campus *B*
Kenyon College *B*
Lake Erie College *B*
Lourdes College *A*
Malone College *B*
Marietta College *B*
Miami University
    Middletown Campus *A*
    Oxford Campus *B, M, T*
Mount Union College *B*
Mount Vernon Nazarene University *B*
Muskingum College *B*
Notre Dame College *B, T*
Oberlin College *B*
Ohio Northern University *B*
Ohio State University
    Columbus Campus *B, M, D*
Ohio University *B, M*
Ohio Wesleyan University *B*
Otterbein College *B*
University of Akron *B, M*
University of Cincinnati *B, M, D, T*
University of Dayton *B*
University of Findlay *B, T*
University of Toledo *B, M*
Walsh University *B*
Wilmington College *B*
Wittenberg University *B*
Wright State University *B*
Xavier University *A, B*
Youngstown State University *B*

Oklahoma

Northeastern State University *B*
Oklahoma Baptist University *B, T*
Oklahoma Christian University of
    Science and Arts *B*
Oklahoma City Community College *A*
Oklahoma City University *B*
Oklahoma State University *B*
Oral Roberts University *B*
Southern Nazarene University *B*
Tulsa Community College *A*
University of Central Oklahoma *B*
University of Oklahoma *B, M, D*
University of Tulsa *B*
Western Oklahoma State College *A*

Oregon

George Fox University *B*
Lewis & Clark College *B*
Linfield College *B*
Linn-Benton Community College *A*
Oregon State University *B*
Pacific University *B*
Portland State University *B, M*
Reed College *B*
Southern Oregon University *B*
University of Oregon *B, M*
University of Portland *B, T*
Western Oregon University *B, T*
Willamette University *B*

Pennsylvania

Albright College *B, T*
Allegheny College *B*
Arcadia University *B*
Bloomsburg University of
    Pennsylvania *B, T*
Bryn Mawr College *B*
Bucknell University *B*
Cabrini College *B*

California University of Pennsylvania *B*
Carlow College *B*
Carnegie Mellon University *B*
Cedar Crest College *B*
Chatham College *B*
Chestnut Hill College *A, B*
Cheyney University of Pennsylvania *B*
DeSales University *B, T*
Dickinson College *B*
Duquesne University *B*
East Stroudsburg University of
    Pennsylvania *B*
Edinboro University of
    Pennsylvania *B, T*
Elizabethtown College *B*
Franklin & Marshall College *B*
Gettysburg College *B*
Grove City College *B, T*
Haverford College *B, T*
Holy Family University *B, T*
Immaculata University *C, A, B*
Indiana University of Pennsylvania *B*
Juniata College *B*
King's College *B, T*
Kutztown University of
    Pennsylvania *B, T*
La Salle University *B, T*
Lafayette College *B*
Lebanon Valley College of
    Pennsylvania *B, T*
Lehigh University *B*
Lincoln University *B*
Lock Haven University of
    Pennsylvania *B*
Lycoming College *B*
Marywood University *B*
Mercyhurst College *B*
Messiah College *B*
Millersville University of
    Pennsylvania *B, M, T*
Moravian College *B, T*
Muhlenberg College *B, T*
Penn State
    Abington *B*
    Altoona *B*
    Beaver *B*
    Berks *B*
    Delaware County *B*
    Dubois *B*
    Fayette *B*
    Hazleton *B*
    Lehigh Valley *B*
    McKeesport *B*
    Mont Alto *B*
    New Kensington *B*
    Schuylkill - Capital College *B*
    Shenango *B*
    University Park *C, B, M, D*
    Wilkes-Barre *B*
    Worthington Scranton *B*
    York *B*
Rosemont College *B*
St. Joseph's University *B*
St. Vincent College *B*
Seton Hill University *B, T*
Shippensburg University of
    Pennsylvania *B, T*
Slippery Rock University of
    Pennsylvania *B, T*
Swarthmore College *B*
Temple University *B, M, D*
Thiel College *B*
University of Pennsylvania *B*
University of Pittsburgh *B, M, D*
University of Scranton *B, T*
Villanova University *B*
Washington and Jefferson College *B*
West Chester University of
    Pennsylvania *B, M*
Widener University *B*
Wilkes University *B*
York College of Pennsylvania *B*

Puerto Rico

Bayamon Central University *B*

Inter American University of Puerto Rico
    Metropolitan Campus *B, M*
Pontifical Catholic University of Puerto
    Rico *B, M*
University of Puerto Rico
    Cayey University College *B*
    Mayaguez Campus *B, M*
    Rio Piedras Campus *B, M, D*
University of the Sacred Heart *B*

Rhode Island

Brown University *B, M, D*
Rhode Island College *B, M*
Salve Regina University *B*
University of Rhode Island *B, M*

South Carolina

Anderson College *B, T*
Charleston Southern University *B*
The Citadel *B*
Clemson University *B*
Coastal Carolina University *B*
Coker College *B*
College of Charleston *B, T*
Columbia College *B*
Converse College *B*
Erskine College *B*
Francis Marion University *B*
Furman University *B, T*
Lander University *B, T*
Newberry College *B*
Presbyterian College *B, T*
South Carolina State University *B*
University of South Carolina *B, M*
University of South Carolina
    Spartanburg *B*
Winthrop University *M*
Wofford College *B, T*

South Dakota

Augustana College *B, T*
Black Hills State University *B*
Northern State University *B*
South Dakota State University *B*
University of South Dakota *B*

Tennessee

Austin Peay State University *B*
Belmont University *B, T*
Bryan College *B*
Carson-Newman College *B, T*
Fisk University *B*
King College *B, T*
Lee University *B*
Maryville College *B, T*
Milligan College *B*
Rhodes College *B, T*
Southern Adventist University *B*
Tennessee State University *B*
Tennessee Technological University *B, T*
Union University *B, T*
University of Tennessee
    Chattanooga *B*
    Knoxville *B, M*
    Martin *B*
Vanderbilt University *B, M, D*

Texas

Abilene Christian University *B*
Angelo State University *B, T*
Austin College *B*
Austin Community College *A*
Baylor University *B, M*
Blinn College *A*
Cisco Junior College *A*
Coastal Bend College *A*
Concordia University at Austin *B, T*
East Texas Baptist University *B*
Galveston College *A*
Hardin-Simmons University *B*
Houston Baptist University *B*
Howard Payne University *B, T*
Kilgore College *A*
Lamar University *B*
Laredo Community College *A*
Lon Morris College *A*
Lubbock Christian University *T*

McMurry University *B, T*
Midland College *A*
Midwestern State University *B*
Northeast Texas Community College *A*
Our Lady of the Lake University of San
    Antonio *B*
Paris Junior College *A*
Prairie View A&M University *B*
Rice University *B, M*
St. Edward's University *B, T*
St. Mary's University *B*
St. Philip's College *A*
Sam Houston State University *B*
South Plains College *A*
Southern Methodist University *B*
Southwest Texas State
    University *B, M, T*
Southwestern University *B, T*
Stephen F. Austin State University *B, T*
Sul Ross State University *B*
Tarleton State University *B, T*
Texas A&M International
    University *B, M, T*
Texas A&M University *B, M*
Texas A&M University
    Commerce *B*
    Corpus Christi *B, T*
    Kingsville *B, M*
Texas Christian University *B, T*
Texas Lutheran University *B*
Texas Southern University *B*
Texas Tech University *B, M, D*
Texas Wesleyan University *B*
Texas Woman's University *B, T*
Trinity University *B*
Trinity Valley Community College *A*
Tyler Junior College *A*
University of Dallas *B*
University of Houston *B, M, D*
University of Mary Hardin-Baylor *B, T*
University of North Texas *B, M*
University of St. Thomas *B*
University of Texas
    Arlington *B, M*
    Austin *B, M, D*
    Brownsville *B, M*
    El Paso *B, M*
    Pan American *B, M, T*
    San Antonio *B, M*
    Tyler *B*
    of the Permian Basin *B*
University of the Incarnate Word *B*
Wayland Baptist University *B, T*
West Texas A&M University *B*
Wharton County Junior College *A*

Utah

Brigham Young University *B, M*
Snow College *A*
Southern Utah University *B*
University of Utah *B, M, D*
Utah State University *B*
Weber State University *B*

Vermont

Bennington College *B, M, T*
Castleton State College *B*
Marlboro College *B*
Middlebury College *B, M, D*
St. Michael's College *B*
University of Vermont *B*

Virginia

Bridgewater College *B*
College of William and Mary *B*
Eastern Mennonite University *B*
Emory & Henry College *B, T*
Ferrum College *B*
Hampden-Sydney College *B*
Hampton University *B*
Hollins University *B*
Liberty University *B, T*
Longwood University *B, T*
Lynchburg College *B*
Mary Baldwin College *B*
Mary Washington College *B*

Randolph-Macon College *B*
Randolph-Macon Woman's College *B*
Roanoke College *B, T*
Shenandoah University *B*
Sweet Briar College *B*
University of Richmond *B, T*
University of Virginia *B, M, D*
University of Virginia's College at
  Wise *B, T*
Virginia Wesleyan College *B*
Washington and Lee University *B*

Washington

Central Washington University *B*
Centralia College *A*
Eastern Washington University *B, T*
Everett Community College *A*
Gonzaga University *B*
Heritage College *B*
Pacific Lutheran University *B*
Seattle Pacific University *B*
Seattle University *B*
University of Puget Sound *B, T*
University of Washington *B*
Walla Walla College *B*
Washington State University *B*
Western Washington University *B, T*
Whitman College *B*
Whitworth College *B, T*

West Virginia

Bethany College *B*
Davis and Elkins College *B*
Potomac State College of West Virginia
  University *A*
West Virginia University *T*
Wheeling Jesuit University *B*

Wisconsin

Beloit College *B*
Cardinal Stritch University *B*
Carroll College *B*
Carthage College *B, T*
Edgewood College *B*
Lakeland College *B*
Lawrence University *B, T*
Marian College of Fond du Lac *B, T*
Marquette University *B, M*
Mount Mary College *B*
Ripon College *B, T*
St. Norbert College *B, T*
Silver Lake College *T*
University of Wisconsin
  Eau Claire *B*
  Green Bay *B*
  La Crosse *B*
  Madison *B, M, D*
  Milwaukee *B*
  Oshkosh *B*
  Parkside *B, T*
  Platteville *B*
  River Falls *B*
  Stevens Point *B, T*
  Whitewater *B, T*
Viterbo University *B, T*
Wisconsin Lutheran College *B*

Wyoming

Casper College *A*
Sheridan College *A*
University of Wyoming *B, M*
Western Wyoming Community
  College *A*

Spanish teacher education

Alabama

Birmingham-Southern College *T*

Arizona

Arizona State University *B, T*
Northern Arizona University *B, T*
Prescott College *B, M, T*
University of Arizona *B, M*

Arkansas

Arkansas State University *B, T*
Harding University *B, T*
John Brown University *B*
Ouachita Baptist University *B, T*
Southern Arkansas University *B, T*
University of Central Arkansas *M*

California

Azusa Pacific University *T*
California State University
  Chico *T*
  Dominguez Hills *T*
  Fullerton *T*
  Long Beach *T*
  San Bernardino *T*
Humboldt State University *T*
Pacific Union College *T*
San Francisco State University *B, T*
San Jose State University *T*
University of the Pacific *T*
Vanguard University of Southern
  California *M, T*
Vista Community College *A*

Colorado

Colorado State University *T*
Colorado State University
  Pueblo *T*
Fort Lewis College *T*
Metropolitan State College of Denver *T*
University of Colorado
  Colorado Springs *T*

Connecticut

Central Connecticut State University *B*
Fairfield University *T*
Quinnipiac University *B, M*
Sacred Heart University *T*
St. Joseph College *T*
Southern Connecticut State
  University *B, T*

Delaware

Delaware State University *B*
University of Delaware *B, T*

District of Columbia

Catholic University of America *B*

Florida

Barry University *T*
Flagler College *B*
Nova Southeastern University *M*
St. Thomas University *B, T*
Stetson University *B, T*

Georgia

Armstrong Atlantic State University *T*
Atlanta Metropolitan College *A*
Georgia Southern University *B, M*
Georgia Southwestern State
  University *B, M, T*
Kennesaw State University *B*
Piedmont College *M, T*
Valdosta State University *T*

Hawaii

University of Hawaii
  Manoa *B, T*

Idaho

Boise State University *T*
Brigham Young University - Idaho *T*
Northwest Nazarene University *B*
University of Idaho *T*

Illinois

Augustana College *B, T*
Benedictine University *T*
Dominican University *T*
Elmhurst College *B*
Greenville College *B*
Illinois College *T*
Loyola University of Chicago *T*
MacMurray College *B, T*
North Central College *B, T*
North Park University *T*
Northwestern University *B, T*

Olivet Nazarene University *B, T*
Rockford College *T*
Roosevelt University *B*
St. Xavier University *B*
Sauk Valley Community College *A*
Trinity Christian College *B, T*
University of Illinois
  Chicago *B*
  Urbana-Champaign *B, M, T*
Wheaton College *T*

Indiana

Anderson University *B, T*
Ball State University *T*
Butler University *T*
Franklin College *B, T*
Goshen College *B*
Grace College *B*
Indiana University
  Bloomington *B, T*
  Northwest *B*
  South Bend *B, T*
Indiana University-Purdue University
  Fort Wayne *B, T*
Indiana University-Purdue University
  Indianapolis *B, T*
Indiana Wesleyan University *T*
Manchester College *B, T*
Saint Mary's College *T*
St. Mary-of-the-Woods College *B*
Taylor University *B, T*
University of Evansville *B*
University of Indianapolis *B, T*
University of Southern Indiana *T*
Valparaiso University *B*
Vincennes University *A*

Iowa

Buena Vista University *B, T*
Central College *T*
Clarke College *B, T*
Cornell College *B, T*
Dordt College *B*
Graceland University *T*
Iowa State University *T*
Loras College *T*
Luther College *B*
Morningside College *B*
Northwestern College *T*
St. Ambrose University *B, T*
University of Iowa *B, T*
Wartburg College *T*

Kansas

Baker University *T*
Benedictine College *B, T*
Bethel College *T*
Friends University *B*
McPherson College *B, T*
MidAmerica Nazarene University *B, T*
Pittsburg State University *B, T*
St. Mary College *T*

Kentucky

Murray State University *B, M, T*

Louisiana

Centenary College of Louisiana *B, T*
Louisiana College *B*
Southeastern Louisiana University *B*
Southern University and Agricultural and
  Mechanical College *B*

Maine

University of Maine *B*

Maryland

Salisbury University *T*
Towson University *T*
Washington College *T*

Massachusetts

Assumption College *T*
Bridgewater State College *T*
Elms College *T*
Framingham State College *B, M, T*
Harvard College *T*
Tufts University *T*

University of Massachusetts
  Dartmouth *T*

Michigan

Alma College *T*
Calvin College *B*
Central Michigan University *B*
Concordia University *B, T*
Eastern Michigan University *B, T*
Grand Valley State University *T*
Hope College *T*
Michigan State University *M*
Northern Michigan University *B, M, T*
University of Michigan *M, D*
University of Michigan
  Flint *T*
Western Michigan University *B*

Minnesota

Augsburg College *T*
Bemidji State University *T*
Bethel College *B*
College of St. Benedict *T*
College of St. Catherine *T*
Concordia College: Moorhead *B, T*
Gustavus Adolphus College *T*
Minnesota State University
  Mankato *B, M, T*
  Moorhead *B, T*
St. Cloud State University *T*
St. John's University *T*
St. Mary's University of Minnesota *B*
St. Olaf College *T*
University of Minnesota
  Duluth *B*
  Morris *T*
University of St. Thomas *B, T*
Winona State University *B, T*

Mississippi

Blue Mountain College *B*
Itawamba Community College *A*
Mississippi College *B, T*
Mississippi State University *T*
University of Mississippi *B, T*

Missouri

Central Missouri State
  University *B, M, T*
College of the Ozarks *B, T*
Lindenwood University *M*
Missouri Southern State College *B, T*
Missouri Western State College *B*
Northwest Missouri State
  University *B, T*
Rockhurst University *B*
Southwest Missouri State University *B*
Truman State University *M, T*
University of Missouri
  Columbia *B*
  St. Louis *T*
Washington University in St.
  Louis *B, M, T*
William Jewell College *T*

Montana

Montana State University
  Billings *B, T*
University of Montana-Missoula *T*

Nebraska

Chadron State College *B*
Concordia University *B, T*
Creighton University *T*
Dana College *B*
Doane College *T*
Hastings College *B, M, T*
Midland Lutheran College *B, T*
Nebraska Wesleyan University *T*
University of Nebraska
  Lincoln *B, T*

New Hampshire

Keene State College *B, T*
Plymouth State College *T*
Rivier College *B, M, T*
St. Anselm College *T*
University of New Hampshire *T*

New Jersey
The College of New Jersey *B, T*
College of St. Elizabeth *T*
Georgian Court College *B*
Monmouth University *B, T*
Rider University *B*
Rowan University *T*
St. Peter's College *T*
William Paterson University of New
   Jersey *T*

New Mexico
Western New Mexico University *B*

New York
Adelphi University *M*
Alfred University *T*
Canisius College *B, M, T*
City University of New York
   Brooklyn College *B*
   City College *B*
   Hunter College *B, M, T*
   Queens College *T*
D'Youville College *M, T*
Daemen College *B, T*
Dowling College *B*
Elmira College *B, T*
Fordham University *M, T*
Hofstra University *B, M*
Houghton College *B, T*
Ithaca College *B, T*
Long Island University
   C. W. Post Campus *B, M, T*
Manhattan College *B, T*
Marist College *B, T*
Marymount College of Fordham
   University *B, T*
Mercy College *T*
Molloy College *B*
New York University *B, M, T*
Niagara University *B, T*
Pace University *B, M, T*
Pace University:
   Pleasantville/Briarcliff *B, M, T*
St. Bonaventure University *M, T*
St. John Fisher College *B, T*
St. John's University *B, M, T*
St. Lawrence University *T*
State University of New York
   Albany *B, M, T*
   Buffalo *T*
   College at Brockport *B, T*
   College at Buffalo *B*
   College at Cortland *B, M*
   College at Fredonia *B, T*
   College at Geneseo *B, M, T*
   College at Oneonta *B, T*
   College at Plattsburgh *B, M*
   College at Potsdam *B, M, T*
   New Paltz *B, M, T*
   Oswego *B*
Vassar College *T*
Wells College *T*

North Carolina
Appalachian State University *M*
Campbell University *B, T*
Davidson College *T*
East Carolina University *B*
Gardner-Webb University *B*
Greensboro College *B, T*
Meredith College *T*
North Carolina Central University *B, M*
North Carolina State University *B, T*
Queens University of Charlotte *T*
Salem College *T*
University of North Carolina
   Charlotte *B*
   Greensboro *B, M, T*
   Wilmington *B*
Wake Forest University *M, T*
Western Carolina University *B, T*
Wingate University *B, T*

North Dakota
Dickinson State University *B, T*
Minot State University *B*

North Dakota State University *B, T*
University of North Dakota *B, T*
Valley City State University *B, T*

Ohio
Ashland University *B, T*
Baldwin-Wallace College *T*
Bluffton College *B*
Bowling Green State University *B, M*
Cedarville University *B, T*
Hiram College *T*
Kent State University *T*
Kent State University
   Stark Campus *B*
Malone College *B*
Miami University
   Oxford Campus *B, T*
Mount Union College *T*
Mount Vernon Nazarene University *B, T*
Ohio Northern University *B*
Ohio University *B*
Otterbein College *B*
University of Akron *B, T*
University of Dayton *B, M, T*
University of Findlay *B, T*
University of Toledo *M, T*
Xavier University *M*
Youngstown State University *B, M, T*

Oklahoma
Northeastern State University *B*
Northwestern Oklahoma State
   University *B, T*
Oklahoma Baptist University *B, T*
Oklahoma City University *B*
Oral Roberts University *B, T*
Southeastern Oklahoma State
   University *B, T*
Southern Nazarene University *B*
University of Central Oklahoma *B*
University of Tulsa *T*

Oregon
Eastern Oregon University *B, T*
Linfield College *T*
Oregon State University *M*
Portland State University *B*
University of Portland *T*
Western Oregon University *T*

Pennsylvania
Albright College *T*
Cabrini College *B*
California University of
   Pennsylvania *B, T*
Chatham College *M*
DeSales University *T*
Dickinson College *T*
Duquesne University *B, T*
Gettysburg College *T*
Grove City College *B, T*
Holy Family University *B, M, T*
Juniata College *B, T*
King's College *T*
La Roche College *B*
La Salle University *B, T*
Lebanon Valley College of
   Pennsylvania *B, T*
Lock Haven University of
   Pennsylvania *B, T*
Lycoming College *T*
Marywood University *B*
Messiah College *T*
Moravian College *T*
St. Vincent College *T*
Seton Hill University *B, T*
Slippery Rock University of
   Pennsylvania *B, T*
Thiel College *B*
Villanova University *T*
Washington and Jefferson College *T*
Widener University *T*
Wilson College *T*

Puerto Rico
Bayamon Central University *B*

Inter American University of Puerto Rico
   Barranquitas Campus *B, T*
   Fajardo Campus *B, T*
   Metropolitan Campus *B*
   San German Campus *B*
Pontifical Catholic University of Puerto
   Rico *B, T*
Turabo University *B*
Universidad Metropolitana *B*

Rhode Island
Rhode Island College *B*
Salve Regina University *B*

South Carolina
Anderson College *B, T*
Charleston Southern University *B*
Francis Marion University *B, T*
Furman University *T*
Lander University *T*
South Carolina State University *B, T*
Wofford College *T*

South Dakota
Augustana College *B, T*
Black Hills State University *B*
South Dakota State University *B*
University of South Dakota *T*

Tennessee
Belmont University *T*
King College *T*
Lee University *B*
Maryville College *B, T*
Southern Adventist University *B*
Union University *B, T*
University of Tennessee
   Martin *B, T*

Texas
Abilene Christian University *B, T*
Baylor University *B, T*
East Texas Baptist University *B*
Hardin-Simmons University *B, T*
Houston Baptist University *T*
Howard Payne University *B, T*
Lamar University *T*
Laredo Community College *A*
Lubbock Christian University *B, T*
McMurry University *T*
St. Mary's University *T*
Southwest Texas State University *M, T*
Texas A&M International
   University *B, T*
Texas A&M University
   Commerce *T*
   Kingsville *T*
Texas Christian University *T*
Texas Wesleyan University *B, T*
University of Dallas *T*
University of Houston *T*
University of Mary Hardin-Baylor *T*
University of Texas
   Arlington *T*
   Pan American *T*
   San Antonio *T*
West Texas A&M University *T*

Utah
Brigham Young University *B, T*
Southern Utah University *B, T*
University of Utah *B*
Weber State University *B*

Vermont
Bennington College *B, M, T*
Castleton State College *B, T*
St. Michael's College *T*

Virginia
Bridgewater College *T*
Eastern Mennonite University *T*
Hollins University *T*
Longwood University *B, T*
Radford University *T*
University of Virginia's College at
   Wise *T*
Virginia Wesleyan College *T*

Washington
Central Washington University *B, T*
Heritage College *B*
Western Washington University *B, T*
Whitworth College *B, T*

West Virginia
Wheeling Jesuit University *T*

Wisconsin
Carroll College *B, T*
Carthage College *T*
Edgewood College *B*
Lawrence University *T*
Marian College of Fond du Lac *B, T*
Marquette University *B, M*
Mount Mary College *B, T*
St. Norbert College *T*
University of Wisconsin
   Green Bay *T*
   La Crosse *B, T*
   Parkside *T*
   Platteville *B, T*
   River Falls *T*
   Whitewater *B*
Viterbo University *B, T*

Spanish/Iberian studies

Colorado
Colorado College *B*

District of Columbia
American University *B*

Iowa
University of Iowa *M, D*

Massachusetts
Elms College *B*

Minnesota
Concordia College: Moorhead *B, T*

New Hampshire
Dartmouth College *B*

New York
Bard College *B*
Columbia University
   Columbia College *B*

Special education

Alabama
Alabama Agricultural and Mechanical
   University *B, M*
Alabama State University *B, M, T*
Athens State University *B*
Auburn University *B, M, D, T*
Birmingham-Southern College *B*
Jacksonville State University *B, M, T*
University of Alabama *B, M, D*
University of Alabama
   Birmingham *B, M*
University of North Alabama *B, M*
University of South Alabama *B, M, T*
University of West Alabama *B, M, T*

Alaska
University of Alaska
   Anchorage *M, T*

Arizona
Arizona State University *B, M*
Central Arizona College *A*
Northern Arizona University *B, M, T*
Prescott College *B, M, T*
University of Arizona *B, M, D*
University of Phoenix *C*

Arkansas
Arkansas State University *B, M, T*
Harding University *B, M, T*
Henderson State University *M*
John Brown University *T*
Philander Smith College *B*

Southern Arkansas University *B, M, T*
University of Arkansas *B, M, D*
University of Arkansas
    Little Rock *M*
    Monticello *B*
    Pine Bluff *B*
University of Central Arkansas *B, M*
University of the Ozarks *B*

California

Azusa Pacific University *M*
California Baptist University *M, T*
California State University
    Bakersfield *M*
    Chico *T*
    Dominguez Hills *M*
    Fresno *M*
    Fullerton *M*
    Hayward *M, T*
    Long Beach *M, T*
    Los Angeles *M, D*
    Northridge *M*
    Sacramento *M*
    San Marcos *T*
    Stanislaus *M*
Cerritos Community College *A*
Chapman University *M, T*
Cuesta College *C, A*
Fresno Pacific University *M, T*
Holy Names College *M*
La Sierra University *B, M*
Loyola Marymount University *C, M*
Mount St. Mary's College *M*
National University *M, T*
Ohlone College *C*
Pacific Oaks College *T*
Point Loma Nazarene University *M*
St. Mary's College of California *M*
San Diego State University *M*
San Francisco State University *M, D, T*
San Jose State University *M*
Santa Clara University *M*
University of California
    Berkeley *D, T*
    Los Angeles *D*
    Riverside *M, D, T*
University of La Verne *M, T*
University of San Diego *M, T*
University of San Francisco *M*
University of the Pacific *D*

Colorado

Metropolitan State College of Denver *T*
Regis University *B, T*
University of Colorado
    Colorado Springs *M*
    Denver *M*
University of Denver *M, D*
University of Northern Colorado *M, D, T*

Connecticut

Central Connecticut State
    University *B, M*
Fairfield University *C, M*
Gateway Community College *C, A*
St. Joseph College *B, M, T*
Southern Connecticut State University *M*
Three Rivers Community College *C, A*
University of Connecticut *B, M, D, T*
University of Hartford *B, M*
Western Connecticut State University *M*

Delaware

Delaware State University *B, M*
University of Delaware *B, M, T*
Wilmington College *M*

District of Columbia

American University *M*
George Washington University *M*
Howard University *M*
Trinity College *M*
University of the District of Columbia *M*

Florida

Barry University *B, M*
Broward Community College *A*

Edward Waters College *B*
Florida Atlantic University *B, M, D*
Florida Gulf Coast University *B, M*
Florida International University *M, D*
Florida State University *C, D*
Gulf Coast Community College *A*
Jacksonville University *B, M, T*
Nova Southeastern University *B, M*
Pensacola Junior College *C, A*
St. Petersburg College *B*
South Florida Community College *A*
Southeastern College of the Assemblies
    of God *B, T*
University of Central Florida *C, B, M*
University of Florida *B, M, D*
University of Miami *B, M, D*
University of North Florida *B, M*
University of South Florida *B, M*
Warner Southern College *B*

Georgia

Albany State University *B*
Armstrong Atlantic State
    University *B, M, T*
Augusta State University *B, M*
Brenau University *B*
Clark Atlanta University *B, M*
Columbus State University *B, M*
Georgia College and State
    University *B, M, T*
Georgia Southern University *B, M, T*
Georgia Southwestern State
    University *B, M, T*
Georgia State University *D*
Middle Georgia College *A*
North Georgia College & State
    University *B, M*
Piedmont College *B, M, T*
University of Georgia *B, M, D, T*
Valdosta State University *B, M*

Hawaii

Brigham Young University-Hawaii *B, T*
Chaminade University of Honolulu *B, M*
University of Hawaii
    Manoa *B, M, T*

Idaho

Boise State University *T*
Brigham Young University - Idaho *A*
Idaho State University *B, M, D*
Lewis-Clark State College *B, T*
Northwest Nazarene University *M*
University of Idaho *B, M, T*

Illinois

Benedictine University *B, T*
Chicago State University *B*
Dominican University *M*
Eastern Illinois University *B, M*
Elmhurst College *B*
Governors State University *M, T*
Greenville College *B, T*
Illinois Central College *A*
Illinois State University *B, M, D, T*
John A. Logan College *A*
Joliet Junior College *C, A*
Kishwaukee College *A*
Lewis University *B, M*
Loyola University of Chicago *B, M, T*
MacMurray College *B, T*
National-Louis University *M*
Northeastern Illinois University *B, M*
Northern Illinois University *B, M, D*
Parkland College *A*
Quincy University *B, M, T*
Sauk Valley Community College *A*
South Suburban College of Cook
    County *A*
Southern Illinois University
    Carbondale *B, M, D*
Southern Illinois University
    Edwardsville *B, M, T*
Trinity Christian College *B, T*
University of Illinois
    Chicago *M, D*
    Urbana-Champaign *B, M, D*

University of St. Francis *B*
Western Illinois University *B, M*

Indiana

Ball State University *B, M, D*
Butler University *M*
Goshen College *B, T*
Indiana State University *B, M, T*
Indiana University
    Bloomington *B, M, D, T*
    South Bend *B, M*
    Southeast *B*
Indiana University-Purdue University
    Indianapolis *M*
Manchester College *B, T*
Marian College *T*
Purdue University *B*
Purdue University
    Calumet *B*
St. Mary-of-the-Woods College *B*
University of Evansville *B*
University of St. Francis *B, M, T*
University of Southern Indiana *B*
Valparaiso University *M, T*
Vincennes University *A*

Iowa

Briar Cliff University *B*
Buena Vista University *B, T*
Central College *T*
Clarke College *B, M, T*
Dordt College *B*
Drake University *B, M*
Iowa State University *M, T*
Loras College *B*
Morningside College *B, M*
Mount Mercy College *T*
St. Ambrose University *M, T*
University of Dubuque *C, T*
University of Iowa *M, D*
University of Northern Iowa *B, M*
Upper Iowa University *B, T*
Waldorf College *A*
William Penn University *B*

Kansas

Benedictine College *B, T*
Bethel College *T*
Central Christian College *A, B*
Emporia State University *M, T*
Fort Hays State University *M*
Fort Scott Community College *A*
Kansas State University *M, D*
Kansas Wesleyan University *T*
Labette Community College *C*
McPherson College *B, T*
Pittsburg State University *B, M, T*
Tabor College *B, T*
University of Kansas *M, D*
Washburn University of Topeka *M*
Wichita State University *M*

Kentucky

Asbury College *M*
Bellarmine University *B, M, T*
Brescia University *B, T*
Cumberland College *B, M, T*
Morehead State University *B, M*
Murray State University *B, M, T*
Union College *B*
University of Kentucky *B, M, D*
University of Louisville *M, D*

Louisiana

Dillard University *B*
Grambling State University *B*
Louisiana College *B*
Louisiana State University
    Shreveport *B*
Louisiana Tech University *B*
McNeese State University *B, T*
Nicholls State University *B*
Northwestern State University *B*
Our Lady of Holy Cross College *B, T*
Southeastern Louisiana University *B, M*
Southern University and Agricultural and
    Mechanical College *B, M, D*

University of Louisiana at Lafayette *B*
University of Louisiana at Monroe *B, M*
University of New Orleans *M, D*
Xavier University of Louisiana *B, M*

Maine

University of Maine *M*
University of Maine
    Farmington *B, T*
University of Southern Maine *M*

Maryland

Bowie State University *M*
College of Notre Dame of Maryland *B*
Community College of Baltimore County
    Catonsville *C, A*
    Dundalk *C, A*
    Essex *C, A*
Coppin State College *B, M, T*
Goucher College *B*
Hood College *B*
Johns Hopkins University *M*
Loyola College in Maryland *M*
McDaniel College *M*
Mount St. Mary's College *B, T*
Towson University *B, T*
University of Maryland
    Baltimore County *T*
    College Park *B, M, D, T*

Massachusetts

American International College *B, M*
Assumption College *M*
Atlantic Union College *M*
Boston University *B, M, D, T*
Bridgewater State College *B, M, T*
Elms College *B, M, T*
Endicott College *M*
Fitchburg State College *B, M, T*
Gordon College *B*
Lasell College *B*
Lesley University *B, M, T*
Northeastern University *M*
Simmons College *B, M*
Springfield College *B*
University of Massachusetts
    Boston *M*
Westfield State College *B, T*

Michigan

Aquinas College *B*
Calvin College *B, T*
Central Michigan University *M*
Eastern Michigan University *M*
Gogebic Community College *A*
Grand Valley State University *B, M, T*
Kellogg Community College *A*
Lansing Community College *A*
Marygrove College *B, M, T*
Michigan State University *B, M, D*
Northern Michigan University *B*
Oakland University *M*
Saginaw Valley State University *B, T*
Schoolcraft College *A*
Wayne State University *B, M, D, T*
Western Michigan University *M, D*

Minnesota

Bemidji State University *M*
Bethel College *M*
Minnesota State University
    Mankato *M*
    Moorhead *B, M, T*
Northland Community & Technical
    College *A*
St. Cloud State University *B, M, T*
University of Minnesota
    Duluth *T*
    Twin Cities *M*
University of St. Thomas *M*
Winona State University *B, M, T*

Mississippi

Alcorn State University *B*
Delta State University *B, M*
Itawamba Community College *A*
Mary Holmes College *A*

Millsaps College *T*
Mississippi College *B*
Mississippi State University *B, M, T*
Mississippi University for Women *B, T*
Mississippi Valley State University *M*
Northwest Mississippi Community
College *A*
University of Mississippi *B, T*
University of Southern Mississippi *B, M*

Missouri
Avila University *B, T*
Central Missouri State
University *B, M, T*
Culver-Stockton College *T*
East Central College *A*
Evangel University *B*
Fontbonne College *B*
Lincoln University *B, T*
Lindenwood University *B, M*
Missouri Baptist University *T*
Missouri Southern State College *B, T*
Missouri Valley College *B*
Northwest Missouri State
University *B, T*
Southeast Missouri State
University *B, M*
Southwest Missouri State
University *B, M*
Stephens College *M*
Truman State University *M*
University of Missouri
Columbia *M, D*
Kansas City *M*
St. Louis *B, M, T*
Webster University *M*
William Woods University *B*

Montana
Carroll College *T*
Montana State University
Billings *A, B, M, T*
University of Great Falls *B*
University of Montana: Western *T*

Nebraska
College of Saint Mary *B, T*
Concordia University *B, T*
Dana College *B*
Doane College *B*
Hastings College *B, M, T*
Nebraska Wesleyan University *B*
Peru State College *B, T*
University of Nebraska
Kearney *B, M, T*
Lincoln *B, M*
Omaha *B, M*
Wayne State College *B, M*
York College *B, T*

Nevada
University of Nevada
Las Vegas *B, M, D, T*
Reno *B, M, T*

New Hampshire
Keene State College *B, M, T*
New England College *B, T*
New Hampshire Community Technical
College
Berlin *C*
New Hampshire Technical Institute *C*
Rivier College *D, T*
University of New Hampshire *M*

New Jersey
Centenary College *M*
The College of New Jersey *B, M, T*
College of St. Elizabeth *B, T*
Felician College *B, T*
Georgian Court College *B, M, T*
Gloucester County College *A*
Kean University *B, M*
Monmouth University *B, M*
New Jersey City University *B, M*
Rider University *M*
Rowan University *B, M*

Rutgers, The State University of New
Jersey
New Brunswick Regional
Campus *T*
Seton Hall University *B, T*
William Paterson University of New
Jersey *B, M, T*

New Mexico
College of the Southwest *B, T*
Eastern New Mexico University *B, M*
New Mexico Highlands University *B, M*
New Mexico State University *B*
University of New Mexico *B, M, D, T*
Western New Mexico University *B, M, T*

New York
Adelphi University *M*
Canisius College *B, M, D*
City University of New York
Brooklyn College *B, M*
College of Staten Island *M*
Hunter College *M, T*
Medgar Evers College *B, T*
Queens College *M*
College of Mount St. Vincent *B, T*
College of New Rochelle *M*
D'Youville College *C, B, M, T*
Daemen College *M, T*
Dominican College of Blauvelt *B, T*
Dowling College *B, M, T*
Fordham University *M*
Hobart and William Smith Colleges *T*
Hofstra University *M, D, T*
Keuka College *B, T*
Le Moyne College *T*
Long Island University
C. W. Post Campus *M, T*
Southampton College *M*
Manhattan College *B, M, T*
Manhattanville College *M, T*
Marist College *B, T*
Marymount College of Fordham
University *B, T*
Marymount Manhattan College *B, T*
Mercy College *T*
Molloy College *B, T*
Mount St. Mary College *B, M, T*
Nazareth College of Rochester *B, M, T*
New York University *B, M, T*
Niagara University *B*
Pace University *C, M, T*
Pace University
Pleasantville/Briarcliff *C, M, D, T*
St. Bonaventure University *M*
St. John Fisher College *B, M, T*
St. John's University *B, M, T*
St. Joseph's College *B, T*
St. Joseph's College: Suffolk
Campus *B, T*
State University of New York
Albany *M*
Binghamton *M*
Buffalo *D*
College at Buffalo *M*
College at Cortland *B*
College at Geneseo *B, M, T*
College at Old Westbury *B, T*
College at Plattsburgh *B, M*
College at Potsdam *M*
New Paltz *B, M, T*
Oswego *M*
Syracuse University *B, M, D, T*
Touro College *B, M*

North Carolina
Appalachian State University *M*
Barton College *B*
Bennett College *B*
Elizabeth City State University *B, T*
Elon University *B, T*
Fayetteville State University *M*
Greensboro College *B, T*
High Point University *B*
Martin Community College *A*
Methodist College *A, B, T*

North Carolina Agricultural and
Technical State University *B*
North Carolina Central University *M*
North Carolina State University *M*
Pfeiffer University *B*
St. Augustine's College *B*
Shaw University *B, T*
University of North Carolina
Charlotte *M, D*
Greensboro *B, M*
Pembroke *B, T*
Wilmington *M*
Western Carolina University *M*
Winston-Salem State University *B*

North Dakota
Minot State University *M*
University of Mary *B, M*
University of North Dakota *M*

Ohio
Ashland University *B, M, T*
Bluffton College *B*
Bowling Green State University *B, M*
Cedarville University *B*
Central State University *B*
Cleveland State University *B, T*
College of Mount St. Joseph *B*
Kent State University *B, M, D*
Kent State University
Stark Campus *B*
Miami University
Oxford Campus *B, M*
Muskingum College *B, T*
Ohio Dominican College *B, T*
Ohio State University
Columbus Campus *B, M*
Ohio University *B, M*
Ohio University
Southern Campus at Ironton *M*
Otterbein College *B*
Sinclair Community College *A*
University of Akron *B, M, T*
University of Cincinnati *M, D*
University of Dayton *B, M, T*
University of Findlay *B, M, T*
University of Rio Grande *B, T*
University of Toledo *B, M, T*
Urbana University *B*
Ursuline College *B, T*
Wilmington College *M*
Wright State University *M*
Xavier University *B, M*
Youngstown State University *B, M*

Oklahoma
East Central University *B, M, T*
Langston University *B*
Northeastern State University *B, M*
Northwestern Oklahoma State
University *B*
Oklahoma Baptist University *B, T*
Oklahoma Christian University of
Science and Arts *B, T*
Oral Roberts University *B, T*
Southeastern Oklahoma State
University *B*
Southwestern Oklahoma State
University *B, M, T*
University of Central Oklahoma *B, M*
University of Oklahoma *B, M, D, T*

Oregon
Eastern Oregon University *T*
Portland Community College *C*
Portland State University *M, D, T*
Southern Oregon University *T*
University of Oregon *M, D, T*
University of Portland *T*
Western Oregon University *T*

Pennsylvania
Albright College *B, M, T*
Arcadia University *B, M, T*
Bloomsburg University of
Pennsylvania *B, M, T*
Cabrini College *B, T*

California University of
Pennsylvania *B, M, T*
Carlow College *B, T*
Cedar Crest College *B*
Chatham College *M, T*
Cheyney University of
Pennsylvania *B, M, T*
DeSales University *C*
Duquesne University *M, T*
East Stroudsburg University of
Pennsylvania *B, M, T*
Edinboro University of
Pennsylvania *A, B, M, T*
Geneva College *B, M, T*
Gwynedd-Mercy College *B, T*
Holy Family University *B, T*
Immaculata University *T*
Indiana University of
Pennsylvania *B, M, T*
Juniata College *B, T*
King's College *B*
Kutztown University of Pennsylvania *B*
La Roche College *C*
La Salle University *B, T*
Lebanon Valley College of
Pennsylvania *T*
Lehigh Carbon Community College *A*
Lehigh University *M, D*
Lincoln University *B*
Lock Haven University of
Pennsylvania *B, T*
Marywood University *B, M*
Mercyhurst College *B, M, T*
Millersville University of
Pennsylvania *B, M, T*
Northampton County Area Community
College *C, A*
Penn State
Abington *B*
Altoona *B*
Beaver *B*
Berks *B*
Delaware County *B*
Dubois *B*
Fayette *B*
Hazleton *B*
Lehigh Valley *B*
McKeesport *B*
Mont Alto *B*
New Kensington *B*
Schuylkill - Capital College *B*
Shenango *B*
University Park *C, B, M, D*
Wilkes-Barre *B*
Worthington Scranton *B*
York *B*
Rosemont College *T*
Seton Hill University *M, T*
Shippensburg University of
Pennsylvania *M, T*
Slippery Rock University of
Pennsylvania *B, M, T*
University of Pennsylvania *M, D*
University of Scranton *B*
Waynesburg College *B*
West Chester University of
Pennsylvania *B, M, T*
Widener University *B, M*

Puerto Rico
Bayamon Central University *B, M*
Inter American University of Puerto Rico
Metropolitan Campus *B*
Pontifical Catholic University of Puerto
Rico *B*
Turabo University *B, M*
Universidad Metropolitana *B, M*
University of Puerto Rico
Rio Piedras Campus *M*

Rhode Island
Community College of Rhode Island *A*
Rhode Island College *B, M*
Salve Regina University *B*

South Carolina

Anderson College *B, T*
Clemson University *B, M*
Coastal Carolina University *B*
College of Charleston *B, M, T*
Columbia College *B, T*
Converse College *B, M, T*
Erskine College *B, T*
Francis Marion University *M*
Furman University *M, T*
Lander University *B, T*
Presbyterian College *B, T*
South Carolina State University *B, M, T*
Southern Wesleyan University *B, T*
University of South Carolina *M, D*
University of South Carolina
    Spartanburg *B*
Winthrop University *B, M, T*

South Dakota

Augustana College *B, M, T*
Black Hills State University *B, T*
Dakota State University *B, T*
Dakota Wesleyan University *B, T*
Northern State University *B, T*
Sinte Gleska University *A, B*
University of South Dakota *B, M*

Tennessee

Austin Peay State University *B, T*
Bethel College *B, M, T*
Carson-Newman College *B, T*
East Tennessee State University *B, M, T*
Fisk University *B*
Freed-Hardeman University *B, T*
Johnson Bible College *T*
Lambuth University *B, T*
Lee University *B*
Middle Tennessee State
    University *B, M, T*
Roane State Community College *A*
Southern Adventist University *M*
Tennessee State University *B, M, T*
Tennessee Technological
    University *B, M, T*
Tusculum College *B, T*
Union University *B, T*
University of Memphis *B*
University of Tennessee
    Chattanooga *B, M, T*
    Knoxville *M, T*
    Martin *B, T*
Vanderbilt University *B, M, D, T*

Texas

Abilene Christian University *B, T*
Angelo State University *M*
Baylor University *B, T*
Del Mar College *A*
Eastfield College *C*
El Paso Community College *A*
Houston Baptist University *B*
Jarvis Christian College *B*
Lamar University *M, T*
Laredo Community College *A*
Lubbock Christian University *T*
McMurry University *T*
Our Lady of the Lake University of San
    Antonio *B, M*
Prairie View A&M University *M*
Sam Houston State University *M*
Southwest Texas State University *M, T*
Southwestern University *T*
Stephen F. Austin State University *M, T*
Sul Ross State University *M*
Texas A&M International
    University *B, M, T*
Texas A&M University
    Commerce *B, M, D, T*
    Corpus Christi *M, T*
    Kingsville *M*
    Texarkana *M, T*
Texas Christian University *M, T*
Texas Southern University *M*
Texas Tech University *M, D*
Texas Woman's University *M, D, T*

University of Houston *M, D*
University of Houston
    Clear Lake *T*
    Victoria *M*
University of Mary Hardin-Baylor *T*
University of North Texas *M, D*
University of Texas
    Austin *M, D*
    El Paso *M*
    Pan American *B, M, T*
    San Antonio *M, T*
    Tyler *M, T*
    of the Permian Basin *M*
University of the Incarnate Word *M*
West Texas A&M University *M, T*

Utah

Brigham Young University *B, M*
Snow College *A*
Southern Utah University *B*
University of Utah *B, M, D*
Utah State University *B, M, D*
Westminster College *B, T*

Vermont

Castleton State College *M, T*
College of St. Joseph in Vermont *B, M*
Green Mountain College *T*
Johnson State College *M*
Lyndon State College *B, M*
St. Michael's College *M, T*
University of Vermont *M*

Virginia

Averett University *M*
Bridgewater College *T*
George Mason University *M*
Hampton University *B, M*
James Madison University *M, T*
Liberty University *M*
Longwood University *B, M, T*
Lynchburg College *M*
Norfolk State University *B*
Old Dominion University *M*
Radford University *B, M, T*
University of Virginia *M, D*
University of Virginia's College at
    Wise *T*
Virginia Commonwealth University *M*
Virginia Intermont College *B, T*

Washington

Central Washington University *B, M, T*
Eastern Washington University *M, T*
Gonzaga University *B, M, T*
Heritage College *M*
North Seattle Community College *C, A*
Northwest College *B*
Pacific Lutheran University *B, M*
St. Martin's College *B, T*
Seattle Pacific University *B*
Spokane Falls Community College *C, A*
University of Washington *M, D*
Walla Walla College *B, M*
Western Washington University *B, M, T*
Whitworth College *B, M, T*

West Virginia

Alderson-Broaddus College *B*
Bethany College *B*
Glenville State College *B*
Marshall University *M*
Ohio Valley College *B*
Salem International University *T*
West Liberty State College *B*
West Virginia State College *B*
West Virginia University *M, D*

Wisconsin

Cardinal Stritch University *M*
Carthage College *B, T*
Edgewood College *B, M, D*

University of Wisconsin
    Eau Claire *B, M*
    La Crosse *M*
    Madison *M, D*
    Milwaukee *M, T*
    Oshkosh *B*
    Superior *M*
    Whitewater *B, T*

Wyoming

Eastern Wyoming College *A*
University of Wyoming *B*

Special education administration

District of Columbia

Gallaudet University *D*

Kentucky

Murray State University *M, T*

Missouri

University of Missouri
    Columbia *M, D*

Ohio

Youngstown State University *M, D*

Pennsylvania

Marywood University *M*

Speech pathology

Alabama

Alabama Agricultural and Mechanical
    University *M*
University of Alabama *M*
University of Montevallo *B, M, T*

Arizona

Northern Arizona University *M*

Arkansas

Arkansas State University *B, M*
Harding University *B*
University of Central Arkansas *B*

California

California State University
    Fresno *M*
    Northridge *B*
Grossmont Community College *A*
Loma Linda University *M*
Orange Coast College *A*
San Diego State University *M*
Stanford University *D*
University of the Pacific *B*

Colorado

University of Northern Colorado *B, M*

District of Columbia

University of the District of Columbia *B*

Florida

Nova Southeastern University *M, D*

Georgia

Armstrong Atlantic State
    University *B, M*
State University of West Georgia *B, M*

Idaho

Idaho State University *M*

Illinois

Eastern Illinois University *B, M, T*
Elmhurst College *B, T*
Governors State University *B, M, T*
Northwestern University *B, D*
Rush University *M*
St. Xavier University *B, M*
Sauk Valley Community College *A*

Indiana

Ball State University *M*
Butler University *B*

Iowa

University of Northern Iowa *B, M*

Kansas

University of Kansas *M, D*

Kentucky

Murray State University *M*

Louisiana

Centenary College of Louisiana *B*
Grambling State University *B*
Xavier University of Louisiana *B*

Maryland

University of Maryland
    College Park *B, M, D*

Massachusetts

Becker College *A*
Boston University *M, D*
Elms College *B*
Emerson College *B, M*
Northeastern University *M*

Michigan

Calvin College *B*
Central Michigan University *M*
Wayne State University *B, M, D*

Minnesota

Minnesota State University
    Mankato *M*
    Moorhead *B*
South Central Technical College *A*

Mississippi

Mississippi University for Women *B, M*

Missouri

Central Missouri State University *B, T*
Southeast Missouri State University *B*

Nebraska

University of Nebraska
    Kearney *B, M, T*
    Lincoln *B, T*
    Omaha *M*

Nevada

University of Nevada
    Reno *B, D*

New Hampshire

University of New Hampshire *B*

New Jersey

The College of New Jersey *M*
Montclair State University *T*
Seton Hall University *M*
William Paterson University of New
    Jersey *B*

New York

City University of New York
    Hunter College *M*
College of New Rochelle *M*
Hofstra University *B, M*
Ithaca College *M, T*
Long Island University
    C. W. Post Campus *M*
Nazareth College of Rochester *B, M, T*
New York University *M*
Pace University:
    Pleasantville/Briarcliff *B*
State University of New York
    Buffalo *M*
    College at Buffalo *B*
    College at Fredonia *M*
    College at Geneseo *M*
    College at Plattsburgh *B, M*
    New Paltz *M*
Touro College *M*

North Carolina

Cape Fear Community College *A*
Southwestern Community College *A*
University of North Carolina
    Chapel Hill *M*

North Dakota
University of North Dakota *M*

Ohio
Case Western Reserve University *M, D*
Kent State University *M, D*
Kent State University
　　Stark Campus *B*
Miami University
　　Oxford Campus *B*
University of Akron *B, M*
University of Toledo *B*

Oklahoma
Oklahoma State University *B, M*
University of Central Oklahoma *M*
University of Oklahoma *M, D*
University of Science and Arts of
　　Oklahoma *B*
University of Tulsa *B, M, T*

Oregon
Portland State University *M*

Pennsylvania
Duquesne University *B, M*
Edinboro University of Pennsylvania *M*
Geneva College *B*
La Salle University *B, M*

Puerto Rico
University of Puerto Rico
　　Medical Sciences Campus *B, M*

Rhode Island
University of Rhode Island *M*

South Carolina
University of South Carolina *M*

South Dakota
Northern State University *B, T*

Tennessee
University of Tennessee
　　Knoxville *B, M*

Texas
Lamar University *M*
Stephen F. Austin State University *M, T*
Texas A&M University
　　Kingsville *B*
Texas Woman's University *M*
University of Houston *M*
University of North Texas *M*
University of Texas
　　El Paso *M*

Utah
Brigham Young University *B, M*
University of Utah *M*

Vermont
University of Vermont *B*

Virginia
James Madison University *B, M, D, T*

Washington
University of Washington *M*
Washington State University *B, M*

West Virginia
Marshall University *B*

Wisconsin
Marquette University *M*
University of Wisconsin
　　Whitewater *B, T*

Speech teacher education

Alabama
Huntingdon College *T*
Samford University *B*

Arizona
University of Arizona *B, M*

Arkansas
Arkansas Tech University *B*

Harding University *B, T*
Ouachita Baptist University *B, T*
University of Arkansas
　　Monticello *B*

California
California State University
　　Hayward *B, M, T*
San Diego Mesa College *A*
San Francisco State University *B, T*

Colorado
Colorado State University *T*
Metropolitan State College of Denver *T*

Georgia
Atlanta Metropolitan College *A*

Hawaii
University of Hawaii
　　Manoa *B, T*

Idaho
Boise State University *T*
Lewis-Clark State College *B, T*

Illinois
Augustana College *B, T*
Greenville College *B*
Lewis University *T*
North Park University *T*
Sauk Valley Community College *A*
University of Illinois
　　Urbana-Champaign *M, T*

Indiana
Ball State University *T*
Indiana University
　　Bloomington *B, T*
Indiana University-Purdue University
　　Fort Wayne *B, T*
Indiana University-Purdue University
　　Indianapolis *B, T*
University of Evansville *B*
University of Indianapolis *B, T*
University of Southern Indiana *T*
Vincennes University *A*

Iowa
Central College *T*
Dordt College *B*
Graceland University *T*
Loras College *T*
Luther College *B*
Maharishi University of Management *T*
Northwestern College *T*
St. Ambrose University *T*
University of Iowa *B, M, T*
Upper Iowa University *T*
Wartburg College *T*

Kansas
Baker University *T*
Bethel College *T*
Emporia State University *B, T*
Fort Scott Community College *A*
McPherson College *B, T*
Pittsburg State University *B, T*

Kentucky
Murray State University *B, M, T*

Louisiana
McNeese State University *T*
Northwestern State University *B*
Southeastern Louisiana University *B*
University of Louisiana at Monroe *B*
University of New Orleans *B*
Xavier University of Louisiana *B*

Massachusetts
Bridgewater State College *M*
Emerson College *B, M*
Northeastern University *B*

Michigan
Alma College *T*
Central Michigan University *B*
Concordia University *B, T*
Lansing Community College *A*

Michigan State University *D*
Northern Michigan University *B, M, T*
University of Michigan *M, D*
University of Michigan
　　Flint *T*

Minnesota
Augsburg College *T*
Concordia College: Moorhead *B, T*
Minnesota State University
　　Mankato *B, M*
　　Moorhead *B, T*
St. Cloud State University *T*
St. Olaf College *T*
Southwest State University *B, T*
Winona State University *B, T*

Mississippi
Itawamba Community College *A*
Mississippi College *B*
Mississippi State University *T*

Missouri
Central Missouri State
　　University *B, M, T*
Culver-Stockton College *B, T*
Lindenwood University *M*
Missouri Southern State College *B, T*
Southeast Missouri State University *B, T*
Southwest Baptist University *T*
William Jewell College *T*
William Woods University *T*

Montana
Montana State University
　　Billings *T*

Nebraska
Creighton University *T*
Dana College *B*
Hastings College *B, T*
Midland Lutheran College *B, T*
Nebraska Wesleyan University *T*
Peru State College *B, T*
University of Nebraska
　　Kearney *B, M, T*
　　Lincoln *B, T*
York College *B*

New Jersey
The College of New Jersey *B, M*
Kean University *B*
Monmouth University *B*

New Mexico
College of Santa Fe *B*

New York
City University of New York
　　Brooklyn College *B*
Elmira College *B, T*
Hofstra University *T*
Long Island University
　　C. W. Post Campus *M*
Marymount Manhattan College *B, T*
Nazareth College of Rochester *T*
State University of New York
　　Buffalo *T*
　　College at Cortland *B*
　　College at Fredonia *B, M, T*
　　College at Plattsburgh *M*
　　New Paltz *B, M, T*
Syracuse University *B*

North Carolina
North Carolina Agricultural and
　　Technical State University *B, T*
University of North Carolina
　　Greensboro *B, T*

North Dakota
Dickinson State University *B, T*
North Dakota State University *B, T*

Ohio
Baldwin-Wallace College *T*
Bluffton College *B*
Bowling Green State University *B*
Defiance College *B, T*

Hiram College *T*
Kent State University *T*
Kent State University
　　Stark Campus *T*
Malone College *B*
Miami University
　　Oxford Campus *B, T*
Mount Union College *T*
Ohio University *T*
University of Akron *B, M, T*
University of Rio Grande *B, T*
Youngstown State University *B, M*

Oklahoma
East Central University *B, T*
Eastern Oklahoma State College *A*
Northeastern State University *B*
Oklahoma Baptist University *B, T*
Oklahoma Christian University of
　　Science and Arts *B, T*
Oklahoma City University *B*
Southeastern Oklahoma State
　　University *B, M, T*
Southern Nazarene University *B*
Southwestern Oklahoma State
　　University *T*

Oregon
Portland State University *T*
Southern Oregon University *T*
University of Portland *T*
Western Oregon University *T*

Pennsylvania
California University of Pennsylvania *M*

South Carolina
Lander University *B, T*

South Dakota
Augustana College *B*
Black Hills State University *B, T*
Northern State University *B, T*
South Dakota State University *B*
University of Sioux Falls *T*
University of South Dakota *B, T*

Tennessee
Tennessee Technological University *T*

Texas
Abilene Christian University *B, T*
Baylor University *B, T*
East Texas Baptist University *B*
Hardin-Simmons University *B, T*
Howard Payne University *B, T*
Lamar University *T*
Laredo Community College *A*
Lubbock Christian University *B, T*
McMurry University *T*
Texas A&M University
　　Commerce *T*
　　Corpus Christi *T*
　　Kingsville *T*
University of Texas
　　Pan American *B, T*
West Texas A&M University *T*

Utah
Southern Utah University *B, T*
University of Utah *B*

Vermont
Johnson State College *M*

Virginia
University of Virginia's College at
　　Wise *T*

Washington
Washington State University *T*
Western Washington University *T*
Whitworth College *B, T*

West Virginia
Concord College *B, T*
Fairmont State College *B*

Wisconsin
Cardinal Stritch University *T*

Lakeland College *B*
Maranatha Baptist Bible College *B*
St. Norbert College *T*
University of Wisconsin
    Green Bay *T*
    Platteville *B, T*
    River Falls *T*
    Whitewater *B, T*

Speech/rhetorical studies

Alabama

Alabama State University *B*
Huntingdon College *B, T*
Samford University *B*
Troy State University *B*
University of Alabama *B, M*
University of Alabama
    Huntsville *B*
University of Montevallo *B, T*
University of North Alabama *B*

Alaska

University of Alaska
    Fairbanks *B*

Arizona

Northern Arizona University *B*
Pima Community College *A*

Arkansas

Arkansas State University *B, M*
Arkansas State University
    Beebe *A*
Arkansas Tech University *B, M*
Henderson State University *B*
Phillips Community College of the
    University of Arkansas *A*
University of Arkansas
    Fort Smith *B*
    Monticello *B*
    Pine Bluff *B*
University of Central Arkansas *B*

California

Cabrillo College *A*
California Polytechnic State University:
    San Luis Obispo *B*
California State University
    Chico *B*
    Fullerton *B, M*
    Hayward *B, M*
    Long Beach *B, M*
    Los Angeles *B, M*
    Northridge *B, M*
Cerritos Community College *A*
Chabot College *A*
College of the Sequoias *A*
Columbia College *A*
Foothill College *C, A*
Golden West College *A*
Grossmont Community College *A*
Humboldt State University *B*
Irvine Valley College *A*
Las Positas College *A*
Long Beach City College *A*
Master's College *B*
Modesto Junior College *C, A*
Ohlone College *C*
Orange Coast College *A*
Palomar College *A*
Pepperdine University *B*
San Diego City College *A*
San Diego State University *B*
San Francisco State University *B, M*
San Joaquin Delta College *A*
Santa Barbara City College *A*
Santa Rosa Junior College *C*
Santiago Canyon College *A*
Southwestern College *A*
University of California
    Berkeley *B, D*
    Davis *B, M*
Ventura College *A*
West Valley College *A*

Colorado

Colorado State University *B, M*
Colorado State University
    Pueblo *B*
Metropolitan State College of Denver *B*

Delaware

Delaware State University *B*

District of Columbia

Catholic University of America *M, D*

Florida

Bethune-Cookman College *B*
Florida Atlantic University *B, M*
Florida State University *M, D*
Gulf Coast Community College *A*
Miami-Dade Community College *A*
Polk Community College *A*
South Florida Community College *A*
University of Central Florida *B*
University of South Florida *B, M, D*

Georgia

Albany State University *B*
Atlanta Metropolitan College *A*
Clark Atlanta University *B*
Clayton College and State University *A*
Darton College *A*
Georgia Southern University *B*
Georgia State University *B*
Morris Brown College *B*
University of Georgia *B, M, D*
Young Harris College *A*

Hawaii

University of Hawaii
    Hilo *B*
    Manoa *B, M*

Idaho

Idaho State University *A, B, M*
Northwest Nazarene University *B*

Illinois

Augustana College *B*
Bradley University *B, T*
Chicago State University *B*
City Colleges of Chicago
    Harold Washington College *A*
Eastern Illinois University *B, M, T*
Illinois Central College *A*
Illinois College *B*
Illinois State University *B, T*
Illinois Valley Community College *A*
Judson College *B*
Lake Land College *A*
Lewis University *T*
Lincoln College *A*
McKendree College *B*
Monmouth College *B, T*
North Central College *B*
Northeastern Illinois University *B, M*
Northern Illinois University *B, M*
Northwestern University *B, M, D*
Richland Community College *A*
Roosevelt University *B*
Southern Illinois University
    Carbondale *B, M, D*
Southern Illinois University
    Edwardsville *B, M, T*
Southwestern Illinois College *A*
Triton College *A*
University of Illinois
    Chicago *B, M*
    Urbana-Champaign *B, M, D*
Wheaton College *B, T*

Indiana

Ball State University *M*
Butler University *B*
Huntington College *B*
Indiana University
    South Bend *B*
Vincennes University *A*
Wabash College *B*

Iowa

Drake University *B*
Graceland University *B, T*
Iowa State University *B*
Mount Mercy College *B, T*
Northwestern College *B*
Simpson College *B*
University of Dubuque *B*
University of Iowa *B, M, D, T*
University of Northern Iowa *B, M*
Wartburg College *B, T*

Kansas

Baker University *B, T*
Bethany College *B*
Butler County Community College *A*
Donnelly College *A*
Kansas Wesleyan University *B, T*
Pratt Community College *A*
University of Kansas *B, M, D*
Washburn University of Topeka *B*

Kentucky

Asbury College *B*
Cumberland College *B*
Morehead State University *B*
Murray State University *B, T*
Thomas More College *B*

Louisiana

Centenary College of Louisiana *B*
Louisiana State University
    Shreveport *B*
Louisiana State University and
    Agricultural and Mechanical
    College *B, M, D*
Louisiana Tech University *B, M*
McNeese State University *B*
Southern University and Agricultural and
    Mechanical College *B*
University of Louisiana at Monroe *B*

Maine

Bates College *B*
New England School of
    Communications *A, B*
University of Maine *B, M*

Maryland

Frederick Community College *A*
Frostburg State University *B, T*
Morgan State University *B*
Mount St. Mary's College *B*
University of Maryland
    College Park *B*

Massachusetts

Emerson College *B, M*
Northeastern University *B*

Michigan

Calvin College *B*
Central Michigan University *B, M*
Concordia University *B, T*
Cornerstone University *B, T*
Eastern Michigan University *B, M*
Hillsdale College *B*
Madonna University *A*
Mid Michigan Community College *A*
Northern Michigan University *B, T*
Spring Arbor University *B*
University of Michigan *B, D, T*
University of Michigan
    Flint *B, T*

Minnesota

Augsburg College *B*
College of St. Benedict *B*
Minnesota State University
    Mankato *B, M*
    Moorhead *B*
St. Cloud State University *B*
St. John's University *B*
Southwest State University *B*
University of Minnesota
    Morris *B*
    Twin Cities *B, M, D*
Winona State University *B*

Mississippi

Blue Mountain College *B*
Mississippi Valley State University *B*

Missouri

Central Missouri State University *B, M*
East Central College *A*
Evangel University *B*
Missouri Western State College *B, T*
St. Louis Community College
    St. Louis Community College at
        Florissant Valley *A*
Southeast Missouri State University *B*
Southwest Baptist University *T*
Three Rivers Community College *A*
Truman State University *B*
William Jewell College *B*

Montana

Miles Community College *A*
University of Montana-Missoula *B, M*

Nebraska

Chadron State College *B*
Doane College *B*
Hastings College *B, T*
Nebraska Wesleyan University *B*
Northeast Community College *A*
University of Nebraska
    Kearney *B, M, T*
    Omaha *B*

New Jersey

The College of New Jersey *B*
Rider University *B*
Rutgers, The State University of New
    Jersey
    Camden Regional Campus *T*

New Mexico

Eastern New Mexico University *B*
New Mexico State University *D*
University of New Mexico *B, M, D*

New York

City University of New York
    Brooklyn College *B, M*
    York College *B*
Hofstra University *B, M*
Ithaca College *B*
Mercy College *B*
New York University *M*
Pace University *B*
Pace University:
    Pleasantville/Briarcliff *B, T*
Rensselaer Polytechnic Institute *M, D*
St. John's University *B*
St. Joseph's College *B*
State University of New York
    Albany *B, M*
    College at Cortland *B*
    College at Oneonta *B*
    College at Potsdam *B*
Syracuse University *B, M*
Touro College *B*
Utica College *B*
Yeshiva University *B*

North Carolina

Appalachian State University *B*
Fayetteville State University *B*
Guilford Technical Community
    College *A*
Methodist College *A, B*
North Carolina Agricultural and
    Technical State University *B*
North Carolina State University *B*
University of North Carolina
    Greensboro *B, M, D*
    Wilmington *B*

North Dakota

Minot State University *B*
North Dakota State University *B, M, D*

Ohio

Bowling Green State University *B*
Defiance College *B, T*

Kent State University *B, M, D*
Kent State University
  Stark Campus *B*
Miami University
  Oxford Campus *B, M, T*
Ohio University *M, D*
University of Akron *B, M*
Youngstown State University *B*

Oklahoma

Carl Albert State College *A*
East Central University *B*
Northeastern Oklahoma Agricultural and
  Mechanical College *A*
Northeastern State University *B*
Northwestern Oklahoma State
  University *B*
Oklahoma Baptist University *B, T*
Oklahoma Christian University of
  Science and Arts *B*
Oklahoma Panhandle State University *B*
Oklahoma State University *B, M*
Redlands Community College *A*
Rose State College *A*
Southern Nazarene University *B*
Tulsa Community College *A*

Oregon

Chemeketa Community College *A*
Multnomah Bible College *B*
Oregon State University *B*
Portland State University *B, M*
Southern Oregon University *B, T*
Western Oregon University *B*
Willamette University *B*

Pennsylvania

Bloomsburg University of
  Pennsylvania *B*
California University of Pennsylvania *B*
Carnegie Mellon University *M, D*
Community College of Philadelphia *A*
Duquesne University *D*
East Stroudsburg University of
  Pennsylvania *B*
Geneva College *B*
Kutztown University of Pennsylvania *B*
La Salle University *B*
Lock Haven University of
  Pennsylvania *B*
Penn State
  Altoona *B*
  Beaver *B*
  Berks *B*
  Delaware County *B*
  Dubois *B*
  Fayette *B*
  Hazleton *B*
  Lehigh Valley *B*
  McKeesport *B*
  Mont Alto *B*
  New Kensington *B*
  Schuylkill - Capital College *B*
  Shenango *B*
  University Park *B, M, D*
  Wilkes-Barre *B*
  Worthington Scranton *B*
  York *B*
Shippensburg University of
  Pennsylvania *B*
Temple University *B, M*
University of Pittsburgh *C, B, M, D*
University of Pittsburgh
  Bradford *B*
West Chester University of
  Pennsylvania *B*
York College of Pennsylvania *B*

South Carolina

Anderson College *B*
Clemson University *B*

South Dakota

Augustana College *T*
Black Hills State University *B, T*
Northern State University *A*
University of Sioux Falls *B*

University of South Dakota *B, M*

Tennessee

Belmont University *B*
Carson-Newman College *B*
East Tennessee State University *B*
Fisk University *B*
Union University *B, T*

Texas

Abilene Christian University *B, M*
Amarillo College *A*
Angelina College *A*
Austin Community College *A*
Baylor University *B*
Blinn College *A*
Brazosport College *A*
Clarendon College *A*
Coastal Bend College *A*
Del Mar College *A*
East Texas Baptist University *B*
El Paso Community College *A*
Galveston College *A*
Grayson County College *A*
Houston Baptist University *B*
Howard Payne University *B*
Lamar University *B, M*
Lon Morris College *A*
Midland College *A*
Northeast Texas Community College *A*
Panola College *A*
St. Philip's College *A*
Sam Houston State University *B*
Southwest Texas State
  University *B, M, T*
Stephen F. Austin State University *B, M*
Sul Ross State University *B*
Tarleton State University *B*
Texas A&M University *B, M, D*
Texas A&M University
  Commerce *B, M*
Texas Tech University *B, M*
Texas Woman's University *D*
Trinity University *B*
Trinity Valley Community College *A*
Tyler Junior College *A*
University of Houston *B, M*
University of Houston
  Downtown *B*
  Victoria *B*
University of Mary Hardin-Baylor *B*
University of North Texas *B, M*
University of Texas
  Arlington *B, D*
  Austin *M, D*
  Pan American *B, M, T*
  Tyler *B*
University of the Incarnate Word *B*
West Texas A&M University *B*

Utah

Southern Utah University *B*
University of Utah *D*
Utah State University *B, M*

Virginia

George Mason University *B*
Hampton University *B*
Old Dominion University *B*
University of Richmond *B*
University of Virginia's College at
  Wise *T*

Washington

Eastern Washington University *T*
Everett Community College *A*
Gonzaga University *B*
University of Washington *B, M, D*

West Virginia

Alderson-Broaddus College *B*
Marshall University *B, M*
West Virginia Wesleyan College *B*

Wisconsin

Beloit College *B*

University of Wisconsin
  Madison *B, M, D*
  River Falls *B, M*
  Superior *M*
  Whitewater *B*

Wyoming

Laramie County Community College *A*

Sports/fitness administration

Alabama

Faulkner University *B*
Huntingdon College *B*
Shelton State Community College *A*
Troy State University *B, M*

Arizona

Arizona Western College *C*

Arkansas

Arkansas State University *B*
Harding University *B*
Henderson State University *M*
John Brown University *B*

California

California State University
  Hayward *C*
Concordia University *B*
Fresno Pacific University *B*
St. Mary's College of California *B*
San Francisco State University *B, M*
University of San Francisco *M*
University of the Pacific *B*

Colorado

Colorado State University
  Pueblo *B*
Fort Lewis College *B*
Front Range Community College *C, A*

Connecticut

Eastern Connecticut State University *B*
Mitchell College *A, B*
Teikyo Post University *B*
University of New Haven *B, M*

Delaware

Delaware State University *B*
University of Delaware *B*
Wilmington College *B*

Florida

Barry University *B, M*
Flagler College *B*
Florida State University *B, M, D*
Manatee Community College *A*
Northwood University
  Florida Campus *A, B*
Nova Southeastern University *B*
St. Leo University *B*
St. Thomas University *B, M*
Stetson University *B*
University of Central Florida *M*
University of Tampa *B*
Warner Southern College *B*
Webber International University *A, B, M*

Georgia

Emmanuel College *B*
Georgia Southern University *B, M*
Georgia State University *M*
South Georgia College *A*
University of Georgia *B*

Idaho

Albertson College of Idaho *B*

Illinois

Elmhurst College *B*
Greenville College *B*
Illinois College *B*
Illinois Valley Community College *A*
Judson College *B*
Lewis University *B*
MacMurray College *B*

Millikin University *B*
North Central College *B*
Olivet Nazarene University *B*
Principia College *B*
Quincy University *A, B*
Sauk Valley Community College *A*
South Suburban College of Cook
  County *C, A*

Indiana

Goshen College *B*
Huntington College *B*
Indiana Institute of Technology *A, B*
Indiana State University *M*
Indiana Wesleyan University *B*
Marian College *B*
Taylor University *B*
Tri-State University *B*
University of Evansville *B*
Valparaiso University *B*
Vincennes University *A*

Iowa

Briar Cliff University *B*
Graceland University *B*
Grand View College *C*
Iowa Wesleyan College *B*
Loras College *B, M*
North Iowa Area Community College *A*
St. Ambrose University *B*
Simpson College *B*
University of Iowa *B, M, D*
Wartburg College *B*
William Penn University *B*

Kansas

Barton County Community College *A*
Central Christian College *A*
MidAmerica Nazarene University *B*
St. Mary College *B*
Southwestern College *B*
Tabor College *B*
Washburn University of Topeka *B*
Wichita State University *B, M*

Kentucky

Asbury College *B*
Kentucky Wesleyan College *B*
Morehead State University *B*
Union College *B*
University of Louisville *B*

Louisiana

Grambling State University *M*
Tulane University *B*

Maine

Husson College *B*
Thomas College *B*
University of New England *B*
University of Southern Maine *B*

Maryland

Community College of Baltimore County
  Catonsville *A*
  Dundalk *A*
  Essex *A*
Towson University *B*

Massachusetts

American International College *B*
Becker College *A, B*
Dean College *A*
Endicott College *B*
Fitchburg State College *B*
Lasell College *B*
Mount Ida College *A*
Mount Wachusett Community College *C*
Nichols College *B*
Northeastern University *M*
Salem State College *B*
Springfield College *B, M*
University of Massachusetts
  Amherst *B, M, D*
Western New England College *B*

Michigan

Aquinas College *B*
Central Michigan University *M*

Cornerstone University *B*
Northern Michigan University *B*
Northwood University *A, B*
Siena Heights University *B*
University of Michigan *B*
Wayne State University *M*

Minnesota
Century Community and Technical
College *C, A*
Crown College *B*
Minnesota State University
Mankato *B, M, T*
St. Cloud State University *M*
University of Minnesota
Crookston *B*
Winona State University *B*

Mississippi
University of Southern Mississippi *M*

Missouri
Lindenwood University *B, M*
Missouri Baptist University *B*
Southeast Missouri State University *B*
Southwest Baptist University *B*
William Woods University *B*

Montana
Montana State University
Billings *B, M*
Bozeman *B*

Nebraska
Bellevue University *B*
Concordia University *B*
Dana College *B*
Hastings College *B*
Nebraska Wesleyan University *B*
Union College *B*
University of Nebraska
Kearney *B*
Wayne State College *B*

Nevada
University of Nevada
Las Vegas *M*

New Hampshire
Colby-Sawyer College *B*
Daniel Webster College *B*
Franklin Pierce College *B*
Hesser College *C, A*
Keene State College *B*
New England College *B*
New Hampshire Technical Institute *A*
Southern New Hampshire University *B*

New Jersey
Rowan University *B*
Seton Hall University *B*

New York
Canisius College *M*
Finger Lakes Community College *A*
Ithaca College *B*
Medaille College *C, B*
New York University *B*
St. John's University *C, B*
State University of New York
College at Brockport *B*
College of Agriculture and
Technology at Morrisville *A*
College of Technology at Alfred *A*
Tompkins-Cortland Community
College *A*

North Carolina
Barton College *B*
Campbell University *B*
Catawba College *B*
Chowan College *B*
Elon University *B*
Greensboro College *B*
Guilford College *B*
High Point University *B*
Lenoir-Rhyne College *B*
Livingstone College *B*
Meredith College *B*

Methodist College *B*
Pfeiffer University *B*
Western Carolina University *B*
Wingate University *B*
Winston-Salem State University *B*

Ohio
Ashland University *B*
Baldwin-Wallace College *B*
Bowling Green State University *B, M*
Cedarville University *B*
Cincinnati State Technical and
Community College *C*
Cleveland State University *M*
Columbus State Community College *A*
Hocking Technical College *A*
Kent State University
Stark Campus *B*
Miami University
Oxford Campus *B, M*
Mount Union College *B*
Mount Vernon Nazarene University *A, B*
Ohio Northern University *B*
Ohio University *B, M*
Otterbein College *B*
Shawnee State University *B*
Tiffin University *B*
University of Akron *C, B, M*
University of Dayton *B*
University of Findlay *B*
University of Rio Grande *B*
Urbana University *B*
Wilmington College *B*
Xavier University *B, M*
Youngstown State University *B*

Oklahoma
Oklahoma Baptist University *B*

Oregon
George Fox University *B*
Portland Community College *C*
Southern Oregon University *B*
Western Baptist College *B*

Pennsylvania
Bucks County Community College *A*
DeSales University *B*
Edinboro University of Pennsylvania *B*
Keystone College *A, B*
Lock Haven University of
Pennsylvania *B*
Mercyhurst College *B*
Millersville University of
Pennsylvania *M*
Neumann College *B, M*
Northampton County Area Community
College *A*
Robert Morris University *B, M*
Slippery Rock University of
Pennsylvania *B, M*
University of Pittsburgh
Bradford *B*
Waynesburg College *B*
West Chester University of
Pennsylvania *M*
York College of Pennsylvania *B*

South Carolina
Coker College *B*
Erskine College *B*
Limestone College *B*
Newberry College *B*
North Greenville College *B*
Southern Wesleyan University *B*
Technical College of the Lowcountry *C*
University of South Carolina *B*
Winthrop University *B*

South Dakota
Dakota State University *B*
Dakota Wesleyan University *B*
Northern State University *B*

Tennessee
Southern Adventist University *B*
Tennessee Wesleyan College *B*
Tusculum College *B*

Union University *B*
University of Memphis *B*
University of Tennessee
Knoxville *B*
Martin *B*

Texas
Abilene Christian University *B*
Baylor University *B*
Hardin-Simmons University *B, M*
Howard Payne University *B*
LeTourneau University *B*
Lubbock Christian University *B*
Midwestern State University *B*
Northwood University: Texas
Campus *A, B*
Southwest Texas State University *B*
Texas Lutheran University *B*
University of Houston *B*
University of the Incarnate Word *B*

Utah
Brigham Young University *B, D*

Vermont
Champlain College *A, B*
Johnson State College *B*

Virginia
Averett University *B*
Eastern Mennonite University *B*
Ferrum College *B*
Hampton University *B*
Liberty University *B*
Longwood University *B*
Lynchburg College *B*
Marymount University *B*
Virginia Intermont College *B*

Washington
Central Washington University *B*
Lake Washington Technical College *C*
Spokane Falls Community College *A*
Washington State University *B*

West Virginia
Bethany College *B*
Davis and Elkins College *B*
Salem International University *B*
West Virginia University *B*
Wheeling Jesuit University *B*

Wisconsin
Marian College of Fond du Lac *B*
University of Wisconsin
La Crosse *B, M*
Parkside *B*

Statistics

Alabama
Auburn University *M, T*
University of Alabama *M, D*
University of South Alabama *B*

Alaska
University of Alaska
Fairbanks *B, M*

Arizona
Arizona State University *M*
Northern Arizona University *M*

Arkansas
University of Arkansas *M*

California
California Polytechnic State University:
San Luis Obispo *B*
California State Polytechnic University:
Pomona *B*
California State University
Chico *B*
Hayward *B, M*
Long Beach *B*
Northridge *B*
Chabot College *A*
Pomona College *B*

San Diego State University *B, M*
San Francisco State University *B*
San Jose State University *B*
Stanford University *M, D*
University of California
Berkeley *B, M, D*
Davis *B, M, D*
Riverside *B, M, D*
San Diego *M*
Santa Barbara *B, M, D*
University of Southern California *M*

Colorado
Colorado State University *B, M, D*
University of Denver *B*

Connecticut
Central Connecticut State University *B*
University of Connecticut *B, M, D*
Yale University *M, D*

Delaware
University of Delaware *B, M, D*

District of Columbia
American University *C, B, M, D*
George Washington University *B, M, D*

Florida
Florida Atlantic University *C*
Florida International University *B, M*
Florida State University *B, M, D*
Manatee Community College *A*
University of Central Florida *C, B, M*
University of Florida *B, M, D*
University of Miami *M*
University of North Florida *B*
University of West Florida *B, M*

Georgia
Georgia Institute of Technology *M*
Oxford College of Emory University *B*
University of Georgia *B, M, D*

Idaho
University of Idaho *M*

Illinois
De Paul University *M*
Lincoln College *A*
Loyola University of Chicago *B*
Northern Illinois University *M*
Northwestern University *B, M, D*
Roosevelt University *B*
University of Chicago *B, M, D*
University of Illinois
Chicago *B*
Urbana-Champaign *B, M, D*

Indiana
Ball State University *M*
Indiana University-Purdue University
Fort Wayne *B*
Purdue University *B, M, D*
Saint Mary's College *B*

Iowa
Iowa State University *B, M, D*
Luther College *B*
University of Iowa *B, M, D*

Kansas
Independence Community College *A*
Kansas State University *B, M, D*

Kentucky
University of Kentucky *M, D*

Louisiana
Louisiana State University and
Agricultural and Mechanical
College *M*
Tulane University *M*
Xavier University of Louisiana *B*

Maine
University of Southern Maine *M*

Maryland
University of Maryland
    Baltimore County *B, M, D*
    College Park *M, D*

Massachusetts
Hampshire College *B*
Harvard College *B*
Worcester Polytechnic Institute *M*

Michigan
Central Michigan University *B*
Eastern Michigan University *B, M*
Grand Valley State University *B*
Kettering University *B*
Michigan State University *B, M, D*
Oakland University *C, B, M*
University of Michigan *B, M, D*
Wayne State University *M*
Western Michigan University *B, M, D*

Minnesota
Minnesota State University
    Mankato *M*
St. Cloud State University *B*
University of Minnesota
    Morris *B*
    Twin Cities *B, M, D*
Winona State University *B*

Mississippi
Mississippi State University *M*

Missouri
Northwest Missouri State University *B*
University of Missouri
    Columbia *B, M, D*
    Kansas City *B, M*
    Rolla *D*
Washington University in St. Louis *B, M*

Montana
Montana State University
    Bozeman *M, D*
Montana Tech of the University of
    Montana *B*

Nebraska
University of Nebraska
    Kearney *B*
    Lincoln *M, D*

New Jersey
The College of New Jersey *B*
Montclair State University *M*
New Jersey Institute of Technology *B, M*
Rutgers, The State University of New
    Jersey
    New Brunswick Regional
        Campus *B, M, D*
Stevens Institute of Technology *B, M*

New Mexico
New Mexico State University *M*
University of New Mexico *B, M, D*

New York
Barnard College *B*
Canisius College *B*
City University of New York
    Baruch College *B, M*
    Hunter College *B, M*
Columbia University
    Columbia College *B*
Cornell University *M, D*
New York University *B, M, D*
Rensselaer Polytechnic Institute *M, D*
Rochester Institute of Technology *B, M*
State University of New York
    Buffalo *B, M*
    College at Oneonta *B*
Syracuse University *M*
University of Rochester *B, M, D*

North Carolina
Appalachian State University *B*
North Carolina State University *B, M, D*
University of North Carolina
    Chapel Hill *M, D*

North Dakota
North Dakota State University *B, M, D*

Ohio
Bowling Green State University *B, M*
Case Western Reserve
    University *B, M, D*
Miami University
    Oxford Campus *B, M*
Ohio Northern University *B*
Ohio State University
    Columbus Campus *M, D*
University of Akron *B, M*
Wright State University *M*

Oklahoma
Oklahoma State University *B, M, D*
University of Central Oklahoma *B*

Oregon
Oregon State University *M, D*
Portland State University *M*

Pennsylvania
Carnegie Mellon University *B, M, D*
La Salle University *B*
Lehigh University *B, M*
Penn State
    Abington *B*
    Altoona *B*
    Beaver *B*
    Berks *B*
    Delaware County *B*
    Dubois *B*
    Fayette *B*
    Hazleton *B*
    Lehigh Valley *B*
    McKeesport *B*
    Mont Alto *B*
    New Kensington *B*
    Schuylkill - Capital College *B*
    Shenango *B*
    University Park *B, M, D*
    Wilkes-Barre *B*
    Worthington Scranton *B*
    York *B*
Temple University *B, M, D*
University of Pennsylvania *B, M, D*
University of Pittsburgh *C, B, M, D*

Puerto Rico
University of Puerto Rico
    Mayaguez Campus *M*

Rhode Island
Brown University *B*
University of Rhode Island *M*

South Carolina
University of South Carolina *B, M, D*

South Dakota
Dakota State University *B*

Texas
Baylor University *M, D*
Rice University *B, M, D*
Sam Houston State University *M*
Southern Methodist University *B, M, D*
Stephen F. Austin State University *M*
Texas A&M University *M, D*
Texas Tech University *M*
University of Houston
    Clear Lake *M*
University of Texas
    Austin *M*
    Dallas *B, M, D*
    El Paso *M*
    San Antonio *B, M*

Utah
Brigham Young University *B, M*
Snow College *A*
Southern Utah University *B*
University of Utah *M*
Utah State University *B, M*

Vermont
Castleton State College *B*

University of Vermont *B, M*

Virginia
University of Virginia *M, D*
Virginia Polytechnic Institute and State
    University *B, M, D*

Washington
University of Washington *M, D*
Washington State University *M*

West Virginia
West Virginia University *B, M*

Wisconsin
University of Wisconsin
    La Crosse *B*
    Madison *B, M, D*

Wyoming
Eastern Wyoming College *A*
University of Wyoming *B, M, D*

Structural biology

New York
State University of New York
    Stony Brook *D*

Structural engineering

Michigan
Michigan Technological University *D*
Western Michigan University *B*

New York
State University of New York
    Buffalo *M, D, T*

Ohio
Youngstown State University *B*

Pennsylvania
Penn State
    Harrisburg *B*

Wisconsin
Milwaukee School of Engineering *M*

Substance abuse counseling

Alabama
Gadsden State Community College *A*
Wallace State Community College at
    Hanceville *A*

Arizona
Pima Community College *C, A*
Rio Salado College *C, A*

California
Bethany College *C, B*
California State University
    Hayward *C*
College of the Redwoods *C*
Diablo Valley College *C*
East Los Angeles College *C*
Glendale Community College *C*
Imperial Valley College *C, A*
Loma Linda University *M*
Modesto Junior College *C*
Mount San Jacinto College *C, A*
San Diego City College *C, A*
Yuba Community College District *C, A*

Connecticut
Asnuntuck Community College *A*
Gateway Community College *C, A*
Housatonic Community College *A*
Manchester Community College *A*
Middlesex Community College *A*
Naugatuck Valley Community College *A*
Northwestern Connecticut Community
    College *A*
Norwalk Community College *A*

Three Rivers Community College *A*
Tunxis Community College *A*

Delaware
Delaware Technical and Community
    College
    Stanton/Wilmington Campus *A*
    Terry Campus *A*

Florida
St. Petersburg College *A*

Illinois
City Colleges of Chicago
    Harold Washington College *C, A*
    Kennedy-King College *C*
College of DuPage *C, A*
College of Lake County *C, A*
Dominican University *B*
Elgin Community College *C*
Governors State University *M*
Moraine Valley Community College *C*
National-Louis University *C, B, M*
Oakton Community College *C*
Prairie State College *A*
Roosevelt University *M*
South Suburban College of Cook
    County *C*
Triton College *C, A*
Waubonsee Community College *C*

Indiana
Indiana University-Purdue University
    Fort Wayne *B*
Vincennes University *C*

Iowa
Des Moines Area Community College *C*
Iowa Western Community College *A*
Southeastern Community College
    North Campus *A*
    South Campus *A*
University of Iowa *M*

Kansas
Dodge City Community College *A*
Kansas City Kansas Community
    College *A*
Pittsburg State University *M*
Washburn University of Topeka *A, B*

Louisiana
Southern University
    Shreveport *C, A*
University of Louisiana at Monroe *M*

Maine
University of Maine
    Augusta *C*
University of Southern Maine *M*

Maryland
Community College of Baltimore County
    Catonsville *C, A*
    Dundalk *C, A*
    Essex *C, A*
Howard Community College *A*
Wor-Wic Community College *C, A*

Massachusetts
Quinsigamond Community College *A*
Springfield College *M*
Stonehill College *C*

Michigan
Washtenaw Community College *A*
Wayne County Community College *C*
Wayne State University *C*

Minnesota
Century Community and Technical
    College *C, A*
Mesabi Range Community and Technical
    College *C, A*
Metropolitan State University *B*
Minneapolis Community and Technical
    College *C, A*
Ridgewater College: A Community and
    Technical College *A*
St. Cloud State University *B, M*

St. Mary's University of Minnesota *M*
University of Minnesota
    Twin Cities *C*

Missouri
Missouri Valley College *B*
St. Charles Community College *A*

Montana
Dawson Community College *A*
Flathead Valley Community College *A*
Fort Belknap College *A*
University of Great Falls *A, B*

Nebraska
Bellevue University *B*
Little Priest Tribal College *A*

Nevada
Truckee Meadows Community
    College *C, A*

New Hampshire
New Hampshire Technical Institute *A*

New Jersey
Mercer County Community College *C*

New Mexico
San Juan College *A*

New York
Broome Community College *A*
Columbia University
    School of Nursing *C*
Corning Community College *A*
Dutchess Community College *C*
Erie Community College
    City Campus *A*
Finger Lakes Community College *A*
Hudson Valley Community College *A*
Marymount Manhattan College *C*
Medaille College *C*
Mohawk Valley Community College *A*
Pace University *M*
Pace University:
    Pleasantville/Briarcliff *M*
St. Joseph's College: Suffolk Campus *C*
State University of New York
    Buffalo *M*
Suffolk County Community College *A*
Tompkins-Cortland Community
    College *A*
Ulster County Community College *A*
Westchester Community College *C, A*

North Carolina
East Carolina University *M*
Guilford Technical Community
    College *C, A*
Roanoke-Chowan Community College *A*
Sandhills Community College *A*
Southwestern Community College *A*

North Dakota
Minot State University *B*
University of Mary *B*

Ohio
Columbus State Community College *A*
North Central State College *C*
Sinclair Community College *C*
Southern State Community College *A*
University of Akron *C, A*
University of Toledo *A*
Wright State University *M*

Oklahoma
Oklahoma State University
    Oklahoma City *A*

Oregon
Chemeketa Community College *A*
Lane Community College *A*
Oregon Health Sciences University *C*
Portland Community College *C, A*
Rogue Community College *A*
Southwestern Oregon Community
    College *A*

Pennsylvania
Community College of Allegheny
    County *C*
Community College of Philadelphia *C*
Drexel University *B*
Marywood University *B*
Montgomery County Community
    College *C, A*
Northampton County Area Community
    College *C*
St. Vincent College *C*
Seton Hill University *C*
University of Scranton *C*

Rhode Island
Community College of Rhode Island *A*

South Dakota
Kilian Community College *A*
University of South Dakota *B*

Tennessee
Cleveland State Community College *C*
Southwest Tennessee Community
    College *C*

Texas
Alvin Community College *C, A*
Amarillo College *C, A*
Angelina College *C, A*
Austin Community College *C, A*
Central Texas College *C, A*
Eastfield College *C, A*
El Paso Community College *A*
Galveston College *C, A*
Grayson County College *C, A*
Howard College *C, A*
Lamar State College at Port Arthur *C, A*
Lee College *C, A*
McLennan Community College *C, A*
Midland College *A*
North Harris Montgomery Community
    College District *C*
Odessa College *A*
St. Mary's University *M*
Texarkana College *C, A*
Tyler Junior College *A*

Virginia
J. Sargeant Reynolds Community
    College *C*

Washington
Bellevue Community College *C*
Clark College *C, A*
Edmonds Community College *C, A*
Lower Columbia College *A*
Peninsula College *A*
Seattle University *C*
Spokane Falls Community College *C, A*
Wenatchee Valley College *C, A*

West Virginia
Mountain State College *A*

Wisconsin
Chippewa Valley Technical College *A*
Fox Valley Technical College *A*
Moraine Park Technical College *A*
Waukesha County Technical College *A*

Arkansas
Arkansas State University *M, T*

Michigan
Saginaw Valley State University *M*

New Jersey
William Paterson University of New
    Jersey *M*

New York
St. Bonaventure University *M*
State University of New York
    Buffalo *M, D, T*

Ohio
University of Dayton *M*
Youngstown State University *D*

Pennsylvania
Marywood University *M*

South Dakota
University of South Dakota *M, D*

Texas
Southwest Texas State University *M*
University of Texas
    Arlington *T*
    Pan American *D*

Vermont
St. Michael's College *T*

Washington
University of Washington *D, T*

Wisconsin
Edgewood College *M*
University of Wisconsin
    Superior *M*

Alabama
Calhoun Community College *C*
Community College of the Air Force *A*
Douglas MacArthur State Technical
    College *C*
Harry M. Ayers State Technical
    College *C*

Arizona
Gateway Community College *C, A*

Arkansas
North Arkansas College *C, A*
Southeast Arkansas College *C, A*
University of Arkansas
    Fort Smith *C, A*
    for Medical Sciences *C, A*

California
Southwestern College *C, A*

Colorado
Front Range Community College *C*

Connecticut
Manchester Community College *A*

Florida
Daytona Beach Community College *C*
Indian River Community College *C*
Palm Beach Community College *C*
Santa Fe Community College *C*

Georgia
Albany Technical College *C*
Athens Technical College *C*
Chattahoochee Technical College *C*
Coastal Georgia Community College *C*
Columbus Technical College *C, A*
Darton College *A*
DeKalb Technical College *C*
Macon State College *A*
Middle Georgia College *A*
Northwestern Technical College *A*
Savannah Technical College *A*
Southwest Georgia Technical College *C*
Waycross College *A*

Idaho
Boise State University *C*
College of Southern Idaho *C*
Eastern Idaho Technical College *A*

Illinois
City Colleges of Chicago
    Malcolm X College *A*
College of DuPage *C, A*
College of Lake County *C*
Elgin Community College *C*
Illinois Central College *C*
John Wood Community College *C*

Kaskaskia College *C*
Parkland College *C*
Prairie State College *C*
Rend Lake College *C*
Richland Community College *C, A*
Southeastern Illinois College *C*
Triton College *C*

Indiana
Ivy Tech State College
    Central Indiana *A*
    Columbus *A*
    Eastcentral *A*
    Lafayette *A*
    Northwest *A*
    Southwest *A*
    Wabash Valley *A*
University of St. Francis *A*
Vincennes University *C*

Iowa
Kirkwood Community College *C, A*
Marshalltown Community College *A*
Mercy College of Health Sciences *C, A*
Western Iowa Tech Community
    College *C*

Kansas
Hutchinson Community College *C*
Johnson County Community College *A*
Seward County Community College *C*

Kentucky
Spencerian College *C*

Louisiana
Delgado Community College *C*
Nicholls State University *A*
Southern University
    Shreveport *A*

Maryland
Chesapeake College *C*
Frederick Community College *C*
Howard Community College *C, A*

Massachusetts
Berkshire Community College *A*
Bunker Hill Community College *C*
Massachusetts Bay Community
    College *C*
Quinsigamond Community College *C*
Springfield Technical Community
    College *A*

Michigan
Baker College
    of Cadillac *A*
    of Clinton Township *A*
    of Jackson *A*
    of Muskegon *A*
    of Port Huron *A*
Lansing Community College *A*
Macomb Community College *C, A*
Northern Michigan University *C*
Oakland Community College *A*
Washtenaw Community College *C*

Minnesota
High-Tech Institute *A*
Lake Superior College: A Community
    and Technical College *C, A*
Rochester Community and Technical
    College *A*
St. Cloud Technical College *C, A*
St. Mary's University of Minnesota *C*

Mississippi
Itawamba Community College *C, A*

Missouri
Mineral Area College *C*
Ozarks Technical Community College *C*
Penn Valley Community College *C*
St. Louis Community College
    St. Louis Community College at
        Forest Park *A*
Three Rivers Community College *C*

Montana

University of Montana-Missoula *A*

Nebraska

Metropolitan Community College *C, A*
Nebraska Methodist College of Nursing
and Allied Health *C*
Northeast Community College *A*
Southeast Community College
Lincoln Campus *C, A*

New Hampshire

New Hampshire Community Technical
College
Manchester *A*
Stratham *A*

New Jersey

Bergen Community College *C*
Ocean County College *C*
University of Medicine and Dentistry of
New Jersey
School of Health Related
Professions *C*

New Mexico

Albuquerque Technical-Vocational
Institute *C*

New York

Nassau Community College *A*
Niagara County Community College *C*
Onondaga Community College *C*
Trocaire College *A*

North Carolina

Blue Ridge Community College *C, A*
Catawba Valley Community College *A*
Coastal Carolina Community
College *C, A*
College of the Albemarle *C*
Durham Technical Community
College *C*
Edgecombe Community College *C*
Fayetteville Technical Community
College *A*
Guilford Technical Community
College *C, A*
Lenoir Community College *C*
Miller-Motte Technical College *A*
Rockingham Community College *C*
Sandhills Community College *C, A*
Wake Technical Community College *A*
Wilson Technical Community College *C*

North Dakota

Bismarck State College *A*

Ohio

Central Ohio Technical College *A*
Cincinnati State Technical and
Community College *A*
Columbus State Community College *A*
Cuyahoga Community College
Eastern Campus *A*
Metropolitan Campus *A*
Western Campus *A*
Lakeland Community College *A*
Owens Community College
Toledo *A*
Sinclair Community College *A*
University of Akron *C, A*
University of Cincinnati
Clermont College *A*

Oklahoma

Northern Oklahoma College *A*

Oregon

Mount Hood Community College *A*

Pennsylvania

'Community College of Allegheny
County *C, A*
Delaware County Community
College *C, A*
Lehigh Carbon Community College *A*
Luzerne County Community College *A*
Mount Aloysius College *C, A*

Pennsylvania College of Technology *C*
University of Pittsburgh
Johnstown *A*
Western School of Health and Business
Careers *A*
Westmoreland County Community
College *C*

South Carolina

Central Carolina Technical College *A*
Florence-Darlington Technical
College *C*
Horry-Georgetown Technical College *A*
Midlands Technical College *A*
Piedmont Technical College *C*
Spartanburg Technical College *C*
Tri-County Technical College *C*

South Dakota

Southeast Technical Institute *A*

Tennessee

Northeast State Technical Community
College *C*

Texas

Amarillo College *C, A*
Austin Community College *C, A*
Del Mar College *C, A*
El Centro College *C*
El Paso Community College *A*
Houston Community College System *C*
Kilgore College *C, A*
Lamar State College at Port Arthur *C, A*
Odessa College *A*
St. Philip's College *C*
San Jacinto College
Central Campus *C*
South Plains College *C*
Tarrant County College *C*
Temple College *C*
Trinity Valley Community College *C*
Tyler Junior College *C, A*
Wharton County Junior College *C*

Utah

Dixie State College of Utah *C*
Salt Lake Community College *A*

Virginia

College of Health Sciences *C*
J. Sargeant Reynolds Community
College *C*
Piedmont Virginia Community
College *C*

Washington

Clover Park Technical College *C*
Renton Technical College *A*
Seattle Central Community College *C*
Spokane Community College *A*

West Virginia

West Virginia Northern Community
College *C*
West Virginia University at
Parkersburg *C*

Wisconsin

Mid-State Technical College *C*
Milwaukee Area Technical College *C, A*
Nicolet Area Technical College *A*
Waukesha County Technical College *A*
Western Wisconsin Technical College *C*

Wyoming

Central Wyoming College *A*

Surveying engineering

Indiana

Vincennes University *A*

Surveying technology

Alaska

University of Alaska
Anchorage *A, B*

Arkansas

University of Arkansas
Monticello *A, B*

California

California State University
Fresno *B*
Chabot College *A*
Coastline Community College *C*
Cuyamaca College *A*
Diablo Valley College *C*
Palomar College *C, A*
Shasta College *C*
Sierra College *A*

Colorado

Metropolitan State College of Denver *B*

Delaware

Delaware Technical and Community
College
Terry Campus *C, A*

Florida

Palm Beach Community College *A*
Polk Community College *A*
South Florida Community College *A*
University of Florida *B*

Georgia

Middle Georgia College *A*
Southern Polytechnic State
University *C, B*

Idaho

Idaho State University *B*

Illinois

Lincoln Land Community College *C*
Morrison Institute of Technology *A*
Parkland College *A*
Waubonsee Community College *C*

Indiana

Purdue University *B*
Vincennes University *A*

Iowa

Kirkwood Community College *A*

Kansas

Kansas State University *A, B*

Kentucky

Murray State University *A*

Maine

University of Maine *B, M, D*

Maryland

Community College of Baltimore County
Catonsville *C, A*
Dundalk *C, A*
Essex *C, A*

Massachusetts

Northeastern University *A*
Wentworth Institute of Technology *C*

Michigan

Ferris State University *C, A, B*
Macomb Community College *C, A*
Michigan Technological University *B*
Montcalm Community College *A*

Minnesota

Rochester Community and Technical
College *A*
St. Cloud State University *B*
St. Paul College - A Community and
Technical College *A*

Missouri

East Central College *A*
Longview Community College *A*

Montana

Flathead Valley Community College *A*
Montana Tech of the University of
Montana *A*

Nevada

Western Nevada Community College *A*

New Hampshire

New Hampshire Community Technical
College
Berlin *A*
University of New Hampshire *A*

New Jersey

Burlington County College *A*
Essex County College *A*
Gloucester County College *A*
Middlesex County College *A*
Ocean County College *A*
Thomas Edison State College *A, B*

New Mexico

New Mexico State University *B*
Santa Fe Community College *C, A*
Southwestern Indian Polytechnic
Institute *A*

New York

Mohawk Valley Community
College *C, A*
Orange County Community College *C*
Paul Smith's College *A*
State University of New York
College of Environmental Science
and Forestry *A*
College of Technology at
Alfred *A, B*

North Carolina

Asheville Buncombe Technical
Community College *A*
Central Carolina Community College *A*
Central Piedmont Community
College *C, A*
Fayetteville Technical Community
College *A*
Guilford Technical Community
College *C, A*
Johnston Community College *A*
Sandhills Community College *A*
Tri-County Community College *A*
Wake Technical Community College *A*

Ohio

Cincinnati State Technical and
Community College *A*
Columbus State Community College *C*
Lakeland Community College *C*
Ohio State University
Columbus Campus *B*
Sinclair Community College *C*
Stark State College of Technology *A*

Oklahoma

Oklahoma State University
Oklahoma City *A*

Oregon

Chemeketa Community College *C*
Oregon Institute of Technology *B*

Pennsylvania

Penn State
University Park *B*
Wilkes-Barre *A, B*
Pennsylvania College of Technology *A*

Puerto Rico

Universidad Politecnica de Puerto
Rico *B*
University of Puerto Rico
Mayaguez Campus *B*

South Carolina

Piedmont Technical College *A*
Trident Technical College *C*

South Dakota

Southeast Technical Institute *A*

Tennessee
East Tennessee State University *B*

Texas
Austin Community College *C, A*
Lamar University *B*
Texas A&M University
Corpus Christi *B*
Tyler Junior College *C, A*

Utah
Salt Lake Community College *C, A*

Virginia
J. Sargeant Reynolds Community
College *C*
Virginia Western Community College *C*

Washington
Centralia College *A*
Grays Harbor College *C, A*
Renton Technical College *C, A*
Walla Walla Community College *C*

West Virginia
Glenville State College *A*

Wisconsin
Nicolet Area Technical College *A*

Wyoming
Sheridan College *A*
University of Wyoming *C*

Swedish

Washington
University of Washington *B*

System administration

Alabama
American College of Computer and
Information Sciences *B*

Arizona
Collins College *A, B*
Paradise Valley Community College *C*
South Mountain Community College *A*

California
Long Beach City College *C*
MTI College of Business and
Technology *C, A*
Ohlone College *A*

Colorado
Colorado Technical University *B*
Jones International University *C, B*
National American University
Denver *B*

Florida
Cooper Career Institute *C*
Florida State University *M*
Schiller International University *B*

Illinois
Parkland College *C, A*
Richland Community College *C*

Indiana
Ancilla College *A*

Iowa
American Institute of Business *C*
Dordt College *B*
Hamilton College
Cedar Falls *A*

Kansas
Bethel College *B*
Tabor College *B*

Kentucky
Louisville Technical Institute *A*
Maysville Community College *C, A*

Maryland
Frederick Community College *A*

Michigan
Cleary University *A*

Minnesota
Academy College *C, A*
Globe College *C, A, B*
University of Minnesota
Crookston *B*

Missouri
Crowder College *A*

New Hampshire
Daniel Webster College *C*

New York
Rochester Institute of Technology *B*
State University of New York
Buffalo *M, D*
College of Agriculture and
Technology at Morrisville *B*

North Carolina
Pitt Community College *C, A*

Ohio
Southeastern Business College *A*
Southeastern Business College:
Jackson *A*

Pennsylvania
Keystone College *C*
Peirce College *C, A, B*
South Hills School of Business &
Technology *A*

Texas
Hallmark Institute of Technology *A*
Temple College *C, A*

Vermont
Champlain College *A, B*

Virginia
ECPI College of Technology *C, A*
ECPI Technical College: Roanoke *A*

Washington
Walla Walla Community College *C, A*

Wisconsin
Viterbo University *B*

Systematic biology

Colorado
University of Colorado
Boulder *B, M, D*

Kansas
University of Kansas *M, D*

Maryland
University of Maryland
College Park *M*

Systems engineering

Arizona
University of Arizona *B, M, D*

Arkansas
University of Arkansas
Little Rock *B*

California
California State University
Northridge *M*
Northwestern Polytechnic
University *B, M*
San Jose State University *B, M*
University of California
San Diego *B, M, D*
University of Southern
California *B, M, D*

Colorado
Colorado State University
Pueblo *M, D*
National Technological University *M*

District of Columbia
Howard University *B, M*

Florida
Florida Atlantic University *M*
Florida International University *B*
University of Florida *B, M, D*
University of West Florida *M*

Idaho
University of Idaho *M*

Iowa
Iowa State University *M*

Louisiana
Louisiana Tech University *M*

Maine
Maine Maritime Academy *B*

Maryland
Johns Hopkins University *M, D*
United States Naval Academy *B*
University of Maryland
College Park *M*

Massachusetts
Harvard College *B*
Massachusetts Institute of Technology *M*
Worcester Polytechnic Institute *B, M*

Michigan
Oakland University *B, M, D*

Minnesota
University of St. Thomas *B, M*

Missouri
University of Missouri
Rolla *M*
Washington University in St.
Louis *B, M, D*

Nebraska
University of Nebraska
Lincoln *M*

New Jersey
Stevens Institute of Technology *M*

New York
Polytechnic University *M*
Rensselaer Polytechnic Institute *B, M, D*
Rochester Institute of Technology *B, M*
State University of New York
Binghamton *M, D*
Buffalo *M, D*
College of Environmental Science
and Forestry *M, D*
United States Merchant Marine
Academy *B*
United States Military Academy *B*

North Carolina
Guilford Technical Community
College *A*

Ohio
Case Western Reserve
University *B, M, D*
Jefferson Community College *A*
Ohio State University
Columbus Campus *B, M, D*

Oregon
Portland State University *M*

Pennsylvania
Lehigh University *M*
University of Pennsylvania *B, M, D*
University of Pittsburgh *M*

Puerto Rico
University of Puerto Rico
Mayaguez Campus *M*

Rhode Island
Providence College *B*

Texas
St. Mary's University *M*
Southern Methodist University *M*
Texas A&M University *M*
Texas Tech University *M*
University of Houston *M, D*

Virginia
George Mason University *B, M*
University of Virginia *B, M, D*
Virginia Polytechnic Institute and State
University *M*

Systems science/theory

California
University of Southern California *B, M*

Connecticut
Yale University *B, M, D*

Florida
University of Central Florida *M, D*
University of Miami *M*
University of West Florida *B*

Idaho
Idaho State University *M*

Indiana
Indiana University
Bloomington *B, D*

Massachusetts
Harvard College *B*

Missouri
Washington University in St.
Louis *B, M, D*

Oregon
Portland State University *D*

Pennsylvania
La Salle University *B*

Rhode Island
Providence College *B*

West Virginia
Marshall University *B*

Talmudic studies

Maryland
Baltimore Hebrew University *B, M, D*

New York
Talmudical Institute of Upstate New
York *B*

Taxation

Alabama
University of Alabama *M*

Arizona
Arizona State University *M*

California
California State University
Fullerton *M*
Hayward *M*
Northridge *M*
Sacramento *M*
De Anza College *C, A*
Golden Gate University *M*
National University *M*
San Diego State University *M*
San Jose State University *M*
Santa Rosa Junior College *C*
University of San Diego *M*
University of Southern California *M*
Yuba Community College District *A*

Colorado
Colorado Technical University *C*
University of Colorado
    Boulder *M*
University of Denver *M*

Connecticut
Manchester Community College *C*
University of Connecticut *C*
University of Hartford *M*

District of Columbia
American University *M*

Florida
Florida Atlantic University *M*
Florida International University *M*
Florida State University *M*
Nova Southeastern University *M*
University of Central Florida *M*
University of Miami *M*

Georgia
Georgia State University *M*
Mercer University *M*

Illinois
De Paul University *M*
Northern Illinois University *M*
St. Xavier University *M*

Louisiana
University of New Orleans *M*

Maine
Thomas College *M*

Maryland
University of Baltimore *M*

Massachusetts
American International College *M*
Bentley College *M*
Boston University *M*
Northeastern University *M*
Suffolk University *M*

Michigan
Grand Valley State University *M*
Walsh College of Accountancy and
    Business Administration *M*
Washtenaw Community College *C*
Wayne State University *M*

Minnesota
St. Cloud Technical College *C, A*
University of Minnesota
    Twin Cities *M*

Mississippi
Mississippi State University *M*
University of Mississippi *M*

Missouri
Fontbonne College *M*

New Jersey
Fairleigh Dickinson University
    College at Florham *M*
    Metropolitan Campus *M*
Rutgers, The State University of New
    Jersey
    New Brunswick Regional
        Campus *M*
    Newark Regional Campus *M*
Seton Hall University *M*

New York
City University of New York
    Baruch College *M*
Hofstra University *M*
Long Island University
    C. W. Post Campus *M*
Pace University *M*
Pace University:
    Pleasantville/Briarcliff *M*
St. John's University *M*
State University of New York
    Albany *B, M*

North Carolina
Cape Fear Community College *C*

Ohio
University of Akron *M*
University of Toledo *M*

Oklahoma
University of Tulsa *M*

Pennsylvania
Drexel University *M*
Duquesne University *M*
Penn State
    University Park *C*
Philadelphia University *M*
Robert Morris University *M*
Temple University *T*
Villanova University *M*
Widener University *M*

Puerto Rico
University of the Sacred Heart *M*

Rhode Island
Bryant College *M*

Texas
Baylor University *M*
Southern Methodist University *M*
Texas A&M University *M*
University of Houston *M*
University of North Texas *M*
University of Texas
    Arlington *M, D*
    San Antonio *M*

Virginia
ECPI College of Technology *C, A*
ECPI Technical College: Roanoke *A*
George Mason University *M*
Virginia Commonwealth University *M*

Taxidermy

New York
Finger Lakes Community College *C*

Teacher assistance

Arizona
Cochise College *C*
Estrella Mountain Community College *A*

California
Antelope Valley College *C, A*
Barstow College *C, A*
Cerritos Community College *A*
Chabot College *A*
College of Alameda *C, A*
Contra Costa College *A*
Diablo Valley College *C*
Long Beach City College *C, A*
Los Angeles Southwest College *A*
Mount St. Mary's College *A*
Ohlone College *C*
Shasta College *C, A*
Sierra College *C, A*

Colorado
Otero Junior College *A*

Connecticut
Manchester Community College *C, A*
Quinebaug Valley Community College *C*
Sacred Heart University *A*

Georgia
Atlanta Metropolitan College *A*
Macon State College *C*

Illinois
City Colleges of Chicago
    Harold Washington College *C, A*
    Malcolm X College *A*
Elgin Community College *C*

Illinois Eastern Community Colleges
    Frontier Community College *C*
    Lincoln Trail College *A*
John A. Logan College *C*
Joliet Junior College *C, A*
Kaskaskia College *C*
Lincoln Land Community College *C*
Moraine Valley Community College *C*
Prairie State College *C*
Sauk Valley Community College *C*
South Suburban College of Cook
    County *C, A*

Iowa
Dordt College *A*
Ellsworth Community College *C, A*

Kansas
Butler County Community College *A*
Seward County Community College *A*

Louisiana
Southern University
    Shreveport *A*

Massachusetts
Greenfield Community College *C*

Michigan
Baker College
    of Cadillac *A*
    of Clinton Township *C*
    of Muskegon *C*
    of Port Huron *C, A*
Bay de Noc Community College *C*
Kirtland Community College *C*

Minnesota
Concordia University: St. Paul *A*
St. Cloud Technical College *C, A*

Missouri
St. Louis Community College
    St. Louis Community College at
        Florissant Valley *A*
    St. Louis Community College at
        Forest Park *A*

New Hampshire
New Hampshire Technical Institute *C*

New Jersey
Brookdale Community College *A*
Middlesex County College *A*
Ocean County College *C*

New Mexico
Clovis Community College *A*
Eastern New Mexico University: Roswell
    Campus *A*
New Mexico Highlands University *A*
New Mexico State University *A*
New Mexico State University
    Alamogordo *A*
University of New Mexico *A*

New York
City University of New York
    Bronx Community College *A*
    Kingsborough Community
        College *A*
Fulton-Montgomery Community
    College *C*
Maria College *A*
St. John's University *A*

North Carolina
Carteret Community College *A*
College of the Albemarle *C*
Craven Community College *A*
Durham Technical Community
    College *A*
Edgecombe Community College *A*
Halifax Community College *C, A*
Isothermal Community College *A*
Lenoir Community College *A*
Martin Community College *C*
Mitchell Community College *A*
Nash Community College *A*
Roanoke-Chowan Community College *A*

Sandhills Community College *A*
Vance-Granville Community College *A*
Wilkes Community College *C, A*

Ohio
North Central State College *C, A*
University of Akron *A*

Oregon
Chemeketa Community College *A*
Clackamas Community College *C*
Portland Community College *C*

Pennsylvania
Bucks County Community College *A*
Cedar Crest College *C*
Community College of Allegheny
    County *C*
Community College of Beaver
    County *C, A*
Delaware County Community College *A*
Montgomery County Community
    College *A*
Reading Area Community College *C*

Puerto Rico
Pontifical Catholic University of Puerto
    Rico *A*
Universidad Metropolitana *C*
Universidad del Este *C*

South Carolina
Forrest Junior College *C, A*
Williamsburg Technical College *A*

South Dakota
Sinte Gleska University *A*
University of Sioux Falls *A*

Tennessee
Johnson Bible College *A*

Texas
McLennan Community College *C*
Midland College *A*
Odessa College *A*
Richland College *A*
St. Philip's College *C, A*

Washington
Clover Park Technical College *C, A*
Edmonds Community College *C*
Green River Community College *C*
Renton Technical College *C, A*
Spokane Falls Community College *A*
Walla Walla Community College *C, A*

Wisconsin
Alverno College *A*
Waukesha County Technical College *C*
Western Wisconsin Technical College *C*

Wyoming
Central Wyoming College *A*
Sheridan College *A*
Western Wyoming Community
    College *C*

Teacher education, multiple levels

Alabama
Alabama State University *M*
Huntingdon College *B, T*
Lawson State Community College *A*
Troy State University *B, M, T*
University of North Alabama *B, M*

Alaska
University of Alaska
    Anchorage *M*

Arizona
Central Arizona College *C, A*
Prescott College *B, M, T*

Arkansas
South Arkansas Community College *A*

California

Azusa Pacific University *B, T*
California State Polytechnic University:
    Pomona *T*
California State University
    Sacramento *T*
Concordia University *B, T*
Glendale Community College *A*
Hope International University *T*
Mills College *M*
National University *T*
Occidental College *M, T*
Pepperdine University *T*
University of California
    Berkeley *T*
    Los Angeles *M, D*
University of San Diego *M*
University of San Francisco *M*
University of the Pacific *B, T*
Whittier College *T*

Colorado

Colorado College *M*
University of Denver *M*

Connecticut

Central Connecticut State University *B*
Quinnipiac University *B, M*

District of Columbia

George Washington University *M*
Howard University *M*

Florida

Edward Waters College *T*
Flagler College *B*
Nova Southeastern University *M*
University of South Florida *M*
University of West Florida *B, M, D*

Georgia

Darton College *A*
East Georgia College *A*
Floyd College *A*
Gordon College *A*
Macon State College *A*
North Georgia College & State
    University *B, M*

Hawaii

Chaminade University of Honolulu *M*
University of Hawaii
    Manoa *M, D*

Idaho

Boise State University *T*

Illinois

Blackburn College *B, T*
Chicago State University *B*
Concordia University *B, M, T*
Dominican University *M*
Judson College *B*
Kankakee Community College *A*
Lewis and Clark Community College *A*
Lincoln College *A*
Monmouth College *B, T*
North Central College *B, T*
North Park University *B, M*
Northwestern University *T*
Quincy University *B, T*
Roosevelt University *B*
Sauk Valley Community College *A*
University of St. Francis *M, T*

Indiana

Ball State University *T*
Earlham College *M*
Indiana University
    Bloomington *B, T*
Manchester College *B, T*
Purdue University
    Calumet *B*
St. Mary-of-the-Woods College *B*
University of Indianapolis *T*
University of Notre Dame *M*
Vincennes University *A*

Iowa

Buena Vista University *B, T*
Ellsworth Community College *A*
Loras College *T*
Morningside College *B*
University of Iowa *B*

Kansas

Bethany College *T*
Central Christian College *A, B*
Friends University *T*
Pittsburg State University *B, M, D, T*
Tabor College *B, T*

Kentucky

Murray State University *B, M*

Louisiana

Xavier University of Louisiana *B, T*

Maine

University of Maine
    Farmington *A, T*
University of New England *T*
University of Southern Maine *T*

Maryland

Carroll Community College *A*
Frederick Community College *A*
Goucher College *M*
Harford Community College *A*
Morgan State University *B, T*

Massachusetts

Anna Maria College *B, T*
Lesley University *B, M, T*
Merrimack College *T*
Northeastern University *B*
Smith College *M*
University of Massachusetts
    Dartmouth *M*

Michigan

Adrian College *B*
Baker College
    of Auburn Hills *B*
    of Muskegon *B*
    of Owosso *B*
Central Michigan University *B, M*
Hillsdale College *B*
Hope College *T*
Madonna University *M*
University of Michigan *B*

Minnesota

Capella University *M, D*
Martin Luther College *B*
Minnesota State University
    Mankato *M*
    Moorhead *B, T*
Ridgewater College: A Community and
    Technical College *A*
St. Mary's University of Minnesota *M*
Winona State University *B, M, T*

Mississippi

Alcorn State University *M*
Mississippi Gulf Coast Community
    College
    Perkinston *A*
Pearl River Community College *A*

Missouri

Central Missouri State University *T*
Culver-Stockton College *T*
Harris Stowe State College *B, T*
Lindenwood University *B, M*
Missouri Baptist University *M, T*
Missouri Southern State College *B, T*
St. Louis University *T*
Washington University in St. Louis *T*
William Jewell College *T*
William Woods University *T*

Montana

Rocky Mountain College *B, T*
University of Montana: Western *B, T*

Nebraska

Concordia University *B, T*

Dana College *B*
Midland Lutheran College *B*
University of Nebraska
    Lincoln *T*
Wayne State College *M*
York College *B, T*

New Hampshire

Keene State College *T*
New Hampshire Community Technical
    College
    Berlin *A*
Plymouth State College *M*

New Jersey

College of St. Elizabeth *T*
Cumberland County College *A*
Fairleigh Dickinson University
    Metropolitan Campus *M*
Felician College *A*
Gloucester County College *A*
Richard Stockton College of New
    Jersey *B*
St. Peter's College *M*

New Mexico

New Mexico Institute of Mining and
    Technology *C*
New Mexico State University *M*
Western New Mexico University *M*

New York

City University of New York
    Medgar Evers College *A*
D'Youville College *B, M, T*
Dowling College *B, M*
Elmira College *B, M, T*
Genesee Community College *A*
Ithaca College *B, M, T*
Mount St. Mary College *B, M, T*
St. Bonaventure University *M*
Schenectady County Community
    College *A*
State University of New York
    Buffalo *M, D, T*
    College at Oneonta *B*
    College at Plattsburgh *B*
    New Paltz *M*
University of Rochester *M*
Wagner College *B, T*

North Carolina

Gardner-Webb University *B*
Halifax Community College *C, A*
North Carolina State University *B*
University of North Carolina
    Asheville *T*
    Charlotte *M*
    Greensboro *B, T*

North Dakota

Jamestown College *B*
North Dakota State University *B*
University of North Dakota *M*

Ohio

Defiance College *B*
John Carroll University *M, T*
Kent State University
    Stark Campus *B*
Marietta College *B*
Mount Union College *T*
Ohio Wesleyan University *B*
Otterbein College *B*
Shawnee State University *B*
University of Akron *B*
University of Dayton *B, M, D, T*
University of Findlay *B*
University of Rio Grande *B, T*
Ursuline College *M, T*
Washington State Community College *A*
Wilmington College *B*
Wright State University *M*
Youngstown State University *B, M*

Oklahoma

Oklahoma City Community College *A*
Oklahoma State University *B, M, D, T*

Oral Roberts University· *M*
Southeastern Oklahoma State
    University *B, M, T*
Southwestern Oklahoma State
    University *M*
University of Central Oklahoma *B*

Oregon

Concordia University *B, M, T*
George Fox University *M, T*
Lewis & Clark College *M*
Linfield College *T*
Warner Pacific College *B, T*
Western Baptist College *B*
Western Oregon University *B, T*

Pennsylvania

Baptist Bible College of Pennsylvania *B*
Cambria County Area Community
    College *A*
Chestnut Hill College *B*
Community College of Allegheny
    County *A*
Delaware County Community College *A*
Duquesne University *M*
Edinboro University of Pennsylvania *M*
Gettysburg College *T*
Keystone College *B*
La Salle University *B, T*
Mercyhurst College *B*
Moravian College *T*

Puerto Rico

Inter American University of Puerto Rico
    Metropolitan Campus *B*

Rhode Island

Rhode Island College *B*

South Carolina

Anderson College *B, T*
Columbia College *B*
Furman University *T*
University of South Carolina *M*
Winthrop University *T*

South Dakota

Dakota State University *B, T*
Northern State University *B, M, T*
University of Sioux Falls *B*

Tennessee

Freed-Hardeman University *B, T*
Southern Adventist University *M*
Tennessee Wesleyan College *B, T*
University of Memphis *B*
University of Tennessee
    Knoxville *M*
    Martin *M, T*

Texas

Abilene Christian University *B, M, T*
East Texas Baptist University *B*
Hardin-Simmons University *B, T*
Howard Payne University *B, T*
LeTourneau University *B*
Lubbock Christian University *B*
McMurry University *B*
St. Edward's University *T*
St. Mary's University *B, T*
Tarleton State University *M, T*
Texas A&M University
    Commerce *B*
Texas Lutheran University *B, T*
Texas Wesleyan University *B, T*
University of Mary Hardin-Baylor *M, T*
University of Texas
    of the Permian Basin *M*
West Texas A&M University *T*

Utah

University of Utah *B, M, D*
Utah State University *B*

Vermont

Bennington College *B, M, T*
College of St. Joseph in Vermont *B*
Goddard College *M*
Johnson State College *B, M*

Virginia
Averett University *B, T*
Longwood University *B, T*
Virginia Union University *B*

Washington
Evergreen State College *M*
Heritage College *B*
Northwest College *B*
St. Martin's College *M*
Seattle University *M*
University of Puget Sound *M*
University of Washington *M*
Washington State University *M, D*
Whitworth College *B, M, T*

West Virginia
Alderson-Broaddus College *B*
Marshall University *M*
Ohio Valley College *B*
Salem International University *B, T*

Wisconsin
Beloit College *T*
University of Wisconsin
 Green Bay *T*
 La Crosse *B, M, T*
 Superior *B, M, T*

Technical/business writing

Alabama
Auburn University *M*
University of Alabama
 Huntsville *C*

Alaska
University of Alaska
 Fairbanks *M*

Arkansas
University of Arkansas
 Little Rock *B, M*

California
California State University
 Chico *C*
 Long Beach *C*
De Anza College *C, A*
Orange Coast College *A*
San Diego State University *C*
San Francisco State University *C, B*
University of Southern California *M*
Woodbury University *B*

Colorado
Colorado State University *M*
University of Colorado
 Denver *M*

Connecticut
University of Hartford *B*

Florida
University of Central Florida *D*
University of West Florida *B*

Georgia
Columbus State University *B*
Kennesaw State University *B*
Southern Polytechnic State
 University *B, M*

Idaho
Boise State University *M, D*

Illinois
Black Hawk College *C, A*
Chicago State University *B*
College of Lake County *C, A*
Dominican University *B*
Illinois Institute of Technology *M*

Iowa
Iowa State University *B*
University of Iowa *M*

Kansas
Independence Community College *A*

Pittsburg State University *B*

Louisiana
Nicholls State University *B*

Maryland
Montgomery College
 Rockville Campus *C*
Towson University *M*

Massachusetts
Clark University *M*
Fitchburg State College *B*
Northeastern University *M*
University of Massachusetts
 Dartmouth *M*
Worcester Polytechnic Institute *B*

Michigan
Grand Valley State University *B*
Kellogg Community College *A*
Madonna University *B*
University of Michigan
 Flint *B*
Washtenaw Community College *A*

Minnesota
Metropolitan State University *B, M*
Minnesota State University
 Mankato *B, M*
Northwestern College *B*
St. Mary's University of Minnesota *B*
University of Minnesota
 Crookston *B*

Missouri
St. Louis Community College
 St. Louis Community College at
 Florissant Valley *A*
 St. Louis Community College at
 Meramec *C*
Southwest Missouri State
 University *B, M*
University of Missouri
 Rolla *B*

Montana
Miles Community College *A*
Montana Tech of the University of
 Montana *B, M*
University of Montana-Missoula *M*

New Jersey
Essex County College *A*
New Jersey Institute of Technology *B, M*

New Mexico
College of Santa Fe *B*
New Mexico Institute of Mining and
 Technology *B*

New York
Clarkson University *B*
Medaille College *B*
New York Institute of Technology *C, B*
Paul Smith's College *A*
Rensselaer Polytechnic Institute *M*
Rochester Institute of Technology *B*
State University of New York
 College of Agriculture and
 Technology at Morrisville *A*

North Carolina
North Carolina State University *M*

Ohio
Bowling Green State University *B*
Cedarville University *B*
Cincinnati State Technical and
 Community College *C, A*
Edison State Community College *C, A*
Miami University
 Oxford Campus *M*
Mount Union College *B*
Ohio Northern University *B*
University of Findlay *C, B*
Youngstown State University *B*

Oklahoma
East Central University *B*

Oklahoma State University *B*

Oregon
Linn-Benton Community College *A*
Portland Community College *C*
Portland State University *M*

Pennsylvania
California University of Pennsylvania *B*
Carlow College *B*
Carnegie Mellon University *B, M*
Drexel University *B, M*
Elizabethtown College *B*
Immaculata University *B*
La Salle University *B*
Penn State
 Abington *B*
 University Park *C*
Pennsylvania College of Technology *B*
University of the Sciences in
 Philadelphia *M*
York College of Pennsylvania *B*

South Carolina
Coker College *B*
Winthrop University *B*

Tennessee
Chattanooga State Technical Community
 College *A*
Maryville College *B*
Tennessee Technological University *B*

Texas
Austin Community College *C, A*
Southwest Texas State University *M, T*
Texas Tech University *M, D*
University of Houston
 Downtown *B*
University of Texas
 El Paso *M*

Utah
Weber State University *B*

Vermont
Champlain College *B*

Virginia
James Madison University *B, M*
Longwood University *B, T*
Thomas Nelson Community College *C*

Washington
Eastern Washington University *B, M*
Everett Community College *A*
University of Washington *B*

West Virginia
Alderson-Broaddus College *B*
West Virginia State College *B*

Wisconsin
Milwaukee School of Engineering *B*
Mount Mary College *B*
University of Wisconsin
 Stout *B*

Technology/industrial arts education

Alabama
Community College of the Air Force *A*

Alaska
University of Alaska
 Southeast *B*

Arizona
Arizona Western College *A*
Eastern Arizona College *A*
Northern Arizona University *B, M, T*
Prescott College *B, T*

Arkansas
Arkansas State University *A, B, T*
University of Arkansas
 Pine Bluff *T*
University of Central Arkansas *A, M*

California
California State University
 Chico *B*
 Stanislaus *M*
San Francisco State University *B, T*

Colorado
Colorado State University *M, T*

Connecticut
Central Connecticut State
 University *B, M, T*

Florida
Hillsborough Community College *A*
Miami-Dade Community College *A*
Nova Southeastern University *M, D*

Georgia
Georgia Southern University *B, M, T*
University of Georgia *B, M*

Hawaii
University of Hawaii
 Honolulu Community College *A*
 Manoa *B*

Idaho
University of Idaho *B, M, T*

Illinois
Chicago State University *B*
Illinois State University *B*
Northern Illinois University *B*
Sauk Valley Community College *A*

Indiana
Ball State University *B, M*
Indiana State University *M, T*
Vincennes University *A*

Iowa
Iowa State University *B, M, D, T*
University of Northern Iowa *B*
William Penn University *B*

Kansas
Central Christian College *A, B*
Fort Hays State University *B*
Fort Scott Community College *A*
Independence Community College *A*
McPherson College *B, T*
Pittsburg State University *B, M, T*

Kentucky
Berea College *B, T*
Morehead State University *B*
Murray State University *B, M, T*

Louisiana
Grambling State University *B*
Northwestern State University *B*

Maine
University of Southern Maine *B, T*

Maryland
Johns Hopkins University *M*

Massachusetts
Fitchburg State College *B, M, T*
Westfield State College *B, T*

Michigan
Andrews University *M*
Central Michigan University *B, M*
Eastern Michigan University *B, M, T*
Madonna University *T*
Michigan State University *M, D*
Northern Michigan University *B, T*
Wayne State University *M*
Western Michigan University *B*

Minnesota
Bemidji State University *M, T*
Minnesota State University
 Mankato *B, M, T*
 Moorhead *B, T*
St. Cloud State University *M*
University of Minnesota
 Twin Cities *B, M, D, T*

Mississippi
Alcorn State University *B*
Mississippi State University *T*
University of Southern Mississippi *B*

Missouri
Central Missouri State
University *B, M, T*
College of the Ozarks *B*
Lindenwood University *B*
Missouri Southern State College *B, T*
Southeast Missouri State
University *B, M, T*
Southwest Missouri State University *B*

Montana
Montana State University
Billings *T*
Bozeman *B*
University of Montana: Western *B, T*

Nebraska
Chadron State College *B, M*
Concordia University *B, T*
University of Nebraska
Kearney *B*
Lincoln *B, T*

Nevada
University of Nevada
Reno *B*

New Hampshire
Keene State College *T*

New Jersey
The College of New Jersey *B, T*
Kean University *B*
Montclair State University *B, M, T*

New Mexico
University of New Mexico *B*
Western New Mexico University *B*

New York
Fashion Institute of Technology *B*
Hofstra University *M, T*
New York Institute of Technology *B, T*
Pace University: *M, T*
Pace University:
Pleasantville/Briarcliff *M, T*
State University of New York
College at Buffalo *B, M, T*
Oswego *B, M, T*

North Carolina
Appalachian State University *B, T*
North Carolina Agricultural and
Technical State University *B, M, T*
North Carolina State University *M, D*

North Dakota
University of North Dakota *B, T*
Valley City State University *B, T*

Ohio
Bowling Green State University *B, M*
Kent State University *B, T*
Kent State University
Stark Campus *B*
Ohio Northern University *B, T*
Ohio State University
Columbus Campus *B*
Ohio University *B, M, T*
University of Toledo *M*
Youngstown State University *M*

Oklahoma
East Central University *B*
Langston University *B*
Northeastern State University *B*
Northwestern Oklahoma State
University *B, T*
Oklahoma Panhandle State University *B*
Rogers State University *A*
Southwestern Oklahoma State
University *B, M, T*
University of Central Oklahoma *B*

Oregon
Chemeketa Community College *A*
Oregon State University *B, M*

Pennsylvania
California University of
Pennsylvania *B, M, T*
Millersville University of
Pennsylvania *B, M, T*
Pennsylvania College of Technology *T*
Pittsburgh Institute of Aeronautics *A*
Waynesburg College *B*

Rhode Island
Rhode Island College *B, M*

South Carolina
Clemson University *B, M*
Coastal Carolina University *M*
South Carolina State University *B, T*

South Dakota
Black Hills State University *B*

Tennessee
Middle Tennessee State University *B*
University of Tennessee
Knoxville *M, D, T*

Texas
El Paso Community College *A*
Prairie View A&M University *M*
Sam Houston State University *M, T*
Southwest Texas State University *M, T*
Sul Ross State University *M*
Texas A&M University
Commerce *M, T*
Kingsville *M*
Texas Southern University *M*
University of Texas
Tyler *M*
West Texas A&M University *M*

Utah
Brigham Young University *M*
Southern Utah University *B, T*
Utah State University *B, D*

Virginia
Old Dominion University *B, M*

Washington
Central Washington University *B, T*
Eastern Washington University *B, M, T*
South Seattle Community College *C*
Western Washington University *B, T*

West Virginia
Fairmont State College *B*

Wisconsin
University of Wisconsin
Platteville *B, T*
Stout *B, M, T*
Viterbo University *B, T*

Wyoming
University of Wyoming *B*

Telecommunications technology

Florida
Palm Beach Community College *C*
St. Petersburg College *A*

Georgia
Southern Polytechnic State University *B*

Illinois
Waubonsee Community College *C*

Indiana
Indiana University-Purdue University
Fort Wayne *C*

Kentucky
Murray State University *B, M*

Louisiana
University of Louisiana at Lafayette *M*

Maryland
Community College of Baltimore County
Catonsville *C*
Essex *C*
Howard Community College *C, A*

Massachusetts
Quinsigamond Community College *C, A*
Wentworth Institute of Technology *A*

New York
Cayuga County Community College *A*
Rochester Institute of Technology *B, M*
Schenectady County Community
College *A*

North Carolina
Fayetteville Technical Community
College *A*

Pennsylvania
Penn State
Abington *B*
Altoona *A*
Beaver *A, B*
Berks *A*
Dubois *A*
Fayette *A*
Hazleton *A*
McKeesport *B*
Mont Alto *B*
New Kensington *A, B*
Schuylkill - Capital College *A, B*
Shenango *A, B*
University Park *B, M*
Wilkes-Barre *A, B*
Worthington Scranton *B*
York *A, B*

Puerto Rico
Inter American University of Puerto Rico
Bayamon Campus *A*

South Carolina
York Technical College *C*

Texas
Texas A&M University *B*
Texas Tech University *B*
University of Texas
Dallas *B, M, D*

Utah
ITT Technical Institute
Murray *B*
Utah Valley State College *A*

Virginia
ECPI College of Technology *C, A*
ECPI Technical College: Roanoke *A*

Washington
Clark College *C, A*

Textile science

Alabama
Auburn University *M*

Georgia
Georgia Institute of Technology *B, M*

Massachusetts
University of Massachusetts
Dartmouth *B, M*

Pennsylvania
Philadelphia University *C, B, M*

Textile sciences/ engineering

Alabama
Auburn University *B*

Georgia
Georgia Institute of Technology *B, M, D*

Massachusetts
University of Massachusetts
Dartmouth *B, M*

New York
Cornell University *B, M, D*

North Carolina
North Carolina State University *B, M*

Pennsylvania
Philadelphia University *B, M*

South Carolina
Clemson University *B, M, D*

Texas
Southwest Texas State University *B*
Texas Tech University *B*

Theater arts management

California
Ohlone College *C*

Georgia
Brenau University *B*

Kansas
Benedictine College *B*

Maine
University of Southern Maine *B*

Missouri
Crowder College *A*
Lindenwood University *B, M*

New Jersey
Seton Hall University *B*

New York
Ithaca College *B*
Niagara County Community College *A*

Ohio
Baldwin-Wallace College *B*

Pennsylvania
Marywood University *B*
Seton Hill University *B*
Waynesburg College *B*

Theater design/technology

Alaska
University of Alaska
Fairbanks *B*

Arizona
University of Arizona *B*

California
California Institute of the Arts *M*
California State Polytechnic University:
Pomona *B*
California State University
Fresno *B*
Hayward *B*
Long Beach *B, M*
College of the Sequoias *A*
Foothill College *C, A*
Gavilan Community College *A*
Glendale Community College *A*
Grossmont Community College *C, A*
Humboldt State University *M*
Irvine Valley College *A*
Long Beach City College *A*
MiraCosta College *C, A*
Ohlone College *C, A*
Palomar College *C*
Pepperdine University *B*
San Diego State University *B, M*
San Francisco State University *M*
Santa Barbara City College *A*
Santa Rosa Junior College *C*

University of California
    Santa Cruz *C, B*
University of Southern California *M*

Colorado
Red Rocks Community College *C, A*

Connecticut
University of Connecticut *B*

Delaware
University of Delaware *B*

District of Columbia
Howard University *B*

Florida
Florida Southern College *B*
Florida State University *B, M*
Lake-Sumter Community College *A*
University of West Florida *B*

Illinois
Columbia College Chicago *B*
De Paul University *B, M*
Lincoln College *A*
Millikin University *B*
Northwestern University *M*
Rockford College *B*

Indiana
Huntington College *B*
Indiana University
    Bloomington *A*
University of Evansville *B*
Vincennes University *A*

Iowa
Drake University *B*
University of Iowa *M*
University of Northern Iowa *B*

Kansas
Central Christian College *A, B*
University of Kansas *B, M*

Louisiana
Centenary College of Louisiana *B*

Maryland
Howard Community College *A*
Montgomery College
    Rockville Campus *A*

Massachusetts
Boston University *B, M*
Brandeis University *M*
Emerson College *B*
Fitchburg State College *B*
Hampshire College *B*
Salem State College *B*

Michigan
Eastern Michigan University *B*
Oakland University *B*
University of Michigan *B*
Western Michigan University *B*

Minnesota
Central Lakes College *A*
Minnesota State University
    Mankato *B, T*
    Moorhead *B*
University of Minnesota
    Duluth *B*

Missouri
University of Missouri
    Kansas City *M*

Montana
Rocky Mountain College *B*

New Hampshire
Franklin Pierce College *B*

New Jersey
Essex County College *A*
Rowan University *B*

New Mexico
College of Santa Fe *B*

New York
Fordham University *B*
Ithaca College *B*
New York University *B, M*
Pace University *B*
Pace University:
    Pleasantville/Briarcliff *B, M*
Sarah Lawrence College *B, M*
State University of New York
    College at Fredonia *B*
    New Paltz *B*
    Purchase *B, M*
Suffolk County Community College *A*
Syracuse University *B, M*
Wagner College *B*

North Carolina
Greensboro College *B*
North Carolina School of the Arts *B, M*

North Dakota
Dickinson State University *B*

Ohio
Clark State Community College *A*
Kent State University
    Stark Campus *B*
Ohio University *B, M*
Otterbein College *B*
Sinclair Community College *A*
University of Akron *M*
University of Cincinnati *B, M*
University of Findlay *B*
University of Rio Grande *A*
Wright State University *B*
Youngstown State University *B*

Oklahoma
Oklahoma City Community College *A*
Oral Roberts University *B*
Southeastern Oklahoma State
    University *B*
University of Oklahoma *M*

Oregon
Chemeketa Community College *A*

Pennsylvania
California University of Pennsylvania *B*
DeSales University *B*
Dickinson College *B*
Penn State
    York *B*
Seton Hill University *B*

Rhode Island
Community College of Rhode Island *A*
Rhode Island College *B*

South Carolina
Coker College *B*

Texas
Baylor University *B*
Lon Morris College *A*
Southern Methodist University *M*
Texas Tech University *B, M*
Trinity University *B*

Utah
Brigham Young University *M*

Vermont
Bennington College *B, M*
Johnson State College *A, B*
Marlboro College *B*

Virginia
Virginia Commonwealth University *B*

Washington
Cornish College of the Arts *B*
North Seattle Community College *C*

Wisconsin
University of Wisconsin
    Madison *B, M*

Wyoming
Casper College *A*

Theater history/criticism

California
Chapman University *B*
College of the Siskiyous *C, A*
Mills College *B*
San Francisco State University *M*
San Jose State University *M*
Scripps College *B*
Whittier College *B*

Connecticut
Naugatuck Valley Community College *A*
University of Connecticut *B*

Delaware
University of Delaware *B*

District of Columbia
George Washington University *B*
Howard University *B*

Florida
Hillsborough Community College *A*
Manatee Community College *A*

Georgia
Oxford College of Emory University *B*

Illinois
De Paul University *C, B*
Northwestern University *B*

Iowa
University of Northern Iowa *B*

Kansas
Seward County Community College *A*

Louisiana
Tulane University *M*

Massachusetts
Boston University *B*
Brandeis University *B*
Emerson College *M*
Hampshire College *B*
Harvard College *B*
Tufts University *B, M, D*

Minnesota
Minnesota State University
    Moorhead *B*

Missouri
Washington University in St. Louis *B, M*

New Jersey
Rowan University *B*

New York
Bard College *B*
Columbia University
    Columbia College *B*
Cornell University *M, D*
Eugene Lang College/New School
    University *B*
Marymount College of Fordham
    University *B*
New York University *B*
Sarah Lawrence College *B, M*
State University of New York
    Purchase *B*

North Carolina
Appalachian State University *B*
Gardner-Webb University *B*

Ohio
Kent State University
    Stark Campus *B*
Ohio University *M*

Pennsylvania
DeSales University *B*

Texas
Lon Morris College *A*
University of Dallas *B, T*

Utah
Snow College *A*

Vermont
Bennington College *B*
Burlington College *B*
Marlboro College *B*

Virginia
Averett University *B*
Mary Baldwin College *B*
Virginia Wesleyan College *B*

Washington
Whitworth College *B, T*

Wisconsin
University of Wisconsin
    Madison *M, D*
    Whitewater *B, T*

Theological studies

Alabama
Faulkner University *B*
Judson College *B*
Oakwood College *B*
Samford University *M*
Southeastern Bible College *A, B*
Southern Christian University *M, D*
Spring Hill College *C, B, M*
University of Mobile *B, M*

Alaska
Alaska Bible College *B*

Arizona
American Indian College of the
    Assemblies of God *B*
Southwestern College *C, A, B*

Arkansas
Harding University *B, M*
John Brown University *B*
Ouachita Baptist University *B*

California
Azusa Pacific University *D*
Bethany College *A, B*
Bethesda Christian University *B*
Biola University *B, M, D*
California Baptist University *B*
Concordia University *M*
Dominican School of Philosophy and
    Theology *M*
Fresno Pacific University *B*
Hope International University *C, A, B, M*
LIFE Pacific College *A, B*
Loyola Marymount University *B, M*
Master's College *B*
Pacific Union College *B*
Pepperdine University *M*
Point Loma Nazarene University *B*
Simpson College *B, M*
Vanguard University of Southern
    California *B, M*

Colorado
Colorado Christian University *B*
Naropa University *M*

Connecticut
Yale University *M*

District of Columbia
Catholic University of America *M, D*

Florida
Baptist College of Florida *A, B*
Barry University *C, B, M*
Florida Christian College *B*
Hobe Sound Bible College *B*
Okaloosa-Walton Community College *A*
Palm Beach Atlantic University *B*
St. Leo University *M*
Southeastern College of the Assemblies
    of God *B*
Warner Southern College *B*

Georgia
Brewton-Parker College *B*
Emmanuel College *B*
LaGrange College *B*
Mercer University *M*
Shorter College *B*
Toccoa Falls College *B*

Idaho
Boise Bible College *A, B*
Northwest Nazarene University *B, M*

Illinois
Dominican University *C, B*
Greenville College *B, M*
Lincoln Christian College and
   Seminary *B, M*
Loyola University of Chicago *M*
Moody Bible Institute *B, M*
North Park University *M, D*
Olivet Nazarene University *B, M*
Quincy University *B*
St. Xavier University *B*
Trinity Christian College *B*
Trinity International University *B*
University of St. Francis *B*

Indiana
Anderson University *B, D*
Bethel College *B, M*
Goshen College *B*
Grace College *B*
Huntington College *M*
Indiana Wesleyan University *B*
Manchester College *A*
Marian College *A, B*
Oakland City University *M, D*
St. Mary-of-the-Woods
   College *C, A, B, M*
Taylor University: Fort Wayne *B*
University of Notre Dame *B, M, D*
University of St. Francis *B*

Iowa
Dordt College *B*
Emmaus Bible College *B*
Faith Baptist Bible College and
   Theological Seminary *B, M*
Loras College *B, M*
St. Ambrose University *M*
University of Dubuque *M, D*
Vennard College *C, A, B*

Kansas
Barclay College *B*
Central Christian College *A, B*
Hesston College *A*
St. Mary College *B*
Southwestern College *B*
Tabor College *B*

Kentucky
Brescia University *C, A, B*
Campbellsville University *M*
Kentucky Christian College *A, B, M*
Kentucky Mountain Bible College *B*
Kentucky Wesleyan College *B*

Louisiana
Loyola University New Orleans *M*

Maryland
Columbia Union College *B*
Mount St. Mary's College *M*
Washington Bible College *B, M*

Massachusetts
Atlantic Union College *B*
Hellenic College/Holy Cross *M*
Merrimack College *A*
St. John's Seminary College *M*

Michigan
Andrews University *B, M, D*
Cornerstone University *M*
Grace Bible College *B*
Madonna University *B*
Reformed Bible College *A, B*
Sacred Heart Major Seminary *C, A, M*

Spring Arbor University *B*

Minnesota
Bethel College *B*
College of St. Benedict *B*
College of St. Catherine *B, M*
College of St. Scholastica *B*
Concordia College: Moorhead *B*
Crossroads College *B*
Crown College *B, M*
Martin Luther College *B*
North Central University *B*
Northwestern College *B*
St. John's University *B*
St. Mary's University of
   Minnesota *C, B, M*
University of St. Thomas *M, D*

Mississippi
Blue Mountain College *B*
Magnolia Bible College *B*
Wesley College *B*

Missouri
Baptist Bible College *B*
Calvary Bible College *A, B, M*
Central Bible College *B*
Central Christian College of the Bible *B*
Global University *C, A, B, M*
Missouri Baptist University *C, B*
Ozark Christian College *C, B*
Rockhurst University *B*
St. Louis Christian College *A, B*
St. Louis University *B, M*
Southwest Baptist University *C, B*

Nebraska
Concordia University *B*
Creighton University *C, A, B, M*
Grace University *B*
Nebraska Christian College *A, B*
Union College *B*
York College *A, B*

New Hampshire
St. Anselm College *B*

New Jersey
Caldwell College *B*
Drew University *M, D*
Seton Hall University *M*

New York
Houghton College *B*
Machzikei Hadath Rabbinical College *B*
Nyack College *B, M*
Roberts Wesleyan College *B*
St. John's University *C, B, M*

North Carolina
Campbell University *M*
Duke University *M*
John Wesley College *C, A, B*
Roanoke Bible College *B*
Southeastern Baptist Theological
   Seminary *A*
Southeastern Baptist Theological
   Seminary: Theological Professions *D*
Wingate University *B*

North Dakota
Trinity Bible College *B*
University of Mary *B*

Ohio
Ashland University *M, D*
Cedarville University *B*
Cincinnati Bible College and
   Seminary *M*
Circleville Bible College *A, B*
God's Bible School and College *B*
Malone College *B, M*
Mount Vernon Nazarene University *M*
Muskingum College *B*
Notre Dame College *A, B*
Pontifical College Josephinum *M*
University of Dayton *M*
University of Findlay *B*
Ursuline College *M*

Walsh University *B*

Oklahoma
Oklahoma Baptist University *A, B*
Oklahoma Christian University of
   Science and Arts *B*
Oklahoma Wesleyan University *B*
Oral Roberts University *B, M, D*
Southern Nazarene University *B*
Southwestern Christian University *B, M*

Oregon
Concordia University *B*
Eugene Bible College *B*
George Fox University *M*
Multnomah Bible College *B, M*
Northwest Christian College *B*
University of Portland *M*
Western Baptist College *B*

Pennsylvania
Baptist Bible College of
   Pennsylvania *B, M, D*
Carlow College *B*
DeSales University *B*
Duquesne University *B, M, D*
Elizabethtown College *B*
King's College *B*
Lancaster Bible College *B, M*
Philadelphia Biblical University *B*
St. Vincent College *B*
Talmudical Yeshiva of Philadelphia *B*
Valley Forge Christian College *B*
Waynesburg College *B*

Puerto Rico
Bayamon Central University *M*
Pontifical Catholic University of Puerto
   Rico *M*

South Carolina
Anderson College *B*
Charleston Southern University *B*
Columbia International University *B, D*
Erskine College *D*
Morris College *B*
Southern Wesleyan University *M*

South Dakota
University of Sioux Falls *B*

Tennessee
American Baptist College of ABT
   Seminary *A, B*
Carson-Newman College *A*
Crichton College *C, B*
Freed-Hardeman University *B, M*
Southern Adventist University *B, M*
Trevecca Nazarene University *B*
Union University *B*
Vanderbilt University *D*

Texas
Abilene Christian University *M*
Arlington Baptist College *B*
Austin Graduate School of
   Theology *B, M*
Baylor University *M, D*
Brazosport College *A*
Dallas Christian College *B*
East Texas Baptist University *C, B*
Hardin-Simmons University *B, M*
Howard Payne University *C, B*
Southern Methodist University *M, D*
Southwestern Adventist University *B*
Southwestern Assemblies of God
   University *B, M*
Southwestern Baptist Theological
   Seminary: Theological
   Professions *M, D*
Texas Christian University *M, D*
University of Dallas *M*
University of St. Thomas *B, M*

Virginia
Eastern Mennonite University *B, M*
Hampton University *B*
Liberty University *M, D*

Washington
Northwest College *B*
Seattle University *M*
Trinity Lutheran College *C, A, B*
Walla Walla College *B*

West Virginia
Alderson-Broaddus College *B*
West Virginia Wesleyan College *B*

Wisconsin
St. Norbert College *M*
Silver Lake College *B*
Viterbo University *B*

Theology/religious vocations

Alabama
Samford University *D*
Southern Christian University *B, M, D*

Arkansas
Arkansas Baptist College *B*
Crowley's Ridge College *A*
John Brown University *B*
Ouachita Baptist University *B*
Williams Baptist College *B*

California
Azusa Pacific University *B*
Bethany College *B*
Bethesda Christian University *B*
California Baptist University *B*
Christian Heritage College *B*
Concordia University *B*
LIFE Pacific College *B*
Loyola Marymount University *B, M*
Master's College *B, M, D*
Mount St. Mary's College *M*
Pacific Union College *B*
Patten University *B*
Queen of the Holy Rosary College *A*
San Jose Christian College *B*
Simpson College *B, M*
Vanguard University of Southern
   California *B, M*

Colorado
Colorado Christian University *B*
University of Denver *M, D*

Connecticut
Holy Apostles College and
   Seminary *B, M*

District of Columbia
Catholic University of America *M*
Trinity College *B*

Florida
Baptist College of Florida *A, B*
St. John Vianney College Seminary *B*
St. Thomas University *M*

Georgia
Young Harris College *A*

Illinois
Concordia University *B, M*
Dominican University *B*
Lincoln Christian College and
   Seminary *C, A, B, M*
MacMurray College *B*
North Park University *M*
Quincy University *B*
Telshe Yeshiva-Chicago *D*
Trinity Christian College *B*
Trinity International University *M, D*
University of Chicago *M, D*
Wheaton College *M*

Indiana
Anderson University *B*
Earlham College *M*
Hanover College *B*
Indiana Wesleyan University *M*
Taylor University: Fort Wayne *B*

University of St. Francis C, B
Valparaiso University B, M

Iowa
Dordt College B
Faith Baptist Bible College and Theological Seminary M
St. Ambrose University B, M
Vennard College C

Kansas
Barclay College B
Central Christian College A, B
Newman University B
St. Mary College B
Seward County Community College A

Kentucky
Bellarmine University B

Louisiana
Xavier University of Louisiana B, M

Maryland
Columbia Union College B
Loyola College in Maryland B
Morgan State University B
Mount St. Mary's College B, M
Washington Bible College C, A, B, M

Massachusetts
Assumption College B
Boston College B, M, D
Boston University M, D
Elms College B, M
Hellenic College/Holy Cross B, M
St. John's Seminary College M

Michigan
Calvin College B
Cornerstone University M
Grace Bible College A, B
Marygrove College B
Reformed Bible College B

Minnesota
Bethel College B
College of St. Benedict B
Concordia University: St. Paul B
Crossroads College B
Crown College B
Martin Luther College B
North Central University B
St. John's University B, M
University of St. Thomas M

Mississippi
Magnolia Bible College B

Missouri
Baptist Bible College M
Calvary Bible College M
Central Bible College A, B
Global University C, A, B
Ozark Christian College B
St. Louis Christian College B
Southwest Baptist University B

Montana
Carroll College B
University of Great Falls B

Nebraska
Concordia University B
Midland Lutheran College B

New Hampshire
St. Anselm College B

New Jersey
Assumption College for Sisters C, A
Caldwell College B
College of St. Elizabeth B, M
Felician College B
Georgian Court College M

New York
Bard College B
Concordia College B
Fordham University B, M, D
Holy Trinity Orthodox Seminary B

Houghton College B
Mesivta Tifereth Jerusalem of America B, M, D
Molloy College B
Nyack College A, B
Ohr Somayach Institutions: School of Theology D
Rabbi Isaac Elchanan Theological Seminary D
Rabbinical College Bobover Yeshiva B'nei Zion D
St. Bonaventure University B, M
St. John's University C, B, M
Sh'or Yoshuv Rabbinical College D
Union Theological Seminary: Theological Professions D
Yeshiva Karlin Stolin Beth Aron Y'Israel Rabbinical Institute D
Yeshivat Mikdash Melech D

North Carolina
Belmont Abbey College B
Lenoir-Rhyne College B
Livingstone College M
Mount Olive College B
Piedmont Baptist College C, B, M
Shaw University M
Southeastern Baptist Theological Seminary A, M, D
Southeastern Baptist Theological Seminary: Theological Professions D

Ohio
Cedarville University B
Cincinnati Bible College and Seminary M
Circleville Bible College B
Defiance College B
Franciscan University of Steubenville A, B, M
Notre Dame College A, B
Ohio Dominican College C, A, B, M
Ohio Wesleyan University B
University of Dayton M, D
University of Findlay B
Xavier University A, B, M

Oklahoma
Oklahoma Baptist University B
Oklahoma Christian University of Science and Arts M
St. Gregory's University B

Oregon
Concordia University B
Marylhurst University M
Multnomah Bible College M
University of Portland B
Western Baptist College A, B

Pennsylvania
Baptist Bible College of Pennsylvania B
DeSales University B
Duquesne University M
Elizabethtown College B
Immaculata University C
Moravian College B, M
St. Charles Borromeo Seminary - Overbrook M
St. Vincent College B
Talmudical Yeshiva of Philadelphia B
Villanova University B, M

Puerto Rico
Inter American University of Puerto Rico Metropolitan Campus D
Pontifical Catholic University of Puerto Rico B, M

South Carolina
Charleston Southern University B
Columbia International University M
Erskine College M
North Greenville College B

South Dakota
University of Sioux Falls A

Tennessee
American Baptist College of ABT Seminary B
Tennessee Wesleyan College B
Trevecca Nazarene University M
Union University B

Texas
Austin Graduate School of Theology M
Houston Baptist University M
St. Mary's University M
Southwestern Assemblies of God University B, M
Southwestern Baptist Theological Seminary: Theological Professions M
Texas Lutheran University B

Vermont
St. Michael's College M

Virginia
Christendom College B, M
Roanoke College B

Washington
Northwest College B
Seattle Pacific University B
Seattle University M

West Virginia
Alderson-Broaddus College B
Appalachian Bible College B
Ohio Valley College B

Wisconsin
Concordia University Wisconsin B
Lakeland College M
Marquette University B, M
Wisconsin Lutheran College B

Theoretical/mathematical physics

Alabama
Southern Union State Community College A

Arkansas
University of Arkansas M

California
San Diego State University B

Georgia
Oxford College of Emory University B

Illinois
Northwestern University B, M, D

Indiana
Indiana University Bloomington D

Massachusetts
Hampshire College B
Harvard College B

Minnesota
Winona State University B

Texas
Southwestern Adventist University B

Vermont
Marlboro College B

Wisconsin
Lawrence University B
University of Wisconsin Madison M, D

Tool and die technology

Alabama
Calhoun Community College C, A
Shelton State Community College C, A

Georgia
Albany Technical College C

Illinois
Black Hawk College C
College of DuPage C
College of Lake County A
John A. Logan College C, A
Southern Illinois University Carbondale A

Indiana
Ivy Tech State College
    Bloomington C, A
    Central Indiana C, A
    Columbus C, A
    Eastcentral C, A
    Kokomo C, A
    Lafayette C, A
    Northcentral C, A
    Northeast C, A
    Northwest C, A
    Southcentral C, A
    Southwest C, A
    Wabash Valley C, A
    Whitewater C, A

Iowa
North Iowa Area Community College A
Western Iowa Tech Community College A

Michigan
Ferris State University A
Jackson Community College C, A
Montcalm Community College C
Oakland Community College C, A

Minnesota
Hennepin Technical College A
Minnesota State College - Southeast Technical C
St. Paul College - A Community and Technical College C

Mississippi
Itawamba Community College A

North Carolina
Davidson County Community College A
Wilson Technical Community College C

Ohio
Muskingum Area Technical College A
North Central State College C, A
Northwest State Community College C, A
Owens Community College
    Findlay Campus C
    Toledo C
Sinclair Community College C, A

Pennsylvania
Lehigh Carbon Community College C
Pennsylvania College of Technology C, A

South Carolina
York Technical College A

Wisconsin
Western Wisconsin Technical College C, A

Tourism promotion

Arizona
Phoenix College C, A

California
Coastline Community College C
Foothill College C, A
Grossmont Community College C, A
Long Beach City College C, A
Los Medanos College C, A
Palomar College C, A
San Diego City College C, A
San Francisco State University B
Southwestern College C, A
Travel University International C, A

Colorado

Arapahoe Community College *A*
Community College of Aurora *C*
Metropolitan State College of Denver *B*
Red Rocks Community College *C, A*

Connecticut

International College of Hospitality
Management *B*
University of New Haven *A, B*

District of Columbia

George Washington University *B, M*

Florida

Florida National College *A*
Miami-Dade Community College *C, A*
St. Thomas University *B*
Schiller International University *A, B*
Webber International University *A, B*

Hawaii

Hawaii Business College *C, A*

Idaho

College of Southern Idaho *A*

Illinois

College of DuPage *C, A*
Danville Area Community College *A*
Elgin Community College *C*
Lincoln College *A*
Midstate College *C, A*
Moraine Valley Community
College *C, A*
Parkland College *C*

Indiana

International Business College *C, A*

Iowa

Des Moines Area Community College *C*
Iowa Lakes Community College *A*
Kaplan College *C, A*
Northeast Iowa Community College *C*

Kansas

Cloud County Community College *C, A*

Kentucky

Sullivan University *C, A*

Maine

Andover College *C, A*
Beal College *A*
University of Maine
Machias *A, B*

Maryland

Allegany College *C*
Chesapeake College *A*
Villa Julie College *A*

Massachusetts

Bay Path College *A, B*
Bay State College *A*
Becker College *B*
Berkshire Community College *C, A*
Fisher College *C, A*
Lasell College *B*
Massasoit Community College *C*
Mount Ida College *A, B*
Newbury College *A*

Michigan

Eastern Michigan University *B*
Grand Valley State University *B*
Lansing Community College *A*

Minnesota

Central Lakes College *C*
Dakota County Technical College *C*
Rasmussen College
Mankato *C, A*

Missouri

Central Missouri State University *B*
East Central College *C, A*
Mineral Area College *A*
Patricia Stevens College *C*

Montana

University of Montana: Western *A*

Nebraska

Lincoln School of Commerce *C, A*
Midland Lutheran College *A*

New Hampshire

New Hampshire Technical Institute *C, A*
University of New Hampshire *B*

New Jersey

Bergen Community College *C, A*
Raritan Valley Community College *C*

New York

Adirondack Community College *A*
Broome Community College *A*
Bryant & Stratton Business Institute
Syracuse *C, A*
City University of New York
Kingsborough Community
College *A*
La Guardia Community College *A*
Corning Community College *A*
Dowling College *B*
Dutchess Community College *A*
Finger Lakes Community College *A*
Genesee Community College *C, A*
Jefferson Community College *C, A*
Marymount Manhattan College *C*
Mildred Elley *C*
Monroe Community College *A*
Paul Smith's College *B*
Rochester Institute of Technology *B, M*
Schenectady County Community
College *C, A*
State University of New York
College of Agriculture and
Technology at Cobleskill *A*
College of Agriculture and
Technology at Morrisville *A*
College of Technology at Delhi *A*
Tompkins-Cortland Community
College *A*
Westchester Community College *C, A*

North Carolina

Blue Ridge Community College *A*
Central Piedmont Community College *A*

Ohio

Columbus State Community College *A*
Davis College *A*
Kent State University
Trumbull Campus *A*
Lakeland Community College *C, A*
Lorain County Community College *A*
Muskingum Area Technical College *A*
RETS Tech Center *C*
Sinclair Community College *A*
Youngstown State University *A, B*

Oklahoma

Oklahoma City Community College *A*

Pennsylvania

Allentown Business School *A*
Butler County Community College *C*
California University of Pennsylvania *B*
Central Pennsylvania College *A*
Community College of Allegheny
County *A*
Consolidated School of Business
Lancaster *C, A*
York *C, A*
Harrisburg Area Community
College *C, A*
Lehigh Carbon Community College *C, A*
Luzerne County Community
College *C, A*
Pittsburgh Technical Institute: Boyd
School Division *A*
Reading Area Community College *A*
Robert Morris University *B*
Westmoreland County Community
College *A*

Puerto Rico

Universidad del Este *C*
University of the Sacred Heart *B*

Texas

Amarillo College *A*
Austin Community College *C, A*
Central Texas College *C, A*
El Paso Community College *C, A*
Texas A&M University *B*

Utah

Salt Lake Community College *C*

Vermont

Champlain College *A, B*

Washington

Edmonds Community College *C, A*

West Virginia

Bluefield State College *A*
Concord College *B*
Mountain State College *A*
Mountain State University *C, A*
West Liberty State College *B*

Wisconsin

Fox Valley Technical College *A*
Lac Courte Oreilles Ojibwa Community
College *C*
Mid-State Technical College *C*
University of Wisconsin
Madison *B, M*

Tourism/travel management

Arizona

Arizona Western College *C, A*
Phoenix College *C, A*
Pima Community College *C, A*

Arkansas

Arkansas State University *B*

California

Chabot College *A*
Coastline Community College *C*
College of the Redwoods *C*
Grossmont Community College *C, A*
Long Beach City College *C, A*
MiraCosta College *C, A*
Mount St. Mary's College *A*
San Diego Mesa College *C, A*
San Diego State University *B*
San Joaquin Delta College *C*
Santiago Canyon College *A*
Southwestern College *C, A*
Travel University International *C, A*
Vista Community College *C*

Colorado

Fort Lewis College *B*
Mesa State College *A*
Metropolitan State College of Denver *B*
Parks College *A*
University of Colorado
Boulder *B*
University of Denver *B, M*

Connecticut

Briarwood College *A*
International College of Hospitality
Management *B*
Three Rivers Community College *C, A*
University of New Haven *A, B, M*

Florida

Broward Community College *A*
Daytona Beach Community College *A*
Florida International University *B, M*
Florida National College *A*
Miami-Dade Community College *C, A*
St. Thomas University *B*
Schiller International University *A, B*
Webber International University *A, B*
Webster College: Holiday *A*

Hawaii

Brigham Young University-Hawaii *A, B*
Hawaii Business College *C, A*
Hawaii Pacific University *B*
Heald College
Honolulu *A*
University of Hawaii
Maui Community College *A*

Illinois

City Colleges of Chicago
Harold Washington College *C, A*
Danville Area Community College *C*
Lincoln College *A*
Midstate College *A*
Northwestern Business College *A*
Parkland College *C*
Robert Morris College: Chicago *C, A*
Rockford Business College *C*
Roosevelt University *B*

Indiana

Indiana Business College *A*
Indiana Business College
Muncie *C, A*
Indiana University-Purdue University
Indianapolis *B*
University of Indianapolis *A, B*

Iowa

American Institute of Business *A*
Hamilton College
Cedar Falls *C, A*
Cedar Rapids *C, A*
Mason City *C, A*
Iowa Lakes Community College *A*
Northeast Iowa Community College *C*

Louisiana

Southern University
Shreveport *A*

Maine

Andover College *C, A*
University of Maine
Machias *B*

Maryland

Villa Julie College *A*

Massachusetts

Becker College *B*
Berkshire Community College *C*
Bunker Hill Community College *C, A*
Fisher College *C, A*
Lasell College *B*
Marian Court College *C, A*
Massasoit Community College *A*
Mount Ida College *A*
Newbury College *C, A*

Michigan

Baker College
of Clinton Township *A*
Grand Valley State University *B*
Lansing Community College *A*
Michigan State University *B*
Northern Michigan University *B*

Minnesota

Rasmussen College
Mankato *C, A*
Minnetonka *C, A*
St. Cloud *C*

Missouri

East Central College *C, A*
St. Louis Community College
St. Louis Community College at
Forest Park *A*

Montana

University of Montana: Western *A*

Nebraska

Lincoln School of Commerce *C*
Nebraska College of Business *C*
University of Nebraska
Kearney *B*

New Hampshire
Hesser College *C, A*
New Hampshire Technical Institute *C, A*
Southern New Hampshire University *B*
University of New Hampshire *B*

New Jersey
Atlantic Cape Community College *C, A*
Cumberland County College *C, A*
Essex County College *A*
Mercer County Community College *C*

New Mexico
New Mexico State University *B*

New York
Adirondack Community College *A*
Broome Community College *A*
Bryant & Stratton Business Institute
    Syracuse *A*
City University of New York
    Kingsborough Community
        College *A*
Corning Community College *C, A*
Dowling College *B*
Dutchess Community College *A*
Elmira Business Institute *C*
Finger Lakes Community College *A*
Jefferson Community College *A*
Katharine Gibbs School
    Melville *A*
Monroe Community College *A*
New York Institute of Technology *B*
New York University *M*
Niagara University *B*
Paul Smith's College *B*
Rochester Institute of
    Technology *A, B, M*
Rockland Community College *A*
State University of New York
    College at Plattsburgh *B*
    College of Agriculture and
        Technology at Cobleskill *A*
    College of Agriculture and
        Technology at Morrisville *A*
    College of Technology at Delhi *A*
Westchester Community College *C, A*

North Carolina
Blue Ridge Community College *A*
King's College *A*
Methodist College *B*

North Dakota
Aaker's Business College *A*

Ohio
Bradford School *C*
Columbus State Community College *A*
Davis College *A*
Lakeland Community College *C, A*
Lorain County Community College *A*
Muskingum Area Technical College *A*
Ohio University *A*
Ohio University
    Southern Campus at Ironton *A*
RETS Tech Center *C*
Sinclair Community College *A*
Tiffin University *B*
University of Akron *C, A*
University of Northwestern Ohio *C, A*
Youngstown State University *A, B*

Oklahoma
Northeastern State University *B*
Oklahoma City Community College *A*
Tulsa Community College *C, A*

Oregon
Central Oregon Community College *A*
Chemeketa Community College *A*
Mount Hood Community College *C, A*
Western Business College *A*

Pennsylvania
Allentown Business School *A*
Bradford School: Pittsburgh *A*
Central Pennsylvania College *A*

Consolidated School of Business
    Lancaster *C, A*
    York *C, A*
Erie Business Center *A*
ICM School of Business & Medical
    Careers *A*
Mercyhurst College *C, A, B*
Newport Business Institute *A*
Pennsylvania College of Technology *A*
Pittsburgh Technical Institute: Boyd
    School Division *A*
Robert Morris University *B*
South Hills School of Business &
    Technology *C*
Westmoreland County Community
    College *A*

Puerto Rico
Huertas Junior College *C*
Inter American University of Puerto Rico
    Fajardo Campus *A*
Pontifical Catholic University of Puerto
    Rico *A, B*
Technological College of San Juan *C*
Turabo University *C*
Universidad del Este *C, A, B*

South Carolina
Clemson University *B*

South Dakota
Black Hills State University *A*

Texas
Amarillo College *C*
Austin Community College *C*
Central Texas College *C*
Del Mar College *A*
El Paso Community College *C, A*
Houston Community College
    System *C, A*
North Harris Montgomery Community
    College District *C, A*
Richland College *A*
St. Philip's College *C, A*
South Texas Community College *C*
Tarrant County College *C, A*
Texas A&M University *B*
University of Texas
    San Antonio *B*

Utah
Salt Lake Community College *C*

Vermont
Champlain College *A, B*
Johnson State College *B*

Virginia
National College of Business &
    Technology
        Roanoke *C, A*
Virginia Highlands Community
    College *C*

Washington
Spokane Falls Community College *C, A*

West Virginia
Concord College *B*
Davis and Elkins College *B*
Mountain State College *A*
Mountain State University *C, A*
West Liberty State College *B*
West Virginia Northern Community
    College *A*

Tourism/travel services

New Hampshire
Hesser College *A*

New York
Dutchess Community College *A*
Schenectady County Community
    College *A*

State University of New York
    College of Agriculture and
        Technology at Morrisville *A*

Pennsylvania
Consolidated School of Business
    York *A*
Newport Business Institute *A*
Northampton County Area Community
    College *C, A*
Pittsburgh Technical Institute: Boyd
    School Division *C*

Utah
Dixie State College of Utah *C, A*

Vermont
Champlain College *A, B*

Washington
Edmonds Community College *C, A*

Toxicology

Arizona
University of Arizona *M, D*

Arkansas
University of Arkansas
    for Medical Sciences *M, D*

California
San Jose State University *M*
University of California
    Davis *M, D*
    Irvine *M, D*
    Santa Cruz *M, D*
University of Southern California *M, D*

Colorado
University of Colorado
    Health Sciences Center *D*

District of Columbia
American University *M*
George Washington University *M, D*

Florida
University of Miami *B*

Georgia
University of Georgia *M, D*

Indiana
Indiana University-Purdue University
    Indianapolis *M, D*

Iowa
Iowa State University *M, D*

Kansas
University of Kansas Medical
    Center *M, D*

Kentucky
University of Kentucky *M, D*

Louisiana
University of Louisiana at Monroe *B*

Maryland
University of Maryland
    Baltimore *M, D*
    Baltimore County *M, D*
    College Park *M, D*

Michigan
Eastern Michigan University *B*
Michigan State University *D*
University of Michigan *M, D*
Wayne State University *M, D*

Minnesota
Minnesota State University
    Mankato *B, M, T*
University of Minnesota
    Duluth *M*
    Twin Cities *M, D*

Mississippi
Mississippi State University *D*

Nebraska
University of Nebraska
    Lincoln *M, D*
    Medical Center *M, D*

New Hampshire
Dartmouth College *D*

New Jersey
Bloomfield College *B*
College of St. Elizabeth *B*
Felician College *B*
Rutgers, The State University of New
    Jersey
        New Brunswick Regional
            Campus *M, D*
St. Peter's College *B*
University of Medicine and Dentistry of
    New Jersey
        School of Health Related
            Professions *B*

New York
Clarkson University *B*
Cornell University *B*
St. John's University *B, M*
State University of New York
    Albany *M, D*
    Buffalo *M, D*
    College of Environmental Science
        and Forestry *B, M, D*
University of Rochester *M, D*

North Carolina
North Carolina State University *M, D*
University of North Carolina
    Chapel Hill *M, D*

Ohio
Wright State University *M*

Oregon
Oregon State University *M, D*

Pennsylvania
Duquesne University *M, D*
University of the Sciences in
    Philadelphia *B, M, D*

South Carolina
Clemson University *B, M*
Medical University of South Carolina *D*

Tennessee
University of Tennessee
    Knoxville *M*

Texas
Prairie View A&M University *M*
Texas A&M University *M, D*
Texas Southern University *M, D*
Texas Tech University *M, D*
University of Texas
    Houston Health Science
        Center *M, D*

Utah
Utah State University *M, D*

Wisconsin
University of Wisconsin
    Madison *M, D*

Trade/industrial education

Alabama
Athens State University *B*
Lawson State Community College *C*
Trenholm State Technical College *A*

Alaska
University of Alaska
    Anchorage *M*

Arizona
Northern Arizona University *B, M*

Arkansas
University of Arkansas *B, M, D*

University of Arkansas
  Pine Bluff *B, T*
University of Central Arkansas *M*

California
California Polytechnic State University:
  San Luis Obispo *M*
California State University
  Los Angeles *T*
  San Bernardino *B*
Humboldt State University *B, T*

Colorado
Colorado State University *T*

Delaware
Delaware State University *B*

Florida
Florida Agricultural and Mechanical
  University *B, M*
Florida International University *B, M, T*
Florida State University *D, T*
University of Central Florida *B, M*
University of North Florida *B*
University of South Florida *B, M*
University of West Florida *B*

Georgia
Darton College *A*
Valdosta State University *B*

Hawaii
University of Hawaii
  Manoa *B, T*

Idaho
University of Idaho *B*

Illinois
Chicago State University *M, D*
Southern Illinois University
  Carbondale *B, M, D*

Indiana
Ball State University *T*
Indiana State University *B, M, T*
Purdue University *A, B*
Vincennes University *A*

Iowa
Iowa State University *B, T*
University of Northern Iowa *B*
William Penn University *B*

Kansas
Central Christian College *A, B*
Fort Hays State University *B, T*
Pittsburg State University *B, T*

Kentucky
Murray State University *B, T*
University of Kentucky *M, D*
University of Louisville *B, M*

Louisiana
Northwestern State University *B*
University of Louisiana at Lafayette *B*

Massachusetts
Fitchburg State College *M*

Michigan
Andrews University *M, T*
Lansing Community College *A*
Western Michigan University *M*

Minnesota
St. Cloud State University *T*

Mississippi
Mississippi Gulf Coast Community
  College
  Perkinston *A*

Nebraska
Chadron State College *B*
Metropolitan Community College *A*
University of Nebraska
  Kearney *B*
  Lincoln *B, T*

Nevada
University of Nevada
  Reno *B*

New York
New York Institute of
  Technology *A, B, T*
New York University *M, D*
State University of New York
  College at Buffalo *B, M, T*
  Oswego *B, M, T*

North Carolina
North Carolina Agricultural and
  Technical State University *B, T*
North Carolina State University *T*
Southwestern Community College *A*

North Dakota
University of North Dakota *M*
Valley City State University *B, T*

Ohio
Kent State University *B, T*
Mount Vernon Nazarene University *B*
Ohio State University
  Columbus Campus *B, M*
Ohio University *B*

Oklahoma
East Central University *B*
Oklahoma State University *B, T*
University of Central Oklahoma *B*

Pennsylvania
Indiana University of Pennsylvania *B, T*
Temple University *B*

Rhode Island
Rhode Island College *B*

South Carolina
Clemson University *D*
South Carolina State University *B, T*

South Dakota
South Dakota State University *M*

Tennessee
University of Tennessee
  Knoxville *B, T*

Texas
Sam Houston State University *M*
Southwest Texas State University *T*
Texas A&M University *D, T*
Texas A&M University
  Commerce *M, T*
University of Houston *B, M*
University of North Texas *M, D*
Wayland Baptist University *B*

Utah
Brigham Young University *B, M*
Southern Utah University *B, T*

Virginia
Norfolk State University *B*
Virginia Polytechnic Institute and State
  University *M, D*
Virginia State University *B, M*

Washington
Central Washington University *B, T*
Renton Technical College *C, A*
South Seattle Community College *C, A*
Western Washington University *M*

West Virginia
Fairmont State College *B*
Marshall University *M*

Wisconsin
University of Wisconsin
  Stout *M*

Wyoming
University of Wyoming *B*
Western Wyoming Community
  College *A*

Traditional Chinese medicine/herbology

Pennsylvania
Academy of Medical Arts and
  Business *C, A*

Transportation

Alabama
Community College of the Air Force *A*

Alaska
University of Alaska
  Anchorage *B, M*

Arkansas
University of Arkansas
  Community College at Batesville *C*

California
California Maritime Academy *B*
California State University
  Dominguez Hills *M*
  Long Beach *C*

Delaware
Wilmington College *M*

Illinois
John Wood Community College *C*
Richland Community College *A*
Triton College *A*

Iowa
Des Moines Area Community College *C*
Indian Hills Community College *C*
Northeast Iowa Community College *C*

Maryland
Morgan State University *M*

Michigan
Baker College
  of Muskegon *C*

Minnesota
St. Paul College - A Community and
  Technical College *C*

Nebraska
Southeast Community College
  Lincoln Campus *C*
Western Nebraska Community
  College *C, A*

Nevada
University of Nevada
  Las Vegas *M*

New Mexico
Mesalands Community College *C*

New York
Nassau Community College *A*
New York Institute of Technology *C*
Niagara University *B*
United States Merchant Marine
  Academy *B*

North Dakota
Lake Region State College *A*

Ohio
Columbus State Community College *A*
Cuyahoga Community College
  Western Campus *A*
John Carroll University *B*
Ohio Technical College *C, A*

Pennsylvania
Robert Morris University *B*

Texas
Brookhaven College *A*
Central Texas College *C*
Texas A&M University
  Galveston *B*
Texas Southern University *B, M*

Virginia
Averett University *B*
J. Sargeant Reynolds Community
  College *C*
University of Richmond *C, A*

Washington
Green River Community College *C, A*
Spokane Falls Community College *A*

Wisconsin
University of Wisconsin
  Superior *B*

Transportation management

Florida
South Florida Community College *A*
University of North Florida *B*

Ohio
North Central State College *C*

Wisconsin
University of Wisconsin
  Superior *B*

Transportation/highway engineering

Arkansas
University of Arkansas *M*

Massachusetts
Massachusetts Institute of
  Technology *M, D*

New Jersey
New Jersey Institute of Technology *M, D*

New York
Rensselaer Polytechnic Institute *M, D*
State University of New York
  Buffalo *M, D*

Pennsylvania
Villanova University *M*

Truck/bus/commercial vehicle operation

Florida
Gulf Coast Community College *C*
Indian River Community College *C*

Idaho
Lewis-Clark State College *C*

Illinois
Black Hawk College *C*
John Wood Community College *C*
Kaskaskia College *C*

Indiana
Vincennes University *C*

Minnesota
Dakota County Technical College *C*
Minnesota State College - Southeast
  Technical *C*

Mississippi
Itawamba Community College *C*

Missouri
Crowder College *C*

New Mexico
Albuquerque Technical-Vocational
  Institute *C*

North Carolina
Cape Fear Community College *C*
Davidson County Community College *C*

Texas
Houston Community College System *C*

Turf management

Virginia
Southside Virginia Community
College *C*

Washington
Clover Park Technical College *C*

Wisconsin
Fox Valley Technical College *C*

Wyoming
Central Wyoming College *C*

Turf management

California
Los Angeles Pierce College *C*
MiraCosta College *C, A*
Monterey Peninsula College *C*
Mount San Antonio College *C*
Mount San Jacinto College *C, A*
San Joaquin Delta College *C*
Southwestern College *C, A*

Florida
Florida Southern College *B*
Indian River Community College *A*
Lake City Community College *C*

Georgia
University of Georgia *B*

Illinois
College of DuPage *C*
College of Lake County *A*
Danville Area Community College *C*
Joliet Junior College *C, A*
Kishwaukee College *C*
Lewis and Clark Community College *A*
Lincoln Land Community College *C*
McHenry County College *C*
Richland Community College *C*
Southwestern Illinois College *A*
William Rainey Harper College *C, A*

Indiana
Vincennes University *C*

Iowa
Des Moines Area Community College *C*
Kirkwood Community College *A*
Western Iowa Tech Community
College *A*

Maine
University of Maine *B*

Massachusetts
University of Massachusetts
Amherst *A*

Michigan
Northwestern Michigan College *A*

Minnesota
Anoka-Ramsey Community College *A*
Rochester Community and Technical
College *C, A*
University of Minnesota
Crookston *B*

Mississippi
Mississippi Gulf Coast Community
College
Perkinston *A*

Missouri
Longview Community College *A*
Ozarks Technical Community
College *C, A*

Nebraska
Central Community College *C*
Nebraska College of Technical
Agriculture *A*
Northeast Community College *A*

New York
State University of New York
College of Agriculture and
Technology at Cobleskill *A*
College of Technology at Delhi *A*

North Carolina
Blue Ridge Community College *C*
Brunswick Community College *A*
Catawba Valley Community College *A*
Central Piedmont Community
College *C, A*
North Carolina State University *A, B*
Sandhills Community College *A*
Wayne Community College *A*

North Dakota
Minot State University: Bottineau
Campus *A*
North Dakota State University *B*

Ohio
Cincinnati State Technical and
Community College *C, A*
Clark State Community College *A*
Kent State University
Salem Regional Campus *A*
Ohio State University
Agricultural Technical Institute *A*
Columbus Campus *B*
Owens Community College
Toledo *A*

Oklahoma
Northeastern Oklahoma Agricultural and
Mechanical College *A*
Oklahoma State University *B*
Oklahoma State University
Oklahoma City *A*

Oregon
Central Oregon Community College *A*

Pennsylvania
Community College of Allegheny
County *C, A*
Delaware Valley College *B*
Penn State
Abington *B*
Altoona *B*
Beaver *B*
Berks *B*
Delaware County *B*
Dubois *B*
Erie, The Behrend College *B*
Fayette *B*
Hazleton *B*
Lehigh Valley *B*
McKeesport *B*
Mont Alto *B*
New Kensington *B*
Schuylkill - Capital College *B*
Shenango *B*
University Park *B*
Wilkes-Barre *B*
Worthington Scranton *B*
York *B*
Pennsylvania College of Technology *A*
Westmoreland County Community
College *A*
Williamson Free School of Mechanical
Trades *C*

South Carolina
Clemson University *B*
Technical College of the Lowcountry *C*
Trident Technical College *C*

South Dakota
Southeast Technical Institute *A*

Tennessee
Chattanooga State Technical Community
College *C*
Walters State Community College *A*

Texas
Grayson County College *A*
Palo Alto College *C, A*

Texas A&M University *B*
Texas State Technical College
Waco *C, A*
Western Texas College *C, A*

Virginia
J. Sargeant Reynolds Community
College *A*

Washington
Clover Park Technical College *A*
Spokane Community College *A*
Walla Walla Community College *C, A*

Wyoming
Sheridan College *A*

Turkish

Texas
University of Texas
Austin *B*

Washington
University of Washington *B*

Ukrainian

Washington
University of Washington *B*

Underwater diving

California
Santa Barbara City College *C, A*

Upholstery

Alabama
Douglas MacArthur State Technical
College *C*
Northwest-Shoals Community College *C*

Washington
Clover Park Technical College *C*

Urban education

California
Holy Names College *M*

Connecticut
University of Hartford *D*

Missouri
Harris Stowe State College *B*

Ohio
Cleveland State University *D*
University of Dayton *B*

Oklahoma
Langston University *M*

Tennessee
University of Tennessee
Chattanooga *M*

Virginia
Norfolk State University *M*

West Virginia
Marshall University *M*

Wisconsin
Marquette University *M, D*

Urban forestry

Pennsylvania
Keystone College *A*

Wisconsin
Mid-State Technical College *A*

Urban studies

Arkansas
Arkansas State University *B*

California
California State University
Long Beach *C*
Northridge *B*
San Bernardino *M*
College of Alameda *C, A*
Loyola Marymount University *B*
San Diego State University *B*
San Francisco State University *B*
San Jose State University *M*
Stanford University *B*
University of California
Berkeley *B*
San Diego *B*
Whittier College *B*

Connecticut
Connecticut College *B*
Trinity College *B*
University of Connecticut *B*

Delaware
University of Delaware *M, D*

District of Columbia
University of the District of
Columbia *A, B*

Florida
New College of Florida *B*
Polk Community College *A*
Rollins College *B*
University of Tampa *B*

Georgia
Clayton College and State University *A*
Floyd College *A*
Georgia State University *B, M*
Morehouse College *B*
Savannah State University *M*

Illinois
De Paul University *B*
Elmhurst College *B*
Loyola University of Chicago *D*
North Park University *B*
Northwestern University *B, M*
Rockford College *B*
Roosevelt University *B, M*
Wheaton College *C*

Indiana
Butler University *B*
Calumet College of St. Joseph *B*
Indiana University-Purdue University
Fort Wayne *C*
Martin University *M*

Iowa
Mount Mercy College *B*
University of Iowa *M*

Kansas
MidAmerica Nazarene University *B*

Kentucky
University of Louisville *D*

Louisiana
Dillard University *B*
Tulane University *B*
University of New Orleans *M, D*

Maryland
Towson University *B*

Massachusetts
Boston University *B*
Hampshire College *B*
Harvard College *B*
Tufts University *M*

Michigan
Aquinas College *B*
Wayne State University *B*

Minnesota

Bethel College *B*
Macalester College *B*
Minnesota State University
    Mankato *B, M*
Ridgewater College: A Community and
    Technical College *A*
St. Cloud State University *B*
University of Minnesota
    Duluth *B*
    Twin Cities *B*
Winona State University *B*

Missouri

St. Louis University *B, M*
University of Missouri
    Kansas City *B*

Nebraska

University of Nebraska
    Omaha *B, M*

Nevada

University of Nevada
    Reno *M*

New Jersey

Rutgers, The State University of New
    Jersey
      Camden Regional Campus *B*
      New Brunswick Regional
        Campus *B, M*
St. Peter's College *A, B*

New York

Barnard College *B*
Canisius College *B*
City University of New York
    Brooklyn College *B*
    Hunter College *B, M*
    Queens College *B, M*
College of Mount St. Vincent *B*
Columbia University
    Columbia College *B*
Daemen College *C*
Eugene Lang College/New School
    University *B*
Fordham University *B*
Hobart and William Smith Colleges *B*
Iona College *B*
Metropolitan College of New York *A, B*
New York University *B*
Sarah Lawrence College *B*
State University of New York
    Albany *B*
    Buffalo *M*
    College of Environmental Science
      and Forestry *B*
Vassar College *B*

Ohio

Cleveland State University *B, M, D*
College of Wooster *B*
Ohio State University
    Columbus Campus *B*
Ohio Wesleyan University *B*
Sinclair Community College *A*
University of Akron *M, D*
University of Cincinnati *B*
University of Cincinnati
    Clermont College *A*
    Raymond Walters College *A*
University of Toledo *B*
Wittenberg University *B*
Wright State University *B, M*

Oklahoma

Langston University *B*
University of Central Oklahoma *B, M*
University of Oklahoma *M*

Oregon

Portland State University *B, M, D*

Pennsylvania

Bryn Mawr College *B*
California University of Pennsylvania *B*
Haverford College *B*

Lehigh University *B*
Penn State
    University Park *M*
Temple University *B, M, D*
University of Pennsylvania *B*
University of Pittsburgh *B*
York College of Pennsylvania *B*

Rhode Island

Brown University *B*
Community College of Rhode Island *A*
Rhode Island College *B*

South Carolina

College of Charleston *B*
Furman University *B*

Tennessee

Rhodes College *B*
University of Tennessee
    Knoxville *B*
Vanderbilt University *B*

Texas

Baylor University *B*
St. Philip's College *A*
Texas A&M International University *B*
Trinity University *B*
University of Houston *B*
University of Texas
    Arlington *M*

Utah

University of Utah *B*

Virginia

Norfolk State University *M*
Old Dominion University *M, D*
University of Richmond *B*
Virginia Commonwealth
    University *C, B, M*
Virginia Polytechnic Institute and State
    University *M*

Wisconsin

Marquette University *B*
University of Wisconsin
    Green Bay *B*
    Madison *M, D*
    Milwaukee *B, M, D*
    Oshkosh *B*

Urban/community/regional planning

Alabama

Alabama Agricultural and Mechanical
    University *B, M*
Auburn University *M*
University of Alabama *B*

Arizona

Arizona State University *B, M*
University of Arizona *B, M*

California

California Polytechnic State University:
    San Luis Obispo *B, M*
California State Polytechnic University:
    Pomona *B, M*
California State University
    Chico *B, M*
East Los Angeles College *A*
Modesto Junior College *A*
San Diego State University *M*
San Jose State University *M*
University of California
    Berkeley *M, D*
    Davis *B, M*
    Irvine *M, D*
    Los Angeles *M, D*
University of San Francisco *B*
University of Southern
    California *B, M, D*

Colorado

University of Colorado
    Denver *M*

District of Columbia

University of the District of
    Columbia *A, B, M*

Florida

Florida Atlantic University *B, M*
Florida State University *M, D*
South Florida Community College *A*
University of Florida *M*

Georgia

Georgia Institute of Technology *M*

Hawaii

University of Hawaii
    Manoa *M, D*

Illinois

Illinois Institute of Technology *M*
University of Illinois
    Chicago *M, D*
    Urbana-Champaign *B, M, D*

Indiana

Ball State University *B, M*
Indiana University-Purdue University
    Indianapolis *M*

Iowa

Iowa State University *B, M*
University of Iowa *M*

Kansas

Fort Scott Community College *A*
Kansas State University *M*
University of Kansas *M*

Louisiana

University of New Orleans *M, D*

Maine

University of Southern Maine *M*

Maryland

Frostburg State University *B*
Morgan State University *M*

Massachusetts

Bridgewater State College *B*
Harvard College *B*
Massachusetts Institute of
    Technology *B, M, D*
Tufts University *M*
University of Massachusetts
    Amherst *M, D*
Westfield State College *B*

Michigan

Eastern Michigan University *B, M*
Grand Valley State University *B*
Michigan State University *B, M*
University of Michigan *M, D*
Wayne State University *M*

Minnesota

Minnesota State University
    Mankato *B, M*
St. Cloud State University *B*

Mississippi

University of Southern Mississippi *B*

Missouri

St. Louis University *M*
Southwest Missouri State
    University *B, M*
Washington University in St. Louis *M*

Montana

University of Montana-Missoula *B, M*

Nebraska

University of Nebraska
    Lincoln *M*

Nevada

University of Nevada
    Las Vegas *B*

New Hampshire

Plymouth State College *B*
University of New Hampshire *B*

New Jersey

New Jersey Institute of Technology *M*
Rutgers, The State University of New
    Jersey
      New Brunswick Regional
        Campus *B*

New Mexico

New Mexico State University *B*
University of New Mexico *M*

New York

City University of New York
    Baruch College *B*
    City College *M*
    Hunter College *M*
Cornell University *B, M, D*
New York Institute of Technology *M*
New York University *M*
Pratt Institute *M*
State University of New York
    Albany *M*
    Buffalo *M*
    College at Buffalo *B*
    College of Environmental Science
      and Forestry *B, M*

North Carolina

Appalachian State University *B*
East Carolina University *B*
University of North Carolina
    Chapel Hill *M, D*

Ohio

Kent State University *C*
Miami University
    Oxford Campus *B*
Ohio State University
    Columbus Campus *B, M, D*
Ohio University *B*
Stark State College of Technology *A*
University of Akron *C, B, M*
University of Cincinnati *B, M*
University of Cincinnati
    Clermont College *A*
Wittenberg University *B*

Oklahoma

University of Oklahoma *M*

Oregon

Portland State University *B, M, D*
University of Oregon *M*

Pennsylvania

Art Institute
    of Pittsburgh *C*
Bryn Mawr College *B*
Haverford College *B*
Indiana University of Pennsylvania *B*
Penn State
    University Park *M, D*
Temple University *B, M*
University of Pennsylvania *M, D*
West Chester University of
    Pennsylvania *M*

Puerto Rico

University of Puerto Rico
    Rio Piedras Campus *B*

Rhode Island

University of Rhode Island *M*

South Carolina

Clemson University *M*

Tennessee

University of Memphis *M*
University of Tennessee
    Knoxville *M*

Texas

Prairie View A&M University *M*
Rice University *M*
Southwest Texas State University *B*
Texas A&M University *M, D*
Texas Southern University *A, B*
University of North Texas *B*

University of Texas
Arlington *M*
Austin *M, D*

Utah
Utah State University *M*

Virginia
University of Virginia *B, M*
Virginia Polytechnic Institute and State
University *M*

Washington
Eastern Washington University *B, M*
University of Washington *B, M, D*
Washington State University *M*

Wisconsin
Northland College *B*
University of Wisconsin
Madison *M, D*
Milwaukee *M*

Wyoming
University of Wyoming *M*

Vehicle parts/accessories marketing

California
Sierra College *A*

Florida
Northwood University
Florida Campus *A, B*

Michigan
Northwood University *A, B*

Texas
Northwood University: Texas
Campus *A, B*

Washington
Spokane Community College *C, A*

Vendor/product certification

Arizona
Estrella Mountain Community
College *C, A*
Paradise Valley Community College *C*

California
Foothill College *C*
Long Beach City College *C*
National University *C*
Santa Rosa Junior College *C*

Colorado
Colorado Technical University *C*

Florida
Herzing College
Orlando *C*
Pasco-Hernando Community College *A*

Illinois
Richland Community College *C*

Kentucky
Jefferson Community College *C*

Michigan
Baker College
of Port Huron *C, A*
Lansing Community College *A*

Missouri
Moberly Area Community College *C*

North Carolina
Beaufort County Community College *A*

Oregon
Pioneer Pacific College *C*

Texas
Temple College *C*

Washington
Bellevue Community College *C*
Clover Park Technical College *C*

Wisconsin
Milwaukee Area Technical College *A*

Veterinary assistant

Alabama
Snead State Community College *A*
Virginia College *A*

Arizona
Pima Community College *C*

California
Foothill College *C, A*
Yuba Community College District *A*

Colorado
Bel-Rea Institute of Animal
Technology *A*
Colorado Mountain College
Spring Valley Campus *A*
Otero Junior College *A*

Connecticut
Northwestern Connecticut Community
College *A*
Quinnipiac University *B*

Delaware
Delaware Technical and Community
College
Owens Campus *A*

Florida
Manatee Community College *A*
Miami-Dade Community College *A*
St. Petersburg College *A*

Georgia
Fort Valley State University *A, B*

Idaho
College of Southern Idaho *A*

Illinois
Joliet Junior College *A*
Parkland College *A*

Indiana
Purdue University *A, B*

Iowa
Des Moines Area Community College *C*
Kirkwood Community College *A*
Waldorf College *A*

Kansas
Johnson County Community College *A*

Kentucky
Morehead State University *A*
Murray State University *B*

Louisiana
Northwestern State University *A*

Maine
University of Maine
Augusta *A*

Maryland
Community College of Baltimore County
Catonsville *A*
Essex *A*

Massachusetts
Becker College *A, B*
Berkshire Community College *C*
Mount Ida College *A, B*

Michigan
Baker College
of Cadillac *A*
of Muskegon *A*
Bay de Noc Community College *C*
Macomb Community College *A*
Michigan State University *C, B*

Minnesota
Globe College *C, A*
Ridgewater College: A Community and
Technical College *A*

Mississippi
Mississippi Gulf Coast Community
College
Perkinston *A*

Missouri
Jefferson College *A*
Maple Woods Community College *A*

Nebraska
Nebraska College of Technical
Agriculture *A*
Northeast Community College *A*
University of Nebraska
Lincoln *B*

New Hampshire
New Hampshire Community Technical
College
Manchester *A*
Stratham *A*

New Jersey
Camden County College *A*
County College of Morris *A*
Sussex County Community College *A*

New York
City University of New York
La Guardia Community College *A*
Medaille College *A, B*
Mercy College *B*
State University of New York
College of Technology at Alfred *A*
College of Technology at Canton *A*
College of Technology at Delhi *A*
Suffolk County Community College *A*

North Carolina
Central Carolina Community College *A*

North Dakota
North Dakota State University *B*

Ohio
Columbus State Community College *A*
Cuyahoga Community College
Western Campus *A*
Stautzenberger College *C, A*
University of Cincinnati
Raymond Walters College *A*

Oklahoma
Oklahoma State University
Oklahoma City *A*

Oregon
Linn-Benton Community College *C*
Portland Community College *A*

Pennsylvania
Lehigh Carbon Community College *A*
Manor College *A*
Median School of Allied Health
Careers *C*
Northampton County Area Community
College *A*
Wilson College *A*

Puerto Rico
University of Puerto Rico
Medical Sciences Campus *B*

South Carolina
Tri-County Technical College *A*

Tennessee
Columbia State Community College *A*

Texas
Houston Community College System *C*
Midland College *A*
North Harris Montgomery Community
College District *A*
Sul Ross State University *A*

Utah
Snow College *A*

Vermont
Vermont Technical College *A*

Virginia
Blue Ridge Community College *C, A*
Mountain Empire Community College *C*

West Virginia
Fairmont State College *A*

Wyoming
Eastern Wyoming College *A*

Veterinary medicine (D.V.M.)

Alabama
Auburn University: College of Veterinary
Medicine *F*
Tuskegee University: School of
Veterinary Medicine *F*

California
University of California Davis: School of
Veterinary Medicine *F*

Colorado
Colorado State University: College of
Veterinary Medicine and Biomedical
Sciences *F*

Florida
University of Florida: College of
Veterinary Medicine *F*

Georgia
University of Georgia: College of
Veterinary Medicine *F*

Illinois
University of Illinois at
Urbana-Champaign: College of
Veterinary Medicine *F*

Indiana
Purdue University: School of Veterinary
Medicine *F*

Iowa
Iowa State University: College of
Veterinary Medicine *F*

Kansas
Kansas State University: College of
Veterinary Medicine *F*

Louisiana
Louisiana State University and
Agricultural and Mechanical College:
School of Veterinary Medicine *F*

Massachusetts
Tufts University: School of Veterinary
Medicine *F*

Michigan
Michigan State University: School of
Veterinary Medicine *F*

Minnesota
University of Minnesota Twin Cities:
College of Veterinary Medicine *F*

Mississippi
Mississippi State University: College of
Veterinary Medicine *F*

Missouri
University of Missouri Columbia: School
of Veterinary Medicine *F*

New York
Cornell University: College of Veterinary
Medicine *F*

North Carolina
North Carolina State University: College
of Veterinary Medicine *F*

Ohio

Ohio State University Columbus
Campus: College of Veterinary
Medicine *F*

Oklahoma

Oklahoma State University: College of
Veterinary Medicine *F*

Oregon

Oregon State University: College of
Veterinary Medicine *F*

Pennsylvania

University of Pennsylvania: School of
Veterinary Medicine *F*

Tennessee

University of Tennessee Knoxville:
College of Veterinary Medicine *F*

Texas

Texas A&M University: College of
Veterinary Medicine *F*

Virginia

Virginia Polytechnic Institute:
Virginia-Maryland Regional College of
Veterinary Medicine *F*

Washington

Washington State University: School of
Veterinary Medicine *F*

Wisconsin

University of Wisconsin Madison: School
of Veterinary Medicine *F*

Violin/viola/guitar/stringed instruments

California

Bethesda Christian University *B, M*
California Institute of the Arts *C, B, M*
University of Southern
California *B, M, D*

Florida

Stetson University *B*

Illinois

Quincy University *B, T*

Indiana

Butler University *B, M*

Kansas

University of Kansas *B, M, D*

Maine

University of Southern Maine *B*

New York

Bard College *B*
Juilliard School *B, D*
Sarah Lawrence College *B*

North Carolina

Meredith College *B*

Ohio

Oberlin College *B, M*
Youngstown State University *B, M*

Pennsylvania

Carnegie Mellon University *B, M*

Texas

Texas Christian University *B, M*

Washington

Central Washington University *B*
University of Washington *B, M, D*

Virology

Illinois

University of Chicago *M, D*

Ohio

Case Western Reserve University *D*
Ohio State University
Columbus Campus *M, D*

Texas

University of Texas
Houston Health Science
Center *M, D*

Utah

Brigham Young University *M*

Vision science

Alabama

University of Alabama
Birmingham *M, D*

Visual/performing arts

Alabama

Birmingham-Southern College *B*
Faulkner University *B*
James H. Faulkner State Community
College *A*
Shelton State Community College *C, A*
University of Alabama
Birmingham *B*
University of Mobile *B*

Alaska

University of Alaska
Anchorage *B*

Arizona

Art Institute
of Phoenix *A*
Central Arizona College *A*
Northern Arizona University *B*
Prescott College *B, M*
University of Arizona *B*

Arkansas

Arkansas State University *B, T*
University of Arkansas
Fort Smith *A*
University of the Ozarks *B*

California

Antelope Valley College *C, A*
Cabrillo College *A*
California Baptist University *B*
California Institute of the Arts *C, B, M*
California State University
Bakersfield *B*
Los Angeles *B, M*
Monterey Bay *B*
San Marcos *B*
Chapman University *B*
College of Alameda *A*
Fashion Institute of Design and
Merchandising *A*
Fashion Institute of Design and
Merchandising
San Diego *C, A*
San Francisco *A*
Glendale Community College *A*
Irvine Valley College *A*
Marymount College *A*
Modesto Junior College *C, A*
Moorpark College *A*
Otis College of Art and Design *B, M*
Pacific Union College *B*
Platt College
Newport Beach *C, A*
Ontario *C, A*
Pomona College *B*
St. Mary's College of California *B*
San Diego City College *A*
San Joaquin Delta College *A*
Sonoma State University *B*
University of California
San Diego *M*
Santa Barbara *B, M, D*

University of San Francisco *B*

Colorado

Art Institute
of Colorado *A*
Colorado Mountain College
Alpine Campus *A*
Spring Valley Campus *A*
Mesa State College *A, B*
Naropa University *B*
Regis University *B*

Connecticut

Albertus Magnus College *B*
Asnuntuck Community College *A*
Connecticut College *B*
Fairfield University *B*
Trinity College *B*
Tunxis Community College *C, A*
University of Connecticut *B*
University of Hartford *B, M, D*

Delaware

University of Delaware *M*

District of Columbia

Catholic University of America *M, D*
Gallaudet University *B*
George Washington University *B, M*
Howard University *B*

Florida

Art Institute
of Fort Lauderdale *A*
Flagler College *B*
Florida Agricultural and Mechanical
University *B*
Full Sail Real World Education *A*
Manatee Community College *A*
Palm Beach Community College *A*
South Florida Community College *A*
Tallahassee Community College *A*
University of Miami *B, M*
University of South Florida *B, M*
University of Tampa *B*

Georgia

Abraham Baldwin Agricultural
College *A*
Andrew College *A*
Atlanta College of Art *B*
Darton College *A*
Georgia Southwestern State University *B*
Kennesaw State University *B*
LaGrange College *B*
Mercer University *B*
Savannah College of Art and
Design *B, M*
Thomas University *B*
Young Harris College *A*

Illinois

American Academy of Art *B*
City Colleges of Chicago
Kennedy-King College *A*
Columbia College Chicago *B*
Illinois College *B*
Illinois Institute of Art *B*
Illinois Valley Community College *A*
Kishwaukee College *A*
Lincoln College *A*
Moraine Valley Community College *A*
North Central College *B*
Northwestern University *B, D*
Parkland College *A*
Richland Community College *A*
Rockford College *B*
Roosevelt University *B, M*
School of the Art Institute of
Chicago *B, M*
University of St. Francis *B*
William Rainey Harper College *A*

Indiana

Goshen College *B*
Indiana State University *B, M*
Indiana University
Bloomington *B, M*

International Business College:
Indianapolis *C*
University of Evansville *B*
Vincennes University *A*

Iowa

Graceland University *B*
Iowa State University *B*
Maharishi University of
Management *B, M*
Marshalltown Community College *A*
North Iowa Area Community College *A*
Waldorf College *A*

Kansas

Central Christian College *A, B*
Cloud County Community College *A*
Garden City Community College *A*
Hutchinson Community College *A*
Kansas City Kansas Community
College *A*
MidAmerica Nazarene University *B, T*
Pratt Community College *A*
St. Mary College *B*
Seward County Community College *A*
Sterling College *T*
Washburn University of Topeka *B*
Wichita State University *B*

Kentucky

Thomas More College *B*

Louisiana

Centenary College of Louisiana *B*
Loyola University New Orleans *B*
Southern University
New Orleans *B*
University of Louisiana at Lafayette *B*

Maine

Bowdoin College *B*
University of Maine
Machias *B*
University of Southern Maine *B*

Maryland

Frostburg State University *C, B*
Johns Hopkins University *B, M, D*
Montgomery College
Rockville Campus *A*
Mount St. Mary's College *B, T*
University of Maryland
Baltimore County *B*
Villa Julie College *A*

Massachusetts

Ai The New England Institute of Art and
Design *A*
Art Institute of Boston at Lesley
University *M*
Assumption College *B*
Berkshire Community College *A*
Boston University *B, M*
Cape Cod Community College *A*
Clark University *B*
Emerson College *B, M*
Hampshire College *B*
Harvard College *B*
Massachusetts College of Liberal Arts *B*
Massasoit Community College *C*
Northeastern University *B*
Pine Manor College *A, B*
Simon's Rock College of Bard *B*
Suffolk University *B*
Tufts University *M*
University of Massachusetts
Dartmouth *B, M*
Lowell *B*

Michigan

Andrews University *B*
Calvin College *B*
Lansing Community College *A*
Mid Michigan Community College *A*
Oakland University *B*
University of Michigan
Flint *B*

Minnesota

Academy College C, A
Concordia University: St. Paul B
Hamline University B
Minnesota School of Business: Brooklyn
    Center C, A
Minnesota State University
    Mankato B
Northland Community & Technical
    College A
St. Olaf College B
Winona State University B

Mississippi

Delta State University B, T
Mississippi College M
Mississippi State University B
University of Southern Mississippi B

Missouri

Drury University B, T
Lindenwood University B, M
Mineral Area College A
St. Louis Community College
    St. Louis Community College at
        Florissant Valley A
Southeast Missouri State University B
Stephens College B
Washington University in St. Louis B, M

Montana

Miles Community College A
University of Montana-Missoula B, M
University of Montana: Western B

Nebraska

Hastings College B
University of Nebraska
    Kearney B, M, T
    Omaha B

Nevada

Art Institute
    of Las Vegas C, A
Sierra Nevada College B

New Hampshire

Franklin Pierce College B
Keene State College B

New Jersey

Bloomfield College B
The College of New Jersey B
County College of Morris A
Fairleigh Dickinson University
    College at Florham B
    Metropolitan Campus B
Mercer County Community College A
Richard Stockton College of New
    Jersey B
Rowan University B
Seton Hall University B, T
William Paterson University of New
    Jersey M

New Mexico

Art Center Design College C
New Mexico Highlands University B

New York

Adelphi University B
Adirondack Community College A
Bard College B, M
City University of New York
    Brooklyn College B, M
    City College B, M
    Queens College B
    Queensborough Community
        College A
Columbia University
    Columbia College B
Cornell University B, M
Dowling College B
Eugene Lang College/New School
    University B
Fulton-Montgomery Community
    College A
Hofstra University B

Ithaca College B, M
Juilliard School B
Medaille College B
New York University M, D
Niagara County Community College A
Pace University B
Pratt Institute B, M
St. Bonaventure University B
Sarah Lawrence College B
School of Visual Arts B, M
State University of New York
    College at Brockport M
    College at Buffalo B
    College at Old Westbury B
    New Paltz B
Union College B
Wells College B
Westchester Community College A

North Carolina

Bennett College B
Brevard College A, B
Carteret Community College A
Central Piedmont Community College A
Fayetteville State University B
Methodist College B
North Carolina Agricultural and
    Technical State University B
St. Andrews Presbyterian College B
St. Augustine's College B
Shaw University B

North Dakota

University of North Dakota B

Ohio

Antioch College B
International College of
    Broadcasting C, A
Kent State University
    Stark Campus B
Lake Erie College B
Lorain County Community College A
Mount Union College T
Notre Dame College B, T
Ohio University D
Otterbein College B
Shawnee State University B
Sinclair Community College A
Union Institute & University M
University of Akron C, B
University of Dayton B
University of Rio Grande B
Wittenberg University B
Youngstown State University B, M

Oklahoma

Oklahoma City University B, M
St. Gregory's University A
Southern Nazarene University B

Oregon

Central Oregon Community College A
Concordia University B
Oregon State University B
Pacific University B
Western Oregon University B

Pennsylvania

Arcadia University B
Art Institute
    of Pittsburgh A
Bucks County Community College A
Cedar Crest College B
Douglas School of Business A
East Stroudsburg University of
    Pennsylvania B
Gettysburg College B
Harrisburg Area Community College A
Kutztown University of Pennsylvania B
Marywood University B, M
Oakbridge Academy of Arts A

Penn State
    Abington B
    Altoona B
    Beaver B
    Berks B
    Delaware County B
    Dubois B
    Fayette B
    Hazleton B
    Lehigh Valley B
    McKeesport B
    Mont Alto B
    New Kensington B
    Schuylkill - Capital College B
    Shenango B
    University Park B
    Wilkes-Barre B
    Worthington Scranton B
    York B
St. Joseph's University B
Shippensburg University of
    Pennsylvania B
University of Pennsylvania B
York College of Pennsylvania A, B

Puerto Rico

Escuela de Artes Plasticas de Puerto
    Rico B
Inter American University of Puerto Rico
    San German Campus B, M
University of Puerto Rico
    Rio Piedras Campus B
University of the Sacred Heart B

Rhode Island

Brown University B
Providence College B
University of Rhode Island B

South Carolina

Charleston Southern University B
Lander University B
Presbyterian College B, T

Tennessee

Carson-Newman College B
King College B
Maryville College B
Nossi College of Art A
Roane State Community College A
Tusculum College B
University of Tennessee
    Martin B

Texas

Angelina College A
Angelo State University T
Coastal Bend College A
College of the Mainland A
Hill College A
Howard College A
Lon Morris College A
Mountain View College C
Rice University B, M
Schreiner University B
Texas A&M University
    Commerce B
    Corpus Christi B
Texas Lutheran University B
Texas Tech University D
Texas Wesleyan University B, T
Trinity Valley Community College A
Tyler Junior College A
University of Texas
    Austin B
    Dallas B

Utah

Brigham Young University B
Weber State University B

Vermont

Bennington College B, M, T
Burlington College B
Castleton State College B
Goddard College B
Green Mountain College B
Johnson State College B

Marlboro College B
Norwich University M
University of Vermont B

Virginia

George Mason University M
Longwood University B, T
Mary Baldwin College M
Norfolk State University M
Old Dominion University M
Shenandoah University B
Virginia State University B

Washington

Centralia College A
Eastern Washington University T
Everett Community College A
Green River Community College C, A
North Seattle Community College C, A
Seattle Pacific University B, T
Western Washington University B
Whitworth College B, T

West Virginia

Bethany College B
West Virginia University B, M

Wisconsin

Carroll College B
Edgewood College B
University of Wisconsin
    Green Bay B
    Milwaukee M
    Stevens Point B
    Superior B, M, T

Wyoming

Casper College A
Western Wyoming Community
    College A

Vocational rehabilitation counseling

Alabama

University of Alabama M

Arkansas

University of Arkansas M, D
University of Arkansas
    Little Rock M

California

California State University
    Fresno B, M

Colorado

University of Northern Colorado M

Florida

Florida State University B, M, D
South Florida Community College A
University of Florida M
University of South Florida M

Georgia

Fort Valley State University M
Georgia State University M
University of Georgia M

Illinois

Illinois Institute of Technology M
Southern Illinois University
    Carbondale M

Kansas

Emporia State University B, M

Kentucky

University of Kentucky M

Massachusetts

Boston University M, D
Springfield College M

Missouri

Maryville University of Saint Louis M

New Jersey

Seton Hall University M

Union County College *A*
University of Medicine and Dentistry of
New Jersey
  School of Health Related
    Professions *M*

New York
Hofstra University *M*
State University of New York
  Buffalo *M*

North Carolina
East Carolina University *B, M*
University of North Carolina
  Chapel Hill *M*

Ohio
Bowling Green State University *M*
University of Cincinnati *M*
University of Cincinnati
  Raymond Walters College *C, A*
Wright State University *B*

Oklahoma
East Central University *B*

Oregon
Western Oregon University *M*

Pennsylvania
Community College of Allegheny
  County *C*
Edinboro University of Pennsylvania *M*

Tennessee
University of Tennessee
  Knoxville *M*

Texas
Stephen F. Austin State University *M*
University of Texas
  Pan American *B, M*
  Southwestern Medical Center at
    Dallas *M*

Virginia
Virginia Commonwealth University *M*

Washington
Edmonds Community College *A*
Spokane Falls Community College *C, A*

West Virginia
West Virginia University *M*

Wisconsin
University of Wisconsin
  Stout *B, M*

Vocational/technical education

Alabama
Auburn University *B, M, D, T*
Northeast Alabama Community
  College *A*
Tuskegee University *B, M*

Arizona
Prescott College *B*

California
San Diego State University *B*

Colorado
Colorado State University *M, D, T*

Connecticut
Central Connecticut State
  University *B, M*
University of Connecticut *D, T*

Delaware
Delaware Technical and Community
  College
    Owens Campus *C*
    Stanton/Wilmington Campus *C*
    Terry Campus *C*

Florida
Palm Beach Community College *A*

University of West Florida *M*

Georgia
University of Georgia *M, D, T*
Valdosta State University *B*

Hawaii
University of Hawaii
  Honolulu Community College *A*

Idaho
Idaho State University *B, T*
University of Idaho *B, M, T*

Illinois
City Colleges of Chicago
  Kennedy-King College *A*
Eastern Illinois University *B, T*
Sauk Valley Community College *A*
University of Illinois
  Urbana-Champaign *M, D, T*

Indiana
Vincennes University *A*

Kansas
Independence Community College *A*
Pittsburg State University *B, M, T*

Kentucky
Murray State University *A, B, T*

Maine
University of Southern Maine *B, T*

Maryland
Johns Hopkins University *M*

Michigan
Andrews University *M, T*
Ferris State University *B, M*
Wayne State University *B, M, T*

Minnesota
Bemidji State University *B*
Minnesota State University
  Mankato *B, M, T*
Ridgewater College: A Community and
  Technical College *A*

Mississippi
Mississippi State University *B, M, T*

Missouri
Moberly Area Community College *A*
University of Missouri
  Columbia *B, M, D*

Nebraska
Chadron State College *M*
Peru State College *B, T*
University of Nebraska
  Lincoln *B*

New Hampshire
Keene State College *B, T*

New Jersey
College of St. Elizabeth *M*

New Mexico
University of New Mexico *M, D, T*
Western New Mexico University *B*

New York
New York Institute of
  Technology *A, B, T*
State University of New York
  College at Buffalo *B, M, T*
  Oswego *B*

North Carolina
East Carolina University *M*
North Carolina State University *M, D, T*

North Dakota
Lake Region State College *A*
Valley City State University *B*

Ohio
Bowling Green State University *B*
Kent State University
  Stark Campus *B*

Ohio State University
  Columbus Campus *M, D*
University of Akron *B, M, T*
University of Findlay *M*

Oklahoma
Oklahoma State University *B, T*

Oregon
Oregon State University *M*

Pennsylvania
Pittsburgh Institute of Aeronautics *A*
Temple University *M*
West Chester University of
  Pennsylvania *M*

Puerto Rico
Inter American University of Puerto Rico
  San German Campus *B*

Rhode Island
Rhode Island College *B*

South Carolina
Florence-Darlington Technical College *A*
Piedmont Technical College *A*
Trident Technical College *A*

Tennessee
Middle Tennessee State University *M*

Texas
Texas A&M University *M*
Texas A&M University
  Commerce *T*
  Corpus Christi *M*
University of North Texas *M, D*

Utah
Brigham Young University *B*
Utah State University *B, M*

Washington
Pacific Lutheran University *B*
Renton Technical College *C, A*
Walla Walla College *B*

Wisconsin
University of Wisconsin
  Platteville *B, T*
  Stout *B*

Voice/opera

Alabama
Birmingham-Southern College *B*
Huntingdon College *B*
Samford University *B*

Arkansas
Harding University *B*
Henderson State University *B*
John Brown University *B*
Ouachita Baptist University *B*
University of Central Arkansas *B*

California
Bethesda Christian University *B, M*
California Institute of the Arts *C, B, M*
California State University
  Chico *C*
  Fullerton *B, M*
  Long Beach *B*
Master's College *B*
Ohlone College *C*
San Diego State University *M*
San Francisco State University *B*
University of Southern
  California *B, M, D*
University of the Pacific *B*

Connecticut
University of Hartford *B, M*

Delaware
University of Delaware *B*

District of Columbia
Catholic University of America *B, M, D*

Howard University *B*

Florida
Florida State University *B, M, D*
Palm Beach Atlantic University *B*
Southeastern College of the Assemblies
  of God *B*
Stetson University *B*

Georgia
Columbus State University *B, M*
Emory University *M*
Georgia College and State University *B*
Georgia Southwestern State University *B*
Shorter College *B*
Toccoa Falls College *B*

Hawaii
Brigham Young University-Hawaii *B*

Idaho
University of Idaho *B*

Illinois
Augustana College *B*
Benedictine University *B*
Columbia College Chicago *B*
Judson College *B*
Lincoln College *A*
Millikin University *B*
Monmouth College *T*
Moody Bible Institute *B*
Northwestern University *B, D*
Olivet Nazarene University *B*
Quincy University *B, T*
Roosevelt University *B, M*
St. Xavier University *B*
Sauk Valley Community College *A*
Trinity Christian College *B*
Trinity International University *B*
University of Illinois
  Urbana-Champaign *B*

Indiana
American Conservatory of
  Music *C, B, M, D*
Ball State University *B*
Butler University *B, M*
Grace College *B*
Indiana University
  Bloomington *B*
Indiana University-Purdue University
  Fort Wayne *B, T*
Indiana Wesleyan University *T*
Saint Mary's College *B*
University of Indianapolis *B*
Valparaiso University *M*
Vincennes University *A*

Iowa
Clarke College *B*
Dordt College *B*
Drake University *B*
Luther College *B*
Simpson College *B*
University of Iowa *B*
Waldorf College *A, B*

Kansas
Allen County Community College *A*
Central Christian College *A*
MidAmerica Nazarene University *T*
Pittsburg State University *B*
Seward County Community College *A*
Tabor College *B*
University of Kansas *B, M, D*

Kentucky
Campbellsville University *B*

Louisiana
Centenary College of Louisiana *B, T*

Maine
University of Southern Maine *B*

Maryland
Columbia Union College *B*
Johns Hopkins University *B, M, D*

Johns Hopkins University: Peabody
  Conservatory of Music *B, M, D*
Washington Bible College *B*

Massachusetts
Anna Maria College *B*
Berklee College of Music *B*
Boston Conservatory *B, M*
Boston University *B, M, D*
Emerson College *B*
New England Conservatory of
  Music *B, M*

Michigan
Calvin College *B, T*
Northwestern Michigan College *A*
Oakland University *B*
University of Michigan *B, M*

Minnesota
Bethel College *B*
Concordia College: Moorhead *B*
Minnesota State University
    Mankato *B, M, T*
    Moorhead *B*
Northwestern College *B*
St. Mary's University of Minnesota *B*

Mississippi
Blue Mountain College *B*
Mississippi College *B, M*

Missouri
College of the Ozarks *B*
Drury University *B*
Hannibal-LaGrange College *B*
University of Missouri
    Kansas City *B, M, D*
Washington University in St. Louis *B, M*
Webster University *M*

Nebraska
Concordia University *B, T*
Hastings College *B*
York College *B*

New Hampshire
University of New Hampshire *B*

New Jersey
Rider University *B, M*

New York
Bard College *B*
City University of New York
    City College *B*
Eastman School of Music of the
    University of Rochester *B, M, D*
Houghton College *B*
Ithaca College *B, M*
Manhattan School of Music *B, M, D*
Mannes College of Music *B, M*
New York University *B*
Roberts Wesleyan College *B*
Sarah Lawrence College *B*
State University of New York
    Binghamton *M*
    College at Fredonia *B*
    New Paltz *B*
Syracuse University *B, M*
University of Rochester *M, D*

North Carolina
Campbell University *B*
Meredith College *B*
Wingate University *B*

North Dakota
North Dakota State University *B, T*

Ohio
Baldwin-Wallace College *B*
Bowling Green State University *B, M*
Cleveland Institute of Music *B*
Kent State University *B*
Kent State University
    Stark Campus *B*
Oberlin College *B, M*
Ohio State University
    Columbus Campus *B*

Ohio University *B*
University of Akron *B, M*
University of Cincinnati *B, M, D*
Youngstown State University *B, M*

Oklahoma
East Central University *B, T*
Northeastern State University *B*
Northwestern Oklahoma State
    University *B*
Oklahoma Baptist University *B*
Oklahoma Christian University of
    Science and Arts *B*
Oklahoma City University *B*
Oral Roberts University *B*
Southwestern Oklahoma State
    University *B*
University of Central Oklahoma *B*
University of Oklahoma *B, M, D*
University of Tulsa *B*

Oregon
Western Baptist College *B*
Willamette University *B*

Pennsylvania
Carnegie Mellon University *B, M*
Curtis Institute of Music *M*
Gettysburg College *B*
Gratz College *C, M*
Marywood University *C*
Mercyhurst College *B*
Penn State
    University Park *M*
Temple University *C, B, M, D*
West Chester University of
    Pennsylvania *M*

Puerto Rico
Conservatory of Music of Puerto Rico *B*

South Carolina
Anderson College *B, T*
Charleston Southern University *B*
Coker College *B*
Furman University *B*
North Greenville College *B*
South Carolina State University *B*
University of South Carolina *M*

Tennessee
Belmont University *B*
Bryan College *B*
Lambuth University *B*
Union University *B*
University of Tennessee
    Knoxville *B*
    Martin *B*

Texas
Abilene Christian University *B*
Alvin Community College *A*
Angelina College *A*
Dallas Baptist University *B*
East Texas Baptist University *B*
Howard Payne University *B*
Lamar University *B, M*
Lon Morris College *A*
McMurry University *B, T*
Prairie View A&M University *B*
Southern Methodist University *B, M*
Texas A&M University
    Commerce *B, M*
Texas Christian University *B, M*
Trinity University *B*
University of Mary Hardin-Baylor *B*
University of Texas
    Arlington *B*
    El Paso *B*

Utah
Brigham Young University *M*
Weber State University *B*

Vermont
Bennington College *B, M*
Johnson State College *B*

Virginia
Virginia Union University *B*

Washington
Central Washington University *B*
Cornish College of the Arts *B*
Eastern Washington University *B, T*
University of Washington *B, M, D*
Whitworth College *B*

West Virginia
Davis and Elkins College *B*

Wisconsin
Carthage College *B, T*
Lawrence University *B*
Northland College *B, T*
University of Wisconsin
    Madison *B, M*

| **Warehousing/inventory management** |

Washington
Clover Park Technical College *C*

| **Watch/jewelrymaking** |

Minnesota
Minneapolis Community and Technical
    College *C, A*
St. Paul College - A Community and
    Technical College *C*

Montana
Flathead Valley Community College *A*

Texas
Paris Junior College *A*

| **Water quality/treatment/ recycling technology** |

Alabama
Northwest-Shoals Community College *A*

Arizona
Gateway Community College *A*

California
Citrus College *C*
College of the Canyons *A*
San Diego Mesa College *C, A*
Santa Barbara City College *C*
Shasta College *C*
Yuba Community College District *C, A*

Colorado
Red Rocks Community College *A*

Connecticut
Three Rivers Community College *C, A*

Illinois
College of Lake County *C, A*

Michigan
Grand Rapids Community College *A*
Northern Michigan University *C, A, B*

New Mexico
San Juan College *C, A*

New York
Rochester Institute of Technology *B*

Ohio
Owens Community College
    Findlay Campus *C*
    Toledo *C*

Oklahoma
Rose State College *C, A*

Texas
Angelina College *C*
Collin County Community College
    District *C, A*

Houston Community College
    System *C, A*

| **Water resource engineering** |

Nevada
University of Nevada
    Reno *B, M, D*

New York
State University of New York
    Buffalo *M, D*

| **Water, wetlands, and marine management** |

Massachusetts
Worcester Polytechnic Institute *B*

North Carolina
Lenoir Community College *C, A*

Ohio
Ohio University *B*

Texas
Texas A&M University
    Galveston *B, M*

Washington
Spokane Community College *A*

| **Web page/multimedia design** |

Alabama
ITT Technical Institute
    Birmingham *A*
Shelton State Community College *C*

Arizona
Collins College *B*
Estrella Mountain Community College *C*

Arkansas
ITT Technical Institute
    Little Rock *A*
Southeast Arkansas College *A*

California
Art Institute
    of California - Orange County *A, B*
Art Institute of California - San
    Francisco *A, B*
Foothill College *C*
ITT Technical Institute
    San Bernardino *A*
MTI College of Business and
    Technology *C*
Ohlone College *C*
Otis College of Art and Design *B*
San Diego Mesa College *C, A*
Taft College *C*

Colorado
Colorado Technical University *C*

Florida
Full Sail Real World Education *A*
Herzing College
    Orlando *C*
ITT Technical Institute
    Ft. Lauderdale *A*
    Maitland *A*
Indian River Community College *A*
Miami-Dade Community College *A*
St. Petersburg College *C, A*
Stetson University *B*

Georgia
Atlanta College of Art *B*
West Georgia Technical College *C, A*

Idaho
Lewis-Clark State College *C*

Illinois
Moraine Valley Community College *A*
Oakton Community College *C*

Indiana
ITT Technical Institute
    Fort Wayne *A*
    Indianapolis *A*
Ivy Tech State College
    Southwest *A*
Sawyer College: Merrillville *M*
Vincennes University *A*

Iowa
Maharishi University of Management *B*
Southeastern Community College
    South Campus *A*

Kansas
Kansas City Kansas Community
    College *C, A*

Kentucky
Maysville Community College *C, A*

Louisiana
ITT Technical Institute
    St. Rose *A*

Maryland
Community College of Baltimore County
    Catonsville *A*
    Dundalk *A*

Massachusetts
Cape Cod Community College *A*
ITT Technical Institute
    Norwood *A*
Quinsigamond Community College *C*
Wentworth Institute of Technology *C*

Michigan
Baker College
    of Jackson *C*
    of Muskegon *A*
    of Port Huron *C, A*
Grace Bible College *B*
ITT Technical Institute
    Troy *A*
Jackson Community College *C, A*

Minnesota
Academy College *C, A*
Globe College *C, A, B*
Hennepin Technical College *C, A*
Hibbing Community College: A
    Technical and Community College *A*
Minneapolis Community and Technical
    College *C*
Minnesota State College - Southeast
    Technical *A*
Rasmussen College
    St. Cloud *C, A*
St. Paul College - A Community and
    Technical College *C*
University of Minnesota
    Crookston *B*

Missouri
ITT Technical Institute
    Arnold *A*
Ozarks Technical Community College *A*
Webster University *C*

Nebraska
ITT Technical Institute
    Omaha *A*
Nebraska Wesleyan University *B*
Vatterott College *A*

Nevada
ITT Technical Institute
    Henderson *A*

New Hampshire
Chester College of New England *B*
New Hampshire Community Technical
    College
    Nashua *C*
    Stratham *A*

New Mexico
New Mexico State University
    Alamogordo *C, A*

New York
Clinton Community College *C*
Jamestown Community College *C*
Marist College *B*
Rochester Institute of Technology *B*
State University of New York
    Buffalo *M, D*
    College of Agriculture and
        Technology at Morrisville *B*
Westchester Business Institute *A*

North Carolina
Carteret Community College *A*

North Dakota
Minot State University: Bottineau
    Campus *C*
North Dakota State College of Science *A*

Ohio
Central Ohio Technical College *A*
Davis College *C*
Lakeland Community College *C, A*
Owens Community College
    Findlay Campus *C, A*
    Toledo *C, A*
University of Cincinnati
    Raymond Walters College *C, A*

Oklahoma
Rose State College *C, A*

Pennsylvania
Albright College *B*
Allentown Business School *C, A*
Art Institute
    of Philadelphia *A, B*
Bradley Academy for the Visual Arts *A*
Bucks County Community College *C*
Community College of Allegheny
    County *C*
Consolidated School of Business
    Lancaster *A*
    York *A*
ITT Technical Institute
    Bensalem *A*
La Salle University *B*
Newport Business Institute *A*
Peirce College *C*
Point Park College *B*

Puerto Rico
Inter American University of Puerto Rico
    Bayamon Campus *C*

South Carolina
York Technical College *C*

South Dakota
Dakota Wesleyan University *B*

Tennessee
Draughons Junior College of Business:
    Nashville *A*
ITT Technical Institute
    Memphis *A*
Pellissippi State Technical Community
    College *C, A*

Texas
Del Mar College *C, A*
Eastfield College *C*
ITT Technical Institute
    Austin *A*
    Houston North *A*
Tyler Junior College *A*

Utah
ITT Technical Institute
    Murray *A*
LDS Business College *C*

Vermont
Champlain College *A, B*

Virginia
Art Institute
    of Washington *A, B*
ECPI College of Technology *C, A*
ECPI Technical College: Roanoke *A*
Piedmont Virginia Community
    College *C, A*

Washington
Bellevue Community College *C, A*
Clark College *C*
Clover Park Technical College *C, A*
ITT Technical Institute
    Bothell *A*
    Seattle *A*
North Seattle Community College *C*
South Seattle Community College *A*

West Virginia
Huntington Junior College *A*

Wisconsin
ITT Technical Institute
    Green Bay *A*

Web/multimedia management

Alabama
ITT Technical Institute
    Birmingham *A*
Shelton State Community College *C*

Arizona
Paradise Valley Community College *C*
University of Phoenix *C*

Arkansas
ITT Technical Institute
    Little Rock *A*
Southeast Arkansas College *C, A*
University of Arkansas
    Fort Smith *A, B*

California
Foothill College *C*
Grossmont Community College *C, A*
Santa Rosa Junior College *C*

Colorado
Colorado Technical University *C*

Florida
Herzing College
    Orlando *C*
St. Petersburg College *C, A*

Idaho
Lewis-Clark State College *C, A*

Illinois
Oakton Community College *C*
Parkland College *C, A*
Rend Lake College *C*

Indiana
ITT Technical Institute
    Fort Wayne *A*
    Indianapolis *A, B*
Sawyer College: Merrillville *C, A*
Vincennes University *A*

Iowa
Hamilton College
    Cedar Falls *A*
Southeastern Community College
    South Campus *A*

Louisiana
ITT Technical Institute
    St. Rose *A*

Maryland
Community College of Baltimore County
    Catonsville *A*

Massachusetts
Cape Cod Community College *A*
Springfield Technical Community
    College *C, A*

Michigan
Oakland Community College *C*

Minnesota
Art Institutes International
    Minnesota *A, B*
Globe College *C, A*
Itasca Community College *A*
Minnesota State College - Southeast
    Technical *A*

Missouri
ITT Technical Institute
    Arnold *A*
Ranken Technical College *A*

Nebraska
ITT Technical Institute
    Omaha *A*

Nevada
ITT Technical Institute
    Henderson *A*

New Hampshire
Daniel Webster College *C*
New Hampshire Community Technical
    College
    Nashua *C, A*

New Jersey
Union County College *C*

New York
Jamestown Community College *C*
Marist College *B*
Mohawk Valley Community
    College *C, A*
Rochester Institute of Technology *B*
State University of New York
    Buffalo *M, D*
    College of Agriculture and
        Technology at Morrisville *B*
Suffolk County Community
    College *C, A*
Westchester Community College *C*

North Carolina
Carteret Community College *C, A*
Fayetteville Technical Community
    College *A*
Pitt Community College *C, A*
Sandhills Community College *C, A*

North Dakota
Minot State University: Bottineau
    Campus *A*

Ohio
ITT Technical Institute
    Youngstown *A*
Owens Community College
    Toledo *C*
University of Cincinnati
    Raymond Walters College *C, A*

Oklahoma
Rose State College *A*

Oregon
Pioneer Pacific College *C, A*
Portland Community College *C*
Southwestern Oregon Community
    College *C, A*

Pennsylvania
Allentown Business School *C, A*
Consolidated School of Business
    Lancaster *A*
    York *A*
Douglas School of Business *A*
ICM School of Business & Medical
    Careers *A*
Montgomery County Community
    College *C, A*
Point Park College *C*

South Carolina
Southern Wesleyan University *B*
York Technical College *C*

Tennessee
ITT Technical Institute
    Memphis *A*

Texas
North Harris Montgomery Community
    College District *C*
St. Philip's College *C, A*
Temple College *C, A*

Utah
LDS Business College *A*

Vermont
Champlain College *A, B*

Virginia
ECPI College of Technology *C, A*
ECPI Technical College: Roanoke *A*

Washington
Everett Community College *A*
ITT Technical Institute
    Bothell *A*
North Seattle Community College *C*
Peninsula College *C*

Wisconsin
Milwaukee Area Technical College *A*

Welding technology

Alabama
Douglas MacArthur State Technical
    College *C*
Harry M. Ayers State Technical
    College *C*
Shelton State Community College *C, A*

Arizona
Arizona Western College *C, A*

Arkansas
University of Arkansas
    Fort Smith *C, A*

California
Antelope Valley College *C, A*
College of the Canyons *C, A*
Long Beach City College *C, A*
Shasta College *C, A*
Victor Valley College *C, A*

Florida
Gulf Coast Community College *C*
Palm Beach Community College *C*

Georgia
Albany Technical College *C*
Southwest Georgia Technical College *C*
West Georgia Technical College *C*

Idaho
Eastern Idaho Technical College *C, A*
Lewis-Clark State College *C, A*

Illinois
Black Hawk College *C*
College of DuPage *C*
College of Lake County *C*
Heartland Community College *C, A*
Kaskaskia College *C*
Moraine Valley Community College *C*
Rend Lake College *C*
Rock Valley College *C*
Waubonsee Community College *C*

Indiana
Vincennes University *C*

Iowa
Indian Hills Community College *C*
Northwest Iowa Community College *C*
Western Iowa Tech Community
    College *C*

Kentucky
Somerset Community College *C*

Louisiana
Delgado Community College *C*
Nunez Community College *C*

Michigan
Ferris State University *A*
Grand Rapids Community College *C, A*
Jackson Community College *C, A*
Montcalm Community College *C*
Oakland Community College *C, A*

Minnesota
Dakota County Technical College *C*
Hennepin Technical College *A*
Northland Community & Technical
    College *C, A*
St. Paul College - A Community and
    Technical College *C*

Mississippi
Itawamba Community College *C*

Missouri
Jefferson College *C, A*
Moberly Area Community College *C, A*
Ozarks Technical Community
    College *C, A*

Montana
Montana Tech of the University of
    Montana *B*

Nevada
Community College of Southern
    Nevada *C, A*
Western Nevada Community
    College *C, A*

New Mexico
Albuquerque Technical-Vocational
    Institute *C*
San Juan College *C, A*

New York
Mohawk Valley Community
    College *C, A*
State University of New York
    College of Technology at
    Alfred *C, A*

North Carolina
Beaufort County Community College *A*
Bladen Community College *C*
Cape Fear Community College *C, A*
Davidson County Community College *C*
Fayetteville Technical Community
    College *C, A*
Isothermal Community College *C*
Lenoir Community College *C, A*
Surry Community College *C*
Tri-County Community College *C*
Wilson Technical Community College *C*

North Dakota
Bismarck State College *C, A*
North Dakota State College of
    Science *C, A*

Ohio
North Central State College *C*
Owens Community College
    Findlay Campus *C, A*
    Toledo *C, A*

Oklahoma
Tulsa Welding School *C, A*

Oregon
Portland Community College *C*

Pennsylvania
Community College of Allegheny
    County *C, A*
Delaware County Community College *C*
Northampton County Area Community
    College *C*
Pennsylvania College of
    Technology *C, A*

South Carolina
Piedmont Technical College *C, A*

York Technical College *C, A*

Texas
Angelina College *C, A*
Houston Community College System *C*
Kilgore College *C*
Midland College *C, A*
North Harris Montgomery Community
    College District *C, A*
Paris Junior College *C, A*
Ranger College *C, A*
St. Philip's College *C, A*
Temple College *C*
Western Texas College *C, A*

Utah
Utah Valley State College *C, A*

Virginia
Eastern Shore Community College *C*

Washington
Centralia College *C, A*
Clark College *C, A*
Clover Park Technical College *C*
Edmonds Community College *C, A*
Lower Columbia College *A*
South Seattle Community College *C, A*
Walla Walla Community College *C, A*

Wisconsin
Nicolet Area Technical College *A*
Western Wisconsin Technical College *C*

Wyoming
Central Wyoming College *C, A*

Western European studies

District of Columbia
American University *B*
Georgetown University *M*

Illinois
Illinois Wesleyan University *B*

Indiana
Indiana University
    Bloomington *M*

Iowa
Central College *B*

Kansas
Central Christian College *A, B*

Maryland
Johns Hopkins University *B*
St. John's College *B, M*

Massachusetts
Amherst College *B*
Harvard College *B*
Tufts University *B, M*

Michigan
University of Michigan *B*

Nebraska
University of Nebraska
    Lincoln *B*

New Hampshire
University of New Hampshire *B*

New York
Bard College *B*
City University of New York
    Brooklyn College *B*
Eugene Lang College/New School
    University *B*
New York University *M, D*
United States Military Academy *B*

Ohio
College of Wooster *B*
Denison University *B*
Ohio State University
    Columbus Campus *B*

Pennsylvania
University of Pittsburgh *C*

Vermont
Bennington College *B*
Marlboro College *B*

Washington
Seattle University *B*

Wildlife biology

Arizona
Eastern Arizona College *A*

California
Feather River College *C, A*

Kansas
Baker University *B*
Barton County Community College *A*
Kansas State University *B*

New Hampshire
University of New Hampshire *B*

Pennsylvania
Keystone College *A*

Texas
Southwest Texas State University *B*

Wildlife/wilderness management

Alabama
Auburn University *B, M, D*

Alaska
Alaska Pacific University *B, M*
University of Alaska
    Fairbanks *B, M*

Arizona
Northern Arizona University *B*
Prescott College *B, M*
University of Arizona *B*

Arkansas
Arkansas State University *B*
Arkansas Tech University *B*
University of Arkansas
    Monticello *B*

California
Cerritos Community College *A*
Feather River College *C, A*
Humboldt State University *B*
Modesto Junior College *C, A*
Napa Valley College *C, A*
San Joaquin Delta College *A*
University of California
    Davis *B*

Colorado
Colorado State University *B, M, D*

Delaware
Delaware State University *B*
University of Delaware *B*

District of Columbia
University of the District of Columbia *A*

Florida
South Florida Community College *A*
University of Florida *B, M, D*

Georgia
Abraham Baldwin Agricultural
    College *A*
University of Georgia *B*

Idaho
College of Southern Idaho *A*
North Idaho College *A*
University of Idaho *B, M*

Illinois
Lake Land College *A*

Shawnee Community College *A*
Southeastern Illinois College *A*

Indiana
Purdue University *B, M, D*

Iowa
Ellsworth Community College *A*
Iowa State University *M, D*

Kansas
Garden City Community College *A*
Pittsburg State University *B*
Pratt Community College *A*
Seward County Community College *A*

Kentucky
Murray State University *B*

Louisiana
Louisiana State University and
 Agricultural and Mechanical
 College *B, M, D*
McNeese State University *B*

Maine
University of Maine *B, M, D*

Maryland
Frostburg State University *B, M*

Massachusetts
University of Massachusetts
 Amherst *B, M, D*

Michigan
Bay de Noc Community College *C*
Michigan State University *B, M, D*
University of Michigan *B, M*

Minnesota
St. Cloud State University *B*
University of Minnesota
 Crookston *B*
 Twin Cities *B, M, D*
Vermilion Community College *A*

Mississippi
Mississippi State University *B, M*

Missouri
East Central College *A*
Northwest Missouri State University *B*
Southwest Missouri State University *B*
University of Missouri
 Columbia *B, M, D*

Montana
Miles Community College *A*
Montana State University
 Bozeman *M, D*
University of Montana-Missoula *B, M, D*
University of Montana: Western *B*

Nebraska
University of Nebraska
 Lincoln *B, M*

Nevada
University of Nevada
 Reno *B*

New Hampshire
University of New Hampshire *B, M*

New Jersey
Rowan University *B*

New Mexico
Eastern New Mexico University *B*
New Mexico State University *B, M*
Western New Mexico University *B*

New York
Paul Smith's College *A*
State University of New York
 College of Agriculture and
 Technology at Cobleskill *A*
 College of Environmental Science
 and Forestry *B, M, D*

North Carolina
Haywood Community College *A*

North Carolina State University *B, M*

North Dakota
Minot State University: Bottineau
 Campus *A*
North Dakota State University *B*

Ohio
Hocking Technical College *A*
Ohio State University
 Columbus Campus *B*
University of Findlay *B*

Oklahoma
Eastern Oklahoma State College *A*
Northeastern Oklahoma Agricultural and
 Mechanical College *A*
Oklahoma State University *B, M, D*
Southeastern Oklahoma State
 University *B*
Western Oklahoma State College *A*

Oregon
Central Oregon Community College *A*
Oregon State University *B, M, D*

Pennsylvania
California University of Pennsylvania *B*
Delaware Valley College *B*
Keystone College *A*
Muhlenberg College *B*
Penn State
 Abington *B*
 Altoona *B*
 Beaver *B*
 Berks *B*
 Delaware County *B*
 Dubois *A, B*
 Erie, The Behrend College *B*
 Fayette *B*
 Hazleton *B*
 Lehigh Valley *B*
 McKeesport *B*
 Mont Alto *B*
 New Kensington *B*
 Schuylkill - Capital College *B*
 Shenango *B*
 University Park *C, B, M, D*
 Wilkes-Barre *B*
 Worthington Scranton *B*
 York *B*

Puerto Rico
University of Puerto Rico
 Humacao *B*

South Dakota
South Dakota State University *B, M*

Tennessee
Roane State Community College *A*
Tennessee Technological University *B*
University of Tennessee
 Knoxville *M*
 Martin *B*

Texas
Southwest Texas State University *B*
Stephen F. Austin State University *B*
Sul Ross State University *B, M*
Tarleton State University *B*
Texas A&M University *B, M, D*
Texas A&M University
 Commerce *B*
 Kingsville *B, M, D*
Texas Tech University *B, M, D*
West Texas A&M University *B*

Utah
Brigham Young University *B, M*
Dixie State College of Utah *A*
Snow College *A*
Utah State University *B, M, D*

Vermont
Sterling College *A, B*
University of Vermont *B, M*

Virginia
Virginia Polytechnic Institute and State
 University *B, M, D*

Washington
Grays Harbor College *A*
Spokane Community College *A*
University of Washington *B*
Washington State University *B*

West Virginia
West Virginia University *B, M*

Wisconsin
Northland College *B*
University of Wisconsin
 Madison *B, M, D*
 Stevens Point *B*

Wyoming
Casper College *A*
Eastern Wyoming College *A*
Western Wyoming Community
 College *A*

Women's studies

Alabama
Huntingdon College *B*
University of Alabama *M*

Arizona
Arizona State University *B*
Prescott College *B, M*
University of Arizona *B, M*

California
California State University
 Chico *B*
 Fresno *B*
 Fullerton *B*
 Long Beach *C, B*
 Monterey Bay *B*
 San Marcos *B*
Claremont McKenna College *B*
Diablo Valley College *C*
Foothill College *A*
Irvine Valley College *A*
Loyola Marymount University *B*
Mills College *B*
Monterey Peninsula College *A*
Occidental College *B*
Pitzer College *B*
Pomona College *B*
St. Mary's College of California *B*
San Diego State University *B, M*
San Francisco State University *B, M*
Scripps College *B*
Sonoma State University *B*
Southwestern College *A*
Stanford University *B*
University of California
 Berkeley *B*
 Davis *B*
 Irvine *B*
 Los Angeles *B, M, D*
 Riverside *B*
 San Diego *B*
 Santa Barbara *B*
 Santa Cruz *B*
University of San Francisco *C*
University of Southern California *B, T*
West Valley College *A*

Colorado
Colorado College *B*
Regis University *B*
University of Colorado
 Boulder *B*
University of Denver *B*

Connecticut
Connecticut College *B*
Manchester Community College *A*
Southern Connecticut State University *M*
Trinity College *B*
University of Connecticut *B*

University of Hartford *B*
Wesleyan University *B*
Yale University *B*

Delaware
University of Delaware *B*

District of Columbia
American University *B*
George Washington University *M*
Georgetown University *B*

Florida
Eckerd College *B*
Florida Atlantic University *M*
Florida International University *B*
Florida State University *B*
Manatee Community College *A*
Polk Community College *A*
University of Miami *B*
University of South Florida *B, M*
University of Tampa *C*

Georgia
Agnes Scott College *B*
Emory University *B, D*
Oxford College of Emory University *B*
Spelman College *B*
University of Georgia *C, B*

Illinois
De Paul University *C, B*
Knox College *B*
Loyola University of Chicago *B, M*
Northeastern Illinois University *B*
Northwestern University *B*
Roosevelt University *C, B, M*
Western Illinois University *B*

Indiana
DePauw University *B*
Earlham College *B*
Goshen College *B*
Indiana University
 Bloomington *B*
 South Bend *B*
Indiana University-Purdue University
 Fort Wayne *C, A, B*
Manchester College *B*

Iowa
Cornell College *B*
Iowa State University *B*
St. Ambrose University *C*
University of Iowa *B, D*
University of Northern Iowa *M*

Kansas
University of Kansas *B*
Wichita State University *B*

Kentucky
Berea College *B*
University of Louisville *B*

Louisiana
Louisiana State University and
 Agricultural and Mechanical
 College *B*
Tulane University *B*

Maine
Bates College *B*
Bowdoin College *B*
Colby College *B*
University of Maine *B*
University of Maine
 Farmington *B*
University of Southern Maine *B*

Maryland
Goucher College *B*
Howard Community College *A*
Johns Hopkins University *B*
Towson University *B, M*
University of Maryland
 College Park *B, M, D*
 University College *C*

Massachusetts

Amherst College *B*
Clark University *D*
College of the Holy Cross *B*
Fisher College *A*
Hampshire College *B*
Harvard College *B*
Mount Holyoke College *B*
Simmons College *B*
Simon's Rock College of Bard *B*
Smith College *B*
Suffolk University *B*
Tufts University *B*
University of Massachusetts
    Amherst *B*
    Boston *B*
Wellesley College *B*
Wheaton College *B*

Michigan

Eastern Michigan University *B, M*
Michigan State University *B*
Oakland University *B*
University of Michigan *B*
Wayne State University *B*
Western Michigan University *B*

Minnesota

Augsburg College *B*
Carleton College *B*
Century Community and Technical
    College *C*
College of St. Catherine *B*
Gustavus Adolphus College *B*
Hamline University *B*
Macalester College *B*
Metropolitan State University *B*
Minneapolis Community and Technical
    College *C*
Minnesota State University
    Mankato *B, M*
St. Olaf College *B*
University of Minnesota
    Duluth *B*
    Morris *B*
    Twin Cities *B*
University of St. Thomas *B*
Winona State University *A*

Missouri

Washington University in St. Louis *B*
Webster University *C*

Montana

University of Montana-Missoula *B*

Nebraska

Bellevue University *B*
Nebraska Wesleyan University *B*
University of Nebraska
    Lincoln *B*

Nevada

University of Nevada
    Las Vegas *B*
    Reno *B*

New Hampshire

Dartmouth College *B*
University of New Hampshire *B*

New Jersey

Caldwell College *C*
The College of New Jersey *B*
Drew University *B, M, D*
Montclair State University *B*
Rowan University *B*
Rutgers, The State University of New
    Jersey
    New Brunswick Regional
        Campus *B, M*
    Newark Regional Campus *B*
William Paterson University of New
    Jersey *B*

New Mexico

University of New Mexico *B*

New York

Barnard College *B*
City University of New York
    Brooklyn College *B*
    College of Staten Island *B*
    Hunter College *B*
    Queens College *B*
Colgate University *B*
College of New Rochelle *B*
Columbia University
    Columbia College *B*
Cornell University *B*
Eugene Lang College/New School
    University *B*
Fordham University *B*
Hamilton College *B*
Hobart and William Smith Colleges *B*
Marymount College of Fordham
    University *B*
New York University *B*
Sarah Lawrence College *B, M*
Skidmore College *B*
State University of New York
    Albany *B, M*
    Buffalo *B, M*
    College at Brockport *B*
    New Paltz *B*
    Oswego *B*
    Purchase *B*
    Stony Brook *B*
Suffolk County Community College *A*
Syracuse University *B*
Tompkins-Cortland Community
    College *A*
University of Rochester *B*
Vassar College *B*
Wells College *B*

North Carolina

Duke University *B*
East Carolina University *B*
Guilford College *B*
Southeastern Baptist Theological
    Seminary *C, M*
University of North Carolina
    Chapel Hill *B*
    Greensboro *B*

Ohio

Antioch College *B*
Bowling Green State University *B*
Case Western Reserve University *B*
College of Wooster *B*
Denison University *B*
Oberlin College *B*
Ohio State University
    Columbus Campus *B, M*
Ohio University *C*
Ohio Wesleyan University *B*
Owens Community College
    Findlay Campus *A*
    Toledo *A*
University of Cincinnati
    Raymond Walters College *C*
University of Toledo *B*
Wright State University *B*

Oklahoma

University of Oklahoma *B*

Oregon

Oregon State University *C*
Portland State University *B*
University of Oregon *B*

Pennsylvania

Albright College *B*
Allegheny College *B*
Bucknell University *B*
Chatham College *B*
Dickinson College *B*
Gettysburg College *B*

Penn State
    Abington *B*
    Altoona *B*
    Beaver *B*
    Berks *B*
    Delaware County *B*
    Dubois *B*
    Erie, The Behrend College *B*
    Fayette *B*
    Hazleton *B*
    Lehigh Valley *B*
    McKeesport *B*
    Mont Alto *B*
    New Kensington *B*
    Schuylkill - Capital College *B*
    Shenango *B*
    University Park *C, B*
    Wilkes-Barre *B*
    Worthington Scranton *B*
    York *B*
Rosemont College *B*
Temple University *B*
University of Pennsylvania *B*
University of Pittsburgh *C*

Rhode Island

Brown University *B*
Rhode Island College *B*
University of Rhode Island *B*

South Carolina

University of South Carolina *B*

Tennessee

University of Memphis *M*
University of Tennessee
    Knoxville *B*

Texas

El Paso Community College *A*
Rice University *B*
South Texas Community College *A*
Southwestern University *B*
Texas Woman's University *M*
University of Texas
    Austin *M*
    Dallas *B*

Utah

University of Utah *B*

Vermont

Burlington College *B*
Goddard College *B*
Marlboro College *B*
Middlebury College *B*
University of Vermont *B*

Virginia

College of William and Mary *B*
Hollins University *B*
Mary Baldwin College *B*
Old Dominion University *B*
Randolph-Macon College *B*
University of Richmond *B*

Washington

Gonzaga University *B*
Pacific Lutheran University *B*
University of Washington *B, M, D*
Washington State University *B*

Wisconsin

Beloit College *B*
Lawrence University *B*
Marquette University *B*
Ripon College *B*
University of Wisconsin
    Whitewater *B*

Wyoming

Casper College *A*
University of Wyoming *B*

Wood science/pulp/paper technology

Massachusetts

University of Massachusetts
    Amherst *B*

Mississippi

Mississippi State University *B, M*

New York

State University of New York
    College of Agriculture and
        Technology at Morrisville *A*

North Carolina

North Carolina State University *B*

Pennsylvania

Penn State
    Abington *B*
    Altoona *B*
    Beaver *B*
    Berks *B*
    Delaware County *B*
    Dubois *B*
    Erie, The Behrend College *B*
    Fayette *B*
    Hazleton *B*
    Lehigh Valley *B*
    McKeesport *B*
    Mont Alto *B*
    New Kensington *B*
    Schuylkill - Capital College *B*
    Shenango *B*
    University Park *B*
    Worthington Scranton *B*
    York *B*
Pennsylvania College of Technology *A*

South Carolina

York Technical College *C*

Woodworking

Alabama

Gadsden State Community College *C*
George C. Wallace State Community
    College
    Dothan *C*
Harry M. Ayers State Technical
    College *C*
Northwest-Shoals Community
    College *C, A*
Shelton State Community College *C, A*
Wallace Community College: Sparks
    Campus *C*
Wallace State Community College at
    Hanceville *C, A*

Alaska

University of Alaska
    Anchorage *C, A*

Arkansas

Phillips Community College of the
    University of Arkansas *C*

California

Bakersfield College *A*
College of the Redwoods *C*
Laney College *C, A*
Palomar College *C, A*
San Joaquin Delta College *C, A*
Sierra College *C, A*

Colorado

Red Rocks Community College *C, A*

Idaho

College of Southern Idaho *C, A*

Illinois

Illinois Eastern Community Colleges
    Olney Central College *A*

Indiana
Ivy Tech State College
Bloomington *C, A*
Central Indiana *C, A*
Columbus *C, A*
Eastcentral *C, A*
Kokomo *C, A*
Lafayette *C, A*
Northcentral *C, A*
Northeast *A*
Northwest *A*
Southcentral *C, A*
Southwest *C, A*
Wabash Valley *C, A*
Whitewater *C, A*

Iowa
Des Moines Area Community College *A*
North Iowa Area Community College *C*

Kansas
Allen County Community College *A*
Fort Scott Community College *A*
Pittsburg State University *A, B*

Michigan
Bay de Noc Community College *C*
Oakland Community College *A*

Minnesota
Dakota County Technical College *C*
Hennepin Technical College *C, A*
St. Paul College - A Community and
Technical College *C*

Mississippi
Northwest Mississippi Community
College *C*

Nebraska
Mid Plains Community College Area *A*

New Mexico
Santa Fe Community College *C*

New York
Rochester Institute of
Technology *A, B, M*
State University of New York
College of Agriculture and
Technology at Morrisville *A*

North Carolina
Haywood Community College *C, A*
Mayland Community College *C*
Rockingham Community College *A*
Tri-County Community College *C*

Ohio
University of Rio Grande *C, A*

Pennsylvania
Bucks County Community College *A*
Pennsylvania College of Technology *A*

South Dakota
Western Dakota Technical Institute *C*

Texas
Austin Community College *C*

Utah
Southern Utah University *A*

Washington
Peninsula College *C, A*
Seattle Central Community College *A*

Wisconsin
Fox Valley Technical College *C*
Western Wisconsin Technical College *C*

Word processing

Arizona
Paradise Valley Community
College *C, A*

Arkansas
East Arkansas Community College *C*

California
Long Beach City College *C, A*
Ohlone College *C*

Illinois
Southeastern Illinois College *C*

Indiana
Sawyer College: Merrillville *C, A*

Iowa
American Institute of Business *C*

Maryland
Frederick Community College *C*

New York
State University of New York
College of Agriculture and
Technology at Morrisville *C*

North Carolina
Beaufort County Community College *C*
Carteret Community College *C*

Ohio
Kent State University *C, A*

Pennsylvania
Consolidated School of Business
Lancaster *C, A*
York *C, A*
Newport Business Institute *A*
Penn State
Lehigh Valley *B*

South Carolina
York Technical College *C*

Virginia
ECPI College of Technology *C, A*
ECPI Technical College: Roanoke *A*

Work/family studies

Arizona
Estrella Mountain Community College *C*

Kentucky
Morehead State University *A, B*

North Dakota
North Dakota State University *B, M*

Ohio
Ursuline College *B*
Youngstown State University *B*

Texas
Lubbock Christian University *B*

Utah
Brigham Young University *B*

Youth ministry

Arkansas
Central Baptist College *B*
Harding University *B*
John Brown University *B*

California
Azusa Pacific University *M*
Master's College *B*
San Jose Christian College *B*
Vanguard University of Southern
California *B*

Colorado
Colorado Christian University *B*

Georgia
Emmanuel College *B*
Toccoa Falls College *B*

Illinois
Lincoln Christian College and
Seminary *B, M*
Trinity International University *B*

Indiana
Goshen College *B*
Grace College *B*

Iowa
Dordt College *B*
Emmaus Bible College *B*

Kansas
Barclay College *B*
Bethel College *C*
Central Christian College *A*
MidAmerica Nazarene University *B*
Tabor College *B*

Maryland
Mount St. Mary's College *C*

Massachusetts
Gordon College *B*

Michigan
Grace Bible College *B*
William Tyndale College *B*

Minnesota
Bethel College *B*
Crossroads College *B*
Crown College *B*
Northwestern College *B*

Missouri
Calvary Bible College *B*

Nebraska
Concordia University *B*

New Jersey
College of St. Elizabeth *C*

North Carolina
Gardner-Webb University *B*
Piedmont Baptist College *B*

Ohio
Circleville Bible College *B*
Malone College *B, M*

Oklahoma
Oklahoma Christian University of
Science and Arts *B*
Oklahoma City University *B*
Southwestern Christian University *B*

Oregon
Multnomah Bible College *B*
Western Baptist College *B*

Pennsylvania
Baptist Bible College of Pennsylvania *B*
Geneva College *B*

South Carolina
Columbia International University *B*

South Dakota
Dakota Wesleyan University *B*

Tennessee
Freed-Hardeman University *B*
King College *B*
Union University *B*

Texas
East Texas Baptist University *B*
Texas Lutheran University *B*

Virginia
Eastern Mennonite University *B*

Washington
Northwest College *B*
Trinity Lutheran College *C, B*

Youth services

Minnesota
Crown College *B*

New York
Dutchess Community College *C*

Zoology

Alabama
Auburn University *B, M, D*

Alaska
University of Alaska
Fairbanks *D*

Arizona
Northern Arizona University *B*

Arkansas
Arkansas State University *B*
Arkansas State University
Beebe *A*

California
California State Polytechnic University:
Pomona *B*
California State University
Stanislaus *B*
Cerritos Community College *A*
Citrus College *A*
East Los Angeles College *C*
Humboldt State University *B*
Palomar College *C, A*
San Diego State University *B, M*
San Francisco State University *B*
San Joaquin Delta College *A*
San Jose State University *B*
University of California
Davis *B*
Santa Barbara *B, M*
Ventura College *A*

Colorado
Colorado State University *B, M, D*

Connecticut
Connecticut College *B, M*
Southern Connecticut State University *B*
University of Connecticut *M, D*

District of Columbia
George Washington University *M, D*

Florida
Palm Beach Community College *A*
Pensacola Junior College *A*
University of Florida *B, M, D*

Hawaii
University of Hawaii
Manoa *B, M, D*

Idaho
Brigham Young University - Idaho *B*
College of Southern Idaho *A*
Idaho State University *B*
North Idaho College *A*
University of Idaho *B, M, D*

Illinois
Black Hawk College
East Campus *A*
Olivet Nazarene University *B*
Southern Illinois University
Carbondale *B, M, D*
Western Illinois University *M*

Indiana
Ball State University *B*
Indiana University
Bloomington *M, D*

Iowa
Iowa State University *B, M, D*
Marshalltown Community College *A*

Kansas
Independence Community College *A*
Pratt Community College *A*

Maine
College of the Atlantic *B*
University of Maine *B, M, D*

Maryland

University of Maryland
  College Park *M, D*

Massachusetts

Harvard College *B*

Michigan

Andrews University *B*
Michigan State University *B, M, D*
Northern Michigan University *B*
University of Michigan *B, D*

Minnesota

Minnesota State University
  Mankato *B, M, T*
St. Cloud State University *B*
University of Minnesota
  Twin Cities *M, D*

Mississippi

Mary Holmes College *A*

Missouri

East Central College *A*
Northwest Missouri State University *B*

Montana

University of Montana-Missoula *B, M, D*

New Hampshire

University of New Hampshire *B, M, D*

New Jersey

Rowan University *B*
Rutgers, The State University of New
  Jersey
  Newark Regional Campus *B*

New Mexico

Western New Mexico University *B*

New York

Cornell University *B, M, D*
State University of New York
  College of Environmental Science
    and Forestry *B, M, D*
  Oswego *B*

North Carolina

Duke University *D*
Mars Hill College *B*
Methodist College *A, B*
North Carolina State University *B, M, D*

North Dakota

North Dakota State University *B, M, D*

Ohio

Kent State University *B*
Kent State University
  Stark Campus *B*
Miami University
  Middletown Campus *A*
  Oxford Campus *B, M, D*
Ohio State University
  Columbus Campus *B*
Ohio University *B, M, D*
Ohio Wesleyan University *B*
University of Akron *B*
Wittenberg University *B*

Oklahoma

Carl Albert State College *A*
Langston University *B*
Northern Oklahoma College *A*
Oklahoma State University *B, M, D*
Southeastern Oklahoma State
  University *B*
University of Oklahoma *B, M, D*

Oregon

Chemeketa Community College *A*
Oregon State University *B, M, D*

Pennsylvania

Juniata College *B*

Rhode Island

University of Rhode Island *B, M, D*

South Carolina

Clemson University *M, D*

Tennessee

Bethel College *B*
University of Tennessee
  Knoxville *B, M, D*

Texas

Hill College *A*
Laredo Community College *A*
South Plains College *A*
Southwest Texas State University *B, T*
Tarleton State University *B, T*
Texas A&M University *B, M, D*
Texas Tech University *B, M, D*
Texas Woman's University *B*
University of Texas
  Austin *B, M, D*

Utah

Brigham Young University *B, M, D*
Snow College *A*
Southern Utah University *B*
Utah State University *B, M*
Weber State University *B*

Vermont

University of Vermont *B*

Washington

Centralia College *A*
Eastern Washington University *B*
University of Washington *B, M, D*
Washington State University *B, M, D*
Western Washington University *B*

Wisconsin

University of Wisconsin
  Madison *B, M, D*

Wyoming

Sheridan College *A*
University of Wyoming *B, M, D*

Special academic programs

Alabama

Alabama Agricultural and Mechanical
University
Alabama Southern Community College
Auburn University
Auburn University at Montgomery
Bevill State Community College
Bishop State Community College
Calhoun Community College
Chattahoochee Valley Community
College
Community College of the Air Force
George C. Wallace State Community
College
Dothan
Selma
Heritage Christian University
Jacksonville State University
James H. Faulkner State Community
College
Jefferson State Community College
Judson College
Lawson State Community College
Lurleen B. Wallace Junior College
Northeast Alabama Community College
Northwest-Shoals Community College
Samford University
Shelton State Community College
Snead State Community College
Southern Christian University
Spring Hill College
Stillman College
Troy State University in Montgomery
University of Alabama
University of Alabama
Huntsville
University of Mobile
University of Montevallo
University of North Alabama
University of South Alabama
University of West Alabama
Virginia College
Wallace State Community College at
Hanceville

Alaska

Alaska Pacific University
University of Alaska
Fairbanks

Arizona

Arizona State University
Arizona Western College
DeVry University
Phoenix
Estrella Mountain Community College
Gateway Community College
Northern Arizona University

Paradise Valley Community College
Pima Community College
Rio Salado College
University of Phoenix
Yavapai College

Arkansas

Arkansas State University
Arkansas State University
Beebe
Lyon College
University of Arkansas
University of Arkansas
Fort Smith
Little Rock
University of Central Arkansas

California

Antelope Valley College
Antioch Southern California
Los Angeles
Art Center College of Design
Azusa Pacific University
Barstow College
California Baptist University
California State University
Bakersfield
Dominguez Hills
Fresno
Fullerton
Hayward
Los Angeles
Sacramento
Stanislaus
Chapman University
Christian Heritage College
Claremont McKenna College
Coastline Community College
Coleman College
College of the Canyons
Concordia University
DeVry University
Fremont
Pomona
West Hills
Diablo Valley College
East Los Angeles College
Fresno Pacific University
Golden Gate University
Golden West College
Grossmont Community College
Holy Names College
Hope International University
Irvine Valley College
La Sierra University
Las Positas College
Long Beach City College
Los Angeles Harbor College
Los Angeles Southwest College
Los Angeles Trade and Technical College
Menlo College
MiraCosta College
Mount St. Mary's College
National University
Occidental College
Pacific Oaks College
Patten University
Pepperdine University
Platt College
Newport Beach
Ontario
St. Mary's College of California
San Diego City College
San Diego Mesa College
San Francisco State University
San Jose Christian College
San Jose State University
Santa Monica College
Scripps College
Simpson College
Sonoma State University
Southern California Institute of
Architecture
Travel University International

University of California
Berkeley
Davis
Riverside
San Diego
Santa Barbara
University of La Verne
University of San Francisco
University of Southern California
University of the Pacific
Vanguard University of Southern
California
Vista Community College
Whittier College
Woodbury University

Colorado

Colorado Christian University
Colorado School of Mines
Colorado State University
Colorado State University
Pueblo
Colorado Technical University
DeVry University
Denver
DeVry University: Colorado Springs
Fort Lewis College
IntelliTec College
Jones International University
Mesa State College
Metropolitan State College of Denver
National American University
Denver
Red Rocks Community College
Regis University
Remington College
Colorado Springs
Trinidad State Junior College
University of Colorado
Boulder
Denver
University of Denver
Westwood College of Technology
South

Connecticut

Albertus Magnus College
Capital Community College
Connecticut College
Eastern Connecticut State University
Gateway Community College
International College of Hospitality
Management
Quinebaug Valley Community College
Sacred Heart University
Southern Connecticut State University
Teikyo Post University
Trinity College
University of Bridgeport
University of Connecticut
University of New Haven
Western Connecticut State University
Yale University

Delaware

Delaware State University
Goldey-Beacom College
University of Delaware
Wilmington College

District of Columbia

American University
Catholic University of America
Gallaudet University
George Washington University
Howard University
Potomac College
Strayer University
Trinity College

Florida

Barry University
Bethune-Cookman College
Broward Community College

Chipola Junior College
DeVry University
Miramar
Orlando
Eckerd College
Edward Waters College
Florida Agricultural and Mechanical
University
Florida Atlantic University
Florida Gulf Coast University
Florida Institute of Technology
Florida Metropolitan University
Orlando College North
Tampa College
Florida State University
Gulf Coast Community College
Hillsborough Community College
Indian River Community College
International Academy of Design and
Technology
International College
Jacksonville University
Jones College
Lake City Community College
Manatee Community College
Miami-Dade Community College
Northwood University
Florida Campus
Nova Southeastern University
Palm Beach Atlantic University
Pasco-Hernando Community College
Pensacola Junior College
Polk Community College
Rollins College
St. Petersburg College
Schiller International University
Seminole Community College
South Florida Community College
Stetson University
Tampa Technical Institute
University of Florida
University of Miami
University of North Florida
University of South Florida
University of West Florida
Warner Southern College

Georgia

Agnes Scott College
Clark Atlanta University
DeVry University
Alpharetta
Atlanta
Emory University
Georgia College and State University
Georgia Institute of Technology
Georgia Perimeter College
Georgia Southern University
Georgia Southwestern State University
Mercer University
Middle Georgia College
Morris Brown College
Oglethorpe University
Piedmont College
Reinhardt College
South University
State University of West Georgia
Thomas University
Truett-McConnell College
University of Georgia
Valdosta State University

Hawaii

Brigham Young University-Hawaii
Chaminade University of Honolulu
Hawaii Pacific University
University of Hawaii
Manoa
West Oahu

Idaho

Brigham Young University - Idaho
Idaho State University
Lewis-Clark State College

Northwest Nazarene University
University of Idaho

Illinois

American Academy of Art
Augustana College
Benedictine University
Black Hawk College
Blackburn College
Bradley University
City Colleges of Chicago
    Malcolm X College
College of DuPage
College of Lake County
De Paul University
DeVry University
    Addison
    Chicago
    Tinley Park
Dominican University
Elgin Community College
Elmhurst College
Greenville College
Illinois Institute of Art
Illinois Institute of Art
Illinois State University
Illinois Wesleyan University
Judson College
Kaskaskia College
Kendall College
Lewis University
Lincoln Land Community College
Loyola University of Chicago
McHenry County College
McKendree College
National-Louis University
North Central College
North Park University
Northwestern University
Olivet Nazarene University
Parkland College
Quincy University
Robert Morris College: Chicago
Roosevelt University
Rush University
St. Xavier University
Shimer College
Southern Illinois University Carbondale
Southern Illinois University Edwardsville
Southwestern Illinois College
Triton College
University of Chicago
University of Illinois
    Chicago
    Urbana-Champaign
University of St. Francis
Waubonsee Community College

Indiana

American Conservatory of Music
Anderson University
Bethel College
Calumet College of St. Joseph
Earlham College
Holy Cross College
Huntington College
Indiana Institute of Technology
Indiana State University
Indiana University
    Bloomington
    Kokomo
    Northwest
    South Bend
    Southeast
Indiana Wesleyan University
Marian College
Martin University
Michiana College
Oakland City University
Professional Careers Institute
Purdue University
    Calumet
Rose-Hulman Institute of Technology
St. Joseph's College
Saint Mary's College

St. Mary-of-the-Woods College
Taylor University: Fort Wayne
University of Evansville
University of Indianapolis
University of Notre Dame
Valparaiso University

Iowa

Buena Vista University
Clarke College
Clinton Community College
Coe College
Cornell College
Drake University
Graceland University
Grand View College
Grinnell College
Hamilton College
Iowa Central Community College
Iowa State University
Kirkwood Community College
Marshalltown Community College
Mount Mercy College
Muscatine Community College
Northwestern College
St. Ambrose University
Scott Community College
Simpson College
University of Iowa
University of Northern Iowa
Upper Iowa University
Waldorf College
Wartburg College
Western Iowa Tech Community College
William Penn University

Kansas

Baker University
Barton County Community College
Bethany College
Butler County Community College
Emporia State University
Fort Hays State University
Kansas City Kansas Community College
Kansas State University
Kansas Wesleyan University
MidAmerica Nazarene University
Ottawa University
St. Mary College
Southwestern College
Tabor College
University of Kansas
Wichita State University

Kentucky

Bellarmine University
Campbellsville University
Cumberland College
Kentucky Christian College
Louisville Technical Institute
Mid-Continent College
Morehead State University
Spalding University
Sullivan University
Thomas More College
Union College
University of Kentucky
University of Louisville

Louisiana

Grantham University
Louisiana College
Louisiana State University and
    Agricultural and Mechanical College
Loyola University New Orleans
McNeese State University
Northwestern State University
Nunez Community College
Remington College
Tulane University
University of Louisiana at Lafayette
University of Louisiana at Monroe
Xavier University of Louisiana

Maine

Andover College
Bates College
Beal College
Bowdoin College
College of the Atlantic
University of Maine
    Farmington
    Presque Isle
University of Southern Maine

Maryland

Baltimore Hebrew University
Baltimore International College
College of Notre Dame of Maryland
College of Southern Maryland
Columbia Union College
Coppin State College
Frostburg State University
Goucher College
Hagerstown Community College
Hood College
Howard Community College
Loyola College in Maryland
Maryland Institute College of Art
McDaniel College
Montgomery College
    Rockville Campus
Mount St. Mary's College
Sojourner-Douglass College
Towson University
University of Baltimore
University of Maryland
    College Park
    University College
Villa Julie College

Massachusetts

American International College
Anna Maria College
Art Institute of Boston at Lesley
    University
Atlantic Union College
Bay Path College
Becker College
Bentley College
Berklee College of Music
Boston College
Boston University
Bridgewater State College
Cape Cod Community College
College of the Holy Cross
Emmanuel College
Endicott College
Fitchburg State College
Hampshire College
Harvard College
Hebrew College
Laboure College
Lesley University
Massachusetts Bay Community College
Massachusetts College of Pharmacy and
    Health Sciences
Northeastern University
Simmons College
Simon's Rock College of Bard
Smith College
Suffolk University
University of Massachusetts
    Boston
    Lowell
Wheaton College
Williams College
Worcester Polytechnic Institute

Michigan

Andrews University
Aquinas College

Baker College
    of Auburn Hills
    of Cadillac
    of Clinton Township
    of Jackson
    of Muskegon
    of Owosso
    of Port Huron
Central Michigan University
Cleary University
Concordia University
Cornerstone University
Davenport University
    Eastern Region
    Midland
Davenport University - Western Region
Eastern Michigan University
Ferris State University
Glen Oaks Community College
Hillsdale College
Kellogg Community College
Kettering University
Kirtland Community College
Lansing Community College
Michigan State University
Monroe County Community College
Northwood University
Oakland University
Reformed Bible College
Saginaw Valley State University
Schoolcraft College
Southwestern Michigan College
Spring Arbor University
University of Michigan
University of Michigan
    Dearborn
Walsh College of Accountancy and
    Business Administration
Wayne State University
Western Michigan University
William Tyndale College

Minnesota

Bemidji State University
Carleton College
College of St. Benedict
College of St. Scholastica
Concordia College: Moorhead
Concordia University: St. Paul
Crown College
Inver Hills Community College
Minneapolis Community and Technical
    College
Minnesota State College - Southeast
    Technical
National American University
    St. Paul
Normandale Community College
St. John's University
St. Mary's University of Minnesota
Southwest State University
University of Minnesota
    Duluth
    Morris
    Twin Cities
Winona State University

Mississippi

Alcorn State University
Blue Mountain College
Itawamba Community College
Mississippi Gulf Coast Community
    College
    Perkinston
Mississippi State University
Northwest Mississippi Community
    College
University of Mississippi
University of Southern Mississippi

Missouri

Avila University
Blue River Community College
Central Bible College

Central Methodist College
College of the Ozarks
Columbia College
DeVry University
    Kansas City
Drury University
Fontbonne College
Hannibal-LaGrange College
Kansas City College of Legal Studies
Lindenwood University
Longview Community College
Maryville University of Saint Louis
Missouri Baptist University
Missouri Southern State College
Missouri Technical School
National American University
    Kansas City
Northwest Missouri State University
Research College of Nursing
Rockhurst University
St. Louis Community College
    St. Louis Community College at
      Meramec
St. Louis University
Sanford-Brown College
Southeast Missouri State University
Southwest Missouri State University
Springfield College
Stephens College
University of Missouri
    Columbia
    Kansas City
    Rolla
    St. Louis
Washington University in St. Louis
Webster University
Wentworth Military Academy
Westminster College
William Woods University

Montana

Montana State University
    Billings
Rocky Mountain College

Nebraska

Bellevue University
Central Community College
Chadron State College
Clarkson College
College of Saint Mary
Concordia University
Creighton University
Doane College
Grace University
Midland Lutheran College
Nebraska Methodist College of Nursing
    and Allied Health
Northeast Community College
University of Nebraska
    Kearney
    Lincoln
York College

Nevada

Career College of Northern Nevada
Las Vegas College
Morrison University
University of Nevada
    Las Vegas

New Hampshire

Colby-Sawyer College
College for Lifelong Learning
Daniel Webster College
Franklin Pierce College
Hesser College
New Hampshire Community Technical
    College
      Claremont
      Laconia
      Stratham
Southern New Hampshire University

New Jersey

Bloomfield College
Caldwell College
Centenary College
College of St. Elizabeth
Cumberland County College
DeVry College of Technology
Drew University
Fairleigh Dickinson University
    College at Florham
    Metropolitan Campus
Felician College
Kean University
Monmouth University
New Jersey City University
New Jersey Institute of Technology
Ramapo College of New Jersey
Raritan Valley Community College
Richard Stockton College of New Jersey
Rowan University
Rutgers, The State University of New
    Jersey
    Camden Regional Campus
    New Brunswick Regional Campus
    Newark Regional Campus
St. Peter's College
Seton Hall University
Stevens Institute of Technology
Union County College
University of Medicine and Dentistry of
    New Jersey
    School of Health Related
      Professions
William Paterson University of New
    Jersey

New Mexico

College of Santa Fe
Eastern New Mexico University
New Mexico Institute of Mining and
    Technology
New Mexico State University
University of New Mexico

New York

Adelphi University
Albany College of Pharmacy
Bard College
Barnard College
City University of New York
    Brooklyn College
    City College
    Hunter College
    Kingsborough Community College
    Queens College
Clarkson University
Colgate University
College of New Rochelle
College of New Rochelle: School of New
    Resources
Columbia University
    Columbia College
    School of Nursing
Concordia College
Cornell University
D'Youville College
Daemen College
DeVry Institute of Technology
    New York
Dominican College of Blauvelt
Dowling College
Elmira College
Eugene Lang College/New School
    University
Excelsior College
Fulton-Montgomery Community College
Hamilton College
Hartwick College
Helene Fuld College of Nursing
Hobart and William Smith Colleges
Hofstra University
Hudson Valley Community College
Iona College
Ithaca College
Juilliard School

Keuka College
Le Moyne College
Long Island University
    C. W. Post Campus
    Southampton College
Manhattan College
Manhattanville College
Marist College
Marymount Manhattan College
Medaille College
Mercy College
Metropolitan College of New York
Molloy College
Monroe Community College
Mount St. Mary College
New York Institute of Technology
New York University
Niagara University
Nyack College
Ohr Somayach Tanenbaum Education
    Center
Pace University
Pace University: Pleasantville/Briarcliff
Parsons School of Design
Plaza College
Polytechnic University
Pratt Institute
Rensselaer Polytechnic Institute
Rochester Institute of Technology
Russell Sage College
St. Bonaventure University
St. John Fisher College
St. John's University
St. Joseph's College
Skidmore College
State University of New York
    Binghamton
    Buffalo
    College at Brockport
    Empire State College
    Institute of Technology at
      Utica/Rome
Syracuse University
Touro College
Union College
Utica College
Utica School of Commerce
Wells College
Westchester Business Institute

North Carolina

Barton College
Bennett College
Campbell University
Cleveland Community College
Craven Community College
Duke University
East Carolina University
Elon University
Fayetteville State University
Greensboro College
Guilford College
High Point University
John Wesley College
Johnson C. Smith University
Lenoir-Rhyne College
Mars Hill College
Meredith College
Methodist College
Montreat College
Mount Olive College
Nash Community College
North Carolina State University
North Carolina Wesleyan College
Pfeiffer University
Piedmont Baptist College
St. Augustine's College
Shaw University
South College
Surry Community College
University of North Carolina
    Charlotte
    Greensboro
    Wilmington
Wayne Community College

Western Carolina University

North Dakota

Dickinson State University
Mayville State University
Minot State University
North Dakota State University
University of Mary
University of North Dakota

Ohio

Ashland University
Baldwin-Wallace College
Bowling Green State University
Case Western Reserve University
Cedarville University
Cleveland State University
College of Mount St. Joseph
Columbus College of Art and Design
Cuyahoga Community College
    Eastern Campus
David N. Myers College
DeVry University
    Columbus
Defiance College
Franciscan University of Steubenville
Franklin University
Heidelberg College
Hiram College
Hocking Technical College
Hondros College
John Carroll University
Kent State University
Kettering College of Medical Arts
Lake Erie College
Lourdes College
Malone College
Marietta College
Miami-Jacobs College
Mount Union College
Muskingum College
Ohio State University
    Columbus Campus
Ohio University
Ohio University
    Eastern Campus
Otterbein College
Pontifical College Josephinum
Tiffin University
University of Akron
University of Cincinnati
University of Dayton
University of Findlay
University of Northwestern Ohio
University of Rio Grande
University of Toledo
Urbana University
Ursuline College
Walsh University
Wilmington College
Wittenberg University
Wright State University
Youngstown State University

Oklahoma

Bacone College
Oklahoma Baptist University
Oklahoma Christian University of
    Science and Arts
Oklahoma City Community College
Oklahoma City University
Oklahoma State University
Redlands Community College
Rose State College
St. Gregory's University
Southwestern Oklahoma State University
University of Central Oklahoma
University of Oklahoma
University of Science and Arts of
    Oklahoma
University of Tulsa

Oregon

Chemeketa Community College

Clackamas Community College
Concordia University
George Fox University
Lane Community College
Lewis & Clark College
Mount Hood Community College
Pioneer Pacific College
Portland State University
Southern Oregon University
Warner Pacific College
Western Baptist College

Pennsylvania

Albright College
Bryn Mawr College
Cabrini College
California University of Pennsylvania
Cambria-Rowe Business College
Carlow College
Carnegie Mellon University
Cedar Crest College
Chatham College
Consolidated School of Business
   Lancaster
   York
DeSales University
DeVry University
   Ft. Washington
Delaware County Community College
Dickinson College
Douglas School of Business
Drexel University
Duquesne University
Franklin & Marshall College
Geneva College
Grove City College
Gwynedd-Mercy College
Haverford College
Holy Family University
Immaculata University
Indiana University of Pennsylvania
Juniata College
King's College
La Roche College
La Salle University
Lafayette College
Lancaster Bible College
Lehigh University
Lincoln University
Lycoming College
Manor College
Marywood University
Mercyhurst College
Messiah College
Millersville University of Pennsylvania
Muhlenberg College
Neumann College
Northampton County Area Community
   College
PJA School
Peirce College
Penn State
   Abington
   Altoona
   Beaver
   Berks
   Delaware County
   Dubois
   Erie, The Behrend College
   Fayette
   Harrisburg
   Hazleton
   Lehigh Valley
   McKeesport
   Mont Alto
   New Kensington
   Schuylkill - Capital College
   Shenango
   University Park
   Wilkes-Barre
   Worthington Scranton
   York
Pennsylvania College of Technology
Philadelphia Biblical University
Point Park College

Rosemont College
St. Charles Borromeo Seminary -
   Overbrook
St. Vincent College
Seton Hill University
Shippensburg University of Pennsylvania
Slippery Rock University of
   Pennsylvania
Temple University
University of Pennsylvania
University of Pittsburgh
University of Pittsburgh
   Johnstown
University of Scranton
Valley Forge Christian College
Villanova University
Washington and Jefferson College
Waynesburg College
West Chester University of Pennsylvania
Widener University

Puerto Rico

Inter American University of Puerto Rico
   Barranquitas Campus
   Bayamon Campus
   Guayama Campus
   Metropolitan Campus
   San German Campus
Pontifical Catholic University of Puerto
   Rico
Turabo University
Universidad Metropolitana
Universidad del Este
University of Puerto Rico
   Cayey University College

Rhode Island

Brown University
Salve Regina University
University of Rhode Island

South Carolina

Anderson College
Benedict College
Charleston Southern University
Claflin University
Coastal Carolina University
College of Charleston
Converse College
Francis Marion University
Limestone College
Morris College
Presbyterian College
Trident Technical College
University of South Carolina
University of South Carolina
   Aiken
   Lancaster
   Spartanburg
Wofford College

South Dakota

Augustana College
Black Hills State University
Mount Marty College
South Dakota State University
Southeast Technical Institute
University of Sioux Falls
University of South Dakota

Tennessee

Aquinas College
Belmont University
Bethel College
Carson-Newman College
Chattanooga State Technical Community
   College
Christian Brothers University
Crichton College
East Tennessee State University
Freed-Hardeman University
Johnson Bible College
King College
Lane College

Northeast State Technical Community
   College
Roane State Community College
South College
Tennessee Technological University
Tusculum College
Union University
University of Memphis
University of Tennessee
   Knoxville
University of Tennessee Health Science
   Center
Vanderbilt University

Texas

Angelina College
Austin Community College
Baylor University
Concordia University at Austin
Dallas Baptist University
DeVry University
   Irving
Del Mar College
East Texas Baptist University
Hallmark Institute of Technology
Hardin-Simmons University
Howard Payne University
Lamar University
Lubbock Christian University
McMurry University
Mountain View College
North Lake College
Northwood University: Texas Campus
Paris Junior College
Prairie View A&M University
Rice University
St. Philip's College
Schreiner University
Southern Methodist University
Southwestern Adventist University
Southwestern University
Stephen F. Austin State University
Tarleton State University
Temple College
Texas A&M University
Texas Tech University
Texas Wesleyan University
Texas Woman's University
Trinity University
Tyler Junior College
University of Houston
University of Mary Hardin-Baylor
University of North Texas
University of Texas
   Austin
   Dallas
   Houston Health Science Center
   San Antonio
University of the Incarnate Word
Wayland Baptist University

Utah

Brigham Young University
University of Utah
Utah State University
Utah Valley State College
Weber State University
Westminster College

Vermont

Champlain College
College of St. Joseph in Vermont
Johnson State College
Lyndon State College
Middlebury College
New England Culinary Institute
New England Culinary Institute
   Essex Junction
Norwich University
Southern Vermont College
Vermont Technical College

Virginia

Averett University

Blue Ridge Community College
Bluefield College
College of William and Mary
Danville Community College
DeVry University
   Crystal City
ECPI College of Technology
ECPI Technical College: Roanoke
George Mason University
Hampton University
Hollins University
James Madison University
Liberty University
Longwood University
Mary Baldwin College
Mountain Empire Community College
Norfolk State University
Old Dominion University
Radford University
Randolph-Macon College
Randolph-Macon Woman's College
Richard Bland College
Roanoke College
Shenandoah University
Southwest Virginia Community College
Sweet Briar College
Thomas Nelson Community College
University of Richmond
University of Virginia
University of Virginia's College at Wise
Virginia Commonwealth University
Virginia Intermont College
Virginia Military Institute
Virginia Polytechnic Institute and State
   University

Washington

DeVry University
   Seattle
Gonzaga University
Grays Harbor College
Henry Cogswell College
Northwest College
Pacific Lutheran University
St. Martin's College
Seattle University
University of Washington
Wenatchee Valley College
Whitworth College

West Virginia

Alderson-Broaddus College
Bethany College
Davis and Elkins College
Glenville State College
Marshall University
Mountain State College
Mountain State University
Potomac State College of West Virginia
   University
Salem International University
University of Charleston
West Liberty State College
West Virginia Northern Community
   College
West Virginia University
West Virginia Wesleyan College
Wheeling Jesuit University

Wisconsin

Bellin College of Nursing
Blackhawk Technical College
Cardinal Stritch University
Carthage College
Columbia College of Nursing
Concordia University Wisconsin
Edgewood College
Fox Valley Technical College
Lakeshore Technical College
Marian College of Fond du Lac
Marquette University
Milwaukee Area Technical College
Moraine Park Technical College
Mount Mary College

Ripon College
Silver Lake College
University of Wisconsin
  Madison
  Oshkosh
  Parkside
  River Falls
  Stevens Point
  Stout
Viterbo University
Waukesha County Technical College
Western Wisconsin Technical College
Wisconsin Indianhead Technical College

Wyoming
University of Wyoming

Combined bachelor's/ graduate program in accounting

Alabama
Alabama State University
Jacksonville State University
Troy State University in Montgomery

Arkansas
University of Central Arkansas

California
Pacific States University
University of San Diego
University of Southern California

Connecticut
Sacred Heart University

District of Columbia
Catholic University of America
Gallaudet University

Florida
Edward Waters College

Georgia
Clark Atlanta University
Georgia Southern University
Thomas University
University of Georgia

Idaho
Albertson College of Idaho

Illinois
Bradley University
Dominican University
Illinois State University
University of Illinois
  Springfield

Indiana
Purdue University
  Calumet

Iowa
Drake University
Grand View College
University of Dubuque

Kansas
Pittsburg State University
Wichita State University

Kentucky
Murray State University
Transylvania University

Louisiana
Herzing College

Maine
Husson College
Thomas College
University of Maine
  Presque Isle
University of Southern Maine

Maryland
Bowie State University
University of Baltimore
Villa Julie College

Massachusetts
American International College
Babson College
Bentley College
Stonehill College

Michigan
Baker College
  of Muskegon
  of Port Huron
Cleary University
Eastern Michigan University
Finlandia University
Grace Bible College
Saginaw Valley State University

Missouri
Drury University
Southeast Missouri State University
Southwest Missouri State University
University of Missouri
  Columbia
Washington University in St. Louis
Webster University

Nebraska
Creighton University

Nevada
Morrison University

New Hampshire
University of New Hampshire

New Jersey
Caldwell College
Fairleigh Dickinson University
  College at Florham
Kean University
Rowan University

New Mexico
College of the Southwest
New Mexico Highlands University

New York
City University of New York
  Baruch College
  Medgar Evers College
Fordham University
Long Island University
  C. W. Post Campus
  Southampton College
Rochester Institute of Technology
St. John's University
State University of New York
  Binghamton
  College at Oneonta
Wagner College

North Carolina
East Carolina University
Meredith College
North Carolina State University
Wake Forest University

North Dakota
University of Mary

Ohio
Case Western Reserve University
College of Mount St. Joseph
Tiffin University
University of Dayton
Xavier University

Oklahoma
Langston University
Oklahoma State University
University of Oklahoma

Pennsylvania
Elizabethtown College
Lock Haven University of Pennsylvania
Philadelphia University
Robert Morris University
University of Pittsburgh
  Greensburg

Puerto Rico
Atlantic College

South Dakota
University of South Dakota

Tennessee
Fisk University
University of Memphis
University of Tennessee
  Knoxville

Texas
Baylor University
Houston Baptist University
Southwestern Adventist University
Stephen F. Austin State University
Texas A&M University
Texas A&M University
  Texarkana
Texas Tech University
Trinity University
University of Houston
  Clear Lake
University of St. Thomas
University of Texas
  Arlington
West Texas A&M University

Utah
Brigham Young University
University of Utah

Virginia
Randolph-Macon College
Virginia Polytechnic Institute and State
  University

Washington
Heritage College
Washington State University

West Virginia
University of Charleston
Wheeling Jesuit University

Wisconsin
Marquette University

Combined bachelor's/ graduate program in architecture

Connecticut
Yale University

District of Columbia
Catholic University of America

Florida
University of Miami

Georgia
Agnes Scott College
Georgia Institute of Technology
Morehouse College

Illinois
Knox College
Monmouth College

Indiana
Earlham College
Goshen College

Iowa
Central College
Coe College
Cornell College

Maine
University of Maine
  Augusta

Michigan
Adrian College
Lawrence Technological University
University of Michigan

Missouri
Washington University in St. Louis
Webster University

Nebraska
Nebraska Wesleyan University

New York
Colgate University
Hobart and William Smith Colleges
New York Institute of Technology

North Carolina
North Carolina State University

Ohio
College of Wooster
Kent State University

Tennessee
University of Tennessee
  Knoxville

Texas
Texas Tech University
University of Dallas

Utah
University of Utah

Vermont
Norwich University

Virginia
Virginia Polytechnic Institute and State
  University

Washington
University of Washington
Washington State University

Combined bachelor's/ graduate program in business administration

Alabama
Jacksonville State University
Spring Hill College
Troy State University in Montgomery

University of Alabama
University of Mobile

Arkansas

Harding University
University of Arkansas
 Monticello
University of Central Arkansas

California

California State University
 Stanislaus
Claremont McKenna College
Harvey Mudd College
Holy Names College
John F. Kennedy University
Monterey Institute of International
 Studies
Pacific States University
Pitzer College
San Francisco State University
Scripps College
Sonoma State University
University of California
 Irvine
University of San Diego

Colorado

Colorado State University
 Pueblo
Jones International University
Mesa State College
Regis University

Connecticut

Fairfield University
Quinnipiac University
Sacred Heart University
St. Joseph College
Teikyo Post University
University of Bridgeport
University of Hartford

District of Columbia

Georgetown University

Florida

Florida Agricultural and Mechanical
 University
Florida Metropolitan University
 Melbourne Campus
Florida Southern College
Northwood University
 Florida Campus
Nova Southeastern University
Palm Beach Atlantic University
Rollins College
St. Leo University
Stetson University
University of Miami
University of South Florida
University of Tampa

Georgia

Thomas University
University of Georgia

Hawaii

Hawaii Pacific University

Idaho

Albertson College of Idaho
Northwest Nazarene University

Illinois

Dominican University
Illinois Institute of Technology
Lewis University
Rockford College
Southern Illinois University Edwardsville
University of Illinois
 Urbana-Champaign
University of St. Francis

Indiana

Earlham College
Indiana Institute of Technology
Indiana University
 Bloomington
Purdue University
 Calumet
Taylor University
Taylor University: Fort Wayne
University of St. Francis

Iowa

Drake University
University of Dubuque
Upper Iowa University

Kansas

Wichita State University

Kentucky

Bellarmine University
Murray State University
Thomas More College
University of Kentucky

Louisiana

Louisiana Tech University
Tulane University
University of Louisiana at Lafayette
Xavier University of Louisiana

Maine

Husson College
Thomas College
University of Maine
University of Southern Maine

Maryland

Bowie State University
Frostburg State University
Johns Hopkins University
University of Baltimore

Massachusetts

American International College
Assumption College
Babson College
Bentley College
Clark University
College of the Holy Cross
Massachusetts Maritime Academy
Nichols College
Suffolk University
University of Massachusetts
 Boston
Wheaton College
Worcester Polytechnic Institute

Michigan

Baker College
 of Auburn Hills
 of Muskegon
Cleary University
Lawrence Technological University
Madonna University
Northwood University
University of Michigan
 Flint

Minnesota

Capella University
St. Cloud State University

Mississippi

Millsaps College

Missouri

Avila University
Culver-Stockton College
Drury University
Maryville University of Saint Louis
Missouri Valley College

Northwest Missouri State University
Southeast Missouri State University
Southwest Missouri State University
Stephens College
University of Missouri
 Kansas City
Washington University in St. Louis
Webster University

Nebraska

Creighton University
Hastings College

Nevada

Morrison University

New Hampshire

Southern New Hampshire University
University of New Hampshire

New Jersey

College of St. Elizabeth
Fairleigh Dickinson University
 College at Florham
 Metropolitan Campus
Rider University
Rutgers, The State University of New
 Jersey
 New Brunswick Regional Campus
 Newark Regional Campus
Seton Hall University

New Mexico

University of New Mexico

New York

Alfred University
Bard College
Canisius College
Clarkson University
Cornell University
Dowling College
Elmira College
Fordham University
Hartwick College
Hobart and William Smith Colleges
Iona College
Ithaca College
Long Island University
 C. W. Post Campus
Marist College
Marymount College of Fordham
 University
Medaille College
Mount St. Mary College
New York Institute of Technology
Niagara University
Nyack College
Pace University
Pace University: Pleasantville/Briarcliff
Rensselaer Polytechnic Institute
Rochester Institute of Technology
Russell Sage College
St. Bonaventure University
St. John's University
St. Lawrence University
Skidmore College
State University of New York
 Albany
 Binghamton
 Buffalo
 College at Cortland
 College at Fredonia
 College at Geneseo
 College at Oneonta
 College at Plattsburgh
 College at Potsdam
 Oswego
Touro College
Union College
University of Rochester
Wagner College
Wells College

North Carolina

Campbell University
Gardner-Webb University
North Carolina State University
Pfeiffer University
University of North Carolina
 Greensboro

North Dakota

University of Mary

Ohio

Baldwin-Wallace College
Case Western Reserve University
Central State University
David N. Myers College
Franciscan University of Steubenville
Franklin University
John Carroll University
Kent State University
Otterbein College
Tiffin University
University of Dayton
University of Findlay

Oklahoma

Cameron University
Southern Nazarene University
University of Tulsa

Oregon

Northwest Christian College
Portland State University
University of Portland
Willamette University

Pennsylvania

Carnegie Mellon University
Chatham College
Duquesne University
Elizabethtown College
Geneva College
Lehigh University
Marywood University
Moravian College
Penn State
 Erie, The Behrend College
Philadelphia University
Point Park College
St. Vincent College
University of Pennsylvania
University of Pittsburgh
 Greensburg
University of Scranton
University of the Sciences in
 Philadelphia
Waynesburg College
Widener University

Puerto Rico

Pontifical Catholic University of Puerto
 Rico
Turabo University
Universidad Metropolitana

Rhode Island

Providence College
Salve Regina University

South Carolina

Coastal Carolina University
Lander University

South Dakota

University of South Dakota

Tennessee

Fisk University

Texas

Angelo State University
Baylor University

Dallas Baptist University
Midwestern State University
Rice University
Sam Houston State University
Southwestern Adventist University
Texas A&M University
    Commerce
Texas Christian University
Texas Tech University
Texas Wesleyan University
University of Dallas
University of St. Thomas
University of Texas
    Arlington
    Brownsville
    Dallas

Utah
Brigham Young University
University of Utah
Westminster College

Vermont
Castleton State College
Champlain College
College of St. Joseph in Vermont
Green Mountain College
St. Michael's College
University of Vermont

Virginia
Hampton University
Liberty University
Old Dominion University
Virginia Polytechnic Institute and State
    University

Washington
Seattle University
Washington State University
Whitman College

West Virginia
University of Charleston
Wheeling Jesuit University

Wisconsin
Lakeland College
Marquette University
University of Wisconsin
    Green Bay
    Whitewater

**Combined bachelor's/
graduate program in
chemistry**

Alabama
Jacksonville State University

California
Chapman University

Connecticut
Sacred Heart University
Wesleyan University

District of Columbia
American University
Gallaudet University

Georgia
Clark Atlanta University
Emory University
Georgia Institute of Technology
University of Georgia

Idaho
Idaho State University

Illinois
De Paul University
University of Illinois
    Springfield

Indiana
Purdue University
    Calumet

Iowa
University of Northern Iowa

Kansas
Pittsburg State University
Wichita State University

Kentucky
Murray State University

Maine
University of Maine

Massachusetts
Clark University
University of Massachusetts
    Dartmouth

Missouri
Southeast Missouri State University
Southwest Missouri State University
University of Missouri
    Rolla

Nebraska
Creighton University

New Jersey
Caldwell College
Rutgers, The State University of New
    Jersey
    Camden Regional Campus

New Mexico
New Mexico Highlands University

New York
Rochester Institute of Technology
St. John's University
State University of New York
    Binghamton
    College at Fredonia
    Stony Brook
University of Rochester
Vassar College

Ohio
Case Western Reserve University
College of Mount St. Joseph

Oklahoma
University of Science and Arts of
    Oklahoma

Oregon
Southern Oregon University

Pennsylvania
Bucknell University
Carlow College
Duquesne University
Lock Haven University of Pennsylvania
University of Pittsburgh
    Greensburg
University of Scranton

South Dakota
South Dakota State University
University of South Dakota

Texas
University of Texas
    Arlington

Utah
Brigham Young University
University of Utah

Virginia
Old Dominion University
Virginia Polytechnic Institute and State
    University

Washington
Washington State University

**Combined bachelor's/
graduate program in
dentistry**

California
University of Southern California
University of the Pacific

Colorado
University of Colorado
    Health Sciences Center

Connecticut
University of Connecticut

District of Columbia
Howard University

Florida
Nova Southeastern University
University of North Florida

Idaho
Idaho State University

Illinois
Southern Illinois University Edwardsville

Iowa
Buena Vista University
Luther College
University of Iowa

Kansas
McPherson College

Kentucky
Murray State University

Maryland
Bowie State University
Coppin State College
Salisbury University
University of Maryland
    College Park

Massachusetts
Boston University
Tufts University

Michigan
University of Michigan

Minnesota
College of St. Benedict
St. John's University

Mississippi
Mississippi College

Missouri
University of Missouri
    Kansas City

Nebraska
Creighton University
Hastings College
University of Nebraska
    Lincoln
    Medical Center

New Jersey
Fairleigh Dickinson University
    Metropolitan Campus
Montclair State University
New Jersey Institute of Technology
Richard Stockton College of New Jersey
Rutgers, The State University of New
    Jersey
        New Brunswick Regional Campus
        Newark Regional Campus
Stevens Institute of Technology

New York
Adelphi University
Alfred University
Barnard College
Canisius College
City University of New York
    Queens College
Le Moyne College
New York University
St. John's University
State University of New York
    College at Fredonia
    College at Geneseo
Utica College
Wagner College

North Dakota
Valley City State University

Ohio
Case Western Reserve University
College of Wooster
Ohio State University
    Columbus Campus

Oregon
Eastern Oregon University
Portland State University

Pennsylvania
Indiana University of Pennsylvania
Juniata College
Lehigh University
Muhlenberg College
Penn State
    Erie, The Behrend College
Rosemont College
University of Pittsburgh
University of Pittsburgh
    Greensburg
Villanova University

South Carolina
Furman University

Tennessee
Fisk University
Union University
University of Tennessee
    Martin

Texas
Lubbock Christian University
McMurry University
Southwest Texas State University
Texas A&M University
    Commerce
University of Texas
    Arlington
    Houston Health Science Center

Utah
University of Utah

Virginia
Old Dominion University

Wisconsin
Marquette University
University of Wisconsin
　　Green Bay

Combined bachelor's/ graduate program in education

Alabama
Alabama State University
Jacksonville State University
Troy State University in Montgomery

Alaska
University of Alaska
　　Southeast

Arkansas
Harding University
University of Central Arkansas

California
Antioch Southern California
　　Los Angeles
Bethany College
Bethesda Christian University
California State University
　　Stanislaus
Holy Names College
Monterey Institute of International
　　Studies
Occidental College
Pacific Union College
Pitzer College
Simpson College
University of San Diego
University of San Francisco

Colorado
Colorado College
Jones International University

Connecticut
Quinnipiac University
Sacred Heart University
University of Bridgeport
University of Connecticut

District of Columbia
American University
Catholic University of America
Gallaudet University

Florida
Edward Waters College
Nova Southeastern University

Georgia
Piedmont College
University of Georgia

Idaho
Northwest Nazarene University

Illinois
Dominican University

Indiana
Earlham College
Oakland City University
Purdue University
　　Calumet
University of St. Francis

Iowa
Emmaus Bible College

Grand View College
St. Ambrose University

Kansas
Pittsburg State University
Wichita State University

Kentucky
Murray State University

Maine
University of Maine
University of Southern Maine

Maryland
Bowie State University
College of Notre Dame of Maryland
Johns Hopkins University
Maryland Institute College of Art

Massachusetts
American International College
Art Institute of Boston at Lesley
　　University
Boston College
Bridgewater State College
Clark University
Hebrew College
Lesley University
Simmons College
University of Massachusetts
　　Lowell

Michigan
Baker College
　　of Cadillac
　　of Port Huron
Finlandia University
Grace Bible College
Reformed Bible College

Minnesota
Capella University

Mississippi
Mississippi Valley State University

Missouri
Avila University
Columbia College
Lindenwood University
Maryville University of Saint Louis
Missouri Valley College
Southeast Missouri State University
Truman State University
Washington University in St. Louis
Webster University

Nebraska
Creighton University
Hastings College

Nevada
Great Basin College
Sierra Nevada College

New Hampshire
University of New Hampshire

New Jersey
Caldwell College
Fairleigh Dickinson University
　　College at Florham
Rutgers, The State University of New
　　Jersey
　　　New Brunswick Regional Campus

New Mexico
College of Santa Fe
College of the Southwest
New Mexico Highlands University

New York
Adelphi University
City University of New York
　　Hunter College
　　Medgar Evers College
Colgate University
College of Mount St. Vincent
D'Youville College
Dominican College of Blauvelt
Fordham University
Hilbert College
Hobart and William Smith Colleges
Long Island University
　　C. W. Post Campus
　　Southampton College
Manhattan College
Manhattanville College
Nazareth College of Rochester
Russell Sage College
St. John's University
State University of New York
　　College at Fredonia
　　College at Potsdam
Utica College
Wagner College

North Carolina
Elon University
Gardner-Webb University

North Dakota
University of Mary

Ohio
Circleville Bible College
College of Mount St. Joseph
Kent State University
　　Salem Regional Campus
Kenyon College
Otterbein College

Oklahoma
Cameron University
Langston University
University of Science and Arts of
　　Oklahoma

Oregon
Northwest Christian College
Pacific University
Portland State University
Southern Oregon University

Pennsylvania
Allegheny College
Arcadia University
Bryn Athyn College of the New Church
Chatham College
Chestnut Hill College
Duquesne University
Gwynedd-Mercy College
Lehigh University
Lincoln University
Lock Haven University of Pennsylvania
Mount Aloysius College
St. Joseph's University
University of Pennsylvania
University of Pittsburgh
　　Greensburg
Valley Forge Christian College

Puerto Rico
Atlantic College
Turabo University
Universidad Metropolitana

South Carolina
Coastal Carolina University
Lander University

South Dakota
South Dakota State University
University of South Dakota

Tennessee
Johnson Bible College

Texas
Concordia University at Austin
Trinity University
University of Texas
　　Brownsville

Utah
Brigham Young University
University of Utah
Westminster College

Vermont
Bennington College
Lyndon State College
University of Vermont

Virginia
Averett University
Hampton University
Liberty University
Old Dominion University
University of Virginia
Virginia Polytechnic Institute and State
　　University

Washington
Heritage College
Trinity Lutheran College
Walla Walla College
Washington State University
Whitman College

West Virginia
West Virginia University
West Virginia University at Parkersburg

Wisconsin
Lakeland College
University of Wisconsin
　　Superior

Combined bachelor's/ graduate program in engineering

Alabama
Huntingdon College

Arkansas
Lyon College

California
Occidental College
San Francisco State University
Santa Clara University
Scripps College
University of California
　　Santa Cruz
University of San Francisco
Whittier College

Colorado
Colorado College
Colorado School of Mines
Regis University
University of Colorado
　　Denver

Connecticut
Fairfield University
Trinity College
University of Bridgeport
Yale University

Florida
Florida Southern College
University of Miami

Georgia
Georgia Institute of Technology
Mercer University
Morehouse College
North Georgia College & State
    University
University of Georgia

Idaho
Albertson College of Idaho
University of Idaho

Illinois
Augustana College
Illinois College
Illinois Institute of Technology
Illinois Wesleyan University
Knox College
Southern Illinois University Edwardsville
University of Illinois
    Urbana-Champaign

Indiana
Anderson University
Earlham College
Goshen College
Purdue University
    Calumet
Taylor University

Iowa
Central College
Cornell College
Grand View College
Iowa State University
Northwestern College
Simpson College
University of Iowa

Kansas
Bethany College
Wichita State University

Kentucky
Murray State University
Transylvania University
University of Kentucky
University of Louisville

Louisiana
Dillard University
Tulane University
University of Louisiana at Lafayette
Xavier University of Louisiana

Maine
Bates College
Colby College
St. Joseph's College
University of Maine

Maryland
Capitol College
Johns Hopkins University
University of Maryland
    Baltimore County

Massachusetts
Clark University
Massachusetts Institute of Technology
Massachusetts Maritime Academy
Mount Holyoke College
Northeastern University
Regis College
Tufts University
University of Massachusetts
    Lowell
Wheaton College
Williams College
Worcester Polytechnic Institute

Michigan
Adrian College
Alma College
Kettering University
Lawrence Technological University
Michigan Technological University

Minnesota
Bethel College
College of St. Scholastica
Hamline University

Mississippi
Mississippi College
Mississippi University for Women

Missouri
Drury University
University of Missouri
    Rolla
Washington University in St. Louis
Westminster College

Montana
Montana Tech of the University of
    Montana
University of Great Falls

Nebraska
Hastings College
Nebraska Wesleyan University

New Hampshire
Dartmouth College

New Jersey
Drew University
Fairleigh Dickinson University
    Metropolitan Campus
Richard Stockton College of New Jersey
Rutgers, The State University of New
    Jersey
        Newark Regional Campus
Stevens Institute of Technology

New York
Bard College
Clarkson University
Colgate University
Cooper Union for the Advancement of
    Science and Art
Cornell University
Fordham University
Hartwick College
Hobart and William Smith Colleges
Ithaca College
Manhattan College
New York Institute of Technology
Polytechnic University
Rochester Institute of Technology
St. Lawrence University
Skidmore College
State University of New York
    Albany
    Binghamton
    Buffalo
    College at Geneseo
    College at Oneonta
    College at Plattsburgh
    Stony Brook
Union College
University of Rochester
Vassar College

North Carolina
Elon University

North Dakota
Jamestown College
University of North Dakota
Valley City State University

Ohio
Case Western Reserve University
College of Wooster
Hiram College
John Carroll University
University of Dayton
Wittenberg University
Xavier University

Oklahoma
Oklahoma Baptist University

Oregon
Eastern Oregon University
George Fox University
Oregon Institute of Technology
Pacific University
Portland State University
Reed College
Willamette University

Pennsylvania
Allegheny College
Arcadia University
Bryn Mawr College
Bucknell University
Carlow College
Dickinson College
Drexel University
Franklin & Marshall College
Gettysburg College
Indiana University of Pennsylvania
Juniata College
Lehigh University
Lock Haven University of Pennsylvania
Millersville University of Pennsylvania
Moravian College
Slippery Rock University of
    Pennsylvania
Thiel College
University of Pittsburgh
    Greensburg
Washington and Jefferson College
West Chester University of Pennsylvania

Puerto Rico
Inter American University of Puerto Rico
    Barranquitas Campus

South Carolina
The Citadel
Furman University
Lander University
University of South Carolina

South Dakota
Augustana College
South Dakota School of Mines and
    Technology
South Dakota State University

Tennessee
Freed-Hardeman University
King College
Rhodes College

Texas
Austin College
Houston Baptist University
Jarvis Christian College
McMurry University
Paul Quinn College
Rice University
Southwest Texas State University
Southwestern University
Texas A&M University
    Commerce
University of Dallas
University of Texas
    Arlington
    Dallas

Utah
Brigham Young University
University of Utah
Westminster College

Vermont
Castleton State College

Virginia
College of William and Mary
Emory & Henry College
James Madison University
Old Dominion University
Randolph-Macon College
Sweet Briar College
University of Virginia
Virginia Polytechnic Institute and State
    University

Washington
Henry Cogswell College
St. Martin's College
Washington State University

West Virginia
West Virginia University Institute of
    Technology

Wisconsin
Beloit College
Marquette University
Milwaukee School of Engineering
Northland College
Ripon College
University of Wisconsin
    Platteville
    River Falls
    Superior

Combined bachelor's/ graduate program in environmental studies

California
Monterey Institute of International
    Studies
San Francisco State University

Connecticut
University of New Haven
Wesleyan University
Yale University

District of Columbia
American University

Georgia
Georgia Institute of Technology
Thomas University
University of Georgia

Illinois
Augustana College

Iowa
Cornell College

Kansas
McPherson College

Kentucky
Murray State University

Louisiana
Southern University and Agricultural and
    Mechanical College

Maine
University of Maine

Maryland
Hood College

Massachusetts
Clark University

Michigan
Lawrence Technological University

Mississippi
Mississippi Valley State University

Nebraska
Creighton University

New Jersey
Caldwell College

New York
Adelphi University
Bard College
City University of New York
    Medgar Evers College
New York Institute of Technology
Rochester Institute of Technology

North Carolina
High Point University
Wake Forest University

Ohio
College of Wooster
Miami University
    Oxford Campus
Ohio State University
    Columbus Campus
Wittenberg University
Xavier University

Oregon
Pacific University
Portland State University
Reed College
Southern Oregon University

Pennsylvania
Albright College
Arcadia University
Carlow College
Chatham College
Duquesne University
Franklin & Marshall College
Gettysburg College
Lebanon Valley College of Pennsylvania
Lycoming College
University of Pittsburgh
    Greensburg

Rhode Island
University of Rhode Island

South Carolina
Furman University

Texas
Hardin-Simmons University
Rice University
University of Texas
    Dallas

Utah
University of Utah

Virginia
College of William and Mary
Old Dominion University
Virginia Polytechnic Institute and State
    University

Washington
Heritage College

Washington State University
Whitman College

Wisconsin
Milwaukee School of Engineering
University of Wisconsin
    Platteville

**Combined bachelor's/
graduate program in fine
arts**

California
Academy of Art College
John F. Kennedy University
San Francisco State University
University of California
    Santa Cruz
University of San Diego

Georgia
University of Georgia

Idaho
University of Idaho

Indiana
University of St. Francis

Kansas
Wichita State University

Maine
Maine College of Art
University of Southern Maine

Maryland
Johns Hopkins University
Maryland Institute College of Art
University of Maryland
    Baltimore County

Massachusetts
Art Institute of Boston at Lesley
    University
Wheaton College

Minnesota
Minnesota State University
    Mankato

Missouri
College of the Ozarks
Northwest Missouri State University
Webster University

Nebraska
Creighton University

New York
City University of New York
    Queens College
Pratt Institute

Ohio
Kent State University

Oregon
Portland State University

South Dakota
University of South Dakota

Tennessee
Memphis College of Art

Utah
Brigham Young University
University of Utah

Vermont
Goddard College

Virginia
Mary Baldwin College
Virginia Polytechnic Institute and State
    University

Washington
Washington State University

Wisconsin
University of Wisconsin
    Madison

**Combined bachelor's/
graduate program in
forestry**

Arkansas
University of Arkansas
    Monticello

Connecticut
Yale University

Florida
Florida Southern College

Georgia
University of Georgia

Illinois
Augustana College
Knox College

Iowa
Cornell College

Kansas
Pittsburg State University

Louisiana
Southern University and Agricultural and
    Mechanical College

Maine
University of Maine

Michigan
Michigan Technological University

New York
Alfred University
Bard College
State University of New York
    College at Geneseo

North Carolina
Guilford College
High Point University
Lees-McRae College
Wake Forest University

Ohio
College of Wooster
Miami University
    Oxford Campus
Ohio State University
    Columbus Campus
Xavier University

Oregon
Portland State University
Reed College
Willamette University

Pennsylvania
Albright College

Allegheny College
Franklin & Marshall College
Gettysburg College
Lebanon Valley College of Pennsylvania
Lycoming College
Moravian College

South Carolina
Furman University

Virginia
Bridgewater College
College of William and Mary
Emory & Henry College
James Madison University
Randolph-Macon College
Virginia Polytechnic Institute and State
    University

Washington
Washington State University
Whitman College

West Virginia
Marshall University

Wisconsin
Northland College
Ripon College

**Combined bachelor's/
graduate program in law**

California
Claremont McKenna College
John F. Kennedy University
Occidental College
University of La Verne
University of San Diego
University of San Francisco
University of West Los Angeles
Whittier College

Connecticut
Quinnipiac University

District of Columbia
Catholic University of America

Florida
Nova Southeastern University
Stetson University

Georgia
Mercer University

Idaho
Albertson College of Idaho
University of Idaho

Illinois
Illinois Institute of Technology
Knox College
Loyola University of Chicago
Roosevelt University

Indiana
Wabash College

Iowa
Drake University
Grinnell College

Kansas
McPherson College

Louisiana
Tulane University

Maine
Bowdoin College
University of Southern Maine

Maryland
University of Baltimore
University of Maryland
    College Park

Massachusetts
Becker College
Newbury College
Northeastern University
Suffolk University
University of Massachusetts
    Dartmouth
Western New England College
Worcester Polytechnic Institute

Michigan
Siena Heights University

Mississippi
Mississippi College

Missouri
Central Missouri State University
Drury University
University of Missouri
    Kansas City
Washington University in St. Louis

Nebraska
Creighton University
Hastings College
University of Nebraska
    Lincoln

New Jersey
The College of New Jersey
Rutgers, The State University of New
    Jersey
        New Brunswick Regional Campus
        Newark Regional Campus
Seton Hall University
Stevens Institute of Technology

New York
Adelphi University
Barnard College
Cornell University
Eugene Lang College/New School
    University
Fordham University
Hamilton College
Hartwick College
New York Institute of Technology
Pace University
Pace University: Pleasantville/Briarcliff
Rensselaer Polytechnic Institute
Russell Sage College
St. John's University
Skidmore College
State University of New York
    Albany
Syracuse University
Union College

North Carolina
Campbell University

North Dakota
Valley City State University

Ohio
College of Wooster
Ohio Northern University

Oklahoma
University of Tulsa

Oregon
Portland State University
Willamette University

Pennsylvania
Dickinson College
Duquesne University
Edinboro University of Pennsylvania
Juniata College
Kutztown University of Pennsylvania
St. Vincent College
Seton Hill University
Slippery Rock University of
    Pennsylvania
Temple University
University of Pennsylvania
University of Pittsburgh
    Greensburg
Villanova University
Washington and Jefferson College
Waynesburg College

Puerto Rico
Pontifical Catholic University of Puerto
    Rico

Rhode Island
Roger Williams University
University of Rhode Island

South Carolina
Voorhees College

South Dakota
University of South Dakota

Tennessee
Lambuth University

Texas
Lubbock Christian University
Rice University
Texas A&M University
    Commerce
Texas Tech University

Utah
Brigham Young University
University of Utah

Vermont
University of Vermont

Virginia
James Madison University
Old Dominion University
Virginia Union University
Washington and Lee University

Washington
Whitman College

Wisconsin
Marquette University
University of Wisconsin
    Green Bay

**Combined bachelor's/
graduate program in
mathematics**

Alabama
Alabama State University
Jacksonville State University

Arkansas
University of Central Arkansas

California
Harvey Mudd College

Pitzer College
University of Southern California

Connecticut
Wesleyan University
Yale University

District of Columbia
American University
Gallaudet University

Florida
Edward Waters College

Georgia
Clark Atlanta University
Georgia Institute of Technology
University of Georgia

Illinois
De Paul University

Indiana
Purdue University
    Calumet

Iowa
Grand View College

Kansas
Pittsburg State University
Wichita State University

Kentucky
Murray State University

Louisiana
Nicholls State University

Maine
University of Maine

Maryland
Bowie State University
Johns Hopkins University

Missouri
Southeast Missouri State University
Southwest Missouri State University
University of Missouri
    Rolla

New Jersey
Caldwell College
Rutgers, The State University of New
    Jersey
        Camden Regional Campus

New Mexico
College of the Southwest

New York
Adelphi University
City University of New York
    City College
    Medgar Evers College
Rochester Institute of Technology
St. John's University
St. Joseph's College: Suffolk Campus
State University of New York
    Buffalo
    College at Fredonia
    College at Potsdam
    Stony Brook
University of Rochester

Ohio
Case Western Reserve University
College of Mount St. Joseph

Oklahoma
Langston University
University of Science and Arts of
    Oklahoma

Oregon
Southern Oregon University

Pennsylvania
Bucknell University
Duquesne University
Lincoln University
Lock Haven University of Pennsylvania
Mount Aloysius College
University of Pittsburgh
University of Pittsburgh
    Greensburg

South Dakota
South Dakota School of Mines and
    Technology
South Dakota State University

Utah
Brigham Young University
University of Utah

Virginia
Old Dominion University
Virginia Polytechnic Institute and State
    University

Washington
Heritage College
Washington State University

**Combined bachelor's/
graduate program in
medicine**

California
University of California
    Riverside
University of Southern California

Colorado
University of Colorado
    Health Sciences Center

Connecticut
University of Connecticut

District of Columbia
Howard University

Florida
St. Leo University
University of Central Florida
University of Miami
University of South Florida

Georgia
Mercer University

Illinois
Bradley University
Illinois Institute of Technology
Knox College
Loyola University of Chicago
Northwestern University
Rush University

Kansas
McPherson College

Kentucky
Murray State University

Louisiana
Tulane University

Maine
St. Joseph's College

Maryland
Johns Hopkins University
University of Maryland
    College Park

Massachusetts
Boston University
Tufts University

Michigan
University of Michigan

Mississippi
Mississippi College

Missouri
Central Missouri State University
Drury University
University of Missouri
    Kansas City

Nebraska
Creighton University
Hastings College
University of Nebraska
    Lincoln
    Medical Center

New Jersey
The College of New Jersey
Fairleigh Dickinson University
    College at Florham
    Metropolitan Campus
Monmouth University
Montclair State University
New Jersey Institute of Technology
Richard Stockton College of New Jersey
Rutgers, The State University of New
    Jersey
    Camden Regional Campus
    New Brunswick Regional Campus
    Newark Regional Campus
Stevens Institute of Technology

New York
Albany College of Pharmacy
Canisius College
City University of New York
    Brooklyn College
    City College
    Queens College
New York University
Rensselaer Polytechnic Institute
Union College
University of Rochester

North Dakota
Valley City State University

Ohio
College of Wooster
Kent State University
Ohio State University
    Columbus Campus

Oregon
Eastern Oregon University
Portland State University

Pennsylvania
Drexel University
Indiana University of Pennsylvania
Juniata College
Lehigh University
Marywood University
Muhlenberg College
Penn State
    Erie, The Behrend College
Rosemont College

Temple University
University of Pittsburgh
University of Pittsburgh
    Greensburg
University of the Sciences in
    Philadelphia
Villanova University
Washington and Jefferson College
Widener University

Rhode Island
Brown University

South Carolina
Furman University
Voorhees College

South Dakota
University of South Dakota

Tennessee
East Tennessee State University
Fisk University
Lambuth University
Union University
University of Tennessee
    Martin

Texas
Lubbock Christian University
McMurry University
Rice University
Southwest Texas State University
Texas A&M University
    Commerce
University of Texas
    Arlington
    Houston Health Science Center

Utah
University of Utah

Virginia
Virginia Commonwealth University

Wisconsin
University of Wisconsin
    Green Bay
    Madison

**Combined bachelor's/
graduate program in
nursing**

Alabama
Birmingham-Southern College
Jacksonville State University
University of Mobile

Arkansas
Harding University
University of Central Arkansas

California
Holy Names College
Loma Linda University
Samuel Merritt College
San Francisco State University
University of San Diego

Colorado
University of Colorado
    Health Sciences Center

Connecticut
Quinnipiac University
Sacred Heart University
St. Joseph College
University of Hartford

Delaware
Wilmington College

Florida
University of Central Florida
University of Miami
University of Tampa

Georgia
Armstrong Atlantic State University
Georgia Southern University
Thomas University

Hawaii
Hawaii Pacific University

Illinois
Knox College
Rush University
St. Xavier University
West Suburban College of Nursing

Indiana
Earlham College
Purdue University
    Calumet
    North Central Campus
University of St. Francis
University of Southern Indiana

Iowa
Cornell College
Dordt College
Graceland University
Grand View College
Mercy College of Health Sciences
Northwestern College

Kansas
Pittsburg State University
Wichita State University

Kentucky
Bellarmine University
Murray State University

Louisiana
Loyola University New Orleans
Southern University and Agricultural and
    Mechanical College
University of Louisiana at Lafayette

Maine
Husson College
St. Joseph's College
University of Maine
University of Southern Maine

Maryland
Salisbury University

Massachusetts
Boston University
Mount Holyoke College
Northeastern University
Regis College
Simmons College
University of Massachusetts
    Boston
    Dartmouth

Michigan
Finlandia University
University of Michigan
University of Michigan
    Flint

Missouri
Culver-Stockton College
St. Luke's College
Southeast Missouri State University
Southwest Missouri State University

University of Missouri
    Kansas City
    Rolla
Webster University

Montana
University of Great Falls

Nebraska
Clarkson College
Creighton University
University of Nebraska
    Medical Center

New Jersey
Fairleigh Dickinson University
    Metropolitan Campus
Felician College
Ramapo College of New Jersey
Richard Stockton College of New Jersey

New York
Adelphi University
City University of New York
    Medgar Evers College
D'Youville College
Daemen College
Excelsior College
Long Island University
    C. W. Post Campus
Molloy College
New York University
Pace University
Pace University: Pleasantville/Briarcliff
Russell Sage College
St. John Fisher College
State University of New York
    Buffalo
    Health Science Center at Stony
    Brook
    Stony Brook
Wagner College

North Carolina
Gardner-Webb University

North Dakota
Valley City State University

Ohio
Circleville Bible College
College of Mount St. Joseph
College of Wooster
Franciscan University of Steubenville
John Carroll University
Kent State University
    Salem Regional Campus
Otterbein College
Ursuline College
Wittenberg University

Oklahoma
Langston University

Oregon
Oregon Institute of Technology
Portland State University
Southern Oregon University

Pennsylvania
Allegheny College
Carlow College
Drexel University
Gwynedd-Mercy College
Juniata College
Lock Haven University of Pennsylvania
Mount Aloysius College
University of Pennsylvania
University of Scranton

South Carolina
Furman University

South Dakota
Augustana College
South Dakota State University

Tennessee
Bryan College
Fisk University
Freed-Hardeman University
Maryville College

Texas
Baylor University
Jarvis Christian College
McMurry University
Southwestern Adventist University
Texas A&M University
    Commerce
University of Texas
    Health Science Center at San
        Antonio
    Houston Health Science Center

Utah
Brigham Young University
University of Utah
Westminster College

Virginia
College of Health Sciences
Liberty University
Old Dominion University

Washington
Washington State University

West Virginia
Mountain State University
West Virginia University at Parkersburg
Wheeling Jesuit University

Wisconsin
Beloit College
Marquette University

Combined bachelor's/ graduate program in occupational therapy

Alabama
Alabama State University
Spring Hill College

Arkansas
University of Central Arkansas

California
Dominican University of California
Loma Linda University

Connecticut
Quinnipiac University
Sacred Heart University

Florida
Nova Southeastern University

Georgia
Brenau University
Columbus State University

Illinois
Augustana College
Dominican University
Illinois College
Knox College
Rush University

Iowa
St. Ambrose University

Kansas
University of Kansas Medical Center

Maine
Husson College
University of Southern Maine

Massachusetts
American International College
Boston University
Springfield College

Michigan
Alma College
Calvin College
Grand Valley State University

Minnesota
College of St. Catherine
College of St. Scholastica

Missouri
Avila University
Culver-Stockton College
Drury University
Maryville University of Saint Louis
Rockhurst University
Stephens College
Washington University in St. Louis

Montana
Rocky Mountain College

Nebraska
Creighton University
Hastings College

New Hampshire
University of New Hampshire

New Jersey
Seton Hall University

New York
D'Youville College
Dominican College of Blauvelt
Ithaca College
Marymount College of Fordham
    University
New York Institute of Technology
Pace University
Pace University: Pleasantville/Briarcliff
Russell Sage College
Touro College
Utica College

North Dakota
University of Mary
Valley City State University

Ohio
University of Findlay
Wittenberg University

Oregon
Pacific University
Portland State University

Pennsylvania
Bloomsburg University of Pennsylvania
Carlow College
Chatham College
Elizabethtown College
Juniata College
Keystone College
La Salle University
Moravian College
Mount Aloysius College
St. Vincent College
University of Pittsburgh
    Greensburg
University of Scranton

University of the Sciences in
    Philadelphia
Villanova University

South Dakota
University of South Dakota

Tennessee
Belmont University

Utah
Brigham Young University
University of Utah

Virginia
College of Health Sciences
Virginia Commonwealth University

West Virginia
West Virginia University

Wisconsin
Carthage College
Concordia University Wisconsin
Lawrence University
Mount Mary College
University of Wisconsin
    Green Bay
    Madison

Combined bachelor's/ graduate program in optometry

Florida
Nova Southeastern University

Indiana
Indiana University
    Bloomington
Purdue University
    Calumet

Kansas
McPherson College

Kentucky
Murray State University

Maryland
Salisbury University

Massachusetts
Assumption College
Wheaton College

New Jersey
The College of New Jersey

New York
Adelphi University
Canisius College
Ithaca College
Le Moyne College
Marymount College of Fordham
    University
Pace University
St. John's University
State University of New York
    Binghamton
    College at Fredonia
    College at Geneseo
    College at Oneonta
    College at Plattsburgh
    College at Potsdam
    New Paltz
    Oswego

North Dakota
Valley City State University

Ohio
Ohio State University
    Columbus Campus

Oklahoma
Northeastern State University

Oregon
Eastern Oregon University
Pacific University
Portland State University

Pennsylvania
Arcadia University
Gettysburg College
Indiana University of Pennsylvania
Juniata College
Lehigh University
Lycoming College
Millersville University of Pennsylvania
Muhlenberg College
University of Pittsburgh
    Greensburg
Villanova University
Washington and Jefferson College
Widener University

Tennessee
Union University
University of Tennessee
    Martin

Texas
Texas A&M University
    Commerce

Virginia
Old Dominion University

Wisconsin
University of Wisconsin
    Green Bay

Combined bachelor's/ graduate program in osteopathic medicine

California
Pitzer College

Florida
Nova Southeastern University

Kansas
McPherson College

Missouri
Drury University

New Jersey
Richard Stockton College of New Jersey

New York
Marist College
New York Institute of Technology
State University of New York
    College at Geneseo
    New Paltz
Touro College
Utica College

Ohio
Kent State University

Oregon
Portland State University

Pennsylvania
Edinboro University of Pennsylvania
Indiana University of Pennsylvania

Juniata College
Kutztown University of Pennsylvania
Penn State
    Erie, The Behrend College
Temple University
University of Pittsburgh
    Greensburg
Widener University

Tennessee
University of Tennessee
    Martin

Combined bachelor's/ graduate program in pharmacy

Arizona
University of Arizona

California
University of Southern California
University of the Pacific

Colorado
University of Colorado
    Health Sciences Center

Florida
Nova Southeastern University
Palm Beach Atlantic University

Georgia
Mercer University

Idaho
Idaho State University

Illinois
Millikin University

Indiana
Butler University
Purdue University
    Calumet

Iowa
Drake University
University of Iowa

Kansas
McPherson College
University of Kansas

Kentucky
Murray State University

Maine
St. Joseph's College

Maryland
Coppin State College
Salisbury University
University of Baltimore
Villa Julie College

Massachusetts
Massachusetts College of Pharmacy and
    Health Sciences
Northeastern University
Western New England College

Michigan
Ferris State University
University of Michigan

Missouri
St. Louis College of Pharmacy

Montana
University of Montana-Missoula

Nebraska
Creighton University
Hastings College
University of Nebraska
    Lincoln
    Medical Center

Nevada
Sierra Nevada College

New Jersey
New Jersey Institute of Technology
Rutgers, The State University of New
    Jersey
    Camden Regional Campus

New York
Albany College of Pharmacy

North Carolina
Campbell University

North Dakota
North Dakota State University
Valley City State University

Ohio
Ohio Northern University
Ohio State University
    Columbus Campus
Xavier University

Oklahoma
Southwestern Oklahoma State University

Oregon
Portland State University

Pennsylvania
Juniata College
Keystone College
St. Vincent College
Temple University
University of Pittsburgh
University of Pittsburgh
    Greensburg
University of the Sciences in
    Philadelphia
Wilkes University

South Carolina
Furman University

South Dakota
South Dakota State University

Tennessee
Fisk University
King College
Lambuth University
Union University
University of Tennessee
    Martin

Texas
Texas A&M University
    Commerce

Utah
University of Utah

Virginia
Old Dominion University
Virginia Commonwealth University

Washington
University of Washington
Washington State University

West Virginia
West Virginia University

Wisconsin
University of Wisconsin
    Green Bay
    Madison

Combined bachelor's/ graduate program in physical therapy

Alabama
Alabama State University
Spring Hill College

Arkansas
University of Central Arkansas

California
Loma Linda University
San Francisco State University

Colorado
University of Colorado
    Health Sciences Center

Connecticut
Quinnipiac University
Sacred Heart University
University of Connecticut
University of Hartford

Florida
Nova Southeastern University
University of Miami

Georgia
Armstrong Atlantic State University

Illinois
Bradley University
Millikin University

Indiana
University of Evansville

Iowa
Clarke College
St. Ambrose University

Kansas
McPherson College
Pittsburg State University
Wichita State University

Kentucky
Bellarmine University

Maine
Husson College

Maryland
Coppin State College
University of Maryland
    College Park
Villa Julie College

Massachusetts
American International College
Boston University
Northeastern University
Simmons College
Springfield College

Michigan
Central Michigan University
Grand Valley State University

University of Michigan
    Flint

Minnesota
College of St. Catherine
College of St. Scholastica

Missouri
Avila University
Maryville University of Saint Louis
Rockhurst University
Washington University in St. Louis

Nebraska
Creighton University
Hastings College
University of Nebraska
    Medical Center

New Jersey
Kean University
Richard Stockton College of New Jersey
Seton Hall University
University of Medicine and Dentistry of
    New Jersey
    School of Health Related
        Professions

New York
Adelphi University
City University of New York
    College of Staten Island
Clarkson University
Concordia College
D'Youville College
Daemen College
Dominican College of Blauvelt
Ithaca College
Marymount College of Fordham
    University
Nazareth College of Rochester
New York Institute of Technology
Russell Sage College
State University of New York
    College at Geneseo
    College at Oneonta
    Health Science Center at Brooklyn
    Oswego
    Upstate Medical University
Touro College
Utica College

North Dakota
University of Mary
University of North Dakota
Valley City State University

Ohio
College of Mount St. Joseph
Ohio University
University of Findlay

Oregon
Pacific University
Portland State University

Pennsylvania
Allegheny College
Arcadia University
Bloomsburg University of Pennsylvania
Cabrini College
Carlow College
Chatham College
Drexel University
Elizabethtown College
Gettysburg College
Indiana University of Pennsylvania
Juniata College
Keystone College
Lebanon Valley College of Pennsylvania
Moravian College
Mount Aloysius College
St. Vincent College

Temple University
University of Pittsburgh
  Greensburg
University of Scranton
University of the Sciences in
  Philadelphia
Villanova University
Widener University

South Carolina
Furman University

South Dakota
University of South Dakota

Tennessee
Belmont University
University of Tennessee
  Chattanooga
  Knoxville

Texas
Hardin-Simmons University
McMurry University
Texas A&M University
  Commerce
Texas Woman's University

Utah
University of Utah

Vermont
University of Vermont

Virginia
Bridgewater College
Marymount University
Old Dominion University

Washington
University of Puget Sound

West Virginia
West Virginia University

Wisconsin
Concordia University Wisconsin
Marquette University
University of Wisconsin
  Green Bay
  Madison

Combined bachelor's/ graduate program in podiatry

Connecticut
Quinnipiac University

District of Columbia
Howard University

Florida
Barry University

Maryland
Salisbury University

Massachusetts
Assumption College

New Jersey
Bloomfield College
Richard Stockton College of New Jersey

New York
Canisius College
Le Moyne College
Pace University

Pace University: Pleasantville/Briarcliff
St. Joseph's College: Suffolk Campus

Oregon
Portland State University

Pennsylvania
Chestnut Hill College
Indiana University of Pennsylvania
Juniata College
Lycoming College
Millersville University of Pennsylvania
St. Vincent College
Washington and Jefferson College
Widener University

Tennessee
Union University
University of Tennessee
  Martin

Combined bachelor's/ graduate program in psychology

Alabama
Troy State University in Montgomery

Arkansas
University of Central Arkansas

California
California State University
  Stanislaus
Claremont McKenna College
John F. Kennedy University

Connecticut
St. Joseph College
Wesleyan University
Yale University

District of Columbia
American University
Catholic University of America
Gallaudet University

Florida
Edward Waters College
Nova Southeastern University

Georgia
Emory University
Georgia Institute of Technology
Thomas University
University of Georgia

Illinois
University of Illinois
  Springfield

Indiana
Purdue University
  Calumet

Iowa
Grand View College
Iowa State University

Kansas
Pittsburg State University
Wichita State University

Kentucky
Murray State University

Maine
University of Maine

Maryland
Bowie State University
Johns Hopkins University
University of Baltimore

Massachusetts
American International College
Lesley University

Minnesota
Capella University
Oak Hills Christian College

Missouri
Avila University

Montana
University of Great Falls

Nebraska
Creighton University

New Jersey
Caldwell College
Fairleigh Dickinson University
  College at Florham
Kean University

New Mexico
College of the Southwest
New Mexico Highlands University

New York
City University of New York
  City College
  Medgar Evers College
Marist College
Mount St. Mary College
Rochester Institute of Technology
St. John's University
State University of New York
  College at Plattsburgh

Ohio
Circleville Bible College
College of Mount St. Joseph
Tiffin University
Walsh University

Oklahoma
Langston University
University of Science and Arts of
  Oklahoma

Oregon
Northwest Christian College
Oregon Institute of Technology
Southern Oregon University

Pennsylvania
Bryn Mawr College
Chestnut Hill College
Geneva College
Gwynedd-Mercy College
Lock Haven University of Pennsylvania
Mount Aloysius College
Rosemont College
St. Joseph's University
University of Pittsburgh
  Greensburg
University of the Sciences in
  Philadelphia
Valley Forge Christian College

Rhode Island
Salve Regina University

South Dakota
South Dakota State University
University of South Dakota

Utah
Brigham Young University
University of Utah

Vermont
Burlington College

Virginia
Old Dominion University
Virginia Polytechnic Institute and State
  University

Washington
Heritage College
Walla Walla College
Washington State University

Combined bachelor's/ graduate program in social work

Alabama
Alabama State University
Jacksonville State University

California
California State University
  Stanislaus
San Francisco State University

District of Columbia
Gallaudet University

Georgia
Thomas University

Idaho
Northwest Nazarene University

Illinois
University of Illinois
  Springfield

Indiana
Grace College
University of St. Francis

Kansas
Pittsburg State University
Wichita State University

Kentucky
Brescia University
Kentucky Christian College
Murray State University

Louisiana
Tulane University

Maine
University of Maine
University of Southern Maine

Maryland
Bowie State University
Salisbury University
University of Maryland
  Baltimore County

Massachusetts
Boston College
Northeastern University

Michigan
Finlandia University

Minnesota
Capella University
St. Cloud State University

Mississippi

Mississippi Valley State University

Missouri

Maryville University of Saint Louis
Washington University in St. Louis
Webster University

Nebraska

Creighton University

New Mexico

New Mexico Highlands University

New York

Adelphi University
Bard College
Concordia College
Fordham University
Marymount College of Fordham
 University
Molloy College
Nazareth College of Rochester
Rochester Institute of Technology
State University of New York
 Albany
 Buffalo
 College at Plattsburgh
 New Paltz

North Dakota

Dickinson State University
Valley City State University

Ohio

Baldwin-Wallace College
Cedarville University
Circleville Bible College
College of Mount St. Joseph
College of Wooster

Oregon

Portland State University

Pennsylvania

Bryn Mawr College
Cedar Crest College
Lock Haven University of Pennsylvania
Marywood University
University of Pittsburgh
 Greensburg

South Dakota

University of South Dakota

Texas

Southwestern Adventist University
University of Texas
 Houston Health Science Center

Utah

Brigham Young University
University of Utah

Virginia

Virginia Commonwealth University

Washington

Heritage College
Walla Walla College

Wisconsin

University of Wisconsin
 Superior

Combined bachelor's/ graduate program in veterinary medicine

Colorado

Colorado State University

Kansas

McPherson College

Maine

St. Joseph's College

Maryland

Salisbury University

Massachusetts

Worcester Polytechnic Institute

Mississippi

Mississippi College
Mississippi State University

New York

Cornell University
Wells College

North Carolina

North Carolina State University

North Dakota

Valley City State University

Ohio

College of Wooster
Kent State University

Pennsylvania

University of Pittsburgh
 Greensburg

Puerto Rico

Pontifical Catholic University of Puerto
 Rico

Tennessee

Lambuth University
Union University
University of Tennessee
 Martin

Texas

Lubbock Christian University
Texas A&M University
 Commerce

Vermont

University of Vermont

Virginia

Bridgewater College
Old Dominion University
Virginia Polytechnic Institute and State
 University

Washington

Washington State University

Combined liberal arts/ career program in accounting

Alabama

Birmingham-Southern College
Calhoun Community College
Jacksonville State University
Remington College
 Southeast College of Technology

Troy State University in Montgomery

Alaska

Alaska Pacific University
University of Alaska
 Southeast

Arizona

Gateway Community College
International Institute of the Americas
 Phoenix
 Tucson
Phoenix College

Arkansas

Harding University
Mid-South Community College
South Arkansas Community College
University of Arkansas
 Community College at Batesville
 Community College at Hope
 Cossatot Community College of the
 Monticello
University of Central Arkansas
University of the Ozarks

California

California State University
 Chico
 Hayward
 Stanislaus
Chapman University
Coastline Community College
College of Alameda
College of the Siskiyous
Columbia College
Diablo Valley College
Foothill College
Gavilan Community College
Hope International University
Long Beach City College
Los Angeles Harbor College
Los Angeles Trade and Technical College
MTI College of Business and Technology
Master's College
Modesto Junior College
Ohlone College
Orange Coast College
Pacific States University
Pacific Union College
San Diego City College
San Diego Mesa College
San Joaquin Delta College
San Jose State University
Santa Rosa Junior College
University of La Verne
University of San Diego
University of Southern California
University of the Pacific

Colorado

Arapahoe Community College
Fort Lewis College
Front Range Community College
National American University
 Denver
Red Rocks Community College
Trinidad State Junior College

Connecticut

Briarwood College
Gateway Community College
International College of Hospitality
 Management
Norwalk Community College
Quinnipiac University
Sacred Heart University
Teikyo Post University
Tunxis Community College
University of Bridgeport

District of Columbia

Gallaudet University

Florida

Edward Waters College
Florida Metropolitan University
 Melbourne Campus
Hillsborough Community College
St. Leo University
Southwest Florida College
Tallahassee Community College
University of West Florida

Georgia

Albany Technical College
Atlanta Metropolitan College
Central Georgia Technical College
Floyd College
Georgia Southwestern State University
Kennesaw State University
LaGrange College
Morehouse College
North Georgia College & State
 University
Paine College
Southwest Georgia Technical College
Thomas University
Waycross College
West Georgia Technical College

Hawaii

Hawaii Business College
University of Hawaii
 Leeward Community College

Idaho

Albertson College of Idaho
Northwest Nazarene University

Illinois

Aurora University
Benedictine University
Chicago State University
City Colleges of Chicago
 Harold Washington College
 Malcolm X College
De Paul University
Dominican University
Illinois College
John A. Logan College
Lewis University
Lewis and Clark Community College
MacMurray College
McKendree College
Olivet Nazarene University
Quincy University
Richland Community College
Rock Valley College
Shawnee Community College
Trinity Christian College
University of Illinois
 Springfield
Waubonsee Community College

Indiana

Ancilla College
Calumet College of St. Joseph
Franklin College
Goshen College
Huntington College
Indiana Institute of Technology
Ivy Tech State College
 Bloomington
 Central Indiana
 Columbus
 Eastcentral
 Kokomo
 Lafayette
 Northcentral
 Northeast
 Northwest
 Southcentral
 Southeast
 Southwest
 Wabash Valley
 Whitewater
Marian College

Oakland City University
Purdue University
    North Central Campus
St. Joseph's College
University of St. Francis

Iowa

Central College
Des Moines Area Community College
Dordt College
Ellsworth Community College
Graceland University
Grand View College
Hamilton College
Hamilton College
    Cedar Rapids
Indian Hills Community College
Iowa State University
Kirkwood Community College
Loras College
Marshalltown Community College
Morningside College
Mount Mercy College
North Iowa Area Community College
Northwestern College
Simpson College
University of Dubuque
Upper Iowa University
William Penn University

Kansas

Allen County Community College
Butler County Community College
Central Christian College
Friends University
Garden City Community College
Kansas City Kansas Community College
Labette Community College
Pittsburg State University
Pratt Community College
Seward County Community College
Tabor College
Wichita State University

Kentucky

Asbury College
Bellarmine University
Cumberland College
Henderson Community College
Madisonville Community College
Murray State University
National College of Business &
    Technology
    Danville
Pikeville College
Southwestern College of Business
Thomas More College
Transylvania University

Louisiana

Centenary College of Louisiana
Dillard University
Herzing College
Louisiana State University
    Eunice
Northwestern State University
Nunez Community College
Remington College

Maine

Andover College
Central Maine Technical College
University of Maine
    Augusta
University of Southern Maine

Maryland

Allegany College
Bowie State University
College of Notre Dame of Maryland
College of Southern Maryland

Community College of Baltimore County
    Catonsville
    Dundalk
    Essex
Coppin State College
Frederick Community College
Hagerstown Community College
Harford Community College
Morgan State University
Mount St. Mary's College
Villa Julie College

Massachusetts

American International College
Anna Maria College
Atlantic Union College
Babson College
Becker College
Bentley College
Berkshire Community College
Bridgewater State College
Emmanuel College
Fisher College
Lasell College
Massachusetts College of Liberal Arts
Mount Wachusett Community College
Newbury College
Stonehill College

Michigan

Adrian College
Alma College
Alpena Community College
Baker College
    of Muskegon
    of Port Huron
Cornerstone University
Glen Oaks Community College
Grace Bible College
Grand Valley State University
Hope College
Jackson Community College
Kellogg Community College
Mid Michigan Community College
Montcalm Community College
Northern Michigan University
Reformed Bible College
University of Michigan
Washtenaw Community College

Minnesota

Bemidji State University
Bethel College
Central Lakes College
Century Community and Technical
    College
College of St. Scholastica
Concordia College: Moorhead
Dakota County Technical College
Globe College
Itasca Community College
Minneapolis Community and Technical
    College
Minnesota School of Business
Minnesota State College - Southeast
    Technical
Normandale Community College
Northland Community & Technical
    College
Rainy River Community College
Riverland Community College: A
    Technical and Community College
Southwest State University

Mississippi

Holmes Community College
Mississippi State University

Missouri

Avila University
Central Methodist College
Central Missouri State University
College of the Ozarks
Culver-Stockton College

Drury University
East Central College
Fontbonne College
Jefferson College
Maryville University of Saint Louis
Mineral Area College
Missouri Baptist University
Missouri Southern State College
Missouri Valley College
Penn Valley Community College
St. Louis Community College
    St. Louis Community College at
        Forest Park
Southwest Missouri State University:
    West Plains Campus
Stephens College
Washington University in St. Louis
Webster University
Westminster College
William Jewell College
William Woods University

Montana

Carroll College
Rocky Mountain College
University of Great Falls

Nebraska

Bellevue University
Concordia University
Creighton University
Dana College
Grace University
Lincoln School of Commerce
Midland Lutheran College
Northeast Community College
Peru State College
Western Nebraska Community College

Nevada

Morrison University
Truckee Meadows Community College

New Hampshire

Franklin Pierce College
New England College
New Hampshire Community Technical
    College
    Laconia
Southern New Hampshire University

New Jersey

Atlantic Cape Community College
Bloomfield College
Caldwell College
The College of New Jersey
College of St. Elizabeth
County College of Morris
Fairleigh Dickinson University
    College at Florham
Hudson County Community College
Kean University
Ocean County College
Passaic County Community College
Rowan University
Union County College
Warren County Community College

New Mexico

New Mexico Highlands University
San Juan College
Santa Fe Community College

New York

Adelphi University
City University of New York
    Baruch College
    College of Staten Island
    Hostos Community College
    Hunter College
    Queens College
Clarkson University
Clinton Community College

D'Youville College
Dominican College of Blauvelt
Genesee Community College
Hartwick College
Houghton College
Jamestown Community College
Keuka College
Long Island University
    Southampton College
Maria College
Marist College
Marymount Manhattan College
Mohawk Valley Community College
Molloy College
Monroe College
Mount St. Mary College
New York Institute of Technology
New York University
Nyack College
Roberts Wesleyan College
St. John Fisher College
St. Joseph's College: Suffolk Campus
Schenectady County Community College
State University of New York
    College at Brockport
    College at Fredonia
    College at Plattsburgh
    College of Agriculture and
        Technology at Morrisville
    Oswego
Tompkins-Cortland Community College
Utica College
Wagner College

North Carolina

Barton College
Beaufort County Community College
Belmont Abbey College
Coastal Carolina Community College
Elizabeth City State University
Elon University
Gardner-Webb University
Lenoir Community College
Mayland Community College
Methodist College
Nash Community College
Pfeiffer University
Queens University of Charlotte
Roanoke-Chowan Community College
St. Andrews Presbyterian College
Sampson Community College
Winston-Salem State University

North Dakota

Aaker's Business College
Dickinson State University
North Dakota State College of Science
University of Mary
University of North Dakota

Ohio

Ashland University
Bluffton College
Cedarville University
Circleville Bible College
Clark State Community College
Cleveland State University
College of Mount St. Joseph
Columbus State Community College
David N. Myers College
Davis College
Franciscan University of Steubenville
James A. Rhodes State College
Kent State University
    Salem Regional Campus
Lakeland Community College
Marietta College
Miami University
    Hamilton Campus
    Middletown Campus
Ohio Business College: Sandusky
Ohio Northern University
Ohio University
Ohio Wesleyan University

Otterbein College
Southwestern College of Business
University of Cincinnati
  Clermont College
  Raymond Walters College
University of Findlay
Ursuline College
Wilmington College

Oklahoma

Cameron University
Carl Albert State College
Langston University
Northern Oklahoma College
Oklahoma Baptist University
Oklahoma Panhandle State University
Oklahoma State University
  Oklahoma City
Oral Roberts University
Redlands Community College
Southwestern Oklahoma State University

Oregon

Blue Mountain Community College
Clackamas Community College
Concordia University
Eastern Oregon University
Lane Community College
Pacific University
Pioneer Pacific College
Southern Oregon University

Pennsylvania

Albright College
Allentown Business School
Arcadia University
Bucknell University
Cambria-Rowe Business College
Cedar Crest College
Community College of Beaver County
DeSales University
Elizabethtown College
Franklin & Marshall College
Geneva College
Gwynedd-Mercy College
Immaculata University
Lebanon Valley College of Pennsylvania
Lehigh University
Lincoln University
Lock Haven University of Pennsylvania
Luzerne County Community College
Marywood University
Moravian College
Mount Aloysius College
Neumann College
Newport Business Institute
PJA School
Penn State
  Dubois
  Erie, The Behrend College
Philadelphia Biblical University
Philadelphia University
Point Park College
Rosemont College
St. Vincent College
Seton Hill University
Temple University
Thiel College
University of Pittsburgh
  Greensburg
  Johnstown
  Titusville
Waynesburg College
Widener University

Puerto Rico

Atlantic College
Columbia College
Inter American University of Puerto Rico
  Barranquitas Campus
  Bayamon Campus
Turabo University
Universidad Metropolitana
Universidad del Este

University of Puerto Rico
  Cayey University College

Rhode Island

Salve Regina University

South Carolina

Anderson College
Columbia International University
Converse College
Florence-Darlington Technical College
Limestone College
Midlands Technical College
Northeastern Technical College
Orangeburg-Calhoun Technical College
Piedmont Technical College
Wofford College

South Dakota

Augustana College
Mount Marty College
University of South Dakota

Tennessee

Belmont University
Christian Brothers University
Draughons Junior College of Business:
  Nashville
Dyersburg State Community College
Fisk University
Freed-Hardeman University
Jackson State Community College
Lambuth University
National College of Business &
  Technology
  Tennessee
Pellissippi State Technical Community
  College
Southwest Tennessee Community
  College
Tennessee Technological University
Tennessee Wesleyan College
University of Tennessee
  Knoxville

Texas

Angelina College
Blinn College
Coastal Bend College
Frank Phillips College
Hill College
Howard College
Lamar State College at Port Arthur
McMurry University
Midwestern State University
North Lake College
St. Edward's University
Sam Houston State University
Schreiner University
Southwestern Adventist University
Southwestern University
Tarrant County College
Texas A&M International University
Texas A&M University
  Texarkana
Texas Lutheran University
Tyler Junior College
University of Texas
  Brownsville

Utah

Brigham Young University
University of Utah
Utah Valley State College
Westminster College

Vermont

Champlain College
College of St. Joseph in Vermont
Lyndon State College
Norwich University

Virginia

Averett University
National College of Business &
  Technology
  Bluefield
  Charlottesville
Norfolk State University
Randolph-Macon College
Rappahannock Community College
University of Richmond
University of Virginia's College at Wise
Virginia Polytechnic Institute and State
  University
Virginia Wesleyan College
Virginia Western Community College

Washington

Gonzaga University
Lake Washington Technical College
Lower Columbia College
Northwest College
Pacific Lutheran University
Renton Technical College
St. Martin's College
University of Washington
Walla Walla College
Washington State University

West Virginia

Bethany College
Bluefield State College
Concord College
Davis and Elkins College
Fairmont State College
Salem International University
Shepherd College
University of Charleston
West Virginia University Institute of
  Technology
Wheeling Jesuit University

Wisconsin

Edgewood College
Lakeland College
Marian College of Fond du Lac
Marquette University
Mount Mary College
University of Wisconsin
  Baraboo/Sauk County
  Green Bay
  Parkside
  River Falls
  Superior

Wyoming

Sheridan College

**Combined liberal arts/
career program in
architecture**

Arizona

Phoenix College

California

California College of Arts and Crafts
Diablo Valley College
Laney College
Long Beach City College
Los Angeles Harbor College
Los Angeles Trade and Technical College
Modesto Junior College
Orange Coast College
Palomar College
San Diego Mesa College
San Joaquin Delta College
Santa Rosa Junior College
University of Southern California

Colorado

Arapahoe Community College
Front Range Community College

Florida

Hillsborough Community College

Georgia

Agnes Scott College
Georgia Institute of Technology
Morris Brown College
Southern Polytechnic State University

Illinois

City Colleges of Chicago
  Harold Washington College
Columbia College Chicago
Knox College
Monmouth College
Waubonsee Community College

Indiana

Earlham College
Goshen College

Iowa

Central College
Coe College
Grinnell College

Kansas

Allen County Community College
Central Christian College
Kansas State University
Seward County Community College

Louisiana

Louisiana Tech University
Southern University and Agricultural and
  Mechanical College
Tulane University
University of Louisiana at Lafayette

Maine

Central Maine Technical College
University of Maine
  Augusta

Maryland

Anne Arundel Community College
Howard Community College
Morgan State University

Massachusetts

Benjamin Franklin Institute of
  Technology
Boston Architectural Center

Michigan

Adrian College
Lawrence Technological University
Montcalm Community College
University of Michigan

Minnesota

Carleton College
Dakota County Technical College
Itasca Community College
Macalester College
Minneapolis Community and Technical
  College
Northland Community & Technical
  College

Mississippi

Mississippi State University

Missouri

Drury University
East Central College
University of Missouri
  St. Louis
Washington University in St. Louis
Webster University

Nevada

Truckee Meadows Community College

New Jersey

Mercer County Community College
Union County College

New York

City University of New York
    City College
    College of Staten Island
Colgate University
Erie Community College
    City Campus
    North Campus
    South Campus
Hobart and William Smith Colleges
Island Drafting and Technical Institute
New York Institute of Technology
Parsons School of Design
Pratt Institute
State University of New York
    College of Agriculture and
        Technology at Morrisville
    College of Technology at Alfred
    College of Technology at Canton
    Maritime College

North Carolina

Coastal Carolina Community College
North Carolina State University
Roanoke-Chowan Community College

Ohio

Columbus State Community College
Lakeland Community College
Oberlin College
Ohio State University
    Columbus Campus

Oklahoma

Langston University
Oklahoma State University
    Oklahoma City
Platt College
    Tulsa

Pennsylvania

Lehigh University
Luzerne County Community College
Penn State
    Dubois
Philadelphia University
Temple University

Puerto Rico

Inter American University of Puerto Rico
    San German Campus
University of Puerto Rico
    Rio Piedras Campus

Tennessee

Southwest Tennessee Community
    College
University of Tennessee
    Knoxville

Texas

Baylor University
Coastal Bend College
Rice University
University of Dallas
University of Texas
    Austin

Utah

University of Utah

Vermont

Norwich University

Virginia

Virginia Polytechnic Institute and State
    University
Virginia Western Community College

Washington

University of Washington
Washington State University

West Virginia

Bluefield State College
Fairmont State College

Wisconsin

Milwaukee Area Technical College
University of Wisconsin
    Baraboo/Sauk County
    Green Bay
    Platteville

Combined liberal arts/ career program in aviation

California

College of Alameda
Foothill College
Gavilan Community College
Long Beach City College
Mount San Antonio College
Orange Coast College
Pacific Union College
San Jose State University

Colorado

United States Air Force Academy

Connecticut

Gateway Community College

Idaho

Idaho State University

Illinois

John A. Logan College
Lewis University
Lincoln Land Community College
Moraine Valley Community College
Rock Valley College
Waubonsee Community College

Indiana

Ivy Tech State College
    Wabash Valley

Iowa

Indian Hills Community College
University of Dubuque

Kansas

Bethel College
Central Christian College
Hesston College
Wichita State University

Louisiana

Northwestern State University

Maryland

Community College of Baltimore County
    Catonsville
    Dundalk
    Essex
Frederick Community College

Massachusetts

Bridgewater State College

Michigan

Baker College
    of Muskegon

Cornerstone University
Jackson Community College
Montcalm Community College

Minnesota

Itasca Community College
Metropolitan State University
Minneapolis Community and Technical
    College
Minnesota State College - Southeast
    Technical
North Central University
Northland Community & Technical
    College

Missouri

Central Missouri State University
College of the Ozarks
Missouri Southern State College
St. Louis Community College
    St. Louis Community College at
        Forest Park

Montana

Rocky Mountain College

Nebraska

Grace University
Western Nebraska Community College

New Hampshire

Daniel Webster College

New Jersey

County College of Morris
Mercer County Community College

New Mexico

San Juan College

New York

College of Aeronautics
Jamestown Community College
Schenectady County Community College
Tompkins-Cortland Community College

North Carolina

College of the Albemarle
Lenoir Community College
Piedmont Baptist College

North Dakota

University of North Dakota

Ohio

Columbus State Community College
Ohio University
University of Cincinnati
    Clermont College

Oklahoma

Langston University
Northern Oklahoma College
Western Oklahoma State College

Oregon

Lane Community College
Multnomah Bible College

Pennsylvania

Community College of Beaver County
Geneva College
Lock Haven University of Pennsylvania
Luzerne County Community College
Marywood University

Puerto Rico

Inter American University of Puerto Rico
    Bayamon Campus

South Dakota

South Dakota State University

Texas

Central Texas College
Hallmark Institute of Aeronautics
Tarrant County College

Utah

Dixie State College of Utah
Utah Valley State College
Westminster College

Virginia

Averett University

West Virginia

Fairmont State College
Salem International University

Combined liberal arts/ career program in business administration

Alabama

Alabama State University
American College of Computer and
    Information Sciences
Birmingham-Southern College
Calhoun Community College
Chattahoochee Valley Community
    College
Community College of the Air Force
Concordia College
Faulkner University
Jacksonville State University
Northwest-Shoals Community College
Remington College
    Southeast College of Technology
Shelton State Community College
Troy State University in Montgomery
University of Alabama
University of Mobile

Alaska

Alaska Pacific University
University of Alaska
    Southeast

Arizona

Gateway Community College
International Institute of the Americas
    Phoenix
    Tucson
Northern Arizona University
Prescott College

Arkansas

Harding University
Mid-South Community College
Philander Smith College
South Arkansas Community College
University of Arkansas
    Community College at Batesville
    Community College at Hope
    Cossatot Community College of the
        Fort Smith
    Monticello
University of Central Arkansas
University of the Ozarks

California

Antioch Southern California
    Los Angeles
    Santa Barbara
Biola University

California State University
  Chico
  Hayward
  Monterey Bay
  San Marcos
  Stanislaus
Chapman University
Coastline Community College
College of Alameda
College of the Canyons
College of the Siskiyous
Columbia College
Concordia University
Diablo Valley College
Dominican University of California
Foothill College
Gavilan Community College
Holy Names College
Hope International University
Imperial Valley College
Long Beach City College
Los Angeles Harbor College
Los Angeles Trade and Technical College
MTI College of Business and Technology
Master's College
Modesto Junior College
Occidental College
Ohlone College
Orange Coast College
Pacific States University
Pacific Union College
San Diego City College
San Diego Mesa College
San Francisco State University
San Joaquin Delta College
San Jose State University
Santa Rosa Junior College
University of La Verne
University of Redlands
University of San Diego
University of Southern California
University of the Pacific
Westwood College of Technology
  Inland Empire
Whittier College

Colorado

Arapahoe Community College
Colorado Mountain College
  Alpine Campus
  Timberline Campus
Fort Lewis College
Front Range Community College
Metropolitan State College of Denver
National American University
  Denver
Red Rocks Community College
Trinidad State Junior College
University of Colorado
  Denver

Connecticut

Asnuntuck Community College
Briarwood College
Gateway Community College
International College of Hospitality
  Management
Quinnipiac University
Sacred Heart University
St. Joseph College
Teikyo Post University
Tunxis Community College
United States Coast Guard Academy
University of Bridgeport
University of Hartford

District of Columbia

Gallaudet University

Florida

Daytona Beach Community College
Edward Waters College
Florida Metropolitan University
  Melbourne Campus

Florida Southern College
Hillsborough Community College
Rollins College
St. Leo University
Southeastern College of the Assemblies
  of God
Southwest Florida College
Stetson University
Tallahassee Community College
University of West Florida

Georgia

Albany Technical College
Atlanta Metropolitan College
Central Georgia Technical College
Clayton College and State University
Emory University
Floyd College
Georgia Institute of Technology
Georgia Southwestern State University
Gordon College
Kennesaw State University
LaGrange College
Macon State College
Morehouse College
North Georgia College & State
  University
Paine College
South University
Southern Polytechnic State University
Thomas University
Waycross College
Wesleyan College
West Georgia Technical College

Hawaii

Hawaii Business College
University of Hawaii
  Leeward Community College

Idaho

Albertson College of Idaho
Lewis-Clark State College
Northwest Nazarene University

Illinois

Aurora University
Benedictine University
Blackburn College
Bradley University
Chicago State University
City Colleges of Chicago
  Harold Washington College
  Malcolm X College
De Paul University
Dominican University
Illinois College
Illinois State University
John A. Logan College
Lewis University
Lewis and Clark Community College
Lincoln Land Community College
MacMurray College
McKendree College
Monmouth College
Moraine Valley Community College
North Central College
Olivet Nazarene University
Quincy University
Richland Community College
Rock Valley College
Shawnee Community College
South Suburban College of Cook County
Trinity Christian College
University of Illinois
  Springfield
University of St. Francis
Waubonsee Community College

Indiana

Ancilla College
Calumet College of St. Joseph
Earlham College
Franklin College

Goshen College
Grace College
Huntington College
Indiana Institute of Technology
Indiana University
  Bloomington
Indiana Wesleyan University
Ivy Tech State College
  Bloomington
  Central Indiana
  Columbus
  Eastcentral
  Kokomo
  Lafayette
  Northcentral
  Northeast
  Northwest
  Southcentral
  Southeast
  Southwest
  Wabash Valley
  Whitewater
Marian College
Oakland City University
Purdue University
  North Central Campus
St. Joseph's College
University of St. Francis
Valparaiso University

Iowa

Briar Cliff University
Central College
Des Moines Area Community College
Dordt College
Ellsworth Community College
Graceland University
Grand View College
Hamilton College
Hamilton College
  Cedar Rapids
Indian Hills Community College
Iowa State University
Kirkwood Community College
Loras College
Maharishi University of Management
Marshalltown Community College
Morningside College
Mount Mercy College
North Iowa Area Community College
Northwestern College
Simpson College
Southeastern Community College
  South Campus
Southwestern Community College
University of Dubuque
Upper Iowa University
Waldorf College
William Penn University

Kansas

Allen County Community College
Barclay College
Bethany College
Butler County Community College
Central Christian College
Friends University
Garden City Community College
Hesston College
Kansas City Kansas Community College
Kansas State University
Labette Community College
McPherson College
Newman University
Ottawa University
Pittsburg State University
Pratt Community College
Seward County Community College
Sterling College
Tabor College
Wichita State University

Kentucky

Alice Lloyd College

Asbury College
Beckfield College
Bellarmine University
Brescia University
Cumberland College
Elizabethtown Community College
Henderson Community College
Kentucky Christian College
Madisonville Community College
Murray State University
National College of Business &
  Technology
  Danville
Pikeville College
Southeast Community College
Thomas More College
Transylvania University

Louisiana

Centenary College of Louisiana
Dillard University
Grantham University
Herzing College
Louisiana State University
  Eunice
Louisiana Tech University
Loyola University New Orleans
Northwestern State University
Nunez Community College
Remington College
Remington College
  Baton Rouge
Southern University and Agricultural and
  Mechanical College
Tulane University
University of Louisiana at Lafayette

Maine

Andover College
Central Maine Technical College
Maine Maritime Academy
St. Joseph's College
University of Maine
University of Maine
  Augusta
  Presque Isle
University of Southern Maine

Maryland

Allegany College
Anne Arundel Community College
Baltimore International College
Bowie State University
Capitol College
College of Notre Dame of Maryland
College of Southern Maryland
Community College of Baltimore County
  Catonsville
  Dundalk
  Essex
Coppin State College
Frederick Community College
Frostburg State University
Hagerstown Community College
Harford Community College
Howard Community College
Morgan State University
Mount St. Mary's College
Villa Julie College

Massachusetts

American International College
Anna Maria College
Atlantic Union College
Babson College
Becker College
Bentley College
Berkshire Community College
Boston University
Bridgewater State College
Clark University
Emmanuel College
Fisher College
Framingham State College

Lasell College
Lesley University
Massachusetts College of Liberal Arts
Massachusetts Maritime Academy
Mount Wachusett Community College
Newbury College
Nichols College
Simmons College
Springfield College
Stonehill College
Western New England College
Wheaton College
Worcester Polytechnic Institute

Michigan

Adrian College
Alma College
Alpena Community College
Baker College
    of Auburn Hills
    of Muskegon
    of Port Huron
Cornerstone University
Finlandia University
Glen Oaks Community College
Grace Bible College
Grand Valley State University
Hope College
Jackson Community College
Kellogg Community College
Lawrence Technological University
Madonna University
Mid Michigan Community College
Montcalm Community College
Mott Community College
Northern Michigan University
Reformed Bible College
University of Michigan
Washtenaw Community College
Wayne State University

Minnesota

Augsburg College
Bemidji State University
Bethel College
Capella University
Central Lakes College
Century Community and Technical
    College
College of St. Catherine
College of St. Scholastica
Concordia College: Moorhead
Crown College
Dakota County Technical College
Fergus Falls Community College
Globe College
Gustavus Adolphus College
Hibbing Community College: A
    Technical and Community College
Itasca Community College
Minneapolis Community and Technical
    College
Minnesota School of Business
Normandale Community College
North Central University
Northland Community & Technical
    College
Riverland Community College: A
    Technical and Community College
St. Cloud State University
Southwest State University
University of Minnesota
    Morris

Mississippi

Millsaps College
Mississippi State University
Rust College

Missouri

Avila University
Central Methodist College
Central Missouri State University
College of the Ozarks

Culver-Stockton College
Drury University
East Central College
Fontbonne College
Jefferson College
Maryville University of Saint Louis
Mineral Area College
Missouri Baptist University
Missouri Southern State College
Missouri Valley College
North Central Missouri College
Northwest Missouri State University
Penn Valley Community College
St. Louis Community College
    St. Louis Community College at
    Forest Park
Southwest Missouri State University:
    West Plains Campus
Stephens College
Three Rivers Community College
Washington University in St. Louis
Webster University
Westminster College
William Jewell College
William Woods University

Montana

Carroll College
Rocky Mountain College
University of Great Falls
University of Montana: Western

Nebraska

Bellevue University
College of Saint Mary
Creighton University
Dana College
Grace University
Lincoln School of Commerce
Little Priest Tribal College
Midland Lutheran College
Northeast Community College
Peru State College
Southeast Community College
    Lincoln Campus
Western Nebraska Community College

Nevada

Great Basin College
Morrison University
Truckee Meadows Community College

New Hampshire

College for Lifelong Learning
Daniel Webster College
Franklin Pierce College
Keene State College
New England College
New Hampshire Community Technical
    College
    Laconia
Rivier College
Southern New Hampshire University

New Jersey

Atlantic Cape Community College
Bloomfield College
Caldwell College
Camden County College
The College of New Jersey
College of St. Elizabeth
County College of Morris
Fairleigh Dickinson University
    College at Florham
    Metropolitan Campus
Hudson County Community College
Kean University
Mercer County Community College
New Jersey City University
Ocean County College
Passaic County Community College
Richard Stockton College of New Jersey
Rowan University
Seton Hall University

Union County College
Warren County Community College

New Mexico

Eastern New Mexico University: Roswell
    Campus
New Mexico Highlands University
New Mexico State University
    Alamogordo
San Juan College
Santa Fe Community College

New York

Adelphi University
City University of New York
    Baruch College
    College of Staten Island
    Hostos Community College
    Medgar Evers College
Clarkson University
Clinton Community College
College of Aeronautics
College of Mount St. Vincent
College of New Rochelle
Concordia College
D'Youville College
Dominican College of Blauvelt
Dowling College
Erie Community College
    City Campus
    North Campus
    South Campus
Genesee Community College
Globe Institute of Technology
Hartwick College
Hobart and William Smith Colleges
Houghton College
Iona College
Jamestown Community College
Keuka College
Long Island University
    Southampton College
Maria College
Marist College
Marymount College of Fordham
    University
Marymount Manhattan College
Medaille College
Mohawk Valley Community College
Molloy College
Monroe College
Mount St. Mary College
Nazareth College of Rochester
New York Institute of Technology
New York University
Niagara University
North Country Community College
Nyack College
Onondaga Community College
Paul Smith's College
Roberts Wesleyan College
Rochester Institute of Technology
Russell Sage College
Sage College of Albany
St. Bonaventure University
St. John Fisher College
St. Joseph's College: Suffolk Campus
Schenectady County Community College
Skidmore College
State University of New York
    Albany
    Binghamton
    College at Brockport
    College at Fredonia
    College at Geneseo
    College at Plattsburgh
    College at Potsdam
    College of Agriculture and
    Technology at Morrisville
    College of Environmental Science
    and Forestry
    College of Technology at Alfred
    College of Technology at Canton
    Maritime College
    Oswego

Tompkins-Cortland Community College
Utica College
Utica School of Commerce
Villa Maria College of Buffalo
Wagner College
Westchester Community College

North Carolina

Barton College
Beaufort County Community College
Belmont Abbey College
Bladen Community College
Central Carolina Community College
Cleveland Community College
Coastal Carolina Community College
College of the Albemarle
Elizabeth City State University
Elon University
Fayetteville Technical Community
    College
Gardner-Webb University
James Sprunt Community College
Lenoir Community College
Mayland Community College
Methodist College
Mount Olive College
Nash Community College
North Carolina State University
Peace College
Pfeiffer University
Queens University of Charlotte
Randolph Community College
Roanoke-Chowan Community College
St. Andrews Presbyterian College
St. Augustine's College
Salem College
Sampson Community College
Southeastern Community College
University of North Carolina
    Asheville
Wilson Technical Community College
Winston-Salem State University

North Dakota

Aaker's Business College
Dickinson State University
Mayville State University
North Dakota State College of Science
Trinity Bible College
University of Mary
University of North Dakota
Valley City State University
Williston State College

Ohio

Antioch College
Ashland University
Bluffton College
Cedarville University
Chatfield College
Circleville Bible College
Clark State Community College
Cleveland State University
College of Mount St. Joseph
Columbus State Community College
David N. Myers College
Davis College
Defiance College
Franciscan University of Steubenville
Hondros College
James A. Rhodes State College
Kent State University
Kent State University
    Ashtabula Regional Campus
    Salem Regional Campus
Lakeland Community College
Lourdes College
Marietta College
Miami University
    Hamilton Campus
    Middletown Campus
Muskingum College
Ohio Business College: Sandusky
Ohio Northern University

Ohio State University
  Columbus Campus
Ohio University
Ohio Valley College of Technology
Ohio Wesleyan University
Otterbein College
Southern State Community College
Southwestern College of Business
University of Cincinnati
  Clermont College
  Raymond Walters College
Urbana University
Ursuline College
Walsh University
Wilmington College
Wittenberg University

Oklahoma

Bacone College
Cameron University
Carl Albert State College
Langston University
Northern Oklahoma College
Oklahoma Baptist University
Oklahoma Panhandle State University
Oklahoma State University
  Oklahoma City
Oral Roberts University
Redlands Community College
Rogers State University
Southern Nazarene University
Southwestern Christian University
Southwestern Oklahoma State University
University of Science and Arts of
  Oklahoma
Western Oklahoma State College

Oregon

Blue Mountain Community College
Clackamas Community College
Concordia University
Eastern Oregon University
Lane Community College
Northwest Christian College
Oregon Institute of Technology
Pacific University
Pioneer Pacific College
Southern Oregon University
Southwestern Oregon Community
  College

Pennsylvania

Academy of Medical Arts and Business
Albright College
Allentown Business School
Arcadia University
Bucknell University
Cambria-Rowe Business College
Cedar Crest College
Community College of Allegheny
  County
Community College of Beaver County
DeSales University
Delaware Valley College
Dickinson College
Douglas School of Business
DuBois Business College
Duquesne University
Elizabethtown College
Franklin & Marshall College
Geneva College
Gettysburg College
Gwynedd-Mercy College
Immaculata University
Lafayette College
Lebanon Valley College of Pennsylvania
Lehigh University
Lincoln University
Lock Haven University of Pennsylvania
Luzerne County Community College
Marywood University
Mercyhurst College
Moravian College
Mount Aloysius College

Neumann College
Newport Business Institute
PJA School
Penn State
  Beaver
  Dubois
  Erie, The Behrend College
  McKeesport
  Mont Alto
  New Kensington
  Wilkes-Barre
  York
Philadelphia Biblical University
Philadelphia University
Point Park College
Rosemont College
St. Vincent College
Seton Hill University
Temple University
Thiel College
University of Pittsburgh
University of Pittsburgh
  Greensburg
  Titusville
University of the Sciences in
  Philadelphia
Valley Forge Christian College
Waynesburg College
Widener University

Puerto Rico

Atlantic College
Columbia College
Inter American University of Puerto Rico
  Barranquitas Campus
  Bayamon Campus
Turabo University
Universidad Metropolitana
Universidad del Este
University of Puerto Rico
  Cayey University College
  Rio Piedras Campus
University of the Sacred Heart

Rhode Island

Salve Regina University

South Carolina

Anderson College
Coker College
College of Charleston
Columbia International University
Converse College
Florence-Darlington Technical College
Lander University
Limestone College
Midlands Technical College
Newberry College
Northeastern Technical College
Piedmont Technical College
Williamsburg Technical College
Wofford College

South Dakota

Augustana College
Mount Marty College
University of South Dakota

Tennessee

Aquinas College
Belmont University
Bethel College
Christian Brothers University
Crichton College
Draughons Junior College of Business:
  Nashville
Dyersburg State Community College
Fisk University
Freed-Hardeman University
Jackson State Community College
King College
Lambuth University
Lane College
Lee University

Maryville College
National College of Business &
  Technology
  Tennessee
Pellissippi State Technical Community
  College
Remington College
  Southeast College of Technology
Roane State Community College
Southwest Tennessee Community
  College
Tennessee Technological University
Tennessee Wesleyan College
Union University
University of Memphis
University of Tennessee
  Knoxville
Walters State Community College

Texas

Angelina College
Blinn College
Central Texas College
Coastal Bend College
Concordia University at Austin
Dallas Christian College
Frank Phillips College
Hill College
Howard College
Howard Payne University
Jarvis Christian College
Lamar State College at Port Arthur
McMurry University
Midland College
Midwestern State University
North Lake College
Northwood University: Texas Campus
Paul Quinn College
Rice University
St. Edward's University
Sam Houston State University
Schreiner University
Southwestern Adventist University
Southwestern University
Tarrant County College
Texarkana College
Texas A&M International University
Texas A&M University
  Texarkana
Texas Lutheran University
Trinity University
Tyler Junior College
University of Dallas
University of Texas
  Arlington
  Austin
  Brownsville
University of the Incarnate Word

Utah

Brigham Young University
University of Utah
Utah Valley State College
Westminster College

Vermont

Castleton State College
Champlain College
College of St. Joseph in Vermont
Community College of Vermont
Green Mountain College
Lyndon State College
Norwich University
St. Michael's College
Southern Vermont College

Virginia

Averett University
Liberty University
Longwood University
Mary Baldwin College

National College of Business &
  Technology
  Bluefield
  Charlottesville
Norfolk State University
Rappahannock Community College
University of Richmond
University of Virginia's College at Wise
Virginia Polytechnic Institute and State
  University
Virginia Union University
Virginia Wesleyan College
Virginia Western Community College

Washington

Clark College
Crown College
Gonzaga University
Henry Cogswell College
Lower Columbia College
Northwest College
Pacific Lutheran University
Peninsula College
St. Martin's College
University of Washington
Walla Walla College
Walla Walla Community College
Washington State University

West Virginia

Bluefield State College
Concord College
Davis and Elkins College
Fairmont State College
Salem International University
Shepherd College
University of Charleston
West Virginia University Institute of
  Technology
West Virginia University at Parkersburg
Wheeling Jesuit University

Wisconsin

Alverno College
Carthage College
Edgewood College
Lakeland College
Marian College of Fond du Lac
Marquette University
Milwaukee Area Technical College
Milwaukee Institute of Art & Design
Milwaukee School of Engineering
Mount Mary College
University of Wisconsin
  Baraboo/Sauk County
  Green Bay
  Parkside
  River Falls
  Superior

Combined liberal arts/ career program in computer science

Alabama

Alabama State University
American College of Computer and
  Information Sciences
Birmingham-Southern College
Calhoun Community College
Chattahoochee Valley Community
  College
Community College of the Air Force
Faulkner University
Jacksonville State University
Northwest-Shoals Community College
Remington College
  Southeast College of Technology
Troy State University in Montgomery
University of Mobile

Arizona

Collins College
Gateway Community College
Rio Salado College

Arkansas

Harding University
Mid-South Community College
Northwest Arkansas Community College
Philander Smith College
South Arkansas Community College
University of Arkansas
    Community College at Batesville
    Cossatot Community College of the
University of Central Arkansas

California

Biola University
California State University
    Chico
    Hayward
    Monterey Bay
    San Marcos
    Stanislaus
Chapman University
Coastline Community College
College of Alameda
College of the Siskiyous
Columbia College
Concordia University
Diablo Valley College
Foothill College
Gavilan Community College
Harvey Mudd College
Hope International University
Laney College
Long Beach City College
Los Angeles Harbor College
Los Angeles Trade and Technical College
MTI College of Business and Technology
Master's College
Modesto Junior College
Mount San Antonio College
Occidental College
Ohlone College
Orange Coast College
Pacific States University
Pacific Union College
Palomar College
Pepperdine University
San Diego City College
San Diego Mesa College
San Francisco State University
San Joaquin Delta College
San Jose State University
Santa Rosa Junior College
Sonoma State University
University of La Verne
University of Redlands
University of San Diego
University of Southern California
University of the Pacific
Vista Community College

Colorado

Blair Junior College
Fort Lewis College
Front Range Community College
Heritage College
IntelliTec College
Metropolitan State College of Denver
National American University
    Denver
Red Rocks Community College
Trinidad State Junior College
United States Air Force Academy

Connecticut

Asnuntuck Community College
Gateway Community College
Quinnipiac University
Sacred Heart University
Teikyo Post University
Tunxis Community College

University of Bridgeport
University of Hartford

District of Columbia

Gallaudet University

Florida

Beacon College
Daytona Beach Community College
Florida Metropolitan University
    Melbourne Campus
Florida Southern College
Hillsborough Community College
St. Leo University
Southwest Florida College
Stetson University
Tallahassee Community College
University of West Florida

Georgia

Albany Technical College
Atlanta Metropolitan College
Central Georgia Technical College
Emory University
Floyd College
Georgia Institute of Technology
Georgia Perimeter College
Georgia Southwestern State University
Gordon College
Kennesaw State University
LaGrange College
Macon State College
Morehouse College
North Georgia College & State
    University
Paine College
Southern Polytechnic State University
Southwest Georgia Technical College
Waycross College
Wesleyan College
West Georgia Technical College

Hawaii

University of Hawaii
    Leeward Community College

Idaho

Albertson College of Idaho
Lewis-Clark State College
Northwest Nazarene University

Illinois

Aurora University
Benedictine University
Blackburn College
Chicago State University
City Colleges of Chicago
    Harold Washington College
    Malcolm X College
De Paul University
Dominican University
Heartland Community College
Illinois College
Illinois State University
Illinois Wesleyan University
John A. Logan College
Lewis University
Lewis and Clark Community College
Lincoln Land Community College
MacMurray College
McKendree College
Monmouth College
Moraine Valley Community College
North Central College
Northwestern University
Olivet Nazarene University
Quincy University
Richland Community College
Rock Valley College
Shawnee Community College
Trinity Christian College
University of Illinois
    Springfield
University of St. Francis

Waubonsee Community College

Indiana

Ancilla College
Calumet College of St. Joseph
Earlham College
Franklin College
Goshen College
Huntington College
Indiana Institute of Technology
Indiana Wesleyan University
Ivy Tech State College
    Bloomington
    Central Indiana
    Columbus
    Eastcentral
    Kokomo
    Lafayette
    Northcentral
    Northeast
    Northwest
    Southcentral
    Southeast
    Southwest
    Wabash Valley
    Whitewater
Marian College
Oakland City University
St. Joseph's College

Iowa

Briar Cliff University
Central College
Des Moines Area Community College
Dordt College
Graceland University
Grand View College
Hamilton College
Hamilton College
    Cedar Rapids
Indian Hills Community College
Iowa State University
Kirkwood Community College
Loras College
Maharishi University of Management
Marshalltown Community College
Morningside College
North Iowa Area Community College
Northwestern College
St. Ambrose University
Simpson College
Southwestern Community College
University of Dubuque
Upper Iowa University
Waldorf College
William Penn University

Kansas

Allen County Community College
Butler County Community College
Central Christian College
Friends University
Garden City Community College
Hesston College
Kansas City Kansas Community College
Kansas State University
Labette Community College
McPherson College
Newman University
Ottawa University
Pittsburg State University
Seward County Community College
Sterling College
Tabor College
Wichita State University

Kentucky

Asbury College
Beckfield College
Bellarmine University
Brescia University
Cumberland College
Elizabethtown Community College
Henderson Community College

Murray State University
National College of Business &
    Technology
    Danville
Pikeville College
Southeast Community College
Thomas More College
Transylvania University

Louisiana

Dillard University
Grantham University
Herzing College
Louisiana State University
    Eunice
Louisiana Tech University
Loyola University New Orleans
Northwestern State University
Nunez Community College
Remington College
Southern University and Agricultural and
    Mechanical College
Tulane University
University of Louisiana at Lafayette

Maine

Andover College
St. Joseph's College
University of Maine
University of Maine
    Augusta
University of Southern Maine

Maryland

Allegany College
Anne Arundel Community College
Bowie State University
College of Notre Dame of Maryland
Community College of Baltimore County
    Catonsville
    Dundalk
    Essex
Coppin State College
Frederick Community College
Frostburg State University
Hagerstown Community College
Harford Community College
Howard Community College
Morgan State University
Mount St. Mary's College
University of Maryland
    Baltimore County
Villa Julie College

Massachusetts

American International College
Atlantic Union College
Becker College
Benjamin Franklin Institute of
    Technology
Bentley College
Berkshire Community College
Bridgewater State College
Framingham State College
Greenfield Community College
Lasell College
Massachusetts College of Liberal Arts
Mount Wachusett Community College
Newbury College
Simmons College
Springfield College
Stonehill College
Western New England College
Wheaton College
Worcester Polytechnic Institute

Michigan

Alma College
Baker College
    of Muskegon
    of Port Huron
Cornerstone University
Glen Oaks Community College
Grace Bible College

Grand Valley State University
Hope College
Kalamazoo College
Kellogg Community College
Lawrence Technological University
Mid Michigan Community College
Montcalm Community College
Northern Michigan University
Reformed Bible College
Washtenaw Community College

Minnesota

Augsburg College
Bemidji State University
Bethel College
Capella University
Central Lakes College
Century Community and Technical
    College
College of St. Scholastica
Concordia College: Moorhead
Crown College
Dakota County Technical College
Globe College
Gustavus Adolphus College
Itasca Community College
Minneapolis Community and Technical
    College
Minnesota School of Business
Normandale Community College
Northland Community & Technical
    College
Rainy River Community College
St. Cloud State University
Southwest State University
University of Minnesota
    Morris

Mississippi

Holmes Community College
Millsaps College
Mississippi State University
Mississippi Valley State University
Rust College

Missouri

Avila University
Central Methodist College
Central Missouri State University
College of the Ozarks
Culver-Stockton College
Drury University
East Central College
Fontbonne College
Jefferson College
Maryville University of Saint Louis
Mineral Area College
Missouri Southern State College
Missouri Valley College
Northwest Missouri State University
Penn Valley Community College
St. Louis Community College
    St. Louis Community College at
        Forest Park
University of Missouri
    Rolla
Washington University in St. Louis
Webster University
Westminster College
William Jewell College
William Woods University

Montana

Carroll College
Rocky Mountain College
University of Great Falls

Nebraska

Bellevue University
College of Saint Mary
Concordia University
Creighton University
Dana College
Grace University

Lincoln School of Commerce
Little Priest Tribal College
Midland Lutheran College
Northeast Community College
Peru State College
Southeast Community College
    Lincoln Campus
Western Nebraska Community College

Nevada

Great Basin College
Morrison University
Truckee Meadows Community College

New Hampshire

College for Lifelong Learning
Daniel Webster College
Franklin Pierce College
Keene State College
New England College
New Hampshire Community Technical
    College
    Laconia
Rivier College
Southern New Hampshire University

New Jersey

Atlantic Cape Community College
Bloomfield College
Caldwell College
Camden County College
The College of New Jersey
College of St. Elizabeth
County College of Morris
Fairleigh Dickinson University
    College at Florham
Hudson County Community College
Kean University
Mercer County Community College
New Jersey City University
Ocean County College
Passaic County Community College
Richard Stockton College of New Jersey
Rowan University
Union County College
Warren County Community College

New Mexico

Eastern New Mexico University: Roswell
    Campus
New Mexico Highlands University
New Mexico State University
    Alamogordo
San Juan College
Santa Fe Community College

New York

Adelphi University
City University of New York
    City College
    College of Staten Island
    Hostos Community College
    Hunter College
    Medgar Evers College
    Queens College
Clinton Community College
College of Mount St. Vincent
D'Youville College
Dominican College of Blauvelt
Dowling College
Erie Community College
    City Campus
    North Campus
    South Campus
Genesee Community College
Globe Institute of Technology
Hartwick College
Houghton College
Iona College
Island Drafting and Technical Institute
Jamestown Community College
Maria College
Marist College

Marymount College of Fordham
    University
Medaille College
Mohawk Valley Community College
Molloy College
Monroe College
Mount St. Mary College
New York Institute of Technology
New York University
Nyack College
Onondaga Community College
Roberts Wesleyan College
Sage College of Albany
St. John Fisher College
St. Joseph's College: Suffolk Campus
Schenectady County Community College
Skidmore College
State University of New York
    Albany
    Binghamton
    College at Brockport
    College at Fredonia
    College at Plattsburgh
    College of Agriculture and
        Technology at Morrisville
    College of Technology at Alfred
    College of Technology at Canton
    Oswego
    Purchase
Tompkins-Cortland Community College
Utica College
Utica School of Commerce
Villa Maria College of Buffalo
Wagner College
Westchester Community College

North Carolina

Barton College
Beaufort County Community College
Belmont Abbey College
Bladen Community College
Carteret Community College
Central Carolina Community College
Cleveland Community College
Coastal Carolina Community College
College of the Albemarle
Elizabeth City State University
Elon University
Gardner-Webb University
Mayland Community College
Methodist College
Mount Olive College
Nash Community College
North Carolina State University
Pfeiffer University
Roanoke-Chowan Community College
St. Augustine's College
University of North Carolina
    Asheville
Wilson Technical Community College

North Dakota

Aaker's Business College
Dickinson State University
North Dakota State College of Science
University of Mary
University of North Dakota
Valley City State University

Ohio

Ashland University
Bluffton College
Bryant & Stratton College
Case Western Reserve University
Cedarville University
Clark State Community College
Cleveland State University
College of Mount St. Joseph
Columbus State Community College
Davis College
Defiance College
Franciscan University of Steubenville
James A. Rhodes State College

Kent State University
    Ashtabula Regional Campus
Lakeland Community College
Marietta College
Miami University
    Hamilton Campus
    Middletown Campus
Muskingum College
Oberlin College
Ohio Business College: Sandusky
Ohio Northern University
Ohio State University
    Columbus Campus
Ohio University
Ohio Valley College of Technology
Ohio Wesleyan University
Otterbein College
Southern State Community College
University of Cincinnati
    Clermont College
    Raymond Walters College
Urbana University
Walsh University
Wilmington College
Wittenberg University

Oklahoma

Bacone College
Cameron University
Carl Albert State College
Langston University
Northern Oklahoma College
Oklahoma Baptist University
Oklahoma City Community College
Oklahoma Panhandle State University
Oklahoma State University
    Oklahoma City
Oral Roberts University
Redlands Community College
Southern Nazarene University
Southwestern Christian University
Southwestern Oklahoma State University
University of Science and Arts of
    Oklahoma
Western Oklahoma State College

Oregon

Blue Mountain Community College
Clackamas Community College
Eastern Oregon University
Lane Community College
Northwest Christian College
Oregon Institute of Technology
Pacific University
Pioneer Pacific College
Reed College
Southern Oregon University
Southwestern Oregon Community
    College

Pennsylvania

Academy of Medical Arts and Business
Albright College
Allentown Business School
Arcadia University
Bryn Mawr College
Bucknell University
Carnegie Mellon University
Cedar Crest College
Community College of Beaver County
DeSales University
Delaware Valley College
Dickinson College
Duquesne University
Elizabethtown College
Geneva College
Gettysburg College
Gwynedd-Mercy College
Immaculata University
Kutztown University of Pennsylvania
Lafayette College
Lebanon Valley College of Pennsylvania
Lehigh University
Lincoln University

Lock Haven University of Pennsylvania
Luzerne County Community College
Marywood University
Mercyhurst College
Moravian College
Mount Aloysius College
Neumann College
Newport Business Institute
PJA School
Penn State
    Beaver
    Dubois
    Erie, The Behrend College
Philadelphia Biblical University
Philadelphia University
Point Park College
Seton Hill University
Temple University
Thiel College
University of Pittsburgh
    Greensburg
    Titusville
University of the Sciences in
    Philadelphia
Waynesburg College
Widener University

Puerto Rico

Atlantic College
Columbia College
Inter American University of Puerto Rico
    Barranquitas Campus
    Bayamon Campus
Turabo University
Universidad Metropolitana
Universidad del Este
University of Puerto Rico
    Rio Piedras Campus
University of the Sacred Heart

Rhode Island

Salve Regina University

South Carolina

Anderson College
College of Charleston
Columbia International University
Converse College
Florence-Darlington Technical College
Forrest Junior College
Lander University
Limestone College
Midlands Technical College
Newberry College
Northeastern Technical College
Orangeburg-Calhoun Technical College
Piedmont Technical College
Williamsburg Technical College
Wofford College

South Dakota

Augustana College
Mount Marty College
South Dakota State University
University of Sioux Falls
University of South Dakota

Tennessee

Belmont University
Bethel College
Christian Brothers University
Draughons Junior College of Business:
    Nashville
Dyersburg State Community College
Freed-Hardeman University
Jackson State Community College
Lambuth University
Lane College
Maryville College
National College of Business &
    Technology
    Tennessee
Pellissippi State Technical Community
    College

Southwest Tennessee Community
    College
Tennessee Technological University
Tennessee Wesleyan College
Union University
University of Memphis
University of Tennessee
    Knoxville
Walters State Community College

Texas

Angelina College
Blinn College
Central Texas College
Clarendon College
Coastal Bend College
Concordia University at Austin
Frank Phillips College
Hill College
Howard College
Jarvis Christian College
McMurry University
Midland College
Midwestern State University
North Lake College
Northwood University: Texas Campus
Paul Quinn College
Rice University
St. Edward's University
St. Mary's University
Sam Houston State University
Southwestern Adventist University
Southwestern University
Tarrant County College
Texarkana College
Texas Lutheran University
Trinity University
Tyler Junior College
University of Texas
    Brownsville

Utah

Brigham Young University
University of Utah
Utah Valley State College
Westminster College

Vermont

Burlington College
Castleton State College
Champlain College
College of St. Joseph in Vermont
Community College of Vermont
Lyndon State College
Norwich University
St. Michael's College

Virginia

Averett University
Liberty University
Longwood University
Mary Baldwin College
National College of Business &
    Technology
    Bluefield
    Charlottesville
Norfolk State University
University of Richmond
University of Virginia's College at Wise
Virginia Polytechnic Institute and State
    University
Virginia Wesleyan College
Virginia Western Community College

Washington

Clark College
Crown College
Gonzaga University
Henry Cogswell College
Lake Washington Technical College
Lower Columbia College
Northwest College
Pacific Lutheran University
Peninsula College

Renton Technical College
St. Martin's College
University of Washington
Walla Walla College
Walla Walla Community College
Washington State University
Whitman College

West Virginia

Bluefield State College
Concord College
Davis and Elkins College
Fairmont State College
Salem International University
Shepherd College
West Virginia University Institute of
    Technology
West Virginia University at Parkersburg
Wheeling Jesuit University

Wisconsin

Carthage College
Edgewood College
Lakeland College
Marquette University
Milwaukee Area Technical College
Mount Mary College
University of Wisconsin
    Baraboo/Sauk County
    Green Bay
    Parkside
    River Falls
    Superior

Combined liberal arts/ career program in criminal justice

Alabama

Alabama State University
Calhoun Community College
Chattahoochee Valley Community
    College
Community College of the Air Force
Faulkner University
Jacksonville State University
Northwest-Shoals Community College

Arizona

Gateway Community College
Northern Arizona University
Prescott College

Arkansas

Harding University
Northwest Arkansas Community College
South Arkansas Community College
University of Arkansas
    Community College at Batesville
    Community College at Hope
    Fort Smith
    Monticello

California

California State University
    Chico
    Hayward
    Stanislaus
Chapman University
College of the Canyons
College of the Siskiyous
Diablo Valley College
Feather River College
Gavilan Community College
Imperial Valley College
Long Beach City College
Los Angeles Harbor College
Loyola Marymount University
Modesto Junior College
Mount San Antonio College
Ohlone College
San Francisco State University

San Joaquin Delta College
San Jose State University
Santa Rosa Junior College
Sonoma State University
University of La Verne
University of Southern California

Colorado

Blair Junior College
Metropolitan State College of Denver
Red Rocks Community College
Trinidad State Junior College

Connecticut

Asnuntuck Community College
Briarwood College
Quinnipiac University
Sacred Heart University
Teikyo Post University
Tunxis Community College

District of Columbia

Gallaudet University

Florida

Daytona Beach Community College
Edward Waters College
Florida Metropolitan University
    Melbourne Campus
Florida Southern College
Hillsborough Community College
St. Leo University
Southwest Florida College
Tallahassee Community College
University of West Florida

Georgia

Albany Technical College
Atlanta Metropolitan College
Central Georgia Technical College
Clark Atlanta University
Floyd College
Gordon College
LaGrange College
Macon State College
North Georgia College & State
    University
Paine College
Thomas University
Waycross College

Idaho

Lewis-Clark State College
Northwest Nazarene University

Illinois

Aurora University
Benedictine University
Blackburn College
Chicago State University
City Colleges of Chicago
    Harold Washington College
    Malcolm X College
Danville Area Community College
Dominican University
Heartland Community College
Illinois State University
John A. Logan College
Lewis University
Lewis and Clark Community College
Lincoln Land Community College
MacMurray College
McKendree College
Moraine Valley Community College
North Central College
Olivet Nazarene University
Quincy University
Richland Community College
Rock Valley College
Shawnee Community College
South Suburban College of Cook County
University of Illinois
    Springfield

Waubonsee Community College

Indiana

Ancilla College
Calumet College of St. Joseph
Franklin College
Grace College
Indiana Wesleyan University
Ivy Tech State College
    Bloomington
    Eastcentral
    Kokomo
    Lafayette
    Northcentral
    Northwest
    Southwest
    Wabash Valley
Oakland City University
St. Joseph's College

Iowa

Briar Cliff University
Des Moines Area Community College
Dordt College
Ellsworth Community College
Graceland University
Grand View College
Hamilton College
    Cedar Rapids
Indian Hills Community College
Kirkwood Community College
Loras College
Marshalltown Community College
Mount Mercy College
North Iowa Area Community College
Northwestern College
St. Ambrose University
Simpson College
Southeastern Community College
    South Campus
University of Dubuque
Upper Iowa University
William Penn University

Kansas

Allen County Community College
Bethany College
Butler County Community College
Central Christian College
Friends University
Garden City Community College
Kansas City Kansas Community College
Kansas State University
Labette Community College
Newman University
Pittsburg State University
Seward County Community College
Wichita State University

Kentucky

Murray State University
Pikeville College
Thomas More College

Louisiana

Dillard University
Louisiana State University
    Eunice
Loyola University New Orleans
Northwestern State University
Nunez Community College
Southern University and Agricultural and
    Mechanical College
University of Louisiana at Lafayette

Maine

Andover College
St. Joseph's College
University of Maine
    Augusta
University of Southern Maine

Maryland

Allegany College
Anne Arundel Community College
Bowie State University
College of Southern Maryland
Community College of Baltimore County
    Catonsville
    Dundalk
    Essex
Coppin State College
Frederick Community College
Frostburg State University
Hagerstown Community College
Harford Community College
Howard Community College

Massachusetts

American International College
Anna Maria College
Becker College
Berkshire Community College
Bridgewater State College
Fisher College
Framingham State College
Lasell College
Mount Wachusett Community College
Newbury College
Springfield College
Stonehill College
Western New England College

Michigan

Adrian College
Alpena Community College
Bay de Noc Community College
Cornerstone University
Finlandia University
Glen Oaks Community College
Grace Bible College
Grand Valley State University
Jackson Community College
Kellogg Community College
Mid Michigan Community College
Montcalm Community College
Mott Community College
Northern Michigan University
Washtenaw Community College

Minnesota

Bemidji State University
Capella University
Central Lakes College
Century Community and Technical
    College
Fergus Falls Community College
Gustavus Adolphus College
Itasca Community College
Minneapolis Community and Technical
    College
Normandale Community College
Northland Community & Technical
    College
Riverland Community College: A
    Technical and Community College
St. Cloud State University
Southwest State University

Mississippi

Mississippi State University
Mississippi Valley State University

Missouri

Avila University
Central Methodist College
Central Missouri State University
College of the Ozarks
Culver-Stockton College
Drury University
East Central College
Jefferson College
Mineral Area College
Missouri Baptist University
Missouri Southern State College
Missouri Valley College

Penn Valley Community College
St. Louis Community College
    St. Louis Community College at
        Forest Park
Three Rivers Community College

Montana

University of Great Falls

Nebraska

Bellevue University
Creighton University
Dana College
Mid Plains Community College Area
Midland Lutheran College
Northeast Community College
Peru State College
Western Nebraska Community College

Nevada

Great Basin College
Truckee Meadows Community College

New Hampshire

College for Lifelong Learning
Franklin Pierce College
New England College
New Hampshire Community Technical
    College
        Laconia

New Jersey

Atlantic Cape Community College
Bloomfield College
Caldwell College
Camden County College
College of St. Elizabeth
County College of Morris
Hudson County Community College
Kean University
Mercer County Community College
New Jersey City University
Ocean County College
Passaic County Community College
Richard Stockton College of New Jersey
Rowan University
Union County College
Warren County Community College

New Mexico

Eastern New Mexico University: Roswell
    Campus
New Mexico Highlands University
New Mexico State University
    Alamogordo
San Juan College
Santa Fe Community College

New York

City University of New York
    College of Staten Island
    John Jay College of Criminal
        Justice
Clinton Community College
Dominican College of Blauvelt
Erie Community College
    City Campus
    North Campus
    South Campus
Genesee Community College
Iona College
Jamestown Community College
Keuka College
Marist College
Medaille College
Mohawk Valley Community College
Molloy College
Mount St. Mary College
New York Institute of Technology
North Country Community College
Onondaga Community College
Roberts Wesleyan College
Rochester Institute of Technology

Russell Sage College
Sage College of Albany
St. John Fisher College
St. Joseph's College: Suffolk Campus
Schenectady County Community College
State University of New York
    Albany
    Binghamton
    College at Brockport
    College at Fredonia
    College at Plattsburgh
    College of Agriculture and
        Technology at Morrisville
    College of Technology at Canton
    Oswego
Tompkins-Cortland Community College
Utica College
Wagner College
Westchester Community College

North Carolina

Barton College
Beaufort County Community College
Belmont Abbey College
Bladen Community College
Carteret Community College
Central Carolina Community College
Coastal Carolina Community College
College of the Albemarle
Elizabeth City State University
Elon University
Fayetteville Technical Community
    College
James Sprunt Community College
Lenoir Community College
Mayland Community College
Methodist College
Mount Olive College
Nash Community College
North Carolina State University
Pfeiffer University
Randolph Community College
Roanoke-Chowan Community College
St. Augustine's College
Sampson Community College
Southeastern Community College
Wake Technical Community College
Wilson Technical Community College

North Dakota

North Dakota State College of Science
University of Mary
University of North Dakota

Ohio

Ashland University
Bluffton College
Cedarville University
Clark State Community College
Cleveland State University
Columbus State Community College
David N. Myers College
Defiance College
Kent State University
    Ashtabula Regional Campus
Lakeland Community College
Lourdes College
Miami University
    Middletown Campus
Ohio Northern University
Ohio State University
    Columbus Campus
Ohio University
Ohio Valley College of Technology
University of Cincinnati
    Clermont College
    Raymond Walters College
Urbana University
Walsh University
Wilmington College

Oklahoma

Cameron University
Carl Albert State College

Langston University
Northern Oklahoma College
Redlands Community College
Rogers State University
Southwestern Oklahoma State University
Western Oklahoma State College

Oregon

Clackamas Community College
Lane Community College
Pioneer Pacific College
Southern Oregon University
Southwestern Oregon Community
College

Pennsylvania

Academy of Medical Arts and Business
Albright College
Allentown Business School
California University of Pennsylvania
Community College of Beaver County
DeSales University
Delaware Valley College
Elizabethtown College
Geneva College
Immaculata University
Kutztown University of Pennsylvania
Lincoln University
Lock Haven University of Pennsylvania
Luzerne County Community College
Marywood University
Mercyhurst College
Moravian College
Mount Aloysius College
Neumann College
PJA School
Penn State
Dubois
Point Park College
Rosemont College
Seton Hill University
Temple University
Thiel College
University of Pittsburgh
Greensburg
Titusville
Waynesburg College
Widener University

Puerto Rico

Inter American University of Puerto Rico
Barranquitas Campus
Turabo University
Universidad Metropolitana
Universidad del Este
University of the Sacred Heart

Rhode Island

Salve Regina University

South Carolina

Coker College
Columbia International University
Florence-Darlington Technical College
Lander University
Limestone College
Midlands Technical College
Newberry College
Northeastern Technical College
Orangeburg-Calhoun Technical College
Piedmont Technical College

South Dakota

Mount Marty College
University of South Dakota

Tennessee

Draughons Junior College of Business:
Nashville
Dyersburg State Community College
Lambuth University
Lane College

Pellissippi State Technical Community
College
Southwest Tennessee Community
College
Walters State Community College

Texas

Angelina College
Blinn College
Central Texas College
Coastal Bend College
Frank Phillips College
Hill College
Howard College
Jarvis Christian College
Lamar State College at Port Arthur
McMurry University
Midland College
Midwestern State University
Paul Quinn College
St. Edward's University
Sam Houston State University
Southwestern Adventist University
Tarrant County College
Texarkana College
Texas A&M International University
Texas A&M University
Texarkana
Texas Lutheran University
Tyler Junior College
University of Texas
Brownsville

Utah

University of Utah
Utah Valley State College

Vermont

Castleton State College
Champlain College
Community College of Vermont
Norwich University
Southern Vermont College

Virginia

Averett University
Longwood University
Norfolk State University
Rappahannock Community College
University of Richmond
University of Virginia's College at Wise
Virginia Union University
Virginia Wesleyan College
Virginia Western Community College

Washington

Crown College
Gonzaga University
Lower Columbia College
Peninsula College
St. Martin's College
Walla Walla Community College
Washington State University

West Virginia

Bluefield State College
Fairmont State College
Salem International University
Shepherd College
West Virginia University at Parkersburg
Wheeling Jesuit University

Wisconsin

Carthage College
Edgewood College
Lakeland College
Marian College of Fond du Lac
Marquette University
Mount Mary College

University of Wisconsin
Baraboo/Sauk County
Green Bay
Parkside
Superior

Wyoming

Sheridan College

Combined liberal arts/ career program in education

Alabama

Alabama State University
Birmingham-Southern College
Calhoun Community College
Chattahoochee Valley Community
College
Community College of the Air Force
Concordia College
Jacksonville State University
Troy State University in Montgomery
University of Mobile

Alaska

Alaska Pacific University
University of Alaska
Southeast

Arizona

Gateway Community College
Prescott College
Rio Salado College

Arkansas

Harding University
Mid-South Community College
Philander Smith College
South Arkansas Community College
University of Arkansas
Monticello
University of Central Arkansas
University of the Ozarks

California

Antioch Southern California
Los Angeles
Bethesda Christian University
California Baptist University
California State University
Chico
Monterey Bay
College of the Canyons
Concordia University
Dominican University of California
Fresno Pacific University
Gavilan Community College
Hope International University
Loyola Marymount University
Master's College
National University
Occidental College
Ohlone College
Pacific Union College
San Diego Mesa College
San Jose State University
Sonoma State University
University of La Verne
University of San Diego
University of San Francisco
University of Southern California
University of the Pacific

Colorado

Colorado Mountain College
Alpine Campus
Fort Lewis College
Front Range Community College
National American University
Denver
Red Rocks Community College

Trinidad State Junior College

Connecticut

Gateway Community College
Quinnipiac University
Sacred Heart University
Trinity College
University of Bridgeport

District of Columbia

Gallaudet University

Florida

Baptist College of Florida
Beacon College
Edward Waters College
Hillsborough Community College
St. Leo University
Tallahassee Community College
University of West Florida
Warner Southern College

Georgia

Albany State University
Albany Technical College
Atlanta Metropolitan College
Central Georgia Technical College
Emory University
Floyd College
Georgia Southwestern State University
Gordon College
Kennesaw State University
LaGrange College
Macon State College
Morehouse College
North Georgia College & State
University
Paine College
Southwest Georgia Technical College
Thomas University
Waycross College
Wesleyan College

Idaho

Albertson College of Idaho
Lewis-Clark State College
Northwest Nazarene University

Illinois

Aurora University
Benedictine University
Blackburn College
Chicago State University
City Colleges of Chicago
Harold Washington College
Malcolm X College
Columbia College Chicago
Danville Area Community College
De Paul University
Dominican University
Illinois College
John A. Logan College
Lewis University
MacMurray College
McKendree College
Monmouth College
North Central College
Olivet Nazarene University
Principia College
Quincy University
Richland Community College
Shawnee Community College
Trinity Christian College
University of Illinois
Springfield
Waubonsee Community College

Indiana

Ancilla College
Calumet College of St. Joseph
Franklin College
Goshen College
Huntington College

Indiana Wesleyan University
Marian College
Oakland City University
St. Joseph's College
University of St. Francis

Iowa

Central College
Dordt College
Drake University
Ellsworth Community College
Faith Baptist Bible College and
    Theological Seminary
Graceland University
Grand View College
Kirkwood Community College
Loras College
Maharishi University of Management
Marshalltown Community College
Morningside College
Mount Mercy College
Northwestern College
St. Ambrose University
Simpson College
University of Dubuque
Upper Iowa University
Waldorf College
William Penn University

Kansas

Allen County Community College
Barclay College
Bethany College
Central Christian College
Friends University
Garden City Community College
Hesston College
Kansas City Kansas Community College
Labette Community College
Ottawa University
Pratt Community College
Seward County Community College
Sterling College
Tabor College
Wichita State University

Kentucky

Alice Lloyd College
Asbury College
Bellarmine University
Cumberland College
Henderson Community College
Kentucky Christian College
Madisonville Community College
Murray State University
Pikeville College
Thomas More College
Transylvania University

Louisiana

Centenary College of Louisiana
Dillard University
Louisiana State University
    Eunice
Loyola University New Orleans
Northwestern State University
Nunez Community College
University of Louisiana at Lafayette
Xavier University of Louisiana

Maine

Maine College of Art
St. Joseph's College
University of Southern Maine

Maryland

Allegany College
Bowie State University
College of Notre Dame of Maryland
College of Southern Maryland
Columbia Union College

Community College of Baltimore County
    Catonsville
    Dundalk
    Essex
Coppin State College
Frederick Community College
Hagerstown Community College
Harford Community College
Howard Community College
Mount St. Mary's College
University of Maryland
    Baltimore County
Villa Julie College

Massachusetts

American International College
Anna Maria College
Atlantic Union College
Becker College
Berkshire Community College
Boston University
Bridgewater State College
Clark University
Emmanuel College
Fisher College
Fitchburg State College
Framingham State College
Greenfield Community College
Lasell College
Lesley University
Massachusetts College of Liberal Arts
Mount Holyoke College
Nichols College
Simmons College
Springfield College
Springfield Technical Community
    College
Stonehill College
Western New England College
Wheaton College

Michigan

Adrian College
Alma College
Alpena Community College
Baker College
    of Auburn Hills
    of Cadillac
    of Muskegon
    of Port Huron
Cornerstone University
Finlandia University
Grace Bible College
Grand Valley State University
Hope College
Jackson Community College
Kellogg Community College
Madonna University
Mid Michigan Community College
Montcalm Community College
Northern Michigan University
Reformed Bible College
University of Michigan

Minnesota

Bemidji State University
Bethel College
Capella University
College of St. Catherine
College of St. Scholastica
Concordia College: Moorhead
Crown College
Itasca Community College
Normandale Community College
North Central University
Northland Community & Technical
    College
Southwest State University
University of Minnesota
    Morris

Mississippi

Holmes Community College
Mississippi State University

Mississippi Valley State University
Rust College

Missouri

Avila University
Calvary Bible College
Central Methodist College
Central Missouri State University
College of the Ozarks
Culver-Stockton College
Drury University
East Central College
Fontbonne College
Jefferson College
Maryville University of Saint Louis
Missouri Baptist University
Missouri Southern State College
Missouri Valley College
North Central Missouri College
Ozark Christian College
Penn Valley Community College
St. Louis Community College
    St. Louis Community College at
        Forest Park
Stephens College
Washington University in St. Louis
Webster University
Westminster College
William Jewell College
William Woods University

Montana

Carroll College
Flathead Valley Community College
Rocky Mountain College
University of Great Falls

Nebraska

College of Saint Mary
Concordia University
Creighton University
Dana College
Grace University
Little Priest Tribal College
Midland Lutheran College
Northeast Community College
Peru State College
Western Nebraska Community College

Nevada

Great Basin College
Truckee Meadows Community College

New Hampshire

Franklin Pierce College
Keene State College
New England College
Rivier College

New Jersey

Atlantic Cape Community College
Bloomfield College
Caldwell College
The College of New Jersey
College of St. Elizabeth
County College of Morris
Drew University
Fairleigh Dickinson University
    College at Florham
Hudson County Community College
Mercer County Community College
Ocean County College
Union County College

New Mexico

New Mexico Highlands University
New Mexico State University
    Alamogordo
San Juan College
Santa Fe Community College

New York

Adelphi University

City University of New York
    City College
    College of Staten Island
    Hostos Community College
    Hunter College
    La Guardia Community College
    Medgar Evers College
    Queens College
    Queensborough Community
        College
Clinton Community College
Colgate University
College of Mount St. Vincent
College of New Rochelle
Concordia College
D'Youville College
Dominican College of Blauvelt
Dutchess Community College
Genesee Community College
Hartwick College
Hobart and William Smith Colleges
Houghton College
Keuka College
Long Island University
    Southampton College
Maria College
Marist College
Marymount College of Fordham
    University
Marymount Manhattan College
Medaille College
Mohawk Valley Community College
Molloy College
Mount St. Mary College
Nazareth College of Rochester
New York Institute of Technology
New York University
Nyack College
Roberts Wesleyan College
Rockland Community College
Russell Sage College
St. John Fisher College
St. Joseph's College: Suffolk Campus
Schenectady County Community College
Skidmore College
State University of New York
    Albany
    College at Brockport
    College at Fredonia
    College at Plattsburgh
    College of Agriculture and
        Technology at Morrisville
    College of Environmental Science
        and Forestry
    Oswego
Syracuse University
Utica College
Villa Maria College of Buffalo
Wagner College

North Carolina

Barton College
Beaufort County Community College
Belmont Abbey College
Bladen Community College
Carteret Community College
Central Carolina Community College
Coastal Carolina Community College
College of the Albemarle
Elizabeth City State University
Elon University
Fayetteville Technical Community
    College
Gardner-Webb University
Lenoir Community College
Mayland Community College
Methodist College
Mount Olive College
Nash Community College
Peace College
Pfeiffer University
Piedmont Baptist College
Queens University of Charlotte
Roanoke Bible College
Roanoke-Chowan Community College

St. Andrews Presbyterian College
St. Augustine's College
Sampson Community College
University of North Carolina
    Asheville
Winston-Salem State University

North Dakota

Dickinson State University
North Dakota State College of Science
University of Mary
University of North Dakota

Ohio

Ashland University
Cedarville University
Circleville Bible College
Cleveland State University
College of Mount St. Joseph
Franciscan University of Steubenville
Kent State University
    Salem Regional Campus
Kenyon College
Lourdes College
Marietta College
Miami University
    Hamilton Campus
Muskingum College
Oberlin College
Ohio University
Otterbein College
University of Cincinnati
    Clermont College
    Raymond Walters College
University of Findlay
Urbana University
Ursuline College
Walsh University
Wilmington College
Wittenberg University

Oklahoma

Cameron University
Carl Albert State College
Langston University
Northern Oklahoma College
Oklahoma Panhandle State University
Oklahoma State University
    Oklahoma City
Oral Roberts University
Redlands Community College
Southwestern Christian University
Southwestern Oklahoma State University
University of Science and Arts of
    Oklahoma
Western Oklahoma State College

Oregon

Blue Mountain Community College
Concordia University
Eastern Oregon University
Eugene Bible College
Multnomah Bible College
Northwest Christian College
Pacific University
Portland State University
Southern Oregon University

Pennsylvania

Albright College
Arcadia University
Bryn Athyn College of the New Church
Bryn Mawr College
Bucknell University
Carnegie Mellon University
Cedar Crest College
Community College of Allegheny
    County
DeSales University
Duquesne University
Elizabethtown College
Geneva College
Gwynedd-Mercy College
Immaculata University

Lebanon Valley College of Pennsylvania
Lehigh University
Lock Haven University of Pennsylvania
Luzerne County Community College
Marywood University
Mercyhurst College
Moravian College
Mount Aloysius College
Neumann College
Penn State
    Beaver
    Dubois
    Erie, The Behrend College
Philadelphia Biblical University
Point Park College
Rosemont College
St. Vincent College
Seton Hill University
Temple University
Thiel College
University of Pittsburgh
    Greensburg
    Johnstown
Waynesburg College
Widener University

Puerto Rico

Atlantic College
Conservatory of Music of Puerto Rico
Escuela de Artes Plasticas de Puerto Rico
Inter American University of Puerto Rico
    Barranquitas Campus
Turabo University
Universidad Metropolitana
Universidad del Este
University of Puerto Rico
    Cayey University College
    Rio Piedras Campus

Rhode Island

Salve Regina University

South Carolina

Anderson College
Converse College
Lander University
Limestone College
Newberry College
Northeastern Technical College
Piedmont Technical College
Wofford College

South Dakota

Augustana College
Mount Marty College
South Dakota State University
University of Sioux Falls
University of South Dakota

Tennessee

Aquinas College
Belmont University
Bethel College
Christian Brothers University
Crichton College
Dyersburg State Community College
Freed-Hardeman University
Jackson State Community College
Lambuth University
Lane College
Maryville College
Pellissippi State Technical Community
    College
Southwest Tennessee Community
    College
Tennessee Technological University
Tennessee Wesleyan College
Union University
University of Memphis
University of Tennessee
    Knoxville

Texas

Angelina College

Central Texas College
Coastal Bend College
Concordia University at Austin
El Centro College
Frank Phillips College
Hill College
Jarvis Christian College
McMurry University
Midwestern State University
North Harris Montgomery Community
    College District
Northeast Texas Community College
Rice University
St. Edward's University
Sam Houston State University
Schreiner University
Southwestern Adventist University
Southwestern University
Texas A&M International University
Texas A&M University
    Galveston
Texas Lutheran University
Trinity University
University of Texas
    Brownsville
    Tyler

Utah

Brigham Young University
University of Utah
Utah Valley State College
Westminster College

Vermont

Bennington College
Castleton State College
Champlain College
College of St. Joseph in Vermont
Green Mountain College
Lyndon State College

Virginia

Averett University
Longwood University
Norfolk State University
Randolph-Macon College
Rappahannock Community College
University of Richmond
University of Virginia's College at Wise
Virginia Polytechnic Institute and State
    University
Virginia Wesleyan College
Virginia Western Community College
Washington and Lee University

Washington

Clark College
Gonzaga University
Lower Columbia College
Northwest College
Pacific Lutheran University
St. Martin's College
Trinity Lutheran College
University of Washington
Walla Walla College
Walla Walla Community College
Washington State University
Whitman College

West Virginia

Bethany College
Bluefield State College
Concord College
Davis and Elkins College
Fairmont State College
Salem International University
Shepherd College
University of Charleston
West Virginia University Institute of
    Technology
Wheeling Jesuit University

Wisconsin

Alverno College

Beloit College
Edgewood College
Lakeland College
Marian College of Fond du Lac
Marquette University
Mount Mary College
University of Wisconsin
    Baraboo/Sauk County
    Green Bay
    Parkside
    River Falls
    Superior

Wyoming

Sheridan College

Combined liberal arts/ career program in engineering

Alabama

Alabama State University
Auburn University
Birmingham-Southern College
Huntingdon College
Northwest-Shoals Community College
Remington College
    Southeast College of Technology
Samford University
Tuskegee University
University of Alabama
    Huntsville
University of Mobile

Arkansas

Harding University
University of the Ozarks

California

Biola University
California Institute of Technology
California State University
    Chico
    Hayward
    Stanislaus
Claremont McKenna College
College of the Siskiyous
Diablo Valley College
Gavilan Community College
Los Angeles Harbor College
Los Angeles Trade and Technical College
Modesto Junior College
Occidental College
Ohlone College
Palomar College
Pomona College
St. Mary's College of California
San Diego Mesa College
San Francisco State University
San Joaquin Delta College
San Jose State University
Scripps College
University of California
    Santa Cruz
University of San Diego
University of San Francisco
University of Southern California
University of the Pacific

Colorado

Arapahoe Community College
Colorado State University
Fort Lewis College
Front Range Community College
Metropolitan State College of Denver
Red Rocks Community College
Trinidad State Junior College
United States Air Force Academy
University of Colorado
    Denver

Connecticut
Fairfield University
Gateway Community College
Norwalk Community College
Trinity College
Tunxis Community College
United States Coast Guard Academy
University of Bridgeport
Wesleyan University

Florida
Daytona Beach Community College
Eckerd College
Florida Southern College
Hillsborough Community College
Jacksonville University
Rollins College
Tallahassee Community College
University of West Florida

Georgia
Agnes Scott College
Albany State University
Armstrong Atlantic State University
Atlanta Metropolitan College
Berry College
Clark Atlanta University
Columbus State University
Covenant College
Emory University
Georgia College and State University
Georgia Institute of Technology
Georgia Southwestern State University
LaGrange College
Macon State College
Morehouse College
Morris Brown College
North Georgia College & State
    University
Paine College
Southern Polytechnic State University
Waycross College
Wesleyan College

Idaho
Albertson College of Idaho
Lewis-Clark State College
Northwest Nazarene University

Illinois
Augustana College
Benedictine University
Blackburn College
Chicago State University
City Colleges of Chicago
    Harold Washington College
Dominican University
Eastern Illinois University
Elmhurst College
Eureka College
Greenville College
Illinois College
Illinois Institute of Technology
Illinois Wesleyan University
Knox College
Lake Forest College
Lewis and Clark Community College
MacMurray College
Monmouth College
Northwestern University
Olivet Nazarene University
Principia College
Quincy University
Richland Community College
Rock Valley College
Rockford College
Shawnee Community College
South Suburban College of Cook County
University of Illinois
    Urbana-Champaign
University of St. Francis
Waubonsee Community College
Wheaton College

Indiana
Butler University
Earlham College
Franklin College
Goshen College
Indiana Institute of Technology
Manchester College
Marian College
Saint Mary's College
Wabash College

Iowa
Briar Cliff University
Buena Vista University
Central College
Clarke College
Dordt College
Ellsworth Community College
Graceland University
Grand View College
Grinnell College
Kirkwood Community College
Loras College
Luther College
Maharishi University of Management
Marshalltown Community College
Morningside College
North Iowa Area Community College
St. Ambrose University
University of Northern Iowa
William Penn University

Kansas
Allen County Community College
Baker University
Benedictine College
Bethany College
Bethel College
Butler County Community College
Central Christian College
Emporia State University
Friends University
Garden City Community College
Kansas City Kansas Community College
Kansas State University
Labette Community College
Pittsburg State University
Seward County Community College
Southwestern College
Wichita State University

Kentucky
Asbury College
Bellarmine University
Berea College
Brescia University
Centre College
Georgetown College
Kentucky Wesleyan College
Murray State University
Transylvania University

Louisiana
Centenary College of Louisiana
Dillard University
Grantham University
Louisiana Tech University
Loyola University New Orleans
Northwestern State University
Southern University and Agricultural and
    Mechanical College
Tulane University
University of Louisiana at Lafayette

Maine
Bates College
Bowdoin College
Maine Maritime Academy
University of Maine
University of Southern Maine

Maryland
Allegany College
Bowie State University

College of Notre Dame of Maryland
College of Southern Maryland
Columbia Union College
Community College of Baltimore County
    Catonsville
    Dundalk
    Essex
Coppin State College
Frederick Community College
Frostburg State University
Goucher College
Hagerstown Community College
Harford Community College
Hood College
Howard Community College
McDaniel College
Morgan State University
Salisbury University
Towson University
University of Maryland
    Baltimore County
Washington College

Massachusetts
Assumption College
Benjamin Franklin Institute of
    Technology
Berkshire Community College
Boston College
Boston University
Clark University
College of the Holy Cross
Emmanuel College
Framingham State College
Franklin W. Olin College of Engineering
Massachusetts Maritime Academy
Mount Holyoke College
Smith College
Stonehill College
Tufts University
Wheaton College
Worcester Polytechnic Institute

Michigan
Adrian College
Alma College
Glen Oaks Community College
Grand Valley State University
Hope College
Kellogg Community College
Lawrence Technological University
Montcalm Community College
University of Michigan
Wayne State University

Minnesota
Augsburg College
Bethel College
Carleton College
Central Lakes College
Century Community and Technical
    College
College of St. Benedict
College of St. Scholastica
Gustavus Adolphus College
Itasca Community College
Macalester College
Northland Community & Technical
    College
St. Cloud State University
St. John's University
University of Minnesota
    Morris

Mississippi
Millsaps College
Mississippi State University
Mississippi University for Women

Missouri
Central Methodist College
Central Missouri State University
College of the Ozarks
Culver-Stockton College

Drury University
East Central College
Fontbonne College
Jefferson College
Lindenwood University
Maryville University of Saint Louis
Missouri Baptist University
Missouri Southern State College
Northwest Missouri State University
Penn Valley Community College
St. Louis Community College
    St. Louis Community College at
        Forest Park
Southwest Baptist University
University of Missouri
    Rolla
    St. Louis
Washington University in St. Louis
Webster University
Westminster College
William Jewell College

Montana
Carroll College
Montana Tech of the University of
    Montana

Nebraska
Concordia University
Dana College
Northeast Community College

New Hampshire
Daniel Webster College
Keene State College
New England College
St. Anselm College

New Jersey
Camden County College
The College of New Jersey
County College of Morris
Drew University
Hudson County Community College
Mercer County Community College
Ocean County College
Passaic County Community College
Richard Stockton College of New Jersey
Rowan University
Rutgers, The State University of New
    Jersey
    Camden Regional Campus
    New Brunswick Regional Campus
    Newark Regional Campus
Union County College

New Mexico
Eastern New Mexico University: Roswell
    Campus
New Mexico Highlands University
New Mexico State University
    Alamogordo
San Juan College
Western New Mexico University

New York
Adelphi University
Alfred University
City University of New York
    Brooklyn College
    City College
    College of Staten Island
Clarkson University
Clinton Community College
Colgate University
College of Aeronautics
Dominican College of Blauvelt
Elmira College
Erie Community College
    City Campus
    North Campus
    South Campus
Genesee Community College
Hamilton College

Hartwick College
Hobart and William Smith Colleges
Houghton College
Ithaca College
Jamestown Community College
Le Moyne College
Mohawk Valley Community College
New York Institute of Technology
New York University
Onondaga Community College
Pace University: Pleasantville/Briarcliff
Roberts Wesleyan College
Russell Sage College
St. Bonaventure University
St. John Fisher College
St. John's University
Skidmore College
State University of New York
    Binghamton
    College at Buffalo
    College at Cortland
    College at Fredonia
    College at Geneseo
    College at Old Westbury
    College at Plattsburgh
    College at Potsdam
    College of Agriculture and
      Technology at Morrisville
    College of Technology at Alfred
    Maritime College
    Oswego
Syracuse University
Tompkins-Cortland Community College
Union College
University of Rochester
Utica College

North Carolina

Barton College
Beaufort County Community College
Bennett College
Campbell University
Central Carolina Community College
Coastal Carolina Community College
College of the Albemarle
Elon University
Gardner-Webb University
Lenoir Community College
Lenoir-Rhyne College
Methodist College
North Carolina State University
Pfeiffer University
St. Andrews Presbyterian College
University of North Carolina
    Asheville
    Greensboro
Wake Forest University
Warren Wilson College
Wilson Technical Community College

North Dakota

Jamestown College
North Dakota State College of Science
University of Mary
University of North Dakota
Valley City State University

Ohio

Baldwin-Wallace College
Bryant & Stratton College
Case Western Reserve University
Cedarville University
Clark State Community College
Cleveland State University
Columbus State Community College
Franciscan University of Steubenville
Heidelberg College
Hiram College
James A. Rhodes State College
Kent State University
    Ashtabula Regional Campus
Kenyon College
Lake Erie College
Lakeland Community College

Marietta College
Miami University
    Hamilton Campus
    Middletown Campus
Muskingum College
Oberlin College
Ohio Northern University
Ohio State University
    Columbus Campus
Ohio University
Ohio Wesleyan University
Otterbein College
Southern State Community College
University of Cincinnati
    Clermont College
    Raymond Walters College
Walsh University
Wittenberg University

Oklahoma

Carl Albert State College
Langston University
Northern Oklahoma College
Oklahoma Baptist University
Oral Roberts University
Western Oklahoma State College

Oregon

Blue Mountain Community College
Eastern Oregon University
George Fox University
Linfield College
Oregon Institute of Technology
Pacific University
Reed College
Southern Oregon University
Southwestern Oregon Community
    College

Pennsylvania

Arcadia University
Bloomsburg University of Pennsylvania
Bryn Mawr College
Bucknell University
California University of Pennsylvania
Carnegie Mellon University
Chatham College
Community College of Beaver County
Duquesne University
Edinboro University of Pennsylvania
Elizabethtown College
Franklin & Marshall College
Geneva College
Gettysburg College
Haverford College
Kutztown University of Pennsylvania
Lafayette College
Lebanon Valley College of Pennsylvania
Lehigh University
Lincoln University
Lock Haven University of Pennsylvania
Luzerne County Community College
Lycoming College
Millersville University of Pennsylvania
Moravian College
Muhlenberg College
Penn State
    Dubois
    Erie, The Behrend College
    Wilkes-Barre
Philadelphia University
Point Park College
Rosemont College
St. Vincent College
Seton Hill University
Swarthmore College
Temple University
Thiel College
University of Pittsburgh
University of Pittsburgh
    Greensburg
    Titusville
Waynesburg College
Widener University

Puerto Rico

Inter American University of Puerto Rico
    Barranquitas Campus
    Bayamon Campus
    San German Campus
Pontifical Catholic University of Puerto
    Rico
Turabo University
University of the Sacred Heart

Rhode Island

University of Rhode Island

South Carolina

Coastal Carolina University
College of Charleston
Erskine College
Florence-Darlington Technical College
Furman University
Lander University
Midlands Technical College
Morris College
Newberry College
Piedmont Technical College
Presbyterian College
Voorhees College
Wofford College

South Dakota

South Dakota State University
University of Sioux Falls

Tennessee

Belmont University
Bethel College
Christian Brothers University
Fisk University
Freed-Hardeman University
Jackson State Community College
King College
Lane College
Maryville College
Middle Tennessee State University
Pellissippi State Technical Community
    College
Southwest Tennessee Community
    College
Tennessee Technological University
Union University
University of Tennessee
    Knoxville
Walters State Community College

Texas

Angelina College
Austin College
Coastal Bend College
Dallas Christian College
Frank Phillips College
Hill College
Huston-Tillotson College
Jarvis Christian College
Lubbock Christian University
McMurry University
Midwestern State University
Northeast Texas Community College
Paul Quinn College
Rice University
St. Mary's University
Sam Houston State University
Schreiner University
Southwest Texas State University
Southwestern Adventist University
Southwestern University
Texarkana College
Texas Lutheran University
Texas Wesleyan University
Trinity University
Tyler Junior College
University of Dallas
University of Texas
    Brownsville

Utah

Brigham Young University
University of Utah
Utah Valley State College
Westminster College

Vermont

Castleton State College
Norwich University
St. Michael's College

Virginia

Bridgewater College
Eastern Mennonite University
Emory & Henry College
Longwood University
Mary Baldwin College
Norfolk State University
Randolph-Macon College
Roanoke College
Sweet Briar College
University of Richmond
Virginia Polytechnic Institute and State
    University
Virginia Western Community College

Washington

Clark College
Gonzaga University
Henry Cogswell College
Lower Columbia College
Pacific Lutheran University
Peninsula College
St. Martin's College
University of Puget Sound
University of Washington
Walla Walla College
Walla Walla Community College
Washington State University
Whitman College

West Virginia

Bethany College
Bluefield State College
West Virginia University Institute of
    Technology
West Virginia University at Parkersburg
Wheeling Jesuit University

Wisconsin

Carthage College
Edgewood College
Lakeland College
Lawrence University
Marquette University
Milwaukee School of Engineering
University of Wisconsin
    Baraboo/Sauk County
    Green Bay
    Parkside
    Superior

Combined liberal arts/ career program in environmental studies

Alabama

Birmingham-Southern College
Northwest-Shoals Community College
University of Mobile

Alaska

Alaska Pacific University
University of Alaska
    Southeast

Arizona

Northern Arizona University
Prescott College

Arkansas

South Arkansas Community College
University of Arkansas
    Cossatot Community College of the
University of Central Arkansas
University of the Ozarks

California

California State University
    Chico
    Hayward
    Monterey Bay
    Stanislaus
Chapman University
Coastline Community College
Dominican University of California
Feather River College
Hope International University
Occidental College
Palomar College
San Francisco State University
San Jose State University
Sonoma State University
University of La Verne
University of Redlands
University of San Diego
University of Southern California
University of the Pacific
Whittier College

Colorado

Colorado Mountain College
    Spring Valley Campus
    Timberline Campus
Fort Lewis College
Front Range Community College
Metropolitan State College of Denver
Red Rocks Community College

Connecticut

Briarwood College
Gateway Community College
Sacred Heart University
Teikyo Post University
United States Coast Guard Academy

Florida

Florida Southern College
Hillsborough Community College
St. Leo University
Stetson University
Tallahassee Community College
University of West Florida

Georgia

Central Georgia Technical College
Emory University
Georgia Institute of Technology
Gordon College
Macon State College
Paine College
Waycross College

Idaho

Lewis-Clark State College

Illinois

Augustana College
Benedictine University
Blackburn College
De Paul University
Dominican University
Illinois College
Illinois State University
Illinois Wesleyan University
Lewis University
Monmouth College
Olivet Nazarene University
Quincy University
Shawnee Community College
University of Illinois
    Springfield
University of St. Francis

Indiana

Earlham College
Franklin College
Goshen College
Huntington College
Marian College
St. Joseph's College
University of St. Francis

Iowa

Central College
Dordt College
Ellsworth Community College
Iowa State University
Kirkwood Community College
Northwestern College
Simpson College
University of Dubuque
Upper Iowa University

Kansas

Kansas State University
McPherson College
Seward County Community College
Tabor College
Wichita State University

Kentucky

Murray State University

Louisiana

Centenary College of Louisiana
Louisiana Tech University
Loyola University New Orleans
Southern University and Agricultural and
    Mechanical College
Tulane University

Maine

St. Joseph's College
University of Maine
University of Southern Maine

Maryland

College of Southern Maryland
Community College of Baltimore County
    Catonsville
    Dundalk
    Essex
Frostburg State University
Harford Community College
Howard Community College
Salisbury University
University of Maryland
    Baltimore County

Massachusetts

Berkshire Community College
Clark University
Framingham State College
Greenfield Community College
Massachusetts Maritime Academy
Mount Holyoke College
Simmons College
Springfield College
Wheaton College
Worcester Polytechnic Institute

Michigan

Adrian College
Alma College
Cornerstone University
Finlandia University
Glen Oaks Community College
Grand Valley State University
Hope College
Lawrence Technological University
Mid Michigan Community College
Montcalm Community College
Mott Community College
Northern Michigan University
University of Michigan

Minnesota

Bemidji State University
Bethel College
Concordia College: Moorhead
Gustavus Adolphus College
Itasca Community College
Rainy River Community College
St. Cloud State University
Southwest State University

Mississippi

Mississippi State University
Mississippi Valley State University

Missouri

Central Methodist College
Drury University
Missouri Southern State College
Northwest Missouri State University
Penn Valley Community College
Stephens College
University of Missouri
    Rolla
Washington University in St. Louis
Westminster College

Montana

Carroll College
Rocky Mountain College
University of Montana: Western

Nebraska

Creighton University
Dana College
Little Priest Tribal College
Midland Lutheran College
Southeast Community College
    Lincoln Campus

Nevada

Sierra Nevada College
Truckee Meadows Community College

New Hampshire

Franklin Pierce College
Keene State College
New England College

New Jersey

Bloomfield College
Caldwell College
Kean University
Richard Stockton College of New Jersey
Rowan University
Warren County Community College

New Mexico

New Mexico Highlands University

New York

Adelphi University
Alfred University
City University of New York
    College of Staten Island
    Hunter College
    Queens College
Clinton Community College
College of New Rochelle
Concordia College
Erie Community College
    City Campus
    North Campus
    South Campus
Genesee Community College
Hartwick College
Houghton College
Jamestown Community College
Le Moyne College
Long Island University
    Southampton College
Marist College
Molloy College
New York Institute of Technology

Paul Smith's College
St. John Fisher College
Skidmore College
State University of New York
    Binghamton
    College at Brockport
    College at Cortland
    College at Fredonia
    College at Plattsburgh
    College of Agriculture and
        Technology at Cobleskill
    College of Agriculture and
        Technology at Morrisville
    College of Environmental Science
        and Forestry
    Maritime College
    New Paltz
    Purchase
Tompkins-Cortland Community College

North Carolina

Barton College
Beaufort County Community College
Bladen Community College
Elon University
High Point University
Lenoir Community College
North Carolina State University
Pfeiffer University
Queens University of Charlotte
Roanoke-Chowan Community College
University of North Carolina
    Asheville

North Dakota

University of North Dakota

Ohio

Antioch College
Ashland University
Cedarville University
Cleveland State University
Columbus State Community College
Defiance College
Kent State University
    Ashtabula Regional Campus
Kenyon College
Marietta College
Muskingum College
Oberlin College
Ohio Northern University
Ohio State University
    Columbus Campus
Ohio University
Ohio Wesleyan University
Otterbein College
University of Cincinnati
    Raymond Walters College
Wilmington College
Wittenberg University

Oklahoma

Northern Oklahoma College
Southern Nazarene University

Oregon

Eastern Oregon University
Oregon Institute of Technology
Pacific University
Southern Oregon University
Southwestern Oregon Community
    College

Pennsylvania

Albright College
Arcadia University
Bucknell University
Cedar Crest College
Community College of Beaver County
DeSales University
Delaware Valley College
Dickinson College
Edinboro University of Pennsylvania
Elizabethtown College

Franklin & Marshall College
Gettysburg College
Immaculata University
Lafayette College
Lebanon Valley College of Pennsylvania
Lehigh University
Lock Haven University of Pennsylvania
Marywood University
Neumann College
Penn State
   Dubois
   New Kensington
Point Park College
Rosemont College
St. Vincent College
Temple University
Thiel College
University of Pittsburgh
   Greensburg
University of the Sciences in
   Philadelphia
Waynesburg College
Widener University

Puerto Rico
Inter American University of Puerto Rico
   Barranquitas Campus
   Bayamon Campus
Pontifical Catholic University of Puerto
   Rico
Universidad Metropolitana
University of Puerto Rico
   Rio Piedras Campus

Rhode Island
Salve Regina University

South Carolina
Furman University
Lander University
Newberry College
Presbyterian College

South Dakota
Mount Marty College

Tennessee
Maryville College
Pellissippi State Technical Community
   College
Southwest Tennessee Community
   College
Tennessee Technological University
University of Tennessee
   Knoxville

Texas
Angelina College
Coastal Bend College
Concordia University at Austin
Frank Phillips College
McMurry University
Midland College
Midwestern State University
Rice University
Sam Houston State University
Southwestern University
Tarrant County College
Texas A&M International University
Texas A&M University
   Galveston
Texas Lutheran University
University of the Incarnate Word

Utah
Brigham Young University
University of Utah
Utah Valley State College
Westminster College

Vermont
Castleton State College
Green Mountain College

Lyndon State College
Norwich University
St. Michael's College
Southern Vermont College
Sterling College

Virginia
Averett University
Longwood University
Randolph-Macon Woman's College
University of Richmond
University of Virginia's College at Wise
Virginia Polytechnic Institute and State
   University
Virginia Wesleyan College

Washington
Gonzaga University
Northwest College
Pacific Lutheran University
University of Washington
Walla Walla College
Washington State University
Whitman College

West Virginia
Davis and Elkins College
Mountain State University
Salem International University
Shepherd College
University of Charleston
Wheeling Jesuit University

Wisconsin
Alverno College
Edgewood College
Lawrence University
Milwaukee School of Engineering
University of Wisconsin
   Baraboo/Sauk County
   Green Bay
   Parkside

Combined liberal arts/ career program in forestry

Alabama
Birmingham-Southern College
Chattahoochee Valley Community
   College
Northwest-Shoals Community College

Arizona
Prescott College

Arkansas
University of Arkansas
   Community College at Batesville
   Monticello

California
Columbia College
Feather River College
Modesto Junior College
Mount San Antonio College
Santa Rosa Junior College

Colorado
Fort Lewis College

Florida
Florida Southern College
Stetson University

Georgia
Albany Technical College
North Georgia College & State
   University
Waycross College

Illinois
Augustana College
Illinois College
Illinois Wesleyan University
John A. Logan College
Knox College
Shawnee Community College

Indiana
Butler University
Franklin College

Iowa
Iowa Wesleyan College
Kirkwood Community College
University of Dubuque

Kansas
Baker University
Kansas State University
Pittsburg State University
Seward County Community College

Kentucky
Murray State University

Louisiana
Louisiana Tech University
Southern University and Agricultural and
   Mechanical College

Maine
University of Maine

Maryland
Allegany College
McDaniel College

Michigan
Montcalm Community College
University of Michigan

Minnesota
Central Lakes College
Itasca Community College
Vermilion Community College

Mississippi
Holmes Community College
Mississippi State University

Missouri
East Central College
William Jewell College

New York
Clinton Community College
Erie Community College
   City Campus
   North Campus
   South Campus
Fulton-Montgomery Community College
Jamestown Community College
Le Moyne College
Mohawk Valley Community College
Paul Smith's College
St. John Fisher College
State University of New York
   College at Cortland
   College at Geneseo
   College of Agriculture and
     Technology at Cobleskill
   College of Agriculture and
     Technology at Morrisville
   College of Environmental Science
     and Forestry
   College of Technology at Alfred
   New Paltz

North Carolina
High Point University
Lees-McRae College

Lenoir-Rhyne College
Mayland Community College
North Carolina State University
University of North Carolina
   Asheville
Warren Wilson College

Ohio
Baldwin-Wallace College
Ohio State University
   Columbus Campus
Wittenberg University

Oregon
Reed College
Southwestern Oregon Community
   College

Pennsylvania
Elizabethtown College
Franklin & Marshall College
Gettysburg College
Lebanon Valley College of Pennsylvania
Moravian College
Muhlenberg College
Penn State
   Dubois
Thiel College

South Carolina
Furman University
Newberry College
Presbyterian College

Tennessee
Middle Tennessee State University
Pellissippi State Technical Community
   College
University of Tennessee
   Knoxville

Texas
Baylor University

Vermont
Sterling College

Virginia
Emory & Henry College
Randolph-Macon College
Virginia Polytechnic Institute and State
   University
Washington and Lee University

Washington
Peninsula College
University of Washington
Washington State University
Whitman College

West Virginia
Davis and Elkins College

Wisconsin
Beloit College
Lawrence University
University of Wisconsin
   Baraboo/Sauk County
   Platteville

Combined liberal arts/ career program in medical technology

Alabama
Community College of the Air Force

Arizona

International Institute of the Americas
 Phoenix
 Tucson

Arkansas

University of Arkansas
 Community College at Batesville
 Cossatot Community College of the
University of Central Arkansas

California

California State University
 Chico
Columbia College
Diablo Valley College
Loma Linda University
Long Beach City College
Modesto Junior College
Pacific Union College
San Diego Mesa College
Santa Rosa Junior College
Sonoma State University

Colorado

Front Range Community College
Red Rocks Community College

Connecticut

Gateway Community College

Florida

Florida Metropolitan University
 Melbourne Campus
St. Leo University
Southwest Florida College
University of West Florida

Georgia

Albany Technical College
Central Georgia Technical College
Floyd College
Georgia Perimeter College
Gordon College
Macon State College
Medical College of Georgia
Mercer University
Waycross College
West Georgia Technical College

Hawaii

Hawaii Business College

Idaho

Lewis-Clark State College
Northwest Nazarene University

Illinois

Benedictine University
Blackburn College
City Colleges of Chicago
 Malcolm X College
Danville Area Community College
De Paul University
Dominican University
Eastern Illinois University
Illinois College
Illinois State University
Knox College
Lincoln Land Community College
McKendree College
Monmouth College
Olivet Nazarene University
Quincy University
Rush University
Shawnee Community College

Indiana

Goshen College

Ivy Tech State College
 Bloomington
 Central Indiana
 Columbus
 Eastcentral
 Kokomo
 Lafayette
 Northcentral
 Northeast
 Northwest
 Southcentral
 Southeast
 Southwest
 Wabash Valley
 Whitewater
St. Joseph's College
University of St. Francis

Iowa

Briar Cliff University
Des Moines Area Community College
Dordt College
Graceland University
Hamilton College
Hamilton College
 Cedar Rapids
Indian Hills Community College
Iowa Wesleyan College
Kirkwood Community College
Loras College
Morningside College
Mount Mercy College
Northwestern College
University of Northern Iowa

Kansas

Allen County Community College
Baker University
Pittsburg State University
Seward County Community College
Tabor College
Wichita State University

Kentucky

Bellarmine University
Brescia University
Cumberland College
Henderson Community College
Kentucky Wesleyan College
Murray State University
Pikeville College
Thomas More College

Louisiana

Northwestern State University
Remington College
Remington College
 Baton Rouge

Maine

Andover College

Maryland

College of Southern Maryland
Howard Community College
University of Maryland
 College Park
Villa Julie College

Massachusetts

Berkshire Community College
Emmanuel College
Massachusetts College of Liberal Arts
Stonehill College

Michigan

Baker College
 of Port Huron
Glen Oaks Community College
Grand Valley State University
Montcalm Community College
Northern Michigan University
Washtenaw Community College

Minnesota

Concordia College: Moorhead
Globe College
Itasca Community College
Minnesota School of Business

Mississippi

Holmes Community College
Mississippi State University
Rust College
University of Mississippi Medical Center

Missouri

Avila University
Central Missouri State University
College of the Ozarks
Culver-Stockton College
Drury University
East Central College
Lindenwood University
Maryville University of Saint Louis
Mineral Area College
Missouri Southern State College
Penn Valley Community College
St. Louis Community College
 St. Louis Community College at
 Forest Park
William Jewell College

Nebraska

Lincoln School of Commerce

New Jersey

Bloomfield College
Caldwell College
College of St. Elizabeth
County College of Morris
Fairleigh Dickinson University
 Metropolitan Campus
Georgian Court College
Hudson County Community College
Passaic County Community College
Union County College
University of Medicine and Dentistry of
 New Jersey
 School of Health Related
 Professions

New Mexico

New Mexico State University
 Alamogordo
San Juan College

New York

Alfred University
City University of New York
 College of Staten Island
Genesee Community College
Hartwick College
Houghton College
Jamestown Community College
Keuka College
Marist College
Monroe College
Mount St. Mary College
State University of New York
 College at Brockport
 College at Fredonia
 College at Oneonta
 College at Plattsburgh
 College of Agriculture and
 Technology at Morrisville
 Oswego

North Carolina

Belmont Abbey College
Bladen Community College
Central Carolina Community College
College of the Albemarle
Elon University
Greensboro College
High Point University
Lenoir Community College

Peace College
Salem College
Winston-Salem State University

North Dakota

North Dakota State College of Science
University of Mary
University of North Dakota

Ohio

Cedarville University
College of Mount St. Joseph
Columbus State Community College
Lakeland Community College
University of Cincinnati
 Raymond Walters College

Oklahoma

Cameron University
Oklahoma Panhandle State University
University of Science and Arts of
 Oklahoma

Oregon

Lane Community College
Oregon Institute of Technology
Pioneer Pacific College

Pennsylvania

Academy of Medical Arts and Business
Cedar Crest College
Chestnut Hill College
DeSales University
Douglas School of Business
Geneva College
Gwynedd-Mercy College
Kutztown University of Pennsylvania
Lebanon Valley College of Pennsylvania
Lock Haven University of Pennsylvania
Lycoming College
Marywood University
Moravian College
Penn State
 Delaware County
 Dubois
Seton Hill University
Thiel College
University of the Sciences in
 Philadelphia

Puerto Rico

Inter American University of Puerto Rico
 Bayamon Campus
University of the Sacred Heart

Rhode Island

Salve Regina University

South Carolina

Anderson College
Columbia International University
Erskine College
Florence-Darlington Technical College
Midlands Technical College
Newberry College
Orangeburg-Calhoun Technical College
Southern Wesleyan University

South Dakota

Augustana College
Mount Marty College
South Dakota School of Mines and
 Technology
University of Sioux Falls

Tennessee

Belmont University
Fisk University
Jackson State Community College
Middle Tennessee State University
Remington College
 Southeast College of Technology
Roane State Community College

University of Tennessee
Knoxville

Texas
Lubbock Christian University
Prairie View A&M University
Sam Houston State University
Southwestern Adventist University
Tarrant County College
Tyler Junior College
University of Texas
Brownsville
San Antonio

Utah
University of Utah
Utah Career College

Vermont
Norwich University

Virginia
Averett University
Bridgewater College
Mary Baldwin College
Norfolk State University
Roanoke College
University of Virginia's College at Wise
Virginia Western Community College

Washington
Lake Washington Technical College
Pacific Lutheran University
University of Washington

West Virginia
Concord College

Wisconsin
Beloit College
Edgewood College
Lawrence University
Marian College of Fond du Lac
Milwaukee School of Engineering
University of Wisconsin
Baraboo/Sauk County
Green Bay

**Combined liberal arts/
career program in natural
resource management**

Alaska
Alaska Pacific University

Arizona
Prescott College

California
California State University
Chico
Columbia College
Feather River College
Modesto Junior College
Mount San Antonio College
San Joaquin Delta College
Santa Rosa Junior College

Colorado
Colorado Mountain College
Timberline Campus
Red Rocks Community College
Trinidad State Junior College

Florida
Rollins College

Georgia
Waycross College

Idaho
Albertson College of Idaho

Illinois
De Paul University
John A. Logan College
Shawnee Community College
Trinity Christian College

Iowa
Ellsworth Community College
Kirkwood Community College
Luther College
Northwestern College
Upper Iowa University

Kansas
Kansas State University

Kentucky
Murray State University

Louisiana
Louisiana Tech University

Maine
University of Maine

Maryland
Allegany College

Massachusetts
Gordon College
Greenfield Community College
Mount Wachusett Community College

Michigan
Grand Valley State University
Montcalm Community College
Northern Michigan University
University of Michigan

Minnesota
Central Lakes College
Itasca Community College
Vermilion Community College

Missouri
Northwest Missouri State University
William Jewell College

New Hampshire
Franklin Pierce College

New Jersey
The College of New Jersey
Mercer County Community College
Richard Stockton College of New Jersey
Rowan University

New Mexico
New Mexico Highlands University

New York
Erie Community College
City Campus
North Campus
South Campus
Iona College
Jamestown Community College
Paul Smith's College
State University of New York
College at Plattsburgh
College of Agriculture and
Technology at Morrisville
College of Environmental Science
and Forestry

North Carolina
Lenoir Community College
North Carolina State University

University of North Carolina
Asheville

Ohio
Cleveland State University
Muskingum College
Ohio State University
Columbus Campus

Oklahoma
Bacone College
Cameron University

Oregon
Eastern Oregon University
Southwestern Oregon Community
College

Pennsylvania
Delaware Valley College
Elizabethtown College
Gettysburg College
Moravian College
Penn State
Dubois

Puerto Rico
University of Puerto Rico
Rio Piedras Campus

South Carolina
Newberry College

Tennessee
Tennessee Technological University
University of Memphis
University of Tennessee
Knoxville

Texas
Coastal Bend College
Texas A&M University
Galveston

Utah
University of Utah

Vermont
Lyndon State College
Sterling College

Virginia
Virginia Polytechnic Institute and State
University

Washington
University of Washington
Washington State University

West Virginia
Shepherd College

Wisconsin
Carthage College
Lac Courte Oreilles Ojibwa Community
College
University of Wisconsin
Baraboo/Sauk County

**Combined liberal arts/
career program in nursing**

Alabama
Birmingham-Southern College
Calhoun Community College
Chattahoochee Valley Community
College
Jacksonville State University
Northwest-Shoals Community College
Shelton State Community College

University of Mobile

Alaska
University of Alaska
Southeast

Arizona
Gateway Community College
Phoenix College

Arkansas
Harding University
Northwest Arkansas Community College
South Arkansas Community College
University of Arkansas
Community College at Batesville
Community College at Hope
Cossatot Community College of the
Monticello
University of Central Arkansas

California
Biola University
California State University
Chico
Hayward
Stanislaus
Chabot College
College of the Canyons
College of the Siskiyous
Dominican University of California
Feather River College
Gavilan Community College
Holy Names College
Imperial Valley College
Loma Linda University
Long Beach City College
Los Angeles Harbor College
Los Angeles Trade and Technical College
Modesto Junior College
Ohlone College
Orange Coast College
Pacific Union College
Palomar College
St. Mary's College of California
Samuel Merritt College
San Diego City College
San Francisco State University
San Joaquin Delta College
San Jose State University
Santa Rosa Junior College
Sonoma State University
University of San Diego

Colorado
Front Range Community College
Metropolitan State College of Denver
Morgan Community College
Red Rocks Community College
Trinidad State Junior College

Connecticut
Quinnipiac University
Sacred Heart University
St. Joseph College
University of Hartford

Florida
Daytona Beach Community College
Florida Southern College
Hillsborough Community College
Tallahassee Community College
University of West Florida

Georgia
Albany Technical College
Armstrong Atlantic State University
Berry College
Central Georgia Technical College
Columbus State University
Covenant College
Emory University
Floyd College

Georgia Southwestern State University
Gordon College
Kennesaw State University
LaGrange College
Macon State College
Medical College of Georgia
Morris Brown College
North Georgia College & State
    University
Paine College
Southwest Georgia Technical College
Thomas University
Waycross College
West Georgia Technical College

Idaho
Lewis-Clark State College
Northwest Nazarene University

Illinois
Benedictine University
Blackburn College
Chicago State University
City Colleges of Chicago
    Harold Washington College
    Kennedy-King College
    Malcolm X College
Danville Area Community College
De Paul University
Dominican University
Heartland Community College
Illinois State University
Illinois Wesleyan University
John A. Logan College
Knox College
Lewis University
Lewis and Clark Community College
Lincoln Land Community College
MacMurray College
McKendree College
Monmouth College
Moraine Valley Community College
Olivet Nazarene University
Quincy University
Richland Community College
Rock Valley College
Rush University
St. Francis Medical Center College of
    Nursing
St. Xavier University
Shawnee Community College
South Suburban College of Cook County
Trinity Christian College
University of St. Francis
Waubonsee Community College
West Suburban College of Nursing
Wheaton College

Indiana
Ancilla College
Earlham College
Franklin College
Goshen College
Indiana Wesleyan University
Ivy Tech State College
    Bloomington
    Central Indiana
    Columbus
    Eastcentral
    Kokomo
    Lafayette
    Northcentral
    Northeast
    Northwest
    Southcentral
    Southeast
    Southwest
    Wabash Valley
    Whitewater
Marian College
St. Joseph's College
University of St. Francis

Iowa
Allen College
Briar Cliff University
Des Moines Area Community College
Dordt College
Ellsworth Community College
Graceland University
Grand View College
Indian Hills Community College
Kirkwood Community College
Marshalltown Community College
Morningside College
Mount Mercy College
North Iowa Area Community College
Northwest Iowa Community College
Northwestern College
St. Ambrose University
St. Luke's College
Southeastern Community College
    South Campus
Southwestern Community College
University of Northern Iowa

Kansas
Allen County Community College
Baker University
Butler County Community College
Central Christian College
Friends University
Garden City Community College
Hesston College
Kansas City Kansas Community College
Kansas State University
Labette Community College
Pittsburg State University
Pratt Community College
Seward County Community College
Tabor College
Wichita State University

Kentucky
Asbury College
Bellarmine University
Elizabethtown Community College
Georgetown College
Henderson Community College
Kentucky Christian College
Madisonville Community College
Murray State University
Pikeville College
Southeast Community College
Thomas More College

Louisiana
Dillard University
Louisiana State University
    Eunice
Louisiana Tech University
Loyola University New Orleans
Northwestern State University
Nunez Community College
Southern University and Agricultural and
    Mechanical College
University of Louisiana at Lafayette

Maine
Central Maine Medical Center School of
    Nursing
Central Maine Technical College
St. Joseph's College
University of Maine
University of Southern Maine

Maryland
Allegany College
Anne Arundel Community College
Bowie State University
College of Notre Dame of Maryland
College of Southern Maryland
Community College of Baltimore County
    Catonsville
    Dundalk
    Essex
Coppin State College

Frederick Community College
Hagerstown Community College
Harford Community College
Howard Community College
Mount St. Mary's College
University of Maryland
    College Park
Villa Julie College
Washington College

Massachusetts
American International College
Anna Maria College
Atlantic Union College
Becker College
Berkshire Community College
Gordon College
Laboure College
Mount Holyoke College
Mount Wachusett Community College
Simmons College

Michigan
Alpena Community College
Aquinas College
Baker College
    of Port Huron
Bay de Noc Community College
Finlandia University
Glen Oaks Community College
Grand Valley State University
Hope College
Jackson Community College
Kellogg Community College
Mid Michigan Community College
Montcalm Community College
Northern Michigan University
University of Michigan
Washtenaw Community College

Minnesota
Bemidji State University
Bethel College
Central Lakes College
Century Community and Technical
    College
College of St. Catherine
College of St. Scholastica
Concordia College: Moorhead
Crossroads College
Fergus Falls Community College
Gustavus Adolphus College
Hibbing Community College: A
    Technical and Community College
Itasca Community College
Macalester College
Minneapolis Community and Technical
    College
Normandale Community College
North Central University
Northland Community & Technical
    College
Rainy River Community College
Riverland Community College: A
    Technical and Community College

Mississippi
Holmes Community College
University of Mississippi Medical Center

Missouri
Avila University
Central Methodist College
Central Missouri State University
College of the Ozarks
Crowder College
Culver-Stockton College
East Central College
Fontbonne College
Jefferson College
Maryville University of Saint Louis
Mineral Area College
Missouri Baptist University
Missouri Southern State College

Northwest Missouri State University
Penn Valley Community College
Rockhurst University
St. Louis Community College
    St. Louis Community College at
        Forest Park
Southwest Missouri State University:
    West Plains Campus
Three Rivers Community College
Webster University
William Jewell College

Montana
Carroll College
Flathead Valley Community College
Montana State University
    Billings College of Technology

Nebraska
College of Saint Mary
Creighton University
Grace University
Hastings College
Mid Plains Community College Area
Midland Lutheran College
Northeast Community College
Southeast Community College
    Lincoln Campus
Western Nebraska Community College

Nevada
Great Basin College
Truckee Meadows Community College

New Hampshire
Rivier College

New Jersey
Atlantic Cape Community College
Bloomfield College
Camden County College
College of St. Elizabeth
County College of Morris
Hudson County Community College
Kean University
Mercer County Community College
New Jersey City University
Ocean County College
Passaic County Community College
Ramapo College of New Jersey
Richard Stockton College of New Jersey
Union County College
Warren County Community College

New Mexico
Eastern New Mexico University: Roswell
    Campus
New Mexico State University
    Alamogordo
San Juan College

New York
Adelphi University
City University of New York
    College of Staten Island
    Hostos Community College
    Hunter College
    Medgar Evers College
Clinton Community College
Cochran School of Nursing-St. John's
    Riverside Hospital
College of Mount St. Vincent
College of New Rochelle
Concordia College
D'Youville College
Dominican College of Blauvelt
Erie Community College
    City Campus
    North Campus
    South Campus
Genesee Community College
Hartwick College
Helene Fuld College of Nursing

Jamestown Community College
Keuka College
Manhattanville College
Mohawk Valley Community College
Molloy College
Mount St. Mary College
Nazareth College of Rochester
New York Institute of Technology
New York University
Phillips Beth Israel School of Nursing
Roberts Wesleyan College
Russell Sage College
St. Elizabeth College of Nursing
St. John Fisher College
St. Joseph's Hospital Health Center
    School of Nursing
Schenectady County Community College
State University of New York
    Binghamton
    College at Brockport
    College at Oneonta
    College at Plattsburgh
    College of Agriculture and
        Technology at Morrisville
    College of Technology at Alfred
    Health Science Center at Brooklyn
Tompkins-Cortland Community College
University of Rochester
Utica College
Wagner College
Westchester Community College

North Carolina

Barton College
Beaufort County Community College
Bennett College
Bladen Community College
Carteret Community College
Central Carolina Community College
Cleveland Community College
Coastal Carolina Community College
College of the Albemarle
Gardner-Webb University
Lenoir Community College
Mayland Community College
Nash Community College
Peace College
Queens University of Charlotte
Randolph Community College
Roanoke-Chowan Community College
Sampson Community College
Southeastern Community College
University of North Carolina
    Asheville
Wake Technical Community College
Wilson Technical Community College
Winston-Salem State University

North Dakota

Dickinson State University
North Dakota State College of Science
University of Mary
University of North Dakota
Valley City State University
Williston State College

Ohio

Ashland University
Bowling Green State University:
    Firelands College
Cedarville University
Circleville Bible College
Clark State Community College
Cleveland State University
College of Mount St. Joseph
Columbus State Community College
Franciscan University of Steubenville
Heidelberg College
James A. Rhodes State College
Kent State University
    Ashtabula Regional Campus
    Salem Regional Campus
Lakeland Community College
Lourdes College

Miami University
    Hamilton Campus
    Middletown Campus
Muskingum College
Ohio State University
    Columbus Campus
Ohio University
Otterbein College
Southern State Community College
University of Cincinnati
    Clermont College
    Raymond Walters College
University of Findlay
Urbana University
Ursuline College
Walsh University
Wittenberg University

Oklahoma

Bacone College
Cameron University
Carl Albert State College
Langston University
Northern Oklahoma College
Oklahoma Baptist University
Oklahoma Panhandle State University
Oklahoma State University
    Oklahoma City
Oral Roberts University
Platt College
    Tulsa
Redlands Community College
Southeastern Oklahoma State University
Southern Nazarene University
Southwestern Oklahoma State University
Western Oklahoma State College

Oregon

Blue Mountain Community College
Clackamas Community College
Eastern Oregon University
Lane Community College
Oregon Institute of Technology
Southern Oregon University
Southwestern Oregon Community
    College

Pennsylvania

Arcadia University
Cabrini College
California University of Pennsylvania
Cedar Crest College
Community College of Allegheny
    County
DeSales University
Elizabethtown College
Geneva College
Gettysburg College
Gwynedd-Mercy College
Immaculata University
Kutztown University of Pennsylvania
Lebanon Valley College of Pennsylvania
Lock Haven University of Pennsylvania
Luzerne County Community College
Marywood University
Moravian College
Mount Aloysius College
Neumann College
Penn State
    Delaware County
    Dubois
    Mont Alto
Rosemont College
Seton Hill University
Temple University
University of Pittsburgh
    Titusville
Waynesburg College
Widener University

Puerto Rico

Columbia College
Inter American University of Puerto Rico
    Barranquitas Campus

Universidad Metropolitana
University of the Sacred Heart

Rhode Island

Salve Regina University

South Carolina

Coastal Carolina University
Columbia International University
Florence-Darlington Technical College
Forrest Junior College
Lander University
Midlands Technical College
Morris College
Newberry College
Northeastern Technical College
Orangeburg-Calhoun Technical College
Piedmont Technical College
Southern Wesleyan University
Voorhees College
Williamsburg Technical College
Wofford College

South Dakota

Augustana College
Mount Marty College
South Dakota School of Mines and
    Technology
South Dakota State University
University of South Dakota

Tennessee

Aquinas College
Belmont University
Bethel College
Bryan College
Dyersburg State Community College
Fisk University
Freed-Hardeman University
Jackson State Community College
King College
Maryville College
Pellissippi State Technical Community
    College
Roane State Community College
Southwest Tennessee Community
    College
Tennessee Technological University
Tennessee Wesleyan College
Union University
University of Memphis
University of Tennessee
    Knoxville
Walters State Community College

Texas

Angelina College
Blinn College
Central Texas College
Clarendon College
Coastal Bend College
Frank Phillips College
Hardin-Simmons University
Hill College
Howard College
Jarvis Christian College
Lamar State College at Port Arthur
McMurry University
Midland College
Midwestern State University
Prairie View A&M University
Southwestern Adventist University
Tarrant County College
Texarkana College
Texas A&M International University
Trinity Valley Community College
Tyler Junior College
University of Texas
    Brownsville
    San Antonio
University of the Incarnate Word

Utah

Brigham Young University

Dixie State College of Utah
University of Utah
Utah Valley State College
Westminster College

Vermont

Castleton State College
Lyndon State College
Norwich University
Southern Vermont College

Virginia

College of Health Sciences
Liberty University
Mary Baldwin College
Norfolk State University
Randolph-Macon Woman's College
Rappahannock Community College
University of Virginia's College at Wise
Virginia Western Community College

Washington

Clark College
Gonzaga University
Lake Washington Technical College
Lower Columbia College
Northwest College
Pacific Lutheran University
Peninsula College
Renton Technical College
University of Washington
Walla Walla College
Walla Walla Community College
Washington State University
Whitworth College

West Virginia

Bluefield State College
Davis and Elkins College
Fairmont State College
Mountain State University
Shepherd College
University of Charleston
West Virginia University Institute of
    Technology
West Virginia University at Parkersburg
Wheeling Jesuit University

Wisconsin

Alverno College
Beloit College
Edgewood College
Lakeland College
Lawrence University
Marian College of Fond du Lac
Marquette University
Milwaukee Area Technical College
Mount Mary College
Ripon College
University of Wisconsin
    Baraboo/Sauk County
    Green Bay
    Parkside
    Platteville

Wyoming

Sheridan College

**Combined liberal arts/
career program in
occupational therapy**

Alabama

Alabama State University
Northwest-Shoals Community College

Arizona

Gateway Community College

Arkansas

South Arkansas Community College

University of Central Arkansas

California
Dominican University of California
Loma Linda University
Samuel Merritt College
San Jose State University
University of Southern California

Colorado
Heritage College
Red Rocks Community College

Connecticut
Briarwood College
Quinnipiac University
Sacred Heart University
University of Hartford

Florida
Daytona Beach Community College
Hillsborough Community College
Tallahassee Community College

Georgia
Columbus State University
Gordon College
Medical College of Georgia
North Georgia College & State
    University

Illinois
Augustana College
Chicago State University
Dominican University
Eureka College
Knox College
Lewis and Clark Community College
MacMurray College
McKendree College
Monmouth College
Moraine Valley Community College
Shawnee Community College
South Suburban College of Cook County

Indiana
Franklin College
Ivy Tech State College
    Central Indiana
University of St. Francis

Iowa
Dordt College
Kirkwood Community College
St. Ambrose University

Kansas
Allen County Community College
Baker University
Friends University
Kansas City Kansas Community College
Kansas State University

Kentucky
Kentucky Wesleyan College
Madisonville Community College
Murray State University

Louisiana
Centenary College of Louisiana
Dillard University

Maryland
Allegany College
Community College of Baltimore County
    Catonsville
    Dundalk
    Essex

Massachusetts
American International College
Berkshire Community College

Gordon College
Springfield College

Michigan
Alma College
Baker College
    of Muskegon
Grand Valley State University
Montcalm Community College

Minnesota
College of St. Catherine
College of St. Scholastica
Gustavus Adolphus College
Hamline University
Itasca Community College
Riverland Community College: A
    Technical and Community College

Mississippi
Holmes Community College
University of Mississippi Medical Center

Missouri
Avila University
College of the Ozarks
Culver-Stockton College
Drury University
Maryville University of Saint Louis
Northwest Missouri State University
Penn Valley Community College
St. Louis Community College
    St. Louis Community College at
        Forest Park
Stephens College
Washington University in St. Louis
William Jewell College

Montana
Rocky Mountain College

Nebraska
College of Saint Mary
Creighton University
Dana College

New Hampshire
New England College

New Jersey
Atlantic Cape Community College
Kean University
Seton Hall University
Union County College

New Mexico
Eastern New Mexico University: Roswell
    Campus

New York
College of Mount St. Vincent
D'Youville College
Dominican College of Blauvelt
Erie Community College
    City Campus
    North Campus
    South Campus
Genesee Community College
Jamestown Community College
Keuka College
Marymount College of Fordham
    University
New York Institute of Technology
Russell Sage College
State University of New York
    College of Agriculture and
        Technology at Cobleskill
    College of Agriculture and
        Technology at Morrisville
    College of Technology at Canton
    Health Science Center at Brooklyn
Touro College
Utica College

North Carolina
Winston-Salem State University

North Dakota
Dickinson State University
University of North Dakota
Valley City State University

Ohio
Cleveland State University
James A. Rhodes State College
Lourdes College
Ohio State University
    Columbus Campus
Ohio Wesleyan University
University of Findlay
Wittenberg University

Oregon
Pacific University
Southern Oregon University

Pennsylvania
Academy of Medical Arts and Business
Cabrini College
Community College of Beaver County
Elizabethtown College
Lebanon Valley College of Pennsylvania
Moravian College
Mount Aloysius College
Penn State
    Delaware County
    Dubois
    Mont Alto
St. Vincent College
Temple University
University of Pittsburgh
    Greensburg
University of Scranton
University of the Sciences in
    Philadelphia

South Carolina
Florence-Darlington Technical College
Newberry College
Piedmont Technical College
Tri-County Technical College

South Dakota
University of South Dakota

Tennessee
Bethel College
King College
Middle Tennessee State University
Roane State Community College
Union University
University of Tennessee
    Knoxville

Texas
Angelina College
Coastal Bend College
Lubbock Christian University

Utah
Brigham Young University
University of Utah

Virginia
College of Health Sciences
Longwood University

Washington
University of Washington

Wisconsin
Carthage College
Lawrence University
Mount Mary College

University of Wisconsin
    Baraboo/Sauk County
    Green Bay
    Platteville

Combined liberal arts/ career program in pharmacy

Alabama
Calhoun Community College

California
Foothill College
University of Southern California
University of the Pacific

Colorado
Front Range Community College
Heritage College
Trinidad State Junior College

Connecticut
Briarwood College
Gateway Community College
University of Connecticut

Florida
Hillsborough Community College
Southwest Florida College

Georgia
Albany Technical College
Central Georgia Technical College
Gordon College
Macon State College
North Georgia College & State
    University
South University
Southwest Georgia Technical College

Illinois
Benedictine University
City Colleges of Chicago
    Malcolm X College
Dominican University

Indiana
Goshen College

Iowa
Dordt College
Drake University

Kansas
Allen County Community College
Baker University
Kansas City Kansas Community College
Seward County Community College

Maryland
Coppin State College
Howard Community College
University of Maryland
    College Park
Villa Julie College
Washington College

Massachusetts
Greenfield Community College
Massachusetts College of Pharmacy and
    Health Sciences
Simmons College
Western New England College

Michigan
Baker College
    of Muskegon
Montcalm Community College
Washtenaw Community College

Minnesota
Century Community and Technical
College
Itasca Community College

Nebraska
Creighton University

New Jersey
County College of Morris

New York
State University of New York
College of Agriculture and
Technology at Morrisville

North Carolina
Bladen Community College

North Dakota
North Dakota State College of Science
Valley City State University

Ohio
Ohio Northern University
University of Cincinnati
Raymond Walters College

Oklahoma
Carl Albert State College
Northern Oklahoma College
Platt College
Tulsa

Oregon
Southern Oregon University

Pennsylvania
Cabrini College
Luzerne County Community College
Penn State
Dubois
Temple University
University of Pittsburgh
Greensburg
University of the Sciences in
Philadelphia

Puerto Rico
Pontifical Catholic University of Puerto
Rico
Universidad del Este

South Carolina
Columbia International University
Florence-Darlington Technical College
Midlands Technical College
Voorhees College

South Dakota
South Dakota State University

Tennessee
Draughons Junior College of Business:
Nashville
Fisk University
King College
Lambuth University
Middle Tennessee State University
Southwest Tennessee Community
College
University of Tennessee
Knoxville

Texas
Angelina College
Lubbock Christian University
Tarrant County College

Utah
University of Utah

Virginia
National College of Business &
Technology
Bluefield
Charlottesville

Washington
University of Washington
Washington State University

Wisconsin
University of Wisconsin
Baraboo/Sauk County
Green Bay

**Combined liberal arts/
career program in physical
therapy**

Alabama
Alabama State University
Birmingham-Southern College
Northwest-Shoals Community College

Arizona
Gateway Community College

Arkansas
Harding University
Northwest Arkansas Community College
University of Central Arkansas

California
Chapman University
Coastline Community College
Hope International University
Loma Linda University
Ohlone College
Samuel Merritt College
San Diego Mesa College
San Francisco State University
Sonoma State University
University of Southern California
University of the Pacific
Whittier College

Colorado
Trinidad State Junior College

Connecticut
Quinnipiac University
Sacred Heart University
University of Hartford

Florida
Daytona Beach Community College
Florida Southern College
Hillsborough Community College
Stetson University
Tallahassee Community College

Georgia
Albany State University
Covenant College
Floyd College
Georgia Perimeter College
Georgia Southwestern State University
Gordon College
Macon State College
Medical College of Georgia
North Georgia College & State
University
Southwest Georgia Technical College
Waycross College

Idaho
Northwest Nazarene University

Illinois
Monmouth College

Indiana
Franklin College
Goshen College
Indiana Wesleyan University
Ivy Tech State College
Eastcentral
Kokomo
Northeast
Northwest

Iowa
Briar Cliff University
Dordt College
Indian Hills Community College
Kirkwood Community College
Northwestern College
St. Ambrose University

Kansas
Allen County Community College
Central Christian College
Friends University
Kansas City Kansas Community College
Kansas State University
Pittsburg State University
Seward County Community College
Tabor College
Wichita State University

Kentucky
Bellarmine University
Kentucky Wesleyan College
Madisonville Community College
Southeast Community College

Louisiana
Centenary College of Louisiana
Dillard University
Louisiana State University
Eunice

Maryland
Allegany College
College of Southern Maryland
Coppin State College
Frederick Community College
Howard Community College
University of Maryland
College Park
Villa Julie College

Massachusetts
American International College
Berkshire Community College
Greenfield Community College
Mount Wachusett Community College
Simmons College
Springfield College

Michigan
Baker College
of Muskegon
Finlandia University
Grand Valley State University
Montcalm Community College

Minnesota
College of St. Catherine
College of St. Scholastica
Itasca Community College
Riverland Community College: A
Technical and Community College

Mississippi
Holmes Community College
Rust College
University of Mississippi Medical Center

Missouri
Avila University
Drury University
Maryville University of Saint Louis
Northwest Missouri State University

Penn Valley Community College
St. Louis Community College
St. Louis Community College at
Forest Park
Washington University in St. Louis

Nebraska
Creighton University
Dana College

New Hampshire
New England College

New Jersey
Atlantic Cape Community College
Kean University
Mercer County Community College
Union County College
University of Medicine and Dentistry of
New Jersey
School of Health Related
Professions

New Mexico
San Juan College

New York
Adelphi University
City University of New York
College of Staten Island
Clarkson University
Clinton Community College
College of Mount St. Vincent
Concordia College
D'Youville College
Dominican College of Blauvelt
Genesee Community College
Le Moyne College
Manhattanville College
Marymount College of Fordham
University
Mount St. Mary College
Nazareth College of Rochester
New York Institute of Technology
Russell Sage College
State University of New York
College at Geneseo
College at Oneonta
College of Agriculture and
Technology at Cobleskill
College of Agriculture and
Technology at Morrisville
Health Science Center at Brooklyn
Oswego
Touro College
Utica College
Villa Maria College of Buffalo

North Carolina
Blue Ridge Community College
Nash Community College
Winston-Salem State University

North Dakota
University of North Dakota
Valley City State University

Ohio
Clark State Community College
Cleveland State University
College of Mount St. Joseph
James A. Rhodes State College
Kent State University
Ashtabula Regional Campus
Ohio University
Ohio Wesleyan University
University of Findlay
Walsh University

Oklahoma
Carl Albert State College

Oregon
Pacific University
Southern Oregon University

Pennsylvania
Academy of Medical Arts and Business
Arcadia University
Cabrini College
Elizabethtown College
Gettysburg College
Lebanon Valley College of Pennsylvania
Lock Haven University of Pennsylvania
Mercyhurst College
Moravian College
Mount Aloysius College
Neumann College
Penn State
    Dubois
    Mont Alto
St. Vincent College
Temple University
University of Pittsburgh
    Greensburg
    Titusville
University of Scranton
University of the Sciences in
    Philadelphia

South Carolina
Florence-Darlington Technical College
Midlands Technical College
Piedmont Technical College

South Dakota
South Dakota School of Mines and
    Technology
University of South Dakota

Tennessee
Bethel College
Jackson State Community College
King College
Lambuth University
Middle Tennessee State University
Roane State Community College
Southwest Tennessee Community
    College
Tennessee Wesleyan College
Union University
University of Memphis
University of Tennessee
    Knoxville
Walters State Community College

Texas
Angelina College
Blinn College
Coastal Bend College
Lubbock Christian University
McMurry University
Texas Woman's University

Utah
University of Utah

Vermont
Lyndon State College

Virginia
Averett University
College of Health Sciences
Longwood University

Washington
University of Washington

West Virginia
Wheeling Jesuit University

Wisconsin
Marquette University

University of Wisconsin
    Baraboo/Sauk County
    Green Bay
    Platteville

Combined liberal arts/ career program in physician assistant

Alabama
Northwest-Shoals Community College

Arizona
Gateway Community College

California
Foothill College
Loma Linda University
Mount San Antonio College
Samuel Merritt College
San Diego City College
University of Southern California

Colorado
Blair Junior College
Red Rocks Community College

Connecticut
Quinnipiac University
Tunxis Community College

Florida
Daytona Beach Community College
Southwest Florida College
Tallahassee Community College

Georgia
Georgia Southwestern State University
Gordon College
Medical College of Georgia
North Georgia College & State
    University
South University
Waycross College

Illinois
City Colleges of Chicago
    Malcolm X College

Indiana
Ivy Tech State College
    Bloomington
    Central Indiana
    Columbus
    Eastcentral
    Kokomo
    Lafayette
    Northcentral
    Northeast
    Northwest
    Southcentral
    Southeast
    Southwest
    Wabash Valley
    Whitewater
University of St. Francis

Iowa
Briar Cliff University
Dordt College
Kirkwood Community College

Kansas
Allen County Community College
Central Christian College
Kansas State University
Seward County Community College
Wichita State University

Kentucky
National College of Business &
    Technology
    Danville
Southwestern College of Business

Louisiana
Centenary College of Louisiana
Dillard University

Maryland
Allegany College
Anne Arundel Community College
University of Maryland
    College Park

Massachusetts
Berkshire Community College
Massachusetts College of Pharmacy and
    Health Sciences
Mount Wachusett Community College
Simmons College
Springfield College
Western New England College

Michigan
Grace Bible College
Grand Valley State University
Montcalm Community College
Wayne State University

Minnesota
Augsburg College
Itasca Community College

Missouri
Drury University

Montana
Rocky Mountain College

Nebraska
Dana College

New Jersey
University of Medicine and Dentistry of
    New Jersey
        School of Health Related
            Professions

New York
City University of New York
    City College
    College of Staten Island
D'Youville College
Le Moyne College
Marymount College of Fordham
    University
New York Institute of Technology
State University of New York
    Health Science Center at Brooklyn
Wagner College

North Carolina
Forsyth Technical Community College
Gardner-Webb University
Greensboro College
High Point University
Lenoir-Rhyne College
Methodist College

North Dakota
University of North Dakota

Ohio
Davis College
James A. Rhodes State College
Marietta College
University of Findlay

Oregon
Clackamas Community College

Pacific University
Southern Oregon University

Pennsylvania
Arcadia University
Carlow College
DeSales University
Lock Haven University of Pennsylvania
Marywood University
Mount Aloysius College
Philadelphia University
St. Vincent College
Seton Hill University
University of the Sciences in
    Philadelphia

South Carolina
Piedmont Technical College

South Dakota
South Dakota State University
University of South Dakota

Tennessee
Bethel College
Draughons Junior College of Business:
    Nashville
National College of Business &
    Technology
    Tennessee
Union University
University of Memphis

Texas
Angelina College
Coastal Bend College
Lubbock Christian University

Utah
University of Utah

Virginia
College of Health Sciences
National College of Business &
    Technology
    Bluefield
    Charlottesville

Washington
University of Washington

West Virginia
Mountain State University

Wisconsin
Marquette University
University of Wisconsin
    Baraboo/Sauk County
    Green Bay
    Platteville

Combined liberal arts/ career program in radiology technician

Alabama
Community College of the Air Force
Northwest-Shoals Community College

Arizona
Gateway Community College

California
Foothill College
Loma Linda University
Long Beach City College
Orange Coast College
San Diego Mesa College
San Joaquin Delta College
Santa Rosa Junior College

Colorado

Red Rocks Community College

Connecticut

Gateway Community College
Quinnipiac University
University of Hartford

Florida

Daytona Beach Community College
Hillsborough Community College
Tallahassee Community College

Georgia

Albany Technical College
Columbus State University
Floyd College
Georgia Perimeter College
Gordon College
Medical College of Georgia
Southwest Georgia Technical College
Waycross College

Idaho

Lewis-Clark State College

Illinois

City Colleges of Chicago
　　Malcolm X College
Danville Area Community College
Heartland Community College
Moraine Valley Community College
Richland Community College
South Suburban College of Cook County

Indiana

Ivy Tech State College
　　Central Indiana
　　Columbus
　　Eastcentral
　　Wabash Valley
University of St. Francis

Iowa

Allen College
Briar Cliff University
Dordt College
Indian Hills Community College
Kirkwood Community College
St. Luke's College
Southeastern Community College
　　South Campus

Kansas

Allen County Community College
Friends University
Kansas City Kansas Community College
Kansas State University
Labette Community College
Newman University
Seward County Community College

Kentucky

Southeast Community College

Louisiana

Northwestern State University

Maine

St. Joseph's College
University of Southern Maine

Maryland

Allegany College
Anne Arundel Community College
College of Notre Dame of Maryland
College of Southern Maryland
Hagerstown Community College
Howard Community College

Massachusetts

Greenfield Community College

Massachusetts College of Pharmacy and
　　Health Sciences

Michigan

Baker College
　　of Muskegon
Glen Oaks Community College
Jackson Community College
Kellogg Community College
Mid Michigan Community College
Montcalm Community College
Washtenaw Community College

Minnesota

Century Community and Technical
　　College
Itasca Community College
Normandale Community College
Riverland Community College: A
　　Technical and Community College

Mississippi

Holmes Community College
University of Mississippi Medical Center

Missouri

Avila University
Drury University
Jefferson College
Missouri Southern State College
Penn Valley Community College
St. Louis Community College
　　St. Louis Community College at
　　　　Forest Park

Nebraska

Dana College
Northeast Community College
Southeast Community College
　　Lincoln Campus
Western Nebraska Community College

Nevada

Truckee Meadows Community College

New Jersey

Mercer County Community College
Passaic County Community College
Union County College

New York

City University of New York
　　Hostos Community College
Clinton Community College
Erie Community College
　　City Campus
　　North Campus
　　South Campus
Iona College
Mohawk Valley Community College
Molloy College
State University of New York
　　College of Agriculture and
　　　　Technology at Morrisville
　　Health Science Center at Brooklyn
　　Oswego
Westchester Community College

North Carolina

Carteret Community College
Greensboro College
Lenoir Community College
Roanoke-Chowan Community College

North Dakota

Jamestown College
University of Mary

Ohio

Columbus State Community College
Kent State University
　　Salem Regional Campus

Lakeland Community College
Ohio State University
　　Columbus Campus
University of Cincinnati
　　Raymond Walters College

Oklahoma

Bacone College
Northern Oklahoma College
Western Oklahoma State College

Oregon

Oregon Institute of Technology

Pennsylvania

Academy of Medical Arts and Business
Community College of Beaver County
Gwynedd-Mercy College
Lebanon Valley College of Pennsylvania
Lock Haven University of Pennsylvania
Mount Aloysius College
Penn State
　　Delaware County
　　Dubois
　　New Kensington

Puerto Rico

Inter American University of Puerto Rico
　　Barranquitas Campus
Universidad del Este

South Carolina

Aiken Technical College
Columbia International University
Florence-Darlington Technical College
Midlands Technical College
Orangeburg-Calhoun Technical College
Piedmont Technical College

South Dakota

Mount Marty College
University of Sioux Falls

Tennessee

Jackson State Community College
Roane State Community College
Southwest Tennessee Community
　　College

Texas

Angelina College
Blinn College
Coastal Bend College
Midland College
Midwestern State University
Tarrant County College
Texarkana College
Tyler Junior College
University of the Incarnate Word

Vermont

Champlain College

Virginia

Averett University
College of Health Sciences
Virginia Western Community College

West Virginia

Bluefield State College
Mountain State University
University of Charleston
West Virginia Northern Community
　　College
Wheeling Jesuit University

Wisconsin

Marian College of Fond du Lac
Milwaukee Area Technical College
University of Wisconsin
　　Green Bay

**Combined liberal arts/
career program in social
work**

Alabama

Alabama State University
Jacksonville State University

Alaska

University of Alaska
　　Southeast

Arizona

Gateway Community College
Northern Arizona University
Prescott College

Arkansas

Harding University
Philander Smith College
University of Arkansas
　　Monticello

California

Antioch Southern California
　　Santa Barbara
California State University
　　Chico
　　Monterey Bay
　　San Marcos
　　Stanislaus
Chapman University
College of the Siskiyous
Foothill College
Hope International University
Long Beach City College
Modesto Junior College
Pacific Union College
Palomar College
San Francisco State University
San Joaquin Delta College
San Jose State University
University of La Verne
University of Southern California
Whittier College

Colorado

Metropolitan State College of Denver

Connecticut

Gateway Community College
Sacred Heart University
St. Joseph College
Tunxis Community College

District of Columbia

Gallaudet University

Florida

Daytona Beach Community College
St. Leo University
Southeastern College of the Assemblies
　　of God
Tallahassee Community College
University of West Florida

Georgia

Atlanta Metropolitan College
Floyd College
Gordon College
LaGrange College
Macon State College
Thomas University

Idaho

Lewis-Clark State College
Northwest Nazarene University

Illinois

Aurora University
Benedictine University

Chicago State University
City Colleges of Chicago
    Harold Washington College
    Kennedy-King College
Illinois State University
Lewis University
MacMurray College
McKendree College
Monmouth College
Northeastern Illinois University
Olivet Nazarene University
Quincy University
Rock Valley College
St. Augustine College
Shawnee Community College
South Suburban College of Cook County
Trinity Christian College
University of Illinois
    Springfield
University of St. Francis
Waubonsee Community College

Indiana

Franklin College
Goshen College
Grace College
Indiana Wesleyan University
St. Joseph's College
University of St. Francis

Iowa

Briar Cliff University
Des Moines Area Community College
Dordt College
Ellsworth Community College
Graceland University
Kirkwood Community College
Loras College
Marshalltown Community College
Mount Mercy College
Northwestern College
St. Ambrose University
Upper Iowa University

Kansas

Allen County Community College
Bethany College
Butler County Community College
Central Christian College
Garden City Community College
Kansas City Kansas Community College
Kansas State University
Pittsburg State University
Seward County Community College
Wichita State University

Kentucky

Asbury College
Brescia University
Cumberland College
Henderson Community College
Kentucky Christian College
Murray State University

Louisiana

Dillard University
Northwestern State University
Southern University and Agricultural and
    Mechanical College

Maine

St. Joseph's College
University of Maine
University of Southern Maine

Maryland

Allegany College
Bowie State University
Coppin State College
Frostburg State University
Hagerstown Community College
McDaniel College
Salisbury University

University of Maryland
    Baltimore County

Massachusetts

Anna Maria College
Atlantic Union College
Berkshire Community College
Bridgewater State College
Lasell College
Massachusetts College of Liberal Arts
Western New England College

Michigan

Bay de Noc Community College
Cornerstone University
Finlandia University
Glen Oaks Community College
Grand Valley State University
Hope College
Kellogg Community College
Montcalm Community College
Mott Community College
Northern Michigan University
Reformed Bible College
University of Michigan
Wayne State University

Minnesota

Augsburg College
Bemidji State University
Bethel College
Capella University
College of St. Catherine
College of St. Scholastica
Concordia College: Moorhead
Itasca Community College
Northland Community & Technical
    College
St. Cloud State University

Mississippi

Mississippi State University
Mississippi Valley State University
Rust College

Missouri

Avila University
Central Missouri State University
Culver-Stockton College
East Central College
Fontbonne College
Maryville University of Saint Louis
Missouri Baptist University
Missouri Valley College
St. Louis Community College
    St. Louis Community College at
        Forest Park
Washington University in St. Louis
Webster University
William Woods University

Montana

Carroll College

Nebraska

Bellevue University
College of Saint Mary
Creighton University
Dana College
Grace University
Western Nebraska Community College

New Hampshire

Daniel Webster College
Franklin Pierce College
New England College
New Hampshire Community Technical
    College
        Laconia

New Jersey

College of St. Elizabeth
Hudson County Community College

Kean University
Mercer County Community College
Ocean County College
Passaic County Community College
Richard Stockton College of New Jersey
Rowan University

New Mexico

New Mexico Highlands University
New Mexico State University
    Alamogordo
San Juan College

New York

Adelphi University
City University of New York
    College of Staten Island
Clinton Community College
College of New Rochelle
Concordia College
Dominican College of Blauvelt
Dowling College
Erie Community College
    City Campus
    North Campus
    South Campus
Genesee Community College
Iona College
Jamestown Community College
Keuka College
Marist College
Marymount College of Fordham
    University
Marymount Manhattan College
Molloy College
Nazareth College of Rochester
New York University
Nyack College
Onondaga Community College
Roberts Wesleyan College
Rochester Institute of Technology
Schenectady County Community College
Skidmore College
State University of New York
    Albany
    Binghamton
    College at Brockport
    College at Fredonia
    College at Plattsburgh
    College of Agriculture and
        Technology at Morrisville
    New Paltz
Wagner College

North Carolina

Barton College
Beaufort County Community College
Central Carolina Community College
Coastal Carolina Community College
Elizabeth City State University
Elon University
Fayetteville Technical Community
    College
Lenoir Community College
Methodist College
Pfeiffer University
Roanoke-Chowan Community College

North Dakota

North Dakota State College of Science
University of Mary
University of North Dakota
Valley City State University

Ohio

Ashland University
Bluffton College
Cedarville University
Circleville Bible College
Clark State Community College
Cleveland State University
College of Mount St. Joseph
Defiance College
Franciscan University of Steubenville

James A. Rhodes State College
Kent State University
    Ashtabula Regional Campus
Lakeland Community College
Lourdes College
Miami University
    Hamilton Campus
Ohio State University
    Columbus Campus
Ohio University
Southern State Community College
University of Cincinnati
    Clermont College
    Raymond Walters College
University of Findlay
Ursuline College
Wilmington College

Oklahoma

Carl Albert State College
Northern Oklahoma College
Oklahoma Baptist University
Oral Roberts University
Southwestern Christian University
Southwestern Oklahoma State University

Oregon

Concordia University
Eastern Oregon University
Pacific University

Pennsylvania

Cedar Crest College
DeSales University
Elizabethtown College
Gwynedd-Mercy College
Immaculata University
Kutztown University of Pennsylvania
Lock Haven University of Pennsylvania
Marywood University
Mercyhurst College
Penn State
    Mont Alto
    New Kensington
Philadelphia Biblical University
Rosemont College
Seton Hill University
Temple University
University of Pittsburgh
    Greensburg
Widener University

Puerto Rico

Turabo University
Universidad Metropolitana
Universidad del Este
University of Puerto Rico
    Rio Piedras Campus
University of the Sacred Heart

Rhode Island

Salve Regina University

South Carolina

Coker College
Florence-Darlington Technical College
Limestone College
Piedmont Technical College

South Dakota

South Dakota School of Mines and
    Technology
University of Sioux Falls
University of South Dakota

Tennessee

Belmont University
Bethel College
Dyersburg State Community College
Freed-Hardeman University
Pellissippi State Technical Community
    College
Tennessee Technological University

Tennessee Wesleyan College
Union University
University of Memphis
University of Tennessee
    Knoxville
Walters State Community College

Texas

Angelina College
Blinn College
Coastal Bend College
Howard Payne University
Midwestern State University
Prairie View A&M University
St. Edward's University
Southwestern Adventist University
Texas A&M International University
Texas A&M University
    Commerce

Utah

Brigham Young University
University of Utah

Vermont

Castleton State College
Champlain College
Lyndon State College
Woodbury College

Virginia

Averett University
Longwood University
Mary Baldwin College
Norfolk State University
Virginia Union University
Virginia Wesleyan College
Virginia Western Community College

Washington

Pacific Lutheran University
St. Martin's College
University of Washington
Walla Walla College

West Virginia

Bethany College
Concord College
Shepherd College
West Virginia University Institute of
    Technology

Wisconsin

Carthage College
Edgewood College
Lac Courte Oreilles Ojibwa Community
    College
Mount Mary College
University of Wisconsin
    Baraboo/Sauk County
    Green Bay
    River Falls
    Superior

Wyoming

Sheridan College

Cooperative education

Alabama

Alabama Agricultural and Mechanical
    University
Alabama State University
Athens State University
Auburn University
Auburn University at Montgomery
Bevill State Community College
Bishop State Community College
Calhoun Community College
Central Alabama Community College

Douglas MacArthur State Technical
    College
Faulkner University
Gadsden State Community College
George C. Wallace State Community
    College
    Dothan
Harry M. Ayers State Technical College
J. F. Drake State Technical College
Jacksonville State University
James H. Faulkner State Community
    College
Lurleen B. Wallace Junior College
Miles College
Northwest-Shoals Community College
Remington College
    Southeast College of Technology
Stillman College
Talladega College
Trenholm State Technical College
Troy State University Dothan
Tuskegee University
University of Alabama
University of Alabama
    Birmingham
    Huntsville
University of North Alabama
University of South Alabama
Wallace Community College: Sparks
    Campus
Wallace State Community College at
    Hanceville

Alaska

Sheldon Jackson College
University of Alaska
    Anchorage
    Fairbanks
    Southeast

Arizona

Arizona State University
Arizona Western College
Cochise College
DeVry University
    Phoenix
Eastern Arizona College
Embry-Riddle Aeronautical University:
    Prescott Campus
Gateway Community College
Glendale Community College
Northern Arizona University
Paradise Valley Community College
Phoenix College
Pima Community College
Rio Salado College
Scottsdale Community College
South Mountain Community College

Arkansas

Arkansas State University
Arkansas State University
    Mountain Home
Harding University
Hendrix College
Mid-South Community College
Philander Smith College
Pulaski Technical College
Rich Mountain Community College
Southeast Arkansas College
Southern Arkansas University
University of Arkansas
University of Arkansas
    Community College at Batesville
    Cossatot Community College of the
    Fort Smith
    Little Rock
    Pine Bluff
University of Central Arkansas
University of the Ozarks

California

Antelope Valley College

Antioch Southern California
    Los Angeles
Art Institute
    of California - Orange County
Azusa Pacific University
Barstow College
Biola University
California Maritime Academy
California Polytechnic State University:
    San Luis Obispo
California State Polytechnic University:
    Pomona
California State University
    Bakersfield
    Chico
    Dominguez Hills
    Fresno
    Fullerton
    Hayward
    Los Angeles
    Monterey Bay
    Northridge
    Sacramento
    San Bernardino
    Stanislaus
Cerritos Community College
Cerro Coso Community College
Chabot College
Chapman University
Citrus College
Coastline Community College
College of Alameda
College of the Canyons
College of the Redwoods
College of the Siskiyous
Columbia College
Cuesta College
De Anza College
DeVry University
    Fremont
    Long Beach
    Pomona
    West Hills
Diablo Valley College
Don Bosco Technical Institute
East Los Angeles College
Feather River College
Foothill College
Glendale Community College
Golden Gate University
Golden West College
Heald College
    Hayward
    Milpitas
Humboldt State University
Irvine Valley College
Laney College
Long Beach City College
Los Angeles Harbor College
Los Angeles Pierce College
Los Angeles Southwest College
Los Angeles Trade and Technical College
Los Medanos College
MTI College of Business and Technology
MiraCosta College
Modesto Junior College
Monterey Peninsula College
Moorpark College
Mount San Jacinto College
Napa Valley College
Ohlone College
Orange Coast College
Otis College of Art and Design
Pacific Union College
Palomar College
Platt College
    Newport Beach
    Ontario
Reedley College
Riverside Community College
San Diego City College
San Francisco State University
San Joaquin Delta College
San Jose State University
Santa Barbara City College

Santa Clara University
Santa Monica College
Santa Rosa Junior College
Shasta College
Sierra College
Sonoma State University
Southwestern College
University of California
    Irvine
    Riverside
    San Diego
    Santa Cruz
University of Southern California
University of the Pacific
Vanguard University of Southern
    California
Victor Valley College
Westwood College of Technology
    Inland Empire
Yuba Community College District

Colorado

Arapahoe Community College
Colorado Christian University
Colorado School of Mines
Colorado State University
Colorado State University
    Pueblo
Colorado Technical University
Community College of Aurora
DeVry University
    Denver
DeVry University: Colorado Springs
Fort Lewis College
Front Range Community College
IntelliTec College, Grand Junction
Mesa State College
Metropolitan State College of Denver
National American University
    Denver
Red Rocks Community College
Trinidad State Junior College
University of Colorado
    Denver
    Health Sciences Center
University of Denver
University of Northern Colorado

Connecticut

Central Connecticut State University
Eastern Connecticut State University
Gibbs College
Holy Apostles College and Seminary
Housatonic Community College
International College of Hospitality
    Management
Manchester Community College
Naugatuck Valley Community College
Northwestern Connecticut Community
    College
Norwalk Community College
Sacred Heart University
Southern Connecticut State University
Teikyo Post University
Three Rivers Community College
University of Bridgeport
University of Connecticut
University of Hartford
University of New Haven
Western Connecticut State University

Delaware

Delaware State University
Delaware Technical and Community
    College
    Owens Campus
    Stanton/Wilmington Campus
    Terry Campus
Goldey-Beacom College
University of Delaware

District of Columbia

American University
Gallaudet University

George Washington University
Howard University
Strayer University
Trinity College
University of the District of Columbia

Florida

Bethune-Cookman College
Broward Community College
Carlos Albizu University
Chipola Junior College
Daytona Beach Community College
DeVry University
    Miramar
Eckerd College
Edward Waters College
Embry Riddle Aeronautical
    University-Extended Campus
Embry-Riddle Aeronautical University
Florida Agricultural and Mechanical
    University
Florida Atlantic University
Florida Gulf Coast University
Florida Institute of Technology
Florida Keys Community College
Florida Metropolitan University
    Orlando College North
Florida National College
Florida State University
Full Sail Real World Education
Gulf Coast Community College
Jacksonville University
Lake City Community College
Lake-Sumter Community College
Manatee Community College
Miami-Dade Community College
Nova Southeastern University
Okaloosa-Walton Community College
Palm Beach Atlantic University
Palm Beach Community College
Pensacola Junior College
Santa Fe Community College
Schiller International University
Seminole Community College
South Florida Community College
Southwest Florida College
Tallahassee Community College
Talmudic College of Florida
University of Central Florida
University of Florida
University of North Florida
University of South Florida
University of West Florida
Valencia Community College

Georgia

Albany State University
Albany Technical College
Armstrong Atlantic State University
Atlanta Metropolitan College
Augusta State University
Berry College
Brenau University
Clark Atlanta University
Clayton College and State University
Columbus State University
Dalton State College
Darton College
DeVry University
    Alpharetta
    Atlanta
Fort Valley State University
Georgia Institute of Technology
Georgia Southern University
Georgia Southwestern State University
Georgia State University
Gordon College
Kennesaw State University
Mercer University
Middle Georgia College
Morehouse College
North Georgia College & State
    University
Oglethorpe University
Paine College

Savannah State University
Southern Polytechnic State University
Southwest Georgia Technical College
State University of West Georgia
University of Georgia
Valdosta State University

Hawaii

Brigham Young University-Hawaii
Chaminade University of Honolulu
Hawaii Pacific University
Heald College
    Honolulu
University of Hawaii
    Hawaii Community College
    Honolulu Community College
    Kauai Community College
    Manoa
    Maui Community College

Idaho

College of Southern Idaho
Lewis-Clark State College
University of Idaho

Illinois

Augustana College
Black Hawk College
Black Hawk College
    East Campus
Blackburn College
Bradley University
Chicago State University
City Colleges of Chicago
    Harold Washington College
    Kennedy-King College
    Malcolm X College
    Olive-Harvey College
    Richard J. Daley College
College of DuPage
College of Lake County
De Paul University
DeVry University
    Addison
    Chicago
    Tinley Park
East-West University
Elgin Community College
Elmhurst College
Eureka College
Greenville College
Illinois Institute of Art
Illinois Institute of Technology
Illinois State University
International Academy of Design and
    Technology
John A. Logan College
Joliet Junior College
Kaskaskia College
Kendall College
Lake Land College
Lewis University
Lewis and Clark Community College
Lexington College
Lincoln Land Community College
North Central College
Northeastern Illinois University
Northern Illinois University
Northwestern University
Parkland College
Rend Lake College
Robert Morris College: Chicago
Rock Valley College
Rockford College
St. Augustine College
Sauk Valley Community College
School of the Art Institute of Chicago
Shawnee Community College
Southern Illinois University Carbondale
Southern Illinois University Edwardsville
Trinity Christian College
Trinity International University
Triton College

University of Illinois
    Chicago
    Urbana-Champaign
University of St. Francis
William Rainey Harper College

Indiana

Ancilla College
Ball State University
Butler University
Calumet College of St. Joseph
Franklin College
Indiana Business College
    Medical
Indiana State University
Indiana University
    Bloomington
    East
    Northwest
Indiana University-Purdue University
    Fort Wayne
Indiana University-Purdue University
    Indianapolis
Ivy Tech State College
    Central Indiana
    Southcentral
    Southwest
Oakland City University
Purdue University
Purdue University
    Calumet
Rose-Hulman Institute of Technology
Tri-State University
University of Evansville
University of Notre Dame
University of Southern Indiana
Valparaiso University

Iowa

Allen College
Central College
Clarke College
Clinton Community College
Des Moines Area Community College
Drake University
Ellsworth Community College
Grand View College
Hamilton College
    Cedar Rapids
Hawkeye Community College
Indian Hills Community College
Iowa Central Community College
Iowa Lakes Community College
Iowa State University
Iowa Western Community College
Kirkwood Community College
Marshalltown Community College
Muscatine Community College
North Iowa Area Community College
Northeast Iowa Community College
Northwest Iowa Community College
St. Ambrose University
Scott Community College
Simpson College
Southwestern Community College
University of Dubuque
University of Iowa
University of Northern Iowa

Kansas

Allen County Community College
Barton County Community College
Benedictine College
Bethany College
Bethel College
Butler County Community College
Central Christian College
Cloud County Community College
Fort Scott Community College
Garden City Community College
Haskell Indian Nations University
Hesston College
Highland Community College
Hutchinson Community College

Johnson County Community College
Kansas City Kansas Community College
Kansas State University
Newman University
Pittsburg State University
St. Mary College
Seward County Community College
University of Kansas
Wichita State University

Kentucky

Cumberland College
Daymar College
Georgetown College
Henderson Community College
Hopkinsville Community College
Jefferson Community College
Kentucky Christian College
Lexington Community College
Louisville Technical Institute
Madisonville Community College
Maysville Community College
Mid-Continent College
Morehead State University
Murray State University
Prestonsburg Community College
Somerset Community College
Spencerian College: Lexington
Thomas More College
Union College
University of Kentucky
University of Louisville

Louisiana

Delgado Community College
Grambling State University
Louisiana State University
    Shreveport
Louisiana State University and
    Agricultural and Mechanical College
Louisiana Tech University
McNeese State University
Nunez Community College
Southern University
    New Orleans
Southern University and Agricultural and
    Mechanical College
Tulane University
University of Louisiana at Lafayette
University of Louisiana at Monroe
University of New Orleans
Xavier University of Louisiana

Maine

Andover College
Husson College
Maine Maritime Academy
University of Maine
University of Maine
    Machias
University of Southern Maine

Maryland

Allegany College
Anne Arundel Community College
Baltimore International College
Bowie State University
Capitol College
Cecil Community College
Chesapeake College
College of Southern Maryland
Columbia Union College
Community College of Baltimore County
    Catonsville
    Dundalk
    Essex
Coppin State College
Frederick Community College
Hagerstown Community College
Harford Community College
Howard Community College
Maryland College of Art and Design
Montgomery College
    Rockville Campus

Morgan State University
Sojourner-Douglass College
University of Baltimore
University of Maryland
    Baltimore County
    College Park
    University College
Villa Julie College

Massachusetts

Anna Maria College
Atlantic Union College
Bay Path College
Bay State College
Becker College
Boston University
Cape Cod Community College
Gordon College
Lasell College
Massachusetts Bay Community College
Massachusetts Institute of Technology
Massachusetts Maritime Academy
Merrimack College
Mount Holyoke College
Mount Wachusett Community College
Nichols College
Northeastern University
Quinsigamond Community College
Simon's Rock College of Bard
Springfield College
Springfield Technical Community
   College
Suffolk University
University of Massachusetts
    Amherst
    Boston
    Dartmouth
    Lowell
Wentworth Institute of Technology
Westfield State College
Worcester Polytechnic Institute

Michigan

Adrian College
Andrews University
Aquinas College
Baker College
    of Cadillac
    of Clinton Township
    of Jackson
    of Muskegon
    of Owosso
    of Port Huron
Bay de Noc Community College
Central Michigan University
Cleary University
Davenport University
    Eastern Region
Davenport University - Western Region
Eastern Michigan University
Ferris State University
Finlandia University
Gogebic Community College
Grand Rapids Community College
Grand Valley State University
Kellogg Community College
Kettering University
Kirtland Community College
Lansing Community College
Lawrence Technological University
Macomb Community College
Madonna University
Marygrove College
Michigan State University
Michigan Technological University
Mid Michigan Community College
Monroe County Community College
Montcalm Community College
Mott Community College
Muskegon Community College
North Central Michigan College
Northwestern Michigan College
Northwood University
Oakland Community College
Oakland University

Saginaw Valley State University
St. Clair County Community College
Schoolcraft College
Siena Heights University
Southwestern Michigan College
University of Michigan
University of Michigan
    Dearborn
    Flint
Washtenaw Community College
Wayne County Community College
Wayne State University
Western Michigan University

Minnesota

Art Institutes International
   Minnesota
Augsburg College
Bemidji State University
Brown College
Concordia College: Moorhead
Concordia University: St. Paul
Crown College
Gustavus Adolphus College
Hibbing Community College: A
   Technical and Community College
Inver Hills Community College
Itasca Community College
Lake Superior College: A Community
   and Technical College
Minnesota State College - Southeast
   Technical
Minnesota West Community and
   Technical College: Worthington
   Campus
Normandale Community College
Oak Hills Christian College
Rasmussen College
    Mankato
Ridgewater College: A Community and
   Technical College
St. Mary's University of Minnesota
Southwest State University
University of Minnesota
    Crookston
    Twin Cities
Vermilion Community College

Mississippi

Alcorn State University
Delta State University
Holmes Community College
Itawamba Community College
Mary Holmes College
Millsaps College
Mississippi Gulf Coast Community
   College
    Perkinston
Mississippi State University
Mississippi University for Women
Mississippi Valley State University
Pearl River Community College
University of Mississippi
University of Southern Mississippi

Missouri

Avila University
Blue River Community College
Central Bible College
Central Missouri State University
Columbia College
DeVry University
    Kansas City
Drury University
Fontbonne College
Lincoln University
Lindenwood University
Longview Community College
Maryville University of Saint Louis
Missouri Southern State College
Moberly Area Community College
North Central Missouri College
Ozarks Technical Community College
Ranken Technical College

Rockhurst University
St. Louis Community College
   St. Louis Community College at
    Florissant Valley
Southwest Baptist University
Southwest Missouri State University
University of Missouri
    Kansas City
    Rolla
    St. Louis
Washington University in St. Louis
Webster University
Westminster College

Montana

Carroll College
Chief Dull Knife College
Miles Community College
Montana State University
    Billings
    Billings College of Technology
Montana Tech of the University of
   Montana
Rocky Mountain College
Salish Kootenai College
University of Great Falls
University of Montana-Missoula
University of Montana: Western

Nebraska

Central Community College
Chadron State College
Clarkson College
College of Saint Mary
Concordia University
Doane College
Metropolitan Community College
Nebraska Indian Community College
Northeast Community College
Peru State College
Southeast Community College
    Beatrice Campus
    Lincoln Campus
    Milford Campus
University of Nebraska
    Lincoln
    Omaha
Wayne State College
Western Nebraska Community College

Nevada

Career College of Northern Nevada
Great Basin College
Morrison University
Truckee Meadows Community College
University of Nevada
    Las Vegas
Western Nevada Community College

New Hampshire

Daniel Webster College
Keene State College
New Hampshire Community Technical
   College
    Claremont
    Laconia
    Manchester
Southern New Hampshire University

New Jersey

Atlantic Cape Community College
Bergen Community College
Bloomfield College
Brookdale Community College
Burlington County College
Camden County College
County College of Morris
DeVry College of Technology
Drew University
Essex County College
Fairleigh Dickinson University
    College at Florham
    Metropolitan Campus
Felician College

Gloucester County College
Kean University
Mercer County Community College
Middlesex County College
Monmouth University
New Jersey City University
New Jersey Institute of Technology
Passaic County Community College
Princeton University
Ramapo College of New Jersey
Raritan Valley Community College
Rider University
Rowan University
Rutgers, The State University of New
   Jersey
    Camden Regional Campus
    New Brunswick Regional Campus
St. Peter's College
Salem Community College
Seton Hall University
Stevens Institute of Technology
Warren County Community College
William Paterson University of New
   Jersey

New Mexico

Clovis Community College
Dona Ana Branch Community College of
   New Mexico State University
Eastern New Mexico University
New Mexico Institute of Mining and
   Technology
New Mexico Junior College
New Mexico State University
New Mexico State University
    Alamogordo
San Juan College
Santa Fe Community College
University of New Mexico
Western New Mexico University

New York

Alfred University
Berkeley College
Briarcliffe College
Broome Community College
Bryant & Stratton Business Institute
   Syracuse
City University of New York
    Borough of Manhattan Community
     College
    Bronx Community College
    Brooklyn College
    City College
    College of Staten Island
    Hostos Community College
    John Jay College of Criminal
     Justice
    La Guardia Community College
    Queens College
    Queensborough Community
     College
    York College
Clarkson University
College of New Rochelle
Concordia College
Cornell University
Daemen College
DeVry Institute of Technology
    New York
Dominican College of Blauvelt
Dowling College
Dutchess Community College
Erie Community College
    City Campus
    North Campus
    South Campus
Finger Lakes Community College
Fulton-Montgomery Community College
Genesee Community College
Hilbert College
Hudson Valley Community College
Iona College
Jamestown Community College
Jefferson Community College

Keuka College
Laboratory Institute of Merchandising
Long Island University
    C. W. Post Campus
    Southampton College
Manhattan College
Marist College
Mercy College
Metropolitan College of New York
Mildred Elley
Molloy College
Monroe College
Monroe Community College
Mount St. Mary College
Nassau Community College
New York Institute of Technology
Niagara County Community College
Niagara University
Onondaga Community College
Orange County Community College
Pace University
Pace University: Pleasantville/Briarcliff
Parsons School of Design
Polytechnic University
Rensselaer Polytechnic Institute
Rochester Institute of Technology
Russell Sage College
Sage College of Albany
Schenectady County Community College
State University of New York
    Buffalo
    College at Buffalo
    College at Cortland
    College at Fredonia
    College at Plattsburgh
    College of Environmental Science
      and Forestry
    College of Technology at Alfred
    Maritime College
    New Paltz
Suffolk County Community College
Syracuse University
Tompkins-Cortland Community College
Ulster County Community College
Union College
Utica College
Vassar College
Westchester Business Institute
Westchester Community College

North Carolina

Alamance Community College
Appalachian State University
Asheville Buncombe Technical
    Community College
Barton College
Beaufort County Community College
Belmont Abbey College
Bladen Community College
Blue Ridge Community College
Caldwell Community College and
    Technical Institute
Campbell University
Cape Fear Community College
Catawba Valley Community College
Central Piedmont Community College
Cleveland Community College
Coastal Carolina Community College
College of the Albemarle
Craven Community College
Davidson County Community College
Durham Technical Community College
East Carolina University
Edgecombe Community College
Elizabeth City State University
Fayetteville State University
Fayetteville Technical Community
    College
Forsyth Technical Community College
Gaston College
Guilford Technical Community College
Haywood Community College
High Point University
Isothermal Community College
James Sprunt Community College

John Wesley College
Johnson C. Smith University
Lenoir Community College
Lenoir-Rhyne College
Louisburg College
Mars Hill College
Martin Community College
Mayland Community College
Meredith College
Mitchell Community College
Mount Olive College
North Carolina Agricultural and
    Technical State University
North Carolina Central University
North Carolina State University
North Carolina Wesleyan College
Pfeiffer University
Piedmont Community College
Pitt Community College
Randolph Community College
Richmond Community College
Roanoke-Chowan Community College
Rockingham Community College
Rowan-Cabarrus Community College
St. Augustine's College
Sampson Community College
Sandhills Community College
South Piedmont Community College
Southwestern Community College
Surry Community College
University of North Carolina
    Charlotte
    Pembroke
    Wilmington
Vance-Granville Community College
Wake Technical Community College
Wayne Community College
Western Carolina University
Western Piedmont Community College
Wilkes Community College
Wilson Technical Community College
Winston-Salem State University

North Dakota

Bismarck State College
Jamestown College
Lake Region State College
Mayville State University
Minot State University
Minot State University: Bottineau
    Campus
North Dakota State College of Science
North Dakota State University
University of Mary
University of North Dakota
Valley City State University
Williston State College

Ohio

Antioch College
Bowling Green State University
Bryant & Stratton College
    Cleveland West
Case Western Reserve University
Central Ohio Technical College
Central State University
Chatfield College
Cincinnati State Technical and
    Community College
Clark State Community College
Cleveland State University
College of Mount St. Joseph
Columbus College of Art and Design
Columbus State Community College
Cuyahoga Community College
    Eastern Campus
    Metropolitan Campus
    Western Campus
David N. Myers College
DeVry University
    Columbus
Defiance College
Franklin University
Hocking Technical College
James A. Rhodes State College

John Carroll University
Kent State University
Lakeland Community College
Lorain County Community College
Malone College
Marion Technical College
Miami University
    Hamilton Campus
    Middletown Campus
    Oxford Campus
Mount Union College
Mount Vernon Nazarene University
Northwest State Community College
Notre Dame College
Ohio Northern University
Ohio State University
    Agricultural Technical Institute
    Columbus Campus
    Mansfield Campus
    Marion Campus
    Newark Campus
Ohio University
Ohio University
    Eastern Campus
Owens Community College
    Toledo
Sinclair Community College
Stark State College of Technology
University of Akron
University of Cincinnati
University of Cincinnati
    Clermont College
    Raymond Walters College
University of Dayton
University of Findlay
University of Northwestern Ohio
University of Rio Grande
University of Toledo
Urbana University
Ursuline College
Wright State University
Xavier University
Youngstown State University

Oklahoma

Carl Albert State College
Eastern Oklahoma State College
Langston University
Northeastern State University
Oklahoma Baptist University
Oklahoma City University
Oklahoma Panhandle State University
Oklahoma State University
Oklahoma State University
    Okmulgee
Redlands Community College
Rogers State University
University of Oklahoma

Oregon

Blue Mountain Community College
Central Oregon Community College
Chemeketa Community College
Clackamas Community College
Clatsop Community College
Eastern Oregon University
George Fox University
Lane Community College
Linn-Benton Community College
Mount Hood Community College
Northwest Christian College
Oregon Institute of Technology
Oregon State University
Pacific Northwest College of Art
Portland State University
Rogue Community College
Southern Oregon University
Southwestern Oregon Community
    College
Umpqua Community College
University of Oregon
Warner Pacific College

Pennsylvania

Arcadia University
Bloomsburg University of Pennsylvania
Bryn Athyn College of the New Church
Bucks County Community College
Butler County Community College
Cabrini College
California University of Pennsylvania
Cambria County Area Community
    College
Carlow College
Carnegie Mellon University
Chatham College
Chestnut Hill College
Cheyney University of Pennsylvania
DeVry University
    Ft. Washington
Dean Institute of Technology
Delaware County Community College
Delaware Valley College
Drexel University
DuBois Business College
Elizabethtown College
Erie Business Center
Geneva College
Gwynedd-Mercy College
Holy Family University
Indiana University of Pennsylvania
Keystone College
La Salle University
Lackawanna College
Lehigh Carbon Community College
Lehigh University
Lincoln University
Mercyhurst College
Millersville University of Pennsylvania
Neumann College
Northampton County Area Community
    College
Peirce College
Penn State
    Abington
    Altoona
    Erie, The Behrend College
    Harrisburg
    Schuylkill - Capital College
    University Park
Pennsylvania College of Technology
Pennsylvania Institute of Technology
Philadelphia University
Pittsburgh Technical Institute: Boyd
    School Division
Reading Area Community College
Robert Morris University
St. Joseph's University
St. Vincent College
Shippensburg University of Pennsylvania
Temple University
Thiel College
University of Pittsburgh
University of Pittsburgh
    Greensburg
    Johnstown
Westmoreland County Community
    College
Widener University
Wilkes University
Williamson Free School of Mechanical
    Trades
Wilson College
York College of Pennsylvania

Puerto Rico

Huertas Junior College
Inter American University of Puerto Rico
    Bayamon Campus
    Guayama Campus
    San German Campus
Technological College of San Juan
Universidad Politecnica de Puerto Rico
University of Puerto Rico
    Bayamon University College
    Mayaguez Campus
    Rio Piedras Campus
    Utuado

University of the Sacred Heart

Rhode Island

Community College of Rhode Island
Providence College
Roger Williams University
University of Rhode Island

South Carolina

Aiken Technical College
Central Carolina Technical College
Charleston Southern University
Clemson University
Coastal Carolina University
Coker College
College of Charleston
Denmark Technical College
Florence-Darlington Technical College
Forrest Junior College
Francis Marion University
Lander University
Midlands Technical College
Morris College
Newberry College
Orangeburg-Calhoun Technical College
Piedmont Technical College
South Carolina State University
Spartanburg Technical College
Technical College of the Lowcountry
Tri-County Technical College
Trident Technical College
University of South Carolina
University of South Carolina
    Aiken
Voorhees College
Winthrop University
York Technical College

South Dakota

Black Hills State University
Dakota State University
South Dakota School of Mines and
    Technology
South Dakota State University

Tennessee

Austin Peay State University
Belmont University
Chattanooga State Technical Community
    College
Cleveland State Community College
Crichton College
Dyersburg State Community College
East Tennessee State University
Fisk University
Freed-Hardeman University
Jackson State Community College
Johnson Bible College
Middle Tennessee State University
Northeast State Technical Community
    College
Pellissippi State Technical Community
    College
Remington College
    Southeast College of Technology
Roane State Community College
Southwest Tennessee Community
    College
Tennessee State University
Tennessee Technological University
Union University
University of Memphis
University of Tennessee
    Chattanooga
    Knoxville
    Martin
Vanderbilt University

Texas

Brazosport College
Brookhaven College
Cedar Valley College
Coastal Bend College
College of the Mainland

Collin County Community College
    District
DeVry University
    Irving
Eastfield College
El Centro College
El Paso Community College
Frank Phillips College
Hill College
Houston Community College System
Howard Payne University
Jarvis Christian College
Kilgore College
Lamar State College at Port Arthur
Lamar University
LeTourneau University
Lee College
MTI College of Business and Technology
MTI College of Business and Technology
Midland College
Mountain View College
North Harris Montgomery Community
    College District
Northeast Texas Community College
Palo Alto College
Paul Quinn College
Prairie View A&M University
Richland College
St. Mary's University
St. Philip's College
Sam Houston State University
San Antonio College
San Jacinto College
    Central Campus
Schreiner University
Southern Methodist University
Southwestern Adventist University
Temple College
Texarkana College
Texas A&M International University
Texas A&M University
Texas A&M University
    Commerce
    Corpus Christi
    Kingsville
Texas College
Texas Southern University
Texas State Technical College
    Waco
    West Texas
Texas Tech University
Texas Woman's University
Tyler Junior College
University of Houston
University of Houston
    Clear Lake
    Downtown
University of North Texas
University of Texas
    Arlington
    Austin
    Brownsville
    Dallas
    El Paso
    Pan American
    San Antonio
    Tyler
University of the Incarnate Word
West Texas A&M University

Utah

Brigham Young University
College of Eastern Utah
Dixie State College of Utah
LDS Business College
Salt Lake Community College
Snow College
Southern Utah University
University of Utah
Utah State University
Utah Valley State College
Weber State University
Westminster College

Vermont

Bennington College
Castleton State College
Goddard College
Lyndon State College
University of Vermont
Woodbury College

Virginia

Bryant & Stratton College
DeVry University
    Crystal City
Ferrum College
George Mason University
Hampton University
J. Sargeant Reynolds Community
    College
Norfolk State University
Old Dominion University
Piedmont Virginia Community College
Rappahannock Community College
Southwest Virginia Community College
Thomas Nelson Community College
University of Virginia
University of Virginia's College at Wise
Virginia Commonwealth University
Virginia Highlands Community College
Virginia Polytechnic Institute and State
    University
Virginia State University
Virginia Union University
Virginia Wesleyan College
Virginia Western Community College

Washington

Art Institute of Seattle
Central Washington University
Centralia College
Clark College
Clover Park Technical College
DeVry University
    Seattle
Eastern Washington University
Edmonds Community College
Everett Community College
Evergreen State College
Grays Harbor College
Green River Community College
Henry Cogswell College
Lake Washington Technical College
Lower Columbia College
North Seattle Community College
Olympic College
Pacific Lutheran University
Renton Technical College
St. Martin's College
Seattle Central Community College
Seattle Pacific University
Spokane Community College
Spokane Falls Community College
University of Puget Sound
University of Washington
Walla Walla College
Walla Walla Community College
Washington State University
Wenatchee Valley College
Whitworth College

West Virginia

Appalachian Bible College
Concord College
Corinthian Schools: National Institute of
    Technology
Davis and Elkins College
Glenville State College
International Academy of Design and
    Technology
Marshall University
Mountain State College
Mountain State University
Shepherd College
University of Charleston
West Virginia State College

West Virginia University Institute of
    Technology
West Virginia University at Parkersburg
Wheeling Jesuit University

Wisconsin

Cardinal Stritch University
Carthage College
Lac Courte Oreilles Ojibwa Community
    College
Lakeland College
Lakeshore Technical College
Marian College of Fond du Lac
Marquette University
Milwaukee Area Technical College
Milwaukee School of Engineering
Northland College
St. Norbert College
University of Wisconsin
    Eau Claire
    Green Bay
    La Crosse
    Madison
    Milwaukee
    Oshkosh
    Platteville
    River Falls
    Stevens Point
    Stout
    Superior
Viterbo University
Waukesha County Technical College
Western Wisconsin Technical College

Wyoming

Casper College
Central Wyoming College
Laramie County Community College
Sheridan College
Western Wyoming Community College

Distance learning

Alabama

Alabama Agricultural and Mechanical
    University
American College of Computer and
    Information Sciences
Athens State University
Auburn University
Auburn University at Montgomery
Bevill State Community College
Calhoun Community College
Chattahoochee Valley Community
    College
Community College of the Air Force
Douglas MacArthur State Technical
    College
Enterprise State Junior College
Faulkner University
Gadsden State Community College
Harry M. Ayers State Technical College
Heritage Christian University
Jacksonville State University
James H. Faulkner State Community
    College
Jefferson Davis Community College
Jefferson State Community College
Judson College
Northwest-Shoals Community College
Snead State Community College
Southern Christian University
Spring Hill College
Troy State University
Troy State University Dothan
Troy State University in Montgomery
University of Alabama
University of Alabama
    Birmingham
    Huntsville
University of North Alabama
University of South Alabama
Virginia College

Wallace Community College: Sparks
    Campus

Alaska

Alaska Pacific University
Prince William Sound Community
    College
University of Alaska
    Anchorage
    Fairbanks
    Southeast

Arizona

Arizona State University
Arizona Western College
Art Institute
    of Phoenix
Central Arizona College
Cochise College
DeVry University
    Phoenix
Eastern Arizona College
Embry-Riddle Aeronautical University:
    Prescott Campus
Gateway Community College
Glendale Community College
International Institute of the Americas
    Phoenix
Northern Arizona University
Paradise Valley Community College
Phoenix College
Pima Community College
Rio Salado College
Scottsdale Community College
University of Arizona
University of Phoenix
Yavapai College

Arkansas

Arkansas State University
Arkansas State University
    Mountain Home
Arkansas Tech University
Henderson State University
Mid-South Community College
Mississippi County Community College
North Arkansas College
Northwest Arkansas Community College
Ouachita Technical College
Phillips Community College of the
    University of Arkansas
Pulaski Technical College
Rich Mountain Community College
Southeast Arkansas College
Southern Arkansas University
Southern Arkansas University Tech
University of Arkansas
University of Arkansas
    Community College at Batesville
    Community College at Hope
    Cossatot Community College of the
    Fort Smith
    Monticello
    Pine Bluff
    for Medical Sciences
University of Central Arkansas

California

Antelope Valley College
Azusa Pacific University
Barstow College
California Maritime Academy
California Polytechnic State University:
    San Luis Obispo

California State University
    Bakersfield
    Chico
    Fresno
    Fullerton
    Hayward
    Long Beach
    Monterey Bay
    Northridge
    Sacramento
    San Bernardino
    San Marcos
    Stanislaus
Cerritos Community College
Cerro Coso Community College
Chabot College
Citrus College
Coastline Community College
Cogswell Polytechnical College
College of the Canyons
College of the Redwoods
College of the Siskiyous
Cuesta College
De Anza College
DeVry University
    Fremont
    Long Beach
    Pomona
    West Hills
Diablo Valley College
Dominican University of California
East Los Angeles College
Feather River College
Foothill College
Fresno Pacific University
Gavilan Community College
Glendale Community College
Golden Gate University
Golden West College
Grossmont Community College
Holy Names College
Hope International University
Humboldt State University
Irvine Valley College
LIFE Pacific College
La Sierra University
Laney College
Las Positas College
Loma Linda University
Long Beach City College
Los Angeles Harbor College
Los Angeles Pierce College
Los Angeles Trade and Technical College
MiraCosta College
Modesto Junior College
Monterey Peninsula College
Moorpark College
Mount San Antonio College
Napa Valley College
National University
Ohlone College
Orange Coast College
Pacific Oaks College
Pacific States University
Palomar College
Reedley College
Riverside Community College
San Diego Mesa College
San Diego State University
San Francisco State University
San Joaquin Delta College
San Jose State University
Santa Barbara City College
Santa Monica College
Santa Rosa Junior College
Shasta College
Sierra College
Simpson College
Sonoma State University
Southwestern College
Stanford University
Taft College

University of California
    Berkeley
    Los Angeles
    Riverside
    Santa Barbara
University of La Verne
University of San Francisco
University of Southern California
Victor Valley College
Westwood College of Technology
    Inland Empire
Yuba Community College District

Colorado

Arapahoe Community College
Art Institute
    of Colorado
Blair Junior College
Colorado Christian University
Colorado Mountain College
    Alpine Campus
    Spring Valley Campus
    Timberline Campus
Colorado State University
Colorado State University
    Pueblo
Colorado Technical University
Community College of Aurora
DeVry University: Colorado Springs
Fort Lewis College
Front Range Community College
Heritage College
Jones International University
Mesa State College
Metropolitan State College of Denver
Morgan Community College
National American University
    Denver
Nazarene Bible College
Red Rocks Community College
Trinidad State Junior College
University of Colorado
    Boulder
    Colorado Springs
    Denver
    Health Sciences Center
University of Northern Colorado
Westwood College of Technology
    South

Connecticut

Asnuntuck Community College
Capital Community College
Central Connecticut State University
Charter Oak State College
Eastern Connecticut State University
Gateway Community College
Holy Apostles College and Seminary
Housatonic Community College
Manchester Community College
Naugatuck Valley Community College
Northwestern Connecticut Community
    College
Quinebaug Valley Community College
Sacred Heart University
St. Joseph College
Southern Connecticut State University
Teikyo Post University
Tunxis Community College
University of Bridgeport
University of Connecticut
University of Hartford
Western Connecticut State University

Delaware

Delaware State University
Delaware Technical and Community
    College
    Owens Campus
    Stanton/Wilmington Campus
    Terry Campus
Goldey-Beacom College
University of Delaware
Wilmington College

District of Columbia

George Washington University
Howard University
Strayer University
Trinity College

Florida

Baptist College of Florida
Barry University
Bethune-Cookman College
Broward Community College
Chipola Junior College
Daytona Beach Community College
DeVry University
    Miramar
    Orlando
Embry-Riddle Aeronautical University
Florida Agricultural and Mechanical
    University
Florida Atlantic University
Florida Christian College
Florida Gulf Coast University
Florida Hospital College of Health
    Sciences
Florida Institute of Technology
Florida International University
Florida Keys Community College
Florida Metropolitan University
    Melbourne Campus
    Tampa College
Florida State University
Gulf Coast Community College
Herzing College
    Orlando
Hillsborough Community College
Hobe Sound Bible College
Indian River Community College
International College
Jacksonville University
Jones College
Lake City Community College
Lake-Sumter Community College
Manatee Community College
Miami-Dade Community College
Northwood University
    Florida Campus
Nova Southeastern University
Okaloosa-Walton Community College
Palm Beach Community College
Pasco-Hernando Community College
Pensacola Junior College
Polk Community College
St. Leo University
St. Petersburg College
St. Thomas University
Santa Fe Community College
Schiller International University
Seminole Community College
South Florida Community College
Southwest Florida College
Tallahassee Community College
Talmudic College of Florida
University of Central Florida
University of Florida
University of Miami
University of North Florida
University of South Florida
University of West Florida
Valencia Community College
Warner Southern College

Georgia

Albany State University
Albany Technical College
Armstrong Atlantic State University
Art Institute
    of Atlanta
Athens Technical College
Bainbridge College
Brenau University
Central Georgia Technical College
Chattahoochee Technical College
Clark Atlanta University
Clayton College and State University
Columbus State University

Columbus Technical College
Darton College
DeVry University
  Alpharetta
  Atlanta
East Georgia College
Floyd College
Gainesville College
Georgia College and State University
Georgia Institute of Technology
Georgia Perimeter College
Georgia Southern University
Georgia Southwestern State University
Georgia State University
Gordon College
Herzing College
Macon State College
Medical College of Georgia
Middle Georgia College
North Georgia College & State
  University
Piedmont College
South Georgia College
Southern Polytechnic State University
Southwest Georgia Technical College
State University of West Georgia
Toccoa Falls College
University of Georgia
Valdosta State University
West Georgia Technical College

Hawaii

Chaminade University of Honolulu
Hawaii Pacific University
University of Hawaii
  Hawaii Community College
  Hilo
  Honolulu Community College
  Kauai Community College
  Leeward Community College
  Manoa
  West Oahu

Idaho

Boise Bible College
Boise State University
Brigham Young University - Idaho
College of Southern Idaho
Eastern Idaho Technical College
Idaho State University
Lewis-Clark State College
North Idaho College
University of Idaho

Illinois

Aurora University
Benedictine University
Black Hawk College
Black Hawk College
  East Campus
Bradley University
Chicago State University
City Colleges of Chicago
  Harold Washington College
  Kennedy-King College
  Malcolm X College
  Olive-Harvey College
  Richard J. Daley College
  Wright College
College of DuPage
College of Lake County
Concordia University
Danville Area Community College
De Paul University
DeVry University
  Addison
  Chicago
  Tinley Park
Dominican University
Eastern Illinois University
Elgin Community College
Finch University of Health Sciences/The
  Chicago Medical School
Governors State University

Heartland Community College
Illinois Central College
Illinois Eastern Community Colleges
  Frontier Community College
  Lincoln Trail College
  Olney Central College
  Wabash Valley College
Illinois Institute of Technology
Illinois State University
John A. Logan College
John Wood Community College
Joliet Junior College
Judson College
Kankakee Community College
Kaskaskia College
Kishwaukee College
Lake Land College
Lakeview College of Nursing
Lewis University
Lewis and Clark Community College
Lincoln Christian College and Seminary
Lincoln Land Community College
McHenry County College
Moody Bible Institute
Moraine Valley Community College
National-Louis University
North Park University
Northeastern Illinois University
Northern Illinois University
Oakton Community College
Olivet Nazarene University
Parkland College
Prairie State College
Quincy University
Rend Lake College
Richland Community College
Robert Morris College: Chicago
Rush University
St. Francis Medical Center College of
  Nursing
Sauk Valley Community College
Shawnee Community College
South Suburban College of Cook County
Southeastern Illinois College
Southern Illinois University Carbondale
Southern Illinois University Edwardsville
Southwestern Illinois College
Spoon River College
Springfield College in Illinois
Trinity International University
Triton College
University of Illinois
  Chicago
  Springfield
  Urbana-Champaign
University of St. Francis
Waubonsee Community College
Western Illinois University
William Rainey Harper College

Indiana

Ball State University
Calumet College of St. Joseph
Grace College
ITT Technical Institute
  Indianapolis
Indiana State University
Indiana University
  Bloomington
  East
  Kokomo
  Northwest
  South Bend
Indiana University-Purdue University
  Fort Wayne
Indiana University-Purdue University
  Indianapolis
Indiana Wesleyan University

Ivy Tech State College
  Bloomington
  Central Indiana
  Columbus
  Eastcentral
  Kokomo
  Lafayette
  Northcentral
  Northeast
  Northwest
  Southcentral
  Southeast
  Southwest
  Wabash Valley
  Whitewater
Oakland City University
Purdue University
Purdue University
  Calumet
  North Central Campus
St. Mary-of-the-Woods College
Taylor University: Fort Wayne
Tri-State University
University of Evansville
University of Indianapolis
University of Notre Dame
University of Southern Indiana
Valparaiso University
Vincennes University

Iowa

Allen College
Buena Vista University
Clarke College
Clinton Community College
Des Moines Area Community College
Dordt College
Drake University
Ellsworth Community College
Franciscan University
Graceland University
Grand View College
Hamilton College
Hamilton College
  Cedar Rapids
Hawkeye Community College
Indian Hills Community College
Iowa Central Community College
Iowa Lakes Community College
Iowa State University
Iowa Wesleyan College
Iowa Western Community College
Kaplan College
Kirkwood Community College
Marshalltown Community College
Morningside College
Muscatine Community College
North Iowa Area Community College
Northeast Iowa Community College
Northwest Iowa Community College
St. Ambrose University
Scott Community College
Southeastern Community College
  North Campus
  South Campus
Southwestern Community College
University of Iowa
University of Northern Iowa
University of Osteopathic Medicine and
  Health Sciences
  Des Moines University -
    Osteopathic Medical Center
Western Iowa Tech Community College
William Penn University

Kansas

Allen County Community College
Barclay College
Barton County Community College
Butler County Community College
Cloud County Community College
Dodge City Community College
Donnelly College
Emporia State University
Fort Hays State University

Fort Scott Community College
Garden City Community College
Hutchinson Community College
Independence Community College
Johnson County Community College
Kansas City Kansas Community College
Kansas State University
Labette Community College
MidAmerica Nazarene University
Newman University
Pittsburg State University
Pratt Community College
St. Mary College
Seward County Community College
Southwestern College
University of Kansas
University of Kansas Medical Center
Washburn University of Topeka
Wichita State University

Kentucky

Campbellsville University
Cumberland College
Elizabethtown Community College
Henderson Community College
Hopkinsville Community College
Jefferson Community College
Lexington Community College
Madisonville Community College
Maysville Community College
Morehead State University
Murray State University
Paducah Community College
Prestonsburg Community College
Somerset Community College
Southeast Community College
University of Kentucky
University of Louisville

Louisiana

Delgado Community College
Grantham University
Herzing College
Louisiana State University
  Alexandria
  Eunice
Louisiana State University and
  Agricultural and Mechanical College
Louisiana Tech University
Loyola University New Orleans
McNeese State University
Nicholls State University
Northwestern State University
Nunez Community College
Our Lady of Holy Cross College
Southeastern Louisiana University
Southern University and Agricultural and
  Mechanical College
University of Louisiana at Monroe
University of New Orleans

Maine

Central Maine Medical Center School of
  Nursing
Husson College
St. Joseph's College
University of Maine
University of Maine
  Augusta
  Farmington
  Machias
  Presque Isle
University of New England
University of Southern Maine

Maryland

Allegany College
Anne Arundel Community College
Bowie State University
Capitol College
Carroll Community College
Cecil Community College
Chesapeake College
College of Southern Maryland

Columbia Union College
Community College of Baltimore County
    Catonsville
    Dundalk
    Essex
Coppin State College
Frederick Community College
Frostburg State University
Goucher College
Hagerstown Community College
Harford Community College
Hood College
Howard Community College
Maryland Institute College of Art
Montgomery College
    Rockville Campus
Morgan State University
Towson University
University of Baltimore
University of Maryland
    Baltimore
    Baltimore County
    College Park
    University College
Wor-Wic Community College

Massachusetts

Art Institute of Boston at Lesley
    University
Atlantic Union College
Becker College
Bentley College
Berkshire Community College
Boston Architectural Center
Bridgewater State College
Bunker Hill Community College
Cape Cod Community College
Elms College
Endicott College
Fisher College
Fitchburg State College
Framingham State College
Greenfield Community College
Hebrew College
Lesley University
Massachusetts Bay Community College
Massachusetts College of Liberal Arts
Massachusetts College of Pharmacy and
    Health Sciences
Massasoit Community College
Mount Wachusett Community College
Nichols College
Northeastern University
Quinsigamond Community College
Springfield Technical Community
    College
Suffolk University
University of Massachusetts
    Amherst
    Boston
    Dartmouth
    Lowell
Westfield State College

Michigan

Alpena Community College
Andrews University
Aquinas College
Baker College
    of Auburn Hills
    of Cadillac
    of Clinton Township
    of Jackson
    of Muskegon
    of Owosso
    of Port Huron
Bay de Noc Community College
Central Michigan University
Cleary University
Davenport University
    Midland
Davenport University - Western Region
Eastern Michigan University
Ferris State University
Finlandia University

Glen Oaks Community College
Gogebic Community College
Grand Rapids Community College
Grand Valley State University
Jackson Community College
Kellogg Community College
Kettering University
Kirtland Community College
Lansing Community College
Lawrence Technological University
Macomb Community College
Madonna University
Michigan State University
Michigan Technological University
Mid Michigan Community College
Montcalm Community College
Mott Community College
Muskegon Community College
North Central Michigan College
Northern Michigan University
Northwestern Michigan College
Northwood University
Oakland Community College
Oakland University
Reformed Bible College
Saginaw Valley State University
St. Clair County Community College
Schoolcraft College
Southwestern Michigan College
Spring Arbor University
University of Michigan
University of Michigan
    Dearborn
    Flint
Walsh College of Accountancy and
    Business Administration
Washtenaw Community College
Wayne County Community College
Wayne State University
West Shore Community College
Western Michigan University
William Tyndale College

Minnesota

Alexandria Technical College
Anoka-Ramsey Community College
Art Institutes International
    Minnesota
Bemidji State University
Central Lakes College
College of St. Catherine
College of St. Scholastica
Concordia University: St. Paul
Crown College
Dakota County Technical College
Fergus Falls Community College
Globe College
Hamline University
Hennepin Technical College
Hibbing Community College: A
    Technical and Community College
Inver Hills Community College
Lake Superior College: A Community
    and Technical College
Metropolitan State University
Minneapolis Community and Technical
    College
Minnesota School of Business
Minnesota State College - Southeast
    Technical
Minnesota State University
    Mankato
    Moorhead
Minnesota West Community and
    Technical College: Worthington
    Campus
National American University
    St. Paul
Normandale Community College
North Central University
North Hennepin Community College
Northland Community & Technical
    College
Northwestern College
Pine Technical College

Rainy River Community College
Rasmussen College
    Minnetonka
    St. Cloud
Ridgewater College: A Community and
    Technical College
Riverland Community College: A
    Technical and Community College
Rochester Community and Technical
    College
St. Cloud State University
St. Cloud Technical College
St. Paul College - A Community and
    Technical College
Southwest State University
University of Minnesota
    Crookston
    Duluth
    Morris
    Twin Cities
Winona State University

Mississippi

Alcorn State University
Coahoma Community College
Delta State University
Holmes Community College
Itawamba Community College
Mississippi Gulf Coast Community
    College
    Perkinston
Mississippi State University
Mississippi University for Women
University of Mississippi
University of Southern Mississippi

Missouri

Avila University
Baptist Bible College
Blue River Community College
Calvary Bible College
Central Methodist College
Central Missouri State University
Columbia College
Crowder College
DeVry University
    Kansas City
Drury University
East Central College
Fontbonne College
Global University
Jefferson College
Longview Community College
Maple Woods Community College
Maryville University of Saint Louis
Mineral Area College
Missouri Baptist University
Missouri Southern State College
Missouri Western State College
Moberly Area Community College
National American University
    Kansas City
North Central Missouri College
Ozark Christian College
Ozarks Technical Community College
Penn Valley Community College
Ranken Technical College
Rockhurst University
St. Charles Community College
St. Louis Community College
    St. Louis Community College at
        Florissant Valley
    St. Louis Community College at
        Forest Park
    St. Louis Community College at
        Meramec
St. Louis University
Southeast Missouri State University
Southwest Missouri State University
Southwest Missouri State University:
    West Plains Campus
Stephens College
Three Rivers Community College

University of Missouri
    Columbia
    Rolla
    St. Louis
Vatterott College: St. Joseph
Webster University

Montana

Dawson Community College
Flathead Valley Community College
Miles Community College
Montana State University
    Billings
    Bozeman
Montana Tech of the University of
    Montana
Rocky Mountain College
University of Great Falls
University of Montana-Missoula
University of Montana: Western

Nebraska

Bellevue University
Central Community College
Chadron State College
Clarkson College
College of Saint Mary
Concordia University
Creighton University
Metropolitan Community College
Mid Plains Community College Area
Midland Lutheran College
Nebraska College of Technical
    Agriculture
Nebraska Methodist College of Nursing
    and Allied Health
Northeast Community College
Peru State College
Southeast Community College
    Beatrice Campus
    Lincoln Campus
University of Nebraska
    Kearney
    Lincoln
    Omaha
Wayne State College
Western Nebraska Community College

Nevada

Community College of Southern Nevada
Great Basin College
Truckee Meadows Community College
University of Nevada
    Las Vegas
    Reno
Western Nevada Community College

New Hampshire

College for Lifelong Learning
Daniel Webster College
New England College
New Hampshire Community Technical
    College
    Berlin
    Laconia
    Nashua
New Hampshire Technical Institute
Southern New Hampshire University

New Jersey

Atlantic Cape Community College
Bergen Community College
Berkeley College
Bloomfield College
Brookdale Community College
Burlington County College
Caldwell College
Camden County College
College of St. Elizabeth
County College of Morris
Cumberland County College
DeVry College of Technology

Fairleigh Dickinson University
    College at Florham
    Metropolitan Campus
Felician College
Georgian Court College
Gloucester County College
Hudson County Community College
Kean University
Mercer County Community College
Middlesex County College
New Jersey City University
New Jersey Institute of Technology
Ocean County College
Passaic County Community College
Raritan Valley Community College
Richard Stockton College of New Jersey
Rutgers, The State University of New
  Jersey
    Camden Regional Campus
    New Brunswick Regional Campus
    Newark Regional Campus
Salem Community College
Seton Hall University
Stevens Institute of Technology
Sussex County Community College
Thomas Edison State College
Union County College
University of Medicine and Dentistry of
  New Jersey
    School of Health Related
      Professions
Warren County Community College
William Paterson University of New
  Jersey

New Mexico

Albuquerque Technical-Vocational
  Institute
Clovis Community College
Eastern New Mexico University
Eastern New Mexico University: Roswell
  Campus
National American University
New Mexico Highlands University
New Mexico Institute of Mining and
  Technology
New Mexico Junior College
New Mexico State University
New Mexico State University
  Alamogordo
San Juan College
Santa Fe Community College
University of New Mexico
Western New Mexico University

New York

Adelphi University
Adirondack Community College
Berkeley College
Berkeley College of New York City
Broome Community College
Bryant & Stratton Business Institute
  Albany
  Syracuse
Cayuga County Community College
City University of New York
    Borough of Manhattan Community
      College
    Brooklyn College
    Hostos Community College
    Hunter College
    John Jay College of Criminal
      Justice
    Medgar Evers College
    Queens College
Clinton Community College
College of Aeronautics
Concordia College
Cornell University
Corning Community College
Culinary Institute of America
D'Youville College
Daemen College
DeVry Institute of Technology
  New York

Dutchess Community College
Erie Community College
  City Campus
  North Campus
  South Campus
Eugene Lang College/New School
  University
Excelsior College
Fashion Institute of Technology
Finger Lakes Community College
Fulton-Montgomery Community College
Genesee Community College
Holy Trinity Orthodox Seminary
Hudson Valley Community College
Iona College
Jamestown Community College
Jefferson Community College
Long Island University
  C. W. Post Campus
  Southampton College
Manhattan College
Manhattanville College
Marist College
Marymount Manhattan College
Mercy College
Mohawk Valley Community College
Monroe College
Monroe Community College
Mount St. Mary College
Nassau Community College
New York Institute of Technology
New York University
Niagara County Community College
North Country Community College
Nyack College
Onondaga Community College
Orange County Community College
Pace University
Pace University: Pleasantville/Briarcliff
Parsons School of Design
Polytechnic University
Rensselaer Polytechnic Institute
Roberts Wesleyan College
Rochester Institute of Technology
Rockland Community College
St. Bonaventure University
St. Elizabeth College of Nursing
St. John's University
St. Joseph's College: Suffolk Campus
Schenectady County Community College
Skidmore College
State University of New York
  Albany
  Binghamton
  Buffalo
  College at Brockport
  College at Buffalo
  College at Cortland
  College at Fredonia
  College at Oneonta
  College at Plattsburgh
  College at Potsdam
  College of Agriculture and
    Technology at Cobleskill
  College of Agriculture and
    Technology at Morrisville
  College of Technology at Alfred
  College of Technology at Canton
  College of Technology at Delhi
  Institute of Technology at
    Utica/Rome
  New Paltz
  Oswego
  Purchase
Suffolk County Community College
Syracuse University
Tompkins-Cortland Community College
Touro College
Ulster County Community College
Utica College
Westchester Community College

North Carolina

Appalachian State University

Asheville Buncombe Technical
  Community College
Beaufort County Community College
Bladen Community College
Blue Ridge Community College
Brunswick Community College
Caldwell Community College and
  Technical Institute
Campbell University
Cape Fear Community College
Carteret Community College
Catawba Valley Community College
Central Carolina Community College
Central Piedmont Community College
Chowan College
Cleveland Community College
Coastal Carolina Community College
College of the Albemarle
Craven Community College
Davidson County Community College
Duke University
Durham Technical Community College
East Carolina University
Edgecombe Community College
Fayetteville State University
Fayetteville Technical Community
  College
Forsyth Technical Community College
Gaston College
Guilford Technical Community College
Haywood Community College
Isothermal Community College
James Sprunt Community College
Johnston Community College
Lenoir Community College
Lenoir-Rhyne College
Mars Hill College
Martin Community College
Mayland Community College
Mitchell Community College
Montgomery Community College
Nash Community College
North Carolina Agricultural and
  Technical State University
North Carolina State University
North Carolina Wesleyan College
Piedmont Baptist College
Piedmont Community College
Pitt Community College
Randolph Community College
Richmond Community College
Roanoke-Chowan Community College
Rockingham Community College
Rowan-Cabarrus Community College
Sampson Community College
Sandhills Community College
South Piedmont Community College
Southeastern Community College
Stanly Community College
Surry Community College
University of North Carolina
  Asheville
  Chapel Hill
  Charlotte
  Greensboro
  Pembroke
  Wilmington
Vance-Granville Community College
Wake Technical Community College
Wayne Community College
Western Carolina University
Western Piedmont Community College
Wilkes Community College
Wilson Technical Community College
Winston-Salem State University

North Dakota

Bismarck State College
Dickinson State University
Lake Region State College
Mayville State University
Minot State University
Minot State University: Bottineau
  Campus
North Dakota State College of Science

North Dakota State University
University of Mary
University of North Dakota
Valley City State University
Williston State College

Ohio

Baldwin-Wallace College
Bowling Green State University
Bowling Green State University:
  Firelands College
Bryant & Stratton College
Bryant & Stratton College
  Cleveland West
  Willoughby Hills
Cedarville University
Cincinnati State Technical and
  Community College
Clark State Community College
Cleveland State University
College of Mount St. Joseph
Columbus State Community College
Cuyahoga Community College
  Eastern Campus
  Metropolitan Campus
  Western Campus
David N. Myers College
DeVry University
  Columbus
Defiance College
Edison State Community College
Franciscan University of Steubenville
Franklin University
Hocking Technical College
James A. Rhodes State College
Kent State University
Kent State University
  Ashtabula Regional Campus
  East Liverpool Regional Campus
  Salem Regional Campus
  Stark Campus
  Trumbull Campus
  Tuscarawas Campus
Lakeland Community College
Laura and Alvin Siegal College of Judaic
  Studies
Lorain County Community College
Malone College
Miami University
  Hamilton Campus
  Middletown Campus
Miami-Jacobs College
Muskingum Area Technical College
North Central State College
Northwest State Community College
Ohio Northern University
Ohio State University
  Columbus Campus
  Lima Campus
Ohio University
Ohio University
  Chillicothe Campus
  Eastern Campus
Owens Community College
  Findlay Campus
  Toledo
Sinclair Community College
Southern State Community College
Stark State College of Technology
Tiffin University
Union Institute & University
University of Akron
University of Cincinnati
University of Cincinnati
  Clermont College
  Raymond Walters College
University of Findlay
University of Northwestern Ohio
University of Rio Grande
University of Toledo
Ursuline College
Washington State Community College
Wright State University
Wright State University: Lake Campus
Youngstown State University

Oklahoma

Cameron University
Carl Albert State College
East Central University
Eastern Oklahoma State College
Langston University
Northeastern Oklahoma Agricultural and
    Mechanical College
Northeastern State University
Northern Oklahoma College
Northwestern Oklahoma State University
Oklahoma City Community College
Oklahoma Panhandle State University
Oklahoma State University
Oklahoma State University
    Oklahoma City
    Okmulgee
Oral Roberts University
Redlands Community College
Rogers State University
Rose State College
Southeastern Oklahoma State University
Southwestern Oklahoma State University
Tulsa Community College
University of Central Oklahoma
University of Oklahoma
University of Science and Arts of
    Oklahoma
Western Oklahoma State College

Oregon

Blue Mountain Community College
Central Oregon Community College
Chemeketa Community College
Clackamas Community College
Clatsop Community College
Concordia University
Eastern Oregon University
Eugene Bible College
Lane Community College
Linfield College
Linn-Benton Community College
Marylhurst University
Mount Hood Community College
Northwest Christian College
Oregon Institute of Technology
Oregon State University
Portland Community College
Portland State University
Rogue Community College
Southern Oregon University
Southwestern Oregon Community
    College
Umpqua Community College
Western Baptist College
Western Oregon University

Pennsylvania

Baptist Bible College of Pennsylvania
Bloomsburg University of Pennsylvania
Bucks County Community College
Butler County Community College
Cabrini College
California University of Pennsylvania
Cambria County Area Community
    College
Career Training Academy
Carlow College
Cedar Crest College
Cheyney University of Pennsylvania
Community College of Allegheny
    County
Community College of Beaver County
Community College of Philadelphia
DeSales University
DeVry University
    Ft. Washington
Delaware County Community College
Drexel University
Duquesne University
Edinboro University of Pennsylvania
Education Direct: Center for Degree
    Studies
Gratz College
Harrisburg Area Community College

Indiana University of Pennsylvania
Juniata College
King's College
Kutztown University of Pennsylvania
La Roche College
Lackawanna College
Lafayette College
Lehigh Carbon Community College
Luzerne County Community College
Manor College
Marywood University
Millersville University of Pennsylvania
Montgomery County Community
    College
Mount Aloysius College
Neumann College
Northampton County Area Community
    College
Peirce College
Penn State
    Abington
    Altoona
    Beaver
    Berks
    Delaware County
    Dubois
    Erie, The Behrend College
    Fayette
    Harrisburg
    Hazleton
    Lehigh Valley
    McKeesport
    Mont Alto
    New Kensington
    Schuylkill - Capital College
    Shenango
    University Park
    Wilkes-Barre
    Worthington Scranton
    York
Pennsylvania College of Technology
Philadelphia University
Point Park University
Reading Area Community College
Robert Morris University
Rosemont College
St. Joseph's University
Seton Hill University
Shippensburg University of Pennsylvania
Slippery Rock University of
    Pennsylvania
Temple University
University of Pennsylvania
University of Pittsburgh
University of Pittsburgh
    Bradford
    Greensburg
    Johnstown
    Titusville
University of Scranton
Valley Forge Christian College
Villanova University
Waynesburg College
West Chester University of Pennsylvania
Westmoreland County Community
    College
Widener University
Wilkes University
York College of Pennsylvania

Puerto Rico

Huertas Junior College
Inter American University of Puerto Rico
    Barranquitas Campus
    Bayamon Campus
    Metropolitan Campus
    San German Campus
Turabo University
Universidad Metropolitana
Universidad del Este
University of Puerto Rico
    Mayaguez Campus
    Utuado

Rhode Island

Community College of Rhode Island
Roger Williams University
Salve Regina University
University of Rhode Island

South Carolina

Aiken Technical College
Central Carolina Technical College
Clemson University
Coastal Carolina University
College of Charleston
Columbia International University
Converse College
Florence-Darlington Technical College
Lander University
Limestone College
Medical University of South Carolina
Midlands Technical College
Northeastern Technical College
Orangeburg-Calhoun Technical College
Piedmont Technical College
South Carolina State University
Southern Wesleyan University
Spartanburg Technical College
Technical College of the Lowcountry
Tri-County Technical College
Trident Technical College
University of South Carolina
University of South Carolina
    Spartanburg
    Sumter
    Union
Williamsburg Technical College
Winthrop University
York Technical College

South Dakota

Black Hills State University
Dakota State University
Dakota Wesleyan University
Kilian Community College
Northern State University
South Dakota School of Mines and
    Technology
South Dakota State University
University of Sioux Falls
University of South Dakota

Tennessee

Austin Peay State University
Belmont University
Chattanooga State Technical Community
    College
Cleveland State Community College
Columbia State Community College
Crichton College
Dyersburg State Community College
East Tennessee State University
Freed-Hardeman University
Jackson State Community College
Johnson Bible College
Lee University
Middle Tennessee State University
Northeast State Technical Community
    College
Pellissippi State Technical Community
    College
Roane State Community College
Southwest Tennessee Community
    College
Tennessee State University
Tennessee Technological University
Union University
University of Memphis
University of Tennessee
    Chattanooga
    Knoxville
    Martin
University of Tennessee Health Science
    Center
Vanderbilt University
Volunteer State Community College
Walters State Community College

Rhode Island

Community College of Rhode Island
Roger Williams University
Salve Regina University
University of Rhode Island

Texas

Abilene Christian University
Alvin Community College
Amarillo College
Amberton University
Angelina College
Angelo State University
Arlington Baptist College
Austin Community College
Blinn College
Brazosport College
Cedar Valley College
Central Texas College
Clarendon College
Coastal Bend College
College of the Mainland
Collin County Community College
    District
Concordia University at Austin
Dallas Baptist University
Dallas Christian College
DeVry University
    Irving
Del Mar College
Eastfield College
El Centro College
El Paso Community College
Frank Phillips College
Galveston College
Grayson County College
Hardin-Simmons University
Hill College
Houston Community College System
Howard College
Howard Payne University
Huston-Tillotson College
Jarvis Christian College
Kilgore College
Lamar State College at Orange
Lamar State College at Port Arthur
Lamar University
Laredo Community College
LeTourneau University
Lee College
Lubbock Christian University
McLennan Community College
Midland College
Midwestern State University
Mountain View College
North Central Texas College
North Harris Montgomery Community
    College District
North Lake College
Northeast Texas Community College
Northwood University: Texas Campus
Odessa College
Palo Alto College
Paul Quinn College
Prairie View A&M University
Richland College
St. Mary's University
St. Philip's College
Sam Houston State University
San Antonio College
San Jacinto College
    Central Campus
Schreiner University
South Plains College
Southern Methodist University
Southwest Texas State University
Southwestern Adventist University
Stephen F. Austin State University
Sul Ross State University
Tarleton State University
Tarrant County College
Temple College
Texas A&M University
Texas A&M University
    Commerce
    Corpus Christi
    Kingsville
    Texarkana
Texas Christian University
Texas Southern University

Texas State Technical College
 Waco
 West Texas
Texas Tech University
Texas Wesleyan University
Texas Woman's University
Trinity Valley Community College
Tyler Junior College
University of Houston
University of Houston
 Clear Lake
 Downtown
 Victoria
University of North Texas
University of St. Thomas
University of Texas
 Arlington
 Austin
 Dallas
 El Paso
 Houston Health Science Center
 Medical Branch at Galveston
 Pan American
 San Antonio
 Tyler
 of the Permian Basin
University of the Incarnate Word
Wayland Baptist University
West Texas A&M University
Western Texas College
Wharton County Junior College

Utah

Brigham Young University
College of Eastern Utah
Dixie State College of Utah
Salt Lake Community College
Southern Utah University
University of Utah
Utah Career College
Utah State University
Utah Valley State College
Weber State University

Vermont

Bennington College
Burlington College
Champlain College
Community College of Vermont
Goddard College
Johnson State College
Norwich University
University of Vermont
Vermont Technical College

Virginia

Blue Ridge Community College
College of Health Sciences
Danville Community College
ECPI College of Technology
ECPI Technical College: Roanoke
Eastern Mennonite University
Eastern Shore Community College
George Mason University
Hampton University
J. Sargeant Reynolds Community
 College
James Madison University
Liberty University
Longwood University
Mary Baldwin College
Mountain Empire Community College
Norfolk State University
Old Dominion University
Paul D. Camp Community College
Piedmont Virginia Community College
Radford University
Rappahannock Community College
Shenandoah University
Southside Virginia Community College
Southwest Virginia Community College
Thomas Nelson Community College
University of Virginia's College at Wise
Virginia Commonwealth University

Virginia Highlands Community College
Virginia Polytechnic Institute and State
 University

Washington

Art Institute of Seattle
Bellevue Community College
Central Washington University
Centralia College
Clark College
Clover Park Technical College
Crown College
DeVry University
 Seattle
Eastern Washington University
Edmonds Community College
Everett Community College
Gonzaga University
Grays Harbor College
Green River Community College
Heritage College
Lake Washington Technical College
Lower Columbia College
North Seattle Community College
Olympic College
Peninsula College
Renton Technical College
Seattle Central Community College
Seattle Pacific University
South Seattle Community College
Spokane Community College
Spokane Falls Community College
University of Washington
Walla Walla Community College
Washington State University
Wenatchee Valley College

West Virginia

Alderson-Broaddus College
Bluefield State College
Glenville State College
Marshall University
Mountain State University
Potomac State College of West Virginia
 University
Salem International University
Southern West Virginia Community and
 Technical College
University of Charleston
West Liberty State College
West Virginia Northern Community
 College
West Virginia State College
West Virginia University
West Virginia University Institute of
 Technology
West Virginia University at Parkersburg
West Virginia Wesleyan College
Wheeling Jesuit University

Wisconsin

Blackhawk Technical College
Bryant & Stratton College
Cardinal Stritch University
Chippewa Valley Technical College
Concordia University Wisconsin
Edgewood College
Fox Valley Technical College
Lac Courte Oreilles Ojibwa Community
 College
Lakeland College
Lakeshore Technical College
Maranatha Baptist Bible College
Marian College of Fond du Lac
Milwaukee Area Technical College
Milwaukee School of Engineering
Moraine Park Technical College
Mount Mary College
Nicolet Area Technical College
Northland College
St. Norbert College

University of Wisconsin
 Baraboo/Sauk County
 Eau Claire
 Fond du Lac
 Fox Valley
 Green Bay
 La Crosse
 Marinette
 Milwaukee
 Oshkosh
 Parkside
 Platteville
 Richland
 River Falls
 Rock County
 Stevens Point
 Stout
 Superior
 Washington County
 Waukesha
 Whitewater
Viterbo University
Waukesha County Technical College
Western Wisconsin Technical College
Wisconsin Indianhead Technical College

Wyoming

Casper College
Central Wyoming College
Eastern Wyoming College
Laramie County Community College
Sheridan College
University of Wyoming
Western Wyoming Community College

Double major

Alabama

Alabama Agricultural and Mechanical
 University
Alabama State University
Athens State University
Auburn University
Auburn University at Montgomery
Birmingham-Southern College
Calhoun Community College
Faulkner University
George C. Wallace State Community
 College
 Selma
Huntingdon College
Jacksonville State University
James H. Faulkner State Community
 College
Judson College
Lawson State Community College
Miles College
Northeast Alabama Community College
Oakwood College
Samford University
Shelton State Community College
South University
Southeastern Bible College
Southern Christian University
Spring Hill College
Stillman College
Talladega College
Troy State University
Troy State University Dothan
Troy State University in Montgomery
Tuskegee University
University of Alabama
University of Alabama
 Birmingham
 Huntsville
University of Mobile
University of Montevallo
University of North Alabama
University of South Alabama
University of West Alabama
Virginia College
Wallace State Community College at
 Hanceville

Alaska

Alaska Bible College
Alaska Pacific University
Charter College
Prince William Sound Community
 College
Sheldon Jackson College
University of Alaska
 Anchorage
 Fairbanks

Arizona

American Indian College of the
 Assemblies of God
Arizona Automotive Institute
Arizona State University
Cochise College
Eastern Arizona College
Embry-Riddle Aeronautical University:
 Prescott Campus
Gateway Community College
Northern Arizona University
Pima Community College
Prescott College
Rio Salado College
University of Arizona

Arkansas

Arkansas Baptist College
Arkansas State University
Arkansas State University
 Beebe
Arkansas Tech University
Harding University
Hendrix College
Lyon College
Mississippi County Community College
Ouachita Baptist University
Southern Arkansas University
Southern Arkansas University Tech
University of Arkansas
University of Arkansas
 Community College at Hope
 Cossatot Community College of the
 Little Rock
 Monticello
 Pine Bluff
University of Central Arkansas
University of the Ozarks
Williams Baptist College

California

Antelope Valley College
Antioch Southern California
 Los Angeles
 Santa Barbara
Art Institute of California - San Francisco
Azusa Pacific University
Bakersfield College
Bethany College
Bethesda Christian University
California Baptist University
California College of Arts and Crafts
California Institute of Technology
California Maritime Academy
California Polytechnic State University:
 San Luis Obispo
California State Polytechnic University:
 Pomona
California State University
 Bakersfield
 Chico
 Dominguez Hills
 Fresno
 Fullerton
 Hayward
 Long Beach
 Los Angeles
 Northridge
 Sacramento
 San Bernardino
 San Marcos
 Stanislaus
Cerro Coso Community College

Chabot College
Chapman University
Christian Heritage College
Citrus College
Claremont McKenna College
Coleman College
College of the Redwoods
Columbia College
Concordia University
Cuesta College
Cuyamaca College
Dominican School of Philosophy and
   Theology
Dominican University of California
East Los Angeles College
Feather River College
Fresno Pacific University
Golden West College
Grossmont Community College
Harvey Mudd College
Holy Names College
Hope International University
Humboldt State University
Imperial Valley College
Irvine Valley College
John F. Kennedy University
La Sierra University
Los Angeles Harbor College
Los Angeles Southwest College
Loyola Marymount University
Master's College
Menlo College
Mills College
MiraCosta College
Modesto Junior College
Monterey Peninsula College
Mount St. Mary's College
Mount San Antonio College
Mount San Jacinto College
Napa Valley College
National University
Occidental College
Ohlone College
Pacific Oaks College
Pacific States University
Pacific Union College
Patten University
Pepperdine University
Pitzer College
Point Loma Nazarene University
Pomona College
Reedley College
Riverside Community College
St. Mary's College of California
Samuel Merritt College
San Diego City College
San Diego Mesa College
San Diego State University
San Francisco State University
San Jose Christian College
San Jose State University
Santa Barbara City College
Santa Clara University
Scripps College
Shasta College
Sierra College
Simpson College
Sonoma State University
Southwestern College
Stanford University
Travel University International
University of California
   Berkeley
   Davis
   Los Angeles
   Riverside
   San Diego
   Santa Barbara
   Santa Cruz
University of La Verne
University of Redlands
University of San Diego
University of San Francisco
University of Southern California
University of the Pacific

Vanguard University of Southern
   California
Victor Valley College
West Valley College
Whittier College
Woodbury University

Colorado

Blair Junior College
Colorado Christian University
Colorado College
Colorado School of Mines
Colorado State University
Colorado State University
   Pueblo
Colorado Technical University
Fort Lewis College
Front Range Community College
Mesa State College
Metropolitan State College of Denver
Morgan Community College
Naropa University
National American University
   Denver
Nazarene Bible College
Red Rocks Community College
Regis University
Rocky Mountain College of Art &
   Design
Trinidad State Junior College
United States Air Force Academy
University of Colorado
   Boulder
   Colorado Springs
   Denver
University of Denver
University of Northern Colorado

Connecticut

Albertus Magnus College
Asnuntuck Community College
Briarwood College
Capital Community College
Central Connecticut State University
Connecticut College
Eastern Connecticut State University
Fairfield University
Holy Apostles College and Seminary
Housatonic Community College
Manchester Community College
Naugatuck Valley Community College
Northwestern Connecticut Community
   College
Norwalk Community College
Quinebaug Valley Community College
Quinnipiac University
Sacred Heart University
St. Joseph College
Southern Connecticut State University
Teikyo Post University
Three Rivers Community College
Trinity College
Tunxis Community College
United States Coast Guard Academy
University of Bridgeport
University of Connecticut
University of Hartford
University of New Haven
Wesleyan University
Western Connecticut State University
Yale University

Delaware

Delaware State University
Delaware Technical and Community
   College
   Owens Campus
   Stanton/Wilmington Campus
   Terry Campus
University of Delaware
Wilmington College

District of Columbia

American University

Catholic University of America
Gallaudet University
George Washington University
Georgetown University
Howard University
Strayer University
Trinity College
University of the District of Columbia

Florida

Baptist College of Florida
Barry University
Bethune-Cookman College
Eckerd College
Edward Waters College
Embry-Riddle Aeronautical University
Flagler College
Florida Agricultural and Mechanical
   University
Florida Atlantic University
Florida Institute of Technology
Florida International University
Florida Keys Community College
Florida Metropolitan University
   Orlando College North
   Tampa College
Florida Southern College
Florida State University
Hillsborough Community College
Hobe Sound Bible College
International College
Jacksonville University
Jones College
New College of Florida
New England Institute of Technology
Northwood University
   Florida Campus
Palm Beach Atlantic University
Palm Beach Community College
Pasco-Hernando Community College
Pensacola Junior College
Polk Community College
Rollins College
St. Leo University
St. Thomas University
Schiller International University
South Florida Community College
Southeastern College of the Assemblies
   of God
Southwest Florida College
Stetson University
Tallahassee Community College
University of Central Florida
University of Florida
University of Miami
University of North Florida
University of South Florida
University of Tampa
University of West Florida
Valencia Community College
Warner Southern College
Webber International University

Georgia

Agnes Scott College
Albany State University
Andrew College
Armstrong Atlantic State University
Augusta State University
Bainbridge College
Bauder College
Berry College
Brenau University
Brewton-Parker College
Clark Atlanta University
Coastal Georgia Community College
Covenant College
Dalton State College
East Georgia College
Emory University
Floyd College
Georgia College and State University
Georgia Institute of Technology
Georgia Military College
Georgia Perimeter College

Georgia Southern University
Georgia Southwestern State University
Georgia State University
Kennesaw State University
LaGrange College
Mercer University
Middle Georgia College
Morehouse College
Morris Brown College
North Georgia College & State
   University
Oglethorpe University
Oxford College of Emory University
Piedmont College
Reinhardt College
Savannah College of Art and Design
Savannah State University
Shorter College
South University
Southern Polytechnic State University
Southwest Georgia Technical College
Spelman College
State University of West Georgia
Thomas University
Toccoa Falls College
Truett-McConnell College
University of Georgia
Valdosta State University
Wesleyan College
West Georgia Technical College

Hawaii

Chaminade University of Honolulu
Hawaii Business College
Hawaii Pacific University
University of Hawaii
   Hawaii Community College
   Hilo
   Manoa
   Maui Community College
   West Oahu

Idaho

Albertson College of Idaho
Boise Bible College
Boise State University
Brigham Young University - Idaho
Idaho State University
Lewis-Clark State College
Northwest Nazarene University
University of Idaho

Illinois

Augustana College
Aurora University
Benedictine University
Black Hawk College
   East Campus
Blackburn College
Blessing-Reiman College of Nursing
Bradley University
Chicago State University
City Colleges of Chicago
   Harold Washington College
College of DuPage
Concordia University
Danville Area Community College
De Paul University
Dominican University
Eastern Illinois University
Elgin Community College
Elmhurst College
Eureka College
Greenville College
Heartland Community College
Illinois College
Illinois Eastern Community Colleges
   Frontier Community College
   Lincoln Trail College
   Olney Central College
   Wabash Valley College
Illinois Institute of Technology
Illinois State University
Illinois Wesleyan University

Judson College
Kaskaskia College
Kendall College
Kishwaukee College
Knox College
Lake Forest College
Lewis University
Lewis and Clark Community College
Lincoln Christian College and Seminary
Lincoln Land Community College
Loyola University of Chicago
MacMurray College
McKendree College
Midstate College
Millikin University
Monmouth College
Moody Bible Institute
Moraine Valley Community College
Morrison Institute of Technology
North Central College
North Park University
Northeastern Illinois University
Northern Illinois University
Northwestern Business College
Northwestern University
Olivet Nazarene University
Parkland College
Principia College
Quincy University
Rockford College
Roosevelt University
St. Augustine College
St. Xavier University
Sauk Valley Community College
School of the Art Institute of Chicago
Shimer College
South Suburban College of Cook County
Southeastern Illinois College
Southern Illinois University Carbondale
Southern Illinois University Edwardsville
Southwestern Illinois College
Springfield College in Illinois
Trinity Christian College
Trinity International University
Triton College
University of Chicago
University of Illinois
    Chicago
    Springfield
    Urbana-Champaign
University of St. Francis
Western Illinois University
Wheaton College

Indiana

American Conservatory of Music
Ancilla College
Anderson University
Ball State University
Bethel College
Butler University
Calumet College of St. Joseph
DePauw University
Earlham College
Franklin College
Goshen College
Grace College
Hanover College
Huntington College
Indiana Business College
Indiana Institute of Technology
Indiana State University
Indiana University
    Bloomington
    East
    Kokomo
    Northwest
    South Bend
    Southeast
Indiana University-Purdue University
    Fort Wayne
Indiana University-Purdue University
    Indianapolis
Ivy Tech State College
    Southcentral

Manchester College
Marian College
Martin University
Michiana College
Oakland City University
Purdue University
Purdue University
    Calumet
Rose-Hulman Institute of Technology
St. Joseph's College
Saint Mary's College
St. Mary-of-the-Woods College
Taylor University
Taylor University: Fort Wayne
Tri-State University
University of Evansville
University of Indianapolis
University of Notre Dame
University of St. Francis
University of Southern Indiana
Valparaiso University
Wabash College

Iowa

American Institute of Business
Briar Cliff University
Buena Vista University
Central College
Clarke College
Clinton Community College
Coe College
Cornell College
Divine Word College
Dordt College
Drake University
Ellsworth Community College
Emmaus Bible College
Faith Baptist Bible College and
    Theological Seminary
Franciscan University
Graceland University
Grand View College
Grinnell College
Hamilton College
    Cedar Rapids
Iowa State University
Iowa Wesleyan College
Kaplan College
Loras College
Luther College
Maharishi University of Management
Morningside College
Mount Mercy College
Muscatine Community College
Northeast Iowa Community College
Northwestern College
St. Ambrose University
Scott Community College
Simpson College
Southwestern Community College
University of Dubuque
University of Iowa
University of Northern Iowa
Upper Iowa University
Vennard College
Waldorf College
Wartburg College
Western Iowa Tech Community College
William Penn University

Kansas

Allen County Community College
Baker University
Barclay College
Benedictine College
Bethany College
Bethel College
Central Christian College
Dodge City Community College
Donnelly College
Emporia State University
Fort Hays State University
Friends University
Highland Community College
Hutchinson Community College

Independence Community College
Johnson County Community College
Kansas City Kansas Community College
Kansas State University
Kansas Wesleyan University
McPherson College
MidAmerica Nazarene University
Newman University
Ottawa University
Pittsburg State University
St. Mary College
Seward County Community College
Southwestern College
Sterling College
Tabor College
University of Kansas
Washburn University of Topeka
Wichita State University

Kentucky

Alice Lloyd College
Asbury College
Bellarmine University
Berea College
Brescia University
Campbellsville University
Centre College
Cumberland College
Daymar College
Georgetown College
Henderson Community College
Hopkinsville Community College
Kentucky Christian College
Kentucky Wesleyan College
Louisville Technical Institute
Madisonville Community College
Mid-Continent College
Morehead State University
Murray State University
National College of Business &
    Technology
    Danville
    Florence
    Lexington
    Pikeville
    Richmond
Pikeville College
Spalding University
Spencerian College: Lexington
Sullivan University
Thomas More College
Transylvania University
Union College
University of Kentucky
University of Louisville

Louisiana

Centenary College of Louisiana
Delgado Community College
Dillard University
Grambling State University
Louisiana College
Louisiana State University and
    Agricultural and Mechanical College
Louisiana Tech University
Loyola University New Orleans
McNeese State University
Northwestern State University
Nunez Community College
Our Lady of Holy Cross College
Southeastern Louisiana University
Southern University and Agricultural and
    Mechanical College
Tulane University
University of Louisiana at Lafayette
University of Louisiana at Monroe
University of New Orleans
Xavier University of Louisiana

Maine

Andover College
Bates College
Beal College
Bowdoin College

Colby College
Husson College
Maine College of Art
New England School of Communications
St. Joseph's College
University of Maine
University of Maine
    Farmington
    Machias
    Presque Isle
University of New England
University of Southern Maine

Maryland

Allegany College
Anne Arundel Community College
Baltimore Hebrew University
Baltimore International College
Bowie State University
Capitol College
Cecil Community College
College of Notre Dame of Maryland
Columbia Union College
Coppin State College
Frostburg State University
Goucher College
Harford Community College
Hood College
Johns Hopkins University
Johns Hopkins University: Peabody
    Conservatory of Music
Loyola College in Maryland
Maryland Institute College of Art
McDaniel College
Montgomery College
    Rockville Campus
Morgan State University
Mount St. Mary's College
St. Mary's College of Maryland
Salisbury University
Towson University
United States Naval Academy
University of Maryland
    Baltimore
    Baltimore County
    College Park
Villa Julie College
Washington Bible College
Washington College
Wor-Wic Community College

Massachusetts

American International College
Amherst College
Anna Maria College
Art Institute of Boston at Lesley
    University
Assumption College
Atlantic Union College
Berklee College of Music
Boston College
Boston Conservatory
Boston University
Brandeis University
Bridgewater State College
Bunker Hill Community College
Clark University
College of the Holy Cross
Elms College
Emerson College
Emmanuel College
Fisher College
Fitchburg State College
Framingham State College
Gordon College
Hampshire College
Harvard College
Hellenic College/Holy Cross
Lasell College
Lesley University
Marian Court College
Massachusetts Bay Community College
Massachusetts College of Art
Massachusetts College of Liberal Arts

Massachusetts College of Pharmacy and
    Health Sciences
Massachusetts Institute of Technology
Massachusetts Maritime Academy
Merrimack College
Montserrat College of Art
Mount Holyoke College
Mount Wachusett Community College
Newbury College
Nichols College
Northeastern University
Pine Manor College
Quinsigamond Community College
Regis College
Roxbury Community College
St. John's Seminary College
Salem State College
Simmons College
Smith College
Springfield College
Stonehill College
Suffolk University
Tufts University
University of Massachusetts
    Amherst
    Boston
    Dartmouth
    Lowell
Wellesley College
Western New England College
Westfield State College
Wheaton College
Williams College
Worcester Polytechnic Institute

Michigan
Adrian College
Alma College
Alpena Community College
Andrews University
Aquinas College
Baker College
    of Auburn Hills
    of Cadillac
    of Clinton Township
    of Jackson
    of Muskegon
    of Owosso
    of Port Huron
Calvin College
Central Michigan University
College for Creative Studies
Concordia University
Cornerstone University
Davenport University
    Eastern Region
    Midland
Eastern Michigan University
Ferris State University
Finlandia University
Glen Oaks Community College
Gogebic Community College
Grace Bible College
Grand Valley State University
Hillsdale College
Hope College
Kalamazoo College
Kellogg Community College
Kettering University
Kirtland Community College
Lansing Community College
Lawrence Technological University
Madonna University
Marygrove College
Michigan State University
Michigan Technological University
Mid Michigan Community College
Mott Community College
Muskegon Community College
Northern Michigan University
Northwood University
Oakland University
Reformed Bible College
Saginaw Valley State University
St. Clair County Community College

Schoolcraft College
Siena Heights University
Southwestern Michigan College
Spring Arbor University
University of Michigan
University of Michigan
    Dearborn
    Flint
Walsh College of Accountancy and
    Business Administration
Wayne State University
Western Michigan University
William Tyndale College

Minnesota
Augsburg College
Bemidji State University
Bethel College
Carleton College
College of St. Benedict
College of St. Catherine
College of St. Scholastica
Concordia College: Moorhead
Concordia University: St. Paul
Crossroads College
Crown College
Dakota County Technical College
Gustavus Adolphus College
Hamline University
Hennepin Technical College
Lake Superior College: A Community
    and Technical College
Macalester College
Martin Luther College
Metropolitan State University
Minnesota State University
    Mankato
    Moorhead
National American University
    St. Paul
North Central University
Northwestern College
Oak Hills Christian College
Rasmussen College
    St. Cloud
Riverland Community College: A
    Technical and Community College
St. Cloud State University
St. John's University
St. Mary's University of Minnesota
St. Olaf College
Southwest State University
University of Minnesota
    Crookston
    Duluth
    Morris
    Twin Cities
University of St. Thomas
Winona State University

Mississippi
Alcorn State University
Blue Mountain College
Delta State University
Itawamba Community College
Millsaps College
Mississippi College
Mississippi State University
Mississippi University for Women
Mississippi Valley State University
Rust College
University of Mississippi
University of Southern Mississippi
Wesley College

Missouri
Avila University
Calvary Bible College
Central Bible College
Central Christian College of the Bible
Central Methodist College
Central Missouri State University
College of the Ozarks
Columbia College

Conception Seminary College
Culver-Stockton College
Drury University
Evangel University
Fontbonne College
Hannibal-LaGrange College
Harris Stowe State College
Jefferson College
Kansas City Art Institute
Lincoln University
Lindenwood University
Maryville University of Saint Louis
Missouri Baptist University
Missouri Southern State College
Missouri Technical School
Missouri Valley College
Missouri Western State College
National American University
    Kansas City
North Central Missouri College
Northwest Missouri State University
Ozark Christian College
Research College of Nursing
Rockhurst University
St. Charles Community College
St. Louis Community College
    St. Louis Community College at
        Forest Park
St. Louis University
Southeast Missouri State University
Southwest Baptist University
Southwest Missouri State University
Stephens College
Truman State University
University of Missouri
    Columbia
    Kansas City
    Rolla
    St. Louis
Washington University in St. Louis
Webster University
Westminster College
William Jewell College
William Woods University

Montana
Carroll College
Chief Dull Knife College
Dawson Community College
Montana State University
    Billings
    Bozeman
Montana Tech of the University of
    Montana
Rocky Mountain College
Salish Kootenai College
University of Great Falls
University of Montana-Missoula
University of Montana: Western

Nebraska
Bellevue University
Central Community College
Chadron State College
Clarkson College
College of Saint Mary
Concordia University
Creighton University
Dana College
Doane College
Grace University
Hastings College
Lincoln School of Commerce
Metropolitan Community College
Midland Lutheran College
Nebraska Christian College
Nebraska College of Technical
    Agriculture
Nebraska Indian Community College
Nebraska Wesleyan University
Peru State College
Southeast Community College
    Beatrice Campus
Union College

University of Nebraska
    Kearney
    Lincoln
    Omaha
Wayne State College
Western Nebraska Community College
York College

Nevada
Community College of Southern Nevada
Morrison University
Sierra Nevada College
University of Nevada
    Las Vegas
    Reno
Western Nevada Community College

New Hampshire
Chester College of New England
Colby-Sawyer College
College for Lifelong Learning
Daniel Webster College
Dartmouth College
Franklin Pierce College
Hesser College
Keene State College
New England College
New Hampshire Community Technical
    College
    Berlin
    Claremont
    Laconia
    Stratham
New Hampshire Technical Institute
Plymouth State College
Rivier College
Southern New Hampshire University
University of New Hampshire
University of New Hampshire at
    Manchester

New Jersey
Atlantic Cape Community College
Bloomfield College
Burlington County College
Caldwell College
Centenary College
The College of New Jersey
College of St. Elizabeth
County College of Morris
Cumberland County College
Drew University
Essex County College
Fairleigh Dickinson University
    College at Florham
    Metropolitan Campus
Felician College
Georgian Court College
Kean University
Mercer County Community College
Middlesex County College
Monmouth University
Montclair State University
New Jersey City University
New Jersey Institute of Technology
Passaic County Community College
Ramapo College of New Jersey
Raritan Valley Community College
Richard Stockton College of New Jersey
Rider University
Rowan University
Rutgers, The State University of New
    Jersey
    Camden Regional Campus
    New Brunswick Regional Campus
    Newark Regional Campus
St. Peter's College
Salem Community College
Seton Hall University
Stevens Institute of Technology
Sussex County Community College
Thomas Edison State College
Warren County Community College

William Paterson University of New
Jersey

New Mexico

Clovis Community College
College of Santa Fe
Dona Ana Branch Community College of
New Mexico State University
Eastern New Mexico University
Institute of American Indian Arts
New Mexico Highlands University
New Mexico Institute of Mining and
Technology
New Mexico State University
New Mexico State University
Alamogordo
Southwestern Indian Polytechnic Institute
University of New Mexico
Western New Mexico University

New York

Adelphi University
Adirondack Community College
Alfred University
Bard College
Barnard College
Broome Community College
Bryant & Stratton Business Institute
Albany
Syracuse
Canisius College
Cayuga County Community College
City University of New York
Brooklyn College
College of Staten Island
Hunter College
Queens College
York College
Clarkson University
Colgate University
College of Aeronautics
College of Mount St. Vincent
College of New Rochelle
Columbia University
Columbia College
School of Nursing
Concordia College
Cornell University
Corning Community College
D'Youville College
Daemen College
Dowling College
Eastman School of Music of the
University of Rochester
Elmira College
Erie Community College
City Campus
North Campus
South Campus
Finger Lakes Community College
Fordham University
Fulton-Montgomery Community College
Genesee Community College
Hamilton College
Hartwick College
Hobart and William Smith Colleges
Hofstra University
Houghton College
Hudson Valley Community College
Institute of Design and Construction
Iona College
Ithaca College
Jamestown Community College
Jefferson Community College
Juilliard School
Keuka College
Le Moyne College
Long Island University
C. W. Post Campus
Southampton College
Manhattan College
Manhattanville College
Mannes College of Music
Marist College

Marymount College of Fordham
University
Marymount Manhattan College
Medaille College
Mercy College
Mildred Elley
Mohawk Valley Community College
Molloy College
Mount St. Mary College
Nazareth College of Rochester
New York Institute of Technology
New York University
Niagara County Community College
Niagara University
North Country Community College
Nyack College
Onondaga Community College
Pace University
Pace University: Pleasantville/Briarcliff
Paul Smith's College
Polytechnic University
Rensselaer Polytechnic Institute
Roberts Wesleyan College
Rochester Business Institute
Rochester Institute of Technology
Rockland Community College
Russell Sage College
St. Bonaventure University
St. John Fisher College
St. John's University
St. Joseph's College: Suffolk Campus
St. Lawrence University
Sarah Lawrence College
School of Visual Arts
Skidmore College
State University of New York
Albany
Binghamton
Buffalo
College at Brockport
College at Buffalo
College at Cortland
College at Fredonia
College at Geneseo
College at Old Westbury
College at Oneonta
College at Plattsburgh
College at Potsdam
College of Agriculture and
Technology at Morrisville
College of Environmental Science
and Forestry
College of Technology at Delhi
Empire State College
Farmingdale
Health Science Center at Stony
Brook
Institute of Technology at
Utica/Rome
New Paltz
Oswego
Purchase
Stony Brook
Syracuse University
Ulster County Community College
Union College
United States Military Academy
University of Rochester
Utica College
Vassar College
Wagner College
Webb Institute
Wells College
Westchester Business Institute
Westchester Community College
Yeshiva University

North Carolina

Alamance Community College
Appalachian State University
Asheville Buncombe Technical
Community College
Barber-Scotia College
Beaufort County Community College
Belmont Abbey College

Bennett College
Bladen Community College
Blue Ridge Community College
Brevard College
Campbell University
Carteret Community College
Catawba College
Catawba Valley Community College
Central Piedmont Community College
Chowan College
Cleveland Community College
College of the Albemarle
Craven Community College
Davidson College
Duke University
East Carolina University
Edgecombe Community College
Elizabeth City State University
Elon University
Fayetteville State University
Forsyth Technical Community College
Gardner-Webb University
Gaston College
Greensboro College
Guilford College
High Point University
James Sprunt Community College
John Wesley College
Johnson C. Smith University
Johnston Community College
Lees-McRae College
Lenoir-Rhyne College
Livingstone College
Mars Hill College
Mayland Community College
Meredith College
Methodist College
Miller-Motte Technical College
Montgomery Community College
Montreat College
Mount Olive College
North Carolina Agricultural and
Technical State University
North Carolina Central University
North Carolina State University
North Carolina Wesleyan College
Peace College
Pfeiffer University
Piedmont Baptist College
Piedmont Community College
Pitt Community College
Queens University of Charlotte
Randolph Community College
Richmond Community College
Roanoke Bible College
Robeson Community College
St. Andrews Presbyterian College
St. Augustine's College
Salem College
Sandhills Community College
Shaw University
South College
South Piedmont Community College
Southwestern Community College
Surry Community College
Tri-County Community College
University of North Carolina
Asheville
Chapel Hill
Charlotte
Greensboro
Pembroke
Wilmington
Vance-Granville Community College
Wake Forest University
Wake Technical Community College
Warren Wilson College
Wayne Community College
Western Carolina University
Wilkes Community College
Wilson Technical Community College
Wingate University
Winston-Salem State University

North Dakota

Dickinson State University
Jamestown College
Mayville State University
Minot State University
Minot State University: Bottineau
Campus
North Dakota State University
Trinity Bible College
University of Mary
University of North Dakota
Valley City State University
Williston State College

Ohio

Antioch College
Antioch University McGregor
Ashland University
Baldwin-Wallace College
Bowling Green State University
Bowling Green State University:
Firelands College
Bryant & Stratton College
Bryant & Stratton College
Cleveland West
Willoughby Hills
Case Western Reserve University
Cedarville University
Central Ohio Technical College
Central State University
Cincinnati State Technical and
Community College
Circleville Bible College
Clark State Community College
Cleveland Institute of Music
Cleveland State University
College of Mount St. Joseph
College of Wooster
Columbus College of Art and Design
Columbus State Community College
David N. Myers College
Defiance College
Denison University
Edison State Community College
Franciscan University of Steubenville
God's Bible School and College
Heidelberg College
Hiram College
Hocking Technical College
James A. Rhodes State College
Jefferson Community College
John Carroll University
Kent State University
Kent State University
Ashtabula Regional Campus
East Liverpool Regional Campus
Stark Campus
Trumbull Campus
Tuscarawas Campus
Kenyon College
Lake Erie College
Lourdes College
Malone College
Marietta College
Marion Technical College
Miami University
Hamilton Campus
Middletown Campus
Oxford Campus
Miami-Jacobs College
Mount Union College
Mount Vernon Nazarene University
Muskingum College
Notre Dame College
Oberlin College
Ohio Business College
Ohio Business College: Sandusky
Ohio Dominican College
Ohio Institute of Photography and
Technology
Ohio Northern University
Ohio State University
Agricultural Technical Institute
Columbus Campus
Marion Campus

Ohio University
Ohio University
   Chillicothe Campus
   Eastern Campus
   Lancaster Campus
   Zanesville Campus
Ohio Valley College of Technology
Ohio Wesleyan University
Otterbein College
Owens Community College
   Findlay Campus
   Toledo
Pontifical College Josephinum
Shawnee State University
Southeastern Business College
Stark State College of Technology
Stautzenberger College
Tiffin University
Union Institute & University
University of Akron
University of Cincinnati
University of Cincinnati
   Clermont College
   Raymond Walters College
University of Dayton
University of Findlay
University of Northwestern Ohio
University of Rio Grande
University of Toledo
Urbana University
Ursuline College
Walsh University
Washington State Community College
Wilmington College
Wittenberg University
Wright State University
Wright State University: Lake Campus
Xavier University
Youngstown State University

Oklahoma

Bacone College
Cameron University
East Central University
Langston University
Northeastern State University
Northwestern Oklahoma State University
Oklahoma Baptist University
Oklahoma Christian University of
   Science and Arts
Oklahoma City Community College
Oklahoma City University
Oklahoma Panhandle State University
Oklahoma State University
Oklahoma State University
   Oklahoma City
   Okmulgee
Oklahoma Wesleyan University
Oral Roberts University
Rose State College
St. Gregory's University
Southeastern Oklahoma State University
Southern Nazarene University
Southwestern Christian University
Southwestern Oklahoma State University
University of Central Oklahoma
University of Oklahoma
University of Science and Arts of
   Oklahoma
University of Tulsa

Oregon

Central Oregon Community College
Chemeketa Community College
Clackamas Community College
Clatsop Community College
Concordia University
Eastern Oregon University
Eugene Bible College
George Fox University
Lane Community College
Lewis & Clark College
Linfield College
Marylhurst University
Mount Hood Community College

Multnomah Bible College
Northwest Christian College
Oregon Institute of Technology
Oregon State University
Pacific University
Portland Community College
Portland State University
Reed College
Rogue Community College
Southern Oregon University
Southwestern Oregon Community
   College
Treasure Valley Community College
Umpqua Community College
University of Oregon
University of Portland
Warner Pacific College
Western Baptist College
Western Oregon University
Willamette University

Pennsylvania

Albright College
Allegheny College
Arcadia University
Baptist Bible College of Pennsylvania
Bloomsburg University of Pennsylvania
Bryn Mawr College
Bucknell University
Cabrini College
California University of Pennsylvania
Carlow College
Carnegie Mellon University
Cedar Crest College
Central Pennsylvania College
Chatham College
Chestnut Hill College
Cheyney University of Pennsylvania
Community College of Beaver County
Curtis Institute of Music
DeSales University
Delaware County Community College
Delaware Valley College
Dickinson College
Douglas School of Business
Drexel University
DuBois Business College
Duquesne University
East Stroudsburg University of
   Pennsylvania
Edinboro University of Pennsylvania
Elizabethtown College
Erie Business Center
Franklin & Marshall College
Geneva College
Gettysburg College
Gratz College
Grove City College
Gwynedd-Mercy College
Harrisburg Area Community College
Haverford College
ICM School of Business & Medical
   Careers
Immaculata University
Indiana University of Pennsylvania
Juniata College
Keystone College
King's College
Kutztown University of Pennsylvania
La Roche College
La Salle University
Lackawanna College
Lafayette College
Lancaster Bible College
Lebanon Valley College of Pennsylvania
Lehigh University
Lincoln University
Lock Haven University of Pennsylvania
Lycoming College
Manor College
Marywood University
Mercyhurst College
Messiah College
Millersville University of Pennsylvania
Moravian College

Muhlenberg College
Neumann College
PJA School
Peirce College
Penn State
   Abington
   Altoona
   Beaver
   Delaware County
   Dubois
   Erie, The Behrend College
   Fayette
   Harrisburg
   Hazleton
   McKeesport
   Mont Alto
   New Kensington
   Schuylkill - Capital College
   Shenango
   University Park
   Wilkes-Barre
   Worthington Scranton
   York
Pennsylvania College of Technology
Pennsylvania Institute of Technology
Philadelphia Biblical University
Point Park College
Robert Morris University
Rosemont College
St. Joseph's University
St. Vincent College
Seton Hill University
Shippensburg University of Pennsylvania
Slippery Rock University of
   Pennsylvania
South Hills School of Business &
   Technology
Swarthmore College
Temple University
Thiel College
University of Pennsylvania
University of Pittsburgh
University of Pittsburgh
   Bradford
   Greensburg
   Johnstown
University of Scranton
University of the Sciences in
   Philadelphia
Villanova University
Washington and Jefferson College
Waynesburg College
West Chester University of Pennsylvania
Westmoreland County Community
   College
Widener University
Wilkes University
Wilson College
York College of Pennsylvania

Puerto Rico

Bayamon Central University
Inter American University of Puerto Rico
   Fajardo Campus
   Guayama Campus
   San German Campus
Pontifical Catholic University of Puerto
   Rico
Technological College of San Juan
University of Puerto Rico
   Bayamon University College
   Mayaguez Campus
   Rio Piedras Campus
University of the Sacred Heart

Rhode Island

Brown University
Bryant College
Community College of Rhode Island
Providence College
Rhode Island College
Roger Williams University
Salve Regina University
University of Rhode Island

South Carolina

Aiken Technical College
Anderson College
Benedict College
Charleston Southern University
The Citadel
Claflin University
Clemson University
Coastal Carolina University
Coker College
College of Charleston
Columbia College
Columbia International University
Converse College
Erskine College
Forrest Junior College
Francis Marion University
Furman University
Lander University
Limestone College
Morris College
Newberry College
North Greenville College
Orangeburg-Calhoun Technical College
Piedmont Technical College
Presbyterian College
South Carolina State University
Southern Wesleyan University
Spartanburg Technical College
Technical College of the Lowcountry
Tri-County Technical College
Trident Technical College
University of South Carolina
University of South Carolina
   Aiken
   Spartanburg
Winthrop University
Wofford College
York Technical College

South Dakota

Augustana College
Black Hills State University
Dakota State University
Dakota Wesleyan University
Kilian Community College
Mount Marty College
Northern State University
Sinte Gleska University
South Dakota State University
Southeast Technical Institute
University of Sioux Falls
University of South Dakota

Tennessee

American Baptist College of ABT
   Seminary
Austin Peay State University
Belmont University
Bethel College
Bryan College
Carson-Newman College
Chattanooga State Technical Community
   College
Christian Brothers University
Crichton College
Draughons Junior College of Business:
   Nashville
East Tennessee State University
Fisk University
Freed-Hardeman University
Johnson Bible College
King College
Lambuth University
Lee University
Maryville College
Memphis College of Art
Middle Tennessee State University
Milligan College
Northeast State Technical Community
   College
Pellissippi State Technical Community
   College
Rhodes College
Roane State Community College

South College
Southern Adventist University
Southwest Tennessee Community
  College
Tennessee State University
Tennessee Technological University
Tennessee Wesleyan College
Trevecca Nazarene University
Tusculum College
Union University
University of Memphis
University of Tennessee
  Chattanooga
  Knoxville
  Martin
Vanderbilt University
Volunteer State Community College

Texas

Abilene Christian University
Angelo State University
Arlington Baptist College
Austin College
Baylor University
College of the Mainland
Concordia University at Austin
Dallas Baptist University
Dallas Christian College
East Texas Baptist University
El Centro College
El Paso Community College
Hardin-Simmons University
Houston Baptist University
Howard Payne University
Huston-Tillotson College
Jarvis Christian College
Lamar State College at Port Arthur
Lamar University
LeTourneau University
Lubbock Christian University
McMurry University
Midwestern State University
Northwood University: Texas Campus
Our Lady of the Lake University of San
  Antonio
Prairie View A&M University
Rice University
St. Edward's University
St. Mary's University
St. Philip's College
Sam Houston State University
San Antonio College
Schreiner University
Southern Methodist University
Southwest Texas State University
Southwestern Adventist University
Southwestern Assemblies of God
  University
Southwestern University
Stephen F. Austin State University
Tarleton State University
Texas A&M International University
Texas A&M University
Texas A&M University
  Commerce
  Corpus Christi
  Galveston
  Kingsville
Texas Christian University
Texas College
Texas Lutheran University
Texas Southern University
Texas Tech University
Texas Wesleyan University
Texas Woman's University
Trinity University
University of Dallas
University of Houston
University of Houston
  Clear Lake
  Downtown
  Victoria
University of Mary Hardin-Baylor
University of North Texas
University of St. Thomas

University of Texas
  Arlington
  Austin
  Brownsville
  Dallas
  Pan American
  San Antonio
  Tyler
  of the Permian Basin
University of the Incarnate Word
Wayland Baptist University
West Texas A&M University

Utah

Brigham Young University
College of Eastern Utah
Salt Lake Community College
Southern Utah University
University of Utah
Utah State University
Weber State University
Westminster College

Vermont

Bennington College
Burlington College
Castleton State College
Champlain College
College of St. Joseph in Vermont
Community College of Vermont
Green Mountain College
Johnson State College
Lyndon State College
Marlboro College
Middlebury College
Norwich University
St. Michael's College
Southern Vermont College
University of Vermont
Vermont Technical College
Woodbury College

Virginia

Averett University
Blue Ridge Community College
Bluefield College
Bridgewater College
Bryant & Stratton College
Christendom College
College of William and Mary
Danville Community College
ECPI College of Technology
Eastern Mennonite University
Emory & Henry College
Ferrum College
George Mason University
Hampden-Sydney College
Hampton University
Hollins University
J. Sargeant Reynolds Community
  College
James Madison University
Liberty University
Longwood University
Lynchburg College
Mary Baldwin College
Mary Washington College
Marymount University
Mountain Empire Community College
National College of Business &
  Technology
  Bluefield
  Charlottesville
  Danville
  Harrisonburg
  Lynchburg
  Martinsville
  Roanoke
Norfolk State University
Old Dominion University
Radford University
Randolph-Macon College
Randolph-Macon Woman's College
Rappahannock Community College

Roanoke College
Shenandoah University
Southwest Virginia Community College
Sweet Briar College
University of Richmond
University of Virginia
University of Virginia's College at Wise
Virginia Commonwealth University
Virginia Highlands Community College
Virginia Intermont College
Virginia Military Institute
Virginia Polytechnic Institute and State
  University
Virginia State University
Virginia Wesleyan College
Washington and Lee University

Washington

Bastyr University
Central Washington University
Centralia College
Eastern Washington University
Evergreen State College
Gonzaga University
Henry Cogswell College
Heritage College
Northwest College
Pacific Lutheran University
Peninsula College
St. Martin's College
Seattle Pacific University
Seattle University
University of Puget Sound
University of Washington
Walla Walla College
Washington State University
Wenatchee Valley College
Western Washington University
Whitman College
Whitworth College

West Virginia

Alderson-Broaddus College
Bethany College
Concord College
Davis and Elkins College
Fairmont State College
Glenville State College
Huntington Junior College
Marshall University
Mountain State College
Mountain State University
Ohio Valley College
Potomac State College of West Virginia
  University
Salem International University
Shepherd College
University of Charleston
West Liberty State College
West Virginia Northern Community
  College
West Virginia State College
West Virginia University
West Virginia University Institute of
  Technology
West Virginia University at Parkersburg
West Virginia Wesleyan College
Wheeling Jesuit University

Wisconsin

Alverno College
Beloit College
Bryant & Stratton College
Cardinal Stritch University
Carroll College
Carthage College
Chippewa Valley Technical College
Concordia University Wisconsin
Edgewood College
Fox Valley Technical College
Lac Courte Oreilles Ojibwa Community
  College
Lakeland College
Lakeshore Technical College

Lawrence University
Maranatha Baptist Bible College
Marian College of Fond du Lac
Marquette University
Mid-State Technical College
Milwaukee Area Technical College
Milwaukee Institute of Art & Design
Milwaukee School of Engineering
Moraine Park Technical College
Mount Mary College
Nicolet Area Technical College
Northland College
Ripon College
St. Norbert College
Silver Lake College
University of Wisconsin
  Eau Claire
  Green Bay
  La Crosse
  Madison
  Milwaukee
  Oshkosh
  Parkside
  Platteville
  River Falls
  Stevens Point
  Stout
  Superior
  Whitewater
Viterbo University
Waukesha County Technical College
Western Wisconsin Technical College
Wisconsin Indianhead Technical College
Wisconsin Lutheran College

Wyoming

Sheridan College
University of Wyoming

Dual enrollment

Alabama

Alabama Agricultural and Mechanical
  University
Alabama Southern Community College
Athens State University
Auburn University
Auburn University at Montgomery
Bevill State Community College
Birmingham-Southern College
Bishop State Community College
Calhoun Community College
Central Alabama Community College
Chattahoochee Valley Community
  College
Enterprise State Junior College
Faulkner University
Gadsden State Community College
George C. Wallace State Community
  College
  Dothan
  Selma
Harry M. Ayers State Technical College
Heritage Christian University
Huntingdon College
J. F. Drake State Technical College
Jacksonville State University
James H. Faulkner State Community
  College
Jefferson Davis Community College
Judson College
Lawson State Community College
Lurleen B. Wallace Junior College
Marion Military Institute
Miles College
Northeast Alabama Community College
Northwest-Shoals Community College
Reid State Technical College
Samford University
Shelton State Community College
Snead State Community College
Spring Hill College
Stillman College

Talladega College
Trenholm State Technical College
University of Alabama
University of Alabama
    Birmingham
    Huntsville
University of Montevallo
University of North Alabama
University of South Alabama
University of West Alabama
Wallace Community College: Sparks
    Campus
Wallace State Community College at
    Hanceville

Alaska

Prince William Sound Community
    College
Sheldon Jackson College
University of Alaska
    Anchorage
    Fairbanks
    Southeast

Arizona

Arizona State University
Arizona Western College
Central Arizona College
Cochise College
Eastern Arizona College
Embry-Riddle Aeronautical University:
    Prescott Campus
Estrella Mountain Community College
Gateway Community College
Glendale Community College
Northern Arizona University
Paradise Valley Community College
Phoenix College
Pima Community College
Rio Salado College
Scottsdale Community College
South Mountain Community College
University of Arizona
Yavapai College

Arkansas

Arkansas State University
Arkansas State University
    Beebe
Arkansas Tech University
Crowley's Ridge College
East Arkansas Community College
Harding University
Lyon College
Mid-South Community College
Mississippi County Community College
North Arkansas College
Northwest Arkansas Community College
Ouachita Baptist University
Phillips Community College of the
    University of Arkansas
Pulaski Technical College
Rich Mountain Community College
South Arkansas Community College
Southern Arkansas University
Southern Arkansas University Tech
University of Arkansas
University of Arkansas
    Community College at Batesville
    Community College at Hope
    Cossatot Community College of the
    Fort Smith
    Little Rock
    Monticello
    Pine Bluff
University of Central Arkansas
University of the Ozarks
Williams Baptist College

California

Academy of Art College
Antelope Valley College
Art Institute of California - San Francisco
Bakersfield College

Barstow College
Bethesda Christian University
Cabrillo College
California Polytechnic State University:
    San Luis Obispo
California State Polytechnic University:
    Pomona
California State University
    Chico
    Dominguez Hills
    Fresno
    Fullerton
    Hayward
    Long Beach
    Los Angeles
    Monterey Bay
    Northridge
    Sacramento
    San Bernardino
    San Marcos
    Stanislaus
Cerritos Community College
Cerro Coso Community College
Chabot College
Citrus College
Coastline Community College
College of Alameda
College of the Canyons
College of the Redwoods
College of the Sequoias
College of the Siskiyous
Concordia University
Contra Costa College
Cuyamaca College
De Anza College
Diablo Valley College
Dominican University of California
Don Bosco Technical Institute
East Los Angeles College
Feather River College
Gavilan Community College
Glendale Community College
Golden West College
Grossmont Community College
Hope International University
Humboldt State University
Imperial Valley College
Irvine Valley College
La Sierra University
Laney College
Las Positas College
Los Angeles Harbor College
Los Angeles Pierce College
Los Angeles Southwest College
Los Angeles Trade and Technical College
Loyola Marymount University
Marymount College
Menlo College
MiraCosta College
Modesto Junior College
Monterey Peninsula College
Mount San Antonio College
Mount San Jacinto College
Napa Valley College
National Hispanic University
Ohlone College
Pacific Union College
Palomar College
Patten University
Riverside Community College
Samuel Merritt College
San Diego City College
San Diego Mesa College
San Diego State University
San Francisco State University
San Joaquin Delta College
San Jose State University
Santa Barbara City College
Santa Monica College
Santa Rosa Junior College
Scripps College
Shasta College
Sierra College
Sonoma State University
Southwestern College

University of California
    Berkeley
    Davis
    Riverside
    Santa Barbara
    Santa Cruz
Vanguard University of Southern
    California
Ventura College
Victor Valley College
Vista Community College
West Valley College
Yuba Community College District

Colorado

Arapahoe Community College
Blair Junior College
Colorado Mountain College
    Alpine Campus
    Spring Valley Campus
    Timberline Campus
Colorado School of Mines
Colorado State University
Colorado State University
    Pueblo
Fort Lewis College
Front Range Community College
Mesa State College
Metropolitan State College of Denver
Morgan Community College
Naropa University
Otero Junior College
Red Rocks Community College
Regis University
Trinidad State Junior College
University of Colorado
    Boulder
    Colorado Springs
University of Northern Colorado

Connecticut

Albertus Magnus College
Briarwood College
Capital Community College
Eastern Connecticut State University
Gateway Community College
Housatonic Community College
Manchester Community College
Middlesex Community College
Mitchell College
Naugatuck Valley Community College
Northwestern Connecticut Community
    College
Norwalk Community College
Quinebaug Valley Community College
Sacred Heart University
St. Joseph College
Teikyo Post University
Three Rivers Community College
Tunxis Community College
University of Bridgeport
University of Connecticut
University of Hartford
University of New Haven
Wesleyan University
Western Connecticut State University

Delaware

Delaware Technical and Community
    College
    Owens Campus
    Stanton/Wilmington Campus
    Terry Campus
Goldey-Beacom College
University of Delaware

District of Columbia

Catholic University of America
Gallaudet University
George Washington University
Howard University
Trinity College
University of the District of Columbia

Florida

Barry University
Broward Community College
Carlos Albizu University
Chipola Junior College
Daytona Beach Community College
Embry-Riddle Aeronautical University
Florida Agricultural and Mechanical
    University
Florida Atlantic University
Florida Christian College
Florida Gulf Coast University
Florida Hospital College of Health
    Sciences
Florida Institute of Technology
Florida International University
Florida Keys Community College
Florida National College
Florida State University
Gulf Coast Community College
Hillsborough Community College
Hobe Sound Bible College
Indian River Community College
Jacksonville University
Lake City Community College
Lake-Sumter Community College
Manatee Community College
Miami-Dade Community College
New England Institute of Technology
Northwood University
    Florida Campus
Nova Southeastern University
Okaloosa-Walton Community College
Palm Beach Atlantic University
Palm Beach Community College
Pasco-Hernando Community College
Pensacola Junior College
Polk Community College
Ringling School of Art and Design
Rollins College
St. Leo University
St. Petersburg College
St. Thomas University
Santa Fe Community College
Seminole Community College
South Florida Community College
Southeastern College of the Assemblies
    of God
Stetson University
Tallahassee Community College
Talmudic College of Florida
University of Central Florida
University of Florida
University of Miami
University of North Florida
University of South Florida
University of Tampa
University of West Florida
Valencia Community College
Warner Southern College
Webber International University

Georgia

Abraham Baldwin Agricultural College
Agnes Scott College
Albany State University
Andrew College
Art Institute
    of Atlanta
Athens Technical College
Atlanta College of Art
Augusta State University
Bainbridge College
Berry College
Brewton-Parker College
Central Georgia Technical College
Chattahoochee Technical College
Clark Atlanta University
Clayton College and State University
Coastal Georgia Community College
Columbus State University
Columbus Technical College
Covenant College
Darton College
DeKalb Technical College

East Georgia College
Emmanuel College
Emory University
Floyd College
Fort Valley State University
Gainesville College
Georgia Institute of Technology
Georgia Perimeter College
Georgia Southern University
Georgia Southwestern State University
Gordon College
Kennesaw State University
LaGrange College
Macon State College
Mercer University
Middle Georgia College
Morehouse College
North Georgia College & State
  University
Oxford College of Emory University
Paine College
Piedmont College
Reinhardt College
Savannah State University
Shorter College
South Georgia College
South University
Southern Polytechnic State University
Southwest Georgia Technical College
Spelman College
State University of West Georgia
Thomas University
Toccoa Falls College
Truett-McConnell College
University of Georgia
Valdosta State University
Waycross College
Wesleyan College
West Georgia Technical College
Young Harris College

Hawaii

Chaminade University of Honolulu
Hawaii Pacific University
University of Hawaii
  Hawaii Community College
  Hilo
  Honolulu Community College
  Kauai Community College
  Leeward Community College
  Maui Community College

Idaho

Albertson College of Idaho
College of Southern Idaho
Eastern Idaho Technical College
Idaho State University
Lewis-Clark State College
North Idaho College
Northwest Nazarene University
University of Idaho

Illinois

Aurora University
Benedictine University
Black Hawk College
Black Hawk College
  East Campus
Blackburn College
Carl Sandburg College
City Colleges of Chicago
  Harold Washington College
  Kennedy-King College
  Malcolm X College
  Olive-Harvey College
  Richard J. Daley College
  Wright College
College of DuPage
College of Lake County
Danville Area Community College
Dominican University
Elgin Community College
Elmhurst College
Eureka College

Heartland Community College
Illinois College
Illinois Eastern Community Colleges
  Frontier Community College
  Lincoln Trail College
  Olney Central College
  Wabash Valley College
Illinois State University
Illinois Valley Community College
John A. Logan College
John Wood Community College
Kankakee Community College
Kaskaskia College
Kendall College
Kishwaukee College
Knox College
Lake Land College
Lewis University
Lewis and Clark Community College
Lincoln College
Lincoln Land Community College
Loyola University of Chicago
MacMurray College
McHenry County College
Midstate College
Moody Bible Institute
Moraine Valley Community College
Northeastern Illinois University
Northern Illinois University
Oakton Community College
Parkland College
Prairie State College
Quincy University
Rend Lake College
Richland Community College
Robert Morris College: Chicago
Rock Valley College
Rockford Business College
Roosevelt University
Sauk Valley Community College
School of the Art Institute of Chicago
Shawnee Community College
Shimer College
South Suburban College of Cook County
Southeastern Illinois College
Southern Illinois University Carbondale
Southwestern Illinois College
Spoon River College
Springfield College in Illinois
Triton College
University of Illinois
  Urbana-Champaign
University of St. Francis
Waubonsee Community College
Western Illinois University
William Rainey Harper College

Indiana

Ancilla College
Butler University
Calumet College of St. Joseph
DePauw University
Goshen College
Grace College
Hanover College
Huntington College
Indiana Institute of Technology
Indiana University
  Bloomington
  East
  Kokomo
  Northwest
  Southeast
Indiana University-Purdue University
  Indianapolis
Indiana Wesleyan University

Ivy Tech State College
  Bloomington
  Central Indiana
  Columbus
  Eastcentral
  Kokomo
  Lafayette
  Northcentral
  Northeast
  Northwest
  Southeast
  Southwest
  Wabash Valley
  Whitewater
Manchester College
Marian College
Oakland City University
Purdue University
Purdue University
  Calumet
  North Central Campus
St. Joseph's College
Taylor University
University of Evansville
University of Indianapolis
University of Notre Dame
University of St. Francis
Valparaiso University
Vincennes University

Iowa

American Institute of Business
Bucna Vista University
Clinton Community College
Coe College
Des Moines Area Community College
Divine Word College
Drake University
Ellsworth Community College
Graceland University
Grand View College
Hawkeye Community College
Indian Hills Community College
Iowa Central Community College
Iowa Lakes Community College
Iowa State University
Iowa Wesleyan College
Iowa Western Community College
Kirkwood Community College
Loras College
Luther College
Marshalltown Community College
Mount Mercy College
Muscatine Community College
Northeast Iowa Community College
Northwest Iowa Community College
Scott Community College
Southeastern Community College
  North Campus
  South Campus
Southwestern Community College
University of Dubuque
University of Iowa
University of Northern Iowa
University of Osteopathic Medicine and
  Health Sciences
  Des Moines University -
    Osteopathic Medical Center
Upper Iowa University
Waldorf College
Wartburg College
Western Iowa Tech Community College
William Penn University

Kansas

Allen County Community College
Barton County Community College
Benedictine College
Bethel College
Butler County Community College
Central Christian College
Cloud County Community College
Dodge City Community College
Donnelly College
Emporia State University

Fort Hays State University
Fort Scott Community College
Friends University
Garden City Community College
Highland Community College
Hutchinson Community College
Independence Community College
Johnson County Community College
Kansas City Kansas Community College
Labette Community College
MidAmerica Nazarene University
Newman University
Ottawa University
Pittsburg State University
Pratt Community College
St. Mary College
Seward County Community College
Southwestern College
Sterling College
Tabor College
University of Kansas
Washburn University of Topeka
Wichita State University

Kentucky

Bellarmine University
Campbellsville University
Daymar College
Elizabethtown Community College
Georgetown College
Henderson Community College
Hopkinsville Community College
Jefferson Community College
Lindsey Wilson College
Madisonville Community College
Maysville Community College
Mid-Continent College
Morehead State University
Murray State University
Paducah Community College
Prestonsburg Community College
St. Catharine College
Somerset Community College
Southeast Community College
Spalding University
Thomas More College
Union College
University of Kentucky
University of Louisville

Louisiana

Centenary College of Louisiana
Delgado Community College
Dillard University
Louisiana College
Louisiana State University
  Alexandria
  Eunice
Louisiana State University and
  Agricultural and Mechanical College
Louisiana Tech University
Loyola University New Orleans
McNeese State University
Nicholls State University
Northwestern State University
Nunez Community College
Our Lady of Holy Cross College
Southern University and Agricultural and
  Mechanical College
University of Louisiana at Lafayette
University of Louisiana at Monroe
University of New Orleans
Xavier University of Louisiana

Maine

Andover College
Thomas College
University of Maine
  Augusta
  Farmington
  Machias
  Presque Isle

Maryland

Allegany College
Anne Arundel Community College
Baltimore Hebrew University
Bowie State University
Carroll Community College
Cecil Community College
Chesapeake College
College of Notre Dame of Maryland
College of Southern Maryland
Community College of Baltimore County
    Catonsville
    Dundalk
    Essex
Coppin State College
Frederick Community College
Frostburg State University
Goucher College
Hagerstown Community College
Harford Community College
Hood College
Howard Community College
Maryland College of Art and Design
Maryland Institute College of Art
McDaniel College
Montgomery College
    Rockville Campus
Morgan State University
Mount St. Mary's College
St. Mary's College of Maryland
Salisbury University
Towson University
University of Maryland
    College Park
    University College
Villa Julie College
Wor-Wic Community College

Massachusetts

American International College
Anna Maria College
Atlantic Union College
Becker College
Berkshire Community College
Boston University
Bridgewater State College
Bunker Hill Community College
Cape Cod Community College
College of the Holy Cross
Emerson College
Fitchburg State College
Framingham State College
Greenfield Community College
Hebrew College
Massachusetts Bay Community College
Massachusetts College of Liberal Arts
Massachusetts Maritime Academy
Montserrat College of Art
Mount Wachusett Community College
New England Conservatory of Music
Northeastern University
Quinsigamond Community College
Roxbury Community College
Simmons College
Simon's Rock College of Bard
Springfield Technical Community
    College
Stonehill College
Suffolk University
University of Massachusetts
    Amherst
    Boston
    Dartmouth
    Lowell
Western New England College
Westfield State College
Wheaton College
Worcester Polytechnic Institute

Michigan

Adrian College
Alma College
Alpena Community College
Andrews University
Aquinas College

Baker College
    of Auburn Hills
    of Cadillac
    of Clinton Township
    of Jackson
    of Muskegon
    of Owosso
    of Port Huron
Bay de Noc Community College
Calvin College
Central Michigan University
Cleary University
Concordia University
Cornerstone University
Davenport University
    Eastern Region
    Midland
Davenport University - Western Region
Eastern Michigan University
Ferris State University
Finlandia University
Glen Oaks Community College
Gogebic Community College
Grace Bible College
Grand Rapids Community College
Grand Valley State University
Hillsdale College
Hope College
Jackson Community College
Kalamazoo College
Kellogg Community College
Kirtland Community College
Lansing Community College
Lawrence Technological University
Macomb Community College
Madonna University
Michigan State University
Michigan Technological University
Mid Michigan Community College
Monroe County Community College
Montcalm Community College
Mott Community College
Muskegon Community College
North Central Michigan College
Northern Michigan University
Northwestern Michigan College
Northwood University
Oakland Community College
Reformed Bible College
Saginaw Valley State University
St. Clair County Community College
Schoolcraft College
Siena Heights University
Southwestern Michigan College
Spring Arbor University
University of Michigan
University of Michigan
    Dearborn
    Flint
Washtenaw Community College
Wayne County Community College
Wayne State University
West Shore Community College
Western Michigan University
William Tyndale College

Minnesota

Anoka-Ramsey Community College
Augsburg College
Bemidji State University
Bethany Lutheran College
Carleton College
Central Lakes College
College of St. Benedict
College of St. Catherine
College of St. Scholastica
Concordia College: Moorhead
Concordia University: St. Paul
Crown College
Fergus Falls Community College
Gustavus Adolphus College
Hennepin Technical College
Hibbing Community College: A
    Technical and Community College
Inver Hills Community College

Itasca Community College
Lake Superior College: A Community
    and Technical College
Macalester College
Mesabi Range Community and Technical
    College
Minneapolis Community and Technical
    College
Minnesota State University
    Mankato
    Moorhead
Minnesota West Community and
    Technical College: Worthington
    Campus
Normandale Community College
North Hennepin Community College
Pine Technical College
Rainy River Community College
Ridgewater College: A Community and
    Technical College
Riverland Community College: A
    Technical and Community College
Rochester Community and Technical
    College
St. Cloud Technical College
St. John's University
Southwest State University
University of Minnesota
    Crookston
    Duluth
    Morris
    Twin Cities
Vermilion Community College
Winona State University

Mississippi

Blue Mountain College
Delta State University
Holmes Community College
Itawamba Community College
Mississippi College
Mississippi Gulf Coast Community
    College
    Perkinston
Mississippi State University
Mississippi University for Women
Mississippi Valley State University
Pearl River Community College
University of Southern Mississippi
Wesley College

Missouri

Avila University
Blue River Community College
Calvary Bible College
Central Methodist College
Central Missouri State University
College of the Ozarks
Columbia College
Cottey College
Crowder College
Culver-Stockton College
Drury University
East Central College
Evangel University
Fontbonne College
Hannibal-LaGrange College
Harris Stowe State College
Jefferson College
Lincoln University
Lindenwood University
Longview Community College
Maple Woods Community College
Maryville University of Saint Louis
Mineral Area College
Missouri Baptist University
Missouri Southern State College
Missouri Valley College
Missouri Western State College
Moberly Area Community College
North Central Missouri College
Northwest Missouri State University
Ozarks Technical Community College
Penn Valley Community College
Ranken Technical College

Research College of Nursing
Rockhurst University
St. Charles Community College
St. Louis Community College
    St. Louis Community College at
      Florissant Valley
    St. Louis Community College at
      Forest Park
    St. Louis Community College at
      Meramec
St. Louis University
Southeast Missouri State University
Southwest Baptist University
Southwest Missouri State University
Southwest Missouri State University:
    West Plains Campus
Stephens College
Three Rivers Community College
Truman State University
University of Missouri
    Columbia
    Kansas City
    Rolla
    St. Louis
Washington University in St. Louis
Webster University
Westminster College
William Woods University

Montana

Carroll College
Dawson Community College
Flathead Valley Community College
Miles Community College
Montana State University
    Billings
    Bozeman
Montana Tech of the University of
    Montana
Rocky Mountain College
Salish Kootenai College
University of Montana-Missoula
University of Montana: Western

Nebraska

Bellevue University
Central Community College
Chadron State College
Clarkson College
Concordia University
Creighton University
Dana College
Doane College
Grace University
Little Priest Tribal College
Metropolitan Community College
Mid Plains Community College Area
Midland Lutheran College
Northeast Community College
Peru State College
Southeast Community College
    Beatrice Campus
    Lincoln Campus
Union College
University of Nebraska
    Kearney
    Lincoln
    Omaha
Wayne State College
Western Nebraska Community College
York College

Nevada

Community College of Southern Nevada
Great Basin College
Truckee Meadows Community College
University of Nevada
    Las Vegas
    Reno
Western Nevada Community College

New Hampshire

Colby-Sawyer College
Daniel Webster College

Franklin Pierce College
Hesser College
New England College
New Hampshire Community Technical
  College
    Berlin
    Nashua
    Stratham
St. Anselm College

New Jersey

Atlantic Cape Community College
Burlington County College
Camden County College
The College of New Jersey
College of St. Elizabeth
County College of Morris
Cumberland County College
Essex County College
Felician College
Gloucester County College
Hudson County Community College
Kean University
Mercer County Community College
Middlesex County College
Monmouth University
Ocean County College
Passaic County Community College
Ramapo College of New Jersey
Raritan Valley Community College
Richard Stockton College of New Jersey
Rutgers, The State University of New
  Jersey
    Camden Regional Campus
    New Brunswick Regional Campus
    Newark Regional Campus
St. Peter's College
Salem Community College
Seton Hall University
Somerset Christian College
Stevens Institute of Technology
Sussex County Community College
Thomas Edison State College
Union County College
University of Medicine and Dentistry of
  New Jersey
    School of Health Related
      Professions
Warren County Community College
William Paterson University of New
  Jersey

New Mexico

Albuquerque Technical-Vocational
  Institute
Clovis Community College
Dona Ana Branch Community College of
  New Mexico State University
Eastern New Mexico University
Eastern New Mexico University: Roswell
  Campus
New Mexico Highlands University
New Mexico Institute of Mining and
  Technology
New Mexico Junior College
New Mexico Military Institute
New Mexico State University
  Alamogordo
San Juan College
Santa Fe Community College
University of New Mexico
Western New Mexico University

New York

Adirondack Community College
Bard College
Barnard College
Broome Community College
Canisius College
Cayuga County Community College

City University of New York
  Borough of Manhattan Community
    College
  Bronx Community College
  Brooklyn College
  City College
  Hostos Community College
  Hunter College
  John Jay College of Criminal
    Justice
  Kingsborough Community College
  La Guardia Community College
  Queens College
  Queensborough Community
    College
  York College
Clinton Community College
Corning Community College
D'Youville College
Daemen College
Dominican College of Blauvelt
Dutchess Community College
Elmira College
Erie Community College
  City Campus
  North Campus
  South Campus
Finger Lakes Community College
Fulton-Montgomery Community College
Genesee Community College
Hilbert College
Hobart and William Smith Colleges
Hofstra University
Hudson Valley Community College
Ithaca College
Jamestown Community College
Jefferson Community College
Long Island University
  C. W. Post Campus
  Southampton College
Maria College
Marist College
Marymount College of Fordham
  University
Marymount Manhattan College
Mohawk Valley Community College
Monroe College
Monroe Community College
Mount St. Mary College
New York Institute of Technology
Niagara County Community College
Niagara University
North Country Community College
Onondaga Community College
Orange County Community College
Pace University
Pace University: Pleasantville/Briarcliff
Parsons School of Design
Rensselaer Polytechnic Institute
Roberts Wesleyan College
Rockland Community College
Sage College of Albany
St. Bonaventure University
St. John's University
Schenectady County Community College
Skidmore College
State University of New York
  Albany
  Binghamton
  Buffalo
  College at Brockport
  College at Buffalo
  College at Cortland
  College at Fredonia
  College at Plattsburgh
  College at Potsdam
  College of Agriculture and
    Technology at Morrisville
  College of Technology at Canton
  College of Technology at Delhi
  Empire State College
  Oswego
  Stony Brook
Suffolk County Community College
Syracuse University

Talmudical Institute of Upstate New York
Tompkins-Cortland Community College
Touro College
Trocaire College
Ulster County Community College
Union College
University of Rochester
Utica College
Utica School of Commerce
Villa Maria College of Buffalo
Yeshiva University

North Carolina

Alamance Community College
Appalachian State University
Asheville Buncombe Technical
  Community College
Barton College
Beaufort County Community College
Belmont Abbey College
Bladen Community College
Blue Ridge Community College
Brevard College
Brunswick Community College
Caldwell Community College and
  Technical Institute
Cape Fear Community College
Carteret Community College
Catawba College
Catawba Valley Community College
Central Carolina Community College
Central Piedmont Community College
Cleveland Community College
Coastal Carolina Community College
College of the Albemarle
Davidson County Community College
Durham Technical Community College
East Carolina University
Edgecombe Community College
Fayetteville Technical Community
  College
Forsyth Technical Community College
Gardner-Webb University
Gaston College
Greensboro College
Guilford Technical Community College
Halifax Community College
Haywood Community College
High Point University
Isothermal Community College
James Sprunt Community College
John Wesley College
Johnston Community College
Lenoir Community College
Lenoir-Rhyne College
Louisburg College
Mars Hill College
Martin Community College
Mayland Community College
Meredith College
Methodist College
Mitchell Community College
Montgomery Community College
Montreat College
Mount Olive College
Nash Community College
North Carolina State University
North Carolina Wesleyan College
Pamlico Community College
Peace College
Pfeiffer University
Piedmont Community College
Pitt Community College
Queens University of Charlotte
Randolph Community College
Richmond Community College
Roanoke-Chowan Community College
Robeson Community College
Rockingham Community College
Rowan-Cabarrus Community College
St. Andrews Presbyterian College
Salem College
Sampson Community College
Sandhills Community College
Shaw University

South Piedmont Community College
Southeastern Community College
Southwestern Community College
Stanly Community College
Surry Community College
Tri-County Community College
University of North Carolina
  Asheville
  Chapel Hill
  Charlotte
  Greensboro
  Pembroke
Vance-Granville Community College
Wake Forest University
Wake Technical Community College
Warren Wilson College
Wayne Community College
Western Carolina University
Western Piedmont Community College
Wilkes Community College
Wilson Technical Community College
Wingate University

North Dakota

Bismarck State College
Dickinson State University
Jamestown College
Lake Region State College
Mayville State University
Minot State University
Minot State University: Bottineau
  Campus
North Dakota State College of Science
North Dakota State University
Trinity Bible College
University of Mary
Williston State College

Ohio

Baldwin-Wallace College
Bluffton College
Bowling Green State University
Bowling Green State University:
  Firelands College
Bryant & Stratton College
  Cleveland West
  Willoughby Hills
Case Western Reserve University
Cedarville University
Central Ohio Technical College
Chatfield College
Clark State Community College
Cleveland State University
Columbus State Community College
Cuyahoga Community College
  Eastern Campus
  Metropolitan Campus
  Western Campus
David N. Myers College
Defiance College
Edison State Community College
Franklin University
Heidelberg College
Hiram College
Hocking Technical College
James A. Rhodes State College
Jefferson Community College
John Carroll University
Kent State University
Kent State University
  Ashtabula Regional Campus
  East Liverpool Regional Campus
  Salem Regional Campus
  Stark Campus
  Trumbull Campus
  Tuscarawas Campus
Kettering College of Medical Arts
Lakeland Community College
Lorain County Community College
Lourdes College
Malone College
Marion Technical College
Miami University
  Hamilton Campus
  Middletown Campus

Miami-Jacobs College
Mount Vernon Nazarene University
Muskingum College
North Central State College
Northwest State Community College
Oberlin College
Ohio Dominican College
Ohio Northern University
Ohio State University
   Agricultural Technical Institute
   Columbus Campus
   Lima Campus
   Mansfield Campus
   Marion Campus
   Newark Campus
Ohio University
   Chillicothe Campus
   Eastern Campus
   Southern Campus at Ironton
   Zanesville Campus
Otterbein College
Owens Community College
   Findlay Campus
   Toledo
Sinclair Community College
Southern State Community College
Stark State College of Technology
Tiffin University
University of Akron
University of Cincinnati
   Clermont College
   Raymond Walters College
University of Dayton
University of Findlay
University of Rio Grande
University of Toledo
Virginia Marti College of Art and Design
Walsh University
Washington State Community College
Wilmington College
Wittenberg University
Wright State University
Wright State University: Lake Campus
Xavier University
Youngstown State University

Oklahoma

Bacone College
Cameron University
Carl Albert State College
East Central University
Eastern Oklahoma State College
Langston University
Northeastern Oklahoma Agricultural and
   Mechanical College
Northeastern State University
Northern Oklahoma College
Northwestern Oklahoma State University
Oklahoma Baptist University
Oklahoma Christian University of
   Science and Arts
Oklahoma City Community College
Oklahoma City University
Oklahoma Panhandle State University
Oklahoma State University
   Oklahoma City
   Okmulgee
Oklahoma Wesleyan University
Oral Roberts University
Redlands Community College
Rogers State University
Rose State College
St. Gregory's University
Seminole State College
Southern Nazarene University
Southwestern Christian University
Southwestern Oklahoma State University
Tulsa Community College
University of Central Oklahoma
University of Oklahoma
University of Tulsa
Western Oklahoma State College

Oregon

Blue Mountain Community College

Central Oregon Community College
Chemeketa Community College
Clackamas Community College
Clatsop Community College
Concordia University
Eastern Oregon University
George Fox University
Lane Community College
Lewis & Clark College
Linn-Benton Community College
Mount Hood Community College
Oregon Institute of Technology
Oregon State University
Pacific Northwest College of Art
Portland Community College
Reed College
Rogue Community College
Southern Oregon University
Southwestern Oregon Community
   College
Treasure Valley Community College

Pennsylvania

Albright College
Baptist Bible College of Pennsylvania
Bloomsburg University of Pennsylvania
Bryn Athyn College of the New Church
Bryn Mawr College
Bucknell University
Bucks County Community College
California University of Pennsylvania
Cedar Crest College
Chatham College
Chestnut Hill College
Community College of Allegheny
   County
Community College of Beaver County
Community College of Philadelphia
Curtis Institute of Music
DeSales University
Delaware Valley College
Duquesne University
Elizabethtown College
Franklin & Marshall College
Geneva College
Grove City College
Harrisburg Area Community College
Holy Family University
Keystone College
King's College
Kutztown University of Pennsylvania
La Salle University
Lebanon Valley College of Pennsylvania
Lehigh Carbon Community College
Lincoln University
Lock Haven University of Pennsylvania
Manor College
Marywood University
Mercyhurst College
Millersville University of Pennsylvania
Northampton County Area Community
   College
Penn State
   Abington
   Altoona
   Beaver
   Berks
   Delaware County
   Dubois
   Erie, The Behrend College
   Fayette
   Harrisburg
   Hazleton
   Lehigh Valley
   Mont Alto
   New Kensington
   Schuylkill - Capital College
   Shenango
   University Park
   Wilkes-Barre
   Worthington Scranton
   York
Philadelphia Biblical University
Reading Area Community College
St. Vincent College

Shippensburg University of Pennsylvania
South Hills School of Business &
   Technology
Swarthmore College
Temple University
University of Pennsylvania
University of Pittsburgh
University of Pittsburgh
   Bradford
   Greensburg
University of Scranton
Valley Forge Christian College
Villanova University
Washington and Jefferson College
Waynesburg College
Widener University
Wilkes University
York College of Pennsylvania

Puerto Rico

Huertas Junior College
Inter American University of Puerto Rico
   Fajardo Campus
   Guayama Campus
   San German Campus
Pontifical Catholic University of Puerto
   Rico
University of Puerto Rico
   Humacao
   Ponce
   Utuado
University of the Sacred Heart

Rhode Island

Community College of Rhode Island
Roger Williams University
University of Rhode Island

South Carolina

Aiken Technical College
Anderson College
Benedict College
Central Carolina Technical College
Charleston Southern University
Claflin University
Clemson University
Coastal Carolina University
Coker College
College of Charleston
Columbia College
Converse College
Erskine College
Florence-Darlington Technical College
Francis Marion University
Lander University
Midlands Technical College
Newberry College
North Greenville College
Orangeburg-Calhoun Technical College
Piedmont Technical College
Presbyterian College
South Carolina State University
Spartanburg Methodist College
Spartanburg Technical College
Technical College of the Lowcountry
Tri-County Technical College
Trident Technical College
University of South Carolina
University of South Carolina
   Aiken
   Lancaster
   Salkehatchie Regional Campus
   Sumter
   Union
Williamsburg Technical College
Wofford College
York Technical College

South Dakota

Augustana College
Black Hills State University
Dakota State University
Dakota Wesleyan University
Kilian Community College

Mount Marty College
Northern State University
Sinte Gleska University
South Dakota School of Mines and
   Technology
South Dakota State University
University of Sioux Falls
University of South Dakota
Western Dakota Technical Institute

Tennessee

Bryan College
Carson-Newman College
Chattanooga State Technical Community
   College
Christian Brothers University
Cleveland State Community College
Columbia State Community College
Crichton College
Dyersburg State Community College
East Tennessee State University
Fisk University
Freed-Hardeman University
Jackson State Community College
King College
Lee University
Memphis College of Art
Northeast State Technical Community
   College
O'More College of Design
Pellissippi State Technical Community
   College
Rhodes College
Roane State Community College
South College
Southern Adventist University
Southwest Tennessee Community
   College
Tennessee Technological University
Tennessee Wesleyan College
Union University
University of Memphis
University of Tennessee
   Chattanooga
   Knoxville
   Martin
Vanderbilt University
Volunteer State Community College
Walters State Community College

Texas

Abilene Christian University
Alvin Community College
Amarillo College
Angelina College
Angelo State University
Arlington Baptist College
Austin Community College
Austin Graduate School of Theology
Blinn College
Brazosport College
Brookhaven College
Cedar Valley College
Central Texas College
Cisco Junior College
Clarendon College
Coastal Bend College
College of Saint Thomas More
College of the Mainland
Collin County Community College
   District
Concordia University at Austin
Dallas Baptist University
Del Mar College
East Texas Baptist University
El Centro College
El Paso Community College
Galveston College
Grayson County College
Hardin-Simmons University
Hill College
Houston Baptist University
Houston Community College System
Howard College
Howard Payne University

Huston-Tillotson College
Jacksonville College
Jarvis Christian College
Kilgore College
Lamar State College at Port Arthur
Lamar University
Laredo Community College
Lee College
Lon Morris College
Lubbock Christian University
McLennan Community College
McMurry University
Midland College
Midwestern State University
Mountain View College
North Central Texas College
North Harris Montgomery Community
College District
North Lake College
Northeast Texas Community College
Northwood University: Texas Campus
Odessa College
Our Lady of the Lake University of San
Antonio
Palo Alto College
Panola College
Paris Junior College
Prairie View A&M University
Ranger College
Rice University
Richland College
St. Philip's College
Sam Houston State University
San Antonio College
South Plains College
Southwest Texas Junior College
Southwest Texas State University
Southwestern Assemblies of God
University
Southwestern University
Stephen F. Austin State University
Tarleton State University
Tarrant County College
Temple College
Texarkana College
Texas A&M International University
Texas A&M University
Texas A&M University
Commerce
Galveston
Texas Lutheran University
Texas State Technical College
Waco
West Texas
Texas Tech University
Texas Wesleyan University
Texas Woman's University
Trinity Valley Community College
Tyler Junior College
University of Houston
University of Houston
Clear Lake
Downtown
University of Mary Hardin-Baylor
University of North Texas
University of Texas
Austin
Brownsville
Dallas
El Paso
Pan American
San Antonio
University of the Incarnate Word
Victoria College
Wayland Baptist University
Western Texas College

Utah

Brigham Young University
College of Eastern Utah
Dixie State College of Utah
LDS Business College
Salt Lake Community College
Utah State University
Utah Valley State College

Weber State University
Westminster College

Vermont

Bennington College
Burlington College
Castleton State College
College of St. Joseph in Vermont
Community College of Vermont
Johnson State College
Lyndon State College
Marlboro College
Sterling College
Vermont Technical College

Virginia

Blue Ridge Community College
Bluefield College
College of William and Mary
Danville Community College
ECPI College of Technology
Eastern Mennonite University
Eastern Shore Community College
Emory & Henry College
Ferrum College
George Mason University
Hampton University
J. Sargeant Reynolds Community
College
Liberty University
Longwood University
Lynchburg College
Mary Baldwin College
Mountain Empire Community College
Old Dominion University
Paul D. Camp Community College
Piedmont Virginia Community College
Radford University
Randolph-Macon College
Randolph-Macon Woman's College
Rappahannock Community College
Richard Bland College
Roanoke College
Southside Virginia Community College
Southwest Virginia Community College
Sweet Briar College
Thomas Nelson Community College
University of Virginia's College at Wise
Virginia Commonwealth University
Virginia Highlands Community College
Virginia Intermont College
Virginia Polytechnic Institute and State
University
Virginia State University
Virginia Western Community College

Washington

Bellevue Community College
Central Washington University
Centralia College
Clark College
Clover Park Technical College
Edmonds Community College
Everett Community College
Gonzaga University
Grays Harbor College
Green River Community College
Heritage College
Lake Washington Technical College
Lower Columbia College
North Seattle Community College
Northwest College
Olympic College
Renton Technical College
St. Martin's College
Seattle Central Community College
South Seattle Community College
Spokane Community College
Spokane Falls Community College
Trinity Lutheran College
University of Washington
Walla Walla College
Walla Walla Community College
Wenatchee Valley College

Whitman College
Whitworth College

West Virginia

Alderson-Broaddus College
Appalachian Bible College
Bethany College
Concord College
Davis and Elkins College
Fairmont State College
Mountain State University
Potomac State College of West Virginia
University
Shepherd College
Southern West Virginia Community and
Technical College
University of Charleston
West Virginia Northern Community
College
West Virginia State College
West Virginia University Institute of
Technology
West Virginia University at Parkersburg
West Virginia Wesleyan College

Wisconsin

Blackhawk Technical College
Cardinal Stritch University
Carthage College
Chippewa Valley Technical College
Concordia University Wisconsin
Edgewood College
Lakeland College
Maranatha Baptist Bible College
Marian College of Fond du Lac
Marquette University
Mid-State Technical College
Milwaukee Area Technical College
Milwaukee School of Engineering
Moraine Park Technical College
Mount Mary College
Nicolet Area Technical College
Silver Lake College
University of Wisconsin
Baraboo/Sauk County
Barron County
Eau Claire
Fond du Lac
Fox Valley
Green Bay
La Crosse
Madison
Manitowoc
Marathon County
Marinette
Oshkosh
Parkside
Platteville
Richland
River Falls
Rock County
Stevens Point
Stout
Superior
Washington County
Waukesha
Viterbo University
Waukesha County Technical College
Wisconsin Lutheran College

Wyoming

Casper College
Central Wyoming College
Eastern Wyoming College
Laramie County Community College
Sheridan College
University of Wyoming
Western Wyoming Community College

ESL program

Alabama

Auburn University

Auburn University at Montgomery
Enterprise State Junior College
Gadsden State Community College
Jacksonville State University
Troy State University
University of Alabama
University of Alabama
Huntsville
University of North Alabama
University of South Alabama

Alaska

Prince William Sound Community
College
University of Alaska
Anchorage

Arizona

Arizona Western College
Central Arizona College
Cochise College
Embry-Riddle Aeronautical University:
Prescott Campus
Estrella Mountain Community College
Gateway Community College
Glendale Community College
Northern Arizona University
Phoenix College
Pima Community College
Rio Salado College
Scottsdale Community College
South Mountain Community College
University of Arizona
Yavapai College

Arkansas

Arkansas State University
John Brown University
Ouachita Baptist University
University of Arkansas
University of Arkansas
Community College at Batesville
Community College at Hope
Cossatot Community College of the
Little Rock
University of Central Arkansas
University of the Ozarks

California

Academy of Art College
Antelope Valley College
Azusa Pacific University
Bethany College
Bethesda Christian University
Biola University
California Maritime Academy
California Polytechnic State University:
San Luis Obispo
California State Polytechnic University:
Pomona
California State University
Bakersfield
Chico
Dominguez Hills
Fresno
Fullerton
Hayward
Long Beach
Los Angeles
Monterey Bay
Northridge
Sacramento
San Marcos
Stanislaus
Cerro Coso Community College
Chabot College
Christian Heritage College
Citrus College
Coastline Community College
College of the Canyons
College of the Redwoods
College of the Sequoias
College of the Siskiyous
Columbia College

Concordia University
Cuesta College
De Anza College
Diablo Valley College
Dominican University of California
East Los Angeles College
Feather River College
Foothill College
Fresno Pacific University
Gavilan Community College
Glendale Community College
Golden Gate University
Golden West College
Grossmont Community College
Holy Names College
Hope International University
Humboldt State University
Imperial Valley College
Irvine Valley College
La Sierra University
Laney College
Las Positas College
Loma Linda University
Long Beach City College
Los Angeles Harbor College
Los Angeles Southwest College
Los Angeles Trade and Technical College
Marymount College
Menlo College
MiraCosta College
Modesto Junior College
Monterey Institute of International
   Studies
Monterey Peninsula College
Mount San Antonio College
Napa Valley College
National University
Northwestern Polytechnic University
Ohlone College
Orange Coast College
Otis College of Art and Design
Pacific States University
Pacific Union College
Palomar College
Pitzer College
Queen of the Holy Rosary College
Riverside Community College
Samuel Merritt College
San Diego State University
San Francisco State University
San Joaquin Delta College
Santa Barbara City College
Santa Monica College
Santa Rosa Junior College
Shasta College
Sierra College
Sonoma State University
Southwestern College
University of California
   Berkeley
   Davis
   Los Angeles
   Santa Barbara
   Santa Cruz
University of La Verne
University of San Francisco
University of Southern California
University of the Pacific
Ventura College
Victor Valley College
Vista Community College

Colorado

Arapahoe Community College
Colorado College
Colorado School of Mines
Colorado State University
Colorado State University
   Pueblo
Community College of Aurora
Fort Lewis College
Mesa State College
Morgan Community College
National American University
   Denver

Red Rocks Community College
Trinidad State Junior College
United States Air Force Academy
University of Colorado
   Boulder
   Denver
University of Denver
University of Northern Colorado

Connecticut

Albertus Magnus College
Briarwood College
Capital Community College
Gateway Community College
Holy Apostles College and Seminary
Housatonic Community College
International College of Hospitality
   Management
Manchester Community College
Middlesex Community College
Mitchell College
Naugatuck Valley Community College
Northwestern Connecticut Community
   College
Norwalk Community College
Quinebaug Valley Community College
Sacred Heart University
Teikyo Post University
Three Rivers Community College
Tunxis Community College
University of Bridgeport
University of Connecticut
University of Hartford
University of New Haven
Western Connecticut State University
Yale University

Delaware

Delaware State University
Delaware Technical and Community
   College
      Stanton/Wilmington Campus
University of Delaware

District of Columbia

Catholic University of America
Gallaudet University
George Washington University
Georgetown University
Trinity College
University of the District of Columbia

Florida

Art Institute
   of Fort Lauderdale
Barry University
Carlos Albizu University
Daytona Beach Community College
Eckerd College
Embry-Riddle Aeronautical University
Florida Atlantic University
Florida Institute of Technology
Florida Keys Community College
Florida Metropolitan University
   Tampa College
Florida National College
Florida State University
Hillsborough Community College
Hobe Sound Bible College
International College
Miami-Dade Community College
Okaloosa-Walton Community College
Palm Beach Atlantic University
Palm Beach Community College
Pensacola Junior College
Polk Community College
St. John Vianney College Seminary
St. Leo University
St. Petersburg College
Santa Fe Community College
Schiller International University
Seminole Community College
South Florida Community College
Tallahassee Community College

University of Central Florida
University of Florida
University of Miami
University of North Florida
University of Tampa
University of West Florida
Valencia Community College
Webber International University

Georgia

Andrew College
Augusta State University
Berry College
Central Georgia Technical College
Chattahoochee Technical College
Dalton State College
DeKalb Technical College
Gainesville College
Georgia College and State University
Georgia Institute of Technology
Georgia Perimeter College
Georgia Southern University
Georgia Southwestern State University
Georgia State University
Kennesaw State University
Morehouse College
North Georgia College & State
   University
Savannah College of Art and Design
Savannah Technical College
University of Georgia
West Georgia Technical College

Hawaii

Brigham Young University-Hawaii
Chaminade University of Honolulu
Hawaii Pacific University
Hawaii Tokai International College
University of Hawaii
   Hawaii Community College
   Honolulu Community College
   Kauai Community College
   Manoa
   Maui Community College

Idaho

College of Southern Idaho
Eastern Idaho Technical College
Idaho State University
Lewis-Clark State College
North Idaho College
University of Idaho

Illinois

Benedictine University
Black Hawk College
Carl Sandburg College
Chicago State University
City Colleges of Chicago
   Harold Washington College
   Malcolm X College
   Wright College
College of DuPage
College of Lake County
Columbia College Chicago
Danville Area Community College
De Paul University
DeVry University
   Chicago
Dominican University
Eastern Illinois University
Elgin Community College
Heartland Community College
Illinois Eastern Community Colleges
   Frontier Community College
   Lincoln Trail College
   Olney Central College
   Wabash Valley College
Illinois State University
John Wood Community College
Joliet Junior College
Kaskaskia College
Kendall College
Kishwaukee College

Lake Land College
Lewis University
Lincoln Land Community College
Loyola University of Chicago
McHenry County College
Moraine Valley Community College
National-Louis University
North Park University
Northeastern Illinois University
Parkland College
Prairie State College
Quincy University
Rock Valley College
Rockford College
Roosevelt University
St. Augustine College
St. Xavier University
Sauk Valley Community College
School of the Art Institute of Chicago
South Suburban College of Cook County
Southern Illinois University Carbondale
Southern Illinois University Edwardsville
Southwestern Illinois College
Triton College
University of Illinois
   Urbana-Champaign
Western Illinois University
William Rainey Harper College

Indiana

American Conservatory of Music
Ball State University
Butler University
Calumet College of St. Joseph
Earlham College
Holy Cross College
Huntington College
Indiana Institute of Technology
Indiana State University
Indiana University
   Bloomington
   South Bend
Indiana University-Purdue University
   Fort Wayne
Indiana University-Purdue University
   Indianapolis
Ivy Tech State College
   Central Indiana
   Northcentral
   Northeast
University of Evansville
University of Indianapolis
University of Southern Indiana
Valparaiso University
Vincennes University

Iowa

Buena Vista University
Clarke College
Clinton Community College
Coe College
Cornell College
Des Moines Area Community College
Dordt College
Drake University
Franciscan University
Graceland University
Indian Hills Community College
Iowa State University
Iowa Western Community College
Kirkwood Community College
Loras College
Marshalltown Community College
Morningside College
Muscatine Community College
Northeast Iowa Community College
Northwestern College
Scott Community College
Simpson College
University of Iowa
University of Northern Iowa
Waldorf College
Western Iowa Tech Community College
William Penn University

Kansas

Barton County Community College
Benedictine College
Butler County Community College
Dodge City Community College
Donnelly College
Emporia State University
Fort Hays State University
Fort Scott Community College
Garden City Community College
Hesston College
Hutchinson Community College
Independence Community College
Kansas City Kansas Community College
Kansas State University
Kansas Wesleyan University
Labette Community College
Ottawa University
Seward County Community College
University of Kansas
Washburn University of Topeka
Wichita State University

Kentucky

Brescia University
Campbellsville University
Hopkinsville Community College
Jefferson Community College
Murray State University
Thomas More College
University of Kentucky
University of Louisville

Louisiana

Delgado Community College
Louisiana College
Louisiana State University and
    Agricultural and Mechanical College
Louisiana Tech University
Loyola University New Orleans
McNeese State University
Nunez Community College
St. Joseph Seminary College
Tulane University
University of Louisiana at Lafayette
University of Louisiana at Monroe
University of New Orleans

Maine

Husson College
University of Maine
University of Maine
    Machias
University of New England
University of Southern Maine

Maryland

Anne Arundel Community College
Baltimore Hebrew University
Carroll Community College
Cecil Community College
Chesapeake College
College of Notre Dame of Maryland
Community College of Baltimore County
    Catonsville
    Dundalk
    Essex
Frederick Community College
Montgomery College
    Rockville Campus
Towson University
University of Maryland
    Baltimore County
    College Park
Washington Bible College
Wor-Wic Community College

Massachusetts

American International College
Anna Maria College
Art Institute of Boston at Lesley
    University
Atlantic Union College
Bay Path College

Bay State College
Benjamin Franklin Institute of
    Technology
Bentley College
Berkshire Community College
Boston College
Boston Conservatory
Boston University
Bridgewater State College
Bunker Hill Community College
Cape Cod Community College
Clark University
Dean College
Elms College
Emmanuel College
Endicott College
Fisher College
Framingham State College
Greenfield Community College
Katharine Gibbs School
Lasell College
Lesley University
Massachusetts College of Pharmacy and
    Health Sciences
Massachusetts Institute of Technology
Massasoit Community College
Merrimack College
Montserrat College of Art
Mount Ida College
Mount Wachusett Community College
New England Conservatory of Music
Newbury College
Northeastern University
Pine Manor College
Quinsigamond Community College
Regis College
Roxbury Community College
Salem State College
Springfield College
Springfield Technical Community
    College
Suffolk University
University of Massachusetts
    Amherst
    Boston
Worcester Polytechnic Institute

Michigan

Adrian College
Andrews University
Central Michigan University
Davenport University - Western Region
Eastern Michigan University
Ferris State University
Finlandia University
Grand Rapids Community College
Grand Valley State University
Kirtland Community College
Lawrence Technological University
Macomb Community College
Madonna University
Michigan State University
Michigan Technological University
Mott Community College
Northwood University
Oakland Community College
Oakland University
Saginaw Valley State University
Southwestern Michigan College
Spring Arbor University
University of Michigan
Washtenaw Community College
Wayne State University
Western Michigan University

Minnesota

Augsburg College
Bemidji State University
Bethel College
Century Community and Technical
    College
College of St. Benedict
Concordia College: Moorhead
Concordia University: St. Paul
Crown College

Dakota County Technical College
Hamline University
Hennepin Technical College
Lake Superior College: A Community
    and Technical College
Martin Luther College
Minneapolis Community and Technical
    College
Minnesota State College - Southeast
    Technical
Minnesota State University
    Mankato
Normandale Community College
North Hennepin Community College
Northwestern College
Rainy River Community College
Riverland Community College: A
    Technical and Community College
St. John's University
St. Mary's University of Minnesota
St. Paul College - A Community and
    Technical College
Southwest State University
University of Minnesota
    Twin Cities
University of St. Thomas

Mississippi

Itawamba Community College
Mississippi State University
Mississippi University for Women
University of Mississippi
University of Southern Mississippi

Missouri

Avila University
Central Methodist College
Central Missouri State University
Columbia College
Conception Seminary College
Crowder College
Drury University
East Central College
Fontbonne College
Jefferson College
Maryville University of Saint Louis
Missouri Southern State College
Missouri Valley College
Northwest Missouri State University
Ozarks Technical Community College
Penn Valley Community College
St. Louis Community College
    St. Louis Community College at
        Florissant Valley
    St. Louis Community College at
        Forest Park
St. Louis University
Southeast Missouri State University
Southwest Missouri State University
Truman State University
University of Missouri
    Columbia
    Rolla
    St. Louis
Washington University in St. Louis
Webster University
Westminster College

Montana

Carroll College
Miles Community College
Montana State University
    Billings
    Bozeman
Rocky Mountain College
University of Montana-Missoula

Nebraska

Bellevue University
Central Community College
Concordia University
Creighton University
Dana College
Doane College

Hastings College
Metropolitan Community College
Northeast Community College
Union College
University of Nebraska
    Kearney
    Lincoln
    Omaha

Nevada

Community College of Southern Nevada
Great Basin College
Morrison University
Truckee Meadows Community College
University of Nevada
    Las Vegas
    Reno
Western Nevada Community College

New Hampshire

Colby-Sawyer College
Franklin Pierce College
Keene State College
New England College
New Hampshire Community Technical
    College
    Nashua
New Hampshire Technical Institute
Rivier College
Southern New Hampshire University
University of New Hampshire
University of New Hampshire at
    Manchester

New Jersey

Assumption College for Sisters
Atlantic Cape Community College
Bergen Community College
Bloomfield College
Brookdale Community College
Burlington County College
Caldwell College
Camden County College
Centenary College
College of St. Elizabeth
County College of Morris
Essex County College
Fairleigh Dickinson University
    College at Florham
    Metropolitan Campus
Felician College
Georgian Court College
Hudson County Community College
Kean University
Mercer County Community College
Middlesex County College
Montclair State University
New Jersey City University
New Jersey Institute of Technology
Ocean County College
Passaic County Community College
Ramapo College of New Jersey
Rider University
Rowan University
Rutgers, The State University of New
    Jersey
    Camden Regional Campus
    New Brunswick Regional Campus
    Newark Regional Campus
Salem Community College
Seton Hall University
Sussex County Community College
Union County College
Warren County Community College
William Paterson University of New
    Jersey

New Mexico

Albuquerque Technical-Vocational
    Institute
Clovis Community College
Dona Ana Branch Community College of
    New Mexico State University
New Mexico Highlands University

New Mexico Junior College
San Juan College
Santa Fe Community College
University of New Mexico

New York

Alfred University
Berkeley College
Berkeley College of New York City
Broome Community College
Canisius College
City University of New York
    Baruch College
    Borough of Manhattan Community
        College
    Bronx Community College
    Brooklyn College
    City College
    College of Staten Island
    Hostos Community College
    John Jay College of Criminal
        Justice
    Kingsborough Community College
    Queens College
    Queensborough Community
        College
    York College
Clarkson University
Clinton Community College
College of Aeronautics
Concordia College
Cornell University
Dowling College
Dutchess Community College
Eastman School of Music of the
    University of Rochester
Elmira College
Erie Community College
    City Campus
    North Campus
    South Campus
Eugene Lang College/New School
    University
Finger Lakes Community College
Fordham University
Fulton-Montgomery Community College
Genesee Community College
Globe Institute of Technology
Hamilton College
Hofstra University
Jamestown Community College
Long Island University
    C. W. Post Campus
    Southampton College
Manhattan College
Manhattan School of Music
Manhattanville College
Mannes College of Music
Marymount College of Fordham
    University
Marymount Manhattan College
Mercy College
Mohawk Valley Community College
Molloy College
Monroe Community College
Nassau Community College
New York Institute of Technology
New York University
Nyack College
Onondaga Community College
Orange County Community College
Pace University
Pace University: Pleasantville/Briarcliff
Parsons School of Design
Paul Smith's College
Pratt Institute
Rensselaer Polytechnic Institute
Roberts Wesleyan College
Rochester Institute of Technology
Rockland Community College
St. Bonaventure University
St. John's University
Schenectady County Community College
School of Visual Arts

State University of New York
    Albany
    Binghamton
    Buffalo
    College at Buffalo
    College at Fredonia
    College at Old Westbury
    College at Plattsburgh
    College of Agriculture and
        Technology at Cobleskill
    College of Agriculture and
        Technology at Morrisville
    Institute of Technology at
        Utica/Rome
    New Paltz
    Purchase
    Stony Brook
Suffolk County Community College
Syracuse University
Tompkins-Cortland Community College
Touro College
Union College
University of Rochester
Utica College
Wells College
Westchester Community College

North Carolina

Appalachian State University
Asheville Buncombe Technical
    Community College
Beaufort County Community College
Bladen Community College
Blue Ridge Community College
Brevard College
Brunswick Community College
Carteret Community College
Cleveland Community College
College of the Albemarle
Davidson County Community College
Durham Technical Community College
Elon University
Forsyth Technical Community College
Gaston College
Greensboro College
Guilford Technical Community College
High Point University
James Sprunt Community College
Lees-McRae College
Lenoir-Rhyne College
Mars Hill College
Methodist College
Nash Community College
North Carolina State University
Pitt Community College
Randolph Community College
Richmond Community College
Rowan-Cabarrus Community College
Sandhills Community College
Stanly Community College
Surry Community College
University of North Carolina
    Charlotte
    Wilmington
Wake Technical Community College
Warren Wilson College
Western Carolina University
Wilkes Community College
Wilson Technical Community College

North Dakota

Lake Region State College
North Dakota State College of Science
North Dakota State University
University of North Dakota
Williston State College

Ohio

Ashland University
Baldwin-Wallace College
Case Western Reserve University
Cedarville University
Central Ohio Technical College

Cincinnati State Technical and
    Community College
Cleveland State University
College of Mount St. Joseph
Columbus College of Art and Design
Columbus State Community College
Cuyahoga Community College
    Eastern Campus
    Metropolitan Campus
    Western Campus
Franklin University
Hiram College
Hocking Technical College
Kent State University
Lorain County Community College
Marietta College
Miami University
    Hamilton Campus
Mount Union College
Muskingum College
Oberlin College
Ohio Dominican College
Ohio State University
    Columbus Campus
Ohio University
Otterbein College
Pontifical College Josephinum
Sinclair Community College
Tiffin University
University of Akron
University of Cincinnati
University of Dayton
University of Findlay
University of Rio Grande
University of Toledo
Wright State University
Xavier University
Youngstown State University

Oklahoma

Oklahoma City Community College
Oklahoma City University
Oklahoma State University
Oklahoma Wesleyan University
Oral Roberts University
St. Gregory's University
Tulsa Community College
University of Central Oklahoma
University of Oklahoma
University of Tulsa

Oregon

Blue Mountain Community College
Chemeketa Community College
Clackamas Community College
Eastern Oregon University
George Fox University
Lane Community College
Lewis & Clark College
Linfield College
Linn-Benton Community College
Marylhurst University
Northwest Christian College
Pacific University
Portland Community College
Portland State University
Rogue Community College
Southern Oregon University
Southwestern Oregon Community
    College
Umpqua Community College
Warner Pacific College
Western Oregon University

Pennsylvania

Albright College
Arcadia University
Bryn Athyn College of the New Church
Bucks County Community College
Carlow College
Carnegie Mellon University
Cedar Crest College
Chatham College
Chestnut Hill College

Community College of Allegheny
    County
Community College of Philadelphia
Delaware Valley College
Dickinson College
Drexel University
Duquesne University
Elizabethtown College
Gwynedd-Mercy College
Harrisburg Area Community College
Immaculata University
Indiana University of Pennsylvania
Juniata College
Keystone College
King's College
La Roche College
Lackawanna College
Lehigh Carbon Community College
Lehigh University
Manor College
Marywood University
Messiah College
Montgomery County Community
    College
Northampton County Area Community
    College
Peirce College
Penn State
    Abington
    Altoona
    Beaver
    Delaware County
    University Park
    York
Point Park College
Rosemont College
St. Joseph's University
Seton Hill University
Temple University
Thiel College
University of Pennsylvania
University of Pittsburgh
University of the Sciences in
    Philadelphia
Valley Forge Christian College
Villanova University
Waynesburg College
Widener University

Puerto Rico

Huertas Junior College
Inter American University of Puerto Rico
    Barranquitas Campus
    Fajardo Campus
    Metropolitan Campus
    San German Campus
Pontifical Catholic University of Puerto
    Rico
University of Puerto Rico
    Bayamon University College
    Mayaguez Campus
    Rio Piedras Campus

Rhode Island

Bryant College
Community College of Rhode Island
Roger Williams University
Salve Regina University

South Carolina

Anderson College
The Citadel
Coker College
College of Charleston
Converse College
Forrest Junior College
Midlands Technical College
North Greenville College
Spartanburg Methodist College
Tri-County Technical College
Trident Technical College
University of South Carolina
University of South Carolina
    Aiken

York Technical College

South Dakota

Dakota State University
Northern State University
University of South Dakota

Tennessee

Carson-Newman College
Chattanooga State Technical Community
College
Cleveland State Community College
Johnson Bible College
King College
Lambuth University
Lee University
Maryville College
Pellissippi State Technical Community
College
Southern Adventist University
Southwest Tennessee Community
College
Tennessee State University
Tennessee Wesleyan College
Union University
University of Memphis
University of Tennessee
Chattanooga
Knoxville
Martin
Vanderbilt University
Volunteer State Community College
Walters State Community College

Texas

Abilene Christian University
Alvin Community College
Amarillo College
Angelo State University
Austin Community College
Baylor University
Blinn College
Central Texas College
Collin County Community College
District
Dallas Baptist University
Del Mar College
East Texas Baptist University
Eastfield College
El Centro College
El Paso Community College
Houston Baptist University
Houston Community College System
Howard College
Howard Payne University
Kilgore College
Lamar State College at Port Arthur
Lamar University
Lee College
Lon Morris College
MTI College of Business and Technology
Midland College
Midwestern State University
Mountain View College
North Harris Montgomery Community
College District
North Lake College
Northeast Texas Community College
Our Lady of the Lake University of San
Antonio
Palo Alto College
Prairie View A&M University
Richland College
St. Mary's University
St. Philip's College
San Antonio College
Schreiner University
Southern Methodist University
Southwest Texas State University
Southwestern Adventist University
Tarrant County College
Texas A&M International University
Texas A&M University

Texas A&M University
Kingsville
Texas Christian University
Texas Tech University
Texas Wesleyan University
Tyler Junior College
University of Dallas
University of Houston
University of Houston
Downtown
University of Mary Hardin-Baylor
University of North Texas
University of Texas
Arlington
Austin
San Antonio
Tyler
University of the Incarnate Word
West Texas A&M University

Utah

Brigham Young University
College of Eastern Utah
Dixie State College of Utah
Salt Lake Community College
Snow College
Southern Utah University
University of Utah
Utah State University
Utah Valley State College
Weber State University

Vermont

Bennington College
College of St. Joseph in Vermont
Community College of Vermont
Green Mountain College
Johnson State College
Landmark College
St. Michael's College
Vermont Technical College

Virginia

Blue Ridge Community College
Eastern Mennonite University
Eastern Shore Community College
George Mason University
J. Sargeant Reynolds Community
College
Liberty University
Mary Baldwin College
Old Dominion University
Piedmont Virginia Community College
Radford University
Roanoke College
Shenandoah University
Thomas Nelson Community College
University of Richmond
Virginia Commonwealth University
Virginia Polytechnic Institute and State
University

Washington

Art Institute of Seattle
Bellevue Community College
Central Washington University
Centralia College
Clark College
Clover Park Technical College
Crown College
Eastern Washington University
Edmonds Community College
Everett Community College
Gonzaga University
Grays Harbor College
Green River Community College
Heritage College
Lake Washington Technical College
Lower Columbia College
North Seattle Community College
Northwest College
Olympic College
Pacific Lutheran University
Peninsula College

Renton Technical College
St. Martin's College
Seattle Pacific University
South Seattle Community College
Spokane Community College
Spokane Falls Community College
Trinity Lutheran College
University of Washington
Walla Walla College
Washington State University
Wenatchee Valley College
Western Washington University
Whitworth College

West Virginia

Bethany College
Concord College
Davis and Elkins College
Fairmont State College
Glenville State College
Marshall University
Mountain State University
Salem International University
West Virginia University
West Virginia Wesleyan College
Wheeling Jesuit University

Wisconsin

Beloit College
Blackhawk Technical College
Cardinal Stritch University
Chippewa Valley Technical College
Concordia University Wisconsin
Fox Valley Technical College
Lakeland College
Lakeshore Technical College
Lawrence University
Marquette University
Milwaukee Area Technical College
Milwaukee School of Engineering
Moraine Park Technical College
Nicolet Area Technical College
St. Norbert College
University of Wisconsin
Eau Claire
Green Bay
La Crosse
Marinette
Milwaukee
Oshkosh
Parkside
Stevens Point
Superior
Waukesha County Technical College
Western Wisconsin Technical College

Wyoming

Central Wyoming College
Eastern Wyoming College
Sheridan College
Western Wyoming Community College

External degree

Alabama

Judson College
Southeastern Bible College
Troy State University in Montgomery
University of Alabama

Alaska

Prince William Sound Community
College

Arizona

Northern Arizona University
Prescott College

Arkansas

Arkansas Tech University
John Brown University
Pulaski Technical College

Rich Mountain Community College

California

Bethany College
Biola University
California Polytechnic State University:
San Luis Obispo
California State University
Bakersfield
Chico
Long Beach
Northridge
Stanislaus
Cogswell Polytechnical College
LIFE Pacific College
Pacific Union College
St. Mary's College of California
Sonoma State University
University of San Francisco
Vanguard University of Southern
California

Colorado

Colorado State University
Pueblo
Metropolitan State College of Denver
National American University
Denver
University of Northern Colorado

Connecticut

Charter Oak State College

District of Columbia

Trinity College

Florida

Embry Riddle Aeronautical
University-Extended Campus
Florida Agricultural and Mechanical
University
Florida Gulf Coast University
Hobe Sound Bible College
Northwood University
Florida Campus
South Florida Community College
University of Florida

Georgia

Abraham Baldwin Agricultural College
Dalton State College
Fort Valley State University
Georgia College and State University
Georgia Military College
Reinhardt College
State University of West Georgia

Idaho

Idaho State University

Illinois

Governors State University
Greenville College
Moody Bible Institute
Northeastern Illinois University
Rock Valley College
Roosevelt University
Western Illinois University

Indiana

Indiana Institute of Technology
Indiana University
Bloomington
East
Kokomo
Northwest
South Bend
Southeast
Indiana University-Purdue University
Indianapolis
Oakland City University
St. Mary-of-the-Woods College
University of Evansville

Vincennes University

Iowa
Allen College
Graceland University
Hawkeye Community College
Iowa Central Community College
Iowa State University
Kirkwood Community College
University of Iowa
Upper Iowa University

Kansas
Donnelly College
Friends University
Kansas City Kansas Community College
Pittsburg State University
Seward County Community College

Kentucky
Murray State University
University of Louisville

Maine
St. Joseph's College
University of Maine
    Machias

Maryland
Columbia Union College
Coppin State College
Howard Community College
University of Maryland
    College Park
    University College

Massachusetts
Atlantic Union College
Bunker Hill Community College
Wheaton College

Michigan
Baker College
    of Cadillac
    of Clinton Township
    of Jackson
    of Muskegon
    of Owosso
    of Port Huron
Central Michigan University
Davenport University
    Eastern Region
Ferris State University
Northwood University
Schoolcraft College
Siena Heights University

Minnesota
Bemidji State University
Bethel College
Metropolitan State University
Minnesota State University
    Moorhead
St. Olaf College
Southwest State University
University of Minnesota
    Morris
    Twin Cities
Winona State University

Missouri
Global University
Hannibal-LaGrange College
Lindenwood University
Missouri Valley College
Stephens College
University of Missouri
    Columbia

Montana
Montana State University
    Billings

Nebraska
Clarkson College
Doane College
University of Nebraska
    Lincoln

New Hampshire
University of New Hampshire at
    Manchester

New Jersey
Caldwell College
County College of Morris
Mercer County Community College
Ramapo College of New Jersey
Thomas Edison State College

New Mexico
San Juan College

New York
City University of New York
    Bronx Community College
Excelsior College
Fulton-Montgomery Community College
Russell Sage College
Skidmore College
State University of New York
    Empire State College
Syracuse University
Utica College

North Carolina
Forsyth Technical Community College
Lenoir-Rhyne College
Mount Olive College
North Carolina Agricultural and
    Technical State University
North Carolina State University
University of North Carolina
    Charlotte

North Dakota
Minot State University
University of Mary
University of North Dakota

Ohio
David N. Myers College
Kent State University
Ohio University
    Chillicothe Campus
    Eastern Campus
Tiffin University
Union Institute & University
University of Findlay
University of Toledo
Walsh University

Oklahoma
Oklahoma City University
Oral Roberts University
Southern Nazarene University
University of Oklahoma

Oregon
Eastern Oregon University
George Fox University
Linfield College

Pennsylvania
Community College of Allegheny
    County
Education Direct: Center for Degree
    Studies
Elizabethtown College
Lehigh University
Luzerne County Community College
Marywood University
Peirce College
Penn State
    Abington
    University Park

University of Pittsburgh
University of Pittsburgh
    Bradford
    Greensburg

Puerto Rico
Inter American University of Puerto Rico
    Guayama Campus
University of Puerto Rico
    Rio Piedras Campus
University of the Sacred Heart

Rhode Island
Roger Williams University

South Carolina
Benedict College
Southern Wesleyan University
University of South Carolina

South Dakota
Northern State University
University of South Dakota

Tennessee
Lee University
University of Memphis

Texas
Concordia University at Austin
El Centro College
Huston-Tillotson College
Lamar State College at Port Arthur
Northwood University: Texas Campus
Southwestern Adventist University
Southwestern Assemblies of God
    University
Texas A&M University
    Commerce
University of North Texas
Wayland Baptist University

Utah
Brigham Young University
Weber State University

Vermont
Burlington College
Community College of Vermont
Goddard College
Johnson State College
Norwich University

Virginia
George Mason University
Liberty University
Mary Baldwin College
Virginia Western Community College

Washington
Seattle Pacific University
University of Washington
Walla Walla Community College
Washington State University

West Virginia
Alderson-Broaddus College
Mountain State University
West Liberty State College
West Virginia State College
West Virginia University
West Virginia University Institute of
    Technology

Wisconsin
Blackhawk Technical College
Cardinal Stritch University
Chippewa Valley Technical College

University of Wisconsin
    Baraboo/Sauk County
    Green Bay
    Platteville
    River Falls
    Stout
    Superior
    Whitewater

Wyoming
University of Wyoming
Western Wyoming Community College

Honors program

Alabama
Alabama Agricultural and Mechanical
    University
Alabama Southern Community College
Alabama State University
American College of Computer and
    Information Sciences
Auburn University
Auburn University at Montgomery
Bevill State Community College
Birmingham-Southern College
Bishop State Community College
Chattahoochee Valley Community
    College
Enterprise State Junior College
Faulkner University
George C. Wallace State Community
    College
    Dothan
Huntingdon College
Jacksonville State University
James H. Faulkner State Community
    College
Jefferson Davis Community College
Jefferson State Community College
Judson College
Lurleen B. Wallace Junior College
Miles College
Northeast Alabama Community College
Oakwood College
Remington College
    Southeast College of Technology
Samford University
Shelton State Community College
Spring Hill College
Stillman College
Troy State University
Troy State University in Montgomery
Tuskegee University
University of Alabama
University of Alabama
    Birmingham
    Huntsville
University of Mobile
University of Montevallo
University of South Alabama
University of West Alabama

Alaska
Prince William Sound Community
    College
University of Alaska
    Anchorage
    Fairbanks

Arizona
Arizona State University
Arizona Western College
Central Arizona College
Cochise College
Estrella Mountain Community College
Gateway Community College
Glendale Community College
Northern Arizona University
Paradise Valley Community College
Phoenix College
Pima Community College
Rio Salado College

Scottsdale Community College
South Mountain Community College
University of Arizona
Yavapai College

Arkansas

Arkansas State University
Arkansas State University
    Beebe
Arkansas Tech University
East Arkansas Community College
Harding University
Henderson State University
John Brown University
North Arkansas College
Northwest Arkansas Community College
Ouachita Baptist University
Phillips Community College of the
    University of Arkansas
Southern Arkansas University Tech
University of Arkansas
University of Arkansas
    Fort Smith
    Little Rock
    Pine Bluff
University of Central Arkansas

California

Academy of Art College
Antelope Valley College
Azusa Pacific University
Barstow College
Biola University
Cabrillo College
California Culinary Academy
California Polytechnic State University:
  San Luis Obispo
California State University
    Bakersfield
    Chico
    Dominguez Hills
    Fresno
    Fullerton
    Hayward
    Long Beach
    Los Angeles
    Monterey Bay
    Northridge
    San Bernardino
    Stanislaus
Cerritos Community College
Cerro Coso Community College
Chapman University
Citrus College
College of Alameda
College of the Canyons
College of the Redwoods
College of the Sequoias
Concordia University
Contra Costa College
Cuesta College
De Anza College
Deep Springs College
Diablo Valley College
Dominican University of California
East Los Angeles College
Feather River College
Foothill College
Gavilan Community College
Glendale Community College
Golden West College
Hope International University
Humboldt State University
Imperial Valley College
Irvine Valley College
La Sierra University
Laney College
Long Beach City College
Los Angeles Harbor College
Los Angeles Pierce College
Los Angeles Southwest College
Loyola Marymount University
Marymount College
Menlo College
MiraCosta College

Modesto Junior College
Monterey Institute of International
    Studies
Moorpark College
Mount St. Mary's College
Mount San Antonio College
Mount San Jacinto College
Napa Valley College
Occidental College
Orange Coast College
Otis College of Art and Design
Pacific Union College
Pepperdine University
Reedley College
Riverside Community College
St. Mary's College of California
San Diego City College
San Diego Mesa College
San Diego State University
San Francisco State University
San Jose State University
Santa Barbara City College
Santa Clara University
Santa Monica College
Scripps College
Shasta College
Sierra College
Sonoma State University
Southwestern College
Stanford University
University of California
    Berkeley
    Davis
    Los Angeles
    Riverside
    San Diego
    Santa Barbara
    Santa Cruz
University of La Verne
University of Redlands
University of San Diego
University of San Francisco
University of Southern California
University of the Pacific
Ventura College
Victor Valley College
West Valley College

Colorado

Arapahoe Community College
Colorado Christian University
Colorado School of Mines
Colorado State University
Colorado State University
    Pueblo
Fort Lewis College
Front Range Community College
Mesa State College
Metropolitan State College of Denver
Red Rocks Community College
Regis University
University of Colorado
    Boulder
    Denver
University of Denver
University of Northern Colorado

Connecticut

Albertus Magnus College
Central Connecticut State University
Eastern Connecticut State University
Fairfield University
Housatonic Community College
Manchester Community College
Northwestern Connecticut Community
    College
Norwalk Community College
Quinnipiac University
Sacred Heart University
St. Joseph College
Southern Connecticut State University
Teikyo Post University
Trinity College
United States Coast Guard Academy
University of Bridgeport

University of Connecticut
University of Hartford
University of New Haven
Wesleyan University
Western Connecticut State University
Yale University

Delaware

Delaware State University
Goldey-Beacom College
University of Delaware

District of Columbia

American University
Catholic University of America
Gallaudet University
George Washington University
Georgetown University
Howard University
Trinity College
University of the District of Columbia

Florida

Art Institute
    of Fort Lauderdale
Barry University
Bethune-Cookman College
Broward Community College
Chipola Junior College
Daytona Beach Community College
Eckerd College
Florida Agricultural and Mechanical
    University
Florida Atlantic University
Florida Gulf Coast University
Florida International University
Florida Southern College
Florida State University
Gulf Coast Community College
Hillsborough Community College
Jacksonville University
Manatee Community College
Miami-Dade Community College
New College of Florida
Northwood University
    Florida Campus
Palm Beach Atlantic University
Palm Beach Community College
Pasco-Hernando Community College
Pensacola Junior College
Rollins College
St. Leo University
St. Petersburg College
St. Thomas University
Santa Fe Community College
Seminole Community College
South Florida Community College
Stetson University
Tallahassee Community College
Talmudic College of Florida
University of Central Florida
University of Florida
University of Miami
University of North Florida
University of South Florida
University of Tampa
University of West Florida
Valencia Community College

Georgia

Abraham Baldwin Agricultural College
Albany State University
Andrew College
Armstrong Atlantic State University
Augusta State University
Berry College
Brenau University
Brewton-Parker College
Chattahoochee Technical College
Clark Atlanta University
Clayton College and State University
Columbus State University
Columbus Technical College
Darton College

East Georgia College
Emory University
Fort Valley State University
Gainesville College
Georgia College and State University
Georgia Institute of Technology
Georgia Perimeter College
Georgia Southern University
Georgia Southwestern State University
Georgia State University
Gordon College
Kennesaw State University
Macon State College
Mercer University
Morehouse College
Morris Brown College
North Georgia College & State
    University
Oglethorpe University
Paine College
Piedmont College
Reinhardt College
Savannah State University
Shorter College
Spelman College
State University of West Georgia
Thomas University
Truett-McConnell College
University of Georgia
Valdosta State University
Wesleyan College

Hawaii

Brigham Young University-Hawaii
Hawaii Pacific University
University of Hawaii
    Hawaii Community College
    Hilo
    Leeward Community College
    Manoa

Idaho

Albertson College of Idaho
Boise State University
Brigham Young University - Idaho
College of Southern Idaho
Idaho State University
Lewis-Clark State College
Northwest Nazarene University
University of Idaho

Illinois

Augustana College
Benedictine University
Blackburn College
Bradley University
Carl Sandburg College
Chicago State University
City Colleges of Chicago
    Harold Washington College
    Kennedy-King College
    Olive-Harvey College
    Richard J. Daley College
    Wright College
College of DuPage
College of Lake County
Concordia University
De Paul University
Dominican University
Eastern Illinois University
Elgin Community College
Elmhurst College
Eureka College
Governors State University
Greenville College
Illinois Central College
Illinois Eastern Community Colleges
    Frontier Community College
    Lincoln Trail College
    Olney Central College
    Wabash Valley College
Illinois State University
Illinois Wesleyan University
Joliet Junior College

Judson College
Kankakee Community College
Kaskaskia College
Knox College
Lake Forest College
Lake Land College
Lakeview College of Nursing
Lewis University
Lincoln College
Lincoln Land Community College
Loyola University of Chicago
MacMurray College
McHenry County College
McKendree College
Midstate College
Millikin University
Monmouth College
National-Louis University
North Central College
North Park University
Northeastern Illinois University
Northern Illinois University
Northwestern University
Oakton Community College
Parkland College
Prairie State College
Quincy University
Rend Lake College
Richland Community College
Robert Morris College: Chicago
Rockford College
Roosevelt University
St. Xavier University
Sauk Valley Community College
Shawnee Community College
South Suburban College of Cook County
Southern Illinois University Carbondale
Southern Illinois University Edwardsville
Spoon River College
Trinity Christian College
Trinity International University
Triton College
University of Illinois
    Chicago
    Urbana-Champaign
Waubonsee Community College
Western Illinois University
William Rainey Harper College

Indiana

Anderson University
Ball State University
Butler University
Calumet College of St. Joseph
DePauw University
Goshen College
Holy Cross College
Indiana State University
Indiana University
    Bloomington
    Kokomo
    Northwest
    South Bend
Indiana University-Purdue University
    Fort Wayne
Indiana University-Purdue University
    Indianapolis
Indiana Wesleyan University
Manchester College
Marian College
Oakland City University
Purdue University
Purdue University
    Calumet
St. Joseph's College
Taylor University
University of Evansville
University of Indianapolis
University of Notre Dame
University of St. Francis
University of Southern Indiana
Valparaiso University
Vincennes University

Iowa

Buena Vista University
Central College
Clarke College
Clinton Community College
Coe College
Des Moines Area Community College
Drake University
Ellsworth Community College
Franciscan University
Graceland University
Grand View College
Indian Hills Community College
Iowa Central Community College
Iowa Lakes Community College
Iowa State University
Kirkwood Community College
Loras College
Luther College
Maharishi University of Management
Marshalltown Community College
Morningside College
Mount Mercy College
Muscatine Community College
North Iowa Area Community College
Northwestern College
Scott Community College
Simpson College
University of Iowa
University of Northern Iowa
Vennard College
Waldorf College
Western Iowa Tech Community College

Kansas

Baker University
Butler County Community College
Donnelly College
Emporia State University
Friends University
Hutchinson Community College
Johnson County Community College
Kansas City Kansas Community College
Kansas State University
Pittsburg State University
Pratt Community College
St. Mary College
Seward County Community College
Southwestern College
Sterling College
Tabor College
University of Kansas
University of Kansas Medical Center
Washburn University of Topeka
Wichita State University

Kentucky

Bellarmine University
Berea College
Brescia University
Campbellsville University
Centre College
Cumberland College
Daymar College
Elizabethtown Community College
Georgetown College
Hazard Community College
Henderson Community College
Hopkinsville Community College
Jefferson Community College
Madisonville Community College
Morehead State University
Murray State University
Paducah Community College
Somerset Community College
Thomas More College
University of Kentucky
University of Louisville

Louisiana

Delgado Community College
Dillard University
Grambling State University
Louisiana College

Louisiana State University
    Eunice
Louisiana State University and
    Agricultural and Mechanical College
Louisiana Tech University
Loyola University New Orleans
McNeese State University
Nicholls State University
Northwestern State University
Nunez Community College
Southeastern Louisiana University
Southern University and Agricultural and
    Mechanical College
Tulane University
University of Louisiana at Lafayette
University of Louisiana at Monroe
University of New Orleans
Xavier University of Louisiana

Maine

Bates College
Colby College
St. Joseph's College
University of Maine
University of Maine
    Augusta
    Farmington
    Machias
    Presque Isle
University of New England
University of Southern Maine

Maryland

Allegany College
Anne Arundel Community College
Baltimore International College
Bowie State University
Carroll Community College
Chesapeake College
College of Notre Dame of Maryland
College of Southern Maryland
Columbia Union College
Community College of Baltimore County
    Catonsville
    Dundalk
    Essex
Coppin State College
Frederick Community College
Frostburg State University
Goucher College
Hagerstown Community College
Hood College
Howard Community College
Loyola College in Maryland
McDaniel College
Montgomery College
    Rockville Campus
Morgan State University
Mount St. Mary's College
St. Mary's College of Maryland
Salisbury University
Sojourner-Douglass College
Towson University
United States Naval Academy
University of Baltimore
University of Maryland
    Baltimore County
    College Park
Villa Julie College
Wor-Wic Community College

Massachusetts

American International College
Amherst College
Art Institute of Boston at Lesley
    University
Assumption College
Atlantic Union College
Babson College
Bay Path College
Bay State College
Bentley College
Berkshire Community College
Boston College

Boston University
Bridgewater State College
Bunker Hill Community College
Cape Cod Community College
College of the Holy Cross
Dean College
Elms College
Emerson College
Emmanuel College
Endicott College
Fisher College
Fitchburg State College
Framingham State College
Gordon College
Greenfield Community College
Harvard College
Lasell College
Lesley University
Marian Court College
Massachusetts Bay Community College
Massachusetts College of Liberal Arts
Massasoit Community College
Mount Ida College
Mount Wachusett Community College
Newbury College
Northeastern University
Pine Manor College
Quinsigamond Community College
Regis College
Roxbury Community College
Salem State College
Simmons College
Smith College
Springfield College
Springfield Technical Community
    College
Stonehill College
Suffolk University
University of Massachusetts
    Amherst
    Boston
    Dartmouth
    Lowell
Wellesley College
Wentworth Institute of Technology
Western New England College
Westfield State College
Wheaton College
Williams College

Michigan

Adrian College
Andrews University
Aquinas College
Calvin College
Central Michigan University
Cornerstone University
Eastern Michigan University
Ferris State University
Gogebic Community College
Grand Valley State University
Hillsdale College
Kellogg Community College
Kirtland Community College
Lansing Community College
Marygrove College
Michigan State University
Mid Michigan Community College
Mott Community College
Muskegon Community College
Northern Michigan University
Northwestern Michigan College
Northwood University
Oakland University
Saginaw Valley State University
St. Clair County Community College
Schoolcraft College
Siena Heights University
Southwestern Michigan College
Spring Arbor University
University of Michigan
University of Michigan
    Dearborn
    Flint
Washtenaw Community College

Wayne County Community College
Wayne State University
Western Michigan University

Minnesota

Augsburg College
Bemidji State University
Bethel College
Century Community and Technical
College
College of St. Benedict
College of St. Catherine
College of St. Scholastica
College of Visual Arts
Concordia College: Moorhead
Crown College
Fergus Falls Community College
Gustavus Adolphus College
Hamline University
Hibbing Community College: A
Technical and Community College
Inver Hills Community College
Macalester College
Minneapolis Community and Technical
College
Minnesota State University
Mankato
Moorhead
North Hennepin Community College
Northwest Technical Institute
Northwestern College
Oak Hills Christian College
Rainy River Community College
Rochester Community and Technical
College
St. Cloud State University
St. John's University
St. Mary's University of Minnesota
Southwest State University
University of Minnesota
Morris
Twin Cities
University of St. Thomas
Vermilion Community College
Winona State University

Mississippi

Alcorn State University
Blue Mountain College
Delta State University
Holmes Community College
Itawamba Community College
Mary Holmes College
Millsaps College
Mississippi College
Mississippi Gulf Coast Community
College
Perkinston
Mississippi State University
Mississippi University for Women
Mississippi Valley State University
Rust College
University of Mississippi
University of Southern Mississippi

Missouri

Blue River Community College
Central Methodist College
Central Missouri State University
College of the Ozarks
Columbia College
Crowder College
Culver-Stockton College
Drury University
East Central College
Fontbonne College
Hannibal-LaGrange College
Harris Stowe State College
Jefferson College
Lincoln University
Lindenwood University
Longview Community College
Maple Woods Community College
Maryville University of Saint Louis

Mineral Area College
Missouri Southern State College
Missouri Western State College
Penn Valley Community College
Ranken Technical College
Research College of Nursing
Rockhurst University
St. Louis Community College
St. Louis Community College at
Florissant Valley
St. Louis Community College at
Forest Park
St. Louis Community College at
Meramec
St. Louis University
Southeast Missouri State University
Southwest Baptist University
Southwest Missouri State University
Southwest Missouri State University:
West Plains Campus
Truman State University
University of Missouri
Columbia
Kansas City
Rolla
St. Louis
Westminster College
William Jewell College
William Woods University

Montana

Carroll College
Montana State University
Billings
Bozeman
Rocky Mountain College
University of Montana-Missoula
University of Montana: Western

Nebraska

Central Community College
Chadron State College
Concordia University
Creighton University
Dana College
Doane College
Metropolitan Community College
Northeast Community College
Peru State College
Union College
University of Nebraska
Kearney
Lincoln
Medical Center
Omaha
Wayne State College
York College

Nevada

Community College of Southern Nevada
Truckee Meadows Community College
University of Nevada
Las Vegas
Reno
Western Nevada Community College

New Hampshire

Colby-Sawyer College
Dartmouth College
Franklin Pierce College
Keene State College
New England College
New Hampshire Community Technical
College
Laconia
Plymouth State College
Rivier College
St. Anselm College
Southern New Hampshire University
University of New Hampshire

New Jersey

Bergen Community College
Bloomfield College

Brookdale Community College
Caldwell College
Camden County College
Centenary College
The College of New Jersey
College of St. Elizabeth
County College of Morris
Cumberland County College
Drew University
Essex County College
Fairleigh Dickinson University
College at Florham
Metropolitan Campus
Felician College
Kean University
Monmouth University
Montclair State University
New Jersey City University
New Jersey Institute of Technology
Ocean County College
Passaic County Community College
Ramapo College of New Jersey
Raritan Valley Community College
Richard Stockton College of New Jersey
Rider University
Rowan University
Rutgers, The State University of New
Jersey
Camden Regional Campus
New Brunswick Regional Campus
Newark Regional Campus
St. Peter's College
Salem Community College
Seton Hall University
Stevens Institute of Technology
Sussex County Community College
Union County College
William Paterson University of New
Jersey

New Mexico

Clovis Community College
Eastern New Mexico University
New Mexico Highlands University
New Mexico Junior College
New Mexico State University
San Juan College
Santa Fe Community College
Southwestern Indian Polytechnic Institute
University of New Mexico
Western New Mexico University

New York

Adelphi University
Alfred University
Barnard College
Broome Community College
Bryant & Stratton Business Institute
Syracuse
Canisius College
Cayuga County Community College
Cazenovia College
City University of New York
Baruch College
Borough of Manhattan Community
College
Bronx Community College
Brooklyn College
City College
College of Staten Island
Hunter College
John Jay College of Criminal
Justice
Kingsborough Community College
Medgar Evers College
Queens College
York College
Clarkson University
Clinton Community College
Colgate University
College of Mount St. Vincent
College of New Rochelle
Concordia College
Cooper Union for the Advancement of
Science and Art

Cornell University
Corning Community College
Daemen College
Dominican College of Blauvelt
Dowling College
Dutchess Community College
Elmira College
Erie Community College
City Campus
North Campus
South Campus
Fashion Institute of Technology
Finger Lakes Community College
Fordham University
Fulton-Montgomery Community College
Genesee Community College
Hartwick College
Hilbert College
Hobart and William Smith Colleges
Hofstra University
Houghton College
Iona College
Ithaca College
Jamestown Community College
Jefferson Community College
Juilliard School
Le Moyne College
Long Island University
C. W. Post Campus
Southampton College
Manhattan College
Manhattanville College
Marist College
Marymount College of Fordham
University
Marymount Manhattan College
Medaille College
Mercy College
Mohawk Valley Community College
Molloy College
Monroe Community College
Mount St. Mary College
Nassau Community College
Nazareth College of Rochester
New York Institute of Technology
New York University
Niagara County Community College
Niagara University
Nyack College
Orange County Community College
Pace University
Pace University: Pleasantville/Briarcliff
Parsons School of Design
Paul Smith's College
Polytechnic University
Rensselaer Polytechnic Institute
Roberts Wesleyan College
Rochester Institute of Technology
Rockland Community College
Russell Sage College
Sage College of Albany
St. Bonaventure University
St. John Fisher College
St. John's University
St. Joseph's College
Schenectady County Community College
Skidmore College

State University of New York
Albany
Binghamton
Buffalo
College at Brockport
College at Buffalo
College at Cortland
College at Fredonia
College at Geneseo
College at Oneonta
College at Plattsburgh
College at Potsdam
College of Agriculture and
Technology at Cobleskill
College of Agriculture and
Technology at Morrisville
College of Environmental Science
and Forestry
College of Technology at Alfred
College of Technology at Delhi
Farmingdale
New Paltz
Oswego
Stony Brook
Suffolk County Community College
Syracuse University
Tompkins-Cortland Community College
Touro College
Ulster County Community College
Union College
United States Merchant Marine Academy
United States Military Academy
University of Rochester
Utica College
Wagner College
Westchester Business Institute
Westchester Community College

North Carolina

Appalachian State University
Barber-Scotia College
Belmont Abbey College
Bennett College
Brevard College
Campbell University
Catawba College
Central Carolina Community College
Central Piedmont Community College
Cleveland Community College
Davidson College
Duke University
East Carolina University
Elizabeth City State University
Elon University
Fayetteville State University
Forsyth Technical Community College
Gardner-Webb University
Greensboro College
Guilford College
Isothermal Community College
Johnson C. Smith University
Lees-McRae College
Lenoir Community College
Lenoir-Rhyne College
Mars Hill College
Meredith College
Methodist College
Montreat College
Mount Olive College
North Carolina Agricultural and
Technical State University
North Carolina Central University
North Carolina State University
North Carolina Wesleyan College
Peace College
Pfeiffer University
Queens University of Charlotte
St. Andrews Presbyterian College
St. Augustine's College
Salem College
Sandhills Community College
Shaw University

University of North Carolina
Asheville
Chapel Hill
Charlotte
Greensboro
Pembroke
Wilmington
Wake Forest University
Warren Wilson College
Western Carolina University
Wilkes Community College
Wingate University
Winston-Salem State University

North Dakota

Jamestown College
Minot State University
North Dakota State University
University of North Dakota

Ohio

Ashland University
Baldwin-Wallace College
Bluffton College
Bowling Green State University
Case Western Reserve University
Cedarville University
Central Ohio Technical College
Central State University
Cincinnati State Technical and
Community College
Clark State Community College
Cleveland Institute of Art
Cleveland State University
College of Mount St. Joseph
Columbus State Community College
Cuyahoga Community College
Eastern Campus
Metropolitan Campus
Western Campus
Defiance College
Denison University
Franciscan University of Steubenville
Heidelberg College
Jefferson Community College
John Carroll University
Kent State University
Kent State University
East Liverpool Regional Campus
Salem Regional Campus
Stark Campus
Trumbull Campus
Tuscarawas Campus
Kenyon College
Malone College
Marietta College
Miami University
Hamilton Campus
Oxford Campus
Mount Union College
Mount Vernon Nazarene University
Oberlin College
Ohio Dominican College
Ohio Northern University
Ohio State University
Agricultural Technical Institute
Columbus Campus
Lima Campus
Mansfield Campus
Marion Campus
Newark Campus
Ohio University
Ohio Wesleyan University
Otterbein College
Owens Community College
Findlay Campus
Toledo
Pontifical College Josephinum
Shawnee State University
Sinclair Community College
University of Akron
University of Cincinnati
University of Dayton
University of Findlay
University of Rio Grande

University of Toledo
Walsh University
Wilmington College
Wittenberg University
Wright State University
Wright State University: Lake Campus
Xavier University
Youngstown State University

Oklahoma

Cameron University
Carl Albert State College
East Central University
Eastern Oklahoma State College
Langston University
Murray State College
Northeastern Oklahoma Agricultural and
Mechanical College
Northeastern State University
Northern Oklahoma College
Oklahoma Baptist University
Oklahoma Christian University of
Science and Arts
Oklahoma City Community College
Oklahoma City University
Oklahoma State University
Oklahoma State University
Oklahoma City
Oral Roberts University
Redlands Community College
Rose State College
St. Gregory's University
Seminole State College
Southeastern Oklahoma State University
Tulsa Community College
University of Central Oklahoma
University of Oklahoma
University of Tulsa
Western Oklahoma State College

Oregon

Clackamas Community College
Eastern Oregon University
George Fox University
Lewis & Clark College
Mount Hood Community College
Oregon State University
Pioneer Pacific College
Portland State University
Southern Oregon University
Southwestern Oregon Community
College
University of Oregon
University of Portland
Western Baptist College
Western Oregon University

Pennsylvania

Academy of Medical Arts and Business
Albright College
Arcadia University
Bloomsburg University of Pennsylvania
Bucknell University
Bucks County Community College
Cabrini College
California University of Pennsylvania
Cambria County Area Community
College
Carlow College
Carnegie Mellon University
Cedar Crest College
Central Pennsylvania College
Chestnut Hill College
Community College of Allegheny
County
Community College of Philadelphia
DeSales University
Delaware Valley College
Drexel University
Duquesne University
East Stroudsburg University of
Pennsylvania
Edinboro University of Pennsylvania
Elizabethtown College

Franklin & Marshall College
Geneva College
Grove City College
Gwynedd-Mercy College
Harrisburg Area Community College
Immaculata University
Indiana University of Pennsylvania
Juniata College
King's College
Kutztown University of Pennsylvania
La Roche College
La Salle University
Lafayette College
Lehigh Carbon Community College
Lehigh University
Lincoln University
Lock Haven University of Pennsylvania
Lycoming College
Marywood University
Mercyhurst College
Messiah College
Millersville University of Pennsylvania
Montgomery County Community
College
Moravian College
Muhlenberg College
Neumann College
Penn State
Abington
Altoona
Beaver
Berks
Delaware County
Dubois
Erie, The Behrend College
Fayette
Harrisburg
Hazleton
Lehigh Valley
McKeesport
Mont Alto
New Kensington
Shenango
University Park
Wilkes-Barre
Worthington Scranton
York
Philadelphia Biblical University
Philadelphia University
Point Park College
Robert Morris University
Rosemont College
St. Joseph's University
St. Vincent College
Seton Hill University
Shippensburg University of Pennsylvania
Slippery Rock University of
Pennsylvania
Swarthmore College
Temple University
Thiel College
University of Pennsylvania
University of Pittsburgh
University of Scranton
Villanova University
Washington and Jefferson College
Waynesburg College
West Chester University of Pennsylvania
Westmoreland County Community
College
Widener University
Wilkes University
Wilson College
York College of Pennsylvania

Puerto Rico

Atlantic College
Inter American University of Puerto Rico
Barranquitas Campus
Bayamon Campus
Fajardo Campus
Guayama Campus
Metropolitan Campus
San German Campus

Pontifical Catholic University of Puerto Rico
Technological College of San Juan
Turabo University
Universidad Metropolitana
Universidad del Este
University of Puerto Rico
 Bayamon University College
 Cayey University College
 Humacao
 Mayaguez Campus
 Medical Sciences Campus
 Ponce
 Rio Piedras Campus
 Utuado
University of the Sacred Heart

Rhode Island

Brown University
Bryant College
Community College of Rhode Island
Providence College
Rhode Island College
Roger Williams University
Salve Regina University
University of Rhode Island

South Carolina

Anderson College
Benedict College
Charleston Southern University
The Citadel
Claflin University
Clemson University
Coastal Carolina University
Coker College
College of Charleston
Columbia College
Converse College
Francis Marion University
Lander University
Limestone College
Morris College
Newberry College
North Greenville College
Presbyterian College
South Carolina State University
Southern Wesleyan University
University of South Carolina
University of South Carolina
 Aiken
 Lancaster
Voorhees College
Williamsburg Technical College
Winthrop University
York Technical College

South Dakota

Dakota State University
Dakota Wesleyan University
Mount Marty College
Northern State University
South Dakota State University
University of Sioux Falls
University of South Dakota

Tennessee

Austin Peay State University
Belmont University
Bryan College
Carson-Newman College
Chattanooga State Technical Community
 College
Christian Brothers University
Cleveland State Community College
Columbia State Community College
Crichton College
Dyersburg State Community College
East Tennessee State University
Fisk University
Freed-Hardeman University
Jackson State Community College
Johnson Bible College
King College

Lambuth University
Lee University
Maryville College
Middle Tennessee State University
Northeast State Technical Community
 College
Pellissippi State Technical Community
 College
Rhodes College
Roane State Community College
Southern Adventist University
Southwest Tennessee Community
 College
Tennessee State University
Tennessee Technological University
Tennessee Wesleyan College
Union University
University of Memphis
University of Tennessee
 Chattanooga
 Knoxville
 Martin
Vanderbilt University
Volunteer State Community College
Walters State Community College

Texas

Abilene Christian University
Alvin Community College
Amarillo College
Angelo State University
Austin College
Austin Community College
Baylor University
Brazosport College
Brookhaven College
Collin County Community College
 District
Concordia University at Austin
Del Mar College
East Texas Baptist University
Eastfield College
El Centro College
El Paso Community College
Galveston College
Grayson County College
Hallmark Institute of Aeronautics
Hill College
Houston Baptist University
Houston Community College System
Howard Payne University
Huston-Tillotson College
Jarvis Christian College
Lamar State College at Port Arthur
Lamar University
Laredo Community College
LeTourneau University
Lee College
Lubbock Christian University
McLennan Community College
McMurry University
Midland College
Midwestern State University
Mountain View College
North Harris Montgomery Community
 College District
Northwood University: Texas Campus
Palo Alto College
Paul Quinn College
Prairie View A&M University
Ranger College
Rice University
Richland College
St. Edward's University
St. Mary's University
St. Philip's College
Sam Houston State University
San Antonio College
San Jacinto College
 Central Campus
Schreiner University
Southern Methodist University
Southwest Texas State University
Southwestern Adventist University
Southwestern University

Stephen F. Austin State University
Sul Ross State University
Tarleton State University
Tarrant County College
Temple College
Texas A&M International University
Texas A&M University
Texas A&M University
 Commerce
 Kingsville
Texas Christian University
Texas College
Texas Lutheran University
Texas Southern University
Texas Tech University
Texas Woman's University
Trinity University
Trinity Valley Community College
Tyler Junior College
University of Houston
University of Houston
 Downtown
University of Mary Hardin-Baylor
University of North Texas
University of St. Thomas
University of Texas
 Arlington
 Austin
 Brownsville
 Dallas
 El Paso
 Pan American
 San Antonio
Wayland Baptist University
West Texas A&M University
Western Texas College
Wiley College

Utah

Brigham Young University
Dixie State College of Utah
Snow College
Southern Utah University
University of Utah
Utah Career College
Utah State University
Utah Valley State College
Weber State University
Westminster College

Vermont

Castleton State College
Champlain College
Green Mountain College
Lyndon State College
Middlebury College
Norwich University
St. Michael's College
Southern Vermont College
Sterling College
University of Vermont
Vermont Technical College

Virginia

Averett University
Blue Ridge Community College
Bluefield College
Bridgewater College
Christendom College
College of William and Mary
Danville Community College
Eastern Mennonite University
Emory & Henry College
Ferrum College
George Mason University
Hampden-Sydney College
Hampton University
James Madison University
Liberty University
Longwood University
Lynchburg College
Mary Baldwin College
Norfolk State University
Old Dominion University

Paul D. Camp Community College
Piedmont Virginia Community College
Radford University
Randolph-Macon College
Randolph-Macon Woman's College
Roanoke College
Southside Virginia Community College
Southwest Virginia Community College
Sweet Briar College
Thomas Nelson Community College
University of Richmond
University of Virginia
University of Virginia's College at Wise
Virginia Commonwealth University
Virginia Intermont College
Virginia Military Institute
Virginia Polytechnic Institute and State
 University
Virginia State University
Virginia Union University
Virginia Wesleyan College
Washington and Lee University

Washington

Bellevue Community College
Central Washington University
Centralia College
Eastern Washington University
Edmonds Community College
Gonzaga University
Heritage College
Olympic College
Pacific Lutheran University
Peninsula College
Seattle Pacific University
Seattle University
Spokane Falls Community College
University of Puget Sound
University of Washington
Walla Walla College
Walla Walla Community College
Washington State University
Western Washington University
Whitman College
Whitworth College

West Virginia

Alderson-Broaddus College
Bethany College
Concord College
Davis and Elkins College
Fairmont State College
Glenville State College
Marshall University
Ohio Valley College
Potomac State College of West Virginia
 University
Shepherd College
West Liberty State College
West Virginia State College
West Virginia University
West Virginia Wesleyan College
Wheeling Jesuit University

Wisconsin

Cardinal Stritch University
Carroll College
Carthage College
Columbia College of Nursing
Edgewood College
Lakeland College
Lakeshore Technical College
Lawrence University
Marian College of Fond du Lac
Marquette University
Milwaukee Area Technical College
Mount Mary College
St. Norbert College

University of Wisconsin
    Baraboo/Sauk County
    Eau Claire
    Fond du Lac
    Fox Valley
    La Crosse
    Madison
    Marathon County
    Milwaukee
    Oshkosh
    Parkside
    Platteville
    River Falls
    Stout
    Superior
    Washington County
    Waukesha
    Whitewater

Wyoming

Central Wyoming College
University of Wyoming
Western Wyoming Community College

Independent study

Alabama

Alabama Southern Community College
American College of Computer and
    Information Sciences
Athens State University
Auburn University
Auburn University at Montgomery
Birmingham-Southern College
Central Alabama Community College
Chattahoochee Valley Community
    College
Community College of the Air Force
Concordia College
Faulkner University
Harry M. Ayers State Technical College
Heritage Christian University
Huntingdon College
Jacksonville State University
James H. Faulkner State Community
    College
Jefferson Davis Community College
Jefferson State Community College
Judson College
Miles College
Northeast Alabama Community College
Northwest-Shoals Community College
Samford University
Snead State Community College
Southeastern Bible College
Southern Christian University
Spring Hill College
Stillman College
Talladega College
Troy State University
Troy State University Dothan
Troy State University in Montgomery
Tuskegee University
University of Alabama
University of Alabama
    Birmingham
    Huntsville
University of Mobile
University of Montevallo
University of North Alabama
University of South Alabama
Virginia College

Alaska

Alaska Pacific University
Prince William Sound Community
    College
Sheldon Jackson College
University of Alaska
    Anchorage
    Fairbanks
    Southeast

Arizona

American Indian College of the
    Assemblies of God
Arizona State University
Arizona Western College
Art Institute
    of Phoenix
Central Arizona College
Cochise College
Eastern Arizona College
Embry-Riddle Aeronautical University:
    Prescott Campus
Estrella Mountain Community College
Gateway Community College
Northern Arizona University
Paradise Valley Community College
Phoenix College
Pima Community College
Prescott College
Rio Salado College
South Mountain Community College
University of Arizona
University of Phoenix
Yavapai College

Arkansas

Arkansas Baptist College
Arkansas State University
Arkansas State University
    Beebe
Arkansas Tech University
Crowley's Ridge College
Harding University
Hendrix College
John Brown University
Lyon College
North Arkansas College
Northwest Arkansas Community College
Philander Smith College
Phillips Community College of the
    University of Arkansas
Southeast Arkansas College
Southern Arkansas University Tech
University of Arkansas
University of Arkansas
    Community College at Batesville
    Community College at Hope
    Cossatot Community College of the
    Fort Smith
    Little Rock
    Monticello
    Pine Bluff
    for Medical Sciences
University of Central Arkansas
University of the Ozarks
Williams Baptist College

California

Academy of Art College
Antelope Valley College
Antioch Southern California
    Los Angeles
    Santa Barbara
Art Center College of Design
Art Institute
    of California - Orange County
Azusa Pacific University
Barstow College
Bethany College
Bethesda Christian University
Biola University
Cabrillo College
California Baptist University
California College of Arts and Crafts
California Institute of Technology
California Institute of the Arts
California Polytechnic State University:
    San Luis Obispo

California State University
    Bakersfield
    Chico
    Dominguez Hills
    Fresno
    Fullerton
    Hayward
    Long Beach
    Los Angeles
    Monterey Bay
    Northridge
    Sacramento
    San Bernardino
    San Marcos
    Stanislaus
Cerro Coso Community College
Chabot College
Chapman University
Christian Heritage College
Citrus College
Claremont McKenna College
Coastline Community College
Cogswell Polytechnical College
College of Alameda
College of the Canyons
College of the Redwoods
College of the Sequoias
College of the Siskiyous
Columbia College
Concordia University
Contra Costa College
Cuesta College
Cuyamaca College
De Anza College
Deep Springs College
Diablo Valley College
Dominican School of Philosophy and
    Theology
Dominican University of California
East Los Angeles College
Fashion Institute of Design and
    Merchandising
Feather River College
Foothill College
Fresno Pacific University
Gavilan Community College
Glendale Community College
Golden West College
Grossmont Community College
Harvey Mudd College
Holy Names College
Hope International University
Humboldt State University
Imperial Valley College
Irvine Valley College
John F. Kennedy University
LIFE Pacific College
La Sierra University
Laney College
Las Positas College
Long Beach City College
Los Angeles Harbor College
Los Angeles Southwest College
Los Angeles Trade and Technical College
Los Medanos College
Loyola Marymount University
Marymount College
Master's College
Menlo College
Mills College
MiraCosta College
Modesto Junior College
Monterey Institute of International
    Studies
Monterey Peninsula College
Moorpark College
Mount St. Mary's College
Mount San Jacinto College
Napa Valley College
National Hispanic University
National University
Occidental College
Ohlone College
Orange Coast College
Otis College of Art and Design

Pacific Oaks College
Pacific Union College
Patten University
Pepperdine University
Pitzer College
Pomona College
Reedley College
St. Mary's College of California
Samuel Merritt College
San Diego City College
San Diego Mesa College
San Diego State University
San Francisco State University
San Jose Christian College
San Jose State University
Santa Barbara City College
Santa Clara University
Santa Monica College
Santa Rosa Junior College
Scripps College
Shasta College
Sierra College
Sonoma State University
Southern California Institute of
    Architecture
Southwestern College
Stanford University
Taft College
University of California
    Berkeley
    Davis
    Irvine
    Los Angeles
    Riverside
    San Diego
    Santa Barbara
    Santa Cruz
University of La Verne
University of Redlands
University of San Diego
University of San Francisco
University of Southern California
University of West Los Angeles
University of the Pacific
Vanguard University of Southern
    California
Ventura College
Victor Valley College
Vista Community College
West Valley College
Westwood College of Technology
    Inland Empire
Whittier College
Woodbury University

Colorado

Arapahoe Community College
Art Institute
    of Colorado
Blair Junior College
Colorado Christian University
Colorado College
Colorado Mountain College
    Alpine Campus
    Spring Valley Campus
    Timberline Campus
Colorado School of Mines
Colorado State University
Colorado State University
    Pueblo
Fort Lewis College
Front Range Community College
Mesa State College
Metropolitan State College of Denver
Morgan Community College
Naropa University
National American University
    Denver
Red Rocks Community College
Regis University
Trinidad State Junior College
United States Air Force Academy

University of Colorado
  Boulder
  Colorado Springs
  Denver
  Health Sciences Center
University of Denver
University of Northern Colorado

Connecticut

Albertus Magnus College
Asnuntuck Community College
Briarwood College
Capital Community College
Central Connecticut State University
Charter Oak State College
Connecticut College
Eastern Connecticut State University
Fairfield University
Gateway Community College
Holy Apostles College and Seminary
Housatonic Community College
Manchester Community College
Middlesex Community College
Naugatuck Valley Community College
Northwestern Connecticut Community
  College
Paier College of Art
Quinebaug Valley Community College
Quinnipiac University
Sacred Heart University
St. Joseph College
Southern Connecticut State University
Teikyo Post University
Three Rivers Community College
Trinity College
Tunxis Community College
United States Coast Guard Academy
University of Bridgeport
University of Connecticut
University of Hartford
University of New Haven
Wesleyan University
Western Connecticut State University
Yale University

Delaware

Delaware State University
University of Delaware
Wilmington College

District of Columbia

American University
Catholic University of America
Gallaudet University
George Washington University
Georgetown University
Howard University
Trinity College
University of the District of Columbia

Florida

Art Institute
  of Fort Lauderdale
Baptist College of Florida
Barry University
Beacon College
Bethune-Cookman College
Broward Community College
Carlos Albizu University
Chipola Junior College
Daytona Beach Community College
Eckerd College
Edward Waters College
Embry Riddle Aeronautical
  University-Extended Campus
Embry-Riddle Aeronautical University
Flagler College
Florida Agricultural and Mechanical
  University
Florida Atlantic University
Florida College
Florida Gulf Coast University
Florida International University
Florida Keys Community College

Florida Metropolitan University
  Melbourne Campus
  Orlando College North
  Tampa College
Florida Southern College
Florida State University
Gulf Coast Community College
Jacksonville University
Jones College
Lake City Community College
Lake-Sumter Community College
Manatee Community College
Miami-Dade Community College
New College of Florida
Northwood University
  Florida Campus
Okaloosa-Walton Community College
Palm Beach Atlantic University
Palm Beach Community College
Pasco-Hernando Community College
Pensacola Junior College
Polk Community College
Ringling School of Art and Design
Rollins College
St. John Vianney College Seminary
St. Leo University
St. Petersburg College
St. Thomas University
Santa Fe Community College
Schiller International University
Seminole Community College
South Florida Community College
Southeastern College of the Assemblies
  of God
Stetson University
Tallahassee Community College
Talmudic College of Florida
University of Florida
University of Miami
University of North Florida
University of South Florida
University of Tampa
Valencia Community College
Warner Southern College

Georgia

Abraham Baldwin Agricultural College
Agnes Scott College
Albany State University
Art Institute
  of Atlanta
Atlanta College of Art
Atlanta Metropolitan College
Augusta State University
Berry College
Brenau University
Brewton-Parker College
Clark Atlanta University
Clayton College and State University
Coastal Georgia Community College
Columbus State University
Covenant College
Dalton State College
Darton College
East Georgia College
Emmanuel College
Emory University
Floyd College
Georgia College and State University
Georgia Institute of Technology
Georgia Military College
Georgia Southern University
Georgia Southwestern State University
Georgia State University
Herzing College
Kennesaw State University
LaGrange College
Mercer University
Morris Brown College
North Georgia College & State
  University
Oglethorpe University
Oxford College of Emory University
Paine College
Piedmont College

Reinhardt College
Savannah College of Art and Design
Savannah State University
Shorter College
South Georgia College
South University
Southern Polytechnic State University
Spelman College
State University of West Georgia
Truett-McConnell College
University of Georgia
Valdosta State University
Waycross College
Wesleyan College

Hawaii

Brigham Young University-Hawaii
Chaminade University of Honolulu
Hawaii Business College
Hawaii Pacific University
University of Hawaii
  Hawaii Community College
  Hilo
  Honolulu Community College
  Leeward Community College
  Manoa
  Maui Community College
  West Oahu

Idaho

Albertson College of Idaho
Boise Bible College
Boise State University
Idaho State University
Lewis-Clark State College
North Idaho College
Northwest Nazarene University
University of Idaho

Illinois

American Academy of Art
Augustana College
Aurora University
Benedictine University
Black Hawk College
Black Hawk College
  East Campus
Blackburn College
Bradley University
Carl Sandburg College
Chicago State University
City Colleges of Chicago
  Harold Washington College
  Kennedy-King College
  Olive-Harvey College
  Richard J. Daley College
  Wright College
College of DuPage
College of Lake County
Columbia College Chicago
Concordia University
Danville Area Community College
De Paul University
Dominican University
East-West University
Eastern Illinois University
Elgin Community College
Elmhurst College
Eureka College
Governors State University
Greenville College
Heartland Community College
Illinois College
Illinois Eastern Community Colleges
  Frontier Community College
  Lincoln Trail College
  Olney Central College
  Wabash Valley College
Illinois Institute of Technology
Illinois State University
Illinois Wesleyan University
International Academy of Design and
  Technology
John A. Logan College

John Wood Community College
Joliet Junior College
Judson College
Kankakee Community College
Kaskaskia College
Kendall College
Kishwaukee College
Knox College
Lake Forest College
Lake Land College
Lakeview College of Nursing
Lewis University
Lincoln Christian College and Seminary
Lincoln College
Lincoln Land Community College
MacMurray College
McHenry County College
McKendree College
Midstate College
Millikin University
Monmouth College
Moody Bible Institute
Moraine Valley Community College
NAES College
National-Louis University
North Central College
North Park University
Northeastern Illinois University
Northern Illinois University
Northwestern University
Oakton Community College
Olivet Nazarene University
Parkland College
Prairie State College
Principia College
Quincy University
Rend Lake College
Richland Community College
Rock Valley College
Rockford Business College
Rockford College
Roosevelt University
St. Augustine College
St. Xavier University
Sauk Valley Community College
School of the Art Institute of Chicago
Shawnee Community College
Shimer College
Southeastern Illinois College
Southern Illinois University Carbondale
Southern Illinois University Edwardsville
Southwestern Illinois College
Springfield College in Illinois
Trinity Christian College
Trinity International University
Triton College
University of Chicago
University of Illinois
  Chicago
  Springfield
  Urbana-Champaign
University of St. Francis
VanderCook College of Music
Waubonsee Community College
West Suburban College of Nursing
Western Illinois University
Wheaton College
William Rainey Harper College

Indiana

Ancilla College
Anderson University
Ball State University
Bethel College
Butler University
Calumet College of St. Joseph
DePauw University
Earlham College
Franklin College
Goshen College
Hanover College
Huntington College
Indiana Institute of Technology
Indiana State University

Indiana University
    Bloomington
    East
    Kokomo
    Northwest
    Southeast
Indiana University-Purdue University
    Fort Wayne
Indiana University-Purdue University
    Indianapolis
Indiana Wesleyan University
International Business College
Ivy Tech State College
    Kokomo
    Southwest
    Whitewater
Manchester College
Marian College
Michiana College
Oakland City University
Purdue University
Purdue University
    Calumet
    North Central Campus
Rose-Hulman Institute of Technology
St. Joseph's College
Saint Mary's College
St. Mary-of-the-Woods College
Taylor University
Taylor University: Fort Wayne
University of Evansville
University of Indianapolis
University of Notre Dame
University of St. Francis
University of Southern Indiana
Valparaiso University
Vincennes University
Wabash College

Iowa

Allen College
Briar Cliff University
Buena Vista University
Central College
Clarke College
Clinton Community College
Coe College
Cornell College
Des Moines Area Community College
Divine Word College
Dordt College
Drake University
Franciscan University
Graceland University
Grand View College
Grinnell College
Hamilton College
Hawkeye Community College
Indian Hills Community College
Iowa Central Community College
Iowa State University
Iowa Wesleyan College
Iowa Western Community College
Kirkwood Community College
Loras College
Luther College
Maharishi University of Management
Marshalltown Community College
Morningside College
Mount Mercy College
Muscatine Community College
North Iowa Area Community College
Northeast Iowa Community College
Northwest Iowa Community College
Northwestern College
St. Ambrose University
Scott Community College
Simpson College
Southeastern Community College
    North Campus
    South Campus
Southwestern Community College
University of Dubuque
University of Iowa
University of Northern Iowa

Upper Iowa University
Vennard College
Waldorf College
Wartburg College
Western Iowa Tech Community College
William Penn University

Kansas

Allen County Community College
Baker University
Barclay College
Barton County Community College
Benedictine College
Bethany College
Bethel College
Butler County Community College
Central Christian College
Cloud County Community College
Dodge City Community College
Donnelly College
Emporia State University
Fort Hays State University
Fort Scott Community College
Friends University
Haskell Indian Nations University
Hesston College
Highland Community College
Hutchinson Community College
Independence Community College
Johnson County Community College
Kansas City Kansas Community College
Kansas State University
Kansas Wesleyan University
McPherson College
MidAmerica Nazarene University
Newman University
Pittsburg State University
St. Mary College
Seward County Community College
Southwestern College
Sterling College
Tabor College
University of Kansas
University of Kansas Medical Center
Washburn University of Topeka
Wichita State University

Kentucky

Alice Lloyd College
Asbury College
Beckfield College
Bellarmine University
Berea College
Brescia University
Campbellsville University
Centre College
Cumberland College
Daymar College
Georgetown College
Henderson Community College
Jefferson Community College
Kentucky Christian College
Kentucky Wesleyan College
Lexington Community College
Lindsey Wilson College
Madisonville Community College
Maysville Community College
Mid-Continent College
Morehead State University
Murray State University
Pikeville College
Prestonsburg Community College
St. Catharine College
Somerset Community College
Spalding University
Spencerian College
Spencerian College: Lexington
Sullivan University
Thomas More College
Transylvania University
Union College
University of Kentucky
University of Louisville

Louisiana

Centenary College of Louisiana
Delgado Community College
Dillard University
Grambling State University
Grantham University
Louisiana College
Louisiana State University
    Eunice
Louisiana State University and
    Agricultural and Mechanical College
Louisiana Tech University
Loyola University New Orleans
McNeese State University
Nicholls State University
Nunez Community College
Our Lady of Holy Cross College
Remington College
Southeastern Louisiana University
Southern University and Agricultural and
    Mechanical College
Tulane University
University of Louisiana at Lafayette
University of New Orleans

Maine

Andover College
Bates College
Beal College
Bowdoin College
Central Maine Technical College
Colby College
College of the Atlantic
Husson College
Maine College of Art
St. Joseph's College
Thomas College
University of Maine
University of Maine
    Augusta
    Farmington
    Machias
    Presque Isle
University of New England
University of Southern Maine

Maryland

Allegany College
Anne Arundel Community College
Baltimore Hebrew University
Bowie State University
Capitol College
Carroll Community College
Cecil Community College
Chesapeake College
College of Notre Dame of Maryland
Columbia Union College
Community College of Baltimore County
    Catonsville
    Dundalk
    Essex
Coppin State College
Frederick Community College
Frostburg State University
Goucher College
Hagerstown Community College
Harford Community College
Hood College
Howard Community College
Johns Hopkins University
Loyola College in Maryland
Maryland College of Art and Design
Maryland Institute College of Art
McDaniel College
Montgomery College
    Rockville Campus
Morgan State University
Mount St. Mary's College
St. Mary's College of Maryland
Salisbury University
Sojourner-Douglass College
Towson University
United States Naval Academy
University of Baltimore

University of Maryland
    Baltimore County
    College Park
Villa Julie College
Washington Bible College
Washington College

Massachusetts

American International College
Amherst College
Anna Maria College
Art Institute of Boston at Lesley
    University
Assumption College
Atlantic Union College
Babson College
Bay Path College
Bay State College
Becker College
Bentley College
Berkshire Community College
Boston Architectural Center
Boston College
Boston Conservatory
Boston University
Brandeis University
Bridgewater State College
Bunker Hill Community College
Cape Cod Community College
Clark University
College of the Holy Cross
Dean College
Elms College
Emerson College
Emmanuel College
Endicott College
Fitchburg State College
Framingham State College
Franklin W. Olin College of Engineering
Gordon College
Greenfield Community College
Hampshire College
Harvard College
Hebrew College
Hellenic College/Holy Cross
Laboure College
Lasell College
Lesley University
Marian Court College
Massachusetts Bay Community College
Massachusetts College of Art
Massachusetts College of Liberal Arts
Massachusetts College of Pharmacy and
    Health Sciences
Massasoit Community College
Merrimack College
Montserrat College of Art
Mount Holyoke College
Mount Ida College
Mount Wachusett Community College
New England Conservatory of Music
Newbury College
Nichols College
Northeastern University
Pine Manor College
Quinsigamond Community College
Regis College
Roxbury Community College
St. John's Seminary College
Salem State College
Simmons College
Simon's Rock College of Bard
Smith College
Springfield College
Springfield Technical Community
    College
Stonehill College
Suffolk University
Tufts University
University of Massachusetts
    Amherst
    Boston
    Dartmouth
Urban College of Boston
Wellesley College

Wentworth Institute of Technology
Western New England College
Westfield State College
Wheaton College
Williams College
Worcester Polytechnic Institute

Michigan

Adrian College
Alma College
Aquinas College
Baker College
    of Auburn Hills
    of Cadillac
    of Clinton Township
    of Jackson
    of Muskegon
    of Owosso
    of Port Huron
Calvin College
Central Michigan University
Cleary University
College for Creative Studies
Concordia University
Cornerstone University
Davenport University
    Eastern Region
    Midland
Davenport University - Western Region
Eastern Michigan University
Finlandia University
Glen Oaks Community College
Gogebic Community College
Grace Bible College
Grand Rapids Community College
Grand Valley State University
Hillsdale College
Hope College
Jackson Community College
Kalamazoo College
Kellogg Community College
Kettering University
Kirtland Community College
Lansing Community College
Lawrence Technological University
Macomb Community College
Madonna University
Marygrove College
Michigan State University
Monroe County Community College
Montcalm Community College
Mott Community College
Muskegon Community College
North Central Michigan College
Northern Michigan University
Northwestern Michigan College
Northwood University
Oakland University
Reformed Bible College
Saginaw Valley State University
Siena Heights University
Southwestern Michigan College
University of Michigan
University of Michigan
    Dearborn
    Flint
Washtenaw Community College
Wayne County Community College
Wayne State University
West Shore Community College
Western Michigan University
William Tyndale College

Minnesota

Alexandria Technical College
Anoka-Ramsey Community College
Augsburg College
Bemidji State University
Bethany Lutheran College
Bethel College
Carleton College
Central Lakes College
College of St. Benedict
College of St. Catherine
College of St. Scholastica

College of Visual Arts
Concordia College: Moorhead
Concordia University: St. Paul
Crossroads College
Crown College
Globe College
Gustavus Adolphus College
Hamline University
Hennepin Technical College
Hibbing Community College: A
    Technical and Community College
Itasca Community College
Lake Superior College: A Community
    and Technical College
Macalester College
Martin Luther College
Mesabi Range Community and Technical
    College
Metropolitan State University
Minneapolis Community and Technical
    College
Minnesota State University
    Mankato
    Moorhead
Minnesota West Community and
    Technical College: Worthington
    Campus
National American University
    St. Paul
Normandale Community College
North Central University
North Hennepin Community College
Northwestern College
Oak Hills Christian College
Pine Technical College
Rainy River Community College
Rochester Community and Technical
    College
St. Cloud State University
St. Cloud Technical College
St. John's University
St. Mary's University of Minnesota
St. Olaf College
Southwest State University
University of Minnesota
    Duluth
    Morris
    Twin Cities
University of St. Thomas
Vermilion Community College
Winona State University

Mississippi

Alcorn State University
Delta State University
Itawamba Community College
Mary Holmes College
Millsaps College
Mississippi College
Mississippi State University
Mississippi Valley State University
Northwest Mississippi Community
    College
Rust College
University of Mississippi
Wesley College

Missouri

Avila University
Blue River Community College
Calvary Bible College
Central Bible College
Central Methodist College
College of the Ozarks
Columbia College
Conception Seminary College
Cottey College
Crowder College
Culver-Stockton College
Drury University
East Central College
Fontbonne College
Global University
Hannibal-LaGrange College
Harris Stowe State College

Jefferson College
Kansas City Art Institute
Lindenwood University
Longview Community College
Maryville University of Saint Louis
Mineral Area College
Missouri Baptist University
Missouri Southern State College
Missouri Technical School
Missouri Valley College
National American University
    Kansas City
Northwest Missouri State University
Ozarks Technical Community College
Research College of Nursing
Rockhurst University
St. Charles Community College
St. Louis Community College
    St. Louis Community College at
        Florissant Valley
    St. Louis Community College at
        Forest Park
    St. Louis Community College at
        Meramec
St. Louis University
Southeast Missouri State University
Southwest Baptist University
Southwest Missouri State University
Stephens College
Three Rivers Community College
Truman State University
University of Missouri
    Columbia
    Kansas City
    Rolla
    St. Louis
Washington University in St. Louis
Webster University
Wentworth Military Academy
Westminster College
William Jewell College
William Woods University

Montana

Carroll College
Dawson Community College
Flathead Valley Community College
Miles Community College
Montana State University
    Billings
    Billings College of Technology
    Bozeman
Montana Tech of the University of
    Montana
Rocky Mountain College
University of Great Falls
University of Montana-Missoula
University of Montana: Western

Nebraska

Bellevue University
Central Community College
Chadron State College
Clarkson College
College of Saint Mary
Concordia University
Creighton University
Dana College
Doane College
Grace University
Hastings College
Lincoln School of Commerce
Little Priest Tribal College
Metropolitan Community College
Mid Plains Community College Area
Midland Lutheran College
Nebraska Christian College
Nebraska Indian Community College
Nebraska Methodist College of Nursing
    and Allied Health
Nebraska Wesleyan University
Northeast Community College
Peru State College
Southeast Community College
    Lincoln Campus

Union College
University of Nebraska
    Kearney
    Lincoln
    Omaha
Wayne State College
Western Nebraska Community College
York College

Nevada

Community College of Southern Nevada
Great Basin College
Las Vegas College
Morrison University
Sierra Nevada College
University of Nevada
    Las Vegas
    Reno
Western Nevada Community College

New Hampshire

Chester College of New England
Colby-Sawyer College
College for Lifelong Learning
Daniel Webster College
Dartmouth College
Franklin Pierce College
Hesser College
Keene State College
New England College
New Hampshire Community Technical
    College
    Berlin
    Claremont
    Laconia
    Manchester
    Nashua
    Stratham
Plymouth State College
Rivier College
St. Anselm College
Southern New Hampshire University
Thomas More College of Liberal Arts
University of New Hampshire
University of New Hampshire at
    Manchester

New Jersey

Assumption College for Sisters
Atlantic Cape Community College
Bloomfield College
Brookdale Community College
Burlington County College
Caldwell College
Camden County College
Centenary College
The College of New Jersey
College of St. Elizabeth
County College of Morris
Cumberland County College
Drew University
Essex County College
Fairleigh Dickinson University
    College at Florham
    Metropolitan Campus
Felician College
Georgian Court College
Hudson County Community College
Kean University
Mercer County Community College
Middlesex County College
Monmouth University
Montclair State University
New Jersey City University
New Jersey Institute of Technology
Ocean County College
Passaic County Community College
Princeton University
Ramapo College of New Jersey
Raritan Valley Community College
Richard Stockton College of New Jersey
Rider University
Rowan University

Rutgers, The State University of New
    Jersey
        Camden Regional Campus
        New Brunswick Regional Campus
        Newark Regional Campus
St. Peter's College
Salem Community College
Seton Hall University
Stevens Institute of Technology
Sussex County Community College
Thomas Edison State College
University of Medicine and Dentistry of
    New Jersey
        School of Health Related
            Professions
Warren County Community College
William Paterson University of New
    Jersey

New Mexico

Clovis Community College
College of Santa Fe
Dona Ana Branch Community College of
    New Mexico State University
Eastern New Mexico University
Eastern New Mexico University: Roswell
    Campus
Institute of American Indian Arts
National American University
New Mexico Highlands University
New Mexico Institute of Mining and
    Technology
New Mexico State University
New Mexico State University
    Alamogordo
San Juan College
Santa Fe Community College
University of New Mexico
Western New Mexico University

New York

Adelphi University
Adirondack Community College
Albany College of Pharmacy
Alfred University
Bard College
Barnard College
Briarcliffe College
Broome Community College
Bryant & Stratton Business Institute
    Albany
Canisius College
Cazenovia College
City University of New York
    Baruch College
    Borough of Manhattan Community
        College
    Bronx Community College
    Brooklyn College
    City College
    College of Staten Island
    Hunter College
    John Jay College of Criminal
        Justice
    Kingsborough Community College
    La Guardia Community College
    Medgar Evers College
    Queens College
    Queensborough Community
        College
    York College
Clarkson University
Clinton Community College
Colgate University
College of Mount St. Vincent
College of New Rochelle
College of New Rochelle: School of New
    Resources
Columbia University
    School of Nursing
Concordia College
Cooper Union for the Advancement of
    Science and Art
Cornell University
Corning Community College

D'Youville College
Daemen College
Dominican College of Blauvelt
Dowling College
Dutchess Community College
Elmira College
Erie Community College
    City Campus
    North Campus
    South Campus
Eugene Lang College/New School
    University
Excelsior College
Finger Lakes Community College
Fordham University
Fulton-Montgomery Community College
Genesee Community College
Hamilton College
Hartwick College
Hilbert College
Hobart and William Smith Colleges
Hofstra University
Houghton College
Iona College
Ithaca College
Jamestown Community College
Jefferson Community College
Keuka College
Laboratory Institute of Merchandising
Le Moyne College
Long Island Business Institute
Long Island University
    C. W. Post Campus
    Southampton College
Machzikei Hadath Rabbinical College
Manhattan College
Manhattanville College
Maria College
Marist College
Marymount College of Fordham
    University
Marymount Manhattan College
Medaille College
Mercy College
Mildred Elley
Mohawk Valley Community College
Molloy College
Monroe Community College
Mount St. Mary College
Nazareth College of Rochester
New York Institute of Technology
New York School of Interior Design
New York University
Niagara County Community College
Niagara University
Nyack College
Ohr Somayach Tanenbaum Education
    Center
Onondaga Community College
Orange County Community College
Pace University
Pace University: Pleasantville/Briarcliff
Parsons School of Design
Paul Smith's College
Pratt Institute
Rensselaer Polytechnic Institute
Roberts Wesleyan College
Rochester Business Institute
Rochester Institute of Technology
Rockland Community College
Russell Sage College
Sage College of Albany
St. Bonaventure University
St. John Fisher College
St. John's University
St. Joseph's College
St. Joseph's College: Suffolk Campus
St. Lawrence University
Sarah Lawrence College
Schenectady County Community College
School of Visual Arts
Skidmore College

State University of New York
    Albany
    Binghamton
    Buffalo
    College at Brockport
    College at Buffalo
    College at Cortland
    College at Fredonia
    College at Geneseo
    College at Old Westbury
    College at Oneonta
    College at Plattsburgh
    College at Potsdam
    College of Agriculture and
        Technology at Cobleskill
    College of Environmental Science
        and Forestry
    College of Technology at Alfred
    College of Technology at Canton
    College of Technology at Delhi
    Empire State College
    Health Science Center at Stony
        Brook
    Institute of Technology at
        Utica/Rome
    Maritime College
    New Paltz
    Oswego
    Purchase
    Stony Brook
    Upstate Medical University
Suffolk County Community College
Syracuse University
Tompkins-Cortland Community College
Touro College
Trocaire College
Ulster County Community College
Union College
United States Military Academy
University of Rochester
Utica College
Vassar College
Wagner College
Webb Institute
Wells College
Westchester Community College
Yeshiva University

North Carolina

Alamance Community College
Appalachian State University
Asheville Buncombe Technical
    Community College
Barton College
Beaufort County Community College
Belmont Abbey College
Bennett College
Bladen Community College
Brevard College
Caldwell Community College and
    Technical Institute
Campbell University
Catawba College
Catawba Valley Community College
Central Carolina Community College
Central Piedmont Community College
Chowan College
Cleveland Community College
Coastal Carolina Community College
College of the Albemarle
Craven Community College
Davidson College
Davidson County Community College
Duke University
East Carolina University
Edgecombe Community College
Elizabeth City State University
Elon University
Fayetteville State University
Forsyth Technical Community College
Gardner-Webb University
Gaston College
Greensboro College
Guilford College
Guilford Technical Community College

Halifax Community College
Haywood Community College
Isothermal Community College
John Wesley College
Johnson C. Smith University
Lees-McRae College
Lenoir-Rhyne College
Livingstone College
Louisburg College
Mars Hill College
Martin Community College
Mayland Community College
Meredith College
Methodist College
Mitchell Community College
Montgomery Community College
Montreat College
Mount Olive College
North Carolina Agricultural and
    Technical State University
North Carolina Central University
North Carolina School of the Arts
North Carolina State University
North Carolina Wesleyan College
Pamlico Community College
Peace College
Pfeiffer University
Piedmont Baptist College
Piedmont Community College
Queens University of Charlotte
Richmond Community College
Roanoke-Chowan Community College
Rockingham Community College
St. Andrews Presbyterian College
St. Augustine's College
Salem College
Sampson Community College
Sandhills Community College
Shaw University
South Piedmont Community College
Southeastern Community College
Southwestern Community College
Surry Community College
Tri-County Community College
University of North Carolina
    Asheville
    Chapel Hill
    Charlotte
    Greensboro
    Pembroke
    Wilmington
Vance-Granville Community College
Wake Forest University
Warren Wilson College
Western Carolina University
Wilkes Community College
Wingate University
Winston-Salem State University

North Dakota

Dickinson State University
Jamestown College
Minot State University
Minot State University: Bottineau
    Campus
North Dakota State University
Trinity Bible College
University of Mary
University of North Dakota

Ohio

Antioch College
Antioch University McGregor
Art Academy of Cincinnati
Ashland University
Baldwin-Wallace College
Bluffton College
Bowling Green State University
Bowling Green State University:
    Firelands College
Bryant & Stratton College
Bryant & Stratton College
    Cleveland West
    Willoughby Hills
Case Western Reserve University

Cedarville University
Central State University
Chatfield College
Cincinnati Bible College and Seminary
Cincinnati State Technical and
 Community College
Circleville Bible College
Clark State Community College
Cleveland Institute of Art
Cleveland Institute of Electronics
Cleveland Institute of Music
Cleveland State University
College of Mount St. Joseph
College of Wooster
Columbus College of Art and Design
Columbus State Community College
Cuyahoga Community College
 Eastern Campus
 Metropolitan Campus
 Western Campus
David N. Myers College
Defiance College
Denison University
Edison State Community College
Franciscan University of Steubenville
Franklin University
Heidelberg College
Hiram College
Hocking Technical College
James A. Rhodes State College
Jefferson Community College
John Carroll University
Kent State University
Kent State University
 Ashtabula Regional Campus
 East Liverpool Regional Campus
 Stark Campus
 Trumbull Campus
 Tuscarawas Campus
Kenyon College
Lake Erie College
Lakeland Community College
Laura and Alvin Siegal College of Judaic
 Studies
Lorain County Community College
Lourdes College
Malone College
Marietta College
Marion Technical College
Miami University
 Hamilton Campus
 Middletown Campus
 Oxford Campus
Miami-Jacobs College
Mount Union College
Mount Vernon Nazarene University
Muskingum College
North Central State College
Northwest State Community College
Notre Dame College
Oberlin College
Ohio Business College
Ohio Business College: Sandusky
Ohio Dominican College
Ohio Institute of Photography and
 Technology
Ohio Northern University
Ohio State University
 Agricultural Technical Institute
 Columbus Campus
 Lima Campus
 Mansfield Campus
 Marion Campus
 Newark Campus
Ohio University
Ohio University
 Chillicothe Campus
 Eastern Campus
 Lancaster Campus
 Zanesville Campus
Ohio Wesleyan University
Otterbein College
Owens Community College
 Toledo
Pontifical College Josephinum

Shawnee State University
Sinclair Community College
Southeastern Business College
Stark State College of Technology
Stautzenberger College
Tiffin University
Union Institute & University
University of Akron
University of Cincinnati
University of Cincinnati
 Clermont College
 Raymond Walters College
University of Dayton
University of Findlay
University of Rio Grande
University of Toledo
Urbana University
Ursuline College
Virginia Marti College of Art and Design
Walsh University
Washington State Community College
Wilmington College
Wittenberg University
Wright State University
Wright State University: Lake Campus
Xavier University

Oklahoma

Cameron University
Carl Albert State College
East Central University
Northeastern State University
Northern Oklahoma College
Northwestern Oklahoma State University
Oklahoma Baptist University
Oklahoma Christian University of
 Science and Arts
Oklahoma City Community College
Oklahoma City University
Oklahoma Panhandle State University
Oklahoma State University
Oklahoma State University
 Oklahoma City
Oklahoma Wesleyan University
Oral Roberts University
Redlands Community College
Rogers State University
Rose State College
Southeastern Oklahoma State University
Southern Nazarene University
Southwestern Christian University
Southwestern Oklahoma State University
Tulsa Community College
University of Central Oklahoma
University of Oklahoma
University of Science and Arts of
 Oklahoma
University of Tulsa

Oregon

Art Institute
 of Portland
Central Oregon Community College
Chemeketa Community College
Clackamas Community College
Concordia University
Eastern Oregon University
Eugene Bible College
George Fox University
Lane Community College
Lewis & Clark College
Linfield College
Linn-Benton Community College
Marylhurst University
Mount Hood Community College
Northwest Christian College
Oregon State University
Pacific Northwest College of Art
Pacific University
Portland State University
Reed College
Rogue Community College
Southern Oregon University
Southwestern Oregon Community
 College

University of Oregon
University of Portland
Warner Pacific College
Western Baptist College
Western Oregon University
Willamette University

Pennsylvania

Albright College
Allegheny College
Arcadia University
Art Institute
 of Philadelphia
Baptist Bible College of Pennsylvania
Bloomsburg University of Pennsylvania
Bryn Athyn College of the New Church
Bryn Mawr College
Bucknell University
Bucks County Community College
Butler County Community College
Cabrini College
California University of Pennsylvania
Cambria County Area Community
 College
Carlow College
Carnegie Mellon University
Cedar Crest College
Chatham College
Chestnut Hill College
Cheyney University of Pennsylvania
Community College of Allegheny
 County
DeSales University
Delaware County Community College
Delaware Valley College
Dickinson College
Drexel University
Duquesne University
Edinboro University of Pennsylvania
Education Direct: Center for Degree
 Studies
Elizabethtown College
Erie Business Center
Franklin & Marshall College
Geneva College
Gettysburg College
Gratz College
Grove City College
Gwynedd-Mercy College
Harrisburg Area Community College
Haverford College
Holy Family University
Immaculata University
Indiana University of Pennsylvania
Juniata College
Keystone College
King's College
Kutztown University of Pennsylvania
La Roche College
La Salle University
Lafayette College
Lancaster Bible College
Lebanon Valley College of Pennsylvania
Lehigh Carbon Community College
Lehigh University
Lincoln University
Lock Haven University of Pennsylvania
Luzerne County Community College
Lycoming College
Manor College
Marywood University
Mercyhurst College
Messiah College
Millersville University of Pennsylvania
Montgomery County Community
 College
Moravian College
Mount Aloysius College
Muhlenberg College
Neumann College
PJA School
Peirce College

Penn State
 Abington
 Altoona
 Beaver
 Berks
 Delaware County
 Dubois
 Erie, The Behrend College
 Fayette
 Harrisburg
 Hazleton
 Lehigh Valley
 McKeesport
 Mont Alto
 New Kensington
 Schuylkill - Capital College
 Shenango
 University Park
 Wilkes-Barre
 Worthington Scranton
 York
Pennsylvania Institute of Technology
Philadelphia Biblical University
Philadelphia University
Point Park College
Reading Area Community College
Robert Morris University
Rosemont College
St. Charles Borromeo Seminary -
 Overbrook
St. Joseph's University
St. Vincent College
Seton Hill University
Shippensburg University of Pennsylvania
Slippery Rock University of
 Pennsylvania
Swarthmore College
Temple University
Thiel College
University of Pennsylvania
University of Pittsburgh
University of Pittsburgh
 Bradford
 Greensburg
 Johnstown
 Titusville
University of Scranton
Valley Forge Christian College
Villanova University
Washington and Jefferson College
Waynesburg College
West Chester University of Pennsylvania
Westmoreland County Community
 College
Widener University
Wilkes University
Wilson College
York College of Pennsylvania

Puerto Rico

Bayamon Central University
Huertas Junior College
Inter American University of Puerto Rico
 Bayamon Campus
 Fajardo Campus
 Guayama Campus
 Metropolitan Campus
 San German Campus
Pontifical Catholic University of Puerto
 Rico
Turabo University
Universidad Metropolitana
Universidad del Este
University of the Sacred Heart

Rhode Island

Brown University
Bryant College
Providence College
Rhode Island College
Rhode Island School of Design
Roger Williams University
Salve Regina University
University of Rhode Island

South Carolina

Aiken Technical College
Anderson College
Central Carolina Technical College
The Citadel
Claflin University
Clemson University
Coastal Carolina University
Coker College
College of Charleston
Columbia College
Columbia International University
Converse College
Denmark Technical College
Erskine College
Florence-Darlington Technical College
Forrest Junior College
Francis Marion University
Furman University
Horry-Georgetown Technical College
Lander University
Limestone College
Newberry College
North Greenville College
Northeastern Technical College
Orangeburg-Calhoun Technical College
Piedmont Technical College
Presbyterian College
Southern Wesleyan University
Spartanburg Methodist College
Spartanburg Technical College
Technical College of the Lowcountry
Trident Technical College
University of South Carolina
University of South Carolina
    Aiken
    Lancaster
    Salkehatchie Regional Campus
    Spartanburg
    Sumter
    Union
Voorhees College
Williamsburg Technical College
Winthrop University
Wofford College

South Dakota

Augustana College
Black Hills State University
Dakota State University
Dakota Wesleyan University
Kilian Community College
Mitchell Technical Institute
Mount Marty College
Northern State University
Sinte Gleska University
South Dakota School of Mines and
   Technology
South Dakota State University
University of Sioux Falls
University of South Dakota

Tennessee

Austin Peay State University
Belmont University
Carson-Newman College
Chattanooga State Technical Community
   College
Christian Brothers University
Cleveland State Community College
Crichton College
Draughons Junior College of Business:
   Nashville
Dyersburg State Community College
East Tennessee State University
Fisk University
Freed-Hardeman University
Johnson Bible College
King College
Lambuth University
Lee University
Maryville College
Memphis College of Art
Middle Tennessee State University
Milligan College

Pellissippi State Technical Community
   College
Remington College
   Southeast College of Technology
Rhodes College
Roane State Community College
Southern Adventist University
Southwest Tennessee Community
   College
Tennessee State University
Tennessee Technological University
Tennessee Wesleyan College
Tusculum College
Union University
University of Memphis
University of Tennessee
   Chattanooga
   Knoxville
   Martin
Vanderbilt University
Volunteer State Community College

Texas

Abilene Christian University
Amberton University
Angelo State University
Arlington Baptist College
Austin College
Austin Community College
Central Texas College
College of the Mainland
Concordia University at Austin
Dallas Baptist University
Dallas Christian College
Del Mar College
East Texas Baptist University
Eastfield College
El Paso Community College
Hardin-Simmons University
Houston Baptist University
Houston Community College System
Howard Payne University
Huston-Tillotson College
Lamar State College at Port Arthur
Lamar University
LeTourneau University
Lee College
Lon Morris College
McMurry University
Midwestern State University
Mountain View College
North Harris Montgomery Community
   College District
Northwood University: Texas Campus
Prairie View A&M University
Rice University
Richland College
St. Mary's University
Sam Houston State University
Schreiner University
Southern Methodist University
Southwest Texas State University
Southwestern Adventist University
Southwestern Assemblies of God
   University
Southwestern University
Stephen F. Austin State University
Texas A&M International University
Texas A&M University
Texas A&M University
   Commerce
   Corpus Christi
   Galveston
   Texarkana
Texas Christian University
Texas College
Texas Lutheran University
Texas Tech University
Texas Wesleyan University
Texas Woman's University
Trinity University
University of Dallas
University of Houston

University of Houston
   Clear Lake
   Downtown
   Victoria
University of Mary Hardin-Baylor
University of North Texas
University of St. Thomas
University of Texas
   Arlington
   Austin
   Brownsville
   Dallas
   El Paso
   Medical Branch at Galveston
   Pan American
   San Antonio
   Southwestern Medical Center at
     Dallas
   Tyler
   of the Permian Basin
University of the Incarnate Word
West Texas A&M University
Western Texas College

Utah

Brigham Young University
Snow College
Southern Utah University
University of Utah
Utah State University
Utah Valley State College
Weber State University
Westminster College

Vermont

Bennington College
Burlington College
Castleton State College
Champlain College
College of St. Joseph in Vermont
Community College of Vermont
Goddard College
Green Mountain College
Johnson State College
Lyndon State College
Marlboro College
Middlebury College
Norwich University
St. Michael's College
Southern Vermont College
Sterling College
University of Vermont
Vermont Technical College
Woodbury College

Virginia

Averett University
Blue Ridge Community College
Bridgewater College
Bryant & Stratton College
Christendom College
College of Health Sciences
College of William and Mary
Danville Community College
ECPI College of Technology
Eastern Mennonite University
Emory & Henry College
Ferrum College
George Mason University
Hampden-Sydney College
Hampton University
Hollins University
J. Sargeant Reynolds Community
   College
James Madison University
Liberty University
Longwood University
Lynchburg College
Mary Baldwin College
Mary Washington College
Marymount University
Mountain Empire Community College
Norfolk State University
Old Dominion University

Paul D. Camp Community College
Piedmont Virginia Community College
Radford University
Randolph-Macon College
Randolph-Macon Woman's College
Rappahannock Community College
Roanoke College
Shenandoah University
Southwest Virginia Community College
Sweet Briar College
Thomas Nelson Community College
University of Richmond
University of Virginia
University of Virginia's College at Wise
Virginia Commonwealth University
Virginia Highlands Community College
Virginia Intermont College
Virginia Military Institute
Virginia Polytechnic Institute and State
   University
Virginia State University
Virginia Union University
Virginia Wesleyan College
Virginia Western Community College
Washington and Lee University

Washington

Central Washington University
Centralia College
Clark College
Eastern Washington University
Edmonds Community College
Everett Community College
Evergreen State College
Grays Harbor College
Green River Community College
Henry Cogswell College
Heritage College
Lower Columbia College
North Seattle Community College
Northwest College
Olympic College
Pacific Lutheran University
St. Martin's College
Seattle Central Community College
Seattle Pacific University
Seattle University
South Seattle Community College
Spokane Community College
Spokane Falls Community College
Trinity Lutheran College
University of Puget Sound
University of Washington
Walla Walla College
Walla Walla Community College
Washington State University
Wenatchee Valley College
Western Washington University
Whitman College
Whitworth College

West Virginia

Alderson-Broaddus College
Appalachian Bible College
Bethany College
Davis and Elkins College
Marshall University
Mountain State University
Ohio Valley College
Salem International University
Shepherd College
Southern West Virginia Community and
   Technical College
University of Charleston
West Liberty State College
West Virginia Northern Community
   College
West Virginia University
West Virginia University at Parkersburg
West Virginia Wesleyan College
Wheeling Jesuit University

Wisconsin

Bellin College of Nursing

Beloit College
Blackhawk Technical College
Cardinal Stritch University
Carroll College
Carthage College
Chippewa Valley Technical College
Columbia College of Nursing
Concordia University Wisconsin
Edgewood College
Lac Courte Oreilles Ojibwa Community
    College
Lakeland College
Lakeshore Technical College
Lawrence University
Maranatha Baptist Bible College
Marian College of Fond du Lac
Marquette University
Mid-State Technical College
Milwaukee Area Technical College
Milwaukee School of Engineering
Moraine Park Technical College
Mount Mary College
Nicolet Area Technical College
Northland College
St. Norbert College
Silver Lake College
University of Wisconsin
    Baraboo/Sauk County
    Eau Claire
    Fond du Lac
    Fox Valley
    Green Bay
    La Crosse
    Madison
    Manitowoc
    Marathon County
    Marinette
    Milwaukee
    Oshkosh
    Parkside
    Platteville
    Richland
    River Falls
    Rock County
    Stevens Point
    Stout
    Superior
    Washington County
    Waukesha
    Whitewater
Viterbo University
Waukesha County Technical College
Western Wisconsin Technical College
Wisconsin Lutheran College

Wyoming

Central Wyoming College
Eastern Wyoming College
Sheridan College
University of Wyoming
Western Wyoming Community College

Internship

Alabama

Alabama Agricultural and Mechanical
    University
Alabama State University
Auburn University
Auburn University at Montgomery
Birmingham-Southern College
Bishop State Community College
Calhoun Community College
Community College of the Air Force
Enterprise State Junior College
Faulkner University
Harry M. Ayers State Technical College
Heritage Christian University
Huntingdon College
J. F. Drake State Technical College
Jacksonville State University
James H. Faulkner State Community
    College

Jefferson State Community College
Judson College
Lawson State Community College
Miles College
Northwest-Shoals Community College
Oakwood College
Samford University
Snead State Community College
South University
Southeastern Bible College
Southern Christian University
Spring Hill College
Stillman College
Talladega College
Trenholm State Technical College
Troy State University
Troy State University Dothan
Tuskegee University
University of Alabama
University of Alabama
    Birmingham
    Huntsville
University of Mobile
University of Montevallo
University of North Alabama
University of South Alabama
Virginia College
Wallace State Community College at
    Hanceville

Alaska

Alaska Bible College
Alaska Pacific University
Charter College
Prince William Sound Community
    College
Sheldon Jackson College
University of Alaska
    Anchorage
    Fairbanks
    Southeast

Arizona

American Indian College of the
    Assemblies of God
Arizona State University
Arizona Western College
Art Institute
    of Phoenix
Central Arizona College
Cochise College
Embry-Riddle Aeronautical University:
    Prescott Campus
Gateway Community College
Glendale Community College
Northern Arizona University
Paradise Valley Community College
Phoenix College
Prescott College
Rio Salado College
Scottsdale Community College
Southwestern College
University of Arizona
Yavapai College

Arkansas

Arkansas State University
Arkansas Tech University
Central Baptist College
East Arkansas Community College
Harding University
Henderson State University
Hendrix College
John Brown University
Lyon College
Mississippi County Community College
Northwest Arkansas Community College
Ouachita Baptist University
Philander Smith College
Phillips Community College of the
    University of Arkansas
Rich Mountain Community College
Southeast Arkansas College
Southern Arkansas University

Southern Arkansas University Tech
University of Arkansas
University of Arkansas
    Community College at Batesville
    Cossatot Community College of the
        Fort Smith
    Little Rock
    Monticello
    Pine Bluff
University of Central Arkansas
University of the Ozarks
Williams Baptist College

California

Academy of Art College
Antelope Valley College
Antioch Southern California
    Los Angeles
    Santa Barbara
Art Center College of Design
Art Institute
    of California - Orange County
    of California: Los Angeles
Art Institute of California - San Francisco
Azusa Pacific University
Barstow College
Bethany College
Biola University
Cabrillo College
California Baptist University
California College of Arts and Crafts
California Culinary Academy
California Institute of the Arts
California Maritime Academy
California Polytechnic State University:
    San Luis Obispo
California State Polytechnic University:
    Pomona
California State University
    Bakersfield
    Chico
    Dominguez Hills
    Fresno
    Fullerton
    Hayward
    Long Beach
    Los Angeles
    Monterey Bay
    Northridge
    Sacramento
    San Bernardino
    San Marcos
    Stanislaus
Cerro Coso Community College
Chabot College
Chapman University
Christian Heritage College
Claremont McKenna College
Cogswell Polytechnical College
College of the Canyons
College of the Sequoias
College of the Siskiyous
Columbia College
Concordia University
Cuyamaca College
De Anza College
Diablo Valley College
Dominican University of California
Fashion Institute of Design and
    Merchandising
Fashion Institute of Design and
    Merchandising
    San Francisco
Foothill College
Fresno Pacific University
Gavilan Community College
Glendale Community College
Golden Gate University
Grossmont Community College
Harvey Mudd College
Heald College
    Hayward
    Milpitas
Holy Names College
Hope International University

Humboldt State University
Irvine Valley College
John F. Kennedy University
LIFE Pacific College
La Sierra University
Las Positas College
Loma Linda University
Long Beach City College
Loyola Marymount University
MTI College of Business and Technology
Marymount College
Master's College
Menlo College
Mills College
MiraCosta College
Modesto Junior College
Monterey Institute of International
    Studies
Moorpark College
Mount St. Mary's College
Mount San Jacinto College
Napa Valley College
National University
Northwestern Polytechnic University
Occidental College
Ohlone College
Orange Coast College
Otis College of Art and Design
Pacific Oaks College
Pacific Union College
Palomar College
Pepperdine University
Pitzer College
Platt College
    Newport Beach
    Ontario
Point Loma Nazarene University
Pomona College
Riverside Community College
St. Mary's College of California
San Diego City College
San Diego Mesa College
San Diego State University
San Francisco State University
San Joaquin Delta College
San Jose Christian College
San Jose State University
Santa Barbara City College
Santa Clara University
Santa Monica College
Santa Rosa Junior College
Scripps College
Shasta College
Sierra College
Simpson College
Sonoma State University
Southern California Institute of
    Architecture
Southwestern College
Stanford University
Travel University International
University of California
    Berkeley
    Davis
    Irvine
    Los Angeles
    Riverside
    San Diego
    Santa Barbara
    Santa Cruz
University of La Verne
University of Redlands
University of San Diego
University of San Francisco
University of Southern California
University of West Los Angeles
University of the Pacific
Vanguard University of Southern
    California
Whittier College
Woodbury University
Yuba Community College District

Colorado

Arapahoe Community College

Art Institute
    of Colorado
Bel-Rea Institute of Animal Technology
Blair Junior College
Colorado Christian University
Colorado College
Colorado Mountain College
    Alpine Campus
    Spring Valley Campus
    Timberline Campus
Colorado School of Mines
Colorado State University
Colorado State University
    Pueblo
Colorado Technical University
Community College of Aurora
Fort Lewis College
Front Range Community College
Mesa State College
Metropolitan State College of Denver
Morgan Community College
Naropa University
National American University
    Denver
Nazarene Bible College
Parks College
Red Rocks Community College
Regis University
Rocky Mountain College of Art &
    Design
University of Colorado
    Boulder
    Denver
    Health Sciences Center
University of Denver
University of Northern Colorado

Connecticut
Albertus Magnus College
Asnuntuck Community College
Briarwood College
Capital Community College
Central Connecticut State University
Connecticut College
Eastern Connecticut State University
Fairfield University
Gateway Community College
Gibbs College
Housatonic Community College
International College of Hospitality
    Management
Manchester Community College
Middlesex Community College
Mitchell College
Naugatuck Valley Community College
Northwestern Connecticut Community
    College
Norwalk Community College
Paier College of Art
Quinebaug Valley Community College
Quinnipiac University
Sacred Heart University
St. Joseph College
Southern Connecticut State University
Teikyo Post University
Three Rivers Community College
Trinity College
Tunxis Community College
United States Coast Guard Academy
University of Bridgeport
University of Connecticut
University of Hartford
University of New Haven
Wesleyan University
Western Connecticut State University

Delaware
Delaware State University
Delaware Technical and Community
    College
    Owens Campus
    Stanton/Wilmington Campus
    Terry Campus
Goldey-Beacom College
University of Delaware

Wilmington College

District of Columbia
American University
Catholic University of America
Corcoran College of Art and Design
Gallaudet University
George Washington University
Georgetown University
Howard University
Strayer University
Trinity College
University of the District of Columbia

Florida
Art Institute
    of Fort Lauderdale
Baptist College of Florida
Barry University
Beacon College
Bethune-Cookman College
Broward Community College
Carlos Albizu University
Daytona Beach Community College
Eckerd College
Edward Waters College
Embry-Riddle Aeronautical University
Flagler College
Florida Agricultural and Mechanical
    University
Florida Atlantic University
Florida Christian College
Florida Gulf Coast University
Florida Institute of Technology
Florida International University
Florida Metropolitan University
    Orlando College North
    Tampa College
Florida Southern College
Florida State University
Full Sail Real World Education
Gulf Coast Community College
Hillsborough Community College
Hobe Sound Bible College
International Academy of Design and
    Technology
Jacksonville University
Jones College
Lake City Community College
Lake-Sumter Community College
Miami-Dade Community College
New College of Florida
New England Institute of Technology
Northwood University
    Florida Campus
Nova Southeastern University
Okaloosa-Walton Community College
Palm Beach Atlantic University
Palm Beach Community College
Pasco-Hernando Community College
Pensacola Junior College
Polk Community College
Ringling School of Art and Design
Rollins College
St. Leo University
St. Petersburg College
Schiller International University
South Florida Community College
Southeastern College of the Assemblies
    of God
Stetson University
University of Central Florida
University of Florida
University of Miami
University of North Florida
University of South Florida
University of Tampa
University of West Florida
Valencia Community College
Warner Southern College
Webber International University

Georgia
Abraham Baldwin Agricultural College

Agnes Scott College
Albany State University
Albany Technical College
Armstrong Atlantic State University
Art Institute
    of Atlanta
Athens Technical College
Atlanta College of Art
Augusta State University
Bauder College
Berry College
Brenau University
Brewton-Parker College
Chattahoochee Technical College
Clark Atlanta University
Clayton College and State University
Columbus State University
Columbus Technical College
Covenant College
Dalton State College
DeKalb Technical College
Emmanuel College
Emory University
Fort Valley State University
Georgia College and State University
Georgia Institute of Technology
Georgia Perimeter College
Georgia Southern University
Georgia Southwestern State University
Georgia State University
Herzing College
Kennesaw State University
LaGrange College
Macon State College
Medical College of Georgia
Mercer University
Morehouse College
Morris Brown College
North Georgia College & State
    University
Oglethorpe University
Oxford College of Emory University
Paine College
Piedmont College
Reinhardt College
Savannah College of Art and Design
Savannah State University
Savannah Technical College
Shorter College
South University
Southern Polytechnic State University
Southwest Georgia Technical College
Spelman College
State University of West Georgia
Thomas University
Toccoa Falls College
University of Georgia
Valdosta State University
Wesleyan College
Young Harris College

Hawaii
Brigham Young University-Hawaii
Chaminade University of Honolulu
Hawaii Business College
Hawaii Pacific University
Heald College
    Honolulu
University of Hawaii
    Hilo
    Honolulu Community College
    Kauai Community College
    Leeward Community College
    Manoa
    West Oahu

Idaho
Albertson College of Idaho
Boise Bible College
Boise State University
Brigham Young University - Idaho
College of Southern Idaho
Eastern Idaho Technical College
Idaho State University
Lewis-Clark State College

North Idaho College
Northwest Nazarene University
University of Idaho

Illinois
American Academy of Art
Augustana College
Aurora University
Benedictine University
Black Hawk College
Black Hawk College
    East Campus
Blackburn College
Bradley University
Carl Sandburg College
Chicago State University
City Colleges of Chicago
    Harold Washington College
    Kennedy-King College
    Malcolm X College
    Olive-Harvey College
    Richard J. Daley College
    Wright College
College of DuPage
College of Lake County
Columbia College Chicago
Concordia University
Cooking & Hospitality Institute of
    Chicago
Danville Area Community College
De Paul University
Dominican University
Eastern Illinois University
Elgin Community College
Elmhurst College
Eureka College
Finch University of Health Sciences/The
    Chicago Medical School
Gem City College
Governors State University
Greenville College
Heartland Community College
Illinois Central College
Illinois College
Illinois Eastern Community Colleges
    Lincoln Trail College
    Olney Central College
    Wabash Valley College
Illinois Institute of Art
Illinois Institute of Art
Illinois Institute of Technology
Illinois State University
Illinois Valley Community College
Illinois Wesleyan University
International Academy of Design and
    Technology
John A. Logan College
John Wood Community College
Joliet Junior College
Judson College
Kankakee Community College
Kaskaskia College
Kendall College
Kishwaukee College
Knox College
Lake Forest College
Lake Land College
Lewis University
Lewis and Clark Community College
Lexington College
Lincoln Christian College and Seminary
Lincoln Land Community College
Loyola University of Chicago
MacMurray College
McHenry County College
McKendree College
Midstate College
Millikin University
Monmouth College
Moody Bible Institute
Moraine Valley Community College
National University of Health Sciences
National-Louis University
North Central College
North Park University

Northeastern Illinois University
Northern Illinois University
Northwestern Business College
Northwestern University
Oakton Community College
Olivet Nazarene University
Parkland College
Prairie State College
Principia College
Quincy University
Rend Lake College
Robert Morris College: Chicago
Rock Valley College
Rockford Business College
Rockford College
Roosevelt University
St. Augustine College
St. Xavier University
Sauk Valley Community College
School of the Art Institute of Chicago
Shawnee Community College
Shimer College
South Suburban College of Cook County
Southeastern Illinois College
Southern Illinois University Carbondale
Southern Illinois University Edwardsville
Southwestern Illinois College
Spoon River College
Trinity Christian College
Trinity International University
Triton College
University of Chicago
University of Illinois
    Chicago
    Springfield
    Urbana-Champaign
University of St. Francis
VanderCook College of Music
Waubonsee Community College
Western Illinois University
Wheaton College
William Rainey Harper College

Indiana

Anderson University
Ball State University
Bethel College
Butler University
Calumet College of St. Joseph
DePauw University
Earlham College
Franklin College
Goshen College
Grace College
Hanover College
Huntington College
Indiana Business College
Indiana Business College
    Medical
Indiana Institute of Technology
Indiana State University
Indiana University
    Bloomington
    East
    Kokomo
    Northwest
    South Bend
    Southeast
Indiana University-Purdue University
    Fort Wayne
Indiana University-Purdue University
    Indianapolis
Indiana Wesleyan University
International Business College

Ivy Tech State College
    Bloomington
    Central Indiana
    Columbus
    Eastcentral
    Kokomo
    Lafayette
    Northcentral
    Northeast
    Northwest
    Southcentral
    Southeast
    Southwest
    Wabash Valley
    Whitewater
Manchester College
Marian College
Martin University
Michiana College
Oakland City University
Professional Careers Institute
Purdue University
Purdue University
    Calumet
    North Central Campus
St. Joseph's College
Saint Mary's College
St. Mary-of-the-Woods College
Sawyer College
Taylor University
Taylor University: Fort Wayne
Tri-State University
University of Evansville
University of Indianapolis
University of Notre Dame
University of St. Francis
University of Southern Indiana
Valparaiso University
Vincennes University
Wabash College

Iowa

Allen College
American Institute of Business
Briar Cliff University
Buena Vista University
Central College
Clarke College
Coe College
Cornell College
Des Moines Area Community College
Dordt College
Drake University
Ellsworth Community College
Faith Baptist Bible College and
    Theological Seminary
Franciscan University
Graceland University
Grand View College
Grinnell College
Hamilton College
    Cedar Rapids
Hawkeye Community College
Indian Hills Community College
Iowa Central Community College
Iowa Lakes Community College
Iowa State University
Iowa Wesleyan College
Iowa Western Community College
Kaplan College
Kirkwood Community College
Loras College
Luther College
Maharishi University of Management
Marshalltown Community College
Morningside College
Mount Mercy College
Muscatine Community College
Northeast Iowa Community College
Northwestern College
St. Ambrose University
St. Luke's College
Scott Community College
Simpson College

Southeastern Community College
    North Campus
Southwestern Community College
University of Dubuque
University of Iowa
University of Northern Iowa
Upper Iowa University
Waldorf College
Wartburg College
Western Iowa Tech Community College
William Penn University

Kansas

Allen County Community College
Baker University
Barclay College
Barton County Community College
Benedictine College
Bethany College
Bethel College
Butler County Community College
Central Christian College
Cloud County Community College
Dodge City Community College
Emporia State University
Fort Hays State University
Fort Scott Community College
Garden City Community College
Haskell Indian Nations University
Hesston College
Hutchinson Community College
Independence Community College
Johnson County Community College
Kansas City Kansas Community College
Kansas State University
Kansas Wesleyan University
Labette Community College
McPherson College
MidAmerica Nazarene University
Newman University
Ottawa University
Pittsburg State University
Pratt Community College
St. Mary College
Seward County Community College
Southwestern College
Tabor College
University of Kansas
University of Kansas Medical Center
Washburn University of Topeka
Wichita State University

Kentucky

Alice Lloyd College
Asbury College
Beckfield College
Bellarmine University
Berea College
Brescia University
Campbellsville University
Centre College
Cumberland College
Daymar College
Elizabethtown Community College
Georgetown College
Jefferson Community College
Kentucky Christian College
Kentucky Mountain Bible College
Kentucky Wesleyan College
Lexington Community College
Lindsey Wilson College
Louisville Technical Institute
Madisonville Community College
Maysville Community College
Morehead State University
Murray State University
National College of Business &
    Technology
    Danville
    Florence
    Lexington
    Pikeville
    Richmond
Pikeville College
St. Catharine College

Somerset Community College
Southeast Community College
Spalding University
Spencerian College
Sullivan University
Thomas More College
Transylvania University
Union College
University of Kentucky
University of Louisville

Louisiana

Centenary College of Louisiana
Delgado Community College
Dillard University
Grambling State University
Louisiana College
Louisiana State University and
    Agricultural and Mechanical College
Louisiana Tech University
Loyola University New Orleans
McNeese State University
Nicholls State University
Northwestern State University
Nunez Community College
Our Lady of Holy Cross College
Southeastern Louisiana University
Southern University
    New Orleans
    Shreveport
Southern University and Agricultural and
    Mechanical College
Tulane University
University of Louisiana at Lafayette
University of Louisiana at Monroe
University of New Orleans
Xavier University of Louisiana

Maine

Andover College
Bates College
Central Maine Medical Center School of
    Nursing
Central Maine Technical College
Colby College
College of the Atlantic
Husson College
Maine College of Art
Maine Maritime Academy
New England School of Communications
St. Joseph's College
Thomas College
University of Maine
University of Maine
    Augusta
    Farmington
    Machias
    Presque Isle
University of New England
University of Southern Maine

Maryland

Allegany College
Anne Arundel Community College
Baltimore Hebrew University
Baltimore International College
Bowie State University
Carroll Community College
Cecil Community College
Chesapeake College
College of Notre Dame of Maryland
Columbia Union College
Community College of Baltimore County
    Dundalk
    Essex
Coppin State College
Frederick Community College
Frostburg State University
Goucher College
Hagerstown Community College
Harford Community College
Hood College
Howard Community College
Johns Hopkins University

Johns Hopkins University: Peabody
   Conservatory of Music
Loyola College in Maryland
Maryland College of Art and Design
Maryland Institute College of Art
McDaniel College
Montgomery College
   Rockville Campus
Morgan State University
Mount St. Mary's College
St. Mary's College of Maryland
Salisbury University
Sojourner-Douglass College
Towson University
University of Baltimore
University of Maryland
   Baltimore County
   College Park
Villa Julie College
Washington Bible College
Washington College
Wor-Wic Community College

Massachusetts

Ai The New England Institute of Art and
   Design
American International College
Anna Maria College
Art Institute of Boston at Lesley
   University
Assumption College
Atlantic Union College
Babson College
Bay Path College
Bay State College
Becker College
Bentley College
Berklee College of Music
Berkshire Community College
Boston Architectural Center
Boston College
Boston Conservatory
Boston University
Brandeis University
Bridgewater State College
Bunker Hill Community College
Cape Cod Community College
Clark University
College of the Holy Cross
Dean College
Elms College
Emerson College
Emmanuel College
Endicott College
Fisher College
Fitchburg State College
Framingham State College
Franklin W. Olin College of Engineering
Gordon College
Greenfield Community College
Hampshire College
Harvard College
Hebrew College
Hellenic College/Holy Cross
Katharine Gibbs School
Lasell College
Lesley University
Marian Court College
Massachusetts Bay Community College
Massachusetts College of Liberal Arts
Massachusetts College of Pharmacy and
   Health Sciences
Massachusetts Institute of Technology
Massachusetts Maritime Academy
Massasoit Community College
Merrimack College
Montserrat College of Art
Mount Holyoke College
Mount Ida College
Mount Wachusett Community College
New England Conservatory of Music
Newbury College
Nichols College
Northeastern University

Pine Manor College
Quinsigamond Community College
Regis College
Roxbury Community College
Salem State College
Simmons College
Simon's Rock College of Bard
Smith College
Springfield College
Springfield Technical Community
   College
Stonehill College
Suffolk University
Tufts University
University of Massachusetts
   Amherst
   Boston
   Dartmouth
   Lowell
Urban College of Boston
Wellesley College
Western New England College
Westfield State College
Wheaton College
Williams College
Worcester Polytechnic Institute

Michigan

Adrian College
Alma College
Alpena Community College
Andrews University
Aquinas College
Baker College
   of Auburn Hills
   of Cadillac
   of Clinton Township
   of Jackson
   of Muskegon
   of Owosso
   of Port Huron
Bay de Noc Community College
Calvin College
Central Michigan University
Cleary University
College for Creative Studies
Concordia University
Cornerstone University
Davenport University
   Eastern Region
   Midland
Davenport University - Western Region
Eastern Michigan University
Ferris State University
Finlandia University
Glen Oaks Community College
Gogebic Community College
Grace Bible College
Grand Rapids Community College
Grand Valley State University
Hillsdale College
Hope College
Jackson Community College
Kalamazoo College
Kellogg Community College
Kirtland Community College
Lansing Community College
Lawrence Technological University
Macomb Community College
Madonna University
Marygrove College
Michigan State University
Michigan Technological University
Mid Michigan Community College
Montcalm Community College
Mott Community College
Muskegon Community College
North Central Michigan College
Northern Michigan University
Northwestern Michigan College
Northwood University
Oakland Community College
Oakland University
Reformed Bible College
Saginaw Valley State University

St. Clair County Community College
Siena Heights University
Southwestern Michigan College
Spring Arbor University
University of Michigan
University of Michigan
   Dearborn
   Flint
Walsh College of Accountancy and
   Business Administration
Washtenaw Community College
Wayne County Community College
Wayne State University
West Shore Community College
Western Michigan University
William Tyndale College

Minnesota

Alexandria Technical College
Anoka-Ramsey Community College
Art Institutes International
   Minnesota
Augsburg College
Bemidji State University
Bethel College
Brown College
Carleton College
Central Lakes College
Century Community and Technical
   College
College of St. Benedict
College of St. Catherine
College of St. Scholastica
College of Visual Arts
Concordia College: Moorhead
Concordia University: St. Paul
Crossroads College
Crown College
Dakota County Technical College
Fergus Falls Community College
Globe College
Gustavus Adolphus College
Hamline University
Hennepin Technical College
Hibbing Community College: A
   Technical and Community College
Inver Hills Community College
Itasca Community College
Lake Superior College: A Community
   and Technical College
Macalester College
Martin Luther College
Mesabi Range Community and Technical
   College
Metropolitan State University
Minneapolis Community and Technical
   College
Minnesota State College - Southeast
   Technical
Minnesota State University
   Mankato
   Moorhead
Minnesota West Community and
   Technical College: Worthington
   Campus
National American University
   St. Paul
Normandale Community College
North Central University
North Hennepin Community College
Northland Community & Technical
   College
Northwestern College
Oak Hills Christian College
Pine Technical College
Rainy River Community College
Rasmussen College
   Mankato
Ridgewater College: A Community and
   Technical College
Riverland Community College: A
   Technical and Community College
Rochester Community and Technical
   College
St. Cloud State University

St. Cloud Technical College
St. John's University
St. Mary's University of Minnesota
St. Olaf College
St. Paul College - A Community and
   Technical College
South Central Technical College
Southwest State University
University of Minnesota
   Crookston
   Duluth
   Morris
   Twin Cities
University of St. Thomas
Vermilion Community College
Winona State University

Mississippi

Alcorn State University
Blue Mountain College
Delta State University
Holmes Community College
Itawamba Community College
Mary Holmes College
Millsaps College
Mississippi College
Mississippi State University
Mississippi University for Women
Mississippi Valley State University
Rust College
University of Mississippi
University of Southern Mississippi
Wesley College

Missouri

Avila University
Blue River Community College
Calvary Bible College
Central Bible College
Central Christian College of the Bible
Central Methodist College
Central Missouri State University
College of the Ozarks
Columbia College
Crowder College
Culver-Stockton College
Drury University
East Central College
Evangel University
Fontbonne College
Hannibal-LaGrange College
Harris Stowe State College
Jefferson College
Kansas City Art Institute
Kansas City College of Legal Studies
Lincoln University
Lindenwood University
Longview Community College
Maple Woods Community College
Maryville University of Saint Louis
Mineral Area College
Missouri Baptist University
Missouri Southern State College
Missouri Technical School
Missouri Valley College
Missouri Western State College
Moberly Area Community College
National American University
   Kansas City
North Central Missouri College
Northwest Missouri State University
Ozark Christian College
Ozarks Technical Community College
Patricia Stevens College
Penn Valley Community College
Ranken Technical College
Rockhurst University
St. Charles Community College
St. Louis Christian College
St. Louis College of Pharmacy
St. Louis Community College
   St. Louis Community College at
     Florissant Valley
   St. Louis Community College at
     Meramec

St. Louis University
Southeast Missouri State University
Southwest Baptist University
Southwest Missouri State University
Springfield College
Stephens College
Three Rivers Community College
Truman State University
University of Missouri
  Columbia
  Kansas City
  Rolla
  St. Louis
Washington University in St. Louis
Webster University
Westminster College
William Jewell College
William Woods University

Montana

Carroll College
Chief Dull Knife College
Dawson Community College
Flathead Valley Community College
Miles Community College
Montana State University
  Billings
  Billings College of Technology
  Bozeman
Montana Tech of the University of
  Montana
Rocky Mountain College
Salish Kootenai College
University of Great Falls
University of Montana-Missoula
University of Montana: Western

Nebraska

Bellevue University
Central Community College
Chadron State College
Clarkson College
College of Saint Mary
Concordia University
Creighton University
Dana College
Doane College
Grace University
Hastings College
Lincoln School of Commerce
Metropolitan Community College
Mid Plains Community College Area
Midland Lutheran College
Nebraska Christian College
Nebraska College of Technical
  Agriculture
Nebraska Indian Community College
Nebraska Methodist College of Nursing
  and Allied Health
Nebraska Wesleyan University
Northeast Community College
Peru State College
Southeast Community College
  Beatrice Campus
  Lincoln Campus
  Milford Campus
Union College
University of Nebraska
  Kearney
  Lincoln
  Omaha
Wayne State College
Western Nebraska Community College
York College

Nevada

Career College of Northern Nevada
Community College of Southern Nevada
Morrison University
Sierra Nevada College
Truckee Meadows Community College
University of Nevada
  Las Vegas
  Reno

Western Nevada Community College

New Hampshire

Chester College of New England
Colby-Sawyer College
College for Lifelong Learning
Daniel Webster College
Dartmouth College
Franklin Pierce College
Hesser College
Keene State College
New England College
New Hampshire Community Technical
  College
  Berlin
  Claremont
  Laconia
  Manchester
  Nashua
  Stratham
New Hampshire Technical Institute
Plymouth State College
Rivier College
St. Anselm College
Southern New Hampshire University
University of New Hampshire
University of New Hampshire at
  Manchester

New Jersey

Atlantic Cape Community College
Bergen Community College
Berkeley College
Bloomfield College
Brookdale Community College
Burlington County College
Caldwell College
Camden County College
Centenary College
The College of New Jersey
College of St. Elizabeth
County College of Morris
Drew University
Essex County College
Fairleigh Dickinson University
  College at Florham
  Metropolitan Campus
Felician College
Georgian Court College
Gloucester County College
Hudson County Community College
Kean University
Mercer County Community College
Middlesex County College
Monmouth University
Montclair State University
New Jersey City University
New Jersey Institute of Technology
Passaic County Community College
Rabbinical College of America
Ramapo College of New Jersey
Richard Stockton College of New Jersey
Rider University
Rowan University
Rutgers, The State University of New
  Jersey
  Newark Regional Campus
St. Peter's College
Salem Community College
Seton Hall University
Stevens Institute of Technology
Sussex County Community College
Union County College
University of Medicine and Dentistry of
  New Jersey
  School of Health Related
    Professions
Warren County Community College
William Paterson University of New
  Jersey

New Mexico

Clovis Community College
College of Santa Fe

College of the Southwest
Dona Ana Branch Community College of
  New Mexico State University
Eastern New Mexico University
Eastern New Mexico University: Roswell
  Campus
Institute of American Indian Arts
New Mexico Highlands University
New Mexico Institute of Mining and
  Technology
New Mexico Junior College
New Mexico State University
San Juan College
Santa Fe Community College
University of New Mexico
Western New Mexico University

New York

Adelphi University
Adirondack Community College
Alfred University
Bard College
Barnard College
Berkeley College
Berkeley College of New York City
Briarcliffe College
Broome Community College
Bryant & Stratton Business Institute
  Albany
  Rochester
  Syracuse
Canisius College
Cayuga County Community College
Cazenovia College
City University of New York
  Baruch College
  Borough of Manhattan Community
    College
  Bronx Community College
  Brooklyn College
  City College
  College of Staten Island
  Hostos Community College
  Hunter College
  John Jay College of Criminal
    Justice
  Kingsborough Community College
  La Guardia Community College
  Medgar Evers College
  Queens College
  Queensborough Community
    College
  York College
Clinton Community College
Colgate University
College of Aeronautics
College of Mount St. Vincent
College of New Rochelle
College of New Rochelle: School of New
  Resources
Columbia University
  Columbia College
  Fu Foundation School of
    Engineering and Applied Science
Concordia College
Cooper Union for the Advancement of
  Science and Art
Cornell University
Corning Community College
Culinary Institute of America
D'Youville College
Daemen College
Dominican College of Blauvelt
Dowling College
Dutchess Community College
Eastman School of Music of the
  University of Rochester
Elmira Business Institute
Elmira College
Erie Community College
  City Campus
  North Campus
  South Campus
Eugene Lang College/New School
  University

Fashion Institute of Technology
Finger Lakes Community College
Fordham University
Fulton-Montgomery Community College
Genesee Community College
Globe Institute of Technology
Hamilton College
Hartwick College
Helene Fuld College of Nursing
Hilbert College
Hobart and William Smith Colleges
Hofstra University
Houghton College
Hudson Valley Community College
Iona College
Ithaca College
Jamestown Community College
Jefferson Community College
Katharine Gibbs School
  Melville
Keuka College
Laboratory Institute of Merchandising
Le Moyne College
Long Island Business Institute
Long Island University
  C. W. Post Campus
  Southampton College
Manhattan College
Manhattanville College
Maria College
Marist College
Marymount College of Fordham
  University
Marymount Manhattan College
Medaille College
Mercy College
Metropolitan College of New York
Mildred Elley
Mohawk Valley Community College
Molloy College
Monroe College
Monroe Community College
Mount St. Mary College
Nassau Community College
Nazareth College of Rochester
New York Institute of Technology
New York University
Niagara County Community College
Niagara University
North Country Community College
Nyack College
Olean Business Institute
Onondaga Community College
Orange County Community College
Pace University
Pace University: Pleasantville/Briarcliff
Parsons School of Design
Paul Smith's College
Plaza College
Polytechnic University
Pratt Institute
Rensselaer Polytechnic Institute
Roberts Wesleyan College
Rochester Institute of Technology
Rockland Community College
Russell Sage College
Sage College of Albany
St. Bonaventure University
St. John Fisher College
St. John's University
St. Joseph's College
St. Joseph's College: Suffolk Campus
St. Lawrence University
Sarah Lawrence College
Schenectady County Community College
School of Visual Arts
Skidmore College

State University of New York
  Albany
  Binghamton
  Buffalo
  College at Brockport
  College at Buffalo
  College at Cortland
  College at Fredonia
  College at Geneseo
  College at Old Westbury
  College at Oneonta
  College at Plattsburgh
  College at Potsdam
  College of Agriculture and
    Technology at Cobleskill
  College of Agriculture and
    Technology at Morrisville
  College of Environmental Science
    and Forestry
  College of Technology at Alfred
  College of Technology at Canton
  College of Technology at Delhi
  Empire State College
  Health Science Center at Stony
    Brook
  Institute of Technology at
    Utica/Rome
  Maritime College
  New Paltz
  Oswego
  Purchase
  Stony Brook
Suffolk County Community College
Syracuse University
Tompkins-Cortland Community College
Touro College
Trocaire College
Ulster County Community College
Union College
United States Merchant Marine Academy
University of Rochester
Utica College
Vassar College
Villa Maria College of Buffalo
Wagner College
Webb Institute
Wells College
Westchester Business Institute
Westchester Community College
Yeshiva University

North Carolina

Alamance Community College
Appalachian State University
Asheville Buncombe Technical
  Community College
Barber-Scotia College
Barton College
Beaufort County Community College
Belmont Abbey College
Bennett College
Brevard College
Brunswick Community College
Campbell University
Cape Fear Community College
Carteret Community College
Catawba College
Central Carolina Community College
Central Piedmont Community College
Chowan College
Cleveland Community College
Coastal Carolina Community College
Craven Community College
Duke University
Durham Technical Community College
East Carolina University
Elizabeth City State University
Elon University
Fayetteville State University
Forsyth Technical Community College
Gardner-Webb University
Gaston College
Greensboro College
Guilford College
Guilford Technical Community College

Halifax Community College
Haywood Community College
James Sprunt Community College
John Wesley College
Johnson C. Smith University
Johnston Community College
Lees-McRae College
Lenoir-Rhyne College
Livingstone College
Mars Hill College
Martin Community College
Mayland Community College
Meredith College
Methodist College
Montgomery Community College
Montreat College
Mount Olive College
North Carolina Agricultural and
  Technical State University
North Carolina Central University
North Carolina School of the Arts
North Carolina State University
North Carolina Wesleyan College
Pamlico Community College
Peace College
Pfeiffer University
Piedmont Baptist College
Piedmont Community College
Pitt Community College
Queens University of Charlotte
Randolph Community College
Richmond Community College
Roanoke Bible College
Roanoke-Chowan Community College
St. Andrews Presbyterian College
St. Augustine's College
Salem College
Sampson Community College
Sandhills Community College
Shaw University
South College
South Piedmont Community College
Southeastern Baptist Theological
  Seminary
Southeastern Community College
Southwestern Community College
Surry Community College
Tri-County Community College
University of North Carolina
  Asheville
  Chapel Hill
  Charlotte
  Greensboro
  Pembroke
  Wilmington
Vance-Granville Community College
Wake Forest University
Warren Wilson College
Wayne Community College
Western Carolina University
Wilkes Community College
Wingate University
Winston-Salem State University

North Dakota

Bismarck State College
Dickinson State University
Jamestown College
Lake Region State College
Mayville State University
Minot State University
Minot State University: Bottineau
  Campus
North Dakota State College of Science
North Dakota State University
Trinity Bible College
University of Mary
University of North Dakota
Valley City State University
Williston State College

Ohio

Antioch College
Antonelli College
Art Academy of Cincinnati

Ashland University
Baldwin-Wallace College
Bluffton College
Bowling Green State University
Bowling Green State University:
  Firelands College
Bradford School
Bryant & Stratton College
Bryant & Stratton College
  Cleveland West
  Willoughby Hills
Case Western Reserve University
Cedarville University
Central Ohio Technical College
Central State University
Chatfield College
Cincinnati Bible College and Seminary
Cincinnati College of Mortuary Science
Cincinnati State Technical and
  Community College
Circleville Bible College
Clark State Community College
Cleveland Institute of Art
Cleveland State University
College of Mount St. Joseph
College of Wooster
Columbus College of Art and Design
Columbus State Community College
Cuyahoga Community College
  Eastern Campus
David N. Myers College
Davis College
Defiance College
Denison University
Edison State Community College
Franciscan University of Steubenville
Franklin University
Heidelberg College
Hiram College
Hocking Technical College
James A. Rhodes State College
Jefferson Community College
John Carroll University
Kent State University
Kent State University
  Ashtabula Regional Campus
  East Liverpool Regional Campus
  Salem Regional Campus
  Stark Campus
  Trumbull Campus
  Tuscarawas Campus
Kenyon College
Lake Erie College
Laura and Alvin Siegal College of Judaic
  Studies
Lourdes College
Malone College
Marietta College
Marion Technical College
Miami University
  Hamilton Campus
  Middletown Campus
  Oxford Campus
Miami-Jacobs College
Mount Union College
Mount Vernon Nazarene University
Muskingum Area Technical College
Muskingum College
North Central State College
Northwest State Community College
Notre Dame College
Oberlin College
Ohio Business College
Ohio Dominican College
Ohio Institute of Photography and
  Technology
Ohio Northern University
Ohio State University
  Agricultural Technical Institute
  Columbus Campus
Ohio University
Ohio University
  Chillicothe Campus
  Eastern Campus
  Lancaster Campus

Ohio Valley College of Technology
Ohio Wesleyan University
Otterbein College
Owens Community College
  Findlay Campus
  Toledo
RETS Tech Center
Shawnee State University
Sinclair Community College
Southern State Community College
Stark State College of Technology
Stautzenberger College
Tiffin University
University of Akron
University of Cincinnati
University of Cincinnati
  Clermont College
  Raymond Walters College
University of Dayton
University of Findlay
University of Rio Grande
University of Toledo
Urbana University
Ursuline College
Virginia Marti College of Art and Design
Walsh University
Washington State Community College
Wilmington College
Wittenberg University
Wright State University
Wright State University: Lake Campus
Xavier University
Youngstown State University

Oklahoma

Cameron University
East Central University
Eastern Oklahoma State College
Langston University
Northeastern Oklahoma Agricultural and
  Mechanical College
Northeastern State University
Northern Oklahoma College
Northwestern Oklahoma State University
Oklahoma Baptist University
Oklahoma Christian University of
  Science and Arts
Oklahoma City Community College
Oklahoma City University
Oklahoma Panhandle State University
Oklahoma State University
Oklahoma State University
  Okmulgee
Oklahoma Wesleyan University
Oral Roberts University
Redlands Community College
Rogers State University
Rose State College
St. Gregory's University
Southeastern Oklahoma State University
Southern Nazarene University
Southwestern Christian University
Southwestern Oklahoma State University
Tulsa Community College
University of Central Oklahoma
University of Oklahoma
University of Science and Arts of
  Oklahoma
University of Tulsa

Oregon

Art Institute
  of Portland
Central Oregon Community College
Clackamas Community College
Concordia University
Eastern Oregon University
Eugene Bible College
George Fox University
Lane Community College
Lewis & Clark College
Linfield College
Linn-Benton Community College
Marylhurst University
Mount Hood Community College

Multnomah Bible College
Northwest Christian College
Oregon Institute of Technology
Oregon State University
Pacific Northwest College of Art
Pacific University
Portland Community College
Portland State University
Reed College
Southern Oregon University
Southwestern Oregon Community
    College
Umpqua Community College
University of Oregon
University of Portland
Warner Pacific College
Western Baptist College
Western Oregon University
Willamette University

Pennsylvania

Academy of Medical Arts and Business
Albright College
Allegheny College
Allentown Business School
Arcadia University
Art Institute
    of Philadelphia
    of Pittsburgh
Baptist Bible College of Pennsylvania
Bloomsburg University of Pennsylvania
Bradley Academy for the Visual Arts
Bryn Athyn College of the New Church
Bryn Mawr College
Bucknell University
Bucks County Community College
Butler County Community College
CHI Institute
Cabrini College
California University of Pennsylvania
Cambria County Area Community
    College
Career Training Academy
Carlow College
Carnegie Mellon University
Cedar Crest College
Central Pennsylvania College
Chatham College
Chestnut Hill College
Cheyney University of Pennsylvania
Community College of Beaver County
Community College of Philadelphia
Consolidated School of Business
    Lancaster
    York
DeSales University
Delaware County Community College
Delaware Valley College
Dickinson College
Douglas School of Business
Drexel University
DuBois Business College
Duquesne University
East Stroudsburg University of
    Pennsylvania
Edinboro University of Pennsylvania
Electronic Institutes: Middletown
Elizabethtown College
Erie Business Center
Franklin & Marshall College
Geneva College
Gettysburg College
Gratz College
Grove City College
Gwynedd-Mercy College
Harrisburg Area Community College
Haverford College
Holy Family University
ICM School of Business & Medical
    Careers
Immaculata University
Indiana University of Pennsylvania
Juniata College
Keystone College
King's College

Kutztown University of Pennsylvania
La Roche College
La Salle University
Lackawanna College
Lafayette College
Lancaster Bible College
Lebanon Valley College of Pennsylvania
Lehigh Carbon Community College
Lehigh University
Lincoln University
Lock Haven University of Pennsylvania
Luzerne County Community College
Lycoming College
Manor College
Marywood University
Median School of Allied Health Careers
Mercyhurst College
Messiah College
Millersville University of Pennsylvania
Montgomery County Community
    College
Moravian College
Mount Aloysius College
Muhlenberg College
Neumann College
Northampton County Area Community
    College
Oakbridge Academy of Arts
PJA School
Peirce College
Penn State
    Abington
    Altoona
    Beaver
    Berks
    Delaware County
    Dubois
    Erie, The Behrend College
    Fayette
    Harrisburg
    Hazleton
    Lehigh Valley
    McKeesport
    Mont Alto
    New Kensington
    Schuylkill - Capital College
    Shenango
    University Park
    Wilkes-Barre
    Worthington Scranton
    York
Pennsylvania College of Technology
Pennsylvania Institute of Culinary Arts
Pennsylvania Institute of Technology
Philadelphia Biblical University
Philadelphia University
Pittsburgh Technical Institute: Boyd
    School Division
Point Park College
Reading Area Community College
Robert Morris University
Rosemont College
St. Joseph's University
St. Vincent College
Schuylkill Institute of Business &
    Technology
Seton Hill University
Shippensburg University of Pennsylvania
Slippery Rock University of
    Pennsylvania
South Hills School of Business &
    Technology
Swarthmore College
Temple University
Thiel College
University of Pennsylvania
University of Pittsburgh
University of Pittsburgh
    Bradford
    Greensburg
    Johnstown
    Titusville
University of Scranton
University of the Sciences in
    Philadelphia

Valley Forge Christian College
Villanova University
Washington and Jefferson College
Waynesburg College
West Chester University of Pennsylvania
Westmoreland County Community
    College
Widener University
Wilkes University
Williamson Free School of Mechanical
    Trades
Wilson College
York College of Pennsylvania

Puerto Rico

Atlantic College
Escuela de Artes Plasticas de Puerto Rico
Huertas Junior College
Humacao Community College
Inter American University of Puerto Rico
    Barranquitas Campus
    Bayamon Campus
    Fajardo Campus
    Metropolitan Campus
    San German Campus
Pontifical Catholic University of Puerto
Rico
Turabo University
Universidad Metropolitana
Universidad del Este
University of Puerto Rico
    Bayamon University College
    Humacao
    Mayaguez Campus
    Medical Sciences Campus
    Ponce
    Rio Piedras Campus
    Utuado
University of the Sacred Heart

Rhode Island

Brown University
Bryant College
Community College of Rhode Island
Providence College
Rhode Island College
Rhode Island School of Design
Roger Williams University
Salve Regina University
University of Rhode Island

South Carolina

Aiken Technical College
Anderson College
Benedict College
Central Carolina Technical College
Charleston Southern University
The Citadel
Claflin University
Clemson University
Coastal Carolina University
Coker College
College of Charleston
Columbia College
Columbia International University
Converse College
Denmark Technical College
Erskine College
Florence-Darlington Technical College
Forrest Junior College
Francis Marion University
Furman University
Horry-Georgetown Technical College
Lander University
Limestone College
Medical University of South Carolina
Morris College
Newberry College
North Greenville College
Piedmont Technical College
Presbyterian College
South Carolina State University
Southern Wesleyan University
Technical College of the Lowcountry

Tri-County Technical College
Trident Technical College
University of South Carolina
University of South Carolina
    Aiken
    Lancaster
    Spartanburg
    Union
Voorhees College
Williamsburg Technical College
Winthrop University
Wofford College

South Dakota

Augustana College
Black Hills State University
Dakota State University
Dakota Wesleyan University
Kilian Community College
Mitchell Technical Institute
Mount Marty College
Northern State University
Sinte Gleska University
South Dakota School of Mines and
    Technology
South Dakota State University
University of Sioux Falls
University of South Dakota
Western Dakota Technical Institute

Tennessee

Austin Peay State University
Belmont University
Bethel College
Bryan College
Carson-Newman College
Chattanooga State Technical Community
    College
Christian Brothers University
Cleveland State Community College
Crichton College
Draughons Junior College of Business:
    Nashville
Dyersburg State Community College
East Tennessee State University
Fisk University
Freed-Hardeman University
Jackson State Community College
Johnson Bible College
King College
Lambuth University
Lane College
Lee University
Maryville College
Memphis College of Art
Middle Tennessee State University
Milligan College
O'More College of Design
Pellissippi State Technical Community
    College
Rhodes College
Roane State Community College
South College
Southern Adventist University
Southwest Tennessee Community
    College
Tennessee Technological University
Tennessee Wesleyan College
Trevecca Nazarene University
Tusculum College
Union University
University of Memphis
University of Tennessee
    Chattanooga
    Knoxville
    Martin
University of Tennessee Health Science
    Center
Vanderbilt University

Texas

Abilene Christian University
Alvin Community College
Angelina College

677

Angelo State University
Austin College
Austin Community College
Baylor University
Brazosport College
Central Texas College
Clarendon College
Coastal Bend College
College of the Mainland
Collin County Community College
   District
Concordia University at Austin
Dallas Baptist University
Dallas Christian College
Del Mar College
East Texas Baptist University
El Centro College
El Paso Community College
Frank Phillips College
Galveston College
Grayson County College
Hardin-Simmons University
Hill College
Houston Baptist University
Houston Community College System
Howard Payne University
Huston-Tillotson College
Jarvis Christian College
Kilgore College
Lamar State College at Port Arthur
Lamar University
LeTourneau University
Lee College
Lubbock Christian University
McLennan Community College
McMurry University
Midland College
Midwestern State University
North Lake College
Northwood University: Texas Campus
Odessa College
Our Lady of the Lake University of San
   Antonio
Palo Alto College
Paul Quinn College
Prairie View A&M University
Remington College
   Houston
Rice University
Richland College
St. Edward's University
St. Mary's University
St. Philip's College
Sam Houston State University
San Antonio College
San Jacinto College
   Central Campus
Schreiner University
South Plains College
Southern Methodist University
Southwest Texas State University
Southwestern Adventist University
Southwestern Assemblies of God
   University
Southwestern University
Stephen F. Austin State University
Sul Ross State University
Tarleton State University
Temple College
Texarkana College
Texas A&M International University
Texas A&M University
Texas A&M University
   Baylor College of Dentistry
   Commerce
   Corpus Christi
   Galveston
   Kingsville
   Texarkana
Texas Christian University
Texas College
Texas Lutheran University
Texas Southern University
Texas State Technical College
   West Texas

Texas Tech University
Texas Wesleyan University
Texas Woman's University
Trinity University
Trinity Valley Community College
Tyler Junior College
University of Dallas
University of Houston
University of Houston
   Clear Lake
   Downtown
   Victoria
University of Mary Hardin-Baylor
University of North Texas
University of St. Thomas
University of Texas
   Arlington
   Austin
   Brownsville
   Dallas
   El Paso
   Health Science Center at San
      Antonio
   Medical Branch at Galveston
   Pan American
   San Antonio
   Southwestern Medical Center at
      Dallas
   Tyler
   of the Permian Basin
University of the Incarnate Word
Wayland Baptist University
West Texas A&M University
Western Texas College
Wiley College

Utah

Brigham Young University
LDS Business College
Salt Lake Community College
Southern Utah University
University of Utah
Utah State University
Utah Valley State College
Weber State University
Westminster College

Vermont

Bennington College
Burlington College
Castleton State College
Champlain College
College of St. Joseph in Vermont
Community College of Vermont
Goddard College
Green Mountain College
Johnson State College
Landmark College
Lyndon State College
Marlboro College
Middlebury College
New England Culinary Institute
Norwich University
St. Michael's College
Southern Vermont College
Sterling College
University of Vermont
Vermont Technical College

Virginia

Averett University
Blue Ridge Community College
Bluefield College
Bridgewater College
Bryant & Stratton College
Christendom College
College of Health Sciences
College of William and Mary
Danville Community College
ECPI College of Technology
Eastern Mennonite University
Emory & Henry College
Ferrum College
George Mason University

Hampden-Sydney College
Hampton University
Hollins University
J. Sargeant Reynolds Community
   College
James Madison University
Liberty University
Longwood University
Lynchburg College
Mary Baldwin College
Mary Washington College
Marymount University
Mountain Empire Community College
National College of Business &
   Technology
   Bluefield
   Charlottesville
   Danville
   Harrisonburg
   Lynchburg
   Martinsville
   Roanoke
Norfolk State University
Old Dominion University
Paul D. Camp Community College
Piedmont Virginia Community College
Radford University
Randolph-Macon College
Randolph-Macon Woman's College
Rappahannock Community College
Roanoke College
Shenandoah University
Southside Virginia Community College
Southwest Virginia Community College
Sweet Briar College
Thomas Nelson Community College
University of Richmond
University of Virginia
University of Virginia's College at Wise
Virginia Commonwealth University
Virginia Highlands Community College
Virginia Intermont College
Virginia Military Institute
Virginia Polytechnic Institute and State
   University
Virginia State University
Virginia Union University
Virginia Wesleyan College
Virginia Western Community College
Washington and Lee University

Washington

Art Institute of Seattle
Bastyr University
Central Washington University
Centralia College
Clark College
Clover Park Technical College
Cornish College of the Arts
Crown College
Eastern Washington University
Edmonds Community College
Everett Community College
Evergreen State College
Gonzaga University
Grays Harbor College
Green River Community College
Heritage College
Lake Washington Technical College
North Seattle Community College
Northwest College
Pacific Lutheran University
Peninsula College
Renton Technical College
St. Martin's College
Seattle Central Community College
Seattle Pacific University
Seattle University
South Seattle Community College
Spokane Community College
Spokane Falls Community College
Trinity Lutheran College
University of Puget Sound
University of Washington
Walla Walla College

Walla Walla Community College
Washington State University
Wenatchee Valley College
Western Washington University
Whitman College
Whitworth College

West Virginia

Alderson-Broaddus College
Appalachian Bible College
Bethany College
Bluefield State College
Davis and Elkins College
Glenville State College
Huntington Junior College
International Academy of Design and
   Technology
Marshall University
Mountain State College
Mountain State University
Potomac State College of West Virginia
   University
Salem International University
Shepherd College
Southern West Virginia Community and
   Technical College
University of Charleston
West Liberty State College
West Virginia Northern Community
   College
West Virginia State College
West Virginia University
West Virginia University Institute of
   Technology
West Virginia University at Parkersburg
West Virginia Wesleyan College
Wheeling Jesuit University

Wisconsin

Alverno College
Beloit College
Blackhawk Technical College
Bryant & Stratton College
Cardinal Stritch University
Carroll College
Carthage College
Chippewa Valley Technical College
Concordia University Wisconsin
Edgewood College
Fox Valley Technical College
Lakeland College
Lakeshore Technical College
Lawrence University
Maranatha Baptist Bible College
Marian College of Fond du Lac
Marquette University
Mid-State Technical College
Milwaukee Area Technical College
Milwaukee Institute of Art & Design
Milwaukee School of Engineering
Moraine Park Technical College
Mount Mary College
Nicolet Area Technical College
Northland College
Ripon College
St. Norbert College
Silver Lake College
University of Wisconsin
   Barron County
   Eau Claire
   Green Bay
   La Crosse
   Madison
   Marathon County
   Marinette
   Milwaukee
   Oshkosh
   Parkside
   Platteville
   River Falls
   Stevens Point
   Stout
   Superior
   Washington County
   Whitewater

Viterbo University
Western Wisconsin Technical College
Wisconsin Indianhead Technical College
Wisconsin Lutheran College

Wyoming
Casper College
Eastern Wyoming College
Laramie County Community College
Sheridan College
University of Wyoming
Western Wyoming Community College

Semester at sea

Alabama
Birmingham-Southern College

Alaska
University of Alaska
 Fairbanks

Arizona
University of Arizona

California
California Polytechnic State University:
 San Luis Obispo
California State University
 Monterey Bay
Chapman University
Marymount College
Sonoma State University
University of California
 San Diego
University of San Diego
Victor Valley College
Whittier College

Colorado
Colorado College
Colorado State University
Red Rocks Community College
University of Colorado
 Boulder
University of Northern Colorado

Connecticut
Connecticut College
Fairfield University
Manchester Community College
Trinity College
University of Connecticut
Wesleyan University

Delaware
Goldey-Beacom College

Florida
Barry University
Eckerd College
Rollins College
University of Florida

Georgia
Agnes Scott College
Morehouse College

Idaho
North Idaho College

Indiana
DePauw University
Franklin College
Indiana University
 Bloomington
University of Indianapolis
Wabash College

Iowa
Cornell College
Drake University

Kentucky
Murray State University

Maine
Bates College
Bowdoin College
Colby College
College of the Atlantic
Maine Maritime Academy
St. Joseph's College
University of Maine
University of Southern Maine

Maryland
Hood College
Salisbury University
University of Maryland
 Baltimore County
 College Park

Massachusetts
Babson College
Boston University
College of the Holy Cross
Lesley University
Massachusetts Maritime Academy
Mount Holyoke College
Northeastern University
Pine Manor College
Simmons College
Smith College
Stonehill College
Tufts University
Wellesley College

Michigan
Central Michigan University

Minnesota
Concordia College: Moorhead
Hamline University
Minnesota State University
 Mankato

Missouri
Maryville University of Saint Louis
Stephens College
Westminster College

Nebraska
Dana College
Nebraska Wesleyan University

New Hampshire
Colby-Sawyer College
Dartmouth College
Keene State College
New England College
University of New Hampshire
University of New Hampshire at
 Manchester

New Jersey
The College of New Jersey
Richard Stockton College of New Jersey
Rowan University

New York
Alfred University
Colgate University
Cornell University
Hobart and William Smith Colleges
Long Island University
 C. W. Post Campus
 Southampton College
State University of New York
 College at Brockport
 Maritime College

Syracuse University
United States Merchant Marine Academy

Ohio
Case Western Reserve University
Denison University
Heidelberg College
Mount Union College
Ohio State University
 Columbus Campus
Otterbein College
University of Dayton
Wittenberg University

Oklahoma
Oklahoma State University

Oregon
Linfield College
Oregon Institute of Technology
University of Oregon
Willamette University

Pennsylvania
Drexel University
Duquesne University
Franklin & Marshall College
Gettysburg College
Lafayette College
Mercyhurst College
Moravian College
University of Pittsburgh
University of Pittsburgh
 Bradford
 Greensburg
 Johnstown
 Titusville
University of Scranton

Puerto Rico
University of the Sacred Heart

Rhode Island
Roger Williams University
Salve Regina University

South Carolina
College of Charleston
Presbyterian College

Tennessee
O'More College of Design

Texas
Rice University
St. Edward's University
Southern Methodist University
Texas A&M University
 Galveston
Texas Christian University
Trinity University
University of Houston

Utah
University of Utah
Weber State University

Vermont
Middlebury College
St. Michael's College
Southern Vermont College

Virginia
College of William and Mary
Hampden-Sydney College
Mary Baldwin College
Mary Washington College
Virginia Commonwealth University

Washington
Western Washington University

West Virginia
West Virginia University

Wyoming
University of Wyoming

Student-designed major

Alabama
Birmingham-Southern College
Huntingdon College
Judson College
Lawson State Community College
Snead State Community College
Spring Hill College
Stillman College
Troy State University in Montgomery
University of Alabama
University of Alabama
 Birmingham
University of North Alabama
University of South Alabama

Alaska
Alaska Pacific University
Sheldon Jackson College
University of Alaska
 Anchorage
 Fairbanks

Arizona
Central Arizona College
Pima Community College
Prescott College

Arkansas
Harding University
Hendrix College
John Brown University
Lyon College
North Arkansas College
Rich Mountain Community College
University of Arkansas
 Cossatot Community College of the
 Little Rock

California
Academy of Art College
Antioch Southern California
 Los Angeles
 Santa Barbara
California College of Arts and Crafts
California Institute of Technology
California Institute of the Arts
California State University
 Bakersfield
 Chico
 Dominguez Hills
 Fresno
 Fullerton
 Hayward
 Long Beach
 Los Angeles
 Monterey Bay
 Northridge
 Sacramento
 San Bernardino
 San Marcos
 Stanislaus
Chabot College
Claremont McKenna College
College of the Sequoias
College of the Siskiyous
Concordia University
Cuesta College
Cuyamaca College
Dominican University of California
Fresno Pacific University
Grossmont Community College
Harvey Mudd College
Holy Names College
Hope International University

Humboldt State University
John F. Kennedy University
La Sierra University
Las Positas College
Los Angeles Pierce College
Loyola Marymount University
Menlo College
Mills College
MiraCosta College
Mount St. Mary's College
Occidental College
Orange Coast College
Pacific Oaks College
Pacific Union College
Pepperdine University
Pitzer College
Pomona College
St. Mary's College of California
San Diego City College
San Diego Mesa College
San Diego State University
San Francisco State University
San Jose State University
Santa Clara University
Scripps College
Simpson College
Sonoma State University
Stanford University
University of California
   Berkeley
   Davis
   Los Angeles
   Riverside
   San Diego
   Santa Barbara
   Santa Cruz
University of La Verne
University of Redlands
University of San Francisco
University of Southern California
University of the Pacific
Whittier College

Colorado

Arapahoe Community College
Colorado Christian University
Colorado College
Fort Lewis College
Heritage College
Metropolitan State College of Denver
Morgan Community College
Naropa University
Red Rocks Community College
Regis University
United States Air Force Academy
University of Colorado
   Boulder
   Denver
University of Denver
University of Northern Colorado

Connecticut

Albertus Magnus College
Central Connecticut State University
Connecticut College
Eastern Connecticut State University
Fairfield University
Manchester Community College
Middlesex Community College
Naugatuck Valley Community College
Quinnipiac University
Sacred Heart University
St. Joseph College
Southern Connecticut State University
Teikyo Post University
Trinity College
University of Bridgeport
University of Connecticut
University of Hartford
University of New Haven
Wesleyan University
Western Connecticut State University
Yale University

Delaware

University of Delaware

District of Columbia

American University
Gallaudet University
George Washington University
Georgetown University
Howard University
Trinity College

Florida

Eckerd College
Florida Atlantic University
Florida National College
Jacksonville University
Jones College
New College of Florida
Okaloosa-Walton Community College
Rollins College
Schiller International University
Stetson University
Talmudic College of Florida
University of Florida
University of Miami
University of North Florida
University of South Florida
University of Tampa
Valencia Community College

Georgia

Agnes Scott College
Atlanta College of Art
Berry College
Clayton College and State University
Covenant College
Fort Valley State University
Georgia College and State University
Georgia Institute of Technology
Georgia State University
Mercer University
Oglethorpe University
Shorter College
Spelman College
University of Georgia
Wesleyan College

Hawaii

Brigham Young University-Hawaii
Chaminade University of Honolulu
Hawaii Pacific University
University of Hawaii
   Hilo
   Honolulu Community College
   Manoa
   West Oahu

Idaho

Albertson College of Idaho
Boise State University
Idaho State University
Northwest Nazarene University
University of Idaho

Illinois

Aurora University
Blackburn College
Bradley University
Carl Sandburg College
Chicago State University
City Colleges of Chicago
   Olive-Harvey College
College of DuPage
College of Lake County
Columbia College Chicago
Dominican University
Eureka College
Governors State University
Greenville College
Illinois College

Illinois Eastern Community Colleges
   Frontier Community College
   Lincoln Trail College
   Olney Central College
   Wabash Valley College
Illinois State University
Illinois Wesleyan University
John Wood Community College
Judson College
Kaskaskia College
Kendall College
Knox College
Lake Forest College
Lewis University
Lewis and Clark Community College
Loyola University of Chicago
McKendree College
Millikin University
Monmouth College
North Central College
North Park University
Northern Illinois University
Northwestern University
Olivet Nazarene University
Principia College
Quincy University
Rock Valley College
Roosevelt University
St. Xavier University
Sauk Valley Community College
School of the Art Institute of Chicago
Southeastern Illinois College
Southern Illinois University Edwardsville
University of Chicago
University of Illinois
   Chicago
   Springfield
   Urbana-Champaign
University of St. Francis
Western Illinois University
Wheaton College

Indiana

Anderson University
Butler University
Calumet College of St. Joseph
DePauw University
Earlham College
Goshen College
Indiana University
   Bloomington
   Northwest
Indiana University-Purdue University
   Fort Wayne
Indiana Wesleyan University
Manchester College
Martin University
St. Joseph's College
Saint Mary's College
St. Mary-of-the-Woods College
Taylor University
Taylor University: Fort Wayne
University of Evansville
University of Indianapolis
University of Notre Dame
Valparaiso University
Vincennes University

Iowa

Briar Cliff University
Buena Vista University
Central College
Clarke College
Coe College
Cornell College
Dordt College
Drake University
Franciscan University
Graceland University
Grand View College
Grinnell College
Iowa State University
Iowa Wesleyan College
Kirkwood Community College
Loras College

Luther College
Morningside College
Mount Mercy College
Northeast Iowa Community College
Northwestern College
St. Ambrose University
Simpson College
University of Iowa
University of Northern Iowa
Upper Iowa University
Wartburg College

Kansas

Allen County Community College
Baker University
Benedictine College
Bethany College
Central Christian College
Emporia State University
Friends University
Garden City Community College
Highland Community College
Kansas Wesleyan University
McPherson College
Newman University
Ottawa University
Pittsburg State University
St. Mary College
Southwestern College
Sterling College
Tabor College
University of Kansas
Washburn University of Topeka

Kentucky

Alice Lloyd College
Berea College
Brescia University
Centre College
Cumberland College
Georgetown College
Morehead State University
Thomas More College
Transylvania University
Union College
University of Louisville

Louisiana

Centenary College of Louisiana
Delgado Community College
Louisiana College
Louisiana State University and
   Agricultural and Mechanical College
Loyola University New Orleans
Northwestern State University
Nunez Community College
Tulane University
University of Louisiana at Lafayette
University of New Orleans

Maine

Bates College
Bowdoin College
Colby College
College of the Atlantic
Husson College
Maine College of Art
New England School of Communications
University of Maine
University of Maine
   Augusta
   Farmington
   Machias
   Presque Isle
University of New England
University of Southern Maine

Maryland

Anne Arundel Community College
Chesapeake College
College of Notre Dame of Maryland
Columbia Union College
Goucher College
Hood College

Johns Hopkins University
Maryland Institute College of Art
McDaniel College
Montgomery College
    Rockville Campus
Mount St. Mary's College
St. Mary's College of Maryland
Salisbury University
Towson University
University of Baltimore
University of Maryland
    Baltimore County
    College Park
Villa Julie College
Washington College

Massachusetts

Amherst College
Anna Maria College
Assumption College
Babson College
Berklee College of Music
Berkshire Community College
Boston College
Boston University
Brandeis University
Clark University
College of the Holy Cross
Dean College
Emerson College
Emmanuel College
Fitchburg State College
Gordon College
Hampshire College
Harvard College
Hebrew College
Massachusetts College of Art
Massachusetts College of Liberal Arts
Merrimack College
Montserrat College of Art
Mount Holyoke College
Mount Ida College
Mount Wachusett Community College
Northeastern University
Pine Manor College
Regis College
Salem State College
Simmons College
Simon's Rock College of Bard
Smith College
Stonehill College
Tufts University
University of Massachusetts
    Amherst
    Boston
    Dartmouth
Wellesley College
Wentworth Institute of Technology
Western New England College
Westfield State College
Wheaton College
Williams College
Worcester Polytechnic Institute

Michigan

Adrian College
Alma College
Andrews University
Aquinas College
Calvin College
Central Michigan University
Concordia University
Eastern Michigan University
Finlandia University
Gogebic Community College
Grand Valley State University
Hope College
Marygrove College
Michigan State University
Michigan Technological University
Northern Michigan University
Oakland University
Saginaw Valley State University
Siena Heights University
Southwestern Michigan College

Spring Arbor University
University of Michigan
University of Michigan
    Dearborn
    Flint
Western Michigan University

Minnesota

Augsburg College
Bethel College
Carleton College
College of St. Benedict
College of St. Catherine
College of St. Scholastica
Crossroads College
Gustavus Adolphus College
Hamline University
Macalester College
Metropolitan State University
Minnesota State University
    Mankato
    Moorhead
Minnesota West Community and
    Technical College: Worthington
    Campus
North Central University
Ridgewater College: A Community and
    Technical College
St. Cloud State University
St. John's University
St. Mary's University of Minnesota
St. Olaf College
Southwest State University
University of Minnesota
    Crookston
    Duluth
    Morris
    Twin Cities
University of St. Thomas
Winona State University

Mississippi

Mississippi State University

Missouri

Calvary Bible College
Central Methodist College
Central Missouri State University
College of the Ozarks
Columbia College
Culver-Stockton College
Drury University
Fontbonne College
Hannibal-LaGrange College
Harris Stowe State College
Lindenwood University
Maryville University of Saint Louis
Missouri Baptist University
Missouri Valley College
Southeast Missouri State University
Southwest Missouri State University
Stephens College
University of Missouri
    Columbia
    St. Louis
Washington University in St. Louis
Webster University
Westminster College
William Jewell College
William Woods University

Montana

Carroll College
Montana State University
    Bozeman
Montana Tech of the University of
    Montana
Rocky Mountain College

Nebraska

Chadron State College
College of Saint Mary
Dana College
Doane College

Hastings College
Midland Lutheran College
Union College
University of Nebraska
    Lincoln
    Omaha
Wayne State College
Western Nebraska Community College

Nevada

Community College of Southern Nevada
University of Nevada
    Las Vegas

New Hampshire

Colby-Sawyer College
College for Lifelong Learning
Dartmouth College
Franklin Pierce College
Keene State College
New England College
New Hampshire Community Technical
    College
    Manchester
    Nashua
Plymouth State College
University of New Hampshire
University of New Hampshire at
    Manchester

New Jersey

Bloomfield College
Caldwell College
Centenary College
College of St. Elizabeth
Drew University
Felician College
Monmouth University
Passaic County Community College
Princeton University
Ramapo College of New Jersey
Richard Stockton College of New Jersey
Rutgers, The State University of New
    Jersey
    Camden Regional Campus
    New Brunswick Regional Campus
    Newark Regional Campus
St. Peter's College
Union County College

New Mexico

College of Santa Fe
Eastern New Mexico University
New Mexico Institute of Mining and
    Technology
New Mexico State University
University of New Mexico

New York

Adelphi University
Alfred University
Bard College
Barnard College
Broome Community College
Canisius College
Cazenovia College
City University of New York
    Baruch College
    College of Staten Island
    Hunter College
    La Guardia Community College
    Queens College
Clarkson University
Clinton Community College
Colgate University
College of Mount St. Vincent
College of New Rochelle
College of New Rochelle: School of New
    Resources
Columbia University
    Columbia College
Concordia College
Cooper Union for the Advancement of
    Science and Art

Cornell University
Daemen College
Eastman School of Music of the
    University of Rochester
Elmira College
Erie Community College
    City Campus
    North Campus
    South Campus
Eugene Lang College/New School
    University
Fordham University
Fulton-Montgomery Community College
Hamilton College
Hartwick College
Hobart and William Smith Colleges
Hofstra University
Hudson Valley Community College
Ithaca College
Jefferson Community College
Keuka College
Long Island University
    C. W. Post Campus
    Southampton College
Manhattanville College
Marist College
Marymount College of Fordham
    University
Medaille College
Mercy College
Mohawk Valley Community College
Molloy College
New York University
Niagara County Community College
North Country Community College
Parsons School of Design
Paul Smith's College
Pratt Institute
Rensselaer Polytechnic Institute
Rochester Institute of Technology
Rockland Community College
Russell Sage College
Sage College of Albany
St. Bonaventure University
St. John Fisher College
St. Lawrence University
Sarah Lawrence College
Skidmore College
State University of New York
    Albany
    Binghamton
    Buffalo
    College at Brockport
    College at Cortland
    College at Fredonia
    College at Plattsburgh
    College at Potsdam
    College of Agriculture and
        Technology at Morrisville
    College of Technology at Alfred
    College of Technology at Canton
    College of Technology at Delhi
    Empire State College
    New Paltz
    Purchase
    Stony Brook
Syracuse University
Touro College
Ulster County Community College
Union College
University of Rochester
Vassar College
Wells College
Westchester Community College
Yeshiva University

North Carolina

Appalachian State University
Bennett College
Brevard College
Catawba College
Catawba Valley Community College
Craven Community College
Davidson College
Duke University

East Carolina University
Elon University
Forsyth Technical Community College
Greensboro College
Guilford College
Lees-McRae College
Lenoir-Rhyne College
Mars Hill College
Meredith College
Methodist College
North Carolina State University
Richmond Community College
Rockingham Community College
St. Andrews Presbyterian College
Salem College
Shaw University
Surry Community College
University of North Carolina
    Asheville
    Chapel Hill
    Greensboro
Warren Wilson College
Western Carolina University

North Dakota

Dickinson State University
Jamestown College
Mayville State University
Minot State University
North Dakota State College of Science
North Dakota State University
University of North Dakota
Valley City State University
Williston State College

Ohio

Antioch College
Antioch University McGregor
Art Academy of Cincinnati
Ashland University
Baldwin-Wallace College
Bluffton College
Bowling Green State University
Bowling Green State University:
    Firelands College
Case Western Reserve University
Cedarville University
Cincinnati State Technical and
    Community College
Circleville Bible College
Clark State Community College
Cleveland State University
College of Wooster
Columbus State Community College
David N. Myers College
Defiance College
Denison University
Edison State Community College
Franklin University
Heidelberg College
Hiram College
Hocking Technical College
James A. Rhodes State College
John Carroll University
Kent State University
Kent State University
    Ashtabula Regional Campus
    East Liverpool Regional Campus
    Stark Campus
    Trumbull Campus
    Tuscarawas Campus
Kenyon College
Lake Erie College
Lourdes College
Malone College
Marietta College
Marion Technical College
Miami University
    Hamilton Campus
    Middletown Campus
    Oxford Campus
Mount Union College
Muskingum Area Technical College
Muskingum College
North Central State College

Northwest State Community College
Notre Dame College
Oberlin College
Ohio Dominican College
Ohio State University
    Agricultural Technical Institute
    Columbus Campus
    Marion Campus
    Newark Campus
Ohio University
Ohio University
    Chillicothe Campus
    Eastern Campus
    Lancaster Campus
    Southern Campus at Ironton
    Zanesville Campus
Ohio Wesleyan University
Otterbein College
Owens Community College
    Findlay Campus
    Toledo
Shawnee State University
Sinclair Community College
Southern State Community College
Stark State College of Technology
Tiffin University
Union Institute & University
University of Akron
University of Cincinnati
    Clermont College
    Raymond Walters College
University of Findlay
University of Rio Grande
University of Toledo
Urbana University
Washington State Community College
Wilmington College
Wittenberg University
Wright State University
Wright State University: Lake Campus
Youngstown State University

Oklahoma

Cameron University
Northeastern State University
Oklahoma Baptist University
Oklahoma City Community College
Oklahoma City University
Oklahoma State University
Oklahoma Wesleyan University
Oral Roberts University
St. Gregory's University
Southern Nazarene University
Southwestern Oklahoma State University
University of Oklahoma
University of Science and Arts of
    Oklahoma
University of Tulsa

Oregon

Central Oregon Community College
Clatsop Community College
Eastern Oregon University
George Fox University
Lewis & Clark College
Linfield College
Linn-Benton Community College
Marylhurst University
Oregon State University
Pacific Northwest College of Art
Southern Oregon University
University of Portland
Warner Pacific College
Western Oregon University
Willamette University

Pennsylvania

Albright College
Allegheny College
Arcadia University
Bryn Athyn College of the New Church
Bryn Mawr College
Bucknell University
Bucks County Community College

Cabrini College
California University of Pennsylvania
Carlow College
Carnegie Mellon University
Cedar Crest College
Chatham College
Chestnut Hill College
Delaware County Community College
Dickinson College
Duquesne University
East Stroudsburg University of
    Pennsylvania
Edinboro University of Pennsylvania
Franklin & Marshall College
Geneva College
Gettysburg College
Grove City College
Harrisburg Area Community College
Haverford College
Juniata College
Keystone College
King's College
Kutztown University of Pennsylvania
La Salle University
Lafayette College
Lebanon Valley College of Pennsylvania
Lock Haven University of Pennsylvania
Lycoming College
Marywood University
Mercyhurst College
Messiah College
Montgomery County Community
    College
Moravian College
Mount Aloysius College
Muhlenberg College
Neumann College
Northampton County Area Community
    College
Penn State
    Abington
    Altoona
    Delaware County
    Dubois
    Fayette
    University Park
    York
Pennsylvania College of Technology
Point Park College
Reading Area Community College
Rosemont College
St. Joseph's University
Seton Hill University
Swarthmore College
Temple University
University of Pennsylvania
University of Pittsburgh
University of Pittsburgh
    Greensburg
    Johnstown
Washington and Jefferson College
West Chester University of Pennsylvania
Westmoreland County Community
    College
Widener University
Wilkes University
Wilson College

Puerto Rico

Atlantic College

Rhode Island

Brown University
Providence College
Rhode Island College
Roger Williams University
University of Rhode Island

South Carolina

Anderson College
Coastal Carolina University
Coker College
Columbia College
Converse College

Furman University
Lander University
Limestone College
Newberry College
North Greenville College
Tri-County Technical College
University of South Carolina
University of South Carolina
    Aiken
    Salkehatchie Regional Campus
    Spartanburg
    Sumter
    Union
Williamsburg Technical College
Wofford College

South Dakota

Augustana College
Dakota State University
Dakota Wesleyan University
Mount Marty College
Northern State University
University of Sioux Falls
University of South Dakota

Tennessee

Belmont University
Bethel College
Carson-Newman College
Chattanooga State Technical Community
    College
Crichton College
Fisk University
Freed-Hardeman University
Lambuth University
Maryville College
Rhodes College
Southwest Tennessee Community
    College
Tennessee Wesleyan College
Tusculum College
University of Memphis
University of Tennessee
    Knoxville
    Martin
Vanderbilt University

Texas

Abilene Christian University
Austin College
Baylor University
Clarendon College
Jarvis Christian College
Lubbock Christian University
Midland College
Rice University
Schreiner University
Southern Methodist University
Southwestern Adventist University
Southwestern University
Stephen F. Austin State University
Texas A&M University
    Texarkana
Texas Tech University
University of Dallas
University of Houston
    Downtown
University of Texas
    Arlington
    Austin
    Dallas
    Tyler

Utah

University of Utah
Utah State University
Utah Valley State College
Weber State University
Westminster College

Vermont

Bennington College
Burlington College
Castleton State College

Community College of Vermont
Goddard College
Green Mountain College
Marlboro College
Middlebury College
Norwich University
St. Michael's College
Southern Vermont College
Sterling College
University of Vermont
Woodbury College

Virginia

Averett University
Bluefield College
College of William and Mary
Emory & Henry College
Ferrum College
George Mason University
Hollins University
Liberty University
Mary Baldwin College
Mary Washington College
Marymount University
Mountain Empire Community College
Old Dominion University
Radford University
Randolph-Macon Woman's College
Sweet Briar College
University of Richmond
University of Virginia
University of Virginia's College at Wise
Virginia Commonwealth University
Virginia Polytechnic Institute and State
 University
Virginia Wesleyan College
Washington and Lee University

Washington

Central Washington University
Centralia College
Eastern Washington University
Evergreen State College
Heritage College
Northwest College
Pacific Lutheran University
Renton Technical College
Seattle Pacific University
Seattle University
Spokane Community College
University of Puget Sound
University of Washington
Wenatchee Valley College
Western Washington University
Whitman College
Whitworth College

West Virginia

Bethany College
Bluefield State College
Concord College
Davis and Elkins College
Glenville State College
Mountain State University
University of Charleston
West Liberty State College
West Virginia University
West Virginia University Institute of
 Technology
West Virginia Wesleyan College
Wheeling Jesuit University

Wisconsin

Beloit College
Blackhawk Technical College
Cardinal Stritch University
Carroll College
Carthage College
Chippewa Valley Technical College
Concordia University Wisconsin
Edgewood College
Lakeshore Technical College
Lawrence University
Marian College of Fond du Lac

Mount Mary College
Nicolet Area Technical College
Northland College
Ripon College
St. Norbert College
Silver Lake College
University of Wisconsin
 Green Bay
 Madison
 Milwaukee
 Oshkosh
 Platteville
 River Falls
 Stevens Point
 Superior
 Whitewater
Viterbo University
Waukesha County Technical College
Wisconsin Lutheran College

Wyoming

Central Wyoming College
University of Wyoming

Study abroad

Alabama

Athens State University
Auburn University
Auburn University at Montgomery
Birmingham-Southern College
Huntingdon College
Judson College
Northeast Alabama Community College
Oakwood College
Samford University
Spring Hill College
Stillman College
Talladega College
Troy State University
University of Alabama
University of Alabama
 Birmingham
University of Montevallo
University of South Alabama

Alaska

Alaska Pacific University
University of Alaska
 Anchorage
 Fairbanks
 Southeast

Arizona

Arizona State University
Arizona Western College
Embry-Riddle Aeronautical University:
 Prescott Campus
Gateway Community College
Northern Arizona University
Phoenix College
Scottsdale Community College
University of Arizona

Arkansas

Arkansas State University
Harding University
Hendrix College
John Brown University
Lyon College
Ouachita Baptist University
Philander Smith College
University of Arkansas
University of Arkansas
 Cossatot Community College of the
 Little Rock
University of Central Arkansas
University of the Ozarks
Williams Baptist College

California

Antelope Valley College

Antioch Southern California
 Los Angeles
 Santa Barbara
Azusa Pacific University
Biola University
Cabrillo College
California Baptist University
California College of Arts and Crafts
California Institute of Technology
California Institute of the Arts
California Polytechnic State University:
 San Luis Obispo
California State Polytechnic University:
 Pomona
California State University
 Bakersfield
 Chico
 Dominguez Hills
 Fresno
 Fullerton
 Hayward
 Long Beach
 Los Angeles
 Monterey Bay
 Northridge
 Sacramento
 San Bernardino
 San Marcos
 Stanislaus
Cerro Coso Community College
Chabot College
Chapman University
Christian Heritage College
Citrus College
Claremont McKenna College
Coastline Community College
College of the Canyons
College of the Sequoias
College of the Siskiyous
Cuesta College
De Anza College
Diablo Valley College
Dominican School of Philosophy and
 Theology
Dominican University of California
East Los Angeles College
Fashion Institute of Design and
 Merchandising
Fashion Institute of Design and
 Merchandising
 San Francisco
Foothill College
Fresno Pacific University
Gavilan Community College
Glendale Community College
Golden West College
Grossmont Community College
Harvey Mudd College
Holy Names College
Hope International University
Humboldt State University
Irvine Valley College
La Sierra University
Loma Linda University
Long Beach City College
Los Angeles Harbor College
Los Angeles Pierce College
Los Angeles Southwest College
Los Angeles Trade and Technical College
Los Medanos College
Loyola Marymount University
Marymount College
Master's College
Menlo College
Mills College
MiraCosta College
Modesto Junior College
Monterey Institute of International
 Studies
Moorpark College
Mount St. Mary's College
Mount San Antonio College
Napa Valley College
Occidental College
Ohlone College

Orange Coast College
Otis College of Art and Design
Pacific Union College
Palomar College
Pepperdine University
Pitzer College
Point Loma Nazarene University
Pomona College
Reedley College
Riverside Community College
St. Mary's College of California
San Diego City College
San Diego Mesa College
San Diego State University
San Francisco State University
San Joaquin Delta College
San Jose State University
Santa Barbara City College
Santa Clara University
Santa Monica College
Santa Rosa Junior College
Scripps College
Sierra College
Simpson College
Sonoma State University
Southern California Institute of
 Architecture
Southwestern College
Stanford University
University of California
 Berkeley
 Davis
 Los Angeles
 Riverside
 San Diego
 Santa Barbara
 Santa Cruz
University of La Verne
University of Redlands
University of San Diego
University of San Francisco
University of Southern California
University of the Pacific
Vanguard University of Southern
 California
Ventura College
Victor Valley College
Vista Community College
Whittier College
Woodbury University
Yuba Community College District

Colorado

Art Institute
 of Colorado
Colorado Christian University
Colorado College
Colorado Mountain College
 Alpine Campus
 Spring Valley Campus
 Timberline Campus
Colorado School of Mines
Colorado State University
Colorado State University
 Pueblo
Community College of Aurora
Fort Lewis College
Front Range Community College
Metropolitan State College of Denver
Naropa University
Red Rocks Community College
Regis University
United States Air Force Academy
University of Colorado
 Boulder
 Colorado Springs
 Denver
University of Denver
University of Northern Colorado

Connecticut

Albertus Magnus College
Central Connecticut State University
Connecticut College
Eastern Connecticut State University

Fairfield University
International College of Hospitality
    Management
Naugatuck Valley Community College
Quinebaug Valley Community College
Quinnipiac University
Sacred Heart University
St. Joseph College
Southern Connecticut State University
Teikyo Post University
Three Rivers Community College
Trinity College
University of Bridgeport
University of Connecticut
University of Hartford
University of New Haven
Wesleyan University
Western Connecticut State University
Yale University

Delaware

Delaware State University
University of Delaware

District of Columbia

American University
Catholic University of America
Corcoran College of Art and Design
Gallaudet University
George Washington University
Georgetown University
Howard University
Trinity College

Florida

Barry University
Beacon College
Bethune-Cookman College
Broward Community College
Daytona Beach Community College
Eckerd College
Embry-Riddle Aeronautical University
Flagler College
Florida Agricultural and Mechanical
    University
Florida Atlantic University
Florida Gulf Coast University
Florida International University
Florida Southern College
Florida State University
Hillsborough Community College
International Academy of Design and
    Technology
Jacksonville University
Lake City Community College
Miami-Dade Community College
New College of Florida
Northwood University
    Florida Campus
Nova Southeastern University
Palm Beach Atlantic University
Palm Beach Community College
Pensacola Junior College
Ringling School of Art and Design
Rollins College
St. Leo University
Schiller International University
Seminole Community College
Stetson University
Tallahassee Community College
Talmudic College of Florida
University of Central Florida
University of Florida
University of Miami
University of North Florida
University of South Florida
University of Tampa
University of West Florida
Valencia Community College
Webber International University

Georgia

Abraham Baldwin Agricultural College
Agnes Scott College

Albany State University
Armstrong Atlantic State University
Art Institute
    of Atlanta
Atlanta College of Art
Atlanta Metropolitan College
Augusta State University
Bainbridge College
Bauder College
Berry College
Brenau University
Clark Atlanta University
Clayton College and State University
Coastal Georgia Community College
Columbus State University
Covenant College
Dalton State College
Darton College
East Georgia College
Emory University
Floyd College
Fort Valley State University
Gainesville College
Georgia College and State University
Georgia Institute of Technology
Georgia Perimeter College
Georgia Southern University
Georgia Southwestern State University
Georgia State University
Gordon College
Kennesaw State University
LaGrange College
Macon State College
Mercer University
Middle Georgia College
Morehouse College
Morris Brown College
North Georgia College & State
    University
Oglethorpe University
Oxford College of Emory University
Paine College
Reinhardt College
Savannah College of Art and Design
Shorter College
South Georgia College
Southern Polytechnic State University
Spelman College
State University of West Georgia
Truett-McConnell College
University of Georgia
Valdosta State University
Waycross College
Wesleyan College
Young Harris College

Hawaii

Chaminade University of Honolulu
Hawaii Pacific University
Hawaii Tokai International College
University of Hawaii
    Hilo
    Kauai Community College
    Manoa

Idaho

Albertson College of Idaho
Boise Bible College
Boise State University
Idaho State University
Northwest Nazarene University
University of Idaho

Illinois

American Academy of Art
Augustana College
Aurora University
Benedictine University
Black Hawk College
Black Hawk College
    East Campus
Blackburn College
Bradley University
Carl Sandburg College

Chicago State University
City Colleges of Chicago
    Olive-Harvey College
College of DuPage
College of Lake County
Columbia College Chicago
Concordia University
Cooking & Hospitality Institute of
    Chicago
De Paul University
Dominican University
Eastern Illinois University
Elgin Community College
Elmhurst College
Eureka College
Governors State University
Greenville College
Harrington Institute of Interior Design
Heartland Community College
Illinois College
Illinois Eastern Community Colleges
    Frontier Community College
    Lincoln Trail College
    Olney Central College
    Wabash Valley College
Illinois Institute of Technology
Illinois State University
Illinois Valley Community College
Illinois Wesleyan University
International Academy of Design and
    Technology
John A. Logan College
John Wood Community College
Joliet Junior College
Judson College
Kankakee Community College
Kaskaskia College
Kendall College
Kishwaukee College
Knox College
Lake Forest College
Lake Land College
Lewis University
Lincoln College
Lincoln Land Community College
Loyola University of Chicago
MacMurray College
McHenry County College
McKendree College
Millikin University
Monmouth College
Moody Bible Institute
Moraine Valley Community College
North Central College
North Park University
Northeastern Illinois University
Northern Illinois University
Northwestern University
Oakton Community College
Olivet Nazarene University
Parkland College
Prairie State College
Principia College
Quincy University
Robert Morris College: Chicago
Rock Valley College
Rockford College
Roosevelt University
St. Xavier University
Sauk Valley Community College
School of the Art Institute of Chicago
Shimer College
South Suburban College of Cook County
Southeastern Illinois College
Southern Illinois University Carbondale
Southern Illinois University Edwardsville
Southwestern Illinois College
Springfield College in Illinois
Trinity Christian College
Trinity International University
University of Chicago
University of Illinois
    Chicago
    Urbana-Champaign
University of St. Francis

Waubonsee Community College
Western Illinois University
Wheaton College
William Rainey Harper College

Indiana

Anderson University
Ball State University
Bethel College
Butler University
Calumet College of St. Joseph
DePauw University
Earlham College
Franklin College
Goshen College
Grace College
Hanover College
Holy Cross College
Huntington College
Indiana State University
Indiana University
    Bloomington
    Kokomo
    Northwest
    South Bend
    Southeast
Indiana University-Purdue University
    Fort Wayne
Indiana University-Purdue University
    Indianapolis
Indiana Wesleyan University
Manchester College
Marian College
Purdue University
Purdue University
    Calumet
Rose-Hulman Institute of Technology
St. Joseph's College
Saint Mary's College
St. Mary-of-the-Woods College
Taylor University
Taylor University: Fort Wayne
University of Evansville
University of Indianapolis
University of Notre Dame
University of St. Francis
University of Southern Indiana
Valparaiso University
Wabash College

Iowa

Briar Cliff University
Buena Vista University
Central College
Clarke College
Clinton Community College
Coe College
Cornell College
Des Moines Area Community College
Divine Word College
Dordt College
Drake University
Faith Baptist Bible College and
    Theological Seminary
Franciscan University
Graceland University
Grand View College
Grinnell College
Hawkeye Community College
Iowa Central Community College
Iowa State University
Iowa Wesleyan College
Kirkwood Community College
Loras College
Luther College
Maharishi University of Management
Marshalltown Community College
Morningside College
Mount Mercy College
Muscatine Community College
Northeast Iowa Community College
Northwestern College
St. Ambrose University
Scott Community College
Simpson College

University of Dubuque
University of Iowa
University of Northern Iowa
Upper Iowa University
Waldorf College
Wartburg College

Kansas

Baker University
Benedictine College
Bethel College
Emporia State University
Fort Scott Community College
Friends University
Johnson County Community College
Kansas State University
McPherson College
MidAmerica Nazarene University
Newman University
Pittsburg State University
St. Mary College
Southwestern College
Sterling College
Tabor College
University of Kansas
Washburn University of Topeka
Wichita State University

Kentucky

Alice Lloyd College
Asbury College
Bellarmine University
Berea College
Brescia University
Campbellsville University
Centre College
Cumberland College
Georgetown College
Kentucky Christian College
Kentucky Wesleyan College
Lindsey Wilson College
Mid-Continent College
Morehead State University
Murray State University
Pikeville College
Spalding University
Thomas More College
Transylvania University
Union College
University of Kentucky
University of Louisville

Louisiana

Centenary College of Louisiana
Dillard University
Grambling State University
Louisiana College
Louisiana State University
    Shreveport
Louisiana State University and
    Agricultural and Mechanical College
Louisiana Tech University
Loyola University New Orleans
McNeese State University
Nicholls State University
Northwestern State University
Our Lady of Holy Cross College
Southeastern Louisiana University
Southern University and Agricultural and
    Mechanical College
Tulane University
University of Louisiana at Lafayette
University of Louisiana at Monroe
University of New Orleans
Xavier University of Louisiana

Maine

Bates College
Bowdoin College
Central Maine Technical College
Colby College
College of the Atlantic
Maine College of Art
Maine Maritime Academy

St. Joseph's College
Thomas College
University of Maine
University of Maine
    Farmington
    Machias
    Presque Isle
University of New England
University of Southern Maine

Maryland

Baltimore International College
Bowie State University
College of Notre Dame of Maryland
College of Southern Maryland
Columbia Union College
Community College of Baltimore County
    Catonsville
    Dundalk
    Essex
Frederick Community College
Frostburg State University
Goucher College
Hood College
Howard Community College
Johns Hopkins University
Loyola College in Maryland
Maryland Institute College of Art
McDaniel College
Montgomery College
    Rockville Campus
Mount St. Mary's College
St. Mary's College of Maryland
Salisbury University
Towson University
University of Baltimore
University of Maryland
    Baltimore County
    College Park
Villa Julie College
Washington Bible College
Washington College

Massachusetts

American International College
Amherst College
Anna Maria College
Art Institute of Boston at Lesley
    University
Assumption College
Atlantic Union College
Babson College
Bay Path College
Becker College
Bentley College
Berklee College of Music
Boston College
Boston University
Brandeis University
Bridgewater State College
Bunker Hill Community College
Cape Cod Community College
Clark University
College of the Holy Cross
Dean College
Elms College
Emerson College
Emmanuel College
Endicott College
Fitchburg State College
Framingham State College
Franklin W. Olin College of Engineering
Gordon College
Hampshire College
Harvard College
Hellenic College/Holy Cross
Lasell College
Lesley University
Massachusetts Bay Community College
Massachusetts College of Art
Massachusetts College of Liberal Arts
Massachusetts Institute of Technology
Merrimack College
Montserrat College of Art
Mount Holyoke College

Mount Ida College
Mount Wachusett Community College
New England Conservatory of Music
Newbury College
Nichols College
Northeastern University
Pine Manor College
Regis College
St. John's Seminary College
Salem State College
School of the Museum of Fine Arts
Simmons College
Simon's Rock College of Bard
Smith College
Springfield College
Stonehill College
Suffolk University
Tufts University
University of Massachusetts
    Amherst
    Boston
    Dartmouth
    Lowell
Wellesley College
Wentworth Institute of Technology
Western New England College
Westfield State College
Wheaton College
Williams College
Worcester Polytechnic Institute

Michigan

Adrian College
Alma College
Andrews University
Aquinas College
Calvin College
Central Michigan University
College for Creative Studies
Concordia University
Cornerstone University
Davenport University - Western Region
Eastern Michigan University
Ferris State University
Finlandia University
Grand Rapids Community College
Grand Valley State University
Hillsdale College
Hope College
Kalamazoo College
Kettering University
Lansing Community College
Lawrence Technological University
Macomb Community College
Madonna University
Marygrove College
Michigan State University
Michigan Technological University
Northern Michigan University
Northwestern Michigan College
Northwood University
Oakland University
Reformed Bible College
Saginaw Valley State University
Siena Heights University
Spring Arbor University
University of Michigan
University of Michigan
    Dearborn
    Flint
Wayne State University
Western Michigan University

Minnesota

Anoka-Ramsey Community College
Augsburg College
Bemidji State University
Bethel College
Carleton College
Central Lakes College
College of St. Benedict
College of St. Catherine
College of St. Scholastica
College of Visual Arts
Concordia College: Moorhead

Concordia University: St. Paul
Crown College
Fergus Falls Community College
Gustavus Adolphus College
Hamline University
Hibbing Community College: A
    Technical and Community College
Inver Hills Community College
Itasca Community College
Macalester College
Mesabi Range Community and Technical
    College
Minnesota State University
    Mankato
    Moorhead
Minnesota West Community and
    Technical College: Worthington
    Campus
Normandale Community College
North Central University
North Hennepin Community College
Northwestern College
Oak Hills Christian College
Ridgewater College: A Community and
    Technical College
Riverland Community College: A
    Technical and Community College
St. Cloud State University
St. John's University
St. Mary's University of Minnesota
St. Olaf College
Southwest State University
University of Minnesota
    Crookston
    Duluth
    Morris
    Twin Cities
University of St. Thomas
Winona State University

Mississippi

Millsaps College
Mississippi College
Mississippi State University
Mississippi University for Women
Rust College
University of Mississippi
University of Southern Mississippi

Missouri

Avila University
Central Methodist College
Central Missouri State University
College of the Ozarks
Columbia College
Crowder College
Culver-Stockton College
Drury University
East Central College
Evangel University
Fontbonne College
Hannibal-LaGrange College
Jefferson College
Kansas City Art Institute
Lindenwood University
Maryville University of Saint Louis
Mineral Area College
Missouri Baptist University
Missouri Southern State College
Moberly Area Community College
Northwest Missouri State University
Research College of Nursing
Rockhurst University
St. Charles Community College
St. Louis Community College
    St. Louis Community College at
        Florissant Valley
    St. Louis Community College at
        Forest Park
    St. Louis Community College at
        Meramec
St. Louis University
Southeast Missouri State University
Southwest Baptist University
Southwest Missouri State University

Stephens College
Truman State University
University of Missouri
  Columbia
  Kansas City
  Rolla
  St. Louis
Washington University in St. Louis
Webster University
Westminster College
William Jewell College
William Woods University

Montana
Carroll College
Montana State University
  Billings
  Bozeman
Rocky Mountain College
University of Montana-Missoula

Nebraska
Bellevue University
Chadron State College
Clarkson College
Concordia University
Creighton University
Dana College
Doane College
Grace University
Hastings College
Midland Lutheran College
Nebraska Wesleyan University
Peru State College
Union College
University of Nebraska
  Kearney
  Lincoln
  Omaha

Nevada
University of Nevada
  Las Vegas
  Reno

New Hampshire
Colby-Sawyer College
Daniel Webster College
Dartmouth College
Franklin Pierce College
Keene State College
New England College
Plymouth State College
Rivier College
St. Anselm College
Southern New Hampshire University
Thomas More College of Liberal Arts
University of New Hampshire
University of New Hampshire at
  Manchester

New Jersey
Bergen Community College
Berkeley College
Bloomfield College
Brookdale Community College
Caldwell College
Centenary College
The College of New Jersey
College of St. Elizabeth
County College of Morris
Drew University
Fairleigh Dickinson University
  College at Florham
  Metropolitan Campus
Felician College
Georgian Court College
Kean University
Middlesex County College
Monmouth University
Montclair State University
New Jersey City University
New Jersey Institute of Technology
Ocean County College

Passaic County Community College
Princeton University
Ramapo College of New Jersey
Richard Stockton College of New Jersey
Rider University
Rowan University
Rutgers, The State University of New
  Jersey
    Camden Regional Campus
    New Brunswick Regional Campus
    Newark Regional Campus
St. Peter's College
Seton Hall University
Stevens Institute of Technology
Sussex County Community College
William Paterson University of New
  Jersey

New Mexico
College of Santa Fe
Eastern New Mexico University
New Mexico Institute of Mining and
  Technology
New Mexico State University
University of New Mexico

New York
Adelphi University
Adirondack Community College
Alfred University
Bard College
Barnard College
Berkeley College
Berkeley College of New York City
Broome Community College
Canisius College
Cayuga County Community College
Cazenovia College
City University of New York
  Baruch College
  Borough of Manhattan Community
    College
  Brooklyn College
  City College
  College of Staten Island
  Hostos Community College
  Hunter College
  John Jay College of Criminal
    Justice
  Medgar Evers College
  Queens College
Clarkson University
Colgate University
College of Mount St. Vincent
College of New Rochelle
Columbia University
  Columbia College
  Fu Foundation School of
    Engineering and Applied Science
Concordia College
Cooper Union for the Advancement of
  Science and Art
Cornell University
Corning Community College
D'Youville College
Daemen College
Dutchess Community College
Elmira College
Erie Community College
  City Campus
  North Campus
  South Campus
Eugene Lang College/New School
  University
Fashion Institute of Technology
Fordham University
Fulton-Montgomery Community College
Genesee Community College
Hamilton College
Hartwick College
Hobart and William Smith Colleges
Hofstra University
Houghton College
Iona College
Ithaca College

Jamestown Community College
Juilliard School
Keuka College
Laboratory Institute of Merchandising
Le Moyne College
Long Island University
  C. W. Post Campus
  Southampton College
Machzikei Hadath Rabbinical College
Manhattan College
Manhattanville College
Marist College
Marymount College of Fordham
  University
Marymount Manhattan College
Mercy College
Metropolitan College of New York
Mohawk Valley Community College
Molloy College
Mount St. Mary College
Nassau Community College
Nazareth College of Rochester
New York Institute of Technology
New York School of Interior Design
New York University
Niagara County Community College
Niagara University
Nyack College
Ohr Somayach Tanenbaum Education
  Center
Onondaga Community College
Pace University
Pace University: Pleasantville/Briarcliff
Parsons School of Design
Paul Smith's College
Pratt Institute
Rensselaer Polytechnic Institute
Roberts Wesleyan College
Rochester Institute of Technology
Rockland Community College
Russell Sage College
Sage College of Albany
St. Bonaventure University
St. John Fisher College
St. John's University
St. Joseph's College: Suffolk Campus
St. Lawrence University
Sarah Lawrence College
School of Visual Arts
Skidmore College
State University of New York
  Albany
  Binghamton
  Buffalo
  College at Brockport
  College at Buffalo
  College at Cortland
  College at Fredonia
  College at Geneseo
  College at Old Westbury
  College at Oneonta
  College at Plattsburgh
  College at Potsdam
  College of Agriculture and
    Technology at Cobleskill
  College of Agriculture and
    Technology at Morrisville
  College of Environmental Science
    and Forestry
  Empire State College
  Farmingdale
  Maritime College
  New Paltz
  Oswego
  Purchase
  Stony Brook
Syracuse University
Tompkins-Cortland Community College
Touro College
Union College
United States Military Academy
University of Rochester
Utica College
Vassar College
Villa Maria College of Buffalo

Wagner College
Wells College
Yeshiva University

North Carolina
Appalachian State University
Barton College
Belmont Abbey College
Brevard College
Campbell University
Catawba College
Chowan College
Davidson College
Duke University
East Carolina University
Elon University
Gardner-Webb University
Greensboro College
Guilford College
John Wesley College
Johnson C. Smith University
Lees-McRae College
Lenoir Community College
Lenoir-Rhyne College
Mars Hill College
Meredith College
Methodist College
Montreat College
North Carolina Agricultural and
  Technical State University
North Carolina State University
Peace College
Pfeiffer University
Queens University of Charlotte
St. Andrews Presbyterian College
St. Augustine's College
Salem College
Shaw University
University of North Carolina
  Asheville
  Chapel Hill
  Charlotte
  Greensboro
  Pembroke
  Wilmington
Wake Forest University
Warren Wilson College
Western Carolina University
Wingate University

North Dakota
Dickinson State University
Minot State University
North Dakota State University
University of Mary
University of North Dakota

Ohio
Antioch College
Art Academy of Cincinnati
Ashland University
Baldwin-Wallace College
Bluffton College
Bowling Green State University
Case Western Reserve University
Cedarville University
Central State University
Clark State Community College
Cleveland State University
College of Mount St. Joseph
College of Wooster
Columbus College of Art and Design
Columbus State Community College
Defiance College
Denison University
Franciscan University of Steubenville
Franklin University
Heidelberg College
Hiram College
Hocking Technical College
John Carroll University
Kent State University
Kenyon College
Lake Erie College

Lorain County Community College
Malone College
Marietta College
Miami University
  Hamilton Campus
  Middletown Campus
  Oxford Campus
Mount Union College
Mount Vernon Nazarene University
Muskingum College
Notre Dame College
Oberlin College
Ohio Dominican College
Ohio Northern University
Ohio State University
  Columbus Campus
Ohio University
Ohio University
  Chillicothe Campus
  Zanesville Campus
Ohio Wesleyan University
Otterbein College
Tiffin University
University of Akron
University of Cincinnati
University of Cincinnati
  Raymond Walters College
University of Dayton
University of Findlay
University of Rio Grande
University of Toledo
Virginia Marti College of Art and Design
Walsh University
Wilmington College
Wittenberg University
Wright State University
Xavier University
Youngstown State University

Oklahoma

Langston University
Oklahoma Baptist University
Oklahoma Christian University of
  Science and Arts
Oklahoma City University
Oklahoma State University
Oklahoma Wesleyan University
Oral Roberts University
St. Gregory's University
Southern Nazarene University
University of Oklahoma
University of Science and Arts of
  Oklahoma
University of Tulsa

Oregon

Art Institute
  of Portland
Central Oregon Community College
Chemeketa Community College
Clackamas Community College
Concordia University
Eastern Oregon University
George Fox University
Lane Community College
Lewis & Clark College
Linfield College
Mount Hood Community College
Northwest Christian College
Oregon Institute of Technology
Oregon State University
Pacific Northwest College of Art
Pacific University
Portland Community College
Portland State University
Reed College
Rogue Community College
Southern Oregon University
University of Oregon
University of Portland
Warner Pacific College
Western Baptist College
Western Oregon University
Willamette University

Pennsylvania

Albright College
Allegheny College
Arcadia University
Baptist Bible College of Pennsylvania
Bloomsburg University of Pennsylvania
Bryn Athyn College of the New Church
Bryn Mawr College
Bucknell University
Cabrini College
California University of Pennsylvania
Carlow College
Carnegie Mellon University
Cedar Crest College
Chatham College
Chestnut Hill College
Community College of Allegheny
  County
DeSales University
Delaware County Community College
Dickinson College
Drexel University
DuBois Business College
Duquesne University
East Stroudsburg University of
  Pennsylvania
Edinboro University of Pennsylvania
Elizabethtown College
Franklin & Marshall College
Geneva College
Gettysburg College
Gratz College
Grove City College
Gwynedd-Mercy College
Harrisburg Area Community College
Haverford College
Holy Family University
Immaculata University
Indiana University of Pennsylvania
Juniata College
King's College
Kutztown University of Pennsylvania
La Roche College
La Salle University
Lafayette College
Lancaster Bible College
Lebanon Valley College of Pennsylvania
Lehigh Carbon Community College
Lehigh University
Lincoln University
Lock Haven University of Pennsylvania
Lycoming College
Marywood University
Mercyhurst College
Messiah College
Millersville University of Pennsylvania
Moravian College
Muhlenberg College
Neumann College
Northampton County Area Community
  College
Penn State
  Abington
  Altoona
  Berks
  Delaware County
  Erie, The Behrend College
  Harrisburg
  Lehigh Valley
  McKeesport
  Schuylkill - Capital College
  Shenango
  University Park
  York
Pennsylvania College of Technology
Philadelphia Biblical University
Philadelphia University
Point Park College
Robert Morris University
Rosemont College
St. Joseph's University
St. Vincent College
Seton Hill University
Shippensburg University of Pennsylvania

Slippery Rock University of
  Pennsylvania
Swarthmore College
Temple University
Thiel College
University of Pennsylvania
University of Pittsburgh
University of Pittsburgh
  Bradford
  Greensburg
  Johnstown
  Titusville
University of Scranton
Valley Forge Christian College
Villanova University
Washington and Jefferson College
Waynesburg College
West Chester University of Pennsylvania
Westmoreland County Community
  College
Widener University
Wilkes University
Wilson College
York College of Pennsylvania

Puerto Rico

Inter American University of Puerto Rico
  Guayama Campus
  San German Campus
Pontifical Catholic University of Puerto
  Rico
Technological College of San Juan
University of Puerto Rico
  Cayey University College
  Mayaguez Campus
  Rio Piedras Campus

Rhode Island

Brown University
Bryant College
Community College of Rhode Island
Providence College
Rhode Island College
Rhode Island School of Design
Roger Williams University
Salve Regina University
University of Rhode Island

South Carolina

Anderson College
Charleston Southern University
The Citadel
Claflin University
Clemson University
Coastal Carolina University
Coker College
College of Charleston
Columbia College
Columbia International University
Converse College
Erskine College
Francis Marion University
Furman University
Lander University
Newberry College
Presbyterian College
South Carolina State University
Southern Wesleyan University
Spartanburg Methodist College
University of South Carolina
University of South Carolina
  Aiken
  Salkehatchie Regional Campus
  Spartanburg
Winthrop University
Wofford College

South Dakota

Augustana College
Dakota State University
Dakota Wesleyan University
Northern State University
South Dakota School of Mines and
  Technology

South Dakota State University
University of Sioux Falls
University of South Dakota

Tennessee

Austin Peay State University
Belmont University
Bryan College
Carson-Newman College
Christian Brothers University
Crichton College
East Tennessee State University
Fisk University
Freed-Hardeman University
King College
Lambuth University
Lane College
Lee University
Maryville College
Memphis College of Art
Middle Tennessee State University
Milligan College
Rhodes College
Southern Adventist University
Tennessee State University
Tennessee Technological University
Tennessee Wesleyan College
Tusculum College
Union University
University of Memphis
University of Tennessee
  Chattanooga
  Knoxville
  Martin
Vanderbilt University

Texas

Abilene Christian University
Alvin Community College
Angelo State University
Austin College
Austin Community College
Baylor University
Brookhaven College
College of Saint Thomas More
Collin County Community College
  District
Concordia University at Austin
Dallas Baptist University
East Texas Baptist University
Hardin-Simmons University
Houston Baptist University
Houston Community College System
Howard Payne University
Huston-Tillotson College
Lamar University
LeTourneau University
Lubbock Christian University
McLennan Community College
McMurry University
Midland College
Midwestern State University
North Harris Montgomery Community
  College District
North Lake College
Northwood University: Texas Campus
Rice University
Richland College
St. Edward's University
St. Mary's University
Sam Houston State University
San Antonio College
Schreiner University
Southern Methodist University
Southwest Texas State University
Southwestern Adventist University
Southwestern University
Stephen F. Austin State University
Tarleton State University
Texarkana College
Texas A&M International University
Texas A&M University
Texas A&M University
  Commerce
  Kingsville

Texas Christian University
Texas Lutheran University
Texas Tech University
Texas Wesleyan University
Texas Woman's University
Trinity University
University of Dallas
University of Houston
University of Houston
    Downtown
University of Mary Hardin-Baylor
University of North Texas
University of St. Thomas
University of Texas
    Arlington
    Austin
    Dallas
    El Paso
    Pan American
    San Antonio
    Tyler
University of the Incarnate Word

Utah

Brigham Young University
Salt Lake Community College
University of Utah
Utah State University
Utah Valley State College
Weber State University

Vermont

Bennington College
Burlington College
Castleton State College
Champlain College
College of St. Joseph in Vermont
Goddard College
Green Mountain College
Johnson State College
Landmark College
Lyndon State College
Marlboro College
Middlebury College
Norwich University
St. Michael's College
Southern Vermont College
Sterling College
University of Vermont

Virginia

Averett University
Blue Ridge Community College
Bluefield College
Bridgewater College
Christendom College
College of William and Mary
Eastern Mennonite University
Emory & Henry College
Ferrum College
George Mason University
Hampden-Sydney College
Hampton University
Hollins University
James Madison University
Liberty University
Longwood University
Lynchburg College
Mary Baldwin College
Mary Washington College
Marymount University
Norfolk State University
Old Dominion University
Radford University
Randolph-Macon College
Randolph-Macon Woman's College
Roanoke College
Shenandoah University
Southside Virginia Community College
Sweet Briar College
University of Richmond
University of Virginia
University of Virginia's College at Wise
Virginia Commonwealth University

Virginia Intermont College
Virginia Military Institute
Virginia Polytechnic Institute and State
    University
Virginia Wesleyan College
Virginia Western Community College
Washington and Lee University

Washington

Central Washington University
Centralia College
Clark College
Eastern Washington University
Edmonds Community College
Everett Community College
Evergreen State College
Gonzaga University
Grays Harbor College
Green River Community College
Lower Columbia College
North Seattle Community College
Northwest College
Olympic College
Pacific Lutheran University
Peninsula College
St. Martin's College
Seattle Central Community College
Seattle Pacific University
Seattle University
South Seattle Community College
Spokane Community College
Spokane Falls Community College
Trinity Lutheran College
University of Puget Sound
University of Washington
Walla Walla College
Washington State University
Western Washington University
Whitman College
Whitworth College

West Virginia

Alderson-Broaddus College
Bethany College
Davis and Elkins College
Fairmont State College
Glenville State College
International Academy of Design and
    Technology
Marshall University
Potomac State College of West Virginia
    University
Salem International University
University of Charleston
West Virginia University
West Virginia Wesleyan College
Wheeling Jesuit University

Wisconsin

Alverno College
Beloit College
Carroll College
Carthage College
Columbia College of Nursing
Concordia University Wisconsin
Edgewood College
Lakeland College
Lawrence University
Maranatha Baptist Bible College
Marian College of Fond du Lac
Marquette University
Milwaukee Institute of Art & Design
Milwaukee School of Engineering
Mount Mary College
Northland College
Ripon College
St. Norbert College

University of Wisconsin
    Baraboo/Sauk County
    Eau Claire
    Green Bay
    La Crosse
    Madison
    Marathon County
    Milwaukee
    Oshkosh
    Parkside
    Platteville
    River Falls
    Rock County
    Stevens Point
    Stout
    Superior
    Washington County
    Waukesha
    Whitewater
Viterbo University
Wisconsin Lutheran College

Wyoming

University of Wyoming

Teacher certification

Alabama

Alabama Agricultural and Mechanical
    University
Alabama State University
Athens State University
Auburn University
Auburn University at Montgomery
Birmingham-Southern College
Faulkner University
Huntingdon College
Jacksonville State University
Judson College
Oakwood College
Samford University
Southeastern Bible College
Spring Hill College
Stillman College
Talladega College
Troy State University
Troy State University Dothan
Troy State University in Montgomery
Tuskegee University
University of Alabama
University of Alabama
    Birmingham
    Huntsville
University of Mobile
University of Montevallo
University of North Alabama
University of South Alabama
University of West Alabama
Wallace Community College: Sparks
    Campus

Alaska

Alaska Pacific University
Sheldon Jackson College
University of Alaska
    Anchorage
    Fairbanks
    Southeast

Arizona

American Indian College of the
    Assemblies of God
Arizona State University
Arizona Western College
Cochise College
Northern Arizona University
Prescott College
Southwestern College
University of Arizona
University of Phoenix
Yavapai College

Arkansas

Arkansas State University
Arkansas Tech University
Harding University
Henderson State University
Hendrix College
John Brown University
Lyon College
Ouachita Baptist University
Philander Smith College
Southern Arkansas University
University of Arkansas
University of Arkansas
    Fort Smith
    Little Rock
    Monticello
    Pine Bluff
University of Central Arkansas
University of the Ozarks

California

Academy of Art College
Antelope Valley College
Antioch Southern California
    Los Angeles
    Santa Barbara
Azusa Pacific University
Bethany College
Biola University
California Baptist University
California Polytechnic State University:
    San Luis Obispo
California State Polytechnic University:
    Pomona
California State University
    Bakersfield
    Chico
    Dominguez Hills
    Fresno
    Fullerton
    Hayward
    Long Beach
    Los Angeles
    Monterey Bay
    Northridge
    Sacramento
    San Marcos
    Stanislaus
Chapman University
Christian Heritage College
Concordia University
Dominican University of California
Fresno Pacific University
Holy Names College
Hope International University
Humboldt State University
John F. Kennedy University
La Sierra University
Loyola Marymount University
Master's College
Mills College
MiraCosta College
Mount St. Mary's College
Mount San Antonio College
National Hispanic University
National University
Occidental College
Pacific Oaks College
Pacific Union College
Patten University
Pepperdine University
Point Loma Nazarene University
Pomona College
St. Mary's College of California
San Diego City College
San Diego Mesa College
San Diego State University
San Francisco State University
San Jose State University
Santa Clara University
Simpson College
Sonoma State University

University of California
  Berkeley
  Davis
  Los Angeles
  Riverside
  San Diego
  Santa Barbara
  Santa Cruz
University of La Verne
University of Redlands
University of San Diego
University of San Francisco
University of Southern California
University of the Pacific
Vanguard University of Southern
  California
West Valley College
Whittier College

Colorado

Colorado Christian University
Colorado College
Colorado State University
Colorado State University
  Pueblo
Fort Lewis College
Mesa State College
Metropolitan State College of Denver
Morgan Community College
Regis University
University of Colorado
  Boulder
  Colorado Springs
  Denver
University of Northern Colorado

Connecticut

Central Connecticut State University
Connecticut College
Eastern Connecticut State University
Fairfield University
Quinnipiac University
Sacred Heart University
St. Joseph College
Southern Connecticut State University
Trinity College
University of Bridgeport
University of Connecticut
University of Hartford
Western Connecticut State University
Yale University

Delaware

Delaware State University
University of Delaware
Wilmington College

District of Columbia

American University
Catholic University of America
Gallaudet University
Howard University
Trinity College
University of the District of Columbia

Florida

Baptist College of Florida
Barry University
Bethune-Cookman College
Edward Waters College
Flagler College
Florida Agricultural and Mechanical
  University
Florida Atlantic University
Florida Christian College
Florida Gulf Coast University
Florida Institute of Technology
Florida International University
Florida Southern College
Florida State University
Gulf Coast Community College
Hillsborough Community College
Hobe Sound Bible College
Jacksonville University

Nova Southeastern University
Palm Beach Atlantic University
Rollins College
St. Leo University
St. Thomas University
Seminole Community College
Southeastern College of the Assemblies
  of God
Stetson University
University of Central Florida
University of Florida
University of Miami
University of North Florida
University of South Florida
University of Tampa
University of West Florida
Warner Southern College

Georgia

Agnes Scott College
Albany State University
Armstrong Atlantic State University
Augusta State University
Berry College
Brewton-Parker College
Clark Atlanta University
Clayton College and State University
Coastal Georgia Community College
Columbus State University
Covenant College
Emmanuel College
Emory University
Fort Valley State University
Georgia College and State University
Georgia Institute of Technology
Georgia Southern University
Georgia Southwestern State University
Georgia State University
Kennesaw State University
LaGrange College
Mercer University
Morris Brown College
North Georgia College & State
  University
Oglethorpe University
Paine College
Piedmont College
Reinhardt College
Shorter College
Spelman College
State University of West Georgia
Toccoa Falls College
University of Georgia
Valdosta State University
Wesleyan College

Hawaii

Brigham Young University-Hawaii
Chaminade University of Honolulu
Hawaii Pacific University
University of Hawaii
  Hilo

Idaho

Albertson College of Idaho
Boise State University
Brigham Young University - Idaho
Idaho State University
Lewis-Clark State College
Northwest Nazarene University
University of Idaho

Illinois

Augustana College
Aurora University
Benedictine University
Blackburn College
Bradley University
Chicago State University
Columbia College Chicago
Concordia University
De Paul University
Dominican University
Eastern Illinois University

Elmhurst College
Eureka College
Governors State University
Greenville College
Illinois College
Illinois Eastern Community Colleges
  Frontier Community College
Illinois State University
Judson College
Kankakee Community College
Kendall College
Knox College
Lake Forest College
Lewis University
Lincoln Christian College and Seminary
Loyola University of Chicago
MacMurray College
McKendree College
Millikin University
Monmouth College
Moody Bible Institute
National-Louis University
North Central College
North Park University
Northeastern Illinois University
Northern Illinois University
Northwestern University
Olivet Nazarene University
Principia College
Quincy University
Rockford College
Roosevelt University
St. Xavier University
School of the Art Institute of Chicago
Southern Illinois University Carbondale
Southern Illinois University Edwardsville
Trinity Christian College
Trinity International University
Triton College
University of Illinois
  Chicago
  Springfield
  Urbana-Champaign
University of St. Francis
VanderCook College of Music
Western Illinois University
Wheaton College

Indiana

Anderson University
Ball State University
Bethel College
Butler University
Calumet College of St. Joseph
DePauw University
Earlham College
Franklin College
Goshen College
Grace College
Hanover College
Huntington College
Indiana State University
Indiana University
  Bloomington
  East
  Kokomo
  Northwest
  South Bend
  Southeast
Indiana University-Purdue University
  Fort Wayne
Indiana University-Purdue University
  Indianapolis
Indiana Wesleyan University

Ivy Tech State College
  Bloomington
  Central Indiana
  Columbus
  Eastcentral
  Kokomo
  Lafayette
  Northcentral
  Northeast
  Northwest
  Southcentral
  Southeast
  Southwest
  Wabash Valley
  Whitewater
Manchester College
Marian College
Oakland City University
Purdue University
Purdue University
  Calumet
  North Central Campus
St. Joseph's College
Saint Mary's College
St. Mary-of-the-Woods College
Taylor University
Taylor University: Fort Wayne
Tri-State University
University of Evansville
University of Indianapolis
University of Notre Dame
University of St. Francis
University of Southern Indiana
Valparaiso University
Wabash College

Iowa

Briar Cliff University
Buena Vista University
Central College
Clarke College
Coe College
Cornell College
Dordt College
Drake University
Emmaus Bible College
Faith Baptist Bible College and
  Theological Seminary
Franciscan University
Graceland University
Grand View College
Grinnell College
Iowa State University
Iowa Wesleyan College
Loras College
Luther College
Maharishi University of Management
Morningside College
Mount Mercy College
Northwestern College
St. Ambrose University
Simpson College
University of Dubuque
University of Iowa
University of Northern Iowa
Upper Iowa University
Vennard College
Waldorf College
Wartburg College
William Penn University

Kansas

Baker University
Barclay College
Benedictine College
Bethany College
Bethel College
Cloud County Community College
Emporia State University
Fort Hays State University
Fort Scott Community College
Friends University
Kansas State University
Kansas Wesleyan University
McPherson College

MidAmerica Nazarene University
Newman University
Ottawa University
Pittsburg State University
St. Mary College
Southwestern College
Sterling College
Tabor College
University of Kansas
Washburn University of Topeka
Wichita State University

Kentucky

Alice Lloyd College
Asbury College
Bellarmine University
Berea College
Brescia University
Campbellsville University
Centre College
Cumberland College
Georgetown College
Kentucky Christian College
Kentucky Wesleyan College
Lindsey Wilson College
Mid-Continent College
Morehead State University
Murray State University
Pikeville College
Spalding University
Thomas More College
Transylvania University
Union College
University of Kentucky
University of Louisville

Louisiana

Centenary College of Louisiana
Dillard University
Grambling State University
Louisiana College
Louisiana State University
    Shreveport
Louisiana State University and
    Agricultural and Mechanical College
Louisiana Tech University
Loyola University New Orleans
McNeese State University
Nicholls State University
Northwestern State University
Our Lady of Holy Cross College
Southeastern Louisiana University
Southern University and Agricultural and
    Mechanical College
Tulane University
University of Louisiana at Lafayette
University of Louisiana at Monroe
University of New Orleans
Xavier University of Louisiana

Maine

Andover College
Bates College
Bowdoin College
Colby College
College of the Atlantic
Husson College
Maine College of Art
St. Joseph's College
Thomas College
University of Maine
University of Maine
    Farmington
    Machias
    Presque Isle
University of New England
University of Southern Maine

Maryland

Baltimore Hebrew University
Bowie State University
Cecil Community College
Chesapeake College
College of Notre Dame of Maryland

Columbia Union College
Community College of Baltimore County
    Dundalk
    Essex
Coppin State College
Frederick Community College
Frostburg State University
Goucher College
Hood College
Howard Community College
Johns Hopkins University: Peabody
    Conservatory of Music
Loyola College in Maryland
Maryland Institute College of Art
McDaniel College
Morgan State University
Mount St. Mary's College
St. Mary's College of Maryland
Salisbury University
Towson University
University of Maryland
    Baltimore County
    College Park
Villa Julie College
Washington Bible College
Washington College

Massachusetts

American International College
Amherst College
Anna Maria College
Art Institute of Boston at Lesley
    University
Assumption College
Atlantic Union College
Bay Path College
Becker College
Berklee College of Music
Boston College
Boston Conservatory
Boston University
Brandeis University
Bridgewater State College
Clark University
College of the Holy Cross
Elms College
Emerson College
Emmanuel College
Endicott College
Fitchburg State College
Framingham State College
Gordon College
Harvard College
Hebrew College
Lasell College
Lesley University
Massachusetts College of Liberal Arts
Merrimack College
Montserrat College of Art
Mount Holyoke College
Mount Ida College
Nichols College
Northeastern University
Pine Manor College
Regis College
Salem State College
Simmons College
Smith College
Springfield College
Stonehill College
Tufts University
University of Massachusetts
    Amherst
    Boston
    Dartmouth
Wellesley College
Western New England College
Westfield State College
Wheaton College
Williams College
Worcester Polytechnic Institute

Michigan

Adrian College
Alma College

Andrews University
Aquinas College
Baker College
    of Auburn Hills
    of Clinton Township
    of Muskegon
Calvin College
Central Michigan University
Concordia University
Cornerstone University
Eastern Michigan University
Ferris State University
Finlandia University
Grand Valley State University
Hillsdale College
Hope College
Kalamazoo College
Lansing Community College
Madonna University
Marygrove College
Michigan State University
Michigan Technological University
Northern Michigan University
Oakland University
Saginaw Valley State University
Siena Heights University
Spring Arbor University
University of Michigan
University of Michigan
    Dearborn
    Flint
Wayne State University
Western Michigan University

Minnesota

Augsburg College
Bemidji State University
Bethel College
Carleton College
College of St. Benedict
College of St. Catherine
College of St. Scholastica
Concordia College: Moorhead
Concordia University: St. Paul
Crown College
Gustavus Adolphus College
Hamline University
Macalester College
Martin Luther College
Minnesota State University
    Mankato
    Moorhead
North Central University
Northwestern College
St. John's University
St. Mary's University of Minnesota
St. Olaf College
Southwest State University
University of Minnesota
    Duluth
    Morris
    Twin Cities
University of St. Thomas
Winona State University

Mississippi

Alcorn State University
Blue Mountain College
Delta State University
Millsaps College
Mississippi College
Mississippi State University
Mississippi University for Women
Mississippi Valley State University
Rust College
University of Mississippi
University of Southern Mississippi

Missouri

Avila University
Calvary Bible College
Central Methodist College
Central Missouri State University
College of the Ozarks

Columbia College
Culver-Stockton College
Drury University
Evangel University
Fontbonne College
Hannibal-LaGrange College
Harris Stowe State College
Lincoln University
Lindenwood University
Maryville University of Saint Louis
Missouri Baptist University
Missouri Southern State College
Missouri Valley College
Missouri Western State College
Northwest Missouri State University
Rockhurst University
St. Louis Community College
    St. Louis Community College at
        Florissant Valley
St. Louis University
Southeast Missouri State University
Southwest Baptist University
Southwest Missouri State University
Stephens College
Truman State University
University of Missouri
    Columbia
    Kansas City
    Rolla
    St. Louis
Washington University in St. Louis
Webster University
Westminster College
William Jewell College
William Woods University

Montana

Carroll College
Montana State University
    Billings
    Bozeman
Montana Tech of the University of
    Montana
Rocky Mountain College
University of Great Falls
University of Montana-Missoula
University of Montana: Western

Nebraska

Chadron State College
College of Saint Mary
Concordia University
Creighton University
Dana College
Doane College
Grace University
Hastings College
Midland Lutheran College
Nebraska Wesleyan University
Peru State College
Union College
University of Nebraska
    Kearney
    Lincoln
    Omaha
Wayne State College

Nevada

Great Basin College
Sierra Nevada College
University of Nevada
    Las Vegas
    Reno

New Hampshire

Chester College of New England
Colby-Sawyer College
Dartmouth College
Franklin Pierce College
Keene State College
New England College
Plymouth State College
Rivier College
St. Anselm College

Southern New Hampshire University
University of New Hampshire
University of New Hampshire at
Manchester

New Jersey

Bloomfield College
Caldwell College
Centenary College
The College of New Jersey
College of St. Elizabeth
Drew University
Essex County College
Fairleigh Dickinson University
College at Florham
Metropolitan Campus
Felician College
Georgian Court College
Kean University
Monmouth University
Montclair State University
New Jersey City University
Princeton University
Ramapo College of New Jersey
Richard Stockton College of New Jersey
Rider University
Rowan University
Rutgers, The State University of New
Jersey
Camden Regional Campus
New Brunswick Regional Campus
Newark Regional Campus
St. Peter's College
Seton Hall University
William Paterson University of New
Jersey

New Mexico

College of Santa Fe
College of the Southwest
Eastern New Mexico University
New Mexico Highlands University
New Mexico Institute of Mining and
Technology
New Mexico State University
University of New Mexico
Western New Mexico University

New York

Adelphi University
Alfred University
Barnard College
Canisius College
City University of New York
Brooklyn College
City College
College of Staten Island
Hunter College
Medgar Evers College
Queens College
York College
Colgate University
College of Mount St. Vincent
College of New Rochelle
Columbia University
Columbia College
Fu Foundation School of
Engineering and Applied Science
Concordia College
Cornell University
D'Youville College
Daemen College
Dominican College of Blauvelt
Dowling College
Eastman School of Music of the
University of Rochester
Elmira College
Erie Community College
City Campus
North Campus
South Campus
Eugene Lang College/New School
University
Fordham University

Hamilton College
Hartwick College
Hobart and William Smith Colleges
Hofstra University
Houghton College
Iona College
Ithaca College
Keuka College
Le Moyne College
Long Island University
C. W. Post Campus
Southampton College
Manhattan College
Manhattanville College
Marist College
Marymount College of Fordham
University
Marymount Manhattan College
Medaille College
Mercy College
Mohawk Valley Community College
Molloy College
Mount St. Mary College
Nazareth College of Rochester
New York Institute of Technology
New York University
Niagara University
Nyack College
Ohr Somayach Tanenbaum Education
Center
Pace University
Pace University: Pleasantville/Briarcliff
Parsons School of Design
Pratt Institute
Roberts Wesleyan College
Rochester Institute of Technology
Russell Sage College
St. Bonaventure University
St. John Fisher College
St. John's University
St. Joseph's College
St. Joseph's College: Suffolk Campus
St. Lawrence University
Sarah Lawrence College
Schenectady County Community College
School of Visual Arts
Skidmore College
State University of New York
Albany
Binghamton
Buffalo
College at Brockport
College at Buffalo
College at Cortland
College at Fredonia
College at Geneseo
College at Old Westbury
College at Oneonta
College at Plattsburgh
College at Potsdam
College of Environmental Science
and Forestry
New Paltz
Oswego
Stony Brook
Syracuse University
Touro College
Union College
University of Rochester
Utica College
Vassar College
Wagner College
Wells College
Yeshiva University

North Carolina

Appalachian State University
Barber-Scotia College
Barton College
Belmont Abbey College
Bennett College
Brevard College
Campbell University
Carteret Community College
Catawba College

Catawba Valley Community College
Chowan College
Davidson College
Duke University
East Carolina University
Elizabeth City State University
Elon University
Fayetteville State University
Greensboro College
Guilford College
John Wesley College
Johnson C. Smith University
Lees-McRae College
Lenoir-Rhyne College
Livingstone College
Mars Hill College
Meredith College
Methodist College
Montreat College
Mount Olive College
North Carolina Agricultural and
Technical State University
North Carolina Central University
North Carolina State University
North Carolina Wesleyan College
Pfeiffer University
Piedmont Baptist College
Queens University of Charlotte
Richmond Community College
Roanoke Bible College
Rowan-Cabarrus Community College
St. Andrews Presbyterian College
St. Augustine's College
Salem College
Shaw University
University of North Carolina
Asheville
Chapel Hill
Charlotte
Greensboro
Pembroke
Wilmington
Wake Forest University
Warren Wilson College
Western Carolina University
Wingate University
Winston-Salem State University

North Dakota

Dickinson State University
Jamestown College
Mayville State University
Minot State University
North Dakota State University
Trinity Bible College
University of Mary
University of North Dakota
Valley City State University

Ohio

Antioch College
Ashland University
Baldwin-Wallace College
Bluffton College
Bowling Green State University
Bowling Green State University:
Firelands College
Case Western Reserve University
Cedarville University
Central State University
Cleveland Institute of Music
Cleveland State University
College of Mount St. Joseph
College of Wooster
Columbus State Community College
Defiance College
Denison University
Franciscan University of Steubenville
Heidelberg College
Hiram College
John Carroll University
Kent State University
Lake Erie College
Lorain County Community College
Lourdes College

Malone College
Marietta College
Miami University
Hamilton Campus
Middletown Campus
Oxford Campus
Mount Union College
Mount Vernon Nazarene University
Muskingum College
Notre Dame College
Oberlin College
Ohio Dominican College
Ohio Northern University
Ohio State University
Columbus Campus
Lima Campus
Mansfield Campus
Marion Campus
Newark Campus
Ohio University
Ohio University
Chillicothe Campus
Eastern Campus
Southern Campus at Ironton
Zanesville Campus
Ohio Wesleyan University
Otterbein College
Shawnee State University
University of Akron
University of Cincinnati
University of Cincinnati
Raymond Walters College
University of Dayton
University of Findlay
University of Rio Grande
University of Toledo
Urbana University
Ursuline College
Walsh University
Wilmington College
Wittenberg University
Wright State University
Xavier University
Youngstown State University

Oklahoma

Cameron University
East Central University
Langston University
Northeastern State University
Northwestern Oklahoma State University
Oklahoma Baptist University
Oklahoma Christian University of
Science and Arts
Oklahoma City University
Oklahoma Panhandle State University
Oklahoma State University
Oklahoma Wesleyan University
Oral Roberts University
St. Gregory's University
Southeastern Oklahoma State University
Southern Nazarene University
Southwestern Oklahoma State University
University of Central Oklahoma
University of Oklahoma
University of Science and Arts of
Oklahoma
University of Tulsa

Oregon

Concordia University
Eastern Oregon University
George Fox University
Linfield College
Northwest Christian College
Oregon State University
Pacific University
Portland State University
Southern Oregon University
University of Oregon
University of Portland
Warner Pacific College
Western Baptist College
Western Oregon University
Willamette University

Pennsylvania

Albright College
Arcadia University
Baptist Bible College of Pennsylvania
Bloomsburg University of Pennsylvania
Bryn Mawr College
Bucknell University
Cabrini College
California University of Pennsylvania
Carlow College
Carnegie Mellon University
Cedar Crest College
Chatham College
Chestnut Hill College
Cheyney University of Pennsylvania
DeSales University
Delaware Valley College
Dickinson College
Drexel University
Duquesne University
East Stroudsburg University of
  Pennsylvania
Edinboro University of Pennsylvania
Elizabethtown College
Franklin & Marshall College
Geneva College
Gettysburg College
Gratz College
Grove City College
Gwynedd-Mercy College
Haverford College
Holy Family University
Immaculata University
Indiana University of Pennsylvania
Juniata College
Keystone College
King's College
Kutztown University of Pennsylvania
La Roche College
La Salle University
Lancaster Bible College
Lebanon Valley College of Pennsylvania
Lincoln University
Lock Haven University of Pennsylvania
Lycoming College
Marywood University
Mercyhurst College
Messiah College
Millersville University of Pennsylvania
Montgomery County Community
  College
Moravian College
Muhlenberg College
Neumann College
Penn State
  Erie, The Behrend College
  Harrisburg
  University Park
Philadelphia Biblical University
Point Park College
Robert Morris University
Rosemont College
St. Joseph's University
St. Vincent College
Seton Hill University
Shippensburg University of Pennsylvania
Slippery Rock University of
  Pennsylvania
Swarthmore College
Temple University
Thiel College
University of Pennsylvania
University of Pittsburgh
University of Pittsburgh
  Bradford
  Greensburg
  Johnstown
University of Scranton
University of the Sciences in
  Philadelphia
Valley Forge Christian College
Villanova University
Washington and Jefferson College
Waynesburg College
West Chester University of Pennsylvania

Widener University
Wilkes University
Wilson College
York College of Pennsylvania

Puerto Rico

Bayamon Central University
Conservatory of Music of Puerto Rico
Escuela de Artes Plasticas de Puerto Rico
Inter American University of Puerto Rico
  Barranquitas Campus
  San German Campus
Universidad Metropolitana
University of Puerto Rico
  Cayey University College
  Humacao
  Mayaguez Campus
  Utuado
University of the Sacred Heart

Rhode Island

Brown University
Providence College
Rhode Island College
Rhode Island School of Design
Roger Williams University
Salve Regina University
University of Rhode Island

South Carolina

Anderson College
Benedict College
Charleston Southern University
The Citadel
Claflin University
Clemson University
Coastal Carolina University
Coker College
College of Charleston
Columbia College
Columbia International University
Converse College
Erskine College
Francis Marion University
Furman University
Lander University
Limestone College
Morris College
Newberry College
North Greenville College
Presbyterian College
South Carolina State University
Southern Wesleyan University
University of South Carolina
University of South Carolina
  Aiken
  Spartanburg
  Sumter
Winthrop University
Wofford College

South Dakota

Augustana College
Black Hills State University
Dakota State University
Dakota Wesleyan University
Mount Marty College
Northern State University
South Dakota State University
University of Sioux Falls
University of South Dakota

Tennessee

Aquinas College
Austin Peay State University
Belmont University
Bethel College
Bryan College
Carson-Newman College
Christian Brothers University
Crichton College
East Tennessee State University
Fisk University
Freed-Hardeman University

Johnson Bible College
King College
Lambuth University
Lane College
Lee University
Maryville College
Middle Tennessee State University
Milligan College
Rhodes College
Roane State Community College
Southern Adventist University
Tennessee State University
Tennessee Technological University
Tennessee Wesleyan College
Trevecca Nazarene University
Tusculum College
Union University
University of Memphis
University of Tennessee
  Chattanooga
  Knoxville
  Martin
Vanderbilt University

Texas

Abilene Christian University
Angelo State University
Austin College
Austin Community College
Baylor University
Collin County Community College
  District
Concordia University at Austin
Dallas Baptist University
East Texas Baptist University
El Centro College
El Paso Community College
Hardin-Simmons University
Houston Baptist University
Howard Payne University
Huston-Tillotson College
Jarvis Christian College
Lamar University
LeTourneau University
Lubbock Christian University
McMurry University
Midwestern State University
North Harris Montgomery Community
  College District
Our Lady of the Lake University of San
  Antonio
Paul Quinn College
Prairie View A&M University
Rice University
Richland College
St. Edward's University
St. Mary's University
Sam Houston State University
Schreiner University
Southern Methodist University
Southwest Texas State University
Southwestern Adventist University
Southwestern Assemblies of God
  University
Southwestern University
Stephen F. Austin State University
Sul Ross State University
Tarleton State University
Texas A&M International University
Texas A&M University
Texas A&M University
  Commerce
  Corpus Christi
  Galveston
  Kingsville
  Texarkana
Texas Christian University
Texas College
Texas Lutheran University
Texas Southern University
Texas Tech University
Texas Wesleyan University
Texas Woman's University
Trinity University
University of Dallas

University of Houston
University of Houston
  Clear Lake
  Downtown
  Victoria
University of Mary Hardin-Baylor
University of North Texas
University of St. Thomas
University of Texas
  Arlington
  Austin
  Dallas
  El Paso
  Pan American
  San Antonio
  Tyler
  of the Permian Basin
University of the Incarnate Word
Wayland Baptist University
West Texas A&M University

Utah

Brigham Young University
Snow College
Southern Utah University
University of Utah
Utah State University
Utah Valley State College
Weber State University
Westminster College

Vermont

Bennington College
Castleton State College
Champlain College
College of St. Joseph in Vermont
Goddard College
Green Mountain College
Johnson State College
Lyndon State College
Middlebury College
Norwich University
St. Michael's College
University of Vermont

Virginia

Averett University
Bluefield College
Bridgewater College
College of William and Mary
Eastern Mennonite University
Emory & Henry College
Ferrum College
George Mason University
Hampton University
Hollins University
James Madison University
Liberty University
Longwood University
Lynchburg College
Mary Baldwin College
Mary Washington College
Marymount University
Norfolk State University
Old Dominion University
Radford University
Randolph-Macon College
Randolph-Macon Woman's College
Roanoke College
Shenandoah University
Sweet Briar College
University of Richmond
University of Virginia
University of Virginia's College at Wise
Virginia Commonwealth University
Virginia Intermont College
Virginia Military Institute
Virginia Polytechnic Institute and State
  University
Virginia State University
Virginia Union University
Virginia Wesleyan College
Washington and Lee University

Washington

Central Washington University
Eastern Washington University
Gonzaga University
Grays Harbor College
Heritage College
Northwest College
Pacific Lutheran University
St. Martin's College
Seattle Pacific University
Seattle University
South Seattle Community College
University of Puget Sound
University of Washington
Walla Walla College
Washington State University
Western Washington University
Whitman College
Whitworth College

West Virginia

Alderson-Broaddus College
Bethany College
Bluefield State College
Concord College
Davis and Elkins College
Fairmont State College
Glenville State College
Marshall University
Ohio Valley College
Salem International University
Shepherd College
Southern West Virginia Community and
   Technical College
University of Charleston
West Liberty State College
West Virginia State College
West Virginia University
West Virginia University at Parkersburg
West Virginia Wesleyan College
Wheeling Jesuit University

Wisconsin

Alverno College
Beloit College
Cardinal Stritch University
Carroll College
Carthage College
Concordia University Wisconsin
Edgewood College
Lakeland College
Lawrence University
Maranatha Baptist Bible College
Marian College of Fond du Lac
Marquette University
Mount Mary College
Northland College
Ripon College
St. Norbert College
Silver Lake College
University of Wisconsin
   Eau Claire
   Green Bay
   La Crosse
   Madison
   Milwaukee
   Oshkosh
   Parkside
   Platteville
   Richland
   River Falls
   Stevens Point
   Stout
   Superior
   Whitewater
Viterbo University
Wisconsin Lutheran College

Wyoming

University of Wyoming

United Nations semester

Arkansas

University of Arkansas

California

Mount St. Mary's College
Occidental College
Point Loma Nazarene University
Scripps College
Sonoma State University
University of Redlands
University of the Pacific

Connecticut

Sacred Heart University
Trinity College
University of Bridgeport

Florida

Barry University
Eckerd College
Florida Southern College

Georgia

Agnes Scott College

Illinois

Illinois Wesleyan University
Lincoln Land Community College
Millikin University
North Central College
Rockford College

Indiana

DePauw University
Franklin College
Indiana University
   Bloomington
University of Indianapolis
Valparaiso University

Iowa

Drake University
Morningside College
Simpson College

Kansas

Fort Hays State University

Maryland

McDaniel College

Minnesota

Hamline University

Mississippi

Millsaps College

Missouri

Westminster College

Nebraska

Dana College
Nebraska Wesleyan University

New Hampshire

Keene State College

New Jersey

College of St. Elizabeth
Drew University

New York

Alfred University
College of New Rochelle
Fordham University
Hobart and William Smith Colleges
Long Island University
   C. W. Post Campus

Marist College
State University of New York
   New Paltz
Syracuse University
Wagner College

North Carolina

Meredith College
Salem College

Ohio

Baldwin-Wallace College
College of Wooster
Muskingum College
Ohio Wesleyan University

Pennsylvania

Gettysburg College
Lycoming College
Seton Hill University
Thiel College
University of Scranton
Wilson College

South Carolina

Furman University
Winthrop University

Texas

Trinity University

Utah

Weber State University

Virginia

Randolph-Macon College

West Virginia

Bethany College

Wisconsin

Carroll College
University of Wisconsin
   Milwaukee

Urban semester

California

Azusa Pacific University
Pitzer College
Scripps College
Sonoma State University
University of Redlands

Colorado

Colorado College

Connecticut

Trinity College
University of Bridgeport
University of Connecticut
Wesleyan University

District of Columbia

Corcoran College of Art and Design

Florida

Florida Southern College
Ringling School of Art and Design

Georgia

Savannah College of Art and Design
Spelman College
State University of West Georgia

Idaho

Brigham Young University - Idaho

Illinois

Greenville College
Illinois Wesleyan University
Knox College
Lake Forest College
Millikin University
Monmouth College
Trinity Christian College
Trinity International University
Wheaton College

Indiana

Anderson University
Bethel College
DePauw University
Earlham College
Goshen College
Manchester College
Purdue University
Valparaiso University
Wabash College

Iowa

Briar Cliff University
Central College
Coe College
Cornell College
Dordt College
Grinnell College
Loras College
University of Dubuque
Vennard College
Wartburg College

Kansas

Bethany College
Bethel College
McPherson College
Southwestern College

Maine

Bates College

Maryland

Maryland Institute College of Art
McDaniel College

Massachusetts

Art Institute of Boston at Lesley
   University
Gordon College
Montserrat College of Art
School of the Museum of Fine Arts

Michigan

Alma College
Calvin College
College for Creative Studies
Hope College
Kalamazoo College
Spring Arbor University

Minnesota

Carleton College
College of St. Benedict
Concordia College: Moorhead
Hamline University
Macalester College
St. John's University
St. Mary's University of Minnesota
St. Olaf College
University of St. Thomas

Missouri

Kansas City Art Institute
Rockhurst University
Westminster College

Nebraska

Dana College
Hastings College
Nebraska Wesleyan University

New Hampshire
St. Anselm College

New Jersey
Berkeley College
Drew University

New Mexico
College of Santa Fe

New York
Alfred University
Bard College
Berkeley College
City University of New York
     Queens College
Clinton Community College
Colgate University
Cornell University
Eugene Lang College/New School
     University
Hamilton College
Hartwick College
Hobart and William Smith Colleges
Manhattanville College
New York University
Niagara University
Onondaga Community College
Pratt Institute
State University of New York
     Buffalo
     College at Brockport
     College at Buffalo
     College at Oneonta
     New Paltz
Syracuse University
Vassar College

North Carolina
Duke University
Gardner-Webb University
Meredith College

Ohio
Baldwin-Wallace College
Cleveland Institute of Art
College of Wooster
Columbus College of Art and Design
Denison University
Kenyon College
Oberlin College
Ohio Wesleyan University
Ursuline College
Wittenberg University
Xavier University
Youngstown State University

Oklahoma
Southern Nazarene University

Oregon
Lewis & Clark College
Pacific Northwest College of Art
Willamette University

Pennsylvania
Albright College
East Stroudsburg University of
     Pennsylvania
Elizabethtown College
Franklin & Marshall College
Gettysburg College
Indiana University of Pennsylvania
Juniata College
Lafayette College
Lehigh University
Mercyhurst College
Messiah College
Seton Hill University

South Dakota
Augustana College
South Dakota State University

Tennessee
Memphis College of Art

Texas
Hardin-Simmons University
Rice University
Southwestern University
Trinity University

Utah
University of Utah
Weber State University

Virginia
Virginia Commonwealth University

Washington
Western Washington University
Whitman College

West Virginia
West Virginia Wesleyan College

Wisconsin
Beloit College
Lawrence University
Milwaukee Institute of Art & Design
Ripon College
Viterbo University

Visiting/exchange student program

Alabama
Alabama Agricultural and Mechanical
     University
Auburn University at Montgomery
Birmingham-Southern College
Miles College
Samford University
University of Alabama
University of Montevallo

Alaska
Alaska Pacific University
University of Alaska
     Anchorage
     Fairbanks
     Southeast

Arizona
Arizona State University
Northern Arizona University
University of Arizona

Arkansas
Hendrix College
Ouachita Baptist University
University of Arkansas
     Cossatot Community College of the
     Little Rock

California
Azusa Pacific University
Biola University
California College of Arts and Crafts
California Institute of Technology
California Polytechnic State University:
     San Luis Obispo
California State Polytechnic University:
     Pomona
California State University
     Bakersfield
     Chico
     Dominguez Hills
     Fresno
     Hayward
     Los Angeles
     Northridge
     San Bernardino
     Stanislaus

Chapman University
Claremont McKenna College
College of the Siskiyous
Concordia University
Dominican University of California
Fashion Institute of Design and
     Merchandising
Fashion Institute of Design and
     Merchandising
     San Francisco
Foothill College
Harvey Mudd College
Holy Names College
Humboldt State University
Mills College
MiraCosta College
Mount St. Mary's College
Occidental College
Otis College of Art and Design
Pitzer College
Pomona College
St. Mary's College of California
San Diego State University
San Francisco State University
San Jose State University
Santa Clara University
Scripps College
Sonoma State University
Southern California Institute of
     Architecture
Stanford University
University of California
     Berkeley
     Los Angeles
     Riverside
     San Diego
     Santa Barbara
     Santa Cruz
University of La Verne
University of Redlands
University of San Diego
University of San Francisco
University of Southern California
Whittier College

Colorado
Colorado School of Mines
Colorado State University
Colorado State University
     Pueblo
Fort Lewis College
Mesa State College
United States Air Force Academy
University of Colorado
     Boulder
University of Northern Colorado

Connecticut
Central Connecticut State University
Connecticut College
Eastern Connecticut State University
Fairfield University
Southern Connecticut State University
Trinity College
United States Coast Guard Academy
University of Bridgeport
University of Connecticut
University of Hartford
Wesleyan University
Yale University

Delaware
Delaware State University

District of Columbia
American University
Corcoran College of Art and Design
Gallaudet University
Howard University
Trinity College

Florida
Broward Community College
Eckerd College

Flagler College
Florida Atlantic University
Florida International University
Lake City Community College
New College of Florida
Palm Beach Atlantic University
Ringling School of Art and Design
St. Petersburg College
Schiller International University
Stetson University
University of Florida
University of Miami
University of South Florida
University of Tampa
University of West Florida
Webber International University

Georgia
Agnes Scott College
Atlanta College of Art
Augusta State University
Brewton-Parker College
Clark Atlanta University
Covenant College
Emory University
Morehouse College
North Georgia College & State
     University
Savannah State University
Shorter College
Spelman College
University of Georgia

Hawaii
Brigham Young University-Hawaii
University of Hawaii
     Hilo
     Manoa

Idaho
Albertson College of Idaho
Boise State University
Idaho State University
University of Idaho

Illinois
Aurora University
Benedictine University
Concordia University
Illinois Institute of Technology
Illinois State University
Illinois Wesleyan University
Lake Forest College
Millikin University
North Central College
North Park University
Northeastern Illinois University
Oakton Community College
Rockford College
St. Xavier University
School of the Art Institute of Chicago
Trinity International University
Triton College
University of Chicago
University of Illinois
     Chicago
     Urbana-Champaign
Wheaton College

Indiana
Ball State University
Butler University
DePauw University
Franklin College
Indiana University-Purdue University
     Fort Wayne
Manchester College
Purdue University
Purdue University
     Calumet
Saint Mary's College
St. Mary-of-the-Woods College
Taylor University: Fort Wayne
University of Evansville

University of Notre Dame
Valparaiso University
Wabash College

Iowa

Buena Vista University
Coe College
Cornell College
Drake University
Grinnell College
Iowa State University
Iowa Wesleyan College
Kirkwood Community College
Maharishi University of Management
Morningside College
University of Iowa
University of Northern Iowa
Upper Iowa University

Kansas

Benedictine College
Bethany College
Emporia State University
Fort Hays State University
Johnson County Community College
Kansas State University
Pittsburg State University
St. Mary College
Southwestern College
Wichita State University

Kentucky

Berea College
Campbellsville University
Morehead State University
Murray State University
Union College
University of Kentucky
University of Louisville

Louisiana

Centenary College of Louisiana
Grambling State University
Louisiana State University and
    Agricultural and Mechanical College
Loyola University New Orleans
Nicholls State University
Northwestern State University
Our Lady of Holy Cross College
Southeastern Louisiana University
Southern University and Agricultural and
    Mechanical College
Tulane University
University of Louisiana at Lafayette
University of New Orleans
Xavier University of Louisiana

Maine

Bates College
Bowdoin College
Colby College
College of the Atlantic
Maine College of Art
Thomas College
University of Maine
University of Maine
    Farmington
    Presque Isle
University of Southern Maine

Maryland

Bowie State University
Hood College
Maryland Institute College of Art
McDaniel College
St. Mary's College of Maryland
Salisbury University
Towson University
University of Baltimore
University of Maryland
    College Park
Washington College

Massachusetts

Amherst College
Anna Maria College
Art Institute of Boston at Lesley
    University
Babson College
Boston College
Bridgewater State College
Elms College
Emmanuel College
Framingham State College
Gordon College
Hampshire College
Harvard College
Hellenic College/Holy Cross
Lesley University
Massachusetts College of Art
Massachusetts College of Liberal Arts
Montserrat College of Art
Mount Holyoke College
Northeastern University
Regis College
Salem State College
School of the Museum of Fine Arts
Simmons College
Simon's Rock College of Bard
Smith College
Suffolk University
Tufts University
University of Massachusetts
    Amherst
    Boston
Wellesley College
Westfield State College
Wheaton College
Williams College
Worcester Polytechnic Institute

Michigan

Adrian College
Alma College
Aquinas College
College for Creative Studies
Concordia University
Ferris State University
Grand Valley State University
Kalamazoo College
Lansing Community College
Michigan State University
Michigan Technological University
Siena Heights University
University of Michigan
Wayne State University
Western Michigan University

Minnesota

Bethel College
College of St. Catherine
Concordia College: Moorhead
Concordia University: St. Paul
Gustavus Adolphus College
Hamline University
Minnesota State University
    Mankato
    Moorhead
North Central University
Northwestern College
Southwest State University
University of Minnesota
    Morris
    Twin Cities
University of St. Thomas
Winona State University

Mississippi

Mississippi State University
University of Mississippi

Missouri

Avila University
Fontbonne College
Kansas City Art Institute
Lindenwood University
Maple Woods Community College

Missouri Southern State College
Northwest Missouri State University
Research College of Nursing
Rockhurst University
St. Louis Community College
    St. Louis Community College at
        Florissant Valley
St. Louis University
Southeast Missouri State University
Southwest Missouri State University
Truman State University
University of Missouri
    Columbia
    St. Louis
Washington University in St. Louis
Webster University
Westminster College
William Woods University

Montana

Montana State University
    Bozeman
University of Montana-Missoula

Nebraska

College of Saint Mary
Concordia University
Creighton University
Doane College
Hastings College
Nebraska Wesleyan University
University of Nebraska
    Kearney
    Lincoln
    Omaha

Nevada

University of Nevada
    Las Vegas
    Reno

New Hampshire

Colby-Sawyer College
Dartmouth College
Franklin Pierce College
Keene State College
New England College
Plymouth State College
St. Anselm College
Southern New Hampshire University
University of New Hampshire
University of New Hampshire at
    Manchester

New Jersey

The College of New Jersey
College of St. Elizabeth
County College of Morris
Drew University
Ramapo College of New Jersey
St. Peter's College
William Paterson University of New
    Jersey

New Mexico

College of Santa Fe
Eastern New Mexico University
Institute of American Indian Arts
New Mexico Institute of Mining and
    Technology
New Mexico State University
University of New Mexico

New York

Alfred University
Bard College
Barnard College
Broome Community College
Canisius College

City University of New York
    Baruch College
    Borough of Manhattan Community
        College
    Brooklyn College
    City College
    Hunter College
    John Jay College of Criminal
        Justice
Colgate University
College of Mount St. Vincent
College of New Rochelle
Columbia University
    Columbia College
Concordia College
Cooper Union for the Advancement of
    Science and Art
Cornell University
D'Youville College
Elmira College
Erie Community College
    City Campus
    North Campus
    South Campus
Eugene Lang College/New School
    University
Fashion Institute of Technology
Fordham University
Hartwick College
Hobart and William Smith Colleges
Houghton College
Juilliard School
Keuka College
Long Island University
    C. W. Post Campus
    Southampton College
Manhattan College
Manhattanville College
Marymount College of Fordham
    University
Marymount Manhattan College
Monroe Community College
Mount St. Mary College
Nazareth College of Rochester
New York University
Niagara University
Parsons School of Design
Pratt Institute
Rensselaer Polytechnic Institute
Rochester Institute of Technology
Russell Sage College
St. Bonaventure University
St. Lawrence University
Sarah Lawrence College
State University of New York
    Albany
    Binghamton
    Buffalo
    College at Buffalo
    College at Cortland
    College at Fredonia
    College at Geneseo
    College at Old Westbury
    College at Plattsburgh
    College at Potsdam
    Oswego
    Stony Brook
United States Military Academy
Utica College
Vassar College
Wagner College
Yeshiva University

North Carolina

Bennett College
Campbell University
Davidson College
Duke University
East Carolina University
Elon University
Forsyth Technical Community College
Johnson C. Smith University
Lenoir-Rhyne College
Mars Hill College
Meredith College

Methodist College
North Carolina State University
St. Andrews Presbyterian College
Salem College
University of North Carolina
    Charlotte
    Wilmington
Wake Forest University
Warren Wilson College
Western Carolina University

Ohio
Art Academy of Cincinnati
Baldwin-Wallace College
Bluffton College
Bowling Green State University
Cleveland State University
College of Wooster
Defiance College
John Carroll University
Kent State University
Kenyon College
Malone College
Marietta College
Miami University
    Oxford Campus
Muskingum College
Notre Dame College
Oberlin College
Ohio Northern University
Ohio State University
    Columbus Campus
Otterbein College
Tiffin University
University of Toledo
Walsh University
Wittenberg University
Wright State University
Youngstown State University

Oklahoma
East Central University
Oklahoma Baptist University
Oklahoma City University
Oklahoma State University
University of Tulsa

Oregon
Concordia University
Eastern Oregon University
George Fox University
Mount Hood Community College
Oregon Health Sciences University
Oregon Institute of Technology
Oregon State University
Pacific Northwest College of Art
Pacific University
Portland State University
Reed College
Southern Oregon University
University of Oregon
Warner Pacific College
Willamette University

Pennsylvania
Albright College
Bryn Mawr College
Cabrini College
California University of Pennsylvania
Carnegie Mellon University
Chatham College
Chestnut Hill College
Dickinson College
Duquesne University
East Stroudsburg University of
    Pennsylvania
Elizabethtown College
Franklin & Marshall College
Gettysburg College
Haverford College
Indiana University of Pennsylvania
Juniata College
La Salle University
Lafayette College

Lehigh University
Lincoln University
Messiah College
Muhlenberg College
Penn State
    Abington
    University Park
Pennsylvania College of Technology
Philadelphia University
Rosemont College
St. Joseph's University
Seton Hill University
Slippery Rock University of
    Pennsylvania
Swarthmore College
Temple University
University of Pennsylvania
University of Scranton
West Chester University of Pennsylvania
Widener University
Wilson College

Puerto Rico
Inter American University of Puerto Rico
    Guayama Campus
Pontifical Catholic University of Puerto
    Rico
Technological College of San Juan
University of Puerto Rico
    Bayamon University College
    Cayey University College
    Humacao
    Mayaguez Campus
    Medical Sciences Campus
    Rio Piedras Campus
University of the Sacred Heart

Rhode Island
Brown University
Rhode Island College
Rhode Island School of Design
Roger Williams University
Salve Regina University
University of Rhode Island

South Carolina
Clemson University
College of Charleston
Columbia College
Horry-Georgetown Technical College
Presbyterian College
South Carolina State University
University of South Carolina
University of South Carolina
    Spartanburg
Winthrop University

South Dakota
Black Hills State University
South Dakota State University
University of South Dakota

Tennessee
Carson-Newman College
East Tennessee State University
Fisk University
Lee University
Memphis College of Art
Rhodes College
Tennessee State University
Union University
University of Memphis
University of Tennessee
    Martin
University of Tennessee Health Science
    Center

Texas
Austin College
Cedar Valley College
Collin County Community College
    District
Concordia University at Austin
Laredo Community College

Rice University
Sam Houston State University
Schreiner University
Southern Methodist University
Southwestern University
Texas Tech University
Texas Wesleyan University
University of Houston
University of North Texas
University of Texas
    Pan American
    Tyler
University of the Incarnate Word

Utah
University of Utah
Utah State University
Utah Valley State College
Weber State University

Vermont
Bennington College
Goddard College
Green Mountain College
Johnson State College
Middlebury College
Sterling College

Virginia
College of William and Mary
George Mason University
Hampden-Sydney College
Hollins University
Longwood University
Mary Baldwin College
Old Dominion University
Radford University
Randolph-Macon College
Randolph-Macon Woman's College
Southside Virginia Community College
Sweet Briar College
University of Richmond
Virginia Commonwealth University
Virginia Military Institute
Virginia Polytechnic Institute and State
    University
Virginia State University
Washington and Lee University

Washington
Central Washington University
Edmonds Community College
Gonzaga University
Pacific Lutheran University
St. Martin's College
Seattle Pacific University
University of Washington
Washington State University
Western Washington University
Whitman College
Whitworth College

West Virginia
Alderson-Broaddus College
Marshall University
West Virginia University
West Virginia Wesleyan College
Wheeling Jesuit University

Wisconsin
Alverno College
Beloit College
Carroll College
Concordia University Wisconsin
Milwaukee Institute of Art & Design
Northland College
Ripon College

University of Wisconsin
    Eau Claire
    Green Bay
    La Crosse
    Parkside
    Platteville
    River Falls
    Stout
    Superior

Wyoming
University of Wyoming

Washington semester

Alabama
Alabama Agricultural and Mechanical
    University
Birmingham-Southern College
Huntingdon College
Judson College
Spring Hill College
University of Alabama

Arizona
Arizona State University
Northern Arizona University

Arkansas
Hendrix College
John Brown University
Lyon College

California
Azusa Pacific University
Biola University
California Baptist University
California State University
    Long Beach
    Stanislaus
Chapman University
Claremont McKenna College
Dominican School of Philosophy and
    Theology
Fresno Pacific University
Master's College
Mills College
Mount St. Mary's College
Occidental College
Pepperdine University
Point Loma Nazarene University
Pomona College
Santa Clara University
Scripps College
Sonoma State University
Stanford University
University of California
    Davis
    Los Angeles
    Riverside
    San Diego
    Santa Barbara
    Santa Cruz
University of Redlands
University of San Francisco
University of Southern California
University of the Pacific
Vanguard University of Southern
    California
Whittier College

Colorado
Colorado Christian University
Colorado College
Mesa State College
Metropolitan State College of Denver

Connecticut
Albertus Magnus College
Connecticut College
Eastern Connecticut State University
Fairfield University

Quinnipiac University
Trinity College
University of Bridgeport
University of Hartford
Wesleyan University

Delaware

University of Delaware

District of Columbia

American University
Catholic University of America
Georgetown University
Trinity College

Florida

Barry University
Eckerd College
Florida Gulf Coast University
Florida Southern College
New College of Florida
Palm Beach Atlantic University
Rollins College
Stetson University
University of Miami
University of North Florida
University of Tampa
University of West Florida

Georgia

Agnes Scott College
Berry College
Clark Atlanta University
Covenant College
Emory University
Oglethorpe University
Oxford College of Emory University
Spelman College
University of Georgia

Idaho

Northwest Nazarene University

Illinois

Blackburn College
Bradley University
Dominican University
Elmhurst College
Eureka College
Greenville College
Illinois College
Illinois State University
Illinois Wesleyan University
Judson College
Knox College
Lake Forest College
Loyola University of Chicago
MacMurray College
McKendree College
Millikin University
Monmouth College
North Central College
North Park University
Northwestern University
Olivet Nazarene University
Rockford College
Southern Illinois University Carbondale
Trinity Christian College
Trinity International University
University of Illinois
    Urbana-Champaign
University of St. Francis
Wheaton College

Indiana

Ball State University
Bethel College
Butler University
DePauw University
Franklin College
Goshen College
Hanover College
Huntington College

Indiana University
    Bloomington
    Northwest
Indiana University-Purdue University
    Fort Wayne
St. Joseph's College
Saint Mary's College
Taylor University
University of Indianapolis
University of Notre Dame
Valparaiso University
Wabash College

Iowa

Briar Cliff University
Central College
Coe College
Cornell College
Dordt College
Drake University
Grand View College
Grinnell College
Iowa State University
Loras College
Luther College
Morningside College
Northwestern College
Simpson College
University of Iowa
University of Northern Iowa
Wartburg College

Kansas

Bethany College
Bethel College
Central Christian College
MidAmerica Nazarene University
Southwestern College
Sterling College
Tabor College
University of Kansas
Wichita State University

Kentucky

Alice Lloyd College
Asbury College
Bellarmine University
Campbellsville University
Kentucky Wesleyan College
Morehead State University
Pikeville College
Transylvania University

Louisiana

Centenary College of Louisiana
Louisiana State University
    Shreveport
Loyola University New Orleans
Tulane University
University of Louisiana at Lafayette
University of New Orleans

Maine

Bates College
Bowdoin College
Colby College
St. Joseph's College
University of Southern Maine

Maryland

Columbia Union College
Goucher College
Hood College
McDaniel College
St. Mary's College of Maryland
Salisbury University
Washington College

Massachusetts

American International College
Anna Maria College
Assumption College
Bay Path College

Boston College
Boston University
Brandeis University
Clark University
College of the Holy Cross
Elms College
Emmanuel College
Framingham State College
Gordon College
Lesley University
Massachusetts College of Liberal Arts
Massachusetts Institute of Technology
Merrimack College
Mount Holyoke College
Nichols College
Pine Manor College
Regis College
Simmons College
Smith College
Stonehill College
Suffolk University
Tufts University
University of Massachusetts
    Dartmouth
Wellesley College
Western New England College
Westfield State College
Wheaton College
Worcester Polytechnic Institute

Michigan

Adrian College
Alma College
Calvin College
Central Michigan University
Cornerstone University
Eastern Michigan University
Grand Valley State University
Hillsdale College
Hope College
Northern Michigan University
Spring Arbor University
University of Michigan
University of Michigan
    Dearborn

Minnesota

Bethel College
College of St. Catherine
Concordia College: Moorhead
Gustavus Adolphus College
Hamline University
Macalester College
Minnesota State University
    Moorhead
Northwestern College
St. Mary's University of Minnesota
St. Olaf College
University of St. Thomas

Mississippi

Millsaps College
Mississippi State University

Missouri

Avila University
Drury University
Evangel University
Maryville University of Saint Louis
Northwest Missouri State University
Research College of Nursing
Rockhurst University
Southwest Baptist University
Stephens College
University of Missouri
    Columbia
Washington University in St. Louis
Westminster College

Nebraska

Creighton University
Nebraska Wesleyan University

Nevada

University of Nevada
    Las Vegas

New Hampshire

Colby-Sawyer College
Daniel Webster College
Dartmouth College
Franklin Pierce College
Keene State College
St. Anselm College
University of New Hampshire
University of New Hampshire at
    Manchester

New Jersey

Caldwell College
Drew University
Fairleigh Dickinson University
    College at Florham
Kean University
Monmouth University
Montclair State University
New Jersey City University
Richard Stockton College of New Jersey
Rutgers, The State University of New
    Jersey
        New Brunswick Regional Campus
        Newark Regional Campus
St. Peter's College
Seton Hall University
William Paterson University of New
    Jersey

New Mexico

University of New Mexico

New York

Adelphi University
Alfred University
Bard College
Canisius College
Cazenovia College
City University of New York
    Brooklyn College
Colgate University
College of New Rochelle
Cornell University
Daemen College
Hamilton College
Hartwick College
Hilbert College
Hobart and William Smith Colleges
Hofstra University
Houghton College
Ithaca College
Jamestown Community College
Keuka College
Le Moyne College
Long Island University
    C. W. Post Campus
    Southampton College
Manhattan College
Manhattanville College
Marist College
Molloy College
Nazareth College of Rochester
New York University
Niagara University
Nyack College
Roberts Wesleyan College
St. Bonaventure University
St. John Fisher College
St. Lawrence University
Skidmore College

State University of New York
   Albany
   Binghamton
   Buffalo
   College at Brockport
   College at Buffalo
   College at Cortland
   College at Fredonia
   College at Geneseo
   College at Oneonta
   Oswego
   Stony Brook
Syracuse University
Union College
United States Military Academy
University of Rochester
Vassar College
Wagner College
Wells College

North Carolina

Barton College
Bennett College
Campbell University
Catawba College
Chowan College
Davidson College
Duke University
Elon University
Guilford College
Johnson C. Smith University
Lenoir-Rhyne College
Meredith College
Methodist College
Montreat College
Pfeiffer University
Queens University of Charlotte
St. Andrews Presbyterian College
Salem College
University of North Carolina
   Greensboro
   Pembroke

Ohio

Ashland University
Baldwin-Wallace College
Bluffton College
Bowling Green State University
Case Western Reserve University
Cedarville University
College of Wooster
Denison University
Heidelberg College
Hiram College
John Carroll University
Kent State University
Kenyon College
Malone College
Marietta College
Miami University
   Oxford Campus
Mount Union College
Mount Vernon Nazarene University
Muskingum College
Oberlin College
Ohio Dominican College
Ohio Northern University
Ohio State University
   Columbus Campus
Ohio Wesleyan University
Otterbein College
University of Cincinnati
University of Dayton
University of Findlay
Wilmington College
Wittenberg University
Xavier University
Youngstown State University

Oklahoma

Oklahoma City University
Oklahoma Wesleyan University
Oral Roberts University
Southern Nazarene University

University of Oklahoma
University of Tulsa

Oregon

George Fox University
Lewis & Clark College
Northwest Christian College
Pacific University
Portland State University
University of Portland
Warner Pacific College
Western Baptist College
Willamette University

Pennsylvania

Albright College
Allegheny College
Arcadia University
Bucknell University
Carnegie Mellon University
Cedar Crest College
Chatham College
Dickinson College
Duquesne University
Elizabethtown College
Franklin & Marshall College
Geneva College
Gettysburg College
Grove City College
Indiana University of Pennsylvania
Juniata College
King's College
La Roche College
Lafayette College
Lebanon Valley College of Pennsylvania
Lehigh University
Lycoming College
Mercyhurst College
Messiah College
Moravian College
Muhlenberg College
Rosemont College
St. Joseph's University
Seton Hill University
Shippensburg University of Pennsylvania
Thiel College
University of Pittsburgh
University of Pittsburgh
   Greensburg
University of Scranton
Villanova University
Washington and Jefferson College
Waynesburg College
Wilson College

Puerto Rico

Inter American University of Puerto Rico
   Barranquitas Campus
   Fajardo Campus
Universidad Metropolitana
University of Puerto Rico
   Rio Piedras Campus

Rhode Island

Providence College
Roger Williams University
Salve Regina University
University of Rhode Island

South Carolina

College of Charleston
Columbia College
Furman University
Presbyterian College
Southern Wesleyan University
Wofford College

South Dakota

Augustana College
Dakota Wesleyan University
Northern State University
University of Sioux Falls

Tennessee

Belmont University
Bryan College
Carson-Newman College
Crichton College
King College
Lambuth University
Lee University
Maryville College
Milligan College
Rhodes College
Union University
Vanderbilt University

Texas

Dallas Baptist University
East Texas Baptist University
Jarvis Christian College
LeTourneau University
Midland College
Rice University
St. Mary's University
Southern Methodist University
Southwest Texas State University
Southwestern University
Texas Christian University
Texas Lutheran University
Trinity University
University of Dallas
University of Houston
University of Texas
   Dallas

Utah

Brigham Young University
University of Utah
Weber State University

Vermont

Middlebury College
St. Michael's College
University of Vermont

Virginia

Averett University
Bridgewater College
College of William and Mary
Eastern Mennonite University
Hampden-Sydney College
Hollins University
James Madison University
Liberty University
Mary Washington College
Randolph-Macon College
Randolph-Macon Woman's College
Roanoke College
Sweet Briar College
University of Richmond
Virginia Commonwealth University
Virginia Polytechnic Institute and State
   University
Washington and Lee University

Washington

Gonzaga University
Northwest College
St. Martin's College
Seattle Pacific University
University of Washington
Western Washington University
Whitman College
Whitworth College

West Virginia

Bethany College
Davis and Elkins College
Fairmont State College
Marshall University
Mountain State University
Salem International University
Shepherd College
University of Charleston
West Virginia University
West Virginia Wesleyan College

Wheeling Jesuit University

Wisconsin

Beloit College
Carroll College
Carthage College
Lawrence University
Marquette University
Mount Mary College
Ripon College
St. Norbert College
University of Wisconsin
   Milwaukee

Wyoming

University of Wyoming

Weekend college

Alabama

Alabama Agricultural and Mechanical
   University
Athens State University
Auburn University at Montgomery
Bevill State Community College
Bishop State Community College
Calhoun Community College
Enterprise State Junior College
Faulkner University
Gadsden State Community College
George C. Wallace State Community
   College
   Dothan
Harry M. Ayers State Technical College
Northwest-Shoals Community College
Trenholm State Technical College
Troy State University Dothan
Troy State University in Montgomery
University of Alabama
University of Alabama
   Birmingham
University of North Alabama
University of South Alabama
Wallace State Community College at
   Hanceville

Arizona

Arizona Western College
Cochise College
DeVry University
   Phoenix
Estrella Mountain Community College
Glendale Community College
Northern Arizona University
Paradise Valley Community College
Pima Community College
Rio Salado College
University of Arizona
Yavapai College

Arkansas

Arkansas Tech University
East Arkansas Community College
Mississippi County Community College
North Arkansas College
Pulaski Technical College
University of Arkansas
   Community College at Batesville
   Little Rock

California

Antelope Valley College
Antioch Southern California
   Los Angeles
Barstow College
Biola University
California Baptist University
California State University
   San Marcos
   Stanislaus
Chabot College
Coastline Community College

College of the Canyons
Cuesta College
Cuyamaca College
De Anza College
DeVry University
 Fremont
 Pomona
 West Hills
Deep Springs College
Diablo Valley College
Dominican University of California
East Los Angeles College
Foothill College
Golden West College
Holy Names College
Irvine Valley College
Laney College
Long Beach City College
Los Angeles Harbor College
Los Angeles Southwest College
Los Angeles Trade and Technical College
Marymount College
MiraCosta College
Modesto Junior College
Monterey Peninsula College
Mount St. Mary's College
Mount San Jacinto College
Napa Valley College
Ohlone College
Orange Coast College
Pacific Oaks College
Palomar College
Patten University
Pepperdine University
Reedley College
Riverside Community College
St. Mary's College of California
San Diego City College
San Joaquin Delta College
Santa Monica College
Shasta College
Sierra College
Simpson College
Southwestern College
University of La Verne
Vanguard University of Southern
 California
Vista Community College
Woodbury University

Colorado

Arapahoe Community College
Colorado Christian University
Colorado State University
 Pueblo
Colorado Technical University
Community College of Aurora
DeVry University
 Denver
DeVry University: Colorado Springs
Front Range Community College
Heritage College
Metropolitan State College of Denver
Morgan Community College
National American University
 Denver
Red Rocks Community College
University of Denver
Westwood College of Technology
 South

Connecticut

Briarwood College
Capital Community College
Eastern Connecticut State University
Housatonic Community College
Manchester Community College
Norwalk Community College
Quinebaug Valley Community College
Sacred Heart University
St. Joseph College
Teikyo Post University
University of Bridgeport

Delaware

Delaware State University
Wilmington College

District of Columbia

American University
Potomac College
Strayer University
Trinity College
University of the District of Columbia

Florida

Baptist College of Florida
Bethune-Cookman College
Broward Community College
Daytona Beach Community College
DeVry University
 Miramar
 Orlando
Edward Waters College
Florida Agricultural and Mechanical
 University
Florida Atlantic University
Florida International University
Gulf Coast Community College
Hillsborough Community College
Indian River Community College
Jacksonville University
Jones College
Lake City Community College
Miami-Dade Community College
Northwood University
 Florida Campus
Palm Beach Community College
Pasco-Hernando Community College
Pensacola Junior College
St. Leo University
St. Petersburg College
Santa Fe Community College
Schiller International University
Seminole Community College
Southwest Florida College
Talmudic College of Florida
University of Florida
University of Miami
University of North Florida
University of South Florida
Valencia Community College
Webber International University

Georgia

Albany State University
Armstrong Atlantic State University
Atlanta Metropolitan College
Bainbridge College
Clayton College and State University
Dalton State College
Darton College
DeVry University
 Alpharetta
 Atlanta
Georgia Perimeter College
Georgia Southern University
Middle Georgia College
State University of West Georgia
Wesleyan College

Hawaii

Hawaii Business College
Hawaii Pacific University
University of Hawaii
 Leeward Community College
 Maui Community College
 West Oahu

Idaho

Boise State University
Eastern Idaho Technical College
Lewis-Clark State College

Illinois

Benedictine University
Black Hawk College

City Colleges of Chicago
 Kennedy-King College
 Malcolm X College
 Richard J. Daley College
 Wright College
College of DuPage
Cooking & Hospitality Institute of
 Chicago
De Paul University
DeVry University
 Addison
 Chicago
 Tinley Park
Elgin Community College
Governors State University
Illinois Central College
Illinois Eastern Community Colleges
 Frontier Community College
 Lincoln Trail College
 Olney Central College
 Wabash Valley College
International Academy of Design and
 Technology
John A. Logan College
Kaskaskia College
Kendall College
Lincoln Land Community College
Moraine Valley Community College
North Central College
Oakton Community College
Parkland College
Prairie State College
Roosevelt University
St. Xavier University
Shimer College
Southern Illinois University Edwardsville
Southwestern Illinois College
Triton College
University of Illinois
 Springfield
University of St. Francis
Waubonsee Community College
Western Illinois University
William Rainey Harper College

Indiana

Bethel College
Calumet College of St. Joseph
Indiana University
 East
 Northwest
 South Bend
 Southeast
Indiana University-Purdue University
 Fort Wayne
Indiana University-Purdue University
 Indianapolis
Ivy Tech State College
 Bloomington
 Central Indiana
 Columbus
 Eastcentral
 Kokomo
 Lafayette
 Northcentral
 Northeast
 Northwest
 Southcentral
 Southeast
 Southwest
 Wabash Valley
 Whitewater
Purdue University
 Calumet
St. Mary-of-the-Woods College
Taylor University: Fort Wayne
University of Indianapolis
University of St. Francis
Vincennes University

Iowa

Briar Cliff University
Buena Vista University
Des Moines Area Community College
Grand View College

Iowa Lakes Community College
Iowa State University
Iowa Western Community College
Kirkwood Community College
Mount Mercy College
Simpson College
University of Osteopathic Medicine and
 Health Sciences
 Des Moines University -
 Osteopathic Medical Center

Kansas

Allen County Community College
Butler County Community College
Donnelly College
Fort Scott Community College
Johnson County Community College
Kansas City Kansas Community College
Pratt Community College

Kentucky

Brescia University
Clear Creek Baptist Bible College
Elizabethtown Community College
Henderson Community College
Jefferson Community College
Lexington Community College
Madisonville Community College
Morehead State University
Murray State University
Paducah Community College
St. Catharine College
Spalding University
Sullivan University
Thomas More College
University of Kentucky

Louisiana

Delgado Community College
Grambling State University
Herzing College
Nunez Community College
University of New Orleans

Maine

Husson College
University of Southern Maine

Maryland

Anne Arundel Community College
Capitol College
Carroll Community College
Cecil Community College
Chesapeake College
College of Notre Dame of Maryland
College of Southern Maryland
Community College of Baltimore County
 Catonsville
 Dundalk
 Essex
Coppin State College
Frederick Community College
Frostburg State University
Harford Community College
Howard Community College
Montgomery College
 Rockville Campus
Morgan State University
Mount St. Mary's College
University of Baltimore
University of Maryland
 University College
Villa Julie College

Massachusetts

American International College
Bay Path College
Becker College
Elms College
Emmanuel College
Marian Court College
Mount Wachusett Community College
Newbury College
Northeastern University

Quinsigamond Community College
Wentworth Institute of Technology

Michigan
Baker College
of Cadillac
Bay de Noc Community College
Central Michigan University
Concordia University
Cornerstone University
Davenport University - Western Region
Eastern Michigan University
Grand Rapids Community College
Jackson Community College
Kellogg Community College
Lansing Community College
Macomb Community College
Madonna University
Mott Community College
Northern Michigan University
Northwood University
St. Clair County Community College
Schoolcraft College
Siena Heights University
Southwestern Michigan College
Spring Arbor University
University of Michigan
Washtenaw Community College
Wayne State University
Western Michigan University

Minnesota
Anoka-Ramsey Community College
Augsburg College
College of St. Catherine
Crown College
Dakota County Technical College
Fergus Falls Community College
Inver Hills Community College
Lake Superior College: A Community
and Technical College
Metropolitan State University
Minneapolis Community and Technical
College
North Central University
North Hennepin Community College
Riverland Community College: A
Technical and Community College

Mississippi
Blue Mountain College
Delta State University
Holmes Community College
Mississippi Gulf Coast Community
College
Perkinston
Mississippi University for Women
Northwest Mississippi Community
College

Missouri
Avila University
Blue River Community College
Central Missouri State University
Crowder College
DeVry University
Kansas City
East Central College
Fontbonne College
Hannibal-LaGrange College
Longview Community College
Maryville University of Saint Louis
Missouri Southern State College
Missouri Western State College
Northwest Missouri State University
Penn Valley Community College
St. Louis Community College
St. Louis Community College at
Florissant Valley
St. Louis Community College at
Forest Park

Montana
Montana State University
Billings

Nebraska
Bellevue University
Central Community College
College of Saint Mary
Metropolitan Community College
Southeast Community College
Lincoln Campus

Nevada
Community College of Southern Nevada
Morrison University
Sierra Nevada College
Truckee Meadows Community College

New Hampshire
New Hampshire Community Technical
College
Nashua
Southern New Hampshire University

New Jersey
Bloomfield College
Brookdale Community College
Burlington County College
Caldwell College
Camden County College
College of St. Elizabeth
County College of Morris
DeVry College of Technology
Fairleigh Dickinson University
College at Florham
Felician College
Hudson County Community College
Mercer County Community College
New Jersey City University
Passaic County Community College
Rider University
Union County College
Warren County Community College
William Paterson University of New
Jersey

New Mexico
Clovis Community College
New Mexico Junior College
New Mexico State University
New Mexico State University
Alamogordo
Santa Fe Community College
University of New Mexico

New York
Adelphi University
Broome Community College
City University of New York
Borough of Manhattan Community
College
Bronx Community College
Brooklyn College
College of Staten Island
John Jay College of Criminal
Justice
Queens College
Corning Community College
D'Youville College
Daemen College
DeVry Institute of Technology
New York
Dominican College of Blauvelt
Dowling College
Elmira Business Institute
Erie Community College
City Campus
North Campus
South Campus
Hofstra University
Iona College
Jamestown Community College
Jefferson Community College

Long Island University
C. W. Post Campus
Maria College
Marist College
Marymount College of Fordham
University
Medaille College
Mercy College
Metropolitan College of New York
Molloy College
Monroe College
Monroe Community College
New York Institute of Technology
New York University
Orange County Community College
Rochester Institute of Technology
Rockland Community College
Sage College of Albany
St. Bonaventure University
St. Elizabeth College of Nursing
St. John Fisher College
St. John's University
St. Joseph's College
St. Joseph's College: Suffolk Campus
St. Joseph's Hospital Health Center
School of Nursing
State University of New York
College of Agriculture and
Technology at Cobleskill
College of Agriculture and
Technology at Morrisville
College of Technology at Delhi
Tompkins-Cortland Community College
Utica College
Westchester Business Institute

North Carolina
Alamance Community College
Barton College
Belmont Abbey College
Bladen Community College
Central Carolina Community College
Central Piedmont Community College
Durham Technical Community College
Edgecombe Community College
Elizabeth City State University
Fayetteville State University
Fayetteville Technical Community
College
Gaston College
Greensboro College
John Wesley College
Lenoir Community College
Louisburg College
Methodist College
North Carolina Wesleyan College
Pfeiffer University
Piedmont Community College
Queens University of Charlotte
Randolph Community College
St. Augustine's College
Sampson Community College
Shaw University
Stanly Community College
Surry Community College
University of North Carolina
Charlotte
Wayne Community College
Wilkes Community College

North Dakota
University of Mary
University of North Dakota

Ohio
Antioch University McGregor
Ashland University
Baldwin-Wallace College
Central Ohio Technical College
Clark State Community College
Cleveland State University
College of Mount St. Joseph
Columbus State Community College

Cuyahoga Community College
Eastern Campus
Western Campus
David N. Myers College
DeVry University
Columbus
Defiance College
Edison State Community College
Franklin University
Heidelberg College
Hiram College
Hocking Technical College
Kent State University
Kent State University
East Liverpool Regional Campus
Tuscarawas Campus
Lake Erie College
Lakeland Community College
Lorain County Community College
Lourdes College
Malone College
Marion Technical College
Miami-Jacobs College
North Central State College
Northwest State Community College
Notre Dame College
Ohio Dominican College
Ohio State University
Agricultural Technical Institute
Mansfield Campus
Marion Campus
Newark Campus
Otterbein College
Owens Community College
Findlay Campus
Toledo
Sinclair Community College
Southern State Community College
Stautzenberger College
Tiffin University
Union Institute & University
University of Cincinnati
University of Cincinnati
Clermont College
Raymond Walters College
University of Findlay
University of Northwestern Ohio
University of Toledo
Ursuline College
Wilmington College
Wittenberg University
Xavier University
Youngstown State University

Oklahoma
Bacone College
Northeastern State University
Oklahoma City Community College
Oklahoma State University
Oral Roberts University
Redlands Community College
Southwestern Oklahoma State University
Tulsa Community College

Oregon
Chemeketa Community College
Eastern Oregon University
Lane Community College
Marylhurst University
Mount Hood Community College
Oregon State University
Pioneer Pacific College
Portland Community College
Western Baptist College

Pennsylvania
Arcadia University
Bucks County Community College
California University of Pennsylvania
Carlow College
Carnegie Mellon University
Cedar Crest College
Community College of Philadelphia
DeSales University

DeVry University
    Ft. Washington
Delaware Valley College
Duquesne University
Gwynedd-Mercy College
Harrisburg Area Community College
Indiana University of Pennsylvania
Keystone College
King's College
Luzerne County Community College
Mercyhurst College
Montgomery County Community
    College
Neumann College
Penn State
    Fayette
    Harrisburg
    York
Pennsylvania College of Technology
Point Park College
Reading Area Community College
Robert Morris University
St. Joseph's University
Seton Hill University
University of Pittsburgh
Valley Forge Christian College
Wilkes University

Puerto Rico

Inter American University of Puerto Rico
    Barranquitas Campus
Turabo University
Universidad Metropolitana
Universidad del Este

Rhode Island

Community College of Rhode Island
Rhode Island College

South Carolina

Benedict College
Claflin University
Forrest Junior College
Midlands Technical College
Piedmont Technical College
University of South Carolina
University of South Carolina
    Sumter
Voorhees College
York Technical College

South Dakota

Southeast Technical Institute

Tennessee

Bethel College
Carson-Newman College
Chattanooga State Technical Community
    College
Crichton College
Miller-Motte Technical College
Northeast State Technical Community
    College
Pellissippi State Technical Community
    College
Roane State Community College
Southwest Tennessee Community
    College
Tennessee State University
Volunteer State Community College
Walters State Community College

Texas

Alvin Community College
Amberton University
Austin Community College
Brookhaven College
College of Saint Thomas More
College of the Mainland
Dallas Baptist University
DeVry University
    Irving
Del Mar College
El Paso Community College

Galveston College
Houston Community College System
Lamar State College at Port Arthur
Lee College
Midland College
Mountain View College
North Harris Montgomery Community
    College District
Northwood University: Texas Campus
Odessa College
Our Lady of the Lake University of San
    Antonio
Palo Alto College
Prairie View A&M University
Richland College
St. Philip's College
Sam Houston State University
San Antonio College
San Jacinto College
    Central Campus
Schreiner University
Southwest Texas State University
Texas Southern University
Texas Wesleyan University
Texas Woman's University
Trinity Valley Community College
Tyler Junior College
University of Houston
University of Houston
    Clear Lake
    Downtown
University of North Texas
University of Texas
    Dallas
    El Paso
    Pan American

Utah

Salt Lake Community College
Southern Utah University
Utah State University
Utah Valley State College
Westminster College

Vermont

Burlington College
Community College of Vermont
Norwich University
Woodbury College

Virginia

Bluefield College
Bryant & Stratton College
DeVry University
    Crystal City
J. Sargeant Reynolds Community
    College
Norfolk State University
Old Dominion University
Piedmont Virginia Community College
Thomas Nelson Community College
Virginia Intermont College
Virginia Western Community College

Washington

Bellevue Community College
Central Washington University
DeVry University
    Seattle
Eastern Washington University
Edmonds Community College
Gonzaga University
Heritage College
Lake Washington Technical College
Seattle Pacific University
Spokane Falls Community College
University of Washington

West Virginia

Fairmont State College
Glenville State College
Ohio Valley College
Potomac State College of West Virginia
    University

Shepherd College
West Virginia State College
West Virginia University

Wisconsin

Alverno College
Carthage College
Concordia University Wisconsin
Edgewood College
Lakeshore Technical College
Marquette University
Milwaukee Area Technical College
Moraine Park Technical College
University of Wisconsin
    Oshkosh
    Parkside
    Rock County
Viterbo University
Waukesha County Technical College
Western Wisconsin Technical College

Colleges in this book

Alabama

Alabama Agricultural and Mechanical University, Normal 35762
Alabama Southern Community College, Monroeville 36461
Alabama State University, Montgomery 36101
American College of Computer and Information Sciences, Birmingham 35205
Andrew Jackson University, Birmingham 35205
Athens State University, Athens 35611
Auburn University, Auburn 36849-5145
Auburn University at Montgomery, Montgomery 36124-4023
Auburn University: College of Veterinary Medicine, Auburn 36849
Auburn University: School of Pharmacy, Auburn 36849
Beeson Divinity School at Samford University, Birmingham 35229
Bevill State Community College, Sumiton 35148
Birmingham-Southern College, Birmingham 35254
Bishop State Community College, Mobile 36603-5898
Calhoun Community College, Decatur 35609-2216
Central Alabama Community College, Alexander City 35011
Chattahoochee Valley Community College, Phenix City 36869
Columbia Southern University, Orange Beach 36561
Community College of the Air Force, Maxwell AFB 36112-6613
Concordia College, Selma 36701
Douglas MacArthur State Technical College, Opp 36467
Enterprise State Junior College, Enterprise 36331
Faulkner University, Montgomery 36109
Gadsden State Community College, Gadsden 35902-0227
George C. Wallace State Community College at Dothan, Dothan 36303-9234
George C. Wallace State Community College at Selma, Selma 36702
Harry M. Ayers State Technical College, Anniston 36202
Heritage Christian University, Florence 35630
Herzing College, Homewood 35209
Huntingdon College, Montgomery 36106-2148
ITT Technical Institute: Birmingham, Birmingham 35242
J. F. Drake State Technical College, Huntsville 35811
Jacksonville State University, Jacksonville 36265-1602
James H. Faulkner State Community College, Bay Minette 36507
Jefferson Davis Community College, Brewton 36427
Jefferson State Community College, Birmingham 35215
Judson College, Marion 36756
Lawson State Community College, Birmingham 35221
Lurleen B. Wallace Junior College, Andalusia 36420
Marion Military Institute, Marion 36756
Miles College, Fairfield 35064
Northeast Alabama Community College, Rainsville 35986
Northwest-Shoals Community College, Muscle Shoals 35662
Oakwood College, Huntsville 35896
Prince Institute of Professional Studies, Montgomery 36117-4231
Reid State Technical College, Evergreen 36401
Remington College: Southeast College of Technology, Mobile 36609-5404
Samford University, Birmingham 35229
Samford University: Cumberland School of Law, Birmingham 35229
Samford University: McWhorter School of Pharmacy, Birmingham 35229
Shelton State Community College, Tuscaloosa 35405
Snead State Community College, Boaz 35957-0734
South University, Montgomery 36116-1120
Southeastern Bible College, Birmingham 35243
Southern Christian University, Montgomery 36117
Southern Christian University, Montgomery 36117
Southern Union State Community College, Wadley 36276
Spring Hill College, Mobile 36608
Stillman College, Tuscaloosa 35403
Talladega College, Talladega 35160
Thomas Goode Jones School of Law--Faulkner University, Montgomery 36109
Trenholm State Technical College, Montgomery 36108
Troy State University, Troy 36082
Troy State University Dothan, Dothan 36304
Troy State University in Montgomery, Montgomery 36103-4419
Tuskegee University, Tuskegee 36088
Tuskegee University: School of Veterinary Medicine, Tuskegee 36088
University of Alabama, Tuscaloosa 35487-0100
University of Alabama at Birmingham, Birmingham 35294
University of Alabama at Birmingham: School of Dentistry, Birmingham 35294
University of Alabama at Birmingham: School of Medicine, Birmingham 35294
University of Alabama at Birmingham: School of Optometry, Birmingham 35294
University of Alabama in Huntsville, Huntsville 35899
University of Alabama: School of Law, Tuscaloosa 35487
University of Mobile, Mobile 36663-0220
University of Montevallo, Montevallo 35115
University of North Alabama, Florence 35632
University of South Alabama, Mobile 36688-2000
University of South Alabama: School of Medicine, Mobile 36688
University of West Alabama, Livingston 35470
Virginia College, Birmingham 35219
Wallace Community College: Sparks Campus, Eufaula 36072-0580
Wallace State Community College at Hanceville, Hanceville 35077

Alaska

Alaska Bible College, Glennallen 99588-0289
Alaska Pacific University, Anchorage 99508
Charter College, Anchorage 99508
Prince William Sound Community College, Valdez 99686
Sheldon Jackson College, Sitka 99835
University of Alaska Anchorage, Anchorage 99508
University of Alaska Fairbanks, Fairbanks 99775-7480
University of Alaska Southeast, Juneau 99801-8697

Arizona

American Indian College of the Assemblies of God, Phoenix 85021-2199
Arizona Automotive Institute, Glendale 85301
Arizona State University, Tempe 85287
Arizona State University: College of Law, Tempe 85287
Arizona Western College, Yuma 85366
Art Institute of Phoenix, Phoenix 85021-2859
Central Arizona College, Coolidge 85228
Cochise College, Douglas 85607-6190
Collins College, Tempe 85281
DeVry University: Phoenix, Phoenix 85201-2995
Eastern Arizona College, Thatcher 85552
Embry-Riddle Aeronautical University: Prescott Campus, Prescott 86301-3720
Estrella Mountain Community College, Avondale 85323
Gateway Community College, Phoenix 85034
Glendale Community College, Glendale 85302
High-Tech Institute, Phoenix 85014-4901
ITT Technical Institute: Phoenix, Phoenix 85008
ITT Technical Institute: Tucson, Tucson 85704
International Institute of the Americas: Phoenix, Phoenix 85019
International Institute of the Americas: Tucson, Tucson 85711
Northern Arizona University, Flagstaff 86011-4084
Paradise Valley Community College, Phoenix 85032
Phoenix College, Phoenix 85013
Pima Community College, Tucson 85709-1010
Prescott College, Prescott 86301
Rio Salado College, Tempe 85281
Scottsdale Community College, Scottsdale 85256
South Mountain Community College, Phoenix 85042
Southwestern College, Phoenix 85032
University of Arizona, Tucson 85721-0066

University of Arizona: College of Law, Tucson 85721
University of Arizona: College of Medicine, Tucson 85724
University of Arizona: College of Pharmacy, Tucson 85721
University of Phoenix, Phoenix 85040-1958
Yavapai College, Prescott 86301

Arkansas

Arkansas Baptist College, Little Rock 72202
Arkansas State University, State University 72467
Arkansas State University: Beebe, Beebe 72012-1000
Arkansas State University: Mountain Home, Mountain Home 72653
Arkansas Tech University, Russellville 72801-2222
Black River Technical College, Pocahontas 72455
Central Baptist College, Conway 72034
Cossatot Community College of the University of Arkansas, De Queen 71832
Crowley's Ridge College, Paragould 72450
East Arkansas Community College, Forrest City 72335
Harding University, Searcy 72149
Henderson State University, Arkadelphia 71999-0001
Hendrix College, Conway 72032
ITT Technical Institute: Little Rock, Little Rock 72204
John Brown University, Siloam Springs 72761-2121
Lyon College, Batesville 72503-2317
Mid-South Community College, West Memphis 72301
Mississippi County Community College, Blytheville 72316
North Arkansas College, Harrison 72601
Northwest Arkansas Community College, Bentonville 72712
Ouachita Baptist University, Arkadelphia 71998
Ouachita Technical College, Malvern 72104
Ozarka College, Melbourne 72556-0010
Philander Smith College, Little Rock 72202-3718
Phillips Community College of the University of Arkansas, Helena 72342
Pulaski Technical College, North Little Rock 72118
Rich Mountain Community College, Mena 71953
South Arkansas Community College, El Dorado 71731
Southeast Arkansas College, Pine Bluff 71603
Southern Arkansas University, Magnolia 71753
Southern Arkansas University Tech, Camden 71711-1599
University of Arkansas, Fayetteville 72701
University of Arkansas - Fort Smith, Fort Smith 72913-3649
University of Arkansas at Little Rock, Little Rock 72204-1099
University of Arkansas at Little Rock: School of Law, Little Rock 72202
University of Arkansas at Monticello, Monticello 71656
University of Arkansas at Pine Bluff, Pine Bluff 71601
University of Arkansas for Medical Sciences, Little Rock 72205
University of Arkansas for Medical Sciences: College of Medicine, Little Rock 72205
University of Arkansas for Medical Sciences: College of Pharmacy, Little Rock 72205
University of Arkansas: Community College at Batesville, Batesville 72503
University of Arkansas: Community College at Hope, Hope 71802-0140
University of Arkansas: School of Law, Fayetteville 72701
University of Central Arkansas, Conway 72035
University of the Ozarks, Clarksville 72830
Williams Baptist College, Walnut Ridge 72476

California

Academy of Art College, San Francisco 94105-3410
American Baptist Seminary of the West, Berkeley 94704
Antelope Valley College, Lancaster 93536-5426
Antioch Southern California at Los Angeles, Marina del Rey 90292
Antioch Southern California at Santa Barbara, Santa Barbara 93101-1581
Art Center College of Design, Pasadena 91103
Art Institute of California, San Diego 92108-4423
Art Institute of California - Orange County, Santa Ana 92794
Art Institute of California - San Francisco, San Francisco 94102
Art Institute of California: Los Angeles, Santa Monica 90405-3035
Azusa Pacific University, Azusa 91702-7000
Azusa Pacific University: School of Theology, Azusa 91702
Bakersfield College, Bakersfield 93305
Barstow College, Barstow 92311

Bethany College, Scotts Valley 95066
Bethesda Christian University, Anaheim 92801
Biola University, La Mirada 90639
Cabrillo College, Aptos 95003
California Baptist University, Riverside 92504-3297
California College of Arts and Crafts, San Francisco 94107
California College of Podiatric Medicine, San Francisco 94115
California Culinary Academy, San Francisco 94102
California Institute of Technology, Pasadena 91125
California Institute of the Arts, Valencia 91355
California Maritime Academy, Vallejo 94590
California Polytechnic State University: San Luis Obispo, San Luis Obispo 93407
California State Polytechnic University: Pomona, Pomona 91768
California State University: Bakersfield, Bakersfield 93311
California State University: Chico, Chico 95929-0722
California State University: Dominguez Hills, Carson 90747
California State University: Fresno, Fresno 93740-8027
California State University: Fullerton, Fullerton 92834-9480
California State University: Hayward, Hayward 94542
California State University: Long Beach, Long Beach 90840
California State University: Los Angeles, Los Angeles 90032
California State University: Monterey Bay, Seaside 93955-8001
California State University: Northridge, Northridge 91330
California State University: Sacramento, Sacramento 95819-2964
California State University: San Bernardino, San Bernardino 92407-2397
California State University: San Marcos, San Marcos 92096-0001
California State University: Stanislaus, Turlock 95382
California Western School of Law, San Diego 92101
Cerritos Community College, Norwalk 90650
Cerro Coso Community College, Ridgecrest 93555
Chabot College, Hayward 94545
Chapman University, Orange 92866
Christian Heritage College, El Cajon 92019-1157
Church Divinity School of the Pacific, Berkeley 94709
Citrus College, Glendora 91741-1899
Claremont McKenna College, Claremont 91711-6425
Claremont School of Theology, Claremont 91711
Cleveland Chiropractic College of Los Angeles, Los Angeles 90004
Coastline Community College, Fountain Valley 92708
Cogswell Polytechnical College, Sunnyvale 94089
Coleman College, La Mesa 91942
College of Alameda, Alameda 94501
College of Marin: Kentfield, Kentfield 94904
College of the Canyons, Santa Clarita 91355
College of the Redwoods, Eureka 95501-9300
College of the Sequoias, Visalia 93277
College of the Siskiyous, Weed 96094
Columbia College, Sonora 95370
Concordia University, Irvine 92612-3299
Contra Costa College, San Pablo 94806
Copper Mountain College, Joshua Tree 92252
Cuesta College, San Luis Obispo 93403
Cuyamaca College, El Cajon 92019
De Anza College, Cupertino 95014
DeVry University: Fremont, Fremont 94555
DeVry University: Long Beach, Long Beach 90806
DeVry University: Pomona, Pomona 91768
DeVry University: West Hills, West Hills 91304
Deep Springs College, Dyer 89010
Diablo Valley College, Pleasant Hill 94523
Dominican School of Philosophy and Theology, Berkeley 94709
Dominican School of Philosophy and Theology, Berkeley 94709
Dominican University of California, San Rafael 94901-2298
Don Bosco Technical Institute, Rosemead 91770-4299
East Los Angeles College, Monterey Park 91754
Fashion Institute of Design and Merchandising, Los Angeles 90015
Fashion Institute of Design and Merchandising: San Diego, San Diego 92101
Fashion Institute of Design and Merchandising: San Francisco, San Francisco 94108
Feather River College, Quincy 95971
Foothill College, Los Altos Hills 94022
Foundation College of San Diego, San Diego 92108-1306
Franciscan School of Theology, Berkeley 94709

Fresno Pacific University, Fresno 93702
Fuller Theological Seminary, Pasadena 91182
Gavilan Community College, Gilroy 95020
Glendale Community College, Glendale 91208
Golden Gate Baptist Theological Seminary, Mill Valley 94941
Golden Gate University, San Francisco 94105
Golden Gate University: School of Law, San Francisco 94105
Golden West College, Huntington Beach 92647
Grossmont Community College, El Cajon 92020
Harvey Mudd College, Claremont 91711
Heald College: Hayward, Hayward 94545
Heald College: Milpitas, Milpitas 95035
Hebrew Union College-Jewish Institute of Religion, Los Angeles 90007
Holy Names College, Oakland 94619
Hope International University, Fullerton 92831
Humboldt State University, Arcata 95521-8299
Humphreys College: School of Law, Stockton 95207
ITT Technical Institute: Anaheim, Anaheim 92801
ITT Technical Institute: Lathrop, Lathrop 95330
ITT Technical Institute: Oxnard, Oxnard 93030
ITT Technical Institute: Rancho Cordova, Rancho Cordova 95670
ITT Technical Institute: San Bernardino, San Bernardino 92408
ITT Technical Institute: San Diego, San Diego 92123
ITT Technical Institute: Sylmar, Sylmar 91342
ITT Technical Institute: Torrance, Torrance 90502
ITT Technical Institute: West Covina, West Covina 91790
Imperial Valley College, Imperial 92251
International School of Theology, San Bernardino 92414
Irvine Valley College, Irvine 92618-4399
Jesuit School of Theology at Berkeley: Professional, Berkeley 94709
John F. Kennedy University, Orinda 94563
John F. Kennedy University: School of Law, Orinda 94563
LIFE Pacific College, San Dimas 91773
La Sierra University, Riverside 92515
Laney College, Oakland 94607
Las Positas College, Livermore 94551
Life Chiropractic College West, San Lorenzo 94580
Loma Linda University, Loma Linda 92350
Loma Linda University: School of Dentistry, Loma Linda 92350
Loma Linda University: School of Medicine, Loma Linda 92350
Long Beach City College, Long Beach 90808
Los Angeles College of Chiropractic, Whittier 90604
Los Angeles Harbor College, Wilmington 90744
Los Angeles Pierce College, Woodland Hills 91371
Los Angeles Southwest College, Los Angeles 90047
Los Angeles Trade and Technical College, Los Angeles 90015
Los Medanos College, Pittsburg 94565
Loyola Marymount University, Los Angeles 90045
Loyola Marymount University: School of Law, Los Angeles 90015
MTI College of Business and Technology, Sacramento 95841
Marymount College, Rancho Palos Verdes 90275
Master's College, Santa Clarita 91321
McGeorge School of Law: University of the Pacific, Sacramento 95817
Menlo College, Atherton 94027
Mennonite Brethren Biblical Seminary, Fresno 93727
Mills College, Oakland 94613
MiraCosta College, Oceanside 92056
Modesto Junior College, Modesto 95350
Monterey Institute of International Studies, Monterey 93940
Monterey Peninsula College, Monterey 93940
Moorpark College, Moorpark 93021
Mount St. Mary's College, Los Angeles 90049
Mount San Antonio College, Walnut 91789
Mount San Jacinto College, San Jacinto 92583
Napa Valley College, Napa 94558
National Hispanic University, San Jose 95127
National University, La Jolla 92037
Northrop-Rice Aviation Institute of Technology, Inglewood 90301
Northwestern Polytechnic University, Fremont 94539
Occidental College, Los Angeles 90041
Ohlone College, Fremont 94539
Orange Coast College, Costa Mesa 92628-5005
Otis College of Art and Design, Los Angeles 90045
Pacific Lutheran Theological Seminary, Berkeley 94708
Pacific Oaks College, Pasadena 91103
Pacific School of Religion, Berkeley 94709
Pacific States University, Los Angeles 90006
Pacific Union College, Angwin 94508

Palmer College of Chiropractic-West, San Jose 95134
Palomar College, San Marcos 92069
Patten University, Oakland 94601
Pepperdine University, Malibu 90263
Pepperdine University: School of Law, Malibu 90263
Pitzer College, Claremont 91711
Platt College: Newport Beach, Newport Beach 92660
Platt College: Ontario, Ontario 91764
Point Loma Nazarene University, San Diego 92106-2899
Pomona College, Claremont 91711
Queen of the Holy Rosary College, Fremont 94539
Reedley College, Reedley 93654
Riverside Community College, Riverside 92506
St. John's Seminary, Camarillo 93012
St. Mary's College of California, Moraga 94556
St. Patrick's Seminary, Menlo Park 94025
Samuel Merritt College, Oakland 94609
San Diego City College, San Diego 92101
San Diego Mesa College, San Diego 92111
San Diego State University, San Diego 92182-7455
San Francisco State University, San Francisco 94132
San Francisco Theological Seminary, San Anselmo 94960
San Joaquin Delta College, Stockton 95207
San Jose Christian College, San Jose 95108
San Jose State University, San Jose 95192-0001
Santa Barbara Business College, Santa Barbara 93111
Santa Barbara Business College: Bakersfield, Bakersfield 93309
Santa Barbara Business College: Santa Maria, Santa Maria 93454
Santa Barbara City College, Santa Barbara 93109-2394
Santa Clara University, Santa Clara 95053-0258
Santa Clara University: School of Law, Santa Clara 95053
Santa Monica College, Santa Monica 90405
Santa Rosa Junior College, Santa Rosa 95401
Santiago Canyon College, Orange 92869
Scripps College, Claremont 91711-3948
Shasta College, Redding 96049-6006
Sierra College, Rocklin 95677
Silicon Valley College: Emeryville, Emeryville 94608
Simpson College, Redding 96003
Sonoma State University, Rohnert Park 94928
Southern California College of Optometry, Fullerton 92631
Southern California Institute of Architecture, Los Angeles 90013
Southwestern College, Chula Vista 91910
Southwestern University School of Law, Los Angeles 90005
Stanford University, Stanford 94305
Stanford University: School of Law, Stanford 94305
Stanford University: School of Medicine, Stanford 94304
Starr King School for the Ministry, Berkeley 94709
Taft College, Taft 93268
Talbot School of Theology of Biola University, La Mirada 90639
Thomas Aquinas College, Santa Paula 93060
Thomas Jefferson School of Law, San Diego 92110
Travel University International, San Diego 92123
University of California Berkeley: School of Law, Berkeley 94720
University of California Berkeley: School of Optometry, Berkeley 94720
University of California Davis: School of Law, Davis 95616
University of California Davis: School of Medicine, Davis 95616
University of California Davis: School of Veterinary Medicine, Davis 95616
University of California Hastings College of the Law, San Francisco 94102
University of California Irvine: College of Medicine, Irvine 92697
University of California Los Angeles: School of Dentistry, Los Angeles 90095
University of California Los Angeles: School of Law, Los Angeles 90095
University of California Los Angeles: School of Medicine, Los Angeles 90095
University of California San Diego: School of Medicine, La Jolla 92093
University of California San Francisco: School of Dentistry, San Francisco 94143
University of California San Francisco: School of Medicine, San Francisco 94143
University of California San Francisco: School of Pharmacy, San Francisco 94143
University of California: Berkeley, Berkeley 94720
University of California: Davis, Davis 95616
University of California: Irvine, Irvine 92697

University of California: Los Angeles, Los Angeles 90095
University of California: Riverside, Riverside 92521
University of California: San Diego, La Jolla 92093
University of California: Santa Barbara, Santa Barbara 93106-3500
University of California: Santa Cruz, Santa Cruz 95064
University of La Verne, La Verne 91750
University of La Verne College of Law at San Fernando Valley, Woodland Hills 91367
University of La Verne: School of Law, La Verne 91750
University of Redlands, Redlands 92373-0999
University of San Diego, San Diego 92110
University of San Diego: School of Law, San Diego 92110
University of San Francisco, San Francisco 94117
University of San Francisco: School of Law, San Francisco 94117
University of Southern California, Los Angeles 90089
University of Southern California: Law School, Los Angeles 90089
University of Southern California: School of Dentistry, Los Angeles 90089
University of Southern California: School of Medicine, Los Angeles 90033
University of Southern California: School of Pharmacy, Los Angeles 90033
University of West Los Angeles, Inglewood 90301
University of West Los Angeles: School of Law, Inglewood 90301
University of the Pacific, Stockton 95211
University of the Pacific: School of Dentistry, San Francisco 94115
University of the Pacific: School of Pharmacy, Stockton 95211
Vanguard University of Southern California, Costa Mesa 92626-9601
Ventura College, Ventura 93003
Victor Valley College, Victorville 92392-5849
Vista Community College, Berkeley 94704
West Valley College, Saratoga 95070-5698
Western State University College of Law, Fullerton 92831
Western University of Health Sciences, Pomona 91766
Westminster Theological Seminary in California, Escondido 92027
Westwood College of Technology, Anaheim 92801
Westwood College of Technology: Inland Empire, Upland 91786
Westwood College of Technology: Los Angeles, Los Angeles 90010
Whittier College, Whittier 90608
Whittier Law School, Los Angeles 90020
Woodbury University, Burbank 91510
Yuba Community College District, Marysville 95901

Colorado
Arapahoe Community College, Littleton 80160
Art Institute of Colorado, Denver 80203
Bel-Rea Institute of Animal Technology, Denver 80231
Blair Junior College, Colorado Springs 80915
Colorado Christian University, Lakewood 80226
Colorado College, Colorado Springs 80903
Colorado Mountain College: Alpine Campus, Glenwood Springs 80487
Colorado Mountain College: Spring Valley Campus, Glenwood Springs 81601
Colorado Mountain College: Timberline Campus, Leadville 80461
Colorado School of Mines, Golden 80401
Colorado State University, Fort Collins 80523
Colorado State University: College of Veterinary Medicine and Biomedical Sciences, Fort Collins 80523
Colorado State University: Pueblo, Pueblo 81001
Colorado Technical University, Colorado Springs 80907
Community College of Aurora, Aurora 80011
DeVry University: Colorado Springs, Colorado Springs 80910
DeVry University: Denver, Denver 80224
Denver Conservative Baptist Seminary, Denver 80250
Fort Lewis College, Durango 81301
Front Range Community College, Westminster 80031
Heritage College, Denver 80212
ITT Technical Institute: Thornton, Thornton 80229
Iliff School of Theology, Denver 80210
IntelliTec College, Colorado Springs 80909
IntelliTec College, Grand Junction, Grand Junction 81506
Jones International University, Englewood 80112
Mesa State College, Grand Junction 81501
Metropolitan State College of Denver, Denver 80217-3662

Morgan Community College, Fort Morgan 80701
Naropa University, Boulder 80302
National American University: Denver, Denver 80222
National Technological University, Fort Collins 80526
Nazarene Bible College, Colorado Springs 80910
Otero Junior College, La Junta 81050
Parks College, Denver 80229
Platt College: Aurora, Aurora 80014
Red Rocks Community College, Lakewood 80228-1255
Regis University, Denver 80221
Remington College: Colorado Springs, Colorado Springs 80918
Rocky Mountain College of Art & Design, Denver 80224
Trinidad State Junior College, Trinidad 81082
United States Air Force Academy, USAF Academy 80840
University of Colorado Health Sciences Center, Denver 80262
University of Colorado Health Sciences Center: College of Pharmacy, Denver 80262
University of Colorado Health Sciences Center: School of Dentistry, Denver 80262
University of Colorado Health Sciences Center: School of Medicine, Denver 80262
University of Colorado at Boulder, Boulder 80309-0026
University of Colorado at Boulder: School of Law, Boulder 80309
University of Colorado at Colorado Springs, Colorado Springs 80933-7150
University of Colorado at Denver, Denver 80217
University of Denver, Denver 80208
University of Denver: College of Law, Denver 80220
University of Northern Colorado, Greeley 80639
Westwood College of Technology: South, Denver 80227
Yeshiva Toras Chaim Talmudical Seminary, Denver 80204

Connecticut
Albertus Magnus College, New Haven 06511-1189
Asnuntuck Community College, Enfield 06082
Beth Benjamin Academy of Connecticut, Stamford 06901
Briarwood College, Southington 06489
Capital Community College, Hartford 06103
Central Connecticut State University, New Britain 06050
Charter Oak State College, New Britain 06053-2142
Connecticut College, New London 06320
Eastern Connecticut State University, Willimantic 06226
Fairfield University, Fairfield 06824-5195
Gateway Community College, New Haven 06511-5970
Gibbs College, Norwalk 06857
Holy Apostles College and Seminary, Cromwell 06416
Holy Apostles College and Seminary, Cromwell 06416
Housatonic Community College, Bridgeport 06604
International College of Hospitality Management, Washington 06793
Manchester Community College, Manchester 06045-1046
Middlesex Community College, Middletown 06457
Mitchell College, New London 06320
Naugatuck Valley Community College, Waterbury 06708-3089
Northwestern Connecticut Community College, Winsted 06098
Norwalk Community College, Norwalk 06854-1655
Paier College of Art, Hamden 06514-3902
Quinebaug Valley Community College, Danielson 06239
Quinnipiac College: School of Law, Hamden 06518
Quinnipiac University, Hamden 06518
Sacred Heart University, Fairfield 06825
St. Joseph College, West Hartford 06117
Southern Connecticut State University, New Haven 06515
Teikyo Post University, Waterbury 06723-2540
Three Rivers Community College, Norwich 06360
Trinity College, Hartford 06106
Tunxis Community College, Farmington 06032
United States Coast Guard Academy, New London 06320
University of Bridgeport, Bridgeport 06601
University of Bridgeport College of Chiropractic, Bridgeport 06601
University of Connecticut, Storrs 06269-3088
University of Connecticut Health Center School of Medicine, Farmington 06032
University of Connecticut: School of Dentistry, Farmington 06030
University of Connecticut: School of Law, Hartford 06105

University of Connecticut: School of Pharmacy, Storrs 06269
University of Hartford, West Hartford 06117
University of New Haven, West Haven 06516
Wesleyan University, Middletown 06459
Western Connecticut State University, Danbury 06810
Yale Law School, New Haven 06520
Yale University, New Haven 06520
Yale University: Divinity School, New Haven 06511
Yale University: School of Medicine, New Haven 06510

Delaware
Delaware State University, Dover 19901
Delaware Technical and Community College: Owens Campus, Georgetown 19947
Delaware Technical and Community College: Stanton/Wilmington Campus, Newark 19713
Delaware Technical and Community College: Terry Campus, Dover 19901
Goldey-Beacom College, Wilmington 19808
University of Delaware, Newark 19716
Widener University School of Law, Wilmington 19803
Wilmington College, New Castle 19720

District of Columbia
American University, Washington 20016
American University: Washington College of Law, Washington 20016
Catholic University of America, Washington 20064
Catholic University of America: School of Law, Washington 20064
Catholic University of America: School of Theology, Washington 20064
Corcoran College of Art and Design, Washington 20006-4804
Dominican House of Studies, Washington 20017
Gallaudet University, Washington 20002
George Washington University, Washington 20052
George Washington University Law School, Washington 20052
George Washington University: School of Medicine and Health Sciences, Washington 20037
Georgetown University, Washington 20057
Georgetown University: Law Center, Washington 20001
Georgetown University: School of Medicine, Washington 20007
Howard University, Washington 20059
Howard University: College of Dentistry, Washington 20059
Howard University: Divinity School, Washington 20017
Howard University: School of Law, Washington 20008
Howard University: School of Medicine, Washington 20059
Howard University: School of Pharmacy, Washington 20059
Potomac College, Washington 20016
Strayer University, Washington 20005
Trinity College, Washington 20017
University of the District of Columbia, Washington 20008
University of the District of Columbia: School of Law, Washington 20008
Washington Theological Union, Washington 20012
Wesley Theological Seminary, Washington 20016

Florida
ATI Health Education Center, Miami 33169-5745
Art Institute of Fort Lauderdale, Ft. Lauderdale 33316
Baptist College of Florida, Graceville 32440
Barry University, Miami Shores 33161-6695
Barry University: School of Graduate Medical Sciences, Miami Shores 33161
Beacon College, Leesburg 34748
Bethune-Cookman College, Daytona Beach 32114
Broward Community College, Ft. Lauderdale 33301
Career Training Institute, Orlando 32804
Carlos Albizu University, Miami 33172
Chipola Junior College, Marianna 32446
Cooper Career Institute, West Palm Beach 33409
Daytona Beach Community College, Daytona Beach 32120
DeVry University: Miramar, Miramar 33027
DeVry University: Orlando, Orlando 32839
Eckerd College, St. Petersburg 33711
Edward Waters College, Jacksonville 32209
Embry Riddle Aeronautical University-Extended Campus, Daytona Beach 32114-3900
Embry-Riddle Aeronautical University, Daytona Beach 32114-3900
Everglades College, Fort Lauderdale 33309
Flagler College, St. Augustine 32085-1027

Florida Agricultural and Mechanical University, Tallahassee 32307

Florida Agricultural and Mechanical University: School of Pharmacy, Tallahassee 32307

Florida Atlantic University, Boca Raton 33431

Florida Christian College, Kissimmee 34744-4402

Florida Coastal School of Law, Jacksonville 32216

Florida College, Temple Terrace 33617

Florida Gulf Coast University, Ft. Myers 33965-6565

Florida Hospital College of Health Sciences, Orlando 32803

Florida Institute of Technology, Melbourne 32901-6975

Florida International University, Miami 33199

Florida Keys Community College, Key West 33040

Florida Metropolitan University: Melbourne Campus, Melbourne 32935

Florida Metropolitan University: Orlando College North, Orlando 32810

Florida Metropolitan University: Orlando College South, Orlando 32809

Florida Metropolitan University: Tampa College, Tampa 33614

Florida Metropolitan University: Tampa College Lakeland, Lakeland 33801-1919

Florida National College, Hialeah 33012

Florida Southern College, Lakeland 33801-5698

Florida State University, Tallahassee 32306-2400

Florida State University: School of Law, Tallahassee 32306

Florida Technical College, Orlando 32807

Florida Technical College: Auburndale, Auburndale 33823

Florida Technical College: Deland, Deland 32720

Florida Technical College: Jacksonville, Jacksonville 32211

Full Sail Real World Education, Winter Park 32792-7429

Gulf Coast Community College, Panama City 32401

Herzing College: Orlando, Winter Park 32792-5509

Hillsborough Community College, Tampa 33631-3127

Hobe Sound Bible College, Hobe Sound 33475

ITT Technical Institute: Ft. Lauderdale, Ft. Lauderdale 33328

ITT Technical Institute: Jacksonville, Jacksonville 32244

ITT Technical Institute: Maitland, Maitland 32751

ITT Technical Institute: Miami, Miami 33126

ITT Technical Institute: Tampa, Tampa 33634

Indian River Community College, Fort Pierce 34981-5596

Institute of Career Education, West Palm Beach 33407

International Academy of Design and Technology, Tampa 33634

International College, Naples 34119

Jacksonville University, Jacksonville 32211

Jones College, Jacksonville 32211

Lake City Community College, Lake City 32025-8703

Lake-Sumter Community College, Leesburg 34788-8751

Manatee Community College, Bradenton 34206

Miami-Dade Community College, Miami 33132

New College of Florida, Sarasota 34243-2197

New England Institute of Technology, West Palm Beach 33407

Northwood University: Florida Campus, West Palm Beach 33409

Nova Southeastern University, Fort Lauderdale 33314

Nova Southeastern University Health Professions Division: College of Optometry, Fort Lauderdale 33328

Nova Southeastern University Health Professions Division: College of Osteopathic Medicine, Fort Lauderdale 33314

Nova Southeastern University of the Health Sciences: College of Pharmacy, Fort Lauderdale 33314

Nova Southeastern University: Shepard Broad Law Center, Fort Lauderdale 33314

Okaloosa-Walton Community College, Niceville 32578

Palm Beach Atlantic University, West Palm Beach 33416-4708

Palm Beach Community College, Lake Worth 33461

Pasco-Hernando Community College, New Port Richey 34654-5199

Pensacola Junior College, Pensacola 32504-8998

Polk Community College, Winter Haven 33881

Ringling School of Art and Design, Sarasota 34234

Rollins College, Winter Park 32789-4499

St. John Vianney College Seminary, Miami 33165

St. Leo University, St. Leo 33574-6665

St. Petersburg College, St. Petersburg 33733

St. Thomas University, Miami 33054

St. Thomas University: School of Law, Miami 33054

St. Vincent De Paul Regional Seminary, Boynton Beach 33436

Santa Fe Community College, Gainesville 32606

Schiller International University, Dunedin 34698-7532

Seminole Community College, Sanford 32773

South Florida Community College, Avon Park 33825

Southeastern College of the Assemblies of God, Lakeland 33801

Southwest Florida College, Ft. Myers 33907-1108

Stetson University, DeLand 32723

Stetson University: College of Law, St. Petersburg 33707

Tallahassee Community College, Tallahassee 32304-2895

Talmudic College of Florida, Miami Beach 33139

Tampa Technical Institute, Tampa 33612

University of Central Florida, Orlando 32816

University of Florida, Gainesville 32611

University of Florida: College of Dentistry, Gainesville 32610

University of Florida: College of Law, Gainesville 32611

University of Florida: College of Pharmacy, Gainesville 32610

University of Florida: College of Veterinary Medicine, Gainesville 32610

University of Florida: School of Medicine, Gainesville 32610

University of Miami, Coral Gables 33124-4616

University of Miami: School of Law, Coral Gables 33124

University of Miami: School of Medicine, Miami 33101

University of North Florida, Jacksonville 32224-2645

University of South Florida, Tampa 33620-9951

University of South Florida: College of Medicine, Tampa 33612

University of Tampa, Tampa 33606-1490

University of West Florida, Pensacola 32514

Valencia Community College, Orlando 32802-3028

Warner Southern College, Lake Wales 33859

Webber International University, Babson Park 33827-0096

Webster College, Ocala 34474

Webster College: Holiday, Holiday 34691

Georgia

Abraham Baldwin Agricultural College, Tifton 31794

Agnes Scott College, Atlanta/Decatur 30030

Albany State University, Albany 31705

Albany Technical College, Albany 31701

Andrew College, Cuthbert 39840-1395

Armstrong Atlantic State University, Savannah 31419

Art Institute of Atlanta, Atlanta 30328

Athens Technical College, Athens 30601-1500

Atlanta College of Art, Atlanta 30309

Atlanta Metropolitan College, Atlanta 30310

Augusta State University, Augusta 30904-2200

Bainbridge College, Bainbridge 39819-0990

Bauder College, Atlanta 30326

Berry College, Mount Berry 30149

Beulah Heights Bible College, Atlanta 30316

Brenau University, Gainesville 30501

Brewton-Parker College, Mount Vernon 30445

Candler School of Theology, Atlanta 30322

Central Georgia Technical College, Macon 31206

Chattahoochee Technical College, Marietta 30060

Clark Atlanta University, Atlanta 30314

Clayton College and State University, Morrow 30260-0285

Coastal Georgia Community College, Brunswick 31520

Columbia Theological Seminary, Decatur 30031

Columbus State University, Columbus 31907

Columbus Technical College, Columbus 31904

Covenant College, Lookout Mountain 30750

Dalton State College, Dalton 30720

Darton College, Albany 31707-3098

DeKalb Technical College, Clarkston 30021

DeVry University: Alpharetta, Alpharetta 30004

DeVry University: Atlanta, Decatur 30030

East Georgia College, Swainsboro 30401-2699

Emmanuel College, Franklin Springs 30639

Emory University, Atlanta 30322

Emory University: School of Law, Atlanta 30322

Emory University: School of Medicine, Atlanta 30322

Floyd College, Rome 30162-1864

Fort Valley State University, Fort Valley 31030-4313

Gainesville College, Gainesville 30503

Georgia College and State University, Milledgeville 31061

Georgia Institute of Technology, Atlanta 30332-0001

Georgia Military College, Milledgeville 31061

Georgia Perimeter College, Clarkston 30021

Georgia Southern University, Statesboro 30460

Georgia Southwestern State University, Americus 31709-4693

Georgia State University, Atlanta 30303

Georgia State University: College of Law, Atlanta 30303

Gordon College, Barnesville 30204

Griffin Technical College, Griffin 30223

Gupton Jones College of Funeral Service, Decatur 30035

Herzing College, Atlanta 30326

High-Tech Institute: Atlanta, Marietta 30067

Interdenominational Theological Center, Atlanta 30314

Kennesaw State University, Kennesaw 30144-5591

LaGrange College, LaGrange 30240

Life College, Marietta 30060

Life University, Marietta 30060

Macon State College, Macon 31206-5144

Medical College of Georgia, Augusta 30912

Medical College of Georgia: School of Dentistry, Augusta 30912

Medical College of Georgia: School of Medicine, Augusta 30912

Mercer University, Macon 31207

Mercer University Southern School of Pharmacy, Atlanta 30341

Mercer University: School of Medicine, Macon 31207

Mercer University: Walter F. George School of Law, Macon 31207

Middle Georgia College, Cochran 31014

Morehouse College, Atlanta 30314

Morehouse School of Medicine, Atlanta 30310

Morris Brown College, Atlanta 30314

North Georgia College & State University, Dahlonega 30597

Northwestern Technical College, Rock Spring 30739

Oglethorpe University, Atlanta 30319

Oxford College of Emory University, Oxford 30054-1418

Paine College, Augusta 30901-3182

Piedmont College, Demorest 30535

Reinhardt College, Waleska 30183

Savannah College of Art and Design, Savannah 31402

Savannah State University, Savannah 31404

Savannah Technical College, Savannah 31405

Shorter College, Rome 30165

South Georgia College, Douglas 31533

South University, Savannah 31406

Southern Polytechnic State University, Marietta 30060-2896

Southwest Georgia Technical College, Thomasville 31729

Spelman College, Atlanta 30314

State University of West Georgia, Carrollton 30118-0001

Thomas University, Thomasville 31792-7499

Toccoa Falls College, Toccoa Falls 30598

Truett-McConnell College, Cleveland 30528

University of Georgia, Athens 30602

University of Georgia: College of Pharmacy, Athens 30602

University of Georgia: College of Veterinary Medicine, Athens 30602

University of Georgia: School of Law, Athens 30602

Valdosta State University, Valdosta 31698

Waycross College, Waycross 31503

Wesleyan College, Macon 31210

West Georgia Technical College, LaGrange 30240

Young Harris College, Young Harris 30582

Hawaii

Brigham Young University-Hawaii, Laie 96762-1294

Chaminade University of Honolulu, Honolulu 96816-1578

Hawaii Business College, Honolulu 96817

Hawaii Pacific University, Honolulu 96813

Hawaii Tokai International College, Honolulu 96826

Heald College: Honolulu, Honolulu 96814

Remington College: Honolulu, Honolulu 96813

University of Hawaii William S. Richardson: School of Law, Honolulu 96822

University of Hawaii at Hilo, Hilo 96720

University of Hawaii at Manoa, Honolulu 96822

University of Hawaii at Manoa: John A. Burns School of Medicine, Honolulu 96822

University of Hawaii: Hawaii Community College, Hilo 96720

University of Hawaii: Honolulu Community College, Honolulu 96817

University of Hawaii: Kauai Community College, Lihue 96766

University of Hawaii: Leeward Community College, Pearl City 96782

University of Hawaii: Maui Community College, Kahului 96732

University of Hawaii: West Oahu, Pearl City 96782

Idaho

Albertson College of Idaho, Caldwell 83605
Boise Bible College, Boise 83714
Boise State University, Boise 83725
Brigham Young University - Idaho, Rexburg 83460
College of Southern Idaho, Twin Falls 83303
Eastern Idaho Technical College, Idaho Falls 83404
ITT Technical Institute: Boise, Boise 83713
Idaho State University, Pocatello 83209
Idaho State University: College of Pharmacy, Pocatello 83209
Lewis-Clark State College, Lewiston 83501
North Idaho College, Coeur d'Alene 83814
Northwest Nazarene University, Nampa 83686-5897
University of Idaho, Moscow 83844-2282
University of Idaho: College of Law, Moscow 83844

Illinois

Adler School of Professional Psychology, Chicago 60601
American Academy of Art, Chicago 60604
Augustana College, Rock Island 61201
Aurora University, Aurora 60506
Benedictine University, Lisle 60532
Bethany Theological Seminary, Richmond 47374
Black Hawk College, Moline 61265-5899
Black Hawk College: East Campus, Kewanee 61443-0630
Blackburn College, Carlinville 62626
Blessing-Reiman College of Nursing, Quincy 62305-7005
Bradley University, Peoria 61625
Brisk Rabbinical College, Chicago 60659
Carl Sandburg College, Galesburg 61401
Catholic Theological Union, Chicago 60615
Chicago State University, Chicago 60628
Chicago Theological Seminary, Chicago 60637
Chicago-Kent College of Law, Illinois Institute of Technology, Chicago 60661
City Colleges of Chicago: Harold Washington College, Chicago 60601
City Colleges of Chicago: Kennedy-King College, Chicago 60621
City Colleges of Chicago: Malcolm X College, Chicago 60612
City Colleges of Chicago: Olive-Harvey College, Chicago 60628
City Colleges of Chicago: Richard J. Daley College, Chicago 60652
City Colleges of Chicago: Wright College, Chicago 60634
College of DuPage, Glen Ellyn 60137-6599
College of Lake County, Grayslake 60030
College of Office Technology, Chicago 60622-3312
Columbia College Chicago, Chicago 60605-1996
Concordia University, River Forest 60305-1499
Cooking & Hospitality Institute of Chicago, Chicago 60610-3050
Danville Area Community College, Danville 61832
De Paul University, Chicago 60604-2287
De Paul University: College of Law, Chicago 60604
DeVry University: Addison, Addison 60101
DeVry University: Chicago, Chicago 60618
DeVry University: Tinley Park, Tinley Park 60477
Dominican University, River Forest 60305
Dr. William M. Scholl College of Podiatric Medicine, Chicago 60610
East-West University, Chicago 60605
Eastern Illinois University, Charleston 61920-3099
Elgin Community College, Elgin 60123-7193
Elmhurst College, Elmhurst 60126
Eureka College, Eureka 61530
Finch University of Health Sciences/The Chicago Medical School, North Chicago 60064
Finch University of Health Sciences/The Chicago Medical School, North Chicago 60064
Garrett-Evangelical Theological Seminary, Evanston 60201
Gem City College, Quincy 62306
Governors State University, University Park 60466
Greenville College, Greenville 62246-0159
Harrington Institute of Interior Design, Chicago 60606
Heartland Community College, Normal 61761
Hebrew Theological College, Skokie 60077
ITT Technical Institute: Burr Ridge, Burr Ridge 60521
ITT Technical Institute: Matteson, Matteson 60443
ITT Technical Institute: Mount Prospect, Mount Prospect 60056
Illinois Central College, East Peoria 61635-0001
Illinois College, Jacksonville 62650
Illinois College of Optometry, Chicago 60616
Illinois Eastern Community Colleges: Frontier Community College, Fairfield 62837

Illinois Eastern Community Colleges: Lincoln Trail College, Robinson 62454
Illinois Eastern Community Colleges: Olney Central College, Olney 62450
Illinois Eastern Community Colleges: Wabash Valley College, Mount Carmel 62863
Illinois Institute of Art, Chicago 60654
Illinois Institute of Art, Schaumburg 60173-4913
Illinois Institute of Technology, Chicago 60616
Illinois State University, Normal 61790-2200
Illinois Valley Community College, Oglesby 61348
Illinois Wesleyan University, Bloomington 61702
International Academy of Design and Technology, Chicago 60602
John A. Logan College, Carterville 62918
John Marshall Law School, Chicago 60604
John Marshall Law School, Chicago 60604
John Wood Community College, Quincy 62305-8736
Joliet Junior College, Joliet 60431
Judson College, Elgin 60123
Kankakee Community College, Kankakee 60901
Kaskaskia College, Centralia 62801
Kendall College, Evanston 60201-2899
Kishwaukee College, Malta 60150-9699
Knox College, Galesburg 61401
Lake Forest College, Lake Forest 60045
Lake Forest Graduate School of Management, Lake Forest 60045
Lake Land College, Mattoon 61938-9366
Lakeview College of Nursing, Danville 61832
Lewis University, Romeoville 60446-2200
Lewis and Clark Community College, Godfrey 62035
Lexington College, Chicago 60607-3534
Lincoln Christian College and Seminary, Lincoln 62656
Lincoln Christian Seminary, Lincoln 62656
Lincoln College, Lincoln 62656
Lincoln Land Community College, Springfield 62794-9256
Loyola University Chicago: School of Law, Chicago 60611
Loyola University Chicago: Stritch School of Medicine, Maywood 60153
Loyola University of Chicago, Chicago 60611
Lutheran School of Theology at Chicago, Chicago 60615
MacMurray College, Jacksonville 62650
McCormick Theological Seminary, Chicago 60637
McHenry County College, Crystal Lake 60012-2761
McKendree College, Lebanon 62254-1299
Meadville-Lombard Theological School, Chicago 60637
Midstate College, Peoria 61614
Midwestern University: Chicago College of Osteopathic Medicine, Downers Grove 60515
Midwestern University: Chicago College of Pharmacy, Downers Grove 60515
Millikin University, Decatur 62522-2084
Monmouth College, Monmouth 61462
Moody Bible Institute, Chicago 60610
Moraine Valley Community College, Palos Hills 60465-0937
Morrison Institute of Technology, Morrison 61270
NAES College, Chicago 60659
National University of Health Sciences, Lombard 60148
National University of Health Sciences, Lombard 60148
National-Louis University, Chicago 60603
North Central College, Naperville 60566
North Park Theological Seminary, Chicago 60625
North Park University, Chicago 60625-4895
Northeastern Illinois University, Chicago 60625
Northern Baptist Theological Seminary, Lombard 60148
Northern Illinois University, DeKalb 60115
Northern Illinois University: College of Law, DeKalb 60115
Northwestern Business College, Chicago 60630
Northwestern University, Evanston 60208
Northwestern University: Dental School, Chicago 60611
Northwestern University: School of Law, Chicago 60611
Northwestern University: School of Medicine, Chicago 60611
Oakton Community College, Des Plaines 60016
Olivet Nazarene University, Bourbonnais 60914
Parkland College, Champaign 61821-1899
Prairie State College, Chicago Heights 60411
Principia College, Elsah 62028-9799
Quincy University, Quincy 62301
Rend Lake College, Ina 62846
Richland Community College, Decatur 62521
Robert Morris College: Chicago, Chicago 60605
Rock Valley College, Rockford 61114-5699
Rockford Business College, Rockford 61103
Rockford College, Rockford 61108
Roosevelt University, Chicago 60605-1394

Rush University, Chicago 60612
Rush University: Rush Medical College, Chicago 60612
St. Augustine College, Chicago 60640
St. Francis Medical Center College of Nursing, Peoria 61603-3783
St. Xavier University, Chicago 60655
Sauk Valley Community College, Dixon 61021
School of the Art Institute of Chicago, Chicago 60603
Seabury-Western Theological Seminary, Evanston 60201
Shawnee Community College, Ullin 62992
Shimer College, Waukegan 60079
South Suburban College of Cook County, South Holland 60473
Southeastern Illinois College, Harrisburg 62946
Southern Illinois University Carbondale, Carbondale 62901
Southern Illinois University Edwardsville, Edwardsville 62026
Southern Illinois University at Carbondale: School of Law, Carbondale 62901
Southern Illinois University: School of Dentistry, Alton 62002
Southern Illinois University: School of Medicine, Springfield 62794
Southwestern Illinois College, Belleville 62221-5899
Spoon River College, Canton 61520
Springfield College in Illinois, Springfield 62702-2694
Telshe Yeshiva-Chicago, Chicago 60625
Trinity Christian College, Palos Heights 60463
Trinity Evangelical Divinity School, Deerfield 60015
Trinity International University, Deerfield 60015
Triton College, River Grove 60171
University of Chicago, Chicago 60637
University of Chicago: Divinity School, Chicago 60637
University of Chicago: Pritzker School of Medicine, Chicago 60637
University of Chicago: School of Law, Chicago 60637
University of Illinois at Chicago, Chicago 60607
University of Illinois at Chicago: College of Dentistry, Chicago 60612
University of Illinois at Chicago: College of Medicine, Chicago 60612
University of Illinois at Chicago: College of Pharmacy, Chicago 60612
University of Illinois at Urbana-Champaign, Urbana 61801
University of Illinois at Urbana-Champaign: College of Law, Champaign 61820
University of Illinois at Urbana-Champaign: College of Veterinary Medicine, Urbana 61801
University of Illinois: Springfield, Springfield 62794
University of St. Francis, Joliet 60435
University of St. Mary of the Lake--Mundelein Seminary, Mundelein 60060
VanderCook College of Music, Chicago 60616-3731
Waubonsee Community College, Sugar Grove 60554-9454
West Suburban College of Nursing, Oak Park 60302
Western Illinois University, Macomb 61455
Westwood College of Technology: O'Hare, Schiller Park 60176
Wheaton College, Wheaton 60187
William Rainey Harper College, Palatine 60067

Indiana

American Conservatory of Music, Hammond 46324
American Trans Air Aviation Training Academy, Indianapolis 46241
Ancilla College, Donaldson 46513
Anderson University, Anderson 46012
Anderson University: School of Theology, Anderson 46012
Associated Mennonite Biblical Seminary, Elkhart 46517
Ball State University, Muncie 47306
Bethel College, Mishawaka 46545
Bethel College, Mishawaka 46545
Butler University, Indianapolis 46208
Butler University: College of Pharmacy, Indianapolis 46208
Calumet College of St. Joseph, Whiting 46394-2195
Christian Theological Seminary, Indianapolis 46208
College of Court Reporting, Hobart 46342
Commonwealth Business College: Michigan City, Michigan City 46360-7362
Concordia Theological Seminary, Fort Wayne 46825
DePauw University, Greencastle 46135
Earlham College, Richmond 47374-4095
Earlham School of Religion, Richmond 47374
Franklin College, Franklin 46131
Goshen College, Goshen 46526
Grace College, Winona Lake 46590
Hanover College, Hanover 47243-0108
Holy Cross College, Notre Dame 46556-0308

Huntington College, Huntington 46750
ITT Technical Institute: Fort Wayne, Fort Wayne 46825
ITT Technical Institute: Indianapolis, Indianapolis 46268
Indiana Business College, Indianapolis 46204
Indiana Business College: Anderson, Anderson 46013
Indiana Business College: Columbus, Columbus 47203-9988
Indiana Business College: Evansville, Evansville 47715
Indiana Business College: Fort Wayne, Fort Wayne 46825
Indiana Business College: Lafayette, Lafayette 47905-4859
Indiana Business College: Marion, Marion 46952
Indiana Business College: Medical, Indianapolis 46239
Indiana Business College: Muncie, Muncie 47303
Indiana Business College: Terre Haute, Terre Haute 47802
Indiana Institute of Technology, Fort Wayne 46803-1297
Indiana State University, Terre Haute 47809
Indiana University Bloomington, Bloomington 47405
Indiana University Bloomington: School of Law, Bloomington 47405
Indiana University Bloomington: School of Optometry, Bloomington 47405
Indiana University East, Richmond 47374-1289
Indiana University Indianapolis: School of Law, Indianapolis 46202
Indiana University Kokomo, Kokomo 46904-9003
Indiana University Northwest, Gary 46408-1197
Indiana University School of Dentistry, Indianapolis 46202
Indiana University South Bend, South Bend 46634-7111
Indiana University Southeast, New Albany 47150-6405
Indiana University-Purdue University Fort Wayne, Fort Wayne 46805-1499
Indiana University-Purdue University Indianapolis, Indianapolis 46202
Indiana University: School of Medicine, Indianapolis 46202
Indiana Wesleyan University, Marion 46953-4999
International Business College, Fort Wayne 46804
International Business College: Indianapolis, Indianapolis 46256
Ivy Tech State College - Bloomington, Bloomington 47404-1511
Ivy Tech State College: Central Indiana, Indianapolis 46206-1763
Ivy Tech State College: Columbus, Columbus 47203-1868
Ivy Tech State College: Eastcentral, Muncie 47302-9448
Ivy Tech State College: Kokomo, Kokomo 46903-1373
Ivy Tech State College: Lafayette, Lafayette 47905-5266
Ivy Tech State College: Northcentral, South Bend 46601-3415
Ivy Tech State College: Northeast, Fort Wayne 46805-1489
Ivy Tech State College: Northwest, Gary 46409-1499
Ivy Tech State College: Southcentral, Sellersburg 47172-1897
Ivy Tech State College: Southeast, Madison 47250-1881
Ivy Tech State College: Southwest, Evansville 47710-3398
Ivy Tech State College: Wabash Valley, Terre Haute 47802-4898
Ivy Tech State College: Whitewater, Richmond 47374-1298
Lincoln Technical Institute, Indianapolis 46202
Manchester College, North Manchester 46962
Marian College, Indianapolis 46222
Martin University, Indianapolis 46218
Michiana College, South Bend 46617
Michiana College: Fort Wayne, Fort Wayne 46815
Mid-America College of Funeral Service, Jeffersonville 47130
Oakland City University, Oakland City 47660
Professional Careers Institute, Indianapolis 46278-1736
Purdue University, West Lafayette 47907-1080
Purdue University: Calumet, Hammond 46323
Purdue University: North Central Campus, Westville 46391
Purdue University: School of Pharmacy, West Lafayette 47907
Purdue University: School of Veterinary Medicine, West Lafayette 47907
Rose-Hulman Institute of Technology, Terre Haute 47803-3999
St. Joseph's College, Rensselaer 47978
Saint Mary's College, Notre Dame 46556

St. Mary-of-the-Woods College, St. Mary-of-the-Woods 47876
St. Meinrad School of Theology, St. Meinrad 47577
Sawyer College, Hammond 46320
Sawyer College: Merrillville, Merrillville 46410
Taylor University, Upland 46989-1001
Taylor University: Fort Wayne, Fort Wayne 46807
Tri-State University, Angola 46703
University of Evansville, Evansville 47722
University of Indianapolis, Indianapolis 46227-3697
University of Notre Dame, Notre Dame 46556
University of Notre Dame: School of Law, Notre Dame 46556
University of Notre Dame: School of Theology, Notre Dame 46556
University of St. Francis, Fort Wayne 46808
University of Southern Indiana, Evansville 47712
Valparaiso University, Valparaiso 46383-6493
Valparaiso University: School of Law, Valparaiso 46383
Vincennes University, Vincennes 47591
Wabash College, Crawfordsville 47933

Iowa

Allen College, Waterloo 50703
American Institute of Business, Des Moines 50321
Briar Cliff University, Sioux City 51104
Buena Vista University, Storm Lake 50588
Central College, Pella 50219
Clarke College, Dubuque 52001
Clinton Community College, Clinton 52732
Coe College, Cedar Rapids 52402
Cornell College, Mount Vernon 52314
Des Moines Area Community College, Ankeny 50021
Des Moines University - Osteopathic Medical Center, Des Moines 50312
Des Moines University - Osteopathic Medical Center, Des Moines 50312
Divine Word College, Epworth 52045
Dordt College, Sioux Center 51250
Drake University, Des Moines 50311
Drake University Law School, Des Moines 50311
Drake University: College of Pharmacy, Des Moines 50311
Ellsworth Community College, Iowa Falls 50126
Emmaus Bible College, Dubuque 52001
Faith Baptist Bible College and Theological Seminary, Ankeny 50021
Faith Baptist Theological Seminary, Ankeny 50021
Franciscan University, Clinton 52733-2967
Graceland University, Lamoni 50140
Grand View College, Des Moines 50316
Grinnell College, Grinnell 50112-1690
Hamilton College, Urbandale 50323
Hamilton College: Cedar Falls, Cedar Falls 50613
Hamilton College: Cedar Rapids, Cedar Rapids 52404
Hamilton College: Mason City, Mason City 50401
Hamilton Technical College, Davenport 52807
Hawkeye Community College, Waterloo 50704-8015
Indian Hills Community College, Ottumwa 52501
Iowa Central Community College, Fort Dodge 50501
Iowa Lakes Community College, Estherville 51334-2725
Iowa State University, Ames 50011
Iowa State University: College of Veterinary Medicine, Ames 50011
Iowa Wesleyan College, Mt. Pleasant 52641-1398
Iowa Western Community College, Council Bluffs 51502-3004
Kaplan College, Davenport 52807
Kirkwood Community College, Cedar Rapids 52404
Loras College, Dubuque 52004-0178
Luther College, Decorah 52101
Maharishi University of Management, Fairfield 52557
Marshalltown Community College, Marshalltown 50158
Mercy College of Health Sciences, Des Moines 50309
Morningside College, Sioux City 51106
Mount Mercy College, Cedar Rapids 52402
Muscatine Community College, Muscatine 52761
North Iowa Area Community College, Mason City 50401
Northeast Iowa Community College, Calmar 52132
Northwest Iowa Community College, Sheldon 51201
Northwestern College, Orange City 51041
Palmer College of Chiropractic, Davenport 52803
St. Ambrose University, Davenport 52803-2898
St. Luke's College, Sioux City 51104
Scott Community College, Bettendorf 52722
Simpson College, Indianola 50125
Southeastern Community College: North Campus, West Burlington 52655
Southeastern Community College: South Campus, Keokuk 52632
Southwestern Community College, Creston 50801
University of Dubuque, Dubuque 52001

University of Dubuque: School of Theology, Dubuque 52001
University of Iowa, Iowa City 52242
University of Iowa College of Dentistry, Iowa City 52242
University of Iowa: College of Law, Iowa City 52242
University of Iowa: College of Medicine, Iowa City 52242
University of Iowa: College of Pharmacy, Iowa City 52242
University of Northern Iowa, Cedar Falls 50614
University of Osteopathic Medicine and Health Sciences: College of Podiatric Medicine and Surgery, Des Moines 50312
Upper Iowa University, Fayette 52142
Vatterott College, Des Moines 50321
Vennard College, University Park 52595
Waldorf College, Forest City 50436
Wartburg College, Waverly 50677-0903
Wartburg Theological Seminary, Dubuque 52003
Western Iowa Tech Community College, Sioux City 51102
William Penn University, Oskaloosa 52577

Kansas

Allen County Community College, Iola 66749
Baker University, Baldwin City 66006
Barclay College, Haviland 67059
Barton County Community College, Great Bend 67530
Benedictine College, Atchison 66002-1499
Bethany College, Lindsborg 67456-1897
Bethel College, North Newton 67117-0531
Butler County Community College, Eldorado 67042
Central Baptist Theological Seminary, Kansas City 66102
Central Christian College, McPherson 67460
Cloud County Community College, Concordia 66901-1002
Dodge City Community College, Dodge City 67801-2399
Donnelly College, Kansas City 66102
Emporia State University, Emporia 66801-5087
Fort Hays State University, Hays 67601
Fort Scott Community College, Fort Scott 66701
Friends University, Wichita 67213
Garden City Community College, Garden City 67846
Haskell Indian Nations University, Lawrence 66046-4800
Hesston College, Hesston 67062
Highland Community College, Highland 66035
Hutchinson Community College, Hutchinson 67501
Independence Community College, Independence 67301
Johnson County Community College, Overland Park 66210
Kansas City Kansas Community College, Kansas City 66112
Kansas State University, Manhattan 66506
Kansas State University: College of Veterinary Medicine, Manhattan 66506
Kansas Wesleyan University, Salina 67401
Labette Community College, Parsons 67357
McPherson College, McPherson 67460-1402
MidAmerica Nazarene University, Olathe 66062
Newman University, Wichita 67213
North Central Kansas Technical College, Beloit 67420
Ottawa University, Ottawa 66067-3399
Pittsburg State University, Pittsburg 66762
Pratt Community College, Pratt 67124
St. Mary College, Leavenworth 66048
Seward County Community College, Liberal 67905
Southwestern College, Winfield 67156
Sterling College, Sterling 67579-0098
Tabor College, Hillsboro 67063
University of Kansas, Lawrence 66045-7576
University of Kansas Medical Center, Kansas City 66160-7116
University of Kansas Medical Center: School of Medicine, Kansas City 66160
University of Kansas: School of Law, Lawrence 66045
Washburn University School of Law, Topeka 66621
Washburn University of Topeka, Topeka 66621
Wichita State University, Wichita 67260

Kentucky

Alice Lloyd College, Pippa Passes 41844
Asbury College, Wilmore 40390
Asbury Theological Seminary, Wilmore 40390
Beckfield College, Florence 41022-0143
Bellarmine University, Louisville 40205
Berea College, Berea 40404
Brescia University, Owensboro 42301
Campbellsville University, Campbellsville 42718
Centre College, Danville 40422-1394

Clear Creek Baptist Bible College, Pineville
40977-9754
Cumberland College, Williamsburg 40769
Daymar College, Owensboro 42301
Daymar College: Louisville, Louisville 40218
Elizabethtown Community College, Elizabethtown
42701
Georgetown College, Georgetown 40324
Hazard Community College, Hazard 41701
Henderson Community College, Henderson 42420
Hopkinsville Community College, Hopkinsville
42241-2100
ITT Technical Institute: Louisville, Louisville 40223
Jefferson Community College, Louisville 40202
Kentucky Christian College, Grayson 41143
Kentucky Mountain Bible College, Vancleve 41385
Kentucky Wesleyan College, Owensboro 42301
Lexington Community College, Lexington 40506-0235
Lexington Theological Seminary, Lexington 40508
Lindsey Wilson College, Columbia 42728
Louisville Presbyterian Theological Seminary,
Louisville 40205
Louisville Technical Institute, Louisville 40218
Madisonville Community College, Madisonville 42431
Maysville Community College, Maysville 41056
Mid-Continent College, Mayfield 42066-0357
Morehead State University, Morehead 40351
Murray State University, Murray 42071
National College of Business & Technology: Danville,
Roanoke 24017
National College of Business & Technology: Florence,
Roanoke 24017
National College of Business & Technology: Lexington,
Roanoke 24017
National College of Business & Technology: Pikeville,
Roanoke 24017
National College of Business & Technology: Richmond,
Roanoke 24017
Northern Kentucky University: Salmon P. Chase School
of Law, Highland Heights 41099
Paducah Community College, Paducah 42002-7380
Paducah Technical College, Paducah 42001
Pikeville College, Pikeville 41501
Prestonsburg Community College, Prestonsburg 41653
RETS Institute of Technology, Louisville 40213-3206
St. Catharine College, St. Catharine 40061
Somerset Community College, Somerset 42501
Southeast Community College, Cumberland 40823
Southern Baptist Theological Seminary, Louisville
40280
Southern Ohio College: Fort Mitchell, Fort Mitchell
41017
Southwestern College of Business, Crestview Hills
41017
Spalding University, Louisville 40203-2188
Spencerian College, Louisville 40216
Spencerian College: Lexington, Lexington 40504
Sullivan University, Louisville 40205
Thomas More College, Crestview Hills 41017-3495
Transylvania University, Lexington 40508-1797
Union College, Barbourville 40906
University of Kentucky, Lexington 40506
University of Kentucky: College of Dentistry,
Lexington 40536
University of Kentucky: College of Law, Lexington
40506
University of Kentucky: College of Medicine,
Lexington 40536
University of Louisville, Louisville 40292
University of Louisville: School of Dentistry, Louisville
40292
University of Louisville: School of Law, Louisville
40292
University of Louisville: School of Medicine, Louisville
40202

Louisiana

American School of Business, Shreveport 71105
Centenary College of Louisiana, Shreveport 71134
Delgado Community College, New Orleans 70119
Dillard University, New Orleans 70122-3097
Dryades YMCA School of Commerce, New Orleans
70119
Grambling State University, Grambling 71245
Grantham University, Slidell 70460
Herzing College, Kenner 70062
ITI Technical College, Baton Rouge 70817
ITT Technical Institute: St. Rose, St. Rose 70087
Louisiana College, Pineville 71360
Louisiana State University Health Sciences Center:
School of Dentistry, New Orleans 70119
Louisiana State University Health Sciences Center:
School of Medicine, New Orleans 70112

Louisiana State University and Agricultural and
Mechanical College, Baton Rouge 70803
Louisiana State University and Agricultural and
Mechanical College: School of Law, Baton Rouge
70803
Louisiana State University and Agricultural and
Mechanical College: School of Veterinary Medicine,
Baton Rouge 70803
Louisiana State University at Alexandria, Alexandria
71302
Louisiana State University at Eunice, Eunice 70535
Louisiana State University in Shreveport, Shreveport
71115
Louisiana State University: School of Medicine,
Shreveport 71130
Louisiana Tech University, Ruston 71272
Loyola University New Orleans, New Orleans
70118-6195
Loyola University: School of Law, New Orleans 70118
McNeese State University, Lake Charles 70609
New Orleans Baptist Theological Seminary, New
Orleans 70126
New Orleans Baptist Theological Seminary: School of
Christian Education, New Orleans 70126
Nicholls State University, Thibodaux 70310
Northeast Louisiana University School of Pharmacy,
Monroe 71209
Northwestern State University, Natchitoches 71497
Notre Dame Seminary School of Theology, New
Orleans 70118
Nunez Community College, Chalmette 70043
Our Lady of Holy Cross College, New Orleans 70131
Remington College, Lafayette 70508
Remington College: Baton Rouge, Baton Rouge 70806
St. Joseph Seminary College, St. Benedict 70457
Southeastern Louisiana University, Hammond 70402
Southern University and Agricultural and Mechanical
College, Baton Rouge 70813
Southern University at New Orleans, New Orleans
70126
Southern University in Shreveport, Shreveport 71107
Southern University: Law Center, Baton Rouge 70813
Tulane University, New Orleans 70118
Tulane University: School of Law, New Orleans 70118
Tulane University: School of Medicine, New Orleans
70112
University of Louisiana at Lafayette, Lafayette 70504
University of Louisiana at Monroe, Monroe 71209
University of New Orleans, New Orleans 70148
Xavier University of Louisiana, New Orleans
70125-1098
Xavier University of Louisiana: College of Pharmacy,
New Orleans 70125

Maine

Andover College, Portland 04103
Bangor Theological Seminary, Bangor 04401
Bates College, Lewiston 04240
Beal College, Bangor 04401
Bowdoin College, Brunswick 04011-8441
Central Maine Medical Center School of Nursing,
Lewiston 04240
Central Maine Technical College, Auburn 04210
Colby College, Waterville 04901-8840
College of the Atlantic, Bar Harbor 04609
Husson College, Bangor 04401
Maine College of Art, Portland 04101
Maine Maritime Academy, Castine 04420
New England School of Communications, Bangor
04401
St. Joseph's College, Standish 04084-5263
Thomas College, Waterville 04901
University of Maine, Orono 04469
University of Maine at Augusta, Augusta 04330
University of Maine at Farmington, Farmington 04938
University of Maine at Machias, Machias 04654
University of Maine at Presque Isle, Presque Isle 04769
University of Maine: School of Law, Portland 04102
University of New England, Biddeford 04005
University of New England: School of Osteopathic
Medicine, Biddeford 04005
University of Southern Maine, Gorham 04038

Maryland

Allegany College, Cumberland 21502
Anne Arundel Community College, Arnold 21012
Baltimore Hebrew University, Baltimore 21215
Baltimore International College, Baltimore 21202-3230
Bowie State University, Bowie 20715
Capital Bible Seminary, Lanham 20706
Capitol College, Laurel 20708
Carroll Community College, Westminster 21157
Cecil Community College, North East 21901
Chesapeake College, Wye Mills 21679

College of Notre Dame of Maryland, Baltimore
21210-2476
College of Southern Maryland, La Plata 20646-0910
Columbia Union College, Takoma Park 20912
Community College of Baltimore County - Catonsville,
Baltimore 21228
Community College of Baltimore County - Dundalk,
Baltimore 21222
Community College of Baltimore County - Essex,
Baltimore 21237
Coppin State College, Baltimore 21216-3698
Frederick Community College, Frederick 21702
Frostburg State University, Frostburg 21532
Goucher College, Baltimore 21204
Hagerstown Community College, Hagerstown
21742-6590
Harford Community College, Bel Air 21015
Hood College, Frederick 21701-8575
Howard Community College, Columbia 21044
Johns Hopkins University, Baltimore 21218
Johns Hopkins University: Peabody Conservatory of
Music, Baltimore 21202
Johns Hopkins University: School of Medicine,
Baltimore 21205
Loyola College in Maryland, Baltimore 21210
Maryland College of Art and Design, Silver Spring
20902-4111
Maryland Institute College of Art, Baltimore 21217
McDaniel College, Westminster 21157-4390
Montgomery College: Rockville Campus, Rockville
20850
Morgan State University, Baltimore 21251
Mount St. Mary's College, Emmitsburg 21727
Mount St. Mary's College: Seminary, Emmitsburg
21727
Ner Israel Rabbinical College, Baltimore 21208
St. John's College, Annapolis 21404
St. Mary's College of Maryland, St. Mary's City
20686-3001
St. Mary's Seminary and University, Baltimore 21210
Salisbury University, Salisbury 21801
Sojourner-Douglass College, Baltimore 21205
TESST College of Technology, Towson 21286
TESST College of Technology: Baltimore, Baltimore
21227-1063
Towson University, Towson 21252-0001
Uniformed Services University of the Health Sciences:
School of Medicine, Bethesda 20814
United States Naval Academy, Annapolis 21402
University of Baltimore, Baltimore 21201
University of Baltimore: School of Law, Baltimore
21201
University of Maryland at Baltimore: School of
Dentistry, Baltimore 21201
University of Maryland at Baltimore: School of Law,
Baltimore 21201
University of Maryland at Baltimore: School of
Medicine, Baltimore City 21201
University of Maryland at Baltimore: School of
Pharmacy, Baltimore 21201
University of Maryland: Baltimore, Baltimore 21201
University of Maryland: Baltimore County, Baltimore
21250
University of Maryland: College Park, College Park
20742-5235
University of Maryland: University College, Adelphi
20783
Villa Julie College, Stevenson 21153
Washington Bible College, Lanham 20706
Washington College, Chestertown 21620
Wor-Wic Community College, Salisbury 21804

Massachusetts

Ai The New England Institute of Art and Design,
Brookline 02445-7295
American International College, Springfield 01109
Amherst College, Amherst 01002
Andover Newton Theological School, Newton Centre
02159
Anna Maria College, Paxton 01612
Art Institute of Boston at Lesley University, Boston
02215-2598
Assumption College, Worcester 01609-1296
Atlantic Union College, South Lancaster 01561
Babson College, Babson Park 02457-0310
Bay Path College, Longmeadow 01106
Bay State College, Boston 02116
Becker College, Worcester 01609
Benjamin Franklin Institute of Technology, Boston
02116
Bentley College, Waltham 02452-4705
Berklee College of Music, Boston 02215
Berkshire Community College, Pittsfield 02101

Boston Architectural Center, Boston 02115
Boston College, Chestnut Hill 02467
Boston College: Law School, Newton 02159
Boston Conservatory, Boston 02215
Boston University, Boston 02215
Boston University Goldman School of Dental Medicine,
  Boston 02118
Boston University: School of Law, Boston 02215
Boston University: School of Medicine, Boston 02118
Boston University: School of Theology, Boston 02215
Brandeis University, Waltham 02454-9110
Bridgewater State College, Bridgewater 02325
Bunker Hill Community College, Boston 02129-2925
Cape Cod Community College, West Barnstable 02668
Clark University, Worcester 01610-1477
College of the Holy Cross, Worcester 01610-2395
Dean College, Franklin 02038
Elms College, Chicopee 01013
Emerson College, Boston 02116-4624
Emmanuel College, Boston 02115
Endicott College, Beverly 01915
Episcopal Divinity School, Cambridge 02138
Fisher College, Boston 02116
Fitchburg State College, Fitchburg 01420-2697
Framingham State College, Framingham 01701-9101
Franklin W. Olin College of Engineering, Needham
  02492
Gordon College, Wenham 01984
Gordon-Conwell Theological Seminary, South
  Hamilton 01982
Greenfield Community College, Greenfield 01301
Hampshire College, Amherst 01002
Harvard College, Cambridge 02138
Harvard School of Dental Medicine, Boston 02115
Harvard University Law School, Cambridge 02138
Harvard University: Divinity School, Cambridge 02138
Harvard University: Harvard Medical School, Boston
  02115
Hebrew College, Newton Centre 02459
Hellenic College/Holy Cross, Brookline 02445
Holy Cross Greek Orthodox School of Theology,
  Brookline 02146
ITT Technical Institute: Norwood, Norwood 02062
ITT Technical Institute: Woburn, Woburn 01801
Katharine Gibbs School, Boston 02116
Laboure College, Boston 02124-5698
Lasell College, Newton 02466
Lesley University, Cambridge 02138
Marian Court College, Swampscott 01907
Massachusetts Bay Community College, Wellesley Hills
  02481
Massachusetts College of Art, Boston 02115
Massachusetts College of Liberal Arts, North Adams
  01247
Massachusetts College of Pharmacy and Allied Health
  Sciences: School of Pharmacy, Boston 02115
Massachusetts College of Pharmacy and Health
  Sciences, Boston 02115
Massachusetts Institute of Technology, Cambridge
  02139
Massachusetts Maritime Academy, Buzzards Bay 02532
Massasoit Community College, Brockton 02302
Merrimack College, North Andover 01845
Montserrat College of Art, Beverly 01915
Mount Holyoke College, South Hadley 01075
Mount Ida College, Newton Centre 02459
Mount Wachusett Community College, Gardner
  01440-1000
New England College of Optometry, Boston 02115
New England Conservatory of Music, Boston 02115
New England School of Law, Boston 02116
Newbury College, Brookline 02445
Nichols College, Dudley 01571-5000
Northeastern University, Boston 02115
Northeastern University: Bouve College of Pharmacy
  and Health Sciences, Boston 02115
Northeastern University: School of Law, Boston 02115
Pine Manor College, Chestnut Hill 02467
Pope John XXIII National Seminary, Weston 02193
Quinsigamond Community College, Worcester 01606
Regis College, Weston 02493-1571
Roxbury Community College, Roxbury Crossing
  02120-3400
St. John's Seminary, Brighton 02135
St. John's Seminary College, Brighton 02135
Salem State College, Salem 01970
School of the Museum of Fine Arts, Boston 02115
Simmons College, Boston 02115-5898
Simon's Rock College of Bard, Great Barrington 01230
Smith College, Northampton 01063
Springfield College, Springfield 01109
Springfield Technical Community College, Springfield
  01105
Stonehill College, Easton 02357
Suffolk University, Boston 02108

Suffolk University: Law School, Boston 02114
Tufts University, Medford 02155
Tufts University: School of Dental Medicine, Boston
  02111
Tufts University: School of Medicine, Boston 02111
Tufts University: School of Veterinary Medicine, North
  Grafton 01536
University of Massachusetts Amherst, Amherst
  01003-9291
University of Massachusetts Boston, Boston
  02125-3393
University of Massachusetts Dartmouth, North
  Dartmouth 02747
University of Massachusetts Lowell, Lowell
  01854-2882
University of Massachusetts Medical School, Worcester
  01655
Urban College of Boston, Boston 02111
Wellesley College, Wellesley 02481-8203
Wentworth Institute of Technology, Boston 02115-5998
Western New England College, Springfield 01119-2688
Western New England College: School of Law,
  Springfield 01119
Westfield State College, Westfield 01086-1630
Weston Jesuit School of Theology, Cambridge 02138
Wheaton College, Norton 02766
Williams College, Williamstown 01267
Worcester Polytechnic Institute, Worcester 01609

Michigan

Adrian College, Adrian 49221
Alma College, Alma 48801-1599
Alpena Community College, Alpena 49707
Andrews University, Berrien Springs 49104
Andrews University Seminary, Berrien Springs 49104
Aquinas College, Grand Rapids 49506
Baker College of Auburn Hills, Auburn Hills 48326
Baker College of Cadillac, Cadillac 49601
Baker College of Clinton Township, Clinton Township
  48035
Baker College of Jackson, Jackson 49202
Baker College of Muskegon, Muskegon 49442
Baker College of Owosso, Owosso 48867
Baker College of Port Huron, Port Huron 48060-2597
Bay de Noc Community College, Escanaba 49829
Calvin College, Grand Rapids 49546
Calvin Theological Seminary, Grand Rapids 49546
Central Michigan University, Mount Pleasant 48859
Cleary University, Ann Arbor 48105
College for Creative Studies, Detroit 48202
Concordia University, Ann Arbor 48105
Cornerstone University, Grand Rapids 49525
Davenport University - Eastern Region, Dearborn
  48126
Davenport University - Midland, Midland 48642
Davenport University - Western Region, Grand Rapids
  49503
Detroit College of Law, Detroit 48201
Eastern Michigan University, Ypsilanti 48197
Ferris State University, Big Rapids 49307
Ferris State University College of Pharmacy, Big Rapids
  49307
Ferris State University: College of Optometry, Big
  Rapids 49307
Finlandia University, Hancock 49930
Glen Oaks Community College, Centreville
  49032-9719
Gogebic Community College, Ironwood 49938
Grace Bible College, Grand Rapids 49509
Grand Rapids Baptist Seminary, Grand Rapids 49505
Grand Rapids Community College, Grand Rapids
  49503-3295
Grand Valley State University, Allendale 49401
Hillsdale College, Hillsdale 49242
Hope College, Holland 49422-9000
ITT Technical Institute: Grand Rapids, Grand Rapids
  49546
ITT Technical Institute: Troy, Troy 48083-1905
Jackson Community College, Jackson 49201
Kalamazoo College, Kalamazoo 49006
Kellogg Community College, Battle Creek 49017-3397
Kettering University, Flint 48504
Kirtland Community College, Roscommon 48653
Lansing Community College, Lansing 48901
Lawrence Technological University, Southfield 48075
Macomb Community College, Warren 48088-3896
Madonna University, Livonia 48150
Marygrove College, Detroit 48221
Michigan State University, East Lansing 48824
Michigan State University: College of Human
  Medicine, East Lansing 48824
Michigan State University: College of Osteopathic
  Medicine, East Lansing 48824

Michigan State University: School of Veterinary
  Medicine, East Lansing 48824
Michigan Technological University, Houghton
  49931-1295
Mid Michigan Community College, Harrison 48625
Monroe County Community College, Monroe 48161
Montcalm Community College, Sidney 48885
Mott Community College, Flint 48503
Muskegon Community College, Muskegon 49442
North Central Michigan College, Petoskey 49770
Northern Michigan University, Marquette 49855
Northwestern Michigan College, Traverse City 49686
Northwood University, Midland 48640
Oakland Community College, Bloomfield Hills
  48304-2266
Oakland University, Rochester 48309-4401
Reformed Bible College, Grand Rapids 49525
Sacred Heart Major Seminary, Detroit 48206
Sacred Heart Major Seminary, Detroit 48206
Saginaw Valley State University, University Center
  48710
St. Clair County Community College, Port Huron
  48061-5015
Schoolcraft College, Livonia 48152
Siena Heights University, Adrian 49221-1796
Southwestern Michigan College, Dowagiac 49047
Spring Arbor University, Spring Arbor 49283-9799
Thomas M. Cooley Law School, Lansing 48901
University of Detroit Mercy: School of Dentistry,
  Detroit 48219-0900
University of Detroit Mercy: School of Law, Detroit
  48226
University of Michigan, Ann Arbor 48109-1070
University of Michigan: College of Pharmacy, Ann
  Arbor 48109
University of Michigan: Dearborn, Dearborn
  48128-1491
University of Michigan: Flint, Flint 48502-1950
University of Michigan: School of Dentistry, Ann Arbor
  48109
University of Michigan: School of Law, Ann Arbor
  48109
University of Michigan: School of Medicine, Ann Arbor
  48109
Walsh College of Accountancy and Business
  Administration, Troy 48007-7706
Washtenaw Community College, Ann Arbor 48106
Wayne County Community College, Detroit 48226
Wayne State University, Detroit 48202
Wayne State University: College of Pharmacy and
  Allied Health, Detroit 48202
Wayne State University: School of Law, Detroit 48202
Wayne State University: School of Medicine, Detroit
  48201
West Shore Community College, Scottville 49454-0277
Western Michigan University, Kalamazoo 49008
Western Theological Seminary, Holland 49419
William Tyndale College, Farmington Hills 48331-3147

Minnesota

Academy College, Bloomington 55425-1554
Alexandria Technical College, Alexandria 56308
Anoka-Ramsey Community College, Coon Rapids
  55433
Art Institutes International Minnesota, Minneapolis
  55402
Augsburg College, Minneapolis 55454
Bemidji State University, Bemidji 56601
Bethany Lutheran College, Mankato 56001
Bethel College, St. Paul 55112
Bethel Theological Seminary, St. Paul 55112
Brown College, Mendota Heights 55120
Capella University, Minneapolis 55402
Carleton College, Northfield 55057
Central Lakes College, Brainerd 56401
Century Community and Technical College, White Bear
  Lake 55110
College of St. Benedict, St. Joseph 56374-2099
College of St. Catherine, St. Paul 55105
College of St. Scholastica, Duluth 55811-4199
College of Visual Arts, St. Paul 55102
Concordia College: Moorhead, Moorhead 56562
Concordia University: St. Paul, St. Paul 55104
Crossroads College, Rochester 55902
Crown College, St. Bonifacius 55375-9001
Dakota County Technical College, Rosemount 55068
Fergus Falls Community College, Fergus Falls 56537
Globe College, Oakdale 55128
Gustavus Adolphus College, St. Peter 56082
Hamline University, St. Paul 55104-1284
Hamline University: School of Law, St. Paul 55104
Hennepin Technical College, Brooklyn Park 55445
Herzing College: Minneapolis Drafting School, Crystal
  55428

Hibbing Community College: A Technical and
Community College, Hibbing 55746
High-Tech Institute, Brooklyn Center 55430
Inver Hills Community College, Inver Grove Heights
55076
Itasca Community College, Grand Rapids 55744
Lake Superior College: A Community and Technical
College, Duluth 55811
Lakeland Medical-Dental Academy, Crystal 55428
Luther Seminary: Theological Professions, St. Paul
55108
Macalester College, St. Paul 55105
Martin Luther College, New Ulm 56073-3965
Mayo Medical School, Rochester 55905
Mesabi Range Community and Technical College,
Virginia 55792
Metropolitan State University, St. Paul 55106
Minneapolis Community and Technical College,
Minneapolis 55403
Minnesota School of Business, Richfield 55423
Minnesota School of Business: Brooklyn Center,
Brooklyn Center 55430
Minnesota State College - Southeast Technical, Winona
55987
Minnesota State University Moorhead, Moorhead 56563
Minnesota State University, Mankato, Mankato 56001
Minnesota West Community and Technical College:
Worthington Campus, Worthington 56187
National American University: St. Paul, Bloomington
55425
Normandale Community College, Bloomington 55431
North Central University, Minneapolis 55404
North Hennepin Community College, Minneapolis
55445
Northland Community & Technical College, Thief
River Falls 56701
Northwest Technical Institute, Eden Prairie 55344
Northwestern College, St. Paul 55113
Northwestern College of Chiropractic, Bloomington
55431
Oak Hills Christian College, Bemidji 56601
Pine Technical College, Pine City 55063
Rainy River Community College, International Falls
56649
Rasmussen College-Mankato, Mankato 56001
Rasmussen College-Minnetonka, Minnetonka 55305
Rasmussen College-St. Cloud, St. Cloud 56301-3713
Ridgewater College: A Community and Technical
College, Willmar 56201
Riverland Community College: A Technical and
Community College, Austin 55912
Rochester Community and Technical College,
Rochester 55904
St. Cloud State University, St. Cloud 56301
St. Cloud Technical College, St. Cloud 56303
St. John's University, Collegeville 56321
St. John's University: School of Theology, Collegeville
56321
St. Mary's University of Minnesota, Winona 55987
St. Olaf College, Northfield 55057-1098
St. Paul College - A Community and Technical College,
St. Paul 55102
South Central Technical College, North Mankato 56003
Southwest State University, Marshall 56258
United Theological Seminary of the Twin Cities, New
Brighton 55112
University of Minnesota Medical School, Minneapolis
55455
University of Minnesota Twin Cities: College of
Veterinary Medicine, St. Paul 55108
University of Minnesota Twin Cities: School of
Dentistry, Minneapolis 55455
University of Minnesota Twin Cities: School of Law,
Minneapolis 55455
University of Minnesota: Crookston, Crookston 56716
University of Minnesota: Duluth, Duluth 55812-2496
University of Minnesota: Morris, Morris 56267
University of Minnesota: Twin Cities, Minneapolis
55455-0213
University of St. Thomas, St. Paul 55105-1096
University of St. Thomas: School of Divinity, St. Paul
55105
Vermilion Community College, Ely 55731
William Mitchell College of Law: Law Professions, St.
Paul 55105
Winona State University, Winona 55987

Mississippi

Alcorn State University, Alcorn State 39096
Antonelli College: Hattiesburg, Hattiesburg 39401
Antonelli College: Jackson, Jackson 39232
Blue Mountain College, Blue Mountain 38610-0160
Coahoma Community College, Clarksdale 38614

Delta State University, Cleveland 38733
Holmes Community College, Goodman 39079
Itawamba Community College, Fulton 38843
Magnolia Bible College, Kosciusko 39090
Mary Holmes College, West Point 39773
Millsaps College, Jackson 39210
Mississippi College, Clinton 39058
Mississippi College: School of Law, Jackson 39201
Mississippi Gulf Coast Community College: Perkinston,
Perkinston 39573
Mississippi State University, Miss. State 39762
Mississippi State University: College of Veterinary
Medicine, Mississippi University 39762
Mississippi University for Women, Columbus 39701
Mississippi Valley State University, Itta Bena
38941-1400
Northwest Mississippi Community College, Senatobia
38668
Pearl River Community College, Poplarville 39470
Reformed Theological Seminary, Jackson 39209
Rust College, Holly Springs 38635
University of Mississippi, University 38677
University of Mississippi Medical Center, Jackson
39216
University of Mississippi Medical Center: School of
Dentistry, Jackson 39216
University of Mississippi Medical Center: School of
Medicine, Jackson 39216
University of Mississippi: School of Law, University
38677
University of Mississippi: School of Pharmacy,
University 38677
University of Southern Mississippi, Hattiesburg
39406-5001
Wesley Biblical Seminary, Jackson 39286
Wesley College, Florence 39073

Missouri

Aquinas Institute of Theology, St. Louis 63108
Assemblies of God Theological Seminary, Springfield
65802
Avila University, Kansas City 64145-1698
Baptist Bible College, Springfield 65803
Blue River Community College, Blue Springs
64015-7242
Calvary Bible College, Kansas City 64147
Central Bible College, Springfield 65803
Central Christian College of the Bible, Moberly 65270
Central Methodist College, Fayette 65248
Central Missouri State University, Warrensburg 64093
Cleveland Chiropractic College of Kansas City, Kansas
City 64131
College of the Ozarks, Point Lookout 65726
Columbia College, Columbia 65216
ConCorde Career Institute, Kansas City 64111
Conception Seminary College, Conception 64433
Concordia Seminary, Clayton 63105
Cottey College, Nevada 64772
Covenant Theological Seminary, St. Louis 63141
Crowder College, Neosho 64850
Culver-Stockton College, Canton 63435
DeVry University: Kansas City, Kansas City 64131
Deaconess College of Nursing, St. Louis 63139
Drury University, Springfield 65802
East Central College, Union 63084
Eden Theological Seminary, Webster Groves 63119
Evangel University, Springfield 65802
Fontbonne College, St. Louis 63105
Global University, Springfield 65804
Hannibal-LaGrange College, Hannibal 63401-1999
Harris Stowe State College, St. Louis 63103-2199
Hickey College, St. Louis 63146
ITT Technical Institute: Arnold, Arnold 63010
ITT Technical Institute: Earth City, Earth City 63045
Jefferson College, Hillsboro 63050
Kansas City Art Institute, Kansas City 64111
Kansas City College of Legal Studies, Kansas City
64131
Kenrick-Glennon Seminary, St. Louis 63119
Kirksville College of Osteopathic Medicine, Kirksville
63501
Lincoln University, Jefferson City 65102-0029
Lindenwood University, St. Charles 63301
Logan College of Chiropractic, Chesterfield 63006
Longview Community College, Lee's Summit 64081
Maple Woods Community College, Kansas City
64156-1299
Maryville University of Saint Louis, St. Louis
63141-7299
Midwestern Baptist Theological Seminary, Kansas City
64118
Mineral Area College, Park Hills 63601-1000
Missouri Baptist University, St. Louis 63141
Missouri College, St. Louis 63122-1583

Missouri Southern State College, Joplin 64801-1595
Missouri Technical School, St. Louis 63132
Missouri Valley College, Marshall 65340
Missouri Western State College, St. Joseph 64507
Moberly Area Community College, Moberly 65270
National American University: Kansas City, Kansas
City 64133
Nazarene Theological Seminary, Kansas City 64131
North Central Missouri College, Trenton 64683
Northwest Missouri State University, Maryville 64468
Ozark Christian College, Joplin 64801
Ozarks Technical Community College, Springfield
65801
Patricia Stevens College, St. Louis 63102
Penn Valley Community College, Kansas City
64111-2429
Ranken Technical College, St. Louis 63113
Research College of Nursing, Kansas City 64132
Rockhurst University, Kansas City 64110
St. Charles Community College, St. Peters 63376
St. Louis Christian College, Florissant 63033
St. Louis College of Pharmacy, St. Louis 63110
St. Louis College of Pharmacy, St. Louis 63110
St. Louis Community College at Florissant Valley, St.
Louis 63135
St. Louis Community College at Forest Park, St. Louis
63110
St. Louis Community College at Meramec, St. Louis
63122-5799
St. Louis University, St. Louis 63103
St. Louis University: School of Law, St. Louis 63108
St. Louis University: School of Medicine, St. Louis
63104
St. Luke's College, Kansas City 64111
St. Paul School of Theology, Kansas City 64127
Sanford-Brown College, Fenton 63026
Southeast Missouri State University, Cape Girardeau
63701
Southwest Baptist University, Bolivar 65613
Southwest Missouri State University, Springfield
65804-0094
Southwest Missouri State University: West Plains
Campus, West Plains 65775
Springfield College, Springfield 65807
Stephens College, Columbia 65215
Three Rivers Community College, Poplar Bluff 63901
Truman State University, Kirksville 63501
University of Health Sciences College of Osteopathic
Medicine, Kansas City 64124
University of Missouri Columbia: School of Law,
Columbia 65211
University of Missouri Columbia: School of Medicine,
Columbia 65212
University of Missouri Columbia: School of Veterinary
Medicine, Columbia 65211
University of Missouri Kansas City: School of
Dentistry, Kansas City 64108
University of Missouri Kansas City: School of Law,
Kansas City 64110
University of Missouri Kansas City: School of
Medicine, Kansas City 64108
University of Missouri St. Louis: School of Optometry,
St. Louis 63121
University of Missouri: Columbia, Columbia 65211
University of Missouri: Kansas City, Kansas City
64110-2499
University of Missouri: Rolla, Rolla 65409-0910
University of Missouri: St. Louis, St. Louis 63121-4499
Vatterott College: St. Joseph, St. Joseph 64506
Vatterott College: Sunset Hills, Sunset Hills 63127
Washington University in St. Louis, St. Louis
63130-4899
Washington University: School of Law, St. Louis 63130
Washington University: School of Medicine, St. Louis
63110
Webster University, Webster Groves 63119
Wentworth Military Academy, Lexington 64067
Westminster College, Fulton 65251
William Jewell College, Liberty 64068
William Woods University, Fulton 65251-2388

Montana

Carroll College, Helena 59625
Chief Dull Knife College, Lame Deer 59043
Dawson Community College, Glendive 59330
Flathead Valley Community College, Kalispell 59901
Fort Belknap College, Harlem 59526
Miles Community College, Miles City 59301
Montana State University: Billings, Billings 59101
Montana State University: Billings College of
Technology, Billings 59102
Montana State University: Bozeman, Bozeman 59717
Montana Tech of the University of Montana, Butte
59701

Rocky Mountain College, Billings 59102-1796
Salish Kootenai College, Pablo 59855
University of Great Falls, Great Falls 59405
University of Montana School of Pharmacy and Allied
   Health Sciences, Missoula 59812
University of Montana-Missoula, Missoula 59812
University of Montana: School of Law, Missoula 59812
University of Montana: Western, Dillon 59725-3598

Nebraska

Bellevue University, Bellevue 68005
Central Community College, Grand Island 68802
Chadron State College, Chadron 69337
Clarkson College, Omaha 68131
College of Saint Mary, Omaha 68124
Concordia University, Seward 68434
Creighton University, Omaha 68178
Creighton University: School of Dentistry, Omaha
   68178
Creighton University: School of Law, Omaha 68178
Creighton University: School of Medicine, Omaha
   68178
Dana College, Blair 68008
Doane College, Crete 68333
Grace University, Omaha 68108
Hastings College, Hastings 68901-7696
ITT Technical Institute: Omaha, Omaha 68127
Lincoln School of Commerce, Lincoln 68501
Little Priest Tribal College, Winnebago 68071
Metropolitan Community College, Omaha 68103
Mid Plains Community College Area, North Platte
   69101
Midland Lutheran College, Fremont 68025
Nebraska Christian College, Norfolk 68701
Nebraska College of Business, Omaha 68134
Nebraska College of Technical Agriculture, Curtis
   69025
Nebraska Indian Community College, Macy 68039
Nebraska Methodist College of Nursing and Allied
   Health, Omaha 68114
Nebraska Wesleyan University, Lincoln 68504
Northeast Community College, Norfolk 68702-0469
Peru State College, Peru 68421
Southeast Community College: Beatrice Campus,
   Beatrice 68310
Southeast Community College: Lincoln Campus,
   Lincoln 68520
Southeast Community College: Milford Campus,
   Milford 68405-8498
Union College, Lincoln 68506
University of Nebraska - Kearney, Kearney 68849
University of Nebraska - Lincoln, Lincoln 68588
University of Nebraska - Omaha, Omaha 68182
University of Nebraska Lincoln: College of Law,
   Lincoln 68583
University of Nebraska Medical Center, Omaha
   68198-4230
University of Nebraska Medical Center: College of
   Dentistry, Lincoln 68583
University of Nebraska Medical Center: College of
   Medicine, Omaha 68134
University of Nebraska Medical Center: College of
   Pharmacy, Omaha 68198
Vatterott College, Omaha 68137
Vatterott College: Dodge Campus, Omaha 68114
Vatterott College: Spring Valley, Omaha 68117
Wayne State College, Wayne 68787
Western Nebraska Community College, Scottsbluff
   69361
York College, York 68467

Nevada

Academy of Healing Arts, Las Vegas 89106
Art Institute of Las Vegas, Henderson 89074
Career College of Northern Nevada, Reno 89502-2331
Community College of Southern Nevada, North Las
   Vegas 89030
Great Basin College, Elko 89801
Heritage College, Las Vegas 89102
ITT Technical Institute: Henderson, Santa Fe 89014
Las Vegas College, Las Vegas 89103
Morrison University, Reno 89503
Sierra Nevada College, Incline Village 89450
Truckee Meadows Community College, Reno 89512
University of Nevada: Las Vegas, Las Vegas 89154
University of Nevada: Reno, Reno 89557
University of Nevada: School of Medicine, Reno 89557
Western Nevada Community College, Carson City
   89703-7399

New Hampshire

Chester College of New England, Chester 03036-4331
Colby-Sawyer College, New London 03257
College for Lifelong Learning, Concord 03301

Daniel Webster College, Nashua 03063
Dartmouth College, Hanover 03755
Dartmouth College: School of Medicine, Hanover
   03755
Franklin Pierce College, Rindge 03461-0060
Franklin Pierce Law Center, Concord 03301
Hesser College, Manchester 03103
Keene State College, Keene 03435
Magdalen College, Warner 03278
New England College, Henniker 03242
New Hampshire Community Technical College: Berlin,
   Berlin 03570
New Hampshire Community Technical College:
   Claremont, Claremont 03743
New Hampshire Community Technical College:
   Laconia, Laconia 03246
New Hampshire Community Technical College:
   Manchester, Manchester 03102
New Hampshire Community Technical College:
   Nashua, Nashua 03063
New Hampshire Community Technical College:
   Stratham, Stratham 03885
New Hampshire Technical Institute, Concord 03301
Plymouth State College, Plymouth 03264-1595
Rivier College, Nashua 03060
St. Anselm College, Manchester 03102-1310
Southern New Hampshire University, Manchester
   03106
Thomas More College of Liberal Arts, Merrimack
   03054
University of New Hampshire, Durham 03824
University of New Hampshire at Manchester,
   Manchester 03101-1113

New Jersey

Assumption College for Sisters, Mendham 07945-0800
Atlantic Cape Community College, Mays Landing
   08330
Bergen Community College, Paramus 07652
Berkeley College, West Paterson 07424
Bloomfield College, Bloomfield 07003
Brookdale Community College, Lincroft 07738
Burlington County College, Pemberton 08068-1599
Caldwell College, Caldwell 07006-6195
Camden County College, Blackwood 08012
Centenary College, Hackettstown 07840
The College of New Jersey, Ewing 08628
College of St. Elizabeth, Morristown 07960-6989
County College of Morris, Randolph 07869
Cumberland County College, Vineland 08362-0517
DeVry College of Technology, North Brunswick 08902
Drew University, Madison 07940-1493
Drew University: School of Theology, Madison 07940
Essex County College, Newark 07102
Fairleigh Dickinson University: College at Florham,
   Madison 07940
Fairleigh Dickinson University: Metropolitan Campus,
   Teaneck 07666-1996
Felician College, Lodi 07644
Georgian Court College, Lakewood 08701
Gloucester County College, Sewell 08080
Hudson County Community College, Jersey City 07306
Immaculate Conception Seminary of Seton Hall
   University, South Orange 07079
Kean University, Union 07083
Mercer County Community College, Trenton
   08690-1099
Middlesex County College, Edison 08818-3050
Monmouth University, West Long Branch 07764-1898
Montclair State University, Upper Montclair 07043
New Brunswick Theological Seminary, New Brunswick
   08901
New Jersey City University, Jersey City 07305-1597
New Jersey Institute of Technology, Newark
   07102-1982
Ocean County College, Toms River 08754
Passaic County Community College, Paterson
   07505-1179
Princeton Theological Seminary, Princeton 08542
Princeton University, Princeton 08544
Rabbinical College of America, Morristown 07962
Ramapo College of New Jersey, Mahwah 07430-1680
Raritan Valley Community College, Somerville
   08876-1265
Richard Stockton College of New Jersey, Pomona
   08240
Rider University, Lawrenceville 08648-3099
Rowan University, Glassboro 08028
Rutgers, The State University of New Jersey: Camden
   Regional Campus, Camden 08102
Rutgers, The State University of New Jersey: Camden
   School of Law, Camden 08102
Rutgers, The State University of New Jersey: College of
   Pharmacy, New Brunswick 08903

Rutgers, The State University of New Jersey: New
   Brunswick Regional Campus, Piscataway
   08854-8097
Rutgers, The State University of New Jersey: Newark
   Regional Campus, Newark 07102-1896
Rutgers, The State University of New Jersey: Newark
   School of Law, Newark 07102
St. Peter's College, Jersey City 07306
Salem Community College, Carneys Point 08069-2799
Seton Hall University, South Orange 07079
Seton Hall University: School of Law, Newark 07102
Somerset Christian College, Zarephath 08890
Stevens Institute of Technology, Hoboken 07030
Sussex County Community College, Newton 07860
Thomas Edison State College, Trenton 08608
UMDNJ-School of Osteopathic Medicine, Stratford
   08084
Union County College, Cranford 07016
University of Medicine and Dentistry of New Jersey:
   New Jersey Medical School, Newark 07103
University of Medicine and Dentistry of New Jersey:
   Robert Wood Johnson Medical School at Camden,
   Camden 08103
University of Medicine and Dentistry of New Jersey:
   New Jersey Dental School, Newark 07103
University of Medicine and Dentistry of New Jersey:
   Robert Wood Johnson Medical School, Piscataway
   08854
University of Medicine and Dentistry of New Jersey:
   School of Health Related Professions, Newark 07107
Warren County Community College, Washington
   07882-4343
William Paterson University of New Jersey, Wayne
   07470

New Mexico

Albuquerque Technical-Vocational Institute,
   Albuquerque 87106
Art Center Design College, Albuquerque 87110
Clovis Community College, Clovis 88101-8381
College of Santa Fe, Santa Fe 87505
College of the Southwest, Hobbs 88240
Dona Ana Branch Community College of New Mexico
   State University, Las Cruces 88003
Eastern New Mexico University, Portales 88130
Eastern New Mexico University: Roswell Campus,
   Roswell 88202
ITT Technical Institute: Albuquerque, Albuquerque
   87109
Institute of American Indian Arts, Santa Fe 87508
Luna Community College, Las Vegas 87701
Mesalands Community College, Tucumcari 88401
Metropolitan College of Court Reporting, Albuquerque
   87110
National American University, Albuquerque 87110
New Mexico Highlands University, Las Vegas 87701
New Mexico Institute of Mining and Technology,
   Socorro 87801
New Mexico Junior College, Hobbs 88240
New Mexico Military Institute, Roswell 88201
New Mexico State University, Las Cruces 88003-8001
New Mexico State University at Alamogordo,
   Alamogordo 88310
St. John's College, Santa Fe 87505-4599
San Juan College, Farmington 87402
Santa Fe Community College, Santa Fe 87508
Southwestern Indian Polytechnic Institute, Albuquerque
   87184
University of New Mexico, Albuquerque 87131-2046
University of New Mexico College of Pharmacy,
   Albuquerque 87131
University of New Mexico: School of Law,
   Albuquerque 87131
University of New Mexico: School of Medicine,
   Albuquerque 87131
Western New Mexico University, Silver City 88062

New York

Adelphi University, Garden City 11530
Adirondack Community College, Queensbury 12804
Albany College of Pharmacy, Albany 12208
Albany College of Pharmacy, Albany 12208
Albany Law School of Union University, Albany 12208
Albany Medical College: School of Medicine, Albany
   12208
Albert Einstein College of Medicine, Bronx 10461
Alfred University, Alfred 14802
Alliance Theological Seminary, Nyack 10960
American Academy McAllister Institute of Funeral
   Service, New York 10019
Bard College, Annandale-on-Hudson 12504
Barnard College, New York 10027
Benjamin N. Cardozo School of Law, New York 10003

Berkeley College, White Plains 10601
Berkeley College of New York City, New York 10017
Briarcliffe College, Bethpage 11714
Brooklyn Law School, Brooklyn 11201
Broome Community College, Binghamton 13902
Bryant & Stratton Business Institute: Albany, Albany 12205
Bryant & Stratton Business Institute: Rochester, Rochester 14606
Bryant & Stratton Business Institute: Syracuse, Syracuse 13203
Canisius College, Buffalo 14208
Cayuga County Community College, Auburn 13021
Cazenovia College, Cazenovia 13035
Central Yeshiva Tomchei Tmimim Lubavitz, Brooklyn 11230
Christ The King Seminary, East Aurora 14052
City University of New York: Baruch College, New York 10010-5285
City University of New York: Borough of Manhattan Community College, New York 10007
City University of New York: Bronx Community College, Bronx 10453
City University of New York: Brooklyn College, Brooklyn 11210
City University of New York: City College, New York 10031
City University of New York: College of Staten Island, Staten Island 10314
City University of New York: Hostos Community College, Bronx 10451
City University of New York: Hunter College, New York 10021
City University of New York: John Jay College of Criminal Justice, New York 10019
City University of New York: Kingsborough Community College, Brooklyn 11235
City University of New York: La Guardia Community College, Long Island City 11101
City University of New York: Medgar Evers College, Brooklyn 11225
City University of New York: Queens College, Flushing 11367
City University of New York: Queensborough Community College, Bayside 11364
City University of New York: School of Law at Queens College, Flushing 11367
City University of New York: York College, Jamaica 11451
Clarkson University, Potsdam 13699
Clinton Community College, Plattsburgh 12901
Cochran School of Nursing-St. John's Riverside Hospital, Yonkers 10701
Colgate Rochester Divinity School-Bexley Crozer Theological Seminary, Rochester 14620
Colgate University, Hamilton 13346
College of Aeronautics, Flushing 11369
College of Mount St. Vincent, Riverdale 10471
College of New Rochelle, New Rochelle 10805
College of New Rochelle: School of New Resources, New Rochelle 10805
Columbia University: College of Physicians and Surgeons, New York 10032
Columbia University: Columbia College, New York 10027
Columbia University: Fu Foundation School of Engineering and Applied Science, New York 10027
Columbia University: School of Dental and Oral Surgery, New York 10032
Columbia University: School of Law, New York 10027
Columbia University: School of Nursing, New York 10032
Concordia College, Bronxville 10708
Cooper Union for the Advancement of Science and Art, New York 10003
Cornell University, Ithaca 14850
Cornell University Medical College, New York 10021
Cornell University: College of Veterinary Medicine, Ithaca 14853
Cornell University: School of Law, Ithaca 14853
Corning Community College, Corning 14830
Culinary Institute of America, Hyde Park 12538
D'Youville College, Buffalo 14201
Daemen College, Amherst 14226-3592
DeVry Institute of Technology: New York, Long Island City 11101
Dominican College of Blauvelt, Orangeburg 10962
Dowling College, Oakdale 11769
Dutchess Community College, Poughkeepsie 12601
Eastman School of Music of the University of Rochester, Rochester 14604
Elmira Business Institute, Elmira 14901
Elmira College, Elmira 14901

Erie Community College: City Campus, Buffalo 14203-2698
Erie Community College: North Campus, Williamsville 14221-7095
Erie Community College: South Campus, Orchard Park 14127-2199
Eugene Lang College/New School University, New York 10011-8963
Excelsior College, Albany 12203
Fashion Institute of Technology, New York 10001
Finger Lakes Community College, Canandaigua 14424
Fordham University, Bronx 10458
Fordham University: School of Law, New York 10023
Fulton-Montgomery Community College, Johnstown 12095-3790
General Theological Seminary, New York 10011
Genesee Community College, Batavia 14020-9704
Globe Institute of Technology, New York 10007
Hamilton College, Clinton 13323
Hartwick College, Oneonta 13820-4020
Helene Fuld College of Nursing, New York 10035
Hilbert College, Hamburg 14075-1597
Hobart and William Smith Colleges, Geneva 14456
Hofstra University, Hempstead 11549
Hofstra University: School of Law, Hempstead 11550
Holy Trinity Orthodox Seminary, Jordanville 13361
Houghton College, Houghton 14744
Hudson Valley Community College, Troy 12180
ITT Technical Institute: Albany, Albany 12205
ITT Technical Institute: Getzville, Getzville 14068
ITT Technical Institute: Liverpool, Liverpool 13088
Institute of Design and Construction, Brooklyn 11201
Iona College, New Rochelle 10801-1890
Island Drafting and Technical Institute, Amityville 11701-2704
Ithaca College, Ithaca 14850-7020
Jamestown Business College, Jamestown 14701
Jamestown Community College, Jamestown 14702-0020
Jefferson Community College, Watertown 13601
Jewish Theological Seminary of America, New York 10027
Juilliard School, New York 10023-6588
Katharine Gibbs School: Melville, Melville 11747
Kehilath Yakov Rabbinical Seminary, Brooklyn 11211
Keuka College, Keuka Park 14478
Kol Yaakov Torah Center, Monsey 10952
Laboratory Institute of Merchandising, New York 10022
Le Moyne College, Syracuse 13214-1399
Long Island Business Institute, Commack 11725
Long Island University: C. W. Post Campus, Brookville 11548-1300
Long Island University: Southampton College, Southampton 11968
Long Island University:Arnold and Marie Schwartz College of Pharmacy and Health Sciences, Brooklyn 11201
Machzikei Hadath Rabbinical College, Brooklyn 11204
Manhattan College, Riverdale 10471
Manhattan School of Music, New York 10027
Manhattanville College, Purchase 10577
Mannes College of Music, New York 10024
Maria College, Albany 12208
Marist College, Poughkeepsie 12601
Marymount College of Fordham University, Tarrytown 10591
Marymount Manhattan College, New York 10021-4597
Medaille College, Buffalo 14214
Mercy College, Dobbs Ferry 10522
Mesivta Eastern Parkway Rabbinical Seminary, Brooklyn 11218
Mesivta Tifereth Jerusalem of America, New York 10002
Metropolitan College of New York, New York 10013
Mildred Elley, Latham 12110
Mirrer Yeshiva Central Institute, Brooklyn 11223
Mohawk Valley Community College, Utica 13501-5394
Molloy College, Rockville Centre 11570
Monroe College, Bronx 10468
Monroe Community College, Rochester 14623
Mount St. Mary College, Newburgh 12550
Mount Sinai School of Medicine of City University of New York, New York 10029
Nassau Community College, Garden City 11530
Nazareth College of Rochester, Rochester 14618
New York Chiropractic College, Seneca Falls 13148
New York College of Osteopathic Medicine of New York Institute of Technology, Old Westbury 11568
New York College of Podiatric Medicine, New York 10035
New York Institute of Technology, Old Westbury 11568
New York Law School, New York 10013
New York Medical College, Valhalla 10595
New York School of Interior Design, New York 10021
New York Theological Seminary, New York 10001

New York University, New York 10003
New York University: College of Dentistry, New York 10010
New York University: School of Law, New York 10012
New York University: School of Medicine, New York 10016
Niagara County Community College, Sanborn 14132
Niagara University, Niagara University 14109
North Country Community College, Saranac Lake 12983-0089
Nyack College, Nyack 10960-3698
Ohr Hameir Theological Seminary, Peekskill 10566
Ohr Somayach Institutions: School of Theology, Monsey 10952
Ohr Somayach Tanenbaum Education Center, Monsey 10952
Olean Business Institute, Olean 14760
Onondaga Community College, Syracuse 13215
Orange County Community College, Middletown 10940
Pace University, New York 10038
Pace University Westchester: School of Law, White Plains 10603
Pace University: Pleasantville/Briarcliff, Pleasantville 10570
Parsons School of Design, New York 10011
Paul Smith's College, Paul Smiths 12970
Phillips Beth Israel School of Nursing, New York 10010
Plaza College, Jackson Heights 11372
Polytechnic University, Brooklyn 11201
Pratt Institute, Brooklyn 11205
Rabbi Isaac Elchanan Theological Seminary, New York 10033
Rabbinical College Beth Shraga, Monsey 10952
Rabbinical College Bobover Yeshiva B'nei Zion, Brooklyn 11219
Rabbinical Seminary M'Kor Chaim, Brooklyn 11219
Rensselaer Polytechnic Institute, Troy 12180
Roberts Wesleyan College, Rochester 14624
Rochester Business Institute, Rochester 14621-3007
Rochester Institute of Technology, Rochester 14623
Rockland Community College, Suffern 10901
Russell Sage College, Troy 12180
Sage College of Albany, Albany 12208
St. Bernard's Institute, Rochester 14620
St. Bonaventure University, St. Bonaventure 14778
St. Elizabeth College of Nursing, Utica 13501
St. John Fisher College, Rochester 14618-3597
St. John's University, Jamaica 11439
St. John's University, Jamaica 11439
St. John's University: College of Pharmacy and Allied Health Professions, Jamaica 11439
St. John's University: School of Law, Jamaica 11439
St. Joseph's College, Brooklyn 11205
St. Joseph's College: Suffolk Campus, Patchogue 11772
St. Joseph's Hospital Health Center School of Nursing, Syracuse 13203
St. Joseph's Seminary and College, Yonkers 10704
St. Lawrence University, Canton 13617
St. Vladimir's Orthodox Theological Seminary, Crestwood 10707
Sarah Lawrence College, Bronxville 10708-5999
Schenectady County Community College, Schenectady 12305
School of Visual Arts, New York 10010
Seminary of the Immaculate Conception, Huntington 11743
Sh'or Yoshuv Rabbinical College, Far Rockaway 11691
Skidmore College, Saratoga Springs 12866
State University of New York College at Brockport, Brockport 14420
State University of New York College at Buffalo, Buffalo 14222
State University of New York College at Cortland, Cortland 13045
State University of New York College at Fredonia, Fredonia 14063-1136
State University of New York College at Geneseo, Geneseo 14454-1471
State University of New York College at Old Westbury, Old Westbury 11568-0210
State University of New York College at Oneonta, Oneonta 13820-4015
State University of New York College at Plattsburgh, Plattsburgh 12901
State University of New York College at Potsdam, Potsdam 13676
State University of New York College of Agriculture and Technology at Cobleskill, Cobleskill 12043
State University of New York College of Agriculture and Technology at Morrisville, Morrisville 13408
State University of New York College of Environmental Science and Forestry, Syracuse 13210

State University of New York College of Optometry, New York 10010

State University of New York College of Technology at Alfred, Alfred 14802

State University of New York College of Technology at Canton, Canton 13617

State University of New York College of Technology at Delhi, Delhi 13753

State University of New York Empire State College, Saratoga Springs 12866

State University of New York Health Science Center at Brooklyn, Brooklyn 11203-2098

State University of New York Health Science Center at Brooklyn: School of Medicine, Brooklyn 11203

State University of New York Health Science Center at Stony Brook, Stony Brook 11794

State University of New York Health Science Center at Syracuse: School of Medicine, Syracuse 13210

State University of New York Health Sciences Center at Stony Brook: School of Dentistry, Stony Brook 11794

State University of New York Health Sciences Center at Stony Brook: School of Medicine, Stony Brook 11794

State University of New York Institute of Technology at Utica/Rome, Utica 13504

State University of New York Maritime College, Throggs Neck 10465

State University of New York Upstate Medical University, Syracuse 13210

State University of New York at Albany, Albany 12222

State University of New York at Binghamton, Binghamton 13902-6000

State University of New York at Buffalo, Buffalo 14214

State University of New York at Buffalo: School of Dentistry, Buffalo 14214

State University of New York at Buffalo: School of Law, Buffalo 14260

State University of New York at Buffalo: School of Medicine, Buffalo 14214

State University of New York at Buffalo: School of Pharmacy, Buffalo 14260

State University of New York at Farmingdale, Farmingdale 11735

State University of New York at New Paltz, New Paltz 12561-2443

State University of New York at Oswego, Oswego 13126-3599

State University of New York at Purchase, Purchase 10577

State University of New York at Stony Brook, Stony Brook 11794

Suffolk County Community College, Selden 11784

Syracuse University, Syracuse 13244

Syracuse University: College of Law, Syracuse 13244

Talmudical Institute of Upstate New York, Rochester 14607

Tompkins-Cortland Community College, Dryden 13053-0139

Touro College, New York 10010

Touro College: Jacob D. Fuchsberg Law Center, Huntington 11743

Trocaire College, Buffalo 14220

Ulster County Community College, Stone Ridge 12484

Union College, Schenectady 12308

Union Theological Seminary: Theological Professions, New York 10027

United States Merchant Marine Academy, Kings Point 11024-1699

United States Military Academy, West Point 10996-5000

University of Rochester, Rochester 14627

University of Rochester: School of Medicine and Dentistry, Rochester 14642

Utica College, Utica 13502-4892

Utica School of Commerce, Utica 13501

Vassar College, Poughkeepsie 12604

Villa Maria College of Buffalo, Buffalo 14225

Wagner College, Staten Island 10301

Webb Institute, Glen Cove 11542

Wells College, Aurora 13026

Westchester Business Institute, White Plains 10606

Westchester Community College, Valhalla 10595

Yeshiva Karlin Stolin Beth Aron Y'Israel Rabbinical Institute, Brooklyn 11204

Yeshiva University, New York 10033

Yeshiva of Nitra Rabbinical College, Mt. Kisco 11211

Yeshivat Mikdash Melech, Brooklyn 11230

North Carolina

Alamance Community College, Graham 27253

Appalachian State University, Boone 28608

Asheville Buncombe Technical Community College, Asheville 28801

Barber-Scotia College, Concord 28025

Barton College, Wilson 27893

Beaufort County Community College, Washington 27889

Belmont Abbey College, Belmont 28012

Bennett College, Greensboro 27401-3239

Bladen Community College, Dublin 28332

Blue Ridge Community College, Flat Rock 28731

Brevard College, Brevard 28712

Brunswick Community College, Supply 28462

Caldwell Community College and Technical Institute, Hudson 28638

Campbell University, Buies Creek 27506

Campbell University: Norman Adrian Wiggins School of Law, Buies Creek 27506

Campbell University: School of Pharmacy, Buies Creek 27506

Cape Fear Community College, Wilmington 28401

Carteret Community College, Morehead City 28557-2989

Catawba College, Salisbury 28144-2488

Catawba Valley Community College, Hickory 28602

Central Carolina Community College, Sanford 27330

Central Piedmont Community College, Charlotte 28235

Chowan College, Murfreesboro 27855

Cleveland Community College, Shelby 28152

Coastal Carolina Community College, Jacksonville 28546

College of the Albemarle, Elizabeth City 27906-2327

Craven Community College, New Bern 28562

Davidson College, Davidson 28035-5000

Davidson County Community College, Lexington 27293-1287

Duke University, Durham 27708

Duke University: Divinity School, Durham 27708

Duke University: School of Law, Durham 27708

Duke University: School of Medicine, Durham 27710

Durham Technical Community College, Durham 27703

East Carolina University, Greenville 27858-4353

East Carolina University: School of Medicine, Greenville 27858

Edgecombe Community College, Tarboro 27886

Elizabeth City State University, Elizabeth City 27909

Elon University, Elon 27244-2010

Fayetteville State University, Fayetteville 28301

Fayetteville Technical Community College, Fayetteville 28303

Forsyth Technical Community College, Winston-Salem 27103

Gardner-Webb University, Boiling Springs 28017

Gaston College, Dallas 28034-1499

Greensboro College, Greensboro 27401-1875

Guilford College, Greensboro 27410

Guilford Technical Community College, Jamestown 27282

Halifax Community College, Weldon 27890

Haywood Community College, Clyde 28721

High Point University, High Point 27262-3598

Hood Theological Seminary, Salisbury 28144

Isothermal Community College, Spindale 28160

James Sprunt Community College, Kenansville 28349

John Wesley College, High Point 27265-3197

Johnson C. Smith University, Charlotte 28216-5398

Johnston Community College, Smithfield 27577

King's College, Charlotte 28204

Lees-McRae College, Banner Elk 28604

Lenoir Community College, Kinston 28502

Lenoir-Rhyne College, Hickory 28603

Livingstone College, Salisbury 28144

Louisburg College, Louisburg 27549

Mars Hill College, Mars Hill 28754

Martin Community College, Williamston 27892

Mayland Community College, Spruce Pine 28777

Meredith College, Raleigh 27607-5298

Methodist College, Fayetteville 28311

Miller-Motte Technical College, Wilmington 28403

Mitchell Community College, Statesville 28677

Montgomery Community College, Troy 27371

Montreat College, Montreat 28757-1267

Mount Olive College, Mount Olive 28365

Nash Community College, Rocky Mount 27804

North Carolina Agricultural and Technical State University, Greensboro 27411

North Carolina Central University, Durham 27707

North Carolina Central University: School of Law, Durham 27707

North Carolina School of the Arts, Winston-Salem 27127

North Carolina State University, Raleigh 27695-7103

North Carolina State University: College of Veterinary Medicine, Raleigh 27606

North Carolina Wesleyan College, Rocky Mount 27804

Pamlico Community College, Grantsboro 28529

Peace College, Raleigh 27604

Pfeiffer University, Misenheimer 28109

Piedmont Baptist College, Winston-Salem 27101

Piedmont Community College, Roxboro 27573-1197

Pitt Community College, Greenville 27835-7007

Queens University of Charlotte, Charlotte 28274

Randolph Community College, Asheboro 27204

Richmond Community College, Hamlet 28345

Roanoke Bible College, Elizabeth City 27909

Roanoke-Chowan Community College, Ahoskie 27910-9522

Robeson Community College, Lumberton 28359

Rockingham Community College, Wentworth 27375

Rowan-Cabarrus Community College, Salisbury 28145

St. Andrews Presbyterian College, Laurinburg 28352

St. Augustine's College, Raleigh 27610-2298

Salem College, Winston-Salem 27108

Sampson Community College, Clinton 28329

Sandhills Community College, Pinehurst 28374

Shaw University, Raleigh 27601

South College, Asheville 28806

South Piedmont Community College, Polkton 28135

Southeastern Baptist Theological Seminary, Wake Forest 27588

Southeastern Baptist Theological Seminary: Theological Professions, Wake Forest 27588

Southeastern Community College, Whiteville 28472

Southwestern Community College, Sylva 28779

Stanly Community College, Albemarle 28001

Surry Community College, Dobson 27017

Tri-County Community College, Murphy 28906

University of North Carolina at Asheville, Asheville 28804-8510

University of North Carolina at Chapel Hill, Chapel Hill 27599

University of North Carolina at Chapel Hill: School of Dentistry, Chapel Hill 27599

University of North Carolina at Chapel Hill: School of Law, Chapel Hill 27599

University of North Carolina at Chapel Hill: School of Medicine, Chapel Hill 27599

University of North Carolina at Chapel Hill: School of Pharmacy, Chapel Hill 27599

University of North Carolina at Charlotte, Charlotte 28223

University of North Carolina at Greensboro, Greensboro 27402-6170

University of North Carolina at Pembroke, Pembroke 28372

University of North Carolina at Wilmington, Wilmington 28403-3297

Vance-Granville Community College, Henderson 27536

Wake Forest University, Winston-Salem 27109

Wake Forest University: Bowman Gray School of Medicine, Winston-Salem 27157

Wake Forest University: School of Law, Winston-Salem 27109

Wake Technical Community College, Raleigh 27603

Warren Wilson College, Asheville 28815-9000

Wayne Community College, Goldsboro 27533-8002

Western Carolina University, Cullowhee 28723

Western Piedmont Community College, Morganton 28655-4511

Wilkes Community College, Wilkesboro 28697

Wilson Technical Community College, Wilson 27893

Wingate University, Wingate 28174

Winston-Salem State University, Winston-Salem 27110

North Dakota

Aaker's Business College, Fargo 58103

Bismarck State College, Bismarck 58506-5587

Dickinson State University, Dickinson 58601-4896

Jamestown College, Jamestown 58405

Lake Region State College, Devils Lake 58301

Mayville State University, Mayville 58257

Medcenter One College of Nursing, Bismarck 58501

Minot State University, Minot 58707-5002

Minot State University: Bottineau Campus, Bottineau 58318

North Dakota State College of Science, Wahpeton 58076

North Dakota State University, Fargo 58105

North Dakota State University: College of Pharmacy, Fargo 58105

Trinity Bible College, Ellendale 58436

University of Mary, Bismarck 58504

University of North Dakota, Grand Forks 58202

University of North Dakota: School of Law, Grand Forks 58202

University of North Dakota: School of Medicine, Grand Forks 58202

Valley City State University, Valley City 58072

Williston State College, Williston 58802-1326

Ohio

AEC Southern Ohio College: Findlay, Findlay 45840
Academy of Court Reporting, Cleveland 44115
Academy of Court Reporting: Akron, Akron 44333
Academy of Court Reporting: Columbus, Columbus 43215
Antioch College, Yellow Springs 45387
Antioch University McGregor, Yellow Springs 45387
Antonelli College, Cincinnati 45202
Art Academy of Cincinnati, Cincinnati 45202
Art Institute of Cincinnati, Cincinnati 45246
Ashland Theological Seminary, Ashland 44805
Ashland University, Ashland 44805
Athenaeum of Ohio, Cincinnati 45230
Baldwin-Wallace College, Berea 44017
Bluffton College, Bluffton 45817-1196
Bohecker's Business College, Ravenna 44266
Bowling Green State University, Bowling Green 43403
Bowling Green State University: Firelands College, Huron 44839
Bradford School, Columbus 43219
Bryant & Stratton College, Cleveland 44114
Bryant & Stratton College: Cleveland West, Parma 44130-1013
Bryant & Stratton College: Willoughby Hills, Willoughby Hills 44092
Capital University: School of Law, Columbus 43215
Case Western Reserve University, Cleveland 44106
Case Western Reserve University: School of Dentistry, Cleveland 44106
Case Western Reserve University: School of Law 44106
Case Western Reserve University: School of Medicine, Cleveland 44106
Cedarville University, Cedarville 45314
Central Ohio Technical College, Newark 43055
Central State University, Wilberforce 45384-1004
Chatfield College, St. Martin 45118
Cincinnati Bible College and Seminary, Cincinnati 45204
Cincinnati College of Mortuary Science, Cincinnati 45224-1428
Cincinnati State Technical and Community College, Cincinnati 45223-2690
Circleville Bible College, Circleville 43113
Clark State Community College, Springfield 45501
Cleveland Institute of Art, Cleveland 44106
Cleveland Institute of Electronics, Cleveland 44114
Cleveland Institute of Music, Cleveland 44106
Cleveland State University, Cleveland 44115
Cleveland State University: College of Law, Cleveland 44115
College of Art Advertising, Cincinnati 45211-4427
College of Mount St. Joseph, Cincinnati 45233
College of Wooster, Wooster 44691
Columbus College of Art and Design, Columbus 43215
Columbus State Community College, Columbus 43215
Cuyahoga Community College: Eastern Campus, Highland Hills 44122
Cuyahoga Community College: Metropolitan Campus, Cleveland 44115
Cuyahoga Community College: Western Campus, Parma 44130
David N. Myers College, Cleveland 44115
Davis College, Toledo 43623
DeVry University: Columbus, Columbus 43209
Defiance College, Defiance 43512
Denison University, Granville 43023
ETI Technical College of Niles, Niles 44446-4398
Edison State Community College, Piqua 45356
Franciscan University of Steubenville, Steubenville 43952-1763
Franklin University, Columbus 43215-5399
Gallipolis Career College, Gallipolis 45631
God's Bible School and College, Cincinnati 45210
Hebrew Union College-Jewish Institute of Religion, Cincinnati 45220
Heidelberg College, Tiffin 44883-2462
Hiram College, Hiram 44234
Hocking Technical College, Nelsonville 45764-9704
Hondros College, Westerville 43081
ITT Technical Institute: Dayton, Dayton 45414
ITT Technical Institute: Norwood, Norwood 45212
ITT Technical Institute: Strongsville, Strongsville 44136
ITT Technical Institute: Youngstown, Youngstown 44509
International College of Broadcasting, Dayton 45431
James A. Rhodes State College, Lima 45804-3597
Jefferson Community College, Steubenville 43952
John Carroll University, University Heights 44118
Kent State University, Kent 44242-0001
Kent State University: Ashtabula Regional Campus, Ashtabula 44004
Kent State University: East Liverpool Regional Campus, East Liverpool 43920

Kent State University: Salem Regional Campus, Salem 44460
Kent State University: Stark Campus, Canton 44720-7599
Kent State University: Trumbull Campus, Warren 44483
Kent State University: Tuscarawas Campus, New Philadelphia 44663
Kenyon College, Gambier 43022
Kettering College of Medical Arts, Kettering 45429
Lake Erie College, Painesville 44077
Lakeland Community College, Kirtland 44094
Laura and Alvin Siegal College of Judaic Studies, Beachwood 44122
Lorain County Community College, Elyria 44035
Lourdes College, Sylvania 435602898
Malone College, Canton 44709-3897
Marietta College, Marietta 45750
Marion Technical College, Marion 43302
Medical College of Ohio, Toledo 43699
Methodist Theological School in Ohio, Delaware 43015
Miami University: Hamilton Campus, Hamilton 45011
Miami University: Middletown Campus, Middletown 45042
Miami University: Oxford Campus, Oxford 45056
Miami-Jacobs College, Dayton 45401
Mount Union College, Alliance 44601
Mount Vernon Nazarene University, Mount Vernon 43050
Muskingum Area Technical College, Zanesville 43701
Muskingum College, New Concord 43762
North Central State College, Mansfield 44906
Northeastern Ohio Universities College of Medicine, Rootstown 44272
Northwest State Community College, Archbold 43502-9542
Notre Dame College, Cleveland 44121-4293
Oberlin College, Oberlin 44074
Ohio Business College, Lorain 44055
Ohio Business College: Sandusky, Sandusky 44870
Ohio College of Massotherapy, Akron 44321
Ohio College of Podiatric Medicine, Cleveland 44106
Ohio Dominican College, Columbus 43219
Ohio Institute of Photography and Technology, Dayton 45439
Ohio Northern University, Ada 45810
Ohio Northern University: College of Law, Ada 45810
Ohio Northern University: College of Pharmacy, Ada 45810
Ohio State University Agricultural Technical Institute, Wooster 44691
Ohio State University Columbus Campus: College of Dentistry, Columbus 43210
Ohio State University Columbus Campus: College of Medicine, Columbus 43210
Ohio State University Columbus Campus: College of Optometry, Columbus 43210
Ohio State University Columbus Campus: College of Pharmacy, Columbus 43210
Ohio State University Columbus Campus: College of Veterinary Medicine, Columbus 43210
Ohio State University: College of Law, Columbus 43210
Ohio State University: Columbus Campus, Columbus 43210
Ohio State University: Lima Campus, Lima 45804
Ohio State University: Mansfield Campus, Mansfield 44906
Ohio State University: Marion Campus, Marion 43302
Ohio State University: Newark Campus, Newark 43055
Ohio Technical College, Cleveland 44103-1269
Ohio University, Athens 45701
Ohio University: Chillicothe Campus, Chillicothe 45601
Ohio University: College of Osteopathic Medicine, Athens 45701
Ohio University: Eastern Campus, St. Clairsville 43950
Ohio University: Lancaster Campus, Lancaster 43130
Ohio University: Southern Campus at Ironton, Ironton 45638
Ohio University: Zanesville Campus, Zanesville 43701
Ohio Valley College of Technology, East Liverpool 43920
Ohio Wesleyan University, Delaware 43015
Otterbein College, Westerville 43081
Owens Community College: Findlay Campus, Findlay 45840-3600
Owens Community College: Toledo, Toledo 43699-1947
Pontifical College Josephinum, Columbus 43235
Pontifical College Josephinum, Columbus 43235
RETS Tech Center, Centerville 45459-2712
Rosedale Bible College, Irwin 43029
St. Mary Seminary, Wickliffe 44092
Shawnee State University, Portsmouth 45662

Sinclair Community College, Dayton 45402
Southeastern Business College, Chillicothe 45601-1038
Southeastern Business College: Jackson, Jackson 45640
Southeastern Business College: Lancaster, Lancaster 43130-1303
Southern State Community College, Hillsboro 45133
Southwestern College of Business, Dayton 45402
Southwestern College of Business: Vine Street Campus, Cincinnati 45202
Stark State College of Technology, Canton 44720
Stautzenberger College, Toledo 43614
Technology Education College, Columbus 43213
Tiffin University, Tiffin 44883
Trinity Lutheran Seminary, Columbus 43209
Trumbull Business College, Warren 44484
Union Institute & University, Cincinnati 45206
United Theological Seminary, Dayton 45406
University of Akron, Akron 44325
University of Akron: School of Law, Akron 44325
University of Cincinnati, Cincinnati 45221-0063
University of Cincinnati: Clermont College, Batavia 45103
University of Cincinnati: College of Law, Cincinnati 45221
University of Cincinnati: College of Medicine, Cincinnati 45267
University of Cincinnati: College of Pharmacy, Cincinnati 45267
University of Cincinnati: Raymond Walters College, Cincinnati 45236
University of Dayton, Dayton 45469
University of Dayton: School of Law, Dayton 45469
University of Findlay, Findlay 45840
University of Northwestern Ohio, Lima 45805
University of Rio Grande, Rio Grande 45674
University of Toledo, Toledo 43606
University of Toledo: College of Law, Toledo 43606
University of Toledo: College of Pharmacy, Toledo 43606
Urbana University, Urbana 43078
Ursuline College, Pepper Pike 44124-4398
Virginia Marti College of Art and Design, Lakewood 44107
Walsh University, North Canton 44720
Washington State Community College, Marietta 45750
Wilmington College, Wilmington 45177
Winebrenner Seminary, Findlay 45839
Wittenberg University, Springfield 45501
Wright State University, Dayton 45435
Wright State University: Lake Campus, Celina 45822
Wright State University: School of Medicine, Dayton 45401
Xavier University, Cincinnati 45207
Youngstown State University, Youngstown 44555

Oklahoma

Bacone College, Muskogee 74403
Cameron University, Lawton 73505
Carl Albert State College, Poteau 74953
East Central University, Ada 74820
Eastern Oklahoma State College, Wilburton 74578
Langston University, Langston 73050
Metropolitan College, Oklahoma City 73118
Metropolitan College, Tulsa 74146
Murray State College, Tishomingo 73460
Northeastern Oklahoma Agricultural and Mechanical College, Miami 74354-6497
Northeastern State University, Tahlequah 74464-2399
Northeastern State University: College of Optometry, Tahlequah 74464
Northern Oklahoma College, Tonkawa 74653
Northwestern Oklahoma State University, Alva 73717
Oklahoma Baptist University, Shawnee 74804
Oklahoma Christian University of Science and Arts, Oklahoma City 73136-1100
Oklahoma City Community College, Oklahoma City 73159
Oklahoma City University, Oklahoma City 73106
Oklahoma City University: School of Law, Oklahoma City 73146
Oklahoma Panhandle State University, Goodwell 73939-0430
Oklahoma State University, Stillwater 74078
Oklahoma State University: College of Osteopathic Medicine, Tulsa 74107
Oklahoma State University: College of Veterinary Medicine, Stillwater 74078
Oklahoma State University: Oklahoma City, Oklahoma City 73107
Oklahoma State University: Okmulgee, Okmulgee 74447
Oklahoma Wesleyan University, Bartlesville 74006
Oral Roberts University, Tulsa 74171

Oral Roberts University: School of Theology and
Missions, Tulsa 74171
Phillips Theological Seminary, Enid 73702
Platt College, Oklahoma City 73128
Platt College: Tulsa, Tulsa 74145
Redlands Community College, El Reno 73036
Rogers State University, Claremore 74017
Rose State College, Midwest City 73110
St. Gregory's University, Shawnee 74804
Seminole State College, Seminole 74818
Southeastern Oklahoma State University, Durant
74701-0609
Southern Nazarene University, Bethany 73008
Southwestern Christian University, Bethany 73008
Southwestern Oklahoma State University, Weatherford
73096-3098
Southwestern Oklahoma State University School of
Pharmacy, Weatherford 73096
Tulsa Community College, Tulsa 74135-6198
Tulsa Welding School, Tulsa 74104-3909
University of Central Oklahoma, Edmond 73034
University of Oklahoma, Norman 73019-0390
University of Oklahoma College of Pharmacy,
Oklahoma City 73190
University of Oklahoma Health Sciences Center:
College of Dentistry, Oklahoma City 73117
University of Oklahoma Health Sciences Center:
College of Medicine, Oklahoma City 73104
University of Oklahoma: College of Law, Norman
73019
University of Science and Arts of Oklahoma, Chickasha
73018
University of Tulsa, Tulsa 74104-3189
University of Tulsa: College of Law, Tulsa 74104
Vatterott College, Oklahoma City 73127
Western Oklahoma State College, Altus 73521

Oregon

Art Institute of Portland, Portland 97209
Blue Mountain Community College, Pendleton 97801
Central Oregon Community College, Bend 97701-5998
Chemeketa Community College, Salem 97309
Clackamas Community College, Oregon City 97045
Clatsop Community College, Astoria 97103
Concordia University, Portland 97211
Eastern Oregon University, LaGrande 97850
Eugene Bible College, Eugene 97405
George Fox University, Newberg 97132-2697
ITT Technical Institute: Portland, Portland 97218
Lane Community College, Eugene 97405
Lewis & Clark College, Portland 97219-7899
Lewis and Clark College: Northwestern School of Law,
Portland 97219
Linfield College, McMinnville 97218
Linn-Benton Community College, Albany 97321
Marylhurst University, Marylhurst 97036
Mount Angel Seminary, St. Benedict 97373
Mount Hood Community College, Gresham 97030
Multnomah Bible College, Portland 97220-5898
Multnomah Biblical Seminary, Portland 97220
Northwest Christian College, Eugene 97401-3745
Oregon Health Sciences University, Portland 97239
Oregon Health Sciences University: School of
Dentistry, Portland 97201
Oregon Health Sciences University: School of
Medicine, Portland 97201
Oregon Institute of Technology, Klamath Falls 97601
Oregon State University, Corvallis 97331
Oregon State University: College of Pharmacy,
Corvallis 97331
Oregon State University: College of Veterinary
Medicine, Corvallis 97331
Pacific Northwest College of Art, Portland 97209
Pacific University, Forest Grove 97116
Pacific University: School of Optometry, Forest Grove
97116
Pioneer Pacific College, Wilsonville 97070
Portland Community College, Portland 97280-0990
Portland State University, Portland 97207-0751
Reed College, Portland 97202-8199
Rogue Community College, Grants Pass 97527
Southern Oregon University, Ashland 97520
Southwestern Oregon Community College, Coos Bay
97420-2956
Treasure Valley Community College, Ontario 97914
Umpqua Community College, Roseburg 97470
University of Oregon, Eugene 97403-1217
University of Oregon: School of Law, Eugene 97403
University of Portland, Portland 97203-5798
Warner Pacific College, Portland 97215
Western Baptist College, Salem 97301-9392
Western Business College, Portland 97204
Western Conservative Baptist Seminary, Portland 97215
Western Evangelical Seminary, Tigard 97281
Western Oregon University, Monmouth 97361

Western States Chiropractic College, Portland 97230
Willamette University, Salem 97301-3922
Willamette University: College of Law, Salem 97301

Pennsylvania

Academy of Medical Arts and Business, Harrisburg
17112-1012
Academy of the New Church, Bryn Athyn 19009
Albright College, Reading 19612-5234
Allegheny College, Meadville 16335
Allentown Business School, Allentown 18103
Antonelli Institute of Art and Photography, Erdenheim
19038
Arcadia University, Glenside 19038-3295
Art Institute of Philadelphia, Philadelphia 19103
Art Institute of Pittsburgh, Pittsburgh 15219
Baptist Bible College and Seminary of Pennsylvania,
Clarks Summit 18411
Baptist Bible College of Pennsylvania, Clarks Summit
18411-1297
Biblical Theological Seminary, Hatfield 19440
Bloomsburg University of Pennsylvania, Bloomsburg
17815
Bradford School: Pittsburgh, Pittsburgh 15219
Bradley Academy for the Visual Arts, York 17402
Bryn Athyn College of the New Church, Bryn Athyn
19009-0717
Bryn Mawr College, Bryn Mawr 19010-2899
Bucknell University, Lewisburg 17837
Bucks County Community College, Newtown 18940
Butler County Community College, Butler 16003-1203
CHI Institute, Southampton 18966
Cabrini College, Radnor 19087-3698
California University of Pennsylvania, California 15419
Cambria County Area Community College, Johnstown
15907-0068
Cambria-Rowe Business College, Johnstown 15902
Cambria-Rowe Business College: Indiana, Indiana
15701
Career Training Academy, New Kensington 15068
Career Training Academy: Monroeville, Monroeville
15146
Carlow College, Pittsburgh 15213-3165
Carnegie Mellon University, Pittsburgh 15213
Cedar Crest College, Allentown 18104-6196
Central Pennsylvania College, Summerdale 17093
Chatham College, Pittsburgh 15232
Chestnut Hill College, Philadelphia 19118-2693
Cheyney University of Pennsylvania, Cheyney 19319
Churchman Business School, Easton 18042
Commonwealth Technical Institute, Johnstown
15905-3902
Community College of Allegheny County, Pittsburgh
15233
Community College of Beaver County, Monaca
15061-2588
Community College of Philadelphia, Philadelphia
19130
Consolidated School of Business: Lancaster, Lancaster
17603
Consolidated School of Business: York, York 17404
Curtis Institute of Music, Philadelphia 19103
DeSales University, Center Valley 18034-9568
DeVry University: Ft. Washington, Fort Washington
19034
Dean Institute of Technology, Pittsburgh 15226
Delaware County Community College, Media
19063-1094
Delaware Valley College, Doylestown 18901
Dickinson College, Carlisle 17013
Dickinson School of Law, Carlisle 17013
Douglas School of Business, Monessen 15062
Drexel University, Philadelphia 19104-2000
DuBois Business College, DuBois 15801
DuBois Business College: Oil City, Oil City 16301
Duquesne University, Pittsburgh 15282-0201
Duquesne University: School of Law, Pittsburgh 15282
East Stroudsburg University of Pennsylvania, East
Stroudsburg 18301-2999
Eastern Baptist Theological Seminary, Wynnewood
19096
Edinboro University of Pennsylvania, Edinboro 16444
Education Direct: Center for Degree Studies, Scranton
18515
Electronic Institutes: Middletown, Middletown 17057
Elizabethtown College, Elizabethtown 17022
Erie Business Center, Erie 16501
Evangelical School of Theology, Myerstown 17067
Franklin & Marshall College, Lancaster 17604-3003
Geneva College, Beaver Falls 15010
Gettysburg College, Gettysburg 17325
Gratz College, Melrose Park 19027
Grove City College, Grove City 16127
Gwynedd-Mercy College, Gwynedd Valley 19437-0901

Harrisburg Area Community College, Harrisburg 17110
Haverford College, Haverford 19041
Holy Family University, Philadelphia 19114-2094
ICM School of Business & Medical Careers, Pittsburgh
15222
ITT Technical Institute: Bensalem, Bensalem 19020
ITT Technical Institute: Mechanicsburg, Mechanicsburg
17055
ITT Technical Institute: Monroeville, Monroeville
15146
ITT Technical Institute: Pittsburgh, Pittsburgh 15220
Immaculata University, Immaculata 19345
Indiana University of Pennsylvania, Indiana 15705
Information Computer Systems Institute, Allentown
18103
Jefferson Medical College of Thomas Jefferson
University, Philadelphia 19107
Juniata College, Huntingdon 16652
Keystone College, La Plume 18440-1099
King's College, Wilkes-Barre 18711
Kutztown University of Pennsylvania, Kutztown
19530-0730
La Roche College, Pittsburgh 15237
La Salle University, Philadelphia 19141-1199
Lackawanna College, Scranton 18509
Lafayette College, Easton 18042
Lake Erie College of Osteopathic Medicine, Erie 16509
Lancaster Bible College, Lancaster 17608-3403
Lancaster Theological Seminary, Lancaster 17603
Lebanon Valley College of Pennsylvania, Annville
17003
Lehigh Carbon Community College, Schnecksville
18078
Lehigh University, Bethlehem 18015
Lincoln University, Lincoln University 19352
Lock Haven University of Pennsylvania, Lock Haven
17745
Lutheran Theological Seminary at Gettysburg,
Gettysburg 17325
Lutheran Theological Seminary at Philadelphia,
Philadelphia 19119
Luzerne County Community College, Nanticoke 18634
Lycoming College, Williamsport 17701
Manor College, Jenkintown 19046
Marywood University, Scranton 18509-1598
McCann School of Business: Pottsville, Pottsville
17901
McCann School of Business: Sunbury, Sunbury 17801
Median School of Allied Health Careers, Pittsburgh
15222
Medical College of Pennsylvania and Hahnemann
University School of Medicine, Philadelphia 19129
Mercyhurst College, Erie 16546
Messiah College, Grantham 17027
Metropolitan Career Center, Philadelphia 19144-3359
Millersville University of Pennsylvania, Millersville
17551-0302
Montgomery County Community College, Blue Bell
19422
Moravian College, Bethlehem 18018
Moravian Theological Seminary, Bethlehem 18018
Mount Aloysius College, Cresson 16630
Muhlenberg College, Allentown 18104
Neumann College, Aston 19014-1928
New Castle School of Trades, Pulaski 16143
Newport Business Institute, Lower Burrell 15068
Newport Business Institute, Williamsport 17701
Northampton County Area Community College,
Bethlehem 18020
Oakbridge Academy of Arts, Lower Burrell 15068
Orleans Technical Institute - Center City Campus,
Philadelphia 19103-4707
PJA School, Upper Darby 19082-1926
Peirce College, Philadelphia 19102
Penn Commercial, Inc., Washington 15301
Penn State Abington, Abington 19001
Penn State Altoona, Altoona 16601-3760
Penn State Beaver, Monaca 15061
Penn State Berks, Reading 19610-6009
Penn State Delaware County, Media 19063-5596
Penn State Dubois, DuBois 15801-3199
Penn State Erie, The Behrend College, Erie 16563
Penn State Fayette, Uniontown 15401
Penn State Harrisburg, Middletown 17057-4898
Penn State Hazleton, Hazleton 18202
Penn State Lehigh Valley, Fogelsville 18051-9999
Penn State McKeesport, McKeesport 15132-7698
Penn State Mont Alto, Mont Alto 17237
Penn State New Kensington, Upper Burrell 15068-1798
Penn State Schuylkill - Capital College, Schuylkill
Haven 17972-2208
Penn State Shenango, Sharon 16146-1597
Penn State University Park, University Park 16802
Penn State Wilkes-Barre, Lehman 18627-0217

Penn State Worthington Scranton, Dunmore 18512-1699
Penn State York, York 17403
Pennsylvania College of Optometry, Philadelphia 19141
Pennsylvania College of Podiatric Medicine, Philadelphia 19107
Pennsylvania College of Technology, Williamsport 17701
Pennsylvania Institute of Culinary Arts, Pittsburgh 15222
Pennsylvania Institute of Technology, Media 19063
Pennsylvania State University College of Medicine, Hershey 17033
Philadelphia Biblical University, Langhorne 19047
Philadelphia College of Osteopathic Medicine, Philadelphia 19131
Philadelphia College of Pharmacy and Science: School of Pharmacy, Philadelphia 19104
Philadelphia University, Philadelphia 19144
Pittsburgh Institute of Aeronautics, Pittsburgh 15236
Pittsburgh Technical Institute: Boyd School Division, Oakdale 15071-3205
Pittsburgh Theological Seminary, Pittsburgh 15206
Point Park College, Pittsburgh 15222
Reading Area Community College, Reading 19603
Reformed Presbyterian Theological Seminary, Pittsburgh 15208
Robert Morris University, Moon Township 15108
Rosedale Technical Institute, Pittsburgh 15217
Rosemont College, Rosemont 19010
St. Charles Borromeo Seminary - Overbrook, Wynnewood 19096
St. Charles Borromeo Seminary-Overbrook, Wynnewood 19096
St. Joseph's University, Philadelphia 19131
St. Vincent College, Latrobe 15650-2690
St. Vincent Seminary, Latrobe 15650
Schuylkill Institute of Business & Technology, Pottsville 17901
Seton Hill University, Greensburg 15601
Shippensburg University of Pennsylvania, Shippensburg 17257-2299
Slippery Rock University of Pennsylvania, Slippery Rock 16057-1383
South Hills School of Business & Technology, State College 16801-4516
South Hills School of Business and Technology, Altoona 16602
Swarthmore College, Swarthmore 19081
Talmudical Yeshiva of Philadelphia, Philadelphia 19131
Temple University, Philadelphia 19122-6096
Temple University: School of Dentistry, Philadelphia 19140
Temple University: School of Law, Philadelphia 19122
Temple University: School of Medicine, Philadelphia 19122
Temple University: School of Pharmacy, Philadelphia 19104
Thiel College, Greenville 16125
Trinity Episcopal School for Ministry, Ambridge 15003
University of Pennsylvania, Philadelphia 19104
University of Pennsylvania Law School, Philadelphia 19104
University of Pennsylvania: School of Dental Medicine, Philadelphia 19104
University of Pennsylvania: School of Medicine, Philadelphia 19104
University of Pennsylvania: School of Veterinary Medicine, Philadelphia 19104
University of Pittsburgh, Pittsburgh 15260
University of Pittsburgh at Bradford, Bradford 16701
University of Pittsburgh at Greensburg, Greensburg 15601
University of Pittsburgh at Johnstown, Johnstown 15904
University of Pittsburgh at Titusville, Titusville 16354
University of Pittsburgh: School of Dental Medicine, Pittsburgh 15261
University of Pittsburgh: School of Law, Pittsburgh 15260
University of Pittsburgh: School of Medicine, Pittsburgh 15261
University of Pittsburgh: School of Pharmacy, Pittsburgh 15261
University of Scranton, Scranton 18510
University of the Sciences in Philadelphia, Philadelphia 19104
Valley Forge Christian College, Phoenixville 19460
Villanova University, Villanova 19085
Villanova University: School of Law, Villanova 19085
Washington and Jefferson College, Washington 15301
Waynesburg College, Waynesburg 15370

West Chester University of Pennsylvania, West Chester 19383
Western School of Health and Business Careers, Pittsburgh 15219
Westminster Theological Seminary, Philadelphia 19118
Westmoreland County Community College, Youngwood 15697-1895
Widener University, Chester 19013
Widener University School of Law, Harrisburg 17106
Wilkes University, Wilkes-Barre 18766
Williamson Free School of Mechanical Trades, Media 19063
Wilson College, Chambersburg 17201
York College of Pennsylvania, York 17405

Puerto Rico
Atlantic College, Guaynabo 00970
Bayamon Central University, Bayamon 00960-1725
Columbia College, Caguas 00726
Conservatory of Music of Puerto Rico, San Juan 00918
Escuela de Artes Plasticas de Puerto Rico, San Juan 00902-1112
Evangelical Seminary of Puerto Rico, San Juan 00925
Huertas Junior College, Caguas 00726
Humacao Community College, Humacao 00792
ICPR Junior College, San Juan 00919-0304
Inter American University of Puerto Rico School of Optometry, San Juan 00919
Inter American University of Puerto Rico: Barranquitas Campus, Barranquitas 00794-0517
Inter American University of Puerto Rico: Bayamon Campus, Bayamon 00957
Inter American University of Puerto Rico: Fajardo Campus, Fajardo 00738
Inter American University of Puerto Rico: Guayama Campus, Guayama 00785
Inter American University of Puerto Rico: Metropolitan Campus, San Juan 00919-1293
Inter American University of Puerto Rico: San German Campus, San German 00683
Inter American University of Puerto Rico: School of Law, San Juan 00936
Ponce School of Medicine, Ponce 00732
Pontifical Catholic University of Puerto Rico, Ponce 00717-0777
Pontifical Catholic University of Puerto Rico: School of Law, Ponce 00731
Technological College of San Juan, San Juan 00918
Turabo University, Gurabo 00778
Universidad Central del Caribe: Medical School, Bayamon 00960
Universidad Metropolitana, Rio Piedras 00928
Universidad Politecnica de Puerto Rico, Hato Rey 00918
Universidad del Este, Carolina 00984
University of Puerto Rico Medical Sciences Campus: School of Dentistry, Rio Piedras 00936
University of Puerto Rico Medical Sciences Campus: School of Medicine, Rio Piedras 00936
University of Puerto Rico Medical Sciences Campus: School of Pharmacy, San Juan 00936
University of Puerto Rico Rio Piedras Campus: School of Law, Rio Piedras 00931
University of Puerto Rico at Humacao, Humacao 00791
University of Puerto Rico at Ponce, Ponce 00732
University of Puerto Rico at Utuado, Utuado 00641
University of Puerto Rico: Bayamon University College, Bayamon 00959
University of Puerto Rico: Carolina Regional College, Carolina 00984-4800
University of Puerto Rico: Cayey University College, Cayey 00736
University of Puerto Rico: Mayaguez Campus, Mayaguez 00681-9021
University of Puerto Rico: Medical Sciences Campus, San Juan 00936-5067
University of Puerto Rico: Rio Piedras Campus, San Juan 00931-3344
University of the Sacred Heart, Santurce 00914

Rhode Island
Brown University, Providence 02912
Brown University: School of Medicine, Providence 02912
Bryant College, Smithfield 02917-1284
Community College of Rhode Island, Warwick 02886
Providence College, Providence 02918-0001
Rhode Island College, Providence 02908
Rhode Island School of Design, Providence 02903
Roger Williams University, Bristol 02809
Salve Regina University, Newport 02840-4192
University of Rhode Island, Kingston 02881-2020

University of Rhode Island: College of Pharmacy, Kingston 02881
Zion Bible Institute, Barrington 02806

South Carolina
Aiken Technical College, Aiken 29802
Anderson College, Anderson 29621
Benedict College, Columbia 29204
Central Carolina Technical College, Sumter 29150
Charleston Southern University, Charleston 29423
The Citadel, Charleston 29409
Claflin University, Orangeburg 29115
Clemson University, Clemson 29634-5124
Coastal Carolina University, Conway 29528-6054
Coker College, Hartsville 29550
College of Charleston, Charleston 29424-0001
Columbia Biblical Seminary and Graduate School of Missions, Columbia 29230
Columbia College, Columbia 29203
Columbia International University, Columbia 29230-3122
Converse College, Spartanburg 29302
Denmark Technical College, Denmark 29042
Erskine College, Due West 29639
Erskine Theological Seminary, Due West 29639
Florence-Darlington Technical College, Florence 29501-0548
Forrest Junior College, Anderson 29624
Francis Marion University, Florence 29501-0547
Furman University, Greenville 29613
Horry-Georgetown Technical College, Conway 29526-1966
ITT Technical Institute: Greenville, Greenville 29615
Lander University, Greenwood 29649-2099
Limestone College, Gaffney 29340-3799
Lutheran Theological Southern Seminary, Columbia 29203
Medical University of South Carolina, Charleston 29425
Medical University of South Carolina, Charleston 29425
Medical University of South Carolina: College of Dental Medicine, Charleston 29425
Medical University of South Carolina: College of Pharmacy, Charleston 29425
Midlands Technical College, Columbia 29202
Morris College, Sumter 29150-3599
Newberry College, Newberry 29108
North Greenville College, Tigerville 29688
Northeastern Technical College, Cheraw 29520
Orangeburg-Calhoun Technical College, Orangeburg 29118
Piedmont Technical College, Greenwood 29648
Presbyterian College, Clinton 29325
Sherman College of Straight Chiropractic, Spartanburg 29304
South Carolina State University, Orangeburg 29117
Southern Wesleyan University, Central 29630
Spartanburg Methodist College, Spartanburg 29301
Spartanburg Technical College, Spartanburg 29305
Technical College of the Lowcountry, Beaufort 29901-1288
Tri-County Technical College, Pendleton 29670
Trident Technical College, Charleston 29423
University of South Carolina, Columbia 29208
University of South Carolina at Aiken, Aiken 29801
University of South Carolina at Lancaster, Lancaster 29721
University of South Carolina at Spartanburg, Spartanburg 29303
University of South Carolina at Sumter, Sumter 29150
University of South Carolina at Union, Union 29379
University of South Carolina: Salkehatchie Regional Campus, Allendale 29810
University of South Carolina: School of Law, Columbia 29208
University of South Carolina: School of Medicine, Columbia 29208
University of South Carolina: School of Pharmacy, Columbia 29208
Voorhees College, Denmark 29042-0678
Williamsburg Technical College, Kingstree 29556
Winthrop University, Rock Hill 29733
Wofford College, Spartanburg 29303-3663
York Technical College, Rock Hill 29730

South Dakota
Augustana College, Sioux Falls 57197
Black Hills State University, Spearfish 57799
Dakota State University, Madison 57042
Dakota Wesleyan University, Mitchell 57301
Kilian Community College, Sioux Falls 57104
Mitchell Technical Institute, Mitchell 57301
Mount Marty College, Yankton 57078

North American Baptist Seminary, Sioux Falls 57105
Northern State University, Aberdeen 57401-7198
Sinte Gleska University, Rosebud 57570
South Dakota School of Mines and Technology, Rapid
  City 57701
South Dakota State University, Brookings 57007
South Dakota State University: College of Pharmacy,
  Brookings 57007
Southeast Technical Institute, Sioux Falls 57107
University of Sioux Falls, Sioux Falls 57105
University of South Dakota, Vermillion 57069
University of South Dakota: School of Law, Vermillion
  57069
University of South Dakota: School of Medicine,
  Vermillion 57069
Western Dakota Technical Institute, Rapid City 57703

Tennessee

American Baptist College of ABT Seminary, Nashville
  37207
Aquinas College, Nashville 37205
Austin Peay State University, Clarksville 37040
Belmont University, Nashville 37212-3757
Bethel College, McKenzie 38201
Bryan College, Dayton 37321
Carson-Newman College, Jefferson City 37760
Chattanooga State Technical Community College,
  Chattanooga 37406
Christian Brothers University, Memphis 38104
Church of God School of Theology, Cleveland 37320
Cleveland State Community College, Cleveland 37320
Columbia State Community College, Columbia 38402
Crichton College, Memphis 38111-1375
Draughons Junior College of Business: Nashville,
  Nashville 37217
Draughons Junior College: Clarksville, Clarksville
  37040
Dyersburg State Community College, Dyersburg 38024
East Tennessee State University, Johnson City
  37614-0000
East Tennessee State University: James H. Quillen
  College of Medicine, Johnson City 37614
Emmanuel School of Religion, Johnson City 37601
Fisk University, Nashville 37208-3051
Freed-Hardeman University, Henderson 38340
Harding University Graduate School of Religion,
  Memphis 38117
ITT Technical Institute: Knoxville, Knoxville 37932
ITT Technical Institute: Memphis, Memphis 38119
ITT Technical Institute: Nashville, Nashville 37214
Jackson State Community College, Jackson 38301
John A. Gupton College, Nashville 37203
Johnson Bible College, Knoxville 37998
King College, Bristol 37620
Lambuth University, Jackson 38301
Lane College, Jackson 38301
Lee University, Cleveland 37320
Maryville College, Maryville 37804-5907
Meharry Medical College: School of Dentistry,
  Nashville 37208
Meharry Medical College: School of Medicine,
  Nashville 37208
Memphis College of Art, Memphis 38104
Memphis Theological Seminary, Memphis 38104
Mid-America Baptist Theological Seminary,
  Germantown 38138
Middle Tennessee State University, Murfreesboro 37132
Miller-Motte Technical College, Clarksville 37040
Milligan College, Milligan College 37682
Nashville Auto-Diesel College, Nashville 37206
National College of Business & Technology: Tennessee,
  Roanoke 24017
Northeast State Technical Community College,
  Blountville 37617
Nossi College of Art, Goodlettsville 37072
O'More College of Design, Franklin 37064
Pellissippi State Technical Community College,
  Knoxville 37933-0990
Remington College: Southeast College of Technology,
  Memphis 38132
Rhodes College, Memphis 38112
Roane State Community College, Harriman 37748
South College, Knoxville 37917
Southern Adventist University, Collegedale 37315-0370
Southern College of Optometry, Memphis 38104
Southwest Tennessee Community College, Memphis
  38101-0780
Temple Baptist Seminary: Theological Professions,
  Chattanooga 37404
Tennessee State University, Nashville 37209-1561
Tennessee Technological University, Cookeville 38505
Tennessee Wesleyan College, Athens 37371-0040
Trevecca Nazarene University, Nashville 37210
Tusculum College, Greeneville 37743-9997

Union University, Jackson 38305
University of Memphis, Memphis 38152
University of Memphis: School of Law, Memphis
  38152
University of Tennessee College of Law, Knoxville
  37996
University of Tennessee Health Science Center,
  Memphis 38163
University of Tennessee Knoxville: College of
  Veterinary Medicine, Knoxville 37901
University of Tennessee Memphis: College of Dentistry,
  Memphis 38163
University of Tennessee Memphis: College of Medicine,
  Memphis 38163
University of Tennessee Memphis: College of
  Pharmacy, Memphis 38163
University of Tennessee: Chattanooga, Chattanooga
  37403
University of Tennessee: Knoxville, Knoxville 37996
University of Tennessee: Martin, Martin 38238
University of the South: School of Theology, Sewanee
  37383
Vanderbilt University, Nashville 37240
Vanderbilt University: School of Law, Nashville 37240
Vanderbilt University: School of Medicine, Nashville
  37232
Vanderbilt University: The Divinity School, Nashville
  37240
Volunteer State Community College, Gallatin 37066
Walters State Community College, Morristown
  37813-6899

Texas

ATI-Career Training Center, Dallas 75220
Abilene Christian University, Abilene 79699
Abilene Christian University: College of Biblical and
  Family Studies, Abilene 79699
Alvin Community College, Alvin 77511
Amarillo College, Amarillo 79178
Amberton University, Garland 75041
Angelina College, Lufkin 75902
Angelo State University, San Angelo 76909
Arlington Baptist College, Arlington 76012
Austin Business College, Austin 78741
Austin College, Sherman 75090-4400
Austin Community College, Austin 78752-4390
Austin Graduate School of Theology, Austin 78705
Austin Presbyterian Theological Seminary, Austin
  78705
Baptist Missionary Association Theological Seminary,
  Jacksonville 75766
Baylor College of Medicine, Houston 77030
Baylor University, Waco 76798
Baylor University: School of Law, Waco 76798
Blinn College, Brenham 77833
Border Institute of Technology, El Paso 79925
Brazosport College, Lake Jackson 77566
Brookhaven College, Farmers Branch 75244
Cedar Valley College, Lancaster 75134
Central Texas College, Killeen 76540
Cisco Junior College, Cisco 76437
Clarendon College, Clarendon 79226
Coastal Bend College, Beeville 78102
College of Saint Thomas More, Fort Worth 76109
College of the Mainland, Texas City 77591
Collin County Community College District, Plano
  75093
Commonwealth Institute of Funeral Service, Houston
  77090-5913
Concordia University at Austin, Austin 78705
Dallas Baptist University, Dallas 75211-9299
Dallas Christian College, Dallas 75234
Dallas Institute of Funeral Service, Dallas 75227
DeVry University: Irving, Dallas 75063-2439
Del Mar College, Corpus Christi 78404
East Texas Baptist University, Marshall 75670
Eastfield College, Mesquite 75150
El Centro College, Dallas 75202
El Paso Community College, El Paso 79998
Episcopal Theological Seminary of the Southwest,
  Austin 78768
Frank Phillips College, Borger 79008-5118
Galveston College, Galveston 77550
Grayson County College, Denison 75020
Hallmark Institute of Aeronautics, San Antonio 78216
Hallmark Institute of Technology, San Antonio 78230
Hardin-Simmons University, Abilene 79601
Hill College, Hillsboro 76645
Houston Baptist University, Houston 77074-3298
Houston Community College System, Houston
  77266-7517
Houston Graduate School of Theology, Houston 77004
Howard College, Big Spring 79720
Howard Payne University, Brownwood 76801

Huston-Tillotson College, Austin 78702
ITT Technical Institute: Arlington, Arlington 76017
ITT Technical Institute: Austin, Austin 78723
ITT Technical Institute: Houston, Houston 77063
ITT Technical Institute: Houston North, Houston
  77090-5818
ITT Technical Institute: Houston South, Houston 77058
ITT Technical Institute: San Antonio, San Antonio
  78249
Jacksonville College, Jacksonville 75766
Jarvis Christian College, Hawkins 75765-1470
Kilgore College, Kilgore 75662
Lamar State College at Orange, Orange 77630
Lamar State College at Port Arthur, Port Arthur
  77641-0310
Lamar University, Beaumont 77710
Laredo Community College, Laredo 78040
LeTourneau University, Longview 75607
Lee College, Baytown 77522
Lon Morris College, Jacksonville 75766
Lubbock Christian University, Lubbock 79407
MTI College of Business and Technology, Houston
  77036
MTI College of Business and Technology, Houston
  77058
McLennan Community College, Waco 76708
McMurry University, Abilene 79697
Midland College, Midland 79705
Midwestern State University, Wichita Falls 76308
Mountain View College, Dallas 75211
North Central Texas College, Gainesville 76240
North Harris Montgomery Community College District,
  Houston 77060-2000
North Lake College, Irving 75038
Northeast Texas Community College, Mount Pleasant
  75456-1307
Northwood University: Texas Campus, Cedar Hill
  75104
Oblate School of Theology, San Antonio 78216
Odessa College, Odessa 79764
Our Lady of the Lake University of San Antonio, San
  Antonio 78207-4689
Palo Alto College, San Antonio 78224
Panola College, Carthage 75633
Paris Junior College, Paris 75460
Parker College of Chiropractic, Dallas 75229
Paul Quinn College, Dallas 75241
Prairie View A&M University, Prairie View 77446
Ranger College, Ranger 76470
Remington College: Dallas, Garland 75041
Remington College: Houston, Houston 77082
Rice University, Houston 77251-1892
Richland College, Dallas 75243-2199
St. Edward's University, Austin 78704
St. Mary's University, San Antonio 78228
St. Mary's University: School of Law, San Antonio
  78228
St. Philip's College, San Antonio 78203
Sam Houston State University, Huntsville 77341
San Antonio College, San Antonio 78212
San Jacinto College: Central Campus, Pasadena 77505
Schreiner University, Kerrville 78028-5697
South Plains College, Levelland 79336
South Texas College of Law, Houston 77002
South Texas Community College, McAllen 78502
Southern Methodist University, Dallas 75275-0221
Southern Methodist University: Perkins School of
  Theology, Dallas 75275
Southern Methodist University: School of Law, Dallas
  75275
Southwest Texas Junior College, Uvalde 78801
Southwest Texas State University, San Marcos 78666
Southwestern Adventist University, Keene 76059
Southwestern Assemblies of God University,
  Waxahachie 75165
Southwestern Baptist Theological Seminary:
  Theological Professions, Fort Worth 76122
Southwestern University, Georgetown 78626
Stephen F. Austin State University, Nacogdoches 75962
Sul Ross State University, Alpine 79832
Tarleton State University, Stephenville 76402
Tarrant County College, Fort Worth 76102
Temple College, Temple 76504
Texarkana College, Texarkana 75599
Texas A&M International University, Laredo
  78041-1900
Texas A&M University, College Station 77843
Texas A&M University-Commerce, Commerce 75429
Texas A&M University-Corpus Christi, Corpus Christi
  78412-5503
Texas A&M University-Galveston, Galveston 77553
Texas A&M University-Kingsville, Kingsville 78363
Texas A&M University-Texarkana, Texarkana 75505
Texas A&M University: Baylor College of Dentistry,
  Dallas 75266

Texas A&M University: Baylor College of Dentistry, Dallas 75246
Texas A&M University: College of Veterinary Medicine, College Station 77843
Texas A&M University: Health Science Center College of Medicine, College Station 77843
Texas Chiropractic College, Pasadena 77505
Texas Christian University, Fort Worth 76129
Texas Christian University: Brite Divinity School, Fort Worth 76129
Texas College, Tyler 75712-4500
Texas Lutheran University, Seguin 78155-5999
Texas Southern University, Houston 77004
Texas Southern University: College of Pharmacy and Health Sciences, Houston 77004
Texas Southern University: Thurgood Marshall School of Law, Houston 77004
Texas State Technical College: Waco, Waco 76705
Texas State Technical College: West Texas, Sweetwater 79556
Texas Tech University, Lubbock 79409-5005
Texas Tech University Health Sciences Center: School of Medicine, Lubbock 79430
Texas Tech University: School of Law, Lubbock 79409
Texas Wesleyan University, Fort Worth 76105-1536
Texas Woman's University, Denton 76204-5587
Trinity University, San Antonio 78212
Trinity Valley Community College, Athens 75751
Tyler Junior College, Tyler 75711
University of Dallas, Irving 75062-4736
University of Houston, Houston 77204
University of Houston: Clear Lake, Houston 77058-1080
University of Houston: College of Optometry, Houston 77204
University of Houston: College of Pharmacy, Houston 77204
University of Houston: Downtown, Houston 77002
University of Houston: Law Center, Houston 77204
University of Houston: Victoria, Victoria 77901
University of Mary Hardin-Baylor, Belton 76513
University of North Texas, Denton 76203-1070
University of North Texas Health Science Center at Fort Worth: Osteopathic Medicine, Fort Worth 76107
University of St. Thomas, Houston 77006-4696
University of St. Thomas: School of Theology, Houston 77024
University of Texas Health Science Center at San Antonio, San Antonio 78229
University of Texas Health Science Center: Dental School, San Antonio 78284
University of Texas Health Science Center: Medical School, San Antonio 78284
University of Texas Health Sciences Center-Dental Branch, Houston 77030
University of Texas Medical Branch at Galveston, Galveston 77555
University of Texas Medical Branch at Galveston: School of Medicine, Galveston 77555
University of Texas Southwestern Medical Center at Dallas, Dallas 75390
University of Texas Southwestern Medical Center at Dallas Southwestern Medical School, Dallas 75235
University of Texas at Arlington, Arlington 76019
University of Texas at Austin, Austin 78712-1111
University of Texas at Austin: College of Pharmacy, Austin 78712
University of Texas at Austin: School of Law, Austin 78714
University of Texas at Brownsville, Brownsville 78520
University of Texas at Dallas, Richardson 75083
University of Texas at El Paso, El Paso 79968
University of Texas at San Antonio, San Antonio 78249
University of Texas at Tyler, Tyler 75799
University of Texas of the Permian Basin, Odessa 79762-0001
University of Texas-Houston Health Science Center, Houston 77225
University of Texas-Houston Health Science Center, Houston 77225
University of Texas: Pan American, Edinburg 78541
University of the Incarnate Word, San Antonio 78209-6397
Victoria College, Victoria 77901
Wayland Baptist University, Plainview 79072
West Texas A&M University, Canyon 79016-0001
Western Technical Institute, El Paso 79901
Western Texas College, Snyder 79549
Wharton County Junior College, Wharton 77488
Wiley College, Marshall 75670

Utah
Brigham Young University, Provo 84602

Brigham Young University: School of Law, Provo 84602
College of Eastern Utah, Price 84501
Dixie State College of Utah, St. George 84770-3876
ITT Technical Institute: Murray, Murray 84123
LDS Business College, Salt Lake City 84111-1392
Salt Lake Community College, Salt Lake City 84130
Snow College, Ephraim 84627
Southern Utah University, Cedar City 84720
University of Utah, Salt Lake City 84112
University of Utah: College of Law, Salt Lake City 84112
University of Utah: College of Pharmacy, Salt Lake City 84112
University of Utah: School of Medicine, Salt Lake City 84132
Utah Career College, West Jordan 84088
Utah State University, Logan 84322
Utah Valley State College, Orem 84058-5999
Weber State University, Ogden 84408-1103
Westminster College, Salt Lake City 84105

Vermont
Bennington College, Bennington 05201
Burlington College, Burlington 05401
Castleton State College, Castleton 05735
Champlain College, Burlington 05402-9847
College of St. Joseph in Vermont, Rutland 05701-3899
Community College of Vermont, Waterbury 05676
Goddard College, Plainfield 05667
Green Mountain College, Poultney 05764
Johnson State College, Johnson 05656
Landmark College, Putney 05346
Lyndon State College, Lyndonville 05851
Marlboro College, Marlboro 05344-0300
Middlebury College, Middlebury 05753
New England Culinary Institute, Montpelier 05602
New England Culinary Institute: Essex Junction, Essex Junction 05452
Norwich University, Northfield 05663
St. Michael's College, Colchester 05439
Southern Vermont College, Bennington 05201
Sterling College, Craftsbury Common 05827
University of Vermont, Burlington 05405-0160
University of Vermont: College of Medicine, Burlington 05405
Vermont Law School, South Royalton 05068
Vermont Technical College, Randolph Center 05061-0500
Woodbury College, Montpelier 05602

Virginia
Art Institute of Washington, Arlington 22209-1802
Averett University, Danville 24541
Blue Ridge Community College, Weyers Cave 24486
Bluefield College, Bluefield 24605
Bridgewater College, Bridgewater 22812
Bryant & Stratton College, Virginia Beach 23462-4417
Christendom College, Front Royal 22630
College of Health Sciences, Roanoke 24031-3186
College of William and Mary, Williamsburg 23187-8795
College of William and Mary: School of Law, Williamsburg 23187
Danville Community College, Danville 24541
DeVry University: Crystal City, Arlington 22202
ECPI College of Technology, Virginia Beach 23462
ECPI Technical College: Glen Allen, Glen Allen 23060
ECPI Technical College: Roanoke, Roanoke 24012
Eastern Mennonite Seminary, Harrisonburg 22801
Eastern Mennonite University, Harrisonburg 22802-2462
Eastern Shore Community College, Melfa 23410
Eastern Virginia Medical School of the Medical College of Hampton Roads: Medical Professions, Norfolk 23501
Emory & Henry College, Emory 24327
Ferrum College, Ferrum 24088
George Mason University, Fairfax 22030
George Mason University: School of Law, Arlington 22201
Hampden-Sydney College, Hampden-Sydney 23943
Hampton University, Hampton 23668
Hollins University, Roanoke 24020
ITT Technical Institute: Norfolk, Norfolk 23502
ITT Technical Institute: Richmond, Richmond 23235
J. Sargeant Reynolds Community College, Richmond 23285-5622
James Madison University, Harrisonburg 22807
Johnson & Wales University: Norfolk, Norfolk 23513
Liberty Baptist Theological Seminary, Lynchburg 24502
Liberty University, Lynchburg 24502-2269
Longwood University, Farmville 23909
Lynchburg College, Lynchburg 24501
Mary Baldwin College, Staunton 24401

Mary Washington College, Fredericksburg 22401
Marymount University, Arlington 22207
Mountain Empire Community College, Big Stone Gap 24219
National College of Business & Technology: Bluefield, Roanoke 24017
National College of Business & Technology: Charlottesville, Roanoke 24017
National College of Business & Technology: Danville, Roanoke 24017
National College of Business & Technology: Harrisonburg, Roanoke 24017
National College of Business & Technology: Lynchburg, Roanoke 24017
National College of Business & Technology: Martinsville, Roanoke 24017
National College of Business & Technology: Roanoke, Roanoke 24017
Norfolk State University, Norfolk 23504
Old Dominion University, Norfolk 23529
Paul D. Camp Community College, Franklin 23851
Piedmont Virginia Community College, Charlottesville 22902-7589
Protestant Episcopal Theological Seminary in Virginia, Alexandria 22304
Radford University, Radford 24142
Randolph-Macon College, Ashland 23005
Randolph-Macon Woman's College, Lynchburg 24503-1526
Rappahannock Community College, Glenns 23149
Regent University: School of Divinity, Virginia Beach 23464
Regent University: School of Law, Virginia Beach 23464
Richard Bland College, Petersburg 23805
Roanoke College, Salem 24153-3794
Shenandoah University, Winchester 22601
Southside Virginia Community College, Alberta 23821
Southwest Virginia Community College, Richlands 24641
Sweet Briar College, Sweet Briar 24595
Thomas Nelson Community College, Hampton 23670
Tidewater Tech, Virginia Beach 23452
Union Theological Seminary in Virginia, Richmond 23227
University of Richmond, University of Richmond 23173
University of Richmond: The T.C. Williams School of Law, University of Richmond 23173
University of Virginia, Charlottesville
University of Virginia's College at Wise, Wise 24293
University of Virginia: School of Law, Charlottesville 22903
University of Virginia: School of Medicine, Charlottesville 22908
Virginia Commonwealth University, Richmond 23284-2527
Virginia Commonwealth University: School of Dentistry, Richmond 23298
Virginia Commonwealth University: School of Medicine, Richmond 23298
Virginia Highlands Community College, Abingdon 24210
Virginia Intermont College, Bristol 24201
Virginia Military Institute, Lexington 24450-0304
Virginia Polytechnic Institute and State University, Blacksburg 24061-0433
Virginia Polytechnic Institute: Virginia-Maryland Regional College of Veterinary Medicine, Blacksburg 24061
Virginia State University, Petersburg 23806
Virginia Union University, Richmond 23220
Virginia Union University: School of Theology, Richmond 23220
Virginia Wesleyan College, Norfolk 23502-5599
Virginia Western Community College, Roanoke 24038
Washington and Lee University, Lexington 24450-0303
Washington and Lee University: School of Law, Lexington 24450

Washington
Art Institute of Seattle, Seattle 98121
Bastyr University, Kenmore 98028
Bellevue Community College, Bellevue 98007
Central Washington University, Ellensburg 98926-7501
Centralia College, Centralia 98531
Clark College, Vancouver 98663-3598
Clover Park Technical College, Lakewood 98499-4098
Cornish College of the Arts, Seattle 98121
Crown College, Tacoma 98444-1836
DeVry University: Seattle, Federal Way 98001-2995
Eastern Washington University, Cheney 99004
Edmonds Community College, Lynnwood 98036-5999

Everett Community College, Everett 98201-1352
Evergreen State College, Olympia 98505
Gonzaga University, Spokane 99258-0001
Gonzaga University: Department of Religious Studies, Spokane 99258
Gonzaga University: School of Law, Spokane 99220
Grays Harbor College, Aberdeen 98520
Green River Community College, Auburn 98092
Henry Cogswell College, Everett 98201
Heritage College, Toppenish 98948
ITT Technical Institute: Bothell, Bothell 98021
ITT Technical Institute: Seattle, Seattle 98168
ITT Technical Institute: Spokane, Spokane 99212
Lake Washington Technical College, Kirkland 98034
Lower Columbia College, Longview 98632-0310
North Seattle Community College, Seattle 98103
Northwest Aviation College, Auburn 98002
Northwest College, Kirkland 98083
Olympic College, Bremerton 98337-1699
Pacific Lutheran University, Tacoma 98447-0003
Peninsula College, Port Angeles 98362
Renton Technical College, Renton 98056-4195
St. Martin's College, Lacey 98503
Seattle Central Community College, Seattle 98122
Seattle Pacific University, Seattle 98119-1997
Seattle University, Seattle 98122-4340
Seattle University: School of Law, Tacoma 98402
Seattle University: School of Theology and Ministry, Seattle 98122
South Seattle Community College, Seattle 98106-1499
Spokane Community College, Spokane 99217-5399
Spokane Falls Community College, Spokane 99224
Trinity Lutheran College, Issaquah 98029
University of Puget Sound, Tacoma 98416-1062
University of Washington, Seattle 98195
University of Washington: School of Dentistry, Seattle 98195
University of Washington: School of Law, Seattle 98105
University of Washington: School of Medicine, Seattle 98195
Walla Walla College, College Place 99324
Walla Walla Community College, Walla Walla 99362-9270
Washington State University, Pullman 99164
Washington State University: College of Pharmacy, Pullman 99164
Washington State University: School of Veterinary Medicine, Pullman 99164
Wenatchee Valley College, Wenatchee 98801-1799
Western Washington University, Bellingham 98225-9009
Whitman College, Walla Walla 99362-2083
Whitworth College, Spokane 99251

West Virginia

Alderson-Broaddus College, Philippi 26416
Appalachian Bible College, Bradley 25818
Bethany College, Bethany 26032
Bluefield State College, Bluefield 24701
Concord College, Athens 24712
Corinthian Schools: National Institute of Technology, Cross Lanes 25313
Davis and Elkins College, Elkins 26241
Eastern West Virginia Community and Technical College, Moorefield 26836
Fairmont State College, Fairmont 26554
Glenville State College, Glenville 26351
Huntington Junior College, Huntington 25701
International Academy of Design and Technology, Fairmont 26554
Marshall University, Huntington 25755
Marshall University: School of Medicine, Huntington 25704
Mountain State College, Parkersburg 26101-3993
Mountain State University, Beckley 25802-9003
Ohio Valley College, Vienna 26105
Potomac State College of West Virginia University, Keyser 26726
Salem International University, Salem 26426
Shepherd College, Shepherdstown 25443-3210
Southern West Virginia Community and Technical College, Mount Gay 25637
University of Charleston, Charleston 25304
Valley College of Technology, Martinsburg 25401
West Liberty State College, West Liberty 26074-0295
West Virginia Business College, Nutter Fort 26301
West Virginia Business College, Wheeling 26003
West Virginia Junior College, Morgantown 26505
West Virginia Junior College: Charleston, Charleston 25301
West Virginia Northern Community College, Wheeling 26003
West Virginia School of Osteopathic Medicine, Lewisburg 24901
West Virginia State College, Institute 25112-1000

West Virginia University, Morgantown 26506-6201
West Virginia University Institute of Technology, Montgomery 25136
West Virginia University at Parkersburg, Parkersburg 26104-8647
West Virginia University: College of Law, Morgantown 26506
West Virginia University: School of Dentistry, Morgantown 26506
West Virginia University: School of Medicine, Morgantown 26506
West Virginia University: School of Pharmacy, Morgantown 26506
West Virginia Wesleyan College, Buckhannon 26201
Wheeling Jesuit University, Wheeling 26003

Wisconsin

Alverno College, Milwaukee 53234-3922
Bellin College of Nursing, Green Bay 54305
Beloit College, Beloit 53511
Blackhawk Technical College, Janesville 53547
Bryant & Stratton College, Milwaukee 53203
Cardinal Stritch University, Milwaukee 53217
Carroll College, Waukesha 53186
Carthage College, Kenosha 53140
Chippewa Valley Technical College, Eau Claire 54701-6162
Columbia College of Nursing, Milwaukee 53211
Concordia University Wisconsin, Mequon 53097
Edgewood College, Madison 53711
Fox Valley Technical College, Appleton 54913
Herzing College, Madison 53718
ITT Technical Institute: Green Bay, Green Bay 54313
ITT Technical Institute: Greenfield, Greenfield 53220-4612
Lac Courte Oreilles Ojibwa Community College, Hayward 54843
Lakeland College, Sheboygan 53082
Lakeshore Technical College, Cleveland 53015
Lawrence University, Appleton 54912-0599
Maranatha Baptist Bible College, Watertown 53094
Marian College of Fond du Lac, Fond du Lac 54935
Marquette University, Milwaukee 53201-1881
Marquette University: School of Dentistry, Milwaukee 53201
Marquette University: School of Law, Milwaukee 53233
Medical College of Wisconsin: School of Medicine, Milwaukee 53226
Mid-State Technical College, Wisconsin Rapids 54494
Milwaukee Area Technical College, Milwaukee 53233
Milwaukee Institute of Art & Design, Milwaukee 53202
Milwaukee School of Engineering, Milwaukee 53202-3109
Moraine Park Technical College, Fond du Lac 54935
Mount Mary College, Milwaukee 53222
Nashotah House, Nashotah 53058
Nicolet Area Technical College, Rhinelander 54501
Northland College, Ashland 54806
Ripon College, Ripon 54971
Sacred Heart School of Theology, Hales Corners 53130
St. Francis Seminary, St. Francis 53235
St. Norbert College, De Pere 54115-2099
Silver Lake College, Manitowoc 54220
University of Wisconsin Madison: School of Law, Madison 53706
University of Wisconsin Madison: School of Medicine, Madison 53706
University of Wisconsin Madison: School of Pharmacy, Madison 53706
University of Wisconsin Madison: School of Veterinary Medicine, Madison 53706
University of Wisconsin-Baraboo/Sauk County, Baraboo 53913
University of Wisconsin-Barron County, Rice Lake 54868
University of Wisconsin-Eau Claire, Eau Claire 54701
University of Wisconsin-Fond du Lac, Fond du Lac 54935
University of Wisconsin-Fox Valley, Menasha 54952
University of Wisconsin-Green Bay, Green Bay 54311-7001
University of Wisconsin-La Crosse, La Crosse 54601
University of Wisconsin-Madison, Madison 53706-1400
University of Wisconsin-Manitowoc, Manitowoc 54220
University of Wisconsin-Marathon County, Wausau 54401
University of Wisconsin-Marinette, Marinette 54143
University of Wisconsin-Milwaukee, Milwaukee 53201
University of Wisconsin-Oshkosh, Oshkosh 54901
University of Wisconsin-Parkside, Kenosha 53141-2000
University of Wisconsin-Platteville, Platteville 53818
University of Wisconsin-Richland, Richland Center 53581

University of Wisconsin-River Falls, River Falls 54022
University of Wisconsin-Rock County, Janesville 53546
University of Wisconsin-Stevens Point, Stevens Point 54481
University of Wisconsin-Stout, Menomonie 54751
University of Wisconsin-Superior, Superior 54880
University of Wisconsin-Washington County, West Bend 53095
University of Wisconsin-Waukesha, Waukesha 53188
University of Wisconsin-Whitewater, Whitewater 53190
Viterbo University, La Crosse 54601
Waukesha County Technical College, Pewaukee 53072
Western Wisconsin Technical College, La Crosse 54602-0908
Wisconsin Indianhead Technical College, Shell Lake 54871
Wisconsin Lutheran College, Milwaukee 53226

Wyoming

Casper College, Casper 82601
Central Wyoming College, Riverton 82501
Eastern Wyoming College, Torrington 82240
Laramie County Community College, Cheyenne 82007
Sheridan College, Sheridan 82801-1500
University of Wyoming, Laramie 82071
University of Wyoming: College of Law, Laramie 82071
University of Wyoming: School of Pharmacy, Laramie 82071
Western Wyoming Community College, Rock Springs 82902-0428

Alphabetical index of majors

— A —

Accounting, 49
Accounting technology/
  bookkeeping, 55
Accounting/business
  management, 56
Accounting/computer science, 56
Accounting/finance, 56
Acoustics, 56
Acting, 56
Actuarial science, 56
Acupuncture, 56
Administrative/secretarial
  services, 57
Adult development/aging, 60
Adult health nursing, 60
Adult/continuing education, 60
Adult/continuing education
  administration, 60
Advertising, 61
Advertising art (*see* Commerical/
  advertising art)
Advocacy (*see* Community
  organization advocacy;
  Consumer services advocacy)
Aeronautical/aerospace
  engineering, 62
Aeronautical/aerospace
  engineering technology, 62
Aesthetician/skin care, 62
African languages, 62
African studies, 62
African-American studies, 63
Agribusiness operations, 64
Agricultural business, 64
Agricultural business
  technology, 65
Agricultural communications, 65
Agricultural economics, 65
Agricultural education
  services, 66
Agricultural equipment
  technology, 66
Agricultural mechanization, 66
Agricultural power machinery
  operation, 66
Agricultural production, 66
Agricultural supplies, 66
Agricultural teacher education, 67
Agricultural/biological
  engineering, 67
Agricultural/food products
  processing, 67
Agriculture, general, 68
Agronomy/crop science, 68
Air conditioning technology (*see*
  Heating/air conditioning/
  refrigeration technology)
Air traffic control, 69
Air transportation, 69
Aircraft mechanics, 69
Aircraft powerplant
  technology, 70
Airline/commercial pilot, 70
Algebra/number theory, 70

Alternative fuel vehicle
  technology, 70
Ambulance attendant (*see*
  Emergency care attendant)
American government/politics, 70
American history (U.S.), 70
American literature
  (Canadian), 70
American literature (U.S.), 70
American sign language
  (ASL), 71
American studies, 71
Analytical chemistry, 72
Anatomy, 72
Ancient Greek, 73
Ancient Near Eastern/Biblical
  languages, 73
Ancient studies, 73
Anesthesiologist assistant, 73
Animal breeding, 73
Animal grooming (*see* Dog/pet/
  animal grooming)
Animal health, 73
Animal husbandry, 74
Animal nutrition, 74
Animal pathology (*see* Pathology,
  human/animal)
Animal physiology, 74
Animal sciences, 74
Animation/video graphics/special
  effects, 75
Anthropology, 75
Apparel/accessories
  marketing, 77
Apparel/textile manufacture, 77
Apparel/textile marketing, 77
Appliance installation and
  repair, 77
Applied economics, 77
Applied mathematics, 77
Aquaculture, 78
Aquatic biology/limnology, 78
Arabic, 78
Archaeology, 78
Architectural drafting/CAD/
  CADD, 79
Architectural engineering, 79
Architectural engineering
  technology, 79
Architectural history/criticism, 80
Architectural technology, 80
Architecture, 80
Architecture/related programs, 81
Archivist (*see* Public history/
  archives)
Area studies, 82
Art, 82
Art history/criticism/
  conservation, 86
Art teacher education, 87
Art therapy, 90
Artificial intelligence/robotics, 90
Artisanry (*see* Crafts/folk art/
  artisanry)
Arts management, 90
Asian bodywork therapy, 90
Asian history, 90
Asian studies, 91
Asian-American studies, 91
Astronomy, 91
Astrophysics, 92
Athletic training, 92
Atmospheric physics/
  dynamics, 93
Atmospheric sciences, 93
Atomic/molecular physics, 94
Audiology/hearing sciences, 94
Audiology/speech pathology, 95
Auditing, 95
Australian/Oceanic/Pacific
  languages, 95
Auto body repair, 96
Automotive engineering
  technology, 96
Automotive technology, 97

Aviation management, 98
Avionics maintenance/
  technology, 99
Ayurvedic medicine, 99

— B —

Bacteriology, 99
Baking/pastry arts, 100
Banking/financial services, 100
Barbering, 101
Bartending, 101
Behavioral sciences, 101
Bible studies, 102
Bilingual/bicultural
  education, 102
Biochemistry, 103
Biochemistry/biophysics and
  molecular biology, 105
Bioethics/medical ethics, 105
Bioinformatics, 105
Biological engineering (*see*
  Agricultural engineering)
Biological immunology, 105
Biological/physical sciences, 105
Biology, 107
Biology teacher education, 112
Biomedical engineering, 114
Biomedical sciences, 115
Biomedical technology, 115
Biometrics, 115
Biophysics, 115
Biopsychology, 116
Biostatistics, 116
Biotechnology, 116
Blood bank technology, 117
Boilermaking, 117
Bookkeeping (*see* Accounting
  technology)
Botany, 117
British literature (*see* English
  literature (British))
Broadcast journalism, 117
Building inspection, 119
Building/property
  maintenance, 119
Bus operation (*see* Truck/bus/
  commercial vehicle operation)
Business administration/
  management, 120
Business communications, 127
Business machine repair, 127
Business statistics, 127
Business teacher education, 127
Business writing (*see* Technical
  writing)
Business/commerce, 129
Business/managerial
  economics, 133
Buying operations (*see*
  Merchandising)

— C —

Cabinetmaking/millwright, 134
CAD/CADD drafting/design
  technology, 134
Canadian history, 135
Canadian literature (*see* American
  literature (Canadian))
Canadian studies, 135
Cardiopulmonary technology, 135
Cardiovascular science, 135
Cardiovascular technology, 135
Caribbean studies, 135
Carpentry, 135
Cartography, 136
Catering (*see* Restaurant/catering
  management)
Cell physiology, 136
Cellular biology/histology, 136
Cellular/anatomical biology, 137
Cellular/molecular biology, 137
Central/Middle/Eastern European
  studies, 137

Ceramic sciences/
  engineering, 137
Ceramics, 137
Chef training, 138
Chemical engineering, 138
Chemical physics, 139
Chemical technology, 139
Chemistry, 139
Chemistry teacher education, 144
Child care management, 146
Child care service, 148
Child development, 148
Child health (*see* Maternal/child
  health)
Child psychology (*see*
  Developmental psychology)
Chinese, 148
Chinese studies, 149
Chiropractic (D.C.), 149
Christian studies, 149
Cinema studies (*see* Film)
Cinematography/film/video
  production, 149
Civil engineering, 150
Civil engineering drafting/
  CAD/CADD, 151
Civil engineering technology, 151
Classical/ancient Mediterranean/
  Near Eastern studies, 152
Classics, 152
Clerical services (*see* Office/
  clerical services)
Clinical child psychology, 153
Clinical genetics technology (*see*
  Cytogenetics)
Clinical laboratory science, 153
Clinical nurse specialist, 155
Clinical nutrition, 155
Clinical pastoral counseling, 155
Clinical psychology, 155
Clinical/medical laboratory
  assistant, 156
Clinical/medical laboratory
  technology, 156
Clinical/medical social work, 158
Clothing/apparel/textiles, 158
Cognitive psychology/
  psycholinguistics, 158
Cognitive science, 159
College counseling, 159
Commerce (*see* Business/
  commerce)
Commercial photography, 159
Commercial pilot (*see* Airline/
  commercial pilot)
Commercial/advertising art, 159
Commerical vehicle operation
  (*see* Truck/bus/commercial
  vehicle operation)
Communication disorders, 162
Communications, 162
Communications engineering (*see*
  Electrical/communications
  engineering)
Communications systems
  installation/repair, 166
Communications technology, 166
Community health services, 167
Community health/preventative
  medicine, 167
Community organization/
  advocacy, 167
Community planning (*see* Urban/
  community/regional planning)
Community psychology, 168
Community services (*see* Family/
  community services)
Community/junior college
  administration, 168
Comparative literature, 168
Comparative/international
  education, 169
Computational mathematics, 169
Computer education, 169
Computer engineering, 170

Computer engineering technology, 171
Computer graphics, 171
Computer hardware engineering, 172
Computer hardware technology, 172
Computer installation and repair, 172
Computer networking/ telecommunications, 173
Computer programming, general, 174
Computer programming, specific applications, 176
Computer science, 177
Computer software technology, 180
Computer systems analysis, 180
Computer systems technology, 181
Computer typography, 181
Computer/information sciences, 181
Computer/systems security, 187
Conducting, 187
Conflict studies (see Peace studies)
Conservation biology, 188
Conservation (see Natural resources/conservation)
Construction engineering, 188
Construction management, 188
Construction trades, 188
Construction/building technologies, 188
Consumer economics, 189
Consumer merchandising, 189
Consumer services/advocacy, 189
Continuing education (see Adult education)
Contracts (see Purchasing/ procurement/contracts)
Correctional facilities administration, 189
Corrections, 189
Cosmetic services, 190
Cosmetology, 190
Counseling psychology, 190
Counselor education, 192
Court reporting, 193
Crafts/folk art/artisanry, 194
Creative writing, 194
Criminal justice studies, 195
Criminalistics/criminal science, 197
Criminology, 197
Critical care nursing, 198
Criticism (see Architectural history; Art history; Theater history)
Crop production, 198
Crop science (see Agronomy)
Culinary arts/related services, 198
Curriculum/instruction, 199
Customer service management, 201
Customer service support, 201
Cytogenetics/clinical genetics technology, 201
Cytotechnology, 201
Czech, 201

— D —

Dairy husbandry, 201
Dairy science, 201
Dance, 201
Dance teacher education (see Drama/dance teacher education)
Dance therapy, 203
Danish, 203
Data entry/applications, 203
Data processing technology, 203

Database design/ management, 204
Demography/population studies, 205
Dental assistant, 205
Dental clinical services, 206
Dental hygiene, 206
Dental laboratory technology, 207
Dentistry (D.D.S., D.M.D.), 207
Design/visual communications, 208
Desktop publishing, 209
Development economics, 209
Developmental biology/ embryology, 209
Developmental/child psychology, 209
Diagnostic medical sonography, 209
Dialysis technology (see Renal/ dialysis technology)
Diesel mechanics, 210
Dietetic technician, 211
Dietetics, 211
Dietician assistant, 211
Digital media, 211
Directing/theatrical production, 211
Distribution (see Sales/ distribution)
Diversity studies (see Intercultural/diversity studies)
Divinity/ministry (B.Div., M.Div.), 211
Drafting and design technology, 212
Drafting (see CAD/CADD drafting)
Drama/dance teacher education, 215
Drama/theater arts, 215
Drawing, 219
Driver/safety education, 219
Dutch/Flemish, 219

— E —

Early childhood education, 220
Early childhood special education, 223
Earth science (see Geology)
Earthmoving equipment operation (see Heavy/earthmoving equipment operation)
East Asian languages, 223
East Asian studies, 224
Eastern European studies (see Central/Middle/Eastern European studies)
Ecology, 224
Econometrics/quantitative economics, 225
Economics, 225
Education, 228
Education of autistic, 231
Education of blind/visually handicapped, 231
Education of brain injured, 231
Education of deaf/hearing impaired, 231
Education of developmentally delayed, 232
Education of emotionally handicapped, 232
Education of gifted/talented, 233
Education of learning disabled, 233
Education of mentally handicapped, 234
Education of multiple handicapped, 234
Education of physically handicapped, 235
Education of speech impaired, 235

Educational assessment/ testing, 236
Educational evaluation/ research, 236
Educational leadership/ adminstration, 236
Educational psychology, 238
Educational statistics/research methods, 239
Educational supervision, 239
Electrical engineering technologies, 239
Electrical transmission (see Power/electrical transmission)
Electrical/communications engineering, 242
Electrical/electronics drafting/CAD/CADD, 244
Electrician, 244
Electrocardiograph technology, 245
Electroencephalograph technology, 245
Electrolysis, 245
Electromechanical technology, 245
Electronic commerce, 245
Electronics/electrical equipment repair, 246
Elementary education, 247
Elementary/middle school administration, 252
Embalming (see Mortuary science/embalming)
Embryology (see Developmental biology)
Emergency care attendant (EMT ambulance), 252
Emergency medical technology (EMT paramedic), 252
Endocrinology, 254
Energy systems technology, 254
Engineering, 254
Engineering mechanics, 256
Engineering physics, 256
Engineering science, 257
Engineering technology, 257
Engineering/industrial management, 257
English, 258
English composition, 263
English language/literature, 263
English literature (British), 264
English teacher education, 264
Entomology, 267
Entrepreneurial studies, 268
Environmental biology, 268
Environmental design, 269
Environmental engineering, 269
Environmental engineering technology, 270
Environmental health, 270
Environmental health nursing (see Occupational/environmental health nursing)
Environmental science, 270
Environmental studies, 271
Environmental toxicology, 272
Epidemiology, 272
Equestrian studies, 272
Equine science (see Horse husbandry)
ESL teacher education, 273
Ethics, 274
Ethnomusicology (see Musicology)
Ethology (see Animal behavior/ ethology)
Eukaryotic genetics (see Microbial/eukaryotic genetics)
European history, 274
European studies, 274
Event planning (see Facilities/ event planning)
Evolutionary biology, 274

Executive assistant, 274
Exercise physiology, 275
Exercise sciences, 275
Experimental psychology, 276

— F —

Facial treatment, 276
Facilities/event planning, 276
Family practice nurse/nurse practitioner, 276
Family psychology, 277
Family resource management studies, 277
Family studies (see Work/family studies)
Family systems, 277
Family therapy (see Marriage/ family therapy)
Family/community services, 277
Family/consumer business sciences, 277
Family/consumer sciences education, 277
Family/consumer sciences/home economics, 278
Farm/ranch management, 279
Fashion merchandizing, 280
Fashion/apparel design, 280
Fashion/fabric consultant, 281
Fiber arts, 281
Film production (see Cinematography)
Film technology (see Photographic/film/video technology)
Film/cinema studies, 281
Finance, 282
Financial planning, 284
Financial services (see Banking)
Financial services marketing (see Personal/financial services marketing)
Fine/studio arts, 284
Fire protection/safety technology, 287
Fire services administration, 288
Firefighting/fire science, 288
Fishing and fisheries, 289
Fitness administration (see Sports/fitness administration)
Fitter (see Marine maintenance/ fitter/ship repair)
Flemish (see Dutch)
Flight attendant, 289
Floriculture, 290
Folk art (see Crafts/folk art/ artisanry)
Food preparation, 290
Food science, 290
Food service, 290
Food technology/processing, 290
Food/nutrition studies, 290
Foreign language teacher education, 291
Foreign languages/literatures, 293
Forensic psychology, 294
Forensic science, 294
Forest engineering, 294
Forest management, 295
Forest resources production, 295
Forest sciences/biology, 295
Forest technology, 295
Forestry, 295
Franchise operations, 296
French, 296
French studies, 299
French teacher education, 299
Functional analysis (see Analysis)
Funeral direction, 300
Funeral services/mortuary science, 300
Furniture design/ manufacturing, 300

— G —

Gay/lesbian studies, 301
Genetic counseling, 301
Genetics, 301
Geochemistry, 301
Geography, 301
Geography teacher education, 303
Geological engineering, 303
Geology/earth science, 303
Geophysics/seismology, 305
Geotechnical engineering, 305
German, 305
German studies, 307
German teacher education, 308
Germanic languages, 308
Gerontology, 309
Geropsychology, 309
Global studies, 309
Government (*see* Political science)
Graphic communications, 310
Graphic design, 310
Graphic/printing production, 310
Greek (*see* Ancient Greek; Modern Greek)
Greenhouse operations, 311
Groundskeeping (*see* Landscaping)
Guitar (*see* Violin/viola/guitar/ stringed instruments)
Gunsmithing, 311

— H —

Hair styling, 311
Hazardous materials information systems, 311
Hazardous materials technology, 311
Health aide, 311
Health care administration, 312
Health communications, 313
Health management/clinical assistant, 313
Health occupations teacher education, 313
Health physics/radiologic health, 313
Health services, 313
Health services administration, 314
Health teacher education, 314
Health unit coordinator, 316
Health unit manager, 316
Health/medical psychology, 316
Health/physical fitness, 316
Hearing sciences (*see* Audiology)
Heating/air conditioning/ refrigeration maintenance, 318
Heating/air conditioning/ refrigeration technology, 319
Heavy equipment maintenance, 319
Heavy/earthmoving equipment operation, 319
Hebrew, 319
Hematology technology, 319
Herbalism, 320
Herbology (*see* Traditional Chinese medicine)
Higher education administration, 320
High-temperature physics (*see* Plasma physics)
Highway engineering (*see* Transportation/highway engineering)
Hispanic-American studies, 320
Histologic assistant, 320
Histologic technology, 320
Histology (*see* Cellular biology)
Historic preservation, 321
History, 321
History of science/ technology, 325

History teacher education, 325
Home economics (*see* Family/ consumer sciences)
Home furnishings, 327
Home health attendant, 327
Horse husbandry/equine science, 327
Horticultural operations, 327
Horticultural science, 328
Hospitality administration/ management, 329
Hospitality/recreation marketing, 330
Hospital/health care facilities administration, 329
Hotel/motel administration/ management, 331
Housing/human environments, 331
Human development/family studies, 331
Human nutrition, 332
Human pathology (*see* Pathology, human/animal)
Human resources development, 332
Human resources management, 333
Human sciences communication, 334
Human services, 334
Humanities, 336
Human/medical genetics, 336
Hydraulics technology, 336
Hydrology/water resources science, 336

— I —

Iberian studies (*see* Spanish/ Iberian studies)
Illustration, 336
Imager (*see* Platemaker)
Industrial arts education (*see* Technology/industrial arts education)
Industrial design, 336
Industrial education (*see* Trade/ industrial education)
Industrial electronics technology, 337
Industrial engineering, 337
Industrial equipment maintenance/repair, 337
Industrial hygiene (*see* Occupational health)
Industrial relations (*see* Labor relations)
Industrial safety technology, 338
Industrial technology, 338
Industrial/organizational psychology, 338
Information resources management, 339
Information sciences (*see* Computer/information sciences)
Information sciences/studies, 339
Information technology, 342
Inorganic chemistry, 342
Institutional food production, 343
Instructional media, 343
Instrumentation technology, 344
Insurance, 344
Intercultural/diversity studies, 344
Interior architecture, 345
Interior design, 345
International agriculture, 346
International business, 346
International economics, 348
International education (*see* Comparative/international education)
International finance, 348
International marketing, 348

International public health, 349
International relations, 349
Inventory management (*see* Warehousing)
Investments/securities, 350
Iranian/Persian languages, 350
Ironworking, 350
Islamic studies, 350
Italian, 350
Italian studies, 351

— J —

Japanese, 351
Japanese studies, 352
Jazz studies, 352
Jewelry arts (*see* Metal/jewelry arts)
Jewish/Judaic studies, 352
Journalism, 353
Junior high education, 355
Juvenile corrections, 357

— K —

Kindergarten/preschool education, 357
Kinesiotherapy, 357
Knowledge management, 357
Korean, 357
Korean studies, 357

— L —

Labor studies, 357
Labor/industrial relations, 357
Land use planning, 359
Landscape architecture, 359
Landscaping/groundskeeping, 359
Language interpretation/ translation, 360
LAN/WAN management, 358
Laser/optical technology, 360
Latin, 360
Latin American studies, 361
Latin teacher education, 362
Law enforcement administration, 363
Law (J.D.), 362
Legal administrative assistance, 364
Legal studies, 366
Leisure studies (*see* Parks, recreation and leisure studies)
Lesbian studies (*see* Gay/lesbian studies)
Liberal arts/sciences, 367
Library assistance, 373
Library science, 373
Licensed midwifery, 373
Licensed practical nursing, 373
Limnology (*see* Aquatic biology/ limnology)
Lineworker, 375
Linguistics, 375
Literature (*see* English language/ literature)
Livestock management, 376
Locksmithing, 376
Logic, 376
Logistics/materials management, 376
Loss prevention (*see* Security/loss prevention)
Low-temperature physics (*see* Solid-state/low-temperature physics)

— M —

Machine shop technology, 377
Machine tool technology, 377
Magyar (*see* Hungarian)
Make-up artist, 377

Management (*see* Business administration)
Management information systems, 377
Management science, 380
Managerial economics (*see* Business/managerial economics)
Manicurist, 381
Manufacturing engineering, 381
Manufacturing technologies, 381
Marine biology, 382
Marine engineering/naval architecture, 383
Marine maintenance/fitter/ship repair, 383
Marine management (*see* Water, wetlands, and marine management)
Marine science/Merchant Marine, 383
Marketing education (*see* Sales/ marketing education)
Marketing management, 383
Marketing research, 386
Marriage/family therapy, 386
Masonry, 386
Massage therapy, 387
Materials engineering, 387
Materials management (*see* Logistics)
Materials science, 387
Maternal/child health, 388
Maternal/child health nursing, 388
Mathematical physics (*see* Theoretical/mathematical physics)
Mathematical statistics/ probability, 388
Mathematics, 388
Mathematics teacher education, 393
Mathematics/computer science, 396
Mechanical drafting/CAD/ CADD, 397
Mechanical engineering, 397
Mechanical engineering technology, 398
Mechanics/repairers, general, 399
Media studies, 400
Medical administrative assistant, 400
Medical claims examiner, 402
Medical ethics (*see* Bioethics)
Medical genetics (*see* Human/ medical genetics)
Medical illustrating, 402
Medical imaging (*see* Radiologic technology)
Medical informatics, 402
Medical insurance coding specialist, 402
Medical insurance specialist, 402
Medical laboratory assistant (*see* Clinical/medical laboratory assistant)
Medical office administration, 402
Medical office assistant, 403
Medical office computer specialist, 403
Medical psychology (*see* Health/ medical psychology)
Medical radiologic technology/ radiation therapy, 403
Medical receptionist, 404
Medical records administration, 404
Medical records technology, 405
Medical scientist, 406
Medical staff services technology, 406
Medical transcription, 406

Medical/clinical assistant, 408
Medication aide, 409
Medicinal/pharmaceutical
    chemistry, 409
Medicine (M.D.), 410
Medieval/renaissance studies, 410
Medium/heavy vehicle
    technology, 411
Mental health counseling, 411
Mental health services
    technology, 411
Merchandising/buying
    operations, 411
Merchant Marine (*see* Marine
    science)
Metallurgical engineering, 412
Metallurgical technology, 412
Metal/jewelry arts, 412
Meteorology, 412
Microbiology, 412
Middle Eastern studies (*see* Near/
    Middle Eastern studies)
Middle school administration (*see*
    Elementary/middle school
    administration)
Military technologies, 412
Millwright (*see* Cabinet making)
Mining technology, 412
Mining/mineral engineering, 413
Ministry (*see* Divinity; Youth
    ministry)
Missionary studies, 413
Modern Greek, 413
Molecular biochemistry, 413
Molecular biology, 413
Molecular genetics, 414
Molecular pharmacology, 414
Molecular physics (*see* Atomic/
    molecular physics)
Molecular physiology, 414
Montessori teacher
    education, 414
Mortuary science/embalming, 414
Motel management (*see* Hotel/
    motel)
Motorcycle maintenance, 414
Movement therapy, 414
Multicultural education, 415
Multimedia, 415
Museum studies, 415
Music, 415
Music history/literature, 419
Music management, 420
Music pedagogy, 420
Music performance, 420
Music teacher education, 422
Music theory/composition, 425
Music therapy, 426
Musical instrument
    fabrication/repair, 426
Musicology/
    ethnomusicology, 426
Mycology, 427

— N —

Native American studies, 427
Natural resource economics, 427
Natural resources
    management/policy, 427
Natural resources/conservation,
    general, 428
Natural sciences, 430
Naturopathic medicine, 430
Naval architecture (*see* Marine
    engineering)
Near/Middle Eastern studies, 430
Neurobiology/physiology, 431
Neuroscience, 431
Nonprofit/public organization
    management, 431
Norwegian, 432
Nuclear engineering, 432
Nuclear engineering
    technology, 432

Nuclear medical technology, 432
Nuclear physics, 433
Nuclear power technology, 433
Number theory (*see* Algebra)
Nurse anesthetist, 433
Nurse midwifery, 433
Nurse practitioner (*see* Family
    practice nurse)
Nursery operations, 433
Nursing administration, 437
Nursing assistant, 438
Nursing (R.N.), 434
Nursing science, 439
Nutrition studies (*see* Food/
    nutrition studies)
Nutritional sciences, 439

— O —

Occupational health/industrial
    hygiene, 440
Occupational safety/health
    technology, 440
Occupational therapy, 440
Occupational therapy
    assistant, 441
Occupational/environmental
    health nursing, 442
Ocean engineering, 442
Oceanic languages (*see*
    Australian/Oceanic languages)
Oceanography, 442
Office management, 442
Office technology/data entry, 444
Office/clerical services, 445
Oncology, 447
Opera (*see* Voice)
Operations management, 447
Operations research, 448
Ophthalmic laboratory
    technology, 448
Ophthalmic technology, 449
Optical technology (*see* Laser/
    optical technology)
Opticianry/ophthalmic
    dispensing, 449
Optics, 449
Optometric assistant, 449
Optometry (O.D.), 449
Organ (*see* Piano)
Organic chemistry, 449
Organization psychology (*see*
    Industrial/organizational
    psychology)
Organizational behavior
    studies, 449
Organizational
    communication, 450
Ornamental horticulture, 450
Orthotics/prosthetics, 451
Osteopathic medicine (D.O.), 451

— P —

Pacific area/rim studies, 451
Pacific languages (*see* Australian/
    Pacific languages)
Painting, 451
Painting/wall covering, 452
Paleontology, 452
Paper technology (*see* Wood
    science)
Paralegal/legal assistance, 452
Paramedic (*see* Emergency
    medical technology)
Parasitology, 454
Parks, recreation and leisure
    studies, 454
Parks/recreational/leisure
    facilities management, 455
Particle physics, 456
Pastoral counseling, 456
Pastry arts (*see* Baking)
Pathology assistant, 457
Pathology, human/animal, 457

Peace/conflict studies, 457
Pediatric nursing, 457
Performing arts (*see* Visual/
    performing arts; Drama/theater
    arts)
Perfusion technology, 458
Persian (*see* Iranian)
Personality psychology, 458
Personal/culinary services, 458
Personal/financial services
    marketing, 458
Pest management (*see* Plant
    protection)
Pet grooming (*see* Dog/pet/
    animal grooming)
Petroleum engineering, 458
Petroleum technology, 458
Petrology (*see* Geochemistry/
    petrology)
Pharmaceutical chemistry (*see*
    Medicinal/pharmaceutical
    chemistry)
Pharmacology, 458
Pharmacology/toxicology, 459
Pharmacy assistant, 459
Pharmacy (PharmD.), 459
Philosophy, 460
Philosophy/religion, 463
Phlebotomy, 464
Photographic/film/video
    technology, 464
Photography, 464
Photojournalism, 465
Physical anthropology, 465
Physical education, 465
Physical fitness (*see* Health/
    physical fitness)
Physical sciences, 468
Physical therapy, 468
Physical therapy assistant, 469
Physical/theoretical
    chemistry, 470
Physician assistant, 471
Physics, 471
Physics teacher education, 475
Physiological psychology (*see*
    Psychobiology)
Physiology, 476
Piano/organ, 476
Pipefitting, 477
Planetary sciences, 477
Plant breeding, 478
Plant genetics, 478
Plant pathology, 478
Plant physiology, 479
Plant protection/pest
    management, 479
Plant sciences, 479
Plasma/high-temperature
    physics, 480
Plastics engineering (*see*
    Polymer/plastics engineering)
Plastics engineering
    technology, 480
Platemaker/imager, 480
Playwriting/screenwriting, 480
Plumbing, 480
Podiatry (D.P.M.), 480
Police science, 480
Polish studies, 482
Political communications, 482
Political science/government, 482
Politics (*see* American
    government; Canadian
    government)
Polymer chemistry, 486
Polymer/plastics engineering, 486
Population biology, 486
Population studies (*see*
    Demography)
Portuguese, 486
Poultry science, 486
Power/electrical
    transmission, 487

Precision production trades,
    general, 487
Predentistry, 487
Prelaw, 489
Premedicine, 491
Pre-ministerial studies, 487
Prenursing, 493
Preoperative/surgical nursing, 494
Prepharmacy, 494
Preschool education (*see*
    Kindergartern)
Preventive medicine (*see*
    Community health)
Preveterinary, 496
Printing management, 497
Printing press operator, 497
Printing production (*see* Graphic/
    printing production)
Printmaking, 497
Probability (*see* Mathematical
    statistics)
Property maintenance (*see*
    Building/property
    maintenance)
Prosthetics (*see* Orthotics/
    prosthetics)
Protective services, 498
Psychiatric nursing, 498
Psychobiology/physiological
    psychology, 498
Psycholinguistics (*see* Cognitive
    psychology)
Psychology, 499
Psychology teacher
    education, 504
Psychometrics/quantitative
    psychology, 504
Psychopharmacology, 504
Public administration, 504
Public finance, 506
Public health, 506
Public health education, 506
Public health nursing, 507
Public history/archives, 507
Public organization management
    (*see* Nonprofit)
Public policy analysis, 507
Public relations, 507
Public services, 508
Publishing, 509
Purchasing/procurement/
    contracts, 509

— Q —

Quality control technology, 510
Quantitative economics (*see*
    Econometrics)
Quantitative psychology (*see*
    Psychometrics)

— R —

Rabbinical studies (M.H.L.,
    Rav.), 510
Radiation biology, 510
Radiation protection/health
    physics technology, 510
Radiation therapy (*see* Medical
    radiologic technology)
Radiologic health (*see* Health
    physics)
Radiologic technology/medical
    imaging, 511
Radio/television, 510
Radio/television
    broadcasting, 510
Ranch management (*see* Farm/
    ranch management)
Range science, 511
Reading teacher education, 511
Real estate, 513
Receptionist, 514
Recording arts, 514

Recreation (*see* Parks, recreation and leisure studies)
Recreational facilities management (*see* Parks/recreational/leisure facilities management)
Recreational therapy, 514
Refrigeration technology (*see* Heating/air conditioning/refrigeration technology)
Regional planning (*see* Urban/community/regional planning)
Regional studies, 514
Rehabilitation engineering (*see* Assistive technology)
Religion/religious studies, 514
Religious education, 517
Religious/sacred music, 518
Renaissance studies (*see* Medieval/renaissance studies)
Renal/dialysis technology, 518
Reproductive biology, 518
Resort management, 518
Respiratory therapy, 518
Respiratory therapy assistant, 520
Restaurant/catering management, 520
Restaurant/food services management, 520
Retailing, 520
Rhetorical studies (*see* Speech/rhetorical studies)
Robotics technology, 520
Romance languages, 521
Roofing, 521
Russian, 521
Russian/Slavic studies, 522

— S —

Sacred music (*see* Religious/sacred music)
Safety education (*see* Driver/safety education)
Sales/distribution, 523
Sales/marketing education, 523
Scandinavian languages, 524
Scandinavian studies, 524
School librarian education, 524
School psychology, 524
Science teacher education, 525
Science technologies, 527
Science/technology/society, 528
Screenwriting (*see* Playwriting)
Sculpture, 528
Secondary education, 529
Secondary school administration, 532
Securities (*see* Investments)
Security services management, 533
Security system installation/repair/inspection, 533
Security/loss prevention, 533
Seismology (*see* Geophysics)
Selling/sales operations, 533
Semitic languages, 533
Sheet metal technology, 533
Ship repair (*see* Marine maintenance)
Sign language interpretation, 533
Sign language linguistics, 534
Skin care (*see* Aesthetician)
Slavic languages, 534
Slavic studies, 534
Slavic studies (*see* Russian/Slavic studies)
Slovak, 534
Small business administration/management, 534
Small engine mechanics, 534
Social psychology, 534
Social science teacher education, 534
Social sciences, 536

Social studies teacher education, 539
Social work, 541
Social/philosophical foundations of education, 543
Sociology, 544
Software engineering, 548
Soil science, 548
Solar energy technology, 549
Solid-state/low-temperature physics, 549
Somatic bodywork, 549
South Asian languages, 549
South Asian studies, 549
Southeast Asian languages, 549
Southeast Asian studies, 549
Spanish, 549
Spanish teacher education, 553
Spanish/Iberian studies, 554
Special education, 554
Special education administration, 557
Special effects (*see* Animation/video graphics/special effects)
Speech pathology, 557
Speech pathology (*see* Audiology)
Speech teacher education, 558
Speech/rhetorical studies, 559
Sports/fitness administration, 560
Statistics, 561
Steiner teacher education (*see* Waldorf/Steiner teacher education)
Stringed instruments (*see* Violin/viola/guitar/stringed instruments)
Structural biology, 562
Structural engineering, 562
Studio arts (*see* Fine/studio arts)
Substance abuse counseling, 562
Superintendency, 563
Surgical nursing (*see* Preoperative/surgical nursing)
Surgical technology, 563
Surveying engineering, 564
Surveying technology, 564
Swedish, 565
System administration, 565
Systematic biology, 565
Systems engineering, 565
Systems science/theory, 565
Systems security (*see* Computer/systems security)

— T —

Talmudic studies, 565
Tattooing (*see* Permanent cosmetics)
Taxation, 565
Taxidermy, 566
Teacher assistance, 566
Teacher education (*see* specific disciplines)
Teacher education, multiple levels, 566
Technical education (*see* Vocational/technical education)
Technical/business writing, 568
Technology and society (*see* Science/technology/society)
Technology/industrial arts education, 568
Telecommunications technology, 569
Television (*see* Radio/television)
Testing (*see* Educational assessment)
Textile manufacture/marketing (*see* Apparel)
Textile science, 569
Textile sciences/engineering, 569
Theater arts (*see* Drama/theater arts)

Theater arts management, 569
Theater design/technology, 569
Theater history/criticism, 570
Theatrical production (*see* Directing)
Theological studies, 570
Theology/religious vocations, 571
Theoretical chemistry (*see* Physical/theoretical chemistry)
Theoretical/mathematical physics, 572
Tool and die technology, 572
Tourism promotion, 572
Tourism/travel management, 573
Tourism/travel services, 574
Toxicology, 574
Trade/industrial education, 574
Traditional Chinese medicine/herbology, 575
Transportation, 575
Transportation management, 575
Transportation/highway engineering, 575
Travel (*see* Tourism)
Truck/bus/commercial vehicle operation, 575
Turf management, 576
Turkish, 576
Typography (*see* Computer typography)

— U —

Ukrainian, 576
Underwater diving, 576
Upholstery, 576
Urban education, 576
Urban forestry, 576
Urban studies, 576
Urban/community/regional planning, 577
U.S. History (*see* American history)

— V —

Vehicle parts/accessories marketing, 578
Vendor/product certification, 578
Veterinary assistant, 578
Veterinary medicine (D.V.M.), 578
Video graphics (*see* (see Animation/video graphics/special effects)
Video production (*see* Cinematography/film/video production)
Video technology (*see* Photographic/film/video technology)
Violin/viola/guitar/stringed instruments, 579
Virology, 579
Vision science, 579
Visual communications (*see* Design/visual communications)
Visual/performing arts, 579
Vocational rehabilitation counseling, 580
Vocational/technical education, 581
Voice/opera, 581

— W —

Wall covering (*see* Painting/wall covering)
Warehousing operations (*see* Parts)
Warehousing/inventory management, 582
Watch/jewelrymaking, 582
Water quality/treatment/recycling technology, 582

Water resource engineering, 582
Water resources science (*see* Hydrology)
Water, wetlands, and marine management, 582
Web page/multimedia design, 582
Web/multimedia management, 583
Welding technology, 584
Western European studies, 584
Wetlands (*see* Water, wetlands, and marine management)
Wildlife biology, 584
Wildlife/wilderness management, 584
Women's studies, 585
Wood science/pulp/paper technology, 586
Woodworking, 586
Word processing, 587
Work/family studies, 587
Writing (*see* Creative writing; Playwriting; Technical/business writing)

— Y —

Youth ministry, 587
Youth services, 587

— Z —

Zoology, 587

Selected Books and Software from the College Board

Annual college directories

The College Board College Handbook with *Real Stuff* CD-ROM, 2004. Over 2 million copies sold. The only one-volume guide to all U.S. two- and four-year colleges. 2,200 pages, paperbound. **Item# 006941** $27.95

The College Board Scholarship Handbook with *Real Stuff* CD-ROM, 2004. Over 2,100 real scholarships, grants, internships, and loans for undergraduate students. 620 pages, paperbound. **Item# 006984** $26.95

The College Board College Cost & Financial Aid Handbook, 2004. Detailed cost and financial aid information at 3,100 two- and four-year institutions; includes indexed information on college scholarships. 800 pages, paperbound. **Item# 006976** $23.95

The College Board Index of Majors and Graduate Degrees, 2004. "A comprehensive, no-nonsense guide"—the *New York Times.* Covers 900 major fields of study at all degree levels: undergraduate, graduate, and professional, including law, medicine, and dentistry. 740 pages, paperbound. **Item# 006968** $23.95

The College Board International Student Handbook of U.S. Colleges, 2004. Provides students with information they need to apply for study at 2,500 U.S. colleges, including costs, required tests, financial aid, ESL programs. 360 pages, paperbound. **Item# 006992** $27.95

Test prep for College Board programs

10 Real SAT®s, Third Edition. 10 real, complete SATs for student practice, with test-taking tips from the test makers themselves. Also includes a mini-SAT on CD-ROM. 700 pages, paperbound. **Item# 006860** $19.95

Real SAT II: Subject Tests. The only source of real SAT II practice questions from cover to cover. 700 pages, paperbound. **Item# 007034** $18.95

APCD® in Spanish Language, 2001. Designed to assist and reinforce classroom teaching, this CD helps students prepare with interactive review and problem-solving strategies. Features audio component. **Item# 201894** $49.00

APCD® in Calculus AB, 2000. A valuable study tool that complements classroom materials and also provides practice exam review with analysis of answers and scores. **Item# 201907** $49.00

APCD® in U.S. History, 1998. This CD augments classroom instruction and materials with multiple-choice practice tests and essay tutorials. **Item# 201865** $49.00

APCD® in European History, 1999. Reinforcement and review of classroom materials includes maps, timelines, practice tests, and essay tutorials. **Item# 201891** $49.00

APCD® in English Language, 1999. Designed to supplement classroom and home assignments, this CD provides essay tutorials, guidelines, and practice tests. **Item# 201889** $49.00

APCD® in English Literature, 1998. A thorough exam review offering essay tutorials and multiple-choice practice, this CD is designed to complement written preparation materials provided in the classroom. **Item# 201864** $49.00

One-on-One with the SAT™. (Version 2.3) Valuable advice and test-taking strategies from the SAT test makers, plus the opportunity to take a real, complete SAT and hundreds of additional practice questions on computer. (Home version—Windows® and Macintosh®) **Item# 006747** $29.95

The CLEP® Official Study Guide 2004–15th Edition. Qualifying scores on CLEP exams can earn credit at over 2,900 colleges. Only guide to cover all 34 CLEP exams with sample questions for all 34 exams. 500 pages, paperbound. **Item# 007026** $22.00

General guidance for students and parents

The College Application Essay, Sarah Myers McGinty. Application essay policies of more than 180 institutions, types of questions asked, plus 40 actual questions and analyses of 6 essays. 131 pages, paperbound. **Item# 005759** $12.95

Campus Visits and College Interviews, Zola Dincin Schneider. Newly revised 2nd edition (2002). Why they are important, when to visit, what to look for, questions usually asked, much more. 162 pages, paperbound. **Item# 006755** $12.95

The College Board Guide to 150 Popular College Majors. One-of-a-kind reference to majors in 17 fields, with related information on typical courses, high school preparation, much more. 377 pages, paperbound. **Item# 004000** $16.00

The Parents' Guide to Paying for College, Gerald Krefetz. Expert advice from a well-known investment analyst and financial consultant on covering college costs, with case studies. 158 pages, paperbound. **Item# 006046** $14.95

Order Form

Mail order form to: College Board Publications, Dept. GSP1103A, P.O. Box 869010, Plano, TX 75074 (*payment must accompany all orders*)
or **phone:** 800 323-7155, M–F, 8 a.m.–9 p.m. Eastern Time (*credit card orders only*)
or **fax 24 hours, 7 days a week to:** 888 321-7183 (*purchase orders above $25 and credit card orders*)
or **online** through the College Board Store at www.collegeboard.com (*credit card orders only*)

Item No.	Title	Price	Amount
	Annual college directories		
006984	Scholarship Handbook with *Real Stuff* CD-ROM, 2004	$26.95	_____
006941	The College Handbook, with *Real Stuff* CD-ROM, 2004	$27.95	_____
006976	College Cost & Financial Aid Handbook, 2004	$23.95	_____
006968	Index of Majors and Graduate Degrees, 2004	$23.95	_____
006992	International Student Handbook of U.S. Colleges, 2004	$27.95	_____
995694	2004 Scholarship 3-book set: *College Handbook, Scholarship Handbook, College Cost & Financial Aid Handbook*	$67.00	_____
995692	2004 Classic 3-book set: *College Handbook, Index of Majors, College Cost & Financial Aid Handbook*	$65.00	_____
	Test prep for College Board programs		
201907	AP® CD-ROM in Calculus AB, 2000	$49.00	_____
201864	AP CD-ROM in English Literature, 1998	$49.00	_____
201865	AP CD-ROM in U.S. History, 1998	$49.00	_____
201891	AP CD-ROM in European History, 1999	$49.00	_____
201889	AP CD-ROM in English Language, 1999	$49.00	_____
201894	AP CD-ROM in Spanish Language, 2001	$49.00	_____
006860	10 Real SAT®s, Third Edition	$19.95	_____
006747	One-on-One with the SAT® (Home version, Windows®/Macintosh®)	$29.95	_____
007026	The CLEP® Official Study Guide, 2004–15th Edition	$22.00	_____
007034	Real SAT II: Subject Tests	$18.95	_____
	General guidance for students and parents		
005759	The College Application Essay	$12.95	_____
006755	Campus Visits and College Interviews, 2nd edition	$12.95	_____
004000	College Board Guide to 150 Popular College Majors	$16.00	_____
006046	The Parents' Guide to Paying for College	$14.95	_____

Subtotal $ _____

Shipping and handling $ _____

Total $ _____

Sales Tax: $ _____
(*IL,CA,FL,GA,TN,PA,DC,MA,TX,VA,Can.*)

Grand Total $ _____

Shipping and Handling
$0	–	$20.00	=	$4.00
$20.01	–	$40.00	=	$5.00
$40.01	–	$60.00	=	$6.00
$60.01+	= 10% of dollar value of order			

❑ Enclosed is my check or money order made payable to the **College Board**   ❑ Enclosed is my purchase order above $25

❑ Please charge my ❑ MasterCard ❑ Visa ❑ American Express ❑ Discover

☐☐☐☐ ☐☐☐☐ ☐☐☐☐ ☐☐☐☐   exp. date: _____/_____   _____
card number   month   year   cardholder's signature

Allow two weeks from receipt of order for delivery.

SHIP TO:

_____   _____
Name   Street Address (no P. O. Box numbers, please)

_____ _____ _____   (_____) _____
City   State   Zip   Telephone

The College Board

The College Board is a national, nonprofit membership association whose mission is to prepare, inspire, and connect students to college and opportunity. Founded in 1900, the association is composed of more than 4,300 schools, colleges, universities, and other educational organizations. Each year, the College Board serves over three million students and their parents, 23,000 high schools, and 3,500 colleges through major programs and services in college admissions, guidance, assessment, financial aid, enrollment, and teaching and learning. Among its best-known programs are the SAT®, the PSAT/NMSQT®, and the Advanced Placement Program® (AP®). The College Board is committed to the principles of excellence and equity, and that commitment is embodied in all of its programs, services, activities, and concerns.

www.collegeboard.com

prepare. inspire. connect.